AMERICAN NATIONAL BIOGRAPHY

AMERICAN
NATIONAL BIOGRAPHY

Published under the auspices of the
AMERICAN COUNCIL OF LEARNED SOCIETIES

General Editors

John A. Garraty

Mark C. Carnes

VOLUME 13

OXFORD UNIVERSITY PRESS

New York   1999   Oxford

OXFORD UNIVERSITY PRESS

Oxford   New York
Athens   Auckland   Bangkok   Bogotá
Buenos Aires   Calcutta   Cape Town   Chennai
Dar es Salaam   Delhi   Florence   Hong Kong   Istanbul
Karachi   Kuala Lumpur   Madrid   Melbourne   Mexico City
Mumbai   Nairobi   Paris   São Paulo   Singapore
Taipei   Tokyo   Toronto   Warsaw
and associated companies in
Berlin   Ibadan

Published by Oxford University Press, Inc.,
198 Madison Avenue, New York, New York 10016
http://www.oup-usa.org

Oxford is a registered trademark of Oxford University Press

Funding for this publication was provided in part by
the Andrew W. Mellon Foundation, the Rockefeller Foundation,
and the National Endowment for the Humanities,
a federal agency.

Library of Congress Cataloging-in-Publication Data

American national biography / general editors, John A. Garraty, Mark C. Carnes
p.   cm.
"Published under the auspices of the American Council of Learned Societies."
Includes bibliographical references and index.
1. United States—Biography—Dictionaries.   I. Garraty, John Arthur,
1920–   .   II. Carnes, Mark C. (Mark Christopher), 1950–   .
III. American Council of Learned Societies.
CT213.A68   1998   98-20826   920.073—dc21   CIP
ISBN 0-19-520635-5 (set)
ISBN 0-19-512792-7 (vol. 13)

Printing (last digit): 9 8 7 6 5 4 3 2 1

Printed in the United States of America
on acid-free paper

KURTZMAN, Harvey (3 Oct. 1924–21 Feb. 1993), cartoonist, was born in Brooklyn, New York, the son of David Kurtzman and Edith Sherman. His father died when he was very young, his mother remarried, and the family moved to the Bronx. Kurtzman's stepfather, a brass engraver, encouraged the boy to develop his emerging artistic abilities, and he attended art classes at Pratt Institute and the Brooklyn Museum. In public school, he was a good student; promoted to a grade a year ahead of his classmates, he was enrolled at the age of thirteen in the High School of Music and Art, where he met several of the people with whom he would later work—chiefly, his frequent collaborator, Will Elder. After graduating in 1939 Kurtzman received a scholarship to study at Cooper Union, which he attended at night. None of Kurtzman's day jobs (printer's apprentice, errand boy in a law office) lasted very long until he found a position with Louis Ferstadt, whose comic book art shop created comic book stories for Ace/Periodical House, Quality, and Gilberton Company, which published Classic Comics, the comic book adaptations of such literary works as *Moby Dick*, *The Three Musketeers*, and the like. After about a year, Kurtzman quit Cooper Union and concentrated on learning how to do comic books. By 1943 his work was being published in several comic book titles; about then, too, he was inducted into the army, which designated him a draftsman, and he spent World War II producing visual training aids in various camps in the United States. Discharged in 1945, he set up an art agency studio with Elder and others.

Kurtzman freelanced for the next several years, placing a short-lived weekly comic strip, *Silver Linings*, with the New York Herald Tribune Syndicate; but his chief client was Timely Comics, for which he produced more than one hundred of his manic one-page gag filler strips called *Hey Look!* and several short stories. He also met Adele Hasan, a Timely staff member, whom Kurtzman married in 1948; they had four children. In 1950 he began working regularly for William C. Gaines's Entertaining Comics (EC), which published a series of horror and science fiction titles. Kurtzman did several stories for these comics and then suggested that EC publish an adventure title; Gaines complied, making Kurtzman editor of *Two-Fisted Tales* in the fall of 1950. But Kurtzman did much more than merely edit the book: he also wrote all the stories, researching their subjects extensively and making detailed page layouts, which he insisted that his artists follow exactly. In the spring of 1951, Gaines assigned Kurtzman a second title, *Frontline Combat*, to capitalize on reader interest in war stories prompted by the Korean War.

In his comic books, Kurtzman concentrated on presenting the truth about war. His stories were not anti-war; in fact, his stories usually acknowledged the necessity of the so-called "police action" in Korea and of wars generally. But against that necessity, he balanced recognition of the overall futility of warfare. Most comic book war stories of the period glorified battlefield action by making bloodshed and death seem patriotic. In his stories, Kurtzman resolutely set about deglamorizing warfare; by focusing on individuals and their usually inglorious and anonymous fates, he dramatized the profligate waste of human life that has characterized wars everywhere in every time. He also produced milestones of comic book artistry. Firmly founded in his research, his comic books resonated with authenticity; and they were distinctively rendered by a stable of EC artists (including regulars John Severin, Will Elder, Wallace Wood, George Evans, and Jack Davis) who took a particular pride in their endeavors because Gaines, unlike most comic book publishers of the day, let them sign their work. Moreover, Kurtzman, controlling narrative pace and the composition of each individual picture with his meticulous layouts, was able to deploy the visual as well as the verbal resources of the medium in ways that expanded its capacity for dramatic expression.

Kurtzman became what he called a behind-the-scenes cartoonist: researching, writing, and laying out four stories a month, he seldom had time to produce the finished art for any of the stories, but when he did, the artwork was a stylistic achievement. Although he could draw in a convincingly realistic fashion, he chose to render his stories in an abstract and telegraphic manner. He used a line of uncommon simplicity and boldness for realistic storytelling, and his figure drawings were exaggerated and contorted, demonstrations of posture as drama rather than reality as perceived. By reducing his visual representations in this way to their absolute narrative essentials, he achieved a reality in his stories that was stark and raw, as uncompromising as truth itself.

In mid-1952 Gaines agreed to let Kurtzman do a third title, a humor comic book, to increase his income, reasoning that the cartoonist could generate funny material quickly without having to do any research. Taking a working title from the editorial persiflage on letters pages of the other EC comics, they called the new comic *EC's Mad Mag*, which Kurtzman soon shortened to just plain *Mad* ("a stroke of genius," Gaines said later). The first issue (cover-dated Oct. 1952) contained genre parodies of horror, crime, science fiction, and western comic books; in the next issues, Kurtzman began parodying specific works, thereby sharpening the satire inherent in the method.

Before long, the distinctive *Mad* approach was in place: by extending a premise of everyday life to its logical and usually ludicrous conclusion, Kurtzman made parody a powerful vehicle for satire and used it to ridicule every phase of American life, particularly such aspects of popular culture as movies, television, comic strips, and, especially, advertising.

In 1955 Kurtzman converted *Mad* from a four-color comic book to a black-and-white magazine, which he saw as a more flexible platform for satire. But he stayed with the new *Mad* for only five issues (until No. 28): his ambitions for the magazine were greater than Gaines was willing to support. In 1956 Kurtzman joined *Playboy* publisher Hugh Hefner in producing a slick, full-color magazine of parody and satire called *Trump*; but it lasted only two issues. Unwilling to abandon the idea of a satirical magazine, Kurtzman subsequently created two low-budget titles (*Humbug* and *Help!*) in succession, but neither was successful. Then with the October 1962 issue of *Playboy*, he and Elder (and occasionally other artists) began producing the most lavish comic strip ever published, *Little Annie Fanny*. Written and laid out by Kurtzman with every panel subsequently painted in full color by Elder and other collaborators, the strip employed Annie, a grown-up, sexy version of Little Orphan Annie, in Candide-like fashion to satirize hip society and sexual mores. After the collapse in 1965 of *Help!*, Kurtzman's principal employment was producing the *Annie* strip and teaching cartoon storytelling at the School of Visual Arts in Manhattan. He also did numerous magazine illustrations and articles.

Writing in the *New Yorker* (29 Mar. 1993, p. 75) at the time of Kurtzman's death in Mount Vernon, New York, Adam Gopnik observed that "Kurtzman saw that the conventions of pop culture ran so deep in the imagination of his audience that you could create a new kind of satire just by inventorying them. . . . Almost all American satire today follows a formula that Harvey Kurtzman thought up." Kurtzman may be the most influential American cartoonist since Walt Disney. Following the patterns that Kurtzman established, *Mad* became one of the most widely circulated magazines, and for generation after generation, the young, at a particular age, read *Mad*, acquiring thereby a certain cynicism about the icons of American popular culture as well as the functioning of its institutions.

• Kurtzman's chief productions are *Two-Fisted Tales* (Nos. 18–35, Nov. 1950–Oct. 1953), *Frontline Combat* (Nos. 1–15, July 1951–Jan. 1954), *Mad* (comic book, Nos. 1–23; magazine, Nos. 24–28, Oct. 1952–July 1956), *Trump* (Nos. 1–2, Jan.–Mar. 1957), *Humbug* (Nos. 1–11, Aug. 1957–Aug. 1958), *The Jungle Book* (1959; repr. 1986), *Help!* (Nos. 1–26, Aug. 1960–Sept. 1965), *Playboy's Little Annie Fanny* (two reprint collections, 1966 and 1972), *Goodman Beaver* (reprint collection, 1984), *Betsy's Buddies* (with Sarah Downs; reprint collection, 1988), *Harvey Kurtzman's Strange Adventures* (1990), *From Aargh! to Zap!* (1991), *Hey Look!* (reprint collection, 1992). All of Kurtzman's EC work has been reprinted by Russ Cochran in the EC Library. Kurtzman's

autobiography, *My Life as a Cartoonist* (1988; with Howard Zimmerman), is written for young readers who might want to be cartoonists, and while it provides insight into the cartoonist's creative processes it is not a detailed or complete life story. Kurtzman gave an extensive interview to the *Comics Journal*, no. 67 (Oct. 1981): 68–99, and the magazine published a chronology of his life and work in no. 153 (Oct. 1992): 47–96, relying for some of its data on Glen Bray's *Illustrated Harvey Kurtzman Index* (1976). An obituary in the *New York Times*, 22 Feb. 1993, is brief and sometimes erroneous.

ROBERT C. HARVEY

KUSCH, Polykarp (26 Jan. 1911–20 Mar. 1993), physicist, was born in Blankenburg, Germany, the son of John Matthias Kusch, a Lutheran missionary, and Henrietta van der Haas. The family immigrated to the United States in 1912, and Kusch became a naturalized citizen in 1922. After receiving his secondary schooling in Cleveland, Ohio, he entered the Case School of Applied Science (now Case Institute of Technology) in 1927 and graduated with a B.S. in physics in 1931. From 1931 to 1936 he was an assistant at the University of Illinois, where he obtained his M.S. in 1933 and his Ph.D. in 1936. Kusch's doctoral dissertation on optical molecular spectroscopy was entitled "The Molecular Spectra of Caesium and Rubidium" and was prepared under the guidance of F. Wheeler Loomis. On 12 August 1935 Kusch married Edith Starr McRoberts; they had three daughters.

In 1936 and 1937 Kusch was a research assistant of John T. Tate at the University of Minnesota. He then accepted an instructorship at Columbia and remained in this position until 1941. During World War II he served as a development engineer at Westinghouse (1941–1942), a research associate in the Division of War Research at Columbia (1942–1944), and as a member of the technical staff at the Bell Telephone Laboratories (1944–1946). Much of his war research was concerned with microwave vacuum tubes as well as high frequency generators, which were needed in the development of radar. Invited by Isidore I. Rabi to return to Columbia, Kusch was an associate professor (1946–1949) and a professor (1949–1972). During this time he was chairman of the physics department for two terms (1949–1952 and 1960–1963), executive director of the Radiation Laboratory (1952–1960), vice president and dean of the faculty (1969–1970), and finally executive vice president and provost (1970–1971). In 1959 Kusch's wife died, and the following year he married Betty Pezzoni. They had two daughters.

Kusch's most significant work was experimental in nature, and it focused on a molecular beam resonance method invented by Rabi in 1937. This spectroscopic procedure, conducted at radio frequencies, was intended to provide a highly accurate measurement of the ground state of an atom or molecule and of the splitting of its spectral lines in the presence of a magnetic field. Kusch participated in this research, and in 1940 he co-authored a paper with Rabi and Sidney Millman on the radio frequency of atoms. After the war he sought to apply it to the determination of the magnetic moment μ_s of a spinning electron. The postulate of Samuel A. Goudsmit and George E. Uhlenbeck, developed in 1925, had said that $\mu_s = \mu_0$ where μfi/0 is the Bohr magneton; this postulate was theoretically confirmed by the early work of Paul A. M. Dirac on quantum electrodynamics. This was unchallenged until Kusch and Henry M. Foley experimentally found that $\mu_s = 1.00119 \, \mu_0$ in 1947 and 1948. Almost immediately Julian Schwinger (1948, 1949), using his new version of quantum electrodynamics, showed that theoretically $\mu_s = (1 + \alpha/2\pi) \, \mu_0 = 1.00116 \, \mu_0$ where α is the fine structure constant. This seemingly small correction was extremely important; it became known as the anomalous magnetic moment of the electron, which demanded an explanation. This constituted not only a remarkable triumph of Kusch's experimental precision, but also a much-needed vindication of the new quantum electrodynamics. Kusch and Herbert Taub (1949) subsequently applied this method to the determination of the magnetic moment of the proton. For his precision determination of the magnetic moment of the electron, Kusch shared the 1955 Nobel Prize in physics with Willis E. Lamb.

In 1972 Kusch joined the University of Texas at Dallas, where he served as a professor of physics (1972–1974), Eugene McDermott Professor (1974–1980), and regental professor (1980–1982). He retired in 1982. A gifted experimental physicist he was noted for his penchant for accurate and precise measurements. In 1955 his mentor Rabi (also a Nobel laureate) described Kusch's analysis as "careful, clever, even brilliant, high precision work." The body of work for which he and Lamb were awarded the Nobel Prize provided a fundamental step in demonstrating the inadequacies of the earlier formulations of quantum electrodynamics. It also verified the new theory of Richard Feynman, Julian Schwinger, and Shinichiro Tomonaga, which was to lead to their shared Nobel Prize in 1965.

Kusch was elected a member of the National Academy of Sciences in 1956. In addition, he received the Great Teacher's Award in 1959 while at Columbia and the Illinois Achievement Award from the University of Illinois in 1975. He died in his Dallas home.

• An autobiographical sketch by Kusch is in *McGraw Hill Modern Scientists and Engineers* 2 (1980). The major paper by Kusch and Foley on the anomalous magnetic moment is "The Magnetic Moment of the Electron," *Physical Review* 74 (1 Aug. 1948): 250–63, and one of his earlier papers together with Schwinger's theoretical calculation is in the reprint volume *Selected Papers on Quantum Electrodynamics*, ed. Julian Schwinger (1958). His Nobel lecture, "The Magnetic Moment of the Electron," reprinted in *Nobel Lectures in Physics* 3 (1964), contains an informal and lucid survey of his research. A more technical physical discussion of these issues, including historical comments, can be found in Steven Weinberg, *The Quantum Theory of Fields*, vol. 1, *Foundations* (1995). Two examples of Kusch's expository writing are "The World of Science and the Scientist's World," *Bulletin of the Atomic Scientists* 24 (Oct. 1988), and "A Personal View of Science and the Future," in *The Future of Science—1975 Nobel Conference Organized by Gustavus Adolphus College*, ed. Timothy C. L. Robinson (1977). Obituaries are in *Physics Today* 47 (Sept. 1994): 114–15, and in the *New York Times*, 23 Mar. 1993.

JOSEPH D. ZUND

KUSKOV, Ivan Aleksandrovich (1765–Oct. 1823), Russian colonial administrator, was born in Totma, Gubernia (province) of Vologda, Russia. Detailed information about his parentage is unavailable, but it is known that he grew up in a family of *meshchanina* (citizens of the town, as opposed to serfs).

In 1790 Kuskov concluded a contract with Kargopol merchant Aleksandr A. Baranov and became his assistant in the management of Russian colonies in North America. Kuskov helped Baranov organize Russian settlements on the islands in the Gulf of Alaska and on the mainland coasts and led hunting parties. He acted as a substitute for Baranov on the ship *Kodiak* in 1796, 1800, and 1804 in Novo-Arkhangelsk (now Sitka) from 1806 to 1808 and was commander of the Konstantin fortress (1798–1799) at Nachek Island. In 1805 Kuskov received a gold medal on a Vladimir ribbon "for diligence," and in October 1806 the Russian government conferred on him the title of "commercial counsellor."

But Kuskov's main achievement was the foundation in 1812 of the fortress and settlement of Ross in California near Romiantsov Bay (now Bodega Bay), only fifty miles from San Francisco. Land for the colony was bought from the Indians for the price of three blankets, three pairs of breeches, two axes, three hoes, and some beads. The colony was planned as an agricultural and cattle-breeding base for Russian America. The construction of the manager's house, barracks, storehouse and storage buildings, bathhouse, leatherworks, windmill, cattleyard, and other services was accomplished in 1814. Later, a chapel was added. Along with fur hunting, Russian colonists raised wheat, vegetables, and fruits. Kuskov became a pioneer in the development of shipbuilding in California. Under his direction two vessels were built, the galliot *Rumiantsev* (1818) and the brig *Buldakov* (1820).

While Kuskov had little trouble in negotiating with the local Indians (on 22 September 1817 Captain Lieutenant L. A. Hagemeister also signed a formal agreement with them in the fortress), establishing relations with Spanish authorities proved much more difficult. At first Kuskov received verbal permission from the governor of Upper California, José Joaquín de Arrilago, to engage in mutual trade, providing the company's vessels did not enter the port of San Francisco without the official consent of the Spanish government. This consent was never given, and in the fall of 1815 the commissioners of the Russian-American Company were detained, and the Aleuts engaged in trapping were taken into captivity. The Spanish authorities renewed their demands for the removal of the

Ross settlement. A prolonged, and in general fruitless, diplomatic correspondence ensued.

Kuskov's wife, Ekaterina Prokhorovna, was, according to E. A. Kichin, "the daughter of an Ustiug meshchanina who lived in India [America]." They had no children. Acquainted to some extent with the languages and customs of the Indians, she helped her husband in his relations with local inhabitants.

In 1821, after more than thirty years in America, Kuskov was replaced at Ross by Carl Schmidt, and in July 1823 he returned to his native Totma, where he died. His house in Totma has been restored, and a museum has opened there. As an assistant to the first Russian governor of Alaska and founder of Fort Ross, Kuskov played an important role in the history of Russian America. The final results of the activities of the Russian-American Company were, however, far from successful. Fort Ross was sold to John Augustus Sutter in 1841, and in 1867 a treaty for the sale of Alaska was signed in Washington, D.C.

• For additional information about Kuskov, see E. A. Kichin, "Ivan Aleksandrovich Kuskov," *Vologodskie gubernskie vedomosti,* 21 Feb. 1848, pp. 83–85; V. A. Potekhin, *Selenie Ross* (Settlement Ross) (1859); Svetlana G. Fedorova, "Russkaiia America i Totma v sudbe Ivana Kuskova" (Russian America and Totma in the life of Ivan Kuskov), in *Problemy istorii i etnografii Ameriki* (1979), pp. 229–54; and Richard A. Pierce, *Russian America: A Biographical Dictionary* (1990), pp. 281–85.

N. N. BOLKHOVITINOV

KUYKENDALL, Ralph Simpson (12 Apr. 1885–9 May 1963), historian and educator, was born in Linden, California, the son of John Wesley Kuykendall, a Methodist minister, and Marilla Persis Pierce. Kuykendall graduated in 1910 with a bachelor of arts degree from the College of the Pacific, where he had been a debater, editor of the college newspaper, and president of the student body. Upon graduation he taught for a year at College Park Academy and then began graduate studies in history at Stanford University, where he served as an assistant in the history department in 1911–1912.

From 1912 to 1918 Kuykendall took a break from his studies, working on a newspaper with his brother in Florida and as a researcher for the California Historical Survey Commission. The commission's director and archivist noted that Kuykendall was "a faithful, conscientious worker . . . a man of keen intellect and . . . great literary ability" and that he "took charge of the field work in the county archives and assisted very materially in bringing into shape for publication the great mass of material contained in our *Guide to the County Archives of California*" (letter from Owen C. Coy to the Hawaiian Historical Commission [1928], Kuykendall Collection).

After serving with the commission for two years, Kuykendall was awarded a scholarship from the Native Sons of the Golden West (NSGW) and returned to his studies at the University of California. In 1919 he married Edith Claire Kelly; they would have two sons.

Also in 1919, Kuykendall completed his M.A. thesis, "History of Early California Journalism," at the University of California at Berkeley. He entered a Ph.D. program at Berkeley (which he never completed) and was a graduate assistant in history there from 1919 to 1921. Kuykendall was awarded another scholarship by the NSGW in 1921 to carry out doctoral research in the archives of Seville, Spain, on early Spanish voyaging along the west coast of the Americas.

While Kuykendall was involved in this research, he was offered a job as executive secretary of the newly created Hawaiian Historical Commission. In 1922 Kuykendall left Seville for Honolulu, Hawaii, where he would serve as a historian for the next forty years. Kuykendall was employed by the Historical Commission from 1922 until its duties were transferred to the University of Hawaii in 1932. He then served with the Department of History at the University of Hawaii, joining the faculty in 1932 as an assistant professor, being promoted to associate professor in 1938 and full professor in 1949, and retiring as an emeritus professor in 1950.

Kuykendall taught courses in the history of the Pacific Coast of North America, the Hawaiian Islands, the Pacific Oceans Area, and the United States in the Pacific, as well as an introduction to the modern history of Oceania. He was one of the first historians of the Pacific, predating the establishment of Pacific Islands history as a formal field of historical inquiry by almost thirty years. His pioneering efforts, along with those of other Pacific historians, including James W. Davidson and Henry E. Maude, helped establish "Pacific History" as a specialization within historical studies.

Kuykendall continued his research into Hawaii's history as emeritus professor until the year of his death. He also served as the secretary (1927–1928, 1931–1938), president (1940–1943), and trustee (1929–1938) of the Hawaiian Historical Society and published sixty works. His meticulous research of English language sources located, preserved, and made accessible a foundation for all future students of the islands' past.

As executive secretary of the Historical Commission, Kuykendall was given three specific assignments to prepare and publish: a high school textbook of Hawaii's history, a history of Hawaii's role in World War I, and a comprehensive and authoritative history of Hawaii for general reading and reference. For his first assignment, Kuykendall used Charles A. Beard and William C. Bagley's *A First Book in American History* as a model and adopted a topical approach that focused on persons, events, or clearly defined lines of development. His *A History of Hawaii*, coauthored with the director of the Bishop Museum, Herbert E. Gregory, was approved by the 1925 legislature for use in the Territory's schools. The second work, *Hawaii in the World War*, written in collaboration with Lorin Tarr Gill, was published in 1928. The agreed-upon third project was intended to include an ancient history of the Hawaiian people; the history of the Hawaiian monarchy from 1778 to 1893; and the history of the Provisional Government, Republic of Hawaii, and the Territorial government. The three-volume *The Hawaiian Kingdom* (1938, 1953, 1967) that Kuykendall produced deals almost exclusively with the second part of the proposed project, the period from 1778 to 1893 (Charles H. Hunter, a University of Hawaii history professor, wrote a final chapter).

Kuykendall worked on this project for more than thirty years. He did however take a couple of years off to coauthor a one-volume history with A. Grove Day, *Hawaii: A History; From Polynesian Kingdom to American Commonwealth* (1948). Following his retirement in 1950, the reserved and meticulously dressed Kuykendall sat at his desk tucked into a corner of the Hawaiian Room at the University of Hawaii Library, working six days a week from 9:00 A.M. to closing time. He continued to work on *The Hawaiian Kingdom* project through the last months of his life.

A memorial to Kuykendall declares that *The Hawaiian Kingdom* "is the definitive work on the subject" and further that "no one in the future will know more, and few will know as much as he did about Hawaii under the monarchy" (*Seventy-Second Annual Report of the Hawaiian Historical Society for the Year 1963*, p. 29). While *The Hawaiian Kingdom* remains nonpareil in its field, the work has drawbacks. The social and cultural history of the monarchy receives short shrift. Kuykendall never developed Hawaiian language skills and makes little use of Hawaiian language sources. Eyewitnesses of the events he describes still lived during Kuykendall's time, and their oral histories could have added much data and enlivened the text. By today's standards Kuykendall's history is open to charges of Eurocentrism but his meticulous methods of research, encyclopedic mind for historical detail, and high standards of scholarship continue to set a goal of excellence in the field, and Kuykendall remains the foremost narrative historian of the Hawaiian Islands.

In January 1963 a frail Kuykendall left the Hawaiian Islands for the last time. That spring, he died at the Tucson, Arizona, home of his son, John R. Kuykendall, a professor of landscape architecture and horticulture at the University of Arizona. The *Honolulu Advertiser* eulogized him as "the nation's most respected and authoritative scholar on Hawaiian history." In 1965 the University of Hawaii named one of its largest classroom buildings Kuykendall Hall in his honor.

• Kuykendall's papers, the Kuykendall Collection, are in the Hawaiian and Pacific Collections, Hamilton Library, University of Hawaii at Mānoa. Kuykendall's fame rests on his three-volume life's work *The Hawaiian Kingdom*, a classic historical study reflecting painstaking research and attention to documentation. Vol. 1, *1778–1854 Foundation and Transformation*, was published in 1938; vol. 2, *1854–1874 Twenty Critical Years*, was published in 1953; and vol. 3, *1874–1893 The Kalakaua Dynasty*, was published posthumously in 1967. The complete publications of Kuykendall are listed in the *Hawaiian Journal of History* 2 (1968): 136–41. Further discussion of his life can be found in Michiko Kodama, "Ralph Simpson Kuykendall, Hawaiian Historian," a manuscript in the Hamilton Library, University of Hawaii at Mānoa.

DAVID W. SHIDELER

KUZNETS, Simon Smith (30 Apr. 1901–9 July 1985), economist, was born in Kharkov, Russia, the son of Abraham Kuznets, a fur dealer, and Pauline Friedman. In 1907 Kuznets's father immigrated to the United States; the First World War and the Russian Revolution intervened before his family could join him. Meanwhile the young Kuznets underwent the traditional Jewish education, entered the Gymnasium in Kharkov, and trained as an economist. After working for a statistical bureau in the Ukraine, Kuznets and his brothers joined their father in New York City in 1922. Kuznets was admitted to Columbia University and studied economics, earning his B.S. in 1923, his M.A. in 1925, and his Ph.D. in 1926.

At Columbia Kuznets's teacher and mentor was the renowned institutional economist Wesley Clair Mitchell. Mitchell not only directed Kuznets's dissertation but also persuaded Kuznets to join him at the National Bureau of Economic Research (NBER). Kuznets's association with the NBER lasted from 1927 to 1961. He married Edith Handler in 1929; they had two children. In addition to his association with the NBER, Kuznets held appointments at the University of Pennsylvania (1930–1954), Johns Hopkins University (1954–1960), and Harvard University (1960–1971; emeritus, 1971–1985). Kuznets was also president of the American Statistical Association (1949) and the American Economic Association (1954).

Kuznets's earliest writings on economics in the United States relate to business cycles and were published as *Cyclical Fluctuations* (1926), *Secular Movements in Production and Prices* (1930), and *Seasonal Variations in Industry and Trade* (1933). Together these three works analyze the cyclical, seasonal, and secular trends in economic data, and they describe the nature, causes, and propagation of business cycles. They also relate business cycles to certain long-term cycles that Kuznets named "secondary secular movements" (also known as "Kuznets cycles") and to seasonal movements. Kuznets's key innovation was to describe the process of the propagation of cycles and to locate their generation and continuation in lags and discontinuities in the response of one sector of the economy to changes in another sector. The discussion of long-term cycles is also significant for connecting changes in population (which had been a neglected endogenous variable until then) with changes in other economic variables, such as consumption, investment, capital formation, immigration, and foreign trade.

During the 1930s Kuznets began developing estimates of the national income of the United States. His theoretical treatment of the appropriate way of measuring national income is most clearly elucidated in his seminal work published in the *Encyclopedia of the Social Sciences* in 1933. In this article Kuznets reviewed alternative uses of national income figures and considered whether economic activity should be measured at the point of production, distribution, or consumption. He further discussed the implications of choices regarding which items and activities should be included in national income figures and how these activities and items might be valued. The article also discussed changes in the distribution of national income among regions, industries, functional shares (service versus property income), and persons.

Kuznets published numerous books extending these estimates and relating them to other measures of economic activity, including *National Income, 1929–1932* (1934), *National Income and Capital Formation, 1919–1935* (1937), *National Income and Its Composition, 1919–1938* (1941), *National Product in Wartime* (1945), *National Income: A Summary of Findings* (1946), and *National Product since 1869* (1946). In the late 1930s Kuznets conducted a series of studies of the extent of American capital formation. These studies provided detailed records of the level and components of capital formation in the U.S. economy. Kuznets's estimates of national income and capital formation were of inestimable value for the economic planners faced with the task of expanding U.S. production to meet the needs of war.

During World War II Kuznets worked for the Planning Committee of the War Production Board. There he participated in studies determining industrial capacity and the availability of resources in an effort to ascertain their suitability for conversion to the needs of war production. As a result of the ensuing reorganization toward war production, the U.S. national output increased by $17 billion in 1942 (Perlman, p. 144).

By the end of the war Kuznets's interests had moved to a new research area: the analysis of the process of modern economic growth. His work comprises some of the most comprehensive and detailed information ever produced about the economic growth of nations. Kuznets distinguished modern economic growth from premodern economic growth, defining the former as a sustained increase in per capita (or per worker) output that is often accompanied by an increase in population and that usually involves dramatic structural changes in the economy and society. Much of his work in this area involved an examination of the growth records of various nations in an effort to describe and understand the nature and cause of changes that occur during the process of growth.

Kuznets's comparative studies revealed the relationship between changes in per capita output and changes in productivity, employment, population, consumption and capital formation, income distribution, and international interdependence. As a result of his work, economists gained a clearer understanding of the complicated phases and interrelationships that comprise growth and of the changes that occur during the process of growth. These findings, and the hypotheses Kuznets developed to explain them, formed the basis of many subsequent theories of economic growth.

Kuznets envisaged these investigations as a necessary stage in an effort to generate a theory of economic growth that would provide a useful model of the essential and common aspects of modern economic growth (*Six Lectures on Economic Growth* [1959], p. 111). In addition he believed that a complete theory would need to analyze the effects of different initial conditions on ensuing patterns of growth and on the resultant mature economy and locate the mechanisms of underlying the spread of modern economic growth throughout the world. Kuznets argued that even if such a theory were never achieved, the quest was worthwhile for two reasons. First, a theoretical schema would be useful for organizing and classifying a vast variety of empirical findings (*Economic Growth and Structure* [1972], pp. 77–78). In addition, this base of empirical knowledge would help economists and policymakers avoid overgeneralization, dogmatism, and reliance on dangerously obsolete theories.

The main contemporary critics of his work—Paul Hohenberg, Edward Denison, and Joan Robinson—emphasized flaws in such an approach to the development of a theory of economic growth. They argued that the collection of large quantities of data would be inadequate for discerning turning points and stages or for discovering mechanisms of initiation and transmission. Thus they criticized an apparently dogmatic rejection of theory. However Kuznets did not reject all theory and often used theoretical constructs extensively in guiding his empirical research. Ultimately it was his thorough, meticulous, and sensitive approach to crude data that impressed reviewers of his work.

In all of his work Kuznets demonstrated a commitment to a sound empirical basis for economic analysis, a willingness to explore myriad hypotheses to understand a correlation or pattern, and an abiding interest in the effect of economic processes on income distribution and welfare. In addition Kuznets was careful to emphasize the importance of technological, social, and institutional factors in hindering or facilitating the process of economic growth.

Kuznets received the Nobel Prize in economics in 1971. The official announcement of the Royal Academy of Sciences for the prize declared that Kuznets had won for "his empirically founded interpretation of economic growth which has led to new and deepened insight into the economic and social structure and process of development." The economic committee of the academy praised Kuznets's careful marshaling of statistical data, his critical examination of abstract theories, his inclusion of institutional and noneconomic elements in his analysis, and his careful delineation of "the margins, uncertainty and lack of precision which arises from qualitative changes in production and consumption."

In the final years of his life Kuznets focused again on population and economic growth, the changing distribution of income, and the income distribution implications of demographic changes. These studies, including *Population, Capital and Growth* (1973) and *Growth, Population and Income Distribution* (1979), sought to determine the patterns of income distribution in developed and developing countries and to relate changes in these patterns to demographic changes and economic growth. Although Kuznets retired from Harvard in 1971, he continued to work and write until his death in Cambridge, Massachusetts.

• Kuznets's papers are at the Harvard University Archives. Other books by Kuznets include *Commodity Flow and Capital Formation* (1938), *Economic Change: Selected Essays in Business Cycles* (1953), *Shares of Upper Income Groups in Income and Savings* (1953), *Capital in the American Economy: Its Formation and Financing* (1964), *Modern Economic Growth: Rate, Structure, and Spread* (1966), *Toward a Theory of Economic Growth* (1968), *Economic Growth of Nations* (1971), *Quantitative Economic Research: Trends and Problems* (1972), *Population, Capital, and Growth: Selected Essays* (1973), and *Growth, Population, and Income Distribution: Selected Essays* (1979). A bibliography of his work, prepared by Robert Fogel, Marilyn Coopersmith, and Kathleen McCauley, was published in *Economic Development and Cultural Change* 31 (Jan. 1983): 433–54. For assessments of his work and career see Erik Lundberg, "Simon Kuznets' Contribution to Economics," *Scandinavian Journal of Economics* 73 (1971): 444–61; Richard A. Easterlin, "Kuznets, Simon," *International Encyclopedia of the Social Sciences*, vol. 18, *Biographical Supplement* (1979), pp. 393–96; Vibha Kapuria-Foreman and Mark Perlman, "An Economic Historian's Economist: Remembering Simon Kuznets," *Economic Journal* 105 (1995): 1524–47; and Mark Perlman, "Political Purpose and the National Accounts," in *The Politics of Numbers*, ed. William Alonso and Paul Starr (1987).

VIBHA KAPURIA-FOREMAN

KYNE, Peter Bernard (12 Oct. 1880–25 Nov. 1957), novelist and short story writer, was born in San Francisco, California, the son of John Kyne, a cattleman, and Mary Cresham. Except for a later half-year in a business school, Kyne received his education in a one-room rural school. He could not resist boasting that a visiting superintendent of schools, reading one of his class assignments, a story on the mercy killing of an infirm horse, told him that he would fail in commerce because "God made you for a writer." He did not graduate but went to work on his father's ranch at the age of fifteen. He then became a clerk in a general store, laboring from 6 A.M. to 9 P.M. for room, board, and twenty dollars a month. He next went to work for a shipping firm for thirty dollars a month. Young Kyne found that he liked the life of a businessman, especially that of a salesman.

Because Kyne was not yet eighteen years old, he had to lie about his age and bribe a corporal to pass the eye exam to enlist in the army. He served in Company L, Fourteenth Infantry, during the Spanish-American War and fought in the Philippine Insurrection. He also served during World War I as a captain in the 144th Field Artillery, the outfit in which fellow writer Stewart Edward White was a major. He would later put his military service to use in his writing. For a half-dozen years after his discharge, he worked at various jobs, even running a haberdashery, his longest-lasting jobs being with a wholesale lumber and shipping firm. From this work and a 1905 stint as a *San Francisco Morning Call* reporter, he came to know the Embarcadero like the palm of his hand, and he salted away waterfront lore for future writing. On 2 February 1910 he married Helene Catherine Johnston. The couple had no children.

When Kyne took a stab at writing in 1909, his first real effort was a short story about salvage that the *Saturday Evening Post* accepted. The *Post* was becoming the most esteemed market for freelance writers and came to be king of the "slicks," popular magazines on better-quality paper. Slicks paid better and were considered more sophisticated than magazines printed on newsprint (pulp paper), which were often descendants of nineteenth-century dime novels. Soon Kyne was a contributor to *Cosmopolitan*, *American Magazine*, *Sunset*, and *Collier's*, but particularly the *Post*, where he placed more than sixty stories.

In 1913 the first of Kyne's twenty-five novels, some of them selling 100,000 copies, appeared. It was *The Three Godfathers*. His next big success was his California lumbering story, *The Valley of the Giants* (1918). *Kindred of the Dust* was second in sales in 1920 only to one of Zane Grey's westerns. *The Pride of Palomar* (1921) was another bestseller; it dwelt on what Kyne saw as the menace of Japanese immigration. He used dialect and other ethnic stereotyping as shorthand characterization. He esteemed—and his main characters personified—the traditional virtues. He had the highest regard for San Francisco's merchant mariners, so many of whom were Swedes or Norwegians that locals referred to the merchant ships calling at the Embarcadero's piers as "the Scandinavian navy."

Kyne's work peaked with *Cappy Ricks* (1916), a collection of tales about an irascible old go-getter of a sea captain with a tender heart hidden by the shrewdness that he displayed in one-upmanship over his son-in-law, Matt Beasley. Kyne patterned his protagonist, in part, after Captain Robert Dollar. This Scot started out with a dinky steam lumber schooner on the Redwood Coast, the *Newsboy*, and ended up a millionaire owner of timber and lumber interests and the world-famous Dollar Steamship Line. Wisely, Kyne had Ricks reappear—*Cappy Ricks Retires* (1922), *Cappy Ricks Comes Back* (1934), and *Cappy Ricks Special* (1935). A (not very successful) play was even adapted from the Cappy Ricks stories by Edward F. Rose in 1919. Ricks remains the only memorable character of Kyne's fiction.

Kyne was very fond of dogs, especially hunting dogs—pointers and setters. When Ray Long, editor of *Cosmopolitan*, asked his best contributors, Kyne, Edna, Ferber, Irwin S. Cobb, and James Oliver Curwood, to select their favorite stories, Kyne chose his "Point," a dog story, for Long's book, *My Story That I Like Best* (1924). In the title of his first collection of short stories, *The Parson of Panamint and Other Stories* (1936), Kyne showed another of his interests, the California desert and Death Valley. He continued to write about ranchers and lumberjacks, troopers and seamen (*Soldiers, Sailors and Dogs*, 1936), and even businessmen, the latter seemingly out of place among his brawny heroes. Kyne referred to himself as a businessman-turned-author. In truth, he remained a businessman all his life; he simply made a very profitable business out of writing. He honestly admired men of commerce and wrote a book on what he saw as the real secret of success. *The Go Getter* (1922) was adopted as a bible by up-and-coming salesmen. Kyne claimed that the world lost a good salesman when he became a writer.

Kyne was prolific, not profound. He wrote formula fiction "to order." With a finely tuned sense of the public's taste, he gave his audience exactly what it wanted. He was a very fast writer, bragging at least once of turning out 13,000 words of copy in just twelve hours. He had no literary pretensions at all and ignored critics, who largely reciprocated. Perhaps because of his lack of education and "polish," the businessman-author in the dedication of his *Never the Twain Shall Meet* (1923), in self-deprecation, called himself just a sufficiently skilled journeyman in a "cockeyed profession," writing, which happened to pay him very well. He saw his stories as salable commodities.

Besides the movies made from his books, Kyne wrote original material for the silent movies (1921–1928) and then turned out scripts for "talkies" by Universal, Columbia, Republic, and 20th Century–Fox (1936–1952), the best-known picture being *Lloyds of London* (1936).

Unfortunately, Kyne squandered much of his wealth in poor investments, speculative manufacturing schemes, inventions, unproductive mines, and oil wells. He owned a string of racehorses. (He served a term as president of the California Jockey Club.) But he was more successful when he imitated his father and bought a ranch to raise cattle and hogs. By the mid-1930s, the well-known Republican author, a member of the Army and Navy Club and San Francisco's elite Bohemian Club, found his popularity fading just as his health began to fail, although a trilogy appeared in 1935, *The Golden West*, containing *Kindred of the Dust, Never the Twain Shall Meet,* and *The Pride of Palomar.* He suffered an economic body blow (1939) in a $30,000 judgment against him for income-tax evasion. His last published novel, *Dude Woman* (1940), did not sell, and he died in San Francisco with his last two novels unpublished. During the 1940s he was able to place only a few articles and short stories in magazines, and the *San Francisco Chronicle* (28 Feb. 1959) reported that his estate was appraised at only $4,390.

Kyne's success was commercial and financial, not literary. His productivity alone, twenty-five novels and hundreds of short stories and articles, what he disdainfully called his "'alleged' literary output," cannot justify immortality. But the best of his fiction has a freshness and truthfulness that rescues him from oblivion. Although his one-time bestsellers are uncollected by bibliophiles and largely unread today, they are useful tools in documenting the culture and the reading tastes of an era. On the other hand, Kyne's importance to the history of American cinema has gone unnoticed. *The Parson of Panamint* was a 1941 film; *The Valley of the Giants* was made into movies in 1919, 1927, and 1938. *The Three Godfathers,* his parable of an outlaw trio of "Wise Men" adopting a desert found-

ling, was made into a movie six times over and into a TV drama retitled *The Godchild.* The 1936 and 1948 cinema versions—the latter directed by John Ford—were important and excellent movies. And Cappy Ricks endures to some extent as a typically American character, guaranteeing Kyne continued respect as a creative writer.

• Kyne's personal papers, including 3,400 letters and 130 literary manuscripts, are in the University of Oregon Library in Eugene. That library's *Occasional Papers No. 6* (1974) included a Kyne bibliography in "Two San Francisco Writers." The best biographical sketch of Kyne and his work is James F. Smith, Jr., "Peter B. Kyne," in *The American Short Story Writers,* Vol. 78 of the *Dictionary of Literary Biography,* ed. Bobby E. Kimbel (1989). Obituaries are in the *San Francisco Examiner* and the *New York Times,* 26 Nov. 1957.

RICHARD H. DILLON

KYNETT, Alpha Jefferson (12 Aug. 1829–23 Feb. 1899), Methodist Episcopal clergyman and church extension executive, was born in Adams County, Pennsylvania, the son of John Kynett, a farmer and cooper, and Polly Peterson, the daughter of a Methodist preacher. His parents were devout members of the Methodist Episcopal church. The family moved to Ohio in 1832, to Indiana in 1838, and finally to Des Moines County, Iowa, in 1842.

At age sixteen Kynett underwent a conversion that confirmed a childhood interest in entering the ministry. He secured a license to exhort in 1850 and a license to preach the next year, when he was admitted on trial to the church's Iowa Conference and appointed to Catfish Station near Dubuque, Iowa. Although Kynett had some early schooling, he was mostly self-taught; he read widely in theology, science, history, law, and literature, and came to be considered among the best thinkers in Methodism.

Kynett was ordained deacon in 1853 and elder in 1855. In 1854 he married Althea Pauline Gilruth of Davenport, Iowa, whom he had met when he was her pastor; they had two children. Kynett's early pastorates included Davenport, Dubuque, Iowa City, and Lyons. He was appointed presiding elder, or supervising pastor, of the Davenport District in 1860, a testimony to his success and leadership. Kynett was dedicated to the Union cause during the Civil War, serving on the Iowa governor's staff, assisting in recruiting and supplying several Union regiments, and leading the work of the Sanitary Commission by organizing auxiliaries across the state.

In 1864 Kynett was elected a delegate to the General Conference, the chief legislative body of his denomination, which met every four years; he was reelected to every successive General Conference until his death. At the 1864 General Conference he was instrumental in introducing legislation and drafting a constitution for the church's first Church Extension Society, intended to organize and build new Methodist churches across the nation. When the important chief executive position of corresponding secretary of the denominational society was vacant in 1867, the bishops appointed Kynett to the post. He had served in a similar position in the Upper Iowa Conference society since 1864. Until his death he carried out the duties of head of the church extension effort from his office in Philadelphia. This included raising more than $6 million, administering building loans to an estimated 12,000 congregations, and facilitating the construction of hundreds of churches, especially in the West. From 1889 until 1899 he also edited a bimonthly periodical, *Christianity in Earnest*, which reported on church growth, financing new churches, and architectural trends. It was also a voice for Methodism's commitment to prohibition. In 1895 Kynett published *The Religion of the Republic, and Laws of Religious Corporations*, a massive survey on church-state relations in the United States, especially in regard to church property; it included fifty-one chapters describing church property laws in the various states and territories.

Believing that his church had to become more representative and democratic, Kynett supported initiatives in the General Conference, including voting rights for lay people, equal lay and clergy representation, and the admission of women as delegates. In *Our Laity: And Their Equal Rights without Distinction of Sex in the Methodist Episcopal Church* (1896) he argued that the church's constitution made women eligible to be elected and to serve in its highest legislative body.

Unlike many of his Protestant peers, Kynett enjoyed friendly relationships with Roman Catholic and Jewish leaders. He was one of those responsible for the renewed life of the Christian Commission, revived during the Spanish-American War under the name National Relief Commission to serve the benevolent interests of Protestants, Catholics, and Jews alike.

From his days as a pastor in Davenport and Dubuque, Kynett had been a stalwart advocate of the temperance movement. He preached, wrote, and organized on behalf of this cause and was influential in the organization of the Anti-Saloon League in America in 1895 and of the Board of Temperance, Prohibition and Public Morals of the Methodist Episcopal Church. The day after he addressed a temperance meeting in Harrisburg, Pennsylvania, he suffered a stroke that resulted in his death.

In the years following the Civil War, no one was more important in northern Methodism than Kynett in organizing and extending the areal growth of the church. Not only was he the successful executive of the agency responsible for church extension, but his views on the structure of the denomination can be seen as prefiguring the network of denominational agencies that became modern corporate Methodism.

• The most complete biographical information is in George Elliott, "Alpha J. Kynett, D.D., LL.D.," *Methodist Review* 81 (1899): 849–64. Additional information about Kynett's work in church extension and temperance is in the memorial issue of *Christianity in Earnest* 11 (1899): 46–75, and in an article by his son, Alpha G. Kynett, "The Real Founder of the Board of Church Extension," *Methodist Review* 85 (1903): 631–34.

CHARLES YRIGOYEN, JR.

KYSER, Kay (18 June 1906–23 July 1985), bandleader, was born James King Kern Kyser in Rocky Mount, North Carolina, the son of Paul B. Kyser and Emily Royster Howell, both pharmacists. During his school years Kyser displayed an outgoing nature that foreshadowed his future career. In his senior year of high school he was class president, a cheerleader, coach of the junior varsity football team, editor of the yearbook, and a member of several academic clubs. Entering the University of North Carolina in 1924 to study law, he again was active as a cheerleader and as an impresario for campus musical productions. In 1926 he began to lead a band of six college musicians. Kyser, who never learned to read music or to play an instrument, functioned as a master of ceremonies. The band was a commercial success, largely because of Kyser's showmanship, and during the next two years the group performed at dozens of college dances throughout the South and Midwest. After graduating in 1928 with a B.A., he completely devoted his time to leading the band.

During an engagement at the Miramar Hotel in Santa Monica, California, in the summer of 1934 Kyser developed a distinctive method of introducing songs: the vocalist would sing the words of the song's title, the musicians played softly in the background while Kyser introduced the vocalist, and then the band would begin the song. This manner of introduction became a hallmark that he kept for the rest of his career. In September 1934 the band, which had grown to fifteen members (using the brass-reeds-rhythm instrumentation typical of dance bands of the era), began performing at the Blackhawk Restaurant in Chicago. Radio exposure of their Blackhawk performances began as early as 1935.

In 1937 the band inaugurated a series of Saturday night broadcasts titled "Kay Kyser's Kampus Klass," which was soon renamed "Kay Kyser's College of Musical Knowledge" (occasionally mistakenly cited as "*Kollege* of Musical Knowledge"). The name derived from the broadcast's quiz-show format. Members of the Blackhawk's audience received prizes if they correctly guessed titles of songs based on questions mailed to Kyser from listeners in the radio audience. Kyser always announced the names of those who submitted questions, and thousands tuned in with hopes that their questions would be read during the broadcast. The "College of Musical Knowledge" rapidly became an immensely successful radio show, and the broadcasts, which can be considered the cornerstone of Kyser's career, continued into the early 1940s.

Kyser's public performances were a popular combination of sweet dance-band arrangements, novelty numbers, quiz-show routines, and comedy bits. Ever the consummate showman, he appeared on stage in an academic gown and mortarboard, and the band's music stands were adorned with drawings typically found on schoolroom blackboards. Trumpeter Merwyn Bogue, who used the stage name "Ish Kabibble" and who sported a comic haircut, was featured on many of the band's most popular novelty numbers.

During World War II the band performed extensively at armed forces training camps and hospitals. In 1942 Kyser recorded what became his most famous number, "Praise the Lord and Pass the Ammunition." The band made dozens of recordings, mostly for the Brunswick and Columbia labels. Among its other hit recordings were the nonsensical novelty tune "Three Little Fishies" (1939), "Who Wouldn't Love You" (1942), "There Goes That Song Again" (1944), "Jingle, Jangle, Jingle" (1946), "On a Slow Boat to China" (1948), and the "Woody Woodpecker Song" (1948).

Kyser and the band appeared in nine motion pictures: *That's Right, You're Wrong* (1939), *You'll Find Out* (1940), *Playmates* (1941), *My Favorite Spy* (1942), *Swing Fever* (1943), *Thousands Cheer* (1943), *Stage Door Canteen* (1943), *Around the World* (1943), and *Carolina Blues* (1944).

From 1949 through 1951 the "College of Musical Knowledge" was presented on NBC television. After the television show was discontinued, Kyser, who was weary of show business and was already a wealthy man, retired and moved back to North Carolina with his wife, the former Georgia Carroll, a Hollywood model whom he had met when they worked together during a USO tour and married in 1944; they had three children. During his retirement years, Kyser was active as a Christian Scientist and contributed much of his time to community affairs. He died in Chapel Hill, North Carolina.

Kyser is remembered more for his showmanship and astute business sense than for any purely musical contribution. George Duning, the band's chief arranger throughout most of its existence, wrote in the sweet, dance-band style that was popular at the time. Models for the band's early style included the music of Guy Lombardo and of Fred Waring. After 1942 the band followed a more swinging style, in part because of additional arrangements by Van Alexander and the presence of jazz musicians such as Herbie Haymer on tenor saxophone and Moe Purtill on drums. Throughout its history, the band had a number of popular vocalists, including Harry Babbitt, Ginny Simms, actress Jane Russell, and Michael Douglas, who later became a well-known television talk-show host.

• A detailed but somewhat hagiographic account of Kyser's early years appears in the *Current Biography Yearbook* for 1941, pp. 481–83. A balanced survey of his career can be found in George Simon, *The Big Bands* (1967). An obituary is in the *New York Times*, 24 July 1985.

MICHAEL COGSWELL

L

LABOUISSE, Henry Richardson (11 Feb. 1904–25 Mar. 1987), statesman and humanitarian, was born in New Orleans, Louisiana, the son of Henry Richardson Labouisse and Frances Devereaux Huger (occupations unknown). Labouisse graduated from Princeton in 1926 and from Harvard Law School in 1929. He practiced law in New York City from 1929 until 1941 and married Elizabeth Scriven Clark in 1935. The couple had one daughter. Elizabeth Labouisse died in 1945. The *New Yorker* (14 Dec. 1957) described Labouisse as "an easy going, slow-speaking cigar smoker, medium-sized, florid and roman nosed, who parts his hair in the middle, in the Ivy League style of the Twenties."

When the country's entry into the Second World War brought many new men into government, Labouisse began a second career with the State Department. He rose quickly in a succession of posts largely concerned with foreign economic policy, becoming chief of the Foreign Economic Administration mission to France and also minister for economic affairs in the Paris embassy (Nov. 1944). The belief by the makers of postwar American foreign policy that the promotion of economic well-being would encourage international peace, political stability, the advance of democracy, and the fulfillment of human aspirations found expression in the generous extension of aid to Western Europe. As a chief deputy to the undersecretary of state for economic affairs, and in his own efforts in coordinating American aid with the various European reconstruction programs, Labouisse played an important, if secondary, role in these efforts, which culminated in the Marshall Plan. For six years Labouisse helped formulate and implement foreign economic policy from a series of positions that concluded with his service as director of British Commonwealth and Northern European Affairs (Oct. 1949–Sept. 1951). Labouisse had long recognized that aid cushioned the European economies from necessary adjustments to market forces and had urged a tougher line on aid since 1949. As head of the aid mission to France from September 1951 to June 1954, during a time when American preoccupations became focused on conflicts in Asia, Labouisse witnessed the shift in American policy in Europe from economic reconstruction toward rearmament. This shift, which threatened to check the recovery of European living standards, replaced the cooperation and progress of the early years with conflict and frustration.

In 1954 Labouisse accepted an offer from United Nations secretary-general Dag Hammarskjöld to become the executive director of the United Nations Relief and Works Agency for Palestine Refugees (UNRWA) in June. In November of that year he married Eve Curie, the daughter of the scientists Pierre and Marie Curie, whom he had met in 1951. This opened his third career, that of an international civil servant concerned with the problems of the developing world. Four years in the Middle East instructed Labouisse on the differences between a powerful state and an impotent international organization. The UNRWA had originally been charged to provide temporary relief until it could rehabilitate the refugees and then integrate them into host states through promoting economic development. Labouisse had come to believe that the best solution to the refugee problem would be to encourage the host countries to absorb the newcomers by transferring responsibility from the United Nations and shifting funding toward development projects. However, the continuing conflict between Israel and the Arab states and the refusal of the refugees to accept final expulsion from their homes raised insuperable barriers to UNRWA's efforts. Labouisse left UNRWA to become a consultant to the International Bank for Reconstruction and Development (May 1959–Mar. 1961), then served the administration of John F. Kennedy during 1961 as director of the International Cooperation Administration, created to coordinate nonmilitary foreign aid programs. When he was squeezed out in an administrative shuffle, Labouisse held the Athens embassy from 1962 to 1965. Here he ably represented the United States in efforts to pacify disputes between Greece and Turkey over Cyprus that threatened to break into war.

In 1965 Labouisse returned to the UN as executive director of the United Nations Children's Fund (UNICEF). He took over an agency with a very high standing—he led the UNICEF delegation that accepted the Nobel Peace Prize in 1965—as it entered a decade of turmoil. International agencies and Western governments had all hoped to make the 1960s the "development decade" for the Third World. Rather than promoting long-term programs, however, Labouisse spent most of his first five-year term dealing with natural and man-made disasters. Discretion and impartiality became watchwords for an international organization dealing with newly independent states that often feared Western aid as a new form of imperialism. Such discretion sometimes brought down severe criticism on UNICEF for the caution and slow pace of its action. Nevertheless, Labouisse strengthened the already well-established reputation of UNICEF by the skill with which he negotiated the supply of aid to the victims of famine in India and of civil war in Nigeria.

During the 1970s UNICEF returned to its efforts to promote development of the Third World by emphasizing the provision of such basic services as better water supply and sanitation, enhanced nutrition for children, improved conditions for women, more accessible medical care, and education adapted to needs. Labouisse served as a facilitator of these efforts, rather than as a development strategist who sought to impose his own vision. Although Labouisse had hoped to retire at the end of his second term in 1975, UN secretary-general Kurt Waldheim prevailed upon him to extend his tour through the end of 1979. Labouisse then found himself organizing yet another international relief effort when the Vietnamese invasion of Cambodia in 1979 raised the possibility of a major famine. The difficult political situation bore a striking resemblance to that of the Nigerian civil war, so once again UNICEF had to proceed with a caution that aroused criticism in Western countries. Nevertheless, UNICEF made an important contribution to mastering the danger of famine by the end of 1979. Labouisse then retired to Manhattan, where he died.

Although an effective negotiator on behalf of organizations, Labouisse was no slave to personal ambition. Rather, he found in his succession of posts in the State Department and the United Nations an outlet for his own fundamental decency, idealism, and desire to help others. All the same, his idealism had a hard edge to it: he sought to make the world a better place, not a perfect place. In this he represented an important strand of "practical idealism" in American foreign policy that sought to create an "empire of liberty and hope," not merely an "American empire," a viewpoint often slighted by the cold warriors who made policy and the historians who interpreted it. For half a lifetime Henry Labouisse devoted his considerable energies and abilities to fostering the success of international cooperative efforts to raise living standards and promote peace around the world.

• Labouisse's personal papers are in the custody of Mrs. Labouisse in Manhattan; some of his official papers for the period 1945–1954 are reprinted in the *Papers Relating to the Foreign Relations of the United States*, a compilation of declassified documents from the State Department. An attractive profile is sketched in the *New Yorker* 33 (14 Dec. 1957): 33–34. For fuller accounts of his work with international agencies see Edward H. Buehrig, *The UN and the Palestinian Refugees: A Study in Nonterritorial Administration* (1971); Maggie Black, *The Children and the Nations: The Story of Unicef* (1986); and William Shawcross, *The Quality of Mercy: Cambodia, Holocaust and Modern Conscience* (1984). His obituary appears in the *New York Times*, 27 Mar. 1987.

J. S. HILL

LACEY, John Fletcher (30 May 1841–29 Sept. 1913), lawyer and congressman, was born in New Martinsville, Virginia, an Ohio River settlement in what later became West Virginia, the son of John Mills Lacey, a brick and stonemason, and Eleanor Patten. In 1853 the family moved to nearby Wheeling, then two years later to Oskaloosa, Iowa. Hard work marked Lacey's passage to adulthood in Iowa. He labored at his father's trade and on the family farm, boarded out to study in a succession of small, lonely academies, and spent two winters as an itinerant schoolmaster. Upon hearing of the firing on Fort Sumter, he immediately joined a volunteer company and, on his twentieth birthday, marched off to war.

As was the case with many public figures of his generation, the Civil War presented Lacey with challenges and opportunities that reshaped his life. Within months of his enlistment, he was captured by Confederate troops on 17 September 1861 at the battle of Blue Mills Landing in Missouri. He was paroled by the rebels, but until formal prisoner exchanges (then suspended) took place he could not again take up arms. Discharged from the army in November 1861, Lacey returned to Oskaloosa and studied law under the tutelage of Samuel A. Rice, the attorney general of Iowa. Rice became a mentor to Lacey and an inspirational model of discipline and professionalism for the younger man. In the summer of 1862 prisoner exchanges resumed, and Lacey reenlisted in the Union army as a private in the Thirty-third Iowa Regiment, commanded by Rice. Lacey rose through the ranks and became a trusted staff officer under Rice. After Rice was killed in 1864, Lacey served on the staff of General Frederick Steele. He saw action in Arkansas, Louisiana, Alabama, and Texas and was mustered out in 1865 with the rank of brevet major. For the remainder of his life he celebrated the achievements of Union veterans and, while in Congress, vigorously defended their pensions.

After the war, Lacey launched his professional career and his family life with characteristic dispatch, opening his law office on 18 September 1865 and marrying Martha Jane Newell the following day. The couple had four children, two of whom died a month apart in 1880. Although he served one term in the Iowa General Assembly beginning in 1869, Lacey was devoted to the law, not public life, during this period. For the next eighteen years he resisted appeals to run for the assembly, bench, or Congress, preferring to work as an attorney. By his own calculation, between 1865 and 1888 he devoted twelve to sixteen hours each day to his practice. He read and traveled widely but with an eye to broadening his mind and preserving his health in order to improve his professional skills and stamina. In trying cases across Iowa, Lacey earned a reputation for courtesy and dignity in personal relations, wit and resourcefulness in debate, and meticulous courtroom preparation. His professional standing was enhanced by the publication in 1870 of the *Third Iowa Digest*, a compilation of state law, and his legal masterwork, the two-volume *Digest of Railway Decisions* (1875, 1884), a compendium of all English language railroad law cases. Renowned as an expert in railroad law, he nevertheless insisted on retaining a general practice in keeping with his belief that the best lawyers were "all around" lawyers.

Lacey's sense of duty and his conservative Republican convictions propelled him into politics in 1888. Following a string of Republican defeats at the hands of a Democratic-Greenback party fusion movement in the Sixth Iowa Congressional District, GOP officials persuaded Lacey to challenge the charismatic fusionist congressman (and future Populist presidential candidate) James B. Weaver. Lacey defeated Weaver in an energetic campaign and embarked upon a lengthy congressional career. Although he was not reelected in 1890, he returned to Congress in 1893 and served seven consecutive terms until 1907. On most issues he was an able but utterly conventional standpat Republican. His defense of party orthodoxy and strenuous opposition to the Iowa Idea, a program of railroad regulation and tariff revision associated with progressive Republican governor Albert B. Cummins, prompted reform-minded Iowans to denounce Lacey as a reactionary and vote him out of office in 1906. In a final act of service to the conservative faction of the Iowa GOP, he unsuccessfully challenged Cummins for a Senate seat in 1908.

Lacey's principal significance as a lawmaker, however, involved a departure from Republican standpattism. During his congressional tenure, he was one of that body's foremost advocates for a national conservation program. Using his position on the House Public Lands Committee, which he chaired from 1895 until 1907, he labored with passion and determination to preserve wildlife, safeguard forests, and create additional national parks. The Lacey Bird and Game Act of 1900 represented his most notable achievement in wildlife preservation. The law banned the interstate shipment of illegally killed birds and game and gave the Agriculture Department greater powers to promote the well-being of native birds and to bar unwanted foreign species. Lacey also worked to set aside game preserves in national parks and forests and to create breeding grounds for the endangered buffalo. In forestry matters, Lacey favored expert supervision of national reserves. Accordingly, he proposed the expansion of national government authority over forests and, within government, the transfer of forest oversight from the use-oriented Interior Department to the Agriculture Department. The 1906 Preservation of American Antiquities Act capped Lacey's efforts to set aside Arizona's Petrified Forest, New Mexico's Cliff Dwellers site, and other locations as protected national monuments.

Despite Lacey's estrangement from progressive reform, his conservation measures did expand the regulatory power of government. Although devised to complement state authority, the Lacey Bird Act still widened the application of the Constitution's interstate commerce clause. In general, Lacey's conservation proposals fit President Theodore Roosevelt's conception of public authority more than they did his own. Lacey justified such actions on practical grounds. "Private owners cannot perform the duty of forestry in America," he argued. "Only the government lives long enough to plant trees extensively" (Pammel, p. 76). Lacey continued his conservation activities and practiced law after he left Congress in 1907. He died in Oskaloosa.

• The Lacey papers, including a manuscript autobiography, are housed at the State Historical Society of Iowa, Des Moines. Many of Lacey's most important speeches and articles as well as a portion of his autobiography are collected in L. H. Pammel, *Major John F. Lacey Memorial Volume* (1915). Lacey's conservation activities are described in Annette Gallagher, C.H.M., "Citizen of the Nation: John Fletcher Lacey, Conservationist," *Annals of Iowa* 46 (1981): 9–24. An obituary is in the *Oskaloosh (Iowa) Daily Herald*, 4 Oct. 1913.

THOMAS R. PEGRAM

LACHAISE, Gaston (19 Mar. 1882–17 Oct. 1935), sculptor, was born in Paris, France, the son of Jean Michel Lachaise, a cabinetmaker and woodcarver, and Marie Barre. Lachaise learned carving in the Paris shop of his father, a master cabinetmaker who had designed the Eiffel apartment in the famed Parisian tower. At the age of thirteen he entered the École Bernard Palissy, then one of France's foremost applied-arts schools, where he studied drawing, modeling, and carving. In 1898 Lachaise enrolled at the Académie Nationale des Beaux-Arts and studied with Gabriel-Jules Thomas. He discovered "primitive," Asian, and preclassical art in galleries and museums. Beginning in 1899 he exhibited works for four years at the annual Salons des Artistes. In about 1902 Lachaise met Isabel Dutaud Nagle, a Canadian-American woman who was to become a lifetime obsession and the inspiration for many of his sculptures. She was ten years his senior, married, and had a young child: it was to be fifteen years before she divorced and they could marry. After serving briefly in the military in 1904–1905, Lachaise worked as a craftsman in Paris for jeweler and glassmaker Rene Lalique.

In 1906 Lachaise arrived in Boston, never to return to Europe. He became an assistant to sculptor Henry Hudson Kitson, who was working on a Civil War commission at the time. When Kitson relocated his studio to New York in 1912, Lachaise moved there also and began working in MacDougal Alley in Greenwich Village. He worked increasingly on his own sculpture, while also employed as an assistant to sculptor Paul Manship from 1913 to 1921. Lachaise exhibited his own work at the Armory Show in 1913 but attracted little notice. As the chief assistant to Manship, he collaborated on the *J. Pierpont Morgan Memorial* (1920, Metropolitan Museum of Art).

In 1917 Lachaise became an American citizen and married Nagle. They had no children together. It was only after his marriage that his independent career began in earnest. Having completed bronze sculptures, marble carvings, and life-sized figures in plaster, he was ready to seek solo exhibitions of his work. Nagle modeled for many of his sensuous female nudes, for which Lachaise received critical recognition. Eroticism was essential to Lachaise's sculptural vision. He created female figures with exaggerated breasts and was interested in unorthodox poses, radically foreshortened limbs, and close-up views of female anatomical parts. *Standing Woman (Elevation)* is generally accepted as one of Lachaise's most important standing figures, and it numbers among many interpretations of his wife, to whom he referred as "Woman." *Standing Woman* is an ambitious work, a larger-than-life representation of the diminutive Nagle, generously proportioned to show his passionate involvement with his subject. The sensuous pose features the massive figure balanced on her tiptoes; the eyes are closed, but the hands are delicately extended in expressive gestures. The monumental proportions of the figure indicate that Lachaise intended to represent more than a likeness of one sitter: the regenerative forces of nature—embodied in Mother Earth—are his true subject. Lachaise conceived the work in 1912; it was shown in a plaster version at New York's Bourgeois Gallery in 1918. The figure was not cast in bronze, however, until 1927, and it was shown later that year at the Brummer Gallery in New York.

In 1918 Lachaise had his first solo exhibition at the Bourgeois Gallery; he was given other one-person exhibitions in subsequent years, including shows at the Kraushaar Galleries and at Alfred Stieglitz's Intimate Gallery. In 1920 Lachaise was appointed to the board of directors of the Society of Independent Artists.

Lachaise had begun a series of sculptures known as "The Mountain" in 1913, producing six different versions over the next two decades. *The Mountain* (1920, Metropolitan Museum of Art), a work carved in sandstone, was exhibited at the Bourgeois Gallery. Poet E. E. Cummings wrote about Lachaise's subject:

The Mountain actualizes the original conception of its creator; who, in contrast to the contemptible conventionally called 'sculptor' thinks in stone . . . and to whom the distinction between, say, bronze and alabaster is a distinction not between materials but, on the contrary, between ideas. In *The Mountain* as it is, Lachaise becomes supremely himself. (*The Dial*, Feb. 1920, pp. 194–204)

It should be remembered that the great carved stone temples of India are intended to represent a mountain, or indeed a range. Not ordinary mountain(s) to be sure, but that mountain which religion and myth would say lies at the center of the universe. "Lachaise extends his metaphor to simplify the forms, generalize the arms, amplify the torso by shaping it like rolling pasture, canyons, creeks and bluffs. The figure appears to sleep—a new presentation of what is perhaps the oldest metaphor in man's memory" (Nordland, p. 114). The series includes a fieldstone version, several cast in bronze, and a final nine-foot study intended for cement casting. Nordland found that the subject "embodies a concept of the reclining woman as an invulnerable absolute, rising from the plain of human experience as a great truth of life. From tiny feet through slender calves to expanding thighs and enormous torso the mountain rises to its idealized head" (Nordland, p. 113).

During the 1920s and early 1930s, Lachaise received commissions for architectural decoration, including four relief panels in limestone for the RCA (now General Electric) Building in Rockefeller Center, New York (1931), and a twenty-foot relief for the Electricity Building at the Chicago World's Fair (1932). His work was frequently illustrated in the *Dial*, and he was championed by a number of American poets and critics. Many portraits were commissioned by members of the staff and contributors to *The Dial*. Subjects of these portraits include John Marin, Georgia O'Keeffe, Alfred Stieglitz, Juliana Force, E. E. Cummings, Marianne Moore, and Edgard Varèse.

In 1934 Lachaise was awarded a second commission for Rockefeller Center: two relief panels for the International Building. Carved on site in limestone, these works include male figures engaged in the construction of a city. Months before his death in 1935, a major retrospective of his sculpture opened at the Museum of Modern Art. The show, which included sixty of his sculptures, received favorable press notices. He died at the age of fifty-three of acute leukemia in New York City.

A sculptor associated with modernism in American art, Lachaise transformed the traditional subject of the nude by seeking sources ranging far beyond the Greco-Roman ideal, fusing Indian temple sculpture and other non-Western art forms into a unique sculptural vision.

• The papers of Lachaise and his wife are in the Archives of American Art, Smithsonian Institution, Washington, D.C. A Lachaise archive can be found in the Beinecke Rare Book and Manuscript Library, Yale University. "A Comment on My Sculpture," *Creative Art* 3 (Aug. 1928): 22–26, is a statement by Lachaise. For a monograph, see Gerald Nordland, *Gaston Lachaise: The Man and His Work* (1974). Exhibition catalogs include Museum of Modern Art, *Gaston Lachaise: Retrospective Exhibition* (1935), with an essay by Lincoln Kirstein; and Carolyn Kinder Carr and Margaret C. S. Christman, *Gaston Lachaise, Portrait Sculpture* (National Portrait Gallery, 1985). For an obituary, see Henry McBride, "The Death of Gaston Lachaise," *New York Sun*, 26 Oct. 1935.

JOAN MARTER

LACKAYE, Wilton (30 Sept. 1862–22 Aug. 1932), actor, was born William Andrew Lackey in Loudoun County, Virginia, the son of James Lackey, an Irish-born officer in the Union army, and Margaret Bagnam. He was educated at the College of Ottawa in Ontario, Canada, and at Georgetown University in Washington, D.C. In 1881 Lackaye was offered a chance to study for the priesthood in Rome but decided he would rather be an actor after seeing a performance of *Esmeralda*, starring Annie Russell and Eben Plympton, shortly before his ship was to sail from New York. When his father expressed opposition to a theatrical career, Lackaye returned to Washington to study law. While a law student, Lackaye became a leading member of the Lawrence Barrett Dramatic Society, an amateur theater group named in honor of a prominent actor of the time. In 1883 Barrett attended some of their performances and asked Lackaye to join his company.

Lackaye made his professional debut in a small role in Barrett's revival of *Francesca da Rimini* at the Star Theatre in New York in August 1883. He stayed with

Barrett for the remainder of the season, playing Salarino in *The Merchant of Venice* and other small parts. Lackaye then acted in a stock company at Dayton, Ohio, and toured in David Belasco's play *May Blossom*, starring Georgia Cayvan, and in *Tad, the Tomboy* with Carrie Swain. Now known professionally as Wilton Lackaye, he spent the 1886–1887 season with the Fanny Davenport company, supporting Davenport in *Fedora* and in several Shakespearean plays.

A tall, heavy-set man with dark hair, large blue eyes, and a handlebar mustache, Lackaye rose to prominence with his work in William Gillette's adaptation of Rider Haggard's novel *She* (1887) and in Steele Mackaye's French Revolution drama *Paul Kauvar* (1887). He then appeared in a succession of plays, most notably *Jocelyn* (1888) with Rose Coghlan, *Featherbrain* (1889) with Minnie Maddern, *Bootle's Baby* (1889), *Roger le Honte* (1889), *The Great Unknown* (1889), *Money Mad* (1890), *The Clemenceau Case* (1890), *Nero* (1890), *The Power of the Press* (1891), Bronson Howard's *Aristocracy* (1892), a major hit that also featured Viola Allen and William Faversham, *The Transgressor* (1894), *The New Woman* (1894), and *The District Attorney* (1895). In September 1896 Lackaye married actress Alice Evans, with whom he had a son.

The role with which Lackaye is most associated is the mysterious genius Svengali in *Trilby* (1895), Paul M. Potter's extremely successful stage version of George du Maurier's bestselling novel. The bug-eyed, pointy-bearded Svengali uses his hypnotic power to turn a beautiful artist's model, Trilby O'Ferrall (Virginia Harned), into a famous opera singer. The part of Svengali was well suited to Lackaye, with his particular skill as a character actor and his reputation as a matinee idol. "Mr. Lackaye's Svengali, at first sight, strikes you as a caricature of du Maurier's pictures; but he soon overcomes your objections by his acting, which is both subtle and strong," said the *New York Times* (21 Apr. 1895). Lackaye appeared in revivals of *Trilby* in 1905, 1915, and 1921.

The versatile Lackaye was known for his lack of pretentiousness and considered acting a "trade," working almost continuously in both serious and comedic parts. He capitalized on his success in *Trilby* by taking another role as a hypnotist in Charles Klein's drama *Dr. Belgraff* in 1897. He then appeared with Joseph Jefferson and Otis Skinner in a production of Sheridan's *The Rivals* (1898) as Sir Lucius O'Trigger. Notable appearances in Lackaye's later career include *Children of the Ghetto* (1899), *Don Caesar's Return* (1901), *A Modern Magdalen* (1902), *The Frisky Mrs. Johnson* (1903), *The Pit* (1903), *The Pillars of Society* (1904), and *The Law and the Man* (1906), a stage version of Victor Hugo's novel *Les Miserables*, adapted and directed by Lackaye himself. He also appeared in *The Battle* (1908), *The Right to Happiness* (1912), *Damaged Goods* (1913), a controversial drama about venereal disease produced by and costarring Richard Bennett, *The Inner Man* (1917), *Palmy Days* (1919), *The Monster* (1922), and *High Stakes* (1924). Lackaye played

James Telfer in an all-star revival of Arthur Wing Pinero's comedy *Trelawny of the Wells* (1927) with John Drew, Mrs. Thomas Whiffen, Pauline Lord, and Henriette Crosman. After suffering from a nearly fatal heart ailment in 1927, Lackaye returned to Broadway to play small parts in the comedies *Ladies of the Jury* (1929) with Minnie Maddern Fiske and *Love, Honor and Betray* (1930) with Alice Brady and Clark Gable.

A celebrated wit whose sharp tongue won him many friends and a few enemies, Lackaye was a member of the Lambs Club, a founder of the Catholic Actors' Guild, and a strong supporter of the Actors' Equity Association. Left a widower by the death of Alice Evans in 1919, Lackaye married his nurse Katherine Alberta Riley in 1928. They had no children. Lackaye died at his home in New York City.

• The New York Public Library for the Performing Arts has clippings files and scrapbooks on Lackaye's career. Other sources of information on Lackaye are "Wilton Lackaye Talks of the Actor's Art," *Theatre Magazine*, May 1904, pp. 119–20; Lackaye, "My Beginnings," *Theatre Magazine*, Oct. 1905, pp. 250–52; and Wendell Phillips Dodge, "The Actor in the Street," *Theatre Magazine*, Feb. 1909, pp. 49–50. Ashton Stevens, "Wilton Lackaye Wit," *San Francisco Examiner*, 11 Sept. 1905, is an interview with Lackaye. See also Lewis Strang, *Famous Actors of the Day in America* (1900), and David Carroll, *The Matinee Idols* (1972). A tribute to Lackaye is in the *Literary Digest*, 10 Sept. 1932, p. 20. An obituary is in the *New York Times*, 22 Aug. 1932.

MARY C. KALFATOVIC

LACLÈDE, Pierre (22 Nov. 1729–May 1778), wholesale merchant and fur trader, was born in Bedous, France. Although his parents' names are unknown, he came from a prominent family of attorneys, scholars, and officeholders, and his father was an *avocat* admitted to practice before the *Parlement* of Navarre. Laclède was well educated and early acquired a fondness for books. Little is known about his youth or eight-year residence in New Orleans, where he arrived in 1755. There he became a wholesale merchant, served as a militia officer, and dealt commercially with the leading members of the business community. Despite economic difficulties caused by the French and Indian War, which began shortly after his arrival, he did reasonably well in business.

During this time he entered into a liaison with Marie Thérèse Bourgeois Chouteau, whose husband, René Auguste Chouteau, departed from the colony after the birth of their son, abandoning them to fend for themselves. From the Laclède–Bourgeois Chouteau liaison, four children were born between 1758 and 1764. They all took the surname Chouteau, and René Chouteau was listed in the baptismal records as their father. Laclède took an avid interest in his stepson Auguste, and the boy acquired a firm education. He soon became a clerk for his stepfather.

As the French and Indian War ended, Laclède formed a partnership with Gilbert Antoine Maxent to establish and manage a trading post in upper Louisiana. Maxent obtained a fur-trading monopoly from acting governor Jean Jacques D'Abbadie despite protests from other New Orleans businessmen and, as senior partner, provided most of the capital for Maxent, Laclède and Company. Laclède departed with Auguste and a large quantity of merchandise in August 1763 for the Illinois country. He left Chouteau, who was then pregnant, and their children in New Orleans; they joined him in 1764. In upper Louisiana in late 1763, Laclède reconnoitered the Mississippi River's west bank for a settlement site because the east bank had been ceded to Great Britain. In February 1764 he dispatched Auguste with workmen to begin the settlement Laclède called St. Louis, named for the patron saint of King Louis XV. Although Laclède later learned that Spain had acquired Louisiana west of the Mississippi, the transfer did not affect life in the upper colony. St. Louis, located on the Mississippi and near the Missouri and Ohio rivers, grew quickly as it attracted settlers who wanted to live in the developing fur-trading emporium.

Initially Laclède did well in the trade and established harmonious relations with the native tribes. He sent agents with goods to their villages to trade, relieving the natives of the need to travel to St. Louis. In 1765, however, the French king annulled the monopoly and opened the fur trade to others. When the partnership ended, Laclède purchased Maxent's 75 percent share of the business in St. Louis for 80,000 livres. The purchase gave Laclède the monopoly's buildings, slaves, merchandise, furs, and other assets in St. Louis. He was to pay Maxent in four installments between 1771 and 1774. But with others in the fur trade, Laclède's volume of business declined considerably, and he failed to make the payments.

Laclède early made Auguste a partner in his business and sent him as his trusted agent to trade in the Indian villages on the Missouri. Later Laclède's own son, Pierre Chouteau, joined the business. Laclède ran the enterprise in St. Louis and often traveled to New Orleans for merchandise. He also served the government, bringing the annual presents for the natives from New Orleans and mounting an expedition in 1773 against the British-based merchant Jean Marie Ducharme, who illegally traded on the Missouri River. Although he was the leading merchant in St. Louis, Laclède often made poor business decisions in outfitting traders who visited the Indian settlements. Many of them failed to repay him with furs and skins.

Maxent, who was not paid at the agreed-upon times, sued Laclède, who delayed the lawsuit by not going to New Orleans. Although in declining health, Laclède finally journeyed to New Orleans in 1777 to settle his financial plight. He was forced to surrender his lands, buildings, and other property in St. Louis. Nevertheless, Maxent provided merchandise for the 1778 trading year to Laclède and his partners, Auguste Chouteau and Sylvestre Labbadie, who was married to Laclède's oldest daughter. On the return trip, Laclède died of natural causes near the mouth of the Arkansas River. When his estate was sold at auction to satisfy the 80,000 livres owed to Maxent, its assets yielded a much smaller sum. The Chouteaus purchased some of his property, which sold at low prices.

The Laclède–Bourgeois Chouteau union learned in 1774 that René Chouteau, who had returned to Louisiana about 1769, was seeking legal action to compel his wife to rejoin him. Governor Luis de Unzaga ordered Lieutenant Governor Pedro Piernas to send her to New Orleans. But neither Piernas nor his successor Francisco Cruzat forced her to go. Nevertheless, in 1775 Madame Chouteau and Laclède were ordered to separate, and she agreed to reside on her farm one league from St. Louis. In reality, however, she continued to live at the house Laclède built and deeded to her and the children in 1768 and where he kept a room. Because of their parents' anomalous relationship, the children never admitted publicly that Laclède was their father. As late as 1847 at a celebration commemorating the founding of St. Louis, an elderly Pierre Chouteau could not acknowledge that Pierre Laclède, dead nearly seventy years, was his father.

Laclède is best remembered as the founder of St. Louis, but he is also known to have possessed a noteworthy collection of books that exceeded 200 volumes. It consisted of many different works that dealt with the grammar of several languages, history, economics, business, agriculture, medicine, horses, and the Enlightenment. It was a remarkable collection for a man living in an embryonic community many hundreds of miles from the nearest city.

• Primary materials on Laclède can be found at the Missouri Historical Society, St. Louis; Archivo General de Indias, Seville; and Archives Nationales, Section Colonies, Series C13A: Correspondence Générale, Louisiana, in Paris. Laclède has received less attention than his stepson Auguste Chouteau, who is often credited as cofounder of St. Louis and who enjoyed more success as a fur trader. More than anyone else, John Francis McDermott has written about Leclède's career. See his "Pierre Laclède and the Chouteaus," *Missouri History Society Bulletin* 21 (1965): 279–83; "Pierre LaClède, the Father of St. Louis," *Missouri Magazine* 9 (1937): 11–13; "The Exclusive Trade Privileges of Maxent, Laclède and Company," *Missouri Historical Review* 29 (1935): 259–71; "Myths and Realities Concerning the Founding of St. Louis," in *The French in the Mississippi Valley*, ed. John Francis McDermott (1965), pp. 1–15; and *Private Libraries in Creole St. Louis* (1938). See also William E. Foley and C. David Rice, *The First Chouteaus: River Barons of Early St. Louis* (1983); Abraham P. Nasatir, "Trade and Diplomacy in the Spanish Illinois, 1763–1792" (Ph.D. diss., Univ. of California, Berkeley, 1926); and Edward F. Rowse, "Auguste and Pierre Chouteau" (Ph.D. diss., Washington Univ., St. Louis, 1936).

GILBERT C. DIN

LACOCK, Abner (9 July 1770–12 Apr. 1837), state and national leader and canal builder, was born on Cub Run, near Alexandria, Virginia, the son of William Lacock and Lovey (maiden name unknown), farmers. Around 1780 his family settled in Washington County in western Pennsylvania; there they bought a 120-acre farm in Amwell Township, and Abner helped his parents in planting and in harvesting crops. Between 1782 and 1786 Lacock attended Thaddeus Dodd's Academy in Amity, Pennsylvania, and studied mathematics, surveying, and the classics. In 1788 he married Hannah Eddy, and the couple had three sons and four daughters.

In 1796 Lacock moved to Beaver Town, Pennsylvania, and became involved in the house-building business. Lacock that year was named as justice of the peace; in 1798 he opened a general store, and in 1800 he operated a tavern. In 1801 he was elected as the first representative to the state legislature from Beaver County and held this position until 1803; he was then named as the first associate judge of Beaver County, a position he gave up one year later.

Between 1804 and 1808 Lacock was elected as the representative from Beaver, Butler, and Allegheny counties to the state legislature. In this capacity he supported bills to construct roads and introduced measures to promote education in western Pennsylvania. By favoring judicial reforms, he also became a radical Republican and emerged as one of "the puppets of [Michael] Leib's machine" (*Freeman's Journal*, 14 Aug. 1807). After Governor Thomas McKean thwarted attempts for judicial reorganization and allegedly violated other provisions of the state constitution, Lacock, along with Leib, engaged in 1807 in unsuccessful efforts to impeach him.

Between 1808 and 1810 Lacock served in the Pennsylvania Senate. There he continued his support of legislation to promote education and road building. In 1810 he voted for the removal of the state capital from Lancaster to Harrisburg.

In 1810 Lacock won election to the U.S. House of Representatives, defeating Pittsburgh Democrat Adamson Tannehill. Called "General" because of his appointment as a brigadier general in the Pennsylvania militia three years earlier, Lacock became an ardent "War Hawk." In 1812 he spoke in favor of the annexation of Canada and supported bills to increase revenues for the army and navy. He also voted for war resolutions against Great Britain in June 1812 and strongly supported the war measures of President James Madison.

Lacock continued his involvement in national politics as a U.S. senator between 1813 and 1819. After difficult financial problems in 1814 forced the resignation of George W. Campbell as secretary of the Treasury, Lacock in October of that year reluctantly gave Madison his consent to appoint his foe Alexander J. Dallas to this position. As the economy began to recover, Lacock championed the cause of the National Republicans; he supported the 1816 tariff to protect American manufacturers from European competition, and he voted that year in favor of the creation of the second Bank of the United States. Moreover, he became known for his support of Henry Clay's American System for internal improvements. In February 1817 Lacock proposed that the $1.5 million bank bonus be used to finance canals and roads. That same year he supported legislation to grant pensions and land to soldiers and a bill to increase the salaries of government employees. He also chaired a Senate committee to inquire into the behavior of General Andrew Jackson during the Seminole campaign; he condemned Jackson's attacks on Spanish territory as being in violation of the Constitution and of international law.

After his departure from the Senate, Lacock played a prominent role in promoting the building of canals in Pennsylvania; he believed that a canal system linking Philadelphia to Pittsburgh would provide competition to Baltimore and New York City for trade in western regions. In April 1825 Lacock was named a commissioner to compile a survey about the construction of canals in Pennsylvania. After this report was completed, he was appointed in 1826 to the state board of canal commissioners. In February 1826 the state legislature allocated funds for the building of the Pennsylvania Canal, and Lacock became the supervisor for the construction of the canal's western division. Under Lacock's guidance the 104-mile Pittsburgh and Johnstown Canal was completed three years later.

On 1 June 1829 Lacock resigned from his position as canal commissioner. In 1831, as a result of his encouragement, the state appropriated funds for the construction of the Ohio, Beaver, and Shenango Canal, taking another important step to link Pittsburgh to Erie.

Transportational developments and politics marked the last years of Lacock's life. Serving as a Whig between 1832 and 1835 in the lower house of the Pennsylvania legislature, Lacock supported bills to fund canals and public schools. He was selected in 1836 as a commissioner to compose a plan for the building of the Pennsylvania and Ohio Canal. After the acceptance of this plan and the allocation of funds for this project in 1836, Lacock that year went to Youngstown, Ohio, to work on the "crosscut canal," which was intended to link the Erie division of the Pennsylvania Canal with the Portsmouth and Ohio Canal. While assisting in the construction of this canal, he became sick from exposure to cold weather and returned to his residence near Freedom, Pennsylvania, where he died.

Lacock's career reflects several important legacies of the early American republic. He embraced reformist causes, and he called for enhancing the powers of justices of the peace, for electing directly the president and vice president, and for establishing public schools. Lacock supported the War of 1812 and thus became an ardent supporter of expansionism. However, Lacock was especially known for attempting to promote the economic interests of western Pennsylvania. Recognizing the importance of both the marketing and transportation revolutions in America during the 1820s and 1830s, he consistently backed internal improvements in his region.

• A few of Lacock's letters are in the library of the Western Pennsylvania Historical Society. Significant primary sources about his political career are in the *Journals of the House of Representatives of the Commonwealth of Pennsylvania* (1801–1803, 1804–1808, and 1832–1835); the *Journals of the Senate of the Commonwealth of Pennsylvania* (1808–1810); and the

Annals of Congress, 1789–1824 (1811–1819). Three older works present sketches of Lacock's accomplishments: J. M. Swank, "General Abner Lacock," *Pennsylvania Magazine of History and Biography* 4 (1880): 202–8; Jacob Fraise and Henry Thomas, *History of Beaver County, Pennsylvania* (1888); and Joseph H. Bausman, *The History of Beaver County, Pennsylvania* (2 vols., 1904). The most detailed profile of his career is Harry Houtz, "Abner Lacock, Beaver County's Exponent of the American System," *Western Pennsylvania Historical Magazine* 22 (1939): 177–87. Sanford W. Higginbotham, *The Keystone in the Democratic Arch: Pennsylvania Politics, 1800–1816* (1952), comments on Lacock's role as a state legislator. His career in national politics is examined in James Kehl, *Ill Feeling in the Era of Good Feeling: Western Pennsylvania Political Battles, 1815–1825* (1956). Victor A. Sapio, *Pennsylvania and the War of 1812* (1970), mentions Lacock's activities as a War Hawk. For assessments of Lacock's investigation of Jackson's attack against the Seminoles, see Robert V. Remini, *Andrew Jackson and the Course of American Freedom, 1822–1832* (1981); and Robert D. Ilisevich, "Henry Baldwin and Andrew Jackson: A Political Relationship in Trust," *Pennsylvania Magazine of History and Biography* 120 (1996): 37–60. Lacock's achievements as a canal builder are mentioned in Phillip S. Klein and Ari Hoogenboom, *A History of Pennsylvania* (1973); and Ronald E. Shaw, *Canals for a Nation: The Canal Era in the United States, 1790–1860* (1990). Obituaries are in the (Beaver, Pa.) *Western Argus*, 19 Apr. 1837; and the (Harrisburg) *Pennsylvania Reporter*, 27 Apr. 1837.

WILLIAM WEISBERGER

LADD, Alan (3 Sept. 1913–29 Jan. 1964), film actor, was born Alan Walbridge Ladd in Hot Springs, Arkansas, the son of Alan Ladd, an accountant, and Ina Rawley. His father died when Ladd was only three years old (1917), and in 1920 his mother remarried and moved the family to California. Ladd attended North Hollywood High School, where he excelled in diving, track, and drama. Upon graduation in 1933, he was recruited by talent scouts for Universal Studios into a program for young actors. This stroke of luck, in the midst of the depression, was short-lived. Ladd was released from the studio after six months and worked as a journalist in the San Fernando Valley, then returned to Los Angeles to work as a studio crew member and as a bit player.

In 1936, discouraged at his lack of progress in movies, he took a job at a local radio station, KFWB, where he read the news and played a wide variety of dramatic roles. That same year he married Marjorie Jane Harrold, with whom he had one child. In 1938 Sue Carol, an agent and former actress in silent films, signed Ladd to a contract after hearing him on the radio. He divorced in 1941 and in March 1942 married Sue Carol, with whom he had two children. In two years Carol placed Ladd in sixteen films, including a bit part in *Citizen Kane* and a sympathetic starring role opposite Veronica Lake in *The Glass Key*, based on the Dashiell Hammett novel. In 1942 he again co-starred with Veronica Lake, this time as a cold-blooded, babyfaced killer in a filmed version of Graham Greene's *This Gun for Hire* (1942). The tension between the nervous, sensitive, but violent Ladd and the

cool, sultry Lake catapulted Ladd into stardom and a long-term contract with Paramount. Early in 1943 he enlisted in the U.S. Army Air Corps but was given a medical discharge for a double hernia late in the year. He returned to Paramount, where he starred as a fast-talking soldier of fortune who discovers patriotism in *China* (1943).

Over the next decade Ladd starred in variations of the sensitive, tough guy theme in a succession of action and western films, most notably with Lake in *The Blue Dahlia* (1946). That string was broken when in 1953 director George Stevens cast Ladd as Shane, a gunfighter who longs for the simple, honest life of a frontier farmer. It was not to be. In one of the most memorable scenes in film history, Ladd guns down the hired killer (played by Jack Palance) of the cattleman who has been running the farmers off their land. *Shane* was the highpoint of Ladd's film career. Despite the tremendous popularity of the film and of Ladd's performance, his career reverted to the kinds of starring vehicles that had brought him to public attention. Not until 1964 did Ladd find another part that earned critical acclaim. Nevada Smith, an ex-cowboy star, in *The Carpetbaggers* proved to be his last role.

Ladd had never been comfortable as a Hollywood star. Insecure about his talent, fearful that his good looks would fade and his public appeal with them, Ladd made only a handful of movies in the early 1960s. He invested heavily, and successfully, in California real estate and formed his own production company: Jaguar Productions. His career as a producer was unsuccessful, however. He died in Palm Springs, California, of a reported heart attack, caused at least in part by the ravages of alcohol and sedatives.

For many, Ladd's movie image was that of a handsome, soft-spoken tough guy in 1940s crime and action films. Yet he is best remembered for his portrayal of a kind, sensitive, and reluctant gunfighter in the classic western *Shane*.

• See Beverly Linet, *Ladd, the Legend: The Legacy of Alan Ladd* (1979). An obituary is in the *New York Times*, 30 Jan. 1964.

GREGORY D. BLACK

LADD, Carl Edwin (25 Feb. 1888–23 July 1943), agriculturist and educator, was born in McLean, New York, the son of Arnold Daniel Ladd and Mary Ellen Mineah, dairy farmers. In 1907 he graduated from the Cortland (N.Y.) Normal and Training School and went on to the New York State School of Agriculture at Cornell University from which he received a bachelor's degree in agricultural science in 1912. He then accepted a post at Cornell as instructor in farm management while working for his doctorate, specializing in farm cost accounting, which he received in 1915.

From 1915 to 1917 Ladd was the director of the New York School of Agriculture at Delhi. After leaving, he worked for the New York State Department of Education in Albany for two years as both the supervisor of the state's agricultural schools and a specialist in agricultural education. In 1920, having directed the state agricultural school at Alfred University for a year, he moved to Cornell as an extension professor of farm management. In 1924 he was promoted to director of extension, and in 1932 he was appointed the dean and director of the agricultural college and the dean of the home economics college.

Through these positions Ladd worked to make agriculture more scientific and businesslike. He kept Cornell researchers working at the cutting edge of agricultural research, dealing with such issues as better packaging, dehydration of foodstuffs, and expanding the market for state produce such as potatoes. He was also concerned with preserving rural communities by keeping farm children on the farm, and thus he promoted the 4-H Clubs throughout the state.

Ladd also was involved with agriculture on a governmental level. In 1929–1930 he was chairman of the New York State Milk Supply Stabilization Committee, and in 1931 he took a leave of absence from Cornell to serve as deputy commissioner in the New York State Conservation Department. He held the post of secretary of the New York State Agricultural Advisory Commission under Governor Franklin D. Roosevelt and chairman under Governor Herbert H. Lehman. He was also a director of the Farm Credit Administration and Federal Land Bank at Springfield, New York, and of the Savings Bank in Ithaca, New York. He headed the state planning council, participated in the state national defense council (and its replacement, the state war council), and held the post of executive director of the state emergency food commission.

Throughout his career Ladd tried to forge good relationships among government, on state and national levels, educational institutions, and farmers. As head of extension at Cornell, he believed his role was to help to transmit the practical information gained at the university to farmers. This worked so well that by the time of his promotion to dean of the Cornell Agricultural College the state extension service had a good and active relationship with farmers and farmers' organizations such as the Dairymen's League. He worked closely with dairy producers, the Agricultural Adjustment Administration (AAA), and extension to stabilize milk production in New York State and played a key role in developing artificial breeding for dairy cattle. He also worked with the canning industry to develop the state's frozen food industry.

Ladd believed that the AAA was basically unsound. He thought the cause of the Great Depression was a breakdown in distribution, not overproduction. He also felt that the program was too intrusive and overcentralized. However, he realized that something had to be done to help the distressed farmers, so he accepted the program as a temporary policy, working with the government to implement it. Despite his frequent professional clashes with Secretary of Agriculture Henry A. Wallace, the two men managed to maintain a close personal friendship; they exchanged long letters on crossbreeding cattle and educating businessmen about agriculture.

Carl Ladd wrote regularly for the *American Agriculturist*, which was edited by his friend Edward R. Eastman, with whom he also coauthored a book, *Growing up in the Horse and Buggy Days* (1943). He also wrote *Dairy Farming Projects*, which was published in 1923.

Ladd was married twice, the first time to Camilla Marie Cox in 1912, with whom he had one daughter. After his wife's death in 1917, he married Lucy Frances Clark the next year; with her he had two sons. He was an active, gregarious man who liked to relax on his own farm in Freeville, New York, with his collection of old and rare books on agriculture and his studies of local colonial history. He was a Presbyterian and a Republican and held membership in numerous organizations, including the American Association for the Advancement of Science, the American Farm Economic Association, the Farm Foundation, the New York State Agricultural Society, the Masons, Acacia, Phi Kappa Phi, Epsilon Sigma Phi, Sigma Xi, and the Ithaca Rotary Club. He died of a heart attack at his home in Freeville.

• Carl Ladd's administrative papers as director of extension and dean are in the Cornell University Archives. For other information see Gould P. Colman, *Education and Agriculture: A History of the N.Y. State College of Agriculture at Cornell University* (1963), and Ruby Green Bell Smith, *The People's Colleges* (1949). See also the following articles in the *New York Times*: "Farmers of State Hear Hopeful Note," 11 Feb. 1936; "Ladd and Heydecker Named to State Jobs," 15 Aug. 1936; "Finds Prices Up 15% in War's 17 Months," 11 Feb. 1941; "Says Food Export May Cut Our Stock," 26 Nov. 1941; and Libby Lackman, "Reminds Growers of '42 Peak Crops," 10 Feb. 1942. An obituary is in the *New York Times*, 24 July 1943.

CLAIRE STROM

LADD, Catherine Stratton (28 Oct. 1808–30 Jan. 1899), educator and writer, was born in Richmond, Virginia, the daughter of James Stratton and Ann Collins. Her father, a native of Ireland, had been in the United States for only two years when, just six months after Catherine's birth, he fell off a boat and drowned. Catherine Stratton was educated in Richmond at the same school attended by Edgar Allan Poe. In 1828 she married George Williamson Livermore Ladd, a portrait and miniature painter, who had studied with S. F. B. Morse in Boston; the couple had two children.

The Ladds first settled in Charleston, South Carolina, where not long after their marriage, she began to write stories, poems, and essays, particularly on art and education. These were published under several different pen names—Minnie Mayflower, Arcturus, Morna, and Alida—in various southern journals, among them, *Floral Wreath*. As reflected in "Unknown Flowers" (by Morna), which was published in the second volume of the *Southern Literary Messenger* (Jan. 1836), her poems focused on nature and exhibited a religious zeal that was characteristic of her era:

Oh! many are the unknown flowers,
By human eyes unseen,
That bloom in nature's woodland bowers,
Of bright and changeless green . . .
And lovely birds, whose brilliant wings
Are bright with hues of brighter things,
Make music in those woodland bowers,
Those Edens of the unknown flowers.

In addition to her poems and sketches, Ladd is said to have contributed articles to the *Charleston News and Courier*, in which she advocated the use of white labor and the development of manufacturing in the South. At least as early as 1851 she argued that South Carolina could not compete with the Deep South in raising cotton and that even with an extensive system of slave labor South Carolina cotton farmers would realize no profit. Ladd also wrote at least two plays, *Grand Scheme* and *Honeymoon*, which were performed by friends and reportedly were locally popular, though this cannot be confirmed.

After living in Charleston, the Ladds moved to Augusta and eventually to Macon, Georgia, where for three years she was principal of Vineville Academy. In 1839, after hearing that an unused building that was suitable for a girls' school had become available, the Ladds returned to Charleston. In 1840 she opened the Winnsboro (also spelled Winnsborough) Female Institute at Winnsboro, South Carolina. The Winnsboro Institute was one of the largest and best-known boarding and day schools for young women in South Carolina. During the Civil War the school had full enrollment; some students were from Winnsboro, but the majority came from other parts of the state. Music, art, literature, dramatics, and the social graces were especially emphasized. The "formal education of women in Winnsboro made a notable advancement" when Ladd opened the institute (Bolick, p. 66). Still successful ten years later, the institute employed nine teachers and had an enrollment of about one hundred students. Over the years her school—and home—became cultural and social centers for the entire community.

In 1861 the Winnsboro Institute was closed by the Civil War. As permanent president of the Ladies' Relief Association of Fairfield County, Ladd spent the war nursing Confederate soldiers, among whom was her son, Albert Washington Ladd, wounded at the battle of Seven Pines (Va). Ladd's husband died in 1864, and in early 1865 her home was burned to the ground by Union troops during General William T. Sherman's march through South Carolina. Winnsboro Institute was not reopened until 1870.

In 1880 Ladd retired to "Buena Vista Plantation," situated nineteen miles from Winnsboro, near Buckhead, South Carolina, and she died there almost two decades later. She had been losing her sight for some time and by 1891 was completely blind, but she continued to write, penning the following verse as late as 1898:

Though our way be dark and dreary,
Though life's trials press us more,
Thou hast mansions for us ready,
Homes where troubles come no more.
O, my Saviour, guide me, watch me,
Lead me by Thy loving hand;
Let me feel that Thou art near me.
Until I reach the Promised Land.

Ladd's ability to organize cultural, social, and educational activities outweighs any modern interest in her minor and now obscure writings. By supporting the arts and by spreading a knowledge and appreciation of music, art, literature, and drama, Ladd provided her region with a center of culture and stability in the years of great social upheaval just before, during, and immediately following the Civil War.

• The *Dictionary of American Biography* refers to a scrapbook of Ladd's, said to contain undated newspaper clippings, family papers, and an autobiographical letter dating probably to 1898, but the scrapbook's present location is unknown. The South Caroliniana Library in Columbia, S.C., contains J. S. Bolick, *A Fairfield Sketchbook* (1963), and Katherine Theus Obear, *Through the Years in Old Winnsboro* (1940; repr. 1980), both of which include various anecdotal references to Ladd. For contemporary views of Ladd see Ida Raymond, *Southland Writers* (2 vols., 1870); Mary T. Tardy, *Living Female Writers of the South* (1872); and Mrs. Thomas Taylor et al., eds., *S.C. Women in the Confederacy* (2 vols., 1903–1907). Also see the *Columbian State*, 7 Mar. 1906, in which Ladd's daughter extols her mother's heroism against invading Yankees, and 12 Apr. 1912, which briefly notes Ladd's caring for Confederate soldiers.

BARBARA KRALEY YOUEL

LADD, Edwin Fremont (13 Dec. 1859–22 June 1925), agricultural scientist and U.S. senator, was born near Starks, Maine, the son of John Ladd and Rosilla Locke, farmers. Reflecting the progressive agricultural notions of his parents, Ladd earned a bachelor's degree in chemistry at the University of Maine in 1884. After graduation he was employed as an agricultural chemist at the New York Agricultural Experiment Station at Geneva, where he worked under Stephen Babcock and E. Lewis Sturtevant, leading agricultural scientists of the day.

In 1890, Ladd became the first agricultural chemist at the new North Dakota Agricultural College, sited at Fargo. As one of a handful of scientists at the institution, Ladd quickly found himself freighted with duties that taxed even his impressive energies. In addition to analysis of soils, fertilizers, and agricultural chemicals, Ladd was charged with meteorological research. The legislature added further to Ladd's duties. By 1905 he was responsible for enforcing pure food legislation, inspecting paint products, and conducting milling and baking studies on wheat. For a time he served as state hotel inspector as well.

Ladd's many jobs made him a well-known and popular figure in the state, as did his editorship of a farm newspaper, the *North Dakota Farmer and Sanitary Home*. Somehow he found time for his wife, Rizpah

Sprogle, whom he married in 1893, and their eight children, as well as service on the Fargo Board of Education and lay leadership in the First Presbyterian Church.

Ladd's regulatory duties pulled him increasingly into reform politics. Enforcement of North Dakota's pure food legislation involved him in frequent litigation and in numerous controversies, climaxed in 1909 by his declaration, upheld in North Dakota courts and by the U.S. Department of Agriculture, that bleached flour was technically adulterated and must be banned from sale. He contended that the poisonous bleaching agent made the flour unfit for human consumption. His milling and baking studies, which raised the ire of grain merchants and millers, laid the foundation for the federal Grain Standards Act of 1916. On the national level, Ladd's alliance with federal food crusader Harvey Wiley in the Association of Official Agricultural Chemists moved that organization to support passage of federal pure food and drug legislation.

Ladd's visibility and popularity resulted in his appointment as college president in 1916 and led the radical Nonpartisan League—a faction of the Republican party favoring public ownership of banks, railroads, grain elevators, and flour mills—to nominate him for the U.S. Senate in 1920. While Ladd's progressive, education- and publicity-oriented reformism was rather conservative by league standards, the agrarian group wanted him on the ticket to boost its flagging popularity. Ladd edged popular incumbent Asle Gronna in the Republican primary and was swept into office by better than 40,000 votes over token Democratic opposition in November.

In the Senate, Ladd aligned himself with the nascent farm bloc and voted for its measures to encourage economic cooperation and regulate middlemen. He was also known for championing early diplomatic recognition of the Soviet Union. His scientific background gained him a degree of respect from his colleagues, but as a junior senator lacking in legislative experience he had minimal impact in shaping legislation. He died in Baltimore.

• Very few Edwin Ladd papers exist, though there is a small collection at the North Dakota Institute for Regional Studies, North Dakota State University. Ladd's activities at the North Dakota Agricultural College are highlighted in Bill G. Reid, *Five for the Land and Its People* (1989), and David B. Danbom, *"Our Purpose Is to Serve": The First Century of the North Dakota Agricultural Experiment Station* (1990). James Harvey Young, *Pure Food: Securing the Federal Food and Drugs Act of 1906* (1989), details Ladd's contributions in that area. A number of his activities are mentioned in Elwyn B. Robinson, *History of North Dakota* (1966). An obituary is in the *New York Times*, 26 June 1925.

DAVID B. DANBOM

LADD, George Trumbull (19 Jan. 1842–8 Aug. 1921), theologian, philosopher, and psychologist, was born in Painesville, Ohio, the son of Silas Trumbull Ladd, a businessman and treasurer of Western Reserve College, and Elizabeth Williams. Ladd graduated from Western Reserve College in 1864 and from Andover Theological Seminary in 1869. Also in 1869 he married Cornelia Ann Tallman of Bellaire, Ohio; they had four children. He was a minister for nearly a decade, spending two years in a small church in Ohio and eight years in the large Spring Street Congregational Church in Milwaukee, Wisconsin. Ladd wrote and read feverishly throughout his life. Having a passion for scholarship, he grew tired of the pastorate and sought freedom in the academic world. He justified this transition by planning a defense of his faith in opposition to the increasingly scientific and secular world. According to his biographer E. S. Mills, "he would serve as the mediator between the old and the new so that the best of both worlds of learning and experience might be preserved." In 1879 Ladd accepted a post in the department of philosophy at Bowdoin College in Brunswick, Maine. Two years later he moved to New Haven, Connecticut, and began his long association with Yale University. At Yale, Ladd was appointed professor of moral and mental philosophy.

Ladd's reputation as a professor grew, and he gave many invited lectures at home and abroad. Most notably, he lectured at Harvard and in Japan, India, and Korea. In 1893 his first wife died. In 1895 he married Frances Virginia Stevens of New York City. In 1899 the emperor of Japan awarded him the Order of the Rising Sun, third class, and later he received the same award, second class. His experiences in Korea are recounted in a book, *In Korea with Marquis Ito*, which proposes a groundwork for lasting peace between Korea and Japan. Ladd's lifelong commitment to the region was demonstrated at his death: half of his cremated remains were flown to Yokohama, Japan, to be buried.

Before 1879 Ladd focused his reading primarily in philosophy, theology, and literature. While at Bowdoin he began an intensive study of the "new psychology," resulting in *Elements of Physiological Psychology* (1887) and *Psychology: Descriptive and Explanatory* (1894), his most significant works. In the latter, he defines psychology as "the science which describes and explains the phenomena of consciousness, as such" (p. 1). Consciousness is an active function of some object, a self. For Ladd, all psychic phenomena are dualistic, consisting of states of consciousness and the self. Active states of consciousness result from a physiologically observable process, and the passive subject of those states is the unobservable self. Consciousness is an activity of the self aiming toward the attainment of an end; it is purposeful, functional, and adaptive. Hence, the term functional psychology is often attached to Ladd's name.

Ladd espoused the teleological character of mind—i.e., that mind is a functioning entity striving to attain some end. In *Psychology* he makes this point clearly: "The whole history of mental evolution depends upon the progressive organization of the elements of mental life under laws or orderly forms of behavior, in accordance with the ends of mental life" (p. 286). The "science" of psychology can apprehend only the observable states of consciousness but can never detail the teleological character of life, much less describe it with any certainty: "All living beings . . . organize themselves according to a plan. This fact cannot be denied, no matter how much our obvious ignorance as to the explanations of the fact may be increased or diminished by the progress of biological science" (*Psychology*, p. 286). Ladd's view promoted the speculative role of the philosopher in a complete psychology, permitting philosophical descriptions of human nature to play a foundational role in psychology.

Throughout Ladd's psychology, the conflict between the "old" and the "new" conceptions of the mind is evident. Physiological and experimental approaches characterize the new approach to psychology while the old approach maintained a speculative philosophical or theological base. Ladd was an "inveterate metaphysician" with theological leanings who also believed in the veracity and usefulness of new scientific advances. As a result, his psychology can best be understood as an attempted synthesis of these two conceptions.

Ladd's struggle with two conflicting approaches to psychology caused difficulties in his Yale laboratory. He rarely conducted any experiments himself, preferring instead to perform the speculative tasks that he thought provided the basis for understanding the experimental evidence. E. W. Scripture (a Wundt student) was hired to run the lab. The relationship between Scripture and Ladd turned out badly. Because of Ladd's theological beliefs and his distaste for the new psychology's materialism, he was in sharp conflict with the approaches of the fervent experimentalist Scripture. The rift between the two forced Ladd into an early "retirement" from Yale in 1905.

Ladd's *Elements of Physiological Psychology* was the first book on the relation between physiology and psychology to appear in the United States—preceding William James's *Principles of Psychology* (1890). The volume was well received in both the United States and Britain and became a standard text that James used in his Harvard course. His later publications, *Primer of Psychology* (1894) and *Psychology: Descriptive and Explanatory*, were not as successful. James called the latter volume "dreary." Irrespective of the failings of his later work, Ladd was an influential figure in the incipient field of experimental psychology. He cofounded and served as second president of the American Psychological Association (G. Stanley Hall was the first and James the third), traveled to the World's Congress of Psychologists as a delegate, and arguably established the first experimental psychological laboratory in the United States. Unfortunately, Ladd lived long enough to witness his own reputation diminish, and he is mostly regarded as a historical and transitional figure. He died in New Haven.

• Ladd's strictly philosophical works are *Philosophy of Mind* (1895), *Philosophy of Knowledge* (1897), and *The Philosophy of Religion* (1905). His last sustained philosophical effort was a series of books for a broader audience: *What Can I Know?* (1914), *What Ought I to Do?* (1915), *What Should I Believe?* (1915), *What May I Hope?* (1915). Ladd also wrote about his travels and published *In Korea with Marquis Ito* (1908), *Rare Days in Japan* (1910), and *Intimate Glimpses of Life in India* (1919), his last published book. Ladd's work appeared in a number of scholarly journals. Among them are *Mind*, *Psychological Review*, *Philosophical Review*, and *Journal of the American Oriental Society*. Finally, Ladd is noted for his work in translating and editing the works of Hermann Lotze. The books that resulted are *Outlines of Metaphysic* (1884), *Outlines of Practical Philosophy* (1885), *Outlines of the Philosophy of Religion* (1885), *Outlines of Aesthetics* (1886), *Outlines of Psychology* (1886), and *Outlines of Logic and of Encyclopaedia of Philosophy* (1887). Eugene S. Mill's biography, *George Trumbull Ladd: Pioneer American Psychologist* (1969), contains the most complete Ladd bibliography. A brief account of Ladd's significance is in Edwin Garrigues Boring, *A History of Experimental Psychology* (1957). Edward Bradford Tichener, *Systematic Psychology: Prolegomena* (1929), provides a description and criticism of Ladd's psychology.

HERMAN J. SAATKAMP, JR.
CLAY DAVIS SPLAWN

LADD, Kate Macy (6 Apr. 1863–27 Aug. 1945), philanthropist, was born in New York City, the daughter of Josiah Macy, Jr., a pioneer in the American oil industry, and Caroline Louise Everit. Ladd was born into a distinguished American family that had prospered for eight generations as coastal and transoceanic merchants. Shortly before her birth, her grandfather and father entered the oil business in Brooklyn, New York. In 1872 John D. Rockefeller acquired the Macy's Brooklyn refinery and oil interests. Four years later, her father died of typhoid fever in New York. Kate's later philanthropic interests derived in part from her father, who gave generously to New York City hospitals and welfare organizations, and in part from her Quaker background (although she later became a Presbyterian). Despite the loss of their father, the family's wealth assured that Kate and her two siblings would be raised in secure, comfortable surroundings. They were educated by private tutors and traveled extensively, as was the custom among upper-class families. In 1883 Kate Macy married Walter Graeme Ladd, a prominent New York attorney and yachtsman; they had no children.

Not long after her marriage, Ladd began to suffer from a series of unspecified, debilitating illnesses, which despite the best medical care, left her an invalid for the rest of her life. In 1905 the Ladds moved to a luxurious, thousand-acre estate, "Natirar," in Far Hills, New Jersey. Confined to the mansion, Ladd became increasingly involved in philanthropy. Shortly after moving to her estate, she established "Maple Cottage," which provided free convalescent care for, as contemporary sources describe, "needy working girls" from New York City. In 1940 Maple Cottage was closed and converted into a shelter for evacuees from New York in case the city came under aerial attack. After the war and Ladd's death, the Kate Macy Ladd fund received over $10 million from her husband's estate, which was used to turn the entire Ladd mansion and grounds into a convalescent home for women. The Kate Macy Ladd Convalescent Home (also known as Maple Cottage) opened in January 1949 and continued to operate into the early 1980s, providing help to thousands of working women.

In 1928 Ladd initiated her most significant contribution to American philanthropy when she commissioned her personal physician, Dr. Ludwig Kast, a professor of clinical medicine at the New York Post Graduate Medical School, to conduct a survey of philanthropy in America. She asked Kast to give particular attention to the accomplishments and promise of medical research and to assess how a private foundation might help realize that promise. Based on the results of the survey, and with Kast as a consultant, in 1930 Ladd established the Josiah Macy, Jr. Foundation, named in memory of her father, with an initial gift of $5 million. Kast became the foundation's first president. In 1931, when the depression reduced the income from her initial gift, Ladd made additional contributions to supplement the foundation's resources. In a letter that accompanied her original gift, she carefully articulated a philosophy and mission for her foundation. She felt that private philanthropy best served the public interest "not by replacing functions which rightfully should be supported by our communities, but by investigating, testing, and demonstrating the value of newer organized ideas . . . from which may gradually emerge social functions which in turn should be taken over and maintained by the public." Underscoring her commitment to new ideas and research, she urged the foundation to "take more interest in the architecture of ideas than in the architecture of buildings and laboratories." She encouraged the foundation to focus its resources on a few fundamental problems in medical science and health care, specifically on "special problems in medical sciences, medical arts, and medical education as required for their solution studies and efforts in correlated fields as well, such as biology and the social sciences."

During the foundation's first decade, its grants contributed to the development of psychosomatic medicine and research on aging. A 1940 foundation grant established a gerontology unit within the National Institutes of Health. Ladd's desire to encourage cross-disciplinary integration resulted in the appointment of Frank Fremont Smith to the foundation in 1936. Smith, a prominent neuropathologist on the Harvard Medical School faculty, initiated a program of interdisciplinary conferences. During World War II, Macy conferences furthered research on traumatic shock, liver injury, and combat neuroses. In the early 1950s, a series of Macy conferences on cybernetics, whose participants included Gregory Bateson, Margaret Mead, and Norbert Wiener, contributed to the development of computer science and cognitive psychology. As federal support for basic research grew, the foundation turned its resources to medical education and faculty development. Throughout the 1950s the foundation supported programs to improve clinical and laboratory training in obstetrics and reproductive

biology and in 1965 helped develop pediatrics programs in developing countries. In the early 1960s the Macy Foundation was among the first to support initiatives to improve the participation of women and minorities in the medical profession, an area in which the foundation is still active.

A 1930 newspaper story described Ladd as an elderly, white-haired woman, often too ill and weak to leave her bedroom, who was generous both with her charitable gifts and with her limited energy and strength. Although surrounded by servants, nurses, and secretaries, she maintained a personal, detailed interest in her extensive charitable interests, only one of which was the establishment of the Macy Foundation. Neither affluence or chronic illness isolated her from the cares of the larger world and the needs of others. She used her wealth and illness to engage in organized philanthropy and thereby maintain an involvement with the larger world and those less fortunate. Upon her death at her New Jersey home, the foundation received an additional $2.5 million from her estate. Between 1930 and 1945, she contributed nearly $19 million to the foundation. Ladd's vision for an effective medical philanthropy has now assisted generations of medical professionals who, as she wished, have helped develop "methods for the relief of suffering."

• The history of the Macy family, Ladd's establishment of the foundation, and a brief history of its programs can be found in "The First Fifty Years: The Foundation since 1930," in the *Josiah Macy, Jr. Foundation, Annual Report* (1982), pp. 21–26. The 1984 foundation report also contains a short history (pp. 13–15). Articles about Mrs. Ladd's initial gift to the foundation appeared in the *New York Times*, 25 Aug. 1930, and the *Yonkers* (N.Y.) *Herald*, 30 Apr. 1930. Obituaries are in the *New York Times*, *New York Sun*, *New York Evening News*, and the *New York Herald Tribune*, all 28 Aug. 1945. The 14 Sept. 1945 editions of the *New York Times* and the *New York Herald Tribune* ran articles on the settlement of Mrs. Ladd's residuary estate.

JOHN T. BRUER

LADD, William (10 May 1778–9 Apr. 1841), reformer, was born in Exeter, New Hampshire, the son of Eliphalet Ladd, a prosperous shipbuilder, sea captain, and merchant, and Abigail Hill. He received an A.B. from Harvard College in 1797, graduating with honors. His parents had planned a medical career for him, but he respectfully demurred and became an ordinary seaman on one of his father's ships. Within two years he commanded one of his father's largest ships. In London, England, in 1799 he married Sophia Ann Augusta Stidolph, admired alike for her piety and intelligence. They had no children.

In 1801 Ladd moved to Savannah, Georgia, where he operated a small mercantile firm for a few months. He then settled in Spanish Florida and experimented in the cultivation of cotton with free white labor. The project failed and cost him a large sum of money. After the death of his father in 1806, Ladd returned to Portsmouth and to the sea. The War of 1812 forced him to retire from sailing permanently. He moved to

Minot, Maine, in 1814, and lived and worked on a large farm that had belonged to his father. In 1818 he experienced a religious conversion that radically altered the course of his life. Now an "experimental Christian," he joined the Congregational church of Minot. He abstained from using tobacco and drinking wine. In short order he became a temperance lecturer, a foe of slavery, a Sunday school teacher, a generous friend to widows and orphans, and finally a licensed preacher.

Ladd committed himself to the cause of peace not long after a visit in 1819 to the bedside of the dying Reverend Dr. Jesse Appleton, the president of Bowdoin College and of the Maine Peace Society. Appleton entreated Ladd to befriend the proliferating benevolent societies that he believed were preliminary to and preparatory for the coming millennium. The newly organized peace societies were singled out and praised by him as unmistakable signs of a new earthly dispensation that was close at hand.

The New York Peace Society, the first of its kind anywhere, was founded by David Low Dodge in August 1815. Four months later the Reverend Noah Worcester organized the Massachusetts Peace Society. In 1814 Worcester had written the *Solemn Review of the Custom of War*, which for decades remained the most widely read and admired book on peace. It made a deep impression on Ladd. He united with the Maine Peace Society and promptly became its most active member and benefactor. His peace lectures and articles appeared regularly in the *Christian Mirror* of Portland, Maine, under the familiar pseudonym "Philanthropos." The best of them were published in his *Essays on Peace and War* (1827). Ladd's lectures were especially well received at the many colleges he visited. And he persistently informed women of his *The Duty of Females to Promote the Cause of Peace* (1836).

After delivering a series of peace lectures from Maine to Pennsylvania, Ladd launched the American Peace Society in May 1828. He contended that the absence of a national society ensured that the "operations of the peace societies" would be "mild," "gentle," "quiet," and "objects of but little notoriety" (*Harbinger of Peace*, May 1828). In the same year he edited and financed the society's monthly periodical, the *Harbinger of Peace*. Ladd supplied all the material for the periodical while residing in Minot and working full time on his farm. The *Harbinger of Peace* was replete with all manner of errata, and Ladd publicly apologized for "the bungling manner in which this only peace periodical . . . has been conducted" (*Harbinger of Peace*, Oct. 1831). The *Harbinger* was succeeded by the *Calumet*, a bimonthly that Ladd left to the direction of the society's executive board. It too bore the unsightly marks of its predecessor.

Peace advocates from the very beginning were divided about the question of whether self-defense, or defensive war, for nations and individuals, was scripturally sound and hence morally permissible. Noah Worcester and probably a majority of peace advocates acknowledged the legitimacy of defensive war. David Low Dodge, on the other hand, wrote an influential pamphlet entitled *War Inconsistent with the Religion of Jesus Christ* (1815). Ladd gradually accepted Dodge's position and led a movement within the society in 1837 to adopt an amendment to the constitution expressly condemning defensive war. Ladd's group carried the day but at the cost of alienating many honest and sincere peace advocates who believed that the amendment was scripturally unsound and theologically insupportable.

Subsequent ambiguous resolutions on the controversial amendment only further obfuscated the issue and polarized the membership even more by upholding the right of individuals to self-defense. Ladd never wavered in opposing defensive war, but he could not countenance the ultraist principles of the New England Non-Resistance Society founded in 1838 by peace extremists embittered by what they considered an unconscionably strict interpretation of the 1837 amendment. The Non-Resistants, led by William Lloyd Garrison and Henry C. Wright, categorically denied the right of governments or individuals to take a life for any reason. Ladd was sympathetic to nonresistance in principle but maintained that it was unreasonable and unrealistic in practice.

Ladd's most enduring legacy to the cause of world peace was his bold conception of a congress and a supreme court of nations. The task of the congress would be to elaborate a code of international law; the supreme court would adjudicate all grave international disputes on the basis of that law. Although the general idea itself was hardly new, Ladd gave it a distinctively "American shaping" by modeling both bodies after the U.S. Congress and the U.S. Supreme Court. In 1840 he published his classic *Essay on a Congress of Nations*, delineating brilliantly his proposal. The "American plan," as the scheme was called, was mainly responsible for engendering the international peace movement of the mid-nineteenth century under the leadership of Elihu Burritt.

William Ladd's health steadily deteriorated after he suffered a mild paralytic stroke in 1833. Even so, he carried on with an onerous lecture schedule. From October 1840 to March 1841 he spoke on peace throughout Massachusetts and New York. On 9 April he returned to his home in Portsmouth, New Hampshire. After readying himself for bed that evening and kneeling in prayer to thank the Lord for his safe return, Ladd lay down and died almost immediately. It is fitting that this apostle of peace died in peace and after prayer.

• Ladd's most important papers are in the Library of Congress, Yale University Library, Brown University Library, Harvard College Library, and the Presbyterian Historical Society in Philadelphia. John Hemmenway, *a Memoir of William Ladd, Apostle of Peace* (1872), and his revised and enlarged manuscript edition of 1890 (reprinted under the same title in 1972), contain many of Ladd's significant letters. The *Memoir*, though rather eulogistic, is informative nonetheless. There is no book-length biography of Ladd. Merle Curti has dealt very judiciously with Ladd in *The American Peace Cru-*

sade (1929). Peter Brock has made pertinent observations about him in *Pacifism in the United States* (1968). See also Arthur Deerin, "The Will to End War," *Advocate of Peace* 86, nos. 4 and 5 (Apr. and May 1924): 228–38, 297–309.

PETER TOLIS

LADD, William Edwards (8 Sept. 1880–19 Apr. 1967), surgeon, was born in Milton, Massachusetts, the son of William Jones Ladd, a merchant, and Anna Watson. Ladd was educated at the Milton Academy and the Hopkinson School in Boston. He entered Harvard University and received his A.B. in 1902. Ladd rowed on the Harvard crew, and association that continued throughout his life, first as a rower and later as the crew's physician. In 1906 he graduated from the Harvard Medical School. After graduation, Ladd served as surgical intern at the Boston City Hospital until 1910. After completing this training, Ladd served a two-year assistantship in Boston with the gynecologist and surgeon Edward Reynolds.

Early in his career Ladd developed an interest in treating surgical problems in children through his attendance on the staff of the old Boston Infant's Hospital from 1909 to 1911. In 1910 he married Katharine Barton; they had three children. That same year he received appointments at the Boston City Hospital and the Children's Hospital. He was appointed chief of the surgical service at Children's in 1927. In addition to his training in gynecology and his work with children, Ladd opened a general practice of surgery in 1912. He was also connected with the Harvard Medical School during this period and progressed from an instructor in 1917 to professor in 1941, a position he held until his retirement in 1947. In 1941 he became the first E. Ladd Professor of Children's Surgery, a professorship established in his honor that year.

In 1911 Ladd published his first paper, "The Treatment of Intussusception in Children." In it he pointed out that the malrotation of the intestines has a fatal outcome if left untreated and he recommended that surgery be performed early to correct the defect. Over the years Ladd published several more papers on the treatment of intussusception and reported a steady decrease in mortality with his suggestions for managing the condition. He also wrote on pyloric stenosis and recommended immediate surgery to relieve the obstruction and reduce mortality to less than 1 percent. In 1939 he devised a treatment for esophageal atresia that in which he exposed the upper end of the esophagus through an incision in the neck, closed the tracheo-esophageal fistula and established a gastronomy for feeding the child. In 1938 he attacked the difficult problem of managing Wilms' tumor and devised an operation in which he removed the tumor from the anterior approach rather than through the flank as was usually done. He reported a drop in mortality over time by his management from 90 percent to 60 percent. He also devised new methods and instruments for harelip operations.

Probably Ladd's best-known contribution to pediatric surgery was his concise, clear, beautifully illustrated Abdominal Surgery of Infancy and Childhood (1941), which he wrote out with his colleague, Robert Gross. One can see the wide variety of childhood conditions he researched and whose treatments he improved. These include biliary atresia, megacolon, omental cysts, intestinal obstruction, existrophy of the bladder, embryoma of the kidney, and branchiogenic anomalies, among many others.

Ladd was a member of the old New England merchant class. Daily he was driven to the hospital by the family chauffeur, but despite his formality, he was approachable and had a fine sense of humor. He enjoyed good health after his retirement in 1947 until 1965, when he fell and fractured his hip. He recovered from this accident and was able to get about with a cane. He died suddenly from an intracranial hemorrhage in Chestnut Hill, Massachusetts.

• Ladd's papers are in the special collections section of the Countway Library of Medicine, Harvard University. Some of Ladd's significant contributions are "The Embryoma of the Kidneys (Wilms' Tumor)," *Transactions of the American Surgical Association* 56 (1938): 390–407, and "Congenital Anomalies of the Esophagus," *Pediatrics* 6 (July 1950): 9–19. Summaries of Ladd's life are "William Edwards Ladd (1888–1967 [should be 1880])," in the *Harvard Medical Alumni Bulletin* 41, no. 5 (Summer 1967), and H. Bill's "William E. Ladd, M.D., Great Pioneer of North American Pediatric Surgery," *Progress in Pediatric Surgery* 20 (1986): 52–59. Other sources to consult are H. William Clatworthy, Jr.'s "William E. Ladd," *Transactions of the American Surgical Association* 85 (1967): 428–32, and Mark M. Ravitch's two volumes of *A Century of Surgery* (1981).

DAVID Y. COOPER

LADD, William Sargent (10 Oct. 1826–6 Jan. 1893), financier, merchant, and mayor of Portland, Oregon, was born in Holland, Vermont, the son of Nathaniel Gould Ladd, a physician, and Abigail Mead. Ladd's father moved the family to New Hampshire in 1830, and at age fifteen William started work on a farm. Four years later he taught school and then became a station agent for the Boston, Concord & Montreal Railroad at Sanbornton Bridge. In 1851 he arrived in San Francisco, responding to reports from a schoolmate, Charles Elliott Tilton. Tilton had written that wealth and opportunity awaited in Portland, Oregon, by supplying miners and prospectors in the area. Portland, Ladd learned, provided the primary source of provisions for the miners in the northern California region, where gold was plentiful. Tilton had moved his own business to San Francisco, specialized in the China trade, and extended his sales network northward. Thus, Ladd had an available supplier in the region, so he acquired a stock of goods and opened a general mercantile business called W. S. Ladd & Company in Portland.

Ladd's business sold eggs, wine, chickens, shovels, and other goods and within a few months had grossed more than $2,000. In 1852 Ladd entered into a partnership with Tilton, who advanced him $60,000 to buy merchandise for his next sales expedition. Ladd soon took on Simeon Reed, another New Englander, as a third partner and renamed the business Ladd & Reed & Company. The company moved into a new location on Front Street in 1853, at which time Ladd started to lend money to and hold deposits of regular customers. In 1854 Ladd married Caroline Ames Elliott; they had five children. In 1854 he was also elected mayor of Portland.

By 1859 Ladd had enough banking business to justify opening a true bank, called Ladd & Tilton, capitalized at $50,000. The bank grew rapidly—$130,000 in deposits at the end of one year—and Ladd's uncle Stephen Mead invested $200,000 worth of new capital in 1869. Ladd & Tilton did a vigorous gold dust exchange business and provided assay reports on gold. In 1880 Ladd and his son William Mead Ladd bought Tilton's share of the bank. That year the Oregon Supreme Court reviewed the state's constitutional prohibition against chartered banking, ruling it unconstitutional. Consequently, Ladd & Tilton, now owned entirely by Oregonians, incorporated under the new interpretation of the law and also started to invest in other Oregon banks, including the Ladd and Bush bank of Salem, Oregon.

Agricultural pursuits represented a second major field of interest for Ladd. He participated in Oregon agricultural circles and stimulated the development of new breeds of hogs, sheep, and horses by importing foreign breeds. His "Broad Mead" farm had the finest herd of Shorthorn cattle on the Pacific Coast, and he was noted for breeding Guernsey cattle. For his endeavors, the Agricultural College at Corvallis (now Oregon State University) elected Ladd to its board of regents. Ultimately, his agricultural interests led him to invest in milling, and in 1883 he founded the Portland Flour Mills, the largest milling operation in the Pacific Northwest.

Ladd established other corporations, including the Oregon Artificial Stone Company (1885), the Oregon Pottery Company (1885), and the Oregon Paving Contracting Company (1884). He held interests in several railroads and was a director of the Portland & Willamette Valley Railroad. In 1862, with John C. Ainsworth, a Portland banker, he founded the Oregon Steam and Navigation Company, which returned such impressive profits that Jay Cooke's Northern Pacific purchased Ladd's shares in 1871. When Cooke went bankrupt in 1873, Ladd reacquired his shares, only to resell them to Henry Villard in 1879.

During the 1870s Ladd suffered a reoccurrence of a spinal injury he had incurred as a young man and was paralyzed from the waist down for the remainder of his life. He spent considerable time in Hot Springs, Arkansas, as a result. Meanwhile, the bank he had built continued under his son, who assumed the presidency upon his father's death in Portland.

Ladd had a reputation as a thrifty man, even eccentric. He replied to letters written to him by returning the original with his comments scribbled in between the lines, and he was known to slice open envelopes to use the inner side of the paper. Yet he had a keen eye

for real estate and obtained large holdings, partially by buying forfeited mortgages and defaulted loans. By 1892 the value of Ladd's landholdings grew at a rate of 20 percent a month. One property of 400 acres, for example, he acquired for $20 an acre; when it was sold in 1909, it brought $5,000 an acre. Consequently, at the time of his death he left a sizable fortune, worth at least $10 million.

Ladd was an active Presbyterian, even though he had been raised a Methodist, and he endowed a chair of theology for the Presbyterians at a San Francisco seminary in 1866. Ladd and fellow bankers Henry Corbett and Henry Failing furnished the grounds for the Riverview Cemetery, and he championed the Portland Library Association.

Ladd was one great contradiction. While he had a public reputation as a man who pinched pennies, he set aside 10 percent of his income for charitable purposes and established a trust fund of half a million dollars for posthumous benefactions. A man who personally abstained from drinking, he sold liquor early in his career. Paralyzed by his injury, his imagination knew no bounds. Most of all, he was early Portland's premier banker.

• The William S. Ladd Papers and corporate records of Ladd & Tilton are at the Oregon Historical Society. See also Larry Schweikart, "William S. Ladd," in *The Encyclopedia of American Business History and Biography: Banking and Finance to 1913*, ed. Schweikart (1990); Orrin K. Burrell, *Gold in the Woodpile—An Informed History of Banking in Oregon* (1967); and E. Kimbark MacColl, *The Shaping of a City: Business and Politics in Portland, Oregon, 1885–1915* (1976).

LARRY SCHWEIKART

LADD-FRANKLIN, Christine (1 Dec. 1847–5 Mar. 1930), psychologist and logician, was born in Windsor, Connecticut, the daughter of Eliphalet Ladd, a farmer and merchant, and Augusta Niles. Soon after the death of her mother, when Ladd-Franklin was twelve, she went to live with her paternal grandmother in Portsmouth, New Hampshire. She graduated from Welshing Academy, a coeducational institution in Wilbraham, Massachusetts, in 1865 as valedictorian of her class. When, because of financial reverses, her father could not afford to send her to Vassar College, a maternal aunt provided the necessary funds. At Vassar she studied astronomy with Maria Mitchell, the premier nineteenth-century American woman scientist, and after two years in residence (1866–1867, 1868–1869) was awarded an A.B. in 1869. For the next nine years, she taught high school science and mathematics in several different localities, while at the same time she submitted mathematical problems and solutions to the *Educational Times* of London.

In 1878 Ladd-Franklin applied for admission to the recently established Johns Hopkins University, the first institution in the United States to be devoted primarily to research and graduate instruction. Although Johns Hopkins was officially closed to women at that time, Ladd-Franklin's contributions to the *Educational Times* gained her an entrée to the university. Her name was recognized by James J. Sylvester, an Englishman and professor of mathematics at Johns Hopkins who urged that she be accepted. In her first year at the school, she was allowed to attend only Sylvester's classes. In subsequent years this restriction was lifted, and for each of the next three academic years she was even awarded a fellow's stipend, but not the title (in order to avoid setting a precedent for awarding fellowships to women).

By 1882 Ladd-Franklin had completed all of the requirements for a doctorate in mathematics and logic, but it was not awarded because Johns Hopkins was still unwilling at that time to grant degrees to women. Not until 1926, as part of its fiftieth anniversary celebration, did Johns Hopkins award Ladd-Franklin the Ph.D. Her dissertation is credited with having contributed to the development of the field of symbolic logic, also known as Boolean logic, which reduced Aristotelian logic to an algebraic calculus. "On the Algebra of Logic" was published in 1883 as part of a collection of works by students of her adviser, Charles Sanders Peirce, entitled *Studies in Logic by Members of the Johns Hopkins University*. In 1882 she married one of her former mathematics professors, Fabian Franklin; they had two children.

By 1887 Ladd-Franklin had developed an interest in theories of vision and was beginning to publish the results of her research on this topic. Her first paper was a report of her investigation of the nature of the horopter, a mathematical question concerned with binocular vision.

During Fabian Franklin's 1891–1892 sabbatical year, the couple traveled to Germany, where Ladd-Franklin studied color vision. She spent the first half of the year in Göttingen in the laboratory of psychologist G. E. Müller and the second half in the laboratory of Hermann von Helmholtz, physicist and physiologist, working under the direction of physicist Arthur König. By the summer of 1892 Ladd-Franklin had come up with her own theory of color vision, which she claimed was able to account for all of the phenomena explained by the two major rival theories of that day. The Hering theory, endorsed by Müller, proposed three opponent color processes in the retina—white-black, yellow-blue, and red-green—and the Young-Helmholtz theory, supported by König, maintained that there were three modes of color excitation in the retina: red, green, and violet. Building on these two theories, which she argued were not contradictory but rather pertained to different stages of the visual process, Ladd-Franklin advanced her own, original contribution: the idea of the evolutionary development of color sensation from achromatic (black and white) to dichromatic (yellow and blue) to tetrachromatic (yellow, blue, red, and green). Although her theory received considerable attention and support during her lifetime, it was eventually superseded by more encompassing theories that included neural mechanisms beyond the retina.

Ladd-Franklin first announced her theory in a paper presented at the Second International Congress of Psychology in London in August 1892. She spent the rest of her life promoting it. In the decade following the invention of her color theory, she published prolifically on the subject of vision and was an associate editor and contributor on that topic for the second volume of the *Dictionary of Philosophy and Psychology* (1902). By the advent of the twentieth century, she had become an internationally recognized authority on vision.

Promoted to professor of mathematics in 1892, Fabian Franklin resigned from Johns Hopkins in 1895 to become editor of the *Baltimore News*. In 1909 he accepted a position as associate editor of the *New York Evening Post*, and the family moved to New York City, where the couple resided for the rest of their lives. Although Ladd-Franklin never held a regular academic appointment, she taught courses at Johns Hopkins on color vision and on logic between 1904 and 1909, and from 1914 to 1929 she had an appointment without salary at Columbia University, where she continued to offer courses on these topics. Between 1912 and 1914 she presented a lecture series on color theory at Columbia, Clark, and Harvard universities and at the University of Chicago. A collection of her articles on color vision, which had originally appeared between 1892 and 1926, were published as *Colour and Colour Theories* (1929).

From her adolescence onward, Ladd-Franklin was a militant supporter of women's rights who championed such causes as equal access to education and the professions and woman suffrage. Beginning in 1912, and for several years thereafter, she assailed Edward Bradford Titchener, an eminent Cornell University psychologist, for excluding women from the elite society he had established in 1904, known as "the Experimentalists." In 1914, when the annual meeting of this group was to be held at Columbia University, as Ladd-Franklin put it in a letter to Titchener, "at my very door," she accused him of holding to a "mediaeval attitude" by refusing to include women psychologists, an attitude that she decried as being "so unconscientious, so immoral,—worse than that—so unscientific!" (Scarborough and Furumoto, p. 126).

Ladd-Franklin lost the distinction of being the first American woman to receive a Ph.D. in mathematics to Winifred Haring Edgerton (who was awarded the degree by Columbia University in 1886) despite having completed all of the requirements for a doctorate in mathematics and logic by 1882. Her major scientific contribution, however, came in the field of psychology, in which, in the 1906 edition of James McKeen Cattell's *American Men of Science*, she was listed as fifteenth among the fifty psychologists judged to be the most eminent in the field. During her lifetime, her theory of color sensation came to rank in importance directly behind the Young-Helmholtz and Hering theories, although mention of the Ladd-Franklin theory can rarely be found in late twentieth-century discussions of the history of color theories. She died in New York City.

• An extensive collection, largely unprocessed, of Ladd-Franklin's papers is in the Rare Book and Manuscript Library of Columbia University. For discussions of Ladd-Franklin's work in logic and mathematics see Judy Green, "Christine Ladd-Franklin (1847–1930)," in *Women of Mathematics: A Biobibliographic Sourcebook*, ed. Louise S. Grinstein and Paul J. Campbell (1987), and Green and Jeanne Laduke, "Contributors to American Mathematics: An Overview and Selection," in *Women of Science: Righting the Record*, ed. G. Kass-Simon and Patricia Farnes (1990). See Thomas C. Cadwallader and Joyce V. Cadwallader, "Christine Ladd-Franklin (1847–1930)," in *Women in Psychology: A Bio-Bibliographic Sourcebook*, ed. Agnes N. O'Connell and Nancy Felipe Russo (1990), for her career and contributions to psychology; Laurel Furumoto, "Joining Separate Spheres—Christine Ladd-Franklin, Woman-Scientist (1847–1930)," *American Psychologist* 47 (1992): 175–82, on gender issues in her life and career; and Elizabeth Scarborough and Furumoto, *Untold Lives: The First Generation of American Women Psychologists* (1987), for an account of her reaction to a policy of exclusion of women psychologists by their male colleagues.

LAUREL FURUMOTO

LADEJINSKY, Wolf Isaac (15 Mar. 1899–3 July 1975), agricultural economist, was born in Ekaterinopol, Ukraine, then part of the Russian empire, the son of a prosperous Jewish miller and trader. His parents' names are unknown. Attracted to learning from an early age, Ladejinsky completed his secondary studies at a nearby Gymnasium. Further university studies were interrupted by the outbreak of the Russian revolution in 1917.

During the Russian revolution and civil war (1917–1921), Ladejinsky's father's mill and property were confiscated, and his brother was killed. In 1920, with his family's approval, Ladejinsky fled to Romania on foot. After an arduous journey and a variety of jobs—selling firewood, working in a flour mill, and apprenticing in a bakery—he found a clerical job with the Bucharest office of the Hebrew Immigrant Aid Society. With their encouragement, in 1922 he emigrated to the United States and settled in New York City.

For the next five years Ladejinsky eked out a living making mattresses, selling newspapers, and washing windows while he learned English and saved enough money to pursue his university studies. In 1926 he enrolled at Columbia University, graduating in 1928 with a B.S. That same year he became a naturalized U.S. citizen. In 1930, as the depression set in, he accepted a well-paying position as an interpreter with the Soviet Union's Amtorg Trading Corporation. Although he was fired without explanation after one year, this brief experience would later trouble him.

Ladejinsky had begun graduate study in agricultural economics at Columbia University; he received an M.A. in 1934 but chose not to pursue a doctorate. Instead, in 1935 he accepted a research position with the Department of Agriculture's Office of Foreign Agricultural Relations, where he worked until 1945. During this period he published several well-regarded articles on Soviet collective farms, including "Collectivization of Agriculture in the Soviet Union" (*Political Science Quarterly* [Mar.–June 1934]: 1–43, 207–52).

He also published numerous articles on Asian agriculture, primarily in official journals of the Department of Agriculture, such as *Foreign Agriculture* and *Journal of Farm Economics*.

By the end of World War II Ladejinsky was considered one of the department's leading specialists on Asian nations, especially Japan. This expertise contributed to his appointment as adviser to General Douglas MacArthur's occupation government in Japan in 1945. Ladejinsky is generally credited as the architect of the sweeping agrarian reform that allowed Japanese farmers to acquire land and that drastically curtailed the power of rural landlords. Ladejinsky was also involved in land reform work in mainland China and Taiwan. In 1950 he was appointed agricultural attaché at the U.S. embassy in Tokyo, a post he held until 1954.

In 1954 Ladejinsky found himself at the center of an unexpected political controversy when the USDA refused to reappoint him to his post on the grounds that he did not meet "security requirements," because of his previous work for Amtorg, an extended trip to the Soviet Union in 1939, and his correspondence with his sisters in Ukraine. Vigorous protests from political, diplomatic, and intellectual circles and behind-the-scenes maneuvering from the White House failed to convince Secretary of Agriculture Ezra Taft Benson to reconsider his position. Several months later, however, Benson retracted his charges and apologized to Ladejinsky. The Ladejinsky affair reflected changing U.S. government attitudes toward the Soviet Union.

In 1955, as a solution to the impasse created by the USDA's decision, Ladejinsky was assigned to work on land reform and refugee resettlement programs in South Vietnam. Initially he worked for the Foreign Operations Administration, the predecessor of the Agency for International Development (AID). Within a year he resigned over a conflict-of-interest case, but he remained as an adviser to President Ngo Dinh Diem. In 1961 he left Vietnam, apparently disillusioned by Diem's lack of commitment to agrarian reform.

For the next three years Ladejinsky worked as a consultant and regional specialist for the Ford Foundation, based primarily in Malaysia. During this time he was concerned mostly with the problems of agrarian reform in Nepal; he also traveled to the Philippines, Indonesia, India, Korea, Mexico, and Iran.

In 1964 Ladejinsky joined other prominent agricultural specialists in a World Bank study of economic development in India. He remained with the World Bank for the next decade, spending most of this period as a member of the bank's permanent resident mission in India. Whereas Japan had been the scene of Ladejinsky's greatest policy triumphs, India provided him with his greatest frustrations. As early as 1950 he had argued for the necessity of land redistribution in India as part of a program of agrarian reform. By the 1970s he felt that the Indian political class had successfully resisted and diluted all attempts at serious, far-reaching reform.

Ladejinsky's legacy rests on his profound and passionate commitment to the idea of agrarian reform and on his belief in the political importance of the conditions of the peasantry in Asian nations. Only by strengthening the principle of private property at the base of the social pyramid by means of far-reaching programs to promote peasant landownership could agrarian societies escape the appeal of communism and the drastic upheavals Ladejinsky had witnessed in his youth. He further believed that politicians, not experts, made successful or unsuccessful agrarian reforms—hence his disappointment with the leaders he saw wavering in their commitment to thorough land reforms.

Ladejinsky's scholarly output is not in monographs or treatises but rather in articles and internal reports for the agencies for which he worked; but, as one obituarist pointed out, his influence extended well beyond the reach of the written word. By all accounts, Ladejinsky was a tireless worker and captivating speaker who felt at home with heads of state as well as with the peasants whom he sought out in his fieldwork. He also collected Asian art, which he donated to the Israeli Museum in Jerusalem. A lifelong bachelor, Ladejinsky died in Washington, D.C.

• Large portions of Ladejinsky's papers are held by institutions such as the Ford Foundation and the World Bank. Louis J. Walinsky, ed., *Agrarian Reform as Unfinished Business: The Selected Papers of Wolf Ladejinsky* (1977), contains excerpts from his most important published and unpublished papers, an assessment of his career, and a complete bibliography. James Rorty, "The Dossier of Wolf Ladejinsky," *Commentary*, Apr. 1955, pp. 326–34, presents a contemporary reaction to the Ladejinsky affair of 1954. Mary S. McAuliffe, "Dwight D. Eisenhower and Wolf Ladejinsky: The Politics of the Declining Red Scare, 1954–55," *Prologue*, Fall 1982, pp. 109–27, discusses the 1954 affair in the broader context of the Eisenhower administration's changing attitude toward security issues. Obituaries are in the *New York Times*, 4 July 1975, and George Rosen, "Wolf Ladejinsky," *Journal of Asian Studies* 36 (Feb. 1977): 327–28.

MAURICIO BORRERO

LAEMMLE, Carl (17 Jan. 1867–24 Sept. 1939), motion picture pioneer, was born in Laupheim, Württemberg, in southwestern Germany, the son of Julius Baruch Laemmle, a businessman, and Rebekka (maiden name unknown). Laemmle, the tenth of thirteen children, attended public school and at age thirteen was apprenticed to a local storekeeper to learn bookkeeping. But he wanted more. An older brother had immigrated to the United States, and Laemmle followed in 1884. He worked in a department store, on a farm, and as a clerk throughout the Midwest before settling in Oshkosh, Wisconsin, where he entered the clothing store business. He became a U.S. citizen in 1889.

In 1898 he married Rasha Stern, the niece of his boss; the couple had two children. The Laemmles moved to Chicago and in February 1906 opened a nickelodeon. To guarantee a regular supply of films for his White Front theater on North Milwaukee Avenue, Carl Laemmle became a film distributor. He had to fight to maintain his new business. The major film producers had set up the Motion Pictures Patents Trust; still, Laemmle was able to successfully expand from film exhibition and distribution into filmmaking. In 1909 he established the Independent Motion Picture Company, with studios in New York City. At this time movies were shot silent, out-of-doors, and were twenty minutes long.

His first feature-length major production was *Hiawatha* (1909), inspired by the Henry Wadsworth Longfellow poem and starring Florence Lawrence. In less than a decade, as Laemmle made longer and more expensive films, he developed several internationally famous stars, including Mary Pickford. Laemmle earned millions, which enabled the newly titled Universal Studios to move to Los Angeles, and in March 1915 he opened Universal City Studios. In his early fifties, the diminutive Laemmle stood atop the new motion picture industry.

During the next decade Universal City Studios functioned as the largest moviemaking operation in the world. Popular Universal films included *Blind Husbands* (1919) and *Foolish Wives* (1922), both directed by Erich von Stroheim, *The Hunchback of Notre Dame* (1923), and *The Phantom of the Opera* (1925). But "Uncle Carl" grew conservative, consolidated his fame and fortune, and never expanded further—as rivals signed away top stars and executives. Laemmle lost such talents as director John Ford and studio executive Irving Thalberg to expanding competitors. Because of his wife's death in 1918 and his own brush with death in 1926 (an appendicitis attack during an Atlantic crossing), Laemmle semiretired in 1929 and placed his son, Carl, Jr., in charge of Universal. Even though the younger Laemmle's only experience had been writing two-reel comedies, he stepped into a position of considerable power as head of production.

The Great Depression brought an end to the Laemmle movie empire. Despite the fact that the company immediately began losing money, Universal under Carl, Jr., earned considerable critical praise for the Oscar-winning *All Quiet on the Western Front* (1930), a daring pacifist tale told from the German point of view. But the studio's bread and butter remained low-budget films—westerns and melodramas—including such horror film classics as *Dracula* (1930), *The Mummy* (1932), *The Invisible Man* (1933), and *The Bride of Frankenstein* (1935).

The Laemmles were never able to develop a strategy to bring customers into theaters during the dark days of the Great Depression. Relentlessly, the corporation moved toward bankruptcy. Eventually, despite all of the senior Laemmle's efforts to hold off creditors, he could not get out from under the mounting debts his profligate son had accrued in trying to make that one saving blockbuster. In March 1936 Laemmle gave up his beloved movie company to a group of Wall Street investment bankers for in excess of $5 million.

Both Laemmles retired, just as their last major effort, a second of three film versions of *Showboat*

(1936), was being released. Ironically *Showboat* proved a hit for the new owners. The senior Laemmle played his role as beloved elder statesman of the film business for a few surviving years; he died in Beverly Hills, California.

• There are no known papers from either Carl Laemmle, Sr. or Jr. Carl Laemmle, Sr., wrote, "From the Inside: The Business of Motion Pictures," *Saturday Evening Post*, 27 Aug. 1927. He also commissioned a laudatory biography, John Drinkwater's *The Life and Adventures of Carl Laemmle* (1931). No scholarly, well-researched biography exists, but details of his life can be found in a number of film industry histories: I. G. Edmonds, *Big U: Universal in the Silent Days* (1977); Douglas Gomery, *The Hollywood Studio System* (1986); and Clive Hirschhorn, *The Universal Story* (1983). A helpful obituary is in the *New York Times*, 25 Sept. 1939.

DOUGLAS GOMERY

LAFARGE, John (13 Feb. 1880–24 Nov. 1963), clergyman, journalist, and civil rights advocate, was born in Newport, Rhode Island, the youngest child of John LaFarge, a painter and art critic, and Margaret Mason Perry, a granddaughter of Commodore Oliver Hazard Perry. Growing up in this distinguished Catholic family, LaFarge was exposed to such famous people as Henry Adams, William James and Henry James (1843–1916), and Theodore Roosevelt (1858–1919). A sickly and introspective child, he was an avid reader and exhibited an early talent for the piano and foreign languages. At the age of eleven he decided that he would become a priest. On the advice of Theodore Roosevelt, LaFarge entered Harvard in 1897, where he majored in Latin and Greek. After graduating in 1901, he traveled to Innsbruck, Austria, to prepare for the priesthood. In 1905 he entered the Society of Jesus and spent the next five years studying theology and philosophy, and teaching at Jesuit colleges. In 1910 he earned an M.A. at Woodstock College in Maryland. LaFarge was seemingly headed for a Ph.D. and a quiet niche in Catholic academia, but his fragile health began to fail. In 1911 his superiors sent him to the Jesuit missions in southern Maryland for pastoral duty and therapy.

His Maryland experience lasted almost fifteen years, and it marked a turning point in his life. He came into contact for the first time with large numbers of poor, uneducated, and oppressed African Americans. He became absorbed in the problem of race. Alarmed by the spiritual and educational neglect of black Catholics, he focused his early efforts on providing equal but separate religious and educational instruction for blacks. His work in southern Maryland culminated in the founding in 1924 of the Cardinal Gibbons Institute in Ridge, which was advertised by LaFarge as the "Catholic Tuskegee."

In 1926 LaFarge became an associate editor of *America*, the influential Jesuit weekly in New York. He served the magazine until his death, acting as executive editor from 1942 to 1944 and editor in chief from 1944 to 1948. A prolific writer, LaFarge penned hundreds of editorials, articles, and book reviews. He also wrote nine books. His interests and writings were broad in scope, treating such topics as the Society of Jesus, communism, fascism, agricultural reform, the liturgy, art, music, education, and ecumenism. He held important offices in the Catholic Association for International Peace, the National Catholic Rural Life Association, and the Liturgical Arts Society.

LaFarge's greatest passion, however, remained the "Negro apostolate." By the 1930s he had become the most prominent Catholic spokesman or black-white relations. More than any other single individual in the first half of this century, he awakened the Catholic church to the moral implications of the race problem. In *Interracial Justice* (1937), his most important book, he proclaimed that racism was a sin and a heresy. Pope Pius XI was so impressed with the book that in 1938 he secretly employed LaFarge to write an encyclical on racism. But the pope died in 1939, and the document was never released. From his arrival in New York in 1926, LaFarge was heavily engaged in interracial activity. In 1928 he founded the Catholic Laymen's Union, a group of black New York businessmen and professionals for whom he acted as chaplain. In 1933 he helped establish the Northeastern Clergy Conference on Negro Welfare. The following year he was the primary mover in the formation of the Catholic Interracial Council of New York. Through its official journal, the *Interracial Review*, the council served as a national clearinghouse of racial information for Catholics, and it provided an organizational model for other cities to follow.

As a pioneer racial reformer, LaFarge adopted a cause that was not popular among American Catholics, lay or clerical. In his autobiography he noted that many of his colleagues saw him as a champion of "lost causes." In the early years of his ministry, many Catholics in fact branded racial reformers like LaFarge as "nigger priests." Nevertheless, he was fiercely loyal to the institutional church and almost blindly obedient to the hierarchy. Ever concerned with the image of his embattled minority church, he was more inclined to conceal certain racial policies of Catholicism than to expose them to the public. His Catholic Interracial Council in New York never advanced beyond the polite, educational stage of racial activism that suited LaFarge's gentle personality and well-mannered intellectualism.

In the late 1920s and early 1930s LaFarge became involved in his most misguided effort when he and William Markoe, a St. Louis Jesuit, became active in the Federated Colored Catholics, a black Catholic lay group founded in 1924 by Dr. Thomas W. Turner. The two Jesuits methodically altered the purpose of the FCC and slowly usurped the authority of Turner, a black protest leader who was the organization's first and only president. LaFarge and Markoe believed that Turner's federation was too race-centered and too anticlerical. LaFarge bemoaned the impatience of the FCC and criticized the fact that it directly placed urgent demands upon the American bishops to integrate Catholic schools and increase the number of black clergy, demands that often were publicized to the embarrassment of the church in the militant black press. LaFarge pressured the FCC to downplay racial protest and shape itself to the broader apostolic mission of the church as exemplified in the concept of Catholic Action, defined by Pope Pius XI as the participation of the laity in the pastoral work of the bishop. In December 1932, when Jesuit activists masterminded a rump session of the FCC's executive committee, which Turner declared illegal and refused to attend, it voted to remove the president from office. The ouster of Turner split the federation into two factions and led to the rapid decline of both. Already suffering from a lack of African-American priests—there were but two in 1933—black Catholic leadership suffered a serious setback with the hobbling of the FCC and its militant lay leaders such as Turner. Moreover, LaFarge soon lost interest in the reformed federation, the National Catholic Interracial Federation, and turned his attention toward the establishment of the Catholic Interracial Council in New York. De-emphasizing black protest and race leadership, the New York council provided the model for the gradualistic interracialism that guided the Catholic church for the next three decades.

Although LaFarge was ahead of his church on the issue of race, he was slow to condemn segregation and unduly optimistic about the South's willingness to end it. Preaching that ignorance caused racism, he was also overly sanguine about the efficacy of education in fighting discrimination. Nor did he support direct, nonviolent action until the early 1960s, and then with the greatest reluctance. Even so, at the age of eighty-three he participated in the famous March on Washington in August 1963 that was highlighted by the "I Have a Dream" speech of Martin Luther King, Jr. LaFarge died in New York City at Campion House, the editorial headquarters of *America*.

• The John LaFarge Papers are housed at Georgetown University, Washington, D.C. Important correspondence can also be found in the Thomas W. Turner Papers, Howard University, Washington, D.C., and in the Josephite Archives in Baltimore, Md. LaFarge's published works include *The Jesuits in Modern Times* (1928); *The Race Question and the Negro* (1943); *No Postponement: U.S. Moral Leadership and the Problem of Racial Minorities* (1950); his autobiography, *The Manner Is Ordinary* (1954); *The Catholic Viewpoint on Race Relations* (1956); *A Report on the American Jesuits*, with photographs by Margaret Bourke-White (1956); *An American Amen* (1958); and *Reflections on Growing Old* (1963). For a significant study of his early career, see Marilyn W. Nickels, *Black Catholic Protest and the Federated Colored Catholics* (1988). Also useful are Edward S. Stanton, "John LaFarge's Understanding of the Unifying Mission of the Church" (Ph.D. diss., Saint Paul Univ., Ottawa, Canada, 1972), and Martin A. Zielinski, "'Doing the Truth': The Catholic Interracial Council of New York, 1945–1965" (Ph.D. diss., Catholic Univ. of America, 1989). George K. Hunton, longtime editor of the *Interracial Review* and a close ally of LaFarge for thirty years, lauded his mentor in his autobiography, *All of Which I Saw, Part of Which I Was* (1967). A balanced assessment of LaFarge can also be found in Cyprian Davis, *History of Black Catholics in the United States* (1990). A comprehensive study of the priest is David W. Southern, *John LaFarge and the Limits of Catholic Interracialism, 1911–1963* (1996). Popular accounts appear in *Time*, 27 July 1942 and 3 Mar. 1952. An obituary is in the *New York Times*, 25 Nov. 1963.

DAVID W. SOUTHERN

LA FARGE, John Frederick Lewis Joseph (31 Mar. 1835–14 Nov. 1910), artist and writer, was born in New York City, the son of John Frederick La Farge, a French émigré, and Louisa Josephine Binsse de Saint-Victor, the daughter of French émigrés. La Farge was raised near Washington Square in New York. His father's success in real estate provided a prosperous home environment. Surrounded by books and fine art, La Farge learned early in life to appreciate his French Catholic heritage. At age six, he took drawing lessons from his maternal grandfather, Louis Binsse de Saint-Victor, a successful miniaturist. Later, at Columbia Grammar School in New York City, La Farge learned to paint with watercolors in the English manner.

Beginning in 1848, La Farge attended the French Catholic college of St. John's in New York, the present Fordham University. In 1850, after being expelled for fighting with another student, he transferred to St. John's parent school, Mount St. Mary's College in Emmitsburg, Maryland. Shortly after graduating in 1853, La Farge apprenticed with a New York law firm in accordance with his father's wishes. By 1855 he had also qualified for a general master's degree from Mount St. Mary's.

Even as La Farge dutifully pursued a law career, he maintained an interest in art. In 1854 he studied in his spare time with an unknown French artist (perhaps Régis Gignoux). A watershed event occurred in April 1856, when he and two of his brothers traveled to France to meet their French relatives. In Paris, La Farge visited the leading literary salons of the day, benefiting from the influence of his mother's cousin, Paul de Saint-Victor, a famous critic. He visited the ateliers of such painters as Jean-Léon Gérôme and Théodore Chassériau and studied drawing for a couple of weeks under Thomas Couture, a teacher popular among Americans. Impatient with studio methods, La Farge followed Couture's advice to stop attending his studio and to instead copy old master drawings at the Louvre.

La Farge traveled extensively throughout Europe. During a tour of northern France and Belgium, altar paintings and stained glass in religious edifices caught his attention. He visited museums in Munich, Dresden, Copenhagen, and Switzerland, copying drawings and paintings by the old masters. In October 1857, La Farge's travels were cut short by news that his father was seriously ill. He returned to the United States via London, and visited the Manchester Art Treasures Exhibition, a massive assemblage of old master and contemporary paintings from British private and royal collections. This final experience of La Farge's stay abroad instilled in him a keen appreciation of artists as diverse as Raphael, Van Dyck, and the British Pre-Raphaelites.

The death of La Farge's father in June 1858 marked a dual liberation for La Farge. He not only found himself independently wealthy under the terms of his inheritance, but he also was freed from parental pressure to practice law. He aspired to a career in art, but he recognized his lack of training in easel painting as a major impediment. He considered returning to Europe for academic study but decided in 1859 to move to Newport, Rhode Island, to work under William Morris Hunt, a former pupil of Couture.

La Farge found Hunt a good teacher in many respects but complained that Hunt had abandoned the realistic figure painting methods of Couture, including modeling, brushstroke, and general technical approach. In their place, Hunt had adopted the more stylized techniques of the French Barbizon artist Jean-François Millet. Given this disappointment, La Farge might well have left Newport shortly after his arrival had he not met Margaret Mason Perry, a member of an illustrious Newport family. Their courtship, begun in late 1859, immediately faced a serious conflict posed by differing religious backgrounds. In the end, La Farge's Catholicism won out over Perry's Episcopalianism. They were married on 15 October 1860, three weeks before she joined the Catholic church. The couple had ten children, seven of whom survived to adulthood.

La Farge's marriage rooted him firmly in Newport for the next fifteen years. Dissatisfied with Hunt as a teacher, La Farge decided to learn easel painting on his own through experimentation and practice. Two ambitious religious subjects, *St. Paul Preaching at Athens* (1860–1862; location unknown) and a triptych of the Crucifixion (1861–1863; side panels in a private chapel in Trujillo, Spain; central panel never executed), occupied La Farge for several years. In both projects, he sought to merge conventional religious imagery with realistic lighting and landscape effects. Similarly, in a number of portraits and figure studies, La Farge sought to replace the mannerisms of conventional figure works with vibrant, atmospheric effects (e.g., *A Bather* [*Woman Bathing*], 1868, Worcester Art Museum; *Portrait of Boy and a Dog*, 1869, private collection).

La Farge began painting landscapes and still lifes from nature, focusing on realistic weather conditions and lighting effects. Although these interests mirrored methods employed by the French impressionists around the same time, La Farge also drew upon Barbizon and Pre-Raphaelite precedents for his plein air work. La Farge was scientific in his approach to painting from nature. Conversant with current color theories, he had studied the principles of optics and made extensive use of photographic reproductions, becoming proficient in the operation of cameras. His studies culminated in two large canvases, *Paradise Valley* (*New England Pasture Land*) (1866–1868, private collection) and *The Last Valley—Paradise Rocks* (1867, private collection). Both paintings were exhibited in major forums for over three decades, including annual exhibitions of the Yale School of Fine Arts (New Haven, Conn., 1871), the London Society of French Artists (1873), the National Academy of Design (New York, 1876), and the Society of American Artists (New York, 1878, 1892), garnering enthusiastic international acclaim. Numerous other works of a more modest scale earned La Farge an avid following in Boston and New York, and the sale of small landscapes and floral pictures supported La Farge and his family throughout their Newport years.

La Farge also earned both income and praise as a result of his book illustrations, a genre he valued as highly as easel painting. His illustrations, which were often inventive and visionary, included designs for the works of Browning, Tennyson, Longfellow, and Emerson. La Farge broke with the prevailing American cartoon-like illustrations by emulating the more realistic British Pre-Raphaelite graphic styles. His most successful book plates, prepared in 1864 for a Christmas gift book edition of Tennyson's *Enoch Arden*, sparked a small revolution in the United States in the field of illustration. Eventually, La Farge's graphic work became central to heated debates over the roles of wood engravers and photomechanical processes in artistic pursuits.

During this so-called "Newport Period," La Farge traveled frequently to Boston and New York, establishing important social and professional contacts. He became intimate with many of the foremost personalities of his day, including the historian Henry Adams; architects William van Brunt, William Ware, and Henry Hobson Richardson; scientist Clarence King; writer William Dean Howells; politician John Hay; artists Elihu Vedder and Winslow Homer; and Henry and William James, brothers he had first met at Hunt's Newport studio. From these associations, La Farge garnered a lifelong reputation as a genial conversationalist with a propensity for hypochondriac complaints. Friends compared him to a venerable oriental sage, at once brilliant, charismatic, and impenetrable.

From the quiet of the Newport years, La Farge emerged in the mid-1870s as a fashionable decorative artist based in New York. The key event in this transition was his commission in 1875 to oversee the interior decoration of Trinity Church in Boston, which was designed by the architect Henry Hobson Richardson. Drawing upon Romanesque church decoration in southern France, La Farge created a design that was carried out by dozens of artisans and artists working in an unheated church still under construction, difficult conditions exacerbated by a short time schedule. The resulting interior was so successful that its completion in 1876 is often heralded as the start of the "American Renaissance," a period of eclectic, monumental achievements in the decorative arts that lasted until the onset of World War I. Virtually overnight, La Farge became one of the most highly regarded decorative artists of his generation.

At this juncture, La Farge realized that his days as an easel painter were numbered. In 1878 and 1879 he sold the contents of his studio at a private auction and announced his intention to devote himself to decorative work. Decorative commissions formed the heart of La Farge's artistic livelihood for the remainder of his life. He completed over a dozen major mural schemes, including the opulent interior of the Cornelius Vanderbilt II house in New York (1880–1882, razed in 1927); a mural of the Ascension in the Church of the Ascension, New York (1886–1888); and lunettes and spandrels for the Minnesota state capitol in St. Paul (1904) and the Baltimore courthouse (1906–1907). He became best known, however, for his work in stained glass in both ecclesiastical and secular contexts.

La Farge's interest in stained glass dated from his earliest travels through European cathedrals. It had been further stimulated in 1873, when, on a brief visit to Europe, he met Edward Burne-Jones and saw numerous Pre-Raphaelite windows. For the next several years, La Farge designed and supervised the construction of several windows, following English techniques and precedents. Dissatisfied with the results, he embarked around 1879 on a more experimental approach that employed opalescent glass of various textures. Using layers of glass, semiprecious stones, and molded glass, La Farge patented in 1880 a method of making windows with opalescent glass that is generally credited as the start of a new stained-glass movement. For his accomplishment, La Farge received the Legion of Honor from the French government in 1889.

La Farge's great success as a decorative artist had several unfortunate consequences. Required by his work to live in Boston or New York while his family remained in Newport (his wife refused to give up her house there), La Farge found himself a virtual bachelor. Even though he eventually employed two of his sons as studio assistants, his relationship with his family became distant. His personal troubles were exacerbated by legal problems that accompanied his rising popularity. In the early 1880s, constantly led by perfectionism to rework windows and continually searching for unusual glasses, La Farge spent more money on commissions than they brought in, resulting in his failure to meet the demands of creditors. In late 1883 he went bankrupt and was forced to take on partners, who formed the La Farge Decorative Art Company as a means of handling La Farge's business matters. Because of conflicting personalities and the efforts of his partners to take artistic control out of La Farge's hands, this enterprise failed in 1885, and La Farge was arrested on trumped-up charges of grand larceny, brought by his partners because La Farge, in retaliation for their trying to take control, had concealed drawings and photographs needed to execute the decorative works encharged to the company. Although later vindicated, La Farge permanently lost the opportunity to pursue the kind of commercial success attained by his rival in opalescent stained glass, Louis Comfort Tiffany. Architects who once provided La Farge with commissions shunned him after his arrest, and he lost some major commissions, including a window for Memorial Hall at Harvard, a project named in the grand larceny lawsuit. La Farge never again enjoyed the wide patronage he had during the early 1880s. He instead became a free agent, executing decorative commissions by contracting with artisans and artists who were formerly employed in his decorative arts company.

La Farge's ultimate failure as a commercial decorative artist left him time to pursue interests that otherwise might have been sacrificed. In the summer of 1886 he fulfilled a long-held ambition and traveled to Japan at the invitation of his old friend from Boston, Henry Adams. For three months, they visited temples and shrines in Tokyo, Nikko, Osaka, and Kyoto, experiences that inspired La Farge to write a series of illustrated articles and a travel book on Japan (*Century Magazine*, 1890–1893; *An Artist's Letters from Japan*, 1897). La Farge and Adams undertook an even more exotic trip in 1890 when, for a year and a half, they visited the island groups of Hawaii, Samoa, Fiji, and Tahiti. Again deeply moved, La Farge expended great efforts to produce illustrated writings documenting the South Seas trip (*Scribner's Magazine*, 1901; *Century Magazine*, 1904; *Reminiscences of the South Seas*, 1912).

La Farge produced nearly 300 watercolors inspired by his travels. Throughout the 1890s, he not only found a lucrative market for these pictures, but he also realized their potential for communicating to the public the substance of his experiences. In 1894 La Farge accepted an invitation from the French government to show his work at the 1895 French Salon. His collection of over 200 travel pictures, gathered under the title "Records of Travel," was shown in both Paris and New York. The exhibition elevated La Farge's reputation as a watercolorist, creating a keen demand for his watercolors that lasted until the end of his life.

La Farge also enjoyed great popularity throughout his life as a teacher, writer, and speaker. His earliest publication, "An Essay on Japanese Art," a chapter in Raphael Pumpelly's *Across America and Asia* (1870), broke new ground in the United States for the study of Asian art. His lectures to aspiring artists delivered at the Metropolitan Museum of Art in 1893 proved so popular that they were published as *Considerations on Painting* (1895). Similarly, his lectures on Barbizon art given at the Art Institute of Chicago in 1903 produced *The Higher Life in Art* (1908). La Farge's essays on old and modern masters such as Van Dyck, Rubens, Rembrandt, Hokusai, and Michelangelo appeared in serial form in *McClure's Magazine* beginning in 1902 and later in his book *Great Masters* (1903). On his death bed, La Farge completed a collection of essays published as *One Hundred and One Masterpieces* (1912), based in part on articles published in *McClure's* (1903–1908). He also left unfinished a book manuscript completed by his executrix Grace Edith Barnes and published as *The Gospel Story in Art* (1913).

Although he remained active until the end of his life, La Farge's later years were overshadowed by declining health and prodigious debts. His wife tried to care for him during his last six months despite his difficult and at times eccentric behavior, but not long before his death she was forced to commit him to Butler Hospital, a mental institution in Providence, Rhode Island. After his death, she not only had to turn over La Farge's estate to his creditors but also had to pay certain debts out of her own pocket.

Dozens of obituaries appearing in newspapers throughout the world eulogized La Farge as a scion of traditional canons of Western art and, as described by his biographer Royal Cortissoz, "America's only old master." But by the 1920s his reputation had tarnished, as avant-garde critics branded him "eclectic" and retrograde. Despite periodic revivals of interest in his works, including a retrospective mounted at the Metropolitan Museum of Art in New York in 1936, it was not until the 1970s that serious scholarship led to a rehabilitation of La Farge's reputation. By the time the Carnegie Institute in Pittsburgh and the Smithsonian Institution organized a traveling retrospective of his work in 1987, La Farge had been firmly reestablished as a "modern old master" who boldly embraced technical innovations and reformed the arts of illustration and stained-glass design in the United States, while simultaneously seeking to preserve traditional artistic prototypes.

• Most documents related to La Farge's artistic production are found in the La Farge Family Papers, Department of Manuscripts and Archives, Sterling Memorial Library, Yale University. This repository will eventually contain all working files for the "Catalogue Raisonné of the Works of John La Farge" by the artist's late grandson Henry A. La Farge. The earliest biography of La Farge, Cecilia Waern's *John La Farge, Artist and Writer* (1896), is of particular interest because of La Farge's extensive direct contributions to the book. Similarly, Royal Cortissoz, *John La Farge: A Memoir and a Study* (1911), is based on La Farge's autobiographical manuscript now housed with the Royal Cortissoz Papers at the Beinicke Library, Yale University. Henry Adams et al., *John La Farge: Essays* (1987), a book published in conjunction with La Farge's 1987 retrospective, contains copious illustrations, extensive discussions of works, a study of La Farge's writings, a detailed chronology, a listing of public decorative projects, and a full bibliography. An obituary is in the *New York Times*, 15 Nov. 1910.

JAMES L. YARNALL

LA FARGE, Oliver Hazard Perry (19 Dec. 1901–2 Aug. 1963), anthropologist, author, and advocate of American Indian reform and welfare, was born in New York City, the son of Christopher Grant La Farge, an architect, and Florence Bayard Lockwood. A descendant and namesake of Oliver Hazard Perry, hero of the battle of Lake Erie in 1813, La Farge was born into a well-known family. Although not wealthy, the La Farges were socially and artistically prominent, numbering among their close friends Theodore Roosevelt (1858–1919) and his wife, Henry Adams, Henry James (1843–1916), and Owen Wister. La Farge's interest in American Indians stemmed in part from his father, an outdoorsman and conservationist, who occasionally wrote about Indians and who did the illustrations for Elsie Clews Parsons's book *American Indian Life* (1922).

La Farge graduated from Harvard in 1924 with a degree in anthropology. While still in college he began to write. He was elected president of the *Advocate*, Harvard's literary magazine, was on the editorial board of the *Harvard Lampoon*, and at graduation was elected class poet by his classmates. He spent the summers of his junior and senior years doing archaeological fieldwork in the prehistoric Anasazi ruins in Arizona. While there, however, he became interested in the Navajos and decided to specialize in contemporary Indians rather than in ancient ones.

In 1925, 1927, and 1932 he studied existing Mayan languages in Guatemala and Mexico. Three ethnographic monographs resulted from these expeditions: *Tribes and Temples* (1927), *The Year Bearers People* (1931), and *Santa Eulalia* (1947). As an anthropologist he specialized in Indian languages, and in the 1930s he helped to transcribe the spoken Navajo language into a written form.

La Farge also turned to Native American themes for his fictional works. In 1929 he published *Laughing Boy*, a novel about a young Navajo couple whose lives are blighted by the white man's world. The novel won the Pulitzer Prize for literature. In that same year he married Wanden Esther Matthews. They were divorced in 1937. In 1939 he married Consuelo Baca. He had two children from each marriage.

La Farge published four more novels—*Sparks Fly Upward* (1931), *Long Pennant* (1933), *The Enemy Gods* (1937), and *The Copper Pot* (1942). He also published an outstanding autobiography entitled *Raw Material* (1945) and numerous short stories, essays, and articles, many of them about American Indians. None of his later works, however, enjoyed the critical and financial success of *Laughing Boy*, a fact that he sometimes complained about with great bitterness. He wrote of this in *Raw Material*:

I have a certain dislike for it because it has been so popular whereas my other books have only done fairly well. I grow sick of smiling fools who tell me, "Oh, Mr. La Farge, I did so love your *Laughing Boy*, when are you going to give us another book?" Having written four other novels, a book of short stories, and two nonfiction books, and being like all writers badly in need of more royalties, one can hardly avoid giving a short answer.

Despite his literary accomplishments a sense of artistic failure followed La Farge throughout most of his life. He wrote in 1949 for the twenty-fifth anniversary report of his Harvard class about "the slow but relentless arrival of the realization that, as one enters middle age, one may be a good writer, competent, skillful, one may have been blessed with a few inspired moments, but one will never be great. The dream one had at the beginning is still achingly real, but it will never be fulfilled."

In 1930 La Farge joined the board of directors of the Eastern Association in Indian Affairs, founded in 1922 by white men and women with an interest in Indian welfare and reform. Originally focusing on southwestern tribes, the association, now called the Association on American Indian Affairs, gradually expanded its activities to other parts of the country. In January 1933 La Farge became its president and remained in that position, save for the years of the Second World War, until his death. La Farge's feelings for Native Americans were caring, even loving, but until the final years of his life he believed they would eventually be assimilated into the larger American society. From about the mid-1950s he began to change his mind and accept the possibility that at least some Indians would retain their cultural identity for the foreseeable future.

For three decades La Farge worked with his colleagues for Indian causes. He promoted the commercial development of Indian arts and crafts, reservation health and educational projects, and economic assistance for the tribes. He lobbied successfully for the Indian Reorganization Act in 1934, providing for the implementation of tribal constitutions and self-governing councils. From 1955 until his death La Farge worked to win the return of the sacred Blue Lake to the Tàos Pueblo Indians of New Mexico, finally achieved in 1970. Other projects of the association involved winning passage in the late 1940s and early 1950s of the Navajo-Hopi Rehabilitation Plan and securing a federally recognized reservation for the Miccosukee Indians in Florida. La Farge died in Albuquerque. He is buried in the military cemetery in Santa Fe.

La Farge's interest in Native Americans consumed his adult life. At least two of his books, *Laughing Boy* and *Raw Material*, are outstanding pieces of literature that reflect that interest. Perhaps his greatest achievement was the preservation of the Association on American Indian Affairs. Without his leadership it most certainly would have disbanded during the depression years of the 1930s. Today, it is a major support group for American Indians. In an editorial the day after his death the *New York Times* wrote of him: "He fought the Indians' battles before many a Congressional committee and the White House advisory group. Others were in the fight, too, but it was La Farge's voice that was heard most frequently and most movingly in behalf of the country's original settlers."

• Most of La Farge's personal papers dealing with his literary career are in the library of the University of Texas at Austin. The most important collection of documents relating to the Association on American Indian Affairs is in the Rare Books Division, Princeton University Library. In 1949 La Farge published *The Eagle in the Egg*, a history of the Air Transport Command, which he served as historian from 1942 to 1946. Among the biographies of La Farge are those by D'Arcy McNickle, *Indian Man: A Life of Oliver La Farge* (1971), and Robert A. Hecht, *Oliver La Farge and the American Indian: A Biography* (1991). An obituary is in the *New York Times*, 3 Aug. 1963.

ROBERT A. HECHT

LAFARO, Scott (3 Apr. 1936–6 July 1961), bass player, was born in Newark, New Jersey. His parents' names are unknown. LaFaro's family moved to Geneva, New York, when he was five. His father played violin in a "society" trio, and Scott was thus exposed to music at an early age. He began to study the clarinet at fourteen and in high school took up the tenor saxophone. He subsequently studied bass at the Ithaca Conservatory beginning in 1953 and then in Syracuse, New York, where he also began to listen to jazz. He was particularly influenced during this formative time by the Miles Davis records he heard on the jukebox and by Davis's bass players at the time, Percy Heath and Paul Chambers.

LaFaro played with a variety of rhythm and blues groups during his apprenticeship. His first significant job in the jazz world came in 1955–1956, when he traveled to Los Angeles with Buddy Morrow's band. He played with Chet Baker in 1956 and 1957, briefly with Ira Sullivan in Chicago, with Sonny Rollins in San Francisco in 1958, and with guitarist Barney Kessel at the Lighthouse Cafe in Hermosa Beach, California. While in California he also heard bassist Ray Brown, one of his most important early influences, and he lived in saxophonist's Herb Geller's house for almost a year, practicing constantly and listening to jazz recordings.

LaFaro made his recording debut on a session led by Tony Scott in 1957. In August of that year he recorded with a group led by clarinetist Buddy DeFranco, already playing "powerful, agile, and legato" solos that combined traditional, walking bass lines with more hornlike figures that reflected the increasingly powerful bop influence on his playing. In 1958 and 1959 he appeared on recordings by Stan Getz and Cal Tjader, pianist Hampton Hawes, and Victor Feldman. In the fall of 1959 he also played briefly with Thelonious Monk, from whom, he later said, he learned a great deal about rhythm. In 1959 LaFaro moved to New York City, a decisive turning point in his career. He toured briefly with Benny Goodman, appeared with Stan Kenton, played on two Booker Little albums in 1960, and recorded twice with Ornette Coleman, on *The Art of the Improvisers* (1960) and *Ornette!* (1961).

By now LaFaro had paid his dues. The pianist Bill Evans invited him to join his trio when Evans had trouble getting a bassist during some early club engagements. LaFaro's brief career with Evans profoundly influenced the future course of jazz, reintroducing the practice of group improvisation in a melodic, lyrical vein that contrasted sharply (at least on the surface) with the similar experiments being concurrently pursued by Coleman. LaFaro's early solos continued to employ traditional walking bass lines in combination with boppish figures drawn from the harmonic vocabulary of Charlie Parker. But he now began to experiment with new rhythmic and melodic approaches. In "Witchcraft," for instance, on Evans's *Portrait in Jazz* (1959), he "interacts rhythmically with Evans rather than playing the usual walking bass lines" (Owens, p. 176). The two furthered this idea of simultaneous improvisation on two other tunes, "Autumn Leaves" and "Blue in Green."

Increasingly LaFaro turned away from the traditional supportive role of the bass. On the classic *Live at the Village Vanguard* sessions recorded in June 1961, he often functioned as a soloist equal to Evans, improvising on the melodies as freely as Evans and "providing rhythmically independent counterpoint to Evans's own octave-doubled improvisations" (Owens, p. 177). LaFaro also contributed certain technical innovations to bass playing. He played closer to the finger board, which produced lower volume and required closer miking but also gave him greater facility in upper ranges and proved highly influential to later bassists. LaFaro, who never married, died shortly after the Vanguard sessions, in a car accident in Geneva, New York. Evans was devastated, musically and personally, and felt the effect of LaFaro's loss for years.

LaFaro once mused that "my ideas are so different from what is generally acceptable nowadays that I sometimes wonder if I am a jazz musician" (Williams, *Panorama*, p. 278). He was greatly interested in classical composers and commented on the "saccharine" harmony that had come to dominate jazz since the days of Charlie Parker. In the Evans trio, he noted, "we were each contributing something and really improvising *together*, each playing melodic and rhythmic phrases. The harmony would be improvised; we would often begin only with something thematic and not a chord sequence" (Williams, p. 280). Or as drummer Paul Motian put it, they were "a three-person voice-one voice."

Thus LaFaro helped free the bass from traditional time-keeping duties, allowing the bassist to play far-ranging counter-melodies in free rhythm, in almost telepathic communication with the other trio members. This approach was not so dissimilar from concurrent and later experiments in free jazz, but with LaFaro, Bill Evans, and Motian, it blended into an improvisatory lyricism rarely equaled in contemporary or later music.

• The literature on LaFaro is scant. Thomas Owens, *Bebop: The Music and Its Players* (1995), provides an excellent, brief introduction to his playing, and Martin Williams, "Introducing Scott LaFaro," in *Jazz Panorama*, ed. Williams (1962), has an informative interview. Much of the best writing on LaFaro is found in work centered on Bill Evans. See in particular Conrad Silvert; liner notes to the LP reissue *Spring Leaves* (1976); and the essay by Williams, "Homage to Bill Evans," in *Bill Evans: The Complete Riverside Recordings* (1984). An obituary is in *Down Beat* 28, no. 17 (1961): 13.

RONALD P. DUFOUR

LAFAYETTE, James (c. 1748–9 Aug. 1830), patriot spy also known to history as James Armistead, was born in slavery; little is recorded of his parentage or early life except that he belonged to William Armistead of New Kent County, Virginia. In the summer of 1781 James was attending his master while Armistead worked as a commissary in Richmond, supplying patriot forces under the command of the Marquis de Lafayette. Lafayette's men had been sent south to counter British units under Charles Cornwallis then operating in eastern Virginia. When it became known that Lafayette was recruiting spies to keep better track of Cornwallis's intentions, James (with his master's consent) volunteered, believing such service might win him his freedom.

By late July James had crossed into the British camp at Portsmouth and apparently was employed as a forager. His work enabled him, in the course of gathering food, to move back and forth through the lines, so that he could both bring information to Lafayette and pass messages from the general to other agents who had been sent amongst the enemy. James's usefulness to Lafayette increased as he earned the redcoats' trust—so much so that he was recruited by them to spy on the patriots. Through his double agent, Lafayette fed Cornwallis either insignificant or misleading information. For example, James brought the British a faked order suggesting that patriot forces had been reinforced by units that had not, in fact, arrived. Ultimately, Lafayette hoped that the British, then pressed against the shores of the Chesapeake Bay, might eventually be snared between patriot armies and the French navy, and James's most important service probably came in helping Lafayette keep abreast of Cornwallis's movements along the Virginia coast. In late July James was able to report that the British were on the verge of leaving Portsmouth by sea. Instead of traveling to New York or to the upper Chesapeake, as expected, however, the British disembarked on the north shore of the peninsula formed by the James and York rivers. In August James informed Lafayette that Cornwallis was fortifying a position at Yorktown. There the English were trapped by an army that by that time included the forces of George Washington and the Comte de Rochambeau and by a French fleet that had won control of the lower Chesapeake. Shortly after his surrender in October 1781, Cornwallis visited Lafayette at his headquarters and was surprised to encounter a slave—probably James—whom he had assumed was one of his own informers.

Wartime spies, when discovered, have always been harshly punished, but if James assumed that he would be immediately rewarded for the risks he had taken, he was mistaken. He returned to William Armistead's household as a slave. Yet in 1786 Armistead proved willing to support the submission to the Virginia legislature of a petition calling for James's manumission—together with appropriate compensation for the master. Evidently swayed by a testimonial Lafayette had written in 1784 praising James for the "Essential Services" he had rendered, legislators passed a bill freeing the slave as of January 1787. The state thereafter paid William Armistead £250 in recompense, an amount considerably above the standard for such reimbursements. The freedman took Lafayette's surname for his own and was subsequently known as James Lafayette.

James Lafayette had gone to heroic lengths to secure his own freedom, but the same year as his emancipation he was listed in New Kent County tax rolls as the owner of three slaves. Such slaves as free people of color were recorded as owning in the antebellum South, however, were most often family members who had not formally been emancipated. Whether or not this was the case with Lafayette, he did have a wife and at least one son by 1816 when he bought forty acres of land adjoining William Armistead's estate in New Kent County. The soil was poor and the return on it small, and two years later Lafayette, citing his service in the Revolution and his poor health, petitioned the Virginia legislature once again, this time for immediate relief and a small pension. Lawmakers awarded him $60 and a stipend of $40 a year. In 1824, when the Marquis de Lafayette returned to Yorktown in the course of his American tour, he recognized his erstwhile spy among the assembled throng and accorded him a very public greeting. James Lafayette died on his farm in New Kent County.

James Lafayette played only a small role in the winning of America's independence. Yet his service was rendered particularly conspicuous by the fact that he, like so many African-American patriots, put himself at risk for a freedom the full benefits of which he could enjoy only by the leave of his master and white authorities.

• John Salmon gathered most of what is known about Lafayette for his article "'A Mission of the most secret and important kind': James Lafayette and American Espionage in 1781," *Virginia Cavalcade* 31, no. 2 (1981): 78–85. Sidney Kaplan and Emma Nogrady Kaplan, *The Black Presence in the Era of the American Revolution*, rev. ed. (1989), reproduces a portrait of James Lafayette painted by John Blennerhasset Martin. See also Luther Porter Jackson, *Virginia Negro Soldiers and Seamen in the Revolutionary War* (1944); *The Letters of Lafayette to Washington, 1777–1799*, ed. Louis Gottschalk (1944); Gottschalk, *Lafayette and the Close of the American Revolution* (1942); and Works Progress Administration, *The Negro in Virginia* (1940).

PATRICK G. WILLIAMS

LAFAYETTE, Marquis de (6 Sept. 1757–20 May 1834), major general in the Continental army and French soldier and statesman, was born Marie-Joseph-Paul-Yves-Roch Gilbert du Motier Lafayette in Chavaniac, France, the son of Gilbert du Motier, marquis de Lafayette, and Julie de la Rivière. After his father, a colonel in the grenadiers, was killed at the battle of Minden in 1759, his mother moved to Paris. The boy was raised at Chateau Chavaniac in the mountains of Auvergne until he was twelve. He then spent four years at the Collège du Plessis in Paris in a curriculum emphasizing the civic virtues of republican Rome.

Lafayette's mother and maternal grandfather died in April 1770. As sole heir of his grandfather's fortune, the orphaned Lafayette was suddenly transformed from a relatively poor provincial nobleman into a rich marquis. In 1773 he became a protégé of the Noailles, a powerful family close to the throne. He and Adrienne de Noailles were married in 1774. As a captain in the Noailles Dragoons he was posted to Metz.

In 1775, having learned about the American "insurgents," like many other young officers Lafayette yearned to win glory in a cause where liberty was opposed to tyranny. When the Crown refused him official permission to join the Americans, he met secretly with the American commissioner, Silas Deane, and in December 1776 contracted to serve as a major general in the Continental army. He bought a ship that took him, Baron de Kalb, and ten other officers who had signed with Deane to serve in America.

Lafayette's ship sailed in April 1777. In letters to his wife written while at sea, Lafayette repeated his desire to be a "defender of that liberty which I idolize," assuring her that "the welfare of America is intimately connected with the happiness of all mankind; she will become the respectable and safe asylum of virtue, integrity, tolerance, equality, and a peaceful liberty." He repeated these themes publicly and privately on every possible occasion until the end of his life.

The party landed in South Carolina near Georgetown in June. After reaching Philadelphia, they learned that their services were not needed and that Deane's commissions were invalid. Lafayette then asked to serve as an unpaid volunteer on George Washington's staff; Congress approved the nineteen-year-old major general's commission on 31 July.

Washington found the tall, red-haired, blue-eyed volunteer grave in demeanor and anxious to learn, unlike too many of the other foreign volunteers. Lafayette found in Washington a mentor and model whom he attempted to imitate for his entire public life. Their close friendship was remarked on regularly.

In September 1777 at the battle of Brandywine, Lafayette received a musket ball in the leg. In December he was given command of a division of Virginians. During the next year he led an abortive expedition to invade Canada and served in actions at Barren Hill, Monmouth Courthouse, and in Rhode Island. He spent 1779 on leave in France, where he prepared for an invasion of England and worked closely with ministers responsible for aid to the Americans. At the end of 1779 his only son, George Washington Lafayette, was born. His other children were Anastasie and Virginie.

Lafayette returned to America early in 1780. From April until September 1781 he led the only Continental forces in Virginia against General Charles Cornwallis, ending by bottling Cornwallis at Yorktown. Then Generals Washington and Jean Rochambeau arrived with their troops from New York and Admiral François de Grasse's fleet came from the Caribbean, forcing Cornwallis's surrender.

After the siege of Yorktown he returned to France on leave. In the fall of 1782 he was named quartermaster general of a Franco-Spanish expeditionary force preparing for the 1783 campaign in the Americas, but he continued to wear the uniform of an American major general, symbolic of his commitment to the American cause.

When peace was declared in 1783, Lafayette accepted a new rank as major general in the French army. He returned to America for five months in 1784. He was feted in ten states, spoke everywhere in favor of a stronger federal union, and was granted citizenship by Maryland; he stayed two weeks at Mount Vernon. Before Congress he proclaimed, "May this immense temple of freedom ever stand a lesson to oppressors, an example to the oppressed, a sanctuary for the rights of mankind!"

Between 1785 and 1789 he spent much of his public life working on behalf of American commerce with the French ministries, in close cooperation with the American minister, Thomas Jefferson, who recalled, "He made our cause his own. . . . In truth, I only held the nail; he drove it." Other claims on Lafayette's time were slave manumission and civil rights for French Protestants.

Houdon's bust of Lafayette was mounted in the state house in Virginia, and a copy was placed in the Hotel de Ville in Paris. In 1787 in the Assembly of Notables, he proposed an elected national assembly, reform of the criminal code, and toleration for Protestants. His actions on behalf of political and religious liberty led admirers to begin to refer to him as the "hero of two worlds."

Elected to the Estates General from Auvergne in 1789, he entered the national assembly in June, and on 11 July he presented to that assembly a draft of "The First European Declaration of the Rights of Man." After the fall of the Bastille, he was named commandant of the new Paris National Guard, and he created the tricolor cockade that soon became the national colors. He was especially proud to be head of a citizen militia answerable to a citizen assembly. After titles of nobility were abolished in 1790 Lafayette never again used his own, stating that if any title were affixed to his name, "General" was the one he preferred.

As head of the Paris National Guard from 1789 to 1791, Lafayette was both guardian and jailer of Louis XVI and keeper of public order until a constitution was approved. He favored a constitutional monarchy, civil liberties, and public order; a moderate centrist, he was despised by both Royalists and Jacobins. He did not appear to be ambitious for political office; when the constitution was approved in the fall of 1791 he resigned as head of the national guard and retired to his estate in Chavaniac.

When war with Austria and Prussia began in 1792 Lafayette was named a commander at the front. On the fall of the king later that year, Lafayette tried to extricate Louis XVI. As a result he was impeached by the revolutionary government. He left France but was captured and spent the next five years in Austrian prisons. His wife sent their son to America as a ward of George Washington. Then, with their daughters, she joined her husband in prison.

Lafayette was released in 1797. Returning to France, he settled at Chateau La Grange, some forty miles southeast of Paris, which became his home until his death. At La Grange he maintained a large acreage in model agricultural practices.

Under Napoleon, Lafayette opposed the regime. Fearing for Lafayette's safety, President Jefferson of-

fered him the governorship of the Louisiana Territory, which he declined. Elected to the Chamber of Deputies in 1814, Lafayette called for Napoleon's resignation after Waterloo and moved for the revival of the national guard to resist the armies of the European coalition.

During the Restoration era (1815–1830), Lafayette served several terms in the Chamber of Deputies, opposing Bourbon policy and citing American political principles and the American experience as a model for France. Chateau La Grange became a mecca for Americans, while at the same time it was often a refuge for exiled revolutionaries from other European states, for Lafayette was supporting liberal revolutions wherever they occurred, from Poland to Latin America.

After President James Monroe invited him to visit the United States, Lafayette toured every state of the union in 1824–1825. He daily received tumultuous welcomes as a hero of the American Revolution, who for a half-century had advocated the principles of the American republic and of its patriarch, Washington, and who had never faltered in his devotion to or faith in the cause of human liberty. During the next decade scores of counties, cities, and other public places were named for him or for his estate at La Grange.

During the French Revolution of 1830, Lafayette once more became head of the national guard. Again he sought to maintain order and peace while a constitutional regime was created. He supported Louis Philipe because the Orleans line seemed to promise "a monarchy with republican institutions," but the performance belied the promise. Lafayette was still in opposition when he died, having spent nearly sixty years of his life as a public figure, always identified with the example of America as a free and prosperous republic.

• The largest collections of Lafayette materials in the United States are the Dean collection, Cornell University Library, and the collection of Lafayetteana in the Louis Gottschalk Papers, University of Chicago Library. Published documents are in Gilbert du Motier Lafayette, *Mémoires, correspondance et manuscrits du générale La Fayette* (6 vols., 1837–1838). Letters to and from Lafayette between 1776 and 1785 are in Stanley J. Idzerda et al., eds., *Lafayette in the Age of the American Revolution, Selected Letters and Papers* (5 vols., 1977–1983); Gottschalk, *The Letters of Lafayette to Washington* (1976); and G. Chinard, *The Letters of Lafayette and Jefferson* (1929). Detailed chronicles of Lafayette's life through the summer of 1790 are in Gottschalk's six volumes beginning with *Lafayette Comes to America* (1935), up to *Lafayette in the French Revolution from the October Days through the Federation* (1973). Other biographical materials include Idzerda et al., *Lafayette, Hero of Two Worlds: The Art and Pageantry of His Farewell Tour of America* (1989); L. S. Kramer, *Lafayette in Two Worlds: Public Cultures and Personal Identities in an Age of Revolution* (1996); S. Neely, *Lafayette and the Liberal Ideal, 1814–1824: Politics and Conspiracy in an Age of Reaction* (1991).

STANLEY J. IDZERDA

LAFEVER, Minard (10 Aug. 1798–26 Sept. 1854), architect, was born near Morristown, New Jersey, the son of Isaac Lefevre, a carpenter, and Anna Stark.

About 1807 the Lefevre family moved to the Finger Lakes region of western New York, where Minard was educated in the public schools of Ovid. By the age of eighteen Lafever (as he always spelled his name) was working at carpentry and building. At that time he also bought his first book on architectural theory, which he supplemented with intensive study of local structures in the Finger Lakes and Genesee area. In 1820 Lafever married Pamelia Laraway with whom he had six children. After Pamelia's death in 1833, Minard married a widow, Ann Delorious Spicer, in 1835. Ann died in 1851, and the following year Lafever married Nancy Kneeland.

In 1824, seeking greater opportunities to advance in the building profession, Lafever moved his family to Newark, New Jersey, where he continued to work as a carpenter and architectural draftsman. Lafever then moved to New York City, about 1828, and immediately participated in the great building boom of the late twenties and early thirties. For the next few years his office was busy providing builders with plans and decorative details for private residences.

Lafever's professional career as an architect began with his competition design (1829) for the Albany City Hall and the publication of his first book, *The Young Builder's General Instructor* (1829). In 1837 Lafever, by now a well-known and respected architect, became a member of the American Institution of Architects (organized in 1836), precursor of the American Institute of Architects.

Forceful and strong willed, Lafever was firm in his demands upon himself and others. "At home his word was law, and he ruled with an iron hand," according to family tradition.

Lafever's most significant contribution to the development of American architecture in the pre–Civil War period was through his extremely influential builders' guides, which spread Greek Revival designs nationwide. Of these, his *Modern Builder's Guide* (1833; repr. 1841, 1846, 1849, 1850, 1853, 1855) and *Beauties of Modern Architecture* (1835; repr. 1839, 1849, 1855) are noteworthy for their personalized variations of Grecian decorative motifs, which were widely copied in the wood and plaster detail of many Greek Revival houses. Lafever's *Modern Practice of Staircase and Handrail Construction* (1838), although strictly technical, also contained two original Grecian villa designs.

In his own early architectural practice, Lafever used the Greek Revival style in only two Greek temple-front structures, both with monumental Ionic eight-column porticoes. One was the main building (1831–1833) for Sailors' Snug Harbor, Staten Island, New York. The other, the First Reformed Dutch Church (1834–1835) in Brooklyn, was done when Lafever was in partnership with James Gallier, Sr.

Gallier had come to New York City from England in 1832. After working as a draftsman for several months in the New York firm of Town, Davis & J. Dakin, Gallier was persuaded in 1833 by Lafever to join him as a partner in an architect's office. In his *Autobiography* (1864), Gallier complained about the "disagreeable" and "badly rewarded . . . routine of grinding out drawings for the builders." Unhappy with Lafever and dissatisfied with his progress in New York, Gallier dissolved the partnership late in 1834 and left for New Orleans to further his architectural career.

Despite the influence of his Greek Revival designs, Lafever's many Gothic Revival churches established his considerable reputation in New York. Early examples were the New Dutch South Reformed Church on Washington Square (1839–1840), the First Baptist Church on Broome Street (1841–1842) and, in Brooklyn, the Pierrepont Street Baptist Church (1843–1844). An unusually sensitive and elegant work is the Church of the Saviour (1842–1844) in Brooklyn Heights. Richer in decorative detail is Lafever's most impressive Gothic structure, the Church of the Holy Trinity (1844–1847), also in Brooklyn Heights.

Lafever was one of the leaders in the movement toward eclecticism, in which architects felt free to select from a wide range of historical styles, sometimes combining them in the same building but more often choosing a particular style for its symbolic association. Lafever used the Egyptian obelisk form in the Ada Augusta Shields tomb (1845) in Greenwood Cemetery, Brooklyn, and in his competition design for a colossal monument to George Washington (1847) in New York. His most famous Egyptian Revival work is the Whalers' (First Presbyterian) Church (1843–1844) in Sag Harbor, Long Island. Examples of Lafever's essays in the Italian Renaissance Revival include the Episcopal Church of the Holy Apostles (1846–1848) in New York, and, in Brooklyn Heights, the old Brooklyn Savings Bank (1846–1847) and the Reformed (Protestant Dutch) Church on the Heights (1850–1851).

Lafever continued the Gothic Revival style in several late works in Brooklyn (where he died). These were the Church of the Neighbor (1848–1850), the Strong Place Baptist Church (1851–1852) and the Packer Collegiate Institute (1854–1856). In his last publication, *The Architectural Instructor* (1856), Lafever included detailed illustrations of a number of his own works, in addition to a variety of eclectic designs for houses, churches, monuments, and public buildings.

A self-taught, gifted architectural stylist, Lafever's ambition and determination enabled him to achieve a widespread professional reputation and nationwide influence and to make a substantial contribution to the New York architectural scene in the pre–Civil War period.

• See Jacob Landy, *The Architecture of Minard Lafever* (1970). For the influence of Lafever's publications, see Talbot Hamlin, *Greek Revival Architecture in America* (1944). There are modern reprints of the two most widely used Lafever books, *The Beauties of Modern Architecture* (1968), with a new introduction by Denys Peter Myers, and *The Modern Builder's Guide* (1969), with a new introduction by Jacob Landy. New documentation for Lafever's early professional career appears in Barnett Shepherd, "Sailors' Snug Harbor Reattributed to Minard Lafever," *Journal of the Society of Architectural Historians* 35 (1976): 108–23.

JACOB LANDY

LAFFAN, William Mackay (22 Jan. 1848–19 Nov. 1909), newspaper editor, publisher, and art connoisseur, was born in Dublin, Ireland, the son of Michael Laffan and Ellen Sarah FitzGibbon. He attended Trinity College of Dublin University and St. Cecilia's School of Medicine. He did not graduate from either institution. Laffan became adept at modeling in clay, etching, and painting in oils and watercolors and was an artist for the Pathological Society of Dublin.

He arrived in the United States at the age of twenty and settled in San Francisco. When the *San Francisco Chronicle* was established in late 1868, Laffan became its first city editor. He also drew the illustrations for the newspaper, a first on the Pacific Coast. He was managing editor of the *San Francisco Bulletin* before moving to Baltimore in 1870. There he became a reporter, then editor, of the *Baltimore Daily Bulletin*, which covered art, literature, science, and general news. Laffan subsequently purchased the paper and its Sunday edition and waged a popular editorial campaign against political corruption. He married Georgiana Ratcliffe of Baltimore in 1872. Soon after, Laffan left newspaper work to become a passenger agent for the Long Island Railroad.

In 1877 Laffan began an association with the *New York Sun* that lasted until his death and was interrupted only by a two-year hiatus when he was a representative for Harper Brothers publishers in London. Laffan began as the *Sun*'s drama critic, then became a general writer on art subjects and a business adviser. Laffan offended some on the *Sun* with his mannerisms and mode of dressing. For example, he would often stare at a person in what was described as an "unpleasant" and "vacuous" manner. He also annoyed staffers with his penchant for wearing formal evening dress to work. However, he quickly became an intimate of its editor, Charles A. Dana. His favor with Dana increased when Laffan began supervising departments of the paper with which he had no official connection. Dana supported Laffan, and it was understood that his opinion was to be considered in all matters affecting the newspaper.

Laffan shared private lunches with Dana and was allowed to walk unannounced into Dana's private office without knocking. His relationship with Dana caused jealousy among some of the staff. In 1896 Laffan and Dana wrote the New York State Republican party platform plank denouncing free silver and declaring for the gold standard. The plank was incorporated into the party's national platform. Frank M. O'Brien called Laffan a "thorough *Sun* man, sympathetic with the ideals" of Dana (p. 427). Candace Stone said Laffan's influence with Dana was so great that some considered it sinister.

Laffan's criticism for the *Sun* was incisive, but at times cruel, even to the point of "smart unkindness" (Stone, p. 44). He became famous for his short, sarcastic editorials. Will Irwin called Laffan "a pugnacious Irishman whose words carry darts" (Stone, p. 44). Commenting on his use of unusual words in editorials, O'Brien wrote that Laffan "never drove a man to drink, but he drove many a man to the dictionary" (p. 198). His supporters and detractors saw him as an aloof and mysterious figure. He disliked publicity and avoided public appearances. He was quick-tempered and capable of blind prejudice, with "hatreds . . . so passionate that he could discern little good in the fiercely hated" (Mitchell, p. 353).

Laffan became publisher of the *Sun* in 1884 and acquired financial control in 1902 with a loan from J. P. Morgan. Laffan founded the *Evening Sun* in 1887 as a one-cent daily. He began a news service in the late 1880s to supplement the *Sun*'s Associated Press franchise. Under the supervision of Chester Lord, it was originally intended to cover news of special interest to the *Sun*, but it eventually supplanted the *Sun*'s Associated Press service in the 1890s. It became known as the Laffan News Bureau, and it lasted until 1916. The *Sun* first listed Laffan on its masthead as proprietor on 22 February 1902, but Edward P. Mitchell, Dana's chief editorial writer, continued to exercise routine editorial direction.

Laffan maintained the paper's policy of disdain for advertisers and often insulted their agents. When the *Sun* was sued for libel by a Wall Street group, he told the city editor to "go ahead and give those men better cause for libel suits" (O'Brien, p. 429). But unlike Dana, Laffan became a "darling" of capitalists, such as Morgan, whom he in turn made "darlings" of the *Sun*. He became an intimate of Morgan and a circle of wealthy capitalists through his expertise in art and his shrewdness as a procurer of art objects. He was named a trustee of the Metropolitan Museum of Art in 1905, while Morgan was president. Laffan wrote three books: *American Wood Engravers* (1883), *Engravings on Wood* (1887), and *Oriental Ceramic Art* (1897). He edited, with Thomas B. Clarke, the *Catalogue of the Morgan Collection of Chinese Porcelains* (1907). Laffan died at his home in Lawrence, Long Island, New York, after an operation for appendicitis. After his death, Morgan established the Laffan Professorship of Assyriology and Babylonian Literature at Yale University.

Laffan's stature faded after his death owing, in part, to his private nature and his failure to publish his memoirs. However, in his time he was a highly influential leader of a major newspaper during a period of significant transformations in American journalism, in particular the changeover from a style of journalism marked by a "personal" approach, of which Dana was a noted practitioner, to a more impersonal or "corporate" style of journalism.

• Laffan's life and career are discussed in Frank M. O'Brien, *The Story of the Sun* (1918), and Edward P. Mitchell, *Memoirs of an Editor: Fifty Years of American Journalism* (1924), which are generally laudatory. A more balanced assessment is found in Candace Stone, *Dana and the Sun* (1938). Laffan's place in the history of American journalism is discussed in Edwin Emery and Henry Ladd Smith, *The Press and America* (1954), and Frank Luther Mott, *American Journalism: A History of Newspapers in the United States through 259 Years,*

1690–1940 (1941). Informative contemporary assessments are in obituaries in the *New York Sun* and the *New York Times*, both 20 Nov. 1909.

JOSEPH P. MCKERNS

LAFFITE, Jean (fl. 1809–1820), pirate, was born in Bayonne, France, the son of a Gascon father and a Basque mother. His name is also spelled Lafitte. Although he is rumored to have captained a French privateer in 1804, nothing definite is known of him until 1809, at which time he and his elder brother Pierre had arrived in New Orleans, Louisiana, and set up a blacksmith shop. This establishment, operated by slave labor, is generally believed to have served as a depot for contraband slaves and goods smuggled into the city by coastal privateers. The shrewd and enterprising Laffite brothers quickly realized that more profit lay in piracy than in the smith's trade, and by 1810 Jean Laffite had become the de facto leader of these outlawed corsairs, directing their operations from a base on the remote island of Grande Terre, in Barataria Bay.

Under Laffite's capable and daring leadership, the Barataria pirates preyed on merchant ships of all nations, seizing their cargoes in the Gulf of Mexico and selling the contraband goods and slaves to Louisiana merchants and planters. Such trade was clearly in violation of the revenue laws of the United States, but it was welcomed by the citizenry and generally ignored by the Louisiana legislature. From time to time, a particularly outrageous act of piracy would inflame Louisiana's governor William C. C. Claiborne to the point that he would raise the price on Laffite's head or send an expedition against the Baratarians, but Laffite's skills in avoiding capture and, more important, the support his actions commanded among the majority of local residents allowed him to remain largely unmolested. In 1814 an indictment against the Laffites, stemming from an incident in which an inspector of revenue had been killed, was presented in a federal court, but the district attorney, John Grymes, resigned his position in order to defend the brothers, and Grymes's associate, Edward Livingston, procured a cessation to the criminal proceedings against them.

After these short-lived legal troubles, Laffite resumed his lucrative privateering activities, but his way was soon blocked again, this time by the British army. Although the United States and Great Britain had officially been at war since 1812, Louisiana had remained relatively untouched by the conflict; by September 1814, though, the British were planning an attack on the crucial port of New Orleans. At that moment, several British officers, led by a Captain Lockyer of the Royal Navy, visited Laffite at Grande Terre and asked for his support in this attack, offering him the sum of $30,000, a captaincy in the navy, title to various lands, and pardon for all his and his followers' past offenses in return, and threatening to destroy the Barataria encampment if the offer were refused. Laffite gathered as much information as possible about the British plan of attack, asked Lockyer for ten days in which to consider his options, and secretly transmitted the information to the Louisiana legislature. Although many might have considered this act a patriotic one, Governor Claiborne and his officers chose to exploit this moment of Laffite's vulnerability and on 16 September 1814 sent an expedition, commanded by Colonel George T. Ross of the U.S. Army, against the Baratarian encampment. Although Laffite himself escaped, as did many of his men, their base was completely destroyed, their ships seized, and a number of their comrades arrested.

Sensing that his options were now limited, Laffite gathered his remaining men at Bayou Lafourche and offered the services of the Baratarian privateers to the newly arrived U.S. army commander, General Andrew Jackson. Jackson had no love for Laffite, considering him and his adherents "hellish banditti," but he was sufficiently in need of extra manpower that he accepted the pirate's offer. The Baratarians were divided into two groups, one manning redoubts on the Mississippi River, the other serving the batteries at New Orleans. Both groups served with considerable skill and were an important element in the American defeat of the British forces at the Battle of New Orleans in January 1815. On 6 February 1815 President James Madison issued a full pardon to Laffite and his men for all previous privateering and smuggling offenses.

As soon as the War of 1812 ended, Laffite returned to his privateering activities; in September 1817 he founded a new smuggling settlement, Campeche, near modern-day Galveston, Texas. His success in this new venture was considerable but short-lived; in 1820 the privateers' capture and scuttling of an American merchant ship in Matagorda Bay brought the full wrath of the U.S. government down upon Laffite's head. Sensing the danger of imminent attack, Laffite loaded his treasure and men onto six vessels, burned Campeche to the ground, and sailed to the Yucatán coast of Mexico. He and his followers were active along the Spanish Main until approximately 1825, but almost nothing is known about these final years of his life. Laffite is generally believed to have died in Mexico in 1826, but the circumstances of his death remain unknown.

Laffite's modern reputation is that of a romantic figure, handsome and charming yet also ruthless and violent. Considering how little is known for sure about him, it is difficult to evaluate the accuracy of such a legend. What can be said of him is that he was in many ways a transitional figure in American commerce and warfare, a man who came of age in the final years of the age of high-seas piracy but was in many ways a successful, if unorthodox, merchant, as well as an important ally of the new United States in its final struggle to free itself from British hegemony.

• Several documents bearing Laffite's signature are in the Rosenberg Library, Galveston; the archives of St. Louis Cathedral, New Orleans, contain the baptismal records of his illegitimate children by his quadroon mistress. Laffite has received little attention from biographers; the standard sources for information about his life remain Charles Gayarre's "Historical Sketch of Pierre and Jean Lafitte, the Famous Smugglers of Louisiana, 1809–1814," *Magazine of American History* (Oct./Nov. 1883), and Lyle Saxon's biography *Lafitte, the Pirate* (1930). Laffite also has an entry in Philip Gosse's *Pirate's Who's Who* (1924).

NATALIE ZACEK

LA FLESCHE, Francis (25 Dec. 1857–5 Sept. 1932), anthropologist, was born on the Omaha reservation in Nebraska, on the western bank of the Missouri River, the son of Estamaza (Iron Eye) and Tainne (Elizabeth Esau). As a child he participated in such tribal rituals as the Wawan (pipe ceremony) and joined in three buffalo hunts, serving once as a runner. Details of his early education at a Presbyterian mission school that accommodated fifty boarding students are recounted in his memoir, *The Middle Five: Indian Schoolboys of the Omaha Tribe* (1900; repr. 1963). The school was called "the house of learning of the White Chests" because of the starched shirts worn by the teachers. Later, while sharing a house in Washington, D.C., with the anthropologist Alice C. Fletcher at 214 First St., he attended the National University School of Law, earning an LL.B. in 1892 and an LL.M. in 1893.

In October 1879, La Flesche began an extended tour of lectures with his sister Susette La Flesche, Ponca chief Standing Bear, and journalist Thomas H. Tibbles to crusade against government removal of Native Americans from their lands. They addressed enormous crowds in Chicago, Pittsburgh, Boston, New York, Philadelphia, Baltimore, and Washington, D.C., and were invited to the White House by President Rutherford B. Hayes. On 13 February 1880 they testified before the Senate. The secretary of the interior, Samuel J. Kirkwood of Iowa, offered La Flesche a position as a copyist in the Office of Indian Affairs, where he worked from June 1881 until 1910. He was then appointed to the Bureau of American Ethnology, where he served until 1929.

According to Margot Liberty, Fletcher used La Flesche "first as field assistant, informant and interpreter, and then as full collaborator in work over many years which culminated in the classic 27th Annual Report of the Bureau of American Ethnology in 1911, *The Omaha Tribe*" (p. 46). Their work together began after she recruited him as her translator in April 1833, when she enforced the apportionment of common tribal land to individual Omaha families. In honor of their arrival on 12 May, the Calumet Dance was performed. Tribal elders granted them permission to record Omaha rituals. A 642-page, two-volume study resulted, in which were transcribed the history, myths, music, government, ethics, and ceremonies of the Omaha.

In 1912, La Flesche collaborated with composer Charles Wakefield Cadman on a three-act opera, *Da-Oma: The Land of Misty Waters*, which was never produced. His first marriage to Alice Mitchell in 1877 ended in divorce a few years later. The dates of his second marriage to Rosa Bourassa, an 1890 graduate of the Indian boarding school at Carlisle, Pennsylvania, who worked at the Indian Office in Washington,

D.C., cannot be ascertained. Apparently the couple separated, however, since by 1915 she was working at the Chilocco Indian School in Oklahoma. Noted for his "flashing wit," La Flesche was widely in demand as a public speaker and contributor of articles to a variety of periodicals such as the *Journal of American Folklore, American Anthropologist,* and *Science.* In 1922 he became president of the Anthropological Society of Washington, which had been founded by his mentor, Alice Fletcher, in 1902.

The final decades of his life were devoted to the compilation of the *Dictionary of the Osage Language* (1932) and to the preservation of Osage rituals. The intricate ceremonies that he rescued from extinction filled over 2,000 pages of four annual reports published by the Bureau of American Ethnology between 1914 and 1939. This work, *The Osage Tribe*, is daunting in its complexity, but its inherent poetic force has profoundly influenced subsequent poets such as Carter Revard and Jerome Rothenberg. Excerpts have been extensively anthologized. Shortly after his retirement, La Flesche died at the home of his brother Carey, on the reservation near Macy, Nebraska.

• The La Flesche Family Papers are held by the Nebraska State Historical Society. Letters, notes, and other documents are in the Schlesinger Library at Radcliffe College and the Peabody Museum of Harvard University. Other manuscripts are in the General Correspondence Files, numbers 1881 and 1886, of the Library of Congress. Biographical information can be found in Alice C. Fletcher and Francis La Flesche, *The Omaha Tribe*, vol. 2 (1911; repr. 1992), pp. 619–38 and in Norma Kidd Green, *Iron Eye's Family* (1969). Obituaries are in the *New York Times*, 10 Sept. 1932, and the *American Anthropologist* 35, no. 2 (1933): 328–31. An assessment of his work can be found in Margot Liberty, *American Indian Intellectuals* (1978), and B. Swann and A. Krupat, eds., *Recovering the Word: Essays on Native American Literature* (1987).

RUTH ROSENBERG

LA FLESCHE, Susette. *See* Bright Eyes.

LA FOLLETTE, Belle Case (21 Apr. 1859–18 Aug. 1931), political activist and magazine editor, was born in Juneau County, Wisconsin, the daughter of Anson Case and Mary Nesbit, farmers. She attended the University of Wisconsin in 1875, taking a modern classical course. She became a member of the Laurean Literary Society and represented it at the junior oratory exhibition. At graduation in 1879 she won the Lewis Oratorical Prize for the best commencement oration. She taught high school near Madison for two years after graduation.

Belle married Robert M. La Follette, then a district attorney, in 1881. They would have four children, including Robert La Follette, Jr., a U.S. senator, and Philip La Follette, a governor of Wisconsin. In 1883 Belle entered the University of Wisconsin Law School. Although she never intended to practice law, she studied it, in her husband's words, as "an intellectual pursuit." In 1885 she graduated from the law school, becoming the first woman to do so. Later that year the La

Follettes moved to Washington, D.C., when Bob became a first-term Wisconsin congressman. Belle worked long hours writing letters, addressing correspondence, and mailing her husband's speeches to interested constituents. She was also intimately involved with her husband's reelection campaigns.

Upon returning to Madison in 1891, Belle began helping Bob in his law practice. She wrote several of his briefs, breaking new ground and helping to win his cases. Bob acknowledged Belle's help with his briefs, noting that they were written by "an unknown but very able member of our bar—altogether the brainiest member of my family." Belle and Bob worked tirelessly to help elect Republican candidates to state and national offices. Belle always joined in strategizing about various elections and her "counsel was always valued" by those present.

In 1900 Robert La Follette was elected governor of Wisconsin. He was reelected in 1902 and 1904 before resigning to become a U.S. senator. During his years as governor, Bob sought Belle's counsel, calling her his "wisest and best counsellor." The Progressive leaders of Wisconsin welcomed her advice and her grasp of the sociological and economic problems of the day. Belle's influence helped to secure appointments of women to positions in state and university offices. She was so involved in the governor's works that Bob often referred to his terms in office as "when we were governor."

Belle La Follette's philosophy of the interdependence of the mind and body led her to believe that a positive mental attitude, when combined with regular exercise, was the best course to achieve mental and physical fitness. She encouraged her children and husband to follow this philosophy. From 1892 Belle was president of the Emily Bishop League, a society devoted to physical education, which she also helped to found. She also spoke in favor of reforming women's clothing to make it lighter and less oppressive.

In 1909 the La Follettes joined friends and supporters to create a national magazine called *La Follette's Magazine*. Belle became associate editor, responsible for articles on women's issues, the home, nutrition, health, and education. She wrote a regular column titled "Home and Education" as well as articles on such topics as the U.S. Senate, marching in a suffrage parade, nutrition for the people, graduate education in home economics, eggless waffle recipes, and having an up-to-date home. She wrote frequently of the need for a fairer division of material wealth and labor and on personal and spiritual issues as well.

Belle La Follette also urged prison reform and opposed capital punishment. She wrote about such health issues as how to combat typhoid and lead poisoning. She worked for the formation of a federal children's bureau that would be concerned with all aspects of children's welfare, including infant mortality, juvenile courts, desertion, accident, and employment.

La Follette advocated the use of women's talents for employment both inside and outside the home, believing that women needed to expand the scope of their responsibilities to include more people than just their families. She was involved in both the National American Woman Suffrage Association and the Wisconsin Woman Suffrage Association. In 1912 she toured Wisconsin campaigning for woman suffrage. Her speeches focused on women's interest in political issues and the need to expand suffrage to protect democracy. Belle argued that the home was the basic unit of society with an inseparable relationship between civic and domestic life. She drew her ideas on suffrage from Progressive ideology, advocating woman suffrage as a move toward a more democratic state. In 1913 she spoke to a Senate committee in favor of woman suffrage, noting that she could not think of a "single important question" that had been before the Congress about which women were not just as concerned as men.

Belle La Follette also wrote and spoke against racial discrimination. One column in 1911, in which she described the life of blacks in Washington during the previous twenty years, cost the magazine numerous subscribers and elicited letters of denunciation. She wrote against segregation in streetcars and federal lunchrooms, noting that its only purpose was racial prejudice. She spoke against the fervor to deport blacks to Africa, noting that such a deportation would cause most homes and businesses in Washington to come to a standstill.

In 1914 the La Follettes became concerned that World War I could jeopardize Progressive legislation in Congress. In her column, Belle argued that giving women the vote would humanize government and promote world peace. In 1915 she helped form the Women's Peace party and the Women's International League for Peace and Freedom. She also helped organize the National Council for the Prevention of War and the Women's Committee for World Disarmament. Recognizing that women were primarily responsible for educating children, Belle argued that the greatest results could be achieved by educating youth in the ideals of peace. She spoke and wrote against congressional measures that would draw the United States into war and against compulsory military training. Once women were granted the right to vote in 1919, she urged them to use their ballots to help achieve world peace.

Robert La Follette died in June 1925. After his death, politicians and women across the country asked Belle to run for his Senate seat. In explaining her decision not to run, Belle stated that she did not conceive it to be her duty to enter the political field and that it would be against her nature to undertake political leadership. She spent the next years working on her husband's biography, which was completed by her daughter, Fola. She worked hard to keep *La Follette's Magazine* viable, and the magazine, renamed *The Progressive*, has continued publishing.

After Belle La Follette died in Washington, D.C., *The Progressive* issued a memorial edition to her on 7 November 1931. La Follette envisioned political action as an instrument to pass social measures that would better the general conditions of human beings.

Although she supported the political aspirations of her husband and sons, she was even more devoted to the ideals of social justice.

• Useful manuscript collections include the Belle Case La Follette Papers and the Robert M. La Follette Papers at the Library of Congress. See also Belle Case La Follette and Fola La Follette, *Robert M. La Follette, June 14, 1855–June 18, 1925* (1953); Lucy Freeman et al., *The Biography of Belle Case La Follette* (1986); Robert M. La Follette, *La Follette's Autobiography: A Personal Narrative of Political Experiences* (1913); Esther Kramer, "Rhetorical Analysis of Three Suffrage Speeches by Belle Case La Follette" (master's thesis, Univ. of Wisconsin, 1988); and Dee Ann Montgomery, "An Intellectual Profile of Belle Case La Follette: Progressive Editor, Political Strategist, and Feminist" (Ph.D. diss., Indiana Univ., 1975).

BARBARA J. COX

LA FOLLETTE, Fola (10 Sept. 1882–17 Feb. 1970), actress and feminist, was born in Madison, Wisconsin, the daughter of Robert Marion La Follette, a progressive politician, and Belle Case, a lawyer and suffragist. Though named Flora at birth, she used her childhood nickname throughout her life. A history major at the University of Wisconsin (1900–1904), La Follette studied under historian of the American West Frederick Jackson Turner. History became a lifelong interest. She also performed in several college plays, beginning an acting career that lasted until 1915. She spent the 1904–1905 season traveling with actress Ada Rehan's company and performing in *The Taming of the Shrew*, *The School for Scandal*, and *The Country Girl*.

La Follette studied with actress Bertha Kunz Baker between 1907 and 1916 and appeared during these years in such productions as Leo Ditrichstein's farce *Button, Button, Who's Got the Button?* (1908–1909) and Percy Mackaye's *The Scarecrow* (Dec. 1911–Jan. 1912), her first opportunity to perform on Broadway. Reviews were lukewarm, however, and La Follette "was delivered finally to the lecture platform" (Weisberger [1994], p. 118). She increasingly lent her dramatic talent to the suffrage cause, appearing in several suffrage plays between 1905 and 1915. In 1910 she played in *How the Vote Was Won* by Cecily Hamilton and subsequently gave readings of the play for woman suffrage organizations in the East and Midwest. A member of Actors' Equity from 1913 to 1928, she carried the banner of the actresses' division in the first woman suffrage parade in New York City in 1911.

She reached the height of her public prominence as a feminist activist during the years 1911–1925. Her decision to retain her maiden name and to continue a public career upon her marriage to dramatist George Middleton in 1911 occasioned considerable attention in the press, which represented the couple as an example of modern marriage. There were no children. In 1912, living in Greenwich Village, La Follette joined New York City's feminist network, the Heterodoxy Club. The following year she played the lead role in Middleton's social problem play *Tradition*, from which the couple also gave a series of joint readings

before various woman suffrage organizations. She spent much of 1914 on the Midland Chautauqua Circuit lecturing on "Democracy of Woman Suffrage."

That same year La Follette spoke at the Second Feminist Mass Meeting at the Peoples' Institute at Cooper Union in New York City on the topic "Should a Man Take His Wife's Name." There she shared the platform with leading feminists of the day. She helped organize the Lucy Stone League, which sought to establish women's legal right to retain their maiden names, and served on the group's executive committee. During World War I she came under public criticism for her pacifist position. While living in Paris between 1920 and 1922, La Follette wrote a series of articles chronicling her experiences for *La Follette's Magazine* and later became a contributing editor. In 1924, reflecting the interest among feminists of the period in psychoanalysis, she became a patient of fellow Heterodoxy member and Jungian analyst Beatrice M. Hinkle. Of her analysis she wrote Middleton, "I am getting something out of it which is very vital. . . . Here one can deal with things in the terms of feeling, at a deeper level." Also in 1924 she campaigned on behalf of her father's independent presidential bid. In that capacity La Follette spoke before African-American audiences in New York and Philadelphia: "As an American citizen I feel humiliated and shamed at the injustice my country and yours has made you suffer. . . . We have no right to talk of this country as a democracy."

Becoming interested in progressive education, La Follette taught from 1926 to 1930 at New York City's progressive City and Country School, where she focused on children's reading and language learning. In 1927 she attended the Fourth International New Education Conference on the meaning of freedom in education in Locarno, Switzerland. The following year she accompanied John and Evelyn Dewey on a tour of schools and summer camps in Moscow and Leningrad.

Beginning in the 1930s La Follette's interest in history reemerged. When Belle Case La Follette died in 1931 she left an unfinished biography of her husband. Fola La Follette carried the narrative forward from her mother's stopping point in 1910 and worked continuously to complete the manuscript, published in two volumes as *Robert M. La Follette* (1953). She also joined historian Mary Beard's effort to establish a world center for women's archives. In a 1939 speech explaining the need for such a repository, she recalled her experience as Frederick Jackson Turner's student. In his interpretation of the West, La Follette said, "something important seemed to be left out—or at least too little emphasized. . . . I asked him why he didn't say more about pioneer women." When Turner suggested she do a paper on the topic based solely on primary sources she "thought it would be easy" but quickly discovered that the documentary record "told only the story of what men had done—only half of the oral history I heard as a child was recorded." As family historian, she spent the years from 1953 until her death organizing the La Follette Family Papers at the Library of Congress—a collection that bears her stamp in many ways. During the most public period of her life (1911–1925), La Follette was committed to many of the important intellectual and social movements of her day—feminism, psychoanalysis, antiracism, and progressive education and politics. She died in Arlington, Virginia.

• La Follette's papers are with the La Follette Family Papers in the Library of Congress. Series A contains family correspondence. Series E contains La Follette's correspondence, typed transcripts of speeches and articles, and other memorabilia. The George Middleton Papers in the Library of Congress contain a valuable scrapbook of newspaper clippings richly detailing the couple's modern marriage and their shared suffrage and feminist activities. La Follette published numerous book reviews in *La Follette's Magazine* throughout the 1920s and edited the memorial issue of *The Progressive*, Nov. 1931, commemorating the life of Belle Case La Follette. Her biography of her father, *Robert M. La Follette*, was reviewed in the *New York Times Book Review*, 20 Dec. 1953; *American Historical Review* 59 (1954): 652–54; and *American Political Science Review* 48 (1953): 167–68. Middleton's autobiography, *These Things Are Mine: The Autobiography of a Journeyman Playwright* (1947), details his and La Follette's involvement in the feminist and woman suffrage movements. The most complete recent account of La Follette's life is Bernard A. Weisberger, *The La Follettes of Wisconsin: Love and Politics in Progressive America* (1994). See also Weisberger, "Changes and Choices: Two and a Half Generations of La Follette Women," *Wisconsin Magazine of History* 76 (1993): 248–70. Obituaries are in the *New York Times* and the *Northern Virginia Sun*, both 18 Feb. 1970.

KATE WITTENSTEIN

LA FOLLETTE, Philip Fox (8 May 1897–18 Aug. 1965), governor of Wisconsin and lawyer, was born in Madison, Wisconsin, the son of Robert M. La Follette (1855–1925), a governor and U.S. senator from Wisconsin, and Belle Case (Belle Case La Follette), a magazine editor and columnist. After serving as a second lieutenant in the army in 1918, La Follette received his B.A. and law degrees in 1919 and 1922, respectively, from the University of Wisconsin. In 1923 he married Isabel Bacon; they had three children.

Groomed as the political successor to his father, whom he resembled in personality and ambition, La Follette was elected district attorney of Dane County in 1924. He also participated in his father's independent Progressive campaign for president that year. After the senior La Follette's death in 1925, Philip La Follette managed the successful campaign of his brother, Robert M. La Follette, Jr. (1895–1953), for election to the U.S. Senate. Philip La Follette returned to private law practice in 1927 and also lectured on law at the University of Wisconsin. In 1930, as a progressive Republican, he handily won election as governor, campaigning against monopoly in banking, retailing, and electric power; corrupt political practices; and high property taxes.

Although the state legislature refused to enact many of his proposals, the vigorous young governor gained

its approval of several significant measures. These included a collective bargaining code; bank stabilization; an improved old-age pension program; more equitable taxation; and broadening the regulation of public utilities. Under La Follette's leadership, Wisconsin pioneered in putting young men to work on forest conservation projects and establishing an unemployment compensation program. He also fostered special railroad crossing work projects for the unemployed. Unfortunately for La Follette, success and innovativeness were not enough to win him renomination as governor in 1932, as many liberal Republicans crossed over to vote in the Democratic primary election.

By 1934 it was clear that the La Follette brothers and their political lieutenants could not regain control of the Wisconsin Republican party. The alternative of joining the state's Democratic party was unattractive because of its conservatism. Thus the La Follettes and their allies formed the Wisconsin Progressive party in 1934. With this political vehicle, Senator La Follette was reelected then, and Philip La Follette regained the governorship. Governor La Follette's chief objective during his second term was to provide "W-O-R-K!" for Wisconsin's unemployed. He sought legislative approval of a comprehensive program of jobs to be financed by federal, local, and state efforts. In the state senate, however, opposition Democrats and Republicans defeated the measure by one vote. Indeed, the legislature defeated all of La Follette's major proposals, including new labor bills and those to facilitate cooperation between the state and federal governments. President Franklin D. Roosevelt, who had approved of Wisconsin experimenting with its own work relief program, then, to the disgruntlement of local Democrats, in effect turned over control of the state's federal Works Progress Administration to Governor La Follette. Wisconsin received, moreover, proportionately more in federal relief funds than other states in its region. In 1936 the La Follette brothers played important roles in siphoning off sentiment for establishing a national progressive–farmer-labor party and in encouraging political independents to support Roosevelt for reelection.

La Follette was reelected governor by a large plurality in 1936. This led to the enactment in Wisconsin of what was dubbed the "Little New Deal," which encompassed reorganization of state government to make it more efficient; a labor relations act; a fair business competition law; legislation to promote sales of the state's agricultural and industrial products; and authorization of a state electric power program. All this renewed La Follette's national reputation as a brilliant governor. Yet his promotion of high-handed legislative tactics such as curtailing debate and hearings also reinforced his local reputation for being autocratic, and he became known as the "Wild Man of Madison." The criticisms were enhanced by the governor's successful promotion of the removal, for incompetence, of Glenn Frank as president of the University of Wisconsin in 1937 and La Follette's launching in 1938 of the National Progressives of America (NPA).

The governor asserted that the NPA would become "THE party of our time," one that would "restore to every American the opportunity to help himself[,] . . . sink or swim." Unfortunately for La Follette, he established the organization without sufficient consultation with other political independents and without anticipating that President Roosevelt might seek a third term in 1940. The NPA was also unveiled with martial pomp and sported the symbol of a cross in a circle, which La Follette's opponents, with obvious reference to Germany's Nazi symbol, called a "circumcised swastika." If all this was not bad enough, 1938 would be a year of Republican resurgence in the United States. It all contributed to a considerable defeat for the Progressives and their allies, including La Follette who lost his bid for a fourth term as governor by almost 200,000 votes.

Roosevelt hoped that La Follette would return to support him, but he never did. Indeed La Follette became a prominent anti-interventionist after the outbreak of World War II in 1939. In 1942, though, he entered the army, serving chiefly on the staff of General Douglas MacArthur in the Pacific. La Follette was discharged in 1945 as a lieutenant colonel. In 1946 Senator La Follette's forces disbanded the Wisconsin Progressive party, which the former governor saw as a great "political blunder." This seemed confirmed by Joseph R. McCarthy's defeat of Robert La Follette, Jr., for the Republican senatorial nomination that year. Growing more conservative, Philip La Follette could only return to the Republican party. In 1948, as he had in 1944, he participated in an unsuccessful effort to gain the Republican presidential nomination for General MacArthur. Four years later, La Follette endorsed the candidacy of Dwight D. Eisenhower for president; afterward the Wisconsinite was all but inactive in politics. He practiced law in Wisconsin after 1945, except for serving as the president of an electronics firm in New York, the Hazeltine Corporation, from 1955 to 1959. La Follette died in Madison.

• The personal papers of Philip F. La Follette are located in the State Historical Society of Wisconsin. The essential printed sources on La Follette are his *Adventure in Politics: The Memoirs of Philip La Follette*, ed. Donald Young (1970); and John E. Miller, *Governor Philip La Follette, the Wisconsin Progressives, and the New Deal* (1982). For related biographical material there are also Belle Case and Fola La Follette, *Robert M. La Follette: June 14, 1855 to June 18, 1925* (2 vols., 1953); and Patrick J. Maney, *"Young Bob" La Follette: A Biography of Senator Robert M. La Follette, Jr., 1895–1953* (1978). See also Lawrence H. Larsen, *The President Wore Spats: A Biography of Glenn Frank* (1965); and regarding the National Progressives of America, Donald R. McCoy, *Angry Voices: Left-of-Center Politics in the New Deal Era* (1958). An obituary is in the *New York Times*, 19 Aug. 1965.

DONALD R. McCOY

LA FOLLETTE, Robert Marion (14 June 1855–18 June 1925), Wisconsin governor, U.S. congressman, and Progressive presidential candidate, was born in Primrose, Wisconsin, the son of Josiah La Follette and Mary Ferguson Buchanan, farmers. Only eight months old when his father died, La Follette throughout his life sought to measure up to an idealized image of the father he never knew. He was seven when his mother married John Z. Saxton, a stern, elderly merchant and Baptist deacon.

In 1873 his again-widowed mother moved the family to Madison, where two years later La Follette entered the University of Wisconsin. He came under the influence of the university's president, John Bascom, who implanted a commitment to public service. As an undergraduate, La Follette devoted himself less to studies than to editing a student newspaper and debating at the Athenean Literary Society. After graduating with a B.S. in 1879, he read law and briefly attended law school before being admitted to the bar the following year. In 1881 he married Belle Case, a fellow student at the university; they had four children. She gave immense assistance to him throughout his career.

During his early political career, La Follette was an ambitious but orthodox Republican. In 1880 he was elected district attorney of Dane County, Wisconsin. Four years later he was elected to the U.S. House of Representatives, where he earned the reputation of being "so good a fellow that even his enemies like him" (*Milwaukee Sentinel*, 30 Mar. 1890). He served on the influential Ways and Means Committee, chaired by William McKinley. La Follette supported the high rates of the McKinley Tariff of 1890, and public reaction against the tariff, together with voter backlash against a state law requiring children to be educated in English, triggered a Democratic landslide that turned La Follette out of office. He returned to Madison to build a successful law practice.

The transforming event of La Follette's life occurred in 1891, when Wisconsin senator Philetus Sawyer, a wealthy lumberman who had always treated him paternally, offered to pay him to intervene in a potentially costly lawsuit over which La Follette's former law partner and brother-in-law, Robert Siebecker, sat as judge. La Follette angrily refused the bribe. Although Sawyer insisted that his proposition had been misconstrued, the incident profoundly shocked La Follette and opened his eyes to the business corruption of government and politics.

La Follette further evolved from party loyalist to insurgent during the national depression from 1893 to 1897, which stirred public anxiety that the economic turmoil of industrialism was eroding American democracy. In the predominantly agricultural state of Wisconsin, reformers confronted railroad and timber interests, but they also had to deal with Milwaukee streetcar and electric power monopolies. Unlike the Populists and William Jennings Bryan, who spoke exclusively for rural America, La Follette absorbed the ideas of both agrarian and municipal reformers and forged a new political coalition of farmers, laborers, small businessmen, and professionals, appealing to them as exploited taxpayers and consumers. "Fighting Bob" La Follette emerged as the embodiment of this new progressive reform movement. In 1897 he addressed a University of Chicago audience on "The Menace of the Political Machine" and then repeated that message at state and county fairs across Wisconsin.

After losing bids for the Republican nomination for governor in 1896 and 1898, La Follette muted his reform themes to win the governorship in 1900. Once in office, he presented the state legislature with an agenda that included fair taxation on railroad property and direct primary elections. When conservative "stalwart" Republicans in the legislature defeated his proposals, La Follette returned to the Wisconsin fairs to "read the roll," telling voters which legislators had voted against his reforms and their interests. He stimulated a grassroots movement to elect a more progressive legislature and to support his own reelection in 1902 and 1904. By 1905 he had a strong majority behind his programs in the legislature.

Winning a firm legislative majority then, Governor La Follette turned Wisconsin into a "laboratory for democracy," enacting direct primary, tax reform, and consumer protection legislation that became models for other states. He promoted the "Wisconsin idea" of using experts, among them University of Wisconsin professors John R. Commons, Richard Ely, and Edward A. Ross, to provide nonpartisan assistance in drafting laws. La Follette was also responsible for creating the Wisconsin Legislative Reference Bureau and later the Legislative Reference Service in the Library of Congress.

While La Follette denounced machine politics, he built a personal political organization that kept him in office and promoted his reforms. The muckraking journalist Lincoln Steffens captured this paradox when he lionized La Follette in *McClure's Magazine*: "There is a machine [in Wisconsin], but it is La Follette's." However, La Follette's suspicion of potential rivals, demand for absolute loyalty, and breaks with his closest lieutenants tended to weaken his organization. The primary elections and civil service reforms that La Follette had championed further limited his control over state politics.

After La Follette won an unprecedented third election as governor in 1904, the state legislature elected him a U.S. senator in January 1905. However, he remained governor for another year until the legislature had redeemed his campaign pledge to create a state railroad regulatory commission. Arriving in Washington, D.C., in 1906 at the beginning of the debate on the Hepburn bill to give the Interstate Commerce Commission power to regulate railroad rates, La Follette ignored an unwritten rule against freshman senators speaking and delivered an address that, with appendices, filled 148 pages in the *Congressional Record*. When other senators left the chamber, he declared, "I cannot be wholly indifferent to the fact that Senators by their absence at this time indicate their want of interest in what I may have to say upon this subject. The public is interested. Unless this important question is rightly settled, seats now temporarily vacant may be permanently vacated by those who have the right to occupy them now." Repeating this message on the Chautauqua lecture circuit, he continued reading the roll of senators who voted for "special privilege."

Although the Hepburn bill had the blessing of President Theodore Roosevelt, La Follette considered it weak and introduced tough amendments. This disagreement marked the beginning of an intense rivalry between Roosevelt, who was willing to compromise to achieve reform, and La Follette, who believed that "in legislation *no bread* is often better than *half a loaf*." Both endorsed government regulation of business, although Roosevelt accepted large-scale industry as necessary for competition in global markets, while La Follette retained a more traditional distrust of big business. Neither one could bring himself to credit the other's contribution to progressive reform.

Relegated to lesser committees and snubbed in the cloakrooms, La Follette worked in relative isolation as a senator, yet he managed to exert considerable influence by filibustering to amend or defeat legislation. He devoted exhaustive research to speeches advocating the direct election of senators, lower tariff rates, income redistribution, worker protection, and stronger antitrust legislation. During his filibuster against the Aldrich-Vreeland currency bill in 1908, La Follette asserted that a handful of wealthy men controlled the nation's industrial and financial system, but he did not direct his attack against individuals. "They but embody an evil," he explained. "Back of these men is the THING which we must destroy if we would preserve our free institutions."

In February 1909 La Follette convened the growing ranks of progressive Republican senators at his Washington home and assumed leadership over the insurgent bloc. During William Howard Taft's administration, La Follette led the insurgents' opposition to the high Payne-Aldrich Tariff, which Taft defended. He further broke with Taft in 1910 over the controversy between Interior Secretary Richard Ballinger and Chief Forester Gifford Pinchot, accusing Taft of siding with the corporations over the conservationists.

In 1909 La Follette launched *La Follette's Weekly Magazine* under the banner "Ye Shall Know the Truth and the Truth Shall Make You Free." In preparation to run for president, he also began publishing installments of his *Autobiography*. The National Progressive Republican League was founded in 1911 as a vehicle for La Follette's campaign for the Republican nomination. However, in February 1912 his campaign collapsed with his disastrous appearance before a Periodical Publishers' Association dinner in Philadelphia. Fatigued from relentless campaigning and writing, La Follette lost his temper and harangued his audience. The press depicted this incident as a nervous breakdown and urged his withdrawal from the presidential race. La Follette's most prominent supporters abandoned him for Theodore Roosevelt. When Roosevelt ran for president on the Progressive party ticket, *La Follette's Weekly Magazine* attacked him with unforgiving ferocity.

La Follette was not unhappy with the election of the Democratic candidate, Woodrow Wilson, in 1912. However, the new president disappointed him by choosing to work through the Democratic congressional caucuses, thereby excluding progressive Republicans from shaping the New Freedom reform program. He voted for Wilson's tariff and banking proposals, and his amendments forced Democrats to set higher income tax rates for upper incomes. In 1915 Congress passed the only bill to bear his name, the La Follette Seamen's Act, which voided longterm binding labor contracts and mandated improved safety for passengers and seamen.

Although La Follette had once defended U.S. economic expansionism, over time he grew critical of corporate involvement in foreign policy. He denounced dollar diplomacy and military intervention in the Caribbean and favored neutrality in the First World War. He preferred Wilson's reelection; but even before Wilson's second inauguration in March 1917, La Follette led a bitter filibuster against the president's efforts to arm the U.S. Merchant Marine, calling it a blank check to permit undeclared naval warfare.

La Follette voted against American entry into the war, opposed conscription, and decried wartime restrictions on free speech and freedom of the press, provoking widespread denunciation of him as pro-German and unpatriotic. The Senate Committee on Privileges and Elections considered his expulsion, but when the 1918 congressional elections gave Republicans a one-vote margin in the Senate, La Follette became indispensable for the party to claim the majority. The Senate dropped the proceedings against him by a vote of 50 to 21. Denouncing Wilson's personal negotiations of the peace treaty without the advice of the Senate as a usurpation of legislative rights, La Follette worked with Henry Cabot Lodge and other nationalist Republicans to defeat the Treaty of Versailles. He warned that the League of Nations would drag the United States into future wars around the world.

Unlike many progressives, La Follette remained unshakably committed to reform during the conservative era that followed the war. Although dismayed over the Harding-Coolidge ticket in 1920, he declined to become the Farmer-Labor party's presidential candidate. In 1922 he convinced the Senate to investigate charges of improper leasing of the naval oil reserves at Teapot Dome, Wyoming, which unearthed evidence of corruption in the Harding administration. La Follette joined journalist Steffens on a well-publicized tour of the Soviet Union in 1923. He had been curious about the Russian Revolution but was appalled at communist suppression of political opposition and civil liberties.

Despite his opposition to communism, La Follette was denounced as a Bolshevik in 1924, when he ran for president on an independent Progressive ticket with Montana Democratic senator Burton K. Wheeler as his running mate. As always, La Follette placed his faith in "the people," counting on their support if they could hear his message. He opened his campaign with the first radio address by a candidate speaking from a broadcast studio. His platform endorsed public ownership of water power and railroads, collective bargaining rights for labor, federal aid to farmers, child labor laws, and the recall of federal judges. La Follette ran a vigorous race against the equally conservative Republican Calvin Coolidge and Democrat John William Davis. He gained 4.8 million votes but carried only Wisconsin.

As punishment for bolting the party, Senate Republicans expelled La Follette from their conference and stripped him of his committee chairmanship in 1925. He died in Washington, D.C., and was succeeded in the Senate by his son Robert La Follette, Jr., who served until 1947. His son Philip La Follette was three times elected governor of Wisconsin. In 1957 the Senate recognized La Follette as one of its five most significant members, together with Henry Clay, Daniel Webster, John C. Calhoun, and Robert Taft. After polling numerous historians and political scientists, the selection committee's chairman, Senator John F. Kennedy, cited La Follette as "a ceaseless battler for the underprivileged in an age of special privilege, a courageous independent in an era of conformity, who fought memorably against tremendous odds and stifling inertia for the social and economic reforms which ultimately proved essential to American progress in the 20th century."

• The La Follette family papers are in the Library of Congress, and La Follette's gubernatorial papers are at the Historical Society of Wisconsin. Robert M. La Follette, *La Follette's Autobiography* (1913), and Belle Case La Follette and Fola La Follette, *Robert M. La Follette* (1953), offer La Follette's perspective. David P. Thelen, *The Early Life of Robert M. La Follette, 1855–1884* (1966), *The New Citizenship: Origins of Progressivism in Wisconsin, 1885–1900* (1972), and *Robert M. La Follette and the Insurgent Spirit* (1976); and Bernard A. Weisberger, *The La Follettes of Wisconsin: Love and Politics in Progressive America* (1994), present more detached assessments. Carl R. Burgchardt, *Robert M. La Follette, Sr.: The Voice of Conscience* (1992), analyzes La Follette's oratorical power. Important studies of La Follette's role in progressive reform are Robert S. Maxwell, *La Follette and the Rise of the Progressives in Wisconsin* (1956); Herbert F. Margulies, *The Decline of the Progressive Movement in Wisconsin 1890–1920* (1968); and Stanley P. Caine, *The Myth of a Progressive Reform: Railroad Regulation in Wisconsin, 1903–1910* (1970). For his Senate years see James Holt, *Congressional Insurgents and the Party System, 1909–1916* (1967); Thomas W. Ryley, *A Little Group of Willful Men: A Study in Congressional-Presidential Authority* (1975); and Ralph Stone, *The Irreconcilables: The Fight against the League of Nations* (1970). Kenneth McKay, *The Progressive Movement of 1924* (1947), chronicles La Follette's last campaign. Briefer but useful profiles can be found in Holmes Alexander, *The Famous Five* (1958), and John Milton Cooper, "Robert M. La Follette: Political Prophet," *Wisconsin Magazine of History* 69 (Winter 1985–1986): 91–105. Obituaries are in the *Wisconsin State Journal*, 18–22 June 1925, and the *New York Times*, 19 June 1925.

DONALD A. RITCHIE

LA FOLLETTE, Robert Marion, Jr. (6 Feb. 1895–24 Feb. 1953), U.S. senator, was born in Madison, Wisconsin, the son of Robert M. La Follette, Wisconsin's renowned progressive governor and senator, and Belle Case (Belle Case La Follette), a lawyer, writer, and reformer. La Follette studied politics almost literally at the feet of his father. He was six when his father became governor of Wisconsin and twelve when the elder La Follette took his crusade for progressive reform to the United States Senate. Politics dominated family life, and "Young Bob," as he was called, became intimately involved in nearly every aspect of his father's career. His formal education was less rigorous than his political training. An indifferent student, he attended the University of Wisconsin between 1913 and 1915 but then withdrew because of chronic health problems. He never returned to complete a college degree.

Despite his early immersion in public affairs, La Follette never would have pursued a career in politics if it had not been for a sense of loyalty to his father. His more ambitious brother Philip hoped to inherit the family's mantle of leadership. But to Phil's everlasting disappointment it was Young Bob whom the elder La Follette groomed as his successor. Between 1916 and 1925, Young Bob served as his father's chief aide in the Senate. Frequently during these years he made plans to strike out on his own, perhaps to pursue a career in journalism or business. Each time his father prevailed upon him to stay. Then, in 1925, the elder La Follette died, and Young Bob, running as a Republican, won a special election to fill his father's unexpired term. At thirty, he became the youngest senator since Henry Clay.

La Follette championed many of the causes that had been his father's stock and trade, such as trust-busting, progressive taxation, and nonintervention in foreign affairs. But he also demonstrated a capacity for innovation. With the onset of the Great Depression he emerged as the leading congressional advocate of bold government action to combat the economic crisis. Having identified the lack of mass purchasing power as the root cause of the depression, he proposed as a solution a massive expansion of public works, direct federal relief to the unemployed, and a modest degree of national economic planning. La Follette's proposals, coupled with the hearings that accompanied them, helped focus public attention on the plight of the unemployed. Late in 1931 he joined Senator Edward P. Costigan of Colorado and Representative David J. Lewis of Maryland to introduce the first major proposal to provide federal relief to the jobless. Although the proposal went down to defeat, it was the progenitor of all subsequent federal relief measures, including the Federal Emergency Relief Act, one of the landmarks of the New Deal.

A relentless critic of Herbert Hoover, La Follette warmly welcomed the election of Franklin D. Roosevelt. Roosevelt, for his part, went out of his way to solicit support from the Wisconsin senator and other progressive Republicans. "If Franklin had not been a Roosevelt," said presidential aide Rexford Tugwell, "I am quite certain he would have liked to be a La Follette." During Roosevelt's first term La Follette played a key role in the formulation and passage of New Deal measures, especially in the areas of relief, public works, and taxation. The Federal Emergency Relief Act, the Wealth Tax Act of 1935, and the Social Security Act all bore the stamp of his influence. But even as he was shaping New Deal legislation he was criticizing Roosevelt for not going far enough to combat the depression or to curb the maldistribution of wealth.

Between 1936 and 1940 La Follette attracted national attention as chairman of the Senate Civil Liberties Committee, which investigated violations of labor's right to organize. Frequently dramatic and always controversial, the committee's hearings exposed the strong-arm tactics some employers used to prevent workers from forming unions. The hearings also enhanced La Follette's reputation as a champion of organized labor.

Although La Follette worked closely with the Roosevelt administration on domestic policy, he and the president parted ways over foreign affairs. Just as his father had opposed American entry into World War I, so La Follette, before Pearl Harbor, opposed American entry into World War II. He was no apologist for Germany, but he believed that World War I had been an unmitigated disaster and that the United States should avoid at almost all costs military intervention in another European crisis. When the Japanese attacked Pearl Harbor, La Follette did support the declaration of war. Before long, however, he was criticizing the administration for not curbing what he considered to be the expansionist tendencies of America's major allies in the war, Great Britain and the Soviet Union.

A transitional figure in the history of twentieth-century reform, La Follette linked his father's brand of progressivism with New Deal liberalism. Yet in his case this linkage was incomplete. He grew increasingly disenchanted with the kind of broker-state approach of the New Deal by which the government mediated among well-organized interest groups, including, ironically, two groups whose interests La Follette had championed, industrial workers and farmers. Nor could he entirely reconcile himself to the expansive role in world affairs that the United States adopted for itself during and after World War II.

Despite his growing unhappiness with public life, La Follette commanded great respect from colleagues on both sides of the aisle, who admired him because of his intelligence, mastery of the issues, parliamentary skills, utter sincerity, and willingness to play by the Senate's "club" rules. Unlike his father, who had delighted in making enemies and who had entitled a chapter of his autobiography "Alone in the Senate," Young Bob was a "senator's senator" who once gave a speech entitled "In Defense of the Senate." La Follette's reverence for the legislative process inspired his last major achievement. Seeking to restore to Congress the power and prestige that had shifted to the presidency during World War II, he sponsored and steered through Congress the Legislative Reorganization Act of 1946, which streamlined the committee system and in other ways modernized the structure and procedures of Congress.

Despite his lofty stature in the Senate, La Follette displayed striking weaknesses as a political leader. In 1934 he and his brother Philip, a three-term governor of Wisconsin during the 1930s, bolted the GOP and formed the Progressive party. But Young Bob never gave the new party the consistent leadership it required to survive, and in 1946 the Progressive party disbanded and La Follette rejoined the GOP. Although La Follette performed well on the stump, he intensely disliked campaigning for office. Consequently, his trips back to Wisconsin became fewer and fewer and his attention to constituent matters more perfunctory. In 1946 his accumulated neglect of Wisconsin affairs finally caught up with him. Running for reelection, but waging only a token campaign, he narrowly lost the Republican primary to Joseph R. McCarthy. Ironically, during his last campaign, La Follette devoted far more attention to the alleged Communist subversion of government than did his opponent, whose name later became synonymous with the issue.

Following his defeat, La Follette continued to live in Washington with his wife, Rachael Young, whom he had married in 1930, and his two sons. He served as a consultant for several large corporations, including Sears Roebuck and United Fruit Company. La Follette apparently found private life even less congenial than public life. In the weeks before his death some friends and family members noticed that he seemed unusually anxious; on one occasion, for example, he expressed fear—groundless as it turned out—that Senator McCarthy might summon him to testify about what he, La Follette, had done to curb communism. But just how unhappy he had become, no one realized until 24 February 1953, when he left his office in the middle of the day and went home and shot himself.

• The principal primary source on La Follette is the rich and voluminous collection of La Follette Family Papers at the Library of Congress. Also essential are the Philip F. La Follette Papers at the State Historical Society of Wisconsin in Madison. The only scholarly biography is Patrick J. Maney, *"Young Bob" La Follette: A Biography of Robert M. La Follette, Jr., 1895–1953* (1978). Important studies dealing in whole or in part with La Follette include Robert T. Johnson, *Robert M. La Follette, Jr. and the Decline of the Progressive Party in Wisconsin* (1964); Jerold S. Auerbach, *Labor and Liberty: The La Follette Committee and the New Deal* (1966); and John E. Miller, *Governor Philip F. La Follette, the Wisconsin Progressives, and the New Deal* (1982). Also valuable are Paul W. Glad, *The History of Wisconsin*, vol. 5: *War, a New Era, and Depression, 1914–1940* (1990); Ronald L. Feinman, *Twilight of Progressivism: The Western Republican Senators and the New Deal* (1981); and Wayne S. Cole, *Roosevelt and the Isolationists, 1932–45* (1983).

PATRICK J. MANEY

LA FOLLETTE, Suzanne (1893–23 Apr. 1983), feminist, writer, and editor, was born Clara La Follette on her family's 1,000-acre ranch near Pullman, Washington, the daughter of William LeRoy La Follette, a rancher, and Mary Tabor. La Follette "grew up on horseback," roaming the unfenced ranges of the Snake River Canyon, an unspoiled area where Jeffersonian lifestyles and values still held sway. A product of this environment, from an early age she placed great value on individual liberty and feared the intrusive power of the state.

In 1910 William La Follette won election to the U.S. House of Representatives and moved the family to Washington, D.C. For the next eight years Suzanne, as she was now known, found herself at the center of various national reform efforts. She joined the woman suffrage crusade and worked part-time both in her father's office and in that of his famous first cousin, Senator Robert M. La Follette of Wisconsin. After graduating from Trinity College in 1915, she determined to pursue an independent life and continued working on Capitol Hill on a full-time basis.

La Follette's long career in journalism began in 1919 when she joined the staff of the *Nation*, a liberal weekly based in New York. There she met the writer and critic Albert Jay Nock, whose radical libertarianism greatly influenced her own thinking. The following year La Follette joined Nock in founding *The Freeman*, a publication dedicated to the extension of individual freedom and the economic principles of classical liberalism. In the pages of *The Freeman* La Follette argued that government-sponsored political reform only enhanced the coercive powers of the state and failed to change underlying economic and social conditions. As the "engine of privilege," the state was "an institution to be protected against and not some form of magical benefactor or neutral umpire." Only when granted complete social and economic freedom could an individual achieve his or her full creative potential and thus improve the general welfare. Celebration of the doctrine of laissez faire did not imply a blanket endorsement of corporate capitalism, however. La Follette considered sprawling business organizations of the 1920s equally threatening to the well-being of American society. "The demands of organization," she declared, "are directly opposed to those of civilization; for whereas organization demands the suppression of individuality, civilization is best promoted by its free development." Though it received contributions from many of the era's best writers and was widely respected among intellectuals, *The Freeman* fell victim to financial insolvency and folded in 1924.

Fully schooled in and fervently committed to libertarianism, La Follette set out to demonstrate its relevance to feminism. In her first book, *Concerning Women* (1926), she argued that government welfare legislation intended to improve the working environment for women only adjusted them to industrial conditions, under which they remained subjugated. Moreover, achieving political or legal equality—such as through suffrage—though a desirable first step, had no significant effect in overcoming feminine subordination. La Follette likewise dismissed feminists who stressed the importance of sexual differences or urged the emancipation of women to improve motherhood.

Women's roles as wives and mothers, she maintained, were secondary to their position as individual human beings. Indeed, the institution of marriage restricted women's individual freedom by keeping them chained to the home, where they were treated as a form of property. Since women's fate was inextricably linked to the larger "social question," women would only achieve true liberation as individuals when both sexes secured complete economic freedom in an unregulated marketplace. Though one historian later referred to La Follette as "the most original feminist writer of the 1920s" (O'Neill, p. 325), the "woman issue" had lost much of its urgency by 1926 and *Concerning Women* received only limited attention at the time.

Shifting her focus to the world of art, La Follette spent a year in France studying with the painter and art critic Walter Pach. Upon her return she published *Art in America* (1929), a survey of American art and architecture from the colonial period to the 1920s. Written for the layperson and well reviewed, the book became a minor classic in its field. In 1930 La Follette launched the *New Freeman*, essentially a revival of the previous *Freeman*, which shared its political outlook. Reflecting the growing influence of Marxism among American intellectuals, the magazine also expressed some sympathy for the "Soviet experiment"—though La Follette herself was primarily interested in the aspect of the experiment involving the "withering away of the state" and would soon become an ardent anti-Stalinist. Once again financial problems intruded, and the *New Freeman* ceased publication in May 1931.

The New Deal years proved especially distressing to La Follette. Contributing frequently to the *Nation*, the *New Republic*, and *Scribner's Magazine*, she warned against welfare-state measures that tied citizens' fates to the beneficence of the government and questioned the motives of New Deal economic planners and social engineers. Even more ominous was the rise of totalitarian societies abroad. In the wake of the Moscow trials, La Follette abandoned any remaining illusions she might have harbored about the nature of the Soviet regime. She accepted the philosopher John Dewey's offer to serve as secretary on the Committee for the Defense of Leon Trotsky, which had been formed to investigate the validity of Stalin's charges against his former comrade. La Follette wrote the committee's final report, *Not Guilty* (1937), which thoroughly exonerated Trotsky. In 1940 La Follette served as managing editor of the *American Mercury*, a conservative periodical critical of the New Deal.

During and after World War II the emphasis of La Follette's libertarianism shifted to a strident anticommunism. From 1943 to 1945 she worked for the American Federation of Labor, ensuring as director of its foreign relief programs that noncommunists would be put in charge of reconstruction operations in Europe. Subsequently, she served as a contributing editor on *Plain Talk*, an unrelentingly anticommunist monthly. In 1950 La Follette initiated yet another reincarnation of *The Freeman*. Though the editors intended to revive the cause of classical liberalism in the tradition of the 1920s *Freeman*, most of the magazine's pages were dedicated to castigating U.S. government officials who were perceived as "soft" on communism. In one issue, La Follette enthusiastically defended Senator Joseph McCarthy's attacks on former secretary of state George C. Marshall. After a staff dispute, she quit *The Freeman* in 1953. Two years later La Follette cofounded the *National Review* with a young protégé she had earlier recruited for *The Freeman*, William F. Buckley. La Follette served four years as managing editor of the conservative journal before retiring in 1959.

While running for Congress from New York's Nineteenth District on the Conservative party ticket in 1964, La Follette denied that her politics had changed radically since the 1920s. "I haven't moved," she insisted. "The world has moved to the left of me." Indeed, she never flagged in her consistent defense of individual liberty against the encroachments of the state. Still, as one biographer has noted, in La Follette's later years, "her libertarian concerns tended more to defend existing freedoms than to strike out for newer or larger ones" (Cooper, p. 273). In this sense her radicalism had turned conservative. She lived her final years in California, dying after a long illness in Menlo Park.

• Suzanne La Follette's papers, including a diary she kept during World War I, are among the La Follette Family Collection at the Library of Congress. James L. Cooper and Sheila McIsaac Cooper, *The Roots of American Feminist Thought* (1973), provides biographical information and a thorough analysis of the relationship between La Follette's political philosophy and her feminism. William L. O'Neill, *Everyone Was Brave: The Rise and Fall of Feminism in America* (1969), places the ideas expressed in *Concerning Women* into a historical context. Susan J. Turner, *A History of the* Freeman (1963), and Charles H. Hamilton, "*The Freeman*, 1920–1924," *Modern Age* 31 (1987): 52–59, address the influence of Albert Nock on La Follette's writing. La Follette herself speaks of this influence in her introduction to Nock's *Snoring as a Fine Art* (1958). John Chamberlain, *A Life with the Printed Word* (1982), recounts La Follette's role in the founding of *The Freeman* of 1950, while John B. Judis, *William F. Buckley, Patron Saint of the Conservatives* (1988), mentions her years of service on the *National Review*. Obituaries are in the *New York Times*, 27 Apr. 1983, and the *National Review*, 13 May 1983.

THOMAS W. DEVINE

LAFON, Thomy (28 Dec. 1810–22 Dec. 1893), real estate broker and philanthropist, was born a free person of color in New Orleans, the son of Modeste Foucher (of Haitian descent) and perhaps Pierre Laralde, who might have been a Caucasian born in France or a free person of color born in Louisiana. Although Thomy Lafon was a devout Roman Catholic, no baptismal record has been found, and there is no birth record. He probably took the name Lafon from Barthélémy Lafon, a prominent architect, engineer, and city planner, who was born in Villepinte, France, and took up permanent residence in New Orleans in 1789 or 1790. The connection between Thomy Lafon and Barthélémy Lafon is still unclear; there was a relationship, however, between the elder Lafon and Thomy Lafon's mother.

Most of what has been written about the early life of Thomy Lafon is based on hearsay and conjecture. He was fluent in French, Spanish, and English, but nothing is known of his formal education. Some have said that he was educated in France and was at one time a teacher, but neither of these assertions can be verified. The first published reference to Lafon that has been found is in the New Orleans city directory of 1842; he is listed as a merchant. He is also listed in several later city directories, but it was not until 1868 that he was identified as a broker. The writer of his obituary for the *New Orleans Daily Picayune* said, "He was careful and shrewd in his speculations in real estate, and this is about the only business that he has been ever known to have engaged in" (23 Dec. 1893). At the time of his death he owned vast amounts of property that were located in almost every section of the city.

Lafon never married. The only sibling acknowledged in his obituary and will, the widow Alfee Lafon Baudin, lived with him at the time of his death, and it was said that she had been his "adviser and companion through life." They lived quietly and simply in a modest cottage, even though Lafon was the owner of pretentious dwellings in the city. He dressed well as befitted a businessman of his stature, but not expensively. He was noted for his courteous and dignified manner. Because of his physical features, he was often taken to be Caucasian, but he never encouraged it and chose to be identified as a Creole of color. He avoided social events, but was a patron of the arts, especially music, and regularly attended concerts and operas. During the Civil War, he favored the Union and later joined Durant's Radical Republican Club. He opposed Andrew Johnson, supported congressional plans for reconstruction, and favored universal male suffrage and racial integration of the public schools.

Lafon's financial success and philanthropy are well documented. He is remembered for the large bequests to institutions in his will, but he was also generous in life. A contemporary, Rodolphe Lucien Desdunes, the Creole historian, wrote in 1897 that "he gave right and left, for every deserving cause. . . . There is not a colored charitable institution established in his days that did not receive a donation from him; not a newspaper started in the interest of human rights that did not obtain assistance from his unmeasured liberality." All the institutions that received bequests in his will had previously benefited from his generosity, but it was said that he derived the greatest satisfaction from private donations, being able to assist deserving destitute families and individuals without regard to race or religion. The *Daily Picayune* announced his death under the headline "A Colored Leader in Charity Passes Away" (23 Dec. 1893).

Lafon's bequests included $49,000 in cash and three pieces of property to relatives and friends and $94,000 in cash and twenty-one properties, valued at approximately $400,000, to twelve institutions. Among the institutions were those operated by or for the benefit of both blacks and whites, Protestants and Catholics. The largest gift, however, was to establish a perpetual trust for the benefit of the Sisters of the Holy Family, an order of African-American nuns, who operated or would assume operation of several of the Catholic institutions that had received special bequests.

In 1894 the lower house of the Louisiana legislature voted to appropriate funds for a bronze bust of Thomy Lafon to be displayed permanently at Tulane University; the bill died in the Senate. However, the Louisiana State Museum possesses a handsome plaster bust of Lafon, sculpted by Achille Peretti in 1894 and acquired by the museum in 1909. The name Lafon lives on in a day-care center and nursing home operated by the Sisters of the Holy Family, a nursing home of the United Methodist Church, a city street, and a New Orleans public school. Charles Barthelemy Rousséve, the historian, has translated from the French into English prose the last lines of an "Ode to Thomy Lafon," written by Desdunes: "We give thanks, for, because thou didst wed principle and good work, no name, Lafon, shall longer live than thine." Lafon died at his home in New Orleans.

• The Thomy Lafon civil court succession records are in the Louisiana Division of the New Orleans Public Library. An English translation of his will and codicil is in the archives of the Sisters of the Holy Family in New Orleans. The Archives Division of Earl Long Library at the University of New Orleans holds the papers of Marcus Christian, which contain collected documents on Lafon, and records of the Louisiana Supreme Court, in which there is documentation on numerous cases concerning the bequests of Barthélémy Lafon. Accounts of aspects of Thomy Lafon's life written by contemporaries are found in the *New Orleans Daily Picayune*, 23 Dec. and 24 Dec. 1893, the *New Orleans Times-Democrat*, 21 Apr. and 25 Apr. 1897, and in Rodolphe Lucien Desdunes, *Nos Hommes et Notre Histoire* (1911). Charles E. Wynes, "Thomy Lafon: Black Philanthropist," *Midwest Quarterly: A Journal of Contemporary Thought* 12 (Winter 1981): 105–12, is based on extensive research and is a reliable assessment. See also Charles Barthelemy Rousséve, *The Negro in Louisiana: Aspects of His History and His Literature* (1937), and Robert Meyer, *Names over New Orleans Schools* (1975).

CLIFTON H. JOHNSON

LA GUARDIA, Fiorello Henry (11 Dec. 1882–20 Sept. 1947), U.S. congressman and mayor of New York City, was born in New York City, the son of Achille La Guardia, an army bandmaster, and Irene Coen. Shortly after La Guardia's father joined the American forces dispatched for Cuba in 1898 he fell ill, probably from the "embalmed beef" sold to the military, and was discharged from the army. He then took the family to Europe, where La Guardia, barely eighteen years old, won a post with the American consular service. On the Continent La Guardia experienced firsthand the intense ethnic hatreds and class antipathies of Central Europe; he also acquired fluency in five languages and a strong ambition to return to the United States.

In New York City, La Guardia took a speedwriting course, registered for night classes at New York University Law School, and within a few months became an interpreter with the immigration service at Ellis Island. To pursue his dreams of a political career, he also joined the Republican party. So hopeless was the Republican effort in New York that the party moved him along a fast path. Although he lost his first race for Congress in 1914, he did well enough to earn another chance, and in 1916 he won a congressional seat from lower Manhattan. Later, in the 1920s, he would represent another equally poor and equally mixed neighborhood, East Harlem.

The short (5′2″) and stumpy "Little Flower" (the literal meaning of Fiorello) served in Congress, with two interruptions, from 1916 until 1932. The first hiatus took him to Europe in 1917 as one of five congressmen to enlist in the military. He later adopted a fashionable pacifism, but combat engaged him as nothing else did. Stationed in Foggia, Italy, he flew fighter planes, trained recruits, carried on propaganda activities, and participated in undercover operations. He left the army as a major, the title thereafter by which his closest friends knew him.

The second interruption in his congressional service came in 1919 when he detoured into municipal politics as president of New York's board of aldermen. He had hoped that this post would lead to the mayoralty, but the combination of electoral defeat in 1921 and the successive deaths of his baby daughter, Fioretta Thea, and his young wife, Thea (Almerigiotti), whom he had married in 1919, threatened to derail his career.

Instead he threw himself into politics with single-minded purpose. His wife and his daughter had died of tuberculosis, the disease of the slums and sweatshops; he transformed their deaths into the cause of assuring common citizens a better life. In politics, crusaders live off villains, and La Guardia's villains were the industrial profiteers, the racists, and the unpitying rich. Them, he pilloried with zest.

Back in Congress in the 1920s La Guardia joined a small band of progressives. He called attention to the suffering of the poor, the exploited, the unemployed. He demanded that the interests be regulated, lashed out at the passage of a racist immigration restriction law, and bristled at the hypocrisy of Prohibition. He supported equal rights for women, freedom of speech for socialists, old-age pensions, unemployment insurance, workmen's compensation, public housing, federal energy development, and an end to child labor. Together with Senator George W. Norris (1861–1944) he helped pass the landmark Norris–La Guardia Act that prevented the use of antilabor injunctions. In 1929 he married his longtime secretary, Marie Fisher. The couple adopted two children.

La Guardia was denounced by conservatives from his own Republican party as a danger to the republic, a disgrace to his race, but he worked hard, made shrewd political deals, ran on any available party line (on different occasions he was a candidate on the Republican, Socialist, and Progressive tickets; once he even won the endorsement of the Democrats) and represented East Harlem, as poor an urban district as ex-

isted. It did not hurt him to be iconoclastic there. It did hurt, though, to be a Republican in 1932, and he was buried by the New Deal landslide.

In 1929 La Guardia had run for the mayoralty against James J. Walker, the Tammany candidate. Charges of corruption and insistence on reform threatened government scandal at a time when New Yorkers seemed satisfied with the good times of Jimmy Walker. La Guardia had been soundly defeated. But the stock market crash, the ensuing economic depression, and the shocking disclosures of systematic municipal corruption made by Samuel Seabury (1873–1958) destroyed Mayor Walker's political career. In 1933 he resigned. After a tough behind-the-scenes struggle, La Guardia persuaded a coalition of Republicans, reformers, socialists, and disaffected Democrats, who had come together under the Fusion banner, that he should lead their crusade against corruption and inefficiency. With the support of a broad coalition, he won in a three-way race.

When he took office on 1 January 1934, the city verged on bankruptcy. A "banker's agreement" gave city creditors a veto over municipal expenditures. More than 230,000 New Yorkers were unemployed, and one in every six New Yorkers subsisted on relief. Public confidence in city government was shattered. "I am," La Guardia lamented, "a captain of a broken ship who must patch and repair and struggle continually to keep it afloat." But he moved into the crisis with a sure-handedness and commitment to good government. Insisting on a degree of honesty and efficiency seldom seen in New York's politics, he expanded the role of municipal government to fit the needs of a modern metropolis. And he accomplished his intentions with a panache that lifted fallen spirits.

La Guardia's first administration was his best in the view of most people. From the first day when he took the Oath of the Young Men of Athens, pledging never to bring disgrace to "our City" but to strive "to quicken the public's sense of duty" and "to transmit this city not less but greater, better and more beautiful than it was transmitted to us," New Yorkers experienced a new era of civic responsibility. He appointed experts, chosen for their skills rather than their political affiliations. "To the victors," he would say, "belonged the responsibility for good government." Every day brought news of some new foe who had been defeated, some new outrage uncovered and eliminated. Before long the city seemed to be overrun with fat little men (all of them La Guardia himself) putting out fires, opening parks, chasing "tinhorns and gangsters" out of town, and running up to Albany to ask for more taxing powers.

La Guardia was the father of modern New York City. Before him, the metropolis was a congeries of antiquated boroughs, divided into political fiefdoms, a city haphazardly administered, with limited social and health services, no public housing, decaying parks, rusting bridges—a city mired in graft. Under La Guardia, New York won a generous portion of federal assistance, making it possible to rebuild the city anew, throwing new bridges over the waters and digging tunnels under them, erecting new reservoirs, sewer systems, parks, highways, schools, hospitals, health centers, swimming pools, and air terminals. For the first time New York offered public housing, a unified transit system, and training and subsidies for the arts and music. Relief was placed on the stable foundation of a sales tax, and government was modernized. The outdated 1898 Charter was replaced by a new compact that centralized municipal powers, consolidated departments, eliminated unnecessary borough and county offices, and streamlined municipal operations.

La Guardia wanted New Yorkers to be happy, to enjoy a sense of ease and security, to live in decent quarters and raise healthy children. But he also wanted them to be morally good. He declared unrelenting war on gamblers, closed the burlesques, and cleared racy magazines from the newsstands (under his powers of "garbage collection"). Beginning in 1942, New Yorkers could tune in every Sunday on to WNYC, the city-owned radio station, to hear the mayor tell them what to buy, how to raise their children, what to wear, how to save money, what to do in case of a German attack, how to resolve family disputes. His tone was strikingly intimate and fatherly. In what became the best-remembered act of his mayoralty, he one Sunday gave a dramatic reading for listeners of the comic strips during a newspaper delivery strike.

La Guardia's forcefulness made him a very powerful mayor, and there were times when he gave his supporters pause. His penchant for abusing subordinates and commissioners made many of them bitterly unhappy. His reputation as a civil libertarian suffered from his campaigns against smut, burlesque, and gambling and from his orders to police to "muss up" racketeers and "chiselers."

La Guardia assumed a far larger role in assuring the social welfare of New Yorkers than previous mayors had. Besides his aggressive approach to problems thrown up by the depression, he changed the reach of local government. Previous mayors had dealt with aldermen and state house politicians; La Guardia took up local needs with the White House. Under him, New York became a leader of a national urban coalition and the linchpin of an emerging federal policy for the cities.

As president of the U.S. Conference of Mayors from 1936 to 1945, La Guardia served as a leading spokesman for urban America, developing an excellent relationship with President Franklin D. Roosevelt. The New Deal valued La Guardia's New York as a showplace for its new programs. In other cities the New Deal was embarrassed by corruption and partisanship in WPA assignments. Not in New York. With the best proposals and the best track record, New York won a consistently disproportionate share of federal funds. "Our Mayor is probably the most appealing person I know," Roosevelt once said. "He comes to Washington and tells me a sad story. The tears run down my cheeks and the tears run down his cheeks and the first thing I know, he has wrangled another $50,000,000."

What La Guardia failed to do was to consider sufficiently the impact of the federal windfall. New York's spanking new infrastructure stood as a powerful testament to its mayor's ability to bargain, and bargain better than any other mayor on behalf of his city. But it was built in unusual times with federal funds. Would the city be able to service all of these new structures? In a broader sense, once citizens came to expect more from the municipal government, where would the money come from? La Guardia wanted a far-reaching benevolent government. He also wanted government to remain unobtrusive. He railed against unfeeling, unthinking, rigid bureaucrats, but the type of big urban government he wanted could exist only with an expanded impersonal bureaucracy. When La Guardia left City Hall in 1945, the city was overburdened and a new budget crisis loomed.

Unrealistic about the city, he also was unrealistic about himself. Toward the end of his second term he began to crave a broader importance. Much of the original Fusion agenda had been accomplished. Marking an end to the years of hardship and despair, he led New York in a great celebration—the 1939 World's Fair dedicated to the World of Tomorrow. There was talk of a cabinet position, the vice presidency on the next national ticket, even the presidency.

Roosevelt's decision to run for a third term foreclosed some possibilities. Nonetheless, Roosevelt understood La Guardia's need for a wider stage. In the spring of 1941, with war on the horizon, the president appointed him to be director of the Office of Civilian Defense, with quasi-Cabinet rank. La Guardia undertook the directorship and simultaneously ran for a third term, persuaded that he could do both jobs equally well. He was wrong, and after the outbreak of hostilities the spectacle of a haggard La Guardia spending three days in Washington on civil defense, then dragging himself back to run the city, grated on New Yorkers' nerves. By February 1942 he was forced to drop OCD, but not before he squandered much goodwill among his supporters.

He was tired of the mayoralty by this time. His original agenda had been accomplished. The rest was, as he used to say, keeping the sewers clean, collecting the garbage, chasing the criminals, and balancing budgets. With his ardor gone, the wonderful energy of the early days gave way to cantankerousness and irascibility. He was a man who always needed some new challenge, and with the nation at war he wanted to be on the front. He badgered Roosevelt to appoint him to a military position, and there was serious talk with General Dwight D. Eisenhower of appointing La Guardia to a generalship either in Italy or North Africa. Roosevelt considered indulging his colleague but in the end dropped the idea. It was La Guardia's greatest disappointment, and he suffered openly. In 1945 he chose not to run again. He died in the Bronx.

La Guardia came to office in hard times. He redefined the role of the modern mayoralty, extending the reach of government, infusing it with integrity, and upgrading its capacity to deliver municipal services.

He worked closely with the New Deal to carve out a national urban policy. Taking full advantage of his access to Roosevelt and New Deal largesse he rebuilt his aging city into a modern metropolis and, in the words of U.S. Supreme Court justice Felix Frankfurter, "translated the complicated conduct of [New York] City's vast government into warm significance for every man, woman and child."

• La Guardia's papers are divided among several collections. The bulk of his congressional papers are held by the New York Public Library. His mayoral papers are in the New York Municipal Archives. Personal papers are in the Fiorello La Guardia and the Robert F. Wagner Archives at La Guardia Community College of the City University of New York. La Guardia wrote a partial autobiography, *The Making of an Insurgent: An Autobiography, 1882–1919* (1948), which is of no more than moderate interest. The most recent and comprehensive scholarly biography is Thomas Kessner, *Fiorello H. La Guardia and the Making of Modern New York* (1989). Lawrence Eliott, *Little Flower: The Life and Times of Fiorello La Guardia* (1983), offers a brief popular account, while August Heckscher, *When La Guardia Was Mayor: New York's Legendary Years* (1978), provides a more penetrating study. Arthur Mann's two volumes, *La Guardia: A Fighter against His Times, 1882–1933* (1959) and *La Guardia Comes to Power: The Mayoral Election of 1933* (1965), are scholarly interpretations of La Guardia's career before he entered City Hall. Howard Zinn, *La Guardia in Congress* (1959), is also useful. Ernest Cuneo, *Life with Fiorello* (1955), is a literate account of Cuneo's early years in La Guardia's congressional office.

THOMAS KESSNER

LAHEY, Frank Howard (1 June 1880–27 June 1953), surgeon, was born Francis Howard Lahey (he later changed his first name to "Frank") in Haverhill, Massachusetts, the son of Thomas Benjamin Pierce Lahey, a contractor, and Honora Frances Powers. Thomas Lahey, partner in the successful bridge-building firm Fletcher and Lahey, thought his son would assume his place in the family business, but young Frank aspired early on to have a career in medicine. After attending Haverhill High, he entered Harvard Medical School, earning the degree doctor of medicine in 1904. He then served as intern and house surgeon at Long Island Hospital before moving on to Boston City Hospital, where he worked as surgeon from 1905 to 1907. He became resident surgeon of the Haymarket Square Relief Station in 1908. That same year he was appointed instructor in surgery at Harvard; he held positions there from 1908 to 1909, then again from 1912 to 1915. In 1909 Lahey married Alice Church Wilcox; they had no children.

Overlapping for several years with his duties at Harvard, Lahey was assistant professor and then professor of surgery at Tufts Medical School from 1913 to 1917. During World War I he served as a major in the U.S. Army Medical Corps and also as director of surgery in the American Expeditionary Forces Evacuation Hospital No. 30. After his tour of duty ended in France, he returned to Harvard and was made professor of clinical surgery at Harvard during the academic year 1923–1924, teaching at Boston City Hospital.

Though he was still a young man when he returned from the war, Lahey realized that a new method of performing surgery, one requiring a team of specialists skilled in asepsis, antisepsis, and anesthesia, was needed. This belief, coupled with his conviction to treat all his patients as individuals with names and not anonymous cases with numbers (as was done with charity cases in the city hospitals), evolved into the idea to form a clinic. Though he later said he could not account for how it all transpired, Lahey remembered the courage it took to resign his Harvard professorship to devote himself full time to starting the clinic.

The original building of the Lahey Clinic was erected in 1926; seven years later, it was doubled in size and soon thereafter doubled again. It went through additional expansions in subsequent years and became well known for its contribution to medical education. Lahey held the chief administrative post, recruiting such medical professionals as Dr. Sara Murray Johnson, gastroenterologist, and Dr. Lincoln Fleetford Sise, anesthetist. The first aim of the clinic, Lahey believed, was to get people well, but he visualized other purposes, including investigating and developing new methods of treatment, providing training in these new methods, and serving as an informal postgraduate center. Always focusing on the team as opposed to the individual, Lahey led his staff to great success in the field of thyroid surgery, reducing the high mortality rate by dividing complicated procedures into two-stage operations. He applied the same techniques to abdominal surgery, pioneering the total removal of the stomach. Whatever the procedure, Lahey was intent on passing along his innovations to colleagues and medical students. He took colored films of some operations, presenting them for study at lectures in this country and abroad. He also opened his operating room to visitors and clinical fellows and provided in-depth speeches on his actions, thus making each operation a lecture and demonstration. As Lahey said frequently, "he [was] devoting his life to the training of young physicians for better service in medicine and surgery" (Fishbein, p. 815). Indeed, by the late 1930s he had gained a reputation as the greatest American teacher of surgery.

In addition to being a leader in the fields of surgery and medical education, Lahey also worked as an honorary consultant to the medical department of the U.S. Navy during World War II. He served as chairman of its medical board and inspected nearly every naval hospital in the States and the Pacific. He opened the Lahey Clinic for training of Navy surgeons during the war and maintained his own practice as well. In 1940 he was elected president of the American Medical Association, serving in this post from 1941 to 1942, when the organization faced a federal suit for fighting health cooperatives. Lahey did not favor group health plans or state medicine and later denounced President Harry S. Truman's proposed compulsory national health insurance plan.

In 1946 the American Gastroenterological Association, of which Lahey was a member, gave him the

Friedenwald medal for his contributions to surgery of the digestive tract. That same year he received the Henry Jacob Bigelow medal from the Boston Surgical Society, the Medal for Merit from the secretary of the navy, and the Certificate of Merit from President Truman. He was also an honorary member of the Royal College of Surgeons of England.

Known as a perfectionist, Lahey constantly pushed himself and his staff to excellence, yet he is remembered by his colleagues for his "inexhaustible kindliness," "delightful personality," and "willingness to give generously of his time and energy" (Deinard, pp. 168, 174). Lahey's slender build and boyish appearance often led people to think him much younger than he was. Once a patient complained about being seen only by a subordinate when it was Lahey himself who had actually attended her. An avid golfer, Lahey also enjoyed fishing and hunting with the dogs he trained and managed in field trials. He died in Boston.

• There is a collection of Lahey's papers at the Lahey Clinic Foundation, Boston, Massachusetts. The archives of Harvard University, Tufts University, and New England Deaconess and New England Baptist hospitals hold material related to Lahey. Lahey published many periodical articles; the most important are contained in the *Lahey Clinic* number of the *Surgical Clinics of North America* series. The best article about Lahey is L. C. Deinard, "Lahey, Perfectionist," in *Postgraduate Medicine*, Aug. 1948. A brief sketch by Walter L. Biering appears in Morris Fishbein, *A History of the American Medical Association* (1947), and obituaries are in the *Journal of American Medical Association*, 11 July 1953, and *Gastroenterology*, Oct. 1953.

LISABETH G. SVENDSGAARD

LAHR, Bert (13 Aug. 1895–4 Dec. 1967), comedian and actor, was born Irving Lahrheim in New York City, the son of Jacob Lahrheim, an upholsterer, and Augusta (maiden name unknown). Lahr detested school and left New York's Public School 40, where he had been funny onstage, simply to take a job, any job. He abandoned fifteen jobs before succeeding in a tryout for the Loew's variety show circuit. At age fifteen he joined the Seven Frolics and traveled to Chicago; later, he was one of the Nine Crazy Kids.

These "kid acts"—one of the era's standard types—satirized classroom behavior. In both acts Lahr was able to use the "Dutch" (comic German) dialect that came naturally to him. The Nine Crazy Kids were organized by Bert Gordon (later famed as the "Mad Russian" of stage and radio). Gordon's original choice for the kids' substitute teacher was Jack Pearl. According to John Lahr, during one of their daily meetings at the Automat in New York, Lahrheim and Jack Pearlman had decided to shorten their names. Pearl remained "Dutch" throughout his stage and radio career, memorably as Baron Munchausen. But Gordon did not believe Pearl's voice strong enough to soar over the "schoolroom" chaos. Lahr's was.

After another kid act and a comedy threesome, Lahr in 1917 followed Pearl onto the Columbia wheel, burlesque's most important circuit. Burlesque, in the United States a low-comedy form, was at the time in transition between its broad, parodic past and its almost exclusively bump-and-grind future. In *The Best Show in Town*, Lahr was the "third comedian," a German-Jewish stereotype with a bulbous nose. Already a worrying perfectionist devoted to "protecting the laugh," he developed his keen eye for human behavior as well as the particular bray of surprise, joy, betrayal, or sexual approval—*gnong-gnong-gnong* has been its best transliteration—that became his career-long trademark. He earned the billing of "the funniest man in burlesque." And, wrote musical theater historian Ethan Mordden, "Burlesque . . . taught him that everything is spoofable because almost everyone is a kind of fool."

In 1921 Lahr formed an act with Mercedes Delpino, a Spanish soubrette and chorus girl in *The Best Show in Town*, who in 1929 became his first wife. As Bert Lahr and Mercedes, the team moved into vaudeville, a "cleaner" form of variety, in 1922. (Delpino gradually became mentally ill, and the marriage was annulled in 1940; they had one child. Lahr's second marriage, to former beauty contest winner Mildred Schroeder in 1940, produced two children.) Lahr and Delpino's one sketch—nominally called "What's the Idea?"—lasted five years. It played the New York Palace (1925) and was listed among the Keith-Albee circuit's all-star acts. According to *Variety*, the low comedy Mercedes and Lahr infused into vaudeville was welcome: "like feeding starving Armenians." Lahr was a blaring, malapropistic, tunelessly singing, rubber-legged, neck-falling "Dutch" policeman and Mercedes the sweetly sexy hootchy-cootchy dancer he attempts to arrest "for shifting her gears" too seductively. "What's the big idea?" and "Some fun, huh kid?" became the earliest of his catchphrases to enrich American English. "What's the Idea?" was incorporated in *Harry Delmar's Revels*, the 1927 revue that marked Lahr's first Broadway appearance and became his entrée to musical comedy.

In 1928 Lahr played the hapless boxer Gink Schiner in *Hold Everything*. Unable to control even the bicycle that propelled him on and off stage, Schiner was capable of any bizarre event in the ring, including knocking himself out. His "sort of broad abandon that is instantly appreciated in the abdomen," according to theater critic Brooks Atkinson, helped *Hold Everything* to run for 413 performances and led to Lahr's first motion picture contract.

Lahr's film career illustrates a charge often leveled at the era's Hollywood studio bosses: buying silk purses, they fashioned sows' ears. *Hold Everything* became a film comedy in 1930, but Joe E. Brown took Lahr's role (and, according to Lahr, a lot of his own "business"). Metro-Goldwyn-Mayer did allow Lahr to star in the 1931 screen version of his 1930 Broadway musical comedy hit *Flying High*, but in general Lahr was relegated to cameos or supporting roles in undistinguished films such as the 1938 *Love and Hisses*, a tale of purported feuding between columnist Walter Winchell and bandleader Ben Bernie.

On Broadway, Lahr's comedy sought loftier targets. In George White's *Music Hall Varieties* (1932) he parodied one of the era's most popular singing and dancing "sophisticates," Clifton Webb. As "Clifton Duckfeet," in Ethan Mordden's words, Lahr "did not subvert the debonair with vulgarity [but] exposed the vulgar in the debonair." Lahr did a similar number on Noel Coward in the revue *Life Begins at 8:40* (1934). In one of the decade's great revues (costarring Beatrice Lillie, one of the rare female stars Lahr respected), *The Show Is On* (1936), Lahr added an operatic parody, "The Song of the Woodman," a tour de force combining burlesqueish lyrics (among the marvelous items made from a tree are comfort seats "all shapes and classes, for little lads and little—lasses") and sharply rendered pretentious singing. *Gnong-gnong-gnong* was refined into an overripe vibrato. Partly because of all the "choppin'," many were reminded of bass Fyodor Chaliapin. The practice in those years did not include "original cast" recordings, but this small masterpiece was preserved in an otherwise forgettable film, *Merry-Go-Round of 1938*.

Composer Harold Arlen and lyricist E. Y. Harburg had written "The Song of the Woodman" for Lahr. Theirs was the score for the 1939 MGM version of *The Wizard of Oz*, in which Lahr's Cowardly Lion, fiddling with his too-long tail, batting his eyelashes coyly, twitching his snout ferociously, shadow-boxing pointlessly, bounded into immortality. The vibrato and the prissily genteel merged like quicksilver in "'f I Were King of the Forest." Awakening to a magical snowstorm from a near-lethal poppy field sleep, he sniffed yawningly, "Unusual weather we're having, ain't it?" a deft parody of his own catchphrases.

Despite *The Wizard of Oz*, one of the most popular films of all time (and his only film success), Lahr escaped typecasting and the curse of being recalled as a one-role actor. He followed the film with his most successful Broadway musical comedy, Cole Porter's *DuBarry Was a Lady* (1939), chasing Ethel Merman around a Louis XV bed (again, he was the eye-rolling monarch of all he surveyed) and being repeatedly shot with arrows in the derriere. "Friendship" ("If they ever put a bullet through your brain, I'll complain"), a duet with Merman, was another small masterpiece. Yet Merman wrote, "Bert worries and broods more than any six worriers or brooders I've known." After the highly successful opening, Lahr remarked, "Yeah, but what about next year?"

In the 1940s musical plays with "serious" themes and greater integration of libretto, dance, and song became dominant, and the services of top bananas like Lahr were not much valued. Red Skelton took Lahr's role in the 1943 film of *DuBarry*. After promising Lahr a film to be called "Oh, You Kid!" to capitalize on another of his catchphrases, MGM gave it to another star and then canceled it. In the 1944 Broadway revue *Seven Lively Arts*, called "a $1.3 million anachronism," Lahr and Lillie did not repeat their earlier success.

In 1946 Lahr revisited his early career, playing a dramatic role as well as directing a revival of Arthur Hopkins's 1927 play *Burlesque*. He toured and appeared in television and films. A rare reprise of earlier revue success came in *Two on the Aisle* (1951). Lahr created Lefty Hogan, a boozing, wenching baseball star who fails to realize he is being interviewed for children's television. One of Lahr's better-remembered film performances came in *Rose Marie* (1954).

Seventeen years after *The Wizard of Oz* and *DuBarry Was a Lady*, Lahr played Estragon in the American premiere of Samuel Beckett's enigmatic play *Waiting for Godot* (1956). The British critic Kenneth Tynan called "Mr. Lahr's beleaguered simpleton, a draughts-player lost in a universe of chess . . . a mighty and blessed clown whose grateful bewilderment . . . bridged for the first time I can remember the irrational abyss that yawns between the world of red noses and the world of blue stockings." Lahr had grasped the humor within Beckett's desolate angst and capitalized on the insecurity underlying his own comic portrayals. His characterization probably helped render Beckett's work accessible to audiences. Subsequent productions of *Godot* have often cast star comedians as Vladimir, Estragon, and Pozzo. The play's most eloquent image and metaphor of humanity is Lahr's: prayerful and pleading, a clown plumbing the depths of pain.

After this breakthrough, with occasional returns to Broadway such as the revue *The Girls against the Boys* (1959), Lahr's career continually demonstrated that, as the Greeks knew, comedy of all latitudes grows from the same human pomposities and insufficiencies and that the great clowns do not need clown makeup. He appeared in the Feydeau farce *Hotel Paradiso* (1957); in Shakespearean repertory, including *A Midsummer Night's Dream* (1960), for which, as Bottom, he was judged best actor of the American Shakespeare Festival; and in Shavian and classic French comedy for television (*Androcles and the Lion* and *The School for Wives*). On Broadway he created a number of satirical roles in S. J. Perelman's series of vignettes *The Beauty Part* (1962). In a 1964 musical adaptation of Ben Jonson's *Volpone* called *Foxy*, still athletic enough to climb the walls of the stage, Lahr won the Antoinette Perry (Tony) award for best actor in a musical. In 1966 he appeared in classic Greek comedy, *The Birds*, in Ypsilanti, Michigan, and commented, "I never knew Aristophanes was a writer of comedy. . . . I did this stuff in burlesque."

Advertising a new brand of potato chips on television in the mid-1960s, grimacing and winking, he delivered one last catchphrase, "Betcha can't eat just one." In 1967 he was in the midst of filming location scenes for *The Night They Raided Minsky's*, another nostalgic visit to his burlesque days, when he died in New York. The film's script was rewritten, but Lahr's role remained intact.

A perfectionist who always feared the worst, Lahr was a great clown in an era that steadily abandoned clowndom. His rubbery, larger-than-life face and the athletic movements of an unlikely body were as eloquent as any dialogue; everything he did was on an increasingly grand scale, increasingly controlled. One more turn of the screw and it might not have worked at all.

• John Lahr's *Notes on a Cowardly Lion* (1969) is an outstanding biography; in addition to insights and analysis, it reproduces in full or in part many of Lahr's sketches and routines. Stanley Green, *The Great Clowns of Broadway* (1984), describes vividly many of Lahr's theatrical performances. Ethan Mordden, *Broadway Babies* (1983), does more of the same, adding comparative analysis. Shirley Staples, *Male-Female Comedy Teams in American Vaudeville, 1865–1932* (1984), shows Lahr and Mercedes Delpino in their historic role in the development of a genre that concludes with George Burns and Gracie Allen. Many books, articles, and television programs have dealt with *The Wizard of Oz*.

JAMES ROSS MOORE

LAINE, Papa Jack (21 Sept. 1873–1 June 1966), musician and bandleader, was born George Vetiala Lane in New Orleans, Louisiana, the son of Francois Laine, a contractor, and Bernadine Wink. "Jack," or "Papa," as he eventually was known, spent his childhood and all of his adult life in the same neighborhood, immediately downriver from the French Quarter, known then as the Eighth Ward and now called by its original name, Faubourg Marigny. His first instrument was a toy drum obtained from bandleader Patrick S. Gilmore's son. His first real instrument, which he received at the age of eleven, was a field drum that his father purchased for him at a salvage sale at the end of the Worlds Industrial and Cotton Centennial Exposition in New Orleans in 1884–1885. He first played in parades with other neighborhood boys with rag-tag homemade instruments. From there he graduated into fife and drum–type bands using tin flutes and penny whistles. Although predominantly a bass drum player, Laine also played snare drum and full trap set. In addition to drums, he played alto horn and string bass.

In 1889, at the age of sixteen, Laine was functioning as a bandleader and began putting together both string bands and brass bands, for all occasions. He had a large drum and bugle corps during the Spanish-American War, but the war ended before the band went into service. One of Laine's early specialties was playing music for funerals, but this aspect of his business was confined to Algiers and Gretna, both of them small towns across the Mississippi River; two other major bandleaders controlled the New Orleans market. However, the practice of having funerals with music for white residents ended shortly after 1900.

In 1895 Laine married Blanche Nunez, whose parents had emigrated to New Orleans from Cuba. They had two children. Laine organized his famous Reliance Brass Band somewhere near the turn of the century, and the market eventually called for three separate units of this group to keep up with the demand. At the same time he also had other bands, the Tuxedo Band, Laine's Band, the Formal Band, and another with no name at all. As the demand for vernacular dance music grew, Laine also had dance bands, using members of the brass bands augmented with pianists, guitarists and string bass players. Laine also had a

children's band with very young musicians. With all these bands booked at the same time, Laine often turned his large house into a dormitory in order to have bands available early in the morning for all-day jobs such as picnics, excursions, and out-of-town parades.

Laine's bands were truly multicultural since they were populated by various ethnic and racial groups including any light-skinned blacks that he could hire without running afoul of the law. The age of his musicians also spanned the full gamut of years. Some of his men had a great deal of formal musical training, and some had none at all. Therefore, his bands were made up of both readers and fakers, which seems to have been a winning combination in playing both the necessary standards and the rapidly evolving new music.

Laine had a band at the St. Louis Exposition in 1904. He combined New Orleans musicians with St. Louis locals, playing with the group until he achieved the sound he wanted. He then left the group to play on its own and headed back to New Orleans to look after the many musical jobs that he had under contract.

During his career as a bandleader, Laine hired somewhere between 100 and 200 New Orleans musicians, 150 of whom are identifiable through various sources. About one third of them became the mainstays of early jazz. Likewise, some of them, such as members of the Tom Brown's Band From Dixie, the Original Dixieland Jazz Band, the Louisiana Five, Jimmy Durante's Original New Orleans Jazz Band, and the New Orleans Rhythm Kings, became internationally famous and retained this fame three-quarters of a century later. This list includes Tom Brown, Nick LaRocca, Larry Shields, Eddie Edwards, Tony Sbabaro, Alcide Nunez, Achille Baquet, George Brunies, and Chink Martin.

One of the last jobs that Laine had before he retired was at Camp Beauregard in Alexandria, Louisiana. Many of his men got drafted during World War I, and a lot of them ended up at Camp Beauregard. Laine was hired by the army to organize and operate bands at the camp, and he considered it to be one of the most enjoyable experiences of his life.

In 1919 Laine retired from the music business, although he apparently continued to play occasional jobs with his son Alfred "Pantsy" Laine's band. He returned full time to his old occupation as a blacksmith, working predominantly for the Dennis Sheen Transfer Company, one of New Orleans's largest drayage firms. However, after years of retirement from the music business, he started to take on the role of an early New Orleans music legend. The first instance of this evolving fame occured in November 1939, when the Sunday *Times-Picayune* newspaper ran a lengthy human interest story titled "Hot Music's Granddad Beats Anvil Instead of Drum."

When the National Jazz Foundation was organized in New Orleans in 1945, interest in Laine was further renewed. This fascination continued to grow when the New Orleans Jazz Club succeeded the foundation as the local jazz society and put out a special issue of their

Second Line magazine on Papa Jack Laine in the May–June 1954 issue. Probably the most important of these revival events occurred in January 1959, when a recording was made of Laine playing bass drum with a band specially picked by cornetist Johnny Wiggs. Laine surprised everyone not only by still being able to play, but by producing an extremely vibrant, driving bass drum sound that definitely kicked the band along.

Laine was interviewed by jazz historians several times between 1951 and 1964, and taken cumulatively these give a fascinating account of his life and the development of jazz over time. On 28 September 1963, a week after his ninetieth birthday, the New Orleans Jazz Club honored him with a Certificate of Merit at a special function at the Royal Orleans Hotel. In late 1963 the National Educational Television network (NET) did a one-hour special on Laine titled "Jack Laine—Patriarch of Jazz." By the time of his death Laine had regained some of the glory of the days when he was at his peak in the New Orleans music scene.

Jack Laine was an extremely important figure in the long and extended development of jazz in New Orleans. As a notable, legendary figure he predated Buddy Bolden, and his career continued long after Bolden became incapacitated. As a bandleader and a musician, his influence touched the lives of many up-and-coming jazz superstars and affected the course of the music even after he himself had been out of the music business for several decades.

• Fortunately, Jack Laine was interviewed several times, and these interviews are available at the Hogan Jazz Archive, Tulane University, New Orleans, La. Additionally, there are interviews with some of Laine's musicians that also mention aspects of Laine's musical career. The NET documentary on Laine is also helpful in tracing his life story. H. O. Brunn's *The Story of the Original Dixieland Jazz Band* (1960), has sections on Laine, as does Frederic Ramsey, Jr., and Charles Edward Smith, eds., *Jazzmen* (1939). Various issues of *Basin Street*, the newsletter of the National Jazz Foundation as well as issues of the *Second Line*, the magazine of the New Orleans Jazz Club, have information on Laine, especially Feb 1951; May–June 1954; Sept–Oct 1963; and July–Aug 1966.

JACK STEWART

LAING, Hugh (6 June 1911–10 May 1988), dancer, was born Hugh Morris Alleyne Skinner on the island of Barbados in the British West Indies, the son of Donald Morris Skinner, a well-to-do merchant of English and Irish extraction and Beatrice Alleyne, also of English extraction. It was his mother who encouraged him in the arts. In his early years Laing played tennis, climbed trees, had a trapeze in his "golden apple tree," and his own pony that he rode bareback. Although he assumed that one day he would become a doctor, he changed his mind and decided to become a commercial artist. In 1931, Laing went to London to study at the Grosvenor School of Modern Art where he remained just eighteen months, preferring his studies of dance at Marie Rambert's Ballet Club. He was rapidly becoming one of the most fascinating and talented performers in the Rambert company. There he met another member of the company, the young dancer and choreographer Antony Tudor, with whom he formed a lifelong partnership that was both personal and artistic.

Laing's commanding stage presence was immediately acknowledged in his first role as the "muscular, mahogany-hued" Vikram, in Tudor's successful ballet, *Atalanta of the East* (1933). Laing's (and Tudor's) fame grew when he played an importunate and passionate lover in *Jardin aux Lilas* (1936). He also developed the pensive and explosive male solo role in *Dark Elegies* (1937), perhaps Tudor's most important ballet. Laing also appeared in several Frederick Ashton ballets for Ninette de Valois's Vic-Wells Company and also as Agnes de Mille's partner in her chamber performances around London.

In 1937, when Tudor left Rambert, he took along Laing, who helped him to establish a new ballet company, the London Ballet. Tudor created for Laing the leading roles in *Gallant Assembly* (1937), *Judgment of Paris* (1938), and *Soirée Musicale* (1938). Laing's first and very successful experiment with stage and costume design came with *Judgment of Paris*, a seedy glimpse of nightclub life and down-and-out women dancers enhanced by the music of Kurt Weill.

Tudor and Laing went to America in October 1939, invited by the newly formed Ballet Theatre in New York, where Laing was for many years one of their most important male dancers. Despite his lack of a pristine classical technique he was able, through his brooding good looks and intensity, to transform his many roles into powerful personal statements. Laing appeared in the first performance of Michel Fokine's *Bluebeard* (1941) and in Leonide Massine's *Aleko* (1942). Laing also shared the startling success of Tudor's *Pillar of Fire* (1942). As the Young Man from the House Opposite, "Laing superbly danced the smoldering and evil youth," the critic John Martin wrote in the *New York Times* (26 Apr. 1942). In a series of inspired portrayals in Tudor ballets, Laing distinguished himself as the "suave and witty" gentleman in *Dim Lustre* (1943), as Romeo in *Romeo and Juliet* (1943), and as the Transgressor in *Undertow* (1945), each time partnering with the great dramatic ballerina Nora Kaye. Robert Sabin in *Dance Observer* (June–July 1945, p. 68) pointed out that "Hugh Laing as the Transgressor comes face to face with the reality of himself. . . . He danced with an emotional vehemence and inner glow which left the spectator completely under the spell of Mr. Tudor's confused ballet."

In 1947, Laing married the ballerina Diana Adams, shortly before moving with her and Tudor to the New York City Ballet. There, Laing and Adams starred together in Tudor's *Nimbus* (1950) and in his touching *Lady of the Camellias* (1951). Laing, in a restaging, also interpreted George Balanchine's *Prodigal Son* (1950) and *Tyl Eulenspiegel* (1951). The couple divorced in 1953; they had no children.

Though the relationship with Tudor became severely strained after Laing's marriage, the partnership was not over. Laing continued to help Tudor restage his ballets in many countries. He was especially insightful and innovative in offering his ideas for costume and scenic design. In addition to the *Judgment of Paris*, he later created the costumes and scenery for *The Divine Horsemen* (1969), and just before his death, he meticulously reconstructed *Gala Performance* (1988). Laing retired from the stage in 1956 and soon afterward became an assistant to well-known studio photographer Ray Jacobs.

Until his death in New York, Laing remained the most powerful voice in the restaging of Tudor's ballets at the American Ballet Theatre. Laing will be remembered as Tudor's éminence grise and a profoundly moving dramatic dancer.

• The Dance Collection at the New York Public Library for the Performing Arts is the best source for correspondence, contracts, articles, reviews, photos, and films in which Laing danced some of his best roles. It also contains a transcription of the Oral History Project interview conducted by Marilyn Hunt (9 May 1986), another transcription of an interview by John Gruen with Maude Lloyd and her husband, Nigel Gosling (13 July 1975), as well as boxes of letters and memorabilia from Laing's estate. Both the Rambert Archives and the Theatre Museum in London are excellent sources for information on Laing's early career with Marie Rambert, Antony Tudor, and Ninette de Valois. No comprehensive book or article discussing the sum total of Hugh Laing's multifaceted and important stage career has been written as yet. Donna Perlmutter has written a superficial biography of Antony Tudor and his relationship to Laing called *Shadowplay, the Life of Antony Tudor* (1991). Judith Chazin-Bennahum, *The Ballets of Antony Tudor: Studies in Psyche and Satire* (1994), includes important discussions of Hugh Laing's professional relationship to Tudor and his ballets.

It is vital to realize that any serious study of Tudor's ballets also includes material about Laing and his performances in the roles that Tudor created for him. Agnes de Mille's *Dance to the Piper* (1958) contains a fine chapter on Tudor and Laing. There are significant references to Laing in Selma Jeanne Cohen's and John Percival's two monographs in *Dance Perspectives* 17 and 18 (1963). Muriel Topaz, ed., "Antony Tudor: The American Years," *Choreography and Dance* 1, part 2 (1989), contains useful information. Marilyn Hunt, "A Conversation with Maude Lloyd," *Ballet Review* 2 (Fall 1983): 5–26, refers to Laing dancing with Rambert. A sensitive obituary appears in *Dance Magazine*, July 1988, p. 32.

JUDITH CHAZIN-BENNAHUM

LAJOIE, Napoleon (5 Sept. 1874–7 Feb. 1959), baseball player and manager, was born in Woonsocket, Rhode Island, the eighth and last child of Québec, Canada, natives John Lajoie, a laborer, and Celina Guertin. Lajoie (pronounced Lah-jway) left school after the eighth grade, going to work in the textile mills and later driving delivery wagons and horse-drawn taxis. He also made a reputation for his ballplaying skills with various Rhode Island semiprofessional teams, and in 1896 he began his professional career at Fall River, Massachusetts, in the New England League. Three months into the season, with Lajoie batting well above .400, the Philadelphia Phillies of the National League (NL) purchased his contract.

A muscular 6′1″ and 195 pounds, the right-handed Lajoie was an instant major league success. His cumulative batting average over his first five seasons in the NL was .362. "Larry" or "Nap," as he was alternately known in baseball circles, played both infield and outfield, although second base became his usual position. Whatever position he assumed, he impressed longtime baseball followers as one of the hardest hitters and most graceful fielders ever to play the game.

Like nearly all his peers, Lajoie chafed under the $2,400 salary limit that had been maintained by the NL clubowners for the past five years. And like many other NL players, Lajoie grabbed at the bigger money offered by Ban Johnson and his associates, who in 1901 proclaimed their American League (AL) the equal of the NL and set up operations in eight cities, including three (Chicago, Boston, and Philadelphia) that were NL bastions. Lajoie was probably the AL's prize catch; signing with manager Connie Mack's Philadelphia Athletics, he proceeded to win the AL's first batting championship with a stunning .422 average, setting a league record that stood throughout the twentieth century.

Early in the 1902 season Lajoie changed teams again. When the Pennsylvania Supreme Court—in response to a lawsuit filed against Lajoie for having signed with the Athletics—upheld an injunction order that prevented Lajoie from playing major league baseball in the state with anybody besides the Phillies, AL president Johnson transferred his contract to the struggling Cleveland franchise. There, in 1903 and 1904, he won more batting titles and became so popular with Cleveland's fans that the team, hitherto known as Blues or Broncos, was renamed the "Naps" in his honor. From 1905 to 1909 Lajoie also managed the Naps, enduring the biggest disappointment of his career in 1908 when his team fell one-half game short of a pennant. Meanwhile, in 1906 he married Myrtle Everturf of Cleveland; they would have no children.

Unburdened of his managerial post by 1910, Lajoie engaged in a dramatic competition for the batting championship with Detroit's brilliant young Ty Cobb, with an expensive Chalmers automobile to be awarded to the winner. Usually affable and easygoing, Lajoie was a favorite of both players and fans around the AL, most of whom also despised the hot-tempered, ferociously competitive Cobb. In a season-closing doubleheader, the St. Louis Browns tried to ensure the Chalmers to Lajoie by giving him seven uncontested bunt hits, but the plot failed when a furious Ban Johnson nonetheless certified Cobb as the batting titlist by a fraction of a percentage point. (The Chalmers company then awarded automobiles to both Cobb and Lajoie.)

Lajoie continued to hammer the ball over the next three seasons, despite being increasingly at odds with Joe Birmingham, who took over as Cleveland's manager in 1912. But after a poor season with a last-place team in 1914, the forty-year-old Lajoie returned to Connie Mack's Athletics, where he spent two more desultory seasons with bad teams before Mack reluctantly gave him his release. Lajoie left the major leagues with a .338 career batting average and 3,244 base hits, including 658 doubles and 161 triples. He scored more than 1,500 runs, and while runs batted in was not an official statistical category in Lajoie's time, later tabulations have given him nearly 1,600. A star of the "dead-ball" era, he totaled eighty-two homeruns; had he played later, in the era of the "lively ball," he would doubtless have amassed several times that number.

For the 1917 season Lajoie signed as player-manager for Toronto, Ontario, Canada, in the International League, a top-level minor circuit. Despite increasingly difficult circumstances in the minor leagues following U.S. entry into World War I, Lajoie spent a thoroughly satisfying season, not only managing the Maple Leafs to the league pennant—the only time he was with a pennant-winner—but also posting a league-leading .380 batting average. The next season Lajoie moved to Indianapolis of the American Association, but in midsummer that league suspended operations because of wartime manpower shortages and attendance woes. After that, Lajoie had finally had enough of the baseball life.

Lajoie's post-baseball years were generally pleasant. Always frugal, Lajoie was comfortably fixed when he quit baseball, and he held a succession of well-paying jobs as a representative for manufacturing firms in the Cleveland area. He also served a term as Cleveland boxing commissioner. In 1937 Lajoie was elected to the National Baseball Hall of Fame; two years later he was present along with the ten other living electees for Hall of Fame inaugural festivities at Cooperstown, New York.

Although the Lajoies were childless, they maintained close contact with a large number of friends and relatives and spent their winters in Florida, finally relocating permanently in 1943. Myrtle Everturf Lajoie succumbed to cancer in 1954; Lajoie died in Daytona Beach, Florida.

• A clipping file on Lajoie is at the National Baseball Library in Cooperstown, N.Y. Lajoie's full career playing record is in Craig Carter, ed., *Daguerreotypes*, 8th ed. (1990), p. 160; some differences in his major league statistics appear in *The Baseball Encyclopedia*, 10th ed. (1996), p. 1246, which are the figures used here. The best biographical treatment is J. M. Murphy, "Napoleon Lajoie: Modern Baseball's First Superstar," special issue of *The National Pastime* (Spring 1988). See also Bob Broeg, *Super Stars of Baseball* (1971); Eugene C. Murdock, *Ban Johnson: Czar of Baseball* (1982); Franklin Lewis, *The Cleveland Indians* (1949); Lee Allen, *The American League Story* (1962); Charles C. Alexander, *Ty Cobb* (1984); and "Triple Play: Cleveland's Hall of Fame Triumvirate," *Timeline*, Apr.–May 1992, pp. 2–17. An obituary is in the *New York Times*, 8 Feb. 1959.

CHARLES C. ALEXANDER

LAKE, Leonora Kearney Barry. *See* Barry, Leonora.

LAKE, Simon (4 Sept. 1866–23 June 1945), inventor and submarine pioneer, was born in Pleasantville, New Jersey, the son of John Christopher Lake and Miriam Adams. Inventiveness ran in the Lake family; Simon's father was the inventor and manufacturer of a window shade roller in Toms River, New Jersey, and later the proprietor of an iron foundry in Ocean City.

When Simon was three his mother died, and his father left him in the care of a step-grandmother while he went west. His father's return in 1874 prompted a move to Camden, New Jersey, and later to Philadelphia. The family settled in Toms River in 1881. Lake briefly attended the Clinton Liberal Institute at Fort Plain, New York, but did not graduate and quit school in 1884. Soon after, he enrolled in and completed a course in mechanical drawing at the Franklin Institute of Philadelphia.

Lake's first patent was granted in 1887, for a steering device for high-wheeled bicycles. He soon modified it into a safety device for the steering gear of boats and found a lively market in Chesapeake Bay. More important for the oyster-fishing trade was his invention of a noiseless winding device for dredges. It prevented kickback of the dredge's winch handle, eliminating a major risk that operators faced. His first attempt at an organized business was the establishment of a company to build a canning machine of his design, but his investors fled at signs of union resistance. Lake, a member of the Congregational church, married Margaret C. Vogel in 1890. They had three children.

Of Lake's more than 200 patents, his most important were those relating to submarines. Jules Verne's *Twenty Thousand Leagues under the Sea* (1873) had entranced him as a child, and as a youth he had made several submarine designs. In 1893 he went to Washington, D.C., to present the secretary of the navy with his plans for the *Argonaut*. His competitors were John Holland and George Baker of Chicago. Lake did not submit a proper bid for his boat's construction, and the contract was given to Holland.

Failure to win a navy contract did not deter him for long. In 1894 he built the *Argonaut Jr.*, which was essentially a sealed pine box that nonetheless could operate submerged for hours at a time. A hand crank propelled it, it had chain-driven wheels, and a hand-pump emptied its ballast tank. Its most novel aspect was Lake's "water gate," essentially an airlock that allowed crew members to step out of the boat onto the sea floor. This vessel was successful enough to attract backing from a wealthy patron and several small investors, allowing Lake to establish the Lake Submarine Boat Company. He contracted to build his *Argonaut I* at the Columbian Iron Works Dry Dock Company in Baltimore, where Holland's *Plunger* was being built. Both were launched in 1897.

Lake's *Argonaut I* was powered by a 30-horsepower gasoline engine that drew air from the surface through a pair of tubes. It also used his water gate and had wheels. The *Argonaut I* sailed more than 2,000 miles and made a successful open sea excursion from Cape

May to Sandy Hook during a storm that destroyed more than a hundred other vessels. This feat prompted a congratulatory telegram from Verne himself. The *Argonaut I* had not met with its inventor's expectations, however, and Lake modified it with another of his innovations: a free-flooding, schooner-shaped superstructure that improved the boat's surface buoyancy and performance. Holland's *Plunger*, however, was abandoned as a failure almost immediately.

The success of the *Argonaut I* allowed Lake in 1900 to organize the Lake Torpedo Boat Company of Bridgeport, Connecticut, to construct the *Protector*. Launched in 1902, this boat pioneered the use of hydroplanes, essentially horizontal rudders, fore and aft to submerge on an even keel. It was also equipped with an omniscope, which was much like the later periscope. After failing to interest the U.S. government in the *Protector*, Lake sold it to Russia. The boat was smuggled to Kronstadt to evade the neutrality laws. Russia bought eleven other submarines from Lake, including the *Lake X*, built to compete for a U.S. Navy contract with Electric Boat Company's *Octopus*. Construction delays prevented the *Lake X* from participating.

Lake lived abroad until 1910, having offices successively in St. Petersburg, Berlin, London, and Vienna. In Russia he received an offer of a new shipyard to produce a defensive submarine fleet. He refused, not wishing to raise his family in Russia. He also received an offer from Germany's Krupp Works for substantial royalties in return for the right to build and market submarines of his type. While he waited for his board of directors to approve the contract, Krupp officials discovered that he had neglected to file patents in Germany. Krupp canceled the offer and appropriated the plans. He then began considering the use of his submarines to recover cargo and as cargo vessels, but while in Austria he learned that the United States was again going to consider building submarines of his type. He returned to Baltimore to try to win this contract.

In 1911 Lake finally sold a submarine to the United States, the 161-foot *Seal*. This boat had four torpedo tubes in its bow and four more on its deck. Over the next eleven years, the U.S. Navy bought twenty-eight more Lake submarines. The disarmament movement that brought about the Washington Conference in 1922 heralded the decline of Lake's fortunes as well. By 1930 the United States had scrapped most of its *Seal*-type boats.

A patented concrete block was the centerpiece of Lake's next commercial venture, the Sunshine Homes Concrete Products Company. Lake intended this enterprise to produce low-cost homes. It did not deliver, and, to pay its debts, Lake sold his Torpedo Boat Company. He built a small salvage submarine in 1932 and then embarked on a quest to recover the treasure reputed to have been lost aboard the frigate HMS *Hussar* in 1780. By 1937 he had recovered no treasure, his fortune was gone, and his bank had foreclosed his home in Milford, Connecticut. He spent his last years trying to interest Congress in cargo-carrying submarines for use in World War II. He died in Bridgeport, Connecticut.

• Lake's *The Submarine in War and Peace* (1918) is a fair-minded appraisal of his work in relation to others. His autobiography, *Submarine* (1938), is primarily useful for information on his early life and does not deal with his last twenty years. Collections of original materials on the *Argonaut* and the *Protector* are in Alan Burgoyne, *Submarine Navigation* (1903), and in the Skarrett Collection, Submarine Library, U.S. Naval Submarine Base, Groton, Conn. See also Richard K. Morris, *John P. Holland, Inventor of the Modern Submarine* (1966), and Lake, "Voyaging under the Sea," *McClure's*, Jan. 1899. An obituary is in the *New York Times*, 24 June 1945.

ERIK M. CONWAY

LAKE, Veronica (14 Nov. 1919–7 July 1973), actress, was born Constance Ockleman in Brooklyn, New York, the daughter of Harry Ockleman, a Sun Oil Company seaman, and Constance Charlotte Trimble. At age eight Lake made her acting debut in the lead role in her school's production of *Poor Little Rich Girl*. In her teen years her family moved to Miami, where Lake's mother enrolled her in several beauty contests. Soon after, Lake landed a nightclub role with the Ritz Brothers, where she was spotted by a talent scout from MGM and encouraged to make a screen test.

With her family, Lake moved to Hollywood and enrolled in acting school, but she began looking for bit parts after MGM indefinitely canceled her test. She landed her first role as an extra in the 1939 Paramount film *All Women Have Secrets* and appeared under the name of Constance Keane in five minor roles for Paramount, MGM, RKO, and 20th Century–Fox. She played her first starring role as Veronica Lake opposite Ray Milland, William Holden, and Brian Donlevy in the 1941 Paramount film *I Wanted Wings*. While her film career spanned four decades, from 1939 to 1973, Lake appeared in only twenty-nine films.

Lake is best remembered for her blonde "peekaboo" hairstyle, which she first wore during the 1940 Busby Berkley film *Forty Little Mothers*. Its introduction created a national fashion trend and quickly established Lake as Hollywood's newest sex symbol. But in early films such as *Sullivan's Travels* (1942) and *This Gun for Hire* (1942), Lake also demonstrated a unique screen combination of beguiling independence and sensuality that served her well in both comedic and dramatic roles.

In spite of Lake's comedic success in *Sullivan's Travels*—a role that cast her as the carefree but lovable "hobo"—Paramount most often sought to cast Lake as a tough-as-nails counterpart to the male hero. In both *This Gun for Hire* and *The Glass Key* (1942), Lake was teamed with the then unknown Alan Ladd, and the screen chemistry between the two ignited one of Hollywood's most memorable pairings. Lake's alluring presence provided the perfect foil to Ladd's icy indifference. Their chemistry and the films' suspenseful storylines appealed to audiences and critics alike and made both films two of the year's top box office attractions.

Lake and Ladd would not appear together again in leading roles until the 1945 film *Duffy's Tavern*. They subsequently appeared in two more films: *The Blue Dahlia* (1946) and the box office flop *Saigon* (1948). During the four-year period between 1942 and 1946, Lake appeared in eight Paramount productions and one United Artists' production. All were well received by moviegoers, but none matched the popularity of the Lake-Ladd films. Also during the war years, like many film stars Lake was recruited to sell war bonds. Because of her immense popularity she became one of the government's best spokespersons; in 1942 alone she sold more than $12 million in bonds.

Lake's relationship with Paramount, however, was continually strained by contract disputes and bad publicity about her personal life. At the height of her popularity Lake was making as little as $750 a week, while similar box office draws such as Bing Crosby and Hedy Lamarr were making $5,000. Added to this were Lake's own personal difficulties. Married to MGM art director John Detlie in 1940, they divorced three years later amid rumors of Lake's infidelity, excessive drinking, and subsequent public outbursts. (They had one child together, who died in infancy.) Her personal problems, while never seriously affecting her box office potential, tarnished her image as the cool, detached, sexy heroine. In 1944 she was married to the film director and producer André de Toth. They had two children.

More upsetting to moviegoers was Lake's change of hairstyle. In the 1944 film *The Hour before the Dawn*, she tied back her hair, and while critics panned the film, the chief complaint came from the viewing public, who preferred Lake's peekaboo look. The trademark hairstyle had become an albatross that she would never be able to shake. Following a series of commercially unsuccessful films, Paramount decided to unite her once again with Alan Ladd in their third and final mystery thriller, *The Blue Dahlia*. It was Lake's last major box office success. In 1948 Paramount chose not to renew her contract. From that time until her death, she appeared in only four independent films.

Between 1949 and 1951 Lake guest-starred on several television shows, including "Your Show of Shows" and "Texaco Star Theater." In 1951, following the dissolution of her seven-year marriage to de Toth, Lake moved to New York and began touring nationally in Broadway productions. For eight years she worked steadily in the theater, but her long absence from Hollywood guaranteed a paucity of screen roles. In 1955 she married Joseph McCarthy, a music publisher and songwriter. They were divorced in 1960.

By 1961 Lake's theater career was also in jeopardy; a severely broken ankle, suffered during a dance routine, sidelined her for nearly two years, and thereafter theater producers were unimpressed with her auditions. Lake, in desperate need of money, took a minimum-wage factory job and later worked as a cocktail waitress at the Colonnade Room in New York's Martha Washington Hotel.

Rediscovered in 1962 by a *New York Post* reporter, Lake was offered a job as a hostess for a Saturday night television program, "Festival of Stars." In 1963 she also appeared in one final New York revival of *Best Foot Forward*. It was a critical success but a commercial flop, and in desperation Lake took to drinking heavily and walking the streets for handouts.

Hoping to revitalize both her health and her career, Lake moved to Florida in 1965. She worked sporadically, starring in two low-budget films, *Footsteps in the Snow* and *Flesh Feast*, before moving to England in 1969. In the same year she published her autobiography, *Veronica*, and starred in two short-lived theater productions, *Madame Chairman* and *A Streetcar Named Desire*.

In 1971 she returned to the United States on a publicity tour for her autobiography but never again appeared in any film or theater production. She was married for a fourth time in 1972, to a sea captain, Robert Carelton-Munro, but they divorced one year later. Lake died in Burlington, Vermont, of acute hepatitis.

• An essay by Veronica Lake, "Starting as an Extra," is included in Charles Reed Jones, *Your Career in Motion Pictures, Radio, Television* (1949). A comprehensive source on Lake is Jeff Lenburg, *Peekaboo: The Story of Veronica Lake* (1983). Additional material can be found in Alain Silver and Elizabeth Ward, eds., *Film Noir: An Encyclopedia Reference to the American Style* (1992); E. Ann Kaplan, *Women in Film Noir* (1980); and Beverly Linet, *Ladd: The Life, the Legend, the Legacy of Alan Ladd* (1979). An obituary is in the *New York Times*, 8 July 1973.

PATRICK BJORK

LAKEY, Alice (14 Oct. 1857–18 June 1935), pure-food crusader, was born in Shanesville, Ohio, the daughter of Charles D. Lakey, a clergyman and, later, an insurance publicist, and Ruth Jaques, who died when Alice was six. The next year her father married Emily Jane Jackson, a painter. After public and private schooling in Chicago, Lakey, with her stepmother, went abroad in 1879 and studied "the art of singing in the old Italian method" in Florence, Paris, and London. Lakey gave concerts in England, where critics complimented her "sympathetic mezzo-soprano voice" and "refined and unaffected manner." Returning to America in 1888, Lakey gave a few performances, but poor health prevented a concert career, although she taught voice for several years. In 1895 the family moved to Cranford, New Jersey.

Lakey's father had always been concerned about his diet, a circumstance that sensitized Lakey to the rising pure-food campaign. In 1903 she wrote Secretary of Agriculture James Wilson (1836–1920) requesting that he send a speaker on this theme to address the Cranford Village Improvement Association, of which she was president. Harvey W. Wiley, himself chief of the Bureau of Chemistry and leader of the growing coalition seeking a national food and drug law, fulfilled the engagement. Impressed by both the man and the message, Lakey joined enthusiastically in Wiley's campaign. Armed by him with exhibits, information, and advice, Lakey lectured to women's groups throughout the nation. She convinced the New Jersey State Federation of Women's Clubs to endorse Wiley's version of a pure-food bill, which would be more rigorous than competing bills sponsored by manufacturing interests in the control of adulteration and misbranding. Lakey persuaded the national General Federation of Women's Clubs to create in 1905 a pure-food committee. She carried her message to the National Consumers League and became head of its pure-food committee (1905–1912). Lakey joined the inner circle of strategists planning how best to lobby for the law. When a committee of six met with President Theodore Roosevelt (1858–1919) in February 1905 to seek his open endorsement of pure-food legislation, Lakey was the only woman member. In the final stages preceding enactment of the Food and Drugs Act in June 1906, women sent one million letters and countless telegrams to members of Congress. Lakey was central in enlisting women, who proved crucial to securing the law.

As Lakey had been Wiley's committed disciple in seeking the law, so was she his unquestioning supporter in the way he sought to enforce it. When business interests challenged Wiley's decisions about benzoate of soda in catsup and canned foods, the use of sulphur dioxide on dried fruit, the denial of the right of rectified whisky to be called whisky, and many other controversial matters, Lakey defended him fiercely in lectures, letters, and print. Indeed, she esteemed the chief chemist as an idol, calling him "a Moses given to the people by God." When Secretary Wilson and presidents Roosevelt and William Howard Taft, upset by some of Wiley's extreme decisions that disturbed farmers and food processors, sought to curb his authority and bar his public expression of his views, Lakey wrote sharp letters to these high officials, which she released to the press. When a thwarted Wiley threatened to resign, she begged him to reconsider. When he finally resigned in 1912, she demanded his reinstatement and urged the ouster of his opponents within the government. "Show the enemies of the law," Lakey demanded of Taft, "that JUSTICE rules in this country and not a few privileged manufacturers. I do appeal to you, Mr. President, with all the earnestness that a woman can who sees dire trouble and CALAMITY falling on the land." Lakey publicly questioned aspiring presidential candidates in 1912 as to what they would do to assure vigorous enforcement of the food law. In 1916, as executive secretary of the new American Pure Food League, Lakey pressed President Woodrow Wilson's administration to strengthen the food and drug law, but without success.

Lakey was appointed in 1906 to the New York Milk Committee (as was Franklin D. Roosevelt) to assure the city a healthful milk supply. When her father died in 1919, Lakey assumed the publishing of his journal, *Insurance*, and this led to her appointment as insurance specialist of the General Federation of Women's Clubs. Lakey helped launch the movement to use insurance as a method of accumulating money for the college education of children. In 1924 Secretary of Commerce Herbert Hoover named her a member of the First National Conference on Street and Highway Safety. In 1926 Lakey took a pioneering step against noise pollution, bringing suit against a man whose radio loudspeaker she deemed a public nuisance.

In 1933 during the early New Deal, a bill was introduced into Congress to revise and update the Food and Drugs Act of 1906. Despite heart problems, Lakey revived the Pure Food League, again serving as executive secretary. The league supported the effort to remedy weaknesses in existing law and kept women's organizations apprised of developments. A coalition of such groups, by opposing crippling amendments and by lobbying vigorously for a strong bill, played a decisive role in achieving the Food, Drug, and Cosmetic Act of 1938. Lakey did not live to see this statute enacted, dying of a heart ailment three years earlier in Cranford, New Jersey.

• Lakey correspondence and texts of her news releases and articles are included in the Harvey W. Wiley Papers and in the National Consumer League Papers in the Library of Congress and in the Department of Agriculture and the Food and Drug Administration Records in the National Archives and the Washington National Records Center. Appraisals of Lakey's activities relating to pure food appear in Mark Sullivan, *Our Times*, vol. 2 (1927); Oscar E. Anderson, Jr., *The Health of a Nation* (1958); Caroline Bird, *Enterprising Women* (1976); James Harvey Young, *Pure Food* (1989); and Wallace F. Janssen, "Clubwomen and Their Fight for Food and Drug Laws," *GFWC Clubwoman* 68 (June/July 1990): 16–18, 44–45. An obituary is in the *New York Times*, 19 June 1935.

JAMES HARVEY YOUNG

LAMAR, Gazaway Bugg (20 Oct. 1798–5 Oct. 1874), business entrepreneur, was born near Augusta, in Richmond County, Georgia, the son of Basil Lamar, a landholder, and Rebecca Kelly. Lamar received little formal education, although he had private Latin instruction. By age twenty-three and married to his first wife Jane Meek Creswell, whom he wed in October 1821, Lamar became a commission merchant in Augusta and, by 1823, in Savannah. Lamar's expanding enterprises included banking and steamboating.

The Georgia legislature appointed Lamar director of the Planter's Bank of the State of Georgia in 1825. He also became the second largest stockholder in the Mechanics' Bank of Augusta by 1836. In 1833 Lamar invested in and experimented with iron steamships for commercial navigation. In 1834 he launched the *John Randolph*, the first commercially successful iron steamboat in the United States, as one of his fleet of eighteen in the Iron Steamboat Company in Augusta.

Lamar advocated free and direct trade between the South and Europe. As a conservative Democrat and constitutionalist, he helped form the State Rights party of Chatham County, Georgia, in February 1834 and entered his first and only foray into elective politics when he lost the aldermen's election in Savannah that fall.

In June 1838 his steamboat *Pulaski* exploded and sank, killing more than one hundred passengers, including Lamar's wife and six of their seven children. Lamar, his eldest son, and his sister survived. Turning to religion and temporarily abandoning shipping, Lamar returned to Augusta to rebuild his life. Within a year he married a Virginian, Harriet Cazenove, with whom he had five children. In 1845 the Lamars moved to Brooklyn, New York, where he resumed business as a commission merchant and invested in commercial vessels. By 1850 Lamar tired of the cotton business and sought other profitable ventures. With several associates, Lamar established in February 1851 the Bank of the Republic in New York City and served as president until 1855, when he resigned to devote more time to shipping and commission activities. He remained a director, resuming the presidency in May 1860. The directors of the Bank of Commerce in Savannah appointed Lamar its first president in May 1856; he resigned four years later.

From banking, Lamar turned his interests to insurance, becoming a director of the Great Western Insurance Company and a trustee of the Republic Fire Insurance Company in 1855. In 1856 he organized the Lamar Insurance Company. Lamar also became the exclusive agent for the American Guano Company in six southern states. Lamar speculated in stocks and bonds, always with an eye to increasing his fortune. Despising ostentatious displays of wealth, Lamar instead gave money to a broad spectrum of charities, from educational, literary, religious, and humanitarian societies to individuals.

In an 1863 letter to New York mayor Fernando Wood, Lamar wrote that "No man ever accused me with being a Southern man *with Northern proclivities*, and if any one were to have the hardihood to do it . . . I do not know that I could restrain my indignation." A late and reluctant convert to secession, Lamar embraced the Confederate cause when disunion became inevitable. Lamar's residency in New York gave him the opportunity to help the southern states on the brink of war in 1860–1861.

As part of Lamar's plan for disunion presented to South Carolina governor William Gist in 1860, he secretly purchased 10,000 guns from the Federal government to stock the South Carolina arsenal. He obtained a printing contract for the first Confederate treasury notes, delivered in April 1861. Lamar also served as a conduit for diplomatic correspondence until threats on his life outweighed his usefulness in New York to the Confederacy. Remaining in the city until shortly after his wife died in May 1861, Lamar returned to Savannah.

Lamar supported the Confederacy, often at the expense of his business interests. Lamar advised Confederate secretary of the treasury Christopher Memminger and other officials, with most of his suggestions unheeded. Lamar's contributions during the war included constructing a floating battery for the Savannah harbor, reorganizing a hospital for war casualties, engaging in a personal crusade against speculators, serving as paymaster of state militia troops (15 Sept. 1861–c. July 1862), helping to formulate fiscal policy for the Confederate government, and convincing bankers to finance the fledgling government.

A year after the first Confederate banking convention in Atlanta (June 1861) chose Lamar as its first president, the bankers' confidence in the Confederacy waned. Lamar advocated a stringent direct tax on people, income, and property, but Memminger rejected the proposal. Lamar realized that cotton would be his best wartime investment. Fearing for the safety of his warehoused cotton, Lamar organized the Importing and Exporting Company in the spring of 1863 to ship the cotton through the Union blockade. A letter to New York congressman Fernando Wood, intercepted and published by the *New York Times* (7 Oct. 1863), suggesting a collaborative effort in blockade running, caused a minor uproar in the North and the South. Ever the practical businessman, Lamar explained his belief that the need for supplies should outweigh the concerns for international law and military strategy.

Lamar, disillusioned by 1864 with the financial confusion in the Confederacy, anticipated southern defeat and sought to protect his business interests. On 6 January 1865 Lamar voluntarily signed the Federal loyalty oath, while stating, "I have the conscientious belief that I did my share in support of the Confederacy, while I was in condition to do it." The Federal government confiscated his stored cotton and personal papers. Lamar was arrested on a charge of stealing U.S. property when he legally moved his own cotton. Found guilty, fined $25,000, and sentenced to three years imprisonment by a military commission, Lamar appealed. Lamar spent his last years in court battling to recoup over $1 million for the cotton. On 2 January 1873 the Court of Claims awarded to Lamar $578,343.51, the largest individual award of the postwar period, which he finally received in April 1874. Six months later he died in New York City; his will directed his heirs to fight for the other half of his claim. The family finally received almost $75,000 from three additional grants in 1919.

An Augusta citizen posthumously described Lamar as "high-toned, honorable, generous, and honest in his convictions." Eschewing a planter's life, Gazaway Bugg Lamar succeeded as a businessman—banker, commission merchant, and shipper—in both the agrarian South and the industrial North, earning respect for his financial acumen.

• The Library of Congress and the University of Georgia hold personal papers of Gazaway Bugg Lamar. Some of Lamar's correspondence can be found in the Howell Cobb Collection, University of Georgia. Robert Neil Mathis, "Gazaway Bugg Lamar: A Southern Entrepreneur" (Ph.D. diss., Univ. of Georgia, 1968), contains the most complete account of Lamar's personal and business life, correcting inaccuracies in earlier articles by Edwin B. Coddington and Thomas Robson Hay. Mathis published two articles from his dissertation: "Gazaway Bugg Lamar: A Southern Businessman and Confidant in New York City," *New York History* 56 (July 1975): 298–313, and "The Ordeal of Confiscation: The Post–Civil War Trials of Gazaway Bugg Lamar," *Georgia Historical Quarterly* 64 (1979): 339–52. Lamar published an undated (c. 1869) pamphlet, *To Andrew Johnson, Ex-President of the United States*, about his postwar travails. An unflattering obituary is in the *New York Times*, 8 Oct. 1874.

SUSAN HAMBURGER

LAMAR, John Basil (5 Nov. 1812–15 Sept. 1862), writer and planter, was born in Milledgeville, Georgia, the son of Zachariah Lamar, a merchant and planter, and Mary Ann Robinson. Lamar attended Nathan S. S. Beman's School at Mt. Zion, Georgia, and the University of Georgia for one year (1827–1828). He never married. After 1830 his main residence was in Macon in a house that he called the Bear's Den. He also had a house in Americus, Georgia, near the plantations that he managed. He owned land in thirteen Georgia counties and Florida.

Lamar served in the Georgia House of Representatives from 1837 to 1838 and as an aide to Governor Charles McDonald from 1839 to 1843. He also served in the Seminole War in Florida in 1840 as a private. He served for five months as a Democrat in the U.S. House of Representatives in 1843 but then resigned. Politics did not appeal to him. He gave as his reason his weak lungs and lack of practice in public speaking.

Besides managing Lamar plantations, he also managed those of his brother-in-law Howell Cobb, who was very active in politics. On the plantation Lamar practiced crop rotation and other intelligent plantation practices and was very successful financially. He understood how to make and keep money.

Despite his success as a planter, Lamar over several years considered selling his plantations and investing in government securities, which he said "would yield me a genteel support, without having to slave myself after scoundrelly overseers." He probably would have preferred to travel and devote himself to literary works. He made at least four trips to Europe and several in the United States. On the eve of the Civil War he was planning a trip to the Holy Land and to Egypt.

Lamar owned an extensive library, which he apparently used regularly and encouraged his nieces and nephews to use. He was very devoted to his sister, Mrs. Howell Cobb, and her children, for whom he did a great deal. He was a vestryman of Christ Episcopal Church in Macon and served as a trustee of the University of Georgia from 1855 to 1858. He did much to aid civic and various public movements to improve conditions in Macon.

Lamar is best remembered as an author of local color sketches, titled "Homespun Yarns." The best known are "Polly Peablossom's Wedding" (Aug. 1842), "The 'Experience' of the Blacksmith of the Mountain Pass" (Sept. 1842), "The Fortune Hunter's Misadventure" (Dec. 1842), and "Cornelius Corntassel's First Affair of Honor" (June 1843). These were all originally published in *The Family Companion*, a Macon literary magazine of 1842–1843. A brief summary of "The Blacksmith of the Mountain Pass" can exemplify his work. A blacksmith in the North Georgia mountains swore he would whip every Methodist minister who came to the area. When a new Methodist minister arrived, he beat up the blacksmith and made him promise to come to church. At camp meeting the blacksmith was converted and soon became a Methodist minister himself. His sketches were widely copied in newspapers, and thus Lamar became well known as an author throughout Georgia. He wrote at least two other sketches that were not published in his lifetime. One of these, "The Devil in the Wolf Pen," was later published in the *Atlanta Constitution* (date unknown). The other has not been located.

Lamar and Cobb were both staunch Unionists and members of the Constitutional Union Party in 1851; they did not advocate secession until Lincoln's election in 1860. Then their views changed. Lamar was an active member of Georgia's secession convention in January 1861.

When war came in 1861, Lamar purchased uniforms for Macon volunteers. He reduced cotton plantings and increased food production on his and Cobb's plantations. He became an aide to his brother-in-law, who served as a Confederate brigadier general. Cobb in September 1862 was ordered to hold his position in Maryland so that Stonewall Jackson could capture Harpers Ferry, where there were considerable supplies and munitions. In this campaign Lamar was wounded in the Battle of Crampton's Gap, Maryland, on 14 September 1862, and died the next day. Cobb wrote Mrs. Cobb that Lamar was "struggling to rally our broken lines" when he was wounded. Lamar was buried in Rose Hill Cemetery in Macon.

Thus Lamar's literary fame rests on only six pieces, but as a southern humorist he showed real talent and great promise. However, he evidently wrote for his own pleasure and not as a professional. During his lifetime and since he has been compared to the better-known Augustus B. Longstreet and his *Georgia Scenes*. Lamar's sketches entitle him to a modest place as a southern humorist.

• The following manuscript collections in the University of Georgia Library, Athens, contain Lamar materials: Howell Cobb Papers; Cobb-Lamar-Erwin Papers; John B. Lamar Papers; and Trustees' Minutes, Demosthenian Society Papers. A typescript copy of "The Devil in the Wolf Pen" from the *Atlanta Constitution* is in the possession of Milton Leathers, Athens. Thomas A. Burke, ed., *Polly Peablossom's Wedding, and Other Tales* (1851; repr. 1972), also includes "The 'Experience' of the Blacksmith of Mountain Pass." Ida Young, Julius Gholson, and Clara Nell Hargrove, *History of Macon, Georgia, 1802–1950* (1950), and Mildred Lewis Rutherford, *The South in History and Literature* (1906) treat Lamar in context.

KENNETH COLEMAN

LAMAR, Joseph Rucker (14 Oct. 1857–2 Jan. 1916), U.S. Supreme Court justice, was born in Ruckersville, Georgia, the son of James S. Lamar, a minister of the Disciples of Christ church, and Mary Rucker. A scion of two prominent planting families in northeast Georgia, Lamar grew up in comfortable circumstances in Augusta, Georgia, where his father held the pastorate of the First Christian Church. After preparatory schooling in Georgia and Baltimore academies, Lamar attended the University of Georgia but took his baccalaureate degree from Bethany College in West Virginia in 1877. He briefly attended the law school of Washington and Lee University but did not take a degree. He read law in the offices of an Augusta attorney and was admitted to the Georgia bar in 1878. At college Lamar met his future wife, Clarinda Pendleton, whom he married in 1879. They had three children, including one who died in infancy.

Lamar taught Latin at Bethany College for a year and then began a successful law practice in Augusta. He served two terms as a Democrat in the Georgia House of Representatives, 1886–1889. In 1893 the governor and state supreme court chose him as one of the revisors of the state's Civil Code, which was adopted in 1895. Lamar was a diligent amateur historian whose contributions on the early legal history of Georgia were well received. A Confederate memorial address he delivered in 1902 that first brought him to national attention extolled the service of Confederate common soldiers and called on white Georgians to provide vocational education to African-American tenant farmers and sharecroppers, "not the mere education of books, but the education that comes from contact with the superior mind." Such opinions, faintly progressive for their time and place, reflected the paternalistic views of Lamar's class.

Lamar was first appointed to the state supreme court in 1903 and was then elected in 1904. During his brief tenure, Lamar wrote opinions upholding the state's regulatory powers over such matters as the sale of cotton seed but restricting its taxing powers, and expanding the fiduciary obligation of corporate directors toward shareholders. After he resigned in 1905, he returned to private practice, representing railroads and other corporations.

When William Howard Taft went to Augusta for a golfing vacation after his successful presidential campaign in 1908, he met Lamar on the links and cultivated a social relationship. In 1910 the president nominated his golfing companion to the U.S. Supreme Court, one of five appointments that Taft made in his one term. Taft sought men who were competent lawyers, preferably with judicial experience, of moderately conservative to mildly progressive political leanings. The Senate promptly confirmed the nominee, and Lamar took his seat in 1911. His distant, more conservative, and better-known cousin, Lucius Quintus Cincinnatus Lamar, had served on the Court from 1888 to 1893.

Lamar's most influential contribution to constitutional development was *United States v. Grimaud* (1911), which upheld congressional delegation of authority for management of federal lands to the secretary of agriculture. His conclusion that "Congress was merely conferring administrative functions upon an agent, and not delegating to him legislative power" long served as a touchstone of congressional power to delegate administrative functions to executive and independent regulatory agencies. *Grimaud* was consistent with other Lamar decisions upholding federal regulatory authority, avoiding a regression to the antiregulatory dogmas of *United States v. E. C. Knight* (1895) and *Adair v. United States* (1908). Lamar was somewhat more suspicious of state regulatory power under the due process and equal protection clauses of the Fourteenth Amendment and even the Contracts Clause of Article I, then far advanced into desuetude. For example, he voted with the majority in *Coppage v. Kansas* (1915) to strike down state prohibition of yellow-dog contracts, which forbade employees from joining unions. On issues of state regulation of race relations and labor unions, his dicta and voting positions suggest that he held conventionally conservative views in matters of labor union activities (*Gompers v. Bucks Stove and Range Company* [1911], upholding the constitutionality of injunctions prohibiting boycotts) and racial segregation (*McCabe v. Atchison, Topeka & Santa Fe Railway* [1914], in which Lamar refused to join the majority's vigorous condemnation of a railroad's refusal to supply luxury accommodations for black passengers).

Woodrow Wilson, a boyhood friend, tapped Lamar for extrajudicial service as a special delegate to the so-called A.B.C. Conference in 1914, at which three South American nations attempted to mediate the disputes between the United States and Mexico resulting from the Mexican Revolution. Lamar served competently in a hopeless task, given Wilson's determination to oust the Mexican caudillo Victoriano Huerta.

Lamar's service on the Court came to an end when he suffered a stroke in September 1915. He died of heart failure in Washington, D.C., the following January and was interred in Augusta. His colleagues and associates unanimously regarded him as amiable, diligent, and learned. His successor on the Georgia Supreme Court, Joseph H. Lumpkin, said of him in eulogy that "he loved his fellowmen, and they loved him. He was thoughtful of others . . . kind without weakness . . . friendly without loss of self-respect" (146 Ga. 845–46).

Joseph Lamar's five years on the Court happened to fall during a period of tranquility in that institution's history. Relatively few great cases came before the Court in those years, and none that either reversed major trends or struck out in radical new directions. Between 1910 and 1915 the Court generally upheld federal regulatory legislation and avoided expanding substantive due process and liberty-of-contract doctrines that inhibited state and federal regulatory power. By temperament and outlook a moderate conservative, Lamar had no occasion to distinguish himself from a bench that differed little from his own orientation. Though he wrote 113 opinions for the Court and eight dissenting opinions, almost none were memorable or had an impact on legal development. Their general tenor suggests that President Taft got just what he hoped for in Justice Lamar, a competent jurist who avoided ideological extremes.

• Lamar's papers are in the University of Georgia Library, Athens. His widow, Clarinda P. Lamar, published a book-length biography, *The Life of Joseph Rucker Lamar, 1857–1916* (1926), which is intimate and domestic in approach, stressing the social and personal relationships of the jurist and his wife. Eulogies containing facts and opinions about him are in 241 U.S. v–xx and 146 Ga. 841–848. Leonard Dinnerstein, "Joseph Rucker Lamar," in *The Justices of the United States Supreme Court, 1789–1969: Their Lives and Major Opinions*, comp. Leon Friedman and Fred L. Israel, vol. 3 (1997), is a modern evaluation. Two studies notice Lamar's contributions in the context of the Court's history: John E. Semonche, *Charting the Future: The Supreme Court Responds to a Changing Society, 1890–1920* (1978), and Alexander M. Bickel and Benno C. Schmidt, Jr., *The Judiciary and Responsible Government, 1910–21* (1984). Some of his contributions to Georgia legal history are in the *Reports* of the Georgia Bar Association, 1892, 1898, 1900, 1907, 1908, 1913.

WILLIAM M. WIECEK

LAMAR, Lucius Quintus Cincinnatus (17 Sept. 1825–23 Jan. 1893), U.S. representative and senator from Mississippi, secretary of the interior, and U.S. Supreme Court justice, was born in Putnam County, Georgia, the son of Lucius Quintus Cincinnatus Lamar, a state judge, and Sarah Williamson Bird. Lamar was educated at Emory College under the guidance of college president A. B. Longstreet, graduating in 1845. Lamar married Longstreet's daughter, Virginia, in 1847; the couple had four children. Virginia Lamar died in 1884, and he married Henrietta Holt in 1887.

After practicing law briefly in Covington, Georgia, Lamar moved to Oxford, Mississippi, when Longstreet accepted the presidency of the state university. He opened a law office and for a short time taught mathematics at the university. He returned to Covington in 1852 and was elected as a Democrat to the state legislature in 1853. Despite this early political success, in 1855 Lamar moved permanently to Oxford, Mississippi, where he again joined the university faculty and simultaneously worked as an attorney. He also acquired land and slaves, but agriculture remained an avocation only. In 1857 Lamar won election to the U.S. House of Representatives, and after that politics was his true vocation.

In Congress Lamar advocated "southern rights" and justified slavery. He stood with Senator Jefferson Davis of Mississippi in trying to avoid separate state secessions from the Union at the Charleston Democratic Convention of 1860, but when the movement gained momentum he wrote Mississippi's secession ordinance. Lamar provided a conservative rationalization that linked the Confederate revolution with the Declaration of Independence of 1776 and with the republicanism of the founding fathers.

After combat as a lieutenant colonel of the Nineteenth Mississippi in Virginia, Lamar fell ill with a debilitating paralysis and resigned from military duty in 1862. Named as Confederate states commissioner to Russia, Lamar traveled to Europe and temporarily undertook desultory duties in England and France in cooperation with other Confederate diplomats and agents. Political circumstances caused the Confederacy to abort the Russian mission, and Lamar was recalled without reaching his destination. During 1864 he did some work for the War Department in Richmond, but mainly he acted as Confederate president Davis's emissary in Georgia, where he conducted a public campaign in favor of the Habeas Corpus Act and other unpopular government actions. In December he rejoined the army and served as a judge advocate to a military court in Richmond.

Following the Civil War Lamar returned to the university and his law office in Mississippi. Eight years later his career took its most important turn of the postwar era. Democrats, including Lamar, had not seriously contended in the election of 1869 while Mississippi remained under federal Reconstruction. A new state constitution, however, granted political rights to former Confederates. To limit Democratic resurgence Republicans redrew congressional district boundaries to isolate the heavily white counties of the northeast and to ensure black majorities elsewhere. Lamar became the nominee in a district that was now 72 percent white, and he easily won election. Congress removed his Confederate disability, and he reentered the U.S. House of Representatives in 1873. This placed him for the first time in the forefront of state politics and ended his apprenticeship behind older antebellum leaders such as Jefferson Davis.

In Congress Lamar was particularly noted for his advocacy of an end to sectional hostility and the Reconstruction policies of the Ulysses S. Grant administration. He presented his reconciliation argument in nationalistic terms and at the same time aggressively sought "home rule" in the South. For Lamar home rule meant that federal government intervention should give way to Democratic control at the state level and to white political supremacy. This combination of patriotic nationalism and partisan objectives in Mississippi became the hallmark of Lamar's career in the House and later in the Senate after 1877.

Lamar's plea for sectional reconciliation and his superb oratorical ability gained him special prominence in 1874 when, in the House, he gave a eulogy on the death of Massachusetts senator Charles Sumner, who was perceived by many to have been a vituperative enemy of the South. Lamar successfully raised the theme of national reunion above personalities and sectional antagonisms and advanced, in the Congress and before a generally admiring news media, the general drift of the country toward fervent nationalism.

Throughout his congressional career Lamar pursued conservative fiscal goals and separated himself from the agrarian wing of his party, which sought economic reform through inflation of the currency. He was especially eloquent in opposition to inflation by silver coinage. He combined his conservatism on the currency issue with consistent support of nationally financed internal improvements, especially those benefiting the economically depressed southern region. In favoring subsidies for Mississippi River and railroad projects, among others, he often voted with Republicans and fellow southern Democrats but against the northern Democrats who favored retrenchment in government spending.

In Mississippi Lamar played a leading role in the state election of 1875. His pronouncements before the state Democratic convention and at various campaign gatherings called for ending racial strife, which he blamed on Republicans, and for implementing the constitutional right of blacks to vote. Meanwhile, on the county level Democratic partisans employed harassment and violence. This strategy of conciliatory rhetoric and intimidation carried the state, and two years later the Democratic legislature sent Lamar to the Senate, where he succeeded Republican James Alcorn.

Before entering the Senate Lamar turned again to national politics and to the crucial issue of the disputed presidential election of 1876. From his House positions as chair of the Democratic caucus and chair of the Committee on the Pacific Railroad he played an important role. After the presidential electoral votes of Louisiana, Florida, and South Carolina were disputed, leaving the outcome of the election in doubt, Lamar concluded that the Republican candidate, Rutherford B. Hayes, would ultimately be confirmed and that civil conflict threatened if Democrats attempted to thwart Hayes's election. From the beginning of the crisis he sought to avoid a constitutional collapse and armed struggle by fashioning an arbitration process satisfactory to both sides. In addition Lamar sought assurance from Hayes that if elected president he would withdraw federal support from the Republican state governments in the South.

Lamar presented to the House an electoral commission bill that provided for a board of senators, representatives, and Supreme Court justices to judge the disputed electoral votes. Later Lamar nominated the House members. When the commission moved to recommend that the electoral votes go to Hayes, however, Lamar joined other Democrats in preventing the count completion. Then he used the threat of obstruction to pressure Republicans into further guarantees of an end to Reconstruction in the south. With assurance gained, Lamar abandoned the Democratic filibuster and joined again with those favoring completion of the vote count. During this controversy Lamar also reported out of committee a Texas Pacific Railroad bill that was used by some southern Democrats as a price for ending the filibuster. Lamar gave energetic justification for this legislation, which would provide a connection between the South and the Pacific Coast, but there is no evidence that he traded support of Hayes for Republican assurances on the Texas Pacific project. A desire for a peaceful succession of the presidency, even a Republican presidency, and home rule in the South shaped his actions throughout this critical period.

In the Senate, which Lamar entered in 1877, he continued to advocate federal subsidies for internal improvements and to oppose silver coinage. A speech against the Bland-Allison Silver Act stands out as one of his most notable oratorical achievements during these years. He suffered much criticism at home in Mississippi, where silver coinage was popular, but won sympathy from the fiscally more conservative northeastern wing of the Democratic party. In addition he espoused traditional Democratic opposition to high tariffs on imports. Lamar's effectiveness suffered however, due to poor Senate attendance as a result of his failing health and his wife's terminal illness. Despite this and the unpopularity of his position on silver coinage, the Mississippi legislature returned him to the Senate in 1882.

A new stage in Lamar's career began in 1885 when Grover Cleveland, the first Democratic president since the Civil War, chose him as secretary of the interior. Lamar's appointment symbolized Cleveland's policy of sectional reconciliation and of rewarding southern leaders. Lamar himself wrote his old comrade Davis, "I think I may go far towards convincing the people that the South desires to serve the best & highest interests of a common country."

As secretary, Lamar attempted, with small success, to implement civil service reforms and to end fraud in the pensions bureau, as well as to buffer Indian lands and tribal organizations from unbridled western development. His reformative policy also opposed unsubstantiated railroad land claims for railroad construction. However, before Lamar completed his full term Cleveland appointed him to the U.S. Supreme Court in 1887.

Lamar won confirmation after a bitter partisan and sectional fight. Lamar was the first Confederate to take a seat on the Court, and he represented there the full reintegration of the South into national governmental institutions, an end that Lamar had long sought. As justice, Lamar generally followed the conservative leadership of the Republican judges, seldom dissenting from the majority view. He argued for expansive federal authority in internal improvement legislation and in interstate commerce, most notably in *Kidd v. Peterson*. Ineffectually he advocated states' rights in matters of social and political authority against a hostile Court majority. His health remained poor while he served on the Court, and he wrote no additional opinions after the spring of 1892. Lamar died in Macon, Georgia.

Appointment to high office signaled personal victory for Lamar and success for the political strategy he had regularly employed since Sumner's death in 1874. In a larger context Lamar's presence in the cabinet and on the Court represented the entry of the United States into a nationalistic era as well as an end to the government's concern with maintaining black voting rights and a two-party system in the South.

• Lamar manuscript collections are located at the University of Mississippi Library, the Southern Historical Collection at the University of North Carolina Library, the Miscellaneous Collection at Emory University Library, the Lunsford Collection at the Georgia State Department of Archives and History, and at the Mississippi State Department of Archives and History. Biographies of Lamar include James B. Murphy, *L. Q. C. Lamar: Pragmatic Patriot* (1973); Wirt A. Cate, *Lucius Q. C. Lamar: Secession and Reunion* (1935); and Edward Mayes, *Lucius Q. C. Lamar: His Life, Times, and Speeches* (1896). Mayes was Lamar's son-in-law and his book includes otherwise unavailable Lamar letters and materials. See also a series of articles on Lamar by Willie D. Halsell in the *Journal of Mississippi History* (1943–1947). An obituary is in the *Atlanta Constitution*, 24 Jan. 1893.

JAMES B. MURPHY

LAMAR, Mirabeau Buonaparte (16 Aug. 1798–19 Dec. 1859), second president of the Republic of Texas, was born near Louisville, Georgia, but grew up near Milledgeville, the son of John Lamar and his wife (and cousin), Rebecca Lamar, farmers. His older brother, Lucius Quintus Cincinnatus, was a noted Georgia jurist whose son of the same name became a Mississippi statesman, senator, and U.S. Supreme Court justice.

Young Mirabeau lacked discipline for scholarly pursuits but was an eclectic reader in history and literature and occasionally wrote poetry. Between 1819 and 1823 he entered mercantile and publishing partnerships in Cahaba, Alabama, then the capital. In 1823 his political career began when his brother secured his appointment as private secretary to Georgia's new governor, George M. Troup. A vociferous supporter of states' rights, Troup opposed President John Quincy Adams's 1825 treaty with the Creek Indians that allowed them to keep a wide strip of land on the Alabama-Georgia border. Mirabeau Lamar's experience with Troup shaped his political course and his anti-Indian policy in Texas. Troup sent Lamar, a descendant of Huguenot immigrants, to Savannah to meet the 1825 tour of the marquis de Lafayette and to escort him to the Georgia capital. Troup's political defeat in 1828 forced Lamar to find another means of livelihood.

Lamar moved his wife Tabitha Jordan (whom he had married in 1826) and daughter to Columbus, Georgia. He began publishing the *Columbus Enquirer*, a states' rights weekly, on 29 May 1828. The following year voters chose him to represent Muscogee County in the state senate; headed for reelection in 1830, he withdrew from politics when his wife died. He overcame his melancholia, a family trait, during the next two years by writing poetry in the romantic style of Lord Byron and by traveling and visiting friends and relatives in Georgia and Alabama.

Unsuccessful in his race for the U.S. House of Representatives in 1832, Lamar joined the Georgia States' Rights party, formed to oppose President Andrew Jackson's threats against South Carolina during the nullification crisis. A second unsuccessful campaign for a seat in Congress ended Lamar's immediate political ambition, and he sold his interest in his newspaper. Despondency returned after the death of his father and young sister, which was followed by the suicide of his brother Lucius in 1834.

As before, Lamar turned to travel, and in June 1835 he left Georgia for Nacogdoches, Texas, to explore the Mexican state then in turmoil. He rode horseback along the old Spanish road to the communities along the Brazos River, talking with people about possible land speculation and the history of early Texas for a future book. He gathered information for the book for several years, but the project was never completed. Recovered, Lamar returned to Georgia in November to settle his affairs before moving to Texas.

Lamar sailed to Texas at the end of March 1836, a few weeks after the Texans had declared independence from Mexico and organized the Republic of Texas. He had $6,000 from Georgia speculators for land, but the interim government could not act amid the crises following the fall of the Alamo and the massacre at Goliad. On 10 April he joined General Sam Houston's army encamped on the Brazos River preparing for a stand against a Mexican force led by President Santa Anna. On 20 April Lamar, a private, helped rescue two men during a short skirmish with the Mexican cavalry at the junction of Buffalo Bayou and the San Jacinto River where both armies were camped. Houston rewarded Lamar's courage by promoting him to colonel in command of the Texan cavalry; the next day the Texans successfully attacked the Mexican line and captured some 600 men. The day after the battle, scouts found Santa Anna, who, in exchange for his life, ordered the remainder of his army to retreat, thus ending the war in Texas.

Lamar, now a war hero, served as secretary of war in interim president David G. Burnet's cabinet from 4 May to 26 May 1836. He resigned in protest over two issues: the plan to return Santa Anna to Mexico, where he was supposed to secure recognition of Texas's independence, and the widespread sentiment among Anglo Texans favoring annexation to the United States. Playing bizarre politics, the unpopular Burnet made Lamar a major general and commander in chief of the army on 29 June; but when he arrived at Victoria in July to take charge, neither the regular army nor the fresh volunteers from the United States would accept him. The election for permanent officers for the republic took place in September 1836, and Lamar was chosen vice president to serve under President Sam Houston for the next two years. Houston could not succeed himself, and Lamar forged a coalition of anti-Houston men and won the presidency at the close of 1838.

During his three-year term, December 1838–December 1841, Lamar abandoned the cautious, frugal course Houston had taken, such as furloughing the army and avoiding trouble with Mexico and the Indians. These steps had reduced the need for issuing large sums of paper money and increasing the national debt. Lamar had been pleased when the United States rejected Texas's bid for annexation in 1837 and, as president, envisioned a grand republic stretching southwest and northwest along the upper Rio Grande. He even contemplated a national bank and state-supported education, financed by public lands. He sent troops to expel the Cherokees and other east Texas Indians and tried to run off the Comanches on the western frontier.

In 1839 Lamar also successfully urged removal (although only temporarily) of the capital from coastal Houston, named for his political adversary, to the frontier town of Austin, which was geographically more central to his grand scheme. Near the end of his term, Lamar sent a doomed expedition to take Santa Fe, where its members were captured and held prisoner near Mexico City. In 1842 Mexico, which had not recognized Texas as independent, sent retaliatory raids to San Antonio and took captives. A punitive Texan expedition was also captured south of the Rio Grande. Lamar had inherited a $2 million debt, but his policies and his issues of paper money left a $7 million debt for his successor, Sam Houston. Lamar retired to his plantation near Richmond, Texas, and busied himself collecting historical material for his book.

The annexation of Texas and the subsequent war between Mexico and the United States allowed Lamar to receive a commission as a lieutenant colonel of Texas Volunteers, and he served the battle of Monterrey. Afterward, he organized the municipal government at Laredo and represented south Texas in the Second Texas Legislature in 1847. He married Henrietta Maffitt in 1851; they had one daughter. In 1857 he received an appointment as U.S. minister to Nicaragua and Costa Rica, where he served for twenty months. Two months after his return to his Richmond home, he died there of a heart attack.

The ambitious Lamar was personally charming and persuasive, but his idealistic vision for Texas was beyond the means of the infant Republic of Texas. Honest but a poor manager of his assets or those of the republic, the romantic poet was able to act the hero in a short military scenario but was unable to guide a frontier nation in need of a firm and practical hand.

• Lamar's papers are in the Texas State Library and Archives in Austin and also are published in Charles Adams Gulick, Jr., et al., eds., *The Papers of Mirabeau Buonaparte Lamar* (6 vols., 1921–1927; repr. 1968). Stanley Siegel, *The Poet President of Texas* (1977), is the most recent biography of Lamar and is strong in details about his presidency; careless editing, however, mars the work. Earlier biographies, Asa Kyrus Christian, *Mirabeau Buonaparte Lamar* (1922), Herbert Gambrell, *Mirabeau Buonaparte Lamar: Troubador and Crusader* (1934), and Philip Graham, *The Life and Poems of Mirabeau B. Lamar* (1938), are more laudatory than analytical. Two articles in the *Southwestern Historical Quarterly*, Nancy Booth Parker, "Mirabeau B. Lamar's Texas Journal," vol. 84 (Oct. 1980–Jan. 1981), and M. Baptista Roach, "The Last Crusade of Mirabeau B. Lamar," vol. 45 (1941), are informative as are the introductions in the first volume of his reprinted papers and in Michael R. Green, ed. and comp., *Calendar of the Papers of Mirabeau Buonaparte Lamar*, published in 1982 by the Texas State Archives. An obituary is in the *Galveston Weekly News*, 27 Dec. 1859.

MARGARET SWETT HENSON

LAMB, Arthur Becket (25 Feb. 1880–15 May 1952), chemist and editor, was born in Attleboro, Massachusetts, the son of Louis Jacob Lamb, a jewelry manufacturer, and Elizabeth Becket. Lamb's youthful interests in chemistry, physics, biology, and mathematics were reinforced by his studies at Tufts College (A.B., A.M. 1900, Ph.D. 1904). Arthur Michael, a leading American organic chemist and professor at Tufts, turned him toward chemistry. Lamb did some research in biology and inorganic and organic chemistry at Tufts, but he decided to concentrate on physical chemistry. After two years of graduate study in chemistry at Tufts, Lamb was attracted to graduate work at Harvard by Theodore W. Richards. His Ph.D. from Harvard (1904) was based on work with Richards on properties of aqueous solutions; his Tufts doctorate was based on his thesis with Michael in organic chemistry.

Lamb spent 1904–1905 on a traveling fellowship in Germany, where his interest in physical chemistry was increased by work in W. Ostwald's laboratory at Leipzig and by Fritz Haber. Lamb translated Haber's monograph, published as *Thermodynamics of Technical Gas Reactions* (1908); this gave the theoretical foundation for Haber's epoch-making work on the combination of nitrogen and hydrogen to form ammonia (the fixation of atmospheric nitrogen). After serving as instructor at Harvard (1905–1906), Lamb moved to New York University, where he had various administrative assignments but little opportunity to do research. In 1912 he returned to Harvard as director of the chemical laboratory and started an active research program.

In 1917 Lamb took part in research on defense against gas warfare, becoming finally a lieutenant colonel in the Chemical Warfare Service. Here he contributed to the development of charcoals for gas masks and became an expert on the adsorption of gases by solids, particularly for the oxidation of toxic carbon monoxide to carbon dioxide. After the war he spent two years organizing the Fixed Nitrogen Laboratory in Washington, D.C., to study the preparation of nitrogen fertilizers from atmospheric nitrogen. In 1917 he also started his major life work, the editorship of the *Journal of the American Chemical Society*, which he retained until 1950. During these years the amount of chemical research conducted in the United States increased greatly, and the journal's size increased accordingly.

Returning to Harvard in 1921, Lamb carried the laborious task of editing the journal in addition to teaching, research, and administrative activity. He extended the referee system for evaluating papers; although he was firm in maintaining good standards for publication, he was very helpful to authors, particularly younger ones. His editorial policies displeased a few established chemists, but it was generally felt that he was fair and unbiased in a very difficult task. The *Journal* became the largest chemical journal in the world and one of the best. In 1923 he married Blanche Anne Driscoll, with whom he would have two children.

Lamb raised funds for and helped design the new chemical laboratories at Harvard, the Mallinckrodt and Converse laboratories, which opened in 1928. He also designed Byerly Hall for science at Radcliffe. His course in freshman chemistry, his only continuing teaching assignment, featured colorful lecture demonstrations and was good, if not inspiring.

Lamb's forty-six scientific papers were on a variety of problems in analytical, inorganic, and physical chemistry and show him to be a good research chemist. He had sixteen patents, mainly resulting from his war work. He arranged patent pools so that his collaborators in the work received a fair share of the royalties. He also acted as a chemical consultant, but his editorial work was his most important scientific activity.

He received the Nichols and Priestley medals from the American Chemical Society, held membership in the National Academy of Sciences and the American Philosophical Society, and was an honorary Fellow of the Chemical Society of London. He was president of the American Chemical Society in 1933.

Quiet, agreeable, and strong-willed if necessary, Lamb possessed both a sense of humor and the ability to inspire devotion in his collaborators. He served as a deacon in the Unitarian Church and enjoyed tennis and mountaineering. His career was an example of unselfish and effective public service in science. He died in Brookline.

• Some of Lamb's papers are in the Harvard archives. Valuable biographical accounts, by people who worked with him for many years, are Allen D. Bliss, *Journal of the American Chemical Society* 77 (1955): 5773–79, and Frederick G. Keyes, National Academy of Sciences, *Biographical Memoirs* 29 (1955): 201–33. The latter contains a list of his scientific publications.

D. STANLEY TARBELL

LAMB, John (1 Jan. 1735–31 May 1800), revolutionary war officer, was born in New York City, the son of Anthony Lamb, an optician and mathematical instrument maker. His mother was a Dutch woman with the maiden name of Ham. In England Anthony Lamb was an accomplice in burglary with the notorious Jack Sheppard. They were tried together for their crimes, and Sheppard was hanged, and Anthony Lamb was sentenced to banishment in the colonies. Arriving in Virginia in 1724, he completed an indentured servitude in that colony and moved to New York City, where he prospered in his craft. John Lamb entered into his father's business. In 1760 he became a liquor merchant, trading principally with the West Indies. Although he probably had only minimal formal education, Lamb was conversant in Dutch, German, and French. In 1755 he married Catherine Jandine; they had three children.

During the Stamp Act crisis of 1765–1766, Lamb was a leader in the New York Sons of Liberty, sharing popularity with Isaac Sears and Alexander McDougall. He fought the Stamp Act in speeches, anonymous broadsides, and articles in the New York and Boston press. He headed the Committee of Correspondence of the Sons of Liberty, which maintained contact with protest leaders in other colonies. On 13 February 1766 he, Sears, and Joseph Allicoke led a mob that forced a New York merchant and the naval officer of the Port of New York to refrain from using stamped documents for the clearance of outgoing vessels. Lamb belonged to the faction of the Sons of Liberty that favored direct action and the improvement of the rights and welfare of the lower-class citizens. He served as an inspector for ensuring merchants' compliance with an agreement not to import British goods.

Lamb orchestrated rioting against Parliament's New York Restraining Act of 1767, which had suspended the New York legislature for violation of the Quartering Act of 1765. The assembly eventually complied with the Quartering Act and had Lamb arrested in December 1769 for publishing two broadsides criticizing it for doing so. Lamb was initially held on a charge of seditious libel, but he was freed by court order for lack of evidence.

With the renewal of rebel fervor resulting from the Tea Act–Coercive Acts crises of 1773–1774, Lamb was back in the thick of anti-British action in New York City. He served on a committee of fifteen of the Sons of Liberty for coordinating protest measures with other colonies. Lamb and his fellow radicals suffered a setback as conservative merchants, fearing disorder, obtained the support of a majority of New York City citizens and assumed direction of the movement. However, with the outbreak of fighting at Lexington and Concord, radicals in New York again had popular support. Lamb and Sears led mobs that unloaded provisions destined for General Thomas Gage's army in Boston, closed New York Harbor, and seized weapons and other military stores at City Hall, at Fort George (in the city), and at Turtle Bay (in the East River).

The New York Provincial Assembly commissioned Lamb a captain of an artillery company on 30 June 1775. Lamb's company linked up with the Canadian invasion army under General Richard Montgomery on 19 September 1775. Lamb and his artillery troops assisted in the capture of St. Johns on 2 November 1775 and Montreal eleven days later. With Benedict Arnold on the Plains of Abraham outside of Quebec during early December, Lamb found that his guns, protected by logs encased with ice, were no match for the heavier British artillery. In the attack on Quebec's citadel at the lower end of the town on 31 December 1775, Lamb's left cheek was hit by grapeshot, which carried away part of the bone and also resulted in the loss of his left eye. Left unconscious on a pile of shavings in a cooper's shop, he was made a prisoner of war.

While Lamb was still a captive, Congress rewarded him for his heroism at Quebec by appointing him, on 9 January 1776, major of the Second Continental Artillery Regiment and commander of artillery of the northern army. Paroled on 2 August 1776, Lamb resided with his family at Stratford, Connecticut. On 1 January 1777 Congress appointed him colonel, and the next day he was exchanged. He joined George Washington's army at Morristown and participated in the defense of an army depot at Danbury, Connecticut, against a raid by governor and colonel William Tryon. At Compo Hill near Danbury on 28 April 1777, Lamb's three guns attempted to break up a British bayonet attack. Grapeshot tore flesh from his left side, but he was rescued. At Fort Montgomery on 5 October 1777, he spiked the American guns and escaped before the British overran the post.

Lamb served as commander of artillery at West Point from 1779 to 1780 and as surveyor of ordnance, a congressional appointment, from 6 March 1779 to 12 August 1780, when the office was abolished. His primary duty as surveyor was inspection of arsenals, with particular attention to the one at Springfield, Massachusetts. Serving under his good friend Arnold at West Point, Lamb never suspected that officer's treason. Lamb questioned Arnold regarding sending men on work details outside the fort, saying, "We shall neither be able to finish the works that are incomplete nor [be] in a situation to defend those that are finished."

Second in rank to General Henry Knox in the artillery corps, Lamb fought at the siege of Yorktown. He had command of the heaviest bombardment of the siege on 17 October, involving some one hundred artillery pieces. He was brevetted a brigadier general on 30 September 1783.

With a revival of a coalition of artisans and small merchants who had been the mainstay of the former Sons of Liberty and who held again the balance of political power in New York City, Lamb was elected to the New York General Assembly in December 1783. He ardently opposed the return of Loyalists and the recovery of their property. Loyalists already residing in the city were intimidated from voting. In the legislature Lamb stood against Loyalist rights and supported a charter for the Bank of New York. He chaired committees on the militia and trade regulation, and he was a member of a joint committee of both houses to consider relations between New York and the future Vermont. He vacated his seat in the legislature in 1784 to become collector of the Port of New York, an appointment made by his friend, Governor George Clinton. Lamb had charge of customhouses in New York City and Sag Harbor, Long Island. He made a fortune speculating in the purchase of confiscated Loyalist estates, buying the estate of John Rapalje at Brookland Ferry and part of the Ten Towns tract, a stretch fifty miles long and twenty miles inland along the St. Lawrence River.

On 30 October 1788 at Fraunces Tavern Lamb organized an antifederalist group, which called itself the Federal Republicans. The group's purpose was to concert plans of antifederalists throughout the nation in opposition to the ratification of the Constitution, and it favored holding a second constitutional convention. In Federalist New York City, a mob prepared to attack his house, but Lamb and three relatives, heavily armed and with the house barricaded, discouraged the crowd from doing any damage.

In respect for Lamb and a display of nonpartisanship, President Washington reappointed Lamb collector of the Port of New York on 6 August 1789. In the 1790s Lamb served as vice president of the Society of the Cincinnati and was an officer in the Humane Society of the City of New York. Suffering from gout, he left his actual customs duties to his son-in-law Charles Tillinghast, the assistant collector. Tillinghast died of yellow fever, and a clerk took over the duties of the customhouse until a new assistant collector could be named. When the clerk embezzled large sums and fled to Europe, Lamb pledged his fortune to cover the losses. The government seized and sold all of his property, and Lamb died in poverty, probably in New York City.

Lamb distinguished himself as a rabble-rouser, a propagandist, and an able artillery officer. Captivity, periodic illnesses, and detached command assignments kept him from most battles engaged in by Washington's army. While Lamb was making the transition from popular leader to soldier, General Montgomery, writing to General Philip Schuyler on 24 November 1775, said of him that he was a brave and intelligent officer but of "bad temper, turbulent and troublesome."

• The John Lamb Papers are in the New York Historical Society. Lamb correspondence is also in the George Washington Papers, Library of Congress; the papers of the Continental Congress, National Archives; and in manuscript collections of prominent revolutionary war figures. Isaac Q. Leake, *Memoir of the Life and Times of General John Lamb* (1850; repr. 1971), contains letters to and from Lamb. For his role in the Sons of Liberty and N.Y. politics, see Roger J. Champagne, "New York's Radicals and the Coming of Independence, *Journal of American History* 51 (1964–1965): 21–40, and Champagne, *Alexander McDougall and the American Revolution in New York* (1975); Herbert M. Morais, "The Sons of Liberty in New York," in *The Era of the American Revolution*, ed. Richard B. Morris (1939; repr. 1965); Edward Countryman, *A People in Revolution: The American Revolution and Political Society in New York, 1760–1790* (1981); and Alfred E. Young, *The Democratic Republicans of New York, 1763–1797* (1967). For Lamb from a Tory view, see Thomas Jones, *History of New York during the Revolutionary War* (2 vols., 1879; repr. 1968). E. Wilder Spaulding covers N.Y. politics during the Confederation period in *New York in the Critical Period, 1783–1789* (1932; repr. 1963). For comment on Lamb's military career, see William E. Birkhimer, *Historical Sketch of the Organization, Administration, Matériel, and Tactics of the Artillery, United States Army* (1884; repr. 1968), and Lynn L. Sims, "The Military Career of John Lamb" (Ph.D. diss., New York Univ., 1975). A brief obituary is in the *New York Daily Advertiser*, 2 June 1800.

HARRY M. WARD

LAMB, Joseph Francis (6 Dec. 1887–3 Sept. 1960), piano ragtime composer, was born in Montclair, New Jersey, the son of James Lamb, a building contractor, and Julia Henneberry. Early ragtime journalists assumed he was an African American from Missouri, like Scott Joplin and James Scott, the other masters of the genre, but Lamb was actually Irish American and never set foot in Missouri. The son of immigrants, he went from elementary school in Montclair to St. Jerome's (c. 1900–1904), a Catholic prep school in Berlin (renamed Kitchener), Ontario, Canada. His mother hoped he would choose the priesthood, but Joe started composing waltzes and two steps, claiming later to have been self taught. H. H. Sparks of Canada published some of these early efforts in 1905 and 1906, shortly after Lamb left Canada.

After spending time with his older married brother, James, in San Francisco, Lamb spent several years at clerical jobs in New York, commuting from Montclair. He became enthralled with ragtime through Scott Joplin's famous "Maple Leaf Rag," published in 1899 by John Stark. Lamb later met Joplin in Stark's New York offices in 1907.

Stark had rejected three of Lamb's rags, probably because of their technical difficulty. Impressed with Lamb's talent, however, Joplin added "arranged by Scott Joplin" to the cover of "Sensation," one of the rags Stark had rejected. Stark honored the endorsement by publishing "Sensation" in 1908.

This was a historic reversal of racial roles at a time when African Americans were at the mercy of a white-dominated music industry that savagely caricatured them on sheet music covers. Lamb inspired an even deeper cultural role reversal by becoming Joplin's protégé. Joplin's espousal of the artistic standards of West European art music and his insistence on the primacy of the notated score transformed Lamb's exuberant, impetuous rag style into a highly lyrical but still virtuosic one. In an age when literacy and European culture presumably flowed from whites to blacks, Joplin and Lamb presented a startling, defiant paradox.

Lamb tried his hand at songwriting for H. H. Sparks and a few Tin Pan Alley publishers, using his own name as well as pseudonyms. In 1910 Lamb worked for several months for publisher J. Fred Helf as an arranger, notating songs of other composers for publication, and as a songplugger, demonstrating the Helf catalog at theaters, beer gardens, and other public gatherings. The following year he married Henrietta "Ettie" Schultz, who demanded that he abandon the idea of a musical career for what was then considered a more respectable livelihood. They settled in Brooklyn and had one son. Lamb joined L. F. Dommerick & Co. Inc., an import/export textile firm, in 1914. He remained there, retiring as an executive in 1957. When Ettie died in 1920 during the great influenza epidemic, the ragtime era was over and Stark had long since retreated to St. Louis. Lamb returned to New Jersey with his son, again commuting to his firm in New York.

He courted Amelia Collins, a Brooklyn neighbor, whom he married in 1922. They built a home in Brooklyn and had three children. Decades later Rudi Blesh and Harriet Janis found him there while researching their book, *They All Played Ragtime* (1950). This catalyst of the ragtime revival established the long-obscure Lamb as one of the "Big Three" composers of classic piano ragtime and romanticized him as a reclusive white emulator of an African-American musical genre. Lamb's inclusion in the inner circle was based on only twelve Stark publications, less than half the output of either Joplin or Scott.

Joplin's death in 1917 and Scott's in 1938 made Lamb the surviving patriarch of classic ragtime. His home became a point of pilgrimage, his interviews and letters crucial documents for the ragtime revival. Neoragtimers, especially Robert "Ragtime Bob" Darch, convinced him to complete partial rags he had carried in his head for decades and also to write new ones, which accelerated a resurgence of ragtime composition decades after its vintage era. Lamb's further development of the genre greatly enhanced his artistic stature and opened creative vistas for even serious composers in academia, such as William Bolcom and William Albright. Lamb thus emerged from personal obscurity shortly before he died. Folksong artist Burl Ives sponsored him in the American Society of Composers, Authors, and Publishers. Folkways Records released *Joseph Lamb: A Study in Classic Ragtime*—Lamb reminiscing and playing his own rags—in 1959. The same year Lamb gave his first public performances in decades on a triumphant return visit to Canada. He died in Brooklyn.

Lamb's artistic and historical reputation have been considerably altered in the decades since his death. A posthumously published collection of thirteen works, *Ragtime Treasures* (Mills Music Co., Inc.), appeared in 1964; a single work, "Alaskan Rag," appeared in the third edition of *They All Played Ragtime* (1966); two recently transcribed rags, "Brown Derby #2," from a homemade audio tape of Lamb performing his own rags in the late 1950s, and "Ragtime Reverie," from a sketchbook discovered in 1993, were premiered at the 1994 Scott Joplin Ragtime Festival in Sedalia, Missouri; and at least thirteen other rags, which have been performed publicly and recorded from manuscript. With many songs and miscellaneous piano pieces, published and unpublished, this legacy transforms Lamb from least to most prolific of the classic ragtime composers.

Until 1977 Lamb's vintage rags were considered his main legacy. *Ragtime Treasures* was looked upon as mere emulations of the vintage rags, and the pre-Joplin works were dismissed as boyhood attempts at composition. A scholarly investigation of Lamb and his music by Joseph R. Scotti revealed a fully matured Lamb style before the actual meeting with Joplin; both "light" and "heavy" rags in the vintage period; a piano novelty style developed in the 1920s; and a highly refined late style of exquisite lyricism and economy of texture.

The recently discovered sketchbook is the only known one for any of the "Big Three" classic ragtime composers. It includes sketches for works in *Ragtime Treasures* and the complete "Ragtime Reverie," which combines vintage style with later ones and contains contrapuntal passages, a rare device in ragtime composition.

The twelve vintage rags published by John Stark include the highly syncopated "heavyweight rags," as

Lamb called them, blending Joplin's lyricism with Scott's virtuosic span of the keyboard. "American Beauty" (1913) and "Ragtime Nightingale" (1915) are the most popular. Rags like "Champagne" (1910) and "Bohemia" (1919), which Lamb called "light" rags, are masterpieces of the milder, tuneful style of the cakewalk. "Sensation" (1908) displays the flamboyant style predating Joplin's influence.

Ragtime Treasures is a kaleidoscope of all five Lamb styles. "Cottontail" and "Ragtime Bobolink" exemplify the expanded harmonic vocabulary, lyrical melodic lines, and exquisitely honed texture of the late style in which every note is crucial. "Hot Cinders" and "Arctic Sunset" alternate strains of 1920s piano novelty style with vintage two-beat ragtime. "Alabama" and "Blue Grass" graft country elements onto the systematic syncopation of ragtime. "Old Home Rag," one of the three rejected by Stark before Joplin's intercession, represents the flamboyant early style. Even more than the vintage rags, *Ragtime Treasures* reveals Lamb's ingenius absorption and blending of widely divergent musical materials.

• Important compositions by Lamb not mentioned in the text include the vintage rags "Ethiopia" (1909), "Excelsior" (1909), "American Beauty" (1913), "Cleopatra" (1915), "Contentment" (1915), "Reindeer" (1915), "Patricia" (1916), and "Top Liner" (1916); and the posthumously published rags "Bird Brain," "Chimes of Dixie," "Firefly," "Good and Plenty," "Old Home," "Thoroughbred," and "Toad Stool" (all from *Ragtime Treasures*). The basic account of Lamb's rediscovery is in Rudi Blesh and Harriet Janis, *They All Played Ragtime* (1950). Joseph R. Scotti, "Joe Lamb: A Story of Ragtime's Paradox" (Ph.D. diss., Univ. of Cincinnati, 1977), investigates Lamb's life and music from a scholarly perspective. Two excellent biographical sources are Russ Cassidy, "Joseph Lamb, Last of the Ragtime Composers," *Jazz Monthly* 7 (Aug., Oct., Nov., and Dec. 1961), which originally appeared in *Jazz Report* (Jan., Feb., Mar., and Aug. 1961), and Marjorie Freilich Den, "Joseph F. Lamb: A Ragtime Composer Recalled" (M.A. thesis, Brooklyn College, 1975). A published analysis of Lamb's rags is Scotti, "The Musical Legacy of Joe Lamb," in *Ragtime: Its History, Composers, and Music*, ed. John Hasse (1985).

JOSEPH R. SCOTTI

LAMB, Martha Joanna R. N. (13 Aug. 1826–2 Jan. 1893), author and editor, was born Martha Reade Nash in Plainfield, Massachusetts, the daughter of Arvin Nash and Lucinda Vinton. She was a precocious child and began to write poems and stories before she was ten. From an early age she enjoyed reading books from her father's library, especially ones devoted to history. She lived for a while in Goshen, Massachusetts, and attended school both in Northampton and in Easthampton, Massachusetts. Tutored in mathematics, she became so adept that she not only taught for a while in a polytechnic institute but also revised a mathematics textbook for use in high schools. She also read widely in English literature and studied foreign languages.

In 1852 she married Charles A. Lamb, who had two children by a previous marriage, and lived with him for some time in Ohio and then, beginning in 1857, in Chicago. Charles and Martha Lamb evidently had no children. In Chicago, where her husband was a furniture salesman, Lamb was prominent in charity work; she helped found the Home for the Friendless and the Half-Orphan Asylum, and in 1863 she was appointed secretary of the first Sanitary Fair, which was held to help medical personnel during the Civil War, and was so successful in her work that she was also active in the 1864–1865 fair.

In 1866 Lamb moved to New York City, and the teeming metropolis fascinated her at once. In the midst of much work as an author and editor, she began painstaking research into the history of New York City. For parts of fourteen years she consulted historians and scholars; interviewed members of important New York families and was given access to many of their private papers; and read in the Library of Congress and the Department of State Library in Washington, D.C., the Astor Library in New York City, the New York City Library, and the libraries at the New York Mercantile Society, the New-York Historical Society, and Yale. Lamb published *The History of the City of New York: Its Origin, Rise and Progress* in two handsome octavo volumes (1877, 1880). The first volume, 786 pages in length and with 158 engravings, illustrations, and maps, summarizes early records kept in the region, discusses Dutch activities in the city, and describes Indian troubles and European political influences, the British presence, and the city government up to the eve of the American Revolution. The 820-page second volume contains 154 pictures and maps and takes up revolutionary activities and the peace following, New York City as the national capital, and the city during the nineteenth century—with emphasis on political institutions, inventions, the War of 1812, and peace and progress. Her enormous work was praised at once by reviewers in the United States and abroad for its exhaustive documentation, its solid historical value, and the charm and variety of its narrative form. In due time, commentators began noting that Lamb's work was a source of information freely used by later scholars without acknowledgment. Some modern historians mention the fact that Lamb insufficiently considered political corruption, economics, and social unrest in her history.

Lamb was honored by membership in at least twenty-six American and European historical and learned societies, including the American Historical Association and the Clarendon Historical Association of Edinburgh. In 1883 she bought and became editor of the *Magazine of American History*, in which capacity she solicited contributions by eminent writers and also published some fifty articles of her own, both signed and unsigned. She reprinted three such essays (May, June, July 1883) in a short book titled *Wall Street in History* (1883), in which she deals with early Dutch and English activities on Wall Street, the function of the street in the eighteenth century as a government and social center, and its emergence as a financial center.

Before, during, and after conducting her extensive historical researches, Lamb was active in New York society and in philanthropic endeavors and at the same time maintained a remarkable writing pace. She wrote a number of moralistic little books for children, including some she called parts of "Aunt Mattie's Library," for example, *Laughing Kittie and Purring Kittie with Other Little Folks at Robinwood* (1868), *The Play School Stories for Little Folks* (4 vols., 1869), and *Fun and Profit* (1870). She edited one book of poems for children actually produced in the form of an owl, titled *The Christmas Owl: A Budget of Entertainment* (1881), another in the form of a basket, titled *The Christmas Basket: Holiday Entertainment* (1882). She also published relatively minor works for adult readers, notably *Spicy: A Novel* (1873), a mystery story featuring the 1871 Chicago fire; "The Coast Survey" (*Harper's New Monthly Magazine*, Mar. 1879), in which she put some of the mysteries of mathematics in simpler terms; *The Homes of America* (1879); and *A Guide for Strangers to General Grant's Tomb in Riverside Park* (1886).

Active and working almost to the end, Lamb caught cold during one of her daily visits to her editorial office, contracted pneumonia, and died in New York City. In 1896 Constance Cary Harrison, the versatile novelist and memoirist, republished part of Lamb's *History of New York* and included a brief supplemental volume titled *Externals of New York*, all of which was an indication of the continuing popularity of Lamb's work.

• Lamb's papers are in the Duke University library; the New Jersey State Historical Society Collections, Trenton; and the Massachusetts Historical Society library, Boston. Frances E. Willard and Mary A. Livermore, eds., *A Woman of the Century: Fourteen Hundred-Seventy Biographical Sketches Accompanied by Portraits of Leading American Women in All Walks of Life* (1893), contains a bibliography of Lamb's works and in addition summarizes her career, as does Daniel Van Pelt, "Mrs. Martha J. Lamb," *Magazine of American History* 29 (Feb. 1893): 126–30. Milton M. Klein, ed., *New York: The Centennial Years 1676–1976* (1976), calls Lamb's history of New York City "magisterial"; David C. Hammack, *Power and Society: Greater New York at the Turn of the Century* (1982), calls it a "classic"; and in Kenneth T. Jackson, ed., *The Encyclopedia of New York City* (1995), it is defined as one of several "laudatory interpretations of the city's history" written late in the nineteenth century. Frank Luther Mott, *A History of American Magazines, 1865–1885* (1967), provides facts concerning Lamb and the *Magazine of American History*. An obituary is in the *New York Times*, 3 Jan. 1893.

ROBERT L. GALE

LAMB, Theodore Lafayette (11 Apr. 1927–6 Sept. 1984), southern liberal, advertising executive, and lawyer, was born in Detroit, Michigan, the son of Foster Lamb, a butcher, and Theodosia Braswell. Lamb's father owned a small farm near Alexander, outside of Little Rock, Arkansas, where Lamb grew up. After attending the local one-room school, he hitchhiked into Little Rock, where he attended high school and served as class president. In 1944 he took classes at both Little Rock Junior College and Louisiana State University before enlisting in the army. He was sent to Yale University and trained as a Japanese linguist. He then served from 1944 to 1947 as a second lieutenant in the army's 441st Counterintelligence Corps. He returned to Yale under the GI Bill and graduated in 1950.

After taking a business training program in accounting from General Electric Company in Syracuse, New York, Lamb settled in Little Rock in 1952 to open his own advertising agency, Ted Lamb and Associates. By 1956 the firm was at its height, with offices in Little Rock, Dallas, Princeton, New Jersey, and Milford, Connecticut. Although bank advertising was his specialty, in 1954 he also did political work for Orval Faubus, a rising Arkansas Democratic politician, who was then viewed as a liberal. Lamb played a key role in Faubus's first gubernatorial race when incumbent governor Francis Cherry charged that Faubus had attended Commonwealth College, a labor school with Communist leanings. Lamb and *Arkansas Gazette* editor Harry Ashmore arranged for a television appearance in which Faubus successfully explained his attendance. Faubus won the election and became governor in 1954.

In 1957 Lamb broke with Faubus when the governor sent the National Guard to bar blacks, who were armed with a court order, from attending Little Rock's Central High School. The next year Faubus invoked new legislation to close the Little Rock schools. The Women's Emergency Committee and a businessmen's group, identified as Southern Moderates, sought to reopen the schools by placing their own supporters on the school board. Lamb had decided to run in opposition to a known segregationist and received the businessmen's endorsement, although his position on integration was far more liberal than theirs. Lamb won his race and remained on the school board until 1964. The board was divided between three segregationists and three moderates. Lamb wrote that he "was the only race liberal member of the Board who . . . believed that racial segregation was immoral as well as illegal." In May 1959 segregationists launched a plan to purge some 100 teachers. The ensuing controversy led to recall elections in which the segregationists were defeated and the purge avoided. During his tenure on the board, Lamb argued for complete integration, opposing such subterfuges as freedom of choice and pupil assignment plans. As a result, he received physical threats, a steady stream of hate mail, obscene telephone calls, and bomb threats. When segregationists tried to prevent the opening of schools in 1959 by alleging the threat of a polio epidemic, Lamb contacted Dr. Jonas Salk and read at the board meeting a telegram from Salk that dismissed the threat.

Lamb's involvement in integration ultimately undermined his advertising business. Segregationists mounted an extensive boycott against integration supporters. One of Lamb's clients, a bakery, had its products boycotted and its drivers threatened. When Lamb's business disappeared, he failed to respond promptly, rejecting offers to leave the state or relocate his satellite offices. In 1965 he decided to retrain as a lawyer. His wife, the former Ardella Bullard, whom he had married in 1948, became a public school teacher and looked after their four children while he liquidated his Texas advertising interests and took one semester of law classes at Southern Methodist University. He then entered the University of Arkansas School of Law, where he twice made the dean's list and graduated seventh in his class in 1967. Establishing his practice in Little Rock, primarily as general counsel for the Teamsters Union in Arkansas, Oklahoma, and East Texas, he remained active in civil rights affairs. From 1965 to 1967 he served as chairman of the Arkansas Advisory Committee to the United States Commission on Civil Rights, but his repeated attacks on segregation in eastern Arkansas aroused such hostility that he was not reappointed. In 1969 he chaired both the Founding Committee of the American Civil Liberties Union of Arkansas and its legal panel. He remained active in legal work and negotiated contracts for basketball player Herbert "Goose" Ausbie.

Although physically small, Lamb was an imposing figure. A true southern liberal, he rejected numerous opportunities to move to the North and instead stayed in Arkansas to fight for racial equality. Happiest on his farm at Alexander, he also savored his connection with Yale University, serving as president of the Yale Club of Arkansas from 1960 until his death. After divorcing his first wife, in 1976 he married Deanna Jones, who had two children of her own. He died of pancreatic cancer at his home in Alexander.

• Lamb's papers, which consist of a scrapbook of newspaper clippings, letters, and telegrams, are in private possession. Shortly before his death, he compiled his own short memoir of the key events in his life, still in private possession. Irving J. Spitzberg, Jr., interviewed Lamb for his book *Race Politics in Little Rock, 1954–1964* (1967). An important interview by newspaperman Harry Pearson appeared in the Pine Bluff *Commercial*, 10 Jan. 1968. Obituaries are in the Little Rock *Arkansas Gazette*, 7 Sept. 1984, and the *New York Times*, 20 Sept. 1984.

MICHAEL B. DOUGAN

LAMB, Thomas White (5 May 1870–26 Feb. 1942), architect, was born in Dundee, Scotland, the son of William Lamb, a "moulder in a foundry," and Sarah Whyte, a "spinner in a factory." The family moved to New York before Lamb was a teenager. Lamb had opened his own architectural office on Fifth Avenue and was doing "general work" by 1892. What training he had received by this time is not known. He entered Cooper Union's general science program only two years later and graduated in 1898 with a bachelor of science degree, having taken only two courses that directly related to his architectural career: mechanical drawing and acoustics.

For five years Lamb was employed by New York City's Bureau of Buildings, first as a building inspector and then as a plan examiner. This hands-on experience provided an important cornerstone of his career, as it presented him with valuable opportunities to encounter all kinds of buildings and construction problems and to meet people like Marcus Loew and William Fox, future clients and moguls of movie theater empires.

Fox and Loew have both been credited with setting Lamb on his career path. One of Lamb's obituaries designated Loew, who in 1908 "called on [Lamb] . . . to draw up specifications for the motion-picture houses of the company, which was then beginning to expand." In a 1927 article in *Motion Picture News*, Lamb acknowledged Fox's City Theater on Fourteenth Street as his pioneering theater designing assignment.

While the 1909 City Theater was Lamb's first large commission, he was not a neophyte in the field. His firm's job book (begun in earnest in 1905) lists thirteen previous theater projects, though these mostly comprised alterations for existing buildings or unsuccessful proposals for new ones. An exception was the 1908 "Nicoland" in the Bronx, now considered to have been the first "purpose-built" movie theater in New York City.

Within a few years, Lamb combined essential characteristics of these inaugural projects—a purpose-built movie theater and a pretentious large-capacity stage house—with unprecedented lobby and lounge space and other creature comforts. In so doing, he created a new building type called the movie palace.

Lamb overturned most of the protocols of commercial theater design by producing huge, extravagantly embellished structures laden with plaster ornament, gold leaf, extravagant furnishings, and glittering marquees. They featured motion pictures, stage spectacles, theater organs, and the most up-to-date technical equipment, all concocted to impress the masses and provide a welcome respite from the humdrum concerns of real life.

Each of Lamb's pathbreaking creations erected between 1913 and 1919 outdid its predecessor in size, luxury, decoration, and appointments. Among these, the most important were built in Manhattan: the 1913 Regent, the first super-deluxe large theater built just for the movies; the 3,000-seat Strand, opened in 1914 and acknowledged as the world's first movie palace; and the 5,300-seat Capitol, whose huge size and magnificence were meant to eclipse any building its patrons had yet seen in 1919.

In this period and during the early 1920s, Lamb's movie palaces tended to adhere to Renaissance, Empire, and Adam styles in their decorative schemes. His special partiality to the low-relief and low-maintenance decorations devised by the eighteenth-century architect Robert Adam was defended in the December 1929 issue of *Architect and Engineer* as the style that he felt "most ably reflected the moods and preferences of the American people." By the mid-1920s, Lamb had detected a change of temperament and "an underlying demand for something more gay, more flashy."

Lamb then obligingly switched to Louis XVI and Italian baroque decorations and was led further afield to a gamut of exotic styles and a few "atmospheric" theaters whose ceilings simulated a semitropical night sky. During the 1930s his firm was equal to another shift in public taste and mood and began designing gleaming "moderne" cinemas festooned with aluminum decorations, zigzag patterns, and frosted glass.

In these later endeavours, Lamb was following rather than leading colleagues like John Eberson, Rapp & Rapp, and S. Charles Lee, movie palace architects who had started in his wake. Nevertheless, in this later period, Lamb's firm continued to contribute many original and glorious excesses to the American cultural landscape. Among these were the Midland in Kansas City and the Albee in Cincinnati (1927); Keith's Memorial in Boston, the Ohio in Columbus, and Loew's State (now called the Landmark) in Syracuse (1928); the San Francisco Fox (1929); and Loew's 175th Street Theater in New York (1930).

Though most of Lamb's commissions were theaters, his firm continued to do "general work." Within this category were a number of banks, Greyhound bus terminals, apartment and office buildings, stores, hospitals, and casinos, as well as such New York landmarks as Madison Square Garden (1925), the Pythian Temple (1927), and the Hotel Paramount (1927).

When engaged on Madison Square Garden, his office numbered about 200 people, including structural and mechanical engineers. The depression saw drastic reductions in staff and a considerable lessening in the pace of commissions. Lamb had time to submit a design for the Palace of the Soviets in Moscow and took great pride in the honorable mention he won in the international competition in 1932.

He remained active in the profession until the day of his death in New York City. He was survived by his third wife, Alfretta (Rhetta) Hurry, and six children. One child was born to his first wife, and three to his second, both of whom had died prematurely (his first wife around 1904 and his second, Elizabeth Jung, in 1919).

Thomas Lamb was one of the most prolific and successful theater architects in America and the originator of a widely dispersed and acclaimed building type. His theaters and movie palaces dotted most large and midsized cities on the North American continent, and they thrilled millions worldwide, in South America, the Caribbean, England, Europe, India, Asia, South Africa, and Australia.

• Thomas Lamb's job book, about 20,000 of his drawings, and other sporadic records of his firm are maintained in the Avery Archives of Columbia University. Information has been derived from birth registers of Dundee, Scotland; from records of the Office of Admissions, Cooper Union, New York; and from some unpublished and private sources (a manuscript by Philip Hamp and interviews with descendants). A few reflections by Lamb on his career are in "Good Old Days to These Better New Days," *Motion Picture News*, 30 June 1927, pp. 29–54, and in "Some High Lights in Motion Picture Theater Design," *Architect and Engineer*, Dec. 1929, pp. 53–54. Much information on Lamb's theaters can be found in most of the issues of *Marquee: The Journal of the Theater Historical Society* (see especially Hilary Russell, "An Architect's Progress: Thomas White Lamb," 21, no. 1 [1989]) and in that society's archive and research center in Elmhurst, Ill. Lamb's career is outlined and many of his theaters illustrated in Ben M. Hall, *The Best Remaining Seats: The Story of the Golden Age of the Movie Palace* (1961); Dennis Sharp, *The Picture Palace and Other Buildings for the Movies* (1969); and David Naylor, *American Picture Palaces: The Architecture of Fantasy* (1981) and *Great American Movie Theaters* (1987). See also Hilary Russell, *Double Take: The Story of the Elgin and Winter Garden Theatres* (1989), for information on Lamb's pre-1914 theaters, and "All That Glitters: A Memorial to Ottawa's Capitol Theatre and Its Predecessors," *Canadian Historic Sites* 13 (1975), for an overview of his Canadian work; and *The American Institute of Architects' Directory* (1892, 1895–1896). Obituaries are in the *New York Times* and the *New York Herald Tribune*, 27 Feb. 1942.

HILARY RUSSELL

LAMB, William Frederick (21 Nov. 1883–8 Sept. 1952), architect, was born in Brooklyn, New York, the son of William Lamb, a builder, and Mary Louise Wurster. After receiving a bachelor of arts degree from Williams College in 1904, Lamb studied architecture at Columbia University from 1904 to 1906. As was the aspiration of the advanced students of architecture of his day, however, Lamb soon left New York for Paris, France, to study at the École des Beaux-Arts, receiving his diploma in 1911.

Returning to New York, Lamb began working with the firm of Carrère & Hastings, a practitioner of the Beaux-Arts style and architects of the New York Public Library. Lamb's Beaux-Arts training was to serve him well throughout his career, particularly in the design aspects of plan and composition. In 1920 Lamb became a partner in the firm, renamed Carrère & Hastings, Shreve & Lamb, which became Shreve, Lamb & Harmon in 1929. With a reputation as a solid design and construction firm, it received commissions from Banker's Trust, General Motors (1927), Bankers Trust (1933), Hunter College (1940), and the *New York Times*. In July 1926 Lamb married Cuthbert Dufour; they had one child.

The most important commission for Lamb and the firm was for the Empire State Building (1929–1931). This commission was exceptional in all aspects: design, construction, height, and historical moment. Built during the Great Depression, the unprecedented 102 stories were completed in less than eighteen months, a feat of efficiency and urgency probably never to be replicated. Lamb's design, steel-framed, limestone-clad with polished steel ornament, is considered a model of dignified restraint, appropriate to the majesty of the building and to its mid-town site at Fifth Avenue and Thirty-Fourth Street. The Empire State Building aesthetically appears to grow, via simple massing and powerful visual vertical thrust, ever upward from street to setback tower to pinnacle, giving fully integrated expression to a distinctly New York architectural type, the setback tall building. Thus the definitive architectural type of the twentieth century, the skyscraper, found in Lamb's design a profound and lucid image.

Shreve, Lamb & Harmon received the gold medal of the American Institute of Architects' New York Chapter in 1931 for the design of the Empire State Building. Lamb's sleek design became an American icon and was made famous even during construction in sketches by architectural renderer Hugh Ferriss and in photographs by Lewis Hine. Recognizing the significance of his work, the American Institute of Architects spoke of the "noble simplicity" of Lamb's building; those words apply equally to Lamb himself.

Having built one of the greatest commercial landmarks in history, Lamb turned his attention to civic pursuits later in life. He aided the city's less fortunate through planning and zoning reform to provide low-income housing for poor families. President Franklin D. Roosevelt recognized Lamb's civic contributions by appointing him to the Federal Commission for Fine Arts (1937–1945). Lamb was also named coordinator of design for the 1939 New York World's Fair. He remains an underappreciated early American modernist, a transitional figure who quietly proceeded to transform American urban architecture from Beaux-Arts classicism into the contemporary skyscraper city. He died in New York City.

• A collection of Lamb's papers is in the Empire State Building Archive of the Avery Architectural Library, Columbia University. Lamb published an illustrated article, "The Empire State Building: The General Design," in *Architectural Forum* 54 (Jan. 1931): 1–8. Material on Lamb is in John Tauranac, *The Empire State Building: The Making of a Landmark* (1995). An obituary is in the *New York Times*, 9 Sept. 1952.

LESLIE HUMM CORMIER

LAMBEAU, Curly (9 Apr. 1898–1 June 1965), professional football player and coach, was born Earl Louis Lambeau in Green Bay, Wisconsin, the son of Belgian immigrants Marcel Lambeau, a building contractor, and Mary (maiden name unknown). His family came to the United States in the 1870s and settled in Green Bay. Because of his curly black hair, Lambeau immediately won the nickname "Curly." He attended East High School in Green Bay, where he competed in track and field and starred as a football halfback. He received his high school diploma in the spring of 1917.

After spending the ensuing summer working for his father's construction business, Lambeau enrolled briefly at the University of Wisconsin. When the school temporarily canceled its football program because of American entry into the First World War, he quickly returned home. He went to work again for his father and played for one of Green Bay's local football teams, the South Side Skidoos.

In the autumn of 1918 Lambeau entered the University of Notre Dame on a football scholarship. The starting fullback on Knute Rockne's first Notre Dame team, he lined up next to the legendary George Gipp in the backfield. At the end of the football season, Lambeau developed tonsillitis and returned to Green Bay for medical treatment. After his recovery he began working as a traffic manager for the Indian Packing

Company at a rate of $250 per month. Now earning a good wage and intent on marrying his high school sweetheart, Marguerite Van Kessel, Lambeau decided to stay in Green Bay rather than return to Notre Dame. He and Marguerite were married in August 1919; they later had one child.

In the fall of 1919 Lambeau convinced his supervisor, Frank Peck, to sponsor a football team. The company contributed $500 to outfit the club, which was captained by Lambeau and staffed with local athletes who had college playing experience. The team was soon called the "Packers," and the players agreed to split evenly any profits from ticket sales. The Packers were among the best teams in Wisconsin, winning eleven games in twelve contests. Lambeau earned $16.75 for his football exploits that year.

By 1921 the Green Bay Packers had entered the American Professional Football Association (APFA), a newly created league consisting of the best professional teams in the eastern and midwestern United States. Lambeau was the team's head coach and star halfback. He instituted an exciting and successful passing attack, a rare strategy because the large oval-shaped ball of that era was difficult to throw. Always looking to find the best players, Lambeau went so far as to hire collegiate players, using pseudonyms, for a late season game. APFA officials, however, discovered this violation of league rules and revoked the Green Bay franchise. Before the 1922 season started, Lambeau asked the association, which had recently renamed itself the National Football League (NFL), to reinstate the Packers. After Lambeau promised to follow league rules, his request was granted. For $1,000, Lambeau purchased the rights to the Green Bay franchise with money accumulated from selling shares in the team and making it a nonprofit and publicly owned corporation. The novel ownership concept saved the Packers, allowing the small-town team to survive in what would soon become a league of large markets.

Lambeau, meanwhile, aggressively pursued the best talent he could find to make the Packers competitive. As a result, from 1921 to 1928 the Packers enjoyed eight consecutive winning seasons. Lambeau became a very demanding coach; he held daily practices and was among the first to show game films to his players. Insisting on discipline, the hot-tempered Lambeau browbeat his team into winning. Newspaper reporters soon referred to him as the "Bellicose Belgian." He continued to emphasize an exciting aerial attack and recruited strong passers and excellent receivers to implement it.

With the acquisition of halfback Johnny Blood in 1929, the Packers blossomed into a championship squad, going undefeated for the season. By this time Lambeau had retired as a player, allowing rising stars like quarterback Red Dunn, end Lavvie Dilweg, and halfback Verne Lewellen to spearhead the Green Bay offense. The Packers again won NFL titles in 1930 and 1931. They continued to be one of the NFL's dominant teams, winning championships in 1936, 1939, and 1944, and producing Pro Football Hall of Fame inductees Cecil Isbell, Arnie Herber, and Don Hutson.

After the Second World War Lambeau and the Packers met with hard times. The Packers' executive committee became concerned about Lambeau's free-wheeling spending habits and the team's declining attendance. In 1947 the committee placed limits on Lambeau's authority, which up to this point had been almost limitless. Continuing disputes with management lessened Lambeau's enthusiasm for coaching the team. He began to spend long periods of time away from Green Bay on his newly acquired ranch in California. His association with film stars further alienated both the Packers' front office and Green Bay fans. The 1948 Packers won only three of twelve games, giving Lambeau only his second losing season since the team's inception. In 1949 the team won just two games.

In 1950 Lambeau finally resigned from the Packers' organization to become head coach of the Chicago Cardinals. After two acrimonious and losing seasons, Lambeau left Chicago to coach the Washington Redskins in 1953. As he had in Chicago, Lambeau feuded with his players, causing some to defect to the Canadian Football League. In the midst of the preseason schedule of 1954, after a shouting match with Redskins owner George Preston Marshall, Lambeau was fired. His NFL career over, he retired to his California ranch. He died in Sturgeon Bay, Wisconsin.

Lambeau coached his NFL teams to 229 victories, including a team-record 212 wins with the Green Bay Packers. The Packers won six league championships under his direction. One of the most successful coaches in NFL history, Lambeau was inducted as a charter member of the Pro Football Hall of Fame in 1963. Green Bay honored him by naming the Packers' home stadium Lambeau Field. Lambeau was instrumental in bringing about the success of one of the great teams of the NFL. Through his efforts, the small city of Green Bay was able to thrive in a business that was soon dominated by large urban franchises.

• Lambeau is featured prominently in many historical accounts of the Green Bay Packers and the National Football League, including Arch Ward, *The Green Bay Packers: The Story of Professional Football* (1946), and Chuck Johnson, *The Green Bay Packers* (1961). Larry Names, *The History of the Green Bay Packers: The Lambeau Years, Part One* (1989), corrects many of the myths and misconceptions about Lambeau's role in the founding of the Packers franchise. Other profiles of Lambeau are in Denis Harrington, *The Pro Football Hall of Fame: Players, Coaches, Team Owners and League Officials, 1963–1991* (1991); Herbert Warren Wind, "The Sporting Scene: Packerland," *New Yorker*, 8 Dec. 1962, pp. 210ff.; and Jim Doherty, "In Chilly Green Bay, Curly's Old Team Is Still Packing Them In," *Smithsonian*, Aug. 1991, pp. 80–89. An obituary is in the *New York Times*, 2 June 1965.

MARC S. MALTBY

LAMBERT, Dave (19 June 1917–3 Oct. 1966), jazz singer and arranger, was born David Alden Lambert in Boston, Massachusetts. His parents' names are unknown. Lambert studied drums for a year at age ten and by the late 1930s was working summers as a drummer with the Hugh McGuiness trio in New England. He was also a tree surgeon in the Civilian Conservation Corps and served in the army from 1940 to 1943, becoming a paratrooper.

Lambert's professional singing career commenced with Johnny Long's dance band (1943–1944). He then joined Hi, Lo, Jack, and the Dame, a vocal group. As a member of drummer Gene Krupa's big band from 1944 to 1945, he sang in the G-notes. Under Krupa's leadership in January 1945 and with fellow G-note singer Buddy Stewart, Lambert made the appropriately titled record "What's This?" which was generally recognized as the first recording of bebop singing. In 1945 he married Hortense Geist; they had a daughter.

After working briefly with trumpeter Harry James's big band, Lambert made recordings as a leader, including "A Cent and a Half" and "Charge Account" (1946), and he led a vocal quartet in the Broadway show *Are You with It?* (1946–1947). At the beginning of 1947 he recorded with Stan Kenton's big band as the featured singer in Kenton's Pastels, a new vocal group that seems to have immediately disbanded. At this point Lambert and his family were living in Manhattan in arranger Gil Evans's basement apartment, an extraordinary bohemian hovel where some of the most creative minds in bebop gathered to sleep and to exchange musical ideas.

Lambert led a small singing group, and in 1949 he broadcast on radio with alto saxophonist Charlie Parker. During the 1950s he was a studio contractor and arranger for radio, film, and television; Carmen McRae and Tony Bennett were among the singers with whom he worked. In 1953, with Evans as arranger and conductor and Annie Ross among Lambert's fellow singers, Parker recorded versions of "In the Still of the Night" and "Old Folks"; the excessively sugar-coated vocal accompaniments document the tasteless side of Lambert's art.

Around 1957 Lambert collaborated with singer Jon Hendricks on an excellent re-creation of bandleader Woody Herman's instrumental hit "Four Brothers," with lyrics matched to lines originally played by Herman's four saxophonists, Stan Getz, Zoot Sims, Herbie Steward, and Serge Chaloff. This device of setting lyrics to instrumental jazz themes and improvisations became known as vocalese.

Later in 1957 Lambert, Hendricks, and Ross were among a large group of singers recording Hendricks's vocalese interpretations of Count Basie's music, sung to the accompaniment of piano, guitar, string bass, and drums. Their master tape was rejected because the other singers lacked a feeling for the nuances of jazz rhythm, and thus Lambert, Hendricks, and Ross decided to remake the vocal parts themselves, overdubbing extra lines as needed. Released early in 1958, the resulting LP *Sing a Song of Basie* was a great success.

Lambert, Hendricks, and Ross established a performing vocal trio with an accompanying instrumental trio, and their sensationally received appearance at the Randall's Island (N.Y.) Jazz Festival in August 1958 marked the start of several years of extensive touring. Their albums included a revised *Sing a Song of Basie*, with Basie's orchestra accompanying them, as *Sing Along with Basie* (1958); *The Swingers* (1958); *The Hottest New Group in Jazz* (1959), including probably their finest performances, "Moanin'," "Gimme That Wine," "Twisted" (on which Ross sang alone), and "Cloudburst"; and *Lambert, Hendricks, and Ross Sing Ellington* (1960), with fine versions of "Cottontail" (despite the absurd Peter Rabbit lyrics), "Main Stem," "Things Ain't What They Used to Be," and "In a Mellow Tone." On later recordings the quality of their material and renditions declined considerably.

In April 1962 Yolande Bavan replaced Ross. In 1964 Lambert left the group for financial reasons, commenting, "It was a good gig for the rhythm section, the agent, the lawyer, the accountants, and the government" (*Down Beat*, 9 Apr. 1964). The group disbanded soon thereafter. He returned to studio work in New York, starred in the film short *Lambert & Co.* (1964), performed in nightclubs as a singer and pianist, and worked as a disc jockey. While changing a tire on the Connecticut Turnpike at Westport, he was struck and killed by a tractor trailer.

Lambert, Hendricks, and Ross popularized vocalese, which had been pioneered in the preceding decade by singer Eddie Jefferson. They had a tendency to sing ballads frightfully out of tune, as heard for example on "All Too Soon" from the Ellington album. Their strength lay elsewhere, in the highly charged and sometimes virtuoso rhythmic delivery of clever lyrics. Lambert was the least accomplished of the three, and appropriately he often took a supporting role on their best recordings. On several tracks from albums cited above, he was featured as a scat singer—that is, improvising nonsense syllables rather than singing vocalese. One such example, "Everybody's Boppin'" from the album *The Hottest New Group in Jazz*, is an extremely fast, retitled version of a test piece for bop musicians, "I Got Rhythm"; Lambert takes the first solo, Hendricks follows, they trade phrases, and finally the two men improvise together. In this context Lambert utilized a deep, smooth-toned, and lightly differentiated approach that was effective but no match for Hendricks's improvisatory brilliance. When singing with Ross, the two men's voices were at times indistinguishable, so closely attuned was their conception of jazz melody.

• Useful sources on Lambert include Gene Lees and Jon Hendricks, "Lambert, Hendricks and Ross and How They Grew," *Down Beat*, 17 Sept. 1959, pp. 16–18, 39; Liam Keating, "The Dave Lambert Singers," *Jazz Journal* 15 (Apr. 1962): 1–2; Robert George Reisner, *Bird: The Legend of Charlie Parker* (1962; repr. 1975); and "Lambert Exits L-H-B: Replacement Set," *Down Beat*, 9 Apr. 1964, p. 13. See also Leonard Feather, *The Encyclopedia of Jazz in the Sixties* (1966); William F. Lee, *Stan Kenton: Artistry in Rhythm*,

ed. Audree Coke (1980); Luciano Federighi, liner notes to the album *I grandi del jazz: Lambert, Hendricks & Ross* (1981); and Bill Crow, *From Birdland to Broadway: Scenes from a Jazz Life* (1992). Obituaries are in the *New York Times*, 4 Oct. 1966, and *Down Beat*, 17 Nov. 1966.

BARRY KERNFELD

LAMBERT, Louis. *See* Gilmore, Patrick Sarsfield.

LAMBERTON, Benjamin Peffer (24 Feb. 1844–9 June 1912), naval officer, was born in Cumberland County, Pennsylvania, the son of James Findlay Lamberton and Elizabeth Peffer. Lamberton attended Dickinson College for three years (1858–1861), and then he was appointed to the U.S. Naval Academy. He graduated from the Naval Academy in 1864 and immediately served aboard the *America* in pursuit of the Confederate steamers *Florida* and *Tallahassee*. He held a variety of assignments in the Atlantic and Pacific squadrons through the late 1860s and early 1870s. His father had died while Lamberton was a young boy, and Lamberton supported his mother out of his naval pay. In 1873 he married Elizabeth Marshall Stedman; they had three children. Aboard the ironclad *Dictator* from 1873 to 1875, Lamberton was attached to the Boston and Portsmouth navy yards in 1876 and then served on the *Alaska* of the Pacific Station, 1877–1879.

Lamberton worked with the Bureau of Equipment, 1879–1882; served as executive officer on the *Vandalia*, 1882–1884; was lighthouse inspector in Charleston, South Carolina, 1885–1888; and was commandant of the Norfolk Navy Yard, 1888–1889. After a tour aboard the training ship *Jamestown*, 1889–1891, he served with the Bureau of Yards and Docks from 1891 to 1894. Altogether his assignments with the lighthouse service over several different terms between 1885 and 1906 added up to about ten years of duty.

In April 1898 Lamberton was ordered to the Asiatic Squadron at Hong Kong to take command of the *Boston*, but he arrived there just before the ship steamed out to participate in the battle of Manila Bay. Captain George F. Wilde retained command of the *Boston*, and Commodore George Dewey made Lamberton his chief of staff. Lamberton accompanied Dewey in the battle on 1 May 1898 on the bridge of the *Olympia*.

"Not until later," said Admiral Dewey in his *Autobiography* (1913), "did I realize how much I owed to the sympathetic companionship of Lamberton's sunny, hopeful, and tactful disposition." At Dewey's command was a fleet of six warships, *Baltimore*, *Raleigh*, *Petrel*, *Concord*, *Boston*, and the flagship *Olympia*. The small force sank or left burning the eleven ships of the Spanish fleet anchored in Manila harbor, including one strong cruiser. The battle lasted exactly six hours and forty-nine minutes, according to Dewey's calculation, leaving 161 Spanish seamen killed and more than 200 wounded. Aboard the American vessels, nine were killed, and only seven were wounded. Lamberton escaped injury, but later problems with his vision were attributed to his proximity to blasts from the big guns of the *Olympia*.

In the immediate aftermath of the battle in Manila Bay, Lamberton performed several valuable services, including going aboard *Petrel* to the arsenal at Cavite to demand the Spanish surrender. He took charge of moving the sick and wounded prisoners to the captured steamer *Isabel* and then oversaw their transfer to Manila. After the defeat of Spanish forces in Manila, Lamberton served as the naval representative on the joint commission that worked out the details of the surrender of the Philippines. Dewey highly commended Lamberton in his report on the battle, and consequently the Navy Department advanced Lamberton seven positions in the promotion list and appointed him captain shortly after the battle in May 1898. Lamberton took over command of the flagship *Olympia*, relieving Captain Charles V. Gridley. He sailed the *Olympia* back to Boston with Dewey aboard in October 1899. The ship was decommissioned in Boston. Congress awarded Lamberton the Dewey Medal in recognition of his service at Manila.

Lamberton had a reputation as a sportsman, and during this period he befriended former president Grover Cleveland, reportedly accompanying him in duck shooting and fishing. Lamberton served on examining boards for the navy after 1900.

In 1903 Lamberton was promoted to rear admiral and was made commander in chief of the South Atlantic Squadron. His vision began to fail during this assignment, and he eventually lost his sight entirely. In 1905, returning to duty ashore, he was chair of the Lighthouse Board. He retired from the navy in February 1906. In retirement he was active in church and community affairs, serving as a vestryman of the Episcopal Church of the Ascension in Washington, D.C. He died in Washington.

The brief Spanish-American War of 1898 saw the only major engagements of the U.S. Navy in the half century between 1865 and 1917. Thus the officers who participated in the battle of Manila on 1 May 1898 and the battle of Santiago on 3 July 1898 received particular attention from their contemporaries and a degree of recognition in history. Although Lamberton was denied the opportunity to command the *Boston* during the engagement at Manila, his fame and achievement derived from his direct assistance to Dewey and his role in the humanitarian and diplomatic work immediately following the battle.

• Sources on Lamberton include L. R. Hamersly, *Records of Living Officers of the U.S. Navy and Marine Corps* (1902), and George Dewey, *Autobiography of George Dewey* (1913). An obituary is in the Washington *Evening Star*, 10 June 1912.

RODNEY P. CARLISLE

LAMBING, Andrew Arnold (1 Feb. 1842–24 Dec. 1918), Roman Catholic priest and author, was born in Manorville, Armstrong County, Pennsylvania, the son of Michael Anthony Lambing and Anne Shields. After attending St. Michael's Seminary in Pittsburgh, he was ordained a priest in 1869. He held a series of parish assignments, including pastorates of St. Mary of Mercy Church in Pittsburgh from 1873 to 1885 and St. James Church, Wilkinsburg, from 1885 until his death.

Early in Lambing's career he began to write popular instructional and apologetic works on themes associated with his ministry as a priest, such as *The Orphan's Friend* (1875) and *The Sunday-School Teacher's Manual* (1877). His later works of this type are *The Sacramentals of the Holy Catholic Church* (1892), *Come Holy Ghost* (1901), *The Immaculate Conception of the Blessed Virgin Mary* (1904), and *The Fountain of Living Water* (1907). These works are reflections of the Catholic mentality of their time and were not intended or considered then as contributions to scholarship.

Lambing's lasting importance lies in his interests in preserving local Catholic history. Without formal training in historical method, he nevertheless recognized the importance of gathering primary sources, as manifested in his works *A History of the Catholic Church in the Dioceses of Pittsburgh and Allegheny from Its Establishment to the Present Time* (1880) and *The Baptismal Register of Fort Duquesne, 1754–1756* (1885). His last work, *Foundation Stones of a Great Diocese* (1912), is a compendium of biographical sketches of Pittsburgh Catholic clergy.

Lambing's historical interests led him to organize a Catholic historical society to sponsor the collection of available data on local Catholic history. His plan resulted in the founding of the Ohio Valley Catholic Historical Society in 1884, similar to the Catholic historical societies formed the same year in New York and Philadelphia. He then opened the Historical Library of the Diocese of Pittsburgh the following year. Beginning in 1884 the Ohio Valley Catholic Historical Society published *Historical Researches in Western Pennsylvania, Principally Catholic*, renamed *Catholic Historical Researches* the following year. The Philadelphia Catholic historian Martin I. J. Griffin purchased the quarterly from Lambing in 1886, and thereafter it became the *American Catholic Historical Researches* and later the *Records of the American Catholic Historical Society of Philadelphia*. The Ohio Valley Catholic Historical Society became inactive shortly after it ceased sponsoring the journal. Lambing also served many years as president of the Historical Society of Western Pennsylvania. The Catholic historian Peter Guilday attributed to Lambing the founding of the first Catholic historical society in the United States, the starting of the first Catholic historical quarterly, and the writing of the first diocesan history according to scientific methods.

Through his literary activities Lambing became acquainted with industrialist Andrew Carnegie and a trustee of the Carnegie Institute and of the Carnegie Technical Institute. In 1915 he was honored with appointment as a domestic prelate with its title of monsignor. He died at his rectory in Wilkinsburg, Pennsylvania.

• Lambing's papers are held in the Archives of the Diocese of Pittsburgh. Martina Hammill, *The Expansion of the Catholic Church in Pennsylvania* (1960), includes a brief account of his activities. Peter Guilday, "Lambing, Historian of Pittsburgh," *America* 50 (16 Dec. 1933): 251–52, evaluates his contributions.

JOSEPH M. WHITE

LAMBRIGHT, Middleton Huger (3 Aug. 1865–21 Mar. 1959), obstetrician, was born near Moncks Corner, South Carolina, the son of freed slaves, John Lambright and Mary Gelzer, farmers. Middleton was one of thirteen children, and although he himself was born free, more than half of his siblings were born into slavery. As a young man he often accompanied his father to Charleston for supplies. Their route took them by the Medical College of South Carolina, and Middleton would question his father about the young men in white coats walking on the campus. This experience established in him the notion of studying medicine. When a life-threatening accident brought him into personal contact with a physician for a period of several months, he became convinced of his life's ambition. With the support of his family, Lambright eventually graduated from Claflin College in Orangeburg, South Carolina, with the A.B. degree. In 1898 he received his M.D. from the Meharry Medical Department of Central Tennessee College (now known as Meharry Medical College). Believing his chances to improve his lot were better outside the South, that fall he migrated to Kansas City, Missouri, where large numbers of blacks and whites were moving to jobs in the shipping and meat-packing industries.

Lambright was joined in Kansas City by James F. Shannon, a friend from his Meharry graduating class, and Thomas Conrad Unthank, another physician who had arrived earlier in the year. They soon encountered some of the same racial divisions that they had hoped to leave behind. Drugstores would not fill prescriptions for black patients, and hospitals would not allow black doctors to practice in them. Finding this situation intolerable, in 1904 the three physicians and one other, John Edward Perry, who had arrived in 1903, opened their own pharmacy and called it The People's Drugstore. The drugstore not only provided medications for black patients, but it brought together four persons dedicated to helping their community. Perry, in his autobiography, *Forty Cords of Wood*, wrote, "It would be difficult to find three men more unselfishly interested in the general welfare of the community as a whole than the late Shannon, Unthank and Lambright." For a number of years Lambright, Shannon, Unthank, and another Meharry graduate, Daniel F. McQueen Carrion, a dentist, shared an office above the pharmacy at Paseo Boulevard and Eighteenth Street. It was the first black-owned business in that part of town, an area that would eventually become the heart of Kansas City's black community.

A second step in unifying the city's black medical profession was the founding of the Kansas City Medical Society in 1909. Lambright, Unthank, Perry, and

Shannon were joined by fourteen others "to promote the science and art of medicine, and to bring close together colored physicians of the city . . . so that they would secure the intelligent unity and harmony in every phase of their labor" (Rodgers, p. 531).

Lambright and his fellow physicians then began to push for access to a public hospital. One particularly persuasive argument for such access was that by neglecting the health of black and Hispanic people, the white citizens were themselves at greater risk for disease. It was a timely request. The city had already decided to build a new public hospital for whites only to replace its old Kansas City Municipal Hospital. It was agreed that local black physicians could use the old vacated hospital to serve black and Hispanic patients, although it would remain under the supervision of white doctors. Kansas City General Hospital No. 2 was opened on 1 October 1911.

In 1910 a prominent Kansas City surgeon, Jabez Jackson, brought together a group of specialists who agreed to offer postgraduate training to interested black physicians. Training never before available to them was offered at the hospital in several fields, including surgery, radiology, pediatrics, ophthalmology, and obstetrics. Lambright selected obstetrics and became proficient in births that were complicated by malposition of the fetus that required manually turning the fetus to ensure safe delivery. He joined the obstetrical staff and soon became its chief, a position he held until he moved to Cleveland in 1923. In the course of his career at General Hospital No. 2, he would train many nurses and doctors in obstetrics.

In 1908 Lambright had married Bartley Smith Oliver, a native of Paxico, Kansas. They had two children, a son, Middleton H. Lambright, Jr., a surgeon who later became the president of the Academy of Medicine of Cleveland, and a daughter, Elizabeth. When his children approached high school age, Lambright decided to move from Kansas City, with its segregated school system, to Cleveland, which at that time was considered one of the least segregated cities in the country. Even so, Lambright arrived in Cleveland in 1923 to find no hospitals available for black physicians to serve their patients. Once again he found himself leading a drive for a racially integrated hospital. It was not until 1939 that Lambright, together with Ulysses G. Mason and thirty-seven other black physicians, succeeded in organizing the Forest City Hospital Association for the purpose of raising funds for and establishing a hospital. Lambright was treasurer and chairman of the finance committee. Pledges of $500 per trustee (to be paid off in installments of $5 and $10) launched the drive.

At Lambright's urging the association solicited successfully from Cleveland's white medical community and industrial leaders. He suggested that a women's auxiliary be formed, a group that was to become a mainstay of the hospital, and he urged that the physicians and their families take their plight to the churches in an effort to involve the entire black community. In 1957 Cleveland's first racially integrated hospital was opened. To honor his contributions to the founding of the hospital, Lambright was asked to choose its name; it became the Forest City Hospital. He died in Cleveland. To honor him further, in 1960 the Middleton H. Lambright Memorial Lectures were established by the medical staff of the hospital. A total of eighteen annual lectures were delivered at various locations. In 1972 a group of black physicians headed by Doris Evans and Edgar Jackson founded the Middleton H. Lambright Society to honor both Lambright and his son and to promote "the right of quality health care for all."

Lambright was instrumental in establishing interracial hospitals in two separate cities, although neither Forest City Hospital nor General Hospital No. 2 remain. Nevertheless he is representative of the first generation of free black physicians who set about breaking down racial barriers in medicine.

• Biographical information on Lambright is in the Historical Division of the Cleveland Health Sciences Library, including a biographical sketch by and an oral history interview with Middleton H. Lambright, Jr. Further information may be found in the Forest City Hospital Archives, also in the Historical Division. See also anonymous, "Old Doc Lambright," *Cleveland Plain Dealer Pictorial Magazine*, 14 Feb. 1954, p. 14. References to Lambright are in John Edward Perry, *Forty Cords of Wood* (1947), and in Samuel D. Rodger, "Kansas City General Hospital No. 2: A Historical Summary," *Journal of the National Medical Association* 54 (Sept. 1962): 525–44, 639. An obituary is in the *Cleveland Press*, 23 Mar. 1959.

GLEN PIERCE JENKINS

LAMER, Victor Kuhn (15 June 1895–26 Sept. 1966), physical chemist, was born in Leavenworth, Kansas, the son of Joseph Secondule LaMer and Anna Pauline Kuhn, occupations unknown. LaMer obtained his A.B. in chemistry at the University of Kansas in 1915 and spent the next year as a high school teacher in Chicago, followed by a summer of graduate work at the University of Chicago. He then accepted a position as a research chemist in Washington, where he was commissioned in 1917 as a first lieutenant in the Sanitary Corps of the U.S. Army. In 1918 he married Ethel Agatha McGreevy; they had three children. After being discharged from the army in 1919, he entered Columbia University and obtained his Ph.D. in 1921. His doctoral research conducted with Henry Sherman was in the area of physical biochemistry and measured the effect of temperature and hydrogen ion concentration on the rate of destruction of the antiscorbutic vitamin, vitamin C. Appointed an instructor at Columbia in 1920, he rose to assistant professor (1924), associate professor (1928), and professor (1935) and became a professor emeritus in 1961.

LaMer was the recipient in 1922 of a two-year traveling fellowship and spent the first year at Cambridge in the laboratory of the colloid chemist Erik Rideal and the second in Copenhagen with J. N. Brønsted where he worked on the study of electrolyte solutions. The research he did with Brønsted established his program for the next fifteen years after his return to Columbia in 1924.

LaMer made major experimental contributions to establishing the validity of the theory of strong electrolytes as proposed in 1923 by Peter Debye and Ernst Hückel. To explain some of the anomalies that occurred within these solutions they proposed that strong electrolytes are completely dissociated into ions. Any deviations are the result of the electrical interactions of these ions in solution, which increase in magnitude as the ions become more highly charged and concentrated. This produces an environment in which each ion's mobility is effectively reduced because of the attraction of ions of opposite charges. Therefore, each ion has an effective concentration or activity much less than its stoichiometric amount. LaMer and his coworkers pioneered in the determination of these activity coefficients for multiply charged ions needed in the Debye-Hückel theory. LaMer also improved the Debye-Hückel theoretical treatment of concentrated solutions.

LaMer in 1933 questioned the prevailing concept in kinetics that the energy of activation is independent of temperature. He experimentally demonstrated that in solution the energy of activation is very much influenced by temperature for reactions in solutions involving ions. This was a definitive investigation in a field that would rapidly develop in the next few decades.

LaMer was one of the first to investigate the properties of solutions in heavy water, particularly acid-base equilibria. When World War II broke out, LaMer, in conjunction with the Chemical Warfare Service, became engaged in research relating to the colloid state. Colloids are a state of matter, intermediate between a solution and a suspension, in which solute particles are large enough to scatter light but too small to ever settle out. Typical colloids are aerosols, sols, gels, and foams. This state of matter would become the major area of LaMer's investigations during the balance of his career.

In collaboration with Irving Langmuir (Nobel Prize in Chemistry, 1932), an early investigator in colloid science, LaMer and his colleagues at Columbia carried out fundamental research on aerosols from 1945. With David Sinclair a device was invented to produce nondispersive aerosols by foreign nucleation. This became a standard technique in the field and was used successfully for several decades. Further contributions were made in light-scattering methods for the purpose of measuring particle size in colloids.

A significant contribution of practical consequence was made by LaMer in his study of how to reduce the evaporation of water by using monomolecular films. From 1955 research was conducted to find the most suitable materials, methods of application, and retention of surface pressure to prevent evaporation.

Studies of flocculation, a phenomenon in which a solid will stay on top rather than forming a precipitate even with centrifugation, were also part of LaMer's postwar research agenda. He found that addition of electrolytes may yield a more granular form by causing the particles to clump together, and thus the resulting precipitate can then be filtered. Practical and theoretical studies of flocculation and precipitation were performed in this period.

In his lifetime LaMer published more than 200 scientific papers. Among his many scientific honors were election to the National Academy of Sciences (1948), Presidential Certificate of Merit (1945), and the Kendall Award in colloid chemistry (1956). He was a founding editor (1956) of the *Journal of Colloid and Interface Science*. He died in Nottingham, England, where he was to speak at a meeting of the Faraday Society.

• There is no known repository of LaMer's papers. A complete list of his scientific work can be found in National Academy of Sciences, *Biographical Memoirs* 45 (1974): 193–214. An obituary is in the *New York Times*, 28 Sept. 1966.

MARTIN D. SALTZMAN

LA MERI (13 May 1898–7 Jan. 1988), dance artist and educator, was born Russell Meriwether Hughes in Louisville, Kentucky, the daughter of Russell Meriwether Hughes, a businessman, and Lily Allen. Russell Hughes and her sister Lilian became acquainted with a broad spectrum of the arts as they were growing up. After the family's move to San Antonio, Texas, around 1902, the girls received public school or private lessons in music, dramatic art, painting, and dance, and from then until Lilian's death in 1965, they often collaborated in performance and teaching. Before she was twenty Russell was active on a number of fronts in San Antonio. In addition to playing violin in the local symphony orchestra and publishing her first two collections of poems, she sang, danced, acted, wrote plays and songs (both lyrics and music), and painted. Between 1921 and 1938 four more collections of her poems were issued by publishing houses in Boston, Philadelphia, and Italy.

Russell began ballet classes at age twelve, also learned some Mexican and Spanish dances, and was soon performing on student programs. Touring companies introduced her to a variety of international dance forms. Performances by notable artists such as Loïe Fuller, Anna Pavlova, the Denishawn company, La Argentina, and Diaghilev's Ballets Russes inspired a passion for dance cultures of the world that would consume her for the rest of her life.

After extensive amateur experience Russell made her professional stage debut early in 1924 at the San Antonio Empire Theater as a dancer, singer, and actress in prologs (live entertainments offered in conjunction with silent movie showings). Her success resulted in a tour of southern movie theaters that eventually led to New York City. She remained there, studying ballet, Spanish dance, and tap while also seeking work on the professional stage.

Russell's early engagements were mainly as a Spanish dancer. She soon acquired an agent-manager, Guido Carreras, who directed her career, organized her tours, and traveled with her from around 1925 to

1944. Under Carreras's management, her first international foray was a three-month stint in Mexico City, where she performed her newly created repertoire and took lessons in Spanish dance, Mexican regional dance, and bull-fighting movement. It was there that she acquired the professional name "La Meri," the invention of a local journalist.

Back in New York City, La Meri was featured as a Spanish dancer in vaudeville, and in the 1927 Shubert revue *A Night in Spain*, which toured for fourteen weeks, she danced, spoke the prolog, sang, played torero, and acted. La Meri's subsequent foreign tours (with sister Lilian in the company) were to the Caribbean (summer 1927), South America (1928–1929), and Europe (1929–1931). In each place she saw and studied dance as well as performed it and met prominent fellow artists, including the German modern dancer Mary Wigman and two dancers who had inspired her many years before in San Antonio, the great ballerina Anna Pavlova and the pioneer Spanish concert dancer La Argentina. Particularly important was her contact in Paris with Indian concert dancer Uday Shankar, who introduced her to the dance of India.

La Meri made her New York City debut as a solo concert dancer at the John Golden Theater on 6 May 1928. Her performances there and on tour typically included ballet, Spanish dance, the incipient modern dance, other Western dance forms, and a growing repertoire of dances from the various cultures with which she came into contact. In *Total Education in Ethnic Dance* La Meri wrote that she introduced the term *ethnic dance* in order to distinguish, from ballet and modern dance, the theatrical presentation of indigenous dance forms that have developed out of the popular or typical dance movements of a particular group or groups—in other words, in order to define a genre. In the early 1930s she gave her first all-ethnic concert in Europe (in Vienna); in 1938, the first of such programs in New York City. By the 1940s she was totally focused on the staging, performance, and teaching of authentic ethnic dances or original works based on one or another of their techniques. La Meri's importance in the field of dance derives from her lifelong achievements in ethnic dance—as performing artist, educator, choreographer, writer, and passionate promoter.

In June 1931 La Meri and Carreras were married in London and from there traveled to Italy, where La Meri wrote her first book on dance and of course continued teaching, choreographing, and performing. They bought a home in Tuscany that served as their base until the outbreak of World War II. Their marriage ended in divorce in 1944; they had no children.

In May 1936 La Meri and Carreras embarked on a tour of Australia, New Zealand, Asia, and the Pacific, which ended in Honolulu in September 1937. Along the way La Meri added to her repertoire dances of India (Bharata Natyam and Kathak), New Zealand (Maori), Burma (the *pwe*), Java, the Philippines, Japan, and Hawaii. After the Asian tour she performed in the United States, Latin America, Italy, and London.

From the late 1930s until 1959, La Meri's base was New York City. In May 1940 she opened the School of Natya with Ruth St. Denis, and out of that developed her own Ethnologic Dance Center (EDC). This unique institution, co-directed with her sister Lilian and after the mid-1940s also with her partner Peter Di Falco, was designed to promote ethnic dance. In 1949 it began to offer a multiyear certificate program to train artists and teachers that included the dance techniques of Spain and India; occasional training in other world dance arts; and a host of corollary courses including choreography, music, Spanish and East Indian culture, production, pedagogy, and writing and speaking.

In addition to her work at the EDC, La Meri was in charge of the ethnic dance program at Ted Shawn's summer dance school and festival at Jacob's Pillow in Lee, Massachusetts, from 1942 until 1953 and also spent part of each summer there from 1959 to 1967. Her work in this venue was particularly influential, as the summer program attracted students from all over the United States. She also taught at the Connecticut College Dance Festival, at Juilliard, and at various universities. A prolific choreographer, La Meri was particularly interested in original compositions based on one or another ethnic dance techniques. Notable works include a version of the ballet *Swan Lake* (1944) and *Bach-Bharata Suite* (1946), both using South Indian Bharata Natyam dance vocabulary, and Manuel de Falla's *El Amor Brujo* (1944, 1953).

In 1956 La Meri closed the EDC and around 1959 moved with Lilian to Cape Cod, where she continued to teach, prepare ethnic dance performances with students, and write. Lilian's death in 1965 deprived La Meri at once of both sister and colleague. In 1970 she founded Ethnic Dance Arts, an incorporated entity that sponsored a summer ethnic dance festival and workshop, provided training and scholarships for promising dance students, and in 1977 established the St. Denis Award for Creative Choreography in the Ethnic Field. Around 1985 La Meri returned to San Antonio, where she died.

Throughout her life La Meri wrote extensively. In addition to her poetry collections she published five books on dance; an autobiography; and numerous articles for *Arabesque*, a New York magazine devoted to ethnic dance, and for other periodicals and encyclopedias. She is credited with spreading knowledge of the world's dance cultures not only throughout the United States but also internationally, particularly through her performances and teaching but also through her writings. In 1972 she received the Capezio Dance Award for her contributions to the field.

• La Meri's papers are in the Dance Collection, New York Public Library for the Performing Arts at Lincoln Center. Her books on dance are *Dance as an Art Form: Its History and Development* (1933), *The Gesture Language of the Hindu Dance* (1941; repr. 1964, 1979), *Spanish Dancing* (1948; 2nd rev. ed., 1967), *Dance Composition: The Basic Elements* (1965; edition in Indonesian, 1975), and *Total Education in Ethnic Dance* (1977). Her autobiography is *Dance Out the Answer* (1977). Her poetry collections are *Poems* (1917), *Marching to France, and Other Texas Rhymes* (1917), *Mexican Moonlight* (1921), *Poems of the Plains* (1922), *The Star Roper* (1925; with sketches by Guido Carreras, 1927, 1928), and *Songs and Voyages* (1938). Interviews by Adam Lahm appear in the two-part "Grand Lady of Ethnic Dance: La Meri," *Arabesque* 4 (Nov.–Dec. 1978): 8–9, 12, and 4 (Jan.–Feb. 1979): 7–9; and in "La Meri: Backwards and Forwards," *Arabesque* 5 (Nov.–Dec. 1979): 12–13, 23. Obituaries are in *Dance Magazine*, Apr. 1988, and the *New York Times*, 21 Jan. 1988.

NANCY LEE CHALFA RUYTER

LAMON, Ward Hill (6 Jan. 1828–7 May 1893), lawyer, was born in Frederick County, Virginia, the son of George Lamon and Elizabeth Ward. He spent his early years in Berkeley County in what is now West Virginia. In 1847 Lamon moved to Danville, Illinois, studied law, and was admitted to the Illinois bar before his twenty-fifth birthday. By 1852 he had become the Danville law partner of Abraham Lincoln and, together with other circuit-riding attorneys, including William Herndon and David Davis, was an intimate friend of the future president. Lamon was described by Stephen Oates as a "legendary boozer, who spent much of his time in the saloon under his office, where he sang lewd and comic songs" and by David Donald as one "famous for his rendition of Southern songs, for his wide assortment of smutty jokes, for his vocabulary of profanity, and for his capacity for liquor." Lamon remained close to Lincoln until his assassination in 1865. He helped organize Lincoln's 1858 senatorial campaign against Stephen Douglas and his 1860 presidential campaign. In February 1861 Lamon undertook to serve as Lincoln's bodyguard, replete with "two revolvers, two derringers, and two large knives," as the president-elect was secretly transported to Washington prior to his inauguration.

Appointed by Lincoln as marshal of the District of Columbia, Lamon relished his various functions, which included introducing the president at a number of formal functions. Yet the exuberance he brought to these responsibilities was marred by an excessive dislike of abolitionists matched only by his hostility toward the expansion of slavery, a duality shared by many of Lincoln's party. As the war expanded, Lamon came into frequent conflict with the officials charged with governing the District of Columbia, especially its military governor.

A major source of conflict was the continued enforcement of the fugitive slave law, even as the war progressed. It would remain valid, Lincoln and Lamon held, until changed by federal legislation. Lamon's conduct as marshal became the subject of partisan congressional wrangling. Indeed, Lincoln received severe criticism from members of Congress for keeping an individual who appeared to be supportive of slavery in a position close to the president. Despite such opposition, Lincoln retained Lamon, and had the hulking, muscular marshal been in Washington on 14 April 1865 instead of on an assignment to Richmond from Secretary of War Edwin M. Stanton, he might well have accompanied Lincoln to Ford's Theater.

After Lincoln's death, Lamon became the law partner of Jeremiah Black, who had served in James Buchanan's administration as both attorney general and secretary of state. Lamon also purchased a number of documents concerning Lincoln that had been collected by Lincoln's former law partner Herndon. In 1872 the first of a projected two-volume Lincoln biography, *The Life of Abraham Lincoln from His Birth to His Inauguration as President*, appeared under Lamon's name. In reality, the book had been written by Black's son, Chauncey F. Black, "by inheritance a Buchanan Democrat, by temperament an anti-Lincoln man." Well before the book's publication, Lamon lost interest in the project, leaving his ghostwriter to integrate the mass of materials purchased from Herndon. The result was a book replete with gossip and unsavory anecdotes about Lincoln's life and career. Possibly because the book gained very limited commercial success, the second volume of the biography never was undertaken.

Lamon ended his partnership with Black in 1879. He spent his final years in desultory travel and practice. He outlived both of his wives (Angelina Turner, who died in 1859, leaving a daughter, and Sally Logan, who died in 1892) and died near Martinsburg, West Virginia. Colorful and controversial during the Civil War, Lamon afterward had drifted, gaining little distinction in the remainder of his life. He frequently reiterated his lasting regret that he had been absent from Washington the night of Lincoln's murder.

• Lamon's papers, including material purchased from Herndon and an uncompleted manuscript about Lincoln's presidential years, are in the Huntington Library, San Marino, Calif. His daughter published a memoir based on these materials, Ward H. Lamon, *Recollections of Lincoln*, ed. Dorothy Lamon Teillard (1911). Comments about his association with Lincoln are in Stephen Oates, *With Malice towards None: The Life of Abraham Lincoln* (1977); David Donald, *Lincoln's Herndon* (1948); and Allan Nevins, *The War for the Union: The Improvised War 1861–1862* (1959). An obituary is in the *New York Herald*, 9 May 1893.

JONATHAN LURIE

LAMONT, Daniel Scott (9 Feb. 1851–23 July 1905), secretary of war and financier, was born in McGrawville, Cortland County, New York, the son of John B. Lamont, a merchant and farmer, and Elizabeth Scott. The youth studied at McGrawville Union School and Cortland Normal College. He entered Union College in Schenectady, New York, in 1868 but left academic life without a degree to enter journalism. Lamont purchased an interest in the *Democrat*, a Cortland County newspaper, and soon became its editor. In 1870 he was appointed by Governor John T. Hoffman as engrossing clerk to the New York State Assembly and shortly thereafter worked as assistant journal clerk in the capitol at Albany, where he met and joined forces with Samuel J. Tilden, governor of New York from 1875 to 1877. In 1872 Lamont obtained a clerkship on the New York Democratic State Central Committee, a po-

sition he held for several years. In 1874 he married Juliet Kinney; they had four daughters. From 1875 to 1882 he was chief clerk in the New York secretary of state's department with John Bigelow, an author and diplomat. Lamont also joined David Manning in editing and publishing the *Albany Argus* from 1877 until 1882.

Lamont's career was closely tied to that of Grover Cleveland. During the 1882 New York gubernatorial campaign, Lamont worked for Cleveland, the Democratic candidate for governor. In 1883 Governor Cleveland placed Lamont on his staff as his private and military secretary with the rank of colonel. This began an intimate personal and professional relationship between the two men that lasted until Lamont's death. After Cleveland won the presidential election in 1884, Lamont in 1885 accompanied Cleveland to Washington, where he served as the president's private secretary for the next four years. Cleveland trusted Lamont implicitly with his most personal thoughts. Acting as an intermediary between the president and others, Lamont lightened the burden for Cleveland, directed memos to appropriate departments, and worked tirelessly to promote the president's agenda. He was the first modern presidential secretary in that he increased the importance of that position to a level it has held ever since his time. He also proved to be indispensable as a political adviser. Admitting that Lamont was extremely useful, Cleveland noted that his secretary had neither friends to reward nor enemies to punish. Lamont's loyalty was to Cleveland, and the president benefited from his association with Lamont. It was he, not Cleveland, who originated the phrase that a public office was a public trust.

Following Cleveland's defeat for reelection in 1888 at the hands of Benjamin Harrison, the Republican presidential standard-bearer, Lamont took a financial position in New York offered by William C. Whitney, Cleveland's secretary of the navy and close friend. In 1889 Lamont joined Whitney and Oliver H. Payne in the consolidation of all the Manhattan streetcar lines under the name of the Metropolitan Traction Company. Whitney wanted Lamont to handle his investments in street railways. Under Whitney's tutelage, Lamont's personal wealth significantly increased, and his family fortune was now secure. When Cleveland again obtained the Democratic presidential nomination in 1892, Lamont was ready to reenter politics.

During Cleveland's second presidential administration, from 1893 to 1897, Lamont served in the cabinet as secretary of war. With this portfolio he once again demonstrated his talents as a good administrator. Assuming an active role, he functioned in some respects as an assistant president. Of all the cabinet officers, only Lamont knew of the president's clandestine surgery on board a private yacht in 1893 to remove a malignant growth from his mouth. In fact, Lamont and his wife were on the yacht with Cleveland at the time of the operation. Vice President Adlai E. Stevenson, who was then in Illinois preparing an Independence

Day address, had not even been informed of Cleveland's condition.

Lamont was involved with several national events during his four years in office. He announced the virtual end of Native American warfare in the country and worked to improve the efficiency of his department. Like Cleveland, he registered disapproval of the annexation of Hawaii, and Cleveland conferred with Lamont on the Venezuelan boundary dispute with Great Britain in 1895. Although at first he opposed sending federal troops to Chicago in 1894 to quell the Pullman Strike, an action called by the American Railway Union under Eugene V. Debs that immobilized railroads in the Midwest, Lamont changed his mind after reading reports from Attorney General Richard Olney. Lamont thereupon strongly supported the president's decision to use force to safeguard the mail, protect interstate commerce, and restore order. As secretary of war, he directed the policing of Chicago during that episode, which met with intense opposition and denunciation from Illinois governor John P. Altgeld.

Lamont was a conservative Democrat committed to the central principles of sound money and tariff reform. In 1896 he vehemently objected to the Democratic presidential nomination of William Jennings Bryan on a free silver platform that also condemned the Cleveland administration. Lamont endorsed the separate presidential ticket headed by Senator John M. Palmer of Illinois, who ran on the National Democratic party's platform supporting the gold standard. On election night Lamont joined a group of conservative Democrats in the White House and rejoiced upon learning of Bryan's defeat.

After Cleveland left office in 1897, Lamont retired to private life. He was elected vice president of the Northern Pacific Railway Company in 1898, serving in this capacity until 1904. He was also president of the Northern Pacific Express Company. In addition, he assumed the directorships in many banks and corporations. During these years, he kept in touch with Cleveland, and the two friends discussed politics. They favored the election of Judge Alton B. Parker, a conservative New York Democrat, for president in 1904. Lamont died of a heart attack at "Altamount," his home in Millbrook, Dutchess County, New York.

• Lamont's papers are in the Manuscript Division of the Library of Congress. This is a valuable collection for information relating to Democratic politics of the period. Some of Lamont's letters are in the manuscript collections of contemporaries, such as Grover Cleveland and William C. Whitney, whose papers are in the Library of Congress. The main work on Lamont is Sister Anne Marie Fitzsimmons, "The Political Career of Daniel S. Lamont" (Ph.D. diss., Catholic Univ. of America, 1965). See also Michael Medved, *The Shadow Presidents* (1979), pp. 75–87. Lamont is mentioned frequently in Allan Nevins, *Grover Cleveland: A Study in Courage* (1941); Robert McElroy, *Grover Cleveland* (1923); and George F. Parker, *Recollections of Grover Cleveland* (1909). Obituaries are in the *New York Times* and the *Brooklyn Daily Eagle*, 24 July 1905.

LEONARD SCHLUP

LAMONT, Thomas William (30 Sept. 1870–2 Feb. 1948), banker and financier, was born in Claverack, New York, the son of Thomas Lamont, a Methodist minister, and Caroline Deuel Jayne. Young Lamont grew up in several small Hudson Valley towns in upstate New York, as his father was posted to a new church every two or three years. The family was not poor, but Lamont's upbringing, described in his *My Boyhood in a Parsonage* (1946), was dominated by financial stringency and moral severity. His education in local schools was enhanced by extensive reading, guided by his father, who had taught Greek before entering the ministry.

A few days before his fourteenth birthday Lamont entered Phillips Exeter Academy. He was not well prepared, but extra hours of study enabled him to catch up with his classmates and then to take part in the extracurricular activities, which included editorship of the student newspaper and yearbook, as well as managing the school's literary magazine. After graduation from Exeter in 1888, Lamont entered Harvard, where he paid his way in part by working for the *Crimson*, the student newspaper, as well as serving as Harvard correspondent for the *Boston Herald*. He graduated cum laude in the spring of 1892 and two days later reported for work at the *New York Tribune* at a salary of $25 per week.

At the *Tribune* Lamont started as a cub reporter and earned extra income by writing features for the Sunday edition. By the following year he had been promoted to assistant night editor; he also helped the financial editor on weekends in making up tables of railway earnings for the Monday business section, an experience that gave him his first exposure to the inside world of finance. Although he found much of the newspaper work interesting, the pay was poor and future prospects were limited, so he left journalism for a career in business. These two years with the press were valuable for Lamont in his future dealings with journalists.

By investing $5,000, which he had to borrow, Lamont in 1894 became secretary of the firm Cushman Brothers, which acted as a New York marketing agent for food manufacturers. By 1898 the company was in such bad financial condition that its creditors asked Lamont to reorganize it, which he did successfully. The result was the new firm of Lamont, Corliss and Co. His partner was his brother-in-law Charles Corliss (in 1895 Lamont had married Florence Haskell Corliss, with whom he had four children).

Lamont's business acumen brought him to the attention of the banker Henry P. Davison, whose biography Lamont would later write. In 1903 Davison asked Lamont to join the Bankers Trust, then being organized. From his starting position as secretary and treasurer, Lamont became vice president in 1905 and progressed to a position as director. In 1909 he became a vice president of the First National Bank; following Davison, in January 1911 he became a partner in J. P. Morgan and Co., where he remained until retirement, becoming chairman of the board upon the death of J. P. Morgan, Jr., in 1943.

During World War I Lamont, as a member of the firm of J. P. Morgan, was involved in arranging for the huge loans to Britain and France that enabled them to fight Germany. In addition, J. P. Morgan established a company through which the Allies could purchase supplies in the United States, a vast improvement over the previous improvised system. When the United States entered the war in 1917, Lamont joined the Liberty Loan committees, which aided the Treasury Department in selling war bonds to American citizens.

As a partner in one of the world's most prestigious investment banking firms, Lamont was witness to and actor in the largest international financial dealings of the interwar years. His career as a financial statesman began in the fall of 1917 with his appointment, at the request of President Woodrow Wilson, as an unofficial adviser to a mission to the Allies headed by Edward M. House. In addition to discussions with British and French government officials, Lamont visited the front. Only days before Lamont got to Britain, the Bolsheviks took power in Russia, and at the suggestion of William B. Thompson, head of the American Red Cross mission in Petrograd, and with the encouragement of British prime minister Lloyd George, Lamont and Thompson tried to persuade the U.S. government to aid the new Bolshevik government in hope of keeping Russia in the war against Germany. This effort came to naught when Wilson not only failed to provide the requested aid but would not even see the envoys upon their return to Washington.

Lamont's experience with the House mission led to his appointment, along with Norman H. Davis, as a Treasury Department representative to the Paris Peace Conference. Both Lamont and Davis were appointed to Sub-Committee No. 2, which was charged with determining Germany's capacity to pay reparations. Lamont regularly attended almost daily meetings during February and March 1919, but because there was no agreement on the size of the reparations, the committee could only recommend that a permanent reparations commission be made part of the final peace treaty. Lamont returned from Paris as a wholehearted supporter of Wilson and the League of Nations, and he publicly supported the League during the Senate debates over U.S. membership in it. So strong was his commitment that in the 1920 election, Lamont voted for James Cox and Franklin D. Roosevelt—the only time this lifelong Republican voted for the Democratic presidential ticket.

The question of German reparations remained an international problem. Lamont was involved in the drafting of the Dawes Plan (1924) and the Young Plan (1929), as well as in the establishment of the Bank of International Settlements called for by the Young Plan. In both these plans German reparations were reduced and the payments rescheduled; both required new loans to Germany, and in both cases J. P. Morgan and Co. headed the syndicate that floated the bonds for the loans. In the end Germany paid about $4.5 billion in reparations (of the original $33 billion); of this more than $2 billion was supplied by private U.S. citizens through the purchase of German bonds, almost none of which were repaid. The reparations ceased in 1932.

During the 1920s Lamont was also involved with the finances of other foreign governments. He headed a commission that tried to straighten out Mexico's foreign debt, accumulated during the revolution of the previous decade, but in spite of strenuous efforts on his part, Mexico's payments remained largely in default. Lamont represented U.S. bankers in an international consortium organized to loan money to China, but because of the Chinese civil war, private bankers found the conditions too risky.

In neighboring Japan prospects were much brighter. Beginning with a loan to help reconstruction after the disastrous earthquake of 1923, J. P. Morgan and Co. became the Japanese government's chief international banker. Lamont's relationship with the Japanese was so close that he became an apologist for Japan's foreign policy, even authoring the statement issued by Japanese finance minister Junnosuke Inouye in the wake of the September 1931 Mukden raid in Manchuria. It would be three more years and several assassinations later (including that of Inouye) before Lamont would turn against his firm's best Asian client. In addition, he was involved in every other international loan made by the firm; during the 1920s this included floating bond issues for Austria, France, Italy, and Argentina.

Lamont's other role during the interwar years was that of spokesman for investment banking in general and J. P. Morgan and Co. in particular. Because of the retiring nature of the junior Morgan, Lamont became the main source of information for journalists covering finance; as one contemporary put it, "Mr. Morgan speaks to Mr. Lamont, and Mr. Lamont speaks to the people." Lamont was particularly able to defend the firm during congressional and other government hearings; from the Pujo hearings of 1912 through the Senate Munitions Committee hearings of 1936, he not only testified and helped others with their testimony, but also handled press relations. In his dealings with the press, Lamont won over all but the most determined adversaries with his easy, informal, seemingly straightforward manner.

Once Lamont commanded significant wealth, he became a generous philanthropist. First among the beneficiaries were his two alma maters; not only did he give large sums to both, but he served on their governing boards as well. In addition, he gave $500,000 to help restore Canterbury Cathedral after World War II, and his will contained a million-dollar bequest to the Metropolitan Museum of Art.

Because of his position with J. P. Morgan and Co., Lamont was considered one of the most powerful men in the United States and perhaps in the world. There can be little doubt that if money is power, then Lamont influenced the destiny of nations. However, in retrospect his stature seems much diminished, and

Ron Chernow's reflection on Lamont and his career seems correct:

Lamont was a man of prodigious gifts . . . as a man of the Diplomatic Age [of finance], he was the architect of huge state loans in the 1920s. As they defaulted in the 1930s, he had to devote his time to fruitless salvage operations, and his gifts were squandered in the general wreckage. For all his power, he seems in retrospect a tiny figure bobbing atop a gigantic tidal wave. His story is a sobering tale of human limitations. (Pp. 480–81)

• The Thomas W. Lamont Papers are held in the Baker Library of Harvard Graduate School of Business Administration. Lamont wrote two useful memoirs, *My Boyhood in a Parsonage* (1946) and *Across World Frontiers* (1951), as well as a biography of his mentor, *Henry P. Davison: The Record of a Useful Life* (1933). A full-length biography, *The Ambassador from Wall Street: The Story of Thomas W. Lamont, J. P. Morgan's Chief Executive* (1994), by Edward M. Lamont (the subject's grandson), is a full and in general fair-minded work largely based on the Lamont papers. Other books that report on Lamont's career include Ron Chernow, *The House of Morgan: An American Banking Dynasty and the Rise of Modern Finance* (1990), and Warren I. Cohen, *The Chinese Connection: Roger S. Greene, Thomas W. Lamont, George E. Sokolsky and American East-Asian Relations* (1978). Thomas Lamont's son Corliss Lamont edited a family history, *The Thomas Lamonts in America* (1962). A sketch in *Current Biography* (1940) gives a contemporary view of his importance, as does the front-page obituary in the *New York Times*, 3 Feb. 1948.

STEPHEN GOLDFARB

LAMOTHE CADILLAC, Antoine Laumet de (5 Mar. 1658–15 Oct. 1730), founder of Detroit and governor of French Louisiana, was born at Les Laumets, department of Tarn-et-Garonne, France, the son of Jean Laumet, a provincial magistrate, and Jeanne Péchagut. Born a commoner, Antoine Laumet invented a noble pedigree, complete with the particle *de* and the alias Lamothe Cadillac by which he has come to be known, in order to enhance his chances of advancement in ancien régime France. Cadillac's early life is veiled in obscurity, in large part because of his conscious efforts to obliterate all traces of his humble origins. Circumstantial evidence suggests that Cadillac received a sound education before seeking his fortune in the New World. Cadillac arrived at Port Royal, Acadia (present-day Nova Scotia), around 1683 and quickly found employment as a sailor aboard a privateer operated by François Guion of New France. In 1687, toward the end of his four years of service, Cadillac married the captain's niece, Marie-Therese Guion. They had thirteen children.

At Port Royal, Cadillac obtained a large land grant encompassing twenty-five square miles along the Union River in modern-day Maine. Cadillac did not develop this small fiefdom, choosing instead to engage in illicit fur trade with the military commandant and royal commissary of Port Royal. Although his collusion with corrupt colonial officials earned the Gascon the enmity of Acadia's governor, Cadillac and his family left Port Royal for Quebec only after the destruction of his Port Royal home by British raiders in 1690. Despite the negative reports circulated about him by the Acadian governor, Cadillac found ready employment in Quebec, thanks to his personal friendship with Governor Frontenac of New France, who requested a military appointment for him.

Shortly after being commissioned lieutenant in the Canadian garrison by the French colonial ministry, Cadillac, who retained extensive knowledge of the New England coastline from his years as a privateer, accompanied cartographer Jean-Baptiste Franquelin during his reconnaissance of that area. Cadillac was promoted to captain in October 1693. In 1694 Governor Frontenac appointed him commandant of Michilimackinac, the strategic center of French military and economic activity in western New France. As commandant, Cadillac spent far more time and energy in pursuit of his profits from his personal—and quite illegal—participation in the brandy and fur trade than in the administration of the post. In August 1697, after royal regulations sharply restricted fur trading in the Great Lakes region, Cadillac returned to Quebec, and in 1698 he traveled to France to petition the Crown for permission to establish a French outpost at present-day Detroit, Michigan.

Cadillac's proposal envisioned Detroit as a haven in which the French-allied tribes who had been decimated by prolonged warfare with the Francophobic Iroquois could regroup under the protection of a small force of French soldiers, missionaries, and fur traders. France's colonial and naval minister warmly embraced the plan, which also protected the fur trade from the English, and in 1700 the project was implemented by the French Crown over the strenuous objections of leading Canadian officials, both because of the project itself and because of Cadillac's profiteering.

During the summer of 1701 Cadillac led a party of 100 Frenchmen to Detroit and established a post there. Three years later he obtained from the Crown full ownership of the installation. Cadillac's ownership of the post elicited the immediate opposition of Philippe de Rigaud de Vaudreuil, the newly appointed governor of New France. A protracted dispute between Cadillac and Vaudreuil quickly erupted and continued until Jérôme Phélypeaux, comte de Pontchartrain, the French Minister of Marine, in charge of the royal navy and colonies, who initially supported the Detroit commander, felt compelled to appoint a special investigator to examine the situation at Detroit. The ensuing report, issued in November 1708, identified Cadillac as a profiteer whose activities threatened the stability of the fur trade as well as French control over the North American interior. Cadillac exercised a tyrannical rule that had earned him the hatred of white and red man alike. He further alienated settlers and Indian allies with his profiteering and by evidently allowing trade with the British in New York. All of these activities, if continued, would have destroyed French hegemony over the Great Lakes region.

Upon receipt of the report, Pontchartrain found himself on the horns of a dilemma. He could not dismiss the charges of malfeasance raised against

Cadillac, but because he had defended Cadillac for so many years, the minister could not publicly humiliate him without acknowledging his own error of judgment. Cadillac was consequently appointed governor of Louisiana, at the time the least desirable posting in the French empire.

Because the former Detroit commandant happened to be in France (instead of traveling directly to Louisiana as ordered), Minister Pontchartrain pressed Cadillac into service as the Crown's public relations agent in a successful attempt to persuade Antoine Crozat, a wealthy French financier, to assume proprietary control of the unprofitable Mississippi Valley colony as a means of removing a major financial burden from the nearly bankrupt French monarchy. Crozat agreed to underwrite a proprietary company, with the Gascon as its principal Louisiana representative.

Cadillac's personal charm, which had proven so effective in the Crown's negotiations with Crozat, was noticeably absent in his dealings with other new appointees to the Louisiana government. While subsequently sailing to Louisiana, Cadillac alienated *Commissaire-ordonnateur* Jean-Baptiste Dubois du Clos, the colony's chief financial officer, by warning his governmental colleague that quarreling with the governor would be dangerous because of the chief executive's "superior intelligence." Upon arrival at Louisiana, Cadillac quickly antagonized Jean-Baptiste Le Moyne de Bienville, the colony's leading political and military figure and a reputed smuggler, by rigorously enforcing Crozat's monopoly on colonial trade. The resulting intragovernmental feuding virtually paralyzed the Louisiana government. Cadillac attempted to salvage his administration by trying unsuccessfully to establish trade with Spanish Mexico and by attempting to locate valuable mineral deposits in the upper Mississippi Valley. Cadillac was consequently recalled to France on 3 March 1716.

Shortly after his return to France in 1717, Cadillac was arrested and imprisoned in the Bastille for his criticism of the attempt by Crozat's successor to promote Louisiana colonization through advertising depicting the colony as an earthly paradise. Following his release from prison, Cadillac pressed the French colonial ministry for back pay and for restoration to his abandoned claim to ownership of Detroit. The ministry allowed him ownership of only a few buildings at Detroit and his pay. In 1723 Cadillac evidently used the money to buy the governorship of the small town of Castelsarrasin in southwestern France. He died there seven years later.

Cadillac remains one of the most complex and controversial figures in the history of French North America. He has variously been described by French colonial historians as a hero and as a scoundrel. The founding of Detroit, Michigan, and Natchitoches, Louisiana—the oldest community in the Louisiana Purchase, founded during Cadillac's attempt to establish trade with Mexico while he was headquartered at Mobile, Alabama—constitute the Gascon's American legacy.

• Agnes C. Laut, *Cadillac, Knight Errant of the Wilderness* (1931), eulogizes the founder of Detroit. Yves F. Zoltvany, "New France and the West, 1701–1713," *Canadian Historical Review* 46 (1965): 301–22; a series of articles by Jean Delanglez in *Mid-America* (1945, 1948, 1950, 1951); and William J. Eccles, *Frontenac, the Courtier Governor* (1959), provide far more balanced views of Cadillac's Canadian career. Marcel Giraud, *Histoire de la Louisiane française* (1953–1993), provides the most insightful look into the Gascon's Louisiana years.

CARL A. BRASSEAUX

LA MOUNTAIN, John (1830–14 Feb. 1870), aeronaut, was born in Lansingburgh, New York. His surname is sometimes rendered as Lamountane. Little is known of La Mountain's childhood, family life, and education. Apparently his father died while La Mountain was young, and he left school to support himself and his mother. There is evidence that he was at one time a seaman.

La Mountain became involved in ballooning with America's most famous antebellum aeronaut, John Wise, and with a scientist named O. A. Gager. After about a half-dozen preliminary flights by La Mountain in balloons provided by Wise, Wise enlisted La Mountain and Gager, with La Mountain superintendent of the project, to help him build the *Atlantic*, a spheroid hydrogen-filled balloon fifty feet in diameter. The intention was to promote the idea of a transcontinental and transatlantic balloon service for mail and passengers. In July 1859 Wise, La Mountain, and Gager, accompanied by a newspaper reporter, made a record American ascension in the *Atlantic* of some 1,100 miles, over 800 air line miles, from St. Louis to the community of Henderson in Jefferson County, New York. The distance and speed of less than twenty hours excited both balloonists and the public to the feasibility of long-distance ballooning. La Mountain, appointed by Wise as aeronaut in charge of the flight, became a celebrity.

La Mountain became a pioneer of early American military aeronautics when General Benjamin F. Butler, in command of the Department of Virginia, solicited his services for early Civil War operations at Fortress Monroe. La Mountain contributed two balloons, one made from parts of and named after the old *Atlantic*. On 31 July 1861 La Mountain laid claim to the first operationally useful reconnaissance by an aeronaut in U.S. military service. Early attempts by the aeronaut James Allen to get a balloon operational had failed, and John Wise's two earlier ascensions from the Washington defenses had provided no significant observations. Thaddeus S. C. Lowe had made an aerial map in late June, but he was at that time only an applicant for military service, and his activities were experimental.

La Mountain performed valuable service at Fortress Monroe until 10 August 1861. He overcame early problems with his inflation apparatus, though the technical details of his experiments with generating apparatus are absent. He had a portable generating apparatus but not one that could inflate a balloon on short notice. Despite this limitation, La Mountain's balloons provided valuable service acknowledged both by those he served and by the enemy. His use of observation balloons attached to an armed transport and a tug has some claim to being the origins of the aircraft carrier.

Butler, though a strong supporter of La Mountain, did not provide adequately for his transfer to General John E. Wool, Butler's successor in command of the Department of Virginia. La Mountain accepted the offer of General Fitz John Porter for employment in the Army of the Potomac as a civilian balloonist on the roll of the Corps of Topographical Engineers. Porter, to whom General George B. McClellan entrusted the infant balloon service, assigned La Mountain to the division of General William B. Franklin. The appointment to Franklin's division was intended in part to keep some distance between La Mountain and his aeronautic rival in the Army of the Potomac, Lowe.

With Franklin, La Mountain contributed free ballooning to Civil War aeronautics. Though his reconnaissance for Butler was from anchored ascensions, La Mountain's principal interest was the military value of free ballooning on favorable westerly winds, rising to catch constant easterly winds. La Mountain advocated free ballooning not only for reconnaissance but also for the bombardment of Confederate cities. But he argued that he needed to return home to bring a larger balloon and improved inflation apparatus. Butler recommended these free-ballooning ideas and their funding to Assistant Secretary of War Thomas A. Scott. Though there is no official documentation, there is evidence that Scott accepted Butler's recommendations. La Mountain returned home to Troy, New York, and retrieved his large balloon *Saratoga* to implement his free-ballooning ideas.

Porter and Franklin inherited and supported La Mountain's idea of free-ballooning reconnaissance, though there was no follow-up on aerial bombardment. La Mountain made his first experimental free excursion for Franklin on 4 October 1861 in the *Saratoga*. He continued to make valuable free-flight reconnaissance with the *Saratoga* until its loss in a mooring accident during a gale on 6 November 1861. Though restricted, La Mountain continued to provide useful free-flight as well as anchored reconnaissance with the deteriorating *Atlantic*.

La Mountain's military career and Civil War free ballooning came to an end over hostilities with Lowe. Lowe had established a reputation in the Army of the Potomac for his use of anchored balloons, including the first use of telegraph to communicate balloon observations. Lowe also had developed the first portable field generator that could quickly inflate a balloon. Lowe rejected the military feasibility of La Mountain's free ballooning, while La Mountain criticized Lowe's use of the telegraph. When La Mountain in his efforts to replace the *Saratoga* launched an intemperate campaign to acquire one of Lowe's balloons, McClellan placed all balloons under Lowe's authority. La Moun-

tain carried on for a time with the *Atlantic*. But when his unjust accusations against Lowe led to open hostilities, McClellan on 19 February 1862 dismissed La Mountain from service. La Mountain continued as a civilian aeronaut until his death at South Bend, Indiana, following an illness complicated by exposure and injuries suffered during a ballooning accident. It is not known if he ever married or had children.

All ballooning declined when General Joseph Hooker took command of the Army of the Potomac and displayed no interest in balloons. Lowe's independence and disrespect for military authority were part of the problem. But when the Army of the Potomac's chief engineer gained direct control over Lowe, he reinforced Hooker's indifference to balloons. After effectively pushing Lowe out of Union service, the engineers turned his balloons over to the Signal Corps, which showed no interest in reviving their use. With the removal of McClellan and his successor, General Ambrose Burnside, these pioneering experiments in military aeronautics appear to have been one technological innovation too many for early Civil War field command and staff organization to absorb.

Though the Union army terminated balloon operations in 1863, after the Chancellorsville campaign, their brief history marked the origins of U.S. military aeronautics. Building on the pioneering experience of the French in the revolutionary wars and the War of Italian Independence, the Civil War aeronauts extended both the technology and application of balloons. The Union army on occasion used balloons not only for reconnaissance but for mapmaking, tactical communications for command and control, and the indirect ranging and firing of artillery. For the first time there was a coordination of balloon and telegraph technology in warfare. The regular use of balloons in early Union field operations was part of an unprecedented military convergence of several industrial technologies that helped make the Civil War the first modern war.

• Primary material on La Mountain's service with Butler is found in the Benjamin F. Butler Papers, Manuscript Division, Library of Congress, and the *Private and Official Correspondence of General Benjamin F. Butler during the Period of the Civil War* (1917). A rare glimpse into La Mountain's mind, pertaining in this instance to the controversies of free ballooning as science and as art, is found in his letter in the 18 July 1863 issue of *Scientific American*, p. 246. The most extensive analysis of La Mountain and his place in Civil War aeronautics is Frederick Stansbury Haydon, *Aeronautics in the Union and Confederate Armies* (1941). Russell J. Parkinson also assesses La Mountain in "Politics, Patents, and Planes: Military Aeronautics in the United States, 1863–1907" (Ph.D. diss., Duke Univ., 1963). To place Civil War aeronautics in the general history of ballooning, see L. T. C. Rolt, *The Aeronauts: A History of Ballooning 1783–1903* (1966). Edward Hagerman, *The American Civil War and the Origins of Modern Warfare: Ideas, Organization, and Field Command* (1988), attempts to place La Mountain and Civil War aeronautics amid other technological and organizational developments in the origins of modern warfare. On La Mountain's antebellum ballooning with John Wise, see Wise's *Through the Air* (1873). See also U.S. War Department, *The War of the Rebellion: A Compilation of the Official Records of the Union and Confederate Armies* (128 vols., 1880–1901).

EDWARD HAGERMAN

L'AMOUR, Louis Dearborn (22 Mar. 1908–10 June 1988), author, was born in Jamestown, North Dakota, the son of Louis Charles LaMoore, a veterinarian, mechanic, deputy sheriff, policeman, and alderman, and Emily Dearborn. In 1923, after a rugged outdoors boyhood during which he received minimal schooling but did much private reading, he moved with his parents to Oklahoma. Immediately thereafter he started what he called his knockabout years. He worked on farms, ranches, and circuses, was a professional boxer, miner, and lumberjack, and shipped as a sailor to ports all around the world. He started using the name L'Amour—rather than his actual family name, LaMoore—when he sold his first short story to *True Gang Life* magazine in 1935. In 1938 he returned to Oklahoma and began writing book reviews, lectured a little, and published a number of short stories about sailors and detectives (sometimes under pseudonyms) in pulp magazines. He also published a book of rather weak poetry (1939). Entering the American army in 1942, he served in France and Germany as an antitank and transportation officer.

In 1946 L'Amour moved to Los Angeles, determined to write popular fiction, mainly westerns. His first novel, *Westward the Tide*, was published in London (1950) and went unnoticed. However, his short story "The Gift of Cochise," which appeared in *Collier's* in 1952, quickly propelled L'Amour to fame, especially when he expanded the story into the novel *Hondo* (1953) and John Wayne appeared in the movie version. Bantam Publishers put L'Amour under permanent contract (beginning in 1955) for two and then three novels a year. In 1956 L'Amour married television actress Katherine Elizabeth Adams, settled into a busy writing schedule, and began to enjoy unparalleled success as a writer of what he termed frontier fiction. The L'Amours and their two children gradually acquired four homes (one in Los Angeles, one on a ranch nearby, and two in Durango, Colorado) and traveled extensively for research and pleasure throughout the United States, Canada, Europe, and the Far East. Over the years L'Amour also amassed a western reference library of about 10,000 books in addition to maps, manuscripts, artifacts, paintings, and other memorabilia.

L'Amour produced ninety novels, seventeen collections of short stories, four books of nonfictional prose, and a book of poetry. He claimed that he wrote more than 400 short stories, but publication has been verified for only 194. L'Amour's fiction has been translated into at least twenty languages, notably French, German, Italian, and Spanish. Twenty-five of his plots have been converted into movies and television shows. Moreover, in 1986 L'Amour entered the audiotape market. Counting those produced after his death, more than three dozen adaptations of his short stories are now available on tape—complete with dialogue, voice-overs, and sound effects. By 1992, sales figures for these tapes passed the one-million mark. L'Amour's book sales, however, best reflect his astounding popular success. By 1977, 50 million copies of L'Amour's books were in print; by 1980, 100 million; and by 1990, more than 200 million.

L'Amour's works include romantic historical fiction, family sagas, and a few miscellaneous items—mostly essays about the West and short critical pieces. The majority of his novels, however, follow the tried-and-true formula invented by Owen Wister and embellished by Zane Grey, Max Brand, Ernest Haycox, and more recent authors. L'Amour's best such work is *Hondo*. In it, an Arizona army scout of the 1870s helps a deserted ranch wife and her son, later reluctantly kills her vicious husband, and finally saves her from Apaches. In *Flint* (1960), an orphan, helped by a New Mexico gunman who is then murdered, moves to the East, becomes rich but unhappy there, returns to the West, and is invigorated not only by participation in violence caused by corrupt railroaders, cattlemen, and a female rancher, but also by a desire for revenge. *Sitka* (1957), L'Amour's best historical novel, is about a daring Alaskan trader in the 1860s. L'Amour's weakest historical novel is *The First Fast Draw* (1959), in which the sordid career of real-life Texas gunman Cullen Baker is altered and sanitized beyond recognition.

L'Amour scored his greatest success with his seventeen-volume series detailing the adventures of his fictitious Sackett family, extending over two continents and three centuries. It begins in Elizabethan England when Barnabas Sackett plans to move to the Carolinas for adventure and profit (*Sackett's Land* [1974], *To the Far Blue Mountains* [1976], etc.). He sires a mighty brood, including three sons who move West (for example, *Jubal Sackett* [1985]). The most active of their nineteenth-century descendants are introduced in *The Daybreakers* (1960) and then followed along various western trails (for example, *The Sackett Brand* [1965]) and into Mexico (*The Lonely Men* [1969]) and Canada (*Lonely on the Mountain* [1980]), from 1866 to about 1880. L'Amour started two more family sagas, respectively featuring Chantrys (often scholars) and Talons (mostly builders). The best of the five Chantry novels is *Fair Blows the Wind* (1978), about a sixteenth-century Irish swordsman/lover; the best of the three Talon novels is *Rivers West* (1975), featuring a Canadian-born shipbuilder not long after the Louisiana Purchase. L'Amour planned to interlock his three family sagas into a mega-saga of perhaps fifty books but did not live to accomplish that task.

Late in his crowded life, L'Amour also sought to break out of the western writer's mold. His first such effort, and also his best, was *The Walking Drum* (1984). It is based on painstaking research and narrates the adventures of an impossibly talented sailor, fighter, merchant, linguist, scientist, and scholar as he searches for his missing father—from Brittany and Spain through Europe to Kiev and the Middle East from 1176 to 1180. Continuing L'Amour's nonwestern experiments, *The Last of the Breed* (1986) details a downed U.S. Air Force jet pilot's escape from the Soviets in Siberia. Finally, L'Amour published *The Sackett Companion: A Personal Guide to the Sackett Novels* (1988) to shed light on his best family saga. His death from cancer, in Los Angeles, prevented his completing *Education of a Wandering Man*, an intellectual autobiography published posthumously (1989).

In addition to entertaining generations of western buffs, L'Amour has educated millions of readers around the world about the history of the American West and much else, in pictorial, didactic, often hastily written, but always fact-crammed fiction. His phenomenal popularity is partly owing to his old-fashioned, infectious respect for nature, country, and traditional family values, but mainly to his uncanny narrative skill. He often said, "I think of myself in the oral tradition—as a troubadour, a village taleteller, the man in the shadows of the campfire. That's the way I'd like to be remembered—as a storyteller. A good storyteller." He will long be so remembered.

• Hal W. Hall, *The Work of Louis L'Amour: An Annotated Bibliography & Guide* (1991), includes primary and secondary material and is thorough and reliable. Robert Weinberg, *The Louis L'Amour Companion* (1992), presents annotated checklists of everything L'Amour published, unreprinted articles and letters by L'Amour, interviews with him, and many critical essays about him, including eight not previously published. Christine Bold, *Selling the Wild West: Popular Western Fiction, 1860 to 1960* (1987), and Loren D. Estleman, *The Wister Trace: Classical Novels of the American Frontier* (1987), separately locate L'Amour in the pop culture tradition. Robert L. Gale, *Louis L'Amour: Revised Edition* (1992), offers the most complete critical and biographical treatment. See also Harold E. Hinds, Jr., "Mexican and Mexican-American Images in the Western Novels of Louis L'Amour," *Latin-American Literary Review* 5 (Spring-Summer 1977): 129–41, for an examination of L'Amour's Mexican and Mexican-American characters; John D. Nesbitt, "Change of Purpose in the Novels of Louis L'Amour," *Western American Literature* 13 (Spring 1978): 65–81, on L'Amour's partial switch from formulary novels to family and historical novels; John G. Hubbell, "Louis L'Amour: Storyteller of the Wild West," *Reader's Digest*, July 1980, pp. 93–98, for a spirited biographical discussion; Michael T. Marsden, "Louis L'Amour," in *Fifty Western Writers: A Bio-Bibliographical Sourcebook*, ed. Fred Erisman and Richard W. Etulain (1982), for a succinct treatment of L'Amour's themes; and Donald Dale Jackson, "World's Fastest Literary Gun: Louis L'Amour," *Smithsonian*, May 1987, pp. 154–70, on L'Amour's methods and achievements.

ROBERT L. GALE

LAMPE, Isadore (16 Nov. 1906–25 Jan. 1982), radiologist, was born Isadore Lampkovitz in London, England, the son of Anna Tamarkin, a Russian, and Joseph Lampkovitz, a cabinetmaker from Poland. He entered the United States when only four and a half months old, wrapped in a tallith, a Jewish prayer shawl. They family settled in Cleveland, Ohio, where they adopted the conservative practices of Orthodox Judaism developed in the United States. Young Isa-

dore attended Mount Pleasant Elementary School and, at the same time, the Hebrew School. In 1923 he graduated with honors from Central High School.

Lampe was admitted within a restricted quota to Adelbert College in Cleveland (the college had an unwritten rule of admitting only 10 percent of eligible Jews), where he became a member of Phi Beta Kappa. At the end of his junior year he was accepted to the School of Medicine of Western Reserve University, which he entered in 1927. His classmates called him "Lamp," and after some thought he legally changed his family name to Lampe. During his second year in medical school he suffered a serious bout of pneumonia, and the resulting long hospitalization forced him to repeat his second year. A member of the Sigma Xi and Alpha Omega Alpha, he received his M.D. in 1931.

That same year Lampe took a position as an intern in St. Vincent Hospital in Toledo, Ohio. There he met an inspiring enthusiast of medical radiology, John Thomas Murphy, and decided to seek training in that field. In 1932 Lampe began serving his residency in the Department of Radiology at the University of Michigan in Ann Arbor. A dedicated and resourceful worker, he was appointed as an instructor in 1934, before the end of his residency a year later. Retained on the staff of the department, he developed an original system of filing and cross-indexing records that was later adopted by other departments. This was important because to that time no standard system of filing had been in use.

At Ann Arbor, like other contemporary centers, the emphasis was on radiodiagnostic excellence. The division of radiotherapy was entrusted to a succession of self-trained amateurs with no special preparation in radiation oncology. In 1939 Lampe was asked to head the division. In 1932 the chargeless atomic particle displaced by proton bombardment was recognized and named *neutron*, and accelerators of atomic particles were developed. Lampe became interested in testing the relative biological effectiveness of neutrons as compared with X-rays. He spent six months at the Radiation Laboratory of the University of California at Berkeley, where Ernest Lawrence had his original cyclotron. When a cyclotron was built in Ann Arbor, Lampe continued his observations there. He concluded that the selective effects of neutrons were inferior to those of X-rays, an important deduction in the process of destroying tumors by irradiation while preserving the normal structures.

In 1944 Lampe published an editorial in the journal *Radiology* that established him as a leader of radiation oncology. His editorial emphasized the preeminence of radiotherapy in the treatment of certain forms of cancer. Malignant tumors of the cerebellum had long been considered incurable by surgery. Lampe irradiated these tumors in children, becoming the first to demonstrate that they were curable with radiotherapy. He was recognized as an original researcher, and his attention to the demanding details of clinical practice, the methodical review of the world's literature on radiotherapy, the accurate reporting of his results, and teaching brought him to the forefront of the development of radiology as a medical specialty. The postwar work in atomic research provided large sources of artificially radioactivated cobalt and cesium, and Lampe fruitfully investigated their possibilities in the treatment of cancer. He pioneered investigation of the use of radioactive isotopes and showed remarkable results in the treatment of cancer of the oral cavity.

An autodidact without an opportunity to serve under an experienced master, Lampe became the outstanding academic radiotherapist in the United States. The Department of Radiology of the University of Michigan was devoted to the training of general radiologists, and although Lampe was exceptionally qualified to train radiotherapists, he was not permitted during his thirty-five year tenure to do so. However, a number of the general radiology residents, who spent six months under him, abandoned the practice of radiodiagnosis and became leaders of the growing specialty of radiotherapy. Lampe was one of the charter members of the International Club of Radiotherapists (1953) and the American Club of Therapeutic Radiologists (1958). He received the gold medal of the American Society of Therapeutic Radiologists in 1979 for his pioneering work in the radiotherapy of cancer, and the Distinguished Teaching and Research Award of the University of Michigan alumni. The University of Michigan created the Isadore Lampe Endowed Chair of Radiation Oncology. A quiet man, he was an amateur photographer with an interest in sports and sports cars. After his retirement in 1980, he suffered from chronic lymphogenous leukemia. On his way to receiving a blood transfusion, he was involved in an automobile accident and died in Ann Arbor as a consequence. He had married Rae Ethel White in 1943; they had two sons.

• Lampe's writings include "The Radiation Therapist in Contemporary Medicine," *Radiology* 43 (1944): 181–83; with R. S. MacIntyre, "Experiences in Radiation Therapy of Medulloblastoma of the Cerebellum," *Arch. Neurol. Psych.* 71 (1954): 659–68; and Lampe et al., *Radiology for Medical Students* (1947). See also J. A. del Regato, "Isadore Lampe (1906–1982)," in *Radiological Oncologists* (1993), and del Regato, "Isadore Lampe," *International Journal of Radiation Oncology, Biology, Physics* 10, no. 2 (Feb. 1984): 173–83.

JUAN A. DEL REGATO

LAMPKIN, Daisy Elizabeth Adams (9 Aug. 1888–10 Mar. 1965), civil and women's rights activist, was born in Reading, Pennsylvania, the daughter of George S. Adams and Rosa Ann Proctor. She attended public schools in Reading and, shortly after graduating, moved to Pittsburgh, Pennsylvania, in 1909. In 1912 she married William L. Lampkin, a restaurant owner. The couple did not have any children, but they raised the daughter of a deceased friend.

Lampkin was an active member of several organizations. She worked with the National Council of Negro Women (NCNW), the National Association of Colored Women, the Links (a community and social group), and the Lucy Stone Civic League. Through the Lucy Stone Civic League she promoted the issue of woman suffrage among the black community, and by 1943 she had raised more than $6,000 in scholarships. Lampkin was a charter member and served as board chair of the NCNW. She also served on the board of the Pittsburgh branch of the National Urban League and as vice president of the *Pittsburgh Courier* Publishing Company from 1929 to 1965. Lampkin actually began her association with the *Courier* in 1913 when she won a prize for selling the most new subscriptions to the paper. She invested the prize money in *Courier* stock, expanding her investment until she was appointed vice president in 1929.

Lampkin was an active member of her church, Grace Memorial Presbyterian, where she served as an elder. In 1947 she became the first individual in twenty years to be inducted as an honorary member of Delta Sigma Theta Sorority.

Like many African Americans during this time, Lampkin was also active in the Republican party, serving as vice chair of the Colored Voters' Division of the Republican National Committee. She chaired the Negro Women's Republican League in Allegheny County and served as vice chair of the Negro Voters League of Pennsylvania. In 1933 she was elected as the first black woman alternate delegate-at-large at the National Republican Convention. Lampkin switched her membership from the Republican party to the Democratic party after the election of Franklin Roosevelt in 1932. However, she returned to the Republican fold in 1952 when an avowed segregationist, John Sparkman of Alabama, was nominated by the Democrats for vice president.

It was Lampkin's work with the National Association for the Advancement of Colored People (NAACP) that would lead to her national acclaim. She was recruited to the organization by Walter White, and her service spanned the executive administrations of James Weldon Johnson, Walter White, and Roy Wilkins. She served on several committees and traveled throughout the country, establishing and revitalizing branches. She was eventually promoted to the positions of regional, then national, field secretary, jobs she held from 1927 to 1947. After her retirement as field secretary, she was appointed to the board of directors.

Lampkin is most well known for her indefatigable efforts at fundraising for the NAACP and as an advocate for civil rights organizations. In 1924 she was one of twelve people, and the only woman, called on by Johnson to meet with President Calvin Coolidge. The purpose of the meeting was to seek justice for black war veterans who had been accused of rioting in Houston, Texas.

Lampkin worked tirelessly to increase the membership of the NAACP. In 1945 she was named Woman of the Year by the NAACP because of her work on the organization's behalf. In 1947 she, more than any other of the organization's executives, increased the membership. The *Pittsburgh Courier* reported that she raised more than $1 million for the NAACP.

Lampkin also raised money for other organizations with which she was affiliated. She spearheaded the drive to found a national headquarters for the NCNW, providing $49,000 for the effort. She was also appointed to lead Delta Sigma Theta's fundraising drive to procure a national headquarters in Washington, D.C.

Lampkin battled against discrimination in its various forms. She promoted integration as a right, not a privilege, for black Americans. She participated in the 1935 meeting of the Association of Southern Women for the Prevention of Lynching, a white women's group. She informed its membership of the horrors of lynching, including its use as a form of political and social control; the implications for black men and boys went beyond the actual murders themselves. Lampkin encouraged the organization's support of the Costigan-Wagner Bill, legislation that would have required federal intervention into lynching cases. The ASWPL did not endorse the legislation, which confirmed Lampkin's belief that the ASWPL was not doing enough to prevent lynchings.

Lampkin used her association with the NAACP and the *Courier* as conduits for pushing forward her views. In an effort to defeat Supreme Court nominee John J. Parker of North Carolina, she embarked on a massive fundraising and membership drive for the NAACP. The NAACP considered Parker an archenemy of black people. The NAACP also worked toward the defeat of all senators who supported Parker's nomination. Lampkin is credited with the defeat of Senator Roscoe McCullough of Ohio, a Parker supporter who was seeking reelection in 1930; she revitalized and energized the Ohio NAACP conference to bring about McCullough's downfall.

In October 1924, while on a membership drive in New Jersey, Lampkin suffered a stroke. She was too ill to attend a ceremony hosted by the NCNW where she was to receive its first Eleanor Roosevelt–Mary Bethune World Citizenship Award. Lena Horne, her good friend, accepted on her behalf. Lampkin died at her home in Pittsburgh. On 9 August 1983 the Pennsylvania Historical and Museum Commission placed a historical marker at the site of her home at 2519 Webster Avenue. She was the first black woman to be so honored by the state.

• The most extensive and complete collection of Lampkin's papers is in the possession of Edna B. McKenzie of Roanoke, Pa. There is correspondence from Lampkin in the Nannie Helen Burroughs Papers, the NAACP Board of Directors Files (1956–1960), and Branch Files of the NAACP (1940–1955) in the Manuscript Division of the Library of Congress. Paula Giddings, *When and Where I Enter* (1984) and *In Search of Sisterhood* (1988), discuss Lampkin's association with the NAACP and Delta Sigma Theta Sorority, respectively.

MAMIE E. LOCKE

LAMY, John Baptist (11 Oct. 1814–13 Feb. 1888), Roman Catholic missionary and bishop, was born in Lempdes, France, the son of Jean Lamy and Marie Dié. Upon graduating from Clermont and the seminary of Montferrand, Lamy was ordained in December 1838. After working briefly as an assistant to a rector in Chapre, France, Lamy and his close friend Abbé Joseph Machebeuf joined Bishop John Purcell in 1839 on a missionary trip to the United States. Sent first to Wooster, Ohio, and then to Danville, Ohio, Lamy built a church in Danville and acted as its pastor for nine years. He was then called to serve in Covington, Kentucky, where he oversaw St. Mary's Church.

When what is now New Mexico became a territory of the United States in 1850, American bishops petitioned Rome to organize it into a vicariate apostolic. The quick approval of the request placed the region in Lamy's care; he was simultaneously consecrated as a bishop by Bishop M. J. Spalding in Cincinnati in November 1850. Lamy's journey from the East to New Mexico was perilous and long: threats from Native Americans necessitated a circuitous route, and the trip took over nine months. After a serious accident en route almost proved fatal, Lamy was forced to spend months recovering in San Antonio.

Lamy's task in New Mexico was a difficult one because the missionary presence in the Southwest had declined after the transfer of the territory from Mexico to the United States and the subsequent withdrawal of the Franciscan order. The initial reaction of his parishioners to a clergyman from elsewhere was hostile. Many still considered Bishop Antonio Zubiria to be in charge of the region because it had never been formally separated from his diocese of Durango, Mexico. Soon after arriving, Lamy traveled to Durango to meet with Zubiria, who welcomed him and wrote a letter to the clergy and parishioners of Lamy's area instructing them to accept their new bishop. With the exception of a few dissident clerics and a lay flagellant society, the Penitentes, the parishioners slowly grew to accept and respect Lamy for his piety, hard work, and willingness to endure difficulties and personal danger. In addition to clearing up existing problems of corruption and the abuse of power within the church, Lamy's priorities as bishop included the establishment of educational institutions and the recruitment of enough clergy to provide for the church's needs in the region. In 1852 he attended the First Plenary Council in Baltimore, returning with four members of the Sisters of Loretto from Kentucky to aid in opening an academy in Santa Fe. The following year he traveled to France and Rome in search of financial assistance. Made bishop of Santa Fe in July 1853, Lamy continued to preach and administer to his growing diocese with the help of fellow missionary Machebeuf, who had accompanied him to New Mexico. The diocese expanded geographically in 1854 when the Gadsden Purchase appended southern Arizona to the territory, and it grew in communicants as Lamy's missionary efforts bore fruit. The number of Catholics under his jurisdiction increased from 68,000 to more than 100,000 in fifteen years. In the same period of time, the diocese expanded from ten to thirty-seven priests, built forty-five new churches and repaired twenty more, and established seven convent schools. Lamy excelled at attracting missionaries to his region, including several members of the Sisters of Charity from Cincinnati in 1865 and a group of Jesuits from Naples in 1867. When Santa Fe was elevated to an archdiocese in 1875, Lamy was made its archbishop. After resigning his position in July 1885, he retired to a ranch north of Santa Fe. In the later years of his life, Lamy oversaw the construction of the French Romanesque Cathedral of San Francisco de Asis, which was dedicated in 1886. He died in Santa Fe.

A popular figure in Southwest history, Lamy has been variously commemorated. Willa Cather's novel *Death Comes for the Archbishop* (1927) is drawn from his life. A U.S. Navy vessel active in World War II was named *Archbishop Lamy* after him. Largely responsible for the spread of Catholicism in frontier Arizona, Lamy was an untiring and remarkably courageous leader and proselytizer in an undeveloped and often dangerous region. Lamy was a significant agent of settlement and growth in New Mexico and Arizona because of his drive to build schools and hospitals.

• For further information on Lamy, see W. J. Howlett, *Life of the Rt. Rev. Joseph P. Machebeuf, D.D.* (1908); J. H. Defouri, *Historical Sketch of the Catholic Church in New Mexico* (1887); J. B. Salpointe, *Soldiers of the Cross* (1898); and J. H. Shea, *History of the Catholic Church in the United States* (1892). An obituary is in the *Cincinnati Commercial Gazette*, 14 Feb. 1888.

ELIZABETH ZOE VICARY

LANCASTER, Burt (2 Nov. 1913–20 Oct. 1994), actor, was born Burton Stephen Lancaster in the Harlem section of New York City, the son of James Lancaster, a postal worker, and Elizabeth Roberts. After graduating from DeWitt Clinton High School at the age of sixteen in 1930, Lancaster attended New York University for two years on a basketball scholarship. An encounter with Australian gymnast Curly Brent (practicing high-bar maneuvers at a local settlement house gym) inspired the nimble Lancaster and a childhood friend, Nick Cravat, to form an acrobatic duo. Lancaster abandoned formal education in 1931 and for the next eight years performed with Cravat in circuses and vaudeville shows. They called their act Lang and Cravat for reasons of marquee brevity. In 1935 Lancaster married circus performer June Ernst, but the union ended in divorce after about a year. They had no children.

A hand injury and general disenchantment with the life of an acrobat prompted Lancaster to seek another occupation in 1940. He worked in Chicago as a department store floorwalker and as a classical music concert promoter before being drafted into the U.S. Army in 1942. His show business background resulted in an assignment to a special services entertainment unit in Europe. While serving in the military Lancaster met his future wife, Norma Anderson, a New York stenographer and sometime entertainer who was performing in a United Services Organization (USO) show.

Just after the end of World War II an associate of Broadway producer Irving Jacobs spotted Lancaster in an elevator in Manhattan's RCA building. The man suggested that the tall, muscular, and graceful Lancaster audition for a part in the new play *A Sound of Hunting*. Though he had no professional acting experience, Lancaster landed the role and, at the relatively advanced age of thirty-two, began his career as an actor. A battle drama with an all-male cast, *A Sound of Hunting* opened at the Lyceum Theatre on 20 November 1945. The play ran for only twenty-three performances but led to Lancaster's signing a contract with movie producer Hal B. Wallis, a longtime Warner Bros. studio executive who was setting up his own independent production company. Their arrangement was not exclusive, and while Wallis lined up projects for Lancaster, the latter sent a screen test to Mark Hellinger, another independent producer. Lancaster made his motion picture debut in Hellinger's *The Killers* (1946), an adaptation of an Ernest Hemingway story. The well-received film made Lancaster a star overnight and was followed by *Brute Force* (1947), a gritty prison drama also produced by Hellinger. Lancaster's first movies for Wallis were similar "film noir" dramas, including *Desert Fury* (1947), *I Walk Alone* and *Sorry, Wrong Number* (both 1948), and *Rope of Sand* (1949). In 1946 he married Anderson, with whom he had his only four children (Lancaster also adopted Anderson's son from a previous marriage).

From the start of his career in Hollywood the ambitious and self-confident Lancaster pushed for dramatically challenging roles despite his limited acting experience. He costarred with Edward G. Robinson in an unsuccessful adaptation of Arthur Miller's play *All My Sons* for Universal Pictures in 1948. That same year Lancaster set up his own production company in partnership with his agent, Harold Hecht. Their first collaboration was *Kiss the Blood off My Hands* (1948), a black-and-white film noir costarring Lancaster and Joan Fontaine. The popular Hecht-Lancaster Technicolor adventures *The Flame and the Arrow* (1950), featuring Lancaster as a medieval Robin Hood–type character, and *The Crimson Pirate* (1952), with Lancaster as an eighteenth-century swashbuckler, allowed him to break out of the somber "tough guy" mold and to show off his brilliant smile and impressive physique. (His athletic skills were also displayed in the 1951 Warner Bros. film *Jim Thorpe—All American*, a biography of the Olympic champion.) After a third partner, screenwriter James Hill, joined them in 1956, Lancaster and Hecht's production company continued to develop interesting but often unprofitable films—usually featuring Lancaster—until 1960, when mounting financial pressures and personal discord among the partners caused the company to disband.

Refusing to be categorized, Lancaster appeared in a wide variety of roles throughout his long career; he willingly took on unflattering, unheroic parts, downplayed his handsome appearance, and shared top billing with costars. In 1952 he grayed his light brown hair and wore baggy clothes to hide his trim waistline in order to perform, opposite Shirley Booth, the role of an unhappily married, disillusioned, alcoholic doctor in Hal Wallis's well-received film version of William Inge's play *Come Back, Little Sheba*. Still in his late thirties, Lancaster was twenty years too young for the part. Wallis, in his 1980 autobiography *Starmaker*, noted Lancaster's curious combination of arrogance and modesty, commenting, "Many male stars would have resisted, fearing that so unattractive an appearance might damage them in the eyes of their fans. But the good side of his cool confidence made any such loss of popularity unthinkable." The following year Lancaster blended into an ensemble cast (and earned his first Best Actor Academy Award nomination) as an embittered drill sergeant in love with an officer's wife (played by Deborah Kerr) in *From Here to Eternity*, one of the most critically and commercially successful films of the early 1950s. He played a supporting role as Anna Magnani's oafish suitor in *The Rose Tattoo* (1955), based on the Tennessee Williams play, and he was a smooth-talking charlatan charming a lonely Katharine Hepburn in *The Rainmaker* (1956). Other notable performances are his roles as Wyatt Earp in *Gunfight at the O.K. Corral* (1957), costarring Kirk Douglas; as a viciously powerful Broadway gossip columnist who blackmails young public relations agent Tony Curtis in *Sweet Smell of Success* (1957); and as an aggressive lieutenant who engages in a battle of wills with his older commanding officer (played by Clark Gable) in the submarine adventure *Run Silent, Run Deep* (1958).

Lancaster was part of another stellar ensemble cast in the film version of Terence Rattigan's play *Separate Tables* (1958), playing Rita Hayworth's ex-husband, an alcoholic writer. He won the Best Actor Academy Award in 1960 for his performance as a flamboyant and unscrupulous evangelist in the film version of Sinclair Lewis's novel *Elmer Gantry*. He was nominated again for the award two years later for his portrayal of Robert Stroud, a long-incarcerated murderer turned ornithologist, in *The Birdman of Alcatraz*. Often derided as a facile actor with more ambition than talent, Lancaster surprised most naysayers with his impressive performance as a nineteenth-century Italian aristocrat in director Luchino Visconti's highly regarded *The Leopard* (1963).

Although his years as a top box office draw had ended by the mid-1960s, Lancaster continued to work regularly. Important roles in the later part of his career include those in *The Swimmer* (1968), based on a short story by John Cheever; *Atlantic City* (1981), for which he earned a fourth Best Actor Academy Award nomination for his melancholic portrayal of an aging, small-time gangster; and *Local Hero* (1983), a rare foray into comedy with Lancaster as an eccentric Texas oil company executive who attempts to build an oil refinery in a remote Scottish village.

Divorced from Norma Anderson in 1969, Lancaster had a lengthy relationship with hairdresser Jackie Bone (they never married). In 1990 he married televi-

sion production coordinator Susan Scherer. Lancaster died at his home in Century City, California.

• The most complete source of information on Lancaster is Gary Fishgall, *Against Type: The Biography of Burt Lancaster* (1995). See also the biographies (all titled simply *Burt Lancaster*) by Robert Windeler (1984), Tony Thomas (1975), and Jerry Vermilye (1971), as well as David Fury, *The Cinema History of Burt Lancaster* (1989), and Allan Hunter, *Burt Lancaster: The Man and His Movies* (1984). There is a detailed article on Lancaster's film career by Mel Schuster in *Films in Review*, Aug.–Sept. 1969, pp. 393–408. An obituary is in the *New York Times*, 22 Oct. 1994.

MARY C. KALFATOVIC

LANCEFIELD, Rebecca Craighill (5 Jan. 1895–3 Mar. 1981), medical bacteriologist, was born in Fort Wadsworth, New York, the daughter of Colonel William E. Craighill, an officer in the U.S. Army Engineering Corps, and Mary Wortly Montague Byrum. She attended Wellesley College, graduating in 1916, and then taught for a year at a girls' school in Vermont.

Nearly all of Lancefield's long career in scientific research dealt with studies of the diverse group of pathogenic bacteria known as the streptococci. In humans, they are responsible for strep throat and a variety of other serious infections, as well as for initiating processes that lead to acute rheumatic fever and glomerulonephritis. Lancefield began working with the streptococci in 1918, just after receiving an M.A. from Columbia University and marrying a fellow graduate student, Donald E. Lancefield. That year she became a laboratory technician at the Rockefeller University for Medical Research. There she worked for two eminent medical microbiologists, Oswald T. Avery and Alphonse R. Dochez, who had initiated studies on a large collection of bacterial strains that had come from an epidemic of streptococcal disease in military camps in 1917.

It was not known whether this collection consisted of a single epidemic strain or of a number of similar but distinct streptococcal strains. It was Lancefield's assignment to try to answer this question with immunological methods, by using antibodies prepared by immunizing rabbits with selected strains and looking for differences in reactivity. Over a year she identified four clearly different serological types of streptococci that made up 70 percent of the organisms in the collection. Her paper with Avery and Dochez reporting these findings in 1919 ushered in the modern era of the study of streptococcal disease.

Lancefield then returned to graduate work in the biology department at Columbia University and in 1922 joined the staff of the Rockefeller Institute and resumed her studies on streptococci. She received a Ph.D. from Columbia in 1925, with work on streptococci forming the basis for her thesis.

It had become clear that there were many more specific types of streptococci causing human infections than the original four reported in 1919, and ultimately Lancefield identified several dozen. She became interested in the nature of the constituent of the streptococcus that was responsible for this diversity and devised ways of extracting the specific substance from the bacterial cells in soluble form. By purification of the soluble material, she was able to establish that it was a protein, which she designated the "M protein."

Further studies revealed that the M protein was essential for the virulence or disease-producing capacity of the organism, and that it acted by preventing white blood cells from engulfing and destroying the bacteria. An antibody specific for the M protein would block this effect and protect experimental animals from infection by the organism. However, the protection was type-specific, and antibody to one type would not neutralize any of the other numerous types of streptococci. Thus the significance of multiple types became clear: it meant that immunity was largely type-specific, and this explained the occurrence of repeated bouts of strep throat in the same individual throughout childhood, as well as the frequent recurrence of acute rheumatic fever.

During these experiments Lancefield was also engaged in other studies that brought some order into the classification of all recognized streptococci, including those from animal species other than man. This was also accomplished by serological means, but the antigen that served to divide streptococci into several well-defined groups was shown to be a carbohydrate rather than a protein. The human streptococci of the different M protein types all proved to fall in the same group, which was designated group A. Organisms in group B were derived primarily from bovine sources, although they were sometimes encountered in human infections, notably in newborns. Groups C through H had other distributions in nature, occasionally also occurring in man.

Lancefield found that group B streptococci also were divided into specific types, though not nearly so numerous as those of group A, and that in this case the type-specific antigens were both a carbohydrate, present as a capsule surrounding the cell, and a protein. Both of these antigens determine the virulence of the organism, much as M protein does in group A.

This summary of the highlights of Lancefield's research gives only a hint of her contributions over several decades. Her classification of streptococci into groups and types brought order into the identification and study of the organisms and at the same time made possible epidemiologic studies and new approaches to the understanding and control of streptococcal disease. Her preeminence was recognized among workers in the field internationally, a fact best illustrated by the action of both the U.S. and the international scientific organizations for study of streptococci and streptococcal disease in changing their official names to the Lancefield Society.

Lancefield received numerous other honors, including election to the National Academy of Sciences and to the presidency of the Society of American Bacteriologists and of the American Association of Immunologists. She was active in laboratory work until shortly before her death and continued her long-established pattern of offering help to others in the field. She provided well-defined bacterial strains and specific antisera to laboratories all over the world for the initiation of streptococcal studies.

Lancefield died in New York City. Her husband, a professor of biology, survived her by only a few months; they had one daughter.

• Nearly all of Lancefield's research was published in the *Journal of Experimental Medicine*. Her summary of the early work on the classification of streptococci appeared in *Harvey Lectures* 36 (1941): 251–90. A more detailed statement on her life and contributions is the entry by Maclyn McCarty in National Academy of Sciences, *Biographical Memoirs* 57 (1987): 227–46, which lists all her papers on the streptococcal studies. An obituary is in the *New York Times*, 4 Mar. 1981.

MACLYN MCCARTY

LANCHESTER, Elsa (28 Oct. 1902–26 Dec. 1986), actress, was born Elsa Sullivan Lanchester in Lewisham, London, England, the daughter of James Sullivan and Edith Lanchester, prominent socialists. By the age of eleven, Lanchester was studying dance with Isadora Duncan and assisting her on lecture tours. While still in her teens, Lanchester gave dance lessons and directed a children's theater. By 1920 she had made her stage debut in a music hall act, and two years later she acted in *Thirty Minutes in a Street*, her first performance in London's West End. In 1924 she founded a London theatrical club, the Cave of Harmony.

Lanchester's first film role was in an amateur production, *The Scarlet Woman* (1924), but soon she was getting parts in short professional releases such as *One of the Best* (1927); *The Constant Nymph, Bluebottles, The Tonic, Daydreams* (all 1928); and *Mr. Smith Wakes Up* (1929). By 1927, when she met Charles Laughton, Lanchester had established a significant reputation: the novelist H. G. Wells had already written three one-act plays for her. She married Laughton in February 1929; they had no children. The couple costarred in several plays and movies, most notably on the stage in *Payment Deferred* (produced in London in 1931 and in New York in 1932), and in *The Private Life of Henry VIII* (1933), the film that made Laughton a Hollywood star. Lanchester gave a stunning performance as Anne of Cleves, one of the king's wives. Although Lanchester was as temperamental as Laughton and the couple often quarreled, they had profound respect for each other's talent.

Lanchester's lack of conventional beauty and her small size did not lend itself to Hollywood stardom. By commercial film standards, her frizzy red hair and stubby nose were not considered photogenic, and she was relegated to character roles.

Lanchester is best remembered for her brilliant performance in *The Bride of Frankenstein* (1935), in which she played both Mary Shelley and the monster's mate. Her unconventional features and hair that looked electrified made her the perfect bride for the man-made monster galvanized into life. The heavily made-up Lanchester put a good deal of her eccentric personality into the role, hissing and screaming, her body wrapped in yards of bandages and wire. Lanchester enjoyed playing this character, especially because she could also show her soberer side in portraying the sedate, well-mannered Mary Shelley. This film was one of her few opportunities to display an acting range that rivaled Laughton's.

Although it may seem strange to call *The Bride of Frankenstein* Lanchester's legacy to the screen, her performance does transcend the limitations of the horror genre. She charged the role of the bride with an almost frightening energy, capturing the strange struggle of a creature coming to life and learning to be human. And her counter role as Mary Shelley showed that she could play more "normal" personalities and had a repertory of skills too infrequently employed because she was not given leading parts.

Indeed, the rest of Lanchester's film career unfolded like the extremes she explored in *The Bride of Frankenstein*. She held her own with Laughton in major films such as *The Beachcomber* (1938) and *Witness for the Prosecution* (1957), for which they both received Academy Award nominations. She also specialized in delightful cameo roles, including a bizarre artist in *The Big Clock* (1948) and a muddled witch in *Bell, Book, and Candle* (1958).

In the 1940s Lanchester revived her nightclub career, singing cabaret at the Turnabout Theatre in Los Angeles, and in the 1960s she created a one-woman show, *Elsa Lanchester—Herself*, that was an extraordinary commercial and critical success. She also received a best supporting actress nomination for *Come to the Stable* (1949) and appeared on television in "The John Forsyte Show" (1965–1966) and "Nanny and the Professor" (1971). She remained active as a film actress until 1980. She died in Woodland Hills, California.

Although unquestionably a brilliant actress, Lanchester labored in the shadow of Laughton, to whom she remained married until his death in 1962. His genius seemed to consume the attention of Hollywood directors and producers, who would offer Lanchester roles almost as an afterthought—creating the impression that she depended on her husband's success. Laughton's fame did not daunt Lanchester, however. Indeed, he represented a steadiness and security that she lacked in her early career. Or as she put it, she had tired of the bohemian life, and her husband offered "middle-class respectability."

Lanchester believed that producers resented the obligation to hire her in order to get Laughton, the real prize. As a result, her bit parts and cameos, no matter how well done, confined her to a niche and conveyed the impression of a minor talent. Yet Lanchester, an ebullient personality, did not allow this shabby treatment to destroy her talent. On the contrary, she determined that every role she played, no matter how small, would be done to her utmost—as if, she said, she were "acting with a pistol at [her] head."

Lanchester worked steadily on the stage and screen in England and in films in Hollywood for many years, receiving excellent reviews. She was admired for her spirited and versatile style, and she was the last Peter Pan to be personally selected by playwright James Barrie. But she did not receive the recognition or popularity that her husband enjoyed as one of the most renowned actors of his period. Lanchester's film roles did not equal her earlier theatrical success. Her contribution to the screen was best captured in *The Bride of Frankenstein*.

• Lanchester published two books, *Charles Laughton and I* (1968) and *Elsa Lanchester Herself* (1983). Her career is discussed in David Shipman, *The Great Movie Stars* (1979). Biographies of Laughton that discuss Lanchester are Kurt D. Singer, *The Laughton Story: An Intimate Story of Charles Laughton* (1954); Charles Higham, *Charles Laughton: An Intimate Biography* (1976); and Simon Callow, *Charles Laughton: A Difficult Actor* (1987).

CARL E. ROLLYSON

LAND, Edwin Herbert (7 May 1909–1 Mar. 1991), inventor, was born in Bridgeport, Connecticut, the son of Harry M. Land, a prosperous scrap and salvage metal dealer, and Martha F. (full maiden name unknown). He attended public schools and then Norwich Academy, a private high school, and showed an early flair for science. After entering Harvard in 1926, Land became increasingly fascinated with the practical possibilities of light polarization. While ordinary light is not polarized—it radiates in all directions—various methods can induce polarization, wherein light rays vibrate primarily in only one direction. Land was seeking efficient means of manufacturing polarizing glass or plastic. He foresaw that such material, in commercial quantities, could have many applications in photographic filtering and scientific research. He spent 1927–1928 in New York City reading in libraries and working in a small ill-equipped laboratory trying to perfect his ideas. He pursued this research for several more years in Cambridge, Massachusetts, while intermittently continuing with courses at Harvard. During this research he married Helen Maislen in 1929. They had two daughters. Feeling he was drawing close to success with his quest for light-polarizing plastic, he left college just one semester shy of graduation and never completed his undergraduate degree. An honorary doctorate from Harvard decades later in 1957 (in addition to others) led to Land's being widely referred to as Doctor Land.

Land and the former Harvard physics faculty member George Wheelwright III formed Land-Wheelwright Laboratories in 1932 and continued their experimentation, working toward a commercially marketable light-polarizing filter. By 1934–1935 the company was providing such material, which they marketed under the trade name Polaroid, for American Optical sunglasses and signed a $10,000 contract with Kodak for photographic filters as well. Further demonstrations of the polarizing principle and its applications (including dimming of automobile headlight glare, a pet project of Land's almost from the beginning) in several cities led to outside investment of

$375,000 to support what in late 1937 became the Polaroid Corporation, which took over all the patents, work, and assets of Land-Wheelwright. *Fortune* published a positive article on the company's prospects as early as 1938.

Land's shaky commercial operation, headquartered then and since in Cambridge, was financially stabilized in 1940–1941 with large military contracts for a small hand-held Personal Angle Finder (used to determine the elevation of an airplane above the horizon), polarized goggles, tank gun sights, three-dimensional air photography, photo-directed bombs, and other projects. During the war years when manufacturing was devoted to military needs, employment peaked at more than 1,200.

Land's chief invention developed out of a 1943 vacation trip to New Mexico when his three-year-old daughter asked why she could not immediately see a photograph he had just taken of her. The question prompted Land to develop instant photography. As he put it in a memoir in a collection of his papers, "Within the hour, the camera, the film, and the physical chemistry became . . . clear to me." But further development had to await the end of wartime manufacturing priorities. After extensive research spearheaded by Land, the first public demonstration of a sepia-and-white Polaroid camera took place at a New York meeting of the Optical Society of America in 1947. The bulky Model 95 cameras were a huge marketing success—despite their steep $89.50 price tag—when introduced in a Boston department store in time for the 1948 Christmas season. But the rolls of film and print paper took sixty seconds to develop and had to be coated to prevent fading. Improvements led to true black-and-white photographs in 1950, though users still had to apply a chemical coating on the finished print to stop further development. By 1956 more than a million of these cameras had been sold. Progressively smaller cameras and faster film appeared regularly. By 1960, with 3,000 people making cameras and film, Polaroid Land cameras produced pictures in ten seconds. Photographer Ansel Adams was a consultant on Land camera applications from 1948 until his death in 1984. His work, and that of others, helped Land cameras enter the photographic mainstream.

For a brief period, three-dimensional movies appeared to be an important and lasting industry. Polaroid produced six million pairs of cardboard-and-plastic viewer glasses a week for theatrical use in 1953 and had 70 million more on order with plans for opening a number of new factories, but the market dried up when the movie fad faded a short time later.

Color Polaroid photography was first announced in 1959 and commercially marketed as Polacolor in 1963. A popular low-cost camera, the Swinger, debuted two years later. By 1968 Polaroid employed some 7,000 people working in numerous manufacturing plants.

The technically elegant SX-70 single-lens reflex folding Polaroid camera (the odd name came from the file designation for the original Land camera project in the 1940s) appeared in 1972, producing dry color prints in less than sixty seconds. The complex technology of its thirteen-layer self-developing color film and intricate optics, perhaps the peak of Land's quest for perfection in instant photography, marked a Polaroid technological high point. Less expensive versions of the camera appeared in subsequent years. Constantly broadening the product line, Polaroid introduced improved self-processing 35mm color slide film as well as black-and-white slide film in the early 1980s.

Continued technical problems with batteries and films forced down company earnings and deflated company stock from record highs in 1972 to record lows just two years later. Under pressure from the company board and financial analysts, both concerned about management succession, Land appointed William McCune, a long-time colleague, as president and became chairman. Though his spirit and technical prowess were central to the company's success, his timing and marketing instincts were not always on target. After a decade of development, in 1977 the company introduced Polavision instant (but silent) motion pictures. In just two years Polavision cost the firm $70 million in losses in a fruitless competition with videotape's ease of use and expanding popularity before the film product was terminated in 1979. Those losses were in part responsible for Land's final retirement as Polaroid's chairman in 1982.

Leaving Polaroid, Land turned to full-time research at the Rowland Foundation, later renamed the Rowland Institute for Science, a Cambridge-based nonprofit research organization that he had founded and funded in 1979 or 1980. He had come full circle, involving himself once again in the pure research on various aspects of optics and light that had fascinated him from the start.

Land developed his working style early on—often 24-hour days when in the initial stages of working out problems. His concentration was legendary—until he got on top of a problem, after which he would rapidly lose interest. His primary fields of knowledge were chemistry, optics, and physics, but he read widely in both general and technical literature. He was shy and diffident and for years had difficulty speaking before large groups. As Polaroid grew, however, he overcame this drawback and became well known for his seeming ease before admiring crowds while demonstrating new products. He conducted experiments and product development along the lines of an academic seminar, which often exhausted younger assistants. He thrived on trying to resolve the unknown or heretofore impossible problems. He wasn't joking when he often repeated that anything worth doing was worth doing to excess. He gave great loyalty to company products, occasionally verging on blindness to suggestions made by others for improvements or modifications. Land eventually held 537 patents (second only to Edison); the first in 1933 was a device for polarizing light. He had little use for market research and less for advertising.

Over the years, Land served as an adviser on numerous government projects. In the 1950s he helped to perfect the U-2 aircraft camera system that for years took aerial photos of the Soviet Union. He was an early proponent of spy satellites. He was appointed to be a member of the 1965–1967 Carnegie Commission that developed the idea for public television. Land remained a part-time adviser to presidents until the Nixon Watergate scandal. He served as a Ford Foundation trustee from 1967 to 1975. Among the many awards he received are the Presidential Medal of Freedom (1963) and the National Medal of Science (1967). He died in Cambridge.

• Land's life and the history of the company he created are detailed in Peter C. Wensberg, *Land's Polaroid: A Company and the Man Who Invented It* (1987), which tells the tale from the inside—from 1958 to 1982 Wensberg was a Polaroid official; and Mark Olshaker, *The Instant Image: Edwin Land and the Polaroid Experience* (1978). There is no scholarly or scientific study of the man or his company. Richard Saul Wurman, *Polaroid: Access Fifty Years* (1989), offers a usefully detailed illustrated chronology of the company. For examples of detailed trade reports on the company and its leader, see "In the Light of Polaroid: Cameras, Sunglasses, Windows, Movies, and Night Driving May Be Different," *Fortune*, Sept. 1938; "Polaroid's Big Gamble on Small Cameras," *Time*, 26 June 1972; "How Polaroid Bet Its Future on the SX-70," *Fortune*, Jan. 1974; and "Polaroid Struggles to Get Back in Focus," *Fortune*, 7 Apr. 1980. For practical aspects of the Polaroid Land Camera, see Ed Hannigan, "Polaroid Photography," *Encyclopedia of Photography*, vol. 16 (1964), pp. 2937–51, and Ansel Adams, *Polaroid Land Photography* (1978).

CHRISTOPHER H. STERLING

LANDER, Frederick West (17 Dec. 1821–2 Mar. 1862), topographical engineer and explorer, was born in Salem, Massachusetts, the son of Edward Lander, a well-to-do factory owner, and Eliza West. Educated at private academies, he later studied engineering privately and at Norwich Military Academy in preparation for a career as an assistant engineer for eastern railroads. Isaac Stevens, another Massachusetts man, tapped Lander as one of his subordinates on the northern railroad survey, one of several western explorations authorized by Congress in 1853.

Stevens viewed his mission as one to find the best route for a transcontinental railroad but also the investigation of a broad band of territory south (and sometimes north) of the forty-ninth parallel. Lander headed one of the parties that made extended reconnaissances, including one into Canada to find the source of the Souris River, which flowed south into the Missouri River. Sent to explore Lewis and Clark Pass in the Rocky Mountains, Lander became lost and then attempted a shortcut through the mountains to the Bitterroot Valley. The party barely survived the venture, adding to Lander's growing reputation as a good engineer, intelligent and courageous, but a hard driver of men and animals. During the several months of the survey Lander revealed another characteristic that marked his career, a dislike of working for others. Failure to follow orders earned him more than one reprimand from Stevens.

When the survey party arrived in Olympia, Lander took issue with his superior's position that the northern route was not only practicable but likely the best alternative, as it provided the closest connection to the markets of Asia. Lander argued that the line would run too close to a potentially hostile Canada as well as crossing inhospitable territory noted for severe weather. The Washington legislature endorsed Lander's proposal to survey a route from Puget Sound to Council Bluffs via the Columbia and Snake rivers and South Pass. All of his six companions but one (who died soon after) were lost or deserted on the trip, during which they were reduced to subsisting on thistle roots and mule meat. Lander extolled the virtues of his route in a report published by Congress (which after Lander's death reimbursed his widow for the self-financed venture). A notable argument made in the report was that first, a wagon road, second, a rough, rapidly built railroad, and finally a permanent rail line should be constructed in successive stages as the needs of the country required.

Lander's western experience, his political standing as a staunch Democrat, his outspoken opinions, and his physical stature recommended the engineer-explorer for the important position of chief engineer for the Fort Kearney, South Pass, and Honey Lake Wagon Road under William M. F. McGraw in 1857. With sectional wrangling holding up federal approval of a transcontinental railroad, Congress appeared to follow Lander's advice by appropriating $300,000 for a wagon road along the central route, which would speed immigrants, the mail, and freight to California. As Lander assumed his duties, he was described by a friend: "Above middle height, and most powerfully built, he looked both active and indolent, both stately and careless. It was something between the complete soldier-likeness of a Knight Templar and the covert agility of a panther on the prowl" (*San Francisco Evening Bulletin*, 15 May 1860?). His physical presence and temperament and his killing of a grizzly bear with a six-shooter earned Lander the sobriquet "Old Grizzly."

In the summer of 1857 Lander, by his account, covered 3,000 miles on horseback in ninety days. The major accomplishment achieved by his party of fourteen was a thorough exploration of the territory lying between South Pass and Salt Lake and the more northerly alternative across present southern Idaho. Lander recommended the latter because of better water and wood, although it was longer and the grades more severe. That year's difficulties between the Mormons and the government also likely influenced Lander's recommendation.

In 1858 Lander was elevated to superintendent of the entire road project, replacing McGraw, who blamed Lander for the dismissal (and later fought him in a much-publicized brawl at Washington's Willard Hotel), although others had characterized the former superintendent as corrupt and incompetent. For the next three summers Lander continued explorations to find the best locations for the route, supervised construction, and attempted to pacify the Paiute Indians. During the winter months he promoted the route by various means, including publication of an "Emigrant Guide" in 1859, which informed prospective travelers that the new road had the advantages of grass, water, wood, no tolls, shortened distance, few hard ascents or descents, and little desert. Lander concluded, "I believe the emigration should take it, and will be much better satisfied with it, even the first season, than with the old road." Lander hired a corps of artists to accompany the road builders, including the then-unknown Albert Bierstadt, whose work would further publicize the route.

In October 1860 Lander married the well-known Shakespearean actress, English-born Jean Margaret Davenport. It was termed by one account the "Union of Mars and Thespis." This, however, was misleading, as Lander during winter months spent in Washington, D.C., or San Francisco wrote and read poetry and delivered public lectures on the fine arts in American life. The couple had no children.

During the 1860 presidential campaign Lander actively supported John Cabell Breckinridge and Joseph Lane but when the secession crises loomed, offered his services to the Lincoln administration. He served first as a secret agent in Virginia and then in Texas, where he had authority to order Federal troops to the support of Unionist governor Sam Houston. In the early weeks of the war he served with George B. McClellan (1826–1885) in West Virginia, receiving appointment as brigadier general of volunteers in May 1861. He took command of a brigade on the Potomac River, where in October he suffered a leg wound at Edward's Ferry the day after the Union disaster at Ball's Bluff. Given command of a division, he remained in the field during the winter of 1861–1862 despite the debilitating effect of the wound. Lander contracted pneumonia at Camp Chase, Virginia, as he prepared to move his troops to join General Nathaniel Banks in the Shenandoah Valley and died there the next day.

An energetic, aggressive man who also embodied the romantic vision of nineteenth-century America, Lander served competently in his chosen field, although he could push others beyond the limits of their physical capacity. His major contribution was the recognition that roads still served a function, even over long distances, during the railroad-crazed era of mid-century. His exploration and improvement of the central route connecting the nation at the very time that secession threatened to tear it apart proved to be a significant practical application of his theory.

• Lander's papers, along with those of his wife, are in the Lander Collection at the Library of Congress. Some of Lander's reports were published by Congress, among them, House, *Report of the Reconnaissance of a Railroad Route from Puget Sound via the South Pass to the Mississippi River*, 33d Cong., 1st sess., H. Ex. Doc. 129, and House, *Emigrant Guide*, 35th Cong., 2d sess., H. Ex. Doc. 108. A biography has yet to be published. The best assessment, which focuses on Lander's years on the central route, is Peter T. Harstad and Max G. Pavesic, *Lander Trail Report* (1966). There is a good account of Lander placed in the context of federal road building in W. Turrentine Jackson, *Wagon Roads West* (1952). Two generally competent articles are E. Douglas Branch, "Frederick West Lander, Roadbuilder," *Mississippi Valley Historical Review* 16 (1929): 172–87, and Carl Schlicke, "Frederick West Lander, Western Road-Builder," *Columbia* 8 (1994): 29–34. An obituary is in the *New York Times*, 3 Mar. 1862.

KENT D. RICHARDS

LANDER, Jean Davenport (3 May 1829–3 Aug. 1903), actress, was born Jean Margaret Davenport in Wolverhampton, Staffordshire, England, the daughter of Thomas Donald Davenport, a lawyer, and Sophy Danby, an actress. Her father was practicing law in Edinburgh when Edmund Kean's performances attracted him to the stage. He eventually succeeded Kean as the manager of the Richmond Theatre, where in 1837 Jean Davenport made her first appearance as Little Pickle in *The Spoiled Child*. Her debut was an artistic and financial success, and she subsequently toured the principle cities in England, Scotland, and Ireland as Little Pickle and in the title role of Shakespeare's *Richard III*. In her childhood Davenport was called "the little Dramatic Prodigy" and is said to have suggested to Dickens the character of the "Infant Phenomenon" in *Nicholas Nickleby*.

Davenport made her American debut as Richard III on 21 May 1838 at James Wallack's National Theatre in New York City. Although generally abominating "premature exhibitions" by child actors, the critic for the *Spirit of the Times* (1838) considered Davenport's performance a "wonderful portraiture" in which "nothing, save the tones of her voice, gave token of the reality that we were actually listening to a child, and every now and then, during the exhibition of some fierce passion, the illusion both of the eye and ear was complete." During her first tour in the United States she also appeared as Shylock, Sir Peter Teazle, Sir Giles Overreach, Young Norval, and as several different character types—including a Yankee boy, a Scotch girl, an Irish lad, and a French minstrel—in *The Manager's Daughter* (1837), a play expressly written for the child actress. In 1842 she returned to Europe and traveled extensively, studying under private tutors and playing engagements in England, Italy, France, Holland, and Germany.

Davenport returned to the United States after a ten-year absence, making her adult debut at the Astor Place Opera House in New York as Shakespeare's Juliet on 24 September 1849. She toured for several years, performing roles that included Julia (*The Hunchback*), the Countess (*Love*), Peg Woffington (*Masks and Faces*), and Pauline (*Lady of Lyons*). In December 1853, during an engagement at the Broadway Theatre in New York, she introduced a version of *La Dame aux Camélias* as well as the first American version of *Adrienne Lecouvreur*. The success she achieved during this second visit prompted Davenport to make America her home. Her father remained her companion and manager until his death in 1851, and her mother continued to perform alongside her daughter. Not considered a transcendent theatrical light, Davenport was nevertheless counted as a rising young actress of great promise, possessing a high order of histrionic talent described variously as "graceful," "refined," and "gentle."

Davenport retired from the stage upon her marriage on 13 October 1860 to Frederick West Lander, a civil engineer. They had no children. With the outbreak of war, Lander joined the Union army and was eventually promoted to general. After his death on 2 March 1862—the result of wounds received in battle—Jean Davenport Lander and her mother joined the nursing corps at Port Royal, South Carolina, and devoted their time to caring for sick and wounded Union soldiers.

On 6 February 1865 Davenport reentered theatrical life at Niblo's Garden, billed as Mrs. Lander, in her own adaptation of *Mésalliance*. Although she achieved her early reputation primarily in original parts, her later fame was based on interpretations of historical characters, principally as a rival of Adelaide Ristori. Lander devoted herself largely to English translations of the Italian actress's successes, bringing a new set of characters into vogue—Queen Elizabeth, Mary Stuart, Marie Antoinette, Charlotte Corday, and Medea. Barely seven months after Ristori had excited American audiences with her interpretation of Queen Elizabeth, Lander performed the role—in her own translation and adaptation of Giacometti's play—for audiences in Washington, Philadelphia, and New York (ironically, at the same theater at which Ristori made her American debut in 1866). Her performance inevitably drew comparison with the Italian actress. One critic for the *Philadelphia Inquirer* noted in 1867: "In Mrs. Lander's able hands the character assumes a magnitude which has seldom invested it, and even Ristori, great and grand as she is in the part, fails at times in comparison with Mrs. Lander in giving it those nice touches of nature. . . . In the 'tempest and torrent' of her passion, perhaps Ristori in a measure excels our favorite tragedienne, but this drawback, if drawback it can be called, is more than compensated for by the finish, fervor and sustained effect characterizing every scene in the play in which Mrs. Lander appears."

Throughout her career, Jean Davenport Lander remained steadfastly faithful to the legitimate drama. Her approach to roles was characteristic of the classic school of acting at a time when the school of emotionalism had begun to gain wide popular appeal. She made her farewell appearance at the Boston Theatre on 1, January 1877 as Hester Prynne, in her own translation of Count de Najac's dramatization of Nathaniel Hawthorne's *The Scarlet Letter*. Thereafter she divided her time between her permanent home in Washington and her summer home in Lynn, Massachusetts, where she died.

• Comprehensive sources on Jean Davenport Lander are G. C. D. Odell, *Annals of the New York Stage*, vol. 4 (1928); T. Allston Brown, *A History of the New York Stage from the First Performance in 1732 to 1901* (1903); Joseph N. Ireland, *Records of the New York Stage from 1750 to 1860* (1867); and William Winter, *Shadows of the Stage* (1892). A promotional pamphlet, *Biographical Sketch of Mrs. F. W. Lander, Formerly Miss Jean Davenport, Tragedienne* (1867), is a valuable source containing newspaper reviews of her performance as Queen Elizabeth; it is located at Harvard University. An obituary is in the *New York Times*, 4 Aug. 1903.

LORIEN A. CORBELLETTI

LANDES, Bertha Ethel Knight (19 Oct. 1868–29 Nov. 1943), reformer and mayor, was born in Ware, Massachusetts, the daughter of Charles Sanford Knight, a painter and Union army veteran, and Cordelia Cutter. Her father moved the family to Worcester and entered the real estate business in 1873. While a student at Indiana University, Bertha Knight lived for a time with her sister Jessie and brother-in-law David Starr Jordan, then university president and later first president of Stanford University. In 1891 she received a degree in history and political science. She then returned to Worcester and taught at Classical High School for three years. In 1894 she married geologist Henry Landes, a fellow student at Indiana. They moved to Seattle after Henry was appointed professor of geology at the University of Washington in the fall of 1895. There they became active in university and community affairs, including the Congregational church. The Landeses had two children; after the death of their daughter Katherine, they adopted a child.

Before World War I Landes's life centered on home and family. Her outside activities involved church, schools and PTA, the Red Cross and other social services, and women's clubs. The consummate club woman, she developed parliamentary and administrative skills heading such Seattle organizations as the Woman's Century Club and the Women's University Club.

In 1921, as president of the Seattle Federation of Women's Clubs, Landes directed the planning and staging of the successful week-long Women's Educational Exhibit for Washington Manufacturers. This brought her to the attention of civic, business, and commercial leaders and introduced her into politics. After the mayor appointed her to the city's commission on unemployment, a fellow commission member suggested she run for the nonpartisan city council. She and four staunch club women friends conducted her 1922 council campaign. They broke the all-male pattern in city government when Landes won election by an unprecedented margin of 22,000 votes.

On the council, Landes spearheaded the move for an ordinance to strengthen cabaret and dance-hall regulation, and she firmly supported municipal ownership of utilities. In 1924 she was elected council president and became acting mayor when Mayor Edwin J. "Doc" Brown went to New York as a delegate to the Democratic National Convention. She received national attention when she fired Brown's police chief for failing to deal with corruption in his department and for insubordination in an exchange of letters with her. She won reelection to the council in 1925.

The following year, though reluctant, she was persuaded to run for mayor against Brown by leaders in women's organizations that had previously backed her and by supporters of efforts to establish city-manager government in Seattle, a change she favored. Her mayoral campaign occurred during the trial of a former Seattle policeman on bootlegging charges. This coincidence kept attention on Landes's concern for morality and law enforcement and tended to corroborate assertions she had made as acting mayor in 1924. She was elected on 9 March 1926 by just under 6,000 votes in a record voter turnout, the first woman to be elected mayor of a major American city.

As mayor she pursued strict law enforcement, sound management for the municipal electric utility, improved traffic safety, and quality appointments based on merit. She succeeded in returning operations of the street railway system to profitability and supported expanded recreation programs and facilities for the park department.

She sought reelection in 1928 with an impressive record in office and with the backing of the Central Labor Council, major newspapers, Prohibition forces, and women's groups. She lost decisively, however. Explanations for her defeat focus on opposition to her moralistic approach to law enforcement, on suspected involvement of private power interests opposed to her when private-versus-public power was a volatile issue in Seattle, and on gender bias in a city boasting a strong masculine image.

Her political career reflected the progressive tenets of efficiency and regulation in public affairs, but her one short term as mayor produced no lasting social change. Unlike other earlier progressives, Mayor Landes built no political machine of her own.

Breaking the gender barrier in politics constituted one of her main contributions. In her 1922 council campaign she stressed the right of women to serve in public office, but she stated clearly that a woman's first duty was to home and family. She reconciled the role of woman-in-the-family with that of woman-in-public-office by combining them. She proclaimed the city a larger home and set about her municipal housekeeping.

She came to relish the power and opportunities of the mayor's office. In an article for *Woman Citizen* (Dec. 1927), she wrote,

Municipal housekeeping means adventure and romance and accomplishment to me. To be in some degree a guiding force in the destiny of a city, to help lay the foundation stones for making it good and great, to aid in advancing the political position of women, to be the person to whom men and women and children look for protection against lawlessness, to spread the political philosophy that the city is only a larger home—I find it richly worthwhile!

After leaving office she made several nationwide lecture tours. She later spoke on behalf of women's economic concerns and early in the depression headed the women's division of the city's Commission for Improved Employment. She also served as president of the American Federation of Soroptimist Clubs and the Washington State League of Women Voters. She was the first woman moderator of the Congregational Church Conference of Washington.

Bertha and Henry Landes conducted summer study tours to the Far East from 1933 to 1936, the year Henry died. In 1941, in part for health reasons, Bertha Landes moved from Seattle to Pacific Palisades, California. She died at her son's home in Ann Arbor, Michigan.

• Bertha Landes's papers, including texts of speeches, letters, clippings, and photographs, are in the University of Washington Library. Her writings include "Does Politics Make Women Crooked?," *Collier's*, 16 Mar. 1929, p. 24; "Steering a Big City Straight," *Woman Citizen*, Dec. 1927, p. 5; and "An Alumna in Politics," *Indiana Alumni Magazine*, Apr. 1939. Two contemporary views of her political career are Blanche Brace, "Well . . . Why Not?" *Woman Citizen*, Sept. 1926, p. 8, and Julia N. Budlong, "What Happened in Seattle," *Nation*, 29 Aug. 1928, pp. 197–98. A study of her final campaign is Florence J. Deacon, "Why Wasn't Bertha Knight Landes Re-elected?" (master's thesis, Univ. of Washington, 1978). Comprehensive works are Doris H. Pieroth, "Bertha Knight Landes: The Woman Who Was Mayor," *Pacific Northwest Quarterly* 75 (July 1984), and Sandra Haarsager, "'The Women Must'": Bertha Knight Landes, the Nation's First Female Big City Mayor" (Ph.D. diss., Washington State Univ., 1990). Obituaries are in the *Seattle Times*, 29 Nov. 1943, and the *Seattle Post-Intelligencer* and the *New York Times*, 30 Nov. 1943.

DORIS H. PIEROTH

LANDIS, James McCauley (25 Sept. 1899–30 July 1964), federal administrator and Harvard Law School dean, was born in Tokyo, Japan, the son of Henry Mohr Landis and Emma Marie Stiefler, missionary-teachers. He first came to the United States at age thirteen for schooling. He graduated from Mercersburg Academy (1916), Princeton University (1921), and Harvard Law School (1924), attaining at each the highest levels of academic achievement and receiving one of Harvard's first doctorates of juridical science.

At Harvard he came under the influence of Professor Felix Frankfurter, with whom he wrote *The Business of the Supreme Court* (1927). Frankfurter arranged for him to clerk for Supreme Court Justice Louis D. Brandeis from 1925 to 1926. Landis's research for Brandeis's dissent in *Myers v. United States* (1926) introduced him to the field of federal regulation, to which he would devote his professional life. While in Washington, he met and married Stella Galloway McGehee, a journalist, in 1926; they had two children. Landis returned to Cambridge in 1926 to join the Harvard Law faculty. By 1928 he had been appointed full professor, a rise that Dean Roscoe Pound called "meteoric, almost unheard of."

The law school proved unable to contain Landis's energies. Brilliant, intense, and ambitious, he dabbled in local public affairs before returning to Washington in 1933 to volunteer his services to Franklin D. Roosevelt's New Deal. Landis, Benjamin Cohen, and

Thomas G. Corcoran—whom the press dubbed the "Happy Hotdogs" after their mentor, Frankfurter—drafted the Federal Securities Act of 1933. Roosevelt then appointed Landis to the Federal Trade Commission to administer the new law, which established the first government regulation over the sale of corporate stocks. Landis, Cohen, and Corcoran played similarly leading roles in preparing the Securities and Exchange Act of 1934.

In recognition of these efforts, Landis became one of the first commissioners of the Securities and Exchange Commission (SEC) and in 1935 succeeded Joseph P. Kennedy as chairman. As a federal regulator, Landis advocated both a promotional and a policing role for the commissions. To restore financial confidence, he adopted an unexpectedly conciliatory attitude toward Wall Street and encouraged the stock exchanges to develop self-policing under SEC supervision. He wove these themes into his seminal book, *The Administrative Process* (1938), portraying federal regulation of industry and finance as a middle ground between government inaction and government ownership. He sought not to overturn capitalism, he explained, but to enable it to "live up to its own pretensions."

In 1937 Landis returned to Harvard as dean of the law school, while continuing to serve as a troubleshooter for Roosevelt. He made himself controversial by endorsing the president's plan to expand the Supreme Court, by supporting the legality of sit-down strikes, and by ruling as a Labor Department judge against the deportation of Longshoremen's Union president Harry Bridges.

During the Second World War Landis returned to government service. In 1942 he succeeded Fiorello La Guardia as director of the Office of Civilian Defense, where he organized a national "block plan" of air-raid wardens and other volunteers to protect and assist civilians in the event of enemy attack. When Allied victories made civilian defense increasingly unnecessary, Landis was dispatched in 1943 to Cairo, Egypt, to represent U.S. economic interests throughout the Middle East. Taking issue with British imperialism in the region, he advocated American support for Arab nationalism and also opposed recognition of Israel as an independent Jewish state.

His return to Harvard after the war was made intolerable by his estrangement from his wife and his desire to marry his secretary, Dorothy Purdy Brown, completely unacceptable actions within his social circles in Cambridge. In 1947 he accepted President Harry Truman's offer to chair the Civil Aeronautics Board (CAB), and he resigned both as dean and professor of law, leaving behind his law books as a symbol of his ultimate break with the school. He divorced Stella that year and married Brown in 1948. There were no children by his second marriage.

Landis found his return to the federal government equally difficult. The Truman administration proved more susceptible to business influence than the New Deal had been and intervened frequently in CAB af-fairs. The board also felt pressure from the major airlines, who protested against competition from a profusion of nonscheduled, limited budget airlines operated by war-veteran pilots. The larger commercial airlines distrusted Landis's independent thinking about airline competition, mergers, government subsidies, and safety precautions. Using Landis's marital and drinking problems as an excuse, and campaign contributions as an inducement, the airlines persuaded President Truman not to reappoint Landis to a second term as chairman.

Thunderstruck by his unexpected dismissal, Landis turned to his old friend Kennedy, who put him on retainer to "Kennedy enterprises." At forty-eight, Landis took his first bar exams and began practicing law, representing clients before many of the federal regulatory agencies, a frustrating experience that heightened his concern over the agencies' bureaucratic delays and inefficiencies. He also served as an unofficial adviser to John F. Kennedy during his congressional career and campaign for the presidency. President-elect Kennedy assigned Landis to reexamine the regulatory commissions. Landis's recommendations in 1960 of increased authority for commission chairmen and streamlined agency procedures formed the core of Kennedy's regulatory policies. Landis helped Kennedy select talented appointees to revitalize the languishing commissions, and he served briefly as special assistant to the president, resigning in 1961 when named co-respondent in his secretary's divorce.

At the same time, the Internal Revenue Service discovered that Landis was five years in arrears with his taxes. Although his psychiatrist was prepared to testify that the failings reflected a long-standing crisis of self-esteem that caused him to become preoccupied with public affairs and to neglect his personal obligations, Landis chose to plead guilty to minimize embarrassment for the Kennedy administration. Expecting only a fine, he was astonished when the judge sentenced him to a thirty-day imprisonment, from 30 August to 27 September 1963, a term he spent in a prison hospital ward for alcoholics. Following his release he was suspended from law practice for one year. Months later he drowned accidentally in the pool at his home in Harrison, New York.

Private tragedies overshadowed Landis's long and productive public career. He was a skilled administrator and a thoughtful student and reformer of federal regulation, which in turn affected nearly every aspect of American economic life. As one colleague noted, he "gave the administrative process, usually so dull and pedestrian, a spark which [was] challenging."

• The papers of James Landis are in the Library of Congress; the Harvard Law School and Harvard Archives; the Roosevelt, Truman, and Kennedy presidential libraries; and in various agency files in the National Archives. Landis also gave a substantial oral history to the Columbia Oral History Research Office. See also Donald A. Ritchie, *James M. Landis: Dean of the Regulators* (1980); Thomas McCraw, *Prophets of Regulation: Charles Francis Adams, Louis D. Brandeis, James M. Landis, and Alfred Kahn* (1984); "The Legend of Landis,"

Fortune 10 (1934): 44–47, 118, 120; and the memorial edition of the *Harvard Law Review* (1964). An obituary is in the *New York Times*, 31 July 1964.

DONALD A. RITCHIE

LANDIS, Kenesaw Mountain (20 Nov. 1866–25 Nov. 1944), federal judge and baseball commissioner, was born in Millville, Ohio, the son of Abraham Hoch Landis, a physician and farmer, and Mary Kumler. He was named after Kennesaw Mountain in Georgia, the site of a Civil War battle in which his father, a surgeon in the Union army, had lost a leg. Kenesaw—his father dropped an "n" when christening his son—moved to Indiana with his family in 1874 and grew up in Logansport. Despite his short stature and slight physique, young Landis gained a statewide reputation as a bicycle racer and played for amateur baseball teams in the Logansport area.

During the 1880s Landis pursued a career in law. Self-taught in shorthand, he first became a county court reporter. Although he had failed to complete high school, he was soon claiming that he could do better than any lawyer practicing in Logansport, and he eventually enrolled at the Y.M.C.A. Law School of Cincinnati. In 1891 he graduated from Union Law School of Chicago (which later merged into Northwestern) and began practicing in Chicago.

The competitive fire that Landis had shown as a bicycle racer propelled his rise in both law and politics. In 1893 Judge Walter Q. Gresham, who had been appointed secretary of state by President Grover Cleveland, hired the young attorney as his personal secretary. Though a Republican in a Democratic administration, Landis prospered in Washington; Cleveland was impressed enough to offer him a ministerial post in Venezuela. Gresham's death in May 1895 ended Landis's tenure at the State Department, and he returned to Chicago, where he married Winifred Reed in July 1895. They had two children.

Landis reestablished his law practice and entered Republican party politics. Although two of his brothers, Charles and Frederick, pursued public office and eventually served in the U.S. Congress, Landis avoided the electoral arena. Instead, he used his friendship with Frank O. Lowdon, whose unsuccessful gubernatorial campaign he had managed in 1904, and an acquaintance with President Theodore Roosevelt to help secure, in March 1905, a position as a federal judge on the U.S. District Court for the Northern District of Illinois.

Landis, always something of a character while an attorney, converted the judicial bench into a full-time stage. Wearing his wavy, graying hair in an unruly mane and developing a flamboyant courtroom style, Landis also gained a reputation for unorthodox jurisprudence. On two occasions, members of Congress were angered enough by his judicial behavior to introduce impeachment resolutions. In 1907 he gained notoriety by fining Standard Oil more than $29 million, a decision that an appeals court quickly overturned because of Landis's "abuse of judicial discretion."

World War I provided Landis with his most controversial cases. He unsuccessfully attempted to secure a murder indictment against Germany's Kaiser Wilhelm II for having caused the death of a Chicago resident during the sinking of the *Lusitania*. In 1918 Landis presided over the successful prosecution of 113 members of the Industrial Workers of the World (IWW) who had been charged with more than 10,000 violations of federal law. After displaying uncharacteristic restraint during the trial itself, he made headlines by levying heavy fines and imposing stiff sentences, including ones against "Big Bill" Haywood and Vincent St. John, that were the maximum allowed under federal law. Landis's bias was more evident in the trial of Victor Berger, a prominent Socialist who was convicted under the Espionage Act. Although Landis sentenced Berger to twenty years, it was not enough, he complained; "the law should have enabled me to have had him lined up against a wall and shot." The U.S. Supreme Court, finding ample evidence of Landis's judicial bias, subsequently overturned Berger's conviction.

Several years earlier Landis had attracted the attention of baseball owners when the new Federal League filed suit in his court against allegedly monopolistic practices by the American and National leagues. The Federal League had strong legal arguments. Landis feared, as he told the litigants, that any decision might "tear down the very foundations of this game." Consequently, he continually postponed his ruling on the Federal League's claim. His eleven-month delay favored the already established leagues, and the undercapitalized Federal League finally folded in December 1915. Landis then dismissed the Federal League's suit as moot.

The demise of the Federal League hardly ended organized baseball's troubles. By 1920 squabbles between owners and players and among owners had become so bitter that the game seemed unable to respond to a grave crisis, allegations that eight members of the Chicago White Sox had thrown the 1919 World Series to the Cincinnati Reds. Even before the "Black Sox scandal" erupted, most baseball owners acknowledged the need for a new governing structure. After some opposition—especially from Ban Johnson, president of the American League—baseball owners asked Landis, still fondly remembered for having pigeonholed the Federal League's lawsuit, to assume the newly created office of commissioner of the complex economic-entertainment enterprise called organized baseball.

Landis assumed office in November 1920 and gained immense authority under baseball's new system of private justice. The owners empowered him to deal with anything that might be "detrimental to the best interests" of the national pastime. In 1931 a federal district court in a lawsuit involving player contracts held that Landis possessed "all the attributes of a benevolent but absolute despot and all the disciplinary powers of the proverbial pater familias" when it came to any issue affecting organized baseball.

Landis enjoyed using his extraordinary power. In his first ruling, he proclaimed that his law, and not that of the nation's courts, would prevail. He decreed that the eight White Sox players who had been acquitted of charges they had thrown the 1919 World Series by a jury in Chicago could not play for any team in organized baseball. The following year, 1921, he suspended Babe Ruth, baseball's greatest hero, for the first forty games of the 1922 season for violating a seldom enforced prohibition against major league players participating in exhibition contests after the World Series and before the next season's spring training. In a series of less publicized cases during the 1920s, Landis permanently banned eleven other players.

A fierce moralist, Landis took credit for "cleaning up" baseball. His well-practiced theatrics, which included watching every World Series from a front row box so that he might personally guard against any repeat of 1919, added to his popular image. Landis also won the plaudits of owners by negotiating lucrative radio contracts during the lean years of the 1930s and by working with Franklin Roosevelt's administration to ensure that World War II would not totally disrupt, or even possibly terminate, organized baseball's operations.

Behind the scenes, however, Landis's high-handed rule produced discord. Until Johnson finally resigned as American League president in 1927, he and Landis feuded constantly. They clashed over both large issues, such as Landis's decision that Ty Cobb and Tris Speaker, two American League legends, had not conspired to throw games, and small ones, such as allowing pitchers to use resin bags.

Although Landis secured several renewals of his contract and remained commissioner until his death, he increasingly became a roadblock to change. He opposed the practice, begun by the St. Louis Cardinals during the 1920s, of big league teams operating a "farm system," a group of minor league affiliates to which they assigned players with whom they had contracts but who were not on their major league rosters. By tying players to a farm system rather than leaving them free to sign with individual minor league teams, Landis argued, major league clubs could prevent talented athletes from advancing to the big leagues. Moreover, the farm system model threatened to force hitherto independent minor league teams to become affiliates of major league franchises. Despite Landis's opposition, every major league team built a farm system during the 1920s and 1930s. Landis could only fight a rear guard action by vigorously enforcing the intricate rules that governed organized baseball's farflung operations. Using his authority to release a number of minor league farmhands from their contracts to major league teams, Landis even gained the title of the "Great Emancipator."

Landis, however, was anything but an emancipator on racial integration, another of the game's controversial issues. Although he publicly insisted that African Americans were not barred, he privately opposed efforts to integrate the national pastime. During the 1930s he prevented owners, beset by depression-era financial woes, from discussing integration. A decade later, he also halted discussions, prompted by a delegation of African-American leaders, on whether or not World War II might be a propitious time for baseball to drop its Jim Crow policies. In 1943 he helped to prevent the sale of the Philadelphia Phillies to Bill Veeck, who hoped to rejuvenate the moribund club with black ballplayers.

By the time Landis died in Chicago, baseball's owners had soured on his style of leadership and absolute authority. They never allowed any of his successors the broad power that Landis wielded in his heyday. Landis, however, was immediately honored by being inducted into the National Baseball Hall of Fame in 1944.

• The National Baseball Hall of Fame in Cooperstown, N.Y., has opened one box of Landis's papers, which holds forty-four folders and several legal briefs, that relate to his career as commissioner. In addition, the archives of the *Sporting News* in St. Louis, Mo., house several files that contain clippings on Landis. J. G. Taylor Spink, *Judge Landis and Twenty-Five Years of Baseball* (1947), is a full-length biography by the long-time publisher of the *Sporting News*. A more critical, scholarly view of Landis appears in Eugene C. Murdock, *Ban Johnson: Czar of Baseball* (1982). Landis's relationship to the broader history of the national pastime is charted in Harold Seymour, *Baseball: The Golden Age* (1971), David Quentin Voigt, *American Baseball: From the Commissioners to Continental Expansion* (1970), and Benjamin G. Rader, *Baseball: A History of America's Game* (1992). New material on Landis's negotiations with organized baseball's magnates in 1920 may be found in John Heylar, *Lords of the Realm: The Real History of Baseball* (1994). Landis's early years are discussed, from a legal-culture perspective, in Norman L. Rosenberg, "Here Comes the Judge! The Origins of Baseball's Commissioner System and American Legal Culture," *Journal of Popular Culture* 20 (1982): 129–46. *Current Biography 1944* contains a lengthy obituary.

NORMAN L. ROSENBERG

LANDIS, Walter Savage (5 July 1881–15 Sept. 1944), metallurgical chemist, was born in Pottstown, Pennsylvania, the son of Daniel Landis and Clara Savage. Landis graduated from Lehigh University in 1902 with a degree in metallurgical engineering and then joined the Lehigh Metallurgy Department's staff as an assistant. In this position he was able to pursue graduate study and in 1906 received a master of science degree. During 1905 and 1906 he traveled abroad to Heidelberg, Germany, to study crystallography and mineralogy, and in 1909 he also worked at the Krupp Institute in Aachen.

Landis remained at Lehigh until 1912, rising through the ranks from instructor (1903–1907), to assistant professor (1907–1910), and finally associate professor (1910–1912). At Lehigh Landis's research was focused primarily on the thermo-chemistry of metallurgical operations, and he published several papers on efficiency improvements for the production of Portland cement as well as on iron and steel metallurgy. He also maintained an extensive industrial consulting practice. During his stay at Lehigh Landis married Antoinette M. Prince, daughter of Bethlehem paint manufacturer Abraham C. Prince, in 1909. They had three children, one of whom died in childhood.

During both his student and faculty years, Landis worked closely with Joseph W. Richards (1864–1921), one of the country's leading metallurgists. Richards was a cofounder and the first president of the American Electrochemical Society, established in 1902, the year of Landis's graduation. Landis himself became the Electrochemical Society's seventeenth president in 1920–1921.

In 1912 Landis elected to change careers, leaving the academic world of Lehigh University to become the chief technologist for American Cyanamid Company, located in Niagara Falls, Ontario, Canada where he began what was to become a distinguished career in industrial research and development and its management. The following year Landis established the company's first industrial research laboratory, and by 1922 he had been elected a director of the company. Just one year later he was appointed vice president, a position he held until his death some two decades later.

Landis was an active researcher himself, ultimately receiving numerous patents involving the development of a number of important processes and the building of their attendant manufacturing plants. One of the earliest and more important of these was Landis's work on the production of sodium cyanide from cyanamid, which resulted in its commercial production by 1916 and subsequent widespread adoption. Landis subsequently developed processes for other derivatives of cyanamid, including the production of ferrocyanides, dicyandiamid and urea, and hydrocyanic acid. In 1914, in conjunction with the General Electric Company in Niagara Falls, he helped to develop a process for the production of argon from residual gases from the cyanamide process. Until liquid air distillation was perfected a year later, this was the only source of commercially available argon for the electric lamp industry.

Landis also worked on nitrogen fixation and the production of fertilizers. The economic electric furnace production of calcium cyanamide from calcium carbide and nitrogen developed in Germany by Albert Frank and Heinrich Caro was the basis upon which the American Cyanamid Company had been formed. However, many problems of technical production as well as applications and uses of the resulting fertilizers remained to be answered by the time Landis came to the company and would occupy much of his time in the years prior to World War I.

With the coming of the war, Landis became involved in several military projects, including the Allies' effort to secure an adequate supply of nitric acid for explosives, which was threatened by German attempts to sink Chilean nitrate ships en route to Europe. At home the Germans were simultaneously experimenting with the development of the Haber ammonia synthesis process. In response, Landis undertook for American Cyanamid the design and building

of several demonstration plants, including one at Warners, New Jersey, for producing ammonia from cyanamide and oxidizing it to nitric acid. Setting up the plant involved obtaining special autoclaves, which had been ordered from Germany. The early outbreak of war necessitated Landis's sailing for Europe on the first available steamer, and, using personal contacts from his student days, he was able to secure and smuggle out several autoclaves, along with associated equipment and plant drawings, before German authorities placed restrictions on the export of chemical apparatus. Landis's groundwork laid the technical foundation for the government's subsequent development of its Muscle Shoals, Alabama, nitrate plant.

Following the war Landis refocused his attention on the production of fertilizers, especially ammonium phosphate. This required extensive research on the production of phosphoric acid from the phosphate rock. A wet process utilizing sulfuric acid for treating the phosphate rock was ultimately settled on and established at the Warners plant, where ammonia was being produced from cyanamide. In addition to the ammonia-phosphate fertilizers produced, various other industrial phosphate processes were developed, making the Warners plant the largest such producing unit in the world by the mid-1930s.

In addition to his work on cyanamide derivatives and nitrogen fixation, Landis also conducted research in the area of electric smelting and distillation. For example, during the 1930s he contributed improvements to the DeLaval electrothermic process for recovering zinc from complex low-grade ores. This work was conducted in plants at Trollhättan, Sweden, and Sarpsborg, Norway. Subsequently, advances in flotation procedures, improvements that had been made at Landis's own cyanamid company, resulted in its supplanting the electrothermic process. Landis subsequently participated in early experiments on the electrothermic production of magnesium, which were carried out in Radentheim, Austria, by the Austro-American Magnesite Company.

Landis utilized the opportunity of his many trips abroad for technical work to also study the cultures and especially the economies of the countries he visited. In this latter subject he became something of an expert. He frequently wrote and published on his perceptions regarding the economic changes overtaking Europe during the 1930s. He was particularly concerned lest political measures override more basic economic laws. In 1937 he discussed the programs of Russia, Italy, and Germany in "A New Planned Economy," and in 1939 he presented an address on "Fascist vs. Democratic Chemical Industry." By 1941 he was warning against a "state socialist system" in America, calling instead for renewal of the free enterprise spirit. In 1944 Landis also published a topically organized, popular treatise on chemistry's contributions to society entitled *Your Servant the Molecule*.

Beyond his research and technical publication interests, Landis also contributed to a wide range of other professional and service areas. In addition to his role in the Electrochemical Society, he was especially active in the American Institute of Chemical Engineers and in the American Chemical Society, for which he served as chairman of its New York section in 1932. He was also a president of the New York Chemists' Club.

Landis received numerous awards and honors during his lifetime for his accomplishments in the field of industrial chemistry. In 1936 the Society of Chemical Industry presented Landis with its annual Chemical Industry Award for his "applied research in the chemistry and economics of the fertilizer industries." Three years later, in 1939, Landis was also the recipient of the society's Perkin Medal. In 1943, a year before his death, Landis received the gold medal of the American Institute of Chemists.

Somewhat unexpectedly, Landis died at his home in Old Greenwich, Connecticut, having overexerted himself by staying up on the previous night trying to protect his home from the effects of a hurricane. Landis's passing marked the end of a career that witnessed dramatic changes in the chemical processing industry, changes that he himself had done much to further.

• Although no personal papers are available, copies of Landis's many published essays are available in the Lehigh Collection of the University Libraries. Through them much of his career can be followed. Among the more important are "Fixation of Atmospheric Nitrogen," *Journal of Industrial and Engineering Chemistry* 7, no. 5 (1915): 433–38; "Production of Ammonia from Cyanamid," *Transactions of the American Institute of Chemical Engineers* 8 (1915): 267–77; "The Oxidation of Ammonia," *Transactions of the American Electrochemical Society* 35 (1919): 283–307; "A New Cyanide," *Transactions of the American Electrochemical Society* 37 (1920): 653–63; "Cyanamid in Some Fertilizer Mixers," *Journal of Industrial and Engineering Chemistry* 14, no. 2 (1922): 143–45; "The International Nitrogen Problem," *Journal of Industrial and Engineering Chemistry* 20, no. 11 (1928): 1144–47; "Joseph W. Richards: The Teacher-The Industry," *Transactions of the American Electrochemical Society* 66 (1934): 6–14; "Trollhättan Electrothermic Zinc Process," *Transactions of the American Institute of Mining and Metallurgical Engineers* 121 (1936): 573–98; "Concentrated Fertilizers," *Journal of Industrial and Engineering Chemistry* 28, no. 12 (1936): 1470–76; "Electrochemical Distillation of Metals," *Transactions of the American Electrochemical Society* 72 (1937): 293–316; "An Early Chapter in Argon Production," *Journal of Industrial and Engineering Chemistry* 31, no. 2 (1939): 241–47; and "Industrial Chemicals in National Defense," *Transactions of the American Institute of Chemical Engineers* 41 (1941): 513–19. No full biography is available, but highlights of his career are noted in Williams Haynes, *American Chemical Industry*, vols. 2 and 3 (1983). Also revealing are the citation essays for the "Perkin Medal Award," *Journal of Industrial and Engineering Chemistry* 31, no. 2 (1939): 240, and the "Chemical Industry Medal Award," *Journal of Industrial and Engineering Chemistry* 28, no. 12 (1936): 1467–70. An obituary is in *Transactions of the Electrochemical Society* 86 (1944): 47–49.

STEPHEN H. CUTCLIFFE

LANDON, Alfred Mossman (9 Sept. 1887–12 Oct. 1987), governor of Kansas and Republican presidential nominee, known as Alf, was born in West Middlesex, Pennsylvania, the son of John M. Landon, an oil and natural gas executive, and Anne Mossman. Landon received a law degree from the University of Kansas in 1908. In 1915 he married Margaret Fleming, who died in 1918. They had a daughter. Landon married Theo Cobb in 1930, and they had a son and a daughter, Nancy Landon Kassebaum, who was elected to the U.S. Senate from Kansas in 1978.

Although Landon was admitted to the Kansas bar in 1908, he did not practice law. He worked instead in banking until 1911, when he became an independent petroleum producer. He served briefly as a first lieutenant in the army in 1918. After 1936 he began developing business interests in addition to oil production, becoming a prominent radio station owner-executive by the 1960s. A shrewd businessman, Landon prospered in his various enterprises, although he never became wealthy. This was largely because of his abiding concern with politics, which had been fostered by his politically active father.

Father and son worked in support of Theodore Roosevelt's 1912 presidential candidacy. In 1914 Alfred Landon was the Progressive party chairman in Montgomery County, but he returned to the Republican party, with most other Progressives, in 1916. In 1922 Landon served as secretary to Governor Henry J. Allen (1868–1950) and in 1924 was an important leader in the independent gubernatorial campaign of William Allen White against the Ku Klux Klan. Landon was the organizer of the successful campaign in 1928 to nominate and elect Clyde M. Reed governor; he himself was chosen chairman of the Republican state committee. In 1930 conservative Republicans denied Reed renomination and ousted Landon from the state chairmanship.

Landon bounced back in 1931, leading a well-publicized movement by independent Kansas oil producers against monopoly and for conservation in their depression-stricken industry. Dealing with Democrats and Republicans in Kansas and elsewhere, he demonstrated that he could work effectively with a broad range of people. Landon was nominated for governor in 1932 as a moderate who could unite the factionalized Republican party, reduce taxes and expenditures, and yet maintain essential state services. He ran for election against the odds, for the Democrats controlled the governorship and seemed destined to sweep the nation at the polls in November. As Landon remarked, though, "There are lots worse things than taking a licking, and one of them is to run away from a fight because it is hard." He ran an energetic campaign against the respected Democratic governor, Harry Woodring, and a colorful independent, Dr. John R. Brinkley, who had gained notoriety for his goat-gland transplantations to restore male virility. Landon won election with a scant plurality, with 34.8 percent of the votes, apparently having convinced people that Brinkley was the "great promiser" and Woodring the "greatest little claimer Kansas has had in a long time."

In 1933, like other American officials, Governor Landon was beset by the challenges of the Great Depression. A champion of governmental economy and efficiency, he declared that one "cannot get something for nothing." Landon advocated action that resulted in further regulation of banks, insurance firms, trucking companies, and utilities; more effective conservation of natural resources; protection of farmers from foreclosures; reform of state and local finances; and reorganization of the state government. All of these measures were accomplished on the basis of a balanced state budget. Moreover, Kansas, under his leadership, obtained proportionately more federal funds than most Plains states to deal with the hardships of both depression and drought, which severely struck the area during his governorship. This reflected Landon's ability often to work successfully with the administration of Democratic president Franklin D. Roosevelt. This cooperation was particularly true in the fields of agriculture, conservation, and unemployment relief. Relying on his own expertise, Landon worked closely with Secretary of the Interior Harold L. Ickes to develop programs to cope with distress in the oil industry.

Landon won reelection in 1934, the only Republican governor who did so that year. In 1935 and 1936 Republican interest in him as a presidential candidate grew steadily. This was not surprising, for after the widespread Democratic victories in the 1932 and 1934 elections there were relatively few Republican state and federal officeholders. Landon alone of these officials had an outstanding record, had no connection with the widely discredited presidency of Herbert Hoover, and occupied the middle ground between Republican insurgents and conservatives. Other Republicans, such as Senators William E. Borah of Idaho, Lester J. Dickinson of Iowa, and Arthur H. Vandenberg of Michigan and Chicago publisher Frank Knox, sought their party's presidential nomination. Landon was able, however, to win the nomination in June 1936 by remaining moderate on the issues and effectively employing his campaign resources. The convention delegates chose Colonel Knox as his running mate.

Landon led a divided as well as a depleted party into the 1936 presidential election campaign. Some Republicans, ferociously attacking the New Deal, assumed positions to his right; others endorsed Roosevelt; and still others remained inactive. Former Democratic presidential nominees John W. Davis (1873–1955) and Alfred E. Smith, among other members of their party, endorsed Landon, although they brought few voters with them. The Kansan ran a vigorous, well-financed, and far-flung campaign. He had considerable success in reorganizing his party and reshaping it along more realistic lines. His chief objective was to champion moderation on the issues, in contrast with what he thought was Roosevelt's immoderation against business and in developing the power of the federal government. Landon advocated resource conservation and the preservation of the family farm. Moreover, he promised to be fair to the needy and to organized labor. He proposed subsistence pensions for the elderly, fair and effective regulation of big business, assistance to tenant farmers, and strict adherence to the Constitution. He forthrightly denounced racial prejudice and religious bigotry. On matters of peace and world trade, the Republican nominee vowed to seek international cooperation. He would also recruit the best people, regardless of party, to staff the government. Landon emphasized the need for efficient administration, a balanced budget, and measures to encourage business expansion in order to bring economic recovery and provide jobs for unemployed Americans. This was, he said, the way to counter the record of Roosevelt's New Deal: "Twenty-five billion dollars spent. Thirteen billion dollars added to the public debt. Eleven million unemployed left."

Contrary to the favorable public opinion polls of the *Literary Digest*, Landon had little chance of winning the presidency from Franklin D. Roosevelt, who was approaching the peak of his popularity. The Kansas governor had neither name recognition, organization, patronage, record, nor speaking ability to match the president. Landon was at his best on issues of minor interest to the electorate at that time, such as opposition to loyalty oaths and prejudice and promotion of international cooperation, and on a popular concern like conservation, on which Roosevelt was equally strong. For the most part Landon's campaign was gallant and kept the Republican party a viable, if diminished, opposition. Roosevelt won reelection in a landslide, polling 27,752,869 votes to Landon's 16,674,665 and 523 electoral votes to 8. The Republicans emerged from the election with only 89 seats in the House of Representatives and 16 in the Senate. The 1936 campaign was heated and often nasty, but neither the governor nor the president indulged in vituperation against each other. Indeed, after the election, whenever Landon visited Washington, Roosevelt invited him to the White House, where they got along cordially.

Although urged to do so, Landon did not run again for public office or accept the Republican national committee chairmanship. He was a vigorous titular head of his party until 1940 and was given much credit for its resurgence in the elections of 1938. Landon was instrumental in the defeat of anti-Semite Gerald Winrod for Kansas's Republican senatorial nomination in 1938. That year he was also the only nationally prominent major party politician to defend the right of Socialist leader Norman Thomas to speak publicly after he had been prevented from doing so in Jersey City. Moreover, the Kansan spoke out against the Nazi persecution of Jews and later served on the board of directors and the executive committee of the National Conference of Christians and Jews.

Landon was a trenchant critic of Roosevelt's policies, although he supported the president on protesting the sinking of the U.S.S. *Panay* by Japan in 1937 as well as on the Ludlow war referendum resolution in 1938 and often on defense measures. Indeed, in 1938 Roosevelt named him vice chairman of the U.S. delegation to the Inter-American Conference in Lima,

Peru. In 1940 the president apparently considered appointing Landon secretary of war, but the Kansan stated publicly that he would not accept the job unless Roosevelt refused to stand for nomination to a third presidential term. By 1941 the two men divided increasingly on foreign policy. The Kansan was not opposed to giving money and goods to Great Britain in its war with Germany and Italy, but he believed that Roosevelt was trying to maneuver the United States into the war, which he opposed and feared would convert the nation into a garrison state. Landon remained a significant opposition spokesman during World War II as an apostle of responsible two-party politics.

Landon's influence declined after the war. He continued to speak out, however, frequently taking independent positions. Among other things, Landon supported President Harry S. Truman often on foreign policy, helped to force the resignation of Republican national committee chairman C. Wesley Roberts in 1953, occasionally criticized Senator Joseph R. McCarthy (1908–1957) and other extreme anti-Communists, opposed right-to-work legislation, favored international control of nuclear weapons, and, beginning in 1953, far in advance of any other prominent Republican or Democrat, advocated American diplomatic recognition of the People's Republic of China. In 1962 he was a leading supporter of President John F. Kennedy's trade expansion legislation. Landon also crusaded regularly over the years against high taxes, inflation, and excessive government regulation. By the end of the 1950s he was widely recognized as an elder statesman. Advancing age slowed Landon's political activities by the late 1960s, but until 1987 he often granted interviews and issued press statements on the issues facing America. He died in Topeka one month after festivities marking his one-hundredth birthday, which included a visit from President Ronald Reagan. To the end Landon remained a remarkably independent political figure, noted for his integrity and sense of responsibility.

• Alfred Landon's personal papers and the records of his governorship are in the Kansas State Historical Society, Topeka. A scholarly biography of him is Donald R. McCoy, *Landon of Kansas* (1966). Frederick Palmer wrote a presidential campaign biography, *This Man Landon* (1936). For a selection of the Kansan's public statements in 1935 and 1936, see Alfred M. Landon, *America at the Crossroads* (1936). Treatments of the 1936 presidential election campaign are William E. Leuchtenburg, "Election of 1936," in *History of American Presidential Elections, 1789–1968*, ed. Arthur M. Schlesinger, Jr., and Fred L. Israel, vol. 3 (1971); Donald R. McCoy, "The Election of 1936," in *Crucial American Elections*, Memoirs of the American Philosophical Society, vol. 99 (1973); and Arthur M. Schlesinger, Jr., *The Age of Roosevelt*, vol. 3: *The Politics of Upheaval, 1935–1936* (1960). Regarding Landon's work as titular head of the Republican party, see George H. Mayer, "Alf M. Landon as Leader of the Republican Opposition, 1937–1940," *Kansas Historical Quarterly* 32 (Autumn 1966). Obituaries appeared in major newspapers on 13 Oct. 1987; the one in the *New York Times* is poor.

DONALD R. McCOY

LANDON, Melville De Lancey (7 Sept. 1839–16 Dec. 1910), wit and humorist, was born in Eaton, New York, the son of John Landon and Nancy Marsh, farmers. Landon was educated at Madison (now Colgate) University and Union College where he earned his B.A. in 1861 and was conferred an honorary A.M. degree in 1862. He worked for U.S. Treasury secretary Salmon P. Chase and served the Union army in Washington, D.C., under the command of Major General Cassius Marcellus Clay. He later served on the staff of Brigadier General Augustus Louis Chetlain in Memphis, Tennessee, who was charged with recruiting black troops in Tennessee and Kentucky. Landon achieved the rank of major in 1863. At the request of Secretary Chase, he resigned the following year to grow cotton in Arkansas and Louisiana. Two years later Landon embarked for Europe where he was eventually appointed secretary at the American Legation in St. Petersburg, Russia, working again for Clay, who had returned to Russia to serve as minister from the United States. While abroad, Landon began a career as a journalist by contributing to a variety of U.S. newspapers. This career later culminated in his serving as president of the New York News Association.

Landon returned to the United States in 1870 and published a book on the Franco-Prussian war, *The Franco-Prussian War in a Nutshell: A Daily Diary of Diplomacy, Battles, and War Literature* (1871). He then turned to journalism full-time and began writing a series of humorous letters set in and concerning Saratoga, New York. Originally published in the *New York Commercial Advertiser*, they were later assembled and published as *Saratoga in 1901* (1872). Described as a "humorous prophecy," it is a compendium of jokes, reminiscences, descriptions of horse racing and gambling, and meditations on walking sticks, gossips, and the social regalia of the resort. This was the first of many collections of humor from the man who was often considered as "the greatest liar in all America."

In 1875 Landon married Emily Louise Smith of Port Chester, New York, with whom he had one child. The following year he was asked by the publishing house G. W. Carleton to edit *The Complete Works of Artemus Ward* (1879), a volume of his friend's humorous writings, to which he also contributed the biographical introduction. It was Ward who gave Landon the pseudonym "Eli Perkins," a name Ward associated with someone having "dry philosophical ideas, original and startling." Landon's career as an editor continued with a volume titled *Wit and Humor of the Age* (1883), which included the writings of such humorists as Mark Twain, Josh Billings, Bret Harte, Ward, Uncle Remus, and Bill Nye. Besides examining wit and humor specific to a variety of professions, including the clergy, medicine, law, and politics, Landon provided chapters on "Irish," "Negro," and "Dutch" wit. He followed this with another collection, *Thirty Years of Wit and Reminiscences of Witty, Wise, and Eloquent Men* (1891). Along with samples of their humor, Landon included biographical and anecdotal information about his fellow humorists.

Much of Landon's humor was inspired by personal experience gained not only during the Civil War and his travels in Europe, but also on his extensive lecture tours. He claimed to have addressed students at every college in the United States and spoke throughout the East and across the West to largely appreciative audiences. In addition to his travels through Europe, he visited Japan and China and was so impressed that he styled his Eaton, New York, summer home as a Japanese bungalow complete with a Shinto shrine. The emperor of Japan is reported to have presented Landon with three sacred dogs and enough vases, dragons, and porcelains to fill the bungalow. He had inscribed over the door to the bungalow his motto: "Truth is Mighty—Scarce!" Landon died in Yonkers, New York.

Throughout his career, Landon spent considerable time developing his "Philosophy of Wit and Humor." In *Thirty Years of Wit*, for example, he argued that both wit and humor depend upon "surprise," or "the magnification or minification of a thought beyond the truth into the imagination." He then distinguished the two by how such surprises are brought about: "I find all humor is pure truth or nature; while all wit is imagination. Humor is the photograph, while wit is an imaginative sketch." Both humor and wit comprise a host of subclasses that Landon went to some pains to describe. Irony, satire, and ridicule, for example, are subclasses of wit because they consist of untruths. Anecdotes and repartee are usually instances of humor as they are generally found in or taken from incidents in real life. His "philosophy," however, is largely an excuse to delight in his examples rather than a detailed examination of his subject.

• Among Landon's humorous writings not mentioned above include *Eli Perkins at Large: His Sayings and Doings* (1875), *Wise, Witty, Eloquent Kings of the Platform and Pulpit* (1890), and *Wit, Humor and Pathos* (1895). He published a more serious book arguing against the free distribution of silver in *Money: Gold, Silver, or Bimetallism* (1895). An obituary is in the *New York Times*, 17 Dec. 1910.

RICHARD HENRY

LANDON, Michael (31 Oct. 1936–1 July 1991), actor, was born Eugene Maurice Orowitz in Forest Hills, Queens, New York City, the son of Eli Orowitz, a manager of movie theaters, and Peggy O'Neill, a former actress and chorus girl. When Landon was a small child he moved with his family to Collingswood, New Jersey, a suburb of Philadelphia. At Collingswood High School Landon excelled at sports, especially javelin throwing, and was elected a class officer. Despite these achievements, Landon always recalled his youth as an unhappy, lonely time because of the anti-Semitism of his peers, his Jewish father and Catholic mother's turbulent marriage, and his own moody, sensitive personality (complicated by a bedwetting problem that persisted into his adolescence).

In 1954 Landon enrolled at the University of Southern California in Los Angeles, which had awarded him an athletic scholarship based on his javelin-throwing talent. When an injury ended his athletic and academic career after one year, Landon remained in Los Angeles working at odd jobs. He drifted into acting when he accompanied a friend to an audition at Warner Bros. studios. Landon attended the Warner Bros. acting school, though he was never placed under contract by the studio or given a salary. He chose Michael Lane as his stage name, but after discovering that another actor was already using that name, he selected Landon, the name above Lane in the Los Angeles telephone directory. In 1956, at age nineteen, Landon married a legal secretary, Dodie Fraser, and adopted her son from a previous marriage. The couple later adopted a second son. Of medium height, with a slim but muscular build, Michael Landon possessed a handsome face and an impressive head of dark, wavy hair. Good looks and a willingness to work hard helped Landon to find small parts on television and to land the title role in the popular low-budget horror movie *I Was a Teenage Werewolf* (1957). After this he appeared in the film version of Erskine Caldwell's novel *God's Little Acre* (1958) and in *The Legend of Tom Dooley* (1959).

Undoubtedly, Landon's big break came when he was cast in the NBC television western "Bonanza." Premiering in the fall of 1959, the hour-long serial program centered around life at the huge Ponderosa Ranch in the High Sierra owned by the widower Ben Cartwright and his three adult sons, the introspective Adam, the "gentle giant" Hoss, and the youthfully impetuous Little Joe, played by Landon, who was clearly intended as the show's sex symbol. Less violent than other westerns, "Bonanza," the first television western to be shot in color, emphasized situations that tested the personal integrity of the upstanding Cartwrights and frequently employed gentle humor. Only a moderate success during its first two seasons on the air, "Bonanza" shot to the number two position in the ratings after being moved to a more propitious Sunday night broadcast time in 1961 and by the mid-1960s was the most-watched television show in the United States. "Bonanza" remained among the top five shows for the rest of the decade. It was also extremely popular in the world market.

Landon was a dedicated family man, though not always a model husband. His first marriage ended in divorce in 1962, and he married the model and actress Lynn Noe the following year. They eventually had four children. He maintained his paternal obligations to his sons from his first marriage and acted as father to his second wife's daughter from her first marriage. Toward the middle of "Bonanza's" run Landon began writing and directing episodes of the series. Although his writing style was frequently cited as clichéd and mawkish, his skill as a director was more generally admired. Landon delivered well-crafted episodes on time and within budget. The long run of "Bonanza" finally came to a close in January 1973, when the show was canceled halfway through its fourteenth season.

Turning down offers to star in typical crime and medical dramas, Landon followed his family-oriented instincts and chose "Little House on the Prairie" as his second television series. Based on the children's books of Laura Ingalls Wilder, "Little House on the Prairie" featured Landon as Charles Ingalls, a stalwart husband, father, and homesteader in late nineteenth-century Minnesota. "Little House on the Prairie," which Landon also produced, ran on NBC from 1974 to 1983. Its success defied conventional wisdom of the time that said contemporary audiences wanted more hard-edged entertainment. There was criticism that the series was a vanity vehicle for an increasingly egotistical and dictatorial Landon (who wrote and directed many of its episodes, in addition to producing and starring) and presented a saccharine view of life on the prairie that was not faithful to Wilder's books. Landon dismissed such comments, claiming that network executives had shown no interest in a "Little House on the Prairie" series until he had become associated with the project and that the ratings proved that the public liked the show's sentimental tone—little matter if the critics did not. Landon created and produced an offshoot series, the equally wholesome "Father Murphy," which starred "Little House" veteran Merlin Olsen as a miner in 1870s Dakota Territory who opens up an orphanage. The show ran from 1981 to 1984 on NBC.

Landon's image as a crusader for "family" entertainment was somewhat tarnished in 1982 when he left his wife of nineteen years to marry a former "Little House on the Prairie" makeup assistant, Cindy Clerico. Landon and Clerico soon had two children. Landon, who retained his trim and muscular physique though his trademark longish, wavy hair had turned grey, returned to television in the fall of 1984 in another NBC series, "Highway to Heaven," in which he played an angel (disguised as an itinerant laborer) who brings love and understanding to the lives of troubled people. Though not as popular as Landon's previous efforts, "Highway to Heaven" was still a solid success and ran until 1989.

The career of Landon was remarkable for its longevity. His success in three television series over a thirty-year period has been rivalled only by that of Lucille Ball. In April 1991 Landon, who was working on a fourth NBC series that was scheduled to air in the fall of that year, was diagnosed with pancreatic cancer. The 54-year-old actor quickly made his almost certainly fatal illness known to the public. He hoped that others might find inspiration in his ordeal and that he, in turn, might gain strength from the support of the public that had been with him for more than thirty years. Landon died several weeks later at his home in Malibu, California.

• The best sources of information on Michael Landon are Marsha Daly, *Michael Landon: A Biography* (1987), which is thorough in regard to his childhood and professional life, and Cheryl Landon Wilson with Jane Scovell, *I Promised My Dad: An Intimate Portrait of Michael Landon by His Eldest*

Daughter (1992), which offers an affectionate but frank look into Landon's private life and personality. An obituary is in the *New York Times*, 2 July 1991.

MARY C. KALFATOVIC

LANDOWSKA, Wanda (5 July 1879–16 Aug. 1959), musician, was born Aleksandra Landowska in Warsaw, Poland, the daughter of Marjan Landowski, a lawyer, and Ewa Lautenberg, a linguist. The Landowskis were formerly Jews who had converted to Roman Catholicism.

Wanda Landowska was a precocious musician who began studying the piano when she was barely out of infancy. She gave her first public recital at the age of four, and from an early age she was especially captivated by the music of Johann Sebastian Bach. She studied privately in childhood and entered the Warsaw Conservatory at the age of fourteen. Her instructors there included Aleksander Michalowski, the noted Chopin interpreter. Following her graduation in 1896, Landowska made her concert debut in Warsaw. She then moved to Berlin, where she studied with Heinrich Urban, the teacher of Padarewski and other renowned performers. Landowska's continued devotion to the music of Bach—which was then infrequently played— earned her the nickname "Bacchante."

In 1900 Landowska eloped to Paris with Henri Lew, a Polish journalist and ethnographer; the couple had no children. There she decided to concentrate on early keyboard literature, especially the music of Bach and its performance on the harpsichord, which had been supplanted by the piano in the nineteenth century. Aided by her husband, Landowska began an intensive study of early classical music and instruments in European libraries and museums. In the course of her research, she met other performers and scholars who were attempting to revive early music performance, including the founders of the Schola Cantorum (Vincent d'Indy, Charles Bordes, and Alexandre Guilmant).

At her first recital in Paris, given in 1903, Landowska played the music of early composers on a small reconstructed harpsichord made by the Pleyel piano company. This instrument proved inadequate, however, and after making a thorough study of harpsichords in museums throughout Europe with the assistance of Pleyel's chief engineer, she commissioned the firm to build her a new instrument that was capable of playing all keyboard music composed between 1500 and 1800, in particular the works of Bach.

While the harpsichord was being constructed, Landowska contributed numerous articles to scholarly journals on the authentic performance of early keyboard music, which nineteenth-century Romantic interpreters had obscured or eliminated altogether. In 1909 she published a book-length work on the subject, *La Musique ancienne*, co-authored with her husband; it was published in English translation as *Music of the Past* in 1924.

The first Pleyel harpsichord built to Landowska's specifications was completed in 1912. The concert-sized instrument had two manuals and included four sets of strings, a coupler, a lute stop, and a second row of jacks for the upper keyboard. Later that year Landowska played it for the first time at a Bach festival in Breslau.

In 1913 the Hochschule für Musik in Berlin hired Landowska to teach its newly created harpsichord class. She and her husband were detained in Germany following the outbreak of war a year later, and in April 1919 he was killed there in an automobile accident. Following his death, Landowska taught master classes in Switzerland before returning to Paris in 1920. She taught for a while at the École Normale de Musique, gave private lessons, and in 1923–1924, at the invitation of Leopold Stokowski, made a concert tour of the United States, playing a large Pleyel harpsichord. During this visit to the United States she began recording for the Victor Company.

During the 1920s, Landowska also toured extensively in Europe, Africa, and South America. Her revival of the harpsichord inspired several contemporary composers, including Manuel de Falla and Francis Poulenc, to write new music for the instrument. In 1925 Landowska took further steps to increase the harpsichord's popularity by establishing the École de Musique Ancienne, a school specializing in early music instruction, on a small estate she purchased at St. Leu-la-Forêt, twelve miles north of Paris. She had a concert hall built on the property and in 1927 began a series of summer concerts that featured performances by herself and her students.

Landowska's summer concerts gained a devoted following and presented many "firsts," including, in 1933, the first complete performance on the harpsichord in the twentieth century of Bach's *Goldberg Variations*. The concerts came to an abrupt end in the summer of 1940, after German troops marched into Paris. Landowska's house, including a collection of harpsichords and other instruments and an extensive library of rare manuscripts, was seized by the Germans. After the war several of the instruments were found in Leipzig; they had previously been hidden in a salt mine in Austria.

After taking refuge in the south of France and giving several harpsichord recitals in Switzerland, Landowska returned to the United States permanently in November 1941. Three months later, on 21 February 1942, she performed Bach's *Goldberg Variations* at Town Hall in New York City, playing a Pleyel harpsichord she had brought from France. She received an ovation from the audience and rave reviews from critics. Landowska lived in New York City for five years, during which time she taught privately, gave concerts, and made recordings for RCA Victor. She continued these activities after moving in 1947 to Lakeville, Connecticut, her home for the remainder of her life.

In 1954, at the age of seventy-five, Landowska completed the recording of Bach's *Well-Tempered Clavier* in its entirety at her home in Lakeville. The recording is considered of great historical significance, and the National Academy of Recording Arts and Sciences included it in its Hall of Fame in 1977. She continued to make recordings—of works by Haydn, Mozart, and Bach—until her eightieth birthday, a month before her death.

In addition to her work as a performer, teacher, and musicologist, Landowska was also a composer of keyboard music. Most of her compositions have been lost, although cadenzas she wrote for concertos by Haydn, Handel, and Mozart are extant. One of her compositions, "Liberation Fanfare," composed in 1943, was frequently played in a band arrangement at outdoor concerts in New York City during the 1940s. Although her primary instrument was the harpsichord, Landowska continued to play the piano as well throughout her life, reproducing the tonal qualities of the eighteenth-century fortepiano.

Landowska was a striking presence on the concert stage. Barely five feet tall, she always wore a long, dark-colored velvet dress and velvet ballet slippers. Her large nose, together with her black hair pulled back in a loose bun, gave her a distinctive profile, and her clawlike fingers attacked the keyboard with precision.

Landowska gave her last public concert in 1954 at the Frick Collection in New York City, but she continued to make recordings until her death, which occurred at her Lakeville home. Her house has been preserved as the Landowska Center and is both a repository for her instruments, books, papers, and memorabilia and a music school that perpetuates her teachings.

• For biographical information on Wanda Landowska, see Roland Gelatt, *Music Makers* (1953). Her musical philosophy is revealed in James Nelson, ed., *Wisdom* (1958), and Denise Restout, ed., *Landowska on Music* (1964), which includes a bibliography of her writings. See also Restout, "Mamusia: Vignettes of Wanda Landowska," *High Fidelity* (Oct. 1960). In addition, Mme. Restout, director of the Landowska Center, provided further information. An obituary is in the *New York Times*, 17 Aug. 1959.

ANN T. KEENE

LANDSTEINER, Karl (14 June 1868–26 June 1943), immunologist and pathologist, was born in Vienna, Austria, the son of Leopold Landsteiner, a journalist and newspaper publisher, and Fanny Hess. He received an M.D. from the University of Vienna in 1891, then spent three years studying chemistry at the Universities of Zurich, Würzburg, and Munich. In 1894 he returned to the University of Vienna and for two years worked as an assistant in the Second Medical University Clinic and the First Surgical University Clinic. In 1896 he became an assistant at the University of Vienna's Institute of Hygiene and began experimenting with the effects of immune blood serum on bacteria cultures. His interest in the nascent field of immunology led him to transfer two years later to the Institute of Pathological Anatomy because its director encouraged him to pursue his work in immunology.

Landsteiner was curious about why blood from one human could rarely be given to another human without resulting in major complications for the recipient. This line of investigation led to the discovery in 1900 that, in every case involving complications, a number of the recipient's red corpuscles had clumped together. However, the fact that clumping did not occur every time blood was transferred suggested to Landsteiner the existence of different types of human blood, and in 1901 he identified three types (which he called A, B, and C). In each type, the red corpuscles contained a distinct set of agglutinogens, which stimulate the production of antibodies, which in turn attack organisms foreign to the body. The red corpuscles in Landsteiner's first group contained only "A" agglutinogens, those in the second group contained only "B" agglutinogens, and those in the third group contained neither "A" nor "B" agglutinogens. In 1902, when two of his associates discovered that some red corpuscles contain both A and B agglutinogens, he identified a fourth group, AB, and renamed the C group 0 (for zero agglutinogens). The importance of this discovery was not widely understood until shortly before the outbreak of World War I, at which time it helped to save the lives of many patients receiving transfusions because doctors now knew to match the blood of both donor and recipient by type. The discovery of the ABO blood groups earned for Landsteiner the 1930 Nobel Prize for Physiology or Medicine.

Between 1902 and 1922 Landsteiner conducted research more closely related to pathology. In 1904 he discovered that paroxysmal hemoglobinuria was caused by exposure to cold, which in turn led to the breakdown of red corpuscles and the release of hemoglobin into the bloodstream. In 1905 he developed a method for viewing the spirochetes of syphilis under a microscope, and the next year he helped to improve the Wasserman test for detecting syphilis. In 1908 Landsteiner joined the pathology staff at Vienna's Royal-Imperial Wilhelmina Hospital; the next year he also began teaching pathology at the University of Vienna. In 1912 he became the first researcher to conclude that poliomyelitis resulted from a viral infection. In 1916 he married Helene Wlasto, with whom he had one child.

Working conditions for research specialists deteriorated rapidly in Austria following that country's defeat in World War I, and in 1919 Landsteiner left Vienna to become a professor of pathology at R. K. Hospital in the Hague, Netherlands. In 1922, with conditions there proving to be no better than in Vienna, he immigrated to the United States at the invitation of the Rockefeller Institute for Medical Research (later known as Rockefeller University) in New York City and became a U.S. citizen seven years later.

Landsteiner's work at the Rockefeller Institute marked a return to his earlier studies of human blood. His first project at the institute involved a comparative study of the blood of humans, monkeys, and apes, and in 1925 he and his colleague C. Philip Miller offered support for zoologists who claimed that humans were not descended from any existing species of primate, but rather that primates and humans were descended

from a common ancestor. Because he remained convinced that each individual's blood was much more unique than the existence of only four blood groups indicated, he and Philip Levine, another Rockefeller colleague, began looking for other distinguishing factors. In 1927 they discovered a new group of agglutinogens (known as M, N, and P); however, these agglutinogens rarely occur in normal blood. In 1936 Landsteiner published *The Specificity of Serological Reactions*, a recapitulation of everything he had discovered at that point about the immune properties of human blood. This work served for many years as the basic text for students of immunochemistry.

In 1940 Landsteiner collaborated with Levine and Alexander S. Wiener to discover the Rh factor in red blood cells. Approximately 85 percent of the population is Rh positive; in the remaining 15 percent, the injection of Rh positive blood can result in the clumping or dissolution of red corpuscles, either of which can cause a number of conditions, including death. This discovery led directly to the development of a treatment for erythroblastosis, the dissolution of red corpuscles in a fetus or newborn infant of an Rh negative mother and an Rh positive father.

Landsteiner served as president of the American Association of Immunologists in 1929. He was made a chevalier in the French Legion of Honor in 1911 and was awarded the Hans Aronson Foundation of Berlin Prize in 1926, the Paul Ehrlich Medal in 1930, the Dutch Red Cross Society Gold Medal in 1933, and the University of Edinburgh's Cameron Prize and Lectureship in 1938. He was elected to membership in the National Academy of Sciences in 1932. He died in New York City.

Landsteiner's discovery of the four human blood groups was one of the critical discoveries that made possible the establishment of the modern blood bank, which in turn permitted operations on the heart, lungs, and circulatory system that had been impossible before because of the large blood loss. His postulation that every individual's blood is unique led to other discoveries that made it possible to settle questions of paternity and criminal guilt by identifying the blood characteristics of the parties involved.

• Landsteiner's papers have not been located. Biographies are P. Mazumdar, *Karl Landsteiner and the Problem of Species* (1976); G. R. Simms, *The Scientific Works of Karl Landsteiner* (1963); and P. Speiser and F. Smekal, *Karl Landsteiner* (1975). An obituary is in the *Journal of the American Medical Association* 122 (1943).

CHARLES W. CAREY, JR.

LANE, Arthur Bliss (16 June 1894–12 Aug. 1956), diplomat, was born in Brooklyn, New York, the son of James Warren Lane, a businessman, and Eva Metcalf Bliss. Lane's maternal grandfather, Eliphalet Williams Bliss, was an inventor; manufacturer of tools, dies, and naval munitions; and real estate investor, who accumulated much of the family fortune. Lane was educated at the Browning School in New York, at the École de l'Ile de France in Liancourt, France, and at Yale University, where he received his B.A. in 1916. He began his diplomatic career as the private secretary to Thomas N. Page, U.S. ambassador in Italy. The following year he was admitted into the Foreign Service and served until 1919 as third secretary in the U.S. embassy in Rome. In 1918 he married Cornelia Thayer Baldwin; they had one child.

Lane served in various subordinate positions in Europe, Latin America, and Washington. He was second secretary of the embassies in Warsaw (1919) and London (1920–1922), and he was secretary to the U.S. delegation to the Supreme Allied Council in Paris (1921). He was then first secretary to the legation in Bern, Switzerland, and assistant to Undersecretary of State Joseph C. Grew. In 1924 he became first secretary to the legation in Mexico City, remaining in that position until 1927, when he was appointed chief of the State Department's Division of Mexican Affairs in Washington. In 1930 he returned to Mexico City as counselor of the U.S. embassy. During these years he worked closely with Ambassador Dwight Morrow, whose efforts to improve relations with Mexico he supported.

In 1933 Lane was appointed minister to Nicaragua and was, at that time, the youngest career minister in the history of the U.S. diplomatic service. Lane arrived in Managua just as the prolonged U.S. occupation ended. It was a difficult appointment, for Lane had to balance requirements of the Franklin D. Roosevelt administration's noninterventionist "Good Neighbor" policy with the consequences of Nicaragua's almost twenty-year experience of U.S. tutelage. The American-trained national guard under Anastasio Somoza Garcia was the most troublesome part of the legacy, for its ambitious leader used the guard to assassinate the Nicaraguan nationalist and anti-American guerrilla leader, Augusto C. Sandino, and eventually to seize power. Many Nicaraguans believed the United States was at least indirectly responsible for these actions and called on Minister Lane to prevent Somoza from toppling the existing government. Lane found it impossible, therefore, not to become involved in internal politics, being frequently urged by Nicaraguans and even other Latin American diplomats in Managua to give friendly, informal advice and pressed to say that the United States would not recognize Somoza if he seized power illegally. Harried by the political pressures, Lane was critical of his predecessors for their interventionist activities and for the formation of the Nicaraguan national guard, which helped to create the situation he confronted.

Lane was not unhappy to leave Nicaragua in March 1936, a few months before Somoza, with Washington's acquiescence, seized power. He took a new post as minister to the Baltic states of Estonia, Latvia, and Lithuania. Unlike Managua, Riga was quiet and relatively unimportant to the United States. His duties were routine, but Lane objected to the presence in the legation of the semiautonomous Russian Section, which had been created to study events in the Soviet Union. Lane disliked the Russian Section's independence and, in his view, its anti-Soviet bias.

In 1937 Lane departed Riga to become the U.S. minister in Yugoslavia, a post of no particular importance to the United States but one that would attract more attention as Nazi Germany moved into Eastern Europe. Soon after his arrival in Belgrade Lane developed a personal relationship with the regent, Prince Paul, who, after the fall of Poland and France, maneuvered to avoid war, even if it meant accommodation with Hitler. Lane understood the regent's dilemma but disapproved of appeasement. Lane tried to discourage his alignment with the Axis by conveying Washington's vague promises of aid through the lend-lease program and warning that, when future peace settlements were made, a nation's action in the face of aggression would be considered. Nonetheless, the Yugoslav government adhered to the Tripartite Pact on 25 March 1941. Two days later the government was overthrown by a military coup d'état in favor of young King Peter. Lane approved of this act as representing the popular will, although he correctly anticipated that the coup would subject Yugoslavia to a German invasion. The invasion came in April. During his last days in Yugoslavia he evacuated Americans from the country amidst mass confusion. German propaganda claimed that he and the U.S. government had conspired to bring the calamity on the country.

Returning to the United States in 1941 Lane lectured and wrote on the threat of Fascism before being appointed minister to Costa Rica. In 1942 he was sent as ambassador to Colombia, where he remained until 1944, when he was appointed ambassador to the Polish government in exile in London. His departure was delayed, however, until the new provisional government was established in Warsaw, and he presented his credentials to that government in 1945. During his tenure in Warsaw he worked single-mindedly to decrease Soviet influence and to use U.S. aid as a means of encouraging free elections, which had been promised in the Yalta and Potsdam agreements. The failure of the Soviet-controlled government to conduct free elections in 1947 led Lane to become increasingly critical of Washington for not doing enough to ensure compliance. His obvious and increasingly anti-Communist hostility and his seeming refusal to recognize the limited realistic choices available to the United States in an area of Soviet dominance lessened his effectiveness as a diplomat. Believing his usefulness in Warsaw had ended, he inquired about other posts. Failing to receive positive responses, he resigned from the Foreign Service on 25 March 1947.

During the next several years Lane became increasingly disillusioned with U.S. foreign policy and wrote and spoke widely about the dangers of Communism, decrying containment, détente, and peaceful coexistence. In 1948 he published *I Saw Poland Betrayed*. He was a member of the board of the National Committee for a Free Europe, cochair of the Committee to Stop World Communism, and chair of the American Committee to Investigate the Katyn Forest Massacre.

In 1952 he helped to write the Republican platform plank calling for independence of the East European nations and campaigned for Joseph McCarthy. He died in New York City.

Lane's career lacked major diplomatic successes. His efforts in Nicaragua, Yugoslavia, and Poland were limited by forces beyond his control. His biographer Vladimir Petrov nevertheless rated him highly, noting that Lane's performance record in both routine and critical situations was outstanding. Yet Lane's unrealistic and inflexible approach to events in Poland and his attendant disillusionment with U.S. policy ended his diplomatic service prematurely.

• The Arthur Bliss Lane Papers, including about 600,000 items, are housed at Yale University. The diplomatic record of his tenure as minister or ambassador at various capitals can be traced in the State Department documents preserved at the National Archives. Selections of these documents are published in the *Papers Relating to the Foreign Relations of the United States* for the appropriate years and countries. For a survey of Lane's diplomatic career see Vladimir Petrov, *A Study in Diplomacy: The Story of Arthur Bliss Lane* (1971). For Lane's role in postwar Poland, the most controversial aspect of his career, John N. Cable, "Arthur Bliss Lane: Cold Warrior in Warsaw, 1945–47," *Polish American Studies* 30 (1973): 66–82, is critical. For a view of Lane in Nicaragua see William Kamman, "U.S. Recognition of Anastasio Somoza, 1936," *Historian* 54 (1992): 269–82. An obituary is in the *New York Times*, 14 Aug. 1956.

WILLIAM KAMMAN

LANE, Franklin Knight (15 July 1864–18 May 1921), interstate commerce commissioner and secretary of the interior, was born on Prince Edward Island, Canada, the son of Caroline Burns and Christopher Lane, a Presbyterian minister who later became a dentist. In 1871 the Lane family migrated to the San Francisco Bay area. Starting in high school, Franklin combined professional newspaper work with his education. He attended the University of California, Berkeley (1885–1886), and Hastings Law School (1886–1888). Although Lane passed the California bar examination in 1888, he continued his journalism career, including two years as *San Francisco Chronicle* correspondent in New York City. In 1891 he purchased the *Tacoma* (Wash.) *Daily News* and in his editorials supported organized labor, a low tariff, Grover Cleveland's candidacy for president, and such reforms as the graduated income tax, direct election of the president, and a heavy tax on unoccupied land.

While in Tacoma, Lane met Anne Wintermute, and they married in April 1893. The couple had two children. In 1894 Lane's newspaper fell victim to the national economic depression, and he returned to San Francisco to work for the weekly *Arthur McEwen's Letter*. Six months later, when it failed, he abandoned journalism and became a partner in his brother's law firm.

In 1897 San Francisco mayor James D. Phelan appointed Lane to a nonpartisan committee to draft a new city charter. Lane's participation in the campaign

to win voter adoption of the new charter led him to run for city attorney in 1898. He proved a popular candidate in his three successful races for the office. In the opinions Lane rendered he demonstrated legally sound judgment. The Supreme Court of California sustained his decisions in every case it reviewed.

Lane attracted national attention in 1902 when, as a Roosevelt Democrat, he lost the California gubernatorial election by 2,549 votes at a time when the Republican party dominated the state. When a mutual friend of Lane and President Theodore Roosevelt (1858–1919), Benjamin Ide Wheeler, president of the University of California, Berkeley, arranged a meeting, Roosevelt took an instant liking to Lane and later made him his second appointee to the Interstate Commerce Commission (ICC). Lane obtained his seat in June 1906 simultaneously with passage of the Hepburn Act, which significantly increased the authority of the ICC. As commissioner Lane won recognition as the dominant member and as a champion of federal regulation, especially of rates and securities. In 1911 President William Howard Taft reappointed him to another term.

The day before Woodrow Wilson's inauguration as president, newspapers announced his appointment of Lane as secretary of the interior, a position Lane owed to his friend and Wilson's closest adviser, Colonel Edward M. House. In Lane's first annual report in December 1913, he summarized the five measures he wanted Congress to enact for the development of natural resources on federal lands. The following year Congress passed laws that fulfilled three of Lane's objectives: the Reclamation Extension Act amended the Reclamation Act of 1902 to encourage more development of semiarid land; the Alaskan Railroad Act authorized the federal government to construct a railroad to improve access to federal lands; and the Alaskan Coal Leasing Act established the terms by which private developers could mine coal on federal lands. The Federal Water Power Act and the General Leasing Act, both passed in 1920, completed the list of Lane's original proposals. Both of these acts encouraged private development through a leasing system under federal regulation with safeguards against monopoly. Passage of the National Park Service Act of 1916 established the National Park System and constituted another milestone of the conservation movement that Lane helped bring to legislative fruition. Although overzealous in specific instances, Lane provided effective, decisive leadership to the conservation movement during a critical period.

Lane's administration of the Indian Bureau, one of the constituent bureaus of the Department of the Interior, rested on his acceptance of the philosophy embodied in the Dawes Act of 1887 and the Burke Act of 1906. The acts called for the government to educate Indians, give each a title to an allotment of the tribal land, and then terminate governmental responsibility and jurisdiction. The Indian Bureau, Lane emphasized, "should be a vanishing Bureau."

Within the cabinet Lane supported Wilson's World War I policies: first neutrality, then preparedness, and finally war, although Lane thought Wilson at times moved too timidly. During the war Lane served on the Council of National Defense, portrayed the war as a crusade for righteousness, and introduced a plan to provide veterans with farms. Although the farms-for-veterans plan generated substantial congressional and public support, farm organizations, fearing overproduction, opposed it, and the Republican-controlled Congress elected in November 1918 had no desire to enact a Wilson administration proposal. Consequently Lane's plan died.

After the war Lane increased his promotion of American values through improved education, an interest he had championed for years through the Interior Department's Bureau of Education. Because he believed that democracy depended upon an educated public, Lane supported higher teacher salaries and the reduction of adult illiteracy. In the Senate he favored compromise in order to obtain ratification of the Treaty of Versailles and, thereby, U.S. membership in the League of Nations. In October 1919 he chaired the Industrial Conference, an unsuccessful attempt to lessen the strong postwar labor-management conflict. Despite House's high opinion of him, Lane never became a close adviser to Wilson, in part because of Lane's garrulous personality and his friendships with reporters and Republicans. Lane remained personally closer to Theodore Roosevelt than to Wilson.

As secretary of the interior, and earlier as interstate commerce commissioner, Lane proved himself a forceful, effective leader in the progressive movement that placed faith in the ability of the federal government to serve as a nonpartisan, regulatory agent representing a broad public interest. He enjoyed favorable press coverage throughout his public career. His views and record as city attorney, ICC member, and secretary of the interior attracted impressive Republic support. Democrats in California urged Lane to run for senator, and both Taft and Wilson considered Lane for possible appointment to the Supreme Court.

In February 1920, for financial reasons, Lane resigned to become vice president of Pan American Petroleum & Transport Company and the Mexican Petroleum Company. At this time the *New York Times* editorialized that he "would be a Presidential probability" were he native-born, and other newspapers made similar assessments. During this period Lane served as chair of the Salvation Army's Second Home Appeal, as treasurer of the European Relief Council, and as trustee of the John D. Rockefeller General Education Board. He died at the Mayo Clinic in Rochester, Minnesota.

• A small collection of Lane manuscripts is at the University of California, Berkeley. Lane published some of his speeches in *The American Spirit* (1918). His widow, Anne Wintermute Lane, and his secretary, Louise Herrick Wall, published a thick volume, *The Letters of Franklin K. Lane: Personal and Political* (1922). The only full-length study is Keith W. Olson, *Biography of a Progressive: Franklin K. Lane, 1864–1921* (1979). An obituary is in the *Washington Post*, 19 May 1921.

KEITH W. OLSON

LANE, Gertrude Battles (21 Dec. 1874–25 Sept. 1941), magazine editor, was born in Saco, Maine, the daughter of Eustace Lane, an organist and piano tuner, and Ella Maud Battles. Lane was educated in Saco, first in the public schools, then at the private Thornton Academy, where she edited the school's literary paper. After graduating in 1892, Lane moved to Boston, where she worked as a private tutor. In 1895, she completed a year-long course at Burdett College of Business and Shorthand. After a brief employment with an insurance company, in 1896 Lane began working for the Cyclopedia Publishing Company as an assistant editor. She held this position for seven years, developing and honing her editorial skills. During this period Lane also contributed poems, essays, and book reviews to the *Boston Transcript* and the *Boston Beacon* and took a class in English composition at Simmons College.

In 1902 financial and management problems at the Cyclopedia Publishing Company caused Lane to search for a new job. She applied for the position of household editor at the *Woman's Home Companion*. The *Companion* was a general, monthly women's magazine, founded in 1874, edited in New York City (though published in Springfield, Ohio), and recently bought by the Crowell Publishing Company. Lane was hired by editor Arthur T. Vance, who had directed the magazine since 1900. She began working at the *Companion* in August 1903; Lane stayed with the publication and the Crowell Publishing Company until her death.

Lane rose steadily at the *Companion*, becoming managing editor in 1909 and editor in chief in 1912. She attributed her success to hard work, but she also possessed both editorial acumen and keen business sense. Under Lane the *Companion* shifted its emphasis firmly back to women and the home (a focus that had extended to the whole family under Vance). However, Lane's view of what the homemaker needed was quite broad. Her magazine gave readers practical service departments, entertaining fiction, and a wide range of general interest features. The formula succeeded, and under Lane circulation grew from 727,764 when she took over in 1912, to 1 million by 1916, more than 2 million in 1923, and over 3.5 million at the time she died. In 1937 the *Companion* took over the lead in circulation from long time leader *Ladies' Home Journal*. Advertising revenues grew commensurately, reaching over $5.9 million in 1941.

Throughout her tenure Lane also ran articles that focused on various social and political issues. A year after she became editor in chief the *Companion* established a Better Babies Bureau to promote improved maternal and infant health care. During Lane's early years, the *Companion* also fought against child labor and unsanitary grocery stores. Later campaigns included a multiyear series in the 1920s to educate women about using the vote, articles arguing for international peace, and support for the Sheppard-Towner bill funding health care for infants and mothers. Informational pieces appeared on topics such as psychology, careers, college education, and politics. Presidents Taft, Wilson, Coolidge, and Hoover all had pieces published in the *Companion*. A page by Eleanor Roosevelt appeared regularly there in the 1930s.

Lane also selected and edited fiction skillfully, and the successful Crowell Publishing Company provided her with the money to pay large author fees. Lane published authors such as Kathleen Norris, Edna Ferber, Sinclair Lewis, Willa Cather, Booth Tarkington, Pearl Buck, and Sherwood Anderson. In the 1930s she paid handsomely for the previously unpublished letters of Robert and Elizabeth Barrett Browning.

Throughout Lane's editorship the *Companion* maintained strong service departments. Lane believed that women wanted a magazine that offered practical, time-saving advice; her image of a housewife was ". . . the woman who wants to do less housework so that she will have more time for other things" (*New York Telegram*, 9 June 1929, p. 9).

During World War I Lane served under Herbert Hoover in the U.S. Food Administration (1917–1918), while continuing to edit the *Companion*. At the Food Administration Lane orchestrated the dissemination of information about food, energy, and clothing conservation to women through magazines and newspapers. She admired Hoover and offered him support and advice throughout the twenties and thirties. Lane served as a member of the 1930–1931 White House Conference on Child Health and Protection under Hoover and was also involved in the 1931 White House Conference on Home Building and Home Ownership.

So successful was Lane as an editor and manager that Crowell chairman of the board Joseph Palmer Knapp called her "the best man in the business." The Crowell Company recognized Lane's editorial and business abilities by first putting her on the board of directors and then, in 1929, making her a vice president of the company.

Lane served as managing director of Crowell's *American* magazine for a time in 1933, in addition to her work on the *Companion*. In 1935 Lane unveiled an innovative plan to gain reader support and feedback for the *Companion*: the reader-editor panel. Composed of 1,500 unpaid readers nationwide, these reader-editors formed one of the first consumer opinion panels. They provided the *Companion* with invaluable information about their buying preferences and habits, as well as their housework needs, by filling out questionnaires on their consumption and reading behavior.

By 1939, Lane was earning $52,000, an amount described by the *New York Times* as one of the highest earned incomes of any woman. As an editor Lane was practical and shrewd yet possessed a vision and passion for her magazine and its readers. In her autobiographical *A Peculiar Treasure* (1939), writer Edna Ferber characterized Lane as "a grand combination of Maine saltines and Latin temperament."

Lane owned a country home in Harwinton, Connecticut, where she entertained and pursued her interest in antiques. She never married and never bore any children but in 1914 adopted a French war orphan who continued to live in France. Lane died in her home in New York City.

• Papers dealing with Lane's career on the *Companion* can be found in the Crowell-Collier Company collection at the New York Public Library; a collection of letters from authors to Lane is at the Lane Library of Congress. Lane's personal papers are held by Mrs. Edward E. Lane, of Wayne, Pa., who is the wife of one of Lane's nephews. Other sources include Frank Mott, *A History of American Magazines*, vol. 4 (1957), pp. 768–70, and Mary Ellen Zuckerman, "Pathway to Success: Gertrude Battles Lane and the *Woman's Home Companion*," *Journalism History* 16 (Spring 1990): 78–87. An obituary is in the *New York Times*, 26 Sept. 1941.

MARY ELLEN ZUCKERMAN

LANE, Harriet Rebecca. *See* Johnston, Harriet Lane.

LANE, Henry Smith (24 Feb. 1811–18 June 1881), representative and senator from Indiana, was born in Montgomery County, Kentucky, the son of James Harding Lane, a farmer, militia colonel, and noted Indian fighter, and Mary Higgins. Lane attended local schools before reading law. In 1832 he was admitted to the bar and married Pamelia Bledsoe Jameson; she died in 1842, and he married Joanna Elston in 1845. He had no children. In 1834 Lane moved to Crawfordsville, Indiana. He served in the Indiana House of Representatives (1838–1839), was elected in 1840 to fill a vacancy in the U.S. House of Representatives, and was reelected later that year, serving from 1840 to 1843. A moderate Whig, an admirer of Henry Clay, and a Clay presidential elector in 1844, Lane disagreed with President John Tyler's bank policy, and he favored colonization of freed blacks in Africa.

Lane endorsed the Mexican War, believing that Mexican Catholicism encouraged ignorance and intolerance, and he commanded the First Indiana Regiment as a lieutenant colonel. Defeated for Congress in 1848, Lane refused several subsequent nominations, partly for health reasons. In 1854 he quit his prominent law practice with Congressman James Wilson and became a banker with his father-in-law, Isaac C. Elston.

Although not an officeholder during the 1850s, Lane's forceful stump speaking and moderate views had made him a major Whig leader in Indiana, and he powerfully affected the creation and success of the Republican party. Although he favored liquor prohibition and a citizenship requirement for voting, Lane was primarily concerned with the interrelated national issues of slavery, economic development, and territories. Thus, he spurned the American (or Know Nothing) party, and he was a leader at the 13 July 1854 meeting that started the People's party. Lane's prominence grew in 1856 when he chaired both the state and national Republican conventions. Although his rough, emotional style did not impress certain easterners at the national convention, he articulated a clear moderate position on slavery, strongly opposing the extension of slavery into the territories, while vigorously rejecting the label of abolitionist.

In 1859 the Indiana legislature chose Lane to replace the sitting U.S. senator whose selection two years earlier the Republicans had disputed, but the U.S. Senate refused to seat him. In 1860 Lane vigorously supported Abraham Lincoln's nomination. Lane was elected governor in that same year, but by prearrangement with Lieutenant Governor Oliver P. Morton, he resigned as governor and was then elected to the U.S. Senate. Throughout his term in the Senate he remained an ardent nationalist, severely critical of war dissenters and demanding the death penalty for traitors. On issues of slavery, race, and property, Lane was one of the moderate Republicans. He supported the Crittenden Compromise in 1861, opposed for several years freeing the slaves of loyal slaveholders, and even after 1865 favored racial separation. Immediately after the war he also favored a somewhat lenient treatment of secessionists, but the pattern of southern behavior after the war moved him to endorse greater governmental activity, and in 1866 he supported all of the major congressional reconstruction measures. Thus, although he introduced few measures and seldom spoke, he occupied a pivotal position in the Senate as a member of the moderate bloc whose votes were essential for the success of Congressional Reconstruction and the Republican party.

After retiring from the Senate in 1867, Lane pursued political activities for only a few more years. A delegate to the 1868 and 1872 Republican National Conventions, he served from 1869 to 1871 as an Indian peace commissioner, and his last post was on a Mississippi River commission in 1872. He died in Crawfordsville.

• Many of Lane's personal papers are held at the Lilly Library at Indiana University and the Indiana Historical Society, with a few items at the Indiana State Library. The best study of Lane is Ronald H. Ridgley, "Henry Smith Lane: Republican Progenitor," in *Their Infinite Variety: Essays on Indiana Politicians*, Indiana Historical Collections (1981). Several dissertations are useful, including Henry A. Hawken, "The Western Oratory of Henry Smith Lane" (Indiana Univ., 1968), and Graham Andrew Barringer, "The Life and Times of Henry S. Lane" (Indiana Univ., 1927). See also James A. Woodburn, "Henry Smith Lane," *Indiana Magazine of History*, Dec. 1931, pp. 279–87, and Robert F. Wernle, *Henry Smith Lane: The Old Warhorse* (1983). Lane's Senate votes are noted in several sources, including Allan G. Bogue, *Earnest Men: Republicans of the Civil War Senate* (1981). The most useful discussion of the Indiana political context in this era is Emma Lou Thornbrough, *Indiana in the Civil War Era, 1850–1880* (1965).

PHILIP R. VANDERMEER

LANE, James Henry (22 June 1814–11 July 1866), U.S. senator, was born in Lawrenceburg, Indiana, the son of Amos Lane, a lawyer and later a congressman, and Mary Foote Howes, a teacher. Lane was tutored by his mother. He became a merchant and a lawyer in his father's practice in Lawrenceburg. In 1841 he married Mary E. Baldridge, with whom he had four children. They later divorced but remarried in 1857. Lane's political career was boosted by his service in the Mexican War. He had been elected colonel of the Third Indiana and later of the Fifth Regiment. He fought at Buena Vista and served as provost marshal of Mexico City.

In 1849 Lane was elected lieutenant governor of Indiana as a Democrat and held this post for four years. He was elected to Congress from the Fourth Indiana District with a majority of 994 votes in 1852. Lane usually adopted the views most likely to please the voters. The historian Alice Nichols labeled him "a perfect specimen of *chameleon politico*," but he was sometimes influenced by prominent politicians. He reluctantly voted for Stephen A. Douglas's Kansas-Nebraska Bill of 1854, which repealed the Missouri Compromise line and allowed proslavery advocates to contend in Kansas Territory. So unpopular was the bill in Indiana that a coalition of anti-Kansas-Nebraska parties won the 1854 election. Lane, sensing defeat, chose not to stand for reelection.

Lane migrated to territorial Kansas in April 1855, apparently intending to establish the Democratic party there with the support of Douglas. He evidently set his sights on the prospective U.S. Senate seat, but he found minuscule support in Kansas for the Democratic party. He quickly joined the emerging Kansas Free State movement, although he still aspired to maintain Douglas's approbation. Lane was supported by many emigrants from the Old Northwest in opposition to the more abolitionist views of Charles Robinson. Lane served the Free State movement by chairing the platform committee of the Big Springs convention in September 1855 and as chair of the so-called Executive Committee of Kansas Territory, which was formed to advocate statehood. In October 1855 he was elected president of a Topeka convention, which framed a constitution that excluded both slavery and free blacks.

In December the Free State town of Lawrence was threatened by proslavery armed forces, assembled as a posse. A "Committee of Safety" was organized. Robinson was chosen commander in chief, but Lane was appointed field commander, and the two united against a common enemy in defense of Lawrence. Territorial governor Wilson Shannon negotiated a peace treaty, but the crisis, according to the historian Wendell Stephenson, "presented a proper background for radical leadership," which Lane, always more fiery and impulsive than Robinson, quickly embraced. Free State partisans, ignoring the legal proslavery territorial legislature, which they labeled "bogus," elected Robinson as governor and Lane as senator in anticipation of statehood. Lane and others were dispatched to Washington to advocate immediate statehood.

When he arrived in Washington to present a memorial to Congress for admission of Kansas as a free state, Lane was rebuffed by Douglas and other Democrats. Lane responded by conducting a speaking tour in Ohio, Indiana, and Illinois on behalf of the Free State movement. Albert Richardson, a contemporary, wrote that Lane's oratory could make "men roar with laughter, or melt into tears, or clench their teeth in passion." During the tour the nation was polarized by reports of violence in "Bleeding Kansas." On 31 May 1856, in Chicago, Lane addressed ten thousand antislavery partisans, who subscribed thousands of dollars toward financing Free State immigration, settlement, and defense. He routed immigrants, arms, and ammunition along the "Lane Trail," which crossed Iowa, thus evading hostile Missourians. Back in Kansas, Lane and his "jayhawking" Free State armed parties terrorized proslavery settlements.

Lane's break with Douglas and the Democratic party was complete when he advocated "Free Territory and [John C.] Frémont," in the presidential election of 1856. In 1857 Free State adherents boycotted an election of delegates to a constitutional convention at Lecompton, and proslavery forces won a large majority. At Lane's urging, however, the Free State proponents participated in the election for territorial legislators and won. The new legislators commissioned Lane as a major general of militia and ordered a referendum on the proslavery Lecompton constitution, which was rejected.

Lane's political career was interrupted on 3 June 1858, when he fatally shot Garius Jenkins over a land dispute. A fifteen-day trial conducted by three justices of the peace found Lane, who had been wounded in the exchange of gunfire, not guilty. In 1859 Lane returned to active politics to claim a U.S. Senate seat in the prospective state through the auspices of the newly formed Kansas Republican party. Kansas's statehood, under the new Wyandotte constitution, which prohibited slavery but did not exclude blacks, was delayed until 29 January 1861. Lane and Samuel J. Pomeroy were chosen as senators.

After the firing on Fort Sumter, Lane and some Kansans visiting Washington, designated as Lane's Frontier Guards, undertook to defend the vulnerable White House. Abraham Lincoln was grateful. Admiring Lane's activism, Lincoln usually cleared patronage matters and army appointments through him rather than through Governor Robinson. Lincoln sanctioned Lane's appointment as brigadier general in the Union army and encouraged his recruitment of "Lane's Brigade." Lane's name was feared in Missouri, where his men captured booty, including slaves of rebels and sometimes of Union loyalists, long before the Emancipation Proclamation. The senator's legal right to serve as an army officer was challenged, and Lane reluctantly relinquished his "shoulder straps" but continued his recruiting activities. He was among the first to recruit black regiments. As a senator, he supported a homestead bill and the expansion of railroads, especially those crossing Kansas. His reputation as a Radical Republican was enhanced by his wartime advocacy of abolition and the enlistment of black soldiers in advance of administration policy.

Lane needed to control the Kansas election in 1864 in order to assure his reelection to the Senate by the legislature. Pomeroy and Robinson opposed Lincoln's nomination, while Lane conspicuously backed the president. Lane supported the nomination of Samuel J. Crawford, the white commander of the Second Kansas Colored Regiment, for governor. In early October 1864 Lane's spokesmen warned of an invasion of Kansas by Confederate general Sterling Price. The alarm was ridiculed by the anti-Lane faction. When Price's army was repulsed at the Missouri-Kansas border in the battle of Westport, 23 October 1864, the Lane party was certain of election. In January 1865 the legislature reelected Lane to the Senate.

Lane had grown accustomed to presidential patronage, and he was reluctant to break with the new Andrew Johnson administration after Lincoln's assassination. Like Lincoln and Johnson, he preferred the rapid return of the Confederate states, especially of Arkansas, where a protégé was waiting to take a Senate seat. When in 1866 he defied the Republican congressional majority by supporting President Johnson's veto of a civil rights bill, he was widely condemned for misrepresenting his Radical constituency. He quickly recognized his mistake, confessing, "I would give all I possess if it were undone." Lane became despondent. He was apparently physically and "mentally deranged" when he returned to Kansas in the summer of 1866. Friends accompanied him, fearing he might harm himself. On 1 July, at a farm near Leavenworth, he slipped away and shot himself in the mouth. He died near Leavenworth ten days later.

Lane was the pivotal political figure in Kansas after the Kansas-Nebraska Act focused America's sectional disputes on that territory. The proslavery attacks made on Free State settlers radicalized him and unleashed his militant disposition. His name came to strike terror into slavery advocates in Missouri and in Kansas. He was a dexterous politician who used the Democratic, Free State, and Republican parties to fulfill his senatorial ambition. After statehood, two parties existed in Kansas, Lane and anti-Lane. Lincoln admired his verve and acumen and allowed him wide latitude in political and military matters in Kansas. A contemporary editor wrote, "Kansas made Lane," but Lane, as the representative of the majority of Kansas settlers who opposed the extension of slavery, did much to make Kansas and sustain the Union.

• The Kansas State Historical Society, Topeka, has numerous clippings on Lane and early Kans. history, including the invaluable "Webb Scrap Book." Personal papers referring to Lane are scattered in various collections, including those of Lane's rival, Charles Robinson, at the Kansas State Historical Society. An early serial publication of the society contains valuable reminiscences, documents, and biographies, including William E. Connelley, "The Lane-Jenkins Claim Contest," *Kansas Historical Collections* 16 (1923–1925): 21–176, and Connelley, "The Lane Trail," *Kansas Historical Collec-*

tions 13 (1913–1914): 268–79. Wendell H. Stephenson, *The Political Career of General James H. Lane* (1930), is a scholarly biography. Albert Castel, *A Frontier State at War* (1958), is useful. John Speer, *Life of James H. Lane, "The Liberator of Kansas"* (1896), is a biased reminiscence that nevertheless contains useful information not available elsewhere. Connelley, *James Henry Lane: The "Grim Chieftain" of Kansas* (1899), is worthwhile. Alice Nichols, *Bleeding Kansas* (1954), paints a brief but colorful portrait of Lane. Albert D. Richardson, *Beyond the Mississippi* (1867), contains a contemporary description of Lane. Lane's reelection is described in Mark A. Plummer, *Frontier Governor: Samuel J. Crawford of Kansas* (1971). See also Kendall E. Bailes, *Rider on the Wind: Jim Lane and Kansas* (1962). The *New York Times*, 3 July 1866, contains an article written after he shot himself but before he died. An obituary is in the *Daily Leavenworth Times*, 12 July 1866.

MARK A. PLUMMER

LANE, James Henry (28 July 1833–21 Sept. 1907), army officer and educator, was born in Mathews Court House, Virginia, the son of Walter Gardner Lane and Mary Ann Henry Barkwell, planters. Educated at private schools and by tutors, Lane entered the Virginia Military Institute (VMI) in 1851 and was graduated three years later, second in a class of fourteen. In 1857 he was graduated from the University of Virginia with a degree in science. He returned to VMI, which accorded him the title of lieutenant and the duties of assistant professor of mathematics and assistant instructor in tactics. Thereafter he taught in several different private schools.

At the outbreak of the Civil War, Lane held the position of professor of natural philosophy and instructor of military tactics at the North Carolina Military Institute. In response to the call of North Carolina's governor for volunteers, Lane enlisted and was promptly elected major of the First North Carolina, a regiment that included much of the corps of cadets of the North Carolina Military Institute. The regiment was sent to the scene of the expected fighting in Virginia. On 10 June 1861 a Union force of about 2,500 men advancing westward from Fort Monroe, Virginia, was met at Big Bethel by Confederate forces, including Lane's regiment. Lane led the scouting patrol that first made contact with the Federals. The fight that followed would hardly have rated as a significant skirmish later in the war, but at this point it was hailed as a great Confederate victory. The First North Carolina took the nickname "the Bethel regiment." That September, when the regiment reorganized for the war, Lane was elected lieutenant colonel. Later that month, when D. H. Hill was promoted to brigadier general, Lane moved up to colonel of the Twenty-eighth North Carolina.

That spring Lane led his regiment in the Confederate defeat at Hanover Court House (27 May 1862) as well as at the battles of Frayser's Farm and Malvern Hill (30 June and 1 July 1862) in the Seven Days' fighting. In both of the latter engagements he was lightly wounded but retained command of the regiment. Lane's regiment was part of Thomas "Stonewall" Jackson's force that made the long flanking march to gain the rear of General John Pope's Union army in the Second Bull Run (Second Manassas) campaign and clashed with northern forces at Cedar Mountain (9 Aug. 1862). After fighting at that battle and participating in the capture of Harpers Ferry and the subsequent battles of Second Bull Run (28–30 Aug.) and Antietam (17 Sept.), Lane's regiment formed the rear guard of the retreating Confederate army. His brigade commander, Lawrence O'Bryan Branch, had been killed at Antietam, and the brigade petitioned to have Lane named to command in his stead. Robert E. Lee, Jackson, and division commander A. P. Hill had already recommended him for such a promotion. Accordingly, he was promoted to brigadier general on 1 November 1862. His new brigade congratulated him by presenting him with a sword, a sash, a saddle, and a bridle. He subsequently led his brigade at the battles of Fredericksburg (13 Dec. 1862) and Chancellorsville (1–5 May 1863).

At the battle of Gettysburg the following summer, Lane's brigade was lightly engaged on the first day of fighting (1 July 1863). His division commander, General William Dorsey Pender, was mortally wounded on the next day, and Lane succeeded to command of the division. In this capacity he interpreted discretionary orders such that he held the division out of the second day's assault. The divisions on its left followed that example. The next day, Lee selected Lane's division to support the desperate assault by General George Pickett's division against the center of the Union line. Believing Lane insufficiently experienced for such duty, Lee gave command of the division to General Isaac Trimble, while Lane led his old brigade. In the assault, Trimble was wounded, and Lane again succeeded to command. In this action the division lost nearly half its personnel, killed or wounded. Once again the duty of guarding the army's retreat fell partially to Lane's men.

The following year Lane took part in the Overland Campaign. In the battle of the Wilderness (4–5 May 1864) he led his brigade in desperate fighting. The armies clashed again at Spotsylvania Court House (8–21 May 1864). At the battle of Jericho Mills, the first engagement of a larger struggle known as the battle of the North Anna, the division of which Lane was a part played a key role in attacking a Federal bridgehead across the North Anna River. After a brief initial success, Lane's and the other brigades were forced back. The next major engagement of the campaign came near the little Virginia crossroads of Cold Harbor. The armies arrived in the vicinity on 1 June and spent that day and the next jockeying for position. On 2 June Lane's and another brigade were assigned to capture Turkey Hill, a key terrain feature near the Chickahominy River. They succeeded, setting the stage for the Confederates' lopsided slaughter of Grant's troops the next day, but in the contest for the hill, Lane was severely wounded. He returned to duty during the siege of Richmond and was present with Lee's army at its surrender at Appomattox. Although Lee seems to have regarded Lane as an adequate brigade commander, he apparently considered him an officer of limited caliber, lacking the capacity to hold higher command.

After the war, Lane returned to civilian life and very hard times. His family's Virginia plantation was in ruins, and his parents were impoverished. He was forced to borrow $150. Returning to teaching, he served the next seven years at various private schools in North Carolina and Virginia. In 1869 he married Charlotte Randolph Meade; they had four children. In 1872 he obtained a position as professor of natural philosophy and commandant of the Virginia Polytechnic Institute. After a year as professor of mathematics at the Missouri School of Mines, in 1882 he became professor of civil engineering at the Alabama Polytechnic Institute in Auburn, Alabama. He was granted emeritus status there in 1907, and there he died.

• For further information on Lane see William C. Davis, ed., *The Confederate General* (8 vols., National Historical Society, 1991); Shelby Foote, *The Civil War: A Narrative* (3 vols., 1958–1974); Douglas Southall Freeman, *Lee's Lieutenants: A Study in Command* (3 vols., 1944); U.S. War Department, *The War of the Rebellion: A Compilation of the Official Records of the Union and Confederate Armies* (128 vols., 1880–1901); and Ezra J. Warner, *Generals in Gray: The Lives of the Confederate Commanders* (1964).

STEVEN E. WOODWORTH

LANE, John (8 Apr. 1789–10 Oct. 1855), Methodist clergyman and a principal founder of Vicksburg, Mississippi, was born in Fairfax County, Virginia, the son of William Lane and Nancy (maiden name unknown), farmers. His father was a revolutionary war soldier who in 1791 moved his family to Elbert County, Georgia. John was the youngest of ten children. His mother died in 1804 but not before she had made a strong impression on him to live a sober and responsible life. Placed in the home of an elder brother until he gained maturity, he subsequently taught school to earn money to attend Franklin College (later the University of Georgia). In this period he resided with the Reverend Hope Hull, a Methodist preacher who influenced Lane toward the ministry and introduced him to the South Carolina Methodist Conference, 12 January 1814.

Lane's first appointment was the Bush River Circuit, and in 1815 he filled the Louisville circuit and was ordained deacon by Bishop William McKendree. That year he and Ashley Hewitt volunteered to go to the Mississippi-Louisiana frontier as missionaries. In 1816 he traveled the Natchez and Claiborne circuit and in 1817–1818 the Wilkinson circuit, and he was ordained elder in 1818. In 1819–1820 he returned to the Natchez circuit, and in 1821 he was appointed presiding elder of the Mississippi District of the Methodist Episcopal Church. On 27 October 1819 he married Sarah Vick, the daughter of the Reverend Newet Vick; they had six children.

Lane relinquished the itinerant ministry in 1821 shortly after marrying Sarah. Due to the death of Sarah's parents, Lane became responsible for the Vick estate and children, a responsibility he fulfilled over

the next ten years while limiting his ministerial services to local needs. His father-in-law, a Methodist preacher in whose home in 1813 the first Methodist Conference in Mississippi was held, had an eye for future development and purchased land on which much of Vicksburg now stands. Lane laid off sections of this land, sold lots, located businesses, and helped to establish a bank. Although Methodists had first met in a blacksmith's shop in this location, Lane donated a lot on which the First Methodist Church in Vicksburg was built. He was a prominent businessman, director of the Railroad Bank, and for many years served as probate judge of Warren County, in which role he was known as a "father of the fatherless and friend of the widow." In spite of litigation, he persisted in his task and successfully handled the responsibilities of a large family. With Newt Vick's sons and a brother-in-law, Charles K. Marshall, John Lane was the center of Methodism in the Hill City.

In 1832 Lane returned to preaching and became an outstanding figure in Mississippi Methodism. As presiding elder he served the Yazoo district (1833–1836 and 1849–1852), the Vicksburg district (1837 and 1839–1842), the Jackson district (1843), the Lake Washington district (1853–1854), the Warren Colored Mission (1838), the Warren circuit (1844–1845 and 1855), and as agent for Centenary College (1846–1847). Elected a delegate to the General Conference in 1820, he opposed a move to have presiding elders elected by the preachers rather than appointed by the bishops. When the Methodist Episcopal church divided into northern and southern denominations in 1844, Lane was a member of the delegation that organized the Methodist Episcopal Church, South. He was also president of the conference's Missionary Society, which advocated religious services among slaves in Mississippi. In 1839 he was a leader in the founding of Centenary College (named for the 100th anniversary of the birth of Methodism) and served for several years as chairman of the board of trustees. Initially located in Clinton, Mississippi, it was removed to Brandon Springs in 1840 but relocated in Jackson, Louisiana, in 1846. In 1908, the college was removed to Shreveport, Louisiana, but the name Centenary College was retained.

At a time when the Mississippi-Louisiana region had yet to be organized and developed, Lane made a foundational contribution to Methodism, Vicksburg, and the state of Mississippi. He was a modest man but known for his zeal in preaching, self-sacrifice as a pastor, and generosity as a churchman. He was credited with having performed more marriage ceremonies in the southwest than any other clergyman and with preaching more than 1,000 funeral sermons. He established his home as a place of hospitality for traveling preachers. Punctuality and integrity characterized his dealings in both church and business. In the wake of the Panic of 1837–1838, Lane paid over $100,000 to meet liabilities he incurred by signing as security for other persons's debts, but he still managed to leave an estate for his family. In 1855 a yellow fever epidemic struck Vicksburg, and Lane died after being exposed to the disease while caring for stricken family members.

• There is no single collection of John Lane papers, but the best resource for material on him is the J. B. Cain Archives of Mississippi Methodism at Millsaps College, Jackson, Miss. Helpful biographical data is in John B. Cain, *Methodism in the Mississippi Conference 1846–1870* (1987), pp. 40, 138–40; *Condensed Minutes of the Mississippi Conference 1855*, pp. 604–5; John G. Jones, *A Complete History of Methodism* (2 vols., 1908); Edward Mayers, *History of Education in Mississippi* (1899), pp. 106–17; Dunbar Rowland, *Mississippi* (4 vols. 1976); William B. Sprague, ed., *Annals of the American Methodist Pulpit*, vol. 7 (1861), pp. 556–61; Thomas O. Summers, *Biographical Sketches of Eminent Itinerant Ministers* (1858), pp. 228–51; *New Orleans Christian Advocate*, 8 July 1854, 24 Nov. 1855, and 25 Jan. 1860; and *The Clarion-Ledger Jackson Daily News*, "Centenary College Founded In State," 25 Aug. 1968.

FREDERICK V. MILLS, SR.

LANE, Jonathan Homer (9 Aug. 1819–3 May 1880), physicist and mathematician, was born in Genesee, New York, the son of Mark Lane and Henrietta Tenny, farmers. After the age of eight, the boy was taught chiefly at home. He was well enough educated to teach in district schools for a year, and in 1839 he entered Phillips Academy in Exeter, New Hampshire, to prepare for college. There he developed an interest in determining absolute zero, the hypothetical lowest limit of temperature.

Lane entered Yale College as a sophomore and graduated in 1846. He became noted for helping fellow students in mathematics and natural science. He taught at a seminary in Vermont for a year, and in 1847 he began work in Washington, D.C., for the U.S. Coast Survey. On the recommendation of Joseph Henry, first secretary and director of the Smithsonian Institution, in 1848 Lane became an assistant examiner in the Patent Office at a time of an increase in its scope and staff. He was promoted to principal examiner in 1851. His biographer Cleveland Abbe said, "As an examiner Mr. Lane was laborious and thorough, cautious and critical, conscientious in the extreme. . . . It may safely be said that no patent approved and endorsed by him has ever been successfully contested." Lane published four articles on mathematical aspects of electricity from 1846 to 1851.

In 1857 a change in administration led to political patronage in the Interior Department, so Lane's superior resigned in protest, and Lane was let go. Sources differ on how he supported himself after that, but he was said to be very frugal. Lane may have served as a consultant in patent cases in Washington. He had a close association with Henry, who often sought his advice on questions in physics and mathematics. In 1859 Lane carried out some studies for Henry concerning the Atlantic telegraph cable. He also tried to develop equipment for determining extremely low temperatures by means of the successive compression and expansion of gases.

In 1860 or 1861 Lane moved to Venango County, Pennsylvania, perhaps to look into opportunities in the new industry of petroleum, but mostly because a brother was a blacksmith there. Lane wanted his help in building the scientific equipment for measuring low temperatures, but that did not happen. He returned to Washington, D.C., in 1866 and was provided with some support by Henry in his pursuit of determining absolute zero.

In 1869 the superintendent of the U.S. Coast Survey, Julius E. Hilgard, who knew Lane, employed him as a "verifier of standards" in the Office of Weights and Measures, predecessor of the National Bureau of Standards. His duties chiefly involved establishing standards for metric units, which are particularly affected by changes in temperature. Lane would continue in this post until his death. While working there he perfected equipment for suppressing the undulations in the mercury artificial horizon, a precision measuring technique for determining horizontal surfaces and the vertical in gravity.

Pursuing other scientific studies, Lane observed a total solar eclipse at Des Moines, Iowa, on 7 August 1869 and reported on it to the U.S. Coast Survey and Naval Observatory. That same year he read a paper to the National Academy of Sciences, which was published in 1870 as "On the Theoretical Temperature of the Sun, under the Hypothesis of a Gaseous Mass Maintaining Its Volume by Its Internal Heat and Depending on the Laws of Gases as Known to Terrestrial Experiments" (*American Journal of Science* 2 [1870]: 57–74). Although he did not provide proof in his paper of the nature of the contraction of a gaseous body, he was credited by Simon Newcomb as having given such proof to him in person. Lane's work offered careful computation of the sun's mass and heat relationships and is considered "a real contribution to the developing evidence of stellar evolution," according to Nathan Reingold.

Lane continued research on determining absolute zero and may have reached significant conclusions by 1870, but he did not publish them. Colleagues noted that he was reluctant to publish until he was certain of all points. Many of his intended projects were not completed, but notes in his personal papers in the U.S. National Archives describe his efforts on ingenious machines for such ideas as determining the quantitative relationship between static and voltaic electricity, a "visual telegraph for transmitting to any visible distance," an electric governor "for very exact, uniform motion, controlled by electro-magnetic break-circuit," and other devices. He did not obtain any patents.

Colleagues noted in memorial tributes that Lane had "little faculty of speech," that it was hesitant and slow, but that his writing was lucid and precise. He was said to be always helpful to colleagues, especially in reviewing mathematical material for them. He was described as of "a most retiring disposition," and he never married. In the late 1850s Lane and Henry were original members of a scientific and social club that in

1871 became the Philosophical Society of Washington. Lane was elected to the National Academy of Sciences in 1872. He died in Washington, D.C.

• Lane's personal papers are in the records of the National Bureau of Standards in the U.S. National Archives in Washington, D.C. His work on the mercury artificial horizon was published in the annual report of the U.S. Coast Survey for 1871, pp. 181–92. A posthumous paper by Lane is "On the Coefficient of Expansion of the British Standard Yard . . . ," *Report of Coast and Geodetic Survey* (1877): 148, 155–66. Biographies are J. E. Hilgard, *Bulletin of the Philosophical Society of Washington* 3 (1880): 122–24; and Cleveland Abbe, National Academy of Sciences, *Biographical Memoirs* 3 (1895): 253–64, with bibliography. A significant account is by historian Nathan Reingold, *Dictionary of Scientific Biography* 8 (1973): 1–3, who reviews Lane's archival material and notes uncertainties and probable errors in some of Abbe's statements.

ELIZABETH NOBLE SHOR

LANE, Joseph (14 Dec. 1801–19 Apr. 1881), soldier and political leader, was born near Asheville, North Carolina, the son of John Lane and Elizabeth Street, farmers. When Lane was three, his family moved to Henderson County, Kentucky. After a rudimentary education, he left home at fourteen and settled in Darlington, Indiana, where he clerked and learned the basics of law in the offices of Warrick County. In 1820 he married Mary Polly Hart and bought land on the Ohio River in Vanderburgh County, where their ten children were born and raised. At age twenty Lane was elected to the state legislature, where, as an admirer and supporter of Andrew Jackson, he served intermittently for the next twenty-five years. Adding military laurels to his political role, he volunteered for service during the Mexican War and was promoted from colonel to brigadier general in command of his Indiana regiment. Placed with Winfield Scott's invading army, he fought against Santa Anna at Huamantla (Oct. 1847). After several key victories, he emerged from the war a hero, and on Lane's triumphal return home, President James K. Polk rewarded him with the governorship of the newly organized Oregon Territory.

Lane traveled overland to his new post, arriving in Oregon City in March 1849. He served only until January 1850, when Whig president Zachary Taylor could name a successor, but during his brief tenure he had a positive impact on the people of Oregon and became a major force to be reckoned with in territorial politics. He was especially popular for his unceremonious handling of Indian affairs. Several Native Americans were tried and hanged, including those found guilty of the murder of Marcus Whitman and his family. Seeking to remove the Indian presence from the areas of white settlement, Lane, in February and again in June and July 1850, successfully negotiated with tribal leaders in the Rogue River area. Despite, or perhaps because of, his brutal directness, Lane gained a measure of respect from Indian leaders, who frequently sought him out in subsequent negotiations.

In 1851 Lane won the first of four two-year terms as Oregon's territorial delegate to Congress, each time proving his political popularity by receiving more than 60 percent of the vote. As a delegate, he served his constituents well, securing money for roads, mail service, and defense against Indians. In 1853 he helped persuade Congress to pass a bill creating the new Washington Territory, thus easing the way for eventual statehood for Oregon. Dispensing territorial patronage in a partisan manner, he rewarded his Democratic friends and denied those at odds with him. Lane became a vital part of the Oregon Democratic machine called the Clique. He was at first closely aligned with editor Asahel Bush, and the two men dominated Oregon politics through the mid-1850s.

National politics finally divided Oregon Democrats and the Clique itself, with Lane at the center of the controversy. Currying southern favor in Congress and at the same time convinced of the slaveholder's right to bring slaves into any territory, the pugnacious Lane showed his hand most dramatically by offering to be Preston Brooks's second when the latter challenged two northern congressmen to duels in 1856. This followed Brooks's vicious caning of the outspoken antislavery senator Charles Sumner of Massachusetts. Lane headed that faction of his party most closely identified with President James Buchanan and his position favoring legalization of slavery in Kansas Territory. Bush in turn aligned his wing of the party with Stephen A. Douglas and his insistence that Kansans be afforded the right to decide, through the process known as popular sovereignty, whether slavery would be permitted in the territory. Lane's outspoken defense of the Buchanan-endorsed, proslavery Lecompton constitution led to the division of the Oregon Democratic party, and the Bush faction allied with the newly formed Republican party of Oregon in support of Douglas and popular sovereignty. When the House of Representatives delayed an Oregon statehood bill in 1858, it was widely believed to be in punishment of Lane and his proslavery allies. Oregon finally achieved statehood in February 1859. Even before Congress acted, Oregon had organized a state government, and Lane again revealed his political influence when the legislature elected him to the U.S. Senate.

As Lane moved ever closer to southern Democrats and their defense of territorial slavery, he alienated an increasing number of Oregon voters, who might approve of his stance on behalf of their interests but could not endorse his support of slavery. Although rarely supportive of abolitionism, Oregonians nevertheless opposed having either slaves or free blacks in their midst. Nonetheless, Lane was chosen by Oregon Democrats to be a delegate to the national nominating convention in Charleston, South Carolina, in April 1860. Although he remained in Washington, he received some votes for the presidential nomination and approved of the southern delegates' decision to leave the convention when it endorsed Douglas's position on popular sovereignty. The convention later reconvened in Baltimore and nominated Douglas, while southern Democrats and their allies met separately in Richmond and nominated John Breckenridge of Kentucky. The Richmond delegates then chose Lane for vice president by acclamation.

The Oregon senator willingly accepted his role on the Breckenridge ticket and campaigned in both the North, which received him with coolness, and the South, which embraced him as one of their own. Horace Greeley spoke for many northern Republicans in accusing Lane of "unbounded servility to the extreme proslavery faction" (*New York Tribune*, 26 June 1860). With Abraham Lincoln the winner, the Breckenridge-Lane ticket placed second in Oregon behind Lincoln and ahead of the Douglas Democrats. Lane, denied reelection to the Senate by the Republican–Bush Democrat coalition, returned to Washington to complete his term in the explosive session before Lincoln's inauguration. Upon the secession of the Lower South, Lane rejected compromise and defended separation, predicting: "When war is made upon that gallant South for withdrawing from a Union which refuses them their rights, the Northern democracy will not join the crusade. The Republican party will have war enough at home" (*Congressional Globe*, 36th Cong., 2d sess., pp. 143–45).

Lane returned to Oregon under a cloud of disapproval, arriving in April 1861 on the same ship that brought news of the opening of the war at Fort Sumter. Rumored to support the formation of a separate Northwest or Pacific republic, Lane professed instead his steadfast loyalty to the Union, but a Union that should not coerce the South to renounce secession. His son John Lane's decision to leave West Point and accept a commission in the Confederate army seemed a reaffirmation of his father's beliefs.

Retired from Oregon politics, Lane lived for twenty years on his farm in the Umpqua Valley near Roseburg, where he died. He is remembered in Oregon and elsewhere for his fierce independence, his vanity, self-confidence, and desire for personal political power, his bitter political partisanship, and his successful advocacy of his constituents' interests. Most of all, Americans recalled his outspoken and controversial defense of southern slaveholders and their peculiar institution.

• Lane's papers are divided between the Oregon Historical Society in Portland and the Lilly Library at Indiana University. His unpublished autobiography, which he related to Hubert Howe Bancroft in 1878, is disappointingly lacking in information, emphasizing his role in the Mexican War and in American Indian relations. Lane's speeches in Congress are in the *Congressional Globe*, 31st–36th Congs., 1851–1861. Biographies include Sister M. Margaret Jean Kelly, *The Career of Joseph Lane, Frontier Politician* (1942), which is a highly favorable interpretation, and James E. Hendrickson, *Joe Lane of Oregon: Machine Politics and the Sectional Crisis, 1849–1861* (1967), which is both scholarly and balanced. Walter C. Woodward, *The Rise and Early History of Political Parties in Oregon, 1843–1868* (1913), is important in its coverage of local issues and Lane's political maneuvering. Robert W. Johannsen, *Frontier Politics and the Sectional Conflict: The Pacific Northwest on the Eve of the Civil War* (1955), develops Lane's role in both Oreg. and Wash. politics. Bancroft, *History of Oregon*, vol. 2 (1888), presents a somewhat negative view of both Lane and his political tactics but does recognize his achievements. Scholarly articles dealing with specific aspects of Lane's career include Henry L. Simms, "The Controversy over the Admission of the State of Oregon," *Mississippi Valley Historical Review* 32 (1945): 255–74; and Eldorah M. Raleigh, "General Joseph E. Lane" *Indiana Historical Bulletin* 4 (Dec. 1926, supp.): 71–82. Obituaries are in the *Daily Oregonian*, 21 and 23 Apr. 1881.

FREDERICK J. BLUE

LANE, Sir Ralph (c. 1528–Oct. 1603), soldier and colonial governor, was the son of Sir Ralph Lane of Orlingbury, Northamptonshire, England, and Maud Parr, daughter of William, Lord Parr of Horton. Lane's place of birth is unknown. Lane was educated at the Middle Temple in 1554 and was elected to Parliament in 1558 and 1563. He went to court in 1563 and, as a client of the earl of Leicester, was an equerry to Queen Elizabeth by 1568. He served in the force sent to quell the northern rebels in 1569.

Lane was the archetypal Elizabethan "projector." During the 1570s and early 1580s he presented to Leicester and Lord Burghley many plans for projects in which he planned to take a leading role, and his success shows the high regard in which he was held. He received a license to search certain Breton ships and seize smuggled goods from them and a commission to suppress piracy in 1571. He served as a captain in the Netherlands in 1572–1573.

In 1574 Lane asked for permission to raise a regiment of 1,000 to 2,000 men to join the army being formed by Philip II of Spain against the Turks. The earl of Leicester urged caution in dealing with Spain, and his secretary, Atye, warned Lane of rumors circulating that the regiment was actually intended for use against the Prince of Orange. Despite the queen's assent, the project did not go forward. In 1579 he presented the first of a series of plans to "encounter" the Spanish in Ireland and (in 1581) in the Low Countries. Also in 1579 he asked, as an alternative, for the queen's letters to "the Kings of Fez and Algiers." Later, possibly in 1584, he claimed to have "prepared seven ships at his own charges, and proposes to do some exploit on the coast of Spain," and asked for a royal commission with the title "General of the Adventurers" (C.S.P. Domestic, 8-16-1579, 12-25-1584?).

However, in 1583 Lane claimed penury and was sent to Ireland with a commission to oversee the construction of fortifications. He asked for and received command of the garrison at Kerry and Clanmorris. His petition asked for support by thirty horse and forty foot and the "houses and demesnes of the Island and Tralee in Kerry," pointing out that he had chosen at the end of twenty years' service "about Her Majesty's person to employ himself in Her desolate Kingdom of Ireland" (C.S.P. Ireland, 1-8-1583, 2-20-1584, 3-12-1584, 4-4-1584). His superiors thought he overvalued his service. Sir Henry Wallop wrote to Lord Burghley: "It seemeth, by some letters that I have seen, that Mr.

Lane expecteth to have the best and greatest things in Kerry, and to have the letting and setting of all the rest. . . . Kerry I account too great a thing for any one man to deal withal, and think Mr. Lane shall do but little good therewith, unless he were of better ability than I conceive him to be" (C.S.P. Ireland 5-21-1585).

By the time Wallop wrote, the queen had already recalled Lane to be governor of Sir Walter Raleigh's colony on Roanoke Island within the North Carolina Outer Banks. The fleet, under the command of Sir Richard Grenville, sailed on 9 April 1585. The flagship, *Tiger*, carrying most of the colony's food supplies for the coming winter, ran aground on approaching the banks; thus the 107 colonists under Lane's command faced the winter dependent on the coastal Carolina Algonquians for sustenance.

Lane had two tasks: to find a better location for the settlement than the treacherous Outer Banks and to find a commodity of sufficient economic power to justify the expense of colonization. He sent a party to explore overland to Chesapeake Bay; the group wintered with the Chesapeake Indians and provided the information on which the later location of Jamestown was selected. Lane himself led an expedition up the Chowan River in search of wealthy tribes of which he had been told. His account of events in Roanoke, published by Richard Hakluyt in his *Principall Navigations* in 1589, reveals Lane's leadership style. He sought the consent of his men for continuing upriver as their food was running out, but he approached the Indians through intimidation, always seizing a high-ranking hostage as his preferred first act. Lane's exploration party was defeated by Indian withdrawal and, with no source of food, quickly returned to Roanoke without results.

Back in the colony in early April 1586 Lane, who had expected to be resupplied from England by then, worried about native resistance to the colonists' continuing need for food. Fearing a conspiracy, he lodged a preemptive strike against the Roanokes in which their chief Wingina was killed. Soon after, when Sir Francis Drake arrived with his privateering fleet, Lane at first accepted the offer of a ship and men. But, when a great storm scattered Drake's ships, Lane decided to take Drake's second offer and bring the colony home to England. He judged the land unpromising: "the discovery of a good mine by the goodnesse of God, or a passage to the Southsea, or someway to it, and nothing els can bring this country in request to be inhabited by our nation" (Quinn, vol. 1, p. 273). Raleigh and his associates sent another colony to Roanoke in 1587, but Lane's association with America was over, although he continued to invest in ventures with Raleigh.

Back in England Lane developed a plan for the coastal defenses and was made captain of Southsea Castle, Portsmouth, and muster master at West Tilbury in 1588. He was muster master over the troops sent to the coasts of Spain and Portugal in 1589. In 1592 he was back in Ireland, where he became muster master general, responsible for certifying the readiness

of all the forces, and clerk of the check of the garrisons. He wrote a book of instructions for musters to be used in Ireland. He was knighted in 1593 but severely wounded in 1594. From that point forward Lane seems to have been unable to perform his duties adequately. In 1596 the Privy Council wrote of him as having been "longe sicke and his recovery doubtfull" and complained repeatedly of his failure to return accurate certificates about the state of the forces, inaccuracies that the council suspected were designed to encourage overpayments. Finally, in 1601 the council wrote frankly about "negligent and corrupt dealing" (A.P.C. 26 [1596–1597]: 176–77; 28 [1597–1598]: 216, 271–72; 32 [1601–1604]: 155). When Lane was forbidden to come to the council table he wrote Burghley of his grief, pointing out that he had "grown gray in Her Majestie's service only" (C.S.P. Ireland, 6-18-1597).

Lane sent many letters asking for sinecures to add to his income, complaining of the "barrenness of his entertainment." He wrote Burghley asking for appointment as chief bell-ringer of Ireland, for which he would pay annually a red rose. At the same time, he wrote directly to the queen asking for the surveyorship of parish clerks of Ireland: "a base place with something, which is better than greater employment with nothing" (C.S.P. Ireland 9-24-1594, 2-16-1595). Complaining against "my perpetual (though undeserved) disgrace," he asked for other employment in England or elsewhere, but it never came. Lane died and was buried in Dublin.

• Sir Ralph Lane's writings on Roanoke, including his "Account of the Particularities of the Employments of the English Men Left in Virginia"; his letters to the two Richard Hakluyts, Sir Francis Walsingham, and Sir Philip Sidney; and his preface to Thomas Hariot's *Briefe and True Report of the New Found Land of Virginia* (1588), are printed in David Beers Quinn, ed., *The Roanoke Voyages, 1584–1590* (2 vols., 1955). Discussion of his participation in the suppression of the northern rebellion and his project for the war against the Turks appears in John Strype, *Annals of the Reformation and Establishment of Religion*, vol. 2, pt. 1 (1824), pp. 455, 517–20, and pt. 2, Appendix of Original Papers, pp. 553–54. Letters and reports by and about Lane are calendared in the *Calendar of State Papers: Domestic* and *Ireland*, and in Historical Manuscripts Commission, *Report* on the Salisbury Manuscripts at Hatfield House, vol. 7 (1899), pp. 310–12, and vol. 13 (1915), p. 468. The Privy Council's discussions of his performance occur in vols. 15, 16, 18, 21, 26, 27, 28, 30, and 32 of *The Acts of the Privy Council of England*.

The most current data on Lane appear in P. W. Hasler, ed., *The History of Parliament: The House of Commons, 1558–1603* (1981). Edward E. Hale published a sketch of Lane's life in *Archaeologia Americana: Transactions and Collections of the American Antiquarian Society* 4 (1860): 317–44. David Beers Quinn, *Set Fair for Roanoke: Voyages and Colonies, 1584–1606* (1985), and Karen Ordahl Kupperman, *Roanoke: The Abandoned Colony* (1984), describe his American career and its background.

KAREN ORDAHL KUPPERMAN

LANE, William Henry (1825?–1852), African-American dancer, also known as "Master Juba," is believed to have been born a free man, although neither his place of birth nor the names of his parents are known. He grew up in lower Manhattan in New York City, where he learned to dance from "Uncle" Jim Lowe, an African-American jig-and-reel dancer of exceptional skill.

By the age of fifteen, Lane was performing in notorious "dance houses" and dance establishments in the Five-Points district of lower Manhattan. Located at the intersection of Cross, Anthony, Little Water, Orange, and Mulberry streets, its thoroughfare was lined with brothels and saloons occupied largely by free blacks and indigent Irish immigrants. Lane lived and worked in the Five-Points district in the early 1840s. In such surroundings, the blending of African-American vernacular dance with the Irish jig was inevitable. Marshall Stearns in *Jazz Dance* (1968) confirms that "Lane was a dancer of 'jigs' at a time when the word was adding to its original meaning, an Irish folk dance, and being used to describe the general style of Negro dancing." Charles Dickens, in his *American Notes* (1842), describes a visit to the Five-Points district in which he witnessed a performance by a dancer who was probably Lane: "Single shuffle, double shuffle, cut and cross cut; snapping his fingers, rolling his eyes, turning in his knees, presenting the backs of his legs in front, spinning about on his toes and heels like nothing but the man's fingers on the tambourine; dancing with two left legs, two right legs, two wooden legs, two wire legs, two spring legs."

In 1844, after beating the reigning white minstrel dancer, John Diamond, in a series of challenge dances, Lane was hailed as the "King of All Dancers" and named "Master Juba," after the African juba or *gioube*, a step-dance resembling a jig with elaborate variations. The name was often given to slaves who were dancers and musicians. Lane was thereafter adopted by an entire corps of white minstrel players who unreservedly acknowledged his talents. On a tour in New England with the Georgia Champion Minstrels, Lane was billed as "The Wonder of the World Juba, Acknowledged to be the Greatest Dancer in the World!" He was praised for his execution of steps, unsurpassed in grace and endurance, and popular for his skillful imitations of well-known minstrel dancers and their specialty steps. He also performed his own specialty steps, which no one could copy, and he was a first-rate singer and a tambourine virtuoso. In 1845 Lane had the unprecedented distinction of touring with the four-member, all-white Ethiopian Minstrels, with whom he received top billing. At the same time, he prospered as a solo variety performer and from 1846 to 1848 was a regular attraction at White's Melodeon in New York.

Lane traveled to London with Pell's Ethiopian Serenaders in 1848, enthralling the English, who were discerning judges of traditional jigs and clogs, with "the manner in which he beat time with his feet, and the extraordinary command he possessed over them." London's *Theatrical Times* wrote that Master Juba was "far above the common [performers] who give imitations of American and Negro character; there is an *ideality* in what he does that makes his efforts at once gro-

tesque and *poetical, without losing sight of the reality of representation.*" Working day and night and living on a poor diet and no rest, Lane died of exhaustion in London.

In England, Lane popularized American minstrel dancing, influencing English clowns who added jumps, splits, and cabrioles to their entrées and began using blackface makeup. Between 1860 and 1865, the Juba character was taken to France by touring British circuses and later became a fixture in French and Belgian *cirques et carrousels*. The image of the blackface clown that persisted in European circuses and fairs continued to be represented in turn-of-the-century popular entertainments as well as on concert stages during the 1920s, in ballets such as Léonide Massine's *Crescendo*, Bronisława Nijinska's *Jazz*, and George Balanchine's "Snowball" in *The Triumph of Neptune* (1926).

In the United States, Lane is considered by scholars of dance and historians of the minstrel as the most influential single performer in nineteenth-century American dance. He kept the minstrel show in touch with its African-American source material at a time when the stage was dominated by white performers offering theatrical derivatives and grotesque exaggerations of the African-American performer. He established a performing style and developed a technique of tap dancing that would be widely imitated. For example, the white dancer Richard M. Carroll was noted for dancing in the style of Lane and earned a reputation for being a great all-around performer; other dancers, like Ralph Keeler, who starred in a riverboat company before the Civil War, learned to dance by practicing the complicated shuffle of Juba. Toward the end of the twentieth century, Lane's legacy continued to be present in elements of the tap dance repertory. Lane's grafting of African rhythms and loose body styling onto the exacting techniques of British jig and clog dancing created a new rhythmic blend of percussive dance that was the earliest form of American tap dance.

• The most comprehensive article on Lane is Marian Hannah Winter, "Juba and American Minstrelsy," in *Chronicles of the American Dance*, ed. Paul Magriel (1948). See also Marshall Stearns and Jean Stearns, *Jazz Dance: The Story of American Vernacular Dance* (1968).

CONSTANCE VALIS HILL

LANEY, Lucy Craft (13 Apr. 1854–23 Oct. 1933), educator, was born in Macon, Georgia, the daughter of David Laney and Louisa (maiden name unknown). Both parents were slaves: they belonged to different masters, but following their marriage they were permitted to live together in a home of their own. David Laney was a carpenter and often hired out by his owner, Mr. Cobbs. Louisa, purchased from a group of nomadic Indians while a small child, was a maid in the Campbell household. One of Lucy Laney's most cherished memories was "how her father would, after a week of hard slave work, walk for over twenty miles

... to be at home with his wife and children on the Sabbath" (*Crisis*, June 1934). After the Civil War and emancipation, David Laney, who had served as a slave lay preacher, was ordained as a Presbyterian minister and became pastor of the Washington Avenue Church in Macon, Georgia. Louisa remained in the Campbell's house as a wage earner. The Laneys' newfound income provided the family some comforts that they shared with numerous cousins, orphaned children, and others in need of shelter.

When missionary teachers opened a school in Macon in 1865 Lucy Laney, together with her mother and her siblings, was among the first to enroll. She graduated from the Lewis High School in 1869 and entered Atlanta University where she received a certificate of graduation from the Higher Normal Department in 1873. In keeping with her strong conviction that "becoming educated [was] a perpetual motion affair" (*Abbott's Monthly*, June 1931), over the course of her career she enrolled in summer programs at the University of Chicago, Hampton Institute, Columbia University, and Tuskegee Institute.

Laney was keenly aware of all the advantages life had afforded her, and she believed that of those to whom much is given much is expected. Emancipation had ushered in new opportunities and responsibilities, and early in life she dedicated herself to her race's advancement. Based on her study of American history, she concluded that the four major components of a realistic program for the "uplift" of blacks were political power, Christian training, "cash," and education. She viewed education as the key to achieving the first three objectives. Her decision to become a teacher was also dictated by the limited employment opportunities available to black women. Following graduation from Atlanta University she accepted a teaching position in Milledgeville, Georgia, and between 1873 and 1883 also taught at schools in Macon, Augusta, and Savannah.

While a student Laney had serious misgivings about the pedagogical practices at the various schools she attended. She had advised her teachers then that "some day I will have a school of my own." Her experience as a teacher in the public school system intensified her desire to establish a school. She had little patience with "dull teachers . . . [who] failed to know their pupils—to find out their real needs—and hence had no cause to study methods of better and best development of the boys and girls under their care." She deplored instructors who underestimated "the capabilities and possibilities" of black students and who did not know and/or teach African-American history ("The Burden of the Educated Colored Woman," 1899). Moreover, she was convinced that black children needed a thorough Christian education and was disturbed by the public school's failure to address moral and religious concerns.

Laney was one of the first educators to recognize the special and urgent needs of black women in light of their central role in the education of their children. She was convinced that ignorance, immorality, and crime among blacks and perhaps some of the prejudice against them were their "inheritance from slavery." In her opinion, "the basic rock of true culture" was the home, but during slavery "the home was . . . utterly disregarded . . . [the] father had neither responsibility, nor authority; mother, neither cares nor duties" ("Educated Colored Woman," 1899). The disregard for homemaking and the home environment resulted in untidy and filthy homes that produced children of dubious character. Moreover, the absence of the sanctity of the marriage vow encouraged immorality and disrespect for black women.

While "no person [was] responsible for [their] ancestor's . . . sins and short-comings," Laney argued that "every woman can see to it that she give to her progeny a good mother and an honorable ancestry." Strengthening the black family and improving its home life was therefore "the place to take the proverbial stitch in time." In addition to their role as wives and mothers, she believed that women were "by nature fitted for teaching the . . . young" and thus were best suited as teachers in the public school system. She was equally convinced that the teacher "who would mould character must herself possess it" and that those who would be mothers, teachers, and leaders needed to be capable in both "mind and character" ("Address before the Women's Meeting," 1897).

Laney's conviction that educated women were a prerequisite for advancement of her race was the major impetus for the founding of the Haines Normal and Industrial Institute. She began her school with six students in the basement of Christ Presbyterian Church in Augusta, Georgia, on 6 January 1886. During the following three years the school, due to increasing enrollment, was moved to various rented buildings around the city. Haines Institute was chartered by the state of Georgia as a normal and industrial school on 5 May 1888. Although the school was sanctioned by the Presbyterian board, the general assembly provided only moral support, which Laney noted "was not much to go on." In 1889, however, the board purchased a permanent site for the school and erected the institution's first building. Despite numerous problems, by 1887 primary, grammar, and normal divisions had been established, and by 1889 she was able to develop a strong literary department as well as a scientifically based normal program and industrial course. By 1892 Haines Normal and Industrial Institute was recognized as one of the best schools of its type in the nation. John William Gibson and William H. Crogman said of Laney in their classic study, *The Progress of a Race* (1897), "There is probably no one of all the educators of the colored race who stands higher, or who has done more work in pushing forward the education of the Negro woman."

Laney was the foremost female member of the generation born into slavery and educated during Reconstruction who rose to leadership and prominence in the 1880s and 1890s. In addition to being a national race leader, she was a pioneer in the struggles for Prohibition and women's rights as well as in the black women's club movement. She was instrumental in establishing the first public high school for blacks in Georgia, organizing the Augusta Colored Hospital and Nurses Training School, and founding the first kindergarten in the city of Augusta. She was also a leader in the battle to secure improved public schools, sanitation, and other municipal services in Augusta's black community. She was a founding member of the Georgia State Teacher Association and a leader within the regional and national politics of the Young Women's Christian Association. She chaired the Colored Section of the Interracial Commission of Augusta and served on the National Interracial Commission of the Presbyterian Church. An eloquent speaker, she was a distinguished member of the lecture circuit between 1879 and 1930.

Laney, who often stated that she wanted to "wear out, not rust out," died in Augusta, Georgia, and was buried on the campus of the school that she built and to which she had devoted most of her life. The most enduring epithet for Laney, who never married or had children, was "mother of the children of the people," and her most profound contributions were the men and women she educated. Writing in the April 1907 issue of the *Home Mission Monthly* she argued that "the measure of an institution is the men and women it sends into the world. The measure of a man is the service he renders his fellows." Judging by this standard Lucy Craft Laney and the school she established were eminently successful.

• There are no known collections of Laney's papers, but a chronology of her life, including both primary and secondary annotated bibliographies and information about her school, is in the Presbyterian Historical Society in Philadelphia. Another useful source is the Lucy C. Laney File in the William E. Harman Collection, Library of Congress. In addition to her annual reports, a number of articles by and about Laney and her school are in Presbyterian church publications such as the *Home Mission Monthly*, the *Church Home and Abroad*, *Women and Mission*, the *Presbyterian Monthly Record*, and the *Presbyterian Magazine* during the years 1886–1933. For general information about Laney's life and work see A. C. Griggs, "Lucy Craft Laney," *Journal of Negro History* (Jan. 1934): 97–102; Sadie Iola Daniel, *Women Builders* (1931); Mary White Ovington, *Portraits in Color* (1927); Lucy Lilian Notestein, *Nobody Knows the Trouble I See* (n.d.); June O. Patton, "Augusta's Black Community and the Struggle for Ware High School," in *New Perspectives on Black Educational History*, ed. Vincent P. Franklin and James D. Anderson (1978); and Benjamin Brawley, *Negro Builders and Heroes* (1937). An obituary is in the *Augusta* (Ga.) *Chronicle*, 23 Oct. 1933.

JUNE O. PATTON

LANG, Benjamin Johnson (28 Dec. 1837–3 Apr. 1909), organist, pianist, and choral conductor, was born in Salem, Massachusetts, the son of Benjamin Lang, a piano teacher and church organist, and Hannah B. Learock. His first teacher was his father, and he later studied with F. G. Hill in Boston. At the age of fifteen he became organist and choir director of the Somerset St. Baptist Church in Boston, but in 1855, at the age of

eighteen, he joined the growing number of young American musicians studying in Europe. There he studied first in Paris with Alfred Jaëll and Gustav Satter and later in Weimar with Franz Liszt, of whom he said, "He was most generous in his artistic advice, which always was given gratis."

Although Lang's early ambition was a career as a concert pianist, on his return to Boston in 1858 he became organist and choir director of the South Congregational Church, a position he held for twenty years, and a year later he was appointed organist of the Handel & Haydn Society under Carl Zerrahn. In 1861 he married Frances Morse Burrage; they had a son and two daughters.

Lang continued to perform as a pianist, and since he was for many years one of the few in Boston who had mastered some of the larger works for piano and orchestra, he occasionally appeared as soloist with the Boston Orchestra under Theodore Thomas. But he also concertized as an organist. In 1863 he took part in the inauguration of the large Walcker organ in Boston Music Hall, and two years later he presided at the memorial service for President Lincoln that was held there. He began teaching as soon as he settled in Boston, gradually building an enviable reputation as an educator. Among his more notable pupils were Arthur Foote, Ethelbert Nevin, William Apthorp, and his daughter Margaret Ruthven Lang, later to achieve prominence as a composer.

It was perhaps his long association with the Handel & Haydn Society that kindled Lang's interest in choral conducting. In 1868 he organized the Apollo Club, a chorus of male voices, and in 1874 he created the Cecilia Society, a mixed-voice chorus that remains active at the end of the twentieth century. He conducted both of these groups until almost the end of his life. As a choral director, Lang boldly introduced Boston audiences to such large-scale works as Berlioz's *Damnation of Faust* and *Requiem*, Bach's *Mass in B minor*, Brahms's *Requiem*, Beethoven's *Missa Solemnis*, Dvořák's *Requiem*, and such esoterica as Mendelssohn's *Comancho's Wedding* and a concert version of Wagner's *Parsifal*.

In 1888 Lang became organist and choirmaster of King's Chapel in Boston, where he directed a mixed quartet composed of some of the best singers in Boston, and during 1898 and 1899 he initiated a series of musical services in which a larger mixed choir performed. In 1895, after many years as its organist, he assumed the direction of the Handel & Haydn Society, holding that position for two years during a period of considerable turmoil. Zerrahn, who had directed the Handel & Haydn for over forty years, was refused reappointment by the board of directors, and Lang was promoted to director in his place. Although Lang had amply proven his skill with choruses, however, it became apparent that he did not have Zerrahn's command of the orchestra. The chorus and its directors were divided into two warring factions, and in the end Zerrahn's supporters gained the upper hand. Zerrahn was reinstated in 1897, only to retire a year later.

While many of his contemporaries were prolific composers, Lang seems to have been inordinately modest about his own efforts in this area. Although he wrote many orchestral, chamber, piano, and choral works, including *David*, an oratorio, most of these remained unpublished. His choir at King's Chapel performed many of his anthems from manuscript, and he is said to have often improvised impressive organ postludes, based on the last hymn in the service.

Lang adroitly balanced his multiple careers, becoming in the process one of the most highly regarded musicians in Boston during his lifetime and associating with many of the other notable artistic figures of the period. One of these, the artist Winslow Homer, was a good friend of the Lang family and in 1895 made a fine pencil drawing of Lang at the organ, now in the Portland Museum of Art, Portland, Maine. Always concerned with the advancement of professional standards, Lang was among the group of prominent organists who in 1896 founded the American Guild of Organists.

In the year preceding his death, Lang collaborated with the up-and-coming young Boston organ-builder Ernest M. Skinner in the design of a large new organ for King's Chapel but died suddenly at his Boston home as it was being completed. The new organ was played for the first time at his funeral, and his son Malcolm succeeded him as organist of the church. Writing just a few years before Lang's death, the music critic Louis C. Elson placed Lang with orchestra conductor Theodore Thomas as a vital influence upon musical taste in Boston: "They have taught the public how to appreciate the best music, and have made it familiar with the modern masterpieces."

• The Boston Public Library houses a large collection of Lang's papers, including programs, correspondence, and manuscripts of music. Major sources of information on Lang's life and work include Louis C. Elson's *American Music* (1904; rev. ed., 1925) and an interview by H. J. Storer in *The Musician* 12 (1907): 475–76. During the period in which it was published (1852–1881) the periodical *Dwight's Journal of Music* often mentioned Lang's performances, particularly as a choral director. His long association with the Handel & Haydn Society is chronicled in H. Earle Johnson's history of that organization, *Hallelujah, Amen!* (1965).

BARBARA OWEN

LANG, Fritz (5 Dec. 1890–2 Aug. 1976), film director, was born in Vienna, Austria, the son of Anton Lang, a prominent architect, and Paula Schlesinger. Lang seemed destined to emulate his father when he took up architecture at the Technical High School of Vienna. But drawn increasingly to painting, he transferred to the Academy of Graphic Arts and then studied at the State School of Arts and Crafts in Munich (1908–1910). At the age of twenty he began traveling the world, working as an itinerant artist and designer in Asia, North Africa, and the South Pacific. Arrested in Paris as an alien at the outbreak of World War I, he returned to Vienna where he entered the Austrian army. Wounded repeatedly (blinded in his right eye), he reached the rank of lieutenant and was decorated for service.

While recuperating from his war injuries, Lang wrote screenplays and acted. In 1918 he moved to Berlin, continuing to compose screenplays and appearing in a few minor film roles. In 1919 he directed his first films. In 1920 he divorced his first wife, Lisa Rosenthal, and married Thea von Harbou. From 1920 to 1933 Harbou collaborated with Lang as author or coauthor of his screenplays.

From the start, Lang's films were distinguished by masterly control of technique and strong graphic images marked by expressionist style. He often employed allegory and symbolism for didactic purposes. For example, in *Der müde Tod* (The tired death, 1921; released in English as *Destiny*), a woman bargains with Death for the life of her boyfriend. In *Dr. Mabuse, the Gambler* (1922), Lang introduced the character of Mabuse, a master criminal who seeks to dominate a world of chaos, crime, and vice by manipulating others. The film was a commercial success, and Lang—who viewed it as a parable of his time—made a sequel in 1932, *The Last Will of Dr. Mabuse*. He reprised the Mabuse character a third time in his last film, *The Thousand Eyes of Dr. Mabuse* (1960).

In 1924 Lang directed *Siegfried* and *Kriemhild's Revenge*, film versions of the Nibelungen epic with impressive effects and architectural settings. He coauthored and directed *Metropolis* (1927), a carefully choreographed and moralistic melodrama with stunning sets and effects—replete with some 30,000 extras. The story, set in the future, depicts the struggle between degraded workers and a technological elite, each class identified with a different level of the city. The film evinces Lang's concern with the deception of visual appearances and their potential for sinister manipulation in a subplot about the construction of a robot designed to lead the workers to violent revolt and their own destruction. Lang himself was dissatisfied with *Metropolis*; it was not a commercial success, and critics have objected to defects in plot and style. Nevertheless the film has appealed to educated audiences for generations and endures as one of the most widely viewed films of the silent era.

Lang mastered sound film in his first effort in the new medium, *M* (1931). His personal favorite, *M* is widely acknowledged as a classic. In it a psychopathic child killer (played masterfully by Peter Lorre) is pursued both by authorities and by an organized underworld of criminals and beggars. Similarities between police and criminals are visually reinforced throughout. Trapped by the underworld, the killer is tried by a kangaroo court. The mob's demand for the killer's death is frustrated only when police break up the mob trial—and the film ends. *M* adapted hitherto unconventional material and employed a greater degree of naturalism: Lang even studied insanity and employed criminals in the cast. The extensive critical literature about—and conflicting interpretations of—*M* testify to its disturbing, ambivalent effect on viewers and its susceptibility to multiple readings.

As they rose to power in the early 1930s, the Nazis banned Lang's most recent films, but, according to Lang, Joseph Goebbels nonetheless asked him to direct films for the Nazis. Although Lang was raised a Roman Catholic, his mother was part Jewish, and he immediately fled Germany. Harbou sympathized with the Nazis—she joined the Nazi party—and stayed in Germany. She divorced Lang in 1933.

After making one film in France, in 1934 Lang moved to Hollywood, where David O. Selznick brought him to work with MGM. His first American film was *Fury* (1936), the story of an innocent man, Joe Wilson, wrongly accused of a crime. Attacked by a lynch mob, Joe escapes but is believed dead. Out for vengeance, Joe allows the mob leaders to be tried for his murder but relents at the end. *Fury* effectively combined familiar Langian themes—the deceptiveness of appearances, the similarities between the criminal order and the legal system, and the self-destructive course of vengeance. To MGM's surprise, it proved a commercial success, and it attracted attention for its timely antilynching message. An immediate classic, *Fury* remains the most popular and most studied of Lang's American works. After completing *Fury*, Lang's contract with MGM expired, and for the next two decades he worked for a variety of producers, sometimes producing his own work alone or in partnership. His films were released by most major companies, including United Artists, 20th Century–Fox, Warner Bros., and Republic.

From 1936 to 1956 he made twenty-two films in the United States—more than half of his total. Among his most highly regarded American films are *You Only Live Once* (1937), a film noir about an ex-con trying to go straight who is wrongly accused of a crime; *Western Union* (1941), a western; *Hangmen Also Die!* (1943), based on a story by Lang and Bertolt Brecht about the Czech resistance; *Ministry of Fear* (1944), an anti-Nazi thriller; *Scarlet Street* (1945), a film noir about the downfall of an amateur artist who kills the woman who tempts him to his ruin; *The Big Heat* (1953), a police melodrama about a detective whose wife is murdered by the mob; *While the City Sleeps* (1956), a thriller about a journalist who traps a sex murderer; and *Beyond a Reasonable Doubt* (1956), a legal drama in which the lover of a writer incriminated of murder searches for exculpating proof.

Lang welcomed the greater technical resources and superior casting opportunities in America but protested against interference with his artistic control. For example, he rightly complained that the kiss inserted at the end of *Fury* in the courtroom was contrived. Yet even while reorienting himself to the more commercial Hollywood system of filmmaking and a wider range of genres, Lang wrote and directed films of high quality and original technique. His innovations in established genres influenced other filmmakers—for instance, his western *Rancho Notorious* (1952) was the first to employ a theme song throughout.

For about a year in 1952, he was blacklisted as a suspected Communist and was unable to get work in Hollywood. He was probably correct in believing this treatment stemmed from his support of antifascist activities in the late 1930s and from his friendship with many Communists. Lang was able to make films again in 1953, but, though he himself was satisfied with several of those works, they did not achieve the commercial success he sought. Growing increasingly frustrated with external interference with his work, in 1957 he accepted an invitation to return to Germany to make a two-part film that he had cowritten in 1920, *The Tiger of Eschnapur* and *The Indian Tomb*. Filmed in India with extravagant scenes, the films were well-received upon their release in Europe in 1959. He returned to Germany to make a third Mabuse film. Lang later told Peter Bogdanovich that he did not make these last three films because of their importance but because "I was hoping that if I made somebody a great financial success I would again have the chance—as I had with *M*—to work without any restrictions. It was my mistake."

Lang returned to Beverly Hills, never to direct another film. During his last years he was recognized as a significant director, especially by younger filmmakers and French New Wave critics. He appeared as himself and commented on film directing in Jean-Luc Godard's film *Contempt* (1963). Yet Lang remained an outsider in Hollywood, suffering from a bad reputation among actors who did not like working with such a perfectionist. He died in Los Angeles.

Lang was one of the few great directors with artistic aspirations whose best films continue to appeal to broad audiences. Critics once dismissed Lang's American work as inferior to the films he directed in Germany, but in the 1950s and 1960s some reevaluated his American films. Accordingly, a division of opinion arose. Luc Moullet insisted Lang's work "is one and indivisible"; some critics argued his Hollywood films equaled or surpassed his more melodramatic and didactic early work; others (like Noël Burch) contended that his early German films attained high artistic levels that he never reached again. He received no major awards from the American film industry.

• Lang's papers are at the University of Southern California. Some correspondence is cataloged in the holdings of the Leo Lania Collection at the State Historical Society of Wisconsin. Lang discussed his views on film in an article in the *Penguin Film Review* (1948) and published the screenplays for *M* (1963) and *Fury* in *Twenty Best Film Plays*, ed. John Gassner (1943). Peter Bogdanovich published edited transcripts of extensive interviews with him about his life and career in *Fritz Lang in America* (1967). There are a number of book-length critical studies of Lang's work and career. Lang's longtime acquaintance, Lotte Eisner, wrote a thorough, sympathetic account, *Fritz Lang* (1976), which includes a good filmography and bibliography, Lang's unfinished autobiography, and excerpts of interviews. Eisner had access to all of Lang's American scripts, and Lang himself read and corrected her text. The most complete bibliography is probably in a critical study of his American work, Reynold Humphries, *Fritz Lang: Cinéast américain* (1982), published in revised English translation by the author as *Fritz Lang: Genre and Representation in His American Films* (1989). An excellent entry on Lang by Philip Kemp is in *World Film Directors*, ed. John Wakeman (1987). Paul M. Jensen, *The Cinema of Fritz Lang* (1969), though programmatic in interpretation and judgmental in evaluation, is well researched and contains particularly helpful discussion of Lang's sources and context. Robert A. Armour, *Fritz Lang* (1978), is a good introduction to Lang's work and treats Lang's major films thematically under different genres. Synoptic, critical studies include Luc Moullet, *Fritz Lang* (1963), with excerpts from critics and contemporaries and a filmography; and Francis Courtade, *Fritz Lang* (1963), with a filmography. Good short studies are: the critical appraisals by Robin Wood and Noël Burch in *Cinema: A Critical Dictionary: The Major Film-Makers*, vol. 2, ed. Richard Roud (1980); the entry by Rolf Badenhausen in *Neue Deutsche Biographie*, vol. 13 (1982); and the entry in Liz-Anne Bawden, ed., *The Oxford Companion to Film* (1976). An obituary is in the *New York Times*, 3 Aug. 1976.

MICHAEL H. HOFFHEIMER

LANG, Lucy Fox Robins (1884–26 Jan. 1962), labor activist, was born in Kiev, Russia, the daughter of Moshe Fox, a silversmith, and Surtze Broche. Seeking to escape the harsh treatment meted out to Russian Jews, her father immigrated to the United States and then returned when Fox was nine years old, moving the whole family to New York City. Not long afterward the family moved to Chicago, where Fox worked in a cigar factory and studied English in night school.

While still a girl, Fox came to know and admire Chicago's great reformer Jane Addams, but she soon grew even more attracted to the local anarchist movement. At fifteen she met and fell in love with Bob Robins, a printer and bookkeeper who shared her radical politics. When they married a few years later, Fox was determined to remain free from the constraints she associated with conventional matrimony, so they married by legal contract instead of a religious ceremony and agreed that the transaction would be binding for only five years. In 1905 the couple moved to New York City, where they soon saved enough to buy a cigar store. At the same time they immersed themselves in the world of radical politics. It was during this period that Robins began her lifetime friendship with the charismatic anarchist Emma Goldman.

After about a year in New York, Robins and her husband moved to San Francisco, where they soon attracted a lively circle of freethinkers and activists to their St. Helena Vegetarian Cafe, a restaurant they opened with the encouragement of author and fellow radical Jack London. When their trial marriage had lasted the agreed-upon five years, the couple separated briefly. This attracted the wrath of the popular press; one paper described Robins scornfully as "the girl on lease for five years." She and her husband soon joined forces again, however, embarking on half a dozen years of wandering that started in a socialist community in Puget Sound and progressed to Seattle, Los Angeles, New York, San Diego, Montgomery, Alabama, and ultimately back to San Francisco. They sustained themselves by taking various semiskilled jobs, some-times living in a trailer they called "The Adventurer." Meanwhile they supported innumerable radical causes, including campaigns on behalf of Big Bill Haywood, the McNamara brothers, several deported radicals, unemployed workers, the International Workers of the World, Joe Hill, and a variety of anarchist projects.

The outbreak of World War I in Europe in 1914 sparked a drive for military preparedness in the United States, along with growing intolerance for dissent. After a bomb exploded at a San Francisco Preparedness Day parade in 1916, Tom Mooney and Warren Billings—labor radicals who had spoken out against the war—were convicted of the crime, even though the evidence against them was flimsy. Robins quickly assumed a leading role on the Tom Mooney Defense Committee. In doing so she sought an audience with Samuel Gompers, the conservative head of the American Federation of Labor. When Gompers refused to see her, she wired him: "I now understand why the great masses of workers despise you, curse you, and eagerly await your death." The wire got her an interview, and the two became fast friends, especially when Robins discovered that he had been working behind the scenes on behalf of Mooney. Soon afterward she joined the AFL staff.

Historians have puzzled over Robins's leap across the political spectrum. Some have speculated that her previous radicalism was a mere youthful enthusiasm that she outgrew; others have explained the change as a shift from one mentor (her husband) to another (Gompers). She does seem to have had a genuine affection for Gompers, but she also had a pragmatic respect for his power. When socialist Eugene V. Debs spoke slightingly of Gompers, she admonished him: "We must admit that the leaders in the American Labor Movement are the leaders of the masses." Until the masses themselves were ready for "a more progressive step," she maintained, it was important to deal with the leaders they recognized.

Robins told friends that Gompers proposed to her after his wife died in 1920; his friends thought it unlikely, and in any case Gompers married someone else the following year. Nevertheless, there was a warm relationship between the two, and Gompers gave her an important institutional base. For instance, beginning in 1918 Robins had chaired the League for Amnesty for Political Prisoners, seeking to free Debs and a number of others who had been imprisoned for protesting U.S. participation in World War I. But the project made little headway until, with Gompers's backing, the New York Central Labor Council established a committee for the same purpose and named Robins executive secretary. She attracted considerable criticism in radical circles for her determination to keep the campaign as clear of left-wing associations as possible, but she made a significant contribution, traveling tirelessly across the country between 1919 and 1921 raising money and support, arranging for labor delegations to be received in Washington, visiting and corresponding with Debs, and personally escorting him when he finally left prison. Debs himself gave her much of the credit for his release, calling her his "noble comrade."

During these years Robins and her husband were growing apart, and when he left for Russia in 1920 they did not expect to see each other again. He returned to New York a few years later, sick and disillusioned, but the marriage was over, and the couple formally divorced in 1924. Eight years later she married Harry Lang, a staff writer on the *Jewish Daily Forward* and a fellow veteran of the campaign to free Debs. She had no children with either Lang or Robins. She remained active in the labor movement for the rest of her life, usually on the progressive side, though in the split between the AFL and the insurgent CIO, she remained loyal to the AFL. The Langs traveled much of each year, though they maintained a base in New York City and later in Croton-on-Hudson, New York. Lang died in Los Angeles.

Gompers was not quite correct when he said that Lang "gave up everything to establish a better understanding between radicals and the labor movement." From the time she met him she cast her lot with the AFL; indeed, her wariness of left-wing associations hardened as she grew older. Nevertheless, she furthered innumerable radical causes with her energy and pragmatism, while she enlivened the AFL with her passion for social justice and her zest for fighting the good fight.

• Lang's papers are in the Indiana State University Library (Terre Haute). Her *War Shadows* (1922) tells the story of the campaign to free Debs, while her *Tomorrow Is Beautiful* (1948) is a memoir of her whole career. Both are lively and informative, though written from her own highly partisan perspective. See also Samuel Gompers, *Seventy Years of Life and Labor* (1925); Bernard Mandel, *Samuel Gompers: A Biography* (1963); and *Letters of Eugene V. Debs*, vol. 3: *1919–1926*, ed. J. Robert Constantine (1990). A *New York Times* obituary appears on 26 Jan. 1962.

SANDRA OPDYCKE

LANG, Margaret Ruthven (27 Nov. 1867–30 May 1972), violinist and composer, was born in Boston, Massachusetts, the daughter of Benjamin Johnson Lang, one of the city's leading organists and choir masters. Her family was socially prominent and musically active in Boston, and as a young girl Margaret received strong musical training from her father. She began writing music at age seventeen. Her family connections aided her artistic visibility and her compositional career. In 1890, for example, she wrote a piece for male chorus entitled *The Jumblies*, a musical setting of poetry by Edward Lear; her father premiered the work.

At age seventeen Lang traveled to Munich to study violin and counterpoint. Back in Boston she studied the finer points of harmony, orchestration, and composition under George Whitefield Chadwick and Edward MacDowell, the most famous composers of late nineteenth-century America. At the World's Columbian Exposition in Chicago in 1893, twenty-one American composers submitted works in a competition. Only four compositions received awards and performances. One of the four was Lang's *Witichis*, op. 10. In 1893 the Boston Symphony Orchestra performed her *Dramatic Overture*, op. 12, the first work by an American woman to be performed by a major symphony orchestra.

Lang's composition style was a mixture of German Romanticism and Impressionism, with relatively conservative use of harmonic dissonance and clear elements of Irish and Scottish folk melodies. Critics praised Lang's music for its unobtrusive spontaneity. Her admirers found her music refreshingly distinct from that of many of the modernists of the early twentieth century whose music was often considered harsh. Champions of the modern styles considered Lang's music old-fashioned, but traditionalists found its focus on pleasing sonorities rather than compositional techniques to be gratifying. Her conservative critics applauded especially.

The Langs were a family of considerable wealth (when Benjamin Lang died in 1909, Margaret Lang received a legacy of $600,000), and throughout her long life Lang never needed to earn a living. She never married and wrote music only until 1917. Through all her years, she was very much a "lady of Beacon Hill," maintaining a social circle of friends and keeping current with the latest intellectual trends. She never moved from the family home at 2 Brimmer Street and attended virtually every performance of the Boston Symphony Orchestra from its founding in 1881. On her hundredth birthday Erich Leinsdorf conducted a concert of the Boston Symphony in her honor. She died in Boston at the age of 104.

• There is no biography of Margaret Lang, nor is there any study of the Lang family. There is one biographical article, E. Syford, "Margaret Ruthven Lang," *New England Magazine*, Mar. 1912, p. 22, and one anthology, T. F. Ryan, *Recollections of an Old Musician* (1899), both of which contemporaneously applaud Lang's musical talent and demonstrate that interest in her is not mere curiosity stemming from either the fact that she lived to such an old age or that she was female. In *Unsung: A History of Women in American Music* (1980), Christine Ammer dedicates a few pages to Lang's life (and celebrates Lang as much for her gender as for her artistry). Ammer summarizes the previous writings about Lang but provides no actual analyses of any of her music. A substantive obituary is in the *Boston Globe*, 4 June 1972.

ALAN LEVY

LANGDELL, Christopher Columbus (22 May 1826–6 July 1906), legal scholar and educator, was born in New Boston, New Hampshire, of Scotch-Irish parents (whose names could not be ascertained). He worked his way through Phillips Exeter Academy and entered Harvard College in 1848, at the age of twenty-two. After eighteen months he left the college, without earning a degree, to work as a tutor and law clerk. In 1851 he entered Harvard Law School, where he stayed twice the conventional term and received his LL.B. in 1854. For the next sixteen years Langdell practiced law in the New York firm of Stanley, Langdell and Brown. Harvard law professor and school historian Arthur E. Sutherland described Langdell as "a lawyer's lawyer" who was greatly respected by the leaders of the bar. Remaining single, he lived in a room above the law offices. In 1870 Charles William Eliot, then the new president of Harvard University, made him Dane Professor of Law. According to Sutherland, Eliot and Langdell shared a "common intellectual commitment to scientism. "Several months after his appointment, the law school faculty elected him dean.

Langdell is credited, and blamed, as the father of the modern form of American legal education. His best-known innovation was the introduction of the case method. Prior to the 1870s law students read scholarly treatises and listened to lectures. Langdell's alternative asked students to read edited versions of appellate decisions and discuss their application to similar, hypothetical, factual situations. By the early twentieth century this became the standard teaching method in American legal education. The adoption of this change, which was widely attributed to Langdell, increased when publishing made judicial decisions available to teachers and students who had previously depended on the treatises. The philosophy underlining the case method asserts that law is a form of science in which general rules can be deduced through the study of particular phenomena, that is, the cases. Since the 1930s most American legal educators have recognized that the case method underestimates the role of history, culture, and human agency in the creation of law. As a method of legal education it devalues legislative and administrative law and the skills of practice. It takes the reported appellate decision as a given datum, from which results in subsequent cases can be deduced.

As the first dean of Harvard Law School, Langdell introduced other reforms that endure in American legal education. In 1870 any white man of good "moral character" could be admitted to the school upon payment of the fee. Langdell instituted admissions standards. By 1875 applicants were admitted only if they had earned a bachelor's degree or passed rigorous exams in Latin and *Blackstone's Commentaries*. Dean Langdell also stiffened requirements for graduation. While in 1870 Harvard Law required only one year of study with no examinations, by 1876 the school required three years of study with demanding exams at the end of each year. This model has, again, become standard. In 1870 the Harvard faculty consisted of three full-time members with extensive practical experience and many part-time judges and practitioners. In 1873 Langdell hired James Barr Ames, a recent graduate and leading disciple of the case method. Even though Langdell had practiced law for many years, he advocated a faculty of full-time teachers, consisting of bright young men with no practical experience. Eliot observed in 1919 that Langdell "was inclined to believe that success at the Bar or on the Bench was, in all probability, a disqualification for the functions of a professor of law." A critical contemporary charged

Langdell with committing a grave error of policy if "his ideal is to breed professors of Law not practitioners." By the end of his deanship, virtually all teaching at Harvard was done by the eight full-time faculty, of whom half had no practical experience. Under his leadership the school also hired for the first time a full-time librarian, who instituted systemic forms of acquisition, cataloging, binding, and storage. By the end of Langdell's term, the Harvard Law School library was rivaled only by the collections of the Library of Congress and the Supreme Court.

An energetic and effective administrator, Langdell raised funds for the construction of buildings for lecture halls, a library, and student residences. Tuition, which had been set at the same rate for fifty years, was increased by 50 percent a year. Both the alumni association and the Harvard Law Review were created under his leadership, and the student body increased from 115 to 750. When he arrived the school was in debt; by the time of his death the school's surplus was nearly half a millon dollars, and the library and physical plant were vastly improved. The Harvard that Langdell created had become the model emulated by the growing number of American law schools. In addition to his work as an educator, Langdell wrote texts that expounded his "scientific" views on equity and contracts. Langdell married late and did not have children. Little is known of his personal life. He retired as dean in 1895. Despite failing eye-sight, he continued to teach part-time. In 1906 Harvard named a new building Langdell Hall. Langdell died at home in Cambridge, Massachusetts.

• Langdell's papers are located at the Harvard Law School Library. His leading works are *A Selection of Cases on the Law of Contracts* (1871), *A Treatise on Contracts* (1873), and *A Summary of Equity Pleading* (1877). A collection of essays, which were composed on the occasion of his death, are in *Harvard Law Review* 20, no. 1 (1906): 1–12. Short biographies appear in James Barr Ames, *Lectures on Legal History and Miscellaneous Legal Essays* (1913); Charles W. Eliot, "Langdell and the Law School," *Harvard Law Review* 33 (1919): 518; Joseph H. Beale, "Langdell, Gray, Thayer and Ames—Their Contribution to the Study and Teaching of Law," *New York University Law Quarterly Review* 8 (1930–1931): 385; Arthur E. Sutherland, *The Law at Harvard: A History of Ideas and Men, 1817–1967* (1967); Robert Stevens, "Two Cheers for 1870: The American Law School," *Perspectives in American History* 5 (1971): 405–548; Anthony Chase, "The Birth of the Modern Law School," *American Journal of Legal History* 23 (1979): 329; Robert Stevens, *Law School: Legal Education in America from the 1850s to the 1980s* (1983); and Richard A. Cosgrove, *Our Lady the Common Law: An Anglo-American Legal Community, 1870–1930* (1987).

SYLVIA A. LAW

LANGDON, Harry Philmore (15 June 1884–22 Dec. 1944), vaudeville and motion picture comedian, was born in Council Bluffs, Iowa, the son of William Wiley Langdon and Levina Lookenbill, both of whom worked for the Salvation Army, an occupation that left the family in a state of poverty almost on the level of the indigents they helped. As a child Harry Langdon had little formal education, spending most of his time taking odd jobs, selling papers, and running errands. In his teens he entered the world of show business, participating in many amateur nights on the local vaudeville stage of the Doheney Theater in his hometown. At the age of twelve Langdon displayed some of the pantomime skills that would develop as the quintessence of his humorous character, and he attempted to be a magician and a ventriloquist. However, he was most adept as a comedian. Mental and physical ineptitude provided the core of a routine that won favor with audiences as early as 1896, thirty years before Langdon became a leading actor for the studios of the producer Hal Roach, a rival of the producer Mack Sennett's Keystone comedy film factory.

Langdon had a much longer career on the stage than did Charles Chaplin, Harold Lloyd, or Buster Keaton—three other comedy kings of the silent era. As a thirteen-year-old, Langdon joined Dr. Belcher's Kickapoo Indian Medicine Show, followed by engagements in circuses and vaudeville shows. It was the longtime stage act, "Johnny's New Car," that eventually, in 1923, caught the attention of Sennett. Langdon introduced this short skit in 1903, using a breakaway car that fell apart, piece by piece, as he tried to fix it—a lampoon of the trouble that plagued the owners at that time. Actress Rose Frances Mensolf, who became Langdon's first wife a year after he created the comedy act, played a shrewish spouse in this routine. By the early twenties the comedian had employed this act thousands of times and had developed a character who would be used best by Roach, because Sennett's writers and directors did not understand Langdon's unusual, low-keyed comic portrait. In *The Crazy Mirror*, a study of the Hollywood comedy, critic Raymond Durgnat suggests that Sennett studios, in their short films, piled situation on situation, while the Roach company had a slower pace that "goes with a genial relish over reactions and character." The move to Roach in 1926 was the beginning of Langdon's brief brush with fame. With director Harry Edwards and writers Frank Capra and Arthur Ripley, the comedian's screen career blossomed. On the eve of his entrance into features, Langdon's popularity was further solidified by *Soldier Man*, a three-reeler released in the spring of 1926. With the assistance of Capra as director and writer, the comedian created two features that year. Capra served as writer for *Tramp, Tramp, Tramp* and director for *The Strong Man*, and in 1927 he would once more guide the comedian in the successful feature *Long Pants*. In these works Langdon employed understated reactions and used a variety of hesitating movements of his legs and arms as he attempted to solve a problem or to take action. However, the character he created would usually fail to confront an obstacle that baffled him.

A popular and critical revisit to the artistry of the silent screen comedy emerged in the sixties. Many of the films were resurrected and shown; books were written praising, most of all, Chaplin and Keaton. Langdon, however, was not given the status he de-

served. For example, Rudi Blesh's 1966 study of Buster Keaton examines the nature of Chaplin's and Lloyd's comedy but does not even mention Langdon. However, the comedian received recognition from one evaluator as early as the late forties. Novelist and journalistic critic James Agee, in his famous 1949 *Life* essay on comedy, rated the comedian as an important contributor to the silent screen tradition. Agee described Langdon as a "virtuoso of hesitation and of delicately indecisive motions" with "a subtle emotional and mental process" similar to Chaplin's. But there was a difference in the two comedians' portraits: the intelligence of the character. Somewhat like the character portrayed by Stan Laurel, Langdon's clown depicted the naive or stupid childlike man, nearly lost in a very sophisticated world of superior people.

The whimsy of Langdon's comic portrait diminished when he dismissed Capra as his director after they completed *Long Pants*. The comedian thought he needed more control over his films like that achieved by the other kings of comedy of the twenties. With neither critical nor popular success, Langdon wrote and directed *Three's a Crowd* in 1927 and *The Chaser* and *Heart Trouble* in 1928. The emotional nature of these pictures moved too much toward the sentimental, suggesting that he could not handle serious scenes in his attempt to rival Chaplin's little tramp. After writing and directing for him, Capra, in his 1971 autobiography, *The Name Above the Title*, indicated that he knew Langdon could not direct himself. The comedian may have had many good comic ideas—later, in 1938, he was a writer for Laurel and Oliver Hardy sound films—but he evidently could not manage the complicated task of the total feature comedy as could his more famous contemporaries Chaplin, Lloyd, and Keaton.

After sound arrived in 1929, Langdon could only manage comic shorts and a few musical film appearances in the thirties and forties. His private life proved to be as chaotic as his career. After he divorced his first wife, he married Helen Walton in 1929, a union that ended in 1934. His third marriage was to Mabel Watts Sheldon; they had one child.

Like Keaton, whose own fame was bankrupt, Langdon became a has-been, struggling to make a comeback. On the slippery slope experienced by too many stars as they faded, Langdon received his last contract in 1941 from the poverty row of movie studios, Monogram. He died of cerebral thrombosis in Los Angeles.

• The most thorough examination of the comedian's life and works is William Schelly, *Harry Langdon* (1982), with an evaluation of the films as the focus of the study as well as a bibliography and a filmography. The first important analysis of Langdon appeared in a popular magazine: James Agee, "Comedy's Greatest Era," *Life*, 5 Sept. 1949, pp. 70–88. See also Walter Kerr, *The Silent Clowns* (1975); Leonard Maltin, *The Great Movie Shorts* (1972); Gerald Mast, *The Comic Mind* (1973); Donald W. McCaffrey, *Four Great Comedians* (1968); Richard Schickel, *The Men Who Made the Movies* (1975); and Mack Sennett (with Cameron Shipp), *King of Comedy* (1954). An effective obituary is in the *New York Times*, 23 Dec. 1944.

DONALD W. MCCAFFREY

LANGDON, John (26 June 1741–18 Sept. 1819), merchant and politician, was born a few miles outside of Portsmouth, New Hampshire, on a modest farm belonging to his parents, John Langdon, Sr., and Mary Hall. He received the finest schooling available for boys in Portsmouth, at Major Samuel Hale's Latin grammar school, where emphasis lay on the classics. It was not there, however, but in Daniel Rindge's countinghouse that Langdon, as a young clerk, gained his lifelong trade and a shrewd eye for the main chance. By the mid-1700s Portsmouth, with its deep-water harbor and easily defended location on the Piscataqua River, buzzed with commercial prosperity. Investing first in some of Rindge's West Indian voyages and then skippering a few himself in the early 1760s, Langdon entered the town's maritime bonanza. Within a few years his own vessels headed out of the Piscataqua laden with lumber, hides, beef, and dried cod and returned carrying sugar and rum. By 1770, having abandoned seafaring, he and Woodbury Langdon, his brother and partner, claimed a tenuous place in Portsmouth's tightly knit mercantile elite.

Though he was hampered by the tightened British trade regulations of the 1760s, it was a personal brush with imperial power that pushed Langdon toward colonial resistance and led him, ultimately, to revolution. In October 1771 British customs agents in Portsmouth seized the *Resolution*, a brig owned by another local merchant but carrying goods that belonged to Langdon. Because the cargo contained 100 hogsheads of allegedly undeclared molasses, port officials under British law condemned the ship along with its entire contents. After an infuriating four months of litigation, the vice admiralty court in Boston finally upheld British customs authority. Becoming more politically radical, Langdon openly protested the Tea Act in 1773. Though British troops did not occupy Portsmouth as they did Boston, Langdon joined in local precautions, and in 1774, responding to a warning from Boston patriots, he helped to lead a raid on Fort William and Mary, at the mouth of the Piscataqua, to secure its munitions from enemy capture. The following year, after being chosen Speaker of the New Hampshire assembly, he was sent to represent the colony in the Second Continental Congress. There his committee assignments related to the acquisition of essential war supplies—the purchase of woolens, the gathering of ordnance, and the processing of lead ore. Langdon remained in Congress until June 1776, when he exchanged his seat in Philadelphia for the more coveted office of Continental agent for New Hampshire.

With its chilling effect on trade, the American Revolution played havoc on the old merchant aristocracy in Portsmouth. Runaway inflation and taxes on speculative lands also diminished many established families, while those who remained loyal to the Crown faced confiscation of their property. Langdon, by contrast, made a fortune on the Revolution, emerging afterward as one of the wealthiest men in the state. To his mind there was nothing wrong with profiting from patriotic deeds. The main task of the Continental agent was to sell the lucrative booty of war that local privateers towed into port, and with each transaction he received a percentage. Langdon guarded his territory like a bird of prey, ever suspicious of incursions by neighboring competitors. In August 1776 he instructed Congress to "by no means let the Agent of any Colony have it in his power to . . . Cruise where he pleases, and to Bring the Prizes into his own Colony when other Harbours are more handy." Mainly through his connection with New Hampshire congressman William Whipple, who sat on the Marine Committee, he also landed contracts to build ships for the Continental navy, including the *Ranger*, which Captain John Paul Jones made famous during the war. In addition, Langdon worked to raise manpower and bring in French supplies for Continental forces. He not only helped to finance, but, as commander of a militia unit, he accompanied General John Stark's summer 1777 expedition that contributed to American victory at Saratoga. His last military service came in the Rhode Island campaign of August 1778. In 1777 he married sixteen-year-old Elizabeth Sherburne; they had two children, only one of whom reached adulthood.

During the war Langdon also gained a dominant position in New Hampshire politics. Between 1777 and 1782 he again served as Speaker of the state house of representatives. He advocated state constitutional reform, especially an independent executive with the power to act decisively. "To have one branch of the legislature . . . execute those laws which they themselves have made is an absurdity," he insisted. A defender of merchant interests against the "levelling spirit" of some fellow legislators, he restrained the more drastic schemes for divesting Loyalists and blocked proposals to aid debtors. Horrified by mounting inflation, he was president of the New Hampshire Convention for Regulating the Currency in 1779. After another short stint in Congress in 1783–1784, he occupied a seat in the state senate until being elected, in 1785, to the presidency of New Hampshire, a one-year post that he lost in 1786 to John Sullivan. A messy controversy over Langdon's appointment of his brother Woodbury as a justice of the superior court generated charges of nepotism that cost him reelection. Voters returned him to the house, where he resumed the Speakership. The following summer, in part because he could pay his own expenses, the legislature dispatched Langdon, along with Nicholas Gilman, to the Philadelphia Constitutional Convention.

One of the richest delegates and the third largest creditor among them, Langdon's conception of nationalism called for ample government protection of American trade and finance. In particular, he wanted Congress vested with exclusive power to regulate commerce, internally and externally. "This once done," he advised Thomas Jefferson in 1785, "Great Britain would soon come into a commercial treaty . . . or they would no doubt be excluded from the Commerce of the Continent; which would be their ruin." Here, Langdon advocated not only self-interest but also the advantage of his key constituents in Portsmouth and the Merrimac Valley, who needed full access to foreign ports and to the Merrimac River, which ran through Massachusetts. He wanted Congress given full authority over slave importation and to have veto power over state laws that conflicted with Union interests. Heavy business connections with nationalists at the convention, mainly Robert Morris, would seem to account for Langdon's voting with them on matters of money. At the time, for example, he was Portsmouth agent for the Bank of North America, headquartered under Morris in Philadelphia. He also held extensive investments in state banks and state securities, along with a massive stake in Continental securities. After signing the Constitution draft at the convention, he led a group of Federalists in campaigning for New Hampshire's ratification of the document, which took place in June 1788.

Again elected president of New Hampshire in 1788, Langdon resigned a year later to accept a seat in the U.S. Senate, which he held from 4 March 1789 until 3 March 1801. Shortly after arriving in New York he was elected the first president pro tempore of the Senate. In the early 1790s Langdon voted consistently with the Federalists, supporting Alexander Hamilton's plans to fund the national debt and establish a national bank. Despite protests in New Hampshire, where most war loans had been paid, he also backed the Hamiltonian plan for federal assumption of state debts. Because he could not support a pro-British foreign policy, however, Langdon switched his political allegiance from the Federalists to the Jeffersonian opposition by 1794. In that year he voted against Jay's Treaty, which denied Americans the commercial sway he expected earlier. At war against France, Britain promised in the treaty to pay reparations for American ships and cargoes seized in 1793–1794, to allow tightly restricted American access to trade in the British West Indies, and to evacuate northwestern posts by 1796. But in return, U.S. special envoy John Jay had outraged Republicans and their commercial supporters by accepting the British definition of neutral rights and by granting Britain most-favored-nation status in American ports. Striking out the insulting West Indies provision, the Senate ratified the treaty by a slim margin, but Langdon nailed his flag to the Republican mast from then on.

Turning down both a third Senate term and an offer from President-elect Jefferson to be secretary of the Navy, Langdon chose comfortable Portsmouth over the swampy new federal capital. He returned to the legislature between 1801 and 1804, including another year as Speaker in 1803. As leader of the Jeffersonian party in the state, Langdon won the governorship in 1805 after three unsuccessful tries. While in office, he persuaded the legislature to locate a permanent state capital at Concord, stopped the importing of slaves through Portsmouth, and steadfastly opposed acceptance of private notes as currency. Except for 1809, when voters punished his loyal support of Jefferson's embargo, he achieved reelection annually until retiring in 1811.

After declining the Republican nomination for vice president in 1812, Langdon's last years afforded him time in his Pleasant Street mansion, built in 1784 and one of the most acclaimed Georgian structures in America. A contemporary described him as "easy, polite, and pleasing in his manners, and social in his habits. . . . liberal, although not lavish of his money." Drawn increasingly to religion, he donated large amounts to Congregational churches in Portsmouth and to the American and New Hampshire Bible societies. He died at home in Portsmouth.

• Large collections of Langdon papers are preserved in the New Hampshire Historical Society, Concord; the Historical Society of Pennsylvania, Philadelphia; the Strawbery Banke Museum in Portsmouth; and the Portsmouth Athenaeum. On Langdon's involvement in the American Revolution, see Jere Daniell, *Experiment in Republicanism: New Hampshire Politics and the American Revolution, 1741–1794* (1970). A full biography of Langdon is Lawrence Shaw Mayo, *John Langdon of New Hampshire* (1937). For background on his role at the Constitutional Convention of 1787, see Forrest McDonald, *We the People: The Economic Origins of the Constitution* (1958). An obituary is in the *New Hampshire Gazette*, 21 Sept. 1819.

JOHN R. VAN ATTA

LANGDON, Samuel (12 Jan. 1723–29 Nov. 1797), Congregational minister, patriot, and college president, was born in Boston, Massachusetts, the son of Samuel Langdon, a house builder, and Esther Osgood. His father died while Samuel was an infant, but despite his impoverished circumstances, Langdon attended Harvard College from 1736 to 1740, earning his A.B. and A.M. degrees.

In 1741 Langdon began his career as a schoolmaster in Ipswich, Massachusetts, where he met his future wife, Elizabeth Whipple Brown. The couple married in 1746 and had eleven children. After initial setbacks, his pursuit of a clerical career was advanced when he accepted a position as schoolmaster in Portsmouth, New Hampshire, with the understanding that he would succeed the incumbent minister upon his imminent retirement. While in Portsmouth, Langdon was named chaplain of the New Hampshire regiment in the 1745 military expedition against Louisbourg, Cape Breton, in French Canada. After his return Langdon was ordained as pastor of the First Church in Portsmouth early in 1747. Over the next quarter century he established himself as the leader of the New Hampshire association of Congregational ministers and promoted religious education throughout the province. Langdon also maintained an avid interest in the natural world; he helped trace the path of comets to aid colonial astronomers like John Winthrop (1714–1779) of Harvard, and together with Joseph Blanchard drew the first accurate map of New Hampshire. Unbeknownst to Langdon, a copy of his map was published in London in 1761 with an inscription to the cabinet minister Charles Townshend, who surprised Langdon by arranging for a doctorate in divinity to be granted to him by the University of Aberdeen.

As a minister in New England's dominant Congregational establishment, Langdon hoped to heal the rifts that the Great Awakening of the 1740s had created within many established churches. Together with Ezra Stiles (later president of Yale College), Langdon became an advocate of what Stiles termed "the Christian Union," a vision of unity among Calvinists, who at the time were splintering into Congregational, Baptist, and Presbyterian churches. Langdon encouraged ministerial associations to promote interdenominational unity, and in 1768 published *A Summary of Christian Faith . . . for the Assistance of Christians of All Denominations in Recollecting the Main Articles of Their Common Professions.*

Langdon's ecumenical vision for New England's religious future had an important political aspect. Implicit in the desire for cooperation among the Calvinist denominations was a growing fear that an Anglican bishop would be established over the colonies. Langdon worried that continuing disputes among New England's dissenting factions would only strengthen the Anglicans' designs. In 1764 the English revivalist George Whitefield informed Langdon of rumors that a secret conspiracy existed within the imperial government to deprive colonists of their religious and civil liberties. The subsequent publication of the Stamp Act and the appointment by the Crown of a Roman Catholic bishop to Canada confirmed Langdon's fears and reinforced his association between the threat of taxation without representation and the impending "plague" of an Episcopal bishop over New England. Langdon became the secretary of the Portsmouth Sons of Liberty, and over the course of the next decade he helped to organize New Hampshire's resistance to parliamentary encroachments on colonial liberties.

In 1774 the presidency of Harvard College fell vacant. Langdon's politics appealed to Harvard's leadership, including the treasurer, John Hancock (1737–1793). After several other candidates declined the position, Langdon was installed in October 1774 and presided over Harvard's difficult adjustment to the Revolution in New England. In 1775 the presence of the Continental army in Cambridge forced the college to evacuate to Concord. When the war moved south in 1776, the college returned to Cambridge, but order could not be restored easily. John Hancock departed for the Continental Congress in Philadelphia and took the college's accounts with him. Langdon and his colleagues in Cambridge could not persuade Hancock to attend to his duties as treasurer, nor could they muster the courage to remove the popular Hancock from office. As a result, the college's finances floundered. Langdon's administrative difficulties were compounded by his inability to discipline and instruct Harvard's young students. The students complained when Langdon abolished Sunday evening singing "to give more time for his harangue" and generally found him "disgusting . . . in his whole deportment." In August 1780 the oblivious Langdon was stunned when a group of

students informed him of their objections. Two days later he resigned. Evidence suggests that student opinion may have been manipulated by other college officers with designs against Langdon, but the source of Langdon's unpopularity remains obscure.

In 1781 Langdon returned to New Hampshire as a Congregational minister in Hampton Falls. Here he continued to preach sermons promoting Christian union and wrote several meditations on apocalyptic themes, including the lengthy *Observations on the Revelation of Jesus Christ to St. John* (1791). In 1788 he represented Hampton Falls in the New Hampshire convention to consider the proposed national Constitution. He played a leading role among the Federalists, and his election sermon of 5 June 1788, *The Republic of the Israelites an Example to the American States,* echoed his earlier themes of Christian union in calling for ratification. His ability to link the proposed Constitution's conciliatory powers with his own long-standing efforts to overcome religious divisions among Americans helped persuade a number of delegates to vote for ratification. Langdon died in Hampton Falls.

Although his brief tenure at Harvard remains the lasting source of his fame, Langdon's strength lay in his work as a minister and political advocate rather than as an administrator. From the parochial viewpoint of Harvard College, Langdon was a failure. But when viewed as a whole, Langdon's career demonstrates remarkable foresight and adaptability and a willingness to see America's denominational fragmentation as a sign of the country's energy and strength, requiring only a vision of unity to reconcile its divisive tendencies.

• Langdon's papers are in the Harvard University Archives, and his correspondence with Ezra Stiles can be found among the Stiles papers, Yale University; selections are printed in F. B. Dexter, ed., *The Literary Diary of Ezra Stiles* (3 vols., 1901). Langdon's career as Harvard president has been reviewed in Josiah Quincy, *History of Harvard University*, vol. 2 (1840), pp. 161–200; F. B. Sanborn's biographical sketch in *Massachusetts Historical Society Proceedings*, 2d ser., 18 (1905): 192–232; and Samuel Eliot Morison, *Three Centuries of Harvard* (1936), pp. 161–63. The most thorough biographical treatment of Langdon's career is Clifford K. Shipton's essay in *Sibley's Harvard Graduates*, vol. 10 (1958), pp. 508–28, which includes a complete listing of Langdon's publications. Langdon's participation in the movement for Christian union in New England is described in Douglas H. Sweet, "One Glorious Temple of God: Eighteenth-Century Accommodation to Changing Reality in New England," *Studies in Eighteenth-Century Culture* 11 (1982): 311–20.

MARK A. PETERSON

LANGDON, William Chauncy (19 Aug. 1831–29 Oct. 1895), Episcopal priest and pioneer ecumenist, was born in Burlington, Vermont, the son of John Jay Langdon and Harriet Curtis. In the second year of Langdon's life his family moved to Washington, D.C., where his father worked in the U.S. Treasury. As his New England family moved around the Old South, both for his mother's delicate health and his father's business ventures, young Langdon demonstrated intellectual and promotional precocity. His father was often absent, but several men took an interest in the boy—teaching, entertaining, and encouraging him. In New Orleans, at the age of ten, Willie learned to set type in a friend's printshop and "became a tolerable compositor." A play he wrote and published himself netted him more than $12, at 18.75 cents a copy. In Tuscaloosa several professors at the University of Alabama, including Frederick A. P. Barnard, awakened in the youth an enthusiasm for science.

In 1845–1846, at age fourteen, Langdon invented, published, and marketed card games illustrating English and American history. That project—"the most significant episode of my young life"—brought him to Boston, where relatives introduced him to leading literary figures. His great-uncle, the historian George Ticknor, arranged for a course in Vermont that would prepare the youth for Williams College and then Harvard. Langdon excelled academically and finished the four-year course in two years, but the headmaster, who had been his father's childhood enemy, found reason in some impetuous behavior to deny him a diploma. Langdon felt crushed and disgraced but not defeated. Through other connections he enrolled in April 1849 in Transylvania University at Lexington, Kentucky, and completed another four-year program in less than two years. His father's business failure ended all family support and accelerated Langdon's already obsessive fury to excel. After graduating second in his class in August 1850, Langdon taught astronomy and chemistry at Shelby College in Shelbyville, Kentucky, and was sent to the Naval Observatory in Washington, D.C., where Matthew Fontaine Maury helped him prepare for the mounting of a large telescope in Shelbyville.

The trip to Washington bore unexpected fruit. In May 1851 Jonathan H. Lane, who had taught Langdon briefly at the preparatory school in Vermont and was now a chief examiner in the U.S. Patent Office, offered him an appointment as assistant examiner. Langdon, not yet twenty years old, resettled in Washington with a good job and the prospect of a productive career. By 1855 he was a chief examiner. The next year he resigned to become a counselor in patent law.

To this point Langdon's career resembled that of many another young American "gentleman of science." Yet his passion for technology and scientific inquiry was matched with a fervent, evangelical, and ecumenical Christianity that befitted the son of an Anglican father and a Unitarian mother. Bishop Leonidas Polk had refused to confirm twelve-year-old Willie in 1843, but Bishop Nicholas H. Cobbs had made him a member of the Episcopal church two years later. Even then his mother's New England piety continued to guide young Langdon's life; he could recall "no distinctively churchly influence" until, at age nineteen, he began teaching Sunday School in Washington's Trinity Church. In the Reverend Dr. Clement Moore Butler, rector of Washington's Trinity Church, he found another valuable mentor who recognized in

Langdon a potential leader of the many young, single men who sought employment in Washington.

In April 1852 Butler handed Langdon a copy of the constitution of the Young Men's Christian Association, recently organized in Boston. With William Jones Rhees and some other young government workers Langdon founded the second local chapter of the YMCA in the United States on 29 June 1852, becoming its corresponding secretary. The New York chapter was organized the next day, and in the next two years the YMCA movement took root in cities throughout the United States and Canada. Even as he met the increasing demands of his patent office posts, Langdon campaigned tirelessly for a North American confederation of YMCAs and became general secretary of the new alliance at its first meeting in 1854. With Henri Dunant of Geneva he promoted a worldwide communication network among local chapters that bore fruit in an international Ecumenical Conference at Paris in 1855. In 1857, after leaving the patent office, Langdon traveled extensively in Europe to cement relations among the associations worldwide. Agnes Courtney, daughter of a "churchly" Baltimore family, had urged him to pursue a religious vocation from their first meeting in February 1852. By May 1856, after Courtney arranged a meeting with Bishop William Rollinson Whittingham, Langdon had committed himself to the church. He was ordained to the diaconate by Bishop Whittingham on 28 February 1858 and married Courtney two months later. They had one son.

Meanwhile, the "prayer meeting revival" that had swept American cities following a financial panic in 1857 was steering the YMCA away from its original mission to "young men" toward a mission of service to the entire community. In Langdon's eyes the YMCA was now doing the work of the church, if indeed it were not becoming a church. The Charleston, South Carolina, convention of 1858 reaffirmed the "true sphere" of the YMCA as "the formation and development of Christian character in young men," but the issue was revisited at Troy, New York, in 1859, and the now Reverend Langdon found himself, according to one observer, "like a lone sheep among three hundred ravenous wolves." Langdon, universally acknowledged to be "the most significant figure of the first decade" of the North American YMCAs, now withdrew from the organization.

During his tour of Europe in 1857 Langdon had observed that the conflict of "patriot elements" in Italy with the papacy would inevitably promote "a catholic reformation in the religious institutions of the land." Conversations with the aging diplomat and lay theologian Baron Christian von Bunsen confirmed these observations and "gave impulse and direction to my Italian policy from that time forward." Having severed his ties with the YMCA, Langdon now responded to the plea of American diplomats in Rome for an Episcopal priest to lead worship. With the support of Bishop Whittingham he organized Grace Church (later St.

Paul's Within the Walls) in the fall of 1859 and remained as a priest there for two years.

Italian church reform, Langdon believed, would lead to reunion of a tragically divided Christendom. He was especially concerned with the nascent agitations that, after 1870, would coalesce into the Old Catholic movement opposed to papal infallibility. The Anglican communion represented, he argued, a model of a worldwide church reformed on ancient "Catholic principles." He did not seek to convert Italians to the American Episcopal church, but rather "to fulfil[l] judiciously the office of a good conductor for the electric currents of Catholic thought and truth, with which I believed my own Church to have been divinely charged." Langdon returned to the United States in 1861, when he became rector of the Episcopal church in Havre de Grace, Maryland.

By 1865, no longer preoccupied with the American Civil War, the General Convention of the Episcopal Church was ready to organize a Joint Committee on the Religious Reform in Italy. Langdon returned to Italy in 1867 as foreign secretary of the committee and its offspring, the Italian Church Reformation Commission. He hoped to establish his headquarters in Florence but came into conflict with the eccentric anti-Catholic Pierce Connelly, now once more an Episcopal priest. Shortly after Langdon's arrival, Connelly formally organized an Episcopal chapel in Florence on his own initiative and otherwise attempted to sabotage Langdon's work among Catholic reformers. Langdon could report many successful contacts and practical efforts to aid the cause of Reform, but the decrees of Vatican I in 1871 drove the reformers toward open schism. Langdon worked in Rome in 1872, and in 1873 he became the first rector of Emmanuel Episcopal Church in Geneva, Switzerland, continuing to widen his communication with reform-minded Catholics in Europe.

After returning to the United States in 1875, Langdon served as rector of Christ Church in Cambridge, Massachusetts, and of St. James Church in Bedford, Pennsylvania, before starting a mission parish in 1890 in Providence, Rhode Island (where his son Courtney was a professor at Brown University). Reunion of Protestants and Catholics on "Catholic principles" remained his ruling passion. He instigated the Sociological Group, which became the League of Catholic Unity, to promote union among the Congregational, Episcopal, and Presbyterian churches.

Langdon brought a warmly received "ecumenical greeting" to open the YMCA international convention of 1895, renewing personal contact with his first and most successful ecumenical endeavor. Time had vindicated his vision of the YMCA's mission. But in that same year, after a decade of ecumenical correspondence with American Protestant denominations, the Episcopal General Convention declined to sponsor a "general conference" of the interested bodies or to initiate further contact. That decision was Langdon's final disappointment; he died nine days later in Providence. At his funeral on the Feast of All Saints, 1895,

more than thirty members of the clergy from eleven denominations honored Langdon's lifelong concern by sharing the Lord's Supper.

• The first and best source for Langdon's early life is an unpublished autobiographical memoir written for his children; a 126-page typescript is available in the YMCA Archives at the University of Minnesota. In his later career Langdon published more than a dozen polemic and apologetic tracts related to his Italian mission and ecumenical projects. Among the more significant of these are *Some Account of the Catholic Reform Movement in the Italian Church* (1868), *The Defects in Our Practical Catholicity* (1871), and *The Conflict of Practice and Principle in American Church Polity* (1882). On Langdon's mission in Florence and his conflict with Pierce Connelly, see Clement W. Walsh, "The Episcopal Church in Florence: A Tale of Two Beginnings," *Anglican and Episcopal History* 56 (Dec. 1987): 423–43. An obituary is in the *New York Times*, 30 Oct. 1895; Langdon's middle name is misspelled in this source.

DON HAYMES

LANGDON, Woodbury (c. 1739–13 Jan. 1805), merchant and judge, was born in Portsmouth, New Hampshire, the son of John Langdon and Mary Hall, successful farmers. Langdon attended the local Latin grammar school and as a young man went to work for Henry Sherburne, one of the leading Piscataqua merchants. He rose quickly to become a ship captain and then Sherburne's partner in business. In 1765 he married his partner's sixteen-year-old daughter, Sarah Sherburne. The couple had nine children. Langdon was building ships as well as trading and had become the fifth highest taxpayer in a community filled with wealthy merchants. He also was involved in imperial politics as an ally of Peter Livius, a recent arrival from England eager to replace Governor John Wentworth.

The coming of the Revolution disrupted Langdon's life. From the start he was ambivalent about the resistance movement. He opposed the Stamp Act in 1765 but refused to sign Portsmouth's resolves against the Tea Act eight years later. Elected to a variety of local committees, the New Hampshire General Court, and even to the revolutionary Provincial Congress, Langdon tried his best to moderate the actions of his associates, including his younger brother John. He continued trading to England after the Continental Congress forbade such activity and helped obtain blankets for British troops stationed in Boston. In late 1774, worried about escalating tensions, he retrenched economically by canceling all of his shipbuilding contracts. Langdon left for England the following September.

Little is certain about Langdon's activities for the next twenty-six months, except that he managed to confuse everyone about his political allegiance. While in England he played the Loyalist, although home officials suspected (probably correctly) that he helped organize trade with France, much of it through his brother John. By 1777 he was ready to return to America. Special pleading and probably bribery—Langdon had turned his English credits into liquid assets—gained him passage to New York. There he was imprisoned at the behest of his old nemesis, Governor Wentworth, but not confined. John Langdon attempted to arrange a prisoner exchange, but when that failed, the ever resourceful Woodbury managed to "escape" his nonconfinement. He was back in Portsmouth by the end of 1777.

Langdon never regained the affluence of his prerevolutionary days. The entire Piscataqua merchant community suffered as long as the war lasted, and only those with impeccable political credentials, like his brother John, managed to thrive. While in England Langdon had bought a share of the Masonian proprietorship. After his return he invested heavily in one of the towns it chartered but seems to have gained little from his effort. He speculated in soldier certificates without success. From the mid-1780s on he had difficulty meeting expenses. He sold his share of the proprietorship in 1795.

Meanwhile, largely through the sponsorship of his brother, Langdon became involved in state politics. In 1778 he was elected to the General Court and appointed as a delegate to the Continental Congress, only to lose both positions when critics, complaining about "late converts," engineered a recall. He helped his brother win the governorship in 1785. John in turn got Woodbury appointed to the Superior Court. The elder Langdon's attendance at sessions was so unpredictable that in 1790 the General Court impeached him. His brother once again came to the rescue, this time by obtaining a lucrative federal appointment for Langdon, who then resigned his state judgeship. After the impeachment, he ran several times for local and state office, twice gaining election to the General Court.

Langdon's style was ill suited to republican politics. Even his admirers—who appreciated his quick-witted incisiveness—considered him arbitrary and haughty. Langdon died in Portsmouth after a long illness.

• Few Langdon papers have survived; the largest number are scattered among collections at the New Hampshire Historical Society and the Historical Society of Pennsylvania. The Public Record Office in London has the original of a memorial Langdon wrote to Lord North in 1777, C.O. 5, vol. 115, folio 253. The best biographical sketch (untitled) is by William Plumer in *Early State Papers of New Hampshire*, ed. Albert S. Batchellor, vol. 21 (1892), pp. 812–15. Records of the impeachment and of Langdon's involvement with the Masonian proprietors are in vols. 22 and 29 of the same series. For coverage of his business and political activities, see Lawrence S. Mayo, *John Langdon of New Hampshire* (1937); Jere R. Daniell, *Experiment in Republicanism: New Hampshire Politics and the American Revolution, 1741–1794* (1970); and Lynn W. Turner, *The Ninth State: New Hampshire's Formative Years* (1983).

JERE R. DANIELL

LANGE, Alexis Frederick (23 Apr. 1862–28 Aug. 1924), educator, was born in Lafayette County, Missouri, the son of Alexander Lange and Caroline Schnegelsiepen. Lange entered the University of Michigan in 1882. In 1883 the university invited selected students about to become juniors, including Lange, to pursue a German university model of higher education, focusing on accelerated and advanced studies. Lange earned both his B.A. and his M.A. in 1885, concentrating in German, English, and Anglo-Saxon. From 1887 to 1888 he studied at the University of Marburg in Germany. Upon his return he became an instructor at the University of Michigan, initially in English (1888–1889) and then in German and Anglo-Saxon (1889–1890).

In 1890 Lange accepted an appointment as an assistant professor of English at the University of California, Berkeley. In 1891 he married Carolyn Crosby Penny. The following year he received his Ph.D. from the University of Michigan. From 1897 to 1900 he was a junior professor of English and then from 1900 to 1907, professor of English and Scandinavian philology. In 1901 he translated Johann Friedrich Herbart's *Outlines of Educational Doctrine* from the German, and in 1903 he edited *The Gentle Craft* by Thomas Deloney, a 1648 book extolling the craft of shoemakers.

From 1897 to 1909, Lange was dean of the College of Letters at California. During that time he reorganized the college, establishing a lower division with general education courses and an upper division focusing on specialized courses. He was dean of the Graduate Division from 1909 to 1910, at which time he organized graduate work into a disciplinary, specialized framework. From 1910 to 1913, he was dean of the faculties at the University of California.

In 1907 Benjamin Ide Wheeler, president of the university, convinced Lange to become head of the department of education. In 1913 he became director of the School of Education, the year of its organization, becoming the dean of the School of Education in 1922. In his role as a professor of education, he urged that schools use both lay control and expert leaders, thus providing an appropriate public administration of education, one reflecting his progressive ideals. He supported the reorganization of the California State Board of Education in 1913 as a lay board (previously it had been a committee of educators that included himself). He also suggested a form of public school financing, which the state eventually implemented. The financing structure included both a formula for minimal assessed valuation of property and state financing of schools, thereby providing equitable financing for schools throughout the state. While Lange was head of the School of Education, he focused the school on educating high school teachers.

By 1885 Lange was already advocating the separation of the first two years and the second two years of college education. By the early 1900s he was an advocate of the junior college, an institution he envisioned as offering the first two years of college work, providing intermediate professional preparation and educating large numbers of students in democratic virtues. His Michigan experience had taught him that secondary schools could offer baccalaureate level courses and universities could accelerate students' higher education. He and Stanford University president David Starr Jordan were instrumental in the development of the junior college movement in California, arguing that high schools could effectively offer the first two years of college.

Lange's vision of the secondary school, however, was not just an extension into college-level work. He also advocated beginning secondary school at the seventh grade, based on his conception of adolescence, thus creating an institution offering instruction in grades seven through fourteen. Lange saw adolescence as beginning in the early teenage years and extending to age twenty. In 1912 he served as chair of a statewide committee in California that argued for a secondary education beginning with seventh grade and ending with the second year of college. His dedicated work with the California Teachers Association gave him the opportunity to argue his ideas at the statewide level and to lobby California politicians. As a result of his efforts, Lange is an important figure in the history of the development of the junior high school and the junior college. He died in Berkeley.

• Lange's collected papers were published posthumously as *The Lange Book: The Collected Writings of a Great Educational Philosopher* (1927), ed. Arthur H. Chamberlain. Edward Gallagher has written several articles about Lange based on his doctoral dissertation, "From Tappan to Lange: Evolution of the Public Junior College Idea" (Univ. of Michigan, 1968). In addition, Steven Brint and Jerome Karabel discuss Lange's views on junior colleges in *The Diverted Dream* (1989).

PHILO A. HUTCHESON

LANGE, Arthur William (16 Apr. 1889–7 Dec. 1956), composer and arranger, was born in Philadelphia, Pennsylvania, the son of Max Lange, an inventor and brushmaker, and Marie Matterne, an accomplished pianist and teacher. His early music studies began with his mother at the age of five; later his father taught him the drums, and a neighbor instructed him on the violin. German was his predominant language until 1895, when he attended a local Lutheran school to learn English.

While working as a cashboy at the Wanamaker Department Store in Philadelphia in 1902, Lange joined the John Wanamaker Commercial Institute Symphony Orchestra as a violinist and cellist. In 1904 he relocated to New York City to work in Tin Pan Alley. Music publisher Charles K. Harris hired him as a switchboard-errand boy for $7.50 a week in 1905, but when Harris discovered him arranging melodies between phone calls, he was fired. Lange studied harmony with songwriter Steve Jones, using Jadassohn's *Manual of Harmony* as a text, and orchestration on his own.

In 1906 Lange joined J. W. Stern & Company as house arranger and pianist. One of his earliest assignments was to arrange for small ensemble Irving Berlin's first published song, "My Sweet Marie from Sunny Italy" (1907). For the next fifteen years Lange was immersed in Tin Pan Alley as a composer, arranger, song-plugger, and conductor for numerous publishing houses. Among the 200 songs he composed were the hits "On the Old Front Porch" (1913), "Virginia Lee"

(1915), "In the Sweet Long Ago" (1916), "America, Here's My Boy" (1917), and "In a Boat" (1921). In 1912 he married Charlotte Borrs; they had two children before divorcing in the early 1930s.

In 1917 he was paid $15 to make a "special arrangement" of Fred Fisher's "Dardanella," which catapulted Lange into the position of premier dance band arranger of the 1920s and revolutionized the music industry since it was the first "dance" arrangement not based on a vocal arrangement and then modified for dance. During the mid-1920s Lange was earning more than $25,000 a year preparing special arrangements for popular dance numbers and scoring Broadway shows; these songs included "Dream Girl" (1919), "Irene" (1919), "Helen of Troy" (1921), "Lulu" (1921), "Honeymoon Lane" (1927), and "Sidewalks of New York" (1928).

He also became an exclusive recording artist for the Cameo Record Company (1922), fronting his own dance band that later evolved into the Roger Wolfe Kahn Band when Lange was too busy to continue. In 1926 his pioneering book *Arranging for the Modern Dance Orchestra* was published by Robbins Music Corporation. It standardized commercial arranging and influenced countless musicians during the next two decades, including the young Glenn Miller and Benny Goodman.

When Hollywood motion pictures converted to sound in the late 1920s, the studios were in desperate need of arrangers and composers. At the request of Irving Thalberg, production chief of Metro-Goldwyn-Mayer Studios, Lange relocated to Hollywood in February 1929 to manage the MGM music department. Within days he realized there were more arranging, orchestrating, and copying chores than skilled employees, so he closed his New York office and brought the entire staff west.

During the two years that Lange was general music director at MGM, he arranged, scored, and recorded music for more than thirty feature films, including *Hollywood Review of 1929*, *Mariane* (1929), *The Mysterious Island* (1929), *The Rogue Song* (1930), *The New Moon* (1930), *Montana Moon* (1930), *Madame Satan* (1930), and *The Wonder of Women* (1929), a part silent–part talkie that required Lange to compose a short symphonic work to accompany the movie.

In May 1931 he became general music director of RKO-Pathe Studios and began to experiment with several new recording procedures that included elevating the roof of the soundstage, installing "adjustable flats" on the soundstage walls to vary the acoustical ambience, and prerecording vocals and music segments and then "dubbing" them later into the film track. This technique became known as the "Lange Process" in the trade journals of the day. However, on New Year's Eve in 1931, RKO closed the unprofitable Pathe Division, and Lange was dismissed. By late 1932 he joined Fox Studios and the following year became general music director for Fox. There he conducted most of Shirley Temple's early films, including *Stand Up and Cheer* (1934), *The Little Colonel* (1935),

Our Little Girl (1935), and *Rebecca of Sunnybrook Farm* (1938). In 1934 he married Marjorie Joesting. Later, at 20th Century–Fox, he continued as musical director for *Thanks a Million* (1935), *On the Avenue* (1937), and *Sally, Irene, and Mary* (1938). In 1936 he was loaned to MGM as music director for *The Great Ziegfeld*, which won the Academy Award for best picture. Unfortunately, no award for music director was given by the academy during those early years.

Lange's contract with 20th Century–Fox was terminated by mutual agreement in 1938, allowing him to freelance at higher fees. Soon afterward he arranged and directed the music for Paramount's *The Great Victor Herbert* (1939) and was nominated for an Academy Award. During the late 1930s Lange began to pursue his interest in serious composition, which dated to 1925 when he was the first to make dance arrangements, or "rhythmic paraphrases," of classical compositions. In 1937 Frank Black and the NBC Orchestra performed over network radio Lange's *Gosling in Gotham*, a large symphonic work that incorporated jazz elements. Other compositions included *Three California Tone Poems*, *Arabesque for Harp and Orchestra*, the *American Symphony*, *Atoms for Peace*, and the symphonic suite *The Fisherman and His Soul*.

In late 1938 he built a recording studio in his Hollywood home and established Co-Art Records, a small West Coast label specializing in unrecorded American music. In addition, Lange issued a monthly magazine, *Co-Art Turntable* (1941–1943), which featured articles on contemporary music and interviews with prominent composers and musicians of southern California. He also serialized his reminiscences of Tin Pan Alley in the publication. When Co-Art Records failed during World War II because of the shellac shortage and the recording ban imposed by James Petrillo, president of the American Federation of Musicians, Lange returned full time to the studios as music director for International Pictures, where he scored *Belle of the Yukon* (1944), *Casanova Brown* (1944), and *The Women in the Window* (1944). That same year he became president of the first West Coast branch of the American Society of Music Arrangers and editor of its monthly bulletin, the *Score*.

After World War II Lange continued to compose and became the founder and then conductor of the Santa Monica Symphony, which gave regular broadcasts over the Voice of America and the Armed Forces Radio Network during the early 1950s. He also taught private composition at the Los Angeles Conservatory of Music (currently the California Institute of the Arts) and completed a harmony book titled *A New and Practical Approach to Harmony*, which was published posthumously in 1958. During his career Lange worked as a composer or arranger on more than 143 known movies, but by the mid-1950s health problems had set in, particularly arthritis. He scored his last film in 1954 and died in Washington, D.C.

• Lange's manuscripts, scrapbooks, personal papers, and private recordings are at the New York Public Library for the Performing Arts. The Society for the Preservation of Film Music devoted the entire Dec. 1990 (vol. 7, no. 4) issue of its journal, the *Cue Sheet*, to Lange's career. An obituary is in the *New York Times*, 8 Dec. 1956.

LANCE BOWLING

LANGE, Dorothea (25 May 1895–11 Oct. 1965), photographer, was born Dorothea Margretta Nutzhorn in Hoboken, New Jersey, the daughter of Henry Nutzhorn, a lawyer, and Joanna (later Joan) Caroline Lange. When she was seven Dorothea contracted the polio that permanently damaged her right leg, leaving her with a lifelong limp. When she was twelve her father abandoned the family; his desertion and her disability helped to form her great capacity to identify with the outsider.

Faced with the task of supporting a family on her own, Dorothea's mother first became a librarian on the Lower East Side of Manhattan and then a social worker. Dorothea attended school in New York, where she became aware of the dispossessed and developed a detached but compassionate sense of observation as she passed through the Bowery on her way home. At the age of eighteen she announced to her family that she wanted to become a photographer and began a series of apprenticeships, among them with Arnold Genthe, then a fashionable society portrait photographer in New York. She also briefly attended classes at the Clarence White School of Photography, which met at Columbia University. She looked upon photography as a trade rather than as an art form.

With a friend, Florence Bates, Dorothea Lange, who by this time had taken her mother's name, left the East Coast in 1918 intending to go around the world, but on their first day in San Francisco they were robbed, and shortly thereafter Lange obtained a job working in a photo finishing business. There she met her lifelong friends, the artist Roi Partridge and his wife, photographer Imogen Cunningham, and determined to stay in the city. By 1919 she established her own studio specializing in portraits of the elite, culturally active families in town. The following year she met and married the artist Maynard Dixon, who was an illustrator of western subjects in the tradition of Frederic Remington. Dixon was a populist, a self-made man involved in the mythology of western individualism who wished to depict his chosen subject in an unsentimentalized, honest way. Dixon and Lange were married for fifteen years, and their union produced two children.

The 1929 stock market collapse affected the couple's professional and private lives: in 1931 they gave up their house, boarded their children, and lived not far from each other in their separate studios. There, with plenty of time on her hands, Lange observed life on the street. She later remembered: "One morning, as I was making a solio proof at the south window, I watched an unemployed young workman coming up the street. He came to the corner, stopped, and stood there for a little while. Behind him were the waterfront and the wholesale districts; to his left was the financial district; ahead was Chinatown and the Hall of Justice; to his right the flophouses and the Barbary Coast. What was he to do? Which way was he to go?" (Reiss, p. 144). Lange resolved to go into the street and photograph the historical moment she sensed was being enacted there. Probably drawn to explore what one woman, Lois Jordan, was doing to feed unemployed men at the docks, she made her first important documentary photograph, *The White Angel Breadline*, sometime in the winter of 1932–1933. The picture shows an older man in a stained hat, cradling a tin cup, leaning against a divider; it is at once compassionate and distant, sympathetic and respectful. Lange became aware of the restive labor activity around the docks and the scores of men, newly impoverished and often hopeless, sitting or standing around waiting for work or sleeping in the parks or in the streets. In 1934 Willard Van Dyke, a photographer, offered her a show of her documentary pictures at his small gallery in Oakland. It was seen there by Paul Schuster Taylor, a professor of agricultural economics at the University of California, Berkeley, who decided that her pictures would serve to complement and illustrate his research and writing on contemporary labor issues.

Taylor, by birth and education a midwesterner, held the Jeffersonian belief that the small farmer was the strength and insurance of the democratic system. Initially involved in the study of sailor's unions, he became interested in the specific issues of western agriculture, where corporate farming practices were causing labor problems through large numbers of seasonal migrant workers needed to tend the fields. It was a system radically different from the family farm tradition he had known in the Midwest. Their situation exacerbated by the depression as well as by years of poor land use, which resulted in the infamous "Dust Bowl," white tenant farm families were migrating into California with the hope of finding work and eventually land, only to find themselves the most recent migrant laborers in California's agribusiness. Taylor was hired by the Franklin D. Roosevelt administration's State Emergency Relief Administration (SERA) in the winter of 1934–1935 to study the migrant problem, and in February 1935 he hired Lange to help him document the pea harvest in Nipomo, California. He and Lange were married the same year; they had no children.

Taylor soon realized that Lange's work was an essential aspect of the reports he was preparing for the government, and, in fact, the illustrated reports may have helped establish the FSA (Farm Security Administration), an agency that she would work for briefly but prominently. Through her association with Taylor, Lange discovered the agricultural history of California, which because of its prominent tradition of agribusiness had hired racial groups as farm workers: the Chinese after the railroads were built, then the Japanese, East Indians, Filipinos, and Mexicans, as well as the single transient workers, called "bindle stiffs," often members of the Industrial Workers of the World (the so-called Wobblies). Lange photographed most of these groups but concentrated primarily on the newest

arrivals: families, mostly white, usually from Oklahoma, Texas, and Arkansas. She discovered, through Taylor, that agriculture in the large and prospering Central Valley area of California was actually an unregulated industry. Lange and Taylor used the indigent, white families to draw attention to the problem, hoping to effect change for everyone. Taylor continued to advocate the cause of family farming in the West for the rest of his life, even as the depression waned.

Lange and Taylor were certainly successful in bringing the condition of the immigrant farming families to local and national attention. In 1935 Lange transferred from the SERA position to the Resettlement Administration (RA), a part of the Department of Agriculture, and in 1937 was again transferred to the FSA (Farm Security Administration), where she worked under Roy Styker.

In 1936 Lange photographed a migrant woman from Oklahoma in the pea fields of Nipomo, near Santa Barbara. In her thirties, widowed, with seven children, the woman had sold the tires to her car for cash and with her children was subsisting off frozen peas in the field and birds the children caught. The *Migrant Mother*, as she has come to be known, became an icon for the FSA and symbolized to many the desperate conditions wrought by the depression. Lange, herself a mother, emphasized the Madonna-like aspect of the subject by concentrating on her concerned distraction and excluding the surrounding circumstance. The publication of this picture in the *San Francisco News* shortly after it was made led to immediate relief for the Nipomo camp and the speedy establishment of federal camps for the workers.

Lange and Taylor often traveled in the South, on assignment from the FSA, documenting the source and cause of the migrant immigration. Lange, sympathetic to the outsider and sensitive to the family as a metaphor of community, found many tenant families still farming the land with mules. She considered southern communities, though divided between black and white, to be culturally rich and operating meaningfully as communities. She was especially attracted to the black community, which, though deeply impoverished, had especially close family ties. Lange photographed women, particularly older women, with great sensitivity. One of them was *Ma Burnham*, whom she met in Arkansas and who embodied the change occurring in rural areas. Burnham said, "Then [before 1920] all owned their farms. The land was good and there was free range. We made all we ate and wore . . . . In 19 and 20 the land was sold and the money divided. Now none of the children own their land. It's all done gone but it raised a family" (*Dorothea Lange Looks at the American Country Woman*, p. 66). A powerful statement about the relationship of class and race was the photograph *Plantation Owner and His Field Hands*, made near Clarksdale, Mississippi, in July 1936. The casual, proprietary way the white man rests his foot on the car and the distance the black men keep from him eloquently describe the social structure of that place and time.

After America entered World War II, Lange was invited by the War Relocation Authority to photograph the controversial, racially motivated relocation of Japanese Americans from California into internment camps in the interior in 1942. She also took a particular interest in the Richmond shipyards, north of Berkeley, a boom town where her brother and oldest son held jobs. There she photographed the former Okies and Arkies, newly employed there, as well as many others recruited from the South. She recorded the energy she found there, the many different racial and ethnic groups, and also the women who were often working outside of their homes for the first time. She represented not the divisiveness that existed there, but the vitality and opportunity.

Although Lange suffered from severe and often debilitating illness from the early 1940s to the end of her life, she continued to pursue two ideas. The first was the transformation of rural communities. In 1940 she received a Guggenheim grant, which enabled her to document Mormon culture with her friend Ansel Adams and her son Daniel Dixon for *Life* magazine in 1955 and finally to work with Pirkle Jones on *Death of a Valley*, a project about the displacement of a rural California village to construct the Berryessa dam. Her other idea was to document the development of the new urban industrial society. The pictures of California postwar development, which she called "The New California," were part of this effort, as well as the energy she put toward developing "Project One," a proposed agency modeled on the FSA and dedicated to documenting city life in the way the conditions of rural living were recorded in the 1930s. She also followed Taylor as he worked for the Ford Foundation and the U.S. Information Agency studying rural agricultural community life in Egypt, South America, and Vietnam, among other places. She produced a great many subtle and moving pictures, which, however, lack the common thematic concerns of her American work. She and her son Daniel went on an extended tour of Ireland and produced an article, "Irish Country People," for *Life* magazine (21 Mar. 1955, pp. 135–43). She died in Berkeley three months before her first major retrospective exhibition at the Museum of Modern Art in New York in 1966.

Lange's work was made with the conviction that it would prove a useful tool in changing the attitudes of her fellow countrymen, that it could cause people to admire the best qualities of their poorer compatriots and help alleviate their suffering. Although she had a difficult time acknowledging the quality of "art" in her pictures, there is nevertheless in her best work a sensitivity to rhythm and pose (which one scholar has related to her disabled condition) and a monumentalizing sensibility, respecting the complex humanness of her subjects. In part, the monumental quality of her figures is the result of the judicious use of a twin-lens reflex camera, normally held at waist level, an instrument awkward enough to require the subject's

complicity to hold still. Lange's forms seem to dance across the picture plane in an ingeniously found choreography. The best of them acknowledge the complexity of the subject, avoid the sentimental, and are informed by the cultural conditions of the time and place in which they were made. She developed the documentary form of photography into a medium of vital visual information and great aesthetic significance.

• The Oakland Museum owns the Dorothea Lange archives, comprising papers, negatives, and some original prints. The Library of Congress has all FSA files, and the National Archives houses work made for the Bureau of Agricultural Economics, the War Relocation Authority, and the Office of War Information. There is also much useful original material at the Bancroft Library, University of California, Berkeley. Interviews with her include Suzanne Reiss, *Dorothea Lange: The Making of a Documentary Photographer*, Regional Oral History Office, Bancroft Library, University of California, Berkeley (1968), and those recorded by Philip Greene and Robert Katz (1962 and 1964) in preparation for the KQED films *Under the Trees* and *The Closer for Me* at the Oakland Museum. Every study of Lange must include notice of the first review of her work by Willard Van Dyke, "The Photographs of Dorothea Lange: A Critical Analysis," *Camera Craft* 41, no. 10 (Oct. 1934): 461–67. Her own books are *An American Exodus*, written with Paul Schuster Taylor (1939), and *Dorothea Lange Looks at the American Country Woman*, commentary by Beaumont Newhall (1967). A consideration of her early work in the context of the FSA is Edward Steichen, *The Bitter Years, 1935–1941: Rural America as Seen by the FSA* (1962), and the catalog of her first exhibition, *Dorothea Lange*, intro. by George P. Elliott (1966). The first thorough biography is Milton Meltzer, *Dorothea Lange: A Photographer's Life* (1978). See also Therese Thau Heyman, ed., *Celebrating a Collection: The Work of Dorothea Lange* (1978), with contributions by Daniel Dixon, Joyce Minick, and Paul Schuster Taylor. See also Heyman et al., *Dorothea Lange: American Photographs* (1994), and Elizabeth Partridge, ed., *Dorothea Lange: A Visual Life* (1994). For consideration of the form of documentary photography, see William Stott, *Documentary Expression and Thirties America* (1973); John Tagg, *The Burden of Representation: Essays on Photographs and Histories* (1981); and Carl Fleischhauer and Beverly W. Brannan, eds., *Documenting America, 1935–43* (1988). An obituary is in the *New York Times*, 14 Oct. 1965.

SANDRA SAMMATARO PHILLIPS

LANGE, Mary Elizabeth (?–1883), educator and founder of both the oldest Catholic school for African Americans and the first order of African-American nuns in the United States, the Oblate Sisters of Providence. The place and date of Lange's birth is unknown. Oral tradition says that she was born on the western part of the island of Saint Domingue (now Haiti). Born Elizabeth Lange, she was the offspring of mixed parentage and was a free mulatto. Her mother was Annette Lange; her father's name is unknown. The revolution on the isle of Saint Domingue coupled with the Napoleonic revolution forced the emigration of many natives; both black and white refugees fled to other parts of the Western Hemisphere. Lange arrived in the United States educated, refined, and fluent in French. When she first came to the shores of Maryland, she encountered major problems. She was a free person of color in a slaveholding state and spoke French in a country whose native tongue was English. She was a black Catholic and a single woman in a foreign male-dominated society. In spite of such difficulties, by 1828 Lange had established a school for children of color in Baltimore, St. Frances Academy, still in existence.

The French revolution also caused an influx of European Catholics into the United States. Among the immigrants was a group of priests known as the Sulpician Fathers. In Baltimore the fathers started a seminary for priests, a college for the laity, and a catechism class for black children. The priest in charge, James Marie Hector Nicholas Joubert de La Muraille, himself a refugee from Saint Domingue, needed someone to help him with the catechism classes. The problem was not doctrine but reading. In volunteering to teach the children to read, Lange also told Father Joubert of her desire to serve God as a religious. Because no such option was open to black women in 1828, the two decided to start a religious sisterhood for women of African descent. In a rented house at 5 St. Mary's Court, Lange began her new Catholic school. Her pupils consisted of eleven day scholars, nine boarders, and three nonpaying poor students who were called "children of the house." From the outset the curriculum was comparable to ones at private schools for white children. Music and the arts played a major role in the program of studies. Several students who graduated from the school eventually started private schools of their own. These endeavors took place where the average black person was still in slavery. In 1829 Lange and her three companions pronounced vows as Catholic nuns. Her name then became Soeur Marie, or Sister Mary. As superior general of the Oblate Sisters of Providence, Lange also became known as Mother Mary Lange.

Soon Lange began taking in homeless children, then widows. Expansion became necessary. Changes in the personnel of the church brought changes into the school and convent of the Oblate Sisters. The reigning archbishop, Samuel Eccleston, suggested that the black women give up the religious life and become good servants in the homes of Baltimore's elite. Lange refused to follow the archbishop's wishes. Poverty and hardship surrounded the infant community. The sisters took in washing, ironing, and sewing to support themselves and their orphans. Then a Bavarian priest, Thaddeus Anwander, asked to help Lange. At first the archbishop asked the priest, "What is the use?" Finally, after much insistence, the bishop gave Father Anwander permission to assist the Oblate Sisters of Providence. Students enrolled at St. Frances, more young black women entered the religious life, and in 1852 a school for African-American males was built. News of the sisters' work soon spread to other cities. The Oblate Sisters opened schools in other sections of Baltimore, including Blessed Peter Claver in Fells Point, St. Joseph's in South Baltimore, and St. Michael's on Lombard Street, as well as Blessed Peter Claver

School in Philadelphia, St. Joseph and St. Frances in New Orleans, Guardian Angel in Kansas, St. Elizabeth's in St. Louis, St. Ann's Academy and St. Augustine's in Washington, D.C., and a mission in Cuba, all in the nineteenth century.

Lange died in Baltimore, the city where she had defied the rules, where she succeeded in establishing an educational system for African-American youths, and where she brought into existence the first permanent African-American Catholic sisterhood. Mother Mary Lange, an immigrant, enriched American culture by enhancing the educational, spiritual, and social structure of nineteenth-century black America.

• Joubert's original diary, started by the priest and continued by the sisters after his death and covering 1828 to 1874, is in the Oblate Sisters of Providence Archives in Baltimore. A comprehensive collection of materials relating to the order, including correspondence, books, maps, and both general and specific information on the history of black Catholics in the United States, is housed at Josephite Fathers of the Sacred Heart, also in Baltimore. Several diaries and writings of the early Sulpician fathers are in the Sulpician Archives, Baltimore. See also Grace Sherwood, *The Oblates Hundred and One Years* (1931).

MARY REGINALD GERDES

LANGER, Susanne K. (20 Dec. 1895–17 July 1985), philosopher, was born Susanne Katherina Knauth in New York City, the daughter of Antonio Knauth, an attorney, and Else Uhlich. Her parents had emigrated from Germany. Susanne attended Veltin School, a private school only a few blocks from her home on Manhattan's West Side, and she was tutored at home. Throughout her youth, German was her primary language. Her childhood was rich with artistic exposure and development, especially in music. She learned to play the cello and the piano, and she continued with the cello for the rest of her life. Susanne acquired the habit of reciting the works of great poets as well as the traditional children's rhymes and tales. She also wrote her own poems and stories, mainly to entertain her younger siblings, and she was an avid reader. "In my early teens, . . . I read *Little Women* and Kant's *Critique of Pure Reason* simultaneously" (quoted in Sargent, pp. 90, 92). Her love of nature began during the summers her family spent in their cottage on Lake George.

Langer enrolled at Radcliffe College in 1916. She earned the bachelor's degree in 1920 and continued with graduate studies in philosophy at Harvard, where she received the master's diploma in 1924 and the doctorate in 1926. She was a tutor in philosophy at Radcliffe from 1927 to 1942. She lectured in philosophy for one year at the University of Delaware and for five years at Columbia University (1945–1950). She also taught philosophy at the University of Michigan, New York University, Northwestern University, Ohio University, Smith College, Vassar College, the University of Washington, and Wellesley College. In 1921 she married William Leonard Langer, a fellow student at Harvard who later became a prominent historian, and in 1921–1922 they studied in Vienna. They had two children; the couple divorced in 1942.

Langer's first book, recalling her childhood literary production, was *The Cruise of the Little Dipper and Other Fairy Tales* (1923). As early as 1924, Langer published articles in such prestigious journals as the *Journal of Philosophy* and *Mind*. Her first book in philosophy was *The Practice of Philosophy* (1930), with a prefatory note by Alfred North Whitehead. *An Introduction to Symbolic Logic* (1937) was one of the best of the early texts in the field. Published in 1942, *Philosophy in a New Key: A Study in the Symbolism of Reason, Rite, and Art* was a signal work in the ontology of absolute originations in experiences. The book quickly became a part of the canon in the history of ideas. For over half a century it has been a required text in graduate and undergraduate courses in philosophy, linguistic and critical studies, the arts and arts education, and the social sciences.

New Key demonstrated the influences on Langer's thought by two living philosophers. The first was her teacher at Harvard, Alfred North Whitehead, and the second was Ernst Cassirer, a German émigré from the Nazi regime. Cassirer was a neo-Kantian thinker who contributed to the field of theories of symbolization. In *New Key*, Langer argued that the making of symbols is the constitutive activity of art, myth, rite, the sciences, mathematics, and philosophy. She stated, "It is a peculiar fact that every major advance in thinking, every epoch-making new insight, springs from a new type of symbolic transformation" (p. 200).

Langer denied the rational/nonrational dualism that is usually ascribed to intellectual versus creative discourses. The wide recognition that *New Key* received (and rightly so) for being a work in aesthetics tends to overshadow the volume's progressivist articulation of a new empiricism, which is enriched in her work with a historical turning and openness to the complexities of actual experiences in creativity and invention. Gilles Deleuze once said of Whitehead that his thought had served to "reunite the two parts of Aesthetics so unfortunately dissociated: the theory of the forms of experience and that of the work of art as experimentation" (*Difference and Repetition*, p. 285). The statement aptly describes Langer's ideas as well, especially her arguments in *New Key*. In her belief that art theory must be interdependent with a theory of mind, she drew from Cassirer's view that Kant's critical epistemology should apply not only to questions about the conditions for reasoning and judgment, but also to the phenomenology of knowledge. She argued in *New Key* that artists engage in the Kantian apperceptive and critical ways of thinking when they create their works; artists, she said, disclose the realm of feeling rather than, as is often assumed, express their own emotions.

Langer's discussion of language was central to her study of symbol in *New Key*. She argued that language is complete, in the sense that all languages have histories that are generated by a universal psychological quality, the desire for expression. All cultures have experienced epochs of drastic change in their languages, sometimes over periods as rapid as a few generations. Before words and as the origination of meaning, there were the cries of ritual. Language, she believed, is not a set of symbols, nor is it mainly propositional; rather it is a function which contextualizes symbols into relationships among ideas. Its purpose is not utilitarian; its evolution and history, like that of the mind itself, have not been naturalistic, but have comprised occasions of sublime sensibility to new insights. Perpetual growth in language demonstrates the increasing liberty to "assign meanings" to life, work, and the metaphysical problems. She said that "the notion that the essence of language is the formulation and expression of conceptions rather than the communication of natural wants (the essence of pantomime) opens a new vista upon the mysterious problem of origins. For its beginnings are not natural adjustments, ways to means; they are purposeless lalling-instincts, primitive aesthetic reactions, and dreamlike associations of ideas that fasten on such material" (p. 118).

Langer concurred with Cassirer's argument that language gives birth to reason and to abstract thought. This claim reverses the positivists' view that language is primarily a behavior or a given set of signs, preceded in ontological importance and in evolutionary development, by the cognitive powers. She argues that "the mind, like all other organs, can draw its sustenance only from the surrounding world; our metaphysical symbols must spring from reality. Such adaptation always requires time, habit, tradition, and intimate knowledge of a way of life." And further, "the transformation of experience into concepts, not the elaboration of signals and symptoms, is the motive of language. Speech is through and through symbolic; and only sometimes signific" (pp. 291, 126).

Langer wrote *Feeling and Form: A Theory of Art* (1953) during her years at Columbia University. In this volume, she elaborated the themes of *New Key* by discussing the specific arts. Philosophically speaking, she postulated such concepts as a "created" and a "virtual" space through her discussions of painting, the dance, and film. She also reflected on the concept of time in her considerations of a "virtual memory" and a "virtual present." Her ideas about the unconscious, in *Feeling and Form* and in her other works as well, are similar to those of Søren Kierkegaard, Henri Bergson, and Deleuze in that she discerned the unconscious as ontological in nature rather than as a psychoanalytic object.

Langer published *Problems of Art*, a collection of her lectures, in 1957 and the edited collection, *Reflections on Art: A Source Book of Writings by Artists, Critics, and Philosophers*, in 1958. *Philosophical Sketches* (1962) introduced the ideas that were to be central in her three-volume work on the philosophy of mind. During the course of her career, she also published essays on world peace and on the philosophy of education.

In 1954 Langer joined the faculty at Connecticut College in New London, where she was a professor of philosophy until 1962. In 1956 she received a research grant from the Edgar Kaufmann Charitable Trust of

Pittsburgh and turned her attention full-time to writing, while sustaining her title and appointment at the college. In the later years, she occasionally taught classes to have intellectual feedback from students with regard to her research and ideas and sometimes to supply a course at the college's request. She worked in her home in Old Lyme, Connecticut, and she often went to her cabin in the woodlands of Ulster County, New York, to work in solitude and to enjoy hiking, canoeing, and camping. In 1961 she visited Japan, where she addressed the Japan Association for the Philosophy of Science.

Langer published *Mind: An Essay on Human Feeling* in three volumes (1967, 1972, 1982). The third volume was concluded in outline form because of Langer's advancing blindness and other health problems. An abridged edition (by Gary Van Den Heuvel, 1988) included a foreword by Arthur C. Danto. *Mind* is primarily a study of evolution. The human brain, argued Langer, is the condensation of many physiological ways of patterning in evolution. For the early humans, language was the phenotype of these complex patternings; the physiology of hand, posture, and central nervous system was the contingent material condition that enabled symbol making to begin in a conscious, enduring way. Once this process was actualized, she speculated, culture and humanization were very fast in coming. Humans were, in effect, fully human from the start.

Langer used a cross-disciplinary approach in her study of evolution. She garnered data from biology, the social sciences, and art as well as from philosophy. In a feature article about Langer in the *New York Times Book Review*, James Lord says of her broader conceptual purposes in *Mind*: "To challenge the existing boundaries of scientific thought! Not by chance, not by the single intuitive tour de force that is occasionally the happy experience of the laboratory scientist, but by the deliberate and rigorous, exercise of intellect" (p. 4).

Langer perceived a continuity among species. Much of the argument of *Mind* is that "feeling," and even the completions of "repertoires" of acts, was constitutive of even the earliest microbes. However, she did not regard the continuations of "feeling" across the span of evolution to consist of obedience to any a priori natural laws. In this, she disagreed with the behaviorists; today's sociobiologists would come under the same Langerian objection. She argued, for example, that animals do not have society or politics; there is no territory, competition, leadership, or goal such as survival except in humans. The instinctive repertoires in animals are best appreciated for their differences from the human for whom symbol making constitutes a transformation of much of the instinctual in animals.

In the philosophical debate on the question of freedom versus determinism, Langer's thought served the "interest" of ontological freedom. In *Mind*, she poignantly refuted two prominent theories about the nature of the mind, both of which are highly deterministic. The first theory is geneticism. Langer did not believe

that evolution is reducible to material units, first causes in an adaptive linear sequence of natural selection. She argued that evolution has been, rather, the process of organisms' making new and unforeseeable responses to one another and to such nonliving events as the elements, seasons, and habitat. The second of the two theories she refuted is cognitivism, the doctrine that consciousness is a projected rationalism, simulable in a totalized way. "Instead of trying to understand the mind as software for the brain," said Melvin Woody in a commentary on her thought at the time of her death, "she conceives of mental life as rooted in sentience, in the feelings that enable the simplest of organisms to adapt to its environment. Then she traces how the evolution of higher forms of life yields expanded awareness of the surrounding world."

Langer died at her home in Old Lyme. Thus far in our nation's history, there have been few great American philosophers, perhaps ten at the most. Interestingly, two of these, Hannah Arendt and Langer, were women. Although she was stubborn in her disavowal of feminism, still, for the women in an intractably male profession, Langer's accomplishments remain a source of pride and assurance. It would even be legitimate to appropriate her thought to feminism as the latter is sometimes defined in philosophy. Feminism is not understood in this case as an ideology about gender. Its meaning is closer to Whitehead's idea of an "event," and accords also with Langer's visionary proposal for philosophical discourses that would create new levels of thinking and indeed negotiate "transformations" in the destiny of values.

Langer contributed to an extraordinary number of areas of philosophy, including philosophy of language, metaphysics, ethics, philosophy of biology, epistemology, aesthetics, theories of creativity, philosophy of mind, and philosophical psychology. Social and political themes also are evident in her texts. As an example of these, one can consider her arguments against the reification that, she believed, afflicted those philosophies of the mid-twentieth century which claimed that common sense was their basis: reification of sense data, of semantic meanings, of the cycle of stimulus and response, of the narrative mode of expression, of motivation and desires, of cognitive faculties.

Langer's distinctive methodology is itself a topic worthy of investigation. Her methods were powerful in their melding of her transcendental understanding of time, movement, and mentation to her poststructuralist interrogation of discursive localities, of nature and life, and of the differences to be constituted in the future. Regarding the two philosophical areas in which she has received the most acknowledgment, namely aesthetics and philosophy of creativity, Langer changed their very directions of inquiry, making them contemporary in their significance, more expansive and inherently originative.

• Langer bequeathed her papers to the Houghton Library, Harvard University, and her library to Connecticut College,

New London. A complete bibliography of primary and secondary sources by and about Langer is by Rolf Lachmann in "Der Philosophische Weg Susanne K. Langers (1895–1985)," *Studia Culturalogica* 2 (1993): 65–114. Meaningful appraisals of her life and thought are in Winthrop Sargent, "Philosopher in a New Key," *New Yorker*, Dec. 1960, pp. 71–96; and in James Lord, "A Lady Seeking Answers," *New York Times Book Review*, May 1968, pp. 5, 32. See also Gilles Deleuze, *Difference and Repetition* (1994). An obituary is in the *New York Times*, 19 July 1985, and a "Commentary" by J. Melvin Woody on the occasion of her death is in *The Day* (New London, Conn.), 28 July 1985.

CONNIE C. PRICE

LANGER, William (30 Sept. 1886–8 Nov. 1959), governor and U.S. senator, was born in Casselton, Dakota Territory, the son of Frank Langer, a homesteader and later a state legislator, and Mary Weber. In 1906 he received an LL.B. from the University of North Dakota but was legally too young to practice law. He also received a B.A. in 1910 from Columbia University, where he was senior class president and valedictorian. After failing in a Mexican land venture, in which he was almost killed by revolutionaries, and losing $34,000 of his father's money, he joined a law firm in Mandan, North Dakota.

While serving as assistant state's attorney and then state's attorney for Morton County from 1914 to 1916, Langer, the "boy prosecutor," won local fame by successfully prosecuting the Northern Pacific Railroad, Standard Oil, and the Occidental Grain Elevator Company—all for unpaid taxes. He was elected state attorney general in 1916 and reelected two years later. Langer entered office as a Republican backed by the agrarian Nonpartisan League (NPL). He strictly enforced prohibition, compulsory school attendance, and blue laws. In a vice crackdown in the town of Minot, he seized the telephone exchange at gunpoint to prevent a tip-off to criminals. When the United States entered World War I, he became legal adviser for the state Council of Defense, in which capacity he protected North Dakota's German Americans from local harassment. In 1918 he married Lydia Cady, daughter of a prominent New York City architect. They had four children.

In 1919 Langer broke with the NPL, accusing its leadership of being too dictatorial and of promoting "socialism and free love." With the support of the conservative Independent Voters Association, he entered the Republican gubernatorial primary in 1920 but lost to incumbent and NPL member Lynn Frazier.

In 1920 Langer returned to a prosperous law practice in Bismarck. Though he held no elective office for the next dozen years, he was appointed to the North Dakota parole board and the board of equalization, and he headed the state's board of health. Making an unsuccessful primary bid for attorney general in 1928, he rejoined the NPL, converting it in time into his own personal political machine.

In 1932, running as a Republican, Langer was elected governor by a landslide. During his campaign he attacked unjust grain-grading, the grain trade monopoly, heavy state expenditures, and corruption in banks, insurance companies, and state government. As in all his statewide campaigns, he was supported strongly in the western part of the state, which had been victimized by sparse rainfall, while pulling less support in the Red River valley and in the cities. In 1933 he proclaimed an embargo on wheat shipments from the state, a measure declared illegal the following year by the federal courts. Trying to ease his constituents' burdens during the depression, he imposed a moratorium on farm mortgages and renters' and small business debts, and he called out the National Guard to prevent foreclosures.

Soon thereafter Langer was charged with "conspiracy to obstruct the orderly operation of an Act of Congress." Indicted by a federal grand jury, Langer was found guilty of forcing state employees to buy subscriptions equal to 5 percent of their salary to the *Leader*, the NPL's newspaper. On 29 June 1934 federal judge Andrew Miller sentenced Langer to eighteen months in the federal penitentiary at Leavenworth and fined him $10,000. While out on bail, he told his constituents that he was "prepared to pay the penalty for being [their] friend." When Lieutenant Governor Ole Olson pointed out that a convicted felon could not hold office, Langer declared martial law, called out the National Guard, and barricaded himself in his office. When the state's adjutant general ruled against him, he finally vacated. That fall the NPL ran Langer's wife for the office. Though Lydia Langer did surprisingly well, she lost the race. A subsequent trial, ordered after he won his appeal, resulted in a hung jury, and on 19 December 1935 a circuit court of appeals found Langer innocent of all charges at his third trial.

In 1936 Langer—running in a three-way race as an independent with NPL backing—was again elected governor. This time opponents pointed to shady state bond transactions and faculty dismissals at North Dakota Agricultural School, while supporters praised his moratoriums on crops and farm eviction. In 1938 he ran for the Senate as an NPL-backed independent but lost to incumbent Gerald P. Nye.

Entering in another three-way Senate race in 1940, this time as a regular Republican supported by the NPL, Langer polled 40 percent of the vote and was elected. In the campaign he endorsed rural electrification, higher price supports for wheat, old-age pensions, and cancellation of feed and seed loans. His opponents brought a host of charges before the Senate Committee on Elections and Privileges, sometimes repeating past accusations, sometimes interjecting new claims such as jury tampering, bribery, and perjury. Though Langer was temporarily seated "without prejudice," the committee submitted a 4,194-page report after which, on 16 December 1941, it ruled thirteen to three that Langer had demonstrated a "continuous, contemptuous, and shameful disregard for public duty." On 27 March 1942, however, the Senate itself overturned its own committee fifty-two to thirty, thereby permitting Langer to retain his seat. Many senators reasoned it was imprudent to question a colleague's past or the will of a state's voters.

In the Senate "Wild Bill" Langer was a maverick par excellence. A large man, six feet tall and weighing two hundred pounds, Langer was best known in the Senate for his frequent and lengthy filibusters, which he delivered in a curious whistling tone, watched in half-bemused, half-fearful amazement by his colleagues. Though formally remaining a Republican, he backed Harry S. Truman for president in 1948 and Adlai E. Stevenson in 1952. But in 1956, when the NPL filed in the Democratic column, Langer broke with his long-time supporters to endorse the reelection of Dwight D. Eisenhower. Yet he never lost popularity with the voters; he won reelection in 1946, captured all counties but three in 1952, and won every county in 1958. In the 1958 race he was too ill to return home to campaign and instead reached voters via a television clip, "A Day in the Life of Senator Langer." When the Republicans gained control of Congress in 1953, he became chairman of the Senate Judiciary Committee. After his wife's death in April 1959, he declined rapidly. He died in Washington, D.C.

An arch-liberal in domestic policy, Langer sought high price supports for farmers, rural electrification, retirement benefits for postal workers, and relief for aliens. He strongly opposed the Internal Security Act of 1950. In foreign affairs he was an outspoken, even flamboyant, isolationist. Bipartisanship, Langer maintained, deprived Americans of any voice in matters of war and peace. He opposed the interventionist legislation of Franklin D. Roosevelt in 1941 and two years later accused the president of leading the country into war. In 1945 he called the collective security proposals of Dumbarton Oaks an "international dope dream" and warned that it would freeze a reactionary status quo. He was one of only two senators to oppose ratification of the United Nations charter, claiming that its adoption would mean "the enslavement of millions of people from Poland to India, from Korea to Java." Instead, he said, there should be a federation of four regions, each possessing a common government, army, currency, and economy. The logical hubs included the United States, the Soviet Union, China, and Brazil; these alone, he believed, had the resources to survive independently.

Langer scorned Truman's Cold War policies and opposed aid to Greece and Turkey, the Marshall Plan, the North Atlantic Treaty, and all conscription proposals. In 1948 he called for an "American Recovery Plan" that would rechannel aid slated for Europe to farm supports, education, reclamation, and pensions. In March 1951 he sought withdrawal of U.S. ground forces from Korea, but in June 1953 he assailed America's allies for opposing action beyond the Yalu River.

Eisenhower's election made little difference to Langer. When in 1954 the president sought a congressional resolution committing the United States to the defense of Formosa, Langer unsuccessfully sought an amendment that would forbid the use of American troops on the Chinese mainland, Quemoy, or Matsu.

A year later, in casting the lone vote against the South East Asia Treaty Organization, Langer warned that some "trigger-happy, war-mongering fascist" president might commit American troops to the "swamps and jungles" of Southeast Asia. Throughout his time in the Senate he continually called for negotiation with mainland China and the Soviet Union.

An outspoken Anglophobe, in 1945 Langer referred to the British Empire as fascist. In 1951 he cabled the vicar of Boston's Old North Church requesting the re-enactment of Paul Revere's warning, namely the hanging of two lanterns in the belfry to warn Americans against Prime Minister Winston Churchill's impending visit.

One exception to Langer's isolationism involved Germany, whose advancement he continually promoted. Ever mindful of his German-American constituency, he opposed the unconditional surrender, the denazification, and the dismantling of war plants. Early in 1936, when Germany was experiencing mass starvation, Langer accused the administration of engaging in "a savage and fanatical plot" to destroy fifteen million women and children. In 1949 he said that "the whole cause of human freedom . . . in Europe, as well as in Asia" depended on Germany.

• Langer's papers are located in the Charles Fritz Library, University of North Dakota. For a favorable comprehensive account, see Agnes Geelan, *The Dakota Maverick: The Political Life of William Langer Also Known as "Wild Bill Langer"* (1975). Glenn H. Smith, *Langer of North Dakota: A Study of Isolationism, 1940–1959* (1979), offers a more analytical picture. Scholarly articles include Lawrence H. Larsen, "William Langer: A Maverick in the Senate," *Wisconsin Magazine of History* 44 (Spring 1961): 189–98, and Robert P. Wilkins, "Senator William Langer and National Priorities: An Agrarian Radical's View of American Foreign Policy, 1945–1952," *North Dakota Quarterly* 42 (Autumn 1974): 42–59. An obituary is in the *New York Times*, 9 Nov. 1959.

JUSTUS D. DOENECKE

LANGER, William Leonard (16 Mar. 1896–26 Dec. 1977), historian and educator, was born in Boston, Massachusetts, the son of Charles Rudolph Langer, a florist, and Johanna Rockenbach, a dressmaker. Reared in a Moravian family, Langer received his A.B. in modern languages from Harvard University in 1915. The same year he began his teaching career at Worcester Academy. With the entry of the United States into World War I, he enlisted in the army and served in the First Gas Regiment as a master engineer. He participated in military engagements at St. Mihiel and Argonne. With the end of the war he published a history of gas weapons originally titled *With "E" of the First Gas* (1919), reissued as *Gas and Flame in World War I* (1965). The obvious failure of European diplomacy sharpened Langer's interest in international issues, and he returned to Harvard, receiving an M.A. (1920) and a Ph.D. (1923) in history. During his graduate school years he studied for a time in Europe. In 1921 he married Susanne Knauth; they had two children.

Clark University offered Langer an appointment as assistant professor of history in 1923. In 1927 he moved to Harvard's history department. Over the years he also had visiting positions at Columbia, Tufts, and Yale, among others. In 1936 he was appointed the Archibald Coolidge Professor of History (named for his revered Harvard mentor) and remained as such until his academic retirement in 1964. Archibald Coolidge was an especially significant role model to Langer because he had served as an adviser to President Woodrow Wilson's "Inquiry" in preparation for the Versailles Treaty negotiations. Langer too functioned as both scholar and government consultant during World War II. He was chief of research and analysis for the Office of Strategic Services (OSS) from 1942 to 1945 and special assistant to the secretary of state in 1946. In that same year he received recognition with the awarding of the OSS Medal for Merit. He was assistant director of National Estimates for the CIA from 1950 to 1951. His marriage to Suzanne Knauth ended in 1941, and in 1943 he married Rowena Nelson.

Langer was also influenced by his mentor, Coolidge, in his association with the Council on Foreign Relations and the council's journal, *Foreign Affairs*, which Coolidge edited. Langer assisted the journal in various capacities, as editor, book reviewer, and bibliographer. His recognized expertise and scholarship in European history led to his appointment as director of the Russian Research Center at Harvard from 1954 to 1959. From 1961 to 1969 he was again called to government service on the president's Foreign Intelligence Advisory Board. He became a trustee of the Carnegie Endowment for International Peace in 1969 and served until 1973.

Langer's first important book was *European Alliances and Alignments* (1931), a study of the evolution of the nation-state system and the role of Bismarck in building the balance of power. His *The Diplomacy of Imperialism* (1935) carried the influence of the European system worldwide in a dynamic interaction with distant societies and cultures. He also edited a long-running series, The Rise of Modern Europe, which brought together talented historians who presented a rich and comprehensive cross section of European culture and history. His own contribution, *Political and Social Upheaval, 1832–1852* (1969), was one of his most distinguished books. World War II inspired three significant works: *Our Vichy Gamble* (1947), a book supportive of Secretary of State Cordell Hull's controversial diplomacy with Marshal Pétain; with S. Everett Gleason, *The Challenge to Isolation: The World Crisis of 1937–1940 and American Foreign Policy* (1952); and, also with Gleason, *The Undeclared War, 1940–1941* (1953), written at the urging of the Council on Foreign Relations to argue in favor of postwar internationalism. The last volume received the Bancroft Prize in history.

In 1957 Langer was chosen president of the American Historical Association. Although his career specialty was European diplomatic history, Langer's presidential address, "The Next Assignment" (*American Historical Review* 63 [Jan. 1958]: 283–304), urged his fellow historians to adapt the modern disciplinary theories and techniques of psychology to the methodologies of history for more insight into historical causation.

Influenced by the work of his brother Walter Langer, who in 1943 had compiled a dossier on Adolf Hitler for psychological warfare purposes at the behest of the State Department, William Langer reached the conclusion that the historian could no longer ignore the findings of psychology. Historians must not only establish the facts of the past but also understand individual and group motives and reactions in their historical contexts. Two decades later, Langer remained committed to the psychohistorical interpretation of history. Citing the work of Erik Erikson on Martin Luther as a primary example of psychobiography, Langer encouraged American historians to engage in similar studies of Karl Marx, Napoleon, and Giuseppe Mazzini.

Langer also urged historians to investigate groups and mass actions in history using the insights of social psychology. He called for the applications of Freudian and humanistic theories of psychology to lay bare the unconscious and irrational elements in human personality while maintaining an appreciation of man as a free agent. Langer's own research on this topic focused on the collective psychology of Europeans during the bubonic plague of the fourteenth century, a watershed period in socioeconomic and political development. Langer never argued that psychology or psychohistory could explain the cause of all past human problems. Rather he hoped to add another methodology for greater insight into the human experience worldwide and across the ages.

A traditional diplomatic historian of the realist school who emphasized narrative history, William Langer was a pioneer in defining European history as a specialty field in the United States, and a revolutionary in the application of psychological causation to historical events and mass movements. Langer died in Cambridge, Massachusetts.

• Langer's personal papers are in the Harvard University Library Archives. In addition to the works mentioned in the text above, he published *The Franco-Russian Alliance, 1890–1894* (1967), another analysis of the nineteenth-century European balance of power, and *Explorations in Crisis: Papers on International History* (1967), a far-ranging volume on international relations, psychohistory, demographics, and epidemiology. Langer edited many books, including *Perspectives in Western Civilization: Essays from* Horizon (1972); *An Encyclopedia of World History*, 5th ed. (1973); *Western Civilization* (1975); and, with Oron J. Hale, *Great Illusion, 1900–1914* (1971). The posthumously published *In and Out of the Ivory Tower: The Autobiography of William L. Langer* (1977) recounts his childhood recollections and his personal and professional accomplishments. Obituaries are in the *New York Times*, 27 Dec. 1977; *Proceedings of the Massachusetts Historical Society* 89 (1977): 187–95; and *American Historical Review* 83 (Oct. 1978): 1150–52.

SALVATORE PRISCO

LANGFORD, Nathaniel Pitt (9 Aug. 1832–18 Oct. 1911), diarist, vigilante, and park superintendent, was born in Westmoreland, Oneida County, New York, the son of George Langford II, a bank cashier, and Chloe Sweeting. After an education in a rural school, young Langford migrated with four of his siblings to St. Paul, Minnesota, in either 1853 or 1854, and followed his father's career, clerking in several banks.

Like many Midwesterners of his day, Langford suffered from fevers and agues and in 1862 decided to go west to improve his health. He not only joined the Northern Overland Expedition, headed for the goldfields of Idaho's Salmon River country, but also demonstrated sufficient leadership for Captain James L. Fisk to appoint him his second assistant and commissary, or third in command. Some 1,600 miles from St. Paul, most of the company wintered in the Prickly Pear Valley. Langford and a few others pushed on, not to Idaho but to the isolated outpost of Bannack in present-day Montana. Gold had been discovered in there in 1861, 400 miles from the nearest settlement. News of the "strike" reached the East and Midwest in late 1862, and by the end of the year and the spring of 1863 thousands of argonauts were hurrying to Bannack or to nearby Virginia City, where Langford relocated that year.

In its early years the area experienced more than a hundred acts of violence, mostly robberies but some homicides, and a number of miners, most or all of them Masons, copied the example of San Francisco in 1849, 1851, and 1856 and formed a committee of vigilance to bring order to a lawless area still without police or judges. Langford served on the executive committee of the Montana vigilantes. His 1890 two-volume reminiscence, *Vigilante Days and Ways (The Pioneers of the Rockies* and *The Makers and Making of Montana, Idaho, Oregon and Washington)*, was a popular book that has become a sort of regional classic in the literature of the northern Rocky Mountains and the Pacific Northwest. Although the author was still secretive about "Judge Lynch" thirty years after the application of lynch law to Montana and refused to name his vigilante colleagues, the book was reprinted (as a single volume) in 1893, 1895, 1912, 1957, 1971, 1973, 1981, and 1996. Langford's vigilantes brought to justice the notorious gang of outlaws headed by the crooked sheriff Henry Plummer, whom they hanged in Bannack on 10 January 1864.

Montana became a U.S. territory in 1864 and Langford accepted the appointment of U.S. collector of internal revenue. During Andrew Johnson's stormy term of office, Langford was twice removed from his post by the president because of political differences but, both times, was reinstated by the Senate, and he served till 1868. In a turnabout of December of that year, President Johnson appointed Langford governor of Montana Territory, but the Senate declined to confirm his appointment.

Langford is best known for his role in the early history of Yellowstone National Park. He was one of the first (after John Colter and other early mountain men

or beaver trappers) to describe the geological wonders of the Yellowstone country. He ventured into the area, still occupied by Indians unfriendly to white trespassers, after David E. Folsom told him and a few other friends of what he had seen with the Folsom-Cook Expedition of 1869 before it was driven from the area by hostiles. General Henry D. Washburn organized a nineteen-man company with the aid of Langford, Lieutenant Gustavus C. Doane, and Judge Cornelius Hedges. The explorers left Helena, Montana, on 17 August 1870 and made the first detailed examination of the Yellowstone district. All four leaders kept diaries that were eventually published, but the most complete and best-written account was Langford's *Diary of the Washburn Expedition to the Yellowstone and Fire Hole Rivers in the Year 1870* (1905). It was retitled *The Discovery of Yellowstone Park* in reprint editions, such as that of 1978 with a foreword by Aubrey Haines, because Langford not only printed his diary but reviewed the history of the area's exploration and the concept of a national park there, refuting the claims of partisans of Ferdinand V. Hayden for honors in this regard.

Folsom and Hedges, as well as Langford, suggested that the Yellowstone region be made into the country's first national park. Indeed, for years it was said that the judge came up with the idea while sitting with Langford and others around an 1870 Yellowstone campfire. But this tale has been discredited by historians and it is Langford, not Hedges, who is considered to be the "father of Yellowstone National Park." It was Langford's skill as a lecturer, lobbyist, and writer that initially sold Congress on the idea, especially his May and June 1871 articles in *Scribner's*. The soundness of his ideas was confirmed by Hayden's Yellowstone explorations of 1871–1872 and the publicity given the area by the works of two of Hayden's aides, the watercolor paintings of Thomas Moran and the dazzling photographs of William H. Jackson. Langford did not accompany Hayden but made another expedition of his own with James Stevenson. They went into country not pictured by Moran and Jackson, exploring the Teton Range and climbing Grand Teton on 28 July 1872. (A later climber with political clout, Rev. Clarence Spencer, persuaded the Wyoming legislature to acclaim him as the first conqueror of the peak because Langford left no proof of his ascent.) Langford and Stevenson then swung into the park proper via today's western entrance.

Langford's key role in Yellowstone, and thus in the eventual system of national parks, was recognized by his appointment as the park's first (unpaid) "commissioner" or superintendent. (Yellowstone was actually administered by the U.S. Army's engineers until the National Park Service took charge in 1916.) Yellowstone was the high point in Langford's career, but he held other Montana offices until 1884. He had married Emma Wheaton in 1876 and after her death married her sister, Clara, but he had no children. By 1885 he was back in St. Paul, where he reentered business. He continued with historical research and writing and was active in the historical societies of both Montana and Minnesota, serving as president of the latter organization from 1905 till his death in St. Paul. (His death date is sometimes given as 1909 because of an error by historian Aubrey Haines.) His most important contribution to historical journals was his study of the Louisiana Purchase in *Collections of the Minnesota Historical Society*, vol. 9 (1900).

• Langford's papers are at the Minnesota Historical Society in St. Paul and at the Montana Historical Society in Helena. A brief account of his life appears in Dan L. Thrapp, *Encyclopedia of Frontier Biography*, vol. 2 (1988), and in the introduction by Dorothy M. Johnson to the 1957 reprint edition of *Vigilante Days and Ways*. He is, of course, mentioned in Thomas J. Dimsdale, *Vigilantes of Montana* (1915); Hiram Chittenden, *The Yellowstone National Park* (1964); and Aubrey Haines, *Yellowstone National Park, Its Expeditions and Establishment* (1974). For general information on Langford's Yellowstone, see Chittenden, especially Richard A. Bartlett's introduction, and Bartlett, *Nature's Yellowstone* (1974). Obituaries are in the *St. Paul Dispatch*, 18 Oct. 1911, and the *St. Paul Pioneer Press*, 19 Oct. 1911.

RICHARD H. DILLON

LANGFORD, Samuel (4 Mar. 1883–12 Jan. 1956), boxer, was born at Weymouth Falls, Nova Scotia, Canada, the son of Robert Langford, a poor black river driver, and Priscilla Robart. He received no formal education, left home at the age of twelve after quarreling with his father, and arrived in the United States on a lumber schooner in 1899. He drifted about New England for several years, working mostly as a stevedore. While panhandling in Boston, he met Joe Woodman, a druggist and small-time boxing promoter. Woodman hired him as a janitor at his gymnasium, and he later became a sparring partner and amateur boxer before making his professional debut in April 1902. He was managed by Woodman until 1919.

Weighing only about 140 pounds at the outset of his boxing career, Langford advanced rapidly. By the end of 1903 he had already defeated lightweight champion Joe Gans and fought the great Jack Blackburn. In 1904 he twice held Blackburn to draws, defeated Willie Lewis and George McFadden, and fought a draw with welterweight champion Joe Walcott. In 1905 he suffered his first serious defeat at the hands of heavyweight Joe Jeannette but defeated Blackburn, George Gunther, and Young Peter Jackson. After beating Jeannette in a return bout, Langford engaged future world heavyweight champion Jack Johnson at Chelsea, Massachusetts, on 26 April 1906 in perhaps the most important bout of his career. Johnson, thirty pounds heavier and much taller, won decisively, but after Johnson won the heavyweight title in 1907, Woodman effectively spread the word that Langford had actually had the better of their fight. For years this story was used unsuccessfully to pressure Johnson into defending the heavyweight title against Langford, but it did have the effect of making Langford famous and seemingly too dangerous for Johnson to fight again.

Langford was at the peak of his career from 1907 to 1912. Although weighing only 165 to 170 pounds, he defeated many outstanding heavyweights and traveled throughout the world to find and meet opponents. At this time few white boxers in the United States would fight blacks, and Langford had to meet several tough opponents many times. Langford fought two black rivals, Jeannette and Sam McVea, a dozen or more times each, usually winning. Two white heavyweights who would fight him were Jim Barry and Jim Flynn; he fought Barry twelve times, losing only once, and defeated Flynn twice in their three meetings. In 1911 he knocked out former light-heavyweight champion Philadelphia Jack O'Brien. Langford traveled to Europe in 1907, 1909, and 1911 and knocked out British heavyweight champion William "Iron" Hague. He fought in Australia from December 1911 to May 1913 with great success.

Langford, nicknamed the "Boston Tar Baby," was a powerfully built, muscular fighter. His shoulders were extremely broad, and his arms were unusually long. Only 5'8" tall, Langford fought aggressively, stalking his foe and throwing short, powerful punches with both hands to head and body. Contemporary descriptions depict him as sleek, pantherlike, and graceful, one of the most impressive fighters in ring history.

Langford is the subject of many legends and stories. He was good-natured and witty. His wit, combined with his awesome reputation, sometimes enabled him to demoralize an opponent with a single remark before the fight even began. It was often said that Langford allowed opponents to stay the distance with him so he could fight them again, but an examination of his record indicates that this could hardly have been true because he won most of his fights by knockout at the peak of his career, and those opponents that he could not knock out were especially formidable.

One of Langford's most interesting fights was a six-rounder in 1910 with the great middleweight champion Stanley Ketchel. This was one of the few times that Langford fought a lighter and faster foe. No official decision was given, but newspaper reporters who witnessed the fight divided about evenly between those who thought Ketchel had won and those who thought it was a draw. Some suggested that Langford held back, but there is no evidence to support this claim.

From 1913 to 1922 Langford, now a heavyweight, declined in his prowess but was still a dangerous opponent. It was in this period that his celebrated series with the much larger Harry Wills took place. They fought sixteen times, including twice in Panama. Their second fight, in Los Angeles in 1914, produced one of Langford's greatest victories, when he came back from eleven knockdowns to knock out Wills in round fourteen. In 1917 he suffered his worst defeat when beaten badly and stopped by Fred Fulton. Langford had impaired vision in his right eye from 1917 onward.

In 1919 Woodman severed his connection with Langford and advised him to retire. But Langford had always quickly spent all the money that he had earned, and boxing was his only income. By 1924 he was blind in his right eye and had developed a cataract in his left eye. Although unable to see his opponents clearly, he continued to have a few fights. Langford's last fight was in 1928 at Shawnee, Oklahoma, with Britt Sims, who battered him badly and then knocked him out cold. He had almost 300 professional fights over a 26-year period, winning approximately 190 times, with 115 knockout victories and about 50 draws.

The story of Langford's later life is one of poverty and an existence dependent on charity. He had married Martha Burell in 1904 and had one child. After leaving the ring he went back to Boston, where they lived, and opened an athletic gymnasium that soon failed. He then went to New York where he was injured in an automobile accident in 1935. Soon afterward an operation performed charitably by a surgeon who remembered and admired him improved his vision, but he was soon reduced to living in squalor. In 1942 he became completely blind. Supported by relief, he spent most of his time in his room listening to a radio.

In 1943 an article by a New York sportswriter resulted in the establishment of a fund that provided Langford with a small monthly income for the rest of his life. In 1947 he returned to Boston to live with his daughter, later going into a nursing home in Cambridge, Massachusetts, where he spent all of his time in one room, alternating between a cot and a wheelchair. Despite the privations of his last thirty years, he retained his wit and good humor until he died in Cambridge.

Langford is considered the greatest professional boxer who never held, or even fought for, a world championship. A combination of factors, including the dominating presence of Jack Johnson during his prime and the limited opportunities available to black boxers of that period, prevented him from winning a title. He was an inaugural inductee into the International Boxing Hall of Fame in 1990.

• A record of nearly all of Langford's fights was published in *The Ring Record Book and Boxing Encyclopedia* (1986–1987), ed. Herbert G. Goldman. A flawed but useful article by Allan Morrison was published in *Ebony*, Apr. 1956. His biography is included in Nat Fleischer, *Black Dynamite*, vol. 4: *The Fighting Furies* (1939). Many articles about Langford have appeared in the boxing magazine the *Ring*, the best of which are Fleischer, "The Forgotten Man," Sept. 1940, pp. 12–13, 44; Nat Loubet, "Langford Is Fair Fighter," Apr. 1954, pp. 18, 44; Ace Foley, "The Weymouth Wizard," Oct. 1954, pp. 29, 47; a three-part series by Fleischer, "The Langford Legend," Mar. 1956, pp. 44–45, 59; Apr. 1956, pp. 38–39, 54; May 1956, pp. 34–35, 41; and Loubet, "Highlights of Sam Langford," Nov. 1963, pp. 10–13. An obituary is in the *New York Times*, 13 Jan. 1956.

LUCKETT V. DAVIS

LANGLADE, Charles-Michel Mouet de. *See* Mouet de Langlade, Charles-Michel.

LANGLEY, Katherine Gudger (14 Feb. 1883?–15 Aug. 1948), U.S. congresswoman, was born in Marshall, North Carolina, the daughter of James Madison Gudger, an attorney, and Katherine Hawkins. Her father was a state senator and state solicitor in addition to being a four-term U.S. congressman from North Carolina, serving from 1903 to 1907 and from 1911 to 1915. The year of Katherine's birth is a matter of speculation. Although her birth certificate states that she was born in 1888, subsequent noteworthy dates in her life suggest that such a listing is inaccurate. After attending school in her hometown, she moved to Virginia in 1899 and enrolled at the Woman's College of Richmond—at the unlikely age of eleven according to the year given on the birth certificate. She graduated two years later with a bachelor of letters degree. She spent one semester at Emerson College of Oratory in Boston, Massachusetts, beginning in January 1902. School records indicate that she was eighteen at the time of her admission, which would mean that she was born in a more-believable 1883.

In 1903 she went to Bristol, Tennessee, to teach expression at the Virginia Institute. She taught for only one year before heading for Washington, D.C., to become her father's secretary. In 1904 she married John Wesley Langley, an attorney who worked for the Census Bureau. They had two children. In 1906 the couple moved to John Langley's home state of Kentucky, settling in the town of Pikeville. That same year John Langley was elected as a Republican to Congress, where he served for nineteen years.

After her husband took office, Katherine Langley worked as his secretary and administrative assistant. As John Langley continued to win what would ultimately be ten consecutive elections, Katherine began to take a more active political role. In 1919 she became the clerk of the House Committee on Public Buildings and Grounds, which her husband chaired. She continued at this post until 1925. Katherine Langley also served on the Republican State Central Committee, earning the distinction as the first woman to do so, and she was chosen as the committee's vice chair in 1920. Additionally that year she was selected as an alternate delegate to the Republican National Convention, and four years later she served as a district delegate.

The Langleys' storybook life as one of Washington's most powerful couples began to unravel in 1925, when John Langley was convicted on charges of conspiring to violate the Prohibition laws or the Volstead Act. After his appeal to the U.S. Supreme Court to overturn his conviction was denied, he resigned from the House of Representatives in January 1926 and began serving a two-year sentence in a federal penitentiary in Atlanta. He was later paroled. Katherine Langley decided to campaign for the House seat representing Kentucky's Tenth District that was vacated by her husband. After winning the Republican primaries later that year, she voiced the opinion that her victory not only proved her fitness for the office but also vindicated the Langley name. In the fall she defeated her opponent in the general election to become only the seventh woman elected to the House.

Representing a constituency of primarily low-income families, Katherine Langley introduced several important, albeit minor, pieces of legislation that addressed the needs of the voters back home in Kentucky. In her first term in office, Langley also served on the Claims, Invalid Pensions, and Immigration and Naturalization committees, and she was chosen to be an at large delegate to the 1928 Republican National Convention. She was elected to a second term in the House in 1928 and in 1930 was chosen for membership on the Republican Committee on Committees, a body that selected the Republican membership for the House's regular standing committees. She was the first woman ever named to that group.

Langley's bid for reelection in 1930 was denied when she was defeated by Democrat Andrew J. May. The effects of the Great Depression eradicated some of the strength of the Republican party in traditionally conservative eastern Kentucky. Langley left Washington and returned to Pikeville, where her husband had set up a law practice upon his release from prison. In her later years, she served as postmistress and was elected two times as the railroad commissioner for the Third District of Kentucky, serving in the latter capacity from 1939 to 1942. She died in Pikeville.

• Biographical profiles of Langley are in *Literary Digest*, 30 Jan. 1926, p. 9, and 21 Aug. 1926, pp. 14–15. For more information, see Duff Gilfond, "Gentlewomen of the House," *American Mercury*, Oct. 1929, and the *Congressional Record* of the 70th and 71st Congs. Obituaries are in the *New York Times* and the *Louisville Courier-Journal*, 16 Aug. 1948.

FRANCESCO L. NEPA

LANGLEY, Samuel Pierpont (22 Aug. 1834–27 Feb. 1906), astrophysicist and aviation experimenter, was born in Roxbury, Massachusetts, the son of Samuel Langley, a wholesale merchant and banker, and Mary Sumner Williams. Langley attended the Boston Latin School and graduated from the Boston High School in 1851. He spent the years 1851–1857 preparing for a career in civil engineering and architecture and worked as a draftsman and merchant in Chicago and St. Louis from 1857 to 1864.

Langley regarded his years in the West as a false start in life. He returned to Boston early in 1864 to seek a career in astronomy, a subject that had fascinated him since childhood. Together with his brother, John Williams Langley, a former medical officer in the Union navy, Samuel embarked on a grand tour of European observatories and laboratories. Joseph Winlock, a leading American astronomer and family friend, hired Langley as an assistant at the Harvard Observatory on Langley's return from Europe. In 1866 Langley was appointed assistant professor of mathematics with responsibility for reestablishing the U.S. Naval Academy observatory. In 1867 he moved to the Western University of Pennsylvania (now the University of Pittsburgh), where he became professor

of physics and astronomy and director of the Allegheny Observatory.

Langley remained at Pittsburgh for twenty years, building a reputation as a pioneer in astrophysics—the "new astronomy"—and establishing himself as a leading American administrator of science. Searching for sources of income for the observatory, he devised a method of distributing precise standard-time signals to railroads, cities, and other interested customers. He also attracted the support of private benefactors, notably William Thaw.

In November 1886 Spencer Fullerton Baird, secretary of the Smithsonian Institution, offered Langley an appointment as assistant secretary in charge of international exchanges, the library, and publications. Langley accepted, explaining to friends that Pittsburgh no longer provided "the companionship that a student of science wants." He became secretary of the institution after Baird's death in 1887.

As secretary, Langley worked to extend the scientific interests of the Smithsonian and to expand its museum and public educational functions. His major administrative accomplishments were the establishment of both the Smithsonian Astrophysical Observatory and the National Zoo. He also played a key role in negotiations leading to the creation of the Freer Gallery of Art.

As an astrophysicist, Langley took little interest in the traditional astronomy of position. He had no taste for the complex mathematical procedures required to reduce observational data and recognized that his own talents lay in the area of instrument design and experimentation. He was particularly interested in the impact of solar radiation on the earth. His chief goal was to arrive at a figure for the "solar constant," a measure of the intensity of solar energy at the earth's mean distance from the sun. The key to his work was the bolometer, an instrument he invented in 1878. Essentially an electrical thermometer, the device employed a thin strip of metallic tape to register differences in temperature as small as one millionth of a degree. Langley coupled his instrument with a spectrograph and began to study temperature distributions across the solar spectrum.

In an attempt to determine the extent to which the atmosphere filtered solar radiation, Langley organized an expedition to Mount Whitney, California, in 1881. With the assistance and support of the War Department, the Pennsylvania Railroad, and his longtime friend William Thaw, Langley established several temporary observing stations on the peak. In the thin, clear mountain air, he and his principal assistant, James Keeler, obtained bolometric readings to compare with the Pittsburgh data and extended their measurements into the far infrared region of the spectrum for the first time.

Langley continued his bolometric studies in Pittsburgh and at the Smithsonian Astrophysical Observatory, which he established in 1890. His interest in solar energy shaped the Smithsonian research agenda in astrophysics for the next two generations. Ironically, in view of the fact that he was a meticulous experimenter and observer, Langley overestimated the value of the solar constant by one-third on the basis of flawed theoretical assumptions. His experimental data was nevertheless of real value to astronomers and physical scientists.

Langley also played an important role as a popularizer. A gifted writer, he published articles on his expeditions in the *National Geographic* and introduced general readers to the latest ideas in astronomy in a series of articles for *Century Magazine* and in his popular book *The New Astronomy* (1888).

A lifelong bachelor, Langley was nonetheless very fond of children and was committed to museum education. He was personally involved in the creation of the Children's Room exhibition in the Smithsonian Castle, complete with carefully crafted labels and low cases designed for viewing by youngsters.

Langley is best remembered as an aviation pioneer. A childhood interest in the subject was reawakened by a discussion of the flying machine problem at an 1886 meeting of the American Association for the Advancement of Science. Within a year he had begun experiments with a whirling arm and other engineering test equipment designed to establish the physical requirements for flight. His report, *Experiments in Aerodynamics* (1891), concluded that "mechanical flight is possible with engines we now possess."

Even before he had published his related study, *The Internal Work of the Wind* (1893), Langley had begun to apply the data he had gathered to the design of actual flying machines. His first aircraft were small models powered by twisted rubber strands driving propellers. By the fall of 1891, he was planning much larger models, with wingspans of up to fourteen feet, that would be powered by lightweight steam engines.

As secretary of the Smithsonian, Langley poured a great deal of time and money into the design and construction of his powered models. He first tasted success on 6 May 1896, when Smithsonian workmen catapulted Aerodrome No. 5 into the air from the roof of a houseboat anchored in the Potomac River. The craft completed two successful flights that day, covering distances of up to 3,300 feet. Other successful flights with this and similar models followed between 1896 and 1902.

In 1898 the U.S. Army Board of Ordnance and Fortification presented Langley with a $50,000 grant to develop a full-sized aerodrome capable of flight with a pilot on board. The airframe of the large machine was patterned after the small aerodromes flown in 1896. Charles Matthews Manly, Langley's chief aeronautical assistant, transformed a less than satisfactory internal combustion rotary engine developed by Stephen Balzer into a radial power plant weighing 200 pounds and developing 50 horsepower.

Like its small predecessors, the Great Aerodrome was designed to be catapulted into the air from the roof of a houseboat. Two unsuccessful attempts were made to launch the craft with Manly as test pilot. On 7 October 1903 the machine shot down the launch rail and

fell into the Potomac. One Washington reporter commented that the Great Aerodrome seemed to have the flying qualities of "a handful of mortar." The second attempt to launch the aerodrome took place on 8 December 1903. This time the rear wings failed as the craft was racing down the launch rail. It nosed straight up into the air and flipped into the water on its back. The Great Aerodrome was destroyed, but Manly escaped with his life.

The failure of the Great Aerodrome exposed Langley to considerable criticism in the press and on the floor of Congress. Representative Gilbert Hitchcock of Nebraska summed up the attitude of the critics in a comment to a reporter from the *Brooklyn Eagle*, "You can tell Langley for me . . . that the only thing he ever made fly was government money." To the end of his life, Langley remained convinced that the Great Aerodrome had not received a fair trial. "Failure in the aerodrome itself or its engines there has been none," he commented in the *Annual Report of the Board of Regents of the Smithsonian Institution, 1904.* The aerodrome, he wrote, "is at the moment of success, and . . . a lack of means has prevented the continuance of the work." Later Smithsonian claims that the Great Aerodrome had been "capable of flight" led to a long and bitter controversy with Orville Wright. Subsequent investigations have demonstrated beyond any reasonable doubt that the structure of the machine was too weak to have withstood the forces that would be imposed on it in flight. Moreover, the control system was inadequate.

Discouraged by the failure of the Great Aerodrome, and stung by the criticism leveled at him, Langley suffered yet another disappointment when a trusted Smithsonian employee was discovered to have stolen a large sum of money from the institution. Langley died at Aiken, South Carolina, after a series of strokes.

• The official papers of Samuel Langley are held by the Smithsonian Institution Archive, which also holds a microform copy of all Langley manuscript material in the collections of the University of Pittsburgh. "Samuel Pierpont Langley Memorial Meeting," *Smithsonian Miscellaneous Collections* 49, no. 4 (1907): 1–47, includes the best available bibliographic guide to Langley's scientific papers and popular articles. Langley provided a general introduction to his own work in *The New Astronomy* (1888). He provided a popular description of his early aeronautical successes in "The Flying Machine," *McClure's Magazine,* June 1897, pp. 647–60. C. M. Manly, *Langley Memoir on Mechanical Flight,* Smithsonian Contributions to Knowledge, vol. 27 (1911), includes detailed information on all the Langley aerodromes. J. Gordon Vaeth, *Samuel Pierpont Langley* (1966), is a popular biographical treatment. Tom D. Crouch, *A Dream of Wings: Americans and the Airplane, 1875–1905* (1981), provides an analysis of Langley's work in aeronautics and his impact on other experimenters. Cyrus Adler, *I Have Considered the Days* (1941), includes personal insights into Langley's character by a close friend.

Much useful biographical information is also to be found in a series of important memoirs published after Langley's death. The best of these are [G. Brown Goode], *The Smithsonian Institution, 1846–1896* (1896); Cyrus Adler, "Samuel

Pierpont Langley," *Annual Report of the Smithsonian Institution, 1906*; C. G. Abbot, "Samuel Pierpont Langley," *Astrophysical Journal*, May 1906; and C. D. Walcott, "Samuel Pierpont Langley," National Academy of Sciences, *Biographical Memoirs* 7 (1913): 247–68.

TOM D. CROUCH

LANGMUIR, Alexander Duncan (22 Sept. 1910–22 Nov. 1993), epidemiologist, was born in Santa Monica, California, the son of Charles Herbert Langmuir, an insurance company executive, and Edith Ruggles. When he was eleven years old, the family moved to Englewood, New Jersey, where he soon came under the influence of his uncle, Irving Langmuir, a physicist and chemist who won the Nobel Prize in chemistry in 1932. Their close association began when his uncle secured a summer job for him in the vacuum tube laboratory of the General Electric Company. Although Langmuir said later that he did not have the vaguest idea what he was doing that summer, he did get a general knowledge of the research process, and for the next fifteen years he absorbed from his uncle "a sense of science at its very best . . . the organization of theories and the interpretation of laws" (Langmuir interview with H. Phillips, 25 Mar. 1964).

Langmuir entered Harvard University at age seventeen where, at his uncle's insistence, he majored in physics. He did not like the subject, however, and decided to become a physician. A guest lecture on a scarlet fever epidemic by George Bigelow, the Massachusetts commissioner of health, set Langmuir on a career in public health. Bigelow advised him to study medicine, finish his internship, get some experience, and then train in public health—advice Langmuir followed to the letter. He received an A.B. from Harvard in 1931 and an M.D. from Cornell Medical School in 1935. From 1935 to 1937 he interned at Boston City Hospital; he then joined the New York State Health Department as an epidemiologist in training. His colleagues there were oriented toward Johns Hopkins, so he chose its School of Hygiene and Public Health for advanced study, receiving an M.P.H. in 1940. That year he married Sarah Ann Harper; they had five children.

Two fortuitous events helped launch Langmuir's career. He investigated an epidemic of five cases of poliomyelitis in New York State soon after his return from Johns Hopkins. That investigation proved the value of field epidemiology and brought him instant fame. Specimens collected from people in the community who showed no sign of illness tested positive, the first proof by laboratory methods that polio had a large proportion of inapparent infections. Polio researchers John R. Paul and Albert Sabin were among those who came to see his work. A promotion to deputy commissioner of the Westchester County Health Department followed shortly, a position Langmuir held during 1941–1942. As the health officer for 35,000 people, he got valuable experience. He also learned to write precisely: his superior officer forced him to write his scientific papers over and over until he got them exactly right. The experience turned Langmuir into a stickler for precision in the use of language.

The second event affecting Langmuir's career occurred during a visit with his uncle, when he met John Dingle of the U.S. Armed Forces Epidemiological Board. The two men established immediate rapport, and Langmuir became a consultant to the board before the United States entered World War II. In February 1942 Dingle asked him to become a member of the newly formed Commission on Acute Respiratory Diseases, whose purpose was to avoid an influenza epidemic like that of 1917. The group had a laboratory at Fort Bragg, North Carolina, and as Langmuir remembered, they went "lickety split" for the next four years. The field experience was invaluable. To hone his writing skills, Langmuir volunteered to write the monthly report for officials in Washington.

When the commission broke up in 1946, Langmuir joined the faculty of the Johns Hopkins School of Hygiene and Public Health as an associate professor of epidemiology, but after the excitement of the camp, the academic world seemed tedious and the students dull. His colleague and former teacher, Kenneth Maxey, provided the most stimulating experience: he introduced Langmuir to the science of biological warfare. He made Langmuir an alternate on the Department of Defense's Committee on Biological Warfare, of which Maxey was a member. Later, after Maxey's retirement, Langmuir became a full-fledged member.

Langmuir made a major career change in 1949, when he accepted an offer from the federal Communicable Disease Center (CDC, later the Centers for Disease Control and Prevention) in Atlanta, Georgia, to organize and develop an epidemiology program. He welcomed the opportunity to get "back on the firing line," where he could assist the states in controlling communicable diseases. His friends thought he was foolish to move to an agency which at that time was concerned almost entirely with malaria and was dominated by engineers and entomologists, but Langmuir saw the "bouncing, thriving, adolescent, gawky, and awkward organization" as "the promised land." He moved quickly to establish a medical dominance at the institution. Just six months after his arrival, he proposed using funds designated for mosquito control to do a surveillance of malaria in the Southeast. He suspected that most of the cases of malaria then reported in the area were false and that the massive control efforts were wasteful.

At that time, Langmuir had no medical epidemiologists on his staff; so he assigned nine nurses to epidemiologic work, and the survey went forward. This was the first surveillance of a disease in America. It confirmed Langmuir's suspicions that malaria had all but disappeared, and more important, it changed the course of public health practice. After 1950 *surveillance* came to mean the systematic collection and evaluation of data and its distribution to all who needed to know, whereas previously it had meant watching people who had been in contact with a serious disease. In

1955, when cases of polio appeared among recipients of the new Salk vaccine, Langmuir used surveillance to track the cause to a contaminated vaccine from a single laboratory. When that problem was eliminated, public confidence in the vaccine returned and its effectiveness was proved. Surveillance was next used during the influenza epidemic of 1957. It became commonplace around the world as a method to analyze patterns of disease outbreaks.

With the onset of the Korean War in 1950, the threat of biological warfare loomed. Langmuir, the U.S. Public Health Service's leading expert in this field, proposed to confront the threat by creating an Epidemic Intelligence Service (EIS) within the CDC. Young physicians, nurses, veterinarians, and other scientists trained as epidemiologists would be the first line of defense. While looking for alien germs, they would be on the alert for domestic ones as well. At the request of the states they would investigate any disease outbreak. Langmuir thus turned a wartime emergency into a peacetime opportunity. His EIS officers became famous as "disease detectives" who practiced "shoe-leather epidemiology" during their two-year stint at the CDC. They quickly became indispensable to the nation's health, and epidemic intelligence, like surveillance, became a foundation of public health practice. The credibility of the EIS also did much to ensure the survival and growth of the CDC as a public agency.

Langmuir was a tall, impressive-looking man with a forceful personality and abundant self-confidence. He relished controversy and was often at odds with state and federal officials, scientists, colleagues in other departments of the CDC, and his own staff, for whom he was a relentless taskmaster. He admitted only "tip-top" young scientists to the EIS program, trained them rigorously, and sent them on epidemic investigations as soon as possible. "We throw them overboard, see if they can swim, and if they can't [we] throw them a life ring, pull them out, and throw them in again." He expected these EIS officers to excel both as scientists and as writers; they produced numerous drafts of their papers.

The techniques of disease investigation that Langmuir introduced saved hundreds of thousands of lives. They speeded the worldwide eradication of smallpox in the 1970s and enabled CDC scientists to identify the causes of Legionnaires' disease and toxic shock syndrome, to issue the first warnings of a mysterious ailment subsequently called AIDS, and to isolate the Hanta virus. The methodology of applied epidemiology was also used to establish the CDC's birth defects database and has been extended to the investigation of problems in population, injuries, and environmental and occupational health. Graduates of the EIS program, almost one-half of whom have pursued careers in public health, have spread these techniques across the nation and around the world. One of these graduates wrote that Langmuir's "application of epidemiological principles to disease investigations serves as the gold standard of how epidemiology should be practiced."

Langmuir retired from the CDC in 1970. His first wife having died, he married that year Leona Baumgartner Elias, the longtime commissioner of public health for New York City; they had no children. He then went to the Harvard Medical School, where until 1977 he was a visiting professor of epidemiology. In 1988 he rejoined the faculty at Johns Hopkins, where his students selected him as an outstanding teacher in 1993. He won numerous awards for his work, including the Bronfman Prize of the American Public Health Association for public health achievement (1965) and the Jenner Medal of the Royal Society of Medicine (1979). Langmuir died in Baltimore.

• Langmuir's papers are at the Johns Hopkins University. Oral history material includes two interviews of Langmuir in the holdings of the National Library of Medicine, Bethesda, Md.: the first by Harlan Phillips, 25 Mar. 1964, George Rosen Transcripts; the second, on videotape, by Donald A. Henderson, Mar. 1979, Leaders in American Medicine series of the Alpha Phi Omega honorary society. Especially important among Langmuir's publications are "The Surveillance of Communicable Diseases of National Importance," *New England Journal of Medicine* 268, no. 4 (24 Jan. 1963): 182–92, and "The Epidemic Intelligence Service of the Centers for Disease Control," *Public Health Reports* 95, no. 5 (Sept.-Oct. 1980): 470–77. Langmuir's role in the evolution of the CDC is in Elizabeth W. Etheridge, *Sentinel for Health: A History of the Centers for Disease Control* (1992). Obituaries are in the *New York Times*, 24 Nov. 1993, and the *American Journal of Public Health* 84, no. 8 (Aug. 1994): 1346–47.

ELIZABETH W. ETHERIDGE

LANGMUIR, Irving (31 Jan. 1881–16 Aug. 1957), chemist and inventor, was born in Brooklyn, New York, the son of Charles Langmuir, an insurance executive, and Sadie Comings. He was one of four brothers, all of whom were very successful in their chosen fields. He attended public schools in Brooklyn, private schools in Paris (where his father served on European assignment) and Philadelphia. His independence, conscientiousness, and interests were bolstered by his parents' provision of scientific equipment, their encouragement to keep regular daily records, and permission to engage independently in a widening round of outdoor activities, such as hiking, mountain climbing, bicycling, and skating. He attended Columbia University School of Mines, graduating with a degree in metallurgical engineering in 1903.

Langmuir earned his Ph.D. in chemistry in 1906 at the University of Göttingen, Germany, working with future Nobel laureate Walther Nernst. Nernst suggested that Langmuir study whether the high temperature in the vicinity of a lamp's light-producing element could sufficiently speed the reactions that oxidized the nitrogen in the air to suggest commercially promising possibilities. Langmuir's experiments in this field of "light bulb chemistry" provided him with a thesis topic and a basis for his most important scientific work.

In 1906 Langmuir joined Stevens Institute of Technology (today the New Jersey Institute of Technology) as an instructor, ready to combine teaching and research. However, in the next three years he found himself overloaded with teaching responsibilities and short of time, equipment, and assistance. In 1909 he learned from a Columbia classmate about a summer job with the General Electric (GE) Research Laboratory in Schenectady, New York. This was the first laboratory in U.S. industry created to combine fundamental and applied science. He got the summer post, was offered at its conclusion a full-time job, and accepted it with no intention of permanence. "While at Schenectady," he wrote his mother, "I will be looking around for a really good job in a university."

Instead, Langmuir was still working at GE at the time of his death nearly fifty years later. Why? Much of the credit goes to the man who hired him, Willis R. Whitney, GE's director of research. He saw a scientist unusually talented and versatile, yet thin-skinned. He quickly made Langmuir a kind of general consultant and sage of the laboratory, permitted him to pick his problems, and equipped him with a highly skilled technician, Samuel Sweetser. Langmuir in turn selected problems related to improving the light bulb. He combined his knowledge of the behavior of gases in light bulbs with heat-transfer studies to invent the gas-filled incandescent lamp, 25 percent more efficient than the vacuum lamp then in use.

Many scientists in the generation of his teachers believed that atoms and electrons were only metaphors. Langmuir moved to the forefront of world science as a person whose work demonstrated that accepting atoms, molecules, and electrons as real objects similar to macroscopic ones, only smaller, provided a very fruitful way of understanding nature. Langmuir's attitude can be best illustrated with a story from his youth. He had weak eyes and finally was fitted with spectacles. To his amazement, the masses of trees suddenly resolved into individual leaves. Similarly, his light bulb studies provided a way to deal with atoms at such low pressures that the behavior of fluids resolved into the behavior of individual atoms and molecules.

Focusing those spectacles on electronics in near vacua cleared up mysteries of thermionic emission and the space-charge effect and developed the high-vacuum tube, a key component in the first electronics revolution. Focusing on chemistry, he developed the theory of heterogeneous catalysis, based on a picture of single layers of atoms occupying spaces on a kind of atomic checkerboard at surfaces, that explained the rates of reactions on surfaces. Focusing on atomic physics, he built on the work of Gilbert N. Lewis, a chemist, to provide a fruitful (but eventually discarded) explanation for valence bonding in terms of stationary shells of electrons around nuclei. Focusing on surface phenomena, he developed a theory that explained a process long important in the mining industry, flotation. Focusing again on surfaces, he built on the work of Agnes Pockels and John William Strutt, Lord Rayleigh, to develop methods of measuring the size of molecules by spreading layers of oil on water until they covered the surface with a uniform thickness of one molecule. His methods provided the foundations for modern biochemical and biophysical studies of cell membranes.

In the course of all this work, he invented important new apparatus. His "Langmuir balance and trough" became a standard tool of surface chemistry. In 1913 he developed two new vacuum gauges, both more sensitive than any previously in use. In 1915 he invented the mercury condensation vacuum pump.

The years from 1912 to 1920 were Langmuir's peak period of productivity. But he maintained for the next three decades a publishing record any scientist would envy, averaging more than ten papers a year. He did not do this merely by sticking to his earlier established specialties. He helped develop methods for the sonic detection of submarines in World War I. He branched out into biological studies and plasma physics (a field he named, based on a somewhat obscure analogy between electrically neutral low-pressure discharges and blood plasma). Building on observations he made in his thesis research, and the work of Robert Wood, he invented the atomic hydrogen welding torch.

He entered his final field of concentration, atmospheric physics, due to some important and militarily useful work undertaken during World War II on smoke screens and the prevention of aircraft icing. In 1946 his associate Vincent J. Schaefer discovered how to seed clouds with dry ice to cause rain or snow. In this field, in the early 1950s, Langmuir would gain his greatest public notoriety with claims that weather modification experiments carried out in the Far West were influencing the weather in the Ohio Valley. The claims have not been confirmed. But the work of Langmuir and his team on "Project Cirrus" became the basis of modern efforts in weather modification and cloud physics.

The full details of his work can be followed in the twelve volumes of his collected works. He received numerous honors for his discoveries, most notably the 1932 Nobel Prize for chemistry, honoring his contributions to surface chemistry.

As the rainmaking episode shows, he did not shrink from controversy or responsible speculation. His address "Pathological Science" (posthumously published) is a devastating critique of scientists who go public with half-baked results; it has been widely referenced in the context of the late twentieth-century cold fusion furor. A less-cited but equally insightful paper, "Science as a Guide to Life," discusses differences between what he termed convergent and divergent phenomena that foreshadowed issues later dealt with in the mathematical study of chaos.

Langmuir married Marion Mersereau in 1912; they adopted two children. His concentration could result in legendary levels of absentmindedness. One story depicts him leaving a tip for his wife after a breakfast in the family kitchen. Another depicts a GE employee collapsing on the stairs in front of him and Langmuir calmly stepping over the prone victim and walking on.

If true, these stories illustrate not an uncaring nature but absorption in his work. He could also be effective outside the laboratory. He organized Schenectady's first Boy Scout troop, ran for city council on a reform ticket, contributed to a book of essays advocating international control of nuclear power, and helped to protect New York State's Adirondack Park from assault by developers. He remained a vigorous outdoorsman, walking over fifty miles in a single day, swimming in the icy waters of Lake George from the dock of his camp, learning to fly a plane, and exploring the Adirondacks.

He died while on vacation on Cape Cod. More than any other individual, Irving Langmuir had demonstrated that support of scientific research by industry could be a good bargain, both for industry and for science.

• Langmuir's personal papers are in the Library of Congress. The best source of information on Langmuir is C. Guy Suits, ed., *The Collected Works of Irving Langmuir* (12 vols., 1962); vol. 12 is a biography by Albert Rosenfeld, who gives an excellent account of the personal events that accompanied Langmuir's scientific productivity. Some of his more accessible papers were published also in *Phenomena, Atoms and Molecules* (1950). The place of Langmuir's work in the understanding of surface phenomena is treated superbly in Charles Tanford, *Ben Franklin Stilled the Waves* (1989).

GEORGE WISE

LANGNER, Lawrence (30 May 1890–26 Dec. 1962), patent agent, playwright, and theatrical producer, was born in Swansea, South Wales, the son of Baruch Bernard Freedman, a businessman, and Cecilia Sarah Langner. (He took his mother's maiden name.) He attended private schools in Swansea and in Margate, England. After a brief stint as a clerk for a theatrical manager in 1903, he was apprenticed to Wallace Cranston Fairweather, a chartered patent agent in London. Langner passed examinations of the British Chartered Institute of Patent Agents in 1910.

In 1911 Langner went to New York to represent Haseltine, Lake & Co., a firm he had joined in 1906. Two years later with his brother Herbert he founded his own firm, which later became Langner, Parry, Card & Langner. The business prospered by specializing in foreign patents and trademarks, representing, for instance, the prolific inventor Charles F. Kettering and his electric automotive self-starter, which replaced cranking. In 1917 Langner became a U.S. citizen. During the First World War he was a consultant on munitions patents and contracts. In 1919 he served as adviser for the preparation of the patents sections of the Treaty of Versailles. He founded and served on an advisory council on patents to the U.S. House of Representatives, and during the Second World War he helped originate the National Inventors Council to screen civilian ideas for military inventions.

Although an expert in the area of patents, Langner was even more famous for his career in theater. In 1914 he and several friends formed the Washington Square Players in Greenwich Village, New York. The Players, dedicated to the production of experimental and noncommercial plays, first mounted a series of one-act plays at the Bandbox Theatre in February 1915. From then until the war halted their activities in April 1918, the group presented sixty-two one-act plays and six full-length works. The productions included works by influential European playwrights such as Maurice Maeterlinck, George Bernard Shaw, and Anton Chekhov, as well as those by emerging American playwrights Eugene O'Neill, Susan Glaspell, and Ben Hecht. Langner also wrote four plays performed by the group. Although not a long-lived group, the Washington Square Players influenced the "little theater" movement in America, popularized new playwrights, and introduced several exceptional performers, including Katherine Cornell.

In 1915 Langner married Texas-born singer Estelle Roege; they had one child. After the war, he and actress Helen Westley, director Philip Moeller, and scene designer Lee Simonson, along with Theresa Helburn and Maurice Wertheim—many of them veterans of the Washington Square Players—founded an even more influential group, the Theatre Guild. Their goal was "to produce plays of artistic merit not ordinarily produced by commercial managers." In 1923 Langner and his wife were divorced, and the following year he married actress Armina Marshall; they had one child. Marshall became a pivotal guild member. The guild began its illustrious career inauspiciously in April 1919 with the production of *Bonds of Interest* by the Spanish Nobel Prize–winner Jacinto Benavente, a project that generated more praise than commerce. The guild's second production, however, *John Ferguson* by St John Ervine, produced on a shoestring of less than $1,000 in May 1919, made more than $40,000 and established the organization both artistically and financially.

Through the 1920s and 1930s the Theatre Guild was the most important theatrical producer in the United States. Langner and Helburn, who became the executive director, eventually supervised the production of more than 200 plays. Langner and other board members were involved in every aspect of production, often attending rehearsals and making artistic suggestions to directors and designers. In its early years the guild specialized in bringing the works of the European theater to the American stage, producing Ferenc Molnar's *Liliom* (1921) and *The Guardsman* (1924); Karel Kapek's robot play *R.U.R.* (1922); Luigi Pirandello's *Right You Are If You Think You Are* (1927); and Georg Kaiser's *From Morn to Midnight* (1922). The guild acted as George Bernard Shaw's American agent—Langner became a close personal friend and frequent correspondent—producing twenty of Shaw's plays, many of them world premieres such as *Heartbreak House* (1920), *Back to Methuselah* (1922), *Saint Joan* (1923), *Caesar and Cleopatra* (1925), *Pygmalion* (1926), and *Major Barbara* (1928). Just as he did with Shaw, Langner established close personal contacts with numerous young writers. Through the guild, he nourished a crop of new American playwrights, producing major works by Elmer Rice, John Howard Lawson, Sidney Howard, S. N. Behrman, Robert E. Sherwood, Maxwell Anderson, and William Saroyan. The guild produced eight of O'Neill's plays, including *Marco Millions* (1928), *Strange Interlude* (1928), *Mourning Becomes Electra* (1931), and *Ah, Wilderness!* (1933).

In 1925 Langner realized a long-term goal when the guild completed its own theater in New York, which it continued to operate until 1944. For several years the guild employed its own company of performers in an "alternating repertory" system that Langner devised. Over the years Theatre Guild productions featured a long list of star performers, a few of whom were Helen Hayes, Katharine Hepburn, Paul Robeson, Frederic March, Jose Ferrer, and John Gielgud. The illustrious team of Alfred Lunt and Lynn Fontanne was associated with the Theatre Guild through twenty-five years and twenty-five plays. In 1928–1929 Langner and the guild instituted a nationwide subscription membership. They sent a series of productions to subscribers in major cities, which in effect replaced the old touring combinations.

Many of the guild's greatest financial and artistic successes were musicals, starting with *Porgy and Bess* (1927), with book by DuBose Heyward and music and lyrics by George and Ira Gershwin. In 1943 the guild produced the trend-setting musical *Oklahoma!* by Richard Rodgers and Oscar Hammerstein II, followed by another Rodgers and Hammerstein success, *Carousel*, in 1945. The national subscription series and the production of popular musical comedies illustrate the change the guild underwent in the 1930s and 1940s as it shifted from the production of primarily avant-garde material to more mainstream fare, although it still produced material such as O'Neill's monumental *The Iceman Cometh* (1946). The guild—with Langner always a major influence in the decisions—remained a significant commercial producer, underwriting plays such as William Inge's *Picnic* (1953) and the musicals *Bells Are Ringing* (1956) and *The Unsinkable Molly Brown* (1960). After Langner's death, his son, Philip, continued the guild as a producing organization. The guild stopped producing its own plays after *Golda* (1977), with Ann Bancroft, and its subscription series ended in 1989, but as it celebrated its seventy-fifth anniversary in 1994, the organization announced plans to revitalize its role as a producer.

Lawrence Langner possessed enormous creative energy, and many of his projects yielded long-lasting results. In 1955, after years of planning, Langner fulfilled his dream for a national Shakespearean theater when the American Shakespeare Festival opened its Globe-style theater in Stratford, Connecticut. The festival spawned a school for training American actors in classical repertory. In 1931 Langner and his wife built Connecticut's Westport Country Playhouse, a summer theater, still in operation, designed to try out plays for New York.

Langner wrote more than two dozen one-act and full-length plays, some of them collaborations or adaptations of classics. About half were produced in New York, with *The Pursuit of Happiness* (1933), like several others written with his wife, garnering the most attention. In later years Langner became involved with electronic media. He coproduced with Armina Marshall the radio drama series "Theatre Guild on the Air" from 1945 to 1954, and between 1947 and 1955 Langner and Helburn produced television plays for "The U.S. Steel Hour" and other outlets. Langner assisted in the formation of the League of New York Theatres in 1931. He was president and chair of the board of the American Academy of Dramatic Arts and a member of the Dramatists Guild as well as patent law associations in New York and Chicago. Langner remained active until his death in New York City.

Langner's accomplishments demonstrate the importance of a creative producer with artistic vision. His founding of the Theatre Guild and his contributions to that organization alone ensured him a prominent place in the history of American theater in the twentieth century.

• Langner's papers are at the Beinecke Library at Yale University. Additional papers of Langer and Armina Marshall (the Theatre Guild Collection) are in the Harry Ransom Humanities Research Center at the University of Texas. Langner's autobiography is *The Magic Curtain* (1951). With his brother Herbert he wrote *Outline of Foreign Trade Mark Practice* (1923). Langner also wrote *The Importance of Wearing Clothes* (1959), *The Play's the Thing* (1960), and *G.B.S. and the Lunatic* (1963). His obituary is in the *New York Times*, 28 Dec. 1962 (western edition) and 1 Apr. 1963 (eastern edition, delayed by newspaper strike).

ROGER A. HALL

LANGSTON, Charles Henry (1817–14 Dec. 1892), abolitionist, temperance advocate, and educator, was born in Louisa County, Virginia, the son of Captain Ralph Quarles, a white plantation owner, and Lucy Langston, Quarles's slave whom he manumitted and with whom he maintained an open relationship. Langston and his brothers were educated by Quarles in their youth. After the death of their parents in 1834 the Langston children were taken by William Gooch, a friend of Quarles and Lucy Langston, to Chillicothe, Ohio, where they were reunited with their half brother and two half sisters, the children of Lucy Langston who were born before her involvement with Quarles. Langston and his brothers took with them to Ohio considerable money bequeathed to them by Quarles. In 1835 Langston and his brother Gideon became the first African Americans enrolled in the preparatory department of Oberlin Collegiate Institute, then a hotbed of abolitionism. After leaving the preparatory department in 1836, Langston worked as a teacher at black schools in Chillicothe and Columbus, Ohio. He reenrolled in the Oberlin preparatory department in 1841 and studied there until the spring of 1843.

In the 1840s and 1850s Langston and his brothers, Gideon and John, were leading activists in the Ohio abolitionist movement. In 1842 and 1843 Langston served on the editorial board of the *Palladium of Liber-*

ty, a black abolitionist newspaper published in Columbus. In 1844 Langston attended the State Colored Convention in Columbus, where he proposed repeal of Ohio's Black Laws, equal education for African-American children in the state's public schools, and Prohibition. In 1848 while on a speaking tour of Ohio with the black abolitionist Martin Delany, Langston narrowly escaped being lynched by a white mob in Marseilles, Ohio. Later that year Langston served on the Business and Organization Committee at the Colored National Convention in Cleveland and was appointed to the convention's National Central Committee. In the early 1850s Langston became increasingly pessimistic about the possibility of improving the condition of African Americans and urged the establishment of an independent black nation in the western hemisphere.

During the 1840s and 1850s Langston was also a leading activist in the national temperance movement, serving as an officer in the Sons of Temperance organization. In 1848 he was appointed western representative of the organization and empowered to charter organizations west of the Alleghenies.

In the late 1850s Langston resumed his educational activities. In 1853 he, along with George Vashon and Charles Reason, proposed the establishment of a vocational college for African Americans. Largely as response to the proposal, in 1856 the Methodist Episcopal church founded Wilberforce University in Wilberforce, Ohio. Langston served as a teacher and in 1856 became principal of the Columbus Colored Schools.

In the 1850s Langston became increasingly active in Ohio Underground Railroad efforts. For his participation in the 1858 rescue of John Price, a fugitive slave, Langston was convicted of violating the Fugitive Slave Act and received a fine and a brief prison sentence. The so-called Oberlin-Wellington rescue became one of the most famous challenges to the Fugitive Slave Act and helped spread antisouthern sentiment in the North. After John Brown's failed raid on Harpers Ferry in 1859, Langston wrote an impassioned defense of it in the *Cleveland Plain Dealer*. Brown's actions "were in perfect harmony with and resulted from the teaching of the Bible and of the revolutionary fathers," he wrote.

During the Civil War Langston helped recruit African Americans in Ohio, Illinois, and Indiana for the Union army. In 1862 Langston resettled near Leavenworth, Kansas, where he taught newly emancipated slaves. After the war he continued his political involvement by advocating civil rights and suffrage for African Americans and women. He also opened a school for freedmen in Leavenworth and actively promoted the Republican party. In 1869 Langston married Mary S. Leary, widow of Lewis S. Leary, one of the participants in the raid on Harpers Ferry in 1859. In 1872 Langston became the principal of the Colored Normal School at Quindaro, Kansas. To support himself he worked as a farmer and a grocer. In September 1872 the Republican State Congressional Convention at

Lawrence nominated Langston as a presidential elector, but in the vote he finished third in a field of five, receiving 66,805 votes.

In the 1880s Langston played a central role in the Convention of Colored Men. At the 1880 meeting of the organization, Langston led a call for reform in the Refugee Relief Board that served as a welfare agency for the so-called "exoduster" black migrants to Kansas. Later that year at another meeting of the Convention of Colored Men a proposal was adopted that Langston should be nominated for lieutenant governor. In 1886 Langston switched his partisan allegiance to the Prohibition party and received the party's nomination for state auditor. He spent the last years of his life living in Lawrence, Kansas, and working as a grocer and editor of a local journal, the *Historic Times*. Langston died in Lawrence.

Langston was a leading intellectual in the African-American abolitionist movement of the antebellum period and one of its most militant spokespersons. As a proponent of African-American nationalist-emigrationist movements and violent opposition to slavery, Langston helped anchor the abolitionist movement's left wing. He is also notable for his lifelong activism as an educator of African Americans, his courageous work on the Underground Railroad, and his advocacy of civil rights in the postwar period.

• The Charles H. Langston Papers are held by the Oberlin College Archives. For substantial biographical treatments of Langston and his brothers, consult William Cheek and Aimee Lee Cheek, *John Mercer Langston and the Fight for Black Freedom, 1829–65* (1989). For an account of Langston's early years, see John Mercer Langston, *From Virginia Plantation to the National Capitol* (1894). Peter C. Ripley et al., eds., *The Black Abolitionist Papers* (1992), contains some of Langston's speeches and writings. See also Eugene N. Berwanger, "Hardin and Langston: Western Black Spokesmen of the Reconstruction Era," *Journal of Negro History* (Spring 1979).

THADDEUS RUSSELL

LANGSTON, John Mercer (14 Dec. 1829–15 Nov. 1897), African-American political leader and intellectual, was born free in Louisa County, Virginia, the son of Ralph Quarles, a wealthy white slaveholding planter, and Lucy Jane Langston, a part–Native American, part-black slave emancipated by Quarles in 1806. After the deaths of both of their parents in 1834, Langston and his two brothers, well provided for by Quarles's will but unprotected by Virginia law, moved to Ohio. There Langston lived on a farm near Chillicothe with a cultured white southern family who had been friends of his father and who treated him as a son. He was in effect orphaned again in 1839, however, when a court hearing, concluding that his guardian's impending move to slave-state Missouri would imperil the boy's freedom and inheritance, forced him to leave the family. Subsequently, he boarded in four different homes, white and black, in Chillicothe and Cincinnati, worked as a farmhand and bootblack, intermittently attended privately funded black schools since blacks were barred from public schools for whites, and in August 1841 was caught up in the violent white rioting against blacks and white abolitionists in Cincinnati.

Learning from his brothers and other black community leaders a sense of commitment, Langston also developed a self-confidence that helped him cope with his personal losses and with pervasive, legally sanctioned racism. In 1844 he entered the preparatory department at Oberlin College, where his brothers had been the first black students in 1835. Oberlin's egalitarianism encouraged him, and its rigorous rhetorical training enhanced his speaking skills. As early as 1848 and continuing into the 1860s, Langston joined in the black civil rights movement in Ohio and across the North, working as an orator and organizer to promote black advancement and enfranchisement and to combat slavery. At one Ohio state black convention, the nineteen-year-old Langston, quoting the Roman slave Terence, declared: "'I am a man, and there is nothing of humanity, as I think, estranged to me.' . . . The spirit of our people must be aroused. They must feel and act as men." After receiving his A.B. degree in 1849, Langston decided to study law. Discovering that law schools were unwilling to accept a black student, however, he returned to Oberlin and in 1853 became the first black graduate of its prestigious theological course. Despite evangelist and Oberlin president Charles Grandison Finney's public urging, Langston, skeptical of organized religion, and especially its widespread failure to oppose slavery, refused to enter the ministry.

Finding white allies in radical antislavery politics, Langston engaged in local politics beginning in 1852, demonstrating that an articulate black campaigner might effectively counter opposition race-baiting; in mid-decade he helped form the Republican party on the Western Reserve. Philemon E. Bliss of nearby Elyria, soon to be a Republican congressman, became Langston's mentor for legal study, and in 1854 he was accepted to the Ohio bar, becoming the first black lawyer in the West. That year he married Caroline Matilda Wall, a senior at Oberlin; they had five children. In the spring of 1855 voters in Brownhelm, an otherwise all-white area near Oberlin where Langston had a farm, elected him township clerk on the Free Democratic (Free Soil) ticket, gaining him recognition as the first black elected official in the nation. Langston announced his conviction that political influence was "the bridle by which we can check and guide, to our advantage, the selfishness of American demagogues."

In 1856 the Langstons began a fifteen-year residency in Oberlin. Elected repeatedly to posts on the town council and the board of education, he solidified his reputation as a competent public executive and adroit attorney. In his best-known case, Langston successfully defended Mary Edmonia Lewis, a student accused of poisoning two of her Oberlin classmates (who recovered); Lewis would become the first noted African-American sculptor. In promoting militant resistance to slavery, Langston helped stoke outrage over the federal prosecution under the Fugitive Slave Law of thirty-seven of his white and black townsmen and others involved in the 1858 Oberlin-Wellington rescue of fugitive slave John Price. Immediately, Langston organized the new black Ohio State Anti-Slavery Society, which he headed, to channel black indignation over the case. While his brother Charles Henry Langston, one of the two rescuers convicted, repudiated the law in a notable courtroom plea, Langston urged defiance of it in dozens of speeches throughout the state. Langston supported the plan by John Brown (1800–1859) to foment a slave uprising, although he did not participate in the 1859 raid on Harpers Ferry. Following the outbreak of the Civil War, once recruitment of northern black troops began in early 1863, he raised hundreds of black volunteers for the Massachusetts Fifty-fourth and Fifty-fifth regiments and for Ohio's first black regiment.

After the war, Langston's pursuit of a Reconstruction based on "impartial justice" and a redistribution of political and economic power elevated him to national prominence. In contrast to Frederick Douglass, the quintessential self-made man, to whom his leadership was most often compared, Langston represented the importance of education and professionalism, joined to activism, for a people emerging from slavery. In 1864 the black national convention in Syracuse, New York, elected him the first president of the National Equal Rights League, a position he held until 1868. Despite rivalries within the league, Langston shaped it into the first viable national black organization. In 1865 and 1866 he lectured in the Upper South, the Midwest, and the Northeast and fought for full enfranchisement not only of the freedpeople, but also of African Americans denied suffrage in the North. In January 1867, on the eve of congressional Reconstruction, he presided over a league-sponsored convention of more than a hundred black delegates from seventeen states to Washington, D.C., to dramatize African-American demands for full freedom and citizenship. That spring Langston assumed a signal role in the South as a Republican party organizer of black voters and the educational inspector-general for the Freedmen's Bureau, traveling from Maryland to Texas. In Virginia, Mississippi, and North Carolina, he helped set up Republican Union Leagues, which instructed freedpeople on registration and voting; in Georgia and Louisiana he advised blacks elected to state constitutional conventions on strategy. In almost every southern state, Langston defended Reconstruction policy in addresses before audiences of both races. Insistent on guaranteeing the citizenship and human rights of freedpeople, he appealed to black self-reliance, self-respect, and self-assertion and to white enlightened self-interest, predicting that interracial cooperation would lead to an "unexampled prosperity and a superior civilization." His charisma, refined rhetorical style, and ability to articulate radical principles in a reasonable tone drew plaudits across ideological and racial lines. Twice, in 1868 and 1872, fellow Republicans, one of whom was white, proposed that

Langston run for vice president on the Republican ticket.

In the fall of 1869 Langston founded the Law Department at Howard University and took up his duties as law professor and first law dean. From December 1873 to July 1875 he was vice president and acting president of the university. He characteristically gained a warm following among students, who were particularly attracted by his manner, which was neither obsequious nor condescending. Despite Langston's accomplishments at Howard, however, the trustees rejected his bid to assume the presidency for reasons that they refused to disclose but that clearly involved his race, his egalitarian and biracial vision, and his nonmembership in an evangelical church. Embittered, he resigned.

Meanwhile Langston continued to function as one of the Republican party's top black spokesmen. In return, President Ulysses S. Grant appointed him to the Board of Health of the District of Columbia in 1871, and he moved his home from Oberlin to Washington, D.C. He served as the board's legal officer for nearly seven years, during which time he helped devise a model sanitation code for the capital. On another front, at the behest of Massachusetts senator Charles Sumner, he contributed to the drafting of the Supplementary Civil Rights Act of 1875, which was invalidated by the U.S. Supreme Court in 1883. As radical Reconstruction crumbled, practicality and personal ambition led Langston in 1877 to endorse President Rutherford B. Hayes's conciliatory policy toward the white South. Two years later, however, he condemned the condition of the freedpeople in the South as "practical enslavement" and called for black migration, the "Exodus" movement, to the North and the West. Langston served with typical efficiency as U.S. minister and consul general to Haiti from 1877 to 1885, winning settlement of claims against the Haitian government, especially by Americans injured during civil unrest, and some improvement in trade relations between the two countries. During his final sixteen months of duty, he was concurrently chargé d'affaires to Santo Domingo.

In 1885 Langston returned to Petersburg, Virginia, to head the state college for African Americans, the Virginia Normal and Collegiate Institute. After his forced resignation less than two years later under heavy pressure from the Democrats who then controlled the state, he announced his intention to run for the U.S. House of Representatives in the mostly black Fourth District, of which Petersburg was the urban center. Running against a white Democrat and a white Republican, Langston waged a ten-month campaign "to establish the manhood, honor, and fidelity of the Negro race." Although the Democratic candidate was initially declared the victor, Langston challenged the election results as fraudulent, and Congress voted in September 1890 to seat him. Within days he was back in Virginia campaigning for reelection to a second term. Again the official count went to the Democrat, a result Langston accepted because he could expect no redress from the new Democratic Congress. The first African American elected to Congress from Virginia, Langston used his three months in the House to put his ideas on education and fair elections into the national record. His most controversial proposal, one intended to head off black disfranchisement, was a constitutional amendment imposing a literacy requirement on all voters in federal elections and a corresponding adjustment in the size of state congressional delegations.

During the remainder of his life, Langston practiced law in the District of Columbia and continued to be active in politics, education, and promoting black rights. He published his autobiography, *From the Virginia Plantation to the National Capitol* (1894), and carried on an active speaking schedule in both the North and the South. He remained hopeful despite legal disfranchisement, segregation, and his own failure to obtain a federal judgeship. In 1896, while raising money to support the filing of civil rights cases, he predicted: "It is in the courts, by the law, that we shall, finally, settle all questions connected with the recognition of the rights, the equality, the full citizenship of colored Americans." He died in Washington, D.C.

• Langston's papers, together with those of his wife, Caroline W. Langston, and son-in-law James Carroll Napier, are in the Fisk University Library. Valuable scrapbooks of newsclippings are in the Moorland-Spingarn Research Center at Howard University. Besides his autobiography, Langston published a collection of his addresses, which includes a biographical sketch by J. E. Rankin, entitled *Freedom and Citizenship* (1883; repr. 1969). The only biography, a study of the first half of his career, is William Cheek and Aimee Lee Cheek, *John Mercer Langston and the Fight for Black Freedom, 1829–65* (1989). His entire career is treated in Cheek and Cheek, "John Mercer Langston: Principle and Politics," in *Black Leaders of the Nineteenth Century*, ed. Leon Litwack and August Meier (1988).

WILLIAM CHEEK
AIMEE LEE CHEEK

LANGWORTHY, Edward (c. 1738–1 or 2 Nov. 1802), teacher and politician, was born near Savannah, Georgia, of unknown parents. Because his parents died when he was young, Langworthy was reared and educated at Bethesda Orphan House, founded by the Reverend George Whitefield near Savannah in 1740. He also read and studied on his own. He married a sister of Ambrose Wright; her first name is unknown. His wife was reported dead in 1771, with no date specified, and Langworthy married again at an unknown date. His second wife, whose name is also unknown, is referred to in a letter of his dated 5 April 1779; she is reported to have died at Christmas time in 1794. No information survives about children from either marriage.

As a young man, Langworthy kept a school in Savannah and in 1771 became the head and teacher of a school of "academical learning" at Bethesda. Little else is known about his activities until the revolutionary troubles erupted in 1774 and 1775.

In September 1774 Langworthy signed objections to a set of resolutions that had been drawn up by a meeting in Savannah and were the first statement of revolutionary sentiment in Georgia. The objections pointed out a number of technical problems at the Savannah meeting and said a dutiful petition to the British Government would have been proper, rather than resolutions questioning its authority. A total of 663 signatures were secured throughout the province, 101 from Christ Church (Savannah) Parish, including several people who later became revolutionaries. The response showed that many Georgians had not yet made up their minds as to how to object to London's actions.

On 11 December 1775 Langworthy became secretary of the revolutionary Council of Safety in Georgia, indicating a change of heart since 1774. He was selected as secretary of the Georgia Provincial Congress on 2 February 1776 and elected by the state legislature to the Continental Congress on 7 June 1777.

He served in Congress from 17 November 1777 to 12 or 13 April 1779. He was absent six weeks in the summer of 1778 and for brief periods otherwise. Several times he was the only Georgia delegate present. He was one of the three Georgia signers of the Articles of Confederation when adopted by Congress in November 1777. He served on the Board of War, the Board of Treasury, the marine committee, the foreign affairs committee, and several other committees, sometimes because he was the only Georgia delegate present. It is difficult to determine how important Langworthy was to the operation of Congress. He seldom entered into debates; his votes, when recorded, give the only indication of his views. He made no motion but seconded a few made by others.

In 1778 Congress split on the argument between Silas Deane and Arthur Lee over the question of whether payment was due for help received from France. Langworthy sided with the Deane party. In 1779 as a member of the foreign affairs committee he opposed the right of the United States to the Newfoundland fisheries as a necessary item in any peace settlement. In both of these matters he opposed Henry Laurens, who in April of 1779 brought up the fact that Langworthy had probably been serving in Congress for the past two months without authorization as he had been elected on 26 February 1778 "for the year ensuing." Langworthy had probably remained in Congress because he was the only Georgia delegate present and thus may have expected to be elected again. But he was not reelected, and he then ceased to attend Congress. Langworthy remained in Philadelphia long enough to be accused, perhaps correctly, of writing several newspaper articles that summer, signed "Americanus," which were critical of Congress on several topics. He seems to have remained in Philadelphia and New York until about the time the war ended, when he probably returned to Georgia briefly.

In 1784 Langworthy moved to Baltimore and was a part owner of the *Maryland Journal and Baltimore Advertiser* in 1785 and early 1786. He also taught at the

Baltimore Academy 1787–1791 and may have headed the school.

In the winter of 1790–1791 the Langworthys moved to Elkton, Maryland, in the northeastern corner of the state. Here he announced his intention of writing "A Political History of the State of Georgia from Its First Settlement with Memoirs of the Principal Transactions Which Happened Therein during the Late Revolution." He was acquainted with many Georgia leaders and a number of happenings in the early revolutionary era in Georgia, and set out to collect documents and memoirs of participants. This work was advertised in the *Georgia Gazette* in the summer of 1791 at two dollars for two proposed volumes. He requested several leading Georgians to solicit subscriptions for the proposed work. The death of his second wife in 1794 and a possible lack of encouragement from Georgia seem to have ended his intention to write the history. Nothing more is heard of it after 1795. It was never published and probably never written.

In the mid-1780s Langworthy acquired the papers of General Charles Lee, a controversial general of the U.S. Continental Army who had died in 1782. There is no evidence that Langworthy and Lee were acquainted. In 1786 Langworthy sent the memoir he prepared to London, where it was published in 1792 as *Memoirs of the Life of the late Charles Lee, Esq., Lieutenant-Colonel of the Forty-fourth Regiment, Colonel in the Portuguese services, Major-General, and Aide de Camp to the King of Poland, and second in command in the service of the United States of America during the Revolution: to which are added his political and military essays; also, letters to and from many distinguished characters, both in Europe and America.* Also issued in New York in 1792 and 1793, the publication consists of a 70-page memoir, 121 pages of miscellaneous writings, and 244 pages of letters. The memoir is essentially factual but favorable to Lee, a controversial position at best.

In 1795 Langworthy returned to Baltimore and a clerkship in the Baltimore Customs House. He held the clerkship until his death in Baltimore. Langworthy's most important activity was his work with the early revolutionary government in Georgia and his service in the Continental Congress.

• There is no collection of Langworthy papers. A few letters and notes are included in Edmund C. Burnett, ed., *Letters of Members of the Continental Congress* (8 vols., 1921–1936), and Paul H. Smith et al., eds., *Letters of Delegates to Congress, 1774–1789* (1976). A full biography of Langworthy has yet to be published. Several short sketches do exist: Charles C. Jones, Jr., *Biographical Sketches of the Delegates from Georgia to the Continental Congress* (1891); Edmund C. Burnett, "Edward Langworthy in the Continental Congress," *Georgia Historical Quarterly* 12 (1928): 211–35; Leonard L. Mackall, "Edward Langworthy and the First Attempt to Write a Separate History of Georgia," *Georgia Historical Quarterly* 7 (1923): 1–17; and Burton Alva Konkle, "Edward Langworthy," *Georgia Historical Quarterly* 11 (1927): 166–70. Incidental references to Langworthy in the *Georgia Historical Quarterly* are in vols. 2, 17, 31, 33, 34, 39, 40, 47, and 56; for details see Barbara S. Bennett and Tracy D. Bearden, *Georgia Historical Quarterly Index, Vols. 1–60, 1917–1976* (1991). A brief obituary in the *Federal Gazette and Baltimore Daily Advertiser*, 2 Nov. 1802, gives the date of his death as "yesterday evening."

KENNETH COLEMAN

LANHAM, Fritz (3 Jan. 1880–31 July 1965), lawyer and U.S. congressman, was born Frederick Garland Lanham in Weatherford, Texas, the son of Samuel Willis Tucker Lanham, a lawyer and politician, and Sarah Beona Meng, a schoolteacher and artist. Lanham's childhood education was divided between public schools in Washington, D.C., and Weatherford College, where he graduated in 1897. He attended Vanderbilt University for the fall semester in 1897 but returned home and taught Greek at Weatherford College in the spring of 1898. That fall he enrolled at the University of Texas, and in 1900 he graduated with a B.A. As a postgraduate student, Lanham was selected as the first editor of the *Texan*, the university student newspaper.

Lanham was secretary to his father, now a U.S. congressman, from 1901 to 1902. In 1902 he worked briefly as a banker in Weatherford and in 1903 returned to Austin, where he entered law school at the University of Texas and worked as a stenographer for his father, who had been elected governor of Texas. He did not complete his final year of law school because he became the governor's secretary (1906–1907). In 1907 Lanham worked as a sports reporter for the *Dallas News* and as an actor with a traveling theater company. He married Beulah Rowe in 1908 and returned to Weatherford, where he entered into the practice of law with Ben G. Oneal, a former law school classmate, and was admitted to the bar in 1909. In 1913 Lanham was named the first editor of the *Alcalde*, the alumni magazine of the University of Texas.

Lanham campaigned unsuccessfully for Parker County attorney in 1916. The following May he took a position in Fort Worth in the Tarrant County attorney's office, where he remained until March 1919. During World War I Lanham offered his talents as a public speaker on behalf of the American Red Cross and the Liberty Loan drive. He was elected to Congress as a Democrat from the Twelfth District in a special election on 19 April 1919 and served until his retirement in 1947.

Lanham entered Congress in the aftermath of World War I ready to support the League of Nations and an expanded role for the United States in foreign affairs. Demonstrating a mixture of political expediency and technological foresight, the Fort Worth congressman encouraged throughout the 1920s and 1930s federal development of helium as a military resource and supported the expansion of the dirigible industry. One of the few facilities devoted to the extraction of helium was located in his district.

Initially a member of the District of Columbia Committee and the Committee of Industrial Arts and Expositions, during his second term he joined the Public Buildings and Grounds Committee and the Committee on Patents, and in 1928 he became a member of the Committee on Expenditures in the Executive Department. He endorsed construction of federal buildings in Washington, D.C., following a plan of architectural conformity, and his support of appropriations for construction of the Departments of Commerce, Justice, and Labor according to the L'Enfant plan helped ensure the passage of the measure. He also helped plan the construction of a new Supreme Court building.

Throughout the 1920s Lanham opposed the tariff policies of the Republicans, believing free trade was crucial to the health of the domestic economy. The congressman also worked on problems associated with copyright and endorsed patent legislation that would protect the intellectual property of authors, asserting that such protections guaranteed the cultural and educational advance of the population. After his first wife died in 1930, Lanham married Hazel Walker Head in 1931; no children were born to either marriage.

Lanham's political philosophy led him to oppose many of the New Deal reform proposals of Franklin D. Roosevelt. Instead of supporting price supports for farmers, Lanham endorsed a plan that included mortgage extensions, lower interest rates, and increased opportunities for foreign trade. In April 1938 he equated the president's efforts at reorganizing government agencies with "the spread of those spurious 'isms' from abroad which seek the destruction of this Nation of ours." Lanham was convinced the depression stemmed from a lack of confidence in government credit and argued that measures such as the Emergency Relief Appropriation Bill of 1937 would only hinder the nation's credit and might trigger another crisis. He charged that federal minimum wage legislation would allow for a dictatorship to control labor and industry in a "decidedly and distinctly un-American" fashion.

While Lanham wanted the United States to take an active role in world affairs, he opposed American involvement in another European war in the mid 1930s. However, as hostilities in Europe heightened in the late 1930s and early 1940s, he endorsed the Roosevelt administration's cash-and-carry policies. The Texas congressman opposed trade with Germany, saying, "Shall we continue being partial to that country which is seeking to wipe from the face of the earth those things most dear to the hearts of the American people?" During the war Lanham defended the military record of the president's sons from the House floor and vehemently opposed strikes, or what he called "communistic outbreaks," in the defense industries.

Lanham gained the chairmanship of the Public Buildings and Grounds Committee in 1939. In 1940 he authored the National Housing for Defense Bill, which funded the construction of temporary housing for civilian war workers. In 1941 his committee passed the Lanham Community Facilities Act, which funded day care for working mothers but concentrated on aid to schools, waterworks, sewers, public sanitary facilities, hospitals, recreational facilities, and streets, with the bulk of the money going to schools. Lanham, however, opposed funding for social services such as day-care centers and fought appropriations for their construction after the bill had passed, rendering the legislation ineffective for two years until Congress amended the law in 1943.

During the early 1940s Lanham sponsored legislation to protect and keep secret the patents on discoveries with military uses. His interest in trademarks and patents culminated with the passage of the Lanham Act in 1947, a measure that increased protection for registered trademarks of businesses. Conservative by nature, he preferred that private industry build housing for returning war veterans.

When he retired from Congress, Lanham remained in Washington as a lobbyist for the National Patent Council, the American Fair Trade Council, and the Trinity Improvement Association of Texas. In 1963 he moved to Austin, Texas, where he died. The congressman, noted for his powerful oratory, carved out a niche for himself as a defender of property and intellectual rights with his support of patent legislation. He served alongside many powerful individuals but never achieved the stature of contemporaries John Nance Garner, Sam Rayburn, or Wright Patman among the Texas power elite in Washington.

• A small collection of Lanham's papers is available at the Center for American History, University of Texas at Austin. Information about Lanham can also be found in the Ben G. Oneal Papers, the Morris Sheppard Papers, and the Martin M. Crane Papers at the Center for American History. The center has a useful biographical file on Lanham. Additional Lanham materials are located in the William Howard Taft Papers, Library of Congress; the Franklin D. Roosevelt Papers, Franklin D. Roosevelt Library, Hyde Park, N.Y.; and the Lyndon B. Johnson Papers and the Wright Patman Papers, Lyndon B. Johnson Library, Austin, Tex. Lanham wrote several pieces himself, including "A Revised Work," *University of Texas Literary Magazine* 16 (Dec. 1900): 106–8; *Putting Troy in a Sack* (1916); and "Helium: Texas Wonder Gas," *Bunker's Monthly*, Mar. 1928, pp. 333–46. For writings about Lanham and his career see "Who's Who at Texas: Fritz G. Lanham," *Alcalde*, Nov. 1916, pp. 43–46; G. A. Holland, *History of Parker County and the Double Log Cabin* (1937); Escal F. Duke, "The Life and Political Career of Fritz G. Lanham" (M.A. thesis, Univ. of Texas, Austin, 1941); Donald S. Howard, "The Lanham Act in Operation," *Survey* 79 (Feb. 1943): 38–40; Neil Borden, "The New Trade-Mark Law," *Harvard Business Review* 25 (Spring 1947): 289–305; William H. Chafe, *The American Woman* (1972); and John M. Blum, ed., *The Price of Vision: The Diary of Henry A. Wallace, 1942–1946* (1973). Obituaries are in the *Austin Statesman*, 2 Aug. 1965, and the *Summer Texan* and the *New York Times*, both 3 Aug. 1965.

NANCY BECK YOUNG

LANIER, James Franklin Doughty (22 Nov. 1800–27 Aug. 1881), lawyer and banker, was born in Washington, North Carolina, the son of Alexander Chalmers Lanier, a farmer and storekeeper, and Drusilla Doughty. The family moved to Kentucky, then to Ohio, and finally to the frontier village of Madison, Indiana, in 1817. Although Lanier's father was a man of modest means, he managed to send his son to an academy in Newport, Kentucky, for a sound education. In 1819 Lanier began to read law with Alexander A. Meek in Madison, and in the same year he married Elizabeth Gardner. They would have eight children. His father died the following year, deeply in debt, and Lanier, an only child, struggled to support his mother while also paying his father's debts.

Lanier completed his legal studies at Transylvania University in Lexington, Kentucky, and graduated in 1823. He soon developed a successful legal practice but found that he lacked the strength for riding the circuit of county courts in southeastern Indiana. From 1824 to 1827 he served as assistant clerk of the Indiana House of Representatives, and from 1827 to 1830 he was the House's chief clerk. He was elected prosecuting attorney on the anti-Jackson ticket in 1830, the only elective office he ever held. Carefully limiting his expenditures, Lanier invested extensively in real estate, both in Madison and in the frontier counties of northern Indiana. After 1833 he turned from the law and politics to concentrate on business, although he was an officer of both the masonic Grand Lodge of Indiana and the State Temperance Society.

Lanier's banking career began about 1830 when he was employed to settle the accounts of the closed Farmers' and Mechanics' Bank in Madison. In 1833 he became president and chief shareholder of the Madison branch of the new State Bank of Indiana. When the state's banking system neared collapse in 1837, Lanier was sent to Washington with $80,000 in gold to persuade the Treasury Department to continue federal deposits in the State Bank; the success of this mission allowed the State Bank to survive the crisis. The following year he ably represented Indiana in a nationwide bankers' meeting in New York, further advancing his reputation. In 1847 he traveled to London and Amsterdam to manage a successful exchange of Indiana's defaulted canal bonds on behalf of the state.

By the early 1840s Lanier was one of the most successful bankers and land speculators in Indiana, and he commissioned Francis Costigan to design and build an elegant mansion for his growing family. His columned home overlooking the Ohio River, completed in 1844, was the largest and most expensive in the state. It remained in the family until it became a state memorial in 1925.

Intrigued by his work for the struggling Madison and Indianapolis Railroad, Lanier saw glowing prospects for western railroads. He moved to New York and in January 1849 joined with Richard H. Winslow to establish Winslow, Lanier and Company, private bankers specializing in railroad securities, as well as county and city issues on behalf of railroads. "We were without competitors for a business we had created," Lanier wrote years later, and as a result, he said, the firm "made money very rapidly." After five highly successful years, Winslow, Lanier and Company withdrew from underwriting railroad securities. Winslow retired in 1859, leaving Lanier in full control of the flourishing Wall Street bank, which continued to act as financial and transfer agent for many railroads.

Lanier's reputation for public service is based on his remarkable efforts to support Indiana's state government during the Civil War. Governor Oliver P. Morton sought his help in 1861 when Indiana needed to borrow quickly in order to equip thousands of recruits. Lanier advanced the state $420,000, which was repaid the following year. When the Democratic majority of the legislature refused to pass any appropriations in 1863, Morton turned to Lanier for loans to sustain the state government. Entirely without security, Winslow, Lanier and Company paid out $629,000 over two years, for which they were reimbursed with interest in 1865.

When Lanier traveled to Europe in 1865 he was asked by Secretary of the Treasury Hugh McCulloch, a friend from banking days in Indiana, to explain the Treasury's confidence in handling the nation's Civil War debts. Lanier delivered a detailed accounting to a meeting of bankers and capitalists in Frankfurt am Main that was subsequently published in both English and German. At McCulloch's request, Lanier met again with European bankers in 1868.

Despite increasingly poor health from the late 1860s, Lanier served as president of the Third National Bank of New York and played a major role in the reorganization of the Pittsburgh, Fort Wayne and Chicago Railroad. He also provided financial aid for the poet Sidney Lanier, a distant cousin. In 1871, Lanier published a 55-page memoir for his family. "I am a business man, from taste as well as from long habit," he wrote, "I have been almost uniformly successful." He took special pride in his support for Indiana during the Civil War. Lanier devoted himself to business in New York, playing no role in either politics or society.

After the death of his wife in 1846, he married Mary McClure two years later. They had three children. In politics he was a Whig and then a Republican, and in religion a Presbyterian. Lanier died in New York after many years of declining health. His estate was reportedly worth almost $10 million.

• A few letters and business papers from Lanier's Indiana years can be found at the Indiana Historical Society, and his correspondence with Governor Morton is in the Indiana State Archives. His autobiography, *Sketch of the Life of J. F. D. Lanier* (1871; rev. ed., 1877), provides the best account of his public life; it is also available in *Two Private Banking Partnerships* (1975). A biography is H. Brooklyn Cull, "James F. D. Lanier, Banker, Patriot" (master's thesis, Indiana Univ., 1952). Lanier's important work in supporting the state's financial position is described by Kenneth M. Stampp, *Indiana Politics During the Civil War* (1949). For information on Winslow, Lanier and Company, see Vincent P. Carosso, *Investment Banking in America: A History* (1970) and Dorothy R. Adler, *British Investment in American Railways, 1834–1898* (1970).

PATRICK J. FURLONG

LANIER, Sidney (3 Feb. 1842–7 Sept. 1881), poet and musician, was born Sidney Clopton Lanier in Macon, Georgia, the son of Robert Sampson Lanier, a lawyer, and Mary Jane Anderson. Early in life, Lanier showed remarkable love and aptitude for music, but this talent was encouraged only as a social grace, for the southern genteel tradition looked with disfavor upon a man's following the arts as a profession. After he graduated in 1860 from Oglethorpe University in Milledgeville, Georgia, his family assumed he would follow his father's example and practice law. Lanier intended instead to follow a scholar's life in Europe, but this dream was cut short by the Civil War. In 1861 he joined the Macon Volunteers, serving in the signal corps and then on a blockade runner until his capture; while imprisoned at a federal camp at Point Lookout, Maryland, he contracted the tuberculosis that eventually killed him.

Upon his return to Macon, he worked as a hotel clerk, tutor, and headmaster, then entered his father's law firm, but found all this unrewarding. During this time he also wrote some lyrical verse and a Civil War novel (*Tiger-Lilies* [1867]), but his unstimulating work, financial worries, and illness made the postwar period a very depressing one for Lanier. The only positive note was his wedding to Mary Day of Macon in 1867; it was a very happy marriage, and the couple had four children. Mary Day Lanier always supported her husband's dreams, even to the extent of raising their sons by herself in Macon for several years while he went to Baltimore to pursue a life in the arts. She and the boys joined him in Baltimore in 1876. The detailed and loving letters between the Laniers during their separation is a rich source of information.

Lanier spent precious and frustrating years trying to resolve the conflict between what his tradition expected of him and his own desires. The resultant tension in his life became one of the major themes in his work: the conflict between the spiritualism of Art and the materialism of Trade. This conflict is best expressed in his long poem "The Symphony." Despite society's expectations of him, his inclinations drew Lanier with increasing intensity to music and poetry. He traveled to New York several times on business and to seek medical care, and attended many concerts while in the city. In 1872 he went for a period to San Antonio, Texas, hoping that the drier climate would provide some relief from his respiratory illness. The large German community of that city impressed him with its love of music. Lanier played there as a flutist in a number of ensembles. Encouraged by his success as a musician, he decided to pursue what he loved. With the understanding of his father and the supportiveness of his wife, Lanier broke with tradition and moved north in the fall of 1873 to attempt entry into artistic circles. As he wrote to his brother Clifford, "An impulse, simply irresistible, drives me into the world of poetry and music."

He went first to New York City, seeking an orchestral position. Lanier was largely self-taught as a flutist. From all contemporary accounts he possessed remarkable natural skill and virtuosity, but he may have underestimated the competition he would face from conservatory-trained musicians in the country's largest city. His "break" actually came in Baltimore, then establishing itself as a cultural center. Stopping here briefly to visit a friend, Lanier met and played for Asger Hamerik, the Danish-born conductor of the orchestra of the newly established Peabody Conservatory of Music. After hearing Lanier play one of his own compositions, Hamerik immediately offered him the position of first flute.

In Baltimore Lanier entered a society dedicated to the enjoyment of the arts, with the European cultural ambience he had dreamed of. He was no amateur among professionals; reviews of the time always praised his musical skill, and the conservatory faculty treated him as an equal, inviting him to play in chamber ensembles and to join them for concert tours. At this point considering himself primarily a musician, he joined the prestigious Wednesday Club's musical rather than literary section. But he was also writing a great deal of poetry, which was profoundly influenced by the music he heard every day at rehearsals.

Hamerik introduced his musicians and audiences to avant-garde music by such contemporary composers as Wagner, Berlioz, and Tchaikovsky; much of this was "program" music in which ideas, stories, or emotions were conveyed through tone. Lanier found this thrilling, for it complemented his idea that poetry ought to convey images through sound as much as through specific words. The influence of program music is evident in his own verse. His early poems are stylistically simple, following the ABAB song concept. But his more mature works, such as "The Marshes of Glynn," mark him as a literary innovator. They blend various voices, lines, and tones; they are symphonic, rich in imagery and in deliberately manipulated sound patterns. Best known for the musicality of his verse, Lanier is the only notable American poet who was also an accomplished musician. This is crucial to an understanding of his poetry, which developed from traditional nineteenth-century verse into a highly individual and innovative form. Lanier's verse is unique in American literature as the only poetry whose musical qualities come from direct, practical, artistic experience.

Though Lanier continued to perform music, and even composed a number of art songs and flute studies, he now began to devote more effort to writing poetry. His national reputation as a poet began in 1874 with the publication of "Corn" in *Lippincott's*. As a result of this success he was asked by the Atlantic Coast Railroad to write a rail travelers' guide to Florida. The assignment paid well, but he was upset because he had to accept such work to put bread on the table. Lanier's intellectual energy, constantly challenged by illness and financial pressures, was pulled in many different directions. He was often forced to waste precious time and strength, and suffer wounded artistic pride, writing "potboilers"—such as a series for Scribner's of classic tales retold for younger readers—to support his family.

An assignment of greater importance came from the U.S. Centennial Commission: to write the words of a cantata for opening-day ceremonies of the national exhibition at Fairmount Park in Philadelphia. This *Centennial Meditation of Columbia*, with music by Dudley Buck of Connecticut (the collaboration was designed to suggest the reconciliation of North and South) was performed on 10 May 1876. This work represented for Lanier the culmination of his idea of a total aesthetic experience, in which words and music were mutually suggestive of each other's meaning. In this year, also, Mary Day Lanier moved to Baltimore with their sons, as Lanier's more steady financial situation made it possible for the family to live together at last.

The only volume of Lanier's poetry to be published during his lifetime appeared in 1877; by the end of that year, his activities had become primarily literary. He delivered a very popular series of private lectures, called "parlor classes," and in 1878 was asked to give a series of lectures on Shakespeare at the Peabody Institute. He wanted very much to teach at the new Johns Hopkins University, established in Baltimore in 1876, and was finally invited to join the faculty in the spring of 1879. He was so well admired and popular as a lecturer in Baltimore that twice as many tickets were requested for his first presentation as were available. At last fulfilled in the academic life he had desired since his college days, Lanier had only a little time left to enjoy it. By early 1881 he was quite weak and had to lecture from a chair. In the summer, accompanied by his family, Lanier went to western North Carolina, hoping to find relief in the cool mountain air. He died there.

Lanier's grave in Baltimore is marked with an inscription from his poem "Sunrise": "I am lit with the Sun." Despite the setbacks of professional frustration and increasingly poor health, Lanier had remained an optimistic man. He was a cheerful companion who enriched the lives of his colleagues and friends and was devoted to his family. He loved the arts and looked to them as beacons to light the path of all humankind. Even in his last days, he was planning new artistic projects and books.

As with any artist who dies prematurely, there is the difficulty of assessing an unfulfilled career. Lanier wrote most of his major poetry late in life; his innovative poetic techniques were just being fine-tuned at the time of his death, so much must be left to speculation. Despite his many accomplishments and his popularity, Lanier has never been granted more than minor literary status. He was not part of any literary "set," nor did he strive to emulate other poets of his day. But although his literary career was brief, he produced a prodigious amount of serious work. His poetry delights the imagination and senses, and his prose (particularly the essays and letters) gives us a rich picture of American intellectual and artistic life in the decade and a half following the Civil War. He was deeply concerned with the power of nature and with science as a progressive force, and had a deep religious faith. The worlds of poetry and music inspired his strongest works. For him music symbolized human harmony: "Music is Love in search of a word" ("The Symphony"). His mature poems—"The Symphony," "The

Marshes of Glynn," and "Sunrise"—are designed for their sound as much as for their literal meaning. Lanier's creation of synaesthetic verse, in which he merged sound and idea into musical poetry, has drawn negative comments from critics who find it lush and "overwritten." But it ultimately has secured his reputation.

• The major collection of Lanier's papers—letters, journals, notebooks, memorabilia, musical manuscripts—is housed at Johns Hopkins University. The standard edition of Lanier's writing is the *Centennial Edition of the Works of Sidney Lanier* (1945), ed. Charles R. Anderson; each of the ten volumes contains detailed introductory material and notes, and there is an extensive bibliography of primary and secondary sources of works up to the mid-1840s. The definitive biography is by Aubrey Harrison Starke *Sidney Lanier: A Biographical and Critical Study* (1933; repr. 1964). See also the section on Lanier in Lewis Leary, *Articles on American Literature 1900–1950* (1954), pp. 174–77, and the Lanier entry and bibliography in *Nineteenth-Century Literary Criticism*, vol. 6, ed. Laurie Lanzen Harris and Sheila Fitzgerald (1984), pp. 230–82. For more recent bibliographic information, see Jack De Bellis, *Sidney Lanier, Henry Timrod, and Paul Hamilton Hayne: A Reference Guide* (1978), De Bellis's entry on Lanier in the *Dictionary of Literary Biography*, vol. 64 (1988), and Jane S. Gabin, "Sidney Lanier," in *Fifty Southern Writers before 1900*, ed. Robert Bain and Joseph M. Flora (1987). Recent full-length studies are De Bellis, *Sidney Lanier* (1972), and Gabin, *A Living Minstrelsy: The Poetry and Music of Sidney Lanier* (1985).

JANE S. GABIN

LANIGAN, George Thomas (10 Dec. 1845–5 Feb. 1886), journalist, was born in Trois Rivières, Quebec, Canada, the son of William Lanigan, a baker, and Emily Juliet Webster. He graduated at the top of his class from the high school of McGill College at Montreal in 1862. He began study for the ministry but soon abandoned the idea and sustained himself as a telegraph operator. He was noted for his speed and accuracy and maintained a cordial rivalry with another young operator, Thomas Edison.

Lanigan began his writing career at age fifteen with a contribution to the *New York Albion*. He continued to publish under the pen name "Allid" in several Canadian and American papers. In 1864 he became an editor for the *Montreal Telegraph*. As Canadian correspondent for the *New York Herald* he earned a scoop by overhearing the clicking of a telegraph instrument that conveyed to the Canadian government a report of the Fenian invasion of Canada in 1866. The Canadian telegraph authorities were less enthusiastic than his American editors, and he was discharged from the service for making unauthorized use of government dispatches. Already in 1865 Lanigan had published at Montreal a small book under the pseudonym Allid called *National Ballads of Canada*, a translation into English verse of seven French-Canadian ballads (six reprinted by Lawrence J. Burpee, *Songs of French Canada* [1909]). Now committed to a career in writing and journalism, he joined a group of Canadian writers to found at Montreal a humorous and satirical journal

called the *Free Lance* (1867). Shortly thereafter, with Hugh Graham and Tom Marshall of the *London Telegraph*, he founded the *Evening Star*, which later became one of Montreal's leading newspapers. Lanigan was the first editor in chief.

In 1870 Lanigan parted company with his associates on the annexation issue, being a supporter of union with the United States, and moved to Chicago, where he worked as an editor for the *Chicago Republican*. He later joined the staff of the *Chicago Tribune* and was western correspondent for the *New York World*. When the Chicago fire broke out in 1871, he made use of his telegraphic experience to be the first to send a report of the disaster to the New York newspapers: "A raging, roaring hell of fire endangers twenty blocks of the city. It is already within a block of the telegraph office where this dispatch is written, sweeping onward, a whirlwind of flames." About 1873 he moved to St. Louis and began work at the *Democrat*; he was quickly promoted to city editor. His account of a smallpox epidemic caused a consortium of local businessmen to threaten a boycott of the paper as injurious to the commercial interests of the city. When the editor in chief printed a retraction, Lanigan resigned in disgust and returned to Chicago.

He moved east to work at the *New York World* in 1874. For the next nine years he was one of the most prolific contributors to that journal. Scarcely an issue appeared without contributions from his pen, many of them unsigned, under pseudonyms, or signed GTL. His Sunday feature, "Crème des Chroniques," often filled eight to ten columns with stories, articles, and reviews translated from the French press. He prepared serialized English translations of contemporary French works by Jules Verne, Victor Hugo, and others. He declined an offer to join the staff of the Paris paper *Le Figaro*.

Lanigan was best known among newspapermen of his day for his intelligence and versatility. In addition to being a keen student of international affairs, he wrote on social issues, history, and literature and was an accomplished sportswriter as well, covering boat races, baseball games, billiard tournaments, cricket matches, and prizefights. In an age before quick access to information, he developed enormous files of newspaper cuttings on diverse subjects, which were admired by his colleagues as the best in the country. His remarkable memory laid to hand anything he had read, and he was happy to put his knowledge and collections at the disposal of other writers.

Lanigan believed that a free, aggressive, competitive press should inform and influence its readership concerning the political, social, and educational issues of its time. Politically he was a Democrat, socially an investigator of abuse and injustice and champion of reform. To him, the reader of the press was entitled to more than reportage, hence the essays, reviews, and verse that flowed from his pen. A passion for exactitude and being first with the facts, an intense idealism, and a satirist's sense of the absurd were important characteristics of the man and his work.

Lanigan regularly contributed light and humorous verse to *Harper's*, *Puck*, *Judge*, and other literary and humorous journals, and wrote for more scholarly undertakings as well, such as *Appleton's Encyclopaedia*. His most popular works proved to be a series of political fables in the style of Aesop, based on issues and personalities of the time, that appeared in the *New York World* and were published in book form as *Fables of G. Washington Aesop, Taken "Anywhere, Anywhere Out of the World"* (1878). Pirated London editions appeared in 1882, 1885, and 1889. A second publication by Lanigan in the "Out of the World" series appeared as *The World's Almanac for 1879, A Compendium of Useless and Interesting Information* (1878). Among Lanigan's innumerable shorter poems and ballads, the best known was his "Threnody for the Death of the Ahkoond of Swat," which appears in most anthologies of American light verse. Based on a news account of the death of the ruler of a principality in India, it was cast as a parody on Tennyson's "Ode on the Death of Wellington." Other poems frequently anthologized include "The Amateur Orlando," "The Rime of the Curious Customer," and "The Plumber's Revenge."

In 1881 Lanigan tried his hand at playwriting and produced at the Detroit Opera House, with A. R. Calhoun, a comedy called *Wanted a Carpenter*, written in only four days. A favorable review appeared in the *Detroit Free Press* (26 Aug. 1881), but when a revised version opened in Chicago, at McVicker's Theater, the reviews were tepid to harsh, and the house was mostly empty.

Lanigan was interested in running an independent newspaper where he could "introduce ideas and try experiments." He tried to raise enough capital to purchase the *Brooklyn Union* in 1882, but the paper was bought from under him by associates of John Foord, then editor of the *New York Times*.

In 1883 Lanigan left New York to carry out his plans for an independent paper at Rochester, assuming the editorship of the *Post-Express*. He opposed James G. Blaine's candidacy for president, however, and the owner would not allow him to support Grover Cleveland, so he resigned in 1884. In 1885 he moved to Philadelphia to write for the *Philadelphia Record*, a post he held until his death there of heart and kidney disease.

In 1866 Lanigan had married Frances Elizabeth Spink, of a journalistic family that had founded the *Sporting News* in St. Louis. The couple had four children. Frances Lanigan in her widowhood sustained herself as a journalist until her death in 1915.

Lanigan was a rubicund, cheerful man. He could write French with one hand and English with the other. His favorite recreations were word games, mathematical puzzles, and whist, of which he was reckoned one of the leading players of his generation. However, his puckish, convivial manner masked strong social and political views.

• Lanigan's few remaining personal papers and the manuscript of his play are in the possession of Benjamin R. Foster, Wallingford, Conn. Information on Lanigan's birth, often incorrectly reported, is from the registers of St. James Anglican Church, Trois Rivières, Quebec. The most important biographical sketches include Lawrence J. Burpee, "George Thomas Lanigan, Canadian Humorist," *Acta Victoriana* 26 (1902): 155–60, and "Canadian Humorists," in *A Little Book of Canadian Essays* (1909), pp. 47–55; and Louis N. Megargee, *Seen and Heard* (1901), pp. 28–32. A portrait and reproduction of a manuscript in Lanigan's hand appears in the third edition of E. S. Caswell, ed., *Canadian Singers and Their Songs* (1925), pp. 90–91. Lanigan's fables were partially reprinted in Mark Twain's *Library of Humor* (1888); in the works of Burpee noted above; in Thomas L. Masson, *Little Masterpieces of American Wit and Humor*, vol. 5 (1904); and in Burpee, *Humor of the North* (1902). The intimation of Charles Kozlay, a Bret Harte enthusiast and collector, that Lanigan plagiarized Harte, "The Piracy of Bret Harte's Fables," in *The Lectures of Bret Harte* (1909), pp. 45–53, was refuted by Burpee, "Literary Piracy," *Queen's Quarterly* 46 (1939): 295–303. Other works are found in Edward T. Mason, ed., *Humorous Masterpieces from American Literature*, vol. 3 (1887), pp. 181, 186, 189. Some of his translations are found in a typescript in the Toronto Public Library; see also R. Renault and B. Sulté, "French-Canadian Songs," *Le Courrier du Livre* 14 (1900): 88–91, 281–90, 327–33. For the literary character of the *New York World* at this time, see Joseph O'Connor in the *Buffalo Courier*, 14 May 1883. Substantial obituaries are in the *New York World*, the *Philadelphia Record*, the *Buffalo Courier*, and the *Rochester Post-Express*, 6 Feb. 1886. A longer memoir, quoting letters by Lanigan on his plans for running his own newspaper, is in the *Philadelphia News*, 7 Feb. 1886; there is a valuable retrospective in the *Rochester Post-Express*, 4 May 1895.

BENJAMIN R. FOSTER

LANING, Edward (26 Apr. 1906–6 May 1981), painter, was born in Petersburg, Illinois, the son of John Laning, a lawyer, and Mabel Smoot. Following the death of his mother when he was about twelve, his father suffered a mental breakdown and abandoned the boy; his prominent and affluent maternal grandparents then raised him.

In 1926, after a year as a student at the University of Chicago, Laning withdrew to enroll at the Art Students League of New York; there he sought out Max Weber, who was noted for his reputation as an avant-garde artist. Laning also studied with Boardman Robinson, Kenneth Hayes Miller, John Sloan, and Thomas Hart Benton, whose essays, "The Mechanics of Form Organization in Painting," led Laning to appreciate baroque composition. During the summer of 1929 he toured Italy and Belgium, and while admiring Peter Paul Rubens's large, baroque *Descent from the Cross*, he resolved to become a muralist.

On his return to New York, Laning studied mural painting with Miller and befriended classmates Isabel Bishop (with whom he and Miller toured London, Paris, and Madrid in 1931) and Reginald Marsh. Because of their shared interest in depicting the urban working class of New York, Bishop, Marsh, Miller, Raphael Soyer, Laning and others formed what John Baur, writing in 1951, called the Fourteenth Street School. Laning's easel paintings of the early 1930s like *Fourteenth Street* and *Unlawful Assembly* employ Miller's doughy figures and rose and lavender palette. The radical John Reed Club's 1932 exhibition, "Hunger, Fascism, and War," included work by Laning. In 1933 he married Mary Fife, and artist, with whom he had no children.

Like many of his peers, Laning rejected radicalism around 1933, the year the federal government began offering grants to artists. Laning cultivated what he imagined was a leftist technique that described the constant flux of social forces; reading the Marxist Nikolai Bukharin's *Historical Materialism* "raised the hair on my head," wrote Laning in 1949, "because it was a description of Rubens. . . . [namely,] *mobility*, or change, or dynamism" (Archives of American Art, Smithsonian Institution).

Laning developed what Reginald Marsh called "a very distinguished mural form" and received a 1935 Works Progress Administration (WPA) commission to decorate the main dining room at Ellis Island. Executed with loose, painterly brushstrokes and energetic figures patterned after Rubens, the 7-by-110-foot mural, completed in 1937, depicts the role of immigrants in the development of the United States, but when Ellis Island closed in 1954, the mural fell into ruin. Salvaged fragments were used to decorate the Immigration and Naturalization Ceremonial Courtroom Number 3 of the Brooklyn Federal Courthouse.

Even as Laning's murals celebrated American ideals, his easel paintings increasingly offered social criticism. Regionalist in setting, the 1937 *Corn Dance* highlights the crass antics of tourists purportedly watching a Santo Domingo pueblo tribal performance in New Mexico; from the same year, *Camp Meeting* depicts the frenzy of repentant sinners in Laning's hometown of Petersburg, Illinois.

The Treasury Department's Section of Painting and Sculpture commissioned Laning to paint post office murals in Rockingham, North Carolina (1937), and Bowling Green, Kentucky (1942). It was the WPA, however, that awarded the artist his most prominent commission, *The Story of the Recorded Word* (1940), for the rotunda of the Central Library of the New York Public Library in New York City. By this time, European artist émigrés had brought their modernist tastes to New York, and Laning's naturalism, along with the Beaux-Arts classicism of the library itself, had fallen out of fashion. Critical reception of the mural was unenthusiastic.

Soon afterward, the entry of the United States into World War II discredited regionalism and its isolationist tendencies. But Laning saw the war as an opportunity. He won approval for an army unit of six enlisted artists to depict the war in the Mediterranean theater, but the project was soon canceled, superseded by George Biddle's comprehensive Army Art Program under the auspices of the Treasury Department. Through the AAP, Laning received a noncommissioned post in the Aleutian Islands. In 1943, when *Time* and *Life* magazines took over the program, he was transferred to Italy. The style of his seventy-five works range from documentary naturalism to a surrealism of desolate public spaces and broken statues reminiscent of the art of Giorgio De Chirico.

Immediately after the war, in 1945, Laning received a Guggenheim Fellowship and accepted an appointment to head the Department of Painting and Drawing at the Kansas City Art Institute. Unhappy there, he resigned in 1950 to take a Fulbright Fellowship in Italy, where he attempted to reinvigorate his art by studying Renaissance painting techniques of three-dimensional representation. Abstract expressionism bored Laning, but he believed that like his own art, it revealed societal forces that increasingly overwhelmed the self-determination of the individual. Writing to Marsh in 1952, Laning asked, "Is your figure not moved rather than moving? And what are the abstract painters doing but concerning themselves directly with these forces, disregarding the irrelevant flotsam and jetsam and painting tide?" (Archives). His easel paintings of the early 1950s such as *Attic*, *Ball of Fire*, and *Everyone Cheers* present dark stage sets for chiaroscuro renderings of weird assemblages of objects and moving figures that Laning later suggested came from his unconscious mind.

In 1952 Laning accepted an instructorship at the Art Students League, where he taught until 1975. Experimenting with mescaline and LSD during the mid-1950s led Laning to appreciate the sensuality of color, which he investigated shortly thereafter in *The Fire Now*, *The Fire Next Time*, *Charity*, and *The Poet*, easel paintings that contrast New York's Union Square monuments celebrating civic ideals with the homeless men beneath them.

After 1958, the year of his election to the National Academy of Design, Laning painted few easel pictures. However, he continued to publish books and articles and to execute murals in his WPA style, including one at the National Bank of Petersburg, Illinois (1976), and the Railroad Museum in Ogden, Utah (1980), based on designs of 1935. Answering the suggestion that some mural painting was "vulgar," Laning wrote in 1980 that "the word derives from the Latin *vulgus*, the *crowd*. Mural painting is, inevitably, painting for the crowd, the public. . . . Let's not be afraid to be public and 'popular'" (Archives). Between 1969 and 1974 Laning served as president of the National Society of Mural Painters. In 1980 the New York Public Library commissioned him to paint murals in the DeWitt Wallace Periodicals Room, but the contract was nullified by the artist's death.

The primacy of abstract expressionism eclipsed Laning's national reputation as a muralist and easel painter, but his art and writings warrant attention for the insights they offer into American society and art movements from the Great Depression to the postwar period.

• Laning's papers are in the Archives of American Art, Smithsonian Institution. Among his other writings are two books on art technique, *Perspective for Artists* (1967) and *The Act of Drawing* (1971). Laning discusses his family, his hometown of Petersburg, Ill., and the town's native son, poet Edgar Lee Masters, in "Spoon River Revisited," *American Heritage*, June 1971, pp. 14–17, 104–107. Laning's own account of his government mural projects appears in "Memoirs of a WPA Painter," *American Heritage*, Oct. 1970, pp. 38–44, 56–57, 86–89. See also Francis V. O'Connor, *The New Deal Art Projects: An Anthology of Memoirs* (1972). For overviews of the artist's life, see Howard E. Wooden, *Edward Laning: American Realist* (1982) and his *Edward Laning*, a 1992 exhibition catalog for Kennedy Galleries in New York, and Andrew Weinstein, "History's Effect on the Realism of American Painter Edward Laning Between 1930 and 1960," a 1984 Younger Scholars Grant report on file at the National Endowment for the Humanities.

ANDREW WEINSTEIN

LANING, Harris (18 Oct. 1873–2 Feb. 1941), U.S. naval officer, was born in Petersburg, Illinois, the son of Caleb Barrett Laning, a banking executive, and Mary Esther Harris. After studying at local schools and the Peekskill (N.Y.) Military Academy, Laning attended the U.S. Naval Academy at Annapolis, graduating in 1895. On a succession of ships, the old *Philadelphia*, the new steel cruiser *Oregon*, and the old second-rate, wooden-hulled *Marion*, Naval Cadet Laning learned his trade in a service in transition from sailing and cruising to steaming and fighting. Serving on the newly rebuilt yet still wooden-walled *Mohican* when war with Spain was declared in 1898, Ensign Laning quickly arranged for passage to the Philippines on the monitor *Monadnock*. After a hellish journey, Laning reached the Philippines to discover that the navy had a new enemy in the Philippine nationalists fighting against American rule. The *Monadnock* provided the U.S. Army forces with support fire in the "battles" of Malate, Parañaque, and Coloocan. Laning then cruised the interisland waters on his first command, the captured Spanish gunboat *Panay*, suppressing trade of and supplies for the revolutionaries. In 1900 he married Mabel Clare Nixon; they had one child.

Posted next to Annapolis, Laning taught in the departments of English, history, and law from 1900 to 1902 and then in the department of ordnance and gunnery, 1905–1907. He was promoted to lieutenant (jg) in 1901, and between 1902 and 1905 he served as watch, then gunnery, officer on the *Dolphin*, a dispatch craft used mostly as a yacht by the navy secretary and his guests. Finally, Lieutenant Laning assumed his first battleship post as navigation officer on the *Nebraska* for its cruise with the "Great White Fleet" around the world, 1907–1909, remaining with that pre-dreadnought until 1910. Returning to Annapolis for a third tour as faculty, Lieutenant Commander Laning headed the athletics and then navigation departments. While there, he shifted emphasis in the latter department from theoretical to practical navigation. In 1906–1907 he had coached the navy rifle team to the national championship, and after resuming these duties, he coached the U.S. rifle team to a gold medal at the Stockholm Olympic Games of 1912.

Laning's second command, the newly completed *Cassin*, came in 1913, and soon afterward Commander Laning was given charge of the Atlantic Fleet's Reserve Destroyer Flotilla, a position he held until 1916. With U.S. entry into World War I, Captain Laning moved to the newly created office of the Chief of Naval Operations (CNO), serving under the conservative leadership of Admiral William Benson. He remained in this office throughout the war and soon headed the Personnel Division of the Bureau of Navigation, charged with mobilizing service people, officers, and ships. By the war's end, Laning was acting director of the Bureau of Navigation. Despite his close working relations with the CNO, Laning was not tainted with the charges of ineptness the former commander of U.S. naval forces in Europe, William S. Sims, leveled against Benson. In fact, after the war Laning followed Sims to sea as chief of staff to the commander, Destroyer Forces Atlantic, and served in that position from 1919 to 1921. In this office he directed the destroyer support network crucial to the first successful transatlantic flight—that of the navy flying boat NC-4 in 1919.

In the interwar years, Laning became one of the leaders in successfully adapting the navy to the lessons of the Great War and preparing for the next major naval war. In 1921 he followed Sims, then president of the Naval War College, to Newport, Rhode Island, first as a student and then from 1922 to 1924 as head of the tactics department. Laning's thesis on destroyer tactics became the model for U.S. tactical doctrine. His emphasis was always on surface fighting ships, sometimes at the expense of the emerging technologies of air and subsurface warfare; in the 1920s he frequently spoke publicly against the "radical" air enthusiasts. Captain Laning's reward for toeing the navy line in favor of battleships was command of the new super-dreadnought battleship *Pennsylvania* (1924–1926) and then of the Naval Training Station in San Diego. From the late twenties on, Rear Admiral Laning put his theory and training experiences to work first as chief of staff to the commander, Battle Fleet, and then as commander of Battleship Division Two, Scouting Fleet (1928–1930).

Laning returned to Newport as president of the Naval War College and oversaw a period of growth in which faculty and students worked to integrate the fast-evolving technologies of air, subsurface, and amphibious warfare into naval strategy and tactics. In 1933 temporary Vice Admiral Laning took command of the Cruiser Division of the U.S. Fleet and experienced one of the few setbacks of his long career, when his flagship *Chicago* collided with a steamer while under the command of his flag captain. Although two officers died, a board of inquiry cleared the navy of responsibility for the accident. The remainder of Laning's tenure proved successful, as the division employed the tactics he designed for a force that included the controversial new eight-inch "treaty" cruisers—so called because they were the most heavily armed ships allowed under the various naval limitation treaties of the 1920s. As a reward for a successful career at sea and on land, Admiral Laning commanded the U.S.

Battle Force, U.S. Fleet, based in Hawaii during 1935–1936.

Admiral Laning served as commandant of the Brooklyn Navy Yard and the Third Naval District from April 1936 until his retirement on 1 October 1937. He was then appointed governor of the Naval Home in Philadelphia. There he wrote his autobiography, and there he died.

For the first third of the twentieth century, Laning played important roles in the nation's defense. He and his messmates rarely embraced the potential of aerial, subsurface, and amphibious warfare, generally preferring to improve on battleships. He typified the hardworking and dedicated people who served and protected, representing and supporting what they saw as the American way.

• Laning's writings as a student, faculty member, and president are in the Naval War College Archives, with a published guide available on request. *An Admiral's Yarn: The Autobiography of Harris Laning*, introduced and annotated by Mark Shulman, includes his student thesis. Laning has not received much comment in secondary works, but he receives some attention in William S. Sims, *The Victory at Sea* (1920), Peter Karsten, *The Naval Aristocracy* (1972), Robert O'Connell, *Sacred Vessels* (1991), and Shulman, *Navalism and the Emergence of American Sea Power* (1995).

MARK RUSSELL SHULMAN

LANMAN, Charles Rockwell (8 July 1850–20 Feb. 1941), college professor, was born in Norwich, Connecticut, the son of Peter Lanman, a textile manufacturer, and Catherine Cook. After receiving his early education at the Norwich Free Academy, he entered Yale, where he was heavily influenced by William Dwight Whitney, a leading American scholar in Indo-European philology. Whitney had studied under Rudolf Roth at Tübingen, and he in turn inspired Lanman, who graduated with a B.A. in 1871, to continue his studies in Sanskrit. Lanman remained at Yale for two more years, earning his Ph.D. in 1873.

Lanman then traveled to Europe, where German universities offered graduate educational instruction far advanced from that available in American colleges. He took full advantage of his time abroad, studying at the Universities of Berlin and Leipzig and with Roth at Tübingen. Roth, who began the scientific study of the Veda, helped to refine his pupil's research interests, and under his guidance Lanman began work on his first paper, *On Noun-Inflection in the Veda* (1880).

Lanman returned to the United States in 1876 and immediately put his scholarly talents to work at the newly founded Johns Hopkins University in Baltimore, Maryland. Under the leadership of President Daniel Coit Gilman, the university strove to provide Americans with the same grade of graduate-level training that had hitherto required overseas study. Lanman remained on the faculty of Hopkins for four years before accepting an invitation in 1880 to join Harvard University as professor of Sanskrit.

Lanman remained at Harvard until his retirement in 1926, and while there he rose to the top of his profession. In 1879 he became secretary of the American Philological Association and gained valuable experience in editing volumes 10 to 14 of the association's *Transactions* (1880–1884). He retained the position of secretary until 1884, when he became corresponding secretary of the American Oriental Society, serving additionally as joint editor of that organization's journal in the process. In 1888 Lanman married Mary Billings Hinckley; they had six children. Following the wedding, Lanman and his wife spent a year in India, during which time Lanman collected numerous Sanskrit and Prakrit manuscripts for the Harvard library. Upon returning to the United States he published the second volume of *Sanskrit Reader, with Vocabulary and Notes* in 1889 (the first volume appeared in 1884) with a view to the needs of language students everywhere. The introductory textbook was well received and was used by instructors for decades following its publication.

Upon returning to the United States, Lanman served as president of the Philological Association in 1889–1890 and then commenced work on the publications for which he is best known, the Harvard Oriental Series. Initiated by Lanman in 1891 and financed by a former student, Henry Clarke Warren, the series eventually reached thirty-six volumes. Consisting of texts, translations, and scholarly examinations of works in Sanskrit and other ancient languages of India, the series showcased the efforts of some of the leading philologists of the day, including Maurice Bloomfield, Arthur Berriedale Keith, Sten Konow, Karl Geldner, Johannes Hertel, Hendrik Kern, and Lanman's mentor Whitney. A landmark set of publications, the Harvard Oriental Series provided the basis for Vedic research. Lanman and Whitney cooperated in producing a translation and annotation of the *Atharva Veda Saṃhitā* in 1905. Lanman also contributed a lively English translation to Konow's *Rāja-çekhara's Karpūra-Mañjarī* (1901), providing him with the opportunity to display his own sense of humor while giving scholarly attention to a famous Prakrit comedy. Among the other standout volumes were Bloomfield's *A Vedic Concordance* (1906), translations of both the *Yajur Veda* (1914) and the *Rig Veda Brāhmanas* (1920) by Keith, and Keith's *The Religion and Philosophy of the Veda and Upanishads* (1925).

Widely honored and recognized for his efforts, Lanman served as president of the American Oriental Society on two occasions (1907–1908 and 1919–1920) and enjoyed membership in more than a dozen foreign learned societies, including the Asiatic Society of Bengal (Calcutta) and the Royal Bohemian Society of Sciences (Prague). He was selected as one of only eight non-Japanese academics to receive the Japanese Medal during celebrations surrounding the 2,500th anniversary of the birth of Buddha.

Lanman enjoyed a long and healthy retirement following his departure from Harvard. Indulging in his twin passions of horseback riding and sculling, he remained active until near the end of his life. His wife died in 1936. Lanman died in Belmont, Massachusetts.

Lanman will long be remembered for his efforts to apply the techniques of modern scholarship to the ancient languages of India. The increased accessibility of these languages to western scholars and the numerous academics who received their training under Lanman remain his greatest legacies.

• Lanman's papers are divided between the Harvard University Archives and the Department of Sanskrit and Indian Studies at Harvard. The best sources of information on Lanman continue to be obituaries in the *Journal of the American Oriental Society*, Sept. 1941, and the *Year Book of the American Philosophical Society*, 1941. An obituary is also in the *New York Times*, 21 Feb. 1941.

EDWARD L. LACH, JR.

LANNUIER, Charles-Honoré (27 June 1779–16 Oct. 1819), cabinetmaker, was born in Chantilly, France, the son of Michel-Cerille Lannuier, an innkeeper, and Marie-Genvieve Malice. He spent his formative years in a France racked by the political and social upheaval of the revolution. Unfortunately, only the barest outline of his life in these tumultuous times can be traced. Baptismal and court records in Chantilly and Paris indicate that he was one of ten children and the considerably younger brother of Nicolas-Louis-Cyrille Lannuier, a Parisian cabinetmaker who attained the guild rank of *maître ébéniste* (master cabinetmaker) on 23 July 1783. By 1791, when Honoré was twelve, his widowed father moved the entire family to Paris, where they resided on the rue des Vielles Thuilleries in the parish of St. Sulpice. Just about this time Lannuier's father, according to custom and tradition, would have sought to apprentice his son to a trade. No record of the master to whom Honoré was apprenticed has been found, however, so it only can be assumed that he learned the "art and mystery" of cabinetmaking from his older brother.

In 1803, after a decade of honing his cabinetmaking skills in Paris, Lannuier left France for New York City, the fledgling American republic's fastest-growing commercial center. If Lannuier's later success there is any measure of his industrious and entrepreneurial nature, then his emigration is not surprising. On the other hand, in 1803 the ranks of Napoleon's army were swelling in preparation for a possible invasion of Great Britain, and the frightening prospect of conscription may also have hastened his departure. Whatever Lannuier's motivation for leaving, his arrival in New York City was probably eased considerably by the established presence there of another older brother, Augustine, who operated a confectionery shop at 100 Broadway from 1799 to 1811. From this address Lannuier launched his American career, heralding his own arrival in an ad placed in the *New-York Evening Post* on 15 July 1803: "Honoré Lannuier, cabinetmaker, just arrived from France . . . takes the liberty of informing the public that he makes all kinds of Furniture, Beds, Chairs, &c., in the newest and latest French fashion. . . . He wishes to settle himself in this city, and only wants a little encouragement. Those who choose to favor him with their custom, may apply to Mr. Augustine Lannuier, Confectioner and Distiller, No 100 Broadway."

It was not long before Lannuier developed a clientele and established his own workshop and wareroom. In 1804 he is listed in the New York City directory at 60 Broad Street in the old but still fashionable first ward. No shop records survive to document the scale of Lannuier's production or the organization of labor within his furniture manufactory. Like several of his competitors, he maintained a store where he stocked furniture of his own make and possibly work by other New York cabinetmakers as well, since subcontracting work was a fairly standard practice in the trade. Additionally it is known that Lannuier sold clocks imported from France, fabrics, and fancy work. Unlike Duncan Phyfe or Michael Allison, two of the city's major operators, however, Lannuier never expanded his establishment substantially in his lifetime, which suggests that he may have been a little less entrepreneurial and less willing to expose himself to risk than some of his major competitors. Lannuier nonetheless seems to have found his niche and captured a significant share of the market. His 1819 estate inventory records more credits than debts, showing him to be not only a man of considerable artistic talents but one of better-than-average business skills as well. He lived and worked at 60 Broad Street for the remainder of his life, making stylish furniture for New York's mercantile and social elite and for wealthy clients as far afield as Philadelphia, Baltimore, Richmond, and Savannah. One of his most important commissions, completed in 1812, was for the seating furniture in the Common Council Chamber of New York's new city hall, one of the grandest public buildings erected in early nineteenth-century America.

Lannuier's furniture is highly distinctive, reflecting not only his superb design training in post-revolutionary France, but also a willingness on his part to incorporate the English Regency-based New York vernacular style, with its prominent use of reeding and stylized water leaf carving. Some of his furniture forms, namely his signature console or pier tables, are more purely French. These tables utilize a wide range of materials—Italian statuary marble, exotic wood veneers, gilded and bronzed carved wooden figures, cast bronze and other metals, and even tôle or tin painted columns in faux malachite—and reveal Lannuier's remarkably inventive approach to design. They have broad platform bases that sit either directly on the floor or are raised on animal feet, mirror-paneled backs, and freestanding front supports in columnar or sculptural forms that bear the weight of their statuary marble tops. This basic form, a staple of the Consulat and Empire periods in France, seems to have been established by Lannuier in New York, where it became the quintessential American Empire form and continued to be manufactured in varying degrees of quality into the 1840s.

Lannuier's career was cut short by his death when he was at the height of his creative powers. His obituary gives no clear indication of the cause, only stating that he died after a "lingering illness." That Lannuier may have savored some of his own success when he was alive is hinted at in a newspaper ad placed about a month after his death by the cabinetmaker John Gruez, who announced to the public that he "has taken the establishment of the late Mr. Lannuier, No. 60 Broad-Street, where he continues to make all kinds of furniture and fancy work for which said establishment was so well known throughout the United States" (*New-York Evening Post*, 8 Nov. 1819). Lannuier's renown continues to this day, with documented examples of his furniture in the permanent collections of many of the nation's leading art museums, including the Metropolitan Museum of Art in New York City, the Art Institute of Chicago, the High Museum in Atlanta, the Henry Francis du Pont Winterthur Museum in Winterthur, Delaware, and the collections of the White House.

Lannuier, whose short but productive career in America lasted only sixteen years, was a contemporary of the renowned furniture-maker Duncan Phyfe and a leading figure in the development of a distinctive and highly refined school of cabinetmaking in New York City during the late federal period. With regard to the history of style and taste, Lannuier's significance resides in the fact that he was a direct transmitter of *le style antique*, or the Greco-Roman revival of Republican and early Empire France, to America. Lannuier traded on his French descent and cachet throughout his career. Even in the carved and gilded card tables and marble-topped consoles made during the last five years of his life—the acknowledged masterpieces of his oeuvre—Lannuier continued to exploit this French connection through a handsomely engraved bilingual label he consistently applied to his finished work. Lannuier's near-obsessive labeling of his work throughout his career is highly significant and has proven to be a great boon to students of New York classical-style furniture. Lannuier's legacy of labeled furniture has allowed him to be identified as a creative, individualistic designer who constantly strove for novelty and innovation, and as a craftsman of the highest caliber. His impact on New York cabinetmaking was considerable in his own lifetime and continued to resonate fully a decade after his demise in the form and ornament of late classical New York furniture.

• Lannuier's life and work are treated in Lorraine Waxman, "French Influence on American Decorative Arts of the Early Nineteenth Century: The Work of Charles-Honoré Lannuier" (master's thesis, Univ. of Delaware, 1958). The earliest published recognition of Lannuier and his work came in two articles by Thomas Hamilton Ormsbee, "A Franco-American Cabinetmaker: Charles-Honoré Lannuier," *Antiques*, May 1933, pp. 166–67, and "The Furniture of Lannuier and His Successor," *Antiques*, June 1933, pp. 224–26. In addition to those mentioned above, Lannuier's furniture is in numerous other museums and historical societies. There are major suites of furniture made for Stephen Van Rensselaer of Alba-

ny in the Albany Institute of History & Art, and for James Bosley, a Baltimore merchant, at the Maryland Historical Society. In addition, a pair of card tables that Lannuier made for John Wickham of Richmond, Va., can be found in Wickham's 1812 house, which is affiliated with the Valentine Museum. In New York City, Lannuier furniture is at the New-York Historical Society, the Museum of the City of New York, and the Brooklyn Museum. Most of the original seating furniture he made for the Common Council Chamber is still at city hall.

PETER M. KENNY

LANSDALE, Edward Geary (6 Feb. 1908–23 Feb. 1987), air force officer and counterinsurgency specialist, was born in Detroit, Michigan, the son of automotive executive Henry Lansdale and Sarah Frances Phillips. He attended the University of California at Los Angeles (UCLA) and obtained an army commission through the Reserve Officers Training Corps (ROTC) program. Leaving UCLA without graduating in 1931, he went to New York City to look unsuccessfully for newspaper work. There he met and married Helen Batcheller in 1932. They had two children.

Moving back to California in 1935, Lansdale began a career in advertising and was working at a San Francisco agency when World War II began. Since he had earlier resigned his army commission, it took him a year to get it reinstated. While Lansdale waited, a business acquaintance, who was now a lieutenant colonel in military intelligence, got him a position with the new Office of Strategic Services (OSS), forerunner of the Central Intelligence Agency (CIA). Ordered to active duty as a lieutenant in February 1943, he was assigned to army intelligence but continued to work for the OSS. This unique dual role began a pattern that he would continue through much of his career. He would work on highly secret projects for civilian intelligence agencies under the cover of doing what appeared to be routine military advising or intelligence work. During the war he worked for the OSS in California and New York, researching and disseminating background information for military intelligence use as well as recruiting and training other agents. What else he actually did and where he did it is not publicly known. All he would say later was that "they kept using me to go out getting new information and meet[ing] new people all the time, which seemed to be my forte."

After the war, Lansdale obtained a regular army commission and went to the Philippines with the rank of major. He was placed in charge of intelligence analysis for the armed forces in the Western Pacific. Still in the Philippines in 1947, he transferred to the newly created air force, which in effect loaned him in 1949 to a highly secret interagency espionage group, the Office of Policy Coordination (OPC), that became part of the CIA in 1952. He served with the OPC in Washington, D.C., on what he termed "cold war duty," and as he had done with the OSS, he operated officially as a military intelligence officer and covertly as a CIA agent. After joining the OPC, Lansdale began studying the techniques of psychological warfare. His experience in the Philippines convinced him that the Cold War battle with communism would be fought not through conventional warfare, but in a struggle for the loyalty and support of the people in so-called Third World countries.

In 1950 Lieutenant Colonel Lansdale went back to the Philippines ostensibly as a military adviser but in fact on a top secret mission to help Philippine defense secretary Ramón Magsaysay create a popular political base. Lansdale had identified the charismatic Magsaysay as the kind of democratic leader he envisioned who could compete politically with a Communist cadre promising radical reforms to poor peasants. Using a wide range of psychological warfare techniques (even including exploiting popular fears of vampires), expediting military and economic assistance, and displaying great personal energy and bravery, Lansdale helped Magsaysay defeat a Communist-influenced and resilient insurgent movement known as the Huks. Magsaysay won election as president of the Philippines in a landslide in 1953, and Lansdale gained a formidable reputation as a counterinsurgency expert. From this victory, Lansdale concluded that governments in developing nations must and could gain popular support through positive propaganda and social services and did not have to rely on oppression. He coined the term "civic action" to describe the programs by which government soldiers "behave as the brothers and protectors of the people."

Early in 1954, the Eisenhower administration sent Lansdale to Vietnam with instructions to do there what he had done in the Philippines. An ardent, even idealistic, champion of democracy, Lansdale accepted the mission with the understanding that he would "help the Vietnamese help themselves" and not assist America's French allies, who had been trying to restore their colonial control over the country. He arrived in Saigon in June, just as the Geneva Conference was preparing to divide Vietnam between the Communist-ruled North and the American-assisted South, and he immediately befriended the new prime minister of South Vietnam, Ngo Dinh Diem. Working independently of the CIA station in Saigon and the U.S. embassy, Lansdale assembled a team, the Saigon Military Mission, which set to work sabotaging facilities in North Vietnam and organizing a mass exodus of Catholics from the North to the South. He tutored the autocratic Diem on the techniques of electoral politics and used financial and other inducements to neutralize Diem's southern political rivals. Lansdale disputed the judgment of President Dwight D. Eisenhower's special representative in Vietnam, General J. Lawton Collins, that Diem would never prove to be a successful leader. Lansdale's assistance helped Diem defeat an armed uprising of religious sects in 1955, and the next year Diem won a one-sided victory as South Vietnam's first president. Lansdale never had the success with Diem, however, that he had had with Magsaysay. The South Vietnamese leader relied too heavily on his clannish family, failed to broaden his base of popular

support, and, in fact, alienated many Vietnamese with his oppressive policies.

Colonel Lansdale left Vietnam in 1956 and went to the Pentagon as an assistant to the secretary of defense for special, that is, covert, operations. Despite Diem's shortcomings, the South Vietnamese president's continued survival in office had added luster to Lansdale's Philippine accomplishments. The mustachioed, harmonica-playing Lansdale had become so mythologized as a secret warrior that he formed the prototype for two fictional characters: the naive Alden Pyle in Graham Greene's *The Quiet American* (1955) and the dashing Colonel Edwin B. Hillandale in William J. Lederer and Eugene Burdick's *The Ugly American* (1958).

Late in 1960 Brigadier General Lansdale returned to Vietnam for a brief inspection. In part he welcomed the trip as a way to divorce himself from what he advised his superiors would be a disaster if their plan to land a force of Cuban exiles at the Bay of Pigs went forward. In January 1961 he informed the incoming Kennedy administration that the U.S. effort to aid South Vietnam was failing, and he recommended emergency assistance to Diem. His report prompted the new president to authorize an expanded counterinsurgency program and to increase the level of U.S. aid to the Saigon government. President John F. Kennedy considered naming Lansdale ambassador to South Vietnam, but officials in the Departments of State and Defense insisted that the general was too controversial and freewheeling to be a diplomat. Instead, late in 1961, after the embarrassing failure of the Bay of Pigs invasion, the president assigned Lansdale to work on a reexamination of U.S. policy toward Cuba. Lansdale became part of Operation Mongoose, an effort to destabilize the government of Cuba and perhaps to eliminate Fidel Castro himself. The planning was abandoned, however, when global tension escalated during the Cuban missile crisis. Always uncomfortable with Lansdale's unconventional approach, the military-diplomatic bureaucracy arranged for his promotion to major general in 1963 and then—with Kennedy's acquiescence—retired Lansdale from active duty on 31 October. The next day (2 Nov. in Saigon) Diem fell victim to an assassin's bullets.

At the suggestion of Vice President Hubert Humphrey, the Johnson administration rehabilitated Lansdale's career and sent him back to Vietnam in 1965 as a special assistant to the U.S. ambassador. His assignment was to work on pacification—improving the political base of the Saigon government—but he had no real authority and accomplished little in the bureaucratic mire that passed for U.S. policy in Vietnam by the middle 1960s. The suspicion and fragmentation within South Vietnam's political structure by that time also frustrated his efforts. He left Vietnam for the last time in 1968 and published his highly self-censored memoirs, *In the Midst of Wars: An American's Mission to Southeast Asia*, in 1972. His wife died in 1972, and the next year he married Patrocinio Yapcinco, whom he had first met in the Philippines in 1945. He died at his home in McLean, Virginia.

Lansdale was one of the architects of the post–World War II military-political strategy known as counterinsurgency. This doctrine developed as a Cold War method of responding to the theory of "people's war" as advocated by Chinese Communist leader Mao Zedong (Mao Tse-tung). In his memoirs Lansdale argued that governments fighting the Communists' revolutionary doctrine must build bridges of friendship with their own people and not rely on bombs, bullets, and big bankrolls to win popular support away from insurgents. He believed that the Communists' self-characterization as popular liberators was a propaganda disguise for oppression and that the new governments of emerging nations had to develop their own unity with their people. Largely because of his success with this strategy in the Philippines, counterinsurgency and civic action came to be accepted by U.S. strategists in the 1960s. The attempted use of Lansdale's theories in Vietnam proved unsuccessful, although Lansdale himself claimed that they were never given a real opportunity to be implemented there. He maintained that U.S. assistance to South Vietnam concentrated almost entirely on military aid and that it sought to win the Vietnamese over to the "American way." He preferred a balance of economic, political, social, and military development pursued in partnership with the South Vietnamese and in sympathy with their history and values. Lansdale understood that the Communist cadre could be ruthless, and he often fought back with his own clandestine operations involving sabotage, disinformation, bribery, and even assassination. French critics dubbed him "Lawrence of Indochina" and claimed that his method was "to defeat the brigands, you must become brigands." Basically, however, he remained an idealist who liked to quote Thomas Jefferson and Thomas Paine and who patterned himself after the patriots of 1776. "Tyranny remains tyranny, whatever its current name," he wrote in 1972, and like Jefferson he swore "eternal hostility against every form of tyranny over the mind of man."

• Lansdale's papers are at the Hoover Institution Archives, Stanford, Calif. The Charles T. R. Bohannon and Samuel T. Williams Papers, also at the Hoover Institution Archives, contain some additional Lansdale papers. Much of the official record of his highly secret activities remains classified in the records of the Department of State and the Office of the Secretary of Defense, Washington, D.C. His memoirs are useful but often do not provide critical details. A concise statement of his views of Vietnam is his "Thoughts about a Past War," the forward to *A Short History of the Vietnam War*, ed. Allan R. Millet (1978). A sympathetic biography is Cecil B. Currey, *Edward Lansdale: The Unquiet American* (1988). See also John Prados, *Presidents' Secret Wars: CIA and Pentagon Covert Operations since World War II* (1986), and David L. Anderson, *Trapped by Success: The Eisenhower Administration and Vietnam, 1953–1961* (1991). Obituaries are in the *Washington Post* and the *New York Times*, 24 Feb. 1987.

DAVID L. ANDERSON

LANSING, John (30 Jan. 1754–12 Dec. 1829?), jurist and politician, often known as John Lansing, Jr., was born in Albany, New York, the son of Gerrit J. Lansing, a trader and minor officeholder, and Jannetje Waters. Lansing's paternal ancestor came from the Netherlands in about 1640. In 1781 John Lansing married Cornelia Ray, and, of their ten children, five daughters lived to adulthood. Three daughters married politically active lawyers, and all three of Lansing's brothers contributed substantially to New York State's political life.

Lansing did not attend college but studied law in Albany with Robert Yates and was admitted to the bar in 1775. During 1776 and 1777 he served as General Philip Schuyler's military secretary. Furthering his knowledge with the law library that James Duane had placed in his charge, Lansing returned to practice in Albany in 1778, appearing frequently before the New York Supreme Court there and later in that court's New York City sittings as well. Meanwhile, he invested in land and securities. In 1780 he became a commissioner to redeem state promissory notes by land sales. He purchased confiscated Loyalist properties and by the end of the decade had also acquired over $7,000 in government bonds and promissory notes.

From 1780 through 1783 Albany County supporters of Governor George Clinton elected Lansing to the assembly. Chosen to the ninth, tenth, and twelfth assemblies, he served as Speaker for the ninth, held in New York City in early 1786, and for the twelfth, which met in Albany in December 1788. Late in 1786, in Hartford, Connecticut, Lansing helped to settle Massachusetts land and jurisdictional claims in western New York. He served in Congress in 1784 and 1787 and was also mayor of Albany from September 1786 through September 1790.

Lansing believed that army recruitment burdens should be distributed evenly among the male population and that the assessment of taxes should take indebtedness into account, but he opposed forcing creditors to accept wartime currency. By 1786 he backed repeal of the 1779 requirement that lawyers certify their loyalty to the patriot cause. He also supported conditional allocation of New York State import duties to the confederation government, but, as an Antifederalist, he opposed substantial changes in the Articles of Confederation.

In 1786 Lansing, along with Alexander Hamilton and Robert Yates, was a delegate to the Constitutional Convention in Philadelphia, Pennsylvania. But he and Yates departed early from the Philadelphia Convention on 10 July 1787. Lansing predicted that the delegates would produce a government that "absorbs all power." He and Yates further developed their objections in a December 1787 open letter to Clinton, arguing that a "consolidation of the states" must destroy "the civil liberty of such citizens who could be effectually coerced" under the new Constitution. In the state convention at Poughkeepsie in mid-1788, Lansing unsuccessfully sought to make New York's ratification of the Constitution contingent upon amendments to protect individual "liberties." In late 1788 and early 1789, trying to check the ascendant Federalists, he led colleagues in the assembly to resist the selection of U.S. senators by means other than a joint ballot.

Lansing was made a judge of the New York Supreme Court in September 1790. In 1790 and 1791 the legislature named him to the commissions to settle the New York–Vermont border and the land claims of New Yorkers in Vermont. He became chief justice of the New York Supreme Court in February 1798 and chancellor in October 1801. He continued to play a role in New York's faction-ridden Republican party. When George Clinton declined to run again for governor, a caucus of 15 February 1804 nominated Lansing, preferred by Alexander Hamilton to the New York City nominee, Aaron Burr. Clintonian concern about Lansing's political reliability led the *Albany Register* to say that Lansing had been picked only after others had declined. Lansing then withdrew. By the next election for governor, in 1807, his resentment of the growing political power of George Clinton's nephew, De Witt Clinton, and De Witt's brother-in-law, Judge Ambrose Spencer, led him to speak out. Openly breaking with the Clintons, he claimed that George Clinton had attempted to commit him to a "particular course" and had suggested that De Witt Clinton be named chancellor.

Lansing, as judge, provided William Coleman, a Federalist lawyer and newspaper editor, with "large extracts from his early minutes written with his own hand" for *Cases of Practice in the Supreme Court of New-York* (1801), which shows how the court, given the availability of land, modified English realty practice. As chancellor, Lansing became a defendant in *John Van Ness Yates v. Lansing*, a well-publicized 1811 case. In 1808 Lansing had jailed Yates, the Clintonian recorder of the city of Albany, for illegally pleading in the name of another lawyer. James Kent of the supreme court released Yates on a writ of habeas corpus. Lansing recommitted him, and the supreme court upheld his order. Yates then won a reversal in the Court of Errors and sued Lansing for a statutory penalty of $1,200; the Court of Errors decided that Lansing did not have to pay. The decision protected judges against civil penalties for their judicial acts in civil suits. Lansing's judgment, however, had been questioned, and this case, along with other reversals, clouded his reputation. In 1812 the Court of Errors, in *Livingston v. Van Ingen*, reversed Lansing's refusal to enjoin a line of steamboats that competed with the Livingston-Fulton monopoly. Lansing had reasoned that the monopoly violated a common right to use navigable waters. As chancellor, he sat on the Council of Revision, where he cast a deciding vote to charter the Bank of America in 1812.

Retiring at the constitutionally fixed age of sixty, Lansing practiced law in Albany and concentrated on the management of his lands and those of his brother-in-law, New York City merchant and banker Cornelius Ray. He allied himself with Martin Van Buren, who in 1822 unsuccessfully supported Lansing's ap-

pointment as postmaster of Albany. In 1824 he lost a heated contest for the mayoralty of Albany and a race for the assembly, but the legislature chose him as one of four presidential electors pledged to William Harris Crawford of Georgia. He published *Reports of Select Cases in Chancery* in 1826, which recorded his efforts to gain value from the Albany and Schoharie County lands that he had mortgaged to the Albany Insurance Company and others. Staying in New York City in 1829, he left his hotel room to visit his nephew Robert Ray and vanished. Thurlow Weed, the political manager, later alleged that foul play brought Lansing's death.

Lansing made his most significant contribution as a moderate Antifederalist who emphasized the need for guarantees that power would not destroy liberty. Having questioned the political dominance of the Clintons, he became in later life a legal eminence to whom anti-Clinton Republicans could turn as they strove to stand for lawful order, the expansion of political rights for white males, and the development of a nationwide party.

• Unpublished correspondence bearing on Lansing's career can be found in the collections of the New York Public Library, Union College in Schenectady, N.Y., the Albany Institute of History and Art, the New-York Historical Society, and the New York State Library. Claude G. Munsell, *The Lansing Family* (1916), is a history of the Lansing family. Joel Munsell, *Collections of the History of Albany*, vol. 2 (1867), documents a portion of Lansing's mayoralty, and the *Journal* of the New York Assembly, fourth through twelfth sessions (1780–1789), records his legislative activity. Joseph R. Strayer, ed., *The Delegate from New York or Proceedings of the Federal Convention of 1787 from the Notes of John Lansing, Jr.* (1939), and James H. Hutson, "Robert Yates's Notes on the Constitutional Convention of 1787: Citizen Genet's Edition," *Quarterly Journal of the Library of Congress* (1978), are valuable for Lansing's contribution to the history of the convention. Jabez D. Hammond, *History of Political Parties in the State of New-York* (2 vols., 1842), offers an early account of Lansing's political role. Lucien Brock Proctor, "Chancellors Livingston, Lansing and Kent," in the "Biographical Department" of the *Albany Law Journal* (Jan.–July 1892): 17–22, outlines Lansing's judicial career, which can be traced more fully in William Johnson, *Reports of Cases . . . in the Court for . . . the Correction of Errors* (20 vols., 1808–1823). *Albany Daily Argus*, 29 Dec. 1829, and Thurlow Weed Barnes, *Memoir of Thurlow Weed* (1884), suggest the circumstances of Lansing's death.

CRAIG HANYAN

LANSING, Robert (17 Oct. 1864–20 Oct. 1928), international lawyer, counselor of the State Department, and secretary of state, was born in Watertown, New York, the son of John Lansing, a lawyer and civic leader, and Marie Lay Dodge. From an early age, Lansing seemed certain to follow his father into a legal career. After obtaining his diploma from Watertown High School, he attended Amherst College, graduating in 1886. Returning to Watertown, he read law in his father's office and was admitted to the New York bar in

1889, whereupon he became the junior partner in the newly formed firm of Lansing & Lansing. He continued in the firm until his father's death in 1907.

In 1890 Lansing married Eleanor Foster, a union that would afford important professional advantages. Eleanor's father, John Watson Foster, was a distinguished American diplomat and international lawyer, who had served as U.S. minister to Mexico, Spain, and Russia. Not long after his daughter's marriage, Foster was appointed secretary of state by President Benjamin Harrison. With his father-in-law's guidance, Lansing quickly turned to the specialized practice of international law, spending an increasing amount of time in Washington, D.C. Although the Lansings were longtime Democrats and Robert continued the partisan affiliation, he showed no reluctance to accept professional favors provided through his father-in-law's Republican party connections.

Beginning in 1892, Lansing accepted appointment as associate counsel for the United States in the Bering Sea Fur Seal Arbitration case. He served as counsel for the United States before the Joint Anglo-American Commission that decided the Alaskan boundary dispute in 1903; the North Atlantic Fisheries Arbitration case in 1908–1910; and the British-American Claims Arbitration in 1911–1914. No other American lawyer served on as many international arbitration cases during the early twentieth century as did Lansing. In addition, he assisted his father-in-law by serving as counsel in the United States, representing such foreign governments as Mexico, Venezuela, Russia, and China. He helped organize the American Society for International Law in 1906, and the next year he participated in establishing the *American Journal of International Law*, for which he was an occasional contributor and reviewer.

When John Bassett Moore resigned as counselor of the State Department in March 1914, President Woodrow Wilson and Secretary William Jennings Bryan settled on Lansing to be Moore's successor. His tenure at the State Department would never be comfortable. Besides being responsible to a secretary of state for whose knowledge, experience, and intuitions in foreign affairs Lansing held little respect, he was constantly aware that the president was directing foreign policy from the White House, relying more often on the advice of his friend Edward House than on the State Department. However, when Lansing personally disagreed with policies being advanced by the White House, he invariably confined the expression of his disagreements to his private memoranda. The European war along with civil strife in China and Mexico generated a host of nearly insoluble legal problems. Lansing's work would be further complicated by his medical condition. Throughout most of his adult life he suffered from *diabetes millitus*, a malady that he managed to conceal from all save his family and his physician. Yet, according to all accounts, Lansing carried an increasing burden of work. Among the numerous legal instruments, he drafted Wilson's pronouncement on neutrality in 1914.

In the spring of 1915, when Bryan resigned over a disagreement with Wilson on the *Lusitania* protest notes, Lansing seemed to be an almost ideal successor—an officer whose demeanor would not likely interfere with the president's determination to direct foreign policy. The diplomatic corps in Washington came quickly to realize, in the words of German Ambassador Johann von Bernstorff, "Since Wilson decides *everything*, any interview with Lansing is a mere matter of form."

Due in part to Lansing's legalistic approach to foreign policy, his tenure as counselor and later as secretary of state was accompanied by frequent disputes with President Wilson, mainly over tactics rather than underlying strategies. A realist and staunch pragmatist, Lansing believed that the United States should assume a predominant role in the Western Hemisphere while seeking a conciliatory posture toward Japan in East Asia and the Pacific region. He was largely instrumental in urging Wilson to dispatch U.S. marines to Haiti and the Dominican Republic in 1915–1916. In order to prevent German influence from growing in the Western Hemisphere, Lansing urged the purchase by the United States of the Danish West Indies in 1917. Lansing was also an important influence on bringing about stabilization in Mexico. During the first years of the European war, while the United States was still neutral, he took the hard line that under no circumstances could Germany and the Central Powers be allowed to emerge triumphant. He believed that this view accorded with the national interests of the United States. Thus Lansing anticipated eventual U.S. intervention in the European war. He persuaded Wilson that it would be well within the legal meaning of neutrality for American citizens, including bankers, to arrange loans on behalf of belligerent governments, chiefly the Allies. On questions concerning whether the U.S. government had responsibility for protecting its citizens who took passage aboard allied ships, Lansing's affirmative advice prevailed. His advice also proved crucial in the eventual arming of U.S. merchant vessels in 1917. What is surprising is that despite Wilson's general distrust of lawyers, the president seems to have maintained a healthy respect for Lansing's advice even on those occasions when Wilson was listening to others. Lansing's influence on foreign policy, at least until the armistice in November 1918, was considerable.

In Lansing's correspondence with the European belligerents, he generally adopted hard legal positions, as he did when criticizing the British application of the naval blockade against neutral shipping to continental Europe. Lansing was much shaken by reports of German atrocities against civilians in Belgium and France. Already by 1915, he came increasingly to believe that America's interests in the European balance of power created for the United States a stake in the outcome of the war. He believed that the United States might be obliged to intervene against Germany and its allies.

Once the United States entered the European war as an associate of the Allied powers, Lansing devoted much time to writing articles and speaking before public forums in order to educate American society to the justifications for belligerency. In part, these activities reflected President Wilson's increasing readiness to delegate responsibilities for foreign affairs to other departments and agencies of government, thus sidetracking Lansing's State Department. Such diversions also reflected the lack of presidential confidence in Secretary Lansing and the Diplomatic Service.

Much of Lansing's attention was directed toward the negotiations he conducted with Japan in November 1917, which resulted in what was popularly known as the Lansing-Ishii Agreement. Intended to deflect expansionist sentiment in Japan toward China and to ease pent-up hostile feelings toward the United States, its ambiguous language recognized Japan's "special interests" in China and denied that the Japanese desired to violate China's territorial integrity or the principle of the Open Door, by which all trading partners would enjoy equal access to the China market. Apparently, the delicate wording succeeded in reducing tensions.

At the end of the war, Wilson appointed Lansing to serve with him as one of the five U.S. commissioners to the peace conference at Paris. Clearly Lansing did not share the president's strong commitment to a proposed world organization later known as the League of Nations. In his memoir of the conference, *The Peace Negotiations* (1921), Lansing declared (p. 162):

The differences between the President's views and mine in regard to the character of the League of Nations and to the provisions of the Covenant relating to the organization and functions of the League were irreconcilable, and we were equally in disagreement as to the duties of the League in carrying out certain provisions of the Treaty of Peace as the common agent of the signatory Powers.

Lansing's memoir recounts fundamental differences between himself and President Wilson over the league as well as other elements of the peace settlement, including mandates, the treaty for the maintenance of French security, and the president's acceptance of Japan's claims in Shantung, China. To a profound extent, Lansing's objections were directed toward what came to be called the Wilsonian doctrine of universalism with its "mutual guaranty of territorial integrity and political independence against external aggression," as set forth in Article X of the Covenant, a responsibility that would clearly fall on the great powers, including the United States. The United States, he believed, would at once be bound to respond to military aggression in Europe, Asia, and Africa. Correspondingly, the European powers would conceivably be able to interfere in the affairs of the Americas. Lansing also resented Wilson's failure to consult him on important matters while at Paris. Nevertheless, following the signing of the Treaty of Versailles with Germany on 28 June 1919, after Wilson returned to the United States, Lansing remained as head of the U.S. delegation to negotiate treaties with the other defeated Central Powers.

By this time, the U.S. role had diminished, and Lansing returned to Washington the next month.

Lansing's position at the State Department became increasingly precarious, as it became clear that his views were not solicited or taken seriously at the White House. During hearings conducted on the Versailles Treaty by the U.S. Senate in the summer of 1919, testimony from William C. Bullitt, a member of the U.S. delegation, revealed Lansing's serious objections to the peace settlement. Although the secretary of state sought to make amends, after the president suffered his paralyzing stroke on 2 October 1919, Lansing proceeded to convene cabinet meetings in Wilson's absence without presidential authorization. Alleging insubordination, the stricken president called for his resignation, and Lansing resigned on 13 February 1920.

After his departure, Lansing joined his erstwhile State Department colleague, Lester Woolsey, in forming the law firm Lansing & Woolsey in Washington. After retiring in 1925, Lansing served as counsel to a number of foreign governments and was the recipient of many honors, including service as trustee and later vice president (1926–1928) of the Carnegie Endowment for International Peace. He died in Washington, D.C.

• The Robert Lansing Papers are located at the Historical Manuscripts Division, Library of Congress. A small collection of Lansing papers reposes at the Princeton University Library. For biographical literature see Thomas H. Hartig, *Robert Lansing: An Interpretive Biography* (1982); Julius W. Pratt, "Robert Lansing," in *The American Secretaries of State and Their Diplomacy*, ed. Samuel Flagg Bemis, vol. 10 (1929), pp. 47–175; and Daniel Smith, "Robert Lansing, 1915–1920," in *An Uncertain Tradition: American Secretaries of State in the Twentieth Century*, ed. Norman Graebner (1961), pp. 101–27.

LAWRENCE E. GELFAND

LANSKY, Meyer (28 Aug. or 4 July 1902–15 Jan. 1983), bootlegger and gambling entrepreneur, was born Meyer Suchowljansky in Grodno, Belorussia (then Russia), the son of Max Suchowljansky, a garment presser, and Yetta (maiden name unknown). Lansky's father emigrated to New York City in 1909 and brought the family over two years later. Meyer, who left school in 1917 at age fourteen, was fascinated by the street life and crap games of the Lower East Side and while still a teenager associated with other hustlers, such as Bugsy Siegel and Charles "Lucky" Luciano.

With the coming of Prohibition in 1920, Lansky and Siegel entered bootlegging, backed initially by Arnold Rothstein and using a car and truck rental company as a front. By the mid-1920s, in partnership with Luciano, Lansky was bringing liquor across the Atlantic directly into New York and New Jersey harbors. Soon his younger brother, Jake Lansky, was an active partner and assistant in his enterprises. The contacts that Lansky made with other bootleggers on the East Coast and in the Midwest provided a network of associations that were central to his later career as a casino owner.

After Prohibition, Lansky became an entrepreneur of illegal and legal gambling casinos, especially in growing tourist centers. As early as the 1920s, he was probably involved in casino operations in Saratoga Springs, New York, during the August racing season, and by the late 1930s he, along with Frank Costello and Joe Adonis, owned the Piping Rock nightclub and casino there. His main focus, though, became the growing tourist trade in the Miami area. In the mid-1930s, along with Vincent "Jimmy" Alo, his closest Italian friend after the jailing of Luciano in the 1930s, Lansky invested in the Plantation casino in Hallandale (near Miami) and in other Florida gambling ventures. He also briefly operated gambling in Cuba through an association with Fulgencio Batista, the country's dictator.

Lansky reached the apex of his casino career in the decade and a half following World War II. In 1945, with Alo, Costello, and other investors, he remodelled and reopened the Colonial Inn in Hallandale; it was one of the most important illegal casinos in the country. Lansky also had interests in the Beverly Club outside of New Orleans, renewed his partnership with Costello in Saratoga Springs, and invested with Siegel and others in the construction of the Flamingo in Las Vegas. In June 1947 Siegel was killed, no doubt because some partners disapproved of his financial management of the Flamingo. Whether or not Lansky approved of the murder of his friend, he continued as an investor in the Flamingo. As the largest and most famous of the fledgling casino/hotels on the Las Vegas strip, the Flamingo helped to launch the city's development as a national center of legal gambling and entertainment. Although Lansky invested in other Las Vegas casinos, he remained in Florida and had little direct involvement in the city.

In October 1950 and March 1951 Lansky was called to testify before the U.S. Senate committee, chaired by Estes Kefauver of Tennessee, that was investigating interstate organized crime. Because the hearings identified Lansky and other criminal entrepreneurs as central to a national coordination of "organized crime," he faced local investigations in Florida and New York (Saratoga Springs) that resulted in indictments and convictions for gambling and conspiracy in 1953 and the closing of his casinos. For the rest of his life, he was the subject of ongoing investigations by the Federal Bureau of Investigation, the Immigration Service, and the Internal Revenue Service.

Lansky's troubles in the United States coincided with the return to power in March 1952 of Cuba's Batista, who had retired in 1944. Lansky became Batista's adviser on the development of Cuban tourism through gambling. In 1955, he and Jake began running the casino at Havana's Hotel Nacional. Soon thereafter, investing his own money, Lansky built the Riviera, perhaps the largest hotel/casino in the world outside of Las Vegas. His days of glory ended abruptly after Fidel Castro took power in 1959. With the nationalization of the casinos in 1960, Lansky lost much of the money he had invested in Cuba.

Back in Florida, Lansky increasingly operated behind the scenes. By this time, he required frequent medical treatment for ulcers and a heart condition and was under the constant surveillance of law enforcement. For a while in the early 1960s he helped organize the skimming of profits from Las Vegas casinos for himself and others. He also arranged for the sale of his Las Vegas casino interests.

In May 1929 Lansky had married Anne Citron; they had three children (one son was physically handicapped). Anne Lansky increasingly soured on the marriage and divorced him in February 1947. In December 1948 Lansky entered into a happier marriage with Thelma "Teddy" Schwartz. Teddy had one child from a previous marriage, but she and Lansky had no children together. During World War II he assisted the U.S. government in contacting the imprisoned Luciano in order to secure his aid in having the New York waterfront unions guard against German sabotage. Although he was not an observant Jew, Lansky recognized a responsibility to Jewish causes and, after the war, gave money to aid the Israeli fight for independence.

Frustrated by what he saw as U.S. government persecution, he moved to Israel in 1970 and applied for citizenship. By the time his application was finally denied in 1972, he faced several indictments in the United States. Leaving Israel on a long and highly publicized international plane trip, he sought asylum in Paraguay but wound up back in the United States. Over the next few years, he underwent a number of federal trials as well as heart bypass surgery. By 1976, he had beaten all charges and then went into retirement in Miami Beach. His medical and legal expenses, combined with the costs of caring for his increasingly handicapped son, drained much of the money he had acquired from selling his interests in Las Vegas casinos. After his death in a hospital in West Miami, the trust fund he had left for his wife and son proved to be almost worthless.

Lansky's importance derives from the central role he played among a group of criminal entrepreneurs, often exbootleggers from the 1920s, who developed illegal casino gambling in a number of American resort areas and who played a critical role in launching Las Vegas as the fastest-growing American city after World War II. It required considerable skill to assemble the capital required to start casinos, to negotiate deals with police and politicians, to hire and supervise a staff so that the casino would not go bankrupt through embezzlement, and to make wealthy customers feel at home while gambling. Although Lansky was often in the news because of a false perception that he was a money manager for an Italian-American mafia, he is properly understood as an independent entrepreneur whose reputation for business acumen and reliability encouraged others to invest in his projects. By the time he died, his world had vanished; the illegal casinos were gone, replaced in Las Vegas, Atlantic City, and other locations with legal casinos to feed America's fascination with gambling.

• The most thoughtful and thoroughly researched biography is Robert Lacey, *Little Man: Meyer Lansky and the Gangster Life* (1991). The footnotes and bibliography of Lacey's biography provide a full guide to the secondary works, government documents, and archival materials on Lansky's career. Also of interest because it is based in part on interviews with Lansky is Dennis Eisenberg et al., *Meyer Lansky: Mogul of the Mob* (1979). Hank Messick, *Lansky* (1971), is useful for understanding Florida gambling because Messick, a reporter, was knowledgeable about the Florida scene. Mark H. Haller, "Bootleggers as Businessmen: From City Slums to City Builders," in *Law, Alcohol, and Order: Perspectives on National Prohibition*, ed. David E. Kyvig (1985), places Lansky within the context of his bootlegging associates. An obituary is in the *New York Times*, 16 Jan. 1983.

MARK H. HALLER

LANSTON, Tolbert (3 Feb. 1844–18 Feb. 1913), inventor, was born in Troy, Ohio, the son of Nicholas Randall Lanston, a tanner and leather merchant, and Mary Jane Wright. His given names were John Tolbert, but he dropped his first name shortly after the Civil War. Until 1856 he lived within forty miles of Troy and grew up in extreme poverty. In 1856 the Lanston family moved to Wapello, Louisa County, Iowa, and remained there until at least 1860. In that year or shortly after the family moved to Dayton, Ohio. In 1861 a noted phrenologist said of him, "He never sees a thing done without at once inquiring of himself, 'Is there not a better way to do it?'" Lanston enlisted for Civil War duty (Company I, Eighty-fourth Ohio Infantry) in Dayton on 31 May 1862, giving his occupation as stencil cutter, and was discharged as a private on 20 September 1862 at Delaware, Ohio. According to family members he reenlisted, became a sergeant, and at the close of the war was mustered out as a sergeant. There is, however, no mention of a reenlistment in his Civil War service or pension records in the National Archives.

In 1865 Lanston moved to Georgetown, D.C., and was appointed a clerk in the U.S. Pension Office. He worked for this office for twenty-two years and eventually became chief clerk. In 1866 Lanston married Beattie Hurdle; they had one child.

Lanston studied law at Columbian College, later called George Washington University, and graduated in 1868. He was admitted to the bar and established his own law office. Presumably he practiced as a patent attorney, but he could not have devoted much time to this profession.

Although without any technical education, Lanston became a fairly prolific inventor. His first invention was a padlock for a mailbag, which was patented on 8 March 1870. Other patents were awarded to him for a hydraulic dumbwaiter, comb and brush, locomotive car coupler, locomotive smokestack, postal scales, sewing machine chair, sewing machine, faucet, window sash, typecasting and setting machine, and adding machine. His adding machine was used in tabulating the 1880 U.S. census, and it was admired by Herman Hollerith, a pioneer in data processing. The patent (No. 622,157) is dated 28 March 1899, and it was assigned to Hollerith, whose punched-card device was used to compile the 1890 census. Although Lanston is said to have derived a moderate income and reputation from his earlier inventions, none of them was nearly as successful as the typecasting and typesetting machine.

Lanston got the idea for his typecasting and setting machine in 1883, applied for patents in 1884, and received six patents in 1887. He then resigned from the Pension Office to devote all his time to this invention. The machine was called the Monotype machine because it cast and set one piece of type at a time. It was by far Lanston's most important invention, and it is this on which his fame rests.

The design of the machine evolved over a period of about ten years, and Lanston and his associates received a number of subsequent patents. Because Lanston was not a trained engineer, he used much outside help. The first prototype was built for him by D. Ballouf, a machinist and modelmaker. One of the early keyboards was built for him by the Incandescent Arc Light Company of Brooklyn, New York, and an improved pneumatic keyboard was designed and built for him by the Taft-Pierce Company of Woonsocket, Rhode Island.

The first Monotype machine, called "The Embossing Type-Maker," produced type from a type-high strip of cold metal. It was in two separate parts. One was a keyboard device that produced two (later one) ribbons of punched paper tape. This tape fed into and controlled the operation of the second part, which cut the metal strip into pieces of the desired width. The pieces were compressed to remove imperfections and stamped on the end with the desired letter form. The machine worked, but it was too slow. Lanston's second model cast type from molten metal and set it into justified lines, and the casting machine was controlled by punched paper tapes as before.

To develop his invention further, Lanston set up the Lanston Type Machine Company on the fifth floor of the Capitol Power House, an electrical generating station in Washington, and there he acted as his own engineer and superintendent of the shops. Five distinct models were built in these shops, and one of them was demonstrated at the World's Columbian Exposition in Chicago in 1893. That machine was one of the first to be powered entirely by electricity. It was to be several more years, however, before a commercially successful machine was designed and built.

In 1896 the Franklin Institute in Philadelphia awarded Lanston its Cresson Medal because the awards committee considered his machine an invention "of the highest order and importance."

About 1897 the building in which Lanston had his shops was destroyed by a midnight fire, and he lost his drawings and just about everything else. The following morning he showed not the slightest sign of emotion and calmly set to work as if nothing had happened. In the same year, to raise capital for a factory, the Lanston firm sold the rights to his invention for Great Britain and its colonies to a group of British investors headed by Lord Dunraven. This group established the Lanston Monotype Corporation, later called the Monotype Corporation, Ltd., a completely independent firm that soon acquired the European rights as well. It was very successful.

With part of this capital Lanston had the firm of William Sellers & Company in Philadelphia build a new model. One of the firm's engineers, John Sellers Bancroft, redesigned the machine, though retaining Lanston's basic principles, and made so many improvements that he is considered almost the coinventor. Other improvements were made by Bancroft's assistant, Mauritz C. Indahl, and by another Philadelphia engineer, Coleman Sellers. The firm built one hundred of the new machines, and the first one to be sold was installed in the printing plant of Gibson Brothers in Washington, D.C., late in 1898. Lanston severed formal ties to the company early in 1898 but continued to act as a consultant. In 1901 the company was renamed the Lanston Monotype Manufacturing Company, and a manufacturing plant was established in Philadelphia. By the end of that year the company had sold ninety-four machines, and by 1911 3,500 Monotype machines were in use in the United States alone.

The Monotype machine had several advantages over its rival, the Linotype machine, which cast a whole line of type as a "slug" and which had been invented in 1886 by German-American Ottmar Mergenthaler. It excelled in setting tabular material, corrections could be made more easily, the operator had much greater control over letter and word spacing and line justification, and type design did not have to yield to the exigencies of the machine nearly as much as with the Linotype machine. Also, the punched tapes could be stored for reuse. The Linotype machine was used in most newspaper offices where typographical refinement was not a high priority. The Monotype machine was used mainly for high-quality book and magazine work. Large printing offices often used both machines. Machines for casting type had been invented earlier, as had some typesetting machines, but until the Linotype and Monotype machines became available, most printing type was hand set. These two inventions revolutionized the printing industry, and they remained in general use until the 1950s, when photographic technology controlled by computers brought about yet another revolution. Today there are still a few printing houses that do high-quality letterpress printing, and virtually all use carefully maintained Monotype machines.

Lanston's wife died in 1908, and the next year he married Alice V. Hieston, a cousin of his first wife. He took no interest in religion until after the death of his first wife, but he then devoted much time to the study of religion in an effort to learn whether he and his wife might be reunited after his own death.

In 1910 Lanston established a trust fund for the benefit of the Children's Hospital, now called the Children's National Medical Center of Washington. Sometime in 1910 or 1911 Lanston suffered a stroke that left him partially paralyzed. From then on he could walk only with difficulty and with the aid of a cane. He died in Washington.

Harold M. Duncan, who knew Lanston well, described him in a letter to Henry Lewis Bullen as "a man of extremely pleasant personality with clearly defined views and much tenacity in upholding them" and as "courteous in manner and lucid and fluent in expression."

• There is very little manuscript material extant by or concerning Lanston except for his Civil War service and pension records in the National Archives and a letter, quoted above, from Harold M. Duncan to Henry L. Bullen of 20 March 1924 at the Butler Library, Columbia University. Lord Askwith, chair of the Monotype Corporation, Ltd., published a letter from Lanston's son in "Mr. Tolbert Lanston (The Inventor of the 'Monotype')," *Monotype Recorder* 25, no. 216 (Nov.–Dec. 1926): 16–18, which in slightly abridged form was reprinted in R. C. Elliot, "The 'Monotype' from Infancy to Maturity," *Monotype Recorder* 31, no. 243 (Jan.–Feb. 1932): 9–39. Henry Lewis Bullen, "Origin and Development of the Lanston Monotype Composing Machine," *Inland Printer*, May 1924, pp. 228–32, is based partly on the reminiscences of Harold M. Duncan. John S. Ritenour, "Master Minds of Type and Press: No. III—Tolbert Lanston," *Inland Printer*, Mar. 1916, pp. 807–8, is mostly about Lanston's personality. Two recent articles describing the history of the Monotype machine are John Randle, "The Development of the Monotype Machine," *Matrix*, no. 4 (1984): 42–53, and Harold Berliner, "The Monotype in America," *Matrix*, no. 4 (1984): 54–56. Seán Jennett, *Pioneers in Printing* (1968), has a chapter, "Tolbert Lanston and the Monotype," pp. 178–91. Two other useful publications are "The Pioneer Days of 'Monotype' Composing Machines," *Monotype Recorder* 39, 1 (Autumn 1949): 3–29, and *The Monotype* (1937), reprinted with additions from *PM* (May 1937): 17–40. An obituary is in the *Washington Post*, 19 Feb. 1913.

PHILIP J. WEIMERSKIRCH

LANUSSE, Armand (1812–16 Mar. 1868), writer, civil rights activist, and educator, was born in New Orleans, Louisiana. Nothing is known of his personal life except that he married and had five children, four sons and a daughter. A brother, Numa Lanusse, also displayed considerable literary talent until his death at the age of twenty-six in a riding accident.

In New Orleans, the nation's nineteenth-century "Creole Capital," Lanusse belonged to a resident coterie of French-speaking Romantic writers whose ranks were reinforced by political refugees of revolutionary upheaval in France and the French Caribbean. Intensely hostile to Louisiana's slave-based racial hierarchy and inspired by the Romantic idealism of the democratic age, Lanusse joined with the native and emigré literati to press for change. In 1843 he played a leading role in the publication of a short-lived, interracial literary journal, *L'Album littéraire: Journal des jeunes gens, amateurs de littérature*, which began as a monthly and contained social commentary, poems, and short stories. Lanusse's work and that of other Afro-Creole writers such as Joanni Questy, Camille Thierry, Mirtil-Ferdinand Liotau, and Michel Saint-Pierre dominated the review, while Jean-Louis Marciacq, a white French emigré and director of a school for children of color, appeared as the publisher. In *L'Album* Lanusse and other black Creole contributors, like Romantic writers in France and the French Caribbean, employed their literary works to attack the evils of contemporary society.

In the short story "Un Mariage de conscience" Lanusse condemned *plaçage* (a French-language term referring to a negotiated agreement between a white suitor and a young woman of color that assured the prospective "wife" of social and financial security). Though French and Spanish law had prohibited interracial marriage, *plaçage* had enabled mixed-race couples to enter into stable, quasi-legitimate partnerships. After 1803, however, the decline of Latin European racial attitudes and the mounting conservatism of American Catholicism destroyed *plaçage*'s institutional viability. *L'Album*'s short stories and poems portrayed *plaçage* as a form of human bondage that reduced free women of color to the status of prostitutes and threatened the stability of the free black community.

L'Album's condemnation of *plaçage*, its fiery attacks "on the awful condition of Louisiana society," and its aggressive advocacy of the rights of "young Louisianians" prompted one critic to charge the journal with fomenting revolution. An anonymous essayist insisted that *L'Album* sought only reform, but the review's content clearly challenged an 1830 state law banning the dissemination of reading materials having a tendency to cause discontent among free blacks and slaves. The periodical apparently ceased publication after only four issues.

With *L'Album*'s demise, Lanusse conceived of the publication of a collection of poems. Appearing in 1845, *Les Cenelles* (the title taking its name from the delectable berries of an indigenous hawthorn bush) contained eighty-five French-language poems by seventeen Afro-Creole authors and conveyed a subdued tone. Lanusse's eighteen contributions, including the dedication and introduction, dominated the book of poetry, and in several of the selections he resumed his attack on the practice of *plaçage*. He also returned to another issue raised in *L'Album*—expanded educational opportunities for the "fine minds" of Louisiana's youth. In *Les Cenelles*'s introduction, Lanusse pointed to education's value as "a shield against the spiteful and calumnious arrows shot at us."

During the 1840s Lanusse acted upon his advocacy of educational reform when he led a campaign to open a free school for impoverished orphans of color, many of whom the illegitimate offspring of interracial liaisons. Free woman of color Justine Firmin Couvent had provided for the establishment of such a school in her 1832 will. Thwarting white opposition to free black education, Lanusse, together with other Afro-Creole leaders, succeeded in executing the terms of Madame Couvent's will. The school, the Sociéte Catholique pour l'instruction des orphelins dans l'indigence, opened in 1848 and became a focal point for some of the city's most radical Afro-Creole activists. In 1852 Lanusse succeeded free woman of color Félicie Callioux as principal of the "Couvent School" and remained head of the facility until 1866.

Threatened with violence and confiscation of their property in the secession crisis of 1861, Lanusse and other free men of color joined the Confederate army in a defensive action. When rebel troops withdrew from New Orleans in April 1862, free black soldiers refused to leave and volunteered their services to federal authorities. Against accusations that free men of color had willingly supported the rebel cause, Lanusse wrote that Afro-Creoles would have been "foolish . . . to offer our cooperation . . . to the preservation of a prejudice which, praise be to God, disappears each day from every civilized country of the earth."

Passionately outspoken in defense of his community, Lanusse engaged in bitter disputes with the free black population's detractors in *L'Union*, a radical, French-language newspaper founded in 1862 by the Afro-Creole intelligentsia. In retaliation, his enemies accused him at one point of desecrating the U.S. flag—a treasonable offense in wartime New Orleans. Cleared of the charge, the irrepressible Louisianian later denounced the U.S. Army after the head of the Department of the Gulf, General Nathaniel P. Banks, forced the resignation of black Union officers in an attempt to appease white conservatives. "Many thought," Lanusse wrote in *L'Union*, "that caste prejudice would disappear with the arrival of federal troops in this city." But, he continued, "in every free state of the Union, prejudice is twice as strong as it is here." Lanusse urged people of color to immigrate to Mexico to escape the nation's stifling racial environment.

Lanusse himself remained in the city, and three years before his death there he helped found an interracial political association, the Friends of Universal Suffrage, to press for black voting rights and proportional representation. The organization's advanced positions helped produce one of the Reconstruction South's most radical state constitutions. Despite the strides forward that had been made, Lanusse's wartime admonitions proved prophetic. By 1900 a nightmare of agrarian peonage, legalized segregation, and disfranchisement that endured for more than fifty years had destroyed Reconstruction's promise of equal citizenship.

• Some of Lanusse's most important editorials are in *L'Union*, 8 Oct. 1862; 12 and 19 July 1864. The best sources for information on Lanusse's life are Rodolphe Lucien Desdunes, *Our People and Our History*, trans. and ed. Sister Dorothea Olga McCants (1973); Charles Barthelemy Rousséve, *The Negro in Louisiana: Aspects of His History and His Literature* (1937); and Edward Maceo Coleman, ed., *Creole Voices: Poems in French by Free Men of Color First Published in 1845* (1945). For an assessment of Lanusse's work, see Caryn Cossé Bell, *Revolution, Romanticism, and the Afro-Creole Protest Tradition in Louisiana, 1718–1868* (1997). Other sources are Régine Latortue and Gleason R. W. Adams, eds. and trans., *Les Cenelles: A Collection of Poems by Creole Writers of the Early Nineteenth Century* (1979); Edward Larocque Tinker, *Les écrits de langue française en Louisiane au XIXe siècle* (1932;

repr. 1970); Auguste Viatte, *Histoire littéraire de l'Amerique française des origines à 1950* (1954) and "Complement à la bibliographie louisianaise d'Edward Larocque Tinker, " *Revue de Louisiane* 3 (1974); and Norman R. Smith, *Etches of Ebony Louisiana* (1996). For a contemporary assessment of Lanusse's writings, see Charles Testut, *Portraits littéraires de la Nouvelle-Orléans* (1850). An editorial in *L'Union*, 6 Dec. 1862, offers an insight into the U.S. flag incident.

CARYN COSSÉ BELL

LANZA, Mario (31 Jan. 1921–7 Oct. 1959), operatic tenor and film star, was born Alfredo Arnold Cocozza in Philadelphia, Pennsylvania, the son of Antonio Cocozza, a decorated U.S. Army veteran disabled in World War I, and Maria Lanza, a seamstress. An only child of Italian immigrants, Lanza was raised in a working-class South Philadelphia neighborhood and educated in the Philadelphia public schools, from which he was expelled shortly before graduation, allegedly for assaulting a teacher who insulted his ethnicity.

An early interest in operatic singing was cultivated by Lanza's virtually constant exposure to recordings of Italian opera during his boyhood, particularly his invalid father's extensive collection of recordings made by Enrico Caruso, the most famous opera singer of his day, with whom Lanza's own singing voice and popularity would become nearly universally compared. Lanza's birth in 1921, the year Caruso died, was a connection that neither Lanza nor studio publicists would miss calling attention to in later years. At age seven the young Lanza once listened to a Caruso record twenty-seven times at a single sitting, and the subsequent Hollywood legend said it was when Lanza's father heard his nineteen-year-old son singing along with the maestro's trademark recording of the aria "Vesti la giubba" from Leoncavallo's *I Pagliacci* that the family decided the boy had an immense natural talent that had to be developed.

After a year and a half of study under Irene Williams, herself a former operatic singer, Lanza had his first professional break in 1942 when an audition for Serge Koussevitzky secured the young tenor a scholarship to that summer's Berkshire Music Festival in Tanglewood, Massachusetts. Lanza shared the limelight there with another alumnus who would also earn a renowned place in American musical history, composer-conductor Leonard Bernstein. The exposure gained the 21-year-old Lanza not only his first recognition in the national press when *New York Times* music critic Noel Straus described his as a "superb natural voice," but a contract with Columbia Concerts, Inc., as well.

Those plans were dashed when Lanza was drafted into the wartime U.S. Army in 1943. After initially training for duty with the military police, Lanza was tapped by the Office of Special Services as a singer, and, billed as "the Service Caruso," he completed his tour of duty, performing first in the Army Air Force musical *On the Beam* and later in its production of Moss Hart's *Winged Victory*. During a furlough in Los Angeles, Lanza regaled Hollywood celebrities with his singing at an all-night party, and, with the help of columnist Hedda Hopper and actor Walter Pidgeon, he wound up landing a recording contract with RCA Victor. A medical discharge from military service in 1945 enabled Lanza to marry Betty Hicks, and he headed off to New York City in the hopes of resuming his interrupted musical career.

Despite these early signs of success, Lanza's life as an operatic tenor languished until New York realtor Sam Weiler, himself a frustrated voice student, underwrote further training for Lanza, who by now had adopted his mother's maiden name as his stage name, with Enrico Rosati, operatic tenor Beniamino Gigli's former vocal coach. "I have waited for you for 34 years—ever since Gigli," Rosati exclaimed upon hearing Lanza's voice.

With Weiler acting as his patron and business manager, within fifteen months Lanza was drawing as many as 76,000 people to a summer concert in Chicago's Grant Park. In 1947 Lanza, as a member of the Bel Canto trio, which also included soprano Frances Yeend and baritone George London, performed a concert at the Hollywood Bowl with Louis B. Mayer in the audience, and Metro-Goldwyn-Mayer signed Lanza to a seven-year film contract.

Put into the hands of producer Joe Pasternak, who was largely responsible for the splashy, polished technicolor film musicals for which MGM was then renowned, Lanza spent his first year as a contract player for the studio losing 100 of his 265 pounds, and it was as a svelte romantic lead alongside Kathryn Grayson that Lanza made his film debut in 1949 in *That Midnight Kiss*, which was followed in 1950 by *The Toast of New Orleans*, also with Grayson. The latter film introduced the hit song "Be My Love," Lanza's first million-seller single recording.

Lanza's proven successes at the box office and with record sales encouraged MGM to take the risk of openly identifying Lanza with his idol Caruso by casting Lanza as the lead in a film biography of the legendary singer. *The Great Caruso*, which was released in 1951, made musical and film history. *Time* magazine, which featured Lanza on its coveted cover, touted him in a story titled "Million-Dollar Voice" as "the first operatic tenor in history to become a fullblown Hollywood star" (6 Aug. 1951). He also was the first recording artist with RCA Victor's venerable Red Seal label, reserved for classical artists, to sell more than a million records, and *The Great Caruso*'s premier at the Radio City Music Hall in Manhattan broke a box-office record by earning $1.5 million in its first ten weeks there.

With another million-seller single, "The Loveliest Night of the Year," to his credit, Lanza embarked a 22-city tour promoting the film before sold-out concert audiences and, along with a weekly radio program sponsored by Coca-Cola, was earning $1 million a year as a performer and traveling with a personal entourage of nine. The title song of his next film, "Because

You're Mine," also became a million-seller single in 1952.

At age thirty-one, when Lanza had established a reputation as a top-draw film star, not to mention as one of the world's great operatic singers, that seemed to be unassailable, the first episode of the kind of temperamental conflict that would eventually scuttle his Hollywood career surfaced. In the effort to lose excess weight for his next film project, *The Student Prince*, Lanza had allegedly been so physically weakened that he failed to appear on the first day of shooting. A prolonged standoff with the studio resulted in MGM's canceling his contract, and a lawsuit was averted only after Lanza agreed to allow the studio to use his recordings of the music mouthed by British actor Edmund Purdom, who starred in the actual film.

Other scandals followed and were seized upon by a press eager to exploit Lanza as the epitome of the star who had risen too high too fast. After a year of inactivity, Lanza was scheduled to appear on the Columbia Broadcasting system (CBS) television program "Shower of Stars" for a fee of $40,000 in October 1954. Once more as a result of dieting in preparation for his appearance, Lanza claimed to be too weak to sing, and earlier recordings were substituted, with Lanza merely mouthing the words in the live performance. Lanza and CBS originally denied the press reports of what was, at the time, regarded as a serious breach of the public's trust. When CBS relented and finally confessed to what the press characterized as a hoax, Lanza returned to seclusion.

When Lanza a short time later walked out on a Las Vegas nightclub booking, rumors began to circulate that he had destroyed his famous voice through abusive overuse. Meanwhile, the Internal Revenue Service sued him for $300,000 in back taxes. In 1956, however, Lanza signed with Warner Bros. Studio to make a comeback in the film *Serenade*, which was based on the James M. Cain novel and costarred film legend Joan Fontaine. He resumed a busy schedule recording albums featuring Broadway showtunes and Neapolitan songs for RCA Victor.

In 1957, apparently disgruntled by his negative press and with the crash dieting that allowed him to maintain his status as a Hollywood star, Lanza, accompanied by his wife and their four young children, resettled in Europe, making their home in Rome, Italy. There he made the 1958 film *The Seven Hills of Rome*, and he later undertook a European tour that included a command performance at London's Royal Albert Hall.

His last film, *For the First Time*, was released in 1959, and Lanza had several record albums and film projects in the works when, in October of that year, he checked into a Rome clinic to lose weight. While there he died suddenly of a heart attack, although subsequent allegations suggest that Lanza was murdered for having embarrassed the racketeer Charles "Lucky" Luciano by reneging on a concert engagement that Luciano had arranged for U.S. military personnel in Na-ples, Italy. The Lanzas' four children were orphaned when the singer's wife, Betty, died five months later.

Lanza occupied a unique place in American musical and popular culture by maintaining a film, concert, and recording career that earned him, despite a repertoire composed to a large extent of what was then generally regarded as highbrow music, the sort of adulation previously reserved only for crooners of romantic melodies. For all the controversy that his short-lived career eventually generated in the media, Lanza's great popularity among film and concert audiences both in the United States and abroad never faltered. Nor did serious music and film critics deny the range, beauty, and sheer robustness of his singing voice, despite Lanza's lack of the proper operatic credentials and, as some saw it, of musical training and artistic discipline.

His indisputable way with a song and his charismatic appeal as a performer aside, Lanza leaves a paradoxical legacy as a romantic leading man who had to contend with chronic obesity, an operatic tenor whose time on the legitimate operatic stage amounted to only two performances as Pinkerton in Puccini's *Madama Butterfly* with the New Orleans Opera early in his career, and a larger-than-life personality who died suddenly in the midst of his career. It is possible to view Lanza as an outstanding example of how fame and fabulous commercial success can overwhelm, if not waste, an incredible artistic gift. However, his obvious love of singing did much to extend the operatic audience, and an impressive discography of operatic, show, and popular tunes assures Lanza an enduring and honored place in American musical history.

• Constantine Callinicos, *The Mario Lanza Story* (1960), by Lanza's friend and frequent accompanist and conductor, includes an extensive discography. Other biographies include Matt Bernard, *Mario Lanza* (1971); Raymond Strait, *Mario Lanza: His Tragic Life* (1980); and Derek Mannering, *Mario Lanza: A Biography* (1993). An obituary is in the *New York Times*, 8 Oct. 1959.

RUSSELL ELLIOTT MURPHY

LAPCHICK, Joe (12 Apr. 1900–10 Aug. 1970), basketball player and coach, was born Joseph Bohomiel Lapchick in Yonkers, New York, the son of Joseph B. Lapchick, a coal miner, hat finisher, trolley motorman, and policeman, and Frances Kassik. Lapchick, the eldest of seven children, was expected to help support the family. As a child he played an improvised form of street basketball, but he most often played baseball. He was a tall boy, 6'3" at age twelve, and his height allowed him to begin caddying when he was only nine. He caddied for many top New York athletes, such as Christy Mathewson and Fred Merkle of the Giants, and a number of well-known entertainers, including Al Jolson and Douglas Fairbanks. He used caddying as an opportunity to learn to play golf.

Lapchick completed grammar school in 1914 and got his first full-time job with an electric company in Bronxville, New York, where he was paid fifteen cents an hour. He spent his free time at Lou Gordon's sports shop in Yonkers; because of his size, Gordon sent him to Jimmy Lee, who managed the Hollywood Inn basketball team, which was sponsored by a businessmen's athletic club. The team was composed of former high school stars. By his own account, Lapchick played poorly for two years, but he learned the game. He developed his own training regimen, consisting of running drills and pivots. As his skills improved, he joined his first professional team, the Yonkers Bantams in an area professional league. He was paid $5 per game, less expenses. In 1916 and 1917 combined, he earned $33.

After World War I, professional basketball, along with other sports, began to attract considerable spectator interest. Lapchick played on four professional teams in four leagues between 1918 and 1922, for which he was paid $75 to $100 per game. He began to emerge as a star. In 1923 he was invited to join the Original Celtics of New York City, the elite of professional basketball, who played at the Central Opera House and later at the Seventy-first Regiment Armory. Founded in 1912 by Frank "Tip" McCormack at the Hudson Guild Settlement House, the team became professional in 1918 under the leadership of Jim Furey. The Celtics' chief rival in the early 1920s was Tex Rickard's Whirlwinds.

When Lapchick joined the Celtics in 1923, he was 6'5". He earned $10,000 the first year, which then was raised to $12,000, making him, along with Nat Holman, the highest-paid professional. Rarely losers, the Celtics played a schedule that took them all over the United States east of the Rockies. Crowds of 10,000 saw them at New York's Madison Square Garden, and in other cities that figure was occasionally surpassed.

Lapchick, who was taller than most opponents, gave the Celtics a tremendous advantage in the center jump, which in the 1920s followed each basket made. In his first year the Celtics compiled a won and lost record of 193–11; in the second year, 204–14. After the Celtics joined the newly formed American Basketball League for the 1926–1927 season, they so dominated the league that fan interest dwindled. League owners moved to break up the team by sending Lapchick, Dutch Denhert, and Pete Barry to the Cleveland Rosenblums, where they played on two more championship teams, in 1928–1929 and 1929–1930. The only team to challenge the dominance of the Celtics and the Rosenblums was the Rens, the Renaissance Big Five of New York, an African-American team led by Jamaican-born Bob Douglas, who named the team after the Renaissance Casino in Harlem, which he managed. The Celtics and Rens are the only two teams to be inducted into the Basketball Hall of Fame.

In 1931 Lapchick married Elizabeth Sarubbi, with whom he had three children. With the coming of the depression and the decline in professional basketball's popularity, Lapchick was ready for another opportunity. It came in 1936 when he was offered the head coaching job in both basketball and baseball at St. John's University.

Never having been to college nor having played for a coach, Lapchick was uncertain of his new position. He took some time to overcome his insecurity, but he eventually became one of the great college coaches. From 1936 until 1947 his teams won 181 games and lost 84, winning National Invitational Tourney titles in 1943 and 1944. St. John's became one of the strongest attractions at Madison Square Garden, where Ned Irish had begun promoting college basketball in the 1930s. The 1944 NIT championship game between St. John's and DePaul University, led by George Mikan, was one of Lapchick's greatest coaching victories. It was also embarrassing when he passed out (from tension and/or fatigue) for ten minutes during the second half.

In 1947 Irish hired Lapchick to coach the New York Knickerbockers, a member of the newly organized Basketball Association of America (BAA). That same year Bob Douglas sought to bring the Rens into the league, but despite Lapchick's support, league members voted against the Rens' admission. The racial integration of professional basketball leagues had to await the merger of the BAA and the National Basketball League into the National Basketball Association in 1949. In 1950 Walter Brown and Red Auerbach in Boston drafted the first black player for the NBA, Chuck Cooper of Duquesne University. That same year Irish and Lapchick signed Nat "Sweetwater" Clifton from the Harlem Globetrotters for the Knicks. Hate mail and threatening phone calls followed their move.

During the nine years of Lapchick's leadership the Knickerbockers won three Eastern Division titles and made the playoffs each season, but in the last two years the relationship between Irish and Lapchick began to deteriorate, with Irish increasingly second-guessing his coach. With deteriorating health and waning confidence, Lapchick resigned as the Knicks' coach in January 1956. During his tenure, the Knicks performed well and the league itself prospered. Red Smith wrote in the New York Herald Tribune: "What the Giants have been to professional football in New York, Joe Lapchick has been to basketball, both college and professional . . . Nobody in any game has lent greater dignity to the American sports scene."

Lapchick returned to St. John's for the 1957–1958 season. He continued to coach there until his mandatory retirement in 1965. During his second round at St. John's, his teams won both Holiday Classic and NIT titles in 1959 and 1965 and continued posting winning seasons. The 1965 NIT championship was his fourth, the most for any coach to that time. His teams won more than 70 percent of their games.

Lapchick twice was voted college coach of the year, and his programs served as a "cradle of coaches," since many of his players became coaches, including eight members of the 1954 Knickerbockers. At St. John's he stressed the importance of a college education for his players, and he personally presided over study halls. He twice was inducted into the Naismith Basketball Hall of Fame, first as a team member with the Celtics in 1959, then as a player in his own right in 1966. He died at a hospital in Monticello, New York, several days after suffering a heart attack.

During his first tenure at St. John's, Lapchick helped to build the popularity of college basketball in New York City, and during his years with the Knickerbockers he helped to create the NBA's popularity. As a player with the Celtics he had a hand in inspiring fan interest in professional basketball across the country. He was proud of his role in the desegregation of basketball, and he worked hard to maintain the integrity of the college game in the face of point-fixing threats from gamblers. At St. John's each basketball season begins with a tournament in his memory, and in 1971 the Joe Lapchick Award was established for the best college senior player in the nation. Sportswriter Leonard Koppett noted that Lapchick had an important effect on the world of basketball at every stage of his career.

• Lapchick's papers and scrapbooks are located at the Naismith Memorial Basketball Hall of Fame in Springfield, Mass., and at St. John's University in Jamaica, N.Y. His insightful autobiography, *50 Years of Basketball* (1968), has an introduction by Clair Bee. Two of the most helpful assessments are by Richard Lapchick, his son, *Broken Promises* (1984) and *Five Minutes to Midnight* (1991), which discuss his views on race, his role in the desegregation of professional basketball, and his views on coaching. A number of secondary works have limited value: Neil Isaacs, *All the Moves* (1975); Sandy Padwe, *Basketball's Hall of Fame* (1970); Al Hirshberg, *Basketball's Greatest Teams* (1965); and Robert W. Peterson, *Cages to Jump Shots* (1990). Accounts of his career can be found in Leonard Koppett's *24 Seconds to Shoot* (1968) and *The Essence of the Game Is Deception* (1973) as well as a column in the *New York Times*, 11 Aug. 1970. That issue of the *Times* also includes an obituary by George Vecsey.

RICHARD C. CREPEAU

LAPHAM, Increase Allen (7 Mar. 1811–14 Sept. 1875), natural historian, was born in Palmyra, New York, the son of Seneca Lapham, a canal contractor and engineer, and Rachel Allen. Lapham, who was formally educated for only several months, began work alongside his father and brothers on the canals of New York, Kentucky, and Ohio at the age of thirteen. He began as a manual laborer but rapidly rose to become a secretary and surveyor. Increase and his brother Darius shared an interest in the geology and paleontology that they saw exposed daily in the canal cuts. In 1828, at the age of sixteen, Lapham had his first scientific article, a note on the geology of the Louisville and Shippingsport Canal, published in the *American Journal of Science*. From 1824 through 1836 he worked on a series of canals, winding up as the secretary of the Ohio Board of Canal Commissioners.

In 1836 Lapham moved to Milwaukee, Wisconsin, where he spent the rest of his life. He married two years later and with his wife, Ann M. Alcott, had five children. His income was derived largely from development, surveying, and land speculation, with occasional income from the natural history work that occu-

pied the bulk of his time. He served Wisconsin as its state geologist and in many other capacities. His *Catalogue of Plants and Shells Found in the Vicinity of Milwaukee* (1836) was the first item published in Wisconsin. He was active as a founder, member, and leader in most of the civic groups in early Milwaukee, most notably the Lyceum, Library Association, and Agricultural Society. He was the moving force behind the creation of the Milwaukee Female Seminary, perhaps because of his closeness to his daughter Julia.

Lapham focused early on geography (publishing the first detailed map of Wisconsin in 1844), on effigy mounds (the origin of which he correctly determined), on the environmental effect of deforestation, and on cataloging the natural history of the state. His interest in both meteorology—as a branch of natural history—and weather—as an important influence on business and agriculture—led him to become one of the driving forces behind the creation of what would become the U.S. Weather Bureau.

Lapham's work on the natural history of Wisconsin was both direct and done through the countless citizens whom he encouraged to collect and observe for him. He had a wide correspondence network within the state with enthusiasts of all branches of natural history. He in turn passed along information and specimens to naturalists in the East, most notably Asa Gray, who used Lapham's data to set the northern and western limits for various species of plants, which Charles Darwin in turn used in his work on the geographical distribution of species. Lapham's work on the role of fire in the creation of prairies arose through his correspondence with Leo Lesquereux, a Swiss émigré living in Columbus, Ohio, who was the country's foremost expert on mosses. His work on the effigy mounds resulted in his "Antiquities of Wisconsin."

Lapham's work to encourage the creation of a national weather bureau was the culmination of nearly thirty years of interest in and observation of meteorology. For years he kept careful observations, which are still consulted by meteorologists trying to study the paths storms typically take, and used them to create climatological tables for the use of farmers and merchants. His position in Milwaukee made him keenly aware of the impact of unexpected storms on shipping and transportation on the Great Lakes, and with the help of the Smithsonian Institution he organized observers across Wisconsin in the late 1850s who were able to telegraph to the East, alerting coastal Wisconsin of imminent storms. In the wake of the Civil War, Lapham proposed that this sort of effort be taken on nationally. The result was the assignment to the Army Signal Corps the tasks of collecting and disseminating meteorological observations and storm warnings. This responsibility was eventually moved from military to civilian control and at that time became the Weather Bureau.

Lapham's greatest contributions came not through his direct scientific work, which was in and of itself noteworthy, but rather through the organizational role he played. Creating and nurturing institutions and fostering the work of many collectors and observers, he accomplished far more than he could have on his own. One of the last self-trained generalists able to participate in science on the national level, Lapham truly shone when he put aside his own work, even his valuable work on prairies, on the distribution of species, on effigy mounds, and on weather, and turned instead to organizing. Lapham was found dead in his rowboat after failing to return from a day of fishing in Oconomowoc, Wisconsin, having apparently suffered a heart attack.

• An extensive collection of Lapham papers, including correspondence and manuscripts, is held in the State Historical Society of Wisconsin. A bibliography of his works was published in the *American Geologist* 13 (1894); 31–38. The major source on Lapham is Graham H. Hawks, "Increase A. Lapham, Wisconsin's First Scientist" (Ph.D. diss., Univ. of Wisconsin at Madison, 1960).

LIZ KEENEY

LAPORTE, Otto (23 July 1902–28 Mar. 1971), physicist, was born in Mainz, Germany, the son of Wilhelm Laporte, an artillery colonel in the German army, and Anna Geyl. The family was of French Huguenot descent and, since the time of Frederick the Great, had been for the most part civil servants in Prussia. Laporte attended the gymnasium in Mainz, where his early interests were in experimental physics. Entering the University of Frankfurt in 1920, he became acquainted with Max Born, whose courses stimulated his interest in theoretical physics. With Born's enthusiastic recommendation, from 1921 to 1924 Laporte attended the University of Munich, whose department of physics, under the leadership of Arnold Sommerfeld, was developing into one of the major European centers of theoretical physics. Laporte received his Ph.D. under Sommerfeld in 1924, with a dissertation on the analysis of the spectrum of iron, "Die Struktur des Eisenspektrums." At Munich he was a classmate and friend of Wolfgang Pauli and Werner Heisenberg, who had received their doctorates under Sommerfeld in 1921 and 1923 respectively. Heisenberg, in his memoirs, *Physics and Beyond* (1971), described Laporte's sober and pragmatic approach to physics as making him an excellent mediator in Heisenberg's stormy encounters with Pauli (p. 28). On graduation, Laporte was awarded an International Education Board Fellowship (1924–1926), which he spent at the National Bureau of Standards in Washington, D.C., with the experimental spectroscopist William F. Meggers. Apparently content in the United States, Laporte accepted the offer in 1926 of Harrison M. Randall to join the faculty of the University of Michigan, which since 1923 had run a Summer Symposia in Theoretical Physics. Randall had overseen the building up of a group of theoretical faculty in the Physics Department, which, including Laporte, David M. Dennison, George E. Uhlenbeck, and Samuel A. Goudsmit, became perhaps the largest theoretical group in the United States at the time. Between 1928 and 1940 the sym-

posia played a key role in bringing modern physics to an American audience. Lecturers included such luminaries as Hans Bethe, Niels Bohr, Paul Dirac, Paul Ehrenfest, Enrico Fermi, Heisenberg, Henrik Kramers, Pauli, Sommerfeld, and Eugene Wigner. Laporte spent virtually his entire academic career at Michigan: as an instructor (1926–1927); an assistant professor (1927–1935); an associate professor (1935–1945); and finally as a professor (1945–1971). Concurrently, he held visiting professorships at Kyoto Imperial University (1928) and Tokyo University (1933 and 1937). He became a naturalized U.S. citizen in 1935. Between 1949 and 1950 he was a scientific intelligence analyst with the U.S. Army of Occupation in Heidelberg. He returned to Japan as scientific attaché at the American Embassy in Tokyo (1954–1956), and as scientific adviser for the U.S. ambassador (1961–1963). Laporte was fluent in Japanese and quite knowledgeable about Japanese culture; in 1956 the U.S. State Department cited his efforts as being instrumental in securing the U.S.-Japan atomic energy agreement.

Laporte's research naturally breaks into two major topics: general theoretical physics and spectroscopy (1923–1945), and fluid dynamics (1946–1971). The first was initiated with a survey paper on the propagation of electromagnetic waves around the earth (1923). This offered a dazzling display of his mathematical expertise, and its solutions included precursors of the so-called Regge poles in nuclear theory. The following two papers (1924), which dealt with his dissertation work on the spectrum of iron, contained the important discovery that the energy levels of atoms consist of two subsets that do not intercombine. This property, called Laporte's rule, was simultaneously discovered by American astronomer Henry N. Russell about titanium. For several years this discovery defied explanation, and it was ultimately recognized to be a general quantum-mechanical selection rule according to which spectral lines produced by electric dipole radiation are generated by transitions between atomic (or molecular) states of opposite parity. However, such an explanation required the general group-theoretical analysis of parity given by Eugene P. Wigner in 1927–1928. Within two years of Bartel L. van der Waerden's introduction of spinor analysis, Laporte and Uhlenbeck produced an important paper containing a spinor discussion of the Maxwell and Dirac equations (1931). Laporte married Eleanor Anders in 1933; they had no children. Following her death in 1957, he married Adele Pond in 1959; they had three daughters.

Laporte's fluid dynamics debut was marked by an ingenious paper on a family of exact solutions for the lift distribution of a class of airfoils of elliptical outline (*Physical Review*, 1946). Subsequently, his interests in fluids broadened to include experimental work on shock waves as director of the Shock Tube Laboratory at Michigan. This work involved the use of reflected shocks to produce high temperatures so that spectroscopic phenomena could be studied. He also produced an important series of research reports for the U.S. Navy on supersonic aerodynamics between 1947 and

1949, in collaboration with his colleague Robert C. F. Bartels. Laporte had been a charter member in 1965 of the Division of Fluid Dynamics of the American Physical Society and was active in its early program and organization. Soon after his death, this division established an annual Otto Laporte Memorial Lectureship.

Laporte was possibly the one student of Sommerfeld who inherited his mentor's taste for mathematical precision and elegance, as well as his interest in classical electrodynamics, fluid dynamics, and atomic structure. While his contributions were not in a class with those of his friends Heisenberg and Pauli, who each won the Nobel Prize—altogether Laporte published fewer than seventy papers and no books—his work is choice and indicates a profound understanding of theoretical physics. He was an inspiring teacher who conveyed to his students his appreciation for the beauty of physics and the need for sound mathematical arguments. His courses were described as being simultaneously both a "high point" and a "hurdle" for graduate students at Michigan.

Laporte was stricken by a rapidly progressing form of cancer and died in Ann Arbor, Michigan. Before this was known, his name had been put forward for membership in the National Academy of Sciences. The election of new members was scheduled for the annual meeting of the academy in April, and in an unprecedented move, in recognition of the high esteem in which he was held, he was posthumously elected a member at that meeting in 1971. In 1973 the National Academy changed its rules to prohibit such elections.

• A collection of Laporte's papers is in the Bentley Historical Library at the University of Michigan. An interview with him (Jan. 1964) is in the Archive for the History of Quantum Physics (available from the American Philosophical Society). Although most of his work is highly technical, he wrote a nice expository article, "Shock Waves," *Scientific American* 181 (Nov. 1949): 14–19, which deals with his interests in fluid dynamics. A memoir by H. R. Crane and D. M. Dennison in the National Academy of Sciences, *Biographical Memoirs* 50 (1979): 269–85, contains a portrait and a list of publications. Obituaries are in the *New York Times*, 30 Mar. 1971, and *Physics Today* 24 (June 1971): 72–73.

JOSEPH D. ZUND

LARAMEE, Jacques (?–1821?), trapper, was probably born somewhere in Canada, the son of unknown parents. Remarkably, next to nothing is known with certainty about his life, leaving biographers to grasp at legends and mere suppositions. Little of LaRamee appears in the documentary record. He seems to have been the descendant of a Frenchman, Jacques Fissiau, dit LaRamee, who migrated to Canada in 1708. Only the trapper's death was recorded in a more or less authoritative contemporary document: Ten years after the fact, John Daughtery, a U.S. Indian agent gathering data on the fur trade for the government, enumerated on his casualty list "J. Loremy . . . a free man . . . killed in 1821 . . . on the Platte by Arapahoes."

Much of the rest of LaRamee's story was constructed from hearsay mixed with ample doses of imagination. According to tradition, LaRamee was in the employ of the Northwest Company, beginning about 1810. He came to the Upper Missouri to trap sometime after 1815. Then, as is told, LaRamee pushed on to the tributaries of the North Platte River in what is now southeastern Wyoming around 1819. He was said to have announced in 1820 to his associates (of indeterminate number) that he was going to trap the headwaters of the river that now bears his name. When LaRamee did not return by the spring of 1821, his companions ascended what is now called the Laramie River to search for him. In three days they discovered his body in a shack he had built on the river's bank. His death, it was assumed, had come at the hands of Arapaho Indians.

With such little material to work with, biographers have been as creative in describing his character as in recounting the events of his life. Some remarked on his fearlessness, and one even closed his eyes to imagine that "Every act of his life commended him as worthy of the friendship of both the white men and natives" (Coutant, p. 297). Yet it is not LaRamee's unknowable attributes or unknown accomplishments that constitute his legacy to the American West, but simply his name. He gave an anglicized version of his name to an unusually large number of places and physical features in the Northern Rockies. The name "Laramie" was attached to rivers, mountains, and a basin in a region of southeastern Wyoming where he was believed to have trapped and to have died; to the trading post established in 1834 at the confluence of the Laramie and North Platte rivers, and later to the famed fort at that site; and to the Wyoming town located by the Union Pacific railroad in 1868.

• There is a Jacques LaRamee biographical file in the Hebard collection at the American Heritage Center, University of Wyoming, Laramie, Wyo. The most reliable sources are John D. McDermott, "The Search for Jacques LaRamee: A Study in Frustration," *Annals of Wyoming* 36 (1964): 169–74, and Dale L. Morgan and Eleanor T. Harris, *The Rocky Mountain Journals of William Marshall Anderson* (1967). Those interested in the legend of LaRamee will find it in Grace Raymond Hebard, "Jacques Laramie," *Midwest Review* 7 (1926): 12–16; Elliott Coues, ed., *Forty Years a Fur Trader on the Upper Missouri: The Personal Narrative of Charles Larpenteur, 1833–1872* (1898); Alice Stevens, "Trapper Jacques Laramie: A Legendary Figure," *Laramie Daily Boomerang*, 13 July 1875; Rufus B. Sage, *Scenes in the Rocky Mountains* (1846); and C. G. Coutant, *The History of Wyoming: From Earliest Known Discoveries* (1899).

GENE M. GRESSLEY

LARCOM, Lucy (5 Mar. 1824–17 Apr. 1893), writer and editor, was born in Beverly, Massachusetts, the daughter of Benjamin Larcom, a sea captain, and Lois Barrett. Her childhood was secure and pleasant until her father's death when she was seven. Mrs. Larcom and her younger children moved to Lowell, Massachusetts, where she managed a boardinghouse and Lucy worked in the mills and went to public school. A precocious child and avid reader, she became a youthful and frequent contributor of verse and prose to the *Lowell Offering.* Her autobiography, *A New England Girlhood* (1889), chronicles these years, contrasting her free and happy childhood with the constriction of the mills, emphasizing the importance of work, and revealing her love of books and learning. In 1846 she went with her sister's family to Illinois, where she first taught at a district school, then was student and teacher at Monticello Seminary. Disenchanted with the West and "pioneer" life, she returned to Massachusetts in 1852. She taught at Wheaton Seminary in Norton, Massachusetts, for nine years.

Larcom's poems appeared first in local newspapers, with several in the *National Era,* then in national magazines, as she built a small but loyal public. Urged on by John Greenleaf Whittier, she published a small book of moral essays entitled *Similitudes* in 1854, followed by three similar books. In 1858 she wrote a story-poem, "Hannah Binding Shoes," for the *Crayon,* a short-lived arts magazine. Although she thought little of the poem and grew to dislike it, it brought her sudden national fame; William Dean Howells later claimed that it conferred immortality upon her. With her fame, her work was welcomed by the *Independent,* the *Atlantic Monthly,* and other quality magazines. From 1865 to 1873 she was associate editor and editor of *Our Young Folks,* a magazine for older children published by James T. Fields, and became part of the New England literary establishment that had its center at the Old Corner Bookstore and the Fieldses' home. After the magazine was sold she supported herself, somewhat precariously, as a freelance writer until her death in Boston.

Though shy and formal in public, she had a gift for friendship, and contemporary accounts stress her warmth, kindness, and humor. She was engaged for many years but finally rejected marriage and pioneer life in California to remain in the East and continue writing. In public, however, she supported marriage, family, and women as homemakers.

Larcom was influenced by Whittier and later by Phillips Brooks, but her poetic model was William Cullen Bryant. Although her early verse was strongly abolitionist and she wrote occasionally about women and children, most of her poetry, characterized by attractive visual imagery and strong lyrical qualities, reflected the nineteenth-century focus on the beauty of nature and its function as a means of discovering God. Collections of her work are *Poems* (1868), *Childhood Songs* (1875), *Wild Roses of Cape Ann* (1881), and *Poetical Works of Lucy Larcom* (1884); her blank verse novel, *An Idyl of Work* (1875), was a story of the Lowell mills. Prose works include *Landscape in American Poetry* (1879; with artist J. Appleton Brown), "Among Lowell Mill-Girls" (*Atlantic Monthly,* 1881), articles for magazines, newsletters for several Boston papers, and her sensitive and evocative autobiography, *A New England Girlhood* (1889), which, like her poems, is rich in visual detail, although more impressionistic than factual. A religious thinker who had moved from the Calvinism of her childhood to a kind of Christian transcendentalism that found a personal God everywhere in nature, Larcom attempted in her last books to share her religious belief: *As It Is in Heaven* (1891), *The Unseen Friend* (1892), and *At the Beautiful Gate* (1892).

• Major collections of Larcom's letters are at the Essex Institute (Salem, Mass.), the Beverly Historical Society and the Beverly Public Library (Beverly, Mass.), the Addison papers at the Massachusetts Historical Society (Boston), and the Clifton Waller Barrett Library, University of Virginia; correspondence with James and Annie Fields is at the Houghton (Harvard) and the Huntington (San Marino, Calif.) libraries. Her work is listed in Jacob Blanck, *Bibliography of American Literature,* vol. 5 (1969), pp. 299–325. Her autobiography, *A New England Girlhood,* which covers her early years, was first published in 1889 and has been twice reprinted, in 1961 and in 1986. Daniel Dulany Addison, *Lucy Larcom: Life, Letters and Diary* (1894), a biography written immediately after her death, emphasizes her religious thought. A more recent biography is Shirley Marchalonis, *The Worlds of Lucy Larcom, 1824–1893* (1989). Her years as a mill girl are discussed in Harriet Hanson Robinson, *Loom and Spindle* (1896), and Benita Eisler, ed., *The Lowell Offering: Writings of New England Mill Women* (1977). See also Shirley Marchalonis, "Profile of Lucy Larcom," *Legacy* 5 (1988): 45–52; and Paul C. Helmreich, "Lucy Larcom at Wheaton," *New England Quarterly* 63 (1990): 109–19.

SHIRLEY MARCHALONIS

LARDNER, Ring (6 Mar. 1885–25 Sept. 1933), writer and journalist, was born Ringgold Wilmer Lardner in Niles, Michigan, the son of Henry Lardner, a prosperous businessman, and Lena Bogardus Phillips, a poet. Lardner's childhood was idyllic. He grew up in a comfortable, upper-class home where nursemaids and other servants supplemented the indulgent, loving care of his parents. As a young child, Lardner, along with the brother and sister nearest him in age, wrote and performed in dramatic recitations, plays, and musical programs in the family home.

Lardner had no formal schooling until high school. His mother first taught the three youngest children at home, then later hired a private tutor for their lessons in Latin, mathematics, and geography. When he graduated from high school in 1901, Lardner had no particular career interests. He worked briefly at office jobs in Chicago, returned to Niles, where he worked for the railroad, and then was sent to Chicago with his brother Rex to study mechanical engineering. After both boys flunked out, they again returned home, and Lardner went to work for the Niles Gas Company. He later remarked that working for the gas company taught him nearly everything there was to know about human nature. In 1905 he took a job as a cub reporter for the *South Bend (Ind.) Times.*

Between 1905 and 1913 Lardner held a succession of reporting and editing jobs. After leaving the *Times* in late 1907, he became a sports writer for the *Chicago Inter-Ocean,* followed by stints as baseball reporter for the *Chicago Examiner,* managing editor and feature writer for the *Sporting News,* based in St. Louis, sports editor for the *Boston American,* copyreader for the *Chi-*

cago *American*, and baseball writer for the *Chicago Examiner*. In 1911 he married Ellis Abbott; they had four sons.

Lardner began writing a daily column, "In the Wake of the News," for the *Chicago Tribune* in 1913. Writing the column not only paid well but allowed him almost free rein in his writing. Critics credit Lardner's expertise in satire and especially his use of the vernacular to the skills he developed in this period. Because of his interest in baseball and his experience as a sports writer, he began putting stories in his column that were purportedly written by unlettered athletes. The pieces were actually written, of course, by Lardner himself, who had an excellent ear for dialogue.

Lardner then began writing short stories in the voice of the fictional rookie ballplayer Jack Keefe, who writes letters to his friend Al Blanchard back home in Bedford, Indiana. First published as a series in the *Saturday Evening Post* in 1914, the stories were so popular that the magazine published another series of them in 1915. In all, Lardner wrote twenty-six Jack Keefe stories, the original six of which were published as a book, *You Know Me Al*, in 1916. Others were collected and published as *Treat 'Em Rough* (1918) and *The Real Dope* (1919). In 1915 he wrote several stories about Fred Gross, a Chicago police detective, which were published in *Redbook* and later collected as *Own Your Own Home* (1919). While the Keefe stories focus on the ballplayer's adventures in his profession, the Fred Gross stories focus on Gross's efforts to get along with his middle-class neighbors in a Chicago suburb and his attempts to move up in society.

Another of Lardner's main characters of this period is Gullible, of *Gullible's Travels, Etc.* (1917). Unlike Keefe and Gross, who relate their stories through the letters they write, Gullible tells his stories in a spoken colorful American vernacular. Walton R. Patrick notes that the Gullible character type, under various names, "appears in a number of Lardner's stories and even serves as an 'in-character' mask for Lardner in much of his nonfiction" (p. 28). This character is that of the "wise boob," who "holds a good opinion of himself and is quite willing to let others share it, particularly those with more money and a higher social status" (p. 28).

Lardner used his own experiences as model or inspiration for the fiction he wrote. When he moved his family to Greenwich, Connecticut, in 1919, he sent three of the children by train with a nurse. The other child traveled with him and Ellis by automobile. The fictionalized account of this road trip was published as *The Young Immigrants* (1920). The story contains an exchange that is probably the most frequently quoted passage of Lardner's works:

"Are you lost daddy I arsked tenderly."

"Shut up he explained."

During the seven years he lived in Great Neck, Long Island, to which he moved in the spring of 1921, Lardner was part of the drinking and partying social scene, playing bridge and golf, and socializing with newspaper and literary figures, including F. Scott Fitzgerald. At Fitzgerald's urging, Lardner published in 1924 a collection of his best stories, called *How to Write Short Stories (with Samples)*. Fitzgerald, who suggested presenting the collection as a parody of a how-to book for writers, believed in the project so strongly that he convinced his own publisher, Scribner's, to publish the book. Unlike Lardner's previous collections, which centered on one main character, the stories in this book were unrelated. With this work, Lardner began to attract the attention of literary critics who previously had dismissed him as a hack. His 1926 collection, *The Love Nest, and Other Stories*, demonstrates Lardner's progress as a writer. Although the best-known story of that collection, "Haircut," is written in the first person, most of the others use third-person narration; only one story is about athletics. More significant than narration or subject matter, however, is the change in tone. In this collection, Lardner is no longer lightly humorous, but darkly satiric.

Lardner continued writing fiction, and by 1929, when his health began to fail as a result of heart trouble and recurring tuberculosis, he had achieved not only popular success but critical acclaim. During his most productive years, he wrote newspaper columns (for the *Chicago Tribune* and then for Bell Syndicate), many short stories, a comic strip based on Jack Keefe, nonfiction, and a satirical autobiography called *The Story of a Wonder Man* (1927). The characters he wrote about included not only athletes and a police detective but also practical jokers, American tourists, suburbanites, social climbers, gold-digging women, heavy drinkers, and bickering couples.

After he was diagnosed with tuberculosis in the summer of 1926, Lardner gave up newspaper writing to write plays. When his first play, written with George M. Cohan, was unsuccessful, he again briefly wrote a newspaper column to earn money. In 1929 he published *Round Up*, his last important collection of short stories. His only successful play was *June Moon*, a 1929 collaboration with George S. Kaufman based on Lardner's short story "Some Like Them Cold." Although he was in poor health and frequently hospitalized the last four years of his life, he continued to write, and in the final year or so, he wrote a weekly radio column for the *New Yorker*. Patrick observes that the radio column was appropriate for Lardner "not only because of his lifelong interest in music but also because he spent his sleepless nights in the hospital listening to radio shows" (p. 37). When Lardner died at the East Hampton, Long Island, home he had built in 1928, he had been working on another play with Kaufman.

Lardner's contribution to sportswriting is that he presented athletes as real people instead of idols. A central question about Lardner is whether he "just doesn't like people," as Clifton Fadiman claimed in a 22 March 1933 essay for *The Nation*, or whether he merely satirized characters who deviated from his own ideal set of human values. Patrick argues that Lardner, in writing about human failings, was motivated "by the idealistic hope that human improvement begins with self-knowledge, with an awareness of one's defects and shortcomings" (p. 148). Regardless of his motivation, Lardner stands as a striking example of the American humorist in the tradition of Mark Twain.

• Lardner's papers are in the Newberry Library, Chicago. For a complete listing of Lardner's works, see Matthew J. Bruccoli, *Ring W. Lardner: A Descriptive Bibliography* (1976). The standard biography is Donald Elder, *Ring Lardner, A Biography* (1956). Maxwell Geismar, *Ring Lardner and the Portrait of Folly* (1972), is also entertaining but more concise and written for the average reader. For a good biography that also provides background about baseball during Lardner's era, see Jonathan Yardley, *Ring: A Biography of Ring Lardner* (1977). An excellent study of Lardner, including a critique of his works, is Walton R. Patrick, *Ring Lardner* (1963). Readers interested in Lardner's witty correspondence should see two books edited by Clifford M. Caruthers: *Ring around Max: The Correspondence of Ring Lardner and Max Perkins* (1973), which contains letters between Lardner and his editor, and *Letters from Ring* (1979), which contains personal letters from Ring to his wife and others. Ring Lardner, Jr., *The Lardners: My Family Remembered* (1976), presents a child's eye view of life in the Lardner family.

CLAUDIA MILSTEAD

LARKIN, James (21 Jan. 1876–30 Jan. 1947), Irish labor leader and charter member of the Communist Labor party in the United States, was born in Liverpool, England, the son of James Larkin (mother's name unknown). Both of his parents were Irish. When Larkin was eleven, his father died of tuberculosis, the death leaving the family in poverty and cutting short Larkin's brief formal education. Larkin was taken on as an apprentice at his father's Liverpool engineering firm, although he soon quit. After hiring on at a series of odd jobs, he landed work as a laborer on the city's docks in 1893. In that same year an injury at work changed the course of his life. For nineteen weeks he spent his days reading at the local library and his evenings attending open-air socialist meetings. This period of study was the beginning of a lifetime commitment to socialism. Interestingly, Larkin also would cultivate a fervent Irish nationalism. These beliefs mixed with a devout Catholicism, which produced his commitment to improving the lives of working people.

By the turn of the century Larkin had become foreman dock porter for T. & J. Harrison, Ltd., where he impressed both his employers and the men under him with his honesty and integrity. In 1903 he married Elizabeth Brown. They had several children, including "young" James, who became a union leader, and Denis, who became Lord Mayor of Dublin. The same year that he married, Larkin also became a member of the National Union of Dock Laborers. It soon became apparent that in trade unionism he had found the vehicle for action.

In 1905 he supported the union in a disastrous walkout and found himself out of a job. The union then offered him a position as an organizer. He immersed himself in his new career, and over the next few years he was involved in major organizing campaigns in the Scottish and Irish ports. During the Belfast strike of 1907 he demonstrated extraordinary organizational abilities, successfully introducing the secondary boycott and the sympathy strike. At one point he managed to bring the Belfast police out in sympathy with the dockworkers. In the end, however, the dockers were abandoned by their allies and forced to return to work without wage concessions or union recognition.

Larkin left the Dock Laborers Union after a personal clash with its general secretary. He did not, however, abandon trade unionism. Angered by the living and working conditions of early twentieth-century Dublin, he was determined to rectify the worst abuses of industrialism, organize the working class, and convert the workers of Dublin to the gospel of socialism. In 1908 he organized the Irish Transport and General Workers Union (ITGWU), and in the next four years he enrolled thousands of carters, dockers, laborers, and factory hands. Further, in organizing the great mass of unskilled workers in Dublin, he inaugurated a new era in the Irish labor movement. These years before World War I would be his most creative and most important as he attempted to lay the foundation for a revolutionary working-class organization.

The city's employers, led by William Martin Murphy and the Employers' Federation Ltd., soon began a counteroffensive against the ITGWU. The inevitable clash came in 1913 as employers attempted to break the union. At first, union and workers found support for their cause throughout the city and from sympathetic unions. However, over the long struggle that support faded, and after eight months the conflict ended without a clear winner. Most transport workers were able to return to their positions without diavowing the ITGWU, as the employers had insisted. But the Irish labor movement was decisively weakened, and Larkin lost his union preeminence. In addition, his vehement personal attacks cost the ITGWU the support of many powerful British and Irish labor leaders.

In 1914 Larkin left on a fundraising and speaking tour of the United States. Although he expected to stay only briefly, he did not return home until 1923. While in the United States, he spoke before socialist, Irish-American, and German-American groups. He also worked, briefly, as an organizer for the Western Federation of Miners. During World War I he was, on several occasions, recruited as a saboteur for the German government. Although he refused to participate in any violence, he did accept payment from the German ambassador for his efforts to encourage strikes and work stoppages and for his attempts to delay American efforts to aid the Allies. Larkin hoped his actions would accomplish two things: through the frustration of British war aims, to speed Irish independence; and by means of an eventual military deadlock, to prompt a workers' revolt in the warring countries.

Larkin was in the United States at the time of the 1916 Irish uprising for independence and throughout the rebellion and civil war that followed. His greatest regret was that after the execution of James Connolly, his compatriot in the labor movement, he believed that the Irish revolution became a rebellion of middle-class nationalists and failed to fulfill its working-class revolutionary potential.

Among American socialists, Larkin was most closely associated with the left wing of the Socialist party. When that group split from the Socialist party in 1919, several members, including Larkin, formed the Communist Labor party. In July 1919 he and the other members of the new party's national council attached their names to a manifesto published in *The Revolutionary Age*. In November 1919, on the strength of this association, Larkin was arrested by order of the New York state legislature's Lusk Committee, which was investigating radical and seditious activities. Although he contended that he was innocent of any illegal or violent activity, Larkin was convicted of criminal anarchy. In May 1920 he began to serve his sentence of five to ten years in Sing Sing prison. Three years later, after much international pressure for his release, he was pardoned by New York Governor Alfred E. Smith and then deported as an undesirable alien.

Back in Ireland, another personal dispute with the leaders of the ITGWU led to Larkin's expulsion from the union. Far from defeated, he and his brother, Peter, organized disenchanted members of the ITGWU into the Workers' Union of Ireland, setting off a long jurisdictional conflict. During these years he also was elected a Dublin city councilor, and from 1927 to 1944 he served three separate terms as a member of Dail Eirann, the Irish parliament. The final decades of his life, however, never matched the creativity and success of his earlier ventures, especially those with the ITGWU. Although the union failed to inspire the social revolution that Larkin had once envisioned, it did become a powerful and significant working-class organization. As his biographer has noted, in terms of advances in wages and working conditions, as well as security and dignity, the Irish working class owed more to Larkin than to anyone else. When he died in Dublin, he was eulogized as the "Lion of Irish Labor," and throughout Ireland, England, and the United States he was mourned by those he had served.

• Contemporary assessments of Larkin include the memoirs of Irish Labour party leader William O'Brien, *Forth the Banners Go* (1969); ITGWU member Frank Robbins, *Under the Starry Plough* (1977); and Bertram Wolfe, *Strange Communists I Have Known* (1965). Emmet Larkin, *James Larkin: Irish Labour Leader, 1876–1947* (1965), offers a thorough biographical treatment. In addition, see John Gray, *City in Revolt: James Larkin and the Belfast Dock Strike of 1907* (1985); Austen Morgan, *Labour and Partition: The Belfast Working Class, 1905–23* (1991); John W. Boyle, *The Irish Labour Movement in the Nineteenth Century* (1987); Charles McCarthy, *Trade Unions in Ireland, 1894–1960* (1977); and obituaries in *Catholic World*, June 1948, and the *New York Times*, 31 Jan. 1947.

TIMOTHY J. HOULIHAN

LARKIN, Thomas Oliver (16 Sept. 1802–27 Oct. 1858), merchant, diplomatic agent, and capitalist, was born in Charlestown, Massachusetts, the son of Thomas Oliver Larkin, Sr., a sea captain, and Ann Rogers Cooper. His spotty education is reflected in his correspondence, which is sprinkled with misspellings and grammatical slips. When Oliver was five, his father died, and in 1813 his mother remarried and moved the family to Lynn, which young Oliver always looked upon as his hometown. At the age of fifteen, he went to nearby Boston "to learn the art of making books," a trade he abandoned two years later for a clerkship in a bookstore. That, too, proved confining, so in October 1821 he set out with a friend for Wilmington, North Carolina, to seek his fortune.

After a brief but disappointing stint as sailors, the two friends opened a small store in Wilmington in June 1822. By 1824 Larkin had his own store, which proved successful. However, in 1827 he sold his store to his former clerks and entered the lumber business, operating a sawmill in Long Creek, North Carolina. A disasterous undertaking, by spring 1831 the sawmill failed.

Influenced by his half brother, John B. R. Cooper, a sea captain engaged in the California trade for some years, Larkin immigrated to that Mexican province in 1831, taking with him a supply of merchandise. On the long voyage he studied Spanish, in which he became fluent, and met a charming young woman, Rachel Hobson Holmes, en route to join her husband, who was involved in the Pacific coastal trade. The two had an affair that produced an illegitimate daughter who died six months later. However, that blight was removed from the child when Mrs. Holmes received news of her husband's death. She and Larkin were married in June 1833; they had eight more children. As the sole heir to her husband's estate, Rachel's inheritance provided her husband with much needed venture capital. Reaching Monterey 13 April 1832, Larkin clerked for Captain Cooper until February 1833, when he went into business for himself, first working as a commission agent and later opening a general store. He built the first flour mill in the region as well as the first sawmill. He had extensive dealings in the hide and tallow market and traded with Mexico and the Sandwich Islands (now Hawaiian Islands) in foodstuffs, lumber, and horses.

Larkin played a prominent role in the acquisition of California by the United States, a goal he had long harbored. Even prior to his formal appointment on 29 January 1844 as U.S. consul at Monterey (the commission was received 24 June), he was involved in the political life of the province and was well known to U.S. naval officers, who frequently called at Monterey. During the critical years 1844 through 1846, which led up to the Mexican War, he was in the diplomatic forefront, working assiduously to thwart any overt British or French designs on the province.

President James K. Polk, who shared that same goal, appointed Larkin "confidential agent in California" on 17 October 1845 in a secret dispatch from Secretary of State James Buchanan. Larkin was instructed to work for an independent California, which would "become one of the free and independent States of this Union," if such could be effected without alienating Mexico. Then "if the People should desire to unite their destiny with ours, they would be received as brethren." To that end, Larkin dedicated all his efforts. However, before the desired objective could be realized, the Mexican War achieved that goal when U.S. naval and military forces occupied California. During the war, Larkin served as the navy's business agent, later storekeeper, providing supplies and needed services. With the Treaty of Guadalupe Hidalgo, 2 February 1848, the United States purchased the Mexican Cession, including present-day California. The treaty also ended Larkin's consular days.

During those eventful years, Larkin prospered by providing the American armed forces with goods, services, and supplies, serving as naval storekeeper, 1847–1848, and naval agent, 1847–1849. At the same time, Larkin early recognized that the halcyon days of the hide and tallow trade were over. Shrewdly, he shifted his business attention to investment in land, which proved a wise choice, particularly with the extraordinary discovery of gold at Coloma on the South Fork of the American River on 24 January 1848. Land values soared, making Larkin a very wealthy man, one of his burning ambitions. The influx of thousands of gold seekers also forced the military authorities to convene a convention in Monterey in the fall of 1849 to address the question of self-government for the territory. As a delegate to that convention, Larkin played a role in drafting California's first state constitution.

In 1850 Larkin decided to return east with his family and chose New York City as their home. For the first six months they traveled often, visiting nearby cities, before settling down at 101 Tenth Street, where they entertained old California friends and New York acquaintances lavishly, as they had in Monterey. Larkin turned to ventures in New York real estate and became an early investor in railroads.

Because of his extensive California holdings, Larkin made two extended trips there to attend to pressing matters. With the ever-increasing squatter problem and the need to protect his land titles, Larkin and his family returned to San Francisco in 1853, taking up permanent residence in a newly built mansion in 1854. Larkin also continued to augment his considerable real estate holdings with new acquisitions. While on a visit to one of his major properties on the Sacramento River, he caught a fever, most likely typhoid. He returned to San Francisco, where he died in less than a week.

• Harlan Hague and David J. Langum, *Thomas O. Larkin: A Life of Patriotism and Profit in Old California* (1990), is the best biography, surplanting the dated study by Reuben L. Underhill, *From Cowhides to Golden Fleece: A Narrative of California, 1832–1858 . . .* (1939). Also useful is Robert J. Parker, *Chapters in the Early Life of Thomas Oliver Larkin . . .* (1939). Invaluable are George B. Hammond, ed., *The Larkin Papers: Personal, Business, and Official Correspondence of Thomas Oliver Larkin, Merchant and U.S. Consul in Califor-*

nia (10 vols., 1951–1968), and John A. Hawgood, ed., *First and Last Consul: Thomas Oliver Larkin and the Americanization of California*, 2d ed. (1970). On Larkin's death San Francisco newspapers carried lengthy articles or extended obituaries: *Alta California, Chronicle, Evening Bulletin, Evening News, Herald,* and *Times,* as well as the Sacramento *Daily Union.*

DOYCE B. NUNIS, JR.

LARNED, Josephus Nelson (11 May 1836–15 Aug. 1913), librarian and social historian, was born in Chatham, Canada West (now Ontario, Canada), the son of Henry Sherwood Larned, a contractor, and Mary Ann Nelson. At the age of twelve Larned and his family moved to Buffalo, New York, where he spent much of the rest of his life. Larned's formal education ended when he was sixteen, and in later years he chided the Buffalo community for not encouraging its young men to strive for higher education.

Larned worked as a bookkeeper and a clerk, and from 1857 to 1859 he traveled in the West. In 1859 the *Buffalo Express* hired Larned as its political editorialist. While there he formed a brief partnership with Samuel Clemens (Mark Twain), who also worked on the paper. Clemens referred all political opinion to Larned and in one memorable editorial deferred all comment about the Annual Republican State Convention until "the other young man [Larned] gets home!" In 1861 Larned married Frances A. K. McCrea. They had three children.

Larned remained at the *Express* until 1872. During those years he also served a term (1871–1873) as superintendent of the Buffalo Schools but was unable to break down the political barriers that hindered school reform and progress. In Buffalo at that time, the business of public education was undertaken by the Common Council, an arrangement that made the schools merely one more agenda item. In his superintendent's report for 1872, Larned bluntly criticized the city, saying: "I know of no other important city in the country in which the government of the schools is not separated from the general organization of municipal government and committed to a board of education." Larned resigned from the superintendency one year later.

Larned's deep concern for education eventually found a productive outlet when he accepted the position of librarian of the Young Men's Association (YMA) in 1877. Although he was primarily charged with the financial integrity of the institution, he used his new position to create a model library for the entire community. During his first year at the YMA, Larned completed the first catalog of its 30,000 volumes, encouraged the reading of good literature by an open-shelf policy, and transformed the library into a mecca of civic responsibility.

Larned was soon primed to make even more strategic changes. At a meeting of the American Library Association, he met Melvil Dewey of Amherst College. Larned was so impressed by Dewey's "System of Relative Location" for books that he implemented the procedure at the YMA, making it the first library outside of Amherst College to use the Dewey Decimal System. Circulation increased greatly, and Larned's support of Sunday reading hours opened the doors of good literature to the working class of Buffalo. Larned was specifically concerned about young people, and his *Catalogue of Books for Young Readers* earned him much respect. Larned's reputation was so impressive that he was asked to create a catalog of 5,000 volumes to be displayed as a model library at the 1893 World's Columbian Exhibition at Chicago.

Throughout his career as a librarian, Larned remained true to his concept of the mission of a library, which he presented to the 1894 American Library Association in his presidential address, saying, "Our tools are not books, but *good* books." Every reform that Larned initiated buttressed his belief that "our schools, churches, museums, art collection, science clubs, literary societies, all find their chief ally in the library, which nurses and nourishes every germ that they throw out."

In 1897 the YMA completed a twofold transition: becoming a public-lending library and moving to a separate facility dedicated to the purpose of education and cultural dissemination. Much to the dismay of the city, Larned resigned from his position as superintendent after this transition was finalized, although he continued to serve Buffalo through his writing, lecturing, and encouragement of educational reform.

A bibliography of Larned's published works must emphasize his *History for Ready Reference* (5 vols., 1894–1895; rev. and enlarged to 7 vols., 1901–1910), which grew out of the multitude of research questions asked by patrons of the YMA. During the early years of the twentieth century, this work was a standard reference, "used everywhere by everybody." Larned's *History of Buffalo* (1911) is also a classic work as are his essays on "Patriotism" and the "Missionaries of the Book." In his essay "Prepare for Socialism," which appeared in the *Atlantic Monthly* (May 1911), Larned called for a reformation of American political parties in order to arm the country against the spread of socialism.

In 1908 Larned became the local standard bearer for the cause of international peace and was the founder and first president of the Buffalo Peace and Arbitration Society, and his essay in the *Atlantic Monthly* entitled "Peace-Teaching of History" (Jan. 1908) provides a very contemporary appraisal of war: "It is the most hideous of historical facts, but its hideousness to us in history as history is too commonly written and taught. It ought to fill us so with horror and pain . . . but it does not."

Larned's contribution to American social education began with his belief that a library serves the needs of the whole community. He was committed to the "educating influence" of books on a community and the training of that community to investigation, study, and intellectual nourishment. For him, a library was a living organism and its resources open to all. Larned thus rightly belongs in the company of influential re-

formers. He died in his Orchard Park, New York, home.

• The Buffalo and Erie County Historical Society houses much of Larned's published work, as well as a catalog of articles written by and about him. Particular attention should be given to vol. 19 of the *Publications of the Buffalo Historical Society*, which contains a brief biographical sketch, several speeches, and complete bibliography of Larned's publications. The Lockwood Library of the State University of New York at Buffalo also contains primary source documents relating to the history of the Buffalo Library. The Buffalo and Erie County Library also contains many materials on Larned. Patricia Myles Hummer, "Josephus Nelson Larned and the Buffalo Library, 1877–1897: A Study in the Emergence of a Modern Public Library" (M. A. thesis, Duke Univ., 1971), gives a wealth of detail about the Young Men's Association. For a general survey of the history of western New York, see John Theodore Horton et al., *History of Northwestern New York: Erie, Niagara, Wyoming, Genesee, and Orleans Counties*, vol. 1 (1947). An older history, Henry Perry Smith, *History of the City of Buffalo and Erie County with Biographical Sketches of Its Prominent Men and Pioneers* (1884), gives a comprehensive look at Buffalo in the nineteenth century and Larned's work at the Young Men's Association.

RUTH F. ADAMS

LARNED, William Augustus (30 Dec. 1872–16 Dec. 1926), tennis player, was born in Summit, New Jersey, the son of William Zebedee Larned, a wealthy Summit landowner and New York lawyer, and Katharine Penniman. Although he did not graduate from Cornell University, while a student he won the 1892 intercollegiate tennis singles championship.

Larned was a great offensive player who used a potent backhand and an attacking style. His graceful yet powerful game was characterized by groundstrokes consistently aimed at the corners of the court combined with volleys and serves hit with mechanical precision and pace. During the two decades between 1892 and 1911, with the exception of 1898 when he rode with Theodore Roosevelt's Rough Riders in the Spanish-American War, he was ranked by the U.S. Lawn Tennis Association among the best six players in the country nineteen times. Included among these were eight years as number one, five years as number two, and four years as number three. He won seven U.S. Lawn Tennis Association men's singles championships (1901–1902 and 1907–1911), a record shared with Richard "Dick" Sears and William "Bill" Tilden. In six years of Davis Cup play between 1902 and 1911, during three of which he served as captain, he won ten and lost five singles matches.

After retiring from competitive tennis in 1911 due to rheumatism, Larned, an independently wealthy lifelong bachelor, continued to pursue his sport interests of golf and other outdoor activities. He enlisted in the aviation section of the Signal Corps as a pilot during World War I and earned the rank of lieutenant colonel prior to his discharge.

Deteriorating health forced him to leave his membership on the New York Stock Exchange in 1922, although he then established the Dayton Steel Racquet

Company to manufacture a racket he had invented. His worsening health and a nervous breakdown led to his suicide in New York City.

Larned, a graceful athlete who hit with pace and accuracy while constantly attacking the lines, played brilliant tennis, although his game was interspersed with impaired effectiveness when he allowed annoyances to affect his concentration. His consistency in rankings and record singles victories earned him selection into the Citizens Savings Athletic Foundation in 1906 and the International Tennis Hall of Fame in 1956.

Tennis during the first decade of the twentieth century remained closely affiliated with its upper-class, private club heritage. Larned's socioeconomic status, like that of most other players at the time, allowed him to develop his tennis skills in the absence of pressures to excel. While he developed an all-court game, many of his contemporaries were content to play a more leisurely baseline style. The choice to attack each ball may have contributed to his not achieving his potential until later in his career. Larned's invincibility in major events between 1907 and 1911 may have motivated opponents to adopt his aggressive, powerful style of play.

• The International Tennis Hall of Fame has a file on Larned. The following four books provide the best overview of Larned's tennis career: Parke Cummings, *American Tennis—The Story of a Game and Its People* (1957); Will Grimsley, *Tennis: Its History, People and Events* (1971); Paul Metzler, *Tennis Styles and Stylists* (1969); and *Fifty Years of Lawn Tennis in the United States* (1931), published by the U.S. Lawn Tennis Association. An obituary is in the *New York Times*, 17 Dec. 1926.

ANGELA LUMPKIN

LAROCCA, Nick (11 Apr. 1889–22 Feb. 1961), cornetist and trumpeter, was born Dominic James LaRocca in New Orleans, Louisiana, the son of Giarolamo LaRocca, a shoemaker and amateur cornetist; his mother's name is unknown. Self-taught at an early age, LaRocca began to play professionally in small groups at the age of sixteen, at which point he dropped out of high school. In 1912 he began playing in Papa Laine's Reliance Brass Band, one of the most famous white marching bands in New Orleans, before moving to Chicago in early 1916. Chicago at that time was a developing center for the new music known as jazz, and many New Orleans musicians, both black and white, were moving there. In May 1916 LaRocca and three other New Orleans colleagues formed the Original Dixieland Jazz (at the beginning, sometimes spelled Jass) Band. They became very successful, culminating in a much publicized engagement at Reisenweber's in New York in January 1917.

The next month the band began to record for Columbia and Victor—the first recordings by a "jazz band." Then followed a lengthy engagement in England (1919–1920) where they made more recordings. Returning to the United States in July 1920, the Original Dixieland Jazz Band continued under the direction of LaRocca until he suffered a nervous breakdown in

January 1925, apparently a result of living in the forefront of the "jazz age."

Returning to New Orleans, LaRocca gave up music and worked as a building contractor for the next eleven years. In July 1936 LaRocca made a comeback with the Original Dixieland Jazz Band as well as a large dance band. In early 1938 he again abandoned music, returning to New Orleans and his contracting business, from which he retired in 1958. He died in New Orleans, survived by his wife and seven children. (His wife's name and the date of the marriage are unknown.)

LaRocca, who switched from cornet to trumpet, probably in the early twenties, did not read music. Coming out of the New Orleans marching band tradition, he was a powerful player, but he was somewhat stiff rhythmically compared with many of the other early jazz trumpeters. LaRocca served as both musical director and manager of the highly successful Original Dixieland Jazz Band. The band's recordings—the only jazz band recordings available between 1917 and 1922—had a widespread influence on younger musicians, among them Bix Beiderbecke. It is not without irony that this white band, playing music largely derived from black New Orleans bands but with little of their improvisational creativity, should have made the first jazz recordings. A number of the pieces recorded, "Livery Stable Blues," "Ostrich Walk," "At the Jazz Band Ball," and "Clarinet Marmalade," have become jazz standards. LaRocca claimed to have composed much of the band's repertoire, but there is evidence that much of this material was common musical language in New Orleans in the early part of the twentieth century. The latter two titles above were probably composed by him, however.

• The best critical evaluations of LaRocca's playing and of the music of the Original Dixieland Jazz Band can be found in M. Williams, *Jazz Masters of New Orleans* (1967), and G. Schuller, *Early Jazz* (1968). H. O. Brunn, *The Story of the Original Dixieland Jazz Band* (1960), is a highly tendentious account, written with LaRocca's cooperation, from which black New Orleans musicians are conspicuously absent, and in which the band is heralded as the "creators of jazz." An obituary is in the *New York Times*, 23 Feb. 1961.

HOWARD BROFSKY

LA ROCHE, René (23 Sept. 1795–9 Dec. 1872), physician, was born in Philadelphia, Pennsylvania, the son of René La Roche, a French émigré physician, and Marie Jeanne de la Condemine. After service as an army officer in the War of 1812, La Roche attended the University of Pennsylvania's medical school, from which he graduated in 1820, and established a practice in Philadelphia. Four years later he married Mary Jane Ellis; they had two children.

La Roche's fascination with fevers, particularly yellow fever, was awakened as early as 1821, when he participated in the survey of yellow fever in the United States undertaken by French physician Nicolas Chervin. He spent 1828 through 1830 studying medicine in France and traveling in Europe. By the 1850s La

Roche had become the leading U.S. authority on yellow fever, having published articles in the *American Journal of the Medical Sciences* and the *Charleston Medical Journal and Review* as well as his best-known treatise, *Yellow Fever Considered in Its Historical, Pathological, Etiological, and Therapeutical Relations* (1855). In 1854 he also published *Pneumonia*. American reception of both texts was favorable, although attention was focused primarily on *Yellow Fever*, which described every known yellow fever epidemic in Philadelphia between 1699 and 1854, and included an extensive bibliography. Throughout his life La Roche opposed the notion that diseases such as yellow fever were contagious, and he intended his book to reinforce the growing inclination of American physicians to question that theory. He believed in anticontagionism, especially the local origin of disease, an important vehicle for sanitary reform.

Yellow Fever came to play a part in the debate over racial hierarchies because many antebellum U.S. physicians had noted the greater resistance to yellow fever among black slaves. La Roche confirmed the fact that slaves rarely suffered from the fever but did not, as southern physicians did, use this fact to bolster conclusions about the appropriate position of blacks in society. He believed that, since blacks were used to laboring in higher temperatures than whites, they were better able to withstand diseases of warmer climates.

La Roche was active in both local and national medical groups, serving as a founding member in 1849 of the American Medical Association, and joining such societies as the American Philosophical Society, the Philadelphia College of Physicians, the Kappa Lambda Association of the United States, and the Pathological Society of Philadelphia. Early in his career he also edited the *North American Medical and Surgical Journal*. La Roche corresponded widely with his colleagues, including physicians Samuel D. Gross, Daniel Drake, and Erasmus Fenner. In addition to his extensive medical library, La Roche had a large collection of music works and wrote a privately published book on the government of ancient Rome. He also purchased several pieces of land in Mississippi and Tennessee with the southern physician A. P. Merrill.

La Roche's last publication, "Remarks on the Origin and Mode of Transmission of Yellow Fever in Philadelphia, . . . " (1871), dealt with the 1870 yellow fever epidemic. At the time of his death in Philadelphia he was writing a new book about fevers.

• Letters to La Roche and assorted other papers are divided between collections at the American Philosophical Society and the College of Physicians, both in Philadelphia. A brief sketch of La Roche is presented in Hubert Kottlove, *René La Roche of Philadelphia (1795–1872) and Yellow Fever* (1965). La Roche's complete bibliography as well as an examination of the American reception of *Yellow Fever* can be found in Smita Dutta, "René La Roche and Yellow Fever" (master's thesis, Johns Hopkins Univ., 1992). La Roche is described in Samuel D. Gross, *Autobiography* (1887). An obituary is in *Transactions of the American Medical Association* 24 (1873): 380–81.

SMITA DUTTA

LA RONDE, Louis Denys de. *See* Denys de La Ronde, Louis.

LARPENTEUR, Charles (8 May 1807–15 Nov. 1872), fur trader and writer, was born five miles from Fontainebleau, France. His father, a Bonapartist, settled in the United States in 1818 and engaged in farming near Baltimore; he may have been one of the two Lewis Larpenteurs listed in the 1840 federal census for Maryland. Charles apparently received only a limited education. He went west when he was twenty-one. At St. Louis he worked as an overseer for retired Indian agent Benjamin O'Fallon. In 1832 he took his first trip up the Mississippi River, an experience that kindled a desire to see more of American-Indian country.

In 1833 he hired on as common hand (and later as clerk) with Robert Campbell and William Sublette of the Rocky Mountain Fur Company and accompanied them to the Green River rendezvous. The partners failed in their efforts to compete with the American Fur Company at the mouth of the Yellowstone River. There, at Fort Union, Larpenteur in 1834 entered the service of the American Fur Company, the firm for which he worked for most of his long career in the fur trade. Being literate, honest, and industrious, he was given the responsible position of clerk. He built and commanded some of the company's other posts and camps along the Missouri River and its tributaries. His employers frequently gave Larpenteur, a man of sober habits, the responsibility of dispensing liquor (illegally) to the American Indians. In addition to French and English, he spoke German and several Indian languages.

Although a capable man, he never rose to the higher ranks of the business, nor did he achieve personal prosperity. With three partners he operated briefly and without success as an independent trader from 1860 to 1863. He returned to Fort Union and employment with the American Fur Company for two years. During 1866–1867 he served as interpreter for the Peace Commission to the Assiniboines. In 1868 he began business as a sutler at Fort Buford, but in 1871 a law permitting only one sutler to an army post forced him to quit what had been a thriving enterprise. That year he retired to, and soon thereafter died on, the farm in Harrison County, Iowa, that he had acquired several years earlier.

Larpenteur was thrice married. His first two wives (whose names are not known) were Assiniboines. The first died in the smallpox epidemic of 1837; the second, the mother of most of his children (numbering at least six), was killed in 1853 or 1854 by a band of Omahas. In 1855 he married Rebecca White, a native of Vermont, with whom he had at least one child. Adding to the unhappiness of his last years were the deaths of three of his children.

Larpenteur's historical significance stems from his published reminiscences of life in the fur trade. Soon after arriving in the West he began keeping regular journals; with these as the basis, in 1871–1872 he wrote a narrative of his experiences. Shortly before his death he gave the completed manuscript to army surgeon and ethnologist Washington Matthews, in the hope that Matthews would prepare it for publication. Several years later Matthews turned it over to Elliott Coues, who "recast" Larpenteur's unpolished prose and supplied many lengthy annotations. Entitled *Forty Years a Fur Trader on the Upper Missouri*, Larpenteur's memoirs appeared in two volumes in 1898. Ever since, it has served as an indispensable firsthand source for the history of the activity to which Larpenteur devoted most of his adult years. Although it is personal, often anecdotal, and emphasizes his own numerous misfortunes, Larpenteur's account is a vivid chronicling of the economics, personalities, physical hardships, depravity, and violence of the fur trade. In the concluding chapters Larpenteur offers his observations on Indian laws and customs and Indian agents and agencies, which conveyed his sympathetic yet unsentimental attitude toward the American Indians. Adding to the book's value is Larpenteur's vantage point from the middle levels of the business; he functioned equally well with the American Indians, the ordinary company employees, and with the upper echelons of the industry.

• Most of what is known of Larpenteur is to be found in the two editions of his memoirs, both bearing the title *Forty Years a Fur Trader on the Upper Missouri: The Personal Narrative of Charles Larpenteur, 1833–1872*. Elliott Coues's two-volume edition (1898) is extensively annotated. Milo Milton Quaife's 1933 edition retains Coues's smooth reworking of Larpenteur's awkward prose, but with Quaife's own less superfluous notes. A verbatim editing of part of Larpenteur's journals is Erin N. Thompson, ed., "Before the Oregon Trail: Charles Larpenteur Goes West in 1833," *Overland Journal* 7 (1989): 29–32. See also the entry for Larpenteur by Louis Pfaller in *Mountain Men and the Fur Trade of the Far West*, ed. LeRoy R. Hafen, vol. 1 (1965).

MICHAEL J. BRODHEAD

LARRABEE, William (20 Jan. 1832–16 Nov. 1912), governor of Iowa, was born in Ledyard, Connecticut, the son of Adam Larrabee, a farmer and banker, and Hannah Gallup. As a youth William attended the common schools of Connecticut and at the age of nineteen began teaching in a country school in that state. In 1853 he joined his brother and sister in northeastern Iowa, where he continued to teach school in Allamakee County until he became foreman of his brother-in-law's farm near Postville. In 1857 Larrabee bought a one-third interest in a flour mill near Clermont, Iowa, becoming sole owner of the business two years later. Moreover, Larrabee began acquiring farmland and purchased shares in several banks. By the 1880s he was purported to be one of the largest landowners in Iowa, and he had an interest in thirteen banks in three states. In 1861 Larrabee married Anna Appelman; they had seven children. Because of the loss of vision in his right eye as a result of a childhood accident, Larrabee was rejected for military service during the Civil War, but he was a strong supporter of the Union cause.

In 1867 Larrabee was elected to the Iowa State Senate, serving in that body for eighteen years. As a senator he chaired the Ways and Means Committee and proved a diligent if unremarkable lawmaker. In 1881, with the backing of Senator William Boyd Allison, Larrabee sought the Republican nomination for governor but lost to State Auditor Buren R. Sherman. After Sherman's four years as governor, Larrabee secured the GOP nomination for the post, and in 1885 he was elected Iowa's chief executive.

The most divisive issue during Larrabee's four-year tenure as executive was the prohibition of alcohol. Iowans had adopted a state constitutional amendment banning the sale of alcohol except by licensed pharmacists for medicinal, sacramental, or industrial purposes. Throughout much of the state, saloons closed their doors. However, Iowans were far from unanimous in support of Prohibition, and in some counties violation of the law was widespread. The Democratic party opposed the dry policy, as did most German-born Iowans, yet the Methodists, Iowa's largest Protestant group, were fervently anti-alcohol. A total abstainer, Governor Larrabee was dedicated to strict enforcement of Prohibition. From throughout the state he collected data on its implementation, and he publicly attacked the laxness of some local officials in suppressing liquor. In 1886 he issued a proclamation in which he exhorted "all citizens to lay aside partisan differences, and by unified and determined efforts banish the dram-shop from Iowa." Moreover, the state legislature adopted his proposals that all Iowa schools be required to teach "the injurious effects of the use of alcohol and narcotics" and that, to prevent illegal purchases, pharmacists be required to keep records of their liquor sales and submit those records to the county auditor.

Larrabee's chief battle as governor, however, was against the railroads. In 1886 Larrabee discovered that the Chicago, Burlington, and Quincy Railroad was charging $1.80 per ton for carloads of coal shipped from Cleveland, Iowa, to the State Institute for the Feeble-Minded at Glenwood, Iowa, whereas the railroad charged only $1.25 per ton for coal shipped from Cleveland to Council Bluffs, almost thirty miles beyond Glenwood. The president of the Burlington line refused to reduce the rate to Glenwood, and the state board of railroad commissioners, with only advisory powers, proved incapable of forcing compliance with the governor's demand for a lower charge. Anti-railroad sentiment had been rising in Iowa for a number of years, and now Larrabee rallied the many farmers and merchants who sought tougher regulation of the rail lines. In 1888 he told the state legislature, "The charges for transportation at present prevailing in the State are by far too high and bear little or no relation to the cost of the service." He recommended "a law fixing reasonable maximum rates of freight on the principal commodities transported by rail." "The whole color and tone of the message on this subject are intense and exceedingly radical," responded the shocked *Des Moines Register* on 13 January 1888, and Larrabee's words angered those Republican leaders who had allied themselves to the railroad companies. Yet most Iowans seemed to embrace the governor's proposal as a declaration of independence, and he became a favorite of the Farmers' Alliance, an agrarian organization antagonistic to the power of railroad corporations. During the legislative session of 1888 the energetic governor worked with Iowa's lawmakers to secure legislation strengthening the state board of railroad commissioners and empowering them to fix maximum freight rates.

The railroads battled unsuccessfully in the courts to overturn this legislation, and by 1890, at the close of his service as governor, Larrabee could claim victory. In his final message to the legislature Larrabee concluded, "It is now generally admitted that our present local freight tariffs are more equitable than any previously in force in the State."

Following his term as governor, Larrabee actively sought no further elective office, but he continued to advocate government curbs on the power of railroad corporations. In 1893 he authored *The Railroad Question: A Historical and Practical Treatise on Railroads, and Remedies for Their Abuses*. In its tenth printing by 1898, this influential book became a reference work for others seeking to replicate the former governor's triumphs over the railroads. In it Larrabee intended "to show that as long as the railroads are permitted to be managed as private property and are used by their managers for speculative purposes or other personal gain, . . . they are not performing their proper functions." He believed that government, either through public ownership or strict regulation of the railroads, needed to protect the interests of the people.

Having crusaded for state regulation of big business, Larrabee welcomed the reforms of the Progressive Era, and during the last years before his death at his home in Clermont, he publicly supported the leading Iowa progressive, Albert Cummins. An outspoken foe of railroad greed, Larrabee was an inspiration for a younger generation imbued with the spirit of reform.

• Larrabee's papers are in the State Historical Society of Iowa. J. Brooke Workman, "Governor William Larrabee and Railroad Reform," *Iowa Journal of History* 57 (1959): 231–66, offers the best account of Larrabee's fight with the railroads. Dan Elbert Clark, "The History of Liquor Legislation in Iowa, 1878–1908," *Iowa Journal of History and Politics* 6 (1908): 503–608, recounts the battle over Prohibition. For further accounts of Larrabee's years as governor, see Benjamin F. Gue, *History of Iowa* (1903); Edgar R. Harlan, *A Narrative History of the People of Iowa* (1931); Cyrenus Cole, *Iowa through the Years* (1940); and Leland L. Sage, *A History of Iowa* (1974). For further information on Iowa politics during the late nineteenth century, see Richard Jensen, *The Winning of the Midwest: Social and Political Conflict, 1888–1896* (1971); and Jeffrey Ostler, *Prairie Populism: The Fate of Agrarian Radicalism in Kansas, Nebraska, and Iowa, 1880–1892* (1993). Obituaries and memorial tributes to Larrabee are in *Annals of Iowa* 11 (1913): 231–33, and *Pioneer Lawmakers Association of Iowa, Reunion of 1913* (1914).

JON C. TEAFORD

LARRAZOLO, Octaviano Ambrosio (7 Dec. 1859–7 Apr. 1930), politician, lawyer, and schoolteacher, was born in Allende, Chihuahua, Mexico, the son of Octaviano Larrazolo, a prosperous landowner, and Donaciana Corral. The Larrazolo family lost everything in the 1860s, when the French invasion force under the emperor Ferdinand Maxmilian crushed the Mexican revolt led by Benito Juarez. An old family friend, the Reverend J. B. Salpointe, the Catholic bishop of Arizona, offered in 1870 to ease the family's financial burdens by taking Larrazolo (who had assisted Salpointe as an altar boy) to the United States. After five years in Tucson, Salpointe, who in the interim had become archbishop of Santa Fe, New Mexico, enrolled Larrazolo in that community's Christian Brothers' preparatory program known as St. Michael's College.

Upon completion of a two-year training program, Larrazolo returned to Tucson to teach for one year and then moved to the border town of El Paso, Texas, where he taught an additional five years in the public schools. Wishing to advance his career beyond the classroom, Larrazolo in 1885 joined the Texas Democratic party, which rewarded him with the job of chief clerk of the U.S. district court. This assignment whetted his appetite for the legal profession, and after three years of reading law with senior El Paso attorneys, Larrazolo was admitted to the Texas bar.

While in El Paso, Larrazolo met and married Rosalia Cobos; they had two children before Rosalia died ten years later. In 1892 Larrazolo married Maria Garcia; they had five children, one of whom, Paul Larrazolo, would become a prominent judge in Albuquerque, New Mexico.

The fluidity of southwestern politics and the need for a more stable income drew Larrazolo in 1895 northward to the New Mexican city of Las Vegas. There he joined Felix Martinez, an old friend who was prominent in Democratic party circles. Larrazolo encountered racism in eastern New Mexico when he campaigned on several occasions for the position of territorial delegate to Congress. When his party showed little interest in Larrazolo's complaints and failed to champion Hispano civil rights, Larrazolo openly opposed his own party.

At the 1910 constitutional convention for New Mexican statehood, Larrazolo, mindful of the segregated schools throughout the United States, demanded protection of the right to an equal education for Hispanos. He also linked with other Hispano delegates to include in the New Mexican constitution the right to conduct public business in both Spanish and English, a condition not guaranteed by law in any other state.

In 1912, upon New Mexico's entry into the Union, Larrazolo dutifully campaigned for Democratic candidates for statewide races, encouraging fellow Hispanos to seek public office. In 1916 his efforts aided Ezequiel C de Baca in becoming the nation's first elected Hispano governor. However, two years later the Democratic party selected Felix Garcia instead of Larrazolo to run for governor, prompting Larrazolo to leave the party that he had served for nearly three decades to register as a Republican. When the GOP named Larrazolo as its choice for governor that year, the *Albuquerque Journal* called him "the ablest Spanish-American in the United States."

In the campaign of 1918 Larrazolo bested his nemesis Garcia, only to face obstacles of environment and economics in the form of a prolonged drought and the Spanish influenza. In light of these crises, Larrazolo pressed for more government involvement in the economy at a time when the nation had grown tired of progressive activism. As governor, he called for a state income tax, child labor laws, pay raises for teachers, and compulsory public education for children ages six to sixteen. Larrazolo in addition asked New Mexico's lawmakers to encourage bilingual education.

While meeting with only mixed successes in these venues, Larrazolo also alienated his own constituency of Hispanos by sending National Guard troops to break the 1919 coal strikes in McKinley and Colfax counties. Then Larrazolo broke ranks with his male Hispano supporters by endorsing the Nineteenth Amendment to the U.S. Constitution, guaranteeing women the right to vote. Evidence of Larrazolo's commitment to growth for all of New Mexico came with his promotion of more state control of public lands. The sale of this "public domain" donated to states by the federal government would generate revenue to provide public services that Larrazolo believed would raise the standard of living for Hispano, American Indian, and Anglo alike.

In 1920, upon completion of his two-year term as governor, Larrazolo lost the support of prominent Republicans, as he had Democrats a decade earlier. Albert Fall, U.S. senator from New Mexico, suggested that Larrazolo run instead for the U.S. Congress, but he declined. Briefly returning to private life, Larrazolo in 1923 attempted a return to public service with an unsuccessful application for the governorship of the territory of Puerto Rico. In 1928 U.S. senator Bronson M. Cutting, a Progressive from New Mexico, asked Larrazolo to run for the junior Senate seat. He was elected and became the first Hispano to serve in that chamber of government. Larrazolo's signal achievement was introduction of a measure to create a "military-industrial school" for Hispanos in Albuquerque at the University of New Mexico, an initiative that unfortunately failed, in part because of Larrazolo's untimely death in Albuquerque.

Two years after his passing, the *New Mexico Historical Review* published an obituary on the life of Larrazolo. Paul A. F. Walter wrote that Larrazolo, "more than any other partisan leader," had demanded that half of the political tickets on every ballot in New Mexico include Hispanos. The necrology also revealed the essential problem facing Larrazolo and other Hispanos in a state moving toward a slim Anglo majority, the tensions that race triggered in the highly charged world of state politics. New Mexico forgot Larrazolo as new generations assumed control of the political process, yet the issues he faced and the criticism he bore touched all aspects of public and private life throughout the Southwest and the nation. The state's lengthy record of Hispano public servants and the awareness of its Anglo majority to accommodate a different political dynamic than experienced elsewhere in the nation owe their existence in part to the struggles of Larrazolo to make all New Mexicans equal before the law.

• No personal papers of Larrazolo are listed with public archives or libraries. His papers from his tenure as governor of N.Mex. are housed in the New Mexico State Records Center and Archives, Santa Fe. A brief mention of Larrazolo is in Ralph Emerson Twitchell, ed., *The Leading Facts of New Mexican History*, vol. 2 (1963). More detailed accounts of Larrazolo's life are in Paul A. F. Walter, "Octaviano Ambrosio Larrazolo," *New Mexico Historical Review* 7, no. 2 (Apr. 1932): 97–104, and Alfred C. Cordova and Charles B. Judah, *Octaviano Larrazolo: A Political Portrait* (1952).

MICHAEL WELSH

LARSELL, Olof (13 Mar. 1886–8 Apr. 1964), medical researcher and educator, was born in Rättvik, Sweden, the son of John Larsell, a railroad worker, and Anna Anderson. Moving to the United States in 1888, Larsell's father established himself in Tacoma, Washington, and sent for his family in 1891. Larsell attended the Edison School in Tacoma and, for high school, the Vashon Military Academy. He enrolled at McMinnville (now Linfield) College in Oregon in 1907 and graduated in 1910 with a B.S. in zoology. While in college he met Leo Dorcas Fleming, whom he married in June 1911; they had three sons. After his graduation, Larsell was an instructor of biology at Linfield College from 1910 to 1913.

Larsell entered graduate school at Northwestern University in the fall of 1913 and received an M.A. in zoology in 1914. He taught at Linfield College for the 1914–1915 academic year but retained his status as a student *in absentia* at Northwestern. During the summer sessions of 1913 and 1914 Larsell took courses at the University of Chicago under the great American neurologist Charles Judson Herrick. As a result of this experience, Larsell's thinking regarding research was from studies on the development and innervation of the lungs to studies in comparative neurology focusing on the central nervous system. He returned to Northwestern as an instructor in zoology in 1915 and pursued studies toward the Ph.D., which he received from this institution in 1918.

After graduation from Northwestern, Larsell took a position as assistant professor of anatomy at the University of Wisconsin in 1918 but returned to Northwestern as associate professor of zoology in 1920 and then became professor and head of the Department of Anatomy at the new medical school at the University of Oregon in 1921. He served in this position, and as dean of the Graduate Division of the Oregon State System (1938–1946), with only brief interruptions, until his retirement in 1952.

During his career Larsell conducted research on the development of the lung and its innervation, on aspects of hemopoiesis (the formation of the various types of blood cells) on the large cells that remove tissue debris, called histiocytes, and on reticulo-endothelial cells, in the field of pathology (general and in the central nervous system), and on embryological topics. He had a lifelong interest in the history of medicine and published extensively in this area. In the field of comparative neurology he published on the anatomy of the cranial nerves and on topics in neurohistology and neurodevelopment. It is, however, Larsell's extensive and seminal research on the cerebellum for which he is widely recognized.

Larsell began his cerebellar studies at Wisconsin and published his first paper on this subject in 1920 on the tiger salamander. There followed (1920–1934) a series of papers on frogs, lizards, snakes and a variety of other reptiles, and newts. Beginning with a publication on the bat cerebellum, Larsell expanded his research (1935–1954) to include a variety of mammals and birds. Through his exhaustive and detailed observations on cerebellar development, and on its morphology in the adult, Larsell identified what came to be recognized as the fundamental plan of cerebellar morphology. He showed that the first furrow (the posterolateral fissure) to appear in the primordial cerebellum divided this structure into a larger part located in front of (rostral to) this fissure and a smaller part located behind (caudal) thereto. This smaller caudal portion is the flocculonodular lobe. Larsell further specified that the second fissure to appear, the primary fissure, divided the larger portion of the primitive cerebellum into anterior and posterior lobes. The subsequent appearance of additional fissures divided the anterior lobe into five smaller units and the posterior lobe into four. Larsell called these individual units "folia" (in birds) or "lobules" (in mammals) and numbered them I–V in the anterior lobe, VI–IX in the posterior lobe, and X (nodulus of the flocculonodular lobe) for the midline structures of the cerebellum. In mammals the midline lobules (i.e., II, III, etc.) have lateral extensions that collectively form the cerebellar hemispheres. These lateral portions were designated by the same corresponding Roman numeral but with the prefix H (i.e., HII, HIII, etc.). Not only did Larsell discover and name this fundamental plan, but in his papers he clarified and simplified the extant terminology used to describe the cerebellum. In addition he showed that this scheme is broadly applicable to all mammals and birds studied to date. First described in birds (1948) and later in mammals (1952–1954), Larsell's interpretation was first adopted by the great Norwegian neuroanatomists Jan Jansen and Alf Brodal in their book *Aspects of Cerebellar Anatomy* (1954) and subsequently endorsed by many influential scientists by the 1960s. "Larsell's lobules" (or folia; I–X for the vermis or midline, and HII–HX for the mammalian hemisphere) are universally recognized, and this terminology is commonly used. A quiet and unassuming man, Larsell expressed concern in letters to C. Judson Herrick that his concept of cerebellar morphology would somehow offend other scientists with whom he did not agree.

During his career Larsell was a visiting professor at Northwestern (1926–1927) and lectured at the University of California (1931, 1932). He shared the Casselbery Prize (1928) and received a Merit Award from Northwestern University (1941). Larsell was a member of Sigma Xi, the Society of Experimental Biology and Medicine, the American Association of Anatomists, the American Association of University Professors, the History of Science Society, Gamma Alpha, Phi Beta Pi, the Western Society of Naturalists, and the Lardonshistoriska Samfundet of Sweden and was a fellow of the American Association for the Advancement of Science. Of particular note is the fact that Larsell served on the editorial board of the *Journal of Comparative Neurology* from 1937 to 1964. A major achievement is Larsell's three-volume *Comparative Anatomy and Histology of the Cerebellum* (1967, 1970, 1972). Conceived by Larsell around 1940 as one monograph, the manuscripts comprising these books went through numerous revisions as the author updated each chapter, incorporated his own new observations, and included the growing body of research from the literature. Published after Larsell's death, these books are the most comprehensive single treatise on the comparative morphology of the cerebellum. In addition, Larsell authored the *Text Book of Neuroanatomy and the Sense Organs* (1939), two editions (1942, 1951) of *Anatomy of the Nervous System*, and the section on "The Nervous System" in two editions of Sir Henry Morris's *Human Anatomy*. He also published *The Doctor in Oregon* (1947), on the history of medicine in the northwest.

After his retirement in 1952, Larsell was professor of neuroanatomy at the University of Minnesota (1952–1954), spent a year at the University of Oslo as a Fulbright Fellow (1954–1955), and was in the Department of Anatomy at the University of South Dakota Medical School. He returned to Oregon and, at the time of his death in Portland, held a research position in the Neurophysiology Research Laboratory at the Good Samaritan Hospital in that city.

• Information on Larsell is in the records of Northwestern University; the Oregon Health Sciences University Library; the University of Chicago; the Bentley Historical Library at the University of Michigan; and in the Herrick Collection at the Spencer Research Library, University of Kansas at Lawrence. Also, especially helpful information was provided in statements by Robert Larsell, Olof Larsell's surviving son. Biographical accounts include D. Hooker, "Olof Larsell 1886–1964," *Anatomical Record* 152 (1965): 360–61; "Olof Larsell 1886–1964," *Journal of Comparative Neurology* 123 (1964): 1–4; A. C. Jones, "Olof Larsell, M.A., Sc.D.," *Proceedings of the Alumni Meeting of the Medical Department of the University of Oregon, 30th Annual Meeting*, University of Oregon Medical School Alumni Association (1942): 5–10; and H. A. Dickel and R. S. Dow, "A Memoriam to Olaf [*sic*] Larsell," *Asklepion* (Spring 1964): 7 (this source incorrectly states that Larsell received a Ph.D. from the University of Chicago). See also C. Bush, "Inside the Black Box: A Biography of Oregon Neuroscientist Robert Stone Dow," unpublished ms., pp. 1–26.

DUANE E. HAINES

LARSEN, Esper Signius, Jr. (14 Mar. 1879–8 Mar. 1961), geologist, was born in Astoria, Oregon, the son of Esper Signius Larsen, a Danish immigrant and grocer, and Louisa Pauly. When Larsen was young, the family moved to Portland, where his father became a wholesale and retail grocer. Larsen attended public schools in Portland. He then worked in a wholesale grocery store for four years to earn money for college.

Larsen entered the University of California at Berkeley in 1902, intending to study mining engineering. Geology professors Andrew Cowper Lawson and Arthur Starr Eakle turned his interests to mineralogy and petrology. After receiving a B.S. in geology in 1906, Larsen was instructor in geology and mineralogy at the University of California for a year.

From 1907 to 1909 Larsen was assistant petrographer at the Geophysical Laboratory of the Carnegie Institution of Washington in Washington, D.C. Following theories proposed by petrologist Joseph Paxson Iddings, that laboratory was especially concerned with the origins of magmas and the variations of rock types during cooling. Larsen worked with Frederick Eugene Wright on determining temperatures in the formation of rocks. Their joint paper ("Quartz as a Geologic Thermometer," *American Journal of Science*, 4th ser., 27 [1909]: 421–27) was "the first systematic attempt to establish criteria for determining temperatures within the earth," said Larsen's biographer C. S. Hurlbut, Jr. In the paper they proposed that granite pegmatite was formed at a temperature of 573 degrees centigrade. Wright had also improved the technique of determining the index of refraction of minerals. At the Geophysical Laboratory, Larsen worked with Herbert Eugene Merwin on this technique, which led him to a long project on recognizing non-opaque minerals.

Because he also wanted to do field studies, Larsen in 1909 joined the U.S. Geological Survey and began studies in the San Juan Mountains region of Colorado and New Mexico. In 1910 he married Eva Audrey Smith; they had two sons.

Larsen was acting associate professor at the University of California at Berkeley in 1915–1916 and earned a Ph.D. in geology there in 1918, with a dissertation on the Creede mining district of Colorado. He was head of the petrology section of the U.S. Geological Survey from 1918 to 1923. During the First World War he searched for tungsten and molybdenum ores, which were critical minerals for defense needs. His laboratory studies, which provided the optical properties of more than 600 minerals through microscopic determination, were published as *The Microscopic Determination of the Nonopaque Minerals* (*U.S. Geological Survey Bulletin 679* [1921]). Larsen's biographer A. F. Buddington called this "the foremost reference work on the subject, found close at hand to the microscope in every petrographic laboratory in the world" (p.

161). Larsen published a revised edition with Harry Berman in 1934 (*U.S. Geological Survey Bulletin 848*). He became an expert on recognizing minerals and described twenty-four new ones, some published with coauthors.

From 1923 until his retirement in 1949 Larsen was professor of petrography at Harvard University. He continued field work in the summers for the USGS for many years and became a consultant to the survey in 1949 in Washington, D.C.

In continuing studies of the San Juan region during many summers until 1930, Larsen concentrated on its extensive unmetamorphosed volcanic rocks. By analyzing samples in the laboratory at Harvard, he was able to determine the chemical relationships of the volcanic rocks and present information on how certain feldspar minerals crystallize from volcanic magma. The entire project, which included many field geologists, was summarized by Whitman Cross and Larsen in 1956 in *The Geology and Petrology of the San Juan Region of Southwestern Colorado* (*U.S. Geological Survey Professional Paper 258*).

From 1930 to 1938 Larsen's field work was primarily in southern California, where, assisted by some of his students, he mapped a portion of the extensive southern California batholith. He determined that the complex system had endured more than twenty separate injections of basaltic magma. His summary was *Batholith and Associated Rocks of Corona, Elsinore, and San Luis Rey Quadrangles, Southern California* (*Geological Society of America Memoir 29* [1948]).

In 1933 Larsen conducted summer field studies on igneous rocks in central Montana with some of his graduate students. In "Petrographic Province of Central Montana" (*Bulletin of Geological Society of America 51* [1940]: 887–948), he defined the rock provinces on the basis of their systematic variation in chemical composition in specific rock series.

In Larsen's view, igneous rocks differed because of slow changes at great depth from fractional crystallization of basaltic magma, but some formed from crystal fractionation as they were erupted toward the surface. He concluded that the southern California batholith and the Idaho batholith were composite bodies that had resulted from successive intrusions. Geologists are still trying to determine the sequence of differentiation of magmatic rocks, and Larsen's carefully detailed studies have been useful in these discussions.

Beginning with his work on the southern California batholith, Larsen wanted to find a method of determining geologic time of rocks and minerals. He observed that radioactivity was concentrated in zircon and some other rarer minerals in the batholith. After what was called "ten years of careful, painstaking and often frustrating work" (Hurlbut, p. 453), Larsen found that a ratio of lead to uranium could be determined from individual zircons, which provided the age of the rock. This technique became called the "Larsen method." It was useful in finding the distribution of certain radioactive elements for the Manhattan

Project in World War II and is still a standard procedure for age determination.

Larsen published about 130 scientific papers. Three papers, written with colleagues, on the San Juan region were published in *American Mineralogist* as "Petrologic Results of a Study of the Minerals from the Tertiary Volcanic Rocks of the San Juan Region, Colorado" (21 [1936]: 679–701; 22 [1937]: 889–905; and 23 [1938]: 227–57). In his later years a number of his papers were on age determination, including "Isotopic Composition and Distribution of Lead, Uranium, and Thorium in a Precambrian Granite," with six coauthors (*Bulletin of Geological Society of America* 66 [1955]: 1131–48). A final paper on that subject was "Distribution of Uranium in Rocks and Minerals of Mesozoic Batholiths in Western United States," with David Gottfried (*U.S. Geological Survey Bulletin 1070-C* [1961]: 63–103).

Larsen was elected to the National Academy of Sciences in 1944. He received the Roebling Medal of the Mineralogical Society of America in 1941 and the Penrose Medal of the Geological Society of America in 1953. He died in Washington, D.C.

• Some correspondence and personal papers of Larsen are in the National Archives (U.S. Geological Survey, RG 57) in Washington, D.C. Biographies are by W. T. Pecora in *Bulletin of Geological Society of America* 73 (1962): 27–33; C. S. Hurlbut, Jr., in *American Mineralogist* 47 (1962): 450–59, with bibliography; and A. F. Buddington in National Academy of Sciences, *Biographical Memoirs* 37 (1964: 160–84), with bibliography.

ELIZABETH NOBLE SHOR

LARSEN, Jakob Aall Ottesen (1 Mar. 1888–1 Sept. 1974), historian of Greece and Rome, was born in Decorah, Iowa, the son of Peter Laurentius Larsen, a pioneer Norwegian Lutheran clergyman and educator and first president (1861–1902) of Luther College in Decorah, and Ingeborg Astrup. Larsen received his B.A. at Luther College in 1908 and an M.A. at the University of Iowa in 1910 with the thesis "A Study of Certain Latin Equivalents for the English Potential Idea." He moved to Yale in 1910 as a fellow in classics to pursue a Ph.D. He stayed only a year, for in the autumn of 1910 he was awarded a Rhodes Scholarship, which he took up in 1911. He was at Queen's College, where his tutor was E. M. Walker, a contributor to the *Cambridge Ancient History* and later provost of the college. Larsen took his B.A. in Literae Humaniores in 1914 and his M.A. in 1920.

Returning to the United States in 1914, he spent three years teaching classics at Park Region Luther College in Fergus Falls, Minnesota, originally founded by Luther College. In 1917 he moved to a position teaching classics at Concordia College in Moorhead, Minnesota. In 1917 he married Celia Clarice Grindeland, also from Decorah, Iowa; they had no children.

In July 1918 he entered the army as a private, receiving his commission as first lieutenant after three months. Because of his fluent Norwegian, he was posted as assistant in intelligence to the military attaché at the American legation in Christiana, Norway, and then at the American legation in Copenhagen. Discharged on 30 August 1919, he returned to Concordia as head of the Department of Greek; he was promoted to captain in the Reserve Corps in February 1920.

He resigned his post at Concordia in 1920 to begin research under William Scott Ferguson in the history department at Harvard. He was in residence for only a year and departed for the University of Washington, where he was assistant professor of history from 1921 to 1926. He spoke of his fondness for the outdoor life in the Northwest and enjoyed climbing Buck Mountain. Tall and strongly built, he also kept fit through tennis. In 1925 he began a steady stream of articles, numbering about fifty (not to mention his many reviews), almost all in the journal *Classical Philology*. The first was "Representative Government in the Panhellenic Leagues," a study based on the dissertation he was writing under Ferguson. He received his doctorate from Harvard in 1928; his thesis was "A Study of Representative Government in Greek and Roman History: Part I, Greek History." Part 2 was never written, and the dissertation was never published, though Larsen returned to the theme and dealt with Roman representative government in his Sather Lectures at the University of California, Berkeley.

In 1926 he became assistant professor of history at Ohio State University, where he obtained tenure as associate professor in 1929. In the same year he published another substantial article in *Classical Philology* titled "Notes on the Constitutional Inscription from Cyrene." He was then appointed associate professor in the Department of History at the University of Chicago in 1930 with responsibility for ancient history. That he became professor only in 1943, at fifty-five, was a scandal of administrative miserliness.

He now settled down to his career of brick-by-brick scholarship. His sober, methodical writings mirrored the man: nothing was flashy or electrifying, and his plain method of teaching resembled what is reported about his father's. He was opposed to writing lectures out; sometimes he would spend an hour over a current piece of research at the cost of the expected topic. Universally called Jake, he was in conversation both congenial and at times crusty about what he considered unimportant work.

His first large production was invited by Tenney Frank for volume four of the *Economic Survey of the Roman Empire* (1938). He contributed a book-length treatment of Roman Greece, beginning with a chapter on the Roman conquest of the region, in which the texts of Livy, Polybius, and other sources are copied out and translated with a surrounding narrative. A large central section of the treatment is a minute analysis of the inscriptions of Delos, in which Larsen sought information on prices, rents, the cost of living, and the like. This study was to lead to one of the most delightful chips from his workshop, an article contradicting F. M. Heichelheim on the price of tiles at Delos. In 1937 he contributed to the mammoth German classical encyclopedia of Pauly-Wissowa an article on the *peri-oikoi* (the villagers around Sparta and on Crete).

Though never a member of the Department of Classics at Chicago, he had an office in its building and from 1939 through 1950 was editor of *Classical Philology*, remaining an associate editor until his death. In 1940 he contributed a long paper to a festschrift honoring his teacher Ferguson, on the founding of the Athens-dominated Delian League; he also wrote its partner discussion of the Spartan system, the Peloponnesian League. From 1948 to 1953 he was on the editorial board of the *American Historical Review*. In 1950 he delivered a report on the state of ancient political institutions to the Ninth International Congress of Historical Sciences, Paris. In 1951–1952 he was president of the American Philological Association; his presidential address was "The Judgment of Antiquity on Democracy," a theme to which he returned in his penultimate article.

World-class scholars (such as Arnaldo Momigliano and F. W. Walbank) sought him out on their visits to America. Among the honors accorded to him was the Sather professorship at Berkeley in 1953–1954, the year following his retirement from Chicago. He returned in his lectures to his earliest work on representative government; three of the eight lectures in fact concern Roman assemblies, the topic he had planned to treat in part 2 of his dissertation.

In 1954 he was a Guggenheim Fellow and was now engaged on his final major work, his comprehensive study of the Greek federal states or leagues, published as *Greek Federal States: Their Institutions and History* (1968). Throughout his work he concentrated on constitutional politics and interstate relations, patiently analyzing the sources in detail but always drawing conclusions from them and asking what each discovery implied. The whole corpus of his work has an enviable solidity.

Larsen held visiting appointments at Northwestern, Rutgers, Columbia, Texas, and Michigan; from 1960 to his second retirement in 1971 he was professor at the University of Missouri, and he continued to live and work in Columbia, Missouri, where he died. His final paper, on the alliance between two of his Greek leagues, appeared in the year after his death.

In the preface to his book on the Greek leagues, Larsen said that he hoped the work would "prove helpful to future students," and he cared greatly about his pupils. Among them were Carl Roebuck, Wilhelmina Feemster Jashemski, J. H. Kent, Lawrence Lee Howe, J. A. McGeachy, and Stewart Irvin Oost. Their work, even beyond Larsen's own writings, is a large portion of his legacy to scholarship, which was recognized in his election as corresponding fellow of the British Academy.

• Larsen's first publication was "Representative Government in the Panhellenic Leagues," *Classical Philology* 20 (1925): 313–29, and 21 (1926): 52–72. There followed two major papers on the system of alliances centered on Sparta: "Sparta and the Ionian Revolt: A Study of Spartan Foreign Policy

and the Genesis of the Peloponnesian League," *Classical Philology* 27 (1932): 136–50, and "The Constitution of the Peloponnesian League," *Classical Philology* 28 (1933): 257–76, and 29 (1934): 1–19. The companion to these was "The Constitution and Original Purpose of the Delian League," *Harvard Studies in Classical Philology* 51 (1940): 175–213.

Meanwhile appeared his book-length chapter, "Roman Greece," in *An Economic Survey of Ancient Rome*, ed. Tenney Frank, vol. 4 (1938), pp. 259–498; an offshoot of this was "The Price of Tiles at Delos from 210 to 180 B.C.," *Classical Philology* 36 (1941): 156–66. His work on Greek leagues led to two major papers, "The Assembly of the Aetolian League," *Transactions of the American Philological Association* 83 (1952): 1–33, and "The Early Achaean League," *Studies Presented to David Moore Robinson*, vol. 2 (1953), pp. 797–815.

His two books were published in his retirement. The first, his Sather Lectures at Berkeley, was *Representative Government in Greek and Roman History* (1955); the second, crowning his career, was *Greek Federal States: Their Institutions and History* (1968).

Among other important papers are some on Greek political theory and practices: "Representation and Democracy in Hellenistic Federalism," *Classical Philology* 40 (1945): 65–97; "The Origin and Significance of the Counting of Votes," *Classical Philology* 44 (1949): 164–81; "The Judgment of Antiquity on Democracy," *Classical Philology* 49 (1954): 1–14; "*Demokratia*," *Classical Philology* 68 (1973): 45–46; "The Boeotian Confederacy and Fifth-Century Oligarchic Theory," *Transactions of the American Philological Association* 86 (1955): 40–50; and "Cleisthenes and the Development of the Theory of Democracy at Athens," in *Essays in Political Theory Presented to George H. Sabine* (1948), pp. 1–16.

Obituaries are in *American Historical Review* 80 (1975): 746, and *Classical Philology* 70 (1975): 126.

MORTIMER CHAMBERS

LARSEN, Nella (13 Apr. 1891–30 Mar. 1964), novelist, was born Nellie Walker in Chicago, Illinois, the daughter of Peter Walker, a cook, and Mary Hanson. She was born to a Danish immigrant mother and a "colored" father, according to her birth certificate. On 14 July 1890 Peter Walker and Mary Hanson applied for a marriage license in Chicago, but there is no record that the marriage ever took place. Larsen told her publisher, Alfred A. Knopf, that her father was "a Negro from the Virgin Islands, formerly the Danish West Indies" and that he died when she was two, but none of this has been proven conclusively.

Larsen was prone to invent and embellish her past. Mary Hanson Walker married a Danish man, Peter Larson, on 7 February 1894, after the couple had had a daughter. Peter Larson eventually moved the family from the multiracial world of State Street to a white Chicago suburb, changed the spelling of his name to Larsen, and sent Nellie away to the South. In the 1910 census Mary Larsen denied the existence of Nellie, stating that she had given birth to only one child. The family rejection and the resulting cultural dualism over her racial heritage that Larsen experienced in her youth were to be reflected in her later fiction.

Nellie Larson entered the Coleman School in Chicago at age nine, then the Wendell Phillips Junior High School in 1905, where her name was recorded as Nellye Larson. In 1907 she was sent by Peter Larsen to complete high school at the Normal School of Fisk University in Nashville, Tennessee, where she took the spelling "Larsen" and began to use "Nella" as her given name. Larsen claimed to have spent the years 1909 to 1912 in Denmark with her mother's relatives and to have audited courses at the University of Copenhagen, but there is no record of her ever having done so. Her biographer, Thadious M. Davis, says, "The next four years (1908–1912) are a mystery . . . , and no conclusive traces of her for these years have surfaced" (p. 67).

In 1912 Larsen enrolled in a three-year nurse's training course at New York City's Lincoln Hospital, one of few nursing programs for African Americans in the country. After graduating in 1915, she worked a year at the John A. Andrew Hospital and Nurse Training School in Tuskegee, Alabama. Unhappy at Tuskegee, Larsen returned to New York and worked briefly as a staff member of the city Department of Health. In May 1919 she married Dr. Elmer Samuel Imes, a prominent black physicist; this childless marriage ended in divorce in 1933.

Larsen left nursing in 1921 to become a librarian, beginning work with the New York Public Library in January 1922 and remaining until her resignation in January 1926. By this time Larsen was working on her first novel, *Quicksand* (1928). Earlier in the 1920s she had published two children's stories in *The Brownies' Book* as Nella Larsen Imes and then two pulp-fiction stories for *Young's Magazine* under the pseudonym Allen Semi. *Quicksand* won the Harmon Foundation's Bronze Medal for literature and established Larsen as one of the prominent writers of the Harlem Renaissance. After her second novel, *Passing*, was published in 1929, she applied for and became the first black woman to receive a Guggenheim Foundation Fellowship. Larsen used the award to travel to Spain in 1930 and to work on her third book, which was never published. After a year and a half in Spain and France, Larsen returned to New York.

Two shocks appear to have ended Larsen's literary career. In 1930 she was accused of plagiarizing her short story "Sanctuary," published that year in *Forum*, when a reader pointed out its likeness to Sheila Kaye-Smith's "Mrs. Adis," a story that had appeared in *Century* magazine in 1922. The editors of *Forum* pursued the charge and exonerated Larsen, but biographers and scholars have concluded that Larsen never recovered from the attack, however unfounded. The second shock was Larsen's discovery of her husband's infidelity early in 1930, although she refrained from seeking a divorce until 1933. Imes supported Larsen with alimony payments until his death in 1941, at which time Larsen returned to her first career, nursing, in New York City. She was a supervisor at Gouverneur Hospital from 1944 to 1961, then worked at Metropolitan Hospital from 1961 to 1964 to avoid retirement. Since her death in New York City Larsen's novels, considered "lost" until the 1970s, have been reprinted and reexamined. While she had always been included in

the few histories of black-American literature, her reputation was eclipsed in the era of naturalism and protest-writing (1930–1970), to be recovered along with the reputations of Zora Neale Hurston and other African-American women writers during the rise of the feminist movement in the 1970s.

Larsen's literary reputation rests on the achievement of her two novels of the late 1920s. In *Quicksand* she creates an autobiographical protagonist, Helga Crane, the illegitimate daughter of a Danish immigrant mother and a black father who was a gambler and deserted the mother. Crane hates white society, from which she feels excluded by her black skin; she also despises the black bourgeoisie, partly because she is not from one of its families and partly for its racial hypocrisy about the color line and its puritanical moral and aesthetic code. After two years of living in Denmark, Helga returns to America to fall into "quicksand" by marrying an uneducated, animalistic black preacher who takes her to a rural southern town and keeps her pregnant until she is on the edge of death from exhaustion.

In *Passing* Larsen writes a complicated psychological version of a favorite theme in African-American literature. Clare Kendry has hidden her black blood from the white racist she has married. The novel ends with Clare's sudden death as she either plunges or is pushed out of a window by Irene, her best friend, just at the husband's surprise entrance. "What happened next, Irene Redfield never afterwards allowed herself to remember. Never clearly. One moment Clare had been there, a vital glowing thing, like a flame of red and gold. The next she was gone" (p. 271).

Larsen's stature as a novelist continues to grow. She portrays black women convincingly and without the simplification of stereotype. Larsen fully realized the complex psychology of the mulatta in America and was able to render this cultural dualism artistically, providing contemporary critics with new ways of reading these texts.

• Larsen's personal papers and books vanished from her apartment at her death, so neither a manuscript archive nor a collection of her private papers exists. The definitive biography of Larsen is Thadious M. Davis, *Nella Larsen, Novelist of the Harlem Renaissance: A Woman's Life Unveiled* (1994), which includes book reviews of *Quicksand* and *Passing* and the complete list of works published by Larsen. Charles Larson (no relation) published *Invisible Darkness: Jean Toomer and Nella Larsen* in 1993 and *An Intimation of Things Distant: The Collected Fiction of Nella Larsen* in 1992. Davis, who did extensive research to unearth the facts of Larsen's life, has corrected misinformation in the introduction to Larson's *An Intimation*, although the work usefully contains Nella Larsen's three adult short stories, including the one that caused the plagiarism scandal, and her two novels. In 1986 Deborah McDowell edited and wrote an excellent introduction for the American Women Writers' combined edition of *Quicksand* and *Passing*, which also contains a selected bibliography of secondary sources including journal articles. Other assessments of Larsen are found in Hazel Carby, *Reconstructing Womanhood: The Emergence of the Afro-American Woman Novelist* (1987); Judith Butler, *Bodies That Matter: On the*

Discursive Limits of "Sex" (1993); Bernard W. Bell, *The Afro-American Novel and Its Traditions* (1987); and Barbara Christian, *Black Women Novelists: The Development of a Tradition* (1980).

ANN RAYSON

LARSEN, Peter Laurentius (10 Aug. 1833–1 Mar. 1915), Lutheran pastor and college president, was born in Christiansand, Norway, the son of Herman Larsen, an army officer, and Elen Else Marie Oftedahl. In 1850 he entered the university at Christiania in Oslo, where he studied theology under Gisle Johnson and Carl Paul Caspari, who greatly influenced him. He graduated in 1855 and, because there was no ministerial position available, tutored in Christiania for the next two years. In July 1855 he married Karen Neuberg; they had four children before her death in 1871. In 1857 Larsen accepted a call to preach among Norwegian immigrants in Rush River, Wisconsin, where he served from 1857 to 1859 and from which he also established new congregations in the area.

In 1859 the Norwegian Synod, which had no seminary of its own, hired Larsen to fill its newly established position of theological professor at the Missouri Synod's Concordia Seminary in St. Louis, Missouri. The outbreak of the Civil War in 1861 finally forced Larsen and the Norwegian students to leave St. Louis, but not before he became embroiled in a bitter theological controversy. Many Norwegian-Americans thought the Missouri Synod was too lenient on the issue of slavery, and Larsen's association with Concordia Seminary made him suspect. When pressed on the issue, he suggested that slavery was an evil but not a sin, and he became the center of an intense controversy that lasted until 1868.

Larsen accepted a call to Half Way Creek, Wisconsin, in 1861, while the synod worked to establish an educational institution of its own. Luther College opened in the fall of 1861, and classes were held in the basement of Larsen's parsonage. In 1862 the college was moved to Decorah, Iowa, where he also served as pastor of a congregation from 1862 to 1889. The first years of the college were difficult because of the poverty of the immigrant community and the pressures of the Civil War, but a main college building was finally completed in 1865. The college grew and prospered; by 1874 enrollment was 200 students, all men. Larsen served as president of the college for forty-one years and as professor of theology for fifty years. His original vision was for Luther to offer a European classical curriculum to train candidates for the ministry, but pressures forced the college to adopt a more American curriculum, with a four-year preparatory program and a four-year college program. In 1872 he married Ingeborg Astrup; they had eight children.

Larsen became a leader within the Norwegian Synod, one of several synods organized among Norwegian Americans. He was vice president of the Norwegian Synod from 1876 to 1893 and editor of several synodical publications, including *Kirkelig Maanedstidende* (1868–1873) and the publication that succeeded this,

Evangelisk Luthersk Kirketidende (1874–1889 and 1902–1912). He was also chairman of the Lutheran Synodical Conference (1881–1883), a national organization of Lutheran synods, of which the Norwegian Synod was a part.

As a leader and editor within the synod, Larsen was no stranger to the theological and ecclesiastical controversies that affected Norwegian-American Lutheranism in his day. In 1861 he became the center of a dispute concerning the question of the nature of forgiveness of sins in the pastoral absolution after the confession. Relying on Missouri Synod theologians, Larsen suggested that there was imputation of forgiveness through the words of the pastor; others strongly disagreed with this, and the controversy continued sporadically until 1906. In the 1880s the theological debate concerned the question of election (predestination). Although Larsen actually supported Ulrik Vilhelm Koren and others who took a position close to that of the Missouri Synod, as editor of the synod's periodical he endeavored to take a balanced position and worked for the reconciliation of the various factions.

In 1889 the main building at Luther College burned to the ground, calling the very existence of the school into question. Larsen immediately began a campaign throughout the Norwegian Synod to keep the college in Decorah and to raise funds for a new college building, which opened in 1890. He was a strong-willed person who kept a tight rein on students and faculty alike, but he was also greatly loved by generations of Luther students. Through the 1890s Larsen faced the complaints of many within the Norwegian Synod who were dissatisfied with the moral and religious conduct of students at the college. At the Norwegian Synod convention in 1902 his reelection as college president was blocked, and Larsen resigned as president, although he continued as professor of theology until 1911. As editor of *Evangelisk Luthersk Kirketidende* from 1902 to 1912, Larsen cautiously urged the various Lutheran factions to discuss their doctrinal differences with the intent of merging.

Larsen stood to the center of his church theologically, holding to a broad confessional Lutheranism and an inclusive Norwegian-American Lutheran church. A man of uncommon energy and learning, he dedicated his life to the growth and development of Norwegian-American Lutheranism. He died in Decorah, Iowa.

• Larsen's papers are in the Archives of Luther College, Decorah, Iowa, and most of his published writings are in the periodicals he edited. Karen Larsen, *Laur. Larsen: Pioneer College President* (1936), is a complete and balanced biography. For his role within Norwegian-American Lutheranism, see E. Clifford Nelson and Eugene Fevold, *The Lutheran Church among Norwegian-Americans* (2 vols., 1960), and J. Magnus Rohne, *Norwegian Lutheranism up to 1872* (1926). For a history of Luther College, see David Nelson, *Luther College, 1861–1961* (1961).

MARK GRANQUIST

LARSEN, Roy Edward (20 Apr. 1899–9 Sept. 1979), publisher, was born in Boston, Massachusetts, the son of Robert Larsen, a newspaperman, and Stella Belyea. Larsen was proud to proclaim himself a "first generation American," for his father and mother had come to this country from Norway and Ireland, respectively. Larsen graduated from the Boston Latin School in 1917 and entered Harvard College. Drafted into the U.S. Army in his freshman year, Larsen served as a second lieutenant in the infantry. After the armistice, he returned to Harvard. Following his graduation in 1921, Larsen went to work for the New York Trust Company.

On 22 November 1921 Larsen attended a meeting at the Harvard Club in New York City, where he conferred with Henry R. Luce and Briton Hadden. These two young Yale men were planning to publish a new kind of magazine that would be called *Time*. Excited by their scheme, Larsen defied the advice of friends and relatives and left banking. He soon became the magazine's first noneditorial employee, and within a decade *Time* had created the modern newsmagazine. Larsen was *Time*'s circulation manager. When *Time* first appeared in 1923, the magazine had 12,000 subscribers; by 1928 that figure had risen to 200,000, and the company was making a profit. Larsen was named a vice president of Time, Inc., in 1927. In that same year he married Margaret Zerbe; the couple had four children.

After cofounder Briton Hadden's death in 1929, Larsen became general manager of Time, Inc., in charge of business operations. Thanks in part to his tireless work, Time, Inc., became one of the great success stories in the history of American publishing. Luce, the editor in chief, and Larsen, the business manager, proved to be a formidable duo. Larsen contributed in 1929–1930 to the founding and success of Luce's *Fortune*, a magazine that revolutionized business journalism.

A great team player, Larsen was also a man open to innovation and risk. Luce was a man of the printed word. By contrast, Larsen embraced new media and pushed Time, Inc., into radio and motion pictures. In the late 1920s Larsen created "Newscasting," a radio quiz spot based on information contained in recent issues of *Time*. This venture evolved into the "March of Time," which first appeared nationwide on CBS on 6 March 1931. Intended to stimulate the magazine's newsstand sales, the program set the stage for the more ambitious newsfilm series of the same name. Working with Louis de Rochemont (sometimes for three days at a time, with little or no sleep), Larsen brought out the first "March of Time" in February 1935. The documentary series, which used theatrical techniques, won an Oscar for "revolutionizing the newsreel." By 1939 the "March of Time" was appearing worldwide in 14,000 theaters.

Where Luce was often brusque and withdrawn, Larsen was personable and gregarious. He represented the corporate personality of Time, Inc.; one observer called him the "average millionaire." Larsen served as the publisher of *Life* in 1936–1946, when America's beloved picture magazine brought Time, Inc., a mass audience and—after a rocky start—vast profits. A staunch opponent of censorship, Larsen was willing to back up words with action. In 1938 *Life* published stills culled from the controversial film *The Birth of a Baby*, which had been banned in the Bronx, New York. Larsen tested the law by publicly selling a copy of the magazine. Arrested, he was acquitted of the charge of selling "indecent" material.

Larsen sometimes played a different kind of role at Time, Inc. He became the chief troubleshooter for the company, and in this capacity Larsen acted vigorously to protect Luce and Time from unfavorable publicity. Behind the scenes, Larsen worked effectively to suppress the publication of material that might offend Luce and his associates. During the early years of the Cold War Larsen worked with a rival publisher and the Federal Bureau of Investigation in two successful attempts to block the publication of valuable material critical of the company's anti-Soviet policies. When Larsen learned that Collier's planned to publish media critic A. J. Liebling's exposé of Time, he intervened to prevent the appearance of the series. When Dorothy Sterling, a leftist and a disenchanted former employee of Time, Inc., completed her manuscript on Time, she discovered that agents and publishers, after a flurry of interest, rejected her work. Behind the scenes, Larsen had worked with the FBI to bury the manuscript. Neither Liebling's articles nor Sterling's book ever saw the light of day. They rest in manuscript archives at Cornell University and the University of Oregon, respectively. Ironically, Larsen usually opposed the kind of McCarthyite redbaiting that disfigured the era.

Larsen served as president of the company in 1939–1960 and was the only employee exempted from Time, Inc.'s age sixty-five retirement rule. By 1950 he was the second largest shareholder in Time, Inc., and a man of great wealth. In 1969 Larsen became vice chair of the board of trustees, a post he retained until his retirement in April 1979. In 1970 he received the Henry Johnson Fisher Award, bestowed by the Magazine Publishers Association. Shareholders and colleagues had confidence in Larsen, and the company continued to prosper. By the time of his death, Time, Inc., enjoyed gross revenues of more than $2 billion annually.

Larsen was an activist who applied his numerous talents and great energy to the fields of education and conservation. He was committed to the improvement of American public education. "I am grateful," he wrote, "for what the American public school system did for me." Larsen served as chair of the National Citizens Commission for the Public Schools. An ardent naturalist, Larsen donated many acres of his Connecticut estate to the cause of conservation. The Roy and Margaret Larsen Audubon Sanctuary in Fairfield, Connecticut, bears witness to this avocation. Larsen also served on the board of the Nature Conservancy and helped to create the Nantucket, Massachusetts, Conservation Foundation, which he chaired.

Larsen died in Fairfield. By ensuring the success and stability of Time, Inc., he had contributed to one of the great publishing enterprises of the twentieth century.

• Valuable information about Larsen may be found in a variety of trade papers and reference works. The most important source is the three-volume history of Time, Inc., written by Robert T. Elson et al., *Time Inc.: The Intimate History of a Publishing Enterprise* (1968–1986). On Larsen's association with Henry Luce and Time, Inc., see Robert E. Herzstein, *Henry R. Luce: A Political Portrait of the Man Who Created the American Century* (1994). See also "Incumbent," *Tide*, 15 Sept. 1939, p. 26; "Too Many Were Out of Touch," *NEA News*, 9 Nov. 1956; "Head of Time Fooled Classmates," *Boston Globe*, 19 Oct. 1958; "Roy E. Larsen of Time, Inc.," *Printers Ink*, 6 Feb. 1959, pp. 48–50; "A Container to Fit the Contained," *Time*, 21 Jan. 1966, p. 64; "Biographical Notes, Roy E. Larsen," Time, Inc., press release, 19 Apr. 1966; and "The First Four Decades," *f.y.i.* (Time, Inc., internal publication), 23 Apr. 1979, pp. 1–8. Obituaries appear in *Time Incorporated News*, 9 Sept. 1979, and the *New York Times*, 10 Sept. 1979.

ROBERT E. HERZSTEIN

LARSON, Leonard Winfield (22 May 1898–30 Sept. 1974), pathologist, was born in Clarkfield, Minnesota, the son of John Larson, a pharmacist, and Ida Anderson. After graduating from St. Olaf Academy in Northfield, Minnesota, he matriculated at the University of Minnesota with the intention of becoming a dentist, but after receiving a B.S. in 1918 he decided instead to pursue a career as a physician. He received an M.D. from Minnesota in 1922 and immediately opened a medical practice in Northwood, Iowa. The practice did not thrive, largely because he spent most of his time traveling from one house call to another. In 1923 he returned to the university to conduct postgraduate research in clinical pathology. That same year he married Ordelia Rebecca Miller; they had two children.

In 1924 Larson returned to private practice as a physician and pathologist with the Quain and Ramstad Clinic in Bismarck, North Dakota; he also became the pathologist at Bismarck Evangelical Hospital. Larson's position with the clinic, a cooperative of physicians and health-care workers who provided medical care throughout North Dakota and parts of South Dakota, Manitoba, and Saskatchewan, was unusual in two respects. Not only was he the only private-practice pathologist in the state and probably one of the few in the country (most worked in hospitals and laboratories), but also he examined patients on a regular basis instead of examining only diseased tissue that had been surgically removed. Because he was interested primarily in the study of tumors, he became involved almost immediately with North Dakota's cancer prevention program; specimens suspected of being cancerous were shipped from around the state to the clinic, where they underwent his expert evaluation. In 1935 he took on the additional duty of pathologist at Bismarck's St. Alexius Hospital, and in 1939 he became one of the clinic's five operating partners.

Larson is remembered chiefly for his involvement in the affairs of the American Medical Association. He first became active in the association in 1926 as a state legislative watchdog and in 1940 he was elected to its house of delegates as a representative for the section on pathology and physiology. Shortly thereafter he became chairman of the correlating committee on lay-sponsored health plans. Steadily increasing health-care costs (in large part the result of more effective methods of diagnosis and treatment) had given rise to a number of prepaid, closed-panel plans that offered a wide range of medical services from a pre-selected group of practitioners for a regular monthly fee. Most AMA members, the vast majority of whom practiced individually, denounced this sort of arrangement as bordering on socialism because it violated the association's longstanding tenets that a physician should receive a fee for every service he provides and that a patient should be free to obtain medical care from the physician of his choice.

Although he personally advocated preserving the status quo on both counts, Larson realized better than most of his colleagues that group practices delivered first-rate health care and that the public's dissatisfaction with rising health-care costs necessitated the development of innovative methods of payment. Moreover, he believed that physicians could best protect their professional interests by trying to manage the coming changes in health-care delivery rather than resisting them. Consequently his committee cooperated with the Group Health Association to develop a set of mutually acceptable principles by which the relationship between physicians and insurers should be governed.

In 1955 Larson was appointed chairman of the AMA's commission on medical care plans. For the next four years the commission analyzed the quality and cost of the medical care delivered by all types of health care plans before issuing in 1959 the so-called Larson Report. The report recognized the high quality of medical care provided by prepaid, closed-panel plans, recommended to the house of delegates that it acknowledge the right of a patient to choose such a plan as well as the right of an AMA member to participate on a closed panel, and urged the AMA to redouble its efforts to assure the competency and affordability of the services offered by private-practice physicians. After six months' debate concerning the report's thirty-nine recommendations, the delegates approved the Larson Report unanimously. In 1961, the same year that the Medicare Act was passed, Larson began serving a one-year term as president of the AMA. In this role he urged physicians to support any financially sound system of tax-supported health insurance as a means of "keep[ing] Government out of the practice of medicine" (*Time*, 7 July 1961, p. 60).

In 1963 Larson relinquished his management role at the clinic but continued to practice medicine there for another seven years. In 1969, the year after his first wife died, he married Esther Knudtson Dagny; they had no children. In 1970 he retired from the clinic and both hospitals to his home in Bismarck, North Dakota, where he died.

Larson served as president of the American Society of Clinical Pathologists (ASCP) from 1939 to 1940, the North Dakota State Medical Association from 1950 to 1951, and the American Cancer Society (ACS) from 1965 to 1966. He also served as co-founder and president of the Joint Blood Council, a four-time delegate to the United Nations World Health Organization, chairman of the Committee on Health and Medical Care at the White House Conference on Aging in 1960, and chairman of the council of the World Medical Association in 1966. He served on the board of trustees of the ACS from 1945 to 1967 and of the AMA from 1950 to 1960 and was awarded the ACS's Gold Medal in 1953, the ASCP's Certificate of Highest Merit, and the University of Minnesota's Outstanding Achievement Award in 1961.

Larson's primary contribution to the development of medicine in the United States involved the major role he played in helping to gain acceptance among physicians for prepaid, government-assisted medical insurance plans.

• Larson's papers are located in the State Historical Society of North Dakota in Bismarck and in the University of North Dakota Library. His contributions to the AMA are discussed in "The A.M.A. & the U.S.A.," *Time*, 7 July 1961, pp. 56–60. An obituary is in the *Bismarck Tribune*, 30 Sept. 1974.

CHARLES W. CAREY, JR.

LA SALLE, René-Robert Cavalier de (21 Nov. 1643–19 Mar. 1687), explorer, was born in Rouen, France, the son of Jean Cavelier, a haberdasher, and Catherine Geest. The family was part of the prosperous bourgeoisie. The sobriquet "de La Salle" referred to an estate they owned outside Rouen. La Salle's initial intention, however, seems to have been to escape his position, for after having studied with the Jesuits in Rouen, he renounced any claim to the family fortunes and entered the novitiate for the order in Paris in 1658. He actually took vows in 1660, continued, apparently rather brilliantly, his studies of mathematics, and taught in Jesuit schools until 1666. Having requested missionary assignments several times and been denied because he had been unable to demonstrate spiritual maturity and submission to the discipline of the order, he was released from his vows in 1667 and only a few months later went to New France, penniless but with many influential connections. There his brother, a Sulpician, was doubtless responsible for his obtaining from that order a grant of a seigneury on Montreal Island, but after two years La Salle sold most of it back to them and began his career of exploration by attaching himself to the Dollier and Galinée missionary party bound for the western Great Lakes. Hearing of the Ohio River from Iroquois Indian guides, he left the party, claiming illness, and virtually disappeared for four years.

What precisely he did between 1669 and 1673 is unknown, although it was probably no more mysterious than what hundreds of other French voyageurs were doing in the interior: trading for furs. His subsequent familiarity with the whole Great Lakes region suggests this, as do his routine yearly visits to Montreal, where he communicated with Governor Jean Talon and dealt with finances. Claims have been made for his having "discovered" the Ohio and even the Mississippi during this time, but if he did so he never personally advanced such a claim.

Returning to Montreal in early 1673, La Salle became allied with the new governor, Louis de Baude de Frontenac, for whom he carried out errands to the Iroquois. During a sojourn in France in 1674–1675 he obtained letters of nobility and a grant of proprietorship of a fort on Lake Ontario, which he renamed for the governor. To expand his plans for a fur-trading empire, he returned to France in 1677–1678 and obtained a license to construct forts at Niagara and south of Lake Michigan and to explore the entire western region of North America, with certain rights to the fur trade in areas he could settle and organize.

La Salle's first efforts to carry out this imperial design met with setbacks. In 1679 he built a ship, the *Griffon*, below Niagara to be used to transport furs from the hinterlands of the western Great Lakes, sending his new lieutenant Henri de Tonti and others westward to organize the collection of furs. Large stocks of peltry were gathered at Detroit and Green Bay, and the *Griffon* was sent back to Fort Frontenac while La Salle and Tonti went with a party southward down Lake Michigan to the Illinois River, where La Salle built Fort Crèvecoeur. He left Tonti in charge when he started in March 1680 for Fort Frontenac.

La Salle arrived to find that the *Griffon* had disappeared, Fort Niagara was burned, a cargo of Indian trade goods had been lost, and the workmen at Crèvecoeur had deserted when the Iroquois attacked the Illinois tribes. La Salle made another trip to the Illinois country in late 1680–1681 and then returned to Montreal to consult with Frontenac. From that meeting he emerged with the resolution to make the voyage of discovery down the Mississippi.

The expedition itself is perhaps most notable for its lack of exciting events. Departing in mid-February of 1682 from the mouth of the Illinois River, the expedition, consisting of twenty-four Frenchmen and twenty-five Indians, reached the Gulf of Mexico on 7 April and executed a formal French claim to the Mississippi Valley on 9 April, having established peaceful relations with the Chickasaw, Quapaw, Taensa, Natchez, and Koroa Indians along the way. There was one hostile encounter with the Chitimachas and some tense moments with the Natchez on the return journey, but the venture was more seriously marred by La Salle's falling ill between the Quapaw villages and the Chickasaw Bluffs. Father Zenobius Membré stayed to nurse La Salle while Tonti was sent ahead to carry news of the discovery of the mouth of the Mississippi. La Salle eventually traveled to meet Tonti at Michilimackinac, but he soon returned to the Illinois country. There he established Fort St. Louis at Starved Rock in the winter of 1682–1683 to serve as a fortified settlement for the Indians of the region against the Iroquois. In the interim Frontenac had been replaced by La Salle's enemy Antoine Le Febvre de La Barre, and Tonti was left to hand over the forts to the new governor's men as La Salle returned to France in the autumn of 1683 to obtain permission to establish colonies to make good the claim to the Mississippi and provide a frost-free port for the fur trade.

La Salle was pursued in France by La Barre's accusations that his explorations had been fruitless and his actions responsible for Iroquois uprisings. But La Salle had his own allies, the abbé Claude Bernou and his circle, and with their help he adapted the schemes of the Spanish deserter Diego de Peñalosa to argue for a settlement at the mouth of the Mississippi as an ideal base of operations for an attack on the Spanish mines of northeastern Mexico. Whether La Salle actually believed that the mouth of the Mississippi was in the vicinity of that of the Rio Grande or falsified evidence to make it seem so, in the end he staked his life on that belief.

In April 1684 La Salle received from Louis XIV command of the whole region between the Illinois country and Mexico and set out with ships and men to reach the coast of the Gulf of Mexico to make a settlement. The expedition included 100 soldiers and their officers, six missionaries (including La Salle's brother the Sulpician Jean Cavelier and Father Membré), nearly fifty indentured workers, and more than twenty other volunteers, including a few women and children. La Salle's constant quarrels with Tanguy Le Gallois de Beaujeu, captain of the convoy's warship, eventuated in the loss of one ship and the expedition's supplies to Spanish pirates near Santo Domingo. The convoy landed at Matagorda Bay on the coast of Texas in mid-February 1685. After a final quarrel Beaujeu returned to France, leaving La Salle and some 180 people to build a settlement and to continue the search for the Mississippi.

The story of La Salle's efforts to find the Mississippi, which lasted nearly two years, is known to us through the account of Henri Joutel, La Salle's closest assistant. Much of the interior of east Texas was explored but without finding what was sought. Supplies dwindled, the last small ship was lost, people died of illness, and some were killed by Indians. As the search apparently grew more hopeless, morale plummeted. La Salle pushed his men deeper and deeper into the interior, and finally members of the expedition turned on one another. La Salle himself was shot to death somewhere in east Texas by Pierre Duhaut as he led yet another party in search of the Mississippi. Some of the survivors of this party, those involved in the killings, remained among the Indians, while the rest did in fact reach European settlements, first finding a small French post established by Tonti among the Quapaws, then reaching Fort St. Louis in the Illinois country and finally Montreal. The survivors were sworn to keep La Salle's death a secret until his brother the priest could collect his debts. The tiny colony left behind on the coast was attacked by the Karankawa Indians, who spared and adopted several children later found and rescued by the Spaniards.

La Salle is best known for his exploration of the North American interior, and to Americans it is his voyage down the Mississippi that is most memorable. Exploration of the interior was being carried out by many Frenchmen at the time; what was unique about La Salle was his vision of empire over the interior and of a fundamental role for Indians as economic participants in that empire. He and his enterprise attracted "loyal Indians," not merely outcasts who found a niche with the white newcomers but whole groups that perceived their fundamental place in his vision. He accumulated enemies because he wanted to circumvent the monopoly of the fur trade by Montreal merchants and Iroquois sachems alike, and for the same reason he was important in opening more direct trading contact between Indians of the Midwest and the French.

La Salle's abortive Texas colony wakened Spain to a serious threat to her unbroken hegemony over southern North America from Florida to California, led to an intensification of both Spanish and British colonial activity in the region, and solidified French resolve to establish a presence there. But it was La Salle's success in establishing peaceful relations with the Indians who dominated the interior that guaranteed at least temporary French success in this contest.

• La Salle himself did not write much that is known to be extant. The first three volumes of Pierre Margry's standard collection of French documents on the early exploration of North America, *Découvertes et établissements des français dans l'ouest et dans le sud de l'amérique septentrionale* (1876–1886), are devoted to La Salle. Included therein are transcriptions (sometimes not very reliable) of the account of the 1682 exploration of the Mississippi by Nicolas de La Salle and of the 1685–1686 journey and its outcome by Joutel. One important account that escaped Margry, by the engineer Minet, is collected, along with other documents relating to the 1685 journey, in Robert Weddle et al., *La Salle, the Mississippi, and the Gulf of Mexico* (1987).

Francis Parkman, *La Salle and the Discovery of the Great West* (1879), is the most widely known account of La Salle's explorations, but it was only in the eleventh and later editions that Parkman was able to exploit the information contained in Margry's documents. Biographies of La Salle include Paul Chesnel, *Histoire de Cavelier de La Salle* (1901); Roger Viau, *Cavelier de La Salle* (1960); and E. B. Osler, *La Salle* (1967), but a definitive scholarly biography has yet to be published. John Vernon's novel *La Salle* (1986) represents a striking modern attempt to evaluate the explorer's motivations. The Jesuit scholar Jean Delanglez published an indispensable group of critical articles in the journal *Mid-America* in the 1930s and 1940s, many now collected in the reprint volume *A Jean Delanglez, S. J., Anthology*, ed. Mildred Mott Wedel (1985). A collection of essays edited by Patricia Galloway, *La Salle and His Legacy* (1982), concentrates on the 1682 voyage down the Mississippi. An important essay by Peter Wood, "La Salle: Discovery of a Lost Explorer," *American Historical Review* 89, no. 2 (1984): 294–323, examines the possible motives behind La Salle's 1685 landfall in Texas.

PATRICIA GALLOWAY

LASATER, Edward Cunningham (5 Nov. 1860–20 Mar. 1930), rancher, dairyman, and land developer, was born at "Valley Farm," near Goliad, Texas, the son of Albert H. Lasater, a rancher, and Sarah Jane Cunningham. The Texas frontier offered Edward only a meager education, but he had dreams of becoming a lawyer. Those dreams were shattered when, his father's health failing, he had to leave school to help with the family's sheep business in Atascosa County. His father purchased a ranch near Oakville in Live Oak County, and after his father's death in 1883, Lasater began buying and selling cattle and establishing his credit. In 1892 he married Martha Patti Noble Bennett. They had two children before Martha died in childbirth in 1900. In 1902 Lasater married Mary Gardner Miller; they had five children.

In 1895 Lasater began to look at the undeveloped land in South Texas, between the Nueces River and the Rio Grande. Where others saw only scrubland, Lasater saw opportunity, and buying land there, he filled it with cattle. Looking for a breed of cattle that could take the hot, dry conditions of South Texas, he first brought in Shorthorn and Hereford stock and crossed them with the rangy native Longhorns. He soon realized that South Texas conditions demanded a stockier and heavier animal that could withstand the frequent droughts. He brought the first Brahman bulls to this area, and the Hereford-Shorthorn-Brahman cross soon made up the bulk of cattle on his ranch. Lasater's efforts to combine the best characteristics of all three breeds represented the first attempts to develop a beef animal specifically adapted to the area's rugged environment. His ranch of over 350,000 acres was stocked with 20,000 head of cattle and was one of the largest in South Texas.

While Lasater made a significant impression on the ranching industry of South Texas, he is best remembered for his endeavors in other fields. In 1909 he decided to establish a herd of purebred Jersey cattle on his ranch near Falfurrias. He bought 100 purebred Jerseys as a foundation stock from a Texas breeder, J. O. Terrell, and developed this stock into the largest in the world. The Lasater herd became internationally famous and was exhibited in all of the major shows in the nation. From 1912 to 1929 he showed his Jerseys at 73 national and state fairs, winning 69 grand championships and 560 first prizes.

Wanting to build a community around Falfurrias, Lasater divided some 60,000 acres of his holdings into small dairy farms in 1911. He attracted many Midwest farmers, and the thriving community of Falfurrias was soon the center of dairy farming in South Texas. To more easily market the products of the dairy farmers, Lasater then established the Falfurrias Creamery. At first a three-room wooden building, the dairy processing plant specialized in sweet cream butter, and Falfurrias became known as the butter capital of the nation. Also in 1911 Lasater was elected president of the Cattle Raisers Association of Texas (now the Texas and Southwestern Cattle Raisers Association).

In the midst of his empire building, Lasater promoted what he called "clean politics" on the Rio Grande, condemning the corruption then widespread in the Texas Valley. In 1912 the Progressive "Bull Moose" party established by Theodore Roosevelt nominated Lasater for governor of Texas, but he lost the election.

On 25 July 1917 Herbert Hoover appointed Lasater to the Food Administration. He only served until March 1918, however, because of his differences with the president over meat policy. Speaking before the Senate Agriculture Committee, Lasater said the administration had been influential in a "conspiracy to break the cattle market to a point below the cost of production. . . . At this date it was costing the producer more than $18 per hundred to produce hogs. A deluge of immature hogs and cattle are being dumped on the market, as a consequence" (Associated Press, 30 Mar. 1918).

After Lasater left the Food Administration he continued to exhibit his winning herd in shows. He also tested and proved that his Jerseys were a better dairy breed than Holsteins. Lasater died in Ardmore, Oklahoma.

• The Lasater papers are at the Eugene C. Barker Texas History Center, University of Texas, Austin, Tex. The center also has a vertical file with several biographical sketches and newspaper articles. A biography by Lasater's grandson is Dale Lasater, *Falfurrias: Ed C. Lasater and the Development of South Texas* (1985). See also Mary Whatley Clarke, *A Century of Cow Business: A History of the Texas and Southwestern Cattle Raisers Association* (1976), and Laurence M. Lasater, *The Lasater Philosophy of Cattle Raising* (1972). An obituary is in the *New York Times*, 22 Mar. 1930.

CHRISTIE BOURGEOIS

LASCH, Christopher (1 June 1932–14 Feb. 1994), historian and social critic, nicknamed "Kit," was born in Omaha, Nebraska, the son of Robert Lasch, a newspaperman and liberal editorialist, and Zora Schaupp, who held a Ph.D. in philosophy and was a part-time social worker. "Both my parents," Lasch later recalled, "were militant secularists," who raised him "in the tradition of Middle Western progressivism, overlaid by the liberalism of the New Deal." (As an adult, however, he quarreled with that tradition; not long before his death, he remarked, "If I seem to spend a lot of time attacking liberalism and the Left, that should be taken more as a mark of respect than one of dismissal.") Shortly after his birth, the family moved to Chicago, and in 1947 Lasch began high school in suburban Barrington, Illinois. He edited the school newspaper, made "impassioned" speeches for presidential aspirant Henry Wallace, and won a statewide Latin contest and a scholarship to the University of Chicago. He went to Harvard, instead, graduating in 1954 with a B.A. in history. In 1955 he earned an M.A. and in 1961 a Ph.D. at Columbia University, and his dissertation, directed by William Leuchtenburg, became his first book, *The American Liberals and* *the Russian Revolution* (1962). While he was at Columbia, he met Nell Commager, whom he married in 1956; they had four children.

After teaching at Williams College and Roosevelt University, Lasch moved to the University of Iowa early in the 1960s as an assistant professor. There, he tested the possibilities of intellectual engagement, helping, for example, to organize—in the wake of the Cuban missile crisis—one of the first teach-ins, while through his courses he sought to demonstrate history's ability to clarify the times. His thinking during his time at Iowa also resulted in *The New Radicalism in America, 1889–1963: The Intellectual as a Social Type* (1965), a collection of thematic essays and intellectual biographies of Jane Addams, Randolph Bourne, and Lincoln Steffens, among others. The book remains provocative. Lasch was already setting forth the terms of his argument with the progressive intellect, which he saw as encumbered by the difficult necessity of maintaining both "provisional loyalty" and "detached engagement." Such qualities required intellectuals somehow to be *in* but not *of* their world, a stance that made extraordinary demands few could meet. According to Lasch, "intellectuals who weren't content to be intellectuals" often fell victim to a fatal "confusion of politics and culture" and fled the rigors of detachment for a consoling immersion in revolutionary and countercultural movements.

The New Radicalism was controversial, and its success opened new venues for Lasch. Chief among them was the *New York Review of Books*, for which he was soon a leading practitioner of the historical essay as social criticism, writing on "The Decline of Populism," "The Revival of Political Controversy in the Sixties," "Divorce and the Decline of the Family," and "The Foreign Policy Elite and the War in Vietnam." These pieces, which gave little comfort to partisans, disdained the ahistorical tendencies of Cold War liberals and New Leftists alike. They nonetheless held wide appeal, especially for younger people fascinated by Lasch's range and attracted to his seriousness and passion. Many of the *New York Review of Books* essays were published in *The Agony of the American Left* (1969) and *The World of Nations* (1972).

Since the early 1960s Lasch had also been trying to conceive a book on women, love, and marriage. He felt that "something in the atmosphere of the late fifties made it seem important to come to terms with the 'woman question.'" After having moved to Northwestern University in 1966 and then to the University of Rochester in 1970, he began what would become *Haven in a Heartless World: The Family Besieged* (1977), which he considered "the most difficult of all the books I ever wrote." Envisioned as a theoretical introduction to the unfulfilled project on women, *Haven* was the first of three books in which Lasch brought the theories of Karl Marx and Sigmund Freud to bear on the contemporary American scene. *The Culture of Narcissism* (1979), widely misunderstood as a jeremiad against American selfishness, won an uncomfortable notoriety. And *The Minimal Self* (1984) opened a re-

consideration of religious tradition, among other things. *Haven*, the most important of the three, examined the implications of the intellectuals' professionalization, their integration within the managerial superstructure of late twentieth-century America. Specifically, it traced the part played by the social sciences and the "helping professions" in abetting corporate capitalism's undoing of the family.

In *Haven*, Lasch observed that in the United States, "defense of an emerging status quo usually takes the form of urgent calls for sweeping reform." Early twentieth-century educators, social workers, and psychologists saw themselves as "doctors to a sick society," who diagnosed the family, especially that of recent immigrants, as a noisome pathology requiring expert intervention. They called for the very "socialization of reproduction" they would soon describe as inevitable. By the 1950s, in Lasch's view, the therapeutic claim to the interior life had been institutionalized within a bureaucratic welfare state. Armed with medical, legal, and academic authority, it comported well with capitalism's shift into an aggressive consumerism. Two halves of the same rationalizing project, each sought the individual's "adjustment" to increasingly manipulative "social forces." Together they undermined individual competence, contributing to the despair, addiction, and dysfunction that each promised to assuage. The citizen had given way to the consumer, the client, and the patient. For many Americans in the 1970s, the brittleness of intimate life had risen to unbearable proportions. Launched, as Lasch saw it, on an era of mass divorce, day care as a way of life, and a pathetic celebration of family "diversity," the "new radicalism" of the American intellectual had attained its apotheosis. The technocratic reconstruction of the American mind and heart was nearly complete, its subversive achievement undeniable.

This line of argument, and the hostile reaction to it, forced Lasch "to think about what had happened to both me and to the Left." Both the right and the left, he concluded, were too deeply invested in the idea of progress to face up to the deterioration of American life; thus neither had "much to contribute to political discussion." In his penultimate book, *The True and Only Heaven: Progress and Its Critics* (1991), he pitted the belief in unlimited progress, whether economic or cultural, against a world steadily piling up evidence against its viability. The idea of progress and the refusal to countenance limits to human aspiration were, Lasch believed, unquestioned features of liberalism and conservatism, the two wings of the single party of managerial capitalism. But the society built on these foundations had all along been parasitic, a proceduralist liberalism living off defeated traditions whose stock of moral capital it had been drawing down for generations. Cleavages of wealth, condition, individual competence, and social trust, so pronounced by the 1990s, reflected this emptying of accounts and signaled the beginning of the end of an epoch.

Lasch thought, however, that Americans might find a fresh basis for hope in reconsidering the defeated traditions of nineteenth-century republicanism, populism, and Protestant moralism. In thinkers ranging from Ralph Waldo Emerson and Orestes Brownson to Reinhold Niebuhr and Martin Luther King, Lasch found a populist alternative to the progressive conception of America. In this populist alternative, democracy rested on civic virtue, itself the product of the self-respect of independent and responsible citizens. Where progress had no answer for the inevitable desolations of life, the populist alternative was a "spiritual discipline" that rejected despair, affirmed hope, and stood up to life, even as it accepted life's tragic limits.

Like *Haven in a Heartless World*, *The True and Only Heaven* won few admirers among defenders of the prevailing orthodoxies. Neoconservatives and others on the right emphasized Lasch's anticapitalism, while they minimized capitalism's complicity in the social breakdown they otherwise so loudly decried. On the left, his dim view of feminism and of faux-radical careerism had already made him anathema. His defense of restraint, self-sacrifice, and a healthy skepticism toward progressive pieties seemed to confirm his apostasy, especially because he hailed the persistence of those qualities within a lower middle class that others saw as blighted by suffocating families, racism, and opposition to unlimited abortion. Lasch saw in these criticisms a worsening anti-intellectualism among the "New Class" of academics and technocratic opinion-shapers. How, he wondered, had the New Class become so impervious to argument, so smug in its self-regarding rectitude? How had contempt become its operative emotion, reserved especially for the mass of Americans who remained unimpressed by affirmative action, gay rights, and the bland conformity of multicultural fashion? How had liberals and the left, once identified with the aspirations of the working classes, developed such a profound disdain for the concerns of ordinary Americans?

Lasch sketched the scope of the problem in his last book, a series of essays titled *The Revolt of the Elites and the Betrayal of Democracy* (1995). He attempted to trace the history of the cult of "objectivity" that had supplanted "the lost art of argument" and undermined the individual American's confidence in forming judgments of one's own. He castigated the cowardice of an "academic pseudo-radicalism" that was conspiring with its right-wing critics to deny its own and "the university's assimilation into the corporate order." Lost to American democracy was the populist principle of "respect," available to all who submit to common standards of judgment: the "misplaced compassion" of progressives and communitarians alike belied a sinister solicitude, "the human face of contempt." The "betrayal of democracy" stemmed above all from the "intensification of social divisions" wrought by global capitalism. By inexorably eroding the economic foundations of the middle class and the social stability it had traditionally provided, late twentieth-century market integration was accelerating the loss of social cohesion even as it consolidated a transnational New Class. That new elite was fatally disconnected from

loyalties to place and memory that gave former elites whatever legitimacy they possessed: it was in "revolt" against the "common life." Having broken the "common frame of reference without which society dissolves into nothing more than contending factions," its rebellion presaged a "war of all against all."

Lasch finished *The Revolt of the Elites* only ten days before his death in Pittsford, New York, from renal cancer. At home, amid family and friends, he devoted much of his final year to the book and to the revision of several essays on women. These latter pieces, fragments of his "many years of inconclusive struggle with the subject," were edited and published by his daughter, the historian Elizabeth Lasch-Quinn, as *Women and the Common Life: Love, Marriage, and Feminism* (1997).

The most important American social critic of the late twentieth century, Lasch personified a heroic conception of the intellectual vocation. He took sides and passed judgment, inspiring and offending many. To some, his writings were too harsh, too idiosyncratic, too redolent of an obsolete moralism. Still, even critics were disarmed on meeting him: they found a gentle man, an amateur musician who enjoyed company and conversation, who strove to see matters from the point of view of others. This effort was for Lasch the essential imaginative requirement of democracy. He challenged the temptations of envy and resentment with the "grateful disposition" of hope. An advocate of "love, useful work, self-respect, honor, and integrity," he aimed to provoke and sustain conversation about "the conduct of life," about "the things that matter."

• Lasch's papers, more than seventy boxes of correspondence, notes, and manuscript drafts covering mostly 1950–1994, are housed in the University of Rochester Library. In addition to the books already noted in the text, Lasch edited *The Social Thought of Jane Addams* (1965) and published numerous articles and book review essays in such periodicals as the *Nation*, *Harper's*, *Salmagundi*, the *New Republic*, *First Things*, *Tikkun*, and *New Oxford Review*. Published interviews include Casey Blake and Christopher Phelps, "History as Social Criticism: Conversations with Christopher Lasch," *Journal of American History* 80 (Mar. 1994): 1310–32; and Richard W. Fox, "An Interview with Christopher Lasch," *Intellectual History Newsletter* 16 (1994): 3–14. Among the many tributes and appreciative essays are Jean Bethke Elshtain, "The Life and Work of Christopher Lasch: An American Story," *Salmagundi*, nos. 106–7 (Spring–Summer 1995): 146–61; Robert Coles, "Remembering Christopher Lasch," *New Oxford Review* 61 (Sept. 1994): 16–19; and Jackson Lears, "The Man Who Knew Too Much," *New Republic*, 2 Oct. 1995, pp. 43–50. An obituary is in the *New York Times*, 15 Feb. 1994.

GUY ALCHON

LASH, Joseph P. (9 Dec. 1909–22 Aug. 1987), biographer, journalist, and political activist, was born in New York City, the son of Samuel Lash and Mary Avchin, grocery store owners. By the time Lash was eleven years old, the metropolitan press had dubbed him a "boy prodigy" because he had scored above college freshmen in the Binet-Simon intelligence test. While helping his Russian-Jewish immigrant parents operate their small store in their Columbia University neighborhood, Lash frequently waited on professors and students, acquiring—as he later recalled—"bookish and academic aspirations by sheer contact." At De Witt Clinton High School, Lash displayed literary inclinations, winning a city-wide essay contest and serving as the student newspaper's book review editor.

As a student at the City College of New York (CCNY), Lash viewed himself as part of the campus literati and began to lean toward political activism. He became a devoted student of the college's most distinguished liberal professor, philosopher Morris Raphael Cohen, whose confrontational approach to teaching shaped Lash's emerging intellectual style. "You could," Lash recalled, "tell a Cohen student by his earnestness, arrogance, and combativeness" (uncompleted autobiography, Lash papers). Lash was also influenced both intellectually and politically by his evolving friendship with Cohen's brilliant son Felix, a recent CCNY graduate who, as the editor of the student newspaper the *Campus*, had spearheaded a campaign to abolish compulsory military training—a struggle that Lash viewed as "dazzling" and whose spirit Lash and his classmates sought to perpetuate. Much like Felix, Lash gravitated toward democratic socialism, chaired CCNY's socialist organization, and served as the editorial chairman of the *Campus*. Lash's iconoclastic editorials enraged CCNY president Frederick Robinson, who refused to sign the distinguished service award the faculty had voted to bestow upon the young editor—a reprisal that angered students and was reported in several New York papers. Lash also received the college's literary prize in recognition of an essay that he wrote on Walt Whitman.

The Great Depression deepened Lash's radicalism, leaving him convinced that capitalism and big business were morally and intellectually bankrupt. In this spirit, Lash and his fellow *Campus* editor Abe Raskin crusaded against CCNY's establishment of a business school. Lash graduated from CCNY in 1931 with an A. B. degree. While a graduate student in English literature at Columbia University, Lash in 1932 joined a student delegation to aid striking coal miners in Harlan County, Kentucky, and experienced firsthand the antilabor violence of coal company vigilantes and police. Lash quickly completed his master's thesis on Christopher Marlowe, gave up on the idea of an academic job, and committed himself to "full-time socialist agitation." From this point in 1932 until almost the end of the depression decade, Lash considered himself "a professional revolutionist."

Although no longer a student, Lash would become the most prominent and persistent campus radical leader in depression-era America. No one did more than Lash to build the first mass student protest movement in American history. From 1932 to 1935 Lash served as the top-ranking national officer of the Socialist-led Student League for Industrial Democracy (SLID). He helped organize the campus campaign for 1932 Socialist presidential candidate Norman Thom-

as, and he worked to publicize the job crisis by founding the Association of Unemployed College Alumni. As a SLID leader Lash originated the student movement's most effective organizing tactic: a national student strike against war, in which students across the nation boycotted classes for an hour. Suck strikes, repeated annually from 1934 to 1941, and the isolationist mood of the campuses mobilized almost half of the entire American undergraduate population in protests against war. Lash also played a key role in the negotiations between the SLID and its Communist-led rival, the National Student League, culminating in their merger in December 1935 into the American Student Union (ASU). He served as the most influential national officer of this united-front organization until 1940.

Lash's involvement in the student movement also led him to sharpen his writing skills. His report on the Harlan expedition, which appeared in the *New Republic* in 1932, represented his first publication in a major national journal. Lash served as the editor of the SLID's national magazine *Student Outlook* (1932–1935) and as the coeditor, with James Wechsler, of the ASU's national magazine *Student Advocate* (1935–1938). It was in the student movement that Lash published his first book, *War Our Heritage* (1936), an antiwar tract and history of the student movement, coauthored by Wechsler. It was also through the student movement that Lash met, and in 1935 married, Nancy Bedford Jones, a UCLA activist; they had no children. The two were separated in 1937 and subsequently divorced.

Lash's foreign policy positions changed dramatically as the Nazi menace grew. By 1937 he had abandoned isolationism and embraced a "Popular Front" position, favoring international action to halt the spread of fascism. In the summer of 1937 he dropped out of the student movement and volunteered to aid the Loyalist forces in the Spanish civil war. Defying U.S. neutrality law, Lash, along with Young Communist League leader Dave Doran, slipped into Spain from southern France and began drilling with the McKenzie Pepinaw battalion. But the International Brigade leadership decided that Lash was most valuable as a leader of the American student movement and ordered him to leave the brigade.

The Spanish civil war drew Lash as close as he ever got to the Communist party. He quit the American Socialist party in 1937 because he thought its pacifism and anti-Communism limited its ability to aid the Spanish republic and to battle fascism. Lash returned from Spain full of admiration for the Communist role in leading the international struggle against fascism. He considered himself a "non-Party Bolshevik" for the rest of the Popular Front era and intended to join the Communist party (and write for its newspaper, the *Daily Worker*) when he completed his work with the student movement.

The Nazi-Soviet Pact of August 1939 ended Lash's brief infatuation with the Communist party. Lash saw the pact as a cynical abandonment of the antifascist principles that he and the American student movement had been championing. The pact provoked heated battles between Communists and non-Communists in the student movement, with Lash playing the lead role in the non-Communist ranks. In the midst of this conflict, which decimated the ASU and the entire American student movement, Lash, in the fall of 1939, was summoned to appear before the House Committee on Un-American Activities (HUAC). Though battling Communist domination within the student movement himself, Lash had no desire to help HUAC in its crusade against leftist and liberal causes.

When Lash finally appeared before HUAC in December 1939, he did so in the presence of Eleanor Roosevelt. In the late 1930s the First Lady had become something of a patron saint of progressive student activism. She attended the HUAC hearing to lend moral support to the young activists and invited several of them, including Lash, to the White House. At the hearing Roosevelt noticed how pained Lash seemed to be as he sought to be fair to the Communists in the student movement while also struggling both to be honest about his differences with them and to avoid giving political ammunition to HUAC. Curious about this troubled and thoughtful young man, Roosevelt kept in touch with him, and a deep friendship evolved that would last until the end of her life and alter the course of Lash's political and professional life.

When Lash lost his leadership position with the ASU as the Communists took control of that organization in 1940, Roosevelt helped ease Lash's transition from the student Left to the New Deal mainstream. She supported him in his effort to broaden the International Student Service (ISS) (for which he served as the general secretary from the fall of 1940 to the spring of 1942) from a refugee aid society to a liberal activist organization and a rival of the ASU. Lash's friendship with the First Lady also led to his involvement in President Franklin D. Roosevelt's third-term presidential campaign, in which he worked as the director of the Youth Division of the Democratic National Committee. In return, Lash became a source of good political advice to Eleanor Roosevelt, particularly with regard to her relationship with youth organizations. Lash helped her see that she had misjudged some of the leaders of the student movement (and in particular the American Youth Congress), who had responded to her friendship with disingenuousness about their links to the Communist party. He also helped her extricate herself from what had become an embarrassingly close relationship with the Youth Congress, an organization covertly dominated by young Communists.

Lash's friendship with the First Lady evoked considerable hostility from both radicals and conservatives. Some of Lash's former colleagues in the student movement publicly denounced him as an opportunist who had sold out his radical principles for New Deal dollars. Conservatives objected to the First Lady socializing with a subversive and depicted her as a dupe or worse. The closeness of the relationship between Lash and the First Lady even led to rumors (and a false Army counter intelligence report) that the two were lovers—although in fact their relationship was one in which she mothered Lash, and he acted, as James Wechsler put it, as her "spiritually adopted son, confidant and counselor." Roosevelt even helped bring him together with Trude Pratt, an ISS organizer whom Lash married in 1944; they had one son. Pratt also became a lifelong friend of the First Lady.

After Lash left the military following World War II, he became active in liberal politics and closely allied with Eleanor Roosevelt. Lash was a founding member of Americans for Democratic Action and headed that organization's New York City branch from 1946 to 1948. In 1948 Lash assisted Elliot Roosevelt in editing a two-volume collection of Franklin Roosevelt's letters. Two years later, Lash went to work for the *New York Post*, covering the United Nations from 1950 to 1960. Lash served as an editorial writer (1961–1963) and an assistant editor (1964–1966) of the *Post's* staunchly liberal editorial page. During his tenure at the *Post*, Lash wrote *Dag Hammarskjold: Custodian of the Brushfire Peace* (1961), and, following the death of Eleanor Roosevelt, he published a memoir of his relationship with the former First Lady titled *Eleanor Roosevelt: A Friend's Memoir* (1964).

Lash's friendship with Roosevelt changed his life once more in 1966 when, on the basis of that friendship, Franklin D. Roosevelt, Jr., asked him to become his mother's official biographer. Lash was the first researcher to gain access to Eleanor Roosevelt's personal papers in Hyde Park. He left the *Post* and spent years pouring through her papers. In a sense Lash was uniquely qualified to portray her life, since he had been close to her for more than a quarter of a century. But such closeness was also a potential liability, since, as Arthur Schlesinger, Jr., put it, Lash's deep affection for Roosevelt "might conflict with the austere obligations of the biographer" and could lead to hagiography rather than critical history. But Lash, as a veteran reporter and a gifted writer, rose to the occasion, producing a masterful 765-page study, *Eleanor and Franklin: The Story of Their Relationship Based on Eleanor Roosevelt's Private Papers* (1971)—which, though sympathetic, humanized rather than canonized Eleanor Roosevelt. The public was startled to learn that her activism sprang in part from the unhappiness she experienced in her personal life—in particular from her troubled relationship with her husband. Lash showed that Eleanor and Franklin's relationship had become more of a political partnership than a conventional marriage. In this partnership he provided her with access to power and she prodded his social conscience through her constant liberal advocacy.

Eleanor and Franklin was the most celebrated book Lash would publish, winning the Francis Parkman Prize, the National Book Award for biography, and the Pulitzer Prize in biography; it was also used as the basis for a nine-hour television docudrama on the Roosevelts. Nonetheless, there were critics who, while admiring the many virtues of *Eleanor and Franklin*, complained that his closeness to Eleanor Roosevelt had helped to produce a book that was more about her than her husband and that viewed their relationship more from her perspective than from his.

The success of *Eleanor and Franklin* ensured that Lash would not return to his work as a journalist but would spend the rest of his life practicing the biographer's art. At the age of sixty-one he had embarked upon a new career as a full-time historian and author. As his friend Robert Caro pointed out, Lash proved enormously productive in this new career despite his advancing age and declining health. Lash wrote or edited nine books in the last sixteen years of his life, most notably his study of Eleanor Roosevelt's final years, *Eleanor: The Years Alone* (1972); his account of another historic relationship, *Roosevelt and Churchill: The Partnership that Saved the West* (1976); a biographical essay on Felix Frankfurter, published in his edited collection *From the Diaries of Felix Frankfurter* (1975); a biography of Helen Keller, *Helen and Teacher* (1980); the two volumes of Eleanor Roosevelt's correspondence that he compiled, *Love Eleanor: Eleanor Roosevelt and Her Friends* (1982) and *A World of Love: Eleanor Roosevelt and Her Friends, 1943–62* (1984); and *Dealers and Dreamers: A New Look at the New Deal* (1988). Lash died in Boston.

Among scholars and the public, Lash is most often cited and remembered in connection with his prize-winning account of the Roosevelts, *Eleanor and Franklin*. Its literary grace and narrative power have made it a classic American biography, and its candor about the private lives of a presidential couple became something of a model for other studies of the presidency. The book has shaped much of the historical profession's understanding of the Roosevelts' relationship.

It was fitting that Lash's final volume, *Dealers and Dreamers* (published posthumously), should focus on the New Deal and on those who like him had been young, idealistic, and reform-minded intellectuals in the 1930s. Almost all of Lash's books illuminated that spirit of reform that had done so much to shape his own life. As John Hersey noted, Lash had taken "the classic journey of our time from left to right" but had "the balance to rest on the middle ground. He did not, like so many others, end up a crabbed and bitter neoconservative. He could not have. The generous spirit of the New Deal never grew old in his mind" (*Joseph P. Lash*, Lash papers).

• Lash's papers are available in the Franklin D. Roosevelt Library in Hyde Park, New York. Among those papers are an uncompleted autobiography and diaries that offer a valuable guide to Lash's early life and a privately published memorial volume, *Joseph P. Lash* (1987), which contains reminiscences about Lash by many of his friends—including Robert Caro, John Hersey, Louis Harris, John Oakes, James Roosevelt, Jr., Arthur Schlesinger, Jr., and Molly Yard. On Lash's role in leading the student movement of the 1930s see Robert Cohen, *When the Old Left Was Young: Student Radicals and America's First Mass Student Movement, 1929–1941* (1993).

ROBERT COHEN

LASHLEY, Karl Spencer (7 June 1890–7 Aug. 1958), physiological and comparative psychologist, was born in Davis, West Virginia, the son of Charles Lashley, a merchant, banker, and town mayor, and Maggie Spencer, a schoolteacher and photographer. He spent most of his early life in Davis, except for an interlude in the Klondike gold rush in 1898. Lashley graduated high school at age fourteen. He attended West Virginia University during 1905–1910, first completing a year of preparatory work, then receiving a B.A. There he was influenced by zoology instructor John B. Johnston and found his life work in the biological sciences, beginning with a desire to trace the neural pathways of the frog in order to discover "how the frog worked."

After an M.S. in bacteriology earned for 1910–1911 work at the University of Pittsburgh, Lashley attended the Johns Hopkins University, receiving a Ph.D. in zoology in 1914. His career as a psychologist interested in the physiology and psychology of learned and instinctive behavior was shaped by his interactions with his doctoral supervisor, H. S. Jennings; behaviorist psychologist John B. Watson; and physiological psychologist Shepherd I. Franz, with whom he did postdoctoral work.

Lashley spent 1917–1918 and 1920–1926 at the University of Minnesota, 1926–1929 at the Institute for Juvenile Research in Chicago, and 1929–1935 as a professor at the University of Chicago. He married Edith Ann Baker, a professional musician, in 1918; their only child, a son, died shortly after birth. The years 1920–1929 were especially productive years for his study of brain functions which culminated in the publication in 1929 of his monograph *Brain Mechanisms and Intelligence*. He moved to Harvard University, first as a professor of psychology (1935–1937), and then as a research professor of neuropsychology (1937–1955). During 1942–1955 he also served as director of the Yerkes Laboratories of Primate Biology in Orange Park, Florida. His wife Edith died in 1948. In 1957 he married Claire Imredy Schiller, widow of Hungarian psychologist Paul Schiller.

In the work for which he is best known, Lashley studied the effects of lesions in the cerebral cortex of rats on their abilities to learn and retain maze-running skills. Lashley found that these abilities were less localized than had been thought; performance depended more on the amount of tissue removed than its location. This led to the principles of equipotentiality—that, within limits, different areas of the cortex could serve similar functions—and mass action—that deficits in function are determined by the amount of tissue removed. At the end of a long search for the specific location of memory traces, the "engram," Lashley concluded that representation in the brain is diffuse rather than localized.

Although a strict materialist, Lashley opposed the simplistic reflexology of the day, believing that animals act with purpose and that attention is a factor in learning. He demonstrated that complex and serially ordered behavior, such as the playing of rapid passages of piano music, could not be explained as governed by sequential reflexes. Rather, he believed that behavior is structured by organized, neural mechanisms; the cerebral cortex functions to integrate behavior. He regarded advances in the methodology for the study of behavior as being as important as those in the study of physiology.

Lashley's contributions to comparative psychology began with his work with Jennings and his studies of the orientation and behavior of terns conducted with Watson in the field in Florida. He returned to the problems of the evolution and control of instinctive behavior throughout his life. Among his last publications was an introduction to Claire Schiller's book, *Instinctive Behavior* (1957), which helped bridge American comparative psychology to European ethology.

Lashley had broad professional interests and experiences. In 1918 he worked with Watson using films in sex education for the U.S. Interdepartmental Social Hygiene Board. As the director of the Yerkes laboratories, he developed programs in growth and development, physiology and psychology of sex, the individual psychology of intelligence and emotion, and brain function in behavior, notably vision. He donated funds to the American Philosophical Society to establish the Karl Spencer Lashley Award in Neurobiology.

Although shy and reserved, Lashley could be informal and unpretentious in small groups. He loved music and played the cello; was an avid and skilled sailor; and also relaxed with skilled shop work.

Professionally, Lashley was regarded as brilliant and incisive, though unsystematic, nonconforming, and unorthodox. He was especially skilled at dismantling the theories of others but did so by building new empirical foundations. He received many honors, including five honorary degrees. Lashley signed the charter book as a member of the Royal Society ten days before his death in Poitiers, France.

• There is no single corpus of Lashley papers. Significant materials are in the library of the Yerkes Regional Primate Research Center of Emory University in Atlanta, Ga., and the Smathers Library of the University of Florida. Selected works by Lashley appear in Frank A. Beach et al., eds., *The Neuropsychology of Lashley* (1960). Lashley wrote no formal autobiography. Biographical sketches were written by Beach, National Academy of Sciences, *Biographical Memoirs* 35 (1961), and D. Bruce, "Integrations of Lashley," in *Portraits of Pioneers in Psychology*, ed. G. A. Kimble et al. (1991). An excellent source is J. Ohbach, *Neuropsychology after Lashley* (1982). Obituaries are in the *American Journal of Psychology* 72 (1959), *Science* 129 (1959), and the Fellows of the Royal Society, *Biographical Memoirs* 5 (1960).

DONALD A. DEWSBURY

LASKER, Albert Davis (1 May 1880–30 May 1952), advertising executive, was born in Freiburg, Germany, the son of Morris Lasker, a merchant and banker, and Nettie Heidenheimer Davis. Both parents, who were American citizens, were in Germany at the time of his birth so that his mother could be treated for poor health. When he was six weeks old, the family returned to Galveston, Texas, where he was raised as one of six children.

Journalism was a fascination and early vocation for Lasker. At the age of twelve, he started his own commercially successful weekly newspaper, the *Galveston Free Press*. He went to work for the *Galveston Morning News* at thirteen and was editor of his high school magazine. Upon graduation, Lasker worked briefly for papers in New Orleans and Dallas and was planning a career in journalism when his father intervened. Morris Lasker opposed his son's interest in the newspaper business and in 1898 arranged for Albert to begin working at the Chicago advertising agency Lord & Thomas.

Beginning as a $10-per-week office boy, Lasker advanced rapidly within the agency. Within a year he was traveling the Midwest as a top salesman, bringing major accounts and much income to Lord & Thomas. By 1904, at the age of twenty-four, Lasker was a full partner and general manager of the agency. In 1910 he became its sole proprietor, and Lord & Thomas grew to become one of the largest and most successful advertising agencies of its time. In 1942 Lasker decided to retire and agreed to sell the company on the condition that the name Lord & Thomas no longer be used. Three of his longtime vice presidents bought the agency and renamed it Foote, Cone, & Belding.

During the first half of the twentieth century, Lasker was arguably the most important person in American advertising. His opinions and business sense had an influence not just on Lord & Thomas and its clients but on the entire industry. Lasker developed the account executive concept, an agency position that would serve as the central link between an advertiser and agency creatives. In many ways, his ideas about effective advertising, agency operations, and the place of advertising in commerce and society guided the evolution of advertising even years after he was no longer a part of it himself. His impact is especially evident in the number of leaders in the advertising business who at one time worked for Lasker, including John Kennedy, Claude Hopkins, and Fairfax Cone.

If there was one thing that characterized the Lasker approach to advertising, it was an emphasis on copywriting as the crucial foundation of any good advertisement. At the time that he began in the business, ad agencies were essentially brokers of newspaper and magazine space, with most advertisers writing their own copy. When Lasker began offering clients copywriting services, Lord & Thomas became one of the first truly full-service agencies.

Lasker's copy philosophy was that advertising should be "salesmanship in print," a notion quite different from the straight descriptive advertising most common at the time. The advertisement must sound like a presentation a salesman would make. It must answer the questions customers raise. His belief in strong, persuasive copy led to the original agency copywriting department, inhouse copywriting classes, and the paying of tremendous salaries to proven copywriters. His concept, a "reason why," became part of Lasker's hard-sell approach. At the same time, Lasker felt that the visual element of an advertisement contributed little and considered art directors subordinate to copywriters and useful only for helping with client presentations. He also disdained research as hindering the instinct and intuition that he was convinced were responsible for good copy, even resigning some large accounts rather than subjecting Lord & Thomas ads to copytesting.

Examples of Lasker's work in advertising included developing the first Sunkist campaign to suggest that oranges might be consumed for their juice, introducing both Kleenex and Kotex to the mass market, and making toothpaste a household product with ads that turned Pepsodent into the top-selling brand. The advertising for Lucky Strike cigarettes, the largest of Lord & Thomas's accounts, broke new ground and more than doubled sales by promoting women's smoking. Lasker was also one of the first to use radio as an advertising medium.

Throughout his life, Lasker involved himself in occasional ventures outside of advertising. President Warren G. Harding appointed him chairman of the U.S. Shipping Board in the early 1920s. He became part owner of the Chicago Cubs baseball team and reorganized the major leagues to include an independent commissioner of baseball following the Black Sox game-fixing scandal. Later in his life he developed a serious interest in collecting art and supported medical research through the establishment of foundations and financial awards. In each of these areas, as in his professional life, Lasker tended to be driven and almost autocratic when it came to pursuing what he saw as important. He experienced at least three nervous breakdowns during his adult life and finally underwent psychoanalysis in the 1940s.

Lasker was married to Flora Warner from 1902 until she died in 1936. They had three children. In 1938 he married actress Doris Kenyon. That marriage ended in divorce after less than a year. In 1940 he married businesswoman Mary Woodward Reinhardt, and they remained married until his death in New York City.

Truly an advertising pioneer, Albert Lasker's lasting influence can be seen still in the structure of the agency business and in the content of modern advertisements.

• The best autobiographical material on Lasker includes *The Lasker Story: As He Told It*, ed. Sid Bernstein and *Advertising Age* (1963), the transcript of a six-hour talk Lasker gave to Lord & Thomas staff. The Oral History Project of Columbia University includes material from Lasker, part of which has been printed in "The Personal Reminiscences of Albert Lasker," *American Heritage*, Dec. 1954, pp. 74–84. John Gunther, *Taken at the Flood* (1960), is an excellent book-length biography of Lasker. The second chapter in Stephen Fox, *The Mirror Makers: A History of American Advertising and Its Creators* (1984), is entitled "The Age of Lasker," and David Ogilvy, *Ogilvy on Advertising* (1985) includes a chapter on "six giants who invented modern advertising," with Lasker listed as the first of these six.

Front-page stories in *Advertising Age* (9 June 1952) and the *New York Times* (31 May 1952) are the most complete obituaries. An editorial in the same issue of the *Times* is also devoted to Lasker's death.

KEVIN L. KEENAN

LASKY, Jesse Louis (13 Sept. 1880–13 Jan. 1958), motion picture pioneer, was born in San Francisco, California, the son of Isaac Lasky, a shoe store owner, and Sarah Platt. The family, including his younger sister Blanche, moved to San Jose, California, when Lasky was eight years old. Because of his father's poor health, the subsequent bankruptcy of his shoe store, and relatives still residing in San Francisco, the Lasky family returned to San Francisco before Lasky could finish high school.

Isaac Lasky became a traveling salesman for a firm from which he had formerly purchased shoes, but it was hard work for a man with such precarious health. Because Jesse Lasky had occasionally played cornet with a professional band in San Jose, the family thought he could earn a living through music. Lying about his age, Lasky became a member of the Musicians' Union, and after weeks of waiting for a job in the union hall he was hired as second cornetist for a traveling medicine show. He quit that job after only two performances, but other low-paying jobs followed, and he began composing music. His father's health deteriorated further until he suffered a stroke and died in 1900.

After trying and failing in several nonmusical enterprises, in 1900 Lasky followed the gold rush to Alaska, where he was also a failure as a prospector. He was able to support himself once again with his cornet, which paid his way back home. Early in 1901 he accepted a job as cornetist with a band at the Orpheum Theatre in Honolulu, Hawaii. Discovering upon his return to San Francisco that his sister had also learned to play the cornet, he decided they should get into vaudeville as a bugle duo (their mother served as their chaperone).

Toward the end of 1903, the Laskys became managers of the magician Hermann the Great while continuing their own performances as part of his show. At the end of the second season, they found another cornetist and his wife to perform their act, and soon they were managing other groups. According to Lasky's own description, they "sent out about 40 acts from 1906 to 1910" (*I Blow My Own Horn*, p. 67), including Ruth St. Denis and Al Jolson.

On a rare vacation (again accompanied by his sister and mother) in the Adirondacks in 1908, Lasky met Bessie Mona Ginzberg, who was "convent-bred" (Notre Dame Academy) and who had studied to become a concert pianist. They married the following December in Boston. After their honeymoon in Atlantic City, Lasky's wife moved into the large apartment in New York City that he shared with Blanche and his mother. Bessie gave up music because of her mother-in-law's objections to it, but after moving to Hollywood, where she and Lasky had their own small house that had no space for other relatives, she became an accomplished artist. The Laskys had one daughter and two sons. One son, Jesse L. Lasky, Jr., became a Hollywood writer and frequently worked for Cecil B. DeMille; the other, William Raymond Lasky, became an assistant director for his father's company.

On one of Lasky's trips to Europe, he realized the potential of an American Folies Bergère. Subsequently, he convinced Henry B. Harris, who leased and managed the Hudson Theatre and had also backed Lasky in previous enterprises, to join him in building an appropriate theater just off Broadway. Although it had a successful opening in 1911, it failed five months later. The building eventually became the Helen Hayes Theatre.

In 1910 Lasky's sister had married glove salesman Sam Goldfish (he later changed his name to Goldwyn), who consistently encouraged Lasky to get into the film business. Knowing little about the motion picture industry, Goldfish, Lasky, and the latter's good friend Cecil B. DeMille formed the Jesse L. Lasky Feature Play Company in 1913. Their first feature-length film was *The Squaw Man* by Edwin Milton Royle, starring matinee idol Dustin Farnum. The first long film produced in Hollywood, it was a hit both when shown at an invitational trade show in New York on 17 February 1914 and in general release the next month.

Realizing they had a financial success, they quickly made more films. Goldfish handled the business problems, DeMille the production and artistic end (they hired other directors and later additional employees such as a technical adviser and property head), and Lasky bought plays and hired the stars. Late in 1914 Lasky purchased ten David Belasco plays, most of which translated well to the silent screen. They were also able to hire DeMille's brother William as one of their writers; he organized the first story department in Hollywood and later became a director for the company. Their typical output was prodigious; in 1915, for example, they released thirty-six feature-length films. *Carmen*, starring Metropolitan Opera star Geraldine Farrar, was their biggest moneymaker to this point.

In 1916 the Lasky group merged with Adolph Zukor's well-known Famous Players Company to become Famous Players–Lasky Corporation with Zukor as president and Lasky as vice president in charge of production. It produced 80 percent of the films that Paramount Pictures, which had been formed in 1915, released. Because of disagreements between Zukor and Goldfish, the latter was asked to leave the company. Not long after, Famous Players–Lasky took control of Paramount, retaining its name for "trademark value." During the 1920s Paramount-Famous-Lasky dominated the motion picture industry; DeMille, however, left in 1924 when his contract was not renewed, owing in part to his hugely overbudget $1 million spectacular *The Ten Commandments*, released the year before.

Paramount survived the first several years of the Great Depression, but in 1932 it went into receivership and Lasky also found himself ousted from the company he had begun. Having once again lost a fortune, he became an independent producer for Fox. Sidney Kent, president of the company, gave him a three-year contract without options, and Lasky produced six films each year.

Lasky passed up the opportunity to continue with the newly merged 20th Century–Fox company. Instead, in 1935 he and Mary Pickford became partners in Pickford-Lasky Productions, Inc., which produced two films, neither of which did well financially—"the total bath of red ink for Pickford-Lasky Productions [was] nearly $200,000" (Eyman, p. 249). For fifty-two weeks toward the end of the 1930s, Lasky produced "Gateway to Hollywood," a CBS radio talent show that gave young people "a chance at show business which might not otherwise have come their way" (*I Blow My Own Horn*, p. 251).

At various times Lasky was an independent producer for Warner Bros. (for which he produced *Sergeant York* [1941], starring Gary Cooper, and *Rhapsody in Blue* [1944]), RKO, and MGM (for which he produced *The Great Caruso* [1951]). During his career he brought "a thousand pictures to the screen" (*I Blow My Own Horn*, p. 252) and launched the careers of many performers who later became major stars.

On 12 September 1951 Lasky became the first person to win the Silver Wreath of Honor from the Screen Producers Guild for "his historic contribution to the American motion picture." His last "pet project" was to produce the film "The Big Brass Band" to honor "the nine million kids who spend their spare time practicing on their instruments instead of running with juvenile gangs, making music instead of mischief" (*I Blow My Own Horn*, p. 269). Before he could begin production of "The Big Brass Band," which he wanted to make more than any other picture (it was to have been released by Paramount), he died in Beverly Hills, California, while promoting his autobiography, *I Blow My Own Horn*.

• Lasky's autobiography, written with Don Weldon, *I Blow My Own Horn*, was published in 1957 (Daniel J. Leab, writing in the *Dictionary of American Biography*, cautions using it with care as he also warns about the use of Bessie Lasky's book, *Candle in the Sun* [1957], but he does not give specifics). The autobiography lacks many dates, and at the time of its writing Lasky may have remembered events differently from the way they actually occurred. However, subsequent researchers like Scott Eyman, who wrote *Mary Pickford* (1990), have happily quoted from Lasky's book. Alva Johnston, "Profiles: A Bugler's Progress," *New Yorker*, 10 July 1937, pp. 18–24, is useful but includes at least one error (e.g., Lasky was not born in San Jose) and other information that differs from Lasky's version in his autobiography. Other sources worth consulting are Benjamin B. Hampton, *History of the American Film Industry from Its Beginnings to 1931* (1970), Anne Edwards, *The DeMilles: An American Family* (1988), Norman J. Zierold, *The Moguls* (1969), and Jesse L. Lasky, Jr., *Whatever Happened to Hollywood* (1975).

DONNA M. PAANANEN

LASSER, Jacob Kay (7 Oct. 1896–11 May 1954), certified public accountant, was born in Newark, New Jersey, the son of Morris Lasser, a merchant, and Rebecca Traub. His parents had emigrated from Austria-Hungary during the 1880s. Lasser's early success was due in part to his academic achievements, which went far beyond the high school education that was the norm among contemporaries who began careers in public accounting in the 1920s. From 1915 to 1917 he studied accounting at New York University part-time while working as a factory bookkeeper. During World War I his training was temporarily interrupted by his induction into the navy, where he served as a crew member on a submarine chaser and later as a compliance verifier for government contracts. After the armistice he resumed his studies at Pennsylvania State University, receiving a bachelor's degree in mechanical engineering in 1920 and a master's degree in industrial engineering in 1923. While pursuing his engineering studies Lasser passed the certified public accountants' licensing examinations in New York and New Jersey in 1921. Later he also became certified in this profession in California and Illinois.

Lasser began his career in public accounting by joining the firm of Touche, Niven & Company (later Deloitte & Touche) in New York in 1921. This connection was fortuitous because it directed the young accountant's career toward specialization in tax consultancy. The firm had been formed in 1900 to serve as a correspondent of the Edinburgh-based chartered accounting firm of George Touche & Company. With the passage of federal income tax legislation in 1913, the head of the American unit, John Ballantyne Niven, a Scot trained in law and accounting, began to develop a strong capacity for tax consultancy as a means for achieving practice growth. In this environment the naturally studious Lasser developed such a strong proficiency in these matters that a rumor gained currency that he had memorized the Revenue Act of 1916.

However, Lasser temporarily left public accounting in 1922 to take a job as a tax consultant with United Publishing (later Chilton Company). The choice may have been conditioned by the limited opportunities for advancement among the leading public accounting firms in the 1920s, especially for a practitioner whose family was of recent immigrant origin. Although many in the business community had begun to appreciate the usefulness of professional accountancy, the demand for its services remained limited and this adversely affected the career opportunities for new entrants. Many firms engaged junior accountants on a seasonal basis, with layoffs after the crush of audit work was completed each spring. Thus, many like young Lasser remained in public accounting only long enough to qualify for a CPA license and to secure more permanent employment at a client business.

At United Publishing Lasser became involved in a tax case that shaped his career in important ways. The company was in litigation with the U.S. Internal Revenue Service arguing that tax assessments levied against it were discriminatory. In this inquiry Lasser developed such a strong competency in tax matters that he decided in 1924 to establish his own company, J. K. Lasser & Co., which soon attracted a substantial clientele from New York's publishing, printing, and allied industries. That year marked a second turning point when he married Terese Traub. They had two children.

Lasser's practice typified a new class of accounting entity emergent in the 1920s, the so-called regional firm. The success of these firms hinged on their ability to develop niche markets for professional accounting services. As was the case with Lasser's firm, the clients were generally small and medium sized businesses in a particular industry whose owner-managers lacked sophistication in finance. Moreover, since these clients had virtually no access to the nation's capital markets, they had little use for the auditing services that were the mainstay of the national public accounting firms, the elite of the profession who served the nation's largest business enterprises. Instead, regional firm clients were more apt to require expert guidance in taxation, budgeting, and other accounting-based services. Lastly, in an era when ascriptive concerns influenced hiring decisions, regional firms like Lasser's served as points of entry for practitioners whose social backgrounds might have otherwise limited their opportunity to pursue professional careers.

Lasser had written extensively on technical accounting topics since the 1920s. His career as an author on taxation, beginning in the following decade, made his name a household word and helped to strengthen the claim of certified public accountants to a significant role in tax practice. For many years the boundaries separating the special spheres of lawyers and accountants in tax practice remained poorly defined. As late as the 1950s, for example, attorneys had initiated legal action against accountants who provided tax services, arguing that the latter were essentially engaged in the unlicensed practice of law. Lasser, however, helped to establish a positive impression among the public of accountants' unique competency in these matters by stressing in his writings the computational and financial dimensions of tax compliance and planning. This aspect of Lasser's career began in 1938 when Leon Shimkin of Simon and Schuster persuaded him to write the popular *Your Income Taxes*. Written in a clear and accessible style, this annual publication made tax concepts and procedures clear to a lay audience. A similar approach was followed in a companion volume titled *Your Corporation Tax*, intended for the nonspecialist managers and proprietors of small businesses. A strong demand developed for these books as Americans tried to minimize their liabilities in the highly progressive tax structure introduced in World War II. Some measure of Lasser's impact is evinced by the fact that more than 13 million copies of his personal income tax book were sold during his career.

Lasser also contributed to the professionalization of tax accounting through his leadership in promoting specialized education. In the 1940s he became active in the formation of tax institutes for the advanced training of accountants and attorneys. In 1942 he helped to found the Institute of Federal Taxation at New York University. Additionally, he served as chairman for the tax schools established at the University of Miami (1946–1947) and at Pennsylvania State University (1947–1950). Besides these affiliations, Lasser was active from 1945 to 1951 as the president of the Tax Institute Inc., a nonprofit organization dedicated to tax and public finance research and education based in Princeton, New Jersey.

Concerns about the growing complexity of tax legislation on both the federal and state levels also induced Lasser to play a more active role in reform. In 1947 he served as a consultant to Governor Ernest W. Gibson of Vermont in a successful drive to simplify compliance procedures and the administration of that state's cumbersome income tax regime. Lasser promoted greater efficiency by reducing calculational complexity in tax liability measurement and by helping to define new state regulations that conformed closely with those of the federal government.

By the time he died of a heart attack in New York City, Lasser's writings, educational endeavors, and participation in reform had done much to solidify the position of accountants in tax practice. The process of winning general acceptance for the specialized skills of this profession in taxation, however, was not completed until after his death, when Congress passed in 1965 Public Law 89-332, which affirmed the right of certified public accountants to practice before the Internal Revenue Service. In addition to his contributions to the professionalization of tax accounting, Lasser was also an early pioneer in the formation of a regional practice. Later, in 1977, Lasser's firm was merged with Touche, Ross & Company (now Deloitte & Touche), the successor to the practice that had originally given him the opportunity to enter the accounting profession in 1921.

• Lasser was a prolific writer and editor with thirty-eight book titles on taxation and business topics to his credit as well as a substantial number of articles. In addition to his great annual compendia on personal and business income taxes, his main works include *Handbook of Accounting Methods* (1943); *Business Executive's Guide* (1945); *How to Speed Up Settlement of Your Terminated War Contract* (1945); *How Tax Law Makes Giving to Charity Easy* (1948); with Sylvia F. Porter, *How to Run a Small Business* (1950); *Estate Tax Handbook* (1951); *Handbook of Tax Accounting Methods* (1951); and *Business Management Handbook* (1952). Lasser served from 1943 to 1954 as the editor of the "Tax Clinic" in the *Journal of Accountancy*, a column created three decades earlier by his former boss, John B. Niven. Lasser reported about the results of the Vermont tax reforms in "Tax Simplification in Vermont," *National Tax Journal* 1 (1948): 62–66. An obituary is in the *New York Times*, 12 May 1954.

PAUL J. MIRANTI
LEONARD GOODMAN

LASSWELL, Harold Dwight (13 Feb. 1902–18 Dec. 1978), political scientist, was born in Donnellson, Illinois, the son of Linden Downey Lasswell, a Presbyte-

rian minister, and Anna Prather, a schoolteacher. Raised in an intellectual household, Lasswell was a precocious student who read the works of Sigmund Freud at the age of fourteen, graduated from the Decatur, Illinois, high school as valedictorian at the age of sixteen, and won a competitive scholarship in history to the University of Chicago. He received his bachelor's degree in philosophy and economics in 1922 and immediately became a graduate student and teaching assistant in the political science department at Chicago. Recipient of several Social Science Research Council fellowships, Lasswell studied at the universities of London, Geneva, and Berlin between 1923 and 1925. After receiving his Ph.D. in 1926, Lasswell became an assistant professor of political science at Chicago, where he remained until 1938.

Once referred to by the American Council of Learned Societies as "the Renaissance person" of American political science, Lasswell wrote more than thirty books, approximately 250 articles, more than 130 book reviews and forewords, and countless unpublished addresses and preliminary works on subjects as diverse as propaganda, empirical political philosophy, international relations, psychoanalysis, semantics, legal education, and the law of outer space. Lasswell's importance came largely from his ability to demonstrate the significance of such areas for a new, interpersonal, and interdisciplinary definition of political science. Rejecting the traditional institutional perspective, Lasswell argued that the proper subject of political science was the allocation of societal resources and the decision-making processes behind it. Lasswell's work was always concerned with questions about which people make the key decisions within a society and how they make them on the basis of what information. According to the title of one of his books, politics was the study of "who gets what, when, and how." The eventual goal of such study, often hidden behind Lasswell's technical vocabulary, was the betterment of the human condition through what he termed "preventive politics," the utilization of social science information and psychoanalytic perspectives as a means of alleviating rather than inflaming personal insecurities. To achieve this, he believed, social scientists required massive amounts of information and sophisticated models of analysis, which would allow successful prediction of future events.

Lasswell's interdisciplinary and contextual perspective reflected the orientation of University of Chicago social science during the 1920s and 1930s. The different departments worked closely together, and Lasswell was a favored student of such sociology faculty as Robert Park and George Herbert Mead. Charles Merriam, chairman of the political science department, who had worked as an Allied publicist in Italy during World War I, encouraged Lasswell to do research in political psychology. Frustrated by the lack of material and methodological sophistication on the subject in Europe as well as the United States, Lasswell turned to the specific study of war propaganda during World War I. In his dissertation, later published as *Propagan-*

da Technique in World War I (1927), he rejected the moralism of previous studies, arguing that propaganda in and of itself was no more moral or immoral "than an ax handle." Rather, he concentrated on the "how" of propaganda: which nations had used which techniques to what effect. Lasswell would return frequently to the subject, most notably in his work for the Office of War Information during World War II.

Lasswell's main interest, however, lay in individual rather than collective psychology, the question of how individuals make decisions. Unhappy with existing models, Lasswell turned to psychoanalysis as a way of comprehending individual behavior. Studying first with the eclectic psychiatrist Elton Mayo, Lasswell later traveled to Europe in 1928–1929 where he immersed himself in psychoanalytic studies and underwent analysis with Theodore Reik, one of Freud's closest disciples. Probably his most famous work, *Psychopathology and Politics* (1930), came out of this experience. Using an orthodox Freudian interpretation, Lasswell argued that all behavior is determined during the oral, anal, and phallic stages of development. In this work Lasswell defined politics as the process by which the irrational bases of society come out into the open. Individuals displace their frustrations and sexual energy onto politics in ways that have no connection with the original impulse. Such a perspective challenged conventional democratic thought; discussion, for example, might lead to increased rather than reduced tensions. In his classic paper "Psychology of Hitlerism" (*Political Quarterly* 4 [1933]: 373–84), Lasswell combined his insights into propaganda and individual psychology to note how German fascism fed on the frustrations and prejudices of the middle class.

Lasswell, however, did not always see politics as individual actions. While in Europe in 1928–1929, he had become influenced by Marxism and the elite analysis of Gaetano Mosca and Vilfredo Pareto as well as Freudianism. His next work *World Politics and Personal Insecurity* (1935), which many consider his most important, sought to demonstrate how competing elite groups use various techniques to appeal to human insecurities. Lasswell moderated the pessimism of such ideas by arguing that certain elites were more likely to share resources and democratic values than others. One such elite was the contemporary middle class and, in such works as the chapter "In Quest of Myth" in *World Politics* and his activist primer *Politics: Who Gets What, When, and How* (1936), Lasswell demonstrated techniques such as manipulation of myths which this group could use to achieve political power and forestall international conflict.

Lasswell left the University of Chicago in 1938 after a dispute with its president, Robert Hutchins, and spent the next eight years as a peripatetic scholar and government consultant dedicated to demonstrating how social scientists could aid policy makers. In this capacity he served a number of government agencies, and for several years he was associated with the Washington School of Psychiatry of Harry Stack Sullivan.

His most significant work was as director of the War Communications Research Division of the Library of Congress, where he demonstrated how content analysis could be used to track international and domestic propaganda. Linking this with his "world attention survey" first advocated in *World Politics*, Lasswell insisted on the need for an analysis of trends that would allow projection of policy alternatives for the future. As early as 1937, Lasswell suggested that the postwar world might be dominated by "garrison states" constantly prepared for war and dominated by military and business elites.

Lasswell hoped that lawyers might be the professional group to lead to increased world democratization and more evenly shared values. In 1943 he and Yale University professor of international law Myres McDougal published "Legal Education and Public Policy" (*Yale Law Journal* 52 [1943]: 203–95), which advocated the restructuring of law schools to produce professionals trained to develop humane public policy. Encouraged by McDougal, Lasswell became in 1946 a professor of law at Yale, where he would remain until 1972. As he began to formulate the emerging new field of policy sciences in such works as his and Daniel Lerner's *The Policy Sciences: Recent Developments in Scope and Method* (1951), Lasswell recognized the need to specify the values and goals cherished by individuals in all cultures. At first, Lasswell split these into classifications of income, deference, and safety but later suggested a more detailed categorization into power, wealth, enlightenment, well-being, respect, skill, affection, and rectitude. In 1950 Lasswell and the philosopher Abraham Kaplan sought in *Power and Society* to codify his conceptual structure for the study of politics.

While Lasswell remained active for close to thirty more years, his influence was exerted increasingly through former students from his Chicago and Washington years, such as Gabriel Almond, Karl Deutsch, Heinz Eulau, Nathan Leites, Ithiel de Sola Pool, Arnold Rogow, and Bruce Smith. American law schools, and Yale Law School in particular, did not follow Lasswell and McDougal's ideas for legal education and continued to turn out individuals trained to win court cases. An individual who enjoyed collaborative projects all his life, Lasswell worked with McDougal on projects in international law and a proposed law of outer space, and with Lerner on *Comparative Study of Elites* (1952) and *World Revolutionary Elites* (1965). He also actively proselytized for the policy sciences and predictive science of future trends. From 1971 to 1976 he served as Distinguished Professor of Law at the John Jay School of Criminal Justice. Afterward he continued to write and lecture until his death from a stroke in New York City. During his lifetime, he received many awards and honors, including the presidencies of the American Political Science Association (1956) and the American Society of International Law (1970–1972) and membership in the National Academy of Science and the American Academy of Arts and Sciences.

• An intensely private individual, Lasswell left no personal papers. The best biographical studies are Bruce Lannes Smith, "The Mystifying Intellectual History of Harold D. Lasswell," and Leo Rosten, "A Memoir," in *Politics, Personality and Social Science in the Twentieth Century: Essays in Honor of Harold D. Lasswell*, ed. Arnold Rogow (1969), pp. 41–106 and 1–14, and Duane Marvick's introduction to his edited collection *Harold D. Lasswell on Political Sociology* (1977), pp. 1–71. Also useful for glimpses of the private Lasswell were presentations by colleagues, friends, and students at two memorial services, *Harold Dwight Lasswell: Statements Made or Prepared for Memorial Services at Yale University and New York Academy of Sciences* (1980). The most insightful assessments of Lasswell's thought include David Easton, "Policy Scientist for a Democratic Society," *Journal of Politics* 12(1950): 450–77, and Heinz Eulau, "Elite Analysis and Democratic Theory: The Contributions of Harold D. Lasswell," *Elite Recruitment in Democratic Politics*, ed. Eulau and Moshe M. Czudnowski (1976), pp. 7–26. Derek McDougall, *Harold D. Lasswell and the Study of International Relations* (1984), explores Lasswell's contribution to that field, while Mark C. Smith, *Social Science in the Crucible: The American Debate over Objectivity and Purpose, 1918–1941* (1994), examines Lasswell's pre–World War II career in relation to his attempt to merge the scientific method with his commitment to normative social science. Barry Karl, *Charles E. Merriam and the Study of Politics* (1974); Martin Bulmer, *The Chicago School of Sociology: Institutionalization, Diversity and the Rise of Sociological Research* (1984); and Lasswell's "The Cross-Disciplinary Manifold: The Chicago Prototype," in *The Search for World Order*, ed. Albert Lepawsky et al. (1971), pp. 416–28, depict Lasswell's intellectual environment of University of Chicago political and social science during the 1920s and 1930s.

MARK C. SMITH

LATHBURY, Mary Artemisia (10 Aug. 1841–20 Oct. 1913), author and illustrator, was born in Manchester, New York, the daughter of English immigrants John Lathbury, a builder and Methodist local preacher, and Betsey Shepherd Jones. While attending school in Manchester, she began sketching pictures and composing stories and poems. At eighteen she went to Worcester, Massachusetts, to spend a year at the School of Design and Academy of Fine Arts. There she was instructed by Elizabeth Gardner (later Bouguereau), who had studied art in Paris. Lathbury then taught drawing, painting, and French at the Methodist seminary in Newbury, Vermont, Fort Edward Institute in Fort Edward, New York, and Drew Ladies' Seminary in Carmel, New York.

She moved to New York City in 1874 after John Heyl Vincent, then secretary of the Methodist Episcopal Sunday School and a leader in the movement for uniform lessons, named her assistant editor of the *Picture-Lesson Paper*, *Classmate*, and *Sunday-School Advocate*. Her verses, stories, and illustrations appeared regularly in these and other specifically religious papers. In the 1870s and 1880s she also contributed to leading juvenile periodicals: the *Youth's Companion*, *Harper's Young People*, *Wide Awake*, and *St. Nicholas*. Her work had wide appeal because it reflected her belief that "a little pure and harmless food for the imagination, and for the fostering of the love of beauty[,] is

quite in the Lord's way of doing with His children" (letter of 3 Dec. 1896 to Amos R. Wells).

Her first book, *Fleda and the Voice* (1876), was a collection of allegorical fairy tales with her own drawings previously published under the pen name "Aunt May." Lathbury's pictures in pen-and-ink and water-color enhanced most of her other collections of verses and stories for children: *Seven Little Maids*, issued also as *The Birthday Week* (1884); *Ring-Around-a-Rosy* (1885); *Idyls of the Months* (1885); *Twelve Times One* (1885); *From Meadow-Sweet to Mistletoe* (1886); *April Skies* (1889); *Bible Heroes* (1898); and *Child's Life of Christ* (1898). *Out of Darkness into Light* (1878), a series of poems cast in the meter of Alfred Tennyson's "In Memoriam" and accompanied by Lathbury's illustrations, narrates a spiritual quest. This book was intended for a mature audience.

She sold illustrations to Harper's, the Century Company, and religious publishers, voluntarily accepting lower pay from the latter. She illustrated *Children of the Year* (1885), a collection of poems by various authors, and furnished pictures of verses for other projects, including books by younger brothers Clarence Lathbury and Albert Lathbury, both clergymen. Some of her drawings of faces were reproduced for framing. Her elegy for Lucy Webb Hayes, a leader in the Woman's Home Missionary Society of the Methodist Episcopal church, was included in an 1890 volume in memory of the former first lady. An assistant editor of Frances E. Willard's *Woman and Temperance* (1883), Lathbury contributed a prose sketch of Willard, leader of the Woman's Christian Temperance Union, that enunciated her own vision of progress and conviction that women do God's work in the world. She endorsed Willard's argument that human development is retarded when women are "dwarfed in the training." She idealized Willard as "a representative, on a spiritual plane, of the new age upon which we are entering" and as "one of the types of the larger and diviner womanhood which our land shall yet produce" (*Woman and Temperance*, pp. 19, 36, 38).

Unmarried, Lathbury formed long-lived relationships grounded in shared commitments and interests. For some time she lived and shared a studio in New York City with her sister, a fellow artist and writer. In correspondence with Amos R. Wells, editor of the *Christian Endeavor World*, she called a nephew her "adopted son," promoted his skill as a journalist, and stated that a niece seemed "almost my own, for I have had to take the place of a father" (letter of 15 July 1899). She was further involved in Christian education through interaction with John Heyl Vincent, who founded Chautauqua to train Sunday school teachers. The movement's campground in southwestern New York became a center for teacher training, general education, and entertainment. She wrote several "carols" that were regularly sung at Chautauqua assemblies. Best known were "Day Is Dying in the West" and "Break Thou the Bread of Life," both written in 1877 at Vincent's request and set to tunes by William F. Sherwin, Chautauqua's first music director. By the late nineteenth century, lyrics by Lathbury were incorporated in hymnals of many denominations.

Lathbury nurtured responsible citizenship and public service as well as piety. In 1874 she proposed the Look-Up Legion, a club for Sunday school youth. Devoted to the principles of kindness and temperance, the legion spread through Sunday schools and Chautauqua meetings, eventually numbering more than 6,000 members. She collaborated with clergyman-journalist Edward Everett Hale in organizing his Ten Times One Clubs, young people's organizations that stressed personal salvation and public spirit. For many years she served as superintendent of a Chinese Sunday school in New York City. A member of the Woman's Christian Temperance Union, she also supported Methodist women's domestic missionary work.

Without alienating her evangelical friends, Lathbury joined the New Church in East Orange, New Jersey, in 1890. This denomination, known also as the Church of the New Jerusalem, was founded by followers of Emanuel Swedenborg. Swedenborgians, a highly literate group, stressed the importance of the printed word—primarily the Bible—and generally discountenanced sectarianism and dogma. After two years of invalidism, Lathbury died at her home in East Orange. In his preface to the posthumous *Poems of Mary Artemisia Lathbury, Chautauqua Laureate* (1915), compiled by her brother Clarence, Bishop Vincent called her "a gifted, self-forgetting, devout spirit" (p. 11). Such terms recur in assessments by her associates.

Lathbury's poems were admired in her time; she was urged to collect them. John Greenleaf Whittier praised *Out of Darkness into Light*, and Edward Everett Hale predicted that her lyrics would be famous for two centuries. Her name remains familiar to hymnologists, and her most popular hymns are still sung. Although her illustrations and children's literature no longer attract attention, she merits recognition for her career as an artist. According to a contemporary, she "share[d] with Mary Hallock Foote the honors of being a [woman] pioneer in the field of book and magazine illustration" (Beede, p. 36). At a time when few American women had access to professional instruction, she managed to support herself, help her family, and work for social reform.

• Twenty-five of Lathbury's letters written in 1896–1899 to Amos R. Wells are in the James O'Neill Collection, University of California, San Diego. The most detailed biography was written by her nephew, Vincent Van Marter Beede: "Mary A. Lathbury: Her Life and Lyrics," *Chautauquan*, Oct. 1899, pp. 35–40. The posthumous *Poems* (1915) contains tributes by her friends John H. Vincent and Frances E. Willard. Willard's *Glimpses of Fifty Years* (1889) includes a sketch of Lathbury. See also Charles S. Robinson, *Annotations upon Popular Hymns* (1893). For information on Lathbury's formal education, consult "American Schools and Colleges for Young Ladies," *Godey's Lady's Book*, Feb. 1859, pp. 176–77, and "Places of Education for Young Ladies," *Godey's Lady's Book*, Sept. 1859, p. 274. An obituary appears in the *New York Tribune*, 22 Oct. 1913.

MARY DE JONG

LATHROP, Francis Augustus (22 Jun. 1849–18 Oct. 1909), artist and decorator, was born at sea two days' sail from the Sandwich Islands, the son of George Alfred Lathrop, a physician, and Frances M. Smith. When Francis was born the Lathrops were heading to Hawaii, where Dr. Lathrop, later a U.S. consul to Honolulu, became administrator of the Marine Hospital. In 1858 the family moved back to the mainland, settling in New York. Francis subsequently attended Columbia Grammar School, and in 1863 he began studying with the American Pre-Raphaelite painter Thomas Charles Farrer.

Lathrop traveled to Dresden in 1867 with his mother and brother, George Parsons Lathrop. He attended the Royal Academy of Fine Arts until, following the advice of painter James Abbott McNeill Whistler, he moved to London in 1870. Lathrop's interest in Pre-Raphaelite painting led him to study under Ford Madox Brown. He also worked in the decorative firm headed by William Morris, the catalyst of the English Arts and Crafts movement. Lathrop became an assistant for J. Roddam Spencer-Stanhope and Edward Burne-Jones, the latter instructing him in English methods of stained-glass design.

Lathrop moved back to New York in 1873. He enjoyed success with a variety of artistic projects, including portraiture, home decoration, and the illustration of books. His interesting vignettes and full-page plates for Clarence Cook's *The House Beautiful* (1878) are competently executed in the current realistic manner. One of the most fortunate episodes of Lathrop's career was his association with the American artist John La Farge, which began during the summer of 1876, when La Farge received a commission from the renowned architect Henry Hobson Richardson to mastermind the interior decoration of the new Trinity Church on Copley Square in Boston. Lathrop was one of La Farge's primary assistants, along with the young Augustus Saint-Gaudens and Will Hicok Low. Several mural lunettes after designs by La Farge are ascribed to Lathrop's hand. He also prepared unexecuted designs for the chancel.

The interior of Trinity Church made La Farge famous and helped Lathrop to emerge as a decorative artist in his own right. During the winter of 1877–1878 Lathrop painted *Moses with the Tablets of the Law* for the Bowdoin College Chapel in Brunswick, Maine. From 1880 to 1883 he assisted La Farge with murals for the Watercolor Room of the mansion of Cornelius Vanderbilt II on the corner of Fifth Avenue and West Fifty-seventh Street in New York. Lathrop soon thereafter found himself the beneficiary of La Farge's misfortune. Vanderbilt and La Farge argued bitterly over delays and cost overruns, leaving Lathrop as the logical choice for decorator during a major expansion of the house in 1892. Lathrop not only provided new glass and painted decorations, but he also reworked those done by La Farge. Lathrop combined two massive glass ceilings from La Farge's original scheme into a new skylight that remains a focal point of the staircase in "The Breakers," Vanderbilt's "cottage" in Newport, Rhode Island.

Lathrop's other decorative work in New York included a mural of Apollo over the proscenium of the old Metropolitan Opera House on Broadway at Thirty-ninth Street (1883; destroyed by fire in August 1892); murals executed in conjunction with Elihu Vedder for the now-razed Fifth Avenue mansion of Collis Potter Huntington (1884); and a marble mosaic of *Widows and Orphans* for the old Equitable Life Insurance Company in New York (1887). Still extant is *The Light of the World*, located in the chancel of St. Bartholomew's Episcopal Church on Madison Avenue at Forty-fourth Street. Completed in 1898, the work is one of the largest murals of the period. With more than 150 figures, it took over five years to paint and cost $65,000.

Lathrop also executed murals and windows in churches, theaters, and residences in Albany, Baltimore, Boston, and other eastern cities. For the William Earl Dodge Memorial Window in the Marquand Chapel at Princeton University, he received a gold medal at an exhibition of decorative art in Philadelphia in 1889 (the window and chapel were destroyed by fire in 1920). Another much-admired window depicts the biblical story of the angel stirring the waters of the pool of Bethesda and is in the chancel of Bethesda Church in Saratoga, New York.

Lathrop was a founding member of the Society of American Artists in 1878, and he served as its secretary in 1879 and its treasurer in 1881. He also belonged to the Architectural League of New York, the Municipal Art Society, the Society of Mural Painters, and the American Institute of Arts and Letters. Three years before his death, Lathrop was elected an associate academician of the National Academy of Design. He also patronized many exclusive clubs, including the Sons of the Revolution, the Players' Club, the Grolier Club, the Calumet Club, and the Century Association. In addition to his gold medal for the Dodge Memorial Window, Lathrop received a silver medal for decorative work contributed in 1901 to the Pan-American Exposition held in Buffalo, New York.

Lathrop never married. He lived most of his adult life at 29 Washington Square, in the artistic heart of New York. In 1907 he suffered the first of several paralytic strokes that forced him to move a year later into the home of a cousin in Woodcliffe Lake, New Jersey, where he died.

The catalog of Lathrop's estate sale of French, English, old master, and Japanese paintings featured a preface by the Brooklyn patron and art collector Hamilton Easter Field. He noted that Lathrop "was one of the rare artists whose appreciation of art was in no way confined to any school nor method of work. His broad taste was a constant source of inspiration and encouragement to his young friends. . . . Lathrop was singularly fortunate in his friendships, having been intimate with most of the prominent painters and authors of his day." Lathrop's importance resides less in his individual works than in his collaborative spirit. His embrace of Arts and Crafts principles and techniques made him an ideal participant in the Aesthetic Movement that swept the United States during the last quarter of the nineteenth century.

• Lathrop's papers, if they survive, have not been located. The New-York Historical Society holds the George Browne Post Papers, containing references to Lathrop's work on the house of Cornelius Vanderbilt II. There is also one autograph letter in the Titus Munson Coan Collection at the same institution. The Preservation Society of Newport County has some minor original documentation pertaining to Lathrop's role at "The Breakers." Writings about Lathrop are scarce. Entries in the *Appleton's Cyclopaedia of American Biography* (1898), the *National Cyclopaedia of American Biography* (1926), the *Dictionary of American Biography* (1934), and Wheeler Preston's *American Biographies* (1940) are the primary published records of his activities. The only substantive assessment of Lathrop's overall character and artistic temperament is the preface by Hamilton Easter Field to the Lathrop estate catalog (Anderson Auction Company, New York, 4–6 Apr. 1911). Obituaries are in the *New York Herald*, 19 Oct. 1909, and in the *New York Times*, 19 and 21 Oct. 1909.

JAMES L. YARNALL

LATHROP, George Parsons (25 Aug. 1851–19 Apr. 1898), author, was born near Honolulu, Oahu, Hawaiian Islands, the son of George A. Lathrop, a physician, and Frances Smith. George A. Lathrop served as U.S. consul in the Hawaiian Islands for much of President Franklin Pierce's term. George Parsons Lathrop was educated in Honolulu until 1859, and thereafter in New York City schools and in Dresden, Germany, where his elder brother, Francis Lathrop, pursued his art career. He returned to New York City in 1870 and studied at Columbia Law School for one year, until 1871. He then worked briefly in a law office but gave that up to pursue a writing career.

In 1868 or 1869, while in Dresden, Lathrop had met Rose Hawthorne, the daughter of author Nathaniel Hawthorne. The Lathrop and the Hawthorne families were active in the Dresden expatriate community. George and Rose married in 1871 in England, where George had come at the request of Rose's brother, Julian Hawthorne, to assist Rose and her sister, Una Hawthorne, after the death of their mother in March. Lathrop's association with the Hawthornes undoubtedly helped him greatly in his literary career, but the joys of being part of this family were mixed with travail.

Lathrop published an article on Nathaniel Hawthorne in the *Atlantic Monthly* in October 1872 and his first book of poems, *Rose and Roof-tree*, in 1875. Later that year he became an associate editor of the *Atlantic* under William Dean Howells. In 1876 he published *A Study of Hawthorne* with Ticknor, Fields and Osgood, a firm directed by three men who had been associated with Nathaniel Hawthorne in other publishing ventures.

The Lathrops' only child was born in November 1876, but shortly afterward Rose entered the McLean Asylum for the Insane, suffering from what we might call today postpartum psychosis. Rose returned home early in 1877, but in the meantime Una Hawthorne's fiancé had died, and Una herself died in September. Then George quarreled with William Dean Howells and resigned from his position with the *Atlantic* on 1 September. Later in 1877 Lathrop became editor of the *Boston Courier*. His writing career continued, with poems in *Galaxy* and one novel, *Afterglow*, in 1877 and two more books in 1878. In the spring of 1879 he and Rose purchased The Wayside, the home her parents had acquired in 1852 and her mother had sold in 1870. Then, early in 1881, their child died of diphtheria.

The marital life of the Lathrops thereafter was marked by separations, for short periods at first, then longer in 1883, and most irrevocably early in 1895, when Rose traveled to Jamaica, ostensibly to see Julian and his family, and began a retreat with the Grey Nuns, in preparation for what she believed would be a useful career in religious service. Both she and George had converted to Catholicism in 1891, in an event well reported in the nation's press. Though his achievements as a Catholic layman did not begin to rival those of Rose, he helped to establish the Catholic Summer School of America in New London, Connecticut, in 1892 and edited, with Rose, *A Story of Courage: Annals of the Georgetown Convent of the Visitation of the Blessed Virgin Mary* (1893).

George's distinguished work as an author must not be overshadowed by the record of his and Rose's marital misfortunes, including their perpetual financial insolvency and George's ill health, bruited at times as alcoholism and reported mostly as "acute gastric distress." He was a talented writer and assumed the lead in the Hawthorne family at the task of utilizing properly its legacy of Hawthorne book contracts, an important source of revenue for all of Nathaniel's survivors.

Lathrop published his first article on Hawthorne when he was only twenty-one, barely a year after his marriage to Rose, and brought out *A Study of Hawthorne* four years later, weathering a public protest from Julian over his use of family documents. Henry James acknowledged his debt to Lathrop's biography in the preparation of his own biography of Hawthorne, though he was not completely satisfied with either his or Lathrop's work.

In 1883 Lathrop brought out the first Riverside Edition of the *Complete Works of Nathaniel Hawthorne*, for which he wrote introductory notes to many volumes and added a biography of over 100 pages. The Riverside Edition remained the principal collection of that author's work until the Ohio State University began publishing its Centenary Edition in the 1960s. Lathrop also produced a number of novels and books of short fiction and poems of his own.

In 1883 Lathrop helped to organize the American Copyright League and became its secretary. In 1894 he produced a poetic text titled *The Scarlet Letter* for a musical composition by Walter Damrosch. They carried that achievement further with a successful opera based on it in 1896. Lathrop was an author of great gifts, a sensitive critic, and a noted personage in the

New York, Connecticut, and Massachusetts societies he frequented. He died in New York City.

• Lathrop's life is discussed in greatest detail in Rose Valenti, *To Myself a Stranger: A Biography of Rose Hawthorne Lathrop* (1991). John L. Idol and Sterling Eisiminger give details on the Lathrop-Damrosch opera in "*The Scarlet Letter* as Opera: The First Settings," *Nathaniel Hawthorne Review* 2 (Fall 1993): 11–16. Earlier studies include Josephine J. Fay (Sister Francis Michael), *George Parsons Lathrop: A Nineteenth Century Critic* (M.A. thesis, St. John's Univ., 1945), and Marie Harte Stafford, *The Literary Theories and Practice of George Parsons Lathrop* (M.A. thesis, George Washington Univ., 1958).

ALFRED H. MARKS

LATHROP, John Howland (6 June 1880–20 Aug. 1967), Unitarian minister and peace advocate, was born in Jackson, Michigan, the son of Arthur D. Lathrop, a banker, and Alice McDora Osborne. At seventeen Lathrop started a two-year stint in a wholesale grocery house in Cleveland, Ohio, where he attended alternately the congregation of Moses J. Gries, a celebrated Reform rabbi, and the Unitarian church of Marion E. Murdoch, the first woman to receive a B.D. degree from Meadville Theological School in Pennsylvania (relocated to Chicago in 1926). Following in Murdoch's footsteps, Lathrop attended Meadville, graduating in 1903. Moving on to Harvard University, where he started as a junior, Lathrop was profoundly influenced by the philosopher William James, met Florence Kelley, a social reformer with whom he later worked in the Consumers' League, of which she was a long-time secretary, and became involved in the peace movement with Fannie Fern Andrews, a pacifist eminent in international relations.

From 1905 to 1911 Lathrop was the minister of the First Unitarian Church of Berkeley, California, and in 1906 he coordinated relief efforts for the 20,000 refugees of the San Francisco Earthquake. On 15 October 1907 he married Lita Schlesinger. They had three children, one of whom died in infancy. From 1911 to 1957 Lathrop was the minister of the First Unitarian Church of Brooklyn, whose public-spirited congregation included the noted housing reformer Alfred T. White.

Balancing "respectability and rebellion" and matching "appreciation of the past" with "resolution for the future," Lathrop was an ideal reformer (Hoogenboom, p. 319). He helped draft the law against racial discrimination in employment, enacted in 1945, making New York the pioneer state in this legislation, and, as a member of the state Tenement House Commission, he convinced Mayor Fiorello La Guardia to sponsor housing in the Fort Greene section of Brooklyn. For many years Lathrop was president of the Brooklyn Urban League, which grew out of a 1916 meeting in his study and, like the national organization, focused on economic and social problems facing migrant blacks. He was the first president of the Brooklyn Council on Social Planning, and, as the president of the Brooklyn Health Council, he improved the lighting in Brooklyn public schools. He was also president of the National Consumers League and of the Euthanasia Society of America.

Lathrop worked to make his church's 1844 Gothic-revival building, designed by Minard Lafever, a "nobler temple of the liberal faith" (Hoogenboom, p. 244). In 1928 he and his congregation completed the Side Aisle Chapel of All Faiths. Inspired by Ralph Waldo Emerson and looking to all the world's religions, this chapel was called the first chapel of all faiths in the nation. Lathrop's second project, to make his congregation's building more Unitarian, traced liberal religion with twenty portrait clerestory windows, including pictures of the Bohemian reformer Jan Hus, the Spanish martyr of liberal theology Michael Servetus, and Ralph Waldo Emerson.

Molding his Brooklyn church in his own liberal and avant-garde image, Lathrop procured counseling services for his parishioners in 1930, when these services had few precedents in the United States. With the help of Beatrice Bishop Berle, who had worked in the psychiatric departments of Cornell Clinic and the Austen Riggs Foundation, he started premarital counseling and a parents' discussion group. The next year Berle was joined at the First Church by Horatio W. Dresser, who had studied with psychoanalytical pioneers Carl Jung and Alfred Adler. Through the Clinic of Religion and Medicine (whose name was later changed to Associated Counseling Service), Dresser counseled Brooklynites until 1953. His Brooklyn clinic combined, for the first time, religion, psychology, and medicine in a unified treatment.

Much of Lathrop's involvement in international affairs was in behalf of world peace and religious freedom. He was president of the National Peace Conference—formed by forty-five national peace organizations—and even though the Federal Council of the Churches of Christ would not accept Unitarians as members, he worked with his cousin John Foster Dulles on its Committee for a Just and Durable Peace. Lathrop's opposition to World War I had placed him at odds with most of his church's trustees. But once the United States had entered the war, he had thrust himself into service, primarily through the Red Cross, which he introduced into the navy—previously the Navy League had excluded the army-oriented Red Cross. Becoming the director of the Bureau of Naval Affairs of the Atlantic Division of the American Red Cross, Lathrop built up sixty Red Cross stations in the Third Naval District and for the duration of the war wore a naval uniform, even while preaching.

Lathrop's work for peace and his leadership of international organizations took him to Europe regularly after World War I. He was president of the International Association for Liberal Christianity and Religious Freedom (IARF) and the American Committee for Religious Rights and Minorities. When in Geneva for the first session of the League of Nations, he sat between Czech statesmen Jan Masaryk and Eduard Beneš at a birthday anniversary luncheon for Jane Addams. Because Masaryk's mother, Charlotte Garrigue, and her family had been part of Brooklyn's First Unitarian Church, Lathrop had a particular interest in and affection for Czechoslovakia. These ties were strengthened in 1927, when he visited that country while heading a five-member commission to report on the treatment of religious minorities in Rumania. Appalled at the growing anti-Semitism that was sweeping Europe, he alerted his countrymen by giving fifty talks on that subject when he returned to the United States.

In 1928–1929 John and Lita Lathrop represented the American Unitarian Association at the centenary celebration of the Brahmo Samaj, a liberal Hindu society. While in India Lathrop embraced the country's new independence and adopted a Brahmo Samaj congregation of outcasts in Alleppey for his Brooklyn congregation to support. In 1934, after attending the IARF convention in Denmark, the Lathrops journeyed by train to the Soviet Union to observe the communist experiment firsthand. While in Moscow, they were the luncheon guests of Ambassador William Bullitt, whom they found outspokenly hostile to the Soviet regime when servants were not in the room.

In 1946 Lathrop spent six months in Czechoslovakia directing a relief project, which gave rise to the Unitarian Service Committee. Part of his many-sided job was to oversee a medical mission headed by Dr. Paul Dudley White of Harvard, which updated Czechoslovak doctors on the medical progress they had missed while under German occupation. Accompanying her husband on his mission, Lita Lathrop established a model orphanage to show what could be done for the million destitute children dumped in Czechoslovakia during World War II. For their relief work, both Lathrops were presented the Czechoslovak Order of the White Lion.

Through 1949 Lathrop made annual visits to Czechoslovakia, and he continued to work for world peace even in his retirement. "No world interests me so much as this world with all of its problems," he reiterated before his death in Berkeley. His only regret, Lathrop insisted, was that he could not live "to see the gradual lines along which those problems are to be solved" (Hoogenboom, p. 318).

• Lathrop's papers are in the First Unitarian Church Collection, Brooklyn Historical Society, Brooklyn, N.Y. See also "The Reminiscences of John Howland Lathrop," Columbia University Oral History Project (1952), and Olive Hoogenboom, *The First Unitarian Church of Brooklyn: One Hundred Fifty Years* (1987). An obituary is in the *New York Times*, 23 Aug. 1967.

OLIVE HOOGENBOOM

LATHROP, Julia Clifford (29 June 1858–15 Apr. 1932), social reformer, was born in Rockford, Illinois, the daughter of William Lathrop, an attorney, and Sarah Adeline Potter. After high school Lathrop attended Rockford Seminary for one year and then went to Vassar College. Returning home after her graduation in 1880, she worked as a secretary in her father's office, spent some time reading law, made several profitable investments, and supported various reform causes, including women's rights.

Lathrop's move to Chicago in 1890 opened a new chapter in her life. Her destination was Hull-House, a settlement that had recently been established in a tenement district by two fellow Rockford alumnae, Jane Addams and Ellen Starr. Following the settlement ideal, Lathrop divided her time between working personally with her immigrant neighbors and pursuing institutional reforms that would improve their lives. During the depression of 1893–1894, for instance, she volunteered to help the county welfare department interview neighborhood families who had applied for public assistance; she then documented the flaws she found in the welfare system in *Hull-House Maps and Papers* (1895). She organized a weekly discussion group called the Plato Club, which met at Hull-House for many years, and in 1908 she helped found the Illinois Immigrants' Protective League, on whose board she served until her death. In 1909 she again combined direct service with broader reform when she cared for the victims of a mining disaster and then used her experience to spark a state investigation of hazardous occupations.

Appointed to the state Board of Charities by reform governor John P. Altgeld in 1893, Lathrop began investigating Illinois' approximately 100 institutions. After visiting the facilities, reviewing their records, and talking with their employees and patients, she made two trips to Europe (1898 and 1900) to study new treatment approaches. She became convinced that instead of gathering all dependent persons—the delinquent, the blind, the mentally ill—under one roof, different kinds of institutions should be established for each group. She also advocated careful selection of facility staff. In 1901, when Altgeld's successor ignored civil service rules, Lathrop resigned in protest. She was reappointed four years later and served until 1909, when the board was reorganized—in accordance with her recommendations—as a nonpartisan body with direct line authority. Lathrop welcomed the emerging mental hygiene movement with its advocacy of more enlightened treatment, and she served on the board of the National Committee for Mental Hygiene.

Addressing the needs of another vulnerable group, Lathrop worked with other women reformers to win passage of a law in 1899 establishing America's first juvenile court. She helped organize a committee that paid the salaries of the court's first probation officers, ran a detention home until the county took it over, and later helped establish a psychiatric clinic in the court.

In 1903 Lathrop helped reformer Graham Taylor organize a series of courses for caregivers. These soon evolved into the Chicago School of Civics and Philanthropy, the second school of social work to be established in the country. Lathrop lectured at the school, organized its pioneering occupational therapy training for mental health staff, established its research depart-

ment in 1907, and served on the board until the school was taken over by the University of Chicago in 1920.

During a world tour with her sister in 1910–1911, Lathrop wrote a report on public schools in the Philippines. Having seen her report and learned of her background, President William Howard Taft appointed Lathrop head of the new U.S. Children's Bureau, part of the Department of Commerce and Labor. This made her the first female bureau chief to be nominated by the president and confirmed by the Senate. Lathrop chose as her first project a study of infant mortality. Because no consistent national data were available, she concentrated on ten industrial cities and then broadened the investigation to include rural communities in twelve states. Concerned by the high death rates revealed, she developed an extensive program to educate mothers about infant care, including a series of popularly written pamphlets that found a wide audience. Simultaneously, the bureau launched a successful campaign to establish birth registration procedures throughout the country.

The bureau's work gradually expanded to include studies of maternal mortality, nutrition, juvenile delinquency, illegitimacy, mental retardation, and mothers' pensions. Two national child labor laws were passed (1916 and 1918), both of which were to be enforced by the bureau. Although each was soon declared unconstitutional, Lathrop and her staff continued to study child labor and to advocate passage of a constitutional amendment.

As more consistent data on births and deaths became available, the bureau was able to show that five other countries were doing better than the United States in terms of infant mortality, that America had the highest rate of maternal mortality of any country that kept such statistics, and that American death rates varied dramatically by social and economic status. Acknowledging the limits of maternal education, Lathrop launched a more ambitious crusade: to establish public medical programs for mothers and infants. During World War I the bureau pressed for government services to soldiers' families, and in May 1919 it organized a national conference on child welfare standards. Finally, in 1921 the bureau won passage of the Sheppard-Towner Act, providing federal funds to the states to establish clinics for mothers and babies.

Lathrop retired from the bureau in 1921 because of a thyroid condition, after ensuring that she would be succeeded by her assistant, Grace Abbott, another Hull-House veteran. Living in Rockford with her sister, Lathrop saw a number of her earlier victories undone; the Sheppard-Towner Act was allowed to lapse after five years, and the constitutional amendment prohibiting child labor, though passed by Congress, failed to win ratification by the states. Moreover, right-wing groups attacked her—along with many other reform leaders—for allegedly converting a whole range of progressive institutions to socialism. Nevertheless, Lathrop continued her public life, serving as president of the Illinois League of Women Voters (1922–1924), member of a presidential commission to investigate overcrowding at Ellis Island, and assessor on the Child Welfare Committee of the League of Nations (1925–1930). She died in Rockford after spending the last months of her life fighting for the reprieve of a local boy who was awaiting execution for murder.

Lathrop displayed a remarkable empathy for individuals, combined with a pragmatic zest for the bureaucratic infighting necessary to achieve administrative and legislative reform. "You felt she enjoyed the game," wrote a colleague, "without losing sight for one moment of the big end she had in view." Lathrop never married; her work was her life. Her appearance was austere, but her warmth and humor captivated those who knew her. Indeed, one of her legacies is the example of her career—proof that the life of a single woman dedicated to social service could be not only productive but lively and satisfying. Beyond that, there is the continuing importance of the many institutions that Lathrop helped to establish, including juvenile courts, the field of occupational therapy, the U.S. Children's Bureau, the University of Chicago School of Social Work, and the national system of birth registration. Finally, there is the broader vision she articulated that still remains to be achieved: an America in which even the most vulnerable members of society have an equal chance for life and happiness.

• Lathrop's papers are at Rockford College, Rockford, Ill. Correspondence with her can be found in the papers of Ethel Dummer and Miriam Van Waters, Radcliffe College; Jane Addams, Swarthmore College; League of Women Voters, Library of Congress; Grace and Edith Abbott, University of Chicago; National Federation of Settlements and Neighborhood Centers, Social Welfare History Archives, University of Minnesota, Minneapolis; Adena Miller Rich and Evelina Belden Paulson, University of Illinois, Chicago; and Nicholas Kelley, New York Public Library. Her published works include *Suggestions for Visitors to County Poorhouses and to Other Public Charitable Institutions* (1905); "The Background of the Juvenile Court in Illinois," in *The Child, the Clinic and the Court: A Group of Papers* (1927); and selections in *Hull-House Maps and Papers* (1895). Jane Addams's *My Friend, Julia Lathrop* (1935) is part of an incomplete biography planned by Addams and Grace Abbott. Most accounts of social reform during the Progressive Era discuss Lathrop's career; see, among others, Ray Ginger, *Altgeld's America* (1958); James A. Tobey, *The Children's Bureau: Its History, Activities and Organization* (1925); Robert H. Bremner, ed., *Children and Youth in America: A Documentary History*, vol. 2 (1971); Allen F. Davis, *American Heroine: The Life and Legend of Jane Addams* (1973); Mary Bryan et al., *100 Years at Hull-House* (1990); "Julia Lathrop and the Public Social Services," *Social Service Review* 6 (June 1932): 301–6; "Twenty Years of the Children's Bureau," *Social Service Review* 6 (Mar. 1932): 140–44; and William Chenery, "A Great Public Servant," *Survey* 46 (1 Sept. 1921): 637–38. An obituary is in the *New York Times*, 16 Apr. 1932.

SANDRA OPDYCKE

LATHROP, Rose Hawthorne (20 May 1851–9 July 1926), writer and founder (as Mother Alphonsa) of the Servants of Relief for Incurable Cancer, was born in Lenox, Massachusetts, the daughter of Nathaniel Hawthorne, a famous novelist, and Sophia Peabody, a painter and sculptor. Most of Rose's childhood was spent in England, where her father had been appointed as consul to Liverpool in 1853. Growing up in a household given to the arts, while she was in England she attended the Kensington Art School. After her father resigned his diplomatic post in 1857, the family traveled on the Continent and spent a final year in England before returning to the United States in 1860. In Massachusetts she attended schools in Lexington, Concord, and Salem. Rose had always had a close relationship with her father, so his death in 1864 on the day before her thirteenth birthday was a great sorrow to her. In the years after her husband's death, Sophia Hawthorne moved the family to Dresden, Germany, where Rose took art lessons and met George Parsons Lathrop, an American who was studying in Dresden. They were married at St. Luke's Church in Chelsea in September 1871, not long after Rose's mother had died.

The young couple returned to the United States to take up residence in Boston. George had initially planned on studying law but had decided instead to be a writer. He became an associate editor of the *Atlantic Monthly* when William Dean Howells was editor in chief. He published his first book in 1875. Rose continued at this time to develop her writing in preference to her painting skills. Her first short story was published in 1874, followed by a poem in 1875. She wrote numerous short stories and poetry for popular magazines, such as *St. Nicholas Magazine*, *Atlantic Monthly*, the *Boston Courier*, the *Cambridge Magazine*, *Ladies' Home Journal*, and the *Catholic World*. In 1888 she published a volume of poetry entitled *Along the Shore*. She and George together published *A Story of Courage: Annals of the Georgetown Convent of the Visitation* (1894). Remembrances of her well-loved father were published in her *Memories of Hawthorne* (1897).

Rose's married life has been of interest to her biographers. In some ways the marriage was a happy one, but several indicators seem to prove that at times it also was not. Their literary efforts failed to bring the couple financial stability. Their only child, a son, died from tuberculosis at age four. Rose suffered from puerperal fever, with its attendant emotional instability, after the child's birth, and for the last ten years of his life George suffered from what has been described as a severe gastric disorder. Some of her early biographers claimed that alcoholism contributed to his chronic ill health, but Patricia Valenti, Rose's biographer, has uncovered no evidence of this. George and Rose lived apart from time to time, sometimes to research or to write. In 1883 she separated from him for a time to go to Europe but then changed her mind and took an apartment first in New York and later in Cambridge. In 1891 both George and Rose (who had been raised as an Episcopalian) converted to Roman Catholicism, to which they had become attracted during their stay in Italy in 1859–1860. Rose's final separation from George came in 1895, when she followed her desire to take care of those suffering from incurable cancer. Rose had always hoped that George would join her in her charitable endeavors, but he was not so inclined. His death in 1898 gave her complete freedom to continue her work on behalf of the terminally ill.

Several influences led Rose to take this step. One was her discovery of her patron saint, Rose of Lima, a third-order Dominican who in the late sixteen and early seventeenth centuries had cared for poor Peruvians, especially those with cancer. She had also heard about the work of a contemporary, Father Damien, a self-sacrificing Catholic priest who had cared for lepers on the Hawaiian island of Molokai. Furthermore, Rose's close friend, poet Emma Lazarus, had died in 1887 of cancer. Also, according to Valenti, Rose was always moved by a particular memory of her father. Once, while visiting an English almshouse, he was approached by an obviously diseased orphan boy who begged for his attention. Hawthorne took the child in his arms, as he would his own child, and gave him the touch of love for which the child begged. Her father's response to the child's suffering was not lost on Rose, who realized that the care given to cancer patients was inadequate to say the least.

Rose began her work for the sick in three small rooms in the slums of New York's Lower East Side, where she offered free respite and care for terminally ill persons who had no resources to provide for themselves; other patients she visited in their homes. Very soon the quarters were too small, so in 1899 she bought a house on Cherry Street and named it St. Rose's Free Home. That same year she and her companion, Alice Huber, were received into the Dominican order as tertiaries. Taking the name Sister M. Alphonsa, she and Alice, now Sister Mary Rose, made their first vows in 1900 and established the Dominican Congregation of St. Rose of Lima, or the Servants of Relief for Incurable Cancer, with headquarters in Hawthorne, New York. In 1901 Rose purchased another property, in Hawthorne; it came to be known as the Rosary Hill Home at Sherman Park. For financial support she depended on those who knew of her work. She wrote as a means of raising funds, and from 1901 to 1904 she published a monthly magazine, *Christ's Poor*, in which she explained the philosophical and theological basis for her work and attracted donations as well as other women who were interested in joining the new order. Proceeds from the reprinting of her *Memories of Hawthorne* in 1922 were used to build a new fireproof structure.

Rose spent the rest her life providing free hospice care and developing her religious order. She spent the last day of her life much like any other day and then died quietly in her sleep at Rosary Hill in Hawthorne. In addition to the first two foundations in Hawthorne and New York City, the Servants of Relief for Incurable Cancer sponsors free hospices in St. Paul, Minnesota; Atlanta, Georgia; Fall River, Massachusetts; Cleveland, Ohio; and Philadelphia, Pennsylvania.

• Materials on Lathrop are collected in the Community Archives, Hawthorne, N.Y. Popular biographies include Katherine Burton, *Sorrow Built a Bridge* (1937); Theodore Maynard, *A Fire Was Lighted* (1948); Marguerite Vance, *On the Wings of Fire: The Story of Nathaniel Hawthorne's Daughter Rose* (1955); James J. Walsh, *Mother Alphonsa: Rose Hawthorne Lathrop* (1930); and Sister M. Josepha, *Out of Many Hearts: Mother Alphonsa Lathrop and Her Work* (1965). Patricia Valenti, *To Myself a Stranger: A Biography of Rose Hawthorne Lathrop* (1991), is the most scholarly biography to date. Short accounts can be found in the standard biographical dictionaries; see also Frances Willard and Mary Livermore, *American Women: Fifteen Hundred Biographies*, vol. 2 (1897), and Vernon Loggins, *The Hawthornes: The Story of Seven Generations of an American Family* (1951).

ELIZABETH KOLMER

LATIL, Alexandre (6 Oct. 1816–Mar. 1851), poet writing in French, was born in New Orleans, Louisiana. His ancestors had come from France. His well-to-do parents' names and occupations are not known. Latil attended classes at Les Écoles Centrale et Primaires of the Ursulines and then at Le Collège d'Orléans. In 1831 he fell in love with a young Creole girl now identified only as "Elm. T." Although the two soon became engaged, both sets of parents persuaded them to wait until they were a little older to marry. But then tragedy befell Latil. While still in his teens, he developed incipient signs of leprosy. Neighbors began to gossip to the effect that one of his ancestors must have had children by a Native American woman. At that time it was a folkloristic canard that unions of French and Indian couples could cause leprosy in their offspring.

As long as possible, Latil remained at home with his admirable parents. Although he urged his beloved Elm. T. to leave him in search of a normal life, her love for him remained strong, and she visited and consoled him devotedly. During his last years he was exiled to a leper colony known as La Terre aux Lepreux, on Bayou Saint-John. He lived in a small cabin, and his fiancée soon joined him, to nurse him in whatever way she could. She finally persuaded the afflicted young man to marry her, after which she continued to act as his selfless nurse, always with a courageous smile. The couple had no children.

Long in agony, the highly intelligent Latil found comfort in serious reading. His favorite authors were French and included the poet and satirist Auguste Marseille Barthélemy, the lyric poet Pierre Jean de Béranger, and the poet and playwright Casimir Delavigne. Latil was inspired by their works, and those of other French poets as well, to compose some poetry in French. Beginning in 1836 he placed several poems in New Orleans and parish newspapers and literary journals. His friends and readers were so impressed by his poetry and his example that they urged him to prepare a book of poems. He did so, and the result was *Les Éphémères, essais poétiques*, which he published in 1841 at his own expense and by subscription, and which contains twenty-four poems. In a foreword Latil refers stoically to his "longue et cruelle maladie" without ever identifying it, explains that only the encouragement of friends persuaded him to publish songs from his "faible et plaintive" lyre, and adds that his foot is "sur le borde de la tombe." He is afraid that modern readers will judge his efforts to be "froides et monotones." He goes on to praise his beloved Louisiana for producing generous men and fine poets. He regrets that his failing eyesight has prevented the inclusion of certain better efforts recently written but necessarily remaining unrevised. He hopes to prepare them for publication later, if health and sight permit. The collection is traditional in content and form because, as Latil asserts, the line supposedly separating the classical and the literary is illusory, the only real line of demarcation being that which divides the true and the false.

Les Éphémères includes several poignant poems. One is a tender "Epithalamie" on the occasion of his sister's marriage in 1838. Another praises Béranger, "barde immortel, noble fils du génie"; another, addressed to Barthélemy, sings the glories of France. One poem beautifully identifies the charms of solitude. Another is a courteous expression of love for his grandfather Lazare Latil. The saddest poem in the book is the undated "La Poète Suffrant," which begins by telling of his fated confinement to obscurity, his sense that love has flown away, and his fear that even God has abandoned him. He concludes the poem, however, not only with thanks to a certain intimate and sincere friend for inspiring his sweet songs, but even with the hope that she will transport him over the ocean of life to the port of a generous deity.

Four poems are given over entirely to expressions of personal love. "Mosaïque" (May 1839) extols an unnamed "amie," who is charming, sweet, virginal, and angelic. The second, "Le Départ: Élégie" (Sept. 1839), though addressed to "une soeur," names "Mlle. Elm . . . T." Latil regrets that time does not permit him to have a beautiful life, but he is nonetheless grateful for peace and innocence. "Mélancolie: Stances Élégiaques" (Oct. 1839), which also names "Mlle. Elm . . . T," expresses the hope that God will recompense both of them for their virtue and innocence. (Most curiously, the epigraph of this poem is a quotation of lines Lord Byron addressed to his sister.) "Mélancolie," perhaps his best poem, contains fifteen 8-line stanzas, rhyming *aaabcccb*. Lines 1, 2, 3, 5, 6, and 7 have three mild accents each; 4 and 8, two. The effect is thoroughly charming. (Most of his other poems have longer lines, often in alexandrine couplets.) Finally, the undated "Hélas!" subtitled "Chère Elm . . . ," is uniquely poignant. The poet says that in his final hour, with his eyes closed to the light, he will bless her, ascend to heaven, and await a "séjour éternal." The final poem from what he called his ephemeral lyre is dated April 1842 and is addressed most formally and respectfully to his parents.

Latil spent nine more years in excruciating pain. His bones partially decomposed, and his fingers fell off at the palms, one by one, so that he could no longer write. He became blind and was bedridden. When he died in early March 1851, his magnificent wife was at his side, after which she disappeared from record.

• Charles Testut discusses Latil in *Portraits Littéraires* (1850), as does Edward Larocque Tinker in *Les Écrits de Langue Française en Louisiane au XIXe Siecle: Essais Biographiques et Bibliographiques* (1932). An obituary is in the New Orleans *L'Orléanais*, 18 Mar. 1851.

ROBERT L. GALE

LATIMER, Elizabeth Wormeley (26 July 1822–4 Jan. 1904), novelist, translator, and historian, was born Mary Elizabeth Wormeley in London, England, the daughter of Rear Admiral Ralph Randolph Wormeley of the English Royal Navy and Caroline Preble of Boston, Massachusetts. Her father was born in Virginia, but as a boy he was taken to England, where he received his education and enlisted in the navy. Elizabeth spent her childhood in England, Boston, Virginia, and France. She was educated mostly by tutors, although she spent a brief time at a boarding school. When she was fourteen, the family moved to London, where she attended the funeral of King William IV and the coronation of Queen Victoria. In Paris she became acquainted with William Makepeace Thackeray and his mother, Mrs. Carmichael Smythe. She witnessed the second funeral of Napoleon and made her debut at the balls of Louis Philippe. In 1842 she traveled to America to visit at the home of friends. Here she met the historian William H. Prescott and Mr. and Mrs. Charles Dickens and became friends with Julia Ward (later Howe), who encouraged her to write. The mixture of literary and historical influence during these years had great impact on the directions her writing took.

When Prescott's *History of the Conquest of Mexico* (1843) was published, included in the appendix was Elizabeth Wormeley's translation of an ancient Mexican poem, her first appearance in print. Her first novel, *Amabel, a Family History* (1853), published in England the same year as *Amabel, the Victory of Love*, was followed by *Our Cousin Veronica, or Scenes and Adventures over the Blue Ridge* (1855). In 1856 she married Randolph Brandt Latimer of Baltimore, Maryland, where they made their home; they had three children. Except during the Civil War when she took part in the care and nursing of sick and wounded soldiers, Latimer devoted the next twenty years to her home, her husband, and the care of her children.

Not until 1876 did Latimer begin seriously to write and publish again. She contributed stories, poems, and essays to *Catholic World*, *Harper's Monthly*, *Critic*, and other periodicals. Three of her novels, *Salvage* (1880), *My Wife and My Wife's Sister* (1881), and *Princess Amélie: A Fragment of Autobiography* (1883), were published anonymously as part of the Roberts Brothers' "No Name Series," but their authorship was soon discovered.

Among Latimer's translations from the French are George Sand's *Nanon* (1890), *Jacqueline* by Marie Therese de Solms Blanc (1893), and *History of the People of Israel* (1898). In 1901 she translated *The Love Letters of Victor Hugo (1820–1822)*, completing the work, with the help of her daughter Caroline Wormeley Latimer, who was also a writer, in three weeks. One of the Chatauqua Literary and Scientific Circle books for the Italian-German year, 1902, was *Men and Cities of Italy* which included a sketch of "The Italian Republics," translated and edited from the Italian by Latimer.

Latimer's most important work was a series of volumes on the history of Europe in the nineteenth century. The first volume, *France in the Nineteenth Century*, was published in 1892, when Latimer was seventy, followed by volumes on Russia and Turkey (1893), England (1894), Italy (1896), and Spain (1897). The volume on Germany was unfinished at the time of her death. Although she was an avid researcher and her work was well respected, Latimer made no claim to be a historian, saying, "My aim has been to tell only what interested myself, and what I hoped might be interesting to other people. I therefore have put many persons, events and other matters into the foreground, which, if I aimed to be an historian, I ought to have relegated to a less prominent position."

Europe in Africa in the Nineteenth Century (1895) was reprinted by the Negro Universities Press in 1969. In the introduction to this volume Latimer says that it is a book of "short yarns," explaining that "short yarn" is the "nautical phrase for a story that has been broken off short—a narrative that has never reached its legitimate conclusion." These stories, she said, "will probably be found to have their ends somewhere in the coming century. Meantime it seems well to know something of the beginnings of what in years to come may interest the world exceedingly." Among the short yarns were stories of Egypt, of Livingston and Stanley, of Liberia and the Maryland colony, of gold mines and diamonds, of Zanzibar and Rhodesia. At the close of the final chapter on Madagascar, Latimer said, "It is sad to close these chapters on 'Europe in Africa in the Nineteenth Century' with a melancholy foreboding. But there are yet five years before the century will end; let us hope that, during that period, the prospects . . . may brighten; . . . sometimes a thunder-storm revives the earth." Latimer died in Baltimore.

• Biographical information and an appreciation of Latimer's work is in Sara Andrew Shafer, "Elizabeth Wormeley Latimer," *Dial*, 1 Feb. 1904, pp. 75–76. The Massachusetts Historical Society holds the "Wormeley-Latimer Papers," including the correspondence of Latimer with her husband, Randolph Latimer, and with friends William H. Prescott and Julia Ward Howe. Correspondence concerning her writing is held by the Maryland Historical Society, and others are in the Cairns Collection in the Rare Books Library of the University of Wisconsin–Madison. A memoir by Latimer, abridged by Katherine Prescott Wormeley, is in the New York Public Library. See also "General Gossip of Authors and Writers," *Current Literature*, May 1901, p. 554. Obituaries are in the *Baltimore American*, 3, 4, and 7 Jan. 1904, and the *Baltimore Sun*, 4 and 5 Jan. 1904.

BLANCHE COX CLEGG

LATIMER, Lewis Howard (4 Sept. 1848–11 Dec. 1928), engineer and inventor, was born in Chelsea, Massachusetts, the son of George W. Latimer, a bar-

ber, and Rebecca Smith, both former slaves who escaped from Norfolk, Virginia, on 4 October 1842. When not attending Phillips Grammar School in Boston, Lewis spent much of his youth working in his father's barber shop, as a paperhanger, and selling the abolitionist newspaper *The Liberator*. Lewis's life changed drastically when his father mysteriously disappeared in 1858. His family, placed in dire financial straits, bound out Lewis and his brothers George and William as apprentices through the Farm School, a state institution in which children worked as unpaid laborers. Upon escaping from the exploitation of the Farm School system, Lewis and his brothers returned to Boston to reunite the family. During the next few years, Latimer was able to help support his family through various odd jobs and by working as an office boy for a Boston attorney, Isaac Wright.

Late in the Civil War, Latimer enlisted in the U.S. Navy. He was assigned to the *Ohio* as a landsman (low level seaman) on 13 September 1864. He served until 3 July 1865, at which time he was honorably discharged from the *Massasoit*.

After returning from sea, Latimer began his technical career in Boston as an office boy for Crosby and Gould, patent solicitors. Through his assiduous efforts to teach himself the art of drafting, he rose to assistant draftsman and eventually to the position of chief draftsman in the mid-1870s. During this time, he met Mary Wilson Lewis, a young woman from Fall River, Massachusetts. They were married in 1873 and had two children.

During his tenure at Crosby and Gould, Latimer began to invent. His first creation, a water closet for railway cars, co-invented with W. C. Brown, was granted Letters Patent No. 147,363 on 10 February 1874. However, drafting remained his primary vocation. One of the most noteworthy projects he undertook was drafting the diagrams for Alexander Graham Bell's telephone patent application, which was approved on 14 February 1876. In 1879 after managerial changes at Crosby and Gould, Latimer left their employment and Boston.

Latimer relocated to Bridgeport, Connecticut, initially working as a paperhanger. He eventually found part-time work making mechanical drawings at the Follandsbee Machine Shop. While drafting at the shop, he met Hiram Stevens Maxim, the chief engineer of the U.S. Electric Lighting Company. In February 1880, shortly after their first meeting, Maxim hired Latimer as his draftsman and private secretary. Latimer quickly moved up within the enterprise, and when the U.S. Electric Lighting Company moved to New York City, it placed him in charge of the production of carbon lamp filaments. Latimer was an integral member of the team that installed the company's first commercial incandescent lighting system, in the Equitable Building in New York City in the fall of 1880. He was on hand at most of the lighting installations that were undertaken by the company, and in 1881 he began to supervise many of their incandescent and arc lighting installations.

Latimer also invented products that were fundamental to the development of the company while directing new installations for the U.S. Electric Lighting Company. In October 1880 Maxim was granted a patent for a filament that was treated with hydrocarbon vapor to equalize and standardize its resistance, a process that allowed it to burn longer than the Edison lamp filament. Latimer began working on a process to manufacture this new carbon filament, and on 17 January 1882 he was granted a patent for a new process of manufacturing carbons. This invention produced a highly resistant filament and diminished the occurrence of broken and distorted filaments that had been commonplace with prior procedures. The filament was shaped into an *M*, which became a noted characteristic of the Maxim lamp. Latimer patented other inventions, including two for an electric lamp and a globe support for electric lamps. These further enhanced the Maxim lamp during 1881 and 1882.

In 1881 Latimer was dispatched to London and successfully established an incandescent lamp factory for the newly founded Maxim-Weston Electric Light Company. In 1882 Latimer left this company and began working for the Olmstead Electric Lighting Company of Brooklyn as superintendent of lamp construction; at this time he created the Latimer Lamp. He later continued his work at the Acme Electric Company of New York.

In 1883 Latimer began working at the Edison Electric Light Company. He became affiliated with the engineering department in 1885, and when the legal department was formed in 1889, Latimer's record of expert legal advice made him a requisite member of the new division. According to Latimer's biographical sketch of himself for the Edison Pioneers, he was transferred to the department "as [a] draughtsman inspector and expert witness as to facts in the early stages of the electric lighting business. . . . [He] traveled extensively, securing witnesses' affidavits, and early apparatus, and also testifying in a number of the basic patent cases to the advantage of his employers." His complete knowledge of electrical technology was exemplified in his work *Incandescent Electric Lighting, a Practical Description of the Edison System* (1890).

Latimer continued in the legal department when the Edison General Electric Company merged with the Thomson-Houston Company to form General Electric Company in 1892. His knowledge of the electric industry became invaluable when the General Electric Company and the Westinghouse Electric Company formed the Board of Patent Control in 1896. This board was responsible for managing the cross-licensing of patents between the two companies and prosecuting infringers. Latimer was appointed to the position of chief draftsman, however his duties went far beyond drafting. He assisted inventors and others in developing their ideas. He used the vast body of knowledge he had acquired over the years in their efforts to eliminate outside competition. He remained at this position until the board was dissolved in 1911, af-

ter which Latimer put his talents to use for the law firm of Hammer and Schwartz as a patent consultant.

In 1918, when the Edison Pioneers, an organization founded to bring together for social and intellectual interaction men associated with Thomas Edison prior to 1885, was formed, Latimer was one of the twenty-nine original members. A stroke in 1924 forced him to retire from his formal position, and he spent much of his last four years engaged in two other activities that were most important in his life, art and poetry. He died at his home in Flushing, New York, which in 1995 was made a New York City landmark. Latimer was one of very few African Americans who contributed significantly to the development of American electrical technology.

• Latimer's papers are in the Lewis Howard Latimer Collection at the Queens Borough Public Library in Queens, N.Y. Copies of many of his papers are located at the Schomburg Center for Research in Black Culture in New York. Good biographical studies of Latimer include Winifred Latimer Norman and Lily Patterson, *Lewis Latimer: Scientist* (1994), Glennette Tilley Turner, *Lewis Howard Latimer* (1991), and Janet M. Schneider and Bayla Singer, eds., *Blueprint for Change: The Life and Times of Lewis H. Latimer* (1995). See also Aaron E. Klein, *The Hidden Contributors: Black Scientists and Inventors in America* (1971), and Louis Haber, *Black Pioneers of Science and Invention* (1970). An obituary is in *Electrical World*, 22 Dec. 1928, p. 1271.

RAYVON DAVID FOUCHÉ

LATIMER, Margery Bodine (6 Feb. 1899–16 Aug. 1932), writer, was born in Portage, Wisconsin, the daughter of Clark Watt Latimer, a sales representative, and Laura Augusta Bodine. Latimer enrolled in Wooster College in Ohio in the fall of 1918; after a semester she returned home, disappointed by the college's social atmosphere, which was dominated by football, fraternities, and sororities. In the autumn of 1919 she entered the University of Wisconsin in Madison, where she majored in English.

In 1921 Latimer moved to New York City, where she attended Columbia University. She worked at the Henry Street Settlement House and, for a brief stint, in the fashion department of the *Woman's Home Companion*. At Columbia she met Blanche Matthias, the Chicago art critic and poet, with whom she developed a lasting friendship. This acquaintance led to others among New York's artistic and literary circles, and Latimer later befriended such figures as Georgia O'Keeffe, Walt Kuhn, Joseph Hergesheimer, Carl Van Vechten, Anita Loos, and Carl and Irita Van Doren.

Since the age of eighteen, Latimer had been mentored by her Portage neighbor, the influential author, suffragist, and journalist Zona Gale, who deemed Latimer "one of the most exquisite centres of intuitive experience imaginable " (Derleth, p. 172). In 1922 Gale established the Zona Gale Scholarship at the University of Wisconsin; its generous terms were tailor-made for Latimer, who returned to the university as its first recipient. While there, she served on the editorial board of the university's literary magazine, to which she also contributed several early pieces. She did not earn a degree; in 1923 she left college to write.

Returning to live in New York City in the autumn of 1924, Latimer supported herself with clerical jobs while continuing to write. Her home was a meeting place for young poets such as Kenneth Fearing, Carl Rakosi, and Horace Gregory, who memorialized it in his first book of poetry, *Chelsea Rooming House* (1930). Rakosi wrote of Latimer: "She wore no make-up, no high heels, no frills of any kind and only the most plain dresses. Her walk was unselfconscious, very straight and direct, without being masculine. What struck one immediately was her radiant presence. Blake would have described her as a cloud of gold" (Loughridge, p. 217). Latimer also formed a close friendship with Meridel Le Sueur, the labor activist and writer, who later claimed that all her writing had been influenced by Latimer's. Le Sueur had also been a protégé of Zona Gale, and both she and Latimer labored in their writing to express women's physicality and sensuality, in rebellion against Gale's prohibitive attitude toward the body.

In the mid-1920s, Latimer began publishing short stories in such journals as the *Century*, the *Bookman*, *Echo*, *transition*, and the socialist literary monthly *New Masses*, as well as reviewing books for periodicals, including the *New York Herald* and the *New York World*. Her work explores themes central to the modernist movement, such as the breakdown of social structures. She often wrote about small towns in the Midwest, offering critiques of traditional family structures and gender roles. She captured the immediacy of experience—transcendent moments, small epiphanies—by means of the carefully rendered physical detail. At its best her work is clever and biting. She employs striking metaphors—a woman's vengeful happiness rises "in her like an actual shawled body rising from mud, smoothly dripping"—and experiments with narrative techniques (such as a melding of first-, second-, and third-person narration in a single story) to jolt and engage the reader. However, her innovations are not always successful: some narratives are uneven, marred by erratic character development and abrupt breaks in the narrative sequence. But the overall critical response was good: her first novel, *We Are Incredible* (1928), met with excellent notices. *Nellie Bloom and Other Stories*, published the following year, was even more widely acclaimed: a reviewer in the *New York Herald Tribune* argued that Latimer had surpassed both Katherine Mansfield and Sherwood Anderson.

In the American tradition of Walt Whitman and the modernist tradition of James Joyce, Latimer reclaims the body as a site for spiritual experience. But in Latimer's case, it is specifically and emphatically the female body that is reclaimed. Latimer's 1930 novel, *This Is My Body*, broke literary barriers by including a tragic description of the protagonist's abortion, but the book's tone was denounced by some reviewers as hys-

terical, and critics generally considered it a failed work by a writer of great talent and promise.

Latimer, whose work often depicted moments of transcendent awareness, had been interested in the Gurdjieff spiritual movement since 1924, attending lectures on the Gurdjieff philosophy in New York and discussing her work with A. R. Orage, the movement's American leader. In 1931 her interest came to fruition when she helped the new leader, Jean Toomer, organize a communal retreat for Gurdjieff students known as the "Portage Experiment." This was misrepresented in the popular press as a haven for radicals. Later that year, she married Toomer, author of the 1923 novel *Cane*, which was widely regarded as the harbinger of the Harlem Renaissance. After their marriage was publicized, Latimer and Toomer (who claimed some African ancestry) were the subjects of a nationwide antimiscegenation scandal. The couple traveled to New Mexico and California before settling in Chicago, where Latimer died of hemorrhaging after delivering a healthy child.

Latimer's final collection of short fiction, *Guardian Angel and Other Stories*, was published posthumously in 1932 to great acclaim; the title story had been previously published in *Scribner's* as a finalist in its $5,000 story competition. Reviews of *Guardian Angel* compared Latimer to Mansfield and D. H. Lawrence and mourned the loss to American literature incurred by her early death.

The feminist project of reviving women's writing led to a renewed interest in Latimer's work, and in 1984 the Feminist Press issued a reprint entitled *Guardian Angel and Other Stories*, which drew stories from both earlier collections. Latimer has been viewed as a minor but important modernist and a forerunner of contemporary women writers.

• The principal collection of Latimer's manuscripts and correspondence is included with the Jean Toomer Collection at the Beinecke Rare Book and Manuscript Library at Yale University. Another important collection that includes Blanche Matthias's unpublished manuscript "My Friendship with Margery Latimer" is housed at the Memorial Library at the University of Wisconsin–Madison in the Department of Special Collections. Nancy Loughridge offers a brief biographical analysis in her "Afterword: The Life" in *Guardian Angel and Other Stories* (1984), and August Derleth devotes a chapter to Latimer's role as protégé in *Still Small Voice: The Biography of Zona Gale* (1940). Daniel P. McCarthy discusses the antimiscegenation scandal in " 'Just Americans': A Note on Jean Toomer's Marriage to Margery Latimer," *College Language Association Journal* 17 (1974): 474–79. For accounts of the marriage, see *Time*, 28 Mar. 1932 ; the *New York Amsterdam News*, 21 Mar. 1932; and the *New York Daily News*, 26 Mar. 1932. For a contemporary view of the author's life and accomplishments, see an obituary in the *Milwaukee Journal*, 17 Aug. 1932.

JOY CASTRO

LATIMER, Wendell Mitchell (22 Apr. 1893–6 July 1955), chemist and educator, was born in Garnett, Kansas, the son of Walter Latimer, a bank manager, and Emma Mitchell. When Latimer was three, the family moved to Kansas City, Missouri. Five years later, his father died of typhoid fever. He and his impoverished mother spent a winter with his uncle at Abingdon, Illinois, and then lived at his grandfather's farm near Greeley, Kansas. There he attended elementary school and a year of high school but then transferred to the much better Garnett High School ten miles away and spent only weekends at the farm.

In 1911 Latimer entered the University of Kansas, intending to become a lawyer, and participated in debating clubs during his first two years. To help meet expenses he took odd jobs, finally working at the University Weather Bureau, where he measured wind velocities and manned the seismograph. Disenchanted with the methods used to win debates, he changed his major to mathematics. He did not take his first chemistry course until the summer session following his sophomore year, but during his final two years he completed majors in both mathematics and chemistry, earning an A.B. in 1915.

Latimer then remained at Kansas for two years as assistant instructor in chemistry. He there received his master's degree under Hamilton P. Cady with the thesis "Dielectric Constant of Liquid Ammonia from $-40°$ to $110°C$.," enabling him to remedy his deficiencies in chemistry and physics caused by his late decision to study science. During the summer of 1916 he attended two courses taught by physical chemist William Draper Harkins at the University of Chicago. Offered a fellowship from department head Gilbert Newton Lewis, Latimer enrolled in the University of California, Berkeley, from which he received a Ph.D. in chemistry in 1919 under George Ernest Gibson's direction with the dissertation "A Test of the Third Law of Thermodynamics." During 1918, while most of the faculty were engaged in World War I, he gave the freshman chemistry lectures.

Latimer remained at Berkeley as instructor (1919–1921), assistant professor (1921–1924), associate professor (1924–1931), and professor (1931–1955). During 1930–1931 he held a Guggenheim fellowship in Munich. He served as assistant dean of the College of Letters and Science (1923–1924), dean of the College of Chemistry (1941–1949), and chairman of the Department of Chemistry (1945–1949). Active in faculty affairs, he served in the Academic Senate. Following the example of Lewis, whom he succeeded as chairman, Latimer was the department's "talent scout." His expertise in detecting signs of originality in prospective graduate students and of creativity in prospective faculty helped maintain the department's preeminent position in research and teaching. Latimer Hall on the Berkeley campus is named in his honor.

Latimer's first article, "Polarity and Ionization from the Standpoint of the Lewis Theory of Valence" (*Journal of the American Chemical Society* 42 [1920]: 1419), coauthored with Worth H. Rodebush, was the first to recognize the hydrogen bond as a general phenomenon in which a proton (hydrogen atom) is held between two highly electronegative atoms. The properties of many substances, including water, are determined largely by hydrogen bonding. It occurs in deoxyribonucleic acid (DNA), the basis of the genetic code. Linus Pauling, who devoted an entire chapter of his classic book, *The Nature of the Chemical Bond*, to examples of the hydrogen bond, claimed that "the significance of the hydrogen bond for physiology is greater than that of any other single structural feature" (3d ed. [1960], p. 450).

Most of Latimer's publications involve the application of thermodynamics to chemistry, but he also worked on such diverse topics as dielectric constants, the thermoelectric effect and electronic entropy, the ionization of salt vapors, radioactivity, and astrochemical processes involved in the formation of the earth. He was the first to recognize the importance of entropies of aqueous ions, which enabled him to use thermal data to calculate free energies so as to predict the directions of most inorganic reactions. When he began his work, not a single ionic entropy was known, but after three decades he and his students had determined entropy values for almost all the stable inorganic aqueous ions, which was of immense value in the general theory of strong electrolytes (salts).

Latimer used much of these data for his book *The Oxidation States of the Elements and Their Potentials in Aqueous Solutions* (1938; 2d ed., 1952), which had a profound influence on the teaching of inorganic chemistry. During the 1930s, together with his former student Willard F. Libby, Latimer initiated a seminar on nuclear chemistry at Berkeley, which interested nuclear pioneers such as Glenn T. Seaborg, Arthur C. Wahl, and Joseph W. Kennedy in that subject and thus helped lay the foundation for the discovery of plutonium. The separation and identification of this element depended on the relative oxidation potentials of the heaviest elements, and Latimer, as the world's leading authority on oxidation potentials, contributed his expertise to the discovery. Latimer also built and operated the first successful hydrogen liquefier in the United States, and William F. Giauque, who won the 1949 Nobel Prize in chemistry for his research on thermodynamics at low temperatures, stated that he learned many of the facts of gas liquefaction from Latimer.

An effective, stimulating teacher, Latimer, in accordance with the policy instituted by Lewis in 1912, participated in the teaching of freshmen in lecture, laboratory, and quiz sections. During World War II he was a member of and a special investigator (oxygen production, chemical warfare, and plutonium research) for the National Defense Research Committee (1941–1945) and a member of War Department missions to England (1943) and Panama, Australia, and New Guinea (1944). He was director of the Manhattan Engineering District project on plutonium chemistry at Berkeley (1943–1947) and played a leading role as associate director (1947–1955) in the chemistry program of the University of California's Radiation Laboratory (now the Lawrence Berkeley Laboratory) from World War II until his death. He was awarded the Presidential Certificate of Merit in 1948 for his wartime activities. In 1954 he was appointed a consultant to the Atomic Energy Commission (AEC). Latimer believed that the consequences for the United States would be disastrous if a potential enemy nation developed a hydrogen bomb first, and during the early stages of the Cold War he strongly advocated the development of thermonuclear weapons.

Latimer was associate editor of the *Journal of Chemical Physics* (1933–1935) and *Chemical Reviews* (1940–1941) and editor of the Prentice-Hall Chemical Series (1937–1955). He was a member of the National Academy of Sciences (chairman of the Chemistry Section, 1947–1950), American Chemical Society, Electrochemical Society, Faraday Society, American Association for the Advancement of Science, American Academy of Political Science, Sigma Xi, and Alpha Chi Sigma. His honors included the Distinguished Service Award from his alma mater, the University of Kansas (1948), the Faculty Research Lectureship at the University of California (1953), and the William H. Nichols Medal of the New York Section of the American Chemical Society (1955).

Latimer married Bertha Eichenauer in 1917; the couple had one son. After the death of his wife and son, he married Glatha Hatfield in 1926; they had two children. During his last years Latimer suffered from poor health and underwent several operations but retained his characteristic sense of humor and continued his research and teaching. He died at the Kaiser Foundation Hospital in Oakland, California.

Latimer made numerous applications of thermodynamics to chemistry, particularly at low temperatures. He was the first to grasp the importance of ionic entropies, which could be used to calculate free energies that make possible the prediction of the feasibility and direction of chemical reactions. He was the first to recognize the principle of the hydrogen bond and the first in the United States to liquefy hydrogen, and his extensive compilation of oxidation potentials had a great influence on the teaching and practice of inorganic chemistry.

• Latimer's letters are in the Bancroft Library of the University of California, Berkeley. Biographical articles include W(illiam) F(rancis) Giauque, "Wendell M. Latimer, Chemist," *Science* 122 (2 Sept. 1955): 406–7, and Joel H. Hildebrand, "Wendell Mitchell Latimer, April 22, 1893–July 6, 1955," National Academy of Sciences, *Biographical Memoirs* 32 (1958): 221–37, which contains an autographed portrait, excerpts from Latimer's autobiographical files, and a bibliography of 108 publications. Obituaries are in the *New York Times*, 7 July 1955; *Chemical and Engineering News* 33 (18 July 1955): 3014; and *Science* 122 (2 Sept. 1955): 406–7.

GEORGE B. KAUFFMAN

LATOURETTE, Kenneth Scott (9 Aug. 1884–26 Dec. 1968), historian, was born in Oregon City, Oregon, the son of Dewitt Clinton Latourette, a lawyer and banker, and Rhoda Scott. Graduating with a B.S. in chemistry from Linfield College of McMinnville, Oregon, in 1904, Latourette studied history at Yale University, receiving a B.A. in 1906, an M.A. in 1907, and a

Ph.D. in 1909. After graduation he served as traveling secretary of the Student Volunteer Movement for Foreign Missions between 1909 and 1910 and then took up missionary work with the Yale Missionary Society in Changsha, China, from 1910 to 1912. Forced to return home because of ill health, Latourette remained interested in Asia and Christian work. He remained active in the Student Volunteer Movement until 1962, the Yale-in-China program until 1952, and for nearly twenty years served as a board member of the American Baptist Foreign Missionary Society. In addition, he served on the boards of many other organizations, including the Oberlin-in-China program, the Nanking Theological Seminary, the International Young Men's Christian Association, the China Medical Board, and the World Council of Churches, of which he was a founding member in 1938.

Although Latourette remained devoted to Christian work, especially missionary activity, teaching history was of equal interest. Between 1914 and 1916 he taught Asian and European history at Reed College, moving to Denison University from 1916 to 1921, where he was also ordained a Baptist minister in 1918, in part to avoid the draft of World War I. In 1921 he became the D. Willis James Professor of Missions at Yale University's divinity school. Here he joined his Christian faith, fascination with Asia, and his training as a historian by teaching and researching Christianity and Asia. Eventually he served as chair of the Department of Religion beginning in 1938, and then as director of graduate studies of the divinity school in 1946. He retired from Yale in 1953 as the Sterling Professor of Missions and Oriental History at the divinity school. He maintained an active publishing career through 1967.

Latourette's contribution to scholarship and teaching was widely recognized. He was president of the American Society of Church History (1945), the American Historical Association (1947), the American Baptist Convention (1951–1952), and, in 1954–1955, the Far Eastern Association (now the Association of Asian Studies). He wrote more than eighty books and innumerable articles and reviews on Christianity, oriental history and customs, and theological subjects; these demonstrate his ability to pursue diverse topics with considerable success. In 1917 he published *The Development of China*, which was in a sixth edition as of 1946; *The Development of Japan* (1918), retitled in its 1947 edition as *The History of Japan*, was still in print in 1957, in its sixth edition. After joining the Yale Divinity School, Latourette wrote *A History of Christian Missions in China* (1929), which has not been replaced or revised since publication and still serves as a standard reference for students of missions and China. In this volume, Latourette argued that China was in the midst of fundamental change and that Christian mission work was a vital, positive force in that process. Latourette's *The Chinese Their History and Culture* (2 vols., 1934) was followed by six editions through 1964. Between 1937 and 1945 Latourette produced a seven-volume work, *The History of the Expansion of*

Christianity, which surveyed sixteen centuries of Christian expansion and gained praise for its sweep of history and freedom from sectarian prejudice. One reviewer called this series "the most monumental work of its kind undertaken, and so successfully completed, in modern times." Latourette returned to the field of Asian history by publishing *The United States Moves across the Pacific* (1946) and *A Short History of the Far East* (1946), the latter standing the test of some twenty years, appearing in a fourth edition in 1964. *A History of Christianity* (1953) was issued as a condensed paperback entitled *Christianity through the Ages* (1965). His *Christianity in a Revolutionary Age: A History of Christianity in the Nineteenth and Twentieth Centuries* (5 vols., 1958–1962) reiterated a theme found in his early theological publications: that Christianity must be seen from a worldwide perspective and as a beneficial force among humanity. Rejecting the view that Christianity was in decline, he found the faith to be more significant to more people than at any other time in history. In addition, he was a continuous contributor on China to the *Encyclopaedia Britannica* from 1926 through 1955, and on missions to its *Book of the Year* between 1936 and 1959. He was also a major participant in the *Dictionary of American Biography*, for which he wrote more than thirty articles, primarily on missionaries.

His presidential address to the American Historical Association in 1948 provides the most succinct statement of Latourette's views. It demonstrates his controversial position as a historian with a reputation for meticulous research who nonetheless always bore Christian witness in his work. This witness, combined with his consistently optimistic view of human progress as being due in part to Christianity, was criticized by some at the meeting as resembling a sermon while others argued that the "theology was perfect." His speech, "The Christian Understanding of History," argued that

The historian, be he Christian or non-Christian, may not know whether God will fully triumph within history. He cannot conclusively demonstrate the validity of the Christian understanding of history. Yet he can establish a strong probability for the dependability of its insights. That is the most which can be expected of human reason in any of the realms of knowledge.

Latourette was killed by an unidentified motorist while in front of his family home in Oregon City, Oregon. A bachelor, he left no known survivors.

• Latourette's papers, including correspondence, diaries, notes, and clippings, are located in the Yale University Divinity Library, Special Collections. For a full autobiography, see Latourette, *Beyond the Ranges* (1967). A shorter sketch can be found in Latourette, "My Guided Life," in *Frontiers of the Christian World Mission since 1938: Essays in Honor of Kenneth Scott Latourette*, ed. Wilbur C. Harr (1962), pp. 281–93. This volume also contains a thorough, although select, bibliography of Latourette's publications. Latourette's presidential address to the American Historical Association appears in the *American Historical Review* 54 (1949): 259–76. William A. Speck, "Kenneth Scott Latourette's Vocation as Christian Historian," *Christian Scholar's Review* 4 (1975): 285–99, discusses Latourette's approach to history from his Christian perspective. Searle Bates, "Christian Historian, Doer of Christian History. In Memory of Kenneth Scott Latourette, 1884–1968," *International Review of Mission* 58 (1969): 317–26, gives a former student's assessment and appreciation of Latourette's contribution. The fullest obituary appears in the *New York Times*, 1 Jan. 1969.

ADRIAN A. BENNETT

LATROBE, Benjamin Henry (1 May 1764–3 Sept. 1820), architect and civil engineer, was born in Fulneck, Yorkshire, England, the son of Benjamin Latrobe, an English Moravian clergyman, and Anna Margaretta Antes, an American born in Pennsylvania. From 1776 until 1783 Latrobe attended Moravian schools in Germany, initially the Paedagogium at Niesky and later the seminary at Barby in Saxony, where he received a broad liberal education in the arts and sciences. Latrobe seems to have traveled extensively in eastern Germany, perhaps visiting Vienna, during his school years. Architectural drawings signed by Latrobe for buildings erected in 1784 and 1785 for a Moravian community near Manchester, England, complement his student architectural drawings of existing Moravian communities. Latrobe held a position in the Stamp Office in London from 1785 to 1794; he received an additional appointment as surveyor of the London police offices in 1792.

On 27 February 1790 Latrobe married Lydia Sellon, (c. 1763–1793), with whom he had two children. Because most of Latrobe's personal and European professional records as well as his library were lost at sea when he was en route to America in 1795–1796, many details of his early life must be pieced together from several sources, including Latrobe's journals and correspondence. Latrobe married his second wife, Mary Elizabeth Hazlehurst (1771–1841) on 1 May 1800, in Philadelphia; three of their six children lived beyond infancy.

About 1786 Latrobe began to work, perhaps as an apprentice, in the office of the leading British civil engineer John Smeaton where he was employed on the Basingstoke Canal (about 1788–1789). Latrobe's most important engineering commission in England was as a surveyor in 1793–1795 for an alternate route in Essex for the Chelmer and Blackwater Navigation system. Sometime after 1786 Latrobe visited Europe to study its great architectural and engineering monuments. He is known to have visited Paris, Naples, and Rome.

Latrobe's professional architectural career began about 1789–1790 as an employee, or perhaps improver (unpaid worker), in the office of Samuel Pepys Cockerell, who had recently inherited the practice of Sir Robert Taylor. The designs of these two leading neoclassical architects profoundly influenced Latrobe's thinking, as did their approach to the practice of architecture. They made fortunes associated with their commissions, a goal that Latrobe attempted unsuccessfully many times during his varied American career. Architecturally Cockerell was among the leaders of a restrained, simplified, and spatial approach to reviving classical architecture, in contrast to many contemporaries who adopted primarily its decorative systems. This circle included Sir John Soane, successor to Taylor as the architect of the Bank of England, with whom Latrobe's work is often compared.

About 1792 Latrobe began practicing architecture independently, receiving at least two major domestic commissions and several probable remodellings. His extant English houses, Hammerwood Lodge (1792) near East Grinstead, Sussex, and Ashdown House (1793) near Forest Row, Sussex, are notable for their early use of Greek Revival columns. They exhibit spatial and decorative themes that Latrobe repeatedly used in his American houses.

In November 1795 Latrobe, a widower for two years, embarked for the United States shortly before bankruptcy notices concerning him appeared in the London *Times* and the *European Magazine*. His illustrated journal of the arduous fifteen-week voyage records his life-long interest in the natural sciences. Latrobe's journals often contained acutely observed watercolors and drawings of animal and plant specimens, as well as geological formations, in addition to man-made structures of all kinds. Latrobe landed in Norfolk, Virginia, in March 1796 and immediately began recording its town plan, buildings, and sanitation requirements. During the next two years he lived and worked in Norfolk and Richmond. His house designs for specific clients are the William Pennock house (1796) in Norfolk, the John Tayloe house design (c. 1796–1799) perhaps for a Washington, D.C. site, and the Harvie-Gamble house (c. 1798–1799) in Richmond. Other drawings of houses from this period were done either as academic exercises, to show to prospective clients, or to record some important monument, such as Mt. Vernon, which he visited on 17 July 1796.

Latrobe's public commissions for Virginia were important for launching his national career as well as being landmark structures for the state and region. His Virginia State Penitentiary (1797–1806) was designed as a panopticon following the humanitarian penological principles of the Englishmen John Howard and Jeremy Bentham. His unexecuted Richmond Theater project (1797–1798), to have included a theater, hotel, and assembly rooms, was the first of several prominent multifunctional structures that Latrobe designed for American cities. His Shockoe Church design (c. 1798–1799), a neoclassical, twin-towered hall church intended for Richmond's Protestant Episcopal community living near the state capitol on Shockoe Hill, was his first known ecclesiatical design. In 1798 Latrobe, as an engineer member of the 1st Regiment of the Virginia Militia, made drawings to complete Fort Nelson (begun in 1779) in Norfolk; much of his design was implemented between 1802 and 1806 by the Army Corps of Engineers.

The second phase of Latrobe's American career was centered in Philadelphia where he lived from 1798 until 1807. He thrived personally and professionally in this cosmopolitan atmosphere, marrying a second time, collaborating with Thomas Jefferson on several federal government commissions, and creating several seminal works for the history of American engineering and architecture. His first Philadelphia commission was the marble Bank of Pennsylvania (1798–1801), America's first Greek Revival temple-shaped building. Latrobe's neoclassicism consisted of synthesizing Greek and Roman traditions, combining Ionic columns derived from the Erectheum in Athens with a circular, domed banking room. His volumetric treatment of the bank's interiors as well as its exterior, achieved by shallow, unadorned niches and unframed windows set directly into the wall, became the identifying hallmark of his style, copied by other architects as well as builders. Other public commissions during Latrobe's Philadelphia years include alterations to the Chestnut Street Theatre (1801), restoration of Nassau Hall for the College of New Jersey (1802) in Princeton, and a design for the Bank of Philadelphia (1807). In 1805 he was involved in planning the towns of Noscopek, Pennsylvania, and Newcastle, Delaware.

Latrobe's most important American engineering project was probably his waterworks for Philadelphia, undertaken late in 1798 shortly after the city had experienced one of several yellow fever epidemics during the 1790s. Steam engines pumped Schuylkill River water through a mile-long tunnel to the Centre Square Engine House, from which it was pumped throughout the city by additional steam engines. Architecturally the engine house was noted for its strong geometries, a three-story, 35-foot-diameter domed rotunda atop a 60-foot-wide cubical base.

For several months in 1801–1802 Latrobe was a commissioner as well as the engineer in charge of a survey for improving navigation on the Susquehanna River from the Pennsylvania border to tidewater. Subsequently he was the engineer for nearly two years in 1804–1805 for an uncompleted canal to link the Chesapeake and Delaware bays. His 1804 plan for the Washington Canal, built between 1810 and 1815, ran from the Potomac River near Georgetown, along the Mall and across Capitol Hill to empty into the Anacostia River (parts of it still exist under Constitution Avenue).

Latrobe introduced Gothic Revival domestic architecture (a few Gothic Revival churches had already been built) to America in Philadelphia with "Sedgeley" (c. 1799–1802), the William Cramond house. His reinterpretation of many European architectural traditions preceded by two or three decades their widespread use in America. Other important domestic works dating from Latrobe's Philadelphia period are the William Waln house (1805–1808) in Philadelphia and "Adena," the Thomas Worthington house (1805–1807; extant) in Chillicothe, Ohio.

Latrobe was often unsuccessful in public competitions for architectural designs and thus condemned the system as a whole. His submissions were chosen for the Virginia State Penitentiary (1797), the Baltimore Exchange (1815), and probably the Louisiana State

Bank, for which he received the commission in 1820. Latrobe lost four major competitions, in three instances to his former pupils: the New York City Hall (1802); the Baltimore Washington Monument (1810); the Richmond Theater Monument and Church (1812); and the Second Bank of the U.S. (1818) in Philadelphia. His surviving drawings for these projects have been critical for the study of American taste in the early nineteenth century.

Latrobe's patronage by the federal government began in 1800 with two projects. A few weeks after George Washington's death in December 1799 Latrobe designed a pyramidal mausoleum as a Washington Monument to be located on the banks of the Potomac River. Set on a base of thirteen steps, the pyramid's interior was decorated with allegorical scenes relating to Washington's civic and military achievements. Although it was never built, Latrobe's choice of an Egyptian form, associated in the nineteenth century with death, influenced his student Robert Mills to choose an obelisk for the Washington National Monument erected on the Mall beginning in 1848.

At the request of Secretary of War James McHenry, Latrobe made an unexecuted design in 1801 for the U.S. Military Academy; its West Point, New York, site was not determined until March 1802. Latrobe's U-shaped building contained under one roof dormitories, professors' lodgings, a library, a dining hall, and a variety of classrooms including laboratories. His subsequent designs for educational institutions include Dickinson College (1803–1805; extant) in Carlisle, Pennsylvania; a wing for the Medical School of the University of Pennsylvania (1805); an unexecuted plan for Transylvania College (1812) in Lexington, Kentucky; and an unexecuted plan for a National University (1816) in Washington.

A covered drydock for the Washington Navy Yard (1802), Latrobe's first executed government project, was commissioned by Jefferson. The president suggested that its wide span be achieved by using curved and laminated wood ribs, a system of construction devised by the French Renaissance architect Philibert de l'Orme. It was later used extensively in the United States to roof large spaces. On 6 March 1803 Jefferson appointed Latrobe surveyor of public buildings, stating that his primary responsibility was completion of the partially built Capitol. For the next six years they collaborated on the redesign of the Capitol and the White House. Latrobe initially visited Washington periodically to oversee these projects and then moved his family to the capital in 1807.

Latrobe replaced the Capitol's original 1790s wood interiors in its three-story north wing with brick and stone vaulted construction, creating new rooms for the Senate, Supreme Court, and Library of Congress. Between 1803 and 1807 he replaced a free-standing wood room for the House of Representatives (erected in 1801) with a south wing to match externally that on the north. It contained Latrobe's famous first hall for the House of Representatives, an oval room lit by 100 skylights. It was destroyed, and many other parts of the Capitol severely damaged, on 24 August 1814, when Washington's public buildings were burned by British troops during the War of 1812.

Latrobe's second tenure as architect of the Capitol began with his reappointment on 14 March 1815. During this building campaign he redesigned and enlarged the House of Representatives in the form of a hemicycle (today's Statuary Hall), enlarged the Senate chamber, proposed a new west wing to house his Egyptian Revival Library of Congress, and designed the center building to contain a domed rotunda. Reconstruction of the north and south wings was well underway when Latrobe resigned his position on 20 November 1817, but the center building and west wing were redesigned and built by his successor, Charles Bulfinch.

Latrobe's most significant contribution to the Capitol's exterior, the wide east portico and stair leading to the rotunda (labeled "Hall of the People" on an 1806 plan), was done with Jefferson's collaboration. Internally Latrobe designed unique but modestly scaled rooms to have a monumental appearance because they were to house the government's most important legislative and judicial bodies. Massive cupolas lit both his second House and Senate chambers, the latter indirectly via a double-roof system to ensure abundant natural light. Latrobe's three invented American orders (columns and their capitals) complement his Greek-inspired columns decorating the Capitol's three major rooms, the Doric Supreme Court, Ionic Senate, and Corinthian House of Representatives. The corn capital vestibule (extant) outside the Supreme Court was the most famous, but the tobacco leaf rotunda (extant) adjacent to the Senate and the magnolia flower order within the Senate chamber also drew on native American flora. Architecturally and symbolically he and Jefferson altered the Capitol's original design to express the role of the country's diverse population within its tripartite governing system.

Latrobe suggested many internal and external changes (1804; 1807; 1809) to James Hoban's design for the President's House, but only his south portico and porte-cochère at the Pennsylvania Avenue entrance were executed (by Hoban in 1824 and 1829, respectively). Latrobe received many other sporadic government commissions, including the Navy Yard (1804–1805; portion built and extant), a lighthouse on Franks Island at the mouth of the Mississippi River (1805–1819), the New Orleans Customs House (1807), a fireproof vault for Treasury Department records (1810–1811), unexecuted designs for a marine hospital in Washington (1812; 1815), plans for the U.S. Arsenal in Pittsburgh (1814), and an unrealized design for the National University (1816) to have been located on the Mall in Washington.

Latrobe's extant, but internally altered, Baltimore Cathedral, the Catholic Basilica of the Assumption of the Blessed Virgin Mary, vies with his work at the Capitol in scale, complexity, and beauty. It too was built during two design and construction campaigns, the first dating 1805–1810, the second 1817–1821. Latrobe preferred alternate designs for a Latin cross-shaped building, one Gothic in style, the other neoclassical. The trustees unanimously chose the latter with its giant Corinthian portico and a Roman Pantheon-inspired dome covering a great circular crossing, a fusion of traditional longitudinal and centralized church forms. Bishop John Carroll discussed with Latrobe the cathedral's final architectural form and details, as Jefferson had done at the Capitol. Latrobe lit the central crossing indirectly, having skylights in the outer dome just below the rim of the oculus opening of the inner dome. Throughout his career Latrobe was concerned with how to increase the spatial drama of his public buildings by manipulating natural light effects.

Public works for other clients after his move to Washington in 1807 include his appointment to build the New Orleans Waterworks (1809–1820), to design and oversee construction of the Baltimore Exchange (1815–1820; in partnership with Maximilian Godefroy), and to design the Baltimore Library Company (1817). None of these works survives. The most significant was the Baltimore Exchange, an early example of a multifunctional building on a very large scale. Ecclesiastical works during this penultimate phase of Latrobe's career were St. John's Episcopal Church (1816) in Washington and St. Paul's Episcopal Church (1817) in Alexandria, Virginia, both extant but considerably altered.

Latrobe continued to receive domestic commissions in many parts of the country after moving to Washington in 1807. His John Markoe house (1808–1811) in Philadelphia was a particularly fine example of his basic formula, with spatially expansive interiors on a relatively small scale. Latrobe intently studied how his public and private buildings would be used, determining their plans before designing their exterior shells. Typically the entrance vestibules of his houses terminated in semicircular walls articulated by symmetrical empty niches. This curved motif was often carried along the central axis to end in octagonal or semicircular bays overlooking gardens. His genius was to create satisfying sculpted volumes out of solid matter and exciting modeled volumes of light and shade out of space. His surface ornamentation was restrained, borrowed from Greek rather than more elaborately decorated Roman buildings, but his spatial types and forms were Roman in inspiration. Combining elements from different historical traditions became the leitmotif of nineteenth-century American architecture.

Little visual data exist on "Clifton" (1808), the James Harris house in Richmond, which an 1885 newspaper account claimed was the finest house ever erected in the city. His Senator John Pope house (1810–1812; extant) in Lexington, Kentucky, a freestanding suburban villa, has a picturesque sequence of spaces along an asymmetrical circulation route culminating in a second-floor domed rotunda from which public rooms and bed chambers radiate outward.

Two substantial Latrobe houses built in Washington after the War of 1812 were among his principal residential designs. The John Peter Van Ness house (1813–1817) and the Commodore Stephen Decatur house (1817–1818; extant) were both located within sight of the White House. The Decatur house is notable for having different floor plans on each of its four stories, each generated by the function of its level. The entrance hall, a sophisticated integration of space and ornament, is the best preserved of Latrobe's domestic spaces. The extent of his involvement with the Ann Casanave house (c. 1815–1817) in southwest Washington is uncertain, as is his authorship of "Brentwood" (c. 1816–1818), the Joseph Pearson house, frequently but probably erroneously attributed to him. These few houses are representative of sixty to seventy Latrobe is known to have designed.

During the interim between his federal appointments in Washington (1813–1815) Latrobe resided in Pittsburgh, where he owned one-third of Robert Fulton's Ohio Steamship Company. There he oversaw construction of shops for the company and supervised the artisans building ships designed by Fulton. The failure of this partnership proved Latrobe to be unsuccessful as a practical engineer and businessman.

Latrobe spent most of 1818 residing in Baltimore, traveling to Annapolis to do a harbor survey, reporting on a canal to divert Jones Falls (which drained into Baltimore harbor) to prevent future flooding of the city, and competing unsuccessfully for a few architectural commissions. He spent nine months in New Orleans during 1819, inspecting the construction of his Franks Island lighthouse, redesigning the main public square, and adding a central tower to New Orleans's Catholic Cathedral of St. Louis. He returned briefly to Baltimore to arrange moving his family to New Orleans. In August 1820 Latrobe won the competition for the Louisiana State Bank (extant) with a plain, cubic exterior but a sequence of vaulted rooms culminating in a domed banking hall, a variant of his 1798 Bank of Pennsylvania. Latrobe's final commission was the New Orleans Waterworks, a project in which he became involved in 1809. Two years later Latrobe sent his eighteen-year-old son Henry (whom he had trained as an engineer) to oversee implementation of his design, conceptually similar to his Philadelphia Waterworks. Henry Latrobe died of yellow fever in 1816 while engaged on the project; his father met a similar fate on 3 September 1820 just after water began flowing through the system.

The bare-bones histories of each of these projects are a poor indication of Latrobe's intellectual range and depth or the complexity of interacting personalities necessary for their construction. Unlike any other American architect of his generation, Latrobe left a paper trail of drawings and textual documents that make it possible to understand some of his intentions. Most of Latrobe's buildings have been destroyed; none survives as it was completed. One of Latrobe's greatest legacies was his education of a few architects, engineers, and craftsmen, principally Robert Mills and William Strickland. He instilled in them professional principles and standards, including the belief that architecture was an intellectual pursuit rather than a skilled craft. In his own work Latrobe fused the three aesthetic philosophies of his era, the picturesque (associated with medieval architecture), the beautiful (associated with classical architecture), and the sublime.

• A microtext edition of *The Papers of Benjamin Henry Latrobe* was issued by the Maryland Historical Society in 1976. Ten subsequent volumes (vol. 9 is divided into two separately bound parts) were prepared by a team of documentary editors led by chief editor Edward C. Carter II. In his lifetime, Latrobe published several treatises on historical and technical topics; essays, including a number that appeared in the *Transactions of the American Philosophical Society* and his "Acoustics," in the *Edinburgh Encyclopaedia* (1812); and pamphlets, such as his *View of the Practicability and Means of Supplying the City of Philadelphia with Wholesome Water* (1798) and *A Private Letter to the Individual Members of Congress on the Subject of the Public Buildings* (1806). Many of his lengthy letters to public officials were published in newspapers, and his play, *The Apology*, was produced in Richmond, Va., in 1798. A large number of his writings were not published in his lifetime, such as his "Essay on Landscape" (1798–1799). A useful biographical account is Talbot Hamlin, *Benjamin Henry Latrobe* (1955). For insightful discussions of Latrobe's place in American architectural history, see Edward C. Carter II et al., eds., *Latrobe's View of America, 1795–1820* (1985); Jeffrey A. Cohen and Charles E. Brownell, *The Architectural Drawings of Benjamin Henry Latrobe* (1994); and Pamela Scott, *Temple of Liberty* (1995).

PAMELA SCOTT

LATROBE, Benjamin Henry (19 Dec. 1806–19 Oct. 1878), civil engineer, was born in Philadelphia, Pennsylvania, the son of Benjamin Henry Latrobe, an architect, engineer, and scientist, and Mary Elizabeth Hazlehurst. Latrobe spent his early years in several cities, including Baltimore, Pittsburgh, Washington, D.C., and New Orleans, following his father's employment. Upon the death of the elder Latrobe in 1820 the family moved to Baltimore, where Benjamin entered St. Mary's College in 1821. After graduating from St. Mary's, he was admitted to the bar in 1825 and practiced law, first in Baltimore and then in Salem County, New Jersey, while also overseeing property owned by his mother. Owing to health problems, Latrobe returned to Baltimore in 1829, where he joined the practice of his brother John, who was a counsel for the Baltimore & Ohio (B&O) Railroad Company.

In the years following the War of 1812, westward expansion and a transportation revolution in the form of steam, rail, canal, and road were accompanied by increases in commercial traffic. While successfully utilizing the clipper ship for coastal and foreign trade, Baltimore was losing commercial ground to New York City on the routes west as a result of the completion of the Erie Canal in 1825. In an attempt to gain a competitive edge in internal trade, the B&O Railroad Company was chartered, and the cornerstone for a line that would run west to the Ohio River was laid in Baltimore on 4 July 1828.

Within a year of returning to Baltimore, Latrobe gave up the law in favor of an engineering career. With his brother's help, he obtained a position with the B&O in 1830, starting at the bottom as a surveyor's rodman on the portion of the line being constructed beyond Ellicott's Mills, Maryland. Moving quickly up the ladder, Latrobe was made a principal assistant to Chief Engineer Jonathan Knight by 1832. He married a cousin, Maria Eleanor Hazlehurst, in 1833; they had six children. Also in 1833, after surveying several routes for the Washington, D.C., branch of the B&O, Latrobe was assigned to design the viaduct that would carry the track over the Patapsco River at Relay, Maryland. At age twenty-six he had no formal engineering education and had never built a bridge before. Latrobe's Thomas Viaduct, named for B&O president Philip E. Thomas but at one time known as "Latrobe's Folly," was a curving granite structure over 600 feet long, with eight sixty-foot arches; upon its completion in 1835 it was the largest bridge in America and the first built on a curving alignment.

Throughout the 1830s Latrobe made a name for himself in railroad surveys and construction, especially through his bridge designs. At Harpers Ferry, West Virginia, in 1834 he designed a six-span, 800-foot covered bridge that was completed in 1837. In 1835 he briefly left the B&O to become chief engineer of the Baltimore & Port Deposit Railroad. Latrobe had several novel ideas for this route from Baltimore to Havre-de-Grace, Maryland: three bridges of considerable length were built over rivers with extremely deep mud by supporting the structures on piles, and at Havre-de-Grace the train cars with freight and baggage were ferried across the river on tracks laid on the upper deck of a steamboat. He returned to the B&O in 1836 under the title of engineer of location and construction. By 1839 Latrobe had located the B&O from Harpers Ferry to Cumberland, Maryland, with a plan that included three tunnels and eleven bridges. During this time Latrobe experimented with various types of locomotive engines, using different kinds of coal and terrain in his tests.

The Baltimore to Cumberland section of the B&O was completed in 1842. Upon its completion, Knight resigned and Latrobe was appointed chief engineer of the B&O. After Knight became the consulting engineer for the city of Wheeling, West Virginia, the two engineers had a disagreement over the route of the B&O to Wheeling, and by 1845 they were waging pamphlet attacks against each other. The section to Wheeling was finally authorized in 1847, but the terrain presented several design challenges to Latrobe. He conquered these through the use of masonry walls to carry the railroad along the slopes, viaducts across gorges supported on slender cast-iron pillars, and twelve tunnels, among them the 4,100-foot Kingwood tunnel. By the time the track was completed to Wheeling on Christmas Eve 1852, Latrobe and colleagues such as Wendel Bollman and Albert Fink had redesigned wooden truss bridges into iron, and according to the *Baltimore & Ohio Annual Report* of 1847, Latrobe had coined the phrase "ton mile" as the railroad unit of work. Latrobe had often been a supporter of

innovation as well as a contributor; in 1843 both La-
trobe and his brother John endorsed Samuel F. B.
Morse's proposal to run a telegraph line alongside the
Baltimore-Washington branch of B&O track.

In his later years Latrobe took on a multitude of duties. In addition to his duties as the chief engineer for
the B&O, he had accepted the job of general superintendent of the railroad, overseeing the track and locomotives. During the 1850s and 1860s he was a consulting engineer for several railroad companies, often in
regard to bridge construction. Latrobe was appointed
president of the Pittsburgh & Connellsville Railroad
Company in 1856 and assumed the additional job of
chief engineer of that railroad in 1858. He retired from
the presidency in 1864 but retained the title of chief
engineer, a dividend of which was the opportunity to
drive the golden spike that connected that railroad to
the B&O in 1871. Between 1866 and 1869 Latrobe
served as a consulting engineer on the Hoosac Tunnel,
and also in 1869 he was brought in as a consulting expert on John Roebling's design for New York City's
East River Suspension Bridge (now the Brooklyn
Bridge).

Latrobe withdrew from active participation in engineering in 1872. He died at his home in Baltimore. Latrobe is among those individuals who literally changed
the face of America. His innovations in bridge design,
track systems, and tunnel construction, and their incorporation into railroad lines, ushered in a new era
for American transportation systems and contributed
to the commercial and social growth of the nation
through the movement of people and goods. Latrobe's
approach to engineering problems, in which he looked
at the system as a whole as well as in parts—including
management of people, energy, and machines—
marked a new era in the engineering profession and
kept the Baltimore & Ohio at the forefront of railroads
for much of the nineteenth century.

• Personal papers of Latrobe can be found in the Latrobe
Family Papers, 1796–1947, at the Maryland Historical Society. Included in this collection is the manuscript copy of John
Edward Semmes, *John H. B. Latrobe and His Times, 1803–
1891* (1917), which although written about his brother, contains information about Latrobe's work and family life. Another primary source are the records of the B&O Railroad
Company, some of which (c. 1826–1951) are located in the
Smithsonian Institution, National Museum of American History, Division of Mechanical and Civil Engineering in Washington, D.C. Various reports by Latrobe are in the Library of
Congress. For information regarding the period during
which Latrobe was with the Pittsburgh & Connellsville Railroad Company, see the collection of letters between Latrobe
and Albert Warfield in the Albert Warfield Gallatin Papers,
Duke University Libraries. Another Biographical sketch is in
Charles B. Stuart, *Lives and Works of Civil and Military Engineers of America* (1871). Works supplying information on the
content and context of Latrobe's career as a railroad engineer
and further bibliographical items include John F. Stover,
History of the Baltimore and Ohio Railroad (1987), and James
D. Dilts, *The Great Road: The Building of the Baltimore and*
Ohio, the Nation's First Railroad, 1828–1853 (1993). Obituar-
ies are in *Railway Age*, 31 Oct. 1878, *Railroad Gazette*, 25
Oct. 1878, and the *Baltimore Sun*, 21 Oct. 1878.

MARY M. THOMAS

LATROBE, John Hazlehurst Boneval (4 May 1803–11
Sept. 1891), lawyer, was born in Philadelphia, Pennsylvania, the son of Benjamin Henry Latrobe, Sr., an architect and civil engineer, and Mary Elizabeth Hazlehurst. His father accepted the post of surveyor of
public buildings for the United States government,
and the family moved to Washington, D.C., in 1807.
Benjamin Latrobe played an active role in the design
and construction of the Capitol, but the War of 1812
diverted funds from the project, and construction temporarily ceased. As a result, the family moved to Pittsburgh in 1813. Benjamin Latrobe resumed his work
on the Capitol in the spring of 1815, and the family
returned to Washington. John and his brother Benjamin enrolled at Georgetown College on 26 June 1815
as boarding students. His father resigned his job as
surveyor and architect of the Capitol in early 1817, and
the family moved to Baltimore. In December 1817
John was appointed a cadet at West Point, then under
General Sylvanus Thayer's superintendency, and reported there in September 1818.

After his father's death due to yellow fever in New
Orleans, Latrobe became the family's sole means of financial support. As a result, he resigned from West
Point in December 1821 although he stood at the head
of his class with five months left before his intended
graduation date. He returned to Baltimore and found
employment as a law student in the office of General
Robert Goodloe Harper, a friend of his father's. Latrobe was admitted to the Maryland bar on 8 May 1824
and to the bar of the United States Supreme Court in
1830. He gained a reputation as a leading railroad and
patent lawyer in his lengthy career. He became chief
counsel of the Baltimore and Ohio Railroad at the time
of its incorporation in 1828, a post he held until his
death. He was instrumental in obtaining an agreement
between Samuel F. B. Morse and the Baltimore and
Ohio Railroad, which allowed Morse to use the railroad's right-of-way to construct the first telegraph
line. Morse sent his celebrated first telegraph message
from Washington to Baltimore over this line in 1844.
Latrobe served as attorney in many telegraph patent
disputes over the next thirty years. Working for Western Union in 1877, he successfully prosecuted the Atlantic and Pacific Telegraph Company for infringing
the former's patent rights to Edison's Quadruplex
transmission system.

Latrobe was an active philanthropist and devoted
much of his time to four causes, African colonization
and the settlement of Liberia; the Maryland Institute,
a mechanics' institute modeled after Philadelphia's
Franklin Institute; the Maryland Historical Society;
and the construction of public parks in Baltimore. He
believed that the only permanent and workable solution to the problems of slavery and race prejudice was
the voluntary emigration of freed blacks to the colony

of Liberia on the west coast of Africa. Active in the African colonization and settlement movement from 1822, he succeeded Henry Clay as president of the American Colonization Society after Clay's death in 1853, holding this post until his own death. Latrobe was influential in establishing the Maryland colony at Cape Palmas on Liberia's far southeastern coast and helped to secure $275,000 from the Maryland legislature to defray transportation costs for the emigrants. He authored the Maryland settlement's constitution and first laws, and he and Harper drew the first map of Liberia and named the first towns. He was active in publicizing the colonization effort, writing several pamphlets to that end.

Latrobe had helped to found the Maryland Institute in 1825. When a fire destroyed the building in February 1835, he actively assisted in the institute's rebuilding, which culminated in its successful 1847 reconstruction and reorganization. He was one of the founders of the Maryland Historical Society in 1844 and served as its first vice president from 1866 to 1871 and as president from 1871 until his death. In 1851 Latrobe became one of Baltimore's first citizens to advocate the construction of public parks. He served as president of the city's park board from 1860 until his death. His other activities included sitting on the board of visitors to West Point after 1847 and serving as president of the American chapter of the Association for the Exploration of Africa.

After a four-year courtship he married Margaret Stuart in 1828; they had one child. She took sick in late 1830 and died in January 1831. He met his second wife, Charlotte Claiborne, while vacationing in the summer of 1832 at Virginia Springs, Virginia; they were married later that year. They had eight children, one of whom died in infancy. While Latrobe himself took no active part in the Civil War, two of his sons fought for the southern cause. A third son served as mayor of Baltimore for seven terms.

Latrobe's various accomplishments include a favorable reputation as an amateur painter and architect. He won a competition in 1825 to design a monument to Thaddeus Kosciuszko, the Polish army officer who assisted the Continental army during the revolutionary war. This monument was installed on the grounds of the U.S. Military Academy at West Point. He also designed several structures in Baltimore, including portions of the Baltimore Catholic Cathedral and monuments in Greenmount Cemetery. He designed and patented an improved stove and fireplace heater in 1846, which met with modest financial success. Latrobe died in Baltimore.

• The Maryland Historical Society in Baltimore houses the papers of both John H. B. Latrobe and his father Benjamin Latrobe, Sr. Latrobe was a prolific author and orator. Of special interest is his edited version of his father's journal, to which he contributed an introduction, *The Journal of Benjamin Henry Latrobe: Being the Notes and Sketches of an Architect, Naturalist and Traveler in the United States from 1796 to 1820* (1905). He also wrote several pamphlets that illuminate the activities and views of the African colonization movement

during the 1850s. One, *Colonization: A Notice of Victor Hugo's Views of Slavery in the United States* (1851), is a refutation of Hugo's abolitionist views. Another, *Colonization and Abolition* (1852), is a polemic against northern abolitionist views and advocates the emigration of freed blacks as the only workable solution to the slavery question. His *African Colonization* (1853) discusses the effects of European immigration on emancipated blacks and contains a useful historical sketch of the colonization movement. A fourth, *The Regina Coeli* (1858), is a defense of the Republic of Liberia against charges of complicity in the French slave trade. His other publications include *A Biography of Charles Carroll of Carrollton* (1824), *The Justices' Practice under the Laws of Maryland* (1826), *Scott's Infantry and Rifle Tactics* (1828), *Picture of Baltimore* (1832), *History of Mason and Dixon's Line* (1854), *Personal Recollections of the Baltimore and Ohio Railroad* (1868), *Hints for Six Months in Europe* (1869), *History of Maryland in Liberia* (1885), and *Reminiscences of West Point* (1887). He also privately published *Odds and Ends*, a collection of verse. The standard biography of Latrobe is John E. Semmes, *John H. B. Latrobe and His Times* (1917). It is largely sympathetic and quotes freely from Latrobe's correspondence; it is weak on analysis and context. Another useful source is Samuel Wilson, ed., *Southern Travels: Journal of John H. B. Latrobe, 1834* (1986). Wilson wrote a brief biographical sketch and an introduction that places Latrobe in his historical context. The journal itself contains a valuable account of the hardships and adventures of contemporary travel, southern manners and society, and New Orleans life.

DAVID HOCHFELDER

LATTIMORE, John Aaron Cicero (23 June 1876?–31 Dec. 1959), physician and civil rights activist, was born near Shelby, Cleveland County, North Carolina, the son of John Carpenter Lattimore and Marcella Hambrick, former slaves and farmers. Lattimore graduated from Bennett College in Greensboro, North Carolina, with an A.B. in 1897. He then attended Meharry Medical College in Nashville, Tennessee, receiving his M.D. in 1901. With a fellow classmate, H. B. Beck, as a partner, he began the general practice of medicine in Louisville, Kentucky; after considerable effort, his practice grew. In 1928 he married Naomi Anthony of Louisville; they had no children.

To provide better care for his patients, Lattimore established the Lattimore Clinic. This effort marked the beginning of a professional lifetime devoted to improving medical care for the black community and presaged similar efforts for improving public health measures, hospital care, and educational opportunities for them. Lattimore served in the Louisville Health Department from 1928 to 1946. His clinical skills were recognized by his election to the John Andrew Clinical Society of Tuskegee Institute.

During the flood of 1937 Lattimore was appointed to the Mayor's Flood Relief Committee. This experience in administering relief and medical care to large numbers of displaced people led to his appointment in 1937 to the advisory committee of the Central District of the American Red Cross.

Lattimore campaigned for the improvement and integration of hospital facilities in the state mental hospitals, resulting in the construction of a new building (begun in 1941) at the Central State Hospital near Louisville. The governor of Kentucky later recognized him for his efforts to obtain the new facilities and to ensure that they were integrated.

By having Kentucky's Day Law amended, Lattimore effected the first step toward obtaining opportunities for professional education for blacks. This law had prohibited blacks and whites from attending school in the same classrooms, but the amendment permitted the integration of professional schools in Kentucky. Lattimore later served on the Governor's Commission on Adult Education.

Through a lifetime involvement in his profession, the African Methodist Episcopal church, and several fraternal organizations, Lattimore became identified as a pillar of the black community. He helped to organize the Louisville chapter of the NAACP and served on its board until his death. Before 1920 he organized, with others, the Louisville Interracial Group; in 1921 he founded a local "Big Brother" movement from which arose the local Urban League (1915–1959), a system for furthering race relations in Louisville. He served for the remainder of his life in this interracial group.

Although he never campaigned for or held an elective office, Lattimore did direct a local political maneuver. Initially a Republican, in 1921 he organized a local third party, the Lincoln party, which assisted black residents in changing their registered political preference to Democrat. It was with some unpleasantness that Lattimore became one of the first black people in Louisville to register as a Democrat.

Lattimore served the black medical profession as an early member, president and vice president of the Blue Grass Medical Association (established in 1899). He helped to organize the Falls City Medical Society, serving as its president and vice president. He also became the president (1947–1948) of the National Medical Association.

Lattimore's many contributions to Louisville and particularly to its black community were recognized over the years. He received the Alpha Phi Alpha Fraternity Award for outstanding leadership (1946 and 1959); he was named Man of the Year by the *Louisville Defender* (1956); the Urban League Guild gave him its Honors Award for initiating health campaigns in Kentucky; and he received an NAACP trophy for outstanding leadership in race relations in Kentucky (1959).

Always modest and unpretentious, Lattimore attributed his numerous contributions to medicine, public health, society, and the civil rights movement to the efforts of others. In an article about him in the *Louisville Courier-Journal* (23 Sept. 1951), in which his accomplishments were summarized, he credited his success to "my confrères, among them the leading white practitioners in the city, without their freely given cooperation in even the tiniest professional matters, I could not have got anywhere." He died in Louisville.

• Some biographical material is contained in the Lattimore papers, Ekstrom Library, University of Louisville, Belknap. Biographical information also appears in the Louisville *Courier-Journal*, 23 Sept. 1951, and in obituaries in the *Louisville Defender*, 31 Dec. 1959, the *Courier-Journal*, 1 Jan. 1960, and the *Journal of the National Medical Association* 53 (Sept. 1961): 536.

EUGENE H. CONNER

LATTIMORE, Owen (29 July 1900–31 May 1989), columnist and Asia expert, was born in Washington, D.C., the son of David Lattimore, a professor of modern languages, and Margaret Barnes. In 1901 the family moved to Shanghai, where Lattimore's father taught in Chinese government schools. In 1912 Lattimore's mother took the children to study in Switzerland. When World War I broke out, Lattimore went to school in England for five years but failed to win a scholarship to Oxford.

Disappointed, Lattimore returned in 1919 to China, where he worked in a treaty port trading firm and newspaper before taking a job in commercial insurance. This work involved extensive travel and permitted him to study Chinese. During this period Owen had his first encounter with caravans from Inner Asia and developed a fascination with Central Asia that colored his whole life.

In 1925 Lattimore met Eleanor Holgate, the daughter of mathematician Thomas Holgate, former president of Northwestern University, who was traveling with her father in China. The couple was married in 1926; they had one child. The Lattimores undertook an extensive adventure across Mongolia, Soviet Central Asia, and Chinese Turkestan (Sinkiang) from August 1926 to September 1927. The trip resulted in his first books, *Desert Road to Turkestan* (1929) and *High Tartary* (1930).

In spite of his lack of a university education, Lattimore began a life of research and writing. From 1928 to 1937 he enjoyed a fellowship at Harvard, assumed the editorship of *Pacific Affairs*, and lived in Peking with the support of the Guggenheim Foundation and Social Science Research Council fellowships. *Pacific Affairs* was intended to voice the opinions of the various nations that made up the journal's advisory body; the editor was to referee the exchange in a responsible manner. As editor from 1933 to 1941, Lattimore led an effort to introduce Soviet participation while still accommodating strong anti-Soviet positions. A man of strong opinions, he opposed Japanese expansionism into Northeast Asia, particularly Manchuria, as was reflected in his book *Manchuria, Cradle of Conflict* (1932). In 1938 Lattimore took a position at Johns Hopkins University as a lecturer in history and in 1939 became director of the Walter Hines Page School of International Relations there.

In Peking, Lattimore had begun to study Mongolian and to undertake his major work, *The Inner Asian Frontiers of China* (1940). Arguing against Ellsworth Huntington's geographical determinism as the shaping force of nomadic life, he maintained that population pressure from the sedentary Chinese civilization had forced border area peoples to take up wholly nomadic ways. He believed the Chinese incapable of abandoning their pattern of settled agriculture. Yet in the ongoing competition between these two different forms of society, the nomadic, horse-riding Inner Asians often won because they were more willing to modify their life styles than were the Chinese farmers and their bureaucratic rulers. This, he reasoned, was how the great empires of nomadic conquest had come about in China. The book remains an important theoretical work on Asian society, and Lattimore's ideas can be said to be thoroughly American in that he focuses on the frontier as the shaper of civilizations.

In 1934 Lattimore's growing fascination with the Mongols resulted in *The Mongols of Manchuria* (1934). At the time, Lattimore endorsed the Soviet's toleration of Mongol society as preferable either to Japanese-style domination or the Chinese pattern of displacement of nomadic peoples. After visiting Mao Tse-tung in Yenan in 1937, Lattimore felt that, although a Communist, Mao was a representative of the Chinese agricultural society that endangered the Mongols. Lattimore later expanded on these notions in *Solution in Asia* (1945) and in a syndicated American newspaper column.

President Franklin D. Roosevelt in May 1941 asked Lattimore to go to China as an adviser to Chiang Kai-shek, the president of Nationalist China. Serving in Chungking from July 1941 until January 1942, Lattimore seems to have formed strongly negative opinions about the Nationalist leader and his government. Later in 1942 he joined the U.S. Office of War Information in San Francisco as deputy director of the Pacific bureau. From April to July 1944 he accompanied Vice President Henry Wallace on a trip through the Soviet Union and China. These activities seemed, to his postwar critics, laden with opportunities to sabotage American policy in China. In 1945 anti-Communist writers began to pillory Lattimore in mainstream publications, such as *Reader's Digest*, for his favorable views toward the Soviet Union, his insistence that Mao was not a tool of Moscow, and his lack of support for Chiang Kai-shek. Lattimore's views were not only a consequence of his attachment to Mongolia, but his concern to preserve Mongolia strongly influenced his attitudes toward Japan, Stalin and the Soviet Union, and China as represented by both Chiang Kai-shek and Mao Tse-tung.

By early 1949 it was clear that the Nationalists were losing China. To the great consternation of the Nationalist government's supporters in the United States, the Department of State increasingly drew away from supporting Chiang Kai-shek. At a State Department policy discussion of early October 1949 (just after the formal proclamation of the Communist government in Peking), Lattimore endorsed the official U.S. policy of waiting for the dust to settle before backing either Peking or Chiang Kai-shek. Lattimore further suggested that U.S. recognition of Peking might at sometime be desirable. A year later, in late 1950, with Peking's ar-

mies attacking American troops in Korea, this advice seemed especially sinister.

After the conviction of Alger Hiss in January 1950, the anti-Communist crusade reached new heights under Republican senator Joseph McCarthy, who announced in February that the State Department was riddled with Communists. Challenged to provide proof, McCarthy named Lattimore as "the top Russian spy" in the American government. Democratic senator Millard Tydings headed a committee to investigate loyalty at the State Department, and Lattimore, who was only an adviser and never a State Department employee, appeared in April 1950 before the Tydings Committee and provided a vigorous defense of himself. The committee cleared Lattimore, who, in his final remarks, publicly excoriated McCarthy.

McCarthy continued into the 1950s to rail from the Senate floor against Lattimore, whom he charged was a Communist. Johns Hopkins University came under pressure to fire Lattimore, a lecturer who lacked both formal tenure and a university degree. Lattimore's income from his newspaper column dried up, as did his lecture invitations. Some of his friends at the State Department were dismissed as security risks. Lattimore faced a second round of hearings before the Senate Internal Security Subcommittee, which ran from July 1951 until July 1952 and ended with charges that Lattimore had been from the 1930s "a conscious articulate instrument of Soviet policy" and had committed perjury in his testimony. The Department of Justice twice tried to bring these charges to trial only to have them dismissed. While these decisions were under appeal, the Department of State denied Lattimore a passport. Although by the end of 1956 the Senate had censured McCarthy, the preceding years had taken an enormous financial, emotional, and intellectual toll on the Lattimores and had doomed his efforts to start Mongolian studies in the United States.

In 1961 Lattimore did obtain a passport to visit Mongolia and in 1963 moved to the University of Leeds in England as professor of chinese studies in the hope of resurrecting there his goal of pursuing Mongol studies.

Following his retirement at Leeds in 1970, Lattimore returned to the United States with his wife, who died en route. Although he continued to work, often assisted by a former student, Fujiko Isono, his life became increasingly disorganized and peripatetic. He spent his last years near his son, David, in New England. He died in Providence, Rhode Island.

Lattimore was one of America's most knowledgeable Asia experts; he was also a liberal and an internationalist. He never favored the isolation of the Soviet Union; he always preferred dialogue. He felt that the Cold War would further harm the Mongols, whose interests would inevitably be overridden by the major powers—the Soviet Union, China, and the United States—as they were locked in larger struggles. Although the U.S. domestic anti-Communist crusade from 1948 to 1956 almost consumed his life and career, he and his wife struggled to retain their focus on Mongolia.

• The Library of Congress contains Lattimore's papers, and the Federal Bureau of Investigation Headquarters in Washington, D.C., holds extensive files on Lattimore. The Hamburger Archives at Johns Hopkins University preserves correspondence from the period of his service there from 1946 to 1952. Lattimore's own reminiscences about his life down to 1945 are found in *China Memoirs* (1941). A full-scale biography is Robert P. Newman, *Owen Lattimore and the "Loss" of China* (1992). James Cotton presents a valuable interpretation of Lattimore's writings in *Asian Frontier Nationalism: Owen Lattimore and the American Policy Debate* (1989). Lionel O. S. Lewis, *The Cold War and Academic Freedom: The Lattimore Case at Johns Hopkins* (1993), details how Lattimore was treated by that university. John T. Flynn makes the anti-Communist case against Lattimore in *The Lattimore Story* (1950). Lattimore's own defense is *Ordeal by Slander* (1950). Thomas C. Reeves, *The Life and Times of Joe McCarthy* (1982), and David M. Oshinsky, *A Conspiracy So Immense: The World of Joe McCarthy* (1983), put the Lattimore case in the context of the McCarthy era. Obituaries are in the *New York Times* and the *Washington Post*, both 1 June 1989, and the *Journal of Asian Studies* 48 (1989): 945–46.

DAVID D. BUCK

LATTIMORE, Richmond Alexander (6 May 1906–26 Feb. 1984), classicist, translator, and poet, was born in Paotingfu, China, the son of David Lattimore and Margaret Barnes, teachers. In 1920 Lattimore came to the United States with his parents from China, where his parents had gone to teach. After attending high school, he received his A.B. from Dartmouth College in 1926 and his M.A. from the University of Illinois in 1927, becoming an assistant professor at Wabash College. He won a Rhodes Scholarship to Oxford in 1929, where he earned a First in Greats in 1932, then returned to Illinois and received his Ph.D. in 1935. In 1934 he was made a Fellow of the American Academy in Rome, where he met Alice Bockstahler, whom he married the following year. They had two children. Lattimore became an assistant professor at Bryn Mawr College where he remained until his retirement, except for military service in World War II (1943–1946) and various visiting fellowships and professorships. He was a Fulbright scholar in Greece in 1951–1952, an award that was won despite the fact that at this time his older brother, Owen Lattimore, was being charged before a Senate committee with having been involved in a Communist conspiracy.

The year at Rome allowed Richmond Lattimore to expand his dissertation on Greek and Latin epitaphs, a taxonomy of ancient grave inscriptions, and he published it in 1942 (*Themes in Greek and Latin Epitaphs*). Lattimore continued producing occasional scholarly articles and later wrote two sensible and perceptive volumes about tragedy, *The Poetry of Greek Tragedy* (1958) and *Story Patterns in Greek Tragedy* (1964), but he had long had an interest in writing and translating poetry himself. He had published an early book of poems, *Hanover Poems* (1927), and had translated selected fragments of the pre-Socratic philosophers for Mat-

thew Thompson McClure's *The Early Philosophers of Greece* (1935). In 1942 he published translations of five of Pindar's odes (*Some Odes of Pindar*) in the series The Poet of the Month. After the war he published a translation of all of Pindar (*The Odes of Pindar* [1947]) and then of other early Greek poets (*Greek Lyrics* [1949]). This was to be the métier for which he would become best known. In 1951 he published his translation of the *Iliad*, and the year after that the first volume of the University of Chicago's *The Complete Greek Tragedies* appeared, with Lattimore and David Grene as coeditors. Lattimore would eventually contribute translations of Aeschylus's *Oresteia* and Euripides' *The Trojan Women*, *Alcestis*, *Helen*, *Rhesus*, and *Iphigeneia in Tauris*. He also translated Hesiod's *Works and Days*, *Theogony*, and *The Shield of Herakles* (1959); the *Odyssey* (1967); and Aristophanes' *Frogs* (1962).

Lattimore's translations sometimes duplicated the complex meters of the original Greek, as in his *Greek Lyrics*. In his *Iliad* and *Odyssey* he did not attempt to reproduce the dactylic hexameter of Homer but worked instead in a meter that required six stressed syllables to the line. Lattimore hewed close to the actual words of the original texts and tried not to import additional words and with them additional meanings. One critic called the versions "tracing paper translations."

At the same time Lattimore was producing poetry of his own, which eventually appeared in five volumes. *Poems* (1957) came first, followed by *Sestina for a Far-Off Summer: Poems 1957–62* (1962) and *The Stride of Time: New Poems and Translations, 1966* (1966). In 1972 these first three collections were published with additional new poems in *Poems from Three Decades*. Lattimore's final volume of poetry was *Continuing Conclusions* (1983). As in his translations, Lattimore's meter is seldom as free as that of his contemporaries, and he often worked in rigid forms such as the sonnet and even the sestina. Still, Lattimore's poetry reveals the intense personal feelings of an educated artist. His topics are sometimes autobiographical ("Wabash Blues," "Memory of a Scholar"), sometimes reflecting a particular moment from which he has taken a powerful image ("A Siding near Chillicothe"), sometimes, appropriately, catching a classical motif in a modern setting ("Sirens in the Aegean"), and sometimes showing the confluence of his extensive travels with his knowledge of history ("Yannina and Ali Pasha," "Krupp's Essen"). Lattimore's combined work gained him many awards, including, just weeks before his death in Rosemont, Pennsylvania, one from the Academy of American Poets.

Lattimore retired from Bryn Mawr in 1971 and turned his hand to a last phase of productivity. He had already published a translation of *Revelation* in 1962, and now he republished it along with new translations of the Gospels (*The Four Gospels and the Revelation* [1979]). In 1982 his *Acts and Letters of the Apostles* appeared. In these final works Lattimore followed the same principle that had guided his translation of classical texts, reproducing in contemporary language the sense and words of the original while not going beyond them.

• Lattimore's papers, including unpublished manuscripts, are in the archives of Bryn Mawr College. The most complete biography of Lattimore is by Emily D. Townsend Vermeule in *The American Philosophical Society Year Book, 1985*, pp. 154–59. For a bibliography of Lattimore's work until 1971, see *Richmond Lattimore: A Bibliography* (1971). An obituary is in the *New York Times*, 28 Feb. 1984.

TIMOTHY LONG

LAUGHLIN, Gail (7 May 1868–13 Mar. 1952), feminist, lawyer, and state legislator, was born Abbie Hill "Gail" Laughlin in Robbinston, Maine, the daughter of Robert Clark Laughlin, an ironworker, and Elizabeth Porter Stuart. After the death of her father, Laughlin's indigent family moved to Saint Stephen, New Brunswick, where her mother's family resided. In 1880 the family settled in Portland, Maine, where Laughlin graduated from Portland High School in 1886, receiving a medal for the highest marks.

After four years of work as a bookkeeper to procure funds to further her education, she entered Wellesley College. There Laughlin founded the Agora Society in 1890 to advance the study of political science and promote debate. She remained president of that organization throughout her four years at Wellesley. Upon graduation in 1894, Laughlin accepted a position as a writer for the *American Economist*. She left that post in 1896, having saved enough money to enroll at Cornell University Law School. Just two years later, she received her LL.B., and after passing the New York bar exam the following year, she opened a firm in New York City. During 1898–1899 she worked as an editorial writer for the *New York Commercial Advertiser* (later *The Globe*).

In 1900 Laughlin was appointed, along with other representatives of business and politics, an expert agent in economics for the U.S. Industrial Commission. In time, Laughlin drafted a report on the plight of minority women as domestic servants, and after two years of work with the commission she abandoned her law practice to dedicate herself exclusively to the cause of women's rights. In 1902 she joined the National American Woman Suffrage Association (NAWSA), and for the next four years she spoke on behalf of NAWSA and organized women throughout the nation.

By 1906 women had gained the right to vote in Colorado, so Laughlin chose Denver as the place to open another law practice. She subsequently passed the Colorado bar and in 1908 established her office. She involved herself intensely in local and state government while residing in Denver. From 1911 to 1914 she was a member of the state board of pardons, and in 1912 she served on the Mayor's Advisory Council for Denver. The same year, she began an association with Colorado's executive committee for the Progressive party, serving as secretary through 1914 and state vice chairperson in 1913–1914. Through her political

work, Laughlin became increasingly aware of the necessity for female jurors because, she argued, unsympathetic all-male juries rendered inequitable decisions.

Later in 1914 Laughlin moved to San Francisco, where she opened her third law firm and again concentrated her efforts on working within the political system to advance the rights of women. She joined the National Woman's Party, eventually becoming vice chairperson, and became an activist in support of suffrage and the Equal Rights Amendment (ERA) and in opposition to the so-called protective laws for women. During the next few years, Laughlin also served as a judge in the police courts, founded and directed the California branch of the National League for Women's Services, and became the vice chairperson of the Women's Council of Defense for San Francisco County. Between 1918 and 1920 she was the president of the California Civic League. Perhaps her greatest accomplishment of this period was writing and lobbying for the law that allowed women to serve on California juries. She was later victorious in her defense of the constitutionality of this law.

In 1919 Laughlin attended the first national conference of the National Federation of Business and Professional Women (NFBPW) in St. Louis, where she gave several speeches and was unanimously voted president of the organization. The goal of the federation was to work for equality for women in business and industry. Under Laughlin's guidance, within a year, the organization evolved to include 287 associations, with nearly every state being represented, comprising a total membership of 26,000 women. Between 1920 and 1922 Laughlin was a member of the statewide Republican Central Committee in California.

In 1924 Laughlin returned to her home state, settling in Portland, where she joined her brother Frederick in legal practice. She became actively involved in both her community and her state. She first ran for the Maine state legislature in 1929, after an appeal by a group of clubwomen convinced her that she could contribute more effectively on a grand scale. She won that race as well as two subsequent ones, serving as a legislator from 1929 to 1935. During her three terms she used her standing to persevere in the fight for justice for women. She proposed several bills that became law, including increasing the marriage age for females from thirteen to sixteen. She also lent her support to the temperance movement, staunchly fighting the repeal of prohibition, a feminist issue based on the belief that restricting the excessive drinking habits of husbands discouraged spousal abuse. Unrelenting in her fight for women, Laughlin was accredited to practice before the U.S. Supreme Court, to which she pled in 1931 for the inclusion of women in jury duty.

In 1935 Laughlin was first elected to the Maine state senate, where she remained faithful to the Republican party and renounced the New Deal. After six years as a senator, she was appointed the first female recorder of court decisions by the governor of Maine. She remained in that position until 1945 and maintained her law practice through 1948, at which point she retired because of a minor stroke. Laughlin died at the home she and her brother shared in Portland. She did not marry.

Laughlin determined from childhood to fight for women's liberty. At the age of twelve she pledged to "dedicate [her] entire life to the freeing of women and establishing their proper place in this 'man's world.'" By working within the existing political structure, she achieved her goal through activism, rewriting and proposing laws, and becoming vigorously involved in committees and organizations on every political level. Distinct from these concrete contributions to the fight for women's equality were more abstract ones, including a capacity for personal influence. The *(Portland) Oregonian* said of her address at the NAWSA national convention of 1905, "Her arguments are the straight, convincing kind that leave nothing for the other fellow to say. She comes to Oregon a lawyer . . . who is proudly boasted of, and justly, by her fellow workers" *(History of Woman Suffrage*, vol. 5, p. 139). Laughlin's life stands as a historical model of all that can be accomplished through education, inspiration, and tenacity.

• Clippings files concerning Laughlin are at the Resources Office of Wellesley College and the NFBPW office in Washington, D.C. Laughlin was the author of "Woman Suffrage and Prosperity," a pamphlet included in her collection entitled *Woman Suffrage Tracts*; a book called *A College Girl on the Wilson Bill*; the "Report of Domestic Service," *U.S. Industrial Commission Reports*, vol. 14 (1901); and "Equal Suffrage and Nevada Prosperity," *Out West*, Aug. 1914. For information regarding Laughlin's involvement in suffrage, ERA activism, and equality for women in professions, see Elizabeth Cady Stanton et al., *History of Woman Suffrage*, vols. 4–6 (1902–1922). Biographical information about Laughlin is in Judith A. Leavitt, *American Women Managers and Administrators* (1985). See also Ruth Sexton Sargent, *Gail Laughlin, ERA's Advocate* (1979). Obituaries are in the *New York Times*, 14 Mar. 1952; *Industry Woman* 31 (Apr. 1952): 128; and the *Portland (Maine) Evening Express*, 13 Mar. 1952.

ELIF Ö. ERGINER

LAUGHLIN, Harry Hamilton (11 Mar. 1880–26 Jan. 1943), eugenicist, was born in Oskaloosa, Iowa, the son of George Hamilton Laughlin, a professor of ancient languages and a preacher, and Deborah Jane Ross. The family moved to Kirksville, Missouri, in 1891. After graduating from the North Missouri State Normal School in 1900, Laughlin was hired as principal of the Kirksville high school (1900–1902). He later took agriculture courses at Iowa State College but did not earn a graduate degree. He was also the high school principal in Centerville, Iowa (1902–1905). From 1905 to 1907 he served as the superintendent of Kirksville public schools, then taught agriculture courses at North Missouri State.

In February 1907, Laughlin's interest in breeding experiments to improve poultry caused him to write to Charles Benedict Davenport, the director of the new Station for Experimental Evolution at Cold Spring Harbor, New York, and one of the first scientists to introduce concepts of Mendelian genetics into the United States. After he persuaded Mary Harriman, widow of the railroad magnate, to underwrite a Eugenics Record Office (ERO), Davenport invited Laughlin to become superintendent. Laughlin and his wife, Pansy Bowen, whom he had married in 1902, moved to Cold Spring Harbor in October 1910 where they resided for the next twenty-nine years. They had no children.

Laughlin, an indefatigable worker, developed a zealous commitment to eugenics. His major tasks in the early years at the ERO were to train field workers (mostly young women) in the procedures for compiling family pedigrees and searching them for evidence of hereditary (usually pathological) traits and to compile and analyze the data that the field workers sent to him from the various state institutions for feebleminded, epileptic, or insane persons to determine the inheritance pattern of these traits.

Laughlin's long-range goals were the curtailing of reproduction by sterilizing mentally retarded and mentally ill persons and the limiting of immigration of "defective persons" to the United States. During the 1920s and 1930s he made great efforts to gain public support for eugenics. He became recognized as an expert on eugenics and influenced the passage of sterilization laws in many states. He was a key witness in congressional hearings concerning the Immigration Act of 1924.

Laughlin's interest in eugenical sterilization was strongly reinforced during his service (1912–1913) on the American Breeders' Association Committee to Study and to Report on the Best Practical Means of Cutting off the Defective Germ Plasm in the American Population, chaired by David Starr Jordan, president of Stanford University. The committee concluded that about 10 percent of the population was "unfit" and that many (including the "pauper class" and "criminaloids") should be sterilized. Laughlin published two monographs discussing the committee's work in 1914.

Working next door to the Station for Experimental Evolution, Laughlin met many leading biologists. This may have stimulated him to pursue doctoral studies at Princeton, where in 1917 he earned a Ph.D. for a thesis on cytology.

From 1917 to 1919 Laughlin devoted himself to writing a manifesto on eugenical sterilization. In part because of its length, he was unable to find a publisher until 1922, when the Chicago Psychopathic Laboratory underwrote it. *Eugenical Sterilization in the United States* clearly established Laughlin as the expert on this topic. From 1922 until 1939 he collected annual statistics on eugenics programs and published many articles and two additional books on sterilization. His model sterilization bills were used by many of the more than thirty states that passed such laws, pursuant to which at least 60,000 persons were sterilized. His greatest single influence may have been as an expert witness for the state in the sterilization petition concerning a Virginia woman named Carrie Buck. She appealed the sterilization order entered against her to the U.S. Supreme Court, which in 1927 upheld the constitutionality of the Virginia eugenic sterilization law (*Buck v. Bell*), a decision that helped influence a number of states to enact similar programs.

Laughlin's studies of the potential dysgenic effects of U.S. immigration policy began as early as 1914. He surveyed hundreds of state institutions of the retarded, the mentally ill, and other groups to compare the percentage of foreign-born residents with their percentage in the general population. This work, entitled *A Statistical Directory of State Institutions for the Defective, Dependent and Delinquent Classes*, was published in 1919. In April 1920 Laughlin testified before the House Committee on Immigration and Naturalization, delivering a warning that delighted the nativist majority on the committee. Albert Johnson (1869–1957), the chairman, appointed him the committee's "expert eugenical agent" and charged him to conduct further studies. In 1922 he completed *Analysis of America's Modern Melting Pot*, which reported that eleemosynary institutions housed disproportionate numbers of persons of Southern and Eastern European origin. He concluded that "recent immigrants, as a whole, present a higher percentage of inborn social inadequate qualities than do the older stocks." The report provided information used to justify a change in the quota system that had been incorporated into the Immigration Act of 1921. The new law (1924) switched the reference year from which country-by-country immigration quotas were calculated from 1910 to 1890, thereby increasing quotas from Northern Europe and decreasing those from Southern and Eastern Europe. This was hailed as a major victory for eugenicists.

During the 1920s and 1930s Laughlin's influence was international in scope. In 1923 he toured Europe for six months to gather material for another report to Congress, *Europe as an Emigrant Exporting Continent and the United States as an Immigrant Receiving Nation* (1924). From 1925 to 1930 he served on the Permanent Emigration Commission of the International Labor Office of the League of Nations. In 1928 he went to Havana to attend the Second International Conference on Emigration and Immigration, and in 1932 he was secretary of the Third International Congress of Eugenics in New York. His publications, especially on sterilization, had considerable influence in Nazi Germany; in 1936 he accepted an honorary degree from the University of Heidelberg, which was awarded largely for developing model laws that rationalized involuntary sterilization of "defective persons" as a valid exercise of the state's power to protect the public health. The 1933 German sterilization law was based in part on his work. His 1934 monograph *Immigration Control* and his 1939 book *Conquest by Immigration* were both published with the assistance of the New York Chamber of Commerce.

Despite his reputation among eugenicists, Laughlin was not well regarded in scientific circles. He rarely published in peer-reviewed journals, and those geneticists who reviewed his writings found significant bias.

As he became involved in lobbying for eugenic causes, Davenport had more and more trouble defending his work to the Carnegie Institution of Washington, which provided much of the ERO's budget. John C. Merriam, its president, repeatedly criticized Laughlin's work. In 1935 he sought an outside opinion from L. C. Dunn, a prominent geneticist, who gave a decidedly negative review of the ERO. In 1938, Davenport having retired, Merriam forced Laughlin to resign and sharply cut the ERO's support, effectively closing it. Laughlin retired to Kirksville, where he died.

• Laughlin's personal papers are in an archive at Northeast Missouri State University in Kirksville. A description of the archive may be found in the *Journal of the History of Biology* 14, no. 2 (1981): 339–53. Many letters from Laughlin to Davenport are at the American Philosophical Society in Philadelphia. Among the most representative of his numerous publications are articles setting out his views on sterilization that appeared in the *Journal of Psycho-Asthenics* 31 (1926): 210–18 and the *American Journal of Sociology* 27 (July 1921). He prepared a major eugenics exhibit for the Century of Progress Exposition in Chicago in 1933, which is described in the *Journal of Heredity* 26 (1935): 155–62.

The archives of the Eugenics Record Office now reside at the Dight Institute at the University of Minnesota.

Francis J. Hassencahl, "Harry H. Laughlin, Expert Eugenics Agent for the House Committee on Immigration and Naturalization, 1921–1931" (Ph.D. diss., Case Western Reserve University, 1970), is an especially valuable resource. A chapter devoted to Laughlin is by Philip Reilly in his *The Surgical Solution: A History of Involuntary Sterilization in the United States* (1991).

PHILIP R. REILLY

LAUGHTON, Charles (1 July 1899–15 Dec. 1962), stage and film actor, was born in Scarborough, Yorkshire, England, the son of Robert Laughton and Elizabeth "Eliza" Conlon, hotelkeepers. Laughton grew up under the strict tutelage of his mother, who was the dominant force in running the family business. He attended a series of Catholic schools, including the Jesuit-run Stonyhurst College, from which he graduated in 1915 and where he was active in school theatricals. After graduation, he briefly considered a naval career, but the family steered him into hoteling. He was duly sent to London to apprentice at Claridge's. While there, he was introduced to London theatrical life, being especially impressed with the brilliant acting style of Sir Gerald du Maurier, who became his lifelong inspiration.

Laughton's hotel career was cut short in 1918 when, just as World War I was drawing to a close, he signed up as a private in the Royal Huntingdonshire Rifles. Sent to Vimy Ridge on the western front in France, he was gassed during the last week of the war, although he suffered only minor effects.

Back in Scarborough, he became increasingly disenchanted with the business world. He had already joined a number of amateur acting groups, and at twenty-four he decided to get formal training. He applied and was accepted at the Royal Academy of Dramatic Arts. George Bernard Shaw, an academy trustee, saw him in several school scenes from *Pygmalion* and predicted "a brilliant career."

Even before graduating from RADA, Laughton began acting professionally in London. Within five years he became one of the most talked-about young actors on the English stage, appearing in classics such as Euripides' *Medea* (1927) as well as in contemporary plays like *Mr. Prohack* (1927) and *On the Spot* (1930). It was during *Mr. Prohack* that he met the young actress Elsa Lanchester, who had a small role. Lanchester, who had a respectable stage and film career, became his wife in 1929. They became U.S. citizens in 1950.

The marriage lasted until Laughton died, but it was not the happy union many people thought it to be. Early on, Laughton revealed to his wife that "he was homosexual partly." Although Lanchester agreed to continue the marriage, she refused to have children. In essence, the couple had a companionate, supporting relationship while Laughton engaged in a series of short- and long-term relationships with younger men.

Laughton appeared in a number of silent films and early English talkies during his years of initial stage success; when *Payment Deferred* was transferred from the West End to Broadway in 1931 with Laughton in his original leading role, he landed a Hollywood contract. Although he returned to the stage occasionally thereafter, he spent the next decade in a series of successful films, winning the first Academy Award given to an Englishman for the title role in *The Private Life of Henry VIII* in 1933. Other hits were *The Barretts of Wimpole Street* (1934), *Les Miserables* (1935), *Mutiny on the Bounty* (1935), *Ruggles of Red Gap* (1935), and *The Hunchback of Notre Dame* (1939).

During the 1940s and 1950s Laughton was still in demand, but he found his film roles declining in importance. More and more, he was accused of relying on his character-actor "tricks." Seeking to revive his sagging career, he began a series of dramatic recitals on radio and on stage. Already having collaborated with Bertolt Brecht on *The Life of Galileo* (1947) for the theater, Laughton and his agent and partner Paul Gregory established the First Drama Quartet with Charles Boyer, Sir Cedric Hardwicke, and Agnes Moorehead to present a staged reading of "Don Juan in Hell" from Shaw's *Man and Superman*. This production toured the United States and England in 1951–1952 with great success. Subsequently, Laughton fashioned a concert staging of Stephen Vincent Benét's *John Brown's Body* (1953) with Tyrone Power, Raymond Massey, and Judith Anderson.

Having established his credentials as a theater director, Laughton was called upon to rewrite and direct *The Caine Mutiny Court-Martial* (1954), adapted for Broadway from Herman Wouk's novel *The Caine Mutiny*. In 1955 Laughton returned to Hollywood to direct a film adaptation of the Davis Grubb novel *The Night of the Hunter*. A startling combination of realism and expressionism, the picture received a lukewarm critical acception and died at the box office, its quirky intermingling of horror and poetry apparently too de-

manding for a mass audience. *The Night of the Hunter*'s failure crushed Laughton; he never directed another film.

After this disappointment, Laughton returned to his readings. He also performed in several more films, giving two of his best performances in *Witness for the Prosecution* (1957) and *Advise and Consent* (1962). He died in Hollywood.

Overweight with a moonlike face, small eyes, a large nose, and fleshy lips, Laughton was highly critical of his looks, suffering through most of his life from a strong sense of inferiority. His consequent sensitivity to physical and emotional pain and his struggle to come to terms with his sexuality enabled him to bring great understanding to his portrayals of men who were separated from society by a special trait or handicap. His performances explore in depth and with great compassion the universal suffering and need that informs the consciousness of society's misfits and that connects such outsiders to the core of humanity.

Laughton's long career on stage and in films had its ups and downs, but during his long acting career he created many unforgettable characters, including Henry VIII, Captain Bligh, Quasimodo, and Rembrandt. He will also be remembered for *The Night of the Hunter*, now seen by many critics as a minor film masterpiece for its haunting combination of visual, musical, and dramatic elements.

• Laughton wrote two books, *Tell Me a Story* (1957) and *The Fabulous Country* (1962), both of them compilations of his favorite stories and anecdotes accompanied by often revealing linking passages. Two comprehensive biographies are Charles Higham, *Charles Laughton: An Intimate Biography* (1976), and Simon Callow, *Charles Laughton: A Difficult Actor* (1988). Callow, an actor and director, analyzes in great detail Laughton's acting development and style. Also insightful is Elsa Lanchester's autobiography *Elsa Lanchester, Herself* (1983). An obituary is in the *New York Times*, 17 Dec. 1962.

MOYLAN C. MILLS

LAUNITZ, Robert Eberhardt Schmidt von der (4 Nov. 1806–13 Dec. 1870), sculptor and monument maker, was born in Riga, Russia (now Latvia). Rejecting family expectations that he would join the Russian military, as four of his brothers did, Launitz went to Rome to study sculpture with an uncle. There he also trained with the Danish sculptor Bertel Thorwaldsen. Launitz was fluent in five languages, but he was said to have lost his hearing after suffering a fever in Rome.

In 1828 Launitz arrived in New York City, where John Frazee employed him as a journeyman in his marble business, which mostly made gravestones, memorial tablets, and mantelpieces. On 6 October 1831 an announcement in the *New York Evening Post* stated that Frazee, a self-taught sculptor, had taken Launitz as a partner to improve the firm's "department of monumental sculpture and statuary." Launitz indeed had aspirations to make ideal sculpture, and soon he began work on a white marble fountain figure of Amphitrite wearing flowing drapery and a pearl diadem. Launitz was elected an associate member of the National Academy of Design in 1832, when he exhibited his *Amphitrite*, and he was elected an academician in 1833. Over the next decade he exhibited six other marbles at the academy, including *Cupid and Psyche* (1834). The *Evening Post* called his bust portrait titled *The Rose of the Alhambra* "the best production of his chisel we have yet seen" (5 May 1843).

Frazee left the partnership in 1837, citing a need to earn greater income to support his family. In departing, he assured Launitz, "I have no complaint to make against you" (letter dated 18 Apr. 1837, Boston Public Library). The pair remained friends as Launitz continued the business and built a reputation with his designs for white marble monuments, which often featured a tall shaft.

Launitz's work in Greenwood Cemetery ensured his early fame. About 1844 he carved a bas-relief of a grieving Indian warrior for the grave of Do-Hum-Mee, a Sac Indian maiden who died after her much-publicized marriage to a brave she had met while two Indian delegations were visiting the region. In 1845 he created a recumbent white marble statue for the grave of Charlotte Canda, who was thrown from a carriage and killed while celebrating her seventeenth birthday. Canda had left drawings for a tribute to a recently deceased aunt, and Launitz was said to have based his figure on those, adding seventeen roses around her hair. "It is safe to say that no private memorial since erected in the United States has aroused so much pathetic interest and curiosity," Truman Bartlett, a student of Launitz's, wrote. Launitz also designed a monument in Greenwood honoring New York firemen; its shaft was topped by the figure of a fireman saving a child from surrounding flames.

Bartlett said sculptors and cemetery sextons from other parts of the country came to Greenwood to study these important examples. The Kentucky legislature commissioned Launitz to make a $15,000 monument to that state's war dead. The 62-foot-high marble monument was surmounted by a goddess of war holding the wreaths of victory in her outstretched arms. It was erected in 1850 in the state cemetery at Frankfort known as the "Bivouac of the Dead" after a poem by Major Theodore O'Hara.

Launitz also created a monument to James Fenimore Cooper in a Cooperstown, New York, cemetery. Constructed on a six-foot granite base, it featured a commander's sword and spyglass on one side of the die, Indian emblems such as a tomahawk and bear's claw necklace on another side, and literary emblems on another. Its shaft was topped by a figure of Leatherstocking loading his rifle while his dog looked on.

Launitz felt that much of his best work was done for the South. In 1852 he won the $17,000 commission for his last major public monument, a tribute to Casimir Pulaski, who died during the 1779 siege of Savannah, Georgia. Erected in Savannah in 1854, it was a 55-foot shaft with a statue of Liberty at the top, the arms of Poland and Georgia on the cornice, inverted cannons on the corners, and bas reliefs of the wounded soldier falling from his horse and of War and History.

Other projects attributed to Launitz included a Greek urn honoring Andrew Jackson Downing in Washington, D.C.; a plaster bust of Peter Augustus Jay, given by a patron to the New-York Historical Society in 1843; and a late statue of Gen. George Thomas in Troy, New York.

Launitz engaged about thirty men, mostly skilled foreigners, at his "monument works" on Broadway before the outbreak of the Civil War. He advertised his business in the *New-York Mercantile Register* (1848–1849) this way:

Robert E. Launitz, Sculptor & Artificer in Marble, No. 536 Broadway, New York, Executes Monuments, Tombs and Headstones of every description, Statues, Busts and Bas-Reliefs, Fountains and Vases. Casts taken from the Dead, and Busts made therefrom, warranted to be perfect likenesses. Mantelpieces in the Louis XIV style, made to order in every variety.

By 1859 he also was selling marble sculptures imported from Italy.

Launitz did not succeed in the heightened competition to build Civil War monuments. Others sometimes copied his designs and underbid him in price. In 1866 L. Prang & Co. published a catalog of some of his conceptions for stone angels, mourning women, lambs, and draped or garlanded architectural forms.

Launitz created influential figurative and architectural monuments in America's cemeteries. Bartlett called him "the father of monumental art in America." In addition, he was a teacher and mentor to younger men, especially Thomas Crawford, who surpassed both him and Frazee after they employed him for two years in the 1830s. Launitz advanced money for Crawford to go to Rome to study and gave him a letter of introduction to Thorwaldsen. Others who served as assistants to Launitz included F. J. Maurer and Caspar Buberl.

Little is known of Launitz's personal life, except that he was married and had at least one son (also named Robert E. Launitz), who worked as a sculptor before his early death. Launitz became a U.S. citizen, but he returned overseas at least twice, in 1846 and 1853, according to passport records. True to his military upbringing, he served as quartermaster of a New York National Guard regiment for many years. He organized the seventh regiment's engineer corps and commanded it until 1860. He died in New York City.

• A few letters from or to Launitz survive in the Manuscript Division, Boston Public Library, and the Frazee papers, Archives of American Art. The best published source about him is Truman H. Bartlett, "Early Settler Memorials," *American Architect and Building News* 22 (6 Aug. 1887 and 3 Sept. 1887): 59–61, 107–9. A letter from Crawford to Launitz was published in the *Crayon* 6 (Jan. 1859): 28. Other useful publications are *Collection of Monuments and Headstones Designed by R. E. Launitz, N.Y.* (1866); *Catalogue of American Portraits in the New-York Historical Society* (1941), p. 157; *National Academy of Design Exhibition Record, 1826–1860*, vol. 1

(1943), p. 286; Richard J. Koke, *American Landscape and Genre Paintings in the New-York Historical Society*, vol. 2 (1982), pp. 268–69; and Frederick S. Voss, *John Frazee: 1790–1852, Sculptor* (1986). Articles on Launitz are in the *New York Evening Post* on 6 Oct. 1831, 25 Nov. 1831, 14 May 1832, 1 Aug. 1837, 5 May 1843, 28 August 1854, 11 July 1859, and 9 Sept. 1871. Also see the *Boston Evening Transcript*, 30 Aug. 1854, 16 Jan. 1856, and 22 June 1867; the *New-York Commercial Advertiser* 25 (Feb. 1836); and the *Knickerbocker* (Mar. 1847), pp. 287–88. Obituaries and a death notice are in the *New York Tribune* and the *New York Evening Post*, both 14 Dec. 1870; and in the *New York Times*, 15 Dec. 1870.

CYNTHIA MILLS

LAURANCE, John (1750–11 Nov. 1810), congressman, senator, and judge, was born near Falmouth in Cornwall County, England. The identity of his parents is not established nor are the circumstances that led him to leave England for New York City in 1767. Apparently he had an independent income or had come into an inheritance. Shortly after his arrival in New York City at age seventeen, he began reading law with Cadwallader Colden, lieutenant governor of New York. He was admitted to the bar in 1772. At age twenty-one he acquired 1,000 acres of land in that part of Albany County that is now in Addison County, Vermont. Laurance supported the Whig patriotic movement, and in late 1774 or early 1775 married Elizabeth McDougall, the daughter of Alexander McDougall, a merchant and the colony's leading radical; the couple had one son.

With the coming of the war, Laurance joined the Fourth New York Regiment as a second lieutenant, commissioned 1 August 1775. In August 1776 he began service in his father-in-law's First New York Regiment, performing as an aide-de-camp and also as a paymaster. Laurance participated in the failed American invasion of Canada. From 11 April 1777 to 3 June 1782 Laurance was a member of George Washington's staff as judge advocate general, reaching the rank of major. In this capacity Laurance was the prosecutor in the spy trial of Major John André in September 1780 before a board of general officers, resulting in André's conviction and execution. In 1783 Laurance was a member of the council "to provide the Temporary Government" for the southern parts of New York during the interim between the British evacuation and the convening of a full state legislature.

Laurance resumed his law practice after the war and, like his close friend Alexander Hamilton, early became a nationalist. Hamilton said in August 1782: "Laurance is a man of good sense and good intentions—has just views of public affairs—is active and accurate in business. He is from conviction an advocate for strengthening the Federal government and for reforming the vices of our interior administration" (*Papers of Hamilton*, vol. 3, p. 140). Laurance was a member of the Society of the Cincinnati, a trustee for Columbia College (1784–1810), and from 1784 served as a regent of the University of the State of New York. He represented New York City and County in the

sixth and eighth sessions of the state assembly (1783 and 1785), and served two terms in the Confederation Congress, April 1785 to January 1787; he sat on the congressional committee for commercial negotiations. He was a state senator from 1788 to 1790. Although not a delegate to the state convention for ratifying the Constitution, Laurance enthusiastically backed the new frame of government. Laurance's wife died on 16 August 1790. He married Elizabeth Allen, a Philadelphia widow, on 30 June 1791.

Nominated by the New York City Federal Committee, Laurance won election to the House of Representatives on 7 April 1789 for the district consisting of New York City and Westchester County. He beat the Antifederalist candidate, John Broome, a city alderman, by a vote of 2,418 to 372. Laurance served in Congress, 4 March 1789 to 3 March 1793 (his reelection in 1792 was uncontested).

A consistent Federalist in Congress, Laurance supported the Hamiltonian program in its entirety. He was one of the most active and vocal members, and sat on thirty-eight committees, including those that dealt with appropriations, import duties, Indian trade, naturalization, salaries, the seat of government, and Vermont statehood. Laurance vigorously debated against most of James Madison's proposals in Congress, opposing lower tonnage duties for French shipping than for that of Great Britain, the location of the nation's capital on the banks of the Potomac River, and discrimination in favor of the original holders of government certificates in funding the national debt. Laurance argued for the establishment of executive departments and Congress's conferring on the president removal power. Laurance also voted for federal rather than state collection of the nation's revenues and against limiting excise taxes to two years. Representing a constituency of merchants, manufacturers, and artisans, Laurance walked a delicate line on import duties; he favored low rates on rum, Madeira wine, and molasses (imports of New York City merchants) and high levies on beer, candles, hemp, and cordage (manufactured by the city's artisans). The caustic senator from Pennsylvania, William Maclay, referred to Laurance as "a mere tool for British Agents & factors" (Maclay, *Journal*, p. 47). Despite looking after his constituents's interests, Laurance held to a broad view of legislative responsibility. In a congressional speech he said: "Every member on this floor ought to consider himself the representative of the whole Union, and not the particular district which had chosen him."

Laurance certainly represented the financial interests of wealthy New Yorkers. One-sixth of the national debt was held by New York investors. Although Laurance preferred to invest almost solely in real estate, he owned three shares in the Bank of New York, and he was a director of the Bank of the United States as well as of its New York branch.

Appointed by President Washington, Laurance served as judge for the U.S. District Court of New York, from 6 May 1794 until 8 November 1796, when he resigned to take a seat in the Senate that had been vacated by Rufus King. Laurance was president pro-tempore of the Senate for the Fifth Congress. He was elected to a full term in the Senate on 27 January 1801 but resigned on 5 February 1802. In the Senate Laurance voted for giving the president permission "to raise a provisional army" and supported an embargo against France, the establishment of the navy department, and the Sedition Act.

Laurance was a huge land speculator after the revolutionary war. Although in his law practice he represented Tories who sought restitution of real estate that had been seized by the New York government, he invested heavily in the purchase of the confiscated estates. Singly or in partnership Laurance put all his capital in land. He also looked for bargains in sales conducted by U.S. marshals and sheriffs and invested substantially in military bounty lands. Laurance subdivided his scattered holdings into small farms and readily found buyers. In 1799 he had an income of $14,000 from his landed investments. Most of Laurance's real estate was located in central New York along the Mohawk Valley and the southern tier of counties. At the time of his death he owned twenty-five of the twenty-eight townships of the Military Tract, 41,000 acres.

After leaving the Senate, Laurance continued in politics as chairman of the Federal nominating meetings, conducted for the purpose of nominating Federalist political candidates. A year after suffering a stroke, from which he recovered, Laurance died at his home in New York City. Laurance was highly regarded for his legal expertise. Of dignified presence and a powerful debater, he had a key role in achieving success for the Federalist program in Congress during the administrations of George Washington and John Adams.

• The Papers of the Continental Congress, National Archives, has documents and letters pertaining to Laurance as judge advocate general of the army and as a member of the Confederation Congress. Small collections of Laurance's papers are found at the New-York Historical Society and the Schaffer Library, Union College, Schenectady, New York. A few letters are located in Charles R. King, ed., *The Life and Correspondence of Rufus King* (1894–1896), and Harold C. Syrett, ed., *The Papers of Alexander Hamilton*, vols. 2–27 (1961–1987). For Laurance's career in the federal Congress, see Linda G. DePauw et al., eds., *Documentary History of the First Federal Congress of the United States of America*, 14 vols. (1972–1995), with a biographical sketch of Laurance in vol. 14, pp. 718–22; *The Debates and Proceedings in the Congress of the United States*, 1st, 2d, 4th, 5th, and 6th Congress (1834–1851); Edgar S. Maclay, ed., *Journal of William Maclay* (1890); and Margaret C. S. Christman, *The First Federal Congress, 1789–1791* (1989). Laurance's record in the Confederation Congress is in Worthington C. Ford, ed., *Journals of the Continental Congress*, vols. 29–31 (1933–1934). For Laurance as land speculator, see Arthur J. Alexander, "Judge John Laurance: Successful Investor in New York State Lands," *New York History* 25 (1944): 35–45. A death notice is in the *New York Evening Post*, 12 Nov. 1810.

HARRY M. WARD

LAUREL, Stan (16 June 1890–23 Feb. 1965), and **Oliver Hardy** (18 Jan. 1892–7 Aug. 1957), comic actors, were born, respectively, in Ulverston, Lancashire, England, and Harlem, Georgia. Stan, born Arthur Stanley Jefferson, was the son of Arthur J. Jefferson, an actor-manager, and Madge Metcalfe, an actress in Jefferson's troupe. Oliver, born Norvell Hardy, was the son of Oliver Hardy, a lawyer, and Emily Norvell. Joining together as Laurel and Hardy in 1927, the duo became the first important comedy team in American film history.

Known as Jefferson until at least 1917, Laurel completed his sporadic and itinerant primary and secondary school education in Glasgow, Scotland, where in 1905 he began working in his father's Metropole Theatre box office. Laurel, who had come to idolize such singing and dancing comedians as Dan Leno, a master of long, wandering anecdotes, appeared in 1906 as "Stan Jefferson—He of the Funny Ways" at Pickard's Museum Music Hall in Glasgow. In 1907 he toured with Levy and Cardwell's Juvenile Pantomimes, a satirical troupe. By 1908 he had performed in small music halls and played his father's variety sketch "Home from the Honeymoon" (later adapted into the Laurel and Hardy film *Another Fine Mess*). In 1909 Laurel appeared in the musical comedy *Gentleman Jockey* and the melodrama *Alone in the World*.

In 1910 Laurel joined Fred Karno's troupe in "Mumming Birds," a portrayal of a variety show beset by such problems as a raucous drunk in the audience. Laurel, often the Comic Singer, understudied the Drunk, played by Charlie Chaplin. Laurel left Karno's touring troupe in the United States in 1911, trying American vaudeville before returning to Britain with another Karno dropout to form the Barto Brothers and write their "The Rum 'Uns from Rome," fifteen minutes of slapstick characterized by lightning timing and explosive effects. After the act broke up, Laurel joined the unsuccessful Eight Comics and then returned to the Karno Troupe.

When Chaplin decided to remain in the States during the Karno Troupe's visit in 1913, so did Laurel, who formed the Three Comiques with Edgar Hurley and Hurley's wife, Wren; the trio performed Laurel's knockabout "The Nutty Burglars," wherein two clumsy burglars pass around a lighted bomb. The Comiques evolved into the Keystone Trio; Laurel, into an exceptional Chaplin impersonator. In 1916 came the Stan Jefferson Trio and "The Crazy Cracksman," a sketch involving flypaper and pratfalls. In 1917 Laurel formed an act with Mae Charlotte Dahlberg, an Australian singer-dancer. They became Stan and Mae Laurel. (Dahlberg later insisted that her partner's superstition about the thirteen letters in "Stan Jefferson" led her to extract the name "Laurel" from a Roman history book.) That same year Laurel had made his first short film, *Nuts in May*, another slapstick venture. In another, *A Lucky Dog* (1917), his character is held up by a bandit played by Oliver Hardy. Laurel made eleven films in 1918, most with Mae and four as

"Hickory Hiram" for Carl Laemmle's Universal Studios.

In 1919 film producer Hal Roach, whose studio had just moved to Culver City, California, saw the Laurels in vaudeville. Beginning in 1921 Laurel made a series of one-reel (ten-minute) comedies for Roach, followed by several parodies of popular films, including *Mud and Sand*, in which Laurel portrayed Rhubarb Vaselino. By 1925 Laurel had made more than forty films but, according to director George Stevens, was still dancing frantically and "laughing and smiling too much." His new producer, Joe Rock, blaming Mae for Laurel's lack of progress, paid her $1,000 to return to Australia, and that same year Laurel married Vitagraph ingenue Lois Neilsor; they had one child before divorcing in 1935. In 1926 Roach persuaded Laurel to join—largely as writer and gag-man—his new Comedy All-Stars, a repertory group that included James Finlayson, Max Davidson, Clyde Cook, Eugene Palette, Edgar Kennedy, Noah Young, Mae Busch, Anita Garvin, and Oliver Hardy.

When Norvell Hardy was eight, his father died and the family moved to Madison, Georgia. His name was legally changed to Oliver Norvell Hardy, and he took his boy soprano voice briefly on the road with Coburn's Minstrels. By the age of fourteen Hardy weighed 250 pounds. His intermittent education included terms at Georgia Military College and the Atlanta Conservatory of Music. In 1910 the family moved to Milledgeville, Georgia, where Hardy worked in a film theater.

Hardy began appearing as the "heavy" in Vim Comedies in Jacksonville, Florida, in 1913, the year of his first marriage, to Madelyn Caloshin. They divorced in 1920 without having any children. He acquired the habit of wearing a derby hat. In 1915 he teamed with Bobby Ray in *The Paperhanger's Helper*, a slapstick comedy in which Hardy played the bumbling boss of a bumbling "fall guy." Some film historians argue that these "team" films created the base for the classic Laurel and Hardy partnership.

In 1916 Hardy moved to California, where he freelanced, appearing with Laurel in the two-reel (twenty-minute) comedy *Lucky Dog* the following year. He continued in short films, usually as a heavy or foil for such leading comics as Billy West, Jimmy Aubrey, and the acrobatic Larry Semon. In 1921 Hardy married actress Myrtle Lee Reeves; their childless marriage ended in divorce in 1937. In 1925 he portrayed the Tin Woodman in a Jazz Age version of *The Wizard of Oz*. By the time Hardy joined Hal Roach's Comedy All-Stars in 1926, he had appeared in several features and more than 100 short films and was regarded as a solid, instinctive performer who could steal scenes from the stars. When Hardy was injured, Laurel substituted for him in *Get 'Em Young* (1926). The following year the two men began to appear together in All-Star Comedies.

Beginning with *Slipping Wives* (1927), Stan Laurel and Oliver Hardy appeared together in thirteen All-Star comedies before becoming a team in *Duck Soup*

(1927). With Hardy, Laurel slowed down, creating deliberate, "holding" sequences and developing a comic situation to unbearable hilarity. He became "Stan," an abstracted reactor to Hardy's various self-destructions. Hardy became "Ollie," large, pompous, courtly, and inept. Both carried gentility to heights of absurdity. The duo's working habits formed quickly. A compulsive worker, Laurel created the gags while the self-indulgent Hardy went to the links or the track. It is said that Laurel was able to provoke one of Hardy's characteristic on-camera reactions—a disbelieving exasperation—by asking for another take when Hardy was headed for golf. Between 1927 and 1932 Laurel and Hardy made sixty-five short films for Roach. Despite the studio's partylike atmosphere, a two-reeler could be turned out in two weeks. The Boys, as they were called, proved to be inspired improvisers, and Roach gave them the time and creative freedom they needed.

Hats Off (1927) introduced one of Laurel and Hardy's standard gags—the "tit for tat" battle, a vignette of studied retaliatory aggression, in this case a wildly burgeoning de-hatting. *The Battle of the Century* (1927) was the climax to film's early obsession with pie-throwing; between three and five thousand pies were hurled in an escalation of communal madness. *Two Tars* (1928) turned one bent fender into a demolition derby. *Big Business* (1929) capped the Boys' fumbling attempts to sell Christmas trees with the decorous destruction of two houses. Another early classic, *Leave 'Em Laughing* (1928), caused the mother of all traffic jams in Culver City after a sudden infusion of laughing gas.

As "Stan" and "Ollie" developed, their work clearly distinguished itself from its vaudeville antecedents. There was no straight man or fall guy. As Scott Nollen wrote, "Laurel and Hardy function as a unit. Stan cannot effectively function without Ollie to tell him what to do, and Ollie cannot get anything done without Stan . . . [yet] as a unit, they never actually accomplish anything."

In *Unaccustomed As We Are* (1929), the team's first sound film, Laurel was first heard to say "Any nuts?" which immediately became a running gag. The Boys made a perfect transition to sound. Their voices—Stan's was squeaky; Ollie's, incongruously prissy—fitted their characters. Sound brought Ollie's mournful wail as he tumbles toward another disaster; their barbed verbal mangles ("You are finally using my brains," "He who filters your good name, steals trash," "Honesty is the best politics," "Now you're taking me illiterally"); Ollie's doublethink, veering from "Don't you ever get anything right?" to the (bemused, in the face of surreal truth) "You know, Stanley, I think you're right"; and Laurel's unexpected eruditions.

Many theaters began to bill their films above the features, but the growing popularity of cartoons began to weaken the audience appeal of short films. However, in *Helpmates* (1931), Laurel and Hardy began to develop an increasingly familiar theme: the relationship between bumbling husbands and overbearing wives. Neither Hardy's bumbling courtliness nor Laurel's immaturity held much appeal for women. In *Twice Two* (1933), their last word on the unequal battle of the sexes, they played their own wives.

Laurel and Hardy's first full-length feature was *Pardon Us* (1931). In the Academy Award-winning three-reel *The Music Box* (1932) the Boys repeatedly move a large piano up the steepest hill in Los Angeles, pausing for a dainty soft-shoe dance on the crate. By this time, Laurel's whimpering baby cry—Roach once said, "Laurel never cried when he was mad . . . when he was hurt . . . when he was scared. He only cried when he was confused; that's why it's so funny"—and his head scratch (which created what biographer John McCabe called "a natural fright wig"), as well as Hardy's delicate "extended pinky, gracious hat tip and tie twiddle," had become world famous. En route to England in 1932, the pair was mobbed in Chicago; at Southampton they were greeted by thousands whistling and singing "The Song of the Cuckoos," their theme.

Beginning with the short film *Thicker Than Water* (1935), surreal elements—prefiguring Hollywood's "screwball comedy" decade—characterized Laurel and Hardy's work. In that film their blood transfusions gradually turn them into each other; as settings change, Laurel pulls the new scene across the screen like a shade. In the feature *Way Out West* (1937) the Boys, dudes in the wilds, dance a decorous buck-and-wing, sing "The Trail of the Lonesome Pine" (it became England's number-two hit song), and work their "triple-gag" to perfection. Stan successfully flicked his thumb to light cigarettes (Laurel called this "white magic"), something Ollie tried thrice before it worked, nearly scaring him to death. In another feature, *Swiss Miss* (1938), they attempt to haul a piano across an Alpine suspension bridge, whereupon they are met by a gorilla.

The biggest Laurel and Hardy money-maker was the less distinguished *Bonnie Scotland* (1935). They broke with Roach after a dispute over salaries—Laurel always made twice as much as Hardy because he did twice as much work—and one more knockabout, *Block-Heads* (1938). Hardy appeared with Harry Langdon rather than Laurel in *Zenobia* (1939). They were unable to produce their own films, and a radio series never materialized. At the 1939 World's Fair in San Francisco, the Boys performed Laurel's "The Driver's License," a triumph of illogicality. In it, Ollie, applying for a license, cannot write; Stan, his helper, can't read. The following year Hardy married Virginia Lucille Jones. They had no children.

In 1940–1941 a Laurel and Hardy stage show toured the nation. The Boys gave more than five hundred performances for servicemen during wartime. Laurel and Hardy's films for MGM and 20th Century–Fox became formulaic after 1940. *The Bullfighters* (1945) was their last American film. Laurel later wrote, "We had no say in those films, and it sure looked it. We had done too many films in our own way for us to keep taking anything like that."

In postwar America the Boys' film career seemed effectively over. They made their first tour of British music halls in 1947 playing "The Driver's License." In 1950 Hardy appeared in two films without Laurel, *The Fighting Kentuckian* and *Riding High*. In 1951–1952 Laurel and Hardy went to France to make an unsuccessful film released under three different titles—*Atoll K*, *Utopia*, and *Robinson Crusoeland*—such was the chaos surrounding the project. During the filming Laurel underwent a prostate operation. In 1953 the Boys toured Ireland and England performing Laurel's "Birds of a Feather," a demented tale of whiskey testers who drive a psychiatrist mad with bird-talk. The tour ended because of Hardy's illness. By this time Laurel and Hardy's old films had become popular on television, and in 1954 they made their last public appearance on the television show "This Is Your Life."

In 1955 Hal Roach, Jr., signed Laurel and Hardy for four, one-hour television films under the series title *Fabulous Fables*, which were to feature Laurel's "white magic" applied to tales such as *Babes in the Woods*. Before the series could begin, Hardy suffered a paralytic stroke. His death in North Hollywood was contemporaneous with *The Golden Age of Comedy* (1957), the first of several archive homages reviving silent film.

Through his long years of partnership with Hardy, Laurel had married and divorced repeatedly. In 1934 he married Virginia Ruth Rogers in Mexico, repeating the ceremony after his divorce from Neilson took effect. This marriage lasted until 1937, though they remarried in 1941 and again divorced in 1946. In 1937 Dahlberg sued Laurel, claiming common-law wife status. (The suit was settled out of court.) In 1938 Laurel married Vera Ivanova Sauvalova, a Russian singer-dancer; they divorced in 1940. In 1946 he married Ida Kataeva Raphael, a singer and film actress.

In later years Laurel, suffering from diabetes, lived in a small apartment, answering all his own mail. In 1961 he won a special award from the Academy of Motion Picture Arts and Sciences. Another followed in 1963 from the Screen Actors Guild. Before his death, he joked with a nurse who was injecting him: "I'd rather be skiing." To the nurse's predictable question, he answered, "No, but I'd rather be skiing than doing this." Laurel died in Santa Monica.

Years after their last performance, the Boys' appeal had hardly faded. After 1978, three attempts were made to produce Laurel and Hardy stage musicals. Laurel and Hardy tours were introduced in Los Angeles. A museum of Laurel and Hardy lore was established in Ulverston. Academic analyses of the Boys' humor began to pile up even before Laurel's death, inspiring him to quote fellow comic Buster Keaton: "When in the name of Christ will these people learn that what we did was gags, gags, gags, and then more gags, and nothing more than gags, set inside a pleasant little story?"

• The definitive biographical-archival work on Stan Laurel and Oliver Hardy has been done by John McCabe, among whose books *Mr. Laurel and Mr. Hardy* (1976) and *The Comedy World of Stan Laurel* (1975) are indispensable. In the latter, McCabe draws upon an unpublished memoir of Laurel, "Turning the Pages," written by Arthur J. Jefferson in 1939. Among critical studies, Scott Allen Nollen, *The Boys: The Cinematic World of Laurel and Hardy* (1989), might have pleased even Laurel. Increasingly complete listings of the Laurel-and-Hardy ouevre can be found in many film encyclopedias. Leonard Maltin, *Selected Short Subjects* (1972), describes all the Boys' short sound films. Among the works on their English tours, Ken Owst, *Laurel and Hardy in Hull* (1990), is fascinating.

JAMES ROSS MOORE

LAURENCE, Baby. *See* Baby Laurence.

LAURENCE, William Leonard (7 Mar. 1888–19 Mar. 1977), science writer, was born in Salantai, Lithuania, the son of Lipman Siew and Sarah Preuss. Raised in a devout Orthodox Jewish family, he spent his boyhood in Lithuania, which was then part of Russia. His intellectual abilities were evident early, and as a young boy he had already resolved to immigrate to the United States. Fleeing a political purge, he escaped to Berlin in 1905 by hiding in a large barrel and from there made his way to the United States. Having earned the money to get to Boston, he found a job working for a florist. While delivering a funeral wreath in Cambridge, he discovered Harvard College and decided he would study there. In 1906 he moved to Roxbury and renamed himself after the elm-lined street where he lived.

In 1908 Laurence enrolled at Harvard, where he studied philosophy. When he ran out of money in 1911, he was forced to drop out, but he reentered in the spring of 1914, finishing his studies the next year. He was awarded the distinction cum laude in philosophy, but he never received a degree because he had not satisfied the university's requirements.

Popular among the Harvard athletes he tutored, Laurence quickly acquired a permanent tutoring job, which he kept until 1917. Naturalized in 1913, he served in the U.S. Army Signal Corps during World War I in France. After the war he studied for a time at the University of Besançon before returning to Cambridge, where he ran his own tutoring school until 1921 when he entered Harvard Law School. Laurence then transferred to Boston University, got a law degree in 1925, and passed the state bar exam, although he never practiced. Instead he worked as a freelance writer and adapted Russian plays for English presentation.

In 1926 Laurence traveled to New York City. Attending a party with a former student, he beat the editor of the *New York World* at a word game and found himself with a job as a general assignment reporter for the paper; he also served as the paper's associate aviation editor. He worked at the *World* until 1930, when the *New York Times* hired him to cover science.

At the *Times* Laurence set his own hours and defined his own beat. He covered scientific meetings and scoured scientific and technical journals. While the scientists at first were skeptical about a reporter's ability to cover their complicated subjects, he won their respect with his intelligence and understanding. In 1931 he married Florence Davidow; they had no children. Attending a scientific meeting in 1934, he and a journalist friend decided to form the National Association of Science Writers. His coverage of the 1936 Harvard Tercentenary Conference of Arts and Sciences won him the 1937 Pulitzer Prize, which he shared with four other science writers who covered the conference.

In 1939 Laurence wrote a number of articles for the *New York Times* on uranium fission but avoided writing about its potential as a weapon. As he interviewed exiled German scientists, however, he began to worry that the Nazis were already working on atomic weapons. In March 1940 he learned that scientists had succeeded in isolating uranium 235. Consequently, he decided the American people and the democratic world needed to be alerted to the implications of atomic power. His story ran in the *Times* on 5 May 1940, and a longer version ran on 7 September in the *Saturday Evening Post*. Only after the war did Laurence learn that the Federal Bureau of Investigation had seized some copies of that issue and asked the *Post* to report the name of anyone who inquired about it. Privately, he bombarded physicists with letters urging them to get busy.

After the Japanese attack on Pearl Harbor, Laurence tried to volunteer for active service, but because of his age he had to content himself with serving as a consultant to the army surgeon general and to the Medical Division of the National Research Council. In April 1945, however, the government called him to prepare the news release about the use of atomic weapons.

That month Laurence disappeared from the *New York Times* and only his editor and his wife knew where he was. He had become the official historian of the Manhattan Project. Flying across the country, he recorded American efforts to develop an atomic bomb. He provided most of the coverage the *New York Times* ran after the first atom bomb was dropped on Hiroshima, and he flew on the plane that dropped the second atom bomb on Nagasaki. His firsthand account of that trip and the series of stories that ran with it—on the development, production, and significance of atomic weapons—won Laurence the 1946 Pulitzer Prize.

In May 1956 Laurence covered the explosion of a hydrogen bomb in the Pacific, and later that year he became science editor for the *Times*. He was known as "Atomic Bill" by his *Times* colleagues, a label that differentiated him from "Political Bill," a writer with a similar name. He retired from the paper in January 1964, and 300 friends gathered for his retirement dinner, sponsored by twenty-seven eminent societies and institutions of science, including the American Association for the Advancement of Science, the American Medical Association, and Harvard University. In 1968 Laurence and his wife moved to Majorca, Spain, where he died.

A pioneer in the field of science writing, Laurence never wrote "down" to his readers. Instead, with a talent for clarity and a sense of the significance and drama of his subject, he made his readers meet him half way. Noted for his historic reporting on atomic developments, Laurence was aware from the early days that the story he was covering would usher in a new era with enormous implications for civilization. With a remarkable memory for scientific detail, he was often able to correlate accidental discoveries of scientists too immersed in their own work to pay attention to what was happening beyond their laboratories.

• An interview with Laurence is included in the Oral History Project of Columbia University. Laurence's account of his time with the Manhattan Project is *Dawn over Zero: The Story of the Atomic Bomb* (1953). That episode is also covered in Meyer Berger, *The Story of the New York Times 1851–1951* (1951). Laurence's other books include *The Hell Bomb* (1951), *Men and Atoms: The Discovery, the Uses, and the Future of Atomic Energy* (1959), and *The New Frontiers of Science* (1964). An interview with Laurence can be found in the *New Yorker*, 18 Aug. 1945. Further information is in Joseph P. McKerns, ed., *Biographical Dictionary of American Journalism* (1989). An obituary is in the *New York Times*, 19 Mar. 1977.

CATHERINE CASSARA

LAURENS, Henry (24 Feb. 1724–8 Dec. 1792), planter-merchant and revolutionary war statesman, was born in Charleston, South Carolina, the son of John Laurens, a saddler, and Esther Grasset. The Laurens family had fled La Rochelle, France, as Huguenot refugees in 1682. After stops in London, Ireland, and New York, they settled in Charleston about 1715. Laurens received in his own words "the best education" that the provincial community could offer. In 1744 he sailed for London to serve a three-year clerkship in James Crokatt's counting house. Laurens married Eleanor Ball in 1750. They had twelve children, but only four survived childhood. John served as an aide to General George Washington and was killed in one of the final actions in the Revolution; Martha married the historian Dr. David Ramsay; Mary Eleanor married statesman Charles Pinckney; and Henry Laurens, Jr., married Elizabeth Rutledge, daughter of Governor John Rutledge.

Laurens joined George Austin in a Charleston-based commission firm in 1749. The firm was Austin, Laurens, & Appleby when George Appleby joined them in 1759, but in 1762 it was dissolved because of Austin's retirement and Laurens's expanding investments in planting and increasing participation in politics. Thus Laurens's interests became centered in South Carolina rather than London and his perspective grew increasingly American rather than English. During this period he adopted as a personal motto Alexander Pope's dictum, "Whatever is, is right," and employed it often in his correspondence with friends and family to explain his way of accepting personal, business, or political reverses.

The exportation of Carolina products such as rice, indigo, deerskins, and naval stores to British, continental European, and West Indian ports and the importation of wine and spirits, textiles, sugar, and slaves made Laurens one of the wealthiest and most respected merchants in Charleston. By 1762 he had changed the focus of his business activities from commerce to planting and the production of staples, especially rice, for export. Despite the fact that much of his wealth as a businessman and subsequently as a planter was derived from the sale and employment of slaves, Laurens quit the trade by 1763. In 1774, when his friend and protégé John Lewis Gervais suggested a venture importing slaves, Laurens clearly stated his position: "Entring [sic] into the African Trade is So repugnant to my disposition & my plan for future Life that it Seems as if nothing but dire necessity could drive me to it." In August 1776, perhaps moved by the ideas of the Declaration of Independence, he wrote his son John that "I abhor slavery" and that he was seeking a means of freeing his slaves. While there is no evidence that he manumitted any of his slaves, his expressions against the institution were employed by abolitionists during the Civil War. In 1766 he held 227 slaves and in 1790, 298.

During the 1760s Laurens became the leading American agent for British investors who sought land in the southern colonies. He also expanded his own land holdings from a single plantation and townhouse in Charleston to three South Carolina plantations ("Wambaw," "Mepkin," and "Wrights Savannah"), two Georgia plantations ("Broughton Island" and "New Hope") and a large tract of land in the South Carolina backcountry that he owned jointly with Gervais. Mepkin, his home plantation, was a 3,143-acre estate on the Cooper River about thirty miles above Charleston. He also purchased a small plantation in 1769 and developed it as the Charleston suburb of Hampstead. As late as 1776 he acquired "Mount Tacitus," a 3,360-acre plantation on the Santee River in South Carolina.

Laurens's public career began during the 1750s when he served in numerous local and church offices. His brief military service as a lieutenant in the militia (1757) and a lieutenant colonel in the provincial regiment (1761) occurred during a conflict with the Cherokees. He participated in an expedition to the backcountry in 1761 after which provincial and British military leaders traded accusations of misconduct. Laurens supported British colonel James Grant in print and enjoyed a brief period of favor with the royal administration, but in 1764 he refused an appointment to the provincial council, preferring to remain an elected member of the assembly. He had begun his long legislative career in 1757 by representing St. Philip Parish in the assembly. He was elected to provincial and state assemblies seventeen times.

Events from 1765 to 1768 helped to make Laurens a moderate patriot in the Anglo-American disputes that grew into the Revolution. During the Stamp Act controversy he felt the fury of the Charleston mob when on the night of 23 October 1765 his home was invaded by radicals in search of stamped paper. He also, however, believed that the British customs officials at Charleston had exceeded their authority. In three celebrated cases in 1767 and 1768 Laurens's schooners *Wambaw* and *Broughton Island Packet*, and ship *Ann* were seized. In each instance, whether dealing with the radicals or the royal officials, Laurens's rigid sense of honor surfaced. In the midst of the Stamp Act mob he challenged "any one man amongst them" to step forward and settle their dispute with "a brace of Pistols." Likewise during his altercation with the customs and vice admiralty officials he tweaked one man's nose and challenged another to a duel. The practice of dueling to force recognition of an impugned reputation or honor led Laurens to challenge or accept on at least five occasions. He survived the two or three duels he actually fought despite his practice of taking fire but not returning it. Laurens also published pamphlets in which he attacked the royal officials responsible for the seizures. He castigated the collector of customs in *A Representation of Facts* (1767) and exchanged printed insults with the vice admiralty judge beginning with his *Extracts from the Proceedings of the High Court of Vice-Admiralty* (1768) and concluding with *Appendix to Extracts* (1769).

After his retirement from commerce and his wife's death in May 1770, Laurens became increasingly occupied with his sons' education. He took them to England in September 1771 to place them in school. He spent the next three years in Europe, mainly in England, where he became disenchanted with the government and society that seemed to him both corrupt and corrupting. He much preferred the more serious and industrious Switzerland, which he visited in 1772 to enroll his two older sons at schools in Geneva. When he returned to South Carolina in December 1774 he found that the people's resolve to resist British taxes and control had advanced to a point "which surpasses all expectations."

Within weeks Laurens was elected to South Carolina's First Provincial Congress, which met in Charleston to govern the province in the waning months of royal authority. In June 1775 he was elected president of the Provincial Congress and president of the Council of Safety, which in effect made him chief executive of the revolutionary government. He helped to devise South Carolina's first state constitution in 1776 and was elected vice president in the new government. Laurens acted as a moderating influence in early revolutionary South Carolina and as a consequence gained the enmity of radicals like Christopher Gadsden and William Henry Drayton. He was especially interested in protecting the individual rights that could be jeopardized by radical excesses. In October 1775 his refusal as a public official to open private mail drew him into a dispute that culminated in a bloodless duel. Elected to the Continental Congress, he left South Carolina in June 1777; he remained away for most of the next eight years.

Laurens took his seat in Congress 22 July 1777, and on 1 November succeeded John Hancock as president. He held the chair until 9 December 1778. Congress sat in York, Pennsylvania, during the first nine months of his presidency because the British occupied Philadelphia. Poor attendance, factionalism, the inability to supply adequately Washington's army, and constant fiscal problems plagued him. Among the accomplishments of Congress during his term were the suspension of the Saratoga Convention governing the disposition of British prisoners of war from General John Burgoyne's army, the completion and submission to the states of the Articles of Confederation, and the formulation and ratification of the Franco-American Alliance.

Laurens was respected but not always popular. He openly criticized and taunted other members as well as the secretary of Congress. Toward the end of his presidency he was drawn into the factional dispute over Silas Deane's recall as a congressional agent in France. Though Laurens planned to serve only one year, the immediate reason for his resignation was the failure of Congress to support him in the Deane controversy. Both as president and as a regular South Carolina delegate, Laurens was regarded as one of the hardest working members as well as a severe critic of the Congress. Massachusetts delegate James Lovell recalled that "Laurens was flush with pen and ink with his candles burning in the morning almost thro the year."

He continued to sit in Congress until November 1779. Appointed a commissioner to negotiate a $10 million loan and a treaty of friendship and commerce with the Dutch, he sailed from Philadelphia in August 1780. The brigantine *Mercury*, on which he sailed, was captured by the British navy off Newfoundland on 3 September. He tried to sink his dispatches, but they were fished from the sea and used to charge him with high treason. He was imprisoned in the Tower of London from 6 October 1780 until 31 December 1781. While in the tower he suspected that he had been abandoned by the American authorities. But efforts by some of his English friends to subvert his loyalty failed. He did, however, in attempts to gain access to pen and ink and to see his son Harry, petition the secretaries of state in submissive tones. These petitions occasioned harsh criticism in America, and James Madison led an unsuccessful move to have his diplomatic commission withdrawn. Initially released on bail, Laurens was exchanged in April 1782 for Lord Cornwallis who had been taken prisoner at Yorktown in October 1781.

The long confinement under poor conditions and his chronic gout prompted Laurens to go to Bath to recuperate after his release. While he was there, Congress appointed him to the peace commission and two days before the 30 November 1782 signing of the preliminary treaty he joined John Adams (1735–1826), Benjamin Franklin (1706–1790), and John Jay at Paris. His influence was felt mainly in the insertion of clauses recognizing American fishing rights off Newfoundland and prohibiting the British from carrying off slaves when they evacuated. He did not sign the final treaty because he was in England discussing commercial matters with British authorities.

Laurens returned to South Carolina in January 1785. Despite repeated attempts to coax him into public service, including his appointment as one of the state's representatives to the 1787 Constitutional Convention in Philadelphia, Laurens refused to serve. The only exceptions he made were to attend the convention at Charleston that ratified the U.S. Constitution in 1788 and to lead the parade held to celebrate the event. His experience in the Continental Congress made him an advocate of the stronger central government promised by the Constitution. He lived out most of his final days at his Mepkin plantation attempting to restore his properties that had been ravaged by the war. On his death at Mepkin, his body was cremated, a practice unheard of among European Americans at that time but ordered in his will.

In both his public and private life, Henry Laurens's commitment to duty and hard work were recognized and admired. Unfortunately, his impatience and criticism of individuals who did not meet his standards made him appear petty and inflexible. As the strongest political figure in South Carolina during the transition from provincial to state government, he worked to protect the rights of Loyalists and moderate the zeal of the radicals. In Congress his constancy during the British occupation of Philadelphia and the trying exile at York may have been his most significant contribution to the national cause. The poor health he endured after confinement in the tower and the emotional shock of his son John's death in August 1782 robbed him of the vigor that had marked his career to that time.

• The largest collections of Laurens's papers are in the South Carolina Historical Society, Charleston; the Kendall Whaling Museum, Sharon, Mass.; the Library of Congress; and the National Archives, Washington, D.C. Philip M. Hamer et al., eds., *The Papers of Henry Laurens* (13 vols. to date, 1968–), will publish all of his papers in letterpress or electronic form. His correspondence while a member of Congress may be found in Edmund C. Burnett, ed., *Letters of Members of the Continental Congress* (8 vols., 1921–1936), and Paul H. Smith et al., eds., *Letters of Delegates to Congress* (20 vols. to date, 1976–). David Duncan Wallace, *The Life of Henry Laurens* (1915), while dated, remains the only full biography. David Ramsay, *The History of South Carolina* (2 vols., 1809) and *Memoirs of the Life of Martha Laurens Ramsay* (1811), contain insightful biographical sketches.

C. JAMES TAYLOR

LAURENS, John (28 Oct. 1754–25 or 27 Aug. 1782), revolutionary war officer and diplomat, was born at the family estate outside Charleston, South Carolina, the son of Henry Laurens, a farmer and merchant, and Eleanor Ball. His father was president of the Continental Congress and one of the wealthiest Americans during the revolutionary period. Having grown up in the fashion of a southern gentleman, Laurens traveled to Europe in 1771 with his father and a brother to be-gin formal education in England and Geneva. He entered law studies at Middle Temple in London in 1772. Four years later he married Martha Manning; they had one child. The ideals of the patriot cause nearly swept him back to America, but at his father's demand he continued his studies until 1777. Returning to America, Laurens volunteered as an aide-de-camp to General George Washington, whom he intelligently served as secretary and translator to French allies. He fought bravely at Brandywine and Germantown later that year and at Monmouth the following year, suffering wounds in the last two battles. Congress voted him a commission as lieutenant colonel, an offer he initially refused but finally accepted in 1779.

Despite his youth, Laurens attempted to demonstrate political sway. In 1777 he convinced the Continental Congress to raise 3,000 soldiers from African-American slaves in South Carolina and Georgia, even offering to pay for equipping a regiment. Laurens's plans were foiled by those states' legislatures, however, because his radical proposal included emancipation as a means to attract black soldiers. He tried to force the issue on two more occasions, but each time it lost on the ballot. Nonetheless, Laurens was elected to the South Carolina Assembly in 1779. He was unable to serve, however, as Washington had sent him to Rhode Island as a liaison to the French. The British invasion of the South soon brought him home. He fought in both Georgia and South Carolina, where he was wounded again at Coosashatchie Pass in the autumn of 1779.

Laurens achieved a reputation as a courageous yet impetuous officer. His passion evinced itself in a troubled relationship with Major General Charles Lee. Lee, not to be confused with the younger brother of Henry Lee by the same name, was disliked by Washington's corps of officers because of his poor performance in battle and negative comments about Washington. Laurens wounded Lee in a duel in December 1778. In another instance, during the siege of Charleston in 1780, Laurens put his light infantry soldiers at risk, resulting in needless loss of life and his capture by General Henry Clinton. He was later exchanged.

Educated in Europe and fluent in French, Laurens was chosen by Washington and commissioned by Congress to travel to France in the spring of 1781 to help Benjamin Franklin negotiate for military supplies. Aged and tired, Franklin had performed poorly recently and had critics both at home and abroad. Washington and Congress hoped that the youthful and aggressive Laurens and his secretary, the renowned Thomas Paine, could succeed where Franklin had begun to falter. Laurens also hoped to find news about his father, who had been captured by the British after he secured a Dutch loan of $10 million.

To Franklin's surprise—and initial approval—Laurens pressed the French ministry hard and even tactlessly bypassed the comte de Vergennes and his cagey associates to appeal directly to King Louis XVI. While this mortified the French and angered Franklin, the ploy worked. Laurens obtained French security for a

$10 million Dutch loan, most of which he left in Europe to purchase military supplies. He returned to the United States with more than $2 million in cash. Congress gave its official thanks upon his presentation.

Laurens rejoined Washington's army during the Yorktown siege in October 1781. Along with Colonel Alexander Hamilton, he led a difficult bayonet attack on British fortifications. Washington chose him to accompany viscount de Noailles in negotiating the British surrender. Laurens pushed an arrangement similar to the conditions General Clinton had forced on Charleston two years earlier, when he had been captured. British general Charles Cornwallis, ironically the constable of the Tower of London, was exchanged for Laurens's father, who had been held in that London prison for more than a year.

After the agreement with Cornwallis was signed, a surrender that eventually ended the war, Laurens, a new member of the state legislature, joined General Nathanael Greene in South Carolina. Tempting fate once again with a daring though insignificant attack against a British search party, Laurens was killed at the Combahee River. The formal peace treaty was agreed on shortly thereafter in Paris, France. Laurens's impulsive and sacrificial nature complemented his father's reasoned leadership to make the Laurens family one of the leading households in the revolutionary South.

• Laurens's published papers, William Gilmore Simms, ed., *The Army Correspondence of John Laurens* (1867), reveal his wholehearted devotion to the American cause. A major biography is Sara B. Townsend, *An American Soldier: The Life of John Laurens* (1958). Laurens's place in the panoply of American heroes is shown in John F. Reed, "The Final Heroes," *Valley Forge Journal* 3, no. 3 (1987): 185–89; and Robert Weir, "Portrait of a Hero," *American Heritage* 27, no. 3 (1976): 16–19, 86–88.

PHILIP K. GOFF

LAURENT, Robert (29 June 1890–20 Apr. 1970), sculptor, was born in Concarneau, France, the son of Louis Laurent and Yvonne Fravaal. In 1902 Laurent became the protégé of visiting American painter, writer, publisher, and critic Hamilton Easter Field, who brought the talented youth and his parents to Brooklyn. Laurent returned to his native Brittany in 1904 to attend school. In Paris from 1905 to 1907 he sold Japanese prints in Ernest Le Véel's shop and studied painting with the modernist Frank Burty (Haviland), who introduced Laurent to primitivism (works by vanguard artists inspired by tribal arts), patrons Gertrude and Leo Stein, and artists Pablo Picasso and Amedeo Modigliani. Laurent later recalled that he also saw "good carvings by Gauguin and Maillol, and Negro sculpture" and that these encounters not only initiated his interest in sculpture but also had an impact on his style of carving. He and Field saw Paul Cézanne's paintings at Charles Loeser's in Florence, and while in Rome, in 1908–1909, Laurent attended classes at the British Academy, his only academic art training, and studied drawing with Field and clay modeling with the

American artist Maurice Sterne. By now aware of his color blindness, Laurent gave up painting to focus on sculpture. In London en route to New York City, Laurent looked at sculpture at the British Museum and met the art curator and critic Roger Fry, who promulgated "pure form," a concept that became essential to Laurent's aesthetics.

Laurent introduced direct carving—cutting the sculpture immediately in and respecting the qualities of the final material—to the United States in 1910 by carving primitivist reliefs on picture frames and cutting flat pictorial reliefs on functional objects (exhibited at Field's gallery, "Ardsley House," in Brooklyn Heights, 1913). Deeply impressed by the Armory Show (1913), he visited it daily. Laurent's *The Priestess* (also known as *The Negress*, 1913, private collection) and other sculptures carved in wood reflect his exposure to tribal art earlier in Paris and between 1914 and 1917, at Alfred Stieglitz's "291" gallery and at Marius de Zayas's Modern Gallery, both in New York. Laurent adopted the simplified forms of American and French folk art, which he collected, and the sculptural abstractions of Constantin Brancusi, Elie Nadelman, and Adelhyde Roosevelt. Like folk sculptors, Laurent whittled, carved, and polychromed his works disregarding representation and academic conventions and favoring reductive geometricized forms and contours. Laurent's four exhibitions in New York in 1917 elicited a review by Helen Appleton Read (*Brooklyn Daily Eagle*, 20 Dec. 1917), who paraphrased him: "He works without models, will often start a piece of a wood without a definite idea of what he is going to do. A chance cut of the chisel will suggest a form and from this he works out his finished design. Some of his finest pieces are merely abstractions, beautiful shapes." As in Brancusi's "portraits," *Muse* and *Mademoiselle Pogany*, eyes are absent from Laurent's *Abstract Head* (1916, Amon Carter Museum, Fort Worth), one of his five nonrepresentational carvings (1916–1917). Convex ribbons of wood spiraling around *Abstract Head* vaguely suggest features and hair; its termination in a solid rectangle enhances the sense of the original block of wood. *The Flame* (1917, Whitney Museum of American Art), a serpentine abstraction of light and fire, changes before the viewer's eyes from woody material to biomorphic abstraction to elemental symbol of warmth and passion.

Laurent, sent to Brittany as a ship carpenter's mate and as an interpreter for the U.S. Naval Aviation Corps, saw no action in World War I. His reunion with family and friends in his native ambience was a positive experience. He returned to America with a Breton bride, Marie "Mimi" Caraes, whom he married in 1919. The couple would have two children.

Plant Form (1924, Amon Carter Museum) is one of Laurent's botanomorphic abstractions that are unique in the history of modern sculpture—other artists abstracted the human figure or animal forms. Laurent completed the paired undulating blades of *Plant Form* as Brancusi was perfecting *Bird in Space* (marble, 1923, private collection, New York) in the aftermath of *Golden Bird* (1919), both of which the pioneering collector John Quinn brought to New York. Laurent's abstracted leaves echo Brancusi's various bird forms, which abstract the quintessence of flight more than they represent a particular flyer. "The best approach of all to Laurent is through his plants," wrote Mary Fanton Roberts (using the pseudonym Guy Eglington, *International Studio*, Mar. 1925). She favored the purity, playfulness, and lyricism of his line, which she observed caressing his inventive forms. Helen Appleton Read, writing in *The Arts*, raved about the "graceful, symbolic flower and plant shapes" on view at Laurent's solo exhibition at the Valentine-Dundensing Gallery in 1926: "No other sculptor . . . has been able to give the delicacy and spirituality of a flower shape. . . . Sometimes these aspiring fecund shapes are realistic, sometimes symbolical, but all of them in their curling leaf, pointed shoot and budding flower, symbolize the essence of plant life." Critic James R. Mellow, in a review of a solo show at Kraushaar Galleries, concurred, noting that Laurent's "most impressive sculptures are the early abstracted wood carvings" (*New York Times*, 16 Jan. 1972).

Laurent carved exclusively until 1927 but thereafter also modeled or carved directly in plaster for bronze casts. He became more versatile in subject, style, materials, and scale. His fifty alabaster sculptures (1920–1970), exemplified by *The Wave* (1926, Brooklyn Museum), unpierced by voids, highlight the translucency of the soft gypseous stone. Laurent chose not to portray the angst and suffering of the twentieth century but rather to concentrate on the enduring qualities of life. His uncomplicated philosophy was tied to an optimistic view of love and of the beauty of natural forms and the materials he carved.

Among the many monumental public sculptures Laurent modeled, cast, or carved are *Goose Girl* (aluminum, 1932, Radio City Music Hall), *Shipping* (limestone relief, 1937–1938, Federal Trade Commission Building, Washington, D.C.), and *Spanning the Continent* (bronze, 1938, Ellen Phillips Samuel Memorial, Philadelphia). From 1910 to 1941 Laurent split his time between Brooklyn Heights and Ogunquit, Maine, an art colony he helped to develop. He taught sculpture in Ogunquit beginning in 1911 and at Indiana University from 1942 to 1960; he then retired to Ogunquit. He died at Cape Neddick, Maine.

• Laurent's papers have been deposited in the Archives of American Art, Smithsonian Institution, Washington, D.C. The largest collection of his work at one site was donated in 1994 to the David and Alfred Smart Museum of Art, University of Chicago, by John N. Stern. Laurent had regular one-man exhibitions in Ogunquit and in New York at the Downtown Gallery (1926–1947) and thereafter at Kraushaar Galleries. Two important early essays are by Henry R. Hope in *Laurent: Fifty Years of Sculpture*, exhibition catalog, Indiana Univ. (1961), and by Peter V. Moak in *The Robert Laurent Memorial Exhibition*, exhibition catalog, Univ. of New Hampshire (1972); the latter cites Laurent's writings. Roberta Tarbell, who interviewed Laurent in 1970, placed him in the context of early twentieth-century vanguard art history in

"Two Modernist Wood Sculptures by Robert Laurent," in *Amon Carter Museum Program 1990*, exhibition catalog (1989); *Vanguard American Sculpture, 1913–1939* (1979); *The Figurative Tradition and American Art*, exhibition catalog, Whitney Museum of American Art (1980); *Robert Laurent and American Figurative Sculpture 1910–1960*, exhibition catalog, David and Alfred Smart Museum of Art, Univ. of Chicago (1994); and "Primitivism, Folk Art, and the Exotic," in *The Human Figure in American Sculpture: The Question of Modernity, 1890–1945*, exhibition catalog, Los Angeles County Museum of Art (1995). See also Doreen Bolger, "Hamilton Easter Field and His Contribution to American Modernism," *American Art Journal* 20 (Summer 1988): 78–107, and Helen Appleton Read, "Robert Laurent," *The Arts* 9 (1926): 251–59. An obituary is in the *New York Times*, 22 Apr. 1970.

ROBERTA K. TARBELL

LAURIE, Annie. *See* Black, Winifred Sweet.

LAURITSEN, Charles Christian (4 Apr. 1892–13 Apr. 1968), nuclear physicist, rocket designer, and national defense science policy adviser, was born in Holstebro, Denmark, the son of Thomas Lauritsen, a sawmill owner, and Marie Nielsen. Lauritsen graduated with a degree in architecture from the Odense Technical School in 1911. In 1915 he married Sigrid Henriksen, a radiologist; they had one child. In 1917 the Lauritsens emigrated to the United States, where Lauritsen worked for six years at a wide variety of jobs—from ship design to professional fishing to the building of radio receivers. In 1923 he took a position as chief engineer with the Kennedy Corporation in St. Louis for the manufacture of household radio sets. There in 1926, after hearing a lecture by physicist and Nobel Prize winner Robert A. Millikan, he decided to undertake formal studies in physics under Millikan at the California Institute of Technology in Pasadena. Lauritsen's association with Caltech would last his entire career.

At Caltech Lauritsen completed his doctoral project under Millikan on the cold-emission effect, the pulling of electrons from metals in electrical fields. Lauritsen published two papers with Millikan on this subject in 1928 and 1929 and received his Ph.D. in the latter year. He joined the Caltech physics faculty in 1930 and became full professor in 1935. He had become a naturalized U.S. citizen in 1928.

The presence of a million-volt cascade transformer at Caltech's High Voltage Laboratory inspired Lauritsen, with R. D. Bennett, to construct a high-voltage X-ray tube that operated initially at 750 kilovolts and later at one million volts, which represented a significant advance over the technology of the time. Originally designed to study the problem of field-emission breakdown, the tube's potential for medicine was quickly recognized by Lauritsen. In collaboration with Seeley G. Mudd and other medical professionals, the million-volt X-ray tube was made available for radiation therapy on cancer patients. For this contribution to medical research, Lauritsen was made a fellow of the American College of Radiology in 1931 and was awarded the college's Gold Medal. In the same year,

Millikan was able to interest W. K. Kellogg, the corn-flakes magnate, in funding the new Kellogg Radiation Laboratory at Caltech. At this facility, cancer patients received treatment during the day, while at night, the lab was given over to physics experiments. This dual use of Kellogg Laboratory continued through 1939, by which time the cancer work was transferred to a clinical setting.

In 1932 John D. Cockcroft and E. T. S. Walton in England announced that atomic nuclei could be disintegrated by being bombarded with artificially accelerated protons. In order to investigate this new field of nuclear physics, Lauritsen and his student H. R. Crane converted one of the old X-ray tubes from the High Voltage Laboratory into a positive-ion accelerator. By bombarding beryllium targets with accelerated helium ions, they were able to report in 1933 the first artificial production of neutrons, a discovery that would revolutionize neutron physics. Not long afterward, in 1934, they discovered that deuteron bombardment produced radioactive nuclei as well as neutrons. Lauritsen's group continued to concentrate on nuclear disintegrations and atomic transformations, studying various kinds of particle interactions with carbon, beryllium, lithium, and other light elements. One significant discovery that would have far-reaching effects was that of nuclear fusion: that atomic nuclei could gain particles as well as lose them. Lauritsen and Crane bombarded carbon 12 with highly energized protons and discovered that the carbon 12 target nucleus could capture a proton, yielding a new combined radioactive isotope, nitrogen 13. The process is known as radiative capture. Lauritsen's discovery provided support for theories propounded by Hans Bethe and others that nuclear fusion powers the sun and stars.

To carry out his research, Lauritsen needed accurate instruments. Always a hands-on scientist, he led his students in the design and construction of high-voltage accelerators and sensitive detection equipment. In particular, Lauritsen's quartz fiber electroscopes for measuring radiation set a standard for accuracy throughout the country.

World War II abruptly interrupted the Kellogg team's research. In August 1940 Lauritsen was called to Washington, D.C., by his Caltech colleague Richard C. Tolman, who was vice chairman under Vannevar Bush of the National Defense Research Committee and head of the section on armor and ordnance. Appointed a vice chairman in Tolman's section, Lauritsen was asked to organize the development of weapons for the armed services and to promote the value of scientific research in the war effort. As his first technical project he took on the development of a proximity fuse for rocket projectiles, which was designed to detonate not through impact or by time but by proximity to its target. Lauritsen soon learned that it was not the fuses but the unreliable rockets themselves that were the problem. His efforts to expand the government's existing rocket program at Indian Head, Maryland, met with considerable frustration, and Lauritsen determined to start up his own rocket development project

at the Kellogg Laboratory at Caltech. Securing funding from the Office of Scientific Research and Development, he launched Section L (L for Lauritsen) in Pasadena on 1 September 1941, approximately three months before the Japanese attack on Pearl Harbor. With a Caltech team that included William A. Fowler, Bruce Sage, Ralph Smythe, Carl Anderson, Frederick Lindvall, Ira Bowen, and administrator Earnest Watson, Lauritsen made major advances in rocket technology and in the development of tactical weapons. Among these were the "Mousetrap" antisubmarine rocket—so-called because of its launcher—the beach barrage rocket, and various types of antiaircraft rockets. Of these, the first to be deployed was the Mousetrap, which was hunting German submarines by the fall of 1942. Lauritsen guided every phase of the rocket project, from designing a dry-extrusion press for propellant powder to supervising testing at sites in the Mojave Desert, to conducting scientific missions to England and Europe. His assistant, Fowler, toured the Pacific in the spring of 1944 to witness the Caltech rockets in combat action.

By late 1944, Lauritsen had decided to turn the rocket project over to the navy, and he was instrumental in the founding of the Naval Ordnance Test Station (NOTS) at Inyokern, California (today the China Lake Naval Weapons Center), to take on the work. He served on the NOTS Advisory Board for twelve years, in 1949–1956, 1958–1961, and in 1963–1964. In 1944 and 1945 Lauritsen turned his attention to the atomic bomb project, working closely with nuclear physicist J. Robert Oppenheimer in both technical and administrative capacities. Toward the end of the war, Lauritsen foresaw the need for continued federal funding of research. To this end, he helped establish the Office of Naval Research in 1946, which played a major part in reinitiating scientific research in the postwar period and was a leading governmental supporter of science for years afterward. For his wartime service, Lauritsen was awarded the Medal of Merit by President Harry S. Truman in 1948.

After the war Lauritsen returned to nuclear physics research at Caltech but remained heavily involved in national defense science policy for the rest of his life. Devoting himself especially to the scientific and strategic aspects of ballistic missiles, he participated in over sixty committees, boards, and defense study groups, and served on numerous panels and advisory groups for the U.S. president and the Department of Defense.

Lauritsen served as president of the American Physical Society in 1951 and received the society's Tom Bonner Prize in 1967. He was elected to the National Academy of Sciences in 1951 and to the American Philosophical Society in 1954. His international recognition included election to the Royal Society of Copenhagen in 1939 and appointment as Kommandor of Dannebrog by the king of Denmark in 1953. He retired from Caltech in 1962 and died in Pasadena.

Lauritsen may be seen as one of three great American pioneers of nuclear physics, in company with Merle Tuve and Ernest O. Lawrence. The discoveries of Lauritsen's research group have been widely influential in the fields of nuclear astrophysics, radiation therapy (specifically, radiation dosimetry), and solid-state physics, as well as in studies of mirror nuclei and charge symmetry, nuclear beta decay, the energy of the sun, atomic spectroscopy, and the time scales of nucleosynthesis. Lauritsen played a key role in placing rockets in the United States's weapons arsenal in World War II. His later presence as a regular and esteemed adviser to the U.S. government on scientific and military matters helped to shape American defense policy during much of the Cold War era.

• Lauritsen's papers were given by his family to the archives of the California Institute of Technology in 1975 and were supplemented in 1981. Encompassing the years 1927 through 1977, they nonetheless lack material from the World War II period, and even the period of the middle and late 1930s is meagerly represented. The bulk of the collection is correspondence. Also included are a small amount of research data, miscellaneous papers relating to Lauritsen's professional activities and government service, and biographical material. A summary of his life and work by his student and close colleague William A. Fowler, as well as a complete bibliography, is in National Academy of Sciences *Biographical Memoirs* 46 (1975): 221–39. For detailed accounts of Lauritsen's research at the Kellogg Laboratory at Caltech and of the Caltech rocket project, see Judith R. Goodstein, *Millikan's School* (1991). Lauritsen's role in American rocketry and naval ordnance is described in the two-volume history of the Naval Weapons Center in China Lake, Calif., by Albert B. Christman, *Sailors, Scientists, and Rockets*, vol. 1 (1971), and J. D. Gerrard-Gough and Christman, *The Grand Experiment at Inyokern*, vol. 2 (1978).

CHARLOTTE E. ERWIN

LAURITSEN, Thomas (16 Nov. 1915–16 Oct. 1973), nuclear physicist, was born in Copenhagen, Denmark, the son of Charles Christian Lauritsen and Sigrid Henriksen. At the time of his birth, his father was employed in an architectural firm in Copenhagen. In 1917 the Lauritsens emigrated to the United States, where Charles Lauritsen would work as an electrical engineer before settling on a career in physics at the California Institute of Technology in Pasadena, starting in 1926. Sigrid Lauritsen earned a medical degree in 1936 from the University of Southern California.

Tommy Lauritsen, as he was called by his friends and colleagues, attended Caltech as an undergraduate, receiving his bachelor's degree in 1936. There he completed his Ph.D. in 1939. During the 1930s the Kellogg Laboratory at Caltech became the locus of many exciting and groundbreaking experiments in the new field of nuclear physics. The Kellogg team, led by Charles Lauritsen and including William A. Fowler, Tommy Lauritsen, and a number of graduate students, focused its work on atomic transformations and particle interactions of carbon and the light nuclei—that is, those nuclides lighter than magnesium on the periodic table. Tommy Lauritsen made his first mark in developing the complex hardware needed to support the Kellogg experiments. For his doctoral project, in collaboration with Fowler, he built a high-

voltage, pressurized Van de Graaff accelerator. This electrostatic accelerator produced a much more constant beam of particles than had the earlier alternating current machines, thus ensuring far greater accuracy in the investigation and measurement of nuclear reactions. For his dissertation, Lauritsen did a study of gamma rays produced from the bombardment of fluorine by protons. During this period he also assisted his father in the development and production of sensitive radiation detection devices, in particular, the quartz fiber electroscope, which the younger Lauritsen built by the dozens.

In 1939 a Rockefeller Foundation fellowship enabled Lauritsen to take a postdoctoral year in Copenhagen at what would later become the Niels Bohr Institute. There he oversaw the construction of an accelerator modeled on that at the Kellogg Laboratory. He also became involved in Bohr's fission research, along with J. K. Bøggild and K. J. Brostrom. This collaboration with Niels Bohr, and subsequently with Bohr's son Aage, cemented a close collegial and personal relationship between the Lauritsen and Bohr families.

While in Copenhagen, Lauritsen met and in 1940 married Else Chievitz, who died in 1944. Their only child was born in 1942. Lauritsen became a U.S. citizen in the same year. He would return to his native Denmark for extended stays in 1952–1953 as a Fulbright fellow (in the first year of the Fulbright program) and again in 1963–1964 as a National Science Foundation senior research fellow.

During World War II Lauritsen joined the Caltech rocket development project. Charles Lauritsen, under the auspices of the National Defense Research Committee (NDRC), had set up this program at Caltech to design, test, and produce rockets for the military. By 1944, when production was turned over to the Naval Ordnance Test Station at Inyokern, California (today the China Lake Naval Weapons Center), the Caltech group had produced more than one million rockets. Lauritsen also participated in the Manhattan Project, working at Los Alamos for periods in 1945. For his war work, Lauritsen received the Naval Ordnance Development Award in 1945 and the President's Certificate of Merit in 1948. In 1946 he received a faculty appointment at Caltech, where he would teach and do research until his death. Also in 1946 Lauritsen married Margaret Laura Solum; they had two children.

The postwar rebuilding of physics at Caltech, in which both Lauritsens—father and son—played a major role, established the Kellogg Laboratory as a world center for basic research in nuclear physics and nuclear astrophysics. Thomas Lauritsen's main research was in the nuclear spectroscopy of the light nuclei. With his skill in instrumentation and in the designing of ingeniously conceived experiments, he brought a wholly new dimension to the investigation of atomic nuclei and their reactions, for example, elucidating basic nuclear symmetries, such as isospin, charge symmetry, and the beta-decay couplings. His unique mastery of the growing body of knowledge on the properties of the light nuclei led him to begin in 1948 the publication of his series of reviews titled "Energy Levels of Light Nuclei." He collaborated at first with Fowler, W. F. Hornyak, C. C. Lauritsen, and P. Morrison and after 1952 with Fay Ajzenberg-Selove, with whom he worked for twenty-one years. Of prime importance for both experimental and theoretical work in the field, these reviews set a standard in presenting an analysis and evaluation of the latest published information on the quantum states of the light nuclei.

Much admired for his clarity and wit, Lauritsen had a highly successful career as a teacher at Caltech. He put substantial effort into the development of the senior physics course and became a coauthor on the principal textbook, *Introduction to Modern Physics* (1955). In an interview conducted for the Center for History of Physics of the American Institute of Physics, Lauritsen summarized his views on the relationship of research and teaching: "I think that discovering new fundamental facts of nature, new basic principles, is obviously the most rewarding business that there can be. But discovering new ways of explaining what we already understand in a vague sort of way is, I think, also a very important enterprise (Interview, p. 34).

Lauritsen served the worldwide physics community devotedly. He played a major role on the National Academy of Sciences' Physics Survey Committee in the years 1969–1972, helping to author *Physics in Perspective* (1972), which provided the first reliable and detailed information on the levels of funding, facilities, and training in American nuclear physics. He was one of the founders of the Division of Nuclear Physics of the American Physical Society and served as its chairman during the last two years of his life. He served on numerous scientific advisory boards and panels, among others, for the Department of Defense, the Institute for Defense Analysis, the National Research Council, the Brookhaven Laboratory, Oak Ridge Laboratory, the Argonne Laboratory, and the National Science Foundation. He served as the U.S. representative to the Nuclear Physics Commission of the International Union of Pure and Applied Physics (1963–1972). He was elected a fellow of the American Physical Society (1949) and of the Royal Danish Academy of Sciences and Letters (1965). He was a member of the American Academy of Arts and Sciences (1969), the National Academy of Sciences (1969), and Sigma Xi.

Lauritsen died of cancer in Pasadena, California. Those who knew him mourned the untimely passing of a man of lively humor, great kindness, and deep dedication to science. His contribution to the knowledge of nuclear reactions, especially those of the light nuclei, remains unique. His imaginative but thorough application of experimental techniques was passed on to many students and colleagues. Lauritsen left his mark on the American physics community through his broad commitment to physics as a profession and to science policy making in the nuclear age.

• Thomas Lauritsen's papers were given to the archives of the California Institute of Technology by his widow. Dating largely after World War II, they consist of personal and scientific correspondence, papers relating to professional and advisory activities, research, and teaching, and biographical material. Included in the latter section is a copy of the oral history interview conducted by Barry Richman and Charles Wiener for the American Institute of Physics (1967), which is an important source for the life, work, and views of Thomas Lauritsen as well as for his father, Charles. The papers of Charles C. Lauritsen, also in the archives of the California Institute of Technology, bear on the life and work of his son as well as elucidate the rise of nuclear physics at Caltech. The development of the Kellogg Laboratory at Caltech is covered in a special issue of *Engineering and Science* 32 (June 1969).

Thomas Lauritsen's life and work is treated by William A. Fowler and Fay Ajzenberg-Selove in National Academy of Sciences, *Biographical Memoirs* 55 (1985): 385–96, which includes a complete bibliography of his writings. Their account can be fleshed out with other biographical sketches found in the T. Lauritsen papers. An obituary, by Thomas Tombrello, a student and later collaborator with Lauritsen, is in *Engineering and Science* 37 (Nov.–Dec. 1973): 19.

CHARLOTTE E. ERWIN

LA VÉRENDRYE, Pierre Gaultier de (17 Nov. 1685–5 Dec. 1749), explorer, military officer, and post commander, was born in Trois-Rivières, Canada, the son of René Gaultier de Varennes, a governor of Trois-Rivières, and Marie-Ursule Boucher, the daughter of Pierre Boucher, a former governor of Trois-Rivières.

From 1696 to 1699 Pierre attended the Petit Séminaire in Quebec City. He entered the military profession as a cadet at the early age of eleven or twelve. He took part in military campaigns against New England in 1704 and Newfoundland in 1705. He left two years later for France to serve in Flanders with the regiment of Brittany. Seriously wounded and taken prisoner at Malplaquet (1709), he was promoted to lieutenant in 1710 and left the service a year later.

La Vérendrye returned to Canada in 1712 and married Marie-Anne Dandonneau du Sablé, the daughter of a seigneur and military officer. They had four sons, who contributed to their father's accomplishments, and two daughters. For fifteen years La Vérendrye lived the life of a seigneur, on his wife's seigneurial lands in the Berthier area, from his seigneurial rights on Du Tremblay, near Boucherville, and his fur trade business at La Gabelle, near Trois-Rivières.

La Vérendrye resumed his military career in 1727, when he was appointed to the Poste du Nord (northern Lake Superior), under his brother, Jacques-René, whom he replaced as commanding officer in 1728. There he gathered information on the Mer de l'Ouest (Western Sea), which he thought would result in the discovery of a French route across the continent to Asia.

In 1731 La Vérendrye was commissioned by Governor Charles de Beauharnois to search for the Mer de l'Ouest and given the command of the posts he would establish in the area. The first three years were used on the route between Lake Superior and Lake Winnipeg. Three posts were built: Saint-Pierre on Rainy Lake in

1731, Saint-Charles on Lake of the Woods in 1732, and Maurepas on Red River in 1734.

The consolidation of his position took priority. La Vérendrye spent a considerable amount of time in maintaining good relationships with the Indian nations, who were not all in favor of the French advance on new territory, especially when it benefited other nations. In 1736, for example, the Sioux massacred a French party under the command of Jean-Baptiste, the eldest son of La Vérendrye, on their way to Michilimackinac.

Once firmly established in the southern part of Lake Winnipeg, La Vérendrye's expeditions took two directions, based on information obtained from the native peoples: toward the southwest and the Mandane country, and toward the north, the lakes, and the Saskatchewan River.

A first expedition left Fort Maurepas in the fall of 1738. La Vérendrye followed the Assiniboine River upstream, established Fort La Reine, and then traveled in a southwest direction. He reached the Mandane country in early December. After a short ten-day stay, he returned to Fort La Reine, arriving on 10 February. He had come to the conclusion that the river of the Mandanes (the Missouri River) did not give access to the Mer de l'Ouest. However, on their return, the two men he had left with the Mandanes to learn the language brought back information relative to white men living at a far distance to the southwest of their territory.

From 1739 to 1741 the explorer directed his efforts toward the north, giving his son Louis-Joseph instructions to explore the "lac des Prairies" (Lake Winnipegosis) and northern Lake Winnipeg. Two posts were built at gathering places for the Crees and the Assiniboines in their fur-trading trips to Hudson's Bay: Fort Bourbon in 1739, on the northwest side of Lake Winnipeg, and Fort Dauphin in 1741, on Lake Winnipegosis.

Southwest exploration resumed in 1742, in order to discover the great sea and the white men mentioned by the Mandanes. La Vérendrye's two sons, Louis-Joseph and François, and two travelers left Fort La Reine with Indian guides on 2 April. The party traveled first to the Mandane country, then to the southwest. They crossed the lands of several Indian nations: "Beaux-Hommes" (Crows?), "Petit Renards" (Little Foxes), "Pioyas" (Kiowas?), "Gens des Chevaux" (Cheyennes?), "Gens de la Belle-Rivière" (Arickaras?), and "Gens de l'Arc" (Bow Indians). They reluctantly took part with the latter in a disastrous war expedition against the "Gens du Serpent" (Snakes). They returned in early February. After meeting with other nations—"Gens de la Petite Cerise" (Little Cherry Indians) and Prairie Sioux—they reached the Mandane villages on 18 May and Fort La Reine on 2 July.

The party had seen mountains, either the Black Hills or the Big Horn Mountains, but they had not reached their intended destination. They had only ascertained that the white men were Spanish and the sea already known. The Mer de l'Ouest was not to be

found in that direction. Once again, La Vérendrye reoriented his search. Fort Bourbon was moved farther to the west in 1743, at the mouth of the Paskoya (Saskatchewan) River.

La Vérendrye's efforts never entirely satisfied the French colonial authorities, who considered his progress too slow and blamed it on too deep an involvement in the fur trade. Their lack of understanding, their continuous criticism, and, last but not least, the lost support of Governor Beauharnois led to his resignation in 1743. Only in 1745 was he granted the rank of captain, in late recognition of his contribution. Reappointed to his former post in 1747, he was unable to go back before his death in Montreal from an epidemic.

Historians have considered La Vérendrye either as an explorer forced by the financial requirements of his expeditions to accept the conditions of the Montreal fur traders or as a post officer taking advantage of his portion and using the search for the Mer de l'Ouest to establish a lucrative and monopolistic fur trade over a very large territory. In fact, La Vérendrye could not ignore the realities of the fur trade. The king of France had refused to fund his expeditions, forcing him to rely on fur trade returns. Moreover, his progress depended on maintaining good relations with the Indian nations, mainly through the exchange of French manufactured goods for furs.

The king's glory and the colony's welfare, La Vérendrye explained in 1744, had always been his only motives. The former was well achieved by the expansion of the French empire and exploration of the Central Plains, the latter by an increase in the fur trade at the expense of the Hudson's Bay Company.

• A large collection of papers relating to La Vérendrye and the Mer de l'Ouest was edited by Lawrence J. Burpee and published by the Champlain Society as *Journals and Letters of Pierre Gaultier de Varennes de La Vérendrye and His Sons* (1927). In his *New France, 1701–1744: "A Supplement to Europe"* (1987), Dale Miquelon presents an up-to-date assessment of La Vérendrye in the context of the fur trade and the general Indian diplomacy. An important bibliographic essay complements Yves F. Zoltvany's entry on the explorer in the *Dictionary of Canadian Biography*. Antoine Champagne's biography, *Les La Vérendrye et le poste de l'Ouest* (1968) and *Nouvelles études sur les La Vérendrye et le poste de l'Ouest* (1971), is still the most extensively documented, though the interpretation needs to be revisited. Other biographies of lesser significance have been written by Martin Kavanagh, *La Vérendrye, His Life and Times* (1967), and Nellis M. Crouse, *La Vérendrye: Fur Trader and Explorer* (1956). G. Hubert Smith, *The Explorations of the La Vérendryes in the Northern Plains, 1738–43*, ed. W. Raymond Wood (1980), contains an interesting discussion of the probable itineraries of the two expeditions to the Plains as well as translations of original journals.

GRATIEN ALLAIRE

LAW, James (13 Feb. 1838–10 May 1921), veterinarian, educator, and public health advocate, was born in Edinburgh, Scotland, the son of John Law and Grace Turner, farmers. In 1857 he graduated from the Veterinary College in Edinburgh and then continued scientific study at the medical school of Edinburgh University and at veterinary schools in France at Alfort (near Paris) and Lyons. Returning to Scotland, he became a protégé of John Gamgee, a cosmopolitan English veterinarian who promoted the view that epizootics (diseases affecting many animals) were caused by minute organisms, not noxious fumes, changes in the weather, or poor ventilation. By siding with the controversial Gamgee, Law abandoned the anticontagionist views held by British veterinarians in general and by his Edinburgh teacher, William Dick. In 1860 Law joined the faculty of Gamgee's New Veterinary College in Edinburgh and taught anatomy and materia medica. In so doing he joined the minority of veterinary educators who sought to improve veterinary education by placing it in a scientific framework. Although he had been certified as a veterinary surgeon by the Highland and Agricultural Society in 1857, he also took and passed the examination of the rival Royal College of Veterinary Surgeons (London) in 1861, thereby becoming a member and in 1877, rising to fellow. In 1863 he married Eliza Crighton in Edinburgh; they had three daughters and one son. When Gamgee reestablished the New Veterinary College in London in 1865 as the Royal Albert Veterinary College, Law moved with him. However, the Royal Albert failed to compete for students with the Royal Veterinary College, and Law left to practice in Ireland.

Gamgee, whose contagionist views and magnetic personality had earned him respect in the United States, recommended Law to Cornell University's president, Andrew Dickson White, who was seeking a veterinarian to teach agricultural students. Law accepted White's invitation, and in 1868 he joined the university as one of its original faculty members. Between 1868 and 1896 Law taught veterinary medicine to undergraduates studying for the bachelor of agriculture degree. Characterized by Veranus A. Moore as "an inspiring and thorough teacher," Law provided instruction in veterinary anatomy, physiology, hygiene, dietetics, breeding, agronomy as it affected the quality of animal fodder, and animal diseases. Law had special students who studied veterinary medicine beyond the year-long course designed for agricultural students. Several earned bachelor of veterinary science degrees and one a doctor of veterinary medicine degree. Among these were Daniel E. Salmon, founder and for twenty-one years director of the Bureau of Animal Industry (BAI); Arthur M. Farrington, organizer of the federal meat inspection service at the BAI; Fred L. Kilborne, who did fundamental research on Texas cattle fever and other animal diseases; Theobald Smith, the leading bacteriologist in the United States before World War II; Pierre Augustine Fish, a physiologist; Grant Sherman Hopkins, an anatomist; Veranus A. Moore, an educator and authority on tuberculosis; Cooper Curtice, a scientist who worked on tuberculosis in cattle and Texas fever; and Leonard Pearson, a leading veterinary educator and advocate for public health in Pennsylvania. Most of these men were connected with the BAI during its formative years.

During the three decades that Law taught Cornell undergraduates, he also became a national leader in veterinary education, public health, and animal health. An unusually clear and forceful writer, he could address politicians, farmers, veterinarians, and scientists with equal success. His survey of continental veterinary schools and his essays advocating higher standards for veterinary education dominated North American discussions of the subject and helped obtain state funding for veterinary education in New York and elsewhere. His two textbooks, one written with Gamgee, became standard in North American veterinary colleges; his essays and pamphlets on the nature and economic costs of epizootics reached a wide audience of veterinarians, physicians, scientists, stock owners, and public officials; and his *Farmer's Veterinary Advisor: A Guide to the Prevention and Treatment of Disease in Domestic Animals* went through sixteen issues or editions between 1876 and his death.

Law was also prominent in advancing the public health and in controlling contagious diseases. In the 1870s he was the veterinarian to whom the American Public Health Association and the National Board of Health turned for advice about animal diseases, and he consulted for the New York State Agricultural Society from 1869 to 1896. In 1882 and 1883 chaired the U.S. Treasury Cattle Commission, which crisscrossed the United States investigating the ravages of lung plague in beef and dairy cattle and observing the successful quarantine station at Point Lévis, Québec, Canada. The commission then published a lengthy and influential report with fifty-two recommendations as to how the federal government could eradicate this dangerous epizootic. In 1884 the commissioner of agriculture named Law the U.S. delegate to the world Veterinary Congress in Brussels and then had him survey veterinary colleges in continental Europe. For federal, state, and local governmental agencies, Law also investigated or supervised the eradication of outbreaks of other diseases, among them, hoof and mouth disease, swine flu, and typhoid fever. (His investigation of swine flu was thorough and methodical but, like the investigations of this epizootic by all other nineteenth-century scientists, inconclusive.) "Always a leader, he often formed public opinion and guided public action in many critical periods," Moore noted.

Even before Cornell University's founding in 1868, Ezra Cornell had planned to create a college for training veterinarians, and twice the university appropriated sums of money for that purpose. However, it was not until March 1894, when the state of New York chartered and funded the New York State Veterinary College at Cornell, that Law felt he had sufficient financial resources to create a veterinary college. New York's support of veterinary education did not come easily; rather, it was the result of years of political work by Law and other Cornell University officials, aided by Law's national reputation as an educator and sanitarian. Between March 1894 and September 1896, when the first class matriculated, Law designed a curriculum, established admission standards, selected a faculty, and designed and supervised the construction of a building. As a result of Law's experience and meticulous planning, the New York State Veterinary College at Cornell became the leading veterinary school in the United States the day it opened. For the next twelve years he served as director of the college while continuing his campaigns for higher matriculation and graduation standards for veterinarians, public funding of veterinary education, and the contagious theory of disease. He retired as director in 1908 and died thirteen years later in Springfield, Massachusetts, while returning to his home in Ithaca.

Law was the most important veterinarian in the United States before the end of World War I. As an educator, he attracted able students and trained more scientists than any other nineteenth- or early twentieth-century veterinarian. He then created at Cornell the strongest and most important veterinary school in the United States. All the while, his advocacy of contagionism reached and persuaded veterinarians, politicians, public officials, and stock owners across the country, preventing millions of dollars in livestock losses.

• Papers and archives relating to Law and his career in the United States are in the Cornell University Archives and the Roswell P. Flower Library of the New York State College of Veterinary Medicine, Ithaca, N.Y. Representative publications are *General and Descriptive Anatomy of the Domestic Animals* (1861–1862), coauthored with John Gamgee; "A Plea for Veterinary Surgery," *American Veterinary Review* 2 (1878–1879): 158–75; *Report of the Treasury Cattle Commission on the Lung Plague of Cattle, or Contagious Pleuro-Pneumonia* (1882); essays on anthrax, rabies, and glanders in William Pepper, ed., *A System of Practical Medicine by American Authors* (1885); *Textbook of Veterinary Medicine* (1896–1903); "Extermination of Texas Fever," *Country Gentleman*, 3 Nov. 1898; and *Tuberculosis in Cattle and Its Control* (1898). Iain Pattison, *The British Veterinary Profession, 1791–1948* (1984), and Lise Wilkinson, *Animals and Disease: An Introduction to the History of Comparative Medicine* (1992), describe the milieu in which Law was educated and developed his views on contagionism and professional education. Wyndham D. Miles's unpublished "History of the National Board of Health, 1879–1893" (1970) in the History of Medicine Division, National Library of Medicine, Bethesda, Md., has a chapter on efforts to regulate animal diseases in the United States. In *A Cornell Heritage: Veterinary Medicine, 1868–1908* (1979), Ellis Pierson Leonard describes Law's veterinary work at Cornell, and in *A History of Cornell* (1962), Morris Bishop recounts Law's place in the history of the university, providing vignettes of how Law's contemporaries saw him. Law himself published an illuminating memoir in *The Report of the Conference at the New York State Veterinary College during the Semi-Centennial Celebration of Cornell University* (1919). Veranus A. Moore, Law's student and successor as dean, wrote an obituary, "A Tribute to Dr. James Law," *Journal of the American Veterinary Medical Association* 59 (1921): 93–96.

PHILIP M. TEIGEN

LAW, Richard (7 Mar. 1733–26 Jan. 1806), legislator and judge, was born in Milford, Connecticut, the son of Jonathan Law, governor of Connecticut, and Eunice Hall Andrew. After graduating from Yale College (1751), he read law with Jared Ingersoll (1722–1781) of New Haven, and was admitted to the Connecticut bar in 1755. Settling in New London in 1757, he married Ann Prentice in 1760, with whom he had twelve children.

His Connecticut political and judicial careers began with his election as a New London deputy to the General Assembly and with his appointment as a justice of the peace, both in 1765. He was often reelected as a deputy until 1776, serving also as a clerk of the General Assembly (1774–1776) when he was elected an assistant, or member of the upper house of the state legislature (1776–1786). His service as a justice of the peace continued until 1775, by which time he had been appointed chief judge of the New London County Court (1773–1784). Appointed to the Connecticut Superior Court in 1784, he became chief judge in 1786, a position he held until 1789, when he was appointed by President George Washington to be district judge of Connecticut (1789–1806). Among his accomplishments as a jurist was the codification of the state's laws, a task he shared with Roger Sherman, also a judge on the superior court. Their work was published in 1784 as *Acts and Laws of the State of Connecticut, in America*.

As the imperial crisis developed, Law was appointed in 1767 to a New London committee in response to the Townshend Acts, and after 1774 served on the town's committee of correspondence. Law was also appointed to several colonywide committees, including Connecticut's committee of correspondence (1774) and council of safety (1776). Because of ill health he was unable to fulfill his appointment as a Connecticut delegate to the Continental Congress in 1774, but he did represent the state in Congress in 1777, and in 1781 and 1782. During these sessions, he served on a variety of committees, including those that dealt with maritime matters, the Indians, the Articles of Confederation, Vermont, and privateers. In February 1781, he was one of several nominees to be secretary for foreign affairs, a position that was eventually filled by Robert R. Livingston (1746–1813) of New York after a protracted contest with Arthur Lee of Virginia.

As a delegate to Connecticut's ratifying convention in early January 1788, Law supported the proposed U.S. Constitution, noting with approval the amendment procedure, the nonhereditary status of the executive and the Congress, and the experiment of a free government over so large a country. In February of the following year, he was one of Connecticut's first seven federal electors, all of whom voted for George Washington's election as president of the United States.

In 1784, while still a judge, Law was elected as the first mayor of the newly incorporated city of New London, a position he held until his death there. Nominated by the Democratic Republican party in 1801 as their candidate for governor, he declined the honor in a state overwhelmingly dominated by the Federalist party. His name remained on the ballot, however, and Law was easily defeated by the incumbent Federalist, Jonathan Trumbull (1740–1809), an unusual moment in a public career otherwise marked by sustained and substantial service and success.

• A small number of Law letters may be found in the appropriate volumes of Edmund C. Burnett's *Letters of Members of the Continental Congress* (1921–1936). Several other Law manuscripts may be found in the papers of the Continental Congress at the Library of Congress. For his government service in Connecticut, see the appropriate volumes in J. Hammond Trumbull and Charles J. Hoadley, eds., *Public Records of the Colony of Connecticut* (1850–1890), and in Charles J. Hoadley et al., eds., *Public Records of the State of Connecticut* (1894–1967). Biographical material is available in Franklin B. Dexter, *Biographical Sketches of the Graduates of Yale College* vol. 2 (1896) and in Frances M. Caulkins, *History of New London, Connecticut* (1852). A description of the revolutionary era and especially Connecticut's efforts in the Continental Congress may be found in Christopher Collier, *Roger Sherman's Connecticut* (1971). One additional, accessible source for Richard Law's jurisprudence is the 1986 facsimile reproduction, edited and with an introduction by Ronald Lettieri and Richard Mandel, of Ephraim Kirby, *Reports of the Cases Adjudged in the Superior Court of the State of Connecticut from the Year 1785 to May 1788* (1789).

THOMAS W. JODZIEWICZ

LAW, Sallie Chapman Gordon (27 Aug. 1805–28 June 1894), Civil War nurse, was born in Wilkes County, North Carolina, the daughter of Chapman Gordon, a revolutionary war veteran, and Charity King. In 1825 she married Dr. John S. Law. The couple lived in Forsythe, Georgia, and Columbia, Tennessee, before John Law's death in 1844. Sallie Law then settled permanently in Memphis, Tennessee, with her seven children. Law was devout and philanthropic in character.

Law and her extended family were deeply involved in the Confederate cause during the Civil War. When her only son enlisted, she told him, "You did right, my son." Her nephew, General John B. Gordon, and her brother, General G. W. Gordon, were two of at least forty male relatives who fought for the Confederacy. Law seized the wartime opportunity to apply her organizational skills and charitable impulses on an expanded level and devoted her energy to the comfort and aid of southern soldiers. When the war broke out, Law and other women formed the Southern Mothers Society with the purpose of assisting Confederate soldiers. The group elected Law president. Shortly thereafter, at the behest of General Thomas Hindman, Law and her associates established the Southern Mothers Hospital in Memphis, which was operational in mid-April 1861. Originally a twelve-bed facility, the hospital expanded to accommodate 400 beds after the battle of Shiloh and eventually served more than 2,000 sick and wounded men during its existence.

Eager to distribute excess hospital stores collected by the Southern Mothers Hospital, Law frequently journeyed behind the lines with supplies, twice taking them to soldiers and hospitals in Columbus, Kentucky, where she witnessed the battle of Belmont. When her hospital closed, following the Union occupation of Memphis in June 1862, Law did not become idle. In her reminiscences she wrote, "Our hospitals all broken up, I felt I must seek a new field in which to work." The Southern Mothers purchased, with the remaining $2,500 in their treasury, quinine, morphine, and opium, which Law smuggled into the Confederacy and delivered to hospitals, mainly in La Grange, Georgia, where she continued her nursing activities. At some point during her stay in La Grange, Law Hospital was named for her.

When Law learned of the destitute state of General Joseph E. Johnston's army at Dalton in December 1863, she was "so greatly troubled to hear of the great suffering of the brave heroes" that she appealed to the Columbus, Georgia, Ladies Aid Society for blankets and clothing, which she personally distributed to the soldiers despite the dangers and hardships of traveling with such a large cargo. Returning to Columbus, she wrote in the local newspapers of the conditions at Dalton and rallied the support of the town. Raising $2,500 from businesses in one hour, she purchased cloth from a textile factory and parceled it out to the women of the city, who quickly produced blankets and socks. After Law's second delivery, in early January 1864, an appreciative General Johnston ordered 30,000 troops to parade before her, an honor probably bestowed on no other southern woman. She continued to nurse in both hospitals and the field, collect supplies, raise money, and convey supplies throughout the war. The combination of her fortitude, her attention to the soldiers' needs, and her family connections enabled Law to efficiently amass and direct much-needed clothing, blankets, and medical supplies to southern fighting men. Moreover, Law emphasized in her reminiscences that her trips were always made at her own expense. Her dedication to the Confederate cause earned her a reputation throughout the South as the "Mother of the Confederacy" and the adoration of southern soldiers.

At the conclusion of the war, the Southern Mothers, often referred to as the Southern Mothers' Association, focused on Confederate memorial work. In 1889, with the Southern Mothers at its core, the Ladies' Confederate Historical Association formed under the auspices of the Confederate Historical Association. Committed to preserving the memory and history of the Confederacy, the group promoted literature relating to the war and the southern cause, aided in marking graves, and commissioned monuments. Until her death, Law served as the sole president of the Southern Mothers, who, in Law's honor, chose to forgo the election of a new leader. The original members retained their title as Southern Mothers for the remainder of their lives.

In 1892, at the age of eighty-seven, Law wrote a sixteen-page pamphlet, *Reminiscences of the War of the Sixties between the North and South*, in which she humbly described several of her experiences during the war. She died two years later in Memphis. The lauda-tory obituaries dedicated to her memory indicate the reverence she inspired in those around her. A journalist for the *Confederate Veteran* wrote in July 1894, "Hers was a character truly deserving of respect and honor from her fellow-men."

Law was one of thousands of women, North and South, who cared for the sick and wounded during the Civil War. The war created many opportunities for patriotic service, and nursing, especially in field conditions, required the strength to handle scenes of suffering, the constant presence of death, exposure to the hazards of war, and a willingness to relinquish comforts. The experience was often significant in women's lives, and their efforts enhanced the efficiency and quality of Civil War medical care. Law's experiences also demonstrate the appreciation soldiers felt for devoted nurses, and the emotional impact of the war upon its participants. The war remained vivid when an aged Law wrote, "Still, memories of suffering, blood, and tears at the bedside of the wounded, dying soldier, is indelibly stamped on my memory."

• Law's pamphlet is at the Memphis / Shelby County Public Library, and the Library of Congress has a photocopy. The *Confederate Veteran* 2 (Apr. 1894) and 5 (July 1894) contains both an obituary and excerpts from her pamphlet. See also Quincealea Brunk, "Caring without Politics: Lessons from the First Nurses of the North and South," *Nursing History Review* 2 (1994): 119–36. Mrs. H. H. Humphreys, "Southern Mothers, Memphis, Tennessee," in *History of the Confederated Memorial Associations of the South* (1904), pp. 262–65, mentions Law's postwar work. Another article in the same book, author unknown, "Ladies' Confederate Memorial Association, Memphis, Tennessee," pp. 266–68, is also useful. Other obituaries are in the *Memphis Commercial*, 29 June 1894; the *Memphis Appeal-Avalanche*, 30 June 1894, repr. in *Southern Historical Society Papers* 22 (1894); and the *New York Times*, 30 June 1894.

LIBRA HILDE

LAWFORD, Peter (7 Sept. 1923–24 Dec. 1984), actor, was born in London, England, the son of Lieutenant General Sir Sydney Turing Barlow Lawford, an officer in the British army, and May Somerville Bunny Aylen. His mother was married to Major Ernest Vaughan Aylen at the time of his birth, and Lawford's birth certificate reads Peter Sydney Ernest Aylen. A year after Lawford's birth, when his parents' respective divorces were final, they married. The family left England for France to avoid the scandal. Since he spent so much time in France, Lawford's first language was French. During Lawford's childhood, the family traveled extensively, first throughout Europe and later around the world. Before he was fifteen, Lawford had been around the world three times. He never attended school and was taught by governesses and then a tutor.

In 1930 Sir Sydney's finances were affected by the worldwide depression, and, to economize, the Lawfords returned to England, staying at their flat in London and the country home in Toddington. Although

the Lawfords were "still shunned by the prissier members of society," they were "welcomed back by most" (Spada, p. 37). Much to his father's dismay, Peter had wanted to be an actor and dancer since he was three, and in 1931 he and his mother visited a film studio, which was then shooting one of the first British talkies, *Poor Old Bill*. The movie had a role for a young boy, but the child who was playing the part did not please the director. When he saw Lawford, the director hired him for the role, and Lawford had his first acting job. After receiving good reviews, Lawford was named "Britain's Jackie Coogan." Although another film, *A Gentleman of Paris*, followed in 1932, the family resumed traveling and Lawford's film career temporarily ended.

In 1937, when Lawford seriously injured his right arm, it was only his mother's insistence that prevented surgeons from amputating the arm at the shoulder. Although the arm gradually improved, Lawford would never have complete dexterity in his right hand or full strength in his right arm. To facilitate healing and escape the damp weather of Aix-les-Bains, France, where they were then living, the family moved to Los Angeles.

Lawford, now fourteen, resumed his film career with a small part in *Lord Jeff* (1938), which starred Freddie Bartholomew and Mickey Rooney. No additional roles followed, and when Lawford's voice began to change, acting assignments were out of the question. At this point the family was again experiencing financial problems and left California for the East Coast to stay with relatives on Long Island and, later, friends in Palm Beach. Running out of relatives and friends, the Lawfords were forced to rent their own small house in Palm Beach and were exposed to life "on the other side of the tracks."

When Lawford turned sixteen, he went to work first pumping gas at a filling station in West Palm Beach and then parking cars. His charming manners earned him good tips, but acting was still his dream, so he joined a small theater workshop and made plans to return to Hollywood. In January 1942 Lawford was back in Los Angeles, working as an usher at the Village Theater. One day Lawford took time off from work to audition for a one-line part in *Mrs. Miniver* (1942). He was hired on the spot, filmed the scene, and went back to work. When he was caught sneaking his friends into the theater, Lawford lost the ushering job, but he continued to get a string of bit parts. His first significant role was in *A Yank at Eton* (1942), in which he played a snobbish, conniving, upper-class Englishman out to get the American, down-to-earth hero, played by Mickey Rooney.

Although he only had a brief, nonspeaking role in *Pilot #5* (1943), Lawford's acting was so impressive that he was offered a contract with MGM. His career was now on its way, and his money problems were over. He had an important role in *The White Cliffs of Dover* (1944) and his first full-length movie role in *Son of Lassie* (1945). Lawford would later note that "Lassie was a vicious bastard" and nicknamed the film "Son of a Bitch." Tasting success, Lawford began to live the life of a playboy movie star and became popular with many major stars. He met Frank Sinatra in 1945, and their friendship led to a role in Sinatra's *It Happened in Brooklyn* (1947). In the film Lawford sang and did a jitterbug routine that had teenage girls screaming in delight. *Good News* (1947), with June Allyson, was a success, and reviews noted that Lawford "fulfills his promise as the most personable romantic lead on the screen" (quoted in Spada, p. 113). In 1948 Lawford's film career was at its peak; he had the third lead in *Easter Parade* and gave Elizabeth Taylor her first screen kiss in *Julia Misbehaves*.

Then roles became scarce. Lawford's one release in 1950 was *Please Believe Me*, in which he was fourth-billed, and his single release in 1951, *Royal Wedding*, gave him little screen time, even cutting his one musical number. When MGM dropped his contract in 1952, Lawford turned to television. He appeared in five teleplays during 1953–1954 and starred and co-produced the sitcom "Dear Phoebe" (1954), which ran only one season. His next television series, "The Thin Man" with Phyllis Kirk, was well received but only ran two seasons, from 1957 through 1959.

In 1958 producer Albert Broccoli offered Lawford the leading role in a series of films based on Ian Fleming's James Bond novels that he planned to make. Broccoli thought Lawford would be perfect for the part but could only pay $25,000 a film and required a commitment for five films. Lawford, whose asking price per picture was $75,000, declined; it was the worst of his "professional" mistakes.

At this time Lawford's personal life seemed to be going better than his career. He became a member of Frank Sinatra's "Rat Pack," and with the other members, Dean Martin, Sammy Davis, Jr., and Joey Bishop, the "Pack" worked together in films, the most successful being *Ocean's 11* (1960). The "Pack" also performed on stage in Las Vegas, played, and did business together; Lawford became a partner with Sinatra in the Cal-Neva Lodge, a Lake Tahoe hotel and casino, and the Beverly Hills restaurant Puccini.

The matinee idol of thousands of teenage girls and the lover of a number of women, Lawford had married Patricia Kennedy in 1954, a match that pleased neither family. The Lawfords would have four children, but the marriage was not a success, and they divorced in 1966. Of all his in-laws, Lawford got along best with Patricia's brother John F. Kennedy and used all his Hollywood contacts to help Kennedy's presidential campaign. Before the significant first televised debate with Richard Nixon, Kennedy sought Lawford's professional advice concerning make-up and how to face the cameras. Lawford even became an American citizen in April 1960 to be able to vote for Kennedy in the election. For the first two years of the Kennedy administration, Lawford's Santa Monica beach house was, in effect, the western White House. When John Kennedy was later assassinated, Lawford was devastated.

On the coattails of the president, Lawford again got some good acting roles. He played Lord Lovat, the Scottish commando, in *The Longest Day* (1962) and the womanizing, playboy senator in *Advise and Consent* (1962). Many thought that Lawford's role was a portrait of John Kennedy, and much of his part was edited out of the picture. In 1961 Lawford formed a production company, Chrislaw, with his friend Milt Ebbins. The company produced the "Patty Duke Show" for television in 1963 and the film *Johnny Cool* (1963). Film roles again dwindled until 1968 when Lawford did *Salt and Pepper*, with Sammy Davis, Jr.; *Buona Sera, Mrs. Campbell*, with Gina Lollobrigida; and *The April Fools* (1969), with Jack Lemmon, a performance that critics described as "excellent."

Lawford appeared on the television show "Laugh-In" once or twice a season from 1968 to 1972 and in 1971 married Mary Rowan, the daughter of Dan Rowan, costar of "Laugh-In." She was twenty-six years younger than he was; they divorced in 1975. A third marriage to Deborah Gould in 1976 lasted only months. During this time in his life, Lawford's over-indulgence in alcohol and drugs can only be called self-destructive. In 1982 he checked into the Betty Ford Clinic for five weeks but resumed taking drugs and alcohol when he was released. Suffering from a bleeding ulcer, in July 1983 he entered the hospital, where, although seriously ill, he married Patricia Ann Seaton, his "common-law wife/companion." Once out of the hospital, Lawford's recovery was slow but steady, and Elizabeth Taylor got him a small role in the television movie *Malice in Wonderland* (1985). However, Lawford resumed drinking and was again hospitalized. He was discharged the morning of filming, but when it was time for him to appear before the cameras he was unable to speak his lines. Lawford died eleven days later at Cedars-Sinai Medical Center in Los Angeles.

Known for his suave good looks, wit, and casual English charm, Lawford appeared in more than sixty films as well as on television. He was once described by critics as a "promising light comedian" but did not live up to that promise. Lawford had many Hollywood friends, but being brother-in-law to President John F. Kennedy was perhaps his most "shining moment."

• Lawford's papers are at Arizona State University Library at Tempe. James Spada, *Peter Lawford: The Man Who Kept the Secrets* (1991), is a scholarly biography, although it focuses on the relationship between the Kennedy brothers and actress Marilyn Monroe, and includes good notes and a selective bibliography for further research. A more "popular" version of Lawford's life by his fourth wife, Patricia Seaton Lawford, ghostwritten by Ted Schwarz, is *The Peter Lawford Story: Life with the Kennedys, Monroe and the Rat Pack* (1988). This book has some incorrect information and includes a selective bibliography and an incomplete filmography. See the chapter on Lawford in James Robert Parish and Ronald L. Bowers, *The MGM Stock Company* (1973). Obituaries are in the *New York Times* and the *Los Angeles Times*, both 25 Dec. 1984, and *People Weekly*, 14 Jan. 1985.

MARCIA B. DINNEEN

LAWRANCE, Charles Lanier (30 Sept. 1882–24 June 1950), aircraft engineer, was born in Lenox, Massachusetts, the son of Francis C. Lawrance and Sarah E. Lanier. He attended Groton School and graduated from Yale University in 1905. In 1910 he married Margaret Dix. They had three children. Lawrance studied architecture for three years at the École des Beaux Arts in Paris, graduating in 1913, before turning to aviation. He designed an experimental aircraft motor and a successful wing section in Paris and worked for several months on a front-wheel drive for an electric automobile in New York City.

During World War I, while doing aeronautical research for the Navy Department, Lawrance began work on a small air-cooled airplane engine in his tiny Manhattan factory, which he had set up as a lab in 1914. Despite the contrary opinion of experts who favored a water-cooled powerplant, Lawrance continued work on his three-cylinder, 60-horsepower engine and developed it into the Whirlwind, which became the Wright Whirlwind in 1923 when Lawrance merged his company, the Lawrance Aero Engine Corporation, with the Wright Aeronautical Corporation of Paterson, New Jersey. Lawrance assumed the presidency of the company in 1925. At 200 horsepower and more, the Whirlwind's first real test came in 1926 with the first flight to the North Pole by *Richard E. Byrd* in a three-engine Fokker.

That feat was overshadowed a year later as the Whirlwind removed for Charles A. Lindbergh (1902–1974) the final obstacle to the first solo transatlantic flight. Several aviators had the courage to set out alone, but until the Whirlwind, a powerplant that could be trusted to go the distance of more than 3,000 miles simply was not available. At a time when engine reliability was by no means a given, the relatively light, powerful, and fuel-efficient Whirlwind "would operate uninterruptedly at peak performance for a period of time measured in days rather than hours" (Morris and Smith, p. 255).

When it arrived for mating with Lindbergh's Ryan monoplane, the young airmail pilot was in awe:

It's like a huge jewel, lying there set in its wrappings. . . . Here is the ultimate in lightness of weight and power— 223 horses compressed into nine delicate, fin-covered cylinders of aluminum and steel. On this intricate perfection, I'm to trust my life across the Atlantic Ocean.

The inner organs of this engine . . . will be turning over many hundred times each minute . . . And I'm demanding that this procedure continue for 40 hours if need be. . . . It seems beyond the ability of any mechanism to withstand such a strain, yet–I force myself back to reality—Whirlwinds are flying on the mail lines for thousands of hours between failures. (Lindbergh, p. 102)

The engine powered many other record-breaking flights, including transoceanic flights by Amelia Earhart and Charles J. Kingsford-Smith. In 1929 three Whirlwinds kept the army's Fokker "Question Mark" aloft for a record 150 hours-plus. Only when a plugged

grease outlet stopped one of the engines did the five-man crew land after forty-three aerial refuelings. The Whirlwind also proved to be popular with the airlines. The 720 of them built in 1928 accounted for more than two-thirds of that year's total engine production in the United States. When the first Douglas DC-3 flew from Chicago to New York in 1936, it was powered by two 900-horsepower Wright Cyclones, derivatives of the Whirlwind. In 1928 President Calvin Coolidge presented Lawrance with the most esteemed aviation award—the Robert S. Collier Trophy of the National Advisory Committee for Aeronautics.

In 1929 Lawrance resigned the presidency of Wright Aeronautical to become vice president in charge of engineering and research for the newly formed Curtiss-Wright Corporation. The next year, he left that firm to organize the Lawrance Engineering and Research Corp. of Linden, New Jersey, remaining president until 1944 and chairman of the board of directors and director of research until he retired in 1946. His research focused on diesel engines for aircraft and marine use. During World War II, the company developed and built thousands of small auxiliary electric generators driven by air-cooled engines for use in large navy and army air force bombers and PT boats.

When Lawrance died in East Islip, New York, it is likely that few remembered his association with an engine that bore the name of aviation's two greatest pioneers, the Wright brothers. Indeed, Lawrance himself was happy to remain the modest engineer. When his associates complained that he had not received due credit, he smiled and asked rhetorically, "Who ever heard the name of Paul Revere's horse?"

• The most detailed account of Lawrance's life and career can be found in *The National Cyclopedia of American Biography*, vol. 38 (1953). Charles A. Lindbergh spells out his admiration for Lawrance's Wright Whirlwind engine in *The Spirit of St. Louis* (1953). Lloyd Morris and Kendall Smith, *Ceiling Unlimited: The Story of American Aviation from Kitty Hawk to Supersonics* (1953), is a valuable source. Also of interest is *The American Heritage History of Flight* (1962). An obituary is in the *New York Times*, 24 June 1950.

DAVID R. GRIFFITHS

LAWRENCE, Abbott (16 Dec. 1792–18 Aug. 1855), manufacturer, philanthropist, and diplomat, was born in Groton, Massachusetts, the son of Samuel Lawrence and Susanna Parker, farmers. Lawrence was educated at the district school and the town academy. In 1808 he went to Boston as an apprentice in the warehouse of his older brother, Amos Lawrence (1786–1852), who was a well-established merchant in the city. In 1814 Abbott was admitted to partnership, and the firm of A. & A. Lawrence was founded, specializing in imports of English goods. Taking advantage of renewed trade following the War of 1812, the firm became one of the wealthiest in Boston. In 1819 Lawrence married Katherine Bigelow, the daughter of

Timothy Bigelow, then Speaker of the Massachusetts House of Representatives. Lawrence and his wife had seven children.

By 1831 Abbott became principal partner, and the firm began to invest its capital directly into the emerging textile industry of New England, having previously sold products from the mills. The Lawrences were part of the interlocking social and economic elite known as the Boston Associates; Abbott emerged as one of the largest textile magnates among this group. He also became a leading proponent of railroad development, arguing that rail transportation was essential for the expanding national economy and for maintaining political unity.

Lawrence's political activities also increased in the 1830s. He served one term on the Boston Common Council in 1831. In both 1834 and 1838 he was elected to the U.S. House of Representatives, where he sat on the Ways and Means Committee. He was an outspoken critic of President Andrew Jackson's veto of the charter for the Bank of the United States. Although as a merchant he had once been a free trader, as a congressman and textile manufacturer he later endorsed higher tariffs to protect American industries. Lawrence opposed the annexation of the Texas republic in 1845 because he feared the extension of slavery, though he was not a supporter of the abolitionist cause. Lawrence thus emerged as a leading figure in the Whig party of New England. He always stood with the more conservative "Cotton" Whigs and the "Lords of the Loom" and argued against antagonizing the South (and its supply of cotton for the textile mills) with threats to the slave system itself.

Lawrence resigned his House seat in 1840 before the conclusion of his second term because of ill health (typhus fever). In 1842, however, he was named by the Massachusetts legislature to serve on a delegation representing the state in complex negotiations over boundary and maritime disputes between the United States and Great Britain. He played a crucial role in drafting the resulting Webster-Ashburton Treaty.

Lawrence expanded his manufacturing holdings, which emerged from the depression of the late 1830s and early 1840s in relatively sound financial shape. In 1845 Lawrence, several of his brothers, and other Boston Associates laid the groundwork for a new industrial city upriver from Lowell, Massachusetts—the new community would bear the name Lawrence and would be a leading textile manufacturing center for decades thereafter. In 1847 Lawrence's growing reputation as a philanthropist was enhanced by his donation of $50,000 to Harvard University to establish a school for what he saw as the practical applications of science in fields such as engineering and chemistry.

Yet Lawrence's interests in politics and the Whig party never abated. In the fall of 1842 he presided over a state convention in Boston, which nominated Henry Clay for president in 1844 and angered Daniel Webster, who thought he should have secured the nomination from his fellow New Englanders. The rift between Lawrence and Webster may well have cost Lawrence the Whig nomination for vice president in 1848, when Webster supporters and young "Conscience" Whigs in the Massachusetts delegation broke rank and denied Lawrence the few votes he needed to secure his place on the ticket. He concealed whatever disappointment he may have felt and campaigned for the election of Zachary Taylor. When Taylor formed his cabinet, he offered Lawrence the secretaryships of the navy and the interior, but Lawrence declined both. When Taylor proffered the premier diplomatic post to the Court of St. James in London, Lawrence finally accepted the position and embarked for England in the fall of 1849.

Lawrence's familiarity with Great Britain—having been there previously as both a merchant and a tourist—combined with his personal wealth—which allowed him to entertain on a grander scale than that permitted by the U.S. government's modest support of the embassy—made him a diplomat of some stature and influence in London. He tackled many delicate and important questions of maritime and fishing rights between two of the world's leading naval powers. He also continued his predecessor George Bancroft's negotiations regarding the possibility of constructing a canal across Nicaragua. Lawrence uncovered, and subsequently published, colonial documents that invalidated Britain's claims on the Central American isthmus. He believed that he could press his case even further in London and was disappointed when the diplomatic talks about the canal were shifted to Washington, D.C.

In October 1852 Lawrence returned to his business interests in Boston. Two years later he contracted a serious liver disease, which doctors thought was related to his previous bout with typhus. He died in Boston, leaving behind a large estate, which included an additional $50,000 bequest to the Lawrence Scientific School at Harvard and $50,000 to build model lodging houses for the poor.

Thus, in death as in life, Lawrence strove to exert his influence in the interrelated spheres of industry, politics, education, and philanthropy. He clung to an ideal of noblesse oblige in a world of rapid economic change. He considered public service and charity not only a moral duty of the rich but essential for preserving his vision of political and social order. Lawrence made his wealth by investing in industrial change; he then used that wealth attempting to control the very changes he had helped to unleash.

• Lawrence's papers from his tenure as ambassador in London are in the Houghton Library at Harvard University. There are letters from Lawrence and his wife in the Nathan Appleton Papers and the John Prescott Bigelow Papers, both of which are also at Houghton. Further correspondence with Appleton is in the Appleton Family Papers at the Massachusetts Historical Society. Several speeches Lawrence gave as a congressman and several of his diplomatic reports as an ambassador were published, including *Letter of the Honorable Abbott Lawrence, to a Committee of the Citizens of Boston, on the Subject of the Currency* (1837) and *Letter from Mr. Lawrence to Mr. Clayton . . . in Relation to Central America*, 32d. Cong., 2d sess., 1853, S. Ex. Doc. 27. The principal biography is Hamilton Andrews Hill, *Memoir of Abbott Lawrence* (1883). Other brief accounts are W. H. Prescott, *Memoirs of the Hon. Abbott Lawrence* (1856); Nathan Appleton's memorial in the Massachusetts Historical Society *Collections*, vol. 4, ser. 4 (1858), pp. 495–507; and F. W. Ballard, *The Stewardship of Wealth as Illustrated in the Lives of Amos and Abbott Lawrence* (1865). See also Frederic Cople Jaher, *The Urban Establishment: Upper Strata in Boston, New York, Charleston, Chicago, and Los Angeles* (1982), on Lawrence and his family; and Robert F. Dalzell, Jr., *Enterprising Elite: The Boston Associates and the World They Made* (1987), on Lawrence as textile magnate and philanthropist.

DAVID A. ZONDERMAN

LAWRENCE, David (25 Dec. 1888–11 Feb. 1973), journalist, was born in Philadelphia, Pennsylvania, the son of Harris Lawrence, a tailor, and Dora Cohen. Both of his parents were recent immigrants from England. The family moved to Buffalo, New York, soon after his birth. While a student at Princeton University, Lawrence worked as an Associated Press campus correspondent. His work earned him a summer job in the AP's Philadelphia bureau in 1908 and 1909 and, after receiving his degree from Princeton, a full-time job there in 1910.

In October 1910 Lawrence was transferred to the AP bureau in Washington, D.C. Among the capital press corps, he quickly earned a reputation for his skill at getting exclusive stories and for his clear and detached writing. Arthur Krock of the *New York Times* recalled that Lawrence "combined the reportorial qualities of a ferret and a beaver. His hazel eyes seemed to reflect at once deep contemplation and a searching eagerness" (Krock, p. 76). Starting in 1911 Lawrence also made several trips to Mexico to cover diplomatic and military developments related to the Mexican Revolution and disputes between Mexico and the United States. He received a gold watch from the AP in 1911 for exceptional service in covering a three-day battle between government forces and rebels.

In 1912 the AP assigned Lawrence to cover Woodrow Wilson's presidential campaign, and in 1913 he was assigned to cover the Wilson White House. He was a charter member and first vice chairman of the White House Correspondents Association, formed in 1914 to accredit White House correspondents. Lawrence also served as an unofficial adviser on Mexican affairs to the Wilson administration. Although many observers saw him as a Wilson confidant, Lawrence insisted he received no favored treatment and gave none. On several occasions, his stories troubled Wilson. One of Lawrence's major exclusive stories came in June 1915, when Secretary of State William Jennings Bryan resigned.

Lawrence took a new job in December 1915 as Washington correspondent for the *New York Evening Post*, where he developed a style of interpretive reporting that was considered an innovation at the time. To his dispatches he added "a shirttail of succinct interpretation," which "set the current happening in the larger canvas of what had gone before and what might reasonably be anticipated in the future" (Phillips, pp. 175–76). In 1916 he traveled to Mexico for the *Post*, which published his articles in a book titled *The Truth About Mexico* (1917). The *Post* also syndicated his Washington dispatches, which dealt with major developments relating to preparedness, diplomacy, the war, and the postwar peace settlement. Lawrence married Ellanor Campbell Hayes in 1918. They had four children.

In 1919 Lawrence left the *Post* after covering the Versailles Peace Conference, Wilson's tour of European capitals, and his cross-country effort to promote support for the Versailles Treaty, which ended with the president's collapse. He then started the Consolidated Press Association in order to sell a Washington column of interpretation and analysis. His column, which by the time of his death appeared in 300 daily newspapers, was among the first modern political columns. His press service also supplied general news and features, financial news, and market quotations, serving about 100 newspapers by late 1920. Lawrence also was a regular contributor to several magazines and became a regular radio commentator in the late 1920s.

By 1926 Lawrence had laid the foundation for his most successful enterprise, his weekly newsmagazine *U.S. News & World Report*. The first step was creation of the *United States Daily*, a newspaper carrying reports of daily activities of all branches of the U.S. government. The motto of the newspaper, which first appeared 4 March 1926, was "All the Facts—No Opinion." It had no editorial page. Lawrence added news about state governments three years later. In 1930 the daily reached its circulation peak of 41,000. Lawrence also made an unsuccessful attempt in 1931 to buy the *Washington Post*.

Lawrence reorganized his enterprises and transformed his daily in 1933. He dissolved the Consolidated Press Association, selling parts of it to the AP and other parts to the North American Newspaper Alliance. He also created the Bureau of National Affairs to provide daily and weekly information services to clients in business and the professions. The daily became a weekly, *The United States News*, beginning on 17 May 1933. It carried a broadened mix of content, including an editorial page, and referred to itself as "America's National Newspaper." Circulation reached nearly 30,000 at the end of 1933 and 85,000 in January 1940, when Lawrence once again transformed his publication, this time into a magazine with expanded coverage of national news. Its circulation passed 300,000 in November 1947. Meanwhile, Lawrence started *The World Report*, "the Weekly Newsmagazine of World Affairs," which first appeared 23 May 1946. In eighteen months its circulation reached 125,000. In January 1948 Lawrence merged his two magazines to create *U.S. News & World Report*. Its first-year circulation was 379,000, and when Lawrence died in 1973, it was nearly two million. In June 1962 Lawrence turned over ownership of the magazine to his employees, staying on as chairman of the board and editor.

Earlier, he had transferred ownership of his other enterprises to employees.

In 1968, marking its thirty-fifth anniversary, the weekly reaffirmed Lawrence's dedication to giving "the information that intelligent people need and want in order that they may make up their own minds and exercise in their own way a proper influence upon national and international policy" (*35 Years of Public Service*, p. 20). Lawrence's editorials at the back of each issue were headed: "This page presents the opinion of the Editor. The news pages are written by other staff members independently of these editorial views." The views Lawrence expressed in his columns and editorials from the 1930s on were consistently conservative. A persistent critic of the New Deal and of subsequent policies and actions, including Supreme Court decisions, that he saw as strengthening centralized government, Lawrence also was a vocal anticommunist and supported U.S. policy in Vietnam.

Lawrence died at his winter home in Sarasota, Florida, a few hours after writing his last column. He maintained an intense lifelong interest in public affairs and tirelessly dedicated himself to the task he saw as being fundamental to the work of journalism—the persistent enlightenment of public opinion about public affairs. The manner in which he performed that task earned him the high regard and respect of colleagues and readers.

• Lawrence's papers are at the Seeley G. Mudd Manuscript Library at Princeton University. His books include *The True Story of Woodrow Wilson* (1924), *Stumbling into Socialism and the Future of Our Political Parties* (1935), *Supreme Court or Political Puppets?* (1937), and *Diary of a Washington Correspondent* (1942). His editorials are collected in *The Editorials of David Lawrence* (6 vols., 1970). In-house histories of Lawrence and his magazine are in "Our 30th Anniversary," *U.S. News & World Report*, 27 May 1963, p. 108, and *35 Years of Public Service* (1968). See also, "'Won Respect of Millions': Life Story of David Lawrence," *U.S. News & World Report*, 26 Feb. 1973, pp. 93–96; "The Lawrence Memorial Service," *U.S. News & World Report*, 26 Feb. 1973, p. 98+; and "Tributes to 'A Giant of Journalism,'" *U.S. News & World Report*, 5 Mar. 1973, p. 84+. For other assessments, see John C. O'Brien, "Custodian of the New Freedom," in *Molders of Opinion*, ed. David Bulman (1945); Cabell Phillips et al., eds., *Dateline: Washington* (1949); F. B. Marbut, *News from the Capital* (1971); "The Durable Wilsonian," *Time*, 26 Feb. 1973, p. 46; and Arthur Krock, "Unforgettable David Lawrence," *Reader's Digest*, Jan. 1974, pp. 75–79. Obituaries are in the *New York Times* and the *Washington Post*, both 12 Feb. 1973.

RONALD S. MARMARELLI

LAWRENCE, David Leo (18 June 1889–21 Nov. 1966), political boss and government official, was born in Pittsburgh, Pennsylvania, the son of Charles B. Lawrence, an unskilled laborer, and Catherine Conwell. Lawrence's early political universe was confined to the Gaelic Irish community located at the juncture of Pittsburgh's three rivers. His maternal grandfather and his father were both involved in ward-level politics and young David's first job at age nine was to run errands for First Ward alderman Steve Toole. Young Lawrence's association with these three men introduced him to Democratic pro-labor politics in a town dominated by Republican manufacturing interests. Political survival for Democrats in Pittsburgh required cooperation, if not collaboration, with the Republican interests.

Lawrence completed a two-year commercial course at St. Mary's High School, and his first full-time job, at age fourteen, as clerk-stenographer to attorney William Brennan added to his political education. Brennan, who had defended the workers' interests at the trials that followed the infamous Homestead Steel Strike, also served as chairman of the Allegheny County Democratic party from 1901 through 1919. Brennan loved to discuss social issues with Democrats and Republicans alike, often into the early hours of the morning, and eventually included Lawrence in these sessions. Brennan took Lawrence to his first Democratic National Convention in 1912. Although Lawrence's favorite, Champ Clark, lost the nomination to Woodrow Wilson, it was here that Lawrence, in his own words, "became devoted to politics." It was in Brennan's law office, however, that Lawrence developed his liberalism regarding social problems such as workmen's compensation, child labor, health care, and education reform, his pragmatic fiscal approach, which demanded that legislation must be accompanied by plans to raise the needed funds, and his ability and willingness to work with members of the opposition party if such cooperation would lead to the desired outcome.

In 1920 Lawrence succeeded Brennan as chairman of the Allegheny County Democratic party. The transition went largely unnoticed throughout western Pennsylvania as the Democratic party had neither numerical nor governmental significance. It had not elected a candidate to a major office for more than four decades, and Democrats were outnumbered by Republicans nearly eight to one. Lawrence's first decade as chairman produced more of the same. In spite of considerable effort to recruit new members and to develop an organizational structure within each precinct of the city and county, the party lost elections at both levels by landslide proportions. The party had difficulty recruiting both candidates and poll watchers. A number of the few remaining Democrats began calling for Lawrence's resignation. The absence of a willing successor, however, spared him. In 1921 he married Alyce Golden; they had seven children, two of whom died at birth.

Lawrence's initial success as a behind-the-scenes political boss occurred during the presidential election of 1932. Stung by his early defeats and the opposition from within his own party, Lawrence reorganized the party, purging a number of ineffective or opposition ward chairmen. He streamlined the executive committee, cutting it in size and establishing new lines of command to the ward level. The possibility of government-sponsored jobs for the ward chairmen and their workers, should Franklin D. Roosevelt win, was held out as the motivational carrot. Republican party squabbling, the depression, which had raised unemployment levels in Pittsburgh to above 25 percent, and the Roosevelt charisma were all factors that produced the century's first Democratic victory in Pittsburgh. Lawrence's leadership guaranteed that the party would not return to its previous ineptness.

Using all the customary tools of the late nineteenth-century political bosses, Lawrence set about consolidating power to guarantee victory at subsequent local elections. Federal patronage was used to provide jobs to party workers and loyal voters. Recalcitrant Democrats were purged from the party. Food and clothing distribution centers were set up in areas where unemployment had hit the hardest. Ethnic leaders were sought or developed to appeal to voters within the cities' various immigrant neighborhoods. In the meantime, the local Republican party disintegrated amidst factional warfare and the conviction of Mayor Charles Klein on numerous charges of malfeasance.

Lawrence personally selected Democratic mayoralty candidate William McNair, educated him on the issues, convinced him to drop his advocacy of Henry George's single-tax ideology, and conducted every facet of his campaign. He was particularly effective in tying the McNair candidacy to the programs of the Roosevelt administration. The *New York Times* observed that "one might think that is Mr. Roosevelt who is running for mayor of Pittsburgh." McNair and all five Democratic candidates for city council won easily. It was a defeat from which the Republicans had not recovered as of the end of the century.

Lawrence spent the remainder of the decade building the party throughout the state and managing Democratic candidates to victory. In 1934, from his new post as state Democratic chairman, Lawrence managed the campaigns of Joseph Guffy and George Earle, the first Democratic candidates elected U.S. senator and governor in Pennsylvania in more than forty years. He also managed the implementation of Earle's "Little New Deal" in Pennsylvania from his appointed post as secretary of the commonwealth from 1935 to 1938. Statewide intraparty battles and two failed indictments for conspiracy to extort campaign contributions failed to dampen his enthusiasm for party politics. Successive Lawrence-managed victories in Pittsburgh and Allegheny County ushered in one of modern America's most durable and efficient urban political machines. David Lawrence, as its head, remained in power until his death, and remnants of his machine continued to dominate political life in the City of Steel many years later.

In 1945 Lawrence abandoned his behind-the-scenes role when he ran for mayor of the city of Pittsburgh and won. He would hold elective office for almost all of the next two decades. Lawrence's term as mayor was characterized by the remarkable redevelopment of one of America's most blighted cities. Working closely with Richard King Mellon and other prominent Pittsburgh industrialists, Lawrence and several Democratic allies cleansed the environment through smoke and flood controls, stimulated new industrial development, and rebuilt the center of the city. Pittsburgh's renaissance and its public-private partnership remained for decades among the nation's most emulated models of urban renewal. In 1958, when Lawrence won election as governor of the commonwealth, he continued to preside over the rebuilding of his beloved Pittsburgh through his influence as head of his party in western Pennsylvania.

Lawrence's single term as governor of Pennsylvania, 1959–1962 (state constitutional law prohibited re-election), was characterized by a four-year effort to produce a balanced budget, a massive highway construction program, and a strict highway safety campaign. The Lawrence administration also launched a comprehensive program of social reform (including fair-housing legislation), education reform (including increasing teachers' salaries, establishing community colleges, and creating scholarships, loan funds, and increased subsidies to school systems), creation of a statewide human relations commission, expansion of minimum wage and workers' compensation laws, and new child labor laws (including protection for children of migratory workers).

When Lawrence left the state office in 1962, he was named the nation's first and only chairman of the President's Council on Equal Opportunity in Housing. He served in this position under Presidents John F. Kennedy and Lyndon B. Johnson until his death. The work of the council was later incorporated in the Civil Rights Act of 1968. Lawrence was stricken with a heart attack in the midst of a campaign speech for Pennsylvania Democratic gubernatorial candidate Milton Shapp on 4 November 1966. He never regained consciousness and died in Pittsburgh seventeen days later.

• Some of Lawrence's papers are available at the Pennsylvania State Archives, Harrisburg, and the Lyndon B. Johnson Library, Austin, Tex. For additional information on Lawrence, see Michael P. Weber, *Don't Call Me Boss: David L. Lawrence, Pittsburgh's Renaissance Mayor* (1988); Sarah Shames, "David L. Lawrence, Mayor of Pittsburgh: Development of a Political Leader" (Ph.D. diss., Univ. of Pittsburgh, 1958); Jon Teaford, *The Rough Road to Renaissance* (1990); Bruce Stave, *The New Deal and the Last Hurrah* (1970); and Andrew Buni, *Robert L. Vann of the Pittsburgh Courier: Politics and Black Journalism* (1974). An obituary is in the *New York Times*, 22 Nov. 1966.

MICHAEL P. WEBER

LAWRENCE, Ernest Orlando (8 Aug. 1901–27 Aug. 1958), physicist, was born in Canton, South Dakota, the son of Carl Gustav Lawrence and Gunda Jacobson, schoolteachers. Both parents were Lutherans of Norwegian ancestry. Lawrence's constant childhood companion, who lived across the street, was Merle A. Tuve, also a teacher's son, who later became a research physicist and geophysicist. The two built and flew gliders and constructed a very early short-wave radio transmitting station, interests reflected in their later work.

Lawrence received his primary and secondary education in the public schools of Canton and Pierre, the state capital. In 1918 he enrolled in St. Olaf College in Northfield, Minnesota, on a one-year scholarship. In 1919 he transferred to the University of South Dakota at Vermillion as a premedical student. He supported himself by selling kitchenware to farmers' wives; in later years he would use this skill and his infectious enthusiasm and belief in his ideas in selling new scientific projects to foundations and government agencies. His unusual aptitude for science was recognized by the university's dean of electrical engineering, Lewis E. Akeley, who tutored him privately and persuaded him to major in physics. Later, in Lawrence's office, Akeley's portrait hung along with those of his other scientific heroes, Arthur H. Compton, Ernest Rutherford, and Niels Bohr. In 1923 Lawrence received his A.M. under W. F. G. Swann's supervision at the University of Minnesota.

In 1924 Lawrence followed Swann to Yale University, where Lawrence completed his research on the photoelectric effect in potassium vapor as a function of the frequency of light (*Philosophical Magazine* 50 (1925): 545–59), which earned him his Ph.D. in 1925. Remaining at Yale as a National Research Council fellow (1925–1927) and then as assistant professor (1927–1928), he gained a reputation as a brilliant experimentalist, especially in photoelectricity. Here he made the most precise determination of the ionization potential of mercury to date (*Journal of the Franklin Institute* 204 [1927]: 91–94) and of the upper limit on the time lag involved in the emission of photoelectrons (with Jesse W. Beams, *Physical Review* 32 (1928): 478–85). Not until decades later would the measurement of such short time intervals become routine, largely because of the use of photomultiplier tubes, wide-band amplifiers, and high-speed oscilloscopes, none of which were available to Lawrence. Lawrence also played an important role in the evolution of the high-speed rotating top that Beams later developed. Except for the mathematics of classical electricity and magnetism, Lawrence made little future use of the skills that he acquired during these days. His approach was intuitive, and he did not like to be bothered with mathematical details.

At that time television was considered to be an impractical dream because its basic element, the rotating scanning wheel, limited the picture quality by restricting the number of "picture lines" to fewer than 100. While still at Yale, Lawrence, using his experience with photoelectricity and the newly developing cathode ray tube, invented a rudimentary all-electronic television system without rotating wheels. After seeing the extensive electronic television equipment at the Bell Telephone Laboratories, he resolved to concentrate on things that he knew the most about rather than dilute his research efforts by competing in the commercial area. He adhered to this resolution until the last decade of his life, when he became fascinated with the technical problems of the field and developed the "Lawrence tube," or "Chromatron," with the support of Paramount Pictures. During his last few years he was issued dozens of patents in the field of color television, but apparently they were never used commercially.

In 1928, despite the misgivings of his friends, Lawrence left Yale for an associate professorship at the University of California, Berkeley, a then little-known state university with a growing reputation in chemistry. Berkeley's subsequent world renown in research was due largely to its physics faculty, which, because of the presence of Lawrence and his contemporaries, including Samuel Allison, Robert B. Brode, and J. Robert Oppenheimer, came to rank with that of Cambridge University. In 1930, largely on the recommendation of Gilbert Newton Lewis, dean and chairman of the chemistry department, Lawrence, at the age of twenty-nine, became the youngest full professor on the Berkeley faculty. In 1936 he was also appointed director of the university's Radiation Laboratory. He held these two positions until his death.

In 1919 physicist Ernest Rutherford at Cambridge University bombarded nitrogen with α-particles (positively charged helium ions) from a natural source and obtained an isotope of oxygen (^{18}O) and protons (hydrogen nuclei). This transmutation of one element into another, the long-sought goal of the ancient alchemists, initiated a new era in the natural sciences. However, as long as such nuclear reactions had to be carried on using α-particles obtained from naturally occurring radioactive substances, strict limits were set to further development with regard to the substances that could be used at the target elements as well as to the quantitative yield of these reactions. The problem was to find some method, other than the use of natural radioactive substances, to produce projectile particles with energies high enough artificially to initiate produced nuclear reactions.

During his early bachelor days at Berkeley, Lawrence spent many evenings in the library. While browsing through scientific journals in 1929, he encountered an article in the German *Archiv für Elektrotechnik* by Norwegian engineer Rolf Wideröe, based on an earlier proposal by the Swedish physicist Gustaf A. Ising, which described the acceleration of potassium ions to 50,000 electron volts (ev) in a linear accelerator. Realizing that in order to produce particle energies of the magnitude of several million electron volts required to initiate nuclear reactions, a linear accelerator would need to be too long to be practical, Lawrence conceived the idea of a circular accelerator, later called the cyclotron, cut in two along a diameter and placed in a vacuum chamber. The cyclotron and other inventions discovered by Lawrence during the 1930s were patented in Lawrence's name, but he assigned them to the Research Corporation, which financially supported his early work. In 1937 he received the Research Corporation Prize and Plaque.

In his cyclotron Lawrence connected a high-frequency oscillator to the two D-shaped halves (called "dees"). He introduced near the center the charged particles, which are forced to travel in a circular path by a magnetic field along the axis of the can. He synchronized the oscillating field so that it imparted successive accelerations to each particle as it repeatedly crosses the gap between the two dees, pushing it outward in an ever-widening spiral path with increasing velocity. As the particle approaches the perimeter, it is deflected at high speed through an opening toward a target, producing a nuclear reaction. Lawrence and co-workers M. Stanley Livingston and David H. Sloan had to develop and build the required vacuum pumps and high-power oscillator tubes because none with the required capacity were then available at reasonable prices. Soon they were using the world's largest high-vacuum pumps, highest-power radio oscillators, and largest magnet.

Lawrence and his doctoral student Niels F. Edlefson first demonstrated the cyclotron magnetic resonance acceleration principle at the fall 1930 meeting of the National Academy of Sciences at Berkeley. Their original apparatus is on permanent display at the Lawrence Berkeley Laboratory, along with the brass vacuum chamber of Lawrence and Livingstone's first four-inch-diameter cyclotron (1931), which accelerated protons to 80,000 ev. In 1931 Lawrence and Livingston built an eleven-inch cyclotron, yielding several hundred thousand ev, which they hoped would be the first accelerator to yield "artificial disintegration" of light nuclei. In 1932 Lawrence, with Livingston and M. G. White, repeated John Cockcroft and E. T. S. Walton's famous disintegration of lithium by protons earlier that year. This was the first of several important discoveries in nuclear physics that could have just as well been made in Lawrence's laboratory. These "missed" discoveries could be attributed to the fact that most of the time Lawrence and his co-workers concentrated on developing the cyclotron, which had been ridiculed as impractical by some physicists, into an efficient tool that was subsequently used in many research areas. This development required the evolution of technologies not then known and was a difficult technological task that only a person of Lawrence's daring and persistence would have undertaken. From his earliest days Lawrence formed the habit of critically examining any scientific results, regardless of their origin, and he applied the same rigid critical standards to his own work, to that of his co-workers, and to reports from other laboratories. During the early 1930s, as leaders of teams of nuclear physicists, Lawrence, with his cyclotron, and Tuve, with his electrostatic accelerator, continued their friendly boyhood rivalry.

This cyclotron was the first in an entire family of circular particle accelerators that made high acceleration energies available with relatively small instruments. Once its principle was proved, progress was rapid. Lawrence's modern group approach inaugurated the advent of "big science" (well-funded projects carried out by large-scale research teams) in the United States, and the old wooden "Rad Lab" (for "Radiation Laboratory"), which was finally torn down in 1959, was the first of the modern nuclear physics laboratories, in which experimentalists collaborated on joint projects or worked on their own projects. Lawrence's enthusiasm for physics permeated the laboratory, which operated around the clock seven days a week except for two hours every Monday night, the time of Lawrence's "Journal Club," a forum in which the rapidly growing staff discussed their own discoveries in radioactivity and related fields.

Lawrence persuaded the Federal Telegraph Company to donate an eighty-ton iron-core magnet that he then used to produce proton energies of 8 million electron volts (mev) with his 27.5-inch cyclotron (later converted to a 37-inch cyclotron). This instrument ushered in the era of high-energy physics and made possible the disintegration of atomic nuclei, artificial isotopes, and the discovery of new elements. Because isotopes are chemically the same elements and undergo the same reactions, artificially radioactive isotopes have been used extensively as "tracer elements" in studying the mechanism of chemical reactions, such as radiophosphorus in biological metabolism and radiocarbon (carbon-14, discovered by Martin D. Kamen and Samuel Ruben in Lawrence's laboratory in 1940), in photosynthesis of plants. Radioisotopes have also been widely used in cancer therapy.

By 1939 Lawrence was operating a sixty-inch cyclotron, and in 1940 the Rockefeller Foundation provided $1.25 million to build a 184-inch cyclotron, which was not completed until after World War II. Although Lawrence is best known for his application of the cyclotron equation to nuclear physics, with his student Frank G. Dunnington he also used it to devise the most precise and accurate method of measuring one of the most important fundamental constants, the specific charge (e/m) of the electron.

From 1931 to 1950 Lawrence's cyclotrons possessed the world's highest energy beams of particles. Radiation intensities corresponding to the α-radiation of 3 kilograms of radium were attained at a time when the entire world stock of radium was about 1 kilogram. Using deuterium (heavy hydrogen) in his cyclotron, by 1939 Lawrence was able to produce daily amounts of radioactive sodium, which, with respect to γ-radiation, were equivalent to 200 milligrams of radium, and by 1939 he was able to produce ten times this amount. One of his concerns with high intensity was his interest in the medical and biological applications of the radiations from the cyclotron and from the radioisotopes that it produced. In medicine, if the radiation levels are too low, the body uses its healing mechanisms to minimize its effects on tumors. In 1938 and 1939 all physics experiments at the 37-inch cyclotron were suspended for a full day each week so that terminal cancer patients could be treated. Lawrence's switch from medical to defense research resulted in increased support for high energy physics. Lawrence was awarded the 1939 Nobel Prize in physics "for the invention and development of the cyclotron and for results obtained with it, especially with regard to artificial radioactive elements." Because of wartime conditions, the prize was presented on 29 February 1940 at Berkeley rather than in Stockholm.

Lawrence was one of the American physicists who in 1940 helped establish another so-called "Radiation Laboratory," at the Massachusetts Institute of Technology, whose actual function was to develop radar. During World War II, he also played a major role in the Manhattan Project. His work on high-beam intensity contributed to the two methods used to produce fissionable material for the nuclear bombs that the United States dropped on Japan. Lawrence spent several of the war years perfecting the Calutron, or mass-spectrometer method of separating the fissionable U-235 isotope (used in the Hiroshima bomb), from ordinary uranium. Glenn T. Seaborg, Edwin M. McMillan, Joseph W. Kennedy, and Arthur C. Wahl used Lawrence's sixty-inch cyclotron to discover and produce the fissionable plutonium isotope Pu-239, used in the Nagasaki bomb, from ordinary uranium. He felt that his arguments to the decision makers in Washington helped convince them to authorize all three approaches simultaneously. From 1941 to 1945 Lawrence and his co-workers worked twelve hours a day, seven days a week. After the war the 184-inch cyclotron (actually a super cyclotron or synchrocyclotron, based on the principle of "phase stability" formulated by McMillan) was completed.

To supplement the Los Alamos, New Mexico, laboratory, where the first nuclear bombs had been assembled and where weapons research continued, Lawrence offered the Rad Lab's Livermore, California, site as a second weapons laboratory, under his and Edward Teller's sponsorship. Both were advocates of the thermonuclear (hydrogen) bomb, which led to the breakup of Lawrence's friendship with J. Robert Oppenheimer, wartime leader of the Los Alamos laboratory. Larger, more powerful, and more efficient accelerators were constructed, such as the "bevatron," which could accelerate particles to billions of electron volts (bev).

Lawrence remained personally involved in these and other postwar developments, but increasing demands on him as a government and industrial consultant frequently took him away from Berkeley. Leaders in government and industry, while respecting his distaste for the limelight, sought his counsel. At President Dwight D. Eisenhower's request, Lawrence was one of a three-member committee to represent the United States at the Conference of Experts to Study the Possibility of Detecting Violations of a Possible Agreement on Suspension of Nuclear Tests at Geneva, Switzerland, in July 1958. Here the ulcerative colitis that had recurrently plagued him for years and the exhaustion caused by the pressures under which he had worked for so long forced him to return home, where major surgery proved unsuccessful. He died in a Palo Alto, California, hospital.

Lawrence had married Mary ("Molly") Kimberly Blumer in 1932; the couple had two sons and four daughters. Their home was famous throughout the physics world for its hospitality and warmth. In 1941 Molly's sister Elsie married Berkeley physicist Edwin M. McMillan, the future (1951) Nobel chemistry laureate, who succeeded Lawrence as director of the "Rad Lab."

An honorary member or fellow of numerous domestic or foreign societies and academics, Lawrence was elected to the National Academy of Sciences in 1934 at the early age of thirty-three. His twenty major awards and medals included the Franklin Institute's Elliot Cresson Medal (1937), the National Academy of Science's Comstock Prize (1937), the Royal Society's Hughes Medal (1937), the Medal of Merit (1946), France's Officier de la Légion d'Honneur (1948), the Institute of Electrical Engineers of London's Faraday Medal (1952), and the Atomic Energy Commission's Enrico Fermi Award (1957). His name is commemorated in the two California "Rad Lab" sites—the Lawrence Radiation Laboratory (later renamed the Lawrence Berkeley Laboratory because of the negative connotations of the word "radiation") and the Lawrence Livermore Laboratory; the Lawrence Hall of Science, a Berkeley museum and research center for science education; the Atomic Energy Commission's annual Lawrence Awards for young scientists; and Lawrencium, the transuranium element 103. Lawrence is remembered not only as the inventor of the cyclotron but also as a pioneer of "big science" and in promoting the uses of radioisotopes throughout the chemical and biological fields, both as tracers and as sources of radiation. Before him, "little science" was carried out largely by lone individuals working with modest means on a small scale. After him, massive industrial, and especially governmental, expenditures of manpower and monetary funding made "big science," carried out by large-scale research teams, a major segment of the national economy.

• Lawrence's scientific and personal papers are preserved in the Bancroft Library at the University of California, Berkeley. The principal biographical source is Herbert Childs, *An American Genius: The Life of Ernest Orlando Lawrence* (1968). Biographical accounts, not uniformly flattering to Lawrence, include Robert Jungk, *Heller als tausend Sonne* (1956), translated by James Cleugh as *Brighter than a Thousand Suns: The Moral and Political History of the Atomic Scientists* (1960); Nuel Pharr Davis, *Lawrence and Oppenheimer* (1968); and Luis W. Alvarez, "Ernest Orlando Lawrence," National Academy of Sciences, *Biographical Memoirs* 41(1970): 251–94, which includes an autographed portrait and a list of honors, distinctions, and publications. The development of the cyclotron is given in Lawrence, "The Evolution of the Cyclotron," in *Nobel Lectures, Including Presentation Speeches and Laureates' Biographies: Physics 1922–1941* (1965), pp. 430–43 (with numerous illustrations); M. Stanley Livingston, "History of the Cyclotron (Part I)," *Physics Today* 12 (Oct. 1959): 18–23; Edwin M. McMillan, "History of the Cyclotron (Part II)," *Physics Today* 12 (Oct. 1959): 24–34; Edwin M. McMillan, "Particle Accelerators," in *Experimental Nuclear Physics*, vol. 3, part 12, ed. Emilio Segrè (1959); M. Stanley Livingstone, *The Development of High-Energy Accelerators* (1966); John L. Heilbron and Robert W. Seidel, *Lawrence and His Laboratory: A History of the Lawrence Berkeley Laboratory* (1989); Glenn T. Seaborg, *Journal of Glenn T. Seaborg, 1942–1958* (1992–); and Emilio Segrè, *A Mind Always in Motion: The Autobiography of Emilio Segrè* (1993). Lawrence's role in the beginnings of the nuclear age is described in Richard G.

Hewlett and Oscar E. Anderson, Jr., *The New World, 1939–1946* (1962). An obituary is in the *New York Times*, 28 Aug. 1958.

GEORGE B. KAUFFMAN

LAWRENCE, Florence (2 Jan. 1886–27 Dec. 1938), motion picture actress, was born Florence Bridgewood in Hamilton, Ontario, Canada, the daughter of George Bridgewood, an actor, and Charlotte Dunn, an actress under the stage name Lotta Lawrence. Her mother led a "tent show" troupe of actors who traveled around small towns performing a repertoire of plays under canvas. "Baby Florence" was a performer in the shows from the age of three. She attended school in Buffalo, New York, living with relatives when her mother was touring. Though small and delicate, she was physically active and learned to ride horseback there. After graduation from high school in Buffalo, she returned to performing with her mother's company and took her mother's stage name of Lawrence.

A series of mishaps caused the tent show to disband in 1906, and mother and daughter looked unsuccessfully for stage work in New York City. Lawrence turned to the fledgling motion picture studios there. On the basis of her ability to ride, she was hired by the Edison company to play in a one-reel film, *Daniel Boone; or, Pioneer Days in America* (1907), and also appeared in a short western for the Vitagraph company, *The Dispatch Bearer* (1907). A chance came for both mother and daughter to tour in a stage drama, *The Seminary Girls*, but after its run Lawrence—desiring a home rather than a traveling actor's hotel room—determined to seek only movie work.

In 1908 Lawrence found steady employment at the Vitagraph studio, where she not only acted in nine one-reel films but sewed costumes. There she met another actor, Harry Solter (sometimes spelled Salter). Through Solter's friendship with director D. W. Griffith, dating from the days both had been struggling stage actors, she was hired to act in Griffith's films at the Biograph movie studio. Her ladylike blond good looks, plus her acting experience and athletic skills, soon led her to leading roles in Griffith's one-reelers. She also played Mrs. Jones in a popular comedy series about a husband and wife. In all, she appeared in thirty-five films at Biograph in 1908. She married Solter at the end of the year.

Griffith's wife, actress Linda Arvidson, later recalled Lawrence's enthusiasm for the medium she had entered: "The movies were the breath of life to her. When she wasn't working in a picture, she was in some movie theater seeing a picture" (Griffith, p. 59). Lawrence rose steadily in public esteem, and since movie companies at that time did not reveal their performers' names, she became a favorite referred to simply as the Biograph Girl. She made thirty-three more one-reel films at Biograph in 1909.

At that point Lawrence and her husband, whose ambition was to become a director, wrote a letter to the Essanay film company proposing that they move, under favorable financial terms, to that studio as an actress/director team. Essanay was one of the members of the Motion Picture Patents Companies, a movie "trust," all of whom were fearful of rising demands from film people as their personal popularity rose. Essanay turned the letter over to Biograph, which fired Lawrence and blacklisted her with all the Patents companies.

Lawrence and Solter went to Carl Laemmle, head of the Independent Motion Picture company (known by its initials as "Imp"), not a member of the movie trust. He hired them both. To make the national public aware that the Biograph Girl was now the Imp Girl, Laemmle staged a major publicity stunt. A story appeared in the press, supposedly issued by Biograph but more likely by Laemmle, that the Biograph Girl had been killed in a streetcar accident. Laemmle immediately took out ads decrying this false information and promising to present the actress alive and well. Before a crowd of avid fans and newspaper reporters, Lawrence made a two-day personal appearance in St. Louis in March 1910. The story, with interviews revealing her true name and details of her personal life, was carried nationwide.

Thus Lawrence was launched as the first star of the movies, someone fans knew by name and felt they knew personally. Her name on a movie sold tickets galore, and other actors were soon starred by name. In about twelve months she made forty-two films for Laemmle's company. The grueling schedule took its toll physically, and at the end of 1910 Lawrence needed three months of rest.

In 1911 Lawrence and Solter went over to the Sigmund Lubin film company, where Lawrence appeared in nearly fifty productions before vacationing in Europe. In 1912 the couple went back to Laemmle, whose company was now known as Universal. They were heads of their own production unit, the Victor Motion Picture Company, at large salaries. A lure for Lawrence was that the studio was located in Fort Lee, New Jersey, and she was able to establish a real home, a fifty-acre estate in nearby Westwood, New Jersey. After marital difficulties in 1912, she announced her retirement early in 1913 and spent some months doing the gardening she loved. Then she was induced to return to moviemaking in longer films of two or three reels directed by Solter.

Early in 1914 Lawrence was working on a film titled *Pawns of Destiny*. A perilous stunt in one scene called for her to carry her leading man, Matt Moore, who weighed 178 pounds, out of a burning building. The fire went out of control, and in leaping to safety with Moore on her back Lawrence suffered burns that left facial scars and serious back injury. She returned to work after a month and managed to complete her contract, but at severe emotional cost. She held Solter responsible for her condition and separated from him. According to Larry Lee Holland, "Universal refused to pay for her medical expenses, and she felt betrayed. For two years she convalesced at her home."

During her absence, Lawrence's career in motion pictures became a thing of the past. There were many other actresses available for film work who were younger, unimpaired, and better able to carry the feature-length films of five or more reels that had become the norm. In 1916 she completed one feature film, *Elusive Isabel*, but while working on a second she collapsed and became paralyzed for some months. It took four years for her to regain her strength. By then Solter had died and audiences had completely forgotten her.

Lawrence was unable to accept that she, the first star of the movies, was finished in movie work. Since the industry had by now moved to California, where she had never been, she left her home and lived in a Los Angeles hotel while seeking a comeback. An interviewer found her "a sad little figure [with a] look of brave, spiritual struggle against overwhelming odds, the look of a woman who knows what it is to fight a losing fight" (*Photoplay*, May 1921). There was no comeback. Lawrence appeared in one feature, *The Unfoldment* (1921), but it was not a success. After marriage in 1921 to Charles Woodbridge, a salesman, she opened a small shop to sell a line of cosmetics bearing her name. In a 1924 article on forgotten stars of the past, she was quoted as saying, "It is hard to feel that you have given the best of your life to motion pictures—and that they have no place for you" (*Photoplay*, July 1924). A movie pioneer, she had appeared in more than 200 films.

Lawrence played bit parts in two more silent movies, *Gambling Wives* (1924) and *The Johnstown Flood* (1926). Her shop failed in 1929; her marriage ended in divorce in 1931. The same year she married Henry Bolton but divorced him after five months, claiming he beat her. There were no children by any of her marriages. She worked occasionally as an extra in films. One of the films was *Secrets* (1933), starring Mary Pickford; Pickford had been an unknown beginner at Biograph when Lawrence was the Biograph Girl, a national favorite. In 1936 Metro-Goldwyn-Mayer gave her, as it did some other movie has-beens down on their luck, a stock contract paying $75 a week. She lived on that in a Los Angeles apartment she shared with two other women. Despondent after learning she had a bone disease, Lawrence committed suicide by swallowing ant paste mixed with cough syrup.

• Some materials on the career of Lawrence are in the Billy Rose Theatre Collection at the New York Public Library for the Performing Arts, Lincoln Center. Autobiographical reminiscences are in Florence Lawrence, with Monte Katterjohn, "Growing Up with the Movies," *Photoplay*, Nov. 1914 through Feb. 1915. Further anecdotes of her early film days are in Linda Arvidson Griffith, *When the Movies Were Young* (1925). A biographical sketch of her life and career with filmography, portraits, and production photographs is Larry Lee Holland, "Florence Lawrence," *Films in Review*, Aug./Sept. 1980. Articles concerning her comeback attempt are Adela Rogers St. John, "The Return of Florence Lawrence," *Photoplay*, May 1921, and Frederick James Smith, "Unwept, Unhonored and Unfilmed," *Photoplay*, July 1924. A report of her suicide is in the *New York Times*, 29 Dec. 1938.

WILLIAM STEPHENSON

LAWRENCE, George Newbold (20 Oct. 1806–17 Jan. 1895), ornithologist and businessman, was born in New York City, the son of John Burling Lawrence, a wholesale druggist, and Hannah Newbold. The younger Lawrence began his serious study of ornithology in 1820, at age fourteen, when his father permitted him to own and use his first gun. Most of his observations were made at the family's summer home, "Forest Hill," on the west side of Manhattan Island near the Hudson River and the present site of the American Museum of Natural History. He became aware of the migration patterns of the various species, and he later noted that large numbers of passenger pigeons and other birds flew overhead in the early fall. Some of these he collected and added to what developed into a substantial private collection of bird skins, ultimately numbering more than 8,000. These he sold to the American Museum of Natural History in 1887.

At the age of sixteen Lawrence became a clerk in his father's firm, and at age twenty he became a partner. Most of his time was taken up with the family business, of which he was in full control by 1835, but vacations and weekends were devoted to his consuming interest in ornithology. When in the 1840s, John James Audubon built a home in what is now the Washington Heights section of the city, some five miles north of Forest Hill, Lawrence became friendly with the naturalist's two sons, John and Victor.

In 1841 Lawrence and Jacob P. Giraud, Jr., later a fellow member of the New York Lyceum of Natural History, and another collector of bird specimens, were invited by John Bell, a local naturalist and taxidermist, to meet the young Pennsylvania ornithologist Spencer F. Baird. Although not yet out of his teens, and only half the age of Lawrence, Baird was already a knowledgeable naturalist, and through their common interest in birds, he and Lawrence soon became good friends. This meeting evidently stimulated Lawrence to begin publishing scientific papers about birds. The first of these, most of which consisted of scientific descriptions of new species found in various parts of the country, was published in 1842. Soon thereafter Lawrence met John Cassin, another pioneering ornithologist who was in the process of building and describing the specimen collections at the Academy of Natural Sciences of Philadelphia.

In 1850 Baird became assistant secretary of the Smithsonian Institution, and within a few years he began attaching young naturalists to the Pacific Railway survey expeditions that were seeking out the most feasible transportation routes to the Pacific Ocean. Many bird skins and other animal specimens were brought back to Washington by these young men and deposited at the nascent National Museum of Natural History at the Smithsonian. At that time there were few individuals in the country who were knowledgeable enough to prepare scientific descriptions of these specimens. When in 1857 the Smithsonian decided to compile a volume summarizing the physical descriptions of all known about North American birds, Lawrence was invited, together with Cassin, to assist Baird with this project. Their two-volume *General Report upon the Zoology of the Several Pacific Railroad Routes . . . Part 2: Birds* (vol. 9 of the Pacific Railroad series) was issued in 1858. Another edition, published two years later as *The Birds of North America*, included some additional descriptions of new species together with a separate volume of 100 plates, illustrating some of the birds described. Lawrence contributed eighty pages to both editions. These included descriptions of such shore and water birds as the albatrosses, petrels, gulls, terns, pelicans, cormorants, tropic birds, loons, and grebes.

Lawrence made no effort to synthesize his ornithological findings at any time in his life, confining himself to listing birds found in various regions of North America and to describing new species. After 1858 he turned his attention to descriptions of Central and South American birds, together with those of Cuba and the West Indies, and earned a reputation as a specialist on the bird fauna of these regions. Virtually all of the birds he described had been collected by others. His principal papers included "A Catalogue of Birds Found in Costa Rica," (1870), *The Birds of Western and Northwestern Mexico* (1874), and *Birds of Southwestern Mexico* (1875).

Around 1862 Lawrence retired from business to devote all of his time to ornithology. His articles and papers, numbering 121 in all, appeared in such publications as *The Annals of the Lyceum of Natural History*, *Memoirs of the Boston Society of Natural History*, the *Auk*, and the *Bulletin of the United States National Museum*. He ultimately described some 323 new species of birds and had one genus and twenty species named in his honor. His last paper, which appeared nearly half a century after his first, was published in the *Auk* in January 1891.

Lawrence was a charter member of the American Ornithologists' Union in 1883, became a fellow and finally an honorary member soon thereafter, and was for some years an active and respected member of its council. He also received honorary memberships from the British Ornithologists' Union, the Zoological Society of London, and the Linnean Society of New York, together with other scientific and scholarly organizations in the United States. When the old Lyceum of Natural History was incorporated in the New York Academy of Sciences, Lawrence was made a member, later a fellow, and ultimately a patron of that organization. He was a founder of the College of Pharmacy of the City of New York, which later became a constituent institution of Columbia University. A kindly, self-effacing person, Lawrence was always held in high esteem by ornithologists because of his pioneering role in the field during the early nineteenth century.

Lawrence had married Mary Ann Newbold of New York in 1834; they had several children. His death in New York City followed hers by a matter of several days.

• There are some Lawrence papers in the Archives of the American Museum of Natural History, New York. The principal biographical sketches are Daniel G. Elliott, "In Memoriam: George Newbold Lawrence," *Auk*, Jan. 1896; L. S. Foster, "The Published Writings of George Newbold Lawrence [includes biographical sketch]," *Bulletin of the United States National Museum* 40 (1892); and W. L. McAtee, "George Newbold Lawrence," *Nature Magazine* 47 (1954). See also sketches in Barbara Mearns and Richard Mearns, *Audubon to Xantus* (1992); Clark A. Elliott, *Biographical Dictionary of American Science: The Seventeenth through the Nineteenth Centuries* (1979); and the obituary in the *New York Tribune*, 19 Jan. 1895.

KEIR B. STERLING

LAWRENCE, James (1 Oct. 1781–4 June 1813), U.S. naval officer, was born in Burlington, New Jersey. His mother, Martha Tallman, died when he was young, and his lawyer and politician father, John Lawrence, a Loyalist, emigrated to Canada. Left in the care of his half-sister in Burlington, Lawrence attended grammar school and studied in preparation to practice law. After his father's death in 1796, he chose a naval career instead and entered the navy with a midshipman's warrant on 4 September 1798. He served in the Caribbean during the Quasi-War against France. Retained under the Peace Establishment Act, he was commissioned lieutenant on 6 April 1802 and appointed to the schooner *Enterprise* for service in the Mediterranean.

Lawrence distinguished himself in the war with Tripoli. He was second in command in a boat attack that burned several feluccas on shore near Tripoli, and he saw close action against a 22-gun corsair. He was Stephen Decatur's (1779–1820) first lieutenant in the ketch *Intrepid*'s successful mission (16 Feb. 1804) to destroy the U.S. ship of the line *Philadelphia*, which had fallen into the hands of the Tripolitans. Lawrence declined as insignificant the award of two month's pay that Congress voted the *Intrepid*'s officers. He commanded the *Enterprise* and gunboat *Number 5* in several attacks on Tripoli that summer. Made first lieutenant of the frigate *John Adams*, he returned to the United States, arriving in March 1805. In May he sailed the 72-foot gunboat *Number 6* across the Atlantic for Syracuse, Italy. At Cádiz, in the presence of the British fleet, he was forced, under protest, to release three crew members who claimed protection of the British flag.

In 1807 Lawrence oversaw the transfer of gunboats built at Portland, Maine, to the Brooklyn Navy Yard, where he was stationed for a time. In January 1808 he sat as a member of the court-martial on the *Chesapeake-Leopard* affair. That same year he married Julia Montaudevert; they had two children, the second born after Lawrence's death. He was first lieutenant of the frigate *Constitution* for six months and then commanded in succession the brig *Vixen*, the sloop *Wasp*, and the brig *Argus*. In 1810, participating in trials of Robert Fulton's experimental spar-torpedo, he used antiboarding netting to foil its effect. On 3 November 1810 he was promoted to master commandant. In November 1811, in command of the sloop of war *Hornet*, he carried to Europe diplomatic messengers who vainly sought to accommodate America's differences with England and France.

The outbreak of the War of 1812 found Lawrence at New York in command of *Hornet*, part of Commodore John Rodgers's (1773–1838) squadron. The squadron set sail on 21 June and returned after a lackluster cruise of two months. Late in October *Hornet* sailed in company with *Constitution* on a cruise off Brazil. At Bahia Lawrence discovered the British sloop of war *Bonne Citoyenne*, laden with £50,000 in specie. The Royal Navy commander ignored Lawrence's challenge to duel ship to ship, and *Hornet* blockaded the *Bonne Citoyenne* in port. *Constitution*, having met and destroyed the HMS *Java*, had departed for the United States when the British ship of the line *Montagu* appeared off Bahia. Lawrence promptly broke off his blockade and sailed north. Continuing the cruise off South America, *Hornet* captured the ten-gun merchant brig *Resolution*. On 24 February 1813, off the Demerara River, *Hornet* took the Royal Navy brig-sloop *Peacock* in a short engagement. *Hornet* suffered few damages or casualties, but *Peacock* was so badly shattered that it sank during the transfer of prisoners.

Sailing *Hornet* into New York Harbor on 24 March, Lawrence was received as a hero and learned that he had been posted captain three weeks earlier, before his victory over *Peacock* was known in Washington. Earlier he had protested the promotion of Lieutenant Charles Morris to the rank of captain over the heads of all the masters commandant. When the secretary of the navy responded coldly to Lawrence's hint of resignation, Lawrence appealed to Congress. Congress postponed Morris's promotion until after Lawrence's, 4 March 1813.

Lawrence took command of the frigate *Chesapeake* in Boston on 20 May with orders for a cruise. On the morning of 1 June, when *Chesapeake* was ready to sail, the frigate *Shannon*, then the sole British vessel blockading Boston Harbor, appeared off Boston Lighthouse. Captain Philip Broke, in command of *Shannon* for seven years, had thoroughly drilled the crew in gunnery. Confident of victory, he sent Lawrence a written challenge. Before receiving the challenge, however, Lawrence sailed, flying his battle flag with its motto "Free Trade and Sailors' Rights."

Broke withdrew into the open sea and then allowed his ship to lay nearly dead in the water so that the *Chesapeake* could overtake it. Instead of seizing the opportunity this offered of crossing *Shannon*'s stern and raking it the length of its deck, Lawrence maneuvered *Chesapeake* alongside to fight yardarm to yardarm. The *Chesapeake*'s gunfire was rapid and accurate, striking the *Shannon* mainly in the hull. However, the *Shannon*'s gunfire was more rapid and accurate as well as deadlier, disabling *Chesapeake*'s rigging and helm, sweeping through the men on deck, and incapacitating the senior officers. A pistol ball entered Lawrence's leg below the knee early in the action, and shortly thereafter a musket ball struck him above the groin. As he was carried below, he gave the famous order, "Don't give up the ship." *Chesapeake*'s men, nonetheless,

gave way before *Shannon*'s boarders, who quickly won control of the American frigate. The entire action lasted a mere quarter of an hour.

Had he heeded the strategic thought of the secretary of the navy, who wanted the seagoing fleet to destroy enemy commerce, not fight Royal Navy warships, Lawrence would have eluded the blockading forces, as had other naval commanders. Nevertheless, the relative equality of force of *Chesapeake* and *Shannon* did not make his seeking battle so rash as its outcome makes it now seem.

Lawrence died of his wounds on board *Chesapeake* at sea, as the British sailed their prize toward Halifax, where they buried Lawrence's body with military honors. Afterward, his corpse was transferred, by a flag of truce, to New York, where it was interred on 16 September. Tenacious of his rights, Lawrence was motivated throughout his career by concern for his reputation, professional pride, and devotion to duty and honor.

• The chief primary sources for Lawrence's career are in the National Archives, Washington, D.C., Record Group 45, in particular in the correspondence of the secretary of the navy. Published documentation of Lawrence's participation in three wars can be found in U.S. Office of Naval Records and Library, *Naval Documents Related to the Quasi-War between the United States and France: Naval Operations from February 1797 to December 1801*, comp. Dudley W. Knox (7 vols., 1935–1983); U.S. Office of Naval Records and Library, *Naval Documents Related to the United States Wars with the Barbary Powers: Naval Operations Including Diplomatic Background from 1785 through 1807*, comp. Dudley W. Knox (6 vols., 1939–1944); and William S. Dudley et al., eds., *The Naval War of 1812: A Documentary History*, vol. 1, *1812*, and vol. 2, *1813* (1985–1992). The standard biography is Albert Gleaves, *James Lawrence, Captain, United States Navy, Commander of the "Chesapeake"* (1904). The most thorough analysis of the *Chesapeake-Shannon* engagement is in Peter Padfield, *Broke and the Shannon* (1968). See also H. F. Pullen, *The Shannon and the Chesapeake* (1970).

MICHAEL J. CRAWFORD

LAWRENCE, John Hundale (8 Jan. 1904–7 Sept. 1991), pioneer in nuclear medicine, was born in Canton, South Dakota, the son of Carl Gustav Lawrence, a teacher and school administrator, and Gunda Jacobson, a mathematics teacher. The Lawrences were a tightly knit family. As youths, John and his older brother, Ernest Orlando Lawrence, were taught the importance of honesty, hard work, and character. In 1911 John's father was elected to the position of state superintendent of public instruction, having served as superintendent for both city and county schools in Canton for some time, and the family moved to Pierre, South Dakota. In 1914 the Lawrences returned to Canton, where John enjoyed fishing and swimming in the river with his father. The family moved to Springfield, South Dakota, in 1918, after Carl accepted the position of president at Southern State Teachers College; the move followed the development of unbearable conditions in Canton resulting from the Lawrences' tolerance for Germans and support of teaching German in the schools, an unpopular position during and following World War I.

Shortly after arriving in Springfield, Lawrence graduated from high school and began studying at Southern State Teachers College. He soon transferred to the University of South Dakota, where he received his B.A. in 1926; he then enrolled in Harvard Medical School, as was his dream. He completed his medical studies in 1930 and carried out his internship at Brigham Hospital in Boston. He accepted a postdoctoral position at Strong Memorial Hospital at the University of Rochester in 1931 and at Yale University and New Haven Hospital a year later. In 1934 Yale hired him as an instructor in medicine, and New Haven Hospital made him an associate physician at the same time.

In the summer of 1935, following a car accident that killed a medical student and left Lawrence hospitalized for over a month, he began his professional association with his brother, who had accepted a position in the physics department at the University of California, Berkeley. Ernest had requested that Lawrence join him in California to determine the effects of the cyclotron and its materials on life. Lawrence spent the first summer evaluating the health effects of neutrons produced by the machine and comparing them to those of X-rays, the safety of which had unfortunately been underinvestigated decades earlier. A healthy respect for the particles was developed following an experimental mishap. A mouse was found dead after only a three-minute neutron irradiation, eliciting rapid development of water shielding between the operators and the cyclotron. Later the mouse was found to have died from suffocation rather than radiation, but the safety precautions were well warranted. Lawrence, H. F. Blum, and Paul C. Aebersold showed that the effect of the particles was as much as five times that of X-rays and varied with the substance irradiated. After arriving in California for the summer of 1936, he intended to remain at Berkeley and the Radiation Laboratory run by Ernest, but contract problems forced him to delay transferring. He returned to Yale in the fall with permission for four months' leave to continue studies at Berkeley. In 1937 Lawrence permanently joined the Berkeley faculty as professor of medical physics and director of Donner Laboratory, the medical division of the Rad Lab, as it was known. Complementing Lawrence, Blum, and Aebersold on the Donner staff were Joseph Hamilton and Robert S. Stone, among approximately seven others. Following completion of the comparative studies, the expanding staff of Donner Laboratory extended their interests to the examination of the therapeutic applicability of cyclotron-produced radioisotopes such as phosphorus-32, iodine-131, and sodium-24, as well as the evaluation of neutron and heavy charged particle beams for therapy.

Lawrence first used P-32 in a polycythemia vera patient in 1936, which was a resounding success referred to by Marshall Brucer as "one of two beginnings of nuclear medicine" (Brucer, p. 225). Donner Laboratory personnel were also using sodium-24, which proved not to be therapeutic in humans. The unpredictable effects of the radioisotopes were a constant source of frustration for Lawrence and his co-workers, but a glimmer of hope came early in their work. In 1937 the Lawrences' mother was diagnosed with inoperable uterine cancer after experiencing severe abdominal pain for several years with no apparent cause. By John Lawrence's recommendation, she was taken to Berkeley for X-ray therapy by Robert S. Stone, which completely ablated the tumor. The doctors at the Mayo Clinic had given her just three months to live, and so the cure by X-rays gave the brothers hope that other radiation methods would prove as promising. Over the next four decades John Lawrence continued to study P-32 in leukemia patients, with varying success. Over time he and others demonstrated that the agent was most successful in polycythemia vera and other chronic forms of leukemia. In 1942 Lawrence married Amy McNair Bowles, with whom he had four children. While other members of the lab were assigned to different locations for government research during World War II, Lawrence was fortunate to remain at Berkeley to continue his investigations.

In addition to radioisotopes, Lawrence focused on the use of cyclotron beams for therapy, utilizing both neutron and heavy ion beams. In 1935 the Lawrence brothers began to evaluate the possibility of charged particle beams (such as protons, deuterons, and alphas) for therapy, the first investigation of its kind. Neutron therapy trials in humans began at the lab in September 1938 but eventually proved to be disappointing. In 1952 Lawrence, C. A. Tobias, and Hal O. Anger first reported the results of their use of proton and alpha beams for therapy. Results of an extended study (1954–1963) of 159 patients who had undergone pituitary gland ablation by heavy ion beam irradiation were reported in 1963. In addition, John's international stature in the treatment of leukemia was clearly indicated by a request in 1953 that he fly to Yugoslavia to treat Aloysius Cardinal Stepinac, who was suffering from polycythemia vera and was under house arrest by order of Communist officials in that country. In 1955 Lawrence served as part of an American delegation to the Atoms for Peace conference in Geneva, focusing on medical aspects of cyclotrons and radioisotopes.

John Lawrence was the recipient of numerous awards and honors from societies in the United States and across the globe. He received the Eugene Wilson Caldwell Medal, as well as the first Marshall Brucer Medal, and delivered many named lectures. The Society of Nuclear Medicine, which he had served as president in 1966, honored him with the Nuclear Pioneer Award in 1970. He was a member of a multitude of professional societies, including the American Nuclear Society, the Society of Nuclear Medicine, and the American College of Nuclear Medicine, which recognized him as a distinguished fellow. Lawrence himself stated that "taking the first step into therapy of human patients was an awesome experience" (Lawrence, p. 527). He died in Berkeley, California.

• The collected works of Lawrence are held by the Bancroft Library at the University of California, Berkeley. A useful source of information for John Lawrence's early life and his family comes from a biography of his brother by Herbert Childs, *An American Genius: The Life of Ernest Orlando Lawrence* (1968). Also focused on Ernest but with a good deal of information regarding John Lawrence is J. L. Heilbron and Robert W. Seidel's *Lawrence and His Laboratory: A History of the Lawrence Berkeley Laboratory* (1989). Marshall Brucer's *A Chronology of Nuclear Medicine* (1990) provides a timeline of important advances and anecdotes regarding scientists and their discoveries. John Lawrence reflects on his own role in the beginnings of nuclear medicine in *Northwest Medicine* 55 (1956): 527–33, a lecture delivered on the occasion of the Society of Nuclear Medicine's twenty-fifth anniversary. The text of that lecture is reprinted in the *Journal of Nuclear Medicine* 20 (1979): 560–64. Two reviews with extensive bibliographies of his scientific accomplishments exist: J. H. Lawrence, *Radiation Research—Supplement* 7 (1967): 360–68, and C. Y. L. Chong et al., *The Radiologic Clinics of North America* 7 (1969): 319–43. Also useful is Ruth Brecher and Edward Brecher's *The Rays: A History of Radiology in the United States and Canada* (1969). An obituary is in the *New York Times*, 9 Sept. 1991.

JOANNA B. DOWNER

LAWRENCE, Marjorie (17 Feb. 1909–13 Jan. 1979), operatic soprano, was born in Dean's Marsh, near Melbourne, Australia, the daughter of William Lawrence and Elizabeth Smith, ranchers. She later became a naturalized American citizen. Her first music lessons were given by the Reverend Alex J. Pearce, her Anglican pastor. Shortly after her eighteenth birthday, Lawrence left home for Melbourne. Supporting herself working as a seamstress, she studied with Ivor Boustead. Lawrence won a number of prizes in the Geelong Musical Competition in Melbourne in 1927 and earned enough money to go to Paris. There she studied with Cécile Gilly, the first wife of French baritone Dinh Gilly.

Engaged by Raoul Gunsbourg to make her operatic debut at the Monte Carlo Opéra as Elisabeth in *Tannhäuser* opposite Georges Thill, Lawrence scored a tremendous success. Immediately thereafter she was hired by the Paris Opéra, where she debuted as Ortrud in *Lohengrin* in February 1933. That same season she sang Brünnhilde in *Die Walküre*, Herodias in *Salome*, Rachel in Halévy's *La Juive*, Aida, and Brünnhilde in *Götterdämmerung*. She was cast in the role of Keltis in the world premiere of Joseph Canteloube's *Vercingétorix* in June 1933. She was a leading dramatic soprano of the Paris Opéra (1933–1936) and maintained an apartment in Montmartre during this period. In 1934 she portrayed Donna Anna in *Don Giovanni*, Brunnhilde in Ernest Reyer's *Sigurd* in Lyon (the latest revival of Reyer's principal work opened in Oct. 1934), and Salomé in Massenet's *Hérodiade*, a work that had received its first Paris performance at the Opéra in 1921. In 1936 she portrayed Brangäne in *Tristan und Isolde* and Valentine in Meyerbeer's *Les Huguenots*.

Lawrence auditioned in Paris for Edward Johnson (1878–1959), general manager of the Metropolitan Opera, who hired her for a Met debut as Brünnhilde in *Die Walküre* in December 1935. During her tenure there she sang a total of eighty-six performances with the Met in New York and on tour, in such diverse roles as Brünnhilde, Tosca, Alceste, Salome, and Thaïs, the latter two roles rather foreign to her conspicuous talents. As Brünnhilde in *Götterdämmerung* in 1936, she was one of the first artists who insisted on riding a horse onto the funeral pyre, as stipulated in Wagner's own stage directions. An outstanding dramatic soprano, she projected an energetic personality and had a powerful and attractive voice. However, she had the misfortune to be continually compared with Kirsten Flagstad, with whom she shared a number of roles and who had debuted at the Met eleven months before as Sieglinde. Flagstad had received rapturous press notices beginning with her debut in New York, and the house was always sold out for her performances.

Lawrence was invited to appear at the Bayreuth Festival in 1939 but declined because of the political situation. In San Francisco she made her debut as Brünnhilde in *Die Walküre*, with Flagstad as Sieglinde; the two artists then exchanged roles, and the second casting was generally accepted as superior. The next San Francisco season featured Lawrence as Carmen, with Ezio Pinza as Escamillo. This production replaced an aborted *La Fanciulla del West* originally planned for Lawrence Tibbett, with Lawrence as Minnie.

In 1941, Lawrence married physician Thomas King. During their honeymoon in Mexico City, where she had been engaged by the National Opera Company, Lawrence was stricken by poliomyelitis and collapsed during the dress rehearsal of *Die Walküre*. All of her performances had to be canceled, and this was the beginning of a major casting problem. With Flagstad unable to return to the United States from Norway, *Tristan und Isolde* was dropped from the repertoire of the Met for the first time since 1920, and the Wagnerian repertoire went into a decline for several decades. Lawrence became paralyzed from the waist down, and there were serious doubts if she would ever sing again. Aided by her husband and the famous Sister Kenny (Elizabeth Kenny), she managed to regain some control of her body as well as a remarkable restoration of her voice. She never openly referred to her affliction; instead, she steadfastly projected an image of enormous courage and inner strength.

Lawrence reappeared for a major recital on 29 November 1942 at Town Hall in New York, seated in a wheelchair. In December she appeared at a "welcome home" concert at the Met, singing the Venusberg duet with Lauritz Melchior. To assist in the staging, a giant medieval huntsman gently lifted her from her wheelchair and placed her on Venus's divan. Among the artists who performed at this tribute to her were Tibbett, Jarmila Novotná, John Brownlee, Pinza, Lily Pons, and Licia Albanese. She returned to the Metropolitan Opera in January 1943 as Venus in *Tannhäuser*, singing eleven performances of the role in a reclining position; the next season she appeared as Isolde, again in a wheelchair. Her Met farewell was as Isolde on 14 March 1944, and she was carried on in the last act by Kurvenal, portrayed by the stalwart Julius Huehn. Throughout the war she gave generously of her time and energy to entertain the servicemen. Following the war, she performed Amneris in *Aida* at the Paris Opéra in 1947, and she appeared in a concert performance of Richard Strauss's *Elektra* in Chicago later that year, during which, according to her autobiography, she stood the entire time. In 1955 her autobiography was made into a Hollywood film, *Interrupted Melody*, with the sound track sung by Eileen Farrell.

From 1956 to 1960 Lawrence was professor of voice at Tulane University in New Orleans. Following that, she was appointed director of the Opera Workshop and professor of voice at Southern Illinois University in Carbondale, where she appeared as Mme. Flora in *The Medium* (1966). In 1976 the TV station in Sydney, Australia, telecast "This Is Your Life," a special program honoring the artist. On 4 October 1978 she was to have joined seven of her colleagues at the inauguration of "Metropolitan Opera Fine Art," a fundraising venture featuring a set of limited-edition graphics in which she represented Isolde. Her final illness, however, made it impossible for her to make the trip to New York. She died at her home in Little Rock, Arkansas. Her life and her performances reflected the down-to-earth, hard-working, positive approach she brought to everything she did.

• Lawrence wrote an autobiography titled *Interrupted Melody: The Story of My Life* (1949). For biographical information, see the sketch on Lawrence in *Current Biography Yearbook* (1940). An obituary by Francis Robinson is in *Opera News*, 7 Apr. 1979, and one by John Rockwell is in the *New York Times*, 15 Jan. 1979.

ROBERT H. COWDEN

LAWRENCE, William (26 June 1819–8 May 1899), U.S. congressman, was born in Mount Pleasant, Ohio, the son of Joseph Lawrence and Temperance Gilchrist, farmers. Educated first in local schools, Lawrence attended Franklin College in New Athens, Ohio, graduating with honors in 1838. For the next year he studied law and taught school in Morgan County, then he enrolled in the Cincinnati Law School and received his degree in 1840. Admitted to the bar, Lawrence briefly served as a reporter for the *Ohio State Journal* and then settled in Bellefontaine, Ohio, where he began to practice law in 1841. He was appointed commissioner of bankruptcy for Logan County the following year. In 1843 Lawrence married Cornelia Hawkins, who died just three months later. In 1845 he wed Caroline M. Miller; they had six children. In 1845 he became prosecuting attorney for Logan County, but he resigned after a year. Remaining active in his community, he was editor and proprietor of the *Logan Gazette* from 1845 to 1847.

As a Whig, Lawrence served in the Ohio House of Representatives from 1846 to 1847 and in the Ohio Senate in 1849, 1850, and 1854. He supported public libraries, reform schools, and improved security for real estate investments, and he drafted the Ohio Free Banking Law of 1851. In 1851, as the reporter for the Ohio Supreme Court, he authored *Reports of Cases Argued and Determined in the Supreme Court of Ohio*, volume 20, and received praise for organizing and analyzing Ohio judicial opinions. In 1852 the Whigs nominated him as a presidential elector, and he was appointed judge of the common pleas and Third District Court of Ohio in 1857. During his eight years on the bench, Lawrence served as an editor of the *Western Law Monthly*. The Civil War temporarily interrupted his tenure on the bench. He was commissioned as colonel in the Eighty-fourth Ohio Voluntary Infantry on 7 June 1862 and served in Maryland for three months.

Lawrence became a Republican at the party's inception in Ohio, and in 1863 President Abraham Lincoln appointed him district judge of Florida, but he declined the post. He remained active in the Republican party, however, and in 1864 was elected to the House of Representatives. Lawrence represented Ohio from 1865 to 1877 with the single exception of the Forty-second Congress (1871–1873). A member of the House Judiciary Committee, he participated in many of the most pressing political issues of his day and consistently supported the expansion of congressional power. In 1868 he advocated a broad interpretation of impeachment in the trial of Andrew Johnson, and he authored "A Brief of Authorities upon the Law of Impeachable Crimes and Misdemeanors." This work was presented by Benjamin F. Butler, a manager of impeachment, in his opening argument favoring Johnson's removal from office. In the brief, Lawrence argued that legal precedent established an impeachable offense as "one in its nature or consequence subversive of some fundamental or essential principle of government or highly prejudicial to the public interest." He also suggested that impeachment could be used "where the public interests imperatively demand it" and deemed Johnson's interference with congressional Reconstruction as such an occasion. The following year Lawrence reported on New York election frauds, prompting passage of a law to preserve the integrity of elections. He championed a law, which passed in 1870, that provided veterans with 160 acres from the alternative sections of railroad grants, doubling the land allowance of the original Homestead Act, and he was instrumental in passing a law prohibiting land sales by authority of American Indian treaties, placing the responsibility for distributing public lands with Congress. Lawrence's greatest accomplishment in Congress, however, was the passage of the Lawrence Bill on 17 July 1876. This act made railroad companies receiving credit through federal bonds responsible for payments into a fund to reduce government liability, which secured a $150 million indemnity for the government. In 1877 he argued the case of the Republican electors of South Carolina before the electoral commission appointed to resolve the contested Hayes-Tilden presidential election and helped secure electoral votes for Rutherford B. Hayes.

During his tenure as in the House of Representatives, Lawrence also argued significant land cases in front of the Supreme Court. In the cases of *Holden v. Joy* (1872), *Morton v. Nebraska* (1874), and *Leavenworth, Lawrence and Galveston Railroad Company v. United States* (1875), he sought to secure congressional control over the sale of public lands, as he had in Congress. In 1880 he was appointed first comptroller of the Treasury Department, and during his five-year tenure, he became the first comptroller to publish his decisions. Upon his resignation from the Treasury Department, Lawrence practiced law in Ohio and was active in the Farmers' National Congress. He served as director of the Ohio National Bank in Washington and as president of both the Ohio and National Wool Growers associations throughout the 1890s. As the leading authority on American wool production, he called for the protection of native wool through a tariff on imports and championed this cause until his death in Kenton, Ohio.

Lawrence helped shape the Republican party as it rose to power in antebellum Ohio. Following the war, he played a prominent role in the House of Representatives both as a man of his party and as an advocate of congressional stewardship of the public lands. Through his speeches, legal briefs, and authoritative works, Lawrence upheld Republican policies and helped define legislative power in the late nineteenth century.

• Lawrence's correspondence with governors and adjutants general of Ohio is in the Ohio Historical Society. His published speeches are in the Library of Congress; the *Congressional Record*, 1865–1871 and 1874–1877; and *Decisions of the First Comptroller in the Department of the Treasury* (1881–1895). The most complete source on Lawrence's political career is Joseph P. Smith, ed., *History of the Republican Party in Ohio* (1898), which includes a comprehensive list of his scholarly works. On the legislatures that Lawrence served in, see Michael Les Benedict, *The Impeachment Trial of Andrew Johnson* (1973); Benedict, *A Compromise of Principle: Congressional Republicans and Reconstruction* (1974); and William Gillette, *Retreat from Reconstruction, 1869–1879* (1980). His obituary is in the *Ohio State Journal*, 9 May 1899.

CHRISTINE DOYLE

LAWRENCE, William (30 May 1850–6 Nov. 1941), Episcopal bishop, was born in Boston, Massachusetts, the son of Amos Adams Lawrence, a merchant and businessman, and Sarah Elizabeth Appleton. He was raised in an atmosphere of wealth and tolerance. His father served as treasurer for the New England Emigrant Aid Company, a group formed to recruit families to settle in Kansas and vote for a free state as against a slave state. He received his B.A. from Harvard in 1871 and continued there for another year to study history. In 1869 he met Phillips Brooks, the rector of Trinity Church in Boston. According to Henry K. Sherrill, "Next to his home, he was influenced most by Phillips Brooks, whose gospel of the love of

God fell like rain upon the parched earth of New England Calvinism" (p. 16). It was while a student at Harvard that Lawrence suffered an attack of what he labeled "nerves." His symptoms manifested themselves in unsteadiness, fear of being alone yet fear of crowds, and dread of heights, and this condition plagued him the rest of his life.

While at Harvard and under the influence of Brooks, Lawrence decided to study for the ministry of the Episcopal church. Lawrence studied at Andover Theological Seminary in Andover, Massachusetts. After two years at Andover (1872–1874), he transferred to the Episcopal Divinity School in Pennsylvania. He spent less than a year there, and then he spent the last three months of his theological studies at the Episcopal Theological School in Cambridge, Massachusetts, from which he received his B.D. (1875).

In May 1874 Lawrence married Julia Cunningham; they had eight children, two of whom became bishops. He was ordained deacon on 20 June 1875 and priest on 11 June 1876. He began his ministry as assistant and then rector of Grace Church in Lawrence, Massachusetts. Grace Church had a large number of working-class people, who were employed in the mills in Lawrence. Here he encountered a point of view different from the capitalist orientation of his upbringing. He spoke out on behalf of workers, protested against child labor, and advocated a better pay system for the workers. Hitherto, the workers had been paid with a monthly check, cashable at banking hours when no employee could leave work. The result was that the grocery stores became the check cashing and credit centers of the city, to the disadvantage of the workers. Lawrence worked to have the monthly check system changed to a weekly payment in cash. Believing in the value of pastoral visitation Lawrence quoted Phillips Brooks, "How is it possible for one to preach to his people if he does not know them, their doubts, sorrows, and ambitions?" (*Memories of a Happy Life*, p. 54). He stressed that "a house-going parson makes a church-going people."

In January 1884 Lawrence became professor of homiletics and pastoral care at the Episcopal Theological School in Cambridge. In 1888 he became vice dean, and the following year he became the fourth dean of the school, a position he held until 1893. One day a visitor inquired for him at his home. "He's not here," said one of his small daughters, "he's over at the Illogical School."

The Episcopal Theological School flourished during Lawrence's deanship. His many leadership qualities, especially "his skill in opening the pocket books of others," contributed greatly to the welfare of the school. Lawrence was also successful in recruiting new faculty members. Bishop Thomas Clark said in the commencement address for 1891, "Professorships are no longer made to serve as a resort and resting-place for retired invalids" (Muller, p. 82).

Phillips Brooks died just fifteen months after his consecration as the sixth bishop of Massachusetts. Lawrence wrote, "The Light is gone out of life." On 4

May 1893 Lawrence was elected the seventh bishop of Massachusetts and was consecrated at Trinity Church in Boston on 5 October 1893. He served as bishop until he retired in June 1927.

During Lawrence's episcopate the diocese grew and developed until there was discussion about ways to reduce the bishop's workload. This was before suffragan bishops were canonically permissible and too early to think about a bishop coadjutor who would be his successor. The decision was made to divide the diocese, which was done in 1901. This opened the way for new growth in the diocese of Massachusetts and in the new diocese of Western Massachusetts.

As Lawrence moved about his diocese, he realized that each parish and mission was a unit in itself, and that there was little sense of belonging to a diocese. He struggled with some way to set before the people "a visible expression of the organization of the church as an Episcopal Church," and decided that a cathedral would be the answer to this need. On 7 October 1912 St. Paul's Church in Boston was set apart as the Cathedral of St. Paul.

Possibly Lawrence's greatest accomplishment was the establishment of the Church Pension Fund; at the time there was no pension plan for clergy and their families, and no disability benefits. He raised over $8,000,000 for the fund, the largest sum of money ever raised at one time by a church for a single cause through voluntary contributions.

When Bishop Lawrence died in Milton, Massachusetts, he was the senior bishop of the Episcopal church in the United States and one of Massachusetts's outstanding citizens. Lawrence was in the Broad Church tradition, with its emphasis on tolerance and ecumenism, and he was a supporter of the "Gospel of Wealth," stating that "it is only to the man of morality that wealth comes."

• Lawrence's papers are in the Archives of the Diocese of Massachusetts, Boston, and the Archives of the Episcopal Divinity School, Cambridge, Mass. His two autobiographical works are *Fifty Years* (1923) and *Memories of a Happy Life* (1926). Lawrence's major writings include *Phillips Brooks, a Study* (1903) and *Life of Phillips Brooks* (1930). The major study of his life and ministry is Henry K. Sherrill, *William Lawrence: Later Years of a Happy Life* (1943). Harold C. Martin, *"Outlasting marble and glass": The History of the Church Pension Fund* (1986), discusses Lawrence's work at length. James Arthur Muller, *The Episcopal Theological School, 1867–1943* (1943), treats Lawrence as a teacher and dean. There is a substantial treatment of Lawrence as bishop in Dudley Tyng, *Massachusetts Episcopalians, 1607–1957* (1960). An obituary is in the *Living Church*, 19 Nov. 1941.

DONALD S. ARMENTROUT

LAWRIE, Lee Oscar (16 Oct. 1877–23 Jan. 1963), sculptor, was born in Rixdorf, Germany. His family emigrated when he was an infant, and he grew up in Chicago. In 1891, after attending public schools in Chicago and the St. Vincent de Paul School in Baltimore, Lawrie entered the studio of sculptor Richard Henry Park, where he learned the rudiments of sculpture and assisted in Park's work for the World's Columbian Exposition held in Chicago in 1893. In the years that followed, Lawrie served as studio assistant to A. Phimister Proctor in Chicago, William Ordway Partridge in Massachusetts, and Philip Martiny and Augustus Saint-Gaudens in New York. His own career was launched when architects Ralph Adams Cram and Bertram G. Goodhue gave him a commission for three marble panels for the public library they designed for Pawtucket, Rhode Island (1901). This was, moreover, his initial effort in architectural sculpture, the field in which he was to become famous.

Lawrie's subsequent career was continuously intertwined with the large architectural commissions of Cram, Goodhue & Ferguson. That firm's additions to the U.S. Military Academy at West Point (1903–1910) contain numerous architectural sculptures by Lawrie, who also executed many ornamental reliefs in the gothic mode for the firm's handsome St. Thomas's Episcopal Church in New York City (1906–1913); the choir loft contains a gigantic reredos (screen) that has approximately sixty life-size figures modeled by Lawrie to represent a variety of religious personages. "In the reredos," one critic wrote, "both architect and sculptor seem imbued with the same aesthetic purpose, revealing all the poetry, the mysticism that is the essence of Gothic architecture" (Tachau, p. 395). Lawrie also modeled the sculptural decorations for St. Bartholomew's Episcopal Church in New York City (1914–1918).

Lawrie was an instructor in sculpture at Yale University from 1908 to 1919 and at Harvard University School of Architecture from 1910 to 1912. From Yale he received a bachelor of fine arts degree in 1910 and an honorary master's degree in 1932. After Goodhue designed the tower and gateway for the Harkness Quadrangle on Yales's campus, Lawrie provided thirty-two statues of famous persons, including Noah Webster, Nathan Hale, James Fenimore Cooper, Eli Whitney, and Samuel F. B. Morse. Goodhue later wrote that Lawrie, "more than any other living sculptor, recognizes the essentially architectonic quality of his art" (p. 40).

In the early 1920s Lawrie created what many would agree was his finest work, the sculptures for Goodhue's Nebraska State Capitol in Lincoln. Although the reliefs bear similarities to classical reliefs, it was here that Lawrie's art began to take on a simplified, stylized, and decorative character that would, especially in its architectonic form, soon transform into one of the foremost manifestations of the art deco style. Lawrie, in fact, came to be known as the "dean" of art deco architectural sculpture. Other works in collaboration with Goodhue date from the early 1920s, among them the National Academy of Sciences in Washington, D.C., and the beautiful gothic portal for the Church of St. Vincent Ferrer in New York City, as well as the Los Angeles Public Library. Lawrie later recalled the importance of those years:

In 1922 . . . Mr. Goodhue and I arrived at a new kind of architectural sculpture, that is essentially a part of the building rather than something ornate and applied. The work on the Los Angeles Public Library . . . is germinated from the same idea. Sculpture, here, is not sculpture, but a branch grafted on to the architectural trunk; forms that portray animate life emerge from blocks of stone and terminate in historical expression. (Quoted in Perry, p. 169)

Lawrie's monumental entrance to the RCA Building and his colossal bronze figure *Atlas* (both 1937) are among the focal points of New York's Rockefeller Center. In 1938 he created a set of bronze doors for the Library of Congress Annex. By then his work had earned him many honors. From the American Institute of Architects he received its gold medal in 1921 and 1927, and he was awarded the Architectural League's Medal of Honor in 1931. Lawrie served as the sculptor member on the Commission of the National Collection of Fine Arts from 1933 to 1937 and from 1945 to 1950. After his retirement in 1940, Lawrie continued to be honored and was active in several sculptural projects. In 1954 he received the Medal of Honor from the National Sculpture Society, of which he had long been a member. He was a member of the American Numismatic Society and in that context is best remembered for the exquisite profile head of Franklin Delano Roosevelt that he modeled for the dime. Lawrie also held memberships in the National Institute of Arts and Letters, the American Academy of Arts and Letters, and the National Academy of Design.

Lawrie's first wife, Ingeborg Jacobsen Frolich, with whom he had five children, died in 1937. He later married Mildred Allen Baker. In his later years Lawrie lived at Locust Lane Farm near Easton, Maryland, where he died.

• There are 5,700 letters, photographs, and other materials in the Lawrie papers, Manuscript Division, Library of Congress; the American Academy of Arts and Letters in New York City has sixty items. For personal statements see "Lawrie's Creed," *Art Digest*, 1 Sept. 1932, p. 29, and Lawrie, "Art and Religious Expression," *National Sculpture Review*, Winter 1968–1969, pp. 8–16. Two small Lawrie monographs with plates are *Lee Lawrie* (1955) and *Sculpture* (1936). Articles on his work include Ernest Peixotto, "St. Thomas's and Its Reredos," *Architecture*, July 1920, pp. 193–98ff; Bertram G. Goodhue, "Lee Lawrie and His Sculpture," *Yale Alumni Weekly*, 29 Sept. 1922, pp. 40–42; Hanna Tachau, "Lee Lawrie, Architectural Sculptor," *International Studio*, Aug. 1922, pp. 394–400; Leon V. Solon, "Architectural Sculpture by Lee Lawrie," *Architectural Record*, Oct. 1923, pp. 388–90; Everett R. Perry, "The Lee Lawrie Sculptures of the Los Angeles Public Library," *American Institute of Architects Journal*, May 1928, pp. 169–73; and Hartley B. Alexander, "The Sculpture of Lee Lawrie: An Appreciation of His Latter Work," *Architectural Forum*, May 1931, pp. 595–600. A study of one of Lawrie's most important sculptural projects is Charles H. Whitaker, *The Architectural Sculpture of the State Capitol at Lincoln, Nebraska* (1926). A brief obituary notice is in the *New York Times*, 25 Jan. 1963.

WAYNE CRAVEN

LAWS, Annie (20 Jan. 1855–1 July 1927), woman's club leader and education reformer, was born in Cincinnati, Ohio, the daughter of James Hedding Laws, a businessman, and Sarah Amelia Langdon. She was educated in Cincinnati's public schools and at Miss Appleton's School for Girls. She also received private instruction in music, art, and literature.

Laws was an activist in reforming nursing education, founding the Cincinnati Training School for Nurses, serving as vice president of Cincinnati's Hospital Social Service Association and secretary-treasurer of Cincinnati's Red Cross, and organizing a home nursing training program.

She supported the kindergarten movement through a number of organizations: the Cincinnati Kindergarten Association (president 1891–1892, 1901–1927), International Kindergarten Union (president 1903–1905), and Committee of Nineteen (dates unavailable). The University of Cincinnati drew on the home economics and teacher training components of these organizations to create its College of Household Arts and Sciences (1914) and the College of Education's Kindergarten Training School (1926).

Active in the women's club movement of her day, she was a founder in 1894 of the Cincinnati Woman's Club, devoted to the study of the arts and civic problems. As first president of the woman's club in 1894, she represented her club at the organizational meeting of the Ohio Federation of Women's Clubs. She also presided over the state federation from 1907 to 1909, overseeing projects devoted to art education, civic improvement, education of children, library extension, literature, industrial and child labor, household and hospital economics, forestry, and health. During her term, she served on the board of director's Legislation and Civil Service Committee, spoke before the Ohio State Federation of Colored Women's Clubs, and invited the General Federation of Women's Clubs to hold its 1910 biennial convention in Cincinnati. She served the Ohio federation in other capacities as well, as recording secretary (1900), National Education Association representative (1909–1915), and, in the 1920s, as historian and member of the Department of Applied Education's Kindergarten Bureau. She compiled and edited a volume on the history of the first thirty years of the Ohio federation, narrating the development of the national and Ohio club movement from her perspective.

Annie Laws was the first woman member of the Cincinnati Board of Education (1912–1916), a member of Cincinnati's Woman's Council of Defense during World War I, and a singer in the Cincinnati May Festival Chorus. She died in Cincinnati.

Laws was an outstanding representative of the modern woman in turn-of-the-century America. She was independent, organized, ambitious, efficient, and responsible. A single woman, she did not disdain the traditional domestic and maternal responsibilities of women. In fact, she worked for more efficient methods of housekeeping to free women for a wider variety of activities and responsibilities. She held high respect for women's capabilities and expected that greater educational opportunities would prepare them to take on new and broad roles in the public arena. She expected women's humane values to improve the social, political, and economic inequities that limited women's contributions to society. Laws understood that individual women could not successfully challenge the system she wished to reform. Rather, she was a firm believer in strength through unity. Confident in women's ability to cooperate for social change, she devoted her life to reform issues of importance to the women of her day, participating in many capacities in a wide variety of women's voluntary organizations.

• Laws was the editor and compiler of the *History of the Ohio Federation of Women's Clubs for the First Thirty Years, 1894–1924* (1924); see pp. 207–14 for her own account of her presidential administration. See also Jane Cunningham Croly, *The History of the Woman's Club Movement in America* (1898), pp. 979–80; Mary I. Wood, *The History of the General Federation of Women's Clubs* (1912), pp. 248–75; James H. Rodabaugh and Mary Jane Rodabaugh, *Nursing in Ohio* (1951); Lavinia L. Dock et al., the *History of American Red Cross Nursing* (1922); and Nina C. Vandewalker, *The Kindergarten in American Education* (1908), pp. 72, 134–35. Obituaries are in the *Cincinnati Enquirer* and *Cincinnati Commercial Tribune*, 2 July 1927; *Childhood Education*, Sept. 1927, and *American Childhood*, Sept. 1927.

KAREN J. BLAIR

LAWSON, Alexander (19 Dec. 1773–22 Aug. 1846), line engraver, was born on a farm at Ravenstruthers, Lanarkshire, Scotland. Little is known of his childhood, not even the names of his parents. He was introduced to drawing by a schoolmaster and apparently sketched in his early workbooks while in school. After his parents died, at age sixteen he moved to Manchester, England, where he was befriended by a bookseller who indulged Lawson's love of illustrated books and art books. He lived near a store where he would have seen printed images for sale. He determined to become an engraver. Like many of his contemporaries in the graphic arts, he was self-taught in his chosen field. His earliest tool was a penknife; later he had a blacksmith make an engraving tool by copying an illustration in an art manual. He experimented with various engraving tools and media—etching, mezzotint, and line engraving. Although he would have preferred to travel to France to perfect his engraving skills, the French Revolution prevented him from doing so.

Lawson left England for the United States in 1794, arriving in Baltimore on 14 July. He settled soon afterward in Philadelphia, a major center of the printing and publishing trades, including engraving. For two years, 1794–1796, he was employed by the firm of Thackara & Vallance. James Thackara was an engraver and stationer of Philadelphia who became the keeper of the Philadelphia Academy after 1826. John Vallance was another native of Scotland who arrived in Philadelphia in 1791. He worked with Thackara from 1791 to 1797 as an engraver. While working for Thackara & Vallance as a journeyman engraver, Lawson did not sign any engravings. The firm was responsible for producing many of the engravings for the American edition of the *Encyclopaedia Britannica*, published by Thomas Dobson. This publication contained almost 550 engraved plates issued over a fifteen-year period beginning in 1789. Dobson monopolized the services of a host of Philadelphia engravers during this period, including Thackara & Vallance.

Having gained some experience, Lawson left Thackara & Vallance and formed a partnership with the Irish immigrant illustrator and engraver John James Barralet about 1797. Together they produced an engraved portrait of William Penn published in 1797 in Robert Proud's *History of Pennsylvania* and one of George Washington published in volume two of Smollett's *History of the British Empire* in 1798, both after drawings by Barralet. Their partnership ended in 1798 after a bitter quarrel. Barralet occasionally received payment for a commission without splitting it with Lawson, and he retouched some engraved plates without Lawson's permission, ruining the plates, in Lawson's eyes. Each continued to work independently.

In 1798 Lawson's signature appeared on engravings executed for the American edition of the *Encyclopaedia Britannica*. Dobson hired Lawson to engrave nine plates in volumes seventeen and eighteen, issued in 1798, and thirty more in the second and third volumes of the supplement issued in 1803. These engravings, although mere copies of British engravings, provided steady employment to Lawson and enabled him to acquire additional commissions.

For many years Lawson worked independently, producing engravings for Philadelphia's leading publishers. Of the generation of engravers working before 1820, he was one of the most prolific. He produced portraits, genre scenes, views, botanical illustrations, literary subjects, maps, charts, and technical and medical subjects. Among separately published prints that he engraved was Thomas Birch's *Perry's Victory on Lake Erie* (1815). This folio engraving was one of his finest efforts. Another very elaborate folio engraving, *Election Day in Philadelphia*, was left uncompleted at his death. His greatest sustained effort was the engraving of fifty of the seventy-six plates for Alexander Wilson's multivolume *American Ornithology* (1808–1814). He was later commissioned to engrave twenty-seven plates for the continuation of Wilson's work, compiled by Charles Lucien Bonaparte and published in four volumes from 1825 to 1833. Although today these works suffer in comparison to the work of John James Audubon, they were considered to be masterpieces by contemporary critics in Europe as well as in the United States.

In 1823 appeared Caspar Wistar's *System of Anatomy for the Use of Students of Medicine* and *An Abridgement of Mr. Heath's Translation of [Jean Louis] Baudelocque's Midwifery* with engravings by Lawson. The latter volume also contains engravings by Robert Scot, another Philadelphia engraver, who died in 1823;

Lawson may have been hired to complete Scot's work. An edition of James Thomson's *Seasons* was published in 1826 with engravings by Lawson. Later engravings include about twenty he produced for gift books and literary annuals published from 1833 through 1845. Some of these images are local genre scenes, recording for posterity the look of the United States at that time. He also engraved for the *American Turf Register and Sporting Magazine*. Lawson's engravings, regardless of the subject matter, were always crisp and expertly done.

In 1805 Lawson had married Elizabeth Scaife, a native of Cumberland, England, who had immigrated to Philadelphia about 1800. They had at least four children, two of whom Lawson trained as engravers and who eventually worked with him. Two of his daughters organized their father's collection of engraved proofs, illustrations, and drawings and presented them to the Academy of Natural Sciences in Philadelphia after his death. This collection (MS Coll. 79) has been microfilmed and described in the *Auk* (43 [1926]: 47–61). His daughter Helen E. Lawson shared her father's expertise in natural history subjects and drew and colored most of the specimens for Samuel S. Haldeman's *A Monograph of the Freshwater Univalve Mollusca of the United States* (1840–1845). This beautifully illustrated natural history contains thirty-one engravings by Alexander Lawson and eight by his son Oscar A. Lawson. This was the last major project that occupied Alexander Lawson, and the work of illustrating the text was shared among the father and two of his children. Helen Lawson was an artist in her own right and exhibited portraits and other paintings at the Pennsylvania Academy from 1830 to 1842.

William Dunlap, the chronicler of American art and artists, wrote in 1834 that Lawson was "a tall, thin man, of large frame, and athletic; full of animation, and inclined to be satirical, but as I judge, full of good feeling and the love of truth." His animated character is revealed in his ability to enliven the engravings for literary subjects; his "love of truth" is exemplified by his faithful and precise rendering into black and white lines the drawings of Alexander Wilson and other naturalists and scientists. This ability, particularly before the advent of photography, was a particularly important skill. Lawson died in his adopted city of Philadelphia.

Lawson was one of the finest engravers of his generation in America. His talent and expertise resulted in a substantial body of carefully executed engravings that ornamented works of literature and provided perfectly rendered diagrams of scientific instruments of lasting usefulness to American mechanics and craftsmen. His engravings for the ornithological works of Wilson and Bonaparte won him immediate recognition and lasting fame.

• The collection of Lawson's work at the Academy of Natural Sciences in Philadelphia is important not only for the study of Lawson but also for the study of several of his contemporaries. There is no complete list of Lawson's engravings. Those

executed before 1821, numbering about 275, are thoroughly described in the *Catalogue of American Engravings* housed at the American Antiquarian Society. William Dunlap's observations were published in his *History of the Rise and Progress of the Arts of Design in the United States* (1834; repr. 1918). Townsend Ward's basic biographical sketch, "Alexander Lawson," in the *Pennsylvania Magazine of History and Biography* 28 (1904): 204–8. Recent studies on Lawson include Judy L. Larson's "Dobson's *Encyclopedia*: A Precedent in American Engraving" and Georgia B. Barnhill's "Publication of Illustrated Natural Histories in Philadelphia, 1800–1850," in *The American Illustrated Book in the Nineteenth Century*, ed. Gerald W. R. Ward (1987). Lawson's work for Wilson is also described in detail in Philadelphia Museum of Art, *Philadelphia, Three Centuries of American Art* (1976). Additional references to his natural history engravings may be found in Ann Shelby Blum, *Picturing Nature: American Nineteenth-century Zoological Illustration* (1993). Lawson's engravings for gift books can be located by using the index for engravers in E. Bruce Kirkham and John W. Fink, *Indices to American Literary Annuals and Gift Books, 1825–1865* (1975).

GEORGIA B. BARNHILL

LAWSON, Andrew Cowper (25 July 1861–16 June 1952), geologist, was born in Anstruther, Scotland, the son of William Lawson, a sailor, and Jessie Kerr, a freelance writer. When he was six, his family moved to Hamilton, Ontario, where Lawson attended public schools. He entered the University of Toronto in 1881 and, on graduating in 1883, went to work for the Geological Survey of Canada.

For the Canadian survey, Lawson investigated the Rainy Lake and Lake of the Woods region of southern Ontario. His work there resulted in a new interpretation of the Precambrian rocks of this area. He found that the Laurentian formation, previously believed to be the oldest in the geological time scale, was actually underlain by another rock formation, which he named the Keewatin. Later research convinced him that below this lay an even older formation, which he named Coutchiching. Much of his work on the Precambrian involved the study of thin sections of rock with the polarizing microscope, a relatively new technique that Lawson studied with George H. Williams at Johns Hopkins University, where Lawson earned a Ph.D. in geology in 1888. Although his conclusions about the age of the rocks of southern Canada were rejected at first by the members of the Canadian survey, they were accepted as authoritative when he reported on his research at the International Geological Congress in London in 1888. In 1911 Lawson reexamined the geology of the Rainy Lake region and discovered two formations within the Laurentian granites, one of which he named Algoman, a name still in use.

In 1889 Lawson married Ludovika von Jansch, with whom he had four children, all sons. Two years after her death in 1929 he married Isabel R. Collins; they had one child, another son, born when Lawson was eighty-seven. In 1890, after a brief stint in Vancouver as consultant on coal fields for the Canadian Pacific Railroad, he accepted an invitation from Berkeley geology professor Joseph LeConte to come to the University of California at Berkeley as assistant professor, to teach the "scientific side" of geology, leaving the "philosophical side" to LeConte (Byerly and Louderback, p. 142). Lawson became full professor in 1899 and served as head of the geology department from 1907 until his retirement in 1928. From 1914 to 1918 he was also dean of Berkeley's College of Mining.

Lawson began his teaching with characteristic vigor, even though he had never taught college geology and had to spend considerable time preparing for his classes. One of his innovations was to establish a systematic course on field geology, the first in the country, to introduce his students not only to methods of investigation but also to habits of thought and analysis. He took the class to Carmelo Bay to study formations that Josiah Dwight Whitney of the California Geological Survey had described in 1865 as Miocene strata metamorphically altered by the intrusion of molten granite. However, Lawson found no evidence of metamorphism, recognizing instead that the Miocene sediments lay unconformably on the eroded surface of the granite. Discovering Whitney's mistake stimulated Lawson to reexamine other sites and to remind his students not to accept uncritically the reports of other geologists.

As department chair, Lawson added several new courses to the curriculum, including microscopic petrography, physical geology, geomorphology, economic geology, and the geology of California. Between 1892 and 1894 he traveled the coast of California by boat and on horseback, observing terraces 500 to 1,500 feet high and concluding that much of the coast had risen from the sea. In cooperation with the United States Geological Survey (USGS) he and his students surveyed and mapped part of the central coast ranges, their years of work culminating in publication of the San Francisco Folio of the *Geologic Atlas* by the USGS in 1914. In an 1895 paper Lawson introduced the term "Franciscan Series" to refer to the complex rock assemblage—now known to have been formed by the collision of the North American and Pacific continental plates—that underlies much of central California's coast. In 1893, to provide a means of publication for the new work being done by himself and others, Lawson brought out the first issue of the *Bulletin of the Department of Geology of the University of California*, which he edited for the next thirty-five years. He also helped organize the western or Cordilleran Section of the Geological Society of America, serving as its first secretary from 1900 to 1905 and as its chairman from 1907 to 1911.

In 1906, immediately following the devastating San Francisco earthquake of 18 April, California's governor appointed an investigating committee of eight members that included Lawson, Grove Karl Gilbert of the USGS, John C. Branner of Stanford, and Harry Fielding Reid of Johns Hopkins University. Lawson was elected chairman and by May had prepared a widely disseminated preliminary report (repr. in *Science* 23 [1906]: 961–67). His organization of the work by twenty-five scientists and his expert editorial supervision resulted in *The California Earthquake of April 18, 1906: Report of the State Earthquake Investigation Commission* (vol. 1, 1908; repr. 1969), which has been called "a milepost in the development of an understanding of earthquake origin" (Byerly and Louderback, p. 143). The report included scientific studies of movement for at least 190 miles along the San Andreas fault, identified for the first time as being one continuous rift probably more than 600 miles long. Also included were descriptions of destruction caused by the quake and many photographs, maps, and seismograms from stations worldwide. Volume two of the commission's report, *The Mechanics of the Earthquake* (1910), by geophysicist H. F. Reid, contained the first full exposition of the elastic rebound theory, which has become the generally accepted explanation of the origin of earthquakes.

As an authority on ore deposition and economic geology, Lawson worked at various times as a mining consultant and served as an expert witness in court cases. He was also consulted on the geological aspects of bridge, dam, and railroad tunnel construction. In later years he became interested in the subject of isostatic adjustment—the process by which adjacent blocks of the earth's crust, which rest on the plastic mantle, achieve equilibrium through vertical displacement. Lawson published eighteen papers on isostasy and its relation to the formation of mountains, the fluctuation of sea level, and other physical phenomena.

Lawson's distinguished career as scientist and educator was recognized with several honorary degrees and medals. He was elected a member of the National Academy of Sciences in 1924 and president of the Geological Society of America in 1926. However, he had a complex and often forbidding personality. He could be cold and quick to criticize what he perceived as shoddy thinking, and yet he inspired a loyal following among his students, who included Charles Palache, Frederick Ransome, and Francis Vaughan. Lawson's ongoing rivalry with Bailey Willis of Stanford University was well known to those who heard them clash verbally at scientific meetings. When Willis challenged Lawson's opinion that the rock under the Golden Gate Bridge was stable, a bitter and well-publicized controversy arose that resulted in their final estrangement. Underneath his severe exterior, however, Lawson was sensitive, tenderhearted, and generous to students in need. In spite of a strict Presbyterian upbringing he was scornful of organized religion and referred to the Bible as "all fairy stories" yet wrote poetry that expressed deep feelings about love and death (Vaughan, pp. 234–36). Active and vigorous almost to the end, Lawson died in a nursing home in San Leandro, California, a year after suffering a cerebral hemorrhage.

• Lawson's papers are in the Bancroft Library at the University of California, Berkeley. Other publications by Lawson include: "The Post-Pliocene Diastrophism of the Coast of Southern California," *Bulletin of the Department of Geology of the University of California* 1 (1893): 115–60; "The Archean Geology of Rainy Lake Restudied," *Geological Survey of Can-*

ada, *Memoir* 40 (1913); and "The Sierra Nevada in the Light of Isostasy," *Geological Society of America Bulletin* 47 (1936): 1691–1712. The only book-length biography is Francis E. Vaughan, *Andrew C. Lawson: Scientist, Teacher, Philosopher* (1970), with bibliography. See also "Memorial to Andrew Cowper Lawson," by colleagues Perry Byerly and George D. Louderback, in *Proceedings Volume of the Geological Society of America, Annual Report for 1953* (May 1954): 141–47 (repeated in slightly different form in National Academy of Sciences, *Biographical Memoirs* 37 [1964]: 185–204).

MARGARET D. CHAMPLIN

LAWSON, James (9 Nov. 1799–24 Mar. 1880), editor, author, and insurance broker, was born in Glasgow, Scotland, the son of James Lawson, a merchant. His mother's identity is not known. Lawson entered the University of Glasgow at the age of thirteen but presumably did not graduate because he left Scotland in 1815. Settling in New York, he worked as an accountant in the firm of Alexander Thomson & Co., which was owned by and named for his maternal uncle. Lawson became a member of the firm in 1822 and remained there until 1826, when the company failed. This turned out to be a rather opportune event; Lawson had been sending submissions of his writing to his long-time friend James G. Brooks, one of the founders of the weekly *New York Literary Gazette and American Athenaeum*, and after Alexander Thomson & Co. closed, he was able to turn his full attention to journalism and literature. Soon thereafter, Lawson reviewed, for the *Literary Gazette*, the New York debut of American-born actor Edwin Forrest, as Iago in *Othello*, and the two subsequently developed a lifelong friendship. One of Lawson's earliest editorial efforts began in 1821 when Edinburgh publisher John Mennon, with whom Lawson had been corresponding, chose him to select the American writers to be included in Mennon's *Literary Coronal*, a collection of miscellaneous verse and prose. (Subsequent editions appeared in 1823 and 1826.) Notable among Lawson's selections were works by William Cullen Bryant, Brooks, and Fitz-Greene Halleck.

All of Lawson's principal works were published anonymously (and some privately). His first work, published simultaneously in Edinburgh and the United States, was *Ontwa, the Son of the Forest* (1822), a poetic narrative chronicling Indian life, with notes by Lewis Cass, secretary of war under President Andrew Jackson, who was then territorial governor of Michigan. (It was reprinted in Glasgow in 1828 in the *Columbian Lyre; or, Specimens of Transatlantic Poetry*.) Also during this period Lawson wrote *Giordano*, a romantic tragedy that was performed only three times at the Park Theatre during November and December of 1828. So unsuccessful was the play that Lawson never again attempted to write for the stage, though *Giordano* was published four years later. He never lost his enthusiasm for the theater, however. In 1829, when Forrest initiated a competition for a play in which the hero was a Native American, Lawson, along with Bryant and Halleck, made up the jury that selected *Metamora*,

John Augustus Stone's play about Philip (Metacom), the great Wampanoag sachem. The production brought Forrest much acclaim.

When the *Literary Gazette* ceased publication in 1827, Lawson, along with Brooks and John B. Skilman, founded the *Morning Courier*; he remained a co-editor of the *Courier* until 1829, when he moved to the *Mercantile Advertiser*, which he comanaged with Amos Butler until 1833. During this time Lawson also wrote *Tales and Sketches, by a Cosmopolite* (1830), a somewhat overly sentimentalized collection of stories set in Scotland.

In 1833 Lawson went into the marine insurance business and in 1837 was named vice president of the Washington Marine Insurance Company, where he remained for the duration of his professional life. During this period he married Mary Eliza Donaldson. Their home in Yonkers, New York, became a gathering place for his literary clique. Lawson's later writings included *Poems: Gleanings from Spare Hours of a Business Life*, published in 1857, followed by *Liddesdale; or, The Border Chief*, a tragedy in blank verse, in 1861 and the domestic drama *The Maiden's Oath* in 1877. His poetry and critical pieces appeared in the *Knickerbocker*, Sargent's *New Monthly*, the *Southern Literary Messenger*, and *American Monthly Magazine*.

Lawson's most significant literary contribution was not as a writer but as a friend and adviser to luminaries such as Edwin Forrest, William Gilmore Simms, James G. Brooks, and Edgar Allan Poe, all of whom were frequent visitors to Lawson's home. After many years of poor health, Lawson died in Yonkers.

• Numerous references to Lawson can be found in W. R. Alger, *Life of Edwin Forrest* (1877), and in Lawrence Barrett, *Edwin Forrest* (1881). Another interesting reference is G. E. Woodberry, *Edgar Allan Poe* (1885). See also J. G. Wilson, *The Poets and Poetry of Scotland* (1876), and W. M. MacBean, *Biographical Register of St. Andrews Society of the State of New York* (1925). An obituary is in the *New York Times*, 25 Mar. 1880.

ALI LANG-SMITH

LAWSON, John (fl. 1700–Sept. 1711), author and surveyor, was born in London, England, the son of Andrew Lawson, a salter (his mother's identity is unknown). In the early twentieth century historians had speculated that Lawson was either a Scotsman, related to scientist Isaac Lawson, or a descendant of the Lawsons of Brough Hall in Yorkshire. More recently, however, Hugh Talmage Lefler has presented a convincing argument on behalf of Lawson's London origins. Lawson's surveying work and his writings on natural history indicate that he had had practical scientific training. An entry in the Court-Book of the London Society of Apothecaries indicates that a John Lawson was apprenticed to apothecary John Chandler in 1675 for a term of eight years. At a later time the John Lawson who was prominent in early North Carolina corresponded with and sent botanical specimens to James Petiver, naturalist and London apothecary. The John Lawson who left England in 1700 signed "Gent."

after his name and possessed sufficient financial resources to travel widely without having to immediately find employment.

According to Lawson, an accidental conversation "with a Gentleman who had been Abroad" led to a spur-of-the-moment decision to take ship for Carolina. He landed at Charles Town in August 1700. On 28 December 1700, in company with six Englishmen and four native guides, Lawson set out to explore the Carolina interior and to make his way by land to Virginia, a journey previously accomplished by only a few dozen Indian traders.

Again a chance meeting redirected Lawson's life. Near modern Hillsborough, North Carolina, Lawson and his traveling companions met several Indian traders who had just come from Virginia. They warned the Carolinians that a dangerous Iroquois war party was active to the north. Rather than turning back, Lawson and his companions headed east toward the North Carolina coast. Lawson ended what he estimated was a journey of "a thousand miles," but which was closer to 550 miles, at an English plantation on the Pamlico River. Being free to settle wherever he might choose, and "being well received by the inhabitants, and pleased with the goodness of the country," Lawson resolved to settle in what was then an isolated and sparsely populated corner of the Carolina colony.

Isolation suited Lawson. He built a cabin at what would become New Bern and apparently lived as something of a recluse for several years. Because Lawson was one of the better-educated residents of the Pamlico Sound region, after a year or two he was engaged to survey and explore on behalf of colonial officials. In 1708, after Lawson had performed successfully as a deputy to the surveyor general of the province, the Lords Proprietors appointed him surveyor general for the portion of the colony that lay north of Cape Fear.

In 1705 Lawson had joined with several Pamlico River residents in purchasing a sixty-acre tract that was then incorporated as Bath, North Carolina's first town. Lawson chose the site, surveyed it, and mapped the town's seventy-one lots. Having relocated to Bath, Lawson served in 1707–1708 as clerk of the court and public register.

While Lawson was in London during 1709 supervising the publication of the work that would establish his reputation, the proprietors of Carolina were ordered by royal authorities to attempt to resolve their boundary dispute with Virginia. Lawson and former surveyor general Edward Moseley were delegated by the proprietors to represent Carolina interests in negotiations set for Williamsburg, Virginia. When the conferees failed during August 1710 to agree on a boundary, Virginia authorities accused Lawson and Moseley of having "no other end than to protract & Defeat the Settling [of] this Affair" in order to protect their own surveying and speculative interests. Not until 1728 would a boundary be agreed upon. It may well have been that because a resolution of the issue was delayed until the population of North Carolina had significantly increased, the northern fifth of the state was retained by North Carolina.

In January 1710 Lawson had supervised the movement from London to North Carolina of 650 Palatines. They were to settle an 18,750-acre tract at the juncture of the Neuse and Trent rivers, which had been purchased by a company headed by Baron Christopher von Graffenried. Lawson led overland from the James River to the Albemarle Sound the some three hundred Palatines who survived the voyage. Near where his first cabin had been located he laid out a town plan for what would become North Carolina's second oldest town, New Bern.

Lawson was not the first Englishman to explore the Carolina interior. Virginia traders had been among the Tuscarora, Occaneechee, Catawba, and other Carolina tribes more than two decades before Lawson's 1701 journey into the interior. Others had explored the Santee, Wateree, and Catawba rivers before him. In traversing central North Carolina from present-day Charlotte to Durham, Lawson traveled over what was already well known in Virginia as the "Occaneechee Path" and in South Carolina as the "Virginia Path." Lawson's contribution to history and ethnohistory lay in his determination to describe for others the topography, plants, animals, and native peoples of his adopted home. He wrote about Carolina, not as a partisan booster, but as a careful observer. His monument is *A New Voyage to Carolina; Containing the Exact Description and Natural History of That Country; Together with the Present State Thereof. And a Journal of a Thousand Miles Travel'd thro' Several Nations of Indians. Giving a Particular Account of Their Customs, Manners & c.*, which was published in 1709. Although reprinted with the title *The History of Carolina* (1714), Lawson's is a natural history and travel account as opposed to a standard history of the colony.

It is ironic that Lawson, who did more than any Carolinian or Virginian of his time to preserve a record of the life and ways of the Indians of the region, should have been executed at native hands. In September 1711 Lawson convinced von Graffenried to join him in an extended exploration of the Neuse River. About forty miles inland Lawson and von Graffenried's small boat was overwhelmed by a Tuscarora war party. The captives were carried to the native town of Catechna, near what is now Snow Hill. According to von Graffenried, Lawson unnecessarily initiated an argument with a native king. Because of this he was sentenced to death while the others were freed. No European witnessed the execution, but native contacts reported that the Tuscarora "stuck him full of fine small splinters of torch wood like hog's bristles and so set them gradually afire."

• John Lawson's *A New Voyage to Carolina* has been reprinted in two modern editions: Frances Latham Harriss, ed., *Lawson's History of North Carolina* (1937; repr. 1952), is based on Lawson's 1714 edition, while Hugh Talmage Lefler edited the 1709 edition as *A New Voyage to Carolina* (1967). Lefler's introduction provides the most complete and most analytical biographical sketch of Lawson. An earlier sketch by Stephen B. Weeks is found in Samuel A. Ashe, ed., *Biographical History of North Carolina* vol. 2 (1905–1907): 212–18. Attempts to identify the route of Lawson's journey through the interior have been made by Douglas L. Rights in "The Trading Path to the Indians," *North Carolina Historical Review* 8 (1931): 403–17; Hugh Talmage Lefler, introduction to *A New Voyage to Carolina* (1967); and Alan Vance Briceland, *Westward from Virginia* (1987).

ALAN V. BRICELAND

LAWSON, John Howard (25 Sept. 1894–11 Aug. 1977), playwright and screenwriter, was born in New York City, the son of Simeon Levy Lawson, the general manager of the Reuters News Agency for the United States and Canada, and Belle Hart. His father added the name Lawson in the 1880s to Levy, his original surname, in the hope of creating a shield against anti-Semitism. After graduating from the Cutler School in Manhattan, young Lawson proceeded to Williams College, from which he graduated in 1914. He then worked for a year for Reuters as a cable editor. Playwriting, however, was his true interest, as it had been since his adolescence. The first of his plays to be produced was *Servant-Master-Lover*, which was staged, unsuccessfully, in Los Angeles in 1916. He suffered a second failure in the same year when his play *Standards*, intended for Broadway, closed after performances in Syracuse and Albany.

During the First World War, Lawson served in France and Italy as an ambulance driver for the Red Cross. In 1918 he married Kate Drain, an American working with the Young Men's Christian Association, whom he had met overseas. The couple had one child. The marriage ended in divorce in 1923, and two years later Lawson married Susan Edwards, with whom he had two children.

Lawson's career began to flourish in the 1920s. His first play to reach Broadway was *Roger Bloomer* (1923), an attack on middle-class society in which workers, moving in unison at their jobs and deprived of individuality, seemed no more than mechanical devices. It is believed to be the earliest American expressionist play. *Processional* (1925) and *Nirvana* (1926) also are expressionist works, the latter, like *Roger Bloomer*, an attack on modern materialism. *Processional*, a satirical comedy with music set against the background of a coal strike in West Virginia, ranks as the best of Lawson's plays.

With these three works Lawson revealed that he had begun to identify with the political left. His career in the theater after *Processional*, which was produced by the centrist, apolitical Theater Guild, was largely spent with liberal-to-left producing units. In 1926 he, John Dos Passos, Michael Gold, and others founded the Workers' Theater, an amateur group. In the following year they and the writers Em Jo Basshe and Francis Edwards Faragoh established the New Playwrights' Theater under the sponsorship of the Wall Street banker Otto H. Kahn. This short-lived company offered eight plays, including two by Lawson: *Loud

Speaker (1927), a truculent satire on American politics accompanied by jazz music, and *The International* (1928), a baffling tragedy mixing jazz and a musical-comedy chorus with the affairs of a wealthy young man who takes a stand with the exploited masses in a revolution. Both were poorly received.

In 1934 articles written by Lawson for the magazines *New Masses* and *New Theatre* hinted strongly that he had joined the Communist party. In *New Theatre* he declared, "As for myself, I do not hesitate to say that it is my aim to present the Communist position and to do so in the most specific manner." Like most left-leaning writers, Lawson abandoned dramatic expressionism for naturalism at that time, a move required by the new Stalinist demand for socialist realism in the arts. Two of his four plays of the decade were produced by the prestigious Group Theater: the ironically titled *Success Story* (1932), a rags-to-riches tragedy in which financial success does not bring happiness to its young protagonist, and *Gentlewoman* (1934), an uneven work concerning the love affair of a beautiful woman and a proletarian novelist. *Success Story* found some admirers, but *Gentlewoman* quickly closed. A similarly unhappy fate overtook *The Pure in Heart* (1934), the story of a young woman and her criminal lover who are presented as the victims of capitalist economy. His final play of the 1930s, *Marching Song* (1937), which is centered in a strike, revealed in its poorly drawn characters that Lawson, the product of a middle-class upbringing, knew less than he imagined about the proletariat.

Lawson began a second, more lucrative career as a screenwriter in 1927, when he was called to Hollywood by Metro-Goldwyn-Mayer to provide a scene of spoken dialogue for Greta Garbo and John Gilbert in the silent film *Flesh and the Devil*. Although nothing came of this project and the film remained silent throughout, it led to many other assignments. His most memorable films are *Blockade* (1938), a drama of the Spanish Civil War that was gripping despite the producers' pusillanimous failure to identify the two warring sides, and *Action in the North Atlantic* (1943) and *Sahara* (1943), both starring Humphrey Bogart. Lawson's screenplay for *Blockade* was nominated for an Academy Award.

Lawson took part in the organization of the Screen Writers' Guild in 1933 and became the guild's first president. He served on the guild's board until 1940. He was also a founder of *Hollywood Quarterly*, a journal devoted to the study of film and other mass media. Between 1937 and 1950 he was the leader of the Communist faction in Hollywood. He conducted a writing clinic whose purpose (seldom achieved) was to ensure that the scripts of screenwriters in his circle were politically correct. In his Stalinist stance, Lawson was stubborn and dogmatic to a degree that often was self-defeating. Those who shared his views, however, looked on him as a brilliant advocate for politically conscious art.

Because of his refusal to answer questions about his political past at a hearing of the House Un-American

Activities Committee in 1947, Lawson was sentenced to a year in prison for contempt of Congress and was blacklisted in Hollywood. After his release he did some ghostwriting on films and wrote three plays, none of which was produced. *Parlor Magic* (1939; originally intended for, but rejected by, the Group Theater) was staged in East Germany and Russia in 1963. Lawson was also the author of *Theory and Technique of Playwriting* (1936; revised and extended in 1949 to include chapters on screenwriting), *The Hidden Heritage* (1950), *Film in the Battle of Ideas* (1953), and *Film: The Creative Process* (1964). He died in San Francisco.

• Lawson's papers are in the collection of Southern Illinois University. No full-scale biography has yet appeared, but a series of twenty articles published (1978–1981) by Leroy Robinson in *Bulletin of Faculty of Liberal Arts, Nagasaki University*, *Keiei To Keizai* (Management and Economy), and *Kyushi American Literature* provides much information about his life. See also Lawson, "Straight from the Shoulder," *New Theatre*, Nov. 1934. On his plays and career in the theater, see Malcolm Goldstein, *The Political Stage: American Drama and Theater of the Great Depression* (1974). On his films and career in Hollywood, see Gary Carr, *The Left Side of Paradise: The Screenwriting of John Howard Lawson* (1984); Edward Dmytryk, *It's a Hell of a Life but Not a Bad Living* (1978); Victor S. Navasky, *Naming Names* (1980); and Nancy Lynn Schwartz, *Hollywood Writers' Wars* (1982). An obituary is in the *New York Times*, 14 Aug. 1977.

MALCOLM GOLDSTEIN

LAWSON, Roberta Campbell (31 Oct. 1878–31 Dec. 1940), clubwoman and collector of Native-American music and artifacts, was born at Alluwe, Cherokee Nation, Indian Territory (now Okla.), the daughter of John Edward Campbell, a rancher and trader, and Emma Journeycake, a Delaware Indian whose parents had gone to live with the Cherokees after white settlers moved into Kansas. Her maternal grandfather was Charles Journeycake, last tribal chief of the Delawares, to whom she was especially devoted and from whom she acquired a lifelong appreciation of her Native-American heritage. Roberta and her younger brother (another brother died in infancy) spent their childhood in a remote rural setting but in a comfortable home where toys, books, musical instruments, and ponies abounded and where guests were always graciously entertained. After being instructed by her parents and a private tutor, Roberta attended a female seminary at Independence, Missouri. A lifelong interest and talent in music (Roberta reputedly assisted her mother as church organist in Alluwe at the age of ten) was complemented with specialized music studies while attending Hardin College, Mexico, Missouri.

In 1901 she married Eugene Beauharnais Lawson, who came to Indian Territory from Kentucky to practice law. The Lawsons settled in the town of Nowata, where their only child, a son, was born in 1905. As the territory approached statehood, Nowata grew rapidly, and the Lawsons were among its important civic and economic leaders. Eugene Lawson's oil interests be-

came the core of the Lawson Petroleum Company, and he was one of the founders of the First National Bank as well as the superintendent of schools. Roberta Lawson helped organize the first women's club in Nowata in 1903 (serving five years as its first president), aided in establishing a town park and public library, was active in the Young Women's Christian Association, and later became a director of the First National Bank.

Lawson's leadership skills soon led her to other women's club responsibilities. With the merging of the Indian Territory and Oklahoma federations of women's clubs in 1908, she became general secretary for all of Oklahoma. During World War I she served as president of the Oklahoma Federation of Women's Clubs and was state chair of the Women's Committee of the Counsel of National Defense. She also rose through the ranks of the General Federation of Women's Clubs, serving as director (1918–1922), music chair (1926–1928), second vice president (1928–1932), first vice president (1932–1935), and finally president (1935–1938).

Expanding oil interests prompted the Lawsons in 1927 to move to Tulsa, where, in addition to her women's club work, Lawson played key roles in educational and civic endeavors. She was the only female trustee of the University of Tulsa, a long-term member of the board of regents of the Oklahoma College for Women, and director of the Oklahoma Historical Society. In 1930 a committee appointed by the governor selected Lawson as one of the twenty-four outstanding women of Oklahoma, and she was later elected to the Oklahoma Hall of Fame. A lifelong friend of Will Rogers (the latter was born on a ranch adjoining her parents' home), Lawson honored his personal request to serve as executive chair of the committee that in the early 1930s dispersed to needy southwestern drought victims the sizable funds realized from his many benefit performances.

Lawson was elected president of the General Federation of Women's Clubs in 1935 in a spirited campaign marred by evidence of prejudice resulting from her Native-American ancestry. The theme of her three-year term was "Education for Living," and she was instrumental in introducing into Congress a bill (never passed) proposing creation of a national academy of public service, similar to West Point and Annapolis, to train personnel for civil and diplomatic service. Other activities during her tenure included a syphilis education program, a concentrated national campaign for the abolition of marijuana, and, with the assistance of the National Broadcasting Company, initiation of a regular series of nationwide radio programs on current events and musical and dramatic productions. Lawson herself gave over 250 public and radio addresses during her presidency. Although she apparently supported the presidency of Wendell Willkie in 1940, Lawson was a Democrat and served under Eleanor Roosevelt on the National Woman's Committee on the Mobilization of Human Needs.

Throughout her life Lawson was an ardent champion of the Native American, regardless of tribe or region. Aware that Indian culture was rapidly disappearing, she and her husband collected and preserved Indian artifacts, amassing a substantial holding of art objects, domestic and war implements, blankets, books, musical instruments, and other materials. Their spacious home in Tulsa became a private museum where visitors were always welcome, and their valuable collection was later donated to the city's Philbrook Art Center. Her particular interest in music led Lawson to preserve Native-American songs, especially the tribal chants and melodies of the Delawares. Lawson compiled a book, *Indian Music Programs for Clubs and Special Music Days* (1926), and she regularly gave lectures and concerts inspired by her Delaware heritage, often in white buckskin attire. Hers was always a striking physical presence, as the *Fort Worth* (Tex.) *Press* observed (21 June 1935) in saluting her election as president of the General Federation of Women's Clubs: "Once seen she is hard to forget because she is so different in appearance from the rank and file of her sex. Her type is rare. Tall, very erect, she has a strange dusky beauty, and a face almost Oriental in its outline and expression which is crowned with a coronet of midnight black braids. Also she has a dignity, a poise, a graciousness which is hard to match." Lawson was staunchly religious and a member of the Presbyterian church.

Roberta Campbell Lawson was a woman of great warmth, boundless energy, and considerable physical ability. She regularly rode horses and golfed, and she held the women's record for tarpon fishing in Texas for some years. Her health declined soon after her tenure as national women's club president ended, however. She died in Tulsa.

• Roberta Lawson also published an article, "The Evolution of Indian Music," *Community Arts and Crafts*, May 1929, pp. 15–17, 28. Biographical information on Lawson may be obtained from Luretta Rainey, *History of Oklahoma State Federation of Women's Clubs* (1939), pp. 53–58; Mildred M. Scouller, *Women Who Man Our Clubs* (1934), pp. 132–35; Mary Hays Marable and Elaine Boylan, *A Handbook of Oklahoma Writers* (1939), pp. 185–86; Marion E. Gridley, *American Indian Women* (1974), pp. 88–93; Mildred W. Wells, *Unity in Diversity: The History of the General Federation of Women's Clubs* (1953), pp. 104–8; and Mary Jean Houde, *Reaching Out: A Story of the General Federation of Women's Clubs* (1989), pp. 210–11. For information on Lawson's Native-American heritage, see Argye M. Briggs, *Both Banks of the River* (1954), and Coe Hayne, "The Only Delaware Voice That Spoke of God on the Trail of Tears," *Missions*, July 1937, pp. 346–49. Other biographical information, newspaper clippings, and documentation of Roberta Campbell Lawson's tenure as president of the General Federation of Women's Clubs may be obtained from files at the federation headquarters, Washington, D.C. See also Marguerite Drennen, "In the Service of Others," *Christian Science Monitor*, 8 Jan. 1936, p. 3. For news accounts of Lawson's support for the Willkie campaign, see two articles by James C. Hagerty: "Douglas and Hanes Join Willkie Ranks," *New York Times*, 23 July 1940, pp. 1 and 13, and "Willkie Counts on Wilson Democrats and Those of 1932," *New York Times*, 30 July 1940, pp. 1 and 14; a photograph of Lawson and Willkie is in the *New York Times*, 31 July 1940, p. 12. An obituary is in the *New York Times*, 1 Jan. 1941.

SIDNEY R. BLAND

LAWSON, Thomas (29 Aug. 1789?–15 May 1861), surgeon general of the U.S. Army Medical Department, was born in Virginia, the son of Thomas Lawson and Sarah Robinson. Nothing is known of his childhood or education, but in all likelihood he attended neither college nor medical school but received his medical education through apprenticeship with a local physician. He never married.

In 1809 Lawson became a surgeon's mate in the U.S. Navy, but in 1811 he resigned, joining the U.S. Army as a garrison surgeon's mate less than a month later. In 1813 he attained the position of surgeon with the Sixth Infantry Regiment, earning praise for his care of the wounded and his courage under fire during the War of 1812. In 1815 he became surgeon with the Seventh Infantry Regiment. By 1818, when the U.S. Army Medical Department was created as a permanent institution, Lawson was one of the department's senior surgeons, and by 1821, when the department was reorganized, he was the army's senior surgeon.

From 1821 until the death of Surgeon General Joseph Lovell in 1836, Lawson served at a number of forts in the West. Unhappy with his assignment to disease-ridden garrisons at isolated posts, he wrote long complaining letters to Lovell in which he displayed a belligerent attitude toward line officers who did not grant him the dignity and respect to which he believed he was entitled; he even became involved in a feud with the commanding officer of his regiment. Subsequently he also began attacking Lovell in a series of increasingly arrogant letters, complaining with especial vehemence about what he believed to be favoritism in assignments.

Lawson demonstrated throughout his career with the army great delight in being part of a unit involved in hostilities. In 1832 his efforts to gain assignment to a regiment involved in the Black Hawk War failed, but in 1836 he managed to be named second in command of a Louisiana volunteer regiment sent to join units fighting the Second Seminole War in Florida. After a few months, however, these duties came to an end, and Lawson was relegated to the position of medical director for the troops serving in Florida.

A few weeks after Lovell's death, Lawson became the new surgeon general. Apparently not enthusiastic about being tied to a chair in the surgeon general's office, Lawson did not at once return to Washington but rather remained in Florida until 1837, when he left briefly to accompany retiring president Andrew Jackson to his home in Tennessee. Lawson returned promptly thereafter to Florida, reporting for duty in the surgeon general's office only in 1838.

As surgeon general, Lawson fought for the rights and prestige of his medical officers and, on occasion, encouraged those he found particularly deserving. At the same time, he took obvious delight in demonstrating his power to any who appeared to question his judgment or authority. Perhaps his most spectacular feud involved surgeon William Beaumont, who apparently considered himself invulnerable as a result of the publicity that had been given to his pioneering research into the secret of human digestion. When Beaumont, who had received many favors from Lovell, threatened to leave the army as a result of Lawson's attitude, Lawson called his bluff and accepted Beaumont's resignation in 1839.

The Mexican War produced another opportunity for Lawson to go into the field of battle with the troops. In 1846 he eagerly accepted an invitation from Major General Winfield Scott, a close friend, to join him when the general led troops into Mexico. Lawson stipulated, however, that he would go to Mexico only in an advisory capacity. His goal was apparently to be able to taste the excitement of military action without being bogged down in the everyday petty details that he had come to despise. This move predictably resulted in confusion concerning the management and distribution of supplies and the direction of medical resources in Mexico.

In 1847 Congress voted rank for medical officers, who to that point had always technically been civilians. At the end of the Mexican War in 1848, Lawson himself was given the rank of brigadier general. The victory Lawson had won in achieving the long-sought goal of rank for medical officers was not complete, however, for the law was interpreted in such a manner as to require medical officers even of the highest rank and longest experience to obey all orders from the greenest of line officers.

Like his predecessor, Lovell, Lawson required his subordinates to submit regular reports concerning the diseases and climate that they encountered at the posts to which they had been sent and to include data on flora, fauna, and geological characteristics. Using the data they sent him, he was able to continue publishing the two series of volumes *Meteorological Registers* and *Statistical Reports*, initiated by Lovell. After 1856, however, Lawson became embroiled in a feud with the Smithsonian Institution about credit for the design of temperature and precipitation charts, and the quarrel led to accusations that the Medical Department had plagiarized the work of the Smithsonian.

In the years before the start of the Civil War, Lawson suffered from some type of arthritic or rheumatic condition. As the possibility of war became increasingly evident, he made no recognizable preparation to ready his department for the challenge. Not long after the attack on Fort Sumter he suffered a fatal stroke while being treated at the home of a physician in Norfolk, Virginia.

Lawson was a man of small talents and great sensitivity to criticism. He was successful in furthering the interests of the Medical Department and its officers, but he took delight in putting down the proponents of newer developments in the field of military medicine. This, together with his penchant for regarding suggestions for improvements in the department as arrogant insults, effectively blocked any progress or preparation in the department for the military struggle whose outbreak immediately preceded his death.

• No collection of Lawson papers exists. He is traditionally given credit for the Medical Department's *Meteorological Register*, vol. 2 (1851) and vol. 3 (1855), and for *Statistical Report on the Sickness and Mortality in the Army of the United States* (3 vols., 1840–1860), although all were actually the work of his subordinates. For more detailed information concerning his career, see Mary C. Gillett, "Thomas Lawson, Second Surgeon General of the U.S. Army: A Character Sketch," *Prologue* 14 (1982): 16–24, and Gillett, *The Army Medical Department, 1818–1865* (1987). Less critical examinations of Lawson's career are James M. Phalen, *Chiefs of the Medical Department, United States Army 1775–1940* (1940), and James E. Pilcher, *Surgeon Generals of the Army of the United States of America* (1905). For briefer discussions of Lawson's accomplishments, see Percy M. Ashburn, *A History of the Medical Department of the United States Army* (1929), and Harvey E. Brown, *The Medical Department of the United States Army from 1775 to 1873* (1873). An obituary is in the *Evening Star*, 20 May 1861.

MARY C. GILLETT

LAWSON, Thomas William (26 Feb. 1857–8 Feb. 1925), stockbroker and financial writer, was born in Charlestown, Massachusetts, the son of Thomas Lawson, a carpenter, and Anna Maria Loring. His father died when Lawson was eight. Lawson left school at twelve to support himself, working as an office boy at a stockbroker's establishment in Boston. He began speculating in stocks on his own and, at the age of seventeen, earned a sizable return from railroad investments. This coup convinced him that he had a talent for finance, even though he lost the money on another investment a few days later. In 1878 he married Jeannie Augusta Goodwillie, with whom he had six children. That same year he began operating as a stockbroker on his own.

In an era when corporate stocks were first being offered as investment instruments, financial advice consisted of advertisements and promotional articles in the press. Lawson's skill in using these devices to publicize the stocks he backed enabled him to attain a following among investors in New England. He became a millionaire by age thirty.

Lawson's first book, a history of the Republican party called *Our Bandanna* (1888), was published privately. His 64-page booklet, *The Krank: His Language and What It Means* (1888), was issued by a commercial publisher. Although his formal education had been curtailed early, he was well read and a capable writer.

Lawson's reputation for financial acumen led to his participation in the struggle over the Bay State Gas Company and control of gas franchises in 1894, in opposition to the Standard Oil Company. During negotiations, Lawson had many meetings with Henry H. Rogers, Standard's strategist, and became recognized as a valuable ally. When Lawson devised a plan to restructure the copper mining industry, he brought it to Rogers in 1897.

The Standard Oil group implemented the plan and bought the Anaconda Copper Company for $39 million, giving its owners a check payable at the National City Bank with the stipulation that the check not be cashed for an agreed period. Lawson and Rogers in 1899 formed the Amalgamated Copper Company and had it purchase Anaconda, issuing $75 million in stock, which was pledged to the bank in return for a loan to make good on the check. Lawson's part of the plan was to sell the stock to the public to repay the loan and make a profit.

As a result of Lawson's promotional skills, the stock offering was over-subscribed. The share price of Amalgamated jumped from the offering price of $100 to $130. Soon thereafter, however, its price fell to $75. Lawson purchased more shares to support the price, but it continued to fall, eventually reaching $33. The Standard Oil group had made a very large profit at virtually no expense, while investors in Amalgamated lost most of the value of their holdings. Lawson claimed to have lost millions and after a few years recognized that he and the investors who had trusted him had been deceived about the worth of Amalgamated's assets.

During this same period, Lawson had built a yacht in order to compete for the America's Cup in 1901. The New York Yacht Club excluded him from the trial competition because he was not a club member. He turned the refusal into a public controversy, writing *The Lawson History of the America's Cup* (1902), which made him prominent in New York City. When he expressed his misgivings about the Amalgamated deal, the editors of *Everybody's Magazine* induced him to write a series about it, which was published in 1904–1905 as "Frenzied Finance." The magazine's circulation soared, and Lawson began writing a regular column, "Lawson and His Critics." He also authored a 31-page booklet, *Getting Even* (1905), under the pseudonym Thomas W. Roastem and published the magazine series as a book, *Frenzied Finance* (1905).

A blend of muckraking, financial information, and autobiography, *Frenzied Finance* elicited mixed reactions. The contemporary journalist Charles Edward Russell found it difficult to determine how much of Lawson "was business acumen, how much megalomania, how much love of the spotlight, how much resentment against his business associates, and how much a sincere desire to expose and correct great evils" (Morris, pp. 293–94). The book went through several printings, and Lawson became a national figure.

Although he laid blame for the Amalgamated debacle on what he called "the system" and not on individuals, Lawson named the individuals responsible, including himself. He traced out the history of the deal and of his association with the Standard Oil group. He offered as evidence letters and his own recollection of conversations with members of the group, especially Rogers. He recounted his efforts to promote Amalgamated stock but included his unusual advertisements warning about the stock when it turned sour. Lawson hoped "that those whose deviltry is exposed . . . may see in a true light the wrongs they have wrought—and repent."

For the remainder of his life, Lawson continued to operate as a stockbroker and to write books. His later books, including a novel, *Friday, the Thirteenth* (1907); *The Remedy* (1912), Lawson's proposal for government regulation of securities; *The High Cost of Living* (1913); and *The Leak* (1919), were not as popular as *Frenzied Finance*. He was never taken to court by the Standard Oil group for his revelations, but his business as a stockbroker declined, and many of his later deals fared poorly, apparently because of the influence of "the system." He died at a low point in his fortunes, in his mansion in Egypt, Massachusetts, where he had dwelled while awaiting its sale at the hands of the bank that had foreclosed on it.

Although the system Lawson exposed would ultimately be reformed during the New Deal of the 1930s, Lawson's writings had little immediate impact on the securities industry. His disclosure of how life insurance companies invested their policyholders' assets in speculative ventures such as the Amalgamated deal did lead to an investigation of that industry in 1905 and subsequent regulation of its practices. *Frenzied Finance* remains of interest as an insider's account of the pecuniary guile of an era filled with stock market machinations.

• Lawson's own writings contain much autobiographical information, but with the exception of *Frenzied Finance*, they are not easily found in libraries. Personal data on him also accompany his writings for *Everybody's Magazine*. A section on Lawson is included in Stewart H. Holbrook, *The Age of the Moguls* (1953), pp. 168–75. See also Lloyd Morris, *Postscript to Yesterday* (1965), pp. 293–99; Louis Filler, *The Muckrakers: New and Enlarged Edition of Crusaders for American Liberalism* (1976), chap. 14; Filler, *Appointment at Armageddon* (1976); and Filler's introduction to David Graham Phillips, *The Deluge* (1905, repr. 1969), a fictionalized account of Lawson. Obituaries are in the *Boston Herald* and the *Boston Transcript*, both 9 Feb. 1925.

DONALD R. STABILE

LAWSON, Victor Fremont (9 Sept. 1850–19 Aug. 1925), newspaper publisher, was born in Chicago, the son of Iver Lawson, a real estate developer, and Melinda Nordvig. Proprietor of the *Chicago Daily News* from 1876 to 1925 and a chief organizer of the Associated Press, Lawson was one of the first major newspaper publishers in the modern twentieth-century mold. He was a business manager, not a journalist. Unlike the great nineteenth-century publishers, Lawson neither wrote nor edited. He managed. And the product of his management was one of the most successful newspapers in the world and the first medium of mass communication in Chicago.

Lawson grew up with Chicago. The son of Norwegian immigrants, he was born into a frontier town of 28,000. Seventy-five years later and only blocks away, he died in a metropolis of three million. The *Chicago Daily News* reflected its proprietor's lifelong devotion to the city. It was quintessentially an *urban* newspaper, committed to private business but also to activist government, to social welfare, and to the broad public life of the city. It was a progenitor of the kind of progressive reform politics that came to flower in many cities during the early twentieth century.

Lawson was the product of Chicago public schools, though in 1869 his family sent him to Phillips Academy in Andover, Massachusetts, to prepare to enter Harvard. Eye troubles and his father's business losses in the Chicago Fire of 1871, however, brought him home. In 1872 Iver Lawson died, and Victor became manager of the family enterprises.

One family business was the *Skandinaven,* a Norwegian-language daily, in whose building Lawson set up his office. Another tenant in the building was the *Chicago Daily News,* a struggling penny paper started in December 1875 by Melville E. Stone. Lawson took an interest in the paper, and in July 1876, with the paper nearly bankrupt, he bought the property for $6,000 and became publisher. Stone remained editor.

Under Stone's editorship, the *Daily News* appealed to middle-class businessmen as well as to working-class laborers. The paper was clean and tasteful, yet cheap and lively. The editorial staff included Eugene Field, the creator of the modern newspaper column. While Stone presided over the merry men of the newsroom, his more austere partner counted pennies and lines of advertising in the business office. The combination clicked. A morning edition, the *Morning News,* was added in 1881. By 1885 the circulation of the afternoon *Daily News* hit 100,000, one of the largest in the world at that time.

The success of the *Daily News* grew from the image it conveyed of its city and its readers. Rather than provide a smorgasbord of information aimed at the disparate tastes of individual readers (in the manner of other large dailies of the time, such as the *Chicago Times*), Stone and Lawson tried to find the common denominator—those interests that bound a heterogeneous population together as citizens of the city. In news and features, this meant a tight focus on a handful of ongoing news stories, as well as a daily short story (fiction), household tips, and consumer protection advice. In editorial advocacy, it meant a concern with streets and sewers, utilities, schools, hospitals, and other public institutions that touched the lives of people across class and neighborhood.

In the early years, Lawson's contributions lay in circulation and advertising. Lawson was considered a genius in promoting newspaper circulation through posters, handbills, premiums, games, contests, and door-to-door solicitations. More important, he was a pioneer of modern newspaper advertising methods. Unlike most publishers of the time, Lawson established an open system of uniform ad rates based upon detailed, sworn statements of circulation. He made deals on his own terms. He frequently wrote to advertising agents that "we wish it distinctly understood that the Chicago *Daily News* does not *receive* propositions from advertisers—it *makes* propositions *to* advertisers."

In 1888 Stone unexpectedly resigned, and Lawson assumed responsibility for the entire operation of the newspaper. Though now editor as well as publisher, Lawson chose to delegate day-to-day editorial authority to a managing editor, while he continued to run the business end. The paper and its proprietor grew rich. Circulation reached 200,000 by 1894. The morning edition (called the *News Record* from 1892 to 1893, the *Record* thereafter) prospered as well.

In the 1890s, Lawson used his newspapers and his private fortune to promote philanthropy and reform, especially the work of nonpartisan "good government" organizations such as the Chicago Municipal Voters' League. In 1898 he began the Foreign Service (first as a service of the *Record,* then transferred to the *Daily News* in 1901), which became one of the most famous networks of overseas correspondents of any American newspaper.

Though Lawson was the enemy of monopoly in other industries, such as railroads and utilities, he was a skilled builder of oligopolies in his own. Most important were the Associated Press and the Daily Newspaper Association of Chicago. Lawson was president of the modern Associated Press, 1894–1900, and a director, 1893–1925. Under his leadership, the New York AP and the Western AP were combined and reorganized. The Daily Newspaper Association, also under Lawson's leadership, organized to coordinate and control business competition and labor relations in the Chicago press. In these activities, Lawson followed principles typical of progressive businessmen. He supported government regulation of private business when it touched the public interest but favored self-regulation of business when, in his judgment, it did not.

Lawson married Jessie Strong Bradley in 1880; she died in 1914 after many years of illness. They had no children. By all accounts, Lawson was a loving husband, a loyal friend, and a generous benefactor of the New England Congregational Church of Chicago.

Lawson's will made no provision for the continuation of the *Daily News*; it was simply to be sold with the rest of the multi-million-dollar estate, the proceeds to go largely to charity. Unlike many other publishers of his era, Lawson believed that his newspaper was greater than himself. Throughout his life, he had never imagined the *Daily News* to be the extension of his own genius or the amplification of his own voice. Rather, he viewed himself as simply a faithful manager of a business enterprise that had its own life. And he was right. Under new ownership, the *Chicago Daily News* maintained the Stone/Lawson tradition and prospered for decades. But like many other venerable afternoon newspapers, the *Daily News* suffered grave advertising and circulation losses in the 1960s and 1970s and finally met its own death on 4 March 1978.

• Lawson's papers, chiefly business correspondence, are in the Newberry Library, Chicago. Charles H. Dennis, *Victor Lawson: His Time and His Work* (1935), is the major biography. Also useful for personal and business details are Melville E. Stone, *Fifty Years a Journalist* (1921), and Henry Justin Smith, *A Gallery of Chicago Editors* (1930). Published studies of the *Chicago Daily News* include David Paul Nord, *Newspapers and New Politics: Midwestern Municipal Reform, 1890–1900* (1981), and Donald J. Abramoske, "The Founding of the *Chicago Daily News*," *Journal of the Illinois State Historical Society* 59 (1966): 341–53. The most detailed studies of the newspaper are three unpublished dissertations: Donald J. Abramoske, "The *Chicago Daily News*: A Business History, 1875–1901" (Ph.D. diss., Univ. of Chicago, 1963); Royal J. Schmidt, "The *Chicago Daily News* and Illinois Politics, 1876–1920" (Ph.D. diss., Univ. of Chicago, 1957); and Robert J. Tree, "Victor Fremont Lawson and His Newspapers, 1890–1900: A Study of the Chicago *Daily News* and the Chicago *Record*" (Ph.D. diss., Northwestern Univ., 1959).

DAVID PAUL NORD

LAWSON, Yank (3 May 1911–18 Feb. 1995), jazz trumpeter and bandleader, was born John Rhea Lawson in Trenton, Missouri, the son of an engineer on the Rock Island Railroad. His parents' names are unknown. His mother played piano and gave him lessons beginning at age five; he also took up saxophone at about age nine or ten. By one account, perhaps erroneous, his nickname came from boyhood comparisons of his playing to that of a local professional saxophonist, Yank Smith; Lawson told interviewer Phil Attebury that the nickname derived from boyhood teasing about his being a New York Yankee fan living in St. Louis Cardinals and Browns' territory. In his early teens he took up cornet and then switched to trumpet, which he studied with Carl Webb.

For two years Lawson took liberal arts courses at the University of Missouri while playing with a college dance band. By this time he had become sufficiently accomplished to be offered an opportunity to join a professional touring group, and around 1931 he dropped out of college. In 1932 he joined trumpeter Wingy Manone's band in Louisiana and then went north to Minneapolis to visit his girlfriend Harriett. In St. Paul he became a member of drummer Ben Pollack's dance band. Lawson married Harriett (maiden name unknown) in 1933; they had four children. Pollack held residencies in New York City and Galveston, Texas, where Lawson is recalled for his heroism in saving the crippled singer Connee Boswell when a flash flood hit the Hollywood Dinner Club.

After a period without work, Pollack brought Lawson to Hollywood, where he appeared in the film short *Ben Pollack and His Orchestra* (1934). But Pollack's activities in Hollywood proved far less lucrative than promised, and the band quit en masse. Early in 1935 Pollack's sidemen went east to New York City, where Lawson worked as a freelancer until Pollack's men reorganized under the leadership of singer Bob Crosby in June. Working elements of Dixieland jazz into a big band context, the Bob Crosby Orchestra became one of the leading groups of the swing era. Lawson was a featured soloist, heard on such recordings as "Dogtown Blues" and "Who's Sorry Now?" (both 1937), the latter with the Bob Cats, Crosby's eight-piece Dixieland band-within-the-band.

Trombonist Tommy Dorsey repeatedly asked Lawson to join his band and finally offered a salary so generous that the trumpeter could not refuse. He worked with Dorsey from August 1938 through November 1939, recording solos on "Hawaiian War Chant" (1938) and "Milenberg Joys" (1939). Initially his wife and child accompanied him on tours with Dorsey. After the birth of twins, this was no longer feasible, and his wife and children settled in New York City. Lawson accepted work with theater and radio orchestras there in 1940 so that he could spend more time with his family, but he became desperately bored after securing a job playing the same Broadway show, *Louisiana Purchase*, night after night for fourteen months. When the show closed in May 1941, he was free to resume touring, and he rejoined Crosby, appearing with the band in the film *Reveille with Beverly* (1943), which was released after Crosby had disbanded in California in the fall of 1942. Lawson returned to his family in New York City after the band's demise, and he briefly joined Benny Goodman's band late that same year.

Lawson then embarked on a long career as a studio musician, playing at sessions like the one at which Frank Sinatra recorded "Stormy Weather" in December 1944. In 1951 he formed the Lawson-Haggart Jazz Band with Crosby's former string bassist Bob Haggart to record new arrangements of classic early jazz recordings. The album *South of the Mason-Dixon Line* (1953) showcases these arrangements. In January 1957 he took the musical role of King Oliver, playing alongside Louis Armstrong on three tracks in the boxed LP set *Satchmo: A Musical Autobiography*. In April 1958 he joined pianists Billy Taylor and Willie "the Lion" Smith for small group performances on the "Ragtime" episode of the educational television series *The Subject Is Jazz*. He performed with Armstrong at the Newport Jazz Festival in 1962 and participated in mid-1960s reunions of the Crosby orchestra that included a tour of Japan and Australia in 1964 and an engagement in 1966 at the Rainbow Grill in New York City. He worked in New York at Eddie Condon's Club intermittently from 1964 to 1966.

During this same period Lawson performed annually in Denver with the Eight (later Nine, and finally Ten) Greats of Jazz. He extended his ongoing New York studio work to television shows, including a long stand as a member of the *Tonight* show band on NBC. Late in 1968 Lawson left the show to return to the jazz life as co-leader with Haggart of an excellent but pretentiously titled group, the World's Greatest Jazz Band of Yank Lawson and Bob Haggart (also the title of their first album, recorded in 1968). Among the band's many distinguished swing and Dixieland members were trumpeter Billy Butterfield, tenor saxophonist Bud Freeman, soprano saxophonist Bob Wilber, pianist Ralph Sutton, and singer Maxine Sullivan. The band toured regularly until 1978, when the leaders continued under their earlier name, the Lawson-Haggart Jazz Band, while also working as freelancers and participating in Crosby's regular reunions. Apart from an ulcer operation that interrupted his career in 1981, Lawson continued performing up until the time of his death in Indianapolis.

Lawson was one of the leading Dixieland and swing trumpeters. He was a fun-loving, conscientious man whose personality evidently transferred directly into his playing, which was characteristically exuberant, powerful, polished, and joyous. As a prominent soloist with Crosby and a subsequent bandleader for decades thereafter, he was one of the leading exponents of a style that incorporated aspects of arranged big-band swing music of the 1930s into a medium- to small-group Dixieland setting. This energetic but "clean-cut" approach to the New Orleans jazz tradition has been enormously influential on white jazz musicians and audiences worldwide, from professionals on the concert stage to amateurs in the pizza parlor.

• The essential survey of Lawson's career is John Chilton, *Stomp Off, Let's Go!: The Story of Bob Crosby's Bob Cats & Big Band* (1983). See also Herb Sanford, *Tommy and Jimmy: The Dorsey Years* (1972); Burt Korall, *The World's Greatest Jazz Band of Yank Lawson and Bob Haggart* (1973); Chilton, *Who's Who of Jazz: Storyville to Swing Street*, 4th ed. (1985); Bob Wilber, *Music Was Not Enough*, ed. Derek Webster (1987); Phil Atteberry, "An Interview with Yank Lawson," *Mississippi Rag* 20 (Dec. 1992): 30–33; James D. Shacter, *Loose Shoes: The Story of Ralph Sutton* (1994); Atteberry, "Yank Lawson Interview," *Cadence* 22 (Apr. 1996): 21–24. For musical analysis, see Gunther Schuller, *The Swing Era: The Development of Jazz, 1930–1945* (1989). An obituary is in the *New York Times*, 21 Feb. 1995.

BARRY KERNFELD

LAY, Benjamin (1681?–3 Feb. 1759), Quaker reformer and abolitionist, was born in Colchester, England, the son of William Lay, a yeoman, and Mary (maiden name unknown), members of the Society of Friends. Some sources cite his year of birth as 1677. Lay, self-taught, spent his adolescence and early adult years working as a glove maker's apprentice, a farmer, and a sailor, careers that were short-lived because of his hunched back and 4′7″ frame. In 1710 he abandoned maritime employment and returned to Colchester, where he married Sarah Smith of Deptford, also hunchbacked and of diminutive stature. The couple had no children. After being expelled from a Quaker meeting for speaking out against "hireling ministers," Lay and his wife left England in 1718 to settle in Barbados, where Lay worked as a merchant.

In Barbados Lay first came in contact with slavery and began his lifelong fight to end it. Lay himself participated in slavery's brutality by whipping two slaves who had tried to steal from his store, a catalytic incident for his activism, "I would give them Stripes sometimes," he wrote in 1737, "but I have been sorry for it many times, and it does grieve me to this day" (Lay, p. 40). Hundreds of slaves from the island's sugar plantations gathered at his home on Sundays to eat his food and listen to his sermons, some of which condemned the evils of human bondage. After intensifying hostility from slave owners compelled him to leave

the island, Lay and his wife returned to England before settling in Philadelphia in 1731. Troubled by Quaker apathy toward slavery in Philadelphia, they moved to nearby Abington a year later. Two years earlier Philadelphia Friends had condemned the antislavery activities of Ralph Sandiford, with whom Lay became good friends, including publication of a pamphlet critical of Quaker slaveholders without the requisite permission from the society. In Abington Lay constructed a home resembling a cave, living like an ascetic in order to demonstrate that one did not need to rely on slave labor, and the couple resumed their crusade against slaveholding. Sarah Lay, a minister in the Society of Friends and a member of the Abington Friends Meeting, provided constant support for his campaign until her death in 1735.

After his wife's death, Lay began to preach in earnest against the practice of slaveholding, which existed, though in a less cruel form than in Barbados, throughout the commonwealth. Lay considered slavery to be antithetical to the teachings of the Quakers, who believed that all humans were equal in the eyes of God. Slavery also encouraged idleness, he argued, and by growing his own food and making his own clothes he demonstrated that one did not need to rely on the labors of the enslaved for sustenance. His attempts to convince his fellow Quakers that slavery degraded both slaves and slave owners were confrontational and dramatic. He staged his protests at various Friends' meetings in New Jersey and in the Philadelphia area, though he did so as an unofficial member of the society; in late 1737 Lay was prohibited from attending the Abington Friends Meeting because he was a "frequent Disturber" and was sanctioned by the Philadelphia Meeting for being a "disorderly person."

Lay was ejected from meetings for speaking his mind and because of his guerrilla theater. In one instance, Lay stood before a meetinghouse with one bare foot in the snow to demonstrate the especially cruel treatment of slaves during the winter months, telling the Friends who expressed concern for him, "Ah you pretend compassion for me, but you do not feel for the poor slaves in your fields, who go all winter half clad" (Vaux, p. 28). In 1738 Lay shocked and angered Quakers attending the Philadelphia Yearly Meeting—held that year in Burlington, New Jersey—which was comprised of some of the most prominent citizens in colonial society and politics. Lay interrupted the meeting by proclaiming that slavery was "in direct opposition to every principle of reason, humanity, and religion. . . . It would be as justifiable in the sight of the Almighty, who beholds and respects all nations and colours of men with an equal regard, if you should thrust a sword through their hearts as I do through this book" (Vaux, p. 27). Lay proceeded to pierce a hollowed-out Bible that he held to his chest, which contained a "bladder" of red pokeberry juice. As the "blood" poured out of the Bible, sprinkling several stunned members in the process, he told the gathering, "Thus shall God shed the blood of those who have enslaved their fellow creatures."

Lay's most important antislavery publication, *All Slave-keepers That Keep the Innocent in Bondage, Apostates Pretending to Lay Claim to the Pure & Holy Christian Religion . . .* , was published by his friend Benjamin Franklin in 1737, though Franklin did so anonymously for fear of earning the wrath of Philadelphia's elite. (Quaker policy prior to 1753 prohibited the publication of abolitionist tracts.) Slavery, Lay wrote in his lengthy title, was the "notorious sin" and a "Practice so Gross and hurtful to Religion, and destructive to Government, beyond what words can set forth." The rambling 278-page document, which tested the editing skills of the young Franklin, enraged influential Quakers because Lay attacked ministers and elders "by whose example the filthy Leprosy and Apostacy is spread far and near" and because he claimed that the book was published at the "request and desire" of his "dear true and tender Friends, called Quakers." Lay attacked the leaders of the society because of the great influence they held in the colonial legislature and with their respective congregations. "The Leaders of the People cause them to Err," he argued. "Do you not consider that you are opening a Door to others, or setting them an Example to do the like by you," he asked (Lay, p. 43). The leading members of the Philadelphia Yearly Meeting had generated their wealth in part by using slave labor, and Lay's campaign depended on the reform of the society's official policy toward the ownership of slaves by its members. Quakers generally opposed the violent treatment of slaves but offered neither public condemnation of slaveholding nor censure of those involved in slave trading. He wrote, "I know no worse or greater stumbling Blocks the Devil has to lay in the way of honest Inquirers, than our Ministers and Elders keeping Slaves" (Lay, p. 85). The leaders of the Philadelphia Yearly Meeting responded by disowning Lay and publishing in Franklin's *Pennsylvania Gazette* the claim that Lay had acted outside "the religious community" in writing the book, which represented, they charged, "gross abuses, not only against some of their members, but against the whole Society" (Drake, p. 46).

After the "bladder of blood" protest and the publication of his book resulted in his alienation from society matters, Lay pursued his campaign in public markets. During one such demonstration in Philadelphia, Lay shattered tea cups to protest the consumption of tea harvested by slaves. Lay also conducted his campaign in the intimacy of neighbors' homes, admonishing families that owned slaves by appealing to their sense of compassion. He told one family that had invited him to eat at their table that he would not "partake with thee of the fruits of thy unrighteousness." One of his most daring acts was to lure to his cave the child of a farmer who ardently defended his right to keep slaves. When the farmer and his wife approached Lay's home at the end of the day's search for their child, he told them, "You may now conceive of the sorrow you inflict upon the parents of the negroe girl you hold in slavery, for she was torn from them by avarice" (Vaux, p. 29).

Lay continued to preach for the abolition of slavery as well as for the end of capital punishment and the religious education of poor children until his death at Abington, Pennsylvania. He was buried in a Quaker cemetery in Abington. Before he died Lay had the satisfaction of knowing that his efforts were not in vain. In 1758 the Philadelphia Yearly Meeting, led by a new generation of Quakers, finally made changes in its policy toward slaveholding by giving monthly meetings the authority to discipline members who bought, sold, or imported slaves into the colony. On hearing of the meeting's decision, Lay told a friend, "I can now die in peace" (Vaux, p. 51). Though the decision did not proscribe or ban Quaker slaveholding, it was the first step toward the eventual prohibition of Quaker slaveholding, which was codified by the Philadelphia Yearly Meeting in 1776.

Benjamin Rush wrote in the 1813 *Annual Monitor* that Lay was "the pioneer of that war, which has since been carried on so successfully, against the commerce and slavery of the negroes" (p. 8). Lay was not the first Quaker activist to assiduously campaign for the abolition of slavery and for the reform of the Society of Friends, but he was the most vocal and insistent; he was a "pertinacious gadfly," as John Greenleaf Whittier called him, hovering over the Quaker's conscience. His dramatic actions inspired a new generation of Quaker abolitionists and helped to impel the leaders of the society to rethink the issue of slave ownership in the context of their faith.

• In Pennsylvania, the Friends Historical Library at Swarthmore College and the Quaker Collection at Haverford College are the best locations for research material on Lay; minutes of the Philadelphia Yearly Meeting are available on microfilm. In London, the Religious Society of Friends in Britain maintains a collection of minutes of Colchester Friends Meetings and other documents in Friends House. Lay's major publication, *All Slave-keepers That Keep the Innocent in Bondage . . .* (1737), can be found on microfiche and contains William Burling's 1718 antislavery tract "An Address to the Elders of the Church." Benjamin Rush, "Biographical Anecdotes of Benjamin Lay," is in *The Annual Monitor; or, New Letter-Case and Memorandum Book* (1815). The standard biography is Roberts Vaux, *Memoirs of the Lives of Benjamin Lay and Ralph Sandiford; Two of the Earliest Public Advocates for the Emancipation of the Enslaved Africans* (1815). Lydia Maria Francis Child essentially reprinted Vaux's work in *Memoir of Benjamin Lay, Compiled from Various Sources*, published by the American Anti-Slavery Society in 1842, with only a few additional anecdotes. John Greenleaf Whittier discusses Lay's activities in his introduction to *The Journal of John Woolman* (1871), pp. 13–15.

For a different view of Lay's Barbados years and coverage of his years in London, see C. Brightwen Rowntree's biographical sketch in the *Journal of the Friends' Historical Society* 33 (1936): 3–19. See also Stanley H. G. Fitch, *Excerpts from Colchester Two Week Meeting, 1705–1741 and from Colchester Monthly Meeting, 1718–1755*. William C. Kashatus III wrote "Abington's Fiery Little Abolitionist," *Old York Road Historical Society Bulletin* 45 (1985): 35–39. For an understanding of Quakers and slavery in the colonial period see

Thomas E. Drake, *Quakers and Slavery in America* (1950), and Jean R. Soderlund, *Quakers and Slavery: A Divided Spirit* (1985).

PAUL ROSIER

LAY, John Louis (14 Jan. 1832–17 Apr. 1899), inventor and engineer, was born in Buffalo, New York, the son of John Lay, a businessman, and Frances Atkins. He was educated in the public schools in Buffalo. Strongly interested in mechanics, he was employed as an engine builder and in other capacities in the Pacific Mail Service. He also worked on various steam vessels on the Great Lakes. For a time he was chief engineer on a steamship operating out of New Orleans that was involved in trading activities in the Gulf of Mexico. Discharged by his employers shortly before the Civil War because he was a northerner, Lay settled in Iowa and, as a licensed first engineer, had charge of a steam vessel plying the Mississippi River.

In April 1861 Lay wrote former congressman William Vandever of Dubuque, Iowa, asking the latter's aid in securing a place as assistant engineer in the U.S. Navy. While at first Lay was deemed ineligible because of his comparative youth, he was advised that, because of his years of experience as a maritime engineer, he might stand for examination by a naval board. Having done so, he was appointed a second assistant engineer in July 1861. For the next seven months he served on blockade duty aboard the *Louisiana*. In February 1862 he participated in an expedition to block the mouth of the Albemarle and Chesapeake Canal. At about this time Lay began work on a naval torpedo of his own devising, using discarded boiler tubes. This activity was periodically interrupted by other duties. In November 1862, for example, he participated in an expedition that resulted in the capture of Greenville, North Carolina. In the spring of 1863 he and his vessel were involved in a naval action, protecting the city of Washington, D.C., from Confederate artillery firing from the Virginia shore of the Potomac.

In October 1863 Lay was promoted to first assistant engineer. Assigned to the command of the torpedo boat *Stromboli* (later the *Spuyten Duyvil*) in December 1863, he worked with chief engineer W. W. W. Wood to develop a new spar torpedo. One torpedo of Lay's devising was used by Lieutenant William Barker Cushing in October 1864 in a daring and successful effort to sink the Confederate ironclad vessel *Albemarle*, anchored on the Roanoke River near Plymouth, North Carolina. In December 1864 Lay was assigned to take the *Spuyten Duyvil* up the James River in Virginia, clear obstructions placed there by the Confederates, and attack other Confederate rams located there. There were several interruptions while Lay went to New York City to secure the necessary projectiles—some newly invented—and other equipment. On 5 January 1865, however, Lay discussed his plans with General Ulysses S. Grant, who recommended that the rams not be attacked until a concerted effort with army units could be organized. Lay accordingly remained on the James with the *Spuyten Duyvil*, removing obstructions and awaiting further instructions, until the war ended.

Lay resigned from the navy in May 1865 on grounds of injured health. His services were later retained by the Peruvian government, which requested his aid in preparing the harbor approaches to the city of Callao against an anticipated attack by a Spanish fleet. Lay worked on mine and torpedo defenses there for several years, returning to his home in Buffalo in 1867. There Lay completed work on several inventions, including a steam engine and locomotive for which he received patents in the summer and fall of 1867. Most of his time was spent on perfecting an electrically propelled moveable torpedo submarine. This device, powered by a stern engine using carbon dioxide gas and controlled by a wire deployed from another vessel or from shore, was built in 16- and 23-foot lengths, containing respectively 100 or 200 pounds of explosives at their forward ends. These weapons had a range of one and a half miles and could travel up to twelve miles an hour. Lay published an undated pamphlet, *Submarine Warfare: Fixed Mines and Torpedos. The Lay Moveable Torpedo: Its Superiority over All Other Implements of Submarine Warfare*, explicating the merits of his invention. Only two were sold to the U.S. Navy, but the Russian and Turkish governments purchased the rights to these devices, for which Lay was paid handsomely.

In about 1870 Lay moved to Europe, were he lived for more than a quarter century. Through unfortunate speculation he lost most of his fortune. Returning to New York in the late 1890s, he attempted unsuccessfully to recoup his finances by marketing some of his later inventions. A former schoolmate found him ill and impoverished in a boarding house and had him admitted to Bellevue Hospital in New York City, where he died. Lay was married and had at least one daughter and one son.

• There is a limited amount of correspondence concerning Lay's enlistment in the navy and a typewritten career summary in the ZB Files of the Early Records Section, Operation Archives Branch, Naval Historical Center, Washington, D.C. Some official correspondence is in various Civil War–era navy letter files, and a transcript of Lay's naval service is in the files of the U.S. Navy's Bureau of Navigation, all at the National Archives. A brief outline of Lay's naval service was published in Thomas H. S. Hamersly, *Complete General Navy Register of the United States of America, from 1776 to 1887* (1888). Published correspondence and other materials concerning his Civil War naval service are in *Official Records of the Union and Confederate Navies in the War of the Rebellion*, ser. 1, vols. 8, 9, 11, and 12, and ser. 2, vol. 1. Cushing's account of his action against the CSS *Albemarle* is "The Destruction of the Albemarle," in *Battles and Leaders of the Civil War*, vol. 4 (1888). Other accounts of this action include Virgil Carrington Jones, *The Civil War at Sea*, vol. 3 (1962), and Ivan Musicant, *Divided Waters: The Naval History of the Civil War* (1995). An obituary is in the *New York Times*, 21 Apr. 1899.

KEIR B. STERLING

LAYDEN, Elmer F. *See* Four Horsemen of Notre Dame.

LAYNE, Bobby (19 Dec. 1926–1 Dec. 1986), football player, was born Robert Lawrence Layne in Santa Anna, Texas, the son of Sherman Cecil Layne, an automobile salesman and farmer, and Beatrice (maiden name unknown). Layne's parents separated early in his life, and he remained with his father, who died when Layne was seven. After his father's death, Layne lived with his adopted parents, Wade and Lavinia Hampton, in Fort Worth, and later in Dallas. At Dallas's Highland Park High School, Layne won renown as a football and basketball player. He also pitched for an American Legion baseball team from Dallas that went to the state championship.

In 1944 Layne entered the University of Texas, where he starred, first, as a football tailback in coach Dana X. Bible's single-wing formation. In late 1944 he joined the merchant marine, and he missed part of the 1945 season. The war ended before he saw active duty, however. In his senior season at Texas he was the quarterback in new head coach Blair Cherry's T formation. Named to several All-America teams, Layne completed 11 of 12 passes to help upend Missouri 40–27 in the 1946 Cotton Bowl. While at Texas he also starred in baseball; he won 28 games without a loss as a pitcher and was offered pro contracts. In 1946 he married Carol Ann Kreuger; they had two children.

Layne rejected a baseball career for one in professional football. In 1948 he joined the Chicago Bears, receiving a $10,000 bonus and a salary of $18,000, but he had to play as a backup to veteran quarterback Sid Luckman and fellow rookie Johnny Lujack. Traded to the lowly New York Bulldogs, he became a starter the next season. After compiling a 1–10–1 won-lost-tied record, the Bulldogs folded, and Layne joined the Detroit Lions for the 1950 season. At Detroit he established himself as one of the premier quarterbacks in the National Football League. Under Layne's fiery direction the Lions missed the 1951 Western Division championship by only half a game and then won league titles in 1952, 1953, and 1957. On three occasions (1953, 1954, 1957), he played in the Pro Bowl. He finished his professional career with the Pittsburgh Steelers, where he played from 1958 through 1962. After retirement, he coached quarterbacks at Pittsburgh (1963–1965) as well as at St. Louis in 1965, and he scouted for the Dallas Cowboys (1966–1967). As a businessman in Texas, Layne earned the sobriquet of the "Texas Tycoon." He dallied in sporting goods and oil and administered his late father-in-law's (pioneer west Texas surgeon Julius T. Kreuger) estate. In the early 1980s he unsuccessfully sought the head football coaching job at Texas Tech University.

In the 1950s Layne helped transform professional football into a major rival of baseball as the nation's favorite spectator sport. Fans loved the colorful quarterback. Dubbed the "Gadabout Gladiator" by sportswriter Sam Blair, he claimed to have survived three head-on auto crashes and to require only five hours' sleep per night. Called the "original bad boy of pro football" for his legendary carousing and off-field exploits, he became best known for his performance when faced with third-down situations or when his team was behind in the closing minutes of a game. "If I wanted a quarterback to handle any team in the final two minutes, I'd have to send for Layne," said George Halas, coach of the Bears. Coach Paul Brown of the Cleveland Browns called Layne "the best third-down quarterback in football." Layne won a reputation for late-game heroics as early as the 1953 title game, when he rallied the Lions for a memorable 17–16 win over Cleveland. In sixty-nine seconds he took the Lions from their own twenty-yard line to score the winning touchdown. He is frequently credited with inventing the "beat-the-clock offense." When Layne died in Lubbock from cancer-induced cardiac arrest, Detroit owner William Clay Ford eulogized, "He led a full life. He was never cheated. He got his full 60 minutes worth."

By the time of his retirement, Layne held nearly every passing record in pro football. In his fifteen seasons with the NFL, he played 175 games, threw 3,700 passes (completing 1,814) for 26,768 yards gained and 196 touchdowns. He also had 243 career interceptions. As a placekicker, he successfully kicked 34 of 50 field goal attempts and 120 of 124 extra-point tries. As a rusher, he averaged 4 yards per carry and scored 25 touchdowns. In 1967 he was named to the Pro Football Hall of Fame. Few quarterbacks in NFL history performed better under pressure or evoked such excitement among fans.

• Personal letters, press releases, and football registers are in the Lions' archives at the Silverdome in Pontiac, Mich. The Canton, Ohio, Football Hall of Fame has a useful clipping file. An autobiography, *Always on Sunday* (1962), was written with Bob Drum. Articles by Layne appeared in *True Magazine*, Oct. 1957, and the *Saturday Evening Post*, 14 Nov. 1959. Representative newspaper accounts are George Puscas, "Greatest Lion of All Returns," *Detroit Free Press*, 14 Aug. 1963; Al Stark, "Bobby Layne—Texas Tycoon," *Detroit News Sunday News Magazine*, 2 Nov. 1975; and Larry Upshaw, "The Heroes of Highland Park High," *Dallas Morning News*, 17 Oct. 1982. Pieces on Layne include "A Pride of Lions," *Time*, 29 Nov. 1954; Sam Blair, "Bobby Layne: Gadabout Quarterback," *Quarterback*, Apr. 1970; Stanley Frank, "Great Rivalries: Bobby Layne vs. Otto Graham," *Sport*, Jan. 1970; Tommy Devine, "Ringmaster of the Lions," *Sport*, Nov. 1953; Jim Klobuchar, "Memory Layne: Life Was a Cabaret for Bobby," *Pro* (1975); Myron Cope's articles in *Sport*, Nov. 1959 and Jan. 1963; and "Bobby Layne: A Leader Then, a Legend Now," *Super Bowl XIV Magazine* (1982). Detroit writer Jerry Green's *Detroit Lions* (1973) includes a vignette on Layne; Green's "The Legend of Layne Lives on in Motor City" appeared in the *Detroit News*, 2 Dec. 1986.

HAROLD L. RAY

LAZAR, Swifty (28 Mar. 1907–30 Dec. 1993), talent agent, was born Irving Paul Lazar on the Lower East Side of Manhattan, New York City, the son of Samuel Mortimer Lazar, a produce wholesaler, and Stari De-

Longpre. Lazar graduated from Fordham University and received a law degree from Brooklyn Law School in 1931. He practiced law in New York, initially specializing in bankruptcies and foreclosures. He soon switched to entertainment law and represented singers and musicians who were clients of the newly formed Music Corporation of America (MCA). In 1935 he abandoned his law practice in favor of representing his clients as an agent. The change enabled him to earn 10 percent of the booking fees, rather than the 1 percent he received as an attorney.

After U.S. entry into World War II, Lazar joined the Army Air Corps, commissioned as a second lieutenant. Although he was stationed at Camp Mitchell, Long Island, he managed to spend most of his time in Manhattan at the Stork Club and the Gotham Hotel. During this period he became acquainted with Broadway producer and playwright Moss Hart. Lazar persuaded Hart to meet his commanding officer, General H. H. "Hap" Arnold and help produce a musical revue comparable to *This Is the Army*, which had been staged by Irving Berlin for the Army Relief Fund. The result was *Winged Victory*, an extravagant stage production that brought in approximately $5 million for the Air Force Emergency Relief Fund. In 1944 20th Century–Fox released two film versions of the show. He was discharged in 1945 with the rank of captain.

After demobilization, Lazar helped organize the Eagle Lion film studio, which soon went out of business. In 1947 he resumed work as an independent talent agent at the advice of his close friend and mentor, Moss Hart. He set up the Irving Paul Lazar Agency in Beverly Hills, California, and soon had a client list of many top writers and stars, including Irwin Shaw, Mario Lanza, Lee J. Cobb, Red Buttons, and Barry Nelson.

Lazar divided his postwar operations between New York and Los Angeles, where he lived in a series of hotels and conducted one-on-one negotiations with the heads of Hollywood movie studios and New York publishing houses. Writer Michael Korda commented that in New York "Lazar became known as the man who could get you bagfuls of money from Hollywood; in Hollywood, he was the man who could bring you the hottest properties before anybody else on the Coast had ever heard of them."

Lazar was very short and bald but created an impressive appearance with expensive handmade shoes and suits from Savile Row and thick, oversized glasses. His eyes were "shrewd and penetrating, with the kind of beady stare that a macaw might bring to bear on you just before lunging to bite your finger" (Korda, p. 43). He spoke in a brusque and rapid-fire manner and frequently made deals in which he represented both the buyer and the seller. Lazar preferred selling books and scripts that were not previously published and had no hesitation in making deals for writers and stars whom he did not officially represent. One famous quip was "Everybody has two agents—his own and Irving Lazar."

Lazar preferred to be known by the nickname he gave himself, the "Prince of Pitch," but he was more frequently called "Swifty." The nickname had been given to him by actor Humphrey Bogart after Lazar won a bet by concluding several deals for Bogart before the end of the day. Lazar was a close friend of both Bogart and Frank Sinatra.

Lazar's own celebrity status was bolstered by his lavish and exclusive parties, particularly the Academy Award night dinner at Hollywood's Spago Restaurant, which became a Hollywood institution during the 1980s. Korda described it as "a kind of homage to Lazar, as well as a potent demonstration of his power to attract both the old guard and the new."

As a deal maker, Lazar was legendary. He got publishers' advances in excess of a million dollars for Richard Nixon and Henry Kissinger as well as for entertainment celebrities like Cher and Joan Collins. Lazar recognized that if a celebrity author later became less popular, the publisher would be tempted to cancel the book and demand return of the advance, so he insisted on special wording in his clients' contracts. Lazar persuaded publishers to replace the traditional "satisfactory performance" clause with a less-binding requirement that the celebrity author need only submit a "complete manuscript" to fulfill the contract (and keep the advance).

In 1963 Lazar had married Mary Van Nuys, a former model and film producer. The couple had no children. His wife died in 1993. After her death, Lazar chose to forgo his daily dialysis treatment, and he died at his home in Beverly Hills, California.

• Some of Lazar's correspondence is in the Howard Lindsay and Russel Crouse Papers and in the Ruth Goodman Geetz Papers, both at the State Historical Society of Wisconsin in Madison. Lazar coauthored an autobiography, in collaboration with Annette Tapert, *Swifty: My Life and Good Times* (1995). A transcript of an oral history interview is at the Kurt Weill Foundation for Music in New York City. Lazar was profiled in Michael Korda, "The King of the Deal," *New Yorker*, 29 Mar. 1993, pp. 42–50; David Brown, "Exit Swifty Lazar," *New Yorker*, 21 Mar. 1994, p. 170; and Kristin McMurran, "Party Animal," *People Weekly*, 27 Mar. 1995, p. 34. His relationship with Bogart is described in Stephen H. Bogart, *Bogart: In Search of My Father* (1995), and his influence on celebrity authors' publishing contracts is described in Mary B. W. Tabor, "Publishers, Joan Collins and That Fine Print," *New York Times*, 12 Jan. 1996, p. D9. Obituaries are in the *New York Times*, 31 Dec. 1993; *Time*, 10 Jan. 1994; and *Womens Wear Daily*, 3 Jan. 1994.

STEPHEN G. MARSHALL

LAZARON, Morris Samuel (16 Apr. 1888–5 June 1979), rabbi, was born in Savannah, Georgia, the son of Samuel Louis Lazaron, a lawyer, and Alice Zipporah de Castro. Lazaron was educated at the University of Cincinnati (B.A., 1909; M.A., 1911) and ordained at the Hebrew Union College, the seminary of Reform Judaism, in 1914. Soon after being ordained, he occupied the pulpit at Congregation Leshem Shomayim in Wheeling, West Virginia. Nine months later, in August 1915, he accepted a position as rabbi at the Baltimore Hebrew Congregation, one of the nation's oldest. He served there until 1947, when he retired to live in Florida. In 1916 he married Pauline Horkheimer; they had three children. Pauline died on 25 April 1933, and twelve years later, in 1945, Lazaron married Hilda Rothschild Rosenblatt. They had no children. Lazaron belonged to the Masons and to the Order of the Scottish Rite, 33 degrees. He was honored with the Gottheil Medal (1934) for contributions to the welfare of the Jewish community.

From the beginning of his rabbinic career, Lazaron was intensely involved in service and interfaith activities. During World War I he served as a chaplain in the U.S. Army Officer's Reserve Corps, eventually earning the rank of major. He stayed in the corps until 1953. In 1921 Lazaron represented American Jewry as one of four officiating chaplains attending the burial of the Unknown Soldier in Arlington National Cemetery. In 1925 he helped found the Military Chaplains' Association, an interfaith organization.

Lazaron was a pioneer of the kind of interfaith liaisons that ultimately produced the National Conference of Christians and Jews (NCCJ) in 1928. His closest friend was Hugh Birckhead, rector of Immanuel Protestant Episcopal Church in Baltimore, with whom he made a pilgrimage to Palestine in 1921. In 1933 and 1935 Lazaron toured the United States with Father John Eliot Ross and the Reverend Everett R. Clinchy, president of the NCCJ, addressing meetings and conducting seminars to promote interfaith dialogue and goodwill. These tours led *Time* to dub the clergymen "the Flying Ministerial Circus" (they were also popularly known as "the Tolerance Trio"). In 1941 Lazaron toured England and Ireland to study interfaith relations, again under the auspices of the NCCJ, with Clinchy and Father Vincent Donovan. During this trip, Lazaron was honored to give a Hebrew blessing to Prime Minister Winston Churchill. Lazaron's 1959 book *Bridges—Not Walls* was introduced by Harry Emerson Fosdick, one of the leading Protestant ministers of the era, who described it as "a book which challenges the great religions, especially Roman Catholicism, Protestantism, and Judaism, in the United States to amend their contentious ways."

Lazaron's other significant books also dwelled on the issue of interfaith cooperation, hence the title of his autobiography, *Common Ground: A Plea for Intelligent Americanism* (1938). In *Seed of Abraham: Ten Jews of the Ages* (1930), Lazaron chose to portray Moses, David, Jeremiah, Mary, Jesus, Baruch Spinoza, Heinrich Heine, Karl Marx, Benjamin Disraeli, and Theodor Herzl. The unorthodox selection of subjects reflected his desire to focus not on people who remained in the Jewish fold but on "Jews whom the world has claimed for its own." The audience he had in mind was clearly ecumenical and not strictly Jewish, as was suggested by his comment, "No one can choose a list of Jews which would be satisfactory to all, Christian and Jew alike."

Lazaron's universalism was interpreted by more traditional Jews as blatantly apologetic, and his fervent anti-Zionism led him into stark conflicts with the Jewish community, including his own Baltimore congregation, with which he had a painful rupture in 1949, ending his status as rabbi emeritus. An enthusiastic advocate of Zionism in the 1910s and 1920s, Lazaron split with the movement in the mid-1930s. In 1942 he emerged as a founder of the explicitly anti-Zionist American Council for Judaism, which aimed to turn back the tide of Zionist tendencies within Reform Judaism. Lazaron was unusual in maintaining a critical position regarding the state of Israel until the early 1970s. He was also an officer of the American Friends of the Middle East, an organization that challenged Israeli policy toward the Palestinian Arabs. In the pamphlet *Mission to the Middle East* (1954), Lazaron applied his universalism to international politics, urging Israel to readmit masses of Arab refugees, to end all forms of discrimination against Israeli Arabs, and to create the conditions for harmony by compensating Arabs for lands that had been occupied by Israelis. In 1973, however, he and his wife contributed $1,000 to the Israel Emergency Fund in the aftermath of the Yom Kippur War.

Lazaron described his "ministry" as having two primary themes: to seek common ground for all Jews regardless of ethnic differences and to advocate Jewish-Christian reconciliation. Although he recognized that his atypical position on Zionism had limited his success at the first objective, Lazaron nonetheless called strenuously for the rededication of Jews in the United States to Judaism and the Jewish tradition. He believed that Jews who assimilated to the point of disregarding their faith were both incapable of helping their people and unwanted by American society. The theme of integrating a universalist present with a particularist past was first enunciated in his rabbinical thesis on "The Tractate Derech Eretz Zutta" (Hebrew Union College, 1914), a 43-page exposition emphasizing that Talmudic wisdom would fit into the modern theological framework of Reform Judaism. Lazaron stated that the contemporary rabbi "must stand with one hand clasped lovingly about the past, while the other, bearing the light of his faith, blazes a way into the future."

A resident of Palm Beach, Florida, Rabbi Lazaron died in London while visiting friends. He had a large significance within the interfaith movement, and his relatively lone voice on the Arab-Israeli conflict would become increasingly resonant in the decades after his death.

• The American Jewish Archives in Cincinnati holds the Morris Lazaron Papers as well as a brief biographical sketch. Some insight into the man can be gleaned from Rabbi David Polish, "The Changing and the Constant in Reform Judaism," *American Jewish Archives* 35, no. 2 (Nov. 1983): 288–89, 292–95, and 298–301. See also Scott Shpeen, "A Man against the Wind: A Biographical study of Rabbi Morris S. Lazaron" (rabbinical thesis, Hewbrew Union College, 1984). An obituary is in the Baltimore *Sun*, 7 June 1979.

ANDREW R. HEINZE

LAZARSFELD, Paul Felix (13 Feb. 1901–30 Aug. 1976), psychologist and sociologist, was born in Vienna, Austria, the son of Robert Lazarsfeld, a lawyer, and Sofie Munk, an Adlerian psychotherapist. Through his mother's friendship with the socialist activist Friedrich Adler—unrelated to the psychologist Alfred Adler—Lazarsfeld became active in socialist student organizations; he edited a newspaper for socialist students, helped found a political cabaret, and ran a children's summer camp based on socialist principles. Married previously to Marie Jahoda and Herta Herzog (the dates of these marriages and the number of children, if any, are unknown), at his death he was survived by his third wife, the former Patricia Kendall, whom he had married in 1950, and two children.

Friedrich Adler was a mathematician and physicist and under his influence Lazarsfeld was trained in applied mathematics; his dissertation, submitted in 1925 for his doctorate degree granted by the University of Vienna, applied Albert Einstein's theory of gravitation to the movement of the planet Mercury. His major interests, however, soon became the development of social research methodology and the establishment of institutes for training and research in the social sciences. Lazarsfeld's family had been active in the intense cultural and political life of turn-of-the-century Vienna. He was, as he once put it, a socialist by birth, and some of his first research was influenced by socialist ideals. A prime example is a 1930s study of unemployed workers in the nearby village of Marienthal that was conducted by the Wirtschaftspsychologische Forschungsstelle, an institute Lazarsfeld had established in Vienna. After he emigrated to the United States, however, his political activism waned.

Lazarsfeld came to the United States as a Rockefeller Fellow in 1933 and soon created a small social research center at the University of Newark. He became director of a Rockefeller-funded study of the social impact of radio, a project that helped establish mass communications research as a field of scholarship. In 1940 the Newark Office of Radio Research was transferred to Columbia University, where in 1944 it became the Bureau of Applied Social Research, with Lazarsfeld as its founding director. Lazarsfeld remained at Columbia until his retirement in 1969; in 1962 he was appointed Quetelet Professor of Social Sciences, a chair created for him.

Most of Lazarsfeld's major writings were collaborations, and most of his work day was spent interacting with students and colleagues. Whether he was at home in New York City or at one of his various rented summer houses, in the classroom or his office or en route, Lazarsfeld was always at work on a variety of projects, and seldom did he work alone. His substantive contributions, issued in a stream of papers and books on the social effects of unemployment, mass communications, voting behavior, and higher education, were not outgrowths of a grand design; rather, for the most part they derived from such external events as the interests of foundations and other sponsors of his research. Lazarsfeld was primarily a methodologist; substantive issues interested him largely because they presented opportunities to develop and test new methodological principles and techniques.

Survey research as a core social science method was in its infancy at the time of the first radio research. Opinion polls were used to measure the popularity or the audience size of radio programs. By creating a range of methods for the multivariate analysis of responses, Lazarsfeld helped transform the opinion poll into a multifaceted research tool. Many opinion surveys report trends over time by using successive samples, a method that cannot reveal what types of people have changed or maintained their opinion. The panel method, in contrast, uses reinterviews with the same sample of individuals at successive points in time. Drawing particularly on the earlier work of Karl and Charlotte Bühler in Vienna and Stuart A. Rice and Theodore M. Newcomb in the United States, Lazarsfeld developed and improved the panel method in studies of voting and other decisions, introducing, for example, control groups into the analysis of panel-derived survey data.

Lazarsfeld's study of the 1940 U.S. presidential election, published in 1944 as *The People's Choice* (co-authored with Bernard Berelson and Hazel Gaudet), focused on the psychological and social processes that affect voting behavior. The study also delineated a process called "opinion leadership," defined as the flow of information from the mass media, first to local opinion leaders and through them to the public at large. In his 1955 book *Personal Influence* (coauthored with Elihu Katz), this process of influence was described as the "two-step flow of communication."

Throughout his career Lazarsfeld worked on the problem of how to study "action" from the standpoint of the person doing the acting. At the heart of this methodology is his concept of an "accounting scheme," a model of the action with which empirical data can be collected and analyzed. He viewed the analysis of action as a means of fusing the study of individual actions with that of the aggregated effects of individual actions; in this way he merged the methodologies of psychology and sociology.

Lazarsfeld was a prime mover in introducing mathematics into survey research. He also encouraged numerous historical studies of empirical social research that documented his thesis that an older European empirical tradition had strongly influenced the American empirical approach to social research. His deep interest in how social science knowledge is used led him, for example, to select "the uses of sociology" as the conference theme during his 1961–1962 presidency of the American Sociological Association.

Lazarsfeld was unusual in the extent to which, throughout his career, he collaborated with his students and colleagues; indeed, many of his students' students came to call themselves Lazarsfeldians. He maintained a particularly intense and mutually rewarding professional relationship with two eminent sociologists who were his contemporaries, the sociological methodologist Samuel A. Stouffer and the social theorist Robert K. Merton. His collaboration with Stouffer was most intense during World War II, when they served together analyzing the impact of films and radio programs on the morale of U.S. soldiers, but it continued until Stouffer's death in 1960. Lazarsfeld and Merton coauthored a few important articles and jointly edited a book on the wartime research among U.S. soldiers, but the most important aspect of their relationship was their almost daily discussions of substantive and professional problems. The Lazarsfeld-Merton relationship lasted for thirty-five years, until Lazarsfeld's death. Rarely in the history of the social sciences have two such accomplished and esteemed colleagues maintained such a productive and cordial working relationship over such a long period of time.

Lazarsfeld was an elected member of both the National Academy of Sciences and the National Academy of Education. He was the recipient of five honorary degrees, three from U.S. and two from European universities. In 1969 the Austrian Republic awarded him its Great Golden Cross, primarily in recognition of his efforts in establishing the Institute for Advanced Studies in Vienna. Shortly after his death in New York City, a memorial fund was established in his honor to sponsor a series of lectures at Columbia University.

• A large collection of Lazarsfeld's books and papers is deposited in Columbia University's Rare Book and Manuscript Library; see Ann K. Pasanella, *The Mind Traveller: A Guide to Paul F. Lazarsfeld's Communication Research Papers* (1994) for a description of its entire contents. The Paul F. Lazarsfeld Archive at the University of Vienna contains copies of all of his books and other writings, published and unpublished. The reports of the Bureau of Applied Social Research are in the archives of the Columbia University Library. A useful compilation of his major papers is *The Varied Sociology of Paul F. Lazarsfeld*, ed. Patricia L. Kendall (1982). For a listing of Lazarsfeld's publications, see Paul M. Neurath, "The Writings of Paul F. Lazarsfeld: A Topical Bibliography," in *Qualitative and Quantitative Social Research: Papers in Honor of Paul F. Lazarsfeld*, ed. Robert K. Merton et al. (1979). Accounts of his career and appraisals up to 1979 are listed in David L. Sills, "Publications about Paul F. Lazarsfeld: A Selected Bibliography," in Merton et al. For additional biographical data and an appraisal of his career and influence, see Sills, "Paul F. Lazarsfeld," in National Academy of Sciences, *Biographical Memoirs* 56 (1987): 251–82. Lazarsfeld's study of the unemployed, conducted by his Vienna institute with Marie Jahoda and Hans Zeisel, is *Die Arbeitslosen von Marienthal: Ein soziographischer Versuch über die Wirkungen langdauernder Arbeitslosigkeit* (1933; English translation, *Marienthal: The Sociography of an Unemployed Community* [1971]). Major results of the radio research project were published in Lazarsfeld, *Radio and the Printed Page* (1940); Lazarsfeld and Frank N. Stanton, eds., *Radio Research* (2 vols., 1941–1944); Lazarsfeld and Harry Field, *The People Look at Radio* (1946); and Lazarsfeld and Merton, "Mass Communication, Popular Taste and Organized Social Action," in *Problems in the Communication of Ideas*, ed. Lyman Bryson (1948). Lazarsfeld's major publication in the field of higher education is *The Academic Mind: Social Scientists in a Time of Crisis*, coauthored by Wagner Thielens, Jr. (1958). *The Language of Social Research*, ed. Lazarsfeld and Morris Rosenberg (1955), and *Continuities in the Language of Social Research*, ed. La-

zarsfeld et al. (1972), contain numerous essays by Lazarsfeld and others on survey design and analysis. Lazarsfeld's other major study on voting behavior that also exemplifies his use of the panel method is *Voting*, coauthored with Bernard Berelson and William N. McPhee (1954). The "two-step flow of communication" is described most fully in Elihu Katz and Lazarsfeld, *Personal Influence: The Part Played by People in the Flow of Mass Communications* (1955). Two collections of papers illustrate Lazarsfeld's contributions to the use of mathematics in social research, *Mathematical Thinking in the Social Sciences*, ed. Lazarsfeld (1954; 2d rev. ed. 1969), and *Readings in Mathematical Social Science*, ed. Lazarsfeld and Neil W. Henry (1966). Lazarsfeld's interest in the empirical study of action and his collaboration with Merton are both described in his "Working with Merton," in *The Idea of Social Structure: Papers in Honor of Robert K. Merton*, ed. Lewis A. Coser (1975). His collaboration with Merton is further described in "Working with Lazarsfeld," by Robert K. Merton (1994, unpublished). A useful obituary is in the *New York Times*, 1 Sept. 1976.

DAVID L. SILLS

LAZARUS, Emma (22 July 1849–19 Nov. 1887), poet and essayist, was born in New York City, the daughter of Moses Lazarus, a well-to-do sugar merchant, and Esther Nathan. The family identified itself as Jewish but was not religiously observant, and Lazarus's early years did not suggest the direction she would later take. "I was brought up exclusively under American institutions, amid liberal influences, in a society where all differences of race and faith were fused in a refined cosmopolitanism," she recalled. Privately tutored, she studied the curriculum for properly educated, young, upper-class ladies.

Lazarus's first volume of poetry was published by her father in 1866 and was republished with some additional poems a year later. These youthful efforts are derivative, sentimental, and full of artificial poeticisms and archaic language. In Lazarus's early years Hebraism was only latent, and as her sister Josephine later noted, it was "classic and romantic art that first attracted her. . . . Her restless spirit found repose in the pagan idea,—the absolute unity and identity of man with nature, as symbolized in the Greek myths."

During her literary career Lazarus struck up tutelary relationships with male writers, the first and most influential of these with Ralph Waldo Emerson, while other mentors included the critics Thomas Wentworth Higginson and Edmund Clarence Stedman, the naturalist John Burroughs, and the novelists Henry James (1843–1916) and Ivan Turgenev. All of these men encouraged her to continue writing and to find her own poetic voice. In 1871 Lazarus published a second volume, *Admetus and Other Poems*. The major poems of this volume—"Admetus," "Orpheus," "Lohengrin," and "Tannheusen"—are curious and suggestive, two Greek myths and two medieval German legends about women who sacrificed themselves for the sake of men. Lazarus, in struggling to find her own voice, seems to have been looking in the wrong place.

As time went on, she revealed a growing interest in the Jewish tradition. She translated the German-Jewish poet Heinrich Heine and the medieval Jewish poets of Spain, studied the Hebrew language, read Heinrich Graetz's seminal *History of the Jews*, and wrote a few poems on Jewish subjects. Still, she remained equivocal, writing in 1877 "my interest and sympathies [are] loyal to our race, although my religious convictions (if such they can be called) and the circumstances of my life have led me somewhat apart from our people" (*Letters of Emma Lazarus*, no. 11). In 1878, however, she corresponded with author William Burroughs on Matthew Arnold's Hellenism as opposed to Walt Whitman's Hebraism. The theme of Hebraism versus Hellenism was to find expression in her own poetry, especially in one of her finest poems, the sonnet "Venus of the Louvre." Written in 1884, the poem begins with a statement of amazement on her first seeing the Venus de Milo. But a shift at the ninth line presents a sudden vision of another figure:

> But at her feet a pale, death stricken Jew,
> Her life adorer, sobbed farewell to love.
> Here Heine wept! Here still he weeps anew,
> Nor ever shall his shadow lift or move,
> While mourns one ardent heart, one poet-brain,
> For vanished Hellas and Hebraic pain.

In the early 1880s, as Lazarus searched for an authentic way to express her increasingly Jewish consciousness, two related events fired her imagination and social conscience: (1) the Russian pogroms of 1881 and the concomitant infamous May Laws of 1882; and (2) the resulting mass emigration of Eastern European Jews to the United States. Until that time, her interest in Judaism was mainly philosophical, but at this crux of Jewish history, she responded passionately as poet, political essayist, and social activist.

In April 1882 Lazarus published in *Century* an essay titled "Was the Earl of Beaconsfield a Representative Jew?" The same issue of the magazine included an article by Madame Z. Ragozin, a Russian journalist who viciously attacked Jewish character and defended the mobs carrying out the pogroms. Before printing the latter article, Richard Watson Gilder, the editor of *Century*, showed it to Lazarus, who immediately wrote an outraged response for the May 1882 issue. "Russian Christianity versus Modern Judaism" was the first of a stream of her polemical pieces in defense of the Jewish people. She had finally hit her stride, and she revealed it in vigorous prose.

Despite the insistence of her sisters and other admirers, Lazarus was not the consummate restrained Victorian woman. All that she lacked was an appropriate object for the moral and aesthetic passion she identified as "late-born and woman-souled." She found it in wedding her own identity with that of her people and her decision to speak and act for them. From that point her poetry abandoned high diction and became charged with the prophetic urgency of the call for a return to Palestine. Her prose, too, became stronger, as exemplified by the series of fourteen essays, ironically

entitled "Epistle to the Hebrews," that she wrote from November 1882 through February 1883. In them she undertook to "bring before the Jewish public . . . facts and critical observations . . . to arouse a more logical and intelligent estimate of the duties of the hour."

In 1883 Lazarus was asked to write a poem for the fundraising project for the Bartholdi Statue Pedestal Art Loan Exhibition. At first she was disinclined to write "anything to order," but when she was reminded of "Russian refugees as recipients of the light of the torch," she agreed. This resulted in the famous sonnet, "The New Colossus," affixed to the pedestal of the Statue of Liberty in May 1903, dedicated to her memory, and on which her entire reputation has rested. Contained in this sonnet, however, is the key to the extraordinary history of Lazarus's personal journey of self-discovery and self-expression. The poem opens with a rejection of the Hellenist heritage of male conquering power, empty ceremony, and aestheticism: "Not like the brazen giant of Greek fame, / With conquering limbs astride from land to land. . . . " In its place is an assertion of the power of womanhood, the comfort of motherhood, the Hebrew prophetic values of compassion and consolation, "a mighty woman with a torch, . . . her name Mother of Exiles."

Lazarus's commitment to social justice was not limited to words, for she helped new immigrants to resettle, and she was among those responsible for founding the Hebrew Technical Institute for Vocational Training located in New York. She sailed to London in 1883 to seek help in her work toward establishing a Jewish national homeland. Thus, a decade before Theodore Herzl's Zionism, she argued for Palestine as a safe haven for oppressed Jews. At no point, however, did she advocate Palestine for all Jews, for she regarded herself as a patriotic American.

Never married, Lazarus died of cancer in New York City.

Lazarus was the first significant American Jewish literary figure and the first internationally celebrated American Jewish woman poet. Her significance lies in her exemplary life and in her impassioned pleas for the poor, for the immigrant, and the oppressed.

• Lazarus's manuscript notebook is located at the Library of the American Jewish Historical Society, Waltham, Mass. In addition to those mentioned in the text, Lazarus's works include *The Spagnoletto* (1876), *Poems and Ballads of Heinrich Heine* (1881), *Songs of a Semite: The Dance to Death and Other Poems* (1882), and *The Poems of Emma Lazarus* (2 vols., 1889). Some of Lazarus's prose can be found in *Emma Lazarus: Selections from Her Poetry and Prose*, ed. Morris U. Schappes (1967). Two important annotated sources are *The Letters of Emma Lazarus, 1868–1885*, ed. Schappes (1949), and *Letters to Emma Lazarus in the Columbia University Library*, ed. Ralph L. Rusk (1939). See also Carole S. Kessner, "The Emma Lazarus–Henry James Connection: Eight Letters," *American Literary History* 3, no. 1 (1991): 46–62. For a personal remembrance, see Philip Cowen, *Memories of an American Jew* (1932), pp. 332–45. The best biography is Daniel Vogel, *Emma Lazarus* (1980), which includes a useful bibliography. For critiques of her standing as a poet, see Joseph Lyons, "In Two Divided Streams," *Midstream* 7 (Autumn 1961): 78–85, and Carole Kessner, "From Mt. Parnassus to Mt. Zion: The Journey of Emma Lazarus," *Jewish Book Annual, 1986–1987* 40 (1986): 1–22.

CAROLE S. KESSNER

LAZEAR, Jesse William (2 May 1866–25 Sept. 1900), physician, was born in Baltimore, Maryland, the son of William Lyon Lazear and Charlotte Pettigrew. Lazear lived with his parents in Baltimore but spent much of his childhood with his grandfather at Windsor Mill Farm near Walbrook in west Baltimore. He received his elementary education at a boy's boarding school in Baltimore. His grandfather and father both died when Lazear was only twelve years old, and his younger brother died two years later. His mother moved the family to live with relatives in Pittsburgh, Pennsylvania, and Lazear switched to a school there. In 1881 he entered Trinity Hall Academy, a preparatory school for boys near Washington, Pennsylvania. In 1884 he began study at Washington and Jefferson College in the same city, but after deciding to study medicine, he transferred to Johns Hopkins University, from which he received his A.B. in 1889.

Because Johns Hopkins did not yet have a medical school, Lazear enrolled in the College of Physicians and Surgeons of Columbia University. After one year at Columbia, Lazear followed an eight-week course in anatomy given by Sir William Turner in Europe. Lazear received his M.D. from Columbia in 1892. Through competitive examinations, he secured a two-year internship at Bellevue Hospital in New York.

The work of Louis Pasteur and of Robert Koch had awakened great interest in the nascent field of bacteriology. As had other young scientists, Lazear decided to study the subject abroad, and in the fall of 1894 he, accompanied by his mother, traveled to the Kaiserliches Gesundheitsamt of Berlin, where he spent five months studying with August Paul Wassermann. Visiting Munich, the Lazears met Martha P. Houston and her daughter Mabel of San Francisco. The two families continued their European visit together, going to Venice, Florence, and Rome, where Lazear lingered to take a course on entomology from Giovanni Batista Grassi. From May to July 1895 he took a course of demonstrations in microbiology given by Emil Roux and Elie Metchnikoff at the Pasteur Institute in Paris.

Offered work at the new medical school developing at Johns Hopkins under the prestigious aegis of William Osler and William Welch, Lazear returned to Baltimore in 1895 and was appointed instructor in clinical microscopy and was put in charge of the school's clinical laboratories. In 1898 he developed an original staining of malarial parasites and diagnosed one of the first cases of gonorrheal endocarditis reported in medical literature. In September 1896 he married Mabel Houston; they made their home in Baltimore, where they had two children.

Upon the declaration of war in Spain in April 1898, Lazear volunteered as a contract surgeon of the U.S. Army. In the winter of 1900 he was sent to take charge of the clinical laboratory of the Columbia Barracks in Quemados near Havana; he was accompanied by his family. Leonard Wood, military governor of Cuba during the American intervention, reported officially that in spite of the efforts of Colonel William Gorgas, who had made of Havana one of the cleanest cities in the world, the occurrence of yellow fever continued to increase. Lazear sent home his pregnant wife and one-year-old son. In June, Surgeon General George Sternberg appointed him as a member of the U.S. Army Yellow Fever Commission.

Lazear, commission chair Major Walter Reed, and the other board members—contract surgeons James Carroll and Aristides Agramonte—first met on 25 June 1900 on the veranda of the officers' quarters and were read their instructions for the study of infectious diseases prevailing on the island. On the same evening Henry Carter of the U.S. Marine Hospital Service approached Lazear and told him that he thought that Carlos Finlay's mosquito theory of yellow fever transmission had merit. Giuseppe Sanarelli of Uruguay had thought that he had discovered the etiologic agent of yellow fever, which he called *Bacillus icteroides*. After five weeks of work on cadavers, the board had proof that Sanarelli's bacillus was, in fact, a common contaminant in cadavers. Next, the board decided to undertake a study of the intestinal flora of victims of the fever, but their direction changed after they met two scientists, Herbert Durham and Walter Myers, from the University of Liverpool, who visited them on their way to Brazil to study yellow fever. The British scientists visited Finlay, who had maintained for twenty years that the mosquito transmitted yellow fever, and were impressed with his work. They frankly admitted that the mosquito theory appeared probable. Members of the board called on Finlay, who received them cordially, gave them reprints of his papers on the transmission of yellow fever by the mosquito and gave them a porcelain soap dish containing the eggs of the species that he had identified as *Culex mosquito*, later renamed *Stegomia fasciata* and now called *Aedes egypti*.

The commission had not been given instructions to look into the mosquito contention and in fact, Surgeon General Sternberg had written against it. While Reed returned to the United States for a vacation, Lazear hatched the eggs, kept them fastened in individual test tubes, and took them to the hospital Las Animas to have them bite yellow fever patients. Cautiously he chose mild cases or patients in recovery. His first seven trials to inoculate volunteers, including himself, were negative. He then had the mosquitoes fill with blood of multiple severe cases. On 27 August, Carroll volunteered to be bitten by one of these mosquitoes, and on 1 September, he was diagnosed as having a severe case of yellow fever from which he recovered. Lazear and Agramonte had the same mosquito bite a volunteer soldier who also developed the fever and recovered. On 13 September Lazear decided to attempt the inoculation on an experimental laboratory animal and, according to his colleagues, inoculated himself possibly in the expectation of recovery and immunity. He had a very severe case, became delirious, and died with convulsions. During his hospitalization Lazear stated that he had been bitten accidentally. He died at the U.S. Army Hospital in the Columbia Barracks near Quemados at the age of thirty-four.

After initial doubts, Reed returned to Cuba to study Lazear's research notebook. By 23 October, he was convinced that Lazear and Finlay were correct, and he proclaimed that the mosquito was the intermediate agent of yellow fever. With the help of Agramonte and Carroll he carried out a controlled experiment with human volunteers that proved to everybody's satisfaction that the mosquito transmitted yellow fever. Colonel Gorgas implemented the preventive measures long advocated by Finlay, and within six months the last case of yellow fever was reported in Havana, where the disease had been endemic for more than 200 years. Lazear's dedication to his research provided the first unquestionable proof of the role of the mosquito when he produced a second case, after Carroll's, using the same contaminated mosquito.

• Lazear's correspondence is in the Hench Yellow Fever Collection at the Claude Moore Science Library at the University of Virginia. Lazear's several important papers include "Pathology of Malarial Fevers: Structure of the Parasites and Changes in Tissues," *Journal of the American Medical Association*. The report of Reed, Carroll, Agramonte, and Lazear was published as "The Etiology of Yellow Fever: A Preliminary Note," *Philadelphia Medical Journal* 6 (1900): 790–96. Other sources include J. A. Del Regato, "Jesse W. Lazear: The Successful Experimental Transmission of Yellow Fever by the Mosquito," *Medical Heritage* 2 (1986): 443–52; Emmett B. Carmichael, "Jesse William Lazear," *Alabama Journal of Medical Science* 9 (1972): 102–14; Howard A. Kelly, *Walter Reed and Yellow Fever* (1906); and the account of the Yellow Fever Commission in *Senate Document 822*, 61st Cong., 3d sess. Obituaries are in the *Journal of the American Medical Association* (6 Oct. 1900): 6, and in *Science* (14 Dec. 1900): 6.

JUAN A. DEL REGATO

LAZEROWITZ, Morris (22 Oct. 1907–25 Feb. 1987), teacher of philosophy and writer, was born in Łódź, now in Poland, the son of Max Laizerowitz and Etta Plochinsky. Lazerowitz's father emigrated to the United States in 1912 with his eldest daughter, and the rest of the family joined them in Omaha, Nebraska, three years later. Although his father, who had been a Yeshiva student, had little formal education and scant preparation for life in a foreign country, he managed by painful saving to secure his family's arrival in the last days before World War I. Resolved to provide an education for his children, he sent his remaining son Morris to study the violin. By the age of nineteen Morris Lazerowitz was substituting in the Chicago Symphony Orchestra. (An elementary school teacher omitted the *i* in Morris's last name, and the change remained.) He was forced by a back injury to leave the profession, and in 1928 he entered the University of Nebraska, where his philosophy teacher, O. K. Bouwsma, who trained a number of students who became philosophers of note, encouraged him to pursue his interest in philosophy. Lazerowitz thereupon entered the University of Michigan, where he received the A.B. in 1933, became a teaching fellow, and took his doctoral degree in 1936. A traveling fellowship, 1936–1937, enabled him to do postdoctorate work at Cambridge University and at Harvard University.

In 1937–1938 Lazerowitz joined the faculty of Smith College, where in 1938 he married Alice Ambrose, who had been a colleague at the University of Michigan. Save for a year as Fulbright lecturer at Bedford College, University of London (1951–1952), he and his wife taught at Smith College for thirty-five years, and for the last nine years they each held the Sophia and Austin Smith Chair of Philosophy. Following retirement in 1972–1973 he and his wife continued to teach, as distinguished professors, at the University of Delaware (1975), Carleton College (1979), and Hampshire College (1977, 1979, 1981). Their productive work, singly and jointly, continued. Each was asked to give the Engel Lecture at Smith College. Lazerowitz died in Northampton, Massachusetts.

Lazerowitz's first published work was in logic and on philosophical questions associated with logic: "Tautologies and the Matrix Method" (1937), "Penumbral Functions" (1937), and "The Null Class of Premises" (1938)—all three in *Mind*—and "Self-contradictory Propositions" in the *Philosophy of Science* (1940). He was coauthor with Ambrose of the logic texts *Fundamentals of Symbolic Logic* (1948) and *Logic: The Theory of Formal Inference* (1961).

The bulk of Lazerowitz's later, and different, work appeared in a number of books and journals, among them *The Structure of Metaphysics* (1955), *Studies in Metaphilosophy* (1964), *Philosophy and Illusion* (1968), and *The Language of Philosophy: Freud and Wittgenstein* (1977). These books had an orientation initiated by the early work of Ludwig Wittgenstein. In the dictated Blue Book and accompanying lectures of 1932–1934 Wittgenstein had turned attention away from questions about the truth of philosophical views purportedly about the world to the language in which they were expressed and supported, maintaining that the traditional treatment had led metaphysicians "into complete darkness." Following this lead, Lazerowitz pioneered a field of research for which he coined the name "metaphilosophy," a name later taken, to his surprise, by a philosophical journal. Metaphilosophy he defined as an investigation of the nature of philosophical theories and their supporting arguments, with the aim of explaining their centuries-long irresolvability. (See *Metaphilosophy* [1990]: 91 and *The Language of Philosophy*, chap. 1.)

Lazerowitz's thesis is that the indicative form of speech, together with the omission of any reference to language, creates the illusion that it asserts facts about the world. This illusion is implemented by a gerrymandered piece of language so used as to appear to be the ordinary use to assert a fact. An example is Parmenides' paradoxical view that change is impossible. However, here and quite generally, supporting argumentation is directed to showing that no fact could possibly refute it, i.e., that it is *necessarily* true. Parmenides' argument, in his poem *On Nature*, is intended to show that change is *inconceivable*. In consequence "change" acquires the nonreferential use of a phrase like "round square." This sort of analysis clearly requires attention to language rather than to what language stands for. Lazerowitz's work thus falls within the analytic tradition of which G. E. Moore in the early and postwar period was the chief representative, insofar as Moore investigated views involving concepts such as causation, time, knowledge, truth, and goodness by examining the *terms* "causation," "time," etc.

Lazerowitz's thesis is that contested views in philosophy are the product of linguistic preferences that introduce linguistic innovations without appearing to do so (e.g., the use of "change" to denote an inconceivability). Lazerowitz's explanation of the altered usage, and the durability of the view, is that it has unconscious determinants. About these determinants he does not speculate, but one can perhaps guess that the appeal of the Parmenidean view is its implied denial of aging and death.

Lazerowitz's explanation of the irresolvability and durability of metaphysical theories is unique to him. The editor of Lazerowitz and Ambrose's *Necessity and Language* (1985), S. G. Shanker of the University of Toronto, predicted that the book would "establish itself as one of the classics of contemporary philosophy."

• Lazerowitz's *The Language of Philosophy: Freud and Wittgenstein* (1977) extends the analysis of the thesis first proposed in *The Structure of Metaphysics* (1955) and carried on in his *Studies in Metaphilosophy* (1964), *Philosophy and Illusion* (1968), and, with Alice Ambrose, in *Essays in the Unknown Wittgenstein* (1984). He was coauthor with Ambrose of *Philosophical Theories* (1976), written for teachers and students of philosophy. He edited a number of anthologies, including, with William Kennick, *Metaphysics: Readings and Reappraisals* (1966); with Ambrose, *G. E. Moore: Essays in Retrospect* (1970) and *Ludwig Wittgenstein: Philosophy and Language* (1972); and with Charles Hanly, *Psychoanalysis and Philosophy* (1970). A collection of essays by Lazerowitz and Ambrose, *Necessity and Language*, ed. S. G. Shanker (1985), contains a complete bibliography of Lazerowitz's work. His later papers include "Wittgenstein: The Nature of Philosophy," *Critica* 19, no. 56 (1987): 3–16, and "A Note on Descartes' *Cogito*," *Metaphilosophy* 17, no. 1 (1986): 85–87.

ALICE AMBROSE

LAZZELL, Blanche (10 Oct. 1878–1 June 1956), painter and printmaker, was born Nettie Blanche Lazzell in Maidsville, West Virginia, the daughter of Cornelius Carhart Lazzell and Mary Prudence Pope. As a result of a childhood illness, Lazzell experienced pronounced hearing loss her entire life. She started her secondary education at West Virginia Conference Seminary (known today as West Virginia Wesleyan) in 1898 and in 1899 attended the South Carolina Co-Educational Institute in Edgefield. The only member of her family to receive a college education, she was a student at West Virginia University from 1901 to 1905 and graduated with three degrees, in literature, liberal arts, and fine arts.

By 1907 Lazzell had moved to New York City to attend the Art Students League, where she studied under William Merritt Chase. However, the death of her father in 1908 forced her to return to West Virginia, where she taught art part-time and painted. In July 1912, with her saved earnings, Lazzell sailed for Europe, where she wanted "to study every room of the famous museums." She traveled to London, Venice, Florence, Rome, Strassburg, Lucerne, and Paris, where she settled and studied at the Académie Moderne. Lazzell immersed herself in French culture. By the fall of 1913, however, she had returned to West Virginia, where she opened her own art school near Maidsville, giving lessons in oil painting, watercolors, pastels, and china (decoration) painting, and exhibited her work in one-person shows in Morgantown.

In the summer of 1915 Lazzell visited artist friends she had known in Paris who had moved to Provincetown, Massachusetts. The thriving artistic community attracted many expatriate American artists fleeing Europe and the turmoil of World War I. She was captivated by the picturesque and nourishing art colony. As she reflected in 1930, "Hundreds of American artists who had been living in Europe before the first World War flocked to Provincetown. . . . To be in Provincetown for the first time, in those days, under ordinary conditions was delightful enough, but that summer of 1915, when the whole scene, everything and everybody was new, it was glorious indeed. . . . Creative energy was in the air we breathed. It was in this quaint setting that the Provincetown Print came into being."

That summer in Provincetown, Lazzell began studying with Charles Hawthorne, a painter and teacher who established the Cape Cod School of Art. By the following year she had learned the "Provincetown print" from Oliver Chaffee and discovered the technique that characterizes her most famous prints. By the summer of 1916 she was exhibiting her prints at the Provincetown Art Association. The Provincetown print was a novel method for producing color woodblock prints invented by B. J. O. Nordfelt, who had become impatient with the labor required to cut several blocks of wood (one for each color) before expressing his idea. He experimented and cut a complete design on a single block of wood. This was done by cutting a groove in the wood to separate each color, and, in printing, this left a white line that emphasized the decorative play of patterns within the design. Each outlined color segment was printed separately, with a combination of impressions making up the finished print. Being able to see the complete picture as one image, like a painting on a canvas, gave new possibilities for creative work in that medium.

The winters of 1916 and 1917 found Lazzell in New York City studying with Homer Boss, a painter and teacher at the Art Students League. She spent the summer of 1917 in Woodstock, New York, painting and printmaking. By the summer of 1918 Lazzell was giving instruction in the medium, and she became a founding member of the Provincetown Printers, the first woodblock print society in America. This group's work was shown in galleries and museums in many cities throughout the United States and in Paris. In 1926 two of her color woodblock prints were chosen for the nationally and internationally selected exhibit Fifty Best Prints of the Year.

In 1923 Lazzell returned to Paris, where she studied with modern painters Albert Leon Gleizes, André Lhote, and Fernan Léger. Under their influence her work became abstract and attracted attention in Paris. While she exhibited at the Salon d'Automne from 1923 until the mid-1930s, she returned to Provincetown in 1925 and resumed teaching classes in block printing as well as in painting and composition. In the late 1920s she extended her artistic energy to the design of hooked rugs.

Frequently returning home to West Virginia to visit family, Lazzell in the 1930s became one of many artists employed by the Public Works of Art Project and the Works Progress Administration. She executed three color prints of historical scenes of Morgantown, West Virginia, in the winter of 1933–1934. In 1934 she finished a mural painting for the courthouse in Morgantown. She continued her work in Provincetown throughout the 1940s and began studying with Hans Hofmann.

Although she considered herself a painter, Lazzell is best known for these Provincetown prints. Her bold shapes, carved in realistic and abstract fashion, are softened by the rainbow-like palette within the decorative white outline. The result is an overall harmonious composition that is distinctive and an ultimately satisfying work of art. In 1930 Lazzell wrote about the print's development: "It appeals to the artist's creative spirit because it is a more direct expression than is the method requiring the use of several blocks. . . . The artist creates his design, carves his block, and does his own printing. The impression is not made by a printing press; but each shape on the block is painted and pressed with the finger or pad, as the shape requires—one shape at a time—until the print is completed. Simplicity in both composition and color is the chief charm of the print."

Between 1916 and 1956 Lazzell created more than 138 blocks and countless impressions through a process that seems to have held a continual fascination for her. Her block prints were technically distinguished by fine cutting and meticulous, sensitive printing. The cutting was made almost exclusively by knife, following a design drawn directly on the block. As she wrote in the foreword to an exhibition catalog, "No two wood-block prints need ever be exactly alike. The variation of color arrangement is inexhaustible. But the limitations of wood-block printing are no less fascinating. The composition must of necessity be simple. There must be a good deal of elimination in drawing."

For more than forty years Lazzell spent almost every summer, and many winters as well, in Provincetown. There she entertained visitors in her wharf studio, displaying her work and demonstrating the techniques of woodblock cutting and printing. Her Color Wood Block Printing course attracted numerous students, many of whom continued to work in the medium throughout their careers. George Ault, Mary Mullineux, Hope Voorhees Pfeiffer, Elizabeth Shuff Tayor, and Grace Martin Taylor are only a few of the artists who benefited from her tutelage and example.

Throughout her long career Lazzell remained open to new experiences and ideas. Her early work in Paris between 1912 and 1914 introduced her to the more radical European movements. By 1925 she had become fully committed to a decorative, geometric cubism, which she defined as "the organization of flat planes of color with an interplay of space, instead of perspective." Abstraction admirably suited her woodcuts and the interpretation of angular patterns of the Provincetown houses, rooftops, and wharves that dominated much of her work. Lazzell was a passionate gardener, and flower images occur repeatedly in her work. Even these images, based on direct observation, were transformed into rhythmic interplays of abstracted shapes. Her mastery of the complexities of the cubist aesthetic is perhaps best represented in a remarkable group of block prints made in 1925 that are among the earliest nonrepresentational prints created in the United States.

• The correspondence, educational and financial records, and exhibition history of Blanche Lazzell are located at the Archives of American Art, Smithsonian Institution, New York, N.Y. For more on Lazzell, see John Clarkson, *Blanche Lazzell*, exhibition catalog by the Creative Arts Center of West Virginia University (1979); Nancy Mallory and Nic Madormo, *Blanche Lazzell: A Modernist Rediscovered*, exhibition brochure, Archives of American Art (1991); and Janet Altic Flint, *Provincetown Printers: A Woodcut Tradition* (1983).

LESLIE NOLAN

LAZZERI, Tony (6 Dec. 1903–6 Aug. 1946), baseball player, was born Anthony Michael Lazzeri in San Francisco, California, the son of Augustin Lazzeri, a boilermaker, and Julia (maiden name unknown). Tony, as he was always called, dropped out of St. Theresa's Catholic School at age fifteen to work with his father in an ironworks in San Francisco. Athletic from his youngest days, he briefly contemplated a boxing career while learning the boilermaker trade. He also found time to play semiprofessional baseball; scouts soon discovered his skills as an infielder, and he was signed to play for Salt Lake City, Utah, in the Pacific Coast League (PCL) for the 1922 season. He was not yet nineteen years old.

At first Lazzeri's minor league experience was disheartening. He batted only .192 in 1922, setting in motion a series of reassignments in lower-level leagues. In the course of three years he was traded back and forth from Salt Lake City to lesser leagues so many times that he threatened to give up the game. He did retire for about ten days before agreeing to join the Lincoln, Nebraska, team. A quiet, introspective boy, he also badly missed his Italian neighborhood in San Francisco. But suddenly his game matured; he stayed with Salt Lake City throughout the 1925 season and performed astonishingly well for his age and experience. He played in 192 games (the PCL had exceptionally long seasons in that era), batted .355 with 252 hits, drove in 222 runs, stole 39 bases, and nearly led the league in batting average. Although the PCL was then considered a hitter's league, his achievement was outstanding, for he led the league in runs scored, runs batted in, and home runs (60), all PCL records. In spite of his youth and the popular belief that the lighter high desert air made home run hitting easier, Lazzeri became the object of much major league interest. The New York Yankees won out, and after the 1925 season they purchased him from the Salt Lake club for $75,000—$55,000 in cash and $20,000 "worth" of players sent from New York to Salt Lake.

Lazzeri was installed at second base for the Yankees at the beginning of the 1926 season and played every game. He became a fixture at that position from 1926 through 1937. (Some managerial experimentation put him at shortstop and third base a few games, but most fans would always associate him as the second baseman during the first years of the Yankee dynasty.) During those twelve seasons the team won the American League pennant six times and the World Series five times. In 1926 the Yankees installed a new shortstop, Mark Koenig, but in general the lineup was the same for the team that finished seventh in 1925 and first in 1926—except for the addition of Lazzeri. "Poosh 'em up Tony," as Lazzeri's fans began to call him, outhit his predecessor Aaron Ward—the Yankees' second baseman in 1925, who was playing at the end of his career—by nearly thirty points, struck 18 home runs compared with Ward's four, and drove in 114 runs compared with Ward's 38. While many teams have had two or three powerful hitters at one time, only the Yankees had such strength at the sixth spot in their batting order. In fan terminology the lineup became known as "Murderers' Row," dreaded by the pitchers of every other American League team. In many cities the team was also designated "Five o'clock lightning," for the Yankees' ability to dishearten pitching staffs in the late innings.

Only his performance in the 1926 World Series against the St. Louis Cardinals could have disappointed Lazzeri that first year in the majors. Perhaps suffering from youthful anxiety, he hit only .192 in the seven games, and he became forever known to fans for being struck out by old Grover Cleveland Alexander, with two outs and the bases loaded in the seventh inning of the last game. The Cardinals won that game and the series, but the Yankees won the World Series in 1927 against the Pittsburgh Pirates and in 1928 against the St. Louis Cardinals, both in four-game sweeps.

Lazzeri's poor—and unfortunately dramatic—first World Series had no effect on his career accomplishments. He averaged nearly 15 home runs and 95 runs batted in during the rest of his career with the Yankees, both exceptional marks for a middle infielder. His lifetime batting average was .292, his highest being .355 in 1929, and he made the first American

League All-Star team in 1933. Lazzeri hit a grand slam home run against the New York Giants in the 1936 World Series and hit .400 the following year against the same team.

In 1938 Lazzeri was sold to the Chicago Cubs, and the next year he was sold again to the Brooklyn Dodgers and then traded to the Giants, but by this time he was only a part-time player. He spent the next four years managing in the minor leagues, after which his baseball career ended. He then returned to San Francisco and ran a tavern.

In 1923 Lazzeri had married Maye Janes; they had one son. Lazzeri was found dead by his wife in their home in Mill Brae, California. A diabetic, he had fallen against a banister, but the exact cause of death may have a been a heart attack.

Probably the quietest as well the smallest (at 170 pounds) of all the Yankees of his generation, Lazzeri was a stabilizing influence and a major producer on one of the most powerful baseball dynasties of all time. He was especially popular with Italian-American societies in the major eastern cities, with huge crowds holding special "days" for Lazzeri when the Yankees were in town. He was inducted into the National Baseball Hall of Fame in 1991.

• A clipping file on Lazzeri is at the National Baseball Library in Cooperstown, N.Y. Material on Lazzeri is scarce, except for numerous accounts of his striking out in a World Series game against Grover Cleveland Alexander, an episode that has fascinated general baseball histories. A reliable source in this regard is Gene Karst, *Who's Who in Professional Baseball* (1973). Frank Graham, *The New York Yankees* (1943), has good background material. John Thorn and Pete Palmer, eds., *Total Baseball*, 3d ed. (1993), contains an abundance of statistical data. An obituary is in the *New York Times*, 8 Aug. 1946.

THOMAS L. KARNES

LEA, Homer (17 Nov. 1876–1 Nov. 1912), writer, was born in Denver, Colorado, the son of Alfred Erskine Lea, a businessman, and Hersa Coberly. After his mother died in 1878, Lea was brought up in Denver by his stepmother, Emma Wilson Lea, a schoolteacher. Most of Lea's uncles were active on the side of the Confederacy, and one, Joseph C. Lea, a captain in the Confederate army, became a founder of the New Mexico Military Academy at Rosewell. Homer Lea, proud of his family's military background, allegedly claimed family ties to General Robert E. Lee, the Civil War hero, but these claims have no basis in reality.

While young, Lea developed an inordinate interest in military affairs. He also had a special interest in the Chinese people, because many had worked for his father in Colorado and California. Thus he later cultivated personal relations with them. When his father's mining business failed, largely because of the panic of 1893, the family moved to Los Angeles. After graduating from Los Angeles High School, Lea wanted to study law at Harvard but settled on Stanford, where he majored in political science, economics, and history. His principal interest in college was to study the history and strategy of the great wars of the world. When the Spanish-American War broke out in 1898, he volunteered to join the army but was rejected because of his physical defects, including a hunchback and a chronic eye disease. He was allowed to join the California National Guard. Since the war ended quickly, he received neither military training nor combat experience. Instead of continuing his education at Stanford, he dropped out after two years (1897–1899) and returned home in Los Angeles to treat his recurring eye disease.

Lea became involved with city politics as an active member of the small group of progressive, reform-minded men, led by Russ Avery, president of the Los Angeles Voters' League, and Marshall Stimson, a Harvard-educated lawyer, determined to break up the political monopoly of the powerful Southern Pacific Railroad Company. However, he left the group because of differences in reform ideas and shifted his political interest to China.

In the wake of the abortive 1898 Hundred Day Reform in China, Lea became interested in reform in that country. He first approached the San Francisco Chinese community, who supported the reform movement, and convinced their leaders of the possibility of successful reform in China through military means. In the summer of 1900 he was commissioned by the president of the newly organized Chinese Empire Reform Association (*Pao-huang-hui*) of San Francisco to go to China to command the reformists' forces. Taking advantage of the chaos resulting from the Boxer Rebellion of 1900 in North China, the reformists staged an armed revolt along the central Yangtze River, but it ended in fiasco. Although he had no formal military training or career, Lea convinced both the Chinese and Americans of his expertise in military affairs. Before his departure for China in June 1900, he attracted national attention because major newspapers, such as the *San Francisco Call* and the *New York Herald*, printed stories about his planned trip. As a result, he received offers of moral or material help from many Americans, both military and civilian. Despite such publicity, however, his military activities in China were shrouded in mystery, because they were largely covert in nature. He returned to California in early 1901 by way of Japan, where he discussed China's reform with Okuma Shigenobu, a leading Japanese politician. In 1903 Lea met Liang Ch'i-ch'ao, a leader of the Hundred Day Reform, in Los Angeles. In 1904 Lea established the Western Military Academy in Los Angeles to train Chinese cadets for the furtherance of China's reform. In many major cities throughout the United States he also created branches of the Chinese Imperial Army, over which he had command as its major general. When K'ang Yu-wei, leader of the abortive Hundred Day Reform and president of the Chinese Empire Reform Association, visited Lea in Los Angeles in 1905, he promoted Lea to the rank of lieutenant general. Lea clashed with K'ang on how to manage the Chinese military establishments and the public funds raised from Chinese Americans. Lea left

K'ang, who was criticized for investing public funds in Mexico for his own personal gains.

In 1908 Lea came in contact with Sun Yat-sen, president of the Chinese Revolutionary Alliance Society (*Chung-kuo Ko-ming T'ung-meng-hui*), organized in 1905 to promote revolution, not reform, in China. Lea and his friends, such as W. W. Allen and Charles B. Boothe, agreed to raise funds for the Chinese revolution, and in 1910 Lea and Sun coordinated military plans with Chinese collaborators in both the United States and China. Nothing came of their joint efforts. In the summer of 1911 Lea married his longtime secretary, Ethel Bryant Powers. The couple had no children. On his way to Europe for his honeymoon, Lea met with American officials, including Senator Elihu Root, a former secretary of state, and Secretary of State Philander Knox, in Washington in an attempt to help Sun diplomatically and financially. With the revolution underway in October 1911, he tried to do the same on behalf of Sun in London and Paris. Although he failed to secure funds, he helped lift the ban on Sun's entry to the British colony of Hong Kong.

Lea was a prolific writer on military affairs. His first novel, *The Vermilion Pencil* (1908), was an indictment of western missionaries who had tried to destroy the Chinese way of life. His second book, *The Valor of Ignorance* (1909), predicted a Japanese attack on the United States facilitated by military unpreparedness on the part of the American government, controlled by what he called "Pacificist politicians." This book became a bestseller during World War II. While in Germany he met with military specialists to discuss his third book, *The Day of the Saxon* (1912), a detailed military analysis that warns of a Slavic threat to the Anglo-Saxons. He also contributed articles related to military affairs in China to such journals as *North American Review* and *World Today* (London).

Lea and Sun returned to China together from France in December 1911. On 1 January 1912 Sun was inaugurated in Nanking as president of the Republic of China, and Lea accompanied Sun as his personal military and diplomatic adviser. Over Lea's objections, Sun gave up his presidency in favor of General Yuan Shih-k'ai in April 1912. Despite Lea's efforts, Sun was unable to keep his political power, largely because of his lack of military power. In early April 1912 Lea fell ill, and his chronic eye disease worsened. He returned to Santa Monica, California, for treatment, but he died at home in Ocean Park of hemiplegia, resulting from complications of his eye disease and poor health.

As a private citizen, Lea devoted his life to promoting military preparedness for the security of the United States through his famous book, *The Valor of Ignorance*, and for the benefit of China's reform and revolution. Publicly he also tried to promote Sino-American relations, diplomatic and economic, for the mutual benefit of the two countries. In failure, his contributions, both personal and public, have been largely ignored by American and Chinese historians. On 20 April 1969 the Republic of China on Taiwan officially honored Lea by transferring his ashes from Los Angeles to Taipei with the stated intention of burying them permanently next to Sun Yat-sen's mausoleum in Nanking upon the recovery of mainland China from the Communists.

• The papers of Lea and his friends and colleagues are in the archives of the Hoover Institution for War, Revolution and Peace, Stanford University. The Joshua Powers and Charles Boothe collections are the primary sources of information on Lea. Eugene Anschel, *Homer Lea, Sun Yat-sen, and the Chinese Revolution* (1984), and Key Ray Chong, *Americans and Chinese Reform and Revolution, 1898–1922* (1984), are the most complete recent assessments of Lea. C. Martin Wilbur, *Sun Yat-sen: Frustrated Patriot* (1976), deals largely with the financial aspect of Lea's relations with the Chinese reformists and revolutionaries. See also Carl Glick, *Double Ten: Captain O'Banion's Story of the Chinese Revolution* (1945), which, though a popular account, is useful for understanding Lea's military assistance in the Chinese reform and revolution. Obituaries are in the *Los Angeles Times*, 1 Nov. 1912, and the *New York Times*, 2 Nov. 1912.

KEY RAY CHONG

LEA, Isaac (4 Mar. 1792–8 Dec. 1886), naturalist and publisher, was born in Wilmington, Delaware, the son of James Lea, a Quaker merchant, and Elizabeth Gibson. His family had been among those who accompanied William Penn on his second trip to America at the end of the seventeenth century. Originally, his family planned for Isaac to become a physician, and with that in mind he was sent to the Wilmington (Del.) Academy. These plans changed when the family moved to Philadelphia, Pennsylvania, when Isaac was about fifteen, and he went to work in the wholesale and importing house run by his oldest brother. His mother fostered Isaac's early interest in natural history. This interest was more fully developed through his friendship with geologist Lardner Vanuxem. The two met as young fellows in Philadelphia, and they made many forays around Philadelphia and eastern Pennsylvania collecting rocks and minerals. As their collections grew, they wanted to learn more about their specimens. However, there was little opportunity to expand their knowledge through formal study because at that time the science of geology was not very organized in the United States. The only collection of rock specimens in Philadelphia at the time was that of Adam Seybert, whom they befriended. In 1814, when British troops controlled Washington, D.C., Lea and Vanuxem joined a volunteer rifle company, which offered its services to the governor of Pennsylvania and which was prepared to march against the British if called. Even though the situation seemed urgent, the company was never called into action. By the act of volunteering, Isaac Lea lost his birthright in the Society of Friends. Lea and Vanuxem both joined the Academy of Natural Sciences (Philadelphia) in 1815 and were among the first members of that organization. They remained lifelong friends.

Lea married Frances Anne Carey, the daughter of publisher Mathew Carey, in 1821. They were married fifty-two years and had two sons and one daughter. With his marriage, Lea backed into the publishing business. Mathew Carey retired from publishing in January 1822 and sold the business to his son Henry Charles Carey and his son-in-law, who formed the company of H. C. Carey and I. Lea. Their publishing house (and its successor companies) was the largest American publishing house during the nineteenth century. They were the first to publish many important American authors and the first to pay foreign authors to gain their American rights. They published the first *Encyclopaedia Americana* and the *American Quarterly Review*; they also introduced literary annuals onto the American scene. In spite of the success of the business, Lea himself was never much of a bookseller or publisher. He took care of the company books and records and acted as the publisher for some natural history books. However, as Henry Carey wrote to his father ten years after the elder's retirement, "[Lea] is scarcely more of a bookseller now than he ever was. . . . He has many good qualities, but is too fond of shells to make a bookseller." Lea retired from business in 1851.

Indeed, Lea was fond of shells, and he remains one of the authorities on the genus *Unio*, freshwater mollusks. He and Vanuxem found mollusca fossils on their collecting expeditions, and Lea felt that to study geology he needed to have a better knowledge of shells. He purchased a collection of Chinese shells to become familiar with Lamarkian systematics. In the process, he discovered his true passion. He was introduced to the genus *Unio* through specimens sent to the Academy of Natural Sciences by Stephen H. Long of the Engineering Corps of the United States from a project along the Ohio River in 1825. At the same time Lea's brother Thomas, who was a Cincinnati merchant and an amateur botanist of note, began sending a steady supply of freshwater shells for Isaac's collection. The description of six of these Ohio Valley shells published in 1827 became his first contribution to conchology. Lea's continuing series *Observations on the Genus Unio* described 901 species and ran to thirteen quarto volumes, issued between 1827 and 1874. He also wrote about and classified more than 900 other species of mollusks, both fossils and those of recent times. In addition to his publications on the subject, he actively corresponded with leading scientists from all over the world and clearly was the recognized authority on freshwater mollusks. In 1832 and again in 1853 Lea made extended visits to Europe and was warmly received in all the important scientific centers. It was not unusual for him to be invited to evaluate and rearrange shell collections in the various institutions and homes in which he was a guest.

In addition to his work in conchology, he also published on subjects as varied as mineralogy, geology, fossils, paleontology, the Northwest Passage, and hibernation. He was one of the first to publish illustrated works on paleontology and particularly on dinosaur footprints. At the time of his death, Lea was also one of the most highly regarded gemologists in the United

States. In addition to his membership in the Academy of Natural Sciences, he was also elected a member of the American Philosophical Society (1828) and of the American Association for the Advancement of Science. He served as president of the Academy of Natural Sciences from 1858 until 1863 and of the American Association for the Advancement of Science in 1860. He was also a vice president of the American Philosophical Society and served in other capacities in various scientific organizations. Benjamin Silliman said that it was Isaac Lea's efforts to secure subscriptions that assured the initial success of the *American Journal of Science*. Harvard bestowed the honorary degree of LL.D. on Lea in 1852.

At the time of his death in Philadelphia, one of his eulogizers referred to the steadfast Lea as the "castor of American naturalists." In addition to his writings, the enduring contribution of Lea can be found in the Museum of Natural History in the Smithsonian Institution. His natural history collections were bequeathed to the National Museum upon his death, and his gem and mineral collection was given to the Smithsonian in 1894 by his daughter. Her husband Leander T. Chamberlain acted as honorary curator of the collection and left an endowment for the collection upon his death. The Lea gem collection forms the nucleus around which the current gem collection has grown.

• An extensive bibliography of all of the writings of Isaac Lea and an extensive biography can be found in Newton Pratt Scudder, "The Published Writings of Isaac Lea, LL.D.," United States National Museum, *Bulletin Number 23* (1885; repr., 1900, 1983). Lea himself produced a catalog of his writings titled *A Catalogue of the Published Works of Isaac Lea, LL.D. from 1817 to 1876* (1876). George W. Tyron, Jr., produced *Publications of Isaac Lea on Recent Conchology: Extracted from a List of American Writers on Recent Conchology* (1861). A description of his shell collection is in the "Check Lists of the Shells of North America," *Smithsonian Miscellaneous Collections*, vol. 2, art. 6 (1860; repr. 1900, 1983). A more modern work discussing Lea's contributions to conchology is Richard Irwin Johnson, *Lea's Unionid Types, or, Recent and Fossil Taxa of Unionacea and Mutelacea Introduced by Isaac Lea including the Location of All the Extant Types* (1974). His gem collection is described in Wirt de Vivier Tassin, "Descriptive Catalogue of the Collections of Gems in the United States National Museum," *United States National Museum Annual Report, 1900* (1902). A history of the Carey and Lea publishing house is in David Kaser, *Messrs. Carey & Lea of Philadelphia: A Study in the History of the Book Trade* (1957). Several obituary notices were written for Lea, but all relied heavily on the Scudder biography.

M. SUSAN BARGER

LEA, Mathew Carey (18 Aug. 1823–15 Mar. 1897), chemist, was born in Philadelphia, Pennsylvania, the son of Isaac Lea, a naturalist and publisher, and Frances Anne Carey. His father, a descendant of an early Quaker family, served as president of Philadelphia's Academy of Natural Sciences (1858) and the American Association for the Advancement of Science (1860). His mother was the daughter of Mathew Carey, the eminent and prolific writer on political economy and

first publisher of the *Encyclopedia Americana*. His younger brother, Henry Charles Lea, became a well-known publisher and renowned philosophical and historical writer. From early on, Carey Lea, as he was called, was intrigued by intellectual and scientific pursuits.

Of frail constitution, Lea attended neither school nor college but received an excellent education at home from the best private tutors available. His keen intellect enabled him to acquire a very broad and thorough knowledge, especially of languages, literature, art, and the natural and physical sciences. In 1832, at the age of nine, he spent six months in England and continental Europe, meeting many of his father's scientific acquaintances.

During his teens Lea joined the Philadelphia firm of Booth, Garrett, and Blair, the first American chemical consulting laboratory, where he studied chemistry under future (1883–1885) American Chemical Society president James Curtis Booth. He studied law at the office of William M. Meredith, the leader of the Philadelphia bar. He was admitted to the bar in 1847 at the age of twenty-four, but continued ill health forced him to abandon his law practice. He then spent several years touring Europe, unsuccessfully seeking relief. He thereafter remained more or less an invalid, and repeated attacks of illness incapacitated him for the more active pursuits of his life.

Lea returned to Booth's laboratory to continue his practical study of chemistry, but he pursued his later experimental work in his private laboratory at his home in the Philadelphia suburb of Chestnut Hill. He was a wealthy, sickly, antisocial recluse, whom few chemists knew personally. Nevertheless, he was considered a brilliant conversationalist. During early manhood an accident in his laboratory seriously injured one of his eyes, which eventually had to be removed. He was able to follow his interest in the current work of foreign scholars by the devotion of his wives, who read to him constantly for many years. He married Elizabeth Lea Jaudon, a cousin, in July 1852. She died, leaving behind one son, in 1881. His second marriage to Eva Lovering, daughter of Harvard professor Joseph Lovering, was childless.

Lea's first scientific paper, "On the First or Southern Coal Field of Pennsylvania" (*American Journal of Science and Arts* [1841]), published in his eighteenth year, presented the results of his coal analyses made in Booth's laboratory. In the field of theoretical chemistry, his article "On Numerical Relations Existing between the Equivalent Numbers of Elementary Bodies" (*American Journal of Science* 29 [1860]: 98, 349) speculated on numerical relations among the elements. Although the germ of some sort of periodic law was in his thoughts, he never clearly enunciated it. In 1895 and 1896 he published ingenious articles on the color relations of atoms, ions, and molecules.

In organic chemistry Lea studied methods for preparing ethylamines, urea, and other compounds. Beginning in 1858 he published a series of articles on picric acid that described a new method for its preparation and many new salts, including urea and quinine picrates. On the outbreak of the Civil War he advised the U.S. government that picric acid was an explosive of greater power than black powder and had the added advantage of being smokeless. The government ignored his observations, and a half-century elapsed before picric acid and picrates were adopted as high explosives.

In analytical chemistry Lea devised a number of new qualitative tests. Some of these tests included picrates to separate primary, secondary, and tertiary ethylamines (1862), a new coloring matter called iononaphthine (1861), a test for gelatin (1865), and an increase of the sensitivity of the starch test for iodine by the addition of chromic acid (1866). Three tests he performed proposed the formation of a purple precipitate (1875), showed that iodoquinone detects traces of sulfuric acid (1893), and developed a new method for detecting the relative affinities of acids (1895). Other significant contributions included, but were not limited to, the proposal of oxalic acid to purify ammonium chloroiridate(III), an iridium purity test (1864), a ruthenium(III) chloride test to detect sodium hyposulfite (1865), and two new methods for the reduction of platinum(IV) chloride to platinum(II) chloride, one with potassium sulfite and one with alkali hypophosphites (1894).

In addition to his chemical articles, Lea published many articles in the field of physics. In 1860 he observed the optical properties of manganese picrate, particularly its dichroism. In 1869 he detected certain phenomena of transmitted and diffused light, and in 1896, shortly before Röntgen's discovery of X rays, he carried out a series of experiments to ascertain if these rays were detectable in sunlight.

However, Lea's most valuable contributions were on the chemistry of photography, and they secured him a worldwide recognition as one of the half-dozen pioneer investigators who laid the scientific foundations of photography. At the time of his death he was the world's acknowledged authority on the chemistry of photography. He primarily studied the chemical and physical properties of the silver halide salts, not only alone, but in combination with each other and with various coloring matters (1887), especially in relation to the action of light on them under different conditions. He also worked on the nature of the photographic process, colloid–silver halide emulsions, developing agents, and the influence of the color of light on the photoreduction of silver salts. His work with the colored compounds formed by the silver salts and aniline dyes foreshadowed color photography.

Perhaps Lea's best-known contributions were his description of what he called "photohaloids" of silver (1885) and his discovery of their identity with the substance of the latent photographic image (1887), as well as his discovery of what he called "allotropic" forms of silver of various colors (described in a series of eight articles published between 1889 and 1891). The importance of his contributions to the new field of photographic chemistry was first recognized by forensic scientists (largely through translation) but was finally recognized in the United States by his election to the National Academy of Sciences in 1895. In the course of photographic investigations Lea also became interested in the relations of energy to chemical changes of matter, and he showed that not only heat, light, electricity, and chemical reactions but also mechanical force are capable of disrupting molecules (1892–1893). He died in Philadelphia.

Lea was a quiet, unostentatious but prolific scientist who not only labored independently on analytical, organic, and inorganic chemistry but also conducted numerous studies of photochemistry. During the last quarter of the nineteenth century these studies were universally regarded as the most important contributions to the relatively new physicochemical field. An acute observer, he was thoroughly acquainted with the past and current literature of chemistry. An undisputed master in his field, he was an indefatigable worker who did not allow his physical infirmities to interfere with his experimental research.

• Lea's only book, *A Manual of Photography* (1868), was widely read in its day. His contributions to photography in the *British Journal of Photography* number nearly three hundred. His papers on others branches of chemistry, which number more than one hundred, appear mostly in the *American Journal of Science*. A biography is Edgar Fahs Smith, *M. Carey Lea—Chemist* (1923); it was reprinted in *Catalyst* 8 (1923). Biographical articles include George F. Barker, "Mathew Carey Lea, 1823–1897," National Academy of Sciences, *Biographical Memoirs* 5 (1905): 155–203 (with a list of 101 of his most important papers); excerpts from this article appear in Smith, *Chemistry in America* (1914; repr. 1972), pp. 277–301; Smith, "M. Carey Lea, Chemist, 1823–1897," *Journal of Chemical Education* 20 (1943): 577–79 (with autographed portrait); and Herbert T. Pratt, "Matthew [*sic*] Carey Lea, 1823–1897," in *American Chemists and Chemical Engineers*, ed. Wyndham D. Miles (1976). Obituaries include *Public Ledger*, 16 Mar. 1897, and Samuel P. Sadtler et al., "In Memoriam: Mathew Carey Lea," *Journal of the Franklin Institute* 145 (1898): 143–47 (with portrait and list of his most important publications).

GEORGE B. KAUFFMAN

LEACH, Robert Boyd (1822–29 July 1863), physician, was born in Virginia to free blacks (names unknown) and moved to Jackson County, Ohio, with his family when he was about five years old. Leach arrived sometime between 1836 and 1844 in Cleveland, where he found seasonal work on the lake steamers.

Leach became interested in medicine while working on the lake steamers. Although, like most African Americans from the southern part of the state, he had no formal education, he was ambitious and industrious. He was described as "pleasing in his address, winning in his manner, upright and trustworthy" (*Cleveland Leader*, 11 Mar. 1958). These characteristics led to his assignment as the nurse for sick patrons on the boats. With only a small medical book at his disposal, he occasionally carried out the responsibilities of ship doctor as well. This work led him to read and study all of the medical texts available, particularly during the off-season, to become more qualified and knowledgeable.

In 1849, when the lake region was plagued with cholera, Leach became quite well known for his concoction of a successful remedy to treat the disease. This event served to make the young man even more determined to become better prepared to treat the sick. In 1856 Leach finally realized his ambition when he began a two-year medical course at the Western College of Homeopathy. After graduation in 1858 he became Cleveland's first African-American medical doctor. An editorial titled "A Man for a' That," in the *Cleveland Leader*, noted that by the time Leach graduated he had "not only secured a fair reputation and acquired an honorable profession . . . but [had] an intelligent, interesting family and a home with all the pleasant surroundings" (11 Mar. 1858). The article undoubtedly referred to his home, valued in 1860 at the very large sum of $10,000, and his wife Imogene, daughter Olivia, and mother (or aunt) Francis, who offered piano lessons for young ladies. At a time when Cleveland's black population numbered somewhat fewer than 800, the article also implies that Leach and his family enjoyed genuine admiration and acceptance from the entire community.

Leach was also well known as an antislavery activist and spokesman for Ohio's black population. As early as 1853 he represented Cleveland and Cuyahoga County at the Ohio State Convention of Colored Freemen in Columbus, where the delegation, including well-known antislavery activists Charles H. Langston and William Howard Day, went on record demanding citizenship rights for all African Americans. In 1860, at the first meeting of the Ohio State Anti-Slavery Society, Leach was elected to the executive board and appointed to a committee to present grievances of the state's black citizens to the legislature.

During the Civil War Leach assisted in the recruitment of black soldiers for the Union cause. However, when he offered his own professional services he was rejected by the War Department because of its objection to homeopathy. Baffled but not discouraged, he immediately began to read texts to qualify to practice the more acceptable allopathic medicine. Sadly, however, after a brief respite early in 1863 in Saratoga, where he went to try to recoup his own failing health, he fell ill and died of liver disease at the home of a friend in Philadelphia en route to Washington, where he hoped to once again volunteer for the army.

• Leach is profiled in Russell Davis, *Black Americans in Cleveland* (1972) and *Memorable Negroes in Cleveland's Past* (1969). The *Cleveland Leader* reprinted an obituary on 7 Sept. 1863 taken from the *Anglo-African*, 15 Aug. 1863.

ADRIENNE LASH JONES

LEACOCK, John (21 Dec. 1729–16 Nov. 1802), Philadelphia silversmith merchant, and revolutionary propagandist, was born in Philadelphia, the son of John Leacock, a pewtersmith and shopkeeper, and Mary Cash. Leacock was born into a prosperous family that had moved from Barbados, where his father had sold his plantations, to Philadelphia to invest in land and in the earliest iron furnaces in the province. Like his two brothers, he was probably apprenticed at a relatively young age to an established gold- and silversmith; he may have worked in a metalworkers' shop owned by his father. In the early 1750s Leacock had evidently worked hard enough to create his own establishment on Walnut Street in Philadelphia. He married Hannah McCally in August 1752; they had two sons, one of whom died in infancy. When his father died late that year, he used his inheritance to move his smithing trade to "the sign of the Golden Cup" on Front Street, the center of Philadelphia's gold- and silversmithing business.

Leacock's metalworking trade prospered and he and his apprentices created objects of finery primarily for upper-class patrons. These included elegant toys, such as sterling whistles, with bells, having coral toothing sticks in one end, one of which was created for Samuel Morris, a well-known merchant, soldier, and civic leader, about 1760. Leacock also worked as an engraver and even occasionally as a printer, probably with his brother-in-law David Hall, partner of Benjamin Franklin. Leacock's family connections favored an affluent trade; he was a brother-in-law of James Read, a prominent lawyer, and a second cousin of Deborah Read Franklin, the wife of Benjamin Franklin. Along with his prosperous business, these connections enabled Leacock to enter high society; in 1759 he was elected to the Schuylkill Fishing Company, which included Philadelphia's most prominent citizens.

When the Stamp Act of 1765 created enough unrest that colonists were ready to rebel, Leacock's signature on Philadelphia's nonimportation agreement of 1765 signified to worried Philadelphians the support of wealthy merchants for the revolutionary effort. Leacock stood to lose everything by such an agreement because as an upper-class tradesman and merchant, he would lose his business with a ban on importation. In addition to signing this ban, Leacock the next year penned and probably paid for the distribution of a broadside (a single-page publication that was handed out or sold in the streets and in shops). The broadside's verse, *A New Song, on the Repeal of the Stamp-Act*, vilified key British ministers of state and celebrated the repeal of the Stamp Act. Given his trade, Leacock's early and consistent support of the revolutionary cause is quite significant indeed.

In the fall of 1767 Leacock gave up his businesses and moved his family to an estate in Lower Merion, just west of Philadelphia. Here he took up the pursuits of a gentleman farmer, working with the American Philosophical Society to promote vineyards in Philadelphia and traveling to Madeira between 1769 and 1771 in an effort to develop connections for wine and grape importation. Hannah McCally died in 1767. Leacock married Martha Ogilby in June 1770; they had three children.

Although life as a man of cultivated leisure evidently appealed to Leacock, he continued to assist in the revolutionary effort. In 1772 he joined the Philadelphia Sons of Liberty in forming a new society, the Society of the Sons of Saint Tammany (named after the legendary Delaware chief, Tamanend). The society, a coalition of upper-class men from differing backgrounds and occupations, seems to have met to sustain social and political cohesion. Leacock more fully clarified his patriot position in his satire, *The First Book of the American Chronicles of the Times*, published during the fall and winter of 1774–1775. This anonymously published, six-chapter pamphlet series used biblical language to ridicule Britain's inept colonial administration. Immensely popular in the colonies, the *American Chronicles* was printed and reprinted from Massachusetts to South Carolina. Leacock followed this satire with a more serious play, *The Fall of British Tyranny* (written and published in 1776 but probably not publicly performed), denouncing the British ministry and Crown as stupid, profligate, and covetous. Leacock was clearly attempting to propagandize the colonial patriot position so that all readers could have access to the thinking of middling and upper-class patriotic whites.

In 1779 Leacock aided the patriot cause by signing bills of credit on behalf of the United States in Easton and Reading, Pennsylvania. In 1780 he moved back to Philadelphia, where in 1785 he received the prominent (and undemanding) post of Philadelphia coroner. Leacock seems to have spent the remainder of his life in social, literary, and political prominence. In the *American Crisis* papers (1776), Thomas Paine called the revolutionary era in which Leacock lived "the times that try men's souls." Leacock might have felt "tried" or tested by the circumstances in his life, but he probably felt as if he had contributed to the key event—the revolutionary war—that would change Anglo-American relations for all time. He died in Philadelphia.

• John Leacock's commonplace book (something like a diary) and some family documents (including the Cash-Leacock family Bible) are located at the American Philosophical Society in Philadelphia. Leacock's family relations are outlined in a genealogical chart printed in Leonard W. Labaree et al., eds., *The Papers of Benjamin Franklin*, vol. 8 (1965), pp. 140–41. Information about John Leacock's life is difficult to find. Norman Philbrick's introduction to the propaganda play, *The Fall of British Tyranny*, which he reprints in *Trumpets Sounding: Propaganda Plays of the American Revolution* (1972), is useful, but Philbrick did not seem to know of a significant article on Leacock that pointed to his authorship of the play: Frances J. Dallett, Jr., "John Leacock and *The Fall of British Tyranny*," *Pennsylvania Magazine of History and Biography* 78 (1954): 456–75. More complete studies of Leacock's life and his writings appear in Carla Mulford, "John Leacock's *A New Song, on the Repeal of the Stamp-Act*," *Early American Literature* 15 (1980): 188–93, and *John Leacock's The First Book of the American Chronicles of the Times, 1774–1775* (1987).

CARLA J. MULFORD

LEAD BELLY (15 Jan. 1888–6 Dec. 1949), folk singer and composer, was born Huddie Ledbetter on the Jeter plantation near Caddo Lake, north of Shreveport,

Louisiana, the only surviving son of John Wesley Ledbetter and Sally Pugh, farmers who were reasonably well-to-do. Young Huddie (or "Hudy" as the 1910 census records list him) grew up in a large rural black community centered around the Louisiana-Texas-Arkansas junction, and he would later play at rural dances where, in his own words, "there would be no white man around for twenty miles." Though he was exposed to the newer African-American music forms like the blues, he also absorbed many of the older fiddle tunes, play-party tunes, church songs, field hollers, badman ballads, and even old vaudeville songs of the culture. His uncle taught him a song that later became his signature tune, "Goodnight, Irene." Though Huddie's first instrument was a "windjammer" (a small accordian), by 1903 he had acquired a guitar and was plying his trade at local dances.

In 1904, when he turned sixteen, Huddie made his way to the notorious red-light district of nearby Shreveport; there he was exposed to early jazz and ragtime, as well as blues, and learned how to adapt the left-hand rhythm of the piano players to his own guitar style. He also acquired a venereal disease that eventually drove him back home for treatment. In 1908 he married Aletha Henderson, with whom he had no children, and the pair moved just east of Dallas, where they worked in the fields and prowled the streets of Dallas. Two important things happened to Huddie here: he heard and bought his first twelve-string guitar (the instrument that he would make famous), and he met the man who later became one of the best-known exponents of the "country blues," Blind Lemon Jefferson. Though Jefferson was actually Huddie's junior by some five years, he had gained considerable experience as a musician, and he taught Huddie much about the blues and about how an itinerant musician in these early days could make a living. The pair were fixtures around Dallas's rough-and-tumble Deep Ellum district until about 1915.

Returning to Harrison County, Texas, Huddie then began a series of altercations with the law that would change his life and almost destroy his performing career. It started in 1915, when he was convicted on an assault charge and sent to the local chain gang. He soon escaped, however, and fled to Bowie County under the alias of Walter Boyd. There he lived peacefully until 1917, when he was accused of killing a cousin and wound up at the Sugarland Prison farm in south Texas. There he gained a reputation as a singer and a hard worker, and it was there that a prison chaplain gave him the nickname "Lead Belly." (Though subsequent sources have listed the singer's nickname as one word, "Leadbelly," all original documents give "Lead Belly.") At Sugarland he also learned songs like "The Midnight Special" and began to create his own songs about local characters and events. When Texas governor Pat Neff visited the prison on an inspection tour, Lead Belly composed a song to the governor pleading for his release; impressed by the singer's skill, Neff did indeed give him a pardon, signing the papers on 16 January 1925. For the next five years Lead Belly lived and worked around Shreveport, until 1930, when he was again convicted for assault—this time for knifing a "prominent" white citizen. The result was a six- to ten-year term in Angola, then arguably the worst prison in America.

In 1933, while in Angola, Lead Belly encountered folk-song collector John Lomax, who had been traveling throughout southern prisons collecting folk songs from inmates for the Library of Congress. Lead Belly sang several of his choice songs for the machine, including "The Western Cowboy" and "Goodnight, Irene." Lomax was impressed and a year later returned to gather more songs; this time Lead Belly decided to try his pardon-song technique again and recorded a plea to the Louisiana governor, O. K. Allen. The following year Lead Belly was in fact released, and though he always assumed the song had done the trick, prison records show Lead Belly was scheduled for release anyway because of overcrowding.

Lead Belly immediately sought out Lomax and took a job as his driver and bodyguard. For the last months of 1934, he traveled with Lomax as he made the rounds of southern prisons. During this time he learned a lot about folk music and added dozens of new songs to his own considerable repertoire.

In December 1934 Lomax presented his singer to the national meeting of the Modern Language Association in Philadelphia—Lead Belly's first real public appearance—and then took him to New York City in January 1935. His first appearances there generated a sensational round of stories in the press and on newsreels and set the stage for a series of concerts and interviews. One of these was a well-publicized marriage to a childhood sweetheart, Martha Promise (it is not known how or when his first marriage ended); another was a record contract with the American Record Company. Lomax himself continued to make records at a house in Westport, Connecticut, a series of recordings that was donated to the Library of Congress and that formed the foundation for the book by John Lomax and Alan Lomax, *Negro Folk Songs as Sung by Lead Belly* (1936). For three months money and offers poured in, but complex tensions stemming in part from Lomax's attempts to mold Lead Belly's repertoire in a way that fit the classic folk music image of the day led to an estrangement between Lomax and Lead Belly, and before long the singer returned to Shreveport.

A year later Lead Belly and his wife returned to New York City to try to make it on their own. He found his audience not in the young African-American fans of Cab Calloway and Duke Ellington (who considered his music old fashioned), but in the young white social activists of various political and labor movements. He felt strongly about issues concerning civil rights and produced songs on a number of topics, the best of which were "The Bourgeois Blues" and "We're in the Same Boat, Brother." Lead Belly soon had his own radio show in New York, which led to an invitation to Hollywood to try his hand at films. He tried out for a role in *Green Pastures* and was consid-

ered for a planned film with Bing Crosby about Lomax. The late 1940s saw a series of excellent commercial recordings for Capitol, as well as for the independent Folkways label in New York. His apartment became a headquarters for young aspiring folk singers coming to New York, including a young Woody Guthrie. Martha Promise's niece Tiny began managing Lead Belly's affairs, and his career was on the upswing when, in 1949, he became ill with amyotrophic lateral sclerosis (Lou Gherig's disease). It progressed rapidly, and in December Lead Belly died in Bellevue Hospital in New York City. His body was returned to Mooringsport, Louisiana, for burial. Ironically, a few months later, his song "Goodnight, Irene" was recorded by the Weavers, a group of his folk-singing friends, and became one of the biggest record hits of the decade.

Lead Belly was one of the first performers to introduce African-American traditional music to mainstream American culture in the 1930s and 1940s and was responsible for the popularity and survival of many of the nation's best-loved songs.

• The basic collection of Lead Belly songs, with rich annotations, is the aforementioned *Negro Folk Songs as Sung by Lead Belly*. The primary biography is Charles K. Wolfe and Kip Lornell, *The Life and Legend of Leadbelly* (1992). Numerous CDs feature reissues of both the singer's commercial and Library of Congress recordings. An example of the latter is the three-volume *Lead Belly: The Library of Congress Recordings* (Rounder 1044–46).

CHARLES K. WOLFE

LEAF, Munro (4 Dec. 1905–21 Dec. 1976), author and illustrator of children's books, was born in Hamilton, Maryland, the son of Charles Wilbur Munro, a printer, and Emma India Gillespie. He married Margaret Butler Pope in 1926 while an undergraduate at the University of Maryland (B.A., 1927); they had two children. He taught and coached football at boys' schools in Belmont, Massachusetts, and Wynnewood, Pennsylvania, and earned an M.A. in English literature from Harvard (1931), where, to compensate for his artistic bent, he also won a boxing championship.

In the fall of 1932 Leaf went to New York City, where he read manuscripts for the Bobbs-Merrill Co., joined the Frederick A. Stokes Co. (1933) as editor and director, and became a part of the intellectual scene at the Algonquin Hotel. His first book, *Lo, the Poor Indian* (1934), was written under the pseudonym "Mun." Within three years Leaf had published two very different kinds of books, each representative of a career direction and a philosophical orientation. *Grammar Can Be Fun* (1934), Leaf's second book, was illustrated by the author with the crude stick figures that would mark the "can be fun" series, and it established Leaf as a committed teacher and socializer of the young. The most important volume in the series was *Manners Can Be Fun* (1936), in which Leaf explained simple manners not as arbitrary customs, but as a requirement of living in society. Other titles in the series include *History Can Be Fun* (1950), *Reading Can Be*

Fun (1953), *Being an American Can Be Fun* (1964), and *Metric Can Be Fun* (1976). Writing in an era characterized by international tension and conflict, Leaf emphasized in books such as *Fair Play* (1939) and *Let's Do Better* (1945) the necessity of getting along with others, the importance of training future generations to be responsible citizens, and the progress of humankind from the "caves" to "civilization." While Leaf's young readers were undeniably entertained by the simple drawings in these books, the written messages were direct, didactic, and judgmental. In *Safety Can Be Fun* (1938), for example, Leaf labeled children who engaged in unsafe behavior "nit-wits" and threatened those who disregarded his advice with extended stays in the hospital. "Watchwords," a long-running monthly feature for *Ladies' Home Journal*, debuted in 1938, with each sketch identifying an unworthy behavioral type, such as the Pouter, the Bragger, or the Tattletale ("no one likes them").

In contrast to the admonitions to conform that were central to these books, *The Story of Ferdinand* (1936) established the integrity of the self, in conflict with social pressures and expectations, as Leaf's seminal thematic contribution to the genre. Written in less than forty minutes, this classic of children's literature—it would sell more than 2.5 million copies—has frequently been interpreted as a pacifist tract or as a commentary on the Spanish civil war, although it was composed before that conflict began. The book features a young bull, Ferdinand, who rejects the roles laid out for him—masculinity, combat, social involvement with peers, sexuality, fatherhood, and progress toward responsible adulthood—for the smell of flowers and a life of leisure. Like the dachshund in *Noodle* (1937) and the Scottish boy in *Wee Gillis* (1938), Ferdinand has only to recognize his own essence—and to shut out the voices of the so-called experts who claim to know what is best for others—in order to make what at first appears to be a difficult, life-determining decision. *The Story of Ferdinand* benefited from the compelling illustrations of Robert Lawson.

In 1942 Leaf enlisted in the army, graduated from the army staff and command school in 1943, and served in the United States and Europe in noncombat capacities until 1946, when he left the service with the rank of major. During the war Leaf wrote a humorous field manual on malaria, *This Is Ann, She's Dying to Meet You* (1943) (Ann was short for anopheles mosquito). Illustrated by Dr. Seuss, it was circulated among American and Australian troops. Among what he called his "other adult performances" were a handbook for the United Nations, *Three Promises to You* (1957), and *You and Psychiatry* (1948), coauthored with psychiatrist William C. Menninger, which analyzed postwar anxieties from a Freudian perspective and advocated the sublimation and control of irrational, dangerous emotions. Leaf's only publication for young adults, *Listen Little Girl: Before You Come to New York* (1938), was a practical guidebook to the potential pitfalls of the big city.

Leaf's efforts at social commentary, though timely, often lacked humor and subtlety. Written at the peak of 1950s prosperity, *Lucky You* (1955) uncritically celebrated synthetic fibers and other benefits of modern science. *I Hate You! I Hate You!* (1968), the product of three extensive trips abroad for the State Department between 1961 and 1964, did little to advance understanding by describing social conflicts around the world as "stupid nonsense." In contrast, Leaf was at his best instructing children in proper conduct and, especially, in exploring the complexities of coming of age. He died in Garrett Park, Maryland.

• Leaf's papers are at the Philadelphia Free Library. His other published works include *Robert Francis Weatherbee* (1935), *The Story of Simpson and Sampson* (1941), *A War-Time Handbook for Young Americans* (1942), *How to Behave and Why* (1946), *Boo: Who Used to Be Scared of the Dark* (1948), *The Wishing Pool* (1960), and *Three-and-Thirty Watchbirds* (1944), one of several published collections of his contributions to *Ladies' Home Journal*. Reviews and commentary on these and other books are in *Children's Literature Review* 25 (1991): 113–36. Anne Commire, ed., *Something about the Author*, vol. 20 (1980), contains a bibliography and comments by Leaf. An obituary is in the *New York Times*, 22 Dec. 1976.

WILLIAM GRAEBNER

LEAHY, Frank (27 Aug. 1908–21 June 1973), college football coach, was born Francis William Leahy in O'Neill, Nebraska, the son of Frank Leahy, the owner of produce and freight hauling firms, and Mary Winifred Kane. Leahy's family moved in 1910 to Winner, South Dakota, where he excelled for three seasons as a halfback on the high school football team. Transferring to Omaha High School for his senior year to take required courses for enrolling at the University of Notre Dame, he was shifted to tackle.

Leahy matriculated at Notre Dame in 1927, becoming freshman class president and center on the freshman team. He started at tackle for the varsity in 1929, when Notre Dame finished undefeated in nine games under coach Knute Rockne and was acclaimed national champion. Leahy suffered a severe knee injury before the start of the 1930 season and missed the entire schedule. When Rockne entered the Mayo Clinic for treatment, he persuaded Leahy to share a room with him and have his knee surgically repaired. Apparently, Leahy profited from their many hours at Mayo discussing football strategies; Rockne proclaimed: "That kid has the greatest football brain I have ever come in contact with."

With a degree in physical education earned in 1931, Leahy spent the next eight years as an assistant coach. He first joined coach Tommy Mills at Georgetown University as line coach, then in 1932 became line coach under Jimmy Crowley at Michigan State College. From 1933 to 1938 Leahy helped develop Fordham University's famed "Seven Blocks of Granite," the heart of a team that lost only two games in three seasons. He married Florence Reilly of Brooklyn in 1936; they had eight children.

In 1939 Leahy became head football coach at Boston College, leading the Eagles that year to nine victories and a postseason appearance in the Cotton Bowl. Boston College in 1940 finished with a perfect 11–0 won-lost record, including an upset victory over Tennessee in the Sugar Bowl, and rated fifth in the nation in the final Associated Press poll.

A release clause in Leahy's multiyear contract with Boston College enabled him to sign as head coach at Notre Dame in 1941. The Irish finished undefeated his first season, ranking third in the AP's national ratings. The following year Leahy broke with the traditional Notre Dame system and adopted the new T formation—to the dismay of alumni and friends. "If Rock [Knute Rockne] were alive, he would be the first to try it," Leahy declared. Notre Dame lost a total of only three games in the 1942 and 1943 seasons, after facing seven of the nation's thirteen top-rated teams. The team won the national championship in 1943. In 1944–1945 Leahy served in the U.S. Navy as a lieutenant commander in charge of recreation programs for submarine crews.

At war's end Leahy returned to Notre Dame and guided the Irish to four consecutive undefeated seasons (1946–1949) and three national titles with such All-Americas as Johnny Lujack at quarterback and Leon Hart at end. Not since 1924 had the coach of a major college team produced four undefeated seasons in succession, an extraordinary feat.

Leahy, however, had his faults and his detractors. His gloomy predictions, even before games that Notre Dame proceeded to win by huge margins, caused ill feeling among opposing coaches. While Rockne could maintain the friendship and admiration of defeated opponents, Leahy could not. He used a "sucker shift" to draw a University of Southern California player offside in 1952, and the following season one of his players faked an injury to stop the clock against Iowa—strategies that other coaches used without the furor that followed Leahy's actions. Yet he was widely admired for his organizational ability, dedication, work ethic, coaching strategy, ability to motivate others, and personal characteristics, including his devotion to his family and church. In 1949 he was appointed by Pope Pius XII to the Knights of Malta, an exclusive worldwide Catholic clergy-lay group, the first football coach so honored.

Often called "The Master" by sportswriters, Leahy drove himself relentlessly, spending long hours reviewing films and preparing for opponents, so consumed that occasionally he forgot to go home at night. He suffered a severe pancreatic attack in 1953 midway through another undefeated football season and was advised to give up coaching for the good of his health. "I have never seen a man who gave himself a worse beating than Leahy does," maintained his attending physician.

Leahy resigned from Notre Dame in 1954. After thirteen seasons at two institutions, he had a composite .864 won-lost percentage that ranks second among all coaches, just behind Rockne's .881. Some felt Notre Dame's administration, sensitive to claims of overemphasis on football and perceptions that Notre Dame was becoming a football factory, was relieved by Leahy's departure. During his Notre Dame tenure, Leahy's teams garnered five national titles, ten top-ten ratings, and included sixteen consensus All-Americas, fourteen Football Hall of Famers, four Heisman, three Maxwell, five Camp, three Rockne, and two Outland award winners. The American Football Coaches Association in 1941 named Leahy coach of the year. He was voted Man of the Year in 1949 by the Football Writers Association of America, and in 1970 he was inducted into the National Football Foundation College Hall of Fame. After his retirement, Leahy became a successful business executive, sports promoter, and football analyst. He spent a year as general manager of the Los Angeles Chargers of the American Football League but resigned because of ill health. In 1960 he sold stock for a Denver oil and gas company; the Securities and Exchange Commission claimed in a legal brief that he gave false and misleading information to prospective buyers, a charge that he denied. An honest man, he apparently was naive enough to allow shady promoters to exploit his name. In approximately 1961 he joined his son in the insurance business in Portland, Oregon, where he died.

Leahy's success in coaching during the 1940s rivaled or surpassed the achievements of such honored figures as Walter Camp, Pop Warner, Percy Haughton, Bob Zuppke, and Rockne. His coaching record of six undefeated seasons in eight consecutive years is unequaled. Notre Dame's four consensus national championships in five years (excluding Leahy's two years of wartime service) had not been seen since 1905–1909. His place in college football history is secure.

• Wells Twombly's *Shake Down the Thunder: The Official Biography of Notre Dame's Frank Leahy* (1974) is the only full-length account of Leahy's career. See also Edwin Pope, *Football's Greatest Coaches* (1956); Arch Ward, *Frank Leahy and the Fighting Irish* (1947); and Jack Clary, *Great College Football Coaches* (1990). Leahy detailed his system in *Notre Dame Football: The T Formation* (1949). His early coaching career is examined in Edward Fitzgerald's "Frank Leahy . . . The Enigma of Notre Dame," *Sport*, Nov. 1949. Other books containing profiles are Francis Wallace, *Notre Dame from Rockne to Parseghian* (1966); Gene Schoor, *A Treasury of Notre Dame Football* (1962); Francis Wallace, *Notre Dame: Its People and Its Legends* (1969); Ken Rappoport, *Wake Up the Echoes: Notre Dame Football* (1975); Dave Condon et al., *Notre Dame Football: The Golden Tradition* (1982). Magazine and newspaper articles that give some insight into the man include John P. Carmichael, "Mr. Notre Dame," *Esquire*, Nov. 1950; "Football's No. 1 Coach: The Going Gets Tougher," *Newsweek*, 7 Dec. 1953; Frank Leahy, with Tim Cohane, "Farewell to Notre Dame," *Look*, 23 Mar. 1954; "Subject: Frank Leahy," *Sports Illustrated*, 31 Oct. 1955; Jim Murray, "Forgotten Man of Notre Dame," *Los Angeles Times*, 14 Dec. 1974. An obituary is in the *New York Times*, 22 June 1973.

JAMES D. WHALEN

LEAHY, William Daniel (6 May 1875–20 July 1959), naval officer, was born in Hampton, Iowa, the son of Michael Arthur Leahy, a lawyer and local politician, and Rose Hamilton. In 1882 the Leahy family moved to Wisconsin, where William lived until he received an appointment to the U.S. Naval Academy in 1893. He married Louise Tennent Harrington in 1904; they had one son, who became a naval officer of flag rank.

Leahy was a mediocre student, graduating in the lower third of his class at the academy in 1897. His first assignment was to the battleship *Oregon*, and he remained a "battleship man" throughout his career. He saw action in the Spanish-American War and during the intervention in China's Boxer Rebellion. He later took part in several interventions in Latin American nations. In 1915 he became an aide to the secretary of the navy, Josephus Daniels, and formed a friendship with Franklin D. Roosevelt, who was assistant secretary. Leahy was given command of his first battleship in 1926. In 1933 Roosevelt appointed him chief of the Bureau of Navigation, a position that enabled him to advance the careers of other battleship officers, known collectively as the "Gun Club." After several important commands during the mid-1930s, Leahy was named chief of naval operations (CNO) by Roosevelt in January 1937. He held this top post until he reached the mandatory retirement age of sixty-four in 1939.

Leahy's tenure as CNO coincided with a period of turmoil in American military preparations in the face of war threats both in Europe and in Asia. He helped raise the prestige and strength of the navy through his personal relationship with Roosevelt and his cultivation of the press and influential congressmen. He was instrumental in getting higher appropriations for the navy, with emphasis on battleships as opposed to aircraft carriers, and in 1939 strongly influenced the drafting of contingency plans in the event of war.

After his retirement, Leahy was appointed governor of Puerto Rico. In November 1940 he received a message from Roosevelt asking him to become ambassador to "Vichy France," the collaborationist regime in that part of the country unoccupied by Germany. The Vichy government was headed by Marshal Henri Philippe Pétain, a military hero of World War I, who Roosevelt thought would be more apt to get along with another person of military background. Roosevelt also hoped Leahy would be influential with high-ranking French naval officers in preventing the French fleet from being turned over to Germany. Leahy did establish a close relationship with Pétain and served ably from January 1941 to May 1942, when he was recalled in protest against the accession to power of pro-Nazi Pierre Laval.

Leahy's next post, a dual one, was his most important. Army Chief of Staff George C. Marshall, Roosevelt's most trusted military adviser, recommended that Leahy be named chairman of the newly created Joint Chiefs of Staff (JCS). The U.S. Army Air Forces, though still technically part of the army, had a representative on the JCS, and Leahy's appointment

would maintain a balance between army and navy. Leahy, Marshall hoped, would serve to mediate service differences and act as a liaison between the JCS and the president. Roosevelt also made Leahy his personal chief of staff.

Leahy's role as chairman of the JCS was not, as it later became, that of first among equals. He presided over meetings but usually said little as Admiral Ernest J. King spoke for the navy. Although partial to his service, Leahy did not hesitate to side with Marshall on a number of matters and generally did act as an honest broker. He supported Marshall on the need for an early cross-channel invasion of France, for instance, and later General Douglas MacArthur's campaign to retake the Philippines, both of which were unpopular with many admirals. As a member of the JCS he also served on the British-American Combined Chiefs of Staff. In 1944 he became the first naval officer to gain a fifth star with the title of Fleet Admiral.

As Roosevelt's chief of staff, Leahy participated in almost all of the top-level discussions and was by Roosevelt's side at the summit conferences with Winston Churchill and Joseph Stalin at Teheran (1943) and at Yalta (1945). Although it is difficult to weigh one person's input in the decision-making process, Roosevelt trusted that Leahy could be relied on to give his honest, often blunt opinions without regard for personal advantage. Leahy thought Roosevelt was too trusting of the Soviets, and he frequently expressed doubts about British intentions.

Harry S. Truman inherited Leahy following Roosevelt's death in April 1945, and the admiral remained as chief of staff until his final retirement in March 1949 owing to poor health. As he did under Roosevelt, Leahy participated in most of the great military and foreign policy decisions Truman had to make. Later referring to his dealings with Stalin at the Potsdam Conference (July-Aug. 1945), Truman wrote of another individual that he was "the only hard boiled hard hitting anti-Russian around except the tough old admiral, Bill Leahy." Leahy not only was anti-Soviet, but he became increasingly suspicious of what he called "pinkies" in the State Department. A myth has been put forward in some historical accounts that Leahy argued against using atomic bombs to defeat Japan on moral grounds. No evidence has been found to support such an assertion. Actually, he did not think they would work. Only a few days before the bombing of Hiroshima he scoffingly referred to the atomic weapon as "a professor's dream."

As relations with the Soviets continued to deteriorate after World War II ended, Leahy was a consistent hardliner. He supported Truman's efforts to pry the Soviets out of Iran in 1946 and promulgation of the Truman doctrine toward Greece and Turkey in 1947. He argued in vain against reduced military budgets in the late 1940s and against the administration's withdrawal of support for the Chinese Nationalists. While Leahy remained a trusted aide until his retirement, his influence probably was greatest during the last months of Roosevelt's life as the latter's health declined and in the Truman administration until James F. Byrnes replaced Edward R. Stettinius (1900–1949) as secretary of state on 3 July 1945.

Following his retirement, Leahy, at Truman's request, published his account of the wartime years. He lived quietly until his death in Bethesda, Maryland.

• Leahy's diary and the bulk of his papers are at the Library of Congress; a smaller collection is at the Wisconsin Historical Society. His own book, *I Was There* (1950), is based on his diary. The George Elsey Papers and Elsey's oral history interviews at the Harry S. Truman Library are valuable. For Leahy's career before he became CNO, see Gerald Thomas, "Admiral Leahy and America's Imperial Years" (Ph.D. diss., Yale Univ., 1973). His impact as CNO is the focus of John Major's essay, "William Daniel Leahy," in *The Chiefs of Naval Operations*, ed. Robert William Love, Jr. (1980). The most detailed account of Leahy's tenure as ambassador to Vichy France is in William Langer, *Our Vichy Gamble* (1947). For his performance on the JCS, see Forrest C. Pogue, *George C. Marshall: Organizer of Victory* (1973), and Grace Person Hayes, *The History of the Joint Chiefs of Staff in World War II: The War against Japan* (1982). A journalistic account of Leahy as the president's chief of staff is Frank Gervasi, "Watchdog in the White House," *Colliers*, 9 Oct. 1948. Scholarly accounts of his role can be found in most standard works on the origins of the Cold War. An obituary is in the *New York Times*, 21 July 1959.

ROBERT JAMES MADDOX

LEAKE, James Payton (4 June 1881–21 Feb. 1973), medical scientist, was born in Sedalia, Missouri, the son of James Leake and Matilda Ann Love. Nothing more is known of his parents or early childhood. Leake attended Smith Academy in St. Louis, Missouri, before going to Harvard University, from which he received an A.B. in 1903. He then attended Harvard Medical School, receiving an M.D. in 1907. He entered the U.S. Public Health Service (PHS) as a medical officer in 1909; he would serve this federal agency with distinction until his retirement more than three decades later.

Leake's superiors in the PHS quickly recognized his affinity for medical investigation, directing the young officer in 1910 to join a team that undertook the first comprehensive study of the epidemiology of poliomyelitis in the United States. Three years later Leake was put in charge of inspecting the nation's supply of serums, vaccines, and other biologics, with the help of several subordinates in a division of the PHS Hygienic Laboratory in Washington, D.C. During Leake's nine-year tenure (1913–1922) as inspector of biologics, he made several outstanding contributions. During World War I, before the United States entered the conflict, Leake's division at the Hygienic Laboratory supplied tetanus antitoxin to the British army. Leake received a formal citation from the British government in recognition of this service.

Leake also made lasting research contributions during his years at the Hygienic Laboratory. In 1916 he resumed his epidemiological interest in polio, which he would study for the rest of his career. PHS historian Ralph Chester Williams wrote a history of the agency

(1951) that "field investigations of poliomyelitis in the Service are largely synonymous with the name of Dr. James P. Leake." Williams's description offers insight into Leake's character: "Leake brought to the problem of poliomyelitis a disciplined, meticulous mind dedicated to the importance of detail. Intertwined with this were a keen clinical sense and an undeviating respect for the patient-physician relationship" (p. 204). In 1921 Leake developed an improved technique for smallpox vaccination. With John N. Force, he established the "multiple pressure" method of vaccination, which resulted in fewer adverse reactions and less scarring than the old scarification technique. Although he did not publish much in his career, Leake prepared a practice manual, *Questions and Answers on Smallpox Vaccination*, which was widely distributed among physicians for decades.

In 1925 Leake was assigned to direct a large study of the health hazards inherent in the use of tetraethyl lead as a gasoline additive. Two years later he joined a team of PHS investigators sent to Montreal at the request of the Canadian government to study an outbreak of typhoid.

Leake began to turn more of his energy to administration of public health work and medical investigations in 1930, when he was chosen to direct the PHS Office of Industrial Hygiene and Sanitation. He held this position for two years and then returned to his preferred field, epidemiology. From 1933 through 1945 he was in charge of the PHS Epidemiology Section. He retired in 1945 when he reached the mandatory federal retirement age. During his long retirement Leake continued to live in Washington, maintaining ties with the PHS community; he was a consultant to Bess Furman when she wrote a history of the agency in the early 1970s. He was preceded in death by his wife, Mary Chase, with whom he had three children.

Leake made several important contributions to medical science; most significantly he was one of a few dozen dedicated PHS investigators of the early twentieth century who established a reputation for excellence in research. This reputation contributed materially to the success of the major post–World War II buildup of medical science within the PHS.

• The best biographical sources on Leake are general histories of the Public Health Service, which give attention to Leake among many other PHS officers: Ralph Chester Williams, *The United States Public Health Service, 1798–1950* (1951), and Bess Furman, *A Profile of the United States Public Health Service, 1798–1948* (1973). Furman credits Leake for assisting with her book (p. 384). A substantive obituary is in the *Washington Post*, 24 Feb. 1973.

JON M. HARKNESS

LEAR, Ben (12 May 1879–1 Nov. 1966), army officer, was born in Hamilton, Ontario, Canada, to Ben Lear, a printer, and Hannah Senden. When Ben was two, the family moved to the United States and settled in Pueblo, Colorado. The elder Lear took employment as shop foreman of the *Pueblo Evening Press*. After high school, young Ben was hired as a printer's assistant for his father. He worked his way up to secretary treasurer and stayed at this position for three years. At the age of nineteen, Ben had his fill of the printer's life and enlisted in the army, enticed by the U.S. declaration of war against Spain in 1898. Lear joined the newly formed First Colorado Volunteer Infantry and was immediately appointed a first sergeant. The unit sailed for the Philippines, where it participated in the capture of Manila and fought gallantly at Marikina and Guadalupe Hill.

Lear proved to be a natural leader, and word of his ability reached the governor of Colorado, who commissioned him a lieutenant in Company A. One of the enlisted men under Lear's command was his own father. Reportedly, father and son served well together with the exception of one disciplinary altercation. Ben Lear, Sr., complained to his son of the long hours he was spending on kitchen detail. After a stern lecture from the commanding officer about duty to his country, the elder Lear returned to the kitchen without further protest.

In July 1899, when the First Colorado Volunteer Infantry mustered out of service, Ben Lear, Jr., remained in the Philippines as a first lieutenant in the Thirty-sixth U.S. Volunteer Infantry Regiment. He served with this regiment during the Philippine insurrection and was placed in command of Aguilar, Pangasinan Province, where he directed the American forces in ridding the country of its menacing guerrilla forces. Lear was mustered out of the volunteer service on 11 June 1901 and was commissioned a second lieutenant of cavalry in the regular army on 2 February 1901.

The commencement of Lear's extensive service in the regular army kept him in the Philippines with the Fifteenth U.S. Cavalry at Davac until 17 April 1903. During this appointment, on 8 April 1903, he fought in the engagement at Bacalod, Mindanao, where a fort held by the Calahui Moros was successfully destroyed by the Americans. As a result of this action, Lear and the men of the Fifteenth Cavalry Regiment garnered praise from their commanding officer, Captain John J. Pershing, for the "excellent service performed in this difficult work directly under the walls and fire from the fort."

Returning to the United States in 1903, Lear eventually reunited with the Fifteenth Cavalry and served with the regiment in a series of assignments as a cavalry commander and instructor. In 1906 he married Grace Russel. They had one daughter, who was born in an army tent in Cuba during Lear's one-year assignment there. Lear made a name for himself as a marksman with both a pistol and a rifle and as an expert horseman. His skill with horses was good enough for him to compete as an equestrian during the 1912 Olympic games in Stockholm, Sweden.

In 1916 the United States sent a punitive expedition to the Mexican border in an attempt to capture the rebel bandit Pancho Villa. Lear served as a captain in the Eighth Cavalry during this fruitless venture. When the United States sent the American Expeditionary Forces to France in 1917, Lear remained behind to serve on the War Department General Staff in Washington, D.C.

An army reduced in size during the interwar years offered few opportunities for junior officers. Lear made the best of this circumstance with service as an instructor and cavalry commander at various posts throughout the United States. On 19 September 1929 he was promoted to colonel during an assignment as chief of the Inspection Division in the Inspector General's Office at Washington, D.C. As a cavalry commander, Lear earned a reputation as a stern disciplinarian with an abrasive but flamboyant personality. Long after the cavalry traded horses for motorized vehicles in 1933, he continued to wear his out of fashion cavalry boots. During his off-duty hours, he was known to be a capable gin rummy player and a serious golfer.

Lear was promoted to brigadier general on 1 May 1936, and he was elevated to major general two years later. His big opportunity came in 1940, when he was assigned to command the Second Army. As World War II raged in Europe, the United States moved to bolster and prepare its military. In September 1941 Lear led 160,000 men of the Second Army against General Walter Kreuger's 240,000-man Third Army during the war games known as the "Louisiana Maneuvers." The "war" between these two forces was one of the most watched and reported events of 1941. During the two phases of the maneuvers, Lear's troops were soundly defeated.

Also in 1941 Lear's disciplinary manner gained him the nickname of "Yoo-Hoo," which remained well after his death. In July he was playing a round of golf near Memphis, Tennessee, when a motorized regiment of citizen-soldiers passed the course on the way to their quarters at Camp Robinson, Arkansas. Also on the golf course that afternoon was a party of young women clad in shorts, who received a rousing "yoo-hoo" from the passing convoy. Although the women appeared to enjoy the attention, Lear was not amused. He had the men retrieved from their camp and returned to Memphis. The following morning Lear forced the 325 officers and men to alternate marching and riding forty-five miles to their camp in the hot sun. The episode generated controversy, and Lear escaped disciplinary action only because of the attack on Pearl Harbor.

In 1943 Lear reached the statutory retirement age with a temporary rank of lieutenant general. He was called back to service in 1944 to take command of the army ground forces after Lieutenant General Leslie J. McNair was killed. In the closing phases of World War II in Europe, Lear served as a deputy commander to General Dwight D. Eisenhower in the European theater of operations. His chief responsibility was to speed up the training of infantrymen in order to move large numbers of soldiers into combat.

Lear returned from World War II in July 1945 as a permanent lieutenant general. He retired on 31 December 1945. After retirement Lear moved to Memphis, where he became active in civic work. He served as chairman of the advisory board of the Salvation Army and chairman of the Disaster Committee of the local Red Cross chapter. He also spent time playing golf and bridge. He died in the Veterans Administration hospital at Murfreesboro, Tennessee. Although the 1941 incident in Memphis clouded Lear's career, it did not overshadow his accomplishments as a professional soldier committed to excellence. This was acknowledged in 1943, when Lear was awarded the Distinguished Service Medal for "his excellent judgement, forceful leadership" as head of the successful Second Army.

• No collections of Lear's personal papers exist, but his military service is documented in a number of primary and secondary sources. Among the Records of the Adjutant General's Office (RG 94) in the National Archives in Washington, D.C., are compiled military service records for the Spanish-American War and a general correspondence file for his service in the regular army from 1899 to 1917. The general correspondence in the War College Division files of the War Department General and Special Staffs (RG 165) contains information on his World War I service. His personnel file for service after 1918 is in the National Personnel Records Center in St. Louis, Mo. Secondary publications documenting Lear's World War II service include John D. Millett, *The Army Service Forces: The Organization and Role of the Army Service Forces* (1954); Bell I. Wiley and William P. Gavon, Historical Section, Army Ground Forces, *History of the Second Army* (1946); and Robert Roswell Palmer et al., *Procurement and Training of Ground Combat Troops* (1948; repr. 1957). Obituaries are in the *New York Times* and the *Washington Post*, both on 2 Nov. 1966.

MITCHELL YOCKELSON

LEAR, Tobias (19 Sept. 1762–11 Oct. 1816), diplomat, was born in Portsmouth, New Hampshire, the son of Tobias Lear, a trader and farmer, and Mary Stillson. After studying at Governor Dummer Academy in Byfield, Massachusetts, Lear entered Harvard College in 1779, graduating in 1783. He then traveled to England and France; many Harvard graduates went to Europe to round out their education, but the decision to send young Lear was probably motivated by a desire on the part of his father and one of his patrons, John Langdon, to obtain information about economic matters. By the time Tobias returned to America, pressure from English creditors compelled his family to declare insolvency, and he was forced to seek employment. General Benjamin Lincoln, with whom he had come into contact at Harvard, recommended Lear as a personal secretary to General George Washington. On 29 May 1786 the young man arrived at Mount Vernon to assume his duties.

Lear built a close personal and professional relationship with Washington and his family. During his service there, he met Mary "Polly" Long, whom he married on 22 April 1790; they had one child before she died on 28 July 1793. Upon his wife's death, Lear left Washington's service and organized a company, with interests in speculation in land near the future national capital on the Potomac River. With an eye to encouraging investment in his company, he published *Obser-vations on the River Potomack—the Country Adjacent, and the City of Washington* (1793), which promoted the idea of the federal city becoming a great center of commercial and manufacturing activity.

In November 1793 Lear left for Europe, armed with letters of introduction from Washington and other prominent government figures, and spent a year there promoting his business interests. In 1795 he returned to America and settled near the Potomac River, where he pursued various business opportunities, mainly associated with the Potomac Canal Company, both for himself and as a proxy for Washington. In August 1795 Lear became president of the Potomack Company, a position he held until Washington requested his services as military secretary when the latter was appointed commander of the U.S. Army in 1798. Lear accepted the position with the rank of colonel. He remained in Washington's service the remainder of the general's life and was with Washington when he died in December 1799. On 22 August 1795 Lear married Washington's niece, Francis Bassett Washington, assuming responsibility for two children she had from a previous marriage. She died less than a year after the wedding, and in 1803 Lear married another Washington niece, Frances Dandridge Henley; their marriage produced no children.

Lear spent nearly two years attending to the affairs of the deceased Washington; controversy over his handling of the general's papers, some of which disappeared during this period, would hound Lear the rest of his life. He then accepted appointment as U.S. consul to Saint Domingue. It was a particularly tricky assignment, because the United States still considered half the island a French colony, in disregard of the regime of Toussaint Louverture. Nonetheless, Lear accepted the unpaid position, hoping he could use it to establish commercial relations that could help mend his ailing financial situation. The horrible violence and racial tensions that persisted on the island, however, rendered futile Lear's efforts to promote American commerce and his own business interests. In January 1802 Napoleon dispatched a large force to Saint Domingue under General Charles Leclerc that brutally reimposed French rule. Lear's subsequent efforts to reach an understanding with Leclerc's regime proved fruitless, and in May 1802 he returned to the United States. His efforts to obtain compensation for the sacrifices he had made in taking the position were rebuffed by the House of Representatives.

Shortly after his return from Saint Domingue, Lear was offered the position of consul general to the Barbary Coast. His task was, with the support of U.S. warships, to negotiate treaties with the Barbary regencies. He experienced success in his dealings with Morocco and Algiers. His negotiations with Tripoli, however, were greatly complicated by the efforts of William Eaton to foment a revolution that would restore the former ruler of Tripoli to his throne and the Tripolitan seizure of the USS *Philadelphia* and her crew of three hundred. After two years of negotiations, Lear signed an agreement with the pasha on 4 June 1805. Among the provisions of the Treaty of Tripoli was an agreement to pay a ransom of sixty thousand dollars for the prisoners. Although the amount was far less than Secretary of State James Madison had authorized, Lear nonetheless came under severe criticism for the ransom provisions of the treaty and its undermining of Eaton's efforts. Lear remained in the Mediterranean until 1812, when on 25 July the dey of Algiers ordered him to leave.

Although the treaties had been defended by Jefferson and had won ratification in the Senate, Lear returned to harsh criticism, generated to a large extent by an embittered Eaton, whose exploits had made him a national hero. During the War of 1812 Lear was sent to northern New York to negotiate with the British over prisoner-of-war exchanges, at which he was successful. He eventually became an accountant at the War Department, a position he held until his death by suicide in Washington.

Despite his prominent diplomatic career, Lear's primary significance was his service with Washington. His ability as an administrator relieved Washington of many of the headaches that accompanied the management of a large plantation and a new nation. Few played so key a role in supporting Washington's ability to provide the United States with the leadership it needed to survive its difficult first years of independence.

• A collection of Lear's papers is at the University of Michigan Library, Ann Arbor. A book-length biography is Raymond A. Brighton, *The Checkered Career of Tobias Lear* (1985). Writings from Lear's time with Washington are in Tobias Lear, *Letters and Recollections of George Washington . . . with a Diary of Washington's Last Days* (1906); *Letters from George Washington to Tobias Lear*, ed. Walter H. Samson (1905); and Stephen Decatur, Jr., *Private Affairs of George Washington from the Records and Accounts of Tobias Lear, Esquire, His Secretary* (1933). Lear is a prominent figure in all works on Washington's later life. See especially Douglas Southall Freeman, *George Washington*, vols. 6 and 7 (1948–1957); and James T. Flexner, *George Washington*, vols. 3 and 4 (1965–1972). Lear's diplomatic career can be traced through *American State Papers: Foreign and Military Affairs*, vol. 2 (1832); R. W. Irwin, *The Diplomatic Relations of the U.S. with the Barbary Powers, 1776–1816* (1931); and Louis B. Wright, *The First Americans in North Africa: William Eaton's Struggle for a Vigorous Policy against the Barbary Pirates* (1945).

ETHAN S. RAFUSE

LEAR, William Powell (26 June 1902–15 May 1978), electrical engineer and aeronautical entrepreneur, was born in Hannibal, Missouri, the son of Reuben Lear, a carpenter and teamster, and Gertrude Powell. His parents separated when Lear was six, and his mother married a plasterer in Chicago. The family's meager income represented a lifelong goad to Lear to become financially secure. After finishing the eighth grade, he left school and found work as a mechanic. At age sixteen Lear decided to leave home and enter military service. Lying about his age, he signed up in 1918 with the navy and was posted to the Great Lakes Naval

Training Station, where he was trained in radio technology. After the armistice, he found employment with a succession of electrical and radio businesses and developed several technical improvements while gaining valuable experience in a rapidly developing industry. During the early 1920s he built and patented the first practical radio for autos but lacked financial support to go into production and sold the design to Motorola in 1924.

Lear continued to work for other firms in the Midwest, becoming chief engineer for the Calvin Manufacturing Company in 1931. The same year he founded his own business, Lear Development Company, which perfected a simplified radio frequency amplifier. In 1934 Radio Corporation of America bought the plans, paying enough for Lear to organize a completely new research, development, and manufacturing company, Lear Avia Corporation, located in Dayton, Ohio.

Lear had learned to fly after World War I, and he continued to own and fly several of his own planes during the 1920s and 1930s; his new radio and electronics company devoted most of its efforts to the aviation industry, especially the private plane sector. Lear Avia's location in Dayton provided important contacts with Air Corps bureaus at McCook Field that were responsible for acquisition of flight equipment. The company's radio receivers and transmitters, direction finders, and navigational equipment not only won a major share of the civil market but also figured in large military orders. In 1939, on the eve of World War II, Lear changed the name of his business operations to Lear Incorporated, a diverse electronics and engineering firm that won more than $100 million in wartime contracts. Meanwhile, in 1942, after three prior marriages and three children, he married Moya Oleson; they had four children.

Lear's work with autopilot controls during World War II led him to develop a highly effective unit for jet fighters that were entering service during the late 1940s. During the 1950s Lear Incorporated produced other electronic products ranging from satellite components to stereo sound systems. In the 1960s Lear played an active role in his company's development of the first eight-track stereo tape systems for automobiles. Patents for his autopilots, stereo equipment, and other systems made Lear a multimillionaire.

In addition to his outstanding record of innovations in electronic equipment and electromechanical units such as the autopilot, Lear was logically drawn to tinker with the growing variety of corporate planes that carried his equipment. After the war, he formed a separate operation to buy used Lockheed Lodestar twin-engine planes; after modifying them and equipping them with state-of-the-art electronics, he marketed them as Learstars. By the end of the 1950s Lear's experience in the executive airplane market had convinced him that he could profitably sell a corporate jet. With at least two such planes available from large established manufacturers, aviation analysts generally agreed that the market for these expensive types was too limited for new competitors to succeed. Lear decided that he would build a much smaller plane for six passengers, arguing that controlling his plane's size would not only keep the price down but would also give it economy and performance that would appeal to time-conscious executives. In 1962, when the directors of Lear Incorporated balked at this risky new venture, Lear sold his personal stake in the company for more than $14 million; the firm subsequently completed a merger to become Lear Siegler Incorporated. Lear's new aviation project finally took the name of Lear Jet Incorporated in 1963.

Realizing that a canceled Swiss jet fighter-bomber had a wing design that matched his requirements, Lear decided to locate his manufacturing center in Switzerland to take advantage of existing tooling. Slow progress and difficulties in parts deliveries prompted him to shift the entire project back to the United States, relocating in Wichita, Kansas, where progress accelerated, and the first Learjet took to the air in 1963. Despite a somewhat cramped cabin for six passengers, the Learjet cruised economically at speeds of over 500 miles per hour. Best of all, its price tag was 30 percent to 50 percent of its competitors. With more than 100 deliveries in its first year of production, the Learjet's affordable cost and impressive performance revolutionized the character of corporate aviation operations. Additional models offered improved performance and more passenger room as Learjet set sales records in North America and elsewhere around the world.

Success eventually created problems in organizing production schedules and setting up a reliable sales organization; a rash of accidents with Learjets during 1965–1966 was traced to icing problems; these difficulties and cash flow troubles in other subsidiaries of Lear's businesses forced him to sell out in 1967. The buyer was Gates Rubber Company, a diversified firm with a background in general aviation operations. The Gates Learjet company that resulted soon worked out the kinks in finances, marketing, and aircraft engineering, making the Learjet a leader in its field. With some $28 million from this transaction, Lear looked for new challenges. Over the next decade he became involved in several airplane development projects, including an advanced pusher-propellor design called the Learfan that featured composite construction. A prototype flew during the 1970s but never garnered support for production. Lear's principal passion centered on his vision of a modern version of the steam-propelled automobile, a program he vigorously promoted as a solution to serious environmental problems from car exhaust.

Winning the prestigious Collier Trophy in 1949 for his work on autopilots reflected Lear's secure position in aviation history; his development of the Learjet marked another major contribution. He held more than 150 patents. Most often remembered for his work in aviation, his legacies in radio and tape equipment also made a permanent mark on the character of the music industry as well as contemporary society. He died in Reno, Nevada.

• The National Air and Space Museum, Washington, D.C., has files on the first Learjet and clippings about Lear. An interview (1960) is in the Oral History Collection at Columbia University. A good review of Lear's electronic career is in *Current Biography* (1966). For an informative summary of his development of the corporate jet and its impact on business aviation, see Robert J. Serling, *Little Giant: The Story of Gates Learjet* (1974). A more comprehensive assessment of Lear's achievements as an innovator in electronics and his role in the field of corporate jets is Richard Rashke, *Stormy Genius: The Life of Bill Lear* (1985).

ROGER E. BILSTEIN

LEARY, John (1 Nov. 1837–8 Feb. 1905), business leader and politician, was born in St. John, New Brunswick, Canada. Virtually nothing is known about his parents or his early life. Apparently relying largely on his own initiative, he prospered in lumber manufacturing and shipping as a young man, and he operated mercantile establishments in his native province. Financial setbacks prompted him to move to Houlton, Maine, where he engaged in the lumber business. In 1858 he married Mary Blanchard. They had no children. In 1869 he followed his interest in lumbering to Seattle, Washington Territory.

Admitted to the Washington bar in 1871, he was one of Seattle's earliest attorneys, a junior partner first in the law firm of McNaught and Leary and, between 1878 and 1882, in Struve, Haines, and Leary. Meanwhile he had become involved in such business and civic enterprises as coal mining, public utilities development, and local politics, and in 1882 he abandoned his law practice to further engage in such activities. After the Northern Pacific Railroad established its northwest terminus at rival Tacoma instead of Seattle, Leary helped organize the Seattle & Walla Walla Railroad. Largely locally financed, it eventually laid no more than twenty miles of track between Seattle and the mining region southeast of town, and the small rail line transported coal for local use and for export. In 1872 Leary and John Talbot opened the Talbot coal mine, and later that decade Leary undertook at his own expense extensive surveys of coal and other mineral resources throughout western Washington and into the eastern portion of the territory. Leary also led in organizing a local gas company and Seattle's water system, and he served as president of both. Moving into journalism, he acquired the *Seattle Post*, merging it in 1882 with the *Intelligencer* to create the *Post-Intelligencer*, which remained more than a century later one of the city's two dailies. In 1883 he and Henry Yesler constructed the Yesler-Leary block, the finest business block in the city; it was destroyed in the great fire that swept through the business district in June 1889.

Throughout the 1880s Leary was a leader and major raiser of capital in Seattle's continuing efforts to secure rail links with transcontinental lines including routes to coal mines and across the Cascade Mountains. He was among the incorporators of the Baker City Railway (1882) and the Seattle, Lake Shore & Eastern Railway (1884). Leary was also involved in local land development and in establishing mail service and general commerce with Alaska. He served as president of the Seattle Land and Improvement Company and the West Coast Improvement Company. In 1890, along with fellow entrepreneurs Thomas Burke and William R. Ballard, he developed the original site of Ballard, a mill town that was annexed to Seattle in 1907. His first wife died sometime around 1890. Leary was president of the Seattle Warehouse and Elevator Company and briefly of the First National Bank. He was on the board of directors of the West Street & North End Electric Railway and of the James Street & Broadway Cable and Electric Line. After acquiring the *Bailey Gatzert*, a steamer that plied Puget Sound waters, he organized the Columbia River and Puget Sound Navigation Company (1891), which built and operated steamers in the Northwest for many decades.

Leary served two terms on the city council and in 1884 was elected to a one-year term as mayor on a ticket organized by business interests to meet a challenge from the newly formed Law and Order League. Led by moralistic elements that included recently enfranchised women, the league sought to end political corruption and to enforce liquor and gambling laws; such actions, the businessmen feared, would interfere with the accustomed manner of conducting civic affairs. Politically conservative, Mayor Leary, in the view of contemporary historian Frederic James Grant (1891), "acted on the principle that property has its duties as well as rights, and that one of its prime duties is to aid and build up the community where the possessor has made his wealth." He converted the largely honorary, unpaid office of mayor to one of commitment and regular office hours; during his administration, major grading and paving of downtown waterfront streets were undertaken. Leary, however, had a falling out with his conservative supporters when he attempted to placate women's and reform groups by allowing raids on saloons and houses of prostitution. His reelection bid failed. In 1885–1886 mounting agitation against the city's Chinese population led to their expulsion. Leary was directly involved in these efforts, unsuccessfully urging the aliens to leave before violence occurred. He also served as president of the Seattle Chamber of Commerce and of the prestigious Rainier Club and was a regent of the University of Washington. On 21 April 1892 he married Eliza P. Ferry, the daughter of Elisha P. Ferry, first governor of Washington State. The couple had no children. Running as a Republican in 1892, Leary was again defeated in a race for mayor.

During the last decade of his life he retired from business interests and was constructing the city's grandest mansion at the time of his death. In his later years, he wintered in southern California and was in Riverside when he died. He left an estate of $2 million.

Frederic James Grant wrote that John Leary's "very presence is stimulating. Buoyant and hopeful by nature, he imparts his own enthusiasm to those around

him." Over three decades, while Seattle grew from a sawmill town of approximately 1,000 residents to the region's dominant city with over 80,000, Leary was involved in most of those civic and business enterprises essential for the burgeoning city.

• Papers of John Leary and of Eliza Ferry Leary are in the Manuscripts and Archives Division, University of Washington Libraries, Seattle. There is no full biography of Leary. The best of several short biographies is in Frederic James Grant, ed., *History of Seattle, Washington with Illustrations and Biographical Sketches of Some of Its Prominent Men and Pioneers* (1891), pp. 457–60. See also Robert C. Nesbit, *He Built Seattle: A Biography of Judge Thomas Burke* (1961), and Margaret Pitcairn Strachan, "Early Day Mansions: No. 3—John Leary," *Seattle Times* magazine section, 17 Sept. 1944, p. 3. An extensive obituary is in the *Seattle Post-Intelligencer*, 9 Feb. 1905.

CHARLES P. LEWARNE

LEASE, Mary Elizabeth Clyens (11 Sept. 1853–29 Oct. 1933), orator and writer, was born in Ridgeway, Pennsylvania, the daughter of Joseph P. Clyens and Mary Elizabeth Murray, farmers. The death of her father, two brothers, and an uncle during the Civil War forced her family into a life of poverty; nevertheless, she received an education at St. Elizabeth's Academy, a Catholic school, and graduated in 1868. She taught in her home county after graduation, and when her attempts to unionize other teachers failed in 1870 she moved to Osage Mission, Kansas, to teach at a parochial school. In 1873 she married Charles L. Lease, a druggist, and the couple moved to an isolated prairie farm in Kingman County. The young couple was plagued with bad luck; they were not successful at farming, and two of their children had died in infancy. When the farm failed, the Leases moved to Denison, Texas, only to fail again. In 1883, while Lease was pregnant, the family moved to Wichita, Kansas. While her husband resumed his career as a druggist, Lease cared for their four children, managed the household, and took in washing. In 1884 she began studying law at home and was admitted to the Kansas bar in 1885.

Lease began her career as an orator that same year, first lecturing for the Irish National League and then campaigning for woman suffrage. She joined the Knights of Labor and, in her capacity as master workman (president) of her local assembly, addressed the 1888 state convention of the newly organized Union Labor party, which was composed largely of former supporters of the Greenback party, in support of woman suffrage. After the convention, she edited a party newspaper, the *Wichita Independent*, campaigned for Union Labor candidates, and began giving speeches for the Farmers' Alliance. Lease had absolutely no training in the art of oratory, and yet she became a public speaker of the first magnitude. She saw herself as "merely a voice, an instrument in the hands of a Great Force," but hers was "a golden voice—a deep, rich contralto, a singing voice that had hypnotic qualities" (White, pp. 218–19). Her speeches, delivered extemporaneously for hours at a time, were "undisciplined, emotional, sarcastic, magnetic, eloquent, torrential" (Nugent, p. 82). She exploded across the Kansas plain during the campaign of 1890, appearing before more than 160 audiences to stump for People's party candidates and lecture on the evildoings of Democrats, railroads, landlords, and loan companies. Although she twice denied saying "What you farmers need to do is to raise less corn and more hell," the radical message inherent in that remark epitomized her political philosophy.

Lease's star reached ascendancy with the triumph of Kansas Populism in 1890. She became a national figure and in 1891 was elected vice president of both the Women's League of America and the Women's Industrial International Congress. She made a speaking tour of Missouri and Iowa and became the first woman to address the Georgia legislature. As a delegate to the People's party national convention in 1892, she seconded the presidential nomination of James B. Weaver. Following the convention, she accompanied Weaver on a canvass of six western states, then joined the "Southern Crusade" with Weaver and prominent Populist orators Jerry Simpson and Annie Diggs in an effort to breathe life into southern Populism.

The Southern Crusade marked the beginning of Lease's political decline. The tour was met by egg-throwing, pro-Democratic crowds at nearly every turn; many of its speaking engagements were canceled, and the crusaders were eventually forced to slink home in defeat. The following year, she opposed unsuccessfully the fusion between Populists and Democrats in the Kansas state legislature, partly because she perceived the Democrats as having been the chief proponents of secession and therefore responsible for the Civil War deaths of her male relatives. Her bitter memories of childhood poverty made it impossible for her to cooperate with Democrats. Lease became a leader of the antifusionist Populists. She demanded that the People's party end its affiliation with the Democrats and run its own candidate for the U.S. Senate.

Lease also became embroiled in an ugly battle with the newly elected governor, Lorenzo D. Lewelling, a Populist turned fusionist. After he appointed her chairwoman of the State Board of Charities and then tried to pressure her to appoint Democrats to key positions, she publicly accused his administration of corruption, whereupon he fired her. Lease took the case to the state supreme court. The court ruled in her favor, but not before a great deal of damage was done to the political fortunes of everyone involved. In 1894 she declared "I hate Democrats" and began writing for the antifusionist newspaper *New Era*. She opposed fusionist candidates on the grounds that their true allegiance was to the Democrats and blamed that year's Populist defeats on the fusion. In 1896 she tried to block the presidential nomination of William Jennings Bryan at the People's party national convention. Lease's disgust with fusion was so complete that, following the convention, she became a Republican and

actively supported the candidacy of William McKinley.

In 1895 Lease began to favor the written word as a means of spreading her political message. She published *The Problem of Civilization Solved*, in which she espoused Caucasian colonization of the tropics, nationalization of the railroads, free trade between the countries of North and South America but high tariffs on the imports of other nations, free coinage of silver, initiative, and referendum. The book, coupled with her decision to leave the People's party, prompted Joseph Pulitzer to hire her as a feature writer for the *New York World* in 1896. When the Leases lost their Wichita home to foreclosure the following year, she moved permanently to New York City with her children to work full-time for the *World*. She filed for bankruptcy and divorce in 1901. For the next thirty years Lease advocated such causes as woman suffrage, Prohibition, and Roosevelt Progressivism and served as president of the National Society for Birth Control. Between 1908 and 1918 she lectured for the New York City Board of Education. She died in Callicoon, New York.

• Lease's autobiography (a manuscript signed "James Arnold" but attributed to her) as well as some of her letters and the texts of some of her speeches can be found in the archives of the Kansas State Historical Society. Betty Lou Taylor, "Mary Elizabeth Lease: Kansas Populist" (M.A. thesis, Wichita State Univ., 1951), is the best biographical study on Lease to date. O. Gene Clanton, *Kansas Populism: Ideas and Men* (1969), and Walter T. K. Nugent, *The Tolerant Populists: Kansas Populism and Nativism* (1963), provide short biographical sketches and assess Lease's importance to the Kansas Populist movement. Her speaking abilities are described in William A. White, *The Autobiography of William Allen White* (1946).

CHARLES W. CAREY, JR.

LEATHERMAN, LeRoy (10 Feb. 1922–9 Apr. 1984), author and arts administrator, was born in Alexandria, Louisiana, the son of LeRoy Sessums Leatherman, a salesman, and Mary Aline Dugger. Educated at Vanderbilt University (1939–1941), Kenyon College (1941–1942), the University of Illinois (1943–1944), and Southern Methodist University (bachelor of arts, 1948), Leatherman held the John Crowe Ransom Creative Writing Scholarship at Kenyon College and wrote many short stories and critical essays. He served in the air force between 1942 and 1946. He first saw Martha Graham, the pioneer of American modern dance, perform in Dallas, Texas, in 1949. Graham hired Leatherman as company manager for her first European performances in 1950, and it was in this capacity that he began writing about her work.

Leatherman became Graham's personal manager in 1953 and also served as director of the Martha Graham School of Contemporary Dance in New York City. He wrote the narration with Graham for her documentary film *A Dancer's World* (1957). This film, which includes superb footage of Graham's dance technique and excerpts of choreography, also explains the artist's philosophical and aesthetic principles. Leatherman was best known for his analytic study of Graham, *Martha Graham: Portrait of the Lady as an Artist* (1966), with photographs by Martha Swope. Leatherman also published two novels, both set in his native South: *The Caged Birds*, written in 1950, and *The Other Side of the Tree*, published in 1954.

During leaves of absence from the Martha Graham Dance Company and School in 1958 and 1961, Leatherman spent time in Yugoslavia and France, where he began writing and directing documentary films on dance and other subjects. From 1966 to 1972 Leatherman served as executive director of the Martha Graham Center of Contemporary Dance. It was during this period that Martha Graham retired from performing. It was also a time of transition in the company, when many of the principal dancers who had worked with Graham from the 1940s and 1950s left. In 1971 Graham became seriously ill. After she recovered late in 1972 she grew to resent those who had managed the company in her absence.

After leaving the Graham organization Leatherman moved to Boston, where he worked from 1972 to 1976 at Boston University. He was assistant dean for the School of Fine Arts, executive director of the Tanglewood Institute, and associate vice president for government and university relations. He also served as vice president of the Boston Fenway Program, Inc.

In 1979 he moved to California, where he served as special assistant to the dean of the University of Southern California's School of Performing Arts. From 1982 until his death he was public information officer for the University of Southern California's School of Music. A lifelong bachelor, Leatherman died in Santa Monica, California.

• The motion picture *A Dancer's World*, with Martha Graham, originally produced by WQED-TV, Pittsburgh, is now available on videocassette. Obituaries are in the *New York Times*, 12 Apr. 1984; *Dance Magazine*, June 1984; and *Ballet News*, Aug. 1984.

ALICE HELPERN

LEAVENWORTH, Henry (10 Dec. 1783–21 July 1834), army officer, was born in New Haven, Connecticut, the son of Jesse Leavenworth, an officer in the revolutionary war, and Catharine Frisbie Conkling. During his childhood the family moved to Danville, Vermont, where his parents separated. Henry and his father moved to Delhi, New York, where he attended the local school. After studying law with Erastus Root, a local attorney, he was admitted to the state bar in 1804. From then until 1812 he practiced law as Root's partner. He also served as the quartermaster, with the rank of major, in Colonel Root's regiment of the state militia. On 25 April 1812 he was appointed a captain in the Twenty-fifth Infantry. He remained on active duty for most of the rest of his life. Leavenworth married three times. He and his first wife, Elizabeth Morrison (marriage date unknown), had two children before divorcing. In 1810 he remarried, this time to

Electa Knapp, who died the next year. Then during the winter of 1813–1814 he married Harriet Lovejoy, with whom he had two more children.

Leavenworth entered an army that was being expanded in preparation for possible war with the British. By August 1813 he was transferred to the Ninth Infantry with the rank of major. That year and the next he served along the New York–Canada border. In July 1814 Leavenworth personally directed a successful charge that helped assure American victory at the bloody battle of Chippewa. Several weeks later on 25 July 1814 he served with distinction at the battle of Lundy's Lane at Niagara Falls. In these engagements he had his horse shot out from beneath him several times; he was honored for bravery by being breveted first a lieutenant colonel and then a colonel. In the May 1815 reduction of the army at the end of the war he was transferred to the Second Infantry at his regular rank of major. Later that year he took a leave to serve one term in the New York legislature.

Leavenworth returned to duty shortly after his term in the legislature and on 10 February 1818 was promoted to lieutenant colonel and transferred to the Fifth Infantry at Detroit. That year the War Department chose the Fifth Infantry along with several other units to help strengthen American presence in the upper Mississippi and Missouri river valleys. The secretary of war wanted to locate forts there to impress the local Indians with American power and to limit incursions by British fur traders from Canada. In early 1819 Leavenworth and his troops sailed west from Detroit to Green Bay. From there they crossed Wisconsin to Prairie du Chien on the Mississippi, and in August 1819 he led the command north to the confluence of that river and the Minnesota River. There the soldiers began work on what became Fort Snelling.

Another round of army reductions took place the next year. In October 1821 Leavenworth joined the Sixth Infantry as a lieutenant colonel, an assignment that brought him to Fort Atkinson, Nebraska, where he was to oversee relations with the Indians of the Missouri Valley. In June 1823 the Arikara Indians in South Dakota attacked fur traders traveling up the Missouri, and the traders called for help. Leavenworth ordered six companies of regulars to move north and gathered other fur traders and 750 Sioux to serve as auxiliaries against the Arikara. On 9 August 1823 his force reached the Arikara villages and the next day fighting began. When his artillery proved ineffective and the rest of the command ran low on ammunition he agreed to a truce. For several days inconclusive talks took place, but during the night of 13 August the Indians fled. The next morning the troops stormed the deserted villages; finding no trace of the Arikara, Leavenworth led his force back downstream to Fort Atkinson. He received much criticism for his leadership of this expedition.

Much of the rest of his career was taken up with administrative duties. On 25 July 1824 he was breveted a brigadier general for having accumulated ten years at the rank of colonel. In 1926 he participated in the construction of what became the first army infantry school, Jefferson Barracks, near St. Louis. In 1827 he led his troops up the Missouri River to build what became Fort Leavenworth. From there he oversaw army dealings with the Indians of the central and southern Plains. In 1834 he led 500 officers and men of the First Dragoons (mounted troops) to meet the Comanches and other tribes of the southern Plains. The expedition was a disaster. Disease swept through the ranks and men died in large numbers. The colonel himself fell off his horse during a buffalo hunt and never fully recovered. A few weeks later he died of fever at a temporary camp on the Washita River.

Leavenworth contributed significantly to the early army despite holding mostly subordinate commands. During the War of 1812 he was one of several junior officers who trained and led troops effectively. He was an influential participant in the postwar shift of the military to the West. The only criticism he received came from his inept handling of the 1823 move against the Arikara villagers. Despite that he came to be known as one of the best officers of his day and was praised for his bravery, good judgment, and concern for the well-being of his troops.

• Except for his official correspondence found in National Archives Record Groups 94 and 107 there is no body of Leavenworth papers. Jeffrey Kimball, "The Battle of Chippewa: Infantry Tactics in the War of 1812," *Military Affairs* 31 (1967–1968): 169–86, considers his early leadership. Roger L. Nichols, *General Henry Atkinson: A Western Military Career* (1965), provides details on some of his actions. See also Marcus L. Hansen, *Old Fort Snelling, 1819–1859* (1918); Elvid Hunt, *History of Fort Leavenworth, 1827–1927* (1926); and Bruce E. Mahon, *Old Fort Crawford and the Frontier* (1926), for his actions at those places. Doanne Robinson, ed., "Official Correspondence of the Leavenworth Expedition of 1823 into South Dakota for the Conquest of the Ree Indians," *South Dakota Historical Collections* 1 (1902): 179–256, focuses on his Arikara campaign, while Brad Agnew, "The Dodge-Leavenworth Expedition of 1834," *Chronicles of Oklahoma* 53 (1975): 376–96, examines his last campaign.

ROGER L. NICHOLS

LEAVITT, Henrietta Swan (4 July 1868–12 Dec. 1921), astronomer, was born in Lancaster, Massachusetts, the daughter of George Roswell Leavitt, a minister, and Henrietta Kendrick. She attended the Society for the Collegiate Instruction of Women (later known as Radcliffe College) in Cambridge, Massachusetts, graduating in 1892. The following year she obtained credits toward a graduate degree in astronomy there for work done at the Harvard College Observatory; she never completed the degree. Leavitt spent the remainder of the 1890s traveling, teaching school, and making measurements of stellar brightness at the Harvard Observatory. In 1900 illness led her to a long stay with family in Wisconsin. Although she lost part of her hearing, she was persuaded to return as a permanent member of the observatory staff in 1902. She continued this work even when poor health forced her to return to Wisconsin for some time in 1908.

Edward C. Pickering, director of the Harvard College Observatory from 1877 until 1919, organized an ambitious systematic program of photographing the sky, measuring stellar magnitudes, and classifying stellar spectra. Stellar photography was still relatively new—William Cranch Bond of Harvard had taken the first photograph of a star other than the sun in 1850—and Pickering wished to take full advantage of the new technology. Photographic plates taken in Cambridge and at Harvard's Boyden Station in Arequipa, Peru, were examined by women hired for the purpose. After 1890 these women were often college-educated. Some, like Leavitt and Annie Jump Cannon, made noteworthy contributions to astronomy.

Leavitt's first research at Harvard concerned the photographic brightness of circumpolar stars. She then began the photometric studies of variable stars for which she is remembered. Superimposing a negative of a photograph taken on one date on a positive made from the same region of the sky taken on another date, she sought places where the white and black images of a star did not precisely coincide. Such stars were suspected of variability and were compared to images of the same star on other plates. Working this way in 1904 and 1905, Leavitt found some 1,054 variable stars in the Magellanic Clouds of the southern hemisphere. In 1908, despite ill health, she published a list of the 1,777 variable stars she had found in these regions in the *Annals of the Astronomical Observatory of Harvard College* (60, no. 2). Moreover, Leavitt was able to find the period of the variability of sixteen stars in the Small Magellanic Cloud that varied like the star Delta Cepheus. She commented in another 1908 article in *Annals* (60, no. 4) that the brighter of these so-called Cepheid variables had longer periods. In 1912 Leavitt returned to the subject of Cepheid variables, plotting the magnitudes of twenty-five Cepheids in the Small Magellanic Cloud at both maximum and minimum brightness against the logarithms of their periods. The longer the period, the greater the brightness at maximum. As all the stars were in the Small Cloud, and hence at roughly equal distances from Earth, Leavitt noted in the *Harvard College Observatory Circular* (1912) that apparent differences in the photographic magnitudes of the stars probably corresponded to real differences in their emission of light. The Danish astronomer Ejnar Hertzsprung soon pointed out that if one knew the actual brightness of Cepheids of given periods, one could estimate their distance from Earth from the apparent brightness. Hertzsprung and later Harlow Shapley used the period-luminosity relationship to estimate the distance of the Small Magellanic Cloud, placing it far beyond our own galaxy. They argued that nebular regions of the sky like the Magellanic Clouds were indeed distant "island universes," outside the confines of our own galaxy. This conclusion was hotly debated at the time. However, both the existence of galaxies not our own and the use of the period-luminosity relationship to find stellar distances, would become widely accepted by astronomers.

Leavitt's quest for variable stars continued. When she died, she had discovered some 2,400—about half of those then known. She increasingly was called on to develop standard sequences of photographic magnitudes. In 1912, for example, she published in the *Harvard Circular* the photographic magnitudes for 96 stars near the North Pole. This sequence combined observations made with thirteen telescopes, both reflecting and refracting, with lenses ranging in size from half an inch to sixty inches. In the following years, she prepared standards of stellar photographic magnitudes for several other regions of the sky. While such work was essential to a general description of the stars, it offered none of the drama of her discovery of the period-luminosity relationship.

Leavitt did not marry. She died of cancer in Cambridge, Massachusetts.

• Some correspondence between Leavitt and Edward C. Pickering is in the Harvard College Observatory Papers, Harvard University Archives. Leavitt's work and significance are covered in Dorrit Hoffleit, *Women in the History of Variable Star Astronomy* (1993), and Pamela Mack, "Straying from Their Orbits: Women in Astronomy in America," in *Women of Science: Righting the Record*, ed. Gabriele Kass-Simon and Patricia Farnes (1990), pp. 102–5. Leavitt is mentioned in Robert Smith, *The Expanding Universe: Astronomy's "Great Debate" 1900–1931* (1982); Bessie Z. Jones and Lyle G. Boyd, *The Harvard College Observatory: The First Four Directorships* (1971); and Solon I. Bailey, *The History and Work of the Harvard Observatory, 1839 to 1927* (1931). Bailey also wrote an obituary in *Popular Astronomy*, 1922, pp. 197–99.

PEGGY ALDRICH KIDWELL

LEAVITT, Humphrey Howe (18 June 1796–15 Mar. 1873), congressman and judge, was born in Suffield, Connecticut, the son of John Leavitt. His mother's given name is unknown, but her maiden name was Fitch. His family moved to the Northwest Territory, near what is now Warren, Ohio, in 1800. He studied at an academy in Western Pennsylvania and later taught school in Warren and Steubenville, Ohio. He served in the U.S. Army in 1812.

Leavitt studied law briefly with Thomas D. Webb of Warren, but he left to become a store clerk. He next read law with Benjamin Ruggles and was admitted to the Ohio bar in 1816. He began a practice in Cadiz, Ohio, where he served as the justice of the peace from 1818 to 1820. He moved to Steubenville in 1820. In 1821 he married Maria Antoinette McDowell; they had three children. Leavitt was an active member of the Presbyterian church.

Leavitt was appointed as the prosecuting attorney for Monroe County (1818–1828) and Jefferson County (1823–1829) by the common pleas courts. He served in the Ohio House of Representatives from 1825 to 1826 and in the Ohio Senate from 1827 to 1828, as the clerk of the Court of Common Pleas of Jefferson County in 1828, and as a Jacksonian Democrat in the U.S. Congress from 6 December 1830 to 10 July 1834. As a congressman he opposed the rechartering of the National Bank, defended President Andrew Jackson's fi-

nancial policies, and made an effort to protect the interests of his constituents by supporting the tariff protecting wool. He did not, however, play a leading role in the House.

Leavitt was said to have been a personal friend of President Jackson, who appointed him as the judge of the U.S. District Court for Ohio on 30 July 1834. The seat of the court was in Columbus. In 1855, when Ohio was divided into two judicial districts, Leavitt was assigned, probably at his request, to the Southern District and moved to Cincinnati. One of the consequences of creating a federal court in Cincinnati was a significant increase in the number of cases filed in the federal courts and in Leavitt's own workload.

In 1843 Leavitt published a book for use by justices of the peace titled *The Ohio Justice's Guide*. As a judge he authored over 128 published opinions, including thirty-three patent opinions, an area in which he was considered an expert. Typical cases that he heard were in the areas of bankruptcy, admiralty, and taxation; he also heard state cases brought before the court because of the diversity of citizenship of the parties. His patent cases were mainly concerned with allegations of infringements of patents for the improvement of inventions to save labor, such as sewing machines, reapers, and steam engines.

One of Leavitt's most important cases was the Methodist church property case *William A. Smith v. Leroy Swormstedt* (C.C.D. Ohio, 1852), which presaged his views on secession. He held that while individuals could withdraw from the church, the general conference of the church had no authority to divide the church between northern and southern wings and that, consequently, those withdrawing from the church had no claim to any of its property. His decision was overruled by the U.S. Supreme Court in *Smith v. Swormstedt* (1853).

Sitting with Justice John McLean on the circuit, Leavitt upheld the constitutionality of the Fugitive Slave Act of 1793 in the John Van Zandt case (1843). He also enforced the Fugitive Slave Act of 1850 and vindicated federal authority in the Green County rescue cases, freeing ten deputy and assistant U.S. marshals who were imprisoned in the Clark County jail for kidnapping alleged runaway slaves (*Ex Parte Sifford*, S.D. Ohio, 1857). This decision was condemned by the 1857 Ohio Republican Convention. In his autobiography, Leavitt said that his actions brought upon him "the bitter denunciations of the entire Abolition Party in the North and West."

Leavitt's most well-known decision involved the denial of the writ of habeas corpus sought by Ohio's leading antiwar Democratic leader, Clement L. Vallandigham, in 1863. Leavitt's opinion gave his reasons for sustaining the action of General Ambrose E. Burnside in arresting Vallandigham; he also took the opportunity to express his hostility to secession and those in the North, such as Vallandigham, whom he believed were assisting the secessionists. But he also made it clear that he felt bound by the prior decision that he and Justice Noah H. Swayne rendered in another unnamed case the year before. Consequently, this case is of historic note, not so much because of the legal principles established (even though the prior case was unreported) but because of the petitioner's standing as a leading antiwar congressman and gubernatorial candidate. In discussing Vallandigham's case, President Abraham Lincoln referred to Leavitt as "a Democrat of better days than these," and indicated that the outcome in the case was worth three military victories.

Leavitt resigned from the court on 31 March 1871 and moved to Springfield, Ohio. He was a member of the World's Convention on Prison Reform, held in London in 1872. He died in Springfield.

• Some of the letters from Leavitt to Supreme Court Justice John McLean are in the McLean collection at the Library of Congress. A sketch of his life appears in *Autobiography of the Hon. Humphrey Howe Leavitt; Written for His Family . . .* (1893). His opinions were originally reported by attorney Lewis H. Bond in Bond's Reports, by Justice McLean in McLean's Reports, and by attorney Samuel S. Fisher in Fisher's Patent Cases. Those opinions were republished in Federal Cases in 1897. An account of the judicial history of the United States during most of Leavitt's service that includes references to Leavitt is in Carl B. Swisher, *The Taney Period, 1836–1864* (1974). Lincoln's discussion of the Vallandigham case is found in his letter to Erastus Corning and others, 12 June 1863, Roy P. Baser, ed., *The Collected Works of Abraham Lincoln* (1953). Accounts of his funeral service are in the *Cincinnati Enquirer,* 17, 18, and 19 Mar. 1873.

RICHARD L. AYNES

LEAVITT, Joshua (8 Sept. 1794–16 Jan. 1873), reformer and newspaper editor, was born in Heath, Massachusetts, the son of Roger Leavitt, a businessman, and Chloe Maxwell. Joshua was raised in a Congregationalist and Federalist household. His father, the wealthiest resident of Heath, held numerous public offices and was active in various reform causes. Joshua attended Yale College between 1810 and 1814. He then taught school in Hartford until 1817, when he began to study law in Northampton, Massachusetts. From 1819 until 1823 Leavitt practiced law in Heath and in Putney, Vermont. In 1820 he married Sarah Williams; they had six children.

Influenced by the expanding religious revivals of the time, in 1823 Leavitt enrolled in Yale Theological Seminary, where he studied under Nathaniel Taylor. Between 1825 and 1828 he was a Congregational minister in Stratford, Connecticut, and began to espouse temperance and the colonization of freed blacks in Africa. He moved to New York City in 1828 as general agent and editor for the American Seamen's Friend Society. Until 1832 he sought especially to advance the missionary cause by preaching religion and morality to sailors.

As editor of the *New York Evangelist* from 1831 until 1837, Leavitt's zealous advocacy of Congregationalism and of Charles Finney's new measures revivalism, with its emphasis on the use of itinerant evangelists, the protracted meeting, the anxious seat, and frequent visitations in the home, made the paper a

powerful force among evangelical Calvinists but also brought him into sharp conflict with conservative Presbyterians. Convinced of the need to combat sin wherever it existed in order to maintain an orderly, moral society, he also actively participated in the manual labor, temperance, and moral reform crusades.

Evangelical doctrines viewing the individual as a free moral agent underlay Leavitt's conversion to immediate emancipation in 1833. In this cause he made his most important contributions as a reformer. His advocacy of immediatism moved him to adopt an increasingly humanitarian and democratic philosophy and to place more emphasis on freedom than on self-control as a prerequisite for moral progress and social justice.

In 1837 Leavitt became editor of the *Emancipator,* the official organ of the American Anti-Slavery Society, which he also served as an executive committee member between 1833 and 1840. Unlike William Lloyd Garrison, one of the society's leaders, Leavitt believed that moral suasion alone could not end slavery, and he thus helped to found the Liberty party in 1839. Often contentious, and at times dogmatic, he defended political abolitionism from attacks by both the Garrisonian and more moderate abolitionists.

Until he resigned as the *Emancipator's* editor in 1848, Leavitt served the Liberty party in several capacities: as the principal abolitionist lobbyist in Washington, D.C., from 1840 until 1845; as a tireless organizer and speaker; as a creative (and increasingly expedient) strategist who effectively developed the Slave Power conspiracy thesis, which branded slaveholders as an aristocratic class that sought to subvert democracy and liberty in the United States; as an outspoken proponent of a liberal antislavery agenda that linked abolition with free trade and cheap postage, which he believed would strengthen the forces of reform and enhance moral progress by facilitating the exchange of goods and ideas, thereby striking a blow at the Slave Power; and as a forceful editor of the party's leading newspaper. Hoping to expand the ranks of political antislavery, he helped to create the Free Soil party in 1848.

After these accomplishments, Leavitt's career as an antislavery activist waned. From 1848 until his death he was managing editor of the *Independent,* a New York newspaper that espoused Congregationalism, antislavery, and various benevolent causes, such as temperance and home missions. He remained an ardent supporter of free trade and abolition, and during the Civil War he argued, with little success, that the Union government must defend U.S. interests by vigorously employing the Monroe Doctrine to remove the French from Mexico. Leavitt died in Brooklyn.

• Letters from Leavitt are in the Joshua Leavitt Papers, the Salmon P. Chase Papers, the Lewis Tappan Papers, and the Elizur Wright Papers at the Library of Congress; in the Amos Phelps Papers at the Boston Public Library; in the John Greenleaf Whittier Papers at the Essex Institute; in the Charles Sumner Papers at Harvard University Library; in the

Joshua Giddings Papers at the Ohio Historical Society; and in the Salmon P. Chase Papers at the Historical Society of Pennsylvania. The best available biography is Hugh Davis, *Joshua Leavitt, Evangelical Abolitionist* (1990).

HUGH DAVIS

LEAVITT, Mary Greenleaf Clement (22 Sept. 1830–5 Feb. 1912), reformer and temperance missionary, was born in Hopkinton, New Hampshire, the daughter of Joshua H. Clement, a Baptist minister, and Eliza Harvey. She received her early education in Hopkinton and Thetford, Vermont. At the age of sixteen she began to teach in schools in New Hampshire and Vermont. After a year of study at the Thetford Academy, she enrolled in the Massachusetts State Normal School at West Newton. She graduated in 1851 and taught in Dover, Massachusetts, then in Boston at the Quincy Grammar School (1852–1854) and the Boylston Grammar School (1854–1857). In 1857 she quit work to marry Thomas H. Leavitt, a land speculator from Greenfield, Massachusetts, with whom she had three daughters. Her husband was a spendthrift and was incapable of supporting his family, so in 1867 Leavitt opened a private school in her home. Opposed to the school, her husband left his family to settle in Nebraska. The couple divorced in 1878.

After her husband's departure, Leavitt became increasingly involved in the temperance movement. The Women's Temperance Crusade of 1873–1874 had interested her, and she helped to organize a chapter of the Woman's Christian Temperance Union (WCTU) in Boston, of which she became president. In 1877 she met the future president of the National WCTU (NWCTU), Frances Willard, who was working with Dwight L. Moody in his revival meetings in Boston. Willard encouraged Leavitt's work with the WCTU, and in 1881 Leavitt gave up her school to take on temperance and sufferage work in Massachusetts full time. She became the first superintendent of the franchise department of the NWCTU in 1882. In 1883, after the death of her father, Leavitt capitulated to the entreaties of Willard to begin organizational work on the Pacific Coast. She resigned the position of organizer in 1884, convinced that local women could do the work better themselves. Later that year, possibly inspired by a call from Mary Livermore for American women to lead the temperance movement around the world, and most certainly urged by Willard, Leavitt prepared to go abroad as the WCTU's first international missionary overseas.

On 15 November 1884 Leavitt left San Francisco on the steamship *Alameda*. She organized a WCTU in Honolulu in early 1885 and proceeded to Auckland, New Zealand, then Australia, Japan, China, Siam, Burma, India, Africa, and Europe. In her travels she organized eighty-six WCTU branches, twenty-four men's temperance societies, and a number of White Cross Societies (dedicated to stricter moral purity laws). She also circulated the WCTU's "Polyglot Petition," which called on world leaders to abolish the trade in alcohol, opiates, and stimulants. In 1885 Wil-

lard organized the World's WCTU (WWCTU) and appointed Leavitt (in absentia) as the union's first corresponding secretary. Leavitt returned to the United States in 1891 and attended the first convention of the WWCTU in Boston. She was appointed honorary president of the WWCTU that year, and Willard became president.

During her seven-year journey, Leavitt visited forty-three countries, employed 229 interpreters in forty-seven different languages, and spent a mere $8,000. All but $1,600 of that money she raised from the people among whom she worked. Soon after her departure, the NWCTU leaders asked their membership to donate to Leavitt's journey, and the initial response garnered $3,000. She returned $1,400 of these contributions to the NWCTU coffers. During and after her initial trip she described her experiences in letters and articles in the *Union Signal*, the official organ of the NWCTU. In these pieces she also drew attention to the volume of European alcohol that was being imported to the non-Western world and criticized American consuls for pushing American rum and whiskey in West Africa. Her experiences included a meeting with the queen of the Hovas in Madagascar, who complained about British and French imports of alcohol to that country, and with King Leopold of Belgium to discuss the problem of European exports of spirits to Africa and Asia.

Although Leavitt continued to be active in the WCTU after her return in 1891, including making a temperance organizational trip to Latin America, she became increasingly critical of the union's leadership throughout the 1890s. During the debates surrounding the building of the Woman's Temple, an office block in Chicago that would become the home of the WCTU and its Woman's Temperance Publishing Association, Leavitt reportedly became one of many critics of the project. Her more vocal criticism was saved for Willard and especially Willard's friend Isabel (Lady Henry) Somerset, the president of the British Woman's Temperance Association (the WCTU's equivalent in Britain) and a vice president of the WWCTU. Somerset first drew Leavitt's anger in 1891 when she rejected Leavitt's request to go to India to help WCTU work there. Leavitt questioned Somerset's dedication to temperance, suggesting that the Englishwoman was more concerned with her own social standing than with social problems. In 1898 Leavitt charged that Somerset served wine to her guests and owned some pubs in England. Leavitt was not alone in her criticism, and several of the policies and activities of Willard and her close circle of friends in the WWCTU leadership increasingly came under scrutiny from the general membership. The socialist proclivities of Willard and her colleagues earned criticism from conservative evangelical women like Leavitt and many of the women she had organized. Willard noted Leavitt's behavior with disdain, at one point suggesting that the international missionary had spent too much time in the hot countries.

Leavitt's influence within the WCTU declined through the 1890s, but she continued to criticize the union. After Willard's death in 1898, possibly frustrated with the leadership's direction of the organization, but likely also out of exhaustion, Leavitt reduced her contact with the formal organization. She died in Boston of pneumonia and arteriosclerosis.

• See Leavitt's letters to the *Union Signal* and her report to the WWTCU in 1891 for further information on her journeys. Leavitt is described in the *Union Signal* by Mary Livermore, 16 July 1885, and by Frances Willard, 27 Jan. 1887. Willard discusses Leavitt's work-in-progress in *Glimpses of Fifty Years* (1889), written while Leavitt was still abroad. Janet Z. Giele's biographical sketch of Leavitt in *Notable American Women 1607–1950*, vol. 2, ed. Edward T. James et al. (1971), provides helpful biographical details and a bibliography. Ian Tyrrell, *Woman's World/Woman's Empire* (1991), is an intense analysis of the WWCTU and includes extensive discussions of the tensions and dynamics within the leadership of the union. See also Ruth Bordin, *Woman and Temperance* (1981), in which Bordin claims that much of Leavitt's correspondence is missing from the WCTU records, and *Frances Willard: A Biography* (1986). For Leavitt's conflict with Willard see also Mary Earhart, *Frances Willard: From Prayers to Politics* (1944). Obituaries appear in the *Boston Transcript*, 5 Feb. 1912, and *Our Message* (published by the Mass. WCTU), Mar. 1912.

DANIEL J. MALLECK

LEBOW, Fred (3 June 1932–10 Oct. 1994), road-racing and track-and-field promoter, was born Fischl Lebowitz in Arad, Romania, the sixth of seven children of an Orthodox Jewish produce merchant. The names of his parents are unknown. In 1942 Nazi soldiers invaded his home town and took his father and older brothers to a concentration camp. Lebow remained at home with his mother and sisters until the Germans ordered all remaining Jews to be sequestered in a nearby abandoned military barracks, which they later learned had been modified into a gas chamber. Disguised as peasants, Lebow, his mother, and sisters left their home in search of a safe haven from the Nazis. Various families hid them from the Nazis until Russian troops liberated the town in 1944. After the Russians imposed a Communist totalitarian regime on Romania, confiscating all private business and property, the Lebowitz family unsuccessfully sought permission to leave the country. The Lebowitzes decided to leave Romania individually instead, with Lebow and one of his brothers joining a group of orphans on a train bound for Czechoslovakia.

The brothers settled in Marienbad, Czechoslovakia, where they attended a Hebrew school and worked various odd jobs to support themselves. Like many other refugee children and teenagers, Lebow became a courier in the growing European black market, smuggling goods from country to country. Lebow specialized in smuggling sugar and diamonds across the European continent and into England through Belgium. After briefly living in England, he settled in Ireland and renewed study at a Hebrew school. In 1951 Lebow became an Irish "stateless citizen," obtained a passport, and emigrated to the United States, having won a scholarship to a talmudic academy in Brooklyn, New York. Brooklyn's ethnic community, however, reminded him too much of Romania, so he transferred to a newly established talmudic school in Kansas City, Missouri. After briefly attending the Kansas City institution, Lebow moved to Cleveland, Ohio, where his brother Morris Lebowitz lived. There he changed his name to Fred Lebow, obtained a social security card, and began working as a salesman for a wholesale television distributor. He also joined a local theater group and became part owner of an improvisational comedy theater, the Left-Handed Compliment. Captured so by the theater, Lebow quit his job selling televisions and managed the comedy club full time for nearly two years.

In the early 1960s Lebow moved to New York City and began working in the garment business, specializing in double-knit fabrics and clothes. He first worked for Tucker Knits, which sent him to the Fashion Institute of Technology. Despite not graduating from FIT, Lebow made a fortune as a consultant in the "knockoff" clothing industry. He was particularly talented in designing a garment that would cost less than $50 based on one that originally retailed for more than $200 by using cheaper fabrics, fewer buttons, imitation pockets (that would not open), and no lining. In the late 1960s and early 1970s, when double-knit fabrics went out of fashion, he went to work for a Long Island fabric company. In his free time Lebow played tennis and competed with moderate success in minor tournaments. By the late 1960s he was so frustrated by losing so often that he began running to improve his stamina. By 1970 Lebow had given up tennis entirely and had begun running competitively. That year he ran thirteen 26.2-mile marathons, recording a personal best of 3 hours, 19 minutes in Syracuse, New York.

In conjunction with the New York Road Runners Club, Lebow spearheaded the organization of the first New York City Marathon in 1970. Run entirely within Central Park, 126 runners started the race, and 72 finished, with Gary Muhrcke, a New York City firefighter, winning in 2 hours, 31 minutes 38 seconds. Lebow, who contributed $300 himself toward the purchase of prizes for the first race, became the president of the New York Road Runners Club in 1973. Through 1975 the New York City Marathon continued to be run within Central Park, receiving minimal attention from even the local media. In 1976 Lebow expanded the race to cover all five boroughs of New York City, starting on Staten Island's Verrazano-Narrows Bridge, running through Brooklyn, Queens, the Bronx, and Manhattan, before ending in Central Park. Manufacturers Hanover, a major New York financial institution, was the largest early sponsor of the race. Since then, other corporations have also financed the marathon. To enhance the race's media appeal, Lebow invited the world's top marathon runners to compete, paying some, such as Bill Rogers, who won the 1976 race, exorbitant appearance fees. A record 2,090 runners started the race that year, with 1,549 finishing, nearly five times as many as the year before. In 1981 Lebow arranged for the American Broadcasting Company to televise the race live, treating the nation to Alberto Salazar's world record performance of 2 hours, 8 minutes, 13 seconds. In 1984 Lebow rewarded both the male and female winners of the New York City Marathon with $25,000 and a new Mercedes-Benz automobile, thereby legitimizing a practice that had been conducted "under the table" since the mid-1970s. In 1984 he published *Inside the World of Big-Time Marathoning*. Coauthored with Richard Woodley, it is partly an autobiography of Lebow, partly an account of the organization of the New York City Marathon, and partly a discussion of the transformation of track-and-field athletes from amateurs to professionals. In addition to the New York City Marathon, Lebow organized and promoted other world-class running events, such as the Fifth Avenue Mile, the World Cross-Country Championships in Belmont Park in 1984, and the New York Games Grand Prix track-and-field meet.

In 1990 Lebow was diagnosed with brain cancer and given six months to live. Defying the odds, he completed the New York City Marathon in nearly five hours, accompanied by close friend Grete Waitz of Norway, who had won the women's division of the race nine times in the late 1970s and 1980s. Four weeks before the twenty-fifth running of the New York City Marathon, Lebow died in New York City. In that year, a record 29,735 runners completed the race.

Lebow stands as one of the most significant sports promoters of the twentieth century, not only for his ability to bring together the world's top performers in the New York City Marathon, but also for his success in promoting marathon racing, one of the most physically demanding athletic events, as a mass participatory sport. Before New York, only a few hundred serious runners gathered to contest the annual Boston Marathon. Although the running boom, which had captured the entire world by the late 1970s, underpinned his success, Lebow ensured the success of the marathon by recasting it as a great urban spectacle, thereby spawning similar events throughout the world.

• For more information on Lebow, see Amby Burfoot, "Across the Finish Line," *Newsweek*, 24 Oct. 1994; Jane Gross, "Inside Fred Lebow's World," *New York Times Biographical Service*, Oct. 1994, pp. 1343–44; Bob Ottum, "The Man Who Runs Running," *Sports Illustrated*, 26 Oct. 1981, pp. 44–45, 50, 52, 57; and Red Smith, "The High Priest of Running," *New York Times Biographical Service*, Nov. 1980, p. 1564. An obituary is in the *New York Times*, 10 Oct. 1994.

ADAM R. HORNBUCKLE

LE BRUN, Napoleon (2 Jan. 1821–9 July 1901), architect, was born Napoleon Eugene Henri Charles Le Brun in Philadelphia, Pennsylvania, the son of the Napoleonic partisan and exile Charles François Eugene Le Brun and the émigré Adelaide Louise de Monmignon Madeleine. Charles Le Brun apprenticed his son

to the architect Thomas Ustick Walter in 1836. The major project in the Walter office at that time was the Girard College for Orphans in Philadelphia, one of the most significant Greek Revival monuments in America. Napoleon Le Brun established his own practice in Philadelphia in 1841; his earliest commissions were local church buildings for both Protestant—Seventh Presbyterian Church (1842), Eighth Presbyterian Church (1843), Church of the Nativity, Episcopal (1844), Church of the Atonement, Episcopal, (1847–1848), Trinity Church, Episcopal (Pottsville, Pa., 1847), and the first Tabernacle Baptist Church—and Roman Catholic congregations. His rebuilding of many Philadelphia Catholic churches damaged in the nativist riots of 1844—among them, Saint Patrick's (1841), Saint Philip Neri's (1841), Saint Peter's (1845), Saint Augustine's (1847), and Saint Vincent's (1847)—earned Le Brun the commission for the Cathedral of Saints Peter and Paul in 1846. Le Brun was replaced as architect in 1850–1851 but was reinstated in 1860, after which the project proceeded to completion according to his plans and was dedicated in 1864. Le Brun undertook the enlargement of the Jefferson Medical College in 1845 and the remodeling of William Strickland's Musical Fund Society Building in 1847.

Also in 1845 Le Brun married Adele Louise Lajus, a daughter of the merchant Paul Lajus. Of their five children, two sons joined their father's practice: Pierre L. Le Brun (1846–1924) in 1870, when the firm became Napoleon Le Brun & Son, and Michel Moracin Le Brun (1856–1913) in 1892, at which time the firm became Napoleon Le Brun & Sons.

Beginning in 1851 Le Brun received commissions to design the Schuylkill County jail at Pottsville (1851–1852) and its extension (1876–1877) and the Montgomery County jail (1851) and court house (1852–1854) at Norristown. The Philadelphia Society for Alleviating the Miseries of Public Prisons had been pressing for prison reform since 1797, and Le Brun, influenced by the movement, based his designs on John Haviland's Eastern State Penitentiary (1823–1836) in North Philadelphia, which became the prototype for enlightened prison design in the United States and abroad. In 1855 Le Brun and an associate, the German Gustav Runge, won the commission for the American Academy of Music (1855–1857), for which Le Brun traveled abroad to inspect exemplary theaters. In 1860 he designed "Chelwood," a country house for Charles Rufus King. Located on the Delaware River at Andalusia, it remains among Le Brun's most important residential commissions.

Le Brun moved from Philadelphia to New York City in 1864 and within three years resumed the practice of architecture. His first undertaking in New York was the Church of the Epiphany (1869–1870; a rectory and sacristy, 1877; and a school, 1887; all but the school were destroyed by fire in 1966). This was followed by seven other area Catholic churches: Saint Ann's (1870), Saint Elizabeth's (1870, demolished), Saint John-the-Baptist (1870–1871), Saint Jean-Baptiste (1882, demolished), Saint Cecilia (1883–1887), the Sacred Heart of Jesus (1884), the Blessed Sacrament (1887, demolished), and, in Brooklyn, the Church of Saint Louis and its rectory (1889). As had been the case in Philadelphia, the Le Brun firm designed churches for Protestant denominations as well: a church for the Stanton Street Baptist Church congregation (1881, demolished); Saint Mary-the-Virgin (1894), and Saint Bernard's Protestant Episcopal Church (1896) in Bernardsville, New Jersey. Le Brun also designed the new Masonic Hall (1870–1875, demolished in 1911) and reproduced a diminutive variation of its granite, four-story and mansard, Second Empire–style facade, in iron, for the Masonic Temple (1876–1877) in Elmira, New York, which has since been greatly altered.

In 1876 Le Brun began renovation of the Wilson B. Hunt building at Church Street and Park Place as company headquarters for the Metropolitan Life Insurance Company. It was the first of several building projects that he and his sons would carry out for the insurance company. For the next thirty-four years the Le Brun firm maintained its offices in buildings it designed for Metropolitan Life, first at Park Place and then at 1 Madison Avenue. Metropolitan Life's original West Coast headquarters (1909) was designed by the Le Brun firm as well.

In 1877 the firm received the first of more than seventy commissions from the city's reorganized Board of Fire Commissioners. Over the course of three decades father and sons perfected a municipal building type that incorporated innovative features in personnel and stabling accommodation as well as sliding poles, sliding doors, and automatic harness. In 1892 the Le Bruns won the competition for the new Home Life Insurance Company Building; the following year they enlarged their design to make the building, already begun, taller than the Postal Telegraph Building rising simultaneously next door. The Le Bruns also received two bank commissions, alterations to the Brooklyn Savings Bank (1881) in Brooklyn and the Hoboken Bank for Savings (1890) in Hoboken, New Jersey. In addition the Le Brun firm designed schools as well as the headquarters of the board of education (1897–1900), tenement buildings, commercial buildings, buildings for the Department of Charities and Correction, and several residences. Inviting comparison with Chelwood is "Evergreens" (1894), designed for Charles S. Shultz in Montclair, New Jersey.

The Le Bruns were instrumental in the establishment of the Willard Collection of architectural casts at the Metropolitan Museum of Art. The will of wealthy businessman Levi Hale Willard stipulated that Napoleon Le Brun act as president of the three-member commission overseeing the collection and that Pierre Le Brun be appointed purchasing agent. The installation of the more than a thousand architectural models and fragments, large and small, was completed in 1896. The casts were intended for both the general public and the architectural profession, and a course in architectural draftsmanship and the systematic study of the casts was included in the museum school's curriculum in association with architectural instruction at Columbia College.

Although his earliest designs had been stylistically dependent on Walter's Greek Revival masterpiece at Girard College, Le Brun's major Philadelphia commissions demonstrate that he recognized the structural and architectural value of other stylistic precedents. For example, an early cathedral facade design—a simplified adaptation in the manner of the church of Saint-Sulpice in Paris as well as a response to the building committee's desire for a twin-towered front—was unbuilt, whereas the interior suggests the works of Renaissance architects Bramante, Alberti, and Alessi. For the Academy of Music Le Brun generalized several of the theater facades represented in Clement Contant's book *Parallele des Principaux Theatres Modernes de l'Europe* but with Runge, improved the capacity and sight-lines of the three-tiered interior by means of an innovative system of iron supports and cantilevers. Extensive iron support also was proposed (1857) for Le Brun and Runge's unbuilt post office alteration to Strickland's Second National Bank interior. Chelwood's low mansard roof is relatively early for Philadelphia; the house's symmetrical river front and integrated three-story rear service wing constitute a well-built synthesis of convenience and comfort.

Pierre Le Brun's three trips abroad in the service of the Willard Commission put the firm's reliance on appropriate prototypes more sharply into focus. Indeed, the historical references that characterize the ornamentation of the Le Bruns' later commissions appear to have been inspired by the Willard Collection and suggest that the sons, especially Pierre, were responsible for the firm's designs from the late 1880s on. The spare Gothic details that characterize the facade of the steel-framed Church of St. Mary-the-Virgin and its flanking auxiliary buildings suggest the collection's French Gothic casts. The terracotta and stone ornamentation articulating the later firehouse facades was based on the Willard casts of Italian and French Renaissance details. Montgomery Schuyler, a contemporary architectural critic and theorist, praised the manner in which the historic motifs were integrated into the facade design of the sixteen-story, steel-framed Home Life Insurance Building, calling it a pioneer in the evolution of the skyscraper aesthetic. In 1910 the firm was awarded a gold medal by the New York Chapter of the American Institute of Architects in recognition of the Metropolitan Life Tower (1909), a steel-framed, marble-veted reference to the great *campanile* in Venice and, at that time, the tallest inhabited building in the world.

Elected a fellow of the American Institute of Architects (AIA) in 1870, Le Brun collaborated in elevating the status and influence of the profession. A member of the founding New York City chapter—which recognized the city's negligence in maintaining reliable standards of building—Le Brun was the chapter's first representative on the new board of examiners of the New York Buildings Department, a post he held for eighteen years, until his professional retirement in 1897. In 1884–1885 Le Brun addressed the issue of a customary schedule of professional charges, and he and his sons actively participated in establishing standards for practice and instruction. He served twice as president of the New York chapter, was a member of the national AIA executive committee in 1883, and was a trustee of the AIA from 1880 to 1887.

In 1910, almost a decade after Le Brun's death in New York City, the firm closed its doors. His sons subsequently established the Le Brun Scholarship, awarded annually by the New York Chapter of the AIA to younger architects and draftsmen for architectural study and travel abroad. The firm's library was donated to the Metropolitan and Montclair art museums. The Le Bruns had shaped a largely municipal practice. Stylistically conservative at a time of stylistic transition, the firm had revived decorative elements and structural systems from the past rather than invent new forms, and the Le Bruns were among the first to adapt these past features to the challenges that first iron and then steel presented in the construction of both old and new building types. In the context of nineteenth-century American architecture, the firm's near seventy-year history embodies a remarkable continuity in the midst of transition: from public monuments in Philadelphia to skyscrapers in New York City, two generations of Le Bruns forged a link between the builder-architect of the early part of the century to the professional architect by century's end.

• Drawings submitted by Le Brun for consideration by the American Academy of Music can be found at the Athenaeum in Philadelphia. Le Brun's work is featured as well in the Collection of the Heinz Architecture Center at the Carnegie Museum of Art in Pittsburgh. For additional biographical information see Joseph Jackson, *Early Philadelphia Architects and Engineers* (1923); Sandra L. Tatman and Roger W. Moss, *Biographical Dictionary of Philadelphia Architects: 1700–1930* (1985); and Jeffrey A. Cohen, "Napoleon Le Brun, FAIA (1821–1901)," in *Drawing toward Building* (1986). On his architectural oeuvre, see Montgomery Schuyler, "The Work of N. Le Brun & Sons," *Architectural Record* 27 (1910): 365–81; Richard Longstreth, "A Country House by Napoleon Le Brun," *Journal of the Society of Architectural Historians* 26 (Dec. 1967): 310–11; "The Masonic Hall, N.Y.," *American Architect & Builders' Monthly*, Apr. 1870, p. 29, and July 1870, p. 69; "The New Masonic Hall, New York," *Technologist* 1 (July 1870): 164–67; and the following reports by Charles Savage for the Landmarks Preservation Commission of the City of New York: "The Free Church of Saint Mary the Virgin" (LP-1562 [1989]), "Metropolitan Life Insurance Company Tower" (LP-1530 [1989]), and "(Former) Home Life Insurance Company Building" (LP-1751 [1991]); other Landmarks Preservation Commission reports on Le Brun's work are "Engine Company 31" (LP-0087 [1966]) and "Saint Cecilia's Church" (LP-0933 [1976]). For Le Brun's work with the American Academy of Music see John Francis Marion, *Within These Walls* (1984). Also see Richard Webster, *Philadelphia Preserved* (1981). An obituary is in the *New York Times*, 30 July 1901.

CHARLES C. SAVAGE

LECHFORD, Thomas (1590s–c. 1643), lawyer and author, was born probably in Surrey County, England. The names of his parents are unknown, but kinsmen (the name Lechford being an uncommon one in England at the time) long resided in Surrey County. Lechford's wife is known only by her first name, Elizabeth; it is unknown whether they had any children.

In England, Lechford had Puritan leanings, and he writes that he was an "auditor" of and "hung upon" the ministry of Reverend Hugh Peters at St. Sepulchre's Church in London. Lechford was a member of Clement's Inn, one of the inns of chancery, in Westminster. He wrote that he was a "Student or Practiser" of the law. In England, however, it appears that he acted as an attorney and solicitor, not as a barrister. He served in some capacity with Sir Thomas Wentworth (earl of Strafford), lord deputy of Ireland.

Lechford offended English authorities because he had "witnessed" against the bishops "in soliciting the cause of Mr. Prynne" (Cotton, p. 265). William Prynne's pamphlet, which attacked episcopacy and cast aspersions on the king and queen, earned the author imprisonment and loss of his ears. Lechford himself was deprived of his "station in England," and he also "suffered imprisonment, and a kind of banishment." He declined employment offers from George Rákóczy, Prince of Transylvania, and the Providence Island Company, the Puritan experiment, chartered in 1630 for colonization in the Caribbean.

Searching for a more compatible religious environment, Lechford sailed for America, arriving at Boston on 27 June 1638. He was the first practicing lawyer in Massachusetts Bay Colony, though others, such as John Winthrop (1588–1649), had been attorneys in England. Lechford did not find the welcome that he had expected. He presented a book that he had written shipboard, "Of Prophecie," to Deputy Governor Thomas Dudley, "the next news I had was, that at first dash he accused me of heresy." Dudley recommended that the book be burned. While Governor John Winthrop did not indicate any special concern, church leaders either condemned or ignored this treatise and another one that Lechford had also written. Dudley set forth his main objections to Lechford's writings: "His tenet beinge that the office of apostleship doth still continew and ought soe to doe till Crist's coming, and that a Church hath now power to make apostles as our Crist had when hee was heere." Indeed for one questioning the New England congregational way, it was not a good time to come to the Massachusetts colony, just after the antinomian controversy over Anne Hutchinson. Lechford was denied church membership, and thus also the right to vote and hold office.

Lechford complained that "I am kept from the Sacrament, and all place of preferment in the Common-Wealth and forced to get my living by writing things, which scarce finds me bread." He unsuccessfully applied to the Massachusetts General Court for employment as clerk and notary, the magistrates had "fear of offending the churches because of my opinions." Lechford, who had skill as a chirographer, worked as a conveyancer, scrivener, and draftsman. He drew up deeds and leases and exercised powers of attorney. He drafted many arbitration bonds for persons settling their differences out of court. He kept a meticulous account of all his legal business in his *Note-Book* (published 1885). Lechford attempted to direct a compromise between the principals in the famous *Sherman v. Keane* case (1636–1643), which divided the colonists politically. Mrs. Richard Sherman, a widow, had sued Robert Keane, a wealthy merchant, over ownership of a sow.

Occasionally Lechford was allowed to act as counsel in court. In summer 1639 he was debarred for "pleading" with the jury "out of Court." He presented the General Court a petition for pardon, which was probably granted.

On 8 June 1639 Lechford presented "A Paper of Certaine Propositions to the general Court made upon request," in which he recommended that all legal judgments, wills, inventories and the like be recorded; his suggestion was not adopted. Though under civil disabilities, Lechford became a member of the Military Company of Massachusetts. In 1640 Lechford was summoned before the Court of Assistants for expressing his views on church government, for which he made public apology, "acknowledging hee had overshot himself, and is sorry for it, promising to attend his calling, and not to meddle with controversies"; the charge was dismissed. Because of his chirographer's skills, the government relented and allowed him to make an official copy of the "Body of Liberties," which was later enacted into law.

Lechford became increasingly disaffected from the arbitrariness of the Massachusetts government as well as from the congregational polity of the churches. He presented a paper in 1640 advocating submission to the king and the Church of England. Lechford considered that the church dominated the government in Massachusetts and that the church neglected its missionary role. He contended that "three parts of the people of the Country remain out of the Church." Though he criticized the democracy of the churches, he felt that in government an aristocracy had gained power.

Leaving his wife, house, and personal property worth £6 13s. 10d., Lechford sailed from Boston on 3 August 1641. In England he returned "humbly" to the Church of England, and by 16 November 1641 he again was a member of Clement's Inn. An order of the Massachusetts General Court in 1647 mentioned that Lechford had been "an ordinary solicitor in England."

After his return to England, Lechford published in 1642 *Plain Dealing; or, Newes from New-England*, reissued two years later as *New-England's Advice to Old England*, the work was also reprinted in 1833, 1867, and 1969. *Plain Dealing*, largely a compilation of letters and documents that he had written earlier, contains valuable information on commonplace life in the Massachusetts colony and even a descriptive narrative of the Indians of New England. The Reverend John Cotton found in it the same theological errors of Lechford's previous writings: denial that any of the New Testament prophecy had been fulfilled and that there should still be persons designated as apostles, "who should by their transcendent authority govern all churches." Cotton also commented that the book had many "false and fradulent" passages, but "I forbear to speak of the man himself, because soon after the publishing of that book, himself was called away out of the world to give account of his book and whole life before the highest judge" (pp. 264–65). Lechford died in England. His New England experience had made him less a Puritan, but he still believed in further reformation of the Church of England, without tampering with episcopal structure.

• The published works of Lechford are J. Hammond Trumbull, ed., *Note-Book Kept by Thomas Lechford, Esq., Lawyer in Massachusetts Bay, from June 27, 1638, to July 29, 1641* (1885) and *Plain Dealing; or, Newes from New-England* (1642; reprint, with an introduction by Darrett B. Rutman, 1969). The latter also contains notes of J. Hammond Trumbull to the 1867 edition. Mention of Lechford is found in Allyn B. Forbes, ed., *Winthrop Papers*, vol. 4: *1638–1644* (1944), Nathaniel B. Shurtleff, ed., *Records of the Governor and Company of the Massachusetts Bay in New England*, vol. 1–2 (1853), and John Noble, ed., *Records of the Court of Assistants of the Colony of Massachusetts Bay*, vol. 1 (1904). John Cotton, "The Way of Congregational Churches Cleared," in *John Cotton on the Churches of New England*, ed. Larzer Ziff (1968), pp. 165–364, comments on Lechford and his views. H. E. Malden, *The Victoria History of the Counties of England: Sussex*, vol. 3 (1911), suggests possible ancestry. For the setting of Lechford's New England years, see Darrett B. Rutman, ed., *Winthrop's Boston: Portrait of a Puritan Town, 1630–1649* (1965).

HARRY M. WARD

LE CLEAR, Thomas (11 Mar. 1818–26 Nov. 1882), painter, was born in Owego, Tioga County, New York, the son of Louis Le Clear, a French émigré who settled in Owego before the War of 1812; his mother's name is unknown. There is little information regarding his formal education as an artist. According to his friend and biographer, Henry Theodore Tuckerman, Le Clear was a self-taught artist who developed a talent for painting at an early age. By the time he was twelve he had produced an image of Saint Matthew painted on rough pine board. The painting proved such a success in his hometown that he was able to sell copies of the work for two dollars and fifty cents each. In 1832 Le Clear's family moved to London, Ontario, where he continued to improve his painting skills. He received several commissions for portraits, including one of John Wilson, a former member of the Canadian Parliament.

Le Clear traveled throughout Ontario and central and western New York while still very young, seeking work. At the age of sixteen he visited Goderich, Ontario, on Lake Huron, where he was employed painting decorative panels for steamboats. Arriving in New York City in 1839, he studied painting with the noted painter Henry Inman. Five years later he opened a studio in Owego. This enterprise, however, was not profitable, and he returned to New York, probably within the year. In 1844 Le Clear married Caroline Wells; they had four children. Le Clear moved to Buffalo and established a studio there sometime between 1845 and 1847. He enjoyed steady patronage and his reputation grew. Le Clear became a leader of Buffalo's artistic community, and with fellow artists William H. Beard and Lars Sellstedt he assisted in founding the Buffalo Fine Arts Academy (now the Albright-Knox Art Gallery) in 1862. He served as one of its directors and was also on the board of managers for the Brooklyn Art Association from 1861 to 1862.

Despite the success he achieved in Buffalo, Le Clear was determined to return to New York City. He had already made his reputation there with his genre scenes of young children; his paintings had been exhibited at the National Academy of Design beginning in 1845 and at the American Art Union in 1846. He continued to paint images of children throughout the 1850s and 1860s. His paintings were not mere representations of childhood anecdote. In *The Little Buffalo Newsboy* (c. 1845, private collection), a small boy with a newspaper under his arm stands alone calling out to unseen buyers. His averted gaze, shadowed face, and isolation within the composition create a sense of tension that is heightened by the disparity in size between the massive architecture behind him and his fragile body. The viewer is left in doubt of the child's survival. A more optimistic view is found in Le Clear's well-known *Buffalo Newsboy* (1853, Albright Knox Art Gallery). A newsboy sits on top of a wooden crate on a deserted street. In contrast to his shabby clothes and surroundings, his expression is one of optimism and determination as he glances beyond the viewer's space as if reflecting on a brighter future. Le Clear's rendering of the boy embodies the Victorian belief that people could achieve their goals through hard work and determination regardless of present economic and social status. Such sentiment as depicted by Le Clear struck a responsive chord with critics and the public.

The early 1860s were tremendously productive years for Le Clear. Beginning in 1861 he exhibited regularly at the Brooklyn Art Association. He was elected to the Century Association in 1862, and that same year he became an associate member of the National Academy of Design (the following year he was made a full academician). In addition to his painting career, he taught at the academy from 1869 to 1870 and from 1872 to 1873; he also served on a committee to improve its educational programs. In 1863 he occupied a studio at New York City's Tenth Street Studio Building, which he maintained until 1880. Following the death of his first wife in 1869 Le Clear married the daughter of James S. King of New York; they had one child.

Throughout his career Le Clear painted genre subjects and portraits; however, during the 1870s he focused his talents on the latter. While his earlier genre paintings depicted hopeful youths dreaming of a better life, his portraits during this period were of successful men who had achieved their goals. Among those who sat for the artist was President Ulysses S. Grant, whose

portrait Le Clear painted twice; a three-quarter length (National Portrait Gallery, Washington, D.C.) and a full length (White House collection). He also painted portraits of leading businessmen including Alexander T. Stewart (National Portrait Gallery), Joseph Henry, the first director of the Smithsonian Institution (National Portrait Gallery), as well as the writer William Cullen Bryant (Metropolitan Museum, N.Y.) and the actor Edwin Booth (Worcester Art Museum, Mass.). In 1873 Le Clear exhibited two portraits at the Royal Academy in London: one of Reverend Frances Vinton (location unknown) and one of Edwin Booth (it is not certain if this is the same painting now in Worcester).

From 1873 until his death Le Clear resided in Rutherford Park, New Jersey. He maintained a successful career as an artist, teacher, and supporter of the arts. A founding member of the Buffalo Fine Arts Academy, he assisted in establishing a permanent public art gallery for that city. Through his association with the National Academy of Design he sought to improve its curriculum. His paintings of young children were immensely popular with the public, and as a leading portraitist of the period, he provided a visual record of this country's leaders in government, business, and the arts.

• An important source for information on Le Clear's career is Chase Viele, "Four Artists of Mid-Nineteenth Century Buffalo," *New York History: The Quarterly Journal of the New York State Historical Association* 43 (1962): 49–78. See also the letters of Chase Viele in the Archives of American Art, National Museum of American Art, Washington, D.C. A contemporary account of Le Clear's life and work can be found in Henry T. Tuckerman, *Book of the Artists* (1867), and his *Sketches of Men of Mark* (1871). For information on Le Clear's early years see Le Roy Wilson Kingman, *Early Owego* (1907). A list of Le Clear's paintings is in James L. Yarnall and William H. Gerdts, *The National Museum of American Arts' Index to American Art Exhibition Catalogues: From the Beginning through the 1876 Centennial Year*, vol. 3 (1986). See also Algernon Graves, *The Royal Academy of Arts*, vol. 5 (1906); and Susan Krane, *The Wayward Muse: A Historical Survey of Painting in Buffalo* (1987), for a history of the artistic community in Buffalo.

PATRICIA BRACK

LECONTE, John (4 Dec. 1818–29 Apr. 1891), scientist and educator, was born in Liberty County, Georgia, the son of Louis LeConte, a planter, and Ann Quarterman. Receiving most of his education at home on a sizable plantation in Liberty County, LeConte imbibed of his father's keen interest in mathematics, chemistry, and natural history. He entered the University of Georgia in 1835 and graduated with an A.B. in 1838. During the following year LeConte enrolled in the College of Physicians and Surgeons, in New York, from which he received his M.D. in 1841. Married to Eleanor Josephine Graham, of New York, in the same year, he moved to Savannah, Georgia, and established a medical practice in 1842. Since he had inherited a large plantation and numerous slaves upon the death of his father in 1838, LeConte did not have to depend upon his medical practice for income. Thus he utilized much of his time in promoting the work of the Georgia Medical Society and in writing articles for scholarly journals. He published a list of Georgia birds and beetles, wrote medical case studies and medical treatises, and conducted experiments to determine "the seat of volition" in the alligator. His publications brought him to the attention of the trustees of the University of Georgia, who appointed him to the faculty in 1846 as professor of chemistry and natural philosophy.

In 1855 LeConte and his brother Joseph LeConte, who had been appointed as a professor at the University of Georgia in 1853, began to take issue with a policy that required the faculty to police students in the dormitory. A highly publicized encounter with the president ensued, and John LeConte resigned. He moved to New York and became a lecturer at the College of Physicians and Surgeons. A few months later, South Carolina College offered him a professorship in natural philosophy. He accepted and moved to Columbia late in 1856. Held in high esteem by his peers in the North, LeConte and his brother, who had also joined the faculty of South Carolina College, received an invitation from Joseph Henry, secretary of the Smithsonian Institution, to develop "a series of tables on the Constants of Nature." Culminating a collaboration begun during their years on the University of Georgia faculty, the LeConte brothers completed the manuscript of a textbook in chemistry, which would be destroyed by Federal troops in 1865. Meanwhile, John LeConte published articles dealing with physical phenomena. In 1850 he published a study of the formation of ice columns extruding from plants and the soil during freezing weather, and in 1858 he published a significant paper on the effects of musical sound upon the flame of a gas jet. Although he devoted more time to physics from 1850 on, LeConte continued to be largely a generalist in his scientific interests, which included medical statistics, ornithology, astronomy, the physical properties of lakes, and the nature of the mind.

Initially, LeConte did not favor the secessionist movement in the South, but eventually he embraced it fully. Thus, he willingly served the Confederacy in various ways as a scientist, ultimately accepting responsibility for supervising the Nitre and Mining Bureau operations in upper South Carolina. Toward the end of the war, he and his brother endeavored to remove the bureau's equipment from the city, but Federal troops intercepted their wagon train, confiscated the valuables, and burned the rest. LeConte and his younger son were captured by Union soldiers, who released his son on the following day. After a march of several days, LeConte was paroled and he made his way back to Columbia, where he found his wife and daughter unharmed from the bombardment and burning of a large portion of the city. He soon learned, however, that all of his papers, which he had sent to the home of the local Catholic priest, had perished in the fire set by Union soldiers.

When South Carolina College reopened as the University of South Carolina in January 1866, LeConte resumed his duties. The loss of his papers and the family's valuables and the freeing of his slaves struck LeConte very hard. The situation became intolerable to him, however, only when he came to believe that the state legislature would be dominated by Republicans and former slaves and freedmen. In addition the loss of his only daughter in 1868 and his fear that blacks would soon overrun the university and its library intensified his desire to leave South Carolina. With the support of prominent northern scientists, he secured the position of professor of physics at the newly established University of California in Berkeley late in 1868. Early in 1869 he left the South forever, declaring that "it is a great relief to escape from this despotism of *ignorance*" and to be free "of the *ignoramuses* who are *now* swelling in our campus."

As the first and most senior member appointed to the new faculty, LeConte was also named acting president, in which capacity he served for several months. The university trustees named him president again in 1875, and he served in that position until 1881, during which time he played a role in securing the Lick Observatory for the university. Unlike his brother Joseph, who also joined the University of California faculty in 1869, John LeConte was not a very productive scholar during his years in California, but he did publish a study of sound shadows on water, a study of the physical properties of Lake Tahoe, and other articles. In 1878 the National Academy of Sciences elected him to its membership. LeConte played a significant role in developing a reputable department of physics and in advancing the standing of the University of California. Both he and his wife suffered from poor health in their later years, and in 1889–1890 LeConte took a leave of absence. He returned to teaching late in 1890 but died at his home in Berkeley a few months later. In commemoration of his and his brother's contributions to the university, a building was named after them at each of the three campuses where they taught (Berkeley, Columbia, and Athens).

• The papers of John LeConte are mainly located in the South Carolina Library, University of South Carolina, Columbia, and the Bancroft Library, University of California, Berkeley. Especially notable among John LeConte's publications are "Experiments Illustrating the Seat of Volition in the Alligator or Crocodilus Lucius of Cuvier," *New York Journal of Medicine and Collateral Sciences* 5 (1845): 335–47; "Observations of a Remarkable Exudation of Ice from the Stems of Vegetables, and on a Singular Protrusion of Icy Columns from Certain Kinds of Earth during Frosting Weather," *Proceedings of the American Association for the Advancement of Science* 3 (1850): 20–34; "Observations on the Freezing of Vegetables, and on the Causes Which Enable Some Plants to Endure the Action of Extreme Cold," *Proceedings of the American Association for the Advancement of Science* 6 (1852): 338–59; "On the Influence of Musical Sounds on the Flame of a Jet of Coal-gas," *American Journal of Science and Arts*, 2d ser., 25 (1858): 62–67; "On the Adequacy of Laplace's Explanation to Account for the Discrepancy between the Computed and the Observed Velocity of Sound in Air and Gases," *London, Edinburgh and Dublin Philosophical Magazine and Journal of Science*, 4th ser., 27 (1864): 1–32; "On Sound Shadows in Water," *American Journal of Science and Arts*, 5th ser., 8

(1882); 98–113; "Apparent Attractions and Repulsions of Small Floating Bodies," *American Journal of Science and Arts*, 3d ser., 24 (1882): 416–25; and "Horizontal Motions of Small Floating Bodies in Relation to the Validity of the Postulates of the Theory of Capillarity," *American Journal of Science and Arts*, 3d ser., 27 (1884): 307–15. The most complete account of his life and career is John Lupold, "From Physician to Physicist: The Scientific Career of John LeConte, 1818–1891" (Ph.D. diss., Univ. of South Carolina, 1970). Useful information is also contained in Joseph LeConte, "Biographical Memoir of John LeConte, 1818–1891," *National Academy of Sciences: Biographical Memoirs* 3 (1895): 371–89. LeConte's close association with his brother Joseph is covered in Lester D. Stephens, *Joseph LeConte: Gentle Prophet of Evolution* (1982).

LESTER D. STEPHENS

LECONTE, John Lawrence (13 May 1825–15 Nov. 1883), entomologist, was born in New York City, the son of John Eatton LeConte, an army topographical engineer and naturalist, and Mary Ann Hampton. Following in the footsteps of his father, a noted naturalist, LeConte began early in life to collect natural specimens, displaying a particular interest in insects, especially in the beetles (order Coleoptera). After attending schools in his native city, LeConte entered Mount St. Mary's College, in Emmitsburg, Maryland, from which he graduated in 1842. Three years later, he enrolled in the College of Physicians and Surgeons, in New York, and in 1846 he received the M.D. degree. While pursuing the study of medicine, LeConte served as an assistant to the botanist and chemist John Torrey. Meanwhile, in 1844, the aspiring young naturalist had already published a paper in which he described twenty-nine species of ground beetles (Carabidae), and, from 1844 to 1846, he had collected specimens in the Rocky Mountains and around Lake Superior.

Like many contemporary naturalists who had trained as physicians, LeConte apparently never had any intention of practicing medicine, and he focused his attention upon collecting, describing, and classifying insect species. When the noted Swiss naturalist Louis Agassiz decided in 1848 to explore the Great Lakes region, young LeConte accompanied him. In 1849 LeConte journeyed to the American West once more, traveling as far as California. He returned to New York in 1851, and a year later he and his father decided to move to Philadelphia because that city was a center of activity in natural history, including entomology. Unlike his cousin Joseph LeConte, of Georgia, with whom he had visited, traveled, collected specimens, and attended medical school, LeConte did not enroll in the Lawrence Scientific School of Harvard University, probably because entomology was not a special concern of Agassiz, the founder of the school. In fact, except for the notable work by Frederick V. Melsheimer in 1806 and by Thomas Say during the following two decades, Americans had described and classified relatively few insects. Many collectors were still sending specimens abroad, especially to England, as late as the mid-1840s, when Le-

Conte set for himself the task of making entomology an important field of study in the United States. He concentrated on the order Coleoptera, for which any effective taxonomic system was lacking. Possessed of sufficient means, LeConte traveled widely, including trips to Central America and Europe; built an extensive collection of beetles; and published a number of descriptions of new species. Active in the affairs of the American Philosophical Society and the Academy of Natural Sciences of Philadelphia and a founding member of the American Entomological Society, he was elected to honorary membership in several European scientific societies.

In 1861 LeConte began a monograph devoted to the classification of the Coleoptera. During the same year he married Helen S. Grier and, to his dismay, watched as his close relatives in Georgia joined heartily in the cause of secession. Only one year earlier he had warned a cousin in Georgia that "the disunion sentiment . . . means civil war . . . and all the attendant horrors." Soon after the Civil War began, LeConte volunteered for service in the U.S. Army medical corps, serving initially as a surgeon and later as a medical inspector. Mustered out of the army in 1865, he resumed his study of natural history. In 1867 he joined a railroad surveying team, serving as a geologist and zoologist to examine landforms and fauna in parts of the Great Plains and the Rocky Mountains. Although he specialized in the taxonomy of the beetles, LeConte possessed considerable knowledge of geology, paleontology, ornithology, and other fields, and he published several dozen articles on topics other than the Coleoptera. In particular, however, he devoted attention to the description and classification of beetles. His studies of the distribution of insects in the American West helped to advance zoogeography as a method of biological inquiry.

Included as a charter member of the National Academy of Sciences in 1863, LeConte served as the president of the American Association for the Advancement of Science in 1874. Widely read in many fields of science, LeConte accepted the theory of evolution but insisted upon design in nature by "the Creator," as he indicated in his AAAS presidential address in January 1875. His impressive record of publications includes at least two hundred articles and two extensive monographs in entomology; almost all those works deal with the Coleoptera. In a monograph on the weevils, or Rhynchophora (now Curculionoidea), of North America, published in 1876, LeConte devoted 460 pages to the study of those fruit and crop pests, and in a monograph on the Coleoptera of North America, which he had begun in 1861 but did not complete until 1883, he offered a nearly 600-page classification of around 11,000 beetles. In both projects, but especially the latter, he was assisted by George Henry Horn. LeConte also published works related to the damage of crops by insects, and in 1877 he made a determined effort to be appointed U.S. Commissioner of Agriculture. Despite letters of endorsement from leading American scientists, however, political patronage prevailed, and President Rutherford B. Hayes chose a less qualified person for that post. Hayes later appointed LeConte to the post of chief clerk of the U.S. Mint in Philadelphia. Despite failing health during the last two years of his life, LeConte continued to be active in the American Entomological Society, in which he had played a leading role for more than fifteen years. Shortly after suffering a stroke, he died at his home in Philadelphia. He was the father of three children, one of whom died in infancy.

The contributions of LeConte to entomology, especially in the taxonomy of the beetles, of which he described or named nearly 5,000 species, significantly advanced descriptive and systematic entomology. As his younger contemporary and fellow entomologist Samuel H. Scudder wrote in 1884, "LeConte was the greatest entomologist this country has yet produced."

• Most of LeConte's manuscripts are in the library of the American Philosophical Society, but others can be found in the library of the Academy of Natural Sciences of Philadelphia, the Smithsonian Institution Archives, and the Bancroft Library, University of California. LeConte's most extensive works are "The *Rhynchophora* of America North of Mexico," *Proceedings of the American Philosophical Society* 25 (1876): i–vi, 1–455, and *Classification of the Coleoptera of North America*, in *Smithsonian Miscellaneous Contributions*, 26 (1883): iii–xxxviii, 1–567. Among the lists of LeConte's publications in entomology are Hermann A. Hagen, *Bibliotheca Entomologica* (1862), and Samuel Henshaw, "Index to the Coleoptera Described by J. L. LeConte, M.D.," *Transactions of the American Entomological Society* 9 (1881–1882): 197–284, but the comprehensive compilation by Alan R. Hardy and Fred G. Andrew, with David H. Kavanaugh, *The Collected LeConte Papers on Entomology* (9 vols., 1982), is indispensable.

A reliable source of genealogical information regarding LeConte is Richard LeConte Anderson, *LeConte History and Genealogy*, vol. 2 (privately printed, 1981). Although uncritical and sometimes inaccurate, the account by Samuel H. Scudder, "Memoir of John Lawrence LeConte, 1825–1883," *National Academy of Sciences Biographical Memoirs* 2 (1886): 261–307 (read as an address in 1884 and published first in the *Transactions of the American Entomological Society* 11 [1884]: i–xxviii), is the most complete biography, but also useful are the tributes to LeConte presented before the American Philosophical Society by J. Peter Lesley only one day after LeConte's death and by his colleague and collaborator George Henry Horn on 7 Dec. 1883, both in the *Proceedings of the American Philosophical Society* 31 (1884): 291–94 and 294–99, respectively. LeConte's association with his southern relatives is discussed in Lester D. Stephens, *Joseph LeConte: Gentle Prophet of Evolution* (1982), and Stephens, "The Appointment of the Commissioner of Agriculture in 1877: A Case Study in Political Ambition and Patronage," *Southern Quarterly* 15 (July 1977): 371–86.

LESTER D. STEPHENS

LECONTE, Joseph (26 Feb. 1823–6 July 1901), geologist and educator, was born in Liberty County, Georgia, the son of Louis LeConte, a planter, and Ann Quarterman. Reared on a large plantation in Liberty County, Georgia, LeConte developed an early interest in natural history, following an example set by his father, an able amateur scientist, and his uncle John Eat-

ton LeConte, a noted naturalist who often visited the plantation and collected faunal specimens in the region. Receiving his preparatory education mainly at home, LeConte entered the University of Georgia in 1838, soon after the death of his father. He graduated with an A.B. in 1841 and three years later enrolled in the College of Physicians and Surgeons, in New York, from which he received the degree of doctor of medicine in 1845.

Married to Caroline Elizabeth Nisbet in 1847, LeConte established a medical practice in Macon, Georgia, during the following year. In 1850 he decided to enroll in the newly established Lawrence Scientific School, at Harvard University, to study with the famed naturalist Louis Agassiz. After completing his work with Agassiz and receiving an S.B. in 1851, LeConte returned to Georgia, and in 1852 he became the professor of natural history at Oglethorpe University in Midway. One year later he accepted the professorship of geology and natural history at his alma mater, joining his brother John LeConte, who had been teaching natural philosophy there for six years. In 1855 the LeConte brothers found themselves at issue with the university's president over the policy that required the faculty to police students in the dormitory. John resigned in 1855, and Joseph left in December 1856. The former joined the faculty of South Carolina College (later, the University of South Carolina) late in 1856, and the latter followed suit in January 1857, as the professor of chemistry and biology.

Until then Joseph LeConte had published only a few articles, on such topics as the gulf stream, the origin of coal, the formation of continents, and the relationship of science to art, education, and sociology, but he began to publish more frequently. With his brother he drafted the manuscript of a textbook in chemistry. Except for the death of one young daughter and the crippling of one of his other three daughters by poliomyelitis, LeConte was immensely happy in Columbia, where he found a congenial society and a stimulating intellectual atmosphere. Although initially opposed to secession, LeConte joined ardently in the cause of the Confederacy in 1861. During the war and after the closing of South Carolina College, he served for a time in manufacturing medicines for the Confederate army and, later, in the Confederate government's Nitre and Mining Bureau. As General William T. Sherman's troops pressed forward after the fall of Atlanta, LeConte was compelled to rescue several relatives in Liberty County and then, with his brother and others, to remove Nitre and Mining Bureau equipment from Columbia. However, Federal troops captured their wagon train, plundered the valuables, and burned the rest, including Joseph LeConte's manuscripts. Circumstances forced John to surrender. Joseph escaped, however, and made his way back to Columbia, where he found that his wife and three daughters had escaped injury during the bombardment and burning of much of the city.

Although LeConte encountered economic difficulties after the war, he patiently persisted in writing a number of articles on the topic of physiological optics, which he later incorporated into a small volume entitled *Sight: An Exposition of the Principles of Monocular and Binocular Vision* (1881), which was the first book on that subject published in the Western Hemisphere. Both he and his brother feared, however, that blacks and Republicans would eventually gain complete control of the state and the University of South Carolina. Thus, each began to search for a position elsewhere, and, when the opportunity arose in 1869, they joined the faculty of the newly established University of California, to be located in Berkeley, John as the professor of physics and Joseph as the professor of geology.

At the age of forty-seven, Joseph began a career at the University of California that would last until his death nearly thirty-two years later. A fifth child, a son, was born shortly after the LeContes moved to California. LeConte readily established himself as an outstanding teacher, and soon he began to publish prolifically, adding to the twenty-three articles he had already published nearly 200 other articles, notes, and reviews, seven books, and two book manuscripts (published after his death). Many of those works dealt with geology, including, in 1877, a highly successful textbook titled *Elements of Geology,* which went through four revised editions. Although he published a number of original articles on geological topics, LeConte was more a theoretical than a field geologist. He was especially interested in rock deformation and in the origin of continents and mountains. His publications in geology helped him win induction into the National Academy of Sciences in 1875, the presidency of the American Association for the Advancement of Science in 1891, and the presidency of the Geological Society of America in 1896.

On the subject of physiology LeConte not only published *Sight,* but also several articles and *Outlines of the Comparative Physiology and Morphology of Animals* (1900). It was as an ardent proponent of the reconciliation of religion and the theory of evolution, however, that he gained his most popular fame. Even before he had left the South, LeConte had begun to teach the theory of evolution to his classes. In *Religion and Science,* published in 1873, he had only hinted at his acceptance of the validity of the theory, but in several articles published soon thereafter and in *Evolution and Its Relation to Religious Thought* (1888); he clearly expressed his belief in the theory. His book became enormously popular and went through several reprintings and a revision in 1891. To LeConte the theory of evolution was "the grandest of all ideas," possessing significance not only for science, but also for every aspect of human culture. Thus, in addition to striving to reconcile the theory with religion, he published many papers in which he related the theory to the physical and cultural differences between the races and the sexes. LeConte's views on these matters were shared by other scientists of the era, and they were not particularly controversial. LeConte's importance on the subject stemmed largely from his ability to articulate his views clearly and reach a varied audience of scientists and other intellectuals.

Recognized as an outstanding teacher, LeConte received numerous accolades from his students. He was also an enthusiastic camper and journeyed to the High Sierras during eleven summers between 1870 and 1901. LeConte was a friend of John Muir and a founding member of the Sierra Club. He died during a trip to Yosemite. Numerous landmarks in the Sierras and a mountain in Tennessee were named for him, and in 1904 the Sierra Club built a memorial lodge in Yosemite that bears his name.

• Most of LeConte's papers are in the Southern Historical Collection, University of North Carolina, Chapel Hill; the Bancroft Library, University of California, Berkeley; and the private collection of a LeConte descendent, but many others are in the archives of the Georgia Historical Society and the South Caroliniana Library, University of South Carolina, Columbia. Additional repositories of LeConte papers are given in Lester D. Stephens, *Joseph LeConte: Gentle Prophet of Evolution* (1982), which is the most comprehensive biography of LeConte. That work also lists all of LeConte's publications. The *Autobiography of Joseph LeConte* (1903), edited by W. D. Armes, is a good source but omits some of the information contained in the original manuscript, which is in the Southern Historical Collection. The journal kept by Joseph LeConte during the final weeks of the Civil War was published by his daughter Caroline in 1937 as *'Ware Sherman: A Journal of Three Months' Personal Experience in the Last Days of the Confederacy.*

LESTER D. STEPHENS

LEDFORD, Lily May (17 Mar. 1917–14 July 1985), folk music singer and musician, was born in the Red River Gorge, Powell County, Kentucky, the daughter of Daw White Ledford, a sharecropper tenant farmer, and Stella May Tackett. The Ledfords had fourteen children, of whom ten survived childhood. The family moved several times to farms within a few miles in the gorge and then around 1920 moved to a farm owned by Daw's uncle in Chimney Top. Lily and her siblings, who sometimes made their own instruments, learned to sing hymns from their mother and to sing and play folk tunes on the fiddle, banjo, and guitar from their father, an accomplished amateur musician. Lily May seemed passionate about music and often stole away from her chores to practice. She attended a single-room schoolhouse a few miles from their home but dropped out in the eighth grade.

Lily May and her older sister Rosie often played and sang together. In 1928, when the family moved from Chimney Top to the more suburban lower gorge area, they performed at parties, dances, revivals, and prayer meetings and learned new songs from Jimmie Rodgers, the Carter Family, and other performers on the radio and from recordings. Lily May usually played fiddle, and she entered and often won local fiddling contests. In 1934 Lily May (fiddle) and Rosie (guitar), with their younger brother Coyen and neighbor Morgan Skidmore, formed a band called the Red River Ramblers. The next year the group traveled to Indiana and Illinois with the Skidmore family and caught the attention of John Lair, who managed several folk music groups and worked for Chicago radio station WLS, home of the successful country variety show "National Barn Dance." He signed a contract with Lily May to be her personal manager, preventing an exclusive contract with the WLS management. On the radio at last in 1936, Lily May was a great success because of her natural acting ability and her rapport with the audience as well as her fine musicianship. Having several good fiddlers available already, Lair switched Lily May to banjo. She became friends with Patsy Montana, Red Foley, George Gobel, Lulu Belle, and others who performed with her. She became a regular on "The Farm Dinnerbell" the "Pine Mountain Merrymakers," and "The Prairie Farmer," as well as the "National Barn Dance" shows. Lily May even became a popular comic strip character in the WLS weekly magazine *Stand By*.

In 1937 Lair took the best of the WLS performers, including Red Foley, the Girls of the Golden West, and Merle Travis, to Cincinnati to start a barn dance show. Lair put four women together—Evelyn Lange on bass, Esther Koehler on mandolin, Rosie Ledford on guitar, and Lily Mae Ledford on fiddle—and called them the Coon Creek Girls. The group was enormously successful, playing at fairs and in movie houses and on other local radio stations. Lisa Yarger described their style: "At WCKY the Coon Creek Girls would storm up to the microphone, break into a hoedown, and begin stomping their feet. Perhaps this youthful energy accounts in part for the enormous popularity of the band" (Yarger, p. 85). Lair promoted the band as a hillbilly group, even over the objections of the women, who had chosen the band name the Wildwood Flowers. In the summer of 1938 the Coon Creek Girls performed in the National Folk Festival in Washington, D.C., where Charles Seeger, father of folk music great Pete Seeger, heard them. When asked by President Franklin D. Roosevelt and Eleanor Roosevelt to arrange a concert of American folk music at the White House to celebrate the visit of King George and Queen Elizabeth of England, Seeger included the Coon Creek Girls on the 8 June 1939 program. Lily May Ledford described the rehearsal the night before:

While we were rehearsing in a White House room, a gentleman came in and stood listening. He told me that he also played the fiddle and wondered if I might fiddle a few tunes with him. He went somewhere and got a fiddle and came back. When I told him my name he said, "You can just call me Cactus Jack." We went to another room and fiddled away for a while. He was pretty good. Later on it turned out that he was the Vice President [John Nance Garner]. (Yarger, p. 67)

The White House appearance led to bookings at the Earl Theater in Washington, D.C., and with Orson Welles at the Stanley Theatre in Pittsburgh. In November 1939 Lair moved his performers to Renfro Valley, Kentucky, and his show, the "Renfro Valley Barn Dance," began broadcasting. Station WHAS in Louisville quickly picked up the show, and then CBS aired it nationally. However, the women discovered that Lair was abusing them financially and had canceled a weeklong booking at the New York World's Fair in order to earn more money playing one-night stands at fairs and theaters. Consequently, Lange and Koehler left to start their own western band on station WLW, and Lily May called on her sisters Susie and Rosie (who had married Red Foley) to form a trio. The sisters sang close harmonies and often switched instruments.

At this time, in 1939, Lily May Ledford married Curt Pearson, a Berea businessman. Although it was not a happy marriage, plagued by her husband's indifference to her and her music, they had a son. Pearson's infidelities added to their marriage problems, and after only a few years Ledford left him and in 1942 received a divorce. In 1945 she married Glenn Pennington, a car dealer who had briefly played bass fiddle on the show. They had three children. They were divorced in 1967.

The three sisters continued as the Coon Creek Girls well into 1950s. However, the advent of television brought new performing stars and made popular new kinds of music, and Nashville's Grand Ole Opry became the country's most popular radio and television venue for country music. One of the group's last major performances was in the 1956 Broadway show *Hayride*, produced by Sunshine Sue of a rival barn dance show in Richmond, Virginia, and featuring Lester Flatt, Earl Scruggs, and the Foggy Mountain Boys. By 1957 the Coon Creek Girls had broken up, left Lair and Renfro Valley, and gone their separate ways to be with their families.

In 1966 Ralph Rinzler, who had been impressed by the group in *Hayride*, called on the women to perform at the Newport Folk Festival in Newport, Rhode Island, and subsequent festivals. These gatherings helped revive interest in the country folk music tradition among college-age fans, and the sisters were again a great success. They participated in many major folk music shows during the next decade, including the Smithsonian Festival of American Folklife (1971), the Man and His World Festival in Montreal (1972), and the touring Oldtime Mountain Music Show (1975).

Susie and Rosie retired in 1975 to be with their families again. With the help of Mike Seeger, Lily May Ledford began a solo career on the Southern Folk Cultural Revival Project tours that performed mostly at colleges and universities throughout the United States and Canada. In February 1979 she began a tour in Santa Monica, California, which took her and the Red Clay Ramblers up and down the West Coast. She gave workshops and recorded an album produced by Voyager Records. The LP *Banjo Pickin' Girl* was issued on the Greenhays label in 1983.

Ledford's solo repertoire included many old standards from her childhood and early years ("How Many Biscuits Can You Eat," "Little Birdie," and "Banjo Pickin' Girl"); Carter Family songs ("Ain't Gonna Work Tomorrow," "John Henry," and "Worried Man Blues"); ballads ("Two Little Orphans" and

"I Have No Mother Now"); and plenty of traditional fiddle tunes ("Ragtime Annie" and "Cacklin' Hen"). At this time she was plagued with arthritis in her fingers and rheumatism, and her health began to fail. Her daughter, Barbara Ledford Greenlief, sometimes traveled with her and assisted in her tours. Ledford made her home in Lexington, Kentucky, with her son Bobby. Into the 1980s she toured with the Reel World String Band, an all-women group from Kentucky, and reveled in their feminist interests. She is recognized as a woman folk music pioneer, and her songs and stories have become an important part of this country's musical and cultural heritage. The song "Banjo Pickin' Girl" became a minor anthem in the country music feminist movement. Lily May Ledford died in Lexington.

• The most important sources documenting the life of Lily May Ledford are numerous personal interviews of Ledford family members and their musician friends, and Lisa J. Yarger, "Banjo Pickin' Girl: Representing Lily May Ledford" (master's thesis, Univ. of North Carolina, Chapel Hill, 1997). The most important interviews are with Barbara Ledford Greenlief (1996), in the Southern Folklife Collection at the University of North Carolina; with John Lair (1975), in the Department of Archives, Hutchens Library, Berea College; and with Ledford (c. 1970), also at Berea College, and in 1966, in the Southern Folklife Collection. Another interview with Ledford by Ellesa High was published in *Adena: A Journal of the History and Culture of the Ohio Valley* 2 (Spring 1977): 44–74. Ledford's autobiography was published in three issues of *Seattle Folklore Society Journal* 8 (Mar. 1977): 17–24; 9 (Dec. 1977): 17–24; and 9 (Mar. 1978): 2–15. Another autobiography, *Coon Creek Girl* (1980), uses material from the *Seattle Folklore Society Journal* series, Barbara Greenlief, and other sources. A thirty-minute videocassette, *Lily May Ledford*, produced by Anne Johnson and others (Appalshop, 1988), shows footage of Ledford performing alone and with several groups. Many articles relevant to Ledford and her performing groups appear in the *John Edwards Memorial Foundation Quarterly*, *Sing Out!*, and the *Journal of the American Academy for the Preservation of Old-Time Country Music*.

STEPHEN M. FRY

LEDYARD, John (Nov. 1751–10 Jan. 1789), explorer, was born in Groton, Connecticut, the son of John Ledyard, a merchant captain, and Abigail Hempstead. He was baptized in Groton on 21 November 1751 and spent the first ten years of his life in that seafaring town. His father died at sea in 1762, and Ledyard went to live with his maternal grandparents in Southold on Long Island. After his mother's remarriage when he was thirteen, Ledyard went to live with his paternal grandparents in Hartford, Connecticut. In 1771 he was recruited by Dr. Eleazar Wheelock to come to the newly formed Dartmouth College and study to become a missionary to the Indians. Ledyard went to Dartmouth in April 1772 but remained there for only one year. Although he was a good student, he resisted discipline, and he became renowned at Dartmouth for his pranks. In April 1773 he hollowed out a canoe, Indian-style, and floated down the Connecticut River as

far as Hartford (his memory is today preserved by the Ledyard Canoe Club at Dartmouth). Having departed from schooling, he commenced a life of high adventure.

Ledyard shipped out of New London, Connecticut, as a common seaman in late 1773. While his ship was anchored off Gibraltar, he had the temerity to desert and join a British regiment there, but he was soon reclaimed by the captain of his ship, Richard Deshon. Ledyard returned to New London in late August 1774 and then went to New York City, whereupon he soon shipped for England. Arriving in Plymouth, he walked to London, where he arrived penniless. Learning that the famous Captain James Cook was about to leave for the third of his voyages of exploration, Ledyard went to Cook and persuaded the captain to take him on as a corporal of marines aboard Cook's ship the *Resolution*.

Cook's expedition, with Ledyard aboard, sailed from England on 12 July 1776. The explorers sailed through many parts of the South Pacific Ocean before they turned northward and reached Nootka Sound on the west coast of Vancouver Island on 28 March 1778. This landfall was apparently a turning point in Ledyard's thinking. Seeing the extreme west side of the North American continent and visualizing the riches that could be made in a fur trade, he dreamed that he might be the first American (though he was at the time in British uniform) to walk across the continent. His dream intensified a few months later when he walked across Unalaska Island to locate a Russian settlement there. Subsequent landfalls on Kamchatka and in southern China increased Ledyard's belief in his vision and possibly expanded it to include the notion of walking across Russia and Siberia to reach the Pacific Ocean.

After Captain Cook died in the Hawaiian Islands on 14 February 1779, Ledyard returned with his ship to England, reaching Deptford on 6 October 1780. He served in army barracks in England rather than serve against his fellow Americans during the remaining two years of the revolutionary war. He then served on a British warship; when that ship went to Long Island, he deserted and returned to his mother and family. He wrote *A Journal of Captain Cook's Last Voyage to the Pacific Ocean* (1783).

Ledyard made futile efforts to interest American merchants in the fur trade that he foresaw in the Northwest and then went to Spain and later to France, where he made the acquaintance of both John Paul Jones and Thomas Jefferson. He proposed several abortive projects having to do with the Northwest and finally came up with an idea that suited his restless nature. He planned to walk across Russia and Siberia, take a ship from there to Nootka Sound, and then walk across North America to reach the American settlements on the East Coast. Thomas Jefferson approved the idea, and Ledyard set out from London to Stockholm and thence to St. Petersburg. He left the Russian capital on 1 June 1787 and reached Irkutsk on 15 August. He then took a boat down the Lena River and reached Yakutsk on 18 September. He returned to Irkutsk on 16 January 1788 and was soon arrested by the police of Czarina Catherine the Great, who brought him back to Moscow by 10 March and then to the border with Poland by 18 March 1788. Ledyard was warned not to repeat his attempt and was barred from entering Russia.

By May 1788 Ledyard was in London, where he won the support of Sir Joseph Banks, who recruited his services for the newly formed Association for Promoting the Discovery of the Interior Parts of Africa. Ledyard went from London to Paris, where he saw Jefferson for the last time, and then to Marseilles, where he took a ship to Alexandria, arriving there on 15 August 1788. Moving to Cairo, Ledyard sought to join a caravan that was to leave for Sennar. The circumstances of his death in Cairo are not certain, but it appears that he went into a violent rage over the delay of the departure of the caravan and that he suffered a broken blood vessel and died after three days. He had never married.

Ledyard was a dreamer and a visionary. Probably the first American to see what would become the American Northwest and British Columbia, he became entranced with those areas in the same manner that many other Americans would in the future. He accurately foresaw the profits that were to be made in the fur trade, and, had the merchants of New York and Philadelphia responded to his invitations, Americans might have cornered the market in furs in the Northwest. As it was, the American claims to the Northwest had to wait until the journey of Lewis and Clark (1804–1806) and the founding of Astoria (1811–1812). Clearly, Ledyard had a manner that could impress some of the notables of his time, Jefferson in particular. But he was ahead of his time in his projects, and his name had to yield place to the explorers who came almost twenty years after him, men such as Lewis and Clark who were better supplied and supported as well as more careful in their journeys than the impetuous man from Groton, Connecticut.

• Ledyard's papers are in the possession of the Ledyard family; the Baker Library at Dartmouth College; and the New-York Historical Society. The modern version of his book on the Pacific is *John Ledyard's Journal of Captain Cook's Last Voyage*, ed. James Kenneth Munford (1963), and his Russian adventure is chronicled in Stephen D. Watrous, ed., *John Ledyard's Journey through Russia and Siberia 1787–1788* (1966). See also Helen Augur, *Passage to Glory: John Ledyard's America* (1946); Henry Beston, *The Book of Gallant Vagabonds* (1925); and Jared Sparks, *The Life of John Ledyard* (1828). Journal articles include Donald Jackson, "Ledyard and Laperouse: A Contrast in Northwestern Exploration," *Western Historical Quarterly* 9, no. 4 (1978): 495–508, and Bertha S. Dodge, "John Ledyard: Controversial Corporal," *History Today* 23, no. 9 (1973): 648–55. Ledyard is mentioned briefly in Richard Hough, *Captain James Cook* (1994).
SAMUEL WILLARD CROMPTON

LEE, Ann (29 Feb. 1736–8 Sept. 1784), visionary, prophetess, and founder of the Shakers (later formally the United Society of Believers in Christ's Second Ap-

pearing), was born in Manchester, England, the daughter of John Lees, a blacksmith, and his wife, a "very pious woman." Lee, one of eight children, was baptized in Christ Church on 1 June 1742. She received little, if any, formal education. Tradition has it that she worked in a cotton factory and also as a cutter of hatters' fur. In 1762 she married Abraham Standerin (also identified as Stanley and Standley), a blacksmith. They both signed the register in the cathedral with only a mark. It is reported that she had four children, all of whom died in infancy or at an early age. The burial record of one daughter, Elizabeth, age six, does exist.

Lee was deeply religious and in 1758 joined a small group of sectarians in Bolton known as "Shaking Quakers," led by James and Jane Wardley. This sect, about which debate exists concerning its link with the Society of Friends, derived its name from the tremors the members experienced during ecstatic worship. The Shaking Quakers were sharply critical of English society and the Church of England. Ann Lee, who experienced visions and revelations, emerged as a leader in this sect. Subsequently she became involved in several incidents with local authorities. In July 1772 Lee and her father were arrested and spent time in prison. The following year in both May and July she was arrested and imprisoned again for disturbing public worship. Years later, according to the testimonies of her followers, she spoke of these times in England as filled with spiritual suffering and tribulation. Yet she was sustained in her labors by a growing sense of direct divine guidance and rising confidence that she could overcome the power of sin, which she associated with carnality and lust.

On 10 May 1774 Ann Lee, her husband, and seven other members of the sect sailed from England to America, arriving in New York City on 6 August. Shaker tradition attributes this move to a vision she received; rising pressure and harassment, no doubt, contributed to the decision. The documentary record for her activities over the next six years is almost nonexistent. It is likely that she worked as a domestic in the city. Tradition tells of her caring for a seriously ill husband, who subsequently proved unfaithful and abandoned her. By late 1776 she and a handful of English followers had relocated to an area northwest of Albany known as Niskeyuna, subsequently named Watervliet. Here the public portion of her American career began.

The spring of 1780 was significant for Lee and the Shaking Quakers. In April they were visited by several individuals from the Hudson River region who had heard about a group of "strange and wonderful Christians." The celebrated "Dark Day" in New England when the sky was darkened, 19 May, combined with widespread evangelical revivals to create an atmosphere of spiritual anxiety and expectation. Residents of nearby New Lebanon, New York, came to visit, including Joseph Meacham and Calvin Harlow, two of the first American converts to the small community. The sect now began to attract increasing attention.

But these were not normal times in America. The English colonies were locked in the struggle for independence. In July 1780 the Shakers were drawn into the conflict when several members, including Ann Lee and her brother William, were arrested on charges that they intended to assist the enemy and were unwilling to take up arms in support of the revolutionary cause. The English Believers opposed the war, but they were not aiding the British forces. Ann Lee was in jail in Albany from 24 July until December, when she was released by George Clinton, governor of New York, provided that she maintain good behavior and not work against the patriot cause. These events spread the word about this "new and strange religion" associated with Lee, identified by her disciples as the "Elect Lady" and also called "Mother." The years of isolation for the Shakers were at an end.

On 4 May 1781 Lee, her brother William, another faithful English follower James Whittaker, and several others set out on a missionary journey that lasted twenty-eight months. She and her companions traveled in the eastern Hudson valley and New England, visiting sites where Shaker converts lived or where they hoped to persuade others to join them. Sometimes they lodged only a few days at the homes of followers; other times they resided for extended stays. For example, they spent several months in Harvard, Massachusetts, where Lee was successful in making converts among the disciples of Shadrach Ireland, a former Baptist elder who had established a celibate communitarian sect there. In fact, Lee and the Shakers purchased his home, the Square House, which became the central outpost for the young society in eastern New England. From this location they traveled to other towns in eastern and southeastern Massachusetts as well as in southern Connecticut.

On this journey Lee and her entourage experienced hardship, frequent persecution, and physical abuse. Mobs assaulted them on more than one occasion. At Petersham, Massachusetts, Lee was dragged out of the house where she was staying and driven away by her abusers, her clothes torn under pretense of discovering whether she was a woman, and she was accused of being a witch. Through all these experiences Lee maintained strength of purpose. At each location she and her companions conducted religious meetings in which they exhorted their followers and potential converts to confess their sins, to flee carnality, and to be resolute in their commitment to the sect. These meetings, which included spiritual labor and ecstatic worship, often lasted several hours. The testimonies of Believers speak of the powerful impression made by Lee on these occasions. Her followers respected, feared, and loved her. Lee and her traveling companions returned to Niskeyuna on 4 September 1783.

Niskeyuna remained the center of the growing community and Lee its principal leader. Over the course of the next year she consolidated the gains that had been made, attracting more converts and teaching her distinctive gospel, a proclamation calling for confession of sin, challenging Believers to strive for perfection,

condemning the established churches, and counseling them to follow the lead of the spirit. Lee and the early Shakers dissented radically from the norms and patterns of the American society at the time.

On 21 July 1784 Lee's brother William, a close companion, died at Niskeyuna. Less than two months later Ann Lee followed him in death. At her burial she was eulogized by James Whittaker, who succeeded her in leadership of the community. The *Albany Gazette* noted her death as follows: "Departed this life, at Nisquenia, Sept. 7, Mrs. Lee, known by the appellation of the *Elect Lady*, or *Mother of Zion*, and head of the people called Shakers." In 1835 the remains of Lee were moved to the "common Burying Ground" at Watervliet. At that time her skull and other bones were reinterred, after being placed on public display for members of the community. Her headstone now reads "MOTHER ANN LEE," accompanied by the dates and locations of her birth and death.

Lee, who was illiterate, forbade her followers to write creeds or confessional statements. She herself wrote nothing. Information about her and her ideas is derived principally from traditions written down by the Believers several decades after her death, or from judgments of her opponents. This source problem complicates reconstruction of her biography. Lee's opponents often depicted her as a demanding, erratic, violent person given to drink, profanity, and promiscuity. An opposite picture emerges from Shaker traditions, in which Lee epitomizes the caring mother who protects, nourishes, and disciplines her children. Her charismatic powers included foresight, miracles, healing, and wisdom. The Believers cherished sayings attributed to Lee, including the most celebrated "Hands to work and hearts to God." The passage of time enhanced the community's view of Lee. In 1808 Shaker leaders formulated a theological assessment of her as the equal of Jesus of Nazareth in the work of redemption, declaring her to be the Beloved Daughter of God. Other Shakers have spoken of her as a "second Christ" and as the embodiment of the spirit of Christ. During the nineteenth century Believers frequently received revelations from the spirit of Ann Lee. Lee retains special importance in the religious life of the small community of Shakers at the close of the twentieth century. She has also attracted widespread interest among scholars working in the field of women's studies.

• The most important published collection of early Shaker traditions concerning Lee is Rufus Bishop and Seth Y. Wells, eds., *Testimonies of the Life, Character, Revelations and Doctrines of Our Ever Blessed Mother Ann Lee, and the Elders with Her* (1816). See also *Testimonies Concerning the Character and Ministry of Mother Ann Lee* (1827). Additional manuscript testimonies are part of the Shaker collections at the Western Reserve Historical Society, the New York State Historical Society, the Winterthur Museum, the Shaker Museum and Library at Old Chatham, N.Y., and the New York Public Library. The earliest published Shaker theological statement concerning Lee is Benjamin Seth Youngs, *The Testimony of Christ's Second Appearing* (1808). Later Shaker biographies of

Lee include Frederick W. Evans, *Ann Lee, the Founder of the Shakers* (1869), and Henry C. Blinn, *The Life and Gospel Experience of Mother Ann Lee* (1882). Mary L. Richmond, *Shaker Literature: A Bibliography* (1977), includes articles inspired by or devoted to Ann Lee. Reuben Rathbun, *Reasons Offered for Leaving the Shakers* (1800), contains an early hostile depiction of Lee. Historical accounts of Lee and her context are contained in Stephen A. Marini, *Radical Sects of Revolutionary New England* (1982); Clarke Garrett, *Spirit Possession and Popular Religion: From the Camisards to the Shakers* (1987); and Stephen J. Stein, *The Shaker Experience in America: A History of the United Society of Believers* (1992). See also Jean M. Humez, "'Ye Are My Epistles': The Construction of Ann Lee Imagery in Early Shaker Sacred Literature," *Journal of Feminist Studies in Religion* 8, no. 1 (1992): 83–103.

STEPHEN J. STEIN

LEE, Archy (1840–1873?), fugitive slave, was born in Pike County, Mississippi. His known family—his mother, two brothers, and a sister—were all slaves. There is no evidence that Lee, the slave of the Stovall family of Pike and Carroll counties in Mississippi, ever learned to read or write.

In the summer of 1857 Charles Stovall took Lee to Missouri, where he left him with friends. In the fall he returned to Missouri and traveled with Lee to California. They arrived in Sacramento in October 1857. Before the year's end Stovall advertised in a Sacramento paper for students to enroll in a school he was opening. He also hired out Lee and used part of those wages to support himself. This he did in a city that had an active and stable free black community of workers, ministers, and businessmen who were in contact with antislavery Sacramento whites.

In January 1858 Stovall decided to return to Mississippi with Lee. At a crucial moment of personal decision-making, Lee fled for sanctuary to a hotel run by free blacks. He was arrested there on 6 January 1858.

The laws pertaining to Lee's case were the national Fugitive Slave Law of 1850 and an 1852 California Fugitive Slave Law that stated that a slaveowner in California was protected in his ownership of a slave for one year. This law was renewed twice and had expired by April 1855.

The first set of legal moves took place in a county court where the opposing attorneys presented their positions before Judge Robert Robinson. Stovall's attorneys held that Lee was his slave in Mississippi and therefore could be returned there without legal interference. Lee's lawyers countered that because California was a free state Stovall had no legal right to hold Lee and, further, that slavery was only protected for slaveowners in transit. Since Stovall had opened a school and also had hired out Lee, he could not be considered in transit. Judge Robinson delayed decision for fifteen days. Unwilling to wait for the judge's decision, Stovall's lawyers tried to get U.S. commissioner George Penn Johnston, a southerner, to take the case, hoping that his regional sympathies would produce a favorable decision for slavery. But the commissioner concluded that the Fugitive Slave Law of 1850 did not apply to the Lee case because Lee did not cross state boundaries in his strike for freedom.

Judge Robinson's delay and the commissioner's decision propelled the Stovall forces to move in another direction even before the anticipated unfavorable decision was handed down by Robinson. They arranged for the supreme court of the state to take the case, and when Robinson freed Lee he was immediately rearrested, to the surprise of all present. The "Archy Case" moved to the highest court in the state. Of the three-member court, two justices were in attendance at the time, both of them southerners with anti–free black and proslavery backgrounds.

Their decision, handed down on 11 February, noted that under existing law Lee was not a fugitive slave, but, inasmuch as, "This is the first case . . . we are not disposed to rigidly enforce the rule." Lee was ordered back into slavery, a decision that was received with journalistic derision from coast to coast. The court had completely set aside the fact that Stovall did not qualify as a traveler once he opened a school. The framers of the state's constitution felt that the sojourner requirement was necessary so that slavery could not be introduced surreptitiously into California.

Stovall now had to transport Lee unobserved from Sacramento to San Francisco and conceal him aboard a ship for the return trip to Mississippi. The theatrics that followed became legal history. From 11 February to 5 March the Stovall forces worked covertly to reach San Francisco Bay without detection by either the white antislavery forces or the well-organized, highly alert black community. Black businessmen and the numerous black maritime workers patrolled the docks night and day during this period. Stovall's forces had every reason to believe that they were not operating in a favorable environment.

When the steamer *Orizaba* left its wharf and moved into San Francisco Bay, a small boat carrying Lee and Stovall moved out from Angel Island to meet it. When the two attempted to board, concealed city police on the ship seized them and brought them to San Francisco, where a new series of court actions began on 8 March. Police officers carried two warrants: one for Archy, to keep him in San Francisco, and the other for Stovall on the charge of kidnapping.

The absurdity of the Archy Lee supreme court decision encouraged the legal and law enforcement community to tolerate the maneuvers that followed Lee's return to San Francisco. The warrants for Lee and Stovall had all the earmarks of ploys to remove Lee from Stovall's control and also to obstruct his efforts to regain control. The pro-Lee forces now had time to position themselves for the next phase of legal struggle.

When the opposing lawyers took their places, representing Lee was one of the most distinguished lawyers in the state, Colonel Edward D. Baker. He was an old friend of Abraham Lincoln and an early member of the new Republican party, and was known as a lawyer who did not fear unpopular causes. Stovall's attorney was James H. Hardy.

After a one-week delay, the case that the press referred to as the "Case of Archy Lee, the Fugitive Slave" resumed on 15 March in a packed courtroom. The lawyers made their opening statements, followed by a variety of arguments by both sides before Judge T. W. Freelon. The fact that Freelon rejected the Hardy request to throw out the entire case suggests that his sympathies were not with the Stovall camp. Baker's strongest statement cast ridicule on the decision of the California Supreme Court to suspend state law because Stovall's obtuseness about the law was a first time offense.

In this round of exchanges Hardy's main point was that even if the state supreme court's decision was faulty, their decision should be honored. Baker's statement made the legal point that the form in which Stovall's attorneys had presented their case to the supreme court was not in the form of an appeal, and the state supreme court was only an appeals court. He then asked the judge to set Lee free. To everyone's surprise, Hardy did not object, and Freelon declared Lee a free man. Within moments a U.S. marshall rearrested Lee. Stovall's attorney, sensing defeat again, had arranged hours earlier for U.S. commissioner George Penn Johnston to once again deal with the case as one coming under the rules of the 1850 Fugitive Slave Law.

Continuances, delays, and adjournments finally concluded on 14 April. By that time Johnston had listened to several Hardy witnesses whose contradictory evidence made it clear that Lee had none of the attributes of a runaway slave from Mississippi. He also heard the Baker ironclad case that Lee was not an interstate runaway and therefore should be freed. Johnston had received by this time the attorney's final briefs and had made his decision. He decreed that the state supreme court had no authority over the Lee case, that Lee's relationship with Stovall en route to California did not support the image of a runaway, and that his strike for freedom was within California state boundaries; therefore, the 1850 National Fugitive Slave Law did not apply. He declared Lee a free man.

Soon on his way to Victoria, British Columbia, Lee joined a large group of California blacks seeking economic opportunity there resulting from the Frazier River Gold Rush. They also feared impending racist legislation in California. Lee reportedly became a drayman and property owner in Victoria. After the Civil War he returned to California and did not come to public notice again until 1873, when a Sacramento newspaper reported that he had fallen very ill. It appears that he died in Sacramento in the winter of that year.

• Rudolph M. Lapp, *Archy Lee, a California Fugitive Slave Case* (1969), has the fullest account. William E. Franklin, "The Archy Case: The California Supreme Court Refuses to Free a Slave," *Pacific Historical Review* 32, no. 2 (May 1963): 137–54, deals with opposing legal and constitutional positions. Paul Finkelman, "The Law of Slavery and Freedom in California," *California Western Law Review* 17 (1989): 427–64, discusses the legal and constitutional issues of the case.

The case is in *California Reports* 9 (1858): 171. A less detailed general account is in Lapp, *Blacks in Gold Rush California* (1977), pp. 148–54.

RUDOLPH M. LAPP

LEE, Arthur (20 Dec. 1740–12 Dec. 1792), polemicist and diplomat, was born at "Stratford Hall" in Westmoreland County, Virginia, the son of Thomas Lee and Hannah Harrison Ludwell, leading Virginia planters. Arthur was one of eleven children. His two eldest brothers, Philip Ludwell Lee and Thomas Ludwell Lee inherited the substantial family wealth (30,000 acres) and prestige when both parents died in 1750. The "Stratford Lees" developed a distinctive family perspective on life; this, combined with the ideals instilled in them by their formal education, propelled them to the highest levels of the provincial elite.

Two aspects of Arthur's childhood marked him for life. In a family noted for its superior training, he became the best schooled. His education included six years (1751–1757) at England's Eton College; study at the University of Edinburgh (1761–1764), where he received an M.D.; and training at London's Inns of Court (1770–1774), which garnered him a law degree. As he recited his Greek, fathomed the history of the Roman republic as etched by Sallust, or fashioned strategy for petitions to the king, Lee craved attention, respect, and praise. Lee gleaned many of his values and goals from his formal training in the classics and from the Real Whigs, who profoundly distrusted power and politicians and who, in English oppositional politics between the 1720s and 1740s, were critics of the monarchy and the court party. Such schooling also channeled his energies toward public controversies. In politics Arthur Lee could exhibit his scholarship and gain distinction.

Lee's perceptions, most prominently his self-image as an ascetic and his profound distrust of others, originated in his youthful experiences. His parents paid little attention to his upbringing. Their deaths further reinforced Arthur's sense of abandonment. Moreover, when Philip Ludwell Lee took charge of family affairs, bitter intrafamilial strife arose. Arthur, learning that he could not trust a brother, was deeply scarred; he came to believe that the world was filled with avaricious and cunning opponents. Some of Arthur Lee's contemporaries were impressed by his upright and bold stances; John Adams (1735–1826) spoke of Lee's "Virtue . . . Honour and Integrity." Others, like Benjamin Franklin (1706–1790), believed that Lee's difficult disposition bordered on insanity.

Lee early sensed his bifurcated identity as an Anglo-American. His response was to value autonomy, for himself and fellow Americans, above all else. While at Edinburgh he was a ringleader of a student protest against lax degree standards. When the faculty voted for stricter regulations, Lee gained a measure of self-righteousness and perhaps undue faith in protest movements.

Lee penned the first of his political pamphlets, *An Essay in Vindication of the Continental Colonies of Amer-*

ica, in 1764. It attacked both slavery and British imperial policy. In 1767 Lee published antislavery essays in both the *Virginia Gazette* and the *Pennsylvania Chronicle*. Later in London he communed with Granville Sharpe, Britain's leading abolitionist. Lee had little sympathy for Africans, but feared that the tobacco trade on which the slave system was based rendered colonials too dependent upon Britain.

From 1764 through 1776 Lee contributed profusely to political journalism on both sides of the Atlantic. From poems to pamphlets, under at least ten identifiable pseudonyms, he lambasted British tax policies and a standing army. His ten American newspaper essays over the signature of "Monitor" were second only to John Dickinson's (1732–1808) in the 1767–1768 counterattack on the Townshend duties that Parliament assessed on colonial imports of basic goods. Lee and Dickinson reputedly wrote "The Liberty Song" that from 1768 onward rallied American resistance to parliamentary taxation.

When Lee returned to Britain in late 1768 he established himself as "Junius Americanus," whose vituperative attacks sought to humiliate the friends of the king. Often these barbs were accorded front-page status by the London press. The Massachusetts Assembly in 1770 subsidized publication of two dozen of his screeds in "The Political Detection." As animosities mounted from 1774 to 1776, Lee produced six more pamphlets. These more mature efforts were less pedantic and more cooly reasoned.

Arthur Lee envisioned himself as the lynchpin between the American resistance movement and the opposition in British politics. In the former sphere he carried on extensive correspondence with the so-called "old Revolutionaries," such as his brother Richard Henry Lee in Virginia and Samuel Adams, firebrand in Massachusetts. Out of these exchanges came the Committees of Correspondence, formed to unify the spirit of resistance. When the Continental Congress met, the Adams-Lee axis formed the most radical camp.

In the British sphere Arthur Lee established friendships with both the earl of Shelburne, whom Lee unrealistically hoped could seize the first ministry and alter imperial policy, and John Wilkes, the London demagogue around whom oppositional forces rallied from 1768 to 1774. Lee also frequented the coffeehouses with Catherine Macaulay, Joseph Priestley, Richard Price, and other radical thinkers in England. He became secretary in the Bill of Rights Society, the radical support group for Wilkes, but failed to place American demands for autonomy high on Wilkes's agenda. Such frustrations led Lee by 1775 to look forward to a war for American independence.

Among Lee's acquaintances in Britain, none was more pivotal than Benjamin Franklin. Both were Fellows of the Royal Society, members of the American Philosophical Society, and noted for their catholic interests. From 1771 to 1774 Lee assisted Franklin in the colonial agency for the Massachusetts House. Lee helped Franklin to obtain the explosive correspondence between Thomas Whately of the British government and colonial representatives of the Crown, which was used to unseat Thomas Hutchinson as governor of Massachusetts. Lee also witnessed Franklin's humiliation in March 1774 when, following the Boston Tea Party, Franklin was charged before the Privy Council with plotting American independence. Yet personal and political differences fatally split Lee and Franklin. Where Lee was an unbending fanatic, the aged sage was pragmatic and conciliatory. Lee always believed Franklin's patriotism was superficial.

In early 1777 Franklin, Lee, and Silas Deane of Connecticut formed the diplomatic corps of the fledgling United States. For more than eighteen months previously Lee had acted as an intelligence agent for Congress. Moreover, in clandestine and chaotic negotiations with a French agent, the playwright Caron de Beaumarchais, he had initiated plans to funnel covert aid to the American rebels. In 1777 Beaumarchais found Deane to be more attuned to the profit-making aspects of the scheme. When Lee alerted Congress that the shipments could best be termed gifts, Beaumarchais was enraged. In turn, the French ministry became convinced that Lee was anti-French, if not still partial to the British.

Lee practiced what become known as militia diplomacy. Ever restless, he chafed as French officials put off American pleas for alliances. In the spring of 1777 he ventured over the Pyrennees to Spain, but the Spanish headed him off at Burgos lest he embarrass them by appearing at the Spanish court to demand recognition. Nevertheless, Lee gained Spanish promises to send funds and supplies to the American rebels via Havana. When he returned to Paris his colleagues suggested he venture to the court of Frederick the Great. On this Prussian mission Lee was further embarrassed when agents of the British minister stole his diplomatic papers. Even in February 1778, as the French came forward to negotiate alliances with the Americans, Lee proved vexing to his colleagues. Adamantly he proclaimed he would never sacrifice American independence, whether to the British or the French. Moreover, he was certain that Deane and Franklin had condoned the activities of their secretary, Dr. Edward Bancroft, whom Lee knew to be a British spy.

In March 1778 Deane was recalled by Congress and replaced by John Adams. Lee sought to unseat Franklin from his position at the center of the American diplomatic corps. Arthur and his brother William created turmoil throughout Europe by claiming that Franklin was overly tolerant of numerous American agents who profited from public accounts. Congress split when Deane and Conrad Alexandre Gerard, the first French minister, arrived in America in July 1778. Ultimately Franklin gained sole possession of the French post, Adams was dispatched to Holland, and John Jay (1745–1829) was named in Lee's stead to Spain. Lee felt defamed.

In 1781 Lee was elected to the Virginia House of Delegates and in turn went to Congress from 1782 to 1785. In congressional debates he was a vociferous opponent of nationalists and commercial-minded folk headed by Robert Morris (1734–1806). In the winter of 1784–1785 he was a member of the negotiating team dispatched to Fort Stanwix and Fort McIntosh to negotiate Indian treaties. Ironically, between 1785 and 1789 he served as the administrative successor to Morris on the Board of Treasury, which tried to direct national finances. In that position he recognized the shortcomings of the Articles of Confederation. Nevertheless, from 1787 to 1789 he was a mild Antifederalist. Failing to gain an appointment in George Washington's presidential administration, Arthur Lee returned to his plantation near Urbanna, Virginia. He designated the place "Lansdowne," in honor of Shelburne. There this energetic and eccentric bachelor died.

• The bulk of Lee's manuscripts may be found at the University of Virginia. Other writings are at Harvard University and the American Philosophical Society. Episodes from his diplomatic career can be traced in Francis Wharton, ed., *The Revolutionary Diplomatic Correspondence of the United States* (6 vols., 1882–1889). Alvin R. Riggs, *The Nine Lives of Arthur Lee, Virginia Patriot* (1976), offers a brief profile. Louis W. Potts, *Arthur Lee, a Virtuous Revolutionary* (1981), covers the public career fully as well as offering a personality profile. Arthur's place in the family is depicted in Paul C. Nagel, *The Lees of Virginia* (1990).

LOUIS W. POTTS

LEE, Bruce (27 Nov. 1941–20 July 1973), motion picture actor, was born in San Francisco, California, the son of Lee Hoi Chuen, a comedian with the Cantonese Opera, and Grace Li. He grew up in Hong Kong, where his family moved when he was three. By the age of eighteen, Lee had become a martial arts master and had appeared in some twenty Chinese-language films. Returning to the United States in 1958, he earned a B.A. in philosophy at the University of Washington in 1964. That year he married an American woman named Linda Emery; they had two children.

In 1964 Lee moved to southern California where he taught martial arts. He was spotted that year by a television producer while participating in karate tournaments. First considered for the role of Number One Son in a prospective Charlie Chan television series, Lee instead was cast as the kung fu houseboy/chauffeur, Kato, in the "Green Hornet" series, which ran for thirty episodes in 1966–1967. Later he was passed over for the lead in the television series "Kung Fu," with the role going to David Carradine. According to some reports, Lee became embittered over the rejection.

Lee began in Hollywood movies with such films as *The Wrecking Crew* (1969), for which he served as karate adviser although he did not appear in the movie, and *Marlowe* (1969), for which he both supervised students and had a supporting role as villain Winslow Wong. He also appeared in other TV series, such as "Longstreet," "Batman," and "Ironside."

"Discovered" by Raymond Chow of Hong Kong's Golden Harvest Studios, Lee garnered his first starring role in *The Big Boss* (1972; released in the West as *Fists of Fury*), which was filmed in Thailand and appeared first in Asia. In movie-mad Hong Kong, the movie quickly outgrossed *The Sound of Music*, until then the most popular film ever shown there, and also became the most popular movie shown to that time in Asia.

With that film Lee gained immense international popularity, becoming a worldwide cult figure among young moviegoers as an icon of the lone, personal quest for justice. He used violence to defeat evil while the official forces of law and order proved incompetent (or at least dilatory). At the same time, as an active, intelligent, aggressive Asian hero, he shattered the western movie tradition of emphasizing Asian stoic passivity.

Amazingly quick (his punches were reportedly timed at one-eighth of a second), Lee developed his own fighting style, which he called Jeet Kune Do (The Way of the Intercepting Fist). Lethal with feet, fists, and a variety of martial arts weapons, Lee has been described hyperbolically as the Fred Astaire of Kung Fu films.

The Big Boss was followed quickly by three other feature films. His second major movie, *Fists of Fury* (1972; known in the west as *The Chinese Connection*), broke *The Big Boss*'s record in Hong Kong. Moreover, his first two films grossed $6 million at the box office in the United States. Next came *Way of the Dragon* (1973), shown in the rest of the world as *Return of the Dragon*. Finally came *Enter the Dragon* (1973), which grossed more than $100 million worldwide, including $18 million in the United States.

Mystery surrounded Lee's sudden death in Hong Kong, one month before *Enter the Dragon* opened in New York. Official records list a brain aneurysm and acute cerebral edema as the cause of death. However, often-bizarre rumors soon began to circulate concerning his death, including the story that he had been murdered by Japanese ninja assassins. Moreover, many of his cult followers believe that Lee did not really die and is still alive.

Lee's death and its aftermath heightened his already legendary status. He was buried in Seattle, with pallbearers including old friends James Coburn and Steve McQueen. Moreover, a crowd estimated at 30,000 turned out for a symbolic funeral in Hong Kong, the largest gathering ever at a funeral there.

Lee's death led to a commercial scramble to patch together old Lee performances into a new format. This resulted in a quickly produced film biography, *The Bruce Lee Story* (1974); a feature film, *Kato and the Green Hornet* (1974), which consisted of three reedited "Green Hornet" episodes; and the release of his fifth starring vehicle, *The Game of Death* (1978), although it had been only partially completed at the time of his death. Nonetheless, it too attained great popularity, becoming Japan's seventh top grossing film of that year.

In an attempt to fill the market void left by Lee, moviemakers launched films in which other stars unsuccessfully tried to capture Lee's magic. *The Clones of Bruce Lee*, for example, featured three actors who resembled Lee and were marketed as Bruce Li, Bruce Le, and Bruce Lei. *Circle of Iron* (1979), based on an outline developed by Lee, provided the final irony, as Lee's role was taken by David Carradine. In recent years, actors such as Chuck Norris have continued the tradition of the martial arts film, while Bruce Lee's son, Brandon, was seeking to assume his father's mantle with such films as *Rapid Fire* (1992), but he died in 1993 when he was shot accidentally during the filming of a scene for *The Crow*.

Lee's continuing popularity seems to reflect his success in simultaneously breaking with and blending with tradition. He broke with western film tradition by creating a charismatic, nontraditional, activist Asian hero. At the same time be blended with the ongoing Hollywood tradition of celebrating individual violence as a legitimate means to achieve justice. A film biography, *Dragon: The Bruce Lee Story*, starring Jason Scott Lee (no relation), was released in 1993, the twentieth anniversary of Lee's death.

• Lee has been the subject of several books, including Felix Dennis, *Bruce Lee, King of Kung Fu* (1974); Alen Ben Block, *The Legend of Bruce Lee* (1974); Chui-ho Hui, *Bruce Lee: The Secret of Jeet Kune Tao and Kung Fu* (1976); Phil Ochs, *The Legend of Bruce Lee* (1977); and Linda Emery Lee, *Bruce Lee, My Husband* (1975). Articles on Lee include Phil Ochs, "Requiem for a Dragon Departed," *Take One* 4, no. 3 (1974): 20–22; Stuart Kaminsky, "Kung Fu Film as Ghetto Myth," *Journal of Popular Film* 3, no. 2 (1974): 129–38; Jack Moore, "I Was Bruce Lee's Voice," *Take One* 4 (1975): 20–21; and Hsiung-Ping Chiao, "Bruce Lee: His Influence on the Evolution of the Kung Fu Genre," *Journal of Popular Film and Television* 9, no. 1 (1981): 30–42.

CARLOS E. CORTÉS
NARORN KEO
MARK ANDERSON

LEE, Canada (3 May 1907–9 May 1952), actor, theater producer, bandleader, and boxer, was born Leonard Lionel Cornelius Canegata in New York City, the son of James Cornelius Canegata, a clerk, and Lydia Whaley. Lee's father came from a wealthy and politically prominent family in St. Croix, Virgin Islands, whose ancestors had adopted a Danish surname. Lee's grandfather owned a fleet of merchant ships; the family also raced horses. James Canegata shipped out as a cabin boy at eighteen, settled in Manhattan, married, and worked for National Fuel and Gas for thirty-one years. Lee grew up in the San Juan Hill section of Manhattan's West Sixties and attended P.S. 5 in Harlem. An indifferent student, he devoted more energy to fisticuffs than to schoolwork. Lee studied violin from age seven with composer J. Rosamund Johnson, and at age eleven he was favorably reviewed at a student concert in Aeolian Hall; his parents hoped he would become a concert violinist.

Lee relished risk and excitement and, like his father, ran away from home, heading for the Saratoga racetracks at fourteen. He worked for two years as a stablehand until a "gyp" (a poor owner who paid his jockeys from winnings only) gave him a chance to race. Lee's unremarkable career as a jockey at the New York tracks (Belmont, Aqueduct, Jamaica) and on a Canadian circuit based in Montreal lasted a further two years, until he grew too tall and too heavy to ride.

Returning to New York penniless, Lee encountered a school friend who had become a professional boxer and whom Lee remembered beating regularly in street fights. With his usual decisiveness, Lee turned to boxing. Within two years, under the training of Willie Powell at the Salem Crescent Athletic Club (in the basement of a Methodist church near his parents' house), Lee had won metropolitan, intercity, state, and national lightweight junior championships. In 1925 he turned professional, managed by Jim Buckley. Lee married his first wife, Juanita Waller, in 1926; their son, actor Carl Vincent (Canegata) Lee, was born in 1928.

When veteran fight announcer Joe Humphries introduced boxer Lee Canegata as "Canada Lee," Lee acquired the name he would use for the rest of his life. In an eight-year career as a welterweight Lee fought some 200 professional bouts, losing only twenty-five. He never won a championship but defeated champions Lou Brouillard, Vince Dundee, and Tommy Freeman in ineligible "over-the-weight" matches shortly before or after they won their crowns. Finally, in a 1931 Madison Square Garden bout intended as a preliminary to a championship bout with Jim McLarnin, Andi Di Vodi landed a blow that left Lee blind in his right eye, which was soon replaced with glass (boxing also left Lee with a broken nose and slightly cauliflowered ears). Always prodigally generous with money, Lee earned more than $80,000 as a boxer and saved none of it.

Lee returned to music, leading his own big band as violinist and singer (he also played piano). He toured domestically and once filled in for Duke Ellington at Harlem's famed Cotton Club. In 1933 or 1934 Lee ran a small Harlem nightclub, the Jitterbug, for about six months, at a loss. (Lee later owned the Chicken Coop, a popular Harlem restaurant he ran from 1941 to 1943, where he fed innumerable prizefighters for free.) Broke again in 1934, in the depth of the Great Depression, and too proud to accept Home Relief but reluctant to take an ordinary job, Lee finally went to the Harlem YMCA employment office. Instead of waiting in line, however, he slipped into the Y's Little Theatre to watch director Frank Wilson's auditions for the "Negro unit" of the Public Works of Art Project theater division. Presuming Lee was an actor, Wilson had him audition; Lee found himself with the role of Nathan in Wilson's *Brother Mose* and a new career.

Lee soon succeeded Rex Ingram in the lead role of Blacksnake in a Theater Union revival of Paul Peters's *Stevedore*, which ran for a year at Chicago's Civic Rep. When the Negro unit became part of the Works Progress Administration Federal Theatre Project in 1935, Lee returned to New York as Banquo in Orson Welles's all-black *Othello*, a role that won critical notice and confirmed his new vocation. Lee's other Federal Theatre roles included parts in Lewis Stiles Gannett's *Sweet Land* and Kenyon Nicholson's *Sailor, Beware* (1935); Yank in an ill-conceived 1937 revival of Eugene O'Neill's four one-act sea plays; Henri Christophe, Haiti's nineteenth-century liberator and king, in William Du Bois's 1938 *Haiti*, again following Ingram; an Irish reporter in Ben Hecht and Charles MacArthur's *The Front Page* (1938); and Victor Mason in Theodore Ward's *Big White Fog* (1940). Lee also appeared in *Brown Sugar*, directed by George Abbott in 1937, and bowed on Broadway as Drayton in the 1938 hit by Dubose Heyward, *Mamba's Daughters*, starring singer Ethel Waters. Despite the varying critical success of these mainly popular productions, Lee was consistently singled out by reviewers.

Lee also worked extensively in radio in the early 1940s. Harlem's WMCA built a 1944 series, "New World a' Coming" ("vivid programs of Negro life" based on the Roi Ottley bestseller), around Lee and made him the voice of the John Kirby Orchestra. He was featured in WNEW's "The Canada Lee Show," narrated a series for CBS, and acted in many radio plays for NBC.

The role of Bigger Thomas in the stage adaptation of Richard Wright's *Native Son*, directed by Welles in 1941, propelled Lee to stardom; overnight he was acclaimed one of the nation's greatest actors. After a 114-show run and extensive New York–area touring, the play returned to Broadway in 1942/43 at popular prices. In 1942 Lee also took lead roles in a bill of two mystical Pirandellian one-acts by William Saroyan, "Talking to You" (in which he played a prizefighter) and "Across the Board on Tomorrow Morning." Lee and his wife were divorced in 1942 after a long separation; Lee continued to raise his son alone.

Lee turned down many stereotypical film parts before accepting the role of Joe, an assistant steward, in Alfred Hitchcock's *Lifeboat* (shot in 1943; released 1944). Lee insisted on rewriting all his dialogue to eliminate its obsequious Hollywood "Negro dialect." While *Lifeboat* was in post-production, Lee returned to New York to produce and star in the controversial *South Pacific*, a didactic melodrama directed by Lee Strasberg that allegorized problems of racial integration in the American military (no relation to the famed Rodgers and Hammerstein musical).

As producer and board member of the American Negro Theater, Lee moved Phillip Yordan's *Anna Lucasta* from Harlem to Broadway for 957 performances in 1944 and triumphed in a role far smaller than his star status warranted. Lee won generally good notices also as Caliban, opposite ballerina Vera Zorina as Ariel, in Margaret Webster's innovative 1944/45 *The Tempest*; and again as the villainous Daniel de Bosola in director Paul Czinner's 1946 production of John Webster's *The Dutchess of Malfi*, said to be the English-speaking world's first "whiteface" role. Lee was also the first African American to produce a straight play on Broadway, when he starred in Maxine Wood's 1946 *On Whitman Avenue*, about a black family

hounded out of a white neighborhood. The crudely written racial melodrama was a critical flop but a great popular success in New York and on its national tour.

In 1947 Lee costarred opposite John Garfield as end-of-the-line champ Ben Chaplin in *Body and Soul*, considered the greatest of the classic boxing films (Lee had previously appeared in 1939's *Keep Punching*). To Lee this role represented "the first time the movies have handled an American Negro like any other human being." Lee often said that boxing remained his greatest love. He denied any interest in the sport's brutal aspect and described boxing as an alloy of music, poetry, dance, and psychology, saying he had "approached fighting from an aesthetic angle." Lee believed boxing had taught him balance, fluidity, and rhythm and given him stage presence. He was praised throughout his career for his physical grace and power, command of stage space, imagination, and directness.

Though Lee often told interviewers he had not suffered from discrimination, every aspect of his career was politicized and viewed through the lens of American race relations. He was seen, and saw himself, as a pioneering black actor dedicated to demolishing racial stereotypes. Throughout his professional life an outspoken and eloquent defender of social justice, Lee lent his name and his gift for public speaking to such progressive causes as a 1946 American Veterans Committee rally to banish Jim Crow from the theater and numerous campaigns against fascism, racism, and anti-Semitism. As early as 1941 Lee took pains to distance himself publicly from any group with Communist affiliations; nonetheless, he was blacklisted, the target of an orchestrated smear campaign in the press, and virtually unable to work in radio, television, or film after 1945. (Stefan Kanfer writes in *A Journal of the Plague Years* [1973] that Lee had been banned from forty radio and television shows by 1952.) The stress Lee endured left him with life-threatening hypertension; he never fully recovered his health.

Lee starred in a production of *Othello* in the summer of 1948 but was unable to secure funding for a Broadway run despite positive notices during the tryout tour, and in 1949 he unsuccessfully attempted to open a school, the Canada Lee Workshop for actors—two of this period's many unfulfilled projects. Lee's last role on Broadway was as George in Dorothy Heyward's 1948 *Set My People Free*. Although Lee was never indicted by the House Un-American Activities Committee, an FBI document introduced in evidence at the 1949 trial of Judith Coplon (a government worker indicted for spying) accused him of being a "fellow traveler." Nearly $18,000 in debt, Lee appealed to variety-show host Ed Sullivan in a letter, declaring himself "no more a Communist than an Eskimo." In a press conference to clear his name, Lee analyzed the racist motive behind HUAC's attack on black leaders, declaring, "Call me Communist and you call all Negroes Communists."

Lee made only two more films, both outside Hollywood. He was powerful in a custom-written role as a

Harlem policeman in Louis de Rochemont's controversial *Lost Boundaries* (1949), based on the true story of a light-skinned black doctor and his family who passed for white in a small New Hampshire community. Novelist Alan Paton, impressed with Lee's performance in that film, insisted he be cast as Stephen Kumalo in the film version of Paton's *Cry, the Beloved Country* (1951), the first film ever made about apartheid, shot in Natal, South Africa, in 1950.

Lee married Frances Pollack, his companion of several years, while in London for retakes of *Cry* in 1951. While there, Lee required two operations to reduce his blood pressure. Retakes were further delayed when Lee had to return to New York after his father's death of a heart attack (the same disease that had killed Lee's mother in 1945), though Lee was too ill to attend the funeral. He traveled in Europe briefly to plan several film projects. He was supposed to return to Italy to begin shooting a film of *Othello* in 1951, but he was not permitted to renew his passport. *Cry* was being shown to capacity houses across the United States when Lee died of uremia in his Manhattan home in 1952 at age forty-five. Lee's memorial service at the Henry Street Settlement House was attended by poet Langston Hughes, among other black leaders, and included a public denunciation of apartheid.

• The above is based partly on the author's 1998 interview with Frances Lee Pearson. The Theater Collection at the New York Public Library for the Performing Arts, Lincoln Center, has a large clippings file (mainly reviews, features, and interviews from Lee's stage career) and large scrapbooks for *On Whitman Avenue* and the O'Neill sea plays. The Manuscripts/Archives and Rare Books Division of the New York Public Library's Schomburg Center for Research in Black Culture possesses collections of production stills from several of Lee's plays and films and all of Lee's personal and professional papers, donated by his widow, including scripts, speeches, correspondence, and photographs. The Schomburg also holds the complete records (1952–1954) of the Canada Lee Foundation, set up after his death to aid talented young African Americans in theater. The microfilm edition of "Communist Activity in the Entertainment Industry: FBI Surveillance Files on Hollywood, 1942–1958," acquired in 1997 by Brandeis University library, includes a dossier and detailed informers' reports on Lee. Samuel L. Leiter, *The Encyclopedia of the New York Stage, 1930–1940* and *1940–1950* (1992), is by far the best source for information on Lee's Broadway and Off-Broadway work. Lee's films are discussed in detail, albeit in a polemical fashion, in Donald Bogle, *Blacks in American Films and Television: An Encyclopedia* (1988); see also Henry T. Sampson, *Blacks in Black and White: A Source Book on Black Films* (1977). An obituary is in the *New York Times*, 10 May 1952.

CHRISTOPHER CAINES

LEE, Charles (26 Jan. 1731–2 Oct. 1782), revolutionary war general, was born in Chester, England, the son of John Lee, a British officer, and Isabella Bunbury. Possessing the important social advantage of gentle ancestry, his education was not neglected. His father, desiring that he familiarize himself with peoples and languages other than English, enrolled him at an early age in an academy in Switzerland. Over the years, Lee became proficient in Greek, Latin, French, Spanish, Italian, and German. In 1746 he entered grammar school at Bury St. Edmunds, where he became lifelong friends with important and well-placed companions such as William Butler and Charles Davers. His father, colonel of the Fifty-fifth Regiment of Foot, also determined that young Lee would continue the family's tradition of military service. Thus when Lee was fourteen years old, Colonel Lee purchased for him an ensigncy in the Fifty-fifth Regiment, soon renumbered the forty-fourth; when young Lee completed his education he reported for active duty. His father died in 1750, and four years later Lee fell out with his mother. Their problems likely stemmed from a strain of eccentricity in the Bunbury family, which Lee inherited, and which manifested itself in moodiness and a choleric temper. As Lee himself later admitted, he suffered from a "distemper of . . . mind." Thereafter, Lee was on close terms only with his unmarried sister, Sidney Lee, who like himself had survived a childhood scarred by the deaths of five siblings.

When Lee joined the Forty-fourth Regiment, it was stationed in Ireland on inactive garrison duty. On 1 May 1751 he purchased a lieutenant's commission and three years later accompanied his regiment to America for service in the French and Indian War. Apparently he was not with the Forty-fourth Regiment in 1755 when it marched toward Fort Duquesne with General Edward Braddock and was ambushed by French and Indians. In the fall he did accompany it to Albany, New York, where he became interested in the Indians. He married the daughter (name unknown) of White Thunder, a Seneca chief, and with her had twins, a boy and a girl. Because of this alliance, he was inducted into the tribe of the Bear under the name Ounewaterika, or "Boiling Water." On 11 June 1756 he purchased a captain's commission in the Forty-fourth Regiment and in 1757 took part in an expedition against the French fort of Louisburg on Cape Breton Island. He was badly wounded in a failed assault on Fort Ticonderoga on 1 July 1758 and was taken to Long Island to recuperate. There he quarreled with an army surgeon, who attempted to assassinate him and almost succeeded. Returning to the Forty-fourth Regiment, he took part in capturing Fort Niagara. On 8 September 1760 he joined General Jeffrey Amherst in the successful assault on Montreal.

Lee went home to England and was promoted major of the 103d Regiment on 10 August 1761. A year later he went to Portugal with the rank of lieutenant colonel in the Portuguese army to fight invading Spaniards. He led a small force against the Spanish at Villa Velha on 5 October 1762 and destroyed large quantities of stores. Publicly thanked by his commander, Count Wilhelm La Lippe, Lee also was promoted to colonel in the Portuguese army. Returning to England at the close of the war in 1763, his regiment was disbanded in November, and he was retired on half pay as a major.

In England during the next decade Lee made numerous enemies as a result of his argumentative nature and was kept from advancement in the army. For a time, he worked on a scheme to found two new colonies in the Illinois country of America but received no support from the ministry. In 1765 he went to Poland and was appointed to the staff of King Stanislaus Augustus on the pro-Russian side in a Polish civil war. The following year, on a trip to Turkey in Polish service, he twice narrowly escaped death, once nearly freezing in the Balkan mountains and another time surviving an earthquake in Constantinople. Returning to England, he spent two fruitless years seeking promotion. In 1769 he went back to Poland to serve as major general with Russian forces in a campaign against the Turks. He fell ill with a violent fever that almost killed him, recuperated in Italy, and lost two fingers in a duel with an officer whom he shot dead. Back in England in 1762 he finally was promoted lieutenant colonel on half pay but by then had become a thoroughgoing Whig republican, ranting about the "dolt," King George III, who was destroying English liberty. He left England in 1773 for America, ostensibly on a business trip to inspect extensive land holdings. In fact, he was musing about settling there and supporting colonials who were quarreling with Britain over taxation.

Lee arrived in New York on 8 October 1773, at the height of agitation over tea duties. He spent the next ten months traveling through the colonies, meeting patriots like George Washington, Patrick Henry, and John Adams. All received him warmly because they knew of his opposition to British coercion of America and of his military abilities, which might prove useful. Lee heartened the patriots at this crucial juncture by arguing that the virtuous, freedom-loving, "vigorous yeomanry" of the colonies could overmaster British redcoats. Also, he wrote a drill manual for militia forces and by December 1774 was training Marylanders for battle. Entering into a pamphlet battle raging between conciliators and hard-liners, he wrote an essay in opposition to the conciliator Myles Cooper. In May 1775 he purchased an estate for £3,000 sterling in Berkeley County, Virginia (now W.Va.), near the home of his friend Horatio Gates, for he believed that Americans would not trust a man "who has no property among them." He resigned his royal commission on 22 June and accepted appointment as second major general in the Continental army, which had been voted by Congress on 17 June, after receiving assurances from Congress that if he lost his property in England he would be compensated. Accompanying General Washington to Boston, he took command of the army's left wing and until December 1775 served brilliantly in constructing entrenchments, training troops, and agitating politicians for American independence. From December to March 1776 he was at Newport, Rhode Island, then New York City, rallying citizens and readying defenses.

In February 1776 Lee was appointed by Congress to command an American army in Canada, but on 1 March these orders were withdrawn. Instead, he was given charge of the Southern Military District, encompassing colonies from Virginia to Georgia. Assuming command at Williamsburg, Virginia, on 29 March he began to organize defenses in the Old Dominion and North Carolina. In early June he proceeded to Charleston, South Carolina, where he commanded patriot forces that repelled a British assault on Fort Moultrie on 28 June 1776. Lee rejoined Washington at New York in August. Commanding the army's left wing in October, during Washington's retreat from Manhattan and the battle of White Plains, he became convinced that the patriots should withdraw immediately to New Jersey. Washington demurred, for Congress was pressuring him to keep a garrison in bypassed Fort Washington on Manhattan. When the fort was lost, along with 2,900 men and huge amounts of supplies, Lee furiously decided that Washington was a weak, cowardly man. Lee dragged his feet when Washington in November and December 1776 ordered him in letter after letter to retreat from New York across New Jersey. On 12 December Lee finally had reached Basking Ridge, New Jersey, where he decided to spend the night in a tavern three miles from camp. That evening, he wrote his friend Horatio Gates that Washington was "most damnably deficient" as a general. The following day, he was seized by a British patrol and was subsequently taken to British headquarters in New York City.

Lee spent the next sixteen months languishing in close captivity, worrying that he might be tried and shot by General William Howe as a deserter and angry that Congress and Washington were not doing enough to free him. Although Howe quickly abandoned any idea of putting Lee on trial, nevertheless Lee, with much time to reflect, came to the conclusion that America could never win the war and that a continuation of the conflict only weakened both the colonies and Britain. Also, the disastrous mauling that the Americans took in the campaign of 1776 convinced Lee to reject his earlier view that the American people loved liberty and were virtuous enough to win and keep it. Therefore, in early 1777 he assisted British efforts to open peace negotiations, and when Congress refused to cooperate he gave Howe advice on how to defeat Washington in the ensuing campaign. Finally exchanged in April 1778, he returned to Continental service only reluctantly, still convinced that the Americans and British ought to negotiate peace. He informed Congress that the Continental army was no match for the redcoats and in June urged Washington to avoid battle with British forces withdrawing from Philadelphia toward New York. Although Washington shared Lee's opinion, he still decided to launch a limited attack on the enemy's rear guard and assigned about 6,000 men to the task. Lee, feeling that the size of this force compelled him to assert seniority rights and lead it, took command reluctantly, for he still did not believe Americans would stand against Britons in open battle.

On 28 June 1778 Lee attacked the British at Monmouth and soon confronted a disaster as the Continentals reeled back in a chaotic retreat. Washington, appearing on the scene with the remainder of his army and without waiting to be apprised of the facts, accused Lee of disobeying orders. Sending Lee to the rear and taking command himself, Washington finally halted the British attack and restored order. A day or two after the battle, Lee angrily wrote Washington, insisting on an apology for the latter's harsh words. When Washington refused to apologize, Lee called for a court-martial to clear his name. Only too glad to oblige, Washington formally charged Lee with disobedience, "making an unnecessary, disorderly, and shameful retreat," and disrespect to a superior officer. Only the last charge had any real merit, but the court and Congress felt compelled to back Washington. On 12 August 1778 Lee's fellow officers on the court found him guilty on all counts, then invoked only a light sentence of suspension from the army for one year; Congress approved the judgment on 5 December.

Vainly, Lee appealed to the legislators and to the people for what he viewed as justice, finally launching venomous attacks on both Washington and the citizenry. Characteristically, in early 1779, while in the midst of all these difficulties, he turned his attention to drawing up a romantic, utopian plan for a military colony to be established in "some happy clime" in America. Later in the year, because of his attacks on Washington, he was called on by Colonel John Laurens to fight a duel and was wounded in the arm. He was saved from a similar rencontre with Anthony Wayne only by a public apology. On 10 January 1780, after writing a particularly impudent screed to Congress, he was dismissed from the army and retired to his home in Virginia. On a visit to Philadelphia, he died from a "refluxion" of the lungs and was buried in the graveyard of Christ Church, although in his will he had requested that he not be interred "in any church, or churchyard."

That Lee's contributions to the American Revolution were important cannot be disputed, but that they were mixed is also beyond question. Early in the war, his military experience and radical Whig republicanism were useful in mobilizing Americans to resist the power of the mighty British Empire. However, as time went on, this same political radicalism, combined with Lee's erratic personality and the growing indications that his military genius was overrated, made him more of a liability than an asset. One thing about this "proud, turbulent, whimsical, unhappy, and valiant spirit" is beyond argument: that he was, in the words of his biographer John Richard Alden, "one of the most remarkable men ever to set foot in America" (pp. 307–8).

• Most of Lee's personal papers have been lost or destroyed but were previously published in *The Lee Papers*, New-York Historical Society, *Collections, 1871–1874* (4 vols., 1872–1876). His public correspondence is in the George Washington Papers, Library of Congress; Papers of the Continental Congress, no. 158, National Archives; Jeffrey Amherst Papers, War Office, 34/36, British Public Record Office; and the Sir Henry Clinton and Nathanael Greene Papers, William L. Clements Library, the University of Michigan. The best biography is John Richard Alden, *General Charles Lee: Traitor or Patriot?* (1951). Others are Jared Sparks, *Lives of Charles Lee and Joseph Reed* (1846), and Samuel White Patterson, *Knight Errant of Liberty: The Triumph and Tragedy of General Charles Lee* (1958). Useful sketches are Edward Robins, "Charles Lee: Stormy Petrel of the Revolution," *Pennsylvania Magazine of History and Biography* 45 (1921): 66–97; Charles W. Heathcote, "General Charles Lee in the American Revolution," *Picket Post* 65 (1959): 7–13; and John Shy, "Charles Lee: The Soldier as Radical," in *George Washington's Generals*, ed. George A. Billias (1964), pp. 22–53. Lee's "treason" is assessed in George H. Moore, *"Mr. Lee's Plan: March 29, 1777": The Treason of Charles Lee, Major General, Second in Command in the American Army of the Revolution* (1860). For Lee's role at Monmouth, see William S. Stryker, "Lee's Conduct at the Battle of Monmouth," New Jersey Historical Society, *Proceedings*, 3d ser., vol. 2 (1900), pp. 95–99; William S. Stryker and William S. Myers, *The Battle of Monmouth* (1927); Thomas J. Fleming, "The 'Military Crimes' of Charles Lee," *American Heritage* 19 (1968): 12–15, 83–89; and Theodore Thayer, *The Making of a Scapegoat: Washington and Lee at Monmouth* (1976).

PAUL DAVID NELSON

LEE, Charles (July 1758–24 June 1815), lawyer and U.S. attorney general, was born at "Leesylvania," in Prince William County, Virginia, the son of planter, burgess, and revolutionary politician Henry Lee (1727–1787) and Lucy Grymes. A younger brother of Henry ("Light-Horse Harry") Lee (1756–1818), Charles Lee followed in his sibling's footsteps and attended Princeton College (then called the College of New Jersey), where he graduated with honors in 1775. Somewhat aimless after graduation, he read law in Philadelphia in 1779; the next year he briefly held the post of secretary to the Board of Treasury. Lee was licensed to practice law at the Virginia bar in 1781 and commenced his profession in the local county courts of northern Virginia. Following the Revolution he expanded his practice into the General Court of Virginia and qualified before the Virginia Supreme Court of Appeals in 1785. During this period Lee gathered brief reports of cases decided by the judges of the superior courts, though his reports were not published until the twentieth century.

Lee held the post of naval officer of the Potomac River District during the Revolution, an appointment he obtained at least as early as 1779. Although deputies carried out the customs inspection duties during Lee's absence in Philadelphia, he apparently retained the position until the creation of the federal government in 1789, when President George Washington appointed him customs collector at Alexandria. The same year Lee wed Anne Lucinda Lee, the daughter of Ricahrd Henry Lee; the couple had six children. In the spring of 1793, Lee resigned his federal post to devote more attention to his law practice in partnership with his younger brother, Edmund Jennings Lee. Also that year he gained election to the Virginia House of Delegates from Fairfax County, where he served for two sessions.

In November 1795 President Washington again called Lee into government service to succeed the deceased William Bradford (1755–1795) as attorney general of the United States. Lee was not Washington's first choice for the post, but he served the president ably and was continued in office by John Adams (1735–1826). A staunch Federalist and vigorous opponent of conciliation with the French, Lee enforced the Alien and Sedition Acts and remained faithful to the president in the tumultuous final days of Adams's tenure. Upon the departure of Timothy Pickering from Adams's cabinet in May 1800, Lee briefly acted as secretary of state and had the pleasure of forwarding a commission to his friend John Marshall as Pickering's permanent successor.

Adams named Lee (as one of his notorious "midnight appointments") to one of the federal judgeships created by the Judiciary Act of 1801, but the Virginian lost the post when Congress repealed the act the following year. Lee then settled in Alexandria to practice law. He was counsel for William Marbury in *Marbury v. Madison*. He also defended Samuel Chase, in his impeachment trial before the U.S. Senate in 1805; and Aaron Burr (1756–1836), in his trial for treason in Richmond in 1807. While practicing law, Lee speculated widely in land on either side of Virginia's Blue Ridge Mountains and in military bounty lands in Ohio. In 1809, five years after his wife's death, Lee married Margaret Christian Scott Peyton of Fauquier County, Virginia, a widow. They had three children. About 1813 he left Alexandria for "Leeton Forest," his country estate in Fauquier County, where he died two years later.

Austere, taciturn, and undemonstrative, Charles Lee was a skilled legal practitioner and a strongly opinionated politician.

• The most recent and most complete biographical sketch of Charles Lee appears in *Princetonians, 1769–1775: A Biographical Directory*, by Richard A. Harrison (1980). Other useful sketches may be found in Robert Sobel, ed., *Biographical Directory of the United States Executive Branch, 1774–1977* (1978); Edmund Jennings Lee, ed., *Lee of Virginia, 1642–1892: Biographical and Genealogical Sketches of the Descendants of Colonel Richard Lee* (1895); and William Hamilton Bryson, ed., *The Virginia Law Reporters before 1880* (1977). The collected law reports of Charles Lee were published by Professor Bryson in the *University of Richmond Law Review* 11 (Summer 1977): 691–741. See also Alfred B. Horner, "Burial Place of Charles Lee," *Fauquier County Historical Society Bulletin*, ser. 1 (1921–1924): 243–45. While no major collection of Lee's personal or professional papers appears to survive, a representative portion of his materials may be found in the Lee family and Peyton family collections at the Virginia Historical Society, Richmond, as well as the Lee family collection at "Stratford Hall," Westmoreland County, Va., and the George Washington papers, Library of Congress.

E. LEE SHEPARD

LEE, Charles Alfred (3 Mar. 1801–14 Feb. 1872), physician and author, was born in Salisbury, Connecticut, the son of Samuel Lee and Elizabeth Brown, farmers.

Lee attended Williams College, from which he received a B.A. in 1822 and later an M.A. After studying medicine under his brother-in-law, Luther Ticknor, he received an M.D. from the Berkshire Medical College in 1825. While a student at Berkshire, he served at times as a demonstrator in anatomy and an instructor in botany.

Lee practiced medicine in Salisbury for two years before taking up a practice in New York City, where he and physician James Stewart were active in the establishment of the Northern Dispensary, a dispensary that cared for thousands of patients annually. During the cholera epidemic of 1832, Lee was appointed physician to the Greenwich Cholera Hospital and attending physician at the New York Orphan Asylum. In 1828 he had married Hester Ann Middleberger. The family genealogy indicates that they had seven children; other sources have reported that there were nine.

In the 1840s Lee's interests turned away from the clinical practice of medicine and he increasingly gained eminence as a teacher and as a medical and scientific editor and writer. In 1844 he became professor of materia medica and general pathology at the Geneva Medical College. His teaching schedule allowed him to teach at more than one school at a time, and in 1849 he gave the valedictory address at both Geneva and the Medical School of Maine of Bowdoin College. Among the other schools at which he taught were the University of the City of New York, the Vermont Medical College, the Berkshire Medical School, and the Starling Medical College of Columbus, Ohio. In 1847 he was on the first faculty of the Buffalo Medical School, where he became professor of pathology and materia medica and from which he retired in 1871 as professor emeritus of materia medica and hygiene.

Versatile as well as peripatetic, Lee taught, as did other medical educators in that period, a variety of subjects: therapeutics and materia medica, general pathology, obstetrics and the diseases of females, and hygiene and medical jurisprudence. As dean of the faculty at Geneva Medical College in 1847, he signed what was in effect the letter of admission of Elizabeth Blackwell, the first woman to obtain an M.D. in the United States.

Throughout his teaching career Lee was a prolific writer. His early efforts included *Human Physiology for the Use of Elementary Schools* (1838), which went through eleven editions, and *Elements of Geology for Popular Use* (1839); the editing of Ralph B. Grindrod's *Bacchus. An Essay on the Nature, Causes, Effects, and Cures of Intemperance* (1840); and the editing of Jonathan Pereira's *A Treatise on Food and Diet* (1843), each of which went through at least six printings.

Lee's efforts were more specifically directed to medicine when he edited James Copland's *A Dictionary of Practical Medicine* which appeared in several formats; the first American edition was issued in nine volumes between 1834 and 1859. In 1844 Lee edited John A. Paris's *Pharmacologia* and in 1845, William A. Guy's

Principles of Medical Jurisprudence. From 1843 to 1862 he edited the second through seventh American editions of Anthony Todd Thomson's *A Conspectus of the Pharmacopoeias of the London, Edinburgh and Dublin Colleges of Physicians*, adding to its title, *and of the United States Pharmacopoeia.* Lee's contributions as editor were considerable. To the Copland work he added an "American Medical Bibliography" at the end of each article; to the Guy work he added "200 pages of original matter"; and his additions to the *Conspectus* "considerably exceeded the original work."

Lee's own later works included *A Catalogue of Medicinal Plants, Indigenous and Exotic, Growing in the State of New-York* (1848), and *On Provision for the Insane Poor of the State of New York, and the Adaptation of the "Asylum and Cottage Plan" to Their Wants; as Illustrated by the History of the Colony of Fitz James at Clermont, France* (1860; repr. 1866), in which he was critical of the use of restraints. He was also a frequent contributor to medical journals. His contributions were remarkable for the diversity of the subjects he covered—epilepsy, smallpox, filaria in a horse's eye, insanity, homeopathy, medical statistics, and the effect of arts and trade on health and longevity. He also wrote on geology, mineralogy, and meteorology for other publications. In 1843 he helped found the *New York Journal of Medicine and Collateral Sciences*, which he edited from 1845 to 1848.

In 1862–1863 Lee contributed a series of forty-three lengthy letters to the *American Medical Times* that described medical affairs, especially of hospitals, observed during a seven-month European tour that he had taken early in the American Civil War. On this tour he had surveyed, on behalf of the Union government, the construction and administration of military and civil hospitals, and he brought back plans, specifications, and models. His thorough report appeared, illustrated with architectural diagrams, in *Transactions of the New York State Medical Society* ([1863], pp. 37–66). In 1863 he became a wartime inspector and visitor of military hospitals for the U.S. Sanitary Commission and, after the war, spent several months in the South as an observer for the commission.

Lee's early interest in the temperance movement continued throughout his life. In 1862 he was invited to lecture before the British Temperance Reform League in London, and in 1871 he published *Remarks on Wines and Alcohol.* Although a member of a panel of scientists that exposed the Fox sisters, notorious spiritualists, he became a believer in spiritual rappings.

Although a member of a number of professional societies—the American Medical Association, the New York Academy of Medicine, and the New York State Medical Society among them—and an honorary member of Ohio and Connecticut medical societies, Lee played no significant role in organizational activities. A bibliophile and collector, he assembled a personal library of between 3,000 and 4,000 volumes, and his herbarium numbered some 1,500 specimens. As a writer, he became one of the most prolific of American medical authors, and as a teacher he was well loved.

One student described him as "greatest of all the professors . . . and worthy of our hearts and warmest emotions." Medical historian and biographer Joseph M. Toner ranked him with the eminent physicians Benjamin Rush, Daniel Drake, and David Hosack, but it must be noted that Lee had named Toner as his literary executor. Lee died in Peekskill, New York, where he had taken up residence in 1850.

• The chief biographical sources are Oliver P. Jones, "Our First Professor of Pathology, Materia Medica, Charles Alfred Lee (1801–1872)," *Buffalo Physician* 8 (1974): 18–21; Joseph M. Toner, "Lee, Charles Alfred, M.D.," *Transactions of the American Medical Association* 32 (1881): 518–23; and [Cato], "Sketches of Eminent Living Physicians—No. XVII. Charles A. Lee, M.D. of New York," *Boston Medical and Surgical Journal* 42 (1850): 467–70. A family genealogy is Leonard Lee and Sarah F. Lee, *John Lee of Farmington, Hartford Co., Conn., and His Descendants* (1897).

DAVID L. COWEN

LEE, Elizabeth Blair (20 June 1818–13 Sept. 1906), letter writer and director of an orphan home, was born in Frankfort, Kentucky, the daughter of Francis Preston Blair (1791–1876), an editor and adviser to presidents, and Eliza Violet Gist (Eliza Violet Gist Blair), a newspaperwoman and political hostess. Lizzie, as Elizabeth Blair was most often called, in 1830 accompanied her parents to Washington, where she was labeled "the little Democrat" and was a special favorite of President Andrew Jackson. She often filled his corncob pipe in the evening and lingered to hear the political discussion he had with her father, who proudly said she was "brought up in caucus." When Blair grew a bit older, she often wrote letters and copied documents for Jackson, who during the last year of his life presented her with his wife's wedding ring. Blair also enjoyed a close relationship with President Martin Van Buren and his family. When Van Buren was defeated for a second term, Blair rode out from Washington on horseback with her father and Martin Van Buren, Jr., to inform the president. When they reached his country retreat, the two men delegated Blair with the unpleasant job and rode on. While helping her from her horse, the president made her task unnecessary. "I saw those two cowards ride past the gate," he told her, "and I know that if their news had been good they would have come with you" (*Evening Star*, 14 Sept. 1906).

Blair's formal education was capped with an 1833–1835 stint at Madame Adele Sigoigne's prestigious school in Philadelphia. Not wanting his daughter to put on airs, Francis Preston Blair carefully outlined what she was to be taught and arranged to have her spend her weekends with Rebecca Gratz, a socially conscious and influential Philadelphian who was a sister of his wife's brother-in-law and who, indeed, became Blair's role model.

On 27 April 1843, after a four-year romance and against the advice of her father and her brother Montgomery Blair, Lizzie Blair married Samuel Phillips Lee, a handsome but quarrelsome naval officer from

Virginia who became a Union admiral during the Civil War. Although Phil, as he was called, chafed at sharing Lizzie with her family, he bowed to the inevitable. Like her father, who refused to relinquish care of her, she had tendencies to tuberculosis, and her health remained delicate, even though she had grown stronger during an 1840–1841 stay in Cuba. Except for brief periods when Lizzie joined her husband at New England or southern naval stations, the Lees and the elder Blairs shared households.

Having long been her family's chief scribe as well as carrying on an extensive correspondence with her numerous friends, Lee now made her husband the chief recipient of her news-packed letters. It is these letters—written with an insider's knowledge of political nuances and following her father's advice to "observe all . . . with an eye that will enable you when you speak of it, to speak accurately"—that assure her a place in history (Francis Preston Blair to Lizzie Blair, 5 Oct. 1833, Blair Family Papers). Even while lamenting "we woman kind can only hold our tongues & pray" (Lizzie Lee to Francis Preston Blair, 12 Sept. 1866, Blair-Lee Papers), Lee was intent on "being seen & heard." She added her own thoughts and pertinent phrases to speeches and articles sketched out by her father and brother Francis Preston Blair (1821–1875), a senator and representative from Missouri who was the Democratic vice presidential candidate in 1868. Her father especially complimented her use of "doughface lackeys" to describe prosouthern, New England politicians Franklin Pierce and Caleb Cushing.

In 1849 Lee joined the board of the Washington City Orphan Asylum, founded by Dolley Madison to shelter orphans of the War of 1812. Working to make it a financially sound institution that proved able to withstand the stresses of the Civil War, Lee also secured jobs for individual orphans and used her influence to integrate them into Washington life. In 1862 she became the orphanage's first director, a title she retained for the rest of her life.

To the delight of the Lees, who had given up on progeny, a son, whom they called Blair, was born to them on 9 August 1857. Aware that she no longer matched her youthful portrait painted by Thomas Sully, Lee seldom allowed her picture to be taken. Her life centered about her son, her family, and her work at the orphanage, but she continued to occupy the exalted position in Washington society she had enjoyed since the days of Jackson. She comforted Mary T. Lincoln after her husband's assassination, and Tad Lincoln's White House goats went to Blair Lee. Spending summers at Silver Spring, Maryland, she returned each winter to Washington, where her parents in 1859 built a home for her, which they shared (now part of Blair House, the nation's guest house).

Instead of being smothered by her overly protective family, Lee thrived in its bosom. She adjusted so well to her irascible husband's long absences that her even temper became ruffled if informed that he would be home earlier than expected. Yet she supported him within the family and worked tirelessly to advance his career and procure the assignments he wished. When he was ordered to California, she badgered President Andrew Johnson with the matron of the orphanage accompanied by sixty to eighty of its children until the assignment was changed.

After her husband's retirement in 1873 and the death of her parents later in that decade, life for Lee was often a tug-of-war. She and Blair, who like her thrived on Washington society, pulled to remain in the city as long as possible, while her husband maneuvered to prolong country living at Silver Spring. Occasionally Lee remained in Washington when the admiral returned to the country, with Blair spending his days with his mother and nights with his father. Outliving her husband and siblings, Lee was a relic of an earlier age as she crossed Lafayette Square, near the statue of Jackson, on the arm of her son each Sunday en route to church. When she died in Silver Spring, she was reputed to have been "conversant with political leaders and movements" for a longer period than any other American woman (*Evening Star*, 14 Sept. 1906). Blindness and deafness in her last years kept Lee from working at the orphanage; but her connection with it continued, and all of its children attended her funeral.

• The primary collections of Lee's letters and papers pertaining to her and her family are in the Blair-Lee Papers, Princeton University, and the Blair Family Papers, Library of Congress. References to her are also in the Woodbury Family Papers, Library of Congress. For her published letters, see Virginia Jeans Laas, ed., *Wartime Washington: The Civil War Letters of Elizabeth Blair Lee* (1991). For biographical material, see Dudley T. Cornish and Virginia J. Laas, *Lincoln's Lee: The Life of Samuel Phillips Lee, United States Navy, 1812–1897* (1986); Elbert B. Smith, *Francis Preston Blair* (1980); and William E. Smith, *The Francis Preston Blair Family in Politics* (2 vols., 1933). For an obituary, see the *Evening Star* (Washington), 14 Sept. 1906.

OLIVE HOOGENBOOM

LEE, Fitzhugh (19 Nov. 1835–28 Apr. 1905), army officer, was born at "Clermont," Fairfax County, Virginia, the son of Sydney Smith Lee, a naval officer, and Anna Maria Mason, a member of a family prominent in Virginia politics. He was the grandson of "Lighthorse Harry" Lee and the nephew of Robert E. Lee. Entering West Point in 1852, Fitzhugh Lee excelled in horsemanship but not in academics or in deportment. Narrowly avoiding dismissal for poor conduct, he graduated forty-fifth of forty-nine in the class of 1856. He was a cavalry instructor at Carlisle Barracks, Pennsylvania, and in January 1858 was appointed second lieutenant in the Second U.S. Cavalry, of which his uncle was lieutenant colonel, and was sent to the Texas frontier. In combat with the Comanches on 19 May 1859, Lee was seriously wounded, but by the following summer he had recovered and was back in combat with the same foes. From 29 December 1860 to 3 May 1861 he served as an assistant instructor of tactics at

West Point. At the end of that time, in consequence of Virginia's secession a few days before, he resigned his commission and offered his services to his native state.

Commissioned in the regular Confederate army as a first lieutenant (the same rank he had resigned in the U.S. Army), he served on the staff of General Richard S. Ewell in the Shenandoah Valley and then transferred to the staff of General Joseph E. Johnston, participating in the first battle of Bull Run (Manassas) on 21 July 1861. The next month he was promoted to lieutenant colonel of the First Virginia Cavalry, and in April 1862 he became colonel of that regiment. During the Peninsula campaign he participated in General J. E. B. Stuart's ride around the Union Army of the Potomac and subsequently became a great favorite of Stuart. For his services in the Peninsula campaign, Lee was promoted to brigadier general on 25 July 1862. Late in getting his troops to the Rapidan the following month, he delayed his uncle's plans for destroying John Pope's Union army until Pope had time to escape. For this Stuart faulted Fitzhugh Lee in his report. In September, however, Lee fought ably, delaying Federal pursuit after the Confederate defeat at South Mountain in Maryland. The time he bought allowed the concentration of the scattered Army of Northern Virginia and helped prevent its annihilation at the subsequent battle of Antietam on 17 September 1862.

That winter Lee continued to perform well, participating in skirmishes at Dumfries and Occoquan, Virginia, in December. He showed resourcefulness in finding forage for his horses, dispersing his units along the upper Rappahannock River. On 17 March 1863 he led a small force of Confederate cavalry against a larger Union mounted force under General W. W. Averell at Kelly's Ford, garnering praise for his skillful tactics. At the battle of Chancellorsville (1–4 May 1863), Lee commanded the only full brigade of cavalry operating with the main army, Stuart having been detached to counter a move by the Union cavalry. Lee's troopers uncovered the fact that the Federal right flank was unprotected and vulnerable to attack. This led to "Stonewall" Jackson's famous flanking march, which Lee's cavalry ably screened. That summer, he was with Stuart again for another ride around the Union army during the Gettysburg campaign, a maneuver that effectively removed the Confederate cavalry from meaningful participation in the campaign and kept them off the Gettysburg battlefield until the third day of fighting. On that day, 3 July 1863, Lee took part in the major clash in which Stuart's forces were bested by the Union cavalry. On 3 August 1863 Lee was promoted to major general, and the following month he was given command of a division of cavalry, which he led under Stuart's overall command until the latter's death in May 1864.

In the 1864 Overland campaign, Lee again performed vital service. On 8 May 1864 his division held off the lead elements of the Army of the Potomac at Spotsylvania Court House until the Confederate main body could come up. This action saved the important road junction and with it Robert E. Lee's lines of supply and retreat. Fitzhugh Lee's division accompanied General Jubal A. Early to the Shenandoah Valley the next month, where Lee was wounded at the third battle of Winchester (19 Sept. 1864). He did not return to duty until January 1865, when his division was back with the main Confederate army, now besieged at Petersburg. In March of that year, after Wade Hampton had been transferred to the Carolinas, Lee became chief of cavalry for the Army of Northern Virginia. On 1 April 1865 he was given the task, along with General George Pickett and his division of infantry, of holding the position of Five Forks on the Confederate right flank. When the position seemed secure that morning, both men went to a shad bake some miles away. They were thus absent when their commands were crushed that afternoon. In the resulting flight of the Army of Northern Virginia, Fitzhugh Lee kept his uncle informed of Union movements and when surrender was imminent led a remnant of cavalry in breaking out of the encirclement that forced the surrender of the rest of the army on 9 April. Lee and his cavalry surrendered two days later at Farmville, Virginia.

After the war Lee took up farming in Stafford County, Virginia. In 1871 he married Ellen Bernard Fowle; they had five children. In November 1885 he ran for governor. The race was boisterous and hotly contested, pitting Lee and the Democrats against the Republicans and their allies the Readjusters (those who advocated a partial repudiation of the state debt and increased educational spending). Lee won overwhelming victory, in part through Democratic party election fraud. His election ended the third party and Republican threat to Democratic supremacy in postbellum Virginia. During his term Virginia prospered, attracting some $100 million in outside capital. Lee, however, was not successful in an 1893 run for the Democratic nomination for U.S. senator. In 1896 he was named consul general to Havana, Cuba, where he served ably in the diplomatic crisis leading up to the Spanish-American War. Returning to the United States upon the outbreak of the war, he was commissioned a major general of volunteers on 5 May 1898 and assigned to the VII Corps. The surprisingly rapid progress of the war meant that he and his troops saw only occupation duty. Subsequently he served from 12 April 1899 to 2 March 1901 as a brigadier general of volunteers, commanding for a time the Department of the Missouri.

Lee retired as a brigadier general and accepted the task of planning for the Jamestown Exposition of 1907. He died in Washington, D.C. Though never the equal of such Confederate cavalry leaders as Nathan Bedford Forrest or Stuart, Lee was nevertheless a competent and effective leader of mounted troops who significantly aided the Confederate cause.

• Lee wrote a biography of his uncle, *General Lee* (1894), and published an account of Chancellorsville in *Southern Historical Society Papers* 7 (1879): 545–85. His Civil War reports and those of his superiors pertaining to him are in *The War of the*

Rebellion: A Compilation of the Official Records of the Union and Confederate Armies (128 vol., 1880–1901). Lee's Civil War service is dealt with in William C. Davis, ed., *The Confederate General* (1991); Shelby Foote, *The Civil War: A Narrative* (1958–1974); and Douglas Southall Freeman, *Lee's Lieutenants: A Study in Command* (1942–1944). Information on his postwar political career in Va. is in Allen W. Moger, *Virginia: Bourbonism to Byrd, 1870–1925* (1968).

STEVEN E. WOODWORTH

LEE, Francis Lightfoot (14 Oct. 1734–17 Jan. 1797), political leader and signer of the Declaration of Independence, was born probably at Machodoc (later Mount Pleasant), Westmoreland County, Virginia, the son of Thomas Lee, a planter and political leader, and Hannah Ludwell. Francis Lightfoot Lee was a member of the third generation of a Virginia family that had already achieved wealth and power. His father was agent for the vast proprietary land grant comprising the whole region between the Rappahannock and Potomac rivers, known as the Northern Neck; a major landowner in his own right and an early investor in new land along the Potomac and to the west; and a member and president of the Virginia Council. Soon after Lee's birth, his father moved the family to a new seat at Stratford and began construction of the house that still stands. Francis Lightfoot was the fifth of his parents' eight children who survived to adulthood. He was in his mid-teens in 1750 when both his parents died and, unlike his three older brothers and his younger brother Arthur, was not sent to England for the completion of his education.

Even before the death of their parents, childhood does not appear to have been easy for the younger Lees. Their mother was, in effect, manager of the estate and concentrated what time and attention she had for the children upon the two eldest, Philip Ludwell and Hannah. Then, Philip Ludwell, who gained a reputation for haughtiness and condescension, did not endear himself to his younger siblings as administrator of the estate, although he did bring Stratford to the height of its prosperity.

Francis Lightfoot, who enjoyed an apparently deserved reputation as a thoroughly gentle and mild-mannered member of an often aggressive and outspoken family, nonetheless in 1754 instituted a suit, which never was decided, to have an uncle named as his guardian in the place of his eldest brother. Instead, in his midtwenties he took up residence on the frontier in newly created Loudoun County, where he had inherited land from his father. In 1758 he won one of the county's two seats in the House of Burgesses, retaining it for the next decade. When he attended his first session of the Burgesses, he was one of five Lees in the membership, including two brothers and two cousins.

In 1769 Lee married a distant cousin, Rebecca Tayloe, daughter of John Tayloe of Mount Airy in Richmond County, and accepted his father-in-law's offer of a thousand acres to return to the Tidewater region. Thereupon he built a residence at his estate, "Menokin," and again won a seat in the House of Bur-

gesses, this time representing Richmond County from 1769 through 1775. Running in absentia and unable to campaign actively, he failed to win a seat in the Virginia Convention of May 1776.

The four youngest Lee brothers, Richard Henry, William, Arthur, and Francis Lightfoot, and an older brother, Thomas Ludwell, remained unusually close to one another before and throughout the American Revolution. The Lees were part of an outspoken minority in the legislature who sometimes opposed the established leadership. Francis Lightfoot never seemed entirely enthusiastic about the give-and-take of politics, sometimes missing whole sessions of the assembly; but, when present, he was an active member, serving on key committees. In the Stamp Act crisis he signed Richard Henry Lee's Westmoreland Association of 27 February 1766. He was a signer, too, of the Virginia nonimportation agreement of 22 June 1770. In 1773 he became a member of the Committee of Correspondence for the colony; and years later Thomas Jefferson specifically recalled that both Francis Lightfoot and Richard Henry had joined him in planning the resolution for a day of fasting and prayer on 1 June 1774 to protest the closing of the Port of Boston.

When the Virginia Convention chose its delegates to the third session of the Continental Congress held in September 1775, it selected Francis Lightfoot Lee to replace the aging and infirm Richard Bland. Reelected in three succeeding years, Lee served until May 1779. He supported Richard Henry Lee's 2 July 1776 resolution that paved the way for adoption of the Declaration of Independence, which Francis Lightfoot signed. When Virginia conservatives denied Richard Henry reelection to Congress in 1777, Francis Lightfoot resigned his seat in protest but resumed it a few months later, after his brother was himself restored to the delegation. In his first years in Congress Francis Lightfoot was especially active as a member of the Board of War, devoting much of his attention to procurement of supplies for the Continental army.

The overshadowing, and ultimately shattering, episode in Lee's congressional career came in 1778, during the bitter controversy that involved his brother Arthur Lee and Silas Deane, both of whom served, along with Benjamin Franklin, as American commissioners to the French government. Arthur Lee, joined by his brother William Lee, who served as Congress's commercial agent in Nantes, found that Deane had personally profited from his administration of funds given in support of the American cause; they also suspected him of supplying intelligence to the British in collaboration with the commissioners' secretary, Edward Bancroft. Having an acerbic personality, and fundamentally suspicious of royalist France, Arthur Lee tangled as well with Franklin, who was willing to tolerate Deane's financial manipulations and to make whatever other compromises were required to win French assistance in the Revolution.

In a Congress in which factional divisions abounded, a group of delegates hostile to Deane had already formed. Richard Henry Lee was an active member, having secured Deane's recall in November 1777 for granting an excessive number of commissions in the American army to French gentlemen. Then, in the spring of 1778, Richard Henry began to hear from his brothers accusations of conflict among the diplomats. In September, after Deane had returned to America, Richard Henry launched an attack against him in Congress and then shortly thereafter left Congress for several months. Francis Lightfoot Lee, who had just returned from a comparable absence, now faced a sharp counterattack from Deane and his supporters that spilled over into the press and created for the first time since independence a widely visible split in the revolutionary leadership. In the end, diplomatic necessity determined the outcome of the controversy. Neither France, an open ally of America since the treaty of alliance of 1778, nor Spain, which by early in 1779 had emerged as a potential ally and agent of a negotiated peace, would accept Arthur Lee, the designated commissioner to Madrid, as a diplomatic representative. Over the next few months, as the members of Congress debated their minimum conditions for peace and a reconstitution of the American diplomatic mission, they voted in successive steps to vacate the appointments of Deane and both Arthur and William Lee.

Even before the final determination of Arthur Lee's fate, Francis Lightfoot Lee and Richard Henry Lee, perceiving the inevitable outcome of the bruising debate, departed Philadelphia, Francis Lightfoot by mid-April 1779. Thoroughly disillusioned and apparently increasingly isolated within the Virginia congressional delegation, the two brothers resigned their seats on 15 May 1779 rather than seek reelection. Even though at the time Francis Lightfoot wrote of his preference for the quiet life of a private station, he won election the next year as a representative of Richmond County in the Virginia House of Delegates, only to be disqualified on a technicality—probably at the instigation of an old family enemy, Carter Braxton—because he had neglected to subscribe to a required oath of allegiance to the state. Lee then won a by-election to the state Senate but served only a single term.

Thereafter Lee turned aside from public life. He spoke in support of the Federal Constitution—one of the few occasions on which he disagreed with Richard Henry—but otherwise took no active part in the ratification contest in Virginia. He and his beloved wife lived quietly at Menokin, assuming responsibility for the upbringing of the two young daughters of his brother William, who returned from Europe as a widower and in poor health. Francis Lightfoot, having outlived all of his brothers, died at Menokin. Although he was never as much a center of controversy as were his more famous brothers, the record of that remarkable group would perhaps be incomplete without taking note of his consistently supportive role.

• Manuscript material on Francis Lightfoot Lee is scattered through a number of Lee collections. A microfilm edition of *The Lee Family Papers, 1742–1795*, ed. Paul P. Hoffman (1966), brings together major collections of Lee papers at the University of Virginia, Harvard University, and the American Philosophical Society. Other major collections of Lee material are at the duPont Library at Stratford and at the Virginia Historical Society, Richmond. Lee's correspondence during his service in the Continental Congress is printed in Paul H. Smith, ed., *Letters of Delegates to Congress, 1774–1789*, vols. 2–12 (1977–1985). Alonzo T. Dill, *Francis Lightfoot Lee, the Incomparable Signer* (1977), provides a brief biography. Paul C. Nagel, *The Lees of Virginia: Seven Generations of an American Family* (1990), is useful for its treatment of the relationship of Francis Lightfoot Lee with his brothers. Chapter eleven of Jack N. Rakove, *The Beginnings of National Politics: An Interpretive History of the Continental Congress* (1979), offers a discerning treatment of the Deane-Lee controversy.

THAD W. TATE

LEE, George E. (28 Apr. 1896–2 Oct. 1958), bandleader, singer, and instrumentalist, was born George Ewing Lee, Jr., in Boonville, Missouri, the son of George Lee, Sr., a violinist who led a string trio, and Katie Redmond. After playing baritone saxophone and piano in an army band in 1917 and working with a vocal quartet, Lee formed a trio that included his sister, singer and pianist Julia Lee, who performed with George regularly until 1933. The group played mainly at the Lyric Hall in Kansas City.

The ensemble gradually grew larger, and Lee himself seems to have performed in many guises. Photos and newspapers testify to his playing tuba, guitar, banjo, ukulele, several sizes of saxophone, and clarinet, in addition to fulfilling his main roles as a singer of ballads and novelty songs, an entertaining master of ceremonies, and the band's manager. By 1927, the year of his first obscure recordings, the eight-piece band included trombonist Thurston "Sox" Maupins, who died in 1928 before documenting the claim of his fellow Kansas City musicians that he was the equal of Jimmy Harrison. When Bennie Moten's band left to tour the East in 1928, Lee found improved opportunities for work. The following year, changes in personnel and an expansion to ten pieces involved the hiring of saxophonist Budd Johnson, who in turn persuaded Lee to ask the temporarily jobless jazz arranger Jesse Stone to update the band's style. Stone became the band's music director, and both he and Johnson contributed substantially to recording sessions made separately under George and Julia's name in November.

The band played for some time at the Reno Club in Kansas City, but it also toured from Texas to the Dakotas. On a visit to Parsons, Kansas, a young Buck Clayton heard Lee: "He sang *Chloe, If I Could Be with You, Eleven-thirty Saturday Night*, and *Mississippi Mud*. He looked so sharp in his Oxford-gray coat, pearl-gray vest and gamble stripe pants. When he sang he snapped his fingers. He had a beautiful voice, a strong voice, that could fill up the hall without a microphone. He used a megaphone. He was really sharp" (Clayton, p. 21). Reports of Lee's personality are contradictory: clarinetist Herman Walder remembers Lee as overbearing and ungenerous; Johnson, as a great guy who let the band take off an hour early when Fletcher Henderson's orchestra was playing in town.

During this period Lee regularly traded jobs with Moten, and after sitting in with Andy Kirk's band in Tulsa at a time when Lee was finishing an engagement at the Pla-Mor Ballroom in Kansas City, he befriended the young Kirk by handing him the job at the Pla-Mor. This sort of arrangement worked to everyone's advantage, because by trading venues, a band could find fresh audiences for its musical routines.

Lee's fortunes slowly began to decline in 1931, though his band had a strong soloist in reed player Tommy Douglas. In 1934 Moten and Lee pooled resources to perform at the new Cherry Blossom nightclub and to produce an elaborate show at the Harlem Club in Kansas City, with dancers, comedians, and a chorus line imported from New York. The show failed, and Moten and Lee resumed working separately. Lee toured with a big band into 1935 and then led small groups until the decade's end, when he retired from music and moved, first to Detroit and then, after World War II, to San Diego. Before retiring he was in some unknown way the overseer of one of the extraordinary events in the history of jazz: When Charlie Parker left Kansas City in the summer of 1937 to work in Lee's small band at a resort in Eldo, Missouri, he had been laughed at as an incompetent; when Parker returned to the city after his months with Lee, he was hailed as a musical genius. Reportedly Lee was completely paralyzed for the last three years of his life. At his death in Los Angeles, he was survived by his wife, Isabelle (maiden name unknown), and his son, George Lee.

Lee's significance was as a pathbreaker. In the first flowering of jazz and dance music in Kansas City during the Prohibition years, his band was the principal rival of Bennie Moten's orchestra. Moten's instrumentalists were superior and his recordings incomparably greater than Lee's, but it was only after hiring Jimmy Rushing that Moten could compete with George and Julia's singing, which gave Lee's band a great popular appeal in the region.

• The pioneering study of Lee's place within the history of Kansas City jazz is by Dave Dexter, Jr., "Moten and Lee Are Patron Saints of Kansas City Jazz," *Down Beat*, 1 Jan. 1941, pp. 8, 18, and "Kaycee Local 627 Prospered during 1930 Boom Days," *Down Beat*, 15 Jan. 1941, pp. 6, 13. The band's most significant alumnus, Budd Johnson, remembers his early years in the first of a two-part interview with Frank Driggs, "Budd Johnson: Ageless Jazzman," *Jazz Review* 3, no. 9 (1960): 6–7. Gunther Schuller supplies a brief description of the band's recordings in *Early Jazz: Its Roots and Musical Development* (1968), pp. 298–99; these are discussed further in Ross Russell, *Jazz Style in Kansas City and the Southwest* (1971), pp. 113–16. Albert McCarthy, *Big Band Jazz* (1974), pp. 138–39, traces the orchestra's personnel through the years. Further reminiscences from Johnson appear in an interview from 1974 that forms a part of Stanley Dance, *The World of Earl Hines* (1977), pp. 208–10. Photos and a capsule history appear in Frank Driggs and Harris Lewine, *Black Beauty, White Heat: A Pictorial History of Classic Jazz, 1920–1950* (1982), p. 152. *Buck Clayton's Jazz World*

(1986) offers impressions of the band at the height of its fame (pp. 20–21) and anecdotes about Lee and his sister in the mid-1930s (pp. 90–92). A short chapter, "George E. Lee and His Singing Novelty Orchestra," in Nathan W. Pearson, Jr., *Goin' to Kansas City* (1988), offers a considerable amount of new material in interviews with musicians who played with or listened to the band. An obituary is in *The Call* (Kansas City), 7 Nov. 1958.

BARRY KERNFELD

LEE, George Washington Custis (16 Sept. 1832–18 Feb. 1913), army officer and educator, was born at Fort Monroe, Virginia, the son of Robert Edward Lee, an army officer, and Mary Ann Randolph Custis. After an early education in local private schools, Custis Lee (as he was commonly called) entered West Point in 1850 and graduated first in the class of 1854. His academic performance entitled him to an assignment in the elite Corps of Engineers, in which he was commissioned second lieutenant. During the remaining years before the Civil War, he worked on river and harbor improvement projects in various parts of the country. When the attack on Fort Sumter brought Virginia's secession, Lee was serving as a first lieutenant and assistant to the chief engineer of the army in his bureau in Washington. Lee resigned his U.S. Army commission on 2 May 1861 and offered his services to Virginia. On 1 July 1861 he was commissioned captain of engineers in the Confederate army, and that month and the next he worked at designing and directing the construction of the fortifications at Richmond. Other duty beckoned, however, when on 31 August he was selected by President Jefferson Davis to serve as his aide-de-camp. For this purpose, Lee was given the rank of colonel of cavalry (though his duties had no more to do with the mounted arm of the service than with any other).

In his new role Lee often performed important duties for Davis. In September 1861 he was sent to inspect the state of the defenses at Norfolk, Virginia—the Confederacy's only real naval base—which was sorely threatened. The next month he was dispatched to Wilmington, North Carolina, to help set in order the defenses of that vital blockade-running port city. During the Peninsula campaign the following spring, he carried messages of the greatest importance from Davis to General Joseph E. Johnston. In June 1863 his faithful service was rewarded with promotion to brigadier general. That fall his father consulted him for advice concerning the reorganization of the Army of Northern Virginia's artillery corps.

Despite all this and other consistent evidence of his position as Davis's most trusted military aide, Lee remained dissatisfied. He urgently desired transfer to a combat command and communicated this desire to Davis. The president, however, believed Lee's services indispensable to him, and so Lee remained trapped in a prestigious, important, and unglamorous assignment. In March 1864 he led a scratch force in opposing a cavalry raid led by Union colonel Ulrich Dahlgren. In October Lee was given the task of organizing Richmond's remaining military-age male population—essentially War Department clerks and skilled workers in war industries—into a Local Defense Brigade. At the same time, he was promoted to major general (20 Oct. 1864). Amid the frequent alarms of the winter of 1864–1865, as the tremors of impending collapse began to shake the Army of Northern Virginia, Lee was frequently called to do duty with his brigade in the Petersburg trenches. When the Army of Northern Virginia was forced to flee Richmond on 2 April 1865, Lee led a division in the retreat. This improvised unit, composed of his own brigade, some regular troops, and various sailors and marines of the now defunct Confederate navy, was attached to General Richard S. Ewell's II Corps. On the fifth day of the retreat, 6 April 1865, this corps became separated from the rest of the army and was beset by the closely pursuing Union infantry and cavalry. At Sayler's Creek, Lee fought his first and last battle in the field. Though his personal valor and skill excited the admiration of his superior, the result was never in doubt. Most of the II Corps, including Lee's division, was captured. While the majority of his comrades would spend a period of captivity at Fort Warren in Boston Harbor, Lee's case was different. The dangerous illness of his mother elicited compassionate treatment from his captors, and he was paroled almost at once.

That October, with the war over, Lee became professor of military and civil engineering at the Virginia Military Institute. After a little over five years in that position, he succeeded his father (who had died on 12 Oct. 1870) as president of Washington College (now Washington and Lee University), 1 February 1871. He is credited with making a number of beneficial reforms and improvements during his more than a quarter-century as president. On 1 July 1897 he resigned, retiring to "Ravensworth" in Fairfax County, Virginia. He died there, never having married.

• For further information on Lee see William C. Davis, *Jefferson Davis: The Man and His Hour* (1991); Davis, ed., *The Confederate General* (1991); Shelby Foote, *The Civil War: A Narrative* (3 vols., 1958–1974); Douglas Southall Freeman, *Lee's Lieutenants: A Study in Command* (3 vols., 1942–1944); E. B. Long and Barbara Long, *The Civil War Day by Day: An Almanac, 1861–1865* (1971); U.S. War Department, *The War of the Rebellion: A Compilation of the Official Records of the Union and Confederate Armies* (128 vols., 1880–1901); Ezra J. Warner, *Generals in Gray: The Lives of the Confederate Commanders* (1959); and Steven E. Woodworth, *Davis and Lee at War* (1995).

STEVEN E. WOODWORTH

LEE, Gypsy Rose (9 Jan. 1914–26 Apr. 1970), striptease artist, burlesque entertainer, and writer, was born Rose Louise Hovick in Seattle, Washington, the daughter of John Olaf Hovick, a newspaper reporter, and Rose Thompson. Lee's parents divorced when she was about four years old. She and her sister June (who later became screen actress June Havoc) lived with their mother's father in Seattle, where Rose Hovick, a prototypical stage mother, drove the girls into a show business career. They began by performing at several lodges to which their grandfather belonged. Lee described herself as a child as being "big for my age and more than just chubby" with the nickname of "Plug." Lee once described her childhood to a reporter: "At that time I wanted to die—just for the vacation."

Lee's mother succeeded in getting her daughters into vaudeville, and Lee and her sister eventually earned as much as $1,250 a week as a song-and-dance act, until June ran off with a chorus boy when she was thirteen. Vaudeville was by then in its last days, and in desperation Lee's mother booked the act, now called Rose Louise and Her Hollywood Blondes, into a burlesque theater. Lee drifted into stripping, obtaining valuable professional advice from an artiste billed as Tessie, the Tassel Twirler. With her mother's approval, she billed herself as Gypsy Rose Lee.

Lee first appeared in New York City in 1931 at Minsky's, where a fortuitous police raid garnered her considerable front-page publicity. She soon emerged as a national celebrity, her intelligence and sophisticated wit distinguishing her from other strippers. *Variety* (29 Apr. 1970) noted that the secret of her stripping was the investiture of a sense of humor; her "peeling was languorous, inviting, and she took distinct pains 'not to stir the animal in men.'" Even though her act featured very little exposure of flesh, she soon became the most famous stripper in America, chatting with her audiences and thereby charming instead of titillating them. Theater manager Florenz Ziegfeld cast her in a small part in *Hotcha* and subsequently used her as a showgirl in his *Follies*. She later appeared in George White's *Scandals* and at Billy Rose's Casino de Paree. H. L. Mencken coined the term "ecdysiast" to describe her act. A tall woman (five feet nine inches), she divested herself of her garments with such panache that the French, avoiding the crass language associated with burlesque, dubbed her "une deshabilleuse." Lee herself said, "Did you ever hold a piece of candy or a toy in front of a baby—just out of his reach? Notice how he laughs. That's your strip audience."

In 1938 Lee made her film debut as Louise Hovick, strippers then considered by the censoring Hays Office as unfit to appear in films, but the *New York Times* reviewer recognized her and suggested it was "the first time a strip-tease artist has appeared before her public without revealing anything, not even her ability." In 1939–1940 she stripped out of a $2,500 costume in the *Streets of Paris* show at the New York World's Fair. During this engagement columnist Walter Winchell asked her to write a guest column for him. She enjoyed the assignment so much that she began a mystery novel. Published in 1941, *The G-String Murders* immediately became a bestseller, and overnight Lee began to participate in the city's varied literary scene. She wrote articles, most of them slightly naughty descriptions of life on the burlesque stage, for the *New Yorker, Harper's Bazaar, American Mercury, Variety*, and *Collier's*, as well as another, less successful mystery novel, *Mother Finds a Body*, published in 1942.

All the while Lee had continued her burlesque career, and after the New York City burlesque houses were closed by order of Mayor Fiorello La Guardia in March 1942, she appeared on Broadway in *Star and Garter*. In 1943 *The G-String Murders* was released as the film *Lady of Burlesque*, exciting considerable controversy and a ban by the National Legion of Decency. That same year Lee's comic play, *The Naked Genius*, a revision of an earlier, unproduced comedy called *Ghost in the Woodpile*, opened and toured to savagely critical reviews. Nevertheless producer Mike Todd, with whom Lee was having an affair, brought the show to Broadway. *The Naked Genius* ran for only one month, the critics having called it "an appalling mess, a silly and vulgar and embarrassing hodge-podge that wastes the time and withers the talent of a great many actors." Nonetheless, 20th Century–Fox purchased the film rights for $150,000. Also in 1943 Lee appeared in the film *Stage Door Canteen*, performing a satire of a striptease. Her success enabled Lee to acquire a house, located at 154 East Sixty-third Street in Manhattan, that had twenty-six rooms and featured marble floors, seven baths, a greenhouse, an elevator, and a small outdoor pool.

In 1957 Lee published her autobiography, *Gypsy: A Memoir*, in which she describes her early life and career in somewhat idealized terms. Bemused critics noted that the main figure was not Lee but her mother and called it a "slickly professional job" of delineation—to be expected from such a practiced hand at circumscribed self-exposure. Others pointed out that Gypsy Rose Lee did not create the public's taste but rather mirrored it with a certain happy elegance. Other reactions included "Fast, funny, tremendously quotable," "an honest, unsparing document, extraordinary Americana, a close-up on a doughty tribe," "friendly, honest, sad, funny and wry. . . . Good stuff." The memoir sold well and in 1959 was adapted by Arthur Laurents into a Broadway musical with lyrics by Stephen Sondheim, score by Jule Styne, staging and choreography by Jerome Robbins, scenery by Jo Mielziner, all under the production of David Merrick and Leland Hayward. Starring Ethel Merman as Lee's mother, *Gypsy* ran for 702 performances. Critic Walter Kerr called it "the best damn musical I've seen in years"; other reviewers were almost unanimously in agreement. Lee's considerable income from the show allowed her to indulge her penchant for filling her Manhattan townhouse with antiques. A film version, starring Rosalind Russell and Natalie Wood, appeared in 1962.

Lee attempted another stage version of her life with her solo show, *A Curious Evening with Gypsy Rose Lee*, which she premiered in Palm Beach in 1958. She revised the show and opened it on Broadway in 1961 to critical and popular indifference. She took the show to Los Angeles later that year and moved permanently to a seventeen-room house in Beverly Hills. For a time she hosted a syndicated television talk show, which was frequently blipped by network censors. She later toured with United Service Organizations (USO) shows, passing out her Kosher Fortune Cookies containing suggestive messages. She died of cancer at age fifty-six in Los Angeles.

Lee had been married three times, first to Arnold R. Mizzy, a dental supply manufacturer, whom she wed in 1937; they divorced in 1941. She married an actor, William Alexander Kirkland, in 1942, separated from him three months later, and divorced him in 1944. Her last marriage was to an artist, Julio de Diego, in 1948; they divorced in 1955. Her son Erik Lee, thought to have been fathered by William Kirkland, was in fact offspring of Lee and film director Otto Preminger, who adopted him in 1971.

As her *Newsweek* obituary (11 May 1970) pointed out, Lee had actually bared less of her body than any other striptease headliner. She delighted audiences with her "polished comic brass," which, combined with her magnetic, statuesque persona, made her the epitome of the stripper for more than three decades. Her sophisticated sexiness was a matter of shrewd packaging. As one co-worker noted, "She had a product to sell, like a car. She could twist any statement into a sexy one. Basically, she knew how to handle men." As Lee put it herself, "You don't have to be naked to look naked. You just have to think naked" (*Life*, 27 May 1957).

• Erik Preminger inherited his mother's collection of scrapbooks; the Billy Rose Theatre Collection at the New York Public Library for the Performing Arts, Lincoln Center, holds a clipping file. Lee's many articles include "My Burlesque Customers," *American Mercury*, Nov. 1942; "Mother and the Man Named Gordon," "Mother and the Knights of Pythias," and "Just Like Children Leading Normal Lives," all in the *New Yorker*, 20 Nov., 10 Apr., and 3 July 1943; "Stranded in Kansas City; or, A Fate Worse Than Vaudeville" and "Up the Runway to Minsky's," both in *Harper's*, Apr. and May 1957; and "Scrapbook Views of a Smart Stripper," *Life*, 27 May 1957. Lee's autobiography, *Gypsy*, remains the single most detailed treatment of her life and career. Erik Preminger published *Gypsy and Me* in 1984, and June Havoc presented her story in *Early Havoc* in 1959. Articles about Lee include Kyle Crichton, "Strip to Fame," *Collier's*, 19 Dec. 1936; John Richmond, "Gypsy Rose Lee, Striptease Intellectual," *American Mercury*, Jan. 1941; J. P. McEvoy, "More Tease Than Strip," *Variety*, 4 June 1941; "Gypsy Rose Lee, a General Collector," *Hobbies*, Oct. 1942; Richard E. Lauterbach, "Gypsy Rose Lee," *Life*, 14 Dec. 1942; "Gypsy Rose and Muse," *Cue*, 12 July 1943; "Gypsy Rose Lee," *House & Garden*, Dec. 1943; "Gypsy Joins the Carny," *Life*, 6 June 1949; "The Men Laugh . . . Hardest with Women in the Audience," *Newsweek*, 29 Apr. 1957; "Tips by an Improbable Pro," *Life*, 29 June 1959; and Stanley Richard, "A Visit with Gypsy Rose Lee," *Theatre*, Jan. 1960. Obituaries are in *National Affairs*, 11 May 1970; the *New York Times*, 28 Apr. 1970, followed by a eulogy on 10 May; *Los Angeles Times*, 27 Apr. 1970; and *Variety*, 29 Apr. 1970.

STEPHEN M. ARCHER

LEE, Henry (29 Jan. 1756–25 Mar. 1818), cavalry officer in the American Revolution popularly known as "Light-Horse Harry" Lee, was born at Leesylvania, Prince William County, Virginia, the son of Henry Lee, a planter, and Lucy Grymes. As the eldest son in an important family, he realized early in life that he was expected to take a leading role in the affairs of his colony. He prepared by studying for three years at the College of New Jersey (now Princeton University), where he enjoyed debate and the Latin classics and graduated at the age of seventeen in 1773. He intended to study law in London, but growing American animosity toward British colonial policies in the 1770s diverted his attention. When the American Revolution began, he declared for America, as did all the Lees of Virginia, and he determined upon a soldier's life. Twice, in 1775 and 1776, he solicited the aid of a neighbor, George Washington, to secure a position as General Charles Lee's aide-de-camp but without success. Finally, on 13 June 1776, upon the nomination of Patrick Henry, he was appointed captain of a company of cavalry in Colonel Theodorick Bland's recently organized regiment.

Summoned by General Washington later that year to join the Continental army, Bland and Lee's cavalrymen reached army headquarters at Morristown, New Jersey, in February 1777 and were reorganized as the First Continental Light Dragoon Regiment. Immediately Lee's company was detached by the commander in chief to forage, picket, and scout, duties that Lee performed so well that he continued them for a year. In March 1778 he was offered by Washington a position as aide-de-camp, but he declined because he preferred to stay with the cavalry. He was promoted to major by Congress on 7 April 1778 and given command of an independent partisan corps consisting of two troops of horse, augmented on 13 July 1779 by a third troop and a small body of infantry. As commander of this corps, which came to be known as "Lee's Legion," Lee acquired the sobriquet Light-Horse Harry. On 19 August, with great skill and bravery, he attacked a British garrison at Paulus Hook, New Jersey, catching it completely off guard and capturing 158 prisoners at a loss of only five of his own men. For this brilliant operation, he was presented a gold medal by Congress.

In February 1780 Lee was ordered to South Carolina to assist Continental forces in attempting to defend Charleston. Before he could depart, the city surrendered, and he remained with Washington throughout the summer. In October he was again ordered south, to join General Nathanael Greene, who was replacing Horatio Gates as commander in that theater. Promoted to lieutenant colonel on 6 November 1780, he rode southward and in January 1781 joined Greene in South Carolina. After conducting an unsuccessful raid on Georgetown, South Carolina, he was with Greene in February during his famous retreat across North Carolina to Virginia, covering the rear of the American army and engaging in spirited skirmishing with Banastre Tarleton's "Tory Legion." On 25 February Lee attacked a body of 300 Loyalist militiamen under Colonel John Pyle, killing one hundred and wounding most of the others, after riding alongside them under the pretense that he was leading a troop of British dragoons. Five days later, at Clapp's Mill, he laid an ambush for Tarleton, killing twenty enemy troopers before withdrawing. He was posted on the left flank of Greene's army at Guilford Court House, 15 March 1781, where he proved himself more than a match for Tarleton's dragoons but could not prevent an American defeat. Following Lee's advice after the battle, Greene adopted the unusual strategy of bypassing British commander Charles, Lord Cornwallis, and marching into South Carolina to attack British posts there. While Greene maneuvered against Lieutenant Colonel Francis, Lord Rawdon's army, Lee was detached to capture enemy positions at Forts Watson, Motte, and Granby and the town of Augusta, Georgia. Successful in all these operations, he rejoined Greene in June at the siege of Ninety-Six. On 8 September, at Eutaw Springs, he likely saved Greene from defeat, and in the pursuit of the enemy that followed he captured large numbers of soldiers. While visiting Washington's camp at Yorktown, Virginia, he observed the surrender of Cornwallis on 19 October 1781, then left the army for a well-deserved furlough home.

Throughout the campaign of 1781, Lee had shown himself a remarkably competent strategist and battlefield leader. Greene recognized his merits, declaring that he was the one soldier most responsible for the successful outcome of the fighting. Lee, however, believed that his contributions had not been adequately recognized and in February 1782 bitterly resigned his commission. A month later he married his second cousin, Matilda Lee, heiress of Stratford Hall. They had four children. Lee entered politics in 1785, when he was elected to the Virginia House of Delegates. That same year he also was chosen to represent Virginia in the Continental Congress, where he served three years. In 1788, as a member of the Virginia convention that ratified the federal Constitution, he earnestly argued for the document and won distinction for his eloquence. Thereafter an ardent Federalist, he was a member of the Virginia legislature, 1789–1791, and governor of the state, 1791–1794. As governor, he was dismayed by Virginians' opposition to the policies of the Washington administration, and for a time he seemed to agree with his constituents. But in the end he supported the president, fearing that partisan bickering was about to result in civil war. Through all these years, Lee's heart was with the military, particularly after his wife's death in 1790. In 1792 he was seriously considered by President Washington to command an army against Northwest Indians but lost the appointment to Anthony Wayne, because the president feared that more senior officers would refuse to serve under him. Feeling "cheated," Lee almost joined the French revolutionary army in 1793 but was talked out of his scheme by Washington. Instead, in 1793 he married Anne Hill Carter; they had five children, the youngest of whom was Robert E. Lee.

In 1794, while Lee was still governor, the Whiskey Rebellion broke out in western Pennsylvania, and in August President Washington offered him command of a militia army to suppress the insurrection. He accepted, leading 15,000 men against the insurgents, who were so overawed that they capitulated in November without bloodshed. In 1798, when war between America and France seemed imminent, Lee was appointed a major general of the U.S. Army, but he never saw active service. A year later he was elected to the House of Representatives as a Federalist. When Washington died in 1799, Lee was assigned the task of drafting a congressional resolution of respect for the president. In it he first inscribed his now-famous description of Washington as "first in war, first in peace and first in the hearts of his countrymen." Later chosen to deliver a memorial oration in Philadelphia commemorating Washington's services, he repeated the statement on 26 December 1799. At the end of his congressional term, in 1801, he retired from public life. Living with his family at Stratford Hall over the next few years, he proved to be an inept plantation manager and was harassed by creditors. He subsisted on a meager income that came nowhere near covering expenses and was constantly humiliated by his inability to maintain his family.

In 1808 Lee was temporarily relieved of these oppressions of spirit by President Thomas Jefferson, who, because of deteriorating relations with Great Britain, mobilized the states' militias, reactivating Lee's army commission as major general. Despite his health, which was poor, and his finances, which were worse, Lee donned his uniform and spent a year organizing the Virginia militia for a war that did not come. Finally bankrupted in 1809, he was sent to debtor's prison, where he languished for a year and almost died of mortification. Desperately seeking diversion, he wrote his *Memoirs of the War in the Southern Department of the United States*, which he published in 1812. Upon his release from prison, he moved his family from Stratford Hall to a small house in Alexandria. He importuned President James Madison to reactivate his commission as a major general upon the outbreak of the War of 1812 but without success. On 27 July 1812 he happened to be in Baltimore when a riot broke out against an antiwar Federalist newspaper, the *Federal Republican*, and its editor, Alexander C. Hanson. Attempting to defend his friend Hanson and his property, Lee was arrested and put in jail. That night he was attacked in his cell by a mob and severely beaten. His health broken, he moved to the West Indies in 1813 but never fully recovered. Trying to return home to Virginia, he died at "Dungeness," on Cumberland Island, Georgia, the home of descendants of Nathanael Greene, his old comrade, and was buried there. In 1913 he was reinterred in the Lee Chapel at Washington and Lee University.

Lee was a great cavalryman, intelligent and resourceful, who provided his commanders with reliable information and provisions. Also, he was adept at surprising enemy detachments and maneuvering rapidly to escape from harm's way. He owed his battlefield triumphs to both his family's military tradition and his own fine moral character.

• Lee's correspondence is in the Lee Family Papers, Stratford Hall and the Virginia State Library in Richmond; the Henry Lee Papers, Alexander Hamilton Papers, James Madison Papers, Thomas Jefferson Papers, and George Washington Papers, the Library of Congress; and the Nathanael Greene Papers, New York Public Library and the William L. Clements Library at the University of Michigan. The best biographies are Thomas E. Templin, "Henry 'Light Horse Harry' Lee: A Biography" (Ph.D. diss., Univ. of Kentucky, 1975); and Thomas Boyd, *Light-Horse Harry Lee* (1931). Less useful are Cecil B. Hartley, *Life of Major General Henry Lee* (1859); and Noel B. Gerson, *Light-Horse Harry: A Biography of Washington's Great Cavalryman, General Henry Lee* (1966). Charles Royster, *Light-Horse Harry Lee and the Legacy of the American Revolution* (1981), is a sophisticated character study. See also Philander D. Chase, "The Early Career of 'Light Horse Harry' Lee" (M.A. thesis, Duke Univ., 1968); and Leonard E. Richardson, "The Military Career of Light Horse Harry Lee in the South, 1781" (M.A. thesis, Univ. of Tennessee, 1966). Lee's place in the Lee family is described in Burton J. Hendrick, *The Lees of Virginia: Biography of a Family* (1935). For background on the southern campaign, see Russell F. Weigley, *The Partisan War: The South Carolina Campaign of 1780–1782* (1970).

PAUL DAVID NELSON

LEE, Henry (28 May 1787–30 Jan. 1837), politician and writer, was born at "Stratford Hall," Westmoreland County, Virginia, the son of Henry "Light-Horse Harry" Lee, a politician and army general, and Matilda Lee. Lee attended Washington Academy (Lexington, Va.) and the College of William and Mary (1807–1808). From 1810 to 1813 he represented Westmoreland County in the Virginia House of Delegates, and he served on the Canadian frontier as a major in the Thirty-sixth U.S. Infantry during the War of 1812. After the war, President James Madison offered Lee the office of assistant inspector general of the southern division, but Lee declined. In 1816 he unsuccessfully ran for a congressional seat.

In 1817 Lee married the wealthy Anne Robinson McCarty and posted a $60,000 bond as guardian of her seventeen-year-old sister Elizabeth. At the birth of his only child, Margaret, in 1818, Lee was described as "a gentleman of great fortune & talents—more distinguished perhaps than any young man in Virginia for excellence of various sorts." After the death of Lee's father in 1818, Francis Walker Gilmer, aware of Lee's predilection toward dissipation, advised him to utilize his talents and the Lee library on a long-term literary project, such as "a history of our country, or of a particular epoch" (Armes, p. 374).

After Margaret's accidental death in 1820, the grief-stricken Anne slipped into opium addiction, and her husband was, in his own words, "surprised into adultery" with Elizabeth. She notified her stepfather in November 1820 of her apparent pregnancy, and Richard Stuart immediately resumed his guardianship over her. Rumors of Lee's adultery and incest, and even infanticide, began to circulate in early 1821, and he mortgaged his estate in March in an attempt to settle his guardianship accounts. He sold the plantation in June to his old classmate, William Clarke Somerville, who also later purchased Stratford Hall's library, furnishings, and some family heirlooms. Lee's father had earned his nickname "Light-Horse Harry" for his military exploits during the revolutionary war, and after the adultery and incest rumors became widespread Henry, Jr., became known as "Black-Horse Harry."

Lee then moved to Fredericksburg and belatedly commenced a literary career with a spirited answer to William Johnson's *Sketches of the Life and Correspondence of General Greene* (1822), which was critical of Light-Horse Harry Lee's revolutionary exploits. While researching *The Campaign of 1781 in the Carolinas: With Remarks, Historical and Critical on Johnson's Life of Greene* (1824) and beginning a new edition of his father's memoirs, Lee began corresponding with the secretary of war, to whom he successfully recommended the West Point application of his youngest half brother, Robert E. Lee. John C. Calhoun agreed to support Lee's proposed newspaper, the *American Gazette and Literary Journal*, but it never saw publication, despite Thomas Jefferson's patronage. After John Quincy Adams's election, Lee obtained, through Calhoun's influence, the position of assistant postmaster general. Secretary of State Henry Clay complained to the president when antiadministration newspaper essays were attributed to Lee.

By 1825 Lee had begun a history of the War of 1812, about which he wrote to Jefferson and Madison. He visited Jefferson at "Monticello" in late June 1826 but was unable to examine his papers before Jefferson's death on 4 July of that year. That summer and fall Lee traveled to New York and Canada to gather materials on the war's northern campaigns. Seeking information on the war in the south, he opened a correspondence with Andrew Jackson, whom he greatly admired.

After *United States Telegraph* editor Duff Green promised in November 1826 to fund Lee's publication of a popular biography of Jackson, Lee decided to relocate closer to the general and his papers. He resigned his government post and wrote to Jackson, "Homer travelled for wisdom from Greece to Egypt, & I may afford to journey from Virginia to Tennessee for truth." Lee and his wife arrived in Nashville in May 1827.

Lee was soon frustrated by Jackson's refusal to divulge confidential letters of living correspondents and by Jackson's commitment to John Henry Eaton's ongoing abridgement of Eaton and John Reid's 1817 biography. But Jackson did provide Lee with enough material to complete preliminary and final drafts of Jackson's life. He also published newspaper pieces, including one by "Jefferson" in the *Nashville Republican*, reprinted as *A Vindication of the Character and Public Services of Andrew Jackson . . .* (1828). Lee accompanied Jackson on his triumphant return to New Orleans in January 1828 and drafted the general's addresses there, according to Adams, who described them as "answers of cold and high-wrought rhetorician eloquence . . . in an ambitious and court-dress style" (Adams, vol. 7, p. 479).

After Jackson's election as president, Lee helped write his first inaugural address and hoped for a major State Department appointment. His chief rival, James A. Hamilton, convinced Jackson that the Senate would oppose Lee's interim appointment to any foreign ministry. Lee was named U.S. consul at Algiers, which he reluctantly accepted. The Lees left New York in August 1829 and arrived at Algiers in October. The Senate unanimously rejected Lee's nomination in March 1830, however, complicating Lee's precarious financial situation.

Upon the arrival in August of Commodore David Porter, Jackson's new appointee, Lee left for Europe after unsuccessfully soliciting the office of negotiator of a Turkish-American treaty. He toured Italy with his wife before settling in Paris in February 1831. There he drafted the mean-spirited *Observations on the Writings of Thomas Jefferson* (1832) in response to Thomas Jefferson Randolph's *Memoir, Correspondence, and Miscellanies from the Papers of Thomas Jefferson* (4 vols., 1829), which included disparagements of Light-Horse Harry Lee.

As Lee finally broke with the administration in 1833 and 1834, he completed the first half of his last major work, *Life of the Emperor Napoleon, with an Appendix, Containing an Examination of Sir W. Scott's "Life of Napoleon Banaparte"; and a Notice of the Principal Errors of Other Writers, Respecting His Character and Conduct*. Published in London in 1834 and in New York in 1835, this work was originally inspired by a chance meeting with Napoleon's mother in Italy. In dire financial need, Lee obtained, on the security of American consul John C. Brent in Paris, a loan to cover the expenses of his second volume, which he did not live to complete. His health broken by impoverishment, Lee succumbed to influenza in Paris during an epidemic. The first volume of his work on Napoleon was republished in London and Paris in 1837, after his death, with corrections and additional material as *The Life of the Emperor Napoleon Bonaparte down to the Peace of Tolentino and the Close of His First Campaign in Italy*. Anne Lee was barely able to gather and send home his remaining papers before her own drug-induced death in 1840. Their executor, Charles Carter Lee, never found Lee's completed life of Jackson but did pass on the draft returned from Paris, from which Amos Kendall drew extensively for his *Life of Andrew Jackson, Private, Military, and Civil. With Illustrations* (1843–1844).

Lee was proud, intemperate, opportunistic, and genuinely talented. Apparently repentant of his 1820 adultery, he appeared to be ever afterward faithful to his wife and was always resentful of his treatment by polite society. His last years were embittered by his perception that he was as much used by his political friends as abused by his enemies. He generally prostituted his rhetorical and literary talents for partisan purposes or wasted them on personal feuds. His historical writings, ranging from forceful and elegant to malicious and extravagant, were soundly based in original sources but too often animated by contemporary controversy and unbridled emotion. Even so, Jackson himself wrote to their mutual friend, William Berkeley Lewis, in May 1839, "I have too great a respect for his memory and high talents as a writer to permit any thing from me that could in the least derogate from either."

• The manuscript draft of Lee's Andrew Jackson biography is in the Jackson papers at the Library of Congress and was printed as *Occasional Pamphlet*, Tennessee Presidents Trust, no. 3 (1992). Some of Lee's correspondence is in the collected papers of Andrew Jackson, James Madison, John C. Calhoun, and John Marshall. Other Lee papers are preserved at the Virginia Historical Society and the Jessie Ball du Pont Memorial Library at Stratford Hall, owned by the Robert E. Lee Memorial Association. Lee's earliest publication was a 28 Oct. 1816 campaign broadside, *To the Electors of the Congressional District Composed of the Counties of Stafford, King George, Westmoreland, Richmond, Northumberland and Lancaster*. The best biographical treatments of Lee are in Ethel Armes, *Stratford Hall* (1936), and Paul C. Nagel, *The Lees of Virginia* (1990). He also appears in Lee family histories by Edmund Jennings Lee, *Lee of Virginia, 1642–1892* (1895), Burton J. Hendrick, *The Lees of Virginia* (1935), and Cazenove Gardner Lee, Jr., *Lee Chronicle*, comp. and ed. Dorothy Mills Parker (1957). Lee's political activities are noted in John Quincy Adams, *Memoirs* (1874–1877), and Jackson biographies by James Parton (1860), Marquis James (1933–1937), and Robert V. Remini (1977–1984). His writings are briefly considered in Merrill D. Peterson, *The Jefferson Image in the American Mind* (1960), and Richard B. Davis, *Intellectual Life in Jefferson's Virginia* (1972). A death notice was printed in the Washington, D.C., *National Intelligencer*, 20 Mar. 1837.

MARK A. MASTROMARINO

LEE, Ivy Ledbetter (16 July 1877–9 Nov. 1934), publicist, was born in Cedartown, Georgia, the son of James Wideman Lee, a Methodist minister, and Emma Ledbetter. He studied at Emory College but finished his A.B. at Princeton in 1898. He attended Harvard Law School for one semester but lacked the finances to continue.

Lee freelanced for newspapers in college and began work as a reporter in 1899 for the *New York Journal*, followed by the *New York Times* and *New York World*. In 1901 he married Cornelia Bigelow. They had three children, two of whom later worked for Lee. In 1903 he quit the *World* to work for Seth Low's losing mayoral reelection campaign, during which he met George Parker, a journalist who was a close associate of Grover Cleveland and the conservative, gold-standard wing of the Democratic party. After working for the Democratic National Committee during the 1904 presidential campaign, the two journalists formed Parker & Lee, the second public relations firm established in the United States. Lee's most important client was the Pennsylvania Railroad. In 1908 he left the firm to work exclusively for the railroad, though he later took a leave of absence to set up the European offices of Harris, Winthrop, & Company, a Wall Street brokerage firm. Lee returned to the railroad in 1912 as executive assistant to the president. Lee advocated openness

to the press, a direct style of press relations to get the company's message across: "Shaping their affairs so that when placed before the public they will be approved and placing them before the public in the most favorable light." In 1914 he won a freight rate increase for the Pennsylvania, Baltimore & Ohio, and New York Central railroads from the Interstate Commerce Commission.

In September 1913 the United Mineworkers of America struck the coal mines of Colorado. The leading firm was Colorado Fuel & Iron, whose principal stockholder was John D. Rockefeller, Sr. The dispute led to the Ludlow Massacre of 20 April 1914 in which company men fired on the workers; twenty-four people died, including twelve children and two women. Public opinion placed responsibility on the Rockefellers, and John D. Rockefeller, Jr., sought Lee's services. Lee began moonlighting for the Rockefellers in the summer of 1914, became a full-time employee on 1 January 1915, and eventually became a director of CF&I.

Lee, using information supplied by the CF&I management, sent out a series of bulletins on the strike to the press and public figures, a tactic he had successfully used to win the rate increase. Intended to sway public opinion to the side of the mine owners, Lee's bulletins contained at least one clear error, reporting the annual salaries paid to UMWA organizers in Colorado as the salaries for only nine weeks of work. The error, of which Lee had prior knowledge, was not corrected until months later. Biographer Ray Eldon Hiebert noted, "Most of the bulletins contained matter which on the surface was true but which presented the facts in such a way as to give a total picture that was false" (p. 101). Lee was criticized by many, including Carl Sandburg, who called him a "paid liar"; Upton Sinclair referred to him in *The Brass Check* as "Poison Ivy Lee." Despite these attacks, Lee became very successful as the Rockefellers' agent. In April 1916 Lee left the exclusive employment of the family to open his own firm that represented the Rockefeller interests until after the death of John D. Rockefeller, Jr., in 1960.

The Rockefellers and other corporate clients benefited from Lee's careful management of the press, a trademark of his method since his days at the Pennsylvania Railroad. He opposed granting exclusive interviews but favored controlling the release of information himself. "He was an anxious gardener of the press, pruning and clipping, urging the growth of strong stories in one plot and stamping out poisonous news in another" (Hiebert, p. 118). The method was used with press releases on Rockefeller charitable contributions, the Rockefeller Foundation, and Williamsburg, Virginia. John D. Rockefeller, Jr.'s speeches on industrial relations, known as the Rockefeller Plan and largely based on advice from Mackenzie King, were widely publicized. (Contrary to popular opinion, Lee was not responsible for John D. Rockefeller, Sr.'s habit of giving away dimes.) As noted by Leonard W. Doob, author of an early work on propaganda, "Lee was able to construct this new image not by advertising the Standard Oil Company, but by making the country's press acquainted with the favorable aspects of that company and of Rockefeller himself" (p. 194). Lee controlled access while he encouraged the Rockefellers and other clients to meet periodically with the press to satisfy some of the demand for stories. His relations with the press were so close that the Associated Press had him review their file on Rockefeller for accuracy in 1923.

Lee, Harris, and Lee (1916–1919), its successor, Ivy Lee & Associates (1919–1933), and then Ivy Lee & T. J. Ross (1933–1960), included as clients many of the major American corporations: Anaconda, Chase National Bank, Phelps Dodge, United States Rubber, Armour, United Artists, Chrysler, and Standard Oil. Bethlehem Steel was another beneficiary, despite a losing campaign against a plan by the government to build its own armor plant in 1916. Bethlehem, under Lee's direction, prepared ads for more than 3,500 newspapers opposing the plan as wasteful and destructive of existing U.S. defense industries. A bill funding the plant was passed but never acted on, and Bethlehem Steel emerged with a new image as an honest and straightforward firm looking out for the public interest. Lee's activities extended to nonprofit agencies as well; he worked for the American Red Cross during the First World War, the Cathedral of Saint John the Divine, and the Henry Street Settlement, serving the last two without charge. A conservative Democrat, Lee continued to be involved in politics, working on John W. Davis's 1924 campaign for the presidency. In 1932, concerned that Franklin Delano Roosevelt was too close to the Left in the Democratic party, Lee promoted Chicago banker Melvin Alvah Traylor for the party's nomination.

Lee also represented foreign governments and interests in the United States, including Poland, Rumania, and American-Cuban sugar companies. He had a private meeting with Mussolini in 1923 and visited the Soviet Union several times. He interviewed every major Soviet leader except Stalin, who did not keep his appointment. Despite being an anticommunist, Lee campaigned hard and long for recognition of the Soviet Union by the United States, leading to charges that the U.S.S.R. was a client, which Lee always denied. The evidence available is inconclusive, and Lee's denials notwithstanding, Representative Hamilton Fish, Jr., investigating communist activities in the United States, labeled Lee a "notorious propagandist for Soviet Russia." In 1933, when recognition was extended, Maxim Litvinov sent Lee a telegram thanking him for his efforts.

Lee also worked for the American subsidiary of the German corporation I. G. Farben beginning in 1929 and, later, for I. G. Farben directly. He traveled to Germany in 1933 and 1934 to meet with several members of Hitler's government and with Hitler himself. He provided advice to I. G. Farben not only on improving the company's image but also the government's image. Lee advised that anti-Semitic and an-tireligious policies would never be viewed favorably in the United States as "it was just foreign to the American mentality." Lee eventually advised I. G. Farben to break with the Nazis and, when this did not occur, ended the relationship. Nevertheless, the House Un-American Activities Committee subpoenaed Lee to testify in a closed session in 1934 about his activities for I. G. Farben. In July HUAC released the transcripts of Lee's testimony. The timing was devastating, following closely Hitler's purge of 30 June. Press reports across the country accused Lee of being Hitler's press agent, though he was cleared of that charge by the committee. The damage was increased when Lee, who had advocated openness to the press, refused to make a statement. In late October he suffered a cerebral hemorrhage. Diagnosed as having a brain tumor, Lee died eleven days later in New York City. Despite all the work he had done for America's wealthiest families and largest corporations, Lee left an estate worth less than $24,000.

Lee is largely a forgotten figure today, despite being the model for many fictional publicity men, including J. Ward Morehouse in John Dos Passos's *The 42nd Parallel*. Modern corporations largely follow Lee's approach to public relations, and foreign governments regularly hire public relations firms to represent their interests, provoking little of the outcry that Lee's work encountered. Despite the fact that Lee began his career as a publicist earlier, advocated the same policies, and sometimes shared clients, Edward Bernays is usually credited with being the father of public relations. Lee's work is probably eclipsed because, unlike Bernays, he never published a book on public relations, though he published numerous articles and pamphlets, and several drafts for a book are among his papers.

• Lee's papers are at Princeton University. Lee's campaign book for Seth Low's 1903 mayoral race is *The City for the People: The Best Administration New York Ever Had* (1903). He also privately published *Memories of Uncle Remus* (1908) and *U.S.S.R.: A World Enigma*, a corrected edition of which was commercially published as *Present Day Russia* (1928). The Colorado bulletins were published as *Facts Concerning the Struggle in Colorado for Industrial Freedom* (1914); the authorship is usually credited to the Committee of Coal Mine Managers despite the fact that it was largely produced by Lee. For a contemporary assessment of Lee's (and Bernays's) work see Leonard W. Doob, *Propaganda: Its Psychology and Technique* (1935). A full-length biography is Ray Eldon Hiebert, *Courtier to the Crowd: The Story of Ivy Lee and the Development of Public Relations* (1966), which is sympathetic and knowledgeable, though largely uncritical. The extensive bibliography omits many works critical of Lee (they often do not deal exclusively with him), though these are cited in chap. 32, "Prosecution by the Critics." H. M. Gitelman, *Legacy of the Ludlow Massacre* (1988), and George S. McGovern and Leonard F. Guttridge, *The Great Coalfield War* (1972), also contain useful information. "The Image Makers" (1984), produced and directed by David Grubin as part of the television series "Walk through the 20th Century with Bill Moyers," is a video documentary on Lee and Bernays. An obituary is in the *New York Times*, 10 Nov. 1934.

ANDREW H. LEE

LEE, James Melvin (16 May 1878–17 Nov. 1929), journalist and journalism educator, was born in Port Crane, New York, the son of James Newell Lee, a Methodist minister, and Emma White. He graduated from Wyoming Seminary, Kingston, Pennsylvania, in 1896 and received his A.B. from Wesleyan University in 1900.

Lee was self-supporting in college, and among his first published articles were several for newspapers on how students were earning money for their college expenses. He later used this material for his first book, *How to Be Self-Supporting at College*, published in 1903.

Lee joined the news staff of the *Springfield* (Mass.) *Union* after his graduation from Wesleyan and taught English at Western Reserve Seminary in West Farmington, Ohio, the following year. In 1902 he became circulation manager of the *Oneonta* (New York) *Star*. He turned to magazine journalism completely in 1906 when he became editor of *Bohemian Magazine*. He was literary editor of *Circle Magazine* from 1907 to 1908, associate editor of *Leslie's Weekly* from 1908 to 1909, and editor of the magazine *Judge* from 1909 to 1912. He was married to Helen Wellner in 1908; and they had one child.

He became a lecturer in journalism at New York University in 1909 and was appointed director of NYU's journalism department in 1911, a position he retained until his death. He thus was one of the pioneers in journalism education, for the NYU program was one of the first, after those at the University of Wisconsin, which began in 1905, and the University of Missouri, which began in 1908. He was secretary of the American Association of Teachers of Journalism (now the Association for Education in Journalism and Mass Communication) in 1913 and president of that group in 1916–1917. He also was secretary of the International Association of Schools of Journalism from 1921 until his death and executive secretary of the Intercollegiate Newspaper Association from 1922 until his death. Lee established an annual lecture in memory of Don Mellett, the editor of the Canton, Ohio, *News*, who was murdered in 1926 after exposing vice in his city. Lee created a number of other scholarship funds as well.

Lee wrote the first textbook on the history of journalism. The book, which grew out of a course he was teaching, was published in 1917 and revised in 1923. William David Sloan, professor of journalism at the University of Alabama, wrote that while it was "not a very good work, it nevertheless incorporated a number of characteristics that became standard items in later textbooks" (p. 68). It thus was an important first step in establishing history of journalism courses as part of the journalism curriculum. Sloan criticizes Lee for explaining the present solely in terms of the past. Lee defended contemporary journalism and viewed the history of American journalism as one of continued progress. He responded to criticism of the press by saying in his history book that "the ethics of journalism to-day are higher than those of any other profes-

sion" (p. 443). *Editor & Publisher*, the trade magazine of the newspaper industry, said in its obituary of Lee that "wherever Dr. Lee went in the last twenty years, whether lecturing at the University of California or visiting in Germany, he preached of the sound ethics of American journalism."

Lee wrote two other books on journalism history: *America's Oldest Newspaper: The New York Globe* (1918) and *James Luby, Journalist* (1930). His other books include *Wordless Journalism in America* (1915), *Newspaper Ethics* (1915), *Instruction in Journalism in Institutions of Higher Education* (1918), *Opportunities in the Newspaper Business* (1919), and *Business Ethics* (1925). He edited *Business Writing* (1920).

Lee died suddenly, apparently from pneumonia, in New York City. In an editorial the day after his death, the *New York World* called him "one of the most distinguished teachers of journalism in the country." The *New York Evening Post* said "he brought a direct inspiration into almost twenty classes of young men and women who went into the profession." The *New York Times* carried a letter from a close friend of Lee's, Henry Edward Warner, a journalist with the Sunpapers in Baltimore and author of much poetry about the press. The letter said "to me as to thousands of others he was Jim, the friend of man, the patient mentor of youth, the continued friend of those who had passed through his institution." This, together with his pioneering in journalism education and authorship of the first history of journalism text, belongs in any assessment of his contributions.

• The best current account of Lee is in William David Sloan, ed., *Makers of the Media Mind: Journalism Educators and Their Ideas* (1990). Other sources are James Melvin Lee, *History of American Journalism* (1923); Edwin Emery and Joseph P. McKerns, "AEJMC: 75 Years in the Making—A History of Organizing for Journalism and Mass Communication Education in the United States," *Journalism Monographs*, no. 104 (Nov. 1987), pp. 11, 12, 82, 84; and the *New York Times*, 17 and 21 Nov. 1929. The 23 Nov. 1929 issue of *Editor & Publisher* has a lengthy obituary.

GUIDO H. STEMPEL III

LEE, Jarena (11 Feb. 1783–after 1849), evangelist and spiritual autobiographer, was born in Cape May, New Jersey. Although her birthplace stood in a free state, Cape May was entwined just enough by commerce and culture with Maryland's Eastern Shore and Virginia's northern borders that Lee probably was exposed at an early age to the inhumanities that characterized southern enslavement. The names and occupations of her parents are unknown. Details of her childhood and education are likewise sketchy. Both parents were free blacks, and poverty forced them to hire out their seven-year-old daughter as a domestic servant for a white family sixty miles away from home.

In the narratives of such nineteenth-century African Americans as Frederick Douglass, Harriet Wilson, and Harriet Jacobs, young African-American children are typically wrested from their parents or indentured to work full time in their master's household or fields. In an era that placed little premium on the education of blacks, most white women, and the landless working classes, Lee's admitted three months of formal schooling was not atypical. Just as the slave narrators are reticent about the processes of their education (often they acquire literacy despite the threat of punishment or death), Lee was likewise taciturn about her own education. Attesting to her intense piety, however, in later years she chiefly criticized her upbringing not for these material or intellectual deprivations but for the absence of religious instruction from her parents.

In 1804, after several months of profound spiritual anxiety, Lee moved from New Jersey to Philadelphia. There she labored as a domestic and worshiped among white congregations of Roman Catholics and mixed congregations of Methodists. On hearing an inspired sermon by the Reverend Richard Allen, founder of the Bethel African Methodist Episcopal Church, Lee joined the Methodists. She was baptized in 1807. Prior to her baptism, she experienced the various physical and emotional stages of conversion: terrifying visions of demons and eternal perdition; extreme feelings of ecstasy and depression; protracted periods of meditation, fasting, and prayer; ennui and fever; energy and vigor. In 1811 she married Joseph Lee, who pastored an African-American church in Snow Hill, New Jersey. They had six children, four of whom died in infancy.

After baptism Lee had received a vision that instructed her to preach the gospel, that is, interpret Scripture. Although she petitioned Allen in 1813 for the Methodists to formally recognize her as an evangelist, Methodist churches did not then ordain women as ministers. They limited female public speakers to affirming the sermons of the male minister by witnessing from their personal experiences or by encouraging their fellow worshipers to admit sin and be saved. Allen denied the request, and Lee checked her resolve to preach. She supported her husband in his life work and taught school after his death in 1817, also holding prayer meetings occasionally in rented rooms or friends' homes.

In an 1821 church service, Lee became so overcome by the Holy Spirit that she sermonized extemporaneously, without the elders' permission. This and subsequent sermons would establish her as an evangelist whose words could heal despairing penitents and embolden dying backsliders of any denomination. Lee's faith and conviction were so great that she could walk up to forty miles and preach at up to four or five assemblages in a day. Resourceful and improvisational, she was comfortable in every outdoor and indoor venue, including camp meetings, town halls, courthouses, and schoolrooms. Although she suffered from chronic infirmities as well as seasickness and exhaustion brought on by the discomforts of sea voyages and cross-country stages, Lee was a tireless steward. In a four-year period, for example, she traveled 1,600 miles, trudging over 200 of them on foot. In 1828 she traveled more than 2,000 miles, preaching over 200 sermons.

Central to Lee's appeal to audiences were her candor, wit, empathy, irony, humor, and willingness to criticize religious orthodoxy, as when she argued in her *Journal* (1849): "If the man may preach, because the Saviour died for him, why not the woman? seeing he died for her also. Is he not a whole Saviour, instead of a half one? as those who hold it wrong for a woman to preach, would make it seem to appear." So moved was Allen by Lee's charisma that he ordained her the first African-American woman to preach in the A.M.E. church. In 1836 she herself published *The Life and Religious Experiences of Jarena Lee, a Coloured Lady*, on her conversion and call to preaching. Her self-published 1849 narrative, *Religious Experience and Journal of Mrs. Jarena Lee, Giving an Account of Her Call to Preach the Gospel*, details this early history, along with specific encounters with congregations from Ohio to Maryland and the sexism and racism she endured.

Lee's work demonstrates how the Great Awakening, with its emphasis on public witnessing, oral expression, and an intimate relationship to God, appealed directly to African-American modes of worship. Her life and writings offer a rare glimpse into how female African-American evangelists during this period resisted religious oppression by traveling together, sharing lodging and provisions, minding each other's families and vicarious finances, and mentoring younger female preachers. Lee's narratives also present realistic portraits of the arduous demands that domestic labor, motherhood, marriage, poverty, poor health, and public censure placed on black women evangelists. Lee's texts and life define black Christianity without divorcing politics from piety. Lee risked her freedom in 1824 to evangelize in a slave state (Maryland). She likewise defied social propriety to comfort prisoners, paupers, and the rich alike, even jeopardizing her health in 1832 by traveling during a cholera epidemic. Throughout her career Lee continuously challenged bigotry by ministering, as she put it, "without distinction of sex, size, or color." In her 1849 narrative she describes Native Americans' attempts to preserve language, dress, and culture in spite of white Americans' endeavors to Christianize them. By combining slave narrative, captivity narrative, and spiritual narrative traditions, Lee's two books reveal the progress of the development of a national literature. The date and location of her death are unknown.

• The most detailed biographical information on Jarena Lee can be found in Phebe Davidson, "Jarena Lee," *Legacy: A Journal of American Women Writers* 10 (1993): 135–40; Constance Killian Escher and Carolyn DeSwarte Gifford, "Jarena Lee," in *Past and Promise: Lives of New Jersey Women*, compiled by the Women's Project of New Jersey, Inc. (1990); and William L. Andrews, *Sisters of the Spirit: Three Black Women's Autobiographies of the Nineteenth Century* (1986). Two important assessments of Lee's contribution to the early American autobiographical tradition are Frances Smith Foster, "Neither Auction Block nor Pedestal: 'The Life and Religious Experiences of Jarena Lee, a Coloured Lady,'" in *The Female Autograph*, ed. Domna Stanton (1984), and Foster, "Adding Color and Contour to Early American Self-Portraitures: Autobiographical Writings of Afro-American Women," in *Conjuring: Black Women, Fiction, and Literary Tradition*, ed. Marjorie Pryse and Hortense J. Spillers (1985). See also Carla Peterson, *"Doers of the Word": African-American Women Speakers and Writers in the North (1830–1880)* (1995), on Lee's erasure of her physical body in her narratives as a strategy to gain authority and to legitimize her preaching.

BARBARA MCCASKILL

LEE, Jason (28 June 1803–12 Mar. 1845), missionary and pioneer, was born near Stanstead, Vermont (now part of Quebec, Canada), the son of Daniel Lee, a farmer and former revolutionary war soldier, and Sarah Whittaker. The Lees had moved from Massachusetts to the vicinity of Stanstead five years before their son's birth, and there Daniel Lee continued his occupation as a farmer. Little is known about Jason Lee's early life and education, but it has been established that he was converted to Methodism in his early twenties. In 1829–1830 he lived in Wilbraham, Massachusetts, where he attended Wilbraham Academy for the purpose of receiving training as a Methodist preacher. With the encouragement of the academy's president, the Reverend Wilbur Fisk, Lee returned to the Stanstead area in 1830 to serve as a minister to Wesleyan Methodists who lived in the region. Two years later he was ordained a deacon in the Methodist Episcopal church, and by 1833 he had become an elder.

Lee was apparently attracted to the missionary activities of his denomination, in particular the church's efforts to convert Native Americans to Christianity. In response to his interest, church officials appointed him to lead a party of missionaries to the so-called Flathead country of what is now British Columbia. Together with his nephew Daniel Lee, also a Methodist clergyman, and three Methodist laymen, Lee joined the second western expedition of Nathaniel J. Wyeth and embarked from Independence, Missouri, on 28 April 1834.

Nearly five months later, on 15 September, Lee's party arrived at Fort Vancouver, but they appear to have encountered resistance to their establishment of a mission in the vicinity. Lee and three members of the group decided to go south, and in early October they settled at a site on the Willamette River, some ten miles northwest of what is now Salem, Oregon. After several years of missionary activity among local Native Americans, the group was joined in June 1837 by a Methodist physician, Elijah White, White's wife, and a young woman named Anna Maria Pittman, all of whom were from New York. Later that summer Lee and Pittman were married.

The activities of the mission expanded, and new outposts were established at two sites along the Columbia River, one near Fort Clatsop and the other at The Dalles. Meanwhile, both U.S. officials and settlers in Oregon had expressed an interest in establishing a territorial government. Such a government moved closer to reality in the winter of 1836–1837, when William Slacum, a U.S. Navy purser, conducted an investigation of the northwest coast. With the aid and encouragement of Slacum, Lee drew up a petition for the creation of a territorial government, and Slacum carried it back to Washington, D.C.

In late March 1838 Lee left his mission on the Willamette and set out for the East Coast, carrying with him a settler's petition for territorial government. En route, he learned that his wife and infant son had died during his absence. That fall Lee arrived in New York City, which he made his base of operations. In the following months he traveled widely through the Northeast and midatlantic region, encouraging support for his mission in Oregon and trying to attract additional participants. He also visited Washington, D.C., where he delivered the settlers' petition and spoke on its behalf to government officials.

By the fall of 1839 Lee had assembled a party of fifty Methodists, later known as "the Great Reinforcement," to accompany him back to Oregon. Among them was Lucy Thomson of Barre, Vermont, whom Lee had married in July. The party sailed from New York in October and arrived at the mouth of the Columbia River in May 1840. Lee resumed his role as director of Methodist missionary activities along the Columbia. Although his tenure presumably had wide support, he had disagreements with at least one mission member, White, who resigned and returned east in the summer of 1840.

Lee's declared main goal was still the same: to Christianize the Native-American population. However, it had now become clear that the population was resisting conversion to such an extent that further efforts in this direction seemed futile. By early 1841 missionary work had been put aside by Lee in favor of strengthening the various settlements, providing for the educational needs of the settlers, and pursuing the establishment of territorial government. Lee had now emerged as the major political figure in the region, and he led efforts in all these areas. He drew up the plan that created the Oregon Institute—later Willamette University—in 1842, and he was largely responsible for the provisional government that finally came into being in July 1843.

To secure further aid for his mission, Lee left Oregon for the East Coast in February 1844. As on his earlier trip east, ill fortune overtook him: en route he learned that the Methodist board of overseers, displeased with his work in Oregon, had relieved him of his post as head of missions there. Upon his arrival in New York in late May, Lee appealed the decision. The board subsequently exonerated him but refused to reappoint him to the post.

Broken in spirit, Lee's health also failed. He now had neither job nor family, for his second wife had died two years earlier and their daughter, the couple's only child, remained in Oregon. Lee left New York and returned to the Stanstead area in the early fall of 1844. That winter he contracted a severe cold and died the following March; he was buried in Stanstead.

More than half a century later, in June 1906, Lee's remains were reinterred in Salem, following a ceremony that hailed him as one of Oregon's leading pioneers.

Despite this public acknowledgment, Jason Lee has always been a controversial figure, and his decade-long role in Oregon's history continues to be debated by scholars. Many see both aspects of his work in a negative light. Although his conversion programs among Native Americans failed, his very efforts in this direction have made him suspect in an intellectual climate that views such attempts as wrongheaded and unethical. As for his political activities, these are criticized on two counts: he is seen by some as a chauvinist for promoting western settlement without regard for the native population that such settlement displaced, while others question the sincerity of his missionary efforts and suggest that colonization—and political power—were his goals from the outset. The debate will likely never be resolved.

• A modern assessment of Jason Lee's life and work is Robert J. Loewenberg, *Equality on the Oregon Frontier: Jason Lee and the Methodist Mission, 1834–43* (1976). Earlier accounts include Reverend A. Atwood, *The Conquerors: Historical Sketches of the American Settlement of the Oregon Country, Embracing Facts in the Life and Work of Rev. Jason Lee* (1907), and Cornelius J. Brosnan, *Jason Lee: Prophet of the New Oregon* (1932). For background information, see H. W. Scott, *History of the Oregon Country* (6 vols., 1924), and C. H. Carey, *History of Oregon* (1922). Details of the 1906 reinterment in Salem, together with the text of speeches made at the ceremony, can be found in the *Oregon Historical Society Quarterly*, Sept. 1906.

ANN T. KEENE

LEE, Jesse (12 Mar. 1758–12 Sept. 1816), Methodist preacher, was born in Prince George County, Virginia, the son of Nathaniel Lee and Elizabeth (maiden name unknown), farmers. Jesse's education was limited, but he learned to read and to respect the prayer book at a neighborhood school. He also cultivated a love and talent for music by attending a local singing school.

Lee's parents, active members of the Church of England, were people of high moral purpose. They came under the influence of Devereux Jarratt, an evangelical Anglican pastor in a nearby parish, and experienced a religious awakening in 1772. In 1774 the Lee family affiliated with a recently formed Methodist society led by Robert Williams, the first Methodist preacher in that area of Virginia. Thereafter, Methodist preachers regularly conducted services at the Lees' home when traveling through the region. Under Methodist tutelage, Jesse experienced a series of religious renewals in which, he later recalled, he "felt greatly quickened, and comforted with the Divine Presence." More than ever, he was devoted to doing the will of God in all things. In 1777 he moved to North Carolina to manage a widowed relative's farm. There he became a Methodist class leader, exhorter, and local preacher, giving his first sermon on November 17 1779.

In 1780 Lee was drafted into the North Carolina militia, but he had great difficulty answering the call. He wrote, "I weighed the matter over and over again, but my mind was settled; as a Christian and as a preacher of the gospel I could not fight. I could not reconcile it to myself to bear arms, or to kill one of my fellow creatures; however I determined to go, and to trust in the Lord. . . . " He discharged his military obligation as a wagon driver, as a sergeant of a small corps of pioneers who cleared and prepared the way for the main body of troops, and as an unofficial chaplain.

In 1782 Lee became a circuit-riding preacher for the Methodists in North Carolina and Virginia. In 1783 he was admitted on trial to the Virginia Conference and continued to preach for the next six years in North Carolina, Virginia, and Maryland. He was the first native Virginian to enter the ministry of the Methodist Episcopal church. In 1785 he became a companion to Francis Asbury, the premier leader and bishop of early American Methodism, on Asbury's southern preaching tour. Although Asbury and Lee had several significant differences of opinion, especially on matters of church organization, their friendship was constant.

A prominent leader in the spread of evangelical religion in the South, Lee is also credited with its expansion in the North. In 1789 Lee began a ministry in New England and was responsible for planting Methodism in that section of the nation. Until 1797 he preached and organized Methodist work in Connecticut, Rhode Island, Massachusetts, Vermont, New Hampshire, and Maine (at that time a part of Massachusetts). In 1790 he was ordained both deacon and elder. Recognizing Lee's gifts, Asbury enlisted him to serve as his traveling assistant in 1797, a position which Lee held until the General Conference of 1800, when he narrowly missed election to the episcopacy. False rumors that he had forced his services on Asbury were a major factor in his defeat. Lee returned to circuit preaching in New England and the South until 1815. In 1809 he was elected chaplain of the U.S. House of Representatives and was reelected at its four succeeding sessions. In 1814 he was elected chaplain of the U.S. Senate. When the House or the Senate were not in session, he was engaged in his itinerant ministry.

Lee was the author of *A Short History of the Methodists in the United States of America* (1810). This was the first published history of American Methodism and remains an invaluable source of information about its early formation. Lee also published two sermons and a biography of his brother titled *A Short Account of the Life and Death of the Rev. John Lee, A Methodist Minister in the United States of America* (1805).

Jesse Lee was a person of large stature; he was over six feet tall and weighed more than 250 pounds. He never married. Lee's death occurred as he was attending a camp meeting near Hillsborough, Maryland.

• For information about the life and accomplishments of Jesse Lee, see William H. Meredith, *Jesse Lee: A Methodist*

Apostle (1909); Leroy M. Lee, *The Life and Times of Jesse Lee* (1848); Minton Thrift, *Memoir of the Rev. Jesse Lee with Extracts from His Journals* (1823); William Warren Sweet, *Virginia Methodism: A History* (1955); and Emory S. Bucke, ed., *The History of American Methodism*, vol. 1 (1964).

CHARLES YRIGOYEN, JR.

LEE, John Doyle (12 Sept. 1812–23 Mar. 1877), Mormon pioneer executed for his role in the Mountain Meadows massacre, was born in Kaskaskia, Randolph County, Illinois, the son of Ralph Lee, a carpenter, and Elizabeth Doyle Reed. At age three, Lee's mother died, and, abandoned by his father, he spent four years under the care of an African-American nurse who spoke only French. In 1819 his mother's sister and her husband, James and Charlotte Conner, became his guardians. At age nineteen he fought in the Black Hawk War and then worked as a clerk in Galena. He moved to Vandalia where he married his first wife, Aggatha Ann Woolsey, on 24 July 1833; eleven children were born to the couple between 1834 and 1856; she died in 1866.

After being introduced to the Book of Mormon, the couple joined the Church of Jesus Christ of Latter-day Saints on 17 June 1838, a few weeks after their move from Vandalia to Far West, Missouri. While in Missouri, Lee became a member of the "Danites," a secret organization of faithful Mormons committed to protect other members by armed force if necessary. Violence visited the Lee homestead when an anti-Mormon mob set fire to his cabin in November 1838. Without a home, Aggatha and their daughter Sarah Jane returned to Vandalia in December while Lee went to Tennessee as a missionary for six months.

In April 1840 Lee moved to the new Mormon city of Nauvoo, Illinois, located on the east side of the Mississippi River. There he worked as a builder, policeman, and bodyguard to the Mormon prophet Joseph Smith (1805–1844) until the spring of 1844, when he left on another mission to assist in Smith's campaign for president of the United States. The campaign ended when Smith and his brother Hyrum were killed by a mob at Carthage Jail on 27 June 1844. Lee returned to Nauvoo and helped construct several public buildings and homes.

On 5 February 1845, Lee entered the practice of plural marriage (polygamy) when he married Nancy Bean. During the next twenty-two years, he married seventeen more wives, and twelve of his nineteen wives bore children. At the time of Lee's death, fifty of his sixty children were still living. Three of his wives preceded him in death; however, of his sixteen other wives, only five remained with him until his death. There were several reasons why. Some of the women found polygamy to be unsuitable, others did not want to leave the Midwest during the exodus west, others resented Lee's headstrong ways, some found more suitable partners, and a few left because of Lee's association with the Mountain Meadows massacre.

Lee was a loyal follower of Brigham Young and, in keeping with nineteenth-century Mormon theological beliefs, was "adopted" by Young into his large family. Because of his prominence in the Mormon community, Lee was named a member of the Council of Fifty, an organization created by Smith in 1844 and charged with establishing the Kingdom of God on earth. The Council of Fifty helped direct the exodus from Illinois and the move to the Valley of the Great Salt Lake in 1847. Lee undertook several assignments in preparing for the move west and completed the trek during the summer of 1848 as the leader of one of the numerous Mormon wagon trains.

After two and a half years in the Salt Lake Valley, Lee was instructed by Young to move south as part of a vanguard of pioneers to establish a Mormon outpost 250 miles south of Salt Lake City. Reluctantly, but obediently, Lee set out on 11 December 1850. For the next quarter of a century, he stood at the center of affairs in southern Utah. He was considered a kind and generous neighbor, a shrewd and exacting businessman, and an aggressive, sometimes quarrelsome and dictatorial leader and family head. His economic enterprises included ranching, farming, operations of mills and a store, and other activities associated with community building on the frontier. In January 1856 Lee was appointed Indian agent. In addition to distributing tools, supplies, and seeds, he represented the U.S. government to the Native Americans of southern Utah. It was in this assignment that he became a central figure in the Mountain Meadows massacre, which occurred in September 1857.

On 7 September, a non-Mormon group of 120 to 150 men, women, and children bound for California with forty wagons and an estimated 900 head of cattle were attacked by Indians while they were camped at Mountain Meadows preparing to cross the desert. After a four-day siege, the Mormon militia arrived, and the migrants, known as the Fancher Party, believing that the Mormon militia had come to save them, agreed to abandon their wagons and goods to the Indians and accompany the militia back to the safety of Cedar City. As the Fancher Party marched under a flag of truce, the group was massacred by Indians and the militia men; only seventeen small children were spared. The reasons for the massacre and Lee's participation in it are complex. The massacre was part of a larger wartime hysteria that was sweeping Utah as the Mormons awaited a threatened invasion of Federal troops marching west under orders of President James Buchanan to put down an alleged Mormon rebellion. Vivid memories of persecutions and mob actions against Mormons in Missouri and Illinois elicited strong sentiments in favor of resistance. In addition, exaggerated and false rumors preceded the Fancher Party, including allegations that the California-bound migrants were stealing from the Saints, poisoning water ponds, boasting of their role in the assassination of Joseph Smith, ridiculing Mormon leaders, and threatening to return from California to attack the Mormons.

Lee's role in the massacre centered on his assignment as Indian agent, which included acting as an intermediary between the Mormon militia and the Indians who had initially attacked and lay siege to the wagon train. Furthermore, as a major in the local militia, Lee was subject to the orders of his superiors, including the area commander, Colonel William H. Dame. Lee and militia man William Bateman, under a flag of truce, met with three members of the besieged wagon train and made arrangements for the migrants to be escorted to safety. After abandoning the wagons, and walking under armed escort, the adult men were shot by Lee and others while the Indians shot the women and older children.

The consequences of Lee's involvement in the Mountain Meadows massacre were not immediate. He remained an active and leading Mormon and for several years continued to expand his family and business enterprises in southern Utah. By the late 1860s, however, stories about his involvement in the massacre increased, and his family was harassed, mostly by their Mormon neighbors. In October 1870 Brigham Young excommunicated Lee from the Mormon church for his role in the massacre. To avoid attention and stay out of the public light, Lee moved in early 1872 to an isolated crossing of the Colorado River, where he established "Lee's Ferry," which served as the main access from southern Utah into Arizona until construction of the Navajo bridge, five miles up river, in 1929. Lee evaded arrest by U.S. officials until November 1874. Following his conviction for murder at Mountain Meadows, he was taken to the massacre site and executed by a Federal firing squad on 23 March 1877. Lee was the only person tried and convicted for the crime, and he considered himself a scapegoat to save the other participants and Mormon leaders from arrest for their role in the conspiracy.

On 20 April 1961 the Mormon church rescinded Lee's excommunication, citing his contributions as a pioneer leader and builder on the Mormon frontier and acknowledging that he had not been solely responsible for the Mountain Meadows massacre.

• The diaries of John D. Lee are in the Huntington Library, San Marino, Calif., and the Archives of the Church of Jesus Christ of Latter-day Saints, Salt Lake City, Utah. Lee's autobiography was dictated to stenographers, edited by W. W. Bishop, and published as *Mormonism Unveiled: The Life and Confessions of John D. Lee* (1877). Lee was a primary topic of study by Juanita Brooks for more than a quarter of a century, and he is the central figure in her ground-breaking study, *The Mountain Meadows Massacre* (1950). She coedited, with Robert Glass Cleland, the diaries of Lee, published as *A Mormon Chronicle: The Diaries of John D. Lee, 1848–1876* (1955). Brooks also wrote a biography, *John Doyle Lee: Zealot, Pioneer Builder, Scapegoat* (1961; repr. 1984), and a biography of one of his wives, *Emma Lee* (1975). Charles Kelly edited the *Journals of John D. Lee, 1846–47 and 1859* (1938), which was reprinted in 1984 by the University of Utah Press with an introduction by Charles S. Peterson.

ALLAN KENT POWELL

LEE, Julia (13 Oct. 1903–8 Dec. 1958), blues singer and pianist, was born in Boonville, Missouri, the daughter of George Lee, Sr., a violinist, and Katie Redmond.

(Most published sources cite her birthdate as 31 Oct., but Harris favors 13 Oct., the date on her death certificate.) She sang with her father's string trio from age four. Around 1913 her parents acquired a piano, and she began studying it with Scrap Harris and Charles Williams. She performed locally from 1916, notably in a group that included bassist Walter Page. After graduating from Lincoln High School in 1917, she studied piano at Western University around 1918. From 1920 to 1933 her career paralleled that of her brother George E. Lee, in whose bands she played and sang. With a group drawn from his orchestra, she recorded "Won't You Come Over to My House? (. . . Nobody Home but Me)" in November 1929. Occasionally during this period she worked on her own, including an engagement in Chicago in 1923. Sometime during the 1920s she married Johnny Thomas; details are unknown. She also was married to Kansas City Monarchs catcher Frank Duncan, with whom she had at least one child, Frank Duncan III.

Julia Lee's career blossomed as her brother's fortunes declined. She held an engagement at Milton's Tap Room in Kansas City from 1933 to 1948, although she left occasionally to perform elsewhere in the Midwest. With Jay McShann playing piano on a session in 1944, she sang a lament, "Trouble in Mind," and a new version of "Come on Over to My House," which included a magnificent alto saxophone solo from Tommy Douglas. In 1945 record producer and *Down Beat* editor Dave Dexter, Jr., included her work in a historical anthology on Capitol Records, and "Trouble in Mind" was so warmly received that she was invited to Los Angeles for further recordings. For the remainder of her career in the studio, Lee herself was the pianist, with occasional featured solos finding her playing variously in blues, boogie woogie, and swing styles. She sang straightforward popular songs, including a moving version of "When the Real Thing Comes Along" (1947), but most of her hit songs were sexually suggestive, delivered in a restrained manner with biting, crystal-clear enunciation, so that the humorous lyrics could be easily understood. The most clever are her bestselling "King-size Papa", "I Didn't Like It the First Time" (ostensibly about spinach but obviously about sex), and "(Come and See Me Baby, but Please) Don't Come Too Soon"; these titles are also from 1947.

While holding engagements in Los Angeles and Denver from mid-1948 through 1950, she continued working in Kansas City, including further recording sessions. In 1949 she was invited to perform for an admirer and fellow Missourian Harry S. Truman at the White House Press Association dinner in celebration of his election victory. She appeared in the film *The Delinquents* in 1957. She died the following year of a heart attack at her home in Kansas City.

Except among devoted fans of rhythm and blues, Lee has been largely forgotten since her death. Carey James Tate described her as "a jolly mother confessor to the depressed spirits of her audiences" (p. 9). Compared to the sexually explicit rap and soul songs of the late twentieth century, Lee's suggestive lyrics seem tame, which makes it difficult to capture the effect they had on audiences of her day. Nonetheless her renditions offer the additional bonus of fine solos from distinguished jazz and rhythm-and-blues musicians, including Douglas, Benny Carter, and Vic Dickenson. When in a serious mood, Lee could convey emotional depth and a plaintive sound.

• Biographies are by Sharon A. Pease, "30 Years in KC, Julia Lee Nabs National Fame," *Down Beat*, 15 Jan. 1947, p. 14, and Carey James Tate, "Julia Lee: (The Last of the Great Blues Singers)," *Second Line* 11 (Jan.–Feb. 1960): 9–12, 20. See also the interview by Max Jones, "Seamy Songs with an Old-Time Beat," *Melody Maker*, 26 Mar. 1949, p. 2. Sally-Ann Worsfold surveys Lee's career and recordings in "Julia's Blues," *Jazz Journal* 25 (Mar. 1972): 23–24, and on liner notes to the album *Julia Lee, Tonight's the Night* (1982). The fullest chronology of her activities is in Sheldon Harris, *Blues Who's Who: A Biographical Dictionary of Blues Singers* (1979).
BARRY KERNFELD

LEE, Luther (30 Nov. 1800–13 Dec. 1889), religious reformer, was born in Schoharie, New York, the son of Samuel Lee and Hannah Williams, pioneer farmers. His father was a revolutionary war veteran, and his mother was raised in the home of Joseph Bellamy, the famous New England divine and protégé of Jonathan Edwards. Lee's family lived in various locations in the Catskill Mountains of upper New York State. His mother became a Methodist; she so impressed young Lee with her enthusiastic religious devotion that at the age of eight he made his own personal Christian commitment.

Lee's mother died when he was thirteen, and the family was scattered. For the next eight years he worked for his room and board at a gristmill and a tannery in Delaware County, New York. He taught himself to read and write. In 1820 Lee sought out the nearest Methodist preaching place, publicly professed the Christian faith, and was baptized. He soon began to speak at worship services, and in 1822 he received a license to preach from the Methodist presiding elder. Designated a "local preacher," Lee was invited to speak at various places throughout the region. In 1825 he moved to Plymouth, New York, where he met and married Mary Miller, the daughter of a prominent farmer; they had seven children. Lee's wife was a schoolteacher, and her tutoring helped him to make up for his lack of formal education. Soon after their marriage they relocated to Cayuga County, where Lee preached and organized a Sunday school. In 1827 he was approved "on trial" as an itinerant minister of the Methodist Episcopal church; his full connection with the Methodist conference and ordination as a deacon was granted two years later.

Lee's appointments as a circuit rider were in the northern section of New York near the Canadian border, and later in central New York. He became well known as a camp-meeting preacher and as a public debater on theological issues. Lee was called on to promote and defend Methodist doctrines against opposing religious views, such as Calvinism, Universalism, and Unitarianism. His highly structured argumentation earned him the nickname "Logical Lee."

In 1837, after the mob killing of abolitionist Elijah Lovejoy, Lee became convinced of the evils of slavery. He began to use his persuasive skills for the antislavery cause, both as a speaker and as a writer of abolitionist articles in the religious press. In 1838 and 1839 he was a full-time traveling agent for the New York State Antislavery Society. He lectured throughout the state, at times attacked by anti-abolitionist mobs. The next year he was an agent for the Massachusetts Antislavery Society. His effectiveness as an antislavery lecturer brought him to the attention of Methodist abolitionists; it also earned him notoriety among Methodist leaders opposed to abolition.

In the split between the supporters of William Lloyd Garrison's "nonresistant" brand of abolitionism and the supporters of political abolitionism, Lee championed the latter position. At an Albany, New York, meeting in May 1839, his arguments on behalf of political action helped to convince many abolitionists of the need for an independent antislavery party as an alternative to the Whigs and the Democrats. The result was soon known as the Liberty party. Lee favored direct church involvement in political campaigning and urged men to vote the Liberty ticket as a religious duty.

In 1842 a group of Methodist antislavery agitators, led by Orange Scott, withdrew from the Methodist Episcopal church. Although Lee was not one of the original seceders, he soon assumed a leadership role among the reformers and assisted them in their 1843 establishment of the Wesleyan Methodist Connection, an explicitly abolitionist denomination. For the twenty years between Scott's death in 1847 and Lee's return to the Methodist Episcopal church in 1867, Lee was the most visible leader of the Connection. He pastored five Wesleyan Methodist congregations in New York and Ohio and helped to organize many others. He edited the church's newspaper, the *True Wesleyan*, from 1844 to 1852, and he was elected presiding officer at three of the first six General Conferences of the denomination. From his influential position in the young church, Lee advocated for a decentralized ecclesiastical polity, enhanced power for the laity, a radical social reform agenda, and the right of individual members to retain their affiliation with secret societies.

During the 1850s and 1860s Lee furthered his academic interests. He wrote a systematic theology text, *Elements of Theology* (1856), received an honorary doctor of divinity degree from Middlebury College in Vermont, and served as professor of theology at two fledgling Wesleyan Methodist colleges in Michigan—Leoni Institute and Adrian College. He also continued his abolitionist activities by assisting runaway slaves on the underground railroad and by preaching a stirring funeral oration at John Brown's gravesite. Lee's support of women's rights was demonstrated by a particularly noteworthy sermon delivered in 1853, "Woman's Right to Preach the Gospel." He was asked to give this sermon at the installation service for Antoinette Brown, who is often considered to be the first ordained clergywoman.

Lee spent the last ten years of his active ministry back in the Methodist Episcopal church. He pastored several congregations before retiring to Flint, Michigan, where he died.

• The best primary source on the life of Luther Lee is his *Autobiography* (1882). Lee's other publications, in addition to those cited in the text, include *Universalism Examined and Refuted* (1836), *The Debates of the General Conference of the M.E. Church, May, 1844* (1845), *Ecclesiastical Manual; or, Scriptural Church Government Stated and Defended* (1850), and *Wesleyan Manual: A Defence of the Organization of the Wesleyan Methodist Connection* (1862). Lee's published sermons (including "Woman's Right to Preach the Gospel") are collected in *Five Sermons and a Tract by Luther Lee*, ed. Donald W. Dayton (1975), which has a fine introduction. Important sources are two books by Lucius C. Matlack, *The History of American Slavery and Methodism from 1780 to 1849, and History of the Wesleyan Methodist Connection of America* (1849) and *Discussion of the Doctrine of the Trinity, between Luther Lee, Wesleyan Minister, and Samuel J. May, Unitarian Minister* (1854). Secondary assessments include Ira Ford McLeister, *History of the Wesleyan Methodist Church of America* (1959); Donald G. Mathews, *Slavery and Methodism* (1965); Donald W. Dayton, *Discovering an Evangelical Heritage* (1976); William C. Kostlevy, "Luther Lee and Methodist Abolitionism," *Methodist History* 20 (Jan. 1982): 90–103; and Paul Leslie Kaufman, "'Logical' Luther Lee and the Methodist War against Slavery" (Ph.D. diss., Kent State Univ., 1994). An obituary is in the *Minutes of the Annual Conferences of the Methodist Episcopal Church, Fall Conferences of 1890* (1890).

DOUGLAS M. STRONG

LEE, Mary Ann (1823–1899), ballerina, was born in Philadelphia, Pennsylvania, the daughter of Charles Lee, an actor, and Wilhelmina (maiden name unknown). She made her first stage appearance at age three with her father. He died when she was small, leaving her mother in financial straits. Lee studied ballet for two years with Paul H. Hazard, a former Paris Opéra dancer, before making her dance debut on 30 December 1837 at age fourteen in François Auber's *La bayadère or the Maid of Cashmere*. She and Augusta Maywood studied together and danced opposite each other in "A Trial Dance" or challenge dance. What had been a fictional situation turned into a reality when audiences began to take sides. As the star of the show, Maywood was accorded a benefit performance; however, Lee was denied one by Maywood's stepfather, the theater's manager, since she was a supporting player for whose lessons he paid. He grudgingly gave way to vociferous public opinion, and on 12 January 1838 jubilant fans packed the theater in what was called "the most crowded house which has been witnessed this season." The *Philadelphia Public Ledger* compared the two this way: "Miss Maywood has the most power, and Miss Lee, the most grace; and at a mature age . . . Miss Maywood will astonish the most, and Miss Lee will please the most" (15 Jan. 1838).

In March, Lee played Flora the nymph to Maywood's *The Dew Drop or La Sylphide*. She was left behind when Maywood set out to conquer Paris, but she inherited title roles in both ballets. By fall she transferred to the Walnut Theatre to dance as Queen Lily of the Silver Stream in a new ballet composed for her, *The Lily Queen*. She was featured in a Tambourine Dance, a *grand pas seul*, and a solo called "The Foundling of the Forest." She also enacted the roles of Little Pickle in *The Spoiled Child* and young Albert in *William Tell*.

Philadelphia theaters were flooded with juvenile dancers, so Lee soon found herself competing for the spotlight. After being demoted to minor roles in *La bayadère*, she compensated by performing a waltz duet, a celebrated hornpipe, and a *cachucha* arranged by her old teacher, Paul Hazard. Lee studied with James Sylvain, who came to America with the great Romantic ballerina Fanny Elssler, and lifted Elssler's entire repertoire of character or national dances: the *Cracovienne*, *Bolero*, *El Jaleo de Jeréz*, and *Cachucha*, which she dared to dance even while the celebrated ballerina was still in town. Madame Stephen Petit arranged Elssler's *Smolenska* "expressly for her."

In her New York City debut on 12 June 1839, Lee appeared with Julia Turnbull in a new ballet, *The Sisters*, a performance attended by President Martin Van Buren. A year later, P. T. Barnum hired her to perform in his Vauxhall Gardens, where she was promoted to the principal role of Zoloe in *La bayadère*. For the next two years she toured extensively; she "turned the heads" of Pittsburgh youth "with her pirouettes" (*Spirit of the Times*, 21 Dec. 1839) and was applauded by university students in Boston. In 1842 she danced in what the playbill described as the "popular Ballet of Action *The Halt of the Caravan*" and the pantomime-ballet *Perpetual Motion*. She arranged an Opium Dance for the play *Life in China* and acted in two melodramas. *La bayadère* was transformed into a burlesque called *Buy It Dear, Tis Made of Cashmere*. In New York in September 1842, she danced under the French ballerina Mme Lecomte in the famous ballet *Robert le Diable* and a year later in *La Muette de Portici*. Lee remained for some time in New Orleans in 1843–1844, where she was described by the newspaper *L'Abeille* as having "the triple merit of being young, pretty and graceful" (11 Feb. 1843, p. 602). Amid all these successes, one sour note was sounded by a New Orleans critic who asserted that "she is a clever girl, and might assume to 'star it' in the *provinces*, but is hardly up to the mark for the principal cities" (*Spirit of the Times*, 11 Feb. 1843).

Despite praise and challenging roles, it must have been apparent to Lee that her rivals were close on her heels, or perhaps she harbored dreams of becoming an international star like Augusta Maywood. Whatever the case, in November 1844 Lee sailed for Paris to study with Maywood's teacher, Jean Coralli, ballet master of the Paris Opéra. American newspapers crowed triumphantly that American legs were on a par with the French. Unlike Maywood, Lee came back within the year: "I much prefer my own dear country," she confessed.

She returned home in 1845 with a vastly improved technique and an enlarged, up-to-date repertoire. The *Spirit of the Times* newspaper now referred to her as "the celebrated danseuse" (11 Oct. 1845), and commented how her dancing "has been much improved by her visit to France" (11 Apr. 1846). Lee quickly appeared in famous ballets imported from the Paris Opéra: *La Jolie Fille de Gand* and *Fleur des champs*. With six *danseuses* and her partner George Washington Smith, an American *danseur noble*, Lee formed her own touring company. The American premiere of the first authentic version of Coralli's *Giselle* was held in Boston at the Howard Atheneum on 1 January 1846. The *Boston Globe* praised her "truthfulness of action" (22 Apr. 1846), and the *New York Herald* critic was smitten with her "beauty, charm, elegance and grace" (14 Apr. 1846). Lee felt *Giselle* to be "such a lovely ballet" that it became a staple of her repertoire for the rest of her career. The *New Orleans Picayune* now crowned her "the best of the American danseuses" (15 Dec. 1846). One critic noted, "There was always something captivating in her style of dancing, from her unaffected native grace and modesty" (*Daily Picayune*, 15 Dec. 1846), but she had been held back by poor training.

At the height of the triumphs for which she had labored long and hard, Lee's health failed. In New Orleans she was forced to stop mid-tour, but, still weak, she continued to Cleveland. In Philadelphia, on 18 June 1847, she last appeared in *La bayadère*, the first ballet in which she ever danced. She retired at age twenty-four, after twenty-one years on the stage. In 1847 she married William F. Van Hook, a dry-goods merchant from Philadelphia; they had three children. She returned under the name of Mrs. Van Hook for a few scattered performances in 1852–1853, with *Masaniello* her last appearance.

Nothing is known of her later years until her death in Philadelphia. Those acquainted with Lee noted her sweet personality, her responsibility to her widowed mother, her modesty, and her loyalty. Critics praised her graceful manner as well as the dogged determination that led her to study the greatest ballets of the Romantic repertoire at their source and to become America's first authentic interpreter of *Giselle*.

• A contemporary account of Lee is found in Charles Durang, "History of the Philadelphia Stage," an unpublished manuscript at the University of Pennsylvania Library. Her career has not been given the full treatment it deserves, other than Lillian Moore's brief study, "Mary Ann Lee, First American Giselle," in *Chronicles of the American Dance*, ed. Paul Magriel (1948), pp. 103–17.

MAUREEN NEEDHAM

LEE, Muna (29 Jan. 1895–3 Apr. 1965), poet, feminist, and specialist in international affairs, was born in Raymond, Mississippi, the daughter of Benjamin Floyd Lee, a druggist, and Mary McWilliams. The eldest of nine children, she spent her childhood both in Raymond and in Hugo, Oklahoma, where her family moved in 1902. In 1909 she returned to Mississippi to attend her mother's alma mater, Blue Mountain College, where she was encouraged to write poetry. She spent a year there and a year at the University of Oklahoma; then she enrolled in the University of Mississippi, earning her B.S. in 1913.

She taught school for several years in Oklahoma, while continuing to advance her career as a poet. She published a poem in *Smart Set* in 1913, and in 1915 she won *Poetry* magazine's Lyric Prize for a group of poems titled "Footnotes." Teaching herself Spanish in order to acquire a government job as a translator, she moved to New York, where she quickly became part of the literary scene. In July 1919 she married Luis Muñoz Marín, a fellow poet, a journalist, and the son of prominent Puerto Rican statesman Luis Muñoz Rivera. The marriage produced two children.

Lee and Muñoz Marín held regular gatherings at their West Side apartment that included Horace and Marya Gregory, Marya Zaturenska, Sara Teasdale, Vachel Lindsay, and William Rose Benét. The wide-ranging literary and political conversations at these events reflected the variety of interests that drove them both, first together and later separately, to their careers. Lee continued to publish poetry throughout the 1920s in a number of magazines. Her only book of poetry, *Sea-Change* (1923), presents her characteristically concise, lyric voice whose subjects include imagist renderings of love and representations of nature forged from Lee's attention to the landscapes of her midwestern and southern past, as well as to the island tropics that became her home.

In 1926 Lee and Muñoz Marín moved their family to San Juan, Puerto Rico. Lee became director of international relations at the University of Puerto Rico, a post she held from 1927 until 1941. But throughout this period, her activities were multiple and varied. In 1928 she was among the speakers from the National Woman's Party (NWP) of the United States who lobbied their way into the sixth Pan-American Conference in Havana, demanding international recognition for the cause of women's rights. Their action resulted in the formation of the Inter-American Committee of Women. In a letter to the *Nation* reporting that event, she wrote, "At least in this hemisphere no more international codes are to be written concerning women without consulting women. The struggle for equal rights has become an inter-American movement" (14 Mar. 1928). She served as director of national affairs for the NWP (1931–1933) and spoke and wrote about women's rights across the United States and in Latin America both during and after her tenure.

She had already begun translating the work of Latin American authors into English, starting with Rafael de Nogales's *Four Years Beneath the Crescent* (1926), and she also wrote an article on the progress of the Inter-American Committee of Women for *Pan-American Magazine* (Oct. 1929). In 1937 she edited *Art in Review*, a special retrospective issue of the *University of Puerto Rico Bulletin* that celebrated a decade of artistic development in Puerto Rico. During the 1930s she also coauthored five mystery novels with Maurice Guinness under the pen name Newton Gayle. These novels featured a wry British sleuth who solved crimes in Britain, the United States, and Puerto Rico, while occasionally referencing broader political themes. *Death Follows a Formula* (1934) concerned the murder of a scientist who created a synthetic substitute for gasoline; *Murder at 28:10* (1937) involved the murder of a Roosevelt New Dealer bent on Puerto Rican reform.

By 1940 her marriage to Muñoz Marín was dissolving. In that year he was elected to the Puerto Rican Senate, later becoming the island's first elected governor. They officially divorced in November 1946. Lee went to Washington, D.C., with her children in 1941 and became a regional specialist for the State Department's Division of Cultural Relations. She was promoted in 1951 to cultural coordinator in the Office of Public Affairs and continued to work for the State Department until 1965. In those capacities she promoted hemispheric cultural exchange involving literature, art, and film; she also served as a delegate to numerous international conferences. Her literary production reflected the concerns of the times, emphasizing that an increased mutual understanding was necessary to maintain peacetime intercultural relations. She published numerous articles that introduced to an English-reading public heroes from Latin American history whom she interpreted as models of democratic struggle.

In 1944 she collaborated with Archibald MacLeish on "The American Story" radio series, producing a handbook for the program that recounted the stories of diverse figures in the European discovery of America. *Pioneers of Puerto Rico* (1945), a book of children's stories, sketched the history of Puerto Rico from colonial times to the poverty-ridden present of Muñoz Marín's efforts to readjust the island's economy. With Ruth McMurry, she wrote *The Cultural Approach: Another Way in International Relations* (1947), which documented the efforts of various nations to promote cultural and intellectual exchange. She was deeply concerned with familiarizing cultural output across national borders, believing that only through knowledge of each other can diverse peoples manage amicable relations. In an article for *The Inter-American* about translation, she likened the sixteenth century to the mid-twentieth: "A world crowded with phenomena surpassing the imaginable had been discovered, changing the everyday lives of ordinary stay-at-home people just as certainly as the invention of the atomic bomb is changing ours" (Nov. 1945, p. 12). Her career was marked by a steady effort to enlarge understanding of the shared and parallel histories of Latin and North American nations. She retired from the State Department in February 1965, returning to San Juan, where she died a few months later.

• Correspondence between Muna Lee and Archibald MacLeish can be found in the papers of MacLeish in the Library of Congress. With Maurice Guinness, Lee also wrote *The Sentry Box Murder* (1935), *Death in the Glass* (1937), and *Sinister Crag* (1939). She translated Jorge Carrera Andrade, *Secret Country* (1946), and Rafael Altamira, *The History of Spain* (1949). Her articles include "Eugenio María de Hostos: After One Hundred Years," *Books Abroad* 14 (1940): 124–28; "José de San Martín," *Pan American Magazine* (Dec. 1930): 386–91; "Pitfalls of a Translator," *The Inter-American* (Nov. 1945): 12–14, 37; "Cuban Literature," *The Americas* 3 (Apr. 1947): 493–501; "Building the Irreplaceable Bridge," *Modern Mexico* (Mar. 1947): 10–11, 24; "Narciso Lopez," *The Pan American* 10 (Nov. 1949): 8–11; "The Port-Au-Prince Bicentennial," *Record* 6 (1950): 1–4; "Some Backgrounds of Latin American Education," *The American Teacher* 35 (Apr. 1951): 10–13; and "Translating the Untranslatable," *Américas* 6 (Sept. 1954): 12–15. Lee is mentioned in Thomas Aitken, Jr., *Poet in the Fortress: The Story of Luis Muñoz Marín* (1964). An obituary is in the *New York Times*, 4 Apr. 1965.

JANE CREIGHTON

LEE, Porter Raymond (21 Dec. 1879–8 Mar. 1939), social worker and teacher, was born in Buffalo, New York, the son of Reuben Porter Lee, a banker, and Jennie Blanchard. He obtained his first experience in social service working at Westminster House, a Buffalo settlement, while he was still in high school. This plus a college course in the methods of modern philanthropy led him to pursue a career in social work. After graduating from Cornell University in 1903 he attended a summer institute at the New York School of Philanthropy, then the only center in the country providing professional social work training. That fall he began work as assistant secretary of the Charity Organization Society (COS) of Buffalo. He later described the six years he spent there under the supervision of secretary Frederick Almy as "the most important single factor" in his education. He married Ethel Hepburn Pollock in 1905; they would have five children.

In 1909 Lee moved to Philadelphia, where he succeeded Mary E. Richmond as general secretary of another COS affiliate, the Society for Organizing Charity of Philadelphia. While there, he also did graduate work at the University of Pennsylvania (1911–1912) and contributed a paper to the National Conference of Charities and Corrections titled "The Social Function of Case Work." In 1912 he moved to the New York School of Philanthropy, where he became an instructor in social work. Lee encouraged his students to respond compassionately to the people they assisted, but he stressed the fact that social workers needed more than ideals and empathy; they must be skilled in the techniques of disciplined and rational investigation. Methodologically he broke new ground by teaching from actual case records instead of from textbooks; his contemporary Karl de Schweinitz called this his most significant contribution to the field of social work education. During these years Lee also pursued further graduate studies at Columbia University.

When Edward T. Devine resigned as school director in 1916, Lee was named to succeed him. (The institution was renamed the New York School of Social Work in 1918 and became an affiliate of Columbia

University in 1940.) Lee significantly expanded the curriculum, adding courses in group work, social psychiatry, and social philosophy, while strengthening the school's offerings in such fields as community organization, statistics, and the study of labor problems. He also helped establish the Bureau of Child Guidance within the school in 1921 as part of the Commonwealth Fund program for preventing delinquency. His book with Marion Kenworthy, *Mental Hygiene and Social Work* (1931), is an account of the bureau's work in integrating mental hygiene approaches with social casework. Under Lee's leadership the school enrollment grew from a few hundred to about 1,500. He was determined, however, to maintain the school's high standards and resisted the opportunity to undertake a major expansion when the social programs of the New Deal triggered a boom in applications.

Lee's influence extended well beyond his own institution. The American Association of Schools of Social Work, for instance, grew out of a meeting of seventeen schools that he convened in 1919. He also chaired the Milford Conference, a study group that met for one week each year between 1923 and 1927 to discuss the theory and practice of social casework. The group's report written by Lee, *Social Case Work, Generic and Specific* (1929), became a classic in the profession, making a strong case for maintaining a general core of social work knowledge rather than succumbing to the growing trend toward specialization. Lee continued to write on this subject in later years, observing that fragmenting a family's care among too many specialists could leave them feeling overwhelmed by a "Hydra-headed authority." The purpose of social workers, he reminded his readers, was not to achieve their own plans, but "to leave the family fit to formulate and work out its own." Lee also served as secretary of the New York COS in 1929 and, as interim director, saw the agency through a critical year of administrative changes in 1933. He was a member of the Joint Committee on Methods of Preventing Delinquency and a trustee of both the Family Welfare Association of America and the Welfare Council of New York City. In his private life, Lee was an accomplished gardener, golfer, and gourmet cook.

In 1929, when Lee was elected president of the National Conference of Social Work, he presented an inaugural address, "Social Work: Cause and Function," that became the best known of his writings. (It later appeared in a volume of the same name, a collection of his papers published in 1937 to celebrate his twenty-fifth year at the New York School of Social Work.) In his speech Lee argued that social work had begun as a "cause," a response of caring amateurs to unmet human need, but that it had evolved into a "function," the responsibility of any well-organized community, which must be carried out by skilled professionals. During the 1930s Lee became concerned that social workers were pressing beyond the limits of their professional expertise. As the depression deepened he spoke out against the growing tendency for members of the profession to serve as advocates for a wide range of social reforms. For example, at a school alumni meeting in 1934 he chided his profession for giving more attention to promoting social change than to technical competence, and he warned that social workers who meddled in areas such as "taxation, industrial organization and political control" were risking harm "both to these programs and to the status of social work."

Lee retired for health reasons in 1938 and died of a heart condition in Englewood, New Jersey. Some contemporaries criticized Lee for his conservative approach to social issues, but he was widely regarded for his personal warmth and for his contributions to the study of family life, the field of social work education, and the profession of social work. Reviewing his career at the New York School of Social Work, one admirer praised him for having made his colleagues "more productive than they knew how to be, more imaginative than they had learned to be, more courageous than they really wanted to be."

• Besides the works cited in the text, Lee coauthored with Walter Pettit and Jane M. Hoey *Report of a Study of the Interrelation of the Work of National Social Agencies in Fourteen American Communities* (1923) and with Pettit *Social Salvage* (1924). For references to Lee's career, see Frank J. Bruno, *Trends in Social Work, 1874–1956* (1957); Helen I. Clarke, *Principles and Practice of Social Work* (1947); John H. Ehrenreich, *The Altruistic Imagination: A History of Social Work and Social Policy in the United States* (1985); and Elizabeth G. Meier, *A History of the New York School of Social Work* (1954). Articles about Lee appeared in *Family*, Jan. 1940, pp. 277–81, and *Bulletin of the New York School of Social Work* (July 1940): 18–20. A biographical sketch appears in the *Encyclopedia of Social Work*, and obituaries are in the *New York Times*, 9 Mar. 1939, and *Social Service Review* 13, no. 1 (Mar. 1939): 122.

SANDRA OPDYCKE

LEE, Richard Bland (20 Jan. 1761–12 Mar. 1827), congressman, was born at "Leesylvania," in Prince William County, Virginia, the son of Henry Lee, a plantation owner, and Lucy Grymes. Scion of the preeminent Virginia political dynasty, his older brothers were the revolutionary war hero Henry "Light-Horse Harry" Lee and Charles Lee, future U.S. attorney general; Arthur and Richard Henry Lee were second cousins. Lee abandoned his studies at the College of William and Mary in 1780. He subsequently settled on the family's Loudon County plantation "Sully" inherited by his father and presently part of Fairfax County. He resided there until debts forced him to sell the property in 1815. Even in the midst of his later congressional career in New York and Philadelphia, Lee corresponded closely with supervisors about the management of Sully and maintained frequent contact with northern Virginia's political and social leaders.

Lee launched his political career as a member of the state House of Delegates from 1784 to 1786 and served again in 1788. Like his brother Henry Lee, one of the leaders at the state convention, Lee was a Federalist during the debate over ratification of the Constitution, playing a notable role in the unsuccessful attempt to steer the ratification ordinance through the legislature without an Antifederalist-inspired circular letter calling for a second constitutional convention. In the first federal election, Lee was one of several candidates seeking to represent the congressional district that boasted both George Washington and the Antifederalist leader George Mason as constituents. Although complete returns are not extant, Lee outpolled his closest Antifederalist opponent in Fairfax County by a ratio of almost four to one.

Lee's recorded votes and speeches on the floor of the House reflect a moderate Federalist's support for a loose constitutional construction favoring a strong central government. He supported the extensive judicial establishment proposed by the Judiciary Act, but his promotion of a strong executive branch was tempered by an ambivalent stance on the president's prerogatives under the Constitution's "advice and consent" clause. A faithful, if reticent, member of the Madison-led coalition for a Bill of Rights devoid of more structural amendments to the Constitution, Lee ardently supported Madison on such broad economic proposals as levying discriminatory impost and tonnage duties that would have favored America's allies. On more parochial economic matters, Lee adequately defended his district's interests. For example, he attacked high duties on steel farm implements, claiming they aimed at protection of northern manufactures rather than revenue.

Lee's overall contributions to the work of the First Federal Congress were admirable, even apart from considerations of his youth and relative inexperience. His numerous committee assignments focused on trade, revenue collection, and appropriations. His other assignments addressed two issues of particular concern to his constituents: western land sales and the location of the federal capital. Lee's pivotal role in resolving the site of the seat of government was perhaps his greatest contribution to the economic welfare of his district. When, near the end of the first session, the first resolution was made for a centrally located site, Lee moved an unsuccessful substitute that stressed the importance of convenient communication between the Atlantic and the West. Although at the time Lee doubted "the practicability for a long time to come of prevailing on the Eastern and Middle States to remove to Potomack," he was the first congressman to make a formal proposal to locate the capital there.

During the second session, the capital city location became tied to the federal assumption of the states' revolutionary war debts, an item in Hamilton's proposed funding program particularly dear to northerners. Under the terms of the crucial Compromise of 1790, southerners pledged to support assumption in exchange for northern pledges not to obstruct passage of a Potomac site for the permanent capital. Lee initially shared his state delegation's majority position against the assumption, although as early as April 1790 he privately confided to his brother Charles that

with a centrally located seat of government to "diffuse the wealth of the Capital in equal measure to the extremes of the Empire . . . the poison of the measure would be very much diminished." By the end of June, he joined the other Virginia representative with a Potomac constituency in promising his vote to the assumptionists. Lee delivered a "very handsome and pathetic speech" when the residence act was first debated on the floor of the House, four days after a Senate committee was ordered to prepare resolutions recommending assumption as part of the funding act.

Lee's alliance with the Hamiltonians was limited to his last-minute switch in favor of assumption and his subsequent vote for duties on distilled spirits to finance it. In the third session he resumed his place in the southern minority that voted against a national bank. His role in the Compromise of 1790 nevertheless continued to haunt him politically; as late as 1797, political enemies were still making reference to "Lee's defection." He won reelection to the Second and Third Congresses, although his support for the administration's foreign policy initiatives led to his increasing political alienation at home. Lee lost his bid for a fourth congressional term after a pamphlet war that focused on Lee's earlier vote for assumption and his later support for Washington's neutrality proclamation and John Jay's unpopular mission to Great Britain.

Lee had married in 1794, and he returned to Sully with his wife, Elizabeth Collins, the daughter of a wealthy Philadelphia Quaker. The couple had six children. He resumed his seat in the Virginia House of Delegates in 1796 and again in 1799–1806, during which time he remained outside the swelling tide of Jeffersonian Republicanism. Lee moved to Washington, D.C., in 1815. He procured an appointment as judge of the orphans' court for the district four years later, serving in that position until his death, in Washington.

• No collection of Richard Bland Lee papers exists, although isolated manuscripts can be found in collections of the Lee Family Papers at the University of Virginia and the Library of Congress. The latter is custodian of a collection of his letters, mostly to Theodorick Lee. Original documentary sources for his national political career are the multivolume House debates in *The Documentary History of the First Federal Congress, 1789–1791* vols. 10–14 (1968–), and Gales and Seaton, *Annals of Congress*, 2d and 3d Cong. Lee's own summary defense of his congressional career can be found in his 8 Dec. 1794 circular letter to his constituents, published in the (Philadelphia) *Dunlap and Claypoole's American Daily Advertiser*, 12 Feb. 1795. His political philosophy emerges in his electioneering pamphlet *Marcellus*, published in the *Richmond Gazette* in Nov. and Dec. 1794. For secondary sources, see Paul C. Nagel, *The Lees of Virginia: Seven Generations of an American Family* (1990), and Robert S. Gamble, *Sully: The Biography of a House* (1973).

WILLIAM C. DI GIACOMANTONIO

LEE, Richard Henry (20 Jan. 1733–19 June 1794), revolutionary, member of the Continental Congress, and U.S. senator, was born in Westmoreland County, Virginia, the son of Thomas Lee and Hannah Ludwell, planters. Lee studied for seven years at an academy in Wakefield, England. In 1757 he married Anne Aylett, with whom he had four children before her death in December 1768. The following summer he married Anne Gaskins Pinckard; they had five children.

Lee had hardly reached maturity when his father included him in the Ohio Company, for which his father, president of the Virginia Council, obtained a grant of up to 500,000 acres in 1749, an event that helped trigger the French and Indian War. After the war Lee joined other Ohio Company investors in the Mississippi Company, whose quest for 2.5 million acres in Kentucky was hamstrung by the postwar British policy restricting western settlement. Around 1760 family attachments moved him to site his home on lands leased from his eldest brother, Phillip Ludwell Lee, a few miles from Stratford Hall.

Lee was elected to the House of Burgesses from Westmoreland County in 1758. In the mid-1760s he emerged as a critic of Speaker John Robinson. The estrangement stemmed from the rivalry between the Ohio Company, composed exclusively of investors from the Northern Neck, and the Loyal Land Company, with members mostly from south of the Rappahannock. During the French and Indian War Northern Neck delegates considered Robinson lukewarm on military policies likely to advantage the Ohio Company. In the spring 1765 session Lee moved to investigate rumors that Robinson, as treasurer, a post he held concurrently with the Speakership, had illegally reissued wartime currency as loans to friends. The auditors, mostly Robinson supporters, reported no wrongdoing, but the Speaker's death in 1766 uncovered loans totaling more than £100,000 to some of the colony's most prominent families. Many never forgave Lee.

Lee's position on the Stamp Act is muddled because he first applied for the post of collector and then withdrew to help compose the burgesses' initial petitions against the proposed tax in the fall of 1764. Lee resented the greater acclaim Patrick Henry received for his similar, but more forceful, resolves in the May 1765 session, implying armed resistance. Lee equally forcefully (some thought hypocritically) led public demonstrations against his neighbor George Mercer who accepted the collector's post. In February 1766 Lee secured his county's support for the Westmoreland Association, which threatened resistance by force.

A hunting accident cost Lee the fingers of one hand and kept him from the forefront of opposition to the Townshend Acts in 1767–1768. In 1769, however, he served on the committee whose attempt to join Massachusetts's protest against the acts led the governor, Norborne Berkeley, Lord Botetourt, to dissolve the Virginia Assembly. The burgesses, Lee among them, marched to a nearby tavern and adopted an association proscribing British imports until repeal.

In February 1773 Lee initiated his long association with Samuel Adams of Massachusetts, and in the spring of that year he called for appointment of committees of correspondence in each colony. A network formed in time to report on the Boston Tea Party in December. Accounts of the British scene from Lee's younger brothers, Arthur, a law student in London, and William, a tobacco importer whom London radicals elected sheriff and then alderman of that city, helped stoke colonial hopes of significant support among the British population.

After Parliament closed the port of Boston in retaliation for the tea party, in May 1774 Lee and other burgesses proposed a public day of fast to signify unity with Massachusetts. Lee pressed further to close Virginia courts and block collection of British debts, but it was the governor, John Murray, earl of Dunmore, who achieved that end by dissolving the legislature before it renewed the statute setting judicial fees. A second time the burgesses met in a neighboring tavern to reestablish the association against British imports. Dissolution precluded Lee submitting additional resolutions calling for a colonial congress and the banning of exports to Britain. A circular from Massachusetts revived these proposals and led to the first Virginia Convention in August, which endorsed the ban on trade and placed Lee on a seven-man delegation to a continental congress in Philadelphia that fall.

In the First Congress Lee gained fame as an orator the equal of Henry. He contributed to a declaration of rights of the colonists; he helped implement a continental association modeled on Virginia's to halt trade with Great Britain; and he moved endorsement of Massachusetts's defiant Suffolk County Resolves.

In July 1775 Lee proposed opening American ports to foreign merchants. In November he discussed establishing independent state governments with John Adams and in the spring of 1776 had Adams's suggestions published in Virginia. In early May the two obtained a congressional resolution advising colonies to form state governments, and on 7 June, in response to the Virginia Convention's instructions of 15 May 1776, Lee moved his famous resolution that Congress should declare the colonies "free and independent states." He left to help Virginia set up its new government before Congress adopted Thomas Jefferson's Declaration of Independence on 4 July.

Six months later Lee returned to Congress, where he remained for the next three years. Day-to-day administration fell to congressional committees, where Lee's oratorical skills and diligent service accorded him considerable influence. His energy and zeal served the new nation well. But his self-appointed role of censor and constant finger pointing at profiteering and lack of patriotism wearied many.

As a member of the Committee of Secret Correspondence, Lee became ensnared in the worst imbroglio of the war. His brother Arthur served as Congress's first agent at the French court, and shortly William Lee also moved to France. They soon charged that another agent, Silas Deane of Connecticut, an associate of Congress's chief financier, Robert Morris, had used his appointment for profit. But the Lees were vulnerable too, for the French court disliked Arthur Lee; and, as continental currency depreciated, Lee pressured his tenants to convert money rents to tobacco, further undermining the currency. Although Deane's accusers forced his recall in November 1777, Lee's opponents nearly defeated him for Congress in 1777 and 1778. A vitriolic newspaper exchange dragged on for years, seriously sapping continental morale.

Lee's first congressional term ended in May 1779 because of a three-year limitation, and for the next four years he concentrated on the state legislature. Henry and Lee emerged as major antagonists during these years, primarily over Lee's hard-money views, although they shared increasingly dour opinions about Congress. After the burning of Richmond in January 1781 by Benedict Arnold and Charles, earl of Cornwallis's arrival in April, Lee's disillusionment with the union grew. His only successful bid to be Speaker came in an emergency session in March after the delegates picked the incumbent Benjamin Harrison over Lee to plea for help from Congress in person. After John Simcoe's and Banastre Tarleton's cavalry raid on Charlottesville in June almost captured the governor and legislature, Lee proposed that George Washington become a dictator in the ancient Roman sense of a military leader temporarily wielding absolute power during a crisis. The decision to mass French and American forces to trap Cornwallis at Yorktown came just as the Virginia supply system disintegrated, and at the call of Jefferson's successor, Governor Thomas Nelson, Lee personally ferreted out food and fodder in his county for the armies. He also struggled, largely unsuccessfully, to fend off raids on Westmoreland plantations long after Yorktown.

Despite victory at Yorktown, Lee's mood toward the union continued to darken. Congress appointed his nemesis, Robert Morris, the superintendent of finance and requested authority to levy an impost. At the height of the British invasion, the Virginia Assembly consented, but, when Rhode Island declined in December 1782, Lee, who had not been present before, succeeded in rescinding the previous vote.

Congress also seemed a tool of special interests in delaying for three years its acceptance of Virginia's 1781 cession of its lands north of the Ohio River, which Maryland had demanded as a condition for ratification of the Articles of Confederation. At issue were conditions that Lee and Arthur Lee vigorously supported to prevent any other claim being recognized if Virginia gave up its own.

Lee returned to Congress in November 1784 and was elected president. Long convinced that revenue from western lands would solve Congress's plight, he supported the Ordinance of 1785, which provided for the survey and sale of Virginia's cessions. His amendment to allow public support of religion failed, and he successfully opposed a ban on slavery in the territory. Poor health kept him from Congress again until 1787, when he served on the committee drafting the Northwest Ordinance, which established government beyond the Ohio. He posed no objection to the ordinance's prohibition of slavery north of the Ohio River,

probably because of the implicit recognition of the institution to the south.

Chosen a delegate to the Philadelphia Convention in 1787, Lee declined because of poor health, nor could he stand for the state ratifying convention the next year. Still, he wielded great influence through one of the most famous antifederalist tracts: *Letters from the Federal Farmer to the Republican* (2 vols., 1787–1788). Lee praised the Constitution for centralizing control of foreign affairs, commerce, money, and the post office, and he approved the planned abolition of the slave trade in 1808. He thought the separate executive and bicameral legislature imitative of the British and undemocratic but justifiable given the Confederation's problems. His complaints centered on the lack of a bill of rights and a time limit on presidential terms and his fear that the number of seats in the House of Representatives was too small for even that branch to be democratic. He urged rejecting the Constitution unless it was revised but acquiesced after ratification occurred.

Reflecting the narrow margin for ratification in Virginia, the legislature elected Lee and another antifederalist, William Grayson, over James Madison as the state's first U.S. senators. Although Lee campaigned on a promise to enact a bill of rights, Madison, who had been elected to the House, preempted him. Lee preferred wording the First Amendment to permit federal support, though not establishment, of religion, and he denounced the Bill of Rights as adopted as incapable of preventing a "tendency to consolidated Empire" (Grayson and Lee to Virginia House of Representatives, 28 Sept. 1789). He seems not to have been privy to Madison's arrangement with Secretary of the Treasury Alexander Hamilton to trade a Potomac site for the national capital for federal assumption of state debts. His objection that apportionment of representatives in 1792 did not follow the census produced the first presidential veto, and he twice tried to reverse the Senate's pre-1794 policy of closing sessions to the public. Lee served, with extensive absences because of illness and a carriage accident, until his resignation on 8 October 1792, the last six months as president pro tempore.

Lee, who had long suffered from gout and frequent bouts of respiratory illness, died at his home, "Chantilly."

• The Lee Family Papers are at the American Philosophical Society, Philadelphia; the Library of Congress; the University of Virginia library; and the Virginia Historical Society. The University of Virginia collection is published in microfilm. See Paul Hoffman, ed., *Guide to the Microfilm Edition of the Lee Family Papers, 1742–1795* (1966). James C. Ballagh, ed., *The Letters of Richard Henry Lee* (2 vols., 1911–1914), is selective. A modern edition of Lee's pamphlet is Walter Hartwell Bennett, ed., *Letters from the Federal Farmer to the Republican* (1978). An older biography is Oliver P. Chitwood, *Richard Henry Lee, Statesman of the Revolution* (1967), and a brief study is John C. Matthews, *Richard Henry Lee* (1978), based on the author's dissertation at the University of

Virginia (1939). The definitive study of the family is Paul C. Nagel, *The Lees of Virginia: Seven Generations of an American Family* (1990).

JOHN E. SELBY

LEE, Robert E. (19 Jan. 1807–12 Oct. 1870), soldier, was born Robert Edward Lee on the Stratford estate in Westmoreland County, Virginia, the son of Henry "Light Horse Harry" Lee, a soldier and political leader, and Ann Hill Carter. The promise of affluence implied by his birth at his father's ancestral estate was not fulfilled in Lee's childhood. Neither family, nor military distinction in the Revolution, nor political success as governor of Virginia (1792–1795) could save Major General Henry Lee from the penalties of financial recklessness, aggravated by broken health. As a result, Robert's childhood was shadowed by the frequent absence of his father, seeking to escape his creditors and to promote his physical rehabilitation, while his mother supported herself and her five children on the income from her Carter legacy, which was adequate but by no means lavish. The family moved to Alexandria, Virginia, in 1810. For an unknown period, Robert attended a school at Eastern View in Fauquier County that was run by the Carters for their children. By 1820 he was a student at Alexandria Academy, where he finished his secondary school education no later than 1823.

A waiting list delayed his admission to the United States Military Academy at West Point until 1 July 1825. He graduated from the academy in 1829, second in his class. Exercising the privilege of a high-ranking graduate, he chose service in the Corps of Engineers, the most prestigious branch of the army. He was commissioned second lieutenant of engineers on 1 July 1829.

The two-month furlough awarded graduates enabled Lee to nurse his widowed mother in the last of many illnesses. After she died on 10 July, he spent time visiting with relatives and frequently called at "Arlington," the home of George Washington Parke Custis, the adopted son of George Washington. There Lee courted Custis's daughter, Mary Anne Randolph Custis, whom he had known since childhood. They were married on 30 June 1831 and had seven children. The marriage linked Lee to Arlington and gave him a symbolic association with the Washington tradition, an association that expanded with the rise of Lee's military fame.

Lee's first army assignments were to help plan the construction of Fort Pulaski on the Savannah River in Georgia (1829–1831) and Fortress Monroe at Old Point Comfort in Virginia (1831–1834). From Fort Monroe, Lee went in August 1834 to Fort Calhoun on the Rip-Raps in adjacent Hampton Roads and then in October to Corps of Engineers headquarters in Washington. While in Washington he was promoted to first lieutenant on 21 September 1836. An excursion into the civil engineering projects historically important to Lee's corps came with his travel to St. Louis in the summer of 1837 to superintend works protecting the harbor of the city from shifts in the channel of the Mississippi. Except for occasional visits to Virginia, Lee remained at St. Louis until October 1840. He found the improvement of the Mississippi intellectually stimulating, and it brought him useful experience in cooperating with civil officials. Meanwhile he rose to captain on 7 July 1838. After another tour at corps headquarters, which included inspection trips to corps work sites, Lee arrived in New York City on 10 April 1841 to superintend the fortifying of the country's most important harbor.

Lee's having won recognition for excellence among the army's engineers was signified by his appointment to a board of officers to attend the West Point final examinations in June 1844 and to membership on the Board of Engineers for Atlantic Coast Defenses on 8 September 1845. Still, for a soldier, greater distinction could be won most readily in combat. Lee's opportunity for such distinction came in the Mexican War, though only after much dull and uneventful marching. He entered Mexico on 12 October 1846 as a staff engineer with the column under Brigadier General John E. Wool. With Captain William D. Fraser, Lee directed the building and repair of roads and bridges from San Antonio, Texas, to near Saltillo, Mexico, a distance of over 600 miles, where Wool's column joined the command of Major General Zachary Taylor.

On 16 January 1847 Lee received orders to join Major General Winfield Scott, commanding general of the U.S. Army, as chief engineer of the main army of invasion. Lee joined Scott at Brazos, Texas, for a planned amphibious assault against Mexico's Gulf coast and a subsequent march to Mexico City. Scott, who had first come to know Lee well on the West Point board in 1844, trusted him completely and accorded him the maximum opportunity to display initiative, allowing him to make decisions just short of the key operational ones of an army commander. Lee responded in a way that virtually assured him of later gaining independent command of a field army.

The enemy held a strong mountainous defensive position around Jalapa, but Lee discovered a feasible route through high hills around the Mexican left; he persuaded Scott to use it and led the vanguard along the route, providing U.S. forces with a victory in the battle of Cerro Gordo on 17–18 April. For this Lee won the brevet rank of major. When the enemy fell back on another strong position in front of Churubusco, Lee again found a feasible route skirting a lava bed known as the Pedregal, to permit another turning of the Mexican defenses. Across the Pedregal, Lee joined with Brigadier Generals Persifor F. Smith and John Cadwalader in deciding to proceed with the turning attack against the Mexican main body in spite of the arrival of enemy reinforcements that threatened the flank of such a move. Then he recrossed the dangerous, mazelike Pedregal with a few men by night to secure from Scott enough additional troops to counter the Mexican reinforcements. Again the outcome was swift American victory, at Contreras across the Pedregal and then at the main enemy position of Churubusco, both on 20 August. In reward, Lee received a brevet as lieutenant colonel. A brevet colonelcy followed on 24 August 1848, for his actions in the previous year's battle of Chapultepec, where Lee's contribution was the more straightforward and less independent one of helping map Mexican strong points to assist Scott in planning the battle. All in all, Lee emerged from the Mexican War a proven combat leader who enjoyed the special confidence of the ranking officer of the U.S. Army.

Arriving back in Washington on 29 June 1848, Lee resumed duties at corps headquarters and on the coast defense board, whose business took him from Boston to Florida and Mobile. In April 1849 he assumed direction of the building of a fort on Sollers's Flats, a shoal in the Patapsco River off Sollers's Point, to defend Baltimore harbor (the work was named Fort Carroll in October 1850). His next assignment demonstrated again that the army regarded Lee as an officer above the ordinary; on 27 May 1852 he was named superintendent of West Point. He held this post from 1 September 1852 to 31 March 1855, restoring cadet discipline, which he found disturbingly lax, but leaving little permanent mark on the academy.

Up to this point, Lee had had little direct contact with the army on the western frontier. While he was superintendent at West Point, Secretary of War Jefferson Davis sought to increase the size of the force patrolling the vast new territories acquired from Mexico. In response Congress authorized the formation of two new cavalry regiments to accompany the existing two of dragoons and one of mounted riflemen. The new Second Cavalry became Davis's favorite; on the same day that it was created, Paymaster Major Albert Sidney Johnston, a close friend of the secretary from their West Point days, was promoted to be its colonel, while Lee became its lieutenant colonel. Lee served with the Second at St. Louis, in the Kansas Territory, and at several posts in Texas before reporting to San Antonio to replace Johnston in command. These tours of duty included a certain amount of chasing after "hostiles" but were more dull than otherwise, and thus typical of the frontier. Lee did, however, learn at firsthand about commanding troops in the field—in small numbers, to be sure, but with difficult logistics.

Lee was at home at Arlington after court-martial service in New York City when, on 17 October 1859, First Lieutenant James E. B. Stuart of the First Cavalry delivered a message ordering him to report immediately to the War Department. The result was that he hastened with Stuart to Harpers Ferry, Virginia, where the abolitionist John Brown (1800–1859) and his followers were holding off Virginia militia and Maryland volunteers after seizing the fire-engine house of the United States Arsenal. Taking command, Lee demanded the surrender of the insurgents early on 18 October and then ordered the storming of Brown's refuge by marines from the Washington Navy Yard. The assault succeeded, and Brown was captured. Lee returned to Texas early the next year, but he was never

to escape the shadow that the Harpers Ferry raid had cast over his state.

He was commissioned full colonel and commander of the First Cavalry on 16 March 1861. By that time, however, seven southern states had seceded from the Union and formed the Confederate States of America. Lee had left Fort Mason and the Second Cavalry on 13 February, under orders to report to Brevet Lieutenant General Scott. Some time in early March, Lee called on Scott in Washington, learned of his coming promotion, and was probably advised by Scott that if the secession crisis erupted into war, he would likely be Scott's second-in-command and the leader in the field. Lee probably warned Scott, in turn, that if Virginia seceded, he would feel obliged to follow his state and resign his commission. He opposed secession, disliked slavery, and never himself owned more than about a half dozen slaves (whom he emancipated before the Civil War), but he believed he must be loyal to Virginia and could not take up arms against the Commonwealth. On 18 April, following the bombardment of Fort Sumter on 12–14 April, Postmaster General Montgomery Blair, on behalf of President Abraham Lincoln, directly asked Lee whether he would take command of an enlarged U.S. Army. But Lee reiterated what he had said to Scott. On 20 April, having learned that Virginia had seceded two days earlier, Lee submitted his resignation. It was a painful decision but one that in its expression of loyalty to home and kindred has commanded sympathy even from those who cannot admire it.

On 21 April Governor John Letcher of Virginia dispatched a messenger offering Lee command of the military and naval forces of the state, with the rank of major general, but the messenger evidently passed Lee while the latter was en route from Arlington to Richmond in response to an earlier invitation from the governor. Lee accepted the commission from Letcher's hand on 22 April. On 10 May the Confederate War Department gave Lee command of its forces in Virginia, though it proceeded to send troops and other officers there apparently without regard to him. Following the voters' ratification of the Virginia Ordinance of Secession on 23 May, the state turned over its forces to the Confederacy on 8 June, while Lee had already been commissioned brigadier general in the Confederate regular army on 14 May.

He also became a confidential military adviser to President Jefferson Davis, who dispatched him to western Virginia in late July to coordinate efforts to recapture the considerable parts of that mountainous region, with its population largely disaffected by secession, that had already been overrun by the Federals. Supervising rather than commanding, displaying a gentlemanly reluctance to offend independent-minded officers of lower rank, Lee saw his first campaign for the Confederacy end in defeat at the battle of Cheat Mountain or Elkwater on 10–15 September, when Confederate columns failed to cooperate enough to drive the Federals from the mountain.

On 31 August Lee had been confirmed as a full general of the Confederate regular army, a rank he had held without formal confirmation since its authorization by the Confederate Congress on 16 May. Confident of Lee's abilities despite Cheat Mountain, Davis next sent him to try to shore up another crumbling front. Unluckily, Lee arrived at Charleston to command the South Atlantic coast defenses on 7 November, the very day that the U.S. Navy captured the defenses of Port Royal Sound in South Carolina. Following this success, the Federal navy had access to the sheltered waters inside the sea islands and could shift vessels and troops up and down the South Carolina and Georgia coasts more rapidly than Lee could respond. He had to concede the bays and inlets south of Charleston to the enemy, permitting the Union to tighten its blockade and hold springboards for further offensive action.

On 2 March 1862 Davis summoned Lee back to Richmond to resume his duties as adviser at an inauspicious moment when the Confederacy confronted an apparently insurmountable challenge posed by Union offensives almost everywhere around its circumference without enough manpower to create an adequate defensive cordon. The defense of Tennessee was already collapsing, and the largest single enemy army, the Army of the Potomac under Major General George B. McClellan (1826–1885), was preparing to advance on Richmond.

Lee had concluded that the Confederacy would continue to suffer reversals if it persisted in a defensive strategy. If the South simply tried to hold its borders, the North could multiply its inherent advantages in manpower and resources by concentrating overwhelming force at the points of attack it chose. The only remedy for the Confederacy was to accept the risks of the initiative by going over to the attack at places of its own choosing. By concentrating force at those places, it might, with good fortune, achieve parity or even superiority of strength at critical points. Following this strategy, Lee arranged to reinforce Major General Thomas J. "Stonewall" Jackson's Army of the Valley sufficiently to permit it to undertake the Shenandoah Valley campaign of 8 May–9 June 1862. The Confederate concentration and initiative produced not only local tactical victories, but also the strategic advantage of diverting Federal troops from McClellan's offensive against Richmond.

Soon Lee confronted that offensive directly. In March, McClellan had moved his main force by sea from Washington to Fort Monroe; then he began an advance toward the Confederate capital by way of the peninsula between the York and James rivers. On 31 May, General Joseph E. Johnston, commanding the Confederate forces opposing him, was wounded at the battle of Fair Oaks or Seven Pines. The next day Lee succeeded to Johnston's command, which he promptly designated the Army of Northern Virginia. Lee applied his principles of concentrating force and seizing the initiative. He had Jackson join him with the Valley Army, and, thus reinforced, he conducted a series of attacks against McClellan just outside Richmond in the Seven Days battles of 25 June–1 July.

The battles saved Richmond and transformed Lee from an apparent failure to the hero of the Confederacy. Lee himself was nevertheless disappointed with the Seven Days, because he had hoped to destroy the Army of the Potomac. Lapses in coordination attributable at least in part to Lee's gentlemanly style of command helped account for the incompleteness of the victory, but for the next year Lee resolutely continued to pursue the goal of the destruction of the enemy army. He progressed in his strategic convictions beyond the belief that the Confederacy must seize the initiative to conclude also that the initiative must be pushed to a decisive, war-ending victory. Otherwise the superior resources of the Union would enable it to outlast local or regional setbacks. The Confederacy must compel the North to recognize its independence rapidly or it would not be able to do so at all.

These convictions carried Lee beyond tactical, battlefield attacks like those of the Seven Days to the strategic offensive. The Seven Days left McClellan's Army of the Potomac inactive, but it was still supported by the Union navy at Harrison's Landing on the James River, while in northern Virginia the Union organized a new Army of Virginia under Major General John Pope for an overland advance from Washington. Trusting in McClellan's by-now frequently demonstrated caution, Lee moved north to meet Pope. The Federals responded by withdrawing the Army of the Potomac from the Peninsula. On 29–30 August, Lee defeated Pope's army, reinforced by part of McClellan's, at the second battle of Manassas or Bull Run. The way was then clear for Lee to invade the North, fully assuming the strategic offensive, in the hope that a southern victory on Union soil would convince the North of the futility of trying to crush the Confederacy and prompt Lincoln's government to concede Confederate independence.

The Army of Northern Virginia had, however, lost casualties of about 25 percent (20,000 killed, wounded, and missing) in the Seven Days and 19 percent (9,000) at Second Manassas. These losses had by no means been completely replenished when Lee's army began crossing the Potomac River into Maryland on 5 September; furthermore, heavy straggling plagued his force, the result both of fatigue and of the disinclination of many Confederate soldiers to depart from a strategy simply of defending their country. Consequently, when the Federals, reunited as the Army of the Potomac under McClellan, brought Lee to battle at Sharpsburg on Antietam Creek on 17 September, Lee had only about 34,000 men to face about 71,500 of the enemy. He felt obliged to fight on the defensive. His men held their positions throughout the bloodiest single day of the war, with losses of some 10,318 or 31 percent (with the Federals losing some 12,400, or 25 percent of the 50,000 actually engaged); but after defying the enemy for one day more, Lee retreated back across the Potomac.

Promptly he importuned President Davis to reinforce his army so that he could resume the strategic offensive. Davis, respectful of Lee but not convinced of the appropriateness of his strategy, did not immediately comply. Therefore Lee's next two major battles were again strategically defensive. At Fredericksburg, Virginia, on 13 December 1862, against the Army of the Potomac now commanded by Major General Ambrose E. Burnside, Lee fought on the tactical defensive also and lost the relatively small total of 5,300 out of 72,000 men (7 percent). At Chancellorsville on 2–4 May 1863 Lee attacked on the battlefield against the latest Federal commander, Major General Joseph Hooker, losing nearly 13,000 men out of about 60,000 (22 percent).

Following Chancellorsville, Davis finally reinforced Lee to the strength the general believed necessary for a new invasion of the North. On 3 June 1863 Lee set out for Pennsylvania, but he did so without Stonewall Jackson, who had died on 10 May of complications from wounds suffered at Chancellorsville. Ever since the Pennsylvania campaign climaxed at Gettysburg on 1–3 July, debate has persisted over whether Jackson's absence accounts for Lee's inability—at Gettysburg or in any of his subsequent battles—to achieve the sort of complete tactical success that the flanking maneuvers led by Jackson at Second Manassas and Chancellorsville had provided. Probably the circumstances of the battle of Gettysburg would have precluded such bold maneuver anyway; in particular, Lee was hampered by a lack of familiarity with the terrain. At Gettysburg less ambitious attempts against both enemy flanks failed on 2 July, and the next day the battle ended with the defeat of Major General George E. Pickett's famous charge against the Union center. The skillful defensive tactics of Major General George G. Meade as Federal commander helped impose on Lee his highest casualties yet: 28,000, about 35 percent.

Lee probably gambled on Pickett's Charge because he recognized that no more throws of the dice of a strategic offensive would be possible. His cumulative casualties were already too great: here lay the fatal flaw in his strategy. He would still, nevertheless, risk attacking on the battlefield in the hope of destroying the enemy army, as he had done from the beginning. In the late summer and the autumn of 1863, he and Meade waged an indecisive campaign of maneuver in northern Virginia. The next spring, Lee faced a different kind of opponent when Lieutenant General Ulysses S. Grant, assuming the post of commanding general of the Union army, took the field in direct supervision of Meade. Grant was determined to end the war by eliminating Lee's Army of Northern Virginia, either by outmaneuvering and trapping it or by exploiting the North's superior manpower to trade casualties with it until Lee's numbers were exhausted. Lee's generalship forced Grant into the second alternative, but that could not save the Confederacy.

In the Wilderness (5–7 May 1864), at Spotsylvania Courthouse (7–20 May), and in lesser actions through Cold Harbor (3 June) and Lee's crossing to the south side of the James River (essentially completed 18 June), Lee's skill and tactical initiatives extracted about 64,000 casualties from the enemy, more than the 61,000 men with which he had begun the campaign against his opponents' 100,000. But the Army of Northern Virginia also suffered about 25,000 casualties during that time, and this arithmetic would inevitably prove fatal unless the Confederacy could maintain its fronts in a way demoralizing enough to the North to prevent Lincoln's reelection in November.

Lee did his part toward that end. On 15–16 June, Meade's Army of the Potomac crossed the James River east of Richmond to join Major General Benjamin F. Butler's (1818–1893) Army of the James in assailing the railroad junction at Petersburg, twenty miles south of the capital, to cut both Richmond and Lee's army off from the lower South. Lee checked the effort and held his opponents to a dreary deadlock of trench warfare around Petersburg through the rest of the summer and into the autumn. He also detached Lieutenant General Jubal A. Early to rescue the Shenandoah Valley from Federals operating there and to threaten Washington, which Early did by marching all the way to the fortifications of the Union capital by 11 July. Unfortunately for the Confederacy, the resources of the North were by this time too fully mobilized to permit Early's triumph to be more than transitory, and Major General Philip H. Sheridan crushed his force in the autumn, doing much to help assure Lincoln of a second term.

Lee persisted in the struggle because he believed himself bound by duty. On 6 February 1865 President Davis appointed him general in chief of the Confederate States Army, while he also remained commander of the Army of Northern Virginia. Hitherto he had derogated the capacities of black troops, but in desperation he urged their enlistment, which the Confederate Congress authorized on 13 March. It did so, however, without the promise of emancipation, which Lee, who now advocated gradual emancipation, thought necessary.

When good campaigning weather returned in the spring, Lee, with 44,000 men, no longer had enough strength to hold some twenty miles of the Petersburg trenches against Grant's force of 128,000. He proposed to withdraw westward and then southward to unite with General Joseph E. Johnston's forces in the Carolinas. Characteristically, he set the stage with an attack, against a vulnerable point in the Federal lines, hoping to compel Grant to weaken his western flank and thus ease the planned maneuver. But it was too late. Lee's assault on Fort Stedman failed on 25 March. Grant then reinforced rather than reduced his left flank, breaking past Lee's own western flank at Five Forks on 1 April. This breakthrough threatened Lee's whole Petersburg position with encirclement, and the next day Lee told Davis that Richmond and Petersburg would have to be evacuated.

Knowing that the chances of joining Johnston were now remote, Lee nevertheless hastened to avoid the enemy's Five Forks spearhead and retreat to the west.

The Federals, better nourished and supplied, paralleled his movements and won several races to key railroad depots. On 9 April Lee's troops attacked southward from Appomattox Courthouse and discovered that all paths of retreat had been closed. Lee decided he must surrender himself and the Army of Northern Virginia to Grant. He did so that afternoon. Only 26,765 men remained to stack arms (and only 7,800 of those on the surrender rolls had actually been bearing arms still).

Under the surrender terms, Lee, like his men, became a paroled prisoner of war. He was, however, among the high Confederate officials excluded from President Andrew Johnston's amnesty proclamation of 29 May, and on 7 June he was indicted for treason by a grand jury of the United States Court for the Eastern District of Virginia sitting at Norfolk. The indictment was not pursued, but neither did Lee receive individual pardon, though on 13 June he wrote to Grant enclosing an application for amnesty.

Still, Lee set his course to lead the South toward accepting reunion. He reiterated his belief that it was the duty of every citizen to work in that direction when he accepted the invitation issued by the Board of Trustees of Washington College on 5 August to become president of that institution. Promptly he traveled to Lexington in the Valley of Virginia to take up the office for the fall term. On 2 October he was formally installed as head of a school whose buildings and library had been looted in 1864 and which found itself short of funds and almost all other necessities, with only fifty students in attendance. Lee succeeded in restoring the college as a model for higher education in the South, and enrollment was up to nearly 400 students in the fall term of 1870.

On 28 September 1870 Lee was stricken by what would now probably be diagnosed as a coronary thrombosis. He died at daybreak on 12 October in Lexington.

In spite of some criticism of his prompt acceptance of reunion, in the South Lee came to be even more revered after Appomattox than he had been before. His reputation continued to grow after his death, and by the turn of the century his cult had spread into the North, signaling a national apotheosis. During the war Stonewall Jackson had probably been more warmly admired; Lee's aristocratic aloofness had earned him more respect than enthusiastic devotion. After the war, however, Lee's apparent remoteness from the usual run of humanity lent itself to his translation into something of a Christ figure: his worldly defeat came to attest to a nobility of character all the more sublime.

Nobility of character Lee surely possessed, in an exemplary personal and family life and in his unswerving devotion to his conception of his duty. As a military commander he demands a more critical appraisal. As a battlefield tactician he was inferior to none in the Napoleonic art of the maneuver against the enemy flank or rear designed to subdue a rival army psychologically as well as physically; Second Manassas and Chancellorsville exhibited masterpieces of such maneuver.

His strategic prescriptions, however, were more questionable. His insistence on seizing the risks of the initiative—attacking in most of his battles and going over to the strategic offensive whenever possible—implied heavy casualties and thus the lavish expenditure of the scarcest of all the Confederacy's scarce resources, its manpower. In addition, Lee inclined toward a parochial view of Confederate strategy. President Davis consulted him about overall strategy through most of the war, but Lee tended consistently to underrate the strategic importance of regions other than his own and the problems of the generals fighting there. In the summer of 1863, for example, reinforcing the West to try to save Vicksburg might have been a more appropriate strategy than invading Pennsylvania.

Nevertheless, Lee's strategic vision was clear when he rejected a passive cordon defense as one that would allow the North, by choosing the points of attack, to multiply its inherent numerical advantage. The true alternative to Lee's strategy was a strategy of flexible defense, yielding territory to trade space for lives and time, counterattacking on opportune occasions to erode the enemy's will and enhance Confederate morale. Such a strategy would have been akin to George Washington's. On the other hand, Lee's risks in pursuing the initiative took into account the probable need for a swift victory if there was to be victory at all. From that perspective, Lee may have chosen the least undesirable strategic option in circumstances that offered little or no hope of winning the war. Combining such a judgment with an appreciation of Lee's mastery as a tactician assures him his rank among the American soldiers most deserving of study and admiration.

• The principal collection of Lee's private papers is in the Library of Congress. His official papers in the National Archives are in Records of the Office of the Chief of Engineers (Record Group 77), Records of the Adjutant General's Office, 1780s–1917 (Record Group 94), and the War Department Collection of Confederate Records (Record Group 109). The National Archives has compiled a "Microfilm of Selected Military Service Records in the Custody of the National Archives Relating to Robert E. Lee."

The United States Military Academy Archives, West Point, N.Y., has formal reports on Lee as a cadet and records of his superintendency. Washington and Lee University, Lexington, Va., has material from Lee's presidency of Washington College not found in his private papers. The Virginia Historical Society, Richmond, has early Lee letters and much material on the Lee family. Additional Lee papers are to be found in the Chicago Historical Society; Manuscript Department, William R. Perkins Library, Duke University, Durham, N.C.; Maryland Historical Society, Baltimore; Missouri Historical Society, St. Louis; Museum of the Confederacy, Richmond; Manuscripts Department and Southern Historical Collection, University of North Carolina at Chapel Hill; New York Public Library; New-York Historical Society; Humanities Research Center Library, University of Texas at Austin; and Western Reserve Historical Society, Cleveland. The Henry L. Huntington Library, San Marino, Calif., has letters to Martha Custis Williams from Lee, published in Avery Craven, ed., *"To Markie": The Letters of Robert E. Lee to Martha Custis Williams from the Originals in the Huntington Library* (1933).

The principal published collections of Lees papers are Clifford Dowdey and Louis Manarin, eds., *The Wartime Papers of R. E. Lee* (1961); *Lee's Dispatches: Unpublished Letters of General Robert E. Lee, C.S.A., to Jefferson Davis and the War Department of the Confederate States of America, 1862–65*, from the private collection of Wimberly Jones De Renne of Wormsloe, Georgia, edited, with an introduction and notes, by Douglas Southall Freeman, new edition, with additional dispatches and a foreword by Grady McWhiney (1957); Robert E. Lee [Jr.], *Recollections and Letters of General Robert E. Lee*, 2d ed. (1924); John William Jones, *Personal Reminiscences, Anecdotes and Letters of General Robert E. Lee* (1874), which together with the book by Lee's son publishes most of the papers in the Library of Congress, though in Jones's book often with errors of transcription; and John William Jones, *Life and Letters of Robert Edward Lee, Soldier and Man* (1906), which includes many antebellum letters.

The standard biography remains Douglas Southall Freeman, *R. E. Lee: A Biography* (4 vols., 1934–1935), of which Richard Harwell, *Lee* (1961), is a one-volume abridgement. Freeman's work should be balanced against the much more critical study by Alan T. Nolan, *Lee Considered: General Robert E. Lee and Civil War History* (1991). Thomas L. Connelly, *The Marble Man: Robert E. Lee and His Image in American Society* (1977), concerns the Lee legend. Noteworthy portraits by those who knew Lee include Walter H. Taylor, *Four Years with General Lee . . .* (1877); the same author's *General Lee: His Campaigns in Virginia, 1861–1865, with Personal Reminiscences* (1906); and Fitzhugh Lee, *General Lee* (1894). Still important as military assessments are Sir Frederick Barton Maurice, *Robert E. Lee, the Soldier* (1925), and John Frederick Charles Fuller, *Grant and Lee: A Study in Personality and Generalship* (1933). For the postwar years, see Marshall W. Fishwick, *Lee after the War* (1963), and Charles Bracelen Flood, *Lee: The Last Years* (1981). A useful reference is Marshall W. Fishwick and William M. Hollis, *Preliminary Checklist of Writings about R. E. Lee* (1951).

RUSSELL F. WEIGLEY

LEE, Rose Hum (20 Aug. 1904–25 Mar. 1964), sociologist, was born in Butte, Montana, the daughter of Hum Wah-Lung, a Chinese immigrant laborer, and Lin Fong. Her father died while Rose was still young. Her mother encouraged Rose and her six siblings to pursue their educations. This early encouragement was an unusual and formative influence in Lee's life, for the idea of a daughter pursuing an American education violated the norms of the small, tightly knit Chinese community in which she was raised.

As a Chinese woman, Lee was expected to raise money for her widowed mother. Instead, she pursued a higher education with her mother's blessings and support. She later wrote that education helped her "escape the domination" of Chinese who sought to make her conform to her expected place. Lee applied herself diligently to her studies and graduated from Butte High School in 1921. Events in her personal life and in China, however, would sidetrack her pursuit of a higher education for two decades.

After graduating from high school, Rose married Ku Young Lee, a Chinese national, in 1921. Her mother was opposed to the union, but Lee left in the late 1920s with her husband to live and work in Canton, China. In 1937 the Japanese invaded Canton, and Lee became an active participant in several Chinese and international relief organizations, including the Canton Red Cross. During her relief work, Lee adopted a child. Soon after the Japanese invasion, Lee returned to the United States with her daughter and decided to resume her education. It is not known what became of her first husband.

Once again Lee's mother defended her efforts against the protests of relatives and other members of the community, and in 1942 Lee received a B.S. in social work from the Carnegie Institute of Technology. She then pursued graduate studies in sociology at the University of Chicago, where she received her A.M. in 1943 and her Ph.D. in 1947. In 1945 Lee joined the faculty of Roosevelt University in Chicago, where she became the chair of the sociology department in 1956. For her entire career Lee was one of the few Asian-American women who held a university position in the humanities, and she was perhaps the most distinguished. In 1951 Lee married lawyer Glenn Ginn, a Chinese American who was a major source of inspiration for her work. She described him as an "undaunted, courageous" advocate for Chinese who wanted to live "the American democratic way of life."

Lee's first major article, "The Decline of China-towns in the United States," was drawn from her dissertation, "The Growth and Decline of Chinese Communities in the Rocky Mountain Region." Published in the *American Journal of Sociology* in 1949, the article examined the status of Chinatowns outside of San Francisco and New York. Using Butte's diminutive Chinatown as a model, Lee argued that economic, legal, and social pressures were slowly but inevitably eroding Chinatowns across America. She theorized that only the Chinese communities of New York and San Francisco, with their greater size and access to trade with China, would survive the coming years. (Lee's dissertation was published in 1978, more than thirty years after it was written, as part of a series titled The Asian Experience in North America: Chinese and Japanese.)

A few years later Lee renounced her own findings. In her 1957 article "Chinese Immigration and Population Changes since 1940," published in *Sociology and Social Research*, she wrote that "predictions made in the mid-forties were invalid by 1950." The predictions were not invalidated by faulty research but by subtle yet important changes in America's immigration laws. Through careful demographic analysis, Lee was one of the first to fully explain how the gradual easing of immigration and citizenship standards during and after World War II had profoundly affected the Chinese population of the United States, reversing the decades-old pattern of decline that she had first identified in her dissertation.

Lee's most important work was *The Chinese in the United States of America* (1960). In this book she portrayed the full breadth of Chinese life in America. She explained that the Chinese population had "often been discussed but seldom understood." Marking the culmination of her career, this study incorporated her own research as well as other sources to become the first significant synthesis of Chinese-American life since Mary Coolidge's *Chinese Immigration* (1909). Lee highlighted the complicated divisions within the Chinese community, not only along generational lines but also according to Chinese views of the larger American society.

This book marked a departure from Lee's precise, analytical writing. Although much of *The Chinese in the United States of America* was a carefully supported sociological study, it was also a personal attempt to define and defend the place of "American-Chinese" in American society. In her candid introduction, she wrote that she expected that the book would be seen as a "betrayal" by some members of the Chinese community. In her previous works, Lee had identified assimilation as an increasingly dominant pattern in Chinese-American life, but in this book she identified assimilation as the correct path. Her strong assimilationist sympathies obfuscated her analysis at times. She unfairly castigated many Chinese in the United States as separatist "sojourners" and overlooked the complexities of life among those who did not fit her category of integrationist "American-Chinese." Yet her bias should not outweigh her impressive synthesis of Chinese-American life. As a Chinese American with a high public profile and as one who did most of her scholarly work after China had become a communist nation, she undoubtedly felt a great deal of pressure to integrate Chinese Americans intellectually into the conservative and conformist American fabric of the late 1950s and early 1960s. Indeed, she wrote that the 1960s would be a "very significant" decade, a time that "may determine whether the Americans of Chinese ancestry will find partial or total integration into American society."

Lee took a leave of absence from Roosevelt University in 1961, taking a position at Phoenix College in Arizona. She died in Phoenix of a brain embolism.

Rose Hum Lee was an important early figure in Asian-American history and studies. Before Lee, few scholars had examined the position of Chinese in America. She was one of the first to point out the implications of the 1940s immigration codes for Chinese communities. Her articles and books remain important starting points for understanding Chinese-American life in the mid-twentieth century.

• The Roosevelt University Library, Chicago, has a small file on Lee, which includes photographs. Among her publications not mentioned in the text are "Chinese Americans," in *One America*, ed. Francis James Brown and Joseph Slabey Roucek (1952); *The City: Urbanism and Urbanization in Major World Regions* (1955); "The Recent Immigrant Chinese Families of the San Francisco–Oakland Area," *Marriage and Family Living* 18 (Feb. 1956): 14–24; "The Established Chinese Families of the San Francisco Bay Area," *Midwest Sociologist* 20 (Dec. 1957): 19–26; and "The Stranded Chinese in the United States," *Phylon* 19 (1958): 180–98. Although she is cited frequently, little is known about Lee and her work. A brief description of her scholarly importance is given by Betty Lee Sung in *Mountain of Gold: The Story of the Chinese in*

America (1967). Obituaries are in the *New York Times* and the *New York Herald Tribune*, both 27 Mar. 1964, the *Chicago Sun-Times*, 26 Mar. 1964, and the *American Sociological Review* 30 (Feb. 1965): 128–29.

JOHN S. BAICK

LEE, Russell Werner (21 July 1903–28 Aug. 1986), photographer, was born in Ottawa, Illinois, the son of Burton Lee, a businessman, and Adeline Pope. The family was financially well off but unstable. Lee's parents divorced when he was five, and his father disappeared from his life. Five years later his mother was killed by a car while crossing a busy street in a rainstorm, leaving Lee, who witnessed the event, to be raised by a succession of relatives and court-appointed guardians. In later life, many of Lee's strongest photographs would be of objects and symbols that evoked "home" or "community."

Educated at Culver Military Academy and Lehigh University, Lee received his B.S. in chemical engineering in 1925, and in 1927 he married Doris Emrick, a painter. The marriage produced no children, but through contact with his wife Russell became acquainted with and attracted to the world of art. In 1929 he took advantage of a legacy from his mother's estate and left his job in engineering, moving with his wife into a life of full-time commitment to art. The couple first spent two years on the West Coast, where they met Diego Rivera. Lee enjoyed Rivera as a person but was not strongly attracted to his work, perhaps because of its monumental character. In 1931 the Lees moved to the East Coast, spending summers at an artists' colony in Woodstock, New York, and winters in New York City.

It was during this time that Lee discovered photography, a medium that allowed him to combine his background in chemistry with his interest in art. Lee was initially attracted to photography because it permitted him to dissect a situation and present its many facets. The camera's ability to record the details of everyday life fascinated him. Never one to look for a single "decisive moment" or a monumental, defining image, Lee took extended series of photographs virtually from the beginning of his photographic career, presaging the later development of the picture story.

In 1936 Lee joined the photographic team of the Resettlement Administration, a small and somewhat maverick farm relief agency of the New Deal that was dedicated to improving the lot of poor farmers, particularly sharecroppers and migrant workers, and that often met opposition from wealthy landowners. Along with a small group of skilled professionals, including Walker Evans, Dorothea Lange, Arthur Rothstein, Marion Post Wolcott, and Gordon Parks, Lee's job was to take pictures that would convince the general public that rural poverty was a grim reality that required federal intervention. Lee's image of ragged children standing around a single bowl of unidentifiable food, titled *Christmas Dinner*, was one of many effective pictures used in the fight to obtain more aid for impoverished farmers. Like all of his pictures, *Christ-*

mas Dinner was simple, honest, and direct. Lee refused to set up photographic situations or to fake pictures in any way, insisting that the truth was far more effective than any created image.

In 1937 the agency was subsumed by the larger and more mainstream U.S. Department of Agriculture, and its name was changed to the Farm Security Administration (FSA). The role of the photographic team was consequently broadened to include a general documentation of rural and small-town life in America. Lee continued to work with the agency through 1942, spending many months out of each year on the road and taking thousands of pictures of everyday life on farms and in towns. He was best known for producing major groups of images illustrating the many facets of life in small towns such as St. Augustine, Texas, and Pie Town, New Mexico. His work was people oriented and generally populistic, like most of the social documentary photographers of the depression era.

In 1938 Lee's first marriage ended in divorce, and he married a newspaper woman from Dallas, Texas, named Jean Smith who traveled with Lee, becoming his companion, notetaker, and assistant. This marriage also produced no children. With the encouragement of the agency's photographic director, Roy Stryker, the Lees developed a sociological approach to photographic documentation, emphasizing the precise rendering of human interrelationships. Lee often approached a community with a series of questions: What do women do during the day? How do they form networks and interact? What do men do? What role does religion play in this community? How do families entertain themselves? How do children cope with loneliness and isolation? As Lee became more skilled in translating such questions into visual form, his work gained both richness and depth. Such a taxonomic approach fit well with Lee's background in the sciences, and it also suited the needs of the agency. His photographs were used in dozens of traveling exhibits, showing the general public the work of the FSA, and many also appeared in major photographic exhibits such as the First International Photographic Exhibition in 1938 in Grand Central Palace, New York City, and later in the Family of Man exhibition assembled by Edward Steichen at the Museum of Modern Art in New York in 1955. Lee's FSA photographs, along with those of Evans, Lange, Wolcott, Rothstein, and others, are preserved at the Prints and Photographs Division of the Library of Congress.

In January 1943 Lee left the FSA and joined the war effort with the rank of captain, serving as head of the Still Photography Section of the Air Transport Command. The Air Transport Command's job was to ferry materials and supplies to hundreds of bases scattered around the world in support of the global war effort. Lee's work consisted of making still photographs of all approaches to every airbase within the ATC structure in order to provide visual guidance to pilots who were often forced to land under radio silence. Lee endured long hours of hard, sometimes dangerous, and often routine work. He was awarded the Air Medal and left the ATC at the end of the war with the rank of major and an ulcer.

The postwar years were a period of relative quiet for Lee, as he and Jean made Austin, Texas, their permanent residence. In 1946 Lee undertook a short-term yet major assignment to document bad living conditions in the bituminous coal industry, working with the U.S. Navy and the Department of the Interior. Six weeks of travel and work in the coal country yielded 4,000 photographs, now located in the National Archives, which were used extensively in the final report of the Coal Mines Administration. This report helped to bring about new federal health and safety regulations, in both the mines and the towns that surrounded them. After completing this project, Russell became more selective about the sort of work he was willing to undertake. He accepted occasional assignments in the field of industrial photography; did work for the *Texas Observer*, a small newspaper that offered a liberal critique of life in Texas in the 1950s; and took long trips with Jean. In 1960 the Lees went to Italy for several weeks, shooting more than 4,000 images of everyday life in rural and small-town Italy, emphasizing the warmth of human interaction that they saw there. From 1965 to 1973 Lee taught creative photography in the art department of the University of Texas. After retirement he remained active in photography, both in the field and in the darkroom, until shortly before his death in Austin.

Lee's life in photography produced a large and profound body of work that has continued to influence the medium. His visual descendants are those who use the camera to investigate the world around them directly, without manipulation, artifice, or self-absorption, who use the detail-gathering ability of the camera to show the world in an intense way, who accept people on their own terms and accord them their dignity; who, in short, do what Russell Lee did.

• Thousands of Lee's photographs are in the FSA File of the Prints and Photographs Division in the Library of Congress and in the Audio-Visual Division of the Archives of the United States. Material relating to Lee's work after 1946 is in the Center for American History at the University of Texas, while many "vintage" prints from the FSA period are at the Photographic Collection of the Southwest Texas Writer's Project at Southwest Texas University, San Marcos. Lee's photographs were used in many state history books produced by the Federal Writers' Project. For example, see *Iowa: A Guide to the Hawkeye State* (1938). Lee worked with Richard Wright to produce illustrations for Wright's *Twelve Million Black Voices* (1941). About 200 of Lee's photographs were used in *A Medical Survey of the Bituminous Coal Industry* (U.S. Government Printing Office, 1947). Lee's photographs of Italy can be seen in William Arrowsmith, ed., *Image of Italy* (1961), and many of his photographs were also published in Thomas H. Garver, ed., *Just before the War: Urban America from 1935 to 1941 as Seen by the Photographers of the Farm Security Administration* (1968). A number of Lee photographs were presented in F. Jack Hurley, *Portrait of a Decade: Roy Stryker and the Development of Documentary Photography in the Thirties* (1972). A book-length treatment of Lee is Hurley, *Russell Lee: Photographer* (1978).

Articles using Lee photographs include Edward Steichen's "The F.S.A. Photographers," *U.S. Camera Annual: 1939* (1938); Lee's "Pie Town, New Mexico," *U.S. Camera*, Oct. 1941; and Hurley, "Pie Town, N.M., 1940," *American Photographer*, Mar. 1983, pp. 76–85. Barry O'Connell, "In the Coal Mines Far Away: Russell Lee's Photographs of Mining Life," in *Prospects II* (1976) shows Lee's photographs for the Coal Mines Administration. For a photographic portfolio see Nicholas Lemann, "Russell Lee's Photos of a Louisiana State Fair Capture the Spirit of the Common Man," *Civilization*, Jan.–Feb. 1995, pp. 58–71. An obituary is in the *New York Times*, 30 Aug. 1986.

F. JACK HURLEY

LEE, Sammy (26 May 1890–30 Mar. 1968), stage and film dance director, was born Samuel Levy in New York City, the son of Harold Levy, a Russian immigrant tailor, and Miriam (maiden name unknown). Although he had little or no training in dance, Lee began performing at the age of eight on street corners and in bars near Henry Street on Manhattan's Lower East Side. In later interviews he mentioned this fact with some pride, stating that he learned everything through "observation and imitation." In 1901 he changed his name to Sammy Lee and made his debut at Miner's Bowery Theatre. Within a few years he became one of Gus Edwards's "Postal Telegraph Boys" and then joined Irene Lee's "Candy Kids," another popular children's song-and-dance act.

At seventeen Lee joined another performer, Harry Kessler, as a "flash" dance act, which meant the steps of the routine consisted of acrobatic combinations with expanded leg and body movements. Despite such tricks, the act was less successful than his next partnership with Ruby Norton; their adagio act eventually brought them to Broadway in Rudolf Friml's *The Firefly* (1912). Norton and Lee continued as a dance act in vaudeville, touring as far as London, until 1916 when Lee enlisted to fight in World War I.

After the war Lee continued to perform with other partners or as a solo act until he got his first chance as a Broadway dance director with *Little Miss Charity* in 1920. However, it was *The Gingham Girl* (1922) that established him as one of the New York theater's more interesting dance directors during the 1920s. Instead of using chorus lines of thirty or forty girls doing simple steps in unison, he worked with smaller groups of eight or twelve; his dancers performed acrobatic, tap, and precision work, developing "distinct personalities who did things that could really interest an audience," as Lee recalled. The critics were delighted with his changes in the standard choreographic routines (which included surprise combinations and patterns), and producers were happy with the lower production costs of a smaller chorus. He continued to elaborate on this style combining versatility with intimacy throughout most of his musicals during the 1920s.

Although Lee took part in occasional lavish revues with large choruses, such as Earl Carroll's *Vanities* in 1923 and 1924, he became especially associated with the Broadway shows of George Gershwin and Ira Gershwin, beginning with *Lady, Be Good!* (1924), where he worked with Fred Astaire and Adele Astaire for the first time and is credited with helping them add faster steps and pattern changes to their tap numbers. He continued to work with the Gershwins on *Tip-Toes* (1925) and *Oh, Kay!* (1926). Both musicals contained elaborate tap routines that often used surprise effects, for example, a chorus tapping while playing prop trombones to "Sweet and Low-Down" in *Tip-Toes* or the intricate hand and thigh clapping for "Clap Yo' Hands" in *Oh, Kay!*

Between these Gershwin shows Lee found time to stage the dances for one of the classic musicals of the decade, *No! No! Nanette!*, which opened on Broadway in 1925 after an extensive tour. His combination of acrobatics, tap, and social dances highlighted numbers such as "I Want to Be Happy" and "Too Many Rings Around Rosie," and he proved to be lyrical as well with the more delicate soft-shoe dancing of the principals and chorus in "Tea for Two."

In 1926 Lee was commissioned by the Metropolitan Opera to choreograph the ballet *Skyscrapers* by John Alden Carpenter, which for a former vaudevillian was a notable honor. By this time he was considered one of Broadway's "Big Four" dance directors along with Busby Berkeley, Bobby Connolly, and Seymour Felix.

The high point of Lee's Broadway career was probably marked by his dances for *Show Boat* in 1927. Jerome Kern's music and Oscar Hammerstein II's book and precise stage directions were well-complemented by Lee's choreography, in which he showed the evolution of dance styles from the cakewalks of the 1890s to the jazz dances of the 1920s. After *Show Boat*, he produced, directed, and choreographed his own musical, *Cross My Heart* (1928), although it was not a success.

Lee was able to make up his losses on this show by accepting a lucrative offer from Metro-Goldwyn-Mayer in Hollywood. Like most of the other studios, MGM was tapping Broadway talent to help stage the "All Talking! All Singing! All Dancing!" motion pictures that audiences craved after the debut of *The Jazz Singer* in 1927. Lee worked on many of the early talkie musicals, including *The Hollywood Revue of 1929*, in which he staged a gamut of numbers starting with the opening minstrel show chorus, a frenetic Charleston for Joan Crawford, an elaborate military tap dance for Marion Davies and male chorus, and a breathtaking acrobatic number for Bessie Love. He again worked with Crawford—and Fred Astaire in his first screen role—in *Dancing Lady* (1933), for which he staged all the tap numbers.

After this film he went to 20th Century-Fox to work on musicals for Alice Faye, such as *King of Burlesque* (1935), which showcased Lee's knowledge of vaudeville routines, or for Shirley Temple, such as *Heidi* (1937), which included an elaborate dream ballet combining pseudo-Swiss folk steps with American tap routines.

At the end of his contract with 20th Century-Fox Lee freelanced from studio to studio for the rest of his career, interspersing choreography for nightclubs, such as the Coconut Grove, with successive films. One of the films in this later period was *Honolulu* (1939) for MGM's tapping star Eleanor Powell. Although Powell always did the choreography for her own solos, Lee was in charge of the chorus numbers and ensembles such as "Hymn to the Sun" for which he surrounded her with hula-skirted young women who echo the star's movements with foot-stomping, clapping, and body sways. *Honolulu* was Lee's last important film. Following it he worked mainly on B musicals such as *Hit the Ice* (1943), an Abbott and Costello vehicle at Universal, or *Carolina Blues* (1944) at Columbia. His last film, *Earl Carroll Vanities* (1945) for Republic, almost took him back to the start of his career; in it Lee used many of the dancers from Carroll's famous club in Hollywood. After a few more nightclub engagements, Lee retired and lived in Hollywood until his death in Woodland Hills, California.

As a dance director, Lee's output was prolific both on Broadway and in Hollywood, although he could not be called a particularly innovative choreographer after the initial changes he made in the early 1920s. However, his Broadway dances represent some of the best of the formula musicals of that decade, and his Hollywood musicals at least record for posterity tap styles, vaudeville routines, and social dances that might otherwise have been lost.

• The most detailed account of Lee's career is Frank W. D. Ries, "Sammy Lee: The Broadway Career," *Dance Chronicle* 9, no. 1 (1986), and "Sammy Lee: The Hollywood Career," *Dance Chronicle* 11, no. 2 (1988). Ethan Mordden's *Broadway Babies* (1983) includes an account of the musical styles of Lee's period, and Mordden's *The Hollywood Musical* (1981) is excellent on the early Hollywood musicals. Clive Hirschorn's *The Hollywood Musical* (1981) includes fairly accurate descriptions of the movies and detailed cast lists. Some of Lee's movies are available on video and laser disc, and the Criterion laser disc of *Show Boat* (1936) includes rare film of the original Broadway cast dancing some of his routines. An obituary is in *Variety*, 10 Apr. 1968.

FRANK W. D. RIES

LEE, Samuel J. (22 Nov. 1844–1 Apr. 1895), politician and lawyer, was born in bondage on a plantation in Abbeville District, South Carolina. A mulatto, he was probably the son of his owner, Samuel McGowan, and a slave woman. When McGowan entered Confederate service, Lee attended him in the camps and on the battlefield. Lee was wounded twice, at Second Manassas in 1862 and later near Hanover Junction, Virginia. After emancipation, he farmed in Abbeville District and then in Edgefield County, South Carolina, having settled in Hamburg. By 1870 Lee had accumulated at least $500 in real estate and $400 in personal property. Sometime before February 1872 he married a woman identified in legal documents as R. A. Lee; her maiden name is unknown.

Though not formally educated as a youth, Lee had learned to read and evidently developed talents as a debater and orator fairly early. When the Reconstruction Acts of 1867 allowed freedmen new opportunities for formal political participation, he made the most of his skills. He served as a registrar in 1867 and became an Edgefield County commissioner in 1868. The same year, he was elected to represent his black-majority county in the South Carolina house of representatives. A Republican, Lee sat in the legislature for the next six years—after 1871 as representative of Aiken County, which had been formed from portions of Edgefield and several other counties. In his early years in the legislature, he was a party regular, consistently voting for legislation that strengthened Republican power and black political rights in South Carolina, but he was somewhat less apt than other black Republicans to support measures pressing integration of transportation facilities. Yet, as a trustee of the University of South Carolina beginning in 1873, he participated in the opening of that college to African Americans (this experiment in biracial education, which prompted the resignation or dismissal of some white faculty members, was ended by Democrats as soon as Reconstruction collapsed).

As African Americans increasingly demanded and won leadership positions in the South Carolina Republican party, Lee rose to become Speaker of the state house of representatives in 1872. He brought a noted polish to the position, being termed by one Yankee journalist an "elegant and accomplished" officer "who would have creditably presided over any commonwealth's legislative assembly" (King, p. 460). Lee did not, however, use his authority as Speaker to increase the number of black committee chairmen. Regrettably, too, at a time when ethical standards were none too high among American politicians, and in a place where opportunities for black Republicans to prosper were few, Lee submitted to abundant temptation. He later admitted to taking money for his vote on a bill and to converting state funds to personal use. Further accusations of corruption were lodged against him, including that he outfitted his home in Aiken with furniture purchased by the state.

Lee resigned the speakership and left the legislature in 1874 to give full time to a second profession, one that would prove less clouded than his political career. He had read law while serving in the general assembly, been admitted to the bar by 1872, and established a practice in Aiken. Initially, though, the baggage he had accumulated as a Reconstruction politician weighed the young attorney down. In 1875 Lee was convicted of fraud in his handling of funds as a county commissioner. Elected solicitor of the second circuit in 1876, he had to resign after Democrats made accusations regarding a large bribe he had allegedly taken as a legislator. After an indictment for conspiracy to defraud the state was brought by the newly installed Democratic administration in 1877, Lee left South Carolina and worked in Alabama, investigating land claims for the federal government.

The conspiracy case seems never to have been brought to trial, and by the following year Lee had returned to settle in Charleston. At first he worked for a white attorney there, but within a few years he established his own firm and became the busiest black lawyer in South Carolina. Chiefly practicing criminal law, Lee attracted more clients and did better by them than any other African-American attorney in the state (forty-six blacks were admitted to the South Carolina bar between 1868 and 1895, the year of Lee's death). Not confining his work to Charleston, he appeared before the state supreme court in Columbia several dozen times between 1880 and 1894.

Lee did not entirely abjure politics and public life after South Carolina was "redeemed" by white conservatives. He was a member of a delegation of black southerners who conferred with President-elect James Garfield in 1881 and the following year competed with Robert Smalls for a Republican congressional nomination (both men lost out to a third candidate, who was white). Having been active in the Reconstruction-era state militia, he served in the early 1890s as general of a black militia brigade in Charleston.

For all his ability and grace in the courtroom, Lee's black clients could not pay him well, if at all, and he did not prosper in his legal practice. At the time of his sudden death from heart failure in Charleston, his estate amounted to some $230 worth of law books and $115 in cash. Though his potential was somewhat dimmed by the temptations of office, the implacability of Democratic opponents, and the poverty of the African-American community he served, Lee remains a conspicuous figure in the opening of politics and the professions to African Americans in the post-emancipation South.

• Eric Foner collected much of the available information for his entry on Lee in *Freedom's Lawmakers: A Directory of Black Officeholders during Reconstruction* (1993). See also Lawrence C. Bryant, *Negro Legislators in South Carolina, 1868–1902* (1967). The most complete discussion of Lee's legal career is in J. R. Oldfield, "A High and Honorable Calling: Black Lawyers in South Carolina, 1868–1915," *Journal of American Studies* 23 (1989): 395–406. Lee's career in politics is touched upon in Thomas Holt, *Black over White: Black Political Leadership in South Carolina during Reconstruction* (1977); Martin Abbott, "County Officers in South Carolina in 1868," *South Carolina Historical Magazine* 60 (1959): 30–40; Vernon Burton, "Edgefield Reconstruction Black Leaders," *Proceedings of the South Carolina Historical Association 1988–1989*, pp. 27–38; and Edward King, *The Great South* (1875). For Lee's testimony on corruption, see *Report on Public Frauds. Report of the Joint Investigating Committee on Public Frauds and Election of Hon. J. J. Patterson to the United States Senate Made to the General Assembly of South Carolina at the Regular Session, 1877–78* (1878). An obituary is in the *Charleston News and Courier*, 2 Apr. 1895.

PATRICK G. WILLIAMS

LEE, Samuel Phillips (13 Feb. 1812–5 June 1897), naval officer, was born at Sully Plantation in Fairfax County, Virginia, the son of Francis Lightfoot Lee (1782–1850), lawyer and planter, and Jane Fitzgerald. He was the grandson of Richard Henry Lee and a cousin of Robert E. Lee. Phillips Lee's mother died in 1816, and his father, because of numerous bereavements and

illnesses, was incompetent after 1820. Thus, Lee and his siblings were reared by relatives who sent him to sea as an acting midshipman at the age of thirteen. When only seventeen he was wounded in a duel. In 1833 he was highly praised for effective action when his ship, the *Brandywine*, lost its tiller twice during a stormy passage around Cape Horn. In 1835–1836 he again won high praise for service as acting lieutenant aboard the USS *Vincennes*. In 1837 he sailed with Charles Wilkes on an exploring expedition to the Antarctic as first lieutenant aboard the USS *Peacock*. According to fellow officers he served admirably, but after bitter quarreling with Wilkes, he was ordered back to Washington in 1839. He was then assigned to the West Indian Squadron but spent most of the next three years on leave in the Washington area.

In 1843 Lee married Elizabeth Blair, daughter of Francis P. Blair (1791–1876), the controversial Jacksonian editor and politician. The Blair family's objections to Lee's profession had delayed the marriage for several years, but the bride's parents soon accepted him as another son and provided the loving family relationship he had been denied as a child. The family connection proved to be both an advantage and a handicap to his career as the Blairs' influence waxed and waned. The Blairs were extremely prominent in Abraham Lincoln's first administration. The Lees' only child, Blair Lee, was destined to become Maryland's first senator elected by the people after the Seventeenth Amendment to the Constitution was ratified.

During the next few years Lee often antagonized senior officers by advocating a steam navy. From 1843 to 1855 he commanded coastal survey expeditions studying winds, currents, depths, tides, birds, shoals, and weather patterns, and his meticulous reports were an important contribution to naval science. In 1855 Congress printed 2,000 copies of his report from a voyage on the USS *Dolphin*. In May 1847 he briefly participated in the Mexican War as commander of the USS *Washington* and was commended by Commodore Matthew Perry for his role in helping capture Fort Iturbide near Vera Cruz.

In 1855 he was promoted to commander and took a three-year leave of absence during which he invested in St. Louis real estate. Returning to active service, he spent from 1858 to 1860 performing various administrative and board duties in the Washington and Annapolis areas.

In 1860, commanding the USS *Vandalia*, Lee was ordered to join the East Indian Squadron, but at Cape Town, South Africa, on 27 February 1861, he learned of southern secession. Disobeying orders, he sailed back to New York, where he was reprimanded but promptly assigned to the Union's inadequate southern blockade. Only three wooden ships blockaded Charleston through the summer of 1861, and Lee's efforts on the *Vandalia* were highly praised by the blockade commander, Admiral Garrett Pendergast, after the *Vandalia* captured two southern ships. In early 1862, as commander of the steamer *Oneida*, he served under Admiral David Farragut in the campaign that captured New Orleans, Baton Rouge, and Natchez and threatened Vicksburg. In various engagements Lee performed with both daring and skill, as the *Oneida* took several hits and suffered numerous casualties.

In July 1862 Lee was promoted to captain, and on 11 August 1862 he assumed command of the North Atlantic Blockade with the rank of acting rear admiral, responsible for stopping Confederate trade along the double coastline of Virginia and North Carolina and their numerous rivers and sounds, cooperating with the army on interior raids, regulating internal trade, and protecting the army's communications. His initial fleet of forty-eight ships, many of them useless, grew to 119 by the end of 1864. He imposed stern discipline and developed effective strategies. He assigned his ships according to the most likely ports of entry, with shallow draft ships close to shore, a second line of heavy ships farther out; and an outside cordon of his fastest ships ready to chase down vessels that might escape the first two lines. In these actions his superior knowledge of the shoals and depths near the inlets was a great advantage. His fleet ultimately captured or destroyed 144 ships. The most difficult port to control was Wilmington, North Carolina, and he argued unsuccessfully for a joint army-navy attack on the city, which was eventually accomplished by others following the plan he had suggested. He advocated a movement up the James River against Richmond and angered General Ulysses S. Grant with his reluctance to sink obstacles blocking the James. Grant considered the armored vessels to be primarily for defense, while Lee was eager to use them in the rivers and did not want to create obstructions for his own ships. He opposed the granting of special trade permits to favored applicants by General Benjamin F. Butler (1818–1893). Officers and crew members divided all captured cargoes, and Lee thereby received some $120,000 in prize money, which caused much jealousy and added to his troubles with other officers. He later gave much of this money to southern relatives impoverished by the war. Meanwhile, the family and political feuds of the Blairs in Washington impeded his promotion to rear admiral, despite the significance of his command.

In July 1864, when Jubal Early invaded Washington, Lee promptly came to the rescue with five ships. The crisis, however, had already abated, and Navy Secretary Gideon Welles condemned Lee's action as a show of panic, even though Lee explained correctly that his post at Hampton Roads was entirely safe, and he had been informed that Washington was in grave danger. In September 1864 Lee was transferred to the command of the Mississippi Squadron of seventy-eight vessels patrolling the Mississippi River and its tributaries. In Tennessee he gave General George H. Thomas significant help in destroying the Confederate army of General John B. Hood. He provided Thomas with important intelligence information and logistical support, and he destroyed Confederate boats, artillery barges, forts, magazines, and bridges, effectively cutting off both the advance and retreat of Confederate soldiers.

After the war, as a member of a special board inspecting yards and docks, Lee wrote a painstaking report on their deficiencies and pleaded in vain for a stronger navy. In 1870 he was promoted to rear admiral and assumed command of the North Atlantic Fleet. He patrolled the Caribbean as a shield for American ships and citizens during revolutions in Cuba and San Domingo (now Dominican Republic). He retired in February 1873 and spent his final twenty-four years managing "Silver Spring," his farm in Maryland, where he died.

Lee was a fearless, able, and duty-bound officer, who usually inspired the devotion of subordinates but occasionally alienated higher authorities with his readiness to disagree with them on matters of principle and strategy. As a naval contribution to the Union victory, his Atlantic blockade was equaled only by the successes of Farragut on the Lower Mississippi.

• The voluminous papers of Admiral and Mrs. Lee are in the Blair-Lee collection at Princeton University. The biography by Dudley T. Cornish and Virginia J. Laas, *Lincoln's Lee: The Life of Samuel Phillips Lee* (1986), is excellent. Virginia J. Laas, ed., *Wartime Washington; The Civil War Letters of Elizabeth Blair Lee* (1991), also reveals much about the admiral's life and career. For those wishing an easily available original source that often reflects opinion and subjective judgments as well as facts, see *The Official Records of the Union and Confederate Navies in the War of the Rebellion* (30 vols., 1894–1922).

ELBERT B. SMITH

LEE, Stephen Dill (22 Sept. 1833–28 May 1908), soldier, educator, and author, was born in Charleston, South Carolina, the son of Thomas Lee, a physician, and Caroline Allison. He was also the grandson of the prominent South Carolina judge Thomas Lee (1769–1839). At the age of seventeen, after attending a boarding school in North Carolina, he entered West Point from which he graduated in 1854, ranking seventeenth in a class of forty-six that included J. E. B. Stuart and Oliver Otis Howard. Commissioned a second lieutenant and assigned to the Fourth Artillery Regiment, during the next six years he saw service, mostly of an administrative nature, in Texas, Florida, Kansas, and the Dakotas, rising in rank to first lieutenant in 1856.

In February 1861, following the secession of his native state, Lee resigned from the U.S. Army and became a captain in the South Carolina Volunteers and then in the Confederate army. In April 1861 he participated, as a member of General P. G. T. Beauregard's staff, in the negotiations with Major Robert Anderson, commander of Fort Sumter, that preceded and succeeded the bombardment of that fort. In June 1861 he became commander of the artillery battery of Hampton's Legion, the most aristocratically elite of all South Carolina military units. Although he arrived in Virginia with his battery too late to participate with the legion in the first battle of Manassas (21 July 1861), he saw considerable action in the Peninsular Campaign (Apr.-July 1862), performing so well that he was placed in command of the artillery of Major General John B. Magruder's division and promoted to colonel (9 July 1862). For awhile following that campaign he headed a cavalry regiment, but when General R. E. Lee's army advanced north late in August 1862, he took command of an artillery battalion in General James Longstreet's corps, in which capacity he distinguished himself at the battle of Second Manassas (29–30 Aug. 1862) and the battle of Antietam (17 Sept. 1862). On the second day of the first of these battles, his cannons played a major role in smashing a Union assault and thus opening the way for a devastating Confederate counterattack.

On 6 November 1862 Lee was promoted to brigadier general and assigned to the defense of Vicksburg, the main Confederate stronghold on the Mississippi. Again he performed well as his brigade, with the aid of another unit, repulsed an attack by a much larger Union force under William T. Sherman at Chickasaw Bayou, Mississippi, on 29 December 1862. In subsequent operations, it prevented the Confederate defeat at Champion's Hill, Mississippi, on 16 May 1863 from turning into a total disaster and held a key position in Vicksburg's fortifications against repeated assaults. Compelled to surrender with the rest of Vicksburg's garrison on 4 July 1863, Lee was paroled and soon exchanged, whereupon he received a well-deserved promotion to major general (3 Aug. 1863) and became commander of all Confederate cavalry in Mississippi. During the latter part of 1863 and the early months of 1864 he opposed a series of Union raids into that state, notably Sherman's Meridian Expedition (3–28 Feb. 1864). On 9 May 1864, as a consequence of the transfer of General Leonidas Polk's Army of Mississippi to Georgia, he replaced Polk as commander of the Department of Mississippi and Alabama. On 23 June 1864 Lee was promoted to lieutenant general, thus becoming at age thirty the youngest man to hold that rank not only during the Civil War but in prior American history. Thanks to General Nathan Bedford Forrest's brilliant victory at Brice's Cross Roads (10 June 1864), Lee repelled one Union foray into Mississippi, but on 14 July 1864 his forces suffered heavy losses at Tupelo, Mississippi, in an ill conceived and poorly executed frontal attack on a larger Federal army holding a virtually impregnable position. Despite their victory, however, the Federals retreated toward Memphis, something they would have done even if Lee had refrained from attacking.

Soon after the Tupelo fiasco Lee was ordered to Georgia where he took command of a corps in General John B. Hood's army defending Atlanta. On 28 July 1864 at Ezra Church he made, contrary to Hood's instructions and without notifying him, another unnecessary, blundering, and futile frontal attack, incurring heavy losses and impairing the morale of his surviving troops. On 31 August 1864 he repeated this performance at the first battle of Jonesboro, Georgia, sending his corps forward prematurely against an entrenched Federal force in an assault that would have been another bloodbath had it not been, as he angrily termed

it in his report, so "feeble." Following this defeat, Hood evacuated Atlanta and withdrew to Palmetto, Georgia, from where late in September he launched a campaign that eventually took him into Tennessee and resulted in the battles of Franklin (30 Nov. 1864) and Nashville (15–16 Dec. 1864), both of them costly Confederate defeats. Lee took no part in the first engagement and only a subsidiary one in the second, but he did help hold off the Union pursuit as Hood's shattered army retreated into Mississippi. Having been wounded at Nashville, Lee then went on sick leave to Columbus, Mississippi, where in 1865 he married Regina Harrison, a union that produced one child. On 31 March 1865 he resumed command of his corps, now in North Carolina as part of a small army under General Joseph E. Johnston, who on 26 April 1865 surrendered to Sherman.

For the next twelve years Lee operated a plantation in Mississippi and took part in activities designed to counter so-called "carpetbag rule." In 1878 he was elected a state senator, and in 1880 he became the first president of the newly established Mississippi A&M College (now Mississippi State University). He held that post until 1899, when he resigned to become a member of a federal commission for the development of a national military park at Vicksburg. In addition he was a delegate to the Mississippi constitutional convention of 1890, a founder and president of the Mississippi Historical Society, author of a number of articles dealing with the Civil War and other matters of historical interest, and in 1904, by which time he was the highest-ranking Confederate general still alive, he became commander in chief of the United Confederate Veterans, a position he held until his death in Vicksburg, Mississippi.

Lee was a superb artillery officer and a superior brigade commander and probably would have done well leading a division. On the other hand, as he demonstrated in 1864, he was not an effective departmental or corps commander, being too impulsive and failing to appreciate that tactically speaking the defense almost totally dominated the offense by the latter part of the Civil War.

• The Southern Historical Collection, University of North Carolina, Chapel Hill, contains most of Lee's military and personal papers. These, however, should be supplemented with his reports and correspondence in *The War of the Rebellion: A Compilation of the Official Records of the Union and Confederate Armies* (128 vols., 1880–1901). Most of his historical writings appear in the *Publications of the Mississippi Historical Society*, the main exception being "The South since the War," in *Confederate Military History*, vol. 13, ed. Clement Evans (1899). The sole but definitive full-length biography is Herman Hattaway, *General Stephen D. Lee* (1976). For a critical view of Lee's role in the Atlanta campaign, see Albert Castel, *Decision in the West: The Atlanta Campaign of 1864* (1992). A brief obituary by W. L. Cabell appears in *Confederate Veteran* 16 (July 1908): 314.

ALBERT CASTEL

LEE, Ulysses Grant (4 Dec. 1913–7 Jan. 1969), educator, army officer, and author, was born in Washington, D.C., the son of Ulysses Lee, a businessman and grocery store owner, and Mattie Spriggs. He graduated from Dunbar High School in Washington in 1931, attended Howard University in Washington, joined the Reserve Officers' Training Corps, earned his B.A. in 1935, and was also a commissioned graduate and a U.S. Army reservist. Remaining at Howard, he taught as a graduate assistant in English in 1935 and 1936 and earned his M.A. in 1936. Lee also studied briefly at the University of Pennsylvania and became a member of the faculty as an instructor and then an assistant professor of English at Lincoln University in Lincoln University, Pennsylvania, from 1936 to 1948. During these years he was twice on leave.

From 1936 to 1939 Lee was a research assistant, a consultant, and an editor with the Federal Writers' Project, for which he helped produce a book on Washington as a city and as the national capital and another book on African Americans in Virginia. During part of the time between 1936 and 1942 he was also a Rosenwald fellow and an Alvia Kay Brown fellow at the University of Chicago as a doctoral student in the history of culture. In 1940 he was a visiting professor at Virginia Union University, in Richmond, Virginia. He coedited, with Sterling A. Brown and Arthur P. Davis, *The Negro Caravan: Writings by American Negroes* (1941), an anthology of 1,082 pages, containing short stories, selections from novels, poems, folk literature, drama, speeches, pamphlets, letters, autobiographies, biographies, and essays (historical, cultural, and personal), together with informative introductory material. It abundantly achieves its announced purpose to present artistically valid writings, to depict African-American character and experience in America, and to assemble in one volume key literary works that have influenced African-American thought and to a lesser degree that of Americans as a whole. *The Negro Caravan* was still a widely used textbook at least fifty years after it appeared.

Called to active duty in 1942 as a first lieutenant, Lee began a distinguished military career. That same year he married Vivian Gill; they had no children. He was one of the first officers assigned to the Information and Education Department of the U.S. Army. During World War II he was an education officer, an editorial analyst in the field, and an Army Service Forces officer. In this last capacity, he wrote parts of and edited the manual *Leadership and the Negro Soldier* (1944). Its purpose was to aid in training African-American soldiers and diminish attitude and disciplinary problems, so as to maximize "efficient troop utilization." It was written in a tactful manner, to avoid the real possibility of public controversy. In 1946 Lee was appointed a staff historian in the Office of the Chief of Military History, Department of the Army. While still in the army Lee found the time and energy to complete his dissertation on the plight and accomplishments of African-American soldiers between World War I and World War II. He retired from the army in 1952 with the rank of major. The University of Chicago awarded him a Ph.D. in 1953 in the field of the history of culture.

Resuming his academic career, Lee taught at Lincoln University in Jefferson City, Missouri, from 1953 until 1956. He then taught at Morgan State College in Baltimore, Maryland. While working enthusiastically at Morgan, he used his dissertation as the beginning of the most significant writing of his career, *The Employment of Negro Troops*, containing twenty-two chapters, in 738 two-columned pages, and with many illustrations and maps. It was published in 1966 by the Office of the Chief of Military History of the U.S. Army as part of the series United States Army in World War II. In his book Lee reviews the experiences of African-American troops in World War I, problems between the wars with respect to their segregation and duty assignments, and military plans for their phased integration and maximum "utilization" in World War II. He discusses problems connected with the requirement that African-American soldiers should have separate facilities, difficulties with regard to training and leading them, their physical fitness and morale, and disturbing incidents connected with use of facilities, "camp town" prejudice, and transportation. He discusses African-American troops overseas, often in menial service units but also dramatically in heroic ground and air combat. To accomplish his research, Lee consulted masses of material, both published and unpublished. The result is a landmark work of enduring historical value; it is scholarly, impressive, and authentic. Without pointing blame, Lee clearly presented evidence of African-American soldiers' patience and bravery despite lingering prejudice both within and outside the army. Reviewers unanimously praised his writing for being dispassionate and judicious.

In 1965 Lee lectured under the auspices of the American Society of African Culture in Nigeria, Sierra Leone, and Cameroon. The most outstanding essay among several he published is "The Draft and the Negro" in *Current History* (55 [1968]: 28–33, 47–48). In it he discusses the African American's historical position with respect to the draft, draft riots and race riots, and African Americans and the draft in World War I, World War II, and later. He concludes that African Americans have been chronically disadvantaged for military service when drafted because of "rankling [social, educational, and vocational] inequities" in the private sector. In 1968–1969 Lee taught concurrently at Morgan State and the University of Pennsylvania. In his limited leisure he studied the art of cooking, classical and jazz music, cocker spaniels, and American railroads. One day as he was leaving the campus at Morgan to return to his home in Washington, he suffered a heart attack and was pronounced dead a few minutes later in a Baltimore hospital.

• Lee's papers are in the Moorland-Spingarn Research Center at Howard University. Limited biographical and bibliographical information is in Robert Ewell Greene, *Black Defenders of America, 1775–1973: A Reference and Pictorial*

History (1974), and Lenwood G. Davis and George Hill, *Blacks in the American Armed Forces, 1776–1983: A Bibliography* (1985). Obituaries are in the *Washington Post*, 9 Jan. 1969, and the *New York Times*, 11 Jan. 1969.

ROBERT L. GALE

LEE, William (31 Aug. 1739–27 June 1795), diplomat, was born in Westmoreland County, in the colony of Virginia, the son of Thomas Lee, a planter and colonial official, and Hannah Harrison Ludwell. The family seat, the commanding "Stratford Hall," symbolized the clan's renown and power. Lee's oldest two brothers were groomed to manage the family's extensive plantations and to assume their father's political clout. His sisters prepared for marriages with other colonial elites. Thus William and his three closest brothers—Richard Henry Lee, Thomas Ludwell Lee, and Arthur Lee—were forced to become more self-reliant, assertive, and more closely connected to each other.

The deaths of both parents in 1750 vastly affected Lee's character and career. His eldest brother, Colonel Philip Ludwell Lee, was named executor of the estate and guardian of the younger siblings. Intrafamilial animosity soon flared as Phil Lee grudgingly withheld bequests, claiming priority for repayment of all family debts. Between 1754 and 1764 the younger Lees brought suit, unsuccessfully, for a prompt and just settlement. William Lee sought a cash settlement, a fund for building a home plus an annual allowance from his father's sinecure. The Lee siblings did succeed in gaining a cousin as replacement as guardian.

Lee's sense of justice was offended; he learned to carry grievances through life. Although less alienated than his other brothers, Lee found himself under his brother Phil's control. The new master at Stratford, following Thomas Lee's instructions, sought to train William and Arthur "to get their living honestly." William, exhibiting a talent for numbers, was groomed first as a clerk and steward at the plantation and then as a budding tobacco merchant. As he was allotted no land of his own, Lee through the age of thirty was dependent on the whim of his erratic and stubborn brother Phil.

In 1760 Lee and his brother Arthur were dispatched to England on dual missions. They were to be schooled in a trade: the former in counting houses, the latter among the professions. Moreover, they were to fashion personal alliances whereby the Stratford Lees could become connected with British aristocrats. Lee returned home in 1763, where he joined his brother Richard Henry in the vanguard of Northern Neck resistance to tighter colonial policies. By 1768 Lee determined to flee Stratford. He aspired to become a merchant prince in India, but as he passed through London his cousin, Hannah Philippa Ludwell, diverted him. They were married in 1769. Hannah Lee, nearly two years older than her husband, experienced much difficulty in childbearing, but three children did survive. Hannah Lee provided astute business counsel and substantial assets. Lee would help divide her father's legacy, valued at £13,000 with her sister. Ulti-mately Lee would garner the Ludwell's impressive James River estate, "Green Spring." Yet as an absentee master he proved inept.

Lee's career in Britain, 1768–1777, followed two paths. In mercantile affairs he experienced early setbacks. He came under the influence of Dennys DeBerdt, an aging Flemish merchant, initially held in high regard in Anglo-American circles. This partnership suffered setbacks. Later as an independent merchant, well connected with Virginia gentry, he prospered amidst a troubled tobacco market. Simultaneously with his brother Arthur and compatriot Stephan Sayre, Lee enlisted in the political circle around DeBerdt. This cohort shared two perspectives: they were critical of British officials who sought to tax the colonies for revenue, and they believed Benjamin Franklin, as an agent for many colonies, was too compliant with such policies.

Lee increasingly plunged into oppositional politics in metropolitan London as his income mounted. Lee, his brother Arthur, and Sayre moved to the front of the popular movement that swirled around the notorious John Wilkes. The Americans believed that Wilkes was the innocent victim of royal resentment and parliamentary disregard for the voters in the city. Moreover, Lee's strategy was to bond those in Britain who had commercial ties in America with the more radical colonists (later known as the Adams-Lee axis) in hopes of maintaining amity by reversing revenue taxes. Arthur Lee became a penman and tactician for the Wilkesites. Sayre and William Lee, by purchasing guild memberships (in the Haberdasher's Livery) and hence the franchise, emerged as electoral candidates. On 3 July 1773 the duo was elected sheriff of London; two years later Lee, representing Aldgate Ward, became the only American elected to a lifetime post as a London alderman. From this position he aspired to a seat in Parliament, but his bid was thwarted in the general election of 1774. Escalating military tensions muffled American influence on British politicians and Lee's candidacy in outlying Surry lacked sufficient Wilkesite support. Both Lee brothers, in petitioning the king and in speeches before metropolitan audiences, enhanced their prominence if not their ability to redress American grievances.

By 1777 Arthur and William Lee had removed to the Continent to assume diplomatic assignments. Both were quick-tempered and confrontational by nature but had powerful friends in Congress. Tumult arose wherever the Lees ventured. Arthur Lee's assignment centered in Paris, yoked with Franklin and Silas Deane. William Lee was named joint commercial agent in the busy port of Nantes. There he was to direct shipping of French supplies to sustain the American war effort and to sell any prizes taken by Americans on the high seas. Lee challenged the entrenched, and none-to-virtuous Thomas Morris, the alcoholic half brother of Robert Morris. The Morris-Deane team frequently put personal profit ahead of patriotism. As irritating to the Lees was wily Benjamin Franklin, who was overly popular by their standards.

In 1778 Lee vied with Franklin's grandnephew, Jonathan Williams, Jr., for control of the Nantes connection.

The Lees' adversaries in Europe spread word that they were too arrogant for diplomatic missions, especially those where Europeans expected Americans to be compliant. When Lee was promoted to the post of commissioner to the courts of Vienna and Berlin in the spring of 1778 he was rebuffed by Emperor Joseph II and Fredrick the Great, both then embroiled in controversy over Bavaria. His prospects were never promising. Moreover when he returned to Paris, Deane and Franklin refused to let him resume duties as a commercial agent. In the following autumn, without authority, Lee fashioned a rough draft of a commercial pact with a (powerless) representative of the merchants of Amsterdam, Jean de Neufville. Although this treaty was never ratified, it became the pretext for the British, in 1780, to declare war on Holland.

The Lees' diplomatic status and efficiency were undercut by rumors of their persistent loyalties to England. For example, Lee's critics questioned why he did not resign his aldermanic post until 1780 and whether his dabblings in the London stock market compromised his public trust. The climax of these animosities, known subsequently as the Lee-Deane imbroglio, reverberated across the Atlantic in the winter of 1778–1779. The crux of the matter was the Lees' charges that Deane had used his diplomatic post to his own personal advantage: playing the London stocks, charging personal losses to the Congress, and engaging in commercial ventures. Deane, having been recalled by Congress, published attacks on the Lees in the American press in December. William Lee fired back in kind in March. On 8 June 1779, with no Lee brothers in Congress, Lee lost his post in an overhaul of the American foreign service. He continued as an agent of Virginia.

For four years, spent largely in Brussels, Lee's finances were precarious. By September 1783 he returned to Green Spring but was beset by misfortune. His wife died in Europe in August 1784 before she could join him. Ill health plagued him for the last decade of life. He briefly held office in the Virginia State Senate and as sheriff of James City County. Increasingly he was haunted by fears of economic insecurity. Yet when he died at Green Spring, wracked by arthritis and blind, he left an opulent estate.

• Lee's papers are scattered in various depositories, but most are at the Virginia Historical Society. There are a number of works about the Lees, none of them fully satisfying, including Worthington C. Ford, ed., *Letters of William Lee, 1766–1783* (1891; repr. 1965); Francis Wharton, ed., *The Revolutionary Diplomatic Correspondence of the United States* (1882); and Paul R. Hoffman and John L. Molyneaux, eds., *The Lee Family Papers* (1966), microfilm. Lee's character and role in the family are etched in Paul C. Nagel, *The Lees of Virginia* (1990). Focused accounts are found in Alonzo T. Dill, *William Lee, Militia Diplomat* (1976), and Karl A. Roider, Jr., "William Lee: Our First Envoy in Vienna," *Virginia Magazine of History and Biography* 86 (1978): 163–68.

LOUIS W. POTTS

LEE, William Carey (12 Mar. 1895–25 June 1948), army general, was born in Dunn, North Carolina, the son of Eldrege Lee, a hardware merchant, and Emma Jane Massengill. Lee attended Wake Forest College, 1913–1915, then he transferred to North Carolina State College and enrolled in the Reserve Officers Training Corps (ROTC). He graduated from N.C. State in 1916 with a B.S. in high school teaching. In World War I he was a reserve second lieutenant of infantry and saw combat in France as a platoon leader and company commander. Lee remained on active duty after the war and received a regular army commission as a first lieutenant in 1920. He married Dava Grey Johnson in 1918; they had no children.

In 1922 Lee graduated from the company officer's course at Fort Benning, Georgia. From 1922 to 1926 he taught military science at North Carolina State College; he then served three years in Panama. In 1930 Lee graduated from Tank School, Fort Meade, Maryland, and taught there from 1931 to 1932. He graduated from the Infantry School's advanced course at Fort Benning in June 1933 and then went to France, where he graduated from the Tank School at Versailles and served a year as an exchange officer with a French armored unit. His observations of German military training during this period, especially the developments of Kurt Student's airborne experiment, impressed him. When he returned to the United States, Lee taught at the Infantry School, Fort Benning, and graduated from the Command and General Staff School in Fort Leavenworth, Kansas, in 1938. He was executive officer of the Second Infantry Brigade, First Division, when he was assigned to the chief of infantry's office in Washington, D.C. Even though he was known as a tank expert, it was there he became the leader of a small group advocating experimentation with airborne. His arguments for the vertical envelopment of troops found a receptive hearing from Major General George A. Lynch, chief of infantry.

In early January 1940 General George C. Marshall, chief of staff, approved a test to ascertain the potential of air infantry. General Lynch was enthusiastic about the project, and he placed Major Lee in charge of the airborne testing. Within two months Lee secured the personnel, aircraft, and materials needed for the test platoon at Lawson Field, Fort Benning, and began immediately testing parachutist equipment, boots, helmets, and parachutes and drops of artillery pieces and ammunition. Although still on Lynch's staff in Washington, Lee closely monitored the test platoon's progress. He made many trips to coordinate testing with Colonel Harris M. Melasky, the Infantry Board's officer at Fort Benning, and Lieutenant William T. Ryder, the test platoon leader. Lee used personal direct diplomacy to expedite equipment, personnel, and materials for his fifty-man test platoon. His efforts proved invaluable since the competition for resources was severe and time limited. To more accurately simulate jumps, Lee took the test platoon to Hightstown, New Jersey, to practice jumps from two parachute towers. In August the test platoon began jumping from planes.

With the test platoon's operations a success, on 16 September 1940 Lynch authorized a tenfold increase in paratroopers and in November established the 501st Parachute Battalion under Major William M. Miley. To assist the 501st and the expected additional battalions, Lee persuaded Washington to build training parachute towers, clear a large jump zone, and construct barracks and mess at Fort Benning. The army subsequently decided to create three new parachute battalions. On 10 March 1941 a specialized organization to administer parachute training, the Provisional Parachute Group, under Lieutenant Colonel Lee was formed at Fort Benning. The 502d, 503d, and 504th battalions were soon established, drawing on Miley's 501st. After Germany's airborne took Crete, all U.S. airborne efforts intensified. To meet the manpower needs of the newly activated battalions, Lee recruited volunteers from the Eighth and Ninth Infantry Divisions.

In late November 1941 General Lee broke his back in a parachute jump. He was hospitalized for weeks and then spent months in a chin to waist cast. After Pearl Harbor, Marshall authorized the creation of additional parachute infantry regiments, and Lee established six in the first half of 1942. By March 1942 organizational changes in the army created the Army Ground Forces under Lieutenant General Lesley J. McNair, who then created the airborne command under Lee. Thus, Lee was placed in charge of all American airborne troops (parachutes, air landing battalions, and yet to be formed glider units). Because of limited space at Fort Benning, Lee had the Airborne Command moved to Fort Bragg, North Carolina, on 9 April 1942. The sequencing of airborne training was jump training at Fort Benning and then tactical training and testing at Fort Bragg. Lee was promoted to brigadier general on 19 April 1942. For his leadership of the airborne during this critical period of development, Lee received the Distinguished Service Medal in 1944.

In the summer of 1942 Lee went to England to coordinate with his British counterpart. Lee's concept of airborne forces at the divisional level coincided with British plans. He strongly recommended divisional airborne units to McNair. McNair authorized two airborne divisions of approximately 8,300 men. The two infantry divisions selected as airborne were the 82d and 101st. The 82d was already on active duty, but the 101st had not been activated. Lee was the logical choice to command the 101st, and he was promoted to major general on 10 August 1942. In twenty-six months Lee had shepherded the American airborne from a test platoon of 50 men to two divisions of 8,300 men. Lee's first order to the 101st charted the division mission. He wrote, "The 101st . . . has no history, but it has a rendezvous with destiny. . . . We have broken with the past and its traditions to establish our claim to the future. Due to the nature of our armaments and tactics . . . we shall be called upon to carry out operations of far-reaching military importance. . . . We

shall go into action when the need is immediate and extreme."

By January 1943 the training of the 101st had been completed. Lee had combined parachutes and glider regiments of the 101st into a cohesive fighting unit, and in March 1943 he went to England to help plan the invasion, returning to England in August 1943 with some elements of the 101st. By January 1944 all of the 101st was in England preparing for the airborne phase of Operation Overlord. Between August and January Lee helped formulate the airborne doctrine and tactical deployment procedures that were used in the airborne invasion on D-Day. He suffered a severe heart attack in early February 1944 and was forced to return to the United States for hospitalization on the eve of the most important airborne operation in history. In March General Maxwell Taylor took command of Lee's "Screaming Eagles."

Lee retired in the fall of 1944. He spent much of his retirement writing about and discussing airborne warfare and its future. He died from heart disease in Dunn, North Carolina.

An appropriate assessment of Lee's contributions to the development of the U.S. airborne was offered on 6 June 1986 at the dedication of the Lee Airborne Museum in Dunn by two of his intimates of World War II. General Taylor wrote, "He [Lee] was truly the 'Father of American Airborne Troops'"; and General A. C. McAuliffe wrote, "General Lee has been called the 'Father of the Airborne.' . . . He organized and commanded the parachute school and trained our first parachutists. . . . By his great character and superior military knowledge [he] set an example for airborne troopers which was reflected in their brilliant combat record during World War II."

• No official collection of Lee's papers exists, and most of his personal papers are in private possession. Three articles by Lee in the *Infantry Journal* show the development of his thinking on armor and airborne warfare: "The Use of Inherent Mobility," Jan.–Feb. 1936, pp. 10–12; "Air Infantry," Jan. 1941, pp. 14–21; and "Air Landing Divisions," Apr. 1941, pp. 20–22. His contemporaries place Lee in historical context in James Gavin, *Airborne Warfare* (1947), for which Lee wrote the introduction; and Maxwell D. Taylor, *Swords and Plowshares* (1972). Gerald M. Devlin, *Paratrooper* (1979), is an excellent secondary source. Another important secondary source is Clay Blair, *Ridgeway's Paratroopers: The American Airborne in World War II* (1985). Other works of importance are Jerry Autry, *General William C. Lee: Father of the Airborne* (1995), John T. Ellis, *The Airborne Command and Center* (1946), James A. Huston, *Out of the Blue: U.S. Army Airborne Operations in World War II* (1972), and Leonard Rapport and Arthur Nosthwood, Jr., *Rendezvous with Destiny: A History of the 101st Airborne Division* (1948). General Lee's widow, Dava J. Lee, provided personal insight concerning the general's career in an interview with the author on 10 Feb. 1978 at Falcon, N.C.

W. LEE JOHNSTON

LEE, William Henry Fitzhugh (31 May 1837–15 Oct. 1891), soldier and congressman, was born in Arlington, Virginia, the son of Robert Edward Lee, the soldier and later Confederate general, and Mary Anne Randolph Custis, the great-granddaughter of Martha Dandridge Custis Washington by her first marriage. He was educated in private schools but failed to gain admittance to West Point. Lee attended Harvard University, where he was a classmate of Henry Adams, the "Rooney" Lee that Adams assessed rather disparagingly, but he left in 1857 without a degree. His shiftlessness and lack of self-control worried his father, who paid his son's college debts. Upon the recommendation of General Winfield Scott, Lee was appointed second lieutenant in the Sixth Regiment, U.S. Infantry. He accompanied this regiment, under Colonel Albert S. Johnston, on an expedition in 1858 to Utah Territory, where a conflict of authority with the federal government resulted in the virtually bloodless Mormon "war." The following year he resigned his commission to return to New Kent County, Virginia, to oversee his estate, "White House," the Custis plantation on the Pamunkey River left him by his grandfather. In 1859 Lee married an orphaned cousin, Charlotte Wickham. Their two children died in infancy.

When the Civil War broke out in 1861, Lee at first thought that secession was a terrible mistake, but he sided with the Confederacy and raised a company of cavalry, with which he joined the Army of Northern Virginia. He was frequently promoted in 1861, earning the ranks of captain, major, and lieutenant colonel. Appointed colonel of the Ninth Virginia Cavalry, Lee served with General J. E. B. Stuart in his first ride around General George B. McClellan in June 1862 during the Peninsular campaign. He subsequently fought at Second Manassas, and during the Antietam campaign he was hurt at Turner's Gap but recovered to participate in the Chambersburg raid. Lee's record of leadership and bravery led to his appointment in 1862 as brigadier general. He commanded his brigade at Fredericksburg in December 1862 and at Chancellorsville in May 1863. Severely wounded in the leg at Brandy Station, the great cavalry battle in June 1863, Lee was convalescing at the Wickham family home, "Hickory Hill," in Hanover County when he was captured on 26 June 1863 during a Federal raid and imprisoned at Fortress Monroe, then commanded by Benjamin F. Butler. He was later transferred to Fort Lafayette, where he remained until an exchange of prisoners occurred in March 1864, three months after the death of Lee's wife from tuberculosis. Mary Boykin Chesnut, a writer whose father and husband served in the U.S. Senate, recorded in her diary: "Rooney Lee says Beast Butler was very kind to him while he was a prisoner. And the Beast has sent him back his war-horse. The Lees are men enough to speak the truth of friend or enemy, unfearing consequences" (*Mary Chesnut's Civil War*, ed. C. Vann Woodward [1981], p. 589).

Following his release from prison, Lee was promoted to major general and served throughout the remainder of the war. He led a newly formed division of cavalry through the Overland and Petersburg assaults in June 1864. He saw action at Globe Tavern, Virginia, in August 1864 and at Five Forks in Virginia on 30 March and 1 April 1865. Lee was with his father in the Appomattox campaign and surrendered with him in 1865. Like his father, he accepted defeat without complaining and advised the South to create a new and better section within the Union. Although not a revered and distinguished officer in the mold of his father, Lee enjoyed the respect of his men and gained recognition for his military skills. The fact that he was the general's son enhanced his reputation.

After the conclusion of the war in 1865, Lee returned to his Virginia plantation, which Union forces had reduced to ruins. In the meantime, he had more fervently embraced Christianity. While not a fatalist, he believed that God directed the daily affairs of people and understood the destruction of his farm and the death of his wife as punishments for his sins. In 1867 Lee married Mary Tabb Bolling; they had five children, two of whom lived to adulthood. In 1874 he moved to Burke's Station, Virginia, where he engaged in farming and raising horses. A noted horseman, he rode virtually every day.

Peace left Virginia prostrate. A major problem confronting the state in the postwar era was a debt of nearly $42 million. The legislature determined that it should be reduced according to the state's ability to pay. During this period of internal controversy over the readjustment of the state debt, Lee entered politics. He served one term, from 1875 to 1879, in the state senate, being its presiding officer during his last year in office. Lee chose not to seek renomination, preferring instead to devote time to his family during a transitional period in the state.

The birth of modern industry in Virginia in the 1880s gave rise to cotton textile plants, shipbuilding plants, and cigarette factories, among others. New railroad lines helped to connect remote areas with the centers of population. Industrialism helped to diversify the state's almost completely agrarian economy, but political and social tensions resulted from these changes. Lee belonged to the conservative Democrats who, under Fitzhugh Lee in 1886, wrested control of the state from William Mahone and the Readjuster party.

Lee returned to politics in 1886, when he was elected as a Democrat to the Fiftieth Congress, representing Virginia's Eighth District. He won reelection in 1888 and 1890, serving in the U.S. House of Representatives from 1887 until his death. Lee's years of congressional service nearly coincided with the gubernatorial term of his first cousin, Fitzhugh Lee, who was the state's chief executive from 1886 to 1890. Congressman Lee favored tariff reductions and a more elastic currency to help relieve agrarian discontent and reduce farm indebtedness. While a member of Congress, Lee died at his home, "Ravensworth," near Alexandria, Virginia.

• The largest aggregation of Lee family papers is held by the Virginia Historical Society in Richmond. Other important collections of family papers are in the Virginia State Library and Archives in Richmond and the Washington and Lee University Library in Lexington. Lee's speeches are in the *Congressional Record* from 1887 to 1891. Biographies of General Robert E. Lee provide some information on his son's life and military activities. These include Emory M. Thomas, *Robert E. Lee: A Biography* (1995), and Douglas Southall Freeman, *R. E. Lee: A Biography* (4 vols., 1934–1935). See also Paul C. Nagel, *The Lees of Virginia: Seven Generations of an American Family* (1990); Stephen Hess, *America's Political Dynasties from Adams to Kennedy* (1966); Freeman, *Lee's Lieutenants: A Study in Command* (3 vols., 1942–1944); and *The War of the Rebellion: A Compilation of the Official Records of the Union and Confederate Armies* (128 vols., 1880–1901). An obituary is in the *Richmond Times-Dispatch*, 16 Oct. 1891.

LEONARD SCHLUP

LEE, William Little (8 Feb. 1821–28 May 1857), jurist and statesman, was born in Sandy Hill, New York, the son of Stephen Lee and Mary Little. Lee graduated in 1842 from Norwich University in Vermont, then studied law at Harvard, thereafter practicing in Troy, New York. Suffering from consumption, he set out by ship from New York to Oregon for his health. When his ship, the brig *Henry*, stopped for an emergency overhaul in Honolulu on 12 October 1846, however, Lee decided to remain in Hawaii. In 1849 he married Catherine E. Newton of Albany, New York.

A transition from absolute monarchy to constitutional monarchy was taking place in the islands, and Lee was to become one of its guiding forces. This devolution of authority had begun with the Declaration of Rights and Laws of 1839, seen as Hawaii's Magna Carta, and the Constitution of 1840, which established a new framework for government. Lee, in his twenties, had arrived just after the passage of a law designed by John Ricord, the attorney general for the Hawaiian Kingdom who himself had arrived in the islands only two years before to expand the court system, establishing for the first time courts of equity, admiralty, and probate. There were not many in Hawaii competent to serve in the judiciary, and, in need of his expertise, the Hawaiian Kingdom appointed Lee on 1 December 1846 a judge in Honolulu to hear civil, criminal, maritime, probate, equitable, and legal cases.

After taking an oath of allegiance to serve the king, Kauikeaouli or Kamehameha III, Lee created, administered, and guided with Ricord a new judicial framework in Hawaii and implemented the court system. Lee and Ricord took the lead in administering the Organic Acts of 1845–1847. The third Organic Act of December 1847 organized the Judiciary Department and established a superior court of law and equity in accordance with the principles of American and British jurisprudence. Prior to its implementation, Lee observed that the highest Hawaiian court had met "in an old grass house, floored with mats, without benches, seats or comforts of any kind, with one corner partitioned off with calico, for judge's office, clerk's office, police court, and jury room." The new law mandated that three judges were to be appointed by the legislature to sit on the superior court. Lee was named chief justice, and his associates were John Ii and Lorrin Andrews. The same act divided the kingdom into sev-

en judicial districts, or circuit courts, and twenty-four district courts presided over by a district justice appointed by the governor of Oahu, Kekuanaoa. The judges of these courts adopted the common and civil law as practiced and administered in the United States and Great Britain in making their decisions, and these decisions became precedents for future cases. The new courts and western law codes administered by Lee and his associates helped protect the independence of the Hawaiian Kingdom from the threat of foreigners eager, had the courts been absent, to take the law into their own hands or to appeal to consular intervention on their behalf.

Lee was also appointed to the king's privy council, where he wielded great influence because of his integrity and law training. After Ricord retired from service to the Hawaiian Kingdom in 1847 and left Hawaii the next year, Lee implemented the new judiciary system in Hawaii along American lines. Lee's appointment marked a new era for the Hawaiian judiciary, as under his leadership the courts won public confidence.

Along with the gradual redistribution of authority from the king and the chiefs to the people, there came a change in land tenure that would obliterate Hawaii's old feudal system. The second Organic Act (1846), which Lee had helped write, authorized a board of commissioners to issue land titles. In 1848 Lee promoted the Great Mahele (Land Division), thus becoming the father of Hawaii's present land laws. Through the Great Mahele, the king gave up his claims to all the lands of Hawaii, retaining only certain parcels as royal estates to be the preserve of the reigning monarch. The remaining lands were granted to the chiefs in fee simple, as they were now permitted to hold outright those lands they formerly held as fiefs from the king. Also, small lots or kuleanas could be purchased by commoners in fee simple. The board of commissioners was to register land titles after the lands were surveyed and after payment of a commutation fee to secure title. The chiefs often paid the commutation fee in land that became government or public land. Foreigners were allowed to lease land for fifty years, but after 1850 legislation they were allowed to purchase land in fee simple on the same terms as citizens of Hawaii. These fee simple lands could now be cultivated, leased, or sold at will. To commoners, over 10,000 kuleana claims were awarded, totaling nearly 30,000 acres, the chiefs were awarded 1.5 million acres, the government received title to over a million acres, and the Crown got not quite a million acres. Many native Hawaiian commoners sold their kuleanas and quickly became a dispossessed segment of the population. By 1900, white settlers in Hawaii owned four times the lands held by native Hawaiians, including the lands held by the Crown. Some of the large tracts of land once owned by the chiefs were bequeathed for public purposes, such as the formation of the Bernice Puahai Bishop Estate, lands held in trust for the education of native Hawaiians.

Lee successfully mediated along with statesman Gerrit P. Judd the threatened seizure of Hawaii by French admiral Legoarant de Tromelin, commander of French naval forces in the Pacific, in 1849 when he attempted to press the demands of the French consul Guillaume Patrice Dillon that Hawaii's trade and tariff laws be changed through threat of military reprisal. In 1850, upon request from the legislature, Lee wrote a penal code that was adopted into law and remained the basis for Hawaii's criminal laws to the present. Lee was also the author of the Act for the Government of Masters and Servants of 1850, which established laws providing for the importation of immigrant labor. This law allowed large numbers of contract laborers from China, Japan, Portugal, the Philippines and parts of Europe to settle in Hawaii, changing the ethnic composition of the islands and helping create a boom in the sugar and, later, pineapple industries. Laborers were sought not only to aid industry, but to repopulate Hawaii. The Hawaiian monarchy cooperated with the planters and encouraged this influx of population because the number of native Hawaiians had declined drastically due to the introduction of foreign diseases to which they had no immunity.

Lee had always been interested in agriculture and was a partner in the firm of H. A. Peirce, which established Lihue Plantation, and was a guiding figure in the Royal Hawaiian Agricultural Society, founded in 1850. In 1851 he was elected to the House of Representatives, a position he held along with his judgeship, and served as House Speaker.

Along with Gerrit Judd and John Ii, Lee drafted the Constitution of 1852 for the Hawaiian monarchy, which incorporated the separation of powers into the executive, legislative, and judicial branches of government. It also provided for the former position of kuhina-nui (coruler) to remain as a type of vice king and regent whenever the throne was vacant or during the minority of kings. The legislature, composed of the House of Nobles and House of Representatives, was fixed in number, with thirty nobles appointed for life and not less than twenty-four or more than forty members of the House of Representatives elected annually by universal male suffrage. As the guiding spirit of the commission that drafted this constitution, Lee, upon its adoption, was appointed chief justice of the Supreme Court.

In 1854 Lee acted as consultant to the Hawaiian Kingdom when the United States considered annexing the Hawaiian Islands, and in 1855 he was appointed Hawaii's minister to the United States. He returned to the islands before his death in Honolulu from tuberculosis.

Lee's efforts in modernizing the judiciary system, ensuring a constitutional monarchy, altering the land laws, and negotiating to meet the demands of foreigners safeguarded Hawaii's independence in the nineteenth century after France in the LaPlace affair (1839) had demanded religious toleration for Catholics under threat of war and Britain in the Paulet affair (1843) actually took control of the islands temporarily, both threatening permanent domination.

• The papers of William Little Lee are located in the State Archives of Hawaii. T. M. Spaulding, "Chief Justice William Little Lee," *Honolulu Mercury* 2 (Mar. 1930): 346–53, offers an excellent overview of Lee's career. Meiric K. Dutton, *William Little Lee* (1953), is an informative biography, and Jane Silverman, "William Little Lee, a Biography," *Kaulike* (History Center of Hawaii), no. 1, May 1989, pp. 2–3, affords a sympathetic view of Lee's career. A native Hawaiian perspective of Lee is Lililaka Kameeleihiwa, *Native Land and Foreign Desires: Pehea La E Pono Ai?* (1992). W. F. Frear, "The Evolution of the Hawaiian Judiciary," *Hawaiian Historical Society Papers*, no. 7 (1894), pp. 1–25, and Ralph Kuykendall, "Constitutions of the Hawaiian Kingdoms," *Hawaiian Historical Society Papers*, no. 21 (1940), pp. 1–60, discuss the changes in Hawaii's court system; Kuykendall, *The Hawaiian Kingdom* (3 vols., 1938–1967), provides the best overview of Hawaiian history and the most informed discussion of Lee's accomplishments. Obituaries are in the *Polynesian*, 30 May 1857, and the *Pacific Commercial Advertiser*, 11 June 1857. S. C. Damon's funeral sermon was published as *A Tribute to the Memory of Honorable William L. Lee* (1857).

BARBARA BENNETT PETERSON

LEE, Willis Augustus, Jr. (11 May 1888–25 Aug. 1945), naval officer, was born in Natlee, Kentucky, the son of Willis Augustus Lee, a local judge, and Susan Ireland Arnold. Reared in Owenton, Kentucky, he was only twenty years old when he graduated from the U.S. Naval Academy in 1908, 106th in his class of 201. Though possessed of a brilliant mind, he applied himself at only those things that interested him.

Following graduation, Lee served on the new battleship *Idaho* and the protected cruiser *New Orleans*. He developed a fondness for China, growing in part from his service on the U.S. Asiatic Fleet gunboat *Helena*, 1910–1913. He was known widely in the navy as "Ching" or "Chink." As a crew member of the battleship *New Hampshire*, he went ashore as part of the U.S. landing at Veracruz, Mexico, in 1914. He spent World War I as a naval ordnance inspector in Illinois. In 1919 he married Mabelle Ellspeth Allen; they had no children. In 1920, after serving on several ships and being a port officer in Rotterdam, he was a member of the U.S. rifle team at the Olympic Games in Antwerp, Belgium. Lee was awarded five gold medals, one silver, and one bronze.

During much of the 1920s, Lee alternated between rifle team duty and command of the destroyers *Fairfax*, *William B. Preston*, and *Lardner*. He also served at the New York Navy Yard and as executive officer of the target repair ship *Antares*. He was in the senior course at the Naval War College, Newport, in 1928–1929, followed by a tour of ordnance inspection on Long Island. His shore duty during the 1930s comprised three separate tours in the Navy Department's Division of Fleet Training.

From 1931 to 1933 Lee was navigator then executive officer of the U.S. Fleet flagship *Pennsylvania*. After a tour in Washington, he commanded the light cruiser *Concord* from 1936 to 1938. He then joined the staff of Rear Admiral Harold R. Stark, who had his flag on the *Concord*. When Stark was chosen chief of naval operations in 1939, Lee accompanied him to Washington as assistant director of the Division of Fleet Training. Lee became director of the division in early 1941, by which time it was actively preparing the fleet for war. Shortly after the attack on Pearl Harbor, Lee became head of the Readiness Division on the U.S. Fleet staff.

Promoted to rear admiral early in 1942, that summer Lee assumed command of Battleship Division Six, the first of the new 35,000-ton fast battleships to operate in the South Pacific. On the night of 14–15 November 1942, Lee was in command of Task Force Sixty-Four, comprised of his flagship *Washington*, the *South Dakota*, and four destroyers. The force turned back a group of heavy Japanese surface ships planning to bombard the Marines on the island of Guadalcanal. Gunfire from the *Washington* resulted in the sinking of the Japanese battleship *Kirishima*. That night action, Lee's finest hour, was decisive and effectively ended Japanese efforts to retake Guadalcanal.

In April 1943, Lee became commander, Battleships Pacific Fleet. From late 1943 onward he was at sea much of the time as his battleships provided the antiaircraft screen for the fast carrier task force engaged in the Central Pacific campaign. Lee's role was to remain ready to assume command of the battle line should it be activated for a surface action. Although he did command the battleships during several shore bombardments, the decisive surface battle that he awaited never came to pass.

In December 1944 Lee's command was split, and he was left as commander, Battleship Squadron Two, the Pacific Fleet fast battleships. During the Iwo Jima and Okinawa campaigns of 1945, Lee remained in a role subordinate to the commanders of the carrier task groups, in which he rode almost as a passenger. In July, after being detached from the battleships, he formed Task Group Sixty-Nine in Casco Bay, Maine, directed to develop countermeasures against kamikaze planes. The war ended before a real solution could be found, and Lee died of a coronary thrombosis a little more than a week later in Casco Bay.

A quiet man with a puckish sense of humor, Lee was casual, even sloppy, in his personal appearance. He had an unpretentious give-and-take manner with juniors, dealing man to man rather than stressing the difference in rank. He was a voracious reader, intellectually curious. He was essentially a scientist in uniform, possessed of the rare quality of being able to operate comfortably in both the theoretical and practical spheres of his profession.

Considering his role in World War II, Lee is a relatively obscure figure half a century later. That he is not well known stems in part from his personality—he was an exceedingly modest man—and in part from the circumstances in which he operated. His work as director of fleet training had substantial effect in preparing the ships of the U.S. Navy to operate tactically against the enemy they would face. However, much of this developmental work was classified and was conducted far from the battle front.

Lee's obscurity is also a product of the tactical organization of the fleet in the Pacific, for it effectively denied his battleships much opportunity to engage in surface actions. In the one big chance he did have, Lee made the biggest contribution of his career: the night battle that led to the eventual success of the Guadalcanal campaign. From then on, however, he experienced a great deal of frustration, for his ships were tied to the protective screens of aircraft carriers during the long months when the American fleet moved ever closer to Japan. He spent himself during his extended period of combat command, and it is likely that his arduous war service was a factor in his death.

• Lee's official navy biographical summary is available in the Operational Archives Branch, Naval Historical Center, Washington, D.C. Other sources useful in tracing Lee's career include Rear Admiral Julius Augustus Furer, USN (Ret.), *Administration of the Navy Department in World War II* (1959); Mariam Sidebottom Houchens, *History of Owen County, Kentucky: "Sweet Owen"* (1976); Vice Admiral Charles A. Lockwood, USN (Ret.), and Hans Christian Adamson, *Battles of the Philippine Sea* (1967); Samuel Eliot Morison, *History of United States Naval Operations in World War II*, vols. 1, 5, 7, 8, 12, 13, 14 (1947–1962); and Clark Reynolds, *The Fast Carriers: The Forging of an Air Navy* (1968).

PAUL STILLWELL

LEECH, Margaret Kernochan (7 Nov. 1893–24 Feb. 1974), historian and novelist, was born in Newburgh, New York, the daughter of William Kernochan Leech, a milkman, and Rebecca Taggert (or Taggart). Leech grew up in the adult world of Newburgh's Palatine Hotel, where, she later recalled, "we were rather nice hotel children" (Nichols, p. 8). After graduating from nearby Vassar College in 1915, Leech went to New York City, where she answered the complaints of subscribers to Condé Nast's magazines and was on the editorial staff of his *House and Garden* before moving into advertising and publicity. During World War I Leech worked for Anne Morgan's American Committee for Devastated France, spent several years abroad, and met Morgan's mentor, Elisabeth Marbury, the legendary theatrical and literary agent.

While still on the staff of Morgan's committee, Leech published her first short story, "The Children" (*Century Magazine*, June 1923). Her whimsical goals in life, revealed in the same issue of that magazine, placed writing "well up on the list of things she wanted to do, coming right after accumulating a lot of money, and buying up most of the hats and dresses in the world, and taking a steamer, whenever she happened to feel like it, for some place far away." Drawing on her own experiences as a young working woman, Leech, when she returned to New York, published *The Back of the Book* (1924), a novel that Robert Benchley found "good front and back" (Giffuni, p. 142). *Tin Wedding* (1926), Leech's second novel, imagined a wife's reflections on ten years of a fashionable marriage with an ill-suited mate, while her last novel, *The Feathered Nest* (1928), explored the effect of a domineering mother on her family. The *Saturday Review of Literature* (20 Oct. 1928) found all three novels "excellent," and reviewers commended Leech's sound characterization, rich detail, and clear style.

During this period Leech came to know the brilliant "vicious circle" of writers that lunched at a round table at the Algonquin Hotel. These writers, many of whom were connected with the *New York World*, appreciated Leech's acerbic wit. When round table member Franklin P. Adams appeared in an opened shirt that revealed the top part of his hairy chest, she quickly remarked, "Well, Frank, I see your fly is open higher than usual today" (Harriman, p. 145). Leech collaborated with Heywood Broun, a *World* columnist and a round-table colleague, on a biography, *Anthony Comstock: Roundsman of the Lord* (1927). A selection of the Literary Guild, the book attacked censorship while giving an amusing account of a crusader who failed to distinguish pornography from art. In 1927 and 1928 Leech "profiled" Morgan, Marbury, and two other women for the *New Yorker*, and in June she covered the "woman's angle" at the Republican and Democratic national conventions for the *World*.

In August 1928 Leech became the second wife of Ralph Pulitzer, the editor and publisher of the *World*. They had two daughters, one of whom died in infancy while they were vacationing in France. In 1930 Pulitzer was forced to retire from the *World* (which was having financial problems), making it possible for him to indulge his passion for big-game hunting and Leech her passion for travel. Apart from conventional trips to Europe, they went to Africa in 1930 to collect specimens for the Carnegie Museum of Natural History in Pittsburgh and to India in 1935 for a tiger and panther hunt that employed fifteen elephants and 500 beaters. In 1934 Leech's bright and amusing play *Divided by Three* failed after running about a month. Written in collaboration with Beatrice (Mrs. George S.) Kaufman, starring Judith Anderson, and produced by Guthrie McClintic, it had all the ingredients of success "except talent," Leech later remarked (Nichols, p. 8).

Feeling that she had neither "enough invention" for future novels nor enough talent for short stories, Leech turned to history. She decided that "fact writing is much the best kind for me, because the material is there and so half the work is done by dredging, by learning the material." To write history, Leech thought, like writing fiction "you must have your own light, your own point of view, for each scene" (van Gelder, p. 18). At the suggestion of Cass Canfield of Harper & Brothers, Leech in 1935 began a study of the city of Washington during the Civil War. With a sick husband and a child to care for, Leech, who wrote as she researched, had many interruptions. Her husband died on 14 June 1939, leaving his estate to her.

When *Reveille in Washington* appeared in the summer of 1941, its timing could not have been better, for the nation was gearing up for World War II. Her careful research in contemporary newspapers coupled with her lively style enabled Leech to paint a colorful and detailed portrait of Civil War Washington with the lid off and to demonstrate the toughness of democracy at a time when totalitarianism was appearing invincible. The historian James G. Randall, while grumbling about the absence of footnotes, appreciated her "technicolor" history. Journalists, novelists, and poets were ecstatic. By "mingling . . . the deep current of history with all the bubbles of rumor and despair and hope," Stephen Vincent Benét observed that Leech made her book fascinating, alive, and contemporaneous (*Saturday Review*, 30 Aug. 1941). Becoming a Book-of-the-Month Club selection and a bestseller, Leech's book won the Pulitzer Prize for history, which, although given by her husband's family, was administered by Columbia University.

For her next project, Leech, who had written when William McKinley was assassinated and she was not quite eight, "I am oh so sorry that our President is dead, / And everybody's sorry, so my father said," determined to re-create McKinley's world and the world of her childhood. Working thoroughly, or in her self-deprecating words, "most ostentatiously" (Nichols, p. 8), she produced *In the Days of McKinley* (1959). A richly detailed, appreciative portrait of the man and the age, it began a reevaluation of McKinley's presidency. Although champions of strong twentieth-century presidents thought Leech had written "a first-rate study of a second-rate President" (John Morton Blum, *New York Times Book Review*, 1 Nov. 1959), subsequent historians are closer to Leech's evaluation of McKinley as a knowledgeable, courageous, independent, effective political leader. Like her earlier history, Leech's *McKinley* was a Book-of-the-Month Club selection and a Pulitzer Prize winner. It also won the Bancroft Prize.

Leech's last project was a biography of another martyred president, James A. Garfield. While doing research on Garfield, she suffered a devastating blow when her surviving daughter died suddenly in 1965, leaving her husband and two young children. Leech proved to be "incredibly strong and resilient, a wonderful grandmother who was always there" (interview with Kate Freedberg, 18 Jan. 1995). She was also self-willed. Rather than take the advice of her doctor, who predicted she would come back in a box if she went to Africa in her late seventies, she switched to a physician who did not object to the trip. In 1972 she was hospitalized with second- and third-degree burns on her hands and feet from a mattress fire in her Fifth Avenue apartment, caused by her smoking in bed. Despite mental anguish and physical pain, she persisted in her research and writing. "There's a challenge in taking something obscure and trying to find out what you can," she explained (Nichols, p. 8). Leech finished eight chapters of *The Garfield Orbit* (1978, completed by Harry J. Brown) before she died in New York. In those chapters, she probes with insight Garfield's earnest, ambitious, self-centered ways, revealing some less-than-admirable character traits (especially in his relationships with women) and providing clues that help to explain his duplicity and indecision as well as his noble qualities.

• Leech's granddaughter, Kate Pulitzer Freedberg, Boston, Mass., has the bulk of Leech's papers except for a few in the possession of Sydney J. Freedberg, Washington, D.C., Leech's son-in-law. Interviews with Sydney Freedberg, 19 Jan. 1995, and Kate Freedberg, 18 Jan. 1995, were helpful. Cathe Giffuni, "A Bibliography of Margaret Leech," *Bulletin of Bibliography* 45 (1988): 142–51, is most valuable. See also "Among Our Contributors," *Century Magazine*, June 1923; Robert van Gelder, "An Interview with Miss Margaret Leech," *New York Times Book Review*, 14 Sept. 1941; Lewis Nichols, "In and Out of Books: Biographer," *New York Times Book Review*, 1 Nov. 1959; and Margaret Case Harriman, *The Vicious Circle: The Story of the Algonquin Round Table* (1951). An obituary is in the *New York Times*, 25 Feb. 1974.

ARI HOOGENBOOM

LEEDS, John (18 May 1705–Mar. 1790), public official, surveyor, and mathematician, was born at Bay Hundred, Talbot County, Maryland, the son of Edward Leeds and Ruth Ball. Leeds, apparently self-educated, developed an expertise in mathematics and an interest in astronomy. He married Rachel Harrison in a Quaker ceremony in 1726; the couple had three daughters. He resided in Talbot County for his entire life and held a variety of public offices, beginning in 1734 as a justice of the peace.

Periodically during his long career, Leeds held several public offices simultaneously, a practice that was not uncommon in provincial Maryland. The positions of county clerk, surveyor and searcher, treasurer, and naval officer provided a steady income over a long period of time with little risk or trouble. Leeds purchased the position of clerk of the Circuit Court, Talbot County, from Tench Francis on 2 August 1738, but he faced criticism in 1739 from a committee of the Lower House for the way the transaction had been conducted. Nominal incumbent Thomas Bullen, Tench Francis's brother-in-law, had tried to buy the office but could not raise the money, whereupon Francis sold the position to Leeds. Leeds served a total of thirty-nine years in this office. Leeds's outspokenness brought him trouble in May 1738 when the Lower House of the Maryland General Assembly arrested Leeds for "expressions insulting the dignity and Honour of this House" and for making several reviling speeches impugning the authority of the House to call him before them. The House demanded an apology and payment of his one-fifth share of £13 17s costs; on 23 May they jailed him in Annapolis until he apologized.

From 7 March 1754 to the end of the colonial period (c. 1774), he held the title Surveyor and Searcher of Oxford. In this position Leeds could enter ships and warehouses, break open packages and trunks, and seize goods for infringements of the law at the port of Oxford. A 1770 report prepared by inspector John Williams for the customs commissioners at Boston indicated that the functions of the surveyor and searcher were useless, but the Treasury Lords refused to reduce patronage; the Revolution abolished these kinds of jobs. The ruling board members of the British treasury controlled customs policy, personnel, and conditions of the service, and manipulated patronage appointments for their own financial and political advantage.

Marking provincial boundaries required men knowledgeable in astronomy to serve as surveyors-general. Leeds's reputation for astronomical knowledge led to Governor Horatio Sharpe's recommendation in 1758 that he be appointed a commissioner of the provincial government. He received provisional appointment in 1760 and permanent appointment in May 1762. Sharpe noted that Leeds had "studied the Mathematicks as much as any Gentlemen among Us," and he considered him "to have the most Mathematical Knowledge of any Person" and "to be by far the best in the province." Leeds and his fellow commissioners oversaw the boundary demarcation between Maryland and Pennsylvania, which was carried out by Charles Mason and Jeremiah Dixon, two professional surveyors, and he signed the minutes of the final meeting and the surveyors' boundary map on 9 November 1768.

Despite his reputation for astronomical knowledge, Leeds's astronomical methodology was somewhat careless. As an amateur astronomer he wrote a letter on 17 June 1769, subsequently published in the *Philosophical Transactions* of the Royal Society (1770), reporting on his observed transit of Venus with the sun using a watch and reflecting telescope. These observations proved inaccurate since he did not know the exact time or the longitude east of Annapolis, Maryland—two factors deemed critical to documenting the event. Although the Royal Society indiscriminately accepted and published any paper submitted, inclusion did not bestow upon the writer the mantle of expertise. Leeds's dabbling in astronomy apparently did not attract the attention of more scientific amateur astronomers such as Benjamin Franklin and David Rittenhouse in Philadelphia; his reputation as a mathematician surpassed his recognition as an astronomer, especially outside Maryland.

From 29 September until 14 October 1766 Leeds was commissioned by Lieutenant Governor Sharpe as the treasurer of the Eastern Shore but resigned to accept the position as naval officer of Pocomoke. He was recommissioned on 28 August 1769 and on 29 April 1773 but resigned in September 1775 in favor of his son-in-law, William Thomas III. As a naval officer, Leeds received commissions on duties he collected and fees for entering and clearing ships, both of which were paid in money rather than in tobacco, which was used to pay most other fees. The Pocomoke office was the least remunerably valuable of the naval offices based on the commissions collected on duties paid.

Among the elite class of Talbot County residents, a strong minority withheld their full support of the American Revolution; some remained silently disapproving, some spoke in favor but did not follow through in action, and still others, like John Leeds, vocally denounced the move for independence. For his avowed toryism, shortly before August 1777 he lost the clerkship that he had held since 1738.

After 1783 Leeds returned to favor and again served as surveyor-general of Maryland until his death at home in Wade's Point, Maryland. John Leeds's reputation as a skilled mathematician in colonial Maryland earned him the confidence of the governor who appointed him as one of the state's six commissioners to supervise the survey of the disputed Maryland-Pennsylvania boundary—the "Mason-Dixon line."

• The personal papers of John Leeds Bozman, Leeds's grandson, at the Maryland Historical Society (Baltimore) and the Library of Congress contain Leeds family correspondence and genealogical papers. Brief biographical information about John Leeds appears in Oswald Tilghman, *History of Talbot County, Maryland, 1661–1861* (1967). His early troubles with the general assembly can be found in *Archives of Maryland: Proceedings and Acts of the General Assembly of Maryland, 1737–1740* (1921). Documentation on the patronage in colonial Maryland and Leeds's various positions is discussed in Donnell MacClure Owings, *His Lordship's Patronage; Offices of Profit in Colonial Maryland* (1953). His reputation as a mathematician and his appointment to the Maryland-Pennsylvania boundary commission are documented in Bernard Christian Steiner, ed., *Archives of Maryland: Correspondence of Governor Horatio Sharpe*, vol. II, 1757–1761 (1890); in William Hand Browne, ed., *Archives of Maryland: Correspondence of Governor Horatio Sharpe*, vol. III, 1761–1771 (1895); and in the Calvert papers at the Maryland Historical Society. Brooke Hindle, *The Pursuit of Science in Revolutionary America, 1735–1789* (1956), invalidates Leeds's "Observations of the Transit of Venus, on June 3, 1769," *Philosophical Transactions* of the Royal Society (1770).

SUSAN HAMBURGER

LEEMANS, Tuffy (12 Nov. 1912–19 Jan. 1979), professional football player, was born Alphonse Emil Leemans in Eloise, Wisconsin, the son of Joseph Leemans, a miner, and Hortense (maiden name unknown). He earned his nickname "Tuffy" when, as a young high school player in Superior, Wisconsin, he flattened two older and larger players on one play. He went on to star for his local high school team, earning a football scholarship to the University of Oregon. When his coach transferred to George Washington University in Washington, D.C., Leemans followed him there for his sophomore year. Midway through the 1933 season he became a regular when, upon entering a game late in the first quarter, he ran for one touchdown, completed five straight passes, and punted for a 48-yard average. For his remaining time at George Washington, he was his team's main offensive threat. In 1934 he set a school record by rushing for 1,054 yards. He completed his career with 2,382 rushing yards and a 40-yard punting average, both school records at the time.

Despite his heroics Leemans received little notice across the country because George Washington was not a national football power. However, Wellington Mara, the teenage son of New York Giants owner Tim Mara, visited Washington in 1935 and witnessed a sensational effort by Leemans in a losing cause against the University of Alabama. Young Mara urged his father to select Leemans when the first National Football League (NFL) draft was held the following year. The Giants took him in the second round of the draft and offered him a contract for $3,500. In his final seasons he earned $12,000, one of the highest salaries in the league.

Before reporting to the Giants, Leemans played in the Chicago College All-Star game, but he received his berth only through a bit of chicanery. At that time the football season opened with the charity exhibition game at Soldier Field between an all-star squad of the previous year's college graduates, chosen by a vote of fans, and the defending NFL champions. Knowing that Leemans would be virtually unknown to most of the nation's fans, *Washington Herald* writer Vincent X. Flaherty plastered ballots with Leemans's name over a bale of hay. As he suspected, the sponsoring *Chicago Tribune* weighed the ballots instead of counting them, thus earning Leemans a spot on the team. Leemans proved worthy of the ruse by playing a major role in the collegians' 7–7 tie with the Detroit Lions.

Leemans enjoyed a terrific rookie year in 1936 with the Giants. Over a 12-game season, the 6′, 185-pound workhorse led the league in rushing attempts with 206 and in rushing yardage with 830. He was the first New York back to ever lead the NFL in rushing. At season's end, he was named to the Official All-NFL Team, an honor he earned again in 1939.

Although he led the Giants in rushing every year from 1937 through 1941, his attempts and yardage totals were fewer than in his rookie season. Oddly enough, the reason for the dropoff was that the Giants became a stronger team. As more good players were added to the squad, Coach Steve Owen instituted his own version of the two-platoon system. Players played both offense and defense at the time, and a substitution rule was in place stating that a player could not leave a game and then reenter during the same quarter. Owen developed two strong squads. Midway through the first quarter, he would send in his "second" team, which would stay on the field until midway through the second quarter. The process would be repeated in the second half. Leemans was a "regular," but he played only about half the time.

Although Owen's system reduced individual statistics, it was effective. The Giants won the 1938 NFL championship by defeating the Green Bay Packers in the title game. They also won Eastern Division championships in 1939 and 1941. During this period Leemans was always regarded as the team's clutch running back and was expected to carry the ball when important yards were needed. In addition, he did much of the passing and punting, served as an occasional pass receiver, returned punts and kickoffs, and called signals from his right halfback position in the Giants' single-wing offense. He was also regarded as a strong defensive back.

Leemans was passed over for military service during World War II after a severe blow to his head in a 1942 game against the Chicago Bears cost him his hearing in one ear. Other injuries took their toll, and in his final two years he was used mostly as a passer. When Leemans retired after the 1943 season, he had rushed for 3,142 yards—the first Giant to top 3,000 yards—passed for 2,324 yards, and gained 442 yards on pass receptions. Such numbers pale in comparison to those achieved in a later, more offense-minded era, but at the time he ranked among the NFL's career leaders. To honor him, the Giants held Tuffy Leemans Day in 1943 and retired his number four jersey.

In 1938 Leemans married Theodora Rinaldi; they had two children. After retiring from football he became a successful businessman in the Washington area. In 1978 his accomplishments were recognized with his induction into the Professional Football Hall of Fame in Canton, Ohio. He died in Hillsboro Beach, Florida.

• The Tuffy Leemans file is at the Professional Football Hall of Fame in Canton, Ohio. See also Dave Klein, *The New York Giants: Yesterday, Today, and Tomorrow* (1973), and Don Smith, "A Real Tuffy," *Coffin Corner* 7, no. 1 (1985). Official statistics for the years 1936 through 1943 are available in David S. Neft and Richard M. Cohen, *The Football Encyclopedia* (1991). An obituary is in the *New York Times*, 20 Jan. 1979.

BOB CARROLL

LEESER, Isaac (12 Dec. 1806–1 Feb. 1868), Jewish religious leader and author, was born in Neuenkirchen, Westphalia, the son of Uri Lippman, a merchant, and Sarah Cohen. Leeser's mother died in 1814, and his father invited his own mother, Gitla, to raise his children. In 1820 Leeser's father and grandmother died. A benefactor took responsibility for the orphaned boy and arranged for him to attend a good school in Münster, where he received an excellent general education. In his Jewish studies, he was greatly influenced by Rabbi Abraham Sutro, a staunch religious traditionalist.

Leeser's maternal uncle Zalma Rehine had left for the United States in 1788 or 1789 and ultimately settled in Richmond, Virginia. In response to his uncle's invitation, Leeser arrived in Richmond in May 1824 and quickly made progress in his studies of English and American history and culture. He worked with his uncle in the dry-goods business.

Leeser became an active member of the congregation of Richmond's Beth Shalome. The synagogue followed the Sephardic mode of worship and its hazan (reader and religious leader) was Isaac B. Seixas. Seixas taught Leeser the synagogue ritual. Leeser was also influenced by Jacob Mordecai, the president of Beth Shalome. The intellectual Mordecai introduced Leeser to significant English-language works dealing with religion and Hebrew grammar.

In 1829 Congregation Mikveh Israel of Philadelphia, having read Leeser's bold defense of Judaism in the *Richmond Constitutional Whig*, invited Leeser to become hazan. With the encouragement of his uncle, he accepted this post and began his duties at Mikveh Israel with diligence. He soon came to see himself not merely as a hazan but as a teacher and communal leader.

Early in his career at Mikveh Israel, Leeser began to instruct his congregants in the basic teachings of Judaism by means of Sabbath discourses. He prided himself on being the first American Jewish religious leader to preach regular sermons in the vernacular. Before Leeser, the hazanim delivered sermons rarely and generally only at the request of the lay leadership. Leeser never married. He suffered from nearsightedness and nearly died of smallpox in 1833. In spite of his physical shortcomings, he pursued his communal work with energy and dignity.

Leeser felt the need to teach Judaism not merely to his own congregation in Philadelphia but to the larger American Jewish audience. In 1830 he published *Instruction in the Mosaic Law* and in 1834, *The Jews and Mosaic Law*. In 1837 he published the first two volumes of his *Discourses on the Jewish Religion*. Through these writings, he established himself as the foremost champion of Jewish tradition in America. In 1837–1838 he published a six-volume set of prayer books according to the custom of Spanish and Portuguese Jews. His book included not only the Hebrew text but his own English translation as well. He also published a Hebrew reader, designed as a guide to the Hebrew language for children and as a self-instruction text for adults (1838).

During this period of significant literary productivity, Leeser also engaged in important communal activities. In 1838 he helped Rebecca Gratz launch the Jewish Sunday school movement in America. In 1840 he organized a large interfaith demonstration in Philadelphia to protest the heinous blood libel charge against Jews in Damascus. In 1841 Leeser presented a plan for the "Union of American Jewry," the first comprehensive attempt to organize the entire American Jewish community. Although this effort failed, it laid the foundation for the future development of American Jewish communal life.

Leeser was a sought-after speaker, whom intellectuals and students of Judaism turned to for guidance. The English Jewish writer Grace Aguilar began correspondence with Leeser in 1840, asking him to be her literary mentor. Indeed, Leeser did edit and annotate several of her works and arranged for their publication.

In 1843 Leeser began publishing the *Occident and American Jewish Advocate*, the first successful Jewish periodical in the United States. He served as editor of this popular monthly for twenty-five years. The pages of the *Occident* were not only a forum for his own ideas but served as the meeting ground for Jews of various opinions.

Leeser was a consistent advocate of unifying the American Jewish community. He was a proponent of a vibrant and creative modern religious Orthodoxy and became a vocal opponent of the incipient Reform movement.

As part of his program to educate American Jews in their religious heritage, Leeser organized the first

American Jewish Publication Society in 1845. His own literary output continued to be impressive. In 1845 he published his English translation of the Torah. In 1848 he published a daily prayer book according to the custom of German and Polish Jews.

Leeser's public and literary life brought him much satisfaction. However, his relationship with Congregation Mikveh Israel was often stormy and unpleasant. In his introduction to the third volume of *Discourses on the Jewish Religion* (1841), Leeser lamented that the position of hazan-minister had serious shortcomings that would deter intelligent young men from seeking a career in Jewish religious leadership.

There is . . . in the usual management of the Synagogue something inconsistent with the appointment of men with endowment to the station of minister, inasmuch as the temporal rulers have too much direct interference with the Hazan in every public act in which he can engage. . . . It is in the nature of man to desire freedom of action; and the same feeling therefore which renders us restive under political subjection, will also create an uneasiness, far from promoting harmony, in the minds of ministers of religion if they are rendered subservient to persons who evidently cannot be more religious and better informed than they are themselves.

Relations between Leeser and his congregation deteriorated so much that in 1850 his contract was ended. Leeser felt that the contract offered to him was not satisfactory and refused to accept it.

With the termination of his position at Mikveh Israel, Leeser supported himself with the *Occident* and his other publications. He continued to work on an English translation of the entire Hebrew Bible, and this work, the first such translation by an American Jew, appeared in 1853–1854. He continued to travel, to lecture, and to fight for the causes he championed: Jewish education, Jewish unity, the centrality of the land of Israel in Jewish life, and traditional Jewish values and observances.

In 1857 a group of his supporters in Philadelphia established a synagogue, Congregation Beth El Emeth, and appointed Leeser as hazan for life. This provided him with a congregational base of support as well as a steady income.

Leeser was concerned that the American Jewish community lacked the educational institutions necessary to produce its own religious leadership. He believed that American-born, English-speaking Jewish preachers could have a powerful impact on American Jewish life. He advocated the establishment of Jewish day schools, which would combine religious and secular studies. His ultimate goal was to establish a rabbinical school. Largely through his efforts, Maimonides College was opened in Philadelphia in 1867—the first rabbinical school in the United States. Leeser served as provost, and the school attracted a respectable faculty including Sabato Morais and Marcus Jastrow. Shortly after the school opened, though, Leeser took ill and died in Philadelphia. Although the school struggled on for a few years, it ultimately failed.

Leeser's accomplishments on the American Jewish scene were monumental. He was a pioneer in elevating the station of the Jewish religious leader in the United States. His numerous publications brought inspiration and enlightenment to thousands of American Jews. Leeser promoted the publication of Judaica works in America on a broad scale. Through the *Occident*, he pioneered in the field of American Jewish journalism. His communal and educational work bore some fruit during the course of his lifetime and motivated others to make contributions of their own. Leeser influenced Hyman Gratz who later established Gratz College in Philadelphia, a college for Jewish education. He also influenced Moses Aaron Dropsie who provided a legacy to found Dropsie College for Hebrew and Cognate Learning in Philadelphia. Leeser's efforts helped lay the foundation for the development of American Jewish life in the generations that succeeded him.

• Leeser's papers are in the Center for Judaic Studies, University of Pennsylvania; the American Jewish Archives, Hebrew Union College; and the American Jewish Historical Society, Brandeis University. Leeser's sermons were published in ten volumes as *Discourses on the Jewish Religion* (1867). The *Occident and American Jewish Advocate* was a monthly periodical, which appeared 1843–1869.

Lance J. Sussman's *Isaac Leeser and the Making of American Judaism* (1995), is the most important book-length biography of Leeser. It includes a good bibliography of Leeser's works as well as studies about him. Among the articles that shed light on Leeser's career are Maxwell Whiteman, "Isaac Leeser and the Jews of Philadelphia," *Publications of the American Jewish Historical Society* 48 (June 1959): 207–44; Maxine Seller, "Isaac Leeser's Views on the Restoration of a Jewish Palestine," *American Jewish Historical Quarterly* 58 (Sept. 1968): 118–35; and Henry Englander, "Isaac Leeser," *Yearbook of the Central Conference of American Rabbis* 28 (1918): 213–52.

MARC D. ANGEL

LEETE, William (c. 1613–16 Apr. 1683), governor of both New Haven and Connecticut colonies, was born in Dodington, Huntingdonshire, England, the son of John Leete and Ann Shute. The Leete family was prominent enough to have a coat of arms. He studied law at Cambridge University, served as clerk to the bishop of Ely's court at Cambridge, and became a Puritan. He married Anne Payne of Hail Weston, Huntingdonshire, in 1636, and the couple had seven children who lived to adulthood.

Leete was a prosperous lawyer and yeoman, living in Keyston in Huntingdonshire, when he, his wife, and four servants sailed for Quinnipiac (New Haven) in May 1639 as part of the Reverend Henry Whitfield's company. Leete was one of the twenty-five persons to sign the covenant of the Whitfield Company on shipboard on 1 June; they arrived at the shores of Long Island Sound on about 10 July 1639. An agreement to purchase land at Menunkatuck, east of New Haven, from the local Indians of that name, was signed by Leete and five other Europeans on 29 September 1639. He also helped negotiate two subsequent purchases of Indian lands in 1641. Until the formal gathering of a church on 19 June 1643, in which Leete was one of the seven pillars, the undivided lands in the new plantation, named Guilford in 1643, were held in trust by the six planters who signed the original Indian deed. On 2 February 1642 the planters voted to entrust all civil and judicial power to four of their number, including Leete. He served in 1643 as a representative from Menunkatuck to a meeting in New Haven that led to the formal organization of the New Haven Colony.

A major landowner in and the leading citizen of Guilford, an area of which is still called Leete's Island, Leete also had a store and experimented in 1654 with raising tobacco. Leete served as clerk of the plantation from 1639 to 1662 and quickly became a major figure in New Haven Colony. He was deputy from Guilford, an elected position, for every session between 1643 and 1649; secretary of the colony in October 1646; magistrate from Guilford during the years 1651–1658; commissioner to Massachusetts Bay in 1653 and 1654, when New Haven was seeking support in case of war against the Dutch at New Amsterdam; and, from 1655 to 1664, commissioner to the United Colonies, a loose confederation formed for defensive purposes by the New England colonies. Leete was elected deputy governor of New Haven in May 1658. He was reelected the following year and, after the death of Governor Francis Newman on 18 November 1660, became acting governor of the colony until his formal election to that position in May 1661. Leete, third and last governor of the colony, served until New Haven was absorbed into Connecticut. Among the other positions Leete held were those of attorney for Guilford in 1647–1649; judge for Southold, Long Island, in 1655; and member of the school committee of what was to become the Hopkins Grammar School in New Haven.

Leete was chief magistrate of New Haven Colony when the consequences of the restoration of Charles II had to be faced. New Haven's position was particularly precarious because of a lack of any legal basis for its existence, its longstanding support for Oliver Cromwell, and its sheltering of the regicides William Goffe and Edward Whalley. Soon after their arrival in New Haven, where they would spend more than three years in hiding, Goffe and Whalley were guided to the home of the deputy governor in Guilford. Leete failed to provide the necessary assistance to the royal agents sent to capture the fugitives. He helped the officials sufficiently to avoid obvious charges of obstructionism but not enough to ensure the regicides' capture.

In August 1661 Leete wrote Connecticut governor John Winthrop seeking a joint charter to extend to beyond the Delaware River, where New Haven agents had been seeking to secure land titles from the Indians. Winthrop, however, declined to support New Haven and the charter he received from the Crown in 1662 provided for the absorption of the smaller colony. On hearing this disagreeable news at a meeting of the United Colony commissioners in Boston, Leete and New Haven magistrate Benjamin Fenn protested that "We cannot as yett say that the procurement of this Pattent wilbe acceptable to vs or our Collonie" (Calder, *New Haven Colony*, p. 232). Resistance, however, proved fruitless, and Governor Leete decided to support a settlement "in a righteous & amicable way" between the two colonies by the summer of 1663. On 5 January 1665 the formal union of the two colonies was achieved.

Some inhabitants of the old New Haven Jurisdiction were so dismayed by union with a colony that failed to adhere to the rigorous Puritan standards of the founders that they left Connecticut. Although lands were laid out for Leete at the site of Newark, New Jersey, he remained in Connecticut and assumed a major role in public affairs. He was one of six men from the former New Haven Colony granted provisional appointments as assistants by the Connecticut General Court in October 1664, prior to the date of formal union; he was also one of eight men nominated in April 1665 to serve on the twelve-man Connecticut Council and was elected to that position the following month along with three other former magistrates from New Haven Colony. He was annually reelected to the upper house until chosen deputy governor of Connecticut in May 1669, replacing Major John Mason. He remained in that position until he was elected governor in May 1676 after the death of Governor Winthrop in Boston on 5 April. Leete was returned as governor by Connecticut freemen each year until his death.

As a reward for his services in the union of the two colonies, Leete was granted 300 acres of land by the General Court in October 1667. He served as Connecticut's commissioner to the United Colonies in 1665, 1667, 1668, 1672, 1673, and 1678 and played an important role in defending the colony in King Philip's War. A special meeting of the General Court on 9 July 1675 appointed a council of war to "haue as full power as the Charter will allow, to consult, conclude and act all matters and things emergent" (Trumbull, vol. 2, p. 261) during the course of the conflict. Between July 1675 and October 1677 Connecticut's council of war held some 180 meetings; Leete presided over more than 120 of them. In May 1678 the General Court asked the governor to move to the seat of government in Hartford, where he lived for the rest of his life. Two years later he was obliged to take an oath on behalf of the colony to enforce England's acts of trade and navigation and to answer a questionnaire sent out by the Lords of Trade.

Leete's first wife, the mother of all his children, died in 1668. He subsequently married Sarah Rutherford, the widow of Henry Rutherford, in 1670. After her death in February 1674, he married Mary Street, the widow of Governor Francis Newman and the Reverend Nicholas Street, in 1678. Leete died in Hartford.

Leete's arrival on the Connecticut shore in 1639 occurred near the end of the great wave of Puritan migration to New England. A well-educated and well-to-do man, he presided as governor of New Haven over the union of that colony with Connecticut. It was his acceptance of the inevitable and his willingness to serve in the Connecticut government that did much to reconcile unhappy New Haveners. The union of the two colonies was symbolically sealed with his accession to the governorship in 1676.

• No significant collection of Leete papers exists. Several Leete manuscripts are located in the Massachusetts Historical Society and a handful of Leete letters are reproduced in Edward E. Atwater, *History of the Colony of New Haven to Its Absorption into Connecticut* (1881); Isabel M. Calder, ed., *Letters of John Davenport, Puritan Divine* (1937); Charles J. Hoadly, ed., *Records of the Colony or Jurisdiction of New Haven, from May, 1653, to the Union* (1858); and J. Hammond Trumbull, ed., *The Public Records of the Colony of Connecticut*, vol. 3 (1859). The largest extant body of Leete letters, numbering twenty-eight, has been published in *The Winthrop Papers*, Massachusetts Historical Society, *Collections*, 4th ser., vol. 7 (1865). Biographical information about Leete can be found in Charles L. Biggs, *William Leete: Co-founder of Guilford* (1940); Stephen J. Knight, "William Leete Settles a Case," New Haven Colony Bar Association, *Bulletin*, no. 21 (May 1938): 28–32; Edward L. Leete, *The Family of William Leete* (1884); Edward L. Leete, *The Descendants of William Leete* (1934); and Bernard C. Steiner, "Governor William Leete and the Absorption of New Haven Colony by Connecticut," American Historical Association, *Annual Report* (1891): 209–22, but none of these works can be considered authoritative. Further information on Leete is in Isabel M. Calder, *The New Haven Colony* (1934); Robert W. Roetger, "New Haven's Charter Quest and Annexation by Connecticut," *Connecticut History*, no. 29 (Nov. 1988): 16–26; Ralph D. Smith, *The History of Guilford, Connecticut* (1877); Bernard C. Steiner, *A History of the Plantation of Menunkatuck* (1897); and the official published records of the New Haven and Connecticut colonies. Given his importance in the history of seventeenth-century Guilford, New Haven, and Connecticut, Leete is deserving of an extended biographical study.

BRUCE P. STARK

LEFEVERE, Peter Paul (29 Apr. 1804–4 Mar. 1869), Roman Catholic missionary and bishop, was born in Roulers, Belgium, the son of Charles Lefevere and Albertine-Angeline Muylle, prosperous farmers. He began his training for the priesthood with the Lazarists in Paris. Volunteering for the American missions, in 1828 Lefevere was sent to St. Louis, where he completed his theological studies in the diocesan seminary. He was ordained to the priesthood on 20 November 1831.

Lefevere spent a year as pastor at New Madrid, Missouri, and was subsequently assigned to the Salt River mission in Ralls County, Missouri, where he served from 1833 until 1840. This vast frontier mission encompassed portions of southern Iowa and western Illinois as well as northeastern Missouri, and Lefevere spent much of his time there on an arduous mission circuit. More than physical stamina was required: Lefevere displayed an enormous self-discipline, capacity for work, and devotion to the pastoral role. These qualities do much to explain his later success as a bishop.

In failing health, Lefevere returned temporarily to Belgium in 1840. During his stay, Roman authorities decided to appoint a coadjutor bishop to the see of Detroit, which Bishop Frederic Rese had unwillingly vacated. Through the mediation of Bishop Joseph Rosati of St. Louis, Lefevere was chosen for the post, despite his youth and want of administrative experience. He was ordained titular bishop of Zela and administrator of Detroit on 21 November 1841 at St. John's Church, Philadelphia.

The diocese of Detroit was in financial crisis as of 1841, with no more than seventeen priests and only eighteen parishes, though the diocese was then coextensive with the states of Michigan and Wisconsin. It was Lefevere's great achievement to lay the institutional foundations for the diocese's eventual extensive development and in so doing to accommodate the needs of a rapidly growing population of Catholic immigrants. At Lefevere's death, the diocese—geographically much smaller—had eighty-eight priests and more than 170 parishes. The first steps had been taken toward what would eventually be a statewide network of Catholic schools. Lefevere recruited three teaching orders into his diocese and oversaw the creation of a fourth, the Sisters, Servants of the Immaculate Heart of Mary, founded in 1845. Under his auspices, the Sisters of Charity established a hospital, an orphanage, and an asylum for the mentally ill.

Lefevere also laid the disciplinary foundations for the future development of his diocese. He promulgated the first diocesan regulations in 1841, presided at two diocesan synods, and established in practice and at state law a bishop's right to ownership of Catholic church properties. His increasingly numerous clergy grew more cohesive and attentive to diocesan rules; they in turn promoted a more disciplined religious practice among the laity. Lefevere was an active proponent of total abstinence from alcohol for clergy and laity alike and a zealous opponent of social dancing. These concerns mark him as a conservative but not radically so for his generation.

Despite his predilection for firm governance, Lefevere encountered relatively little conflict in his tenure as bishop. His pastoral orientation probably best accounts for this: he was widely admired for the hours he spent in the confessional and for his tireless visitation of parishes throughout the diocese, including distant Indian missions. He seems to have had a pastor's instinct for tempering discipline with compassion: deeply opposed to mixed marriages, for example, he nonetheless maintained "that we cannot oppose them with harshness without doing an immense injury to religion." Letters from his priests bespeak an affection and trust that was not invariably the lot of his episcopal contemporaries.

Lefevere played only the most limited role in Detroit and Michigan politics and in the politics of the American hierarchy. He campaigned aggressively but without success in 1852–1853 for public funding of Michigan's Catholic schools, and in so doing he helped to intensify anti-Catholic sentiment in the state. With Louisville's Bishop Martin Spalding, Lefevere was a moving force in the 1857 founding of the American College at Louvain, whose first four rectors were priests who had served in the diocese of Detroit. The college was an important source of clergy for the American missions in the second half of the nineteenth century and significant over the longer term in the training of American-born seminarians. Lefevere died at St. Mary's Hospital in Detroit.

• Most of Lefevere's surviving papers are in the archives of the archdiocese of Detroit, though a small number of letters and documents bearing on his Detroit years can be found in the archives of the University of Notre Dame. Correspondence relating to his ministry in Mo. is housed in the archives of the archdiocese of St. Louis; some is reprinted in John E. Rothensteiner, *History of the Archdiocese of St. Louis* (2 vols., 1928). On Lefevere's Detroit career, see George Paré, *The Catholic Church in Detroit, 1701–1888* (1951; repr. 1983), and Leslie Woodcock Tentler, *Seasons of Grace: A History of the Catholic Archdiocese of Detroit* (1990). See also Richard H. Clarke, *Lives of the Deceased Bishops of the Catholic Church in the United States* (3 vols., 1888).

LESLIE TENTLER

LEFFEL, James (19 Apr. 1806–11 June 1866), inventor and manufacturer, was born in Botetourt County, Virginia, the son of John Leffel, a sawmill operator, and Catherine (maiden name unknown). About all that is known of his parents is that they moved from Virginia before his first birthday, settling near Springfield, Ohio, on Donnel's Creek, where his father erected and operated a sawmill and gristmill. In Leffel's youth, he worked in his father's mills and developed an interest in waterpower. He received a limited formal education. In the 1820s, just outside Springfield on the Mad River, he built a sawmill, installing a waterwheel of his design. It operated well and brought Leffel further millwrighting jobs in the region. Leffel's success as a millwright, a career he pursued for around fifteen years, enabled him to marry Mary A. Croft in 1830. They were to have six sons and three daughters.

In 1838 Leffel decided to diversify his interests by erecting a foundry, the first in Clark County, Ohio, to manufacture axes, knives, sickles, scythes, and other iron agricultural and domestic implements, relying on water for power. The success of this venture, which began operations in January 1840, led Leffel to diversify further. In 1843 he took on two foundrymen as partners, increased production, and simultaneously introduced several new products, especially mill gearing and stoves. Stove castings soon accounted for much of the firm's output.

In 1845–1846 Leffel terminated his first partnership and with a new partner, William Blackeney, erected a larger foundry in Springfield. When it was completed they began manufacture of an improved cast-iron stove and maintained their general foundry business.

Leffel's interest in waterpower persisted through these ventures. In the early 1840s he persuaded two local flour manufacturers to construct a 1.5-mile-long canal to bring water for power from nearby Buck Creek to Springfield. He oversaw the work and purchased 1/12 of the power developed by the project himself, building a sawmill to use it. In 1845 he patented a form of water turbine and, confident of its success, devoted a portion of his foundry to its production. In 1846, when he and Andrew Richards, another Springfield manufacturer, built a cotton mill and machine shop, Leffel drew on the waterpower canal he had promoted and installed his new wheel to provide the cotton mill and machine shop with power.

When sales of the water turbine did not live up to expectations, however, Leffel had to shift his attention back to agricultural and domestic iron goods. In addition, the Leffel and Richards cotton mill proved disappointing, and by 1850 Leffel had sold out. His foundry and machine shop, however, continued to prosper. Their prosperity was aided by Leffel's inventiveness. In 1849 he patented an improved "double oven" stove, and in 1850 he patented a lever jack. The oven gained a good regional reputation and sold well, and the lever jack was marketed by Leffel and his son Wright nationally. In addition, in the 1850s Leffel began manufacturing horse-powered threshing machines.

As the foundry and machine shop continued to prosper, Leffel turned more and more to waterpower experiments. He improved his experimental facilities, developing a miniature flume with glass sides to observe the behavior of model wheels he designed. Even though he knew the rudiments of physics, Leffel was a typical nineteenth-century practical inventor, operating mainly by patient trial and error. He constructed and tested more than one hundred forms of water turbine, modifying each form dozens of times during the course of experiments and utilizing the skills developed by years of foundry casting to make detailed improvements.

On the basis of this work, Leffel in 1862 took out his second water turbine patent, the "American Double Turbine." On the success of this design Leffel's fame largely rests. Leffel's new wheel was unique. It combined two turbine wheels, or runners, in a single casing. The upper had inward flow buckets; the lower wheel had buckets that curved inward and then downward. Leffel claimed 92–95 percent efficiency for his double turbine wheel and demonstrated its effectiveness, first, by erecting a linseed oil mill to showcase it and then through public competition with a rival wheel design in May 1862.

For the remaining four years of his life Leffel was totally absorbed in promoting, demonstrating, producing, and marketing his American Double Turbine, talking about it at the least provocation and dispatching his son Frederick to solicit orders all over the country. In late 1862 orders began to flow in, leading Leffel and his partners to increase the number of employees working on wheel production. In 1863 Leffel erected a large flour mill to further demonstrate the effectiveness of his new wheel. That same year he reorganized his business, and in December he purchased additional property to house a new foundry to be devoted solely to the production of the new turbine. Orders for turbines increased, jumping from 47 in 1862 to 153 in 1864, by which time the wheel was selling in the West and Canada as well as in the Midwest and

East. James Leffel & Company, the firm formed to manufacture the wheel, by 1866 had become one of the first companies to initiate quantity production of standardized water turbines and pioneered in stocking standardized waterwheels as hardware stores stock ordinary tools and implements.

Throughout his business career, Leffel seems to have had little trouble attracting partners for his enterprises, perhaps because he early established a reputation for unshakable integrity and tremendous mechanical ingenuity. He was also known for his energy and was considered a great talker, characteristics that probably also helped. Leffel had few interests other than his businesses, but he did engage in poultry breeding as a hobby, winning prizes in regional county fairs for his breeds.

Leffel died in Springfield, Ohio, just as his turbine business was penetrating national markets on a major scale. On his death the business was continued by his son-in-law John W. Brookwalter, his wife, and a partner, William Foos. By 1880 James Leffel & Company had put more than 8,000 Leffel turbines into operation. The company continued to be a major producer of water turbines for more than a century after its founder's death.

• Some primary materials on Leffel can be found in the Leffel collection at the Clark County Historical Society, Springfield, Ohio, and the Leffel papers at the Ohio Historical Society, Columbus, Ohio. The best source of information on Leffel is Carl M. Becker, "James Leffel: Double Turbine Water Wheel Inventor," *Ohio History* 75 (1966): 200–211, 269–70. An adulatory biographical sketch can be found in James Leffel & Co., *Illustrated Descriptive Pamphlet and Price List of Leffel's American Double Turbine Water Wheel for 1870* (1870). In addition, there are brief notes on Leffel in *The History of Clark County, Ohio* (1881) and "Personal Recollections of Early Springfield," told by Squire J. J. Snyder in *Yester Year in Clark County* 2 (1948): 22–23. Louis C. Hunter, *A History of Industrial Power in the United States, 1780–1930*, vol. 1: *Waterpower in the Century of the Steam Engine* (1979), provides good context for Leffel's contribution to the development of waterpower technology.

TERRY S. REYNOLDS

LEFFINGWELL, Christopher (11 June 1734–7 Nov. 1810), businessman and civic leader, was born in Norwich, Connecticut, the son of Benajah Leffingwell, one of the town's wealthiest residents, and Joanna Christophers, the daughter of a New London merchant. Born to wealth and social position, Leffingwell used his advantages to increase his own fortune and to serve the community into which he was born and where he died.

Leffingwell's ancestors had founded Norwich at the headwaters of the Thames River in the 1660s and had grown wealthy as the town developed into a busy commercial center. By the eighteenth century a large, extended Leffingwell family was involved in a wide array of successful agricultural and mercantile enterprises. In 1756, upon the death of his father, Christopher Leffingwell became the capable head of a flourishing family business with assets that included ships, land, shops, and slaves. He continued and expanded his father's operations and was throughout his life one of the richest men in Norwich.

In 1760 Leffingwell married Elizabeth Harris (they had no surviving children); after her death in 1762 he married Elizabeth Coit in 1764, with whom he had ten children. Both of his wives were daughters of prominent merchants and further connected Leffingwell with business associates throughout eastern Connecticut.

Leffingwell took an early and active part in the protest against Parliament. He petitioned against the Stamp Act in 1765, helped organize the Norwich Committee of Correspondence in 1774, served on the local Committee of Inspection and Safety, and extended his credit to finance Benedict Arnold's expedition to Fort Ticonderoga in 1775. He also invested in manufacturing enterprises after the boycott of English imports stimulated the desire for American self-sufficiency. Most notably, he began to produce paper in 1765 and chocolate in 1770. A militia lieutenant before the war, Leffingwell was appointed captain of the Norwich Light Infantry, a unit composed of businessmen and clerks. Although engaged in no battles, Leffingwell led three expeditions to Long Island in 1776 to take away supplies before the British army could seize them, and he volunteered his company to maintain a constant patrol of the Long Island shore to prevent enemy raids. He eventually won promotion to colonel of his regiment. Of even greater value to the war effort, Leffingwell sent out vessels to prey on British shipping and served the Continental army as a purchasing agent, advancing his own money to buy food, clothing, and other material.

After the war Leffingwell continued his diverse business operations, investing in land, Continental securities, a hotel, turnpikes, insurance, and banking. In 1799, three years after his second wife died, Leffingwell married Ruth Petit, the widow of a neighbor. He remained actively engaged in his business affairs until a short illness ended his life.

Although Leffingwell operated successful manufactures, he belonged to the preindustrial age. He introduced no technological innovations in his mills and when he built "Leffingwell's Row" in Norwich in order to bring together different manufacturing operations under one roof with a common source of power, he built not a factory but a building divided up into ten shops rented out to individual artisans. In 1792 he organized an artisan protest against Connecticut's system of taxation because, he claimed, it benefited large-scale industry at the expense of the traditional master craftsmen. Leffingwell's own manufactories were too small-scale and too personally managed to survive his death. His oldest son, as executor of the estate, auctioned off all of his father's property, including the paper and chocolate mills.

Leffingwell's character and career were shaped by his birth into the responsible aristocracy of a small Connecticut community. A man of great personal honor, integrity, and self-righteousness, he recognized no distinction between his own self-interest and the public good. His anger at Parliament's new trade regulations after 1764 mixed Whig principles with the irritation of a merchant who found it harder to smuggle molasses. When he began to manufacture paper, he successfully lobbied the Connecticut General Assembly for a subsidy because he was performing a public service. When he advanced his own money to buy supplies for the Continental army, he expected eventually to realize a profit, and he prospered during the war. When he emancipated his slaves in 1778 he required that they work fifty days each year for him for the rest of their lives. He perfectly combined the "republican" ideal of virtuous self-sacrifice with a keen sense of economic self-interest.

Above all, Leffingwell lived a life of local responsibilities. He operated a farm in western Massachusetts and owned lands in Vermont, New Hampshire, and Ohio, but the center of his life remained Norwich. He represented the town in the general assembly for nine terms between 1770 and 1790 and held many local offices, such as selectman, alderman, and justice of the peace. In 1784 he was appointed by Congress as naval officer for Norwich. He was a member of the First Congregational Church in Norwich, raised a large family there, invested most of his capital there, and is buried there in the Old Burying Ground, with three wives and six daughters, amid the Tracys, Lathrops, and Huntingtons with whom he had shared the political, social, and economic leadership of Norwich.

• The largest and most important collection of Leffingwell manuscripts is the Leffingwell Family Papers in the Manuscript and Archives Room, Sterling Memorial Library, Yale University. The collection comprises eight boxes and three folios of business and personal items, such as account books, correspondence, and diaries. The Connecticut Historical Society has a small collection, of which the most important piece is a copy of the 46-page inventory of Leffingwell's estate. The Connecticut State Library also has a small collection, including a journal kept by a member of the lower house of the general assembly during its October 1783 session and attributed, probably correctly, to Leffingwell. The New Haven Colony Historical Society and the Western Reserve Historical Society, Cleveland, also hold some Leffingwell manuscripts.

Marvin G. Thompson has published a good topical study of Leffingwell's business and civic activities, *Connecticut Entrepreneur: Christopher Leffingwell* (1979). The basic genealogical data have been compiled by Albert Leffingwell and Charles Wesley Leffingwell in *The Leffingwell Record, a Genealogy of the Descendants of Lieutenant Thomas Leffingwell, One of the Founders of Norwich, Connecticut* (1897). Because Leffingwell's life was so centered in Norwich, see the definitive town history by Frances Caulkins, *History of Norwich, Connecticut: From Its Possession by the Indians to the Year 1866* (1874). Leffingwell figured prominently in an episode described by James P. Walsh, "'Mechanics and Citizens': The Connecticut Artisan Protest of 1792," *William and Mary Quarterly* 42 (Jan. 1985): 66–89.

JAMES P. WALSH

LEFLORE, Greenwood (3 June 1800–31 Aug. 1865), chief of the Choctaws, planter, and member of the Mississippi legislature, was born near the present site of the old state capitol in Jackson, Mississippi, the son of Louis LeFlore, a French Canadian who lived among the Choctaws as an agent and trader, and Rebecca Cravat, a young girl from an important Choctaw family. When Greenwood was twelve years old, Major John Donley, who handled mail along the Natchez Trace, took the boy to his home near Nashville, Tennessee, where he stayed for five years attending school. At seventeen Greenwood asked permission to marry Donley's fifteen-year-old daughter, Rosa, but Donley did not consent to the marriage because they were too young. Greenwood and Rosa slipped away to a friend's home to get married, and Greenwood thereafter took his bride home to Mississippi, where two children were born.

Throughout the 1820s LeFlore became an active tribal leader, promoting the establishment of schools, organizing a mounted patrol known as the "light horsemen," and spearheading a movement for a national council to frame a tribal constitution. In 1828, as pressure for the removal of the Choctaws to lands west of the Mississippi grew, the tribesmen, fearing that their old chiefs might be tempted to sell out their nation, deposed Mushulatubbee and Robert Cole and elected the young chiefs (*mingos*), Greenwood LeFlore and another of mixed blood, David Folsom.

In June LeFlore led the Choctaw expedition to survey the new territory provided for the tribe. LeFlore's party, however, found the country mountainous and the soil vastly inferior to that in the Mississippi home, and by the time the expedition returned in December, LeFlore had decided to remain in Mississippi even if his nation was forced to emigrate. On the question of removal, by September 1829 the Choctaws had divided into two political factions: the moderate Republicans led by the old leaders such as Mushulatubbee, who had resisted removal before but were now willing to discuss a "fair solution," and the Christian party headed by LeFlore and Folsom, who proposed to hold fast to their homeland. The death of his wife on 3 October prevented LeFlore from taking an active role in the crucial period, and Mushulatubbee won the struggles and agreed, after consulting his full-blooded supporters, to emigrate. To counter the move, Folsom proclaimed himself chief for life.

In January 1830 Mississippi announced the extension of its laws over the tribe. The tribesmen, fearful of the effect of state laws on tribal society, formally deposed LeFlore and reinstated Mushulatubbee, and Folsom quickly adopted a more moderate stand on removal to avoid the same fate as LeFlore. In March, while the Choctaw leaders assembled to decide on a united policy, LeFlore, convinced that the Choctaw council could not agree on anything, opened separate negotiations with the Indian Bureau head, Thomas McKenney, for an equitable settlement.

By 7 April LeFlore's removal treaty was ready and was immediately dispatched to Mushulatubbee, but it did not satisfy him. When LeFlore quickly added another stipulation (the United States would defend the emigrants with soldiers and give the nation $50,000 annually forever), the old chief agreed to submit it to the council. LeFlore then appeared before the council and defended his treaty, pointing out its merits. His colleagues praised his treaty and unanimously elected him not only chief of the northwestern district but also chief of the entire nation—an honor never before bestowed on a Choctaw chief. LeFlore immediately had his treaty drafted and delivered it to President Andrew Jackson, but LeFlore at the time proposed a bribe to the War Department, promising that he would see to it that the Choctaw Indians left the state if the department would give him enough land to maintain himself as a planter in Mississippi.

Jackson considered the demand unreasonable (costing $50 million to remove some 40,000 Indians). He realized the Choctaws were shrewd businessmen, trying to strike a hard bargain, and sent the treaty to the Senate with the recommendation that it be rejected. The Senate acted accordingly. After some maneuvering, in September Jackson sent Secretary of War John H. Eaton and John Coffee to meet with the Choctaws at Dancing Rabbit Creek (in Noxubee County), where nearly 6,000 Choctaws attended under the leadership of LeFlore, Mushulatubbee, and Nitakechi.

On 27 September the Choctaws reluctantly signed the treaty, which was definitely less favorable to them than the earlier one. By the terms of the treaty, the Choctaws would sell all their Mississippi lands and would receive money, farm and household equipment, subsistence for a year, and payment for the improvements they had made to the land in Mississippi. The United States would also pay $20,000 in the first year and $10,000 for another twenty years. For each head of a family electing to remain in Mississippi, 640 acres would be provided, and U.S. citizenship would be granted. Supplementary articles were added to give lucrative extra land grants to prominent tribal families: four sections of land either in Mississippi or in Indian Territory for each of the three chiefs, one section for each captain, and one-half section for each subcaptain and principal man.

The Treaty of Dancing Rabbit Creek was the most important treaty LeFlore negotiated, but ironically it was his large role in the treaty that destroyed his influence over the tribe. LeFlore, who insisted that he had signed the treaty for the good of his people, is reported to have said, "Kill me if you wish; shoot me here," placing his hand over his heart. The tribesmen did show their displeasure by replacing LeFlore with George W. Harkins as the new *mingo* for the northwestern district.

While the Choctaws moved to the Indian Territory, LeFlore remained in Mississippi and became a citizen of the United States. In 1831 LeFlore married Elizabeth Cody, a Cherokee, the niece of Chief Ross, and a cousin to William "Buffalo Bill" Cody, but she lived only about twelve months; they had no children. A year later he married sixteen-year-old Priscilla James Donley, the younger sister of his first wife, and a daughter was born four years later. Also in 1831 LeFlore was elected as representative from his district to the Mississippi House and was reelected in 1835. He became a state senator in 1841 and served for three years.

His plantation grew extensively and came to comprise at its greatest 15,000 acres, on which 400 slaves worked. It produced cotton—together with the corn, oats, hay, and other feed for his cattle, horses, sheep, and goats—and vegetables and fruits. He also acquired a part interest in 60,000 acres in Texas. Being dissatisfied with the way his cotton was handled at the loading point on the Yazoo River, he built a small town, Point LeFlore, and constructed a $75,000 turnpike to divert business to his town. In 1854 LeFlore had a stately mansion ("Malmaison") built by a young Georgian architect and builder, James Harris, who did not charge for his services but married, instead, LeFlore's eighteen-year-old daughter, Rebecca.

During the Civil War LeFlore's enterprises languished and his Texas lands were lost. He deplored secession and remained loyal to the Union. After the war LeFlore lost his cotton, his slaves, and the greater part of his valuable property. LeFlore's anxiety during the Civil War caused his health to deteriorate rapidly. He went to places seeking healing for his body, which was afflicted with paralysis. When he died at Malmaison, his body was wrapped in the flag of the United States as he requested and was buried in the family cemetery. After his death his wife remained in seclusion for forty-five years, until she died in her ninety-third year in 1910.

• Greenwood LeFlore's speeches, correspondence, and other personal papers are in Records of the Office of Indian Affairs, Letters Sent, 1824–1833, MSS in the Records of the War Department, National Archives; Choctaw Agency, 1824–1833, Letters Received, MSS, Choctaw Emigration, 1826–1833, Letters Received, MSS, and Unsigned Journal of Commrs. Eaton and Coffee, 15–27 Sept. 1830, Ratified Treaty File No. 160, Choctaw, Dancing Rabbit Creek, 27 Sept. 1830, MSS in the Records of the Bureau of Indian Affairs, National Archives; and Governor's Documents, Series E, Letters Received (24 vols.), 1817–1833), MSS in the Mississippi State Archives and History. Major secondary works are W. David Baird, *Peter Pitchlynn: Chief of the Choctaws* (1972); Thelma V. Bounds, *Children of Nanih Waiya* (1964); Angie Debo, *The Rise and Fall of the Choctaw Republic*, 2d ed. (1961); Arthur H. DeRosier, Jr., *The Removal of the Choctaw* (1970); Pearl Vivian Guyton, *Our Mississippi* (1952); Lee J. Langley, "Malmaison: A Palace in a Wilderness, Home of General LeFlore," *Chronicles of Oklahoma* 5, no. 4 (Dec. 1927): 371–81; Jesse O. McKee and Jon A. Schlenker, *The Choctaws: Cultural Evolution of a Native American Tribe* (1980); Florence Rebecca Ray, *Chieftain Greenwood LeFlore and the Choctaw Indians of the Mississippi Valley* (1927); Allene DeShazo Smith, *Greenwood LeFlore and the Choctaw Indians of the Mississippi Valley* (1951); and Vera Alice Toler, "Greenwood LeFlore, Choctaw Chieftain and Mississippi Planter" (M.A. thesis, Louisiana State Univ., 1936).

YASUHIDE KAWASHIMA

LEFSCHETZ, Solomon (3 Sept. 1884–5 Oct. 1972), mathematician, was born in Moscow, Russia, the son of Turkish citizens Alexander Lefschetz and Vera (maiden name unknown). Lefschetz's father was an importer who raised his children in Paris, France. After attending Parisian public schools, Lefschetz studied for three years at the École Centrale des Arts et Manufactures, from which he graduated with the degree of mechanical engineer in 1905. Seeking practical engineering experience, he immigrated to the United States in November 1905 and took a job with the Baldwin Locomotive Works outside Philadelphia. Finding himself attracted to the emerging field of electrical engineering, he became an apprentice at Westinghouse Electric and Manufacturing Company in Pittsburgh, Pennsylvania, in January 1907. This choice turned tragic in November of that year when, during his rotation through the transformer testing section, Lefschetz was caught in an explosion that caused him to lose both of his hands and forearms. Following his convalescence, he came back to Westinghouse and in 1909 joined a group studying alternating current generator design.

Dissatisfied with this routine work, Lefschetz took up investigations in pure mathematics—a field he had abandoned while a student in Paris, fearing its dismal career prospects in France for those who, like himself, were not French citizens. Because, however, his early mathematics training had been excellent, when Lefschetz entered the graduate program at Clark University in 1910, the mathematics faculty recognized immediately that he was prepared to begin work on a research topic. Lefschetz received a Ph.D. summa cum laude in 1911; his thesis, supervised by William E. Story, was on finding the largest number of cusps that a plane curve of given degree may possess. While at Clark, Lefschetz also met mathematician Alice Berg Hayes, whom he married in 1913; they had no children.

Lefschetz left Clark for an assistantship in the mathematics department at the University of Nebraska in 1911, which was soon followed by an instructorship. In 1913 he joined the faculty at the University of Kansas, where he moved steadily through the ranks to full professor in 1923. Though isolated from most active mathematical researchers while in these midwestern positions, Lefschetz was able, in this atmosphere of mathematical solitude, to pursue successfully his own creative investigations in algebraic geometry. In 1919 he produced seminal results, which he published as "On Certain Numerical Invariants of Algebraic Varieties with Application to Abelian Varieties" (*Transactions of the American Mathematical Society* [1921]), a definitive account of his complete topological theory of algebraic surfaces. He extended this work in a 1924 monograph, *L'analysis situs et la geometrie algébrique.* During the same period Lefschetz also broke important new ground in algebraic topology. This work led during the 1920s and 1930s to celebrated results on fixed-point theorems (theorems about mappings of spaces under certain general conditions).

Lefschetz was invited to Princeton University, home to one of the nation's leading mathematics departments, as a visiting professor in 1924. He joined Princeton's faculty as an associate professor in 1925, was made full professor in 1927, and in 1933 became the second occupant of the Henry Burchard Fine Research Professorship. He served as chair of the mathematics department from 1945 until his retirement in 1953. While at Princeton, Lefschetz assumed the editorship of the *Annals of Mathematics* from 1928 to 1958 and helped to bring that journal, which was founded in 1884, to the highest ranks of research publications. He also served as president of the American Mathematical Society in 1935–1936.

Lefschetz's topological investigations formed the basis for many fundamental results in algebraic topology. In addition to the fixed-point theorem that bears his name, he developed fundamental concepts of singular-chain complexes, cocycles, relative homology, and duality. His influence in the field was further extended by his publication of several important textbooks, including *Topology* (1930) and *Algebraic Topology* (1942), and expository works. As the author of these volumes, he is credited with establishing the modern name of "topology" for the field previously known as "analysis situs." Lefschetz was celebrated by his colleagues and students not only for this highly original and creative mathematical research but also for his remarkable personal influence. One fellow mathematician observed that "the influence of Professor Lefschetz will long be spread by the mathematical organizations he established, and the students of all levels he inspired by his courageous enthusiasm, humane leadership, and critical scholarship" (Markus, p. 663).

Lefschetz carried his investigations to yet another area of mathematics after 1943, when he became a consultant to the U.S. Navy at the David Taylor Model Basin near Washington, D.C. Working closely with specialists on guidance systems and ships' stability, Lefschetz recognized the need for further study of the geometrical theory of ordinary differential equations and its applications to control theory and nonlinear mechanics. From 1946 until his retirement in 1953 Lefschetz directed a research project on differential equations, supported by the Office of Naval Research, at Princeton. He continued this work at Princeton from 1953 to 1957, then at the Research Institute for Advanced Study at the Glen L. Martin Aircraft Company in Baltimore until 1964, and finally at the Center for Dynamical Systems (later renamed the Lefschetz Center for Dynamical Systems) of the Division of Applied Mathematics at Brown University until 1970. As part of this work, Lefschetz helped found the *Journal of Differential Equations* in 1965. During his later years he also frequently visited the Institute de Mathematicas of the National University of Mexico in Mexico City, where he was a part-time visiting professor from 1944 through 1966, and helped to stimulate mathematical activity in Mexico.

Widely recognized during his lifetime as one of his generation's leading mathematicians, Lefschetz received many honors for his mathematical work, including the Bordin Prize (1919) from the French Academy of Sciences, and the Bôcher Memorial Prize (1924) and the Steele Prize (1970) from the American Mathematical Society. He received the Antonio Feltrinelli International Prize of the Accademia Nazionale dei Lincei, Rome, in 1956; the Order of the Aztec Eagle of Mexico in 1964; and the National Medal of Science of the United States in 1964. He was awarded several honorary degrees and was a member of mathematical societies throughout Europe and the United States, as well as of the American Philosophical Society, the National Academy, L'Académie des Sciences of Paris, the Academia Real de Ciencias in Madrid, the Reale Instituto Lobardo of Milan, and of the Royal Society of London. He died in Princeton.

• Lefschetz's most significant mathematical papers, as well as his monograph *L'analysis situs*, are collected in *Selected Papers by Solomon Lefschetz* (1971). A complete bibliography of Lefschetz's work is appended to the memoir by Phillip Griffiths et al. in the National Academy of Sciences, *Biographical Memoirs* 61 (1990): 271–313. Other memoirs include those by Sir William Hodge in *Biographical Memoirs of Fellows of the Royal Society* 19 (1973): 433–53, reprinted in *Bulletin of the London Mathematical Society* 6 (1974): 198–217; and by Lawrence Markus in *Bulletin of the American Mathematical Society* 79 (1973): 663–80.

LOREN BUTLER FEFFER

LE GALLIENNE, Eva (11 Jan. 1899–3 June 1991), actor, director, and translator, was born in London, England, the daughter of Julie Norregaard, a Danish journalist, and Richard Le Gallienne, an English poet. Her parents separated when she was four, and Eva was raised by her mother and schooled in Paris and London. Her feminist mother, who had been influenced by literary critic Georg Brandes and playwright Henrik Ibsen, gave her daughter an aesthetic education and taught her independence. By the time she was seven, Eva knew Paris, London, and Copenhagen and read and spoke French, English, and Danish. After seeing Sarah Bernhardt perform and then meeting her, Eva decided to dedicate her life to the theater.

In 1915 mother and daughter moved to New York City, where Le Gallienne pursued a theater career. From 1915 to 1920 she played fifteen roles in a variety of plays on Broadway and on national tours, and she was a member of Ethel Barrymore's company for two years. Her first Broadway success was the lead in Arthur Richman's *Not So Long Ago* (1920), followed by two starring roles in Broadway hits: Julie in Ferenc Molnar's *Liliom* (1921) and Alexandra in Molnar's *The Swan* (1923). Not content with acting, during the long-running *Swan* she produced, directed, and played in matinee performances of *The Assumption of Hannele* (1924), and the following year she translated and starred in Mercedes de Acosta's play *Jehanne d'Arc* at the Theatre de l'Odeon in Paris. She returned to America, where she formed an acting company and

produced, directed, and starred in Ibsen's *The Master Builder* (1925) and *John Gabriel Borkman* (1926) on Broadway and on tour.

In 1926, the same year that she became an American citizen, Le Gallienne turned her back on the commercial theater. "Too much cake," she declared, "not enough bread." She founded the nonprofit Civic Repertory Theatre on Fourteenth Street in New York City, where she functioned as leading actor, director, and producer. The Civic Repertory formed the philosophical bedrock for off-Broadway and the nonprofit resident theater movement, united a young American theater tradition with a rich European heritage, and left a legacy of artistic achievement. Notable productions included Anton Chekhov's *The Three Sisters* (1926), *The Cherry Orchard* (1928), and *The Seagull* (1929) and Ibsen's *The Master Builder* (1926), *John Gabriel Borkman* (1926), and *Hedda Gabler* (1928). In *Peter Pan* (1928), Le Gallienne became the first Peter Pan to fly out over the audience to the balcony. She presented *Romeo and Juliet* (1930), and critics called her the Juliet of her generation. In addition to the plays of Shakespeare, Molière, Dumas, and Barrie, she premiered new American work, including Susan Glaspell's Pulitzer Prize–winning *Alison's House* (1930). She adapted Lewis Carroll's *Alice in Wonderland* (1932). At the Civic, she kept almost forty productions alive in rotating repertory. She started an apprentice company and discovered and trained a generation of actors, including Burgess Meredith, Howard da Silva, Robert Lewis, Norman Lloyd, J. Edward Bromberg, and writer May Sarton.

Following the fifth Civic season in 1931 (which ended with Le Gallienne playing the title role in *Camille*), she sustained life-threatening burns in a gas explosion at her Weston, Connecticut, home, which left her hands permanently scarred. She recovered and returned to the Civic in 1932 for two more seasons, but following a national tour in 1934 the Civic was forced to close, a victim of the depression. During the 1930s Le Gallienne's most notable work in acting and direction was the title role in Rostand's *L'Aiglon* (1934–1935), Rebekka West in her own translation of Ibsen's *Rosmersholm* (1935), and the title role in *Hamlet* (1937). In 1939–1940, with her own company, she toured the country in *The Master Builder* and *Hedda Gabler*. In 1941 and 1942 she joined with the Theatre Guild to direct *Ah, Wilderness* and *The Rivals*. She played Lettie opposite Joseph Schildkraut in the long-running Broadway hit *Uncle Harry* (1942) and directed, translated, produced, and starred in *The Cherry Orchard* (1944) and *Therese* (1945).

In 1946, twenty years after the founding of the Civic Repertory, with director Margaret Webster and producer Cheryl Crawford, Le Gallienne founded and served as leading actor of the American Repertory Theatre, producing *Henry VIII*, *What Every Woman Knows*, *John Gabriel Borkman*, *Androcles and the Lion*, and *Alice in Wonderland*. Although the ART discovered the talents of Eli Wallach, Anne Jackson, Julie

Harris, and Efrem Zimbalist, Jr., the repertory company failed after one season.

In the 1950s Le Gallienne devoted more time to writing, but she acted in *The Corn Is Green* (1950), *The Starcross Story* (1953), and *The Southwest Corner* (1955); performed in her first movie, *The Prince of Players* (1955), starring Richard Burton; acted on television in *Alice in Wonderland* (1955); and had a distinguished success with her portrayal of Queen Elizabeth in the Phoenix Theatre production of *Mary Stuart* (1957), directed by Tyrone Guthrie.

During the 1960s Le Gallienne acted and directed with two nonprofit theater companies, the National Repertory Theatre and the Association of Producing Artists. With the NRT she toured the country in *Elizabeth the Queen* (1961–1962), *Mary Stuart* (1961), *Ring around the Moon* (1963–1964), *The Seagull* (1963), *The Madwoman of Chaillot* (1965–1966), and *The Trojan Women* (1965–1966). With the APA, she directed and starred in *Ghosts* (1962) and *Exit the King* (1968) and directed Uta Hagen in *The Cherry Orchard* (1968).

Despite her advancing age, during the 1970s and 1980s Le Gallienne played Countess Roussillon in *All's Well That Ends Well* (1970) at the American Shakespeare Festival, directed her translation of *A Doll's House* (1975) at the Seattle Repertory Theatre, and played Mrs. Woodfin in Barbara Wersba's *The Dream Watcher* in 1975 at the White Barn Theatre and in 1977 at the Seattle Repertory. She played Fanny Cavendish in a critically and commercially successful production of Kaufman and Ferber's *The Royal Family* on Broadway and on a national tour (1975–1976). She won an Emmy in 1978 for best supporting actress in *The Royal Family* on PBS. For costarring with Ellen Burstyn in the movie *Resurrection* (1980) she was nominated for an Academy Award. She starred in Joanna Glass's *To Grandmother's House We Go* (1981) on Broadway and on tour, and in 1982 she made her last Broadway appearance, directing and playing the White Queen in her adaptation of *Alice in Wonderland*. Her final professional engagement was in "The Women" (1984) on NBC's "St. Elsewhere" television series.

Since she spent most of her life as a working actor, Le Gallienne's record of written work is extraordinary. Her translations of twelve of Ibsen's plays published by Modern Library in two volumes in 1951 and 1961 were the standard texts for years. She also wrote prefaces to *Hedda Gabler* (1953) and *The Master Builder* (1955) and translated Chekhov's *The Three Sisters*, *The Cherry Orchard*, and *The Seagull* (which were performed but never published). She wrote two autobiographies, *At 33* (1934) and *With a Quiet Heart* (1953); *Flossie and Bossie*, a children's story (1949); and bestselling translations of Hans Christian Andersen stories, including *Seven Tales* (1959), *The Nightingale* (1965), and *The Little Mermaid* (1971). Her biography of Eleonora Duse, *The Mystic in the Theatre* (1966), was based on her own observations of Duse's acting, which greatly influenced her own.

Five foot four, slender, with fine-boned features, large blue eyes, and a musical voice, Le Gallienne was a consummate character actor, able to transform herself into another person. "All acting is character acting," she told her students, whom she taught informally and in classes at the White Barn Theatre in Westport, Connecticut (where she discovered Peter Falk and Mariette Hartley). Most critics acclaimed her work. In the 1920s John Mason Brown wrote that she "has the quality of courage combined with vision and extraordinary talents that has made her one of the most exciting figures of today." Sixty years later Alan Rich in *New York* magazine said, "Watch her, and you learn volumes about simplicity, economy, and directness." Jack Kroll in *Newsweek* observed that Le Gallienne "makes you believe that the theater does breed people of unique beauty, grace, and human richness." Walter Kerr pointed out that Le Gallienne's long career symbolized Broadway stardom and "the movement to diversify Broadway."

Throughout her life, Le Gallienne championed the nonprofit theater. She called the lack of government support for the arts "a national scandal." In her public and personal life, Le Gallienne smashed stereotypes. Long and loyal relationships with women, both as friends and lovers, were important to her. She was a woman of great passion, who believed that her homosexuality was natural and beautiful.

Born in 1899, Le Gallienne liked to say that she was a "step ahead of the century," and her life spanned the century. In 1928 President Calvin Coolidge selected her as one of the most outstanding persons of the year. At thirty she appeared on the cover of *Time* magazine. She won the 1947 Outstanding Woman of the Year citation from the Women's National Press Club; she was awarded Norway's highest honor, the Grand Cross of the Order of Saint Olav in 1961; the American Theatre Wing honored her with a special Tony award in 1964; New York City awarded her the Handel Medallion in 1976; and in 1986 she received the National Medal of Arts. She died at her home in Weston, Connecticut.

• Le Gallienne's Civic Repertory papers are held at the Beinecke Library, Yale University. Her personal papers, diaries, and correspondence are at the Library of Congress in Washington, D.C. Important sources for Le Gallienne include her two autobiographies and Robert A. Schanke, *Eva Le Gallienne: A Bio-Bibliography* (1989). A complete and comprehensive source, which draws on Le Gallienne's diaries and thousands of unpublished letters and manuscripts, is Helen Sheehy's biography *Eva Le Gallienne* (1996). An obituary is in the *New York Times*, 5 June 1991.

HELEN SHEEHY

LE GALLIENNE, Richard (20 Jan. 1866–14 Sept. 1947), writer, was born Richard Thomas Le Gallienne in Liverpool, England, the son of John Le Gallienne and Jane (maiden name unknown). He attended local schools, including Liverpool College, which he left at the age of sixteen to become a clerk in a shipping office. He found the work tedious, and to pass the time he began writing verse for self-amusement. The pastime grew into a serious avocation, and he decided to pursue a writing career. Le Gallienne began contributing verse to local newspapers and magazines, and in 1887 his first book, *My Lady's Sonnets*, was privately printed. A year later he moved to London to write full-time.

Le Gallienne quickly found employment as a private secretary to the famous British actor Wilson Barrett; he also worked briefly as a literary critic for the *London Star*. Le Gallienne found a receptive audience for his verse among members of the so-called decadent movement, which included Aubrey Beardsley and Oscar Wilde. With their encouragement, he began contributing verse and short stories to John Lane's *Yellow Book* and other literary magazines and in 1889 published his second book of poetry, *Volumes in Folio*. Other books followed—a total of twenty-two between 1890 and 1903, the year he moved to the United States. Many were collections of verse; of these, *English Poems* (1892) and *Robert Louis Stevenson: An Elegy, and Other Poems* (1895) were the most notable. Le Gallienne achieved his first popular success with his novel *The Quest of the Golden Girl*, published in 1896.

Le Gallienne lived in New York from 1903 until 1927, supporting himself as a freelance journalist and through a variety of publishing jobs while continuing to write books. During those years he published seventeen additional collections of poetry, stories, and essays; he also edited several anthologies of verse and compiled a nostalgic tribute to the Mauve Decade (*The Romantic Nineties* [1925]). Although Le Gallienne had moved beyond the style of the decadents to develop a voice of his own, his work still reflected a nineteenth-century sensibility that seemed increasingly dated as the years passed. Several of his books published during his stay in America enjoyed a modest popularity—notably *New Poems* (1910), *The Lonely Dancer* (1913), *The Junk Man and Other Poems* (1920), and *A Jongleur Strayed* (1922)—but critics became increasingly scornful of his recourse to sentimentality in an age whose spirit seemed more accurately captured in T. S. Eliot's *The Waste Land*.

Discouraged by his failure to win critical acclaim in New York and yearning to recapture the romantic spirit of the past, Le Gallienne moved to Paris in 1927. He did not associate with the avant-garde, however, whose works he dismissed as "modern nonsense." To Le Gallienne, James Joyce and his followers were obsessed with what he called "dirtomania." In Paris, Le Gallienne continued to write his romantic stories and verse while supporting himself as a freelance journalist for American newspapers, primarily working as an essayist for the *New York Times Book Review* and the *New York Times Magazine*, with which he had become associated in 1924. He also wrote a weekly column for the *New York Sun* called "From a Paris Garret"; a selection of these columns was published in 1936 under the same title and is considered one of his best books.

In 1938 Le Gallienne published his last book, a collection of essays, *From a Paris Scrapbook*, in which he described his favorite city in his characteristically sentimental style. The work received an award from the French government for the best book about France written that year by a foreigner.

Le Gallienne was married three times. His first wife, Mildred Lee, whom he married in 1891, died three years later; they had one daughter, Hesper Le Gallienne, who later became a poet. In 1897 he married Julie Norregaard, a Danish writer with whom he had another daughter, Eva Le Gallienne, who became a celebrated actress; they were divorced in 1911. That same year he married Irma Hinton Perry, an American divorcée.

In June 1940, as German troops began their occupation of Paris, Le Gallienne and his third wife fled to Menton, in the south of France. They moved to Monte Carlo in 1943 and lived there in seclusion until the end of the war, at which time they returned to Menton. Le Gallienne died at his villa there.

• For biographical information on Le Gallienne, see Richard Whittington-Egan and Geoffrey Smerdon, *The Quest of the Golden Boy: The Life and Letters of Richard Le Gallienne* (1960); Stanley Kunitz and Howard Haycraft, eds., *Twentieth Century Authors* (1942); Kunitz, ed., *Twentieth Century Authors*, 1st suppl. (1955); *Dictionary of Literary Biography*, vol. 4 (1980); *Contemporary Authors*, vol. 107 (1983); and Le Gallienne's entry in *Who Was Who in America*, vol. 2 (1950), which includes an incomplete but still lengthy list of his many publications. Obituaries are in the *New York Times* and *The Times* (London), both 16 Sept. 1947.

ANN T. KEENE

LEGARÉ, Hugh Swinton (2 Jan. 1797–20 June 1843), jurist and attorney general of the United States, was born on John's Island, South Carolina, the son of Solomon Legaré, a planter, and Mary Splatt Swinton. Legaré's father died when Legaré was two years old. Fortunately his paternal grandfather, a South Carolina planter of Huguenot heritage, provided Legaré's mother with the means for his upbringing. Legaré's life was marked by many medical maladies, the first of which was an injurious childhood smallpox inoculation that not only left him scarred but also led, it seems, to a disproportionate shortness of his limbs. Nevertheless, he was a precocious child and in 1814 graduated first in his class from South Carolina College in Columbia, where he received a thoroughly classical education.

Having chosen law for his profession, Legaré decided on an unusual route. While most of his contemporaries chose to apprentice to lawyers, Legaré instead read law independently with the aid of a tutor. He then went to Europe to continue his studies. He had intended to spend a few months in Paris and then go on for formal studies to Germany, which he felt had "the greatest—indeed, . . . the only fit schools" in his branch of education (*Writings*, vol. 1, p. xlviii). But in Paris Legaré learned of recent disturbances in his chosen university, Göttingen. Receiving a recommendation from William Campbell Preston, an American in Paris who had only recently arrived from studies in Edinburgh, Legaré decided to go to Scotland and to postpone study in Germany.

At Edinburgh, according to Preston, Legaré spent eight to ten hours a day reading Latin law treatises and attending lectures (in Latin) on law. It was there that he developed the love for the civil law that was to mark his career. The civil law and the common law are the two great divisions into which the world's developed legal systems are commonly classed. Common law systems, which include the American, have roots in the English common law. Civil law systems, which included the Scottish and all Continental systems, have their roots in Roman law. The two systems are profoundly different in how they create and apply law. According to Legaré:

It is certain that the civil law has greatly the advantage of ours in the manner in which it has been expounded and illustrated. . . . In comparing what the Civilians have written upon any subjects that have been treated of by English text writers, or discussed in the English courts, it is, we think impossible not to be struck with the superiority of their truly elegant and philosophical style of analysis and exposition. Their whole arrangement and method—the division of the matter into its natural parts, the classification of it under the proper predicaments, the discussion of principles, the deduction of consequences and corollaries—every thing, in short, is more luminous and systematic—every thing savors more of a regular and exact science. (*Writings*, vol. 2, p. 110)

Typical common law texts, he noted elsewhere, have "a total absence of all philosophical analysis, and systematic exposition" (*Writings*, vol. 1, p. 517).

After his return from Europe in 1820, Legaré completed his studies and was admitted to the bar. He entered state politics that year through a courtesy election without opposition to the state legislature, where he served for two years as representative from his home of John's Island, which was a so-called rotten borough where disenfranchised slaves outnumbered whites by about fourteen to one. After moving to Charleston and starting a law practice, Legaré represented the city in the state legislature from 1824 to 1830. In the pre–Civil War political struggles that characterized Charleston politics then, he was an unenthusiastic defender of the Union. In 1830 the state legislature elected him state attorney general.

When the *Southern Review* was founded in 1827 as a political quarterly counterpart to Boston's *North American Review*, Legaré quickly became a prolific contributor of both legal and nonlegal articles, including "Classical Learning"; "Roman Literature"; "Codification"; a review of the first edition of the leading American legal treatise of the nineteenth century, James Kent's four-volume *Commentaries on American Law*; "Education in Germany"; "Jeremy Bentham and the Utilitarians"; and a discussion of the French jurist "D'Aguesseau." In his writings Legaré was not timid; for example, in his essay on Bentham's *Principles of Legislation*, he criticized Bentham's style as "full of a quaint pedantic affection of simplicity" and of self-conceit.

When pleading a case in Washington, D.C., before the Supreme Court in 1829, Legaré and his interest in the civil law became known to Secretary of State Edward Livingston. Livingston, who is best known for his proposed penal code for Louisiana, was devoted to the civil law and, according to Preston, exhorted Legaré to "prosecute the study of it for great national purposes" (*Writings*, vol. 1, p. lix). In 1832 Livingston offered Legaré the position of chargé d' affaires to newly independent Belgium. This position permitted Legaré to observe the civil law in its leading centers.

To "engraft the Civil Law upon the jurisprudence of this country," according to Justice Joseph Story, the most renowned member of the Supreme Court of the day and himself a student of the civil law, became the "darling object" of Legaré's ambition. Legaré and Livingston both, as Preston observed, saw that much of the spirit of the civil law might be adapted to the peculiar conditions of the United States, where so much was new and so many modifications of the old were necessary. Legaré himself was convinced that the most important part of the civil law "is suitable not only to other countries, but to all other countries—that it is as applicable at Boston as at Paris, and has served equally to guide the legislation of Napoleon, and to enlighten the judgment of Story" (*Writings*, vol. 1, p. 525). He sought in his professional life to use it to inform all aspects of law from legislation to court decisions.

In 1836, upon Legaré's second return to the United States, his ambiguous position on the Union made possible his election to the House of Representatives with Unionist support. Although a true supporter of the Union in Congress, Legaré lost the support of South Carolina's most prominent Unionist, Joel Poinsett, and with it, reelection. During John Tyler's presidency, in September 1841, Legaré was appointed attorney general. Since this was then a part-time cabinet position, he continued to practice law. As attorney general, he argued fifteen cases before the Supreme Court. When Daniel Webster resigned as secretary of state, Tyler offered Legaré the position, but Legaré declined, apparently uncertain of the administration's future. Legaré did, however, in May 1843 assume the duties of interim secretary of state. He was fulfilling those duties when he died unexpectedly of an abdominal ailment while in Boston to attend ceremonies marking the anniversary of the battle of Bunker Hill. He had never married.

Legaré's place in American history is established as one of very few holders of high legal office thoroughly conversant in the civil law. His modern biographer, Michael O'Brien, called him "that unusual creature, a philosophical politician eager to extract general truths from particularities" and counted the Supreme Court as Legaré's natural destination blocked only by a premature death. Legaré's efforts notwithstanding, the American legal system has been largely immune to civil law influences such as he, Livingston, Story, and some of their contemporaries promoted. Late in his short life, Legaré recognized the futility of his efforts when he wrote in a private letter, "I have found *my studies in Europe* impede me at every step of my progress. They have hung round my neck like a dead weight. . . . Our people have a fixed aversion to every thing that looks like foreign education" (*Writings*, vol. 1, p. 236). His failed campaign for reelection to Congress in 1838 was one instance where his broad knowledge was cause for ridicule and not acclaim.

• Legaré's personal papers are largely found in the South Caroliniana Library of the University of South Carolina in Columbia, while his public papers are in the National Archives. Most of Legaré's published works and many unpublished materials are collected in Mary S. Legaré, ed., *Writings of Hugh Swinton Legaré, Edited by His Sister* (2 vols., 1845; repr. 1970). Studies of Legaré include Michael O'Brien, *A Character of Hugh Legaré* (1985), and Linda Rhea, *Hugh Swinton Legaré: A Charleston Intellectual* (1932), both of which include bibliographic references and manuscript source information. Volume 1 of the *Writings* includes a biographical sketch by Edward Johnston. A modern assessment of Legaré's jurisprudential work is in Michael H. Hoeflich, *Roman and Civil Law and the Development of Anglo-American Jurisprudence in the Nineteenth Century* (1997). For an assessment of his career by one of the leading American jurists of his day, see Joseph Story, "Tribute to the Memory of Mr. Legaré," *The Miscellaneous Writings of Joseph Story*, ed. William W. Story (1852; repr. 1972).

JAMES R. MAXEINER

LEGGETT, Mortimer Dormer (19 Apr. 1821–6 Jan. 1896), soldier, educator, and commissioner of patents, was born near Ithaca, New York, the son of Isaac Leggett and Mary Strong, farmers. When he was fifteen, his parents moved to Montville, Ohio, where for the next three years he helped his father clear and tend farmland. After attending night school, Leggett graduated first in his class from a teacher's college in Kirtland, Ohio. He then studied law at Western Reserve College (later part of Case Western Reserve University). After being admitted to the bar, he attended medical school so that he could specialize in medical jurisprudence; he received an M.D. in 1844. That same year he married Marilla Wells of Montville; they had four sons and a daughter.

Becoming interested in elementary education, Leggett in 1846 moved to Akron, where he helped establish the first free grade-school system west of the Alleghenies, of which he became superintendent. Three years later he moved to Warren, Ohio, and organized a school district there. He also began practicing law in partnership with future Union general Jacob D. Cox. In 1856 he joined the faculty of the Ohio Law College in Poland. The following year the peripatetic Leggett settled in Zanesville, Ohio, where he worked as an attorney and school superintendent.

When the Civil War erupted in 1861, Leggett laid aside his many peaceful pursuits in order to assist a friend, Union major general George B. McClellan. Joining McClellan's staff as a civilian aide de camp, he accompanied "Little Mac" during the early operations in western Virginia. Returning to Zanesville late in the year, he accepted a commission from Ohio governor William Dennison, who authorized him to raise a regiment of volunteer infantry. In a little over a month Leggett induced more than 1,000 recruits to join the Seventy-eighth Ohio, of which he became colonel.

When the outfit went south early in 1862 to join Brigadier General Ulysses S. Grant's Military District of West Tennessee, Leggett, although lacking military experience, served ably in the 16 February capture of Fort Donelson. After the battle, Grant appointed him provost marshal in charge of the surrendered garrison. Under Major General Lew Wallace, Leggett saw limited action on the second day at Shiloh but won praise for exemplary leadership. By mid-1862 his martial abilities had gained him command of a brigade in Major General James B. McPherson's XVII Corps, Army of the Tennessee. That September he led detachments of several regiments—fewer than 1,000 troops all told—in repulsing six times as many Confederates who had attacked one of Grant's supply lines, the Mississippi Central Railroad. The following month, in recognition of Leggett's "meritorious service," Grant recommended him for a brigadier generalship of volunteers. The appointment came through on 29 November.

During the Vicksburg Campaign, Leggett served with distinction in several actions, most notably on 16 May 1863, when his brigade, part of Major General John A. Logan's division, drove a Rebel force from a well-entrenched position outside Port Gibson, Mississippi. On 25 June, after Grant's army had begun to besiege Vicksburg, Leggett's brigade gallantly but unsuccessfully charged an enemy position known as Fort Hill in the wake of a mine explosion. Although wounded, Leggett remained with his command through the balance of the siege, which culminated in the 4 July surrender of the enemy stronghold.

By December 1863 Leggett had assumed provisional command of Logan's division. On Major General William T. Sherman's Meridian Expedition of February–March 1864, designed to cut enemy communications east of Vicksburg, Leggett's troops marched 350 miles and wrecked 24 miles of railroad track. On 22 May the Ohioan gained permanent command of the Third Division, XVII Corps, which he led throughout the Atlanta Campaign. As a brevet major general of volunteers, he was conspicuous at Kennesaw Mountain on 27 June, driving a Confederate force from a line of works and holding an advanced position for two hours under a crossfire of artillery.

Leggett's most famous exploit of the war occurred after Sherman's armies reached the outskirts of Atlanta. On 21 July 1864 his division seized an elevation known as Bald Hill, opposite the Union left flank outside the city. The next day the command maintained its strategic position—afterward called Leggett's Hill—against counterattacks from two directions, fighting first on the east side, then on the west, and again east of its captured works. Sherman gave Leggett "great credit" for this feat, which hastened the fall of the Gate City.

In mid-November 1864 the Third Division accompanied Sherman on his "March to the Sea," which Leggett called the "most pleasant" journey his command had ever made. After briefly besieging Savannah in late December, the division followed Sherman into South Carolina. The following month, having played a major role in capturing Pocotaligo, Leggett took an extended sick leave. He saw little service in the closing operations under Sherman but returned to duty in time to command the XVII Corps on its march to Washington, D.C., and in the Grand Review of 24 May 1865. The following month he joined the corps in Louisville, Kentucky, where it did occupation duty in the Department of the Ohio. On 21 August 1865, five weeks before leaving the volunteer army for civilian life, Leggett won promotion to the full rank of major general.

After completing his military service, Leggett returned to his legal practice in Zanesville. He also developed an interest in business and political pursuits, and in later years he became an officer in several manufacturing concerns. In January 1871 President Grant appointed him commissioner of patents. Moving to Washington, Leggett reorganized and expanded the Patent Office and supervised a long overdue reclassification of patents. He resigned his position in November 1874 to practice law in Cleveland with two of his four sons. A decade later he founded an electronics firm, the Brush Electric Company, that later merged with General Electric; the merger made Leggett a wealthy man. He died in Cleveland, survived by two sons, one daughter, and his second wife, the former Weltha Post of Sandusky, Ohio, whom he had wed in 1879.

Leggett was one of many volunteer officers in the Civil War who, without benefit of military education or training, rose to high rank through inherent leadership skills. While an aggressive combat commander, the burly, bushy-haired westerner was also a prudent tactician ever mindful of the welfare of his troops; after Shiloh, General Wallace commended him not only for courage under fire but for "avoiding unnecessary exposure of his soldiers." Leggett knew how to get the most from those soldiers; his experience as an educator enabled him to motivate his regiments and elevate their morale. He was one of the first division leaders to institute peer competitions, awarding prizes to outfits that demonstrated the highest proficiency in drill, discipline, camp sanitation, and "all these qualities which characterize the efficient, soldierly, and model regiment" (*War of the Rebellion*, 1st ser., vol. 52, pt. 1, p. 499).

Leggett's service was limited by his fragile health, which forced him onto the sick list on several occasions. He never absented himself from his command, however, when battle loomed; his personal courage was attested to by the commendations of commanders as diverse as Grant, Sherman, McPherson, Logan, and Major General Frank P. Blair, commander of the XVII Corps in the Atlanta Campaign. During the Grand Review of Sherman's armies it was said that "no

general officer was more warmly received by the president [Andrew Johnson] than was Gen. Leggett, who was that day recognized as a national hero" (*National Cyclopaedia of American Biography*, vol. 2, p. 350).

• The Western Reserve Historical Society, Cleveland, Ohio, houses a collection of Leggett's papers that includes unpublished accounts of his service at Shiloh and Vicksburg. Some of his postwar correspondence can be found in the papers of one of his subordinates, General Manning F. Force, in the library of the University of Washington, as well as in the Amelia High Jeffreys Papers at Duke University. For Leggett's reports of Vicksburg, the Atlanta Campaign, the Meridian Expedition, and other operations, see *War of the Rebellion: A Compilation of the Official Records of the Union and Confederate Armies* (128 vols., 1880–1901). An undated broadside, a copy of which reposes in the Library of Congress, contains the *Official Report [of] Col. M. D. Leggett of the Engagement Near Bolivar, [Tennessee,] Aug. 30th, 1862*. Leggett also wrote and published *The Battle of* Atlanta (1883) and *The Military and the Mob* (1884).

An interesting character study forms part of William H. Withington, "The West in the War of the Rebellion, as Told in the Sketches of Some of Its Generals," *Magazine of Western History* 4 (1886): 814–22. Leggett's stint as regimental commander receives attention in *History of the 78th Regiment O. V. V. I. [Ohio Veteran Volunteer Infantry]* (1865). Modern-day campaign studies that mention him prominently include Albert Castel, *Decision in the West: The Atlanta Campaign of 1864* (1992), and James Lee McDonough and James Pickett Jones, *War So Terrible: Sherman and Atlanta* (1987).

EDWARD G. LONGACRE

LEGGETT, William (30 Apr. 1801–29 May 1839), journalist, was born in New York City, the son of Abraham Leggett, a merchant, and Catherine Wylie. After a childhood in New York, Leggett enrolled in Georgetown College in 1815 but did not graduate. In 1819 he joined his family's trek to Illinois, where he wrote sentimental poetry for the *Edwardsville Spectator*; some of the pieces were reprinted in *Poems* (1822). Leggett joined the navy in 1822 and subsequently published a volume of poems titled *Leisure Hours at Sea: Being a Few Miscellaneous Poems by a Midshipman of the United States Navy* (1825). His naval career ended in a court-martial for dueling; he resigned his commission in 1826 and returned to New York. There he wrote stories for magazines, some of which were collected in *Tales and Sketches by a Country Schoolmaster* (1829). The most popular of these stories, "The Rifle," nicely captured the cadence of life and speech in frontier Illinois. After a brief venture into theater, he joined the *New York Mirror* in 1827 as literary critic.

In 1828 Leggett married Almira Waring of New Rochelle, New York, and launched a literary magazine, *The Critic*. The marriage endured, but the magazine failed in the following June. In 1829 Leggett was hired by William Cullen Bryant to write literary criticism and theatrical notices as assistant editor on the *New York Evening Post*. Though he soon moved into political journalism on the *Post*, Leggett continued to write short stories in the early 1830s, some later appearing in *Naval Stories* (1834).

When Leggett joined Bryant, he enlisted with a leading voice of Jacksonian Democracy in New York. In the late 1820s, Bryant had made the *Post* a crusader against protective tariffs, monopolies, and federal support for internal improvements, and in the early 1830s, the paper joined the war on the Second Bank of the United States. In these battles over political economy, Leggett found his medium and his genre in the form of the daily newspaper editorial. Writing at a desk in the *Post*'s printing plant, amid the chatter of machinery and "political loungers," he churned out a steady stream of polemic. Though contending with the controversies of the day, his chief interest lay with abstract ideas. As Bryant put it in his memoir of Leggett, "He boldly and invariably brought public measures to a rigid comparison with first principles."

For Leggett, the most important of these "first principles" was liberty. "He was for liberty every where and in all things," the poet John Greenleaf Whittier wrote of him, "in thought, in speech, in vote, in religion, in government, and in trade." His love of liberty fired within him an intense devotion to equal rights and laissez-faire. In 1834 he wrote, "If we comprehend the nature and principles of a free government, it consists in the guaranty of EQUAL RIGHTS to all free citizens. We know of no other definition of liberty than this. Liberty is, in short, nothing more than the total absence of all MONOPOLIES of all kinds, whether of rank, wealth, or privilege." Reasoning from this principle, Leggett opposed all special legislation establishing banks and corporations, bridge and ferry monopolies, and even state asylums. If banks and corporations were useful economic devices, then everyone should be free to enter the field, and the laws of the marketplace would sort among them.

Leggett's radical understanding of equal rights was denounced as lunatic "ultraism" by Whigs and regular Democrats. But to him it was merely the logical application of commonplace American ideals. "The only material difference between the present system, and the system we propose," he explained, "is that instead of exclusive privileges, or particular facilities and immunities, being dealt out to particular sets of individuals by the legislature, all kinds of business would be thrown open to free and full competition. . . . If this is lunacy, it is at all events such lunacy as passed for sound and excellent sense in Thomas Jefferson." Such thinking made Leggett a favorite theoretician of the Locofoco (Equal Rights) party then emerging in New York.

Though Leggett denounced combinations that grew from special government privilege, he believed in purely voluntary association, and he supported the right of workers to organize unions and of abolitionists to plump for their cause. In 1834–1835, following antiabolition riots in New York, Leggett stridently defended the abolitionists' right to speak. He especially opposed post office suppression of abolition materials in the southern mails. "If the Government once begins to discriminate as to what is orthodox and what heterodox in opinion, what is safe and what is unsafe in its tendency, farewell, a long farewell to our freedom," he wrote. He eventually became an abolitionist, though he remained—true to his ideal of limited government—opposed to federal antislavery legislation.

Leggett had his greatest influence while chief editor of the *Evening Post* from June 1834 to October 1835, while Bryant was in Europe. The intensity of his struggles, however, sapped his health and the health of the newspaper. For defending the abolitionists, the *Post* lost political patronage, advertising, and subscribers. Meanwhile, Leggett fell seriously ill in October, and Bryant rushed home to rescue the paper. Leggett, who had long suffered from yellow fever he had contracted while in the navy, could not return to work for a year. Soon afterward, in November 1836, he left the *Post* forever.

To support himself and his wife (they had no children), Leggett started a weekly newspaper, *The Plaindealer*, in December 1836, but it failed in 1837. Still in poor health, he was appointed diplomatic agent to Guatemala in 1839, and friends hoped the change of climate would restore his health. Leggett never made the trip; he died in New Rochelle. In an obituary on the next day in the *Post*, Bryant wrote warmly of Leggett's devotion to equal rights: "He espoused the cause of the largest liberty and the most comprehensive equality of rights among the human race." Richard Hofstadter captured Leggett's style and his contribution to American political journalism: "It was not so much the substance of Leggett's thought as his exceedingly broad sympathies, his rhetorical excesses, and the severe logic with which he applied commonly accepted principles to political reality that made him seem profoundly revolutionary."

• Leggett's manuscripts have not survived. The most important published compilation of his work is *A Collection of the Political Writings of William Leggett*, 2 vols., ed. Theodore Sedgwick, Jr. (1840), reprinted in facsimile in 1970. Another collection is William Leggett, *Democratick Editorials: Essays in Jacksonian Political Economy*, ed. Lawrence H. White (1984). Important contemporary biographical sketches are William Cullen Bryant, "William Leggett," *United States Magazine and Democratic Review* 6 (July 1839): 17–28, and John Greenleaf Whittier, "William Leggett," in *Old Portraits and Modern Sketches* (1850). See also Bryant's poem "William Leggett," *United States Magazine and Democratic Review* 6 (Nov. 1839): 430. Other biographical and critical sketches include Richard Hofstadter, "William Leggett, Spokesman of Jacksonian Democracy," *Political Science Quarterly* 58 (1943): 581–94; Charles I. Glicksberg, "William Leggett, Neglected Figure of American Literary History," *Journalism Quarterly* 25 (1948): 52–58; and Page S. Procter, Jr., "William Leggett (1801–1839): Journalist and Literator," *Papers of the Bibliographical Society of America* 44 (1950): 239–53. Studies that place Leggett in the political and intellectual life of his times include Allan Nevins, *The Evening Post: A Century of Journalism* (1922); Edward K. Spann, *Ideals & Politics: New York Intellectuals and Liberal Democracy, 1820–1880* (1972); and Thomas Bender, *New York Intellect: A History of Intellectual Life in New York City, from 1750 to the Beginnings of Our Own Time* (1987).

DAVID PAUL NORD

LEGINSKA, Ethel (13 Apr. 1886–26 Feb. 1970), concert pianist, conductor, and composer, was born Ethel Liggins in Hull, Yorkshire, England, the daughter of Thomas Liggins and Annie Peck. A child prodigy, Leginska gave her first public piano recital at the age of seven. In 1900 she won a scholarship to study the piano at the Hoch Conservatory in Frankfurt under James Kwast and theory under Bernhard Sekles and Ivan Knorr. In 1904 she began a three-year period of study with Theodor Leschetizky in Vienna and in Berlin. In 1907, the year of her London debut, she married Roy Emerson Whittern, an American who was studying composition; he later changed his name to Emerson Whithorne.

Leginska gave many recitals in Europe beginning in 1906. She made her New York debut on 20 January 1913 in Aeolian Hall in a solo recital that was commended for its brilliance, vigor, and diverse tonal colors. She was soon dubbed the "Paderewski of women pianists" and toured the United States each season in recitals and with orchestras. By 1916–1917 Leginska was an exceedingly popular performer standing at the "summit of achievement" as a pianist.

Leginska's bobbed hair and severe concert attire in lieu of evening gowns attracted attention. She defended the use of the trim skirt and black velvet jacket with white shirt by referring to her practical dress as a uniform that enabled her to "forget my appearance and concentrate on my art" (*Minneapolis Journal*, 11 Oct. 1915). Leginska believed that women performers were handicapped in their artistic efforts by fashions in women's clothing as well as by unequal education and childbearing. Her sensitivity on the child care issue is understandable given her own painful experience during the course of obtaining a divorce in the winter of 1917–1918. She lost the custody suit for her son even though she offered to give up her concert career and teach piano instead.

Between 1915 and 1920 Leginska became known for her stance on a number of problems confronting professional women, and she stressed the need for women to pursue new directions. In 1926, after repeated nervous breakdowns resulted in the cancellation of a number of recitals, Leginska announced her permanent retirement as a concert pianist in order to devote herself to composition and conducting.

Leginska had continued her theoretical work when she came to the United States, studying harmony under Rubin Goldmark in 1912 and composition under Ernest Bloch in New York in 1918. As early as 1914 she was composing her own songs and piano music. Her compositions, dating mainly from the late 1910s and early 1920s, include chamber music, orchestral music, and two operas. They are characterized by rhythmic display and a modernistic style. Leginska's orchestral and stage works were performed by major organizations at a time when women's compositions were rarely acknowledged.

Leginska studied conducting with Eugene Goossens in London and Robert Heger in Munich in 1923. She was the guest conductor with major orchestras in London, Paris, Munich, and Berlin in 1924, frequently appearing as the pianist in a concerto on the programs. Her American conducting debut was with the New York Symphony Orchestra on 9 January 1925. She went on to conduct the Boston People's Symphony Orchestra that spring and was hailed as the first female to conduct at the Hollywood Bowl in the summer of 1925. Skeptically viewed by the press at first as a curiosity, Leginska won over the majority of her critics. She is recognized as the first woman in musical history to be a guest conductor with most of the world's major orchestras.

Leginska was also the first female to be engaged as a grand opera conductor. She conducted *Madame Butterfly*, *Tosca*, *Rigoletto*, *Carmen*, *Louise*, *Thaïs*, and *Werther* in London, Salzburg, New York City, Boston, and elsewhere. She was also the regular conductor of the Montreal Opera Company during its 1932–1933 season. She conducted the world premiere of her one-act opera, *Gale*, in 1935, given by the Chicago City Opera with an all-American cast including John Charles Thomas.

Leginska is known as a pioneer for her work as organizer and conductor of three women's symphony orchestras in Boston, Chicago, and New York. She founded and conducted the Boston Philharmonic Orchestra (1926–1927) of one hundred players and the Boston Woman's Symphony Orchestra (1926–1930). She also established and directed the Boston English Opera Company and directed the Chicago Women's Symphony Orchestra (1927–1929). After guest conducting in a number of European opera houses in Europe in 1930, Leginska returned to the United States in 1931 and organized the short-lived National Women's Symphony Orchestra in New York.

Leginska's celebrity had faded by 1935, and conducting opportunities diminished. She went abroad and taught piano in London and Paris in 1938 and 1939, returning in 1940 to set up a studio in Los Angeles, where she continued to teach into the 1950s. In 1941 she set up an annual series of orchestra concerts at the Wilshire Ebell Theatre in Los Angeles, where her students were featured as piano soloists with the Leginska Little Symphony Orchestra. In 1943, with concert manager Mary V. Holloway, Leginska founded New Ventures in Music in Los Angeles, where her students played a series of programs and recitals.

Leginska made inroads for all women musicians in a world that was traditionally male. Her varied repertoire in her concert programs did much to educate the general public. The women's orchestras that she founded paved the way for the inclusion of women in major orchestras. Her own career as a conductor and composer opened up the fields to women who followed in her footsteps. Ethel Leginska died in Los Angeles, a devoted teacher and promoter of her piano students' careers.

• In addition to *Gale*, Leginska composed the opera *The Rose and the Ring* (1932), which premiered in Los Angeles on 23 Feb. 1957. For orchestra she composed *Beyond the Fields We*

Know (1921), *Fantasy for Piano and Orchestra* (c. 1922), *Quatres sujets barbares* (1923), and *Two Short Poems* (1924). Her chamber works include *String Quartet*, after four poems by Rabindranath Tagore; *Triptych*, for eleven instruments (1928); *The Gargoyles of Notre Dame*, for piano (c. 1920); *Scherzo*, after Tagore, for piano (c. 1920); and *Three Victorian Portraits* (1959). Her songs include "At Dawn" (1919), "Bird Voices of Spring" (1919), "The Frozen Heart" (1919), "The Gallows' Tree" (1919), "Six Nursery Rhymes" (1928), and "In a Garden" (1928). Carol Neuls-Bates's extensive research on Leginska appears in her articles in the *New Grove Dictionary of American Music* (1986) and the *New Grove Dictionary of Women Composers* (1994). See also Historical Records Survey, District of Columbia, *Bio-Bibliographical Index of Musicians in the United States of America from Colonial Times* (1941), Adrienne Fried Block and Carol Neuls-Bates, *Women in American Music: A Bibliography of Music and Literature* (1979), Aaron I. Cohen, *International Encyclopedia of Women Composers* (1981), Judith Lang Zaimont, *The Musical Woman: An International Perspective* (1983), George Kehler, *The Piano in Concert* (1982), and Susan Stern, *Women Composers: A Handbook* (1978). An obituary appears in *Opera News*, 5 Sept. 1970.

PAULA CONLON

LEGLER, Henry Eduard (22 Feb. 1861–13 Sept. 1917), librarian and author, was born in Palermo, Sicily, the son of Henry Legler and Raffaela Messina. Some biographical sources erroneously give his birthdate as 22 June 1861. His father was Swiss-German; his mother was Italian and died when he was still an infant. When he was quite young, his family settled in La Crosse, Wisconsin. His father's death in 1878 interrupted his education. Legler worked as a printer, a reporter for the *La Crosse Republican-Leader*, and then as an editor for the *Milwaukee Sentinel*.

In 1888 Legler was elected to the state legislature. When his term expired, he became secretary of the Milwaukee school board for fourteen years but started to become interested in librarianship, then a relatively undeveloped field. In 1895 the Wisconsin legislature created the Free Library Commission, and Legler was appointed its secretary and executive officer (1904–1909); he was a resourceful organizer. Under his direction the *Wisconsin Library Bulletin* was begun (1905); a library school (later part of the state university) was set up in Madison (1906) along with the University of Wisconsin Extension Division; traveling libraries were sent out to book study clubs, to lumber camps, and to remote and isolated communities; and a legislative reference bureau was established. With other historically minded citizens, Legler founded the Parkman Club, a historical society for Milwaukee citizens who were interested in the early days and origins of their city and, subsequently, the state of Wisconsin. Legler contributed two essays to its publications.

In 1909 Legler became librarian of the Chicago Public Library ("a mansion which many people were afraid to enter"); it was the first appointment of a major public library director under civil service regulations, and he held the position until his death. It was a most remarkable period of development. Among his many accomplishments, Legler made the library more accessible and extended its usefulness; increased circulation to almost six million; expanded branch libraries from one to forty; doubled library staff; set up the Educational Division that assisted with programs in schools and in adult education; improved the publications program; reclassified the 800,000-volume general collection; provided library service to businesses, corrections institutions, and hospitals in Chicago; and inaugurated a staff retirement system, a significant advancement at that time.

However, a major shortcoming in Legler's mostly progressive directorship was a program instituted in 1911 that censored fiction being considered by the library acquisitions committee. Believing that many novels published that year contained "sex complications," he asked the staff to screen personally all fiction added to the library collection. Legler's views were shared by most of American society and were sincerely stated. He considered the public library the best institution to develop "an enlightened and humane society," but he reflected a conservative attitude toward society and a nostalgic longing for a pastoral American democracy. Legler exhorted fellow librarians to uplift the urban working classes, whom he considered a threat to the nation's welfare. He considered World War I the disintegration of civilization and charged public librarians to influence schools to rekindle the American mission to work "the miracle of human evolution" for a better civilization, an impossible burden for librarians.

Legler was a member of the Bibliographical Society of America, American Library Institute, Caxton Club of Chicago, American Historical Association, State Historical Society of Wisconsin, Milwaukee Press Club, Chicago City Club, and the American Library Association (president, 1912–1913). He founded the ALA *Booklist* in 1904 and edited it until 1916. His other publications, which reflected his interest in history and literature, included *Chevalier Henry de Tonty, His Exploits in the Valley of the Mississippi* (1896); *Moses of the Mormons*, a biography of James Strang (1897); *Leading Events of Wisconsin History* (1898); *James Gates Percival* (1901); *Early Wisconsin Imprints* (1904); *Poe's Raven* (1907); *Of Much Love and Some Knowledge of Books* (1912); *Walt Whitman, Yesterday and Today* (1916); and various historical and bibliographical pamphlets.

Legler married Henrietta M. Clark in 1890; they had three children. Strict and pragmatic but a romantic at heart, Legler was deeply dedicated to his beliefs. Overwork contributed to his death from an apparent heart attack in Chicago.

• Legler's papers (1833–1909) are in the State Historical Society of Wisconsin. The Chicago Public Library has information in its *Annual Report, 1910–1917*, and a brief biographical sketch by Legler's successor, Carl Roden, is in the library's *Book Bulletin* (Sept. 1917). The American Library Association Archives (ALA), University of Illinois, Urbana-Champaign, has photographs and two signed letters in the James I. Wyer Autograph Collection. Executive board minutes and transcripts cover his tenure as ALA President (1912–1913).

The League of Library Commissions File has no specific correspondence by or to Legler, but it does contain material relating to the league during his tenure as chairman. There is also pertinent information on Legler in the Annual Conference record series, especially Attendance Registers (1890–1900) and Cumulative Attendance Registers (1876–1939). The ALA Headquarters Library, Chicago, has a bibliography of Legler's writings and of writings about him. Henry M. Legler compiled and edited his father's most significant writings in *Library Ideals* (1918). See also "Henry Eduard Legler: In Memoriam," *Library Journal* 42 (Dec. 1917): 951–54; Carl B. Roden, "Henry Eduard Legler," *Bulletin of Bibliography* 14 (1930): 21–22; and Althea Warren and Pearl I. Field, "Henry Eduard Legler, 1861–1917," in *Pioneering Leaders in Librarianship*, ed. Emily M. Danton (1953). Rudolf Engelbart, *Librarian Authors* (1981), has a bio-bibliography. References to Legler's periodical articles are in *Library Literature*. Obituaries are in the *Chicago Daily News*, 13 Sept. 1917, and the *Chicago Tribune* and the *Milwaukee Sentinel*, both 14 Sept. 1917.

MARTIN J. MANNING

LEHMAN, Arthur (1 June 1873–16 May 1936), investment banker, was born in New York City, the son of Mayer Lehman, a businessman, and Babette Newgass. Lehman's father and two uncles in 1850 established Lehman Brothers, a merchandising business that later turned to banking. Lehman earned an A.B. from Harvard in 1894 and acquired business experience by working for four years at Lehman, Stern & Company in New Orleans. The company, one of the many southern cotton concerns controlled by his family, profited early by buying cotton and storing it in warehouses until its price peaked.

Lehman Brothers originated in Montgomery, Alabama, but in 1858 Lehman's father opened its New York office, which in 1868 became its headquarters. His father was one of the 132 cotton merchants who formed the New York Cotton Exchange in 1870, was on its first board of governors, and headed its first finance committee. In 1898 Lehman left the South to join Lehman Brothers in New York. He became a partner in the firm in 1901, the same year he married Adele L. Lewisohn; they had three children. Her father Adolph Lewisohn brought mining interests to Lehman Brothers.

For the rest of his life Lehman was a wheelhorse in Lehman Brothers, helping to transform it from a family business into a major investment institution. He was its most important partner during most of the first two decades of the twentieth century (the time between the periods when his older cousin Philip and that cousin's son Robert exerted their influence on the business). Although commodity trading and commission business remained Lehman Brothers' main concern into the twentieth century, after coming to New York the firm also lent money to industries. While working with its new clients, Lehman Brothers' partners realized that companies that distributed and manufactured consumer goods were practically shut out of the public investment market.

In meeting its clients' needs by "sponsoring the introduction of merchandising and consumer-goods securities to the investing public," Lehman Brothers ushered in "a new era in investment banking" (Manheim, pp. 35, 37). Its first underwriting was $10 million of preferred Sears, Roebuck & Company stock in 1906. Another pioneering effort by Lehman Brothers that proved successful was the marketing of F. W. Woolworth Company securities in 1912, the first time that the stock of a variety chain was sold publicly. By 1925 the New York Stock Exchange listed thirty companies whose marketing had resulted from the activities of Lehman Brothers, sometimes in conjunction with Goldman, Sachs & Company. Among these listings were department stores, such as the May Company, Gimbel Brothers, and R. H. Macy, and other corporations of a more diverse character, including Studebaker (1911), Continental Can (1913), B. F. Goodrich (1920), Campbell Soup (1922), and Anglo-Chilean Nitrate (1925). Although Lehman Brothers underwrote its first corporate bond issue in 1909, it did not have a separate bond department until 1922.

So significant had Lehman Brothers' new activities become that by the end of World War I investment banking was its primary business. During the thirty-five years that Lehman was a leader in the firm, it publicly financed over 100 companies. The firm outgrew family management, which included Lehman's brothers Sigmund and Herbert, and was forced to accept and train those outside the family for leadership. The first partner who was not a Lehman, John M. Hancock, was named in 1924. In 1929 Lehman Brothers formed Lehman Corporation as its own investment company, with capital funds of $100 million and with Lehman remaining its president until his death. Its first offering, shares of $100 par value stock, sold immediately. By employing a flexible investment policy and by trading most of its stocks and bonds on the New York Stock Exchange, this corporation weathered the Great Depression and proved so successful over many decades that Lehman Brothers termed it "the most important single chapter in its history" (Manheim, p. 60). Lehman was a director of many commercial and banking organizations, including the American Natural Gas Company and Federated Department Stores. He continued his firm's close relationship with commercial banking by helping to organize the Marine Midland Trust Company. He was also an organizer of the Southern States Land & Timber Corporation, which opened up the lower part of Florida by reclaiming nearly two million acres in the upper Everglades.

As a member of the branch of the Lehman family known especially for its public service, Lehman was appointed a commissioner in the Department of Public Welfare by his brother Herbert, who became the governor of New York State in 1933. Lehman was also a trustee of the New York City Housing Corporation, the New School for Social Research, and the Museum of the City of New York. To mark the thirtieth anniversary of his graduation from Harvard, he gave that university $200,000 to erect Lehman Hall, an administration building. He helped organize the Federation of Jewish Philanthropies of New York and served as its president and as the treasurer of its Joint Distribution Committee. Remaining an optimist even during the Great Depression, he stated that "the constructive acts" of the Franklin Roosevelt administration had "overbalanced those adverse factors" resulting from its "enlarged participation . . . in the affairs of business" (*New York Times*, 16 May 1936).

Like other members of their family, Lehman and his wife became important collectors of art. Aided at first by Lehman's Harvard classmate Paul J. Sachs of the Fogg Art Museum, they assembled a "very personal" collection over a fifty-year period. Terming their Saturdays "collector's days," they searched in galleries for art objects—primarily paintings, tapestries, and porcelains of the fifteenth and sixteenth centuries. Lehman's wife later gave most of their collection to the Metropolitan Museum of Art (twenty-four works, including thirteen paintings) and the Fogg Art Museum (seven works). These items were exhibited together at the Metropolitan Museum in 1966.

Lehman was the active senior partner at Lehman Brothers when he died in New York City.

• Approximately forty letters from Arthur and Adele Lehman are in the Herbert H. Lehman Suite and Papers, Columbia University. The most helpful books on Lehman Brothers and Lehman's part in it are Frank Manheim, *A Centennial: Lehman Brothers, 1850–1950* (1950), and Roland Flade, *The Lehmans, from Rimpar to the New World: A Family History* (1996). Also of use are Stephen Birmingham, *"Our Crowd": The Great Jewish Families of New York* (1967), and Elliott Ashkenazi, "Jewish Commercial Interests between North and South: The Case of the Lehmans and the Seligmans," *American Jewish Archives* 43 (1991): 24–39. For information concerning Lehman's art collection see Claus Virch, *The Adele and Arthur Lehman Collection* (1965). An obituary is in the *New York Times*, 16 May 1936.

OLIVE HOOGENBOOM

LEHMAN, Herbert Henry (28 Mar. 1878–5 Dec. 1963), investment banker and politician, was born in New York City, the son of Mayer Lehman and Babette Newgass, German immigrants. Lehman was reared in the prosperous surroundings of German-Jewish society in midtown Manhattan. His father was a founding partner of Lehman Brothers, a cotton-trading company that developed into a leading investment banking firm.

After earning a bachelor's degree from Williams College in 1899, Lehman took a job with J. Spencer Turner, a New York textile firm, eventually rising to become vice president and treasurer of the company in 1906. Two years later he joined Lehman Brothers as a full partner. There he participated in the creation of several large corporations, including F. W. Woolworth and Studebaker, on whose boards of directors he also served. In 1910 he married Edith Altschul, a banker's daughter; the couple subsequently adopted three children.

After securing his place in business, Lehman devoted increasing time to a variety of philanthropic activities. As a young man he did volunteer work at Lillian Wald's Henry Street settlement house on Manhattan's Lower East Side. Among his many other charitable activities, the closest to his heart was the Joint Distribution Committee (JDC), which was organized by American Jews during World War I to aid co-religionists, especially in Eastern Europe. Lehman helped the group raise over $43 million for relief efforts during the war, and in the 1920s he became vice chairman of the JDC, directing disbursement of aid to reconstruct Jewish communities in Eastern Europe. Lehman's work with the JDC strengthened his identification with Judaism. "If anything has made me feel the value of Jewish spirituality," he observed in 1928, "it is my connection with the cultural and religious activities of the Joint Distribution Committee." Although Lehman attended a Reform synagogue, he also worked closely with Conservative and Orthodox Jews, and he contributed to synagogues identified with all three groups. Lehman gave regularly to hundreds of other charities as well, including Catholic and Protestant groups and a myriad of civic causes from the Boy Scouts to the National Association for the Advancement of Colored People. He once estimated that he had donated over $7 million to charities.

Lehman entered government service during World War I. He applied for a direct commission in the army and rose from captain to colonel while serving with the General Staff Corps in Washington, D.C.

A lifelong Democrat, Lehman was brought into politics by New York governor Alfred E. Smith, who selected Lehman for numerous posts in the Democratic party after the two met in 1922. Lehman became treasurer of the governor's reelection campaign in 1924, headed Smith's campaign committee in 1926, and directed the finance committee in Smith's 1928 presidential bid. Smith rewarded Lehman's generous and faithful service by backing him for lieutenant governor in 1928. Teamed with Franklin D. Roosevelt, Lehman was expected to assist the governor who was still adjusting to the paralysis caused by his polio. During his first year as governor, Roosevelt traveled frequently to the rehabilitation center at Warm Spring, Georgia. In his absence, Lehman served as acting governor, and crises inevitably arose. On one occasion Lehman ordered state police and National Guardsmen to put down a prison riot. Although he originally looked on the two-year term as a brief hiatus in his business career, Lehman never returned to banking. Reelected lieutenant governor in 1930, Lehman worked closely with Roosevelt, who called Lehman "my good right arm." In addition to helping win support for Roosevelt's legislative program, Lehman worked on policies to deal with bank failures and growing unemployment.

Having earned a reputation as a conscientious public official, Lehman was elected governor by a record margin of over 800,000 votes in 1932. Reelected in 1934 and 1936, he became New York's longest serving governor when he was elected in 1938 to a four-year term, the first mandated by a recent constitutional amendment. Lehman's popularity with New York voters rested on his apolitical qualities. Humorless and colorless, he won respect for his single-minded devotion to the public interest rather than to party or person. As an upstate farm leader recalled, Lehman "lacked the radiant personal charm of Franklin Roosevelt, but he was virtually nonpartisan in his thinking and he seemed to be devoid of what we think of as the wiles of the politician." This reputation for political independence was enhanced in 1932, when Lehman successfully sought the Democratic nomination for governor over the opposition of party bosses, including the head of Tammany Hall. Even Lehman's poor speaking ability seemed to work in his favor. "The Governor is not a good speaker," noted a Republican newspaper. "But, on the other hand, he gives an impression, often lacking in presidential speeches, of sincerity and honesty of purpose."

As a Wall Street banker committed to political reform, Governor Lehman appealed to a wide spectrum of New Yorkers. Under his leadership New York adopted the "Little New Deal," a collection of state programs for relief and reform that closely resembled Roosevelt's federal New Deal. In addition to expanding state relief for the unemployed and initiating state aid to farmers, Lehman sponsored reforms that established public housing, a minimum wage system, unemployment insurance, collective bargaining rights for labor, and social security for the elderly, physically disabled, and fatherless families. Enacted between 1933 and 1938, these state measures paralleled federal efforts, but they benefited groups, such as intrastate workers, often excluded from federal legislation. Although both the depression and Roosevelt's New Deal gave impetus to reform, the adoption of New York's Little New Deal was mostly the result of Lehman's character and leadership. Genuinely interested in the plight of less fortunate people, he saw no inconsistency between being a businessman and a liberal. The governor relied heavily on the advice of social workers and union leaders to frame government-sponsored remedies for economic exploitation and dependency, and then he fought doggedly for legislative approval.

During World War II Lehman turned his attention once again to international relief. Eager to join the war effort, he resigned as governor in December 1942, a month before the end of his fourth term, in order to accept President Roosevelt's request that he immediately become head of the Office of Foreign Relief and Rehabilitation Operations (OFRRO), a new agency in the State Department. Designed to aid liberated countries until an international relief effort was organized, OFRRO provided food, clothing, and medical supplies to needy civilians in North Africa and the Middle East during 1943.

On 9 November 1943 representatives of forty-four nations signed an agreement to establish the United Nations Relief and Rehabilitation Administration (UNRRA). Two days later its council elected Lehman

director general. He dedicated himself to creating an organization that transcended national interests; he also set a high standard of selflessness by serving without pay. UNRRA was designed as a temporary agency to provide basic necessities to war victims in countries liberated from Axis occupation. This required building a staff (eventually numbering some 20,000), raising funds (ultimately $3.8 billion), and securing supplies (totaling twenty-four million tons from thirty-one nations). UNRRA ultimately provided relief to sixteen countries and initiated the rehabilitation of industry and agriculture. Lehman devoted much of his time to persuading member nations, led by the United States and Great Britain, to provide needed supplies and transportation to assist civilian victims of the war. Through an effective lobbying effort at home he helped win congressional approval of significant American contributions, which continued even after the Allied victory brought increased resistance to foreign aid. As postwar relations between the United States and the Soviet Union deteriorated, Lehman sought to transcend political considerations, dispensing relief to countries on the basis of need rather than political orientation. Physically exhausted and discouraged by increasing U.S. opposition to international cooperation, Lehman resigned from UNRRA on 12 March 1946. He soon reentered domestic politics.

In 1946 Lehman ran unsuccessfully for the U.S. Senate, suffering the only election defeat of his career in a year when the Republicans recaptured control of Congress. Three years later an unexpected opportunity arose to run again as the result of a special election created by the resignation of Senator Robert F. Wagner. Lehman's opponent was John Foster Dulles, who had been appointed by New York's Republican governor to fill the seat temporarily. Lehman's victory was followed by election to a full six-year term in 1950. His career in the U.S. Senate was marked by his staunch defense of liberal principles. While supporting President Harry Truman's Cold War policies in international affairs, Lehman was a member of a small group of liberal senators who tried to expand the New Deal by enacting Truman's Fair Deal proposals. Faced with a conservative majority in Congress, however, Lehman spent much of his time fighting unsuccessfully against repressive legislation, such as the 1950 Internal Securities Act and the 1952 McCarran-Walter Immigration Act, both of which were opposed by President Truman because they went too far in abridging the rights of citizens and aliens. From 1950 to 1954 Lehman distinguished himself as an outspoken critic of the worst abuses of domestic anticommunism. In Senate debates he repeatedly confronted Senator Joseph R. McCarthy of Wisconsin, demanding proof of reckless charges and defending innocent victims against false accusations of disloyalty. In 1954 Lehman voted for the Senate resolution that condemned McCarthy's conduct and effectively destroyed his power.

Disillusioned by his experience in the Senate, Lehman announced in 1956 that he would not run for reelection. The last years of his life were spent fighting for liberal causes, including a three-year battle to remove New York City's Tammany Hall boss, Carmine De Sapio, who was finally defeated by reform Democrats in 1961. Two years later Lehman died at his home in New York City as he prepared to go to the White House to receive the Presidential Medal of Freedom. The country's highest civilian award carried a citation that accurately described Lehman's contribution: "Citizen and statesman, he has used wisdom and compassion as the tools of government and has made politics the highest form of public service."

• Lehman's papers are housed at Columbia University's School of International Affairs. His records as director general of UNRRA are in the United Nations Library. The Oral History Collection at Columbia University contains memoirs by Lehman and a number of his closest associates. The only biography is Allan Nevins, *Herbert H. Lehman and His Era* (1963). For Lehman's years as governor, see Robert P. Ingalls, *Herbert H. Lehman and New York's Little New Deal* (1975). An obituary is in the *New York Times*, 6 Dec. 1963.

ROBERT P. INGALLS

LEHMAN, Irving (28 Jan. 1876–22 Sept. 1945), lawyer and jurist, was born in New York City, the son of Mayer Lehman, a cotton broker, and Babette Newgass. His older brothers went into the family business, but Irving, the grave, studious one, was not interested in business. While still attending the preparatory school of Julian Sachs he became interested in law and legal history, read accounts of court cases in the newspapers, and was determined to become an expounder and interpreter of the law. He began his studies at Columbia College in 1892, earning an A.B. (1896), an A.M. (1897), and the LL.B. (1898). In his senior year he was awarded the Toppan prize for excellence in constitutional law. Throughout his long career he remained keenly interested in preparation for the bar. At a joint conference on legal education in June 1937, he urged the cooperation of bench, bar, and law school to "keep the unfit from an overcrowded profession." He was a member of the Board of Visitors of Columbia Law School.

In 1898 Lehman joined the law firm of Marshall, Moran, Williams and McVicker, becoming a partner in 1901. He also married Sissie Straus that year. They had no children. After 1906 the firm became Worcester, Williams and Lehman. Lehman's wife was very active in charitable causes, as was he, and he manifested a keen interest in the work of the Henry Street Settlement, serving as a volunteer social worker between his graduation from Columbia and elevation to the bench.

In 1908 Lehman, a Democrat, was elected to the New York Supreme Court as a compromise candidate; he served a fourteen-year term. On the basis of merit it is unlikely that a better selection could have been made, but in later years he gave a frank explanation of his swift rise in the profession: "I was a very young lawyer, in practice only a short time; I was deaf, and I was Jewish. None of these helped. But I was married

to Nathan Straus's daughter, and Mr. Straus was a friend of Al Smith, and Smith knew the governor of New York. So I became a judge." Campaign contributions to the party by his father-in-law helped smooth the way.

In 1922 Lehman was endorsed for reelection to the supreme court by both major parties, and a year later he was elected for a term of fourteen years to the court of appeals, New York state's highest court. He was reelected in 1937, having been nominated by the Democratic, Republican, and Labor parties, and in the autumn of 1939 he was nominated for chief judge, to succeed retiring judge Frederick E. Crane. He was sworn in on the last day of the year after a series of congratulatory dinners. His term was to have run from 1940 to 1946, but he died less than three months before the next general election.

Judge Lehman was a man of immense dignity who enforced strict decorum in the courtroom. His rise came as the culmination of long study of legal history and all branches of common and statue law. He may have lacked the literary flair that would make his opinions fully effective, but he had touches of profundity and a strong grasp of the fundamental principles of law and government. He could not be considered a seminal thinker in the law, as was his close friend, Justice Benjamin Cardozo, but the judicial system of the country had no more conscientious officer. Such was his impartiality that it was often necessary to read through his entire opinion, perfectly balanced between pros and cons, to learn his final judgment. As he had become very deaf he wore a hearing aid, which enabled him to pick up the faintest whisper in any part of the courtroom, so that in the midst of a trial he was at times seen to smile suddenly and inexplicably. And when he became bored he would abruptly snap off the electrical device.

Lehman's reputation as a jurist came to rest on a double foundation. He was known to the general public as a liberal, whose interpretation of the law made it a living force, subject to change and development with the appearance of new problems and new outlooks. And he was known to lawyers for his ability to slash through legal verbiage and go straight to the heart of complex legal, commercial, or economic problems. If his mastery of these complex problems often escaped general public notice, his decisions in cases involving social and economic issues did not.

An opinion Lehman wrote almost a decade before labor's right to collective bargaining was given statutory recognition won wide public attention. The 1928 ruling, *Interborough Rapid Transit Co. v. Lavin, New York Reports* 247, voided an injunction obtained by New York City's Transit Authority in a dispute with its employees. The reasoning set forth in the opinion was influential in shaping New York's labor policy for many years. He wrote the opinion for the court of appeals in 1930 denying New York City transit an increase in fares from 5 to 7 cents. His later ruling upholding the validity of a statute requiring owners of old-law tenements to make their buildings conform to improved standards gave an impetus to better housing in the city. Broadly interpreting the state's police powers, Lehman insisted that the legislature could fix prices of certain commodities.

Lehman's most famous dissent was registered in a case testing the authority of New York's Industrial Commission to set minimum wages for women and children, *People ex rel. Tipaldo v. Morehead, New York Reports* 270 (1936). The U.S. Supreme Court had held similar federal legislation unconstitutional in 1923 and would do so again, invalidating the New York law in *Morehead v. New York ex rel. Tipaldo, United States Reports* 298 (1936). Lehman strongly believed that the judge must seek the reasons for old precedents and then determine whether law based on old reasons is in reality law in harmony with the needs of today. In this instance he was vindicated when the U.S. Supreme Court overruled both its Adkins (*Adkins v. Children's Hospital*, 1923) and Tipaldo decisions in *West Coast Hotel v. Parrish, United States Reports* 300 (1937). It was incumbent upon the judge, he said, to follow within constitutional limits legislative policy, as laid down in remedial legislation, to meet recognized economic and social evils such as sweatshops, unhealthy tenements, and the exploitation of women and children.

Lehman's decisions reflect a strong confidence in the flexibility of the law to meet new conditions. In a speech in 1925 before the Association of the Bar of the City of New York he said, "As a judge . . . I can conceive of no justice except justice according to law. But law is not so removed from human affairs that its application to a particular case can fail totally to take into consideration the merits of that case as distinguished from other cases." Although these would be considered liberal views, he always preferred to be called a libertarian rather than a liberal.

Lehman's zealous championship of civil liberties found various illustrations, notably in defending the rights of religious groups, including Jehovah's Witnesses. In 1944 he wrote the unanimous opinion for the court of appeals denying state power to require peddler's licenses of religious proselytizers who sold Bibles or religious tracts door to door (*People v. Barber, New York Reports* 289). A contrary decision by the U.S. Supreme Court (*Lovell v. Griffin*, 1938) that limited the scope of the guarantees of religious freedom in such cases was not, according to Judge Lehman, binding on New York under its constitution. His court was bound to exercise its independent judgment. He defended the refusal by children of Jehovah's Witnesses to salute the flag in school in *People v. Sandstrom, New York Reports* 279 (1939). This case was decided a year before Justice Felix Frankfurter for a U.S. Supreme Court majority ruled that a Pennsylvania district school board could mandate the flag salute of all children, regardless of their religious beliefs. But three years later the Court, with a new majority, reversed itself, holding a similar West Virginia flag-salute statute unconstitutional. In three separate opinions, in-

cluding a dissent, Lehman condemned the employment of third-degree tactics in police interrogations.

As a person, Lehman was courteous, kindly, and gentle, resembling his intimate friend and predecessor on the court of appeals, Benjamin Cardozo. At the same time he was a forceful, uncompromising presiding judge. Brought up in the Reform tradition of Judaism, for years he served as president of Temple Emanu-El, a post to which he was elected shortly after the death of Louis Marshall. Like the Schiffs, Warburgs, and Marshalls, he saw the need to supply Jews who followed the Conservative tradition with training and enlightened spiritual leadership. All his life Judge Lehman was active in the improvement of Jewish educational institutions, and he devoted time and resources to Jewish affairs and philanthropy. He served as president of the board of trustees of the Jewish Welfare Board (1921–1940), whose policies he helped shape from its inception. In 1942 he was vice president of the American Jewish Committee. He supported many projects for the development of the new state of Israel, although the Lehmans were not Zionists.

Lehman's tenure as chief judge was not without controversy. His brother Herbert Lehman served as governor of New York from 1932 to 1942, and for the first time in the history of any state two brothers headed the executive and judicial, two of the three coordinate branches of the government. Some were critical of this situation, seeing it as a conflict of interest and a concentration of too much power in a single family. Upstate figures objected to the fact that the city of New York was unduly represented in the government of the state. Carmine De Sapio wondered why Governor Lehman was so critical of the New York system of judicial nominations when he had acquiesced without any objection to the elevation of his brother by that method.

Early in 1939 Governor Lehman had written to Franklin D. Roosevelt asking the president to consider his brother Irving for the Supreme Court. But Roosevelt replied that geographical considerations made the appointment impossible. There were other unstated reasons. Irving Lehman, however, was well satisfied in the post of chief judge, one of great dignity and opportunity.

Lehman died unexpectedly at his home in Port Chester, New York. On a woodland walk he fell and broke his leg. An embolism developed, and the tall, grave, kindly man was gone before any of his fellow judges on the court of appeals even knew he was ill.

• Lehman's court of appeals decisions are in vol. 237–294 of the *New York Reports*. His papers were destroyed at the time of his death, but there are surviving items in the Herbert Lehman Papers on deposit in Special Collections at Columbia University Library. A monograph devoted to his legal work is Edmund H. Lewis, *The Contribution of Judge Irving Lehman to the Development of the Law* (1951). See also William M. Wiecek, "The Place of Chief Judge Irving Lehman in American Constitutional Development," *American Jewish Historical Quarterly* 60 (Mar. 1971): 280–303; Bernard Shientag, *Meno-*

rah Journal (Spring 1947); and Allan Nevins, *Herbert H. Lehman and His Era* (1963). Obituary notices are in the *New York Times*, 23, 24, and 25 Sept. 1945.

MARIAN C. MCKENNA

LEHMAN, Robert (29 Sept. 1891–9 Aug. 1969), investment banker, was born in New York City, the son of Philip Lehman, the most influential second-generation partner in Lehman Brothers, and Carrie Lauer. In 1913 Lehman graduated with a B.A. from Yale University, where he studied art history and was managing editor of the *Yale Daily News*. At first Lehman worked full time augmenting the art collection his father had begun two years earlier. In 1917 he enlisted in the army and served in France as a captain in the 318th Field Artillery of the Eighty-first (Wildcat) Division. In 1919, with World War I over, he joined his family's banking concern, where his colleagues called him Bobbie. Two years later he became a partner. In 1923 he married Ruth Rumsey; their marriage ended in 1931 without progeny, and the next year he married Ruth Owen Meeker. They had one child before their marriage also ended in divorce. In 1952 Lehman married Lee Anz Lynn; they had no children.

Following in his father's footsteps in both finance and art collecting, Robert Lehman has been called "the last of the imperiously rich men." He became Lehman Brothers' most important partner and amassed the greatest private art collection of his time. Lehman maintained his firm's interest in retail merchandising, and like his father and his father's cousin Arthur, Lehman backed issues which other bankers failed to handle. Proving himself to be, in the words of a colleague, "one of the truly imaginative minds of the financial community," Robert Lehman became especially noted for financing and consolidating firms in the entertainment and air transportation industries. In the mid-1920s he financed B. F. Keith Corporation, which after consolidations became Radio-Keith-Orpheum (RKO). Later he financed other motion-picture studios, including Paramount Pictures and 20th Century–Fox. In 1928 he consolidated 700 theaters into the Keith-Albee and Orpheum chain, the country's largest grouping of theaters. In 1932 Lehman Brothers invested in the Columbia Broadcasting System; subsequently the firm financed the Radio Corporation of America, and in the late 1930s Lehman Brothers was the first investment company to publicly underwrite a television company, Allan B. DuMont Laboratories. Lehman Brothers also acquired a firm footing in the telegraphic and radio communications field by reorganizing the Postal Telegraph Company, merging it with the Western Union Telegraph Company, and gaining seats on its board of directors as well as on that of the American Cable & Radio Company.

Extremely interested in aviation and himself a certified pilot, Lehman early realized the importance of air transportation. Joined by his friend W. Averell Harriman, he organized in 1929 the Aviation Corporation, a holding company, and served as the chair of the executive committee of this first integrated unit of the new industry. In 1931 some eighty of its subsidiary airlines were consolidated as American Airways (which became American Airlines). Although Lehman and Harriman lost control of the Aviation Corporation two years later, Lehman was still very much in the industry as the banker of Pan American, whose board he had joined in 1929. Besides helping that airline and those that became Trans World Airlines to expand, he financed Capital, Continental, and National Airlines.

Lehman Brothers in 1929 formed Lehman Corporation, its own early investment company, with capital funds of $100 million; Robert Lehman served as president after Arthur Lehman's death in 1936. Keeping a flexible investment policy and usually trading its stocks and bonds on the New York Stock Exchange, this corporation proved Lehman Brothers' most successful creation. Other innovations included their Industrial Department, where individual employees specialized in and concentrated on the development of one or more industries, and an Economic Service, which constantly analyzed the American economy while compiling important data.

Lehman Brothers was the first investment bank to tap the cash reservoirs of insurance companies and pension funds to finance enterprises during the Great Depression. In 1936 the firm established a branch office in Chicago and ten years later opened one in Los Angeles. In 1950, when the nation's twenty largest retailing concerns were listed, Lehman Brothers was or had been the investment banker for more than half of them. Three years later when the organizers of Litton Industries approached Lehman for financing, he launched their conglomerate with $1.5 million, telling them, "I bet on people," making it clear that management was more important to him than financial statements.

The Investment Advisory Service Lehman built up for persons wishing to invest half a million or more controlled $2 billion, and his Industrial Advisory Service shared information compiled by the firm's specialists. Lehman was a superb matchmaker, who not only paired corporations in mergers but paired people and companies needing money with those wanting to lend it for a fee. Working out of a nine-by-fifteen-foot, pie-shaped office, he made his family's firm what many believed to be the biggest profit maker "in the business." In 1965 he co-managed a Chase Manhattan Bank offering that alone raised $250 million.

Along with collecting art, Lehman began collecting thoroughbred race horses in the 1940s, and by the 1960s he had acquired more than sixty of them. One of his last winners was Flit-to, who won the $100,000 United Nations Handicap at Atlantic City in 1967. Occasionally Lehman's art collecting and his horse interest coincided, as could be seen in the red and orange racing horses in the Kees van Dongen painting over his desk. Other paintings were displayed in the Lehman office building and in Lehman's eighteen-room Park Avenue apartment, but most of his collection remained in his parents' five-story stone mansion on

West 54th Street, where it had been assembled. There, protected by a twenty-four-hour guard, his vast collection, representing every major period and style of western painting from the thirteenth to the twentieth century, as well as tapestries, Renaissance furniture and jewelry, ceramics, bronzes, and Venetian glass, could be viewed by art students and experts.

Believing that important art, even when in private hands, should be available to the public, Lehman was generous in lending his treasures, including his collection's cornerstones—an early Rembrandt, a rare pair of Francesco del Cossa portraits, El Greco's *St. Jerome*, and Goya's *Countess of Altamira and Her Daughter*. Lehman exhibited large selections from his collection at the Metropolitan Museum [of Art] in 1954, at the Louvre's Musée de l'Orangerie in 1957, and at the Cincinnati Art Museum in 1959. In Paris, during the first two weeks of his paintings' tour, 17,000 people viewed the 293 paintings chosen by the Louvre from Lehman's collection of 1,000.

Before his death at his country home in Sands Point, New York, Lehman established the Robert Lehman Foundation and arranged for the Metropolitan Museum to house his unparalleled private art collection, amassed over a seventy-year period with the help of experts. Planned as a tranquil area "of human and classical proportions" within the larger museum, the Robert Lehman Wing opened in 1975.

Lehman's final years were filled with honors. His firm, with underwritings of $3.5 billion in 1967, was listed as one of the nation's top four investment banks. Also in that year he gave $1 million to New York University's Institute of Fine Arts and was made chair of the Metropolitan Museum's Board of Trustees (of which he had been a member since 1941). In 1968 his alma mater, Yale University, where in 1963 he had endowed a chair in the history of art, made him an honorary doctor of humane letters, observing that he had "enhanced the civic life, the culture, and the artistic development of our civilization."

• Lehman's papers are at the Metropolitan Museum. For Lehman's part in his family's firm, see Frank Manheim, *A Centennial: Lehman Brothers, 1850–1950* (1950), and for information on him, his family, and its firm, see Joseph A. Thomas, "Foreword," in George Szabo, *The Robert Lehman Collection: A Guide . . .* (1975); Stephen Birmingham, *"Our Crowd": The Great Jewish Families of New York* (1967); Ken Auletta, *Greed and Glory on Wall Street: The Fall of the House of Lehman* (1986), whose chronology, however, should be used with caution; and Roland Flade, *The Lehmans: From Rimpar to the New World, a Family History* (1996). On Lehman as a collector, see Metropolitan Museum of Art, *Robert Lehman Collection* (13 vols., 1987–), a catalog of this "most variegated" collection by noted art historians, each an expert with a worldwide reputation in one of the numerous fields represented in the collection. See also Cincinnati Art Museum, *The Lehman Collection, New York* (1959), and Robert Lehman's catalog of his father's collection (1928). A very full obituary is in the *New York Times*, 10 Aug. 1969.

OLIVE HOOGENBOOM

LEHMANN, Lotte (27 Feb. 1888–26 Aug. 1976), operatic soprano and lieder recitalist, was born in Perleberg, Germany, the daughter of Carl Lehmann, secretary of a national benevolent society, and Marie Schuster. Her childhood was uneventful and relatively happy. Everyone in the family sang but only as amateurs. Lotte's father had intended to enroll her in a commercial course, but he was persuaded by her vocal talent to allow her to accept a scholarship at the Royal High School of Music in Berlin. Later study included a discouragingly counterproductive period at the Etelka Gerster School of Singing from which she was expelled for a perceived lack of talent, and then a year (1909–1910) of very satisfying progress with Mathilde Mallinger, who had been Richard Wagner's first Eva in *Die Meistersinger*.

Lehmann began her professional career at the Hamburg Opera, starting with very small roles. She made her debut as the Second Boy in *The Magic Flute* on 2 September 1910. Although her voice was admired from the beginning, her acting was at first considered clumsy and self-conscious; only gradually did she emerge as one of the great singing actresses of her era. Her breakthrough role, first performed on 29 November 1912, was Elsa in *Lohengrin* (coached and conducted by Otto Klemperer). With that role Lotte Lehmann became a beloved star of the Hamburg Opera.

In the summer of 1914 Lehmann made an inconspicuous debut in London (at the Drury Lane Theatre) as Sophie in *Der Rosenkavalier*, her first appearance outside of Germany, and cut her first recordings, two arias from *Lohengrin*, for Pathé in Berlin. On 30 October 1914 she made her debut at the Vienna Court Opera as a guest Eva in *Die Meistersinger*. Two seasons later she became a regular member of that company, opening the season with Agathe in *Der Freischütz* on 18 August 1916. Two months later she created a sensation as the "Composer" in the premiere on 4 October 1916 of the revised version of *Ariadne auf Naxos* by Richard Strauss, who had personally insisted on Lehmann after she had substituted for an absent colleague at one of the rehearsals. Lehmann quickly became a favorite of the Viennese public. Strauss cast her in the premieres of his next two operas and personally coached her at his villa in Garmisch.

Giacomo Puccini greatly admired Lehmann's Mimi, Manon Lescaut, and, especially, Sister Angelica. He wrote that her interpretation of Sister Angelica was the finest he had experienced. Her first appearance in her most celebrated role, the Marschallin in *Der Rosenkavalier*, took place at Covent Garden, London, on 21 May 1924, under the direction of Bruno Walter, whom she considered her greatest teacher of interpretation. In 1926 Lehmann married Otto Krause, who had four children from a previous marriage. She was a leading attraction at the Salzburg Festival every summer from 1926 until 1937. In 1928 she made debuts in Paris, Stockholm, and Brussels. She was decorated by the king of Sweden; France made her, first, a chevalier, later an officer of the Legion of Honor.

Lehmann's North American debut was with the Chicago Opera on 28 October 1930 as Sieglinde in *Die Walküre*. A phenomenally successful Town Hall recital in New York on 7 January 1932 established Lehmann's reputation in the United States as a lieder singer, and, with annual concert tours all over the country, she remained the most influential interpreter and popularizer of the German lied in America until her final recitals in 1951. Some seasons she gave as many as eight song recitals in New York City alone. Lehmann made her triumphant debut at the Metropolitan Opera as Sieglinde on 11 January 1934 and remained a member of the company until 1945.

A love affair with Arturo Toscanini began in 1934 with their first concert together and lasted several years. In 1935 their performances of *Fidelio* made history in Salzburg; the following summer she was also his Eva in *Die Meistersinger* there. They remained close friends until his death.

In 1938, when Hitler annexed Austria, Lehmann's four stepchildren, Jewish through their mother, managed an adventurous escape on the Orient Express. Meanwhile, Lehmann, uncertain of their fate, collapsed on stage at Covent Garden during the first act of *Der Rosenkavalier*. The family moved to the United States, where Otto Krause, her husband, died in 1939. After his death Lehmann made her home with Frances Holden, who had been a devoted fan for many years. Holden encouraged Lehmann to take up painting, an avocation she pursued energetically for the rest of her life. She wrote an autobiography and a novel, both published in 1937; later she published valuable books on the interpretation of lieder and on her operatic roles.

Having made her permanent home in the United States, Lehmann applied in 1939 for U.S. citizenship, which was finally granted on 13 June 1945 after the defeat of Germany. (During World War II she was classified as an enemy alien, although as an outspoken opponent of the Nazis she had been forbidden to sing in Germany and was warmly welcomed at American army camps and canteens when she sang for U.S. troops.) Lehmann's last appearance in opera was as the Marschallin in Los Angeles on 1 November 1946. In 1948 she played the mother of Danny Thomas in a Hollywood film, *Big City*. During the 1940s, many well-known opera and concert singers, among them Rose Bampton, Eleanor Steber, Risë Stevens, Dorothy Maynor, and Jeanette MacDonald, studied opera and/or lieder with Lehmann.

As her operatic career was drawing to a close, Lehmann came fully into her own as a supreme interpreter of the German lied. Her "farewell recital" at New York's Town Hall on 16 February 1951 was an emotional experience for the audience as well as for the singer, who made a touching speech and then choked up in her final encore, Schubert's song of thanks to the art of music. There were more "farewells" in California, her home since 1940, the very last in Pasadena on 11 November 1951.

After her retirement as a singer, Lehmann had an extraordinarily successful new career as a teacher, not of singing as such but of interpretation. Her master classes at the Music Academy of the West, Santa Barbara, became famous, as did those in Pasadena, California, at Northwestern University and Mills College, and later in England, Canada, Austria, Kansas City, and New York. Among many other honors and tributes, Lehmann was awarded several honorary doctorates, the Honor Cross of the Austrian government, the Ring of Honor of the city of Vienna, and another special Ring of Honor, created for her by the soloists of the Vienna State Opera. A promenade in Salzburg and a concert hall at the University of California, Santa Barbara, were named after her.

As a teacher Lehmann was gifted with the ability to articulate her artistic vision in words; she inspired a generation of young singers to surpass themselves. As a singer she moved audiences all over the world through the very distinctive and haunting quality of her voice, through her total identification with what she was singing, and through the mastery with which she communicated her feeling for both words and music to her listeners. Lehmann never felt that she had a perfect vocal technique as such; she was often short of breath, and in later years her highest notes lost much of their earlier beauty. But she never lost her hold on the audience. Every song became a personal experience brought to new life. With Lehmann nothing was ever "routine"; no matter how often she had sung a particular role or a particular song, it was always communicated as spontaneously, as freshly, and with as eloquent an inspiration as if she had only just discovered its secrets.

Lotte Lehmann died quietly in her sleep at her home in Santa Barbara. Her ashes were sent to Vienna and given a place of honor near the graves of Schubert and other great musicians. What Richard Strauss had said of her was carved upon the stone: "When she sang she moved the stars."

• Much of Lehmann's voluminous correspondence, including letters from Richard Strauss, Giacomo Puccini, Bruno Walter, Arturo Toscanini, Otto Klemperer, and Thomas Mann, is housed in the Lotte Lehmann Archive of the library of the University of California, Santa Barbara. The private collection of Lehmann's heir, Dr. Frances Holden, who died in 1996, will be housed either in the Lotte Lehmann Archive or at the Music Academy of the West, Santa Barbara. The archive also includes many articles by and about Lehmann, manuscripts, press books, taped interviews, art works, and recordings, both commercial and noncommercial. Her autobiography is *Anfang und Aufstieg* (1937); the U.S. edition in English is *Midway in My Song* (1938). Lehmann published two books on song interpretation, *More than Singing* (1945; repr. 1985) and *Eighteen Song Cycles* (1971), and two on her operatic roles, *My Many Lives* (1948; repr. 1974) and *Five Operas and Richard Strauss* (1964; repr. 1982). Two biographies (with extensive discographies) are Beaumont Glass, *Lotte Lehmann: A Life in Opera and Song* (1988), and Alan Jefferson, *Lotte Lehmann, 1888–1976* (1988). An obituary is in the *New York Times*, 27 Aug. 1976.

BEAUMONT GLASS

LEIB, Michael (8 Jan. 1760–28 Dec. 1822), physician and politician, was born in Philadelphia, Pennsylvania, the son of Johann George Leib, a German immigrant of modest means, and Margaretha Dorothea Liebheit. After a common school education he studied medicine under Benjamin Rush. In 1780, during the American Revolution, Leib was commissioned as a surgeon in the Philadelphia militia. Following the Revolution he entered medical practice in Philadelphia and soon became known as one of the leading physicians of the city. He was one of the incorporators of the College of Physicians of Philadelphia in 1789 and was on the staffs of the Philadelphia Dispensary and the Philadelphia Almshouse and Hospital. During the great yellow fever epidemic of 1793 he was among the physicians coordinating medical efforts, and he supervised the Bush Hill Hospital, where many victims of the epidemic were treated.

Leib's passage from medical practice to an all-consuming occupation with politics began in 1793, when he took part in the organization of some of the first Democratic-Republican societies, founded originally to support the French Revolution and advance "republican" principles throughout the world. In April 1793 he was a founding member and secretary of the German Republican Society in Philadelphia. Leib also became an active member of the Democratic Society of Pennsylvania, formed in May 1793, and was a member of its three-person correspondence committee, along with the newspaper editor Benjamin Franklin Bache and the scientific farmer George Logan. The trio was regarded in a satirical poem by the federalist editor John Fenno as "the leaders of the Demon frantic club." By 1796 these societies had emerged as the basis for the new national opposition party that was forming around Thomas Jefferson. In July 1796, when Philadelphia Republicans organized a campaign supporting Jefferson's presidential candidacy, Leib was chosen as the chair.

In 1795 Leib had begun the first of three consecutive one-year terms in the Pennsylvania House of Representatives; he quickly became known as a staunch advocate of Jeffersonian principles. In 1798 he was elected to represent a Philadelphia district in the U.S. House of Representatives and held that seat until 1806. Leib gave strong support to Jefferson's administration. He also emerged as a dominant force in Philadelphia city politics. He gained a reputation as an uncompromising, power-hungry, and autocratic politician. His control over federal patronage and his relentless pursuit of any opposition were principal sources of a factionalism among Philadelphia's Democratic Republicans that persisted until his death. The emerging party split in Philadelphia pitted Leib and William Duane (successor to Bache as editor of the Philadelphia *Aurora*) against former political associates such as Logan, Pennsylvania governor Thomas McKean, and the economist Tench Coxe. In the 1805 campaign, Governor McKean referred to the Leib-Duane opposition as "a set of clodpoles and ignoramuses," which led to the faction's adopting for itself the title "clodpoles."

After close factional battles over his seat in the U.S. House of Representatives in 1802 and 1804, Leib declined to run again in 1806 and was returned instead by his district to the Pennsylvania legislature. Until 1808 he led a strident legislative opposition to Governor McKean, culminating in an unsuccessful effort to impeach the governor in 1807. Pennsylvania Republicans united in 1808 to support James Madison's election to the presidency, and in December 1808 the legislature elected Leib to the U.S. Senate, where he served until 1814. Also in 1808, Leib married Susan Kennedy; they had two children.

During Leib's absence in Washington the Leib-Duane "Old School" Democrats (as they were now called) lost influence in Philadelphia politics to the rival faction, led by the journalist John Binns and associated with Pennsylvania's new governor, Simon Snyder. The "Old School" faction became alienated from the Madison administration and from its secretary of the Treasury, Albert Gallatin, who was from western Pennsylvania and who controlled much federal patronage. The Snyder faction, on the other hand, preserved its ties with Madison and Gallatin. The division among Democrats allowed Federalists to win local offices in Philadelphia in 1810 and 1811. In 1812 Leib privately opposed Madison's course toward war with Great Britain, but when a vote for a declaration of war came he bowed to public opinion in Pennsylvania and supported it. In that year's presidential election, he supported New York's DeWitt Clinton against Madison. In 1814, despite his continuing conflict with the Madison administration, Leib was appointed postmaster at Philadelphia; outcries from the Binns faction eventually led to his resignation from the Senate in 1814 and his removal from the postmastership in 1815. In 1815 Leib found a new political base as president of the board of commissioners of Northern Liberties, adjoining the city of Philadelphia.

Leib's influence declined in the fluid and disorganized conditions of party politics after 1815. The Old School Democrats made alliances with some remnants of the rapidly disappearing Federalist party, and this combined support brought Leib one final term (1817–1818) in the state house of representatives. His further attempts at elective office were unavailing. Leib and his faction continued to attach their allegiances to the presidential candidacy of Clinton, whose presidential hopes waned as those of Andrew Jackson began to strengthen in the early 1820s. Leib's final political office was an appointive one, one month before his death, as prothonotary of the Philadelphia county court. When Leib died at Philadelphia and William Duane left the country, the Old School faction disappeared into the maelstrom of the new Jacksonian political system.

Leib entered the political world as a strong Jeffersonian ideologue, but this career became increasingly governed by opportunism, intrigue, and an incessant search for political power. He played a role in the political revolution of Jefferson's presidential administration, but his principal legacy was the faction-ridden, patronage-driven style of urban politics he fostered in Philadelphia.

• Manuscripts concerning Leib are in various political collections in the Historical Society of Pennsylvania. His role in the early 1790s is documented in Philip S. Foner, ed., *The Democratic-Republican Societies, 1790–1800: A Documentary Sourcebook* (1976). See also Roland M. Baumann, "The Democratic-Republicans of Philadelphia: The Origins, 1776–1797" (Ph.D. diss., Pennsylvania State Univ., 1970). Leib's political career can be traced in Harry M. Tinckom, *The Republicans and Federalists in Pennsylvania, 1790–1801* (1950), Sanford W. Higginbotham, *Keystone in the Democratic Arch: Pennsylvania Politics, 1800–1816* (1952), and Philip S. Klein, *Pennsylvania Politics, 1817–1832: A Game without Rules* (1940). For Leib's role in the War of 1812, see Victor A. Sapio, *Pennsylvania and the War of 1812* (1970). For details on Philadelphia politics, see J. Thomas Scharf and Thompson Westcott, *History of Philadelphia, 1609–1884* (1884). An obituary is in *Poulson's American Daily Advertiser*, 30 Dec. 1822.

JAMES M. BERGQUIST

LEIDESDORFF, William Alexander (1810–May 1848), pioneer, diplomat, and businessman, was born in St. Croix in the Danish Virgin Islands, the son of William Leidesdorff, a Danish planter, and Anna Marie Sparks, an Afro-Caribbean slave. He was educated by his owner, who reportedly treated him more as a son than as a slave. As a young man he was sent to New Orleans to work for his uncle's cotton business as a master of ships sailing between New York and New Orleans. Both his father and uncle died soon after, leaving Leidesdorff a sizable inheritance. His newly acquired wealth allowed him to propose to a woman he had been courting, Hortense, who accepted. The engagement ended painfully shortly before the marriage date when Leidesdorff told his fiancée that through his mother he was of African descent. She called off the wedding, and he, heartbroken, left New Orleans.

Arriving in California in 1841 aboard his schooner the *Julia Anna*, Leidesdorff settled in San Francisco, then known as Yerba Buena. In addition to using the *Julia Anna* to make regular visits to the West Indies until 1845, Leidesdorff ran a shipping route between California and Hawaii. In 1843 he obtained two large land grants on the corner of Clay and Kearney streets in San Francisco from the Mexican government, which then controlled California. On this land he constructed an adobe building that served as both his home and a retail store. He became a Mexican citizen in 1844 and with his citizenship acquired a third grant, the Rancho Rio de los Americanos, a 35,500-acre lot on the American river at what is now Folsom. His pro–U.S. sentiments caused his appointment in October 1845 as U.S. vice consul of San Francisco, his Mexican citizenship notwithstanding. American interest in California was growing quickly, and preparations for war with Mexico were beginning. John Frémont, the explorer and surveyor, was sent to the region by the U.S. government ostensibly to survey the Sacramento River valley, but in reality as a political and military leader in the event of a U.S. invasion. Leidesdorff met with and advised Frémont. He obtained a fourth land grant from the Mexican government in 1846, a lot on California Street and the street that would later be named Leidesdorff Street, where he built a warehouse.

In July 1846 U.S. marines, led by Captain John Montgomery, landed in California and declared the region the property of the United States. Leidesdorff translated his declaration into Spanish. As a prominent Mexican citizen, he was given care of the Mexican flag that had flown over the plaza of the city, and of certain official papers. As an American sympathizer and government official, two months after the invasion he hosted a grand ball in honor of U.S. naval commander Commodore Robert Field Stockton. Leidesdorff continued to develop his land. He constructed a hotel on one lot and bought a house in which he would live permanently. In 1847 he launched his boat the *Sitka* into the San Francisco Bay, the first steamer ever to sail there.

In addition to his business involvements, Leidesdorff was active in city politics. He was elected to the city council in 1847 and served as town treasurer in 1848. He became chair of San Francisco's school board, presiding over the opening of the first public school in California in April 1848. He died in San Francisco of typhus.

Shortly before his death, gold was discovered on his land at the Rancho Rio de los Americanos. Captain Joseph Folsom, negotiating to buy the stake, traveled to the West Indies to bargain directly with Leidesdorff's mother. Not until meeting her did Folsom, or anyone in San Francisco, realize that Leidesdorff was of African descent. Having no way of knowing the value of her son's estate, she sold the claim to Folsom for $75,000. When Folsom returned, he registered the property with the deed listing its value as $1.5 million. Leidesdorff is thus sometimes cited as the first African-American millionaire, although since the wealth did not materialize until after his death the claim is debatable. Unquestionably, he was one of the most affluent and influential African Americans of his time, leading in the economic and political development of California. His diplomacy and leadership during the transition from Mexican to U.S. government smoothed a potentially turbulent takeover.

• The best source for Leidesdorff's life is "The First Negro Millionaire," *Ebony*, Nov. 1958, pp. 50–54. See also William L. Katz, *Black People Who Made the Old West* (1977), Edgar A. Toppin, *Biographical History of Blacks* (1971), and Olive W. Burt, *Negroes in the Early West* (1969).

ELIZABETH ZOE VICARY

LEIDY, Joseph (9 Sept. 1823–30 Apr. 1891), comparative anatomist, paleontologist, and microscopist, was born Joseph Mellick Leidy in Philadelphia, Pennsylvania, the son of Philip Leidy, a hatter, and Catherine Mellick, who died twenty months later in childbirth.

Soon thereafter, Leidy's father married Christiana Taliana Mellick, Catherine's first cousin, a determined, intelligent woman who raised Leidy. German was spoken in the Leidy (Leydig) home. As a young boy, Joseph developed an intense interest in plants, animals, and minerals, and he showed an unusual talent for drawing. He was an indifferent student at a private, classical school, spending most of his time following his interest in nature, exploring the creeks and parks of Philadelphia.

Leidy graduated from the Medical School of the University of Pennsylvania in 1844, and at the insistence of his father he practiced medicine, only to abandon it in 1847 to become a full-time investigator. In 1844 he was appointed prosector, or dissecting assistant, to William Horner, the professor of anatomy at the University of Pennsylvania, where he was introduced to microscopy. His career in research was launched in 1845 with the dissection and drawing of snails for Amos Binney's *The Terrestrial Air-breathing Mollusks of the United States and the Adjacent Territories of North America*, edited by Augustus A. Gould and published in 1851. The work earned him immediate membership in the Boston Society of Natural History and the Academy of Natural Sciences of Philadelphia. An astonishing amount of work of a descriptive, anatomical nature on a wide range of life followed, including the discovery of rhinoceros teeth in the West and the transplantation of fragments of human cancer to a frog (1851).

Leidy in 1845 was appointed librarian and then in 1846 curator of the academy, a position he held for the rest of his life. His rise was rapid at the medical school, and upon the death of Horner in 1853, he became professor of anatomy, which he taught to medical students for the next thirty-eight years. In 1861 he published *An Elementary Treatise on Human Anatomy*, the standard text used by medical students for many years. His work on the fibrillar structure of cartilage, the anatomy of the liver, the temporal and intermaxillary bones, and the larynx made him the foremost anatomist in the United States. In 1871 he established the Department of Natural History at Swarthmore College and taught there until 1885, relinquishing the position to help found and then direct the Department of Biology at the University of Pennsylvania. He directed the department until his death. In 1885 he was elected president of the Wagner Free Institute of Science of Philadelphia. He expanded and maintained the natural history museums at both the university and the institute. He was the first president of the American Association of Anatomists (1888–1889).

At mid-century Leidy was the foremost microscopist in America. No one could approach his output of papers on numerous subjects involving the microscope. He was probably the first to use the instrument in forensic medicine when he showed that the blood on a suspected murderer's clothing was not that of a chicken, as the murderer claimed, but could be that of a human since the red blood cells were not nucleated. Leidy observed that small organisms of a plant and animal nature lived in and on a wide range of species, from insects to humans. In most instances, such organisms caused no observable damage, while in some the host was harmed. He discovered cysts of *Trichina* larvae in ham, critical information leading to an understanding of the life cycle and spread of this parasite in humans, and he advocated that meat be cooked to destroy the larvae (1853). His earlier studies on parasites, which included a large number of newly described organisms, was summarized in *Flora and Fauna within Living Animals* (1853) and *A Synopsis of Entozoa and Some of Their Ectocongeners Observed by the Author* (1856), highly praised works for which he was called the founder of American parasitology and of protozoology.

In 1847, on examining teeth and fossilized bones of the horse, he showed that the animal had existed in North America in prehistoric times, contrary to common belief. The horse had become extinct for unknown reasons and was reintroduced by the Spanish in the sixteenth century. In 1858 he assembled and described the first fairly complete dinosaur fossil found in America (in New Jersey), *Hadrosaurus foulkii*, correctly adducing its present familiar image—a kangaroolike, bipedal reptile with small forelimbs, which provided evidence for biologist Thomas H. Huxley's theory of the reptilian origin of birds. Leidy had earlier described the teeth of a dinosaur. Between 1850 and 1870 he examined virtually all fossils from the West sent by collectors, two of whom were Ferdinand V. Hayden and Spencer Baird, secretary of the Smithsonian Institution. Leidy himself was not primarily a collector. Among the many extinct animals he was first to describe were several ancestors of the horse; *Titanotherium*, elephant-sized monsters; *Poëbrotherium wilsonii*, an ancestor of the camel; *Camelops kansanus*, the camel; *Merycoidodon*, the first oreodont, which looked like a cross between a pig, a deer, and a camel; *Uintatherium*, a great, horned beast; *Hyracodon*, a relative of the rhinoceros; and fossils of numerous other species and genera. His work on completely unknown Tertiary fossils was summarized in more than two hundred of his publications, including *The Ancient Fauna of Nebraska* (1854), *Cretaceous Reptiles of the United States* (1865), *The Extinct Mammalian Fauna of Dakota and Nebraska Including an Account of Some Allied Forms from Other Localities* (1869), and *Contributions to the Extinct Vertebrate Fauna of the Western Territories* (1873). His monographs were ground-breaking, and he is generally recognized as the founder of American vertebrate paleontology. He left paleontology, however, in the early 1870s to avoid the bitter Marsh-Cope controversy over priority in the discovery and naming of several fossil species and returned to microscopy, his first love. His later work was summarized in his classic *Fresh-water Rhizopods of North America* (1879). In the last few years of his life, Leidy studied fossils from Florida such as *Smilodon*, the saber-toothed cat. A prodigious worker, he was busily engaged in research to the very end of his life.

Leidy was aware of extinction and the appearance of new species, of variation and change within species, and the lack of a clear demarcation between some species, especially of small organisms. Some of his writing, years before Charles Darwin's, is remarkably prescient on notions of evolution. It is not surprising that he was an early and ardent supporter of Darwinism, for natural selection provided a mechanism and explanation for his own observations and thoughts. After his own notions on the subject were clarified for him by Darwin's published findings in 1859, the direction and nature of Leidy's research continued unchanged. He was aware of the evolutionary implications of his work, especially that on the horse, and he had a remarkable talent for discerning affinities between fossil structures, yet he refused to speculate and write about the possible phylogenetic implications of his findings. It was left to Leidy's juniors, Othniel Charles Marsh and Edward Drinker Cope, to outline the phylogenies of known fossil vertebrates and modernize the taxonomy so that specimens could be understood in the context of evolutionary theory. Cope and Marsh, in their fierce antagonism, rarely, if ever, mentioned Leidy's critically important contributions, one of the reasons for the eclipse of Leidy's name.

Some consider Leidy the finest American naturalist of the century. A modest man, without pretense, and revered by his colleagues, he avoided conflict at any price. A naturalist of the old school, Leidy never changed from his descriptive, nonexperimental, nonspeculative mode of research. His work was graced by his beautiful illustrations, and he was famous for being almost always correct in his observations and conclusions. During the Civil War he was surgeon at the Satterlee General Hospital, performing autopsies, and he was a member of the Sanitary Commission. In 1864 he married Anna Harden; they had one adopted daughter.

Leidy was a member of more than fifty societies, including the American Philosophical Society and the College of Physicians, but he rarely went to meetings other than at local, familiar institutions in Philadelphia. A charter member of the National Academy of Sciences, he soon resigned in order to avoid political controversy. He won several awards and honors, including the medal of the Royal Microscopical Society (1879), the Walker Prize, Boston (1880), the Lyell Medal of the Geological Society of London (1884), and the Cuvier Medal, Academy of Sciences of Paris (1888). He died in Philadelphia.

• A collection of Leidy's letters and holographs is at the Academy of Natural Sciences of Philadelphia. Leidy published more than 600 papers, many only brief notes, but several of his monographs are considered seminal in their respective disciplines. He also edited Quain's *Human Anatomy* (1849) and translated and annotated Gottlieb Gluge's *Atlas of Pathological Histology* (1853). A complete list of publications is in W. S. W. Ruschenberger, "A Sketch of the Life of Joseph Leidy, M.D.," *Proceedings of the American Philosophical Society* 30 (1892): 135–84; and Henry F. Osborn, "Biographical Memoir of Joseph Leidy, 1823–1891," National Academy of Sciences, *Biographical Memoirs* 7 (1913). The first full biography of his life is Leonard Warren, *The Last Man Who Knew Everything: A Biography of Joseph Leidy* (1997). Also see Ronald Rainger, "The Rise and Decline of a Science: Vertebrate Paleontology at Philadelphia's Academy of Natural Sciences, 1820–1900," *Proceedings of the American Philosophical Society* 136 (1992): 1–32, for Leidy's scientific activities and community building. An obituary is in the *Philadelphia Inquirer*, 30 Apr. 1891.

LEONARD WARREN

LEIF ERIKSSON (c. 975–c. 1025), explorer and discoverer of America, was born probably in Eiríkssta ir/ Haukadal, Iceland, the son of Erik the Red, a farmer and the discoverer of Greenland, and Thiodhild. Though Leif Eriksson (Old Norse: Leifr Eiríksson) is one of the most famous persons in Western history, little is known about his life except his discovery and exploration of Vinland/America. He is mentioned briefly and mostly in connection with Vinland in several historical sources of the twelfth and thirteenth centuries, such as the *Landnámabók* (Book of the settlement of Iceland), Abbot Nikuláss's *Landalýsing* (Itinerarium), Snorri Sturlusson's *Heimskringla* (History of the Norwegian kings), the Kristni saga, and the long version of Ólafs saga Tryggvasonar.

Fortunately, Leif's story is told in more detail by two Old Icelandic sagas, the Eiríks saga rau a (Eirík's saga) and the Groenlendinga saga (Saga of the Greenlanders). The older of these manuscripts dates from the fourteenth century but both build on an earlier tradition. The difficulty is that these two sagas differ decisively in their details on Leif's life. Although Jón Jóhannesson has demonstrated in "The Date of the Composition of the Saga of the Greenlanders" (*Saga-Book of the Viking Society for Northern Research* 16, no. 1 [1962]: 54–66) that, in contrast to former opinions, the Groenlendinga saga is older and historically more trustworthy than the Eiríks saga, all the biographical hints have to be taken cautiously.

Leif was born probably in the 970s at the farm Eiríkssta ir in southwestern Iceland. His father, Eiríkr Thorvaldsson, surnamed "the Red" because of the color of his hair, originally was a farmer in Jaeren in southern Norway but had to flee to Iceland because of his involvement in some killings. At first Eiríkr and his father settled in the poor northwestern region of the island. After having married the wealthy Thorhild (later, after the conversion, called Thiodhild), a descendant of one of the first settlers, he moved to Eiríkssta ir. Charged with murder, Eiríkr was sentenced to outlawry for three years and used this time to explore the Gunnbjarnar skerries, islands west of Iceland whose identity is unknown today. He discovered and explored Greenland between 982 and 985 and moved there in 985 or 986 together with several hundred other people. He settled at Brattahlí at the Eiríksfjord (present-day Tunukdliarfik).

Thus, Leif grew up as the son of the leading lord at the manor farm in the so-called Eastern Settlement together with his brothers Thorvald and Thorstein and his half-sister Freydis. He was obviously trained well, among other things as a seaman. Eiríks saga tells us that Leif, sailing to Norway in 999 or 1000, was driven off course to the Hebrides, where he begot an illegitimate son, Thorgils, whom he later acknowledged. He resumed his voyage to Norway, where he stayed with King Ólaf Tryggvason, who had him baptized and ordered him to Christianize Greenland. On his way home he is said to have found Vinland and rescued fifteen shipwrecked people. He persuaded the Greenlanders to become Christian, among them his mother Thiodhild, who built the first church on the island. His father Eiríkr is said to have stuck to his old faith in Thor.

According to the research of Jón Jóhannesson, this whole story of Leif being involved in the conversion of Greenland is due to an invention of the Icelandic monk Odd Snorrason around 1200. The older Groenlendinga saga and other sources make no mention of Leif as a converter of Greenland, and it positively states that his father died before the Christian faith came to Greenland. Leif assumed the leading position in Greenland, married, and fathered at least one son. He must have died before 1025, since the Fóstbroe ra saga states that in that year Leif's son Thorkel was chief in Greenland.

The most important event in Leif's life and the reason he is still so famous is the discovery or at least the exploration of Vinland, Wineland the good, that is, America. Eiríks saga reports that Leif's ship, on the way home from Norway to Greenland, was driven off course to a land then unknown. He explored the land and finally came home to Brattahlí . The more trustworthy Groenlendinga saga account gives the credit for the discovery to Bjarni Herjólfsson, who is not even mentioned in Eiríks saga. According to the Groenlendinga saga, Bjarni was driven off course while sailing from Iceland to Greenland. He sighted three different lands—green and grassy, woody, and stony, respectively—but did not go ashore. Finally he reached Greenland (possibly in 986 or 987). Telling about his discovery at the court of King Ólaf Tryggvason in Norway, Bjarni was blamed for not having explored the newly found land.

Leif heard about this discovery in Greenland and decided to equip an expedition. He bought Bjarni's seaworthy ship and, circa 1000, started his voyage with thirty-five men. The first land they found was the one Bjarni had sighted last. Full of glaciers and large flat stones, the land seemed uninhabitable. Leif called it Helluland (Slab-land). It was probably Baffin Island. The second land they sighted was flat and woody, with sandy beaches, and Leif called it Markland (Forest-land). It was probably Labrador. The third landfall was made at an island with meadows and a river full of salmon. The group decided to winter there and built large houses, the so-called Leifsbú ir (Leif's booths), which later were made available to explorers and settlers who followed. After having discovered wild grapes, Leif called this land Vinland (Wineland). The following year he sailed back to Greenland.

The rather unclear remark that on the shortest day of the year the sun at Vinland was up by 9 A.M. and set later than 3 P.M. indicates that Vinland must have lain between the fortieth and fiftieth north parallels. But unlike Markland and Helluland, Vinland has not yet been identified unequivocally, though in 1960 the Norwegian Helge Ingstad discovered an impressive Viking settlement at L'Anse-aux-Meadows, Newfoundland.

Leif's discoveries led to several attempts at settlement, all finally unsuccessful because of the increasing hostility of the indigenous people. All of these voyages were undertaken by members of Leif's family: the first by Leif's brother Thorvald, who was the first white settler killed by the skraelingar (Indian tribes); the second by Leif's brother Thorstein, who did not even reach the New World; and the next by Thorfinn Karlsefni, who had married Gudrid, the widow of Thorstein. Gudrid gave birth to Snorri Thorsteinsson, the first American-born European. Finally, even Freydis, Leif's half-sister, tried to settle in Vinland, a voyage that ended with murder and dishonor. Astonishingly enough, Leif's family vanishes from the historic record after the Vinland intermezzo.

Leif's personal characteristics remain somewhat shadowy in the sources. We know he was surnamed *inn heppni* (the Lucky) because of his rescue of the fifteen shipwrecked people. The Groenlendinga saga gives only the following short characterization: "Leif was tall and strong and very impressive in appearance. He was a shrewd man and always moderate in his behavior."

• The two main sources, Eiríks saga rau a and the Groenlendinga saga, were edited in Old Icelandic by Matthías Þór arson in the Icelandic saga series *Íslenzk fornrit*, vol. 4, *Eyrbyggja saga* . . . (1935; rev. ed., 1957). Both sagas are well translated into English and published with an introduction and annotations by Magnus Magnusson and Herman Pálsson as *The Vinland Sagas: The Norse Discovery of America* (1965). The secondary literature is vast. See especially Gwyn Jones, *The Norse Atlantic Saga* (1964; enl. ed., 1986); Tryggvi J. Oleson, *Early Voyages and Northern Approaches 1000–1632*, Canadian Centenary Series, vol. 1 (1964); Helge Ingstad, *Land under the Pole Star* (1966); Ingstad, *Westward to Vinland* (1969); Eric Wahlgren, "Fact and Fancy in the Vinland Sagas," in *Old Norse Literature and Mythology*, ed. E. C. Polomé (1969); Samuel E. Morison, *The European Discovery of America: The Northern Voyages 500–1600* (1971); Magnusson, *Vikings!* (1980); Anne Stine Ingstad, *The Norse Discovery of America*, vol. 1, *Excavations of a Norse Settlement at L'Anse-aux-Meadows, New Foundland, 1961–1968* (1985); Erik Wahlgren, *The Vikings and America* (1986); and Hans-Jürgen Krüger, *Erik der Rote und Leif der Glückliche: Eine Biographie der Eriksfamilie* (1990).

UWE SCHNALL

LEIGH, Benjamin Watkins (18 June 1781–2 Feb. 1849), lawyer, court reporter, and politician, was born in Chesterfield County, Virginia, the son of William Leigh, an Episcopalian minister, and Elizabeth Watkins. Benjamin attended the College of William and Mary, where he studied under St. George Tucker. He began practicing law in Petersburg, Virginia, in 1802.

Leigh became interested in politics and represented Dinwiddie County in the House of Delegates from 1811 to 1813. He left the legislature but made Richmond his permanent address to pursue his legal career, becoming one of Virginia's prominent attorneys.

Leigh was requested by the legislature to direct the compiling and publishing of the Code of Virginia of 1819, a systematic collection of the statutes of Virginia currently in operation. He was assisted in this project by William Waller Hening and William Munford.

In 1822 Leigh was commissioned by the legislature to represent Virginia in meetings with Henry Clay of Kentucky to negotiate a political solution to the legal controversy over conflicting claims resulting from Kentucky having been originally a part of Virginia. Their compromise plan, however, was not accepted by either state's legislature.

The partisan politics of his age disturbed Leigh, and he objected to the movement toward democracy. He was also a longtime enemy of the man who most represented the new age of the common man, Andrew Jackson. Leigh opposed absolute or arbitrary government, whether by a tyrant or a democracy, and he believed the former could easily result from the latter. Beginning with the raid into Spanish Florida, Leigh condemned Jackson for placing himself above the law. Leigh wrote essays against Jackson, which were printed in 1818 and 1819 in the Richmond *Enquirer*, the state's leading newspaper, under the pseudonym of "Algernon Sidney" and were published again during Jackson's presidency. Leigh contended that the popular support for Jackson's actions undermined stable government, law and order, and the protection of property. Because of his opposition to Jackson and the Democrats at the national level and in Virginia, Leigh associated himself with those who eventually became the Whigs, but he tried to remain independent and stay out of party politics. He believed that any party in government would abuse its power.

Leigh emerged in the 1820s as one of Virginia's leading defenders of the status quo. He wrote the leading work in opposition to the Democratic Reform movement, developed in the north and west of the state, which called for a convention to alter the state's constitution to end the dominance of the eastern gentry. In his *Substitute . . . on the Subject of a Convention* (1824), he defended Virginia's constitution as having passed the test of time: In "forms and principles of government, *Experience* alone can detect what is evil and approve what is good. That is our only sure guide." He contended that government would be unable to protect life, liberty, and happiness if it was made more democratic, because it would then change with the whims of the populace.

Leigh defended property qualifications for voting and the geographic representation of counties in the legislature. Voting, he stated, was not a right. Property gave a citizen a "manly independence." Noting that

only fifty acres were needed to qualify, Leigh declared, "If this be an aristocracy, it is the most open and most unguarded that ever existed: every man is free to acquire the patent of nobility."

Leigh resisted the idea of electoral districts and proportional representation. Not only were the people of Virginia distinct from the people of other states, the people in long-established counties each formed a separate and distinct community as well. The "people of every county" had their own "peculiar county character," and their local interests needed representation in the legislature.

In the state constitutional convention of 1829–1830, Leigh represented a district including Petersburg and the counties of Amelia, Chesterfield, Cumberland, Nottoway, and Powhatan. He became a leader of the conservatives, who succeeded in preserving an apportionment system that favored the planters.

In 1830–1831 Leigh again served in the House of Delegates, representing Henrico County. In 1833 he again represented Virginia in discussions with another state, this time trying to dissuade South Carolina from taking its nullification stance.

In 1834 the legislature chose Leigh to finish out a term in the U.S. Senate. In the Senate he denounced Jackson's actions of withdrawing government deposits from the Bank of the United States. Leigh narrowly won the next Senate election in the state legislature, in 1835, by two votes. After the legislature was firmly under the control of the Jackson Democrats, it instructed the state's senators to support Jackson in his "bank war." Leigh had supported the right of a state legislature to instruct its senators, but he believed a senator did not have to abide by the instructions if to do so would be a violation of the Constitution. In *Letter from B. W. Leigh to the General Assembly of Virginia* (1836), he contended that Jackson's actions against the Bank of the United States were unconstitutional, and it would be unconstitutional for congressmen to give the president their support. Leigh was censured by the legislature. Citing personal reasons, he resigned and left politics.

Leigh continued his law practice. Since 1829 he had been the court reporter for the Virginia Supreme Court of Appeals. He compiled volumes of the court reports, Leigh 1–12, to 1841. In 1835 he was honored with a doctorate in laws from the College of William and Mary.

Leigh was married three times: first to Mary Selden Watkins; second to Susan Colston, a niece of Chief Justice John Marshall; and third to Julia Wickham, a daughter of the highly successful Richmond lawyer, John Wickham. No other details about his marriages are available. Leigh had numerous children. He died in Richmond.

Prominent in the legal profession of his day, Leigh is known for his court reports. What distinguished him most, however, was his early articulation of a southern conservatism. He believed that the reform and changes he witnessed from the James Monroe presidency through the era of Jackson could only serve to destroy the foundation of government established by the Revolution.

• The Benjamin Watkins Leigh Papers are in the Virginia Historical Society. Along with the Virginia Court Reports, known as Leigh 1–12, several of the speeches Leigh delivered in the U.S. Senate in connection with Jackson's "bank war" were published. Leigh supervised the compiling of *The Revised Code of the Laws of Virginia: Being a Collection of All Such Acts of the General Assembly, of a Public and Permanent Nature, as Are Now in Force* (1819). He also wrote *The Letters of Algernon Sidney, in Defense of Civil Liberty and against the Encroachments of Military Despotism* (1830) and *Essays on the American System* (1831). See the biographical essay by Philip M. Grabill, Jr., in *The Virginia Law Reporters before 1880*, ed. William Hamilton Bryson (1977); and Earl G. Swem and John Williams, *A Register of the General Assembly of Virginia, 1776–1918, and of the Constitutional Conventions* (1911).

F. THORNTON MILLER

LEIGH, Vivien (5 Nov. 1913–8 July 1967), actress, was born Vivian Mary Hartley in Darjeeling, India, the daughter of Ernest Richard Hartley, a junior partner in a brokerage firm, and Gertrude Robinson. The family spent half the year in India and the other half in England until 1920, when they moved back to England permanently. Leigh was enrolled in the Convent of the Sacred Heart in Roehampton. There she discovered her lifelong passion for acting when, at age eight, she appeared as a fairy in a school production of *A Midsummer Night's Dream*. Academic classes held little appeal for her, but over the next few years she reveled in extra music and ballet lessons as well as appearing in school productions.

When Leigh was thirteen, her parents took her on an extended European tour that lasted five years and included finishing schools in Italy, Bavaria, and France. She acquired poise, an intimate acquaintance with international fashion design, and fluency in Italian, German, and French, and her knowledge of the arts expanded through visits to art galleries, opera, ballet, concerts, and theater. Included in her formal studies was time spent under the tutelage of Mlle Antoine at the Comedie Française.

At age eighteen she returned to England, richly endowed with every attribute likely to attract theatrical attention. Her physical grace, assurance, and vibrant but delicate beauty enabled her eventually to land her first big stage role. Meanwhile she continued her stage education by enrolling at the Royal Academy of Dramatic Art.

Theatrical aspirations came to a swift and abrupt end when, in December 1932, she married a rising young barrister, Herbert Leigh Holman. She assumed the role of fashionable wife until the arrival of her only child in October 1933. By the following year Leigh's acting ambitions were too strong to resist, and she was actively seeking theatrical work.

Her first break came in 1934, when she had one line in the film *Things Are Looking Up*. More small film parts followed, and she chose as her theatrical name

her husband's middle name and a variation of her own first name, Vivien Leigh.

The following year she had a small role in *The Green Sash* in the London suburbs. The play did not reach the West End, but Leigh attracted the attention of producer Sydney Carroll. When a beauty was needed for the leading role in Carroll's production of Carl Sternheim's *The Mask of Virtue*, the producer cast her. The play was not a success, but she was widely noticed and tagged by the press as an actress to watch.

Leigh's rave reviews caught the attention of Alexander Korda, who signed her to a five-year film contract. Despite her youth and inexperience, she was a true professional in her dedication to hard work and improving her craft, and throughout 1936 and 1937 she played a series of major stage roles.

In 1937 Korda finally cast her in the film *Fire over England*, which marked another major turning point. Acting with Laurence Olivier led to both love and valuable help and guidance in her theatrical development. By June 1937 Leigh was working for the Old Vic, acting Ophelia to Olivier's Hamlet. Working with the company, she received first-rate vocal tutelage and improved her rather light voice, gaining strength and authority. She costarred with Robert Taylor in *A Yank in Oxford* (1938), a joint British-American production and box-office hit.

In 1938, while both Leigh and Olivier were awaiting divorces so they could marry each other, Leigh followed Olivier to Hollywood, where he was filming *Wuthering Heights*. Through Olivier's influence, Leigh was allowed on the MGM set where David O. Selznick was filming the burning of Atlanta for *Gone with the Wind*. Again, as with her first stage break, Leigh's appearance deeply impressed the producer, and she won one of the most coveted roles in movie history, Scarlett O'Hara.

The 1939 film brought Leigh both an Oscar and international standing as a major film star, but the stage remained her first love and primary theatrical arena. In 1940, with both divorces final, she and Olivier married and began their exceptional theatrical collaboration with the 1941 film *Lady Hamilton*. She made her New York stage debut playing Juliet to Olivier's Romeo. The Second World War was raging in Europe, so they returned home, where Olivier joined the armed forces, and Leigh became a homemaker. In 1942 she appeared in George Bernard Shaw's *The Doctor's Dilemma*, and a year later she was off on a three-month tour of North Africa to entertain servicemen. In 1945 she began to suffer bouts of tuberculosis.

With the end of the war and the return of Olivier from his navy service, Leigh's stage career blossomed, and critics began to appreciate the authority and maturity she had gained. In 1945 she showed her capability to fill the stage with her presence in Thornton Wilder's *The Skin of Our Teeth*. Olivier was knighted in 1947, and the following year they both embarked on a grueling ten-month tour of Australia and New Zealand with the Old Vic company in a variety of classical roles. When they returned to London in 1949, Leigh appeared in *Antigone*, garnering critical plaudits for her maturity, vocal command, and force of character. She had become an international star of real stature.

Vivien Leigh was now in her theatrical prime, appreciated by audiences and critics alike. In October 1949 she thrilled audiences in another historic role, that of Blanche DuBois in the London production of *A Streetcar Named Desire*. Her subsequent film performance of the same role (1951) opposite Marlon Brando earned her a second Oscar. However, she preferred acting on stage with her husband. The years 1951 through 1955 yielded a series of challenges and triumphs for the two. Under their own joint management they performed *Caesar and Cleopatra* and *Anthony and Cleopatra* on alternate nights in London. They continued the arrangement in New York. This challenge enabled Leigh to show her extraordinary range, going from coy, kittenish adolescent in the Shaw play to smoldering, treacherous, sensual, intelligent adult in Shakespeare's work. They performed a season at Stratford-upon-Avon in 1955 and in 1957 a prestigious tour of European capitals in Peter Brook's production of *Titus Andronicus*. For her exceptional work Leigh received the knight's cross of the Legion of Honour in 1957.

After this strenuous decade her health began to suffer. At times she became hyperactive, lost control of herself, and berated Olivier in public. These episodes were reported to be an incurable physiological condition that could be expected to increase over time. The last straw came in 1957 when they were attending a debate in the House of Lords and she rose to protest the destruction of the St. James Theatre so violently that she had to be ushered out. Olivier gave up on the relationship, and they appeared on stage together for the last time in 1957. They were divorced in 1960.

Working without Olivier, Leigh continued to give fine performances. Despite her brilliance in classic and tragic roles, she was famous for her comic style and sense of timing. Her performances included roles in plays by Jean Giraudoux and Noël Coward, among others, and she won a new reputation in the Broadway musical *Tovarich* in 1963. Her last film appearance was in Stanley Kramer's *Ship of Fools* (1965). Her delicate constitution was unable to cope with the pace she set for herself, however, and her career suffered interruptions from nervous collapse and recurrences of tuberculosis. She was in rehearsal for the London production of Edward Albee's *A Delicate Balance* when she finally succumbed to tuberculosis. That night all the exterior lights of London's West End theaters were blacked out for an hour, and news of her death made the front page of the *New York Times*.

• Works on Leigh include Gwen Robyns, *Light of a Star* (1968); Alan Dent, *Vivien Leigh: A Bouquet* (1969); Anne Edwards, *Vivien Leigh: A Biography* (1979); Alexander Walker, *Vivien: The Life of Vivien Leigh* (1987); John Russell Taylor, *Vivien Leigh* (1984); Angus McBean, *Vivien: A Love Affair in Camera* (1989); and Hugo Vickers, *Vivien Leigh* (1988). There are also a number of works that deal with Leigh in relation to Olivier: Felix Barker, *The Oliviers* (1953); Jesse L. Lasky, with Pat Silver, *Love Scene: The Story of Laurence Olivier and Vivien Leigh* (1978); and Garry O'Connor, *Darlings of the Gods: One Year in the Lives of Laurence Olivier and Vivien Leigh* (1984). A brief critical view of Leigh's work in the role of Blanche DuBois is in Jordan Yale Miller, *Twentieth Century Interpretations of A Streetcar Named Desire* (1987). There is an extensive bibliography, Cynthia Maryle Molt, *Vivien Leigh: A Bio-bibliography* (1992), and a journal article, Derek Cross, "A Lass Unparallel'd: A Tribute to Vivien Leigh," *Performing Arts* 24, no. 12 (1 Dec. 1990): 21. Since Leigh was an actress, it might also be noted that there are biographical videos. An extensive obituary is in the *New York Times*, 8 July 1967.

CARY CLASZ

LEIGH, William Robinson (23 Sept. 1866–11 Mar. 1955), illustrator and artist, was born at Falling Waters, West Virginia, the son of William Leigh, a Confederate officer and plantation owner, and Mary White Colston. In the aftermath of the Civil War the family's fortunes did not permit him to have a private tutor or attend grammar school while he was growing up at "Maidstone," the family's plantation in West Virginia. His mother became his tutor, and she encouraged him to develop his artistic interests. Her careful stewardship of the family's limited resources allowed Leigh to study art at the Maryland Institute of Art in Baltimore. Because he showed promise as an artist, two of Leigh's uncles provided support for him to study at the Royal Academy of Fine Arts in Munich, Germany. Although Leigh wanted to study in Paris, the expenses of living in the French capital exceeded his resources. From 1883 until 1896 he studied in Munich and acquired the characteristics of that school, mastering draftsmanship, acquiring a lasting taste for realism and genre paintings, and developing a romantic, yet disciplined approach to subject matter. At the academy in Munich he frequently won bronze medals for his work; and although he could not afford live models, he became proficient in drawing and painting from photographs, a practice that was useful to him throughout his career. When resources from home began to wane, he maintained himself by painting six large-scale, revolving cycloramas including the *Battle of Waterloo* and the *Crucifixion of Christ*.

Unable to support himself by painting when he returned to the United States in 1896, Leigh became an illustrator. Although he initially had little interest in preparing sketches and drawings for magazines, his well-defined and distinctive skills as a draftsman and his attention to detail enabled him to become within a decade one of the nation's most successful illustrators. His work appeared in *Collier's*, *Harper's*, and *McClure's Magazine*, and he also began to receive occasional commissions for portraits. In November 1899 Leigh married Anna Seng; they had one child but were divorced in 1903.

In 1906 Leigh made his first trip to New Mexico and entered a region that nourished his artistic imagination for the rest of his life. His visits to the pueblos of Laguna, Acoma, and Zuñi introduced him to the beauty and interest of Native Americans and their villages and the majestic topography of the Southwest. He returned to the Southwest each summer from 1906 to 1909 and completed landscape paintings of this area commissioned by the Santa Fe Railroad to promote travel and to adorn railroad publications, marketing materials, and dining car menus. These landscapes included *Grand Canyon at Sunset*, *Grand Canyon at Sunrise*, and *The Grand Canyon of the Colorado*. Until his death he made almost yearly trips into this region to make sketches, studies, and photographs that he later developed into paintings in his studio. Although he had been trained at Munich as a genre painter, the majority of his paintings from 1906 to 1914 were landscapes.

In 1910 Leigh began to shift the focus of his western trips, and he traveled into the northern Rocky Mountains and the Yellowstone country. In 1912 he painted one of his most famous works, a classic of American hunting art titled *A Close Call*, a meticulous and detailed delineation of a fallen hunter threatened by a grizzly bear held at bay by the hunter's pack of dogs.

Seeking opportunities to exhibit his paintings, Leigh joined with other struggling artists in 1914 to form the Allied Artists of America. With the outbreak of World War I Leigh encountered difficulties supporting himself by selling his paintings and illustrations, so he worked for a while painting backdrops for theater and stage productions. In 1916 he visited Arizona, spending time at Hubbell's Trading Post near Ganado and exploring Canyon de Chelly. Sketches and photographs from this trip were the basis of most of his paintings for the next five years. This trip introduced him to the world of the Navajo and the Hopi. They became so prominent in his paintings that he became identified with them for the remainder of his career. This region and its natives nurtured not only his painterly passions but also his literary instincts; by 1922 he was publishing short stories about the peoples of this region. He became a prolific author, writing plays, poems, essays, short stories, and articles, many of which are extant but unpublished. As the economy improved with the conclusion of the war, Leigh gained prominence once more as an illustrator.

In 1921 Leigh married Ethel Traphagen; they had no children. Each contributed to the professional success of the other. Leigh helped his wife establish the Traphagen School of Fashion and Design in New York City and taught there, and she aggressively promoted his career and paintings through the magazine that she published, *Fashion Digest*. In 1926 Leigh joined an American Museum of Natural History expedition to Africa. Led by Carl Akeley, this fourteen-month expedition collected specimens, artifacts, sketches, and photographs for ten habitat groups it was preparing for the museum's African Hall. From 1932 until 1935 Leigh supervised the preparation of the large murals for the African Hall exhibits. Talented in his portrayals of animals, he revealed his skill in capturing both African animals and the environmental setting for the wildlife of that continent in these habitat dioramas.

In 1930 Leigh published his play *Clipt Wings*. Although never produced despite his best efforts, this work proposed that Shakespeare's plays and sonnets were written by Francis Bacon. Painting became less important to Leigh in the 1930s as he sought to support himself both by painting and writing. He published two books: *The Western Pony* (1933) examined the role of the mustang in the life of the Navajo, while *Frontiers of Enchantment* (1938) was a carefully crafted description of his African experiences.

In spite of his interest in literature, in the 1940s Leigh enjoyed more success and artistic recognition than he had yet known. He became identified as a popular western painter and was often praised as a peer of Frederic Remington and Charles M. Russell. He received commissions for large murals whose prices exceeded those he was receiving for his largest paintings, which sold for about $10,000. Even in his eighties, he was a remarkably active painter, producing more than seventy-five paintings from 1948 to 1950. In 1955 he was elected to full membership in the National Academy of Design. Dynamic in his approach to life and energetic in confronting what he believed were the inadequacies of modern art and the limitations of capitalism, he had become a popular dinner speaker and lecturer. Strongly individualistic, he criticized the nation's founding fathers, the U.S. Constitution, and contemporary artists who produced a work that he maintained "disfigured the wall on which it hung." Suspicious of religion and committed to nonconformity, he had become in 1915 a charter member of the Freethinkers of America and even developed his own Ten Commandments, which argued that "Thou shalt have no other God but Commonsense" and concluded with "Thou shalt not destroy thy self-respect." Leigh died in New York City after a day of work at his easel.

Painting almost every subject found in the American Southwest, Leigh created works that are characterized by a warm palette, strong lines, romantic definition, and graphic realism. He had received more academic training than any other western artist of his era and possessed the most highly developed technical skills of those painters who sought to portray the final phases of the frontier West. Leigh refused to acknowledge contemporary movements in American art, and as a result, there are few impressionistic or abstract themes in his paintings. His work contributed significantly to the artistic discovery of the beauty of canyon lands and deserts of the Navajo and Hopi and their people.

• The most extensive collection of his manuscript materials may be found in the Thomas Gilcrease Institute of American History and Art in Tulsa, Okla., which acquired his studio and contains the most extensive holding of his paintings, drawings, sketches, and unpublished articles, books, and poems. D. Duane Cummins, *William Robinson Leigh, Western Artist* (1980), presents a detailed and scholary examination of his life. June DuBois, *W. R. Leigh* (1977), provides not only a survey of his life but also numerous examples of his paintings. See also David C. Hunt, "W. R. Leigh, Portfolio of an American Artist," *American Scene* 7, no. 1 (1966); Donnie D.

Good, "W. R. Leigh, the Artists Studio Collection," *American Scene* 9, no. 4 (1968); and Michael Kennedy, "W. R. Leigh, Sagebrush Rembrandt," *Montana: Magazine of Western History*, Winter 1956, pp. 38–54. An obituary is in the *New York Times*, 13 Mar. 1955.

PHILLIP DRENNON THOMAS

LEINSDORF, Erich (4 Feb. 1912–11 Sept. 1993), conductor and pianist, was born Erich Landauer in Vienna, the son of Julius Ludwig Landauer, a pianist, and Charlotte Lobl. His father died when Erich was three. Erich began his music education during his elementary school years and became a serious piano student by the age of seven. Later he took specialized music training at the University of Vienna, graduating in 1930, and at Vienna's Music Academy, where he obtained his diploma in 1933. His courses included studies of the piano and cello, as well as composition classes.

From 1932 through 1934 Leinsdorf became Anton Webern's rehearsal pianist at the time when Webern was conductor of the Singverein der Sozialdemokratischen Kunstelle and with them made his professional debut performing Stravinsky's *Les Noces* in 1933. After his debut he became Bruno Walter's assistant at the Salzburg Music Festival in 1934, and when Arturo Toscanini needed a pianist, he called on Leinsdorf to play Kodaly's *Psalmus Hungaricus*, which Leinsdorf had studied and performed with Webern. He continued to assist Walter and Toscanini at Salzburg until 1937, when he was recommended for a conducting position with New York's Metropolitan Opera. Leinsdorf made his American debut in 1938 at the Metropolitan Opera (the Met) performing Wagner's *Die Walkure* when he was just twenty-five years old. In 1939 he married Anne Frohnknecht, with whom he had five children. He continued to perform in New York, conducting Strauss's *Elektra* and other Wagner operas, and because of his reputation and experience, he was appointed head of the Met's German repertory. He remained at the Met until 1943 at the insistence of management, though Leinsdorf's reputation for long rehearsals and his lack of restraint in criticizing a performance won him few supporters among singers and orchestra members.

In 1943 Leinsdorf was hired to direct the Cleveland Orchestra in Ohio, but his fiery temperament and insistence on tight control of musical matters led the orchestra to seek someone more to their liking a year later. After this, Leinsdorf searched for permanent conducting positions, mainly with United States orchestras. He worked again briefly with the Metropolitan Opera after leaving the Cleveland Orchestra and accepted several guest appearances before moving to Rochester, New York, and becoming director of the Rochester Philharmonic in 1946. During his tenure there, Leinsdorf and the Philharmonic made a series of recordings that brought the city much musical notoriety. He directed the Rochester Philharmonic until 1956.

After leaving Rochester, Leinsdorf once more turned to the world of opera, accepting directorships, which again were of short duration. He became director of the New York City Opera in 1956, but in 1957 he returned to the Metropolitan Opera as conductor. He stayed in New York until 1962, when the Boston Symphony asked him to succeed Charles Munch as their musical director. Along with this post came the responsibility for the orchestra's summer concerts at the Tanglewood Music Festival, among which were some of Leinsdorf's greatest successes with the orchestra. Though there were clear objections from members of the orchestra, Leinsdorf continued his directive for discipline and hard work from all performers. He increased both the number and duration of rehearsals and expected more discipline from the orchestra members. This drive and discipline made it possible for Leinsdorf to introduce many new works to the public, including Benjamin Britten's *War Requiem* in 1963. These attempts to expand the orchestra's repertory with new material and to require more exacting performances from the players, however, contributed to the scarceness of the praise that he received from members of the orchestra and the press. When it became clear that he was no longer welcome, Leinsdorf left the Boston Symphony in 1969 to tour and make guest appearances with orchestras and opera companies in other parts of the world. Leinsdorf and his first wife were divorced in 1968, and later that year he married Vera Graf, a violinist.

After leaving Boston, Leinsdorf made his living primarily as a guest conductor, touring with the world's major orchestras for several weeks at a time. During these years he focused his energies on concert music rather than opera, and except for a brief tenure as the principal conductor of the (West) Berlin Radio Symphony Orchestra from 1978 to 1980, he avoided the burdens of a permanent appointment. He also accepted contracts during this time to record Debussy and Stravinsky in 1985 with the Los Angeles Philharmonic as well as the Mozart Symphonies with the Los Angeles Philharmonic in 1988.

Leinsdorf also authored two books after leaving his post at Boston. The first, *Cadenza: A Musical Career*, written in 1976, was a look at his conducting career and a candid description of his musical strengths and administrative weaknesses in dealing with orchestra management and performers' unions. The second, *The Composer's Advocate: A Radical Orthodoxy for Musicians*, published in 1981, outlined his methodical approach to conducting, describing what a conductor needs to know and do to lead a symphony orchestra. Both books were warmly received, and Leinsdorf was praised by critics for his clarity, wit, and forthrightness.

Leinsdorf remained active in the world of music until his death at his home in Zurich. He was best known for his systematic approach to conducting and for a strident, sometimes offensive intelligence. He combined a thorough learning of the music with a disdain for the melodramatic effects and shortcomings of some of his contemporaries. A leading conductor of both American and European orchestras, Leinsdorf's rigorous standards for the conductor's podium, recording studio, and written word won him many honors, including a fellowship in the American Academy of Arts and Sciences.

• For the most complete work on Leinsdorf, see his autobiography, *Cadenza: A Musical Career* (1976). A biographical sketch is in the *Atlantic Monthly* 210 (1962): 111–14. An obituary is in the *New York Times*, 12 Sept. 1993.

DONNA H. LEHMAN

LEIPZIGER, Henry Marcus (29 Dec. 1854–1 Dec. 1917), educator and Jewish civic leader, was born in Manchester, England, the son of Marcus Leipziger, a small businessman, and Martha Samuel. He immigrated to New York City in 1865 with his father, stepmother (Harriet Solomon), and sister. He attended New York's public schools (1865–1868), the College of the City of New York (A.B. and B.S., 1868–1873), and Columbia Law School (LL.B., 1875). In 1882 he earned an M.A. from the College of the City of New York, and in 1888 he received his Ph.D. from Columbia University with a dissertation entitled, "The Philosophy of the New Education."

Leipziger started his full-time teaching career at Grammar School No. 16 in the city's 9th Ward (1874–1880). After admission to the bar (1875) he also did part-time legal work. In the winter of 1880–1881 he took gravely ill, most probably with tuberculosis. His three-year illness left him permanently frail.

In 1884, when Leipziger resumed his career, it was as an ardent advocate of the New Education (precursor of progressive education), which was concerned with the whole child—hand and eye as well as mind. In 1884 he convinced several prominent Jewish philanthropists to found the Hebrew Technical Institute and became its first director (1884–1891). The institute served boys of the rapidly growing East European Jewish immigrant community, preparing them for productive work as artisans and craftsmen. The instructional program that Leipziger developed, influenced by the New Education, became a model for technical schools.

In 1890 Leipziger returned to the New York City schools as part-time supervisor of adult lectures, and from 1891 to 1896 he was full-time assistant superintendent of schools in charge of organizing, administering, and supervising the lecture program.

The Adult Free Lectures were founded in 1889 with 186 lectures presented to 22,000 auditors. From this modest base Leipziger, a meticulous administrator who headed this free public-lecture system until his death, developed a program that at its height (1902–1909) reached well over a million listeners at over 5,000 lectures. The lectures served all economic classes and all neighborhoods. In 1903, after years of lobbying, Leipziger convinced the Board of Education to offer lectures in Yiddish, Italian, and German. The lectures spread knowledge of America, encouraged immigrants to learn English, and helped them cope with their new environment.

Lectures were given on health, hygiene, cultural, social, literary, and scientific topics, some in conjunction with leading colleges and charitable and cultural institutions. Later, in addition to single lectures, Leipziger organized courses of lectures with their own syllabi, final examinations, and certificates. Several of these courses, including one for elementary teachers, were given in collaboration with the College of the City of New York. They became the base on which the college built its extension program.

Leipziger insisted that lectures be illustrated when possible with slides, scientific experiments, books, pamphlets, and music, and he was an early champion of moving pictures for instruction. Just before the turn of the century he initiated the highly successful "platform library" in conjunction with the New York Free Circulating Library so that books related to a lecture could be borrowed at the close of a session. Lecturers were drawn from the city's colleges, universities, and museums, and in a break with tradition, he employed women. Among occasional lecturers were Theodore Roosevelt (1858–1919), Woodrow Wilson, G. Stanley Hall, William R. Harper, and Seth Low.

To realize his "university of the people," a "university without walls," Leipziger pressed for the wider use of the schoolhouse. The five-hour day, five-day week school had to go. "Why should the people have to hire a hall when they have these buildings built by their own money for their own use?" (quoted in Frankel, pp. 118f.) In the quest for lifelong learning, "the adult must continue to go to school and the schoolhouse thus becomes the chief factor in the civic life of our community. Here all divisions of race and religion are obliterated. Here citizens meet to discuss the welfare of the neighborhood or the policy of the nation" (quoted in Frankel, p. 144.)

Leipziger was also an active participant in New York's Jewish community. He considered entering the rabbinate and for much of his life guest lectured in the pulpits of leading Reform congregations; he was a longtime Sunday School teacher at Temple Emanu-El and a member of the board of Hebrew Union College. He participated in the founding of the Young Men's Hebrew Association (1874) and was a founding member (1886) and officer of the Aguilar Free Library, which served immigrant Jewish districts of Manhattan, a director and chairman of the library committee of the Educational Alliance, and a founding member and vice president of the Jewish Publication Society of America. He was founding president from 1897 until his death of the Judeans, intellectual and professional leaders who sought to represent the interests of Jewish culture in the broader community.

Leipziger never married. He lived with his stepmother and sister, a librarian, and maintained close ties with his two nieces, the children of his younger brother. He died in New York City.

The "Leipziger Lectures," as they came to be called, barely outlived their namesake. Their demise was brought about by budget cuts during World War I, the absence of a dynamic successor, lack of interest among board members confronted with a rapidly growing school system, and new technologies, especially motion pictures and later radio, which competed for the free time of adults. Leipziger's influence on the education of adults, however, was reflected in the growth of evening division and extension programs at public schools, colleges, universities, and cultural institutions. Leipziger combined the American progressive's faith that education could materially and morally improve individuals and society with the Jewish Enlightenment's belief in the liberating and redemptive value of modern learning.

• Leipziger's papers are in the Rare Books and Manuscripts Collection, New York Public Library. Documents and official reports of the Adult Free Lectures are located in the New York City Board of Education Archives, Special Collections, Milbank Memorial Library, Teachers College, Columbia University. Ruth L. Frankel, Leipziger's niece, provides a flattering portrait of him in the only book-length treatment of his life and work, *Henry M. Leipziger, Educator and Idealist* (1933). For a discussion of the Adult Free Lectures, especially those intended for immigrants, see chapter 7 of Stephan F. Brumberg, *Going to America, Going to School: The Jewish Immigrant Public School Encounter in Turn-of-the-Century New York City* (1986). An obituary is in the *New York Times*, 2 Dec. 1917; a eulogy is in the *City College Quarterly*, Mar. 1918.

STEPHAN F. BRUMBERG

LEISEN, Mitchell (6 Oct. 1898–28 Oct. 1972), film director, was born in Menominee, Michigan, the son of a brewery owner. Leisen's parents (names unknown) were divorced within a few years of his birth, and he was raised by his mother and her second husband in St. Louis, Missouri. Leisen was born clubfooted, which may have caused him to become a solitary child. Early on, he designed floral arrangements and model theaters, but his parents considered such interests effeminate and sent him to military school.

Leisen subsequently enrolled at Washington University in St. Louis, where he studied fine arts and architecture, graduating before he reached twenty-one. His first job was in the *Chicago Tribune* advertising department, after which he worked for a Chicago architectural firm and spent his free hours acting with a local theater group.

In 1919 Leisen traveled to Hollywood to take a stab at film acting, but only a single minor part came his way. However, the stage sets he designed for the Hollywood Community Theatre interested the important director Cecil B. De Mille, who invited him to design clothing for rising star Gloria Swanson. From that point Leisen went on to create the wardrobes for several De Mille films.

In 1922 action star Douglas Fairbanks hired Leisen to design the costumes for such period films as *Robin Hood* (1922) and *The Thief of Bagdad* (1924). During that period Leisen became romantically linked with actress Marguerite De La Motte, although they never married. He did marry aspiring opera singer Sondra Gahle around that time and formally remained her husband until their divorce in 1942. They had no children. Over the span of his marriage, Leisen, a bisexual, rarely lived with Gahle and carried on affairs both with men and with other women.

Leisen returned to De Mille's production staff in 1925. Within two years he was chief art director for all of the filmmaker's projects—some twenty major motion pictures. On four films Leisen served as an assistant director. Finally, in 1933, he broke free of De Mille and directed several well-crafted apprentice films for Paramount, his employer for most of his career.

In 1934 Leisen directed *Murder at the Vanities*, a bizarre movie melding murder detection, bawdy comedy, implied nudity, and lavish musical production numbers. Featured in the film—remarkably—was the song "Sweet Marijuana."

Hands across the Table (1935), starring Carole Lombard, marked the first time that Leisen's best directorial qualities came together to form a captivating, socially insightful romantic comedy. In it Leisen revealed an eye for stunning visuals, a sure use of details and pacing, and an intimate rapport with his female star. Along with *Easy Living* and *Swing High—Swing Low* (both 1937), *Hands across the Table* anticipated the superb films that he directed from 1939 through 1946.

The first of these, *Midnight* (1939), is considered by many critics to be Leisen's finest picture and one of the three or four best screwball comedies of the 1930s. One reviewer called it "a genuinely great film . . . the swansong of Thirties comedy." On the heels of *Midnight* came the glowing *Remember the Night* (1940), written by Preston Sturges, and *Arise My Love* (1940), scripted by the team of Charles Brackett and Billy Wilder. In addition, 1941 saw one of Leisen's biggest box-office hits, *I Wanted Wings*, which contained breakthrough aerial photography and introduced the wartime sensation Veronica Lake and her peekaboo hairdo.

Hold Back the Dawn (1941) was a departure for Leisen, a moving drama in the form of a love story focusing on the plight of Nazism's European victims. *No Time for Love* was one of a trio of light comedies in 1942–1943 that flowed from Leisen's sharp-edged views on the battle of the sexes. *Kitty* (1945), a satire of the Pygmalion theme, embodied Leisen's most confident direction in the film's lively ensemble acting, its tour de force use of the camera, and what one British critic called the most authentic rendering of Regency England ever achieved in a Hollywood movie. *To Each His Own* (1946) was that decade's quintessential "woman's picture"; it stayed clear of easy sentimentality through the script's perceptive characterizations, Leisen's beautifully composed screen images, and the assured acting of Olivia De Havilland in her first Oscar-winning role.

Besides De Havilland, some of the finest actresses in the Hollywood of that era responded to Leisen's guidance with their best work, including Jean Arthur, Marlene Dietrich (twice), Joan Fontaine (twice), Lombard (twice), Barbara Stanwyck (twice), and Claudette Colbert (five times). Leisen even managed to coax better-than-routine performances from Paulette Goddard, admittedly a mediocre actress, in *Hold Back the Dawn* and *Kitty*. He tried his best with Ginger Rogers, too, but they repeatedly quarreled on the set of *Lady in the Dark* (1944), his most ambitious but his own least favorite picture, which, ironically, was his greatest commercial success.

In the later 1930s Leisen had become exclusively homosexual, entering an affair with youthful dancer Billy Daniels; their intimate relationship lasted until the mid-1950s. Some of Leisen's longtime friends warned him that Daniels was using him to advance his own ambitions. Whether those claims were true or not, it was apparent by the postwar years that the relationship was taking a disturbing toll on Leisen's creative talents. This and other factors undermined his career. For instance, his style of thoughtful, subtle romantic comedy no longer was in vogue with audiences. Also, the quality of scripts he was asked to direct declined. But something ineffable, possibly stemming from his private life, was also missing from Leisen's directorial palette.

After *To Each His Own* Leisen directed an unlucky thirteen films. A handful of them showed the earmarks of his distinctive craft, but only a striking film noir, *No Man of Her Own* (1950), matched his better efforts of earlier years. After leaving Paramount in 1954 Leisen turned to television work for a time in addition to directing two independently contracted films. He soon was devoting all of his attention to a men's clothing store in Beverly Hills and the design of residential interiors. By the early 1960s his health was deteriorating. He was plagued with ulcers, failing eyesight, and emphysema, and in 1970 one of his legs had to be amputated. He died in Woodland Hills, California.

Until the 1980s Leisen was a forgotten man among Hollywood's front-line directors. Since then, however, his reputation has risen steadily, until today many critics value him as one of the finest filmmakers of his era. His directorial legacy includes two minor masterpieces (*Midnight* and *Hold Back the Dawn*), six or seven first-rank romantic comedies, a classic woman's picture, and a memorable film noir. Leisen's long-lasting critical standing seems assured.

• David Chierichetti, *Hollywood Director: The Career of Mitchell Leisen* (1973), based on lengthy interviews with Leisen, is essential. Unfortunately, the book is out of print and difficult to find, even in major research libraries. In its stead an insightful article by Dennis Drabelle, "Swing High, Swing Low: Mitchell Leisen in Perspective," *Film Comment*, Sept.– Oct. 1994, pp. 8–18, tries to fill in some of the pieces missing from other survey studies of Leisen's life and career. Interesting and useful general articles on Leisen can be found in John Wakeman, ed., *World Film Directors*, vol. 1: *1890–1945* (1987); the Yann Tobin entry in Jean-Pierre Coursodon, *American Directors*, vol. 1 (1983); and David Thomson, *A Biographical Dictionary of Film*, 3d ed. (1994). See also the John Baxter entry on Leisen in *The International Dictionary of Films and Filmmakers*, vol. 2: *Directors/Filmmakers*, ed.

Christopher Lyon (1984), and Baxter's *Hollywood in the Thirties* (1968). A sketchy though largely accurate obituary is in the *New York Times*, 1 Nov. 1972.

ROBERT MIRANDON

LEISLER, Jacob (bap. 31 Mar. 1640–16 May 1691), merchant and de facto lieutenant governor of New York, was born in Frankfurt-am-Main, Germany, the son of Rev. Jacob Victorian Leisler, minister of the Frankfurt French Reformed congregation, and Susanna Adelheid Wissenbach. The family was of the magisterial class. In 1637 Rev. Leisler fled the imposition of the Inquisition in Spanish-occupied Frankenthal, in which city he was minister to the Huguenot community. He sought refuge in Kreuznach. The following year he was called to be minister of Frankfurt's French congregation. Because the Lutheran Frankfurt council forbade the practice of the Reformed religion within city walls, the French congregation gathered in the nearby suburb of Bockenheim. Leisler's youth was thus shaped by his family's social position, his father's Calvinist convictions, and the turmoil of the Thirty Years' War.

In 1653 Rev. Leisler died. Shortly thereafter the family moved to Hanau, and Jacob was sent to a Protestant military academy. In the winter of 1658–1659 he moved to Amsterdam. In June 1659 he appears in the Dutch West India Company records as a verifier of Dutch-English translations for company shareholder Cornelis Melyn. The following year the West India Company named him an officer of the troops being sent to New Netherland, and on 27 April 1660 he sailed for the New World.

Shortly after his arrival in New Amsterdam, Leisler entered into the fur and tobacco trade. He later added salt, grain products, fish, whale oil, and horses to his export trade and spices, human cargoes (indentured and slave), finished cloth, and trade goods to his import business. With his 1663 marriage to Elsie Tymens van der Veen, the widow of a ship's carpenter, Leisler united with an evolving elite in New Netherland. They had seven children. By this time he was one of the wealthiest men in the colony.

After his marriage Leisler began to invest his excess capital in land; by the 1680s he was one of New York's largest property holders. His single-gabled renaissance-style town house, built adjacent to Petrus Stuyvesant's town house, was one of New York City's most impressive residences. In addition to numerous rental properties scattered throughout the city, one of the city's bolting mills, and a large farm encompassing present-day City Hall Park, Leisler acquired through marriage, outright purchase, or partnership shares in extensive properties on Long Island, in Westchester County, and in East Jersey, as well as in England and on the Continent.

Leisler's wealth and social position made him a prominent member of the New York community. In August 1664 he was among the signatories of a remonstrance urging Petrus Stuyvesant to surrender New Netherland to the English, and a month later he was one of the first to swear allegiance to the new regime. Thereafter he frequently served as a juror and court-appointed arbitrator in the English legal system. With the Dutch recapture of New York in 1673, Dutch governor Anthony Colve appointed Leisler to make a survey of the province's fortifications, named him a tax assessor, and used him in other advisory capacities. Leisler remained active in the government after the Treaty of Westminster restored New York to the English in 1674. In 1677 Maryland governor Thomas Notely named him as the Maryland government's New York agent. While on a voyage to Europe in the fall of that year, Leisler was captured by Algerians but swiftly obtained the ransom for his release and returned to New York in 1678. Under Roman Catholic governor Thomas Dongan Leisler's appointments increased. Dongan appointed him a commissioner to the admiralty court (1683), a New York County justice of the peace (1685), and asked him to prepare the king's evidence in cases appearing before the court of sessions (1684). Leisler also acted as Suffolk County's agent to the provincial government. Moreover, he served under both Dutch and English administrations as a militia captain and by the 1680s was recognized as the senior captain in command.

Despite his various commissions, Leisler does not appear to have been politically motivated except on behalf of Calvinist orthodoxy. A member of the New York City Dutch Reformed Church since 1661, he was by 1670 a deacon and a member of the New York consistory. Leisler's religious activism came to the fore in 1676 when Albany minister Rev. Nicholas Van Rensselaer sued him, along with New York City merchant Jacob Milborne, for having declared that Van Rensselaer's preaching did not conform to Reformed tenets. At issue was the government's appointment of Van Rensselaer to the pulpit—an act repugnant to Calvinists, who held that a minister must be called by the congregation. The suit divided the province before ending by command of the governor. When Louis XIV revoked the Edict of Nantes in 1685, Leisler became well known for his efforts on behalf of Huguenot refugees, founding the town of New Rochelle on their behalf. In that year he left the Dutch church, and it is said he became a founding elder of New York City's first French Reformed congregation.

When in July 1688 James II annexed New York to the Dominion of New England, New Yorkers' simmering discontent with the Catholicizing and centralizing tendencies of the Stuart monarchy intensified. The province was therefore ripe for rebellion when word arrived the following winter that William, the Protestant Prince of Orange, had invaded England. While it does not appear that Leisler instigated rebellion in New York, he apparently knew in advance of the Prince of Orange's plans. The family firm of Leisler, Sarasin und Leisler served as banker to the duchy of Württemburg, and a sister was married into the court of Brandenburg-Prussia, and indications are that Leisler was kept well informed of European events. Boston's April 1689 overthrow of James II's dominion governor, Sir Edmund Andros, left New York lieutenant governor Francis Nicholson to continue alone. Nicholson appointed Leisler to an expanded council to protect New York from foreign invasion in the wake of the unrest. Leisler's subsequent discovery that Nicholson was continuing to receive directives from the imprisoned Andros caused him to withdraw his allegiance from Nicholson, but he did not join with the rebels.

On 31 May 1689, the New York militia revolted and seized Fort James. Leisler's role in the revolt is unclear, but two days later he emerged as the leader of the Orangist faction. Nicholson's subsequent flight from the province and the continuing reluctance of James II's three New York dominion councilors—Stephanus Van Cortlandt, Nicholas Bayard, and Frederick Philipse—to declare for the new Protestant monarch left a governmental vacuum. A provincial committee of safety was called, and on 27 June representatives from several East Jersey and all New York counties except Ulster and Albany began to meet in New York City. On 28 June the committee designated Leisler captain of the fort and on 16 August appointed him commander in chief of the province.

Leisler vigorously undertook the strengthening of the province's fortifications, struck a seal, called for local elections, and began the first codification of New York's laws. In the meantime, Bayard and Van Cortlandt fled to Albany where they organized a government in exile and issued a torrent of anti-Leisler propaganda. In October Leisler sent troops under the command of Jacob Milborne to subdue Albany. The expedition met with defeat when Mohawks loyal to that city threatened to attack Milborne's troops.

In December 1689 royal letters addressed to Francis Nicholson, "or in his absence, to such as for the time being takes care for preserving the peace and administering the laws" arrived. Notified by Massachusetts governor Simon Bradstreet that he was the intended recipient, Leisler seized the letters and assumed the title of lieutenant governor. Dismissing the committee of safety and forming a council, Leisler undertook a purge of his opposition (including the imprisonment of archrival Nicholas Bayard), issued hundreds of new commissions, and called a provincial assembly. In February 1690 a French and Indian massacre of the frontier community of Schenectady realized the worst fears in Protestant New York of a Catholic menace. While Leisler oversaw relief efforts, he began imprisoning all suspected "Papists" and their sympathizers. Shortly thereafter Albany capitulated to Leisler. To deal with French Quebec, Leisler then called for a convention of all the colonial governments. On 1 May 1690, delegates from Massachusetts, Plymouth, Connecticut, and New York met in New York City, while Maryland and Barbados responded by letter. This would be the first attempt by the colonies to create an independent military union. Leisler's plan for a two-pronged attack against Quebec was adopted by the convention, with Leisler recognized by all the participating governments as commander in chief.

In the meantime, Leisler suffered a series of setbacks that would have dire consequences. His initial letters to William III had been captured by the French, and Francis Nicholson was able to present his case to the government first. In September 1689, Henry Sloughter, who viewed Leisler unfavorably, was appointed governor, and Nicholson's old council was reappointed. The mission of Leisler's ambassador, Joost Stol, was a disaster. Stol managed to present his papers to the king who turned them over to the Tory-dominated Lords of Trade before leaving for the Continent. At that time a growing reaction in England to William's "Dutch Invasion" caused the Tories to look with hostility on all foreigners, and the government's impartial directives regarding Leisler were altered by the Lords in the king's absence because Leisler was "a Walloon." The arrival in June 1690 of news that Nicholson had been appointed lieutenant governor of Virginia gave encouragement to Leisler's enemies, and a riot ensued in New York City in which Leisler was personally attacked. Shortly thereafter the land campaign against Quebec under the command of Fitz-John Winthrop (1638–1707) collapsed. Leisler imprisoned Winthrop for failing to follow orders, thus alienating his New England allies. By the fall of 1690 Leisler's increasingly autocratic government was bitterly dividing the population.

Administrative difficulties delayed the sailing of Henry Sloughter and two companies of regular soldiers. The latter, separated from Sloughter, arrived in New York in January 1691 under Captain Richard Ingoldesby. Ingoldesby, with no authority other than a military commission, demanded that Leisler turn over the fort, which Leisler refused to do without proper orders. For nearly two months New York hovered on the brink of civil war, with Leisler's adherents in the fort and Ingoldesby's soldiers, joined by Leisler's enemies, in the town. On 17 March shots were exchanged, during which six persons were killed. Two days later, Sloughter arrived, proclaimed his commission, and again demanded the fort's surrender. As it was night, Leisler, following Continental rules of war, refused to do so until daylight. When he surrendered the following morning, Sloughter had him arrested. A court consisting of Leisler's enemies was hastily convened, and Leisler along with his council were brought to trial. Leisler refused to plead during the trial until the question of his authority was settled. Thus, tried as a mute, he was found guilty of treason and on 16 May 1691 hanged and then beheaded along with Jacob Milborne, who three months previously had become his son-in-law.

The executions of Leisler and Milborne shocked many in America and Europe, and an international campaign was undertaken to clear their names. In August 1691 the Court of Holland held an inquest into the executions and began to apply pressure on the English government. At the instigation of William III, Parliament in 1695 reversed the New York court's sentences and legitimized Leisler's administration. In 1702 the New York assembly voted an indemnity of £2,700 to his heirs. Nonetheless, bitter divisions between Leislerians and anti-Leislerians continued to divide New York's politics well into the eighteenth century.

Leisler was a man of deep convictions and stubborn disposition. The passions he aroused in both his admirers and his enemies have ensured that he remains a topic of controversy.

• Major collections of Leisler's papers are in the New York State Archives, the New-York Historical Society, the Pennsylvania Historical Society, and the Connecticut State Library. European collections include the Public Records Office, Kew Gardens, and the Amsterdam Gemeentearchiv. Related family materials may be found in the Franzosich-reformierte Gemeinde collections of the Frankfurt Stadtarchiv and Staatsarchif des Kantons Basel-Stadt. Published collections of Leisler's correspondence include Edmund B. O'Callaghan et al., eds., *Documentary History of the State of New-York*, vol. 2 (1849), and the *Collections of the New-York Historical Society* (1868). Three tracts dealing with Leisler's administration are in Charles M. Andrews, ed., *Narratives of the Insurrections 1675–1690* (1915). No adequate biography of Leisler exists. For biographical data see Else Toennies-Volhard, *Die Familie Leissler in ihrer Beziehung zu den familien Volhard und Waechter* (1930); David William Voorhees, "European Ancestry of Jacob Leisler," *The New York Genealogical and Biographical Record* 120 (October 1989): 193–202; and Edwin R. Purple, *Genealogical Notes Relating to Lieut.-Gov. Jacob Leisler, and His Family Connections in New York* (1877). Also see Jerome R. Reich, *Leisler's Rebellion: A Study of Democracy in New York 1664–1720* (1953); Thomas J. Archdeacon, *New York City, 1664–1710: Conquest and Change* (1976); Robert C. Ritchie, *The Duke's Province: A Study of New York Politics and Society, 1664–1691* (1977); and Charles Howard McCormick, *Leisler's Rebellion* (1989).

DAVID WILLIAM VOORHEES

LEITER, Levi Zeigler (2 Nov. 1834–9 June 1904), merchant, was born in Leitersburg, Washington County, Maryland, the son of Joseph Leiter and Anne Zeigler. He attended common school and later worked as a clerk in a local store. In 1853 he moved to Springfield, Ohio, securing a comfortable position with merchant Peter Murray. But Leiter saw more opportunity in Chicago and by 1855 he was there with Downs & van Wyck. In January 1856 Cooley, Wadsworth & Co.—second only to Potter Palmer among Chicago's mercantile houses—hired Leiter as a bookkeeper, and his prodigious financial skill and fierce integrity brought him rapid promotion; he was soon head bookkeeper and accountant.

Leiter soon began to make his distinctive contribution to American enterprise. He recognized that the then-current reliance by wholesalers on long, easy credit, running four months or more and offered to virtually any retailer, was costly and diminished the ability of wholesalers to offer competitive prices. Critically, wholesalers risked failure if a sudden contraction (like that of 1857) left retailers unable to pay. Leiter's solution was twofold: he cut credit to no more than sixty days, offering sharp discounts for early payment; he was fanatical in determining both the reliability of a merchant, keeping at hand volumes from every credit-rating agency, and economic conditions in a merchant's region. For such information he relied heavily on the firm's salesmen, bankers, and even railway agents. Leiter was strikingly successful at improving cash flow and cutting losses on credit sales.

In 1857 the Cooley-Wadsworth partnership expired and a new partnership emerged, that of Cooley & Farwell. Leiter continued handling finances, with Marshall Field, "the most capable salesman in Chicago," responsible for sales. In 1860 Field became a junior partner, and Cooley moved to New York to handle purchasing while Farwell supervised business in Chicago. Field took responsibility for hiring, sales, and credits, and Leiter began working with him almost daily.

The partnership was initially enormously successful; in 1863 its sales probably surpassed longtime leader Palmer. But Cooley, believing his health was declining because of business pressures and fearing that the Civil War boom was ending, turned conservative. Palmer continued expanding, reaping huge profits while Cooley & Farwell stagnated. Frustrated by Cooley's behavior, Farwell forced creation of a new partnership, with Field joining as full partner and with two junior partners, one "the bushy-whiskered and dynamic Levi Z. Leiter." Field and Farwell were, however, uneasy partners; the partnership lasted one year.

Field and Leiter, with principal employees, wanted to start their own firm, but their capital (Field and Leiter had mustered $300,000 between them) was only half that needed for a strong start. Propitiously, Potter Palmer wanted to retire and offered to sell "on very handsome terms." Critically, he agreed to leave $330,000 in the firm, giving Field and Leiter capital of $750,000. Palmer's brother Milton also invested and was made a general partner, creating Field, Palmer & Leiter in January 1865. In 1867 Palmer sold his interest, and in 1869 Field and Leiter reorganized, each taking a one-third interest, dividing the remainder among four junior executives.

Palmer had in many ways transformed merchandising in the 1850s. He had been among the first to appreciate the potential of heavy newspaper advertising; understood the importance of visually appealing displays; had introduced the idea of guaranteed satisfaction, backed by full refund or equal exchange; and offered unprecedented variety and quality of goods. Field, with his passion for merchandising, and Leiter, with unmatched financial skills, were perfectly suited to take over Palmer's business and to build on his techniques.

Leiter continued to improve financial controls and was meticulous in paying bills on time to maximize discounts, even keeping mail schedules to assure timely arrival of payments. Field exploited this reputation for prompt payment by securing even lower initial bids. This combination permitted Field and Leiter to offer customers—retail and wholesale—lower prices than any other merchant.

After the great Chicago Fire in 1871, Leiter was active in assuring rebuilding and securing aid for victims. He personally persuaded leading insurer Liverpool & London & Globe Insurance Company, of which he was a director, to commit publicly to not only reestablishing itself in the city but also expanding its presence. He supported generously the Chicago Relief and Aid Society, for which he was a director from 1874 to 1880.

Field & Leiter itself quickly opened a temporary store, then after two years moved into a grand facility at State and Washington. In 1877 it burned, and the Singer Company, the owner of the site, rebuilt but decided it wanted to sell for a stiff fee of $700,000. Leiter, responsible for the purchase, delayed, believing he could talk Singer's price down. Annoyed, Singer leased the building to Field & Leiter's arch rival, Carson, Pirie & Co. Immediately, Field and Leiter personally paid Singer the $700,000 and Carson another $100,000 to break the lease, saving their prized location. Leiter's failure in this matter, however, exacerbated existing tension between the partners. Leiter thought the future lay with wholesale; Field believed retailing was the right direction. Field declared that he would not extend the partnership, which expired in January 1881. When Leiter discovered the junior partners and lesser officers supported Field, he sold his share for $2.7 million, and in 1886 Field bought Leiter's half interest in the State Street store.

Leiter was a changed man on retiring. No longer focused on the daily effort to manage, he and his wife—Mary Theresa Carver, whom he had married in 1866—with their four children traveled widely, to Paris, London, Moscow, Monaco, and Cairo. They built a pretentious summer house—"Linden Lodge," with thirty-seven rooms and nineteen fireplaces—at Lake Geneva, Wisconsin. They later bought another mansion, in Washington, D.C., where Leiter assembled an impressive collection of Americana. He was prominent in the Illinois Humane Society, supported the Newsboy Home, served as the second president of the Chicago Art Institute, founded and served as first president of the Commercial Club of Chicago, and led efforts to build a new home for the Chicago Historical Society. He was also instrumental in establishing Chicago's Public Library and in 1893 contributed $100,000 toward establishing a national museum in Chicago.

Leiter, wealthy when he parted from Field, enjoyed continued success. He was a principal owner in the Comstock Lode, invested heavily in railroads and the Pullman Company, bought extensive lands in the West (principally in Wyoming, Montana, Colorado, Utah, Nebraska, and South Dakota), and was the second largest individual investor in land (holding over $10 million worth in 1895) on Chicago's South Side. In 1898 he covered his son's near $10 million loss from a failed corner of the wheat market. Leiter died at the Vanderbilt summer cottage in Bar Harbor, Maine, leaving a $10 million estate.

• There are four collections of Leiter family papers: the Levi Z. Leiter Collection, the Mary Theresa Leiter Collection, and the Mary Victoria Leiter Collection, all at the Chicago Historical Society; and the Levi Z. Leiter Collection at the University of Wyoming. There is material on Leiter in the Marshall Field Corporate Archives, Chicago, and in the Lyman Lobdell Collection at the Chicago Historical Society. See also *The Leiter Library, a Catalogue of the Books and Maps Relating Principally to America, Collected by Levi Z. Leiter. With Collations and Bibliographic Notes by Hugh Alexander Morrison* (1907); Robert W. Twyman, *History of Marshall Field & Co. 1852–1906* (1954); Lloyd Wendt and Herman Kogan, *Give the Lady What She Wants!* (1952); and Debra L. Walker, "Accumulation to Speculation: The Careers of Levi and Joseph Leiter 1865–1932" (master's thesis, Rosary College, 1975). Obituaries are in the *Chicago Daily News*, 9 June 1904, and the *Chicago Daily Tribune*, 10 June 1904.

FRED CARSTENSEN

LEITH, Charles Kenneth (20 Jan. 1875–13 Sept. 1956), geologist, teacher, and consultant, was born in Trempealeau, Wisconsin, the son of Charles Augustus Leith, a newspaper publisher and civil servant, and Martha Eleanor Gale, a schoolteacher. In 1883 the family moved to Madison, Wisconsin, where he attended public school. During his senior year in high school Leith also attended the local business college and graduated from both in 1892.

That fall Leith entered the University of Wisconsin to study modern classics but found he needed a job to meet expenses. He secured a job as a part-time stenographer and typist to Charles R. Van Hise, who had just been appointed professor of geology and head of the department. Leith soon became, in effect, Van Hise's private secretary and professional associate, as he decided to pursue his career in geology. Van Hise had broad interests ranging from metallurgy to mineralogy, pre-Cambrian geology, iron ore in the Lake Superior region, and later, conservation of mineral and natural resources. His correspondence, much of which was handled by Leith, brought Leith in contact with many of the scientists and geologists of the time. Until his death in 1918, Van Hise continued to influence Leith's career. While Leith was an undergraduate, he also became involved with the U.S. Geological Survey in the process of conducting studies of the Michigan and Minnesota iron districts. He received his B.S. in 1897 and remained at the university for graduate work. He married Mary E. Mayers of Madison in 1898; they had two sons. In 1900 he was assigned by Van Hise to study the newly discovered Mesabi, a range of low hills in northeastern Minnesota known for deposits of iron ore, and in 1901 he received a Ph.D.

In 1903, when Van Hise became president of the University of Wisconsin, Leith was picked to succeed him as professor of geology and head of the department. He remained head of the department until 1934 and after that was a member of the faculty until his retirement in 1945. Over the years Leith taught classes in structural geology, metamorphic geology, pre-Cambrian geology, and ore deposits at Wisconsin and

sometimes taught at other universities. His lectures were always carefully prepared in advance and delivered just from notes. Leith was remembered for starting his lectures with the opening statement, "Now this is the broad, general set up of this problem," and ending them with, "Well, has anyone any questions to ask?" Students usually looked forward to his annual spring and fall geology field trips and his yearly graduate student open house at his home. He also made an effort to see to it that his graduate students were well placed in industry or academe after they received their degree.

Leith always maintained a heavy schedule of research, writing, and reviewing and relied heavily on a personal secretary and the assignment of assistants and experts to help him with his work. Many of his early works on iron ores were published by the U.S. Geological Survey as reports, and several became standard texts in the field. Leith was soon recognized as the authority on iron ores in the Lake Superior region and eastern shore of Hudson Bay, and he became a consultant to many companies who were then exploiting these areas. From these experiences he wrote a book, *A Summer and Winter on Hudson Bay* (1912), with his brother who also was a geologist. In addition to his faculty salary, Leith acquired a modest income from several private mining ventures he formed in association with some of his former students.

With the advent of World War I, Leith's interests increasingly turned toward public service in an effort to conserve national and world mining and mineral resources. Before World War I, the United States was fairly self-sufficient in meeting its demands for minerals and metals and was even the leader in some mineral exports. It also, however, had to rely on imports for most of its manganese, chrome, tungsten, and sulphur. Early in the war the U.S. Shipping Board was formed to monitor such imports and exports. In 1917 the Committee on Mineral Imports and Exports was formed under the agency, and Leith was appointed as the chairman of its Mineral Committee. Later he became an adviser to Bernard Baruch, who was then chairman of the War Industries Board. This association lead to the opportunity to attend the 1919 Paris Peace Conference, where he offered his plan for a world balance sheet for each of the basic mineral commodities. His plan was not successful, but the experience made him even more aware of the international implications of mining and mineral resources.

The period between World War I and World War II was notable for the activity of professional mining, metal, and minerals associations, such as the American Institute of Mining Engineers, the Society of Economic Geologists (SEG), and the Geological Society of America (GSA). During this period Leith served as president of SEG (1925) and GSA (1933). Notable in this period was the publication of his book *World Minerals and World Politics* (1931), which was the first to emphasize the place and influence of minerals in world affairs. With the approach of World War II in Europe, the United States became more aware of the need to stockpile critical minerals, and Leith was active in advising and chairing various government planning committees and boards. In 1940 he was appointed chairman of the Advisory Committee on Metals and Minerals, whose job it was to supply data on specific mineral problems to the Office of Production Management and, later, after the United States entered the war, to the War Production Board. In 1943, in anticipation of the role minerals would play in the future, he published *World Minerals and World Peace* (1943), in which he presented his views on the relationship between mineral control and peace.

With the close of the war in 1945, Leith retired from the University of Wisconsin but he continued to divide his time between Madison and Washington, D.C. He continued his role as a government consultant, serving as a member of such groups as the Combined Development Agency of the U.S. Atomic Energy Commission, the National Security Resources Board, the Research and Development Board of the Department of Defense, and the Minerals and Metals Advisory Board of the National Research Council. Throughout the years he received many honors, including the Penrose Medal (SEG, 1935, GSA, 1942) and membership in the American Academy of Arts and Sciences and the National Academy of Sciences.

Leith died suddenly while on a trip to Madison. Through his efforts, the United States and the world have become aware of both the international and the political importance of the earth's mining and mineral resources.

• Leith's correspondence, notes, memoranda, drafts of reports, and personal papers are somewhat scattered. The bulk of the material dating before 1940 may be found in the University Archives, University of Wisconsin. Most of his government papers, if not still classified, may be in the National Archives, with a few in the Library of Congress. Others are scattered. Leith wrote more than 200 technical articles and fourteen books. The best source of information on Leith, including an essay on the sources of his papers, may be found in Sylvia Wallace McGrath, *Charles Kenneth Leith: Scientific Adviser* (1971). Short biographies of Leith appear in numerous collective biographies of scientists and geologists. The best memoirs are D. F. Hewett, "Charles Kenneth Leith," National Academy of Sciences, *Biographical Memoirs* 33 (1959): 180–204, and Richard J. Lund, "Memorial to Charles Kenneth Leith," *Proceedings Volume of the Geological Society of America, Annual Report for 1956.* An obituary is in the *New York Times*, 15 Sept. 1956.

ROBERT J. HAVLIK

LEITZEL, Lillian (1891?–15 Feb. 1931), circus performer, was born Lillian Alize Elianore in Breslau, Germany, the daughter of Edward Elianore, a Hungarian army officer turned theatrical impresario, and Elinor Pelikan, a Bohemian circus aerialist. There is much dispute over her birth date and name. The year of her birth is variously recorded somewhere between 1891 and 1895. There are also half a dozen variations on her given names and their spelling, although Leitzel never used her father's name for any length of time during her life. If the facts of Leitzel's life are clouded

in controversy it is because she, herself, made it a habit to change the facts of her story each time she told it to a different reporter. Being exceedingly vain, she would also have taken care to present herself as being as young as possible.

Leitzel's mother's family had been circus performers for several generations before Leitzel was born. Because her mother was actively pursuing her career at the time of Leitzel's birth, she was raised by her maternal grandparents in Breslau, receiving what amounted to a classical education pointed toward a career in music or dance. She was fluent in five languages and well on her way to becoming a concert pianist when she joined her mother's acrobatic troupe known as Leamy's Ladies, which presented an aerial ballet. Although the exact date is uncertain, she was only around nine years old.

Leitzel came to America in 1910 with the Leamy Ladies. A year later the act disbanded, but its youngest member, who had by then taken the professional name of Lillian Leitzel (the latter being a corruption of her middle name), decided to remain and try her luck with a solo aerial routine in vaudeville. She was discovered by an agent for the Ringling Brothers in South Bend, Indiana, and made her debut with that circus in April 1915. Leitzel was immediately elevated to stardom, a position she enjoyed for the remainder of her life. When the Ringling Brothers and Barnum and Bailey circuses combined in 1919, her fame and popularity reached an unprecedented level.

Neither her physical appearance nor her specialty offer any explanation of the adulation Leitzel enjoyed. She was just 4'9" tall, weighed ninety-five pounds, and had an over-developed upper body; her act was merely a series of arm dislocations in which she threw her body over her right shoulder 100 to 150 times. Her performance, essentially a display of physical endurance rather than danger, was a perfect example of style over content.

No other acts were permitted to intrude on Leitzel's flirtation with the audience. This was the first instance of a solo act in the multiple ring format of "The Greatest Show on Earth." She was escorted into the arena by a giant major-domo whose immense size served to accentuate her diminutive stature. A uniformed maid stood in attendance nearby. The performer wore a spangled two-piece costume that was uncommonly brief for the time, and she projected what has been described as a "legitimate nonchalance." She shamelessly played to the audience, blowing kisses and waving, giggling with girlish glee at any unusually enthusiastic response. By the time she had finished her act, her long, golden hair had become unpinned and was whipped about as she completed her final gyrations. As a fitting finale she often pretended to faint when she had descended the rope on which she performed and fell into the arms of her attendant.

But it was not just Leitzel's performance in the big top that captivated her fans and admirers. Offstage she was the very essence of a tempestuous prima donna, often refusing to work until some imagined slight was placated, toying with an endless stream of well-heeled suitors who plied her with extravagant gifts. Her private dressing tent, another Ringling first, was carpeted with oriental rugs, bedecked with floral tributes, and—if not crowded with reporters and admirers—filled with numerous children of the circus, whose company she particularly favored and on whom she showered lavish gifts. Leitzel was similarly attracted to stray or wounded animals, which she often tried to rescue. Management also accorded her the singular honor of a private Pullman car on the circus train, furnished with a piano on which she played pieces from the classical repertoire.

Despite her urbane tastes in art and music and the numerous wealthy men who sought her attention, she first married an anonymous stagehand (date of marriage unknown) and then Clyde Ingalls, the circus's side show manager in 1920. Both marriages ended in divorce, the second in 1924. Her final marriage, in 1928, was to Alfredo Codona, the circus's star flyer. She had no children.

On Friday, 13 February 1931, Leitzel fell to the floor of an indoor circus in Copenhagen when her rigging suddenly snapped apart. Two days later she died. Her body was brought back to the United States by Codona and buried in Ingelwood Park, California. Six years later, Codona committed suicide after murdering the woman he had married following Leitzel's death.

A remarkable tribute that attests to the depth and range of Leitzel's popularity was held a few days after her death in Madison Square Garden in New York City during a New York Rangers ice hockey game. The notoriously rowdy hockey fans stood in bowed silence as a solitary rope was lowered and then raised in her honor. No wonder she has been called the "Bernhardt of the Circus."

• Individual clipping files for Leitzel can be seen at the Billy Rose Theatre Collection at the New York Public Library for the Performing Arts, Lincoln Center; the research library of the Circus World Museum, Baraboo, Wis. (which also possesses several biographical summaries that compare the discrepancies in dates and information relative to the subject culled from various sources); and the Hertzberg Circus Museum, San Antonio, Tex. The most reliable firsthand account of Lillian Leitzel's performance and offstage lifestyle is *The Big Top* (1952), the autobiography of the circus's equestrian director, Fred Bradna. He witnessed her act twice a day for twelve years, lived on the circus lot, and trained with her during that time. Robert Louis Taylor devotes a lengthy section of his book *Center Ring* (1956) to a profile of the star that first appeared in the *New Yorker* magazine. An obituary is in the *New York Times*, 16 Feb. 1931.

ERNEST ALBRECHT

LE JAU, Francis (1665–15 Sept. 1715), Anglican clergyman, was born in Angers, France, of Huguenot parents whose names are unknown. Little is known of his early life, but he emigrated to England in 1685, probably to escape the religious persecution associated with the revocation of the Edict of Nantes. He attended Trinity College, Dublin, earning an M.A. in 1693, a B.D. in 1696, and a D.D. in 1700. He also served as a canon in St. Paul's Cathedral in London.

At that time the Church of England, to which Le Jau converted and in which he was ordained, was seeking to expand at home and abroad, as evidenced by the creation of the Society for the Propagation of the Gospel in Foreign Parts (SPG) in 1701. Henry Compton, bishop of London, aided a number of foreign-born Anglican clergymen to find offices in the American colonies, which were loosely under his control. Le Jau was one of these agents of Anglican expansion, serving first in the West Indies, and then accepting an appointment and salary from the SPG to be a missionary in South Carolina, where he arrived in October 1706.

South Carolina was just developing permanent institutions. There were about 4,000 white settlers in the colony, less than half of whom were Anglicans, and nearly as many slaves. Rice had become a lucrative staple crop, and the Indian trade, which included both deerskins and Indian slaves, was already a source of great wealth. After a bitter political struggle, in which they were aided by the Huguenots and fought by the Presbyterians, Baptists, and Quakers, the Anglicans had established the Church of England, largely because of support from the proprietors.

Le Jau was elected rector by the parishioners of St. James, Goose Creek, which lay to the west of Charles Town, and he served that parish until his death. He was a capable and kindly clergyman who earned the respect and affection of his parishioners. Although he supported the Anglican party in South Carolina politics, he was also aware that religion was not the only thing at issue: "Revenge, self interest, engrossing of trade, places of any profit and things of that nature are the Mobile . . . of our affairs" (*Carolina Chronicle*, p. 29). While he was critical of the Anglican gentry, Le Jau relied on their support for his own efforts, such as improving the morals of his parishioners and promoting education. His religious views illustrate both the rational latitudinarianism of the Church of England and his French Calvinistic heritage. He taught the basic elements of Christianity with a naive faith that anyone who understood them would be converted, but he also believed that an outbreak of smallpox in 1712 was God's judgment on a sinful South Carolina.

Le Jau was interested in the Indians, some of whom lived nearby, in part because he hoped that their religious beliefs and practices would show some correspondence to Christians ones and thus validate the idea of a universal religion. He also saw and lamented the white traders' cruelty toward the Indians. In 1715, however, when abuses associated with the Indian trade led to the Yamasee War, Le Jau joined other Anglican clergymen in condemning the Indians as savages.

Similarly, Le Jau manifested a paternalistic concern for the growing slave population of South Carolina, but he never challenged the nature of servitude itself. He carried on an active ministry among the slaves of St. James, Goose Creek, despite the opposition of the planters to such religious instruction, teaching many African Americans but baptizing only a few. Le Jau condemned extreme cruelty toward slaves, but his chief concern was for the souls of the African Americans. He worried more about the behavior of the slaves, the parties they enjoyed on Sundays, and the looseness of their sexual behavior than he did about the harshness or injustice of their labor.

Le Jau married Jeanne Antoinette Huguenin in 1690, and she bore them four children before her death on Christmas Day 1700. He later married Elizabeth Harrison of Westminster; they had two children. His son, also Francis Le Jau, provided a commemorative plate that was placed in St. James, Goose Creek, shortly after the elder Le Jau was buried near the altar of the church.

Francis Le Jau was an important member of the Huguenot immigration that enriched the American colonies at the end of the seventeenth century. An effective clergyman, he was also a sensitive and articulate social critic, albeit with important prejudices of his own.

• The best source on Francis Le Jau is his own letters, which have been collected in *The Carolina Chronicle of Dr. Francis Le Jau, 1706–1717*, ed. Frank J. Klingberg (1956). See also S. Charles Bolton, *Southern Anglicanism: The Church of England in Colonial South Carolina* (1982); Frederick Dalcho, *An Historical Account of the Protestant Episcopal Church in South Carolina* (1820); Peter H. Wood, *Black Majority: Negroes in Colonial South Carolina from 1670 through the Stono Rebellion* (1974); John Frederick Woolverton, *Colonial Anglicanism in North America* (1984); and Jon Butler, *Awash in a Sea of Faith: Christianizing the American People* (1990).

S. CHARLES BOLTON

LEJEUNE, John Archer (10 Jan. 1867–20 Nov. 1942), Marine Corps officer, was born in Pointe Coupee Parish, Louisiana, the son of Ovide Lejeune, a sugar planter, and Laura Archer Turpin. The perilous economic times following the Civil War resulted in the loss of the family plantation, "Old Hickory." Educated at Louisiana State University, in 1884 Lejeune accepted an appointment to the U.S. Naval Academy when his family could no longer fund his education. He graduated thirteen in his class in 1888, and he was commissioned a second lieutenant in the U.S. Marine Corps two years later.

As a junior officer, Lejeune displayed few of the traits that caused him to stand out in later years. His religious devotion, temperance, and preference for the Democratic party made him almost unique among officers of the naval services during that era. In 1895 he married Ellie Harrison Murdaugh; they had three children.

For the next decade, Lejeune's naval service differed little from contemporaries: stints ashore in barracks at various Navy yards alternated with tours at sea in command of marine detachments in the ships of the fleet. During the Spanish-American War, he saw action in a ship deployed to Cuban waters. Thereafter, Lejeune commanded a battalion embarked on the *Dixie*, which participated in President Theodore Roosevelt's (1858–1919) seizure of the Panama Canal in 1903–1904. Following a tour in the Philippines, 1907–1909, Lejeune received orders to attend the Army War College.

At this juncture in his career, Lejeune's performance had not been characterized by either dash or brilliance. At the Army War College, however, he earned a reputation as an articulate student of the military arts. His next major assignment involved command of a regiment in the Advance Base Maneuvers, held in Puerto Rico in 1913. The following year he was the commanding officer of the First Provisional Regiment during the imbroglio with Mexico. His steady and reliable performance captured the attention of his superiors. President Woodrow Wilson's secretary of the navy, Josephus Daniels, considered Lejeune briefly as a candidate for commandant of the Marine Corps but passed him over because of seniority. Nonetheless, Daniels and Lejeune began a lifelong, close friendship. The successful candidate, George Barnett (1859–1930), ordered Lejeune to Washington, D.C., to serve as his assistant. By then civilian and naval leaders had begun to recognize Lejeune as an exceptional officer.

With U.S. entry into World War I, Lejeune besieged his superiors for an assignment to the American Expeditionary Forces (AEF). Arriving in France in June 1918, Lejeune led infantry brigades briefly but then assumed command of the Second Division, AEF, and led it through the offensives of St.-Mihiel, Mont Blanc, and Meuse Argonne. He was advanced to the rank of major general on 31 July 1918. After returning home with the division, Lejeune commanded the marine base at Quantico from October 1919 through June 1920. During that tour, however, the personal and professional relationship between Secretary Daniels and Commandant Barnett grew increasingly estranged. In a decision that stunned official naval circles, the secretary of the navy ousted the commandant of the Marine Corps and replaced him with Lejeune.

Throughout the 1920s Lejeune enjoyed cordial relations with the three secretaries of the navy of that decade. He nonetheless suffered the debilitating retrenchment shared by all of the armed forces. The traditional commitments of the Marine Corps remained, and deployments to Haiti and Santo Domingo continued to demand marines. Late in the decade, more leathernecks were ordered to Nicaragua and then to China. By 1929 two-thirds of the Marine Corps was stationed outside the United States or at sea.

Even more frustrating than the burden of many postings outside the country were the disputes among Lejeune's officers. Before the war most officers came from the Naval Academy. The few who did not resented the apparent preference shown Annapolis graduates. During the war, however, the size of the officer ranks grew from 431 to more than 2,400. Most of the new second lieutenants consisted of men selected from the ranks or graduates of Reserve Officers Training Corps (ROTC) programs. In the 1920s selection boards faced the unsavory prospect of deciding which should remain in uniform. Junior officers with distinguished records of conduct under fire or tropical campaigning retained their commissions, while others received dismissal. Lejeune arbitrated the disputes among his officers judiciously, but this problem frustrated him throughout his tenure as commandant of the Marine Corps. The service desperately needed a system of officer promotion and retention based on merit and selection rather than seniority. While the House Naval Affairs Committee agreed with Lejeune each year, its counterpart in the Senate refused to consider such legislation.

Throughout his tenure, Lejeune persisted in his belief that the Marine Corps must be of service to the fleet. Although the Advanced Base Force had proven successful in the years just before the war, its emphasis had been on the defense of forward bases. Lejeune argued persuasively that in the next war the seizure of enemy-held bastions by amphibious assault should be the primary mission of his corps. In 1927 the Joint Army-Navy Board agreed and codified this role, effectively separating the Marine Corps that Lejeune had joined in 1890 from that which led the amphibious assaults in the Pacific during World War II.

By late 1928 the frustrations of his position began to wear on Lejeune. Failure to gain passage of legislation affecting the corps and the increasing commitments overseas without necessary increases in manpower caused him to consider stepping down. The election of President Herbert Hoover (1874–1964) in 1928 prompted Lejeune to relinquish his command. He worried about the retrenchment promised by Hoover and Charles Francis Adams (1866–1954), the secretary of the navy designate. Moreover, Lejeune wanted his good friend, Major General Wendell Cushing Neville, to succeed him. To facilitate that goal, he resigned as commandant and left office in March 1929, replaced by Neville.

Lejeune became the superintendent of the Virginia Military Institute that same March. While in Lexington, he employed his leadership skills and his folksy, down-home manner successfully. Using his friendship with President Franklin D. Roosevelt, he obtained funds through various public works programs to significantly refurbish the campus.

Failing health forced Lejeune to retire to Norfolk in 1937. He was advanced in rank to lieutenant general on the retired list by act of Congress in 1942, a few months before his death in a Baltimore hospital. Lejeune left a legacy of uncompromising professionalism and dedication to the naval services. The legislative retrenchment of the 1920s prevented most of his programs from reaching fruition, but the adoption of the amphibious assault mission as the Marine Corps's raison d'être meant a significant role for the smaller branch of the naval services in the next war.

• Lejeune's personal papers are held by the Manuscripts Division, Library of Congress; the collection of Josephus Daniels's correspondence may also be located there, including his diary. Lejeune's fitness reports are found in his Officers' Qualification Record, Marine Corps Headquarters, Washington, D.C.; and in Entry 62, Records of the Navy Judge Advocate General, RG 130, Federal Records Center, Suitland, Md. Correspondence germane to his career is held in RG 127, Records of the U.S. Marine Corps, National Archives and Records Administration; RG 120 in the same repository contains useful material on Lejeune and the Second Division, AEF, in World War I.

Lejeune's memoir, *The Reminiscences of a Marine* (1930), provides a useful version of his life and times. Merrill L. Bartlett, *Lejeune: A Marine's Life, 1867–1942* (1991), is the most recently published secondary study, and the bibliography contains a compendium of published materials on Lejeune's life and times.

MERRILL L. BARTLETT

LELAND, Charles Godfrey (15 Aug. 1824–20 Mar. 1903), poet and journalist, was born in Philadelphia, Pennsylvania, the son of Charles Leland, a prosperous commission merchant, and Charlotte Godfrey. Leland graduated from the College of New Jersey (now Princeton University) in 1845 and then studied abroad for three years at the Universities of Heidelberg and Munich and the Sorbonne. He manned the barricades in Paris for three days during the revolution of 1848.

Leland returned to Philadelphia to study law, but with only two clients in six months, his practice failed. He turned to journalism, writing art and drama criticism in *Drawing-Room Journal* as well as reviews of literature from six foreign languages. In 1853 he joined P. T. Barnum's *Illustrated News* in New York, soon becoming its sole editor. Never well paid, the prolific Leland took numerous jobs over the next ten years, editing the *Evening Bulletin* and *Graham's Magazine* in Philadelphia and *Appleton's Cyclopaedia* in New York City. In 1856 he married Isabel Fisher; the couple had no children.

During the Civil War Leland edited *Vanity Fair* (1860–1861), writing aggressive pro-Union tracts such as "Woe for the South" and converting the northerners' rallying cry from "abolition" to "emancipation." For two years he edited the Republican party vehicle *Continental Magazine* in Boston. After President Abraham Lincoln was assassinated, Lincoln's oft-read copy of Leland's *Ye Book of Copperheads* (1863) was given to the author. During the Gettysburg campaign, when Philadelphia was threatened, Leland saw action as a private in the Union army. Soon after the war, Leland represented the *Philadelphia Press* on a railway promotion tour, riding to the end of the line at Fort Riley, Kansas. His meetings with the Kaw Indians and with General George Armstrong Custer were published in the *Press* and as *The Union Pacific Railway, Eastern Division; or, Three Thousand Miles in a Railway Car* (1867).

His first book, *Meister Karl's Sketch-Book* (1855), contained travel sketches and light verse but more important at this time were his humorous pieces in *Knickerbocker Magazine*, some written in a Yankee dialect. In May 1857, to fill out the pages of *Graham's*, he casually established his claim to literary posterity: "In a hurry I knocked off 'Hans Breitmann's Barty.' I gave it no thought whatever." Over the years he published

Breitmann poems in magazines or enclosed them in letters; after the war he collected and published them serially in five pamphlets (1868–1870), then as *The Breitmann Ballads* (1871; repr. as *Hans Breitmann's Ballads*, 1914).

To understand Leland's enormous popularity for the remainder of his life is to know Hans Breitmann. Even his *Memoirs* affixed Hans Breitmann to the author's name. The humor of these ballads derived from both the German-English interlanguage and the persona, a robust, beer-guzzling, giant of a man who matched the American spirit. His life was an adventure and a "barty" (that is, party):

> Hans Breitmann gife a barty,
> I dells you it cost him dear;
> Dey rolled in more ash sefen kecks
> Of foost-rate lager beer.

His rowdiness was the envy of many:

> Und den I gissed Madilda Yane,
> Und she shlog me on de kop,
> Und de gompany vighted mit daple-lecks
> Dill de coonshtable made oos shtop.

The collection of fifty-four poems included "A Ballad Apout de Rowdies," "Breitmann in Kansas," "Breitmann in Battle," "Brietmann in Forty-eight," "Breitmann in Munich," and even "Breitmann Interviews the Pope":

> Next tay in *Vaticano*, while he shtared
>   at frescoes o'er him,
> Hans toorned und mit amazemend saw
>   der Pabst was shoost pefore him!
> Down on his knees der Breitmann vent—
>   for so de law it teaches;
> He proke two holes in de bavement—
>   und likevise shblit his preeches.

Some ballads, such as "Breitmann's Going to Church" and "Schnitzerl's Philosopede," invoked pathos and the sublime.

Americans acclaimed. In 1866 James Russell Lowell wrote, "I do not know when I have enjoyed anything more highly. . . . I read it aloud at breakfast, so well as laughing would let me. . . .Why do you not collect them?" Oliver Wendell Holmes in 1867 declared that he "read with huge delectation the travels and adventures of Hans Breitmann. . . . The whole is good as it can be." Four thousand copies sold quickly. English readers responded even more enthusiastically, with nine editions (plus pirated versions) published in London within two years. Both William Dean Howells (*Atlantic*, Oct. 1868) and Leslie Stephens (*British Quarterly Review*, 1 Oct. 1870) approved "the genuineness of the humor." The *Athenaeum* (12 Feb. 1870) proclaimed the ballads "a new kind of humorous poetry."

The rambunctious Breitmann with his macaronic lexis begat both humor and inspiration, which the author's preface described as "Teutonic philosophy and sentiment, beer, music, and romance." Leland's biographer, Elizabeth Pennell, asserted that no satire on Americans was intended and that Breitmann was clearly a foreigner. Americans, however, could laugh at themselves, and her theory cannot support the European enthusiasm for Breitmann; as Leland in 1870 wrote, "Why, the Germans all admit the truth of Hans—why the deuce can't the Americans?" For comparison to other dialect humorists, readers must look to Artemus Ward, Petroleum V. Nasby, and Lowell's Hosea Biglow, as well as Bret Harte's "Plain Language from Truthful James" and "The Heathen Chinee."

From 1870 on Leland was an expatriate, living first in London and then in Italy for many years. During that time he was initially preoccupied with introducing industrial and decorative arts into the public schools. He returned to Philadelphia and Washington, D.C., for three years, taught, and published *Industrial Art in Schools* (1882). He also continued his abiding interest in languages and folklore. He discovered and recorded Shelta, a Gaelic-gypsy language, and published a number of works on slang, legends, and gypsy lore (*The English Gipsies and Their Language* [1873], *The Algonquin Legends of New England* [1884], and *Etruscan Roman Remains in Popular Tradition* [1892]). For his gypsy work, Leland was hailed as "The Rye," signifying Romany king. Leland died in Florence, Italy.

Breitmann's popularity ebbed about the time Leland died. People stopped asking, "Vhere ish dot barty now?" More than twenty-six editions of the ballads were published. His fifty-plus books included translations of Heinrich Heine, philosophical poems in *The Music-Lesson of Confucius* (1872), humor in *Pidgin-English Sing-Song; or, Songs and Stories in the China-English Dialect* (1876), numerous volumes on industrial arts, and social views in *The Alternate Sex; or, The Female Intellect in Man, and the Masculine in Woman* (1904).

• Leland's papers, letters, and clippings are mainly at the Historical Society of Pennsylvania; smaller collections are also at the Princeton, Harvard, and Yale libraries. His own *Memoirs* (1893) is an important source. His niece, Elizabeth Pennell, published the biography *Charles Godfrey Leland* (1906), two informative and charming volumes that include many letters. David Sloane, "Charles G. Leland," in *Dictionary of Literary Biography* 11 (1982), is an accessible life. The long gaps have been filled only by Marianne Thalmann, "Hans Breitmann," *PMLA* (June 1939): 579–88, in German with English footnotes, and Sculley Bradley, "'Hans Breitmann' in England and America," *Colophon* 2 (Autumn 1936): 65–81, on copyright problems and Leland's success in England. Joseph Jackson, *A Bibliography of the Works of Charles G. Leland* (1927), clarifies the dates and editions of the Breitmann poems published as pamphlets and as collected works. An obituary is in the *New York Times*, 21 Mar. 1903.

JOEL ATHEY

LELAND, Henry Martyn (16 Feb. 1843–26 Mar. 1932), pioneer automobile manufacturer, was born in Danville, Vermont, the son of Leander B. Leland, a teamster, and Zilpha Tilft. When he was a teenager, Leland moved with his family to Worcester, Massachusetts, and he found work as an apprentice mechanic at Worcester's Crompton and Knowles Loom Works. During the Civil War Leland worked for three years at the federal arsenal at Springfield, Massachusetts. This job and later employment at Colt's gun works at Hartford, Connecticut, introduced Leland to controlled, precise manufacturing work. It also taught him the importance of precision in achieving truly interchangeable parts.

In 1867 Leland married Ellen Rhonda Hull of Millbury, Massachusetts. They had one son and two daughters. One son, Wilfred, became an important partner in Leland's automobile career.

Leland's next job was in Providence, Rhode Island, in 1872 with the Brown and Sharpe Manufacturing Company, renowned as makers of machine tools as well as of high-quality precision micrometers. Work here further exposed Leland to precision manufacturing standards, and he worked with tolerances as low as $1/100,000$ to $1/270,000$ inches. While working for Brown and Sharpe, Leland also served as a traveling salesman and consultant, visiting the growing industries of the American Midwest to introduce the firm's tools and instruct buyers in their use. During these travels, for the first time he visited Detroit, the city where he later settled.

Leland determined to start his own factory and selected Chicago as the city in which to set up shop. However, he arrived in 1886 on the day of the Haymarket riots; the labor unrest and violence he witnessed curdled his confidence in the city and persuaded him to leave. It is possible that the Haymarket riots cost Chicago a position as a preeminent city for American automobile manufacturing, because Leland proved to be one of the industry's most successful and innovative leaders.

Leland instead settled in Detroit and in 1890 founded the firm of Leland, Faulconer and Norton (which was shortened to Leland and Faulconer when Norton withdrew in 1895). Robert Faulconer was a Michigan lumberman looking for a new investment; Charles Norton was the inventor of an automatic grinding machine and a former employee of Brown and Sharpe. The firm quickly built a reputation for high-quality precision manufacture of gears and machine tools and later of gasoline engines. Its products were engineered with tolerances of $1/2,000$ inch, production standards almost unheard of in that era. When Ranson E. Olds opened the country's first major automobile company in Detroit and began building cars in 1900, he bought transmissions and later engines from Leland. Leland's engine increased the horsepower and enhanced the performance of Olds's car.

Leland's work attracted the attention of the Detroit Automobile Company, which used his engines in its cars and hired Leland as an adviser. In 1902 the company reorganized as the Cadillac Automobile Company (named after the French general, Antoine de la Mothe Cadillac, who founded Detroit in 1701; his coat of arms was adopted as the car's emblem). In 1904 Leland took over the firm, merging it with his Leland and Faulconer concern to form the Cadillac Motor Car Company. Leland served as the first general manager of the new company. Wilfred, his son, was assistant treasurer.

The first Cadillac car had been completed two years earlier, in 1902. It was a simple, one-cylinder car, but its light weight and high ground clearance were well suited to handle the harsh conditions of America's unpaved roads. The car also offered a steering wheel instead of a tiller, which represented a significant advance over most cars on the road. Various models of the single-cylinder Cadillac were offered between 1905 and 1908, with prices ranging from $750 to $1,400.

What set Leland's Cadillac car apart from others was its exceptional quality. Leland demanded engine tolerances far more precise than industry standards at the time, and his manufacturing processes used specially designed machine tools that led to first-class workmanship. Leland used high-quality alloy steels in the frame and axles, as well as specially designed self-locking nuts. His unwavering devotion to precision mechanics gave rise to the Cadillac motto, "Craftsmanship a creed, accuracy a law."

In 1908 the Cadillac Motor Car Company received worldwide attention with a dramatic demonstration of its cars' interchangeable parts. At the Brooklands circuit in England, officials of the Royal Automobile Club (RAC) selected three Cadillacs at random from a group of eight, completely stripped them down, and scrambled all the parts. Within seventy-two hours mechanics reassembled the three cars, which all started on the first attempt and then ran 500 miles at Brooklands with no trouble. As a result of this impressive feat, the RAC awarded the Cadillac Motor Car Company the coveted Dewar Trophy, the Nobel Prize of the automobile industry, given to the company that made the industry's greatest innovation in that year. It was the first time that a foreign company had won the prestigious award. Just as important, Cadillac's interchangeability of parts shattered the tired old standard of hand production, demonstrating that precision and high quality could be achieved in cars made through mass production techniques. Cadillac adopted the slogan, "The Standard of the World," because it was the first company to ensure standardization of its automobile parts.

Leland soon introduced two more important innovations that revolutionized the automobile industry. In 1910 he began producing closed sedans, offering passengers protection from the elements. The next year Cadillac began using a self-starting motor in its cars, an advancement that Leland especially advocated because a friend of his had died from injuries sustained while cranking a car. By 1912 Cadillac cars featured as standard equipment a combination of electric starting, lighting, and ignition, developed by electrician Charles Kettering at Dayton Engineering Labs Corporation (DELCO). For this advancement the Royal Automobile Club awarded Cadillac the Dewar Trophy in 1914, making Cadillac the first two-time winner of the award.

In 1914 Cadillac announced its first production V-8 engine, and from 1915 onward all Cadillacs featured the engine, the success of which was partly attributable to Leland's advanced engine manufacturing methods. Another advancement that Leland pioneered at this time was thermostatic control of engine temperature.

In 1909 Cadillac had joined William C. Durant's General Motors (GM) Company, and six years later Cadillac became a division of GM when the company was recognized as a corporation. Cadillac, GM's prestige line, was one of the most independent of GM's divisions. When the United States entered World War I, Leland wanted to convert the Cadillac factory to produce Liberty airplane engines, but Durant turned him down. As a result, Leland and his son Wilfred resigned from Cadillac in August 1917 and founded the Lincoln Motor Company to produce Liberty engines.

Leland brought to the new company his sterling reputation as well as many Cadillac employees. He also acted with dispatch; within two days of founding the company he secured a government contract, and within ten months his company had 6,000 employees and was turning out an amazing fifty engines a day, which equalled the weekly production output of top British manufacturers.

After the war Leland geared up to produce a new luxury car, the Lincoln, named for the president, and in 1920 he and son Wilfred formed the Lincoln Motor Company of Delaware. Leland was already seventy-seven years old at the time he began this new venture. He received 1,000 orders for his new V-8 Lincoln car even before it went into production, a testimony to his outstanding reputation.

Leland's new company fell upon hard times almost immediately, in part because of a postwar depression, in part because the car's styling was disappointingly effete, and in part because Leland was still strapped with government loans from the war years and bank loans he had taken out in order to start the company. He was put further in arrears because of the cost of converting from airplane engine manufacture to luxury motor car manufacture. The fledgling company's financial difficulties were compounded when the U.S. Treasury Department assessed an enormous $4.5 million tax bill, which was grossly in error. The financial crisis allowed Henry Ford to purchase the company for $8 million. Leland and Ford clashed immediately; Leland and his son found themselves intensely dissatisfied with Ford's heavy-handed leadership and with what they considered the interference of Ford's staff with their operation. Ford and the Lelands were unable to resolve their differences, and in 1923 Ford fired Wilfred, after which Henry promptly resigned. By 1924 the company was in the black, and Lincoln cars gained a sound reputation and especially found favor among law enforcement officials because of their powerful engines and reliability.

After leaving Lincoln, Leland remained active in Detroit's business and civic affairs and maintained an office in downtown Detroit. A tall man with a shock of white hair and a bushy moustache and goatee beard, Leland cut a striking figure. He attributed his physical and mental fitness even during his advanced years to a life of moderation and even asceticism. Leland said he never tasted liquor or used tobacco in his life and instead channeled his time and energy into hard work and a mastery of his business. He died at Grace Hospital in Detroit.

Leland adhered to firm business principles throughout his life. He preached honesty in his business dealings, maintaining that a reputation for honesty is priceless. "Honesty is not only the best policy. One should aim to be honest because it is eternally right," he once said. Leland was leery of trade unions, an attitude arising from his having witnessed the Haymarket riots and from his awareness that strikes threatened the ideal of efficient production that he so cherished. Still, he recognized that trade unions were workers' only refuge against unscrupulous employers, and his sense of fairness led him to defend workers' right to organize. But to help forestall labor unrest, Leland paid and treated his workers well, and worker discontent was conspicuously absent in his factories.

Leland's greatest legacy was the creation of the Cadillac and Lincoln Motor Car Companies, whose automobiles reflected the precision manufacturing and rigorous engineering standards that he brought to the nascent American automobile industry.

• The National Automotive History Collection of the Detroit Public Library maintains a file on Leland. A biography that captures the recollections of Leland's daughter-in-law, Ottilie M. Leland, is *Master of Precision: Henry M. Leland* (1966), with Minnie Dubbs Millbrook. H. D. Hendry, "The Great Precisionist: Henry M. Leland," appeared in *Car Life*, July 1965, pp. 58–66. A comprehensive obituary is in the *Detroit Free-Press*, 27 Mar. 1932; an obituary is in the *New York Times* on the same date.

YANEK MIECZKOWSKI

LELAND, John (14 May 1754–14 Jan. 1841), Baptist clergyman, was born in Grafton, Massachusetts, the son of James Leland and Lucy Warren. His education consisted of reading the Bible, John Bunyan's *Pilgrim's Progress*, and Philip Doddridge's *The Rise and Progress of Religion in the Soul*. In 1772, at the age of eighteen, he heard a voice from heaven admonishing him to replace the "frolicks or evening diversions" with "the work which you have got to do" (Butterfield, p. 160). Leland was baptized in June 1774 in the Baptist church in Bellingham, Massachusetts, which licensed him to preach in the spring of 1775. During the winter and spring of 1775–1776 he preached in churches stretching from New England to Virginia. In September 1776 he married Sally Divine of Hopkinton, Massachusetts, and returned to Virginia. The couple had seven children.

Arriving in Culpeper County, Virginia, in early 1777, Leland secured ordination by the local Baptist church. During the winter of 1777–1778 a preaching tour took him to the Peedee River in South Carolina. In 1778 he settled in Orange County, Virginia, where he remained until 1791. There he served churches in Orange, Louisa, Culpeper, and Spotsylvania counties, a ministry that grew by 1779 to form a 120-mile circuit.

Leland believed that the recently disestablished Episcopal church in Virginia retained the vices of an established church in the sense that it occupied a privileged place in the social order and employed learned clergy to improve the moral tone of society rather than preaching a simple gospel to ordinary folk. During an impromptu debate, he accepted the challenge of an Episcopal minister to preach extemporaneously on an assigned text, which turned out to be Numbers 22:21, "And Balaam saddled his ass." Without missing a beat, Leland explained that Balaam, as a false prophet, represented "a hireling clergy," the saddle the bloated salaries paid to clergy of an established church, and the dumb ass "the people who will bear such a load" (Butterfield, p. 169).

Like other evangelicals, Leland seized on fiddle playing and dancing as emblems of a spiritually heedless life style. Stopping outside a farmhouse in 1787 where a wedding party was in progress, Leland declined the groom's invitation that he share a glass of "sling" but pointedly inquired about the musical noise coming from the house. Told it was a fiddle, Leland asked to examine the instrument. The music stopped. A few days later the family invited Leland to return to their home and preach to them. In a few days several members of the family and their neighbors "turned to the Lord" and were baptized in a nearby creek (Greene, p. 28).

Leland's precise role in the campaign to defeat public subsidizing of religious instruction in Virginia is not known, but the record does show that on three occasions he served on committees lobbying the Virginia General Assembly: in 1786 to repeal the legal incorporation of Episcopal churches and in 1788 and again in 1790 to sell former Episcopal glebe lands. Between 1787 and 1789 he baptized some 400 new converts. Leland also helped collect source material for a history of Baptists in Virginia, some of which he published in 1790. His sermons reflected his wide reading, powerful memory, and intellectual vigor. He worked hard to dissuade fellow Baptist ministers from resorting to "odd tones, disgusting whoops and awkward gestures," preferring dignified, pious presentation of the gospel (Butterfield, p. 180). He persuaded the Baptist General Committee in 1789 to condemn slavery as "a violent deprivation of the rights of nature" and "inconsistent with a republican government," which the legislature ought to "extirpate" in a manner "consistent with the principles of good policy," a stance from which Baptists retreated in 1793 (Butterfield, p. 182).

Tradition holds that James Madison visited Leland on his return from the Constitutional Convention to allay Baptist fears that the proposed Constitution would not sufficiently protect religious liberty and that it would not render the new government responsive to the people. If such a meeting did occur, it would explain why Leland's Orange County neighbors elected Madison as a delegate to the Virginia ratifying convention by a vote of 202 to 187 over his nearest rival. In 1789 Leland congratulated Madison on his election to Congress and urged him to remember, amid legislative work on the national debt and taxation, the protection of "religious Liberty, . . . anywise threatened" (Butterfield, p. 194). If true, Leland's appeal was part of the constituent pressure that led Madison to propose the addition of a Bill of Rights to the Constitution during the first Congress.

In Connecticut and Massachusetts, Baptists still struggled under the yoke of established Congregationalism, and this struggle beckoned Leland north. In 1791 he left Virginia and returned to Massachusetts. Once there, he published a tract, *The Rights of Conscience Inalienable, and Therefore Religious Opinions Not Cognizable by Law; or, The High-Flying Churchman, Stript of His Legal Robe, Appears a Yahoo* (1791). It drew on John Locke's *Essay on Toleration* and on Thomas Jefferson's Statute on Religious Freedom to argue that every individual must face God and be held accountable for the integrity of his worship of the Almighty. "If government can answer for individuals at the day of judgment, let men be controlled by it in religious matters; otherwise let men be free" (Butterfield, p. 199).

In July 1791 Leland settled in Conway, Massachusetts, where his father lived, and the following year accepted a call to lead the new Baptist society in Berkshire County, where he remained for most of the remainder of his life. A leader in the struggle over church-state relations in Massachusetts, he published *The Yankee Spy, Calculated for the Religious Meridian of Massachusetts . . .* in 1794. That pamphlet called for a revision of the Massachusetts constitution of 1780, providing for public support for Christian churches in the commonwealth—in practice the Congregationalists. In 1801 he published a fast-day sermon attacking the Massachusetts law that fined towns not financially supporting Christian ministers.

Leland strongly supported Jeffersonian democracy. He exercised enormous political influence over his Cheshire, Massachusetts, parishioners, who voted almost to the man for Republican congressman Elbridge Gerry. Leland never tired of defending Jefferson's reputation nor of equating the Republican cause with the will of God. He arranged for the ladies of Cheshire to send a huge cheese—six feet in diameter and twenty-one inches thick—to President Jefferson in 1801. The delivery of the cheese was a major post-inauguration media event. Jefferson's son-in-law, Thomas Mann Randolph, called it "an ebullition of the passion of republicanism in a state where it has been under heavy persecution" (Butterfield, p. 223).

A combative purist on religious liberty all his life, Leland opposed, during the 1830s, both organized mission work as unscriptural bureaucracy and Sabbatarian laws—especially closing post offices on Sunday—as government infringement into matters of conscience. He died in North Adams, Massachusetts.

• Virtually all of Leland's extant writings, including an autobiographical sketch written in 1835, are collected in *The Writings of John Leland*, ed. L. F. Greene (1845). His sermon *The Rights of Conscience Inalienable . . .* is reprinted in Ellis Sandoz, ed., *Political Sermons of the American Founding Era, 1730–1805* (1991). L. H. Butterfield, "Elder John Leland: Jeffersonian Itinerant," *Proceedings of the American Antiquarian Society* (1952): 151–242, is the standard biography of Leland.

ROBERT M. CALHOON

LELAND, Waldo Gifford (17 July 1879–19 Oct. 1966), historian and archival theorist, was born in Newton, Massachusetts, the son of Luther Erving Leland and Ellen Maria Gifford, public school teachers. Leland attended Newton High School and Brown University, graduating with a B.A. in sociology in 1900. While at Brown he studied with history professor J. Franklin Jameson. He continued his studies at Harvard, receiving an M.A. in history in 1901, and then worked as a teaching assistant in the history department. In 1903 Jameson asked Leland to come to Washington, D.C., to help him and Claude H. Van Tyne on an archival study financed by the Carnegie Institute of Washington. Leland and Van Tyne co-wrote *The Guide to the Archives of the Government of the United States in Washington* (1904). Three years later, Leland published a revised version, establishing his reputation as an authority on federal records. His next project was collecting letters written by the delegates to the Continental Congress, a job that required him to travel extensively in the eastern United States. In April 1904 Leland married Gertrude Dennis, a violionist; they had no children.

Leland moved to France in 1907, where he served as the principal representative of the Carnegie Institute of Washington in that country. While in France he began work on his exhaustive *Guide to Materials for American History in the Libraries and Archives of Paris*. He also supervised the copying of French manuscripts relevant to the United States for inclusion in the Library of Congress. He served as the American delegate to the International Congress of Historical Sciences in 1908 and 1913. In 1909 Leland helped to organize the first Conference of Archivists and gave its keynote address. That same year, he was hired as general secretary of the American Historical Association (AHA), a post that he obtained partly with the help of J. Franklin Jameson, who had used his position in the Carnegie Institute to ensure funding of the AHA. Leland performed this job largely in absentia, editing the association's annual reports and prize essays from Paris. During the academic year 1910–1911, Leland attended the École Nationale des Chartes in Paris.

Leland returned to the United States in 1914, where he remained throughout the First World War. His mentor Jameson was deeply involved in the National Board for Historical Services, and Leland again worked with him as the board's secretary-treasurer. The board's program and methodology was largely derived from Leland's 1912 essay "The National Archives:

A Program" published in the *American Historical Review*. In 1919, again at Jameson's suggestion, Leland served as organizing secretary of the American Council of Learned Societies, a group of six national scholarly organizations convened to represent the U.S. in the International Academic Union. Returning to France in 1922, Leland continued his work as a representative of the Carnegie Institute. During the academic year 1923–1924 he taught as the Hyde Exchange Lecturer at several French universities. In 1926 Leland published the bibliographical work he had written with Newton D. Mereness, *Introduction to American Official Sources for the Economic and Social History of the War*. Leland also helped Jameson lobby Congress to establish National Archives in 1926. In the same year, Leland's long-time work with the International Congress of Historical Sciences came to fruition in the formation of the International Committee of Historical Sciences. This committee was Leland's creation, designed to remedy two major problems that he saw in the ICHS: the lack of continuity between yearly congresses and the exclusion of Germans from participation in the ICHS's work. He served as the International Committee's treasurer.

Leland went back to the United States in 1927 to become secretary of the American Council of Learned Societies, which he had helped begin eight years earlier. The ACLS had grown to include twelve national professional scholarly organizations and had received a major grant from the Rockefeller Foundation to provide for full-time administration. Leland administered the council's affairs as secretary from 1927 to 1939 and as director from 1939 to 1946. His leadership developed the ACLS from a loose constellation of twelve organizations recommending projects for foundation support to a stable federation of twenty-four societies with its own programs in support of scholarship. His major projects at the ACLS included sponsoring the publication of the *Dictionary of American Biography* (1927–1936) and the *Handbook of Latin American Studies*, which appeared beginning in 1935. Leland's fundraising enabled the ACLS to distribute grants directly to scholars and to fund academic conferences. The ACLS was especially active in encouraging the development of regional area studies, including programs focusing on China, Japan, India, Iran, the Slavic countries, the Near East, and Latin America. The first volume of his *Guide to Materials* concerning material in libraries, appeared in 1932 and the second, on papers in the archives of the French Ministry of Foreign Affairs, in 1943. The final three volumes were never published, but the unfinished manuscripts are housed in the Leland papers at the Library of Congress.

In 1938 Leland became president of the International Committee of Historical Sciences. From 1939 to 1941 he presided over the Society of American Archivists. During the Second World War, he served on many war advisory councils. After the war, he was a delegate to a 1945 London conference that laid the groundwork for the United Nations Educational, Scientific, and Cultural Organization (UNESCO). He served on UNESCO's U.S. National Committee as vice chairman from 1946 to 1949. A long-time interest in the Park Service culminated in 1945 in his five-year membership on the U.S. Department of the Interior's Advisory Board on National Parks, Historical Sites, Buildings, and Monuments. This work won Leland the Pugsley Gold Medal from the American Scenic and Historic Preservation Society and the Distinguished Service Award with Gold Medal from the Department of the Interior one year later. In 1958 he chaired the United States delegation to the Eighth International Congress of Historical Sciences held in Zurich, Switzerland. Leland died in Washington, D.C.

Jameson's summons to Washington in 1903 stopped Leland's progress toward a Harvard Ph.D. But with his modest bearing and irenic temperament, Leland became a key figure in the creation and growth of the national and international infrastructure for the scholarship in history and the humanities.

• The Library of Congress houses the Leland papers. A bibliography of his writings appears in American Council of Learned Societies, *Studies in Modern Culture* (1942). For further information on Leland, see his reminiscences of his early career, "Some Early Recollections of an Itinerant Historian," *Proceedings of the American Antiquarian Society*, Oct. 1951; and an Oral History Project transcript at Columbia University, 24 May 1955. See also two articles by Rodney A. Ross: "Waldo Gifford Leland: Archivist by Association," *American Archivist*, Summer 1983, and "Waldo Gifford Leland and Preservation of Documentary Resources," *Federalist*, Summer 1986. Obituaries appear in the *New York Times* and *Washington Post*, both 20 Oct. 1966, and a posthumous tribute is in the *Washington Post*, 23 Oct. 1966.

ELIZABETH ZOE VICARY

LEMAY, Curtis Emerson (15 Nov. 1906–1 Oct. 1990), airman, was born in Columbus, Ohio, the son of Erving LeMay, an ironworker, and Arizona Carpenter. Desiring a military career yet unable to gain appointment to West Point, he enrolled in Reserve Officers Training Corps (ROTC) while attending Ohio State University. LeMay left school without graduating to accept a commission as second lieutenant in the field artillery reserve on 14 June 1928. Inspired by Charles Lindbergh's flight across the Atlantic Ocean the previous year, LeMay volunteered for training at the Army Air Corps School at March Field, California, and received his wings on 12 October 1929. He subsequently toured with the Twenty-seventh Pursuit Squadron at Selfridge Field, Michigan, and by 1934 had completed his degree in civil engineering at Ohio State. LeMay married Helen E. Maitland in 1934; they had one daughter.

LeMay rose to first lieutenant in March 1935 and gained a reputation as a first-rate pilot and navigator. His career reached a turning point in 1937, when he transferred to the Forty-ninth Bombardment Squadron, Second Bomb Group, at Langley Field, Virginia, becoming one of the first qualified pilot/navigators of the new B-17 heavy bomber. In this capacity LeMay

skillfully conducted the overwater interception of the USS *Utah* (1937) and the Italian liner *Rex* (1938), clearly demonstrating air power's utility to American defense. During this period he also commanded a squadron of B-17s on a goodwill tour of Latin America to underscore air power's potential for hemispheric defense. He gained promotion to captain in January 1940 and returned to Langley commanding the Forty-first Reconnaissance Squadron, and the following year he received command of the Seventh Squadron, Thirty-fourth Bomb Group. Promoted to major in 1941, LeMay next flew several experimental, long-range ferry missions to England and North Africa in another demonstration of strategic air power. He consequently received a Distinguished Flying Cross.

The advent of World War II propelled LeMay dramatically in rank and responsibility. His exploits quickly established him as a leading exponent of aerial warfare. A lieutenant colonel as of January 1942, he was assigned to the 305th Bombardment Group in Muroc, California. LeMay advanced to colonel that March and accompanied his men to England as part of General Ira C. Eaker's Eighth Air Force. His innovative and daring tactics, such as restricting evasive maneuvers on approach to a target, resulted in significant improvements in accuracy. On 17 August 1943 LeMay personally conducted the first shuttle raid from England to Regensburg, Germany, before landing in North Africa. Audacious leadership culminated in his promotion to brigadier general in September 1943 and to major general in March 1944. At thirty-seven, he was the youngest three-star general since Ulysses S. Grant. LeMay continued on as commander of the Third Bombardment Division until August 1944, when he was ordered to the China-Burma-India theater (CBI) as head of Twentieth Bomber Command.

In China LeMay encountered the B-29 Superfortress, a technologically advanced aircraft still experiencing developmental problems. Overcoming tremendous logistical and operational challenges, he debugged the massive bomber and directed the first air raids against the Japanese mainland. LeMay concluded that the extreme ranges involved, coupled with a necessarily light bomb load, rendered these efforts negligible. When General Haywood S. Hansell of Twenty-first Bomber Command, operating from the much closer Marianas Islands, also failed to produce results, LeMay became his successor. Dissatisfied with high-altitude daylight bombing, he ordered his B-29s stripped of armament, laden with incendiaries, and sent in low at night. The results were devastating. The 9 March 1945 raid torched sixteen square miles of Tokyo, killing an estimated 100,000 people. In rapid succession, LeMay's bombers gutted several Japanese cities, gravely crippling their ability to resist. He briefly assumed control of the newly created Twentieth Air Force in August 1945 before transferring to the staff of General Carl A. Spaatz, head of U.S. Strategic Air Forces. There he helped orchestrate the atomic bombings of Hiroshima and Nagasaki that ended the war. He thereafter returned to the United States on a record-breaking nonstop flight from Tokyo to Chicago.

Between 1945 and 1947 LeMay functioned as deputy chief of staff for air force research and development in Washington, D.C., and helped introduce the first jet bombers into the American arsenal. When the U.S. Air Force became a separate entity in 1947, he received temporary promotion to lieutenant general and command of all air forces in Europe. The rapidly unfolding Cold War afforded LeMay new opportunities for distinction. Between June 1948 and May 1949 he organized Operation Vittles to counter the Soviet ground blockade of Berlin. He personally remarked at one point to Secretary of State George C. Marshall that the blockade should have been run by force, but LeMay's aircraft nonetheless successfully delivered 2 million tons of supplies in 300,000 flights, thereby thwarting Soviet intentions. Before the airlift concluded, however, he was recalled stateside to replace General George C. Kenney as head of the Strategic Air Command (SAC). In that position LeMay was one of the prime movers of American nuclear policy and a powerful influence in the debate over national defense.

LeMay's task of turning SAC into the world's finest strategic bomber force was daunting. In 1948 it consisted of only 610 obsolete aircraft, a handful of atomic weapons, and poorly trained, demoralized personnel. However, he proved himself a genius at procuring both modern, complicated weapons systems, like the all-jet B-47 Stratojet, and top-rate flight and ground crews to man them. Discipline was tightened, training became relentless, and SAC crews were deployed on a constant, around-the-clock basis. Furthermore, LeMay instituted his unique Management Control System (MCS), whereby subordinates would detect potential breakdowns in SAC and correct them before they occurred. By 1954 LeMay had succeeded in a dramatic fashion. Within six years he commanded a fleet of 1,000 jet bombers carrying sufficient megatonnage to annihilate the Soviet Union within days of a conflict. For the remainder of the Cold War, the United States possessed a strategic air force second to none that functioned as both a deterrent to hostilities and a guarantor of national security.

In April 1957 LeMay departed SAC to serve as air force vice chief of staff under General Thomas White. In June 1961 President John F. Kennedy elevated LeMay to full chief. Unfortunately, his tenure was an unhappy one on account of differing perceptions with Secretary of Defense Robert S. McNamara. LeMay, as purveyor of the "bomber cult" in the scheme of national defense, held manned aircraft at a premium and opposed any new technologies threatening that eminence. McNamara, by contrast, argued for lavish expenditures on highly sophisticated and expensive missile systems to enhance nuclear deterrence. LeMay also denounced Joint Chiefs of Staff general Maxwell Taylor's concept of "flexible response" toward communism and instead advocated a confrontational policy of rollback. LeMay's dissatisfaction crested with President Lyndon B. Johnson's policy of gradual esca-

lation during the Vietnam War, and he resigned on 1 February 1965, concluding thirty-seven years of military service. LeMay served as an executive with an electronics firm, but in 1968, still concerned with Vietnam, he ran as vice president on the ticket with segregationist governor George C. Wallace of Alabama. LeMay's call to bomb North Vietnam "back into the Stone Age" was repudiated at the polls. However, his general view on the application of air power against North Vietnam was vindicated when Operation Linebacker II, a concentrated air assault upon Hanoi, brought the Communists back to the negotiating table in December 1972. LeMay died at March Air Force Base, Riverside, California.

LeMay was a tough-minded and effective proponent of American air power. His seemingly gruff and blunt exterior belied first-rate analytical and administrative abilities. The Strategic Air Command and the high efficiency standards it set were his greatest efficacies. Conversely, LeMay's inflexible strategic disposition and imperious style alienated civilian superiors and undoubtedly cost him the chair on the Joint Chiefs. Nonetheless, vision, innovation, and dogged determination to succeed were hallmarks of LeMay's leadership and mark him as the twentieth century's foremost aviation strategist.

• Collections of LeMay's papers are at the Manuscripts Division, Library of Congress; the National Air and Space Museum, Smithsonian Institution; the Air Force Academy Library, Colorado Springs; and the Air Force Historical Research Agency, Maxwell Air Force Base, Montgomery, Ala. Oral histories are at the Office of Air Force History, Bolling Air Force Base, Washington, D.C.; the Lyndon B. Johnson Library, Austin, Tex.; and the libraries of Princeton and Columbia Universities. LeMay's own writings include *Superfortress* (1988); *Mission with LeMay* (1965), with MacKinlay Kantor; and *America Is in Danger* (1968), with Dale O. Smith. A printed interview is in Richard H. Kohn and Joseph P. Haraham, eds., *Strategic Air Warfare* (1988). The best biographical treatment is Thomas M. Coffey, *Iron Eagle: The Turbulent Life and Times of General Curtis LeMay* (1986). Analysis of his military contributions is in Robert F. Futrell, *Ideas, Concepts, Doctrine* (2 vols., 1989); Walton S. Moody, *Building a Strategic Air Force* (1996); and Carroll Zimmerman, *Insider at SAC* (1988). Other facets of his career are addressed in Harry R. Borowski, "Capability and the Development of the Strategic Air Command, 1946–1950" (Ph.D. diss., Univ. of California, Santa Barbara, 1976); William S. Borgiasz, "Struggle for Predominance: Evolution and Consolidation of Nuclear Forces in the Strategic Air Command" (Ph.D. diss., American Univ., 1991); and James M. Doyle, "The XXI Bomber Command: Primary Factor in the Defeat of Japan" (Ph.D. diss., St. Louis Univ., 1964). Less flattering assessments are in Richard Rhodes, *Dark Sun: The Making of the Hydrogen Bomb* (1995), and Michael S. Sherry, *The Rise of American Air Power* (1987).

JOHN C. FREDRIKSEN

LEMKE, William Frederick (13 Aug. 1878–30 May 1950), agrarian leader, congressman, and presidential candidate, was born in Albany, Minnesota, and raised in Towner County, North Dakota, the son of Fred Lemke and Julia Anna Klier, pioneer farmers who were successful enough to accumulate some 2,700 acres of land. The young Lemke worked long hours on the family farm, attending a common school for only three months in the summers. The family did, however, reserve enough money to send William to the University of North Dakota, where he was a superior student. Graduating in 1902, he stayed at the state university for the first year of law school but moved to Georgetown University, then to Yale, where he finished work on his law degree and won the praise of the dean.

Lemke returned to his home state in 1905 to set up practice at Fargo. His clients were farmers and farm organizations, and eventually he became associated with most major farm groups in the Northwest. In 1910 he married Isabelle McIntyre, with whom he had three children. He suffered a disastrous financial setback when his extensive speculation in Mexican lands, begun in 1906, was wiped out by the effects of the Mexican revolutions. Impoverished by this failure, he wrote an angry book, *Crimes against Mexico* (1915), attacking President Woodrow Wilson for not supporting the Victoriano Huerta government.

These troubles, however, were soon eclipsed by a series of successes as a leader of the Nonpartisan League, a movement of agrarian protests organized in North Dakota in 1915. The following year Lemke became the attorney for the league, which grew to a membership of 200,000 and spread into four neighboring states. When the league gained control of the North Dakota Republican party in 1916, Lemke became the party chairman and trained newly elected farmer-legislators in the state capital. There he wrote much of the Nonpartisan League legislative program that was enacted into law. In 1920, having become a rising star in the state, Lemke was elected attorney general, but good fortune was not of long duration.

Opponents of the Nonpartisan League soon charged that Lemke and others had caused the state-owned central bank to deposit funds in a private institution they knew to be insolvent. The subsequent indictments were quashed, and his political enemies were never able to provide evidence of personal dishonesty. However, Lemke's reputation was damaged, and he suffered the humiliation of defeat—along with his friend, Governor Lynn Frazier—in a recall election in 1921. When he failed in a race for the gubernatorial nomination the following year, he retired in bitterness to private law practice for the next decade. During the critical election of 1932, in the depths of the Great Depression, he returned to public life and was elected to one of North Dakota's two at-large congressional seats.

At first a strong supporter of Franklin D. Roosevelt, Representative Lemke turned against the president when the New Deal failed to support Lemke's plans to alleviate the problems faced by western farmers. The administration opposed the legislation for which he became most noted, the Frazier-Lemke Farm Bankruptcy Act, originally enacted in 1934, subsequently struck down by the Supreme Court, and then reenacted in modified form in 1935. Although this legislation was successful in liberalizing bankruptcy proceedings for debt-ridden farms, it never received the support of the White House. More important was Roosevelt's rejection of Lemke's central scheme for saving desperate agrarians menaced by foreclosure, the Frazier-Lemke Farm Refinance Bill.

Lemke's ambitious plan called for the federal government to supply the cash farmers required to pay off their mortgages or buy back farms lost to foreclosure since 1928. The scheme would cost $3 billion and would be financed by simply printing the money. New Dealers dismissed it as an unworkable and hyperinflationary "pipe dream," but the North Dakotan was convinced that his plan would not only save the farmers but would also solve the economic problems of the land. "It will put into circulation sufficient money," he wrote, to cure the depression. Unpersuaded, the administration mobilized its forces to inflict a crushing defeat on Lemke when he forced a floor vote on the bill in early 1936.

Lemke became an embittered foe of the White House, claiming, "Truth is on the scaffold, wrong is on the throne . . . the money changers are trying to destroy the farmer." He turned to other figures offering inflationary panaceas, men who also had become disenchanted with Roosevelt. One was Father Charles E. Coughlin, the famous "radio priest" who had organized the National Union for Social Justice and was now planning a new political party to challenge Roosevelt in the fall campaign. Coughlin had endorsed Lemke's failed bill, and now the congressman agreed to be the presidential candidate for the new Union party. When Dr. Francis E. Townsend, creator of the Old Age Revolving Pension Plan, and Gerald L. K. Smith, organizer for the late senator Huey Long's Share Our Wealth Plan, endorsed Lemke at the huge National Union Convention in Cleveland, a coalition was created of angry outsiders who had become leaders of mass movements built around neopopulist critiques of the corporate order and the New Deal state.

Short and chunky, lantern-jawed and almost completely bald, his face a maze of freckles and pock marks (the result of a youthful case of smallpox), and his features defined by the loss of an eye in a childhood accident, candidate Lemke was an unimpressive figure on the hustings. His speaking style was flat and monotonous, and his voice could be shrill in emphasis. Yet the real obstacles he faced in the national race in 1936 had less to do with his personal qualities than other factors. Lemke had to deal with strains developing in the alliance of radical leaders, as first Smith, whose self-serving schemes alienated his allies, and then Townsend lost interest in the Union ticket. Coughlin's increasingly strident and intemperate speeches also injured the Union cause and overshadowed the Lemke candidacy as election day neared. In addition, the Union party faced insuperable obstacles to getting on the ballot in several states, and many American voters proved reluctant to "throw away" their votes on the third-party candidate in those states where the Union name appeared. In the end, Lemke polled 892,378 votes, just under 2 percent of the national total. He did not come close to carrying any single state, as the president scored a resounding reelection victory with more than 27 million votes.

Following the election, Lemke was a diminished public figure, but he did remain active. While he was defeated by his archenemy in North Dakota politics, William Langer, in a close race for senator in 1940, he stayed on in Congress for the rest of his life, serving from 1936 to 1940 and from 1942 to 1950. He continued to advocate the interests of his state and region but without making a major impact on events and in ways largely unmarked by controversy. Until his death in Fargo, he remained what he had been all his adult life, a dedicated spokesman for the farmers of the American West.

• The best sources for any study of the life of Lemke are the William Lemke Papers in the Orrin G. Libby Historical Manuscripts Collection, University of North Dakota, Grand Forks. Other manuscript materials are in the Franklin D. Roosevelt Papers (Official File 300, Democratic National Committee, and Official File 1038, Frazier-Lemke Bill); the Franklin D. Roosevelt Library, Hyde Park, N.Y. and the Democratic National Campaign Committee: Correspondence of James A. Farley, Chairman, 1936, in the Roosevelt Library. Edward C. Blackorby, *Prairie Rebel: The Public Life of William Lemke* (1963), is a study of Lemke's career. David H. Bennett, *Demagogues in the Depression: American Radicals and the Union Party, 1932–1936* (1969), traces Lemke's career and describes the origins and activities of the Union party campaign in 1936. Contemporary views of Lemke and his Union party candidacy are in Walter Davenport, "Mr. Lemke Stops to Think," *Collier's*, 17 Oct. 1936, pp. 7–8, 25–26; and Jonathan Mitchell, "Liberty Bill Lemke," *New Republic*, 12 Aug. 1936, pp. 8–10.

DAVID H. BENNETT

LEMNITZER, Lyman Louis (29 Aug. 1899–12 Nov. 1988), U.S. Army general, was born in Honesdale, Pennsylvania, the son of William L. Lemnitzer, a shoe manufacturer, and Hannah Blockberger. Lemnitzer graduated from the U.S. Military Academy at West Point in 1920, a product of the accelerated program of World War I. In 1923 he married Katherine Mead Tryon; they had two children. The next twenty years followed a familiar pattern: slow advancement as artilleryman, punctuated by service as instructor at West Point (1926–1930, 1934–1935) and at the Coast Artillery School (1936–1939). That he was chosen to attend the Command and General Staff School at Fort Leavenworth, Kansas, in 1936 and the Army War College at Carlisle, Pennsylvania, in 1940 attested to the promise that his early career showed.

World War II provided an opportunity for him to utilize his talents as organizer and administrator, which had been evidenced early in his career through his successful teaching experiences. General Dwight D. Eisenhower recognized his special abilities in handling staff issues and serving as a mediator in dealing with conflicting interests in an army of allies. Lemnitzer was preeminently a staff officer and served Eisenhower with distinction as assistant G-3 for Allied Forces Headquarters in London and in Algiers. Subsequently, he was deputy chief of staff to General Mark Clark and to Field Marshal Sir Harold Alexander in Italy. While he also served as commanding general of an antiaircraft brigade in 1943 in the Tunisian campaign, he made his mark as a planner and organizer, not as a field general or strategist.

His easy relations with European military leaders combined with his experience as a military planner made Lemnitzer an attractive choice as an observer and supporter of the new Western Union that the United Kingdom, France, and the Benelux countries created in 1948. He was appointed in 1949 to be director of European military assistance in the Department of Defense and as such was the most influential American military supporter of the North Atlantic Treaty Organization (NATO), which grew out of the Western Union.

His European orientation notwithstanding, Lemnitzer left Washington in 1951 to serve in Korea. To advance to the highest ranks he needed the credentials of leadership. He acquired them as commanding general of the Eleventh Airborne Division and the Seventh Infantry Division in 1951 through 1952 during the Korean War. He was commander of the Eighth Army in Japan and Korea in 1955. His last post in Asia was commander in chief of the Far Eastern Command (1955–1957).

When he returned to Washington in 1957, his attention once again was directed to Europe in his roles as vice chief of staff of the army (1957–1959), army chief of staff (1959–1960), and chairman of the Joint Chiefs of Staff (1960–1962). His tenure at the Pentagon involved him primarily but not exclusively in European issues, such as the impact of Sputnik and the crises over access to Berlin in 1958 and 1961. His most difficult time was in the spring of 1961 when, as chairman of the Joint Chiefs of Staff, he took some of the blame for the abortive invasion of Cuba at the Bay of Pigs.

When the administration of John F. Kennedy looked for a successor to General Lauris Norstad as supreme Allied commander, Europe (SACEUR), Lemnitzer was a logical choice. No military figure, not even Eisenhower, had a longer association with NATO than Lemnitzer. As SACEUR from 1963 to 1969, he helped implement the new doctrine of "flexible response," which was intended to reduce NATO's dependence on nuclear weapons by increasing the deterrent power of conventional forces, and he steered the organization through such challenges as the Warsaw Pact's invasion of Czechoslovakia in 1968. His greatest service was keeping intact the military organization of the alliance when de Gaulle's withdrawal of France in 1966 might have destroyed it.

Lemnitzer achieved the objectives toward which every professional soldier aspires. He lacked the commanding presence of Eisenhower and the political instincts of Norstad, but from 1963 to 1969 he used Paris and Brussels as arenas for the realization of his administrative and diplomatic talents. In his years of retirement he was a tireless advocate for the Atlantic alliance, lecturing at universities in every part of the country. In 1982 Kent State University named its Center for NATO Studies in his honor. He died in Washington, D.C.

• General Lemnitzer's correspondence, official and private, has been deposited in the library of the National Defense University in Washington, D.C. Some material may be found as well in the Dwight D. Eisenhower Library, Abilene, Kan. The Lyman L. Lemnitzer Center for NATO and European Community Studies at Kent State University contains memorabilia, particularly of his NATO years. Kathleen A. Kellner, "Broker of Power: General Lyman Lemnitzer, 1946–1969" (Ph.D. diss., Kent State Univ., 1987), concentrates on his connections with NATO. See also Lawrence S. Kaplan and Kathleen A. Kellner, "Lemnitzer: Surviving the French Military Withdrawal," in *Generals in International Politics: NATO's Supreme Allied Commander, Europe,* ed. Robert S. Jordan (1987).

LAWRENCE S. KAPLAN

LE MOYNE, Jean-Baptiste (baptized 23 Feb. 1680–7 Mar. 1767), French soldier, explorer, and governor of colonial Louisiana, was born in Montréal, New France, the son of Charles Le Moyne, sieur de Longueuil et de Châteauguay, a provincial nobleman, and Catherine Thierry Primot. Jean-Baptiste Le Moyne inherited the title *sieur de Bienville* on the death of his brother François in 1691. Following the death of his parents early in his childhood, Bienville looked to his elder brothers for guidance, following them into the French military service and, like them, serving with distinction as a naval and colonial officer. Bienville entered the navy as a midshipman in 1692, a rank he held until 1699. During this period, Bienville served under his brother Pierre Le Moyne d'Iberville, a Canadian military hero, in campaigns along the New England coast, in Hudson Bay, and in Newfoundland. After sustaining severe head injuries in a 1697 engagement, Bienville accompanied Iberville to France where, the following year, he was assigned to participate in the colonization of Louisiana, serving once again under his brother.

Bienville sailed for Louisiana on 24 October 1698. After arriving along the Gulf Coast, Bienville participated in an expedition sent to explore the lower reaches of the Mississippi River in February and March 1699. Following his return to his ship, Bienville was appointed second in command of Fort Maurepas, an outpost constructed near present-day Biloxi, Mississippi, to safeguard France's claims to the Mississippi Valley.

In the succeeding months, Bienville led diplomatic missions to area tribes and commanded small exploratory expeditions to the lower Mississippi Valley. While engaged in one of the latter missions in 1699, Bienville, who had only five men and two canoes at his disposal, encountered a British warship carrying Huguenot colonists in the Mississippi and audaciously ordered its commander, Captain William Louis Bond, to withdraw or face destruction at the hands of superior French forces. Unwilling to test Bienville's bravado, Bond departed, forever linking the event to the bend in the Mississippi known thereafter as English Turn.

In 1700 Bienville explored the lower Tensas, Black, Ouachita, and Red river valleys, before taking command of the newly established Fort de Mississippi in present-day Plaquemines Parish, Louisiana. The following year he became acting commandant of Fort Maurepas, a position that, because of Iberville's absence, made him the highest-ranking officer in the embryonic colonial government. The Canadian was formally commissioned royal lieutenant and commandant in 1702. Bienville continued to serve in this capacity until 1712, and, over the course of this decade, he was forced to confront numerous major problems, including prolonged neglect by the mother country throughout the War of the Spanish Succession; factional political strife within the colonial government; charges of malfeasance, corruption, and immorality leveled by his Louisiana detractors among the clergy, colonial bureaucracy, and the garrison; and the hostility of the strategic Alabama tribe. In 1702 the colony moved to Mobile in search of better land for farming, deeper harbors for shipping, and a healthier environment. The move was also the first step in Iberville's effort to contain British expansion into the Trans-Mississippi region.

Bienville was replaced as de facto governor of Louisiana in 1712. Louis XIV, facing major economic difficulties in the metropole, relinquished control of Louisiana to wealthy French financier Antoine Crozat. Crozat named Antoine Laumet, alias Lamothe Cadillac to govern the colony, and Bienville was reduced to garrison commandant.

Stung by the humiliation of his demotion and alienated by Cadillac's arrogance and acerbic personality, Bienville joined with Louisiana's new commissioner of justice, finance, and administration to effectively paralyze the colonial government. At the height of the intragovernmental feuding, Cadillac assigned Bienville to quell an incipient conflict incited by the new governor with the powerful Natchez tribe. Put into the field with only thirty-four soldiers and facing an armed contingent of eight hundred Natchez, Bienville nevertheless managed, through subterfuge and kidnapping, to coerce the tribe into executing warriors charged with the deaths of several Frenchmen and into erecting a French fortress on their tribal lands.

Following his return to Mobile and Cadillac's subsequent recall to France, Bienville again became acting governor of Louisiana, pending the arrival of royal appointee Jean-Michel de L'Epinay. In 1718 Bienville, who again became governor of Louisiana following L'Epinay's recall to France, played a pivotal role in the establishment of New Orleans as an entrepôt and administrative center for the colony's most rapidly developing region. The Canadian also supervised the generally successful French military campaign against Spanish West Florida (1719–1720), despite a woeful lack of resources.

Bienville's military and governmental successes were deemed less significant to Louisiana's new proprietary company—the Company of the Indies—than his tendency to spawn factionalism and conflicts. The company consequently recalled Bienville to France in 1724, ostensibly for "consultations," but on 9 April 1726 the proprietary regime stripped Bienville of military and governmental rank, the 1729 Natchez massacre plunged Louisiana into a full-scale Indian war, destroying the colony's emerging profitability and creating the need for a governor experienced in colonial warfare and Indian diplomacy.

In 1732, the Company of the Indies having retroceded control of Louisiana to the Crown, the French monarchy rehabilitated Bienville and named him governor of Louisiana. During the 1730s Bienville grappled with the perennial problems of colonial administration in the lower Mississippi Valley: contraband commerce, the slave trade, land grants, the search for profitable staple crops, inflation, construction and maintenance of fortifications, troop desertions, natural disasters, and inadequate funding by the French colonial ministry. The landmark events of this last gubernatorial administration were two ill-starred military campaigns against the Chickasaws, stemming from the Chickasaw refusal to surrender fugitives given safe haven during the recently concluded Natchez war. Bienville's first Chickasaw campaign, mounted in 1736, was poorly coordinated. Tired of waiting for Bienville's army, then slowly wending its way to Chickasaw territory from New Orleans, the impetuous commander of the second French contingent mounted an ill-advised and ultimately disastrous offensive against the main Chickasaw villages. On 26 May 1736 Bienville's army attacked the Chickasaw village of Ackia, only to be repelled with heavy losses. The French army was compelled to withdraw.

Ordered by the French colonial ministry to mount a second campaign, Bienville led an equally unsuccessful offensive against the Chickasaws in 1739–1740. When his engineers proved unable even to chart a road to the Chickasaw villages, Bienville wisely chose to sue for peace, extracting only token concessions from the Chickasaws.

Following the second defeat, Bienville chose to step down from office rather than await the inevitable letter of recall. He requested permission to go to France to rehabilitate his allegedly failing health. The colonial minister authorized Bienville's retirement in October 1741. His replacement—Pierre Rigaud de Vaudreuil—did not arrive at New Orleans until May 1743. Bienville departed the colony the following August.

After debarking at Rochefort, France, in October 1743, Bienville made his home along Rue Vincennes in Paris, where he spent his twilight years in obscurity until his death there. He never married.

Jean-Baptiste Le Moyne de Bienville has been frequently called "the father of Louisiana" with more than a little justification, for he was unquestionably the most important figure in the eighteenth-century French colonization of the Gulf Coast and lower Mississippi Valley. He governed Louisiana through most of its most difficult formative period and left an indelible mark on the course of the colony's political, economic, and military development.

• No cache of personal papers is known to exist. Much of Bienville's official correspondence has been transcribed and translated in Albert Godfrey Sanders et al., eds. and trans., *Mississippi Provincial Archives* (6 vols., 1927–1984). The original correspondence and miscellaneous documents relating to Bienville's Louisiana land grants can be found in the following French documentary collections: Archives Nationales, Archives des Colonies, série C 13a (Louisiane: correspondance générale), vols. 1–54; série G1 (état civil), vols. 412, 464, 465. Bienville has attracted surprisingly little scholarly attention. E. Grace King, *Jean Baptiste Le Moyne, Sieur de Bienville* (1892), and Georges Oudard, *Bienville, le père de la Louisiane* (1900), constitute the only full-length biographies of this colorful and controversial personality, but their now badly outdated works constitute little more than apologia. Marcel Giraud, *Histoire de la Louisiane française/History of French Louisiana* (1953–1993), provides a much more balanced and factually accurate account of Bienville's life and contributions.

CARL A. BRASSEAUX

LE MOYNE, Pierre (baptized 20 July 1661–9 July 1706), French soldier, explorer, and governor of colonial Louisiana, was born at Ville-Marie de Montréal, New France, the son of Charles Le Moyne, sieur de Longueuil et de Châteauguay, a provincial nobleman, and Catherine Thierry Primot. The early life of Pierre Le Moyne, known as the sieur d'Iberville, is veiled in obscurity. It is known that he was groomed for naval duty by his influential father through service aboard his father's ship. In 1683 he was entrusted with Governor Le Febvre de La Barre's dispatches for the French Crown. It was also in that year that Jeanne-Geneviève Picoté de Belestre's guardians brought a paternity suit against Iberville, claiming that the young Canadian officer was responsible for her pregnancy. The Conseil Souverain, Canada's court of last resort, concurred with the plaintiffs and ordered Iberville to support the child until its fifteenth birthday.

Iberville's maritime experiences served him well in his military career, which began in 1686, when he participated in Chevalier de Troyes's expedition against English installations on James Bay. As a result of his valorous conduct during the French assault against Moose Fort, he was made one of the leaders of the ensuing French campaign against Charles Fort. He subsequently led a party of only thirteen men in the capture of the *Craven*, a British trading vessel anchored near Charles Fort.

Following these exploits, Iberville returned to Moose Fort and then participated in the French campaign against Albany Fort on James Bay. After the fort's capture, Troyes placed Iberville in command of the forty soldiers assigned to occupy the post and in August 1686 appointed him "governor" of the captured British installations. One year later, having received neither expected reinforcements nor supplies, Iberville traveled to Quebec, whence he sailed to

France. In France during the winter of 1687–1688, Iberville secured royal support—including the *Soleil d'Afrique*, a small man-of-war—for the captured outposts along James Bay. He returned to James Bay via Quebec during the summer of 1688. The *Soleil d'Afrique*, however, was blockaded in the Albany River by two British warships in September 1688. During the following months, Iberville ordered his men to prevent the British crews from hunting, thereby guaranteeing an outbreak of scurvy aboard the enemy vessels. By spring the surviving British sailors were unable to offer resistance to Iberville and his sixteen French-Canadian crewmen. Iberville's forces captured a third British vessel in James Bay in July 1689 and triumphantly returned to Quebec on 28 October 1689, with a large cargo of British prisoners and captured pelts.

Iberville participated in the French campaign against present-day Schenectady, New York, during the winter of 1690. Armed with a 1689 commission as commander of the "northern sea," Iberville subsequently sailed from Quebec to Hudson Bay in command of three small ships. After skillfully avoiding capture by three British vessels in August 1690, Iberville's forces captured the British trading post of New Severn, seizing there 100,000 *livres'* worth of pelts. Iberville returned to Quebec in October 1691 after wintering at James Bay.

Iberville subsequently sailed for France to petition the French monarchy for additional naval support for his anticipated 1692 campaign against the remaining British installations along Hudson Bay. The Crown, however, required Iberville to engage in escort duty for Canadian-bound supply ships. Iberville's vessels arrived at Quebec too late to undertake the proposed Hudson Bay expedition. His vessels were again employed in escort duty in 1692 and 1693. On 8 October 1693 Iberville married Marie-Thérèse Pollet de la Combe-Pocatière. Five children are known to have been born of this union. In 1694 Iberville mounted an expedition against York Fort on Hudson Bay, capturing the outpost on 13 October after a brief siege. The following spring and summer he supervised the lucrative fur-trading operations there. After acquiring approximately 450 canoe-loads of prime pelts, Iberville installed a seventy-man garrison at York Fort and set sail for La Rochelle, France.

After his arrival in France on 9 October 1695, Iberville was given command of two naval frigates and assigned to lift the British siege of French Newfoundland. En route to Newfoundland, his unit engaged and defeated a British flotilla near the mouth of the St. John River, in present-day New Brunswick. His forces subsequently laid siege to and captured Fort William Henry in Newfoundland. In November 1696 the French-Canadian's troops captured St. John's after a brief siege.

After the fall of St. John's, Iberville led his naval squadron to Hudson Bay to prevent British reinforcements from reaching York Fort, which had been recaptured in 1696. During the voyage his flagship, the *Pélican*, became separated from the rest of the squadron. On arrival at the Hayes River, the *Pélican* encountered British frigates. Through a series of brilliant tactical maneuvers in the ensuing combat, Iberville's vessel sank one enemy ship, captured one, and forced the third to flee. With the subsequent arrival of the remainder of the squadron, Iberville laid siege to York Fort, and on 13 September 1697 the British garrison surrendered. Following the conclusion of hostilities through the Treaty of Ryswick (1697), Iberville departed York Fort for France later in September.

Arriving in France in November, Iberville was named to lead an expedition to the mouth of the Mississippi River, where he was to lay the foundation for a French colony. He sailed for the Mississippi River from Brest, France, in command of four naval vessels in October 1698. His squadron anchored at a roadstead off the present Mississippi coastline in February 1699. Leading a small party of Frenchmen and Canadians, he located and explored the lower Mississippi Valley. He then supervised construction of Fort Maurepas, near present-day Biloxi, Mississippi, to safeguard France's claim to the area before sailing for France on 3 May 1699.

When he arrived in France, Iberville was awarded the Cross of St. Louis for meritorious career service. He was the first native Canadian to receive the honor.

Iberville led a second expedition to Louisiana in the fall of 1699. Arriving at Fort Maurepas in January 1700, he forged alliances with the region's major Native American groups and ordered construction of an outpost along the lower Mississippi River. He then sailed for France in May 1700.

After his return to the Gulf Coast in February 1702, Iberville supervised construction of a French outpost near present-day Mobile, Alabama. In April 1702 he returned to France, where he was formally appointed governor of Louisiana in 1703; Iberville, however, would never return to Louisiana.

In late 1703 Iberville's eight-ship naval squadron was diverted from an expedition to Louisiana because of more pressing military needs. He spent 1703–1706 in France, some of the time gravely ill. In 1706 Iberville commanded a twelve-ship fleet sent to raid British installations in the West Indies. The task force captured the British island of Nevis in April 1706, and Iberville permitted his troops to pillage the sugar island. Iberville died of yellow fever at Havana, Cuba, where his fleet had put in for supplies.

Iberville, sometimes called the Canadian Cid, is widely considered Canada's greatest colonial hero. He is also rightfully considered the founder of Louisiana. Since the 1950s Iberville's once sterling reputation has been tarnished by the fact that he was tried posthumously and found guilty of embezzlement of a large amount of provisions intended for the Nevis expedition; his widow was forced to make restitution to the Crown.

• Most of the primary resources pertaining to Iberville's career can be found in France's Archives Nationales, Archives des Colonies, series C 11 (general correspondence for New France) and C 13 (general correspondence, Louisiana). Some of these manuscripts were transcribed and published by Pierre Margry in *Découvertes et établissements des français dans l'ouest et dans le sud de l'Amérique septentrionale, 1614–1754* (6 vols., 1876–1886). Iberville's Louisiana journals have been translated and published in Carl A. Brasseaux, trans., ed., and annot., *A Comparative View of French Louisiana: The Journals of Pierre Le Moyne d'Iberville and Jean-Jacques-Blaise d'Abbadie, 1699 and 1762* (1979), and Richebourg Gaillard McWilliams, trans. and ed., *Iberville's Gulf Journals* (1981). Readers wishing to investigate more fully Iberville's life and military career should consult Nellis M. Crouse, *Lemoyne d'Iberville: Soldier of New France* (1954); Guy Frégault, *Iberville le conquerant* (1944); L.-M. Le Jeune, *Le Chevalier Pierre Le Moyne, Sieur d'Iberville* (1937); and Marcel Giraud, *Histoire de la Louisiane française*, vol. 1 (1953).

CARL A. BRASSEAUX

LE MOYNE DE MORGUES, Jacques (c. 1533–May 1588), artist and cartographer, was born in Dieppe, France. Nothing is known of Le Moyne's early life. In 1564 he was recruited by Gaspard de Coligny, admiral of France and sponsor of the French Florida colonization expeditions (1562–1565), to chart the coast and rivers of northeastern Florida. It is possible that Le Moyne was Charles IX's cartographer and was chosen by Coligny for this reason. Because Jean Ribault, who had commanded the first expedition (1562–1563), was being detained in England, it was under René Goulaine de Laudonnière's leadership that the French left Le Havre in April 1564. Shortly after their arrival in Florida in June, they founded Fort Caroline (near present-day Jacksonville) at the mouth of the St. John's River, where they remained for fifteen months. During that time Le Moyne traveled extensively and took an active role in establishing contact with the native Timucuans.

The Spaniards, determined to drive the French out of Florida, established a settlement in St. Augustine, a few miles south of Fort Caroline, under the leadership of Pedro Menéndez de Avilés in September 1565. Ribault had arrived in Florida the previous week, on 29 August, with reinforcements and decided to seize St. Augustine by sea with most of the French troops, leaving Fort Caroline poorly defended. At dawn on 20 September 1565, the Spaniards successfully stormed the French fort. Le Moyne and René de Laudonnière were among the fifteen who managed to escape. After walking two days and nights, they reached the French ships anchored at the mouth of the river. They set sail for France but arrived in England by mistake in mid-November. In the early months of 1566 they arrived in Moulins, in the south of Paris, where the French court was residing. There they gave a report of the expedition to Charles IX, and Le Moyne presented his map of Florida to the king.

Sometime before 1581, during the Wars of Religion, Le Moyne fled to England, where he was granted denization, a status close to naturalization. Like most Huguenot refugees in London, Le Moyne took up residence in Blackfriars with his younger wife Jeane (maiden name unknown), whom he had married either before leaving France or once in England. There they had a child, who presumably died at an early age. In the mid-1580s Le Moyne became associated with a group concerned with the colonization of Virginia. He had met the draftsman John White probably between 1584 and 1586; White introduced Le Moyne to Sir Walter Raleigh, who was to become their patron. Through the latter, Le Moyne probably met his other patron, Lady Mary Sidney, and began a series of plant watercolors. In 1586 he published some of them in a collection entitled *La clef des champs*, with a sonnet and dedication to her. On 16 May 1588 Le Moyne wrote his will, which was probated on 1 June, implying that he died between these two dates. Shortly thereafter Theodor de Bry, a Protestant publisher originally from Liège but established in Frankfurt, bought Le Moyne's account and paintings of the Florida expeditions from his widow. His narrative, entitled *Brevis narratio eorum quae in Florida Americae provincia Gallis acciderunt*, engravings after his drawings, and his map of Florida were then published in 1591 as the second volume of de Bry's collection of voyages.

Le Moyne contributed to Europeans' knowledge of North America through his paintings and his map of Florida more than through his narrative, which adds little information to Laudonnière's *Histoire notable de la Floride*. Le Moyne's pictorial work entitled *Florida Americae provincia descriptio et eicones* contains a general introduction about Florida and forty-two hunting, agricultural, and battle scenes, as well as portraits of the Timucuans, accompanied by descriptive captions. These illustrations are the only ones to portray the Timucuans and give the earliest detailed descriptions of Native American life. However, the ethnographic significance of these illustrations is subject to controversy, for they were probably reconstructions based on memory (it is not known whether Le Moyne managed to escape Fort Caroline with his work) and were considerably altered by de Bry himself, who was unfamiliar with the subject. One of them is deposited in the New York Public Library, but historians are still debating whether it is an original or a contemporary reproduction. Despite their ethnographic inaccuracies, Le Moyne's engravings remain a precious iconographic source of early southeastern Native American history. The map, which represents the Floridian peninsula and Cuba, is based on Ribault's reports and charts as well as Le Moyne's own observations and fills an important gap in southeastern North America cartography.

• Le Moyne's *Brevis narratio* and *Florida descriptio et eicones* are available in Latin in Theodor de Bry, ed., *Historia Americae sive novi orbis* (6 vols., 1590–1634), which is located in the libraries of Arizona State University, University of Georgia, and Southern Methodist University. Paul Hulton, ed., *Jacques Le Moyne de Morgues: A Huguenot Artist in France, Florida, and England* (1977), contains a biography of Le Moyne along with an English translation of *Brevis narratio* and *Florida descriptio et eicones* and reproductions of his pictorial work. On Le Moyne and his influence on John White's work, see Paul Hulton, "The Images of the New World: Jacques Le Moyne de Morgues and John White," in *The Westward Enterprise* ed. K. H. Andrews et al. (1978), pp. 195–214. For a discussion on the authenticity of Le Moyne's watercolor deposited in the New York Public Library, see Christian F. Feest, "Jacques Le Moyne Minus Four," *European Review of Native American Studies* 2 (1988): 33–38. For reproductions of Le Moyne's illustrations, see also William C. Sturtevant, "First Visual Images of Native America," in Fredi Chiappelli, ed., *First Images of America* (2 vols., 1976), and Gloria Deak, ed., *Picturing America, 1497–1899: Prints, Maps, and Drawings Bearing on the New World Discoveries and on the Development of the Territory That Is Now the United States* (2 vols., 1988). For a general background on the French Renaissance and the New World, see Frank Lestringant, *Mapping the Renaissance World: The Geographical Imagination in the Age of Discovery* (1994).

BERTRAND VAN RUYMBEKE

L'ENFANT, Pierre Charles (2 Aug. 1754–14 June 1825), engineer and architect, was born in Paris, France, the son of Pierre L'Enfant, painter of military subjects for the French Crown, and Marie-Charlotte Leullier. In 1771 he was listed as his father's student at the Royal Academy of Painting and Sculpture, the only known record of his education. L'Enfant arrived in Portsmouth, New Hampshire, in April 1777 aboard the *Amphitrite*, with Major General Jean-Baptiste Tronson de Coudray's contingent of French engineers to participate in the American Revolution. No extant French military records document his prior military training or experience as an engineer or architect.

In December 1777 L'Enfant was sent to Boston to join the staff of the newly arrived acting inspector general of the Continental army, Friedrich Wilhelm von Steuben. Steuben's entourage arrived at Valley Forge, Pennsylvania, on 23 February 1778. Their major occupation was training and drilling the soldiers. L'Enfant drew eight illustrations for Steuben's *Regulations for the Order and Discipline of the Troops of the United States*. As a result of this work L'Enfant was appointed a captain in the corps of engineers on 3 April 1779 (retroactive to 18 Feb. 1778). On 5 May 1778 he was assigned to work with General Johann de Kalb.

L'Enfant was wounded at the battle of Savannah on 9 October 1779, taken prisoner at Charleston on 12 May 1780, and exchanged in November. On 2 May 1783 he was breveted a major and received an honorable discharge on 1 January 1784. George Washington often employed him as a courier, a job that took L'Enfant to many sections of the country. L'Enfants's portrait of Washington done at Valley Forge is lost, but his panoramic view of West Point showing Washington directing operations is now in the Library of Congress.

L'Enfant's architectural career in America commenced with designing and decorating the temporary pavilion to celebrate the birth of the French dauphin, Louis XVII, erected by the French minister Anne-César La Luzerne in Philadelphia in 1782. Descriptions of its interior focused on its allegorical symbolism, the rising sun and thirteen stars representing America at one end of the room and the sun at its zenith representing France at the opposite end.

L'Enfant was a founding member of the Society of Cincinnati and was selected to design the society's membership diploma, badge, and a medal. He sent drawings and a description of the eagle badge to the society's president, Steuben, on 10 June 1783. As an emissary of the society he traveled to France in late 1783, where he spent ten weeks arranging to have the society's diploma engraved and eagle insignias made and meeting with the society's French members. The Society of Cincinnati eagle was the first adaptation of the heraldic eagle of the Great Seal of the United States for nongovernmental use.

In May and June 1787 L'Enfant supervised the erection of Jean Jacques Caffieri's Richard Montgomery Monument at St. Paul's Church in New York. The following year a banqueting pavilion designed by L'Enfant was built to seat 6,000 people who would participate in New York's federal procession to celebrate the ratification of the Constitution.

In September 1788, L'Enfant's design for "additions, alterations, and repairs" to convert New York's city hall into Federal Hall to house the U.S. Congress was accepted. Its facade of a pedimented, two-story Doric portico set above an arcade faced Broad Street where it intersected with Wall Street. The octagonal-ended room for the House of Representatives was located at the rear of the ground floor, while the rectangular room for the Senate on the second story opened onto the balcony from which Washington took the oath of the presidency on 30 April 1789.

On 15 December 1784, L'Enfant had submitted to Congress a plan for the country's general defense that included the suggestion that the government create a separate territory held by the states for their common use. On 11 September 1789, L'Enfant applied directly to President Washington for the job of planning a capital city on the Susquehannah River; the construction of a capital city had been approved four days earlier by the House of Representatives. In January 1791 Washington selected L'Enfant to design the federal city, as well as all of its public buildings, to be located on the Potomac River.

The architect arrived in Georgetown, Maryland, on 9 March, and by the twenty-sixth he had conceptualized the entire nature of the city. His preliminary plan of the city was publicly displayed in Georgetown on 2 July. L'Enfant's report to Washington on 19 August was accompanied by a more complete map that included numerous plans for proposed buildings. Washington placed L'Enfant's plan before Congress on 13 December.

L'Enfant's unwillingness to subordinate himself to the authority of the federal city commissioners led to his dismissal on 27 February 1792. The first engraved map, published in the March 1792 issue of a Philadelphia journal, the *Universal Asylum and Columbian Magazine*, did not carry L'Enfant's name as the city's designer. The accompanying description credited the plan to the surveyor Andrew Ellicott, who had worked with him.

L'Enfant's design of the city of Washington was large in scale (6,111 acres). The architect saw it as a microcosm of "this vast empire." Its dual system of street patterns, an orthogonal grid underlying a series of wider diagonal avenues, simultaneously addressed practical, aesthetic, and symbolic issues. The diagonals directly connected squares chosen for their prominence on the landscape; fifteen of them were named for the states (Vermont and Kentucky were added to the Union in 1791) and clustered within the city according to their geographic location within the country. L'Enfant's "Congress House," renamed the Capitol by Thomas Jefferson, was one and a quarter miles from his president's house, a separation probably intended to reflect the organization of the federal government as set out in the Constitution.

While working in the federal city, L'Enfant had been approached on 11 October 1791 by Governor Thomas Mifflin of Pennsylvania to design a president's house in Philadelphia in an attempt to retain Philadelphia as the national capital. However, after L'Enfant left Washington he was hired by his friend Alexander Hamilton (1755–1804) in July 1792 to design the hydraulic system (including an aqueduct and canals), town plan, and buildings for the Society for Establishing Useful Manufactures in Paterson, New Jersey. Peter Colt carried out a simplified version of L'Enfant's scheme between 1792 and 1796.

Under the aegis of Secretary of War Henry Knox, L'Enfant was appointed in 1794 to rebuild Fort Mifflin on Mud Island in the Delaware River off Philadelphia and to build a fort for the defense of Wilmington, Delaware. His services were terminated early in 1795 because his designs were too grand and complex. The work was completed by Stephen Rochefontaine, a fellow French engineer.

L'Enfant's designs for domestic architecture in New York during the 1780s were said to have been numerous but remain unknown. His famous house for Robert Morris (1734–1806) in Philadelphia was designed and partially constructed between 1793 and 1795. Huge in scale, multifaceted with a mansard roof and constructed of brick with pale blue marble window frames and porticoes, its French character, lavishness, and cost were widely discussed at the time. It was never completed because Morris went bankrupt, and it was demolished in 1801. In the summer of 1812 L'Enfant was offered a professorship at West Point, which he declined. In 1814 and 1815 he began reconstructing Fort Washington after it failed to protect the city of Washington from invasion by British troops.

L'Enfant died and was buried in an unmarked grave at "Green Hill," a Digges family estate in Prince George's County, Maryland. He was later disinterred and lay in state in the Capitol rotunda, then reinterred in Arlington National Cemetery on 28 April 1909.

L'Enfant always conceived his projects on a grand scale, and his inability to adjust his expectations to American circumstances led to repeated dismissals.

However, the visionary character of his design for the city of Washington is considered the decisive factor in its greatness.

• The majority of L'Enfant's papers are in the Library of Congress and National Archives. The pioneering work was J. J. Jusserand, *With Americans of Past and Present Days* (1916), followed by Elizabeth S. Kite, *L'Enfant and Washington, 1791–1792* (1929). See also H. Paul Caemmerer's biography, *The Life of Pierre Charles L'Enfant* (1950). Recent evaluations of his work are found in John W. Reps, *Monumental Washington* (1967); Daniel Reiff, *Washington Architecture 1791–1861* (1971); Pamela Scott, "This Vast Empire: The Iconography of the Mall, 1791–1848," in *The Mall in Washington, 1791–1991*, ed. Richard Longstreth (1991); and Richard W. Stephenson, *"A Place Wholy New." Pierre Charles L'Enfant's Plan of the City of Washington* (1993).

PAMELA SCOTT

LENNON, John (9 Oct. 1940–8 Dec. 1980), rock music singer and composer, was born John Winston Lennon in Liverpool, England, the son of Alfred Lennon, a merchant seaman, and Julia Stanley. Alfred soon abandoned the boy and his mother, and from the time Lennon was five, he was raised by an aunt, Mimi Smith. When Lennon was seventeen, his mother was killed in a car accident. He later referred to these biographical facts in songs. He formed his first band, the Quarrymen, at Quarry Bank High School when he was sixteen, and he invited schoolmate Paul McCartney to join.

Lennon attended the Liverpool College of Art from 1957 to 1959 but left to work full time with his band, the name of which was changed in 1960 to the Beatles, a reference to Buddy Holly's band the Crickets. The group honed their style in tough clubs on the waterfront in Hamburg, Germany, in 1961–1962, then toured northern England, performing nightly for months at a time. In 1961 the Beatles signed with manager Brian Epstein, a Liverpool businessman who helped organize their rise to fame and fortune. The Beatles recorded their first hit, "Love Me Do," a simple Lennon/McCartney composition, in 1962. The same year Lennon married schoolmate Cynthia Powell, who gave birth to Julian, their only child, the following year.

"Beatlemania" hit Britain in 1963, when a vast legion of fans went wild for the "Fab Four." It spread to the United States the following year, when the group appeared several times on the popular Ed Sullivan television variety show and when "I Want to Hold Your Hand," another Lennon/McCartney composition, topped the U.S. charts. The song was a raucous and passionate expression of teenage sexual frustration.

That year the Beatles transformed pop music permanently. In place of the conventional three- and four-chord rock songs, Lennon/McCartney music had a richer and more musically complex structure, incorporating minor chords and unexpected sevenths over a rough rhythm-and-blues beat. "A Hard Day's Night" had eleven different chords, unprecedented for a rock song. The Beatles sounded new and exciting because their songs used innovative musical forms and harmonies.

Lennon's exhilarating vocal style incorporated the screams, shouts, and falsetto cries of black gospel-rooted rhythm and blues. The Beatles also sang in the sweet, close harmonies of popular black vocal groups. Lennon worked with a degree of artistic autonomy rare in the world of rock music. Because he and McCartney wrote and performed their own songs, the Beatles were free from the grip of hack producers. The Beatles' triumph was part of a larger change in popular culture, in which a new black music was gaining a white audience and the more complex and expressive personal songs of Lennon, Bob Dylan, and other innovative songwriters were on the rise.

The film *A Hard Day's Night* (1964) told the story of an exuberant day in the life of the Beatles. It established Lennon as "the clever Beatle," sardonic and sharp tongued. The same year saw the publication of *John Lennon in His Own Write*, a collection of brief stories filled with sophisticated puns, skeptical satire, and vicious political wit. It became a bestseller in England and won admiring reviews in mainstream publications like the *Times Literary Supplement* and the *Sunday Times*.

Lennon's music advanced by giant steps in 1965–1966. The albums *Rubber Soul* and *Revolver* contained more serious music than ever before, with complex rhythms, lyrics that were studied, and innovative use of musical instruments. They included introspective biographical songs like "In My Life" and songs of psychedelia like "Tomorrow Never Knows." The single "Strawberry Fields Forever" (1966) marked another breakthrough in rock music. It was nothing like the conventional rock single, as it expressed childhood feelings of isolation and hopelessness in a dizzy, dreamy tour de force of sound.

The Beatles found themselves at the center of a political storm when they began their second U.S. tour in 1966. Lennon had stated that the group was "more popular than Jesus." This provoked outrage in the Bible Belt, and the Ku Klux Klan picketed their concert in Memphis. On the same tour the Beatles criticized the war in Vietnam, a first for a rock group. The tour turned out to be their last; henceforth the Beatles played together only in the recording studio.

Sgt. Pepper's Lonely Hearts Club Band (1967) marked the high point of the Beatles' career, although not of Lennon's musical development. The album took modern recording to its limits. The first rock album to be unified around a single theme, it had the most memorable album cover to date—band members superimposed before a crowded montage of lifesize cultural icons, including the four "dead" Beatles—and was the first to include lyrics printed on the sleeve. It ended with Lennon's "A Day in the Life," a song of dreamy journalism, with concise and chilling images of the disconnectedness, loneliness, and quiet horrors of daily life. *Time* magazine put a picture of the album on its cover. That summer Lennon's single "All You Need Is Love" served as the anthem of the "summer of love." A hippie manifesto, the song called for liberation from the traditional bourgeois virtues of individualism, competition, acquisitiveness, and achievement.

How I Won the War (1967), a dramatic film that incorporated strategies of the modernist theater, starred Lennon without the Beatles and without music. It was a bitterly satirical critique of war movies. Panned by critics, it nevertheless represented a giant step for Lennon—the start of his engagement with the peace movement and the avant-garde.

In May 1968 Lennon spent his first night with Japanese-American conceptual artist Yoko Ono, and the two were henceforth inseparable. Ono showed Lennon how avant-garde art strategies could express the personal and the political. She soon replaced McCartney as his partner in artistic collaboration. Beatle fans never forgave her, and Ono, blamed for breaking up the Beatles, became the target of their hostility. The Beatles continued to record as a group, however. On *The Beatles* (1968) (usually called the white album because of its blank cover), Lennon played his hardest rock in years. "Happiness Is a Warm Gun" ridiculed the American obsession with weapons and expressed Lennon's wild love for Ono. On this album he sang his most tender song, "Julia," to his dead mother.

Lennon and Ono were arrested and charged with possession of cannabis resin in London in 1968. They claimed they had been framed, but Lennon agreed to plead guilty to a misdemeanor. The conviction would later be cited by President Richard Nixon as the basis for an order to deport him from the United States.

John and Cynthia Lennon were divorced in November 1968. He and Ono married in 1969 and declared their honeymoon at the Amsterdam Hilton a weeklong "bed-in for peace," "our protest against all the suffering and violence in the world." The bed-in was a media event that combined performance art with radical politics in an effort to liberate antiwar politics from its traditional forms, particularly the protest march. At a second bed-in in Montreal, Lennon wrote and recorded the cheerful "Give Peace a Chance," which became the anthem of the peace movement with its refrain, "All we are saying . . . ." At the Vietnam Moratorium Day in Washington, D.C., in 1969, Pete Seeger led half a million antiwar demonstrators in singing the song. Lennon later called this "one of the biggest moments of my life."

The Beatles officially broke up in 1970. Lennon released his first solo album, *Plastic Ono Band*, in many ways his greatest work. It presented stark songs of shattering personal intensity that went far beyond the established conventions of pop music. The album opened with "God," in which Lennon declared he did not believe in the Beatles, that "the dream is over," and that he could not—or would not—serve as a pop hero anymore. In the bitter "Working Class Hero" Lennon described his personal and political oppression, and in "Mother" he screamed out his childhood terrors. The album was accompanied by the publication of an extensive interview, "Lennon Remembers," in *Rolling Stone* magazine, in which Lennon spoke with a candor and venom unprecedented in the world of celebrities. Working to destroy his own status as a superstar, he attacked the Beatles as a cultural ideal of joy and fun.

Lennon and Ono moved to New York City in 1971. *Imagine* (1971) expressed a warmer Lennon; the title song, a gently lyrical call to restore the utopian imagination of the peace movement, became his most popular work. The album also included "Gimme Some Truth," a torrent of thrilling political outrage, and "Oh, Yoko!," a playful and passionate up-tempo love song.

In New York Lennon eagerly joined with antiwar leaders, seeking to develop a strategy that would use his power as a pop star to mobilize young people against the continuing war in Vietnam. Lennon talked about scheduling a national concert tour to coincide with the 1972 election campaigns, in which Nixon was running for reelection. It would have been the first American tour by an ex-Beatle since the group waved farewell at San Francisco's Candlestick Park in 1966. The plan called for an unconventional tour that would combine rock music with radical politics, raise money at each stop for local antiwar organizing projects, and include antiwar speakers as well as other musicians. Lennon and friends talked about ending the tour at what they called a Political Woodstock outside the Republican National Convention, where Nixon was to be renominated.

Only one such concert was ever held: a trial run in Ann Arbor, Michigan, in December 1971. Lennon appeared along with Stevie Wonder and several other groups, plus antiwar and black leaders. Lennon played a new song written for the occasion, "John Sinclair," about a local radical activist who had been sentenced to ten years in jail for possessing two joints of marijuana. Two days later authorities released Sinclair from prison, and Lennon and friends proclaimed the experimental concert a complete success.

Republican senator Strom Thurmond of South Carolina wrote Nixon's attorney general in February 1972 informing the White House of Lennon's tour plans and suggesting that "deportation would be a strategic counter-measure." The immigration service promptly ordered Lennon deported, citing his 1968 misdemeanor conviction for cannabis possession.

Lennon spent the next several years in a desperate and exhausting legal battle. A national campaign of support was endorsed by leading mainstream political figures as well as the art world and myriad fans, who rallied to the cry "Let him stay in the USA." Nevertheless, during this period Lennon's music deteriorated. He paid a heavy price for his political commitments and remains the only rock star the U.S. government ever tried to deport because of the political power of his music.

In retrospect, Nixon's belief that Lennon posed a threat to the White House seems unfounded. After all, Nixon defeated George McGovern in a landslide. Lennon's plan had a logic that Nixon apparently understood, however; 1972 was the first year in which eighteen-year-olds had the right to vote in a presidential election. The election served as a referendum on Nixon's conduct of the war in Vietnam, which continued without an end in sight. It was widely assumed that eighteen-year-olds formed the country's strongest antiwar constituency but that they were the least likely age group to register and vote. Lennon's plan sought to harness the power of rock music to mobilize young people to vote against the war. When the Nixon administration ordered Lennon deported, it was not clear that Nixon would easily win. The president had won the narrowest of victories in 1968 and vowed to use the full power of the White House to assure his reelection.

The Nixon administration's campaign against Lennon is supported by documents in FBI files released under the Freedom of Information Act. Although many files were withheld, the released documents seem to support Lennon's view that the deportation order was an effort to silence him as a spokesman for the antiwar movement.

Although Lennon canceled his plans for a national concert tour on the advice of his attorneys, he did headline the One to One benefit concert at New York's Madison Square Garden in 1972. He sang "Cold Turkey," "Instant Karma!," and a reggae version of "Give Peace a Chance" with special intensity, captured on film and recordings.

The immigration battle took its toll on Lennon's personal life. At the end of 1972 he separated from Ono and moved to Los Angeles, where he became notorious for drunken scenes in nightclubs. In Los Angeles he recorded three albums: *Mind Games*, on which he took few musical risks; *Rock 'n' Roll*, a collection of favorite oldies; and then a number-one album, *Walls and Bridges*. From *Walls and Bridges*, "Whatever Gets You Thru the Night" (1974), which he later called "one of my least favorites," became a hit single. He sang it that year at an Elton John concert at Madison Square Garden. This was Lennon's last live performance. In the meantime, Nixon had resigned from office, and the immigration service had finally granted Lennon permanent residency. Lennon and Ono reunited and moved into New York's Dakota Apartments on Central Park. The next year a son, Sean, was born.

Lennon now made a radical break with his past: after pulling together a greatest-hits album, *Shaved Fish*, he announced his withdrawal from the music business and from public life. He declared he would become a househusband. For the next five years Lennon devoted himself to raising their son while Ono supervised their extensive business affairs. In a series of interviews just before his death, Lennon spoke warmly about the sheer ordinariness of daily life with his young son. He was giving him everything he felt he had been denied in his own childhood.

When Sean reached age five, Lennon returned to the studio and, with Ono, recorded *Double Fantasy*, an album that returned to the risk-taking that had been at the heart of his best music. He sang about life as a househusband. "Watching the Wheels" was a gentle manifesto about rejecting the rock world. "I'm Losing You," the strongest song on the album, expressed anger and despair as a couple fights. On the single "(Just Like) Starting Over," Lennon played a deep-voiced suitor proposing a week of lovemaking. In a series of lengthy interviews, Lennon insisted that *Double Fantasy* was not a hymn to private life but, rather, a continuation of his long-standing project to link his personal life with his political ideals. "The thing the sixties did was show us the possibility and the responsibility that we all had," he said in his last interview. "It wasn't the answer. It just gave us a glimpse of the possibility." Six hours later he was shot and killed outside the Dakota by Mark David Chapman, a deranged fan.

A massive worldwide outpouring of grief followed, underscoring Lennon's significance for those who had grown up with him. In an age of cynical superstars, he had struggled to speak honestly not only about his wish for peace and love but about his own anger and misery. A dreamer, a fighter, a working-class wit, and a proud father, Lennon provided an exemplary figure for the sixties generation.

• Lennon's music is widely available on recordings, including posthumous releases *Milk and Honey* (1984), *Menlove Avenue* (1986), and *The Beatles Anthology* (1995–1996), a three-part CD series that includes previously unreleased material. A major documentary, *Imagine: John Lennon* (1988), is available on video, and the companion volume is richly illustrated. Several interviews have been published as books—notably, *Lennon Remembers* (1971) and *The Playboy Interviews with John Lennon and Yoko Ono* (1981). Mark Lewisohn has written two remarkable reference works, *The Beatles: Recording Sessions* (1988) and *The Beatles: Day by Day* (1990). Harry Castleman has compiled a series of Beatles discographies: *All Together Now: The First Complete Beatles Discography, 1961–75* (1975), *The Beatles Again?* (1977), and *The End of the Beatles?* (1985). Elizabeth Thomson and David Gutman, *The Lennon Companion* (1987), draws from selected journalism. Biographies include Ray Coleman, *Lennon* (1984), and Jon Wiener, *Come Together: John Lennon in His Time* (1984).

JON WIENER

LENNOX, Charlotte Ramsay (1729?–4 Jan. 1804), author, was born probably in Gibraltar, the daughter of James Ramsay, a member of the Coldstream Guards; her mother's name is unknown. The date and place of Charlotte Lennox's birth, as well as the rank of her father, is the subject of some dispute. Though she has been called "The First American Novelist," it appears that she lived in America only between 1739 and 1743, while her father was stationed as captain of an Independent Company of Foot in New York. Early biographical accounts name James Ramsay as either the governor or the lieutenant governor of New York and place Lennox's birth in New York. There is no foundation for either claim. Little is known about Lennox's childhood and education, though her novels *The Life of Harriot Stuart* (1751) and *Euphemia* (1790) give lavish descriptions of the New York she knew. Lennox

left New York for England alone in 1743, probably the year her father died. In October 1747 she married the Scotsman Alexander Lennox, who worked for the printer William Strahan. The marriage was neither happy nor profitable. The couple was short on money, perhaps the reason that Charlotte Lennox turned to professional writing. A daughter was born in 1765 and a son in 1771. By 1792 the Lennoxes were separated.

Charlotte Lennox's life and works reflect the position of an eighteenth-century woman who must support herself. Lennox came to London alone, possibly to live with a female relation. Some critics have surmised that on her arrival, Lennox found this relative incurably insane. That this is the story line of Lennox's first novel, *Harriot Stuart*, suggests that critics have chosen to read Lennox's work autobiographically. Certainly Lennox, like the heroines of her novels, did face the problem of finding female protection and patronage. Early in her career she had the support of various gentlewomen in England, though later she was generally shunned by her fellow women writers, as Fanny Burney notes: "Mrs. Thrale says that tho' her books are generally approved, nobody likes her." Lennox produced *Poems on Several Occasions, Written by a Young Lady* (1747), and her poetry later met with the disapproval of her contemporary women readers. Lennox appeared on the stage in 1748, and Horace Walpole remembered one performance enough to write to a friend that she was "a deplorable actress." By 1750 Lennox was writing novels and did attain a degree of success. Samuel Johnson held an all-night party to celebrate the publication of *Harriot Stuart*. Johnson, Samuel Richardson, and Henry Fielding all encouraged Lennox in her literary pursuits. Johnson praised Lennox above her fellow female authors: "I dined yesterday at Mrs. Garrick's, with Mrs. Carter, Miss Hannah More, and Miss Fanny Burney. Three such women are not to be found: I know not where I could find a fourth, except Mrs. Lennox, who is superior to them all."

Johnson is also credited with writing a chapter of Lennox's best-known novel, *The Female Quixote* (1752). As the name suggests, *The Female Quixote* is an imitation of Cervantes's *Don Quixote*. In this novel, the heroine Arabella, who has grown up in isolation, believes that the romances she has read are accurate depictions of modern society. When Arabella does enter society, her assumptions propel her into many comic adventures. The success of *The Female Quixote* has been enduring: it has been almost constantly in print since it was first published, and Jane Austen used it as a prototype for her *Northanger Abbey*.

Lennox was very much a woman of letters; besides her novels, she published translations of French works, including Voltaire's *The Age of Louis XIV* (1752), plays, and *Shakespear Illustrated; or, The Novels and Histories, on Which the Plays of Shakespear Are Founded, Collected and Translated* (1753–1754). She also edited the *Lady's Museum*, a periodical, from 1760 to 1761. Lennox's popularity as a novelist, however, began to decline after *Henrietta* (1758). *Sophia* (1762) was not received well, and Lennox stopped writing novels for almost thirty years. Lennox met with varied success as a playwright: David Garrick would not produce her *Philanderer* (1757), though he later produced her *Old City Manners* (1775) on Drury Lane. After this production, very little is known about Lennox's life. For a while, in the 1780s, she was reduced to working as a governess. With *Euphemia* Lennox returned to literature, but this effort did not bring her the recognition she once enjoyed. Though this novel was extremely unpopular, it does have the appeal of unusual subject matter. *Euphemia* presents a bleak picture of life after marriage at a time when most novels dealt solely with the drama of courtship.

Euphemia, like the earlier *Harriot Stuart*, was set in America. While neither novel is explicitly about America, Lennox fills each with local color and presents a compelling picture of 1740s New York. In both novels the heroines travel from New York City up the Hudson to Albany and later to Schenectady. In *Harriot Stuart* much attention is paid to the renewal of the peace treaty between Great Britain and the five Indian nations. Lennox, who probably witnessed such an event as a child, carefully describes her impressions:

These people, when they travel, carry with them the materials for building their houses, which consist of the bark of trees, and two or three wooden poles, with some bear skins to lye on: thus a square of ten feet will serve to contain a very large family; and it being now in the middle of summer, their hutts were decorated with the boughs of trees on the outside, to keep out the sun, which (on account of their different verdure) formed a new and beautiful prospect.

In *Euphemia* Lennox recounts Dutch and English cultural differences as well as the French Jesuit treatment of Indians. Lennox is at her most descriptive when she writes about the Hudson River Valley, natural cataracts, and the harshness of a New York winter.

Charlotte Lennox's vivid descriptions of early New York are an important cultural legacy. However, it is as a valued member of London's most prestigious literary circle, and as an influential novelist, that she remains a significant literary figure. In her later years Lennox was dependent on the Royal Literary Fund for subsistence. She died a very poor woman in Dean's Yard, Westminster, London.

• Lennox's letters are at the British Library, the Victoria and Albert Museum (Forster collection), and the Pierpont Morgan Library; a more extensive collection is at the Houghton Library at Harvard University. Manuscript copies of Lennox's plays *The Sister* (1769) and *Old City Manners* are in the Larpent collection at the Huntington Library. The most extensive biography of Lennox is Miriam Rossiter Small, *Charlotte Ramsay Lennox: An Eighteenth Century Lady of Letters* (1935). See also Gustavus Howard Maynadier, *The First American Novelist?* (1940), on her novels set in America. See Jane Spencer, *The Rise of the Woman Novelist* (1986), and Margaret Anne Doody's introduction to *The Female Quixote* (1989) on the novel's significance. Jerry C. Beasley's entry on Lennox in the *Dictionary of Literary Biography* (1985) gives a concise biography and plot summaries of Lennox's major works.

KIMBERLY DAWN LUTZ

LENOIR, J. B. (5 Mar. 1929–29 Apr. 1967), blues singer and songwriter, was born near Monticello, Lawrence County, Mississippi, the son of Dewitt Lenoir and Roberta Ratliff, farmers. He grew up in a musical family, in which both parents played guitar. He was particularly inspired by his father's blues singing and later claimed that he could play his first song, "Jim Jackson's Kansas City Blues," before he was big enough to sit in a chair and hold the guitar. His father quit blues after dreaming that he was chased by the devil, but J. B. carried on the family musical tradition, sharpening his performance skills at house parties and picnics. Although he recalled few local influences besides his father, he was clearly influenced by the style of Mississippi-born Arthur "Big Boy" Crudup, whose records in the late 1940s helped to bring the electric guitar to the forefront as a blues instrument.

In his early teens Lenoir left home, ending up in New Orleans, where, sometime around 1944, he encountered guitarist Elmore James and harmonica player Aleck Miller, better known as Sonny Boy Williamson, possibly sitting in with them at the New York Inn. Unhappy with conditions in the South, Lenoir moved from job to job, ranging as far north as New York City and eventually settling in Chicago in the late 1940s. Working as a meat packer by day, he began to check out the city's music scene by night, thus becoming a younger protégé of guitarist and fellow Mississippian Big Bill Broonzy, who allowed Lenoir to sit in with his band and helped him to meet other artists such as Memphis Minnie and Muddy Waters. As he began to gain recognition, Lenoir formed his own band and in 1951 made his first recordings, cutting four sides, including the topical commentaries "Korea Blues" and "Deep in Debt Blues," for the J.O.B. label. Other J.O.B. sessions in fall 1951, late 1952, and early 1953 yielded four more singles, but they did little for him financially. In October 1954 he switched to Parrot, a label owned by Chicago disk jockey Al Benson. Among the sides cut for Parrot in 1954 and 1955 was another topical single, "Eisenhower Blues," which was summarily pulled off the market—legend has it that "government interference" prompted the action—and recut as "Tax Paying Blues," minus any direct references to President Dwight Eisenhower. Of greater significance to his career, Lenoir cut "Mama, Talk to Your Daughter" in 1954. It became his signature piece, his only song ever to make the R&B charts, and a continuing classic in the Chicago blues tradition. He would rework variations of the piece throughout his career. At a 1955 recording session, Lenoir brought together the two saxophone players he would work with for the next three years, Alex Atkins and Ernest Cotton. The two-horn, guitar-boogie combination produced a distinctive sound that became Lenoir's musical trademark. In 1955 he began a three-year affiliation with Checker, a subsidiary of Chess Records, where he teamed up with bassist, songwriter, and producer Willie Dixon. However, their material was out of sync with current R&B tastes and did not sell.

In the late 1950s Lenoir operated and partially owned a blues club, the Club Lolease, but the club went under along with his investment. In the summer of 1958 he recorded a single with harmonica player Junior Wells, but the record did not sell—nor did a 1960 Vee-Jay single. In the early 1960s, however, Lenoir recorded for a European label and played acoustic guitar on a documentary album compiled by British researcher Paul Oliver, foreshadowing a shift into the folk and blues-revival markets. After one final R&B single, a 1963 venture produced by Willie Dixon, Lenoir recorded almost exclusively for European, documentary, and revival-era labels. He began to play white or mixed clubs such as Big John's and the Fickle Pickle on the North Side. He traveled to Europe in 1965 as part of the American Folk Blues Festival, being particularly well received in England, where he inspired blues rocker John Mayall. A second tour with the American Folk Blues Festival in 1966 reinforced his status in Europe, but back in Chicago he struggled to make a living with music. He moved downstate to take a job as a kitchen worker at the University of Illinois in Champaign. Commuting between Champaign and Chicago in April 1966, he was involved in an auto accident and apparently sustained injuries that were more serious than first believed. Three weeks after the accident he suffered an apparent heart attack and was pronounced dead at Mercy Hospital in Urbana, Illinois. His wife Ella Louise and his three children had his body shipped to his birthplace, where he was buried in the Salem Church Cemetery.

Though he was unappreciated during his lifetime, J. B. Lenoir was a gifted blues composer who drew inspiration from the social and economic ills of the 1950s and 1960s. His stark protest compositions covered hard times, poverty, taxes, war (both Korea and Vietnam), and racial discrimination. Some critics likened Lenoir to blues artists who switched from ethnic material to "folk songs" in the 1950s and 1960s, but his songs were more personal than so-called folk material and at times were even surreal. Moreover Lenoir wrote protest material throughout his career, not as a response to changing public tastes in music.

Lenoir delivered his material in a keen, high-pitched voice that could be as boisterous as the saxophones in his band or as sensitive as the subject matter in his social commentaries. A competent guitarist, he initially used variations of a walking bass boogie figure for his upbeat numbers. Later he developed a style that he referred to as "African hunch," which he often used on acoustic guitar.

In seeming contrast to his talent for sensitive composition, Lenoir had a real flair for showmanship, wearing imitation tiger-skin tails, matching bow tie and a gold earring; Lenoir often used a harmonica rack to hold his microphone so he could jump off stage to dance and sing at a club patron's table. Lenoir's long-time friend Willie Dixon, writing in his autobiography, recalled, "He was a helluva showman, because he had this long tiger-striped coat with tails. We used to call it a two-tailed peter."

• For additional information on Lenoir see John Broven, "J. B. Lenoir," in *Nothing but the Blues*, ed. Mike Leadbitter (1971); Sheldon Harris, *Blues Who's Who: A Biographical Dictionary of Blues Singers* (1979; repr. 1989); Mike Rowe, *Chicago Blues: The City and the Music* (1975); and Willie Dixon (with Don Snowden), *I Am the Blues* (1989). For brief interview material see Paul Oliver, *Conversations with the Blues* (1965); and for a discography see Mike Leadbitter et al., *Blues Records 1943–1970: "The Bible of the Blues"*, vol. 2 (1994); to sample his music, try *Mama Watch Your Daughter*, Charley Blues Masterworks CD BM47; *J. B. Lenoir, the Topical Bluesman: From Korea to Vietnam*, Blues Encore CD 52017; and *J. B. Lenoir: Vietnam Blues*, Evidence ECD 26068-2.

BILL McCULLOCH
BARRY LEE PEARSON

LENROOT, Irvine Luther (31 Jan. 1869–26 Jan. 1949), member of the U.S. House of Representatives and the U.S. Senate, was born in frontier Superior, Wisconsin, the son of Swedish immigrants Lars Lenroot, a blacksmith, and Fredrika Larsdötter (later changed to Larson). After graduating from Parsons Business College in 1889, Lenroot worked as a stenographer and read law in Superior, where he was admitted to the bar in 1897. He married Clara Clough McCoy in 1890; the couple had two children.

In 1900 Lenroot was elected to the state assembly as a Republican and a supporter of the new governor, Robert M. La Follette. He became La Follette's ally in the factional conflict that ensued, displaying energy, ability, and judgment. In 1903 and 1905 Lenroot served as Speaker of the assembly. He helped draft Wisconsin's landmark primary election and railroad commission laws. As La Follette's candidate for the gubernatorial nomination in 1906, he was defeated; but in 1908 he won election to Congress, having pledged to oppose the reelection of Joseph Cannon as Speaker. His district was progressive but divided on foreign policy when war came in Europe.

In the House Lenroot sought to democratize the institution's rules and secured liberalizing amendments to the Mann-Elkins Act of 1910, extending regulation of railroads. Cooperating with Gifford Pinchot, he defended the conservationist view in a ten-year struggle for the Mineral Lands Leasing Act of 1920 and the Federal Waterpower Act of 1920. He became the leader of the progressive Republicans in the House and their candidate for party leader in 1916. Even so, he cooperated with Minority Leader James R. Mann against Democratic practices, such as rules precluding amendments and proposals like the Underwood low tariff bill, after the Democrats won control of the House in 1911.

The Lenroot–La Follette friendship cooled gradually and ended in 1917 when Lenroot supported war against Germany while La Follette opposed it. After the death of Senator Paul Husting in 1918, Lenroot ran on the issue of vindicating Wisconsin's loyalty after statements by La Follette drew national criticism as unpatriotic. In the Republican primary election Lenroot defeated La Follette's candidate, James Thompson. Then he won the general election against Joseph E. Davies, Democrat; and Victor Berger, Socialist. In 1920 Lenroot was again opposed by Thompson, acting for La Follette, in both the primary and the general election. Lenroot won renomination and reelection to the Senate and headed a coalition in Wisconsin of progressives and conservatives who had supported the war.

At the Republican National Convention in 1920, many party leaders favored Lenroot as the vice presidential nominee. He delayed accepting their support, however, and Calvin Coolidge was nominated. Lenroot thereby lost the opportunity to become president in 1923.

As a senator, Lenroot was prominent in the battle over approval of the Treaty of Versailles and consequent adherence to the League of Nations. He was a leader of the mild reservationist faction. As such, he helped defeat proposed amendments to the treaty in order to avoid time-consuming renegotiation with signatories. He promised reservations to protect the United States from unwanted obligations, and he wrote several of the "Lodge reservations" that the Senate adopted, including refusal of American assent to Japan's acquisition of privileges in the Chinese province of Shantung and refusal to be bound by league decisions in which the British benefited from votes of its dominions or colonies. President Woodrow Wilson would not accept them, however, and Lenroot's efforts for treaty passage failed.

During the administrations of Warren Harding and Calvin Coolidge, Lenroot was a moderate progressive and close ally of Secretary of Commerce Herbert Hoover. He led in adoption of the Agricultural Credits Act of 1923 to provide for federally assisted loans to farmers. In 1926 Lenroot had charge of the resolution of adherence to the World Court. The Senate approved the resolution, but one of its five reservations proved unacceptable to court members, so the United States did not then join the court.

First as a member of the Committee on Public Lands, then as its chairman, Lenroot was slow to detect corruption in the leasing by Secretary of the Interior Albert Fall of federal oil lands at Teapot Dome, Wyoming, and Elks Hills, California. Lenroot was attacked as too close to the administration in the Teapot Dome investigation, a factor in the senatorial primary election of 1926, in which he was defeated for renomination by Wisconsin governor John J. Blaine.

Lenroot remained in Washington and practiced law. In 1929 he accepted Coolidge's nomination to a judgeship on the U.S. Court of Customs Appeals. The nomination was not acted on before the Congress adjourned, but the new president, Herbert Hoover, resubmitted the nomination. Lenroot served on the court, renamed the court of patent and customs appeals, until 1944, when he resigned. His wife died in 1942, and a year later he married Eleonore von Eltz; he and his second wife did not have children. Lenroot continued to reside in Washington, where he died.

Lenroot was overshadowed in politics and history by the more flamboyant La Follette. Some of his best legislative efforts, such as those in connection with the Treaty of Versailles, came to nothing. In conservation matters and on progressive issues, he was a gifted and constructive legislator and an important factional political leader within the Republican party in Wisconsin and the nation.

• The Irvine L. Lenroot Papers are in the Library of Congress. There is Lenroot correspondence in many other collections. The most useful are the Robert M. La Follette Papers and the Gifford Pinchot Papers at the Library of Congress; the William Kent Papers at the Yale University Library; the James A. Stone Papers and another segment of the Robert M. La Follette Papers at the State Historical Society of Wisconsin, Madison; and the Herbert Hoover Presidential Library, West Branch, Iowa. Lenroot's political career is described in Herbert F. Margulies, *Senator Lenroot of Wisconsin: A Political Biography, 1900–1929* (1977). An unpublished longer account by the same author, "Progressivism, Patriotism and Politics: The Life and Times of Irvine L. Lenroot," may be found with the Lenroot papers and at the State Historical Society of Wisconsin. Lenroot's role as a mild reservationist leader is most fully described in Margulies, *The Mild Reservationists and the League of Nations Controversy in the Senate* (1989). Two of his political campaigns are treated in Padraic C. Kennedy, "Lenroot, La Follette and the Campaign of 1906," *Wisconsin Magazine of History* (Spring 1959): 163–74, and Robert Griffith, "Prelude to Insurgency: Irvine L. Lenroot and the Republican Primary of 1908," *Wisconsin Magazine of History* (Autumn 1965): 16–28.

HERBERT F. MARGULIES

LENS, Sidney (28 Jan. 1912–18 June 1986), independent radical and trade union leader, was born Sidney Okun in Newark, New Jersey, the son of Charles Okun, an unsuccessful pharmacist and newsstand owner, and Sophie Horowitz, both Jewish immigrants from czarist Russia. Following the death of his father in 1915, Lens moved with his mother to the Lower East Side of New York City, where she found work as a garment worker and he attended a Jewish parochial school and a public high school. Although he grew up in an atmosphere where labor radicalism competed with religious orthodoxy among the Jewish working class, Lens's involvement with the labor movement began after he was beaten by local police when he attempted to organize a union of waiters and busboys at a resort in the Adirondacks on 4 July 1930.

Drifting into Communist politics in the early 1930s but critical of the Communist party, USA (CPUSA), Lens (who changed his name in the mid-1930s after he was blacklisted for his labor organizing) gravitated to the Trotskyist movement and became something of a roving radical. As the decade advanced, Lens participated in Marxist discussion groups in Washington, D.C., with radicalized lower New Deal officials, joined in a CPUSA-led seizure of the New Jersey legislature in June 1936 to demand jobs and relief benefits for the unemployed, and, most of all, attempted to organize unions of autoworkers in Detroit and other industrial and service workers. Lens also developed a relationship with the Reverend A. J. Muste, a prominent Marxist and pacifist, that continued for decades and strongly influenced his postwar activities.

As a member since the mid-1930s of a small Trotkyist group, the Revolutionary Workers League, Lens opposed U.S. involvement in World War II, which he defined as an imperialist war. In 1941 Lens, now centered in Chicago, organized retail clerks and waiters and led them into gangster-dominated local 329 of the United Service Employees Union, freeing the local from underworld control and taking it into the Congress of Industrial Organizations (CIO). Becoming director (chief administrative officer) in 1942, he led the local until his retirement in 1966 to engage in full-time political work. In 1946 he married Shirley Rubin. They had no children.

In the postwar period Lens, while remaining an opponent of the CPUSA, saw U.S. imperialism as the main danger to the working class of the United States and to the burgeoning socialist and progressive movements of the world. Furthermore, he had come to believe by the early 1950s that an eventual American revolution would develop in stages and be led by a coalition of mass movements, something closer to the Populists of the 1890s than to the French Jacobins or the Russian Bolsheviks.

In 1949 his first book, *Left, Right, and Center*, was published. Although he wrote anti-Communist works such as *The Counterfeit Revolution* in the early 1950s, the State Department refused on a number of occasions to renew his passport, at one point informing him that he had no right to appeal, since appeals were only for Communists and he was not a Communist.

With the help of the American Civil Liberties Union, Lens won his passport and visited ninety-four countries between 1950 and 1970, interviewing figures such as Gamal Abdel Nasser of Egypt, and Mohammad Mossadegh of Iran. After the publication of *Crisis of American Labor* (1959), Lens was recognized as a major critic of the AFL-CIO's conservatism. Lens also spoke and debated frequently on college campuses and was a part-time lecturer on labor and international affairs at the University of Chicago, the University of Illinois, Roosevelt University, and other colleges and universities in the Chicago area.

In the 1950s Lens was a founder of *Dissent* magazine with Irving Howe, although he was later removed by Howe from its editorial board because he disagreed with its negative anti-Communist direction and isolation from practical struggles. With A. J. Muste and civil rights activist Bayard Rustin, he helped to found *Liberation* magazine, a radical pacifist journal, and worked with Muste in the late 1950s to bring socialists and Communists together in an American forum to reunify the left.

Working with a variety of prominent liberals, such as Supreme Court Justice William O. Douglas, Lens

wrote for publications such as the *Nation*, the *New Republic*, the *New York Times*, and the *Christian Science Monitor* and became a regular contributor to the liberal journal the *Progressive*, serving as a senior editor after 1978. From the 1950s on, as he saw it, he was something of a "political fireman," seeking to put out factional fires and build coalitions on the labor and peace movement left.

Lens also supported the Cuban Revolution and led the Chicago Fair Play for Cuba Committee in 1960, ran as an independent peace candidate for Congress in Chicago in 1962 (actions that brought him before the Senate's Internal Security Committee in 1963), and deepened his involvement in a variety of antiwar and political independence movements in the middle 1960s. In 1968 he initially sought to organize an independent protest presidential ticket of Martin Luther King and Benjamin Spock. Later that year he led an international peace delegation to Stockholm and met with Vietnamese delegates at a conference concerning the Vietnam War. He fought during the 1968 Democratic National Convention in Chicago to defend the rights of demonstrators and the right to hold demonstrations.

Emerging as a voice of political reason in opposition to the Weathermen and others in the fragmenting protest movements, Lens was a leader of the New Mobilization Committee to End the War in Vietnam and, most significantly, the 15 October 1969 Vietnam Moratorium, a one-day national strike that produced rallies throughout the country and symbolic strikes and protest meetings by many union locals. Lens also published *Radicalism in America* (1966), a historical work; *Poverty: America's Enduring Paradox* (1969); *The Military Industrial Complex* (1970); and *The Labor Wars* (1973), popular works that influenced both an emerging progressive scholarship and ongoing struggles.

As the New Left waned, Lens, who can be seen as an amalgamation of the Old Left and the New, remained very active. He organized the Illinois Impeach Nixon Committee during the Watergate crisis and in 1976 became a founder of Mobilization for Survival, a leading force in the 1970s and 1980s against both nuclear weapons and nuclear power. He also wrote *The Day before Doomsday: An Anatomy of the Nuclear Arms Race* (1977) and *The Bomb* (1982), a work aimed at youth.

Lens also continued his commitment to independent political action, supporting leading environmentalist and socialist Barry Commoner's attempt to organize a Citizens party in 1980 and serving as its candidate for the U.S. Senate in 1980.

In his memoir, *Unrepentant Radical*, published in 1980, Lens looked forward to a political upsurge in the 1980s and took pride in his fifty years of activism. Although the upsurge failed to materialize, Lens was never disillusioned, remaining active in campaigns to mobilize peace and social justice coalitions until his death in Chicago. His many books and articles provide a legacy of insight and experience for activists of future generations.

• Sidney Lens, *Unrepentant Radical: An American Activist's Account of Five Turbulent Decades* (1980), is the best source for those interested in Lens's life and point of view. Of his many works, *Left, Right, and Center, Crisis of American Labor, Radicalism in America, The Promises and Pitfalls of Revolution* (1974), and *The Day before Doomsday* show the development of his interests and thought and his attempt to speak to the major issues, as he saw them, of his time. An obituary is in the *New York Times*, 20 June 1986.

NORMAN MARKOWITZ

LENYA, Lotte (18 Oct. 1898–27 Nov. 1981), singing actress, was born Karoline Wilhelmine Charlotte Blamauer, in Vienna, Austria, the daughter of Franz Blamauer, a carriage driver, and Johanna Teuschl, a laundress. "Linnerl," as she was nicknamed, spent her childhood in a Roman Catholic but impoverished and abusive family in the working-class district of Penzing. At fourteen she left the Bürgerschule for gifted children in Hietzing to begin a four-year apprenticeship in a small hat factory. In 1913, however, an aunt took her to Zurich, where she worked as a domestic helper while studying dance part-time and playing small roles in productions at the Stadttheater.

During her second season in Zurich, the principal stage director, Richard Révy, accepted her as a private acting student. He guided her technical training and introduced her to the classics of dramatic literature. Inspired by the character Yelena in *Uncle Vanya*, Révy also gave her a new but still private nickname, "Lenja." She appeared as Lotte Blamauer in productions at the Stadttheater and the Pfauen-Theater, where she came into contact with many notable artists, including Elisabeth Bergner, who recalled Blamauer as "only a bit player" though "often seen in the company of officers, but each time it was a different one." Lenya later explained, "I wanted to know how it feels to have everything, to be driven to the theater by a chauffeur, to have beautiful jewelry and not a worry anymore."

In autumn 1921 Blamauer and a friend set out for Berlin, where they tried unsuccessfully to make a career as dancers. In 1922, during an audition for a children's Christmas pantomime, *Zaubernacht*, she was introduced, now as "Lotte Lenja," to its composer, Kurt Weill. She was cast, but out of loyalty to Révy, who was not hired to direct, she declined the offer. Although unemployed, Blamauer managed to stay on in Berlin by selling her jewelry. In 1923, while playing the role of Maria in a suburban production of *Twelfth Night*, Lenya met Georg Kaiser, the leading German Expressionist dramatist, who invited her to live with his family in Grünheide. Lenya was reintroduced to Weill, who then was collaborating with Kaiser on a one-act opera. Two years later they married.

After appearing as Fanny in Shaw's *The Shewing Up of Blanco Posnet* at a minor theater in Berlin and Juliet in *Romeo and Juliet* at the Wallnertheater, in 1927 Lenya performed publicly in one of Weill's works for the first time, the role of Jessie in the Songspiel *Mahagonny* at the Baden-Baden music festival. Although her inimitable but untrained soprano voice already set her apart from the opera singers who composed the rest of the cast, she did not achieve a secure position in Berlin's vibrant theatrical scene until she created the decidedly secondary role of Jenny in *Die Dreigroschenoper* in 1928. Critic Ernst Bloch vividly described her waifish voice as "sweet, high, light, dangerous, cool, with the radiance of the crescent moon." For the next several years she enjoyed an active stage, recording, and film career in Berlin. Although her efforts centered on her husband's collaborations with Bertolt Brecht, she also appeared in nearly a dozen other productions. She recorded songs from *Die Dreigroschenoper, Happy End*, and *Mahagonny* and recreated her original role in G. W. Pabst's 1930 film version of *Die Dreigroschenoper*, in which she first sang the "Ballad of Pirate Jenny," which soon became her signature number.

In 1931, after all the state-subsidized opera houses in Berlin had rejected *Aufstieg und Fall der Stadt Mahagonny*, Weill rewrote the role of Jenny so that Lenya could sing it in a commercial production at the Theater am Kurfürstendamm, which ran for fifty performances. Several months later she performed the role in Vienna, where she fell in love with tenor Otto von Pasetti. Although she and Weill divorced in 1933 and Weill fled Germany alone, that did not dissuade him from casting both Lenya and Pasetti in the Paris and Rome productions of *Mahagonny* and the Paris and London productions of *Die sieben Todsünden*, which was choreographed by Balanchine. After Pasetti absconded with money from Weill's accounts, Lenya had an intense affair with painter Max Ernst before reconciling with Weill during the summer of 1935. In September they sailed to New York for what was to be a short stay while working on Max Reinhardt's production of Franz Werfel's and Weill's biblical spectacle *The Eternal Road*.

By the time the production finally opened in January 1937, with Lenya playing the role of Miriam, Weill already had a musical play, *Johnny Johnson*, running on Broadway. They decided to stay in the United States, remarried, and reentered the country as immigrants (Lenya gained U.S. citizenship in June 1944). Lenya tried intermittently to establish a career in America as Suicide in Marc Blitzstein's radio drama *I've Got the Tune* (1937), as a singer at Le Ruban Bleu, a club in New York, and in 1941–1942 with Helen Hayes in Maxwell Anderson's play *Candle in the Wind*. In 1943 she recorded *Six Songs by Kurt Weill* and in 1945 received disastrous reviews as the Duchess in Weill's and Ira Gershwin's operetta *The Firebrand of Florence*. She reluctantly retired from the stage to their eighteenth-century farmhouse in Rockland County, New York, which remained her primary residence for the rest of her life.

Weill's sudden death in April 1950 left Lenya without a livelihood. She resumed her career at the urging of George Davis, the erstwhile editor of *Mademoiselle* and *Flair*, whom she married in 1951. She appeared in several memorial concerts for Weill (Town Hall, 1951–1952), as Xantippe in *Barefoot in Athens* (a role that Maxwell Anderson had written for her), and then as Jenny in Blitzstein's adaptation of *The Threepenny Opera*, first under Leonard Bernstein in concert at Brandeis (1952) and then in the off-Broadway production at the Theatre de Lys, which ran for 2,611 consecutive performances (1954–1961) and for which she won a Tony Award in 1956. With Davis's assistance, a new Lenya—with the trademark Toulouse-Lautrec red hair and a voice that she described as "an octave below laryngitis"—launched an international career on stage, television, film, and disk. She returned to Berlin for the first time in 1955, singing privately for Brecht before beginning her first recording sessions. He responded, "Lenya, anything you do is epic enough for me," and invited her to join the Berliner Ensemble. She declined, "valuing her American passport too much for that."

After playing Jenny for more than 600 performances, Lenya left the cast of *The Threepenny Opera*, but thereafter she commanded a loyal New York following for her concert appearances at Town Hall and Carnegie Hall. Meanwhile, she supervised and performed on recordings, including *The Threepenny Opera* (1954), *Berlin Theater Songs* (1955), *Johnny Johnson* (1955), *Die sieben Todsünden* (1956), *Aufstieg und Fall der Stadt Mahagonny* (1956), *September Song and Other American Theatre Songs of Kurt Weill* (1957), *Die Dreigroschenoper* (1958), and *Happy End* (1960). In 1958 she recreated the role of Anna I in Balanchine's production of *The Seven Deadly Sins* at the City Center in New York and two years later for the German premiere in Frankfurt—in both instances singing an unacknowledged arrangement accommodating her lower vocal range at age sixty.

Lenya's performances and recordings fueled the Weill renaissance of the late 1950s, but her considerable administrative responsibilities as executrix of his estate proved onerous. After Brecht's death in 1956, she and Helene Weigel resumed their amicable rivalry as actresses but fought bitter battles in the so-called "widow wars" over contractual matters concerning their deceased husbands' joint works. After Davis's death from a heart attack in November 1957, in a conscious attempt to free herself from the "Widow Weill" image, Lenya recorded *The Stories of Kafka* (1958) and *Invitation to German Poetry* (1958), and she played the Countess in the film *The Roman Spring of Mrs. Stone*, for which she received Academy Award and Golden Globe nominations (1961). She also appeared in the New York and national touring companies of *Brecht on Brecht* (1961–1963). During its run in London in 1962, she married Russell Detwiler, a painter twenty-seven years her junior. The following year she created one of her most memorable screen characters, the lesbian, stiletto-shoed Colonel Rosa Klebb in the James Bond film *From Russia With Love*. In 1965 she played the title role in Brecht's *Mutter Courage und ihre Kinder* in Recklinghausen, Germany, also broadcast on German television, and during the 1960s she starred in a number of television specials about Weill. In 1966 Harold Prince cast her as Fräulein Schneider in the musical *Cabaret*, a role she played for most of its

Broadway run of 1,165 performances and which earned her a Tony nomination as best actress in a musical play. In 1968 she appeared in Metro-Goldwyn-Mayer's *The Appointment* with Omar Sharif, and the following June the West German government awarded her its "grosse Verdienstkreuz," complementing the Freedom Bell awarded her by West Berlin in 1958.

After the accidental death of Detwiler (which involved an overdose of alcohol and tranquilizers) in October of 1958, Lenya's public appearances became less frequent, though her commitment to Weill's legacy was undiminished. In June 1971 she married filmmaker Richard Siemanowski; they maintained separate residences and divorced in 1973, with few of even her closest friends having been aware of the relationship. She appeared in *Der Silbersee* at the Holland Festival and in *Mother Courage* at the University of California, Irvine. She continued to grant radio and television interviews and to appear on daytime television, talk shows, and documentaries. In 1977 she accepted her final film role, as Burt Reynolds's sadomasochistic masseuse in *Semi-Tough* (1977). She was elected to the Theater Hall of Fame in November 1979, the same month the Metropolitan Opera mounted its first production of *Aufstieg und Fall der Stadt Mahagonny*, an event she deemed final confirmation of the long-term impact of her efforts for Weill. Having first undergone surgery for abdominal cancer in 1977, she spent her final months establishing the Kurt Weill Foundation for Music, to which she would entrust Weill's legacy upon her own death. She died in the Manhattan apartment of her friend, sculptor Margo Harris.

During a fifty-year public career, Lenya's stage persona evolved from that of youthful victim to worldweary survivor, yet she remained always the *femme fatale*. The authority of her later interpretations—widely distributed, broadcast, and telecast as the "authentic" performing style for Weill-Brecht—has inadvertently encouraged others to mimic her vocal handicaps rather than to match her interpretive gifts. Despite sporadic efforts to carve out an independent identity, Lenya's long career was linked inextricably with Weill's. Though Lenya never learned to read music and avoided formal vocal training, she became Weill's muse and most influential interpreter and thus one of the outstanding *diseuses* of the century.

• Lotte Lenya's papers are housed in the Weill/Lenya Archives of the Yale University Music Library and the Weill-Lenya Research Center, New York, N.Y. *A Guide to the Weill-Lenya Research Center* (1995) includes as Appendix B "Lotte Lenya: A Chronological List of Live Performances, Recordings, Films, Radio Plays, Television Appearances, and Awards." Donald Spoto's *Lenya: A Life* (1989) is a brash and breezy biography intended for the general reader. A composite of Lenya's attempts at autobiography is included as the prologue to *Speak Low (When You Speak Love): The Letters of Kurt Weill and Lotte Lenya*, ed. and trans. Lys Symonette and Kim H. Kowalke (1996), and a biographical account of her career after Weill's death comprises its epilogue. "That Was a Time!," an essay written by George Davis based on interviews with Lenya and Elisabeth Hauptmann, was published under Lenya's byline in the May 1956 issue of *Theatre Arts* and reprinted as the foreword to the Grove Press edition of Desmond Vesey and Eric Bentley's translation of *The Threepenny Opera* (1964). The most extensive and reliable profile published during her lifetime is David Beams, "Lotte Lenya," *Theatre Arts* 46 (June 1962): 11–18, 66–72. See also Susan Borwick, "Perspectives on Lenya: Through the Looking Glass," *Opera Quarterly* 5, no. 4 (1987–1988): 21–36, and Guy Stern, "Lotte Lenya's Creative Interpretation of Brecht," in *Brecht Unbound*, ed. James Lyon and Hans-Peter Breuer (1995). The catalog of the Weill-Lenya Exhibition at the New York Public Library in 1976, edited by Henry Marx, contains a wealth of visual material. The most complete published discography of Lenya's work is Richard C. Lynch, "For the Record—Lotte Lenya," *Show Music* 5 (Nov. 1986): 32–35. The Hessischer Rundfunk in Frankfurt produced an hour-long television documentary by Barrie Gavin and Kim H. Kowalke, *Lenya: An Invention* (1994). See also David Drew, *Kurt Weill: A Handbook* (1987); Jürgen Schebera, *Kurt Weill: An Illustrated Life* (1995); Stephen Hinton, ed., *Cambridge Opera Handbook: The Threepenny Opera* (1990); and Kim H. Kowalke, ed., *A New Orpheus: Essays on Kurt Weill* (1986). An obituary is in the *New York Times*, 29 Nov. 1981.

KIM H. KOWALKE

LEONARD, Benny (7 Apr. 1896–18 Apr. 1947), professional boxer, was born in New York City, the son of Gershon Leiner, a tailor, and Minnie (maiden name unknown), Eastern European Jewish immigrants. Although Leonard's real name was Benjamin Leiner, he boxed professionally, and was known to the public, as Benny Leonard. Initially, he adopted the pseudonym in a futile attempt to keep his parents from knowing that he was a boxer. Even as a boy, however, poverty and ethnic rivalries led to his involvement in street fights. The working-class Leiner family lived near the public baths on Manhattan's Lower East Side. When Irish and Italian boys from nearby neighborhoods came to use the baths, fighting often occurred, with Leonard taking part. At age eleven, he first donned boxing gloves and began to spar at a local athletic club. Despite his frail appearance, he was acknowledged as the best fighter in his street gang. Abandoning his attempt to learn the printing trade, he began to box for money in 1911.

Many of Leonard's early fights took place at athletic clubs with floating memberships. In Leonard's matches, promoters often exploited ethnic rivalries. From 1914 to 1925, Billy Gibson, proprietor of the Fairmont Athletic Club and influential in Bronx politics, served as his manager. Gibson hired trainer George Engel to develop Leonard's strength. Under Engel's tutelage, the 5'5" lightweight developed into a great defensive fighter and a strong puncher. On 28 May 1917, at the Manhattan Casino in New York City, Leonard knocked out Freddie Welsh in the ninth round to win the lightweight championship of the world.

During World War I, Leonard held the rank of lieutenant in the Athletic Activities branch of the U.S. Army. As an army boxing instructor in 1917 and 1918, he trained thousands of men. Leonard also encouraged enlistments, participated in war bond drives, and fought exhibition bouts to help purchase athletic equipment.

Unlike his contemporary, Jack Dempsey, who had only six bouts in seven years as heavyweight champion and refused to fight black challengers, Leonard, during his eight years as the lightweight titleholder, fought more than eighty times, facing all authentic contenders, regardless of race. Feinting, bobbing, weaving, throwing combination punches, chattering as he fought, Leonard always put on a good show. He synthesized technical brilliance with a colorful style.

Many of Leonard's matches were notable. On 25 July 1917 in Philadelphia he knocked out Johnny Kilbane, the featherweight champion of the world, in the third round. After suffering a knockdown in the first round of his 14 January 1921 fight with Richie Mitchell, Leonard recovered, scoring a knockout over Mitchell in the sixth round. He lost on a disqualification to welterweight champion Jack Britton on 26 June 1922. After retaining his title in a 27 July 1922 no-decision bout with Lew Tendler, Leonard defeated the southpaw challenger in a 24 July 1923 fight that went the distance. Reflecting Leonard's appeal, boxing's new legitimacy, and innovative strategies for promoting sports in its 1920s' "Golden Age," the two Leonard-Tendler fights produced gate receipts of $368,000 and $453,000. Famous and wealthy, but aware that his great skills were beginning to fade, and yielding to the concerns of his mother, Leonard, still the lightweight champion, announced his retirement in 1925.

Celebrity brought opportunities. During the 1920s Leonard acted in several motion pictures and appeared in vaudeville. He taught boxing at the City College of New York. In addition, he invested in stocks, an automobile accessory business, and real estate. The Great Depression, however, put his finances in a precarious state, leading him to attempt a boxing comeback in 1931. Additional weight made him a welterweight. Although he lost only two of his eighteen comeback fights, he was a shadow of his former self. After being knocked out in the sixth round of a 7 October 1932 bout with Jimmy McLarnin, he permanently retired from boxing.

Nat Fleischer, the preeminent chronicler of boxing, ranked Leonard as the second best lightweight of all time. In 209 bouts, he registered 88 victories (68 by knockout), 1 draw, 115 no-decisions, and 5 losses. Under the present system of scoring, most of Leonard's no-decisions would be classified as victories because contemporary newspaper accounts suggest that he dominated most of the no-decision contests, which, under New York's Frawley Law, were matches that went the distance.

American boxers traditionally have come from lower-income ethnic and racial groups living in urban areas. So it was with sons of Jewish immigrants who turned to boxing in the early decades of the twentieth century as a means of escaping poverty. By the 1920s a number of Jewish boxing contenders and champions had emerged, including bantamweight Harry Harris, featherweight Abe Attell, middleweight Al McCoy, and light-heavyweight Battling Levinsky. Leonard, as the most talented of these Jewish fighters, became the protagonist of apocryphal stories about his defense of Jewish neighborhoods from anti-Semites, thus serving as a standard-bearer for Jews resentful of canards that portrayed them as passive in the face of physical assault.

After retiring for a second time, Leonard invested in a Pittsburgh professional hockey team, a dress business, and a camp for boys. Active in Jewish organizations, he supported Zionism and the Maccabiah movement, which promoted Olympic-style competition between Jewish athletes throughout the world. On 1 January 1936 he married his secretary, Jacqueline Stern; they had no children. During World War II, he enlisted in the U.S. Maritime Service, again taught thousands of men to box, and reached the rank of lieutenant commander. In his later years he refereed a number of boxing matches. While officiating a bout at New York's St. Nicholas Arena in 1947, Leonard, felled by a fatal heart attack, collapsed in the ring.

• Information concerning certain significant areas of Leonard's life is not easily accessible, but the International Boxing Hall of Fame Museum in Canastota, New York, plans to establish research files on Leonard and other major figures in boxing history. The only book-length biography, Nat Fleischer's *Leonard the Magnificent* (1947), is incomplete and uncritical. Steven A. Riess, "A Fighting Chance: The Jewish-American Boxing Experience, 1890–1940," *American Jewish History*, Mar. 1985, analyzes Leonard's career within the context of ethnic history. Riess's entry on Leonard in the *Biographical Dictionary of American Sports: Basketball and Other Indoor Sports* (1989), ed. David L. Porter, provides an overview of his life. See also Ken Blady, "Benny Leonard," *The Jewish Boxer's Hall of Fame* (1988); Peter Levine, "Oy Such a Fighter!: Boxing and the American Jewish Experience," in *Ellis Island to Ebbets Field* (1992); and Harold U. Ribalow and Meir Z. Ribalow, "Benny Leonard," in *The Jew in American Sports* (1985). An obituary is in the *New York Times*, 19 Apr. 1947.

WILLIAM M. SIMONS

LEONARD, Charles Lester (29 Dec. 1861–22 Sept. 1913), physician, was born in Easthampton, Massachusetts, the son of M. Hayden Leonard and Harriet Moore. Leonard received his early education at the Rittenhouse Academy in Philadelphia. He attended the University of Pennsylvania and received his A.B. in 1885; in 1886 he received an additional A.B. from Harvard. He graduated from the University of Pennsylvania Medical School in 1889, and in 1892 he was awarded an A.M.

While a student at the medical school, Leonard became interested in photography and worked for a short time with Eadweard Muybridge, serving as a subject for time-sequenced pictures of human motion. As his studies of medicine progressed, Leonard started working with the microscope and taking pictures of the microstructures of bacteria. To learn more about photomicroscopy, he spent the years between 1889 and 1892 observing photomicrographic work in Europe. On his return to the United States in 1892, he continued his studies of photomicrography at the University of Pennsylvania and designed an electrically operated lens shutter that allowed him to obtain pictures of bacteria in various stages of their life cycle. In late 1892 he was appointed assistant instructor in clinical surgery. In 1895, when the William Pepper Clinical Laboratory opened, he was given space for his research in the new building adjacent to the hospital. In 1893 Leonard married Ruth Hodgson; they had one daughter.

In 1895, after Wilhelm Roentgen announced his discovery of X rays, Arthur Goodspeed, professor of physics at Pennsylvania, realized that he and William Jennings had obtained an X-ray image in 1890. He approached J. William White, the John Rhea Barton Professor of Surgery, about the use of X rays in clinical surgery. Once the physicians at the university realized that X rays allowed them to visualize structures within the body, the use of this new technique caught on rapidly. White enlisted Leonard to work with Goodspeed because of his experience in photography and surgery, assigning Leonard to aid in taking and developing the plates. By September 1896 Leonard had been given a small area near his laboratory on the upper floor of the Pepper Laboratory and was operating a "skiagraphy" service for the entire hospital. In 1897 the X-ray operation was moved to a small area in the new Agnew Pavilion near the surgical dispensary, and Leonard was given another small room under the surgical amphitheater for a darkroom. With these inadequate facilities, in 1897 he worked out a method for visualizing the lining of the stomach by instilling an emulsion of bismuth, a radiopaque substance. In 1898 Leonard became the first to demonstrate kidney stones by X ray. In 1899 he was appointed skiagrapher to the Hospital of the University of Pennsylvania. He left the university in 1902 and became director of the X-ray laboratories of the Methodist Hospital and the Polyclinic Hospital.

Leonard was president of the American Roentgen Ray Society (1904–1905). In 1905 he founded the Philadelphia Roentgen Ray Society. He was a member of the British and German roentgenological societies and served on the editorial boards of the *Archives of Roentgen Ray* (London), the *Zeitschrift für Roentgenkunde* (Leipzig), and the *Journal de Radiologie* (Brussels).

When Leonard first worked with X rays he did not believe they were harmful and employed no protection for his hands and body. By 1908, however, his hands had been so badly burned by X-ray exposure that he was forced to admit that X rays were harmful to tissues. Now he began searching for ways to prevent X-ray damage to the body. His X-ray burns were treated by amputation first of an injured finger, next his left hand and forearm, and finally his upper arm. Despite the discomfort from these severe injuries, Leonard remained cheerful and never asked for sympathy. He died in Atlantic City from metastatic carcinoma at the age of fifty-one.

Leonard was a pioneer in photomicroscopy who was swept to fame by being present at the introduction of X rays in medicine.

• Leonard's papers on skiagraphy include "Cases Illustrative of the Practical Application of the Roentgen Rays in Surgery" (with White and Goodspeed), *American Journal of Medical Sciences* 112 (1896): 125–47; "The Diagnosis of Calculus Nephritis by Means of the Roentgen Rays," *Philadelphia Medical Journal* 2, no. 8 (1898): 389; and "The Influence of the X-Ray Method of Diagnosis upon the Treatment of Fractures," *Therapeutic Gazette* 14 (1898): 178. A fairly complete account of Leonard's work as skiagrapher appears in Lynne Allen Leopold, *Radiology at the University of Pennsylvania 1890–1975* (1981). A memoir of Leonard by his colleague George Pfahler is in the *Transactions and Studies of the College of Physicians of Philadelphia*, 4th ser., 5 (1938). There are brief biographies in Howard A. Kelly and Walter L. Burrage, *American Medical Biographies* (1920), and John Welsh Crosky, *History of Blockley* (1929). Leonard's contributions to radiology are also described in Ruth Brecher and Edward Brecher, *The Rays: A History of Radiology in the United States and Canada* (1969). An obituary is in the *New York Times*, 24 Sept. 1913.

DAVID Y. COOPER

LEONARD, Daniel (18 May 1740–27 June 1829), lawyer, Loyalist, and chief justice of Bermuda, was born in Norton, Massachusetts, the son of Ephraim Leonard, an ironmonger, and Judith Perkins. His family had enjoyed social and political prominence in southern Massachusetts for more than a hundred years, their wealth having come from the iron industry, which they established in Taunton, Massachusetts. In 1760 Leonard entered Harvard College and was ranked second among his class. His scholastic achievement merited his selection as a commencement speaker, and he delivered his speech in Latin. Returning to Taunton he practiced law alongside Samuel White, Speaker of the Massachusetts Assembly. In 1767 Leonard married White's daughter Anna White, who died at the birth of their daughter in 1768. Leonard, like his father-in-law, became the king's attorney for Bristol County in 1769. In 1770 he married Sarah Hammock; they had three children.

While serving as lieutenant colonel of the third Bristol County Regiment, Leonard initially spoke out against King George, but in 1774 Governor Thomas Hutchinson appointed him a mandamus councilor, which swayed his allegiance. Leonard denied that his views had changed, saying he was still interested in expanding the colonists' share of Englishmen's liberty but, unlike his former colleagues, he would not commit treason. His acceptance of a royal appointment coincided with the dismissal of the Massachusetts legislature. Once in support of the Crown, Leonard found that the Whig community in Taunton would not tolerate his position as a Tory. An armed mob attacked his house, firing shots and breaking windows, and he was forced to abandon his country home to seek refuge in Boston, which was occupied by the British.

In 1774 and 1775, under the name "Massachusettensis," Leonard published a series of articles in support of the royal cause. John Adams replied to these writings with commentaries of his own, signed "Novanglus." Unlike most conservative authors of the period who expressed public opposition to the radicals, Leonard wrote his letters in the security of Boston. He followed the tradition of political writers of the day and often included elaborate metaphors in his essays. "I saw a small seed of sedition," he wrote, "when it was implanted, it was a grain of mustard. I have watched the plant, until it has become a great tree; the vilest reptiles that crawl upon the earth are concealed at the root; the foulest birds of the air rest in its branches." He became most impassioned when he wrote of the possible consequences of the impending rebellion. He asked, "[Could anyone be] so deluded [as to think that Great Britain], who so lately carried her arms with success to every part of the globe," would not be victorious against the disorganized American colonies? To Leonard it was apparent that, "with the British navy in the front, Canadians and savages in the rear, the regular army in our midst," the provinces would be crushed, "our houses be burnt to ashes, our fair possessions laid waste."

While within British lines, Leonard served as a customs officer. Following the Declaration of Independence, he was proscribed, and like that of other Loyalists, his property was confiscated. When British troops evacuated Boston, Leonard left and joined the community of exiles residing in Halifax, Nova Scotia. Soon the casual relationships among the Massachusetts refugees was formalized by the founding of the New England Club. Members met to socialize while playing cards and to soften their time in exile.

Once he realized he would not be able to return to Massachusetts for quite a while, Leonard began to look for a permanent position outside of the colonies. Leaving Halifax, he sailed to England and was admitted to the bar. With time the British also recognized that the exiles would not be filling the positions that they had once held, so the various ministries began to consider Loyalist applications to fill appointments in many other locations in the British empire. In 1781 Leonard was chosen to be the chief justice of Bermuda, a position he held from 1782 to 1806. Although he would never again reside in his home province, he did return to Massachusetts in 1799 and 1808. His son Charles Leonard remained in the United States throughout the conflict and maintained his rights as heir to his grandfather's ironworks. Leonard's wife died in 1806 while en route to Bermuda. Leonard died of a pistol wound at his daughter Harriet Leonard's home in London. As to whether Leonard committed suicide, his family would not confirm.

• Primary source material is in *The Works of John Adams*, ed. C. F. Adams (10 vols., 1850–1856), and *The American Colonial Crisis: The Daniel Leonard–John Adams Letters to the Press 1774–1775* (1972). Secondary sources include Ralph Davol, *Two Men of Taunton, in the Course of Human Events, 1731–1829* (1912); W. R. Deane, *A Genealogical Memoir of the Leonard Family* (1851); and H. E. Egerton and D. P. Coke, *The Royal Commission on the Losses and Services of the Ameri-*

can Loyalists, 1783–1785 (1915). The most recent assessments of Leonard are Mary Beth Norton, *The British-Americans: The Loyalist Exiles in England 1774–1789* (1972), and Christopher Moore, *The Loyalists: Revolution, Exile, Settlement* (1984).

CAROL BERKIN

LEONARD, Harlan Quentin (2 July 1905–1983), jazz saxophonist and bandleader, was born in Butler, Missouri, not Kansas City, as is commonly given. Nothing is known of his parents. Leonard's nickname was "Mike," for reasons unknown. He attended public schools in Butler and Kansas City, where at age thirteen he enrolled at Lincoln High School, playing clarinet in a school band. Later he studied alto saxophone with George Wilkenson and Eric "Paul" Tremaine. He worked briefly with bandleader George E. Lee in 1923, the year that he graduated. Leonard married in the mid-1920s. His wife's name is unknown; the couple had two children.

Leonard was the lead alto saxophonist, doubling on clarinet and soprano sax, in Bennie Moten's ensemble from 1923 to late 1931, as it evolved from a small dance band into one of the pioneering jazz big bands. His first recorded solo with Moten was on "She's Sweeter Than Sugar," from May 1925. Among numerous subsequent solos, he played jaunty, sweet-toned melodies on "The Jones Law Blues" and "Small Black," both recorded in October 1929, and he led the saxophone section through their featured portions of "Oh! Eddie" and "That Too, Do" in October 1930. After a slow-growing dispute over finances and stylistic direction, Leonard and several other members of Moten's band, including trombonist Thamon Hayes, became part of a new band, Hayes's Kansas City Sky Rockets. In forming the band, Leonard received financial help from his mother-in-law.

In May 1932 Hayes's group defeated Moten's reorganized ensemble in a battle of the bands at the El Paseo Ballroom. As a consequence of this victory Hayes obtained a booking for the summer at Fairyland Park, on the outskirts of Kansas City. In 1932 and 1933 they worked at the Pla-Mor, a ballroom for whites only, while also performing in many African-American social clubs. They left Kansas City for brief tours of the Midwest and the South.

After an abortive job in Chicago, Hayes, disgusted, went home, and Leonard took over leadership of the band. They performed at the Cotton Club in Chicago in 1935 and then in Kansas City until 1937, when Leonard disbanded the group and formed a new ensemble that included sidemen who had previously played with tenor saxophonist Jimmy Keith and clarinetist Tommy Douglas.

With Moten dead, George E. Lee's big band disbanded in 1935, Count Basie's big band having set off for New York in 1936, and Andy Kirk's band touring nationally from 1937, Leonard's Kansas City Rockets became the leading jazz band in the city. In January 1937 young alto saxophonist Charlie Parker joined the group, but he was always late to the job, and Leonard,

who at this point was serving mainly as conductor, was obliged instead to play the lead alto saxophone part. Hence he soon fired Parker. In September, when tenor saxophonist Henry Bridges joined, the band signed with the Music Corporation of America (MCA). Their first recordings, made in January 1940, included a version of "My Gal Sal" on which both Bridges and trombonist Fred Beckett make something special of improvisations on this potentially corny tune. Among four titles recorded on 11 March were "Ride My Blues Away," featuring blues shouter Ernest Williams and Bridges on tenor saxophone, "Parade of the Stompers," with Bridges in especially fine form. In this same period, the band performed in Chicago and New York.

Arranger Tadd Dameron and string bassist Billy Hadnott joined that summer; they would later have distinguished careers of their own respectively in jazz and in rhythm and blues. Leonard told writer Leonard Feather, "One day I ran into Tadd Dameron at the Woodside Hotel [in Harlem]. He was broke, and looking for work. I took him along with me to Kansas City and for a while he played piano in the band as well as writing a lot of our arrangements." Recordings of Dameron's work include "Rock and Ride" and the ballad "A-la-Bridges," both from 15 July 1940. That same year Leonard's band toured the East and Midwest.

Over the next three years Leonard alternated between engagements at Kansas City venues and regional touring. Moving to the Los Angeles area, he worked at local clubs from May 1943 until early in 1945. He then disbanded, being no longer able to secure enough musical work to support his family. To avoid the temptation to resume playing, he sold his instruments. In January 1949, after working in a defense job for Lockheed and at the post office, he joined the cashier's section at the Los Angeles office of the Department of Internal Revenue. He eventually became chief of the section. He retired around 1970 and did some unspecified interracial work in Los Angeles, where he died. The date of his death is unknown.

As an alto saxophonist, Leonard was admired for his beautiful tone, his feeling for lyrical melodies, his accurate reading skills, and his confident manner of leading ensemble passages. He was not a significant jazz improviser and never claimed to be. Leonard's big band recordings from 1940 are modeled after Basie's, with an emphasis on repeated riffs and improvised solos. But the riffs lack the special creative spark heard in Basie's pieces, and the improvisations are far inferior, with the exception of the consistently excellent tenor saxophonist Bridges, who alone assures Leonard's importance as a bandleader. Many other solos, including those of the perhaps overrated trombonist Beckett, suffer from stiff, sloppy, or awkward moments, including a number of melodic clunkers as an instrumental soloist fails to accord with the accompanying harmony. If anything, a reasonably good band such as Leonard's makes us realize how difficult it actually was for Basie's state-of-the-art ensemble to achieve its seemingly effortless perfection.

• There are no detailed sources on Leonard. Bits and pieces of his story may be culled from a variety of interviews and surveys involving Leonard or his sidemen, including Dave Dexter, Jr., "Moten and Lee Are Patron Saints of Kansas City Jazz," *Down Beat*, 1 Jan. 1941, pp. 8, 18; "Kaycee Local 627 Prospered during 1930 Boom Days," *Down Beat*, 15 Jan. 1941, pp. 6, 13; Frank Driggs, "Kansas City and the Southwest," in *Jazz: New Perspectives on the History of Jazz*, ed. Nat Hentoff and Albert J. McCarthy (1959; repr. 1974); George Hoefer, "The Hot Box," *Down Beat*, 12 Oct. 1961, p. 21; Johnny Simmen, "Harlan Leonard and His Rockets," *Jazz Journal* 16 (Aug. 1963): 4–6; Gene Fernett, *Swing Out: Great Negro Dance Bands* (1970); Ross Russell, *Jazz Style in Kansas City and the Southwest*, rev. ed. (1973; repr. 1983); McCarthy, *Big Band Jazz* (1974); Jan Evensmo, *The Tenor Saxophones of Henry Bridges, Robert Carroll, Herschal Evans, Johnny Russell* (n.d.); John Chilton, *Who's Who of Jazz: Storyville to Swing Street*, 4th ed. (1985); Dave Penny and Tony Burke, "'Rockin' with the Rockets': Harlan Leonard and His Kansas City Rockets," *Blues & Rhythm: The Gospel Truth*, no. 22 (Sept. 1986): 10–11; Les Mallows, "The Forgotten Ones: Harlan Leonard," *Jazz Journal International* 40 (July 1987): 19; Nathan W. Pearson, Jr., *Goin' to Kansas City* (1988); and Gunther Schuller, *The Swing Era: The Development of Jazz, 1930–1945* (1989).

BARRY KERNFELD

LEONARD, Robert Josselyn (5 Feb. 1885–9 Feb. 1929), educator, was born in San Jose, California, the son of Joseph Howland Leonard, a physician, and Ella Isabelle Clark. A Vermont native, his father was involved in local political and literary pursuits in addition to his medical practice; he also invested heavily in real estate. Poor property investments depleted much of the family's wealth, and after his father's early death, the responsibility for supporting the family fell upon Robert and his brother. Despite this burden, Leonard managed to complete his early education in local schools. He entered the State Normal School (now San Jose State University) following a year at San Jose High, and he graduated in 1904.

Early interests in both automobiles and drawing led him to enter the growing field of vocational education. After teaching at the Belmont School in California, Leonard taught at schools in both Berkeley and Fresno before deciding to attend college. He entered Columbia University and graduated with a B.S. in 1912. In August of that same year he married Eugenie Ann Andruss of Seattle, Washington; they had two children. Following his marriage, Leonard returned to Columbia for graduate studies, earning an M.A. in 1914. After receiving his graduate degree, he received an appointment in 1914 to the chair of vocational education (the first of its kind in the nation) at Indiana University.

Leonard committed himself to a career in vocational education at a time when the movement to advance the cause of the field had been steadily gaining momentum since the turn of the century. With the passage by the U.S. Congress of the Smith-Hughes Act of 1917, which provided federal financial support for the curriculum, its future looked particularly bright. In 1914 Leonard undertook an extensive survey of the paper box industry in New York City at the request of the New York Factory Investigation Commission. The first extensive occupational study of its kind, it attempted to determine the educational needs of a variety of laborers within the industry. In the following year, Leonard surveyed the total range of occupations in the state of Indiana and conducted similar studies for the cities of Hammond and Richmond, Indiana. Four books resulted from this work: *An Investigation of the Paper Box Industry to Determine the Possibility of Vocational Training* (1915), *A Study of the People of Indiana and Their Occupations* (1915), *Some Facts Concerning the People, Industries and Schools of Hammond, Indiana* (1915), and *Report of the Richmond, Indiana, Survey for Vocational Education* (1916).

Upon the entry of the United States into World War I in 1917, Leonard became a special agent of the Federal Board for Vocational Education. As the supervisor for an eleven-state region in the Midwest, he was responsible for administering the provisions of the Smith-Hughes Act. He also established and supervised numerous teacher-training schools that were charged with providing trained instructors for the United States armed services.

After the end of the war in 1918, Leonard returned to his native state as professor of education and director of the division of vocational education at the University of California. He remained at Berkeley until 1923, serving in his last two years as university representative in educational affairs and in his last year taking on the duties of acting dean of the school of education as well. While in California, Leonard served as an adviser to both the university president and the regents in policy matters, and he also formulated a proposed plan of reorganization for the school. Leonard did not neglect his own scholarship in the face of teaching and administrative duties, authoring *An Introductory Course on Part-Time Education* (joint effort, 1920), *Data Sheets for Teachers' Course on Part-time Education* (1920), and *The Co-ordination of State Institutions for Higher Education Through Supplementary Curricula Boards* (1923), his published Ph.D. dissertation.

Leonard's final career move came in 1923, when he became professor of education and director of the school of education in Teachers College at Columbia. Receiving his Ph.D. from Columbia in that same year, he drew upon his administrative experiences at Berkeley to develop the first formal course in the newly emerging field of college administration studies. By now a well-recognized educational consultant, he undertook surveys of higher education facilities in the states of Maine and Florida. He conducted a similar survey for the colleges under the control of the United Lutheran Church in America and also investigated conditions at individual institutions, such as Howard University, Fisk University, and Hampton Institute. Instrumental in the founding of the American Association for Adult Education, he was also a director of the National Junior Personal Service, as well as a member of the National Education Association, the National Society for the Study of Experimental Education, and the Child-Study Association of America. His death occurred in New York City where, after recovering from a two-month illness, his premature return to work caused a relapse. He died days later in a delirium-induced fall from his apartment window.

An early death at the age of forty-four cut short a promising career for Robert Josselyn Leonard. Nevertheless, he deserves to be remembered as an early pioneer in the fields of vocational and adult education, both of which are now mainstays of the American educational system. His efforts in the development of formal coursework in collegiate administration also helped secure a place of leadership in the field of education for Columbia.

• While Leonard's papers have apparently not survived, a collection of his speeches, *An Outlook on Education*, was published posthumously in 1930. Leonard has received very little scholarly attention in recent years; the best sources of information on his life and career are memorials published in *Kadelphian Review* and the *Industrial Educational Magazine*, both in Mar. 1929. Overviews of the development of vocational education can be found in Arthur F. McClure et al., *Education for Work: The Historical Evolution of Vocational and Distributive Education in America* (1985), and Marvin Lazerson and W. Norton Grubb, eds., *American Education and Vocationalism: A Documentary History, 1870–1970* (1974); both works ignore Leonard's contribution to the field. Obituaries are in the Washington, D.C., *Evening Star*, 9 Feb. 1929, and the *New York Times*, 10 Feb. 1929.

EDWARD L. LACH, JR.

LEONARD, Sterling Andrus (23 Apr. 1888–15 May 1931), educator and linguist, was born in National City, California, the son of Cyreno Nathaniel Leonard, a dentist, and Eva Andrus, a teacher. From 1904 to 1907 Leonard attended Simpson College in Indianola, Iowa. He received an A.B. from the University of Michigan in 1908, an A.M. from Michigan in 1909, and a Ph.D. from Columbia University in 1928. An assistant in the English department at Michigan while earning his A.M., Leonard held several jobs during the subsequent decade, including positions at the Milwaukee Normal School, the Gymnasium at Danzig, Germany, and the Horace Mann School of Teachers College, Columbia University. In 1913 he married Minnetta Sammis, a graduate of Teachers College, and they had one child.

Leonard was appointed an assistant professor of English at the University of Wisconsin in 1920 and promoted to associate professor in the teaching of English in 1925. In addition to his professorship, Leonard was chair of the English department at the Wisconsin High School and a leader in the National Council of Teachers of English (NCTE). As long-term chair of NCTE's committee on essentials and president of the organization in 1926, he significantly contributed to the body's philosophical direction.

Leonard trained teachers and actively conducted scholarship that focused on both the teaching of English and research on matters of usage. His work was influenced specifically by the thinking of Fred Newton Scott, a composition expert who was chair of the Rhetoric department at Michigan, and by George Philip Krapp, a historical linguist and Leonard's dissertation adviser at Columbia. More generally, Leonard's scholarship was shaped by and contributed to the outlook broadly defined as progressive education. His major writings on pedagogy included *English Composition as a Social Problem* (1917) and *Essential Principles of Teaching Reading and Literature* (1922). In the progressive tradition, these and his other works on teaching English stressed the making of meaning rather than the mastery of a priori rules. In doing so, Leonard subordinated instruction in the niceties of grammar to activity that promoted clear and persuasive writing, and he eschewed literary criticism for an approach to literature that enlarged students' experience.

Leonard's work belies the widely held assumption that progressive education necessarily was antagonistic to standards and strenuous effort. Leonard believed that young people would take writing seriously if topics sprang from their desire to express themselves in social situations. Feedback from the class and individual conferences with the teacher would help students navigate the demanding process of transforming conversation about topics into refined essays. Although Leonard rejected the teaching of elaborate rules of punctuation and grammar that, he maintained, could be learned only superficially, he demanded mastery of those essentials that would enhance communication. Furthermore, his emphasis on the experiential value of literature and his recognition that readings should relate to the interests of students were not tantamount to affirming the value of whatever literature students enjoyed. Rather, an understanding of students' interest would help teachers guide them to "books with real fineness of material and of presentation" (*Essential Principles*, p. 88).

Leonard's argument that conventions of writing matter only insofar as they facilitate thoughtful expression led him to valuable research on issues of usage. His dissertation was published as *The Doctrine of Correctness in English Usage, 1700–1800* (1929). This study maintained that efforts by eighteenth-century scholars to standardize the English language typically were motivated more by abstract concern with logic than by the goal of effective communication. In contrast to the rigid rules these grammarians prescribed, Leonard held that "the occasion, the speaker or writer, the subject, the purpose, the audience—all help to determine the place of any form at a given time" (p. 240). Further, presaging work in sociolinguistics, Leonard noted that "most matters of so-called correctness are related slightly to clarity and intelligibleness of communication, most largely to demarcations of social difference" (p. 245). Finally, Leonard decried the presence in modern grammar books of many gratuitous prescriptions made by eighteenth-century scholars.

He advocated "a cleaning out of this ancient purist muddle" (p. 238) so that composition could be taught properly.

To better define the essentials of usage, Leonard surveyed educated opinion about various contemporary practices involving punctuation and grammar. This work, published as *Current English Usage* (1932), found that many constructions censored in grammar books had become established practice among educated people and consequently should not be tampered with by English teachers. Correct usage, Leonard believed, was not "something fixed and static but merely the organized description or codification of the actual speech habits of educated men" (p. 188).

Before *Current English Usage* was completed, Leonard drowned in Madison's Lake Mendota in a canoeing accident that literary critic I. A. Richards survived. An obituary in the *English Journal* noted that *English Composition as a Social Problem* and *Essential Principles of Teaching Reading and Literature* were "two of the most-quoted books on the teaching of English" (Sept. 1931, p. 597). Yet, as scholar John Brereton has pointed out, Leonard's two major works on usage more firmly established his long-term reputation. Although *Current English Usage* was castigated in the popular press for its perceived hostility to standards, and even scholars partial to its perspective pointed out methodological flaws, it nonetheless went through two editions by the late 1930s, inspired more definitive research on the topic, and helped shape NCTE's policy on usage. The less controversial *Doctrine of Correctness*, reprinted in 1962, remained essential reading for understanding efforts to codify English during the eighteenth century.

Leonard's reputation was well established during his brief lifetime, and his research on language and his formulations about teaching contributed to widening and deepening the stream of progressive education. His writings were thoughtful, persuasive, elegant, and abundant, but his ideas were not particularly original. Not only did Leonard build on the more seminal scholarship of his former teachers, Scott and Krapp, but he also rightly acknowledged a major intellectual debt to John Dewey. In addition, much of his thinking was shared by other educational reformers, including many members of the NCTE. Collectively, the ideas of these reformers anticipated and to some extent informed the perspectives and practices of that revival of progressive education that by the early 1980s became known as "whole language." Leonard's largely applied scholarship significantly helped shape and sustain a tradition that laid groundwork for a new movement that would much more broadly influence the teaching of English. Yet it is perhaps not surprising that few educators active in this progressive revival have been familiar with Leonard himself. Following his premature death, a comment in the *Saturday Review of Literature* offered a succinct and apt assessment of Leonard: "The science of linguistics has lost in him an earnest worker, and American scholarship one of its most promising members" (30 May 1931, p. 858).

• The most thorough treatment of Leonard is John Brereton, "Sterling Andrus Leonard," in *Traditions of Inquiry*, ed. Brereton (1985), pp. 81–104. This valuable essay focuses on Leonard's writing, viewing his scholarly work as especially pathbreaking, and it provides an annotated bibliography that includes most of Leonard's books, articles, and edited volumes. Leonard receives only occasional mention in histories of the National Council of Teachers of English, among them Arthur N. Applebee, *Tradition and Reform in the Teaching of English: A History* (1974), and J. N. Hook, *A Long Way Together: A Personal View of NCTE's First Sixty-seven Years* (1979). Two books that note Leonard's importance in the movement to alter the way usage was taught suggest that this reform effort had little immediate influence on the actual practice of teachers: Edward A. Krug, *The Shaping of the American High School, 1920–1941* (1972), and Edward Finegan, *Attitudes toward English Usage: The History of a War of Words* (1980).

ROBERT LOWE

LEONARD, William Ellery (25 Jan. 1876–2 May 1944), philologist, poet, and dramatist, was born in Plainfield, New Jersey, the son of the Reverend William James Leonard and Martha Whitcomb. Named after the famous Unitarian minister William Ellery Channing (1780–1842), he dropped Channing by the time he reached college. Reverend Leonard, himself a native of Plainfield, had been a Baptist minister in Chicago but suddenly resigned his pastorate when he could no longer accept the religious beliefs of his congregation. At the time of Ellery's birth he was editor of the *Weekly New Jersey Times* in Plainfield.

At the age of two and a half, Leonard received a traumatic shock from a railroad locomotive, which he later interpreted in his autobiography, *The Locomotive-God* (1927), as the primary cause of an acute phobia of space and enclosure at intervals throughout his life. By the time he reached high school, however, he seemed to be a normal boy, socially adjusted, fond of swimming, playing tennis, and serving as star catcher on a winning baseball team. He studied Latin and Greek under a capable teacher. Beginning Virgil in his second year was "The magic of Dawn on earth," and the *Aeneid* in his junior year was "the radiant light and music that transformed" his days. He knew at that point that he wanted to be a college teacher of the classics.

Leonard feared that his dream had been shattered when in 1893 his father suddenly resigned his editorship and accepted the pastorate of a Unitarian church in Bolton, Massachusetts, a small village southwest of Concord. No high schools in or near Bolton had advanced courses in Latin or Greek, though public libraries had good collections of the standard British and classical authors. Leonard continued his studies alone and learned by correspondence that he was outdistancing his former classmates. Yet in his loneliness he felt exiled like Lord Byron and fancied himself a Don Juan.

Leonard knew that his father could not send him to college, but by a lucky accident on a trip to Boston he met officials of Boston University and was offered a scholarship. His father managed to pay for his room and board, enabling him to matriculate. He had such an excellent record at Boston University that on his graduation in 1898 he was admitted to Harvard as a graduate student, though officially a Harvard A.B. was a prerequisite. By almost superhuman effort he managed both to teach Latin at Boston University and to earn an M.A. in one year at Harvard. In that same year, 1899, his father left Bolton for a smaller church in Bath, New Hampshire, where he was to stay for only two years before moving to Boston to serve as supply pastor in nearby towns and to help edit a New Thought magazine. Leonard in the meantime served one year as principal of the high school in Plainville, Massachusetts, before embarking in 1900 for Europe. Harvard had rewarded him with a fellowship for two years of study in a German university, and Boston University promised him an instructorship in Latin on his return. However, he decided to switch from Latin to Germanic philology, thus sacrificing a sure position at Boston University. Enrolled in the University of Göttingen in 1900–1901 and the University of Bonn in 1901–1902, he spent the two happiest years of his life in Germany.

After returning to the United States, Leonard was awarded a fellowship for 1902–1903 in the English Department of Columbia University. In New York he longed for Germany and began to have emotional problems that caused his professors to regard him as unstable. His only intimate friend was Ludwig Lewisohn, whose parents had emigrated from Germany to South Carolina, where Lewisohn had experienced less anti-Semitism than at Columbia.

Leonard was awarded a Ph.D. in 1904 after completing a routine thesis titled "Byron and Byronism in America," published the following year at his own expense. Columbia had made little effort to find an academic position for him, and after an unsatisfactory fall term teaching at a boys' school in upper New York state, he substituted in the spring term of 1904 as the German teacher at the Classical High School in Lynn, Massachusetts. Later that year he found employment in Philadelphia as associate editor on *Lippincott's English Dictionary* until the project was terminated for lack of funds in March 1906. He worked briefly as a reporter on the Philadelphia *Public Ledger* before securing an instructorship in English later that year at the University of Wisconsin, where he remained the rest of his life. An eye problem he had experienced in Philadelphia disappeared, and he felt the first peace he had known for four years.

On 23 June 1909, Leonard married Charlotte Freeman, daughter of English professor John Freeman, former ambassador to Denmark. The marriage was a happy one until Charlotte's father died suddenly on 10 April 1911, and three weeks later she committed suicide. Leonard was desolate and had to ask for a leave from his teaching. He would experience panic attacks at intervals for the remainder of his life, but he managed to resume teaching and writing. In 1914 he married Charlotte Charlton, one of his graduate students.

He was a visiting professor at New York University in 1916–1917, but otherwise he was not able to attend professional meetings or accept invitations to lecture at other universities. He was a good teacher, however, and his scholarly and literary writings finally won him a professorship at the University of Wisconsin at Madison in 1926. Leonard's emotional problems eventually proved too much for Charlotte, and she divorced him in 1934. A year later, he married another graduate student, Grace Golden. Two years later she also divorced him but remarried him in 1940 and remained with him in Madison until his death.

Leonard's scholarly work consists chiefly of interpretations of Old English prosody and Middle English alliterative verse as well as a study of the metrics of the *Cid* (*La métrica del Cid* [1928–1930] and in *Publications of the Modern Language Association* [June 1931]). His translations include *The Fragments of Empedocles* (1908), *Beowulf: A New Verse Translation for Fireside and Class Room* (1923), *Gilgamesh, Epic of Old Babylonia: A Rendering in Free Rhythms* (translated from a German version, 1934), and Lucretius's *Of the Nature of Things: A Metrical Translation* (1921 in Everyman's Library; followed in 1942 by an edition of *De rerum natura* with Stanley B. Smith). He translated a play by Hermann Sudermann in *The Vale of Content* (1915) but also wrote plays of his own for production in Madison, *Glory of the Morning* (collected in *Wisconsin Plays*, ed. Thomas H. Dickinson [1912]) and *Red Bird, A Drama of Wisconsin History* (1923).

During his lifetime Leonard published ten volumes of poems, many of them having first appeared in such magazines as *American Mercury*, *Prairie Schooner*, and *Double Dealer*. In spite of their conventional rhyme and accented verse, they contributed to the revolution in American poetry that began in 1912. Leonard's first volume of verse, *Sonnets and Poems*, appeared in 1906 and was followed by *The Poet of Galilee* (1909), *The Vaunt of Man and Other Poems* and *Aesop and Hyssop, Being Fables Adapted and Original with the Morals Carefully Formulated* (both 1912), *Poems 1914–1916* (1917), *The Lynching Bee, and Other Poems* (1920), *Two Lives* (1925, reprint of a private printing in 1923), *Tutankhamen and After: New Poems* (1924), and *This Midland City* (1930). His poems also appeared in musical settings composed by Louis Adolphe Coerne and Cecil Burleigh. A substantial collection of previously published poetry appeared in 1928 as *A Son of Earth*. *A Man against Time: An Heroic Dream*, sonnets written in midlife but published posthumously (1945), contains some of his finest love poems. His most famous volume of poetry is *Two Lives*, which the critic Howard Mumford Jones praised at the time as "probably the best poem that has ever come out of America." *Two Lives* is a sonnet sequence on the suicide of his first wife and the aftermath. The love poems are followed by bitter denunciations of those acquaintances who blamed him for his wife's suicide and spread slanders about him. They resembled the small-town Americans whom Sinclair Lewis satirized in *Main*

Street and Edgar Lee Masters in *Spoon River Anthology*.

Leonard's best-known work is his psychoanalytical autobiography *The Locomotive-God* (1927), in which by self-analysis he sought the origins of his panic fears. As therapy the book was a failure, yet it is an intense narrative with the emotional impact of Greek tragedy that received wide critical acclaim and went rapidly through four printings.

Leonard championed liberal causes: he defended both the labor leader Tom Mooney and Socialist Eugene Debs, protested the persecution of German Americans during World War I, and condemned the treatment of African Americans in *The Lynching Bee* and the Wisconsin Indians in the drama *Red Bird*.

• In addition to works named above, Leonard published an edition of Francis Parkman's *The Oregon Trail* (1910) as well as *Socrates, Master of Life* (1915), *Lucretius, the Man, the Poet, the Thinker* (1941), and *Belgium and Germany* (1916, a translation from Dutch of Johan Lebberton's *De Belgische neutraliteit geschonden*). He also contributed a chapter in the *Cambridge History of American Literature* on Bryant and the minor poets. Contemporary criticism of Leonard's poetry appears in essays by Howard Mumford Jones in *Double Dealer* (1926), by Ludwig Lewisohn in *Cities and Men* (1927) and *Expression in America* (1932), by Ernest Meyer in *American Mercury* (July 1934), and by Clarence Cason in *Virginia Quarterly Review* (1928).

GAY WILSON ALLEN

LEONARD, Zenas (19 Mar. 1809–14 July 1857), trapper, was born in Clearfield County, Pennsylvania, the son of Abraham Leonard and Elizabeth Armstrong, farmers. Leonard's formal education was limited to grade school, and by the time he was twenty-one, he had rejected life as a farmer and set out for Pittsburgh to work in his uncle's store. Eager for adventure, Leonard quickly moved on to St. Louis, then the center of the western fur trade, and eventually signed on as clerk for the trading company of Gantt and Blackwell.

On 24 April 1831 Leonard departed St. Louis and began his career as a trapper and explorer in the American West. As recorded in his firsthand account, *Narrative of the Adventures of Zenas Leonard* (1839), the Gantt and Blackwell party traveled to the Laramie River in present-day Wyoming and spent a disastrous winter avoiding hostile American Indian tribes and searching for game. After Gantt and Blackwell's dissolution in 1832, Leonard joined a new partnership with fifteen other trappers and started for the headwaters of the Humbolt River in what is now Nevada. On the way he participated in the battle of Pierre's Hole, 18 July 1832, in which a large company of mountain men, joined by Flathead and Nez Percé Indians, engaged a group of hostile Gros Ventres. By April 1833, after many difficulties and intermittent success, Leonard and his companions had moved back to the territory of the Platte River, where he was attacked and wounded by hostile Arikaras.

After recovering from his arrow wound, Leonard joined the party of Captain Benjamin Louis Eulalie de Bonneville ("Bowville" in Leonard's *Narrative*). On 24 July 1833 he left the Green River rendezvous in a group led by Bonneville's assistant, Joseph Reddeford Walker. The Walker party, as Leonard notes in his *Narrative*, "was ordered to steer through an unknown country, towards the Pacific, and if he did not find beaver, he should return to the Great S. L. in the following summer." Accordingly, the party passed the northern edge of the Great Salt Lake and followed the course of the Humbolt across present-day Nevada. This portion of the journey proved especially difficult; twenty-four of the group's horses died from lack of food and water, and the party was forced to eat, as Leonard records, "the best parts" of seventeen of these. Such hardship soon ended, however, when the Walker party crossed the Sierras and descended into the Yosemite Valley. Leonard was among the first white men to see the now-famous valley, and in his *Narrative* he calls the initial view "one of the most singular prospects in nature; from the great height of the mountain the plain presents a dim yellow appearance; but on taking a view with the spy glass we found it to be a beautiful plain stretched out towards the west until the horizon presents a barrier to the sight."

Refreshed by the abundant game of the valley, the party soon worked its way down the Merced River to the San Joaquin Valley, trapping for beaver along the way. They reached the Pacific at the mouth of the San Joaquin and traveled south to Monterey, the capital of Upper California. Leonard and the others remained in California for several months, exploring the Spanish territory and observing such local "games" as bull-baiting.

Early in 1834 the party left California for the Great Salt Lake and their rendezvous with Bonneville. The return trek proved even more difficult than the original journey, but by summer they had rejoined Bonneville near the banks of the Bear River in what is now northern Utah. From there Leonard continued in the company of Captain Walker, moving northeast toward the headwaters of the Missouri River. In November 1834 Walker left Leonard and two others in the company of the Crow Indians "for the purpose of instigating them in the business of catching beaver and buffalo." Leonard remained with the Crow until December, observing with great interest their customs and even witnessing a gruesome clash between the Crow and a smaller band of Blackfeet.

After several more months of trapping, Leonard, "anxious to . . . visit the States lest [he] should also forget the blessings of civilized society," reached Missouri in the company of Captain Bonneville. In the fall of 1835 he returned to Clearfield but only for about six months, after which he moved west again and established a store at Sibley, Missouri, the former site of Old Fort Osage. There he supplied local settlers and traded with Indians for furs that he shipped to St. Louis. He married Isabel Harrison, and they had three children, Zenas, Martha, and Elizabeth. He died in Sibley.

Leonard's importance rests exclusively upon his *Narrative*, which was first published in serial form in *The Clearfield Republican* and then later reprinted by D. W. Moore, the paper's publisher. Despite some chronological errors, Leonard's sober and clear first-hand account of the Walker party's journey continues to be an indispensable source of information about the important expedition, while the *Narrative* as a whole contains valuable information about the life of the mountain men and the customs and peoples of Spanish California and the Upper Missouri.

• The original edition of Leonard's *Narrative* is in the Library of Congress. John C. Ewers, "Editor's Introduction," *Adventures of Zenas Leonard Fur Trader* (1959), provides good basic information and historical context. LeRoy R. Hafen, ed., *Mountain Men and the Fur Trade of the Far West* (10 vols., 1965–1972), and Robert Glass Cleland, *This Reckless Breed of Men: The Trappers and Fur Traders of the Southwest* (1950), contain useful related information.

CLARK DAVIS

LEOPOLD, Aldo (11 Jan. 1887–21 Apr. 1948), conservationist and author, was born in Burlington, Iowa, the son of Carl Leopold, the principal manager of an office furniture manufacturing firm, and Clara Starker. (His first name, Rand, was rarely used.) Leopold came of age during the ascendancy of the progressive conservation movement of the early 1900s. His father (whom he would later describe as "a pioneer in sportsmanship") and mother nurtured his early interest in the outdoors and in conservation and supported him in his decision to enter the emerging field of forestry. Leopold entered Yale University in 1905, graduating from the Sheffield Scientific School in 1908. In 1909 he received his Master of Science degree from the Yale Forest School, the training ground for many foresters entering the recently established U.S. Forest Service.

Following graduation, Leopold accepted a Forest Service appointment to the Apache National Forest in the Arizona Territory, one of the many national forests established during the administration of Theodore Roosevelt (1858–1919). In 1912 he married Estella Bergere of Santa Fe, whose family had long been prominent in the settlement of Mexico and the Spanish Southwest. Their own family would eventually include five children.

Leopold spent fifteen years in a series of field and administrative positions in the American Southwest. During these years he became a pioneering figure in many aspects of conservation science, policy, and administration, including forest and range management, soil conservation, recreation, and wildlife management. In the early 1920s he began to act on his growing concern over the loss of wilderness lands in the national forests. In articles, speeches, and official meetings, Leopold described the aesthetic, scientific, and historic values of wilderness (which he defined at the time as "a continuous stretch of country preserved in its natural state, open to lawful hunting and fishing,

big enough to absorb a two weeks' pack trip, and kept devoid of roads, artificial trails, cottages, or other works of man"). His efforts resulted in the designation in 1924 of the Gila Wilderness Area in New Mexico, the first such protected area in the world to be so established.

An increasingly sophisticated understanding of the dynamic processes of population ecology and landscape change in the arid Southwest underlay all of Leopold's diverse interests. Drawing on his extensive field experience and his enthusiastic personal interest in all aspects of natural history, Leopold detailed his scientific findings as well as his emerging conservation philosophy in popular and professional publications, gaining wide professional recognition for his forthright advocacy, his literary skill, and his critical approach to difficult conservation issues.

In 1924 Leopold became assistant director of the Forest Products Laboratory in Madison, Wisconsin, the main research facility of the Forest Service. Although confined by the demands of the position, Leopold devoted much of his extracurricular time to two of his primary interests: wilderness protection and game management. By the mid-1920s he was a leading spokesman in the movement for wilderness protection, and he provoked the Forest Service to assume a more active role in the systematic appraisal and reservation of the remnants of wilderness within the national forests. (In 1935 Leopold would become a charter member of the Wilderness Society, the first conservation organization devoted solely to the protection of wilderness.) As a proponent of game management, he sought to place the conservation of game animals and other wildlife on a more scientific foundation, arguing that restrictive measures would be insufficient and ineffective if not informed by a basic understanding of wildlife biology and ecology and if not oriented primarily toward the protection, management, and, where necessary, restoration of habitat.

In 1928 Leopold left the Forest Service to devote his full energies to the establishment of game management as a profession. His ecological approach to wildlife conservation was revolutionary for the time, and for the rest of his life he would work to develop and put into practice these new ideas. Supported at first by private funds, he embarked on an unprecedented, three-year effort to understand the wildlife habitat conditions of the American Midwest, an effort that resulted in the 1931 publication of his *Report on a Game Survey of the North Central States*. Two years later, he summarized the philosophy, theory, science, and practice of the new profession in his landmark book *Game Management*, the first text in the field. Shortly thereafter he joined the University of Wisconsin as the nation's first professor of game (later wildlife) management, a position he would hold until his death.

As a teacher, researcher, and writer, and as a policymaker in a wide variety of government agencies and conservation organizations, Leopold through the remainder of the 1930s and the 1940s continued to explore the ecological foundations of conservation, to communicate his findings, to train students in the land management professions, and to alter policy to reflect the new scientific understanding and philosophical approach. Responding to new conservation dilemmas—the Dust Bowl of the mid-1930s, the accelerated pace of habitat destruction, the decline and unpredictable explosion of wildlife populations—and to personal experiences in landscapes from Wisconsin to Germany to Mexico to the American West, Leopold gradually rejected many of his early convictions on such issues as predator control and the capacity of managers to control wildlife populations. Outgrowing the utilitarian foundations of the progressive conservation movement, his thinking during these important years evolved to reflect his ever-deepening ecological insights. Although concentrating primarily on wildlife management, he continued to seek a general understanding of all aspects of conservation and to synthesize them in an approach that stressed the functional integrity (or "health," as he termed it) of ecosystems, the retention of biological diversity within the "land community," and the harmonious integration of human economic activities within that community.

Throughout these years, Leopold detailed the progress of his thinking in an outpouring of professional publications. During World War II, however, he began to produce more of the literary essays that he had only occasionally published before. Eventually gathered and published posthumously as *A Sand County Almanac and Sketches Here and There* in 1949, these essays drew on the combined elements of traditional natural history, modern ecology, personal narrative, and conservation philosophy. Leopold's wry style, light touch, pervasive sense of history, scientific expertise, and unusual literary skill would make *A Sand County Almanac* one of the critical sourcebooks of the modern environmental movement. Its capstone essay, "The Land Ethic," became an important early expression of the philosophy underlying that continuing movement.

One week after learning that his essay collection would be published, Leopold suffered a fatal heart attack while fighting a grass fire on a neighbor's property near his own "sand county" farm in central Wisconsin. As a pioneer in diverse technical fields, a revered practitioner and teacher, and an eloquent articulator of a new and more enlightened attitude toward the natural world, Leopold stands as one of the most significant figures in twentieth-century conservation. Underlying his experience was a belief best expressed in his own introduction to *A Sand County Almanac:* "We abuse land because we regard it as a commodity belonging to us. When we see land as a community to which we belong, we may begin to use it with love and respect."

• The Aldo Leopold Papers of the University of Wisconsin Archives in Madison contain the bulk of Leopold's personal and professional correspondence, as well as his published and unpublished manuscripts, scientific records, field notebooks, journals, teaching materials, and photographs. Other relevant records are found in the archival collections of the institutions, agencies, and organizations with which Leopold worked, including the University of Wisconsin, the U.S. Forest Service, and the Wildlife Management Institute. Correspondence may also be found in the papers of the many prominent conservation figures with whom Leopold associated. These and other sources are listed in the bibliography of Curt Meine's full-length biography, *Aldo Leopold: His Life and Work* (1988). Susan Flader, *Thinking Like a Mountain: Aldo Leopold and the Evolution of an Ecological Attitude toward Deer, Wolves, and Forests* (1974), provides a detailed analysis of Leopold's intellectual development, focusing on the evolution of his ideas on wildlife ecology and management. Various aspects of Leopold's life, thought, and impact are explored in two anthologies: Thomas Tanner, ed., *Aldo Leopold: The Man and His Legacy* (1987), and J. Baird Callicott, ed., *Companion to A Sand County Almanac* (1987). Portions of Leopold's unpublished and previously published works have been collected in three books: *Round River: From the Journals of Aldo Leopold*, ed. Luna B. Leopold (1953), *Aldo Leopold's Wilderness*, ed. David E. Brown and Neil B. Carmony (1990), and *The River of the Mother of God and Other Essays by Aldo Leopold*, ed. Susan Flader and J. Baird Callicott (1991).

CURT MEINE

LEOPOLD, A. Starker (22 Oct. 1913–23 Aug. 1983), wildlife biologist, conservationist, and educator, was born Aldo Starker Leopold, Jr., in Burlington, Iowa, the son of Aldo Leopold, a forester, naturalist, and ecologist, and Estella Bergere. His achievements as a scientist and conservationist paralleled those of his father, a dominant figure in the development of scientific wildlife management.

Starker Leopold enrolled at the University of Wisconsin in 1929, but youthful indiscretion (in which a friend damaged his father's new car) and poor grades prompted his father to remove him from college temporarily. Starker was dispatched to work at a state game farm but returned to Wisconsin and received a B.S. in 1936. He married Elizabeth Weiskotten in 1938; they had two children.

After a year of graduate study in the Yale School of Forestry, Leopold transferred to the University of California, Berkeley, where he received his Ph.D. in zoology in 1944. His predoctoral employment included the positions of junior biologist with the U.S. Soil Erosion Service (1934–1935) and field biologist for the Conservation Commission of the State of Missouri (1939–1944); for the latter he worked on managing deer and wild turkeys in the Ozarks. After receiving his doctorate, he spent the period from 1944 to 1946 in Mexico as director of field research for the Conservation Section of the Pan American Union, working under William Vogt.

In 1946 Leopold joined the faculty of the University of California, Berkeley, as assistant professor of zoology and conservation in the Museum of Vertebrate Zoology. He was promoted to associate professor in 1952 and to professor in 1957. In 1959 he was appointed associate director, and in 1965 acting director, of the Museum of Vertebrate Zoology. He moved in 1967 to the Department of Forestry and Conservation, where he was professor of zoology and forestry until his retirement as professor emeritus in 1978. He was also director of the Sagehen Creek Field Station (1969–1979) and served a term as assistant to the chancellor (1960–1963) at Berkeley.

Leopold was a gifted and popular teacher. He had an unusual ability to clarify complex subject matter for young scholars. Although his students knew him as a demanding taskmaster, they respected his infectious enthusiasm for his field. His lack of pedantry and his obvious interest in the students' welfare also contributed to his popularity. His courses attracted nonmajors too, many of whom rated Leopold as among the best teachers at Berkeley.

Leopold also took an effective part in academic affairs. With colleagues from other departments, he developed an interdepartmental Ph.D. program in natural resources conservation. Following his transfer to the Department of Forestry and Conservation, he strove for the further development of professional education in wildlife biology and management and for closer integration of wildlife, range management, and forestry.

Despite his teaching and administrative responsibilities at Berkeley, Leopold, an ardent outdoorsman, conducted extensive field research that resulted in the publication of more than 100 articles and five books. His books *Wildlife of Mexico: The Game Birds and Mammals* (1959) and *The California Quail* (1977)—a detailed treatment of the ecology and management of California's state bird—both received the Wildlife Publication Award, given annually by the Wildlife Society to the book judged the best of that year. He also wrote, with F. F. Darling, *Wildlife in Alaska: An Ecological Reconnaissance* (1953), and *The Desert* (1961). His last book, *North American Game Birds and Mammals* (1981), summarized available information on the habits, distribution, and status of significant game species.

As impressive as Leopold's attainments as an educator and wildlife biologist were his contributions to the conservation of animals and the ecosystems they occupy. Most of his published works include reasoned arguments for wise human use of animal populations—including hunting where appropriate—and their environments. As a group of colleagues pointed out in a memorial recollection, "He kept his eyes on his main goal, a world suited to wildlife and therefore fit for people."

Leopold was an active member of a number of committees and organizations dedicated to conservation. He was on the governing board or served as an officer of the Nature Conservancy, the Sierra Club, the Wilderness Society, the National Wildlife Federation, and the California Academy of Sciences. He was also a consultant to the California Water Quality Control Board, the Conservation Commission of the State of Missouri, and the Tanzania National Parks, and he was a presidential appointee to the U.S. Marine Mammal Commission.

Especially notable was his service during the 1960s and 1970s as chairman of three influential committees that investigated and made recommendations to the

secretary of the interior in the areas of predator and rodent control, management of the national wildlife refuge system, and perhaps most important, wildlife management in the national parks. In the last case, the committee concluded (1963) that the goal of managing the nation's parks and monuments "should be to preserve, or where necessary to recreate, the ecological scene as viewed by the first European visitors." In 1967 Leopold was appointed by Secretary of the Interior Stewart L. Udall as chief scientist of the National Park Service.

Leopold was the recipient of many honors, including the California Academy of Sciences Fellows Medal (1970), the Winchester Award for Outstanding Accomplishment in Wildlife Management (1974), and a Distinguished Service Award from the American Institute of Biological Sciences (1980). He was elected to the National Academy of Sciences in 1970. He died at his home in Berkeley, California.

• Some of Leopold's correspondence and other papers are held in the Aldo Leopold Collection at the University of Wisconsin–Madison Archives. There are also letters of his in the Paul Lester Errington Papers in the Iowa State University Library, Ames. The best account of Leopold's career is the obituary by Robert J. Raitt in *Auk: A Quarterly Journal of Ornithology* 101 (Oct. 1984): 868–71. A memorial recollection, *In Memoriam* (1985), by his colleagues at the University of California, Berkeley, contains observations on Leopold as a teacher, administrator, scientist, and colleague. See also Robert A. McCabe, National Academy of Sciences, *Biographical Memoirs* 59 (1990): 237–55. Some sense of the relationship between Starker and his famous father can be gathered from passages in Curt Meine, *Aldo Leopold: His Life and Work* (1988).

RICHARD HARMOND

LEOPOLD, Nathan Freudenthal, Jr. (19 Nov. 1904–29 or 30 Aug. 1971), and **Richard Albert Loeb** (11 June 1905–28 Jan. 1936), criminals, were both born in Chicago, Illinois. Leopold was the son of Nathan Leopold, millionaire box manufacturer, and Florence Foreman; Loeb of Albert H. Loeb, the vice president of Sears, Roebuck and Company, and Anna Bohnen. As a child and young man, "Babe" Leopold enjoyed the customary comforts and advantages that derive from wealthy parentage. Yet he also suffered from glandular disorders that may have contributed to his psychological problems. Endowed with great intelligence—Clarence Darrow would claim that Leopold possessed "the most brilliant intellect I have ever met in a boy"—he early developed a passion for natural sciences, especially botany and ornithology. Like many other intellectually alert young persons of his time, he was also drawn to the philosophy of Friedrich Nietzsche. In 1923 at age eighteen he became the youngest graduate in the University of Chicago's history. In the ensuing months he studied for and passed the requisite entrance examination for the Harvard Law School, which he planned to enter in the fall of 1924. Loeb had graduated from the University of Michigan, also at age eighteen, the youngest graduate in the history of that institution, and was also planning to study law in the months ahead. Instead, the two friends were arrested on 31 May 1924 for the cold-blooded murder of fourteen-year-old Robert Franks in what soon came to be called "the crime of the century."

Unprepossessing in looks and demeanor, Leopold had met the more attractive, even wealthier, and much more self-assured "Dickie" Loeb while both were in their early teens. Although Leopold was the older of the two by nearly a year, he worshipped Loeb as a sort of Nietzschean superman. For several years, largely through the urgings of Loeb, the two committed petty crimes and misdemeanors but escaped apprehension. In late 1923 they began to plot a "perfect" crime that would involve kidnapping, ransom, and murder, although Leopold was reluctant to go as far as killing someone.

On the afternoon of 21 May 1924, Leopold and Loeb, after having rejected several prospective victims, lured Bobby Franks into their rented car. Since the Leopold and Loeb families were neighbors and friends of his own wealthy family, Franks was not suspicious. While Leopold was driving the car, Loeb suddenly killed the unsuspecting Franks with a chisel. They buried their victim near some deserted railroad tracks and later that evening called his parents, assuring them that their son was safe and that ransom instructions would follow. They did not receive the money, however, and the naked body of Bobby Franks was discovered the next day. A week later authorities arrested them largely because a pair of Leopold's glasses was found at the scene of the crime and the alibi the two had used was faulty. (The chauffeur for the Leopold family disputed the murderers' account of the whereabouts of Nathan's car on the day of the murder and also told authorities that he had seen the two friends trying to eradicate some red matter from the interior of the car the next day.)

The families of Leopold and Loeb retained Clarence Darrow, the nation's most famous trial lawyer, to defend their sons. Their guilt was never in serious question: both had confessed not long after their arrest. (Loeb briefly contended that Leopold had perpetrated the murder.) But their 67-year-old lawyer was determined to save their lives. Long an adamant foe of the death penalty, Darrow chose not to risk trial by jury for fear that the publicity and anger surrounding the crime would doom his clients. Instead, when the trial began on 24 July 1924, he entered a plea of guilty for them and asked for mitigation on the grounds that the defendants, while not insane, were mentally abnormal. Both the prosecution and the defense subpoenaed numerous witnesses, including psychiatrists. On 10 September Judge John R. Caverly rendered his decision. Announcing that he was moved more by the defendants' age than by other arguments, he sentenced them each to life imprisonment and 99 years for the respective crimes of murder and kidnapping.

Between 1924 and 1958, Nathan Leopold remained incarcerated, occasionally at the Illinois State Penitentiary at Joliet, but mainly at nearby Stateville. During these years he received regular visits from family members. He also continued to see Loeb, until the latter's murder in early 1936 by a fellow prisoner who claimed that Loeb had made homosexual advances. More importantly, Leopold managed to fill these years with a variety of projects. He studied languages (including hieroglyphics), mathematics, and physics. (While involved with the last he wrote to Albert Einstein for advice on how best to study the subject; he received a reply that contained suggested readings.) Additionally, Leopold, who admitted that he had only begun to feel genuine remorse for his crime after serving some time in prison, worked zealously to benefit others. He brought organization to the Stateville library, for instance, and encouraged fellow inmates to pursue their education. At one point he learned Braille in order to teach it to a young inmate. During the mid-1930s he helped with an ambitious statistical study for predicting recidivism among parolees. Published as *Predicting Criminality* (1936), by Ferris F. Laune, a Stateville prison official, it drew recognition from both sociologists and criminologists. (Leopold originally was to be cited as coauthor, but the notoriety surrounding Loeb's murder earlier that year altered the decision.) During World War II, when fighting in the Pacific theater of operations raised public concern about malaria, Leopold immersed himself, both as a volunteer subject and as a technician, in an Army project that ultimately yielded pentaquine, one of the cures for the disease. A decade later, he wrote *Life plus 99 Years* (1958), an autobiography that recounted the Franks murder and subsequent trial but focused primarily on his prison experiences.

As the years went by, Leopold hoped that his exemplary prison record might earn him parole or a pardon from the state governor. After several rejections, however, he began to fear that "the crime of the century" would never be forgotten, thanks to periodic bouts of publicity about the event, most notably Meyer Levin's *Compulsion* (1956), an enormously popular fictionalized account of the crime. Nonetheless, in 1958 Leopold's fifth attempt at securing parole proved successful. Moving to Puerto Rico, he spent his remaining years most notably as the administrator of the island's sole leprosy hospital. In 1961 he married Trudi Feldman Garcia de Quevado, the widow of a local physician. Leopold died in San Juan.

• Helpful accounts of the crime, trial, and personalities can be found in Hal Higdon, *The Crime of the Century: The Leopold and Loeb Case* (1975); Maureen McKernan, *The Amazing Crime and Trial of Leopold and Loeb* (1924); Maurycy Urstein, *Leopold and Loeb: A Psychiatric-Psychological Study* (1924); Richard Loeb, *The Leopold-Loeb Case: With Excerpts from the Evidence of the Alienists and Including the Arguments to the Court by Counsel for the Defense* (1926); Clarence Darrow, *Clarence Darrow's Sentencing Speech in* State of Illinois v. Leopold and Loeb (in the *Classics of the Courtroom* series, foreword by Irving Younger, 1988); Elmer Gertz, *A Handful of Cases* (1965); Frederick Arthur Mackenzie, *Twentieth Century Crimes* (1927); Clarence Darrow, *The Story of My Life* (1932); and Irving Stone, *Clarence Darrow for the Defense*

(1941). *Swoon* (1993), a film treatment of the Leopold-Loeb story, is distributed by New Line Home Video/Columbia Tristar Home Video. An obituary for Leopold is in the *New York Times*, 31 Aug. 1971, as is one for Loeb, 29 Jan. 1936.

ROBERT MUCCIGROSSO

LERNER, Abba (28 Oct. 1903–27 Oct. 1982), economist and democratic socialist, was born Abba Ptachya Lerner in Bessarabia, Russia, the son of Eastern European socialists who moved to the Jewish quarter of London's East End in 1912. His earliest influences included a diverse collection of leftist intellectuals and movements, from Maurice Dobb to Thorstein Veblen, from Marxists and Social Democrats to Labor Zionists. After a series of false starts—he was for brief periods a capmaker, rabbinical student, Hebrew school teacher, and (failed) businessman—he accepted the London School of Economics's offer in 1930 of its famous Tooke Scholarship. He received a B.Sc. in economics in 1932, winning both the Gonner and Gladstone Memorial Prizes, and his Ph.D., also from LSE, in 1943, some time after he had moved to the United States.

Lerner's first contribution to the academic literature, "A Diagrammatical Representation of the Cost Conditions in International Trade," was published in *Economica* (12 [Aug. 1932]: 346–56) even before he had assumed his residential fellowship (1932–1934) at LSE, but it foreshadowed, in form if not in substance, much of the six decades of research that followed. The paper demonstrated Lerner's soon renowned methods and analytical powers: he became one of the few modern economic theorists whose reputation for precision and sophistication did not rely on the use of abstract mathematics. As the restatement of an "established" economic principle, the work was also the first manifestation of Lerner's durable commitment, unusual in an economist of his stature, to the clarification and dissemination of the work of others, including that of Gottfried Haberler. To the extent that his often became, and sometimes remained, the "textbook" versions of fundamental economic principles, his influence on the evolution of the discipline is sometimes difficult to demarcate. Furthermore, the paper revealed an intellectual commitment to the methods, if not the politics, of mainstream economics, an obvious tribute to his conservative mentors at LSE, Lionel Robbins and Friedrich von Hayek.

In 1933 Lerner became one of the founders and editors of the *Review of Economic Studies*, which soon established a reputation as an influential forum for concise theoretical research. He also contributed an important article to the inaugural volume, "The Concept of Monopoly and the Measurement of Monopoly Power" (1 [June 1934]: 157–75), which opened one of the several lines of research that later culminated in his dissertation and magnum opus, *The Economics of Control* (1944). The paper's principal contribution was its clear account of the formal requirements for allocative efficiency, familiar to most economists as the "Pareto conditions."

Lerner's second contribution to the *Review of Economic Studies*, "Economic Theory and Socialist Economy" (2 [Oct. 1934]: 51–61), was the first of several influential papers he published on the theoretical foundations of "market socialism" between 1934 and 1938. With Oskar Lange, his LSE classmate and, later, vice president of Poland, and American economist Frederick M. Taylor, Lerner soon acquired a reputation as one of the most prominent and formidable advocates of the proposition that socialist economies could exploit the "market mechanism" to realize desirable and efficient allocations. (Although this is often called the Lange-Lerner Theorem, it was Taylor's "The Guidance of Production in a Socialist State" [*American Economic Review* (Mar. 1929)] that breathed new life into Enrico Barone's vision of "rational" socialist planning.) The simple but elegant rules outlined in these papers were then modified and extended in Lerner's *Economics of Control*.

Lerner will also be remembered for his contributions to the establishment of a "Keynesian tradition" in the United States, and his "conversion" might be traced to the publication of Joan Robinson's "The Theory of Money and the Analysis of Output" in the remarkable first volume of the *Review of Economic Studies* (Oct. 1933). In 1934–1935 a Leon Fellowship allowed Lerner to spend six months in Cambridge, England, where he became one of the first and few Cambridge outsiders to participate in the deliberations of the "Political Economy Club," the "circus" of economists that, including Robinson and John Maynard Keynes himself, devoted much of its time to the discussion of the principles and policies that would later become the foundation of Keynes's *The General Theory of Employment, Interest and Money* (1936). Lerner's review of Keynes's landmark treatise, published a few months later in the *International Labor Review* (34 [Oct. 1936]: 435–54), was both enthusiastic and, in the judgment of most historians of economic thought, faithful.

After a brief period (1935–1937) as an assistant lecturer at LSE, Lerner then traveled on a Rockefeller Fellowship (1937) to the United States, where, with the exception of several brief interludes in Switzerland (1950–1951) and Israel (1953–1956), he remained until his death. Soon after his arrival, he published a number of articles on the "new macroeconomics," which became so closely identified with Keynesian principles that David Colander, who would collaborate with Lerner on a "market anti-inflation plan" in the late 1970s, could wonder "Was Keynes a Keynesian or a Lernerian?" (*Journal of Economic Literature* [Dec. 1984]).

One of Lerner's best-known contributions to this tradition was the "doctrine of functional finance." In his often-reprinted *Social Research* (10 [Feb. 1943]: 38–51) paper, "Functional Finance and the Federal Debt," he offered this definition:

The central idea is that government fiscal policy, its spending and taxing, its borrowing and its repayment of loans, its issue of new money and its withdrawal of money, shall all be taken with an eye only to the *results* of these actions on the economy and not to any established traditional doctrine about what is sound or unsound.

In practice, Lerner believed, this called for the state to (a) ensure that the level of effective demand that was "appropriate" in each period, which required increases in net (of taxation) public expenditure in recessions and decreases in booms, and (b) support the interest rate(s) consistent with the optimal level of investment in new plant and equipment, which required the state to lend funds when interest rates were excessive and to borrow when interest rates were too low. In this context Lerner also introduced his famous "steering wheel" metaphor for the role of fiscal and monetary policies and also articulated his still relevant critique of economists' "conventional wisdom" concerning the burdens of an internal public debt.

Well before this paper was published, however, Lerner had moved from the University of Kansas City (assistant professor, 1940–1942), his first permanent U.S. academic appointment, to the New School for Social Research (associate professor, 1942–1946; professor, 1946–1947). In a remarkable but peripatetic career, he would also hold positions as professor at Roosevelt University (1947–1959), Michigan State University (1959–1965), and the University of California at Berkeley (1965–1971) and, as distinguished professor, at Queen's College (1971–1978) and Florida State University (1978–1980).

"The Essential Properties of Interest and Money" (*Quarterly Journal of Economics* [May 1952]) was another important, if less influential, contribution to the literature on Keynesian economics. It explored some of the most difficult and problematic sections of Keynes's *The General Theory*, namely, those concerned with the failure, either in principle or in practice, of the so-called self correction mechanism, the centerpiece of classical macroeconomics. In the still standard characterization of the mechanism, the downward wage and price adjustments that should be associated with depressed product and labor markets stimulate, through a number of indirect channels, the demands for both. When economies failed to self-correct, however, or when the self-correction mechanism proved slow or unreliable, macroeconomists were forced to consider whether this was a consequence of "wage and price stickiness," or the absence of an "invisible hand." Keynes himself seemed to endorse both positions—that is, wages were inflexible downward but even if this were not the case, no self-correction mechanism existed—but his rationale for the second position was both opaque and controversial. In Lerner's careful restatement, it is the expectation of further deflation, in a world where, as an institutional matter, wages' and prices' deflation is never smooth, that "short circuits" the self-correction mechanism.

Lerner was also the first of Keynes's disciples to be concerned about the possible "inflation bias" of active stabilization policies. In particular, he became convinced, even if he failed to convince Keynes himself, that upward pressure(s) on wages and prices would materialize, even in the absence of "labor force bottlenecks," before economies achieved "full employment" in the conventional sense of the word. In his *Economics of Employment* (1951), Lerner drew the distinction between "low full employment" and "high full employment" and warned that, without policies to complement the standard tools of demand management, wage and price inflation would materialize at the former, not the latter. The distinction is perhaps not as contrived as it first seems: almost two decades later, Milton Friedman's influential "The Role of Monetary Policy" (*American Economic Review* [Mar. 1968]) would introduce the notion of the "natural rate of unemployment," a version of Lerner's "low full employment."

From the 1950s onward, inflation became the principal focus of Lerner's research, a reflection of his intellectual commitment to discover the particular combination of policies that would maintain both "high full employment" and stable prices. In the process, he contributed much to the modern understanding of the phenomenon, including its now familiar classification into "overspending inflation," "administered inflation," and "expectational inflation," all of which were reviewed in his *Flation* (1972). He was one of the first to understand that the classification of inflation mattered inasmuch as the cure for the first type was the obvious (demand reduction) one, while remedies for the second and third would prove more elusive. He expressed the view that, because administered, or cost-push, inflation arises from the inconsistent claims of workers and capitalists on national income and expectational inflation tends to be self-fulfilling, both can (and sometimes do) manifest themselves well below full employment, in which case reductions in public and private expenditure would reduce inflation, but at the cost of increased joblessness.

Lerner's own solution, the product of joint research with David Colander, is described in its most complete form in their *MAP: A Market Anti-Inflation Plan* (1980), the last of Lerner's major contributions to economics. Lerner and Colander proposed the use of "tradeable permits"—an approach often associated with environmental economists who deal with "externalities" of another kind—that would in effect establish a market for permits to increase prices faster than some predetermined rate. Whatever the practical merits of their proposal, it exhibited Lerner's lifelong commitment to the reliance on market-based ends to achieve constructive social ends. He died in Tallahassee, Florida. He was survived by his second wife and by two children from his first marriage, which ended in divorce.

• A fraction of Lerner's archives are available at the University of California at Berkeley. The standard introduction to Lerner's work is *Selected Economic Writings of Abba P. Lerner*, ed. David C. Colander (1983), a collection that includes his most influential articles, brief selections from the books mentioned here as well as *Everybody's Business* (1961) and, with Haim Ben-Shahar, *The Economics of Efficiency and Growth* (1975), and a number of unpublished papers. The most comprehensive evaluations of Lerner's place within the discipline are Tibor Scitovsky, "Lerner's Contribution to Economics," *Journal of Economic Literature* 22 (1984): 1547–71, and Irwin Sobel, "Abba Ptachya Lerner, 1903–1982: Six Decades of Achievement," *Journal of Post-Keynesian Economics* 6 (1983): 3–19. For Lerner's own assessment of his role in the Keynesian revolution, see David Colander and Harry Landreth, eds., *The Coming of Keynesianism to America* (1996). For a critical review of the Lange-Lerner literature on "market socialism," see Joseph E. Stiglitz, *Whither Socialism?* (1994). An obituary is Martin Bronfenbrenner, "Abba, 1903–1982," *Atlantic Economic Journal* 11 (Mar. 1983): 1–5.

PETER HANS MATTHEWS

LERNER, Alan Jay (31 Aug. 1918–14 June 1986), lyricist, librettist, and author, was born in New York City, the son of Joseph Lerner, a dentist who became part owner of a chain of clothing stores, and Edith Edelson. Schooled in New York, England, and Connecticut, Lerner studied music at Juilliard and in 1940 received his A.B. in French and Italian literature from Harvard, where he wrote for the Hasty Pudding club revues.

In a 1939 college boxing match, Lerner suffered a detached retina that disqualified him from the military. In 1940, while writing special theatrical material and three weekly radio programs, Lerner was befriended by lyricist Lorenz Hart, then near the end of his life, whom he met at New York's Lambs Club. Of the major popular lyricists of his century, Lerner proved closest in wit and verbal inventiveness to Hart. Lerner's subsequent collaboration with composer Frederick Loewe, another Lambs member, echoed Hart's with Richard Rodgers: brilliant lyrics, at once wistful and cynical, and enlivening sweet melodies.

Lerner and Loewe first collaborated on a 1942 touring show; for their first Broadway show, *What's Up?* (1943), Lerner co-wrote the libretto with Arthur Pierson. Beginning with *The Day before Spring* (1945) Lerner wrote both lyrics and book. This tale of reliving the past as it should have been foretold a favorite Lerner theme: love overcoming time. The sale of its film rights introduced Lerner to Hollywood.

The next Lerner-Loewe collaboration, *Brigadoon* (1947), a love-against-time story involving Americans in a Scottish town that awakened once each century, established the partners as rivals and heirs to Rodgers and his later collaborator, Oscar Hammerstein II. Lerner and Loewe became their era's most successful team. Biographer Stephen Citron likened Lerner to Hammerstein, who also wrote libretti and lyrics. Both advanced the musical's art and craft by attaching songs firmly to plot and character. Although this attachment eventually limited the appeal of theater music, many of *Brigadoon*'s songs were extremely popular, particularly "Almost Like Being in Love." Loewe and Lerner made a great deal of money from the show. However, the fun-loving Loewe and the nervous perfectionist

Lerner were not always compatible, and Loewe temporarily dropped out of the partnership.

Lerner teamed with another German immigrant, Kurt Weill, for *Love Life* (1948), a stylistically innovative fantasy covering 150 years of a marriage beginning in the 1790s. It indirectly examined the Freudian belief that love between man and a woman was impossible in the modern world.

In 1949 Lerner signed a three-film contract with Metro-Goldwyn-Mayer, where he wrote scripts and lyrics for producer Arthur Freed. *Royal Wedding*, a musical comedy for Fred Astaire, and *An American in Paris*, based on George Gershwin's music, were both released in 1951. Lerner's *Royal Wedding* score with composer Burton Lane included an Academy Award–nominated song "Too Late Now"; *An American in Paris* dominated the Academy Awards, including Lerner's award for best screenplay.

Paint Your Wagon (1951) reunited Lerner and Loewe on a boisterous Broadway tale of the California gold rush. Much altered, it became an unsuccessful film in 1969 with additional songs by Lerner and Andre Previn. Like *Brigadoon*, the show ran successfully in London. When the partnership again lapsed, Lerner returned to Hollywood. A remarkable series of events made the musical rights to George Bernard Shaw's *Pygmalion* available after Rodgers and Hammerstein had previously worked on it without success. Lerner and Loewe took up the challenge, and the result, *My Fair Lady* (1956), broke the New York long-run record with 2,717 performances. Perhaps the best of Lerner's character-evoking lyrics were the conflicted soliloquies ("A Hymn to Him" and "An Ordinary Man") of Professor Henry Higgins, originally sung-spoken by Rex Harrison. Lerner's book altered Shaw, revealing that the Cockney girl Higgins had trained to perfection finally became Higgins's mentor. *My Fair Lady* rapidly became known as a classic of the musical theater.

Lerner owed MGM another film, and collaborating again with Loewe, created *Gigi* (1958), which became the most honored film musical of all time, earning eight Academy Awards, including Lerner's award for best screenplay and both partners' award for the title song, another character-investigating soliloquy.

The last Lerner-Loewe stage musical was *Camelot* (1960). Adapting the Arthurian novels of T. H. White, Lerner told the comic-tragic tale of Arthur, Guinevere, and Lancelot amidst the brilliance of Camelot and how its perfection was lost through human greed, jealousy, and betrayal. Few musical plays had attempted so much. President John Kennedy's widow revealed after his 1963 assassination that the musical was her husband's favorite and that he saw his administration as a Camelot.

Lerner became dependent on vitamin-and-methedrine stimulation while working on *Camelot*. In 1961 Loewe resigned from the partnership after the play, and Lerner briefly worked with Rodgers (Hammerstein had died in 1960) on projects that came to nothing.

Lerner's last memorable stage musical was *On a Clear Day You Can See Forever* (1965), written with Burton Lane. The play examined two of Lerner's most cherished beliefs: love and reincarnation. The mystical title song ("The Glow of Your Being Outshines Ev'ry Star") and a raucously spellbinding call across the centuries "Come Back to Me" proved popular. Its film version (1970) as well as that of *Camelot* (1967) were curiously unmusical, despite Lerner's participation.

By 1969, when Lerner and Previn wrote *Coco*, a musical biography of couturier Coco Chanel, the outside world was involved with war and protest, and show music no longer led the recording industry. *Coco*'s year-long run depended on curiosity about star Katharine Hepburn's ability to sing. Biographer Gene Lees's claim that Lerner did not understand ordinary people may explain the string of expensive failures (Lerner insisted on lavish staging) that followed, particularly *Lolita, My Love* (1971), Lerner and John Barry's adaptation of Vladimir Nabokov's novel. Further failures were a stage version of *Gigi* (1973) and a film fantasy *The Little Prince* (1975), both with Loewe; a bicentennial musical with Leonard Bernstein, *1600 Pennsylvania Avenue* (1976); and a last pairing with Lane, *Carmelina* (1979).

In 1971 Lerner, an engaging raconteur with a light, attractive singing voice, had led an evening of his songs at the Young Men's Hebrew Association in New York. In later years he regularly gave such performances in various media. In 1978 Lerner issued his partial autobiography, *The Street Where I Live*, one of the most readable and quotable of the genre. By 1979 Lerner had moved to London, where in 1981 he married Liz Robertson, the star of his last New York failure (with Charles Strouse) *Dance a Little Closer* (1983). "Brocades and Coronets," a song written with Gerard Kenny, was published and recorded by Robertson in England in 1984.

In 1985 Lerner and Loewe were among the first six Americans given Kennedy Center honors. Suffering from cancer, Lerner died in New York City before the publication of his *The Musical Theatre* (1986), a history that was distinctive in its analysis of the interplay between the British and American musical.

Lerner was married seven times before his marriage to Liz Robertson. In 1940 he married Ruth Boyd; they had one child and divorced in 1947. That same year Lerner married singing actress Marion Bell; they had no children and were divorced in 1949. In 1950 Lerner married actress Nancy Olson. They had two children and were divorced in 1957, when Lerner married Micheline Muselli Pozzo di Borgo. They had one child before their divorce in 1965. The following year Lerner married Karen Gundersen; they had no children and were divorced in 1973, when Lerner married actress Sandra Payne. They had no children and were divorced in 1976. In 1977 Lerner married Nina Bushkin; they had no children and were divorced in 1979.

• Lerner's papers are privately held, though some manuscripts are at the New York Public Library for the Performing Arts, Lincoln Center. Aside from Lerner's autobiography, Gene Lees, *Inventing Champagne: The Musical Worlds of Lerner and Loewe* (1990), and Stephen Citron, *The Wordsmiths: Oscar Hammerstein 2nd and Alan Jay Lerner* (1995), are very useful. Ethan Mordden, *Broadway Babies* (1983), is helpful on *Love Life*. An excellent chapter on Lerner and Loewe is in Benny Green, *Let's Face the Music* (1989). All the major newspapers of Lerner's era carried extensive obituaries.

JAMES ROSS MOORE

LERNER, I. Michael (14 May 1910–12 June 1977), geneticist, was born Israel Michael Lerner in Harbin, Manchuria, the son of Russian parents, Michael Lerner, a merchant, and Cecilia Sudja. During the Russian revolution in 1917, waves of émigrés, including university professors, musicians, and actors, sought work in Harbin. As a result, Lerner was exposed to specialized subjects, such as political economy, philosophy, literary criticism, and history, from a particularly early age and developed a deep and lasting interest and love for the performing arts, especially opera. Lerner attended the Harbin Public Commercial School from 1922 to his graduation in 1927. Deciding to immigrate to Canada for his higher education, he landed in Vancouver, British Columbia, without a passport, visa, or funds.

Lerner's first job involved digging ditches and caring for chickens on the poultry farm of the University of British Columbia. This experience with chickens would develop into a lifelong interest in poultry genetics through the initial encouragement of a young university professor, Vigfus F. Asmundson. Continuing his studies at the University of British Columbia, Lerner received a B.S. in 1931 and an M.S. in 1932. On the advice of Theodosius Dobzhansky, who was visiting Vancouver, Lerner moved to Berkeley, California, choosing genetics for his graduate studies. In 1936 he received a Ph.D. in genetics from Berkeley, where he would become a professor in the Departments of Poultry Husbandry and Genetics and, in 1973, emeritus professor.

Lerner's early research dealt with the inheritance of a number of components underlying egg production, balancing selection with inbreeding, and developing empirical tests of theoretically predicted gains from simultaneous selection for several inherited characteristics. These studies resulted in the construction of selection indices, which were exploited by the commercial poultry producers to boost egg production. Many of his studies were conducted in collaboration with his longtime colleague Everett R. Dempster, who provided excellent analytical and mathematical analyses, and his assistant Dorothy Lowry. Two of Lerner's books, *Population Genetics and Animal Improvement* (1950) and *Genetic Basis of Selection* (1958), were highly influential in putting animal breeding on a firm basis of multifactorial Mendelian inheritance.

Lerner's most interesting work was his theory of genetic homeostasis, an extension of the concept of physiological homeostasis advanced earlier by Claude Bernard and Walter B. Cannon. Both processes involve the regulation of self-stabilizing properties that maintain the norm against fluctuating internal and external environments. Examples of properties maintained by physiological homeostasis include body temperature and pulse rate. Lerner's theory—a combination of elements of population genetics and evolutionary theory with some practical aspects of poultry breeding—arose initially from an attempt to explain the occurrence of a certain proportion of deviant individuals (*phenodeviant*) in every generation. One such deviant Lerner analyzed was the trait "crooked toes" in the poultry. Lerner's concept of genetic homeostasis, later applied to the human species by J. V. Neel, demonstrated that even though the incidence per generation of individuals with certain congenital defects is variable, the total frequency of all congenital malformations in human populations remains nearly constant. Several of these anomalies, such as cleft lip and palate, show great variation in phenotypic expression, suggesting different degrees of liability at varying threshold levels. Although the effect of inbreeding is rarely demonstrated, genetic etiology involving multiple recessive genes and their interaction with various environmental influences are often discerned. Defects due to recessive genes can only be manifested when there are two copies of the gene present, i.e., homozygous condition, a situation that occurs more frequently in children whose parents are blood-related. Lerner suggested that, in every generation of a species, a certain proportion of individuals, whose genotype falls below the obligatory level of heterozygosity required for normal development, will be deviant or defective. In the human species, one example, cleft lip and palate, fits the criteria for a phenodeviant as defined by Lerner (Dronamraju [1986], p. 119). However, partly because of the difficulty of obtaining a "proof" in mathematical models, some geneticists have not completely accepted Lerner's concept of genetic homeostasis.

A popular professor and a gifted teacher, Lerner strove to follow a strict code of ethics but showed much kindness and compassion for his colleagues and humanity at large. He was greatly interested in teaching genetics and its impact on society, especially to lay audiences. One of his books, *Heredity, Evolution and Society* (1968), was specially written for this purpose. In his preface, Lerner wrote:

This book has grown out of a course in genetics that I have been teaching for several years to students not majoring in biology. . . . For the student who must live through the last third of the twentieth century, the most important facts are those that have social implications; those bits of information that demonstrate the involvement of every human being in the ethical, social, and political problems of this age of science problems that are multiplying in geometrical progression in the wake of scientific and technological advances.

Lowry observed that Lerner's "freedom from animosity in the conflict of ideas was remarkable. His teaching . . . was of the highest order."

In his later years, Lerner turned his attention to a study of selection and behavior in the common flour beetle, *Tribolium*. Through a series of elegantly designed experiments, Lerner showed that the outcomes of his experiments were almost entirely deterministic when the experimental conditions as well as the genetic compositions of the competing entities were carefully controlled. He showed further that some of the characteristics involved in competitive ability were behavioral. During his later years at Berkeley, Lerner turned his attention increasingly to behavioral studies and was associated with the Institute of Personality Assessment on that campus. He died in Berkeley, California.

• Among Lerner's works not already mentioned is *Genetic Homeostasis* (1954). His work is treated in K. R. Dronamraju, *Cleft Lip and Palate: Aspects of Reproductive Biology* (1986).

KRISHNA R. DRONAMRAJU

LERNER, Max (20 Dec. 1902–5 June 1992), scholar, teacher, and newspaper columnist, was born Maxwell Alan Lerner near Minsk, Russia, the son of Benjamin Lerner, an itinerant scholar, and Bessie Podel. His father emigrated to the United States the next year, and Max followed with his mother and siblings in 1907. After brief jobs in New York and New Jersey, his father moved to New Haven, Connecticut, in 1913 and entered the dairying business.

Lerner attended Yale on a scholarship for local Jewish students, graduating in 1923. He studied law for one year in the Yale law school and then went to St. Louis for graduate study in economics, receiving his master's degree from Washington University in 1925. Following completion of his doctorate at the Robert Brookings Graduate School of Economics and Government in Washington, D.C., in 1927, he took a position with the editorial staff of the *Encyclopedia of the Social Sciences*, based in New York City. He also began his writing and teaching careers, publishing book reviews and essays and holding a teaching position at Sarah Lawrence College (1932–1935). He married Anita Marburg in 1928, with whom he had three daughters.

Lerner was at heart a political meliorist who favored a "via media between violent change and no change" (*Political Science Quarterly* [Sept. 1928]: 458). He admired the achievements of the American capitalist democracy; it is "more important to arrive than to avenge; better to become general manager than Spartacus," he wrote in 1932 ("The Shadow of Capitalism," *Our Neurotic Age*, ed. Samuel D. Schmalhausen [1932], p. 366). But the business establishment failed to respond effectively to the Great Depression. As Franklin D. Roosevelt's New Deal advocated affirmative change but encountered resistance and as the rise of Nazism in Germany became a cause of political instability in Europe, Lerner became a Marxian liberal. In the "campaign of history" he fought to make the promise of American life constitutional and to advance the cause of labor unions. He gave voice to this position as a member of the editorial staff of *The Nation* magazine (1935–1937). He also became a master of the biographical profile in the intellectual style of V. L. Parrington. He took a stand at the center of *The Nation*'s significant editorial shift to support Roosevelt's "court-packing" plan in 1937. He also wrote the often anthologized law review article, "The Constitution and Court as Symbol and Myth" (1937), as this political and cultural crisis subsided.

In 1938 Lerner published his first book, *It Is Later Than You Think: The Need for a Militant Democracy*, which argued for democratic collectivism that both supported the social goals of the New Deal and made a Marxian liberal critique of the American capitalist society. *Ideas Are Weapons: The History and Use of Ideas*, his first collection of essays from journals of opinion, appeared in 1939. He took his first full-time teaching post at Williams College in 1938. With the fall of France in 1940 he reentered the fray of political journalism, particularly as a contributor to the *New Republic*, which was strongly supportive of an American role in World War II in Europe in the struggle for democracy. Ever interested in "the actions and passions" of his time, Lerner left Williams in 1943 to become editorial director for the Marshall Field adless newspaper, *PM*, in New York City. In this position he originated a column that continued in newspapers for the rest of his life. After he and his first wife divorced in 1940, he married Edna Albers, a psychologist, in 1941, with whom he had three sons.

Shortly before the conclusion of the war in Europe in 1945, Lerner became a correspondent at the front. Drawing contrasts between the ruins of war there and America's industrial might and democratic goals, he began work on the book *America as a Civilization*. Using the framework and insights of the social sciences for his interpretation, he tried "to grasp—however awkwardly—the pattern and inner meaning of contemporary American civilization and its relation to the world of today" (*America as a Civilization*, p. xv). The book took more than a decade to complete; published in 1957, it is the book for which Lerner is best known.

While writing *America as a Civilization*, Lerner also continued his column and resumed teaching. His work on the book, along with the course of events in the immediate postwar years, led him to reevaluate his basic thinking. In his *PM* column Lerner was critical of President Harry S. Truman but more critical of Henry Wallace's progressivism. He eventually declared himself for socialist Norman Thomas in 1948. By then, however, *PM* had folded, having been replaced by the short-lived *New York Star*. With Truman's victory, Lerner began to examine what was happening in the country both politically and socially. In 1949 his column moved to the *New York Post*, and he began teaching at Brandeis University.

Lerner supported Truman's response to the threat of Russian aggrandizement in Eastern Europe. He was frequently critical of Dwight Eisenhower's leadership and was harshly critical of Vice President Richard Nixon, whom he characterized as a political pygmy. He chided Eisenhower and John Foster Dulles for ignoring or misreading the revolutionary ferment abroad in the world. In *The Age of Overkill* (1962) he argued for democratic forms of revolution and for structures to foster economic development around the globe and to contain the real threat of nuclear conflagration. He argued a few years later that Vietnam was a necessary fight but that Lyndon B. Johnson failed to provide proper leadership.

By the mid-1960s Lerner moved from a role as an engaged intellectual activist to a less partisan role as a cultural commentator. There was a new generation undergoing rapid social changes, but there was no new social movement akin to the New Deal. In this environment he became supportive of the judicial activism espoused by the Supreme Court under Chief Justice Earl Warren. He objected to the too narrowly defined social goals of the Democratic party in the 1970s. He supported Ted Kennedy in 1980 but then voted for Republicans Ronald Reagan and George Bush through the rest of the decade. Calling himself late in life a "civilization watcher," Lerner sought the balancing forces that would maintain the promise of our complex, dynamic polity. This quest for equilibrium is fully evident in his later writings on the courts, collected into *Nine Scorpions in a Bottle* (1994), in which he noted the strengths and limits of both judicial activism and judicial restraint.

Ever feisty, Lerner moved to the United States International University in San Diego shortly after retirement from Brandeis in 1973 and continued teaching until shortly before his death. Beginning at age seventy-eight he had bouts with two forms of cancer, compounded by a heart attack. His book *Wrestling with the Angel* (1990) is a memoir of this "triumph over illness." He battled for Robert Bork's nomination to the Supreme Court in 1987, in much the same way that he supported Hugo Black's nomination in 1937. Ultimately, the cancer returned, and he died in New York City.

Lerner lived to write an update for a thirtieth anniversary edition of *America as a Civilization* in 1987. He had been lucky, he reflected, on his timing in 1957. As with individual lives, he wrote, "there are phases of a civilization when it is in conflict with itself, and other phases when its energies are in some kind of balance." "Once again" in the 1980s, he continued, "even with deep divisions and scarring scandals, the civilization is moving toward a working equilibrium which may give its watchers a chance to view it in action as a new whole, for however long it may last."

Of Lerner's place in American thought, Daniel Bell termed him an "intellectual nestor" for the liberal thinking dominant in mid-20th century America. Lerner's *Ideas Are Weapons*, Jacques Barzun wrote, not only preached democracy but also was a "sign of intellectual democracy working in our midst and on a very high level." A British reviewer termed the work a stimulating contribution to democratic thought, "a work of scholarship though its style is the very reverse of scholastic." Gilbert Seldes stated that "it is the placing of facts and knowledge and ideas in relation to one another" that made *America as a Civilization* significant, a one-man effort possibly comparable to Diderot's encyclopedia nearly two centuries before. Stephen Shaw's review of *Nine Scorpions in a Bottle* argued that Lerner's effort "to distinguish judicial review from judicial supremacy" was largely persuasive and of special significance.

Lerner was a talented and incisive thinker who could pare issues to the core. He wrote of John Stuart Mill in 1961 that "while his passion grew out of the events of his day, he gave his thoughts and values the imprint of the universal"; this characterization applied equally to Lerner himself.

• The Max Lerner Papers are at Yale University. The collection includes a useful bibliography of early articles and book reviews and his unsigned editorials in *The Nation* and the *New Republic*. He used the pseudonym "Maxwell Alan Lerner" in the 1923 Yale yearbook and on a few writings but on none after 1930. In addition to the books specifically mentioned, Lerner wrote *Ideas for the Ice Age: Studies in a Revolutionary Age* (1941), three collections of selected newspaper columns: *Public Journal: Marginal Notes on Wartime America* (1945), *Actions and Passions: Notes on the Multiple Revolution of Our Time* (1949), and *The Unfinished Country: A Book of American Symbols* (1959), as well as *Education and a Radical Humanism* (1962), *Tocqueville and American Civilization* (1969), *Values and Education* (1976), and *Ted and the Kennedy Legend* (1980). He also wrote introductions to many books, particularly Oliver Wendell Holmes, *The Mind and Faith of Justice Holmes* (1943); Thorstein Veblen, *The Portable Veblen* (1948); and *The Essential Works of John Stuart Mill* (1961). These and other essays on historical figures have been collected in *Magisterial Imagination* (1994). Many of these have remained in print through reprint editions. Two books, *Thomas Jefferson: America's Philosopher-King* and *Wounded Titans: American Presidents and the Perils of Power*, were released in 1996. For analyses of Lerner, see George W. Bain, "Liberal Teacher: The Writings of Max Lerner, 1925–1965" (Ph.D. diss., Univ. of Minnesota, 1975). For a more recent assessment, see Robert Schmuhl, "The Wit and Wisdom of Max Lerner," *The Quill* 76 (Nov. 1988): 34–41, and his introduction to *Magisterial Imagination*. Schmuhl has become Lerner's literary executor. An obituary is in the *New York Times*, 6 June 1992.

GEORGE W. BAIN

LERNOUX, Penny (6 Jan. 1940–8 Oct. 1989), journalist, was born Mary Lernoux in Los Angeles, California, the daughter of Maurice Lernoux, a chemist, and Beatrice (maiden name unknown). Like Carey McWilliams, the *Nation* editor who was her model of the engaged journalist, she studied at the University of Southern California, receiving her B.A. in 1961. From the beginning, Lernoux's career was focused on Latin America. Immediately after her graduation, she worked for the U.S. Information Agency in South America, serving in Bogotá and Rio de Janeiro. She remained in the region as a reporter for the Copley News Service, heading its bureaus in Caracas (1964–1967) and Buenos Aires (1967–1970), then was a South American correspondent based in Bogotá from 1970 to 1974. Thereafter, she worked as a freelance writer, doing investigative reporting and social analysis of events in Latin America. During this period, she was also Latin American editor of the *Nation*. Lernoux married businessman Denis Nahum in 1972, and the couple and their adopted daughter, Angela, lived in Colombia until the last year of Lernoux's life, when they returned to the United States with plans to settle in Connecticut.

In 1979, after fifteen years of writing about the region, Lernoux wrote, "My principal motivation has always been to try to explain to and interest U.S. readers in the peoples of Latin America. My principal areas of interest are human rights, political, economic, and social matters in the form of investigative reporting." Once she became a freelance writer, she applied her investigative and analytic skills to the writing of books as well as magazine articles. Her first book, *South America* (1974), coauthored with Mari Wesche and Rolf Wesche, is essentially an introductory textbook about the region and its problems. Thereafter, her books concentrate on the specific interaction of social, religious, and political issues in Latin America.

A deeply committed Catholic, Lernoux threw in her lot with her coreligionists who believed social activism informed by liberation theology could empower the poor in Latin America. She sided with the church when, as in *Notes on a Revolutionary Church: Human Rights in Latin America* (1978) and *Cry of the People* (1982), her subject is the "martyrdom" of Catholicism under Latin American dictatorships. She also questioned the church as an institutional force when, as in *People of God: The Struggle for World Catholicism* (1989), she criticized its opposition to Catholic liberation movements that challenged the traditional hierarchy.

As George Black, another writer who specialized in Latin American issues, later wrote in Lernoux's obituary for the *Nation*, "Her primary loyalty was . . . to the kind of Christianity represented by men like Brazilian Cardinal Paul Evaristo Aras and women like the Maryknoll Sisters [socially engaged missionary nuns] . . . brave, humorous, battle-scarred women like Penny herself." The link Lernoux saw between religion and her work as a journalist is reflected in the fact that she called the Maryknoll Sisters her "spiritual family" and constantly referred to McWilliams as "Saint Carey."

In addition to books that focus on the church in contemporary Latin America, Lernoux also wrote analyses of the political and economic forces at work in the region. *In Banks We Trust* (1984) is a penetrating exposé of economic dependency enforced through the international debt structure. *Fear and Hope*, published the same year, considers the political future of the region, as embodied in the subtitle of the book, *Toward Political Democracy in Central America*.

As was perhaps inevitable, Lernoux was assailed in the course of her career from both the left and the right. Lernoux's disagreements with the left originated in the assumption on the part of secular radicals that the church's official rejection of liberation theology made Catholicism the enemy of social justice in Latin America, part of the problem, whereas Lernoux continued to believe in some version of Catholicism as a vehicle of liberation.

The attack from the right was at once more focused and extravagant. In 1978, for instance, the year before the Sandinistas took power in Nicaragua, Ronald Reagan, then preparing to run for president, named Lernoux in a radio broadcast as a "leader" of the "conspiracy" to unseat Anastasio Somoza. It was in Latin America itself, however, that Lernoux faced criticism from the right backed with military or paramilitary force. Her career was notable for the courage she displayed in getting at and publishing the truth as she saw it, despite threats to herself, her family, and her sources. Her sense of the danger her work entailed is reflected in the fact that she retained the Spanish translation rights to her books and did not allow some of them to appear in Spanish at all, lest people and projects she cared about be harmed.

Lernoux returned to the United States when her final illness, lung cancer, was in a fairly advanced stage. She died in Mount Kisco, New York, where she was writing a history of the Maryknoll Sisters. Completed by Arthur Jones and Robert Ellsberg, *Hearts on Fire: The Story of the Maryknoll Sisters* (1993) was published posthumously. She is buried in the Maryknoll cemetery overlooking the Hudson Valley.

• Lernoux's papers are housed at Marquette University. Macalester College is developing a memorial collection in her name, focusing on Latin American affairs. Biographies other than entries in standard reference works are contained in obituaries like those in the *Nation*, 30 Oct. 1989, and the *Utne Reader*, Jan./Feb. 1990.

LILLIAN S. ROBINSON

LE ROUX, Bartholomew (1663–Aug. 1713), silversmith, was born in Amsterdam, Holland, the son of Pierre Le Roux, a goldsmith, and Jannetje (maiden name unknown). The son of French Huguenot exiles, Pierre emigrated to London in 1680 and became a naturalized citizen in 1682. Jane and the children followed in 1683, possibly remaining in Amsterdam until Bartholomew completed his apprenticeship.

Bartholomew and his three brothers sailed to America, apparently in 1687, the year in which Bartholomew became a freeman in New York City. The following year he married Geertruyd van Rollegom in the Reformed Dutch church. They had eleven children.

In 1693 Le Roux purchased a house in New York's West Ward, an average neighborhood in economic and social terms. Like most craftsmen at the time, he operated his business out of his home. In 1694 he purchased land in New Rochelle, New York, a Huguenot community where his brother Pierre lived.

Le Roux was a highly talented silversmith who produced a variety of forms. He worked in the contemporary Dutch and emerging New York styles, meeting the tastes of his local patrons. His greatest contribution was training apprentices in fine-quality crafts-

manship and in the characteristics of contemporary Huguenot silver made in both Holland and London. Le Roux was the only French silversmith working in New York City until 1710, and French stylistic features first appear in America in the work of his apprentices. These included Peter Van Dyck, who married his daughter Rachel in 1711, possibly his wife's nephew, Tobias Stoutenburgh, and most likely his sons Charles and John. Charles became a leading craftsman, serving as official silversmith and sealmaker for the city of New York from 1720 to 1743.

Silversmiths were among the most socially and politically elite craftsmen of New York, and Le Roux was a particularly prominent member of the community. He held terms as constable (1691–1692), collector (1699–1700), assessor (1698–1699, 1707–1708), and assistant alderman (1702–1704, 1708–1713) on the Common Council, the city's governing body.

While serving in the New York City militia under Captain Gabriel Minvielle, Le Roux joined other French Protestant and Dutch residents in supporting Jacob Leisler's famous seizure of Fort James at the southern tip of Manhattan in 1689. Le Roux was chosen to present the insurgents' complaints to local officials. His signed affidavit explains that they had seized the fort because the French population felt threatened by papists from Staten Island and Boston, they feared that the fort was poorly defended, and they were anxious since former New York governor Thomas Dongan's brigantine appeared to have been preparing for military action against the city of New York. By mid-1691 Leisler's domineering and demagogic style had caused most of his followers to withdraw their support, including Le Roux. Leisler was eventually convicted of treason and murder.

Prominent in church life as well, in 1703 Le Roux chose to join Trinity Church, the Anglican house of worship, rather than the Reformed Dutch church that his family attended or the French Protestant church. He held the post of vestryman, the highest lay position of the Anglican church, from 1703 through 1709.

Le Roux died in New Rochelle. His few surviving works are in the collections of the Henry Francis du Pont Winterthur Museum, the Metropolitan Museum of Art, the Minneapolis Institute of Art, the Yale University Art Gallery, and the Heritage Foundation.

• Information on the Le Roux family is available at the Huguenot Society of America in New York City and in Morgan H. Seacord, *Biographical Sketches and Index of the Huguenot Settlers of New Rochelle, 1687–1776* (1941). References to Le Roux can be found in various volumes of the *Collections of the New-York Historical Society* and the *Collections of the New York Genealogical and Biographical Society*. Le Roux's affidavit in support of Leisler's rebellion is published in Edmund Bailey O'Callaghan, *The Documentary History of the State of New York*, vol. 2 (1849).

KRISTAN H. MCKINSEY

LEROY, Mervyn (15 Oct. 1900–13 Sept. 1987), film director and producer, was born in San Francisco, California, the son of Harry LeRoy, a department store owner, and Edna Armer. In 1905 Mervyn's mother left the family to marry Percy Teeple, a salesman. When the 1906 earthquake destroyed Harry LeRoy's store, Mervyn was forced to work, first as a newspaper boy, but later as a vaudeville actor and singer. By the time he was fifteen he was being dubbed "Mervyn Le-Roy, the boy tenor of the generation." By 1916, the year of his father's death, LeRoy had teamed with pianist Clyde Cooper to tour the country as "LeRoy and Cooper, Two Kids and a Piano."

In 1919 the act broke up, and LeRoy joined his cousin Jesse Lasky at Famous Players-Lasky in Hollywood. LeRoy quickly advanced from wardrobe assistant (at $12.50 per week) to lab assistant to assistant cinematographer. In 1922 he briefly resumed acting (appearing as a chariot rider in Cecil B. DeMille's *Ten Commandments* in 1923). LeRoy stopped performing altogether in 1924 and then became a gag writer for First National pictures, working on films such as *Sally* (1925) and *Ella Cinders* (1926), both of which starred Colleen Moore.

In 1927 Moore convinced Jack Warner, the owner of First National, that LeRoy should be a director. After LeRoy made his first film that year, *No Place To Go*, he was immediately called a "Boy Wonder" because, at twenty-seven, he was the youngest director working in Hollywood. The short (5′7″), gregarious LeRoy began chomping cigars regularly to toughen his youthful image, and he was married for the first time, to Edna Murphy, an actress, although they soon divorced.

Throughout the late 1920s and early 1930s, LeRoy cranked out low-budget silent and sound comedies, but in 1930 Warner asked LeRoy to film *Little Caesar* (1931), a gangster picture starring Edward G. Robinson as a ruthless Al Capone type. The highly popular film won critical raves for its brutal but realistic depiction of mobster life. LeRoy's 1931 film *Five Star Final*, about a newspaper editor, was hailed as an exposé of yellow journalism. LeRoy continued to make light comedies, but in 1932 Warner and Darryl Zanuck, production chief of Warner Bros., asked LeRoy to film his most harrowing "social conscience" picture to date, *I Am a Fugitive from a Chain Gang* (produced by Warner's new Warner Bros. studios). So successful was this depiction of chain gang life that LeRoy's film helped force reform on the state of Georgia's penal code.

By 1932 LeRoy was a top director at Warner Bros., earning $2,750 a week. After filming a production number without credit in the backstage musical *42nd Street* (1933), LeRoy was assigned his own fast-paced, "let's-put-on-a-show" musical, *Gold Diggers of 1933* (1933), starring his girlfriend Ginger Rogers. Just as his affair with Rogers hit the tabloids in 1933, LeRoy married Doris Warner, the daughter of Harry Warner and the niece of Jack Warner. With his marriage, LeRoy joined the ranks of Hollywood royalty: he went into the horse-racing business with his in-laws and worshipped with them at the Wilshire Boulevard Temple. The couple had two children.

In the mid-1930s LeRoy was still making both light entertainments like *Sweet Adeline* (1935), a Jerome Kern musical, and socially relevant films like *They Won't Forget* (1937), an indictment of mob justice. In 1936 LeRoy founded Mervyn LeRoy Productions, releasing his films through Warner Bros., but in 1938 he moved his production unit to Metro-Goldwyn-Mayer, where he produced such films as *At the Circus*, starring the Marx Brothers, and *The Wizard of Oz* (both 1939). Despite his new eminence as a producer (earning a record $300,000 a year), LeRoy wanted to direct again. Over the next few years he directed a number of hugely successful films, including the glossy but artful war romances *Waterloo Bridge* (1940) and *Random Harvest* (1942), the latter nominated for an Academy Award for best picture.

During World War II LeRoy produced twelve shorts for the U.S. government on such topics as putting out fires and contending with bombs. In 1945 LeRoy won an Oscar for the RKO short subject *The House I Live In*, a powerful condemnation of ethnic prejudice starring Frank Sinatra. That year LeRoy divorced Doris Warner, and in 1946 he married Katherine Spiegel, the widow of a midwestern theater-chain executive. They had no children.

In 1947 LeRoy returned to MGM to film the appropriately titled post–World War II drama *Homecoming* (1948), a stylish, modern-day version of *Ulysses*. Next, LeRoy remade *Little Women* (1949) in Technicolor, but he was becoming increasingly frustrated with the cost-conscious Dore Schary, the mogul who had joined the studio in 1948 and eventually replaced Louis B. Mayer in 1951. In 1951 LeRoy made the three-hour Roman epic *Quo Vadis*, which later won both the Christopher and the Brotherhood awards (the latter for LeRoy's "25 years of distinguished service to greater world understanding"). In 1953 LeRoy wrote his first autobiography, *It Takes More Than Talent*.

In 1954 LeRoy left MGM and returned to Warner Bros., where he finished John Ford's *Mister Roberts* (1955) when Ford became ill and adapted from the stage *The Bad Seed* (1956), the chilling story of a homicidal child. LeRoy also made *Home before Dark* (1958) starring Jean Simmons. Over the next decade LeRoy produced and directed films that made money but were considered artistic misfires: *The F.B.I. Story* (1959), for example, paid homage to his *Little Caesar* salad days, but with an apologia to J. Edgar Hoover. However, LeRoy's last signed film, *Moment To Moment* (1966), was a haunting melodrama that revamped the amnesia motif from *Random Harvest*. LeRoy then worked on one last film, but without credit, codirecting John Wayne's controversial Vietnam war recruiting poster *The Green Berets* (1968).

In his post-Hollywood years LeRoy was honored with a major retrospective at New York's Museum of Modern Art in 1967, wrote his second autobiography, *Mervyn LeRoy: Take One*, in 1974, and won the Irving G. Thalberg Memorial Academy Award in 1975. Diagnosed with Alzheimer's disease in the early 1980s, LeRoy died of heart failure at his Beverly Hills home.

LeRoy was a gifted, versatile director-producer who made many entertaining movies during Hollywood's "Golden Age." Auteur scholars are critical of him for not having an identifiable style, but he is esteemed for the work he did that embraced topical social issues. In 1974 LeRoy said, "I never made a picture the same. You know that's why they can't define the LeRoy touch." Nevertheless, LeRoy's touch can be identified by its solid craftsmanship and positive spirit. Many of his films are fondly remembered and remain popular with audiences.

• Personal papers are still held by the LeRoy family, but the American Museum of the Moving Image, New York, holds LeRoy's collection of stills, and the University of Southern California holds the Mervyn LeRoy–Sol Lessor Collection of Historical Motion Picture Devices. The two best sources about LeRoy's life are LeRoy's two autobiographies, *It Takes More Than Talent* (1953, as told to Alyce Canfield) and *Mervyn LeRoy: Take One* (1974, as told to Dick Kleiner). Several books about the film *The Wizard of Oz* contain information about LeRoy, including Doug McClelland, *Down the Yellow Brick Road: The Making of the Wizard of Oz* (1976), and Aljean Harmetz, *The Making of the Wizard of Oz* (1977). Articles on LeRoy's work include Raymond Rohauer, "Mervyn LeRoy," *A Tribute to Mervyn LeRoy* (1967), pp. 2–4, 13–14; Mike Snell, "Mervyn LeRoy: The Director as Audience," *Quirk's Reviews*, Oct. 1983, pp. 5–6; "Les immortals du cinéma: Mervyn LeRoy," *Cine revue* (2 Sept. 1982): 20; "Mervyn LeRoy Revisited," *Revue du Cinéma* 378 (Dec. 1982): 119–20; Bill Hare, "Mervyn LeRoy: The Wizard behind *The Wizard of Oz*," *Hollywood Studio Magazine* 17, no. 3, pt. 2 (Apr. 1984); and Richard Chatten, "Mervyn LeRoy," *Film Dope* 35 (Sept. 1986): 4–7. An informative interview by director William Friedkin was published in *Action* 9, no. 6 (Nov.–Dec. 1974): 4–14. Obituaries are in the *New York Times*, 9 Sept. 1987, and *Revue du Cinéma* 432 (Nov. 1987): 77.

ERIC MONDER

LESCAZE, William Edmond (27 Mar. 1896–9 Feb. 1969), architect, was born in Onex (now part of Geneva), Switzerland, the son of Alexandre Lescaze, a professor of German language and literature, and Marthe Caux. Lescaze attended the College of Geneva from 1910 to 1914, pursuing a technical course of study. He had begun painting and drawing at an early age, and these remained creative outlets for him. By the time he graduated Lescaze had decided to pursue an architecture career, but he rejected the traditional training of the École des Beaux-Arts in Paris. In 1915 Lescaze entered the École Polytechnique Federale in Zurich to study with leading modern architect Karl Moser; he received the master of architecture degree in 1919.

After graduating Lescaze moved to France, where he initially worked on the reconstruction of the war-damaged town of Arras. Then he went to Paris, where he worked for Henri Sauvage, an architect known for his low-cost housing designs. Lescaze arrived in the United States in August 1920. He spent the next three years in Cleveland, Ohio, working briefly for Hubbell and Benes and then for Walter R. MacCornack. In 1923 Lescaze established his own office in New York City after receiving his first independent commission,

the remodeling of a house on Sutton Square. For the next six years Lescaze was occupied with a series of interior remodeling projects in New York. He made frequent trips to western Europe and stayed abreast of the latest architectural developments, particularly in the Netherlands, France, and Germany. Lescaze's use of his own furniture designs brought a degree of unity to his interior design projects, and total involvement in all aspects of a design characterized his work throughout his career.

The year 1929 marked a turning point for Lescaze both personally and professionally. In March Lescaze became a naturalized U.S. citizen, and in April he became partners with George Howe. This partnership resulted in several of Lescaze's most distinguished designs. Howe was a Beaux-Arts trained Philadelphia architect who had practiced with the firm of Mellor, Meigs and Howe designing historically based houses in the Philadelphia area that Howe later termed "Wall Street pastoral." Howe left his partnership with Mellor and Meigs in 1928 to pursue modern design, and he sought out Lescaze, ten years his junior, as a partner familiar with new European design. Despite their partnership, the two continued to work separately. Lescaze's New York office became the primary address for the firm, while Howe maintained a Philadelphia office.

The Philadelphia Saving Fund Society Building in Philadelphia, known as the PSFS Building (1929–1932), was the most important project Howe and Lescaze designed. From his previous office, Howe brought this commission to design a new bank hall and office tower for the conservative Philadelphia institution. After joining the partnership Lescaze contributed his experience with European modernism to the collaborative effort; support from the forward-looking bank president, James M. Willcox, made the innovative design a reality.

The PSFS Building was the first International Style skyscraper built in the United States and is considered an important landmark of modern American architecture. Its design drew on precedents of leading modernist architects in Europe, including Le Corbusier, Ludwig Mies van der Rohe, Walter Gropius and J. J. P. Oud. The work of these European modernists was characterized by an emphasis on spatial volume rather than mass, on regularity rather than axial symmetry, and by the absence of applied decoration. These characteristics were codified as the principles of the International Style in the 1932 Museum of Modern Art exhibition of modern architecture and in the accompanying catalog and book, written by Henry-Russell Hitchcock, Jr., and Philip Johnson. The exhibit and publications all featured the work of Howe and Lescaze.

The PSFS Building combines a rectilinear office tower set asymmetrically above a curvilinear podium base containing ground floor shops and a second-floor banking hall. The design features a cantilevered corner in the base, horizontal ribbon windows, expressed vertical structural members in the tower, and neon let-tering on the roof announcing the company's monogram. The finished structure is noteworthy not only for its architectural design but also as one of the first U.S. high-rises to incorporate air conditioning. The rich interior finishes and furnishings were also designed by the firm.

Never a close relationship, the partnership between Howe and Lescaze had begun to disintegrate by 1933 and finally dissolved in 1935. In his independent designs during the partnership period, however, Lescaze introduced the International Style to other building types. For the nursery school building of the Oak Lane Country Day School (1929) in Philadelphia, Lescaze integrated modern design with progressive education ideas. The Frederick Vanderbilt Field House (1930–1931) in New Hartford, Connecticut, was the first house in new style on the East Coast. Lescaze also received commissions for several buildings at Dartington Hall in Devon, England, from 1930 to 1935, including the Headmaster's House (1930–1932). In 1935 Lescaze established a firm under his own name; he maintained this New York practice until his death.

On 29 September 1933 Lescaze married Mary Connick Hughes of New York. They had one child. The house and studio he designed for his family (1933–1934) was the first International Style townhouse in New York, a modern reinterpretation of the traditional brownstone. The incorporation of glass block and an air conditioning system were among first such uses in American residential architecture. This design led to three more New York townhouse commissions. At this time Lescaze also began a fifteen-year association with the Columbia Broadcasting System. Through his consultation on graphic designs and field equipment, as well as his architectural and interior designs, Lescaze helped the company to develop a corporate image.

Following European trends, Lescaze's work of the 1930s began to incorporate vernacular materials and a greater variety of color and textures, creating "domesticated modern" designs. Examples include the Roy F. Spreter studio and garage (1933–1934) in Ardmore, Pennsylvania and the Kimball Glass Company Administration Building (1936–1937) in Vineland, New Jersey.

Ten Eyck Housing, Brooklyn, New York (later Williamsburg Housing, 1935–1938), was Lescaze's first realized large-scale public housing project. Drawing on English and German models, as well as on his own designs for the Chrystie-Forsyth project in lower Manhattan (1931–1933), Lescaze and an associated group of architects created the first federally financed public housing in New York.

Lescaze designed two buildings for the New York World's Fair in 1939, the Aviation Building and the Swiss Pavilion. The same year he also designed the Longfellow Building (1939–1941) in Washington, D.C. This was important as an early modern-style building in Washington, but it was later radically altered by several remodelings. A slow period followed during World War II, at which point he turned his at-

tention again to housing issues. In 1942 he published *On Being an Architect*, which describes his own practice and his experience in architecture.

Renewed building activity after the war brought new commissions for large-scale commercial and public buildings during the 1950s and 1960s. Lescaze incorporated new steel and glass technology in buildings such as the offices at 711 Third Avenue in New York (1952–1956). His last works reflected the classicizing tendencies of Mies van der Rohe's later projects. Symmetry, clear structural expression, and a return to cubic forms are characteristics of his High School of Art and Design, New York (1953–1960, with Kahn and Jacobs); the Swiss Embassy, Washington, D.C. (1959); 777 Third Avenue Office Building, New York (1961–1965); and his last major commission, One New York Plaza Office Building, New York (1965–1969).

Lescaze was a leading figure of the modernist movement. The PSFS Building, his best-known work, introduced the International Style to the United States. In subsequent projects Lescaze continued to adapt European models to American building types and to incorporate technological developments into his work. Lescaze died in New York after fifty years of progressive architectural practice.

• Lescaze's papers are in the George Arents Research Library for Special Collections at Syracuse University. Records of his English projects are in the Records Office of Dartington Hall in Devon, England. *On Being an Architect* (1942), contains Lescaze's own account of his career. The fullest assessment of his architectural career is Lorraine Welling Lanmon, *William Lescaze, Architect* (1987). The exhibition catalog *William Lescaze* (1982), with essays by Christian Hubert and Lindsay Stamm Shapiro, is an important source, and it contains bibliographies compiled by Lanmon of writings on and by Lescaze. See Robert M. Coates, "Profile," *New Yorker*, 12 Dec. 1936, pp. 28–34, for a contemporary discussion of Lescaze and his work. William H. Jordy has assessed the role of the PSFS Building in "PSFS: Its Development and Its Significance in Modern Architecture," *Journal of the Society of Architectural Historians*, May 1962, pp. 47–83; and in his book *American Buildings and Their Architects: The Impact of European Modernism in the Mid-Twentieth Century* (1972). See also Robert A. M. Stern, "PSFS: Beaux-Arts Theory and Rational Expressionism," *Journal of the Society of Architectural Historians*, May 1962, pp. 84–102; and *George Howe: Toward a Modern American Architecture* (1975). Obituaries are in the *New York Times* and the *Washington Post*, both 10 Feb. 1969.

ANN C. HUPPERT

LESCHI (?–19 Feb. 1858), western Washington Indian leader, was the son of a Nisqually father and a Klickitat or Yakima mother. He grew to maturity among his father's tribe in the vicinity of the Nisqually River near present-day Yelm, Washington. When the first American settlements appeared in the area around 1850, he was perhaps about thirty years of age. Leschi, who may have had two wives, quickly adapted to the agricultural practices of the settlers, growing crops and tending livestock. He was seen by his American neighbors as a model for the course all Indians should adopt. Washington territorial officials, as well as his own people, recognized Leschi as a charismatic leader. Leschi lived in a native culture (Coast Salish) in which, with few exceptions, there were no political leaders in the European-American sense of the term. Leschi, however, was able to extend his influence over not only the Nisquallies but also neighboring bands and tribes.

At the Medicine Creek council in December 1854, where a treaty was negotiated by Governor Isaac I. Stevens with the Nisquallies, Puyallups, and other bands, Leschi was a prominent figure. There is no evidence, as asserted many years later, that he refused to sign the treaty. He did argue, both at the council and at a subsequent meeting with the governor's interpreter, that the reservation set aside on the Nisqually River was too small because he and others needed more land for their horses. The treaty (ratified on 3 Mar. 1855) allowed for adjustments in the reservations that were intended to be temporary. However, before changes could be made, war broke out east of the Cascade Mountains, a conflict in which the Yakimas took a prominent role. Leschi, apparently upset by the failure of the government to react quickly to his demands and pressured by his relatives among the Yakimas and Klickitats, agreed to lead the Indian war effort in the Puget Sound country.

From the fall of 1855 through the spring of 1856 Leschi instigated a series of raids and guerilla activities. Although the white population was thrown into a state of near hysteria, the warfare, including the much-publicized attack upon Seattle at which Leschi may have been present, had relatively little impact. Despite concerted efforts by the U.S. Army and territorial volunteer forces working with Indian allies, Leschi eluded capture or a major battle. As the hostilities drew to a close, the army under the command of General John E. Wool took a conciliatory approach, offering pardons to those who had participated in the conflict. However, Governor Stevens and the civilian leadership demanded that the alleged perpetrators of the war, including Leschi, be captured and brought to trial. In response to a reward offer, members of Leschi's band seized him on 13 November 1856 and turned him over to the authorities.

Three days after his capture Leschi was charged in the territorial courts with participating in the murder of two territorial volunteers early in the conflict. The trial involved two issues: was Leschi present when the men were ambushed—he and others said he was not—and, if he had been a participant, was the attack a legitimate act of war? The first jury was hung, with ten men supporting a guilty verdict. A second trial in March 1857, in which a different judge charged the jury to consider only whether or not Leschi participated in the incident, returned a guilty verdict; he was sentenced to be hanged.

While the verdict was appealed to the territorial supreme court, the case became a cause célèbre in the region. The first execution date was voided when lawyers and other citizens defending Leschi arranged to have the sheriff responsible for carrying out the sentence arrested by a U.S. marshall on charges of illegal liquor trafficking. Public demonstrations followed this seeming frustration of the judicial process. A second execution date was set for 19 February 1858. This time the sentence was carried out. Leschi, who had remained in jail at Fort Steilacoom (where he converted to Catholicism), went to his death calmly, maintaining his innocence as he had throughout the long proceedings.

Leschi was an able, respected leader who nevertheless was betrayed by his own men. To many European Americans he became a symbol of a native leader who at first appeared to welcome settlers and to accept their ways but who then treacherously betrayed them. To others he was a man of principle who led a gallant but vain effort to stem the tide of settlement. To them he died as a martyr for his people.

• There is no biography of Leschi, but Ezra Meeker's 1905 account *Pioneer Reminiscences of Puget Sound: The Tragedy of Leschi* contains a good deal of information on the Indian leader. Meeker served as a member of the first jury that tried Leschi and was an ardent defender whose facts and conclusions are often open to question. Two articles are Cecelia S. Carpenter, "Leschi: Last Chief of the Nisquallies," *Pacific Northwest Forum* 1 (1976): 4–11, and Martin Schmitt, "The Execution of Chief Leschi and the 'Truth Teller,'" *Oregon Historical Quarterly* 50 (1949): 9–39.

KENT D. RICHARDS

LESLEY, J. Peter (7 Sept. 1819–1 June 1903), geologist and topographer, was born in Philadelphia, Pennsylvania, the son of Peter Lesley, a cabinetmaker, and Elizabeth Oswald Allen. He was christened Peter Lesley but adopted the initial J. to avoid confusion with his father. Lesley graduated from the University of Pennsylvania in 1838, planning to enter the Princeton Theological Seminary to prepare for a career as a Presbyterian minister. Poor health delayed his plans, and in an effort to rebuild his health through vigorous outdoor life he joined the first state geological survey of Pennsylvania under Henry Darwin Rogers in 1838. His principal activities with Rogers included extensive fieldwork in Pennsylvania's coal regions and the preparation of topographic and geologic maps. He remained with the survey until late in 1841, at which time he began his theological studies. He continued to work for Rogers as time permitted, preparing maps that were intended to accompany the final report of the state survey.

In 1844 Lesley visited Europe, spending much of his time in Germany, to further his theological studies. He returned to a ministry among the poor Pennsylvania German people of the Appalachian Mountains. In 1847 he moved to Boston, where Rogers was living, to work again on maps for the final report of the state survey. In that same year he became the pastor of a Congregational church in Milton, Massachusetts, near Boston. When he completed his work for Rogers, probably in 1848, the church became his full-time activity. In February 1849 he married Susan Inches Lyman; the couple had two children. In 1850 he returned to work once again for Rogers while continuing his pastoral work, but in 1852, after a prolonged disagreement with Rogers over the extent of credit for the survey work that should be given to each of the assistants, Lesley left the survey. At about the same time he decided to leave his church and devote his full attention to geology. He returned to Pennsylvania and settled in Germantown.

He found that he could earn a living by doing geological surveys and mapping Pennsylvania's iron and coal regions. One of his employers was the Pennsylvania Railroad Company, which he began working for in 1852. He was always fond of drawing and engineering, and among his responsibilities for the railroad was the design of a depot in Pittsburgh. A map that he prepared for the railroad company in 1853–1854 represents one of the earliest uses of topographic contour lines on a geologic map.

Lesley made use of his extensive knowledge of Pennsylvania's coal fields in a *Manual of Coal and Its Topography* (1856), which summarized the important geological and topographical features connected with the coal lands of Pennsylvania. He also used the book to give instruction in making geological and topographical maps. In 1856 he was appointed secretary of the American Iron Association, and in 1859 he published the *Iron Manufacturers' Guide,* a publication of more than 700 pages based extensively on his own visits to sites of iron production and manufacture.

In 1859 Lesley was appointed secretary and librarian of the American Philosophical Society and professor of mining at the University of Pennsylvania; in 1863 he was selected as an original member of the National Academy of Sciences; in 1869 he was appointed editor of the *United States Railroad and Mining Register,* a weekly newspaper published in Philadelphia; in 1872 he became professor of geology and mining engineering and dean of the science faculty at the University of Pennsylvania. In 1875 he became dean of the New Towne Scientific School.

In response to a burgeoning oil industry in Pennsylvania and a general need for new and more extensive information on the state's geology than was provided by the first survey, a second state survey was authorized in 1874. It continued until 1889, and Lesley served as its director during its entirety. By the standards of the first survey, this one was enormous, employing over eighty assistants and covering the various areas of the state in greater detail than had been possible in the earlier survey. A total of 124 progress reports, volumes, and atlases were published. Lesley wrote or prepared eight of these, including *A Geological Hand Atlas of the 67 Counties of Pennsylvania* (1885), a three-volume *Dictionary of the Fossils of Pennsylvania* (1889–1890), two volumes and part of a third entitled *A Summary Description of the Geology of Pennsylvania* (1892–1895), and a *Historical Sketch of Geological Exploration in Pennsylvania and Other States* (1876). Other volumes were prepared by Lesley's assistants. Unlike the first survey, which was characterized by annual reports and a final report all written by Rogers, Lesley arranged for volumes on each district or county to be prepared by the geologists working in those areas. These volumes were published under the names of the assistants who compiled them, and twenty-nine of his assistants thus received credit for all or part of the volumes. Lesley chose to operate in this fashion so that the assistants responsible for the fieldwork would receive full credit for it. After leaving Rogers in 1852, Lesley had become increasingly bitter toward him over the issue of credit and vowed that this situation would not be repeated in the second survey. This method of operation, however, failed to produce a synthesis of the total work. For this reason, a legislative act of 1891 called for a final report. Lesley had completed two and a half volumes of this report (the summary description cited above) when he suffered a complete mental and physical breakdown in 1893 from which he never recovered.

Lesley was a tireless worker and writer. Although fully occupied with the administration of the survey, he continued teaching at the University of Pennsylvania until 1878. His professional activities continued unabated, and in 1884–1885, he served as president of the American Association for the Advancement of Science. He found time for several trips to Europe but always worked while there. Often exhausted by the stress of his work, he suffered periodic illnesses for many years. After his breakdown in 1893, he spent his remaining years as a semi-invalid, cared for by his wife until his death in Milton, Massachusetts.

Throughout his career Lesley played a significant role in directing attention to the importance of topographical studies and mapping. His most important contribution, however, was his leadership and organization of the Second Pennsylvania Survey, which enhanced and expanded the work of the first survey and delineated in detail the economic mineral resources of the state.

• The principal collection of Lesley papers is at the American Philosophical Society and is available on microfilm in the society's History of Science series. Lesley's daughter, Mary Ellen Ames, prepared the *Life and Letters of Peter and Susan Lesley* (1909), which contains both an extensive selection of letters and helpful personal comments by Ames regarding her father. Several short biographies exist; principal among them is B. S. Lyman, *Biographical Notice of J. Peter Lesley* (1903). This and other biographical sketches are reprinted in the *Life and Letters.* William M. Jordan, "J. Peter Lesley and the Second Geological Survey of Pennsylvania," *Northeastern Geology* 3 (1981): 75–85, is an especially helpful summary of Lesley's work with the survey.

PATSY GERSTNER

LESLEY BUSH-BROWN, Margaret White (19 May 1857–17 Nov. 1944), painter and etcher, was born in Philadelphia, Pennsylvania, the daughter of J. Peter Lesley, a professor of geology and mining engineering at the University of Pennsylvania, and Susan Inchus Lyman, a writer and social reformer. During her childhood, Margaret Lesley's Unitarian parents encouraged her to develop her artistic skills. In 1869 she entered the antique class at the Pennsylvania Academy of the Fine Arts but was soon told by officials at the school that she was too young. They referred her to the Philadelphia School of Design for Women, where she is listed on the school register for 1870. Lesley was probably a student of Peter Moran, who was the painting and drawing instructor at that time. In 1871 her parents arranged for her to spend a few months studying with sculptor Henry Kirke Brown at his Newburgh, New York, studio.

Following a summer trip to Europe with her parents, Lesley returned to the Pennsylvania Academy in 1876 and entered the ladies' life class. She studied with Christian Schussele and Thomas Eakins at the academy until January 1880. During these years she earned money by making models for her father's geological survey of Pennsylvania. Her father urged her to specialize in making models for him, but, supporting Lesley's desire to become a painter, her mother gave Lesley her family inheritance so she could study painting in Paris.

In Paris in 1880 Lesley studied with Émile-Auguste Carolus-Duran for a few months, made a brief visit home, then spent the next year studying at the Académie Julian with Tony Robert-Fleury, Jules Lefebvre, and Gustave Boulanger. During the summer of 1881 she joined Ellen Day Hale and Helen Knowlton to travel and sketch in Belgium and the French provinces. In 1882 she made another trip home, took classes at the Pennsylvania Academy for a few months, then went back to Paris until some time in 1883. Her oil painting *Nantucket Farmer* was accepted for exhibition in the Paris Salon that year. In Philadelphia in October 1883, Gabrielle DeVaux Clements taught Lesley to etch. She exhibited an etching, *Study of a Girl's Head*, a portrait of the artist Ellen Day Hale, with the New York Etching Club for the first time in 1884, when she also reentered the Pennsylvania Academy. During the 1880s Lesley exhibited paintings and etchings regularly at the Pennsylvania Academy, in the Paris Salon, at the Art Institute of Chicago, and with the Boston Art Club, the New York Etching Club, and the Salmagundi Club, New York. She showed her work at the 1887 Massachusetts Charitable Mechanic Association and in the Women Etchers of America exhibition at the Union League Club in 1888.

Considering marriage to sculptor Henry Kirke Bush-Brown, the nephew and adopted son of her former teacher, Henry Kirke Brown, Lesley asked that he read English writer Elizabeth Gaskell's novel on male-female relationships, *Wives and Daughters*, and he did. She sent him a marriage oath she proposed they use. His 1886 letters to her reveal that the oath was "entirely new" to him and that he liked it "very much." He wrote that "it shall be ours." There is no record of what the oath contained because, at her request, he destroyed her letters to him (she saved his letters). He also agreed to respect her intention to work as an artist after their marriage. They married in April 1886, moving to his home in Newburgh-on-the-

Hudson in New York. Her interest in women's issues continued. In the 1890s she occasionally recorded in her diaries her attendance at suffrage rallies and Unitarian women's meetings.

Lesley Bush-Brown and her husband spent three years in France and Italy, where their daughter and first son were born in 1887 and 1888, and her professional activities temporarily stopped. Two more sons were born in 1890 and 1892, after their return from Europe.

Back in Newburgh, Lesley Bush-Brown again began to paint. For a few years she and Henry shared a studio in their home, but in 1894 they rented a studio in Manhattan and spent several days a week working there. A cook and nurses cared for the children. In August 1898 they resettled their family in New York City.

Lesley Bush-Brown continued to specialize in oil and pastel portraits, often in a landscape setting; she never returned to etching. She also painted narrative scenes and miniatures. Around the turn of the century her paintings were included in shows at the Pennsylvania Academy; the National Academy of Design, New York; the Boston Art Club; the Salmagundi Club; the New York Water Color Club; the Woman's Art Club of New York; the St. Botolph Club, Boston; the Charcoal Club, Baltimore; and the National Arts Club, New York. She painted a mural, *Spring*, for the Pennsylvania State Building at the World's Columbian Exposition, Chicago, in 1893.

In 1910 Lesley Bush-Brown and her husband moved to Washington, D.C., where Henry had a commission for a monumental equestrian sculpture. They each set up a studio and helped to found the Arts Club of Washington, which housed artists' studios and exhibition galleries. Assisting him in drawing for his sculpture designs, she continued to paint and quickly established herself as a prominent figure painter in Washington. The Corcoran Gallery held a solo exhibition of thirty of her paintings in 1911. Her traditional miniatures and large paintings in oil and pastel representing "the long study and thorough knowledge that . . . commands the respect of the discriminating cultured public" hung in almost every Washington exhibition for years. The Doll & Richards Gallery in Boston held an exhibition of her portrait drawings in 1923. Group shows included the 1915 Panama-Pacific Exposition, San Francisco. In 1924 the Atlanta Art Association sponsored an exhibition of works by Margaret, Henry, and their daughter Lydia.

In addition to the Arts Club of Washington, Lesley Bush-Brown was a member of the Woman's Art Club, New York; the National Association of Women Painters and Sculptors; the National Society of Miniature Painters; the Philadelphia Arts Club; the Society of Washington Artists; the Washington Water Color Club; the Washington Society of Mural Painters; and the National Arts Club, New York.

Because portrait painting and sculpture had been displaced by photography, Lesley Bush-Brown and her husband had a difficult time making a living in the

early twentieth century. Her early determination to work as a professional after she married particularly paid off when her portrait painting supported her and her husband once he could no longer obtain commissions for sculpture. In the 1920s she took several lengthy trips alone to the Midwest in search of portrait commissions. Her earnings she sent home to Henry, who spent his time seeking funding for his monumental, idealized sculptures.

Lesley Bush-Brown's prominence as a highly esteemed artist whose life crossed two cultures, women's traditional homemaking and that of the predominantly male art world, helped to set the precedent for increasing choices for women and women's inclusion in professional life. In her 1901 lecture titled "Address before New York Unitarian Club on the Relations of Women to the Artistic Professions," she advocated that women's first responsibility was to their families but encouraged artists also to pursue their careers for fulfillment and with earning money as a goal. Her diaries suggest that she was happy putting aside her painting while her babies were very young, but she nevertheless lived an active professional life, demonstrating an extraordinary degree of independence for a married woman of her time. She died in Ambler, Pennsylvania, at the home of her son James.

• Lesley Bush-Brown's papers and some of her etchings are in the Sophia Smith Collection, Women's History Archive, at Smith College in Northampton, Mass. These papers include diaries for 1869, 1876, 1879, 1880–1881, 1894–1898, and 1902–1903. The letters are mostly from the 1920s until her death. The archives also contain letters to Margaret from her husband. The National Museum of American Art, the Smithsonian Institution, and the Arts Club, Washington, D.C., own paintings by Lesley Bush-Brown. Her 1914 self-portrait is in the Pennsylvania Academy. The New York Public Library has a small collection of her etchings. For catalogs from her solo exhibitions, see the Corcoran Gallery of Art, *Exhibition of Portraits and Pictures by Mrs. Henry K. Bush-Brown* (1911), and Doll & Richards Gallery, *Portrait Drawings by M. Lesley Bush-Brown* (1923). The most thorough sources are Phyllis Peet, "The Emergence of American Women Printmakers in the Late Nineteenth Century" (Ph.D. diss., UCLA, 1987) and *American Women of the Etching Revival* (1988). An obituary is in the *New York Times*, 18 Nov. 1944.

PHYLLIS PEET

LESLIE, Amy (11 Oct. 1855–3 July 1939), actress and drama critic, was born Lillie West in West Burlington, Iowa, the daughter of Albert Waring West, a banker and sometime publisher, and Kate Content Webb. She was educated at several Catholic schools, including St. Joseph's Academy in St. Joseph, Missouri, and the conservatory of music at St. Mary's Academy near South Bend, Indiana, from which she graduated in 1874. West's love of music led her to attend the Chicago Conservatory of Music for a short time and then to join the Grayman Comic Opera Company in 1879. In the early 1880s light comic opera and operetta came

into vogue, and West capitalized on the trend, touring the country with the Norcoss, the Grau, and a number of other light opera companies.

While on tour in 1880, West met and married Harry Brown, a fellow performer. After their marriage the couple continued to tour, and they had a son. On 5 May 1881 West made her debut in New York City as Fiametta in Edmond Audran's *La Mascotte* at the Bijou Theatre. *La Mascotte* ran for more than 100 performances to enthusiastic audiences. West became known for her portrayal in *La Mascotte* and for Amelia in *Olivette*. She also performed in a series of light operettas by Gilbert and Sullivan, including the starring roles in *The Mikado*, *H. M. S. Pinafore*, and *The Pirates of Penzance*. In 1889 Lillie West Brown began to prepare for the leading role in DeWolf Hooper's production of Gustave A. Kerker's *Castles in the Air*. During rehearsal, her son died of diphtheria; devastated, West quit the stage and never returned. Shortly after their son died the Browns separated, and West moved back to Chicago to be with her mother.

West's mother encouraged her to try writing professionally since she was now without a husband and an income. Writing about what she knew, West wrote a review of *Castles in the Air*—the production in which she had been slated to star—and sold it to the *Chicago Daily News* using the name Amy Leslie. The editor of the paper, T. H. White, hired Leslie as the drama critic. She remained with the paper for the next four decades.

As a critic, Leslie was known for a rhapsodic writing style. A fellow critic called her writing "ornate and endless. . . . Given half an excuse Amy gave birth to a sunrise of words. No drama critic I have read since, not even Alexander Woollcott, could swoon as madly in front of the footlights as our Amy Leslie" (Hecht, p. 13). Although she is remembered for her adulatory reviews, she felt strongly that her job was to help improve the theater, and thus she was not hesitant to criticize such stars as Viola Allen, Cissy Fitzgerald, or John Barrymore. She was often accused of "puffing" her reviews—making the show sound better than it really was—in order to help sell tickets at the box office. Because of Leslie's early career as a performer, she knew personally many of the stars she reviewed. She became popular with her readers by relating stories about such friends as Edwin Booth, Sarah Bernhardt, Julia Marlowe, Lillian Russell, and John Drew.

In 1896 Leslie developed a friendship, and some say a romantic relationship, with the novelist Stephen Crane. Nothing came of the relationship, however, and in 1901, while living in Chicago's Virginia Hotel, she met and fell in love with the bellboy, Franklin Howard Buck, twenty-five years her junior. After a courtship that held the attention of all Chicago, the couple married in July. In his autobiography, *All in a Lifetime*, Buck wrote that he "gave strength, protection, and vitality to Amy, and she gave [to him] of her fine intelligence and knowledge." The couple had no children. Leslie loved the theatrical nightlife of the city while her husband loved adventure. Despite the friendly words in his autobiography, in the 1916 divorce suit Buck listed "cruelty," "nagging," and "humiliation in public" as his complaints against Leslie. Buck later gained notoriety, as Frank "Bring 'em Back Alive" Buck, for his jungle expeditions.

In addition to her newspaper work, Leslie published *Amy Leslie at the Fair* (1893), her account of her trip to the World Exposition; *Some Players* (1899), reminiscences and sketches about a number of popular stars; and *Gulf Stream* (1930), her memoirs. She died in Chicago.

Leslie's position as an arts critic was unique in the 1890s. Women in journalism were rare, especially at major metropolitan newspapers like the *Chicago Daily News*. Although journalism was considered by many a man's world, she not only held her own with her male competitors but often exceeded them in popularity and insight. For forty years Leslie influenced the Chicago theater scene with her candid and scrutinizing reviews. Her own professionalism both on stage and in her journalistic career led to her dissatisfaction with what she believed was the lowering of standards and expectations regarding live performance, especially tragedy and light opera. She spoke out against commercialism, the star system, and the developing film industry to which she attributed this loss of professionalism. As a possible solution, through her writing and influence Leslie encouraged the redevelopment of small amateur theatres on a regional as well as a metropolitan scale. In essence, she wanted to educate theater goers—to raise *their* standards and expectations after which the theatre would follow or falter.

As a woman in the male-dominated world of journalism, Leslie became a pioneer whom other women would follow. As a critic, she saw herself as more than a reviewer, as a guide helping to raise the quality of entertainment available to the public.

• Memorials of Leslie are Ben Hecht, "Wistfully Yours," *Theatre Arts*, July 1951, p. 13, and Alexander Woollcott, "In Memoriam: Rose Field," *Atlantic Monthly*, May 1939, p. 645. Obituaries appear in the *New York Times* and the *Chicago Daily Tribune*, both 4 July 1939, and in the *Chicago Daily News*, 5 July 1939.

MELISSA VICKERY-BAREFORD

LESLIE, Charles Robert (19 Oct. 1794–5 May 1859), artist and author, was born in London, England, the son of Robert Leslie, a Philadelphia clock and watch store owner, and Lydia Baker; one of his sisters was the author Eliza Leslie. Leslie's father, who was also a draftsman, musician, and member of the American Philosophical Society, had taken his family to London on an extended business trip. The family returned to Philadelphia in 1800 after a traumatic journey in which their ship was forced to lay over in Lisbon after being severely damaged during an attack by a French man-of-war. After attending the University of Pennsylvania, Leslie was apprenticed to a bookseller in 1808.

Inspired by the theatrical illustrations he saw in the bookstore, Leslie began to sketch portraits of noted actors and was soon considered a prodigy. He exhibited five watercolor drawings at the Pennsylvania Academy of the Fine Arts in 1811, and he was granted permission to study there. Thomas Sully also gave him lessons in oil painting. Financed by a group of Philadelphians and a contribution from the academy, Leslie went to London in 1811. There he met Benjamin West and Charles Bird King, studied under Henry Fuseli and John Flaxman at the Royal Academy, became a protégé of Washington Allston, roomed with Samuel F. B. Morse, and met many of the leading intellectuals of the day.

The subjects of Leslie's most significant early paintings were taken from Shakespearean drama: the neoclassical *Timon of Athens* (1812, the Athenaeum of Philadelphia) reflects the artist's studies in anatomical drawing at the Royal Academy, and both the unusual *The Personification of Murder* (1813, damaged by fire) from *Macbeth* and *The Murder of Rutland by Lord Clifford* (1815, Pennsylvania Academy of the Fine Arts) from *Henry VI* are exceptionally melodramatic examples of the romantic sublime. Leslie also quickly became an accomplished portraitist, as is evidenced by his early pendant portraits of Mr. and Mrs. John Quincy Adams (1816, U.S. Department of State).

Encouraged by the success of the British genre painter David Wilkie and attracted to the seventeenth-century Dutch and Flemish pictures he saw in London, Leslie soon abandoned grand academic historical painting in favor of contemporary literary illustration. He specialized in such subjects after his *Sir Roger de Coverley Going to Church* (1819, private collection) received a favorable critical reception. In 1821 he was elected an associate of the Royal Academy, and he was made a full academician in 1826. In 1825 he married Harriet Stone of London. In 1833 he accepted a position as drawing master at West Point Military Academy, but resigned after a few months and returned to England, where he remained for the rest of his life. His first literary effort was *Memoirs of the Life of John Constable, Esq., R.A.* (1843). In 1847 he became a professor of painting at the Royal Academy; he later published his teachings in *A Hand-book for Young Painters* (1855), and his *Life and Times of Sir Joshua Reynolds* was published posthumously in 1865. Leslie died in London.

Leslie's best work is distinguished by his highly capable draftsmanship, brilliant use of color, and increasingly free use of paint. His writings reveal him to have been an amiable character, but the artist John Neagle found him "of a very cold temperament and of a cautious and politic turn on a first acquaintance." These personality traits assured Leslie's professional success. Unlike the tragic figures Allston and Morse, who returned to America and unsuccessfully attempted to interest an unsophisticated public in grand manner historical painting, Leslie remained in England and was content to paint popular genre scenes and lucrative high society portraiture. Although Leslie was greatly admired by his American contemporaries, he had a negligible influence on the art of the United States and in historical retrospect is best classified as a British painter.

• For further accounts see Tom Taylor, ed., *Autobiographical Recollections by the Late Charles Leslie, R.A.* (1860); William Dunlap, *A History of the Rise and Progress of the Arts of Design in the United States* (1834); Henry T. Tuckerman, *Book of the Artists* (1867); George Johnston, *History of Cecil County, Maryland* (1881). Dorinda Evans, *Benjamin West and His American Students* (1980), pp. 161–180, provides an excellent summary and assessment of Leslie's career as an artist. See also P. G. Hamerton, *Fortnightly Review*, Jan. 1866; Henry Tuckerman, *Christian Examiner*, Sept. 1860; R. C. Waterson, *North American Review*, Jan. 1861.

ROBERT WILSON TORCHIA

LESLIE, Eliza (15 Nov. 1787–1 Jan. 1858), writer, was born in Philadelphia, Pennsylvania, the daughter of Robert Leslie, a watchmaker, and Lydia Baker. Like many female children of her time, Leslie was privately tutored in French and music and attended school only for a few months, to learn needlework. From 1793 to 1799 the family lived in London, where her father exported watches and clocks to Philadelphia. Meanwhile, the American side of the business was sorely mismanaged, and after the death of her father in 1803, Eliza and her mother were forced to open their home to boarders. While her brother Charles Robert Leslie achieved artistic fame in England, Eliza taught drawing, sold her faithful copies of masterworks, and attempted to sell her poetry, although she commented that "at thirteen and fourteen, I began to despise my own poetry, and destroyed all I had," and that she abandoned "the dream of my childhood, the hope of one day seeing my name in print" (Haven, pp. 348–49).

In the early 1820s, perhaps to improve the food at their boarding house, Eliza Leslie attended Mrs. Goodfellow's cooking school in Philadelphia, the first American culinary school, and soon began copying Goodfellow's recipes for her friends. Apparently at the urging of her brother Thomas Jefferson Leslie, then treasurer of the U.S. Military Academy at West Point, Eliza turned these recipes into her first publication, *Seventy-five Receipts for Pastry, Cakes, and Sweetmeats* (1827).

With the success of this volume, Leslie's publisher urged her to try juvenile stories, which launched the Mirror Series. The success of *The Young Americans; or, Sketches of a Sea-Voyage* (1829) led her to cease publishing anonymously, and in 1831 her *American Girl's Book*, a collection of riddles, games, and handiwork, appeared under the name "Miss Leslie." Some of her stories for children are collected in *Atlantic Tales* (1833). At the same time, Leslie began writing fiction for magazines such as *Graham's* and *Godey's Lady's Book*. For the next twenty-five years she wrote children's books, compiled tomes on behavior and etiquette, wrote magazine articles, and edited *The Gift*,

an annual, and *The Violet*, a juvenile "souvenir"—all in spite of weak eyes and debilitating headaches.

The most striking examples of Leslie's fiction are the stories collected in *Pencil Sketches* (1833–1837) and the novel *Amelia; or A Young Lady's Vicissitudes* (1848). Leslie had a satiric style, an ability to pen quick if broad-stroked character sketches, and a flair for didactic domestic anecdotes. Typified by "Mrs. Washington Potts" (1831), for which *Godey's* awarded her a prize, Leslie's stories satirize pretension and feature intelligent, modest women who, with the help of sensible men, recover the values of domesticity and propriety after forays into self-indulgence or upper-class affectation. Quite different is "The Travelling Tin Man" (1833), the story of a young black girl who is kidnapped from her free parents and ultimately bound over as a servant to the farmer who rescues her.

Leslie's literary perspective is summed up in "Conduct to Literary Women" in *The Ladies' Guide to True Politeness* (1864):

Be it understood that a woman of quick perception and good memory can see and recollect a thousand things which would never be noticed or remembered by an obtuse or shallow, common-place capacity. . . . When in company with literary women, make no allusions to "learned ladies," or "blue stockings," or express surprise that they should have any knowledge of housewifery, or needle-work, or dress; or that they are able to talk on "common things." It is rude and foolish, and shows that you really know nothing about them, either as a class or as individuals.

Leslie's domestic books, including *Domestic French Cookery* (1832) and *The House Book* (1840), provided her greatest source of income. She published the *Indian Meal Cookbook* (1846) to help with relief work during the potato famine. *Directions for Cookery* (1837), which the *Ladies National Magazine* claimed "no woman ought to be without," was the most popular cookbook of the nineteenth century; it went through fifty printings.

Leslie mostly wrote for the middle class—those, she explained, who keep "elegant tables" as well as those "who live well, but moderately." Stressing health, patriotism, practicality, newness, and efficiency, she put less emphasis on thrift and self-reliance than did Lydia Maria Child, who addressed *The Frugal Housewife* (1829) to "the poor" and to "those who are not ashamed of economy." Leslie's popularity perhaps stemmed from the era's population dispersal, which forced many women who might otherwise have sought domestic advice from family and neighbors to turn to written sources.

Leslie's recipes and instructions provide a compelling window into the household economies, domestic labors, and cross-cultural influences of the mid-nineteenth century. Her books reveal what Louisa May Alcott called "our national plenteousness"—the tremendous variety of foods raised, shot, trapped, prepared, preserved, cooked, and served at the time. Leslie offered recipes for mussels, hare, turtle, duck, pigeon, plover, bobolink, broccoli, artichokes, asparagus, spinach, cauliflower, corn, okra, eggplant, sweet and white potatoes, rice, and rutabagas. These suggest the vast amounts of food, time, and labor required to serve large families, servants, and guests; not atypical are a recipe calling for 400 oysters and one for roast pork that begins with a pig killed that morning. At a time when almost all cooking was done over an open hearth, and baking in a flueless oven built into the wall of a fireplace or in a dutch oven hanging over the fire, and before the invention of refrigeration, baking powder (1856), or commercial yeast (1868), Leslie tried to give approximate cooking times for cooks who lacked kitchen clocks and worked over fireplaces. She also gave suggestions for measuring tools and for alternative ingredients.

Leslie's cookbooks reflect the impact of Native-American and African-American foods on Anglo-American cuisine. Her recipes include such ingredients as wild greens, herbs, and cornmeal: "You might like a little Indian in your bread" (*Directions for Cookery*, p. 376). They assume access to herbs and spices imported from India and the Caribbean, pineapples and coconuts from the West Indies, and lemons and other citrus fruits from the South. Leslie incorporated stylish French tastes for salads and champagne as well as foods discovered through international shipping and travel, such as mulligatawny soup and curries. Many recipes include aromatic herbs as preservatives, spices, or possibly camouflage, among them turmeric, cassia, coriander, cayenne pepper, cloves, and cinnamon. Similarly, her readers learned to preserve meats, make sausages, produce cheese, prepare flavored vinegars and "cathcups"—catsups of tomato, lemon, anchovy, or oyster—and to brew beer, fruit wines, cordials, and brandies.

Although most of Leslie's recipes were directed toward wealthy households with servants, there are some suggestions for budgetary management for working-class wives. She claimed that all her recipes were carefully tested. Significantly, in her prefaces she reiterated that "the receipts in this little book are, in every sense of the word, American; but the writer flatters herself that [these dishes] will not be found inferior to any of a similar description made in the European manner."

Leslie resided during the last decade of her life at the United States Hotel in Philadelphia. An invalid, apparently overweight and with a walking difficulty, she was treated as a celebrity. She had the reputation of a brilliant woman with a sarcastic wit and heady opinions who frequently offended strangers but was warmly affectionate to relatives and friends and generous to the needy. The focus of her later writings was increasingly middle-class. Late editions of the cookbooks include directions on when to switch the fork to right hand and how to use a finger bowl, as well as the policy that a salad should be dressed by "the gentleman." In the same edition that advises how to feed a pig and keep the pen clean ("No animal actually likes dirt, and even pigs would be clean if they knew how"), Leslie specifies how a woman should drink wine in public: "When both glasses are filled, look at him [your drinking partner], bow your head, and taste the wine. . . . It is not customary, in America, for a lady to empty her glass."

Leslie died in Gloucester, New Jersey. Her extensive written record shows that the United States' national cuisine was conceived, developed, penned, and preserved almost entirely by women; it also illustrates the creative and enduring role of food as an instance of women's participation in both the public and domestic economies of the nineteenth century.

• Leslie's papers are scattered and are available, among other locations, at the Beinecke Library, Yale University; the Houghton Library, Harvard University; the Alderman Library, University of Virginia; and the Historical Society of Philadelphia. The fiction of Eliza Leslie is collected in *Pencil Sketches; or, Outlines and Manners* (1833, 1835, 1937) and in *Atlantic Sketches; or, Pictures of Youth* (1833). Her best-known novel is *Amelia; or, A Young Lady's Vicissitudes* (1848). Other fiction includes *Althea Vernon* (1838) and "The Batson Cottage" (1847). Her principal domestic books include *Seventy-five Receipts for Pastry, Cakes, and Sweetmeats* (1827), *The American Girl's Cookbook* (1831), *Domestic Cookery Book* (1837), *The House Book* (1840), and *The Behavior Book* (1853). The most important contemporary biographical source is Alice B. Haven, "Personal Reminiscences of Miss Eliza Leslie," *Godey's Lady's Book* 56 (1858), which includes Leslie's autobiographical sketch. See also R. W. Griswold, *The Prose Writers of America* (1847), and the *New York Times*, 4 Jan. 1858. Modern commentary includes Ophia Smith, "Eliza Leslie's Impressions of New York and West Point," *New York Historical Society Quarterly* 35, no. 4 (1951), and "Charles and Eliza Leslie," *Pennsylvania Magazine of History and Biography* 74, no. 4 (1950); Waverley L. Root and Richard de Rochemont, *Eating in America: A History* (1976; repr. 1981); and Mary Anna DuSablon, *America's Collectible Cookbooks: The History, the Politics, the Recipes* (1994).

JEAN PFAELZER

LESLIE, Frank (29 Mar. 1821–10 Jan. 1880), engraver and publisher, was born Henry Carter in Ipswich, England, the son of Joseph Leslie Carter and Mary Elliston. Spurning his father's efforts to bring him into the family's prosperous glove-manufacturing business, young Carter took up wood engraving in London and assumed the name Frank Leslie for the signing of his woodcuts. In 1842 he joined the engraving department of the *Illustrated London News*, one of the first illustrated newspapers. Soon he was put in charge of its engraving department.

Leslie had married Sarah Ann Welham at the age of twenty, and during the years in London the couple had three sons. But Leslie's career was advancing slowly, and in 1848 he took his family to New York City, where woodcut engravers were few and the demand for his skills was greater. He set up shop on Broadway as "F. Leslie, engraver," and soon landed a major client in P. T. Barnum, who hired Leslie to illustrate the tour by the renowned soprano Jenny Lind, of which Barnum was the sponsor. Then Leslie went to Boston to prepare woodcuts for the new illustrated weekly, *Gleason's Pictorial and Drawing Room Companion*. Returning to New York in 1852, he became head of the engraving department of Barnum's *Illustrated News*. The venture lasted only a year, and Barnum sold out to *Gleason's*. But Leslie stayed in New York and set up his own publishing company, launching *Frank Leslie's Ladies' Gazette of Fashion* in January 1854.

Later that year Leslie purchased the *New York Journal of Romance*, an amply illustrated story paper, but this and the fashion paper were intended to provide quick profits while he prepared for his major venture. In December 1855 he introduced *Frank Leslie's Illustrated Newspaper*, a weekly publication featuring news pictures. His decision to introduce the new journal as a "newspaper" marked a milestone. Although the weekly was not always his (and eventually his second wife's) most profitable venture, it served as the flagship Leslie publication for forty-four years and continued under other publishers until 1922.

Events up to and including the Civil War created a growing demand for news and unprecedented opportunities for pictorial reporting. In 1857 *Harper's Weekly* entered the arena, followed two years later by the *New York Illustrated News* (no kin to the Barnum venture). From 1861 to 1865 the images of the war were largely seen through these three publications. Later generations would view the war through Mathew Brady's photographs as well, but at the time there was no halftone engraving, and the only way war scenes could be published was in woodcuts such as those of the three illustrated weeklies.

Leslie had the New York legislature ratify his name change (legally he was still Henry Carter until 1857); when he launched a German-language news weekly in 1857 and a humor magazine in 1859, both bore his now-legal name in the nameplate. More important to the history of journalism was Leslie's use of his illustrated newspaper in 1858 to launch a pioneer crusade, an investigation into the New York "swill milk" scandal. His artists portrayed dying cows fed brewery waste to produce milk unfit for the city's children, and legislative reform followed the press crusade in events that predated the muckraking movement by half a century.

But Leslie's personal life and his compulsion to start new projects and publications caused his journalistic leadership to slip away from him during the war. His marriage began to disintegrate in the late 1850s, and in 1860 he left his family. He then rented rooms from a contributor to the *Illustrated Newspaper* named Squier, whom Leslie appointed in 1861 to be editor of the paper. Meanwhile, Leslie evidently became enamored of Squier's wife, Miriam, and increasingly turned his attention to the literary publications that she fancied. While Leslie was distracted by his personal affairs and work on other publications, the *Illustrated Newspaper* declined in circulation from a high of around 200,000 at the start of the Civil War. The paper was also the victim of some bad luck in its reporting of events in the field. As a result, *Harper's* pulled

ahead as the leading news pictorial, which it remained to the end of the century.

In the 1860s Leslie continued to start new periodicals, several of which were successful. At the same time he reused his Civil War woodcuts to produce such nonperiodical publications as *Frank Leslie's Pictorial History of the War of 1861* (1861–1862), *Frank Leslie's Pictorial Life of Abraham Lincoln* (1865), and *Frank Leslie's Pictorial History of the Great National Peace Jubilee* (1869). In addition to fourteen of these pictorials, he published ten annuals and almanacs as well as forty-six books, ranging from classics to juvenile adventure stories.

Leslie obtained a divorce in 1872 and helped Miriam Squier get her own divorce in 1873. The two married in that year and pursued a lavish way of life for the rest of the decade. In the last few days of 1879, a fast-growing tumor appeared in Leslie's throat. He died suddenly in New York City, but not before he put the reins of his sizable enterprise firmly into the able hands of his wife. She eliminated the company's unprofitable titles, reorganized and revitalized the others, had her own name legally changed to "Frank Leslie," and soon earned the unofficial title of America's "Empress of Journalism." When she died in 1914, she left her $2 million estate to the cause of woman suffrage.

With his own name prominent in the titles of most of his twenty-eight periodicals, Frank Leslie symbolized the American era of personal journalism. He also pioneered investigative reporting and developed numerous new ways of marketing popular culture. Most important he, more than anyone else in the United States, launched the shift from words to pictures in the media's portrayal of the news—a trend that continues today.

• For discussion of Leslie's contributions to journalism, see Budd Leslie Gambee, Jr., *Frank Leslie and His Illustrated Newspaper, 1855–1860* (1964). Historical sketches of several Leslie publications are given in Frank Luther Mott, *A History of American Magazines*, vols. 2–3 (1938). His innovations in popular literature are covered in Madeleine B. Stern, ed., *Publishers for Mass Entertainment in Nineteenth-Century America* (1980). Leslie's life and career as an American publisher are given considerable attention in Stern's *Purple Passage: The Life of Mrs. Frank Leslie* (1953), and his Civil War coverage is detailed in W. Fletcher Thompson, Jr., *The Image of War* (1959). In addition to the obituary in the *New York Tribune*, 11 Jan. 1880, much biographical detail is to be found in tributes published that winter in the various Leslie publications.

GEORGE EVERETT

LESLIE, Lew (15 Jan. 1890–10 Mar. 1963), theatrical producer, was born Lev Lessinsky in New York City, the son of Michel Lessinsky and Mary (maiden name unknown). Graduating from public schools in New York, he entered vaudeville as an impressionist and singer. By 1909 he had a double act with future wife Belle Baker (originally Becker), later a "red hot mama," belting earthy and sentimental songs. They were divorced in 1919, and he later married Irene Wales. This marriage also failed. No children were born to either marriage.

Leslie, who served in the National Guard during World War I, became in 1920 the manager of the cabaret at Broadway's Café de Paris, where his ability to spot talent and trends emerged. Among his claimed discoveries were the "yowsah" bandleader Ben Bernie, comic actor Frank Fay, and comic accordionist Phil Baker. In 1921 Leslie understood the impact of *Shuffle Along*, an all-black musical show by Eubie Blake and Noble Sissle that became Broadway's biggest hit and, according to poet-dramatist Langston Hughes, the inspiration for the literary Harlem Renaissance. Early in 1922 Leslie presented at the Café de Paris his first all-"Negro" show, *The Plantation Revue*; when a few months later he added Florence Mills from the cast of *Shuffle Along*, she became the rage of the town and the heart of the show, which quickly transferred to Broadway's 48th Street Theatre.

Leslie's shows were the vanguard of a wave of "colored" successes in Europe. Much of *The Plantation Revue* became the sensational second half of *From Dover to Dixie* (1923) staged in London. The *Dixie* half continued to Paris. Mills's showstopper "I'm Just a Little Black Bird (looking for a little blue bird)" eventually named an entire Leslie series. *Dixie* returned to New York in 1924 within *From Dixie to Broadway*, commanding an unprecedented $3.30 for a top ticket. One reviewer summarized Mills's impact: "My God! Man, I've never seen anything like it! I never imagined such a tempestuous blend of passion and humor could be poured into the singing of a song." *Variety* remarked that the show's success "shatters some deeprooted theories heretofore existing relative to colored musical companies"—mainly that they could not succeed financially on Broadway.

Even more than *Shuffle Along*, Leslie's lavish, sophisticated shows set the pattern for the next generation of all-black shows. As a revue, *Shuffle Along* differed from shows such as Will Marion Cook's *Clorindy* (1898) and *In Dahomey* (1903), both broad musical comedies more or less following the lines of their "white" counterparts. Like these shows, however, *Shuffle Along* was the creative effort of African Americans. Especially after *From Dixie to Broadway*, virtually all "black" Broadway shows were revues conceived and directed by whites. Leslie's views were unregenerate. He preferred white songwriters, saying, "They understand the colored man better than he does himself. . . . The two greatest Negro songs now sung were written by white men—'Ol' Man River' and 'That's Why Darkies Were Born.'"

Few producers controlled details of production more thoroughly than Leslie, who cast his shows, wrote their books, oversaw every performance, and frequently conducted the orchestra. A Leslie show's trademark was its breakneck "briskness," adopted because of his belief that blacks were generally lazy. Despite racist sketches, Leslie's revues did dilute plantation-centered stereotypes. Often as lavish as the *Follies*

of Florenz Ziegfeld, they stirred many hopes. Mills had envisioned "a permanent institution . . . for the colored artists and an opportunity . . . for the glorification of the American High-Browns."

Black Birds opened in London in 1926. More than twenty years earlier, the English had afforded a sensational welcome to *In Dahomey*, and *Black Birds* confirmed Leslie's belief that "the average Englishman . . . thinks of a Negro show in terms of art." A *Daily Mail* reviewer lauded Pullman porters "who dance as if they had oiled their feet and were performing on smooth ice. . . . But," he added, "life in Dixie Land must be terribly exhausting."

In 1927 Mills's sudden death from appendicitis in New York preceded several flops. *White Birds*, which lost £60,000 in London for a youthful British backer, was a classic of disorganization, wasting the talents of a cast that included Maurice Chevalier and Ninette deValois, later British ballet's grande dame. *White Birds* accounted for at least one nervous breakdown and a possible suicide. One star later said no money could compensate for the humiliation the "arrogant, dictatorial" Leslie wrought.

But Leslie rebounded with *Black Birds of 1928*, which evolved from his Fifty-seventh Street New York club, Les Ambassadeurs. The show made a star of Adelaide Hall, a "scat-singer" who improvised nonsense syllables like a jazz instrumentalist. The show also afforded the legendary tapdancer Bill "Bojangles" Robinson a mainstream Broadway opportunity and introduced the one-legged tapper Peg Leg Bates; its 518 performances were the most of any black show of the decade. Leslie hired a hundred performers and songwriters Jimmy McHugh and Dorothy Fields, whose score included "I Can't Give You Anything but Love," "Diga Diga Doo," and "Doin' the New Low Down." In 1929 *Black Birds* was the last show to play the original Moulin Rouge in Paris; it returned to Broadway success. Leslie was at the pinnacle of his career.

In 1930 the infighting and mishandling of Leslie's new (virtually all-white) show, the *International Revue*, recalled *White Birds*. Despite another McHugh-Fields score, despite Gertrude Lawrence, Harry Richman, and Argentinita, the dancer of the moment, the show sank in three months, losing $200,000 in a depression year. A new *Black Birds* folded in one month, leaving its cast stranded and unpaid, despite Ethel Waters and a score by African Americans Blake and Andy Razaf.

Rhapsody in Black (1931), staged minimally, was nearly vaudeville, mixing musical styles from spirituals through Victor Herbert to Gershwin. It made a star of Waters but ran only eighty performances. For the rest of the decade, *Black Birds* recycled earlier ideas. Despite Robinson and sophisticated parodies of Noël Coward and Eugene O'Neill, the 1933 version was called "not funny, not musical and not original." Two hybrids in 1934–1935 at London's Coliseum were better received. There Valaida Snow (later interned by the Nazis) sang, played the trumpet, and directed a choir, and the "Black Beauty" chorus paraded vitality, swagger, and short shorts. The 1936 London versions boasted Johnny Mercer's score, bass Jules Bledsoe (the originator of "Ol' Man River"), and the Nicholas Brothers, the era's great acrobatic dancers. Thoroughly in the democratic spirit of the New Deal, it included a stirring Jamestown-to-Harlem "Negro Cavalcade" by the Rosamond Johnson choir. It did not impress New York.

When *Blackbirds of 1939* opened in New York, the critic Brooks Atkinson wrote, "There is nothing quite so remarkable as the sight of Mr. Leslie, tired and gloomy, working his head off in the orchestra pit. . . . He puts his heart and soul into making the pace hot and terrific . . . singing all the words to himself, signalling ferociously to the drummer, changing his melted collar between acts." Once Leslie had to be revived by the house physician and was sent home by ambulance. The show closed after nine performances. Leslie never produced another show; he became a theatrical agent and lived in Manhattan until his death in Orangeburg, New York.

• There is a clipping file on Leslie at the New York Public Library for the Performing Arts, Lincoln Center. Allen Woll, *Black Musical Theatre: From Coontown to Dreamgirls* (1989), is invaluable and contains many useful references to Leslie's life and work. Many works by Stanley Green, including *Broadway Musicals of the '30s* (1982), help to bring Leslie's New York shows to life. A significant sourcebook on early African-American musicals is Henry T. Sampson, *Blacks in Blackface* (1980). Leslie's London ventures are detailed in a number of British show business autobiographies, as well as in the programs and clippings in the files at the Victoria and Albert Theatre Museum, London.

JAMES ROSS MOORE

LESLIE, Miriam Florence Follin (5 June 1836–18 Sept. 1914), editor and publisher, was born in New Orleans, Louisiana, the daughter of Charles Follin, commission merchant, and his common-law wife, Susan Danforth. She attended school briefly in New Orleans but was educated primarily by her father, an accomplished linguist. In Cincinnati, where the family moved in 1846, she attended Mrs. Lloyds's Seminary for Girls. By 1850 the Follins moved to New York, where Miriam continued her language studies at home. After her father's business failed, her uncle Adolphus Follin was appointed her guardian in 1850. Four years later she married a jeweler's clerk, David Charles Peacock, but the marriage was annulled in 1856.

In 1857, with actress Lola Montez, she took a theatrical tour in Albany, Providence, and Pittsburgh, using the stage name "Minnie Montez." A brief affair in 1857 with William M. Churchwell, former congressman from Tennessee, was followed that same year by her second marriage, to archeologist Ephraim George Squier. All of her marriages were childless.

Miriam Squier's first published book appeared in 1858: a translation of a play by Alexandre Dumas the Younger, *The "Demi-Monde": A Satire on Society*. The following year she assisted her husband in the publication of a short-lived Spanish newspaper, *Noticioso de Nueva York*. Squier's appointment in 1861 as editor of *Frank Leslie's Illustrated Newspaper* began an association that would involve her in the profession of publishing. Already a power on Publishers' Row with his fleet of monthlies and weeklies, Frank Leslie appointed Squier editor of *Frank Leslie's Lady's Magazine* in 1863. In 1865 she planned and edited *Frank Leslie's Chimney Corner*, explaining her purpose in her florid style: "We give a story a day all the year around, some to touch by their tragic power, some to thrill with love's vicissitudes, some to hold in suspense with dramatic interest, some to convulse with humor."

As the Frank Leslie Publishing House expanded, relations between Miriam Squier and Leslie intensified. In 1871 her translation of Arthur Morelet's *Voyage dans l'Amérique Centrale* was published as *Travels in Central America*; the same year she began work on another Leslie periodical, *Once a Week: The Young Lady's Own Journal*, the title of which was changed to *Frank Leslie's Lady's Journal*. In 1872 Leslie obtained a divorce from his wife, and in 1873 Miriam Squier divorced her husband. The following year she married Leslie, combining her career as Leslie editor with that of salon leader. Spending two days a week in the publishing office, she familiarized herself with every department, serving as literary critic, consultant, writer, and editor.

In 1877 the Leslies took a highly publicized transcontinental railroad journey that resulted in numerous sketches of the West for Leslie newspapers and Mrs. Leslie's *California: A Pleasure Trip from Gotham to the Golden Gate* (1877). Her disparagement of Virginia City, Nevada, in that book triggered a damaging exposé of her personal life from that town's newspaper *Territorial Enterprise*. Upon their return, the Leslies faced mounting debts, and Leslie was forced to assign his property, for the benefit of his creditors, to Isaac W. England, publisher of the *Sun*. On 10 January 1880 Leslie died, leaving to his widow a bankrupt business.

Miriam Leslie assumed complete control and soon restored the publishing house. Having borrowed $50,000 to pay debts, she repaid the loan by boosting circulation of *Frank Leslie's Illustrated Newspaper* with early illustrated reports of the assassination of President James A. Garfield. In addition, she changed her name legally to "Frank Leslie." She then proceeded to reorganize the business, which now employed three-to four-hundred and boasted art and electrotyping departments, editorial and engraving rooms, publication and business offices. Her editorial policy was "The public shall have the newest news." She encouraged women interviewers, believing them "born disseminators of news." Where her husband had favored twenty periodicals with a circulation of 1,000 each, Leslie preferred one periodical with a circulation of 20,000, and she began to cut down on the number of publications. Hailed as "The Empress of Journalism," she narrowed her periodical list by 1885 to two weeklies and four monthlies, concentrating upon *Frank Leslie's Popular Monthly*.

Leslie also found time to make numerous trips abroad and to preside over her weekly New York salon. Her "conquests" included Joaquin Miller, the "Poet of the Sierras"; William Redivivus Oliver de Lorcourt, Anglo-French marquis de Leuville; and a Russian prince, George Eristoff de Gourie. In 1888 she published *Rents in Our Robes* on the "social successes or solecisms" of the day.

The Frank Leslie Publishing House was incorporated with $1 million in capital in January 1889. The next month Leslie sold her weeklies to Judge Publishing Co., retaining her *Popular Monthly*. Her book, *Beautiful Women of Twelve Epochs*, appeared in 1890, and that year she began touring the country with lectures on "Royal Leaders of Society." In 1891 she married the 39-year-old William Charles Kingsbury Wills Wilde, older brother of Oscar Wilde. In January 1892 they joined the International League of Press Clubs in a tour to San Francisco. The next year Leslie's *Are Men Gay Deceivers?* was published (followed in 1899 by a similar volume of essays, *A Social Mirage*), and her dramatized version of Dumas's *Demi-Monde* was performed as *The Froth of Society*. In June 1893 her marriage to Wilde was dissolved.

In 1895 the decline of the Leslie Publishing House began, as Leslie withdrew from the management of its affairs. In that year she leased her interest in the Leslie publications to a syndicate managed by Frederic L. Colver; three years later the syndicate formed a stock company, of which she became president and editor of the *Popular Monthly*. In 1900 she surrendered half her stock to Colver, and by 1905 the former Frank Leslie Publishing House was out of existence.

Leslie died in New York. She bequeathed an estate of nearly $2 million to Carrie Chapman Catt for furtherance of woman suffrage. A colorful and flamboyant personality, she was an effective editor and publisher of news and story papers, women's magazines, and mass-marketed periodicals.

• The Leslie Estate Papers, deposited in the offices of the law firm Sullivan & Cromwell in New York City, and the *Squier v. Squier* divorce records in the Superior Court of the City of New York contain valuable biographical materials. The only full-length biography is Madeleine B. Stern, *Purple Passage: The Life of Mrs. Frank Leslie* (1953), which includes a bibliography of her writings and a checklist of Leslie publications. Information on the Leslie Publishing House appears in Madeleine B. Stern, *Imprints on History: Book Publishers and American Frontiers* (1956). The files of Leslie journals, especially *Frank Leslie's Illustrated Newspaper* and *Frank Leslie's Popular Monthly*, contain much useful information. Of interest for the Leslie bequest is Rose Young, *The Record of the Leslie Woman Suffrage Commission, Inc.* (1929). Death notices are in the *New York Daily Tribune* and the *New York Times*, 19 Sept. 1914.

MADELEINE B. STERN

L'ESPERANCE, Elise Strang (Jan. 1878?–21 Jan. 1959), physician and clinic founder, was born in Yorktown, New York, the daughter of Albert Strang, a physician, and Kate Depew. Her father had longed for a son to follow in his profession, but after the birth of three daughters he prophesied that Elise was the one who "will be my doctor." Elise graduated from St. Agnes Episcopal School in Albany, New York, before enrolling in courses at the Woman's Medical College of the New York Infirmary for Women and Children in 1896. She greatly admired women colleagues and educators who taught her to have persistence, dedication, and courage. Although a bout with diphtheria prevented her graduation in 1899, she received her M.D. in 1900. She married David A. L'Esperance, Jr., a lawyer, that year; they had no children.

In 1900–1901 Elise L'Esperance served her internship in pediatrics at New York Babies Hospital before entering into private practice. She was a pediatrician for two years in Detroit and for five years in New York City. Realizing the great need for advancement in clinical studies, L'Esperance quit her practice to become a member of the Tuberculosis Research Commission in New York.

In conjunction with the commission, L'Esperance worked with the New York Department of Health, where her interest in pathology steadily grew. In 1910 she applied to work as an assistant to James Ewing, a prominent pathologist at Cornell University Medical School. Although Ewing had adamantly refused to hire a woman in the past, he employed L'Esperance. Under Ewing she became proficient in clinical research. In her two years at Cornell, she studied malignant tumors and discovered the crucial importance of recognizing the early warning signals of cancer.

From 1910 to 1917 L'Esperance worked as a pathologist, and she was director of laboratories from 1917 to 1954 (with the exception of 1928) of the New York Infirmary for Women and Children. In 1912 she became an instructor in the pathology department at Cornell. She took a six-month leave of absence in 1914 to travel to Germany as a Mary Putnam Jacobi Research Fellow. While in Munich she studied malignant hepatomia. She returned home following the outbreak of World War I, finishing her research at Cornell. Her findings were published as "Primary Atypical Malignant Hepatomia" in the *Journal of Medical Research* (1915). In articles she wrote for numerous publications, she detailed the early signs of some cancers, especially Hodgkin's disease and cancers affecting females.

In 1920 L'Esperance became the first woman to be promoted to an assistant professorship at Cornell, a position she retained for twelve years. From 1919 until 1932 she also was an instructor of surgical pathology on the second surgical division of Bellevue Hospital, and she served as a pathologist at various New York hospitals between 1917 and 1920.

In 1930 the death of her mother to cancer had a tremendous impact on L'Esperance. Rather than commemorating their mother's memory with a token gesture, L'Esperance and her sister used an inheritance from an uncle to open the Kate Depew Strang Tumor Clinic at the New York Infirmary for Women and

Children in 1933. After hearing women tell of their fears of being stricken with cancer, L'Esperance realized there was a need to open a clinic to have exams for healthy women—not only to assure those women but to uncover in the earliest stages the small percentage of women who did have cancer. In 1937 the clinic became a center for prevention, the first permanent cancer detection facility in the world.

The clinic, staffed by female physicians, provided complete physical exams and referred women to specialists if any sign of cancer was found. Only seventy-five women came to the clinic the first year, but the numbers rose dramatically each year following. Ewing, seeing L'Esperance's success, suggested that she open a second clinic at New York's Memorial Hospital for Cancer and Allied Disease. The Strang Cancer Prevention Clinic opened in 1940 and was directed by L'Esperance for the next ten years. At first the clinic operated in whatever examining rooms were open, but in 1946 patients were seen at a permanent site. Men were added to the patient list. The number of patients soon exceeded 30,000 a year. By 1950 the patient load had increased so greatly that 6,000 men and women were placed on a waiting list. Noting this success, other clinics, patterned after the Strang clinic, opened across the country.

L'Esperance considered the facilitation of training and education of physicians, especially women, of primary importance. She invited would-be physicians to come and study at the clinic, and her encouragement brought students from all over the world for specialized training. She deflected objections that women did not want to be subjected to routine pelvic examinations by explaining that once women understood that their risks would be minimized by the exam, they would submit to it. Education of the public on the importance of examinations, she believed, was the best method and had to be stressed.

A number of technological advances originated from research and clinical studies done at the Strang clinics, such as the Pap smear for signals of cervical cancer and the proctoscope in detection of abnormalities of the colon and rectum. These advances, combined with L'Esperance's emphasis for the need of complete physicals, helped advance the understanding of women's particular health problems.

In 1942 L'Esperance became the first woman recipient of the Clement Cleveland Medal of the New York City Cancer Committee. She received the Lasker Award for Medical Research in 1951. In 1935–1936 she served as president of the Women's Medical Society of New York State, and in 1948–1949 she was president of the American Medical Women's Association. As editor of the *Medical Women's Journal* from 1936 to 1941, and the first editor of the *Journal of the American Medical Women's Association* from 1946 to 1948, she directed more attention on elevating the status of women physicians.

Following her ten-year absence, L'Esperance returned to Cornell in 1942 as assistant professor of preventive medicine. She became a full clinical professor before leaving in 1950. In 1954–1955 she served as a consultant in pathology at the New York Infirmary. She enjoyed her hobbies of raising and showing hackney horses and collecting carriages. She died in Pelham Manor, New York.

A remarkable woman, L'Esperance saved countless women from the anxiety of not knowing the state of their health. Her program of early detection and education enabled many women to live longer lives. While promoting advances in women's health, she championed continued progress of women in medicine by encouraging them to remain in the profession.

• Some of L'Esperance's publications are in a collection at the Medical Archives of Cornell University Medical Center, Ithaca, N.Y. Her work and her beliefs are also detailed in numerous articles by her, including "The Advantages of Women's Medical Societies," *Medical Woman's Journal* (June 1936): 150–51; "Early Carcinoma of the Cervix," *American Journal of Obstetrics and Gynecology* (Oct. 1924): 461–74; and "Embryonal Carcinoma of the Ovary," *Archives of Pathology* (Mar. 1928): 402–10. Other sources with information on her life and career are "Prevention Is Her Aim," *Time* 55, 3 Apr. 1950, pp. 78–80; Miriam Zeller Gross, "Men of Medicine," *Postgraduate Medicine* (Aug. 1952): 187–90; and Esther Pohl Lovejoy, *Women Doctors of the World* (1957). Details of her clinic are in the infirmary's publication, *The New York Infirmary: A Century of Devoted Service, 1854–1954* (1954). An obituary is in the *New York Times*, 22 Jan. 1959.

MARILYN ELIZABETH PERRY

LESQUEREUX, Leo (18 Nov. 1896–25 Oct. 1889), teacher, student of mosses, and paleobotanist, was born in Fleurier, Switzerland, the son of V. Aimé Lesquereux, who made watchsprings, and Marie Anne (maiden name unknown). At age ten, while climbing near his home, the young Lesquereux suffered a major fall; after being in a coma for several weeks, he was found to have lost hearing in one ear. At age thirteen he was sent to Neuchâtel to begin an academic course. He was a classmate of Arnold Guyot (later a geographer and geologist in the United States) and August Agassiz, younger brother of Louis Agassiz (later a prominent biologist at Harvard). The curriculum was mainly in the classics, with long hours, made more arduous by Lesquereux's economic necessity to tutor younger students.

After graduation at age twenty, Lesquereux was able to obtain a position in Saxony, tutoring in French. There he met his future wife, Sophia von Wolfskeel, the daughter of a general, but he had no means of support. Returning to Switzerland, he first became a teacher and then won a competitive examination of a week to become a high school principal. He married Sophia (he and his wife were to have five children) and taught for several years, but then he began to lose more of his hearing. He went to a doctor in Paris; but as a result of the treatment, he suffered a brain fever and became totally deaf.

Lesquereux worked as a laborer to support his family, then as a mechanic; the family was so poor that his wife's piano was sold to buy a lathe. He was a skilled operator of this machine, but his ill health resumed. His father offered him a partnership in the family watchspring factory, provided he would spend a year as an apprentice; Lesquereux had no other options. Shortly after he began work in the factory, he became interested in botany and was soon drawn to the study of mosses. What scant time he had was absorbed by this new passion.

The Swiss government became interested in peat bogs as a fuel source and offered a prize for an essay on how they were formed and could be preserved. Lesquereux devised an auger to sample the bogs and worked overtime in the factory to obtain daylight hours for his research. He determined the temperature within the bogs, the amount of moisture absorbed by mosses, and other critical data. Despite the difficulties that he encountered, including ridicule by local inhabitants, his essay won the prize. Louis Agassiz was a member of the committee to test the recommendations in Lesquereux's report and recognized his ability.

As a result, Lesquereux was commissioned to write a textbook on the bogs and later was appointed to a government office to direct their study and exploitation. He received a commission to study similar bogs in Germany, Sweden, France, and the Netherlands and spent two months on travel. He examined a lignite mine and also conjectured that amber was formed from pine tree resin.

However, the political climate in Switzerland changed. In 1847 at age forty, Lesquereux emigrated to America with his wife and five children in steerage; the trip took sixty days. As a result of his experience, Lesquereux later wrote a book of advice for those coming to the New World. For a year, he worked with Louis Agassiz on plants of the Lake Superior region. He then settled in Columbus, Ohio, and started a business manufacturing watchsprings. Fortunately, W. S. Sullivant, an independently wealthy man with a keen interest in mosses, lived there. Lesquereux and Sullivant collaborated in bryological research and published two editions of *Musci Americani Exsiccati* (1856). They also worked together on *Icones Muscorum* (1864), for which Lesquereux wrote the Latin descriptions; he produced the entire second volume on his own after Sullivant's death.

About the time he began his study of mosses, Lesquereux chanced on a remark by an earlier French writer suggesting that coal seams had originated under conditions similar to those that formed peat bogs. Inspired by this speculative idea, he took to identifying and describing plants associated with coal; commonly these fossils are found in the roof shale above the coal seams. Soon Lesquereux became the leading taxonomist of such fossil plants in the United States. He described material from the beds of Pennsylvanian (late Paleozoic) for the geological surveys of Kentucky, Pennsylvania, Indiana, Illinois, Alabama, and Arkansas.

In addition, Lesquereux described much younger Cretaceous and Tertiary western plants for F. V. Hayden's Geological and Geographical Survey west of the 100th meridian. In California he studied living mosses and Tertiary floras associated with gold-bearing gravel. His work on the seeds and fruits of the Tertiary Branden Lignite in Vermont was far in advance of that field.

Although Lesquereux wrote many papers in paleobotany, his magnum opus was "Description of the Coal Flora of the Carboniferous Formation in Pennsylvania and throughout the United States," published in the *Second Geological Survey of Pennsylvania*, vol. 2 (1880–1884), with two volumes of text and a companion volume of plates. More than 250 species were described, about one-third of them new to science. To his good fortune, he again found a collaborator, R. D. Lacoe, who was able to hire professional collectors to supplement Lesquereux's efforts and provide money to underwrite the cost of the illustrations. "Coal Flora" has remained a standard work and a necessary item in any paleobotanical research library.

Despite the difficulties of beginning a new career in mid-life with no financial or institutional support combined with the need to learn to lip-read English, Lesquereux was remarkably productive. His ability and versatility were widely recognized; after the National Academy of Sciences was organized, he was the first member elected. A cofounder of the discipline of Paleozoic paleobotany in North America, Lesquereux died in Columbus.

• Biographical information on Lesquereux's life and work can be found in H. N. Andrews, *The Fossil Hunters: In Search of Ancient Plants* (1980); Edward Orton, "Leo Lesquereux," in *The American Geologist* (1890); and J. P. Lesley, "Leo Lesquereux," in National Academy of Sciences, *Biographical Memoirs* 3 (1895): 189–212.

ELLIS L. YOCHELSON

LESUEUR, Charles Alexandre (1 Jan. 1778–12 Dec. 1846), artist and naturalist, was born in Le Havre, France, the son of Jean-Baptiste-Denis Lesueur, an officer in the admiralty, and Charlotte Geneviève Thieullent, the daughter of a naval captain. At the age of nine Lesueur entered the Royal Military School at Beaumont-en-Auge. In 1793 he enrolled in a military school in Le Havre called the "Batillon de l'Esperance," and from 1797 to 1799 he was an underofficer in the National Guard of Le Havre. For a few months in 1798 he served aboard the dispatch boat *Le Hardy* in the English Channel. It is not known where Lesueur learned his drawing skills (Bonnemains, p. 18).

In 1800 Lesueur joined the First Consul, a geographic and scientific expedition sent out by Napoleon to explore and study the coasts of Australia and Tasmania. Under the command of Nicolas Baudin, twenty scientists, including botanists, zoologists, astronomers, mineralogists, and geographers, were selected to accompany the expedition. Among these men were some of great promise, including a student of zoology and medicine, François Péron, who would become Lesueur's close friend and collaborator. Two corvettes, the *Géographe* and the *Naturaliste*, were fitted out in Le Havre for the voyage. Lesueur, an excited witness of these preparations, signed on as a gunner's assistant after his application to enlist as an artist had been turned down because that post had already been filled. But his artistic skills were discovered on the voyage, and he was soon included among the scientific staff.

Lesueur and Péron, after surviving the terrible hardships that decimated the scientists and the crew, returned with the diminished expedition in 1804, bringing back 100,000 zoological specimens, including some 2,500 new species, to the Museum of Natural History in Paris. Péron wrote accurate descriptions while Lesueur made hundreds of detailed drawings of their discoveries. When a committee from the French Academy of Sciences, composed of the eminent naturalists Pierre Simon Laplace, Louis Antoine de Bougainville, Bernard Lacepede, and Georges Cuvier, examined the collection, they reported that "Péron and Lesueur alone have discovered more new animals than all the traveling naturalists of latter times" (*Voyage*, vol. 1, preface).

The two friends set out to publish their finds, but tragedy intervened in 1810 with the death of Péron from tuberculosis, contracted on the voyage. One volume *of Voyage de découvertes aux terres Australes pendant les années 1801, 1802, 1803, 1804* had been published during Péron's lifetime (1807), but the second was completed in 1816 by Louis de Freycinet, a fellow member of the expedition.

Brokenhearted by his friend's death and discouraged by the fall of Napoleon in 1815, Lesueur at that time met in Paris William Maclure, a wealthy Scotsman and enthusiastic geologist who offered him a two-year position as his artist and assistant-naturalist on a trip to America. The two men left France in August 1815 and, after visiting many of the Caribbean Islands, landed in New York on 10 May 1816. They spent a short time in Philadelphia and then set out on a journey of exploration through Delaware and Maryland, across the Allegheny Mountains to Pittsburgh, north to Lake Erie, to Niagara Falls, and into New York State to Lake George and Lake Champlain. They traveled down the Hudson River by steamboat to Newburgh, New York, and then by carriage to Philadelphia.

Lesueur was welcomed by the scientific community and elected a member of the Academy of Natural Sciences of Philadelphia in December 1816. He served as curator at that institution from 1817 to 1825. His contacts with the naturalists of France were of great benefit to the academy scientists in opening up important European channels. Before coming to America, Lesueur had been elected a member of the Société Philomatique of Paris, the Linnean Society of Paris, the Linnean Society of Calvados, and the Natural History Society of Paris. In 1822 he was made a corresponding member of the French National Museum. In America, he was elected a member of the American Philosophical Society in January 1817.

When the inaugural issue of the *Journal of the Academy of Natural Sciences of Philadelphia* appeared in May 1817, the first article, by Lesueur, described six new species of mollusks of the genus *Firola* that he and Péron had observed in the Mediterranean Sea in 1809. Lesueur's contract with Maclure ended at this time, and for the next nine years he supported himself by teaching drawing and painting at several women's schools around Philadelphia and by printing and engraving his own plates. Aside from the numerous drawings he made and engraved for various articles by academy members in the *Journal*, he drew many of the illustrations for naturalist Thomas Say's pioneering *American Entomology*. Lesueur was one of the first in the United States to use lithography. His lithographs of fish that appeared in the *Journal* in 1822 were among the first lithographic book illustrations published in America (Jackson, p. 388).

Between 1819 and 1822 Lesueur spent part of his time as one of the cartographers of the United States and Canadian Boundary Commission engaged in mapping the northeastern boundary between the United States and Canada. He visited Kentucky in 1821 and the upper Hudson River in 1822 and 1823.

In late 1825 Maclure persuaded Lesueur to accompany him, Thomas Say, and Dutch mineralogist and academy founding member Gerard Troost to New Harmony, Indiana, a small town on the frontier where Maclure planned to put into practice his educational theories based on the teachings of Johann Heinrich Pestolozzi, a Swiss educator who believed in *unfolding* the powers and faculties of children rather than *grafting* knowledge onto them. Maclure entered into this venture with the Welsh philanthropist Robert Owen, who had purchased the entire town from a German religious group. Owen's "utopian" experiment failed, but the community of some 800 persons continued after 1827, and Lesueur stayed on with Thomas Say. Maclure, who left to live in Mexico because of his health, bought a printing press for the scientists and valuable European books.

Lesueur acted as surveyor, architect, and physician in New Harmony and taught natural history and drawing to pupils over age twelve, but mostly to adults, in the school Maclure had established (Lockwood, p. 242). He drew several plates for Say's *American Conchology* and produced five plates for his own *American Ichthyology; or, The Natural History of the Fishes of North America*, which was abandoned in 1827 and never completed. For the next ten years he lived at New Harmony, making frequent trips to New Orleans, St. Louis, and Nashville, where Troost moved in 1827, and to many small communities in the surrounding countryside. During these journeys he made notes and sketches of the various specimens he gathered, the geological formations, the landscape, and the people. Also during his years in New Harmony, Lesueur undertook the first scientific investigation of the ancient mounds of Indiana. Some of the artifacts he uncovered can be found in the American Museum of Natural History in New York, the Smithsonian Museum of Natural History, and the Museum of Natural History of Le Havre.

In 1837, overcome with loneliness from the loss of his friends, who had either moved away or died, like Say in 1834, and threatened with the fact that his small pension of 1,500 francs, granted to him by Napoleon, would cease if he did not return, Lesueur sailed for France. He lived for a while in Paris near the Jardin des Plantes, working on his manuscripts and sketches and earning a marginal living teaching drawing. Chosen in March 1846 as "Conservateur" (director) of the newly formed natural history museum in Le Havre, Lesueur, who never married, died suddenly of heart failure less than a year later in Le Havre.

Lesueur's numerous drawings and valuable specimen collections from his voyage to Australia with Péron, from his journey to the West Indies with Maclure, and from his wide-ranging travels in North America formed the basis of the Le Havre museum. Although the building was destroyed during World War II, and Lesueur's specimens lost, his magnificent drawings of the fauna of Australia, many on vellum, and his countless North American sketches are housed in the rebuilt museum.

Lesueur was the first scientist to study the fishes of the Great Lakes of North America. In addition to papers on reptiles, amphibians, and crustaceans, he published twenty-nine papers on American fishes (all listed in Dean [1917]). The most important of these articles is a monograph on the family of suckers, or Catostomidae, in the *Journal of the Academy of Natural Sciences of Philadelphia* (1 [1817]). Louis Agassiz considered Lesueur's accomplishments in ichthyology second only to his own in the United States.

• Lesueur's drawings and paintings are in the Musee D'Histoire Naturelle du Havre in Le Havre, France. Several museum publications reproduce Lesueur's sketches of America, with careful annotations by Jacqueline Bonnemains, whose short account of his life and of his Australian expedition, "Les Artistes Du Voyage De Decouvertes aux Terres Australes (1800–1804)," is in *Bulletin Trimestriel de la Société Geologique de Normandie et des Amis du Muséum du Havre* (1989). Mention of his work in lithography is in Joseph Jackson, "Bass Otis, America's First Lithographer," *Pennsylvania Magazine of History and Biography* 37, no. 4 (1913): 385–94. Biographical studies are Gilbert Chinard, "The American Sketchbooks of C-A. Lesueur," *Proceedings of the American Philosophical Society* 93 (1949): 114–18; Bashford Dean, *A Bibliography of Fishes*, vol. 2 (1917); E. T. Hamy, *Les voyages naturaliste Ch. Alex. Lesueur dans l'Amérique du Nord (1815 a 1817)* (1904; trans. by Milton Haber as *The Travels of the Naturalist Charles A. Lesueur in North America: 1815–1837* [1968]); Adrien Loir, *C-A. Lesueur, artiste et savant français en Amerique de 1816–1839* (1920); and George Ord, "A Memoir of Charles Alexandre Lesueur," *American Journal of Science*, 2d ser., 8 (1849): 189–216. Lesueur figures prominently throughout *Partnership for Posterity: The Correspondence of William Maclure and Marie Duclos Fretageot, 1820–1833*, ed. Josephine Mirabella Elliott (1994), and Patricia Tyson Stroud, *Thomas Say: New World Naturalist* (1992). For information on Lesueur's stay in New Harmony, see George B. Lockwood, *The New Harmony Movement* (1905); Maximilian Prince de Wied, *Travels in the Interior of North America*, ed.

Reuben Gold Thwaites (1905); and Arthur Bestor, *Backwoods Utopias: The Sectarian Origins and the Owenite Phase of Communitarian Socialism in America, 1663–1829* (1950).

PATRICIA TYSON STROUD

LE SUEUR, Marian (2 Aug. 1877–26 Jan. 1954), teacher and radical politician, was born Marian Lucy in Bedford, Iowa, the daughter of (first name unknown) Lucy, a lawyer, and Antoinette McGovern. Le Sueur's parents apparently had nontraditional views and strong streaks of independence. Her father reportedly fled home for long periods preceding the birth of each child. Her mother eventually reared the children alone, going west in 1899 to claim land in Oklahoma, where she built a house and became a temperance leader.

Le Sueur left home at age sixteen and went to Chicago, where she found a job. She then attended Drake University in Des Moines, Iowa, around 1893. She was outstanding in mathematics, but the only courses open to women were domestic arts and language. In 1895, at age eighteen and a year from graduation, she married William Wharton, a Drake divinity student. The couple went immediately to a parish in Boise, Idaho, where society, the church, and Wharton, described by their daughter as deeply patriarchal, imposed many strictures on the young bride. Le Sueur had no legal standing: she could not own property, she could not vote, and her husband could claim any money she earned. She found her situation untenable, but divorce was difficult. They had three children; one of whom, Meridel Le Sueur, became a well-known radical and feminist activist and writer.

In 1910 Le Sueur left Wharton and took the children to Perry, Oklahoma, where she began her public career. Wharton later divorced Le Sueur in Texas on grounds of desertion and her interest in dangerous literature. Le Sueur spoke on the Chautauqua circuit on "Love and Bread," advocating labor reforms and feminist positions, such as a nine-hour working day, sex education, and reproductive choice. She was charged at least once with illegally providing birth-control information. It was a time of political turmoil and labor unrest. Le Sueur participated by organizing children's health clinics and teaching workers at night. Agrarian socialism was at its peak, and Le Sueur was an adherent.

Le Sueur became head of the English department at the People's College in Fort Scott, Kansas. The college, a workers' school launched by the Socialist party in 1914, was a hub of radicalism and a stopover for activists. The school's philosophy was that education should not require a "student" and a "teacher." Rather, "reality" would be revealed through group thinking. Le Sueur edited a weekly publication for correspondence students entitled *People's News*. Its slogan was, "To remain ignorant is to remain a slave." She wrote a book entitled *Plain English, for the Education of the Workers* (1917) and instigated the Little Blue Books, a series that ultimately embraced 2,203 titles. The books (most have faded to tan), published by

Emanuel Haldeman-Julius in Girard, Kansas, were very small (3½″ × 5″) in response to Le Sueur's request for inexpensive, portable texts for workers. In 1917 she married Arthur Le Sueur, a lawyer, Industrial Workers of the World (IWW) supporter, and Socialist who had been mayor of Minot, North Dakota, before joining the college's law department. They had no children.

As Europe went to war, the Le Sueurs, like many midwestern progressives, generally opposed U.S. intervention. After American entry into the war, antiwar activists came under attack. Established institutions, fearing organized farmers, laborers, and Socialists, also used the potential of domestic unrest and the resulting advantage to external enemies as an excuse to attack radicals and reformers. Patriotic hysteria led to persecution of dissenting groups in the name of "loyalty," and the People's College was destroyed.

The Le Sueurs moved in 1917 to St. Paul, Minnesota, where the National Nonpartisan League (NPL) had its headquarters. Marian served as NPL education director, and Arthur was legal representative. They led an antiwar faction at the 1917 Socialist party convention. The league favored neutrality and ran Charles A. Lindbergh, Sr., a noninterventionist, as its Minnesota gubernatorial candidate in 1918. The notorious Commission of Public Safety, Minnesota's World War I loyalty watchdog, harassed Socialists and league leaders and even banned their meetings. In 1923 the Le Sueurs moved to Minneapolis, where their home, which housed the extended family, visiting politicians and activists, and the homeless and needy, was subjected to threats and surveillance. Marian worked outside the home and also cooked, cleaned, and tended to all.

By 1920 the NPL's uneasy coalition of farm, labor, small-town business, and reform interests disintegrated. The more left-wing faction went to the Farmer-Labor Association, formally organized in 1924. Le Sueur was on the executive committee and headed the education department. Minnesotans reelected Farmer-Laborite Floyd B. Olson governor in 1934, and Olson appointed Le Sueur to the Minnesota Board of Education to fill a vacancy. Despite a petition on her behalf organized by the Hennepin County Farmer-Labor Women's Club, the state legislature rejected a full-term appointment. Her radical past, the taint of communism and bolshevism in the Farmer-Labor party, and a charge that she and cohorts on the board had made changes at the State Department of Education to impose a curriculum requiring the teaching of communism and socialism were used against her, and she served only from 1934 to 1936. Her supporters blamed the defeat on sexism as well. She also served on the State Planning Board, 1934–1936, where she pressed for rural electrification.

In 1944 the Farmer-Labor party joined with Minnesota's struggling Democratic party to form the Democratic-Farmer-Labor party, of which Le Sueur was state chairwoman, 1944–1948. However, Le Sueur disagreed with the anti-Communist, liberal (not radical) policies of the dominant Hubert H. Humphrey wing. She bolted to the Progressive party in 1948 to support Henry Wallace for president on the basis of his internationalist, idealistic platform. In 1952, at the age of seventy-six, Le Sueur ran for office as Minnesota's Progressive candidate for U.S. senator. She came in a poor third in a field of four, polling 7,917 votes.

Le Sueur died in Minneapolis. She summed up her own life in two pieces written for use at her memorial service. She said to her children and grandchildren, "I've had a wonderful life of struggle and growing. . . . My life has been a rich life lived . . . to help build a world where every man and woman could have equal opportunity to be his rich full self." She wrote a hopeful essay "to the people" extolling the beauty of American destiny and American democracy while still calling for them to bring vision and courage to the fight to achieve the American dream as they saw it, not as decreed by "the kings of power." "As women, mothers, and homemakers, we want peace and a world without hunger."

Examining Le Sueur's ideas and career is an education in radical midwestern politics. Her rich and full life stands as a symbol of the ways many women have both served and led in building a political tradition of reform.

• The Hennepin County Farmer-Labor Women's Club letter, to which is attached a brief against Le Sueur, is in Correspondence and Other Papers Relating to the Minnesota Legislature, 1933–39, at the Minnesota Historical Society. The Arthur Le Sueur Papers at the Minnesota Historical Society provide no substantive information on Marian; however, the inventory by John Wickre provides some biographical data. The folder prepared for Marian Le Sueur's memorial service, 14 Feb. 1954, is in the Joseph Gilbert Papers at the Minnesota Historical Society. Published material on Le Sueur is scant. The most important source is Meridel Le Sueur, *Crusaders: The Radical Legacy of Marian and Arthur Le Sueur* (1955; repr. 1984). The Le Sueurs' daughter powerfully portrays her parents' backgrounds and beliefs, but some of the biographical facts remain elusive. James M. Youngdale, *Third Party Footprints: An Anthology from Writings and Speeches of Midwest Radicals* (1966), gives more detail of Le Sueur's political activities and publishes excerpts of her writings and speeches (also scarce). For a description and analysis of Minn. politics 1890–1989, see John E. Haynes, "Reformers, Radicals, and Conservatives," in *Minnesota in a Century of Change: The State and Its People since 1900*, ed. Clark E. Clifford, Jr. (1989). Other useful background sources are Mari Jo Buhle et al., eds., *Encyclopedia of the American Left* (1990), especially regarding the Little Blue Books and "Agrarian Radicalism"; Richard J. Altenbaugh, *Education for Struggle: The American Labor Colleges of the 1920s and 1930s* (1990); and Deborah K. Neubeck, "Historical Background," in *Guide to a Microfilm Edition of the National Nonpartisan League Papers* (1970). Obituaries are in the *Minneapolis Morning Tribune* and the *Saint Paul Pioneer Press*, 19 Jan. 1954.

SUE HOLBERT

LETCHER, John (29 Mar. 1813–26 Jan. 1884), congressman and governor of Virginia, was born in Lexington, Virginia, the son of William Houston Letcher, a merchant, builder, and general self-made business-man, and Elizabeth Davidson. He grew up in the comfortable southern middle class and briefly attended Washington College (now Washington and Lee University) before becoming a lawyer. Soon he was active in the Democratic party, and for several years he edited its local newspaper, the *Valley Star*. Intelligent, industrious, and ambitious, Letcher gradually advanced, a typical small-town lawyer-politician of his age. In 1843 he married Susan Holt; over the years their large, two-story brick house in Lexington became the home for eleven children, seven of whom reached maturity.

In 1847, during a passionate debate at the Franklin Society and Library Company, Letcher advocated gradual emancipation. By this time white southerners were closing ranks in the face of the rising abolition movement in the North, and Letcher quickly recanted his political heresy. The people in his area of the Shenandoah Valley, never as sensitive on the issue of slavery as their fellow Virginians in the East and aware that Letcher himself owned a few house servants, accepted his disclaimer and in 1850 elected him a delegate to the state constitutional convention of 1850–1851.

Letcher was one of the leaders of the successful western drive for reform, operating most effectively behind the scenes on committees and relying more on facts and statistics than emotion and eloquence. Finally the conservative East yielded, and Virginia accepted popular election of the governor and many other state officials; universal white manhood suffrage; gradual reapportionment of the legislature, which would soon give control to the white majority living west of the Blue Ridge Mountains; and other aspects of the democracy that had already swept through most of the rest of the nation.

The voters of Letcher's area of the valley quickly rewarded him for his performance by electing him to Congress in 1851, and he easily won reelection three more times. In Washington Congressman Letcher operated as a typical conservative southern Democrat, stressing strict construction of the Constitution, a limited and frugal federal government, and states' rights. As chairman of a special committee, he strongly criticized the rising power of wealthy lobbyists and over time won the nickname "Honest John Letcher, Watchdog of the Treasury." Basically a moderate, he sometimes spoke out for southern rights but never for secession. Occasionally he denounced the abolitionists with great passion, but he always eventually supported restraint and compromise. Unimpressed with the southern aristocracy, he was socially and politically most comfortable with middle-class folks like himself, northerners as well as southerners, and he remained a stubborn optimist as the nation stumbled toward catastrophe.

Late in the decade the shifting tides of Virginia politics gave Letcher an opening, and after winning the Democratic gubernatorial nomination at a rather raucous convention in December 1858, he was elected governor in May 1859. His brief flirtation with emancipation in 1847 hurt him in the conservative East. However, the white majority west of the Blue Ridge remembered his success at the reform convention of 1850–1851 and gave him enough votes to win a hard-fought victory. On 1 January 1860 he became Virginia's leader for four crucial years.

Still an optimistic moderate, Governor Letcher championed sectional compromise. In his inaugural address, he fruitlessly urged the legislature to quickly call a convention of all the states. When the legislators finally acted a year later, it was far too late. In the fateful presidential election of November 1860, he supported Stephen A. Douglas, the candidate of the northern Democrats, and after Abraham Lincoln's victory, he resisted pressure to call a state convention that could carry Virginia out of the Union by a simple majority vote. When that pressure grew irresistible, he supported moderate candidates, who gained control of the new convention, which in February 1861 voted against joining the deep South's secession crusade. Even when the war started he held back, waiting five days for the convention's formal vote to secede on 17 April 1861.

Then Governor Letcher acted decisively and led Virginia into the Confederate States of America. Now he was the leader of the most powerful state in the new nation, and he had a new mission, victory in modern war. Practical and pragmatic, he realized that the rebels had to abandon many old states' rights and personal liberties and close ranks to win, so he collaborated with the other southern states and strongly backed President Jefferson Davis and the Confederate government. This acceptance of Confederate supremacy was the main theme of his wartime administration, making him one of the most cooperative and reliable state governors.

From the start Governor Letcher moved fast to mobilize Virginia and to integrate its armed forces into the burgeoning Confederate military machine. Later, in April 1862, when many rebel troops prepared to return home after a year in the field, he publicly supported the Confederate government's enactment of the first national draft in American history. This controversial policy stirred up a storm of protest, and although he privately felt it was unconstitutional and rather impractical, publicly Letcher fully backed President Davis's dramatic new plan. Governor Letcher led a state constantly being invaded by powerful Union forces, so he quite realistically favored winning first and then arguing over constitutional refinements.

Letcher continued to cooperate with every Confederate call-up of state militia units, notwithstanding rising objections from the affected counties. In May 1862, increasingly concerned about local defense, Letcher began organizing a small state force called the Virginia State Line, for once ignoring Confederate complaints. The Line, understaffed, poorly equipped and ineptly led, as often got in the way of regular Confederate forces as the enemy, so in February 1863, despite the governor's protests, the legislature disbanded it.

Letcher was particularly anxious about the vulnerability of saltworks in southwestern Virginia because this mineral was used to preserve food. In the fall of 1862 the legislature made him the virtual salt czar of Virginia, with sweeping powers over production, distribution, and pricing, but the governor failed to establish an efficient system, so early in 1863 the legislature transferred the program to other state officials, who did no better. At every level inexperienced southern officials had difficulty administering complex new programs, especially relating to the economy, and soon inflation was undermining the rebel home front. Governor Letcher discussed this growing problem in many of his rather dull, tedious speeches, which contained dashes of passion when he denounced "speculators" and "extortioners," but like the other rebel leaders he had no lasting solutions.

Clearly he had weaknesses as a popular leader in a great people's war, but he did continue to support President Davis and the Confederate government, even as the southern masses began to waver. Personally he detested the Confederate policy of impressing civilian property, including slaves, but officially he backed this harsh but necessary action in the face of increasing complaints from his Virginia constituents. He did ease up a little in 1863, the last year of his administration, as criticism intensified in the legislature, but basically he continued to cooperate with the Confederates and to demand an all-out war effort from Virginians.

An experienced politician like Letcher knew the risks of ignoring public opinion in this manner, but he stayed the course and soon paid the price. During 1863 some of his duties were assumed by the growing Confederate government and, to a lesser extent, by a more assertive state legislature. With more time to spare Letcher laid plans to move on to the Confederate Congress from his old district in the Shenandoah Valley as soon as his gubernatorial term ended in December. He had been unbeatable in this district in the 1850s, but when the election was held in May 1863 he lost amid a light turnout. He held a slight majority in the army vote, but the people at home rejected him decisively. The civilian voters disapproved of his policy of vigorously cooperating with the Confederates and diluting traditional rights and privileges until victory—and they too would soon pay the price.

Disappointed by his defeat and nearly bankrupted by the roaring inflation in Richmond, Letcher returned his family to Lexington in January 1864. The ex-governor continued to support the rebel war effort as a private citizen, optimistically hoping that Robert E. Lee could somehow still salvage victory. In May 1864 the Letchers' sixteen-year-old eldest son marched off to war with the Virginia Military Institute cadet corps, and the following month an invading Union army destroyed their home. When the Confederacy finally collapsed in the spring of 1865, Letcher was arrested and confined in a prison in Washington for almost seven weeks. Clearly the enemy appreciated his contributions to the rebel war effort, even if many of his own constituents had not.

Paroled in July, Letcher went home and resumed the practice of law, slowly but surely rebuilding his shattered finances. He also contributed to the revival of two local institutions: he helped persuade General Lee to become president of Washington College, and for fourteen years he served as president of the Board of Visitors of Virginia Military Institute. He even returned briefly to politics, serving as a Democrat in the Virginia House of Delegates from 1875 to 1877. As soon as the war ended he reverted to his habitual moderation and tirelessly championed sectional reconciliation until he died peacefully at his home in Lexington, once again what he had always genuinely wanted to be, a Virginian, a southerner, and an American.

• The executive papers of Governor Letcher are located in the Virginia State Library in Richmond. An extensive collection of his private papers remains the property of the Letcher family in Lexington, and smaller collections are at the Library of Congress, Duke University, the Virginia Historical Society in Richmond, Virginia Military Institute, and the Rockbridge County Historical Society in Lexington. The definitive biography of Letcher is F. N. Boney, *John Letcher of Virginia: The Story of Virginia's Civil War Governor* (1966); the same author wrote the "Virginia" chapter in *The Confederate Governors*, ed. W. Buck Yearns (1985), and "John Letcher: Pragmatic Confederate Patriot," in *The Governors of Virginia: 1860–1978*, ed. Edward Younger and John Tice Moore (1982). See also the pen portrait of Letcher in Boney, *Southerners All* (1984; rev. ed., 1990). An obituary is in the Richmond *Daily Dispatch*, 27 Jan. 1884.

F. N. BONEY

LETCHER, Robert Perkins (10 Feb. 1788–24 Jan. 1861), congressman and governor of Kentucky, was born in Goochland County, Virginia, the son of Stephen Giles Letcher, a brickmaker, and Betsey Perkins. Young Letcher moved with his family to Kentucky about 1800, settling first near Harrodsburg and soon after that in Garrard County. While working in his father's brickyard, the young man taught himself reading, writing, and arithmetic. He then gained admission to a private academy operated by Joshua Fry near Danville. He subsequently studied law in the Frankfort office of Humphrey Marshall. Working to support himself, he assisted another future Kentucky governor, Thomas Metcalfe, in constructing the executive mansion in Frankfort.

After finishing his legal studies, Letcher returned to Garrard County to open his practice. During the War of 1812 he served briefly as judge advocate in the Kentucky Mounted Volunteer Militia, commanded by James Allen. Returning home in the fall of 1812, he embarked on a career in politics. He was elected to the Kentucky House of Representatives in 1813, 1814, 1815, and 1817. From 1819 to early 1820, he served as a judge for the Arkansas Territory. In 1822 he was elected to the U.S. House of Representatives, where he served from 1823 to 1835.

Letcher's wit and genial personality won him many friends in Congress, despite his strong partisanship for the National Republican party and later the Whig party. When debate turned bitter, he would often throw in a joke that returned his colleagues to good humor. He also enlivened many parties and campaign appearances with his fiddle-playing.

An intimate friend of House Speaker Henry Clay, Letcher played a key role in the election of John Quincy Adams by the House of Representatives in 1825. He helped Clay carry the Kentucky delegation's vote for Adams, in spite of legislative instructions to support Andrew Jackson. His actions also were questioned when the "corrupt bargain" charge was leveled against Clay and Adams following the new president's appointment of Clay as secretary of state. Attempting to sound out Adams about what role he planned for Clay if he became president, Letcher had held several private conversations with Adams before the House vote, but he always maintained that he did so on his own initiative and not as Clay's emissary. Nevertheless, it was an issue that would be raised every time Clay ran for president.

Throughout Adams's term Letcher remained his strong supporter; he was equally adamant as an opponent of the Jackson administration. He ushered through the House the Maysville Road Bill, which Jackson subsequently vetoed. This would have extended the National Road from Maysville, Kentucky, to Lexington. He also engineered the passage of Clay's Compromise Tariff of 1833 when, during a discussion of the administration bill, he moved an amendment to strike out the entire bill and substitute Clay's compromise, which was then being debated in the Senate. This was done, and the compromise measure was passed.

As the House elections of 1833 approached, Letcher's reelection was viewed by Whig leaders as crucial to successful passage of the bill to recharter the Second Bank of the United States. The election between Letcher and Democrat Thomas P. Moore proved to be so close that each presented himself to the House as the duly elected representative. After a six-month investigation, the House declared neither man qualified and called for a new election. In August 1834 Letcher defeated Moore in a second contest by a majority of less than three hundred votes.

After leaving Congress in 1835, Letcher again represented Garrard County in the Kentucky house from 1836 to 1838, serving the last two years as speaker. At the Whig convention in Harrodsburg in August 1839, he was nominated for governor. In the 1840 election he defeated Democrat Richard French by more than 15,000 votes, and the Whigs had a comfortable majority in both houses of the legislature.

Letcher was inaugurated 2 September 1840. One of his first acts was to meet with the newly elected Whig president, William Henry Harrison, as he passed through Frankfort. Letcher urged Harrison to appoint his friend John J. Crittenden to a cabinet post, which he did.

Letcher's message to the Kentucky General Assembly in December called attention to an expected deficit in state revenues, resulting largely from a national depression as well as from substantial expenditures on internal improvements. Blaming the country's economic woes on the failure of Congress to recharter the Bank of the United States, the new governor made it clear that Kentucky would not repudiate its debts, as many states were doing. Rather, major cuts had to be made in internal improvement projects. Letcher recommended that no new projects be started and that those under way be postponed until the state had money to pay for them. The governor opposed major measures for relief of debtors but approved some minor acts to hold off foreclosures. By June 1842 state banks resumed specie payment on their notes, which had been suspended in 1839. Each full year of Letcher's term witnessed a small surplus in the state treasury, and at the end of his term Kentucky bonds, worth eighty cents on the dollar when he took office, were above par. This was accomplished, however, at the cost of needed improvements.

After leaving office in 1844, Letcher practiced law in Frankfort. He remained active in politics and in 1847 ran for a seat in the U.S. Senate, but he was defeated by Joseph R. Underwood.

One of the greatest disappointments of Letcher's gubernatorial term had been Clay's failure to win the presidency in 1844. In 1848, however, Letcher joined with Crittenden in opposing Clay's nomination, instead supporting Zachary Taylor. He was rewarded by the new Whig president with an appointment as minister to Mexico, which he held from 1850 to 1852. He hated life in Mexico City, and the treaties he negotiated there were eventually rejected by the Mexican government. After returning home, he opposed Democrat John C. Breckinridge in a doomed attempt to return to the U.S. House, his last race.

As the Whig Party disintegrated in the 1850s, Letcher supported Know-Nothing candidates; in 1860 he favored the Constitutional Union candidate, John Bell, for president. Letcher died in Frankfort. He married twice; first to Mary Oden Epps, who died early, and second to Charlotte Robertson, who survived him. He had no children.

• A sizable collection of Letcher's gubernatorial papers, including letterbooks and ledgers, are in the Kentucky Department for Libraries and Archives, Frankfort. Many of his letters were published in James F. Hopkins et al., eds., *The Papers of Henry Clay* (11 vols., 1959–1992), and in Mrs. Chapman Coleman (Ann Mary Butler Crittenden), ed., *The Life of John J. Crittenden with Selections from His Correspondence and Speeches* (2 vols., 1871). The most comprehensive analysis of his gubernatorial administration is Will D. Gilliam, Jr., "Robert Perkins Letcher: Whig Governor of Kentucky," *Filson Club History Quarterly* 24 (1950): 6–27. Two older but useful sources are Jennie C. Morton, "Governor Robert Letcher," *Register of the Kentucky Historical Society* 3 (1905): 11–17; and Lewis Collins and Richard H. Collins, *History of Kentucky* (2 vols., 1874; repr., 1966).

MELBA PORTER HAY

LETCHWORTH, William Pryor (26 May 1823–1 Dec. 1910), industrialist and philanthropist, was born in Brownville, New York, the son of Josiah Letchworth, a harnessmaker, and Ann Hance. Raised in a strict Quaker home, he was educated at primary school and then went to work for his father in the harnessmaking business. His parents were Hicksite Quakers who were strongly opposed to slavery. Young William frequently attended the Unitarian church and nurtured a social conscience of his own. At fifteen he went to Auburn, New York, to work in the firm of Hayden and Holmes, manufacturers and merchants of saddlery hardware; his salary was forty dollars per year. His personal frugality and industrious attitude impressed his employer, who sent him to New York City in 1845 as a confidential secretary to Peter Hayden, the senior partner who also ran another business in the city, the P. and T. Hayden Company. In 1848 the hardware merchants Samuel and Pascal Pratt of Buffalo offered Letchworth a partnership; he accepted and became the managing partner in a new company, Pratt and Letchworth. Many innovations characterized Letchworth's business, including the organization of a modified assembly line, which he employed at the Erie County Penitentiary. In the 1860s he experimented with processes to produce malleable iron, and as the Civil War concluded, his new company, the Buffalo Malleable Iron Works, made a significant contribution to the war effort.

In the mid-1850s Letchworth expanded his personal horizons and became more socially active. He joined and became president of the Buffalo Academy of Fine Arts, and he was a prominent trustee of the Buffalo Female Academy, one of the first collegiate level institutions for women in New York State. From 1856 to 1857 he toured the British Isles and western Europe, partly on business but also to broaden his life experiences; he took particular note of old world architecture and Italian landscapes. A founder of the Buffalo Children's Aid Society and a prominent donor to the Thomas Orphan Asylum on the Cattaraugus Indian Reservation, he was a delegate to the first National Conference on Charities and Correction in 1871. From his connections in the Young Men's Association, he gathered friends and business associates in 1863 to found the Buffalo Historical Society. These and other organizations brought Letchworth into close contact with significant leaders in the state, including personal friendships with Millard Fillmore and William H. Seward.

In 1869 Letchworth retired from business to engage in various health care and philanthropic ventures. Over the years he supported the work of Dr. Cordelia Greene of Castile, New York, a close personal friend who operated a hydrotherapy sanitorium for invalids. He accepted a commissionership on the state board of charities, and he worked to resettle children from the Erie County poorhouse into local asylums. In 1870 he founded the Wyoming Benevolent Institute to provide a respite from the city's hot summer streets for the destitute children of Buffalo. From 1875 to 1876 he was instrumental in having legislation passed to prevent the confinement of children between three and sixteen in state poorhouses. Known as the "Erie County System," his concept came to include a plan for the adoption of children. In 1878 he was made president of the State Board of Charities, on which he served until 1893.

In 1880 Letchworth's interests turned to insane and delinquent children. He toured Europe for a year, visiting the places of which Dorothea Dix had written, to observe methods in various kinds of asylums. His findings were published in *The Insane in Foreign Countries* (1889). In 1884 he helped to introduce a manual labor program to the Western House of Refuge at Rochester, New York (later renamed the State Industrial School). At about the same time as his European observations, he advocated statewide control of the care of the insane and also established farm colonies, which he frequently supervised. Turning his focus to epileptics, he established a colony for the care of epileptics at a defunct Shaker community in Sonyea, near Mount Morris, New York. In 1896 this center was officially opened by the state as Craig Colony. In 1900 he published a groundbreaking work, *The Care and Treatment of Epileptics*.

Letchworth made a trip on the Erie Railroad across the Genesee River Gorge near Portageville, New York, in 1858, and, admiring the beauty of the gorge and waterfalls in the area, he determined to buy the site. Between 1859 and 1860 he purchased 700 acres, which included three waterfalls and the surrounding lumber and farm operations. For the remainder of his life he devoted personal energy and funds to reforestation and historical projects in his reserve. On the adjacent valley lands he operated successful farms raising livestock and grains using experimental techniques. He refurbished a house near the falls, naming it "Glen Iris," which became a woodland retreat and a center of hospitality for western New York. His interest in native peoples and local history led to the relocation of the last surviving Seneca Council House from Caneadea on the Upper Genesee to the park, as well as the grave of famed Mary Jemison, a white woman who married a member of the Seneca tribe and lived as one of them. In 1906 Glen Iris and its preserve were threatened by electric power advocates. To forestall the construction of a dam, Letchworth deeded his estate to the state of New York; thereafter it was known as Letchworth Park, the "Grand Canyon of the Genesee."

Although he suffered a stroke in 1903 that left him partially paralyzed, Letchworth continued to read widely and to write on concerns ranging from local history to charitable enterprises. He was easily the most influential person in his state and wielded great political power for the causes he espoused. He was honored many times, including an honorary LL.D. by the Board of Regents of the State University of New York, an honor that required the unanimous vote of the board and had previously been conferred only twenty times. In 1872 the Wolf clan of the Seneca Nation adopted Letchworth into their clan as Hai-wa-ye-if-tah (The man who always does the right thing). In 1909 the Eastern New York State Custodial Asylum at Rockland, New York, was renamed "Letchworth Village" in his honor.

Gentle in spirit and sympathetic in nature, Letchworth was one of the most beloved philanthropists of his era. He never married and died at Glen Iris.

• The personal papers and memorabilia of Letchworth are at Milne Library, State University of New York at Geneseo; the Buffalo and Erie County Historical Society in Buffalo; and the Genesee Valley Museum in Letchworth Park, Portageville, N.Y. Letchworth published sixty-five papers and reports in the general field of charities and corrections, in addition to his books, which include *A Sketch of the Life of Samuel Pratt* (1898) and an edition of James E. Seaver's *Narrative of the Life of Mary Jemison* (1898). Biographical studies include Stephen Smith, *An Appreciation of the Life of William Pryor Letchworth* (1911), J. N. Larned, *The Life and Work of William Pryor Letchworth* (1912), and Irene A. Beale, *William P. Letchworth: A Man for Others* (1982). Obituaries are in the *New York Herald Tribune* and the *New York Times*, both 3 Dec. 1910.

WILLIAM H. BRACKNEY

LEUSCHNER, Armin Otto (16 Jan. 1868–22 Apr. 1953), astronomer and educator, was born in Detroit, Michigan, the son of Richard Otto Leuschner, a German immigrant, and Caroline Humburg (occupations unknown). His father died when Leuschner was less than a year old, and his mother, born in America of German parents, took him back to Germany. In 1886 he graduated from a Gymnasium in Cassel (Kassel in what is now the German state of Hesse), and he and his mother then returned to the United States. Leuschner entered the University of Michigan and completed his A.B. after only two years, in 1888. Then he went to Lick Observatory, of the University of California, as its first graduate student in astronomy. He moved to the Berkeley campus in 1890 as an instructor in mathematics, working on his thesis there, but gradually dropped it after he was promoted to assistant professor in 1892, then appointed assistant professor of astronomy and geodesy (the first faculty member in astronomy on the campus) in 1894. Even before there was an astronomy department at Berkeley, or he had his Ph.D., Leuschner taught two graduate students, each on an individual basis. They were Frederick H. Seares, who went on to a long and distinguished research career at Mount Wilson Observatory, and William H. Wright, who did the same at Lick, each without the benefit of an earned Ph.D. In 1896 Leuschner married Ida Louise Denicke, the daughter of an important regent of the University of California. They had three children. She accompanied him to Berlin when he went on leave for the year 1896–1897. In that year he wrote a completely new thesis on the determination of the orbits of comets and received his Ph.D. "in testimony of his signal acumen." Returning to Berkeley, Leuschner became associate professor of astronomy and geodesy and later professor of astronomy. He single-handedly built up the Berkeley Astro-

nomical Department and its Students' Observatory and was its chairman and director from 1898 until he retired in 1938.

Leuschner's whole research interest was in celestial mechanics, and especially in the determination of the orbits of asteroids and comets. He had not gotten along well with Edward S. Holden, the first director of Lick Observatory and his first thesis adviser, but he was very close to James E. Keeler, who took over as the second director in 1898. Leuschner had worked as Keeler's assistant at Lick in 1888–1890 and had studied and worked with him for a time at Allegheny Observatory before going to Berlin. Keeler and Leuschner collaborated closely in setting up the University of California graduate program in astronomy, under which the students took graduate courses at Berkeley (especially in the winter and spring, the poor observing season on Mount Hamilton) and learned research by doing it, as assistants at Lick Observatory (especially in the summer and fall). In 1901 Leuschner hired the first Ph.D. from this program, R. Tracy Crawford, as the second member of the Berkeley Astronomical Department faculty. All the faculty members subsequently appointed in the department until after Leuschner's retirement—Sturla Einarsson, William F. Meyer, and C. Donald Shane—were also products of the California Ph.D. program.

After Keeler's unexpected death in 1900, W. W. Campbell became the Lick director, a post he held until 1930. He continued the close collaboration with Leuschner, and California became the outstanding graduate school in astronomy in America. Campbell often urged Leuschner to let the students take more physics and especially spectroscopy courses, but Leuschner insisted that celestial mechanics, particularly "Leuschner's method" (for determining an orbit rapidly and accurately from the minimum number of observations) was too important to give up. As a result, the California Ph.D.s were very well trained in both the astronomy and astrophysics of their day, and a considerable number of them became the research leaders of American astronomy well into the generation after Leuschner's. In a report he prepared at the end of 1938, Leuschner summarized the careers of the astronomers his department had trained. Counting Seares and Wright, who had not earned Ph.D.s, and Frank E. Ross and Charles W. Smiley, whose degrees were in mathematics, although they had studied astronomy and were working in it, there were sixty-three graduates. Fifty-one were men; twelve were women. All but one were still alive. Five had been elected to the National Academy of Sciences, ten were starred as "most distinguished astronomers" in *American Men of Science*, and fourteen were directors of observatories. It was a record of which Leuschner was justifiably proud.

Leuschner had a driving dedication to research and promoted it tirelessly. As dean of the graduate school from 1913 until 1923, and chairman of the university-wide Board of Research from 1916 until 1935, he played a key role in building up the University of California into a great research university. On the national scene he helped to found the Association of American Universities and was for many years the chairman of its Committee on Academic and Professional Higher Degrees. In all these posts Leuschner strove always for high standards of research and recognition and funding for it. Campbell, who became president of the University of California in 1923, supported Leuschner completely in this. During their regimes, for instance, Ernest O. Lawrence was recruited to Berkeley from Yale, and Leuschner was pivotal in making it possible for him to start the Radiation Laboratory on the Berkeley campus.

During World War I Leuschner, who spoke with a pronounced German accent throughout his life and had an appreciation for the culture of Goethe and Schiller (as well as the science of Gauss and Bessel), was widely perceived as "disloyal." Campbell, a superpatriot whose son was a pilot in the little American Air Corps in France, was one of the leaders in the anti-"Teutonic" campaign. Leuschner, an American citizen by birth, quieted this criticism by seeking and receiving a commission in the Chemical Warfare Service. His commission did not come through until just as the armistice was concluded, and as a major he spent the first six months of 1919 in Washington as an organizer of science. There he worked, under George Ellery Hale, as the executive secretary of the National Research Council and chairman of its Division of Physical Sciences.

Leuschner continued his own research, mostly on the orbits of asteroids, all his life. However, his contributions as an educator of research scientists and as a promoter of research were far more important to science. He died in Berkeley.

• The most complete collection of Leuschner's papers is in the Department of Astronomy Papers, University of California Archives, and the Armin O. Leuschner Papers, Bancroft Library, both at the University of California, Berkeley. There are also many of his letters, especially concerning graduate students, in the Mary Lea Shane Archives of the Lick Observatory, University Library, University of California, Santa Cruz. Copies of his Ph.D. thesis, "Beiträge zur Kometenbahnbestimmung," are in the Berkeley and Santa Cruz libraries of the University of California. The best memorial biography is Paul Herget, "Armin Otto Leuschner 1868–1953," National Academy of Sciences, *Biographical Memoirs* 49 (1978): 129–47. It contains a full bibliography of his published scientific papers and also lists several of his more important publications in the educational field. Leuschner recounted the early history of the Berkeley Astronomical Department himself in "History and Aims of the Students' Observatory," *Publications of the Astronomical Society of the Pacific* 16 (1904): 68–77, and a longer account, including the chairmanships of his immediate successors Crawford, Shane, and Einarsson, is given in Donald E. Osterbrock, "Armin O. Leuschner and the Berkeley Astronomical Department," *Astronomy Quarterly* 7 (1990): 95–115. An obituary is Dinsmore Alter, "Armin Otto Leuschner," *Publications of the Astronomical Society of the Pacific* 65 (1953): 269–73.

DONALD E. OSTERBROCK

LEUTZE, Emanuel Gottlieb (24 May 1816–18 July 1868), painter, was born in Gmünd, Württemberg, the son of Gottlieb Leutze, an artisan, and his wife, whose family name is unknown. Verses addressed to the elder Leutze at the time of the family's immigration to the United States, which took place in 1825, suggest a political motive for leaving the Swabian principality, and it may be that the Leutze family was associated with one of the dissident movements that preceded the 1848 revolution.

Settling first in Fredericksburg, Virginia, and then in Philadelphia, young Leutze and his family were soon on their own when Gottlieb Leutze died. Legend has it that the boy sold his artwork to support his mother and siblings. In any event, he enrolled in John Rubens Smith's art classes in 1834 and, hired to make likenesses for James Barton Longacre and James Herring's *National Portrait Gallery of Distinguished Americans*, could call himself a professional artist by the age of twenty. After his association with the project ended in 1837, he began to earn his living as an itinerant portraitist, concentrating his efforts in the Fredericksburg region of Virginia. In portraits from this period, such as *Colonel Byrd Charles Willis and His Son*, dated May 1837, Leutze's style bears no evidence of the dramatic flair that informs his most famous history paintings, though he demonstrated flashes of the sensitivity to color and to character with which his later productions were imbued.

Financially supported by Edward Carey and Joseph Sill, two of his Philadelphia patrons, Leutze went to Europe and entered the Düsseldorf Art Academy in 1841. At that time on a par with academies in Paris, Florence, and Munich, the Düsseldorf academy boasted a distinguished faculty including Wilhelm von Schadow, Karl Friedrich Lessing, and Johann Hasenclever, all well known for their meticulous attention to realistic detail in figure painting and for their predilection for narrative in genre and historical subjects. In 1843 Leutze traveled to Italy via southern Germany, a trip crucial to the direction his future career would take—not so much because of the art he saw as because of a revelation he experienced:

The romantic ruins of what were once free cities . . . led me to think how glorious had been the course of freedom from those small isolated manifestations of the love of liberty to where it has unfolded all its splendor in the institutions of our own country. Nearly crushed and totally driven from the old world it could not be vanquished, and found a new world for its home. This course represented itself in pictures to my mind, forming a long cycle, from the first dawning of free institutions in the middle ages, to the reformation and revolution in England . . . to the Revolution and Declaration of Independence [in the United States]. (Henry T. Tuckerman, *Artist-Life* [1847], p. 177)

When he returned to Düsseldorf and embarked on the program inspired by this vision, he commenced to strengthen the name he had made earlier for himself in America with his 1842 painting of *The Return of Co-*

lumbus in Chains from Cadiz (Masco Corporation). In rapid succession he painted and sent to the United States *Columbus before the Queen* (1843, Brooklyn Museum) and several scenes drawn from English history, especially the Cromwellian era.

From his letters, it would appear that Leutze did not intend to reside permanently in Düsseldorf, but his marriage in 1845 to a German woman, Juliane Lottner, altered his plans. A daughter was born to the Leutzes in 1846 and a son the following year. In addition to his domestic life, Leutze's growing political involvements kept him tied to Düsseldorf. He became president of the Union of Düsseldorf Artists, an organization founded to offset the domination of the academy. He was a cofounder, along with Lessing, Hasenclever, Andreas Achenbach, Ludwig Knaus, and other painters and poets, of the Malkasten, a democratically oriented club predominantly comprised of members known for their liberal politics but dedicated to consensual solutions: "As all colors in our palette [*Malkasten*] are in peaceful co-existence, so should we also be united," proclaimed the club's charter.

Formation of the Malkasten also should be seen as an important public sign of the Düsseldorf artists' involvement in the events of 1848. In March of that year, a brief outbreak of fighting in Berlin gave vent to the frustrations many liberals were beginning to feel with the fractured, petty monarchies that kept German-speaking peoples divided. Various political factions, with interests that were for the most part irreconcilable except for a common desire to unite the German states, forced the creation of the Frankfurt Parliament, and this legislative body, in turn, proposed a new constitution in which the German states would be united under King Friedrich Wilhelm IV of Prussia. He refused the crown in August 1849 and vigorously suppressed an uprising of the far Left the following month.

Artists in Düsseldorf who championed unification of the German states joined people's militias during this trying period or supported the Frankfurt Parliament in other ways, but it was Leutze who originated the idea of forming the Malkasten during the "Festival of German Unity," which the fledgling legislative body had designated as 6 August 1848. In a watercolor still in the possession of the Malkasten, he recorded the moment when a torchlight parade of artists, with himself as one of the leaders, ended at the foot of a statue of Germania they had erected; cannons were fired, and the banner bearing the ancient imperial eagle of the Holy Roman Empire was raised. The esprit de corps that so clearly infused the Malkasten's founding remained an essential ingredient of the organization and contributed to its success. It and not the academy became the real center of Düsseldorf artistic life, and Leutze, during the years he lived in Germany, always played a guiding role in Malkasten affairs.

Even though the major part of his career took place abroad, it also may be said that Leutze occupied an important position in the artistic life of the United States. A large number of American would-be painters, some of whom later became quite famous, came to Düsseldorf for training, especially in draftsmanship. They congregated around Leutze, who taught them or found them instructors, introduced them to the Malkasten membership, advised them, lent them money, sent them on long tours of the Rhine, and behaved in every way toward them like a father and a friend. Eastman Johnson was one of the most able of the American students; he wrote in an 1851 letter to his family in America that he belonged to the Malkasten, "the smartest [club] in town," and painted in Leutze's studio, "a large hall where six of us paint with convenience, three on large pictures." His fellow pupil Worthington Whittredge remembered in later years, "Writers and art students have not known what the [Düsseldorf School] really was, especially in Leutze's day. The 'school' never meant merely the influence of the professors of the Academy, but has always meant the influence of the whole body of artists. . . . Leutze had a tremendous influence upon the School when I was there . . . [The academicians] spoke of Leutze as genius." Other American painters who benefited from Leutze's presence in Düsseldorf include Albert Bierstadt, Charles Wimar, and John Adams Elder.

Leutze's reputation in the United States, as well as his fame in European circles, rests today mainly on his history paintings featuring George Washington and Christopher Columbus; in his own time his popularity resulted from the general, if not critical, acclaim that greeted all of his productions, from English Puritan subjects to scenes of westward expansion. From any perspective, his paintings of the 1850s represent the zenith of his talent, his verve, and—a quality that served him well in the dispirited atmosphere of post-1848 Germany, where ideals of unity and republicanism were not entirely extinguished—his alertness to the relationship between historical subject matter and contemporary political issues. His ability to organize a large number of figures on a broad field and to paint an episode from the past with the conviction of an eyewitness is the hallmark of his best work, in particular *Washington Crossing the Delaware* (Metropolitan Museum of Art).

In October 1849 Leutze began his portrayal of one of the revolutionary war's most pivotal moments, the sneak attack on Hessian troops camped on the New Jersey side of the river on Christmas Eve 1776. American military fortunes, then at a low ebb, received much-needed encouragement from the subsequent victory, and Washington was perceived as having demonstrated in the battle not only strategic brilliance but also heroic leadership. Not surprisingly, the encounter had attracted earlier artists, such as John Trumbull and Thomas Sully, but only Leutze's image has attained lasting and almost universal recognition.

Two versions of the painting existed, as the canvas begun in 1849 was damaged by fire in November 1850. This painting was repaired and after exhibition in several German cities became the property of the Bremen Kunsthalle, where it was destroyed by Allied bombers in 1943. A second canvas, described by Eastman Johnson as "two-thirds finished" in March 1851, was purchased by Goupil and Company for the International Art Union. In September of that year, the painting was exhibited in New York, and early in 1852 Leutze showed it at the U.S. Capitol. Marshall Roberts bought the painting from Goupil shortly thereafter, and it remained in his collection until 1897, when it was sold to John S. Kennedy, who gave it to the Metropolitan Museum.

Leutze proposed as a pendant to *Washington Crossing the Delaware* a painting of Washington rallying the troops at the battle of Monmouth, a topic revealing Washington's superlative qualities less than his ordinary flaws. At Freehold, New Jersey, in 1778, Washington intercepted retreating American soldiers under the command of Major General Charles Lee, whom he publicly excoriated. Although Washington regathered the troops and repelled the British, Leutze chose to paint the moment the commander in chief lost his temper. The large canvas of the subject he completed in 1854 garnered few admirers in America; *The Crayon*, a respected art journal in the United States, declared the painting was not "in the slightest degree heroic." In contrast, the *Augsburg Allgemeine Zeitung* praised the picture because it emphasized that "not . . . heroism, but truth, energy, and intelligence turn the odds of battle," a reading that seems in keeping with the artist's loyalty to the cause of democracy. Leutze hoped in vain that Congress would purchase this work. After it was exhibited in Berlin and Brussels, *Washington Rallying the Troops* was bought by a private collector and subsequently entered the collection of the University of California, Berkeley.

In 1858 Leutze left Düsseldorf and the following year took up residence in Washington, D.C., where he continued to paint historical subject matter but was rather more successful as a portraitist. Among the leading figures of the day who sat for Leutze were Chief Justice Roger B. Taney (1859; Harvard Law School, Cambridge, Mass.), William Seward (1859; Union League Club, New York), Nathaniel Hawthorne (1863; National Portrait Gallery, Washington, D.C.), and Frederic Church (1865; private collection). Leutze was elected to membership in the National Academy of Design in 1860. In 1861 he received a commission from the U.S. Congress, and after a trip to the Rockies to observe firsthand the terrain he was to delineate, Leutze painted *Westward the Course of Empire Takes Its Way*, a 20 × 30-foot mural on the walls of the Great Stairway in the House of Representatives in 1862.

Leutze spent his remaining years in the United States (he made one short trip to Düsseldorf in 1863) and was noted here as he had been in Germany for his congenial nature and hearty good spirits. Hawthorne wrote to a friend that his sittings with Leutze would endow the finished portrait with "an aspect of immortal jollity and well-to-doness, for Leutze . . . gives me a first-rate cigar, and when he sees me getting tired, he brings out a bottle of splendid champagne; and we quaffed and smoked yesterday, in a blessed state of

mutual good will . . . Leutze . . . is the best of fellows." Although Leutze was troubled in his last months by money and health problems, he did not appear to be daunted. The cartoon for a very large painting to be entitled *The Emancipation of the Slaves* was underway when Leutze died of heatstroke in Washington, D.C., where he is buried.

In Germany Leutze has always been admired as a sterling example of the Düsseldorf school. In the United States, on the other hand, though he has always been considered an American painter, his association with Düsseldorf has been the source of fluctuating esteem among art historians. By the late twentieth century the newly acknowledged importance of history painting in American art of the nineteenth century had restored his reputation, though it should be added that, as an icon equaled by few others in American popular culture, *Washington Crossing the Delaware* remains for the lay audience unrelated to its author. Whatever the critical assessment of his paintings, Leutze's significance for the German and American artist communities is unquestioned.

• Of nineteenth-century accounts of Leutze and his work, Wolfgang Müller von Königswinter, *Düsseldorfer Künstler aus den letzten 25 Jahren* (1854); Moritz Blanckarts, *Düsseldorfer Künstler: Nekrologie aus den letzten zehn Jahren* (1877); Friedrich von Bötticher, *Malerwerke des neunzehten Jahrhunderts* (2 vols., 1891–1901); and Henry T. Tuckerman, *Book of the Artists* (2 vols., 1867), are the most useful. Contemporary treatments of the artist include Raymond Stehle, "Washington Crossing the Delaware," *Pennsylvania History* 31 (July 1964): 269–94; Barbara Groseclose, *Emanuel Leutze, 1816–1868: Freedom Is the Only King* (1976); William Gerdts and Mark Thistlethwaite, *Grand Illusions: History Painting in America* (1988); and Barbara Gaehtgens, "Fictions of Nationhood: Leutze's Pursuit of History Painting in Düsseldorf," in *American Icons* (1992).

BARBARA GROSECLOSE

LEVANT, Oscar (27 Dec. 1906–14 Aug. 1972), pianist, actor, and composer, was born in Pittsburgh, Pennsylvania, the son of Max Levant, a jeweler, and Annie Radin, both Russian Jewish immigrants. Levant left high school after the early death of his father in 1921. A brilliant but rebellious student, he was a child prodigy on the piano. At the age of fifteen he was sent to New York City to study with Sigismond Stojowski. He played in dance bands and roadhouses to pay for his lessons. Levant's father had opposed a concert career, but his strong-willed mother encouraged her youngest of four sons. Later in life, when asked what he had wanted to be when he grew up, quick-witted Levant answered, "An orphan."

Levant began and abandoned several careers (pianist, songwriter, composer, actor, television and radio personality), but his most enduring contributions have been as an interpreter of George Gershwin's piano works; as the creator of a witty, sardonic, and sometimes hypochondriacal film persona in thirteen films; and as a wit whose barbed comments about his contemporaries and his own frail mental and emotional health shocked television audiences in the 1950s and 1960s. ("I knew Doris Day before she became a virgin," he once said. And "Self-pity? It's the only pity that counts.")

Levant first became known around Broadway for his streetwise personality and humor. Walter Winchell often included Levant's quips in his gossip column. Levant was trying his hand at writing Tin Pan Alley pop songs during this time. He wrote eighty popular songs over fifteen years, including two big hits, "Lady Play Your Mandolin," written with Irving Caesar for the 1930 Broadway musical *Ripples*, and "Blame It on My Youth," written in 1934 with Edward Heyman, a song that has become a standard.

Levant met his idol, George Gershwin, around 1925 and became the first pianist after Gershwin to record *Rhapsody in Blue* (with the Frank Black Orchestra on the Brunswick label, 1925). He became an acolyte in Gershwin's circle of composers, songwriters, and arrangers centered around the preeminent music publisher of the day, Max Dreyfus of Harms, Inc.

Levant went to Hollywood in 1929 to appear in the film version of the 1927 Broadway musical *Burlesque*, retitled *The Dance of Life* (Paramount Pictures, 1929), an early "talking and musical" picture starring Hal Skelly and Nancy Carroll. While there he began writing songs for the new "talkies" and was paired with lyricist Sidney Clare. In the space of six months Levant and Clare composed tunes for six RKO films.

Levant made his Broadway debut as one of the composers of *Ripples* (1930). Although the show closed after only eight weeks at the New Amsterdam Theatre, it nevertheless brought him back into the Gershwin circle. He began to spend so much of his time at the adjoining penthouse apartments of Gershwin and his brother Ira that Levant referred to himself as "a penthouse beachcomber." George Gershwin's forays into the concert hall inspired Levant to compose concert music, and he began work on a piece called *Sonatina for Piano*.

Levant met composer Aaron Copland at a Gershwin gathering and played for him the first movement of his *Sonatina*. Copland invited Levant to perform the piece at the First Festival of Contemporary American Music at Yaddo, the artist's retreat in Saratoga Springs, New York. Levant's piece was favorably reviewed at the festival, which took place on 30 April and 1 May 1932, but Levant was uncomfortable among serious composers and fled the event. He believed that his Broadway background made him suspect in the eyes of European-trained composers. That same year he both married and divorced showgirl Barbara Smith, known by her stage name, Barbara Wooddell.

Levant faced a tug-of-war between high and low culture. He was as much in love with Tin Pan Alley and Hollywood as he was with the concert stage. While studying composition with Arnold Schoenberg in Los Angeles in 1935–1938, Levant composed a truncated opera called "Carnival" for the 20th Century–Fox film *Charlie Chan at the Opera* (1936).

Levant's stint as the youngest—and funniest—member of the three-man panel of experts on the "Information, Please!" radio quiz show (along with Franklin P. Adams and John Kieran, with Clifton Fadiman as the program's moderator) brought him national celebrity. It was this popularity, combined with his brilliant renditions of Gershwin's *Rhapsody in Blue* and Concerto in F at two Gershwin memorial programs following the composer's death in 1937, that prompted concert managers to seek out Levant as a guest artist. From 1940 through 1953 Levant toured the country specializing in Gershwin's piano works, drawing tremendous crowds and praise from the critics. His annual all-Gershwin summer concerts at Lewisohn Stadium in New York City drew audiences of 18,000 to 22,000. During this period Levant was the highest-paid concert performer in the nation and the first concert pianist to receive a percentage of the house. He had remarried in 1939, to actress June Gilmartin, who used the stage name June Gale. They had three children.

Important critics like the composer Virgil Thomson believed that Levant had limited himself to "a provincial career" by specializing in Gershwin's piano music. The composer David Diamond, however, thought that Levant's gifts as a pianist were "in the genius category," but that forging a world-class reputation as a concert artist did not mean enough to Levant so he never entered the echelon inhabited by pianists such as Vladimir Horowitz and Artur Rubinstein. Again, Levant's conflicting allegiances to high and low culture may have kept him from the rigors of attaining the highest achievement as a concert artist.

During the late 1930s and early 1940s Levant continued to pursue serious composing. Most of his compositions reflected his dual allegiances to opposite ends of the spectrum: Schoenberg's serial music and Gershwin's Broadway-inspired melodies. Of the ten compositions Levant completed, the three most performed have been his "Dirge" (the second movement of an uncompleted suite for piano and orchestra), which was written to commemorate Gershwin's death; *Caprice for Orchestra*, recorded in 1993 on Angel Records; and *Sonatina for Piano*. Los Angeles Symphony conductor Michael Tilson Thomas conducted Levant's *Dirge* in the 1970s and described the piece as a work "of high seriousness," noting, however, that Levant always made light of his own compositions. Levant suffered horribly from stage nerves and never enjoyed concertizing.

Levant appeared in thirteen Hollywood films from 1929 through 1955. His roles capitalized on his popularity as a wisecracking piano player. Invariably he played a version of himself. In the biographical film about Gershwin, *Rhapsody in Blue* (Warner Bros., 1945), Levant literally played Oscar Levant, George Gershwin's "best friend." The films in which he appeared uncannily reflected Levant's real life. In *Dance of Life* (Paramount, 1929), he played a piano player and man-about-town, the best friend of a rising star (not unlike his relationship with Gershwin). In 1946

Humoresque (Warner Bros.) also depicted a friendship between two musicians: Levant's role as pianist/best friend to John Garfield's struggling, Lower East Side violinist. Levant provided much of his own dialogue in his films, and his comments on the life of a concert artist in *Humoresque* are revealing of his misgivings about the musician's life. ("Who goes to debuts? Relatives and enemies," he bitterly tells Garfield in one scene.)

Levant appeared in a trilogy of Arthur Freed musicals, beginning with *The Barkleys of Broadway* (MGM, 1949), written by his friends Betty Comden and Adolph Green. He played Ezra Millar, a dyspeptic pianist and hypochondriac. In *An American in Paris* (MGM, 1951), directed by Vincente Minnelli and starring Gene Kelly, Levant played an expatriate composer and pianist. He invented the "ego fantasy" scene in which he plays every instrument in the orchestra in a performance of the third movement of Gershwin's Concerto in F—a fantasy sequence often cited as one of the most original scenes of this landmark musical. *The Band Wagon* (MGM, 1953), also directed by Minnelli from a screenplay by Comden and Green, began filming six weeks after Levant suffered a heart attack; he was barely able to make it through some of the more arduous song-and-dance numbers, such as the famous "That's Entertainment" scene.

A grueling concert schedule and run-ins with James C. Petrillo, the autocratic head of the American Federation of Musicians, probably contributed to Levant's heart attack, which virtually ended his concert career and led to his decade-long addiction to Demerol and other prescription drugs. He was repeatedly hospitalized for drug addiction and for bipolar illness, which erupted during the 1950s. His final film, *The Cobweb* (MGM, 1955), also directed by Minnelli, was set in a private psychiatric hospital and again mirrored the life Levant was living as a psychiatric patient in various Los Angeles institutions.

Levant emerged from retirement between hospital stays to appear in 1958 on his own weekly television talk show, "The Oscar Levant Show," a local program on KCOP-TV and then on KHJ-TV that grew out of a handful of earlier appearances on similar shows. The show was a chaotic but stimulating affair; Levant invited a heady mix of figures from high and low culture as his guests—from writers such as Christopher Isherwood and Aldous Huxley to sports figures Gene Tunney and Maxie "Slapsie" Rosenbloom. Levant even had one of his psychiatrists as a guest. Because he was simultaneously undergoing treatment for drug addiction, depression, and mania while doing his program, Levant's behavior and remarks were sometimes bizarre. He was twice thrown off the air: once for insulting the show's sponsor and once for an unprintable comment about Marilyn Monroe.

Levant never planned his remarks. His wit was spontaneous and often surprised even him. When his program went off the air in 1958, he was invited to appear on Jack Paar's "The Tonight Show" and later on "The Jack Paar Show" as a guest. But his poor health and his uncontrolled blinking and facial grimaces shocked many people, as did his frank remarks about his struggles with drug abuse and mental illness. Levant holds the dubious honor of being the first celebrity to talk about his emotional and mental problems on television, a behavior that later became commonplace. "I was thrown out of a mental hospital. I depressed the other patients," he joked. "I used to suffer from deep apathy. Then I relapsed into deep depression. Gee, how I longed for those deep apathy days!" Levant died in Los Angeles of a heart attack.

Though Levant's approximately 100 recordings for Columbia Masterworks are out of print, his performances of Gershwin's works for piano have been released in compact disc format as *Oscar Levant/Gershwin* (Sony Masterworks). The singer and archivist Michael Feinstein has compiled additional recordings of Levant on *Oscar Levant Plays Levant and Gershwin* (DRG Records), which includes Levant's playing of his *Sonatina for Piano* and his Piano Concerto. Levant's witty remarks continue to be quoted and to appear in print in places such as *The Curmudgeon Calendar* and other compilations of quotes on various subjects.

Levant's final legacy is as an "American original," a personality produced by the striving of concert music–loving Jewish immigrants new to this country, cross-fertilized by the burgeoning pop culture of the 1930s, 1940s, and 1950s. Levant may have been the last major cultural figure who was completely at home in both high and low culture.

• Levant's papers are in the Cinema Special Collections of the Cinema-Television Archive at the University of Southern California in Los Angeles. The original transcripts that made up his second book, *The Memoirs of an Amnesiac* (1965), are housed in the Oscar Levant Archive at the Music Division of the Library of Congress, Washington, D.C. The first complete biography is Sam Kashner and Nancy Schoenberger, *A Talent for Genius, the Life and Times of Oscar Levant* (1994). Levant's own three books are *A Smattering of Ignorance* (1940), *The Memoirs of an Amnesiac* (1965), and *The Unimportance of Being Oscar* (1968). Articles written with particular insight into Levant's character are Jonathan Lieberson, "The Unimportance of Being Oscar," *New York Review of Books*, 20 Nov. 1986, pp. 36–38; Irving Kolodin, "The Trouble with Oscar," *Saturday Review*, 9 Sept. 1972; Adolph Green's eulogy, "Oscar Levant, 1906–1972," *New York Times*, 27 Aug. 1972, sec. 2, p. 3; and Maurice Zolotow, "Lucky Oscar, Sour Genius of the Keyboard," *Saturday Evening Post*, 21 Oct. 1950, pp. 24–25ff. On Levant's relationship with Arnold Schoenberg, see Walter B. Bailey, "Oscar Levant and the Program for Schoenberg's Piano Concerto," *Journal of the Arnold Schoenberg Institute* 6, no. 1 (June 1982): 56–79. A lively account of Levant's behavior in Hollywood in the 1930s is recounted in Harpo Marx and Roland Barber, *Harpo Speaks!* (1961; repr. 1985). An obituary is in the *New York Times*, 15 Aug. 1972.

NANCY SCHOENBERGER

LEVENE, Phoebus Aaron Theodor (25 Feb. 1869–6 Sept. 1940), organic and biochemist, was born Fishel Aaronovitch Levin in Sagor, Russia, the son of Solom Levin, a shirtmaker, and Etta Brick. In 1873 the family moved to St. Petersburg, where in 1886 Levene became one of the few Jewish students admitted to the Imperial Medical Academy. Faced with rising anti-Semitism, the family immigrated to New York City in 1891. Levene returned to St. Petersburg to complete his examinations and received an M.D. in 1891. For the next four years he practiced medicine in the Russian Jewish colony of New York.

An interest in organic and physiological chemistry prompted Levene to become a special student at the Columbia School of Mines and the College of Physicians and Surgeons. In 1896 he abandoned medical practice for a research career at the New York State Hospital Pathological Institute. He soon contracted tuberculosis and entered the Saranac Lake sanitarium; he then spent two years recuperating in Davos, Switzerland. In 1899, shortly after resuming his career, the Pathological Institute closed for reorganization. From 1900 to 1902 he was a chemist investigating the tubercle bacillus and began study of nucleic acids at the Saranac Lake Laboratory for the Study of Tuberculosis and from 1902 to 1905 at the reopened Pathological Institute. He had published eighty-four papers on protein and nucleic acid chemistry when the new Rockefeller Institute for Medical Research selected him in 1905 for its first group of scientists. In 1907 he became a life member and director of the division of chemistry. On a 1919 visit to Saranac Lake he met Anna Margaret Erickson. They married in 1920; the couple had no children.

Levene, a prolific scientist, produced more than 700 publications. He devoted his career to the isolation, characterization, synthesis, and structure of the chemical constituents of tissues. He was best known for his research on conjugated proteins—proteins with a nonprotein prosthetic group. From 1900 to 1940 he examined glycoproteins, mucoproteins, and nucleoproteins to discern the nature of their nonprotein constituents. He discovered that the glycoproteins, the substances responsible for blood group specificity, contained two nitrogenous carbohydrates, chitosamine and chondrosamine, which he isolated and characterized between 1914 and 1924. This was a new field, requiring him to develop his own methods of isolation, synthesis, and structure determination. Especially important were his spatial configuration studies of these optically active substances. These sugars existed in mirror image forms. Levene thus had to determine not only their composition but also which form was present in the natural product by correlating their optical activity from the rotation of polarized light when passed through their crystals, with structure. In lengthy and tedious research lasting ten years he established a series of relationships leading to the spatial configuration of chitosamine and chondrosamine as 2-amino-2-deoxy-D-glucose and 2-amino-2-deoxy-D-galactose, respectively. The mucoproteins were found in connective tissues, membranes, and cell walls. Levene demonstrated that the nonprotein prosthetic group consisted of amino sugars and uronic acids, the latter being carbohydrates with a carboxylic acid group. During

the 1920s and 1930s he synthesized these and established their structures. His investigations represented fundamental carbohydrate chemistry and also proved essential to his other lifelong task, the chemistry of the nucleic acids.

In 1900 much was unclear about the nucleic acids. Albrecht Kossel in Germany had shown that these nonprotein components of nucleoproteins found in the cell nucleus contained purine and pyrimidine bases (compounds containing carbon and nitrogen in a ring), a carbohydrate, and phosphoric acid. No one knew how these entities were linked in the nucleic acid or the nature of the carbohydrate. Through a brilliant use of organic chemical methods, Levene unraveled the details of structure and bonding. In 1909 he isolated from beef muscle nucleic acid a carbohydrate of unknown nature, subsequently proving it to be the five-carbon sugar, D-ribose, the mirror image of the known L-ribose. He also revealed the nature of the linkages between base, sugar, and acid, naming this tripartite unit a "nucleotide" and the base-sugar portion a "nucleoside." In 1912 he isolated from yeast nucleic acid four nucleotides, each one having D-ribose linked to either adenine, cytosine, guanine, or uracil base, a finding that became the basis for his erroneous belief that nucleic acids were tetranucleotides or small multiples thereof. Later scientists demonstrated that nucleic acids were giant molecules and had no fixed, repeating sequence of nucleotides.

In 1929 Levene isolated from thymus nucleic acid a pentose different from D-ribose. In 1930 he proved it was 2-deoxy-D-ribose, a hitherto unknown carbohydrate. Thenceforth, he classified nucleic acids by their carbohydrate entity as either ribonucleic acid (RNA) or deoxyribonucleic acid (DNA). By 1935 he established that the structural form of the carbohydrate in nucleosides was a furanose ring, the five-membered ring structure of carbohydrates. Levene thus provided biochemists with reliable methods to isolate and characterize nucleic acid components, discovered the two sugars of nucleic acids, established the notion of nucleotide subunits, and distinguished nucleic acids into DNA and RNA types.

Levene retired in 1939. He was a short, thin person, with a long, heavy shock of hair, a mustache, deepset eyes, and dark complexion. Of strongly liberal views, he had a wide circle of friends from both the scientific and artistic worlds. He had a keen interest in contemporary art and purchased paintings from young artists he hoped had a future. He played the violin, attended the New York Philharmonic concerts and the New York theater, and was well read in literature. He traveled extensively and frequently to Europe but never in the United States. He died in New York City.

Levene was a pioneer in the application of organic chemical methods to the materials found in tissue. A charter member in 1906 of the American Society of Biological Chemists, he helped establish biochemical research in America, leaving a legacy to biochemists of important findings and methods concerning the constituents of tissue.

• Levene's correspondence and other unpublished material are in the Rockefeller University Archives. Among his more important monographs and reviews are *Hexosamines, Their Derivatives and Mucins and Mucoids* (1922); *Hexosamines and Mucoproteins* (1925); *Nucleic Acids*, with Lawrence W. Bass (1931), the first major exposition of the subject; "The Chemistry of the Carbohydrates and the Glycosides," *Annual Review of Biochemistry*, with A. L. Raymond, 1 (1932): 213–46; and "Rotatory Dispersion," *Organic Chemistry*, ed. Henry Gilman (1938), pp. 1779–1849, an important review of optical rotation and spatial configuration. Biographical essays and analyses of his contributions by his Rockefeller associates include those by Donald D. Van Slyke and Walter A. Jacobs in National Academy of Sciences, *Biographical Memoirs* 23 (1945): 75–126, which has a bibliography of his publications; R. Stuart Tipson in *Advances in Carbohydrate Chemistry* 12 (1957): 1–12; and Melville Wolfrom in *Great Chemists*, ed. Eduard Farber (1961), pp. 1313–24. Joseph S. Fruton, *Molecules and Life* (1972), contains a fine study of Levene's nucleic acid research, and his "P. A. Levene and 2-deoxy-D-ribose," *Trends in Biochemical Science* 4 (Feb. 1979): 49–50, is a fiftieth anniversary commemoration of the carbohydrate of DNA. George W. Gray, "The Mother Molecules of Life," *Harper's Magazine*, Apr. 1952, pp. 51–61, is a popular account of nucleic acid research and includes a lucid exposition of Levene's findings. An obituary is in the *New York Times*, 7 Sept. 1940.

ALBERT B. COSTA

LEVENE, Sam (28 Aug. 1905–28 Dec. 1980), actor, was born Sam Levine in Russia, the son of Harry Levine and Bethsheba Weiner. In 1907 the family immigrated to the United States, where Sam was educated at Stuyvesant High School in New York City, graduating in 1923. Levene planned to join the family garment business but felt his heavy accent and self-consciousness hindered his salesmanship. In order to advance his sales career, Levene enrolled in night classes at the American Academy of Dramatic Art. Encouraged by Levene's progress, his instructor, Charles Jehlinger, offered him a full scholarship, and Levene began his formal training.

Levene studied at the academy until 1927, making his professional debut in New York as William Thompson in *Wall Street* in April of that year. His early career was marked by a string of short-lived, unsuccessful productions, including *Jarnegan* (Sept. 1928), *Tin Pan Alley* (Nov. 1928), *Solitaire* (Mar. 1929), *Street Scene* (May 1929), and *The Wonder Boy* (Oct. 1931). Levene (who had to change the spelling of his last name to join Actor's Equity because another Sam Levine was already on the roster) also appeared as Max Kane in George S. Kaufman's *Dinner at Eight*, which opened in October 1932 at the Music Box Theatre and ran for 232 performances. After his success in *Dinner at Eight*, Levene worked steadily in well-received productions for the next three years, including performances as Gabby Sloan in *The Milky Way*, which opened in May 1934, and as Patsy, one of his most successful roles, in *Three Men on a Horse*, which opened in January 1935 and ran for two years.

After *Three Men on a Horse* closed, Levene made his film debut in the cinematic version of the play in 1936,

the success of which led to his next film, *After the Thin Man*, released that same year. Although he appeared successfully on stage as Gordon Miller in *Room Service* in May 1937, for the next few years Levene worked primarily in film. From 1938 until 1979 Levene appeared in more than forty films, often playing the role of the somewhat successful gambler, a character type he had made popular in *Three Men on a Horse*, in movies such as *Shopworn Angel* (1938), *Golden Boy* (1938), *The Big Street* (1942), *Boomerang* (1947), *Brute Force* (1947), *Crossfire* (1947), *Designing Woman* (1957), *Sweet Smell of Success* (1957), *Act One* (1963), and *Last Embrace* (1979). Levene also played the role of the typical New Yorker in a number of World War II films, including *Destination Unknown* (1942), *Action in the North Atlantic* (1943), *Gung Ho!* (1943), and *The Purple Heart* (1944).

Never becoming a "star" on the stage or on the screen, Levene traveled frequently between New York and Hollywood in order to secure roles. In addition to his film credits, he appeared in more than fifty stage productions in New York and often on tour. Other than his role in *Three Men on a Horse*, Levene is best known for his performance as Sidney Black in *Light up the Sky*, which he originated in 1948 and also played during revivals in 1970, 1974, and 1975; Nathan Detroit in *Guys and Dolls* (1950); and Al Lewis in Neil Simon's *The Sunshine Boys* (1972–1974). Although the last two roles were his most popular, Levene lost the movie roles to bigger stars. Levene was nominated for a Tony Award for best actor for his portrayal of Dr. Aldo Meyer in *The Devil's Advocate* in 1961. Levene married Constance Hoffman in 1953; the couple had one son. Levene died in New York City.

When asked to describe his acting technique, Levene replied, "Hard work, hard work, and more hard work" (*New York Times*, 29 Dec. 1980); however in the later years of his career he blamed his inability to gain commercial success on his lack of study, which he believed made it impossible for him to have the range other star actors possessed. As a result he was often typecast into the "hustling, fast-talking, street-wise ethnic roles" for which he is best known. A perfectionist who seemed rarely satisfied with his own performances, Levene remained his toughest critic. Although he enjoyed acting, Levene called the theatre "a heartbreaking business at best." The insecurity of the profession weighed heavily on him, especially in his final years, prompting him to say, "So I've been an actor . . . So what? . . . If I had invented penicillin, then I might be able to say something" (*New York Times*, 29 Dec. 1980). Commenting on Levene's performance in the 1969 revival of *Three Men on a Horse*, a critic for the *New York Times* said Levene was "still looking like a man whose eyes have been allocated the wrong size eyelid [Levene was known for his bushy eyebrows and mustache], still mugging, double taking, offering his celebrated impersonation of an actor impersonating a character who has based himself on Damon Runyan, Mr. Levene is great. No one else plays Mr. Levene like Mr. Levene does" (29 Dec. 1980).

• Biographical and professional information on Levene may be found in *Who's Who in the Theatre* (1981); *Annual Obituary* (1980); Evelyn Truitt, *Who Was Who on Screen* (1983); David Ragan, *Who's Who in Hollywood* (1992); and *The Cambridge Guide to American Theatre* (1993). Levene's obituary is in the *New York Times*, 29 Dec. 1980.

MELISSA VICKERY-BAREFORD

LEVENSON, Sam (28 Dec. 1911–27 Aug. 1980), comedian, author, and educator, was born Samuel Levenson in New York City, the son of Hyman Levenson, a tailor, and Rebecca Fishelman. Levenson attended Brooklyn College (now part of the City University of New York), graduating with a B.A. in 1934. From that year until 1946 he taught Spanish in Brooklyn high schools, also serving as a guidance counselor for the final five years. In 1936 he married his childhood sweetheart, Esther Levine, with whom he had two children. His former students and academic advisees still remember him as a warm and funny teacher who took a personal interest in them and their future.

These qualities of warmth and wit were also reflected in Levenson's work as a humorist, a career he at first pursued on a part-time basis while continuing to teach. From 1940 to 1946 Levenson took jobs as an entertainer, doing stand-up ethnic folk humor at Catskill Mountain resorts and in New York City nightclubs and serving as a master of ceremonies at community events until he could find enough personal appearance and television work to allow him to leave his teaching job. The live monologues Levenson did during these years were designed and performed for people whose background and social status were very much like his own; he brought out the funny side of growing up poor and Jewish for people who had been there themselves and whose culture valued the ability to laugh at one's own condition. The themes of these early monologues included family relationships, straitened economic circumstances, school, and neighborhood, all informed with a nostalgic warmth that only a dry wit kept from degenerating into sentimentality.

After a very successful debut on Ed Sullivan's "Toast of the Town" (1949), Levenson became a television personality, performing on most of the major variety and comedy shows of the 1950s, as well as his own program, "The Sam Levenson Show" (1951–1952). In common with many other comedians of his generation, he faced the problem that, in order to continue to be funny, he had to translate the in-group specifics of his brand of ethnic humor into a form accessible to a predominantly Gentile middle-American audience. The monologues continued their gentle approach to the lighter side of life in a poor family, but the experience was now universalized so that Jewish references—as well as the rich sprinkling of Yiddish words and phrases—disappeared. Levenson's style, however—his body language, gestures, and accent—remained those of a Jewish New Yorker raised in an environment where Yiddish was the first language. As a panelist and game show participant on such shows as "The Match Game" and "To Tell the Truth," he tended to rely on one-liners and wisecracks, bolstered by the warm persona that had come through in the monologues.

Levenson's first book, *Meet the Folks* (1948), published just before the comedian made the transition from nightclubs and other local venues to national television, is subtitled *A Session of American-Jewish Humor*. The rest of his books were published between 1966 and 1979, after retiring from his career as a regular television performer. In these books, Levenson gives evidence of having taken a further step in his development, from "wit" to "wisdom." Although family, observed from the point of view of someone who has played the roles of son, brother, and father, remains central, there are fewer obvious ethnic references than in the first book and a greater tendency to generalize, even to moralize. Levenson's tone always remains good-humored, but the themes of his later writings often involve a curmudgeonly rejection of modern permissiveness in favor of old-fashioned self-control and external discipline. His approach is that of a cheery teacher, but the content of his philosophizing was likely to have its strongest appeal among those who already believed, like the author, that the culture of the 1960s and 1970s had gone too far and that the values of their own youth were really the best guide for the world of their maturity.

The personality that came across on stage and screen and in print was an accurate reflection of the personal warmth and humor commented on by almost everyone who knew Levenson. Offstage, he was active in organizations concerned with mental health, particularly that of children, and, through the B'nai Brith Anti-Defamation League, in Jewish community affairs. Levenson's last book, *You Don't Have to Be in Who's Who to Know What's What*, was published in 1979. He died in New York City.

• In addition to the books mentioned above, Levenson also published *Sex and the Single Child* (1969), reissued as *A Time for Innocence: A Kid's-Eye View of the Facts of Life* (1977); *In One Era and Out the Other* (1973); and *You Can Say That Again, Sam* (1975). *Everything but Money* (1966) was Levenson's closest approximation to a "regular" autobiography. An obituary is in the *New York Times*, 29 Aug. 1980.

LILLIAN S. ROBINSON

LEVENTHAL, Albert Rice (30 Oct. 1907–6 Jan. 1976), publisher, reporter, and author, was born in New York City, the son of Philip F. Leventhal and Ida Rice. Leventhal graduated from the University of Michigan with an A.B. in 1928. In that same year he joined the *Brooklyn Times-Union* as a reporter, where he wrote a column about one of his favorite activities, contract bridge. His ambitious nature led him to become the Sunday editor of the paper just two years later. In 1933 he was hired by Dick Simon as an assistant in the sales department of Simon's publishing company, Simon and Schuster. There are two versions of the story about how Leventhal came to be employed by Simon and Schuster. One claims that it was because of the skill he demonstrated when he agreed to play as a "fourth" in a game of bridge with Richard Simon. Another says that Jack Goodman, after completing a mediocre job interview with Simon, mentioned to Simon that he was on his way to the Cavendish Club for a game of contract bridge with his partner, Albert Leventhal. Simon was so impressed with the fact that both Goodman and Leventhal played at the Cavendish Club that he hired them both. In either case, Leventhal seemed to be a natural in the sales promotional field and quickly advanced to sales manager after five years with the company.

Leventhal married Janis H. Hilpp in 1934; they had three children. Shortly after his marriage, Leventhal became involved in developing the Golden Books division of Simon and Schuster (known today as Little Golden Books), which specialized in children's books. Initially Simon and Schuster was approached by Georges Duplaix, who was heavily involved in the mass production of low-cost comic-strip books from Western Printing and Lithographing Company. Duplaix's original idea was for full-color children's books, though he did not envision as low a price for the product as Leventhal proposed or such high-volume production. The production and marketing concept for Golden Books was largely based on the success of Pocket Books, the Simon and Schuster division that mass produced affordable books for adults. Leventhal believed that more parents would buy their children books if they were durable and yet inexpensive enough that it would not seem a great loss if the book were dropped in the bathtub accidentally. In 1942 Western Printing and Lithographing Company began producing the Golden Books division's full-color children's books for only a fraction of the cost of other children's books of the time. Little Golden Books soon became an international publishing phenomenon, appearing in nearly every language and country. In 1945 Leventhal became a partner in Sandpiper Press, the editorial end of Golden Books. In the years after World War II, as Dick Simon's health declined, Leventhal became increasingly involved with the daily operations of Simon and Schuster sales. He eventually became an executive vice president at Simon and Schuster in 1952.

In 1957, the same year that Leventhal resigned from Simon and Schuster, he wrote a review attributing the success of the Little Golden Books not only to their low price but also to their quality assembly, use of color, and well-known children's characters. However, Leventhal also noted that the market for Little Golden Books seemed to be reaching a point of saturation. Whether as a direct result of Leventhal's analysis or Western Printing's lucrative offer, Simon and Schuster sold Golden Books to Western Printing, effective as of 1958. In seeming contradiction to his market prediction for Little Golden Books, Leventhal joined Western Printing and Lithographing Company in 1958 and became the president of Golden Press Incorporated and Artists & Writers Press Division until 1968.

Leventhal's interests were not limited to the business aspect of publishing and to playing bridge. He was also a Civil War buff, and in 1973 his book *War* was published by Playboy Press. In this book Leventhal examines the effects of war and developing war technology on mankind through the use of carefully edited photographs of war scenes, beginning with the Crimean War and concluding with Vietnam. Each chapter is plainly titled for the war that it covers and is introduced by well-written, thought-provoking narratives that document the major historical events portrayed in the chapter. In his introduction Leventhal states that *War* is more a book of pictures than of words, relying on the age-old adage that a picture is worth a thousand words. Leventhal also published *War: The Camera's Battlefield View of Man's Most Terrible Adventure, from the First Photographer in the Crimea to Vietnam* (1975). He published *I Wish I'd Said That* (1934), *False Colors* (1941), and *Book Publishing in America* (1973) under the pseudonym Albert Rice.

Although he was successful as both a writer and an editor, Leventhal is most remembered for his remarkable career in the publishing industry, which influenced the direction of children's book publishing in the United States. His marketing and sales skills, contagious enthusiasm, and interpersonal skills led to many successful business ventures for the companies of which he was a part. Peter Schwed, author of *Turning the Pages*, remembers Leventhal and credits his energy, drive, and ambition for his ability to make a success of virtually any project he worked on. His first major success, the launching of Little Golden Books, occurred during his mid-thirties. Leventhal continued to remain actively involved in the publishing industry and was still demonstrating his keen ability to develop a sound project when he founded Vineyard Books in 1973, at the same time serving as president of the company until his death. He was a member of the board of directors of the American Book Publishers Council and a member of Phi Beta Kappa, Phi Kappa Phi, Zeta Beta Tau, and the Regency Club. Leventhal died in New York City.

• Although little has been written regarding Albert Rice Leventhal, some excellent biographical information about his career with Simon and Schuster may be found in Peter Schwed, *Turning the Pages* (1984). His obituary in the *New York Times*, 8 Jan. 1976, includes relatively detailed highlights of his life and career in the publishing industry.

L. ANNE CLARK DOHERTY

LEVER, Asbury Francis (5 Jan. 1875–28 Apr. 1940), congressman and agricultural policy maker, was born near Spring Hill, in Lexington County, South Carolina, the son of Asbury Francis Washington Lever and Mary Elvira Derrick, farmers. Educated in local schools, Lever graduated with honors from Newberry College in 1895. After teaching school for two years, he served from 1897 to 1901 as a private secretary to U.S. representative J. William Stokes, developing a reputation as someone who actively sought answers to constituent inquiries on agricultural issues. Lever graduated from Georgetown University Law School in 1899. He was a delegate to the South Carolina Democratic state conventions in 1896 and 1900 prior to his election in 1900 to the South Carolina House of Representatives from Lexington County.

Following Stokes's death in 1901, Lever was elected to his seat in Congress and was continuously reelected until his resignation on 1 August 1919 to become a member of the Federal Farm Loan Board on which he served until 1922. Highlights of his congressional career include chairing the House Committees on Education and Agriculture. In 1911 he married Lucille Butler; they had two children. In 1918 he made an abbreviated run for the U.S. Senate.

Lever's greatest contributions stem from agricultural legislation produced and enacted during his congressional tenure. The most prominent is the Smith-Lever Act of 1914, on which he collaborated with Georgia senator Hoke Smith. This statute established the Cooperative Extension Service within the U.S. Department of Agriculture to disseminate agricultural research knowledge from land-grant universities to farmers in the form of field demonstrations, publications, and instruction. The initial appropriation for this legislation was $600,000, with each state receiving $10,000 annually. Federal funds were responsible for only 50 percent of the cost of extension service; the rest was provided by state, county, and local authorities. Implementation of this legislation saw county extension agents established in agriculturally important areas nationwide. The Extension Service played a particularly important role in expanding food production to meet American and European needs during World War I.

Lever's other prominent legislation includes the Cotton Warehouses Act (1914), which licensed cotton futures exchanges; the Cotton Futures Act (1914), which sought to regulate cotton speculation; and the Federal Farm Loan Act (1916), which created the Farm Credit Administration, federal land banks, the Productive Service Corporation, and other aspects of the rural credit system.

In 1922 Lever served as president of the First Carolinas Joint Stock Land Bank and on the boards of trustees for Clemson College and Newberry College. In 1930 he ran for governor but was forced to drop out of the campaign for health reasons. In 1933 he became director for the Farm Credit Administration, Southeast Region, and held that position until his death. In early 1940 former president Herbert Hoover appointed him South Carolina director of the Finnish Relief Fund. Lever's interest in agricultural issues and the development of the Cooperative Extension Service remained throughout his life.

Lever died at his home near Charleston, South Carolina. He was a major figure in pre–New Deal federal agricultural policy making. The Smith-Lever Act is still a cornerstone of the land-grant university system, benefiting American farmers and the interests of domestic and international consumers.

• Lever's personal papers are in the Special Collections Department of Clemson University's Robert Muldrow Cooper Library. Secondary sources include Congressional Research Service, *A Brief History of the Committee on Agriculture, Nutrition, and Forestry, United States Senate, and Landmark Agricultural Legislation: 1825–1986* (1986); Dewey W. Grantham, Jr., *Hoke Smith and the Politics of the New South* (1958); John K. Campbell, *Reclaiming a Lost Heritage: Land Grant and Other Higher Education Initiatives for the Twenty-first Century* (1995); and USDA, Cooperative Extension Service Circular 335, *Asbury Francis Lever: A Tribute* (1940). Obituaries are in the Columbia, S.C., *State* and the *Congressional Record*, both 29 Apr. 1940.

BERT CHAPMAN

LEVERETT, John (July 1616–16 Mar. 1679), Puritan leader and governor of Massachusetts, was born in Boston, Lincolnshire, England, the son of Thomas Leverett and Anne Fisher. Thomas Leverett was a landowner and a protector in England of the great Puritan minister John Cotton. Through an appearance before a bishop's court that had suspended Cotton from his pulpit, Thomas Leverett succeeded in having him restored to his church. Leverett, his wife, and three children came to New England in 1633 and settled in Boston, where Cotton preached. John Leverett married Hannah Hudson in 1639, four years after she emigrated to Massachusetts with her parents. This marriage, which brought John a sizable dowry, produced four children. Hannah Hudson Leverett died in 1646, and the next year John married Sarah Sedgwick, with whom he had fourteen children.

To vote in Massachusetts and to take part in political and governmental life, one had to be a freeman; to become a freeman one had to be a church member. John Leverett joined the Boston Church in 1639 and the next year was made a freeman. Sometime in these years, probably early in the 1640s, he became a merchant, trading outside of New England, an occupation that brought him modest wealth. Public life proved to be more important to him, if his public service revealed his inclinations, than commerce and land owning. Certainly he made his name in the military and governmental service. In 1642 the Massachusetts government sent him on a mission to the Narrangansetts led by Chief Miantonomo, to discover whether the Indians were in fact about to attack English settlements. The mission was successful—no plot was discovered, and no military operation followed. Shortly after the civil war began in England, Leverett returned to the home country, where he served as a commander in the army fighting Charles I. After four years of service Leverett came back to Massachusetts in 1648. Three years later he was elected in the General Court.

In 1653 Leverett was in England again, this time with Robert Sedgwick in search of military aid against the Dutch in New Netherland. England was at war with the Netherlands at this time, and the Puritan colonies at New Haven, Plymouth, and Connecticut were expected by Oliver Cromwell's government to join Massachusetts in an attack on the Dutch colony. Massachusetts, however, lagged in the effort, and Leverett and Sedgwick, apparently in dismay, decided to seek English aid: Cromwell obliged by supplying them with four ships, 200 soldiers, and a commission to raise other forces in New England for an expedition against New Netherland. The war ended in 1654 at the time Cromwell sent out these ships and troops. His purpose must have been to remind the Massachusetts Bay Colony of its allegiance to the protectorate. Ships and troops arrived in Boston just before the news of peace and soon discovered that they had no war to fight. Sedgwick, not one to sit idle, sailed the fleet to the north against the French, capturing their forts at Penobscot, St. John, and Port Royal. Leverett held a command in this effort and with his colleague received reimbursement from Cromwell for his services.

Leverett's public life intensified in the next twenty-five years, and his land holding increased as the General Court rewarded him for his efforts. The variety of assignments he was asked to take on reflects the public trust in his abilities. In 1655 the General Court appointed him colonial agent to England. His instructions in 1660 at the accession of Charles II included strangely inconsistent orders to argue strongly for Massachusetts's privileges but to deny that he had power to negotiate. Leverett reported to the General Court that "the general vogue of the people is that a governor will be sent over," a warning that the Crown intended to assert its control over the colony. In the argument with royal officials over the division of authority between England and Massachusetts, Leverett may have threatened at one point to deliver Massachusetts to the Spanish. Leverett came back to Boston in 1662, before such matters were resolved—the resolution was achieved long after his death—and the next year took up his duties in the General Court, where he was elected Speaker. Between 1665 and 1670 he sat in the upper house, the Council, and in 1671 was made deputy governor. He also held the rank of major general in the Massachusetts forces for ten years (1663–1673). His final service was as governor, a position to which he was elected in 1673 and held until his death. In office, Leverett soon faced a major uprising of Indians in King Philip's War. His response was to give direction to local forces and to hold New England together.

In June 1676, when Edward Randolph, an agent sent out by Charles II's ministers, demanded that Massachusetts officials enforce the Navigation Acts and acknowledge English supremacy, Leverett and all but three of the magistrates resisted. Randolph delivered a letter to the governor and the magistrates in a meeting in which he was snubbed by the refusal of all but three of the Massachusetts men to remove their hats. And during his stay, Leverett, who refused to take an oath to administer the Navigation Acts, told Randolph in effect that Parliament's laws bound Massachusetts only when the colony decided that its interests were served by the laws.

Leverett's life illustrates much of the strength and purpose of Puritans in Massachusetts. The seventeenth-century disposition was to cling to the original Massachusetts Bay Company charter of 1629, which the first settlers brought with them to New England. These people were determined to establish a church and state that kept largely free of England's control. Leverett accepted the vision of the Puritan founders and placed himself in its service throughout his career.

• Important sources included Jacob B. Moore, *Lives of the Governors of New Plymouth, and Massachusetts Bay* (1851); N. B. Shurtleff, ed., *Records of the Governor and Company of the Massachusetts Bay in New England, 1628–1686* (5 vols., 1853–1854; repr. 1968), especially vols. 1 and 4; and R. N. Toppan and A. T. Goodrick, eds., *Edward Randolph, . . . Letters and Official Papers* (7 vols., 1898–1909). There is no complete modern life, but important information and insights are available in Michael G. Hall, *Edward Randolph and the American Colonies, 1676–1703* (1960), and Richard Dunn, *Puritans and Yankees* (1962).

ROBERT MIDDLEKAUFF

LEVERETT, John (25 Aug. 1662–3 May 1724), president of Harvard College, was born in Boston, Massachusetts, the son of Hudson Leverett, an attorney, and Sarah Payton (or Peyton); he was the grandson of John Leverett, a governor of Massachusetts (1672–1679). Leverett studied at the Boston Latin School under the renowned master Ezekiel Cheever. He graduated from Harvard College with an A.B. in 1680, at which occasion he delivered the salutatory oration in Latin. He read theology and irregularly preached for several years.

In September 1685 Leverett and William Brattle were appointed the two resident fellow tutors at Harvard; Leverett held this position for a dozen years. While President Increase Mather took leave to secure a new colony charter in England (1688–1692), Leverett and Brattle managed the affairs of the college. They revived the practice of disputations, whereby students debated topics in the great hall, and they introduced the reading of Anglican authors. Henry Newman, a pupil under Leverett, later wrote that Leverett and Brattle "made more Proselytes to the Church of England than any two men ever did that liv'd in America" (Kenneth Silverman, *The Life and Times of Cotton Mather* [1984], p. 216). In 1692 Harvard granted Leverett a bachelor of divinity degree.

While a fellow tutor, Leverett studied law. He left Harvard in 1696 to become a practicing attorney, and he also went into politics. From 1696 to 1702 he served in the Massachusetts House of Representatives, representing Cambridge; in 1700 he was elected Speaker of the House. He was also a justice of the peace and briefly a judge in the Court of Admiralty. In 1702 Leverett became a judge of the Superior Court and of Probate Court for Middlesex County. He owed these appointments to his close friend Governor Joseph Dudley. In 1706 Leverett became a member of the Council, the upper house of the General Court (legislature).

In 1697 Leverett married Margaret Rogers Berry, the daughter of former Harvard president John Rogers. They had nine children, six of whom died in infancy, before she died in 1720. Not long after her death, Leverett married Sarah Crisp Harris; they had no children.

Leverett, as an Indian commissioner from Massachusetts, attended a conference with the Iroquois at Albany in 1704; the meeting failed to produce an Iroquois entry into the war on the side of the British. He was a lieutenant in the Ancient and Honorable Artillery Company, but his only active military service was to raise and command a company of volunteers for an unsuccessful expedition against the French at Port Royal in Nova Scotia in 1707. Finding Port Royal reinforced, the New England force turned around and went home. In 1709 Leverett served as Governor Dudley's emissary to negotiate with Governor John Lovelace of New York for military cooperation between Massachusetts and New York on the frontier and for an invasion of Canada.

To fill the vacant office of president of Harvard upon the death of Samuel Willard, the Harvard Corporation, consisting of the fellows and officials of the school, voted on 28 October 1707 to recommend Leverett for the position; he received eight votes, Increase Mather three, Cotton Mather one, and William Brattle one, with one person not voting. He also had the backing of the governor as well as thirty-nine ministers. Cotton Mather, who opposed any layman in the presidency, led his own campaign against the appointment of Leverett. The General Court, which had to ratify the decision, split, with the Council in favor of Leverett and the House against. With Governor Dudley announcing that the Harvard charter of 1650 would be revived (thus denying royal control over the institution), the House reversed itself and on 6 December 1707 agreed with the Council for Leverett's appointment. Leverett was inaugurated president in January 1708.

Leverett is credited with transforming Harvard from a divinity school into a secular institution. He showed an affinity for the Anglican "Cambridge Platonists," who sought to fuse together reason and God and to demonstrate faith by devotion and purity in living. Representative of this group was Henry More, whose *Enchiridion Ethicum* was introduced into the Harvard curriculum. Leverett kept close ties with the Anglican missionary agency in America, the Society for the Propagation of the Gospel; moreover, the Anglican church recruited ministers from Harvard graduates. Cotton Mather, the strict Puritan, commented that Leverett might as well have handed over Harvard to the bishop of London. Leverett introduced the study of French and Hebrew and revived a former exercise of having students translate scripture from one ancient language to another; he also reinstated evening prayers. Although Leverett continued to allow the boxing of ears of delinquent students, Harvard came under criticism for laxity in discipline and the often "riotous behaviour" of the pupils. The first college periodical, the *Telltale*, began publishing in 1721. Leverett expanded enrollment and the endowment. By 1718 124 students were in residence at the college. Massachusetts Hall was erected in 1720.

Leverett's distancing Harvard from the influence of the Congregational clergy prompted the philanthropy of Thomas Hollis, a London merchant and devout Baptist. Hollis provided books for the library, funds for scholarships for poor students, and a large gift to endow a chair for a professor of divinity, with a candidate for this position not to be discriminated against because of "his belief and practice of adult baptism." The chair gift was accepted on Hollis's terms and named after him.

As president of Harvard, Leverett lived on the verge of poverty, being provided for only by his salary. He inherited, through his great-grandfather Thomas Leverett, a share of the huge Muscongus Patent in Maine, between the Kennebec and Penobscot rivers. Leverett helped to form the Lincolnshire Company for the development of the Maine lands, but nothing was accomplished during his lifetime, and the grant later wound up under the control of Samuel Waldo.

Leverett published no works (Cotton Mather referred to him after his death as an "infamous drone"), but he was elected a fellow of the Royal Society, London, on 11 March 1713. He died in Cambridge.

• The Harvard University Library has the John Leverett Papers and John Leverett's diary, 1703–1723. The *Harvard College Records, Publications of the Colonial Society of Massachusetts*, vols. 15–16 (1925), Robert W. Lovett, ed., *Documents from the Harvard University Archives, 1638–1750* (2 vols., 1975), and *Publications of the Colonial Society of Massachusetts*, vols. 49–50 (1975), have archival material for the period of Leverett's association with the college. A summary of Leverett's life is John L. Sibley, "John Leverett," *Biographical Sketches of Graduates of Harvard University*, vol. 3 (1885), pp. 180–98. For the family see "Genealogical Memoir of the Family of Rev. Nathaniel Rogers," *New England Historical and Genealogical Register* 6 (1851): 105–52, and Nathaniel B. Shurtleff, "Genealogical Notice of the Family of Elder Thomas Leverett," *New England Historical and Genealogical Register* 4 (1850): 121–36. The relationship of the college to the legislature during Leverett's administration (after 1715) is considered in *Journals of the House of Representatives of Massachusetts*, vols. 1–6 (1919–1925). Relevant studies of the college are Margery S. Foster, *"Out of Smalle Beginnings . . . ": An Economic History of Harvard College in the Puritan Period, 1636–1712* (1962); Samuel E. Morison, *Three Centuries of Harvard* (1936); and Josiah Quincy, *The History of Harvard University*, vol. 1 (1885). Leverett in a social context is discussed in M. Halsey Thomas, ed., *The Diary of Samuel Sewall* (2 vols., 1973). For Leverett's relative conservatism in religion and the Anglican connection, see Arthur D. Kaledin, "The Mind of John Leverett" (Ph.D. diss., Harvard Univ., 1965), and Norman Fiering, "The First American Enlightenment: Tillotson, Leverett, and Philosophical Anglicanism," *New England Quarterly* 54 (1981): 307–44. An obituary is in the *Boston Gazette*, 4–11 May 1724.

HARRY M. WARD

LE VERT, Octavia Celeste Walton (11 Aug. 1811–12 Mar. 1877), socialite and author, was born at the plantation home of her grandfather, "Bellevue," just outside Augusta, Georgia, the daughter of George Walton II, a wealthy lawyer and senior statesman, and Sally Minge Walker. (Le Vert's birth year has appeared in some sources as 1810 and 1820 and her death date as 13 March. The dates given here are the official dates printed on her tombstone and cemetery records.) Le Vert came from a family with generations of distinguished history. Her paternal grandfather, General George Walton, was a signer of the Declaration of Independence, and one of her grandmothers was the daughter of a British nobleman. Her family background, along with her upbringing, provided Le Vert with the status to be the socialite that she eventually became. While she was still a child, her father gained political prominence akin to that of his father. He moved the family to Pensacola, Florida, in 1921 so that he could assume the position of secretary of state under General Andrew Jackson, governor of Florida, whom he later succeeded. Under her father's governorship, Le Vert was given the task of naming the capital of Florida. She chose Tallahassee, the Seminole word for "beautiful land."

Having never attended an established school, Le Vert was cultivated intellectually and socially at home by her mother, her grandmother, and a Scottish tutor. She became proficient in French, Spanish, and Italian, with knowledge of Greek and Latin. In her youth her father relied on her to translate foreign papers. At fourteen Le Vert was presented to the marquis de Lafayette in place of her grandmother, and she conversed with him in French, charming him so that he called her a "truly wonderful child" and predicted for her a "brilliant career." In 1833–1834 she traveled to Washington, D.C., and attended sessions of Congress, taking such careful notes that Henry Clay, John C. Calhoun, and Daniel Webster sought her documentation of their speeches.

In 1835 the family moved to Alabama, and in 1836 Octavia married Henry Strachey Le Vert, a physician whose distinguished background was reminiscent of her own. They made their home in Mobile, Alabama, and had five children, of whom only two survived childhood.

Better known as Madame Le Vert, she had the breeding, poise, and ease of conversation that enabled her to become a worldwide celebrity. After her first trip to Europe in 1853, Le Vert turned her home into a place for social gatherings reminiscent of French "salons." Every Monday from eleven in the morning until eleven in the evening, guests and dignitaries visited. During her visit to Paris as the Alabama representative (named by the state's governor) to the great Paris Exposition of 1855, her hotel room became a meeting place for the international elite, a veritable "Tower of Babel." Washington Irving exhorted Le Vert to keep a journal, and the French poet Lamartine urged her to write an account of her travels, "a few souvenirs" to allow others to vicariously participate in her adventures. As she compiled her journals and her letters to her mother from trips taken to Europe in 1853 and 1855, she formed her only published work, *Souvenirs of Travel* (1858).

Although there are other travel narratives about Europe written by American women of prestige, Le Vert's ability to infiltrate the ranks of the political and literary front-runners of her day and to make the acquaintance of notables such as Queen Victoria, Pope Pius IX, Napoleon III, Empress Eugénie, Millard Fillmore, and Robert Browning and Elizabeth Browning set her account apart from others. Her vivid and enthusiastic prose style, combined with her social prominence, renders her text valuable as a historical record of manners and class privilege, as well as an insightful view of famous persons. A light, almost childish enthusiasm accompanied by erudition and an awareness of etiquette fills her pages, as in her description of the eruption of Mount Vesuvius: "Glorious news I write you, glorious news indeed! . . . the mountain! It was perfectly wonderful! Blazing and flaming like—but to what shall I compare it? In truth, it was like Shakespeare's Richard, 'itself alone'" (pp. 188–89). Her personal sketches are insightful and lucid, with the king of Naples described as "stern, hard, and cruel-looking" and Pope Pius IX, by contrast, as "an exceedingly handsome man" with a "genial manner, so honest and truthful."

During the Civil War, Le Vert openly opposed secession (although she always traveled with her mulatto slave) and aided both Yankee and Confederate soldiers in her home. By 1865 her husband had succumbed to illness, her family had fallen from riches, and her popularity had waned significantly. Under suspicion of being a Yankee spy, Le Vert moved north to New York and worked on two other manuscripts that were never published: "Souvenirs of Distinguished People" and "Souvenirs of the War." In her final years, having returned to Georgia, she made appearances as a public reader; helped found Sorosis, a pioneer women's club; and was instrumental in the preservation of "Mount Vernon," George Washington's beloved home. She died at the family plantation in Bellevue.

Written by the "magnolia flower of the South," Le Vert's book was one of the first from Alabama to gain national recognition. Her roles as social hostess and author/translator were complementary, creating in her person one who was emblematic of the southern belle—a First Lady of the South—and a distinguished contributor to America's history. Le Vert's reputation as a socialite often overshadowed her popularity as an author; yet it is precisely her position as a representative of the best that American society could offer that makes her two-volume work important.

• Colonel D. B. Dyer, owner of "Bellevue" in the late twentieth century, renamed the estate "Chateau Le Vert"; many scrapbooks with hundreds of letters from notable persons to Le Vert are kept there. A few selections from Le Vert's correspondence and diary have been published: Mrs. Thaddeus Horton, "Letters from Henry Clay to Madame Le Vert," *Uncle Remus's Magazine*, June 1907; "Madame Le Vert and Her Friends," *Uncle Remus's Magazine*, Aug. 1907; and "Madame Le Vert's Diary," *Alabama Historical Quarterly*, Spring 1941. Biographies include Frances Gibson Satterfield, *Madame Le Vert* (1987); C. Delaney, "Madame Octavia Walton Le Vert, 1810–1877" (M.A. thesis, Univ. of Alabama, 1952); and Corine Chadwick Stephens, "Madame Octavia Walton Le Vert"

(M.A. thesis, Univ. of Georgia, 1940). For biographical entries that include selections from her work, see *Library of Southern Literature*, vol. 8 (1907), and Mary Forrest, *Women of the South Distinguished in Literature* (1861). Fredrika Bremer recounts several days spent visiting Le Vert in Mobile in *Homes of the New World* (1853). Elizabeth F. Ellet, *The Queens of American Society* (1867), includes quotes about Le Vert by Lady Emmeline Stuart Wortley, a Turkish ambassador, personal slaves, Rev. John Pierpont, and various anonymous friends and writers. Other informative references include Virginia Peacock, *Famous American Belles of the Nineteenth Century* (1901); James Wood Davidson, *Living Writers of the South* (1869); and Benjamin Buford Williams, *A Literary History of Alabama* (1979).

SUSIE LAN CASSEL

LEVIN, Louis Hiram (13 Jan. 1866–21 Apr. 1923), social worker and journalist, was born in Charleston, South Carolina, the son of Harris Levin, a merchant, and Dora Levine, daughter of a rabbi. The Levin family moved to Maryland in 1871 and settled in Baltimore by 1876. Levin graduated in 1881 from Bryant and Stratton College. He later attended Baltimore University School of Law and graduated in 1896.

At first Levin worked as a bookkeeper and at night wrote poems, essays, and short stories. Then he met the Szold family, prominent in Baltimore's socially conscious Jewish community. When Rabbi Benjamin Szold's daughter Henrietta Szold (founder of Hadassah, a women's organization that sent nurses to Palestine) suggested in 1889 that the newly arrived East European Jews needed English classes, Levin offered to teach bookkeeping. Thus began his active commitment to meet the needs of Baltimore's Jewish community. With Henrietta Szold's encouragement, Levin became editor, in 1899, of the *Jewish Comment*, a newspaper published in Baltimore. Under his direction the paper became an outlet for Anglo-Jewish literature and commentary. His wife, Bertha Szold (Henrietta Szold's sister), whom he married in 1901, assisted him with the *Comment*. They had five children.

An early advocate of intra-ethnic harmony, Levin suggested the federation of all the German Jewish charities into one organization. When the merger occurred in 1906, Levin served as the first executive secretary of the Federated Jewish Charities of Baltimore. The following year he was elected vice president of the United Hebrew Charities, a federation of mostly East European Jewish groups. Attending the fifth biennial session of the National Conference of Jewish Charities in 1908, he then advocated the merger of these two charitable groups, a feat he accomplished by 1921, when he was elected executive secretary of the combined Associated Jewish Charities of Baltimore. Levin also led the way in advocating the professionalization of social work in a 1910 paper he delivered at the sixth biennial session of the National Conference of Jewish Charities in St. Louis. He championed preventive social work, a system that divided the city into beats in which a resident social worker would disseminate useful information to families and direct people to the proper agencies.

In 1913 he established the Baltimore Jewish Court of Arbitration in which mediators familiar with talmudic law settled many disputes among the Jewish residents. The Jewish court alleviated the heavy volume of cases in the civil courts and also provided a social control mechanism that reflected the cultural values of the Jewish community. Also in 1913 he persuaded the Baltimore Association of Jewish Women to establish and maintain a school for training Jewish social workers. For this program, Levin arranged practicum that included student observation and participation in the activities of Jewish, non-Jewish, and public charitable organizations in Baltimore and also courses in sociology and philanthropy at Goucher College. The association offered scholarships to two applicants and purchased a library of social literature for use by the students taking these courses. He also instituted social service work at Baltimore's Hebrew Hospital Sinai. In 1914 he established the Jewish Big Brothers Bureau in Baltimore, and in 1915 he was chosen to head a delegation to bring food and supplies to people in Palestine suffering from the war.

Levin drew upon his daily welfare work to write short stories that appeared in the *Forum* (1914) and were reprinted as "Little Tragedies" in the *Best Short Stories of 1915*. He also edited *Jewish Charities*, a monthly published in New York, and *Helping Hand*, a weekly issued by the Federated Jewish Charities of Baltimore, which printed human interest stories of families under the organization's care.

Levin questioned the concept of the melting-pot theory as applied to immigrant groups when he attended a performance of Israel Zangwill's play *The Melting Pot* in 1908. In a review that appeared in the magazine *Journal Intime* (Jan. 1909), Levin maintained that immigrants did not have to give up their ethnic identity to become Americans. "We must Americanize in the best sense, in self reliance, fair play and social cooperation, but we must not lose our identity. The Jews are a unique element in our civilization with a unique contribution."

Levin gave a series of lectures on immigration in 1915 for Goucher College's course in philanthropy. Again he stressed the importance of fostering appreciation of the heritage and traditions of immigrants among the second generation. Grace Abbott echoed his sentiments and endorsed Levin's efforts in her address in 1917 at the National Conference of Charities and Social Work.

In 1919 Levin initiated the first tri-city gathering of Jewish social workers from New York, Philadelphia, and Baltimore. He proposed a plan to legalize the profession by having state commissions pass on all applicants. In 1920 the governor of Maryland appointed him to a commission to survey mental health conditions in the state.

His 1921–1922 lectures at Johns Hopkins University incorporated the two major themes of professional training and education for future social workers. Levin's contributions to the development of Jewish social services in particular, and his pioneering efforts to encourage a sensitivity and understanding of immigrant culture and beliefs, influenced his contemporaries who directed the training of social workers in the United States. Levin died in Baltimore.

• Levin's papers are deposited in the Jewish Historical Society of Maryland. In addition to the newspapers, he edited the 1910 conference publication for the National Conference of Jewish Charities. His daughter-in-law, the writer Alexandra Lee Levin, has described Levin's life and work in *Dare to Be Different: A Biography of Louis H. Levin of Baltimore, a Pioneer in Jewish Social Service* (1972). J. Vincenza Scarpaci's article, "Louis H. Levin of Baltimore: A Pioneer in Cultural Pluralism," *Maryland Historical Magazine* 77 (Summer 1982): 183–92, focuses on Levin's interest and support of ethnic identity. Obituaries are in the Baltimore *Morning Sun*, 22 Apr. 1923, and the *Jewish Times*, 27 Apr. 1923.

VINCENZA SCARPACI

LEVINE, Joseph Edward (9 Sept. 1905–31 July 1987), motion picture distributor and producer, was born in Boston, the son of a Russian immigrant tailor. (His parents' names are unknown.) He grew up in a poor Jewish neighborhood; when he was four, his father died. From then on, when not in school, Joseph worked on the streets, shining shoes, carrying luggage, and hawking newspapers. At age fourteen he gave up his studies to take a full-time job in a dress factory, which eventually led to his owning his own dress shop.

In 1938 Levine made his first venture into movie exhibition when he purchased the Lincoln Arts Theater in New Haven, Connecticut. In an attempt to increase day-to-day profits, he borrowed $4,000 to obtain New England distribution rights for a collection of second-run westerns. Also in 1938 he married Rosalie Harrison, a singer with the Rudy Vallee orchestra; they had two children. Over the next half-dozen years Levine expanded his holdings from a single theater to a small chain of cinemas. Until 1949 he continued to distribute what he called "exploitation pictures," which ranged from a sex hygiene primer to a documentary on Admiral Richard E. Byrd's fourth Antarctic expedition.

Soon after World War II, Levine made a quantum leap from his ragtag beginnings when he bought the U.S. rights to such outstanding Italian neorealist pictures as *Open City* (1945), *Paisan* (1946), and *The Bicycle Thief* (1948). These were enthusiastically greeted by audiences in American art cinemas.

Another decade passed before Levine raised his financial stakes by exhibiting exploitation pictures to mass audiences on a national scale. His first wager backed a low-budget Japanese monster movie, *Godzilla: King of the Monsters* (1956). He bought the film's U.S. rights for $12,000, borrowed $400,000 to be spent on a widespread advertising campaign, and more than doubled his investment—grossing $1 million. With *Godzilla*, Levine established a marketing pattern that he used two years later on *Attila* (originally produced in 1954), a sloppily-made Italian historical spectacle starring Anthony Quinn and then little-known Sophia Loren. This time Levine invested $700,000 and cleared $2 million in receipts.

The Hollywood film industry started to pay real attention when Levine sent $150,000 for the rights to a "spears and sandals" extravaganza, *Hercules* (1959), which starred an unknown California bodybuilder, Steve Reeves. Every major U.S. studio had rejected the picture, but Levine put up $120,000 for English-language dubbing and opening credits. He added $1 million for promotion and advertising and another $375,000 for extra color prints. He then opened *Hercules* simultaneously in about six-hundred cinemas and drive-in theaters throughout the country. It was seen by 24 million ticket buyers in thousands of theaters, allowing Levine to gross almost $5 million, a satisfying vindication of his unprecedented saturation booking strategy. He followed this success with *Hercules Unchained* and *Jack the Ripper* (both 1960).

Levine next—almost characteristically—shifted his focus again by distributing the Italian import *Two Women* (1961). The picture, starring Sophia Loren in a challenging dramatic role, received strong advertising support and bookings into art houses and selected first-run theaters. Levine campaigned vigorously to win an Academy Award for Loren, an honor no actress in a foreign-language film had ever received. "I nursed that picture like a baby," Levine said. When Loren did win an Oscar, Levine was poised to place *Two Women* in theaters where only Hollywood staples normally played. By the end of 1962 the picture had earned $3 million. Levine followed up this success by continuing to distribute outstanding imported films, including *Divorce Italian Style* (1962), *8½* (1963), *Yesterday, Today and Tomorrow* (1963), and *Darling* (1965). All netted substantial profits.

With his distribution arm solidly established, Levine turned to producing his own films. Embassy's first production, *The Carpetbaggers* (1964), was an immediate hit, bringing in the year's second-highest U.S. financial return. It led to a string of similar films aimed directly at the box office, including *Where Love Has Gone* (1964), *Harlow* (1965), *Nevada Smith* (1966), and *The Spy with the Cold Nose* (1966).

Levine's principal production of 1967 became his greatest commercial success and did more than any other film to define and create the youth (under-thirty) film market of the 1970s and beyond. With the unknown Dustin Hoffman as the male lead, *The Graduate* was the biggest box office winner of 1968 and one of the two most profitable films of the 1960s.

Embassy now was a powerful Hollywood corporate player, and in 1968 Levine sold the company for $40 million to Avco Corporation. Avco-Embassy came into being, and Levine stayed on as chief executive officer. During his tenure he produced and distributed a number of fine motion pictures, such as *The Lion in Winter* (1968), his own favorite; *Carnal Knowledge* (1971), a major commercial hit; and *The Ruling Class* (1972).

Levine, however, was anything but a corporate team player. "I'm not the executive type," he said.

"I'm a wheeler-dealer who wants to buy or make movies and promote them." After six years he severed his connection with Avco-Embassy and established his own company, Joseph E. Levine Presents. Although not his final picture, *A Bridge Too Far* (1977), a World War II combat spectacular, served as his last hurrah. Filmed at 146 locations at a cost of $25 million, with a staggering roster of stars, the movie failed to make back its costs. The kindest thing any reviewer said of it was "technically impressive."

Levine ceased producing movies after 1981, having played a hand in the U.S. release of more than 500 pictures during his career. He died in Greenwich, Connecticut.

Levine was a loner in the midst of the faltering Hollywood studio system of his era. His innovations—intensive advertising and saturation booking—revolutionized motion-picture promotion and distribution. His risk-taking and sincere love for movies inspired him to bring some of the finest films of the 1940s and 1960s to American audiences. "This is no business for big business," he once said. "It's an art form."

• Levine is mentioned briefly in most histories of the film industry. Articles on aspects of his career or on individual films appear in *American Film*, Sept. 1979; the *New Yorker*, 16 Sept. 1967; and *Variety*, 28 June and 1 Nov. 1978. Reliable biographical articles are in *Current Biography 1979* and *Annual Obituary 1987*. An obituary is in the *New York Times*, 1 Aug. 1987.

ROBERT MIRANDON

LEVINE, Lena (17 May 1903–9 Jan. 1965), gynecologist, psychiatrist, and pioneer of the birth control movement, was born in Brooklyn, New York, the daughter of Morris H. Levine, a clothing manufacturer, and Sophie Levine. Her parents, Jewish émigrés from Russia, had come to the United States in the 1890s. Her father's business did well enough that the family lived relatively comfortably compared to their neighbors. Levine received a bachelor's degree from Hunter College in 1923, and then went on to earn her M.D. from University and Bellevue Hospital Medical College in 1927. Two years later she married Louis Ferber, another medical student, but decided to retain her maiden name. They both did their residencies at Brooklyn Jewish Hospital.

Levine, who was a supporter of the idea of legalized contraception, chose to specialize in obstetrics and gynecology. She set up a practice with her husband, a general practitioner. In the 1930s she became involved in the birth control movement by working for the Birth Control Federation of America (the precursor of the Planned Parenthood Federation of America) and the Margaret Sanger Research Bureau, a women's clinic. In addition, Levine became the medical secretary for the International Planned Parenthood Association. Her first book, *The Doctor Talks with the Bride* (1936), was the beginning of a long career in writing books, articles, and pamphlets on various topics relating to sex and women, including marriage, birth con-

trol, menstruation, menopause, and sexual fulfillment.

Levine and her husband had two children, one of whom was rendered severely brain damaged by an attack of viral encephalitis in infancy. To add to her family tragedy, Levine's husband died of a heart attack in 1943. This prompted Levine to reevaluate her life, and she decided to focus solely on gynecology, since practicing obstetrics would mean having to leave her children in order to deliver babies at a moment's notice. Her own personal experience with psychoanalysis led her to study psychiatry, especially Freudian theory, at the College of Physicians and Surgeons of Columbia University. After becoming a certified psychiatrist, Levine added psychiatry and marriage counseling to her practice.

Although she continued to practice gynecology and psychiatry for the rest of her life, in the 1950s she began to concentrate more on her work in the birth control movement. She continued to write books, appeared on radio and television shows, and traveled, giving lectures and advice to both expert and popular audiences. Her beliefs included the fact that marriage is a partnership and that to achieve strong marriages a society should start training its children for marriage from an early age. According to her, most couples could benefit from marriage counseling which entailed a frank and open exchange of attitudes about sex. Levine promoted the ideas that women had the right to be sexually fulfilled and that birth control should be freely available.

In the 1940s Levine, along with other members of the birth control movement, conducted marriage counseling at the Community Church of New York. She and Dr. Abraham Stone ran what is thought to be one of the first group counseling programs on sex and birth control—they had originally started the program to try to help as many individuals as possible but then realized that group counseling could allow the participants to learn from and reassure each other. In 1941 Levine moved up to become the associate director of the Margaret Sanger Research Bureau and offered women advice and (sometimes) assistance in getting abortions through her Special Consultation Bureau. She decided not to publicly discuss abortion, however, since it might have moved the focus of debate away from the movement to legalize birth control.

Levine continued this work and her practice until her death in New York City. Always a champion for birth control, she became an important member of the movement through her work organizing, lecturing, writing, and counseling. She was a strong promoter of sexual education and spoke out hoping to change people's conservative attitudes about sex. In an attempt to encourage stronger marriages, she worked to teach people about how their bodies worked and how to express their feelings and emotions. Her practices in psychiatry and gynecology complemented her work in the birth control movement and helped her to stay current with people's needs and questions about sex. Levine worked tirelessly to promote her beliefs and helped women gain control of their lives and their bodies.

• Levine's papers relating to her work in the birth control movement are part of the Planned Parenthood Manuscripts of the Sophia Smith Collection, Smith College. The rest of her papers are privately held. Her major published books are *The Menopause* (1952), with Beka Doherty; *The Pre-Marital Consultation* (1956), with Abraham Stone; *The Modern Book of Marriage: A Practical Guide to Marital Happiness* (1957); *The Frigid Wife: Her Way to Sexual Fulfillment* (1962), with David Loth; and *The Emotional Sex: Why Women Are the Way They Are Today* (1964), with David Loth. *Notable American Women: The Modern Period. A Biographical Dictionary* (1980) contains a biographical sketch that includes information that was obtained from Levine's daughter and is not published elsewhere. A brief section on Levine can be found in Brooke Bailey, *The Remarkable Lives of 100 Women Healers and Scientists* (1994). Information relating to Levine's work in counseling and as part of the birth control movement is in Linda Gordon, *Woman's Body, Woman's Right: A Social History of Birth Control in America* (1976). An obituary is in the *New York Times*, 11 Jan. 1965.

KATHLEEN SHANAHAN

LEVINSON, Richard Leighton (7 Aug. 1934–12 Mar. 1987), writer, creator, and producer of television programs, was born in Philadelphia, Pennsylvania, the son of William Levinson, a businessman, and Georgia Harbert. He received a B.S. in economics from the University of Pennsylvania in 1956 and served in the U.S. Army during 1957–1958. Levinson developed a lifelong partnership with William Link, his boyhood friend and college roommate. The two began collaborating on class skits and mystery stories as junior high school students. Levinson continued his personal and professional alliance with Link for over four decades.

After leaving military service, Levinson returned to Philadelphia, where he worked for the CBS–owned television station WCAU as a stagehand, director of weather programs, and jack-of-all-trades. In 1959 Levinson and Link moved to Los Angeles together to pursue writing careers and broke into television by selling an original teleplay, "Chain of Command" to *Desilu Playhouse*, a CBS anthology drama series. This led to work as contract writers at Four Star Productions, a television studio. In 1961 their stageplay *Prescription: Murder* was mounted for a seven-month national tour. The script contained a police detective who would eventually become the basis for their most successful television character—the rough-hewn but brilliantly deductive Lieutenant Columbo.

Levinson and Link returned to television writing during the early 1960s, contributing episode scripts to successful dramatic series, including *Dr. Kildare*, *Alfred Hitchcock Presents*, *The Fugitive*, and *Mannix*, for which they wrote the pilot. In 1966 they went under contract to Universal Television, where they adapted *Prescription: Murder* for television as a two-hour film starring Peter Falk as Lieutenant Columbo. Levinson married Rosanna Huffman, an actress, in 1969, and the couple had a daughter. In 1971 a second film featuring the Columbo character, *Ransom for a Dead*

Man, served as a pilot for the *Columbo* series (NBC, 1971–1977). *Time* (2 Jan. 1972) lauded it as "at once the most classic and original" of crime narratives, comparing the Los Angeles homicide detective to Sherlock Holmes. Falk continued to play the title role in periodic telefilms for more than twenty years. Other successful Universal detective series created, produced, and written by Levinson and Link (in some cases along with other collaborators) include *McCloud*, *The Name of the Game*, and *Murder, She Wrote*. In the latter, which ran on CBS more than a dozen years, Angela Lansbury starred as a New England crime-story writer who cannot help but get involved in real-life cases.

In 1978 Levinson and Link formed their own production company, and their names became synonymous with the made-for-television movie. The partners shared multiple credits in more than two dozen such projects. In addition to the detective mysteries for which they were known, they wrote and produced telefilms focusing on relevant social issues. *That Certain Summer* (ABC, 1972) starred Hal Holbrook and Martin Sheen as gay lovers. Though a tepid treatment of homosexuality by later standards, the movie was considered so controversial that NBC, which originally held the rights, declined to broadcast it. The writer Merle Miller commended the handling of the previously taboo subject as "beautifully written, superbly acted and directed and produced with tender care." *The Gun* (ABC, 1974) took on the hotly debated topic of gun control by following the life of a handgun as it is passed from owner to owner over the years. In the final scene a child finds it and accidentally shoots himself to death.

The most celebrated of the many Levinson and Link telefilms is *The Execution of Private Slovik* (1974), a historical drama concerning the 1945 firing squad execution of Eddie Slovik, the first execution of an American soldier for treason since the Civil War. The film was a success both in the ratings and with critics. It won numerous awards, including a Peabody and several Emmys.

In addition to their television scripts, Levinson and Link also collaborated on two novels: *Fineman* (1972) and *The Playhouse* (1984), as well as more than thirty short stories that appeared in mystery magazines and genre collections. Theater projects included *Killing Jessica*, which ran in both New York and London during the 1980s, and the script for *Merlin*, a 1983 Broadway production. They wrote two nonfiction books: *Stay Tuned: An Inside Look at the Making of Prime-Time Television* (1981), a backstage look at the television production process; and *Off-Camera: Conversations with the Makers of Prime-Time Television* (1986), in which they interviewed their colleagues. In 1983 the partners offered a series of seminars on television writing at the Museum of Broadcasting in New York City.

Levinson was a member of the Academy of Television Arts and Sciences; the Caucus for Writers, Producers, and Directors; the Writers Guild of America; and the Actors Studio West, where he served as chairperson of the playwrights committee. He was the corecipient, with Link, of multiple Emmy and Peabody awards. In 1973 the pair received both a Golden Globe Award and a Writers' Guild of America Award. Other accolades include the Image Award from the NAACP for *My Sweet Charlie* (1970), a telefilm on interracial friendship; the Silver Nymph Award from the Monte Carlo Film Festival for *That Certain Summer*; and a Christopher Award for *Crisis at Central High* (1981), a docudrama on the landmark Little Rock school desegregation crisis of 1957. The team also received a record four Edgar awards from the Mystery Writers of America for their short stories. *Merlin* was nominated for a Tony in 1983.

Levinson died of a sudden heart attack at his home in the Brentwood section of Los Angeles.

• *Contemporary Authors*, vols. 73–76 (1962–), offers biographical information. See also *Contemporary Theatre, Film and Television*, vol. 5 (1988). Obituaries are in the *New York Times*, 13 Mar. 1987; the *Hollywood Reporter*, 16 Mar. 1987; *Daily Variety*, 13 Mar. 1987; and *Time*, 23 Mar. 1987.

DAVID MARC

LEVINTHAL, Israel Herbert (12 Feb. 1888–31 Oct. 1982), rabbi, was born in Vilna, Russia, the son of Rabbi Bernard Levinthal and Minna Kleinberg. Descended from twelve generations of rabbis, Levinthal immigrated to the United States in 1891 with his family. He grew up in Philadelphia, where his father became spiritual leader of the Orthodox congregation of his father-in-law, Eleazar Kleinberg, and helped to found the Union of Orthodox Rabbis (*Agudat ha-Rabbanim*) in 1902. Levinthal attended Columbia University and the Jewish Theological Seminary in New York City. In 1908 he married May Rahel Bogdanoff, with whom he would have two children. He received his B.A. in 1909 and his ordination as rabbi in 1910.

Levinthal's experience with his first congregation, Temple B'nai Shalom in Brooklyn, discouraged him from the rabbinate because of the constant pressure on him to raise funds. As an optional vocation he decided to study law and earned a J.D. from New York University in 1914. Unlike his brothers, however, he never practiced. Choosing instead to remain on a more obviously spiritual course, in 1915 he left for Temple Petach Tikvah in Brownsville, Brooklyn.

His second congregation allowed Levinthal to experiment with religious services and expand synagogue-sponsored activities. Among the innovations he introduced and supervised were late Friday night services after the sabbath meal, youth clubs, a Hebrew school that met daily, and organizations affiliated with the congregation. Levinthal's efforts, designed to establish a synagogue-center that was responsive to American urban life in ways that were comparable to the institutional church, provoked internal opposition; the congregation also disapproved of his involvement in Zionist and communal activities outside of Temple Petach Tikvah. For these reasons, in 1919 he left to become rabbi of the newly formed Brooklyn

Jewish Center. In 1920 he received his Doctor of Hebrew Letters degree from the Jewish Theological Seminary, published his thesis on the Jewish Law of Agency, and coauthored *Song and Praise for Sabbath Eve*, a volume of Hebrew songs and English readings for late Friday night services.

Levinthal helped to shape the Brooklyn Jewish Center into a model synagogue-center that implemented Mordecai M. Kaplan's understanding of Judaism as a civilization embodying high cultural ideals as well as folkways, responded to pragmatic concerns of an emerging Jewish urban middle class seeking a modern structure for their religious life, and embodied Levinthal's interpretation of what an American rabbi should be. Levinthal merged his rabbinical career with the Brooklyn Jewish Center, which he geared to serving Jews comprehensively, from birth to death. The imposing building on Eastern Parkway contained a swimming pool and gym, an auditorium with stage, a library, a dining room and kosher kitchen, and classrooms as well as a two-story synagogue. Levinthal expected that Jews would come to play and pray, study and learn, spend leisure time and celebrate family life cycle events. During the Brooklyn Jewish Center's heyday, it included an all-day elementary school, Center Academy, and an institute of adult education that offered extension courses for college credit and conducted a popular lecture series.

A gifted preacher, Levinthal extended his influence through speaking and writing. Preaching to him was central to the modern American rabbinate, the means to show the Jewish way of understanding the world. Although he spoke extemporaneously from notes, Levinthal developed the art of preaching on contemporary issues through traditional homiletics that linked each thought to a rabbinic text or midrash (a form of exegetical rabbinic text). The popularity of his sermons led to their publication, the first volume, *Steering or Drifting—Which?*, appearing in 1928. A *New York Times* (21 July 1935) review of a subsequent volume, *Judaism—An Analysis and an Interpretation* (1935), observed that Levinthal's "knowledge of the vast range of Jewish literature is so exact as to permit him to find the text" that best fits contemporary needs. In 1937 the Jewish Theological Seminary invited Levinthal to teach homiletics for a year; ten years later he returned as visiting professor of homiletics, a position he held until 1962.

Levinthal's congregational achievements earned him a place of leadership within the Conservative movement as well as among Brooklyn Jews. In 1930–1932 he served a term as president of the Rabbinical Assembly, the association of Conservative rabbis; from 1932 to 1935 he chaired a campaign of the United Synagogue, the union of Conservative congregations, to build a synagogue-center in Jerusalem. Levinthal was also a founder and first president of the Brooklyn Board of Rabbis (1929–1931), chairman of the Brooklyn Region of the Zionist Organization of America (1933–1935), and president of the Brooklyn Jewish Community Council (1940–1944), the last of which addressed increasing incidents of anti-Semitism in the borough. He recognized and accepted the responsibilities of communal leadership as integral to the rabbi's role.

A committed Zionist, Levinthal interpreted the Jewish renaissance in the land of Israel—especially the revival of Hebrew—as the real hope for Judaism's future in the modern world, where secularism undermined Jewish civilization. American Jews, he believed, needed Zionism as an inspiration to help them focus on religious rituals that had always sustained Judaism. Levinthal rejected secular Zionism, however, insisting on the continued centrality of religion to Jewish civilization. As the Brooklyn Jewish Center stood as a model synagogue-center, so Levinthal's blend of religious faith and Zionist ideology characterized an entire generation of Conservative rabbis.

Levinthal's only daughter, Helen Hadassah, wanted to enter the rabbinate, and in 1939 she became the first woman in the United States to complete the full rabbinic course leading to ordination at the liberal Jewish Institute of Religion. She was not ordained, however.

Levinthal's success as rabbi, preacher, and Jewish leader depended on the maturation of a second generation, the children of Jewish immigrants, whom he inspired to develop an American Judaism tailored to the realities of urban life. In the 1960s, however, as Jews left Brooklyn for the suburbs, they left the Brooklyn Jewish Center behind. Despite Levinthal's efforts to maintain the synagogue-center rather than relocate it, by 1973 he had to curtail activities, abandon the Hebrew school, and even cancel Friday night services, the initial innovation that had marked his departure from Orthodox Judaism and had heralded his future path. Yet he helped write a significant chapter in the growth of American Judaism by shaping an institution, revitalizing preaching, and creating a new role for rabbis in communal and civic life. Although he never officially retired, his last years were spent quietly living with his daughter in New Rochelle, New York, where he died.

• Materials from the Brooklyn Jewish Center and Levinthal's papers are in the archives of the Joseph and Miriam Ratner Center for the Study of Conservative Judaism at the Jewish Theological Seminary. His publications include his doctoral thesis, *Jewish Law of Agency, with Special Reference to Roman and Common Law* (1920), and seven volumes of sermons. *A New World Is Born* (1943) and *The Hour of Destiny* (1949) address contemporary political issues, whereas *Point of View—An Analysis of American Judaism* (1958) and *The Message of Israel* (1973) present interpretations of Judaism for the modern world. Deborah Dash Moore, "A Synagogue Center Grows in Brooklyn," in *The American Synagogue*, ed. Jack Wertheimer (1987), discusses the formative years of the Brooklyn Jewish Center and Levinthal's role as rabbi. Pamela S. Nadell, ed. *Conservative Judaism in America* (1988), offers a brief biography that complements the obituary in the *New York Times*, 4 Nov. 1982.

DEBORAH DASH MOORE

LEVITT, Abraham (1 July 1880–20 Aug. 1962), lawyer and housing contractor, was born in Brooklyn, New York, the son of Rabbi Louis Levitt and Nellie (maiden name unknown), immigrants form Russia. Little is known about his parents. Levitt grew up in the Williamsburg section of Brooklyn. Because his family was very poor, he was forced to drop out of school at the age of ten to become a newsboy on Park Row. Later he worked as a dishwasher and held other menial positions, such as dock worker and waiter. Nevertheless, he educated himself by avidly reading books, newspapers, and magazines. He later said that by the time he was sixteen years old, he read some part of some book every day; his favorite subjects were history, economics, and philosophy. He also frequently attended lectures at Cooper Union and joined and regularly attended the meetings of various literary and scientific societies. When he was twenty years old, he took and passed a New York's regents examination to gain entrance to the New York University Law School. Specializing in real estate law, he wrote an outstanding student manual on his specialty when he was a sophomore, the profits from which helped him finish his LL.B. Admitted to the New York bar in 1903, he established a private practice that soon flourished. Three years later he married Pauline A. Biederman; the couple had two sons, William Jaird and Alfred Stuart.

After twenty-five years of practicing real estate law, Levitt, with his sons, founded a construction company in 1929, just before the stock market crash. In the firm—Levitt and Sons—Abraham came to specialize in landscaping as well as in legal issues. He also had the maturity and the broad vision that stabilized the company while Alfred and William were gaining experience. Alfred studied and became a building designer, while William served as the company's president and focused on "business" aspects, such as management, finances, and sales.

Although the company grew slowly during the depression, it did have various successes. With developments in Rockville Centre and Manhasset, New York, Levitt and Sons built 2,500 custom-designed homes during the 1930s. During World War II the Levitts built 2,300 homes under government contract for military and civilian personnel near Norfolk, Virginia. As the company finished its last few hundred homes there, the Levitts had a chance to experiment with the building process, especially in standardization and cost reduction. When they soon put their new knowledge to work, they began a process that would revolutionize the housing industry in the United States.

Levitt and Sons was well situated financially in 1945, poised for the tremendous economic boom in housing construction that occurred immediately after World War II. A majority of civilians had made relatively good money during the war; many had deferred their desires to have new homes of their own until after the war. Millions of veterans also demanded decent housing when they returned home, and the GI Bill made these expectations possible by extending long-term, low-interest home loans. Despite occasional economic slumps, there was general prosperity in the country from World War II into the 1950s and 1960s. In this positive environment for new construction the

Levitts introduced a plan that they had tried in Norfolk, one, that they believed would make their fortune and help potential home buyers at the same time.

The Levitts understood that single-family dwellings were relatively expensive to build because they were essentially being custom-made out of at least 2,000 separate items. The company decided to apply assembly-line techniques to housing construction. First, the Levitts developed one basic floor plan for a small, two-bedroom, 800-square-foot house. Next, the company made or ordered as many prefabricated items as possible, such as kitchen cabinets, shower stalls, window sills, and other housing components. Finally, specialized work crews were hired to move from house to house following a standardized sequence, with each crew devoted to one limited aspect of construction. With their assembly-line techniques (the moving crews), the Levitts could build thirty-six houses per day, a number that astounded executives of other construction companies.

To initiate their first "Levittown" project on Long Island, New York, the company bought 7.3 square miles of land in Nassau County, and the Levitts and their construction teams went to work. Together, they built 17,500 Cape Cod-style homes in their first project. As housing rows were finished, the company put them on the rental market, asking $65 per month. Each renter had an option to buy for $6,990, and the Levitts charged veterans no down payment. Demand was such that prices soon rose to $7,990 per unit. After 1949 the homes were no longer available for rent but were offered for sale only.

Later the company also built larger homes, some with four or five bedrooms, which were more expensive; still, their popular "ranch-style" homes sold for under $10,000. Within given neighborhoods, most houses had essentially similar floor plans, but some variety was achieved by changing the facades, by locating the homes at different distances from the curb, and by using winding streets that gave certain homes a different look from curb-side.

The major secret of the company's success was, of course, that it constructed houses that average Americans could afford to buy in more spacious, private, and healthier environments than the cities where many had grown up. Levittown, as the new suburban community was called, showcased its builder's emphasis on community planning. "Green" areas in each neighborhood contained playgrounds for children, swimming pools for the families, and shopping centers for everyone. In person and in letters, Levitt consulted often with homeowners about the upkeep of their property, including even the care of the yards. For a time he had a regular column in the *Levittown Tribune* that emphasized order, cleanliness, and nature's beauty. In sum, Abraham Levitt and his sons built neighborhoods, not just houses. After completing the successful Long Island project, the company constructed similar "Levittowns" in Pennsylvania, New Jersey, Florida, and Puerto Rico. Overseas communities included housing projects in Israel and France. By the time of Abraham Levitt's death, Levitt and Sons had constructed more than 100,000 homes.

The Levitts and their housing projects were not without critics. The first 800 square-foot houses, each with the same floor plan, were called little "ticky-tacky" homes, or worse, by their detractors; and the units really were all in a row. However, historians like Kenneth T. Jackson were kinder and more positive. Jackson held that the Levitts had a greater impact on twentieth-century housing than any other one company. "Ticky-tacky" or not, the inexpensive homes accomplished their purpose: thousands and later millions of people escaped the inner cities when they bought one of those little houses all built in a row. In their own estimation the purchasers' standards of living improved. Finally, the Levitts' success encouraged other construction companies to use their methods when building houses; as a result, countless developments of moderately priced housing cropped up around the nation.

Abraham Levitt, probably the most innovative developer of modern American housing, died in Great Neck, New York.

• The Levittown, N.Y. Public Library houses the Levittown Collection. A bibliography published by the library is Joseph E. Spagnoli, *Levittown, New York: An Annotated Bibliography, 1947–1972* (1972). For more information on Abraham Levitt's concept of "Levittowns" and the housing industry, see Boyden Sparkes, "They'll Build Neighborhoods, Not Houses," *Saturday Evening Post*, 28 Oct. 1951, pp. 43–45. A book-length treatment of Levittown, N.J., is Herbert J. Gans, *The Levittowners* (1967), and see William Dobriner, *The Suburban Community* (1958). An obituary is in the *New York Times*, 21 Aug. 1962; a minor correction of the obituary is in the *New York Times*, 5 Sept. 1962. Also see the obituary for William Jaird Levitt in the *New York Times*, 29 Jan. 1994.

JAMES M. SMALLWOOD

LEVITT, William Jaird (11 Feb. 1907–28 Jan. 1994), real estate developer and building contractor, was born in Brooklyn, New York, the son of Abraham Levitt, a lawyer and building contractor, and Pauline A. Biederman. After attending Brooklyn's public schools, Levitt studied at New York University for three years but, eager to make money, did not graduate. Although he once aspired to a career in commercial aviation, when he was twenty-two he joined with his father and brother Alfred to create Levitt and Sons, a construction company that specialized in single-family housing. That same year he married Rhoda Kirsher; they had two children.

For the new company, Abraham, whose specialty was real estate law, handled legal matters along with landscaping and, more important, community planning. He also contributed maturity and wisdom. Alfred became an expert on building design. William became the company's president and occupied himself primarily with management and financial matters, including sales. Founded in 1929 just before the stock market crash signaled the nation that a depression was under way, the company had modest success during the 1930s. From 1930 to 1934 the company built approximately 600 homes. In 1934 it developed Strathmore-at-Manhasset, building 200 houses that ranged in price from $9,100 to $18,500. During the decade, inclusive, the Levitts built 2,500 homes.

World War II interrupted Levitt's business career. He served in the Pacific as a lieutenant with the Seabees, the U.S. Navy's "can do" combat construction teams. He acquired a reputation for intelligence and willingness to bend rules or even disobey orders if such actions allowed him to accomplish his objectives. While Levitt was getting valuable experience in rapid, safe construction under unsafe conditions, the family company made much progress. It received a federal war contract in 1942 to build 1,600 homes near the Norfolk, Virginia, naval base for military and civilian personnel. In the last 750-odd homes, Abraham and Alfred experimented with building processes, especially with standardization and cost reduction.

Shortly after Levitt returned to the family business, the company entered its greatest era of success. The Levitts correctly forecasted the tremendous economic boom that occurred in housing construction immediately after World War II. They analyzed the factors that caused single-family domiciles to have such relatively high costs. One major factor was that homes were, largely, custom-made and required building or installing at least 2,000 separate items. The Levitts decided to apply assembly-line techniques to housing construction. First, Alfred developed one basic floor plan for a two-bedroom, 800-square-foot house (the company would build larger homes later). Next, the company had made to order as many prefabricated items as possible. And third, specialized workers, individuals doing just one basic job, would go from house to house—ahead of another crew, behind yet another. With their assembly line, the Levitts could build thirty-six houses per day.

The crews finished their work so fast that the Levitts created almost instant suburbs. Levitt later said that "bigness" was one secret for success. Further, since approximately 20 percent of the work had to be done by skilled artisans, he held that by organizing properly he could save $1,000 per unit on labor costs alone. And there was a market; potential home buyers were legion, especially since the federal government made millions of dollars for mortgages available to veterans under the popular GI Bill.

The first "Levittown," on Long Island, New York, begun in 1947 and completed in 1951, included 17,500 Cape Cod–type homes spread over 7.3 square miles of land. What had once been potato fields became homes for buyers. The many features of the mass-produced dwellings included up-to-date kitchen equipment, laundry rooms, and televisions. Each unit had two bedrooms and an expansion attic that could become a third bedroom, an office, or a utility room, as needed.

As workers finished the housing rows, Levitt and Sons immediately put them on the rental market, asking $65 per month, with an option to buy for $6,990

and with no down payment for veterans. Demand became such that the company quickly raised its price to $7,990 per unit; after 1949 the homes were no longer rented. They were available for sale only. Later, the company also built larger homes, some with four and five bedrooms. Still, the most expensive ranch-style houses sold for under $10,000.

Within their various neighborhoods, most of the houses had little variety, but some heterogeneity was achieved by changing the facades of the identical floor plans; by locating the homes at different distances from the curb; and by using winding streets that gave certain homes a different look from the curb. Most homeowners helped give their places an individual "look" with different painting schemes, trim colors, lawn decorations, and all manner of personal touches. They added garages, terraces, extra rooms, dormers, and other innovations to create a bit of individuality.

In the first Levittown, the company made a profit of approximately $5 million. In 1949 alone, the Levitts built 4,600 homes and sold them for more than $42 million. Clearly, their mass production technique was the key to the company's future. The team next built in Bucks County, Pennsylvania, near both a new U.S. Steel plant and a new Kaiser Metal Products Corporation factory. With the work begun in 1951, they developed a 5,500-acre tract near the Delaware River, part of which had once been only swampland, that contained 16,000 homes. The Levitts made most of the homes in the ranch design and sold them for $9,000 to $17,500. Other Levittowns were built later in New Jersey, New York, and Florida.

In each new area, when the houses were completed, young families—many including a veteran, his wife, and one or two small children—quickly bought all the project's housing. Why? First, the homes were relatively inexpensive. Second, postwar American society placed great stress on the family unit and its quality of life. This was especially true of families that had been separated or otherwise disrupted by the war. Third, families with several growing children could afford larger suburban homes more easily than they could afford (or even find) homes in the inner cities. Suburban homes also gave families more privacy than people had in city apartments.

Suburban areas also had something other than miles of concrete and high-rise buildings. Suburbia had green grass and front and back yards; more open space generally; and, most likely, better quality air and water. Above all was the space for individual families to have all the consumer goods that postwar Americans craved—the automobiles, boats, appliances, outdoor patio furniture, swing sets and other recreational items for growing children, space in the garage for dad's workshop and storage for his golf bag, the ever-present barbecue grills, and other products too.

In addition to housing affordability, another key to Levitt and Sons' success was community planning, usually supervised by Abraham Levitt. "Green" areas in each neighborhood contained playgrounds, swimming pools, and shopping malls. Personally and in print, Abraham consulted often with homeowners about upkeep of their property, including the care of yards, which, as designed by Abraham, originally had a set quota of trees and shrubs.

From the late 1940s to the late 1960s Levitt and Sons remained phenomenally successful with its new projects, including some overseas. William assumed more control in the mid-1950s when Alfred left the company. With Abraham retiring in 1962 and dying later that year, William took yet more control. By the late 1960s he had become one of the richest men in the United States. Although sources disagree, his net worth may have been in excess of $100 million. By the 1960s he lived lavishly in a thirty-room mansion on his estate "La Coline" on Mill Neck, Long Island. He and his family spent much time on his 237-foot yacht, *La Belle Simone*, named after his third wife. Active in community affairs, Levitt worked with the Boy Scouts, the North Shore Hospital on Long Island, and the United Jewish Appeal. For recreation, he played golf.

William Levitt did not escape controversy in his career. As late as the 1950s he refused to sell houses to African Americans. He argued that whenever blacks came into a suburb, white flight began, and the homes began to lose their value. In 1955 the National Association for the Advancement of Colored People filed suit against Levitt's whites-only policy. A federal district court refused to force integration, holding that neither the Federal Housing Administration nor the Veterans Administration had a duty to prevent discrimination in home sales. Various housing experts, urban historians, and sociologists criticized Levitt. Among others, Lewis Mumford complained about the uniformity, conformity, and "ticky-tacky" houses all in a row. Levitt responded to Mumford by citing sales statistics. Even if the homes were ticky-tacky, suburban Americans still had a higher standard of living and a better quality of life than the generations before them.

In retrospect, it appears that Levitt made a major mistake in 1968 when he sold Levitt and Sons to International Telephone and Telegraph for $492 million. The contract barred Levitt from engaging in the U.S. construction industry for ten years. Apparently becoming restless, he tried to build new Levittowns in France, Iran, Venezuela, Israel, and Nigeria. Most of the projects failed, and Levitt lost money. In the late 1970s he tried two more ventures, both in Florida, where he had earlier found success. Again failing, he had to refund the deposits of thousands of potential buyers because no houses were ever finished.

Shortly thereafter, New York attorney general Robert Abrams launched an investigation of the Levitt Foundation, a nonprofit philanthropic organization created years before when Levitt was still working with his father and brother. He had apparently "borrowed" heavily from foundation funds, for he later settled by repaying $5 million to the foundation. Levitt's mismanagement also alarmed the federal government. Ultimately, in 1987, a federal court ordered him to re-

fund $11 million in judgments to former customers who suffered because of his misuse of the funds.

By 1982, with much of his large estate and yacht gone, Levitt had settled into a restless retirement. He died at North Shore University Hospital in Manhasset, New York.

Despite his financial problems in his later years, William Levitt, along with Abraham and Alfred, had revolutionized the housing industry. Most construction companies adopted all, or at least some, of the methods that Levitt and Sons used to lower the cost of housing for the mass market. Millions of middle-class and working-class Americans became homeowners and lived in relatively modest, inexpensive housing without even knowing that they had Levitt and Sons to thank. Perhaps appropriately, Levitt's heirs divided his estate into ten lots and built luxury homes, all of which sold for about $3 million.

• The Levittown, N.Y., Public Library houses the Levittown collection. The library also published Joseph E. Spannoli's *Levittown, New York: An Annotated Bibliography, 1947–1972* (1972). For more information on William Levitt's concept of Levittowns and the housing industry, see Boyden Sparkes, "They'll Build Neighborhoods, Not Houses," *Saturday Evening Post*, 28 Oct. 1951, pp. 11, 43–45. A book-length treatment of Levittown, N.J., is Herbert J. Gans, *The Levittowners* (1967). William Dobriner, *The Suburban Community* (1958), is also worth consulting. Also see Alexander Boulton, "The Buy of the Century," *American Heritage* 44 (July 1993): 62–69. Short articles on Levitt and the Levittowns appear in the *Christian Science Monitor*, 16 Apr. 1948, and the *New York Times*, 29 Jan. 1950. An obituary is in the *New York Times*, 29 Jan. 1994.

JAMES M. SMALLWOOD

LEVY, Uriah Phillips (22 Apr. 1792–22 Mar. 1862), U.S. naval officer and philanthropist, was born in Philadelphia, Pennsylvania, the son of Michael Levy, a merchant, and Rachel Phillips. He was drawn early to the sea and at age ten ran away to be a cabin boy. After his return two years later, he was apprenticed for four or five years to a Philadelphia ship owner to learn navigation and other maritime skills. By age eighteen he had made several profitable voyages as a mate from Philadelphia to the West Indies.

In 1811 Levy purchased a one-third share in a new schooner, which he then commanded on behalf of his partners and himself. Shortly afterward the crew mutinied and stole the vessel. Levy pursued the mutineers, brought them to court, and saw them convicted of piracy.

The War of 1812 was just starting, and Levy, an experienced mariner, but without a ship, entered the U.S. Navy on 21 October 1812 as a sailing master, the rank just below lieutenant. He was one of five or six Jewish officers in the navy at that time.

Levy served first aboard the *Alert* in New York Harbor but was detached from it in January 1813. After a period of leave in Philadelphia, he was ordered to the brig *Argus*, reporting aboard on 11 May as a "supernumerary," or extra, sailing master. In June the *Argus* carried the new American minister, W. H. Crawford, to France and then raided British shipping around the south of Ireland. On 11 August Levy was put on board one of their captures, the *Betsey*, as prizemaster, but the ship was recaptured the next day by a British frigate. On 14 August the *Argus* was captured by the brig *Pelican*. Levy and the other officers of the *Argus* lived as prisoners of war on parole in the town of Ashburton, Devon.

Levy was released in November 1814 and sent home to the United States. After a year at the Philadelphia Naval Station he was ordered to duty aboard the USS *Franklin* and on 5 March 1817 was promoted to lieutenant. It was during this period that he was involved in the first of a series of controversies that were to blight much of his life in the navy. At a ball he was insulted and kicked by another officer. Levy struck back and was challenged to a duel. At the dueling ground Levy tried to settle the quarrel peaceably, but when his antagonist refused, Levy shot him dead. This was Levy's only duel, but the incident established a pattern for the future: petty incidents often ended in serious altercations. Levy was combative and intense. He had the ardent sense of personal honor common in his time, was sensitive to slights and insults, and never let one pass without responding as forcefully as he could.

Most of Levy's problems in the navy resulted from prejudice and his strong-minded reaction to it. Throughout his career he faced the attitudes, common in the officer corps, that those promoted to lieutenant from the rank of sailing master were socially and professionally inferior to officers who had entered as midshipmen. Further, although there seems to have been little or no bias against Jews in the pre-1815 navy, in the following years Levy was increasingly the object of anti-Jewish bigotry. He refused to accept any of this biased treatment and always fought back vigorously.

From his promotion to lieutenant in 1817 until mid-1827, Levy served first aboard the 74-gun ship *Franklin*, followed by the frigate *United States* and the brig *Spark*, then ashore at the Charleston Naval Station, and later aboard gunboat number *158* and the ship sloop *Cyane*, each for a period of a few months to two years. He left each ship (except gunboat *158*) after some petty altercation had blown into a major quarrel. Gunboat *158* was shipwrecked and lost while under Levy's command.

Levy underwent five courts-martial during this period and was found guilty in all of them, but usually his accuser was also reprimanded. He faced a court of inquiry over the loss of gunboat *158*, but that incident was blamed on the civilian pilot handling the vessel.

After he left the *Cyane* in 1827, Levy was not given another duty assignment for eleven years. He had become wealthy from real estate investments in New York and did not need continuous navy assignments to support himself. Levy's accomplishments during this period give him a firm place in history. He had long admired Thomas Jefferson, and while in France in 1832 he commissioned the celebrated sculptor Pierre-Jean David d'Angers to create a larger-than-life bronze statue of Jefferson in modern dress. The statue was finished in 1834, and Levy presented it to Congress as a gift to the people of the United States. It stands today in the Rotunda of the U.S. Capitol.

In 1836 Levy made a pilgrimage to visit Jefferson's home at Monticello, where he found the house and grounds in bad repair and rapidly deteriorating. He bought the Monticello property, and it became his purpose to bequeath it to the nation. He performed much useful restoration work and often lived there. The Levy family owned and maintained Monticello for eighty-seven years, finally selling it in 1923 to the Thomas Jefferson Memorial Foundation.

In 1837 Levy was promoted to commander and the next year was assigned to command the sloop *Vandalia*. By now he was much interested in humane treatment for sailors and the abolition of flogging, and he wrote many letters and pamphlets urging this. During his fourteen months in command he made the *Vandalia* into an efficient, effective ship with minimal use of the lash. However, an incident in which he sentenced a boy to having his trousers pulled down and a spot of tar and some feathers put on his buttocks, in lieu of a flogging, was viewed as "scandalous" by other officers and resulted in Levy's sixth court-martial. He was found guilty, relieved from command, and sentenced to be dismissed from the navy. His dismissal was later remitted by President John Tyler (1790–1862).

Following this incident Levy was not given another assignment for over eighteen years. He was promoted to captain in 1844 but in 1855 was cashiered from the navy by the secret "Board of Officers" without an opportunity to defend himself, apparently because of his many courts-martial and long periods of inactive service. After much effort, he was reinstated in 1858 and assigned to command the sloop *Macedonian*, bound for the Mediterranean. He had in 1853 married his 18-year-old niece, Virginia Lopez, and she accompanied him, living on board. (They did not have children.) In January 1860 he was ordered to take command of the Mediterranean Squadron with the title of flag officer. He was ordered home on 15 May 1860. This was his last duty except for a few months in charge of the court-martial at Washington. He died at his home in New York.

Levy was creative in introducing humane discipline on board the ships he commanded, and through his speeches, letters, and pamphlets he unofficially contributed to the abolition of flogging in the navy. His career in the navy spanned fifty years, but he served on active duty, at sea or ashore, for only fifteen years of that time. His lasting accomplishments were elsewhere, in his preservation of Monticello for future generations and in the gift to the nation of the magnificent bronze statue of Jefferson.

• Sources for Levy's early life and his time in merchant vessels include Abram Kanof, *Uriah Phillips Levy: The Story of a Pugnacious Commodore* (1949). Levy's navy service in the War of 1812 aboard the *Argus* is documented in two journals kept by *Argus* officers, the *Log of the "Argus"* and the *James Inderwick Journal*, both in the Rare Books and Manuscripts Division, New York Public Library; the *Muster Table of the "Argus,"* HCA 32/1793, PRO, London; and the listing of *Argus* officers, prisoners of war on parole in Ashburton (May 1814), RG 45, National Archives. For Levy's post-1815 navy service see letters between the secretary of the navy and officers, RG 45, *Abstracts of Service of Naval Officers*, RG 45, and *Records of Officers*, RG 24, National Archives; Benjamin F. Butler, *Defense of Uriah P. Levy, Before the Court of Inquiry* (1858); and Harold D. Langley, *Social Reform in the United States Navy, 1798–1862* (1967). For Levy and the Jefferson statue and Monticello, sources include *Journal of the Senate of the United States*, 23d Cong., 1834; Mary T. Christian, "The Capitol Sculpture of David d'Angers," *Capitol Dome* 25, no. 3 (Aug. 1990): 5; and Charles B. Hosmer, Jr., *Presence of the Past* (1965). An obituary is in the *New York Herald*, 28 Mar. 1862.

IRA DYE

LEWELLING, Lorenzo Dow (21 Dec. 1846–3 Sept. 1900), Populist governor of Kansas, was born in Salem, Iowa, the son of William Lewelling, a Quaker minister, and Cyrena Wilson. Lewelling's grandfather freed his slaves after moving from North Carolina to Indiana in 1825. William Lewelling, a noteworthy public speaker, followed his uncles to Salem, Iowa, before Lorenzo's birth and died while touring as an antislavery speaker when Lorenzo was two years old. Lorenzo's mother died when he was nine. Subsequently, he lived with a sister and worked for neighboring farmers. Manual labor, poverty, and transience characterized most of his youth.

Lewelling enlisted in the Union army in 1861, but his Quaker family forced his discharge on religious grounds. He then joined the Quartermaster Corp of the Union Army of Tennessee as a cattle drover. Later, Lewelling worked for a Union army bridge-building unit at Chattanooga. At the end of the war, he briefly taught for the Freedman's Aid Society in Missouri. In 1866 Lewelling entered Knox College at Galesburg, Illinois, and then attended Eastman's Business College in Poughkeepsie, New York. After graduating in 1866 or 1867, he worked his way back to Iowa at various common labor jobs, including a bridge-building project for the Burlington and Missouri River Railroad at Ottumwa, Iowa. Afterward, Lewelling attended and taught at Whittier College in Salem, Iowa. After graduation in 1868, he became principal of the Iowa State Reform School for Boys. Lewelling quickly rose to assistant superintendent, but resigned and relocated to Red Oak, Iowa, in 1870, to marry Angeline M. Cook, a local schoolteacher he had met in college. That same year Lewelling farmed briefly before founding the *Salem Register*, a weekly Republican party newspaper. Lewelling sold the paper in 1872 when he and his wife became the first superintendent and matron of the Iowa State Reform School for Girls. They retained these positions until 1886, with the exception of two years. In 1880 Lewelling founded the Des Moines *Iowa Capital*, an "anti-ring" Republican paper. But he returned to the state

reform school for girls in 1882 because of his wife's failing health. She died in 1885, and Lewelling married her cousin, Ida Bishop, shortly afterward. He had three children with his first wife and one with his second.

Lewelling was a prominent penologist and represented Iowa at several meetings of the National Conferences of Charities. He also served on the board of directors of the State Normal School of Iowa. Lewelling was president of the board when he relocated to Kansas in 1886, where he became a Wichita dairy and produce merchant.

Lewelling became interested in economic issues during the turbulent 1880s and developed a great concern about the growing conflict between capital and labor. Because of the hardships of his own youth, Lewelling's sympathies lay with the cause of labor and other underdogs. In 1884 he unsuccessfully sought the Republican nomination for secretary of state of Iowa as an anticorporation candidate. Subsequently, his zeal for the GOP waned rapidly. After moving to Kansas, Lewelling ceased to affiliate with the Republican party.

Although Lewelling was not a member of the Farmers' Alliance, many of the patrons at his Wichita dairy and produce store were. When the Kansas Alliance turned to partisan politics in 1890, he joined the People's party and delivered the keynote address at the party's 1892 state convention in Wichita. In this speech Lewelling, who came from a town with a significant Democratic party vote, advocated welcoming "honorable allies" for the upcoming election. Populists who favored fusion rallied behind Lewelling's successful bid for the gubernatorial nomination. Democrats subsequently endorsed the 1892 Populist state ticket, which was victorious.

Although Populists carried the executive offices and organized the 1893 Kansas Senate, both Republicans and Populists claimed to have elected a majority in the house of representatives. Each side organized its own supposedly constitutional chamber, which paralyzed state government for more than a month. The controversy became known as the "Kansas Legislative War." Eventually, Republicans seized the house chamber. Lewelling ordered the state militia to clear the chamber, but the militia commander, a partisan Republican, refused. When each side's supporters began arming themselves, Lewelling agreed to a compromise that allowed a Republican victory and avoided bloodshed. Friends attributed Lewelling's aversion to violence to his Quaker background. The Legislative War took up all but eleven days of the session and destroyed Populist hopes for enacting their platform, which included a call for a maximum freight rate law, the popular election of railroad commissioners, an end to free railroad passes for politicians, woman suffrage, and the secret ballot. Only the secret ballot measure passed the 1893 Kansas legislature. Lewelling was particularly disappointed by the failure to tighten the regulation of railroads.

In December 1893, after economic depression had caused significant transience, Lewelling issued his famous "Tramp Circular," which suggested that metropolitan police commissioners, who were gubernatorial appointees, let poverty "cease to be a crime" and ignore vagrancy laws. Lewelling had briefly been a homeless transient himself as a youth. The governor particularly denounced sending those unable to pay fines to "rock piles" and "bull pens," which he labeled municipal slavery. "The first duty of the government is to the weak," he proclaimed. Opponents ridiculed Lewelling's argument that vagrancy laws unconstitutionally deprived the poor of their liberty.

Populists renominated Lewelling for governor in 1894. Democrats, however, made separate nominations. Despite Lewelling's generosity toward Democrats with patronage, the Populist endorsement of woman suffrage alienated their fusion partners. Republicans won a plurality victory in the subsequent three-way race. Sedgwick County (Wichita) voters elected Lewelling to the state senate in 1896 and 1898. He served as chairman of the Ways and Means Committee in the former legislature and concurrently as a member of the State Board of Railroad Commissioners in 1897 and 1898. Lewelling was particularly active as a floor leader for his party and influential in the passage of a bill creating a court of visitation, which replaced the railroad commission in 1898.

Lewelling sold his creamery business and converted his farm to orchards in 1898. He was leaning toward socialism when he died from heart failure after a brief illness at a relative's home in Arkansas City, Kansas.

Lewelling was an eloquent spokesman for the moral humanism of Populism and a leading exponent of fusion with Democrats, a position that drove Kansas Republicans from power in 1892 and 1896.

• A brief autobiographical sketch (c. 1893) can be found in Lewelling's personal papers at the Kansas State Historical Society in Topeka, which are not extensive. The society also has his official governor's papers. For Lewelling's ancestors see O. A. Garretson, "The Lewelling Family—Pioneers," *Iowa Journal of History and Politics* 37 (1929): 548–63. W. J. Costigan, "Lorenzo D. Lewelling," *Transactions of the Kansas State Historical Society* 7 (1902): 121–26, is a biographical synopsis by a close political associate. O. Gene Clanton, *Kansas Populism, Ideas and Men* (1969) and *Populism: The Humane Preference* (1991), deal with Lewelling's term as governor. Other sources are *The Kansas Blue Book* (1899); Hill P. Wilson, *A Biographical History of Eminent Men of the State of Kansas* (1901); and Benjamin F. Gue, *History of Iowa*, vol. 4 (1903). Obituaries are in the *Topeka Daily Capital* and the *Wichita Daily Eagle*, both 4 Sept. 1900.

WORTH ROBERT MILLER

LEWIN, Kurt (9 Sept. 1890–11 Feb. 1947), social psychologist, was born in Mogilno, Prussia (now Poland), the son of Leopold Lewin, a store owner and leader in the local Jewish community, and Recha Engle. In 1905 the family moved to Berlin, which offered better educational opportunities for the Lewin children. After completing his term at Gymnasium in 1909, Lewin spent a semester each at the Universities of Freiberg and Munich. In the spring of 1910 he enrolled at the University of Berlin. Influenced early on by courses with philosopher Ernst Cassirer, Lewin developed an interest in the theory of science, which led him to the study of psychology at Berlin's Psychological Institute. He earned his doctorate in 1916 under the experimental psychologist Carl Stumpf.

Lewin served as a lieutenant in the German Army during World War I and earned an Iron Cross. In his paper "The War Landscape" (1917), which was based on his army experience, he noted that objects took on different meaning according to whether they were seen in the context of peace or of war. He later came to call the subject of this work "life space" or psychological field, and his use of personal experience to frame scientific problems characterized much of his later work. In 1917 Lewin married Maria Landsberg, a high school teacher. They had two children and were divorced in 1928. That same year he married Gertrud Weiss, with whom he had two children.

After the war Lewin returned to the Psychological Institute, which brought him into close association with the Gestalt psychologists Wolfgang Köhler (who succeeded Stumpf as director), Kurt Koffka, and Max Wertheimer. Though not strictly Gestalt, Lewin's thinking and his field theory were compatible with Gestalt ideas and focused on complete psychological acts rather than on the association of behaviors. Lewin's academic position was that of *privatdozent*, an untenured faculty member without civil service rank. He later rose to the position of *ausserordentlicher* (extraordinary) professor, the highest then open to him as a Jew.

At the Psychological Institute, Lewin attracted students from around the world, the first four of whom were women from the Soviet Union. This attraction was both intellectual and personal. Among Lewin's greatest contributions was his influence on the subsequent work of these talented students. As he attracted students from the United States, articles on his work began to appear in English. Invited to speak in 1929 at the International Congress of Psychology at Yale, he illustrated his ideas about conflicting forces in a field by showing a film of an eighteen-month-old child attempting to sit down on a flat stone. Because perception depends on motivation, the stone took on a valence only when the child wanted to use it to sit: the stone hadn't changed, the child had. Lewin's presentation forced several American psychologists to reconsider their own thinking on learning and behavior. Invited to contribute a chapter, "Environmental Forces in Child Behavior and Development," to Carl Murchison's *A Handbook of Child Psychology* (1931), he became known in the United States as a child psychologist.

Lewin was traveling between lecture engagements in Tokyo and Moscow when Hitler became chancellor of Germany on 30 January 1933. Upon reaching Moscow, Lewin wired friends in the United States, where he had just spent six months as a visiting scholar at

Stanford University, about job possibilities. Resigning from the Psychological Institute in August 1933, he and his family left for the United States. In his resignation letter to Köhler, Lewin reviewed his lifelong experience with anti-Semitism in Germany and described his feeling about the growing repression. Some scholars believe that these experiences explain Lewin's shift of interest from individual dynamic processes to group processes, which took place after his move to the United States. There he became increasingly interested in applying field theory to practical situations and developed ingenius experimental techniques for that purpose. In one notable series of experiments at the University of Iowa, Lewin and his colleagues successfully manipulated group structure in the laboratory, comparing the effect on young boys of either democratic or authoritarian leadership styles. The results of the study were first published in 1939 (*Journal of Social Psychology* 10:271–99).

Lewin's first position in the United States was a two-year appointment in the School of Home Economics at Cornell, which was funded by the Emergency Committee in Aid of Displaced Scholars. There he worked in the nursery school on a series of studies of social pressures on the eating habits in children and produced two of his major works, *A Dynamic Theory of Personality* (1935) and *Principles of Topological Psychology* (1936).

In 1935 Lewin took a position at the Iowa Child Welfare Research Station (later the Institute of Child Behavior and Research) at the State University of Iowa in Iowa City, where he remained for nine years. There his work began to focus on group interaction. During World War II he conducted research for the U.S. government on the effects of group decisions on the food habits of housewives, which was commissioned in anticipation of wartime food rationing. He became an American citizen in 1940 and changed the pronunciation of his name from the German "La-veen" to an Americanized "Lewen."

In 1944 Lewin established the Research Center for Group Dynamics at the Massachusetts Institute of Technology to study the functioning of groups in the laboratory and in the field. Studies were designed and carried out on such issues as leadership, group cohesiveness, group productivity, the effects of group membership on its members, cooperation and competition, intergroup relations, communication and the spread of influence within groups, and social perception. He developed a technique for field research that he called action research (a three-step process of program planning, execution, and evaluation, which then fed into the next level of planning). Many of the field studies, which were conducted for the Council of Community Interrelations for the American Jewish Congress, investigated problems of minority groups in society and framed these problems in field theoretical terms.

Lewin died suddenly of a heart attack in Newtonville, Massachusetts. In a 1984 survey he was named, along with Freud, as the greatest influence on the thinking of contemporary psychologists. Taking into account the broad social determinants of behavior, in particular the interdependence of group process and individual psychology, his field theory was an early form of systems theory. The influence of Lewin's thinking can be seen today in the fields of communication, business management, organizational development, and education.

• Lewin's books that are not already mentioned in the text are *Resolving Social Conflicts* (1948) and *Autocracy and Democracy: An Experimental Inquiry*, with R. Lippitt and R. White (1960). The only biography is A. J. Marrow, *The Practical Theorist: The Life and Work of Kurt Lewin* (1969); Materials collected during the writing of Marrow's biography are now at the Archives of the History of American Psychology at the University of Akron in Ohio. Works that present Lewin's theory and work are J. F. Brown, "The Methods of Kurt Lewin in the Psychology of Action and Affection," *Psychological Review* 36 (May 1929): 200–21; and D. Cartwright, ed., *Field Theory in Social Science: Selected Theoretical Papers* (1951). Discussions of Lewin's working style and subsequent influence are L. Festinger, ed., *Retrospections on Social Psychology* (1980), and S. Patnoe, *A Narrative History of Experimental Social Psychology: The Lewin Tradition* (1988). An obituary is E. C. Tolman, "Kurt Lewin 1890–1947," *Psychological Review* 55, no. 1 (1948): 1–4.

SHELLEY PATNOE

LEWIS, Alfred Henry (20 Jan. 1857–23 Dec. 1914), lawyer, journalist, and author, was born in Cleveland, Ohio, the son of Isaac Jefferson Lewis, a carpenter, and Harriet Tracy. He attended Cleveland public schools, read for the law, and passed the Ohio bar in Columbus in 1876, placing first among those examined. He practiced law, dabbled in politics, became prosecuting attorney in the Cleveland police court (1880–1881), and moved to Kansas City, Missouri, with his parents and brothers. He turned to cowboy hobo-ing on ranches in Meade County, Kansas, along the Cimarron River and into Oklahoma Territory, driving cattle up to Dodge City, Kansas, and riding in Texas and Arizona. He was a journalist in New Mexico Territory—as the *Mora County Pioneer* editor, then on the *Las Vegas Optic* staff—and in 1885 returned to Kansas City to resume the practice of law.

To augment his income, Lewis turned to politics and wrote for local newspapers. He married Alice Ewing, a Richmond, Ohio, physician's daughter, in 1885 (the couple had no children), speculated in Kansas City real estate, and accepted the advice of the city editor of the *Kansas City Times* to write short stories. The first one took the form of an interview conducted in a local hotel by Dan Quin, the third-person narrator, with the "Old Cattleman," a crusty bachelor in his seventies who does most of the talking. Published anonymously in the *Kansas City Times* in 1890, the story earned Lewis no pay but was reprinted nationwide and became such a hit that his second "Old Cattleman" yarn, under the pen name "Dan Quin," earned him $360 and a job on the *Kansas City Star*. In 1891 he went to Washington, D.C., as the *Chicago Times* and the *Kansas City Times* correspondent. When the *Chi-*

cago Times was sold to the *Chicago Herald* in 1894, he declined an invitation to edit the *Chicago Times-Herald* and instead became manager of the Washington bureau of William Randolph Hearst's *New York Journal* (to 1898). Theodore Roosevelt, who was a civil-service commissioner when Lewis met him in 1893, read Lewis's early Wolfville stories, encouraged him to publish a book-length collection of them, and even persuaded Frederic Remington to provide illustrations. The result, dedicated to Hearst, was *Wolfville* (1897). The stories narrate events in the lives of residents of Wolfville, a town patterned after Tombstone, Arizona, and in rivalry with the nearby town of Red Dog. Lewis also wrote a number of "news novelettes" for Hearst's *Journal*. These pieces treated not only the action of current events but their background and foreground as well. Many were of the vicious muckraking variety.

In 1898 Lewis and his wife moved to New York City, where he wrote many editorials and essays for Hearst's newspapers and magazines, often in criticism of Republican politicians Mark Hanna and President William McKinley. Lewis also edited a pair of magazines—*The Verdict* (1898–1900), a humorous Democratic weekly, and *Human Life: The Magazine about People* (1905–1911), a Boston journal publishing miscellaneous pieces, including Lewis's own "Confessions of a Newspaperman" (Nov. 1905–Dec. 1906). Lewis wrote five essays as part of a series bitterly entitled "Owners of America" and published in Hearst's *Cosmopolitan* (June–Nov. 1908). Of the six chapters, devoted to Andrew Carnegie, Thomas F. Ryan, J. Pierpont Morgan, the Vanderbilts, Charles M. Schwab, and John D. Rockefeller, Lewis wrote all but the one on the Vanderbilts (prepared by Charles P. Norcross). Lewis's muckraking essays are factual, thorough, corrosively critical, and also virtually unique among muckraking pieces because they rebuke the victims of ruthless robber barons for being pusillanimous and thus deserving to be trampled on. Lewis, who grew even more acrimonious in his last years, suddenly died in New York of an intestinal disorder.

Author of some eighteen books in all, Lewis is of current value to literary historians only because of the seven books growing out of his "Old Cattleman" stories. In addition to *Wolfville*, they are *Sandburrs* (1900), *Wolfville Days* (1902), *Wolfville Nights* (1902, with a preface entitled "Some Cowboy Facts"), *The Black Lion Inn* (1903), *Wolfville Folks* (1908), and *Faro Nell and Her Friends: Wolfville Stories* (1913). These stories helped legitimize cattle-frontier fiction appearing early in the twentieth century in magazines such as the *American, Collier's, Cosmopolitan, McClure's, Everybody's,* and the *Saturday Evening Post.* The stereotype of the dried-up, talkative sidekick who populates innumerable western short stories, movies, and television series derives directly from Lewis's "Old Cattleman." An unfortunate feature of his yarns is his pervasive racism. A source of reader tedium is the phonetically spelled vernacular lingo in which they are too often narrated.

The remainder of Lewis's work is mostly forgotten. *The Sunset Trail* (1905) is his novelized life of real-life western lawman Bat Masterson, whom Lewis knew and to whom he dedicated the book. It started a trend of sanitized depictions of western lawmen who in real life were often unsavory. *The Throwback: A Romance of the Southwest* (1907) is significant mainly for helping another western stereotype evolve: the eastern tenderfoot who develops into a western veteran. Zane Grey later capitalized on this "dude" type. Lewis also published romantic novels (*The Old Plantation Home: A Story of Southern Life Just after the War* [1899] and *Peggy O'Neal* [1903]); a political novel (*The President* [1904]); books about historical figures (Andrew Jackson, Aaron Burr, John Paul Jones); two collections of short stories about crime; a book about sensational New York murders; a 1901 biography of Tammany Hall boss Richard F. Croker; and for good measure a novel based on Croker (*The Boss, and How He Came to Rule New York* [1903]). Lewis also edited a 1906 book of Theodore Roosevelt's 1901–1905 messages and speeches.

Lewis's Wolfville stories have endured, engaging the attention of traditional lovers of literature of the Old West. Some of their plots provided the basis for two plays: *Wolfville: A Drama of the Southwest* (1905), by Clyde Fitch and Willis Steell, and *The Heart of Peggy O'Neill* (1924), by Stephen Vincent Benét and John Farrar. Three movies based on Lewis's Wolfville characters are *Dead Shot Baker* (1917), *The Tenderfoot* (1917), and *Faro Nell, or in Old Californy* (1929).

• Letters by Lewis are in the Huntington Library, San Marino, Calif.; the Alderman Library, University of Virginia; and the Fales Library, Special Collections, New York University. An exhaustive bibliography of Lewis's works is in Jacob Blanck, *Bibliography of American Literature*, vol. 5 (1969), pp. 399–404. Lewis expresses aspects of his hopelessly bleak naturalistic philosophy in "What Life Means to Me," *Cosmopolitan*, Jan. 1907, pp. 293–98. Louis Filler, "Wolfville," *New Mexico Quarterly Review* 13 (Summer 1943): 35–47, presents a brief biography of Lewis and observes that his Wolfville stories combine primitivism and sentimentality. Both Ferdinand Lundberg, *Imperial Hearst: A Social Biography* (1936), and W. A. Swanberg, *Citizen Hearst: A Biography of William Randolph Hearst* (1961), criticize Lewis for being Hearst's hatchetman. The best detailed study of Lewis and his literary accomplishments is Abe C. Ravitz, *Alfred Henry Lewis* (1978). Jon Tuska and Vicki Piekarski, eds., *Encyclopedia of Frontier and Western Fiction* (1983), provides data on movies made from Lewis's fiction. An informative obituary is in the *New York Times*, 24 Dec. 1914.

ROBERT L. GALE

LEWIS, Andrew (9 Oct. 1720–26 Sept. 1781), military, political, and economic leader, was born in County Donegal, Ireland, the son of John Lewis and Margaret Lynn, farmers. Lewis's mother was a cousin of James Patton, who would also play a leading role in the development of southwestern Virginia. During Lewis's childhood, the family left their substantial farm, migrated first to Pennsylvania, and reached Augusta County, Virginia, by about 1732. They were among the area's earliest white settlers. Lewis married Elizabeth Givens; they settled, with their children, along the Upper Roanoke River.

Lewis invested heavily in real estate on the Virginia frontier, serving as an agent and surveyor for the company that received a 100,000-acre grant on the Greenbrier River in 1745 and acquiring much land on his own and in collaboration with others. By the early 1760s he owned at least 1,420 acres in the Beverley Manor area near Staunton, and he also held substantial amounts of land in the Greenbrier Valley, the area surrounding his home near present-day Salem, and elsewhere in southwestern Virginia. Not surprisingly, in the fluid setting of the southern frontier, Lewis's quest for wealth and position often led him into quarrels with other leaders. In the 1750s and 1760s, for example, he engaged in a long struggle with John Buchanan over their ranks in the Augusta County militia. Since Buchanan was the son-in-law and protégé of Patton, this quarrel was in some respects a continuation of the earlier conflicts between Patton and Lewis's father.

Lewis gained his greatest prominence as a frontier military leader. In addition to holding positions of authority in the local militia, he served as an officer in the disastrous expedition led by George Washington against the French fortifications on the Upper Ohio River near present-day Pittsburgh at the beginning of the Seven Years' War in 1754. Two years later he led the Sandy Creek expedition, which attempted to reach the Ohio River from southwestern Virginia. Unfortunately his army exhausted its food supply, and despite the efforts of Lewis and other officers, most of the men deserted and returned home. In 1758, on another expedition against the French on the Upper Ohio, he was captured while participating in an advance party, under the command of Major James Grant, that reconnoitered the enemy fortifications.

During Dunmore's War in 1774, Lewis commanded the forces that won an important victory over the Shawnee Indians. Fearing that the encroachments of Virginia and Pennsylvania settlers on Shawnee territories might intensify Indian attacks, Virginia authorities planned a two-pronged offensive against the Shawnee towns beyond the Ohio River. Governor John Murray Dunmore was to lead an army westward from northwestern Virginia while Lewis marched with militia forces numbering about 1,000 men from southwestern Virginia toward an anticipated rendezvous at Point Pleasant, the junction of the Ohio and Kanawha rivers. The two forces were then to advance together across the Ohio toward their objective. Upon arriving at Point Pleasant, however, Lewis learned that the governor's forces had already moved beyond the Ohio, leaving instructions for him to meet them at the Shawnee towns. On 10 October Cornstalk and a large Shawnee force who had secretly crossed the Ohio River, attacked Lewis's army at Point Pleasant. The victory ended the Shawnees' resistance, and nine days later they signed a treaty conceding all of their territory south of the Ohio to Virginia.

The victory at Point Pleasant assured Lewis a prominent role in Virginia's defensive efforts during the early revolutionary war years. In March 1776 the Continental Congress appointed him a brigadier general, and that summer he commanded the troops that attacked Governor Dunmore's Loyalist forces on Gwynn's Island in the Chesapeake Bay near the mouth of the Piankatank River. Ultimately this campaign forced Dunmore to give up his challenge to Virginia patriot authorities and remove his followers from the colony. Disappointed that he had not been appointed major general, Lewis resigned from the Continental army in April 1777.

Lewis also played an important role in the political life of his region and of Virginia. At various times he served Augusta and Botetourt counties as sheriff, member of the county court, colonial legislator, and member of the 1775 revolutionary conventions. In addition he represented Virginia in several negotiations with Native American groups in the Trans-Appalachian West, and in 1780 he was appointed a member of Virginia's Executive Council, on which he served until he died the next year in Bedford County while returning to his Botetourt County home.

Throughout his life Lewis's reputation as an aloof and authoritarian leader made him controversial. While some other leaders admired him, ordinary settlers who preferred more consensual leadership styles often resented his manner and actions. Thus on the Sandy Creek expedition of 1756, Lewis's vigorous assertion of his own authority apparently further embittered his underfed soldiers: many deserted by marching off in company formation at the conclusion of his speech that warned of the consequences of such actions. Similar antagonisms developed during Dunmore's War. One popular ballad about the battle of Point Pleasant portrayed Lewis as not merely aloof but also cowardly for remaining well behind the line of combat. In contrast the ballad celebrated the more dramatic and democratic leadership styles of other officers, including Lewis's brother Charles Lewis, who was killed in the battle.

Andrew Lewis's career shaped and was shaped by several broader patterns of change in eighteenth-century America and the Atlantic world. He was a part of the migration of settlers from Ulster to Pennsylvania and the southern colonial frontier, and his military, political, and land speculation activities encouraged the continued westward expansion of Euramerican settlement. Moreover, like many other leaders on the frontier and throughout revolutionary America, he encountered substantial difficulties in attempting to sustain traditional styles of political and military leadership.

• The most detailed study of Lewis is Patricia Givens Johnson, *General Andrew Lewis of Roanoke and Greenbrier* (1980). He is also discussed in Freeman H. Hart, *The Valley of Virginia in the American Revolution* (1942), John E. Selby, *The*

Revolution in Virginia, 1775–1783 (1988), and Albert H. Tillson, Jr., *Gentry and Common Folk: Political Culture on a Virginia Frontier, 1740–1789* (1991).

ALBERT H. TILLSON, JR.

LEWIS, Augusta (c. 1848–14 Sept. 1920), journalist and labor leader, was born in New York City, the daughter of Charles Lewis and Elizabeth Rowe, occupations unknown. Having lost both her parents while still an infant, Lewis was raised by Isaac Baldwin Gager, a commission merchant in Brooklyn Heights. She received her early education at home, after which she lived for several seasons with one of her private teachers in Cold Spring, New York. Returning to New York City, she studied at Brooklyn Heights Seminary and then entered the Sacred Heart Convent School in Manhattanville, New York, from which she graduated with honors.

Because of reverses suffered by Gager in the depression of 1866–1867, Lewis suddenly found it necessary to support herself. Capitalizing on her flair for writing and conversation, she started contributing articles to various periodicals and working as a reporter for the *New York Sun*. Then she embarked on a new occupation: typesetting. Women were in the minority in the printing field, and they were paid considerably less than men for the same work; nevertheless, they were among the best-paid working women in the city, earning far more than those who entered the dominant female occupations of domestic service and the needle trades. Lewis began as an apprentice typesetter at the *New York Era*; then when her training was complete, she moved to the *New York World*. She also continued working as a reporter.

Because of her skill at typesetting as well as her personal qualities, Lewis came to be recognized as a leader among the women printers. In December 1867 the male members of the trade launched a strike against the *World*. The female typesetters, who were excluded from the International Typographical Union (ITU) because of their gender, chose to continue working. When the strike ended ten months later, one of the returning workers' demands was that the women "scabs" should be fired; the managers of the *World* promptly complied. Although Lewis herself was not dismissed, she quit her job to protest the firing of the others. She managed to find work in various small printing firms, but her experience at the *World* convinced her that women typesetters must have a union of their own.

Lewis arrived at this idea just as two other formidable women were coming to the same conclusion by a different route. Elizabeth Cady Stanton and Susan B. Anthony had been campaigning for woman suffrage for a number of years. Having been rebuffed by the male leaders of both major political parties, Stanton and Anthony began looking for allies in the labor movement. Their newspaper, *Revolution*, championed the cause of the fired women typesetters, and this stand led to an alliance with Lewis. In September 1868 the three established the New York Working Women's Association (WWA), based at the *Revolution* office. With a membership of about one hundred women, most of them typographers, the WWA announced its intention to look out for the interests of female workers "in the same manner as the associations of workingmen now regulate the wages, etc. of those belonging to them."

A month after the WWA was founded, Lewis took a leading role in organizing the Women's Typographical Union Local 1, of which she became president. In this effort she received important backing from Alexander Troup, who was secretary-treasurer of the ITU and corresponding secretary of ITU's New York Local 6. Recognizing—more clearly than many ITU members—that excluding women only created a potential pool of strikebreakers, Troup promised to provide the local with a hall for its meetings, books, and stationery and with enough money to cover expenses until it could stand on its own.

Anthony hailed the founding of the women's union, assuring Lewis and her colleagues that they had taken "a great, a momentous step forward in the path to success." But despite its shared commitment to women's rights, the alliance between Lewis and the suffragists began showing strains almost as soon as it got underway. Stanton and Anthony hoped that the WWA would endorse woman suffrage because they saw the vote as the critical first step in securing other rights. Lewis, on the other hand, felt that "business purposes" must come first; she warned that tying the fledgling WWA to woman suffrage would frighten off potential members by identifying the association with "short hair, bloomers and other vagaries." She insisted that the solidarity among women workers was too new and fragile to risk introducing so divisive an issue. Her view prevailed and the three women continued to work together while carrying on a friendly debate about the issue in the pages of the *Revolution*.

A more serious break emerged early in 1869, when many New York printers went on strike. Lewis, who put union and class loyalty first, made every effort to discourage WWA members from taking the strikers' jobs. Meanwhile, Anthony, who saw only an opportunity for women to get work experience they were usually denied, encouraged WWA members to break the strike and pled with employers to hire them. Anthony's punishment came a few months later, when she tried to attend the annual convention of the National Labor Union in Philadelphia as a WWA delegate. Lewis wrote a letter to the convention maintaining that the WWA was not a true labor organization, since by then most of its working members had withdrawn. Middle-class women now dominated the group, she said, and "either the want of knowledge or the want of sense renders them, as a working-woman's association, very inefficient." Backing her up, the New York delegation urged that Anthony be barred from the proceedings. The convention as a whole voted to admit her, but when the ITU threatened to bolt if she was seated, the vote finally went against her. This ended Lewis's association with Anthony and Stanton.

Though Lewis remained a firm supporter of woman suffrage the rest of her life, her organizational ties from 1869 were with the ITU.

In 1870 Lewis attended the national ITU convention as a delegate from Women's Local 1. On that occasion the ITU took the unprecedented step of electing Lewis to serve as corresponding secretary, an important position that involved significant administrative responsibility. The following year she presented to the convention a comprehensive report on wages and working conditions in the printing trades in a dozen cities; this paper represented the first such report in American labor history produced by a woman. Acknowledging Lewis's achievements as corresponding secretary, the convention president praised her for displaying "industry, zeal and intelligence in the position rarely met with."

Despite Lewis's importance in the parent organization, her own Women's Local No. 1 faced formidable odds and never grew to more than forty members. The crux of the problem was that employers refused to pay female typesetters the same wages as men. As a result, the women were seen as a threat to the standard wage scale, and ITU members often opposed their being hired even though Lewis's organization had received an ITU charter in 1869 (the first ever granted to a women's local) and faithfully respected every strike. On the other hand, the women's status as union members made anti-union shops unwilling to hire them. By the time Lewis left the organization in 1874 (some sources say 1871 or 1872) to marry Alexander Troup, the women's local was falling into decline, demoralized by its inability to win equal pay for equal work. When the union finally dissolved in 1878, the ITU decided not to charter any more separate locals for women. It later began admitting female members to its existing locals, but they remained a minority and did not have the opportunity for leadership that Women's Local No. 1 had provided to Lewis and her fellow members.

Lewis settled in New Haven, Connecticut, where her new husband had become the publisher of a labor-oriented newspaper, the *New Haven Union*. While he built a career in journalism and Democratic party politics, Lewis raised five children, wrote for her husband's paper, and took an active interest in local charities, especially those in the city's Italian neighborhood. After her death in New Haven, a local junior high school named in her honor included a plaque paying tribute to her as the "Little Mother of the Italian Community."

As long as she was a typesetter, Lewis dedicated much of her energy to the cause of unionism, but she and her women's local gave the male printers in their union more loyalty than they received in return. Indeed, if Lewis were to be faulted, it would be for underestimating the importance of gender in shaping labor relations. Yet doing so helped her to persevere, and, as she said, "to add a link to the chain that would span the chasm that has heretofore divided the interests of the male and female printers." Her most basic aspirations—equal pay for equal work and equal status within the union—were not realized in her lifetime. But important progress has been made, and Lewis helped to set the agenda for it.

• Lewis left no personal papers, but writings by and about her appear in *Revolution*, 24 Sept. and 1, 8, 15 Oct. 1868 and 4, 11, Feb., 24 June, and 9 Sept. (1869). Accounts of her career are in George A. Stevens, *New York Typographical Union No. 6: A Study of a Modern Trade Union and Its Predecessors* (1913); George A. Tracy, *History of the Typographical Union* (1913); Eleanor Flexner, *Century of Struggle: The Woman's Rights Movement in the United States* (1959); Susan Estabrook Kennedy, *If All We Did Was to Weep at Home: A History of White Working Class Women in America* (1979); Philip S. Foner, *Women and the American Labor Movement: From the First Trade Unions to the Present* (1979); David Montgomery, *Beyond Equality: Labor and the Radical Republicans, 1862–1872* (1967); Ellen DuBois, *Feminism and Suffrage: The Emergence of an Independent Women's Movement in America, 1848–1869* (1978); and Joyce Maupin, *Labor Heroines: Ten Women Who Led the Struggle* (1974). An obituary is in the *New York Times*, 15 Sept. 1920.

SANDRA OPDYCKE

LEWIS, Charles Bertrand (15 Feb. 1842–21 Aug. 1924), humorist, was born in Liverpool, Ohio, the son of George C. Lewis, a contractor and builder, and Clarissa (maiden name unknown). At age fourteen Lewis began to learn the printer's trade as an apprentice at the *Jacksonian* in Pontiac, Michigan, and he worked as a compositor, press-hand, and local reporter for a small newspaper in Lansing, Michigan. He continued his career in journalism as a war correspondent for the Union army during the Civil War.

After the war Lewis began working at the *Pontiac Jacksonian*, where he occasionally inserted his own paragraphs of humor to fill empty space. These space fillers attracted the attention of the *Detroit Free Press*, and in 1868 Lewis was hired by the paper as a legislative reporter. In 1869 he wrote his first humorous article, which was based on a true incident. Earlier that year, Lewis had been aboard a steamer that exploded. Under the pen name "M. Quad," Lewis wrote an article titled "How It Feels to Be Blown Up." The article was very popular and resulted in Lewis writing numerous others.

Still writing as M. Quad, Lewis became known for the characters he created. The feuding Mr. and Mrs. Bowser and Brother Gardner, leader of a black social club, were his most memorable creations. Some of Lewis's most popular writings for the *Free Press* were later revised, collected, and appended to form several book-length works: *Brother Gardner's Lime Kiln Club* (1882; repr. 1887); *Goaks and Tears* (1875); *Trials and Troubles of the Bowser Family* (1889; repr. 1902); and *Quad's Odds* (1875). Lewis also tried his hand at writing plays but with less success: only one of his five comedies, *Yakie* (1883), was ever produced, and it received bad reviews. In addition to his efforts at humor, a few of Lewis's writings were more serious in content, such as *Field, Fort and Fleet* (1885) and *Under Five*

Lakes (1886), which sketched scenes from Civil War battles.

In 1891, after twenty-two years at the *Free Press*, Lewis took a position with the *New York World* and *Evening World* and moved to Brooklyn. As a New York columnist, Lewis continued to write about some of the characters that he created while at the *Free Press: The Life and Troubles of Mr. Bowser* was published in 1902 and *The Humorous Mr. Bowser* in 1911. For the rest of his life, Lewis contributed to the *World* and the *Evening World*, and also wrote for the *New York Herald* syndicate. As late as 1922 he was still contributing six columns of humor to the *Herald* syndicate every week.

Lewis was married, but his wife died approximately seventeen years prior to his death. They had one son. Lewis suffered from severe rheumatism during the final years of his life and rarely left the grounds of his son's home, where he resided. Lewis died at his son's home in Brooklyn, New York.

During the height of his career as a humorist, Lewis was known as a writer whose knowledge of human nature transferred to his writings; it was this element of Lewis's works that made them so popular. Many of his stories and sketches dealt with the poor and the black population. In 1897 Art young noted that Lewis "spends much of his time studying human nature in the slums of the great East Side of New York City" (p. 197). Lewis himself admitted that in his works dealing with the Bowser family, he "simply relate[d] what might and what [did] transpire in the average household" (*Mr. and Mrs. Bowser and Their Varied Experiences*, preface [1899]).

The reading public also knew Lewis as a boisterous writer whose stories produced almost uncontrollable laughter. In 1922 Thomas L. Masson wrote that Lewis's writing was "filled with the most robust humor, side-splitting often in its primitive revelings" (p. 232). Unlike this characteristic of his work, Lewis's personality was quite different. In an interview after Lewis's death, James A. Robison, who worked with Lewis at the *Free Press*, noted that "Lewis was the reverse of the popular conception of a humorist. He was reserved in conduct, and made few friends, though he was extremely observant" (*Detroit Free Press*, 24 Aug. 1924).

• Other works by Lewis include *Bessie Bane; or, The Mormon's Victim* (1880) and *Sparks of Wit* (1885). For a thorough list of Lewis's writings see the entry on Lewis in the *Dictionary of Literary Biography*. For reviews of his play *Yakie* see the *New York Times*, 18 Sept. 1883, and *Life*, 27 Sept. 1883. A chapter in Thomas L. Masson's *Our American Humorists* (1922) provides Lewis's reflections on his start in journalism. See Art Young, *Author's Readings* (1897), for a short history of Lewis's life up to that year. Several articles found in the *Detroit Free Press*, 24 Aug. 1924, are important for seeing how Lewis's contemporaries remembered him. Obituaries are in the *New York Times* and the *Detroit Free Press*, 23 Aug. 1924.

JESSICA LEXIE HOLLIS

LEWIS, Charlton Thomas (25 Feb. 1834–26 May 1904), classical scholar and lawyer, was born in West Chester, Pennsylvania, the son of Joseph Jackson Lewis, a lawyer, and Mary Sinton Miner. At Yale College he excelled in languages and mathematics. Upon graduating in 1853 he began to study law at West Chester but in 1854 prepared for the Methodist ministry. In 1857 he took up teaching, first at the Normal University of Illinois at Bloomington, and from 1859 to 1862 at the short-lived university at Troy, New York, where he taught Greek and mathematics. At this time he wrote, with Marvin Richardson Vincent, an English translation of John Albrecht Bengel's *Gnomon of the New Testament* (2 vols., 1860–1862). In July 1861 Lewis married Nancy Dunlop McKeen; they had four children. After briefly resuming his work in the Methodist church, he was appointed deputy commissioner of internal revenue late in 1862, serving under his father, who had been made commissioner by President Abraham Lincoln. In 1865 Lewis took up the practice of law in New York, but after two years the stress of his varied and demanding career caused him to suffer from "overwork," and he went to Europe to rest for a year.

When Lewis returned to New York in 1868, he joined the editorial staff of William Cullen Bryant's New York *Evening Post*, of which he became managing editor in 1871, writing frequently for the editorial page. After a year at this post, Lewis began to practice law again, and this remained his principal professional occupation for the rest of his life. His specialty was corporation law, but he became known as an expert on insurance and as an advocate of prison reform.

From this time on, Lewis also executed an impressive amount of literary work, especially on assignments for the publisher Harper & Brothers. As early as 1872 he gave the firm legal advice on a matter of copyright infringement involving *A Copious and Critical Latin-English Lexicon* (1851), edited for Harper & Brothers by Ethan Allen Andrews. In 1874 the firm published Lewis's *History of Germany from the Earliest Times*, based on David Müller's *Geschichte des Deutschen Volkes*. In the same year it engaged him to rewrite a large portion of Andrews's *Lexicon*, following the plan laid down by the classical philologist Charles Short (1821–1886), who had already begun the revision but whose work had been proceeding slowly. With remarkable rapidity Lewis completed letters *B* through *Z* of the new lexicon by 1878, and it appeared the next year as *Harpers' Latin Dictionary*, widely known as "Lewis and Short." This, Lewis's most lasting achievement, became the standard Latin-English dictionary throughout the English-speaking world, in spite of shortcomings (such as omissions of words and citations), many of which have been remedied in the comprehensive *Oxford Latin Dictionary* (1968–1982).

In 1885, two years after his first wife died, Lewis married Margaret Pierce Sherrard; they had two children. Among his later publications are *A Latin Dictionary for Schools* (1889) and *An Elementary Latin Dictionary* (1891). He also edited *Harper's Book of Facts*

(1895), supervised a translation of *The Love Letters of Bismarck* (1901), and wrote numerous reviews and articles on law, insurance, and prisons. He died in Morristown, New Jersey.

• A list of Lewis's writings appears in *The Class of 'Fifty-three in Yale College, A Supplementary History Concluding the Fifth Decade* (1903). See also the list of his writings on prisons in the *Fifty-ninth Annual Report of the Prison Association of New York for the Year 1903* (1904). A biographical account appears in *Harper's Weekly* 48 (11 June 1904): 890–91. For a fully documented discussion of his part in the compilation of the lexicon known as "Lewis and Short," see F. J. Sypher, "A History of *Harpers' Latin Dictionary*," *Harvard Library Bulletin* 20, no. 4 (1972): 349–66.

F. J. SYPHER

LEWIS, Clarence Irving (12 Apr. 1883–3 Feb. 1964), philosopher, was born in Stoneham, Massachusetts, the son of Irving Lewis, a shoemaker, and Hannah Carlin Dearth. His father was blacklisted for union activities, which constrained the family to living in a number of small towns in Massachusetts and New Hampshire as the father sought work. With savings from after-school and summer jobs, Lewis entered Harvard in 1902 and graduated in three years to save on tuition. After teaching high school English for one year, Lewis taught English and philosophy at the University of Colorado from fall 1906 until January 1908. He returned briefly to Massachusetts in January 1907 to marry Mabel Graves, whom he had known since high school. They had four children, two of whom died at young ages.

In 1908 he returned to the Harvard philosophy department. William James had just retired, and Josiah Royce was the dominating intellectual figure. Again for economic reasons, Lewis completed his Ph.D. in two years, presenting a thesis in 1910 synthesizing concerns of the idealist Royce and the critical realist Ralph Barton Perry. In the following year he was an assistant to Royce in his logic course. In the fall of 1911 he went to the University of California at Berkeley as an instructor in philosophy. He was made an assistant professor at Berkeley in 1914. Lewis enlisted in the army as a private when the United States entered World War I. He served as a gunnery instructor in the coast artillery at Fort Monroe, Virginia. When he returned to Berkeley in 1918, he had risen to the rank of captain. He stayed at Berkeley until he returned to Harvard as a one-year lecturer in 1920.

While at Berkeley he wrote his first book, *A Survey of Symbolic Logic* (1918). This provided the background that would enable a student to appreciate Alfred N. Whitehead and Bertrand Russell's monumental *Principia Mathematica* (1910–1913). It also contained material critical of some approaches of Whitehead and Russell, which Lewis formulated in an alternative logic system of "strict implication." These ideas were more fully developed in subsequent publications and received the most thorough treatment in *Symbolic Logic* (1932), which he wrote with Cooper Harold Langford. Much of the field now known as modal logic, which studies the interrelations of statements about what is possible and necessary, can be directly traced to Lewis's work.

At Harvard he became assistant professor in 1921, associate professor in 1924, and full professor in 1930. In 1946 he succeeded Perry to the Edgar Pierce professorship, which he held until his retirement in 1953. During this period he wrote his two most important works, *Mind and the World Order* (1929) and *An Analysis of Knowledge and Valuation* (1946).

Lewis took seriously the Kantian distinction between a priori knowledge, such as that 2 + 2 = 4, which we can have without specific experiences, and empirical knowledge, which depends on the occurrence of specific events, such as that Caesar crossed the Rubicon. He was concerned with the problem of how we can have knowledge of either sort. Royce had argued for an absolute mind that includes and coordinates the sum of experiences of both the self and others, providing the arena in which our ideas relate to a single world. Lewis took his cue from the pragmatism of James and Charles S. Peirce to define the content of our empirical beliefs as the sum of experiences that would result from possible actions. For Lewis, the belief that there is a cup in front of one consists in (among other things) the visual experiences and the touch sensations that one would have if one reached to pick up the cup. The fact that these experiences can be coordinated for different observers constitutes the objectivity of one's knowledge that a cup is before one.

For a priori knowledge, Kant had argued that it results from activities of the mind that structure our experiences in certain inevitable ways. Lewis accepted that there is a conceptual structure the mind provides to organize experience and that our a priori knowledge expresses this. But he argued that this conceptual structure could change when our actions in pursuit of what we value fail to produce the expected satisfactions. That such changes do not produce a chaos of shifting concepts, that 2 + 2 = 4 remains true over time, showed Lewis that our conceptual structures were grounded in an enduring, but not inevitable, order of human experience.

Widely regarded as the most important American philosopher of his day, he received numerous honors and was invited to lecture at many universities. He was president of the Eastern Division of the American Philosophical Association in 1934, and Columbia University awarded him a Butler medal in 1950.

After his retirement from Harvard, Lewis taught for a year at Princeton. He then moved to Menlo Park, California, where he periodically gave courses at Stanford; occasionally he also lectured and taught elsewhere. In these years he devoted himself to ethics, publishing *The Ground and Nature of the Right* (1955) and *Our Social Inheritance* (1957). He argued that statements about values are objectively true or false. This was in contrast to the "emotivist" view, common at that time in American philosophy, that statements about value simply express personal approval or disapproval and so are not true or false. He died in Menlo Park.

Lewis is an important link in the historical chain of American philosophers. Uniting the systematic concerns of his mentor Royce with the vague suggestions offered by James, he produced the most developed version of pragmatism. Although the style of argument in *Mind and the World Order* echoes that of Royce, Perry, and James, his later work achieves the precise formulation and detailed elaboration of consequences that was to become the norm in subsequent American philosophy. Many of his themes were congenial to the logical positivism that became influential during the last phase of his career, but he remained distant from the trend. He was convinced that philosophic problems could not be solved or avoided by clarification of language systems, as the logical positivists promised, but that they have their root in the nature of human experience.

• Lewis's papers are at the Stanford University Library. There are two autobiographical articles by Lewis. One is in *The Philosophy of C. I. Lewis*, ed. Paul A. Schilpp (1968), which also contains articles about his work by other philosophers and a complete bibliography. Another autobiographical article, "Logic and Pragmatism," is reprinted along with a selection of published and unpublished papers in *Collected Papers of Clarence Irving Lewis*, ed. John D. Goheen and John L. Mothershead (1970). There is also a collection of ethics papers by Lewis in *Values and Imperatives: Studies in Ethics*, ed. John Lange (1969). Two biographical articles about him are Donald C. Williams, "Clarence Irving Lewis, 1883–1964," *Philosophy and Phenomenological Research* 26 (1965): 159–72, and William T. Parry, "In Memoriam: Clarence Irving Lewis (1883–1964)," *Notre Dame Journal of Formal Logic* 11 (1970): 129–40. A chapter in Elizabeth Flower and Murray G. Murphey, *A History of Philosophy in America*, vol. 2 (1977), analyzes his philosophy. His philosophy, along with biographical context, is also given a chapter in Bruce Kuklick, *The Rise of American Philosophy* (1977). An obituary is in the *New York Times*, 4 Feb. 1964.

MICHAEL SCANLAN

LEWIS, David Peter (1820?–3 July 1884), governor of Alabama, was born in Charlotte County, Virginia, the son of Mary Smith Buster and Peter C. Lewis. In the 1820s the family moved to Madison County, Alabama, where Lewis's father became a county commissioner but died soon thereafter. His mother remarried. After attending the University of Virginia and reading law in Huntsville, Alabama, Lewis moved to Lawrence County in 1843 and practiced law. He never married and until 1860 was not involved in politics.

In 1860 Lewis owned $20,000 in real property and $42,185 in personal property (including thirty-four slaves). He was a Douglas Democrat and represented Lawrence County in the 1861 Alabama constitutional convention, where he opposed secession. However, he signed the ordinance under instructions from his constituents. In 1861 he was elected to the Provisional Confederate Congress and was appointed to the Patents and Indian Affairs committees. He resigned his office on 29 April and joined a volunteer company,

which was soon disbanded. In 1862 Lewis and other North Alabama Unionists organized a secret Peace Society, and he declined appointment as lieutenant colonel in Colonel Philip Roddey's command. In 1863 Governor John Gill Shorter appointed Lewis as judge of the Fourth Alabama Judicial Circuit Court. Lewis resigned on 1 January 1864. Although exempt from conscription as the owner of a public mill, he was ordered to report for military service in the fall of 1864. He refused and crossed through the Federal lines to Nashville, where he remained for the duration of the Civil War.

Lewis returned to Alabama in July 1865, began a law practice in Huntsville, and soon applied for a pardon under the clause in Andrew Johnson's plan of Reconstruction that required men with over $20,000 to apply individually. In 1868 he attended the Democratic National Convention as a delegate but the next year quietly joined the Republican party in Alabama. By this time Lewis had established a reputation as a man of "firm but not obtrusive" opinions, a learned and respected attorney.

As a native white Republican (scalawag), Lewis joined others of his background to battle for control of the party in Alabama. Unlike many other states in the Reconstruction South, in Alabama white natives managed to control their party even though they were outnumbered by blacks and newcomers. Nevertheless, Lewis was outraged, because Alabama Unionists were insufficiently rewarded for their prewar opposition to secession. Especially offensive was the officeholding disability, whereby men who had sworn to uphold the federal Constitution and subsequently broke that oath by aiding the Confederacy could not hold office until Congress voted to remove this disability. Lewis was furious that those who had "sincerely grieved at the success of secession, and whose only crime was a fatherly sympathy for his son, who joined the rebel army to avoid the disgrace of conscription," were deemed as guilty as those who had concocted the scheme of secession. He advocated general amnesty and removal of the disabilities from all who had opposed secession in 1860. Other than these occasional outbursts over political neglect of Unionists, Lewis was not embroiled in Republican party quarrels.

As a man with few political enemies, Lewis was a desirable candidate for governor in 1872. Having lost the Alabama governorship in 1870, Republicans now recognized how essential for their party's success was the support of the conservatives of 1860. Lewis was elected governor of Alabama over Democrat Thomas Hord Herndon in 1872; however, the outcome of the election of the legislature was disputed. Both parties claimed control of the general assembly, and both parties organized legislatures. Although Lewis recognized the Republican-controlled legislature, U.S. attorney general George Henry Williams resolved the impasse by creating a fusion legislature, with Republicans holding a slight majority.

The resulting configuration of the legislature produced a stalemate; in addition, the panic of 1873 wreaked economic havoc on the state, then suffering from earlier reckless railroad development. Lewis has been unfairly blamed for Alabama's economic crisis. Actually, the damage had been done between 1868 and 1872, when first a Republican and then a Democratic government appropriated the state's credit to build first a Republican-backed railroad and then a Democratic-backed one. Lewis remained aloof from the most important legislative action of his administration, the efforts made by his party to pass a civil rights bill. Stormy debates in both houses revealed the division within the Republican party regarding racial issues, and the bills died.

In 1874 Alabama Republicans hoped to repeat their 1872 success and nominated Lewis for a second term. However, Republican internal quarrels and congressional debate over a federal civil rights bill doomed his prospects. Furthermore, Alabama Democrats made race the issue of the 1874 campaign and resorted to widespread intimidation and violence to win the election. Democrats ostracized white Republicans and employed economic reprisals against members of the black population who did not respond to physical intimidation and violence. Black Republicans, angry that their white colleagues had not supported passage of a civil rights bill in Alabama, attacked their white party leaders, calling Lewis a man of "utter lack of backbone" who had betrayed black Republicans. As Democrats waved the flag of white supremacy, whites deserted the Republicans, and the Democrats won in a landslide.

After he tried and failed to receive an appointment as a federal district judge in 1874, Lewis retired from active politics. In 1875, when Democrats rewrote the Alabama constitution, he supported ratification of the new document. By the fall of 1876 Lewis, like many other Alabama scalawags, had quietly returned to the Democratic party. He explained that Republican Reconstruction had been a "disgraceful failure" and that he saw no hope among Republicans for southern men of conservative views. After leaving public office Lewis resumed his law practice in Huntsville until his death there.

• A small collection of Lewis manuscripts is in the Governor David P. Lewis Papers, Alabama Department of Archives and History (ADAH), Montgomery. Other letters are widely scattered in manuscript collections. For example, see Records of the Judiciary, Disabilities, Alabama, 42d Cong., Committee on the Records of the U.S. House of Representatives (RG 233), National Archives; Records of the Adjutant General's Office (RG 94), National Archives; William E. Chandler Papers and Andrew Johnson Papers, Library of Congress; and William Hugh Smith Papers, ADAH. Two Lewis letters are published in Sarah Van V. Woolfolk, "Amnesty and Pardon and Republicanism in Alabama," *Alabama Historical Quarterly* 26 (1964): 240–48. Another appears in the Montgomery daily *Alabama State Journal*, 8 Sept. 1872. His 1865 amnesty and pardon application is in Register of Applications for Amnesty and Pardon, vol. 2, p. 174, ADAH; and a sworn statement (12 Aug. 1865) is in Records of the Adjutant General (RG 94). The legal affairs of Peter C. Lewis, David P. Lewis, and Mary Lewis Webb can be followed in Pauline Jones Gandrud, *Alabama Records* (probate records of Lawrence and Madison counties, n.d.), Special Collections, University of Alabama Library.

Two biographical sources are Thomas McAdory Owen, *History of Alabama and Dictionary of Alabama Biography* (1921), and W. Brewer, *Alabama: Her History, Resources, War Record, and Public Men* (1872). Ezra J. Warner and W. Buck Yearns, *Biographical Register of the Confederate Congress* (1975), and Kenny A. Franks, "David Peter Lewis," in *Encyclopedia of the Confederacy*, ed. Richard N. Current (1993), are critical of Lewis. See also Sarah Woolfolk Wiggins, *The Scalawag in Alabama Politics, 1865–1881* (1977), and Malcolm C. McMillan, ed., *The Alabama Confederate Reader* (1963). Obituaries are in the *Huntsville Advocate*, 4 July 1884; the *Montgomery Daily Advertiser*, 5 July 1884; and the *Huntsville Weekly Democrat*, 9 July 1884.

SARAH WOOLFOLK WIGGINS

LEWIS, Dioclesian (3 Mar. 1823–21 May 1886), temperance reformer and pioneer in physical education, was born near Auburn, New York, the son of John C. Lewis and Delecta Barbour, farmers. A product of the "Burned-Over District," America's most fertile ground for revivalism and reform during the Second Great Awakening (1800–1830), Dio Lewis absorbed revivalism's lesson of individual improvement through self-discipline and applied it to social problems created or exacerbated by urbanization and industrialization. His first exposure to the new world of industry came as a boy, when he was hired by a cotton mill near his home. After spending several years in his late teens as a teacher, Lewis turned to the study of medicine, at first with a local doctor, then for a short time at Harvard. While practicing in Port Byron, New York, he was converted by his partner to homeopathy, and as a result of his efforts in publicizing homeopathic principles Lewis was awarded an honorary M.D. in 1851 by the Homeopathic Hospital College of Cleveland, Ohio.

Influenced by his mother's teachings, Lewis had always been a supporter of temperance. During the 1850s he became a popular lecturer for a new fraternal order, the Sons of Temperance. By all accounts, he was a formidable and compelling figure on the platform, a large man whose performance manifested the vitality promised by his gospel of health. At the same time as he maintained his medical practice and nurtured his new lecturing career, he was seeking to cure the tuberculosis of his wife, Helen Cecilia Clarke, whom he had married in 1849, using therapies that minimized the use of drugs and relied heavily on exercise. Lewis's treatments seem to have been successful (his wife outlived him), and the experience helped to convince him of the necessity of physical activity for a healthy lifestyle. With sedentary occupations on the increase, middle-class urban Americans were becoming concerned with finding ways to foster physical fitness. In contrast to advocates of strength-building regimes dependent on heavy and expensive fixed equipment designed for the use of young men, Lewis created an exercise program that employed light, portable, and easily fabricated aids, such as wands, dumb-bells, rings, and the beanbag, suitable for persons of both sexes and all ages.

During the 1860s Lewis turned his considerable energies to publicizing his system. Thomas Wentworth Higginson described him at this time: "So hale and hearty, so profoundly confident in the omnipotence of his own methods and the uselessness of all others, with such a ready invention, and such an inundation of animal spirits that he could flood any company, no matter how starched or listless, with an unbounded appetite for ball-games and bean-games" (*Atlantic Monthly*, Mar. 1861, p. 300). He also wrote a book, *The New Gymnastics for Men, Women, and Children* (1862), which went through twenty-five editions; published in 1861 a journal, the short-lived *Gymnastic Monthly and Journal of Physical Culture*, notable as the first American physical education periodical; and in the same year established the Boston Normal Institute for Physical Education, the nation's first school to train teachers in physical education. Through his efforts and those of his followers, many schools in the United States and abroad adopted or expanded programs of physical education. In 1864 Lewis founded a girls' school in Lexington, Massachusetts, to put into practice his ideas on physical education as well as his pedagogical philosophy, according to which students were regarded as "reasonable and intelligent beings, who would naturally choose the right and accept the opportunities of mental and physical culture offered them" (Eastman, p. 104); the school encouraged close and relatively informal relations between teachers and students, banned corporal punishment, and de-emphasized grades.

After his girls' school burned in 1867, Lewis returned to the lecture circuit to champion the twin causes of women's health (to be achieved through exercise and loose, comfortable clothing) and women's autonomy (to be gained through entry into all respectable occupations, equal pay for equal work, and "voluntary motherhood," i.e., freedom from unwanted pregnancy). He also extolled his mother's success many years before in closing saloons through prayer at the saloonkeepers' doorsteps. The latter message struck a responsive chord during the winter of 1873–1874 in small towns in western New York and southern Ohio, where women inspired by Lewis began to mount nonviolent marches on local retail liquor outlets. These women launched the Women's Temperance Crusade, which gave birth to the Woman's Christian Temperance Union (WCTU), the largest American women's reform organization of the century. When the WCTU turned to advocacy of prohibition and linked its fortunes with the Prohibition party, however, Lewis found himself in a minority among temperance reformers, as his individualistic ethos precluded measures more coercive than mass prayer and specifically rejected prohibition, which he wrote a book to oppose (*Prohibition a Failure* [1875]).

No original thinker, Lewis gave voice to the faith in individual improvement and social progress that resounded so confidently through the northern states in the years after the building of the Erie Canal. Essentially an enthusiast and promoter, he was unable to understand the class divisions and social conflict of his times in any terms but those of personal vice or virtue. Lewis's individualistic solutions to social problems were increasingly rejected in favor of collectivist or organizational approaches. Just as his insistence on moral suasion became a minority position among temperance reformers, physical education after the Civil War gravitated toward a model of military drill given new appeal by the wartime experience. By the time he died, in Yonkers-on-the-Hudson, New York, he was a spokesman for causes that were ultimately to flourish, but one whose voice no longer commanded assent.

• A laudatory biography of Lewis is Mary F. Eastman, *Biography of Dio Lewis* (1891). In addition to works cited above, his many books include *Our Girls* (1871) and *Chastity; or, Our Secret Sins* (1874). A discussion of his contributions to physical education is in Mabel Lee, *A History of Physical Education and Sports in the U.S.A.* (1983). Jack S. Blocker, Jr., "*Give to the Winds Thy Fears*": *The Women's Temperance Crusade, 1873–74* (1985), analyzes Lewis's ideas and his relation to the Women's Crusade.

JACK S. BLOCKER, JR.

LEWIS, Dixon Hall (10 Aug. 1802–25 Oct. 1848), U.S. representative and senator, was likely born in Hancock County, Georgia, the son of Francis Lewis, a planter, and Mary Dixon Hall. In Hancock County Lewis graduated from Mount Zion Academy, founded by the Reverend Nathan S. S. Beman. Lewis graduated from South Carolina College in Columbia in 1820, then joined his parents, who had settled in Autauga County, Alabama, while he finished college. He studied law under Henry Hitchcock, attorney general, in Cahaba, then the capital of Alabama. He secured admission to the bar in 1823 and opened a law practice in Montgomery in 1825. In 1823 Lewis married Susan Elizabeth Elmore; they had seven children, six of whom survived infancy. They resided in the part of Montgomery County that later became Lowndes County.

Lewis succeeded in his law practice, but he decided to concentrate his energies on politics. He represented Montgomery County in the Alabama House of Representatives for three terms, from 1826 through 1828, becoming the leader of states' rights Democrats. He developed his views under the influence of his maternal uncle Bolling Hall, Republican member of Congress from Georgia from 1811 to 1817, who had voted against chartering the second Bank of the United States. Upon retirement from office, Hall relocated in 1818 to a plantation near Montgomery, Alabama, where he frequently discussed politics with his nephew.

In the 1827 legislative session Lewis successfully sponsored a resolution that reduced taxes to the amount required for the necessary expenditures of the state rather than continuing to place surplus funds in the state bank. In the 1828 session his proposal to extend the state's jurisdiction over all American Indian territory within its boundaries initiated a debate over states' rights. Lewis defended his bill, maintaining state territorial sovereignty within its limits, and ultimately the bill passed. Members esteemed Lewis so highly that they selected him to chair the legislative committee to nominate Andrew Jackson for the presidency. His colleagues respected his intellect and his "uniform courtesy to all others—but particularly to the very old and the very young members." He readily proffered advice to fellow members, who sought his counsel on ways to achieve passage of particular bills.

In 1829, when congressional elections in Alabama centered around federal aid for internal improvements, Lewis ran for the southern district seat. Challenging federally financed internal improvements, he suggested to voters that government could become despotic if not restrained by the people. The district that Lewis sought to represent contained fifteen counties from Montgomery to Mobile on both sides of the Alabama River. Residents in counties on the river heavily favored federal aid for a canal to connect the Coosa and Tennessee rivers to facilitate commerce between the Tennessee Valley and the seaport of Mobile. His two opponents strongly supported the project as well, and while they primarily campaigned in counties along the river, Lewis traveled to the back counties, delivering witty and humorous "stump speeches" in open-air meetings. He won that election to Congress and seven successive ones.

In his first term in Congress, which coincided with Jackson's first term as president, Lewis supported the administration's policy of Indian removal. Later Lewis, who allied with John C. Calhoun and the Nullifiers, opposed the president on nullification. In his eight terms in Congress, from 1829 to 1844, Lewis opposed the national bank, protective tariffs, and federal internal improvements, all indications of his states' rights constitutional positions. Lewis eventually became a member of an inner circle of advisers to Calhoun who tried unsuccessfully to get him the Democratic presidential nomination in 1844 and 1848.

In April 1844, when William R. King resigned his Senate seat to accept President John Tyler's appointment as minister to France, Governor Benjamin Fitzpatrick appointed Lewis, his brother-in-law, to the seat. In December 1844 the legislature elected Lewis to serve the remainder of King's term to 1847. In a bitter contest with King, a Union Democrat who had returned from France, and A. F. Hopkins, a Whig, Lewis won reelection by the legislature to a full term beginning 4 March 1847. To prevail, Lewis agreed to the demands of North Alabama Democrats that he pledge to support all measures of the James K. Polk administration and to refrain from participating in the selection of the Democratic presidential candidate in 1848.

In the Senate Lewis was chairman of the Committee on Finance, and during the Mexican and American War he maneuvered passage of a free trade measure, the Walker Tariff of 1846. Late on the last night of the session before adjournment, 10 August 1846, Lewis

presented an appropriations bill passed by the House that included the Wilmot Proviso, which would have prohibited slavery in any territory acquired from Mexico, but he, as a senator from a slave state, moved to strike the proviso from the bill. While senators discussed the issue, the House adjourned, so Lewis's actions in the Senate helped filibuster the bill to death, thus leaving unsettled the fate of slavery in the territory to be won from Mexico. Senator Daniel S. Dickinson of New York, whose seat adjoined Lewis's,

found him kind, frank, and sincere; a ready and able counsellor; firm and decided in his opinions, yet yielding and conciliatory, and regardful of the opinions and motives of those with whom he differed. . . . [T]hough he seldom spoke publicly, he gave evidence in his intercourse of the mature strength of the statesman and the cultivated taste of the scholar. (*Congressional Globe*, p. 16)

Throughout his life Lewis's excessive weight required him to make numerous adjustments for his comfort and safety, especially when visiting, traveling, and campaigning. At age twenty Lewis weighed 350 pounds and at the time of his death at least 430 pounds. When visiting friends near his home in Alabama, he carried along his own specially built chair. While he served on the Board of Trustees of the University of Alabama from 1828 to 1831, the board had a chair built for his use at its meetings. On public conveyances he purchased and used two seats. Both houses of Congress had chairs constructed for him.

While visiting New York City to address a free trade group, Lewis became ill and died there of ischuria renalis. The mayor and common council of New York gave him a public funeral at City Hall. Lewis was born into one family and married into another whose men had quickly assumed political leadership during the early statehood of Georgia and Alabama. He personally championed sometimes unpopular causes on constitutional grounds, yet he managed to persuade voters to support his states' rights positions long enough to have an unbroken record of state and federal legislative service from 1826 to 1848.

• Some Dixon H. Lewis Papers are in the Library of the University of Texas in Austin, and other letters plus an obituary biographical sketch are in the Dixon H. Lewis Letters, Alabama Department of Archives and History. Some correspondence has been published in the *Papers of John C. Calhoun*, ed. Clyde Wilson, vols. 14–21 (1981–1993). Conflicting information about his birthplace in interment records and the memorial monument at his gravesite at Green-Wood Cemetery in Brooklyn, N.Y., can be resolved by the 1805 Ga. state census. Recollections of contemporaries appear in W. Brewer, *Alabama: Her History, Resources, War Record, and Public Men* (1872), and William Garrett, *Reminiscences of Public Men in Alabama* (1872). The most helpful modern political analysis of Lewis in state politics is J. Mills Thornton III, *Politics and Power in a Slave Society: Alabama, 1800–1860* (1978). Also useful is Thomas M. Williams, *Dixon Hall Lewis*, Alabama Polytechnic Institute Historical Studies, ed. George Petrie, 4th ser. (1910). For Lewis's role among political intimates of Calhoun, the most informative volumes are

Charles M. Wiltse, *John C. Calhoun, Nullifier, 1829–1839* (1949) and *John C. Calhoun, Sectionalist, 1840–1850* (1951). An obituary is in the *Montgomery Flag and Advertiser*, 4 Nov. 1848, and a tribute is in the *Congressional Globe*, 30th Cong., 2d sess., 7 Dec. 1848.

HARRIET E. AMOS DOSS

LEWIS, Edmonia (c. 1840–after 1909), sculptor, was born Mary Edmonia Lewis near Albany, New York, the daughter of a part African-American, part Chippewa woman whose name is not known, and Samuel Lewis, a black man, employed as a valet, who came to this country from the West Indies, probably from Haiti.

There is little reliable information about Lewis's early life. She was often inconsistent in interviews even with basic facts about her origins, preferring to present herself as the exotic product of a childhood spent roaming the forests with her mother's people. Lewis and her older stepbrother, Samuel, born in 1832, were orphaned early in life, Lewis's mother dying in 1844, her father three years later. At the time of the parents' deaths, the family was living in Newark, New Jersey. Young Samuel arranged for his sister to board with a Captain S. R. Mills and went west to seek his fortune.

With financial support from her stepbrother, who became a successful prospector during the California gold rush, Lewis was sent to school at the preparatory division of New York Central College at McGrawville and later at the Ladies' Preparatory Division at Oberlin College in Ohio, both pioneering coeducational abolitionist institutions.

At Oberlin, Lewis's studies included painting and drawing. Her earliest known work, a drawing entitled *The Muse Uranus* (1862), was done as an engagement present for a friend there. It is signed, as is her later work, Edmonia Lewis. In a dramatic incident, Lewis was accused in 1862 of attempted murder—by poisoning—of two Oberlin classmates who were stricken shortly after enjoying a hot drink she had prepared. While the young women lay ill, Lewis was abducted by a white mob and severely beaten. Following her recovery and subsequent vindication in the courts, she ended her studies and moved to Boston in early 1863 to pursue a career in the arts.

With the encouragement and support of William Lloyd Garrison, Lydia Maria Child, and the sculptor Edward Brackett, among others, Lewis established a reputation for her portrait busts and medallions of such prominent abolitionists as John Brown, Maria Weston Chapman, and Garrison himself. A clay model, now lost, of the African-American sergeant William H. Carney of the Massachusetts Fifty-fourth Regiment, wounded but holding aloft the flag at Fort Wagner, was her first attempt at a full-length figure. Lewis's bust of Robert Gould Shaw, the Boston Brahmin and Civil War martyr who died leading his black troops into battle, was such a success that sales of copies and photographs of the work helped finance the artist's 1865 trip to Europe. Following travels through England, France, and Italy, Lewis settled in a studio on the Via della Frezza in Rome.

A friend of Anne Whitney, Harriet Hosmer, and Charlotte Cushman, Lewis was a member of a group of expatriate British and American women artists in Italy dubbed by Henry James "the white marmorean flock." About Lewis he wrote in *William Wetmore Story and His Friends* (1903), "one of the sisterhood . . . was a negress, whose colour, picturesquely contrasting with that of her plastic material, was the pleading agent of her fame" (p. 357). James's opinion notwithstanding, Lewis's work was much in demand. Her studio, listed with those of other artists in the best guidebooks, was a fashionable stop for Americans on the Grand Tour, many of whom ordered busts of literary or historical figures to adorn their mantels or front parlors. Her figures based on Henry Wadsworth Longfellow's *Song of Hiawatha* were particular favorites, coming as they did from the hand of a woman known to be part Indian.

Even in her depictions of Hiawatha and Minne-Ha-Ha, however, the public saw themes from African-American life. Following the Civil War, the two Indian lovers from warring tribes were thought to represent hope for reconciliation between North and South. Similarly, one of her masterworks, *Hagar*, an 1875 depiction of the biblical bondwoman and outcast, was understood as an allegory of the black race.

Lewis first came to the attention of the American public at large with the exhibition of her monumental statue, *The Death of Cleopatra*, at the Philadelphia Centennial Exposition in 1876 (currently in the collection of the National Museum of American Art at the Smithsonian Institution). Described by one journalist as "perhaps the most remarkable piece of sculpture in the American section," the work was praised for the horrifying verisimilitude of the moment when the snake's poison takes hold and for Lewis's attempt to depict the "authentic" Egyptian queen from the study of historic coins, medals, and other records. The statue, in gleaming Carrara marble, drew a steady stream of viewers.

Lewis's triumph at Philadelphia was a milestone in a career begun more than a decade earlier and pursued against enormous odds as she struggled to make a respected name for herself in the world of fine arts. A prolific artist, she is known to have executed at least sixty works, exploring themes from history, mythology, and the Bible as well as from African-American and Native American subjects; fewer than half of these sculptures have been located.

Among her best-known works, *Forever Free* (1869) shows a slave couple hearing the news of emancipation. Beyond the moment of liberation, however, the kneeling woman, ostensibly prayerful, deftly suggests the continuing subjugation of African-American women in various spheres of postemancipation domestic and public life. Her supplicating posture echoes the famous antislavery emblem that read "Am I Not a Woman and a Sister?" and suggests a possible irony in the title of the piece.

Although little is known about the later years of Lewis's life, she was mentioned by Frederick Douglass who visited her when he and his second wife, Helen, toured Europe in 1887. They were welcomed in Rome by Lewis who lent them books on Roman history and accompanied them on day trips to museums and other sites. Douglass was impressed with the life Lewis had made for herself. He wrote in his diary that he "found her in a large building. Near the top in a very pleasant room with a commanding view. No. 4 via XX Settembre, Roma. Here she lives, and here she plies her fingers in her art as a sculptress. She seems very cheerful and happy and successful." She never married.

Recognized today as a talented, pathbreaking, and determined pioneer in the history of African Americans and women in the fine arts, Edmonia Lewis worked in a style that combined the idealized forms of late neoclassicism with elements of realism and naturalism, Her finest body of work is thought to be her portrait busts, in particular those of Shaw (1864) and Longfellow (1871).

The date and place of Lewis's death are not known. In its February 1909 issue, *The Rosary* magazine reported that Lewis, who was a convert to Catholicism and a devout Roman Catholic, was still living in Rome. According to Italian records, she did not die in that city. In a January 1915 letter the African-American sculptor Meta Warwick Fuller, writing to critic Freeman H. M. Murray, suggests people whom Murray might contact in the United States and abroad to ascertain whether Lewis was still alive. No later documentation has come to light.

• Useful contemporary information about Edmonia Lewis is in the published letters of Anne Whitney at the Wellesley College Library and in *Lydia Maria Child: Selected Letters, 1817–1880*, ed. Milton Meltzer et al. (1982). A thorough discussion of the Oberlin poisoning incident is in Geoffrey Blodgett, "John Mercer Langston and the Case of Edmonia Lewis: Oberlin, 1862," *Journal of Negro History* 53 (July 1968): 201–18. Lewis's work was well represented in the 1985 National Museum of American Art exhibition *Sharing Traditions: Five Black Artists in Nineteenth-Century America* in Washington, D.C.; see the essay by Lynda R. Hartigan in the catalog published for the exhibition in 1985. Marilyn Richardson, "Edmonia Lewis's *The Death of Cleopatra*: Myth and Identity," *International Review of African American Art* 12 (Summer 1995): 36–52, includes previously unpublished biographical information.

MARILYN RICHARDSON

LEWIS, Edwin (18 Apr. 1881–28 Nov. 1959), theologian, was born in Newbury, England, the son of Joseph Lewis, a carpenter, and Sarah Newman. At the age of nineteen, Lewis went as a Methodist missionary to Labrador and later pursued his higher education at Sackville College (Canada), Middlebury College, Drew Theological Seminary (B.D., 1908; Th.D., 1918), United Free Church College (Scotland), and New York State College for Teachers (B.A., 1915). In 1904 he married Louise Newhook Frost, with whom

he had five children. She died in 1953, and he later married Josephine Stults. Lewis was ordained as an elder in the Methodist Episcopal church in 1910 and early in his career served as a minister to Methodist churches in New York and New Jersey. He became a naturalized citizen of the United States in 1916. In 1920 Lewis was appointed professor of systematic theology at Drew Theological Seminary in Madison, New Jersey, succeeding his esteemed teacher Olin Curtis, an eminent Methodist theologian of the time. After his retirement from Drew in 1951, Lewis served for three years as a visiting professor at the Temple University School of Theology in Philadelphia. He died in Morristown, New Jersey.

Lewis lectured widely at churches, colleges, and theological schools in North America, and during 1936–1937 he made a lecture tour to Japan, Korea, China, and India. He represented his Troy Methodist Conference at the national Methodist assemblies in 1928, 1932, and 1936. He also became a leader in the movement for the establishment of professional standards for the Protestant ministry, a movement that culminated in the formation in 1936 of the American Association of Theological Schools, the accrediting agency for American seminaries. Most of Lewis's life work, however, was devoted to theological scholarship. He required of his ministerial students, and of himself, the diligent mastery of the sources of the Christian tradition since his approach to Christian theology entailed both careful attention to biblical texts and wide acquaintance with the history of Western thought. Students remembered him as a demanding teacher who took great interest in them personally and infused his instruction with an evangelical spirit.

Lewis's lasting contribution appeared in the development of his published theology. That development was marked by a movement from Protestant liberalism to Protestant neo-orthodoxy. Unlike some thinkers who revolted against liberalism, however, Lewis continued to manifest an interest in the philosophical implications of Christian faith and doctrine. In his first book, *Jesus Christ and the Human Quest* (1924), Lewis proposed a view of Christianity that was typical of much Protestant liberalism in early twentieth-century America: all persons by nature seek goals that will bring them individual and social satisfaction, and Jesus Christ, by virtue of his own supreme moral achievement, best embodied that human quest. To conservative Protestants, including a large group of American Methodists who responded negatively to the book, Lewis had reduced Jesus to a mere moral example, had located the power of Christianity in the impulses of human nature rather than in the initiative of God's act of revelation, and had obscured the unique character of salvation through Jesus.

Lewis offered hints in that first book that he might move beyond such liberal views. He exalted Jesus Christ as the one hope of the world's salvation, and he alluded to the limits of human reason and the need to accept certain religious mysteries by faith. Shortly after the appearance of *Jesus Christ and the Human*

Quest, however, Lewis began to depart decisively from the liberalism of his early theology. In 1926 he became a coeditor of the *Abingdon Bible Commentary*, and he later claimed that his daily work on the Christian Bible revolutionized his thinking by turning him from a preoccupation with speculative philosophy to a concern for biblical doctrines. In a book published in 1931, *God and Ourselves*, Lewis indicated what his immersion in the world of the Bible had come to mean: the initiative in human salvation belongs to God. In 1933 he wrote a review of William Ernest Hocking's *Re-Thinking Missions* in which he criticized the "futilities of modernism" in the book for not giving centrality to Jesus Christ within the Christian faith and for failing to portray Christianity "in its biblical and historical self-presentation." In the early 1930s Lewis also was reading the works of the prominent Swiss neo-orthodox theologian Karl Barth. Although he criticized the absolutism and authoritarianism of Barth's theology, he sympathized with Barth's claim that modern, liberal theology had abandoned the teachings of the historic Christian tradition, and he later professed that Barth gave him the courage to insist on revelation in Jesus Christ as the central and organizing feature of Christian theology. Despite his reservations about some features of European neo-orthodox thought, Lewis—along with other American thinkers such as Reinhold Niebuhr and H. Richard Niebuhr—clearly was caught up in a postwar, broadly neo-orthodox mood. It was a mood that led many theologians to emphasize the mysteries of divine grace and the ubiquity of human foibles, their high liberal hopes for human progress having been dashed by a world war and a great economic depression.

Lewis's break with liberalism and the statement of his own neo-orthodox position came with his *A Christian Manifesto* (1934). The book insisted that Christianity is neither an answer to a human yearning nor a solution to a philosophical quest but is an affirmation of God's resolute love of the sinner. The manifest consequence of that atoning divine love was now for Lewis supernaturalism: *"Christianity means supernaturalism: this is the inescapable logic alike of the history and of the experience."* Lewis meant by the supernaturalism of Christianity that the core of the Christian message eludes all the natural capabilities of human reason and that the action of God in human affairs cannot be exhaustively defined by naturalistic philosophical categories.

Although accused by some critics of fundamentalism because of his supernaturalist claims, Lewis never embraced fundamentalism's biblical literalism, nor did he abandon philosophical reflection on the Bible. Lewis's insistence on the useful, if limited, role of philosophical thinking was apparent in his other two major books. In *A Philosophy of the Christian Revelation* (1940), he argued that the meaning of Christ cannot be derived from a study of Scripture alone—that would be to move in a closed circle of understanding. Rather, human reason can make use of the signs, symbols, and meanings in creation to elaborate on and interpret the revelation of God in Christ. And in *The Creator and the Adversary* (1948), he explicated philosophically what he believed to be the central scriptural claim about evil: evil derives neither from God nor simply from the human will but is an opposition to God's love that "goes down to the very roots of existence." In order to ascribe metaphysical status to demonic reality, Lewis divided existence into three parts: the creative work of God, a neutral structure outside of God, and the evil adversary who emerges from that structure and struggles against God for control of creation.

The evolution of Edwin Lewis's theology from a Protestant liberal confidence in human religious potential to a neo-orthodox affirmation of the primacy of the God of the Bible to philosophical reflections on biblical teachings reflected the course of much American Protestant thought from the early twentieth century through the 1950s. Disappointed in his earlier hopes for the progressive realization of the liberal values of Western civilization, Lewis, like so many other postwar theologians in England and the United States, turned to the mysteries of the biblical God. But in doing so, Lewis and many of his theological cohort refused to abandon philosophical reflection on biblical doctrines. Lewis's theology became one of several alternatives to both the anthropocentrism of Protestant liberalism and the biblical literalism of fundamentalism.

• For studies of Lewis's life and work see "Bibliography of the Works of Edwin Lewis," *Drew Gateway* 21 (Spring 1951): 63–66; Charley D. Hardwick, "Edwin Lewis: Introductory and Critical Remarks," *Drew Gateway* 33 (Winter 1963): 91–104; Smith Jameson Jones, Jr., "Three Representative Leaders in Contemporary American Methodist Theology" (Ph.D. diss., Vanderbilt Univ., 1965); Carl Michaelson, "The Edwin Lewis Myth," *Christian Century*, 24 Feb. 1960; and David Wesley Soper, *Major Voices in American Theology* (1952). An obituary is in the *New York Times*, 30 Nov. 1959.

CONRAD CHERRY

LEWIS, Estelle Anna Blanche Robinson (Apr. 1824–24 Nov. 1880), author, was born near Baltimore, Maryland, the daughter of John N. Robinson. Her mother, whose name is unknown, was the daughter of an American revolutionary war officer. Estelle's father, of Cuban birth and independently wealthy, died during her infancy. She attended Emma Willard's Female Seminary in Troy, New York, and studied science and law as well as belles lettres. She published a few stories in an Albany magazine. She left the academy in 1841 and during that same year married Sylvanus D. Lewis, an attorney. The couple, who had no children, lived in a comfortable Brooklyn residence in which they established a literary salon. Estelle Lewis maintained a program of independent home study in classical and modern languages, literature, and history, and she wrote steadily under the following names: Estelle Anna Lewis, Estella Anna Blanche Lewis, Estelle Anna Robinson Lewis, and Stella.

Lewis published *Records of the Heart*, her first book of poetry, in 1844. In 1845 or 1846 she and her husband first met Edgar Allan Poe, with whose name hers is now always associated. He often dined at their home, played whist with them and with fellow guests, and read aloud his poetry in draft stages. By 1847 Lewis was often visiting Poe, his wife, Virginia Poe, and his mother-in-law, Maria Clemm, in their Fordham cottage. Both Lewises helped Poe socially and financially, and Sylvanus Lewis once advised him in connection with a libel suit. Mostly in return for such favors, Poe flattered and helped Estelle Lewis greatly. He may have intended his 1847 "To ——— Ulalume: A Ballad" to appear to be dedicated to her. He spells out the name "Anna Lewis" in his 1848 acrostic sonnet "An Enigma." In addition, he showed her how to make her poetry more forceful and varied, certainly revised one of her poems and probably others as well, commended her work in his 1848 lecture "The Poets and Poetry of America," and puffed her 1848 *Child of the Sea, and Other Poems* in several reviews. Early in 1849 he evidently tried to persuade publisher George Palmer Putnam to issue a second edition of her poetry and to include her most recent verse in it, and he definitely asked editor Rufus Griswold to substitute a short essay by Poe about her in place of Griswold's own commentary in later editions of *The Female Poets of America*, his 1849 anthology. (Sylvanus Lewis even agreed to pay Griswold for the typesetting and proofreading of Poe's essay. Griswold declined all such overtures but did include Poe's sketch of Estelle Lewis in his 1850 edition of Poe's works.) The Lewises attended Virginia Poe's funeral in 1847 and offered Poe what comfort they could. After Poe's death in 1849, they provided Maria Clemm much hospitality. The famous daguerreotype of Poe taken in Lowell, Massachusetts, in 1849 is now known as the "Stella" portrait because Lewis gave a copy of it to Poe's English biographer, John Henry Ingram, who saved it. Marie Louise Shew, a rival of Lewis's among Poe's several poetizing female friends, thought "Ulalume" was dedicated to her and not Lewis. In an 1875 letter to Ingram, Shew described Lewis as a "fat gaudily dressed woman whom I often found sitting in Mrs. Clemm's little kitchen, waiting to see the man of genius, who had rushed out to escape her."

Lewis published her third volume of poetry, *Myths of the Minstrel*, in 1852. She and her husband were divorced in 1858, after which she traveled widely in Europe, studied in the Vatican Library and in the Bibliothèque Impériale in Paris, revisited America, and then settled permanently in London in 1865. She studied at the British Museum. Her most complex work is *Sappho: A Tragedy in Five Acts*, published in 1868. It was performed on stage that year; was favorably reviewed in England, France, and the United States; was translated into modern Greek and staged in Athens; and went into a fourth edition in 1878 (and subsequent ones after Lewis's death). Never in the least self-effacing, Lewis in 1877 sent some clippings from London to a friend back home with the following comment:

"The British press has placed me on a plane with Shakespeare—the highest position accorded to a woman since the Greeks seated Sappho by the Side of Homer on the pinnacle of fame." Lewis's *The King's Stratagem; or, The Pearl of Poland: A Tragedy in Five Acts* (1869) was less popular than *Sappho*. Her last efforts were a series of sonnets in praise of Poe. At the time of her death in London, her *Records of the Heart* was in its eleventh edition.

Estelle Lewis is remembered more for her friendship with Poe than for any of her writings. Her short fiction, travel sketches, and translations, though featured in popular periodicals such as the *Democratic Review*, *Godey's Lady's Book*, *Graham's Magazine*, and the *Literary World*, now interest only specialists in Victorian culture. Some of her verse still has a measure of charm. "Child of the Sea," a long poem in four cantos, which Poe effusively praised, is a narrative in precise stanzas but stilted language. The hero, a castaway on the Mediterranean Sea, is led to believe that his beloved is the daughter of his own father (who is the object of his revenge), learns she is not, marries her, and becomes a happy poet. The heroine of Lewis's *Sappho* is limned as subtly intelligent but defeated by her own dictatorial manner, shaken by uncontrollable though unspecified passions, and seeking fulfillment of impossible desires. Lewis was too conventional even to hint at lesbianism here. "The Angel's Visit" blatantly capitalizes on "The Raven" by Poe. Early lines describe a tapping on the persona's door and are followed thus: "Trembling, shivering, timid-hearted, / From that holy dream I started." The spectral visitor advises her to prefer reason to love. She ignores the advice, is soon abandoned, and then decides to keep her "heart locked evermore." The persona of "The Forsaken," though hoping that someone will leave "halls of glee" to mourn at her grave, is certain that she will lie "Lone and forgot." "Laone: The Student's Story" depicts a girl sorry too late for telling her tutor and would-be lover that she thinks of him only as a brother. The central figure in "The Prisoner of Peroté" is a captured freedom fighter who dreams of his beloved Andalusia. Lewis catered to readers enamored of sentimentality and represents a once-popular type of romantic poet.

• Most of Lewis's few extant papers are at the Houghton Library of Harvard University and the Historical Society of Pennsylvania, Philadelphia. David M. Robinson, *Sappho and Her Influence* (1924), pays Lewis's *Sappho* brief but respectful attention. Pertinent information concerning Poe and Lewis is in Dwight Thomas and David K. Jackson, *The Poe Log: A Documentary Life of Edgar Allan Poe, 1809–1849* (1987), and Kenneth Silverman, *Edgar A. Poe: Mournful and Never-ending Remembrance* (1991). An obituary is in the *London Daily News*, 26 Nov. 1880.

ROBERT L. GALE

LEWIS, Francis (21 Mar. 1713–31 Dec. 1802), merchant and member of the Continental Congress, was born in Llandaff, Glamorganshire, Wales, the son of Reverend Francis Lewis, a rector, and Amy Pettingal of Caernarvonshire, Wales, whose father was also a Church of England clergyman. Orphaned at a very early age, Lewis lived with relatives in Wales and Scotland (learning both the Cymric and Gaelic languages), and finally came under the care of his maternal uncle, who was dean of St. Paul's in London. Lewis attended Westminster School in London. After finishing his education, he worked in a countinghouse of a London merchant.

On receiving his inheritance at age twenty-one, Lewis decided to go into business on his own, forming a partnership with Richard Annesley. The two men shipped goods to America, where Lewis arrived in 1738. After spending about two years in Philadelphia, Lewis then resided in New York City. The partnership broke up, and Annesley died in 1743, leaving most of his property to his sister, Elizabeth. A brother, Edward Annely, prepared to contest the will, claiming that Elizabeth Annesley had sought "to defraud the Estate in hopes to bribe Lewis for a husband." Edward Annely and Lewis published advertisements against each other in New York newspapers, and Annely drew up "Instructions" for counsel for use in a lawsuit, but a case seems not to have been brought to trial, and the will was allowed to stand. Lewis and Elizabeth Annesley were married in 1745. Of seven children, three survived infancy; one son, Morgan Lewis, became governor of New York, and their daughter Ann was disinherited because of her marriage to a British naval captain.

Lewis's mercantile ventures took him to the British Isles, northern Europe (including Russia), and Africa. Twice he was shipwrecked off Ireland. During the French and Indian War, Lewis secured a contract to supply clothing to British troops at Fort Oswego. He also served as an aide to Colonel James Mercer, who was killed when the French attacked the post. At the surrender, 14 August 1756, Lewis was one of thirty prisoners allotted to the Indians. He avoided ill treatment and even death by communicating in the Cymbric language, which somehow his captors were able to grasp. Turned over to the French at Montreal, Lewis was sent to France, and eventually exchanged. The British government awarded him 5,000 acres for his war service. In New York City, he continued to build a fortune through commerce. During the Stamp Act crisis of 1765, Lewis retired from business and moved from New York City to Whitestone (now in Flushing, Queens). From 1771 to 1775 Lewis was back in New York City, where he established a dry goods firm with his son Francis, Jr. He again gave up business and returned to Whitestone.

Lewis was regarded as a good Whig at the start of the Revolution, although it was alleged that, through his son, he attempted to become the contractor of supplies for the British army in Boston. In 1774 he was a delegate to the Provincial Convention and a member of the Committee of Fifty-one in New York City, from which he resigned because the group had become too conservative. On 22 April 1775 the Provincial Convention elected Lewis a delegate to the Continental Congress; he sat in this assembly May 1775–November 1779. In fall 1776 a British detachment plundered his property and destroyed his home at Whitestone. His wife was detained and then imprisoned in New York City, an ordeal that contributed to her death in 1779. Elizabeth Annesley Lewis was freed only after George Washington had two Tory women seized in Philadelphia as retaliation. Throughout the remainder of the war Lewis's family resided in Baltimore.

In Congress Lewis avoided participation in major decision making but went quietly about the numerous tasks that Congress assigned him. He did, however, press for a military invasion into the Iroquois country. His mercantile background and executive ability served him well as a member of numerous standing and temporary committees dealing with all phases of military procurement. He served on the Committee of Claims, which provided groundwork for eventual liquidation and settlement of the nation's debts. He was a member of a committee on Indian trade and also one on prisoners. His major contributions came from membership on two powerful committees: the Secret Committee (renamed the Committee of Commerce, 5 July 1777), which contracted for the importation of powder and munitions, and the Marine Committee, which handled a broad spectrum of naval affairs, including ship construction and procurement. His work called for visits to major ports and to Washington's headquarters. With the New York government finally giving authorization, Lewis and his fellow state delegates signed the Declaration of Independence on 2 August 1776.

Defeated for reelection to Congress in November 1779, Lewis accepted an appointment by Congress as a member, and then chairman, of a three-man commission forming the Board of Admiralty. Congress, on 28 October 1779, created this body, which had responsibility for all naval administration, to replace the Marine Committee. On 7 Feb. 1781 Congress voted to dissolve the Board of Admiralty and, in its stead, appointed a Secretary of Marine. Lewis resigned on 17 July 1781; the Board of Admiralty was formally terminated on 29 August 1781.

For the remainder of his life, Lewis retired from both business and public service. He served as a vestryman for Trinity Church, 1784–1786. He resided with his sons. According to his great-granddaughter, shortly before his death in New York City Lewis suffered a fall that affected his nervous system. He was buried in the Trinity Church yard. When his estate was settled, it was worth only $15,000. Lewis certainly made a sacrifice for independence; if nothing else, he took on work in the Congress that others were reluctant to assume. Benjamin Rush referred to him as a "moderate Whig, but a very honest man, and very useful in executive business."

• Francis Lewis's congressional career is fully documented. Papers of the Continental Congress, National Archives, microfilm; Worthington C. Ford, ed., *Journals of the Continental Congress*, vols. 1–21 (1904–1912); and Paul H. Smith, ed.,

Letters of Delegates to Congress, vols. 1–18 (1976–1991). *The Public Papers of George Clinton*, vols. 1–6 (1899–1902), contain Lewis correspondence during the revolutionary war period. A family tribute to Lewis by his great-granddaughter is found in Julia Delafield, *Biography of Francis Lewis and Morgan Lewis*, vol. 1 (2 vols., 1877). A strong dislike of Lewis is evident in a work by a Tory justice of the New York Supreme Court, Thomas Jones, *History of New York during the Revolutionary War*, ed. Edward F. deLancey (2 vols., 1879). This history contains a sketch of Lewis, vol. 2, pp. 357–61, and Edward Annely's "Instructions" regarding preparation for a lawsuit against Lewis, vol. 2, pp. 628–36.

Brief appraisals of Lewis's life include Charles C. Burlingham, *Francis Lewis: one of the New York Signers of the Declaration of Independence* (pamphlet, 1926), B. J. Lossing, *Biographical Sketches of the Signers of the Declaration of American Independence* (1854), pp. 71–73; and John Sanderson, *Sanderson's Biography of the Signers to the Declaration of Independence*, 1846 ed., pp. 276–81. Walker Barrett, *The Old Merchants of New York City*, vols. 2 and 4 (1885), comments on Lewis's business activity; for a sketch of Lewis, see vol. 4, pp. 96–105. The *New-York Evening Post*, 3 Jan. 1803, contains a notice of Lewis's death.

HARRY M. WARD

LEWIS, Fulton, Jr. (30 Apr. 1903–20 Aug. 1966), radio commentator, was born in Washington, D.C., the son of Fulton Lewis, Sr., a lawyer, and Elizabeth Saville. Lewis, Jr., was to live in Washington all his life. He had considerable musical talent, which his family encouraged. He studied piano, voice, harmony, and composition for fourteen years while growing up. Two of his musical comedies were performed at his public high school, and at the University of Virginia he wrote the fight song for the Cavaliers. (The words to the song were composed by a fellow student and friend, Harry J. Taylor, who, curiously enough, also became a political commentator.)

After leaving the university, Lewis married Alice Huston, the daughter of a Republican National Committeeman, in June 1924. The Lewises had two children. The same year he married, Lewis began his newspaper career at the *Washington Herald*, where he reported on the news and also wrote a fishing column. In 1928 he left the *Herald* to become the assistant bureau manager of Hearst's Universal News Service in Washington. He rose to bureau head before he left in 1937. At the same time he worked for Hearst he also wrote a newspaper column, "The Washington Side Show." This column was in print from 1933 to 1936.

In 1937, gambling on his future, Lewis resigned his job at the Universal News Service, which had consolidated with International News Service and which offered considerable promise, to take a $25-a-week job as a temporary replacement for a broadcaster on WOL, a local radio station. The gamble paid off; by December he was a regular commentator on the Mutual Broadcasting System.

From the beginning of his radio career, Lewis was a right-wing commentator described by one critic as having a "voice with a snarl." He attacked President Franklin D. Roosevelt and the New Deal and was quick to identify government programs as socialistic or communistic. In addition to his own show, he acted as chairman of the "American Forum of the Air" in January and February 1939. By this time, his own fifteen-minute program, "The Top of the News from Washington," was carried by 130 to 150 radio stations around the country.

Lewis was a founder and first president of the Radio Correspondents Association. He created a furor when he invited Charles Lindbergh to speak on his program in August 1939. Many listeners opposed to American isolationism objected vehemently. The complaints did not deter Lewis from controversial issues. During World War II in his radio shows; in a weekly column, "Fulton Lewis, Jr., Says," syndicated by King Features; and in a daily column, "Washington Report," both published in 1944–1945, Lewis attacked the Office of Price Administration, the building of government housing for war workers, and such labor leaders as Sidney Hillman of the Congress of Industrial Organizations.

After the war Lewis's targets shifted to Harry Truman and his Fair Deal. He became a red-baiter and supported Senator Joseph McCarthy in his early campaigns. In 1949 he interviewed a former army major who claimed that Henry A. Wallace and Harry Hopkins both had helped the Russians by giving them atomic bomb secrets. The accusations resulted in the House Un-American Activities Committee taking testimony from Wallace before dismissing the charges as unfounded.

In 1950 Lewis was extremely active in McCarthy's campaign against Senator Millard Tydings of Maryland, whom he attacked almost every night in his program. As a result of his militant anti-Communism, Lewis received the American Jewish League against Communism's Award in 1958 and the American Legion's Fourth Estate Award in 1962.

Lewis supported Barry Goldwater in the election of 1964. At the time of his death in Washington two years later, he was still active in radio, and his program aired on 460 stations. His influence had faded somewhat, however, because of the advent of TV. His tumultuous career illustrated the polarization of American politics stimulated by the New Deal and the Cold War.

• For one who was so notorious in his own time, Lewis left few permanent traces. Herndon Booton, *Praised and Damned: The Story of Fulton Lewis, Jr.* (1954), is a short, hero-worshiping work that contains little of interest for serious readers. Lewis appears in the 1942 edition of *Current Biography*. Bits and pieces of his activities during the post–World War II years can be found in accounts of the McCarthy years. William F. Buckley and L. Brent Bazell use one of Lewis's reports to deny the veracity of Senator Tydings in their *McCarthy and His Enemies* (1954), while Roger Burlingame's biography of Elmer Davis, *Don't Let Them Scare You: The Life and Times of Elmer Davis* (1961), portrays Lewis as a villain. An obituary is in the *New York Times*, 22 Aug. 1966.

DWIGHT HOOVER

LEWIS, Furry (6 Mar. 1893–14 Sept. 1981), blues musician, was born Walter Lewis in Greenwood, Mississippi. His parents' names are unknown. Lewis began his career as a performer in Memphis, Tennessee, the thriving musical center to which he moved at a young age from his family's home in the Mississippi Delta. After teaching himself to play the guitar, by 1910 Lewis was earning a meager living by performing for traveling minstrel and medicine shows that took him around the South and up the Mississippi River. In 1916 he lost a leg in an accident on a train track, and for the rest of his life he wore an artificial limb that undoubtedly added to his allure as a stage performer.

Lewis eventually settled in the Memphis area, scraping out a living from tips from street-corner performances and house parties. He played briefly as a member of the Memphis Jug Band in the late 1920s and accompanied the equally legendary Memphis Minnie in the early part of that decade. Lewis allegedly performed alongside W. C. Handy, the so-called "Father of the Blues," who Lewis claimed gave him his first guitar. In 1922 Lewis took a job as a street cleaner for the Memphis Sanitation Department. He held this job for more than forty years, later boasting facetiously that he had "cleaned up in the music business." During this phase of his career Lewis recorded twenty-three sides for the Victor and Vocalion labels in Chicago, all of which were later rereleased and received warmly by blues critics. Lewis was credited with amalgamating several blues styles distinctive to Memphis on these recordings, and several musicians of the 1960s folk revival, including Joni Mitchell, Don Nix, and Leon Russell, would later cite Lewis's recordings as an important influence.

In 1929, after the last of his Chicago recording sessions, Lewis stopped playing professionally, although he continued to practice his craft for the enjoyment of his family and a few select friends. He opened an antique shop and continued to clean the streets of Memphis until he was rediscovered in 1959 by blues and jazz enthusiast Sam Charters. Lewis then resumed his recording career, becoming a colorful and popular spokesman for the Memphis blues scene almost overnight. Fully appreciating the spotlight that had eluded him for some thirty years, Lewis made up for lost time by joining the touring circuit of coffeehouses and blues festivals spawned by the folk revival of the 1960s. An accomplished storyteller, Lewis delighted audiences—which were composed mainly of white college students—and created a stage persona that gave them exactly what they expected from an old African-American bluesman. Lewis appeared in several documentaries in the 1960s and 1970s; his presence contributed to the popular perception that the only "real" blues musicians were old, grizzled, street-corner veterans who had survived difficult lives and performed their music to express their "blues."

Lewis's success in the folk revival market propelled him to more mainstream popularity. In a sublime example of truth being stranger than fiction, Lewis—only recently an anonymous street-sweeper—appeared several times on the "Tonight Show" with Johnny Carson, became the first African American to be named an honorary Tennessee colonel by the governor of the state, was featured in a 1970 *Playboy* magazine article, and landed a substantial role in the motion picture *W. W. and the Dixie Dance Kings* (1975), which starred Burt Reynolds. Lewis deeply enjoyed the attention and took every opportunity to extol the wonders of Memphis blues and blues performers to increasingly wider audiences. He continued to perform in Memphis and advertise the Memphis blues scene elsewhere until he died in his adopted hometown.

Music writers consider Lewis an "accomplished if unconventional guitarist and an intriguing songwriter" (Santelli, p. 253), particularly adept at challenging slide-guitar riffs and complex finger pickings, and noteworthy for the wit that shone through his songwriting. Critics found in some of Lewis's earliest recorded lyrics the profound sense of rage that characterized much of the recorded blues of the 1920s. But he won enduring fame not for his considerable talents as a musician and songwriter but as an affable showman and raconteur with a wonderful sense of humor who helped to introduce a generation of Americans to the rich cultural heritage of Memphis and the Mississippi Delta.

• Two collections of Lewis's recordings are *Furry Lewis in His Prime*, Yazoo Records 1050, and *Back on My Feet Again*, Prestige Records 7810. Eric Sackheim, ed., *The Blues Line: A Collection of Blues Lyrics from Leadbelly to Muddy Waters* (1993), contains the lyrics to six of Lewis's early songs. Robert Santelli, *The Big Book of Blues* (1993), features a brief biographical sketch of Lewis and an evaluation of his historical importance. James C. Cobb, *The Most Southern Place on Earth: The Mississippi Delta and the Roots of Regional Identity* (1992), examines Lewis's lyrics and places him in the context of the cultural history of the Mississippi Delta.

J. TODD MOYE

LEWIS, George (13 July 1900–31 Dec. 1968), jazz clarinetist, was born Joseph François Zeno in New Orleans, Louisiana, the son of Henry Louis Zeno, a fisherman, and Alice Williams, a domestic servant. He was called George from birth, and the Louis of his father's name became Lewis. He used this name throughout his life. He had a sketchy education. His family home was located behind Hopes Dance Hall, and he grew up hearing the sounds of the bands that played there. At the age of seven he bought his first instrument, a fife; at about age seventeen he bought his first clarinet. Like other New Orleans clarinetists he played the Albert System clarinet throughout his life because he preferred the larger bore and more flexible tone of these instruments over the Boehm System.

Although he was probably influenced by people like Sidney Bechet, a family friend, Lewis taught himself to play clarinet, and in the summer of 1917 he played with his first band, the Black Eagles, in Mandeville. Throughout the 1920s he played with various dance band leaders, including trumpeters Buddy Petit and Henry "Kid" Rena and trombonist Edward "Kid"

Ory. He also worked in brass bands like the Eureka, primarily playing the E-flat clarinet. At the time parades, funerals, and festivals provided regular employment for New Orleans musicians. From 1923 on Lewis led his own groups, which early on included Henry "Red" Allen on trumpet. From 1929 to 1932 he played with the Olympia Band of drummer Arnold DuPas. He then went to Crowley, Louisiana, to join trumpeter Evan Thomas. After Thomas was murdered on the bandstand, Lewis returned to New Orleans. In 1929 Lewis had married Emma (maiden name unknown), with whom he had four children. They separated in 1932, and in about 1934 Lewis married Geneva (Jeannette) Stokes; they had one child.

The 1930s were lean years for playing work. Lewis appeared with Kid Howard's brass band and with Billie and De De Pierce but worked days loading ships on the river. Musical styles changed as swing gained popularity, but Lewis always held to his personal style, which was rooted in the New Orleans tradition. Although it evolved over time, that tradition stressed direct expression of feeling and close interaction among a group of improvisers. In 1942 William Russell, an important early jazz researcher, came to New Orleans hoping to record that early jazz sound. Although the assembled group centered around trumpeter Bunk Johnson, who had been a member of Thomas's band, Lewis played clarinet on the session. This led to a number of recordings over the next five years, some with Johnson and others, and some under Lewis's own name. *Burgundy Street Blues*, recorded in Lewis's home, demonstrates his full tone and lyricism and is considered a classic in the New Orleans jazz style. These sessions for Russell were pivotal for Lewis's career, as they introduced him to listeners outside of New Orleans.

In 1945 a band including Lewis, Bunk Johnson, trombonist Jim Robinson, and drummer Baby Dodds appeared in New York at the Stuyvesant Casino. It was a huge success, owing to a revived interest in New Orleans music. After a year Bunk Johnson parted ways with Lewis and the others, who returned to New Orleans and played regularly at Manny's Tavern. The New Orleans revival, sparked by an intellectual interest in the true roots of jazz and the direct, personal style of playing typical of New Orleans musicians, continued into the 1950s, and Lewis was at the center of it. His playing at this time was characterized by much ornamentation, as well as his usual sincere expressiveness. He toured with his band around the United States in the 1950s and went to England, Denmark, and Sweden in 1957 and 1959. In the early 1960s he toured Japan. From 1961 on he appeared frequently at Preservation Hall, his last performance being less than three weeks before his death in New Orleans.

Lewis's manner was quiet and polite, but he held strong views about his music. He told his biographer Tom Bethell, "I like my music peppy, and I like four beats to a bar. Something should be going all the time. It's a conversation" (p. 281). Lewis was referring to collective improvisation, which is the hallmark of the New Orleans style. While some listeners may find fault with his technique and his intonation, enthusiasts savor his direct enthusiasm and the unique personality that comes through in a self-taught, natural talent. Regarded as one of the best and most influential clarinetists in the New Orleans tradition, Lewis's name is synonymous with New Orleans style jazz.

• Tom Bethell, *George Lewis (A Jazzman from New Orleans)* (1977), is an indispensable source of information on Lewis, including personal interviews, a detailed discography, and exhaustive bibliography. Bethell includes citations for many interviews, voice transcripts, and short articles by Lewis. "Play Number Nine" from the *Jazz Record*, reprinted in *Selections from the Gutter: Jazz Portraits from "The Jazz Record,"* ed. Arthur Hodes and Chadwick Hansen (1977), gives valuable insight into the culture and music scene in New Orleans from 1916 to 1945. Also of interest are the diaries of William Russell, which began to be published in *New Orleans Musician* in 1995. A thorough discography was written by Lennart Faelt and Håkan B. Haakaansson and published as *Hymn to George: George Lewis on Record and Tape* in 1985. Other books on Lewis include *Call Him George* (1961), by Jay Allison Stuart (a pseudonym for Dorothy Tait); and Eberhard Kraut, *George Lewis: Streifzug durch ein Musiker-Leben* (1980). Although dated, Samuel Charters, *Jazz: New Orleans* (1963), is still a good source for information on New Orleans musicians.

JAMES KALYN

LEWIS, George William (10 Mar. 1882–12 July 1948), aviation pioneer, was born in Ithaca, New York, the son of William Henry Lewis and Edith Sweetland, merchants. During his early childhood his family moved to Scranton, Pennsylvania, and there he received his elementary and high school education. In 1908 he married Myrtle Harvey; the couple had six children. Also in 1908 he graduated from the Sibley College of Engineering; he received the degree of M.E. from Cornell University in 1908 and the degree of Master Mechanical Engineer (M.M.E.) in 1910. He was a faculty member of the Department of Mathematics at Swarthmore College from 1910 until 1917 and then became engineer in charge at Clarke-Thompson Research, Philadelphia, where he remained until 1919.

Lewis, already interested in aviation, joined the National Advisory Committee for Aeronautics (NACA), a federal agency created in 1915 to foster aeronautical technology, as executive officer in 1919 and became its director of aeronautical research in 1924. His work in that position helped to shape in a fundamental way the course of aeronautical research and development in the United States for the next quarter century. In 1919 the NACA staff totaled only forty-three people, including the research staff of NACA's Langley Memorial Aeronautical Laboratory, located at Hampton, Virginia.

Lewis set about to expand and remake the NACA into a premier research organization by recruiting and inspiring young scientists, engineers, and mathematicians to enter federal service, usually for less pay than they could find elsewhere. He promised them, however, an opportunity to perform cutting-edge research and to try sometimes hare-brained ideas that had little immediate commercial application. His efforts worked, and by the time of his retirement in 1947 the NACA enjoyed an exceptionally positive reputation for innovative aeronautical research and development. Under his leadership the NACA built an effective and balanced research team that pioneered novel methods of flight research; new ideas for recording instruments; and new methods and facilities for research on engines, propellers, structures, seaplanes, ice prevention, helicopters, and many other branches of aerodynamics. He developed and made use of variable-density, full-scale, refrigerated, free-flight, gust, transonic, supersonic, and other types of wind tunnels, the core instruments the NACA engineers employed to advance aerodynamic knowledge.

Lewis's greatest challenge came in a radical expansion of the NACA in response to the rearmament of Europe beginning in the mid-1930s. Lewis personally traveled to Europe in 1936 via the *Hindenburg* to investigate the aeronautical development then underway. He visited Nazi Germany and was both impressed and disquieted by its aeronautical research and development activities. He learned that Luftwaffe chief and Hitler stalwart Hermann Göring was "intensely interested in research and development." With Göring's force, Germany greatly expanded aeronautical research and development, decentralizing it at three major stations: one for research on new aircraft, one for fundamental research without application to specific aircraft designs, and one for the development of new propulsion systems. It was a powerful combination, especially when Reichmarks were flowing to fund accelerated experimentation. In his "Report of Trip to Germany and Russia, September–October, 1936," Lewis remarked:

It is apparent in Germany, especially in aviation, that everyone is working under high pressure. The greatest effort is being made to provide an adequate air fleet. Every manufacturer is turning out as many airplanes as possible, and the research and development organizations are working on problems that have an immediate bearing on this production program.

To maintain American primacy in aviation, Lewis advised, the nation should immediately start the NACA's expansion.

Lewis followed this trip with another in 1939 that confirmed his initial impressions. He found that in just three years Hitler had multiplied German air research facilities until they were five times the magnitude of those available in the United States. In testimony on Capitol Hill and in the NACA annual reports Lewis clearly presented to the president and Congress this challenge to American leadership, and Lewis arranged also to spend May 1939 in Germany, touring the new air research facilities. In June he testified before Congress in detail and reported the opinion of nu-

merous German scientists and professors that war would start before the next snow fell.

Congress approved the doubling of the NACA's facilities and staff at Langley and the construction of a second major NACA station, the Ames Aeronautical Laboratory (later the Ames Research Center) at Moffett Field, California. A year later Congress authorized the NACA Aircraft Engine Research Laboratory at Cleveland, Ohio, later renamed the Lewis Research Center in honor of George Lewis.

NACA research facilities built during Lewis's regime cost about $80 million and, although often new in concept and design, proved exceptionally useful in enabling the United States to place into the air combat aircraft on a par with or superior to Axis equipment. When failing health caused him to resign as director of aeronautical research in 1947, the seventeen members of NACA signed a testimonial praising Lewis for "inspiring leadership" and declared: "The Committee's research organization has won the confidence and respect . . . of the aeronautical world, and made scientific and technical contributions of inestimable value to the national security. . . . Our heartfelt thanks for all he has done . . . and congratulations for 28 years of exceptionally meritorious service to his country."

Lewis remained in NACA service as a research consultant thereafter. But his health was poorer than even he understood at the time. He died at his summer home near Scranton, Pennsylvania.

• The best collections of George W. Lewis Papers are located at the National Air and Space Museum, Smithsonian Institution, Washington, D.C., and at the National Archives, but some material is also available in the NASA Historical Reference Collection, NASA Headquarters, Washington, D.C. Longer biographies are William F. Durand, "George William Lewis, 1882–1948," National Academy of Sciences, *Biographical Memoirs* 25 (n.d.): 297–312; Jerome C. Hunsaker, "George William Lewis (1882–1948)," *Year Book of the American Philosophical Society* (1948), pp. 269–78. Additional information can be found in Alex Roland, *Model Research: A History of the National Advisory Committee for Aeronautics, 1915–1958* (1985); James R. Hansen, *Engineer in Charge: A History of the Langley Memorial Aeronautical Laboratory, 1917–1958* (1987); Virginia P. Dawson, *Engines and Innovation: Lewis Laboratory and American Propulsion Technology* (1991). Obituaries are in *Wing Tips*, 23 July 1948, and in the "George William Lewis Commemoration Ceremony," 28 Sept. 1948, at the NACA's Lewis Flight Propulsion Laboratory.

ROGER D. LAUNIUS

LEWIS, Gilbert Newton (23 Oct. 1875–23 Mar. 1946), physical chemist, was born in Weymouth, Massachusetts, the son of Francis Wesley Lewis, a lawyer, and Mary Burr White. In 1884 the family moved to Lincoln, Nebraska. Lewis enrolled in the University of Nebraska in 1891, transferring after his sophomore year to Harvard. He received bachelors, masters, and doctoral degrees in chemistry in 1896, 1898, and 1899, respectively. He was a Harvard instructor for one year and then a postgraduate fellow in Germany. He resumed his instructorship in 1901, but disenchantment with Harvard prompted him in 1904 to become a chemist at the Bureau of Science in the Philippines.

On returning to the United States in 1905 Lewis joined a group of young physical chemists headed by Arthur A. Noyes at the Massachusetts Institute of Technology. He rose from assistant to full professor in 1911 and published thirty articles on physical chemistry during his MIT years, gaining a reputation as the leading young American physical chemist. In 1912 he married Mary Hinckley Sheldon, daughter of a Harvard professor; they had three children. In that same year Lewis became professor of chemistry, chair of the department, and dean of the college of chemistry at the University of California in Berkeley. He remained there for the rest of his life, except during 1917–1918 when he was director of training for the Chemical Warfare Service in France.

Lewis's career at Harvard, MIT, and California had important consequences for American chemistry. Under the direction of Theodore W. Richards at Harvard, he became a superb experimentalist in physical chemistry. Richards, however, was an authoritarian and an empiricist who would not tolerate speculations about atoms, valence, and the chemical bond. These were the very things that fascinated the shy, quiet Lewis. His mind was full of unorthodox conjectures, and when Richards and others at Harvard expressed disdain for his ideas, a long-lasting resentment grew, which manifested itself in 1929 with his rejection of an honorary degree from Harvard. In contrast, he found at MIT a progressive spirit with Noyes encouraging him to explore unconventional ideas. On moving to Berkeley in 1912 with the freedom to reform a backwater department, he put into place all that he missed at Harvard, such as free discussion, cooperation, full contact between faculty and students, no division of professors by rank, and an intense weekly conference for all faculty and graduate students to discuss the latest topics and ideas. To accomplish these innovations, he hired the brightest young chemists he could find. The department became the most renowned in the world, setting new standards for all areas of chemistry.

Lewis also effected a major reform of physical chemistry. In two unpublished theoretical papers in 1900–1901, he discussed the limitations of thermodynamics for chemistry. Being derived from the behavior of ideal gases and solutions, thermodynamic equations were inexact when applied to actual systems and required complex corrections. He proposed the concept of fugacity to express the tendency of a substance to pass from one chemical phase to another and also revived the little-used concept of free energy as an expression of the tendency of a chemical change to occur. He believed that these concepts could transform chemical thermodynamics into an exact science applicable to real systems.

In 1907 Lewis introduced the concept of activity. It had the dimensions of concentration and was thus especially relevant to solution chemistry. He derived new thermodynamic equations using fugacity and activity, arriving at relationships that applied to real gases and solutions. He also developed free energy experimentally by determining free energy values for elements and compounds. His investigations culminated in the 1923 treatise *Thermodynamics and the Free Energy of Chemical Substances*, written with Merle Randall. The book made chemical thermodynamics relevant to all branches of chemistry, and its equations and tables of free energy data made possible the calculation of a wide range of information about hundreds of reactions.

The 1897 discovery of the electron, a mobile, subatomic particle in the atoms of all elements, intrigued Lewis. Suggestions soon appeared that electron transfer between atoms was the basis for the chemical bond. In 1902, doodling on the back of an envelope, Lewis drew a series of cubic atoms in which two cubes shared electrons along a common edge rather than transferring them. The model stemmed from his wondering about the cycle of eight elements in the periodic table and asking what geometric form corresponded to the number eight. His answer was the eight corners of the cube at which he placed eight electrons to represent the stable rare gases.

Over the next fourteen years theories of the chemical bond proliferated, at first employing polar bonds formed by electron transfer, followed by theories of two types of bonds, one for polar substances and another for nonpolar ones. In 1916 Lewis formulated a bold, new synthesis that repudiated all dualistic theories. The shared electron pair between atoms was the chemical bond, the sharing ranging from completely equal to various degrees of unequal sharing in a continuous series of bonds from nonpolar to polar. He represented the electrons by dots and the shared electrons by a colon. Because American chemists were among the chief proponents of polar theories, the reaction to his article was negative.

World War I disrupted the debate on chemical bonds for Lewis. In 1919 a prominent American chemist, Irving Langmuir, adopted Lewis's theory and wrote several papers amplifying the ideas, including renaming the electron pair bond the "covalent bond." So successful was his advocacy that the theory became known as the "Lewis-Langmuir theory." Rivalry between the two chemists led Lewis to write the definitive *Valence and the Structure of Atoms and Molecules*, his second masterpiece of 1923. He not only explained and applied his ideas on electron sharing but also included two major new conceptions. He proposed a generalized concept of acids as any substance capable of accepting an electron pair, thereby divorcing acids from limitations such as having hydrogen ions, and defined bases as electron pair donors. He also introduced the concept of the hydrogen bond, a notion that Linus Pauling found essential to his protein structures of the 1930s. The book became the backbone of modern chemical and structural theory with Pauling deepening the theory by translating it into the new language of quantum mechanics. Organic chemists were especially enthusiastic, finding in the electron pair bond the central theme of their science and in the Lewis acid a key to understanding organic reaction mechanisms.

After 1923 Lewis searched for new fields to conquer. In the mid-1930s he made substantial contributions to the separation of isotopes. But only in his last seven years did he find a field in which he could combine experiment and theory again to produce important results. In 1938 he noted that some Lewis acids existed in a variety of colored forms and began to explore the relation between color and molecular structure. In a 1939 review of photochemistry with Melvin Calvin, he successfully explained the ultraviolet absorption spectra and color of organic molecules in terms of a theory that combined elements of classical wave theory and quantum theory.

From 1940 to 1946 Lewis investigated the spectra of fluorescence and phosphorescence. He found evidence for two excited electronic states in his absorption spectra and interpreted his findings by using the triplet and singlet states of quantum theory, wherein the absorption of a quantum of light not only raises a molecule to an excited state but also decouples electron pair spins resulting in two excited states, one with two unpaired electrons (triplets) and another with the electrons paired (singlets). Having detected the triplet state by means of very difficult measurements, he demonstrated that phosphorescence is the emission of light during the return to the ground state from the excited triplet state. These studies became the starting point for a rapid development of photochemistry and molecular spectroscopy.

Lewis died in Berkeley, probably as the result of an accident while he was engaged in research on fluorescence. Many chemists and historians of science regard him as the most important American chemist since Josiah Willard Gibbs. He was more responsible than anyone for the development of a vigorous tradition of physical chemistry in the United States, and he also left a legacy of important concepts that affected all branches of chemistry, including the shared electron pair bond, one of the most fruitful ideas in the history of chemistry.

• The Lewis archive is at the University of California at Berkeley. The Harvard University Archives has a collection of Lewis's correspondence with Theodore W. Richards and records of his Harvard years. Joel H. Hildebrand contributed the biography and analysis of Lewis's achievements for the National Academy of Sciences, *Biographical Memoirs* 31 (1958): 209–35, which includes a bibliography of his publications. William F. Giauque wrote the biography of Lewis for the *American Philosophical Society Yearbook 1946*, pp. 317–22. Melvin Calvin provided an excellent account of the research career of Lewis in "Gilbert Newton Lewis," *Proceedings of the Robert A. Welch Conferences on Chemical Research* 20 (1977): 116–49. An absorbing symposium covering all aspects of Lewis's career appeared as a fourteen-article series in the *Journal of Chemical Education* 61 (1984). There is a popular, anecdotal biography by Arthur Lachman, *Borderland of the Unknown: The Life Story of Gilbert Newton Lewis, One of the World's Great Scientists* (1955). Essential to the understanding of the development of the Lewis theory of the chem-

ical bond are three articles by Robert E. Kohler in *Historical Studies in the Physical Sciences*: "The Origin of G. N. Lewis's Theory of the Shared Electron Pair Bond," 3 (1971): 343–76; "Irving Langmuir and the Octet Theory of Valence," 4 (1972): 39–87; and "The Lewis-Langmuir Theory of Valence and the Chemical Community," 6 (1975): 431–68. A superb monograph on the development of American physical chemistry with valuable insights on Lewis is John W. Servos, *Physical Chemistry from Ostwald to Pauling: The Making of a Science in America* (1990). An obituary is in the *New York Times*, 25 Mar. 1946.

ALBERT B. COSTA

LEWIS, Henry Clay (26 June 1825–5 Aug. 1850), physician and humorist, was born in Charleston, South Carolina, the son of David Lewis, a merchant, and Rachel Salomon. The family relocated to Cincinnati, Ohio, around 1829. After his mother's death in 1831, Lewis went to live with an older brother, Alexander, whose wife, Lewis felt, treated him poorly. In 1835, he stowed away on a steamboat bound for New Orleans. Quickly finding work as a scullery boy, Lewis remained on the Mississippi and Yazoo rivers for about a year. In 1836, he went to live with Joseph, another brother who was established as a prosperous merchant in Manchester, Mississippi (renamed Yazoo City in 1839). The financial panic of 1837 ruined Joseph, however, and young Henry was sent to work picking cotton for several years.

In 1841 Lewis's fortunes improved, for in that year Joseph arranged for a local physician, Dr. Washington Dorsey, to take Henry on as an apprentice. After two years of apprenticeship, Lewis enrolled in the Louisville (Ky.) Medical Institute in the fall of 1844. Shortly thereafter, he fell in love with a Louisville girl named Lucy. This romance, apparently the only serious one in his short life, ended when Lucy's father forbade her to see Lewis. Following the conclusion of his first course of lectures in March 1845, Lewis returned to Yazoo City. That summer he published his first humorous sketch, "Cupping on the Sternum," in William T. Porter's *Spirit of the Times*, a New York–based sporting weekly that published many of the important humorists of the day, including Thomas Bangs Thorpe, Charles F. M. Noland, and Johnson Jones Hooper. The popular and widely reprinted sketch, which recounts an incident from Lewis's early days as a physician's apprentice, turns on the novice's mistaken equation of "sternum" and "stern"—a likely mistake for a young man who had spent time on riverboats. Medical anecdotes, often of an autobiographical nature, would prove a fertile ground for the budding humorist.

In the fall of 1845 Lewis returned to Louisville for his second and final round of lectures. After receiving his M.D. in March 1846, he returned to Yazoo City, where his youthful age and appearance prevented the townsfolk from taking him seriously as a physician. Discouraged, Lewis took a job as "swamp doctor" in Madison Parish, Louisiana, on the banks of the Tensas River. A combination of these place names would provide his eventual pseudonym, Madison Tensas. Following his initial success with "Cupping on the Sternum," Lewis published several sketches in the *Spirit*, most notably "A Tight Race Considerin'," a farcical dialect tale that concludes with a respectable woman being pitched naked over her horse's head into a church.

By 1847 Lewis had adopted the swamp doctor persona that would inform most of his later work. As his biographer, John Q. Anderson, notes, the swamp doctor is, on the one hand, a literary device; Madison Tensas appears more as a grizzled veteran than a young physician in his early twenties. This persona was not, however, fully imaginative; by all accounts, Lewis was a serious physician whose work put him in contact with a wide range of social types, including planters, pseudo-aristocrats, slaves, poor whites, and rugged backwoodsmen. Surely the most memorable of the last category is Mik-hoo-tah, the "Indefatigable Bear Hunter," a character based on Michael Hooter, a Yazoo City resident who also served as a model for Lewis's fellow humorist, William C. Hall. Crippled in a fight with a grizzly, Mik gains new life when he beats a bear unconscious with a wooden leg the swamp doctor has fashioned. Writing in a genre often characterized as being hostile to the lower class, Lewis demonstrates his respect for unpolished characters such as Mik and the Hibbs family of "A Tight Race Considerin'," whom he describes as "plain, unlettered people, honest in intent and deed, but overflowing with that which amply made up for all their deficiencies of education, namely, warm-hearted hospitality, the distinguishing trait of southern character." Lewis's views of African Americans, however, were typical for his day and age; his black characters are convenient and conventional racial stereotypes.

In 1848 Lewis moved from his log cabin on the Tensas River to the plantation of Caswell T. Foster; in addition to caring for Foster's slaves, he continued to serve the local community. In 1849 he moved to Richmond, the largest town in Madison Parish, where he became the partner of Dr. George D. Shadburne, a socially prominent physician. Owing to fertile cotton lands, the area had seen a rapid growth in population, a fortunate circumstance for a young doctor who had begun to purchase land, sport a refined wardrobe, and move in fashionable circles.

By April, Lewis had submitted the manuscript of *Odd Leaves from the Life of a Louisiana "Swamp Doctor"* to the Philadelphia publishing house of A. Hart. Consisting of twenty-two sketches, *Odd Leaves* was published in March 1850. In addition to sketches dealing with swamp life, the work contains autobiographical material and anecdotes from Lewis's life as a physician's apprentice and medical student. More than most humorists, Lewis confronted the grim realities of decay, disease, and death; in "A Struggle for Life," a sketch that would be anomalous even in the exploits of George Washington Harris's Sut Lovingood, a drunken black dwarf chokes the swamp doctor into unconsciousness before burning to death in a campfire. As he lies near death, Tensas wonders, "What will my friends say when they hear that on a visit to the sick, I disappeared in the swamp and was never heard of more?—drowned or starved to death?" (p. 201). These words would prove prophetic. Less than half a year after the publication of his only book, Lewis drowned in Madison Parish while attempting to cross a river on horseback during a cholera epidemic.

Dead at twenty-five, Lewis had nevertheless contributed a minor classic to the annals of American humor. Like Joseph Glover Baldwin in *The Flush Times of Alabama and Mississippi* (1853), he also contributed an important historical document describing the frontier culture of the Old Southwest. Lewis was unique, moreover, in his insightful examination of the doctor's role within that culture.

• For biographical material, see *Louisiana Swamp Doctor: The Life and Writings of Henry Clay Lewis*, ed. John Q. Anderson (1962), which also includes the collected writings. See also Milton Rickels, "The Grotesque Body of Southwestern Humor," *Critical Essays on American Humor* (1984): 155–66; Charles Israel, "Henry Clay Lewis's *Odd Leaves*: Studies in the Surreal and Grotesque," *Mississippi Quarterly* 28 (1975): 61–69; Mark A. Keller, "'Aesculapius in Buckskin': The Swamp Doctor as Satirist in Henry Clay Lewis's *Odd Leaves*," *Southern Studies* 18 (1979): 425–48; Alan H. Rose, "The Image of the Negro in the Writings of Henry Clay Lewis," *American Literature* 41 (1969): 255–63; and Edwin T. Arnold's introduction to Louisiana State University Press's 1997 edition of *Odd Leaves*, pp. xi–xlviii.

SCOTT ROMINE

LEWIS, Howard Bishop (8 Nov. 1887–7 Mar. 1954), biochemist, was born in Southington, Connecticut, the son of Frederick Austin Lewis and Charlotte Ruth Parmelee, farmers. After finishing his secondary education in 1903, he studied classical Greek while waiting to meet the minimum age requirement for admission to Yale University. He excelled in the classics and the physical sciences at Yale and received his B.A. in 1908; he then spent the next two years teaching at the Hampton (Va.) Institute and the Centenary Collegiate Institute in Hackettstown, New Jersey. In 1910 he enrolled in George Washington University's graduate chemistry program, where he met Isaac Phelps, a faculty member and fellow Yale alumnus.

At the time, physiologists were debating about the amount of protein required in the daily human diet. The debate was occasioned in 1904, when Yale physiologist Russell H. Chittenden asserted that the high-protein diet espoused in 1866 by German physiologist Carl Voit as essential to human growth and development was potentially dangerous; he argued that this diet necessitated the elimination of large amounts of nitrogen in the form of urine and therefore overtaxed the kidneys. Phelps believed that a proper understanding of the way in which the body processes amino acids, its primary source of nitrogen, during protein metabolism might determine the outcome of the debate; therefore, he convinced Lewis that a bright future awaited him in biochemical research. Thus inspired, Lewis returned to Yale as a graduate student later that year and in 1911 became a laboratory assistant at both Yale and the Connecticut State Hospital in Middletown. His first venture into protein metabolism involved the study of several of the heterocyclic nitrogen compounds derived from urea, a primary constituent of urine and the final byproduct of protein metabolism.

In 1913 Lewis received his Ph.D. in physiological chemistry and accepted a position as an instructor at the University of Pennsylvania. His work with urea led him to study the synthesis in rabbits and humans of hippuric acid, another byproduct of protein metabolism that is formed in the kidneys from benzoic acid and glycine, the simplest amino acid. In 1915 he married Mildred Lois Eaton; they had two children. That same year he joined the faculty of the Department of Chemistry of the University of Illinois as an associate and the head of the division of physiological chemistry. Yale's Thomas B. Osborne and Lafayette B. Mendel had recently demonstrated that cystine, at the time the only known sulphur-containing amino acid, was essential to growth and development in white rats. In 1916 Lewis, realizing that high-protein diets also result in high concentrations of sulphur in urine (suggesting that sulphur itself is not essential to protein metabolism), embarked on a thirty-year investigation into the metabolism of sulphur in general and the nutritional role of sulphur-containing amino acids in particular.

In 1917, the same year he was promoted to assistant professor, Lewis offered further support for the universality of the findings of Osborne and Mendel by demonstrating that cystine was also essential to the growth and development of dogs. Two years later he was promoted to associate professor. In 1922 he joined the faculty at the University of Michigan School of Medicine as a full professor and the head of the Department of Biological Chemistry. That year, by studying the oxidation of cystine in animal organisms, Lewis concluded that cystine converts during metabolism into the sulphur-containing amino acid cysteine. Having become one of the foremost authorities on sulphur metabolism, he authored in 1924 the first of his six reviews that appeared over the next sixteen years in *Physiological Reviews* and *Annual Review of Biochemistry*, addressing current research in the chemistry and metabolism of the compounds of sulphur. In 1926 and 1927 he determined the suitability of a number of individual sulphur-containing compounds such as taurine, a substance derived from bile, as replacements for cystine in the diets of young white rats. In 1929 Lewis determined the rate of oxidation of ingested cystine in rabbits and discovered that when moderate doses were fed to rabbits for several days, renal casts, a sign of kidney failure, began to appear in their urine, thereby offering support for Chittenden's critique of the high-protein diet.

In 1933 Lewis assumed the additional duties of the director of Michigan's College of Pharmacy. His investigations into sulphur metabolism now included the study of methionine, another sulphur-containing amino acid discovered in 1923 by John H. Mueller. In 1934 he conducted a comparative study of the metabolism of cystine and methionine in rabbits, in which he demonstrated that, although a certain amount of methionine is indispensable to the rabbit's growth and development, cystine can replace methionine as a source of sulphur to a considerable degree. In 1947 Lewis resigned as director when he was appointed as the John Jacob Abel University Professor of Biological Chemistry. He retired from his teaching and administrative duties in 1948 but remained at the university an additional year as a Henry Russell Lecturer.

Lewis served as the president of the American Society of Biological Chemists from 1935 to 1937 and the American Institute of Nutrition Commission's executive committee from 1947 to 1952, and for many years he managed the Federation of American Societies for Experimental Biology's Placement Service. He served on the editorial boards of the *Proceedings of the Society of Experimental Biology and Medicine* from 1927 to 1938, *Physiological Reviews* from 1935 to 1940, the *Journal of Nutrition* from 1935 to 1939 and from 1941 to 1945, *Chemical Reviews* from 1938 to 1940, and the *Journal of Biological Chemistry* from 1938 to 1954. He was a member of the National Board of Medical Examiners from 1935 to 1950, the American Medical Association's Council on Foods and Nutrition from 1936 to 1954, and the National Research Council's Division of Medical Sciences from 1945 to 1948. He was elected to membership in the National Academy of Sciences in 1949. He died in Ann Arbor, Michigan.

Although Lewis conducted research in a number of areas pertaining to protein metabolism and nutrition, he was most concerned with the metabolism of sulphur and sulphur-containing amino acids. His pioneering efforts in this regard led to a better understanding of the role played in protein metabolism by cystine, methionine, and other sulphur-containing compounds.

• Lewis's papers are in the University of Michigan's Michigan Historical Collection. He discusses his contribution to the understanding of sulphur metabolism in "Fifty Years of Study of the Role of Protein in Nutrition," *Journal of the American Dietetic Association* 28 (1952): 701–6. A biography, including a bibliography, is William C. Rose and Minor J. Coon, National Academy of Sciences, *Biographical Memoirs* 44 (1974): 139–73. Obituaries are in the *New York Times*, 9 Mar. 1954, and *Science*, 3 Sept. 1954.

CHARLES W. CAREY, JR.

LEWIS, Ida (25 Feb. 1842–24 Oct. 1911), first female lighthouse keeper in the United States, was born in Newport, Rhode Island, the daughter of Captain Hosea Lewis, a coast pilot, and his second wife, Idawalley Zoradia Willey. The couple named their eldest daughter Idawalley Zoradia, but she was known throughout her life as "Ida" or "Miss Lewis."

After her father was appointed keeper of the Newport Harbor lighthouse on Lime Rock in 1853, Ida attended school in Newport, Rhode Island, while an appropriate home was being built at the lighthouse for the family. In 1857 Captain Lewis moved his wife and four children to the island, ending Ida's formal education. She continued, however, to row her younger sister and brothers to the mainland each day for school and developed the strength and discipline that would enable her in the future to help others who encountered imminent death in the bay. Ida was only fifteen years old when she became her father's assistant in maintaining the lighthouse. Three years later he suffered a stroke that left him partially paralyzed, and Ida assumed most of his duties as keeper of the lighthouse. After his death in 1872, she continued to maintain the Lime Rock light but was not officially appointed light keeper until 1879, after her heroic rescues had brought her national fame.

Lewis's first rescue came in 1858 or 1859, when she spotted four young men who had been thrown into the waters of Narragansett Bay when their boat capsized. She immediately went to their aid, hauled all four into her little skiff, and rowed them to safety. In 1866 she pulled a drunken soldier from the harbor and in 1867 rescued three sheepherders who had ventured too far from the shore in pursuit of a sheep that had fled into the bay. She saved the animal as well as its three disheveled and frightened pursuers.

The event that brought Lewis national attention occurred in March 1869. In the midst of a blizzard, she and her brother Hosea managed to reach two soldiers whose small boat had capsized in the choppy, windswept waters as they were being rowed from Newport back to their station at Fort Adams. (The boatman apparently drowned before the Lewises arrived on the scene.) Both men were unconscious by the time Lewis and her brother got them into the dinghy and back to Lime Rock. She worked over the two for an hour before she felt confident that they were out of danger. Lewis's previous exploits had gone unnoticed except in local articles, but this time a New York reporter in search of a good human-interest story emblazoned her name in the newspapers and proclaimed her the rescuer of the two soldiers. The resulting publicity catapulted her into the national limelight. The editor of *Harper's New Monthly Magazine* (June 1869) praised her heroism and criticized any who would question the femininity of a woman who could row a boat with such strength and skill. None but a donkey, the editor proclaimed, would call unfeminine an action that saved lives. Susan B. Anthony joined the *Harper's* editor in her own journal, the *Revolution* (July and Sept. 1869), in complimenting Lewis on her competence and bravery.

Now twenty-seven, Lewis was showered with gifts and letters of adulation. During the summer of 1869 the citizens of Newport held a special celebration in her honor and gave her a new lifeboat, appropriately christened the *Rescue*. Colonel James Fisk of the Fall River Line readily recognized Lewis's heroism and presented her with a silk flag for her new vessel and a new boathouse in which to shelter the skiff. The soldiers at Fort Adams rewarded her with a gold watch and other gifts.

The admiration showered upon Lewis included a number of marriage proposals, one of which she accepted. On 23 October 1870 she married William Heard Wilson, a sailor and fisherman from Black Rock, Connecticut, but lived with him only a short time before deciding she had erred. They were never divorced, but Lewis resumed her duties at Lime Rock and remained there for the rest of her life, caring for her invalid siblings as well as for the lighthouse.

In 1878 Lewis's rescue of three inebriated musicians brought her case to the attention of General Ambrose E. Burnside, U.S. senator from Rhode Island. Impressed by Lewis's bravery, and hearing of her dedication as lighthouse keeper, the general looked into her record, noted the many times she had come to the aid of mariners in need, and was astonished that she had for such a long time held no title at the Lime Rock Lighthouse. Burnside determined that she should be officially appointed and persevered until she was named custodian for life.

Lewis continued her lifesaving activities and is credited with having saved at least eighteen people from the waters of Narragansett Bay. She also continued to garner awards and honors for her deeds. Congress bestowed a gold medal upon her after the rescue of yet two more waterlogged wayfarers. Other gold medals came from the state of Rhode Island and from the American Cross of Honor Society. She was awarded silver medals by the Life Saving Benevolent Association, the American Life Saving Society, and the Massachusetts Humane Society, as well as a silver rudder yoke and boat hook presented to her by the Narragansett Boat Club of Providence. Perhaps of most importance, in 1906, on the fiftieth anniversary of her service to the Lime Rock Lighthouse, she received a life pension of $30 a month from the Carnegie Hero Fund.

Lewis lived out her life with her brother Rudolph on the little island that cradled the lighthouse. By 1911 there were hints in the newspapers, however, that Lime Rock might be abandoned. Such a prospect, her brother claimed, caused Lewis to suffer a paralytic stroke in October. She soon died of a cerebral hemorrhage. So esteemed had she become that as she lay in a coma in the last days of her life, still at the lighthouse, the Department of War ordered the cessation of target practice in the Narragansett Bay defense district lest she be disturbed by the firing of the guns. She was buried in the "common ground" on Farewell Street in Newport.

• The Newport Historical Society has preserved the lifeboat *Rescue* and Lewis's medals. The society's *Bulletin* (Jan. 1930) includes extracts from the *New York Tribune*, 15 Apr. 1869, and the *Newport Daily News*, 5 July 1869, recounting Lewis's lifesaving exploits that year and the ensuing celebration held in her honor. George Brewerton also described the event in *Ida Lewis, the Heroine of Lime Rock* (1869), approved by Ida herself. See also her interview with J. Earl Clausen, "A Half-Forgotten Heroine," *Putnam's Magazine*, Feb. 1910. Obituaries are in the *New York Times* and the *Newport Daily News*, 25 Oct. 1911, and the *Newport Mercury*, 28 Oct. 1911. See also the full-page pictorial article, "The Passing of Ida Lewis, the Heroine of Newport," the *New York Times*, 29 Oct. 1911, p. 9.

ROSANNA LEDBETTER

LEWIS, Isaac Newton (12 Oct. 1858–9 Nov. 1931), soldier and inventor, was born in New Salem, Pennsylvania, the son of James H. Lewis and Anne Kendall. Little is known of his childhood because of his own reticence and the destruction of many of his personal papers in a fire. The family moved to Kansas, where Lewis was educated. Beyond that there is no information on family life, parental occupations, or even exact location. At twenty Lewis taught school, a task he found unpleasant. In 1880 he received an appointment to the U.S. Military Academy, from which he graduated in 1884 and was commissioned a second lieutenant into artillery. After several short postings, he attended the Torpedo School at Willet's Point, New York, in 1885 and 1886. In 1886 he married Mary Wheatley; they had four children.

Lewis was posted to Fort Leavenworth, where he began his career as an inventor in 1888 with a range and position finder for artillery. Other inventions followed, including a quick reading vernier and a clock-interval and bell signal system for artillery fire control. All received military adoption. He also produced civilian devices, such as a car axle–powered dynamo to provide electric lighting for railroad cars and a device whereby rural windmills could generate electricity. His reputation grew within the service, and in 1894 he was made a member of the Board for Regulation of Coast Artillery Fire in New York. From 1898 to 1902 he was recorder and member of the prestigious Board of Ordnance and Fortification in Washington.

In 1900 Secretary of War Elihu Root, who was working on sweeping military reforms, sent Lewis to Europe to examine ordnance manufacturing and supply systems. Lewis's report to the secretary led Root to direct him to devise the new organization for the artillery. At the time the United States had no units larger than regiments, and Lewis's plans for an artillery corps were adopted in 1902. Borrowing from the French 75-millimeter gun, Lewis, by making several improvements, including strengthening the breech and designing a light carriage, created the first modern artillery piece adopted by the U.S. Army. From 1904 through 1911 he commanded the Artillery District of the Cheasapeake and also served as director of the department of enlisted specialists, which included responsibilities in charge of training and management of technical personnel, as acting commandant of the Coast Artillery School, and as commandant at Fortress Monroe. During this period he devised artillery fire control systems for fortifications and invented a gas-powered torpedo.

In 1910 Lewis became associated with the weapon that would bring him fame, wealth, and controversy—his light machine gun. The financially troubled Automatic Arms Company of Buffalo, New York, approached Lewis to design a machine gun based on an existing patent or one of his own design. He chose a weapon designed by Samuel N. McLean and patented in 1906. Lewis, with more than a year of work, improved on a basically sound firing mechanism and created or modified the cooling system, rate of fire regulator, and spring system, all of which he patented. The completed design was a 26-pound, gas-operated (the gases produced by fired cartridges are fed back to operate the weapon), air-cooled, magazine-fed light machine gun that could be carried and operated by one soldier. A pan-shaped magazine above the receiver contained forty-seven cartridges and was easily changed for rapid reloading. The weapon contained only sixty-two parts and could not be assembled or loaded incorrectly. This fit not only Lewis's technical concept but also his tactical views of large volumes of fire during assault and maneuver. His retirement from the army in 1913 allowed him more time to press the army for adoption of the weapon. General Leonard Wood, the chief of staff, was impressed, but tests in 1913 with tool room–produced models suffered more than 200 failures owing to improperly hardened parts. The Ordnance Department chief, General William Crozier, refused to allow any correction of the problem or to admit the arm to the next round of tests. Personal animosity between Lewis and the department dating back more than a dozen years may have played a role in the decision. All appeals failed.

The controversy between Lewis and the Ordnance Department continued into U.S. participation in the First World War, with Lewis charging, as he had a dozen years before, contract fixing, cronyism, and test rigging. Angered and disgusted, Lewis went to Belgium. His gun received favorable reviews and Belgian army adoption, and operations began under *Armes Automatique Lewis* in Liège. When the German army invaded the country, machinery and personnel from the firm were removed to England. Production of the Lewis gun was carried on by the Birmingham Small Arms Company, then the largest such facility in the world. Officials were impressed with the weapon's reliability and lightness and by a rapid production rate. Five Lewis guns could be manufactured in the time it took to produce one standard heavy machine gun. The British purchased large numbers of the gun, and the government paid for expansion of the facilities. By 1917 the British had more than 40,000 Lewis guns in use in the trenches of France and in the Middle East, many of these manufactured in the United States. In the United States the Ordnance Department objections were demolished by further demonstrations. Journalists and public figures entered the fight. So disruptive was the debate that the War Department ordered the controversy ended. With certain modifications, the arm was accepted by the army in 1917 but saw only limited use by American ground forces. Troops who had them prized them and found ways to acquire more by trading with the British or by smuggling Lewis guns used in training to France. Most Lewis guns purchased by the United States were mounted on aircraft. Its success in the air came as no surprise to Lewis. In 1912, at his request, the gun became the first machine gun to be fired from an airplane at ground targets. In August 1914 two British aviators used a Lewis gun to fire the first machine gun in aerial combat. The weapon was modified for aircraft and a 96-round magazine was introduced. In addition to air combat and strafing, the Lewis gun is credited with destroying the German zeppelin threat over Britain. The gun was acknowledged as the best light machine gun of the war, and more than 100,000 were produced in Britain, France, and the United States during the conflict. In addition, the Germans, using some of the Belgian machinery, produced a significant but unknown number of the Lewis guns in their own caliber. Lewis, who had offered his gun royalty free to the United States, returned his royalties of more than $1 million from American purchases to the Treasury.

Lewis contributed more than his weapon. The idea of volume fire and movement is the concept of modern assault tactics. In 1916 the French developed a light machine gun of a design much inferior to the Lewis but based on the same tactical concepts. To a degree the Lewis gun was the first forerunner of the modern assault rifle. Like the Lewis, the assault rifle is a machine gun capable of assault fire that can be carried by the individual soldier and reloaded rapidly with precharged magazines. Unlike the Lewis, the assault rifle is light in weight, usually fires less powerful, lightweight ammunition, and can fire a single round with each separate pull of the trigger if desired. Lewis recognized some of these latter qualities. In 1916 he wrote Commander J. P. Jackson of the U.S. Navy that he was designing a machine gun in the same shape as the individual service rifle that could fire single rounds also—ideal, Lewis said, for marine assault parties. Had such a weapon actually been built, it would have been the world's first assault rifle. Others later recognized these principles, but Lewis was a generation ahead of his time.

After World War I Lewis led a quiet life in retirement at his home in Montclair, New Jersey. A member of a number of professional and social clubs, he often traveled to New York to attend meetings or to dine with friends. He was returning home from a lunch with friends in the city when he suffered a fatal heart attack on the train platform at Hoboken, New Jersey.

• The most detailed technical treatment of Lewis's invention, including test results and other government documents, is in George M. Chinn, *The Machine Gun* (4 vols., 1951). C. H. Claudy, "The Romance of Invention—VIII: The One Man Machine Gun and Its Inventor," *Scientific American* 122 (14 Feb. 1920): 120, 172, gives a detailed contemporary view. Coverage of the Lewis gun controversy is in David A. Armstrong, *Bullets and Bureaucrats: The Machine Gun and the United States Army, 1861–1916* (1982), and William H. Hallahan, *Misfire: The History of How America's Small Arms Have Failed Our Military* (1994). For a defense of the Ordnance Department see William Crozier, *Ordnance and the World War* (1920). See also J. David Truby, *The Lewis Gun* (1988). Obituaries are in the *New York Times*, 10 Nov. 1931, and *Army Ordnance*, Dec.–Jan. 1931–1932.

CARL L. DAVIS

LEWIS, James (c. 1837–10 Sept. 1896), actor, was born in Troy, New York, and is generally accepted to be the son of William Hoadley Deming and Arabella Benson. Lewis remained reticent about his birthdate, parentage, and childhood throughout his life. A reference to Lewis as James Lewis Deming is in J. K. Deming's *A Genealogy of the Descendants of John Deming* (1904).

Lewis embarked on his stage career in his hometown at the Troy Museum company. The story goes that an actor friend of Lewis's had left the company without notice, and Lewis—then seventeen—agreed to fill in, playing a small part in *The Writing on the Wall*. His performance earned him an engagement as a utility player for the rest of the season. A short stint at the Green Street Theatre in Albany and a subsequent four-year Georgia circuit tour followed. When the Civil War broke out and Lewis found himself south of the Mason-Dixon line, he headed north.

From the beginning, Lewis was cast almost exclusively in comic roles. Self-described as an "eccentric comedian," he became a versatile comic performer. He played seasons of stock in Rochester and in Cleveland (as the principal low comedian with John Ellsler's Theatre) and then moved in 1865 to New York City. There, he was hired at Matilda Vining (Mrs. John) Wood's Olympic Theatre, where he made his New York debut in *Your Life's in Danger*, as John Strong. Lewis's working relationship with Matilda Wood was apparently not happy, foreshadowing his later difficulties with another manager, Augustin Daly.

Daly saw Lewis in Eliza Holt's burlesque troupe, in travesty roles (satirical burlesques), which included those of Lucretia Borgia and Rebecca in *Ivanhoe*. Impressed, he hired the comedian for his stock company at the Fifth Avenue Theatre on West Twenty-fourth Street. Lewis appeared there for the first time on 6 September 1869, playing John Hibbs in *Dreams*. The critics' responses were good, and Lewis continued to work with Daly until a falling out in 1877, when Daly fired Lewis.

Lewis had no difficulty finding other work and was a hit in burlesques and other light entertainments in Chicago, including *White Fawn!*, a fairy extravaganza under the management of J. B. Booth, Jr., in which he played the role of King Dingdong. He also received his first starring engagement in 1877 as Archibald Meek in *Marriage*, with the Boucicault Comedy Company at the Brooklyn Academy. A series of successes followed when Lewis joined Mrs. G. H. (Anne Hartley) Gilbert in Henry Abbey's company at New York's Park Theatre. Soon, Augustin Daly rehired Lewis's friend, Mrs. Gilbert (as she was known), who convinced Daly to take Lewis back.

Though they continued to work together until Lewis's death, a strong rapport eluded the two men, who differed both in temperament and opinion. The most consistent source of conflict between them appears to have been Lewis's casting. Daly assigned a wide variety of parts to Lewis, even casting the homely comedian in the romantic role of Leonardo Tompkins, opposite Ada Rehan in *Our First Families.* The critics were unkind, and thereafter any role that Lewis did not want to take became "a Leonardo Tompkins role." Perhaps Daly was occasionally guilty of miscasting, but Lewis may have gone too far in the other direction, overreacting to Daly's assigning him roles outside his usual range. James Burge notes the existence of no fewer than sixty letters from Lewis to Daly, "most of them vitriolic" (p. 270), in which he questions his casting.

Whatever their differences, both Lewis and Daly profited from their association. Lewis is best remembered as one of the "Big Four" actors around whom Daly planned his seasons. Joining Ada Rehan, Gilbert, and John Drew, Lewis completed a highly successful ensemble of actors. Within the company, Lewis became famous for his line of eccentric characters, especially old men. With his sharp features, bulging eyes, slight stature, and dry delivery, he teamed up with Gilbert to contrast with the striking John Drew and Ada Rehan.

James Lewis was best in contemporary comedies—especially farces with Gilbert, who played comic old women to his eccentric old men. Some of their most successful collaborations were in *Red Letter Nights* (1884), *A Wooden Spoon* (1885), and *A Night Off* (1885). Lewis could also turn in a respectable performance in the classics, but he never enjoyed them. Though he performed in *As You Like It, Love's Labour's Lost,* and a landmark production of *A Midsummer Night's Dream,* as well as other classic comedies, he would often say, "Hey! Shakespeare is no friend of mine!" (Skinner, p. 67). Instead, he preferred adaptations of French and German comedies and was successful in such big hits as Bronson Howard's *Saratoga,* as well as in the now-obscure plays *Americans Abroad, Needles and Pins,* and *An International March.*

A private man, Lewis died suddenly in West Hampton, Long Island. Married twice, he was survived by his second wife, Medora Frances Herbert, whom he married in 1871. Neither marriage produced any children.

Aside from his obvious popularity as an eccentric comedian, Lewis is important for his contribution to a shift in acting styles that occurred toward the end of the nineteenth century. With William Gillette and others, Lewis's characterizations show a departure from the more presentational work of earlier comedians. One *New York Daily Graphic* critic, identified only as "T," summed up Lewis's part in this shift: "While the old like of caricaturing comedians is running down . . . a new style of comedy—in much adapted from the French, conventional, chatty, played without grimace, and extending its effects in harmonious relations with the general movement of the play—has come into vogue. The master of conversational comedy is Mr. Lewis, of the Fifth Avenue Theatre, New York" (Billy Rose Theatre Collection).

• The Billy Rose Theatre Collection at the New York Public Library for the Performing Arts, Lincoln Center, has numerous clippings on Daly and Lewis, as well as scrapbooks in the Robinson Locke Collection. Correspondence from Lewis to Daly is in the Folger Shakespeare Library, and other materials are in the James Lewis file in the Harvard University Theatre Collection. See James C. Burge, *Lines of Business* (1986), for an excellent comparison of Lewis's repertoire with that of other nineteenth-century low comedians. Other useful sources include Joseph Francis Daly, *The Life of Augustin Daly* (1917); Arthur Hornblow, *History of the Theatre in America,* vol. 2 (1919); Otis Skinner, *Footlights and Spotlights* (1924); J. R. Towse, *Sixty Years of the Theatre* (1916); and George C. D. Odell, *Annals of the New York Stage* (1927–1949; repr. 1970), especially vols. 8 through 13. Obituaries appear in the *New York Times* and the *Boston Herald,* 11 Sept. 1896; the *New York Dramatic Mirror,* 19 Sept. 1896; and the *Troy (N.Y.) Northern Budget,* 13 Sept. 1896.

CYNTHIA M. GENDRICH

LEWIS, John Francis (1 Mar. 1818–2 Sept. 1895), politician and farmer, was born at his family home, "Lynwood," near Port Republic in Rockingham County, Virginia, the son of Samuel Hance Lewis and Nancy Lewis, farmers. An active youth, he found his studies in an old-field school confining, and his father applied the son's energies to work on the large family farm. Lewis excelled in this area and became an innovative, successful, and wealthy farmer himself. His interests expanded into other ventures as well. He became superintendent of the Mount Vernon Iron Works in Rockingham County before the Civil War, and he apparently continued in the iron business for many years. He married Serena Helen Sheffey in 1842, and they raised seven children.

A supporter of the Whig party throughout the antebellum era, Lewis demonstrated little passion for politics until the secession crisis of 1860–1861, when his strong attachment to the Union led him to campaign for and win a seat in the Virginia secession convention. Despite public denunciation and threats of physical violence, he quietly refused to support the secession movement, voted twice in the convention against separation, and was the only member from east of the Allegheny Mountains who refused to sign the secession ordinance after it was adopted. During the Civil War, while his brother Charles H. Lewis (b. 1816) became secretary of the commonwealth under the wartime Unionist governor, Francis H. Pierpont, John Lewis remained quietly on his farm in Rockingham County. Some evidence exists that he was pressured into selling iron to the Confederate government.

In the state's first postwar elections in October 1865, Lewis ran for a seat in the U.S. House of Representatives from the Sixth District. Defeated by another former Whig, Alexander H. H. Stuart, who had initially opposed secession but then supported the Confederacy once war came, Lewis nevertheless pressed on with his new political ambitions and became a leading member of the state's Republican party. As one of forty-nine witnesses who testified on Virginia before the Joint Committee on Reconstruction in early 1866, he reiterated his strong Unionist views and emphasized his regret that some former Confederates still harbored disloyal sentiments. He helped to organize the national Republican convention that met in Philadelphia in September 1866 to offset the impact of the recent National Union Convention ("Arm-in-Arm Convention") of conservative Unionists and Democrats. A year later he joined Governor Pierpont, the moderate Republican leader John Minor Botts, and northern party leaders in an effort to patch up differences between radical and centrist wings of the state's Republican party in preparation for elections to the 1867–1868 state constitutional convention mandated by the congressional plan of Reconstruction. When radical Republicans refused to cooperate, Lewis, unlike some centrist Republicans who abandoned the party in disgust, announced his candidacy as a Republican for a seat in the convention. While he failed to win election, his reputation as a friend of the Union and of the freedmen earned him the ballots of 304 of the 314 black voters in Rockingham County.

In the 1869 state elections required by the congressional Reconstruction plan, the more radical regular Republicans nominated interim governor Henry H. Wells for the governorship and J. D. Harris, a prominent black physician, for lieutenant governor. Centrist Republicans, including Lewis, wanted to build a biracial party and broke from the regulars, who preferred more fundamental reform of Virginia laws. The centrists formed a new, third party, the True Republicans. This new group nominated New York–born Gilbert C. Walker for governor and Lewis for lieutenant governor. Rather than split the anti-radical vote, the state's Conservative party withdrew their nominations and finally gave their lukewarm support to the True Republicans as the lesser of two evils. In a hard-fought campaign in the summer of 1869, the True Republican–Conservative coalition crushed the regular Republicans. Lewis won the race for lieutenant governor by a margin of 120,068 to 99,400. He served only a few months before the new legislature elected him as a Republican to the U.S. Senate, where he served from 1870 to 1875.

Lewis was as quiet and unassuming in the Senate as he had been in the secession convention. He was chairman of the Committee on the District of Columbia and authored a bankruptcy law that was generous to debtors, but otherwise he made few speeches or comments on Senate proceedings. When his term expired, as a reward for his fidelity to the Republican party, President Ulysses S. Grant appointed him U.S. marshal for the Western District of Virginia. President Rutherford B. Hayes renewed the appointment in 1878. Lewis retained that position until the early 1880s, when he returned to politics as one of the leading figures in the emerging coalition of Virginia Republicans and a new insurgent party, the Readjusters, headed by his old True Republican colleague, former Confederate general William Mahone. Elected lieutenant governor for a second time in 1881, Lewis served through the stormiest years of Readjuster-Republican control of

state politics (1882–1886) and was regarded by Democrats as a friend of Virginia blacks. Mahone was more flexible in his principles, more willing to trim and compromise, and Lewis broke with him in 1889, preferring a straight Republican ticket, and played a key role in the decline of Mahone's political fortunes.

Lewis returned to Lynwood after serving as lieutenant governor and fought a long, painful fight against cancer before dying there of the disease. His personal courage and gentlemanly demeanor apparently earned him the respect of political foes as well as friends, and he lived up to his family's long tradition of public service. Lewis's political career placed him among that small group of mid-nineteenth-century southern whites who swam against the tide of public opinion, supported the Union, and became staunch and consistent Republicans in the Reconstruction and post-Reconstruction eras.

• No sizable body of Lewis's personal papers exists. Some insight into the man and his career may be gained from a small collection of his papers at the Virginia Historical Society in Richmond; scattered letters in other collections at the Virginia Historical Society; and documents in the Francis Harrison Pierpont Letters and Papers (West Virginia University Library), the Francis H. Pierpont Executive Papers (Virginia State Library and Archives), the John C. Underwood Papers and Scrapbook (Library of Congress), and the William Mahone Papers (Duke University Library). Lewis's activities during the Reconstruction and Readjuster eras are covered in Richard Lowe, *Republicans and Reconstruction in Virginia, 1856–70* (1991); Jack P. Maddex, Jr., *The Virginia Conservatives, 1867–1879: A Study in Reconstruction Politics* (1970); and James Tice Moore, *Two Paths to the New South: The Virginia Debt Controversy, 1870–1883* (1974). Obituaries are in the *Richmond Dispatch*, 3 Sept. 1895, and the *Rockingham* (Va.) *Register*, 6 Sept. 1895.

RICHARD LOWE

LEWIS, John Henry (1 May 1914–14 Apr. 1974), boxer, was born in Los Angeles, California, the son of John E. Lewis and Mattie Drake. His father had been a boxer, runner, and jockey, later operating a gymnasium in Los Angeles and training the track team of the University of Southern California. In 1918 the family moved to Phoenix, Arizona, where Lewis's father operated another gymnasium and served as trainer to Arizona university teams. John Henry graduated from Armstrong High School in Phoenix and later attended Arizona State University.

As a child, Lewis often boxed his older brother Christy in public exhibitions. When he was only fourteen years old, he fought professionally for the first time, as a welterweight; by the end of 1931 he had twenty-one fights in Arizona rings, winning twenty and boxing one draw. In 1932 the Lewis family moved to Oakland, California, and John Henry, who had grown into a light heavyweight, immediately began to meet tougher opposition in San Francisco Bay area rings. Before the year ended, he defeated light heavyweight contenders Yale Okun, Fred Lenhart, and Lou Scozza and outpointed future heavyweight champion

James Braddock, losing only a nontitle fight to light heavyweight champion Maxie Rosenbloom.

By this time, although he was only eighteen years old, the 5′11″, 175-pound Lewis was a highly skilled fighter and had developed the style that he would use throughout his career. To quote Nat Fleischer:

As a defensive boxer, he had few equals. He moved with the speed of a welterweight . . . He was versatile in his attack, capable of switching from head to body with no loss of effectiveness, and was a sharp, damaging puncher with either hand, though not a one-punch knockout artist. A boxer, rather than a slugger, he was forever pressing forward with a continuous blinding two-handed attack, and much of his effectiveness was due to the speed and relentlessness of his pace, which gave his ring foes very little rest. (*Black Dynamite*, p. 206)

In 1933 and 1934 Lewis continued to box in the western states, managed by Frank Schuler, a San Francisco boxing promoter. In return fights he twice outpointed Rosenbloom and defeated many lesser opponents, with only three draws to interrupt his series of successes. In November 1934 he went east under the management of Gus Greenlee of Pittsburgh, owner of a black professional baseball team, and made his debut at Madison Square Garden in New York City on 16 November 1934 against Braddock. The well-trained, greatly improved Braddock gave Lewis his second defeat and became the first opponent to knock him down.

Lewis quickly rebounded from the Braddock defeat and won his next eleven fights, including a decision over Bob Olin, who had succeeded Rosenbloom as light heavyweight champion. In July 1935 he lost decisions to Rosenbloom and Abe Feldman, but he then fought Olin for the world light heavyweight championship in St. Louis on 31 October. Although the fight went the full fifteen rounds, Olin was badly beaten and Lewis became the champion.

In the years that followed, Lewis fought often and seldom lost, defending his title successfully five times. In 1936 he decisively outboxed Englishman Jock McAvoy in New York; he then traveled to London, England, and easily beat another Englishman, Len Harvey. In 1937 he knocked out Olin in eight rounds of a title rematch in St. Louis, Missouri. In 1938 he knocked out Emilio Martinez in four rounds in Minneapolis, Minnesota, and defeated Al Gainer in fifteen rounds in New Haven, Connecticut. He fought and defeated many highly ranked heavyweights, including Johnny Risko, Al Ettore, Patsy Perroni, and Tony Shucco.

Despite his successes, Lewis's ring earnings were comparatively small. The light heavyweight championship was not especially prestigious. In general, attendance at boxing events, and hence ring earnings, were low during the Great Depression. Furthermore, although Lewis was the first African American to win the light heavyweight title, he was greatly overshadowed by Joe Louis, whose career began in 1934. While the bigger and much harder-hitting Louis fought important battles in New York and Chicago before enormous crowds, Lewis defended his title and fought nontitle bouts mostly either in smaller cities or in large cities before small crowds.

On 25 January 1939 Lewis and Louis met for the world heavyweight title. Although the two men were said to be friends, the heavyweight champion showed no mercy; he quickly launched a devastating attack that ended the fight in the first round. Landing only two light punches himself, Lewis suffered three knockdowns and a bad beating before the referee stopped the fight. It was the first time he had ever been knocked out and proved to be his last fight. In March 1939 he was refused permission to box in Michigan when it was discovered that he was blind in one eye and had very poor vision in the other. An attempt to set up a light heavyweight championship rematch with Harvey in England failed when the British Boxing Board of Control banned him from boxing there. Unable to arrange fights, Lewis lost recognition as light heavyweight champion when the New York State Athletic Commission declared the title vacant on 27 July 1939.

Lewis was well liked by all who knew him. Quiet and gentlemanly, he was devoutly religious, abstained from using alcohol and tobacco, and pursued sports and music as hobbies. After his retirement he lived in the Bay Area with his wife Florence Anita Reid, with whom he had two children. He died in Berkeley, California.

Lewis fought 117 times, winning 103, 60 by knockout, boxing six draws, and losing only eight times. He was elected to the International Boxing Hall of Fame in 1994.

• A full record of Lewis's boxing career is available in Herbert G. Goldman, ed., *The Ring 1986–87 Record Book and Boxing Encyclopedia* (1987). The principal source of information on his career is Nat Fleischer, *Black Dynamite*, vol. 5: *Sockers in Sepia* (1947). Articles entitled "Nat Fleischer Says," in *The Ring*, June, July, Sept., and Dec. 1939, give details of Lewis's vision problems and his attempt to continue his career after losing to Joe Louis. An obituary is in the *New York Times*, 19 Apr. 1974.

LUCKETT V. DAVIS

LEWIS, John L. (12 Feb. 1880–11 June 1969), labor leader, was born John Llewellyn Lewis in Lucas County, Iowa, the son of Thomas Lewis, a coal miner and policeman, and Ann Louisa Watkins. Both parents were Welsh-born. Through the 1880s and into the early 1890s, the family lived in ill-constructed, company-owned houses with an outdoor privy.

When John was in his early teens, the family moved to Des Moines. There John attended high school, completing almost the full four-year course. Family ties were strong, and, while he did not embrace his mother's Reorganized Church of the Latter Day Saints faith, John did adopt her rigid views regarding alcohol and sexual propriety.

In the late 1890s the family returned to Lucas County. There John worked in the mines and in 1901 became a charter member and secretary of the United Mine Workers of America (UMWA) local. He acted in talent shows and served as manager of the opera house.

In 1901 Lewis left home, spending the next four years working at mining and construction sites in the West. Throughout his subsequent career he invoked his memories of mining disasters and heroic deeds to lend authenticity to his claim to speak for the working class, although virtually no independent evidence has ever turned up to document some of his more dramatic accounts.

In 1905 he returned to Lucas. In 1907 he ran for mayor and launched a feed-and-grain distributorship. Both endeavors, however, failed, and, shortly after, all the Lewises left Iowa for the coalfields of south-central Illinois, settling in the new mining town of Panama. The Lewis men quickly established themselves among the largely immigrant work force. By 1910 he had been elected president of Local 1475, one of the largest in the state's heavily unionized mining region.

Shortly before leaving Iowa, Lewis had married Myrta Edith Bell, the daughter of a local physician. She provided a stable home life and bore three children. Myrta Bell Lewis shared little of her husband's concern with public affairs and labor politics, and Lewis kept his home life rigidly separate from his professional affairs.

Lewis's leadership in the Panama local led to advancement in the labor movement. He soon became a legislative agent for UMWA District 12 (Illinois) in nearby Springfield. He supported the incumbent administration in the district's internal conflicts. In 1911 he gained appointment as a field representative for the American Federation of Labor (AFL) and for the next six years roamed the country, serving as observer and troubleshooter for AFL president Samuel Gompers. In the UMWA he was a key supporter of international president John White in the recurrent battles for leadership of the expanding Mine Workers' union. His reward came in 1917 with appointment as statistician, a key office in the UMWA's collective-bargaining apparatus. Before the year was out, Lewis became vice president when White resigned, and his replacement, Frank Hayes, named Lewis to fill the now-vacant slot. Since Hayes was physically unwell, Lewis quickly assumed de facto leadership of the union, now the largest in the AFL with a war-engorged membership of about 400,000. On 1 January 1920 Hayes resigned, leaving Lewis officially in charge. Later that year he was elected president, a position he held for the next forty years.

During the 1920s the UMWA declined rapidly. Bituminous coal operators drove it from the footholds it had achieved in the Appalachian South. Through the mid-1920s in strikes and negotiations with traditional bargaining partners in the Central Competitive Field (Illinois, Indiana, Ohio, and parts of Pennsylvania), Lewis pursued a policy of "no backward step." Operators, however, insisted that competition from southern mines required wage and tonnage reductions. Lewis, an active Republican, appealed fruitlessly to Secretary of Commerce Herbert C. Hoover to help the UMWA in its efforts to maintain a high-wage policy. A protracted strike in the Central Fields in 1927–1928 further crippled the UMWA in its former area of greatest strength. In the hard-coal, or anthracite, region of northeastern Pennsylvania, which employed more than 100,000 UMWA members, conditions were little better. Recurrent strikes and competition from fuel oil led to shrinking markets and resultant unemployment. During the 1920s and early 1930s, UMWA membership shrank by 80 percent.

Critics blamed Lewis for the union's tribulations. Socialists and militants such as John Brophy of Pennsylvania and Adolph Germer of Illinois accused the Lewis regime of failing to press organization of the South and engaging in collaborative relations with favored operators. Convinced that the disputatious miners' union could no longer afford internal division, Lewis consolidated his control. He placed the once-autonomous UMWA districts under centralized receivership, packed the union bureaucracy with men directly beholden to him, and used UMWA conventions and publications to discredit his critics. In 1926 Brophy ran against him for the union's presidency, enlisting a broad coalition of reformers, radicals, and anti-Lewis district leaders. Lewis, however, employed armed force, red-baiting, and ballot-box stuffing to crush Brophy's bid.

The UMWA's tribulations caused Lewis to look to governmental action. His chief advisor, W. Jett Lauck, had long urged a break with traditional AFL voluntarism. Lewis's 1925 book *The Miner's Fight for American Standards*, most of which was actually written by Lauck and UMW publicists, combined a grim depiction of miners' poverty with a call for the extension of modern standards of income and consumption to mining communities. Only through a powerful union, Lewis argued, could miners (and by extension, other workers) claim a place by right in the expanding consumer economy. In 1928 Lewis supported the promulgation of a code of fair competition for the bituminous industry that would regulate wages, prices, and competitive practices and protect the workers' right to organize.

This initiative failed, but the onset of the depression and the coming to power in 1933 of Franklin D. Roosevelt revived interest in such an approach to economic stability. Initially, of course, the depression deepened Lewis's and the UMWA's problems. Membership totals and financial resources further shrank, and rivals contested Lewis for the allegiance of coal miners. Lewis survived these challenges through ruthless suppression of his opponents and tightened control of the union apparatus.

Although it is likely that Lewis supported Hoover in 1932, as he had done in 1928, he exploited the opportunity that the incoming Roosevelt administration presented. Through Lauck, a Washington insider, Lewis played a significant role in formulating the labor provisions of the National Industrial Recovery Act (NIRA). Even before it became law on 16 June 1933, Lewis launched a campaign to rebuild the UMWA and to extend it into the formerly nonunion southern fields. Exploiting both the smoldering militancy of the coal miners and the widespread public enthusiasm for FDR, Lewis gambled the union's slender resources on a spectacularly successful campaign of reorganization.

Throughout the rest of the decade, Lewis built upon this initial success. He proved both an effective negotiator and a brilliant maneuverer in complex government-labor-operator relations. In both code hearings during the life of the National Recovery Administration (1933–1935) and in collective bargaining, the UMWA boosted wage rates, reduced or eliminated regional differentials, and gained strong union security provisions. The revived UMWA quickly built up a huge treasury, and Lewis moved toward a larger role in the labor movement generally.

Lewis believed that the NIRA and the union-mindedness it encouraged among industrial workers represented an unparalleled opportunity for the AFL to expand from its craft-union base into the industrial core. Such expansion was particularly important for the UMWA because thousands of coal miners toiled in so-called "captive" mines, pits owned and operated by the big steel producers. Organization of the nation's 400,000 steelworkers, whose unions had been crushed repeatedly over the previous forty years, was critical for the UMWA if it was to unionize these captive mines. More generally, Lewis believed that the UMWA and the AFL could not prosper in a largely nonunion economy. As a member of the AFL's executive council, he pressed for aggressive campaigns to organize mass production workers.

AFL president William Green (1870–1952), a former associate of Lewis in the UMWA, acknowledged the opportunity to extend organization. Federation traditionalists, however, were skeptical of the ability of mass production workers to sustain unions. Moreover, they insisted that industrial workers be organized into separate crafts rather than, as the workers themselves overwhelmingly desired, in all-inclusive units. Thus, in fact the AFL did little to exploit union sentiment.

At the AFL's 1935 convention in Atlantic City, Lewis castigated the AFL leadership for its lethargy and provocatively identified with frustrated industrial unionists. Toward the end of the convention, a shouting match between Lewis and President William L. Hutcheson of the Carpenters escalated into a brawl, with the Mine Workers' chief delivering a punch that sent his antagonist from the hall streaming blood.

The day after the convention, Lewis convened a meeting of AFL leaders interested in industrial unionism. Joining him were UMWA vice president Philip Murray; Sidney Hillman, president of the Amalgamated Clothing Workers (ACWA); and David Dubinsky of the International Ladies' Garment Workers' (ILGWU). On 9 November the group formally constituted itself as the Committee for Industrial Organiza-

tion (CIO). Lewis selected former rival John Brophy to serve as director. The CIO was to operate within the AFL, providing support to workers seeking to organize along industrial lines.

For the next five years, Lewis and the CIO dominated the American labor scene. With Lewis serving as its eloquent spokesman and often conducting key negotiations with corporate officials, the CIO established permanent unions in the automobile, steel, rubber, and electrical appliance industries. The passage of the National Labor Relations Act (Wagner Act) in July 1935 underscored the importance to organized labor of having a friendly administration in Washington and in industrial state capitals. Thus, Lewis led in creating Labor's Non-Partisan League in 1936, through which he channeled more than $500,000 in UMWA-CIO funds to Roosevelt's reelection campaign. He played a critical role in the United Automobile Workers' (UAW) dramatic February 1937 victory against General Motors in the Flint, Michigan, sit-down strike. Three weeks later, Lewis and U.S. Steel president Myron Taylor announced an agreement between the giant corporation and the CIO's Steel Workers Organizing Committee (SWOC). Other successes in the longshoring, rubber, electrical appliance, and general industrial sectors soon made the CIO synonymous with militant unionism and made Lewis a central figure in the nation's political, economic, and journalistic arenas. The $7 million in loans, gifts, and services that the UMWA poured into the CIO represented at least 70 percent of its financial resources during this period.

By the time of the CIO's 1938 constitutional convention, however, the magic aura had begun to fade. In the spring of 1937, SWOC had suffered a bloody defeat in a strike against the "Little Steel" companies. Resurgent AFL unions increasingly experienced success in the escalating rivalry between the two labor bodies. The recession of 1937–1939 slowed CIO gains, and internal conflict ravaged the new UAW. Lewis's critics charged that he had permitted Communists to gain influence in the CIO and that his elevation of daughter Kathryn, brother Dennie, and other family members in the CIO hierarchy weakened the organization. CIO membership totals and financial resources eroded; an organizing drive in textiles bogged down.

Driven from the AFL by action of its executive council, in November 1938 the CIO reconstituted itself as the Congress of Industrial Organizations, an autonomous labor federation. Lewis's own course began to shift. He was increasingly at odds with the other leading figures in the early CIO, Hillman and Dubinsky, both of whom hoped for rapid healing of the rift with the AFL. They and many others in the CIO remained ardent supporters of the Roosevelt administration, but Lewis grew ever more critical of the president. He regarded Roosevelt's support for the western allies and his program of stepped-up defense production as dangerous, charging that the United States was in danger of being dragged into war at the behest of the British Empire. In a dramatic radio broadcast a week before the November 1940 election, Lewis declared his support for Republican candidate Wendell Willkie and urged union members to uphold him.

At the CIO convention the following month, Lewis stepped down as CIO president in favor of SWOC director Philip Murray, his long-term associate in the UMWA. As the military and diplomatic situation darkened over the next year, Murray, Hillman, and most other CIO leaders drew ever closer to the administration, seeing its military and diplomatic programs as essential for the defeat of fascism. The defense boom, moreover, provided jobs and organizing opportunities, which the CIO exploited successfully. Lewis, however, intensified his criticism both of the president and of laborites who backed him. He charged that the CIO's dependence on the administration threatened to destroy its status as an autonomous organ of workers' interests. A protracted UMWA strike over union recognition in the captive mines in the fall of 1941, while dutifully supported by Murray and the CIO, added to the strain, as did moves by the UMWA to expand its jurisdiction into the construction and general industrial sectors. By the spring of 1942, Lewis had in effect taken the UMWA out of the CIO.

Lewis and the UMWA formally supported the war effort and endorsed organized labor's December 1941 No Strike Pledge. Coal production mounted enormously, as did accident rates. Lewis, however, soon came to regard the National War Labor Board (NWLB), created in January 1942 to resolve wartime disputes, as inept and the Roosevelt administration as duplicitous in its treatment of workers' legitimate claims for wage relief in the face of soaring inflation. Miners' dissatisfaction grew, and in 1943 Lewis led the nation's half-million soft-coal miners out in a series of strikes. Although these walkouts were short in duration and never seriously affected the nation's coal stocks, they were almost universally condemned by politicians and the press. Congress's passage in June 1943 of the Smith-Connally Act, which subjected unions to tighter regulation, was a direct result of the walkouts. Lewis also aroused the enmity of fellow labor leaders, many of whom faced rank-and-file challenges because of their adherence to the pledge and their support for the NWLB.

With the end of the war, Lewis continued his confrontational stance vis-à-vis the federal government. Soft-coal strikes became virtually annual affairs in the late 1940s. Lewis skillfully used several episodes of temporary federal takeover of the mines to achieve pioneering health care and pension benefits for UMWA members. His defiance in 1946 of a federal injunction, however, brought down upon him and the union massive fines. Apart from a brief period of reaffiliation with the AFL in 1946–1947, the UMWA remained outside the labor establishment. Lewis frequently voiced his disdain for Green and Murray and for such rising younger men as the UAW's Walter Reuther and the AFL's George Meany.

After 1950, with bituminous coal demand diminishing, Lewis's relations with the coal operators became ever more collaborative. He sanctioned deals with financially troubled employers that undercut the standard UMWA contracts. Since the UMWA's pension and health care programs were financed by a royalty charge for each ton of coal produced, the union cooperated in job-destroying mechanization programs. There were no national coal strikes in the 1950s, and as he approached his eightieth birthday, industry leaders lionized him as one of the industry's most honored figures.

By now the UMWA had degenerated internally into a corrupt and violent satrapy. With the elderly Lewis concentrating on high-level coal statesmanship, much of the ongoing direction of union affairs fell to his administrative assistant, W. A. "Tony" Boyle. After Lewis's retirement as UMWA president in January 1960, Boyle assumed the post. He took over a union that retained few of its once-proud democratic tendencies, and he used the authoritarian and often-corrupt administrative apparatus that Lewis had created to increase his own power. As the coal industry slide continued, once-generous pension and health fund benefits were slashed, often in arbitrary and heartrending ways. Lewis remained a director of the welfare and retirement fund and shared responsibility for unwise investments and banking arrangements that further reduced its viability. On several occasions Lewis privately expressed concern about Boyle's course, but he made no public statements. Lewis died in Washington, D.C.

Throughout his long career in the labor movement, Lewis exhibited seemingly contradictory tendencies. No labor leader thundered more eloquently against capitalist excess, yet few more ardently upheld the basic tenets of the business system. At various times he advocated and exploited the involvement of the federal government in labor affairs, while at other times he espoused extreme voluntarism and engaged in harsh conflicts with federal authorities. Heavy-handed in his rule of the UMWA, Lewis was the key figure in the creation of the CIO, which spawned some of America's most democratic mass labor organizations.

Beyond these apparent paradoxes, however, lay inner consistency of character and ambition. Lewis never held any integrated political or economic philosophy, nor did he embrace nationalist or socialist movements. Constantly, he sought to acquire and exercise power. Confident of his personal ability and intelligence, he believed he merited positions of authority that required others to defer to him. Suspicious of intellectuals, politicians, and radicals, he relied only on his family and a few trusted subordinates. Although he exhibited an interest in public office, he came to understand that his only real chance for success, power, and influence lay in the labor movement. Believing that social change occurred in sudden and unforeseeable shifts, Lewis often adjusted his course abruptly in light of changing circumstances.

• Few of Lewis's personal papers survive. The small John L. Lewis Collection at the State Historical Society of Wisconsin contains little revealing material. The Brophy and Murray collections (Catholic University of America), the Hillman–Amalgamated Clothing Workers and Dubinsky–International Ladies' Garment Workers collections (Cornell), and the Germer collection (State Historical Society of Wisconsin) are rich in UMWA, AFL, and CIO material of the Lewis era. The CIO Files of John L. Lewis, available as are the Germer, Lewis, and the Hillman-ACWA papers in microfilm, are drawn from the partially processed UMWA collections. The pages of the *United Mine Workers Journal* and the proceedings of the UMWA, AFL, and CIO conventions contain Lewis's most important statements and speeches. The standard biography is Melvyn Dubofsky and Warren Van Tine, *John L. Lewis: A Biography* (1977). See also Robert H. Zieger, *John L. Lewis: Labor Leader* (1988), which contains a substantial bibliography. Lewis's obituary appeared in the *New York Times*, 12 June 1969.

ROBERT H. ZIEGER

LEWIS, Mary (29 Jan. 1897–31 Dec. 1941), opera singer, was born in Hot Springs, Arkansas, the daughter of Charles Kidd and Hattie Lewis, occupations unknown. Her early life was spent in poverty; her parents were soon separated, and her mother married Ed Maynard. Lewis and her brother were placed in an orphanage and a series of foster homes until being reunited with their mother. While living in the slums of Dallas, Texas, Lewis attracted the attention of Mrs. Frank F. Fitch, the wife of a Methodist minister. The Fitches took Mary into their home and nurtured her musical talent, teaching her the song "Jesus Wants Me for a Sunbeam." In 1908 the Fitches were called to a pastorate in Judsonia, Arkansas, and the following year moved to Little Rock. Their extreme strictness led to revolt. Lewis's singing had attracted the attention of H. F. Auten, a prominent Arkansas lawyer, real estate developer, and Republican politician, who moved Lewis into his household and arranged for formal music lessons under Alice Henniger.

Lewis disappointed Auten by falling in love, and in 1915 she married J. Keene Lewis. This marriage did not last, and in 1918 Mary left Little Rock as a member of a touring company. After several years of chorus work and minor singing engagements, she joined the Fanchon and Marco vaudeville company, made films for Christie's Comedies, and in 1920 moved to New York, appearing in the Village Follies. The following year she was engaged by Florenz Ziegfeld for his Follies.

Unsatisfied with a Broadway career, Lewis took singing lessons with William Thorner, the former teacher of Rosa Ponselle. Banker Otto H. Kahn recommended her to Metropolitan Opera general manager Giulio Gatti-Casazza, who suggested Lewis go to Europe. She intended to study with the renowned tenor Jean de Reszke, but there is no evidence that she did. She did work with Jean Perier of the Paris Opéra Comique before making her debut as Marguerite in *Faust* in Vienna on 19 October 1923. Aware of the value of publicity, Lewis made sure the event was well-reported in the American press. She then sang in Bratislava and Monte Carlo before signing with the British National Opera Company in London, where she starred in *La Bohème* and an English version of *Les contes d'Hoffman, The Tales of Hoffman*. Her most notable role was that of Mary in the premiere of Ralph Vaughan Williams's great English folk opera, *Hugh the Drover*. During her European stay she made records for the Gramophone Company, including highlights from *Hugh the Drover*.

Lewis debuted as Mimi in *La Bohème* at the Metropolitan Opera on 28 January 1926. Warmly greeted by her friends, she received mixed critical notices. Shortly thereafter came the debut of Marion Talley, and the two Americans were often compared and sometimes cast together. Lewis then undertook an extensive concert tour, which included a stop at Little Rock, where she was welcomed by Governor Thomas J. Terral. In addition, she recorded arias and songs for the Victor Talking Machine Company. Her southern accent, which she had labored to remove, was useful for the song "Dixie."

In the summer of 1926 she sang at the Opéra Comique in Paris, returning to the United States, her concert tours, and the Metropolitan Opera in 1927. That year she married the German bass-baritone Michael Bohnen. The first hint of trouble came in 1927 when Vitaphone sued her, claiming drunkenness had rendered her film work unusable. She and Bohnen separated in 1929 and were divorced in 1930. In her last performance at the Metropolitan Opera in 1930, she reportedly was "as drunk as a lord" (John C. Sicignano to author, 12 Feb. 1975). Despite considerable fanfare, a motion picture career failed to materialize in 1930. Although Lewis sued Pathé, the company cited her drinking and invoked the "morals clause." After an unsuccessful trip to Europe, she returned to the United States and married Robert L. Hague, a millionaire marine architect for Standard Oil of New Jersey. She had no children in any of her marriages.

She continued her career, giving a well-received Town Hall concert in New York in 1934, and sang frequently on the radio. She made some additional records in New York, but at least one recording session was marred by her arriving in an intoxicated state. In 1936 she returned to Arkansas to participate in the state's centennial and sang at the inauguration of New York governor Herbert Lehman. She and Hague quarreled and were separated prior to his death in 1939. In 1939 she undertook a concert tour of Puerto Rico, but a swelling in her throat led to its cancellation. Her illness continued, and she died at the Roy Sanitarium from what the *New York Times* called a heart attack and the *Arkansas Gazette* a bladder ailment. It is highly probable that radiation poisoning was the cause of her death, for during her Broadway days she had worn a dress decorated extensively with radium that glowed in the darkened theater.

Lewis's life embodied many elements of the Roaring Twenties. Although she never became a major operatic figure, she managed at the time to capture extensive newspaper coverage. Considered by Ziegfeld to be the most beautiful of his prima donnas, Lewis was, in the judgment of her contemporary, singer Jessica Dragonette, "a touching enigma, evidently bent on destroying herself in spite of her excelling gifts" (*Faith Is a Song* [1951], p. 75).

• Still unlocated are the records Mary Lewis made in the late 1930s. Miscellaneous scrapbooks are in the private possession of Lawrence F. Holdridge. Lewis is mentioned in most operatic reference books, notably K. J. Kutsch and Leo Riemens, *A Concise Biographical Dictionary of Singers* (1969); Oscar Thompson, *The American Singer: A Hundred Years of Success in Opera* (1937); and Irving Kolodin, *The Story of the Metropolitan Opera* (1953). Much published data about her early life is in error. The first scholarly treatment exists in two versions: Michael B. Dougan, "A Touching Enigma: The Opera Career of Mary Lewis," *Arkansas Historical Quarterly* 36 (Autumn 1977): 258–79, contains footnotes; the same text appears in *Record Collector* 23 (Dec. 1976): 172–91, without footnotes but with a discography by W. R. Moran. In addition, an unpublished (1994) full-length study of Mary Lewis was done by Alice Zeman of Paw Paw, Ill. Obituaries include the *New York Times* and the Little Rock *Arkansas Gazette*, both 1 Jan. 1942.

MICHAEL B. DOUGAN

LEWIS, Meade Lux (4 Sept. 1905–7 June 1964), jazz pianist, was born Meade Anderson Lewis in Chicago. His parents' names are unknown. His father, a Pullman porter, played guitar. Lewis spent a part of his childhood in Louisville, Kentucky. In Chicago he studied violin for about six months, but he lacked interest in it. At age sixteen, when his father died, he left school to go to work. He was interested in becoming an automobile mechanic, but he preferred music. Lewis was a teenage friend of future pianist Albert Ammons. They learned to play piano by listening to such musicians as Hersal Thomas and Jimmy Yancey and by copying the action of player pianos. Both were strongly attracted to "The Fives," a blues involving strong, repetitive, percussive patterns in the left hand, set against equally strong and percussive but less rigorously repetitive counterrhythmic patterns in the right; this piano blues style came to be known as "boogie woogie." At some point during this period Lewis acquired his nickname: in imitating characters in the comic strip "Alphonse and Gaston," he would stroke his chin as if he had a goatee and mustache; from this gesture he came to be called "the Duke of Luxembourg," hence "Lux."

Around 1925 Ammons found Lewis a job playing at and supervising the Paradise Inn, a whorehouse in South Bend, Indiana. Lewis regularly returned to Chicago during this time. He played for parties in Detroit for several months in 1927, and he again returned home, where at the end of the year he was given an opportunity to record his greatest boogie-woogie piano piece, "Honky Tonk Train Blues," which features fabulous tensions between oscillating chords in the left hand and counterrhythmic patterns in the right.

Having worked with Ammons at the Silver Taxi Cab company, while also playing when opportunities arose, Lewis left Chicago around 1930 or 1931 to entertain in whorehouses in Muskegon Heights, Michigan, and then in Muskegon. Later, he had fond memories of the area because he had an opportunity to go fishing every day, and the catch was substantial. He recalled that he was well liked on the job. Although his pianistic skills were limited, he had a good ear and could play any tune from memory if a few bars could be hummed to him.

Lewis stayed in Muskegon until 1932, went back to Chicago, returned to Muskegon, and then returned to Chicago again in 1934. He also worked as a WPA laborer during this period. In Chicago he took a job traveling as a chauffeur for several months. After this job ended, Ammons found him work with a drummer and trumpeter. This trio was working at Doc Huggins's club late in 1935 when record producer John Hammond came looking for Lewis. Ammons directed Hammond to the club (not to a car wash, as is often said; Lewis explained that Hammond made up the story of discovering Lewis at a car wash to make the return from obscurity seem even more colorful). Hammond requested "Honky Tonk Train Blues," and after hearing it, he returned the next night with Benny Goodman and Teddy Wilson, who played with the trio. Lewis began recording on a regular basis, including the first of several renditions of "Honky Tonk Train Blues"; early in 1936 he recorded "Yancey Special," based on a piece by his forerunner in the boogie-woogie style, Jimmy Yancey; at this same session he played boogie-woogie on celeste rather than piano. In 1937, Lewis tried a different sort of novelty, "Whistlin' Blues," on which while playing he whistled with the phrasing of a New Orleans jazz cornetist.

With Hammond's support, Lewis made forays to New York to play at the Imperial Theatre in 1936 and at Nick's club in 1937, but the breakthrough to a general audience came only with the appearance of Lewis, Ammons, and Pete Johnson as a boogie-woogie piano trio at the Spirituals to Swing concert on 23 December 1938 at Carnegie Hall. With Joe Turner, the trio worked at Café Society in New York's Greenwich Village and at the Hotel Sherman in Chicago; there also were national radio broadcasts.

In 1940 Lewis recorded his sixth solo piano rendition of "Honky Tonk Train Blues," together with "Bass on Top" and "Six Wheel Chaser." The next year, as a member of clarinetist Edmond Hall's quartet with Charlie Christian on acoustic guitar, he again recorded on celeste, including "Jammin' in Four" and "Profoundly Blue," playing a blues solo on the latter in a delicate, transparent, tuneful manner, rather than in his usual two-handed percussive style. From August 1941 he lived in Los Angeles, where he devoted considerable time to fishing and golfing, while playing in clubs, for parties, on soundtracks for movie shorts and cartoons, in the movie *New Orleans* (1947), and on television. He toured in 1952 with the Piano Parade, which included Erroll Garner, Art Tatum, and Pete Johnson. Lewis was killed in an automobile accident in Minneapolis.

Many critics regard Lewis and Ammons, after Yancey, as the best of the boogie-woogie pianists. A technically narrow blues and jazz piano style, their approach was worn out within a few years, but it took on a new vitality as one of the strongest influences on rhythm and blues, urban blues, and rock and roll.

• An unsigned interview appeared as "Meade Lux Lewis: A Blues Man's Story," *Down Beat*, 19 Feb. 1959, pp. 16–17. An interview by Dave Mangurian and Don Hill, taken in 1961, was published by Hill, "Meade Lux Lewis," *Cadence*, Oct. 1987, pp. 16–28. A survey by Leonard Feather, "Piano Giants of Jazz: Meade Lux Lewis," *Contemporary Keyboard*, Apr. 1980, p. 74, includes a musical excerpt, "The First Two Choruses of 'Honky Tonk Train Blues,'" notated by Jim Aikin; the whole piece is notated in Eric Kriss, *Barrelhouse and Boogie Piano* (1974). Eli H. Newberger, "Archetyes and Antecedents of Piano Blues and Boogie Woogie Style," *Journal of Jazz Studies* 4 (Fall 1976): 84–109, includes a notated musical example and discussion of an excerpt from Lewis's "Far Ago Blues."

Lewis figures prominently in surveys of his chosen style: William Russell, "Boogie Woogie," in *Jazzmen*, ed. Frederic Ramsey, Jr., and Charles Edward Smith (1939), pp. 183–205; Ernest Borneman, "Boogie Woogie," in *Just Jazz* vol. 1, ed. Sinclair Traill and Gerald Lascelles (1957); Max Harrison, "Boogie Woogie," in *Jazz*, ed. Nat Hentoff and Albert J. McCarthy (1959), pp. 105–35; Martin Williams, "Cuttin' the Boogie," in *Jazz Heritage* (1985), pp. 160–72; and Mike Rowe, "Piano Blues and Boogie-Woogie," in *The Blackwell Guide to Blues Records*, ed. Paul Oliver (1989), pp. 112–38. Obituaries appear in *Down Beat*, 16 July 1964, p. 11, and the *New York Times*, 8 June 1964.

BARRY KERNFELD

LEWIS, Mel (10 May 1929–2 Feb. 1990), jazz drummer and band leader, was born Melvin Solokoff in Buffalo, New York, the son of Samuel Solokoff and Mildred Brown. His father was a vaudevillian drummer who paved the way for his son's early playing career with local dance bands at the age of fifteen. In 1946 he traveled to New York City with the Lenny Lewis Band and a year later joined Boyd Raeburn's band. In 1948 he played in the Alvino Rey (Al McBurney) band.

Mel Lewis worked with several swing-and-dance bands in the late 1940s and early 1950s, including ensembles led by Ray Anthony (1949–1950 and 1953–1954) and saxophonist Tex Beneke, leader of the Glenn Miller Band (1950–1953). On Anthony's recommendation he used his brother's name (Lewis) for drum advertisements in which he appeared. He recorded extensively with Anthony from 1949 to 1954 and with Beneke in early 1951. In late 1952 Lewis married Doris Sutphin, a bank clerk from Washington, D.C., with whom he had three children. From 1954 to 1956 he toured with Stan Kenton, whose innovative arrangements helped shape and solidify Lewis's unique big-band style of drumming. In 1957 he stopped extensive traveling and took up permanent residence in Los Angeles.

From the late 1950s into the early 1960s, Lewis performed with ex-Kentonites (Frank Rosolino, Bill Holman, Gerry Mulligan, Shorty Rogers) and other well-known California-based jazz musicians (Hampton Hawes, Terry Gibbs, Gerald Wilson) while working as a Hollywood studio musician for both the American

Broadcasting Company (1960) and the National Broadcasting Company (1962). In the early 1960s, he toured with big bands led by Dizzy Gillespie (Europe, 1961) and Benny Goodman (Russia, 1962).

Lewis left California and returned in 1963 to New York, where two years later, in December 1965, he formed and co-led with trumpeter Thad Jones one of the country's foremost big bands, the Thad Jones–Mel Lewis Orchestra. This eighteen-piece ensemble was composed of some of New York's finest studio musicians, and for the next twenty-four years the band played Monday nights at the Village Vanguard in Greenwich Village. During this time the band not only served as a training ground for young, talented jazz musicians, but the group's published compositions and arrangements (mainly written by Jones) also became a repertory wellspring for public school and college jazz ensembles. The experimental nature of the ensemble and its status as a working "rehearsal band" allowed for the sometimes free expression of musical ideas that might have been suppressed in more commercial settings. In this way the Thad Jones–Mel Lewis band remained on the cutting edge of big-band jazz for nearly a quarter century.

Although the band maintained its appearances at the Village Vanguard, it toured frequently. From 1968 well into the 1980s, the group traveled to Europe, Russia, and the Far East. It was quickly recognized for its accomplishments and received numerous awards, including the International Jazz Critics Poll (1966), several Grammy nominations, and a Grammy Award (1978).

Lewis took over sole leadership of the band when Jones left in 1979 to conduct the Radioens Big Band in Denmark. Later, trombonist, Bob Brookmeyer filled the position vacated by Jones. Lewis continued to front big bands (the Mel Lewis Jazz Orchestra and the American Jazz Orchestra) and recorded with these ensembles until his death from cancer in New York City.

Although Lewis was a product of the Swing Era, his playing style in both small groups and big bands was firmly rooted in those techniques developed by bebop drummers of the 1940s. His earliest influences were derived from the subtle playing of Dave Tough and later the innovative bop style of Shadow Wilson. Lewis's playing, like that of Tough, Sid Cattlett, Jo Jones, and Wilson, demonstrates an emphasis on creative musicality rather than ostentatious technique. And although his drumming could at times be complex, technically difficult, and startling, it was his odd rhythmic twists and bold metric permutations that set him apart from his contemporaries. Lewis was not a flashy soloist, but he did what few drummers were able to do: he successfully brought small-group bop-drumming techniques into the big-band setting. Unlike his rival big-band drummers (Sonny Payne, Buddy Rich) who spawned a generation of soundalikes, Lewis had no imitators. However, like Shelly Manne, his unique style formed the basis for experimentation by future jazz drummers.

Lewis's earliest recordings, with Anthony (1949), demonstrate his controlled swing style, while those he made with Stan Kenton (*Contemporary Concepts*, Capitol T666, 1955, and *Cuban Fire*, Capitol T731, 1956) provide excellent examples of his adaptation of bop-drumming techniques to a large jazz ensemble. His unbridled, straight-ahead swing style can be heard on his album with trumpeter/arranger Shorty Rogers in 1959 (*Wizard of Oz and Other Harold Arlen Songs*, RCA Victor LPM, 1997). Several recordings he made with Thad Jones demonstrate his continued growth in both large- and small-group settings (*Live at the Village Vanguard*, Solid State 18016, 1967 and *Thad Jones–Mel Lewis Quartet*, Artists House 3, 1977). Nearly every recording by the Thad Jones–Mel Lewis Orchestra is on *The Complete Solid State Recordings of the Thad Jones–Mel Lewis Orchestra* (Mosaic MD5-151, 1994). For numerous examples of his versatile style, see also *The Mel Lewis Orchestra, Twenty Years at the Village Vanguard* (Atlantic 81655, 1985), and *Mel Lewis Sextet: The Lost Art* (Musicmasters 60222F, 1989).

The most informative interview with Lewis is by Rick Mattingly, "Mel Lewis," *Modern Drummer* 9, no. 2 (Feb. 1985): 8ff. Several articles in *Down Beat* magazine provide substantial background information about Lewis's musical experiences, including Joseph Tynan, "Time Is the Quality Mel Lewis Has" 24, no. 24 (1957): 22; A. J. Smith, "Mel Lewis: Staunch but Swinging" 45, no. 11 (1978): 16–17, 37; and John McDonough, "Footsteps in the Cellar" 57, no. 3 (1990): 26-27. See also Ira Gitler, "Jazz: Mel Lewis and His Dream Band," *Wall Street Journal*, 23 Jan. 1990. Lewis appears on the following videocassettes: "Mel Lewis in Jerusalem" (V.E.I.W., Inc. [1986]) and "Mel Lewis and the Jazz Orchestra" (Adler Enterprises [1983]). Obituaries are in *Down Beat* 57, no. 4 (1990): 12, and the *New York Times*, 4 Feb. 1990.

T. DENNIS BROWN

LEWIS, Meriwether (18 Aug. 1774–11 Oct. 1809), explorer and soldier, was born in Albemarle County, Virginia, the son of William Lewis, a planter, and Lucy Meriwether. The family was prominent in the area, and moved in circles that included Thomas Jefferson. William Lewis died when his son was five. His mother remarried, and Lewis spent part of his childhood in Georgia. He returned to Virginia in his early teens and attended a number of local schools. His formal education ended at the age of eighteen. From that time on, he was in charge of "Locust Hill," the family plantation in Albemarle County.

In 1794, when President George Washington called out militia to suppress the Whiskey Rebellion in western Pennsylvania, Lewis volunteered and served as private. He enjoyed army life and on 1 May 1795 entered the regular army as an ensign. In August 1795 he was present at Anthony Wayne's Treaty of Greenville with the northwestern Indians. Three months later Lewis was court-martialled for insulting a lieutenant when drunk but was acquitted. For a time he was in a rifle company commanded by William Clark, who was also from Albemarle County and who later accompanied Lewis on his expedition to the Pacific coast.

From 1795 to 1801 Lewis continued to serve on the western frontier, gaining experience in Indian relations that he later used as an explorer. Most of his service was in the Old Northwest, but for a time in 1797 he was at Fort Pickering at Chickasaw Bluffs in Tennessee (the site of modern Memphis), and in 1798–1799 he was in Charlottesville engaged in recruiting. He was promoted to lieutenant in March 1799 and to captain in December 1800. In 1800 and early 1801 he was at Detroit.

In February 1801, Thomas Jefferson, who had recently been elected president, asked Lewis to be his private secretary. Jefferson later said that the position was more that of aide-de-camp than secretary. He wrote to Lewis that he was being offered the position not simply to aid "in the private concerns of the household," but also because his knowledge of the western country and the army would be useful to the administration. Jefferson stated that although the pay was not great, Lewis would save the expense of subsistence and lodgings "as you would be one of my family." Jefferson also arranged that Lewis would remain on the active army list as a captain. Lewis arrived in Washington in April 1801, moved into the White House, helped in managing Jefferson's domestic arrangements, and acted as Jefferson's personal representative in talking to members of Congress and others in the city.

Jefferson had long hoped that an exploring expedition could cross the American continent, and he involved Lewis in planning for this ambitious undertaking. Jefferson was interested in the possibility of a water route to the Pacific and in trade with the Indians, but he also had a scientific interest in the trans-Mississippi West. He thought that Lewis, a trusted old Virginia neighbor, had the qualities of leadership and the experience necessary to lead the expedition. In January 1803, Jefferson gained the necessary approval from Congress and sent Lewis to Philadelphia and to Lancaster, Pennsylvania, for a quick tutoring in map-making and related skills.

Lewis chose William Clark to join him in leading the expedition. Early in July 1803 Lewis left Washington for the West and in the winter of 1803–1804 camped near St. Louis, across the Mississippi from the mouth of the Missouri. The exploring party of less than fifty men set off up the Missouri on 14 May 1804. Progress was slower than expected, and, after reaching the Mandan Indian villages, they spent the winter of 1804–1805 in temporary Fort Mandan, near the site of present Bismarck, North Dakota.

The expedition set out again in April 1805. Some men returned to St. Louis, but the Shoshoni Indian Sacagawea joined the party with her husband, a fur trader. After an arduous journey up the Missouri, across the Continental divide, and into the Rockies, the expedition followed the Clearwater River, the Snake, and the Columbia, reaching the Pacific in November. The winter of 1805–1806 was spent just north of present Astoria, near the mouth of the Columbia in hastily constructed Fort Clatsop.

Lewis started the return journey in March 1806. For a time the party split, with Lewis investigating the Marias River, a tributary of the Missouri, and Clark exploring the Yellowstone. Lewis's party skirmished briefly with the Piegan (Blackfeet) Indians; this proved to be the only fighting in which the expedition members engaged during their long journey through Indian country. Before the two parties rejoined at the junction of the Yellowstone and the Missouri, Lewis was accidentally shot in the leg by one of his own men and temporarily disabled. The expedition finally reached St. Louis on 23 September 1806.

Lewis's leadership of the expedition was all that Jefferson could have desired. Although technically he outranked Clark, Lewis showed no hesitation in sharing his leadership with his companion. The expedition lost only one man (a death from natural causes) and generally maintained good relations with the numerous Indian tribes it encountered.

Jefferson's careful instructions regarding the acquisition of scientific knowledge and the keeping of journals enhanced the importance of the expedition. Both Lewis and Clark kept daily journals, and they attempted to follow Jefferson's instructions by entering all possible information on the geography of the areas through which they traveled, commenting on Indian life, the terrain, animals, plants, minerals, and climate. They also encouraged other members of the expedition to keep journals; four of these other journals survived and eventually were published. The leaders of the expedition also satisfied Jefferson's instructions by bringing back a variety of botanical, zoological, and ethnological specimens, and they compiled Indian vocabularies of the tribes they encountered. Although full publication of the journals was delayed for a century, the expedition drew American attention to opportunities beyond the Mississippi. With the additional stimulus provided by the Louisiana Purchase, American interest in the trans-Mississippi West soared.

After the triumph of the Lewis and Clark expedition, the rest of Lewis's career was anticlimactic. Although Lewis had sufficient ability to win the admiration of Thomas Jefferson, he apparently had a troubled personality. Jefferson later wrote that Lewis was a hypochondriac, and there are a number of indications that he was an excessive drinker. Also, although Lewis expressed admiration for several women, he never married.

Lewis returned to Washington in December 1806. Congress rewarded both Lewis and Clark with grants of 1,600 acres, and late in February 1807 Jefferson nominated Lewis as governor of the territory of Upper Louisiana. Although the appointment was confirmed by the Senate early in March, Lewis did not reach St. Louis to take up his new post until a year later, and his stay there was short and unhappy. He clashed frequently with the territorial secretary, Frederick Bates, and also experienced financial difficulties. These increased when Washington officials balked at reimbursing him for what he viewed as legitimate expenditures.

In September 1809 Lewis decided to return to Washington to resolve questions regarding the details of his administration. He intended to travel down the Mississippi to New Orleans, and by sea to the East Coast, but when he went ashore at Chickasaw Bluffs he was very ill and incoherent. It was later said that twice on the journey he had attempted suicide. Apparently recovered, he decided to continue his journey overland. On 10 October he stayed at Grinder's Stand, some seventy miles from Nashville, again showing signs of agitation. During the night shots were heard, and in the early morning Lewis was found dying. It was assumed at the time, and for many years after, that he had committed suicide. In more recent years some writers have suggested that Lewis, traveling on the dangerous Natchez Trace, might have been murdered, but there is no solid evidence for this conclusion. There seem to be far stronger indications that Lewis committed suicide.

Lewis had one great triumph in what was generally an undistinguished career, but that triumph has given him a permanent place in American history.

• Manuscript materials relating to Lewis are in the Missouri Historical Society in St. Louis and the American Philosophical Library in Philadelphia. Among the most useful published primary materials are Donald Jackson, ed., *Letters of the Lewis and Clark Expedition: With Related Documents, 1783–1854* (1962), and Reuben G. Thwaites, *Original Journals of the Lewis and Clark Expedition, 1804–1806* (8 vols., 1904–1905). The two most useful biographies are Richard Dillon, *Meriwether Lewis: A Biography* (1965), and John Bakeless, *Lewis and Clark: Partners in Discovery* (1947). See also Stephen E. Ambrose, *Undaunted Courage: Meriwether Lewis, Thomas Jefferson, and the Opening of the American West* (1996).

REGINALD HORSMAN

LEWIS, Morgan (16 Oct. 1754–7 Apr. 1844), soldier and politician, was born in New York City, the son of Francis Lewis (1713–1802), a merchant, and Elizabeth Annesley. Lewis's father, a prominent political figure in New York, served in the Second Continental Congress and was a signer of the Declaration of Independence. Young Lewis's early life showed promise of a brilliant future. He graduated with high honors in 1773 from the College of New Jersey (now Princeton University). Afterward, he studied law in the offices of John Jay (1745–1829). When the revolutionary war began, Lewis joined a rifle company in June 1775. In August 1775 he became commander of a company of volunteers, rising in November to first major of the Second Regiment, commanded by Jay. Because of Jay's other duties, the command devolved upon Lewis. Later Lewis accompanied General Horatio Gates to the North as his chief of staff with the rank of colonel. At Saratoga Lewis received the surrender of the British army. Later he participated in expeditions into the Mohawk Valley in 1778 and against Crown Point in 1780. Appointed assistant quartermaster general, he performed his duties faithfully and efficiently to the end of the war.

During the war, in 1779, Lewis married Gertrude Livingston, the daughter of Robert R. Livingston (1718–1775). She brought to the marriage not only a connection with the powerful Livingston family, but also a vast estate of 20,000 acres, which assured Lewis a comfortable income from rents for the rest of his life. They had one child.

After the revolutionary war, Lewis returned to the practice of law. He was a solid but plodding lawyer, and while he was successful, he was not one of the most outstanding members of the New York bar. Nevertheless, he was elected to the New York Assembly in 1789 and again in 1792. As a colonel of a volunteer militia company, his troops escorted General George Washington at his first inauguration as president.

Through a series of fortuitous events, Lewis advanced rapidly in New York politics. He became attorney general of New York in November 1791 when Aaron Burr (1756–1836) went to the U.S. Senate. Then Lewis was appointed to the Council of Appointment by the tie-breaking vote of Governor George Clinton (1739–1812), and the council made Lewis a New York Supreme Court justice in December 1792. In 1801 Lewis became chief justice when John Lansing moved up to chancellor.

Lewis had aspirations to be mayor of New York, but in 1804, when Burr returned to run for governor, Lewis was the available gubernatorial candidate for the Livingston-Clinton wing of the Republican party. Lewis defeated Burr handily. Lewis was, however, temperamentally unsuited to the governorship. He was quickly accused of nepotism when he appointed his son-in-law, Maturin Livingston, as recorder of New York, a position for which he was not qualified. Lewis's proscriptive removal policy, such as removing Peter B. Porter as clerk of Ontario County, angered many, and his support for the incorporation of the Merchants Bank of New York, which benefited Federalists more than his fellow Republicans, led to a split with De Witt Clinton and his followers in the Republican party. Followers of Lewis were called "Quids" and later "Martling Men" because of a gathering at a popular meeting place by that name. Lewis overstepped the bounds of partisanship when he removed De Witt Clinton as mayor of New York, which was extremely unpopular. Republican members of the legislature responded by supporting Daniel D. Tompkins for governor, and Tompkins defeated Lewis by a little over 4,000 votes in 1807. In 1810, however, Lewis was elected a senator in the New York Assembly.

In 1812 Lewis was appointed quartermaster general with the rank of brigadier general. His authority, however, was limited to the Northern Department. In 1813 he was appointed major general and was briefly in command of the northern army when Major General Henry Dearborn became ill after successful assaults on York (now Toronto) and Fort George on the Niagara peninsula. Lewis was criticized for failing to follow up on the latter victory, which allowed the British to regroup and defeat an American force sent belatedly by Lewis at Stoney Creek in June 1813. Although General Dearborn was later supplanted as commander of the northern army, Lewis was not given the command. Lewis served under Major General James Wilkinson in the abortive campaign against Montreal late in 1813, and in 1814 he was assigned to a relatively less important command, the defense of New York City, until the end of the war.

After the war, Lewis held no further political offices. He did become the grand master of the Masonic Order of the State of New York in 1830 in the midst of the anti-Masonic movement, a position he held until his death. He was president of the New-York Historical Society from 1832 to 1836, and he served as president general of the Society of the Cincinnati from 1839 until his death in New York City. Although Lewis never quite achieved the promise of his youth, he was a prominent figure in his time, and his contributions to his country were not insignificant. He was one of the builders of the young American Republic.

• The only biography of Lewis is Julia Delafield, *Biographies of Francis Lewis and Morgan Lewis* (1877), but it is thinly researched and partial to its subject. Two older but useful works are Jabez Delano Hammond, *The History of Political Parties in the State of New York . . .* (2 vols., 1842), and De Alva Stanwood Alexander, *A Political History of the State of New York* (4 vols., 1906–1923).

C. EDWARD SKEEN

LEWIS, Oscar (25 Dec. 1914–16 Dec. 1970), anthropologist, was born Oscar Lefkowitz in New York City, the son of Chaim Leb Lefkowitz and Broche Biblowitz, immigrants from a village near Grodno in what is now the Republic of Belarus. Lewis's father, a Yeshiva graduate, worked as a temple sexton and Hebrew teacher during his early years in New York City. In the early 1920s the family opened a summer hotel in Liberty, New York. The business often floundered, and the family's economic circumstances were never more than modest.

Lewis (who legally changed his name in 1940) spent much of his childhood in the countryside doing farm chores and working in the family hotel. He entered the City College of New York in 1930, received a bachelor's degree in history in 1936, and began his graduate work in the history department of Columbia University the same year. Through his future brother-in-law Abraham Maslow, who was then doing postdoctoral work in psychology at Columbia, Lewis met Ruth Benedict and shortly thereafter transferred to the anthropology department to work with her. In 1937 he married Ruth Maslow, who, as Ruth Lewis, became his major collaborator in field work and the editing of field materials for publication. They had two children.

At Columbia, Lewis studied anthropology under Alexander Lesser, Gene Weltfish, Ralph Linton, William Duncan Strong, and Ruth Bunzel. He also did work in the new field of culture and personality with Benedict, the psychologist Otto Klineberg, and the psychiatrist Abram Kardiner. His principal academic interests, however, were the relationship between economics and culture, and issues of class stratification and mobility.

In 1939, under Benedict's supervision, Lewis undertook his first field investigation on the Brocket Reserve of the Northern Piegan Blackfoot in Alberta,

Canada. From the field data that he and Ruth Lewis collected, he published his first article, "Manly-Hearted Women among the Northern Piegan" (*American Anthropologist* 43 [1941]: 173–87). Lacking funding for additional field work, Lewis based his dissertation on library research and received a Ph.D. in 1940. Published as *The Effects of White Contact upon Blackfoot Culture, with Special Reference to the Role of the Fur Trade* by the American Ethnological Society in 1942, the study reflected his interest in the relationship between economic and cultural processes, and became one of his most cited works.

During World War II, Lewis (who as a father was not draft eligible until late in the war) worked for the Justice and Interior Departments. In 1943 he and his wife were hired by Commissioner of Indian Affairs John Collier to do research in Mexico as part of a comparative study of "Indian personality." Lewis chose the village of Tepoztlán as a research site because an earlier study by anthropologist Robert Redfield had provided a basis on which the project could build. He supervised the village study while Ruth Lewis, who had been trained in psychology, coordinated the program of psychological testing. From this work came *Life in a Mexican Village: Tepoztlán Restudied* (1951), a finely drawn work of ethnography that established Lewis's place in anthropology. The book drew immediate attention for its criticism of Redfield's folk-urban continuum and a depiction of village life that was at odds with Redfield's description of a nonconflictive pastoral society. The two studies came to be used as textbook examples of how field objectives and methods, and personalities, can affect the outcome of research.

In 1945 Lewis moved to the Department of Agriculture, where during 1945–1946 he worked as a field investigator for the Bureau of Agricultural Economics and applied his village study techniques to an evaluation of land use in Bell County, Texas (*On the Edge of the Black Waxy* [1948]).

In 1946 Lewis left government service for an academic position at Washington University, where he served in the Department of Sociology and Anthropology with Jules Henry, another of Benedict's students. Lewis moved to a similar position at the University of Illinois in 1948 and became professor of anthropology when the department was founded in 1960. During his twenty-two years at Illinois he conducted field investigations in Spain (1949), Mexico (1950–1952 and 1956–1962), India (1952–1953), Puerto Rico and New York City (1963–1968), and Cuba (1969–1970).

Lewis was socialist in his sympathies, but any political content in his work was implicit. His interest in Marxian theory informed his research but never played a central role in its conceptualization or analysis. He was not politically active after his college years and had no party or other formal political affiliations. He preferred to find expression for his political values in his work. For this reason he was drawn early on to applied anthropology and took an interest in research that had policy implications. In India, as a project

evaluator for the Ford Foundation in 1952, he initiated a village study (*Village Life in Northern India* [1958]) to show its "relevance . . . for action programs."

During the course of the Tepoztlán project, Lewis began to develop his field method for doing family studies through taped interviews and a form of household observation he called day studies. The first such study appeared as a chapter in his first book of family studies, *Five Families* (1959), and later as the independent volume *Pedro Martínez* (1964), the culmination of twenty years of observations. Other volumes, which centered on families in Mexico City (*Children of Sánchez* [1961]) and in San Juan, Puerto Rico (*La Vida* [1966]), brought Lewis fame far beyond his academic reputation. *La Vida* won the 1966 National Book Award for nonfiction.

Lewis also became widely known for his writing on the culture of poverty. His thesis that poverty is perpetuated in families over generations through cultural factors first appeared in a 1959 article, and in its fullest form in *Scientific American* (Oct. 1966). Lewis hypothesized the existence among the poorest people in capitalist societies of a shared subculture that had "distinctive social and psychological consequences for its members." Early versions of the thesis stressed the social consequences, especially the way the urban poor were articulated into class-stratified societies, while the later versions emphasized the psychological consequences, specifically the formation of a distinctive personality configuration and high levels of psychopathology.

The culture of poverty concept was given broad exposure in the United States by Michael Harrington in *The Other America* (1962). This work brought Lewis to the attention of War on Poverty policymakers. He became a consultant to Head Start and engaged in a public dialogue with Senator Robert Kennedy about the causes of poverty in America (*Redbook*, Sept. 1967). The concept became a focal point of War on Poverty arguments over whether government or individuals bear greater responsibility for ending poverty.

In 1969, after many years of seeking permission to study culture change in a revolutionary system, Lewis received an invitation from the Cuban Academy of Sciences to undertake a field project in Cuba. After receiving Fidel Castro's personal assurances of investigative freedom and the right to remove unreviewed research materials from the country, Lewis and a field team that included his wife, two Mexicans, and ten Cuban students began a three-year project that was to be divided into urban and rural phases. Working against the project from its inception, some Cuban officials accused Lewis of being a spy because he had received Ford Foundation funding. By intervention of Cuban State Security, the project ended midway, field materials were confiscated, and one informant was arrested and imprisoned.

After leaving Cuba, Lewis, who suffered from hereditary heart disease, died in New York City. The taped interviews and other field notes from the first fifteen months of the Cuban investigation formed the basis of the three-volume series *Living the Revolution: An Oral History of Contemporary Cuba* (1977–1978), coauthored by Ruth M. Lewis and Susan M. Rigdon. Lewis's former student and colleague Douglas Butterworth wrote a fourth volume, *The People of Buena Ventura* (1980), on relocated slumdwellers, which had been undertaken as a test of Lewis's culture of poverty thesis.

Because of the implicit criticisms of society and government policies in his work, and the fact that he had received his greatest public attention in the politically volatile 1960s, Lewis was surrounded by political controversy throughout the last decade of his life. His brief writings on the culture of poverty, because of their focus on culture and personality, were seen by many on the Left as an attempt to hold the poor responsible for their poverty. For his depiction of life in one San Juan slum he was accused of slandering all Puerto Ricans, and for his work in Cuba he was called both a CIA agent and an uncritical admirer of Fidel Castro.

The greatest public fury over any of Lewis's writings came with the publication of *Children of Sánchez* in Spanish in 1964. Its appearance triggered a highly publicized scandal in Mexico, where, for publishing graphic details of poverty in Mexico City, Lewis was accused of sedition and the fabrication of data, and the government-owned publishing house was threatened with legal action. The Mexican attorney general cleared all parties the following year. The housing project where the Sánchez family study was conducted became a symbol of poverty in Mexico. In 1976 the state film industry partially financed a filmed version of the book.

Lewis is best remembered in anthropology as a prodigious fieldworker with a great gift for establishing rapport. His first village study in Tepoztlán is arguably his greatest contribution to anthropological literature as narrowly defined. The volumes that were produced from tape-recorded biographies and household observations are notable for their innovative presentation of field data as literature. His writing on culture of poverty helped further the debate over poverty policy in the United States. By capturing broad reading audiences in North and South America for his biographical studies, he gave a public voice to the rural and urban poor.

• The Oscar Lewis Papers are in the Archives of the Graduate Library at the University of Illinois, Urbana-Champaign. They contain most of Lewis's raw field data and more than half of his professional correspondence but none of his personal letters. Lewis's doctoral thesis and most of his major articles were reprinted in *Anthropological Essays* (1970). An intellectual biography that includes correspondence and a complete bibliography is Susan M. Rigdon, *The Culture Facade: Art, Science and Politics in the Work of Oscar Lewis* (1988). An obituary is in the *New York Times*, 18 Dec. 1970.

SUSAN M. RIGDON

LEWIS, Reginald Francis (7 Dec. 1942–18 Jan. 1993), arbitrager and business executive, was born in Baltimore, Maryland, the son of Clinton Lewis, a skilled worker and small businessman, and Carolyn Cooper. Lewis was strongly influenced by his mother, especially since his African-American parents divorced during his childhood. His mother married Jean S. Fugett, Sr., in 1951. An elementary school teacher, he was a graduate of Morgan State College and had five sons and daughters.

Lewis attended a Catholic grade school but was not admitted to a Catholic high school because of low test scores and discrimination against blacks. Instead, he attended the black Paul Lawrence Dunbar public high school, where he starred in three sports: football, baseball, and basketball. Academically below the median because of his weakness in the sciences, Lewis received a football scholarship from Virginia State College in Petersburg, Virginia, a black public institution. After his freshman year, Lewis withdrew from football because of a shoulder injury; moreover, he had not quite shown star quality in college. His freshman year grades were good but not outstanding. Losing his athletic scholarship, Lewis held a variety of jobs while a student. Rescue from obscurity came in the form of a Harvard Law School summer program for blacks upon his graduation in 1965. Although many of his age cohort entered military service, Lewis was classified 4-F as a diabetic. He maintained a B average at Harvard Law School, graduating in 1968. In 1969 he married Loida Nicolas, a graduate of the University of the Philippines law school whose father was an entrepreneur. The couple had two daughters.

Lewis worked at the well-known liberal New York firm of Paul, Weiss, Rifkind, Wheaton & Garrison from 1968 to 1970. He then became a partner in Wallace, Murphy, Thorpe and Lewis, a black Wall Street law firm. This firm mostly did legal work for the New York Urban Coalition but was gradually adding major corporate clients. As the other partners withdrew, the firm slowly became identified with Lewis. In 1978 the firm became Lewis & Clarkson, but Lewis had recruited Clarkson. Under Lewis's direction, the firm oriented itself more and more to business, specializing in venture capital work. Lewis adamantly insisted on being paid what his legal services were worth and not less because he was black. Similarly, he did not like receiving legal work for the reason that he was a black attorney.

Becoming ever more deeply involved in arbitrage, Lewis made the transition from lawyer to financier. In 1975 he tried to buy Parks Sausage, a black-owned publicly traded Baltimore company, but he failed because he lacked a credible financial background and a track record of success, which caused Parks to not take his promises seriously. Typically Lewis sought low-tech, high-cash-flow, well-managed companies for acquisition. He next unsuccessfully tried to buy Almet, a manufacturer of leisure furniture. In 1983 Lewis formed TLC Group, a holding entity, and success came his way soon after. The same year he sought a leveraged buyout of the McCall Pattern Company for $22.5 million. McCall was owned by Esmark, a conglomerate that had purchased McCall Pattern from

Norton Simon Industries. Through experience as a corporate lawyer and through preparation, Lewis established his credibility with leading financial intermediaries such as Bear, Stearns, who managed the transaction; Drexel Burnham Lambert and others competed for the business, and Bankers Trust lent $19 million. Lewis paid $20 million and a note for $2.5 million in addition to a warrant for 7.5 percent of TLC Pattern Inc. He invested a million in cash, much of it borrowed or obtained from other investors. Lewis netted $50 million for the McCall deal. A highly leveraged acquisition, Lewis doubled McCall's profits in 1985 and 1986. Under his management, McCall did not compete on the basis of price and conceded market share for profit, stressing cash flow to reduce debt. Lewis shared McCall equity with management but he himself owned more than 80 percent of the equity when McCall went public. Lewis's creative financing and strength as a negotiator obtained him a ninety-to-one gain on equity. A year after Lewis sold McCall for three times his cost, it went bankrupt. Its new owners sued Lewis alleging fraudulent conveyance, but the suit was dismissed; such cases customarily fail for insufficient evidence and are often a form of legal blackmail.

Lewis's crowning coup was a leveraged buyout in 1987 of Beatrice International Food Company, a multinational conglomerate holding the international operations of Beatrice Foods. He paid almost $1 billion to the owners, Kohlberg, Kravis and Roberts, which had pioneered leveraged buyouts in the late 1970s and early 1980s. Michael Milken of Drexel Burnham Lambert acted as the principal financier, and Drexel received 35 percent of the equity for its financial services; Manufacturers Hanover Trust furnished additional credit. Although Lewis did not want to be portrayed as an African American, after the buyout he selected a black-dominated board composed of longtime friends. The closing in December was complicated by the sharp stock market decline the previous October; however, Lewis obtained no price concession. Lewis immediately sold Beatrice assets to finance the buyout and reduce the Beatrice debt, selling units in Canada, Australia, and Spain for $430 million. By 1989 Lewis had disposed of enough assets to cover 88 percent of the Beatrice buyout. The divestitures left Beatrice with a core food business focused in Western Europe. Having invested $15 million of his own money in the Beatrice buyout, Lewis ended with TLC Beatrice as one of America's largest corporations in his control.

Living in New York and Paris, Lewis, fluent in French, moved to Paris after acquiring Beatrice. An art collector, he owned paintings by Picasso, Matisse, and others. Lewis became one of the country's wealthiest businessmen with an estimated net worth of $400 million. He donated $1 million to Howard University; $100,000 to his wife's school, the University of the Philippines; $3 million to the Harvard Law School; and $2 million to the National Association for the Advancement of Colored People. Incidentally, he backed various black politicians, including Jesse Jackson in 1984, and he contributed significantly to Jackson's 1988 presidential campaign.

Doctors diagnosed brain cancer in 1992 but the news was withheld from Beatrice. The public was notified only shortly before Lewis's death in New York a year later. The Lewis family owned 51 percent of Beatrice; his wife, who was chairman and chief executive officer, and his half-brother, Jean S. Fugett, Jr., assumed the helm of TLC Beatrice. During the 1980s Lewis capitalized on the merger mania; his significance transcends race because he did not build a black enterprise catering to the black market. Similarly, while donating both time and money to African-American causes, his philanthropic role reached out to the larger society.

• Reginald Lewis's personal and business papers are not currently publicly accessible. Reginald F. Lewis and Blair S. Walker, *"Why Should White Guys Have All the Fun?": How Reginald Lewis Created a Billion-Dollar Empire* (1995), a partial autobiography supplemented by interviews conducted by Walker, a journalist with a law degree, remains the single best source. The review in the *Wall Street Journal*, 12 Jan. 1995, notes that Walker, who completed this book after Lewis's death, avoided controversy and tried to balance homage and objectivity. Harry C. McDean, "Beatrice: The Historical Profile of an American-Styled Conglomerate," in *American Business History: Case Studies*, ed. Henry C. Dethloff and C. Joseph Pusateri (1987), pp. 381–412, stops in 1985 before Lewis acquired Beatrice but does provide invaluable background. A. Edmond, "Reginald Lewis Cuts the Big Deal," *Black Enterprise*, Nov. 1987, pp. 9, 42–46; Edmond, "Dealing at the Speed of Light," *Black Enterprise*, June 1988, pp. 150–52, 154, 156–58, 160, 162; N. J. Perry, "Reg to Riches," *Fortune*, 14 Sept. 1987, pp. 122–23; A. Kupfer, "The Newest Member of the LBO Club," *Fortune*, 4 Jan. 1988, pp. 32–33; and Erik Calonius, "For Reg Lewis: Mean Streets Still," *Fortune*, 15 Jan. 1990, pp. 123–24, trace the emergence of one of America's richest men. The *New York Times* obituary, 20 Jan. 1993, and a related article on 26 Sept. 1993 supply useful information.

SAUL ENGELBOURG

LEWIS, Rhoda Valentine (31 Aug. 1906–12 Sept. 1991), lawyer and judge, was born in Chicago, Illinois, the daughter of Charles Tobias Lewis, an engineer, and Josephine Valentine Spitzer. During her childhood, Lewis lived in Chicago and Honolulu, Hawaii. She graduated from Stanford University in 1927 and from Stanford Law School in 1929, proving her command of the law early by graduating first in a seventy-member class and completing her studies in two years instead of the usual three. Despite being the only woman in her class, Lewis had a congenial law school experience, which did not prepare her for the gender obstacles that she would encounter after graduation.

Lewis passed the California bar examination in 1929 and applied for employment in private law firms. In spite of her strong academic record and admission to the state bar, firms only offered her nonattorney, secretarial positions. This treatment, however, was not unusual in an era in which gender discrimination was rampant. Legal jobs were difficult, if not impossible, for women lawyers to obtain. The depression also gave firms another reason not to hire women. As one woman commented, "At every single interview, I was asked how I could possibly expect to be considered when there were men out there with families to support" (*UCLA Women's Law Journal* 7:138). Lewis began to face the fact that she would not soon find a position as a lawyer. Thus, she worked for a law professor for two years and then became a nonlegal secretary to the California Committee of the Bar Examiner.

Determined to acquire legal experience, Lewis applied for a job with a Buffalo, New York, firm on a trip to visit her sister in New York. The firm hired her, and in 1933 Lewis passed the New York bar examination. After four years of practice in Buffalo, however, she returned to Hawaii, where she had not been since childhood.

In 1937 Lewis passed the Hawaii bar examination and subsequently worked at the prosecutor's office. After six months she moved to the attorney general's office, where she became an assistant attorney general. In this role she drafted the Hawaii Defense Act, which Governor Joseph B. Poindexter had wanted in anticipation of a wartime emergency. The act, which gave the governor broad powers while safeguarding basic civil liberties, passed in the legislature, and the governor signed it shortly after the 7 December 1941 bombing of Pearl Harbor.

Lewis was known as the "engine" of the attorney general's office. She frequently worked nights, proving her dependability to the entire staff, and she developed a reputation as the office's best legal technician. Lewis wrote over fifty opinions and hundreds of memoranda from 1940 to 1958; she also prepared crucial research for the oral argument in the U.S. Supreme Court case *Duncan v. Kahanamoku* (1946) for the Hawaii attorney general. Governmental departments also benefited from her expertise in tax and property law. Lewis resolved issues regarding the tax-exempt status of a hospital and the taxation of property condemned for use as a public road, and she helped define what constituted a "business" for tax purposes. These questions were especially significant since Hawaii had begun to open its doors to U.S. mainland investors, who challenged the territory's right to tax them. The Tax Department used Lewis's expertise so much that it requested that she be permanently assigned to their office. Even the Statehood Commission and the Constitutional Convention's Standing Committee on Agriculture, Conservation, and Land consulted with Lewis on land and tax issues. For her contributions and hard work, Lewis received little public credit.

In 1959, the year Hawaii gained statehood, Governor William F. Quinn appointed Lewis to the state supreme court as its first female justice. Lewis's appointment received widespread acceptance as due recognition for her capabilities and for her twenty-three years of contributions to the Hawaii community. The appointment of a woman to Hawaii's highest court was unprecedented.

Lewis wrote over forty opinions and nine dissents. A chronological record of her decisions does not reveal a specific pattern because of the court's varied docket. However, during Lewis's eight-year tenure, she commonly reviewed issues of procedure—such as questions involving evidence and jury instructions, as well as those defining the jurisdiction of courts; many of these issues rose out of Hawaii's 1954 adoption of the Federal Rules of Civil Procedure. She also ruled on the rights of defendants, an issue that was also before the U.S. Supreme Court at this time (under Chief Justice Earl Warren). In one case, Lewis wrote the court's opinion, which reversed a default judgment entered against the defendant (see *Stafford v. Dickison and Stuart, dba Airway Hawaii*, 1962). In *Stafford*, the Hawaii Supreme Court held that the defendant was deprived of due process of law because the lower court had allowed his defense attorney to withdraw, knowing that the defendant was out of the state and had not been notified of the withdrawal. Lewis, for the majority, wrote that, "though an attorney be warranted in withdrawing from a case, he should do so only on reasonable notice to the client, allowing him time to employ another lawyer" (p. 671). In another decision, Lewis's principled stance against misconduct resulted in a scathing dissent (see *Kealoha v. Tanaka*, 1962). In *Kealoha*, a bailiff had bought jurors alcoholic drinks while the jurors were sequestered. The defendant-driver in this wrongful death suit had been drinking before the accident occurred. Lewis, in her dissent, argued that because the defendant's negligence involved drinking alcohol, the drinks that the bailiff had provided to jurors had minimized that important issue: "What concerns me is the impression left with the jury that the use of intoxicants was sanctioned by the court. . . . The reason is that the consumption of intoxicating liquor does tend to affect the deliberate judgment of the jurors. Any indulgence by members of a jury, particularly when occurring during deliberation, is bound to cast suspicion on its verdict" (p. 478). Lewis's opinions reveal her sensitivity to improper influences affecting the administration of justice.

In 1967 Lewis's term expired, and the newly elected governor, John A. Burns, did not reappoint her. Most believed that the Democratic governor wanted his party supporters on the supreme court. One year later Lewis was elected to the Hawaii State Constitutional Convention, which was called every ten years to review the state constitution. This was Lewis's only elective position. During this time she was also the reporter for the Committee on Coordination of Rules and Statutes in 1971–1972 and revised the state's rules on civil procedure by eliminating inconsistencies and making technical improvements. Lewis's recommendations were readily accepted by the legislature, which signified their trust in her work.

Lewis is remembered for her outstanding legal talent and her unconditional love for the law, qualities that she shared without resentment while supporting the more publicly acclaimed careers of her male counterparts. Lewis never married, did not have children, and died in Honolulu.

• For a complete biography of Lewis, see Mari Matsuda, ed., *Called from Within: Early Women Lawyers of Hawaii* (1992).

TERRI ANN MOTOSUE

LEWIS, Richard (1699?–Mar. 1734), poet, was born in Llanfair, Montgomery County, Wales, the son of Richard Lewis and Elizabeth (maiden name unknown). Lewis matriculated at Balliol College, Oxford, 3 April 1718 at the age of nineteen but left after thirteen weeks without a degree; that same year Lewis emigrated to Maryland. There, Lewis succeeded Michael Piper as schoolmaster of King William's School in Annapolis. On 15 March 1723 Lewis married Betty Giles; they had at least one child. Between 1723 and 1728 Lewis's responsibilities as schoolmaster, which he described as "very fatiguing Employment," probably occupied much of his time. Lewis's interest in nature and natural philosophy is evident in the report he sent to the Royal Society regarding an explosion in the air he heard on 22 October 1725, while in Patapsco, where his father-in-law, John Giles, owned property.

In 1728 Lewis published a translation of Edward Holdsworth's *Muscipula* entitled *The Mouse-Trap; or, The Battle of the Cambrians and Mice*. This publication, especially the dedicatory poem, indicates the close relationship Lewis had with his patron and friend, Benedict Leonard Calvert, lieutenant governor of Maryland. Calvert sent a copy of the translation to Thomas Hearne, calling the publication "one of our first" to come from the Annapolis press and identifying Lewis as a schoolmaster educated at Eton and "a man realy of Ingenuity, and to my Judgment well versed in Poetry." In the following year, "To *Mr. Samuel Hastings (Ship-wright of Philadelphia) on his launching the Maryland-Merchant, a large Ship built by him at* Annapolis," a poem attributed to Lewis, appeared in the *Maryland Gazette* of 30 December 1729.

In the spring of 1730, Lewis served as clerk on a committee considering revision of the Maryland tax laws, and in May, his poem "A Journey from Patapsco to Annapolis, April 4, 1730," probably appeared in the *Maryland Gazette*. This, Lewis's most frequently reprinted poem, has been called the "best neoclassic poem of colonial America" (Lemay, p. 138). The poem, in which the poet announces that his life has run "a Course of thirty Years / Blest with few Joys, perplex'd with num'rous Cares," presents the poet's diurnal journey from Patapsco to Annapolis as an allegory for the individual's journey through life and focuses on the tension between traditional theology and the new science. Lewis reflects the new science primarily by making detailed observations of the natural world throughout the poem, and builds to a profound questioning of man's place in the new universe. Calling out to "TREMENDOUS GOD!" The poet wonders whether he may not "justly fear":

> . . . that my Notions of the World *above*,
> Are but Creations of my own *Self-Love*!
> To feed my coward Heart, afraid to die,
> With *fancied* Feasts of Immortality.

Given such thoughts, he then wonders: "And must I, when I quit this Earthly Scene, / Sink total into *Death*, and never rise again?" But the poet immediately dismisses doubt and affirms traditional theology by concluding: "Patient let me sustain thy wise Decree, / And learn to know *myself*, and *honour* Thee." Despite the poem's affirmation of traditional theology, Alexander Pope satirized it in Book IV of the *Dunciad* and associated it with scientific deism (Lemay, pp. 149–50).

During the next several years, Lewis wrote and published a number of poems. "Food for Critics" appeared in the *Maryland Gazette* in the spring of 1731; *A Rhapsody* was first published as a folio sheet on 1 March 1732 and then reprinted in the *Maryland Gazette*, 9 February 1733, and in the *Gentleman's Magazine* for July 1734. Both poems continue Lewis's interest in nature poetry, but only *A Rhapsody* addresses the theological issues raised by "A Journey," though in much more muted fashion. Two poems known only from a manuscript copy in the library of the U.S. Naval Academy date from 1732: "Verses, to Mr. Ross, on Mr. Calvert's Departure from Maryland, May 10th 1732" and "Verses, To the Memory of his Exclly [*sic*] Benedict Leonard Calvert; Late Governour of the Province of Maryland who died at Sea, June—1732." Two other poems from 1732 saw publication: "Congratulatory Verses, wrote at the Arrival of Our Honourable Proprietary," which appeared in the *Pennsylvania Gazette* for 21 August 1732, and *Carmen Seculare*, printed in Annapolis, dated 25 November 1732, and reprinted in the *Gentleman's Magazine* for April and May 1733.

During these years Lewis also continued an interest in science and nature. In December 1730 Lewis wrote to Peter Collinson, a member of the Royal Society, reporting that he had witnessed the Aurora Borealis from Annapolis. In October 1732 Lewis wrote an "Account of a remarkable Generation of Insects; of an Earthquake; and of an explosion in the Air." The following summer, Lewis wrote a final time to Collinson. On 10 August 1733 Lewis sent two insect specimens of which he writes: "They seem fond of Man, and when taken on the finger will raise their forefeet and gaze earnestly on the person that holds them and use many freakish contorsions with their head, as if they endeavour'd to divert one." Lewis concludes that "for this their singular behaviour I have given them the name of Mangazers" (quoted in Lemay, p. 172). At about this time, Lewis may have written a proposal "For founding An Academy at Annapolis for the Education of the Youth of this Province."

In the months prior to Lewis's death, two poems appeared. One, entitled "Upon Prince Madoc's Expedition to the Country now called America, in the 12th century" and signed "Philo-Cambrensis," was published in the *American Weekly Mercury* for 26 February

1734. The other was named "An ELEGY on the much lamented Death of the Honourable Charles Calvert, Esq.; formerly Governour in Chief of the Province of *Maryland*; and at the time of his Decease, Commissary-General, Judge of the Admiralty, Surveyor-General of the *Western* Shore, and President of the Council. Who departed this Life, February 2, 1733–4" and appeared in the *Maryland Gazette* 15 March 1734. Lewis died intestate in Annapolis.

Lewis was one of the most widely reprinted American poets in the early eighteenth century and the first important American nature poet.

• The only manuscripts of Lewis's work exist in a scrapbook in the U.S. Naval Academy, containing two poems by Lewis, "To John Ross Esqr Clerk of the Council" and "Verses, To the Memory of his Exclly [*sic*] Benedict Leonard Calvert; Late Governour of the Province of Maryland who died at Sea, June—1732." These poems are reprinted in Walter B. Norris, "Some Recently Found Poems on the Calverts," *Maryland Historical Magazine* 32 (1937): 112–35. Lewis's contributions to the Royal Society can be found in *Philosophical Transactions of the Royal Society of London* 37 (1731–1732): 69–70 and 38 (1733–1734): 119–21. The proposal "For founding An Academy" can be found in *Maryland Archives* 38: 456–61. The best modern assessment of Lewis is J. A. Leo Lemay, *Men of Letters in Colonial Maryland* (1972), pp. 126–84. See also C. Lennart Carlson, "Richard Lewis and the Reception of His Work in England," *American Literature* 9 (1937–1938): 301–16; Pierre Marambaud, "'At Once the Copy,—and the Original': Richard Lewis's 'A Journey from Patapsco to Annapolis,'" *Early American Literature* 19, no. 2 (1984): 138–52; and Christopher D. Johnson, "A Spiritual Pilgrimage through a Deistic Universe," *Early American Literature* 27 (1992): 117–27. An appreciation is in the *Pennsylvania Gazette*, 5 Dec. 1734.

DUANE H. SMITH

LEWIS, Samuel B. (17 Mar. 1799–28 July 1854), first superintendent of common schools in Ohio, was born in Falmouth, Massachusetts, the son of Samuel Lewis, a sea captain and farmer, and Abigail Tolman. A large and loving family of moderate means provided him with love, home education, and strong religious convictions. Lewis left school at the age of ten and continued his education at home under the direction of his aunt and his minister. He credited his grandfather, who taught him farming, with imbuing him with the love of learning and teaching him high moral standards. Lewis also had the benefit of going out to sea with his father, but the eclectic nature of his education troubled him greatly. He stated, "I feel the defect of early education and discipline so much that I often blush and mourn over myself." The inferiority complex was overcome by his optimism and his "compelling sense of stewardship of his fellow men" (Petit, p. 5).

Lewis's character has been described by one of his biographers as "uncompromising inflexibility, humorless, self-righteousness, and ostentatious embracing of the hair shirt and martyrdom" (Petit, p. 1). All described him as a man with deep conviction who was not always well liked but who was always convincing.

With Lewis, 'principle took priority.' Lewis developed his strong character early in life when the family of eleven moved, primarily on foot, to Cincinnati, Ohio. The move was made because family fortunes had changed for the worse during the War of 1812. In Ohio, Lewis worked as a farm laborer, mail carrier, surveyor's assistant, and carpenter. In 1819, continuing to work during the day, he began to study law at night with the Honorable Jacob Burnet. This became a turning point in his life, as he passed the bar in 1822 and ended the search for a career and his life of poverty. Lewis practiced law for twelve years until physical overexertion and chronic tuberculosis forced him to retire at the age of thirty-five.

In 1823 Lewis married Charlotte Kerr Goforth, the well-educated daughter of a Cincinnati physician. They had six children, three of whom lived to maturity. This family, too, provided love and support for the reform spirit of Lewis, who was often away from home because of his illness and his activities on behalf of the common school. His interests included formation of high schools, improvement of teacher training, improvement of school finance, and creation of districts and administrative structures.

The friendship and mentoring of William Woodward, a wealthy and respected citizen of Cincinnati, gave Lewis his first opportunity to support free public education when he recommended that Woodward give his money for the founding of Woodward High School in Cincinnati. Ohio, where, at this time, education was available in a very limited way, provided fertile ground for Lewis's educational reforms. Along with his friends Woodward, Asa Lord, William McGuffey, and Salmon P. Chase, Lewis worked first as a philanthropist and then full time as an educator toward the goal of providing free public education for all the citizens of Ohio. Lewis's association with the Western Literary Institute and College of Professional Teachers propelled him into the position of superintendent. This organization was dedicated to the promotion of fusion of knowledge relating to education. At the annual meetings, Lewis found a platform to promote his educational ideas, and the organization found an effective speaker on such topics as "The Best Method of Establishing and Forming Common Schools in the West" and the "Expediency of Adapting Common School Education to the Entire Wants of the Community." Lewis reported, "General education cannot be sustained except in an enlightened, free and religious community; nor can such a community exist without such an education" (Galbreath, p. 15).

The membership of the Western Literary Institute and College of Professional Teachers convinced the Ohio legislature of the need for a state superintendent. The legislature acted on the recommendation and on 30 March 1837 appointed Lewis to the post with a salary of $500. Lewis accepted the position despite his poor health and the fact that he had earned ten times more in his law practice. He brought to the position his conviction of the need for free public education and a high regard for hard work. The *Methodist West-*

ern Christian Advocate praised Lewis: "The man's soul is in his work. . . . He cannot be idle anywhere" (Petit, p. 95).

Ohio did not have a free public school system but had, instead, schools ranging from private to quasi-public that served 468,812 students, some for as little as two months of the year. In his first year of work, Lewis traveled more than 1,200 miles on horseback, visiting more than 300 schools, speaking at public meetings, and conversing with interested parties. Recommendations made in his first annual report were passed into law in the 1838 Ohio School Law, which allowed for more money for schools, the appointment of district superintendents, and the writing of school reports by teachers and superintendents. Lewis also began in 1838 the publication of a journal to assist teachers, the *Ohio Common School Director.*

Many of Lewis's educational ideas were shared by such men as Horace Mann. Lewis felt that the education of teachers was of critical importance to the success of schooling and advocated the founding of state normal schools. He was concerned, however, that only one school for teachers exist until the correct way to teach children was known. He also supported women teachers for the education of young children. Here his Yankee frugality won out; he believed women were less expensive and "had a natural fondness for children." In his three annual reports, Lewis advocated reforms that provided for the modern system, including the creation of township high schools, county supervisors, adequate school buildings, and free libraries. The position of superintendent of common schools of Ohio came to an end in 1840, when Lewis resigned in February because of poor health.

At the time of his resignation, the public, concerned about taxes, did not support Lewis's views. The office of superintendent was abolished and the function was transferred to a clerk in the office of the secretary of state. Public schools in Ohio fell into a steady decline, and not until the new state constitution was adopted in 1851 did Lewis's ideas for better-funded schools with additional grades and more highly trained teachers become a reality.

Regaining his health, Lewis moved into the abolition movement through politics. He ran as a Liberty party candidate for Congress in 1843 and 1848, for governor in 1846, 1851, and 1853, and for the state senate in 1842. He was also the vice presidential candidate of the Liberty party in 1843, running with presidential candidate Leicester King. Even though Lewis lost all of the elections in which he ran, his friends continued to urge him to run, undoubtedly because of his campaign fervor and his personal courage in the face of certain defeat.

Lewis is known for his accomplishments for free public education in Ohio, typifying the struggles of antebellum school reformers. The ultimate irony of Lewis's life was that a man remembered for his contributions to education had little formal education himself. His Methodist religious beliefs, reform spirit, and strength of character allowed him to become politically influential and the first superintendent of common schools in Ohio. He died of bilious-typhoid fever.

• Lewis's papers are duplicated in the biography by his son, William G. W. Lewis, *Biography of Samuel Lewis: First Superintendent of Common Schools for the State of Ohio* (1857). A contemporary account is Charles B. Galbreath, *Samuel Lewis, Ohio's Militant Educator and Reformer* (1904). Mary Loretta Petit completed a critical work, "Samuel Lewis, Educational Reformer Turned Abolitionist" (Ph.D. diss., Case Western Reserve Univ., 1966). A helpful history of education in Ohio is James J. Burns, *Educational History of Ohio* (1905).

RITA S. SASLAW

LEWIS, Sinclair (7 Feb. 1885–10 Jan. 1951), novelist and first American winner of the Nobel Prize for literature, was born Harry Sinclair Lewis in Sauk Centre, Minnesota, the son of Edwin J. Lewis, a physician, and Emma F. Kermott, a former teacher. Lewis's father, a stern and practical man, was a major influence on his son. After attending Yale University (1903–1908), where he earned an A.B. degree, Lewis worked as a newspaper reporter in Iowa and California and as a junior editor and advertising manager for publishers in New York City. Between 1912 and 1920 he published a children's book, *Hike and the Aeroplane* (1912), and five modestly successful novels, including *Our Mr. Wrenn* (1914), *The Trail of the Hawk* (1915), *The Job* (1917), and *Free Air* (1919). During that same decade, Lewis became a popular short-story writer, frequently publishing in the *Saturday Evening Post.* In 1914 he married Grace Livingston Hegger, who bore him a son.

Lewis attained fame with the publication of *Main Street* (1920). The book's protagonist, Carol Kennicott, a quixotic young woman determined to adopt a small prairie town and bring culture to it, moves to Gopher Prairie, Minnesota, a town not unlike Sauk Centre, and is dismayed by the small-minded people who live there. *Main Street* is an exposé of midwestern small-town life, depicting the prejudices of America's villagers and expressing the quintessential statement of the "revolt against the village" introduced by nineteenth-century novelists such as E. W. Howe and Joseph Kirkland. Lewis's satirical wit and his skill at creating memorable characters, however, set him apart from his literary predecessors.

The novel was not only a bestseller, but a cultural phenomenon, inspiring a host of similar books, jokes about small towns, a popular song ("Main Street: A Fox Trot Song"), and fan mail from a variety of readers ranging from housewives who recognized themselves in the book's protagonist to fellow authors such as F. Scott Fitzgerald and Sherwood Anderson. The novel was controversial, however, some reviewers seeing it as unfair to the small town and even unfair to the American character. In part because of its controversial nature, the novel was passed over for the Pulitzer Prize, for which it was a major contender in 1921.

As *Main Street* was in press, Lewis was at work on another novel with which he planned to consolidate his success. *Babbitt* (1922) was greeted with an intensification of the dispute that had resulted from the publication of *Main Street*. George F. Babbitt is a realtor with flexible morality: while he demands the highest standards of others, he is not too scrupulous to profit from insider information about which areas of town will benefit from new highways or to inflate the value of decaying property when he markets it. Babbitt loudly defends his way of life throughout the novel, but at the end he confesses to his son—and to himself—that his self-confidence has been a sham and that he has never done anything he wanted to do in his life.

Although, like *Main Street*, *Babbitt* became a bestseller and many reviewers praised the book, it won only hostility from a large segment of the popular audience. This animosity was perhaps best represented by an editorial campaign, launched by *Nation's Business*, that characterized Lewis not only as antibusiness, but as anti-American. Once again Lewis was a runnerup in the competition for the Pulitzer Prize, losing to Willa Cather, whose World War I novel, *One of Ours*, was seen as a reaffirmation of positive American values rather than an attack on decaying moral standards.

In *Arrowsmith* (1925) Lewis critically examined the medical profession. While depicting his protagonist Martin Arrowsmith as a general practitioner in a small town, an officer of the public health service, and a scientist in a major medical research institute, Lewis satirized the faults of doctors, from intellectual laziness—the failure to keep up with the latest developments in their fields—to blatant materialism. Although some reviewers rejected the scientific subject matter of the book, Martin Arrowsmith's idealism obviously pleased the selection committee for the Pulitzer Prize, and Lewis was chosen to receive the award.

In a carefully worded letter that he released to the press in May 1926, Lewis refused the prize. His anger at having been passed over twice was undoubtedly a major factor in causing him publicly to reject the honor, but Lewis stated that he did so because of the stipulation that the prize should be awarded to the novel "which shall best present the wholesome atmosphere of American life." Such an inhibiting charge, Lewis claimed, prevented the writer who aspired to literary awards from pursuing pure excellence in fiction, which should be the aim of all authors. Lewis's rejection of the Pulitzer Prize was widely viewed as a calculated ploy to achieve even greater notoriety. If this was true, the ruse worked. So did the publication of his next major novel.

Elmer Gantry (1927) attacked hypocrisy in the church. Gantry begins his career as a relatively sincere divinity student who is troubled by his strong sexual nature, but he becomes a hypocritical minister and, later, a jackleg traveling evangelist. Some ministers of the day approved of the book as an attack on genuine abuses within their profession, and literary gadfly H. L. Mencken praised its satire of corrupt fundamentalism. Many critics, however, viewed the book as obscene and its satire as overdone.

In 1928 Lewis was divorced by Grace Hegger Lewis and soon married Dorothy Thompson after a determined romantic courtship during which he pursued her throughout Europe. Thompson, a lecturer and journalist, was a foreign correspondent for the Philadelphia *Public Ledger* and the New York *Evening Post*. She bore Lewis the second of his two sons.

Lewis capped his literary achievements of the 1920s with a different type of novel. *Dodsworth* (1929) returns to the subject of the businessman, but Sam Dodsworth possesses a larger soul than George F. Babbitt. An inventor as well as a manufacturer of automobiles, Dodsworth is a pioneer in auto body design, ushering in an era of streamlining that actually anticipates developments in the 1930s, such as the Cord and the Auburn. In Sam Dodsworth, Lewis recognizes that the twentieth-century American businessman could still live up to the ideals of Benjamin Franklin (1706–1790).

However, *Dodsworth* is less about its hero's business life than about his personal life. Near the beginning of the novel Dodsworth sells his automobile manufacturing business and embarks on a Jamesian quest for self-knowledge. His wife, Fran, has persuaded Sam to take a trip to Europe, but ironically Sam profits most from the trip. While Fran is distracted by the false standards of the decadent aristocracy on the Continent, Sam begins to examine his life and to change many of his attitudes about American pragmatism and European culture. Cast off by Fran, who unsuccessfully attempts to marry a German nobleman, Sam drifts through Europe, finds a new mate, and at the end of the novel plans to export European architecture to the United States. He is still a businessman, but he has become enlightened.

When Lewis was awarded the Nobel Prize for literature in 1930, the honor generated a major literary controversy in his own country. Some critics believed that Lewis had been rewarded by the European academy for his negative depiction of Americans in his satirical novels, while others applauded the award as an American achievement. His detractors were quick to point out that Lewis, claiming he feared that awards affected the integrity of authors, had taken the high ground in refusing the Pulitzer Prize, yet he had readily accepted the more prestigious—and lucrative—Nobel Prize. Lewis intensified the battle with his acceptance speech, "The American Fear of Literature," in which he decried the timidity of the old American literary establishment and of American critics and readers.

A long-term consequence of the prize, however, was the attention given to Lewis's major fiction of the 1920s. Critics such as Henry Seidel Canby and Howard Mumford Jones examined his collected works with care, assessing their good and bad points: Lewis's realistic depiction of American speech and manners and his analytical perception as a social critic were noted as major assets, while his tendency toward repetition was considered a liability. During his most successful decade he had interspersed writings of lesser quality among his major novels. Such works as his satire of westerns, *Mantrap* (1926), and his tour de force, *The Man Who Knew Coolidge* (1928), were clearly written with his left hand, just as most of his short stories had been in the period preceding the publication of *Main Street*.

The 1930s were a busy decade for Lewis, but his career was obviously in decline, despite the fact that he attempted to grow by writing in a new genre, drama, while he continued to publish controversial fiction. If his first post-Nobel novel, *Ann Vickers* (1933), seemed to have some affinity with his previous work—it introduced a strong feminist heroine, investigated prison conditions, and unearthed scandals in penology—both *Work of Art* (1934), which explored the world of a hotel keeper, and *The Prodigal Parents* (1938), which attacked the self-centered nature of the younger generation, while satirical, seemed to retreat from Lewis's earlier portraits of businessmen as materialistic anti-intellectuals. *The Jayhawker* (1935), Lewis's first play, met with little success, as did his collection of short stories published that same year.

Of his works from the 1930s, only *It Can't Happen Here* (1935) achieved success comparable to that which Lewis had enjoyed before he won the Nobel Prize. Based on the premise that European fascism could take root in American soil, the novel describes one newspaper editor's fight against American fascists. Lewis had not lost his satirical technique, although some reviewers felt that he was heavy-handed in his depiction of his American Nazis. Because the topic was timely, the novel was adapted into a play that proved even more influential than the novel. The Federal Theater Project of the Works Progress Administration staged the play simultaneously in eighteen cities across the country. Metro-Goldwyn-Mayer (MGM) bought film rights to the book and assigned Sidney Howard to write a screenplay, although the studio later decided not to film the story, supposedly because Hollywood considered the work too controversial. Lewis took advantage of the situation by publicly claiming that the book was being suppressed.

Lewis's marriage to Dorothy Thompson officially broke up in 1942, but the couple had separated in 1937, and Lewis began seeing Marcella Powers, an aspiring actress who was just eighteen. Before he met Powers, Lewis had already tried his hand at acting, appearing in a production of *It Can't Happen Here* and in *Angela Is Twenty-Two*, a much less successful play that he had written with actress Fay Wray. Lewis and Powers appeared in several plays together, and Lewis, never one to waste material, employed his theater experience in his first novel of the new decade, *Bethel Merriday* (1940).

During his later years, Lewis also experimented briefly with the role of the man of letters, first writing a weekly column for *Newsweek*, "Book Week," during 1937 and 1938 and later producing a series of book reviews for *Esquire* in 1945.

Unfortunately for Lewis, the 1940s were much like the 1930s: although he continued to publish, his work was not as impressive as it had been before he won the Nobel Prize. Of his six novels published from 1940 to 1951, only *Kingsblood Royal* (1947) achieved a celebrity similar to the success that had come so routinely during the 1920s. *Gideon Planish* (1943), the story of a professional fundraiser, is another of Lewis's anatomies of a profession, but it lacks the fire of *Babbitt*, *Arrowsmith*, and *Elmer Gantry*. *Cass Timberlane* (1945), considered by some reviewers the best novel Lewis had written since the 1920s, was judged superficial by others. In *Cass Timberlane* Lewis returned to the basic situation he had treated in *Main Street*, but he evoked the reader's sympathy for the husband rather than for the wife. Jinny Timberlane's rebellion is more the result of the flightiness of a young woman who fails to appreciate the strengths of her husband, Cass, a judge from Grand Republic, Minnesota. Even sympathetic reviewers pointed out that Lewis had advanced no new ideas in the novel, and some suggested that Lewis's once legendary ear for the American idiom seemed out of date, as if the author had last heard American slang twenty years before. In spite of the book's sale to MGM and its selection by the Book-of-the-Month-Club, it did not effect Lewis's return to the first ranks of American novelists.

Kingsblood Royal was different, however. Beginning with Richard Wright's *Native Son* (1940), a school of African-American novelists began to attract the attention of the reading public, and Lewis capitalized on that growing interest with the story of Neil Kingsblood, World War II veteran and respected banker, who discovers while doing genealogical research that he is one–thirty-second black. Neil naively announces his newly discovered racial identity, believing that his old friends will continue to accept him and will even abandon their prejudices against black people. Instead, his friends and even his relatives turn against him, he loses his job, and his house is attacked by white gangs. His wife, Vestal, a solid member of the middle class, asks Neil why such quixotic sacrifices are necessary. At the same time, Neil is unable to integrate himself into the black community of Grand Republic, whose members are suspicious of a fair, red-haired man who seems to be pushing himself on them. Lewis ends the novel ambiguously, with Vestal supporting her husband as the couple is taken to jail for defending their home against a mob. Critical opinion of *Kingsblood Royal* was divided. While reviewers generally recognized that the book was less a novel than a propaganda piece, some compared it to *Uncle Tom's Cabin*, suggesting that the good it might do would outweigh its lack of art. In this spirit, Lewis was recognized by *Ebony* magazine with a special award for promoting interracial understanding.

Lewis's long-term affair with Marcella Powers came to a definite end in 1947, when she announced her intention to marry another man. Lewis found solace in his work as he had done before, writing a historical novel about Minnesota, *The God-Seeker* (1949). Although it differed from most historical novels by satirizing American history, and early missionaries in particular, it was not a successful work, and reviewers' opinions ranged from a charitable characterization of the book as "uneven" to assertions that Lewis had finally reached the end of his long career.

Only Sinclair Lewis refused to believe that his life as a novelist was over. Treating his disappointment with two methods he had used before, he began to drink heavily and fled to Europe, where he embarked on his twenty-second novel, which would be published posthumously. This time, however, his attempt at a comeback failed. Much as *The Prodigal Parents* was seen as revisiting the subject matter of *Babbitt*, and *Cass Timberlane* was viewed as a reappraisal of the theme of *Main Street*, *World So Wide* (1951) was generally conceded to be a pale re-creation of *Dodsworth*. Its protagonist, architect Hayden Chart, travels to Europe to find himself—and, incidentally, a new mate—after his wife is killed in an automobile accident.

Sinclair Lewis, who had been claimed by the state of Minnesota because he was born there, died in Rome, Italy, of heart failure. His death in a foreign country was appropriate, since Lewis was a literary nomad who seldom settled anywhere for long. He had begun his travels when he left Sauk Centre for New Haven, had worked his way to England on cattle boats during summers while he was enrolled at Yale, and had consistently roamed the world, occasionally buying houses or farms but never finding the ideal place to make a home. Even brief sojourns in Minnesota proved unsatisfactory.

Compared with most other American winners of the Nobel Prize for literature, Sinclair Lewis was not one of his country's greatest novelists, but the best of his work endures. The strongest novels of his great decade—*Main Street*, *Babbitt*, *Arrowsmith*, *Elmer Gantry*, and *Dodsworth*—remain in print and still speak to today's readers. Even selected works from the unproductive years after he won the Nobel Prize—especially *It Can't Happen Here* and *Kingsblood Royal*—achieve new relevance for generations that were not born when those novels first appeared, as the American Right asserts itself or racism resurfaces. His trenchant satire of various facets of American life from business ethics to evangelism coupled with his talent for depicting American social history and his skill in delineating character have kept his work alive even though many of his contemporaries have receded into the annals of literary history.

• Lewis's papers are in the Beinecke Rare Book Room and Manuscript Library, Yale University. Some short stories appear in *The Selected Short Stories of Sinclair Lewis* (1935), and his essays are collected in Harry E. Maule and Melville H. Cane, eds., *The Man from Main Street* (1953). The standard biography is Mark Schorer, *Sinclair Lewis: An American Life* (1961). His letters are collected in Harrison Smith, ed., *From Main Street to Stockholm: Letters of Sinclair Lewis, 1919–1930* (1952). The standard bibliography is Robert E. Fleming and Esther Fleming, *Sinclair Lewis: A Reference Guide* (1980). See also Sheldon N. Grebstein, *Sinclair Lewis* (1962); D. J. Dooley, *The Art of Sinclair Lewis* (1967); James Lundquist, *Sinclair Lewis* (1973); Martin Light, *The Quixotic Vision of Sinclair Lewis* (1975); and Martin Bucco, *Critical Essays on Sinclair Lewis* (1986).

ROBERT E. FLEMING

LEWIS, Strangler (30 June 1891–7 Aug. 1966), professional wrestler, was born Robert H. Friedricks in Nekoosa, Wisconsin, the son of Jacob Friedricks, a lumberman and farmer. His mother's name is unknown. In his childhood the family moved to Lexington, Kentucky. By the age of fourteen he weighed 200 pounds and was a skilled all-around sportsman, especially at wrestling. That year he won his first professional match in Madison, Wisconsin. Because his parents disapproved of wrestling as a profession, he changed his name to Ed Lewis in order to hide his occupation from them. Later he added "Strangler" to his professional name in honor of a famous old-time matman, Evan "Strangler" Lewis. After graduating from Lexington High School, he moved back to Wisconsin, where he soon made a name for himself in matches throughout the West and Midwest. His powerful headlock soon gave fans a real reason to call him "Strangler" Lewis.

Early in 1911 Lewis entered the University of Kentucky, where he lettered in football, baseball, basketball, track, and wrestling, in addition to coaching various sports. Apparently, he never graduated. In 1915 he wrestled to a two-hour draw with world champion Joe Stetcher. The two men followed on 4 July 1916 with a 5½-hour draw in front of 15,000 spectators in Omaha, Nebraska. From this point on Lewis was acknowledged as one of the top wrestling professionals, either the champion or a leading contender. After serving as a physical instructor in the U.S. Army during World War I, he won his first world title on 3 December 1920 by defeating his old rival Stetcher in a 2½-hour struggle at New York City. He then lost and regained the title a number of times (perhaps six times) between 1920 and 1933. In addition to Stetcher, Stanislaus Zbyszko, Wayne "Big" Munn, Jim Londos (whom Lewis defeated in their first fourteen contests), and Jim Browning were among his major opponents.

Professional wrestling was very popular during this period, both in the United States and throughout the world. Indeed, it fully equaled professional boxing in terms of both the number of fans and the financial take. For the first time, big money was available for the most successful practitioners. Matches moved up from burlesque theaters and ratty dives to the finest auditoriums. Lewis became one of the so-called "Gold-Dust Trio," along with promoter Joe "Toots" Mondt and manager Billy Sandow. This threesome, with Lewis as the "champion," controlled the title during most of the 1920s. Rival promoters sprang up with the growth of the sport, however, and a number of very good wrestlers (Jack Sherry, Fred Grubmier, Hans Steinke, and John Pesek, among others) tried by various means to function as "trust-busters" to get near to the title and thus the big money. While many of the matches may not have been strictly on the level, they were filled with basic wrestling moves and holds. Such terms as "shooting match" (an honest bout), "working" (a fixed match), and "heat" (getting the fans worked up) came into being, at least within the profession.

A very large wrestler for his day, Lewis weighed 240 pounds in his prime, although late in his career he often came in at 260–270 pounds. He had a massive torso and a 21-inch neck. He possessed exceptional strength, especially when he applied his favorite hold, the headlock. Because of his size and the deadly mystique of this hold—he was often photographed squeezing a wooden block in the shape of a human head—Lewis often inspired great enmity in the crowds and occasionally had to have the police escort him safely from the ring. Fans often came to see him defeated, something that rarely occurred during his heyday. At one time he attempted to arrange a mixed wrestling-boxing match with heavyweight boxing champion Jack Dempsey, but the contest never took place.

Returning from a European tour in 1928, Lewis found that the game had changed during his absence. A former football star from Dartmouth College, Gus Sonnenberg, had created a sensation with his new tumbling style, which included flying tackles, dropkicks, and headbutts—a foretaste of what the game eventually became. Lewis detested the new style, but the fans were delighted. Nevertheless, he continued to be a power in the sport for several more years. He semi-retired in 1934 but wrestled sporadically until 1947, when he was well into his fifties. During his later years Lewis was paunchy and nearly blind from trachoma.

In his career Lewis made some $4 million, most of which he squandered. As of 1933 he had unofficially lost only six matches as top matman and, according to his own optimistic calculation, lost just 33 matches overall in a lengthy career that included some 6,200 contests. He was nearly invincible in the handful of "shooting" matches that were held in the 1930s.

Lewis's marriage to Ada Morton, a physician, ended in divorce in 1924. Shortly thereafter he married Bessie McNair, supposedly locking his manager Sandow in his room to prevent Sandow from stopping the wedding. Lewis had one adopted son. During his retirement Lewis appeared in a number of "B" movies, ranched for a time, and operated a restaurant and a health club. For a time he lived comfortably in a large home near Los Angeles but was totally blind and poverty-stricken at the end. Nevertheless, he was content with life through gaining religion. Lewis died at the Veterans' Administration hospital in Muskogee, Oklahoma.

• Information about Lewis and professional wrestling in general can be found in Nat Fleischer, *From Milo to Londos* (1936); Marcus Griffith, *Fall Guys* (1937); Joe Jares, *Whatever Happened to Gorgeous George?* (1974); "Sports Hall of Fame: Strangler Lewis," *Sport*, Aug. 1961; and Charles Morrow Wilson, *The Magnificent Scufflers* (1959). A lively account of professional wrestling in the 1930s is Herman Hickman, "Rasslin Was My Act," *Saturday Evening Post*, 6 Feb.

1954. In the 1920s the *New York Times* sporting section often reported important Lewis matches in considerable detail. An obituary is in the *New York Times*, 8 Aug. 1966.

FRANK P. BOWLES

LEWIS, Ted (6 June 1890–25 Aug. 1971), entertainer, musician, and bandleader, was born Theodore Leopold Friedman in rural Circleville, Ohio, the son of an owner of a dry goods store whose name cannot be ascertained. Young Theodore began his show business career performing in a nickelodeon in his hometown and learned to play the clarinet in his school band. As a beginning clarinetist, Lewis was something of a prodigy. Although he was never regarded seriously as a musician, he played easily and improvised naturally. Having no desire to go into the dry goods business and still in his teens, he went to Columbus, Ohio, where for a time he demonstrated instruments in a music store. His freewheeling improvisations amused customers but eventually caused him to lose the job.

His earliest theatrical experiences were in local tent shows, small-time vaudeville, and a stint as a member of Earl Fuller's Band, a group that attained some modest success on the provincial circuit. In 1911 Lewis tried to break through into the New York music scene playing in a trio in vaudeville at Hammerstein's Theater. He also secured employment in New York's Palace Theatre pit band. Once again, however, he was dismissed for improvising. This firing was a good thing, for Lewis began to tour in vaudeville on his own. He played medicine and minstrel shows, carnivals, and small-time vaudeville before returning to New York, where he formed the Ted Lewis Nut Band with some modest success. During this time Lewis began to develop his distinctive style as an entertainer, which included the jaunty wearing of a battered top hat that he had won in a crap game from a taxi driver named "Mississippi." At Rector's Restaurant in 1917 Lewis first used his famous expression, "Is ev'rybody happy?" to the delight of the audience. From this time forward Lewis steadily ingratiated himself with café society audiences.

Lewis met and married Adah Becker in 1915. They had no children. Adah served as Lewis's secretary and business manager (after Lewis's death, she started a museum dedicated to his memory in his hometown of Circleville, Ohio). In 1918 Lewis owned his own nightclub, the Bal Tabarin, in New York and subsequently ran the Montmartre Club and the Ted Lewis Club. Lewis also played a successful vaudeville engagement at New York's Palace Theater in 1919, only the first of numerous appearances that he would make as a headliner at the legendary theater throughout the 1920s. He sang in his raspy, declamatory voice, led his band in playing what was then described as "jazz," and appeared in outrageous comedy sketches as part of an act that was a whole show unto itself.

In the 1920s Lewis scored a triumph with the song "Me and My Shadow," written in 1927 by Billy Rose, Al Jolson, and Dave Dreyer, with vaudevillian Eddie Chester as the first of many "shadows." The memorable routine involved Lewis singing the song and dancing a light soft-shoe step that was matched by his "shadow." Over the years in various performances, the "shadow" was replaced by one or another great star making a surprise appearance. Lewis also made a standard of the song "When My Baby Smiles at Me" (1920) and had successes with such other songs as "All By Myself" (1921), "O! Katharina" (1924), "Just a Gigolo" (1930), "In a Shanty in Old Shanty Town" (1932), and "Lazybones" (1933). His busiest and most successful era was during the 1920s when *Variety* proclaimed that "Lewis is in a class by himself as an entertainer" (10 Sept. 1924).

While continuing his prolific vaudeville career, Lewis also appeared in revues, including Florenz Ziegfeld's *Midnight Frolic of 1919*, the *Greenwich Village Follies of 1919*, the *Greenwich Village Follies of 1921*, *Ted Lewis's Frolic* (1923), and *Artists and Models* (1927). In 1925 he played London's Kit Kat Klub, sharing the bill with the legendary Dolly Sisters. During the 1930s Lewis played with such outstanding musicians as Muggsy Spanier, Georg Brunis, Frank Teschemacher, Jimmy Dorsey, Benny Goodman, and Fats Waller. Although he was not their equal in musical talent, Lewis made up the difference on stage with his warm, lighthearted personality. On recordings Lewis led his own band and frequently backed other entertainers, like Sophie Tucker and Ruth Etting. Lewis also appeared in London in the mid-1920s, introducing his particular brand of American jazz to European audiences at the Hippodrome and the Kit Kat Klub.

In movies Lewis debuted with little success appearing in the primitive early talkie *Is Everybody Happy?* (1929). He also appeared, usually in specialty spots, in *Show of Shows* (1929), *Here Comes the Band* (1935), *Manhattan Merry-Go-Round* (1937), *Hold That Ghost!* (1941), and *Follow the Boys* (1944). Another film called *Is Everybody Happy?* (1943) featured Lewis in a highly fictionalized version of his own life and career.

Lewis continued to lead his band through the mid-1960s, usually playing in nightclubs and resorts, with occasional television guest spots. When he played the Las Vegas nightclubs in this era, one critic wrote that he "sings in his own peculiar fashion, he dances, he struts, he is both funny and sentimental. And after an hour and ten minutes, the audience refused to let him get off the stage." Lewis never altered his schmaltzy vaudevillian style, even decades after the last vestiges of that era had long since died. In 1962 he appeared at Roseland in New York and once again demonstrated his familiar style. As John S. Wilson, the *New York Times* music critic, wrote, Lewis "is still slim and agile, gracefully pirouetting, jigging and strutting, twirling a cane and rippling out the mannered gestures that seem to start at his shoulders and flow slowly out to his finger tips" (26 Aug. 1971). The entertainer Eddie Cantor, a contemporary and friend of Lewis's, wrote, "As one of his ardent admirers, I can tell Ted everybody will always be happy while he's around doing what he's doing, which is great entertainment with ac-

cent on the nostalgia" (Cantor, p. 73). Lewis's last major appearance was a 1965 engagement at the Latin Quarter nightclub in Manhattan. He died in New York with his wife by his side.

• For information on Lewis, see David Brown and Ernest Lehman's biographical article, "Is Everybody Happy?" *Collier's*, 27 May 1939, pp. 16, 62, 64. Eddie Cantor, *As I Remember Them* (1963); Brian Rust, *The Dance Bands* (1972); and L. Walker, *The Wonderful Era of the Great Dance Bands* (1972), also describe aspects of Lewis's career. An obituary is in the *New York Times*, 26 Aug. 1971.

JAMES FISHER

LEWIS, Warren Harmon (17 June 1870–3 July 1964), anatomist, embryologist, and cell physiologist, was born in Suffield, Connecticut, the son of John Lewis, a lawyer, and Adelaide Harmon. Early in his life Lewis's family moved to Chicago, where he began his education in the public schools of Oak Bank. From 1886 until 1889 he attended the Chicago Manual Training School. While Lewis was a teenager, his mother stimulated his interest in anatomy when she gave him a book by the famous anatomist Henry Gray.

Lewis entered the University of Michigan and received his B.S. in 1896. After graduation he remained at the university for two years as an assistant in the zoology department. Deciding to study medicine, in 1896 he entered the fourth class of the Johns Hopkins Medical School, in Baltimore, Maryland, and received his M.D. in 1900. At Johns Hopkins Lewis was significantly influenced by Franklin Mall, John J. Able, and William Henry Howell. He was particularly attracted to Mall's department, anatomy, where he was befriended by two senior members of the department, Charles R. Bardeen and Ross G. Harrison. The first project Lewis undertook was with Bardeen and resulted in the publication of his first paper, "Observations on the Pectoral Muscle in Man," in the *Bulletin of the Johns Hopkins Hospital* 12 (1901): 172–77. That same year a paper by Bardeen and Lewis on the development of muscles in the limbs and trunk was the lead article in the first issue of the *Journal of Anatomy*.

Around 1901 Lewis started spending his summers at the Marine Biological Laboratory in Woods Hole, Massachusetts, and was fortunate enough to assist Jacques Loeb with his experiments. Lewis's findings formed the basis of Loeb's explanation of cell life.

In 1902 Lewis went to Europe and worked in the laboratory of Moritz Nussbaum in Bonn, Germany. Here he demonstrated that pigment cells originated in the ectoderm, not in the mesoderm as previously thought. In 1903 he returned to Baltimore and continued this work, investigating the dependence or independence of certain tissues on other tissues for their origin, differentiation, and growth. In this work he extended the experiments of Hans Spemann of the Kaiser Wilhelm Institute, Dahlem, who had shown that the formation of the lens of the eye in the embryo of the European newt *Triton* depended on the previous development of the optic cup. Spemann had suggested that definitive confirmation of this finding would depend on whether the lens could be shown to form from an optic cup transplanted to another site in the embryonic body. Lewis performed this difficult experiment by using the newly developed dissecting microscope to transplant ectoderm from a distant site to an area over the optic cup. The transplanted ectoderm formed a lens, proving embryonic induction. In carrying out these delicate operations, Lewis was the first to succeed in refined operations on a microscopic scale. Subsequently, he was able to transplant the optic cup to another area of ectoderm, and lenses also developed, adding further proof.

Lewis's technical and experimental skills made him a valuable member of Mall's department. He was promoted to assistant instructor in 1901, to the Johns Hopkins equivalent of assistant professor in 1903, and to associate professor in 1904. In 1907 Lewis became Mall's senior staff member. Later, to keep Lewis at Johns Hopkins, the university created a second chair in anatomy with the title professor of physiological anatomy. During the year 1910 Lewis's time was largely taken up with preparing a chapter on the development of human muscles for Kriebel and Mall's *Manual of Human Embryology*, a review of the field that is still a classic.

In 1913 Mall received a grant from the Carnegie Institute in Washington, D.C., which allowed him to build a research staff for intensive study of embryology. To aid Mall with this research, Lewis undertook the project of making a full description of a human embryo that was twenty-one millimeters in length. Lewis's problem was to construct a large model of the embryo's internal and external structure. In making this model he devised a number of ingenious techniques. Instead of making line drawings, he used enlarged photographs to obtain the embryo's shape. After cutting out the embryo form from wax sheets, he stacked the sections. A permanent plaster-of-Paris model was obtained by the lost-wax process. This technique became the standard procedure for making comprehensive series of models of the stages of development of the embryo.

In 1918 Lewis took over the editorship of *Gray's Anatomy*. For twenty years he guided the publication of revised editions 21, 22, 23, and 24, issued at six-year intervals.

Lewis's work took a dramatic turn in 1910, when he married Margaret Reed, an accomplished biologist trained by Thomas Hunt Morgan at Bryn Mawr College. They began to work together with tissue culture. Although Ross Harrison is credited with originating tissue culture, Margaret Lewis was actually the first to grow mammalian cells in culture. Between 1910 and 1920 the Lewises carried out extensive experiments to determine what cells could be grown in tissue culture and the ideal conditions for their growth. This work resulted in the development of systems that allowed them to observe the morphological changes of growing under the microscope. In 1923 Lewis applied the tissue culture technique to the study of cancer cells, and over the next decade he described the cytological features of malignant cells in various stages of growth. Next Lewis introduced the use of time-lapse photography to record the events of cell growth. By screening and rescreening these motion pictures, as well as speeding them up and slowing them down, he could study events impossible to evaluate by direct visualization under the microscope. One of the many things he discovered in this way was pinocytosis, the process by which cells engulf fluid from the surrounding medium.

When Lewis reached retirement age in 1940, he accepted an invitation to join the staff of the Wistar Institute of Anatomy in Philadelphia. Here he and his wife continued their scientific work for more than twenty years. Their laboratory at the Wistar Institute was located on the third floor, and in their last decade they always climbed three flights of stairs to their laboratory because they were afraid they might not have the strength to open the elevator door. Lewis had always been athletic, engaging in ice-skating in winter and swimming and sailing in summer. Archaeology interested him, and he made several trips to southern Europe to view prehistoric caves and to the Yucatan and Guatemala to see Maya ruins. He had three children. Lewis's long life ended in Philadelphia.

• A collection of Lewis's papers is at the American Philosophical Society, Philadelphia. Information on Lewis is in George Washington Corner, "Warren Harmon Lewis," in National Academy of Sciences, *Biographical Memoirs* 39 (1967): 322–58. An obituary is in the *Baltimore Sun*, 4 July 1964.

DAVID Y. COOPER

LEWIS, Warren Kendall (21 Aug. 1882–9 Mar. 1975), chemical engineer, was born in Laurel, Delaware, the son of Henry Clay Lewis and Martha Ellen Kinder, farmers. Lewis's early education was in the public schools of Laurel. His parents, hoping to give him better educational opportunities, sent him to relatives in Newton, Massachusetts, to complete his high school education. He entered the Massachusetts Institute of Technology (MIT) in 1901, studying in the Department of Chemistry and Chemical Engineering and receiving a B.S. in 1905. Upon graduating he became an assistant to William Hurtz Walker, a chemistry professor at MIT, who soon established the Research Laboratory of Applied Chemistry (1908). With this background, Lewis went to Germany under an Austin Traveling Fellowship, receiving a doctorate in chemistry in 1908 from the University of Breslau (now Wroclaw, Poland).

After returning to the United States, Lewis married Rosalind Denny Kenway in 1909; they had two sons and two daughters. He worked briefly as a chemist for the tannery W. H. McElwain Co. in Merrimack, New Hampshire, before joining MIT in 1910 as an assistant professor of chemistry. In 1912 he was appointed an associate professor of chemical engineering, and in 1914 he was promoted to full professor. From 1917 to

1918 he worked with the Bureau of Mines and the Chemical Warfare Service on poison gas defense. He then returned to MIT, where he became the first head of the Department of Chemical Engineering (1920), a position he held until 1929. With Walker and William Henry McAdams, Lewis coauthored *Principles of Chemical Engineering* (1923), one of the first chemical engineering textbooks. It was organized around "unit operations," a concept that was introduced in the first decades of the century and that simplified complex chemical processes into generic process operations like distillation and heat transfer. Previously chemical processes had been organized according to products such as petroleum, paper, glass, and so forth. The effectiveness of the concept of unit operations, "a wholly American achievement," was a major factor leading to the professionalization of chemical engineering as a discipline distinct from applied or industrial chemistry.

From 1929 until his retirement in 1948, except for his years of government service, Lewis was a professor of chemical engineering devoted to teaching, research, and consulting. From 1940 to 1943 he was the vice chairman of the Chemistry Division of the National Defense Research Committee (NDRC) and also a member of the Senior Advisory Committee for the Manhattan Project. During these war years he served as an experienced engineer asked to troubleshoot and advise on production matters in a capacity similar to consulting for petroleum, rubber, and chemical companies.

At MIT Lewis directed research in diverse areas of chemical engineering, resulting in approximately 100 papers and two coauthored monographs, *Industrial Stoichiometry* (1926), with Arthur H. Radasch, and *Industrial Chemistry of Colloidal and Amorphous Materials* (1942), with Lombard Squires and Geoffrey Broughton. In their role as consultants to Standard Oil Development Company (N.J.), Lewis and Edwin Richard Gilliland (also a professor of chemical engineering at MIT) invented in 1938 the fluidized-bed method of cracking petroleum, which was of particular importance during the war for the production of high-octane aviation gasoline. The dimensionless "Lewis number," which is equal to the ratio of mass diffusivity to thermal diffusivity, honors Lewis's research in the field of mass transfer.

Among Lewis's doctoral students, three eventually served as the head of the MIT chemical engineering department: Walter Gordon Whitman, Gilliland, and Raymond Frederick Baddour. Lewis was also a strong supporter of the School of Chemical Engineering Practice, established in 1916 by Walker as a means of giving students industrial experience under the supervision of the chemical engineering faculty. This program was strongly supported by industry and is an example of early cooperative education programs.

Lewis received numerous awards, including the Perkin Medal of the American Section of the Society of Chemical Industry (1936), the Priestley Medal of the American Chemical Society (1947), the Founders Award (1958) of the American Institute of Chemical Engineers, the John Fritz Medal (1966) of the engineering societies, the President's Medal for Merit (1948), and the National Medal of Science (1965). He was a member of many professional societies, including the National Academy of Sciences and the National Academy of Engineering.

The citation accompanying the 1966 Fritz Medal noted Lewis's contributions to "establishing the modern concept of chemical engineering, developing generations of leaders in engineering and science, and pioneering industrial problems that have contributed immeasurably to the progress of mankind." He is memorialized by the Warren K. Lewis Award of the American Institute of Chemical Engineers (established in 1963) and the Warren K. Lewis Professorship of Chemical Engineering at MIT (established in 1969). Lewis died in Plymouth, Massachusetts.

• Papers related to Lewis are in the Institute Archives at MIT. Upon his retirement from MIT, students privately published a collection of anecdotes resulting from his legendary adversarial style of teaching as *A Dollar to a Doughnut: The Lewis Story* (1953). This contains biographical information about Lewis's early years and education. A biographical article written by Lewis's son and emphasizing his teaching principles is H. Clay Lewis, "W. K. Lewis, Teacher," in *History of Chemical Engineering*, ed. William F. Furter (1980), pp. 129–40. Two papers by MIT chemical engineering professors that contain brief summaries of Lewis's contributions to the profession are also published in this symposium volume; they are H. C. Weber, "The Improbable Achievement: Chemical Engineering at MIT," pp. 77–96, and Glenn C. Williams and J. Edward Vivian, "Pioneers in Chemical Engineering at M.I.T.," pp. 113–28. A scholarly paper on the founding of chemical engineering containing references to Lewis is John W. Servos, "The Industrial Relations of Science: Chemical Engineering at MIT, 1900–1939," *ISIS* 71 (1980): 531–49. The Lewis and Gilliland method of cracking petroleum is described in John Lawrence Enos, *Petroleum Progress and Profits: A History of Process Innovation* (1962).

KENNETH G. HELLYAR

LEWIS, W. Arthur (23 Jan. 1915–15 June 1991), economist, development expert, and Nobel laureate, was born William Arthur Lewis on St. Lucia in the West Indies, the son of George Lewis and Ida Barton, teachers. When Lewis was only seven, his father died and his mother opened a shop to help support her family of five sons. Financially assisted by the Anglican church and inspired by his mother's unrelenting determination, the precocious youngster completed the studies required for university admission at fourteen and worked as a government clerk for four years. At eighteen, Lewis won the St. Lucia government scholarship for study in Britain and elected to attend the London School of Economics (LSE). Although he had wanted to be an engineer, Lewis knew that neither local industry nor the British government hired blacks in that field. Interested in business and curious about the nature of economics, he chose instead to pursue a bachelor of commerce degree.

In London, Lewis discovered his exceptional talent and future career. After receiving his B.Com. in 1937, he received an LSE scholarship for a Ph.D. in economics and rapidly became interested in applying the field's knowledge to practical dilemmas. Especially concerned with the way that institutional structures influenced economic problems, he wrote a doctoral thesis on the organization of British industry. The first black at LSE ever appointed as a lecturer, Lewis completed the Ph.D. in 1940, taught at the school (1938–1948), and continued to test economic theory against concrete historical situations.

During the fifteen years following his doctorate, Lewis set in place a basic pattern that would last half a century. Maturing as an intellectual of remarkable range and deep political convictions, he combined his academic endeavors with constant service in government and public administration. Joining the Fabian Society, the intellectual ally of Britain's Labour party, he wrote pamphlets on the exploitation of indigenous labor in the West Indies and the problems of administering Britain's mixed economy. Working through the United Kingdom's Colonial Office, he argued that Britain should grant political independence and economic assistance to the nations comprising its empire. In 1947 Lewis married Gladys Jacobs, a teacher from Grenada whom he met through the League of Colonial Peoples, an organization much like the American National Association for the Advancement of Colored People (NAACP); they had two daughters.

In 1948 Lewis accepted a position as professor of political economy at the University of Manchester. In addition to publishing his dissertation, he also published two more books before the end of the decade, *Economic Survey 1918–1939* and *Principles of Economic Planning* (both 1949). Where other scholars described the late 1920s as a period of global prosperity, Lewis's *Survey* noted the weakness of agricultural prices on the world market and provided new answers to questions that historians had typically explored without the benefit of economic analysis. In his treatment of planning, written before Cold War tensions made such accounts much more common, Lewis provided a critical argument regarding the problems produced when a central state attempted to control a nation's economy. Noting that centralized planning demanded that a government direct not only the production of a specific good but also all the component parts of its manufacture, as well as its substitutes and complements, he argued that coordination would require an army of functionaries and, in the end, result in highly standardized, low quality goods. A social democrat with an optimistic view of the potential for long-term capitalist growth to improve popular welfare, Lewis rejected both laissez faire and centralized control in favor of manipulation of the price mechanism and money flows to harness market forces and ensure that the benefits of economic expansion be widely shared.

Lewis's historical analysis and research in problems of political economy won critical acclaim, but his work in development theory made him one of the most influential economists of his generation. In a 1954 article, "Economic Development with Unlimited Supplies of Labour," published in the journal *Manchester School*, he made an intellectual breakthrough that profoundly changed the way both academics and policy makers came to understand the nature of growth in the poorer countries of the world. Where equilibrium models accepted the neoclassical assumption of a limited supply of labor, he argued that many poor nations, unlike the industrialized countries of Western Europe, were characterized by "dual economies." Although the marginal productivity of labor might be high in the small capitalist industrial and commercial sectors of these countries, he claimed that the population engaged in subsistence agriculture, "petty retail trading," domestic service, and informal, sporadic work in urban areas was so large, relative to available resources, that marginal productivity in these areas was negligible. This "disguised unemployment," however, presented a hidden opportunity because workers, including women kept in the home by social mores, could be moved into the commercial and industrial sectors at a wage set by the subsistence level plus an increment just large enough to encourage the transfer. Once this shift started to take place, employment and productivity in the dynamic, capitalist sectors rose and, as long as the labor surplus existed, wages remained constant. As the share of capitalist profits in the nation's income increased, reinvestment and savings promoted rapid economic growth in the poor country until, finally, the labor surplus was exhausted, demand for more workers led to wage increases, and expansion slowed.

Placing that model of development in an open system, Lewis cautioned that attempts to improve productivity in the commercial sector, if directed toward export purposes, could erode the terms of trade. Increasing efficiency in producing crops for foreign markets, he commented, often only lowered prices by raising international supply. Profits and investment, he argued, were the engines of growth; but applying capital to many export industries would only benefit the foreign consumer.

Lewis's dual economy model met with criticism from a range of sources. Many colleagues objected to the idea of a labor surplus so large that a negligible marginal productivity in "subsistence" sectors would allow for labor transfers without output loss. Others claimed that he ignored the fact that the gap between urban and rural wages often grew dramatically and attacked his claim that industrial wages would stay close to rural income. Critics on the left also rejected his assumption that a nascent capitalist class would automatically reinvest profits and lamented the apparent policy implication, later accepted by some African and Asian countries, that import-substituting industrialization could be pursued without attention to problems of rural development.

Lewis did not solve all the problems critics raised. He did argue, however, that he had never meant to endorse an exclusive focus on industrial growth. The path to development, he explained, could be pursued in rural, capitalist agriculture or mining as well as urban industry. His work, moreover, opened up new avenues of inquiry, inspired a massive literature on growth patterns, and was soon applied by economic historians working on India and Japan, for example, and even such problems as illegal immigration in the United States. In elaborating on the problem of foreign capital investment in export sectors, Lewis provided a compelling explanation of the means by which colonialism had helped create a world divided into poorer agricultural nations and wealthy urban industrial ones. In 1955 he expanded on his insights in *The Theory of Economic Growth*, one of the first textbooks in the field of development economics.

Over the next thirty years, Lewis continued to play a major role both in academia and in formulating public policy. After leaving Manchester in 1958, he became principal of the University College of the West Indies in 1959 and was appointed vice chancellor of the institution when it was enlarged and made autonomous from the University of London in 1962. In 1963 he moved to the United States to become a professor of economics and international affairs at Princeton University, until retiring in 1983. He also continued to dedicate himself to the problems of economic policy making in West Africa and the Caribbean. Between 1957 and 1970 he complemented his academic duties by working as economic adviser to Ghanian prime minister Kwame Nkrumah, deputy managing director of the United Nations Special Fund, and director of Jamaica's Industrial Development Corporation. Taking a leave from Princeton, he also served as president of the Caribbean Development Bank from 1970 to 1973. Hoping to foster rural development, he argued for democratic institutions over single-party systems.

In later life, Lewis continued to publish and from 1978 to 1980 was a member of the Economic Advisory Council of the NAACP. By the time he died Lewis had become one of the most respected social scientists of his generation. Knighted by Queen Elizabeth II in 1963, he shared the 1972 Nobel Prize in economics with Theodore Schultz. A thinker and policy maker whose belief that market forces could be harnessed for progressive, reformist goals, Lewis was often at the center of contentious debate. He died in Barbados.

• Lewis's papers are in Princeton University's Seeley G. Mudd Manuscript Library. Over the course of his career, Lewis published twelve books and over eighty articles. In addition to those works mentioned above, Lewis authored *Economic Problems of Today* (1940), *The Economics of Overhead Costs* (1949), *Politics in West Africa* (1965), *Development Planning* (1966), *Reflections on the Economic Growth of Nigeria* (1967), *Some Aspects of Economic Development* (1969), *The Evolution of the International Economic Order* (1978), *Growth and Fluctuations, 1870–1913* (1978), and *Racial Conflict and Economic Development* (1985). Lewis himself prepared a reflective essay for Gerald M. Meier and Dudley Seers, eds., *Pioneers in Development* (1984), and a short autobiographical memoir for William Breit and Roger W. Spencer, eds., *Lives of the Laureates: Seven Nobel Economists* (1986). An essay by Jagdish N. Bhagwati, "W. Arthur Lewis: An Appreciation," in *The Theory and Experience of Economic Development*, ed. Mark Gersovitz et al. (1982), and the introduction to *Perspectives on Development: Essays in the Honour of W. Arthur Lewis*, ed. T. E. Barker et al. (1982), provide brief reviews of Lewis's accomplishments and life. P. F. Leeson's "The Lewis Model and Development Theory," *Manchester School* 47 (1979): 196–210, and Ronald Findlay's essay on Lewis in *Contemporary Economists in Perspective*, ed. Henry W. Spiegel and Warren J. Samuels (1984), offer more critical, though still appreciative, analyses of Lewis's theoretical work. Obituaries are in the *Washington Post* and the *New York Times*, both 17 June 1991. A *New York Times* editorial on 18 June 1991 also praised Lewis's lifelong combination of scholarship with concern for the human problems of poverty and development.

MICHAEL E. LATHAM

LEWIS, William Berkeley (23 June 1784–12 Nov. 1866), planter and politician, was born in Loudoun County, Virginia, the son of John Lewis. He arrived in Nashville as a young man in his mid-twenties, but little is known of him prior to that time, including anything about his forebears except that his mother was a member of the prominent Berkeley family. Shortly after his arrival in Nashville he obtained a position in the state land office and soon married Margaret Lewis (no relation), a daughter of William Terrell Lewis. They had one child. One of the richest men in Tennessee, boasting Andrew Jackson as his nearest neighbor and John Eaton as a son-in-law, the old man died very shortly before his daughter married, and Eaton and William B. Lewis soon divided up the vast estate. Lewis, overnight, became a country squire with large land holdings and took over ownership of the Nashville Inn and the old farmhouse, "Fairfield," twelve miles down the road from Jackson's "Hermitage." In the following year Margaret died, and Lewis was soon married to Adelaide Stokes Chambers, a widowed daughter of General Montfort Stokes of North Carolina, a U.S. senator and governor. They had two children. Despite his remarriage, Lewis continued to live at Fairfield for the rest of his life, except when in Washington.

Lewis lost little time in ingratiating himself with Jackson and others of prominence in Nashville. He was indeed an imposing figure in frontier society and is described by historian James Parton as standing well over six feet "with shoulders as broad as a door." Like most of the free men of the time, he joined the state militia, and in December of 1812 Major General Jackson appointed him assistant deputy quartermaster of the Tennessee troops. From the time of the Creek War until after Jackson's victory at New Orleans in January 1815, Lewis expended considerable energy in keeping Jackson's troops well supplied. Indeed, he won completely the confidence of the "Old General" who commended him publicly for his work.

Lewis returned to Nashville after the war and, as a gentleman planter with slaves and thousands of acres, had time to spare. He was among the first to perceive Jackson as a possible candidate, and he soon became associated with the wealthy judge John Overton, brother-in-law Senator John Eaton, and perhaps a few others in exploring possibilities. Encouraged by Jackson's actions against the Seminole Indians in Florida in 1818, the "Nashville Junto" talked of presenting Jackson as a presidential candidate in 1820 but thought better of the matter when President James Monroe's popularity became all too apparent. Some talked of Jackson for governor but presidential hopes brightened after Monroe's second inauguration. The Federalist party faded, the Republican party exploded into several strong factions, the West expanded, the "common man" demanded more influence in government, and the caucus was ignored and became ineffective. An added factor was the American people's devotion to military heroes. Lewis persuaded Jackson to enter the race in 1823 for U.S. Senate, and when he defeated veteran senator John Williams handily, Lewis and others prepared Jackson for the presidential race of 1824. After Jackson lost the presidency in the House of Representatives (though winning a plurality of the popular vote), they labored daily during the next four years to secure victory in 1828.

Lewis was at the Old General's side when the president-elect headed for Washington for the 1829 inaugural. Rachel Jackson had died a few weeks earlier, and Lewis took rooms in the White House as one of the president's closest friends and advisers. Lewis played a major role in the selection of the cabinet, including Martin Van Buren as secretary of state, and in other matters influenced Jackson in his decisions. Taunted by some politicians as servile and sycophantic, Lewis was undaunted in his loyalty to the "Old Chief." He soon secured a position as second auditor of the Treasury, but he conceived of his prime task as advising the president.

Lewis's influence on Jackson probably was at a peak in 1831–1832 as he sought to smooth things over among various cabinet officers during the Eaton-O'Neill affair. It declined in Jackson's second term as the chief came to depend more on his regular cabinet for advice and as his confidence in Lewis's judgment diminished. (Lewis had disagreed with the president over the issues of the U.S. Bank and the spoils system, and Jackson may also have felt that Lewis had nothing else innovative to offer.) Jackson urged Lewis to return to Fairfield in 1837 when Jackson left the White House, but Lewis preferred to remain on under Van Buren. However the new president—although Lewis had supported him vigorously—had little or no need for the Nashville politician. Van Buren permitted him to continue as second auditor of the Treasury but otherwise treated him with indifference and perhaps distrust. When Lewis was continued on the payroll during the Whig administration of William Henry Harrison and John Tyler (1841–1845), Democratic leaders criticized him. James K. Polk, soon after his inauguration in 1845, summarily dismissed him, and Lewis, feeling discredited, could do nothing else but return to Nashville. Arriving in June, he came just in time to be at the bedside of the Old General, who lay dying at the Hermitage.

Lewis lived in the seclusion of Fairfield for the remainder of his life. His wife, a son, and a daughter had died, and another daughter resided in France. But Lewis corresponded with many old friends and supported the Union at the outbreak of the Civil War. When the Tennessee Union Convention assembled in Nashville in January 1865, he was nominated and subsequently elected to the state house of representatives, where he worked as a Conservative Republican. He resigned in the following year but was reelected without campaigning. He then was denied his seat by the Radical majority.

Lewis's death at Fairfield brought a day's adjournment of the state house of representatives and flattering obituaries in the Nashville press.

• Lewis corresponded with the great and the small among politicians of the country, and some of his letters are included in John Spencer Bassett, ed., *Correspondence of Andrew Jackson* (7 vols., 1926–1935), and in Sam Smith et al., *The Papers of Andrew Jackson* (1980–). Various clippings and papers about Lewis may be found in the State Library and Archives in Nashville. By far the most perceptive of the accounts of Lewis is Louis Harlan, "Public Career of William Berkeley Lewis," *Tennessee Historical Quarterly* 7 (1948): 3–37, 118–51. Lewis figures prominently in all of the Jackson biographies. He was responsible for much of the content of James Parton's *Life of Andrew Jackson* (3 vols., 1860), and naturally receives frequent mention. Jackson biographies published subsequently follow Parton. Also, the principal biographies of James K. Polk, Felix Grundy, John Bell, Henry Clay, and others of the time discuss the influence of Lewis on the politics of the Jackson era. An obituary is in the (Nashville) *Daily Gazette*, 14 Nov. 1866.

ROBERT E. CORLEW

LEWIS, William Henry (28 Nov. 1868–1 Jan. 1949), lawyer and public official, was born in Berkeley, Virginia, the son of Ashley Henry Lewis, a Baptist minister, and Josephine Baker. His parents were former slaves who had been freed through manumission shortly before the Civil War. Lewis worked his way through the Virginia Normal and Collegiate Institute, a black preparatory school, before entering Amherst College in 1888. An excellent student and star athlete, he became the first African American to serve as captain of an Ivy League football team. After graduating with a B.A. in 1892, he studied law at Harvard Law School (1892–1895) and continued to play football for the Harvard team. Named to Walter Camp's All-American team in 1892 and 1893, he retained a life-long interest in the sport and even published an early manual, *A Primer of College Football*, in 1896.

As a law student Lewis developed a strong interest in civil rights, which was based on his own experience of racial bigotry. When a local barber refused to serve him, he and black attorney Burton R. Wilson successfully lobbied the state legislature to expand the coverage of an 1865 equal rights statute. The original law applied only to licensed establishments; the new one forbade racial discrimination in any public facility, whether licensed or not. After receiving his LL.B. in 1895, Lewis practiced for a time in a Boston law office and then founded the firm of Lewis, Fox, and Andrews. In 1896 he married a Wellesley student, Elizabeth Baker; they had three children.

Lewis's student activism carried over to his early professional career. At first a vigorous opponent of Booker T. Washington's accommodationist policies, he gradually adopted a more conciliatory stance, in response to his wife's conservative sympathies and because of his increasing need for Washington's political support. Elected three times to the Cambridge common council (1899–1901), Lewis also served one term in the Massachusetts House of Representatives (1902–1903) but failed to win reelection. By that time blacks were being systematically excluded from elective offices in Massachusetts and other northern states as a wave of Anglo-Saxon chauvinism swept the nation after the Spanish-American War. Through Washington's influence with Theodore Roosevelt (1858–1919), however, Lewis secured an appointment as assistant U.S. attorney for Massachusetts (1903–1906) and became chief of the Naturalization Bureau for New England from 1907 to 1911. He attained national prominence when William Howard Taft appointed him in 1911 to be the first African-American assistant attorney general of the United States.

While Lewis had achieved political advancement by cooperating with the white establishment, he was painfully reminded of his unequal status when friends proposed that he and two other black attorneys be admitted to the lily-white American Bar Association in 1911. The executive committee initially approved the nominations but, on learning the race of the applicants, it rescinded its action. After a bitter debate at the annual meeting in 1912, the ABA agreed to allow the candidates to retain their membership but resolved that future applicants must disclose their race and sex in order to avoid a recurrence of such situations.

With the advent of Woodrow Wilson's Democratic administration in 1913, Lewis left government service and returned to private practice. He formed a new partnership in Boston with Matthew L. McGarth, a genial Irishman with a talent for recruiting clients. A forceful courtroom advocate noted for his rugged good looks and oratorical skills, Lewis gained his greatest reputation as defense counsel in criminal cases. His skillful defense of a black man charged with the murder of a white physician in Providence, Rhode Island, won praise from the *New York Times* in 1916. During the following decade he earned large fees through his representation of accused bootleggers. In his most famous case, in 1941, he served as defense counsel at the impeachment trial of Daniel H. Coakley, who was charged with influence peddling while a member of the Massachusetts executive council.

Despite Lewis's strategic endorsement of Booker T. Washington's views, he remained on friendly terms with more militant African-American leaders. In 1923 he used his influence with Calvin Coolidge, a fellow Amherst alumnus, to help secure the appointment of W. E. B. Du Bois as special minister to the 1924 inauguration of President C. D. B. King of Liberia. He also participated actively in the early civil rights movement, joining with other African Americans in a well-orchestrated, but unsuccessful, protest against the showing in Boston of D. W. Griffith's blatantly racist film, *The Birth of a Nation* (1915). His most important civil rights case was *Corrigan v. Buckley* (1926), in which he assisted white NAACP lawyers in attacking the constitutionality of racially restrictive covenants before the U.S. Supreme Court. Although the Court rejected their arguments at the time, it eventually ruled in *Shelley v. Kraemer* (1948) that such covenants were unenforceable.

Lewis retired from practice in 1948, after a series of heart attacks. He died in Boston. His record of public service and commitment to the defense of unpopular clients made him a role model for later generations of African Americans.

• Letters from Lewis are in the Booker T. Washington Papers, the Theodore Roosevelt Papers, and the Calvin Coolidge Papers in the Library of Congress. The Harvard University Archives contain a folder of clippings on Lewis. For valuable appraisals of his early career, see John Daniels, *In Freedom's Birthplace* (1914); August Meier, *Negro Thought in America, 1880–1915* (1963); and Stephen R. Fox, *The Guardian of Boston* (1970). Geraldine R. Segal discusses the ABA incident of 1912 in *Blacks in the Law* (1983). On the significance of the *Corrigan v. Buckley* case, see Loren Miller, *The Petitioners* (1966). An obituary is in the *Boston Globe*, 2 Jan. 1949.

MAXWELL BLOOMFIELD

LEWISOHN, Irene (5 Sept. 1892–4 Apr. 1944), theater patron and practitioner and philanthropist, was born in New York City, the daughter of Rosalie Jacobs and Leonard Lewisohn, a German-Jewish immigrant who made his fortune in the mining and processing of copper and other minerals. The deaths of Lewisohn's parents before she was ten years old left her older sister Alice and her with considerable wealth—and the social burden of such wealth. The daughter of a philanthropist, Lewisohn was impressed by the Henry Street Settlement, one of her father's causes. After attending the Finch School in New York, she studied dance independently and eventually found her calling in the unique combination of social service and the arts.

Lewisohn and her sister brought the arts to the East Side residents who frequented the settlement house; more importantly, they elicited from the neighborhood the culturally diverse arts of its many representative ethnic groups. As early as 1907 the sisters had trained a company of dancers and mounted a festival in the Henry Street gymnasium. In 1912 they gathered a group to perform under the title "Neighborhood Players," from which the famed school of theater that Irene later founded gained its name. In 1913 the young Lewisohns were responsible for organizing and staging a gigantic street festival in celebration of the Henry Street Settlement's twentieth anniversary.

In 1915, having purchased the land the preceding year, the sisters had built and donated to the settlement a fully equipped theater, located on nearby Grand Street. By 1920 a resident professional company was operating in the space, and the Neighborhood Playhouse joined the ranks of such prestigious theater companies as the Provincetown Players in spearheading the "little theater" movement. Beginning in 1923 a series of yearly parodies of the contemporary theater scene, the Grand Street Follies, complimented the company's already busy seasons. The company's most famous and critically acclaimed productions were the Hindu classic *The Little Clay Cart* (1924) and the Yiddish folk play *The Dybbuk* (1925). European, Middle Eastern, and Asian influences characterized many of the Neighborhood's productions.

From the beginning of their involvement in these projects, the mining heiresses seem to have possessed a natural instinct for accomplishing social work with dignity and respect for its recipients. In his introduction to Alice Lewisohn Crowley's 1959 book on the sisters' experiences, Joseph Wood Krutch wrote, "They saw that it need be no mere matter of anything condescendingly handed down. Those who came to the settlement were not to be merely instructed and presented with 'culture.' They were to be helped to become the creative artists they potentially were" (p. xii). Their success at coupling social service and the arts far surpassed that of many public agencies in New York or elsewhere, and a number of their productions met with critical acclaim. Theater professionals and avid theatergoers consistently made the trip to the East Side, far "Off Broadway," to attend productions, and heavy traffic to the Neighborhood necessitated the creation of a subway stop there. Attendance figures substantiate the neighborhood's positive response to all of these programs.

It is easy to consider the work of the "Misses Lewisohn"—an epithet with which they are often cited—as inseparable because as girls and young women Alice and Irene *were* inseparable, working together and traveling to Europe and the Middle East in 1910 and 1922–1923. However, although they shared responsibility for their joint theatrical venture and possessed similar artistic sensibilities, each had her own specific areas of expertise and domain in the Neighborhood's organizational structure.

Irene Lewisohn designed and choreographed for the festivals, training the festival dancers and teaching classes. Alice said, "If a festival is in the making, Irene is in command." Irene was responsible for the children's component of the programming as well. Her talent and interest lay in the areas of folk expression and lyric productions, and she was particularly fascinated with Asian and Middle Eastern ritual. When on occasions she herself performed, it was in roles that required the sort of precise movement characteristic of the Japanese Nōh theater that she so greatly admired. She played a variety of roles, including "Waki" in Zeami's *Tamura*, which the company staged as early as 1917–1918. She also codirected the Hindu play *The Little Clay Cart*.

Lewisohn's lifelong artistic pursuit was to explore the relationship between movement and music. She was a true "interdisciplinarian" long before the phrase was coined. No doubt her 1910 visit to Germany, where she experienced the techniques of Dalcroze, deeply influenced her work. When praising her sister, Alice Lewisohn Crowley wrote in retrospect, "Today the dance has achieved an art form in and of itself, but at the Playhouse . . . the relation of free movement to music was a pioneer adventure, for dance in this country still had no distinctive form" (Crowley, p. 21). After the Neighborhood's closing in 1927, Irene Lewisohn created a series of orchestral dance dramas. Her dancers appeared in concert with a full symphony orchestra and on occasions included Martha Graham.

Education was another of Lewisohn's passions. She founded New York's Neighborhood Playhouse School of the Theatre, which produced numerous actors of merit and was led by actor-director Sanford Meisner for a number of years.

Lewisohn pioneered the concept of costume as "artifact," valuable not only for costume research but as evidence of material culture. She formed the Costume Institute, which began with her private collection of world costumes and was later placed under the auspices of the Metropolitan Museum, where it was greatly expanded.

In the last years of her life, Irene Lewisohn returned to social work, founding the Spanish Child Welfare Association in response to the Spanish Civil War and working with the American Theatre Group's Stage Door Canteen and the Club for Merchant Seamen during World War II. Lewisohn died of lung cancer in New York City.

• Neighborhood Theatre papers are available at the New York Public Library for the Performing Arts, Lincoln Center. While personal in its style, Alice Lewisohn Crowley's *The Neighborhood Playhouse* (1959) is the most complete source of information on Irene Lewisohn, for from it can be inferred the delineation of responsibilities and talents between the sisters. See also Robert L. Duffus, "The Neighborhood Playhouse," in *Lillian Wald* (1938).

ANNE FLETCHER

LEWISOHN, Ludwig (30 May 1883–31 Dec. 1955), writer and translator, was born to acculturated Jewish parents, Minna Eloesser and Jacques Lewisohn, in Berlin. His father, a ne'er-do-well businessman, settled the family in a South Carolina village, where Minna Lewisohn had relatives, in 1890. But Lewisohn spent most of his childhood in Charleston where, he recalled, he strove to "forget his Jewish and his German past" and be accepted as "an American, a Southerner, and a Christian." Graduating in 1901 from the College of Charleston with both a B.A. and an M.A., he began graduate studies in English literature at Columbia University in New York City, where in 1903 he earned another M.A. In New York he began to affirm his German and, ultimately, his Jewish origins. He was plagued by the anti-Semitism and xenophobia of American university life at that time, but as instructor of German at the University of Wisconsin (1910–1911) and subsequently as professor of German language and literature at Ohio State University (1911–1919) he established his credentials as a prime interpreter of modern European, especially German, literature.

From 1912–1917, seven volumes of *The Dramatic Works of Gerhart Hauptmann* appeared under Lewisohn's editorship. This was the first time that the work of the German playwright became widely accessible to Anglo-American readers, and H. L. Mencken applauded Lewisohn for "undertaking the extremely arduous enterprise." Lewisohn's reputation was further enhanced by his masterly studies, *The Modern Drama* (1915), *The Spirit of Modern German Literature* (1916), and *The Poets of Modern France* (1918). His pacifist and Germanophile opposition to U.S. participation in World War I precipitated his departure from Ohio State University. Lewisohn became the *Nation's* drama editor in 1919, served from 1920 to 1924 as associate editor, and in *A Book of Modern Criticism* (1919), *The Drama and the Stage* (1922), *The Creative Life* (1924), and *Cities and Men* (1927) continued his critical defense of modern, post-Victorian literature in the United States, a literature that eschewed the Puritan heritage and its insistence on "a correct sentiment to which human nature must be made to conform." Even Alfred Kazin, no partisan of Lewisohn, later characterized his criticism as "a force for progress" and endorsed his approach to art as "a spiritual vocation." Lewisohn's *Expression in America* (1932) was probably the first attempt at a Freudian reading of American literature.

By the mid-1930s Lewisohn had undergone radical changes. He had left the United States for an expatriate decade (1924–1934) in Europe. He had abandoned his first wife, Mary Childs, whom he had married in 1906; Childs was herself an accomplished playwright who used the nom de plume Bosworth Crocker (their marriage was not legally dissolved until 1937). He had fathered a son with the singer Thelma Spear, a liaison American law never recognized as legal, and was on the way to finding this relationship a failure. He had become a champion of Jewish identity and of Zionism (while still at Ohio State University he had begun an association with the Intercollegiate Menorah Society, and in the early 1920s he had met and been influenced by Zionist leaders Kurt Blumenfeld and Chaim Weizmann). He had also published three striking autobiographical volumes, *Up Stream* (1922), *Israel* (1925), and *Mid-Channel* (1929), and his first unabashedly Jewish novels, *Roman Summer* (1927), *The Island Within* (1928), and *The Last Days of Shylock* (1931)—all this in addition to the even better known and more controversial novel evoking his disastrous first marriage, *The Case of Mr. Crump* (1926), in which Thomas Mann detected "a high determination after compact and direct truth." In 1940 he published another autobiographical volume, *Haven*, with journalist Edna Manley, whom he married that year; the marriage collapsed in 1943, and they were divorced the following year.

In the pre–World War II years, Lewisohn retained his pacifist sympathies and, as a publicist for Zionism, urged a rather utopian bi-nationalist program, "the divorcement of nationalism from power." Assaults on Jews and Judaism by Hitler and Stalin during the 1930s made him anticipate "a mounting world conjuration" against the Jews, and with the outbreak of war in 1939 he repudiated "empty pacifism," including the bi-nationalist commitment in Palestine. Zionism became for Lewisohn a means of politicizing Jewry and expressing "a will to political power"; he saw no other way to save the Jews and Jewish values. As editor of the Zionist *New Palestine* between 1944 and 1947, he espoused Jewry's right to "an undiminished and undivided" Palestine.

In 1948 Lewisohn joined the faculty of newly founded Brandeis University near Boston and until his death lived there with Louise Wolk, whom he had married in 1944. The radical anti-Puritan of earlier years had become a precursor of the neoconservatives and also a spokesman for traditional Judaism; especially in the young State of Israel, he believed, there must arise "Jews in the classical sense," their "continuity with the whole of Jewish history . . . unhurt and unbreached." Lionel Trilling charged him with a neurotic "willingness to be provincial and parochial," but in fact Lewisohn never relinquished his loyalty to western civilization. Preoccupation with Jewish concerns did not mean indifference to other cultural perspectives: in the postwar years he produced not only *The American Jew: Character and Destiny* (1950), but also *Goethe: The Story of a Man* (a biography and compilation in two massive volumes, 1949) and *The Magic Word: Studies in the Nature of Poetry* (1950).

If only for his masterly style and his achievement as a writer of fiction (well over a dozen novels, many of them notable for a frank, though never tasteless, expression of sexuality) and as a translator (of Hauptmann, Sudermann, Rilke, Buber, Wassermann, Werfel, Morgenstern, Picard, and Goethe, among others), Lewisohn would deserve to be remembered as a litterateur of great distinction. In addition, however, his many volumes of criticism and his passionate struggle for Jewish survival greatly enriched not only Jewish, but American culture in the twentieth century. He died in Miami Beach, Florida.

• The American Jewish Archives on the Cincinnati campus of Hebrew Union College has an extensive collection of Lewisohn papers. See Stanley F. Chyet, "Lewisohn and Hauptmann," *Proceedings of the Sixth World Congress of Jewish Studies* 2 (1975): 205–13; Adolph Gillis, *Ludwig Lewisohn: The Artist and His Message* (1933); Milton Hindus, "Ludwig Lewisohn: From Assimilation to Zionism," *Jewish Frontier*, Feb. 1964, pp. 22–30; Seymour Lainoff, *Ludwig Lewisohn* (1982); the entry on Lewisohn by Ralph Melnick in *Dictionary of Literary Biography*, vol. 4 (1984); David F. Singer, "Ludwig Lewisohn: A Paradigm of American-Jewish Return," *Judaism* 14 (1965): 319–29; and Saul Spiro, *The Jew as Man of Letters, Being Some Notes on Ludwig Lewisohn* (1935).
STANLEY F. CHYET

LEWY, Hans (20 Oct. 1904–23 Aug. 1988), mathematician, was born in Breslau, Germany, the son of Max Lewy, a merchant, and Margarete Rösel. Lewy attended the Johannes Gymnasium in Breslau from 1910 to 1922. He was gifted in both mathematics and music, and, deciding to pursue the former as a profession, he entered Göttingen University in 1922. He earned his doctorate there in 1926 with a dissertation on differential equations, "Über die Methode der Differenzengleichungen zur Lösung von Variations und Randwert-Problemen," directed by Richard Courant. He then became a privatdozent at Göttingen (1927–1933), and during the winters of 1929–1930 and 1930–1931 he studied in Rome and Paris, respectively, on a Rockefeller International Fellowship.

Upon the Nazi accession to power, Lewy left Germany and was a research associate at Brown University from 1933 to 1935. He then joined the faculty as a lecturer at the University of California at Berkeley, serving successively as assistant professor (1937–1939), associate professor (1939–1946), and professor (1946–1972). In 1950 his career at Berkeley was interrupted when he, among others, refused to sign a new loyalty oath imposed by the state legislature and was fired. This action was later revoked by the courts (as a violation of his civil rights), and he was reinstated with back pay and full privileges in 1952. During his dismissal he held visiting one-term positions at Stanford (1950–1951) and Harvard (1951–1952) Universities.

Lewy became a naturalized U.S. citizen on 26 January 1940 and served as a civilian consultant at the Balistic Research Laboratory at the Aberdeen Proving Ground in Maryland during 1942–1943. He was a visiting professor at New York University (1959–1960) and the University of Pisa (1964–1965), and Professor Linceo at the Accademia Nazionale dei Lincei in Rome (1969–1970). An accomplished linguist and seasoned traveler, he gave lectures on his research in the Soviet Union, the People's Republic of China, Japan, Czechoslovakia, and literally all the countries of western Europe. He married Helen Pratt Crosby in 1947; they had one child.

Lewy received numerous honors in his lifetime. In 1964 he was elected a member of the National Academy of Sciences, and he was also a member of the Accademia dei Lincei and the Göttingen Akademie der Wissenschaften. He won the Steele Prize of the American Mathematical Society in 1979, and in 1985 he shared the Wolf Foundation Prize in mathematics with the Japanese mathematician Kunihiko Kodaira.

Almost all of Lewy's research centered on partial differential equations, one of the most difficult areas in mathematics. Although the subject has been of paramount importance for mathematics and mathematical physics for almost three centuries, theoretically it remains in an embryonic and incomplete state. Lewy deeply probed the theoretical foundations of the subject, with the result that his work revealed many new features—even surprising aspects—that have profoundly altered our view of the area. Much of his work was of a highly technical character, but roughly speaking his contributions can be divided into four main periods. The first period (1925–1931) dealt with basic existence / uniqueness questions and initial value problems and included his fundamental work with Courant and K. O. Friedrichs on the partial differential equations of mathematical physics (1928). This work reformulated the problem in terms of difference equations, and during the war years Lewy recognized that the method could be employed to obtain numerical solutions of certain classes of equations. The resulting use of it on computers has been of crucial importance, and quite literally thousands of research articles have been based on this pioneering work.

Lewy's second period (1935–1938) was devoted to the differential geometry of surfaces in ordinary Euclidean space. There, employing his investigations of the Monge-Ampere systems of equations (1935, 1937), he was able to solve the Minkowski and Weyl problems (1938), which was a seminal contribution to differential geometry in the large. His third period (1946–1956) was concerned with the theory of free boundary problems, and in particular with the theory of water waves and hydrodynamics. He developed a theory of water waves on sloping beaches (1946), and in collaboration with Friedrichs solved the so-called "Dock Problem" (1948).

In the final period (1957–1972), Lewy focused on fundamental problems concerning the local solvability of linear partial differential equations. For almost a century, based on the celebrated Cauchy-Kowalewski theorem, experts had anticipated that any "reasonable" partial differential equation was solvable and that the hypothesis of analyticity in this theorem could be relaxed. In 1957 Lewy exhibited an example of a simple partial differential equation with nonanalytic coefficients that was unsolvable. Hence, in one dramatic stroke he destroyed a common belief and forced a reinterpretation of a classical result. In subsequent papers he showed that his example had important implications for the theory of several complex variables and microlocal analysis. The ultimate ramifications of the Lewy example are still a topic of investigation.

Lewy was a quiet, gentle man who directed his energy into his research and teaching and shunned the allure of academic politics and stardom. He was independent in his choice of research problems and published only results that, in his judgment, were of importance and sufficiently polished. Consequently, for a mathematician of his stature and longevity, the number of his publications was relatively small (fewer than sixty papers). But the results that met his standards were choice and highly original, and his work was unusually rich in its content and depth. In 1962 he was invited to write an introduction to the reissue of Bernhard Riemann's *Gesammelte Mathematische Werke*. This contained a moving tribute to Riemann's superb craftsmanship, his self-effacing nature and modesty, and indefatigable search for hidden truths. Prophetically, contemporary mathematicians now feel that Lewy's assessment of Riemann is also an appropriate characterization of Lewy himself.

Lewy remained active in mathematics after his 1972 retirement and lectured in Cortona, Italy, only ten weeks before his death. He died in Berkeley, California.

• A collection of Lewy's personal and professional papers is in the Manuscript Division of the Bancroft Library at the University of California, Berkeley. An interview containing numerous pictures, with some personal comments, is given in *More Mathematical People*, ed. Donald J. Albers et al. (1990); and a biographical sketch by Constance Reid appears in *Miscellanea Mathematica*, ed. Peter Hilton et al. (1991). Brief obituary notices are in the *California Monthly* (Nov. 1988) and *In Memoriam* (1988), both publications of the University of California at Berkeley.

JOSEPH D. ZUND

LEY, Willy (2 Oct. 1906–24 June 1969), science journalist and spaceflight publicist, was born in Berlin, Germany, the son of Julius Otto Ley, a wine merchant, and Frida May. Educated in primary and secondary schools in Berlin, he studied paleontology, physics, and astronomy at the Universities of Berlin and Königsburg. While he did not obtain a degree, Ley developed a broad command of the sciences and became fluent in a variety of languages.

Ley was nineteen years old when he read the book that would change his life, *Die Rakete zu den Planetenräumen* (1923), by the Rumanian physicist Hermann Oberth. Ley immediately decided that this treatise, filled with dense mathematical equations proving the possibility of spaceflight and outlining the means by which it might be accomplished, should be made available to an audience of general readers. Ley's first two books, *Fahrt ins Weltall* (*Trip into Space*) (1926), and *Die Möglichkeit der Weltraumfahrt* (*The Possibility of Interplanetary Travel*) (1928), achieved that goal and marked the author as an emerging leader in the field.

The work of Oberth, Ley, and other writers, including the rocket experimenter Max Valier, sparked a flurry of interest in spaceflight. In June 1927 a small group of enthusiasts formed the Verein für Raumschiffahrt (Society for Space Travel). The members of the VfR, Ley later explained to an American correspondent, were determined "to spread the thought that the planets were within reach of humanity, if humanity was only willing to struggle a bit for that goal." Ley was elected vice president of the organization early in 1929.

The members of the VfR conducted pioneering experiments with liquid propellant rockets between March 1931 and April 1932. According to Ley's account, they completed 270 static engine tests; 87 flights; 23 demonstrations for other organizations; and 9 presentations for the press. Their rockets reached altitudes of up to 4,922 feet. Ley, the single most visible member of the VfR, communicated news of the organization's research program to other rocket enthusiasts around the world. He wrote articles, lectured, corresponded widely, and hosted young rocketeers from other nations, such as G. Edward Pendray of the American Rocket Society.

By 1933, a series of problems brought an end to the golden age of VfR rocketry. The death of several rocket experimenters, including Valier and Reinhard Tilling, underscored the dangers inherent in liquid propellant rockets. Moreover, Rudolph Nebel, the man in charge of VfR rocket experiments, was creating problems for the organization. In the spring of 1933 Ley and VfR president Major Hans-Wolf von Dickhuth-Harrach discovered that Nebel had signed a contract with the city fathers of Magdeburg, promising to launch a man-carrying rocket to high altitude. Fearing that the VfR might be charged with fraud, Ley and Dickhuth-Harrach attempted to force Nebel out of the organization. Failing that, the two men announced their own resignations and attempted, unsuccessfully, to establish a new society.

Split by internal dissension, the VfR finally succumbed to government pressure. German army interest in rocket weapons had resulted in the creation of a small military rocket research team headed by the young Wernher von Braun, whom Ley had drawn into VfR membership. A curtain of military secrecy was drawn across all rocket experiments. Private individuals were forbidden to build or launch rockets, or to write articles on the subject.

By the end of 1934, Ley, barred from writing on his favorite subject, had decided to leave Germany. He made use of his broad contacts in the international astronautical community, traveling first to England in January 1935. There he stayed at the Liverpool home of Phillip Cleator, a member of the British Interplanetary Society, while waiting for passage to the United States. He arrived in the United States in late February and lived for a time with Pendray, whose letters of support had convinced U.S. officials to provide Ley, who was almost blind in one eye, with a tourist visa.

With the assistance of Pendray and other American friends, Ley made the acquaintance of a number of important engineers interested in rocket propulsion, including Alexander Klemin of New York University. As a result of these contacts, Ley was hired to serve as flight operations supervisor for an experimental winged rocket designed to carry small packets of mail across frozen Greenwood Lake, in upstate New York. Two of the rockets were flown on 23 February 1936. The first rocket climbed to an altitude of 1,000 feet, then spun to the ground when the combustion chamber burned through. The wings of the second rocket ripped off after only fifteen seconds in the air.

Forbidden by immigration regulations from accepting full-time employment, Ley made his living as a freelance writer and lecturer. He spent the years 1936 to 1940, as he later explained to a *New York Times* reporter, "writing day and night, turning out articles for scores of publications both here and in Europe." A friend estimated that he contributed at least ninety articles to science fiction magazines alone between 1935 and 1950. Most of these treated aspects of science, although he did write a few science fiction stories under the pseudonym Robert Wiley.

Ley joined the staff of the liberal tabloid newspaper *PM* as science editor in 1940. The following year he married ballet dancer Olga Feldman, a Russian immigrant who wrote a physical fitness column for *PM*; they were to have two children, both daughters. The year 1941 also marked Ley's emergence as an author of popular books on science. His earliest such books included *The Lungfish, the Dodo, and the Unicorn* (1941); *Bombs and Bombing* (1941); *Shells and Shelling* (1942); and *The Days of Creation* (1941).

In 1944 Ley became a naturalized U.S. citizen and published the first edition of his best-known and most influential book, *Rockets*. Based on the author's twenty-year search for material on the subject, his own experience in Germany, and his correspondence with virtually all of the pioneering figures in the field, the book traced the history of rocketry from the black powder era through the 1930s and explained the basic physical principles that would govern spaceflight. Over the next twenty-eight years, Ley would produce three major new editions of the book: *Rockets and Space Travel* (1948); *Rockets, Missiles and Space Travel* (1951); and *Rockets, Missiles and Men in Space* (1968). In all, the book went through twenty printings during Ley's lifetime.

For all of his expertise, the advent of the space age took Ley by surprise. A. V. Cleavor, a British weapons expert visiting the United States in the fall of 1944, remembered that Ley refused to believe reports that long-range German rockets were falling in London. His old colleagues, Ley argued, "were most unlikely to have developed such a weapon, which would be inaccurate and uneconomical, and probably impossible to achieve at that date, in any case."

Ley had underestimated the German rocketeers. During the nine years since his departure from Germany, the Nazi government had established a great research center at Peenemunde, on the Baltic Coast. There the rocket team headed by von Braun had succeeded in developing the A-4, or V-2, the world's first large ballistic missile.

The wartime record of the V-2, and well-publicized postwar rocket tests at White Sands, New Mexico, fueled public interest in spaceflight. Ley remained a leading commentator on the subject for the rest of his life. He held a variety of positions during the early postwar years, serving for a time as a research engineer with the Washington Institute of Technology in College Park, Maryland; a lecturer on scientific topics at Farleigh Dickinson University; an information specialist with the Office of Technical Services, U.S. Department of Commerce; a technical consultant to the producers of the pioneering science fiction television series "Tom Corbett, Space Cadet"; and, from 1950 to the end of his life, as science editor of the science fiction magazine *Galaxy*.

In 1951 Ley and Haydon Planetarium director Robert Coles organized the First Annual Symposium on Space Travel. Held in New York on 12 October 1951, the symposium featured papers on spaceflight by leading American scientists and engineers. Intrigued by the gathering, Cornelius Ryan, a writer for *Collier's* magazine, began work on what would become a series of eight feature articles on spaceflight. Ryan drew on the expertise of a large number of leaders in the field, but Ley and von Braun were the central figures in the project. With illustrations by artists Chesley Bonestell, Fred Freeman, and Rolf Klep, the articles, which appeared between March 1952 and April 1954, were an enormous success.

Viking Press, which had published Ley's *The Conquest of Space* (1949), transformed the *Collier's* articles into three bestselling books, *Across the Space Frontier* (1952); *The Conquest of the Moon* (1953); and *The Exploration of Mars* (1956). Ley was also an important contributor to three Walt Disney television programs on spaceflight that were inspired by the *Collier's* article. "Man in Space," "Man and the Moon," and "Mars and Beyond" aired on the "Disneyland" television program beginning in September 1955.

Ley continued to produce popular books on science and aspects of spaceflight, including *Dragons in Amber* (1951); *Lands Beyond* (1952); *Salamanders and Other Wonders* (1955); *Exotic Zoology* (1959); *Harnessing Space* (1963); *Beyond the Solar System* (1964); *Watchers of the Skies: An Informal History of Astronomy from Babylon to the Space Age* (1963); *Ranger to the Moon* (1965); and *Mariner IV to Mars* (1966). He served as an adviser to the National Aeronautics and Space Administration and was preparing to leave for the launch of Apollo 11 at Cape Kennedy, Florida, when he died of a heart attack at his home in Jackson Heights, Queens, New York.

Reporting his death, the *New York Times* remarked that Ley had "helped usher in the age of rocketry and then became perhaps its chief popularizer." Captivated as a youth by the dream of spaceflight, he communicated that dream to others in the more than thirty books and countless articles that he produced during his forty-year career as a writer. He was the first important historian of the space age, and one of its most eloquent spokesmen.

• The papers of Ley are in the archives of the National Air and Space Museum, Smithsonian Institution. The Special Collections Department of the library at the University of Alabama, Huntsville, has preserved the 5,000 books and journals that made up Ley's private library. Both institutions maintain additional extensive biographical and bibliographic files on Ley. Additional files of Ley correspondence are in the papers of G. Edward Pendray at Princeton University, and of Wernher von Braun at the University of Alabama, Huntsville. Biographical material appears in "Willy Ley," *Die Rakete*, 15 Aug. 1928, p. 128; Steve Bland, "Sky Guy," *Philadelphia Inquirer Magazine*, 9 Sept. 1951, p. 12; P. E. Cleaton, "A Tribute to Willy Ley," *Spaceflight* 11, no. 11 (Nov. 1969): 408–9; and Lester del Rey, "The First Citizen of the Moon," *Galaxy Magazine*, Sept. 1969, pp. 151–57. An obituary is in the *New York Times*, 25 June 1969.

TOM D. CROUCH

LEYDA, Jay (12 Feb. 1910–15 Feb. 1988), translator, writer, filmmaker, and photographer, was born in Detroit, Michigan. His parents' names are not known.

Leyda grew up in Dayton, Ohio, where he spent his youth experimenting with photography, acting, painting, and sculpture. After high school, Leyda worked on a punch press in Dayton and apprenticed in the studio of the photo-secessionist Jane Reece. He arrived in New York City in 1929 to work as a darkroom assistant for the photographer Ralph Steiner and made a living photographing portraits for small magazines such as *Arts Weekly*. He continued to write and to publish poetry and short stories and to spend time with Walker Evans and other young photographers.

In 1930 Leyda started working as a recording engineer at the Bronx Playhouse, where he first saw the films of Russian director Sergei Eisenstein. With the profits from selling a thrift-shop folk sculpture Leyda bought a sixteen-millimeter camera that he used in his work at the Workers Film and Photo League and to make *A Bronx Morning* (1931). The film was shown by Alfred Stieglitz at An American Place, in addition to being screened at the New School for Social Research and in London. In October 1932, while searching for funding for a second film, Leyda exhibited his portrait photographs at the Julian Levy Gallery. This show accompanied Leyda to Moscow after he was accepted into Eisenstein's directing course at the Moscow State Film School in September 1933.

Between 1934 and 1936, Leyda worked on location for Joris Ivens and Dziga Vertov in the Soviet Union. Leyda provided moral support to Vertov in the wake of the Soviet government's negative reaction to *Three Songs of Lenin* (1934) and assisted in making the minor travelogue films to which Vertov was assigned, particularly *Leningrad*. Leyda also worked with Eisenstein as an apprentice director, still photographer, and production historian for the unfinished *Bezhin Meadow* (1935–1937). During this time Leyda acted as theater correspondent for *Theatre Arts Monthly* and *New Theatre* and maintained close contact with friends in the intellectual left in New York City, such as Steiner, Evans, Paul Strand, Lee Strasberg, Harold Clurman, Stella Adler, Aaron Copland, Joseph Losey, Iris Barry, and Lincoln Kirstein. His intimate connection with Soviet film and theater during this crucial time allowed him to assist Alfred Barr in securing works by Tatlin, Rodchenko, and Stepanova for a show at the Museum of Modern Art (MOMA).

In 1935 Leyda married dancer and choreographer Si-Lan Chen, whom he had met through her sister who attended the Moscow Film School. Shortly thereafter, Leyda accepted the position of assistant curator in MOMA's new film department, to which he brought Eisenstein's only complete print of *The Battleship Potemkin* (1925). While Si-Lan continued to dance abroad before coming to New York in 1937, Leyda shared an apartment in New York City with James Agee, Ben Shahn, and Evans. Between 1936 and 1940 Leyda wrote program notes at MOMA for Russian and Soviet films, titling Ukrainian films, and lecturing on film at Harvard, Columbia, New York University, and the New School. During this time he also worked with Frontier Films as an editor and ad-

viser on both *People of the Cumberland* (1938) and *China Strikes Back* (1937); edited the journal *Films* with Kirstein, Strasberg, and Mary Losey; and edited the film *Youth Gets a Break* (1941) for Joseph Losey. Like other left-wing artists working at this time, Leyda adopted a pseudonym; he called himself Eugene Hill in homage to the early photographers Eugene Atget and David Octavius Hill. This period of Leyda's life ended when he was asked to resign from MOMA in 1940 after Seymour Stern's political attack on his work in *The New Leader*.

In 1941 Eisenstein requested that Leyda translate the four essays that became *Film Sense* (1942); the work that was to become *The Melville Log* (1951) was started at this time as a birthday present for Eisenstein. Leyda moved to Hollywood in 1942 as a technical adviser to MGM and Warner Bros. for Russian-oriented films such as *Mission to Moscow* (1943), *Song of Russia* (1943) and *The Bridge of San Luis Rey* (1944). After being inducted into the army in 1943, then released on honorable discharge following a bout of pneumonia, Leyda found that his left-wing associations were preventing him from working in Hollywood. Leyda continued research on Melville in Boston in 1944, speaking with Eisenstein for the last time in 1945 before returning to Hollywood. He collaborated with Sergei Bertensson on *The Musorgsky Reader* in 1947, then completed *Film Form*, the second series of translations of Eisenstein's essays, in 1949.

Leyda's completion of *The Melville Log*, *The Portable Melville*, and *The Complete Stories of Melville* between 1949 and 1951 reinvigorated Melville scholarship; his continuing interest in Melville led him to begin writing a libretto based on "Bartleby the Scrivener." In 1954 Leyda prepared a story film from the negative of Eisenstein's unfinished *Que Viva Mexico*, and in 1956 he worked again with Bertensson on *Sergei Rachmaninoff: A Lifetime in Music*. In addition, after receiving a Guggenheim award Leyda initiated his research on Dickinson by cataloging the Folger Library's collection, which resulted in *The Years and Hours of Emily Dickinson* in 1960. During this period Leyda started working and living abroad, writing for the BBC in London in 1955 and completing *Kino: A History of Russian and Soviet Film* while in residence at the Cinémathèque Française under Henri Langlois between 1957 and 1958. In 1959 Leyda traveled to China with Si-Lan and found work cataloging non-Chinese films at the Chinese Film Archive. In what had become a pattern, Leyda then assembled a book in 1962 that he described as an "account" of film in China called *Dianying: Electric Shadows*. He continued his indispensable work on Eisenstein by translating *Film Essays with a Lecture* (1968).

Leyda and Si-Lan left China just before the Cultural Revolution reached full swing. They returned to the United States in 1964 for the premiere of the opera *Bartleby the Scrivener*, with libretto by Leyda and music by Walter Aschaffenburg, and the publication of Leyda's *Films Beget Films: A Study of the Compilation Film* (1964). The years 1964–1969 were spent lecturing at the Staatliches Filmarchiv in East Berlin, marked the beginning of Leyda's continued presence as a member of the Venice Film Festival Jury (1965–1969), and found him at the biennial International Film Festival in the Union of Soviet Socialist Republics (1965–1981). During the 1970s Leyda taught classes on Soviet film and D. W. Griffith's films at Yale University, York University, and finally at New York University, where he was named Pinewood Professor of Cinema Studies. In 1977 he published *Voices of Film Experience* and in 1980, *Eisenstein at Work*, with Zina Voynow. The last years of Leyda's life were no less full: he was the voice of Thomas Alva Edison in Charles Musser's *Before the Nickelodeon* of 1982; he began major revisions of *The Melville Log* in 1985; and worked on *Before Hollywood*, a major retrospective of early American cinema, in 1986. Leyda was publicly recognized in 1976 by his election as president of the Melville Society and in 1981 by his receipt of the New York University Great Teacher Award. After a brief illness, Leyda died in New York City. He left a legacy of precise, unflagging, and selfless scholarship.

• The catalog for "Jay Leyda: A Life's Work," by Elena Pinto Simon and David B. Stirk for the exhibition at New York University's Tisch School of the Arts Photography Department Gallery, shown from 29 Jan. to 27 Feb. 1988, has been the crucial source for this biography. Leyda is mentioned to various degrees in the biographies of many twentieth-century artists and intellectuals, most notably in *Footnote to History*, written by Si-Lan Chen Leyda in 1984. Annette Michelson and Rosalind Krauss published a special edition of *October* 11 (Winter 1979), containing essays in honor of Leyda, photographs by Leyda, and a Leyda bibliography. An obituary is in the *New York Times*, 18 Feb. 1988.

ROBIN BLAETZ

LEYENDECKER, J. C. (23 Mar. 1874–25 July 1951), artist and illustrator, was born Joseph Christian Leyendecker in Montabaur, Germany, the son of Peter Leyendecker, a coachman, and Elizabeth Orselfen. In 1882 the family immigrated to Chicago, where his father became a brewer. His parents, like many immigrant families, poured their resources into financing the education of their oldest son, in the Leyendeckers' case, Joseph. His younger brother, Frank Xavier, with whom he was very close, also became a fairly prominent artist and illustrator.

At sixteen Leyendecker apprenticed as an engraver to J. Manz and Company, an engraving firm in Chicago. He used the money he saved while working for the firm to study for close to five years at the Art Institute of Chicago. In 1896 he won first prize in the *Century* magazine poster contest, and the reproduction of his drawing on the cover of the magazine launched his career. By 1897, the prominent *Inland Printer* magazine had reproduced more than a dozen of his drawings on its covers. With his winnings from the contest, his savings, and his parents' financial assistance, he set off for Paris to study art, taking his younger brother with him.

The two studied at the Académie Julian in Paris under Adolphe William Bouguereau. A stringent academic painter (that is, one who paints in accordance with teachings of the established European art academies), Bouguereau was contemptuous of the extremely fashionable "popular art" of Toulouse-Lautrec, Mucha, and Chevet. The brothers Leyendecker were not interested in contemporary artists and, following their teacher, worked diligently to perfect their academic skills, which well served Joseph Leyendecker throughout his career. He became regarded as one of the most gifted artists ever to attend the Académie, and his student art portfolio was placed on permanent exhibition at the Académie until it was destroyed by bombing in World War II.

In 1898 the brothers returned to Chicago and opened a studio in the Stock Exchange Building. Success came quickly, leading to a clientele that eventually included the Carson, Pirie and Scott Department Store, A. B. Kirschbaum Clothiers, and McAvoy Brewery. In 1900, barely a year after Leyendecker's first cover was published by the *Saturday Evening Post*, the brothers moved to New York. Leyendecker's work would grace the cover of the *Post* 322 times. The only artist to exceed that number was Norman Rockwell, an ardent admirer and beneficiary of Leyendecker's work.

In 1905, now firmly established in New York, Leyendecker was hired by Cluett, Peabody, and Co. to create the advertising art for a line of shirts. Out of this project the Arrow Collar Man was born. Soon becoming a common epithet for any handsome, neatly dressed fellow, the Arrow Collar Man was a cultural phenomenon, the subject of poems, songs, even a Broadway play. Arrow collar sales soared, by 1918 to more than $32 million. For Leyendecker, the frenzy gave way to other advertising campaigns, including ones for B. Kuppenheimer and Co.; Hart, Schaffner, and Marx; and Interwoven Socks. In the meantime, his work for the *Post* continued unabated. Between 1903 and 1943 he produced all of the holiday covers for the *Post* as well as many nonseasonal covers. His creation of the New Year's baby and his strutting characters inspired Norman Rockwell's first cover for the *Post*. During World War I and II, but especially World War I, when he worked as an artist for the navy's Division of Pictorial Publicity, Leyendecker created an abundance of posters in support of the war effort.

Meticulous about his work, Leyendecker lived in a perpetual state of nearly missed deadlines because he had the habit of reworking and reworking a sketch. He left behind a copious amount of oil sketches, some work related but many not. He also kept many sketches on hand in the event that an assignment warranted one. Leyendecker normally began his pencil and charcoal drawings with a 2 × 3 sketch—his oils were somewhat larger—that later was transferred to a larger canvas. Relying on the method of "squaring up," he used a pencil to draw a gridlike pattern of lines across the sketch and then bisect the squares with diagonal lines.

He repeated this process over and over, changing diagonals and moving figures or parts of figures to better relate to the total composition, until he was satisfied with the result. The final product was always a combination of fragments that never lost sight of the whole. A "consummate pictorial designer," Leyendecker was a master of composition.

Leyendecker's monumental success yielded generous financial rewards, but he spent his money as quickly as he earned it. He once told Rockwell, "Buy more than you can afford, and you'll never stop working or fret so over a picture that it never gets done. If every day you have to save yourself from ruin, every day you'll work. And work hard." In 1914 Leyendecker built a large mansion in New Rochelle, New York, that he shared with his brother. Inseparable in childhood, they remained just as close well into adulthood. Neither married, and they lived together for most of their lives. Frank, a talented artist in his own right, never escaped his brother's shadow long enough to shine. Yet he was the more social of the two. Whereas Joseph was quiet and withdrawn, Frank was friendly and outgoing. Their relationship became strained, however, in 1901, the year that Charles Beach became Leyendecker's Arrow collar model. There is no conclusive evidence that the relationship was homosexual in nature, but the two men cohabited for over fifty years. Apparently resentful of their relationship, Frank moved out of the house around 1923. He died the following year of a drug overdose.

After his brother's death, Leyendecker retreated even further into his shell. He rarely left the grounds of his house and spent a great deal of time gardening. Nonetheless, his output did not appear to suffer. He continued to produce art and illustration work into the early 1940s and earned more than $50,000 a year. It was in the early 1940s, however, that he began to lose commissions to more "popular" illustrators. Having adhered to a reckless financial credo for much of his life, he eventually had to let his entire staff go and manage his house with the help of Beach. He died of a heart attack on the patio of his house.

For forty years, Leyendecker was the foremost illustrator in America. His famous Arrow Collar Man and his hundreds of *Saturday Evening Post* covers are exemplary illustrations of early twentieth-century commercial art. His solitary existence and withdrawn manner did not detract from his popularity, and people often remarked on his own "natty" appearance. Though not as well remembered as Norman Rockwell, Leyendecker laid the foundation for early to middle twentieth-century illustrative art.

• The main source of information on the Leyendeckers is Norman Rockwell's *My Adventures as an Illustrator* (1960). The only biography of Leyendecker is Michael Schau, *J. C. Leyendecker* (1974). For useful information and several illustrations see Susan E. Meyer, *America's Great Illustrator* (1978), and Walt Reed and Roger Reed, *The Illustrator in America 1880–1980* (1984). For Leyendecker's influence on Rockwell see *Norman Rockwell: A Sixty-year Retrospective* (1972). Useful obituaries are in the *Saturday Evening Post* and the *New York Times*, 26 July 1951.

THOMAS E. TOONE
MICHELLE OSBORN

L'HOMMEDIEU, Ezra (30 Aug. 1734–27 Sept. 1811), lawyer and legislator, was born in Southold, New York, the son of Benjamin L'Hommedieu, a sea captain, and Martha Bourne, prominent members of their community. L'Hommedieu's first name came from his maternal grandfather, Ezra Bourne, who was a distinguished jurist of Sandwich, Massachusetts. His surname was derived from an early ancestor who had fought in the Crusades and received the title "L' Homme de Dieu" (the man of god). Benjamin L'Hommedieu, Ezra's Huguenot grandfather, fled France following the revocation of the Edict of Nantes in 1685 and arrived in America by February of the next year. Within a few years he was a naturalized citizen and had moved to Southold, one of the oldest settlements on Long Island, where he resided until his death in 1748.

L'Hommedieu received his earliest education at home through the help of a private tutor. He then attended Yale College and graduated in 1754. Less than a year later L'Hommedieu's father died, bequeathing him a large estate. Opting for a profession in the law, he studied under a prominent judge in Southold and passed the bar. Eventually he established a successful practice in his hometown and in New York City. At the age of thirty-one L'Hommedieu married Charity Floyd, whose brother, William Floyd, was a future signer of the Declaration of Independence.

As the imperial crisis with Great Britain deepened in the years preceding the American Revolution, L'Hommedieu became radicalized by the oppressive measures levied on the colonists by King George III and his ministers. He was an active patriot during the early 1770s and among the first in Suffolk County to sign the Agreement of the Association, pledging his support to the Continental Congress. His name was placed in nomination at the New York Convention, where he was elected a delegate to the First Provincial Congress in 1775 and subsequently reelected to the next three Provincial Congresses. During the fourth Congress, meeting in Kingston in 1777, L'Hommedieu participated in the drafting of his state's constitution.

When the Provincial Congress was out of session, L'Hommedieu participated on numerous committees, including the Committee of Safety. He also helped to distribute equipment and supplies to the Eastern Militia of Suffolk County. The capable L'Hommedieu was also appointed loan officer, charged with garnering subscriptions for the loans Congress had authorized for the war effort. In this capacity he handled the receipt of funds, ensuring that they were safely deposited. During the evacuation of Long Island in 1776, L'Hommedieu saw to it that guns that had been mounted in his hometown were transported to Saybrook. When funds from the Congress failed to materialize, L'Hommedieu spent his own funds to help other refugees.

As the war continued, L'Hommedieu's name continuously appeared on legislative rolls. Aside from his work with the provincial congresses, he traveled to Philadelphia to serve as a delegate to the Continental Congress from 1779 to 1783. During this time he kept in close touch with New York's governor, George Clinton, advising him of the progress of the war and of his contacts with General George Washington. When peace negotiations began in the war's aftermath, L'Hommedieu kept Clinton apprised of the proceedings, noting on one occasion how property rights for Loyalists remained a key issue: "They observe that the British were very unwilling to make use of any terms that might give uneasinesse to the Refugee Tories." On a matter of key relevance to Clinton, L'Hommedieu informed him in a letter dated 16 October 1783 that "General Washington told me yesterday that he expected the Evacuation of New York would take Place about the Middle of next Month."

L'Hommedieu's service to the Continental Congress was one of many positions he held during the war. At the local level he was clerk of Suffolk County from 1784 until 1811, an office he held successively except for one year. L'Hommedieu also served in the state assembly from 1777 to 1783 and in the senate from 1784 to 1792 and from 1794 to 1809. During his tenure in the state senate, L'Hommedieu served as chairman of the judiciary committee. His advice proved invaluable in 1801 when he was chosen a member of a convention charged with interpreting parts of the constitution, including determining the apportionment of members to each house of the legislature. L'Hommedieu was particularly familiar with this aspect of the constitution because of his service from 1784 to 1798 on the Council of Appointment, which oversaw the election of almost every judicial, civic, and military officer in the state.

Possessing a keen interest in education, and believing particularly in the importance of higher education, L'Hommedieu in 1787 played an important founding role in the reestablishment of the University of the State of New York. Furthermore, he held the office of regent of the state university from its first establishment in 1784 until 1811. L'Hommedieu also envisioned himself an agriculturalist, conducting numerous experiments and then publishing his findings.

L'Hommedieu's wife died in 1785, and in 1803 he married Mary Catherine Havens. Theirs was a happy marriage that resulted in one daughter. L'Hommedieu would not live to see his progeny marry a prominent New York attorney; he died in Southold. "Through a long life," it was inscribed on his tombstone, "[he had] faithfully served in the councils of his country during the arduous struggles of the Revolution and the calm of Independence."

• Valuable primary material that traces L'Hommedieu's involvement in the Revolution appears in the George and James Clinton Papers and the Hugh Hughes Papers, both housed at the Library of Congress. Volume two of the published town records of Southold (1884) also are helpful. Important legislative information appears in the *Journals of the Provincial Congress of New York* (1842). A praiseworthy sketch of his life was written by a relative, William L'Hommedieu, and appears in *Americana*, July 1933. Another dated version of his life, written by C. B. Moore, is in the *New York Genealogical and Biographical Record*, Jan. 1871. For a general treatment of the war, refer to Stephen Conway, *The War of American Independence* (1995); Colin Bonwick, *The American Revolution* (1991); and Edward Countryman, *The American Revolution* (1987).

ELIZABETH T. VAN BEEK

LIBBEY, Edward Drummond (17 Apr. 1854–13 Nov. 1925), business executive in the glass industry, was born in Chelsea, Massachusetts, the son of William L. Libbey, a glass manufacturer, and Julia M. Miller. He was educated in Boston and attended lectures at Boston University. Libbey spent his early career in eastern Massachusetts, a nineteenth-century glass-manufacturing center, where he learned the business of glassmaking from his father. The senior Libbey's experience included executive positions with several Boston-area glass importers and manufacturers, including Jarvis and Commeraiss, the Old England Glass Company, and the New England Glass Company. In 1874 Libbey joined his father in the management of the New England Glass Company, taking charge of the firm at his father's death in 1883. Libbey inherited a shaky firm, and his attempts to put the company on solid footing with innovative product lines, including Amberina, failed in the light of changing consumer tastes and tough competition from factories in the growing western glassmaking center of Pittsburgh.

By 1888 the ambitious Libbey had moved west to Toledo, Ohio, and two years later he married Florence Scott; their one child died in infancy. In Toledo natural gas was abundant and cheap and thus a good source of energy for the company—W. L. Libbey and Son—that Libbey established in 1888 for the manufacture of expensive cut and engraved glassware. In 1892 the name of the company was changed to the name by which it was commonly known, the Libbey Glass Company. Shortly after his arrival in Ohio, Libbey's fortunes became entwined with those of his plant supervisor, Michael J. Owens, a glassworker-turned-inventor who was determined to mechanize the labor-intensive craft of glassblowing. Over the next four decades Libbey became Owens's stalwart supporter and financial backer, ignoring his bankers' advice and agreeing to provide the demanding mechanic with capital for his experiments. The partners' first venture was the Toledo Glass Company, created in 1896 to build and license Owens's semiautomatic equipment for making tumblers and lamp chimneys. Their most important venture was the Owens Bottle Machine Company, established in 1903 to construct and market Owens's automatic bottle-blowing machine. Libbey's other quantity-production companies were geared primarily toward making bulb envelopes for the electrical manufacturers or drawing sheets of window glass for the construction trades. During his long Ohio career, Libbey also held executive positions in the Owens European Bottle Machine Company (established in 1905); the Westlake Machine Company (established in 1907); the Libbey-Owens Sheet Glass Company (established in 1916); and a complex network of other companies designed to further his rapidly expanding Toledo-based glassmaking empire.

The greatest irony of Libbey's career is that his passion for efficiency on the shop floor—manifested in his support of Owens's inventions—eroded the very skills of his craft that were celebrated in the products of his pet firm, the Libbey Glass Company. As the president of this cut-glass factory, Libbey ignored the criticisms of his directors and invested personal funds in an elaborate display at the World's Columbian Exhibition in Chicago in 1893. The investment paid off, for publicity surrounding the miniature glassworks on the Midway Plaisance pushed Libbey's firm to the forefront of the highly competitive cut-glass trade. Again and again, Libbey spared little expense in publicizing his firm's artistic cut-glass products—expensive handcrafted ornaments for middle-class and upper-class tables and whatnot shelves—through national advertising campaigns and elaborate exhibits at local, regional, and national fairs. Libbey continued to encourage glassworkers on his payroll to push their skills to the limit with projects such as the world's largest punch bowl and an elaborate crystal table, both of which brought acclaim to his favorite factory and goodwill to his adventures in mechanization.

Following the perfection of Owens's automatic bottle machine in the early 1900s, Libbey spent considerable time in Europe engaged in intensive negotiations with English and Continental glass manufacturers who sought licenses to use the equipment. During these travels Libbey and his wife also canvassed the European art market, collecting paintings, sculpture, and other works for the Toledo Museum of Art, which they founded in 1901. The Libbeys established the museum's extensive glass holdings between 1913 and 1917, when they purchased important European and American collections for the institution. The couple left the bulk of their fortune to the museum.

Libbey's other business ventures included an executive position with the MacBeth-Evans Glass Company, a Pittsburgh manufacturer of lighting equipment. After Libbey's death in Toledo, the Owens Bottle Machine Company merged with the Illinois Glass Company to form the Owens-Illinois Glass Company, the world's largest manufacturer of glass containers.

Throughout his career, Libbey tried to balance his passion for business with his love of beauty. In his association with inventor Owens, he helped establish Toledo as one of the world's most important glassmaking centers at the turn of the twentieth century. In collaboration with his wife, Libbey made significant contributions to the cultural life of his adopted city.

• Libbey's business and personal papers are at the Corporate Archives of the Owens-Illinois Glass Company in Toledo, Ohio. For accounts of Libbey's career, see Warren Candler Scoville, *Revolution in Glassmaking: Entrepreneurship and Technological Change in the American Industry, 1880–1920* (1948); Carl U. Fauster, *Libbey Glass since 1818* (1979); and Lura Woodside Watkins, *Cambridge Glass, 1818 to 1888: The Story of the New England Glass Company* (1930). Libbey is placed in the context of his industry in Pearce Davis, *The Development of the American Glass Industry* (1949). See also Susan E. Maycock, *Survey of Architectural History in Cambridge: East Cambridge*, rev. ed. (1988).

REGINA LEE BLASZCZYK

LIBBEY, Laura Jean (22 Mar. 1862–25 Oct. 1925), writer, was born probably in Brooklyn, New York, or Springfield, Massachusetts, the daughter of Thomas H. Libbey, a surgeon, and Elizabeth Nelson. Libbey spent most of her life in Brooklyn, where she attended public schools as a child before spending three years at Vassar College from which she never graduated. Her father apparently died when she was very young, and her domineering mother insisted that Libbey remain unmarried despite numerous proposals. Her mother exerted such a strong influence over Libbey that she was able to marry only after her mother's death in 1898.

Libbey's literary talents first came to the attention of a schoolteacher, who directed a composition written by the precocious fourteen-year-old to the desk of Robert Bonner, editor of the *New York Ledger*. Bonner paid Libbey five dollars for her piece but advised her to wait until she was eighteen to submit more work to him. Libbey followed his advice and at the age of eighteen became a regular contributor to the *Ledger* as well as the *Fireside Companion* and the *Family Story Paper*. Libbey wrote numerous serial stories for these journals, and they were later reprinted in cheap paperbound editions costing between fifteen and twenty-five cents by publishers such as George Munro and Street & Smith's. Libbey's melodramatic stories of labor and love contain young heroines named little Leafy or pretty Guelda who attempt to overcome the dangers that independent life in a modern city poses. In addition to her income from these stories, Libbey supported herself by editing Munro's New York *Fashion Bazaar* from 1891 to 1894 and by writing special articles for the *Evening World* and the *Chicago Tribune*. At the height of her popularity Libbey boasted an income of over $60,000 a year, $10,400 of which came from her editorship of the New York *Fashion Bazaar*.

Libbey wrote the bulk of her novels in this serialized fashion and reached the height of her popularity in the 1880s and 1890s, but her career came to a temporary halt with her marriage to Van Mater Stilwell, a Brooklyn lawyer, in 1898. Despite her assumption of a traditional domestic role as a wife, she resumed writing nine years later when a theatrical manager, Charles E. Blaney, solicited a dramatization of one of her novels, *Miss Middleton's Lover* (1888), for a series of melodramas that he was presenting. Libbey collaborated with James R. Garey, and the resulting play, *Parted on Her*

Bridal Tour, was produced in March 1907 at Blaney's Theater in Brooklyn. Although Libbey would go on to write over 120 plays at the prodigious rate of two or three per week, none of her subsequent plays was produced during her lifetime. She continued to write novels until 1923, but despite the fact that her older titles still sold relatively well in urban centers, Libbey had to publish her later novels herself. By the time she died in Brooklyn, Libbey had faded into near obscurity, and none of the major New York papers even carried her obituary. Her tombstone was inscribed with her maiden name, the name she had kept throughout her professional life.

The formulaic character of Libbey's stories was commented on both during and after her brief heyday; indeed, Libbey quit writing for the *New York Ledger* in 1914 because Bonner complained about the similar plots in all her serialized stories, and modern critics, despite their differing assessments of Libbey's work, always emphasize the structural similarities in her plots. Today Libbey is perhaps best known for her contribution to the working-girl novel. Her version of the familiar theme depicts a working-class heroine, bereft of the comforts of her family and rural home, who must negotiate an always menacing urban public space as she struggles to earn a living working in a factory. This heroine must keep her virtue intact in the face of unwanted advances by the upper-class villain, who abuses the working girl and often resorts to violence and trickery in order to accomplish a seduction that is usually figured as a marriage plot. Despite these predicaments, the working girl always emerges unscathed, due to some technicality or circumstance that renders her marriage invalid. This plot contrivance makes it possible for the working girl to marry the hero of the story, the wealthy young man who is usually the factory owner's son. Through her marriage to the wealthy heir at the end of the story, the working girl is forever lifted from the toils of the factory floor. In addition, her marriage is often accompanied by the disclosure that she herself is an heiress, and her newfound status becomes a correlative of the noble nature that she had demonstrated while still apparently a member of the working class.

During Libbey's lifetime, critics reviewed her books with condescension and equated the appreciation of her novels with a lack of educated taste. The few literary critics who wrote about her work after her death echoed that judgment, dismissing her books as mass-market pulp without any literary value. Some critics have also argued that her novels served the dominant socioeconomic interests of her day by providing working-class women with fantasies of class mobility that obscured their actual conditions. While it is true that Libbey's novels invoke the setting of the workplace only to leave it, and that their depictions of orphaned working women marrying wealthy young heirs were improbable, some recent critics have attempted to rethink the relationship between Libbey's novels and her audience. These critics refute the notion that such works of popular culture foster a passivity inimical to class consciousness or feminist solidarity in the workplace. On the contrary, these critics ascribe significance to the fact that Libbey shifted the settings of her novels from the domestic interiors that characterized so much of nineteenth-century fiction to the public workplaces that predominate in her stories. Through this shift, Libbey helped redefine the boundaries of young womanhood to include paid wage labor outside the home. In addition, her novels always posit a realm of possibility for young women beyond the factory floor, and therefore these working-girl novels act as a utopian protest against the working conditions of these newest urban laborers.

• Some of Libbey's best-known working-girl novels include *Leonie Locke: The Romance of a Beautiful New York Working Girl* (1889); *Willful Graynell; or, The Little Beauty of the Passaic Cotton Mills* (1890); *Little Leafy, the Cloakmaker's Beautiful Daughter: A Romantic Story of a Lovely Working Girl in the City of New York* (1891); *A Master Workman's Oath; or, Coralie the Unfortunate: A Love Story Portraying the Life, Romance, and Strange Fate of a Beautiful New York Working Girl* (1892); and *Only a Mechanic's Daughter: A Charming Story of Love and Passion* (1892). Other noteworthy novels not explicitly about the working girl include *A Fatal Wooing* (1883); *Madolin Rivers; or, The Little Beauty of Red Oak Seminary: A Love Story* (1885); *Parted at the Altar* (1893); and *Wooden Wives: Is It a Story for Philandering Husbands?* (1923). The one anomaly of Libbey's career remains *A Forbidden Marriage; or, In Love with a Handsome Spendthrift* (1888), as Libbey ended her story not with the marriage of heroine and hero, but with the death of the heroine in a train wreck and the subsequent death of the lovesick hero on the frosty grave of his beloved. The vociferous response by Libbey's readership ensured that this departure from formula was never again repeated.

For an interview with Libbey, see Victor Rousseau in *Harper's Weekly*, 23 Jan. 1909, pp. 12–13. An insider's view into Libbey's literary production is given by her secretary, Louis Gold, in the *American Mercury*, Sept. 1931, pp. 47–52. The most useful appraisals of Libbey's career and significance are Joyce Shaw Peterson, "Working Girls and Millionaires: The Melodramatic Romances of Laura Jean Libbey," *American Studies* 24, no. 1 (1983): 19–35, and chapter 10 of Michael Denning, *Mechanic Accents: Dime Novels and Working-Class Culture in America* (1987). Libbey's marriage and death certificates can be found in the New York City Dept. of Health.

MICHAEL MAIWALD

LIBBY, Orin Grant (9 June 1864–29 Mar. 1952), historian, was born on a farm near Hammond, Wisconsin, the son of Asa B. Libby and Julia W. Barrows, farmers. Following his graduation from River Falls State Normal School in 1886, Libby taught high school until 1890. He then entered the University of Wisconsin at Madison.

After completing his B.Litt. degree in 1892, Libby stayed at Wisconsin to study history with Frederick Jackson Turner. Three years older than Libby, Turner guided the younger man for the next decade. The two men shared an analytical approach to history and an interest in geography. Libby's 1893 master's thesis, "De Witt Clinton and the Erie Canal—A State Enterprise," displayed his interest in economics. Libby's doctoral dissertation, "The Geographical Distribution of the Vote of the Thirteen States on the Federal Constitution, 1787–8" (1894), impressed Turner. The originality of Libby's approach, his careful numerical calculations, and his detailed map linking geographic and economic variables to Federalist and Anti-Federalist voting gradually attracted widespread attention, particularly after his map was published in several leading U.S. history textbooks.

Beginning in 1895 Libby taught alongside Turner as an instructor in the Department of History at Wisconsin. Libby expanded his research to include both Wisconsin history and voting behavior in the early U.S. Congresses. He also pursued his lifelong fascination with ornithology. In 1900 he married Eva Gertrude Cory; they had two children. Unfortunately, Libby's initially cordial relationship with Turner deteriorated. Once his student's enthusiastic advocate, Turner developed doubts about Libby's ability to synthesize the results of his research. In 1902 Turner terminated Libby's appointment. Understandably, Libby thereafter believed that his former mentor had treated him unfairly.

Libby immediately moved to the Department of History at the University of North Dakota, where he initially served as an assistant professor and the department chair. Although he later made at least one serious attempt to secure a position at the State Historical Society of Wisconsin, Libby spent the remainder of his career in Grand Forks. North Dakota and its developing state university offered the hardworking young scholar considerable opportunity. His students found him well prepared, stimulating, and demanding. Libby turned the focus of his historical research to the upper Missouri and upper Mississippi river valleys as well as to his adopted state. He maintained that the region he defined as "the New Northwest" properly included the northern plains of the United States together with those of southern Canada. His multiple publications on the eighteenth-century travels of the La Verendrye family challenged Francis Parkman's interpretation of their ventures. In 1912 Libby conducted oral history interviews with nine surviving Arikara Indian scouts who had served with General George A. Custer. His *Arikara Narrative of the Campaign against the Hostile Dakotas, June 1876* appeared in 1920. The Arikara named the diligent professor "Long-Man who-gets-things-right."

Libby's indefatigable work and distinctive accomplishments in public history overshadowed his effective teaching and valuable publications in western history. He generously employed his organizational skills for the benefit of both North Dakota and regional historical associations. Beginning in 1903 he helped revitalize the North Dakota Historical Society. As its secretary (1903–1945) and president (1903–1909), Libby built its collections and expanded its programs. He supervised the systematic acquisition of territorial and state newspapers. Libby repeatedly crisscrossed North Dakota and Minnesota in order to collect artifacts, pioneer narratives, and Native-American history. His interviews with Mandan and Hidatsa Indians helped preserve their past. In 1906 Libby initiated publication of the society's annual *Collections*, editing the first nineteen volumes. In 1926 Libby was responsible for starting the *North Dakota Historical Quarterly*, which he edited until 1944.

Libby consistently promoted the study of North Dakota history, including the history of Native Americans, in his state's public schools. Libby also oversaw the development of a system of six state parks. He advocated the reestablishment of indigenous grasses and trees in these parks and suggested that park visitors ought to be able to converse with resident Indian families.

In 1907 Libby helped organize the Mississippi Valley Historical Association, which he served as president in 1909–1910. When the association met in Grand Forks in 1914, its members viewed an outdoor historical pageant written under Libby's supervision. Libby also served two terms on the editorial board of the *Mississippi Valley Historical Review* (1914–1917 and 1924–1927).

A committed progressive, the outspoken Libby alienated conservatives on his campus. The public admiration he had earned proved particularly useful to him in 1920, when his open support for the controversial Non-Partisan League nearly cost him his faculty position. The university president found it impossible to fire the well-known professor but reduced his departmental responsibilities.

Libby's research on the Constitution and his articles on politics continued to interest scholars in the twentieth century. His most persistent critic, Charles Beard, praised Libby's dissertation but rejected Libby's later arguments denying the existence of political parties prior to 1798. Libby, in turn, charged that Beard overstated the effect of economic issues on political behavior. In his *Economic Origins of Jeffersonian Democracy* (1915), Beard dismissed Libby's "mathematical" politics. Beginning in the 1950s, however, innovative political historians applauded Libby's emphasis on social science history and appropriated his quantitative techniques. Since the 1960s New Left historians have reevaluated both Libby and Beard and renewed scholarly debate over the relationship between economic interests and the rise of political parties in the new nation. Libby's work in Native-American history also found a fresh audience in the 1980s among some members of the rising generation of "new" western historians.

Recognized as Turner's ablest early student and as the father of North Dakota history, Libby retired in 1945 after a university career of fifty years. Precise and often blunt, he had intimidated or antagonized some professional peers but had also charmed civic groups and earned the affection of schoolchildren. He died in Grand Forks.

• Libby's incomplete papers are housed in the Orin G. Libby Manuscript Division of the library of the University of North Dakota. A paper that Libby delivered at the 1895 meeting of the American Historical Association was published as "A Plea for the Study of Votes in Congress," *American Historical Association, Annual Report* 1 (1896): 321–34. Libby's Mississippi Valley Historical Association presidential address, published as "Professional Ideals," *Mississippi Valley Historical Association, Proceedings* 3 (1909–1910): 86–95, outlines his values. Libby's analysis of the rise of the Democratic-Republican party appears in "A Sketch of the Early Political Parties in the United States," *Quarterly Journal of the University of North Dakota* 2, no. 3 (April 1912): 205–42, and "Political Factions in Washington's Administration," *Quarterly Journal of the University of North Dakota* 3, no. 4 (July 1913): 293–318. His critical review of Beard's *An Economic Interpretation of the Constitution* (1913) is in the *Mississippi Valley Historical Review* 1, no. 1 (June 1914): 113–17. Important to understanding Libby's research interests are his articles "Some Verendrye Enigmas," *Mississippi Valley Historical Review* 3, no. 2 (Sept. 1916): 143–60, and "The New Northwest," *Mississippi Valley Historical Review* 7, no. 4 (Mar. 1921): 332–47. The most useful introduction to Libby's work is Robert P. Wilkins, "Orin G. Libby: His Interests, Ideas, Opinions—An Annotated Bibliography," *North Dakota Quarterly* (Summer 1956): 71–93. See also Wilkins, "Orin G. Libby: His Place in the Historiography of the Constitution," *North Dakota Quarterly* (Summer 1969): 5–20.

JULIENNE L. WOOD

LIBBY, Willard Frank (17 Dec. 1908–8 Sept. 1980), chemist and university professor, was born in Grand Valley, Colorado, the son of Ora Edward Libby and Eva May Rivers, farmers. When Libby was five his family moved to Santa Rosa, California. After graduation from high school in Sebastapol, he entered the University of California at Berkeley, where he majored in chemistry. He received a B.S. in 1931 and a Ph.D. in chemistry two years later.

From 1933 to 1941, Libby taught chemistry at the University of California at Berkeley, where he rose from instructor to tenured associate professor. In 1940 he married Leonor Hickey, a schoolteacher; they had twin daughters. His research on how neutrons work, on the chemistry of radioactive elements, and on chemical elements in gaseous states, attracted national recognition and resulted in a Guggenheim Fellowship that enabled him to spend the 1941–1942 academic year at Princeton University. Shortly after U.S. entry into World War II in December 1941, Libby joined the Manhattan Project at Columbia University, where until 1945 he worked on a team that devised a gaseous-diffusion process for separating uranium isotopes, a process that was fundamental to producing an atomic bomb.

In 1945 Libby was appointed professor of chemistry at the University of Chicago. There he served as a member of the university's Enrico Fermi Institute for nuclear studies until 1954, when President Dwight D. Eisenhower appointed him to the Atomic Energy Commission, on which he served actively for five years. Upon completing his term on the AEC in 1959, Libby was appointed professor of chemistry at UCLA. The following year, he received the Nobel Prize in chemistry for his pioneering work in radiocarbon dating.

Libby remained at UCLA until his retirement in 1976. From 1962 he was also director of UCLA's Institute of Geophysics and Planetary Physics, in which capacity he was concerned with studying the atmosphere of planets, earthquake control, space and lunar research, and a range of related fields. His first marriage ended in divorce in 1966, and in the same year Libby married Leona Woods Marshall, professor of environmental engineering at UCLA. They had no children.

Libby had far-ranging interests, an insatiable intellectual curiosity, and a broad intellect. Yet, as Glenn Seaborg, 1951 Nobel laureate in chemistry, observed, he was "a painstaking, patient, and effective teacher," always approachable and firmly committed to undergraduate education, in which he actively engaged as frequently as he could.

Radiocarbon dating was Libby's most celebrated scientific contribution. In the 1930s chemists knew that the nuclei of radioactive isotopes are unstable and emit alpha, beta, and gamma rays during decay. Earlier researchers had used radioactive nuclei to trace chemical reactions. Walther Bothe, 1954 Nobel laureate in physics, had developed in the 1930s a coincidence counter whose various electrical detectors measured simultaneous discharges of radiation. Working from Bothe's measuring techniques, Libby created in 1953 a measurement chamber with both internal and external radiation detectors that, by reducing the effects of background radioactivity, made it possible to measure extremely low-level radiation more accurately than ever before.

In 1939 a New York University research group headed by Serge Korff discovered that cosmic rays, when they strike atoms in the upper atmosphere, produce cascades of neutrons that nitrogen, which comprises some 80 percent of the atmosphere, absorbs, causing it to decay into a radioactive isotope of carbon, carbon 14. Intrigued by these findings, Libby speculated that, through the cosmic ray activity that Korff and his colleagues had described, the nitrogen in the upper atmosphere was converted to radioactive carbon, which, when it bonded with oxygen in the air, became carbon dioxide, a major element in photosynthesis. Organisms nourished by plants would necessarily contain radioactive carbon, whose half-life is 5,730 years.

Libby further contended that all living organisms through the uptake of carbon dioxide maintain a constant level of radioactivity, but that when they die, the level decreases in predictable amounts based upon the half-life of carbon 14. Using this information, Libby found that accurately measuring the amount of radioactivity in organic material would provide a reliable means of dating it. The implications for archaeologists, anthropologists, historians, paleontologists, geologists, and other scholars were tremendous. In time Libby's method, now widely validated, changed conclusively humankind's perceptions of many historical contentions, such as the dates of the Ice Age or of the Dead Sea Scrolls. He died in Los Angeles.

Libby's method of dating had a profound effect on the interpretation of history. Among other findings, he provided convincing evidence that the Ice Age in North America ended about 10,000 years ago rather than 25,000 years ago, as had been the previous conjecture. By 1961 forty radiocarbon dating laboratories had been established throughout the world that, according to Professor Goodwin of Cambridge University, attempt to act in cooperation with one another and publish annual definitive data lists in the *American Journal of Science*. Although it cannot date organic material over 70,000 years old, Libby's method has remained the best measurement to date of organic matter within that limit.

• Many of Libby's papers are at UCLA and at the University of Chicago. Among Libby's most notable publications are *Radioactive Dating* (1952), and *Isotopes in Industry and Medicine* (1955), which updates the work of chemist George de Hevesy, who in 1922 was at the forefront of devising ways to use radioactive nuclei to trace chemical reactions, in the light of Libby's own research with radioactive elements. Libby's broader interests are reflected in *Solar System Physics and Chemistry: Papers for the Public* (1981), a collaboration with Leona Marshall Libby, and in his *Collected Papers* (1981). A full account of Libby's most celebrated work is found in the Nobel Prize Committee's report, *Le Prix Nobel en 1960* (1961), along with his acceptance speech, in which Libby details his work in radiocarbon dating. H. Goodwin presents an informed and appreciative account of Libby's scientific contributions in *Proceedings of the Royal Society, London* (1961). Theodore Berland, *The Scientific Life* (1962), considers Libby within the context of the scientific era in which he flourished. A more recent appreciation and analysis of Libby's work appears in Glenn T. Seaborg, "Willard Frank Libby," *Physics Today* 34 (Feb. 1981): 92–93. An obituary is in the *New York Times*, 10 Sept. 1980.

R. BAIRD SHUMAN

LIBERACE (16 May 1919–4 Feb. 1987), entertainer, was born Wladziu Valentino Liberace in West Allis, Wisconsin, the son of Salvatore (Sam) Liberace, an often unemployed french horn player, and Frances Zuchowski, a coproprietor of a mom-and-pop grocery store. Liberace, called Walter at home, was a sole-surviving twin and the third of four children. By the age of four he could play by ear and at seven performed Paderewski's Minuet in G for the composer, who advised the family to take the boy's talent seriously. A scholarship to the Wisconsin College of Music in Milwaukee was awarded him in 1926.

Liberace was a sickly child, prone to bouts of pneumonia. His frail health caused him to miss school, but at age eleven his piano jobs began to help support the family during the depression. He gave his first professional concert at age thirteen. In his mid-teens he had a band that played school dances, and he soloed in Milwaukee night clubs for twenty-five dollars a week plus tips. He also played at style shows, stag parties, and weddings, as well as for a dancing school. During this time, his mother preserved his future career by nursing a gangrenous finger that doctors wanted to amputate.

He appeared as a soloist with the Chicago Symphony in 1936 as Walter Liberace, displaying his classical side, but he earned most of his money playing popular music in clubs as Walter Buster Keys. After graduating from Milwaukee West High School, Liberace left home to earn a living as, alternately, a classical pianist and a popular musical performer. The two pursuits came together in 1939 at a classical recital when a member of the audience requested a popular novelty song for an encore. Liberace played it in a mock-serious classical style, to the delight of the audience, as reported in a wire service story titled "The Three Little Fishies Swim in Sea of Classics." In 1940, as the intermission pianist at the Persian Room in New York, Liberace learned to disarm audiences by saying out loud what he thought they were thinking—to heckle himself. This part of his act would turn out to have enormous popular value: it was futile to mock Liberace since he enjoyed the joke so much himself.

A spinal injury kept Liberace out of World War II. In 1945 he dropped his first name and began to establish himself as a major piano act, with his brother, George, as his conductor, violinist, and business manager. By the late forties, his act featured stage props, including an imitation Louis XIV candelabrum. By 1950 Liberace was earning $60,000 a year as a performer.

What propelled him to stardom was television. Beginning with a local show on Los Angeles KLAC-TV, Liberace was the summer replacement for Dinah Shore. By 1953, he was the host of a filmed half-hour syndicated show that was seen on more stations than *I Love Lucy*. Liberace began each program looking directly into the eyes of the audience and winking wantonly. His personal warmth, the living room-like nature of his stage conversation, and his willingness to share his personal feelings with his viewers made him not only America's first television matinee idol but, by 1954, the nation's biggest solo attraction, earning, according to *Billboard*, "the highest grosses ever attained by a pop concert artist."

Liberace—this was now his legal name—was a popular-culture phenomenon in 1954, his television show seen by an estimated 35 million viewers and his 230,000 registered fans helping him break box office records in every venue, from the Hollywood Bowl to Madison Square Garden. At one point he was also the number one seller of record albums. Critics complained that his audience consisted primarily of middle-aged and older women. But while the big-city newspapers were harsh, small-town papers were friendly. "Nobody loves me but the people," Liberace observed.

In an era of mindless masculinity, Liberace brought romance and sentimentality to middle America. Women dressed up to watch his television show and left lipstick marks on the screen. Men, especially married men, resented the affection. What did women see in Liberace? "Pleasant relief from what I have to look at every day: Loudmouths! Chest-beaters!" a Bronx housewife told *Collier's*. Like Elvis Presley, Liberace made women feel beautiful, made them feel as if they had been alone with him at his concert. As early as 1954 Liberace was followed from city to city by women fans known only by their wardrobes: the Green Hornets, the Ladies in White.

During these concerts Liberace wore white tails and white shoes. He played the Minute Waltz in 37 seconds, sang "September Song" and "I'll Be Seeing You," talked for twenty minutes between numbers, presented his mother to the audience and wept (along with the audience), played "*Reader's Digest* versions" of classical compositions, parlor favorites, and popular ballads, performed "The Rosary" and "Beer Barrel Polka" back to back, and invariably introduced a handsome man as his "chauffeur and friend."

Liberace's popularity faded in 1955. *Sincerely Yours*, a movie in which he played a deaf pianist, bombed, but he found new audiences in Europe. Though he was enthusiastically received in London in the fall of 1956, the sexual ambiguity he displayed onstage led the *Daily Mirror* to attack him as a "Neuter," an "It," and "the biggest sentimental vomit of all time." Liberace alleged that the paper had called him a homosexual and sued, successfully, for libel, proving that in the 1950s you could call someone a communist even if he weren't, but not a homosexual even if he were. "I cried all the way to the bank," Liberace used to joke, but in fact the homosexual accusation seriously damaged his career at the time. In 1958 he went conservative with his stage persona until deciding that his fans wanted him to be flamboyant and outrageous.

Throughout the 1960s Liberace was on the road for thirty to forty weeks a year. In 1963 he collapsed on stage; kidney failure caused by the carbon tetrachloride used to clean his costumes almost killed him. In the 1970s he developed his Las Vegas act and subsequent reputation as the world's highest-paid entertainer. In 1976 he established the Liberace Foundation and in 1979 opened the Liberace Museum. That year, his contract with the MGM Grand Hotel was reported to be worth $3 million a year.

After his mother died in 1980, Liberace began to tour extensively, traveling with sixty wardrobe cases full of exotic and expensive costumes. In 1982, a former "chauffeur and friend" sued him, unsuccessfully, for $113 million, alleging that Liberace had broken his promise of lifelong financial support in exchange for sexual favors. In 1984, the entertainer drew 82,000 fans in fourteen performances at Radio City Music Hall. For his entrance he wore a $300,000 rhinestone-studded Norwegian blue-fox cape with a sixteen-foot train and was driven on stage in a silver-mirrored Rolls-Royce. The ten costumes for the engagement cost over $1 million. The next year he set a Radio City house record: 21 standing-room-only performances for 103,000, with a gross of $2.4 million. At his last engagement in New York in the fall of 1986 everything was red, white, and blue: the Rolls-Royce, the sequined and feathered robe, the hotpants suit underneath, and the baton he used to lead the Rockettes in "The Stars and Stripes Forever." Outrageous and

flamboyant to the end, he went out on top, having been "Mr. Showmanship" for an unprecedented four decades.

His health deteriorating, Liberace canceled his 1987 engagements to go on vacation. He was sixty-seven years old when he died of AIDS at his vacation home in Palm Springs, California. *Newsweek* estimated that for more than twenty-five years his average earnings had been $5 million a year. *Time* observed that the gaudy excess of his performances paved the way for Elvis and glitter rock, and that his androgynous stage personality prefigured the careers of Mick Jagger, Elton John, David Bowie, and Boy George.

Liberace always remained coy about his sexual orientation. Though he never acknowledged his homosexuality, he never hid it either. When he emerged on the scene in the homophobic 1950s, he said he refused to worry about "lavender-tinted innuendoes," and indeed in later years his stage banter became bolder and his show took on a distinct homosexual aura. Despite his relative openness about his sexual orientation, he perpetuated the stereotype that gay males were effeminate. His fans in middle America either refused to believe what they saw or looked beyond it to the man they loved. "Remember that bank I used to cry all the way to?" he used to tell them. "I bought it."

• Liberace's famous costumes, stage jewelry, pianos, and other artifacts are on exhibit at the Liberace Museum in Las Vegas, attracting an estimated 200,000 visitors a year. As author, Liberace published, with Carol Truax, *Liberace Cooks!* (1970); his autobiography, *Liberace* (1973); *The Things I Love*, ed. Tony Palmer (1976); and *The Wonderful Private World of Liberace* (1986). For references to Liberace's early career, see Richard G. Hubler, "Liberace," *Cosmopolitan*, Dec. 1954, pp. 104–11, and Richard Donovan, "Nobody Loves Me But the People," *Collier's*, 3 Sept. 1954, pp. 28–32, and "Liberace: The Power of Love," *Collier's*, 17 Sept. 1954, pp. 72ff. An interview published in Karl and Anne Taylor Fleming's *The First Time* (1975) presents Liberace's frankest attempt to explain his sexual orientation. For an analysis of his concerts see Edward Rothstein, "Liberace, the King of Kitsch," *New Republic*, 2 July 1984, pp. 25–29. Richard Corliss, "The Evangelist of Kitsch," *Newsweek*, 3 Nov. 1986, p. 96, reviews Liberace's last engagement at Radio City Music Hall. The most comprehensive account is the 1986 *Current Biography Yearbook*, pp. 307–11. Scott Thorson's *Behind the Candelabra: My Life with Liberace* (1988) is a tell-all book by a former chauffeur and friend who sued him. Useful obituaries may be found in the *New York Times*, 5 Feb. 1987; *Newsweek* 16 Feb. 1987; and *Time*, 16 Feb. 1987.

JAMES M. SALEM

LIBMAN, Emanuel (22 Aug. 1872–28 June 1946), physician and medical researcher, was born in New York City to Fajbush Libman and Hulda Spivak, a prosperous middle-class couple. Libman acquired most of his education in New York City, attending local public schools and the City College of New York. From an early age he was drawn to medicine. After he graduated from City College in 1891, Libman entered medical school at the Columbia University College of Physicians and Surgeons, receiving his M.D. in 1894. He then accepted an internship at New York's Mount Sinai Hospital, beginning an association with that institution that would endure for the remainder of his life.

During his internship, Libman encountered Abraham Jacobi, the founder of modern pediatrics. Inspired by this mentor, he first considered a career in pediatrics. When he completed his internship, he traveled to Europe for postgraduate training in that specialty. (Many young doctors in Libman's position went overseas to study.) Among the world-renowned physicians Libman encountered in Austria and Germany was the Austrian Theodor Escherich, with whom he studied enteritis in infants. During his time in Escherich's laboratory, Libman became adept in bacteriology and was successful in isolating streptococcus from the blood of a live patient. Many of his colleagues later credited this early success for Libman's change of heart about his specialty. When he returned to New York at the end of 1897, he accepted the post of assistant pathologist of Mount Sinai.

Libman entered the field of pathology at a heady time for medicine. Confirmations of the germ theory, first postulated by Robert Koch in 1875, had revolutionized medical research, and pathologists were among the pioneers who, on a seemingly daily basis, were uncovering new knowledge about the human body. Libman continued to apply the research methods he had learned abroad, studying the bacteriology of blood and performing autopsies to determine the cause of death. With his home located a scant three blocks from his hospital laboratory, Libman in the early years of his career was able to devote most of his time to his scientific investigations.

Much of the work that Libman did related to endocarditis, an infection of the inside of the heart that can lead to death. By the end of his career, Libman had become an unquestioned authority on this disease. Along with his colleague Benjamin Sacks in 1924, Libman isolated a new form of endocarditis, which they originally termed atypical verrucous endocarditis. Unlike most other varieties of endocarditis, this disease occurs in the absence of bacteria as a byproduct of the body's immune system.

His research triumphs aside, Libman was also known among his colleagues for his clinical diagnostic skills. He often asserted to medical students that he could determine what disease was present in a patient by his acute sense of smell, and he was known for predicting disease in strangers just on the basis of their appearance. In 1903 Mount Sinai Hospital appointed him as an adjunct physician; he was promoted to an attending physician in 1915 and a consulting physician in 1925. He saw a number of distinguished patients in his New York private practice, including Chaim Weizmann, the first president of Israel, and Albert Einstein. Shortly before Gustav Mahler's death in New York City in 1911, Libman diagnosed the great composer as having bacterial endocarditis.

Libman's professional contacts extended beyond his hospital to the world of clinical research, in which he was a well-respected figure. In 1908 he was one of the founding members of the American Society for Clinical Investigations. Libman published extensively in medical journals throughout his life. Libman was also a committed medical educator, lobbying for federal funds to improve Mount Sinai's education programs.

In 1931 Libman established the New York Academy of Medicine's "Graduate Fortnights" to encourage people to share their own work. This program brought together his colleagues and their students in a workshop setting. Libman was also instrumental in establishing a number of fellowships for medical education and research, including one at the Tuskegee Institute in Alabama. During World War II he established the Henry Dazian Foundation for Medical Research, an organization that gives Latin-American doctors an opportunity to come to America.

Reared in a Jewish household, Libman retained his ties to the faith, joining the Hadassah Medical Advisory Board in 1917. In 1921 he became the treasurer and later the chairman of the American Jewish Physicians Committee, which helped spearhead the effort to build Hebrew University in Jerusalem. In 1927 Libman realized a lifelong goal and visited Palestine.

Remembered by his colleagues as a brusque man, Libman also had his softer side. Although he was never well compensated for his work at the hospital, he paid his secretary a salary three or four times greater than his own out of his own pocket. Libman, who never married, also maintained a fondness for music, from Strauss to symphonic tunes, and was himself a piano player. In 1942 the American Medical Association awarded him a Silver Medal for his work on nonbacterial endocarditis, which by this time had been renamed Libman-Sacks disease in tribute to the two researchers who first identified it.

Upon Libman's death in his beloved New York City, two of his colleagues wrote: "He was steeped in medicine throughout his life." Indeed, this devoted clinician and introspective researcher witnessed an incredible evolution in his own field. When he first started, no one had identified the numerous causes of endocarditis; by shortly before his death, doctors had developed chemotherapy and surgical techniques not only to diagnose the disease but also to cure it.

• Libman's research interests are described in Edward Hook, "Emanuel Libman and Infective Endocarditis: Comments on *The Etiology of Subacute Infective Endocarditis*," *American Journal of the Medical Sciences* 309 (1995): 71–73. Information on Libman's days at Mount Sinai can be found in Joseph Hirsh and Beka Doherty, *The First Hundred Years of the Mount Sinai Hospital of New York* (1952). For an account of his trip to Palestine, see Manfred Waserman, "Dr. Emanuel Libman Visits Palestine: An Historical Note," *Israel Journal of Medical Sciences* 26 (1990): 713–18. A description of his encounter with Mahler occurs in David Levy, "Gustav Mahler and Emanuel Libman: Bacterial Endocarditis in 1911," *British Medical Journal* 293 (1986): 1628–31. For a perspective on the world of clinical research in which Libman worked, see A. McGehee Harvey, *Science at the Bedside: Clinical Research in American Medicine, 1905–1945* (1981). Obituaries include Bernard S. Oppenheimer, "Emanuel Libman," *Bulletin of the New York Academy of Medicine* 23

(1947): 116–17; Bernard Sutro Oppenheimer and Charles Friedberg, "Emanuel Libman," *Journal of the Mount Sinai Hospital* 13 (1946–1947): 215–23; and the *New York Times*, 29 June 1946.

SHARI RUDAVSKY

LICHINE, David (25 Oct. 1910–26 June 1972), dancer and choreographer, was born at Rostov-on-Don, Russia, the son of Michael Liechtenstein, a musician and composer known professionally as Mikhail Olshansky, and Anna Egorova. Lichine's family left revolutionary Russia when he was nine. They lived in Bulgaria and Turkey and eventually joined the large Russian émigré community in Paris. Lichine began law studies at the Sorbonne, and simultaneously, in his late teens, he began to study ballet. His principal teachers were Lubov Egorova and Bronislava Nijinska, who brought him into the company of Ida Rubenstein, where she was the choreographer and where he debuted in 1928. He danced briefly in Anna Pavlova's company, and Léonide Massine hired him for a ballet at La Scala, Milan.

Lichine was one of the young dancers chosen to complement several seasoned performers for a new company to be based in Monte Carlo, codirected by René Blum and Colonel Wassily de Basil with George Balanchine as the choreographer, which would continue the lineage of the Diaghilev Ballets Russes. In a memoir published in the *Dancing Times* (Sept. 1939), Lichine wrote, "I remember the day. . . . It was the year 1932, one morning at the Egorova studio in Paris. Colonel de Basil, George Balanchine, and Boris Kochno were sitting watching the class. It was the beginning of a new era for the Russian ballet." Their first performances were in Monte Carlo and Paris in the spring of 1932 with three new ballets by Balanchine, *Le Bourgeois Gentilhomme*, *Concurrence*, and *Cotillon*, and one by Massine, *Jeux d'Enfants*. That winter Massine was hired to replace Balanchine as the company's choreographer. He created four new works, among them *Les Présages*, the first of his controversial symphonic ballets, with the leading roles of the lovers in the second movement for Irina Baronova and Lichine. The company performed during the summer of 1933 in London, where a season planned for three weeks was triumphantly extended to four months and concluded with the premiere of *Choreartium*, a second symphonic ballet by Massine, again with a leading role for Lichine.

The company traveled to New York for its first U.S. tour, sponsored by Sol Hurok. Little ballet had been seen in America since the mid-1920s, and Hurok was taking a sizable risk in presenting a Russian ballet company during the Depression. The visit began with a Christmas 1933 season at the Saint James Theater, New York. Then the company split, and Lichine, Baronova, and Tatiana Riabouchinska headed a troupe for two months of New York performances while the rest of the company embarked on a cross-country tour. The units reunited in Chicago for February 1934 performances, and the tour was extended

through the spring. For their second London season the company moved to the prestigious Royal Opera House. The next North American tour began in Mexico City with the inauguration of the Palacio de Bellas Artes, proceeded to Canada, and continued with seasons in large American cities and five months of touring smaller cities and towns by train. The 1935–1936 season followed the same pattern. In America, helped by Hurok's excellent publicity and well-organized touring apparatus, the Ballet Russe built an American audience for ballet. An article in *Time* (20 Apr. 1936) reported, "Ballet had suddenly become a rage . . . 100 U.S. cities visited by [Ballets Russes de] Monte Carlo dancers since last October . . . capacity audiences in Little Rock, El Paso, Portland" on a tour of twenty thousand miles. Similarly, in England the Ballets Russes was a feature of the Royal Opera House seasons until 1939 and an integral aspect of London artistic life.

Throughout the 1930s Lichine was the young male star of the Ballets Russes de Monte Carlo, sharing the spotlight with the so-called "baby ballerinas"—Tatiana Riabouchinska, Tamara Toumanova, and Irina Baronova—and the established star dancers Massine and Alexandra Danilova. Lichine was noted for his performances in the Massine ballets, particularly *Les Présages*, and in many ballets in which Nijinsky had been famous, such as *Schéhérazade*, *Les Sylphides*, *Le Spectre de la Rose*, and *L'Après-midi d'un Faune*. The critic Edwin Denby wrote of his Faun, "Lichine excelled. It is a part that demands exceptional imagination, as well as a great plastic sense. And Lichine had besides these a fine simplicity" (Osato, p. 118). In Danilova's autobiography *Choura* (1986), she called him "a capable, handsome artist, rather temperamental. . . . His dancing wasn't classical, but it was dynamic: he became the role he was dancing" (p. 119).

Lichine was ambitious to create ballets, and he was encouraged by de Basil and aided by Massine. After two minor apprentice works, he had his first success with *Francesca da Rimini* (1937), a ballet to Tchaikovsky's *Romeo and Juliet* score that was based on the Dante story of the love affair of Paolo and Francesca. *Protée* (1938) was also well received. That fall, in the gathering shadow of European war and embroiled in a messy split between de Basil and Massine (which resulted in a competing Ballet Russe company), the de Basil company departed for Australia, where it opened a historic tour in September and remained until April 1939. Lichine had injured a knee and danced sparingly in Australia, concentrating on choreography. His *Prodigal Son* premiered in Melbourne to glowing reviews. When the company returned to London for the summer 1939 season, Lichine was officially billed as choreographer in chief. The company was booked to return to Australia in the fall. The dancer Sono Osato wrote, "When war broke out, Massine's company was as widely scattered throughout Europe on holiday as de Basil's. . . . Massine and Hurok had left for America. . . . Stranded and jobless, the many men who had Nansen passports could not hope to escape the draft [and be sent, perhaps, to the Maginot line]. . . . In desperation, Massine's dancers turned to de Basil for help . . . de Basil added nearly 20 dancers to the company" (pp. 167–68). They safely reached Australia in December. It was during this tour that Lichine created *Graduation Ball*. Centered on a cadet and a young girl, roles danced by Lichine and Riabouchinska, the ballet offered a cascade of technically challenging duets, trios, solos, and group dances and an ebullient atmosphere. It premiered on 1 March 1940 in Sydney and was an immediate hit.

The company left Australia in September and opened an October–March American tour in Los Angeles. Lichine's *Graduation Ball* had become the company's signature piece and during a nine-week season in New York was given thirty-seven times. The company was facing financial crises, and the long tour ended in Havana in a dancers' strike. Lichine was among those who were stranded in Cuba, and he created an Afro-Cuban dance act that played several months at the Tropicana nightclub. Back in New York in 1942, he staged the jazz dances in a George Abbott musical, *Beat the Band*.

Lichine affiliated himself with the new Ballet Theatre company during the early 1940s and made a folk ballet, *Fair at Sorochinsk* (1943). Michel Fokine had started *Helen of Troy* but was taken ill; unable to continue, he left the completion of the ballet to Lichine.

Lichine was one of the many European artists who gravitated to Hollywood. As early as 1939 he had been filmed in an Adolph Zukor short, *Spring Night*. Sequences in Walt Disney's *Fantasia* (1940) were based on Ballets Russes dancers: Hyacinth Hippo and Ben Ali Gator were Riabouchinska and Lichine. Lichine appeared in and staged conga production numbers for *Something to Shout About* (Columbia Pictures, 1943) and danced with Eleanor Powell in *Sensations of 1944* (United Artists), with Tatiana Riabouchinska in *Make Mine Music* (Disney, 1946), and with Tamara Toumanova in *Tonight We Sing* (Twentieth Century–Fox, 1953). In addition, he was the dance director for *North Star* (Goldwyn, 1943) and *The Unfinished Dance* (MGM, 1947), with Cyd Charisse and the ten-year-old Margaret O'Brien.

Lichine and Riabouchinska married sometime in the 1940s; they had been a couple for many years. He had been married once before, in 1933, to another dancer, Lubov Rostova. That relationship had ended in divorce. As a young man Lichine had a reputation as a womanizer, as mentioned in several published accounts. Danilova wrote, "There were innumerable intrigues, little scenes, many tears on his account" (p. 119).

Lichine and Riabouchinska rejoined the de Basil company one last time in 1946 in Mexico City, where she danced *Les Sylphides* despite being five months pregnant with their daughter, his only child. The company, which had survived World War II in South America, was in serious decline. Lichine and Riabouchinska continued to appear as guest artists, and Lichine restaged his ballets or created new works for numerous companies, including the London Festival Ballet, Le Grand Ballet du Marquis de Cuevas, the Netherlands Ballet, and the ballet troupe of the Teatro Colón in Buenos Aires. Lichine created two ballets in 1948 for Les Ballets des Champs-Élysées, *La Création*, danced without music, and *Le Rencontre*, which made an instant star of Leslie Caron, whom Lichine had chosen from the corps.

Beginning in the early 1950s, Lichine and Riabouchinska operated a ballet studio in Beverly Hills. Their concert groups, named in several variations of the wording Ballet Society of Los Angeles, were part of numerous attempts to establish a viable classical ballet company in southern California. Lichine became an American citizen in 1956. He died in Los Angeles.

In the absence of films of his concert works, it is difficult to evaluate Lichine's choreographic contributions. Choreography depends for its survival on a continuous performing tradition, and Lichine was working during the upheavals of international war. His *Graduation Ball* remained a favorite for two decades and is still occasionally revived, but contemporaries remember *Protée* and *The Prodigal Son* as outstanding. As a dancer, Lichine was a leading star of the Ballets Russes de Monte Carlo, which in the 1930s brought the art to a receptive public. The seasons in London and Australia and tours to hundreds of communities across the North American continent established a national audience for ballet.

• Lichine published an article, "Ballet Milestones," on the history of the de Basil Ballets Russes in *Dancing Times*, Sept. 1939, pp. 629–30, and "Thoughts of a Choreographer" in *Ballet*, Sept. 1947, pp. 13–15. The principal sources for this account are oral histories with Tatiana Riabouchinska and Irina Baronova in the Dance Collection of the New York Public Library for the Performing Arts; recollections in published autobiographies of Sono Osato (1980), Léonide Massine (1968), Alexandra Danilova (1986), and Cyd Charisse (1976); Kathrine Sorley Walker, *De Basil's Ballets Russes* (1982); and Vicente Garcia-Marquez, *The Ballets Russes: Colonel de Basil's Ballets Russes de Monte Carlo, 1932–1952* (1990). Brief (and somewhat fanciful) biographical sketches appear in books by Gladys Davidson and by Margaret F. Atkinson and May Hillman. Additional material may be found in an unsigned obituary in *Dance Magazine*, Aug. 1972, and in Irving Deakin, *Ballet Profile* (1936), and four books by Arnold Haskell, *Balletomania* (1934), *The Balletomane's Scrapbook* (1936), *Dancing around the World* (1938), and *Balletomane's Album* (1939). An obituary is also in the *New York Times*, 21 July 1972.

MONICA MOSELEY

LICHTENSTEIN, Tehilla Rachael (16 May 1893–23 Feb. 1973), Jewish spiritual leader, was born in Jerusalem, Palestine, the daughter of Chaim Hirschenson, an Orthodox rabbi, and Chava Cohen. She came to the United States at the age of eleven and grew up in Hoboken, New Jersey, where her father served as spiritual leader of a small, Orthodox congregation. Like her sisters Esther (Taubenhaus), Nima (Adlerblum), and Tamar (de Sola Pool), Tehilla Hirschenson received an exceptionally good secular education, earning a

B.A. in classics from Hunter College in 1915 and then an M.A. in literature from Columbia University. She had begun to study for her doctorate in English literature at Columbia when she left school in 1919 to marry Reform Rabbi Morris Lichtenstein. She soon gave birth to two sons. The Lichtensteins spent most of their married life in New York City, where Tehilla remained until her death.

Tehilla Lichtenstein saw herself as religious by nature and actively tried to cultivate a personal relationship with God. From 1922 to 1938 she worked closely with her husband in developing a movement known as Jewish Science. Initiated as a Jewish alternative to Christian Science, Jewish Science, according to the Lichtensteins, was nothing more than "Applied Judaism," that is, the application of Jewish teachings to everyday life. Although theologically it differed greatly from Christian Science, espousing, for example, the reality of matter and evil and the benefits of modern medicine, Jewish Science, like Christian Science, emphasized God's immanence, goodness, and healing power. It also drew upon many of Christian Science's prayer techniques, including affirmation and visualization, which served as the primary distinction between Jewish Science services and services conducted in Reform congregations throughout the United States.

During the society's early years, Tehilla Lichtenstein served as principal of its religious school and editor of its monthly periodical, *The Jewish Science Interpreter*. She later wrote articles that appeared in the *Interpreter* and lectured widely. Her assumption of religious leadership came about by circumstance rather than by design. Morris Lichtenstein died in November 1938. In his will, he specified that should neither of their sons be willing to succeed him, his wife should do so. After her sons declined, Lichtenstein agreed to become leader of the society in order to ensure the continuation of her husband's religious vision. In so doing, she became the first American woman to serve as spiritual leader of an ongoing, Jewish congregation. According to the *New York Times*, more than 500 people attended the first service at which Tehilla Lichtenstein preached, on 4 December 1938. The numbers gradually lessened, yet she retained a loyal following of several hundred persons, many of whom remained in the society long after her death. In 1956 the society completed the building of a synagogue in Old Bethpage, Long Island. Often employing a local rabbi to lead services there, Lichtenstein continued to preach at the society's "home center," that is, the hall in New York City that housed services held by the society on Sunday mornings.

Lichtenstein continued to identify herself as her husband's disciple, yet many of the images she used and the ideas she espoused in her sermons clearly were her own. Having spent much of her adult life as a wife and mother, her sermons, for example, frequently drew on images related to motherhood, marriage, and the home. Thus, while she spoke of God as a kind, benevolent, loving, and accessible father, she often compared the love that God feels toward humanity with the love a mother feels for her children. Without explicitly identifying God as a female divinity, she maintained that "God has given each one of us . . . this same equalizing gift—our mother's love, which is, on this earth, the nearest thing, the closest thing, to the love that God bears for mankind. Mother's love is of the same substance, it is of the same divine fabric, and expresses itself in the same boundless way."

Like Morris Lichtenstein, Tehilla Lichtenstein envisioned Judaism as a communal religion. Yet, while her husband minimized the concept of divine election, Tehilla stressed the importance of Jews viewing themselves as members of a chosen people. She insisted that, despite what others might believe, "there is no arrogance involved in that claim; only a sense of destiny . . . [and] great responsibility." She also had a greater attachment than he to the land of Israel and before 1948 spoke frequently and passionately about the founding of a Jewish state. Afterward, she continued to voice her support, maintaining the hope that Israel would enrich the world by incorporating into its notion of statehood the ideals and teachings of Judaism.

The Lichtensteins believed that Judaism was a practical religion and that all prayer was efficacious. Yet perhaps because by the late 1930s American Jews were drawn less to the teachings of Christian Science than to those of Norman Vincent Peale, Tehilla Lichtenstein placed greater emphasis than her husband on the power of positive thinking, which she identified as the power of positive prayer. Many of her sermons and weekly radio broadcasts in the 1940s focused on specific "how to's": How to Acquire a Sense of Self-Worth, How to Achieve Happy Human Relationships, How to Influence Your Enemies and Make Them Your Friends, and so on. She retained a keen interest in psychology and wrote numerous sermons detailing the relationship between psychology and religion. Although she once referred to psychoanalysis as "hokum," she recognized that psychology can help a person overcome fear and worry and that psychology, together with religion, can help one conquer feelings of self-doubt and self-renunciation.

Yet Tehilla Lichtenstein felt that the practicality of Judaism's teachings extended far beyond the development of an effective personality. In numerous sermons, especially during the Second World War and the Cold War of the 1950s and early 1960s, she applied Jewish teachings, as understood by Jewish Science, to national and international problems. Tackling such issues as Nazi aggression, Soviet foreign policy, and anti-Semitism in postwar America, she underscored that Judaism can meet, and provide an answer to, any and all situations. Illness forced her to step down from the pulpit in 1972, but she continued to serve as spiritual leader of the society until her death.

Tehilla Lichtenstein remains historically significant for the religious leadership role she assumed thirty-four years before the ordination of women as rabbis. The more than 500 sermons she wrote serve as an important resource for those interested in Jewish Science, and they offer a rare view of Jewish spirituality as seen through the eyes of an exceptional, early twentieth-century Jewish woman.

• Tehilla Lichtenstein's papers, including her sermons and recordings of her radio broadcasts, as well as copies of the *Jewish Science Interpreter*, are housed in the offices of the Society of Jewish Science, Plainview, N.Y. Copies of her sermons can also be found in the American Jewish Archives, Cincinnati, Ohio. More easily accessible is Doris Friedman, ed., *Applied Judaism: Selected Jewish Science Essays by Tehilla Lichtenstein* (1989). For a description of the first service at which she preached see the *New York Times*, 5 Dec. 1938, p. 25. An obituary is in the *New York Times*, 26 Feb. 1973.

ELLEN M. UMANSKY

LIEB, Frederick George (5 Mar. 1888–3 June 1980), sportswriter, was born in Philadelphia, Pennsylvania, the son of George August Lieb and Theresa Zigler (occupations unknown). Lieb grew up in South Philadelphia and became interested in writing when his parents gave him a toy printing press as a Christmas gift. He attended Philadelphia public schools, graduating from Central Manual High School in 1904. Although an avid baseball fan, following the Phillies in local papers, Lieb did not attend his first professional game until 1904. Following high school, he went to work as a clerk for the Norfolk and Western Railroad from 1904 to 1910. While employed there he unsuccessfully sought a job with Philadelphia newspapers as a sportswriter. Finally, in 1909, *Baseball Magazine* agreed to publish biographies that he wrote on Honus Wagner, Fred Clarke, Ty Cobb, and Hugh Jennings. Soon he was also writing baseball fiction for *Short Stories*.

After six months with the Philadelphia News Bureau reporting financial news, in 1910 Lieb began a full-time sportswriting career that lasted until shortly before his death. His big break came when the *New York Press* hired him to cover the New York Giants baseball team for the 1911 season at $35 a week. With incentives, including duty as official scorer, Lieb was making about $60 a week. At age twenty-three he was working at a job that combined his two loves, baseball and writing. In April 1911 he married his high school sweetheart, Mary Ann Peck; they had one daughter.

Lieb joined a New York sportswriting scene that included Damon Runyon, Grantland Rice, and Heywood Broun. In 1920 he became a nonvoting member of baseball's rules committee and was instrumental in the rule change that awarded a batter a home run when the game-winning hit cleared the fence in the last half of the home inning. Earlier, the batter was awarded only a single. Lieb also was a member of the Baseball Writers Association, serving as president from 1922 until 1924 and as the chief scorer for the World Series. He remained a sportswriter in New York until 1943, writing for the *Press*, the *Post*, and the *Morning and Sunday Telegram*. In 1935 he began thirty-five years of writing for the *Sporting News*. Also in 1935, the Liebs bought a winter home in St. Petersburg, Florida, and in 1965 he began writing a column, "The Hot Stove League," for the *St. Petersburg Times*.

While in New York, Lieb became friends with many of baseball's greatest players, among them Babe Ruth and Lou Gehrig. In 1923, the year Yankee Stadium opened, Lieb dubbed it "The House that Ruth Built," a name that has stuck. His friendship with Ruth lasted until Ruth's death when Lieb served as an honorary pallbearer. He also established friendships with Yankees manager Miller Huggins, Philadelphia Athletics manager Connie Mack, and baseball commissioner Kenesaw Mountain Landis. Landis encouraged Lieb to tour Japan with a team of baseball stars in 1931, the first such tour in major league history.

In a career that spanned sixty-eight years Lieb witnessed much baseball history. In that time he attended sixty-six World Series—more than 200 games. He was in the press box when the Yankees' Carl Mays felled Ray Chapman of the Indians with a fastball that resulted in Chapman's death, the only onfield fatality in major league history. Lieb was one of the first writers to suspect that first baseman Hal Chase of the Yankees was throwing games in 1913. By 1918 the evidence against Chase was too strong, and he was banished from baseball, playing his final season in 1919 with the New York Giants.

Lieb wrote eighteen books, most under his own name, but also ghostwrote J. G. Taylor Spink's *Judge Landis and Twenty-five Years of Baseball* (1947) and Bob Considine's *The Babe Ruth Story* (1948). He wrote team histories of the Baltimore Orioles (1955), Boston Red Sox (1947), Philadelphia Phillies (1953), Pittsburgh Pirates (1948), and St. Louis Cardinals (1945), as well as a biography of Connie Mack (1945). His most important work was his 1977 autobiography. During his lifetime he was referred to as baseball's greatest historian, and over the course of his career he received many accolades. He became a member of the Old Timers Committee for the National Baseball Hall of Fame in 1965 and was inducted into the Hall in 1972.

Lieb was a tall, lanky man with a quick wit. His understated writing style relied more on fact than on flash. He wrote in his autobiography, "I did try to inject humor into my stories but I was never an iconoclast. . . . I took baseball seriously as a profession, despite its being a game, and I took baseball writing seriously as a profession. I think I wrote first of all to satisfy Fred Lieb the reader of sports pages."

• Material regarding Lieb is available in his files at the Baseball Hall of Fame in Cooperstown, N.Y., and the *Sporting News* archives in St. Louis, Mo. For more information on Lieb, see his autobiography, *Baseball As I Have Known It* (1977). Obituaries are in the *New York Times*, 5 June 1980; the *St. Petersburg Times*, 4 June 1980; and the *Sporting News*, 21 June 1980.

BRIAN S. BUTLER

LIEB, John William (12 Feb. 1860–1 Nov. 1929), electrical and mechanical engineer, was born in Newark, New Jersey, the son of John William Lieb, a leather worker, and Christina Zens. Both sides of Lieb's family immigrated to the industrial city of Newark from Württemberg, Germany, his mother's family after first spending a number of years in Antwerp, Belgium. While growing up, Lieb learned German and French as well as English. He acquired his formal education in the local public school and at the Newark Academy, a private high school, from which he graduated in 1875. Perhaps influenced by his father's interest in chemistry and mechanical technology, Lieb entered the preparatory high school connected with the Stevens Institute of Technology in nearby Hoboken, New Jersey, in September 1875. A year later Lieb became a student in mechanical engineering at the Stevens Institute.

While at the Stevens Institute Lieb first became interested in the newly emerging electrical industry. Among his class assignments he assisted with tests of the Brush arc light system in fall 1877 at the Coney Island pier. In early 1880 he and his classmates also visited Thomas Edison's Menlo Park Laboratory to see the newly invented incandescent electric lighting system. Lieb's practical experience with the Brush arc light led to his joining the Brush Electric Company in Cleveland after graduation. Hired as a draftsman, Lieb was soon being trained as a central station constructor and manager. However, while visiting his family over the Christmas holidays, he met with Edison to ask for a job and in January 1881 began his long association with the Edison electric light interests.

Lieb joined the staff of the Edison Electric Light Company at its 65 Fifth Avenue headquarters in New York City. He initially worked as a draftsman in the company's engineering department but was soon transferred to the Edison Machine Works on Goerck Street, where he assisted in the development of generators and other equipment for the Pearl Street central generating station. When this station opened in September 1882, Lieb was placed in charge.

Lieb's knowledge of central station technology as well as his facility with French impressed Italian professor Giuseppe Colombo during the latter's visit to the Edison Machine Works to observe tests of dynamos for the central station his Italian Edison Company was building in Milan. As a result, Colombo requested that Lieb be sent to Milan to supervise the installation of the Milan station. He became chief electrician of the plant, which was put into service in March 1883. Lieb, who soon became fluent in Italian, was appointed chief electrician of the Italian Edison Company when it was reorganized later in the year as the Societa Generale Italiana di Elettricita Sistema Edison. As the company began to erect other central power stations in the second half of the decade, Lieb took on increasing technical responsibilities, supervising both the company's power plant business and its manufacturing facilities.

During his years in Italy Lieb was an innovative leader of the electrical industry. The Milan station was among the first to install an alternating current distribution system in 1886, and in connection with this he conducted some of the earliest experiments with direct-driven alternators connected in parallel. The same year he also introduced the Thomson-Houston arc light system for street lighting in the city. In 1892–1893 Lieb directed the installation of Milan's first electric trolley line and one of the earliest in Italy.

Lieb continued to maintain close ties to the United States and married Minnie F. Engler while visiting New York in 1886. (The couple had three children.) In 1894 he returned permanently to the United States when he became assistant to R. R. Bowker, vice president of the Edison Electric Illuminating Company of New York (later New York Edison). As general manager, and later vice president, Lieb was in charge of all the company's technical operations, including the installation and operation of its central stations and electrical distribution system and supervision of all research and development efforts. At the time of his death, Lieb was senior vice president of New York Edison and president of the Electrical Testing Laboratories, which he had helped to found.

Lieb led an active professional life as a member and officer of several technical and scientific societies and congresses in the United States and Europe and also served on many industry associations and public commissions related to the energy industry. Honored for his work by both the Italian and French governments, Lieb also received the Edison Medal of the American Institute of Electrical Engineers. After becoming a member of the Raccolta Vinciana of Milan during his stay in Italy, Lieb retained a lifelong interest in Leonardo da Vinci, collecting a large library of Vinciana. Lieb died at his home in New Rochelle, New York.

Lieb was a major figure in the early electric utility industry. As station manager at Pearl Street in New York City and then of the Edison plant in Milan, Italy, he was responsible for the operation of two of the most important early electric central stations in the world. He was an innovative leader of the Edison company in Italy, introducing a number of major improvements. Finally, during his years with the Edison Electric Illuminating Company of New York, he became a leader of the electric utility industry in the United States.

• Letters and other documents by Lieb appear in Thomas E. Jeffrey et al., eds., *Thomas A. Edison Papers: A Selective Microfilm Edition* (1985–); other material, including some of Lieb's articles and speeches and an obituary sketch, may be found in the Edison Pioneers Collections at the Edison National Historic Site, West Orange, N.J., and the Henry Ford Museum, Dearborn, Mich. A book-length biography of Lieb has yet to be published, but the Electrical Testing Laboratories published *John William Lieb: An Appreciation* (1930), and an article-length biographical sketch appeared in the *Stevens Indicator* 37 (1930): 6–15. An obituary is in the *New York Times*, 2 Nov. 1929.

PAUL B. ISRAEL

LIEBER, Francis (18 Mar. 1798 or 1800–2 Oct. 1872), educator and political writer, was born in Berlin, Germany, the son of Friedrich Wilhelm Lieber, an iron merchant. (His mother's name is not known.) Raised in a large middle-class family of nationalistic sentiments, Lieber witnessed the conquering of Berlin by

Napoleon in 1806. He fought in the Colberg militia and was wounded in the Waterloo campaign in 1815. An adherent of the educator Friedrich Ludwig Jahn, active in secret patriotic societies, and (falsely?) implicated in the assassination of August von Kotzebue, Lieber was spied on and twice imprisoned by the police. He received a Ph.D. in mathematics from Jena in 1820 and also studied at Halle, Dresden, and Berlin. Under the influence of Barthold Niebuhr, Friedrich E. D. Schleiermacher, and Alexander von Humboldt, he was drawn mainly to the study of politics, law, and history. Fearing further persecution, in 1826 he left Germany for England where, as a tutor, he met his future wife, Mathilda Oppenheimer. In 1827 he emigrated to the United States. He married Mathilda in 1829 and became a naturalized citizen three years later.

In America, Lieber's career turned principally on higher education and political writing. His lifelong dedication to educational reform found early outlets in presiding over the new Boston Gymnasium in 1827, in preparing a plan for Girard College in 1834, and in organizing and editing the first *Encyclopaedia Americana* (1829–1833). He assisted Alexis de Tocqueville and Gustave de Beaumont in their gathering of statistics on the penitentiary system in the United States and then translated and annotated their finished volume in 1833. He also wrote his own pamphlets on penology and prison reform—including *Education and Crime* (1835)—that posited education as a deterrent to crime and favored the Pennsylvania system of solitary confinement. In these efforts Lieber was assisted and befriended by some of America's most influential thinkers and political activists, including Joseph Story, James Kent, Charles Sumner, John C. Calhoun, Daniel Webster, Edward Livingston, Jared Sparks, John Pickering, and George Ticknor.

Failing to find permanent academic employment in the North, Lieber accepted a chair in history and political economy at South Carolina College in Charleston in 1835. During his 21-year stay there, he wrote his three principal theoretical works in political science: *Manual of Political Ethics* (1838), *Legal and Political Hermeneutics* (1839), and *On Civil Liberty and Self Government* (1853). The last of these proved to be a popular college textbook. During this period, Lieber also wrote numerous shorter studies in history, linguistics, philology, and political economy, including *Essays on Property and Labour* (1841).

In these works, Lieber pioneered a theory of the modern state that incorporated the sentiments of liberal nationalism and republican constitutionalism. He favored a strong national union and opposed the doctrines of states' rights, nullification, protectionism, utilitarianism, and communism. He maintained the principle of popular sovereignty but rejected social contract theory on the basis that the natural and historical condition of men and women is found in society. The state, for him, is a "jural society," that is, a society understood in terms of its legal sovereign identity. The government is simply the administrative organization of the state, the principal concern of which is to promote individual development and free trade. Believing that citizens are under ethical obligations and the duties of liberty to participate in institutional self-government, Lieber formulated (in various works) his most famous phrase: "No Right without its Duties; no Duty without its Rights." He also thought that citizens in their varying capacities are bound to take upon themselves the task of interpreting important texts and actions. Lieber contributed to this latter task, especially in *Hermeneutics*, by developing a set of principles for interpretation and construction. Drawing upon statistical and historical sources for all his works, Lieber displayed the sort of empirical understanding of modern states and political processes that became known as the historical, comparative method.

Sensing the pending breakup of the Union and tired of suppressing his sympathies for the nation and against slavery, Lieber left South Carolina in 1856 and moved to New York. He accepted Columbia College's offer of a chair as well as the honor of titling it. By his own design he became professor of history and political science, thereby becoming the first officially named political scientist in America. He made clear in his inaugural address that he took his field to be "the very science for nascent citizens of a republic." During the Civil War he advised the U.S. government in legal matters and organized the voluminous output of the Loyal Publication Society. He also wrote an important pamphlet on *Guerilla Parties Considered with Reference to the Laws and Usages of War* (1862) as well as *A Code for the Government of Armies in the Field, as Authorized by the Laws and Usages of War on Land* (1863). Solicited by General Henry Halleck, Lieber's code was turned into a set of instructions issued by President Abraham Lincoln as General Orders No. 100. These instructions were later influential on the accords that emerged from The Hague Conference of 1899 and 1907. As chief of the bureau of rebel archives, Lieber also investigated the papers of Jefferson Davis and other Confederate leaders for possible trials of treason. The Civil War exacted a great personal toll on Lieber's family. Two of his three sons fought for the Union, one losing an arm; the third died a Confederate soldier at the battle of Williamsburg.

After the war, Lieber returned to active scholarly work at Columbia, in the School of Law, writing monographs and pamphlets on nationalism, international law, and constitutional reform. He became a founding member of the reformist American Social Science Association and helped to lay the groundwork for Columbia's School of Political Science, which was formally established in 1880 by Lieber's successor, John W. Burgess. Because of his preeminence as a writer on international law, Lieber also presided as umpire over the Mexican Claims Commission in 1870.

Lieber died in New York City while Matilda read to him. Eulogies that compared him to Tocqueville and Montesquieu were generous indeed. More sober remembrances were later made by Elihu Root, who praised Lieber as "a patron saint" of the study of international law, and by Merle Curti, who deemed him "the most significant figure" in developing a theory of American nationalism. Lieber also continues to deserve remembrance as one of the principal architects of the academic study of politics in the United States.

• The main body of Lieber's voluminous papers and manuscripts is to be found in the Henry E. Huntington Library, San Marino, Calif. Significant collections are to be found also at Johns Hopkins University, Columbia University, and the Library of Congress. Lieber's personal library is now shelved amid the volumes at the University of California at Berkeley. Lieber's other published works include *The Stranger in America* (1835), *A Popular Essay on Subjects of Penal Law* (1838), and several shorter works collected in *Miscellaneous Writings: Reminiscences, Addresses, and Essays*, ed. Daniel C. Gilman (2 vols., 1881). Early uncritical biographies by Thomas Sergeant Perry, *The Life and Letters of Francis Lieber* (1882), and Lewis R. Harley, *Francis Lieber: His Life and Political Philosophy* (1899), were rendered obsolete by Francis Freidel, *Francis Lieber: Nineteenth Century Liberal* (1947), which remains the major work about Lieber. Aspects of Lieber's political thought are interpreted in Elihu Root, "Francis Lieber," *American Journal of International Law* 7 (1913): 453–69; Merle Curti, "Francis Lieber and Nationalism," *Huntington Library Quarterly* 4 (1941): 263–92; Bernard E. Brown, *American Conservatives: The Political Thought of Francis Lieber and John W. Burgess* (1951); Wilson Smith, *Professors and Public Ethics: Studies of Northern Moral Philosophers before the Civil War* (1956); James Farr, "Francis Lieber and the Interpretation of American Political Science," *Journal of Politics* 53 (1990): 1027–49; Peter Knupfer, *The Union As It Is: Constitutional Unionism and Sectional Compromise, 1787–1861* (1991); and John G. Gunnell, *The Descent of Political Theory: The Genealogy of an American Vocation* (1993).

JAMES FARR

LIEBERMAN, Saul (25 May 1898–23 Mar. 1983), Jewish scholar, was born in Motol, Poland, the son of Moshe Lieberman, a scholar in rabbinics, and Liba Katzenellenbogen-Epstein. He received his ordination from the Slobodka yeshiva (rabbinical seminary) in Kovno, Lithuania, in 1916. He then studied talmudic philology and Greek language and literature at the Hebrew University of Jerusalem, which awarded him an M.A. in 1931. After lecturing in Talmud at the Hebrew University and teaching at the Mizrachi Teachers Seminary in Jerusalem, in 1940 he moved to the United States, where he spent the next forty-three years at the Rabbinical School of the Jewish Theological Seminary of America in New York City. He was appointed professor of Palestinian literature and institutions and became, in 1971, the Distinguished Service Professor of Talmud. He led numerous teaching and research institutions, including the Harry Fischel Institute for Talmudic Research in Jerusalem (1935–1940), the Rabbinical School of the Jewish Theological Seminary of America (1949–1983), and the American Academy for Jewish Research (various times in the 1950s and 1960s). Lieberman married Rachel Rabinowitz in 1922; they had no children. Rachel Lieberman died in 1930, and two years later Lieberman married Dr. Judith Berlin, who predeceased him.

Although his early education was in the yeshiva, Lieberman became convinced that the most effective method of clarifying and explaining rabbinic literature was the scientific study of the rabbinic texts in light of their contemporary cultural context. Thus he grounded his research in the Palestinian Talmud and the Tosefta within the context of the classical world, its languages and cultures. His profound knowledge of philology, archaeology, and Semitics became important elements of this pioneering cross-cultural approach. The Palestinian Talmud (compiled approximately in the middle of the fourth century and primarily at Tiberias on the Sea of Galilee), although important to the development of Jewish oral law, had been the subject of few commentaries and considerably less study than had its more-compendious counterpart, the Babylonian Talmud. Similarly, the Tosefta (compiled approximately between the third and fourth centuries), the vast collection of tannaitic material that was not included by the redactor of the Mishnah, had never been exposed to a thorough, systematic exposition by anyone who was as familiar with the Jewish and the classical sources as was Lieberman. The first fruits of Lieberman's methodology appeared in *Al ha-Yerushalmi* (1929), which explained for the first time several obscure passages in the Palestinian Talmud. This was followed by a number of other works on the Palestinian Talmud, including *Talmuda Shel Keisarin* (1931), in which Lieberman challenged several fundamental assumptions about the dating and origin of major portions of the Palestinian Talmud. During this period he also wrote *Hayerushalmi Kifshuto* (1934), a comprehensive commentary on three tractates of the Palestinian Talmud—Shabbat, Eruvin, and Pesachim.

Lieberman next turned his attention to his other lifelong preoccupation, the Tosefta. In this enterprise as well Lieberman succeeded in producing a masterful commentary in which textual errors were systematically exposed and corrected in convincing fashion, primarily by reference to talmudic quotations found in the texts of the Rishonim, the early commentators on the Talmud (*Tosefet Rishonim*, 4 vols., 1936–1939). The publication of this work created a sensation among scholars and provided a preview of his later masterwork on the Tosefta.

In the meantime, Lieberman produced two important historical works, *Greek in Jewish Palestine* (1942) and *Hellenism in Jewish Palestine* (1950), in which he demonstrated a keen understanding of the dynamics of the Greek and Roman world and of the impact of the Hellenization of the Mediterranean world on the Jewish community in Palestine. Topics as diverse as manners, customs and superstitions, physical exercise, and natural science are discussed, and the role of Greek proverbs in rabbinic literature is explored, as is the approach to temple worship taken by the heathens in contrast to that of the Jews. Before discussing how the rabbis integrated certain Hellenistic practices into Judaism without compromising the integrity of their own religion, Lieberman wrote that the cultural impact of Hellenism on the Jews in Palestine "was even larger and deeper than could be inferred from the facts recorded in Rabbinic literature." In the larger cities of Roman Palestine, more affluent Jews lived, worked, and traded among Christians and Pagans. Although the rabbis did their best to keep them focused on the spiritual path, the "people could not help admiring the beautiful and the useful; they could not fail to be attracted by the external brilliance and the superficial beauty of Gentile life" (*Greek in Jewish Palestine*, p. 91).

From the 1950s to the end of his life Lieberman devoted most of his time and energies to writing and publishing what would become his magnum opus: the *Tosefta Kifshutah* (1955–1988), twelve volumes of which were published during his life and three of which were published posthumously. The work, which has taken its place among the standard talmudic reference works and is rightly regarded as the definitive commentary on the Tosefta, has been called by Dov Zlotnick the most important edition of a rabbinic text produced in the twentieth century. Representing the full flowering of all of the methods that Lieberman had developed in his earlier works, this masterpiece draws on diverse disciplines, including philology, history, literature, and economics, to elucidate the obscure origins of the text. It includes extensive references to, among other things, early rabbinic works, other texts that contain quotations from long-lost sources, exegetical material preserved in rarely studied manuscripts, and a diverse range of other Greek, Roman, Christian, and Jewish writings that shed new light on the meaning of the Tosefta in its cultural and historical context. Lieberman was thus able to demonstrate, in convincing fashion, that portions of the manuscripts that had been long relied on and considered accurate were, in fact, seriously flawed and had been revised several times over. By finding and analyzing the original version of the text he was able to resolve long-standing textual difficulties and to reveal the underlying logic that informed the rabbinic mind. His multidisciplinary perspective enabled Lieberman to offer a fresh, persuasive, and historically sound approach to understanding the Tosefta. In addition, because the scope of the Tosefta is so far-reaching, he was able to use it as a framework for the explanation of complex and difficult passages throughout all of rabbinic literature. His solutions to textual problems were both profound and creative, rendering simple and obvious that which had appeared complex and convoluted, and thereby made a significant and lasting contribution to the study of Talmud and Midrash generally.

In addition to his commitment to his own scholarship, Lieberman encouraged and assisted scholars with guidance and personal advice as well as with funding to enable them to contribute to Jewish scholarship. Alexander Marx, in an address delivered to the 1948 convention of the Rabbinical Assembly of America, described his colleague's ability to combine a variety of critical approaches and to search out unexplored sources in his attempt to interpret as well as correct inaccurate interpretations of rabbinic texts as "really astounding. We admire the sound method which he applies to textual criticism, together with his excellent philological equipment which leads him, in practically all his writings, to give illuminations of a linguistic character and to offer very unexpected interpretations of words in every branch of Talmudic literature." Lieberman's scholarship is respected even by those elements within the Orthodox community that might have been reluctant to embrace his contributions both because of the scientific approach he brought to bear on the study of the ancient texts and because of his position within the Conservative movement.

Within that movement, Lieberman was the leading authority on Jewish law. His knowledge and erudition were so well respected that his views on the development of Jewish law carried enormous weight. For example, the problem of the "chained woman" (*agunah*) had long presented extraordinary difficulties for many women leaving Jewish marriages. If a man refused to deliver a Jewish bill of divorce (*get*) to his wife, she would be precluded from remarrying under Jewish law. In the early 1950s Lieberman proposed that a provision be added to the Jewish marriage contract (*ketubah*) that would address this issue. The new clause provided that the couple would appear before a Jewish divorce tribunal (*bet din*) for binding arbitration in the event of a civil divorce. This new provision, referred to as the "Lieberman clause," was adopted by the Rabbinical Assembly of America in 1954. Its enforceability was affirmed by the New York Court of Appeals in 1983.

Lieberman was awarded several honorary degrees by leading universities. He was honored with a number of prizes, including the Bialik, Israel, and Harvey prizes, the last for his "research in the cultures of the Middle Eastern countries in the Hellenistic and Roman periods and his great and profound commentaries on the sources of the Oral Law." Lieberman died on an airplane flying from the United States to Israel.

• In addition to the publications referred to in the text, a collection of Lieberman's essays, reviews, and addresses covering a period of approximately fifty years can be found in *Studies in Palestinian Talmudic Literature* (in Hebrew), ed. David Rosenthal (1991). Lieberman's *Texts and Studies* (1974) includes essays originally published in Hebrew and translated for publication in that volume. For a comprehensive bibliography of Lieberman's publications (prepared by Tovia Preschel) see *Saul Lieberman Memorial Volume* (in Hebrew), ed. Shamma Friedman (1993). Eliezer Shimshon Rosenthal's "Hamoreh" is a detailed evaluation of Lieberman's work that appeared in the *Proceedings of the American Academy for Jewish Research* 31 (1963). A one-volume reprinted edition of Lieberman's two classics, *Greek in Jewish Palestine* and *Hellenism in Jewish Palestine* (1994), includes an introduction by Dov Zlotnick in which he describes Lieberman's contribution to Jewish scholarship. Following Lieberman's death, a number of his students and colleagues published articles on his personal impact on rabbis and scholars along with assessments of his methods and techniques. Zlotnick's tribute appeared in the *Rabbinical Assembly Proceedings 1983*; that of David Weiss Halivni was included in *Conservative Judaism* 38

(Spring 1986): 5; those of Ephraim Urbach, Shraga Abramson, Chaim Zalman Dimitrovsky, and Shamma Friedman are included in the volume (in Hebrew) *Le-Zikhro Shel Shaul Lieberman* (1983). A survey and description of Lieberman's books and essays is included in Phillip Sigal, "The Scholarship of Saul Lieberman: Reflections on His First Yahrzeit," *Judaism* 33 (Spring 1984): 135. Solomon Spiro's article "The Moral Vision of Saul Lieberman," *Conservative Judaism* 46 (Summer 1994): 64, analyzes the ethical foundations of Lieberman's work. For essays that touch on his role within the Jewish Theological Seminary, see Jack Wertheimer, ed., *Tradition Renewed: A History of the Jewish Theological Seminary of America* (1997). An obituary is in the *New York Times*, 24 Mar. 1983.

SOLOMON SPIRO

LIEBLING, A. J. (18 Oct. 1904–28 Dec. 1963), journalist, was born Abbott Joseph Liebling in New York City, the son of Joseph Liebling, a furrier born in Austria, and Anna Slone, who was from San Francisco. He went with his parents to Europe (1907, 1911) and early in life learned to love fine food, newspapers, and books. He attended public schools in Manhattan and Queens but because of precocity never graduated from high school. He attended Dartmouth (1920–1921), was temporarily expelled for avoiding compulsory chapel (spring 1921), returned to Dartmouth (fall 1921), but was expelled for again not attending chapel (1923). Without much enthusiasm, he attended the Pulitzer School of Journalism at Columbia (1923–1925). While at Columbia, however, he enjoyed not only a course in Old French but also preparing as class assignments crime reports at lower Manhattan police headquarters. He went to Europe with his parents once more (1924) before graduating from Columbia (B.Lit., 1925). He hated the name Abbott, was called Joe, and signed his writing A. J. Liebling.

He vacillated for a few years after graduation. He worked as a dilatory sports-report copy reader for the *New York Times* (1925–1926), then wrote for the *Providence Evening Bulletin* and then the *Providence Journal* in Rhode Island (1926). He went to Paris at his parents' expense, supposedly to study history and French at the Sorbonne (1926–1927), but mainly to dine, wine, work out (jogging, boxing, rowing), attend the cinema, write, and consort with women along the Left Bank. After another stint with the *Providence Journal* (1927–1930), he returned to his beloved New York City as a staff writer for the *World* (1930–1931), then as a feature writer for the *World-Telegram* and the *Journal* (1931–1935).

Then came two major events. First, in 1934, Liebling married Anna Beatrice McGinn, an Irish-Catholic orphan from Providence and a schizophrenic, who was sometimes institutionalized. They had no children. Next, in 1935, he joined the staff of the *New Yorker* (1935), became a lifelong friend of its eccentric editor Harold Ross, and began to write what became a large number of articles, essays, and reviews—308 in all—for that magazine. His main topics were the social scene (including politics), sports (mainly boxing and horseracing), and gastronomy. His style evolved into a unique blend of wit, sarcasm, irony, edginess, close-up details, and low-keyed superciliousness.

The advent of World War II was the making of Liebling. The *New Yorker* sent him as a war correspondent to France (1939–1940), England (1941, 1942), North Africa (1942–1943), and England again and then the Continent (1943–1944). In inimitable dispatches, he covered the fall of France, the London blitz, American infantry advances across Africa, the Normandy invasion, and the liberation of Paris. He assembled much of his war writing in *The Road Back to Paris* (1944). He had published three minor books earlier, a Tin Pan Alley memoir and two books about New York sharpers and con men.

For a short while after the war, Liebling was at loose ends. He wrote again for the *New Yorker* and in 1946 took over its "Wayward Press" column, which Robert Benchley had popularized. For the next two decades and more, Liebling made it an organ for bitter criticism of establishment journalism. He coedited *La République du silence* (1946), a huge anthology of French Resistance materials. (*The Republic of Silence*, the English translation by Ramon Guthrie and others of this heartbreaking book, appeared the following year.) Liebling published two books of his "Wayward Press" articles, *The Wayward Pressman* (1947) and *Mink and Red Herring: The Wayward Pressman's Casebook* (1949).

In 1949 he and Anna were divorced, and he married Harriet Lucille Hille Barr Spectorsky, a beautiful, twice-divorced model whom he had known since 1946. The couple had no children. For a little less than a year in 1949–1950 he resided in Chicago, mainly to write three *New Yorker* essays reworked for an unnecessarily critical book about the sprawling Illinois metropolis, called *Chicago: The Second City* (1952). Liebling's book *The Honest Rainmaker: The Life and Times of Colonel John R. Stingo* (1953) is about the author of a *New York Enquirer* racing column whom Liebling knew and admired. *The Sweet Science: A Ringside View of Boxing* (1956) contains his insightful, multistyled observations on his favorite sport. *Normandy Revisited* (1958) is a set of revised *New Yorker* essays comparing and contrasting old memories and fresh observations occasioned by recent trips back to France (1955, 1956).

The year 1959 was a busy one for Liebling: he was divorced from his long-estranged Lucille and married the novelist Jean Stafford, who was the ex-wife of the poet Robert Lowell and whom Liebling had first met in London three years earlier. They had no children. Liebling also visited New Orleans to observe and criticize Louisiana's controversial governor, Earl Long, Huey Long's younger brother. But, coming to believe in Earl Long, Liebling wrote essays assembled into a generally complimentary book titled *The Earl of Louisiana* (1961). *The Press* (1961) is a popular collection of Liebling's press articles. His *Between Meals: An Appetite for Paris* (1962) gathers his eight exuberant essays from the *New Yorker* on Parisian food, wine, women, and actors.

The Most of A. J. Liebling was published earlier in the year of Liebling's sudden death in New York City and therefore turned out to be an impressive hail-and-farewell collection of much of his most superb writing. For years he had gorged himself on too much food and drink. Only 5′9½″ in height, he ballooned to 243 pounds, suffered from chronic gout, and succumbed to bronchial pneumonia. Anna, his first wife, committed suicide a little less than five months later.

A. J. Liebling has become known as the gadfly of American journalism because of his stinging comments about the news industry. More lasting, however, are his superpatriotic war dispatches, which crisply present only what he personally saw, are without heroics, concentrate on little details, and are therefore uniquely memorable. For example, he describes the effect of a German shell that hit a landing craft he was on off Normandy on D-Day: human blood and the contents of condensed-milk cans quickly ran together on the crowded deck. The best of Liebling's writings express his undying love of both Paris, his favorite foreign city, and New York, which as he repeatedly said, was "where I came from."

• Liebling's papers and letters, filed with the E. B. White Papers, are in the Cornell University Library. Robert Owen Johnson, *An Index to Literature in the "New Yorker"* . . . (3 vols., 1969–1971), lists 264 articles and 44 reviews by Liebling. A thorough biographical study of Liebling is Raymond Sokolov, *The Wayward Reporter: The Life of A. J. Liebling* (1980). Dale Kramer, *Ross and the "New Yorker"* (1951), briefly discusses Liebling's relations with Harold Ross. Edmund M. Midura, *A. J. Liebling: The Wayward Pressman as Critic* (1974), concentrates on Liebling's opinions. Curt Riess, ed., *They Were There: The Story of World War II and How It Came About by America's Foremost Correspondents* (1944), reprints, as "Christmas in the Maginot Line," Liebling's "They Defend Themselves" (*New Yorker*, 10 Feb. 1940). Robert William Desmond, *Tides of War: World News Reporting, 1931–1945* (1984), frequently mentions Liebling's *New Yorker* reporting from North Africa and France. L. Moody Simms, Jr., in *Encyclopedia of American Humorists*, ed. Steven H. Gale (1988), offers brief coverage of Liebling, pp. 284–86. An extended obituary is in the *New York Times*, 29 Dec. 1963.

ROBERT L. GALE

LIEBMAN, Joshua Loth (7 Apr. 1907–9 June 1948), rabbi and author, was born in Hamilton, Ohio, the son of Simon Liebman and Sabina Loth. His parents were divorced when he was two years old, and he lived with his paternal grandfather, Rabbi Lippmann Liebman, and grandmother in Cincinnati during his formative years. A child prodigy, Liebman began his studies at the University of Cincinnati at age fifteen and completed his bachelor's degree in 1926. He simultaneously attended Hebrew Union College for rabbinical training and was ordained in 1930. While completing his rabbinical studies, he served as Taft Teaching Fellow in Philosophy, 1926–1929, at the University of Cincinnati, and it was in that capacity that he became acquainted with his student and first cousin, Fan

Loth, whom he married in 1928. He spent 1929–1930 as a student at Hebrew University in Jerusalem, where he became an ardent Zionist.

After his ordination, Liebman took a position as a weekend rabbi in Lafayette, Indiana. On weekdays he returned to Cincinnati to teach courses in Bible and exegesis at Hebrew Union College. In 1934 Liebman succeeded Solomon Freehof as the rabbi of Congregation Kehillath Anshe Maarab, a major Reform congregation in Chicago. During his stay there, he completed his work for a doctor of Hebrew letters degree at Hebrew Union College under the direction of Zvi Diesendruck. His topic was the religious thought of medieval philosopher Aaron ben Elijah. In Chicago, Liebman became interested in psychology and underwent psychoanalysis. He later became a pioneer in the study of psychological awareness in Reform Judaism.

Liebman's last and most significant position was as rabbi of Temple Israel in Boston, Massachusetts, where he began serving in 1939. While at Temple Israel, Liebman gained fame as a radio preacher and author of the popular book on religion and psychology, *Peace of Mind* (1946), which led the *New York Times* bestseller list for over two years. Originally parts of sermons that were presented as lectures at the Jewish Institute of Religion in 1946, the book was rewritten for a popular audience with the help of Henry Morton Robinson, novelist and editor of *Reader's Digest*. Liebman had two goals in writing *Peace of Mind*. As a popular work, it was designed to bring comfort and healing to individuals, and in particular to American Jews, who were devastated by the Nazi destruction of European Jewry. It also sought to foster new respect for the insights of psychology among liberal Jewish and Christian institutions, refocusing the energies of liberal religion on the emotional needs of individuals.

Like other works of popular religion, *Peace of Mind* focused on ways in which individuals could achieve a sense of personal well-being. Unlike other authors of the genre, Liebman did not believe that faith alone could enable someone to achieve this goal. Rather, he focused on attaining emotional health through psychological insight. His book showed that the insights of Freudian psychology and liberal religion are compatible. Liebman sought to discourage liberal churches and synagogues from fostering the repression of feelings, especially feelings of grief. He asserted that they should teach the value of self-love and self-acceptance, along with the message "love thy neighbor." Rather than ignoring the emotional problems of congregants, he claimed, the clergy should function as pastoral counselors, and he encouraged congregants to seek out clergy as sympathetic listeners who could help them deal with problems of fear and faith.

Liebman's concept of God reflected his optimistic philosophy. Following American Jewish philosopher Mordecai Kaplan, Liebman described God as "the Power that makes for righteousness." He considered this a mature concept of God, one in which God is not confused with the childhood notion of the omnipotent parent. *Peace of Mind* began a trend of popular self-help books written by clergy of various faiths, such as Norman Vincent Peale's *The Power of Positive Thinking* (1952) and Bishop Fulton Sheen's *Peace of Soul* (1949).

During World War II Liebman served as a member of the Committee on Army and Navy Religious Activities, directing the work of Jewish chaplains. He himself was disqualified from army chaplaincy in 1944 due to "essential hypertension." In 1947, shortly before his death, Liebman and his wife adopted Leila Bornstein, a Polish-born refugee whose parents had been killed in the Auschwitz concentration camp.

As a visiting professor in the graduate school of Boston University and at the Andover-Newton Theological Seminary, Liebman was reputed to be the first rabbi to teach on the faculty of a Christian seminary. After the publication of *Peace of Mind*, he began to lecture widely. Although he had many opportunities to occupy more prestigious positions (such as president of Hebrew Union College and senior rabbi of Temple Emanuel in New York City), he remained at Temple Israel until his death from a heart attack in Boston at age forty-one. His most notable accomplishment was bridging the gap between the realms of psychology and religion in American Jewish life.

• Liebman's papers and correspondence are in the Twentieth Century Archives at the Boston University Library. His sermons are collected at the American Jewish Archives in Cincinnati. Liebman edited *Psychiatry and Religion* (1948); his essays are collected in Fan Loth Liebman, ed., *Hope for Man* (1966). More detailed biographical information may be obtained in Arthur Mann, "Joshua Loth Liebman: Religio-Psychiatric Thinker," in *Growth and Achievement: Temple Israel, 1854–1954*, ed. Arthur Mann (1954). Also see Rebecca T. Alpert, "Joshua Loth Liebman: The Peace of Mind Rabbi," in *Faith and Freedom: A Tribute to Franklin H. Littell*, ed. Richard Libowitz (1987), and Bernard Mehlman, "Joshua Loth Liebman," in *Reform Judaism in America: A Biographical Dictionary and Sourcebook*, ed. Kerry M. Olitzky et al. (1993). An obituary is in the *New York Times*, 10 June 1948.

REBECCA T. ALPERT

LIEBMAN, Max (5 Aug. 1902–21 July 1981), stage and television director and producer, was born in Vienna, Austria, the son of Harry Liebman, a furrier, and Sarah Glazer. Brought to the United States as an infant, Liebman was raised in New York City, where his father entered the fur business. Liebman graduated in 1917 from Boys' High School in Brooklyn, where he was a member of the drama club and the debate society. Following graduation, Liebman moved to Texas, where he worked in the oil fields and, for a short period of time, as a "front man" for a magician.

Returning to New York City in 1920, Liebman began his show business career as a vaudeville sketch writer and, over the next five years, director and producer. In the summer of 1925 Liebman worked as a social director at the Log Tavern, a Pennsylvania summer camp. Seven years later, in 1932, Liebman began a long association with the Hotel Tamiment, a resort in Pennsylvania's Pocono Mountains, where he worked

as theater director for fifteen seasons. In 1935 he married Sonia Veskova. They had no children.

Every week at Tamiment, Liebman would produce and direct a completely new musical revue, using the same stock company idea he would later employ in television. In 1939 his musical *The Straw Hat Revue* appeared on Broadway. First tested at the Tamiment Playhouse, the musical introduced Danny Kaye, Imogene Coca, and Anita Alvarez. Liebman would eventually bring other celebrities from the Poconos to Broadway, including Sid Caesar, Betty Garrett, and choreographers Jerome Robbins and Lee Sherman.

Throughout the 1930s and 1940s Liebman worked as an "additional dialogue writer" for motion pictures, spending several years traveling across the country to theaters, film studios, and nightclubs. He became known chiefly as a "play-doctor," re-writing scenes, skits, and dialogue for faltering music shows, some on Broadway, where he gained a growing reputation as a producer. During World War II he served as a civilian director and sketch writer for USO camp shows. In 1945 he produced and directed *Tars and Spars* for the coast guard; during this production Liebman first joined with Sid Caesar in shaping the air force movie-parody routine that ignited the comedian's career. After touring the country the show was bought by Columbia Pictures and filmed in 1946. The same year, Liebman produced *Shooting Star* in Boston, a musical based on the life of Billy the Kid, and continued producing musicals with his Tamiment troupe of performers. He also composed material, with "literary partner" Sylvia Fine, exclusively for Danny Kaye in two motion pictures, *Up in Arms* (1944) and *The Kid from Brooklyn* (1946).

In January 1949 Liebman made his television debut with "The Admiral Broadway Revue," which was broadcast live by the National Broadcasting Company. Hired by NBC president Pat Weaver to produce "spectaculars" as a method of getting top stars on television, Liebman produced a "full fledged musical show." According to a source close to the production, as quoted by Frank Sturcken in his study *Live Television* (1990), Liebman set out his aims for his shows: "Some of these were to be completely original, some would be revivals. Some would have a book; some would be revues. All of them would be loaded with big names and given lavish productions in . . . color." The format of "The Admiral Broadway Revue" was similar to Liebman's Tamiment productions: sophisticated comedy, a large amount of music and dance, solos, and ensemble efforts. Liebman brought in two of his most talented writers from the Poconos for the show, Mel Tolkin and Lucille Kallen; he also brought in Imogene Coca and paired her with Sid Caesar for the first time. For the dancing sequences, Liebman presented the talented couple of Marge and Gower Champion. "The Admiral Broadway Revue" ran for nineteen weeks before its cancellation.

However, by February 1950 the triumvirate of Caesar, Coca, and Liebman was back on the air with one of the most historic shows of television's early years.

The ninety-minute live broadcast of "Your Show of Shows" was essentially an expanded, improved version of the earlier Admiral production and is regarded as early television's best written variety show. The series, which ran until 1954, had a guest star every week as well as guest artists from opera, ballet, modern dance, and classical music. "Your Show of Shows" was done as a legitimate Broadway-style revue and received a great deal of critical praise as well as a large audience following. It, like all of Liebman's television shows, was treated as a Broadway production, with the cameras kept off the stage and stagehands hidden from the studio audience. The series established Caesar and Coca as television icons and Liebman as a dominant force in the comedy-variety vogue of early television. He was often credited as the behind-the-scenes inventor of the genre. Liebman's genius for presenting talent on-screen was only outstripped by his ability to gather it off-screen. For example, the remarkable writing staff of "Your Show of Shows" included Woody Allen, Selma Diamond, Neil Simon, Mel Brooks, and Larry Gelbart as well as on-screen personalities such as Carl Reiner and Howard Morris.

Liebman produced dozens of musical comedy specials, including Bob Hope's 1950 television debut, and many television spectaculars that appeared under the banner of "Max Liebman Presents," which ran on NBC from 1954 until 1956. However, he is best remembered for his masterpiece, "Your Show of Shows," the success of which secured his reputation as "the Ziegfeld of TV" and a place in the history of the television medium.

After the demise of "Your Show of Shows" in 1954, Liebman continued to produce and direct television variety specials. By the late 1960s, however, Liebman was unable to survive the growing decline of the comedy-variety format; eventually there was little work left for him in prime-time television. In 1973 he compiled a film anthology titled *Ten from Your Show of Shows* that reawakened interest in the famous Caesar-Coca sketches.

Liebman was honored with many awards for his television productions, most notably the Michaels Award of the Television Academy of Arts and Sciences in 1952. He died in New York City.

• Liebman's role and importance in the careers of Sid Caesar and Imogene Coca is discussed in Karin Adir, *The Great Clowns of American Television* (1988). His importance in the early history of television is assessed in Harry Castleman and Walter J. Podrazik, *Watching TV: Four Decades of American Television* (1982), and his relationship with Pat Weaver is discussed by Frank Sturcken in *Live Television: The Golden Age of 1946–1958 in New York* (1990). Ted Sennett offers a comprehensive examination of the series in his *Your Show of Shows* (1977). An overview of Liebman's life until 1953 is presented in *Current Biography*, April 1953, and his obituary is in the *New York Times*, 24 July 1981.

JAMES YATES

LIELE, George (c. 1751–1828), pioneering Baptist clergyman and African-American émigré to Jamaica, said of his slave origins, "I was born in Virginia, my father's name was Liele, and my mother's name Nancy; I cannot ascertain much of them, as I went to several parts of America when young, and at length resided in New Georgia" (*Baptist Annual Register*, p. 332). Liele's master Henry Sharp took him to Burke County, Georgia, as a young man. Liele wrote that he "had a natural fear of God" from his youth. He attended a local Baptist church, was baptized by Matthew Moore, a deacon in the Buckhead Creek Baptist Church about 1772, and was given the opportunity to travel, preaching to both whites and blacks. Liele preached as a probationer for about three years at Bruton Land, Georgia, and at Yamacraw, about a half mile from Savannah. The favorable response to Liele's "ministerial gifts" caused Sharp, who was a Baptist deacon, to free him. Liele remained with Sharp's family until Sharp's death as a Tory officer during the revolutionary war when the British occupied Savannah.

Upset over his status as a free man, some of Sharp's heirs had Liele imprisoned. Liele produced his manumission papers and with the aid of a British colonel named Kirkland resumed his public activities. He gathered a small congregation that included African Americans who had come to Savannah on the promise by the British of their freedom. One of Liele's converts was Andrew Bryan, who was later responsible for the development of African-American Baptist congregations in Savannah. David George, the pioneering organizer of black Baptist congregations in Nova Scotia and Sierra Leone, also was one of Liele's converts. Despite increasing anxiety over escalating American-British hostilities, Liele continued to hold worship services.

When the British evacuated Savannah in 1782, Liele went as an indentured servant with Kirkland to Kingston, Jamaica. After working two years to satisfy his indebtedness to Kirkland, Liele received a certificate of freedom, and about 1784 he began to preach in a small house in Kingston to what he called a "good smart congregation." It was organized with four other blacks who had come from America. The congregation eventually purchased property in the east end of Kingston and constructed a brick meetinghouse. Liele reported that raising money to pay for the new building was difficult because his congregation was composed mostly of slaves whose masters allowed "but three or four bits per week" out of which to pay for their food. The free people who belonged to Liele's church were generally poor.

Despite initial opposition from some whites, Liele's congregation grew to about 350 members by 1790. It included a few whites. Liele accepted Methodists after they had been baptized by immersion, but in a pragmatic move he did not receive slaves as members without, as he wrote, "a few lines from their owners of their good behavior toward them and religion." Liele assisted in the organization of other congregations on the island and promoted free schools for slaves as well as free black Jamaicans. On his ministerial activities Liele wrote in the early 1790s, "I have deacons and elders, a few; and teachers of small congregations in the town and country, where convenience suits them to come together; and I am pastor. I preach twice on the Lord's Day, in the forenoon and afternoon, and twice in the week, and have not been absent six Sabbath days since I formed the church in this country. I receive nothing for my services; I preach, baptize, administer the Lord's Supper, and travel from one place to another to publish the gospel and settle church affairs, all freely." By 1797 Liele had reason to be more pessimistic. Originally charged with "seditious preaching" because he was the leader of so many slaves, he was thrown into prison where he remained for three years, five months, and ten days. The charge of seditious preaching was dismissed, but his inability to satisfy debts incurred in the building of his church kept him in prison. During Liele's imprisonment his eldest son conducted preaching services.

When Liele was about forty years old he reported that he had three sons and one daughter. His four children ranged in age from nineteen to eleven. His wife, whose name is unknown, had been baptized with him in Savannah. Liele worked as a farmer and teamster besides conducting regular worship services and conducting church business. George Liele has the distinction of being the first regularly ordained African-American Baptist minister in America. He is also noteworthy as the founder of the first Baptist church in Jamaica. Liele reported in 1790, "There is no Baptist church in this country but ours." An article sent to British Baptists in 1796 said of Jamaican Baptists whom Liele led: "They preach every Lord's day from 10 to 12 o'clock in the morning, and from 4 to 6 in the evening; and on Tuesday and Thursday evening, from seven to eight. They administer the Lord's supper every month, and baptism once in three months. The members are divided into smaller classes which meet separately every Monday evening, to be examined respecting their daily walk and conversation." Details regarding the last few decades prior to Liele's death in Jamaica are not known.

Liele's pioneering work in establishing the Baptist church in Jamaica set the foundation for a denominational tradition that continued until the late twentieth century. Apart from being the spiritual father of the Jamaican black Baptist churches, he was the first missionary from any African-American church body to the island and may well have been the first African American to be ordained a Baptist preacher. Although nothing is known of his political and social views, he seems to have considered his primary work that of preaching the Christian Gospel and caring for the spiritual welfare of his members.

• Primary materials about Liele's life are extremely limited. The principal sources are the letters written from Jamaica by fellow Baptists and published in 1793 in *The Baptist Annual Register* by the English Baptist John Rippon. The letters, which include citations from nonextant reports written by Liele, are most conveniently found in "Letters Showing the Rise and Progress of the Early Negro Baptist Preachers," *Journal of Negro History* 2 (Apr. 1918): 119–27. Secondary sources, such as Edward A. Holmes, "George Liele: Negro Slavery's Prophet of Deliverance," *Foundations* 9 (Oct.–Dec. 1966): 333–45, and John W. Davis, "George Liele and Andrew Bryan, Pioneer Negro Baptist Preachers," *Journal of Negro History* 3 (Apr. 1918): 119–27, are dependent on Rippon's work. In 1796 "The Covenant of the AnaBaptist Church" appeared in a supplement to the first volume of the *General Baptist Repository*. G. W. Rusling reprints and discusses this early Jamaican Baptist church covenant in "A Note on Early Negro Baptist History," *Foundations* 11 (Oct.–Dec. 1968): 362–68.

MILTON C. SERNETT

LIENAU, Detlef (17 Feb. 1818–29 Aug. 1887), architect, was born in Ütersen, Schleswig-Holstein, Germany, the son of Jacob Lienau, a wine merchant, and Lucia Catherine Heidorn. He trained in carpentry and cabinetmaking in Berlin from 1837 to 1840 and in Hamburg in 1840–1841. Because of his skill in draftsmanship, he continued his studies at the Royal Architectural School (Königliche Baugewerksschule) in Munich in 1841–1842. Relocating to Paris in 1842, he began working under Henri Labrouste, whose design for the Bibliothèque Sainte-Geneviève was in progress, and traveled extensively in Bavaria, France, and Italy, making many sketches. In 1847 he became a designer and draftsman for the Chemin de Fer de Paris à Lyon and won first prize in a design competition for a municipal hospital in Altona, Germany.

The following year, at a time of great political unrest in Europe, Lienau immigrated to the United States, joining his older brother Michael, a merchant in New York City, who had been there since 1839. Michael gave Detlef his first American commissions and introduced him to wealthy clients who were able to take advantage of the talents of a professionally trained architect, a relative rarity at that time in New York City. Lienau's first American work was a board-and-batten house (1849) for Michael in Jersey City, New Jersey, followed by the Grace (Van Vorst) P.E. Church (1850–1853) in Jersey City, with stained-glass windows donated by Michael Lienau. This brownstone Gothic Revival structure first opened for worship on 11 May 1853 on the occasion of Detlef Lienau's marriage to Catherine Van Giesen Booraem Diedrichs; the couple had three children before her death in 1861.

Shortly before his marriage Lienau had established a reputation with his first major city residence (1850–1852), a house for banker and financier Hart M. Shiff at 32 Fifth Avenue that introduced the mansard roof to New York City. Other notable residential work from this decade includes "Beach Cliffe," the DeLancey Kane villa (1852), which, with its monumental, banded, rusticated facade, is an early instance of French influence in Newport, Rhode Island; "Nuits," the very grand Italianate Francis Cottenet villa (1852), Dobbs Ferry, New York; and, for Cottenet's daughter and son-in-law, the William C. Schermerhorn house (1853–1859), 49 West Twenty-third Street, with brownstone detail and a mansard roof creating a pavilion effect.

Lienau brought his expertise to the design of other building types, including banks, loft buildings, and factories. Among these were the Mechanics' and Traders' Bank (1859) and the First National Bank (1864), both in Jersey City; the New York Life & Trust Co. building (1865), 52 Wall Street; a trio of marble-faced Italianate loft buildings with cast-iron store fronts (1859–1860) for the Langdon estate, 577–581 Broadway; and the F. O. Matthiessen & Weichers Sugar Refinery (1862–1870), Jersey City, which housed centrifugal machines, the newest technology in sugar refining, with the layout determined by the sequence of operations. The Noel & Saurel French and Belgian Plate Glass Co. (1863–1864), Howard and Crosby, has a massive arcaded base in granite supporting a brick facade with stone arches and banding in the Néo-Grec style (a French utilitarian style, popular in the 1850s and 1860s, that used abstracted Greek forms and ornament to emphasize the building's structure).

Lienau continued to evoke praise for his residential designs. "Elm Park," the LeGrand Lockwood mansion (1864–1868), South Norwalk, Connecticut, was one of the most grandiose houses of the period, as befitted the broker–railroad magnate client; it was designed around an octagonal court, with interiors executed by decorator Léon Marcotte, who had been a partner of Lienau's in 1851–1853. For William Schermerhorn's brother, Edmund H. Schermerhorn, Lienau designed a grand French-inspired double house (1867–1869), 45–47 West Twenty-third Street, with a center entrance pavilion, a mansard roof, and a carriage drive that led through the house to West Twenty-fourth Street. Precedent setting in both location and design was a group of eight attached houses (1868–1870) for Rebecca Jones located on Fifth Avenue between East Fifty-fifth and East Fifty-sixth streets. Faced in light-colored Ohio stone, the houses were designed as a unified ensemble with a series of pavilions and a continuous mansard roof. He received another residential commission from his brother for Schloss Duneck (1872) in the family's home town of Ütersen, Germany. In 1866 Lienau married Harriet Jane Wreaks, with whom he had two children.

William Schermerhorn and his father-in-law, Francis Cottenet, provided Lienau opportunities to design other residential building types: the Schermerhorn Apartments (1870–1871) on Third Avenue, built in four sections designed to look like a single unit with shops at street level and rear courtyards between the units; and Grosvenor House (1871–1872), an apartment hotel with all modern conveniences, including an elevator. Lienau also explored the constraints of tenement house design in 1879 with a so-called dumbbell tenement at 162 Elm Street in the Five Points section of Manhattan.

Lienau undertook substantial work for institutions, designing Odenheimer Hall (1868) for St. Mary's Hall, Burlington, New Jersey; Suydam Hall (1871–1873) and Sage Library (1873–1874) for the General Theological Seminary, New Brunswick, New Jersey; and the fireproof Hodgson Hall (1873–1876) for the Georgia Historical Society, Savannah. Very late in his career, he designed the picture gallery (1885–1886) of the Telfair Academy of Arts and Sciences, Savannah, employing a classicism that related successfully to the earlier house, which had become an academy building.

Lienau continued to design commercial buildings, often of a rather conservative character. Among them were an office building (1881–1882) at 67 Wall Street and a loft building (1883–1884) at Broadway and East Seventeenth Street, both for Daniel Parish's estate; and a loft building (1873–1874), 676 Broadway, and an office building (1876), 62–64 Cedar Street, for DeLancey Kane.

Lienau's last executed work was a row of houses (1886) at 48, 50, 52, and 54 West Eighty-second Street, each house with a large central stair hall on the parlor floor. Lienau and his family moved into number 48 in January 1887, just a few months before his death.

In 1857 Lienau was a founding member of the American Institute of Architects. His office was a training ground for other architects, most notably Paul Pelz, who subsequently designed the Library of Congress, and Henry Hardenbergh, whose northern European design sensibility owes much to Lienau. Additionally, one of Lienau's sons, J. August Lienau, had joined his architectural practice in 1873.

Lienau had the good fortune to establish himself in New York City at a time of rapid expansion and growth. The opportunities for skilled, well-trained architects were great. Lienau set standards for architects who followed, both in the quality of his work, with its respect for rational planning and its emphasis on sound principles of construction, and in expectations for professional practice and conduct.

• The major collection of Lienau material, consisting of some 700–800 drawings of projects by Lienau, manuscript notes, photographs of works by Lienau, and a brief typewritten biography by J. Henry Lienau, is in the Avery Architectural and Fine Arts Library, Columbia University. In conjunction with the collection, one may consult a typescript by Ellen W. Kramer, "Detlef Lienau: Catalog of Student Drawings and Early European Commissions" (rev. 1954). An assessment of Lienau by his fellow architects is recorded by Sadakichi Hartmann, "A Conversation with Henry Janeway Hardenbergh," *Architectural Record* 19 (May 1906): 376–80. See also Talbot F. Hamlin, "The Rise of Eclecticism in New York," *Journal of the Society of Architectural Historians* 11 (May 1952): 7–8.

For more recent scholarship, see Kramer, "Detlef Lienau, an Architect of the Brown Decades," *Journal of the Society of Architectural Historians* 14 (Mar. 1955): 18–25; and Kramer, "The Domestic Architecture of Detlef Lienau, a Conservative Victorian" (Ph.D. diss., New York Univ., 1958). An assessment of Lienau's role in the advancement of the architectural profession is offered in Lockwood-Matthews Mansion, *Nineteenth-century Architects: Building a Profession* (1990). Obituaries are in *American Architect and Building News*, 17 Sept. 1887, p. 129, and *Building*, 3 Sept. 1887, p. 80.

MARJORIE PEARSON

LIGGETT, Hunter (21 Mar. 1857–30 Dec. 1935), soldier, was born in Reading, Pennsylvania, the son of James Liggett, a tailor, and Margaret Hunter. Liggett's father served from 1879 to 1882 in the Pennsylvania House of Representatives but had no military experience. Two of Liggett's uncles died in the Civil War, however, which may have influenced his decision to enter the U.S. Military Academy at West Point in 1875. He ranked forty-first out of sixty-seven in the class of 1879 and was commissioned a second lieutenant of infantry.

Like most of his classmates, Liggett was assigned to a western outpost. From 1879 to 1892 he served in Montana, Dakota, and Texas. The monotony and tedium of garrison duty was interrupted by sporadic Indian skirmishes, and although he did not participate in any large Indian campaigns, Liggett did earn the Indian Campaign Badge. Throughout his years in the West, Hunter maintained his interest in military history and tactics, subjects that never lost their appeal. On 30 June 1881 he married Harriet R. Lane; they had no children. Initially his promotions were limited: he became a first lieutenant in 1884 and a captain in 1897. When his regiment, the Fifth Infantry, left the frontier for service in Florida and Georgia in 1892, he became regimental adjutant, the principal staff and administrative officer.

In 1898 Liggett obtained a volunteer commission as a major and assistant adjutant general with the Thirty-first Infantry during the Spanish-American War, but he missed the Santiago campaign. He finally arrived in Cuba for a brief stay in 1899 but soon returned to Florida to recover from typhoid fever. In December 1899 he journeyed to the Philippines to begin service in Mindanao and Luzon. There he met John J. Pershing, with whom he developed a lasting friendship. His final Philippines staff assignment was as brigade adjutant at Dagupan during the first half of 1902. Liggett returned to the United States in May 1902 and was posted to Fort Snelling, Minnesota, at his new permanent rank of major. The following year he became adjutant general of the Department of the Lakes in Chicago. In September 1907 he was transferred to Fort Leavenworth, Kansas, as battalion commander with the Thirteenth Infantry.

Liggett's scholarly inclinations became apparent when, from 1909 to 1910, he attended the newly created Army War College. Upon graduation he stayed on as director (1910–1913) and then president (1913–1914). In these capacities Liggett strengthened military education, developing the curriculum in military history, operational planning, and general staff duties, and seeking to improve the overall quality of officer education. Believing that military education should not be restricted to lessons found in books, he led tours of the Civil War battlefields with his students, including such future military leaders as George C. Marshall and Robert L. Bullard. Simultaneously, Liggett served as chief of the War College Division, the principal planning agency of the War Department General Staff, producing war plans for interventions in Mexico and the Caribbean. His promotions came more quickly: to lieutenant colonel in 1909, to colonel in 1912, and to brigadier general in 1913.

In 1914 Liggett left the War College and returned to Chicago to assume command of the Department of the Lakes. From there he went to Texas City, Texas, to lead the Fourth Brigade of the Second Division, and in April 1916 he returned to the Philippines as commander of the Philippines Department, the largest overseas command at the time. In March 1917 he was promoted to major general (one of only seven then in the army). In May, after the United States became involved in World War I, he returned to the United States as commander of the Western Department in San Francisco. In September 1917 he assumed command of the Forty-first Division and a month later embarked for France.

At this crucial stage in his career, Liggett's liabilities, his age sixty and weight (200 pounds on a 6-foot frame), were balanced by Pershing's respect for Liggett's military knowledge, strength of character, and command experience. Pershing, as commander of the American Expeditionary Force (AEF), recommended Liggett to represent the United States on the newly created Supreme War Council, but the War Department selected General Tasker Bliss. In January 1918 Liggett took command of the I American Army Corps. As part of the French Sixth Army, Liggett's corps occupied the area west of Château-Thierry, engaged in the second battle of the Marne in late July and early August, and drove back the German forces some twenty miles across the Ourcq and Vesle rivers.

In mid-September 1918 Liggett's I Army Corps, now part of the newly formed First Army, effectively reduced the St. Mihiel Salient, an action followed ten days later by the Meuse-Argonne campaign (26 Sept.–11 Nov.). Faced with exceedingly difficult terrain in the Argonne Forest, the I Corps steadily pressed northward and westward against stubborn German positions and by 10 October had captured the Argonne. Pershing rewarded Liggett with a new assignment on 16 October—command of the entire First Army and its more than one million men. Liggett carefully rebuilt his forces in preparation for the next assault, which began ten days later. His efforts proved effective as the American assault broke the German resistance, forcing them into retreat all along the First Army front. Only the 11 November armistice halted Liggett's advance.

After the war Liggett retained his command of the First Army until it was dissolved in April 1919. From April until July he commanded the American Third Army, which occupied the Rhineland. Returning to San Francisco, he resumed command of the Western Department until he retired in March 1921 as a major general. In 1930 Congress voted to restore his wartime rank of lieutenant general. He died in San Francisco.

Begun on the Northern Plains fighting Indians, Liggett's career reflected the evolution of the American military officer corps as it emerged from the ragged force scattered across the western frontier, gained discipline and character from the educational curricula of its newly established service schools, and ultimately fought effectively in World War I. While president, he shaped the academic programs at the Army War College thus influencing the future course of military education in the United States. During World War I he commanded the largest single military force up to that time. Unflappable in crisis, level-headed, unselfish, and loyal, Liggett earned the respect of his troops and the confidence of his superiors. His knowledge of military history and tactics, which he generously shared with his students and colleagues, his ability to work effectively within the chain of command, and his finesse in managing a large army in the field justify his reputation as one of the nation's foremost military leaders.

• Record Group 120 in the National Archives contains materials relating to the AEF. The George C. Marshall Research Foundation Library in Lexington, Va., contains the diary of Major Pierpoint L. Stackpole, Liggett's aide, covering the period from Jan. 1918 to Aug. 1919. Liggett wrote two books about his wartime experiences: *Commanding an American Army: Recollections of the World War* (1925) and *A.E.F.: Ten Years Ago in France* (1928). No comprehensive biographies of Liggett exist. Of use is B. H. Liddell Hart's chapter on Liggett in *Reputations Ten Years After* (1928). Because biographical information is so sparse, the obituaries in the *New York Times*, the *San Francisco Examiner*, and the *San Francisco Chronicle*, 31 Dec. 1935, should be consulted.

EDWARD A. GOEDEKEN

LIGGETT, Louis Kroh (4 Apr. 1875–5 June 1946), drugstore chain founder and executive, was born in Detroit, Michigan, the son of John Templeton Liggett and Julia Kroh. He attended public school until age sixteen, after which he worked for the *Detroit Journal*, then for Wanamaker's. He soon showed a flair for sales and, while still a teenager, was sent to close up a bankrupt store. Though his advertising—bright red footsteps painted on sidewalks leading to the store—got him arrested briefly, the sale was a smash success. In 1895 he married Musa Bence; they had three children.

Liggett soon began his own business, a brokerage that sold goods—from buttons to carpets—from thirty-two mills direct to retailers. He then began selling a headache remedy, P.D.Q. (Pain Destroyed Quickly) and created the "Handy Lunch Box"—a business selling fresh box lunches each morning to business district workers. But he contracted typhoid and could not work from October 1896 until the following spring; by then his businesses were ruined. In December 1897 he learned of a new proprietary tonic, Vinol. He persuaded its marketer, Chester Kent & Company, to hire him as salesman; he began in Boston on 1 January 1897. Among his first sales were to two druggists in Salem; one soon used Vinol to promote sales, pricing it below cost; the other, a better account for Liggett, refused to reorder. Thus Liggett discovered the importance of exclusive agency; he successfully argued to change sales policy and initiated a company reorganization.

As a result, in 1898 he was general manager of Kent, at a salary of $3,500.

For the next four years Liggett traveled the entire country, visiting hundreds, perhaps thousands, of druggists; he recognized that few of them were good businessmen. Although there was the National Association of Retail Druggists, there was no organization to help druggists as businessmen. Liggett had learned to help retailers of Vinol with clever advertising and window displays; to this he added a national marketing plan, beginning with the creation of "the Vinol Club" in 1899, and extended with publication of the "Vinol Notice" in 1900. At the Vinol Club's third meeting, in Buffalo, New York, in 1901, Liggett presented his idea for creating a new company, the Drug Merchants of America, through which local druggists would collectively buy virtually all their goods directly from manufacturers, thereby securing better quality and lower prices (the same thing Liggett's brokerage had done). Liggett already had a corporate charter; United Drug Merchants opened immediately in New York.

Liggett quickly recognized cooperative buying was inadequate; druggists should have a manufacturing company to make many of the goods they sold, and these goods should have a shared brand name. In 1903 he founded United Drug and created the Rexall brand name. Liggett leased a small factory in Boston for this purpose; he had $160,000 from forty investors but just one product, a dyspepsia tablet. He added products quickly, including Rexall Cherry Juice Cough Syrup, an asthma remedy, and liver pills. In February 1903 he opened a candy department and was shipping by April. Liggett also spent heavily to advertise the Rexall name.

United Drug was almost too successful. Liggett struggled to meet demand for several years as member druggists surged to 700 in 1904, over 1,000 in 1906, and a remarkable 15,500 in 1914. Sales grew similarly, from under $62,000 in 1902 to $1 million in 1907 and to $15.6 million in 1914; manufacturing space grew from 300,000 to more than 4 million square feet. Liggett constantly looked for ways to expand the business and strengthen his associated druggists. He created National Cigar Stands to help them compete with United Cigar Stores, bought Gruth Chocolate and Chocolate Refiners to strengthen their candy offerings, acquired importers Deitsch Brothers to get better access to European goods, created United Druggists Mutual Fire Insurance to assure proper coverage, added Seamless Rubber to supply Rexall-branded rubber goods, and bought a string of paper and stationary producers to get high quality paper goods into Rexall stores. To combat expanding chains, United created its own retail chain under the Louis K. Liggett name.

Liggett was equally innovative in retailing, developing specially packaged "Saturday only" candy boxes and introducing the "one cent sale"—a second one for just one penny more. He also opened subsidiaries in Canada and then England in 1912. In 1920 United Drug bought out the English chain Boots, creating an enormous multinational drugstore conglomerate. Liggett's Drug Merchants, United Drug, and Rexall brand were all so successful that at least fifty-seven companies tried to imitate its approach, without success.

In 1921 Liggett nearly lost his company and his personal fortune when a speculator began driving down United's stock price; Liggett kept buying in an effort to support the share price. He hid the extent of his borrowing by securing loans from sixty different banks, but on 21 July he was forced to declare personal bankruptcy. His friends and Rexall retailers quickly organized and put up the money to restore Liggett. He paid them back in less than three years.

United Drug continued to expand through the 1920s. In 1928 Liggett led in creating a holding company, Drug, Inc., through which United Drug joined five manufacturing companies—Sterling Products, Vick Chemical, Bayer, Bristol-Myers, and Life-Savers—and three drug retail chains, the largest being Owl in the far west, to create what was intended to be a fully integrated manufacturing and retailing conglomerate. The holding company brought together many leading brands, including Vick's Vaporub, Vitalis, Life Savers, Ipana Tooth Paste, and Phillips Milk of Magnesia. But the trust failed, and in 1933 the five manufacturing companies withdrew, leaving Liggett and Drug, Inc. with just the retail chains and United Drug.

The Great Depression hit the 700-store Liggett chain particularly hard; it had taken long leases on retail locations, often subletting space to other retailers. As business contracted, reducing Liggett's own sales, many of these subletters failed, throwing the whole rent back onto Liggett. Despite renegotiating rents to secure nearly $1.5 million in rent reductions, on 31 March 1933 the Liggett chain went into bankruptcy, taking United Drug with it. Liggett himself had carefully laid the groundwork with creditors—of which his own Drug, Inc., was the largest—to avoid a court-appointed receiver. He had also anticipated the implications of the growing crisis in America, and from September 1932 he had worked to sell the Boots chain in England. In January 1934 he succeeded in completing the sale, bringing Drug, Inc., nearly $30 million. This money permitted Drug, Inc., to buy out the Liggett chain, paying $7.3 million, and assume its remaining liabilities of $2.6 million.

Liggett himself again took over as president of United Drug, and in 1941 he moved to the post of chairman and in 1944 to honorary chairman. Justin M. Dart, who had been married to Ruth Walgreen and headed that arch-rival's store operations, but who had then had a bitter falling out with the Walgreen family, succeeded Liggett as chairman. Dart, building from the United Drug manufacturing base, created Dart Industries, producers of brands such as Tupperware, West Bend pans, and Duracell batteries. The last pieces of Liggett's original Rexall business were sold in 1978.

Liggett pursued few activities outside of business. In 1915–1916 he organized the Republican League of Young Men in Massachusetts and played an important role in introducing newspaper advertising to political campaigns. He also served as a trustee for the Eastern States Exposition, was an active member of the League for the Preservation of American Independence, was for a single term president of the Boston Chamber of Commerce, and from 1928 to 1932 represented Massachusetts on the Republican National Committee. He enjoyed yachting for recreation, and for a time he had a camp in Maine.

One of America's most creative retailers and business managers between 1900 and 1920, Liggett shaped both the style of marketing and the development of the chain store concept. He lived his last few years in Washington, D.C., with one of his daughters; he died there of intestinal cancer.

• Liggett apparently left no business or personal papers. Samuel Merwin, *Rise and Fight Againe: The Story of a Life-Long Friend* (1935), provides a useful if uncritical biography. George F. Redmond, *Financial Giants of America*, vol. 1 (1922), pp. 367–75, offers a reasonably complete summary of Liggett's career to 1921. For a general history of the development of American chain stores, see Godfrey M. Lebhar, *Chain Stores in America: 1859–1962*, 3d ed. (1963). There is a trove of information in the industry's periodical, *Chain Store Age*, published since 1925 by Chain Store Publishing.

FRED CARSTENSEN

LIGHTNIN' SLIM (13 Mar. 1913–27 July 1974), guitarist and blues singer, was born Otis Hicks in St. Louis, Missouri, the son of Jerry Lee Hicks. Except for his father's name, there is little verified information about his parents, both of whom died young, or about his early life. After his mother's death—probably around 1926—he moved with his father to a farm near St. Francisville, Louisiana, where his father became a tenant farmer. After his father died, Hicks dropped out of school (he later recalled going as far as the tenth grade) and went to work to help support his three older siblings. By that time he had learned a little music from his father, an amateur guitarist, but did not develop a serious interest in music until later.

After eking out a living as a farmer during the depression, Hicks moved to Baton Rouge in 1946 to work at a fertilizer plant. Within two years, he was interested in guitar again, learning the basics from his brother Layfield. He began playing at house parties, working with such local artists as Cleve "Schoolboy Cleve" White and James Moore (later known as "Slim Harpo"), and eventually joined a Baton Rouge band, Big Poppa and the Cane Cutters.

According to Hicks, his recording career began when he was approached by Ray Meaders, a radio disc jockey whose on-air name was "Diggy Do." Meaders supposedly noticed Hicks playing on a porch one day and asked him if he would like to make records. Meaders then set up an audition in early 1954 with entrepreneur J. D. Miller, who recorded country and Cajun music at a studio in nearby Crowley.

In May 1954 Hicks cut his first sides for Miller's Feature label, accompanied by harmonica player Wild Bill Phillips, who had been bailed out of jail for the session, and disc jockey Meaders, who was pressed into service as a drummer. Miller decided that Hicks should be dubbed "Lightnin' Slim," and the artist's first single, the plaintive "Bad Luck" backed by "Rock Me, Mama," became a minor hit in the South. There were two more sessions for Feature, and two apparently illegal sessions for Chess in Opelousas, Louisiana, and Ace in Jackson, Mississippi—the latter creating permanent bad blood between Miller and the head of Ace Records.

By 1955 it was clear that Lightnin' Slim needed wider distribution than he could get from Feature. So Miller worked out a lease arrangement with Ernie Young's Excello Records in Nashville, Tennessee. Although Lightnin' continued to record in Miller's studio, songs and publishing rights went to Excello. The early releases on Excello had the same old-time sound as "Bad Luck," but a more distinctive sound was soon to evolve. In 1956, while riding a bus to a recording session in Crowley, Lightnin' met harmonica player Leslie Johnson. Johnson went along to the session, and when the scheduled harmonica player failed to show, he filled in, launching a nine-year recording partnership. Miller, ever fond of coining nicknames, dubbed Johnson "Lazy Lester."

Backed by Lazy Lester, Lightnin' Slim became a commercial success throughout the South by 1958 with such blues as "Hoo Doo Blues," "I'm a Rollin' Stone," "I'm Grown," and "My Starter Won't Work." And in 1959 his up-tempo "Rooster Blues" climbed to number twenty-three on *Billboard* magazine's rhythm and blues chart. A decade later, Miller told researcher Mike Leadbitter:

The way I used to get Lightnin' Slim to cut blues was this. Two or three days before I'd call him for a session I'd give his woman twenty-five dollars to give him hell. If at the session he really sang the blues . . . I'd give her another twenty-five. If she really made a good job of it, I'd give her the prettiest dress she'd ever seen on top of that.

Miller wore many hats: A-and-R man, producer, manager, and booking agent. He released sixty-six Lightnin' Slim sides and kept the artist active with engagements throughout the South, often as part of package tours with other Excello blues musicians such as Slim Harpo, Whispering Smith, and Lazy Lester. In the mid-1960s, however, only a year or two after the peak of his popularity, Lightnin' Slim's record sales declined as his partnership with Lazy Lester faded and the market for down-home blues dwindled. In 1965 he went to visit relatives in the Detroit area and remained a Michigan resident the rest of his life. Miller later claimed that Lightnin' stayed in the North because he had wrecked a borrowed van and feared prosecution if he returned to Louisiana. For whatever reason, he dropped out of show business briefly and took a job on an assembly line.

That same year, Slim Harpo, Lightnin' Slim's former sideman and protégé, scored the biggest rhythm-and-blues hit ever on Excello, "Baby Scratch My Back," which launched Slim Harpo on extensive tours through the late 1960s, with Lightnin' touring as a sideman between industrial jobs.

In the early 1970s Lightnin' Slim began a modest comeback of his own, playing at the Chicago Folk Festival in 1971 and the Ann Arbor Blues Festival in 1972. He picked up club bookings and traveled to Europe with American blues revues in 1972 and 1973. Within a year of the second European tour, however, he was diagnosed with stomach cancer. He died in Detroit.

Lightnin' Slim is often called the father of Louisiana "swamp blues." Influenced early by Texas blues guitarist Sam "Lightnin'" Hopkins, Hicks developed into a seminal regional stylist whose primitive guitar arpeggios and raspy vocals, embellished by Lazy Lester's harmonica, were strongly evocative of Louisiana's bayou country. Lightnin' Slim was also the first graduate of the Baton Rouge blues scene to make an impact as a recording artist. And he was the first commercially successful blues artist to be recorded by J. D. Miller, sparking Miller's emergence as a leading producer of regional, down-home blues. The distinctive sound produced by Miller's collaboration with Lightnin' was described by *Cashbox*, a trade magazine, as "straight from the swamp."

Although he did not achieve national success, Lightnin' Slim was an influential regional artist with a strong following in the South. He was considered by Miller and others to be the deepest of the Baton Rouge blues stylists.

• For more biographical information and excerpts from interviews with Lightnin' Slim, J. D. Miller, Lazy Lester, and others, see John Broven, *South to Louisiana* (1983); Fred Reif, "Lightnin' Slim: Wanderin' and Goin'," *Blues Unlimited*, no. 81 (Apr. 1971): 4–5; Jimmy Beyer, *Baton Rouge Blues: A Guide to the Baton Rouge Bluesmen and Their Music* (1980); and Sheldon Harris, *Blues Who's Who: A Biographical Dictionary of Blues Singers* (1989). For discographical information, see Mike Leadbitter et al., *Blues Records 1943–1970: "The Bible of the Blues,"* vol. 2: *L–Z* (1994); and for a sample of his music, try *Rooster Blues, Lightnin' Slim*, Excello 8000.

BILL MCCULLOCH
BARRY LEE PEARSON

LIGON, Thomas Watkins (1 May 1810–12 Jan. 1881), congressman and governor of Maryland, was born into a locally prominent family in Prince Edward County, Virginia, the son of Thomas D. Ligon, a farmer, and Martha Watkins, daughter of Colonel Thomas Watkins, who had served as an officer in the Revolution and founded a political dynasty in Prince Edward County. Although his father died when Ligon was a still a boy and his mother remarried, young Watkins grew up in relatively affluent surroundings and graduated from nearby Hampden-Sidney in 1830. During the next three years, he pursued the study of the law at the University of Virginia and at Yale. He returned to Virginia and was admitted to the bar but moved within a year to Baltimore, where he established a law practice in 1833. In 1840 Ligon married Sallie Dorsey and set up residence at "Chatham" near Ellicott's Mill—later called Ellicott City—southwest of Baltimore, where he maintained his law offices. They had two children before Sallie died in 1847. By 1850 he had amassed $80,000 in property, owned seventeen slaves, and was becoming that ubiquitous figure in the Old South—a lawyer/planter/politician of modest but quite sufficient means. In 1854 Ligon married his first wife's sister Mary; they had three children.

Ligon's career followed a common trajectory for one connected by birth and marriage to the political and social elite. Soon after settling in the Baltimore area, he became active in political affairs as a vigorous supporter of Andrew Jackson and his administration. Throughout his life, he was a strongly partisan Democrat and was elected to the Maryland House of Delegates in 1843. That year, although the Whigs swept to victory in the legislative elections by advocating a protective tariff, Ligon bucked the tide and supported "Van Buren and Free Trade." He served only a single term, however, before the Democrats nominated him to run for Congress in 1845.

Following the uprising over taxes that precipitated the calling of a convention to "reform" the constitution, the Maryland voters turned against the Whigs, cutting the party's huge majority in the House of Delegates to a mere four members and electing Ligon and three other Democrats to replace Whigs in Congress. Ligon's personal popularity with his constituents enabled him to gain a second term in 1847, although that year the Whigs strengthened their hold on the legislature and regained a majority in the state's congressional delegation. While in Congress, the Maryland Democrat stood as a loyal supporter of the Polk administration, advocating the adherence to a strict construction of the constitution and laissez faire in matters of political economy that constituted the domestic program of the "New Democracy" while also defending Manifest Destiny and the Mexican War. Although he supported southern rights, defended the peculiar institution, and advocated the removal of free blacks, Ligon shied away from extreme sectionalism.

When he returned to politics in the 1850s, Ligon emphasized his opposition to the abolitionists, a position shared by most of his fellow Marylanders. He won the governorship in 1853 rather handily against the demoralized Whigs, who had lost the state in the presidential election of 1852 for the first time in the party's brief history. However, as governor, Ligon soon found himself embroiled in a battle with the strong temperance/nativist coalition that seemed to emerge out of nowhere to dominate the state's legislature and control the city of Baltimore.

Ligon's administration was marked primarily by his ongoing conflict with the "secret political societies"— the Know Nothing or American party—that he singled out for criticism in his annual message of 1856.

Subsequently, he attempted to use the state militia to quell electoral violence in Baltimore, which led to contention over jurisdiction with the city's strong-willed, Know Nothing mayor, Thomas Swann. In 1856 the American party candidate, former president Millard Fillmore, carried Maryland's electoral votes in part because of Baltimore's rough-and-tumble electoral politics that featured gangs of nativist toughs like the Rip Raps, Blood Tubs, Pug Uglies, and Black Snakes, whose violent activities directed against naturalized voters and silk-stocking Democrats were winked at by the sympathetic constabulary. As many working-class Protestants converted from the Democrats to the new party, joining middle-class ex-Whigs, the Americans seized control of the state and in 1857 elected former Whig Thomas Hicks to replace Ligon. Eventually, however, Ligon's attempts to pacify the city led to the "reform" movement that ejected the Baltimore members of the House of Delegates chosen in the particularly violent election of 1859 and established a new Police Commission for the city in 1860.

Ligon chose not to run for a second term and withdrew from politics. He had given up his law practice in 1853 when he became governor, and he retired to the life of a gentleman farmer and a supporter of various local charitable and educational institutions. Ligon endured the Civil War (opposing both abolition and secession), emancipation, and what passed for Reconstruction in Maryland, living at Chatham until his death there in 1881.

A typical border-state Democrat of the antebellum period, Ligon was a staunch supporter of his party as a legislator and as a member of Congress during the 1840s. In the 1850s as governor he stood solidly against the Know Nothings, as he believed they were fomenting violence at the polls and corrupting the political system. Although he probably would have been defeated if he had run for reelection in 1857 against the American party candidate, Ligon was remembered by Democrats and the state's historians for his forthright stance against political bigotry and "ruffian rule."

• J. Thomas Scharf, *History of Maryland from the Earliest Period to the Present Day* (1879), includes a sympathetic account of Ligon's governorship and reprints numerous documents. There is a brief sketch in Heinrich Ewald Buchholz, *Governors of Maryland from the Revolution to the Year 1908* (1908). W. Wayne Smith, *Anti-Jackson Politics along the Chesapeake* (1989); Jean Baker, *The Politics of Continuity: Maryland Political Parties from 1858 to 1870* (1973); and William J. Evitts, *A Matter of Allegiances: Maryland from 1850 to 1861* (1974), present modern studies of Md. politics during Ligon's active years. Baker, *Ambivalent Americans: The Know-Nothing Party in Maryland* (1977), is the best study of his vociferous opponents, although Laurence F. Schmeckebier, *History of the Know-Nothing Party in Maryland* (1899), is still useful. Obituaries are in the *Baltimore Sun* and the *Baltimore American*, 13 Jan. 1881.

WILLIAM G. SHADE

LIGUTTI, Luigi (21 Mar. 1895–26 Dec. 1984), Roman Catholic priest, rural life advocate, and ecumenist, was born in Romans near Udine, Italy, the son of Spiridione L. Ligutti and Teresa Ciriani, farmers. He attended primary school in his native village and high school and one year of college in the Petit Seminary in Cividale and Udine. After immigrating to the United States in 1912, he attended St. Ambrose College in Davenport, Iowa, receiving his A.B. in June 1914. In 1917 he completed theological studies at St. Mary's Seminary in Baltimore, Maryland, receiving an S.T.B. He was ordained a Roman Catholic priest for the Diocese of Des Moines on 23 September 1917. After his ordination, he attended the Catholic University of America in Washington, D.C., where he majored in Latin and Greek and graduated in June 1918 with an M.A. Later he took postgraduate classes at Columbia University and the University of Chicago.

For eight years, Ligutti served as the pastor of small rural churches in Iowa, where he refined his philosophy of Catholic rural sociology. A practical man he did not romanticize rural life, but he was convinced that it was the most beneficial environment for families. Holding a personalist philosophy, he believed that the total development of the individual can best be achieved through decentralization of landholdings, wider distribution of property ownership, and a breakup of the heavy population concentrations in metropolitan areas.

In 1925 Ligutti was assigned to Assumption Parish in Granger, Iowa. The plight of his parishioners, who were unemployed coal miners, moved him to confront some of the problems caused by the depression. He saw the miners languishing without work while surrounded by untilled acres of rich, arable farmland. With the help of funding from the National Recovery Act and the personal interest of First Lady Eleanor Roosevelt, he sponsored and organized Granger Homesteads, the first national program of housing for lower-income families. Initiated in 1933, the program gave fifty families a home and five acres of land to farm. The families were given a 49-year lease. In 1942 the families formed the Granger Homestead Cooperative Association and took over the indebtedness that remained.

In 1934 Ligutti was appointed the diocesan director of rural life in the Diocese of Des Moines and became a member of the executive committee of the National Catholic Rural Life Conference (NCRLC). This organization, founded in 1922 by Edwin V. O'Hara, served Catholics in the primarily Protestant rural areas of the United States. In 1937 Ligutti was elected as the president of the NCRLC. In 1940, as executive secretary, he took on the day-to-day operation of the conference and moved the national headquarters from St. Paul, Minnesota, to his own diocese of Des Moines. Once Ligutti became a full-time executive secretary, he challenged national agricultural policy and the growth of corporate farming. Historian John Tracy Ellis characterized his leadership as "intelligent and dynamic" (Ellis, p. 125).

Over the next twenty years, Ligutti wrote and traveled extensively throughout the United States on behalf of rural life. In a typical year in the 1940s, Ligutti gave several hundred lectures in the United States and other parts of the world. His avid interest in land reform and cooperatives took him to Nova Scotia, the Scandinavian countries, the British Isles, Iran, and the United Arab Republics.

Ligutti joined forces with leaders in the Liturgical Movement, the National Conference of Catholic Charities, and Catholic Relief Services to make American Catholics more aware of the importance of rural life and the gravity of its problems. He felt that the gradual disappearance of the small family farm was endangering a way of life that had helped form the American character. He also worked with his counterparts in other Christian churches, becoming one of the earliest overt Catholic ecumenists in the United States.

Beginning in 1947, the NCRLC, under Ligutti's leadership, published the *Christian Farmer*, a journal aimed at the farmer and his family rather than the conference leadership. Unable to sustain itself, the periodical was succeeded by several other short-lived journals until in 1958 the magazine *Catholic Rural Life* took hold and gained a following.

On 26 July 1948 Ligutti was appointed as the Vatican observer to the Food and Agriculture Organization (FAO) of the United Nations, the first Vatican appointment to any office of this body. The following year he became the official permanent observer for the Holy See with the FAO, and in 1978 he was awarded the FAO's Agricola Medal. This medal is reserved for "men of our time who have made important international contributions."

After World War II, Ligutti went as a member of a commission representing Catholic War Relief Services to make a survey of displaced persons in Germany, Austria, Italy, Switzerland, France, Belgium, and England. This experience led to a new interest in the problems of migrants and to the eventual formation of the International Catholic Migration Commission. An emigrant himself, Ligutti had an active sympathy for the problems of refugees.

In 1960 the board of directors of the NCRLC relieved Ligutti of the office of executive secretary and asked him to accept a newly created position as the director of international affairs. Subsequently, he moved his residence to Rome and spent most of his time there. One of his most significant accomplishments had been the organization, beginning in 1950, of international rural life conferences. After 1950 he sponsored nine international conferences of rural Catholic leaders. As a direct result, in 1962 the International Catholic Rural Association, which included 124 organizations from forty-nine countries, was founded.

From 1962 to 1965, Ligutti served as a consultant to three preparatory commissions for Vatican Council II and to the conciliar commission on the laity. The council's statements on rural life, tithing, and migration often expressed Ligutti's ideas. He helped draft the sections on agriculture in two of Pope John XXIII's encyclicals, *Mater et Magistra* (1961) and *Pacem in Terris* (1963). In these documents, John XXIII echoed Ligutti's concern that throughout the world there existed an imbalance between the amount of arable land and the number of inhabitants as well as between the richness of the resources and the instruments of agriculture available. The pope called upon nations to enter into collaboration with each other and facilitate the circulation of goods, capital, and manpower. After the council, Ligutti established Agrimissio, an organization to foster collaboration among religious leaders, developmental agencies, the FAO, and others to promote higher standards of living for rural people by "helping them to help themselves."

In 1973 Ligutti was a moving force in the planning and implementation of an International Stewardship Seminar in Rome. His interest in stewardship, especially stewardship of the soil, presaged the manifold ecological concerns that later developed worldwide. In recognition of his efforts on behalf of stewardship, the National Catholic Stewardship Council in 1975 presented him with their first Christian Stewardship Award.

The last years of Ligutti's life were spent in retirement at his home, Villa Stillman, in Rome. Following his death in Rome, his body was returned to the United States and interred, as he had requested, in the cemetery of Assumption Church in Granger, Iowa.

During his lifetime, Ligutti was widely recognized for his contributions to international peace and justice. He was a member of the Pontifical Commission for Justice and Peace. He also received the 1961 Peace Award of the Catholic Association for International Peace and the Leon d'Oro in 1967 from the Lions Club International, Venetian Region.

• Ligutti's papers are preserved at the Archives of the Diocese of Des Moines, Iowa. Ligutti's articles and lectures are scattered in countless periodicals, magazines, and conference proceedings; these include "Catholic in Finland," *Commonweal*, 12 June 1940, pp. 256–57; "Cities Kill," *Commonweal*, 2 Aug. 1940, pp. 300–301; and "Religion and Poverty in Latin America," *America*, 25 June 1955, pp. 327–28. He coauthored, with John Rawe, *Rural Roads to Security* (1939). A biography of Ligutti, written during his lifetime, is Vincent A. Yzermans, *The People I Love: A Biography of Luigi Ligutti* (1976). Raymond Philip Witte, *Twenty-five Years of Crusading: A History of the National Catholic Rural Life Conference* (1948), contains a record of Ligutti's early work with the NCRLC. Ligutti's contributions are described in David S. Bovee, "Luigi Ligutti: Catholic Rural Life Leader," *U.S. Catholic Historian* 8, no. 3 (Summer 1989); John Tracy Ellis, *American Catholicism* (1956); Donald McDonald, "Priest on the Land," *Today* (Apr. 1951); and Francis X. Murphy, "Cardinal Pietro Pavan: Inveterate Optimist," *America*, 10 Feb. 1996.

MARY ROGER MADDEN

LIHOLIHO. *See* Kamehameha II.

LIKERT, Rensis (5 Aug. 1903–3 Sept. 1981), social scientist, was born in Cheyenne, Wyoming, the son of George Herbert Likert, an engineer for the Union Pacific Railroad, and Cornelia Zonne, a former teacher. After spending several years as a civil engineering student, Likert received his bachelor's degree in sociology at the University of Michigan in 1926. He then enrolled at Columbia University, from which he received a Ph.D. in psychology in 1932. In 1928 he married Charlotte Jane Gibson, with whom he had two children.

At Columbia, Likert's interests turned from experimental to social psychology. For his dissertation under Gardner Murphy he carried out a number of attitude studies of college students. Experimenting with different ways of measuring attitudes, he developed in 1932 a new method of "summated ratings," which asked respondents to choose a position from a five-point scale between "strongly agree" and "strongly disagree" for each of a set of attitude statements. Likert found that the resulting attitude scores correlated highly with the established "Thurstone," or "equal-appearing interval" scale, which had been derived from psychophysical measurement procedures but was much more laborious to construct as well as to administer to respondents. The "Likert scale," which lays out a pro/con continuum from "strongly agree" to "strongly disagree" for the respondent, became Likert's legacy to social science research and a major data-gathering tool for the next sixty years. Although Likert's future contributions may have been much more important, the sophistication of the deceptively simple-appearing scale has often been ignored. His name as attached to this scale is usually mispronounced (as if it rhymed with "hiker" instead of with "kicker").

Moving from teaching at New York University to heading the research department at the Life Insurance Agency Management Association in Hartford, Connecticut, in 1935, he began to work on a problem that was to occupy him for the rest of his life, the study of management styles and work organization. In 1939 he became head of the Division of Program Surveys at the U.S. Department of Agriculture. In this capacity he played a major role in the innovative development of scientific survey research techniques beyond the then current opinion polling. Some of the lasting contributions of this period were the "probability sampling" method, the "open-ended question" format (where respondents have to formulate their own answers instead of selecting from the fixed alternatives typical of commercial polls), and the "funnel technique" (a sequence of progressively more focused questions) for use in intensive interviews in smaller but more precise random samples.

After the outbreak of World War II, the topics of Likert's surveys shifted from agriculture to matters of concern to other government agencies, such as the sale of war bonds or public reactions to rationing. By the end of the war, Likert had overseen the development of the "morale" study of the U.S. Strategic Bombing Survey, an attempt to evaluate the effects of large-scale strategic bombing on civilian populations in Germany and Japan. Likert received the Medal of Freedom for this survey, the complex results of which, revealing differences between Germany and Japan and at the personal and aggregate level in Germany, indicated the problematic outcomes of such massive bombing strategies.

When Congress abolished the Program Surveys Division after the war, Likert took a core group of researchers from government into academia. In 1946 his optimism and persuasive skills succeeded in establishing a Survey Research Center at the University of Michigan at Ann Arbor. In 1949 this center was combined with the former Research Center for Group Dynamics of the Massachusetts Institute of Technology to become the new Institute for Social Research, with Likert as director. His enthusiasm, interpersonal skills, and managerial style helped to make ISR one of the three major academic social research institutions, along with Paul F. Lazarsfeld's Bureau of Applied Social Research at Columbia University and the National Opinion Research Center at Denver and later at Chicago.

Under Likert's direction, ISR experienced impressive growth and expansion together with an amazing stability in the outstanding senior personnel he had recruited. By the time he retired in 1970, the institute, a semi-autonomous, self-supporting organization, had developed several unique programs. These included a political behavior program with major national election studies; an economic behavior program, which included periodic national surveys of consumer confidence for the Federal Reserve Board; an organizational behavior program, which studied the effectiveness of major businesses from the United Parcel Service to health service organizations and others; and a program for the development and improvement of various aspects of survey methodology.

Likert's own theoretical interests lay in the development of a social psychological theory of organizations. In several books beginning with *New Patterns of Management* (1961), he argued that a decentralizing, participatory organizational structure would be more effective as well as more humane than traditional hierarchical organizations. He also promoted a process of human resource accounting, in which the costs and benefits of investment in employees and their productivity would be added to the standard methods of business accounting.

After his retirement Likert set up a consulting firm for organizational management, Rensis Likert Associates, and continued research on the effectiveness of participatory organizational styles. He died in Ann Arbor. One of his longtime co-workers described him as having been a warm and supportive person, an entrepreneur always open to new ideas, "a pragmatic sort of visionary."

The continued flourishing of both the organizations he founded, the ISR and Rensis Likert Associates, attest to Likert's skills in institution building as well as to the soundness of his theoretical insights. His influence on the academic parent discipline appears more limited, however, as postwar social psychology soon turned its back on survey research on social problems in favor of more scientist laboratory experimentation and honored Likert most for the minor technical contribution of the "Likert scale." Ironically, recent discussions of the problems of American business and the need for organizational change often advocate a Japanese model when in fact many of the ideas represented in this model were formulated in this country by Likert and his co-workers from the 1930s to 1970s.

• Some of Likert's professional papers are in the Bentley Historical Library at the University of Michigan, Ann Arbor. Additional published books by Likert include *The Human Organization: Its Management and Value* (1967) and *New Ways of Managing Conflict*, with Jane Gibson Likert (1976). A thumbnail sketch of Likert is in Ernest R. Hilgard, *Psychology in America* (1987), pp. 724–25. See also J. M. Converse, *Survey Research in the United States: Roots and Emergence, 1890–1960* (1987). An obituary by S. E. Seashore and Daniel Katz is in the *American Psychologist* 37 (1982): 851–53.

FRANZ SAMELSON

LILIENTHAL, David Eli (8 July 1899–14 Jan. 1981), attorney and government official, was born in Morton, Illinois, the son of Leo Lilienthal, a merchant, and Minnie (or Minna) Rosenak, who were both Czech immigrants. After attending local public schools, Lilienthal studied at DePauw University in Greencastle, Indiana, receiving a bachelor's degree and election to Phi Beta Kappa in 1920. In college he also excelled as a light heavyweight boxer, developing a skill he had been taught as a teenager. That fall he entered Harvard Law School, where the teachings of one of his professors, Felix Frankfurter, later a U.S. Supreme Court justice, encouraged Lilienthal's interest in the conservation of natural resources.

Following graduation from law school in 1923, Lilienthal married a DePauw classmate, Helen Marian Lamb; they had two children. Lilienthal began the practice of law in Chicago with the firm of Donald Richberg. He specialized in utility law, and his victory in several cases challenging rates charged by large utility companies led to his appointment by Governor Philip La Follette to the Wisconsin State Utility Commission (later the Wisconsin State Public Service Commission) in 1931. In that post he enforced rate reductions by telephone companies and other utilities. Two years later President Franklin D. Roosevelt appointed him as a director of the newly established Tennessee Valley Authority (TVA), a federal electric power and flood-control program.

The TVA was a depression-engendered project created to improve living standards in a poor and long-neglected region of the United States. To control flooding and at the same time make electric power widely available for area residents, government workers cleared 175,000 acres of land and built more than twenty dams on the Tennessee River and its major tributaries during the 1930s. The first chair of the TVA was Arthur Morgan, an engineer who was in charge of dam construction, while Lilienthal had responsibility for the power program. A third director, Harcourt Morgan, was in charge of a fertilizer-production program.

Morgan and Lilienthal clashed almost from the outset. The chair wanted to maintain peaceful relations with existing power companies in the region by charging similar rates. Lilienthal strongly disagreed, arguing that the TVA should offer power at a cheaper rate to area municipalities. When Lilienthal's term expired in 1936 and Roosevelt reappointed him to the post, Morgan protested. Their feud continued until 1938, when Roosevelt removed Arthur Morgan from office for "contumacy" and appointed Harcourt Morgan to succeed him.

Lilienthal's difficulties were not over, however. His plans were also opposed by Wendell L. Willkie, the future presidential candidate who headed the Commonwealth and Southern Corporation, the major utility holding company in the Tennessee Valley. Willkie publicly questioned Lilienthal's ethics and further suggested that he was acting illegally. Lilienthal, Willkie charged, had refused to consider arbitration to settle the rate dispute between the power companies and the TVA. Willkie also disclosed that Lilienthal had used government funds to build power-distribution facilities in the valley that duplicated existing privately held facilities. These actions, Willkie claimed, would unfairly force private power companies to lower their prices to remain in business.

Congressional Republicans seized upon the dispute and used it as a vehicle to attack Roosevelt's New Deal programs, which they said were designed to destroy capitalism. Lilienthal was vituperatively denounced in the House and Senate. One leading Republican, Senator Styles Bridges of New Hampshire, called him "a Führer" who was trying to set up "an authoritarian state in the heart of America." Despite persistent criticism, however, Lilienthal persevered in his post. He turned the tables on the private utilities by negotiating the government's purchase of Commonwealth and Southern properties for $78 million in early 1939. Soon afterward he was named vice chair of the TVA and proclaimed that the organization was now "an established institution."

Lilienthal became chair of the TVA on 15 September 1941. Sensing that U.S. participation in World War II was imminent, he began expanding the TVA's power program to serve the needs of both private and government plants producing ammunition and other war-related materials. By 1943 the TVA had become what Lilienthal publicly called "the largest producer of power for war in the Western Hemisphere." In 1944 the TVA was the nation's leading producer of electric power, with an annual output of 10 billion kilowatt-hours. One major customer of the TVA, however, only became known after the war ended in 1945: the U.S. Army–sponsored Manhattan Project, which developed the atomic bomb, had been secretly headquartered in Oak Ridge, Tennessee, to take advantage of TVA power.

In May 1945 President Harry S. Truman reappointed Lilienthal to another term as TVA chair, but he served only eight more months in that post. In January 1946 Truman named Lilienthal as chair of an advisory committee to the U.S. Department of State on the postwar production and uses of atomic energy. Later that year the committee drew up a plan, called the Acheson-Lilienthal Report after its principal authors, the chair and then Under Secretary of State Dean Acheson, which became the basis for U.S. government policy on atomic energy control.

Not long after the report was issued, Truman named Lilienthal chair of the new Atomic Energy Commission (AEC), created to remove atomic energy production from military control and place it under civilian auspices. Once again, Lilienthal found himself the subject of controversy as the Senate debated his confirmation to the post. A wave of anticommunism was engulfing the nation—the early stages of what would later be called "McCarthyism"—and conservative politicians, Democratic as well as Republican, accused Lilienthal of being a communist sympathizer because of his controversial views on public power and his parents' births in Czechoslovakia, a nation that had come under domination by the Soviet Union.

Outraged at these accusations and attacks on Lilienthal's loyalty, many prominent men and women came to his public defense, including leading nuclear scientists and the president himself. During widely publicized congressional hearings, Lilienthal eloquently defended his patriotism and became a heroic figure to millions when he warned that "hysteria . . . innuendo and smears, and other unfortunate tactics" might "cause a separation among our people, cause one group and one individual to hate another, based on mere attacks, mere unsubstantiated attacks upon their loyalty."

Lilienthal was finally confirmed in April 1947 after three months of hearings. He immediately began expanding the production of atomic bombs, expressing his belief that the United States was falling behind in the international race to develop atomic energy. While spearheading nuclear weapons development, Lilienthal also encouraged the use of atomic power in private industry. Many members of Congress continued to oppose him, however, and when President Truman reappointed him chair of the AEC in the spring of 1948, Truman was forced to extend his term of service only two years, to June 1950.

In 1949 Lilienthal was forced to fight congressional charges of mismanagement at the AEC, and by the time he was absolved of blame later that year he had decided to resign as chair. He remained only long enough to participate in the conclusion of a debate among himself and the four other commissioners over whether or not to develop a hydrogen bomb. Although not opposed in principle to developing the bomb, Lilienthal expressed concern that if scarce resources were diverted to the project, then crucial atomic bomb production would lag.

Following the AEC's decision to pursue development of a hydrogen bomb, Lilienthal resigned as chair, effective 15 February 1950. He went on a lecture tour and traveled widely in Europe, Africa, and Asia before joining the banking firm of Lazard Frères

& Company as an industrial consultant. In 1952 he became president of Minerals Separation, an industrial minerals producer. Three years later he was named chair and chief executive officer of the Development and Resources Corporation, an international resource-development organization, and held that post until 1979, when the company was dissolved.

In addition to his roles as an attorney, government official, and businessman, Lilienthal was also a writer and a member of the Authors Guild. His books include *TVA: Democracy on the March* (1944), *This I Do Believe* (1949), *Big Business: A New Era* (1953), *The Multinational Corporation* (1960), *Change, Hope and the Bomb* (1963), *Management: A Humanist Art* (1967), and *Atomic Energy: A New Start* (1980). He also oversaw the publication of the first six volumes of *The Journals of David E. Lilienthal* (1964–1976), an edited version of his diaries; a seventh volume, edited by his widow, was published posthumously in 1983.

Lilienthal received many awards during his lifetime, including the Public Welfare Medal of the National Academy of Sciences, election to the American Academy of Arts and Sciences, and commendations from the governments of Peru and Brazil for his contributions to resource development in those countries. In retirement Lilienthal lived with his wife in Princeton, New Jersey. He died in New York City.

• Lilienthal's papers, including the journals in their entirety, are deposited in the Seeley G. Mudd Manuscript Library at Princeton University. The Lilienthal collection also includes the records of the Development and Resources Corporation. Biographical information on Lilienthal is in *Current Biography Yearbook 1944* (1945), pp. 413–15; and Willson Whitman, *David Lilienthal: Public Servant in a Power Age* (1948). See also G. Bromley Oxnam, "The Administrator as Social Reformer: David E. Lilienthal," in his *Personalities in Social Reform* (1950). An obituary is in the *New York Times*, 16 Jan. 1981.

ANN T. KEENE

LILIENTHAL, Max (6 Nov. 1814?–5 Apr. 1882), rabbi and educator, was born in Munich, Germany, the son of Loew Seligmann Lilienthal, a merchant, and Dina Lichtenstein. He achieved a brilliant record at the University of Munich (Ph.D. 1837) and received his rabbinic ordination from Munich's chief rabbi, Hirsch Aub. In 1839, upon the recommendation of Ludwig Philippson, editor of the *Allgemeine Zeitung des Judentums*, Germany's most important Jewish newspaper, he was invited to head a German-style modern Jewish school, established on Haskalah (Jewish enlightenment) principles by the small Jewish community of Riga, Russia. After serving in that position for just over a year (1840–1841), he was summoned by S. S. Uvarov, Russia's minister of national enlightenment, to oversee a proposed reform of the educational system of Jews throughout the Russian empire to promote greater rapprochement between Jews and their neighbors. Lilienthal toured Russian Jewish communities seeking support for the plan, but he met with stiff resistance, especially in Lithuania. In 1842 he published

Maggid Yeshu'ah, translated into Hebrew by S. Y. Fin, that both defended the proposal to create government-sponsored Haskalah-oriented Jewish schools and warned against interference and opposition. Two years later a new law "establishing special schools for the education of Jewish youth" was promulgated.

Lilienthal left Russia on holiday in July 1845 and never returned. While many claim that he had become disillusioned with the government's program or had been made aware of its alleged conversionist aims, recent scholarship suggests that he actually left to marry his fiancée, Babette "Pepi" Nettre, and that his subsequent resignation owed much to family pressure to abandon what had become a frustrating and underpaid position. Whatever the case, Lilienthal and his wife, with whom he would have seven children, soon left for New York City, where they arrived in November 1845.

Lilienthal was among the first college-trained and properly ordained rabbis to reach America's shores, and in order to secure his services New York's three leading German Orthodox synagogues, Anshe Chesed, Rodeph Shalom, and Shaarey Hashamayim, formed a "United German-Jewish Community" and elected him their chief rabbi. In addition to supervisory and pastoral duties, he preached every Sabbath, alternating among the three synagogues, ran a school, and for a brief period presided over a rabbinical court along with Rabbi Isaac Mayer Wise and Herman Felsenheld. In 1848, however, the congregational union ended, owing partly to friction between Lilienthal and a group of trustees and partly to tensions over ritual innovations that Lilienthal had championed, including confirmation, rules of order, and slight liturgical changes. As a result, he withdrew from his position and founded a private Jewish boarding school, which he and his wife ran with great success until he left the city. He continued to carry on some rabbinic functions during most of this period, but as a member of the radical society for liberty and freedom of thought known as the "Friends of Light" (*Verein der Lichtfreunde*), he became increasingly sympathetic toward religious reforms and withdrew from active communal involvements.

In 1855, upon the recommendation of Wise, Lilienthal was elected rabbi of K. K. Bene Israel, the oldest synagogue in Cincinnati. He came in as a moderate reformer, prompting a split in the congregation, and after the more traditional members departed, Bene Israel adopted many of the changes previously accepted by Wise's own Cincinnati congregation, K. K. Bene Jeshurun. Lilienthal was sharply attacked for his moderate role in the Rabbinical Conference in Cleveland (1855) and thereafter focused much of his attention on local Cincinnati affairs. He served on the city's board of education (1860–1869); became a regent of McMicken College, which later became the University of Cincinnati (1872–1882); actively participated in local philanthropic, social, and cultural organizations; and was the first rabbi to preach in Christian pulpits. He also worked closely with Wise on behalf of religious reforms, church-state separation, the Union of American Hebrew Congregations, and especially Hebrew Union College, where he taught history.

Lilienthal was beloved by his congregation, community, and students and like his teacher Aub was acclaimed as a man of peace. A contemporary describes how Lilienthal and Wise, working side by side, complemented one another: "What Wise suggested, Lilienthal supported, and what Lilienthal pacified, Wise promoted. What Wise wounded, Lilienthal healed, and what Lilienthal whitewashed, Wise exposed. Where Wise wanted to lead, Lilienthal gracefully followed, and where Lilienthal wisely warned, Wise laudably obeyed" (*American Israelite*, 11 June 1883).

Lilienthal published a volume of poems entitled *Freiheit, Fruehling und Liebe* (1857) and numerous addresses, sermons, and journalistic pieces. He also coauthored with Robert Allyn a textbook entitled *Things Taught: Systematic Instruction in Composition and Object Lessons* (1862), which applied the educational theories of Johann Heinrich Pestalozzi to the study of composition. In addition, he edited the journals *Sabbath School Visitor* and *The Hebrew Review*, contributed regularly to the Anglo and German Jewish press, and organized the short-lived Rabbinical Literary Association. He died in Cincinnati, and his funeral was reputedly "one of the most impressive ever held" in the city. The modern American Reform rabbinate owes much to the conception of the rabbi's role that Lilienthal pioneered and taught.

• Small collections of Lilienthal's correspondence may be found at the American Jewish Archives in Cincinnati, which also houses the papers of Congregation Bene Israel. The Western Jewish History Center in Berkeley, Calif., houses an important collection of Lilienthal family papers, some of which are reprinted in Sophie Lilienthal, *The Lilienthal Family Record* (1930). Other primary sources bearing on Lilienthal's career are published in Hyman B. Grinstein, *The Rise of the Jewish Community of New York, 1654–1860* (1945) and "The Minute Book of Lilienthal's Union of German Synagogues in New York," *Hebrew Union College Annual* 18 (1944): 321–53; Sefton D. Temkin, "Rabbi Max Lilienthal Views American Jewry in 1847," in *A Bicentennial Festschrift for Jacob Rader Marcus*, ed. B. W. Korn (1976); and Temkin, "A Beth Din for America," in *Perspectives on Jews and Judaism*, ed. A. A. Chiel (1978). Isaac Mayer Wise published anonymous and revealing reminiscences of Lilienthal in "Reminiscences," *Hebrew Review* 2 (1881–1882): 184–90. Lilienthal's student and successor, Rabbi David Philipson, authored the only full-length biography, *Max Lilienthal, American Rabbi Life and Writings* (1915), which contains valuable excerpts from Lilienthal's articles and memoirs. For his Russian period, the best modern treatment is in Michael Stanislawski, *Tsar Nicholas I and the Jews* (1983), which cites earlier publications. Two articles by Morton J. Merowitz, "Max Lilienthal (1814–1882)—Jewish Educator in Nineteenth-Century America," *Yivo Annual* 15 (1974): 46–65 and "A Note on the Dating of Dr. Max Lilienthal's Birth," *American Jewish Archives* 26 (1974): 78–79, fill in data not otherwise available.

JONATHAN D. SARNA

LILIUOKALANI (2 Sept. 1838–11 Nov. 1917), last sovereign queen of Hawaii, was born in Honolulu, the daughter of high chief Kapaakea and the chiefess, Keohokalole. Her father had been a close adviser of King Kamehameha III. Lydia, as she was named, was *hanaied* (adopted) at birth, which was a custom of goodwill to solidify relationships, by Abner Paki and his wife, Konia, and she lived in their home "Haleakala." Paki was a councilor of Kamehameha III. The Pakis had one natural daughter, Bernice Pauahi, and throughout her life Liliuokalani, or Lydia Kamakaeha Paki as she was then known, was closer to Bernice than to her own siblings.

When Liliuokalani was four years old, her adoptive parents enrolled her in the Royal School, originally the Chiefs' Children's School founded in 1839, which was administered by American missionaries. At the Royal School she became fluent in English, and her moral values were shaped by the influence of the missionaries. She was also an outstanding member of Kawaiahao Church, built under the direction of Hiram Bingham (1789–1869), the leader of the first company of missionaries to Hawaii in 1820. As a young girl she was part of the royal circle attending Kamehameha IV and Queen Emma. In 1862 she married John Owen Dominis, the son of an American sea captain. They had no children.

Being primed for the crown's inheritance, Liliuokalani (her royal name) made several visits throughout the islands to impress her subjects. "It became proper and necessary for me to make a tour of the islands to meet the people, that all classes, rich and poor, planter or fisherman, might have an opportunity to become acquainted with the one who some day should be called upon to hold the highest executive office." She and her husband also journeyed in 1887 to England in celebration of Queen Victoria's golden jubilee and were received as royalty. On the way they visited Washington, D.C., where they were received by President Grover Cleveland.

King Kalakaua died in San Francisco in January 1891, and Liliuokalani assumed the throne. One of her first acts was to suggest that there should be a new constitution for Hawaii, because Kalakaua had been forced to submit to the "Bayonet Constitution" of 1887. The Bayonet Constitution had weakened the powers of the monarchy and had forced Kalakaua to relinquish numerous powers to the American members of his cabinet. Liliuokalani attempted this constitutional change during an economic slump after the McKinley Tariff of 1890. American interests in Hawaii began to think of the annexation of Hawaii by the United States in order to reestablish an economic competitive position for the sugar interests. But native Hawaiians desired more detachment from American influences and supported the queen's new constitution. Economic circumstances plus her willful and stubborn character caused Liliuokalani to lose her throne.

Several members of the queen's own cabinet, which had not been accepted by the legislature, refused to sign the new constitution, which she attempted to promulgate in January 1893. After she had attempted to rule by edict, a committee of public safety made up of revolutionaries against the queen had been established. This committee sought protection of military forces aboard an American ship in port, the USS *Boston*. The American minister in Hawaii, John L. Stevens, had ordered the *Boston*'s troops ashore to defend the interests of Americans and to take control of various governmental buildings. The revolutionaries' Committee of Public Safety then deposed the queen, abrogated the monarchy, and established a government that later became the Republic of Hawaii (1894). This group then petitioned to be annexed by the United States.

Historically, it was Queen Liliuokalani's right to issue a new constitution through an edict from the throne as had been done in the past. But the group against her, led by Sanford B. Dole, thought they were protecting themselves against a capricious monarch who had precedent on her side but was politically inexperienced. She wished to restore the balance between local island interests and those of the foreigners who had come increasingly to control large parts of the Hawaiian economy and land. Liliuokalani lost the political battle. Her opponents established a republic and waited for a favorable time to press for annexation to the United States.

During Grover Cleveland's second term (1893–1897), one of his first acts was to withdraw a treaty of annexation of Hawaii that had been negotiated by his predecessor, Benjamin Harrison (1833–1901), with the annexationists who had deposed the queen. Cleveland believed Liliuokalani to have been wronged and urged the annexationists to restore the queen to her throne. Sanford B. Dole and the republican-annexationists politely refused to do so. Through Cleveland's support, Liliuokalani hoped to be enthroned again and restored to full power.

In March 1893, James H. Blount arrived, representing President Cleveland, to seek a solution to the problem. He listened to both the annexationists and the restorationists and concluded that the Hawaiian people were on the side of their queen. Blount's final report also implicated the American minister Stevens in the overthrow of Liliuokalani. Cleveland then instructed Albert S. Willis, the new American minister, to offer to support the queen if she would grant a general amnesty to the annexationists who had dethroned her. Liliuokalani, out of stubbornness, initially refused to grant general amnesty, but by mid-December she changed her mind and offered clemency for her political enemies. Because of her delay, however, she had compromised her political position. President Cleveland had turned the Hawaiian question over to Congress.

On 4 July 1894, the Republic of Hawaii with Sanford B. Dole as president was proclaimed. It was recognized immediately by the U.S. government. In 1895 Liliuokalani was arrested and, after a cache of weapons was found in the gardens of her home, was forced to reside in Iolani Palace. She denied knowledge of this cache, which in fact was intended to be used by her supporters to restore her. After her imprisonment in the palace, her supporters kept her abreast of the news in Hawaii by sending flowers to the palace wrapped in newspapers of the day. In November 1896 she was released and allowed to speak freely. She journeyed to Washington, D.C., in December 1896 to speak directly to Cleveland, but by this time Cleveland was a lame-duck president. The Spanish-American War period witnessed the complete triumph of her enemies. Hawaii was now seen as a strategic bastion to protect other U.S. interests in the Pacific. Hawaii was annexed to the United States through a joint resolution of Congress in 1898.

Liliuokalani lived on for nearly two decades in Honolulu, receiving an annual pension from the legislature, which by 1917 was $15,000. She also received income from various properties, including a 6,000-acre sugar plantation. She was present at most state occasions but had declined the offer to watch the annexation ceremonies as she could not bear to see the Hawaiian flag lowered and the Stars and Stripes put in its place.

In her gracious old age, Liliuokalani became a model Hawaiian who forgave her enemies and stood for all that was virtuous in Hawaii's grand past. She sought to preserve the Hawaiian traditions. She also continued to write songs, of which her earlier "Aloha Oe" is the best known. She was the most outstanding member of the Kalakaua dynasty in composing music. She also played the piano with a high level of skill as well as the ukulele, guitar, zither, and organ.

Most modern American historians cast Liliuokalani as "the Polynesian chiefess of olden times, in whom centuries of tradition bred a belief in the sacred bond between a people and their land" or as "the strong-willed, well-educated Victorian monarch who valiantly defended her inherited sovereignty and made it her overriding duty to safeguard and preserve Hawaiian independence." Both characterizations are correct.

Before her death, she established the Liliuokalani Trust to be used for destitute or orphaned Hawaiian children. She died in Honolulu.

• The diaries, letters, and documents in regard to Queen Liliuokalani's personal life are located in the Liliuokalani Collection in the State Archives of Hawaii and also in the Bishop Museum manuscript collection. Additional records related to Liliuokalani and Princess Kaiulani (heir apparent) are to be found in the A. S. Cleghorn Collection, State Archives of Hawaii. Published sources of information include Liliuokalani, *Hawaii's Story by Hawaii's Queen* (1898); William D. Alexander, *History of the Later Years of the Hawaiian Monarchy and the Revolution of 1893* (1896), a contemporary view; Lorrin A. Thurston, *Memoirs of the Hawaiian Revolution* (1936); William A. Russ, *The Hawaiian Revolution (1893–94)* (1959); Merze Tate, *The U.S. and the Hawaiian Kingdom* (1965); Julius A. Pratt, *The Expansionists of 1898* (1936); Gavan Daws, *The Shoal of Time: A History of the Hawaiian Islands* (1968); Alfons L. Korn and Barbara Peterson, "Liliuokalani," in *Notable Women of Hawaii*, ed. Barbara Bennett Peterson (1984); Ralph S. Kuykendall, *The Hawaiian Kingdom, 1874–1893* (1967); Helena G. Allen, *The Betrayal of Queen Liliuokalani*

(1982); and the Hawaii State Foundation on Culture and the Arts pamphlet titled "A Sculpture of Queen Liliuokalani" (1977). An obituary is in *Paradise of the Pacific*, Jan. 1918, pp. 11 and 15.

BARBARA BENNETT PETERSON

LILLIE, Frank Rattray (27 June 1870–5 Nov. 1947), scientist, was born in Toronto, Canada, son of accountant George Waddell Lillie and Emily Ann Rattray. Both Lillie's grandfathers were clergymen, and his family expected him to follow in their footsteps. Instead, upon entering the University of Toronto in 1887, Lillie majored in the natural sciences. His interest in biology, especially embryology and physiological perspectives, blossomed under faculty members R. Ramsay Wright and A. B. Macallum. Lillie received his A.B. in 1891 and immediately left to attend his first summer session at Woods Hole Marine Biological Laboratory (MBL) in Massachusetts. He spent the next fifty-five summers at the MBL.

That first summer, Lillie met Charles Otis Whitman, became a member of the Corporation of MBL, and obtained a graduate fellowship at Clark University under Whitman, who was professor of morphology there. In 1892, Whitman was invited to join the faculty of the new University of Chicago as head of biology by President William Rainey Harper. Whitman accepted and brought along most of the Clark zoology faculty and students. At Chicago Lillie became a fellow in morphology and reader in embryology while working on his doctorate. In 1894, at the age of twenty-four, Lillie received his Ph.D. in zoology *summa cum laude*.

That same summer, Lillie met Frances Crane, a student in his embryology course at Woods Hole, and they married in 1895. The Lillies had six and adopted three children. Both Mrs. Lillie and her brother Charles R. Crane became active contributors to the MBL and the University of Chicago, providing personal financing for several important projects, including construction of the University's Whitman Laboratory.

Upon graduation, Frank Lillie became instructor of zoology at the University of Michigan, remaining until 1899, when he served as professor of biology at Vassar College for one year. He returned to the University of Chicago in the fall of 1900 as assistant professor of embryology and remained there for the rest of his career. In 1906 he became a full professor and, upon Whitman's death in 1910, Lillie succeeded him as chair of the department of Zoology. Lillie held this position until 1931, when he was appointed dean of the Division of Biological Sciences. In 1935, he was honored as the Andrew MacLeish Distinguished Service Professor of Embryology and became a professor emeritus. Lillie achieved significant national stature both as a researcher and as a scientific statesman and fundraiser par excellence.

Lillie's research centered around a series of subtly linked problems across his scholarly career. The first set of problems, based in classic turn-of-the-century embryology especially as practiced at Woods Hole, concerned cell lineage, which he studied first in the freshwater mussel *Unio* at Whitman's suggestion for his dissertation, and later in the marine annelid (worm) *Chaetopterus*. Running against the biological tide in cleavage studies, which then emphasized similarities in cleavage patterns *across* species, Lillie's research emphasized the distinctive features of cleavage *within* each species and how these might functionally serve the future larva. These projects established Lillie's stature as a biologist.

Like Whitman and other Chicago biologists who emphasized organizational phenomena, Lillie often sought to understand connections across biological processes. Thus it is not surprising that he turned next to a temporally prior set of biological problems, those of fertilization, which he studied most extensively in sea urchins and the annelid *Nereis*. With his student Ernest Everett Just, one of the first black biologists, Lillie developed the theory that fertilization is precisely timed, irreversible, species specific, and involves *fertilizin*, biochemical substances borne by the sperm and the egg that interact in a lock-and-key fashion. He pioneered in diagramming this interaction. This research led to publication of *Problems of Fertilization* (1919 and, with Just, in 1924).

Lillie's long-standing interest in embryology then led him to his third major line of research, the hormonal basis of sex development and sex characteristics in mammals. He came to this work through providing a groundbreaking new explanation of the freemartin in cattle as an infertile female co-twin to a normal male. The freemartin may or may not have perceptibly ambiguous sex characteristics. Lillie's painstaking research was conducted largely on twin embryos collected from the Chicago stockyards and a family ranch. He found that the bloodstreams of the embryos were connected through the placentae, that the freemartin was a genetic female (via estimates based on the sex ratio), and that circulating male hormones generated by the male fetus were responsible for the female's sterility and other abnormalities. From this major early reproductive endocrinological investigation, Lillie went on to serve as founder, contributor, and sponsor of that field for the rest of his life.

Lillie's last major line of research centered on the effects of hormones on developing structures, specifically regenerating fowl feathers in the brown leghorn. He worked on these problems with research assistants Mary Juhn and Hsi Wang until his death. Lillie's "General Biological Introduction" to the many editions of the core volume in reproductive sciences, *Sex and Internal Secretions* (Edgar Allen, ed., 1932), stands as a model of synthesis and problem formulation for an emergent field. It continues to be read.

Lillie's considerable administrative skills benefited many organizations, not least the Woods Hole Marine Biological Laboratory, which he served as assistant director after 1900 and as director from 1908 until 1926. Lillie most successfully stewarded the fledgling institution into a financial security comparable to its scholarly renown, increasing its assets a hundredfold, from

$35,000 to $3.5 million. Lillie was especially instrumental in the establishment in 1930 of the Woods Hole Oceanographic Institute and the MBL Library, and was managing editor of the MBL's *Biological Bulletin* from 1902 to 1926. Lillie himself wrote the major early history of the MBL, *The Woods Hole Marine Biological Laboratory* (1944).

Among his many offices, Lillie was president of the Central Branch of the American Society of Zoologists (1905–1908) and of the American Society of Naturalists (1915). Elected a member of the National Academy of Sciences in 1915, he served as a founding member of the National Research Council's Committee for Research in Problems of Sex after 1921. Lillie was the only person ever to serve simultaneously as chairman of the National Research Council (1935–1936) and as president of the National Academy of Sciences (1935–1939). Here Lillie helped establish the National Research Fellowships in Biological Sciences, a fitting institutionalization of his career-long shepherding of the biological sciences into the modern era of foundation and federal support for scientific scholarship and research. Lillie died in Woods Hole, Massachusetts.

• Most of Lillie's scientific and personal papers are housed in the library of the Woods Hole Biological Laboratory. Some additional papers are in the Special Collections of the Regenstein Library at the University of Chicago, both under Lillie's name and in the papers of the Department of Zoology. The surveys of his life and contributions include Carl R. Moore, "Frank Rattray Lillie, 1870–1947," *Science*, 9 Jan. 1948, pp. 33–35; Ray L. Watterson, "The Striking Influence of the Leadership, Research, and Teaching of Frank R. Lillie (1870–1947) in Zoology, Embryology, and Other Biological Sciences," *American Zoologist* 19 (1979): 1275–87; Ray L. Watterson, "Lillie, Frank Rattray," *Dictionary of Scientific Biography* (1974), 8:354–60; B. H. Willier, "Frank Rattray Lillie, 1870–1947," *National Academy of Sciences of the United States of America Biographical Memoirs* 30 (1957): 179–236; B. H. Willier, R. G. Harrison, H. B. Bigelow, and E. G. Conklin, "Frank Rattray Lillie, 1870–1947," *The Biological Bulletin* 95, no. 2 (1948): 151–62.

ADELE E. CLARKE

LILLY, Josiah Kirby (18 Nov. 1861–8 Feb. 1948), pharmaceutical manufacturer, was born in Greencastle, Indiana, the son of Eli Lilly, a soldier, and Emily Lemon. Born at the beginning of the Civil War, Lilly spent his early years with his grandparents in Greencastle while his father served as a colonel with the Union army's Ninth Indiana Cavalry. Following the war's end, Lilly's father relocated the family to Mississippi and attempted to raise cotton. The experiment ended in disaster; Lilly's mother died and both father and son contracted malaria. Lilly's father returned with his son to Indiana in 1866 but three years later moved to Paris, Illinois, where he entered the retail drug business. Josiah Lilly enrolled in the preparatory department at nearby Asbury College (now Depauw University) in 1875. He dropped out the following year to join his father's newest endeavor, a drug manufacturing firm in Indianapolis that established the family fortune.

After joining his father's company as an errand boy and the firm's fourth employee, Lilly remained with it until 1880. In that year, recognizing the need for additional training, Lilly traveled east and entered the Philadelphia College of Pharmacy. After graduating with a Ph.G. cum laude in 1882, he returned to Indiana and resumed working with his father, whose firm had been incorporated in 1881 as Eli Lilly and Company. In 1882 he married Lilly Marie Ridgely; they had two sons.

Upon his return to Indianapolis, Lilly organized and became director of the firm's manufacturing and research laboratory. Eli Lilly and Company at the time consisted of some two dozen employees and was busily producing elixirs, fluid extracts, syrups, and sugar- and gelatin-coated pills. From its beginnings the business had concentrated on producing so-called "ethical" or prescription medicines in lieu of the more widely known and lucrative, if less reliable, "patent" medicines. Convinced by his pharmaceutical training that the future lay in maintaining rigorous standards in both research and production, Lilly and Ernest G. Eberhardt, a recent graduate of Purdue University's College of Pharmacy, created a scientific division within the firm in 1886. Rewarded for his initiative with a directorship in 1887, Lilly founded a botanical department in 1890 and a year later added a company library.

Upon his father's death in 1898, Lilly succeeded him as company president. Temporarily shifting his focus from research and development to marketing and sales, he oversaw extensive company expansion during the early years of his presidency. By 1903 Eli Lilly and Company had established branch offices in St. Louis, Chicago, New Orleans, Kansas City, and New York City, and sales rose accordingly, reaching $1 million annually by 1905. His aggressive marketing even extended to disaster relief. Following the 1906 San Francisco earthquake, the corporation rushed medicines to the area before survivors even had a chance to place orders. The company also expanded its field force, which by 1909 consisted of a hundred sales representatives operating in every state. In the years before World War I Lilly returned to research and development, opening in 1908 a biological department called the Lilly Biological Laboratories on a 156-acre tract of land in Greenfield, Indiana. With the advent of hostilities, the Lilly Company threw its resources into producing vitally needed wartime pharmaceuticals. Production of the antispasmodics stramonium and belladonna at Greenfield helped to alleviate wartime drug shortages. The firm also equipped and organized, as a memorial to Eli Lilly, the Lilly Base Hospital No. 32, which operated in France between December 1917 and April 1919.

In the years after the war, Lilly renewed his efforts to keep his enterprise in the forefront of the pharmaceutical world. Following the discovery of insulin by Dr. Frederick Grant Banting of the University of Toronto, the Lilly Company, at Banting's request, spent several hundred thousand dollars in the preparation and development of the product. Lilly oversaw the production of the first commercially prepared insulin, vital in controlling diabetes, in the United States in 1923. Not content to rest on its laurels, the firm continued to produce additional new products, including Merthiolate (an antiseptic), epidrine, liver extracts (used in treating pernicious anemia), and a number of barbituric acids (which were later used to produce medications used in obstetrics and surgery). Owing to Lilly's insistence on quality products, the firm enjoyed a widespread reputation for reliability in the medical profession. The tightly knit company management had either direct ties to Eli Lilly or midwestern origins. Paternalistic in outlook, Josiah Lilly managed to guide the business through the Great Depression without any layoffs, preferring to use make-work jobs to tide its labor force through slow periods. He resigned from the presidency in 1932 but remained chairman of the board of directors until his death. Following the death of his first wife in 1933, Lilly married Lila Allison Humes in 1935. They had no children.

In 1934 Lilly opened a new research facility in Indianapolis large enough to accommodate up to 400 research technicians and engineers. The company expanded overseas in the face of the worldwide depression, opening its first European subsidiary, Eli Lilly and Company, Ltd., in 1934. Another division was established in Canada in 1938, followed later by branches in Brazil, Mexico, India, and Argentina.

Lilly also contributed to his community, particularly through the Lilly Endowment, Inc., established in 1937. Created by Lilly and his two sons, the endowment served a variety of educational, charitable, and religious causes. Possessing only modest assets at the onset, the endowment became one of the largest foundations of its type in the country. In addition to serving as the endowment's first president, Lilly cofounded and for many years served as chairman of the Indianapolis Foundation. A charter member of the Indianapolis Chamber of Commerce, he cofounded and from 1930 to 1948 chaired the board of the Purdue Research Foundation. A major benefactor of Purdue, Lilly served as a trustee of the school for ten years. Modeling his fondness for research and development, he gave the Remington Memorial Manufacturing Laboratory to his alma mater, the Philadelphia College of Pharmacy. Among his hobbies, Lilly cultivated orchids and collected music and memorabilia of Stephen Collins Foster, establishing perhaps the largest Foster collection in the world. In 1936 Lilly donated the collection, consisting of more than 10,000 items, to the University of Pittsburgh, where it was housed in Foster Memorial Hall, which was built with contributions from both Lilly and the local citizenry. For Lilly's efforts to popularize Foster's music, the National Committee for Music Appreciation presented him with an award in 1940. In 1939 he received the insignia of Yugoslavia's Order of St. Sava, and in 1942 he was awarded the Remington Medal from the New York section of the American Pharmaceutical Association.

Lilly's eldest son, Eli Lilly II, succeeded him as president, and the Lilly Company continued to enjoy phenomenal growth. Sales increased from $13 million in 1932 to $117 million in 1948. During World War II the firm produced more than two hundred different pharmaceuticals, including Merthiolate, penicillin, and atabrin, for the American war effort and processed without charge over one million quarts of blood plasma. Following the end of the war, the corporation expanded again, acquiring additional land in Lafayette, Indiana, on which to build an antibiotics manufacturing facility. Lilly died in Indianapolis and was succeeded by Eli Lilly II as chairman of the board.

Lilly's legacy is twofold. He guided his company's growth and expansion through both depression and world war, and he founded with his sons an endowment that became a major source of revenue for a variety of educational and charitable endeavors.

• Materials relating to Lilly's presidency are at the Lilly Corporate Center in Indianapolis, Ind. The best secondary source on Lilly's life and career is Roscoe C. Clark, *Threescore Years and Ten: A Narrative of the First Seventy Years of Eli Lilly and Company* (1946). Obituaries are in the *Indianapolis News Star*, the *Indianapolis Times*, and the *New York Times*, 9 Feb. 1948.

EDWARD L. LACH, JR.

LIMÓN, José (12 Jan. 1908–2 Dec. 1972), dancer and choreographer, was born José Arcadio Limón in Culiacán, Sinaloa, Mexico, the son of Florencio Limón, a musician, and Francisca Traslaviña. The family immigrated to the United States in 1915, eventually settling in Los Angeles. Limón attended the University of California for a year, but in 1928 he left school to pursue a career as a painter in New York. This proved to be an unhappy choice, when Limón realized his own painting would never match that of his idol, El Greco.

In 1929, when he was twenty-one, he attended a concert of the German dancers Yvonne Georgi and Harald Kreutzberg and immediately decided, in spite of his age and lack of previous training, to become a dancer. He enrolled in the classes of Doris Humphrey and Charles Weidman, soon becoming a member of their company. Humphrey encouraged his interest in choreography, and Limón began to show some pure movement pieces at the Humphrey-Weidman Studio. In 1937, he received one of the first choreographic fellowships awarded by the Bennington School of the Dance, where he prepared his first group work, *Danza de la Muerte*, dealing with the civil war in Spain. Two years later he returned to his ethnic heritage with *Danzas Mexicanas*.

In 1940, Limón toured the West Coast with May O'Donnell, performing dances they had created together. The following year, he rejoined the Humphrey-Weidman company as a leading dancer with occasional opportunities to choreograph. During World War II he staged dances in camp shows for servicemen at Camp Lee, Virginia, while creating further works in New York during leaves from the army. In 1946 the

José Limón Company was formed, with Humphrey as artistic director. Here Humphrey created some of her greatest works, which showed Limón at the height of his performing powers. He portrayed the heroic death of a bullfighter in *Lament for Ignacio Sánchez Mejías* and the simple dignity of the life of man in *Day on Earth*.

Invaluable to him in the development of his career were two women: Humphrey, the mentor who guided and abetted his creative efforts, and Pauline Lawrence, whom he had married in 1941 and who designed the costumes for his dances and also managed the company business. They had no children. While continuing to dance, Limón was also developing as a choreographer. He returned to his Mexican background in *La Malinche* (1949), in which village performers tell the story of Cortez and his Indian mistress, who is accused of being a traitor. The same year he produced one of his most important works, *The Moor's Pavane*. For a distillation of Shakespeare's *Othello*, Limón used only four characters: Othello, Desdemona, Iago, and Emilia, who tell their story of passionate love and jealousy to the formal music of Henry Purcell. *The Moor's Pavane* won Limón a Dance Magazine Award in 1950.

The next year the Instituto Nacional de Bellas Artes invited Limón to Mexico City to choreograph and perform. Here he worked for the first time with large groups, using both local Mexican dancers and his own company members in dances with Mexican themes and rhythms. He taught classes in New York during most of the time he lived there, at the American Dance Festival at Connecticut College from 1948 on, and in the Dance Department of the Juilliard School of Music from 1951 to 1968. He worked on refining the Humphrey teaching technique, eventually building a system of his own that involved isolation of weight in various body parts and successional lifts in the spine and limbs, as well as fall, rebound, and suspension. He retired from teaching in 1968.

Important works created in the 1950s included several dances based on biblical themes: *The Exiles* (1950), which portrayed Adam and Eve's ouster from the Garden of Eden; *The Visitation* (1952), about the Virgin Mary; and *The Traitor* (1954), about the betrayal of Christ. *There Is a Time* (1956) used the words of Ecclesiastes: "To every thing there is a season, and a time to every purpose under the heaven." A suite of dances visualized the words "a time to be born and a time to die; a time to plant and a time to pluck up that which is planted." It was Limón at his noble best and most poetic.

This period also witnessed the company's first performances abroad. A tour of South America in 1954 made it the first modern dance company to participate in the U.S. State Department's Cultural Exchange Program. Further international tours were to follow. Upon visiting devastated Poland in 1957, Limón was inspired to create *Missa Brevis*, a testimony to the strength and nobility of the human spirit.

With Humphrey's death in 1958, Limón turned to more abstract themes. His tribute to her, "A Choreographic Offering" (1964), invoked her spirit through movement phrases characteristic of her works. *The Winged* (1966), about birds and flight, used a collage of electronic sounds, chirping, and a jazz score. His experimentation with sound continued with *The Unsung* (1970), a tribute to Native Americans in which eight men danced solos in silence, except for the sound of their feet running, leaping, and stamping. His last work, *Carlota* (1972), which told the story of the Spanish conquest of Mexico, also was rendered in silence. He died in Flemington, New Jersey.

For many years the Limón company was a stable entity, its members consisting of Ruth Currier, Lucas Hoving, Letitia Ide, Betty Jones, and Lavina Nielsen. In the 1960s the original members left to pursue independent careers while the younger dancers—Sarah Stackhouse, Louis Falco, Jennifer Muller, and Daniel Lewis—remained. Limón himself performed until April 1969. Other modern dance companies began to acquire Limón's works for their own use, and in time classical companies also became interested. Limón dances were added to the repertories of the American Ballet Theatre, the Joffrey Ballet, the Pennsylvania Ballet, the Royal Danish Ballet, and the Royal Swedish Ballet.

Along with recurring themes drawn from the Bible and from his Mexican heritage, Limón's choreography favored portrayals of man's dignity. The citation for his 1964 Capezio Award called him "a man of dignity." For an essay in *The Modern Dance: Seven Statements of Belief* (1966) he wrote: "I try to compose works that are involved with man's basic tragedy and the grandeur of his spirit. I want to dig beneath empty formalisms, displays of technical virtuosity, and the slick surface; to probe the human entity for the powerful, often crude beauty of the gesture that speaks of man's humanity." While most choreographers of the postmodern era that followed Limón's death rejected his noble intentions in favor of dances designed to exhibit movement for its own sake, by the 1990s some choreographers had turned their attention once again to depicting the enduring grandeur of man's spirit.

• Limón's unpublished writings and letters are in the files of the Juilliard School and in the Dance Collection of the New York Public Library for the Performing Arts at Lincoln Center. Scores of some of his dances are held by the Dance Notation Bureau. Barbara Pollack and Charles H. Woodford have written a brief biography, *Dance Is a Moment: A Portrait of José Limón in Words and Pictures* (1993). The reviews of Limón's works by John Martin in the *New York Times* are especially valuable. A most important appraisal is Doris Hering, "José Limón: Midstream Vintage Years in Retrospect," *Dance Magazine*, Nov. 1973, pp. 42–47.

SELMA JEANNE COHEN

LIN Yutang (10 Oct. 1895–26 Mar. 1976), novelist, linguist, and philosopher, was born Lin Ho-lok in Amoy, Fukien Province, China, the son of Lin Chi-shing, a

Presbyterian minister, and Young Shun-min. At age seventeen, he changed his given name, meaning peaceful and happy, to Yutang, meaning elegant language, and came to be known as Lin Yutang. Lin attended English-language schools and graduated from St. John's University, a private western-oriented institution in Shanghai, in 1916. In the same year he became a teacher at Tsing Hua College in Peking. In January 1919 he married Liu Tsui-fung, a wealthy classmate of his sister; eventually the union produced three children. In the fall of 1919 he embarked with his wife to study comparative literature at Harvard.

After a year's residence, Lin completed his work for the M.A., with the exception of a course in Shakespeare, which he made up at Jena, Germany. On the way to Germany, he worked briefly with the American YMCA in Le Creusot, France. He then transferred to Leipzig, receiving his Ph.D. in linguistics in 1923. He immediately accepted a position in the English department of Peking National University (now Peking University). During this period he wrote articles supporting the Kuomintang (National Peoples' Party) against independent generals or war lords. To avoid arrest by the reactionary regime, he moved in 1926 to Hsiamun University in his native Amoy, where he became dean of humanities and secretary of graduate studies.

Lin considered humor to be one of humanity's most precious gifts, the function of which he regarded as the criticism of one's dreams and bringing them in touch with the world of reality. In 1924 he published "A Study of Humor" in the Peking *Morning Post*, and in 1932 he founded a bimonthly magazine, *Lun Yu* (Analects), specializing in comic writing. More than one hundred of his own essays in the same facetious vein appeared between 1930 and 1936 in a Shanghai-based English-language weekly, the *China Critic*, a selection from which was later published as *The Little Critic, Essays, Satires and Sketches on China* (1935).

When Pearl Buck, visiting China on a world tour, made Lin's acquaintance in 1933, they admired each other's literary works and soon became friends. Dissatisfied with the writings of American missionaries about China, Buck persuaded him to record his own perspective, a task that he completed in ten months. The book, *My Country and My People* (1935), containing a preface by Buck, became first on the bestseller list. In rapid succession Lin brought out English translations of earlier Chinese works, a humorous drama and a collection of essays published jointly as *Confucius Saw Nancy and Essays about Nothing* (1936).

As Japan and China were on the brink of war in 1936, Lin moved with his family to New York City. In the next year he published his second bestseller, *The Importance of Living*, a blend of philosophy and humor justifying a moderate hedonism. This was followed in 1938 by an edition of *The Wisdom of Confucius*. In the same year he revisited France, where nearly twenty years earlier he had unsuccessfully sought to uncover lost relatives. He incorporated fictional references to these family members in his first novel, *A Moment in Peking* (1939), which some critics consider his best. Although it has some resemblance to the Chinese scholar-beauty romance, it also sketches the origins of the Sino-Japanese war. The book immediately had three editions in Japanese, the first of which, to Lin's chagrin, preceded the one in Chinese. In a semi-continuation, *A Leaf in the Storm* (1941), Lin openly protested the Japanese invasion, the male and female protagonists symbolizing the rebirth of Chinese patriotism. After the entry of the United States into World War II, Lin published a political work, *Between Tears and Laughter* (1943), criticizing the Far East policy of the United States and England, which, he charged, was predicated on the West dominating the East. In the midst of the war he returned to China for a propaganda trip throughout the area controlled by the Kuoming-tang. On his return to America he published an account of his travels, *The Vigil of a Nation* (1944), and broadcast an appeal for overseas Chinese to support Chiang Kai-shek.

His personal life deteriorated in 1945, as his eldest daughter eloped with a nondescript American, and his bank account was almost wiped out. He had invested in a Chinese typewriter of his own invention that proved to be unmarketable because of the Chinese civil war, and he was forced into bankruptcy. Although the typewriter was never produced commercially, its keyboard and character classifications were later adopted for Chinese computers. In 1947 Lin was offered the post of head of the Arts and Letters Division of UNESCO in Paris, but before leaving the United States he was required to pay a debt to the Internal Revenue Service of $30,000. He obtained this amount through sales of another novel, *The Gay Genius: The Life and Times of Su Tungpo* (1947).

Almost as soon as he arrived in Paris, Lin resigned his position in order to pursue his literary career. In Cannes he wrote his most notable fictional work about America, *Chinatown Family* (1948), a lighthearted portrayal of ordinary domestic life flavored by oriental philosophy. The pioneer work in the genre of Asian-American fiction, it presents an idealistic vision of marriage and the family among Chinese and Italian immigrants.

In 1949 Lin and his wife moved back to the United States to be close to their daughters. He soon published two more works of popular philosophy, *Wisdom of Lao Tse* (1948) and *On the Wisdom of America* (1950). In a related modernization of classical texts, he rewrote several Chinese narratives, *Miss Tu* (1950), *Widow, Nun, and Courtesan* (1951), and *Famous Chinese Short Stories* (1952). Returning to the theme of war, he published in 1953 a fictional love story, *The Vermilion Gate*, set in the midst of the Chinese-Moslem conflict twenty years earlier.

In 1953 Lin broke his connection with the John Day Company, which had published most of his books in the United States. He was dissatisfied with the percentage of royalties he was being paid, and Pearl Buck, who was married to Richard J. Walsh, president of the

Day company, had refused to lend him money during his period of financial difficulties.

In 1954 Lin became vice chancellor of Nangyang University in Singapore, but he resigned after six months, donations to the university having declined radically because of his ties with the Kuomintang. In 1955 he returned to Cannes and combined aesthetic, political, and religious topics in a utopian novel, *Looking Beyond*, also called *Unexpected Island* (1955). In 1957 he reverted to Chinese themes with an English translation of Chuangtze, published under the philosopher's name, and a historical biography of the T'ang Dynasty, *Lady Wu*. His final work explaining China to the West was *Chinese Theory of Art: Translations from the Masters of Chinese Art* (1967).

In 1959 Lin published his spiritual autobiography, *From Pagan to Christian*, a modern pilgrim's progress revealing his early links with Christianity, his doubts during middle age, and his eventual return to a nominal Christianity. That he never embraced orthodoxy, however, is amply revealed in his *The Pleasures of a Nonconformist* (1962). In 1961 he published a volume of straight history, *Imperial Peking: Seven Centuries of China*, and a somewhat erotic novel, *The Red Peony*. These were followed in 1963 by *Juniper Loa*, an autobiographical novel concerning a young man's attraction to a girl who marries someone else. In 1964 he brought out his last work of fiction, *Flight of Innocents*.

In 1965 Lin began writing a newspaper column for the news agency of the Republic of China under the rubric "Anything That Comes to Mind," later collecting the columns in two volumes published in 1965 and 1967. In 1966 he moved to Taiwan and was elected vice president of the local branch of the International P.E.N. Club. In the following year he accepted a professorship from the Chinese University of Hong Kong to edit a modern Chinese-English dictionary. Linguists consider its publication in 1972 to be his crowning achievement. In 1975 he was elected vice president of the World P.E.N. and nominated for the Nobel Prize in literature.

Lin's private life during his final years was not happy, in large measure because his eldest daughter, distraught by divorce from a husband whom she still loved, committed suicide. After the completion of his dictionary, moreover, he was forced to shuttle back and forth between Taipei, where he felt more comfortable, and Hong Kong, which his family preferred. He died in Hong Kong but is buried in the garden of his Taipei home, which has been converted into the Lin Yutang Memorial Library.

• An extensive collection of the manuscripts of Lin's published works is housed in the Palace Museum in Taipei, Taiwan. A smaller manuscript collection at the Lin Yutang Memorial Library includes a large number of private letters. In 1973 Lin wrote *Eighty: An Autobiography* (1975), first published in *Chinese Culture University Journal* 9 (1974): 263–324, as "Memoirs of an Octogenarian." Both the book and the journal contain a complete bibliography of his writings in Chinese and English. Personal reminiscences of his daughter Adet Lin are found in *Our Family* (1939). She provides an extended view in Chinese in *Lin Yutang chuan* (The life of Lin Yutang) (1990). A twelve-page *Biographical Sketch of Lin Yutang* (1937) has a profile by Pearl Buck. More biographical information is in Diran John Sohigian, "The Life and Times of Lin Yutang" (Ph.D. diss., Columbia Univ., 1992). Notable quotations from Lin's works are collected by Arthur James Anderson as *The Best of an Old Friend* (1975). Anderson has also prepared "Lin Yutang: A Bibliography of His English Writings and Translations," *Bulletin of Bibliography* 30 (1973): 83–89. Considerable overlapping exists in four books in Chinese by Chien-wei Shih: *Lin Yutang tsai ta lu* (Lin Yutang in China) (1991); *Lin Yu Tang zai hai wai* (Lin Yutang overseas) (1992); *Yu mo ta shih: Lin Yutang chuan* (Master humorist: The life of Lin Yutang) (1994); and *Lin Yutang tsou hsiang shih chieh ti yu mo ta shih* (Lin Yutang: The humorist faces the world) (1994). An obituary is in the *New York Times*, 27 Mar. 1976.

A. OWEN ALDRIDGE

LINCECUM, Gideon (22 Apr. 1793–28 Nov. 1874), naturalist and frontiersman, was born in Hancock County, Georgia, the son of Hezekiah Lincecum and Sally Hickman, farmers. Because of his family's frequent moves along the frontier in Georgia and South Carolina, Gideon completed only five months of formal schooling. He read avidly, however, from volumes he earned by selling books for Mason L. Weems (George Washington's biographer), and he also learned the lore of his Muskogee Indian neighbors. This eclectic background prepared him for lifelong inquiries into natural history, Indian languages and traditions, and other subjects. As a young man he served one term as a schoolmaster and two tours of duty in the War of 1812. In 1814 he married Sarah Bryan; they had thirteen children, ten of whom survived infancy.

In 1818 Lincecum moved his family to a new frontier on the Tombigbee River above what is now Columbus, Mississippi. He served as a commissioner in the organization of Monroe County, Mississippi, and helped develop the communities of Cotton Gin Port and Columbus. He prospered as a trader with the Choctaw and Chickasaw nations, taking time to record the legends and traditions of the Choctaw in the tribe's own language. Lincecum's manuscript "Chahta Traditions" is regarded as the most extensive record of southeastern Indian lore dating from the early nineteenth century. His ethnographic notes later served as the basis of two posthumous publications, "Choctaw Traditions about Their Settlement in Mississippi and the Origin of Their Mounds" (*Mississippi Historical Society Publications* 8 [1904]) and "Life of Apushimataha" (*Mississippi Historical Society Publications* 9 [1906]).

In 1830, following a long illness, Lincecum determined to take up medicine. At first he practiced the allopathic system, but suspecting that frequent bleeding and the administration of potent drugs did more harm than good, he undertook a six-week apprenticeship with a Choctaw herbal doctor, and after much study he adopted the botanical system of Samuel Thompson. From 1830 to 1848 his practice grew steadily, first at Cotton Gin Port and then in Columbus to which he moved in 1841.

In 1835 Lincecum led a party to Texas to scout the prospects for settlement. When his companions returned to Mississippi, Lincecum explored alone from the Aransas Bay to the Edwards Plateau. He found desirable land in Stephen F. Austin's land grant, and in 1848 he moved his family to the community he founded at Long Point, Washington County, Texas. Having sold his medical practice and having seen his children grow up, Lincecum devoted the remainder of his life largely to exploring and studying the natural history of Texas. He corresponded with naturalists in the East and in Europe, collected weather data as an observer for the Smithsonian meteorological project, and sent large collections of plants, mammals, fossils, shells, birds, and insects to the Smithsonian Institution and the Academy of Natural Sciences of Philadelphia. In 1868 Elias Durand of Philadelphia included more than 1,000 of Lincecum's plant specimens in a collection he sent to the Jardin des Plantes in Paris.

Lincecum wrote articles on various natural history topics, but he is best known for his studies of the agricultural, or harvester, ant (*Pogonomyrmex molefaciens*). Various species of these ants that gather seeds and store them in their mounds were known from the Old World, but Lincecum was the first to report on agricultural ants in America. He related his observations to S. B. Buckley, who in 1860 published the first account of the Texas harvester ants in the *Proceedings of the Academy of Natural Sciences*. Lincecum also wrote to Charles Darwin, who sponsored his communication on harvester ants in the *Journal of the Proceedings of the Linnaean Society of London* in 1862. Lincecum's descriptions of the harvesting activities of these ants and of their migration—which involves the transplanting of entire colonies—have been corroborated by later investigators. His controversial claim that the ants planted seeds for crops that were harvested the following season, although initially supported by Darwin, has since been rejected. Lincecum's attribution of intelligence to ants and other animals added zest to his writings but diminished the credibility of his generally reliable observations.

His observations and opinions ranged beyond animal societies to religion, sociology, and philosophy. As a self-styled free thinker and agnostic, he scoffed at the idea of a deity and opposed organized religion. He advocated the castration of hardened criminals and other social misfits as a means of improving human society.

A patriotic southerner and slave owner, Lincecum considered the Confederate demise his personal defeat, one intensified by the death of his wife in 1867. He abandoned Texas from 1868 to 1873 to join a colony of former Confederates in Texpan, Veracruz, Mexico. There he established a banana and sugar cane plantation, studied Indian ruins, and continued his correspondence with naturalists. In 1874 he returned to Long Point, where he spent his final year finishing his autobiography.

Running through Lincecum's many-sided career as a naturalist, a physician, an Indian trader, and an ethnologist is the theme of the American frontier. From the days of the early republic to the post–Civil War era, Lincecum helped shape events on the southern and western frontier, and he was in turn shaped by the frontier. A rugged individualist and a self-made man who began without contact with established centers of science and learning in the East, Lincecum attained genuine stature as an interpreter of animal and Indian societies. His insistence that ants exhibited organization and intelligence that rivaled that of humans encouraged the myth of agricultural ants that sowed seeds in anticipation of the harvest, but this idiosyncratic side of his personality detracts but little from the achievements of a remarkable frontier naturalist. He died in Long Point, Texas.

• Lincecum's papers are in the Eugene C. Barker Texas History Center at the University of Texas, Austin. The Smithsonian Institution has a number of accession records and correspondence relating to collections sent there by Lincecum, and the Academy of Natural Sciences of Philadelphia has some original Lincecum correspondence and manuscripts. Portions of Lincecum's autobiography appeared in the *American Sportsman* (1874–1875). Another portion was published as "The Autobiography of Gideon Lincecum," *Mississippi Historical Society Publications* 8 (1904): 443–519. These and other biographical sources are combined in Jerry Bryan Lincecum and Edward Hake Phillips, eds., *Adventures of a Frontier Naturalist: The Life and Times of Dr. Gideon Lincecum* (1994). Selected letters from the Lincecum papers in the University of Texas collection are printed with commentary in Jerry Bryan Lincecum et al., eds., *Science on the Texas Frontier: Observations of Dr. Gideon Lincecum* (1997), which includes a comprehensive bibliography of Lincecum publications. An earlier account of his life, with bibliography, is Lois Wood Burkhalter, *Gideon Lincecum, 1793–1874: A Biography* (1965). Lincecum's ethnological work is evaluated in Cheri Lynne Wolfe, "The Traditional History of the Chahta People: An Analysis of Gideon Lincecum's Manuscripts" (Ph.D. diss., Univ. of Texas, Austin, 1993). His studies of harvester ants are placed in historical and scientific context in W. M. Wheeler, *Ants: Their Structure, Development, and Behavior* (1910). An obituary is in the *Dallas Daily Herald*, 12 Dec. 1874.

W. CONNER SORENSEN

LINCOLN, Abraham (12 Feb. 1809–15 Apr. 1865), sixteenth president of the United States, was born in Hardin County, Kentucky, the son of Thomas Lincoln and Nancy Hanks, farmers. Thomas Lincoln had come to Kentucky from Virginia with his father Abraham in 1782. He acquired only enough literacy to sign his name but gained modest prosperity as a carpenter and farmer on the Kentucky frontier. He married Nancy Hanks, also illiterate, in 1806. Abraham was born in a log cabin on "Sinking Spring Farm" three miles south of Hodgenville. When he was two years old the family moved to another farm on Knob Creek about seven miles northeast of Hodgenville. On this farm of 230 acres (only thirty of which were tillable)

Abraham lived for five years, helped his parents with chores, and learned his ABCs by attending school for a few weeks with his older sister Sarah.

In December 1816 the Lincolns again moved, this time to the newly admitted state of Indiana. The tradition that the Lincolns moved because of dislike of slavery may have some truth; they belonged to a Baptist denomination that broke from the parent church on the slavery issue. However, the main reason for the move was Thomas's uncertainty of Kentucky land titles. Indiana offered secure titles surveyed under the Northwest Ordinance. The Lincolns lived in a rude, three-sided shelter on Pigeon Creek sixteen miles north of the Ohio River. There Abraham learned the use of axe and plow helping his father carve a house and farm out of the hardwood forest. The growing youth also snatched a few more months of schooling in the typical one-room schoolhouses of the frontier. In late 1817 or 1818 the Lincolns were joined by Nancy's aunt Elizabeth Hanks Sparrow and her husband, Thomas Sparrow, and Abraham's cousin Dennis Hanks. In the fall of 1818 the Sparrows and Nancy Hanks Lincoln all died of "milk sick," probably caused by drinking the milk of cows that had grazed on white snakeroot.

After a year of rough homemaking, Thomas Lincoln returned to Kentucky, where on 2 December 1819 he wed the widow Sarah Bush Johnston and brought her and her three children to Pigeon Creek. His stepmother provided the teenage Abraham with more affection and guidance than his natural mother or his father ever did. With a desire for learning and ambition for self-improvement, he devoured every book he could borrow from the meager libraries of friends and neighbors. Thomas Lincoln neither understood nor encouraged his son's intellectual ambition; quite the contrary, he chastised Abraham's "lazy" preference for reading over working.

Abraham's thinly veiled disdain for the life of a backwoods farmer doubtless irritated his father. Abraham in turn resented the requirement of law and custom that any wages he earned before he came of age—by hiring out to neighbors to split rails, for example—must be given to his father. One historian has suggested that Abraham Lincoln's hatred of chattel slavery, which denied to slaves the "fruits of their labor," may have originated in Thomas Lincoln's expropriation of the teenage Abraham's earnings (Burlingame, pp. 37–42). In any event, relations between Abraham and his father grew increasingly estranged. When Thomas lay dying in January 1851, he sent word that he wanted to say goodbye to his son. Abraham refused to make the eighty-mile trip, stating, "If we could meet now, it is doubtful whether it would not be more painful than pleasant" (Basler, vol. 2, p. 97). He did not attend his father's funeral.

In 1828 Lincoln and a friend took a flatboat loaded with farm produce down the Ohio and Mississippi rivers to New Orleans. He repeated the experience in 1831. These trips widened his horizons and, by tradition, shocked him with the sight of men and women being bought and sold in the slave markets of New Orleans. Although he came of age in 1830, he did not immediately strike out on his own. Once more his father sold the farm and set forth to greener pastures, this time in central Illinois. After helping his father clear land, Abraham hired out to split rails for other farmers, and he kept his earnings. In the summer of 1831 he settled in New Salem, a village on the Sangamon River bluff about twenty miles northwest of Springfield.

Lincoln's six years in New Salem were a formative period. For a time he drifted from one job to another: store clerk, mill hand, partner in a general store that failed, postmaster, surveyor. Six feet four inches tall with a lanky, rawboned look, unruly coarse black hair, a gregarious personality, and a penchant for telling humorous stories, Lincoln made many friends. Among them were Jack Armstrong and his gang of young toughs, "the Clary Grove boys." As the new boy in town with a reputation for great physical strength, Lincoln had to prove his mettle in a wrestling match with Armstrong. Winning the match, Lincoln also won the loyalty of the Clary Grove boys despite his refusal to participate in their drinking and hell-raising.

In 1832 the Sac and Fox Indians under Chief Black Hawk returned to their ancestral homeland in Illinois, precipitating the short-lived Black Hawk War. Lincoln volunteered for the militia and was elected captain of his company, which included the Clary Grove boys. They saw no action, but Lincoln later recalled his election as captain as the most gratifying honor of his life.

Another side of Lincoln's complex personality was a deeply reflective, almost brooding, quality that sometimes descended into serious depression. Lincoln described this condition as "the hypo," for hypochondria, as medical science then termed it. This recurring ailment, coupled with Lincoln's almost morbid fondness for William Knox's lugubrious poem "Mortality" (1824) and his later self-reported dreams in which death figured prominently, may have resulted from the deaths of loved ones: his mother, his sister Sarah in childbirth in 1828; and Ann Rutledge in 1835. Lincoln met Rutledge at her father's tavern in New Salem, where he boarded in 1833. Their story has taken on so many layers of myth and antimyth that the truth is impossible to determine. For half a century, until the 1990s, professional historians discounted the notion of their love and engagement, but new scholarship revived the credibility of a Lincoln-Rutledge romance (Walsh, *The Shadows Rise*). In any event, Rutledge died in August 1835, probably of typhoid fever, and Lincoln apparently suffered a prolonged spell of "hypo" after her death.

During the New Salem years Lincoln developed new purpose and direction. The local schoolmaster, Mentor Graham, guided his study of mathematics and literature. Lincoln joined a debating society, and he acquired a lifelong love of William Shakespeare and Robert Burns. He also acquired a passion for politics and in 1832 announced his candidacy for the legislature. Although he failed of election, he received 92 percent of the vote in the New Salem district, where he was known. When he ran again in 1834, he campaigned throughout the county and won decisively.

Lincoln was a Whig, a devotee of Henry Clay, whom Lincoln described as his "beau ideal of a statesman." Clay's American System, with its emphasis on government support for education, internal improvements, banking, and economic development to promote growth and opportunity, attracted him. In the legislature Lincoln came under the wing of John T. Stuart, a Springfield lawyer and Whig minority leader in the house. Stuart encouraged Lincoln to study law and guided him through Sir William Blackstone's *Commentaries on the Laws of England* (1765–1769) and other books whose mastery was necessary to pass the bar examination in those days. On 9 September 1836 Lincoln obtained his license. In 1837 he moved to Springfield and became Stuart's partner.

Lincoln won reelection to the legislature in 1836, 1838, and 1840. He became floor leader of the Whigs and a prominent member of the "Long Nine," Whig legislators from Sangamon County who averaged more than six feet in height. Legislative logrolling enabled the Long Nine to get the state capital moved from Vandalia to Springfield in 1837. During the same session Lincoln and one colleague from Sangamon County entered a protest against a resolution passed overwhelmingly by the legislature that denounced antislavery societies in such a way as to imply approval of slavery. Declaring slavery to be "founded on both injustice and bad policy," Lincoln and his colleague nevertheless criticized the abolitionists, whose doctrines tended "rather to increase than to abate [slavery's] evils" (Basler, vol. 1, pp. 74–75).

Although ill at ease with women, Lincoln in 1836 began a half-hearted courtship of Mary Owens, whose sister lived in New Salem. A year later she broke off the relationship, to the probable relief of both parties. In 1839 Lincoln met Mary Todd, who had come from Kentucky to live with her married sister in Springfield. Despite the contrast between the educated, cultured, and socially prominent daughter of a Lexington banker and the socially awkward, rough-hewn son of an illiterate farmer, Mary and Abraham fell in love and became engaged in 1840. What happened next remains uncertain. Lincoln seems to have developed doubts about his fitness for marriage and broke the engagement. In January 1841 he succumbed to the worst case of hypo he had yet experienced. "I am now the most miserable man living," he wrote to Stuart on 23 January. "If what I feel were equally distributed to the whole human family, there would not be one cheerful face on earth" (Basler, vol. 1, p. 229).

After a series of twists and turns, the courtship revived. Lincoln's closest friend, Joshua Speed, married in 1842; Speed's assurance that matrimony was not so frightening after all seems to have encouraged Lincoln. On 4 November 1842 he and Mary were wed. The quality of their marriage has been much debated. It produced four sons. Mary shared Abraham's lively interest in public affairs, he often sought her advice, and she encouraged his political ambition. In personality, however, they were in many ways opposites. He was disorganized, careless in dress, and indifferent to social niceties; she was quick-tempered, sometimes shrewish, dressed expensively, and lived by the strict decorum of Victorian conventions. He got along with almost everybody; she quarreled with servants, workmen, merchants, and some of Lincoln's friends. He was absent from home on the legal or political circuit for weeks at a time, leaving her to cope with the trials of household management and child rearing. His moodiness sometimes clashed with her fits of temper. Over time her mental stability became more fragile.

After retiring from the legislature in 1841, Lincoln devoted most of his time to his law practice. In 1841 he formed a partnership with Stephen T. Logan, who helped him become more thorough and meticulous in preparing his cases. The Springfield courts sat only a few weeks a year, requiring Lincoln to ride the circuit of county courts throughout central Illinois for several months each spring and fall. Most of his cases involved damage to crops by foraging livestock, property disputes, debts, and assault and battery, with an occasional murder trial to liven interest. By the time of his marriage Lincoln was earning $1,200 a year, income equal to the governor's salary. In 1844 he bought a house in Springfield—the only home he ever owned. In 1844 he also dissolved his partnership with Logan and formed a new one with 26-year-old William H. Herndon, to whom Lincoln became a mentor.

Lincoln's ambitions were not fulfilled by a successful law practice. He wanted to run for Congress from this safe Whig district, but the concentration of Whig hopefuls in Springfield meant that he had to wait his turn under an informal one-term rotation system. When his turn came in 1846, Lincoln won handily over Democratic candidate Peter Cartwright, a well-known Methodist clergyman who tried to make an issue of Lincoln's nonmembership in a church (Mary later joined Springfield's First Presbyterian Church, which Abraham also occasionally attended).

Lincoln's congressional term (1847–1849) was dominated by controversies over the Mexican War. He took the standard Whig position that the war had been provoked by President James K. Polk. On 22 December 1847 Lincoln introduced "spot resolutions" calling for information on the exact "spot of soil" on which Mexicans shed American blood to start the war, implying that this spot was actually Mexican soil. Lincoln also voted several times for the Wilmot Proviso, declaring that slavery should be prohibited in any territory acquired from Mexico. On these issues Lincoln sided with the majority in the Whig House of Representatives. In addition, Lincoln introduced a bill (which was buried in committee) for compensated abolition of slavery in the District of Columbia if approved by a majority of the District's voters.

Lincoln's opposition to the Mexican War was not popular in Illinois. "Spotty Lincoln," jibed Democratic newspapers, had committed political suicide. "What an epitaph: 'Died of Spotted Fever'" (Thomas, p. 120). When Lincoln campaigned in 1848 for the Whig presidential nominee Zachary Taylor, the "Spotty Lincoln" label came back to haunt him. The Whig candidate for Congress who succeeded Lincoln under the rotation system, his former partner Stephen T. Logan, went down to defeat—perhaps because of voter backlash against the party's antiwar stance. Taylor nevertheless won the presidency, but Lincoln did not get the patronage appointment he expected as commissioner of the General Land Office.

Lincoln returned to Springfield disheartened with politics and gave full time to his law practice. During the 1850s he became one of the leading lawyers in the state. His annual income reached $5,000. The burst of railroad construction during the decade generated a large caseload. Lincoln at various times represented railroads. In two of his most important cases he won exemption of the Illinois Central from county taxation and successfully defended the Rock Island from a suit by a shipping company whose steamboat had hit the Rock Island's bridge over the Mississippi (the first such bridge ever built). Yet it would be misleading to describe Lincoln as a "corporation lawyer" in the modern sense of that term, since he opposed corporations with equal frequency. In one important case he represented a small firm in a patent infringement suit brought against it by the McCormick Reaper Company. Lincoln continued to ride the circuit each spring and fall; the great majority of cases handled by Lincoln and Herndon (some 200 each year) concerned local matters of debt, ejectment, slander and libel, trespass, foreclosure, divorce, and the like.

In 1854 a seismic political upheaval occurred that propelled Lincoln back into politics. The Kansas-Nebraska Act, rammed through Congress under the leadership of Illinois senator Stephen A. Douglas (an old acquaintance of Lincoln and once a rival for Mary Todd's affections), revoked the ban on slavery in the Louisiana Purchase territory north of 36° 30′. This repeal of a crucial part of the Missouri Compromise of 1820 opened Kansas Territory to slavery. It polarized the free and slave states more sharply than anything else had done. It incited several years of civil war between proslavery and antislavery forces in Kansas, which became a prelude to the national Civil War that erupted seven years later, and it gave birth to the Republican party, whose principal plank was exclusion of slavery from the territories.

Before 1854 Lincoln had said little in public about slavery, but during the next six years he delivered an estimated 175 speeches whose "central message" was the necessity to exclude slavery from the territories as a step toward its ultimate extinction everywhere (Waldo W. Braden, *Abraham Lincoln: Public Speaker* [1988], pp. 35–36). That had been the purpose of the Founding Fathers, Lincoln believed, when they adopted the Declaration of Independence and enacted the Northwest Ordinance of 1787, barring slavery from most of the existing territories; that was why they did not mention the words "slave" or "slavery" in the Constitution.

"Thus, the thing is hid away, in the constitution," said Lincoln in 1854, "just as an afflicted man hides away a wen or cancer" (Basler, vol. 2, p. 274). By opening all of the Louisiana Purchase territory to slavery, the Kansas-Nebraska Act had reversed the course of the Founding Fathers. That was why Lincoln was "aroused," he later recalled, "as he had never been before" (Basler, vol. 4, p. 67).

Lincoln ran for the state legislature and took the stump for other "anti-Nebraska" Whigs. The fullest exposition of Lincoln's philosophy occurred in a speech at Peoria on 16 October 1854. Slavery was a "monstrous injustice," he said, that "deprives our republican example of its just influence in the world—enables the enemies of free institutions, with plausibility, to taunt us as hypocrites." With the Kansas-Nebraska Act, "our republican robe is soiled, and trailed in the dust. Let us repurify it. . . . Let us re-adopt the Declaration of Independence, and with it, the practices, and policy, which harmonize with it" (Basler, vol. 2, pp. 247–83). These sentiments were Lincoln's lodestar for the rest of his life.

That same year a coalition of anti-Nebraska Whigs and Democrats, including Lincoln, appeared to have gained control of the legislature. Their first task in February 1855 was to elect a U.S. senator, and Lincoln resigned from the legislature to become the Whig candidate. Through six ballots he led other candidates but fell short of a majority. To prevent the election of a regular Democrat, Lincoln then threw his support to Lyman Trumbull, an anti-Nebraska Democrat, who was elected on the tenth ballot.

Deeply disappointed, Lincoln picked up his law practice again. In 1856 he helped found the Republican party in Illinois. With his speech at the new party's state convention in Bloomington on 29 May (the famous "lost speech"—so called because newspaper reporters were supposedly so entranced by its eloquence that they neglected to take it down), Lincoln emerged as the state's Republican leader. At the party's national convention he received 110 votes in a losing bid for the vice presidential nomination. Lincoln campaigned for the Republican ticket headed by John C. Frémont, giving more than fifty speeches in all parts of Illinois. However, while Frémont won a plurality of the northern popular vote in the three-party contest, he lost Illinois and the other crucial lower North states of Pennsylvania and Indiana, which the Democrat, James Buchanan, added to the Solid South to win the presidency.

By the time Senator Douglas came up for reelection in 1858, he had broken with the Buchanan administration over the Lecompton constitution in Kansas and thus appeared vulnerable to a Republican challenge. The party nominated Lincoln (an almost unprecedented procedure in that time, when state legislatures elected U.S. senators), who set the theme for his campaign with his famous "House Divided" speech at Springfield on 16 June 1858. "'A house divided against itself cannot stand,'" said Lincoln, quoting the words of Jesus recorded in the Gospel of Mark. "I believe this government cannot endure, permanently half *slave* and half *free*. . . . It will become *all* one thing, or *all* the other." The Dred Scott decision in 1857 had legalized slavery in every territory on a principle that Lincoln feared would legalize it in every state as well if the southern-dominated Supreme Court had its way. But when Republicans gained national power and had a chance to reconstitute the Court, they would ban slavery from the territories, thus stifling its growth and placing it "where the public mind shall rest in the belief that it is in course of ultimate extinction" (Basler, vol. 2, p. 461).

Lincoln challenged Douglas to a series of debates. Douglas accepted, and the two met in seven three-hour debates in every part of the state. Why could the country not continue to exist half slave and half free as it had for seventy years? asked Douglas. Lincoln's talk about the "ultimate extinction" of slavery would drive the South into secession. Douglas also upbraided Lincoln for his alleged belief in "negro equality." Sensing a winning issue in Illinois, Douglas shouted questions to the crowd: "Are you in favor of conferring upon the negro the rights and privileges of citizenship?" Back would come the response, "No, No!" "Do you desire to turn this beautiful state into a free negro colony ('no, no') in order that when Missouri abolishes slavery she can send one hundred thousand emancipated slaves into Illinois, to become citizens and voters on an equality with yourselves? ('Never,' 'no')" (Basler, vol. 3, p. 9).

Douglas's demagoguery put Lincoln on the defensive. A "Black Republican" would have no chance of election in Illinois. Lincoln replied with cautious denials that he favored the "social and political equality" of the races, but he preferred the higher ground of principle. The problem with Douglas was that he "looks to no end of the institution of slavery," said Lincoln. "That is the issue that will continue in this country when these poor tongues of Judge Douglas and myself shall be silent" (Basler, vol. 3, p. 315).

The popular vote for Republican and Democratic legislators was virtually even in 1858, but because apportionment favored the Democrats, they won a majority of seats and reelected Douglas. Lincoln once again swallowed his disappointment and continued to speak for Republican candidates in the off-year elections of several midwestern states in 1859.

In retrospect, Lincoln was the real winner of the Lincoln-Douglas debates. His famous question at Freeport forced Douglas to enunciate the "Freeport Doctrine" that settlers could keep slavery out of a territory despite the Dred Scott decision by refusing to enact and enforce a local slave code. The Freeport Doctrine further alienated Douglas from southern Democrats and kindled their demand for a federal slave code in the territories. This issue split the Democratic party in 1860, virtually assuring the election of a Republican president. The national visibility achieved by Lincoln in the debates caused his name to be increasingly mentioned as the possible Republican nominee.

While deprecating his qualifications for the presidency, Lincoln admitted privately, "The taste *is* in my mouth a little" (Basler, vol. 4, p. 45). Lincoln's prospects were enhanced by the favorable impact of his speech on a large crowd, including several prominent eastern Republicans, at Cooper Union in New York City on 27 February 1860. On the basis of thorough research, Lincoln explicated the parallels between the Republican position on slavery and that of the Founding Fathers. His success at Cooper Union brought Lincoln numerous invitations to speak in New England on his way to visit his oldest son Robert, who had enrolled at Phillips Exeter Academy for a year of preparatory work before entering Harvard.

Lincoln used these occasions to focus on what has been called the "free labor ideology," which was at the core of the Republican value system. All work in a free society was honorable. Slavery degraded manual labor by equating it with bondage. Free men who practiced the virtues of industry, thrift, self-discipline, and sobriety could climb the ladder of success. "I am not ashamed to confess," Lincoln said in New Haven, "that twenty-five years ago I was a hired laborer, mauling rails, at work on a flat-boat—just what might happen to any poor man's son." But in the free states an ambitious man "can better his condition" because "there is no such thing as a freeman being fatally fixed for life, in the condition of a hired laborer." The lack of hope, energy, and progress in the slave states, where most laborers were "fatally fixed" in the condition of slavery, had made the United States a house divided. Republicans wanted to keep slavery out of the territories so that white workers and farmers could move there to better their condition without being "degraded . . . by forced rivalry with negro slaves." Moreover, said Lincoln, "I want every man to have the chance—and I believe a black man is entitled to it—in which he *can* better his condition" (Basler, vol. 4, pp. 24–25; vol. 3, p. 478). The symbolism of Lincoln, the "poor man's son," visiting his own son at New England's most elite school was not lost on his audiences.

Lincoln returned from his eastern tour to find Illinois friends mounting a concerted effort for his nomination as president. As the 16 May opening date approached for the Republican National Convention in Chicago (a fortunate location for Lincoln's cause), circumstances converted him from a favorite son to a serious contender. The leading candidate was William H. Seward of New York. Seward's long and prominent public career was a source of both strength and weakness. His chief liability was a reputation as an antislavery radical who could not carry the crucial lower North states of Illinois, Indiana, and Pennsylvania that the Republicans had lost in 1856. Though Seward's current position was in some respects more conservative than Lincoln's, he suffered from the image created by his Higher Law speech of 1850 and Irrepressible Conflict speech of 1858. Lincoln's campaign managers worked feverishly to persuade delegates that Lincoln was more electable than Seward and to line up second-choice commitments to Lincoln from several states. Lincoln's promoters also skillfully exploited the "rail-splitter" image to illustrate the party's free labor theme. The strategy worked. Seward led on the first ballot; Lincoln almost caught up on the second and won on the third.

The ensuing four-party campaign was the most fateful in American history. The Democrats split into northern and southern parties, while a remnant of Whigs, mostly from the border states, formed the Constitutional Union party. Lincoln carried every free state except New Jersey, whose electoral votes he divided with Douglas, and thereby won the election despite garnering slightly less than 40 percent of the popular votes—no popular votes at all in ten southern states. Seven of those states enacted ordinances of secession before Lincoln's inauguration.

Between the election and his inauguration, Lincoln remained in Springfield, putting together an administration. He made no public statements despite panicky advice that he say something to reassure the South. He was already on record many times saying that he had no constitutional power and no intention to interfere with slavery in the states where it existed. "I could say nothing which I have not already said. . . . If I thought a *repetition* would do any good I would make it" (Basler, vol. 4, pp. 139–40).

Lincoln gave private assurances to southern moderates and Unionists of his purpose to go no further against slavery than the Republican platform's pledge to keep it out of the territories. To Alexander Stephens of Georgia, who opposed secession until his state went out, Lincoln wrote in December that the slave states had nothing to fear, but he added: "I suppose, however, this does not meet the case. You think slavery is *right* and ought to be extended; while we think it is *wrong* and ought to be restricted. That I suppose is the rub" (Basler, vol. 4, p. 160).

It was indeed the rub. Southerners had read Lincoln's House Divided speech, in which he had said that restriction of slavery was a first step toward "ultimate extinction." Whether ultimate or imminent, the demise of slavery portended by the South's loss of the national government to an antislavery party was the reason for secession. For most secessionists there was no turning back.

Nevertheless, a host of compromise proposals emerged during the 1860–1861 session of Congress. The most important were embodied in constitutional amendments sponsored by Senator John J. Crittenden of Kentucky. The centerpiece of the Crittenden Compromise was a proposal to allow slavery south of 36°30′ in all territories "now held, *or hereafter acquired*" (italics added). Such a compromise would not only negate the chief plank of the Republican platform but would also step up the drive to acquire Cuba and other tropical territories suitable for slavery. Seward (whom Lincoln had designated as secretary of state) and some other Republicans seemed prepared to tilt toward compromise, but from Springfield came admonitions to stand firm. "Entertain no proposition for a compromise in regard to the *extension* of slavery," Lin-

coln wrote to Seward and to other key Republican leaders. "We have just carried an election on principles fairly stated to the people. . . . If we surrender, it is the end of us. . . . A year will not pass, till we shall have to take Cuba as a condition upon which they will stay in the Union" (Basler, vol. 4, pp. 150, 172).

The Crittenden Compromise went down to defeat, but there is no reason to believe that the seven seceded states would have returned even if it had passed. These states had seized all federal property within their borders except Fort Pickens on an island off Pensacola and Fort Sumter in Charleston harbor. A month before Congress adjourned (and before Lincoln was inaugurated), delegates from the seven seceded states met at Montgomery, Alabama, and formed the Confederate States of America. As he departed Springfield for Washington on 11 February 1861, "with a task before me greater than rested upon Washington," Lincoln faced the reality of a divided nation (Basler, vol. 4, p. 190).

Lincoln's inaugural address offered both a sword and an olive branch. The sword was an unconditional affirmation of the illegality of secession and his intention to execute the laws in all states, to "hold, occupy and possess" federal property, and to "collect the [customs] duties and imposts." The olive branch was a reiteration of Lincoln's pledge not "to interfere with slavery where it exists" and to enforce the constitutional provision for the return of fugitive slaves. Wherever "in any interior locality" hostility to the federal government was "so great and so universal, as to prevent competent resident citizens from holding the Federal offices," Lincoln would suspend federal operations "for the time." In an eloquent peroration suggested by Seward, Lincoln spoke of the "mystic chords of memory," which he hoped would "yet swell the chorus of the Union, when again touched, as surely they will be, by the better angels of our nature" (Basler, vol. 4, pp. 262–71).

Lincoln hoped that his inaugural address would buy time for passions to cool in the South and enable the seven states to "reconstruct" themselves back into the Union. This hope was founded on an erroneous but widely shared assumption in the North that a silent majority of southerners were Unionists who had been swept along by the passions of the moment. But time was running out. The day after his inauguration, Lincoln learned that Major Robert Anderson, commander of the besieged federal garrison at Fort Sumter in Charleston harbor, had only supplies enough to last a few more weeks.

Fort Sumter was the flash point of tension. Charleston was proud of its reputation as the cradle of secession. Insisting that a sovereign nation could not tolerate a foreign fort in one of its harbors, Confederate leaders demanded the transfer of Fort Sumter to the Confederacy. For a month Lincoln endured sleepless nights and conflicting advice on what to do. To give it up would constitute de facto if not de jure recognition of the Confederacy. On the other hand, it would preserve peace and keep the upper South in the Union.

On 15 March a majority of the cabinet, with Seward as the strongest voice, counseled Lincoln to yield Fort Sumter. Lincoln explored the possibility of pulling out in return for an assurance from Virginia that it would remain in the Union. Playing an independent role as the putative "premier" of the administration, Seward informed Confederate commissioners that Lincoln would withdraw the garrison. By the end of March, however, Lincoln had made the opposite decision. He let Seward know in no uncertain terms that he would be premier of his own administration.

A majority of the cabinet now supported Lincoln's decision to resupply Fort Sumter (as well as the less controversial Fort Pickens). The problem was how to do it. To send reinforcements prepared to shoot their way into the bay would surely provoke a war that Lincoln would be blamed for starting. Lincoln hit upon an ingenious solution. Instead of sending reinforcements, he would send only provisions—"food for hungry men"—and he would notify southern authorities in advance of his peaceful intention. On 6 April Lincoln sent a message to the governor of South Carolina, "An attempt will be made to supply Fort Sumpter [*sic*] with provisions only; . . . no effort to throw in men, arms, or ammunition, will be made, without further notice, or in case of an attack upon the Fort" (Basler, vol. 4, p. 323).

With this message Lincoln in effect flipped a coin and told Confederate president Jefferson Davis, "Heads I win; tails you lose." If the Confederates allowed the supplies to pass, the American flag would continue to fly over Fort Sumter as a symbol of sovereignty. If the Confederates attacked the supply ships or the fort, they would suffer the onus of starting a war and would unite a divided North. Davis did not hesitate; he ordered the Confederate guns to fire on Sumter. They did so on 12 April. And the war came.

On 15 April Lincoln called out 75,000 militia to quell the rebellion, prompting four more states to secede. On 19 April Lincoln proclaimed a naval blockade of the Confederate coastline. From there the war escalated step by step on a scale of violence and destruction never dreamed of by those who fired the guns at Sumter.

On the Union side Lincoln was the principal architect of this escalation. He insisted on a policy of unconditional surrender. Sovereignty, the central issue of the war, was not negotiable. As Lincoln put it late in the war, Davis "cannot voluntarily reaccept the Union; we cannot voluntarily yield it. Between him and us the issue is distinct, simple, and inflexible. It is an issue which can only be tried by war, and decided by victory" (Basler, vol. 8, p. 151).

Because "all else chiefly depends" on "the progress of our arms," as Lincoln said in 1865, he devoted more attention to his duties as commander in chief than to any other function of the presidency and spent vast amounts of time in the War Department telegraph office. He borrowed books on military history and strategy from the Library of Congress and burned the midnight oil mastering them. Eleven times he visited troops at the front in Virginia or Maryland. The greatest frustrations he experienced were the failures of Union generals to act with the vigor and aggressiveness he expected of them. Perhaps one of the greatest satisfactions he experienced was the ultimate victory of commanders who had risen to the top in large part because Lincoln appreciated their vigor and aggressiveness.

In 1861 Union armies achieved limited but important successes by gaining control of Maryland, Missouri, part of Kentucky, and also much of western Virginia, which paved the way for the later admission of West Virginia as a new state. Union naval forces gained lodgments along the South Atlantic coast. But in the year's biggest battle, at Bull Run (Manassas), 21 July 1861, the Union suffered a dispiriting defeat. Lincoln then appointed 34-year-old George B. McClellan commander of the Army of the Potomac and, from 1 November, general in chief of all Union armies. McClellan's minor victories in western Virginia had given him a newspaper reputation as the "Young Napoleon." He proved to be a superb organizer and trainer of soldiers but a defensive-minded and cautious perfectionist in action. He repeatedly exaggerated enemy strength as an excuse for postponing offensive operations.

Lincoln grew impatient with McClellan's inaction during the eight months after he took command, while Republicans in Congress grew suspicious that McClellan, a Democrat, did not really want to strike the "rebels" a hard blow. When McClellan finally began a glacial advance up the Virginia peninsula toward Richmond in the spring of 1862, Lincoln admonished him on 9 April: "Once more let me tell you, it is indispensable to *you* that you strike a blow. . . . I have never written you, or spoken to you, in greater kindness of feeling than now, nor with a fuller purpose to sustain you. . . . *But you must act*" (Basler, vol. 5, p. 185).

Lincoln already had his eye on a commander who had proved he could act. His name was Ulysses S. Grant, and he had captured Forts Henry and Donelson on the Tennessee and Cumberland rivers and then beat back a Confederate counteroffensive in the bloody battle of Shiloh, 6–7 April 1862. Other Union forces in the West also scored important victories in the spring of 1862, capturing New Orleans and Memphis and gaining control of most of the Mississippi River. In the East McClellan finally advanced to within five miles of Richmond by the end of May. The Confederacy seemed doomed.

Then the Union war machine went into reverse. By September 1862 Confederate counteroffensives in Virginia, Tennessee, and Kentucky took southern armies across the Potomac into Maryland and almost north to the Ohio River. This inversion stunned the northern people and caused home-front morale to plummet, but Lincoln did not falter. He issued a new call for volunteers and declared, "I expect to maintain this contest until successful, or till I die, or am conquered, or my term expires, or Congress or the country forsakes me" (Basler, vol. 5, p. 292).

The Confederate tide ebbed after the limited Union victories at Antietam in Maryland on 17 September 1862 and Perryville in Kentucky on 8 October. But the failure of Union commanders to follow up these victories caused Lincoln's frustration to boil over. He could not "understand why we cannot march as the enemy marches, live as he lives, fight as he fights" (*Complete Works of Abraham Lincoln*, ed. John G. Nicolay and John Hay [1905], vol. 8, pp. 63–64). On 24 October he replaced sluggish General Don Carlos Buell with William S. Rosecrans as commander of the Army of the Ohio (renamed the Army of the Cumberland). A week later he removed McClellan from command of the Army of the Potomac. McClellan had "the slows," the president told one of the general's supporters (Elbert B. Smith, *Francis Preston Blair* [1980], p. 328).

Lincoln did not have any better luck with the next two commanders of the Army of the Potomac. Ambrose Burnside lost the disastrous battle of Fredericksburg, 13 December 1862, and his successor Joseph Hooker fumbled several opportunities and lost the battle of Chancellorsville, 1–5 May 1863. Lincoln finally found a general who remained in command of that army for the rest of the war, George G. Meade, whose skillful defensive tactics won the crucial battle of Gettysburg, 1–3 July 1863. Meade gravely disappointed Lincoln, however, with his failure to follow up that victory with a vigorous effort to trap and destroy Robert E. Lee's Army of Northern Virginia before it could retreat across the Potomac. "My dear general, I do not believe you appreciate the magnitude of the misfortune involved in Lee's escape," Lincoln wrote Meade on 14 July. "As it is, the war will be prolonged indefinitely" (Basler, vol. 6, p. 328). Upon reflection, he did not send this letter, but it expressed his sentiments, sharpened by contrast with his attitude toward Grant, who had captured Vicksburg on 4 July 1863. Grant's star had alternately dimmed and brightened since the spring of 1862. Unfounded rumors of excessive drinking and the appearance of aimless floundering in the early stages of the Vicksburg campaign had generated much criticism. Lincoln nevertheless retained his faith in Grant. "I think Grant has hardly a friend left, except myself," said Lincoln in the spring of 1863. "What I want . . . is generals who will fight battles and win victories. Grant has done this, and I propose to stand by him" (Shelby Foote, *The Civil War: A Narrative*, vol. 2: *Fredericksburg to Meridian* [1963], p. 217). Grant followed up his victory at Vicksburg by driving the Confederates away from Chattanooga and into the mountains of northern Georgia. Congress created the rank of lieutenant general (last held by George Washington). Lincoln promoted Grant to this rank in March 1864 and made him general in chief of all Union armies.

For the first time Lincoln had a commanding general in whom he had full confidence, one who could take from his shoulders some of the burden of constant military oversight. On the eve of the military campaigns of 1864, Lincoln wrote Grant: "The particulars of your plans I neither know, or seek to know. You are vigilant and self-reliant; and pleased with this, I wish not to obtrude any constraints or restraints upon you" (Basler, vol. 7, p. 324).

Lincoln wrote thus because he and Grant saw eye to eye on military strategy. In this war the Confederates had the advantage of fighting on the strategic defensive with interior lines that enabled them to shift reinforcements from inactive to active fronts unless the Union employed its superior numbers to attack on several fronts at once. Lincoln grasped this point better than many of his generals. As early as 13 January 1862 Lincoln instructed the hapless Buell, "I state my general idea of this war to be that we have *greater* numbers, and the enemy has the *greater* facility of concentrating forces upon points of collision; that we must fail, unless we can find some way of making *our* advantage an overmatch for *his*; and that this can only be done by menacing him with superior forces at *different* points, at the *same* time" (Basler, vol. 5, p. 98). Grant agreed. He devised simultaneous Union advances on several fronts to prevent Confederates from shifting troops from one point to another. In the end this strategy won the war.

An issue related to military events also absorbed much of Lincoln's time: internal security. Confederate sympathizers in the border states and antiwar activists in the North (the "Copperheads") constituted a "fire in the rear" that Lincoln feared "more than our military chances" (Edward L. Pierce, *Memoir and Letters of Charles Sumner*, vol. 4 [1893], p. 114). Early in the war he suspended the privilege of the writ of habeas corpus in limited areas, which he kept expanding until a proclamation of 24 September 1862 extended the suspension to the whole country. In his capacity as a circuit court judge in Maryland, Chief Justice Roger B. Taney had ruled in May 1861 that the president could not suspend the writ without congressional authorization (Ex parte Merryman, 17 Fed. Cas. 144). Lincoln disagreed and exercised this power before as well as after congressional authorization in March 1863.

Under these suspensions of the writ, Union officials arrested and detained without trial at least 15,000 civilians during the war, mostly in the border states. Military courts also tried several civilians, most notably the Copperhead leader, Clement L. Vallandigham, for "treasonable" activities. Some of these arrests and trials, as in the case of Vallandigham, came dangerously close to infringing First Amendment rights. Lincoln was embarrassed by the Vallandigham case, which aroused a storm of criticism. Nevertheless, he justified the detention of those who undermined the struggle for national survival. He made his case in pungent prose that everyone could understand. "Under cover of 'Liberty of speech,' 'Liberty of the press' and 'Habeas Corpus,'" wrote the president, the rebels "hoped to keep on foot amongst us a most efficient corps of spies, informers, suppliers, and aiders and abettors of their cause." If anything, he believed he had arrested too few rather than too many. "Must I shoot a simple-minded soldier boy who deserts, while I must not touch a hair of a wiley [*sic*] agitator who induces him to desert? . . . I think that in such a case, to silence the agitator, and save the boy, is not only constitutional, but, withal, a great mercy" (Basler, vol. 6, pp. 263, 266–67). Scholars disagree about Lincoln's record on civil liberties, but one thing can be said with certainty: compared with the enforcement of espionage and sedition laws in World War I and the internment of Japanese-Americans in World War II, the curtailment of civil liberties during the far greater internal crisis of the Civil War seems quite mild.

Another matter bound up with Lincoln's powers as commander in chief, but involving many other considerations as well, was slavery. Lincoln's decision in 1862 to issue an emancipation proclamation freed himself as much as it freed the slaves—freed him from the agonizing contradiction between his antislavery convictions and his constitutional responsibilities. Lincoln had said many times that he considered slavery "a social, moral, and political wrong. . . . If slavery is not wrong, nothing is wrong." Yet, he added, "I have never understood that the Presidency conferred upon me an unrestricted right to act officially on this judgment and feeling" (Basler, vol. 3, p. 92; vol. 7, p. 281). The Constitution he swore to preserve, protect, and defend sanctioned slavery in states that wanted it. Moreover, Lincoln conceived his primary duty to be preservation of the Union. In 1861 he believed that to preserve it he must maintain the support of Democrats and border state Unionists, who would be alienated by any move toward emancipation. That is why he revoked General Frémont's military order freeing the slaves of Confederate sympathizers in Missouri. If he had let Frémont's order stand, Lincoln explained to a critic, it would have driven Kentucky into secession. "To lose Kentucky is nearly the same as to lose the whole game. Kentucky gone, we can not hold Missouri, nor, as I think, Maryland" (Basler, vol. 4, p. 532).

For the next year Lincoln adhered publicly to this position despite growing pressure from his own party to move against slavery. To a powerful emancipation editorial by Horace Greeley in the New York *Tribune*, Lincoln replied on 22 August 1862 with a letter published in the *Tribune*: "My paramount object in this struggle *is* to save the Union, and is *not* either to save or to destroy slavery. If I could save the Union without freeing *any* slave I would do it; and if I could save it by freeing *all* the slaves I would do it; and if I could save it by freeing some and leaving others alone I would also do that" (Basler, vol. 5, pp. 388–89).

Lincoln had already drafted an emancipation proclamation but was awaiting a Union military victory to announce it. His letter to Greeley was designed to prepare the public, especially conservatives, for the announcement by making it clear that freeing *some* of the slaves was necessary to achieve his, and their, main goal of preserving the Union.

Earlier in 1862 Lincoln had tried to persuade border state Unionists to accept an offer of federal compensation for emancipation in their states. They refused, while Union military fortunes took a turn for the worse in the summer of 1862. By then Lincoln agreed with the Radical Republican argument that a proclamation of emancipation would strike a blow against the Confederate economy and war effort that would more than counterbalance the damage it might do by alienating Democrats and border state Unionists. Slaves constituted the principal labor force of the Confederacy. Escaped slaves (labeled "contrabands") had been coming into Union lines since the outset of the war; an official proclamation of emancipation would accelerate this process. In his capacity as commander in chief, Lincoln believed he had the constitutional power to seize enemy property (slaves) being used to wage war against the United States. On 22 September 1862, five days after the battle of Antietam, Lincoln issued a preliminary proclamation, declaring that all slaves in any state or part of a state still in rebellion against the United States on 1 January 1863 "shall be then, thenceforward, and forever free" (Basler, vol. 5, pp. 433–36). New Year's Day came, and Lincoln issued the Emancipation Proclamation, which exempted Tennessee and parts of Louisiana and Virginia (as well as the slave states that had remained in the Union), because they were occupied by Union forces or deemed loyal to the Union and therefore not subject to the war powers under which Lincoln acted.

Despite cavils that the Emancipation Proclamation did not in and of itself free a single slave, it did broaden northern war aims to include emancipation. Union armies became armies of liberation. As a corollary of the proclamation, the Lincoln administration began recruiting black soldiers and sailors, mostly freed slaves—189,000 in all by the end of the war. In August 1863 Lincoln stated in a widely published letter, "The emancipation policy, and the use of colored troops, constitute the heaviest blow yet dealt to the rebellion." Referring to critics of emancipation and opponents of the war, Lincoln said pointedly that, when the war was won, "there will be some black men who can remember that, with silent tongue, and clenched teeth, and steady eye, and well-poised bayonet, they have helped mankind on to this great consummation; while, I fear, there will be some white ones, unable to forget that, with malignant heart, and deceitful speech, they have strove to hinder it" (Basler, vol. 6, pp. 408–10).

As a war measure the Emancipation Proclamation would cease to have any effect when the war was over. While many slaves would have gained freedom, the institution of slavery would still exist. Thus Lincoln and his party pledged to adopt a constitutional amendment to abolish slavery. Antislavery Unionists gained control of the state governments of Maryland and Missouri and abolished slavery in those states. The wartime "reconstruction" governments in the occupied parts of Louisiana, Arkansas, and Tennessee did the same. With a skillful use of patronage and arm-twisting, Lincoln nurtured these achievements.

Lincoln did not live to see the final ratification of the Thirteenth Amendment. Yet the future shape of a disenthralled United States was clear enough by 19 November 1863 for Lincoln to proclaim "a new birth of freedom" in the brief address he delivered at the commemoration of a cemetery at Gettysburg for Union soldiers killed in the battle there.

Lincoln is best known for his brief speech at Gettysburg, but on many other occasions also he gave voice to the purpose for which 360,000 northern soldiers gave their lives. "The central idea pervading this struggle," he said as early as 1861, "is the necessity . . . of proving that popular government is not an absurdity. We must settle this question now, whether in a free government the minority have the right to break up the government whenever they choose. If we fail it will go far to prove the incapability of the people to govern themselves" (Tyler Dennett, ed., *Lincoln and the Civil War in the Diaries and Letters of John Hay* [1939], pp. 19–20).

Abraham Lincoln's eloquence and statesmanship were grounded in his skills as a politician. He was not only president and commander in chief but also leader of his party. Some of the party's fractious members in the cabinet and Congress gave Lincoln almost as many problems as fractious and incompetent generals. Four members of his cabinet had been his rivals for the presidential nomination in 1860. Some of them as well as some congressional leaders continued to think of themselves as better qualified for the presidency than Lincoln. Yet he established his mastery of both cabinet and Congress. He generally deferred to cabinet members in their areas of responsibility and delegated administrative authority to them to run their departments. Although he listened to advice, Lincoln made the most important decisions himself: on Fort Sumter, on emancipation, on appointing or dismissing generals, on Reconstruction. Secretary of the Treasury Salmon P. Chase, who thought of running for president in 1864, convinced Republican senators that Lincoln was too much influenced by Secretary of State Seward. At a low point in the Union cause after the battle of Fredericksburg in December 1862, the Senate Republican caucus pressed Lincoln to dismiss Seward. If he had "caved in" (Lincoln's words), he would have lost control of his own administration. In an exhibition of political virtuosity, he confronted Chase and the senators in the presence of the cabinet and forced them to back down. Chase offered his resignation, which Lincoln refused to accept, thereby keeping both Seward and Chase in the cabinet and maintaining the separation of executive and congressional powers.

Another contest of power and policy between Lincoln and congressional Republicans occurred in 1864 over the issue of Reconstruction. Lincoln conceived of this process as primarily an executive responsibility, a part of his duty as commander in chief to win the war by "reconstructing" southern states back into the Union. On 8 December 1863 he issued a "Proclamation of Amnesty and Reconstruction," offering pardons to most categories of Confederates who would take an oath of allegiance to the United States. When the number of those pardoned in any state equaled 10 percent of the number of voters in 1860, Lincoln authorized them to form a Union state government, to which he promised executive recognition. Congressional leaders, however, viewed Reconstruction as a legislative process in which Congress would mandate the conditions for restoration of states to the Union and readmission of their representatives to Congress. The showdown in this struggle came in the summer of 1864, when Lincoln killed the Wade-Davis Reconstruction Bill, which was more stringent than his own policy, by a pocket veto. The bill's cosponsors, Representative Henry Winter Davis and Senator Benjamin Wade, thereupon issued a blistering "Manifesto," charging Lincoln with executive usurpation.

This imbroglio became entangled with Lincoln's campaign for reelection. The party's national convention had unanimously renominated him, after an initial token vote for Grant by the Missouri delegation, on 7 June. But beneath this surface unanimity seethed hostility to Lincoln by Republicans who opposed him on Reconstruction. The main issue in 1864, however, was not Reconstruction but the war itself. Union offensives, especially in Virginia, bogged down in a morass of carnage that made victory appear more distant than ever. War weariness and defeatism corroded the will of northerners as they reeled from the staggering cost in lives. Lincoln came under immense pressure to open peace negotiations. Unofficial envoys met with Confederate agents in Canada and with Jefferson Davis at Richmond in July to make clear Lincoln's terms for peace: reunion and emancipation. Davis spurned these conditions, insisting on Confederate independence, but somehow northern Democrats convinced much of the electorate that only Lincoln's requirement of emancipation blocked a peace settlement.

Lincoln refused to back down. "No human power can subdue this rebellion without using the Emancipation lever as I have done," he said. Black soldiers would not continue fighting for the Union if they thought the North intended to "betray them. . . . If they stake their lives for us they must be prompted by the strongest motive . . . the promise of freedom. And the promise being made, must be kept" (Basler, vol. 7, pp. 500, 507).

When Lincoln said this, he fully expected to lose the election. On 23 August he wrote his famous "blind memorandum" and required cabinet members to endorse it sight unseen: "This morning, as for some days past, it seems exceedingly probable that this Administration will not be re-elected. Then it will be my duty to so co-operate with the President elect, as to save the Union between the election and the inauguration; as he will have secured his election on such ground that he can not possibly save it afterwards" (Basler, vol. 7, p. 514). A week later the Democrats nominated McClellan for president on a platform that branded the war a failure and demanded an armistice and peace negotiations.

The war did indeed seem a failure. Two days later, on 2 September, came a telegram from General William T. Sherman, however, saying "Atlanta is ours and fairly won." Northern opinion turned 180 degrees almost overnight. Then came news of spectacular military victories by General Philip Sheridan's army in the

Shenandoah Valley. Lincoln's tarnished reputation as commander in chief turned to luster. He was triumphantly reelected in November, carrying every Union state except New Jersey, Delaware, and Kentucky.

As Sherman marched through Georgia and South Carolina, Union armies advanced on other fronts, and Grant tightened the vise near Richmond. The end of the war seemed only a matter of time. In his second inaugural address, on 4 March 1865, Lincoln looked forward to a peace "with malice toward none; with charity for all." He also suggested that "this terrible war" may have been God's punishment of the whole nation for the wrong of slavery. "Fondly do we hope—fervently do we pray—that this mighty scourge of war may speedily pass away," said Lincoln. "Yet, if God wills that it continue, until all the wealth piled by the bond-man's two hundred and fifty years of unrequited toil shall be sunk, and until every drop of blood drawn with the lash, shall be paid by another drawn with the sword, as was said three thousand years ago, so still it must be said 'the judgments of the Lord, are true and righteous altogether'" (Basler, vol. 8, p. 333).

During the last winter of war, Lincoln and congressional Republicans came closer together on a postwar Reconstruction policy. After Lee's surrender at Appomattox, Lincoln spoke to a large crowd of celebrants at the White House on 11 April. He hinted that his Reconstruction policy would enfranchise literate blacks and black army veterans. "That means nigger citizenship," muttered a member of the crowd, the actor John Wilkes Booth. "Now, by God, I'll put him through. That is the last speech he will ever make" (William Hanchett, *The Lincoln Murder Conspiracies* [1983], p. 37).

A native of Maryland and an unstable egotist who supported the Confederacy and hated Lincoln, Booth headed a shadowy conspiracy with links to the Confederate secret service, which had intended to kidnap Lincoln and hold him hostage in Richmond. The fall of Richmond had ruined that plot, so Booth decided to kill the president. While the Lincolns watched a comedy at Ford's Theatre in Washington, D.C., on 14 April, Booth gained entrance to their box and shot Lincoln in the head. Lincoln died at 7:22 the next morning.

Scorned and ridiculed by many critics during his presidency, Lincoln became a martyr and almost a saint after his death. His words and deeds lived after him and will be revered as long as there is a United States. Indeed, it seems quite likely that without his determined leadership the *United* States would have ceased to exist. Union victory in the Civil War resolved two fundamental, festering problems that had been left unresolved by the Revolution of 1776 and the Constitution of 1789: whether this republic, "conceived in Liberty, and dedicated to the proposition that all men are created equal," would "long endure" or "perish from the earth"; and whether the "monstrous injustice" of slavery would continue to mock those ideals of liberty. The republic endured, and slavery perished. That is Lincoln's legacy.

• The principal collection of Lincoln's papers is the Robert Todd Lincoln Collection in the Library of Congress. Most of the 18,000 items in this collection are incoming letters. The fullest collection of Lincoln's own letters, speeches, and other writings is *The Collected Works of Abraham Lincoln*, ed. Roy P. Basler (8 vols. and an index, 1953–1955), with the addition of *The Collected Works of Abraham Lincoln: Supplement 1832–1865*, ed. Basler (1974). The most important of Lincoln's letters and other writings have been selected by Don E. Fehrenbacher and published in two volumes titled *Abraham Lincoln: Speeches and Writings* (1989). Another valuable selection of Lincoln writings is *Lincoln on Democracy*, ed. Mario M. Cuomo and Harold Holzer (1990), which has been translated into several languages.

The number of biographies and other books about Lincoln is huge—far greater than for any other figure in American history. Lincoln's law partner William Herndon spent several years after Lincoln's death interviewing people who had known him and gathering other material about the first fifty years of Lincoln's life. Herndon collaborated with Jesse W. Weik to present this material in *Herndon's Lincoln: The True Story of a Great Life* (3 vols., 1889), which has been reprinted in whole or in part in many subsequent editions. Herndon's account distorted some aspects of Lincoln's life and accepted as true some information that may have been apocryphal. Nonetheless, all subsequent biographers are indebted to Herndon for most of what we know about Lincoln's early life. A year after the appearance of *Herndon's Lincoln*, Lincoln's wartime private secretaries, John G. Nicolay and John Hay, published a ten-volume biography, *Abraham Lincoln: A History*, which focused mainly on the presidential years.

Until the Robert Todd Lincoln Collection was opened to the public in 1947, the Nicolay and Hay biography was the only one based on full access to Lincoln's papers. Before 1947, however, other important biographies appeared: Lord Charnwood, *Abraham Lincoln* (1917), which was notable for its sympathetic British perspective; Albert J. Beveridge, *Abraham Lincoln 1809–1858* (2 vols., 1928), whose author died before he could continue the biography into the war years; and Carl Sandburg, *Abraham Lincoln: The Prairie Years* (2 vols., 1926) and *Abraham Lincoln: The War Years* (4 vols., 1939), a powerful evocation of Lincoln and his times, which, however, piles up dubious as well as authentic evidence in a mixed profusion. The fullest scholarly biography, part of it written after the Lincoln papers were opened, is James G. Randall, *Lincoln the President* (4 vols., 1945–1955), with the fourth volume completed after Randall's death by Richard N. Current, who has also written a volume of incisive essays, *The Lincoln Nobody Knows* (1958). Randall's interpretation is marred by a tendency to squeeze Lincoln into a conservative mold that fails to appreciate the depth of his antislavery convictions. The same fault is shared in part by Benjamin Thomas's one-volume biography *Abraham Lincoln* (1952), but is corrected by another readable one-volume biography, Stephen B. Oates, *With Malice toward None: The Life of Abraham Lincoln* (1977). The best biography within the covers of a single volume is David Herbert Donald, *Lincoln* (1995). A concise thematic biography is Mark E. Neely, Jr., *The Last Best Hope of Earth: Abraham Lincoln and the Promise of America* (1993). Neely has also written a comprehensive and valuable reference work, *The Abraham Lincoln Encyclopedia* (1982), as well as *The Fate of Liberty: Abraham Lincoln and Civil Liberties* (1991).

Other valuable studies of specific aspects of Lincoln's life and career include: Gabor Boritt, *Lincoln and the Economics of the American Dream* (1978); Boritt, ed., *The Historians' Lincoln* (1988); Michael Burlingame, *The Inner World of Abra-*

ham Lincoln (1994); David Donald, *Lincoln Reconsidered*, 2d ed. (1961); Fehrenbacher, *Lincoln in Text and Context: Collected Essays* (1987); Fehrenbacher, *Prelude to Greatness: Lincoln in the 1850's* (1962); James M. McPherson, *Abraham Lincoln and the Second American Revolution* (1991); Phillip Shaw Paludan, *The Presidency of Abraham Lincoln* (1994); Charles B. Strozier, *Lincoln's Quest for Union* (1982); John E. Walsh, *The Shadows Rise: Abraham Lincoln and the Ann Rutledge Legend* (1993); T. Harry Williams, *Lincoln and His Generals* (1952); Kenneth P. Williams, *Lincoln Finds a General* (5 vols., 1949–1959); and LaWanda Cox, *Lincoln and Black Freedom* (1981).

The *New York Times* ran an obituary on 17 Apr. 1865.

JAMES M. McPHERSON

LINCOLN, Benjamin (24 Jan. 1733–9 May 1810), revolutionary war soldier, was born in Hingham, Massachusetts, the son of Colonel Benjamin Lincoln, a farmer and maltster, and Elizabeth Thaxter. His family was well established in Massachusetts, for some of his ancestors were among the first settlers, and his father was a member of the politically important governor's council. Although his education was only in the common schools, he learned to write well and also became a prosperous farmer. In 1756 he married Mary Cushing, with whom he had eleven children. Over the next few years he held the offices of magistrate and justice of the peace, and he was elected a member of the colonial legislature. He also joined his father's militia regiment, the Third Suffolk, as adjutant and was promoted through the ranks to succeed his father as colonel and commander. As tensions between Britain and America rose in the mid-1770s, he was dismayed with Britain's policies, for he believed they threatened the "peace, liberty, and safety" of the colonists. Hence he gave his "interest in support of the present struggle with Great Britain" by serving on the Hingham Committee of Safety and attending sessions of the Massachusetts Provincial Congress. In the latter body he acted as secretary, member of the committee of correspondence, and commissary. As commissary, he reorganized the Massachusetts militia and purged Loyalist officers. He marched with his regiment in April 1775 to the siege of Boston but arrived after the fighting had ceased.

With war underway, Lincoln was appointed muster master of the Massachusetts army and in July was elected president of the Provincial Congress. He spent the winter of 1775–1776 at home, then on 23 May 1776 was appointed head of a committee to instruct the Provincial Congress to support independence if the Continental Congress voted for it. Promoted to major general of the Massachusetts militia, he commanded an expedition in June to clear Boston harbor of enemy blockading vessels. In August he was ordered by the Massachusetts government to reinforce General George Washington's army in New York, and on 28 October he commanded the American right wing at the battle of White Plains. Lincoln found in Washington a congenial spirit, and he and the Virginian soon became fast friends. In early January 1777 he served under General William Heath during a disastrous at-tack on Fort Independence on the Hudson River above New York City and a month afterward joined Washington for the winter at Morristown, New Jersey. On 19 February he was promoted to major general in the Continental line. Two months later, while stationed at Bound Brook, New Jersey, he was surprised by an enemy detachment under Charles Lord Cornwallis and James Grant and barely escaped capture. This military action, although embarrassing to Lincoln personally, had no strategic or tactical consequences for the American cause.

In July Lincoln and Benedict Arnold were dispatched by Washington to join General Philip Schuyler's army in upstate New York to oppose an advance by John Burgoyne out of Canada. Taking post at Manchester, Vermont, Lincoln rallied frightened citizens and raised a body of New England militia. He just missed the battle of Bennington on 16 August but quickly seized posts on Lake George to sever Burgoyne's communications with Canada. In September he joined General Horatio Gates, who had replaced Schuyler, at Stillwater and took command of the American right wing. In the battle of Bemis Heights on 7 October he commanded defensive works behind the lines. The following morning, at the head of a small party, he fell in with an enemy force, was severely wounded in his right ankle, and was almost captured. Invalided home, he recuperated until the following summer but never completely recovered from his wound.

In August 1778 Lincoln rejoined the army, and on 25 September he was appointed by Congress to command the Southern Department. Arriving in Charleston, South Carolina, on 4 December 1778, he reorganized his troops and four months later marched into Georgia to challenge a British force commanded by General Augustine Prevost. Instead of overwhelming Prevost, however, he soon found Prevost challenging him. Outmaneuvered by the enemy commander, Lincoln was soon compelled to rush north to defend Charleston. But Prevost in turn ran into problems, and after he retreated to Savannah, a sort of stalemate emerged between him and Lincoln. With the arrival of a French fleet under Count d'Estaing off Savannah in September, the stalemate was broken in Lincoln's favor, and the American commander quickly joined the French in besieging the city. But when d'Estaing proved unwilling to stay in Georgia long enough to effect Savannah's surrender, Lincoln had to abandon the siege and return to Charleston. In February 1780 his own situation became precarious, for Sir Henry Clinton landed a large English army thirty miles below Charleston and advanced upon him. Knowing that it was militarily unwise to linger with his army in Charleston but under intense political pressure to remain, he finally allowed himself to be besieged. Although he obstinately defended his post, he was compelled on 12 May to surrender the city and an army of 3,371 soldiers.

Paroled in June, Lincoln hastened to Philadelphia and demanded a court of inquiry, to examine his conduct at Charleston. No court ever sat, for none of Lincoln's compatriots found reason to fault his behavior. Exchanged for British major general William Phillips in early 1781, he was welcomed back to Washington's army on the Hudson River north of New York City. When word arrived in August that Cornwallis had taken post at Yorktown and might be trapped, Lincoln was ordered by Washington to lead the march of patriot forces to Virginia. During subsequent siege operations, he commanded the American right wing, and when Cornwallis surrendered on 19 October was appointed by Washington to receive the British officer's sword as partial compensation for his humiliation at Charleston. After Yorktown he assumed the office of secretary of war under the new national government and held that position with distinction until October 1783. Thereupon he resigned public life and returned to Hingham. Elected president of the Massachusetts Society of the Cincinnati, a postwar organization of Continental army officers, he held that office until his death.

At the outbreak of Shays's Rebellion in 1786, Lincoln was persuaded to leave his retirement and once again take up military service. Because of his popularity in western Massachusetts, where Daniel Shays's followers mostly were located, Governor James Bowdoin appointed him commander of the Massachusetts militia to do battle with the insurgents. By early 1787 he had organized his forces in Boston, and on 20 January he marched westward toward Springfield to relieve General William Shepard, who was defending the federal arsenal and courts there. He arrived at Springfield on the twenty-seventh and easily routed the insurgents but was unsuccessful in negotiating with Shays for a total surrender. He struck at the rebels again on the night of 3 February, attacking their headquarters at Petersham and chasing them into the cold darkness. Moving on to Pittsfield, he sent numerous militia detachments in all directions to apprehend Shays's followers and soon had the insurgency in Massachusetts under control. Thereafter he faced only a few holdout refugees in Vermont and New York who loomed on the borders but mostly sought a means of submission. While cooperating with the governors of these neighboring states to contain the insurgency, Lincoln urged Bowdoin to adopt a policy of moderation toward the refugees in order to encourage their surrender. This "delicately cautious" program of the general's, Bowdoin decided, was exactly right for the situation, and so in March he had the General Court appoint Lincoln head of a commission to travel through the disaffected regions to hear complaints. That duty done, Lincoln resigned his extraordinary militia commission on 10 June 1786 and returned to his home. Lincoln's military effectiveness and subsequent conciliatory policy in large measure ended Shays's Rebellion quickly and almost bloodlessly.

In 1787 Lincoln was elected lieutenant governor of Massachusetts and one year later served as a member of the state convention to ratify the new federal Constitution. In 1789 Washington appointed him collector of the Port of Boston and a member of a commission to make peace with the Creek Indians in the South. In 1793 he was sent on a similar mission to the Northwest Indians in an unsuccessful attempt to avert war. Losing political influence after Thomas Jefferson's election to the presidency, the Federalist Lincoln was forced in 1809 to resign the office of collector while under partisan attack. During his final years, he lost interest in politics and turned instead to scientific and literary matters. As a member of the American Academy of Arts and Sciences and of the Massachusetts Historical Society, he wrote papers on topics as diverse as the Indian tribes, religion, soil, topography, and history of his native New England. His remarkably diverse career closed at his death in the house in which he had been born.

• The major collection of Lincoln papers is in the Massachusetts Historical Society. Lincoln's correspondence with George Washington is in the Washington papers, Library of Congress, and his letters to Congress are in the Papers of the Continental Congress, nos. 149 and 157, National Archives. Some of Washington's letters to Lincoln are calendared in A. J. Bowden, *Fifty-five Letters of Washington to Benjamin Lincoln 1777–1779* (1907). The best biography, and the only full-length one, is David Bruce Mattern, "A Moderate Revolutionary: The Life of Major General Benjamin Lincoln" (Ph.D. diss., Columbia Univ., 1990). Useful sketches are Francis Bowen, "Life of Benjamin Lincoln, Major-General in the Army of the Revolution," in *The Library of American Biography*, ed. Jared Sparks, 2d ser., vol. 13 (1847), and Clifford K. Shipton, "Benjamin Lincoln: Old Reliable," in *George Washington's Generals*, ed. George A. Billias (1964). Lincoln's revolutionary war career is assayed by John Carroll Cavanagh in "The Military Career of Major General Benjamin Lincoln in the War of the American Revolution, 1775–1781" (Ph.D. diss., Duke Univ., 1969) and in "American Military Leadership in the Southern Campaign: Benjamin Lincoln," in *The Revolutionary War in the South: Power, Conflict, and Leadership*, ed. W. Robert Higgins (1979). Further background is provided by Hoffman Nickerson, *Turning Point of the Revolution* (1928); John S. Pancake, *1777: The Year of the Hangman* (1977) and *This Destructive War: The British Campaign in the Carolinas, 1780–1782* (1985); and Alexander A. Lawrence, *Storm Over Savannah* (1951). Charles Martyn, *The Life of Artemas Ward* (1921), describes Lincoln's part in suppressing Shays's Rebellion. The most comprehensive survey of the rebellion is Robert A. Feer, *Shay's Rebellion* (1988).

PAUL DAVID NELSON

LINCOLN, Enoch (28 Dec. 1788–8 Oct. 1829), politician and lawyer, was born in Worcester, Massachusetts, the son of Levi Lincoln, a lawyer, politician, and governor of Massachusetts, and Martha Waldo. Enoch entered Harvard with advanced standing in 1806 but left college in 1808 without completing his degree. He returned to Worcester to study law at his older brother Levi's office and became a member of the Massachusetts bar in 1811.

Lincoln began his legal career in Salem but soon returned to Worcester, where he briefly edited the pro-Republican newspaper *Aegis*. In the spring of 1813 Lincoln relocated to Fryeburg, District of Maine, to practice law. Lincoln's new home inspired many new interests that became lifelong pursuits. He indulged his literary interests in 1816 when he wrote "The Village," a poem that celebrated the beauty of his new home. The frontier-like setting of the area also enabled him to meet several Indian inhabitants of the region; these contacts inspired an intense curiosity about Native-American languages and history. Lincoln remained in Fryeburg until 1819, when he moved his official residence to the local shire town of Paris.

As a member of one of Massachusetts's most prominent Republican families, Lincoln rose quickly through the party ranks in Maine. In 1815 he was appointed an assistant U.S. district attorney for Maine, a position he held until 1818. That year he left Maine for Washington, D.C., to complete the remaining congressional term of Albion K. Parris. Lincoln remained a member of the U.S. House of Representatives until January 1826. His congressional career was generally undistinguished, but he earned widespread respect in his home state when he defied local party leaders by opposing Maine statehood as a condition for Missouri's admission to the Union as a slave state.

In 1826 deep divisions in Maine's Republican ranks enabled Lincoln, a compromise candidate, to become the gubernatorial nominee. He was elected in September of that year and held the office until 1829. The most pressing issue confronting him during his three years as governor was the northeastern boundary controversy. The dispute resulted from ambiguities in the 1783 Treaty of Paris that left the boundary between the United States and British North America, including Maine's northern frontier, undetermined. Efforts to resolve the issue immediately after the War of 1812 had failed, leaving millions of acres of valuable timberland in dispute. Lincoln was eager to assert Maine's claim to the territory, partly to defend state interests but also because of his own speculation in timberlands. As governor he sent fact-finding teams into the area, encouraged the exercise of American sovereignty in the region, and ignored federal pleas for restraint. When an American citizen was arrested in 1827 for defying British authority in the disputed territory, Lincoln urged the federal government to take action. During the crisis that followed, Lincoln worked closely with Massachusetts officials, including his older brother Levi, then serving as governor of the Bay State. (Massachusetts maintained a proprietary interest in the territory as part of the terms of Maine's separation.) In pressing for a settlement, Lincoln consistently denied the federal government's constitutional authority to cede territory without the consent of the state, a stance consistent with the philosophy of many fellow Republicans. His assertion of Maine's right to the area in dispute became an article of faith for the state's politicians in ensuing years. Despite his efforts, he was unable to gain a settlement. Instead, the boundary was submitted for arbitration to King William of the Netherlands and would remain unsettled until the Webster-Ashburton Treaty (Treaty of Washington) of 1842.

Lincoln, a conciliatory politician who had always enjoyed amicable relations with the various Republican factions, finally fell victim to political infighting and did not run for governor in 1829. Weary of politics, he looked forward to becoming a gentleman farmer and hoped that the respite from public life would afford him the opportunity to spend more time on his historical interests. His "Remarks on the Indian Languages" and "Some Account on the Catholic Missions in Maine" were both published posthumously. Following an address at the Female Academy in Augusta, Maine, Lincoln fell ill and died. Lincoln was a lifelong bachelor, although he had been betrothed for many years to Mary Chadbourne Page.

Lincoln's most important contribution came as governor, when he sought to assert Maine's claim to territory under dispute with Great Britain. His aggressive stance on his state's right to the territory and his proclamation that the federal government could not relinquish the territory without Maine's consent captured the defiant mood of the young state but only served to prolong settlement of the boundary.

• A fairly extensive collection of Lincoln's papers can be found in the Lincoln Family Papers at the American Antiquarian Society in Worcester, Mass. The papers of important contemporaries, such as Francis O. J. Smith, Albion K. Parris, John Holmes, and John Chandler, are available at the Maine Historical Society in Portland. His historical writings are in William Willis, ed., "Late Gov. Lincoln's MSS. Papers," *Collections of the Maine Historical Society*, vol. 1 (1831; 2d ed., 1865). The best accounts of Lincoln's life are brief treatments, including Waldo Lincoln, *History of the Lincoln Family: An Account of the Descendants of Samuel Lincoln of Hingham, Massachusetts, 1637–1920* (1923); "The Late Governor of Maine," *Yankee and Boston Literary Gazette* 2, no. 5 (1829): 225–32; William Lincoln, *History of the Lincoln Family* (1837); and Louis C. Hatch, *Maine: A History* (1919). Lincoln's role in the northeastern boundary controversy has been examined by several historians. The best accounts appear in Henry S. Burrage, *Maine in the Northeastern Boundary Controversy* (1919), and Howard Jones, *To the Webster-Ashburton Treaty: A Study of Anglo-American Relations, 1783–1843* (1977). Thomas L. Gaffney, "Maine's Mr. Smith: A Study of the Career of Francis O. J. Smith, Politician and Entrepreneur" (Ph.D. diss., Univ. of Maine, 1979), ably recounts Maine's political landscape during the period.

J. CHRIS ARNDT

LINCOLN, Joseph Crosby (13 Feb. 1870–10 Mar. 1944), writer and editor, was born in Brewster, Massachusetts, the son of Joseph L. Lincoln, a sea captain, and Emily Crosby. Although Lincoln lived in other places during his life, Cape Cod was forever a part of who he was. In a conversation with the poet Joyce Kilmer, Lincoln stated, "I am a Cape Codder." His heritage of generations of Lincolns and Crosbys living on Cape Cod became the bedrock on which his poems, sketches, short stories, and novels were based.

Lincoln's father, grandfather, and uncles were ships' captains, and his mother sailed with her husband, as was common during that time, to Europe, South America, and Asia. When Joseph was ten months old, his father died of a fever on a voyage south in Charleston, South Carolina. Emily Lincoln brought up her only child in Brewster until they relocated to Chelsea, Massachusetts, so she could work as a dressmaker. Joseph was thirteen years old when they left Cape Cod, but he continued to spend his summers in Brewster and Chatham, visiting his grandmother and cousins.

In Chelsea, Lincoln edited his school paper and graduated from the Williams Grammar School (ninth grade) in 1885. He was sixteen years old when he took his first full-time job in 1886 as a runner for George T. Sears, a wholesale salt dealer in Boston. In 1887 he took a position as a clerk in a brokerage house in Boston, followed by another clerking job. By 1895 he had moved to a bookkeeping position for the Swift Desk Company in Boston.

These jobs paid the bills, but they were not what he wanted to do with his life. From 1894 to 1896 Lincoln was a pupil of Henry (Hy) Sandham, a well-known Boston artist who specialized in painting historical events. In 1896 Lincoln and Howard Reynolds, a fellow student at Sandham's, set up a commercial art studio in Boston. Lincoln gave up his bookkeeping job, determined to become a full-time artist.

Lincoln and Reynolds also collaborated on a short story, "The Studio Puzzle," which was published in the ten-cent magazine *The Owl*, and worked together on some verses and sketches. After the partners split at the end of 1896, Lincoln moved to his own studio. He did not have much success, and when he was asked to come on staff as an illustrator for the League of American Wheelmen's *L. A. W. Bulletin*, he accepted. The magazine, with a circulation of more than 100,000 bicycle enthusiasts, published both his poetry and his sketches.

In 1897 Lincoln married Florence Elry Sargent, of Chelsea, a bookkeeper. That year he became an associate editor of the magazine and had shifted his focus from commercial art to poetry. But with the increasing use of the automobile, the bicycle was becoming less important in American life, a fact that was reflected in declining sales of the magazine.

Lincoln left the *L. A. W. Bulletin* at the end of 1898, and he and Florence moved to Brooklyn, New York. His objective was to become a professional writer, and Lincoln saw the greatest opportunities in New York City. However, finances dictated that he write by night and on weekends and earn money by day as the editor of a banking magazine.

His first major breakthrough as a writer was the publication of the short story "Mrs. Phidgit's System" in *Harper's Bazaar* in January 1900. This year also saw the publication of three of Lincoln's short stories and two of his poems in the *Saturday Evening Post*, and Joseph and Florence's move to Hackensack, New Jersey. Their only child was born that year as well.

Lincoln's first book, *Cape Cod Ballads and Other Verse* (1902), with drawings by Edward W. Kemble, included all the poems previously published in a variety of magazines. These poems were based on recollec-

tions of his boyhood on Cape Cod. But it was the almost overnight success of his first novel, *Cap'n Eri, a Story of the Coast* (1904), that allowed him to give up his day job at the bank and devote his time exclusively to writing.

Cap'n Eri tells the story of three retired sea captains who flip a coin to decide which of them will advertise for a wife, not for romantic reasons but rather to keep house for them. The story is filled with the dry humor and memorable characters that would become earmarks of Joseph C. Lincoln's style. Although the plot works out predictably, the complications are entertaining, as are such characters as M'lissy Busteed: "She'd be a good one to have on board in a calm. Git her talkin' abaft the mains'l and we'd have a twenty-knot breeze in a shake."

Lincoln was a prolific writer. He wrote forty-six books, including five short story collections, two collections of poetry, a play, two books of essays, and thirty-seven novels. Three of the novels were coauthored with his son Freeman: *Blair's Attic* (1929), *The Ownley Inn* (1939), and *The New Hope* (1941). All Lincoln's manuscripts were written by hand on yellow, ruled legal paper. He did not type or dictate to a secretary, yet he managed to write about a book a year until his death. His last novel, *The Bradshaws of Harniss*, was published in 1943.

The focus of Lincoln's work was Cape Cod, centering on places he knew well, although he did not give them their true names. For example, Orleans and Eastham become Orham in Lincoln's world. The books are filled with typical Cape Cod activities. His second book of essays, *Cape Cod Yesterdays* (1935), includes information about the cranberry industry, stagecoach rides, even recipes, evoking a way of life in a unique location. All Lincoln's books sold very well, and his novel *The Portygee* (1920) made the annual bestseller list for that year. This was the first of his novels to be published in serial form; it ran in the *Delineator* from October 1919 to June 1920. Later the *Ladies' Home Journal* would serialize four Lincoln novels: *Fair Harbor* (1922), *Queer Judson* (1925), *Silas Bradford's Boy* (1928), and *Blowing Clear* (1930).

In addition to being a writer, Lincoln was a popular lecturer and would read from his own works to church groups and at dinners. When his son was at Harvard, he lectured there about being a writer and read poems and told Cape Cod tales to the dramatic club.

Lincoln was also interested in the theater. He sponsored the Unitarian Dramatic Club in Hackensack and wrote and directed many of the productions, which played to capacity audiences. Lincoln even acted in some of these plays. The only play that was published was *The Managers, a Comedy of Cape Cod* (1925) in one act. His novel *"Shavings"* (1918), however, was dramatized by Pauline Phelps and Marion Short and played in Boston and on Broadway in 1920.

Several novels were made into films. *Rugged Water* (1925) starred Wallace Beery; *Cap'n Eri* was filmed in Rhode Island in 1915, as was *Partners of the Tide* (1905), Lincoln's second novel, in 1916. *Partners* was filmed again in 1921. *Mary 'Gusta* (1916) became the film *Petticoat Pilot* in 1918. *The Rise of Rosco Paine* (1912) was produced in 1922 as *No Trespassing* with Irene Castle. And *Doctor Nye of North Ostable* (1923) became the film *Idle Tongues* in 1924. Lincoln completed only the ninth grade, but in 1935 his literary achievements were recognized with an honorary degree of doctor of literature from Rollins College.

Although Lincoln lived in Hackensack until 1925 when he moved to Villa Nova, Pennsylvania, and wintered from 1930 to 1944 in Winter Park, Florida, he always returned to Cape Cod for the summers. In 1916 he built "Crosstrees" in Chatham as his permanent summer home. He died in Winter Park and is buried in the Union Cemetery in Chatham.

Lincoln's novels evoke a world that is now lost. Although he did not use the actual names of the Cape villages, he did recreate their essence. The sense of place and of the people living there, the ship's captains, storekeepers, coach drivers, and spinsters, are depicted with their idiosyncracies and their "Yankee" virtues of hard work, ingenuity, honesty, and thrift. Lincoln himself was concerned about the future of a changing Cape Cod, and in a letter to the editor of the *Boston Traveler* on 26 December 1935 he stressed the "preservation of Cape Cod as Cape Cod is" and stated: "how important it is to save our towns and villages from becoming mere copies of towns and villages elsewhere." Sadly, the old Cape Cod of Joseph C. Lincoln's memory lives only within the pages of his books.

• Lincoln manuscripts and memorabilia are housed in the Old Atwood House Museums in Chatham, Mass. A complete list of his writings can be found in the descriptive bibliography, edited by Stephen W. Sullwold, appended to Percy F. Rex's biography of Lincoln: *The Prolific Pencil* (1980). *The Joseph C. Lincoln Reader* (1959) is edited and introduced by his son Freeman Lincoln. Loring Holmes Dodd includes a chatty sketch of Lincoln in his *Celebrities at Our Hearthside* (1959). An obituary is in the *New York Times*, 11 Mar. 1944.

MARCIA B. DINNEEN

LINCOLN, Levi (15 May 1749–14 Apr. 1820), Jeffersonian politician, was born in Hingham, Massachusetts, the son of Enoch Lincoln and Rachel Fearing, farmers. In his youth he was apprenticed by his father to a blacksmith, but he showed such a penchant for scholarship that he was later allowed to enroll in Harvard. After graduation in 1772, he studied law in Northampton until the outbreak of the revolutionary war. Thereupon he evinced such a zeal for independence that he joined the Minutemen for a time then turned his hand to writing a series of appeals to patriotism entitled "Farmer's Letters." During the remainder of the war, he practiced law in Worcester and steadily rose to prominence in the community that was to be his permanent home. He served as clerk of the court and judge of probate of Worcester County, commissioner for confiscated estates, and delegate to a convention in Cambridge to frame a state constitution. In 1781 he was elected to the Continental Congress but

declined to serve. That same year he helped litigate a number of court cases that argued against the legality of slavery in Massachusetts, which were subsequently upheld by the state supreme court. Hence, he did a great deal to abolish slavery in Massachusetts. Also in 1781 he married Martha Waldo, with whom he had nine children. Two of his sons, Levi Lincoln (1782–1868) and Enoch Lincoln, distinguished themselves later as governors of Massachusetts and Maine, respectively.

During the two decades after the Revolution, Lincoln established himself as a leader of the Jeffersonian party in Massachusetts while also consolidating his position as head of the state's bar. In 1796 he served in the Massachusetts House of Representatives and a year later in the senate. After a bitterly fought contest, he was elected in 1800 to Congress to replace Dwight Foster, who had resigned. Although winning a term of his own for the next congressional session, he resigned when President Thomas Jefferson appointed him attorney general of the United States. In the few months before the arrival of James Madison (1751–1836) in Washington, he also acted as provisional secretary of state. Over the next four years, the inactive office of attorney general allowed him little scope for his talents. When asked by Jefferson to give his views on the constitutionality of the Louisiana Purchase, he suggested that the president simply avoid the issue by getting France to allow the boundaries of Georgia and the Mississippi Territory to be extended westward. After the president had rejected that idea, Lincoln declared that the safest way of going about the business was to amend the Constitution specifically to allow the purchase.

Although Lincoln was not overwhelmed with government business while serving on Jefferson's cabinet, he did not waste his time. He was constantly engaged in party battles with Federalists, receiving from his opponents abuse that he returned with interest. He was particularly effective as a political polemicist in *Letters to the People, by a Farmer* (1802), wherein he attacked the Federalists for politicizing the clergy. That Jefferson thought highly of Lincoln and relied on him to advance Republican interests in New England is shown by his entrusting the latter with patronage distribution in that region. Albert Gallatin, Jefferson's secretary of the treasury, also had a high regard for Lincoln, describing him at this time as "a good lawyer, a fine scholar, a man of great discretion and sound judgment, and of the mildest and most amiable manners" (quoted in Malone, p. 57).

It was with regret, therefore, that Jefferson accepted Lincoln's resignation from the attorney general's post at the end of Jefferson's first term of office. If the president was concerned about losing Lincoln's talents, however, he had nothing to fear, for Lincoln had not abandoned Jeffersonian politics. In 1806 he was elected to the Council of Massachusetts, and a year later, when his party gained control of the governorship, he succeeded to the office of lieutenant governor. He became governor upon the death of James Sullivan

(1744–1808), but because the voters abhorred Jefferson's Embargo, he lost the election in 1809 when he ran for a full term of his own. After serving two more years on the Governor's Council, he was offered a seat on the U.S. Supreme Court by President Madison. Jefferson, seconding the president's choice of a man who would at last give the Republicans a majority on the Court, praised Lincoln's "firm republicanism, and known integrity"—although Jefferson did not consider Lincoln "a correct common lawyer," trained as he was in the New England "system of Jurisprudence [which was] made up from the Jewish law, a little dash of common law, & a great mass of original notions" (Ford, vol. 9, pp. 282–83). Lincoln declined the offer, however, because of failing eyesight and retired to his farm in Worcester.

During the remaining years of his life, Lincoln cultivated his acres, lived happily with his wife and children, and, to the degree that his vision allowed, read classical literature. He continued his membership in many learned societies, including the American Academy of Arts and Sciences, kept up his interest in the law, and survived long enough to see his sons successfully launched in their political careers. He died on his farm in Worcester.

• Lincoln's letters are in the Massachusetts Historical Society and the American Antiquarian Society. His correspondence with Jefferson is in the Thomas Jefferson Papers, Library of Congress, and some of it is published in Paul Leicester Ford, ed., *The Writings of Thomas Jefferson*, vols. 8–9 (1892–1899). Information on the Lincoln family is in Waldo Lincoln, *History of the Lincoln Family* (1923), and Alonzo Hill, *Memorial Address on Levi Lincoln, Jr.* (1868). For Lincoln's antislavery litigations, see Emory Washburn, "The Extinction of Slavery in Massachusetts," *Collections of the Massachusetts Historical Society* 4, ser. 4 (1858): 337–44. His role as attorney general in the Jefferson administration is delineated in Dumas Malone, *Jefferson the President: First Term, 1801–1805* (1970).

PAUL DAVID NELSON

LINCOLN, Levi (25 Oct. 1782–29 May 1868), lawyer and politician, was born in Worcester, Massachusetts, the son of Levi Lincoln, a lawyer and later attorney general of the United States in the first Thomas Jefferson administration, and Martha Waldo. Levi Lincoln was admitted to the Massachusetts bar in 1805, three years after graduating from Harvard College. He established a practice in Worcester, and in 1807 he married Penelope Winslow, with whom he had eight children.

Lincoln became politically active as a Jeffersonian Republican. After serving from 1812 to 1813 in the Massachusetts Senate, he won election in 1814 to the Massachusetts House of Representatives, which Federalists and opponents of the War of 1812 dominated. He quickly established himself as the leader of the pro-war Republican minority and consistently opposed the policies of Federalist governor Caleb Strong. When the Federalists passed an act authorizing participation in the Hartford Convention, an antiwar gathering, Lincoln wrote the minority protest that was signed by

seventy-six members of the house and distributed statewide. The Hartford Convention, followed closely by the end of the war, discredited the Federalists and elevated Lincoln to prominence in the state. Lincoln further enhanced his reputation in the state constitutional convention of 1820–1821 by actively supporting the abolition of apportionment of seats in the senate based on tax assessments by districts. He advocated apportionment by population solely, a position that won him substantial approval from reformers, while his restrained manner preserved the respect of conservatives and his friends among the social and economic elite. Lincoln enjoyed a broad and increasing base of support, and members of the house chose him to serve as Speaker in 1822.

In 1823 Lincoln resigned from the house to accept appointment as lieutenant governor of Massachusetts. Two years later Federalists, suffering a clear and steady decline in their political power and authority, decided to endorse the moderate Lincoln for governor on an "amalgamation" ticket. With Marcus Morton, a highly partisan Republican, as Lincoln's running mate, the ticket drew support from both parties, and Lincoln won 94 percent of the votes cast. He served as governor until 1834 and was never seriously challenged in the annual elections.

As governor Lincoln laid the basis for the progressive economic development of the state. He carried out a survey of state geological resources and topography, promoted the charter of Massachusetts's first railroad companies, and endorsed protective corporation laws through legislative adoption of a principle of limited liability. He eased laws on imprisonment for debt and bankruptcy and reformed prison administration, and he promoted public education with the establishment of normal schools throughout the state and support for the programs of Horace Mann. Also highly regarded was his appointment of Lemuel Shaw as chief justice of the Massachusetts Supreme Court in 1830.

Lincoln made an easy transition from a Jefferson Republican into a National Republican and was indirectly instrumental in organizing the Massachusetts Whig party. In 1824 he supported John Quincy Adams's election to the presidency and in 1827 declined appointment, which Adams promoted, to the U.S. Senate, partly out of concern that his departure from the state house would jeopardize the fragile Republican-Federalist coalition. With Lincoln representing former Jeffersonian Republicans, Daniel Webster representing former Federalists, and both coalescing behind Adams, the Massachusetts National Republican party was now fully organized.

Whereas subsequently Adams flirted with Antimasonry and Webster courted various coalitions in his pursuit of the presidency, Lincoln remained steadfast in the new political organization and held it together. In 1827 his veto of a bill permitting construction of a non-toll bridge across the Charles River that would have ended the monopoly of a toll bridge owned by Harvard College and conservative Bostonians won him conservative support. However, this concern for property rights and his associations with former Federalists and conservative Republicans alienated the Jacksonian elements in the state. By 1834 Lincoln's party evolved into the Massachusetts Whig party, which remained dominant in the state until the party collapsed nationally in 1854.

In 1834 Lincoln won election as a Whig and ally of Webster to the U.S. House of Representatives. He replaced John Davis, who in turn replaced Lincoln as governor. Lincoln served in the House from 17 February 1834 to 16 March 1841 and loyally supported Whig programs. He did not distinguish himself in the House, although he stood as an effective champion of American claims in the dispute with England over the Maine boundary.

Lincoln resigned from the House to accept appointment by President William Henry Harrison as collector of the Port of Boston, replacing Democrat George Bancroft. He served for two years, until President John Tyler replaced him with Democrat Robert Rantoul, Jr., in a bid for Massachusetts Democratic support. Lincoln's dismissal marked his only involuntary political retirement in his career. He returned to the Massachusetts State Senate in 1844 and 1845 and served as president of the senate in 1845. In 1848 Lincoln was an elector for Zachary Taylor and Millard Fillmore and was elected the first mayor of the newly incorporated city of Worcester, a largely ceremonial post he held for one year only. Following that service, at the age of sixty-seven and after thirty-five years in public office, Lincoln retired from politics.

Between 1849 and 1868 Lincoln devoted himself to philanthropic, charitable, and community affairs. He was a founder of the American Antiquarian Society, served on its council from 1817 to 1854, and was a vice president of the society from 1854 to his death. Although Lincoln's career is most associated with Massachusetts, his nationalism was deep and constant throughout his life. He supported Jefferson and James Madison through the War of 1812, condemned South Carolina's nullification ordinance in 1833, and as his last political act, cast electoral votes for Abraham Lincoln and Andrew Johnson in the election of 1864. Neither a scholar, great legislator, nor charismatic public speaker, Lincoln was a stable and highly respected public official during a politically chaotic time. After an illness of two years, he died in Worcester.

• Lincoln's papers are housed in the Massachusetts Historical Society in Boston and the American Antiquarian Society in Worcester. The latter contains an extended contemporary eulogy, Charles Hudson, "Life, Services, and Character of Hon. Levi Lincoln of Worcester." Information can be drawn from several older publications and general histories of Mass., such as Waldo Lincoln, *History of the Lincoln Family* (1923), written by his son; and a collection of eulogies in *A Memorial of Levi Lincoln, the Governor of Massachusetts from 1825 to 1834* (1868). Lincoln's activities are also described in Arthur B. Darling, *Political Changes in Massachusetts, 1824–1848: A Study of Liberal Movements in Politics* (1925); and Ronald P. Formisano, *The Transformation of Political Culture: Massachusetts Parties, 1790s–1840s* (1983).

KINLEY BRAUER

LINCOLN, Mary Johnson Bailey (8 July 1844–2 Dec. 1921), educator and culinary writer, was born in South Attleboro, Massachusetts, the daughter of the Reverend John Milton Burnham Bailey and Sarah Morgan Johnson. Although raised with limited means, Bailey felt that the prestige of being in a ministerial household helped form her strong, industrious character. Her father died when she was seven, and she began to earn money for her own expenses by taking factory work in Attleboro, sewing hooks and eyes on cards, and setting stones in jewelry. Her mother then moved the family to Norton, Massachusetts, so that her daughters would be educated at Wheaton Seminary while she served as a housemother there. While a student Bailey continued to do her share of the housework and made hair nets for the seminary girls.

Following graduation from Wheaton in 1864 Mary Bailey assumed a teaching position in a Vermont country school for one year. Back in Norton she met David A. Lincoln, a businessman, and happily exchanged teaching for homemaking when the couple married in June 1865. The couple had no children. After moving to Boston, Mary Lincoln once again had to work outside the home because of her husband's career woes and related failing health. Employed as a domestic, she credited good health and a happy disposition for her ability to cope.

In November 1879 the Woman's Education Association (WEA) hired Mary Lincoln to teach in the newly opened Boston Cooking School at a salary of $75 a month, although her employers made it conditional that she take a few free cooking classes. The cooking school movement was founded by middle-class women to benefit poor women who were ignorant of the best way to cook the cheapest foods. They were highly successful in accomplishing this goal, but, unfortunately, their male counterparts refused to support the cause.

The school's first instructor, Joanna Sweeney, taught Lincoln the basics, but it was the charismatic Maria Parloa whose ease at lecturing gave her confidence. Parloa's connection with the school brought it renown, but her fee was high, her expenses higher, and she attracted society matrons instead of the "poorest classes" as was originally intended by the WEA. Because charitable funds did not materialize, Lincoln taught basic courses to homemakers, teachers, Harvard medical students, handicapped students, cooks, nurses—anyone who could afford to pay tuition. She provided concise instructions for everything from fire building to baking a perfect blueberry pie and helped develop lessons in complementary subjects such as chemistry and hygiene.

Lincoln was named principal of the Boston Cooking School, but she was not involved with management. Instead, she began compiling a thorough textbook based on the lessons and recipes used in classes so that students would not have to spend so much time copying. *Mrs. Lincoln's Boston Cook Book* (1884) was the result, followed by an abridgment, *The Boston School Kitchen Text Book* (1887), which after scores of revisions and editions came to be known simply as *The Boston Cook Book*. Advertisers helped keep production costs down as this highly successful manual found its way beyond American cooking schools to England and to missions in China. Lincoln was one of the first to tabulate ingredients at the head of a recipe and require exact measurements, thus marking a distinct change in food literature.

The Boston Cooking School thrived under Lincoln's direction and prepared women to face any challenge as a homemaker, as a competent worker outside the home, or as a servant manager. Lincoln herself continued to cultivate the down-to-earth, respectful attitude for which she achieved celebrity. In January 1885 she resigned, stating that the death of her sister was the reason, although it may have been because of her growing interest in journalism and public speaking. In April 1894 Lincoln, Anna Barrows, and Estelle Merrill cofounded the *New England Kitchen Magazine*, later called *American Kitchen Magazine*. As culinary editor, Lincoln ran a popular column, "From Day to Day"; by 1898 many articles were syndicated in newspapers nationwide. Numerous other cooking publications were attributed to her expertise. Lincoln went on to teach classes at Lasell Seminary in Auburndale, Massachusetts.

Lincoln was also an active member of the prestigious New England Woman's Press Association that met at the Parker House in Boston; she cochaired the program and finance committees from 1889 to 1909. The club maintained an energetic agenda and kept track of various causes including suffrage; indeed, according to one historian of the association, Mary Lincoln was singled out with luminaries Lucy Stone and Julia Ward Howe as members who had "won distinction in the literary field." She died in Boston.

Always a stickler for facts, Lincoln attempted throughout her life to give credit where credit was due. In "The Pioneers of Scientific Cookery" (*Good Housekeeping*, Oct. 1910), she gave evidence of the bittersweet choice women had to make between helping the needy and making money as professionals. She argued that advancement opportunities for women were stymied; for instance, it was not an option for a skilled female cook to enter the workforce as a chef. Instead, culinary experts justified them as "domestic scientists" in order to gain approval from the advertising industry that controlled women's consumer choices for many decades. Mrs. Lincoln's Baking Powder, a short-lived item, was among the many products she endorsed.

Although Mary Lincoln's culinary talent was modest, she was able in her articles and books to lift the morale of brides and young mothers performing difficult and unappreciated household tasks. She developed a striking skill that enabled her to lecture while preparing food on stage. She taught women to build their self-esteem and nurtured her own by associating with other high-caliber, high-profile women leaders. She ranks highly with those pioneers who recognized and paid tribute to women's work.

• Some of Lincoln's papers and correspondence are in the archives of Wheaton College, Norton, Mass.; Simmons College, Boston, Mass.; and the Woman's Education Association, Boston. Genealogical and other important information about Lincoln is in Julia Ward Howe, ed., *Representative Women of New England* (1904), and Mary J. Lincoln, "How I Was Led to Teach Cookery," *New England Kitchen Magazine*, May 1894, pp. 67–69. See Katherine Golden Bitting, *Gastronomic Bibliography* (1939), and Janice Bluestein Longone, *American Cookbooks* (1984), for details on Lincoln's cooking publications. See also Myra Lord's charming *History of the New England Woman's Press Association, 1885–1931* (1932). Laura Shapiro, *Perfection Salad* (1986), is a valuable but overly critical account of America's female culinary professionals. An obituary is in the *Boston Herald*, 3 Dec. 1921.

MARY ANNA DUSABLON

LINCOLN, Mary Todd (13 Dec. 1818–16 July 1882), first lady, was born in Lexington, Kentucky, the daughter of Robert Smith Todd, a well-known Whig politician and, at various times in his life, a banker and partner of a dry-goods firm, and Eliza Parker. Both of her parents were descendants of a large, wealthy, influential family, whose earlier members had founded the town of Lexington.

Mary Todd, the third daughter in a family of six surviving children, was six when her mother died. Her father remarried, and the family eventually increased to fifteen children. Unhappy at home with her stepmother, Mary Todd enjoyed school, spending twelve years in John Ward's local academy and Mme Victorie Mentelle's boarding school. She joined her married sister Elizabeth Todd Edwards in Springfield, Illinois, in 1837. After returning to live there permanently in 1839, Mary Todd met Abraham Lincoln, and, after a courtship that was stormy due to the couple's differences in class and temperament and the opposition of her sisters, they married on 4 November 1842. The couple had four children, three of whom died during Mary Lincoln's lifetime.

In addition to her role as a mother and housewife, Lincoln was absorbed in politics and worked to promote her husband's career. She wrote patronage letters, advocated his election, and even followed legislative choices in his senatorial campaigns. After Abraham Lincoln was elected president in 1860, she ambitiously sought for herself the role of an influential first lady. Wearing stunning gowns and shawls, she tried to define American fashion. She tastefully renovated the White House, especially the downstairs public rooms, and entertained at parties designed to display to foreign ambassadors the power of the Union. She established an informal American salon, where public men and literary figures discussed the topics of the day. Besides these extensions of domestic roles, Lincoln sought a controversial voice in her husband's patronage appointments, including his cabinet.

Mary Lincoln's tenure as a first lady coincided with the Civil War. During her first days in the White House, when Confederate units were unopposed in northern Virginia, army officials encouraged her to leave the city, but she insisted on staying and even accompanied her husband on tours of the Washington defenses. Like many other women, she nursed soldiers in hospitals, often inscribing their dictated letters to relatives in the North. Lincoln was unusual in her commitment to raising money for the support of impoverished former slaves ("contraband"), who crowded into Washington. However, her good works never stilled the criticism of her extravagance when the allowance for the White House was exceeded, nor did she ever shake the gossip that, because her half brothers fought for the Confederacy, she was a spy.

On 14 April 1865 Mary Lincoln accompanied her husband to Ford's Theatre and witnessed the shooting that took Abraham Lincoln's life. Thereafter, as a widow, she wandered from Europe to the health spas in the United States and Canada. She also sought out the centers of spiritualism, which attracted her after her second son Willie died in 1862 of typhoid fever. In 1870 Congress voted her a pension of $3,000, which was raised to $5,000 in 1881.

In 1875, on the complaint of her only surviving son, Robert Todd Lincoln, Mary Lincoln was taken without warning to a courtroom, where she was found guilty of being insane. Her supposedly insane behavior included spending too much money and consulting with spiritualists. A conservator was appointed to manage her finances, and she was committed to an institution. Within months, after the intervention of Myra Bradwell, one of the few female lawyers in the United States, she was released. After a second trial she was adjudged capable of managing her estate. Mary Lincoln subsequently lived in Pau, France, but she returned to Springfield shortly before her death. She died in Springfield.

A vivacious belle in her youth, the short, plump Lincoln was an important and controversial first lady who expanded that role's authority. Stepping outside of the traditional female role of homemaker into the male-dominated world of public affairs, she was often criticized for her behavior. Extravagant, high-strung, and tempestuous, she nonetheless played an important role in her husband's ascent to the presidency and made the unpaid but demanding position of first lady into a post of influence.

• Most of Mary Todd Lincoln's letters are published in Justin Turner and Linda Levitt Turner, *Mary Todd Lincoln: Her Life and Letters* (1972). Other letters are available in the microfilm edition of the Robert Todd Lincoln Collection of Abraham Lincoln Papers at the Library of Congress. Family remembrances are published in Katherine Helms, *The True Story of Mary, Wife of Lincoln* (1928). See also Ruth Randall, *Mary Lincoln: Biography of a Marriage* (1953); and Jean H. Baker, *Mary Todd Lincoln: A Biography* (1987).

JEAN H. BAKER

LINCOLN, Robert Todd (1 Aug. 1843–26 July 1926), secretary of war and minister to Great Britain, was born in Springfield, Illinois, the son of Abraham Lincoln, an attorney and future president of the United States, and Mary Todd. Only seventeen years old when his father became the sixteenth president of the

United States, Robert Lincoln was "subjected to almost constant attention from the press and the population in general" (Goff, p. 39). He attended Harvard and graduated in 1864; then he studied briefly at Harvard Law School, while the Civil War entered its final months. President Lincoln may have felt an obligation to have his own son serve in the Union army, but the president did not want to send his son into combat. Thus, Robert Lincoln left law school and accepted a commission, serving during the last two months of the war as a captain on the staff of General Ulysses S. Grant.

The assassination of his father in 1865, combined with the increasing mental instability of his mother, Mary Todd Lincoln, left Robert Lincoln the head of the family while only twenty-one years old. He handled the burden flawlessly, establishing the reputation that the Chicago *Tribune* described about a quarter of a century later: "In all walks of life, public and private, he has been conspicuous for his good judgment, tact, prudence, and discretion" (Goff, p. 174). Lincoln practiced law in Chicago over the next forty-five years. He married Mary Harlan, daughter of Senator James Harlan (1820–1899) of Iowa, on 24 September 1868. They had three children. Lincoln was determined to remain a private person and to prevent others from using his name for political or financial gain. Perhaps these were unrealistic objectives for Abraham Lincoln's only surviving child. Building on a substantial inheritance, he accumulated great wealth. Newspapers across the nation publicized the trying experience of having his mother declared mentally incompetent in 1875. Lincoln's law practice attracted many corporate clients, some undoubtedly hoping to capitalize on his name.

Lincoln sided with the "Stalwart" wing of the Republican party and supported Grant's bid for a third presidential nomination in 1880, thereby identifying with those determined to thwart the presidential aspirations of the leader of the "Half-Breed" wing of the party, Senator James G. Blaine. The wheeling and dealing, which broke the deadlock at the Republican National Convention and produced the nomination of Representative James A. Garfield on the thirty-sixth ballot, continued after the election, when Garfield constructed his cabinet. Garfield included Blaine as secretary of state and the 37-year-old Lincoln, representing both Illinois and the "Stalwarts," as secretary of war. Reluctant to hold high public office, Lincoln nevertheless remained in the cabinet after the assassination of President Garfield, the only member of the cabinet to serve the full four-year term in the administration of President Chester A. Arthur.

While Lincoln served as secretary of war the army of only 25,000 officers and soldiers entered the last decade of its continuing campaign against the Indians and took the first small steps into the modern era. As of 1881, the army launched a program of specialized training for cavalry and infantry officers at Fort Leavenworth. The following year the army began to try to bring meaningful change to the composition of the officer corps, making retirement mandatory at sixty-four years of age. Though Lincoln spent most of his time performing what have been described as "routine" duties, he added to his reputation among the intellectuals in the Northeast—the "Mugwumps"—and other Republicans who favored any candidate except Blaine for the presidential nomination in 1884. Lincoln, who refused to campaign for the nomination and received only four votes on the first ballot, once again supported Blaine's most serious rival for the nomination, President Arthur.

In 1888, private citizen Lincoln received only three votes on the first ballot for the presidential nomination, and the delegates chose Benjamin Harrison (1833–1901), former senator from Indiana, on the eighth ballot. Harrison's victory in the presidential election produced the inevitable invitation for Blaine, a Harrison supporter, to serve once again as secretary of state. Harrison, however, was determined to demonstrate his independence from the start, filling the remaining cabinet positions and the most important diplomatic posts without consulting Blaine. A former Civil War general, he chose the son of Abraham Lincoln to represent the United States as minister to Great Britain. Lincoln served with great dignity over the next four years, stoically enduring yet another family tragedy, the death of his son, Abraham Lincoln II, from "blood poisoning." While Secretary of State Blaine and President Harrison took charge of the drawn-out dispute with Great Britain over the seal herd in the Bering Sea, Lincoln did little more than relay correspondence back and forth. Service in London marked the end of his public career.

Lincoln was special counsel to the Pullman Palace Car Company through the depression that began in 1893 and the labor unrest that soon followed. He may have tarnished his image by serving as legal advisor to company president George Pullman during the Pullman strike of 1894, ended only by the controversial intervention of federal troops. After the death of Pullman in 1897, Lincoln was president of the company until 1911. He had acquired an estate in Manchester, Vermont, in 1902 and upon retirement from the Pullman Company moved his residence to Washington, D.C., dividing his time between the nation's capital and his Vermont retreat. He died in Vermont.

• Lincoln's papers covering 1865–1912 are on eighty reels of microfilm in the Henry Horner Lincoln Collection of the Illinois State Historical Library. The library holds an additional 170 letters covering 1859–1924, and there are some forty letters at the Manuscript Division of the Library of Congress. John S. Goff has written the only biography, *Robert Todd Lincoln: A Man in His Own Right*, 2d ed. (1990). See also Herbert Eaton, *Presidential Timber: A History of Nominating Conventions, 1868–1960* (1964).

ALLAN BURTON SPETTER

LINCOLN, Victoria Endicott (23 Oct. 1904–13 June 1981), author, was born in Fall River, Massachusetts, the daughter of Jonathan Thayer Lincoln, a textile machinery manufacturer, and Louise Sears Cobb. As a child she knew fellow Fall River resident Lizzie Borden, who became the subject of Lincoln's 1967 novel *A Private Disgrace: Lizzie Borden by Daylight*. She was educated in Fall River and at Radcliffe College. Upon graduating in 1926, she married Isaac Watkins, a classmate at nearby Harvard. They had one child. The couple separated in 1932 and divorced in the following year. In 1934 she married Victor Lowe, then a graduate student in philosophy. They had two children. Lowe would eventually teach philosophy at Johns Hopkins University in Baltimore, where the couple lived for the better part of their lives. Although Lincoln finished work for an M.A. at Radcliffe and at the University of Marburgh in Germany, she never completed her thesis; instead, as she noted, "I wrote a detective story and lived happy ever after as an AB." A full-time writer, she also taught writing courses and summer school at Johns Hopkins.

Of her literary career, Lincoln noted, "From the time I could first hold a pencil and print words, I have taken it for granted that it was my business in life to be a writer. As a poet I have had an appreciative audience of one, namely Victoria Lincoln. As a novelist and short-story writer I have communicated with a considerably wider field." This "wider field" first emerged in 1930 with the publication of *Swan Island Murders*, which was followed by her most famous novel, *February Hill* (1934), later made into both a play and a movie under the name *The Primrose Path*. In 1967 she was awarded the Mystery Writers of America's Edgar Award for best fact crime book for *A Private Disgrace*. She wrote biographies of Charles Dickens (*Charles* [1962]) and St. Teresa of Avila (*Teresa: A Woman* [1984]). A great percentage of her writings appeared in various popular magazines, such as *Harper's*, *Vogue*, and the *New Yorker*. These pieces were generally humorous sketches, profiles, or vignettes, many based on her own experiences. One piece, published in the *New Yorker*, tells of a nightmare she experienced while weekending with friends. The dream was so frightening, she awoke screaming. Her husband, taken by surprise, also began to scream. As she wrote, "I woke up to see my husband sitting at his desk, screaming. So then I screamed again, louder. At that, seeing that I was wide awake and still screaming, he became really disturbed. We were both shouting 'Stop, stop, darling, stop! Stop!' at the top of our lungs when everybody in the house began to hammer at the door." Although her short stories were frequently anthologized during her lifetime, only the posthumously published *Teresa* remains in print.

Lincoln's style mixes traditional romantic themes with social realism. *February Hill* exemplifies this unique blend. The *Saturday Review of Literature* review (10 Nov. 1934) notes that "it is a book of the new realism, not 'grim' like the realism of yesterday, but cordially and even blithely acceptant of life in any of its vital manifestations." Although her characters' faults often outweigh their strengths, and their dreams are not always fulfilled, they do not despair; rather, they accept their fates, comfort others in theirs, and go about their lives. The novel is set in Rhode Island in the 1930s and, like similar novels and films of the period such as *Mildred Pierce*, tells the stories of lower-class women and their ambivalent struggles to rise above their station through the aid of wealthy men. Early on, the protagonist, Minna Harris, reflects on her marriage to Vergil, a seemingly excellent match because of his Harvard education. From the outset, however, Minna knows that Vergil will never be a success because of his alcoholism, but "her heart betrayed her." Minna recognizes her own weakness, yet she allows her life to continue on the trajectory it has taken, despite the problems that are certain to arise.

Lincoln was an insightful and sensitive storyteller who was never willing to reduce her writing to formulaic clichés or her characters to two dimensions. It is her ability to give voice to women's stories that is Lincoln's most lasting contribution. Elias L. Rivers, the editor of *Teresa: A Woman*, notes, "Miss Lincoln discovered in Teresa a kindred spirit, a semi-liberated woman who seemed never to have been properly understood from a human point of view." The final decades of Lincoln's life were spent researching and retelling the story of this kindred spirit. Lincoln died in Baltimore, Maryland.

• Lincoln's most notable works are *Grandmother and the Comet* (1944), *The Wind at My Back* (1946), *Out from Eden* (1951), *The Wild Honey* (1953), *A Dangerous Innocence* (1958), and *Everyhow Remarkable* (1967). Rivers's comments are taken from the editor's note for *Teresa: A Woman* (1984). All quotes by Lincoln herself are taken from *Contemporary Authors* and Stanley Kunitz, ed., *Twentieth Century Authors* (1942; rev. ed., 1973). See also "Stranger than Fiction, at Least," *New Yorker*, 29 Apr. 1944, pp. 20–21. A brief sketch of Lincoln's life and art is in "American Novelists of Today," *Good Housekeeping*, Oct. 1947. Also see reviews of *February Hill* in the *New York Times Book Review*, 28 Oct. 1934; the *Saturday Review of Literature*, 10 Nov. 1934; and the *New Republic*, 28 Nov. 1934. A review of *Out from Eden* appears in the *New York Times Book Review*, 2 Dec. 1951. Obituaries appear in the *New York Times*, 22 June 1981, and *AB Bookman's Week*, 27 July 1981.

MICHAEL HEUMANN

LIND, John (25 Mar. 1854–18 Sept. 1930), congressman, governor, and diplomat, was born in Kånna parish in the southern province of Småland, Sweden, the son of Gustav Lindbacken and Katherina Jonasson, farmers. Lind immigrated with his parents to the United States in 1867, and at the same time his father changed the family surname to Lind. Lind's left hand was amputated following a hunting accident in December 1868, so as a young immigrant boy, he faced the challenges of learning English and overcoming a physical disability.

Educated in the common schools of Sweden and Goodhue County, Minnesota, Lind received training as a teacher and lawyer. In the spring of 1869 he studied briefly at St. Ansgar's Academy (now Gustavus Adolphus College) in Carver County, Minnesota, but returned to Red Wing schools in 1869–1870. Lind

taught from 1870 to 1875 in country schools in Goodhue County and in Sibley County, where his parents homesteaded in 1872. At the same time he studied law and worked at the office of J. Newhart in New Ulm, a German-settled community in southern Minnesota. In 1875–1876 he took preparatory classes, including German language, at the University of Minnesota and studied for the state law exam. Revealing his family loyalty and character, Lind postponed his studies when he gave his modest savings to his father to help save the farm during the grasshopper plague of 1877. He was admitted to the bar in 1877.

That year Lind established his own law practice in New Ulm, and he also served as Brown County superintendent of schools in 1878 and 1879. In 1879 he married Alice Shepard of Mankato, Minnesota; they had two sons and two daughters. From 1881 to 1885 Lind served as agent and receiver for the U.S. Land Office in Tracy, Minnesota, then returned to his law practice in New Ulm. In 1887 the Linds built a comfortable Queen Anne style home, the "Lind House," which became a Minnesota state historic site.

Lind entered politics as a Republican and won three terms in the U.S. House of Representatives, 1887–1893, becoming the first Swedish-born member of Congress. Of independent political leanings, during the 1890s he embraced the agrarian revolt. He ran three times for governor of Minnesota as a Democratic-People's party candidate with support from Fusionists and Silver Republicans. He narrowly lost in 1896 to Governor David Clough (165,706 to 162,254). In 1898 Lind won and served one term as governor, 1899–1901, defeating William Eustis (131,980 to 111,796) and becoming the first non-Republican to head the Minnesota state government in forty years and the first Swedish-born U.S. governor. On his third attempt in 1900 he lost a close race to Samuel Van Sant (152,905 to 150,651). As governor Lind had difficulty implementing his reform program because of a hostile legislature, but he led the Progressive movement in Minnesota by advocating strong educational, social, tax, state administrative, and railroad regulatory reforms. In his 1899 inaugural address he outlined specific needs for state-printed, free textbooks for schoolchildren; improvement of penal institutions and those for the mentally ill and retarded; continued support of normal schools to train teachers, saying, "No branch is more important in itself"; and strong funding for the University of Minnesota. During the Spanish-American War Lind served as first lieutenant and quartermaster with the Twelfth Regiment, Minnesota Volunteers.

After his governorship, Lind remained active in political and educational affairs. He served twice on the Board of Regents of the University of Minnesota (1893–1895 and 1908–1914) and as chairman during the latter term. He observed, "To enable professors to do even the elementary work of the university properly the size of the classes must be reduced . . . and a standard of salaries established and maintained that shall attract and hold the best men on the faculty."

From 1903 to 1905 "Honest John" Lind served one more term in the U.S. House of Representatives as a Democrat, but in 1904 he announced his retirement from politics. In 1907 the Linds moved to Minneapolis, where he continued his law practice and declined a gubernatorial run in 1910.

Lind was an admirer and friend of William Jennings Bryan and a supporter of the policies of Woodrow Wilson. In June 1913 Wilson offered Lind the position of minister to Sweden, but he declined because he was a native-born Swede. Lind achieved national prominence when he was chosen by President Wilson, somewhat surprisingly since he had no diplomatic experience, as his personal representative to Mexico in 1913 and 1914. Lind faced the difficult task of calling for free elections, demanding that Victoriano Huerta not run for president, and promoting an armistice with U.S. mediation backed by the threat of intervention. When Huerta agreed not to run for office in August 1913, Lind wrote to Secretary of State Bryan, "From a diplomatic standpoint the mission is a success." Bryan replied that "the crisis is passed" (Link, *Wilson: The New Freedom*, p. 362). But the fighting continued, and Lind, who returned to Washington, D.C., in April 1914, remained there for five months as an adviser supporting intervention during the Tampico incident and the U.S. occupation of Veracruz. Clearly Lind's commitment as a loyal progressive Democrat, despite his lack of knowledge of Mexican history and the Spanish language, coincided well with the ideals of Wilson, and he could be trusted. In Mexico, Lind saw the same corrupt politics and privileged business interests that he had fought in his own country. In the end, however, his mission failed, and he was dismissed for being too pro-Carranza and for his controversial views toward the Catholic church. Ultimately Wilson's ill-conceived moral diplomacy led to further intervention in Mexico.

During World War I Lind, a strong American patriot, served as a member of the Minnesota Commission of Public Safety, a wartime watchdog agency, but in December 1917 he resigned because of disagreement with chairman John McGee. Lind symbolized success in U.S. immigrant politics, especially to Scandinavian-Americans, even though he did not openly court this support. His major contributions were as a progressive reform politician and as a diplomat. Stubbornly independent, honest, direct, and widely popular in Minnesota, he put issues before party loyalty. He once called himself a "political orphan" with no party. His career demonstrated his maverick politics as did his later support of Minnesota Farmer-Labor party candidates and Robert La Follette for president in 1924. Lind died in Minneapolis.

• The John Lind Papers, including his gubernatorial papers, are at the Minnesota Historical Society, St. Paul. For his Mexican mission papers see Deborah Neubeck, ed., *A Guide to the Microfilm Edition of the Mexican Mission Papers of John Lind* (1971). The John Lind File at the Brown County Historical Society, New Ulm, Minn., includes letters and early background. Documents on Lind's diplomatic activities are in the Woodrow Wilson Papers and the William Jennings Bryan Papers at the Library of Congress and the U.S. State Department Papers at the National Archives. Lind wrote "The Mexican People" *Bellman* 18 (12 Dec. 1914). A biography on Lind is George M. Stephenson, *John Lind of Minnesota* (1935). On Lind's Minn. political career see James H. Baker, *Lives of the Governors*, vol. 13 of *Collections of the Minnesota Historical Society* (1908); William Watts Folwell, *A History of Minnesota*, vol. 3 (1926; repr. 1969); Theodore C. Blegen, *Minnesota: A History of the State*, rev. ed. (1975); Carl H. Chrislock, *The Progressive Era in Minnesota, 1899–1918* (1971); Chrislock, *Watchdog of Loyalty: The Minnesota Commission of Safety during World War I* (1991); and Bruce L. Larson, "Scandinavian and Scandinavian-American Governors of Minnesota and Education," *Scandinavian Immigrants and Education in North America*, ed. Philip J. Anderson et al. (1995). On Lind's diplomatic career, see Arthur S. Link, *Wilson: The New Freedom* (1956) and *Wilson: The Struggle for Neutrality, 1914–1915* (1960); and Paolo E. Coletta, *William Jennings Bryan: Progressive Politician and Moral Statesman, 1909–1915* (1969); Kenneth J. Grieb, *The United States and Huerta* (1969); Robert E. Quirk, *An Affair of Honor: Woodrow Wilson and the Occupation of Veracruz* (1962); and Larry D. Hill, *Emissaries to a Revolution: Woodrow Wilson's Executive Agents in Mexico* (1973). A contemporary account is "John Lind as a Strong Personality," *American Review of Reviews* 48 (Sept. 1913).

BRUCE L. LARSON

LINDBERGH, Charles August (20 Jan. 1859–24 May 1924), congressman and lawyer, was born in Stockholm, Sweden, the son of August Lindbergh (Ola Månsson in Sweden), a farmer and member of the Swedish parliament, and Louisa Carline. Some documents date his birth 1858, and his middle name is often incorrectly given as Augustus. Lindbergh immigrated to the United States with his parents in 1859 and grew up on the central Minnesota frontier near Melrose in Stearns County. He attended grammar school and Grove Lake Academy in the same area and graduated from the University of Michigan with a law degree in 1883. He joined the St. Cloud law firm of Searle, Searle, and Lohman for about a year, and in 1884 he established his own law practice in nearby Little Falls, Minnesota.

As a young lawyer, Lindbergh specialized in real estate and land sales. His younger brother Frank Lindbergh was a partner in the firm from 1892 to 1899, and C. A. Lindbergh served one term as county attorney, 1891–1893. He was also a modestly successful business entrepreneur, purchasing land and eventually building thirty-five houses and three commercial buildings in Little Falls. In 1887 he married Mary "May" LaFond; they had three daughters, one of whom died in infancy. In 1898 Mary died following surgery to remove an abdominal tumor. In 1901 Lindbergh married Evangeline Lodge Land, a young chemistry teacher. They had one son, Charles Augustus Lindbergh, the aviator. C. A. and Evangeline Lindbergh were estranged early in their marriage but never divorced. As Eva Lindbergh Christie, C. A.'s daughter from his first marriage, said in 1967, "They were attuned mentally, but not emotionally." In 1901 Lindbergh built a three-story house on a 110-acre farm along the Mississippi River near Little Falls. That house burned in 1905, and he built a smaller structure. The farm later became Lindbergh State Park, including the Lindbergh House and Lindbergh Interpretive Center, operated by the Minnesota Historical Society.

Lindbergh entered Minnesota congressional politics in 1906 and won five terms as a Republican in the U.S. House of Representatives, serving from 1907 to 1917. A staunch progressive, he was unwavering in his belief that the productive parts of the U.S. economic structure—farmers, laborers, and legitimate businesses—were not receiving just rewards after being bilked by Wall Street and the "profiteers." His whole range of reforms was in essence an attempt to bring back to farmers and workingpeople those profits taken unfairly by big business, bankers, and "special interests." He introduced resolutions that ultimately led to the Pujo investigation of the money trust in 1912 and 1913, and his expertise made him a valuable member of the House Committee on Banking and Currency, which drew up the Federal Reserve Act. He voted against the Payne-Aldrich Tariff and supported the insurgent revolt in Congress against "Cannonism." Opposed to the European war, he attacked the munition makers and called for a referendum on war. His voting record consistently reflected his backing of the interests of midwestern farmers, his support of woman suffrage, and his concern for preserving natural resources.

As a political independent, Lindbergh put issue before party, running at various times as a progressive Republican, as a Nonpartisan League candidate, as an Independent, and as a Farmer-Laborite. When Robert La Follette, a fellow reformer whom he supported, faltered in the 1912 campaign, Lindbergh wrote Theodore Roosevelt, "I expect you to succeed Taft." In 1916 Lindbergh entered the Minnesota Republican primary for the U.S. Senate. Frank B. Kellogg, who took a preparedness stand on the war and was well financed, won by a plurality over former governor Adolph O. Eberhart and the antipreparedness progressives, incumbent senator Moses Clapp and Lindbergh.

Lindbergh's 1918 campaign in the Republican gubernatorial primary against Governor Joseph A. A. Burnquist brought his earlier antiwar stand into sharp focus. In a bitter race Burnquist defeated Lindbergh, largely because of wartime hysteria and organized political opposition against the powerful farm protest Nonpartisan League movement, which endorsed Lindbergh. Even though he declared his loyalty after U.S. entry into the war in 1917, Lindbergh's antiwar comments in Congress, his book attacking big business for promoting the war, and his association with the league, with its large German-American membership, led to charges of disloyalty and bolshevism. Local officials, supported by the wartime Minnesota Commission of Public Safety, viciously attacked Lindbergh, and he was refused the right to speak in many communities, hanged in effigy, arrested on a charge of conspiracy, and shot at in southwestern Minnesota. Understandably, his daughter Eva Lindbergh was worried, but Lindbergh warned: "I am not so cowardly as to be afraid for myself. . . . You must prepare to see me in prison and possibly shot." President Woodrow Wilson appointed Lindbergh to the War Industries Board later in 1918, but Lindbergh voluntarily resigned after the appointment met with a storm of protest in the press.

In 1920 Lindbergh ran as an Independent for his old congressional seat but lost by a wide margin. He also helped found Minnesota's unique Farmer-Labor party, which had its beginnings after Lindbergh's 1918 loss, when the Nonpartisan League and labor groups joined together. In 1923 Lindbergh entered the Farmer-Labor primary for the U.S. Senate but finished last behind the winner, Magnus Johnson, and New Ulm mayor L. A. Fritsche. During the campaign Lindbergh flew briefly with his son Charles in his barnstorming Curtiss "Jenny" airplane. In 1924 he entered and became a major contender in the Farmer-Labor primary for governor, but by April his final illness due to a brain tumor forced his withdrawal from the race.

As was typical of many progressive reformers, Lindbergh was also an author and journalist. He wrote three books. In *Banking and Currency and the Money Trust* (1913) he stressed the need for financial reform, stating, "We must get away from the idea that money is created to serve any other purpose than that of an exchange agent." In *Why Is Your Country at War and What Happens to You after the War and Related Subjects* (1917) he accused big business of promoting war for profit and declared, "The war hysteria has so unbalanced the world that it is even considered traitorous to suggest terms of peace." In *The Economic Pinch* (1923) he emphasized humanitarian concerns as they related to economics and his hatred of "privilege," asserting, "We must substitute reason for tradition—if we are ever to unshackle ourselves from the arbitrary domination of property privilege over human right." His other reform writings include three magazines, *The Law of Rights* (1905), *Real Needs* (1916), and *Lindbergh's National Farmer* (1919–1920); and *This Pamphlet Tells Who and What Caused the Panic . . .* (n.d., likely 1924).

Lindbergh made substantial contributions to American protest politics and progressive thought. Politically, the image of the stubborn Swede was true, and he was often uncompromising. Influenced by Darwinism and evolutionary thinking, he argued for government control of banks and government ownership of transportation facilities and utilities. But he opposed pure socialism, placing value on individual and societal competition. Above all, he sought to improve economic and social conditions for the average citizen. Personally, he was reserved, honest, and direct, an individual of strong conviction and courage. This description was true also of his father, who challenged majority opinion in the Swedish Riksdag, and of his son, who flew across the Atlantic in 1927. Lindbergh loved to roam and think while near woods and water, which seemed to sharpen both the competitiveness and gentleness of the man. He died in Crookston, Minnesota, and his ashes were distributed over the old Lindbergh homestead near Melrose, Minnesota, by his son from an airplane.

• The Charles A. Lindbergh, Sr., and Family Papers are in the Minnesota Historical Society, St. Paul. Important materials are also in the Charles A. Lindbergh, Jr., Papers at Sterling Memorial Library, Yale University; and the Charles A. Lindbergh Collection at the Missouri Historical Society, St. Louis. Other informative collections include the Lynn Haines and Family Papers and the Knute Nelson Papers at the Minnesota Historical Society and the Theodore Roosevelt Papers and the Woodrow Wilson Papers at the Library of Congress. The most complete biography is Bruce L. Larson, *Lindbergh of Minnesota: A Political Biography* (1973). A sympathetic account by progressive journalists is Lynn Haines and Dora B. Haines, *The Lindberghs* (1931). Richard B. Lucas, *Charles August Lindbergh, Sr.: A Case Study of Congressional Insurgency, 1906–1912* (1974), covers Lindbergh's early tenure in Congress. Significant insights on career and family are in Charles A. Lindbergh, *The "Spirit of St. Louis"* (1953), *The Wartime Journals of Charles A. Lindbergh* (1970), *Boyhood on the Upper Mississippi: A Reminiscent Letter* (1972), and *Autobiography of Values* (1978); and in the five volumes of *Diaries and Letters of Anne Morrow Lindbergh* (1971–1980), covering the years 1922–1944. See also Kenneth S. Davis, *The Hero: Charles A. Lindbergh and the American Dream* (1959), and Joyce Milton, *Loss of Eden: A Biography of Charles and Anne Morrow Lindbergh* (1993). On Minnesota see Carl H. Chrislock, *The Progressive Era in Minnesota, 1899–1918* (1971); Robert L. Morlan, *Political Prairie Fire: The Nonpartisan League, 1915–1922* (1955); Carol Jenson, "Loyalty as a Political Weapon: The 1918 Campaign in Minnesota," *Minnesota History* 43 (Summer 1972): 42–57; and Larson, "Swedish Americans and Farmer-Labor Politics in Minnesota," in *Perspectives on Swedish Immigration*, ed. Nils Hasselmo (1978). For contemporary comment on Lindbergh see Ida M. Tarbell, "The Hunt for a Money Trust," *American Magazine*, May 1913, pp. 3–17.

BRUCE L. LARSON

LINDBERGH, Charles Augustus (4 Feb. 1902–26 Aug. 1974), aviator, was born in Detroit, Michigan, the son of Charles August Lindbergh, a lawyer and congressman, and Evangeline Lodge Land, a science teacher. He was reared on a farm near Little Falls, Minnesota, where his father practiced law. Of Swedish descent, his father was a progressive Republican who served for ten years in the U.S. House of Representatives. Young Lindbergh was tall, lean, bright, quick, and well coordinated. He wanted to become a flyer in World War I but was not old enough. He enrolled in engineering at the University of Wisconsin, but he stayed only three semesters before leaving to become an airplane pilot.

He bought his first airplane in 1923 and barnstormed through the South and West. He enlisted in the Army Air Service, graduated at the top of his class as a pursuit pilot in 1925, and became a captain in the Missouri National Guard. While flying mail between

St. Louis and Chicago, he persuaded St. Louis businessmen to finance the construction of an airplane to compete for a $25,000 prize Raymond Orteig had offered to the first person to fly nonstop from New York to Paris. The single-engine monoplane (soon named the *Spirit of St. Louis*) was powered by a Wright radial engine. On 20–21 May 1927, flying alone in his *Spirit of St. Louis* through clouds, icing, storms, and sleepiness, Lindbergh traveled from New York to Paris in thirty-three hours and thirty minutes. He landed at night to claim the prize before an enthusiastic crowd of 100,000 cheering Frenchmen at Le Bourget Aerodrome.

Though not the first to fly across the ocean, Lindbergh was acclaimed as one of America's great heroes. Hundreds of thousands cheered his accomplishment in rousing receptions in London, Washington, New York, and St. Louis. He was awarded the Congressional Medal of Honor, and accolades were showered upon him from all over the world. He used his fame to advance the cause of aviation. His *Spirit of St. Louis* now hangs in an honored place in the Smithsonian Institution Air and Space Museum.

In 1929 Lindbergh married Anne Spencer Morrow, the daughter of the U.S. ambassador to Mexico. The couple had six children. Making flights across the United States, South America, Canada, Alaska, China, Greenland, Europe, and Africa, Lindbergh continued to promote the development of commercial aviation by exploring potential air routes.

Constantly hounded by newsmen, hero-worshipers, and crackpots, Lindbergh and his wife found it impossible to live normal lives. The most shocking evidence of this came when their infant son was kidnapped from his crib in the Lindbergh home in New Jersey and murdered. The tragedy and the trial of the kidnapper, Bruno Richard Hauptmann, received sensational worldwide publicity.

To escape newsmen and crackpots, the Lindberghs and their second son quietly slipped out of the country late in 1935, seeking temporary refuge first in England and later in France. The U.S. military attaché in Berlin invited Lindbergh to inspect aviation developments in Germany. As a consequence of his inspection visits (as well as similar visits in Poland, the Soviet Union, Czechoslovakia, and France), Colonel Lindbergh became convinced that German military aviation surpassed that of all other European states and might soon approach that of the United States. He urged Britain, France, and the United States to step up their military aviation preparations. At the same time he urged avoiding war. He thought Britain and France could not defeat Hitler's Nazi Germany and feared that a war could destroy western civilization.

As war drew closer in Europe, Lindbergh, his wife, and their children returned to the United States in the spring of 1939. At the invitation of Army Air Corps chief General Henry H. Arnold, Lindbergh helped speed American air preparations. That fall, when World War II erupted in Europe, Lindbergh began to speak out against American involvement in the conflict. He thought aid short of war for Britain and France would slow America's military preparations and would not enable those countries to defeat Germany. He feared that American involvement in the war could cost the lives of over a million young Americans, and he was persuaded that the United States could successfully defend itself in the Western Hemisphere. In April 1941 he joined the America First Committee and became the leading spokesman for that noninterventionist organization.

Lindbergh was not pro-Nazi and did not want Hitler's Germany to triumph in either Europe or America. But interventionists called him an isolationist and charged him with serving the Nazi cause. He brought down a torrent of criticism when he contended in a speech at an America First rally in Des Moines, Iowa, that "the three most important groups who have been pressing this country toward war are the British, the Jewish, and the Roosevelt Administration." He denied charges of anti-Semitism, but his reputation never recovered from allegations that he was pro-Nazi and anti-Semitic.

When the Japanese attacked Pearl Harbor and the United States declared war on the Axis powers, Lindbergh ceased his noninterventionist activities, pledged to support the war effort, and volunteered his services to the Army Air Force. Unable to regain his military commission, he helped the war effort as a civilian by testing and developing military aircraft. In 1944, although a civilian, he flew fifty combat missions in the South Pacific, shooting down a Japanese plane in the process. In May 1945, when the war ended in Europe, he traveled with a naval technical mission to learn about German jet and rocket propulsion for military aircraft. Though he supported the American war effort during World War II, Lindbergh never apologized for his prewar noninterventionist efforts and never retracted his statements.

After World War II, Lindbergh performed a variety of services for the U.S. Air Force and the Defense Department. In 1954 President Dwight D. Eisenhower restored his commission in the Air Force Reserve and promoted him to the rank of brigadier general. He wore the silver wings of a command pilot. His autobiography, *The Spirit of St. Louis* (1953), was awarded the Pulitzer Prize for biography in 1954. Lindbergh also became active in conservation and in efforts to save endangered species, working through such organizations as the World Wildlife Fund. For many years he served on the board of Pan American Airways and traveled all over the world pursuing his various interests. He continued to pilot airplanes even when he passed the age of seventy and during his lifetime accumulated more than 8,000 hours as a pilot in more than 250 types of airplanes—both piston and jet powered. Lindbergh died on the island of Maui in Hawaii.

Lindbergh's reputation never recovered from the damaging charges made against him as a consequence of his efforts to keep the United States out of World War II. Nonetheless, he was the most acclaimed aviator in American history and contributed much to the development of commercial and military aviation. He was a man of character, courage, patriotism, self-discipline, and independence (some called it stubbornness), with an obsession for factual and technical accuracy and a high sense of integrity. In his diary he once wrote, "I prefer adventure to security, freedom to popularity, and conviction to influence." Such a man was bound to have difficulties in public life.

• Lindbergh's papers have been deposited at the Sterling Memorial Library at Yale University in New Haven, Conn. Though there are many published biographies of Lindbergh, most have factual errors and are marred by hero worship or hostility. The best place to start is in his own books, particularly *The Spirit of St. Louis* (1953), *The Wartime Journals of Charles A. Lindbergh* (1970), *Boyhood on the Upper Mississippi: A Reminiscent Letter* (1972), and *Autobiography of Values* (1978). Also superb are Anne Morrow Lindbergh's variously autobiographical books, particularly the five-volume *Diaries and Letters of Anne Morrow Lindbergh* (1972–1980). Among the many biographies of Lindbergh, the best may be Walter S. Ross, *The Last Hero: Charles A. Lindbergh* (1976). The best book on Lindbergh's noninterventionist activities, based on research in relevant manuscripts, is Wayne S. Cole, *Charles A. Lindbergh and the Battle against American Intervention in World War II* (1974). For a concise collection of essays by qualified authorities compiled to commemorate the fiftieth anniversary of his transatlantic flight, see Tom D. Crouch, ed., *Charles A. Lindbergh: An American Life* (1977).

WAYNE S. COLE

LINDEBERG, Harrie Thomas (10 Apr. 1879–10 Jan. 1959), architect, was born Harry Thomas Lindberg at Bergen Point, New Jersey, the son of Theodore Lindberg and Augusta Osterlund. Both of his parents were born in Sweden and had emigrated to the United States before their children were born. The family was counted in the 1880 census as residing in Hoboken, where Theodore Lindberg's occupation was listed as "dealer, neck ties." Virtually nothing is known of Harrie Lindeberg's education or upbringing until the age of twenty-two, when he appears in the office books of the architectural firm of McKim, Mead & White in New York. He worked there from February 1901 until March 1906.

Lindeberg (who later altered the spelling of his first and last names) served as an assistant to the flamboyant Stanford White, absorbing not only some of his architectural ideas but also his dandyish mannerisms. While working on prestigious residential commissions such as the home of James Breese at Southampton, he also rubbed elbows with the rich. Shortly before White was killed in 1906, Lindeberg and another employee, Lewis Colt Albro, seized the opportunity to open a firm catering to the same high-society clientele.

Albro and Lindeberg established their reputation with the success of their very first commission, the 1907 country estate of National City Bank president James A. Stillman at Pocantico, New York, formerly a McKim, Mead & White client. This widely published design in the manner of a Cotswold cottage helped to popularize a more rustic, English vernacular mode for American mansions. The *Architectural Record* called it a "Thatched Palace." But Lindeberg was also adept at taking models from his old firm and updating them to fit current tastes; another early work, the Tracy Dows farm in Rhinebeck, New York (1909), was a Mount Vernon–style takeoff on White's Breese house.

Lindeberg changed partners as easily as he switched from style to style. Following the untimely death of his wife, Eugenie Lee Quinn, only six months after their June 1906 marriage, he remained a widower until July 1914. He then split with Albro and married Lucia Hull (from the patrician Livingston family of the Hudson Valley), with whom he had two children. This gave him a social pedigree with New York's old money and garnered him commissions in the most fashionable upper-class circles. In 1937 he divorced his second wife to marry Angeline Krech James, climbing a further rung in the social ladder. By this time he was well removed from his roots and a member of exclusive clubs such as the Piping Rock, Players, Coffee House, and Knickerbocker. Indeed, it is likely that Lindeberg sought to obscure his Swedish heritage and identify with the WASP society that dominated the United States. Like his mentor White, he relished his association with high-society figures and increasingly donned their patrician mannerisms. A dapper dresser, he often boasted that he had never learned to drive, since there was always a chauffeur and car on hand to take him wherever he wished to go.

Thus a second-generation immigrant, largely self-taught, transformed himself into a successful residential architect specializing in lavish country houses for America's foremost families. Lindeberg anticipated the tastes and wants of his society clients and worked effectively in all the popular domestic styles, giving each his characteristic flair for massing and surface treatment. He also made sure he was near the enclaves of wealth, building a house for his family in Locust Valley, Long Island (1927), and designing the prestigious Onwentsia Country Club (1912) in Lake Forest, Illinois. Among the interwar generation of academic eclectic architects following the precepts of McKim, Mead & White, he was the most prolific residential architect of his time, with a client list straight out of *Who's Who*. When *Vanity Fair* made up its June 1934 pantheon of significant Americans, the fashionable Lindeberg was cited as "a scholar and a traditionalist," who had "achieved fame in twenty-six states." Two years later *Arts & Decoration* called him "perhaps the world's most independent and original exponent of the traditional form in architecture."

Lindeberg designed crisp, suave country houses throughout the United States for notable patrons such as Dayton's Frederick B. Patterson, president of National Cash Register; opera star Amelita Galli-Curci; meat-packing czars P. D. and Laurance Armour of Chicago; publisher Nelson Doubleday; New York surgeon Ernest Fahnestock; Minnesota's flour king, John S. Pillsbury; Eugene Du Pont of the Delaware chemical dynasty; and Harry F. Knight, the St. Louis millionaire. In Houston Lindeberg helped to develop "Shadyside," a fashionable enclave of 1920s oil millionaires, and his work is well represented in Short Hills, New Jersey; East Hampton, New York; and Lake Forest, Illinois. Characteristic of his best work are the colonial revival house of corporate mogul Gerard F. Lambert, near Princeton, New Jersey (1914), and the imposing seaside estate of Michael Van Buren, "Glencraig" (1926), in Middletown, Rhode Island. During an era in which a corporate oligarchy ruled American business and society, Lindeberg's name became synonymous with the rich man's country estate. A number of younger residential specialists, such as John F. Staub of Houston, Maurice Fatio of Palm Beach, and William Warren of Birmingham, Alabama, trained in his office.

In 1940 Lindeberg published a lavish folio of his designs titled *Domestic Architecture of H. T. Lindeberg*, amending the smaller 1912 volume of work done with Albro, *Domestic Architecture*. In the introduction, the noted critic Royal Cortissoz cited Lindeberg's distinctive artistic personality as a key to his success and placed him "on the same high ground" as Charles McKim, Charles Platt, Henry Bacon, Stanford White, and John Russell Pope. Nevertheless, the fact that Lindeberg did virtually nothing but residential work has not helped his subsequent reputation. Although in 1935 he was appointed adviser to the U.S. State Department, and although he designed handsome classical consulates for Helsinki, Moscow, and Manila, the war intervened to halt the projects and effect his retirement. He rapidly slipped into obscurity. His death at Locust Valley did not occasion the customary laudatory obituaries in professional publications; by this time modernism had come to dominate U.S. architecture, and Lindeberg was associated with a retrograde mode of design. Honors awarded him included membership in the National Academy of Design, the Beaux-Arts Institute of Design, and the National Institute of Arts and Letters.

• Biographical information on Lindeberg is scant, and no office records appear to exist. In addition to the two photographic monographs mentioned above, Lindeberg's writings include "The Design and Plan of the Country House," *American Architect* 94 (12 Apr. 1911): 133–37, and "The Return of Reason in Architecture," *Architecture Record* 74 (Oct. 1933): 252–56. For assessments of his architecture, see Russell Whitehead, "Harrie T. Lindeberg's Contribution to American Domestic Architecture," *American Architect* 146 (Apr. 1935): 33–48; C. Matlack Price, "The New Spirit in Country House Design as Expressed by the Work of Harrie T. Lindeberg," *House Beautiful*, Feb. 1925, pp. 128–32; and A. H. Forbes, "The Work of Albro and Lindeberg," *Architecture* 26 (15 Nov. 1912): 207ff. A short biography may be found in Mark Alan Hewitt, *The Architect and the American Country House, 1890–1940* (1990), p. 278. An obituary is in the *New York Times*, 11 Jan. 1959.

MARK ALAN HEWITT

LINDEMAN, Eduard Christian (9 May 1885–13 Apr. 1953), educator and writer, was born in St. Clair, Michigan, the son of Frederick Lindeman, a laborer, and Frederecka Johanna Von Piper. Lindeman's parents died when he was young, and he worked as a manual laborer until the age of twenty-two, when he entered Michigan Agricultural College. He graduated in 1911, and the next year he married Hazel Charlotte Taft, the daughter of one of his professors; they had four daughters.

From 1912 to 1915 Lindeman was a pastor's assistant at the Plymouth Congregational Church in Lansing, Michigan, where among other activities, he developed youth clubs. This position gave him appropriate experience for his next job working for the Michigan Cooperative Extension Service, organizing student groups which developed into 4-H clubs (1915–1918). He became state director of the program but left in 1918 to work briefly with the War Camp Community Service in New York City. In 1919 he taught at the YMCA College in Chicago. He then became director of the sociology department at North Carolina College for Women in Greensboro, where he remained until 1924. In both of these teaching positions he was the center of controversy for his liberalism, and the Ku Klux Klan had a role in forcing him from his North Carolina position.

Lindeman wrote his first book, *College Characters: Essays and Verse*, published in 1912. His 1922 article for the *New Republic* may have brought him to the attention of editor Herbert Croly, who invited him to make more contributions to that influential intellectual journal. It was probably Croly who introduced Lindeman to Dorothy Whitney Straight, a liberal philanthropist who assisted him financially between 1922 and 1924 while he worked for a social research project called "The Inquiry." The Inquiry was a group of progressive researchers who examined and discussed critical issues such as race relations, international affairs, and community development, and wrote monographs and articles about them. He wrote articles for the *New Republic*, *Survey*, *Review of Reviews*, and other journals, drawing on his work for The Inquiry. He also became Croly's friend and wrote eighteen articles and reviews for the *New Republic* between 1922 and 1945. A contributing editor of the *New Republic*, in 1928 he edited a special section on adult education for the journal.

Lindeman actively participated in the intellectual life of American progressivism through the *New Republic* group that Croly led. Croly's biographer David Levy wrote that Lindeman was "Croly's closest intellectual companion during the last years of his life." Croly himself said of Lindeman: "He and I are more closely allied intellectually than I have ever been with any previous friend" (Levy, p. 281).

The Republic Publishing Company, associated with the *New Republic*, published three of Lindeman's twelve books: *Social Discovery: An Approach to the Study of Functional Groups*, with an introduction by Croly (1924); *The Meaning of Adult Education* (1926); and *Social Education: An Interpretation of the Principles and Methods Developed by the Inquiry During the Years 1923–1933* (1933). Lindeman also wrote over 400 journal articles during his prolific writing career.

In 1924 Lindeman joined the faculty of the New York School of Social Work of Columbia University, where he taught social philosophy and other subjects until his retirement in 1950. He also taught at and was a trustee of Alvin Johnson's New School for Social Research, a leading institution in progressive adult education. At various times he was a visiting lecturer at the University of Delhi, the University of California, Stanford University, Temple University, and other institutions. While continuing his writing and teaching at Columbia, Lindeman served from 1935 to 1938 as director of the Department of Community Organization for Leisure in the Works Progress Administration, a New Deal agency.

Lindeman was an activist as well as a scholar and held many leadership positions in organizations devoted to education, civil liberties, racial equality, housing, child welfare, and social change. He was a director of the American Civil Liberties Union and a member of the executive committees of the Public Education Association, the Progressive Education Association, and the American Association for Adult Education. He was active in the National Council of Parent Education, the Urban League, the Institute for Propaganda Analysis, the Council of Churches, the Federation of Protestant Welfare Agencies, the National Child Labor Committee, the National Conference of Social Work, the Association on American Indian Affairs, and the National Sharecroppers Fund.

Despite his consistent opposition to communism, Lindeman's liberal activism brought on right-wing attacks. McCarthyites and American Legionnaires identified him as a "controversial educator who is a notorious advocate of 'Progressive Education' which is the entering wedge of Socialism in our school systems." Lindeman maintained a lifelong opposition to such rightwing groups. Shortly before his death he said to members of his family: "This is a beautiful country. Don't let the demagogues spoil it" (Stewart, pp. 218, 221).

Lindeman's chief influence was through his work in progressive adult education. John Elias and Sharan Merriam wrote that "it was not until Eduard Lindeman's book, *The Meaning of Adult Education*, appeared in 1926 that the ideas of the progressives were fully applied to the field of adult education. Lindeman was directly influenced by the ideas of John Dewey and other progressives" (Elias and Merriam, p. 53).

The Meaning of Adult Education was Lindeman's most widely read book and was reprinted in 1961. Lindeman's biographer, David Stewart, says that Lindeman was "the earliest major conceptualizer of the progressive-pragmatic tradition in American adult education. . . . It is this tradition that is still mainstream within the world of adult education in the United States in the latter days of the twentieth century" (Stewart, p. 225). Lindeman was clearly America's most influential and innovative educator of adults. He died in New York City.

• Lindeman's papers and letters are in the Rare Book and Manuscript Library, Columbia University; the Archives and Historical Collections, Michigan State University; the Social Welfare History Archives, University of Minnesota; the Dorothy Whitney Straight Elmhirst Papers, John M. Olin Library, Cornell University; the Max Otto Papers, Wisconsin Historical Society; and the Dartington Hall Trust, Totnes, Devon, England.

Lindeman's books, in addition to those mentioned, include *The Community: An Introduction to the Study of Community Leadership and Organization* (1921), *Dynamic Social Research* (1933), *Wealth and Culture* (1936), and *Leisure—A National Issue* (1939). He edited *Emerson, The Basic Writings of America's Sage* (1947), and *Plutarch's Lives: Life Stories of Men who Shaped History* (1950). He also wrote several books with other authors: with Nels Anderson, *Urban Sociology: An Introduction to the Study of Urban Communities* (1928); with John Hader, *Dynamic Social Research* (1933); and with T. V. Smith, *The Democratic Way of Life* (1951).

The definitive biography of Lindeman is David W. Stewart's *Adult Learning in America: Eduard Lindeman and His Agenda for Lifelong Education* (1987). Stewart corrects the errors of some earlier writers about Lindeman. His notes and bibliography include most of Lindeman's writings but overlook "Getting Ready for Social Change," in *Capitalizing Intelligence: Eight Essays on Adult Education*, ed. Warren Seyfert (1937), and three essays in the *Encyclopedia of the Social Sciences*: "Adult Education," "Discussion," and "Public Welfare" (1930). Stewart also identifies much published and unpublished material about Lindeman.

Lindeman's daughter, Elizabeth Lindeman Leonard, wrote a more intimate biography, *Friendly Rebel: A Personal and Social History of Eduard C. Lindeman* (1991). Other useful sources are Max Otto's "Foreword" and Robert Gessner's "Introduction," in *The Democratic Man: Selected Writings of Eduard C. Lindeman*, ed. Gessner (1956); Gisela Konopka, *Eduard C. Lindeman and Social Work Philosophy* (1958); and John Elias and Sharan Merriam, *Philosophical Foundations of Adult Education* (1980). On Lindeman's relationship with Croly, see David W. Levy, *Herbert Croly of The New Republic* (1985). Lindeman's obituary is in the *New York Times*, 14 Apr. 1953.

JAMES WALLACE

LINDENTHAL, Gustav (21 May 1850–31 July 1935), civil engineer, was born in Brunn, Moravia (renamed Brno after becoming part of the Czechoslovak Socialist Republic following the First World War), the son of Dominik Lindenthal, a cabinetmaker, and Franciski Schmutz. He received practical training as a mason and carpenter and worked in a machine shop before leaving home at about the age of twenty to seek work in the capitol city of Vienna. There, despite obtaining engineering work on the staff of the Austrian and the Swiss national railways, he found that his lack of a formal engineering education handicapped his career in Europe and decided to emigrate to the United States, where self-educated engineers could still rise to considerable heights in the profession. Arriving in 1874, Lindenthal landed his first job, as a stone mason for the 1876 World's Fair in Philadelphia. His talents soon were recognized, and he advanced to the design offices of the Fair Commission. After the exposition closed, Lindenthal continued his apprenticeship, working for several bridge-fabricating companies and

railroads before establishing his own office in Pittsburgh, where he completed the Smithfield Street Bridge in 1883, his first important commission. A century later, the bridge was rehabilitated carefully to preserve not only Lindenthal's lenticular trusses, but the decorative portals that mark the entrance and celebrate one's arrival to the former steel-making city.

The renowned Brooklyn Bridge was completed in the same year as Smithfield Street, eclipsing Lindenthal's hope of gaining national notoriety or prominence for the project but not frustrating his spirit. Two years later, Samuel Rae, assistant to Pennsylvania Railroad president George B. Roberts, approached Lindenthal to explore the feasibility of a railroad bridge over the Hudson River. Rae desired direct entry for the railroad into New York City, which rail traffic could only reach by transferring at the Hudson to barges and ferries. Thus began for Lindenthal a 45-year quest to construct a railroad-suspension bridge across the Hudson River and a professional relationship with New York City.

Appointed bridge commissioner in 1902–1903, when the city was in the process of linking Manhattan with its burgeoning boroughs, Lindenthal oversaw completion of the Williamsburg Bridge, a suspension bridge designed by Leffert L. Buck with exposed steel towers that many considered to be the ugliest bridge in New York. When the bridge was dedicated the year after Lindenthal's arrival, the new commissioner was careful not to denigrate a fellow engineer and described the bridge as "the heaviest suspension bridge in existence, and the largest bridge on this continent." He personally prepared plans for two others, one adjacent to the Brooklyn that became known as the Manhattan Bridge and another further upstream at Blackwell's Island that became known as the Queensboro Bridge. His design for the Manhattan Bridge, an eye-bar-chain suspension bridge with rocker towers, was rejected by the succeeding administration in favor of a wire-cable span with fixed towers, but his design of a double cantilever without suspended spans for the Queensboro Bridge was accepted and built in 1909.

Lindenthal's Pennsylvania Railroad connection paid off shortly after his term as bridge commissioner ended in 1903 when he was appointed in 1904 chief engineer of the New York Connecting Railroad to design a bridge and viaduct system providing a rail linkage between New England and the rest of the country via the New York, New Haven & Hartford Railroad. The Pennsylvania had resolved the Hudson River barrier by boring a tunnel under the river that eventually would be linked with Lindenthal's bridge and viaduct system. The crowning achievement was the mighty Hell Gate Bridge, one of the great steel-arch bridges of all times. Completed in 1917, it was a two-hinged arch, the longest yet, at 977 feet, and the heaviest, at 80,000 tons, in the world. All great engineering projects required assistance to provide detailed design and supervision. By hiring Othmar Ammann and David B. Steinman as assistants on the Hell Gate and on subsequent projects, Lindenthal fulfilled another function of master builder by providing apprenticeship opportunities to the next generation of engineers. Both later became master engineers. In 1902 Lindenthal had married Gertrude Weil; she died in 1905. He then married Carrie Herndon in 1910; they had one daughter.

Before Hell Gate was completed, Lindenthal was approached by the Norfolk & Western Railroad to design a bridge over the Ohio River that linked the Allegheny coal fields with the Great Lakes. This was the Sciotoville Bridge, which when completed in 1917, the same year as the Hell Gate, was the longest continuous truss and whose twin spans, 775 feet each, remain the ultimate expression of that bridge form.

Lindenthal was profilic not only in bridge building, but in writing as well. Papers on two of his most famous projects, the Smithfield Street Bridge in Pittsburgh and the Sciotoville Bridge over the Ohio, won the Rowland Prize from the American Society of Civil Engineers, one of the society's most prestigious awards. He also studied engineering formally at the polytechnical schools in Dresden (1911), Brunn (1921), and Vienna (1926). Lindenthal's last group of bridges, three spans over the Willamette River in Portland, Oregon—the Burnside, Sellwood, and Ross Island—was completed in the mid-1920s. In designing these bridges Lindenthal continued his propensity to never design two bridges alike. At this time, great suspension bridges were being planned in large cities across the United States, and Lindenthal still held out hope that his dream span of the Hudson River at Fifty-seventh Street might be built. For the rest of his life he spent a good portion of his time promoting this project. Although this bridge was never built, Lindenthal was recognized as the "Dean of American Bridge Engineers" for the many outstanding spans he built and for helping create a period in American bridge engineering that was the foremost in the world. He died in Metuchen, New Jersey.

• The Division of Mechanical and Civil Engineering, National Museum of American History, Smithsonian Institution, Washington, D.C., maintains the Biographical Archive of American Civil Engineers, from which *A Biographical Dictionary of American Civil Engineers* (2 vols.; 1972, 1991) was compiled by the American Society of Civil Engineers. The entry for Lindenthal appears in volume 1, pp. 81–82. Lindenthal's papers on the Smithfield Street and Sciotoville bridges appear in *Transactions of the American Society of Civil Engineers* 12 (1883): 353–85, 386–92; and 85 (1922): 910–53, 954–75. His associates at ASCE published a memoir of his life and work in the *Transactions of the American Society of Civil Engineers* 105 (1940): 1790–94. On his works, especially his masterpiece, the Hell Gate Bridge, see Tom Buckley, "A Reporter at Large (the Eighth Bridge)," *New Yorker*, 14 Jan. 1991, pp. 37–59. Henry Petroski devotes a chapter to Lindenthal (pp. 123–216), in his *Engineers of Dreams* (1995). An obituary is in the *New York Times*, 1 Aug. 1935.

ERIC DE LONY

LINDERMAN, Frank Bird (25 Sept. 1869–12 May 1938), author and advocate for American Indians, was born in Cleveland, Ohio, the son of Mary Ann Brannan and James Bird Linderman, a merchant. Linderman was educated in the public schools of Cleveland and Elyria, Ohio. But he yearned to go west. When he was just sixteen and a student at a business college in Oberlin, Ohio (1884–1885), he decided that he wanted to become a fur trapper. With his parents' consent Linderman traveled to the Flathead Lake region of Montana Territory, where he hunted and trapped for six years. He formed valuable friendships with frontiersmen and among the Flathead Indians. He prized the freedom of the Indians' life and felt the injustices they suffered.

When he met Minnie Jane Johns in 1890, Linderman realized that he would have to give up trapping. He learned assaying, became an assistant assayer in Victor, Montana (1892), and then an assayer in Butte (1893). Linderman married Johns in 1893; they had three children. They moved in 1896 to Sheridan, where Linderman opened his own assaying office and became increasingly active in politics. But assaying did not pay well, and so in 1899 he purchased the *Sheridan Enterprise*, a newspaper. Thus it was that he discovered his gift for writing. He sold the paper in 1905.

He was elected to the state legislature, where he served from 1901 to 1904; he rose to become assistant secretary of state and, briefly, acting secretary of state (1905–1907). He was an active advocate for Indians throughout his political career—and after. In 1916, for example, he took the leading role in winning for Little Bear's homeless and impoverished band of Crees and Chippewas a parcel of land that was to be named Rocky Boy's Indian Reservation. Linderman was fluent in the sign language, and so he could converse easily with Indians throughout the Northwest.

In 1910 Linderman became state agent for the Guardian Life Insurance Company. In his first year he sold more insurance than any other agent in the United States. But Linderman still wanted to write. In 1915 he published his first book, *Indian Why Stories*, illustrated by his friend Charles M. Russell. This was a book of etiological legends gathered from Cree, Chippewa, and Flathead friends in the course of Linderman's travels. In 1917 Linderman sold his lucrative insurance business, built a large log house on Flathead Lake, and devoted himself to his writing: *Indian Lodge-Fire Stories* (1918), *Indian Old-Man Stories* and *On a Passing Frontier* (1920), *How It Came About Stories* (1921), *Lige Mounts, Free Trapper* (1922), and *Kootenai Why Stories* (1926).

These books won consistently good reviews, but Linderman was discouraged by their poor sales. Then he decided to write the life story of his old friend Plenty Coups, Crow warrior and chief; *American* (1930; later editions were titled *Plenty-Coups, Chief of the Crows*) was one of the first Indian as-told-to autobiographies—and certainly one of the best. This book sold quite well, and Linderman followed it with *Red Mother* (1932; later editions were titled *Pretty-Shield: Medicine Woman of the Crows*), the as-told-to autobiography of Plenty Coups's sister. This was the first as-told-to autobiography by an Indian woman. In the next few years he published several other books, including novels, such as *Beyond Law* (1933), and history, such as *The Blackfeet Indians* (1935).

Late in life Linderman enjoyed clay modeling and bronze casting. He died in Santa Barbara, California, where he had moved for his health. Linderman is remembered mainly for his writings, and of these the most important are the two as-told-to Indian autobiographies, which are among the earliest and the best of such books.

• Collections of Linderman's papers are at UCLA's University Research Library, Department of Special Collections, and the Museum of the Plains Indian, Browning, Mont. For biographical information, see Hugh A. Dempsey's introduction to his edition of Linderman's *Wolf and the Winds* (1986) and Linderman's autobiography, *Montana Adventure: The Recollections of Frank B. Linderman* (1968). See H. David Brumble, *American Indian Autobiography* (1988), for discussion of Linderman's two as-told-to Indian autobiographies; for Linderman's relations with the Crow chief, see "Linderman and Plenty-Coups," in William W. Bevis, *Ten Tough Trips: Montana Writers and the West* (1990), pp. 76–91. An obituary is in the *New York Times*, 13 May 1938.

H. DAVID BRUMBLE

LINDGREN, Waldemar (14 Feb. 1860–3 Nov. 1939), economic geologist, was born in the village of Vassmölösa near Kalmar, Sweden, the son of Johan Magnus Lindgren, a judge of the provincial court, and Emma Bergman, of a celebrated Swedish family. He graduated with the degree of mining engineer from the Royal Mining Academy at Freiberg, Saxony, in 1882 but continued on for an additional year of graduate work in metallurgy and chemistry, specializing on the mineralogy of Långban, Sweden.

In June 1883 Lindgren satisfied his dream of participating in the extensive mining activity in the western part of the United States by joining Professor Raphael Pumpelly in charge of the Northern Transcontinental Survey and working as an assistant to Professor W. M. Davis. When the Northern Transcontinental Survey disbanded in 1884, he took a position first as an assayer near Helena, Montana, and then as a designer of smelting furnaces at Anaconda, Montana. Late in 1884 Lindgren joined the U.S. Geological Survey under George F. Becker, who was undertaking a systematic study of the gold belt of the Sierra Nevada. Lindgren married Ottolina Allstrin of Göteborg, Sweden, in 1886; they had no children.

Lindgren remained with the Survey for thirty-one years except for the academic year of 1897–1898, when he served as associate professor of geology at Stanford University. Among his students was Herbert C. Hoover, who previously had served as Lindgren's first assistant for three field seasons. After a continuous period of field studies, mainly in California, Idaho, New Mexico, Arizona, Utah, and Oregon, he was appointed head of a section in the Division of Mineral Resources of the Survey in 1905, then chief of the Division of Metalliferous Geology in 1908, and chief

geologist in 1911. Administrative duties interfered with his scientific interests, and he resigned in 1912 as chief geologist; after completing projects in progress, he resigned from the Survey entirely in 1915.

As a result of a series of lectures on ore deposits over a period of five weeks in 1908 at the Massachusetts Institute of Technology (MIT), repeated again in 1909, 1910, and 1911, Lindgren was invited to be the William Barton Rogers Professor of Geology and head of the MIT Department of Geology in 1912. He developed the department into a world-class training center for economic geologists. While at MIT he supervised sixty-four theses in addition to his teaching and administrative duties, and he took on consulting assignments in Mexico, Chile, Bolivia, Cuba, and Canada as well as in the United States. He took part in the celebrated Utah-Apex legal case as an expert witness. The Lindgren Library at MIT was named after him in 1932. He retired from active teaching in 1933 as professor emeritus.

Lindgren is best known around the world for his book *Mineral Deposits*, which has appeared in four editions (1913, 1919, 1928, 1933). It synthesizes his vast experience as recorded in more than 135 journal articles in economic geology. His principal thesis was that igneous processes dominated ore formation and that it was necessary to have a regional geological understanding to interpret ore deposits. His studies on hot springs were related to ore-forming processes. He classified the metasomatic processes in fissure veins and was the first to recognize contact metamorphic ore deposits in North America. The "Lindgren law" resulted from his observation of the constancy of volume in replacement phenomena. On the other hand, his strong advocacy of the importance of colloids in some ore-forming processes has not stood the test of time. Because of his detailed attention to the mineralogy of ore deposits, he extracted a large amount of information from their textures, sequence, composition, and chemical stability. From these data he was able to classify ore deposits genetically into several ranges of temperature using geological thermometers, characterize the zoning of ore minerals both with depth and radially, and recognize the broad metallogenic provinces essential to mineral exploration.

The journal *Economic Geology* was established in 1905 by a small group under the leadership of Lindgren, who also served as one of its associate editors. During his administration as chairman of the Division of Geology and Geography of the National Research Council he helped establish the *Annotated Bibliography of Economic Geology*, which abstracts the enormous volume of literature on all phases of economic geology.

Lindgren served as president of the Mining and Metallurgical Society of America (1920), the Society of Economic Geologists (1922), and the Geological Society of America (1924), and he was honorary chairman of the Sixteenth International Geological Congress held in the United States in 1933. In addition to being honored with membership in the societal "triple crown" (National Academy of Sciences, 1909; American Philosophical Society, 1917; and American Academy of Arts and Sciences, 1912), he received the Penrose Gold Medal from the Society of Economic Geologists in 1928, the Penrose Medal from the Geological Society of America in 1933, the Gustave Trasenster Medal of the University of Liége, Belgium, in 1936, and the Wollaston Medal of the Geological Society of London in 1937. In the centennial commemorative number of *Economic Geology* (55 [1960]: vii) Lindgren is described as the "world's foremost economic geologist." The mineral lindgrenite was named in his honor by Charles Palache. Lindgren himself named two new minerals, coronadite (with W. F. Hildebrand) and violarite (with W. M. Davy).

Lindgren was well read, a linguist in at least seven languages, and probably read an equal number of other languages. He is described as a modest man with quiet dignity, easily approached, and a "good fellow" to students. Contrary to the stern expression of his photographs, he was considered a most engaging conversationalist with knowledge in history, art, and world politics.

Lindgren laid the foundations for modern concepts in the physical chemistry of ore deposition, making major contributions in theory, field observations, and in pioneering the application of both transmitted and reflected light microscopy to the laboratory study of ore minerals. He died in Brookline, Massachusetts, after about a year of illness that had left him an invalid.

• Some of Lindgren's papers are held in the Archives of the Massachusetts Institute of Technology. The most complete bibliography is given in Robert Rakes Shrock, *Geology at M.I.T., 1865–1965* (1977), pp. 385–468, which includes the details of Lindgren's early life in Sweden as well as his tenure at MIT. An especially noteworthy inclusion in Shrock's volume is appendix A, "Waldemar Lindgren Goes West," which consists of translations by Anders Martinsson of four letters Lindgren sent to his parents in 1883 and which originally appeared in the Swedish journal *Geologiska Föreningens i Stockholm Förhandlingar* 95 (1973): 280–87. His years at the U.S. Geological Survey are described by Mary C. Rabbitt in *Minerals, Lands, and Geology for the Common Defence and General Welfare*, vols. 2 and 3 (1986). An extensive biography and partial bibliography is "Life and Scientific Work of Waldemar Lindgren," *Ore Deposits of the Western States: Lindgren Volume* (1933), ed. L. C. Graton, an early field assistant. Biographical information is in the memorial written by one of his students, M. J. Buerger, in *American Mineralogist* 25 (1940): 184–88.

H. S. YODER, JR.

LINDNER, Richard (11 Nov. 1901–16 Apr. 1978), painter, was born in Hamburg, Germany, the son of Jüdell (Julius) Lindner, a salesman, and Mina (or Minna) Bornstein, an American of German parentage. When he was four his family resettled in the Bavarian city of Nuremberg. Raised in a modest, Jewish household, he never revealed much about his background other than to mention his supposedly brief career as a pianist, an account that cannot be confirmed.

Lindner attributed his choice of profession to a casual encounter with an artist friend, whose bohemian lifestyle lured Lindner at age twenty-one to enroll in the Kunstgewerbeschüle Nürnberg (Nuremberg School of Applied Arts) for four years of training in commercial art. Moving to Berlin in 1927, Lindner commenced his career as a freelance graphic artist. In 1930, when he was hired as art director for the Munich publisher Knorr and Hirth, he married Elsbeth Schülein, an aspiring fashion illustrator, and the couple settled in the Schwabing district of Munich.

In 1933, with the ascendancy of National Socialism, Lindner and his wife (Social Democrats as well as Jews) fled Germany for an uncertain life as refugees in prewar Paris. Although his wife succeeded as a fashion illustrator for *Vogue*, Lindner was unable to continue his commercial career. Instead he began to familiarize himself with French modern art, particularly surrealism.

At the outbreak of World War II in September 1939, Lindner and his wife were separated involuntarily when the French interned them as enemy aliens in separate concentration camps. Elsbeth Lindner was released first, emigrated to the United States after a seven-month ordeal in Casablanca, and settled in New York City early in 1941. Assigned to a forced labor company with the British expeditionary forces, Lindner was released in June 1940, when Paris fell. Fleeing first to Lyons and then to Lisbon, he entered the United States with his wife's help in March 1941, and they settled in Manhattan.

Joining a close-knit group of wartime émigré artists such as René Bouché, Saul Steinberg, Hedda Sterne, and photographer Evelyn Hofer, Lindner resumed his career as a freelance illustrator. His fine line drawings and tinted watercolors were published in major journals ranging from *Mademoiselle* to *Fortune*. The Lindners' marriage, however, was a casualty of wartime disruptions; the couple had divorced by the time Lindner was naturalized in 1948.

Dissatisfied with commercial art, Lindner began painting in 1950 after his first trip to Paris since his immigration. While he continued to produce illustrations until 1962, he supported himself by teaching part time at the Pratt Institute from 1952 until 1966.

During the 1950s Lindner developed a symbolic figure style completely at odds with current vanguard trends, particularly the expressionist abstractions of the New York School. Childhood memories and youthful experiences in Weimar Germany had undoubtedly shaped Lindner's symbolic art. For example, when he was twelve, his mother began operating a custom-fitted corset business from the family home, and the corset later became a recurring motif in Lindner's figure paintings. Blending machine-like precision and brutal naiveté, he invented three figure types: the portrait caricature, the Wunderkind or child prodigy, and the corset-clad woman. He invested each with the alienation and absurdity that he considered the essence of the human condition. In his masterpiece group portrait, *The Meeting* (1953, Museum of Modern Art), Lindner juxtaposed these figure types with likenesses of family and friends to create an allegory of his experience as an artist-immigrant. Although Lindner was represented by the prestigious dealer Betty Parsons, he had little recognition or financial success during the 1950s.

Both his art and his fortunes changed in the 1960s. Inspired by observations of Manhattan street life and American mass culture, Lindner transformed his machinist figure style into a visual satire of the modern urban spectacle. Gangsters, pimps and prostitutes, and estranged couples predominated in his bold, large-scale paintings from that decade. His masterful fusion of hard-edge abstraction and popular culture icons brought him belated recognition. Lindner's success, supported by his new dealer Cordier and Ekstrom, coincided with the advent of pop art. Although he was often identified with that movement, he denied the connection and instead contended that his was the art of an outsider: "My figures are the impressions of a tourist visiting New York," he told dealer Wolfgang Fischer in 1973. While Lindner reintroduced personal symbolism into his work from the 1970s, urban alienation and sexual estrangement remained predominant themes for the balance of his career.

In 1969 Lindner married a young French artist, Denise Kopelman, and the couple maintained dual residences in New York and Paris. When he died in his New York studio, Richard Lindner had attained international renown as one of the premier figurative artists of the postwar era.

• Lindner's papers are in private hands and are closed to scholars. Transcripts of two unpublished interviews by Dorothy Seckler (1962) and John Jones (1965) and a tape recording of a radio interview by Colette Roberts (1965) are in the Archives of American Art, Smithsonian Institution, Washington, D.C. Three monographs published during the artist's lifetime remain useful: Sidney Tillim, *Lindner* (1961), Dore Ashton, *Richard Lindner* (1969), and Hilton Kramer, *Richard Lindner* (1975). A special issue of *XXe Siècle Review, Homage to Richard Lindner* (1980), includes articles and memoirs, as well as interviews by Wolfgang Fischer and John Gruen. Of the many solo exhibition catalogs, the most significant are *Richard Lindner* (Städisches Museum Schloss Morsbroich, 1968), *Lindner* (University Art Museum, Univ. of California, Berkeley, 1969), *Richard Lindner* (Musée National d'art moderne, 1974), *Richard Lindner: A Retrospective Exhibition* (Museum of Contemporary Art, Chicago, 1977), and *Richard Lindner* (Fondation Maeght, Saint-Paul, 1979). Claudia Loyall, *Richard Lindner, ein Emigrant in New York: Zum Selbstverständnis des Künstlers, 1950–1953* (1995), includes important new research. The most substantial monograph is Judith Zilczer, *Richard Lindner: Paintings and Watercolors, 1948–1977* (1996).

JUDITH ZILCZER

LINDSAY, Bertha (28 July 1897–3 Oct. 1990), Shaker eldress, was born Goldie Ina Ruby Lindsay in Braintree, Massachusetts, the daughter of Lloyd E. Lindsay, a mechanic, grocer, and photographer, and Abbie H. Smith. Goldie arrived at the Canterbury Shaker Village (United Society of Believers in Christ's Second Appearing) in 1905, after the death of her parents. Her sister May, in her mid-twenties at the time, was about

to marry and head west. The family, Baptists, had worshiped at the village; the Shakers were known to take in young children, and so they were asked to care for her. Years later, when she signed the covenant in 1918, Goldie took the name "Bertha" as a way of honoring Sister Bertha Lillian Phelps, in whose care she had been as a teenager and whom she considered her spiritual mother.

According to Lindsay, there were two times that she wanted to leave the Shakers. The first was the day that her sister left. The second, as she described it, occurred during World War I. She wondered then about marriage, or a career in music. Both times, the nondirective love and support of the other sisters convinced her that she was in the right place.

While Lindsay did well in the Shaker school, her eyesight was poor, and at fifteen she began to spend more of her time learning housekeeping skills and cooking. At the age of twenty her talents in the kitchen were recognized, and she was given the position of head cook for the business leaders of the community and their guests. Although Lindsay was primarily associated with the processing and serving of food at the village throughout her life, she was also in charge of the fancywork trade from 1944 until 1958.

Lindsay enjoyed elocution and participated regularly in the skits, mostly religious, that the community of sisters put on and that the public attended. Later in her life she spent a considerable amount of time reading books on religion and spirituality. She had an ecumenical interest in a variety of religious and philosophical perspectives. With fellow enthusiasts, she formed a study group for the discussion of books such as Richard Maurice Bucke's classic *Cosmic Consciousness* and the works of Edgar Cayce. She read the Bible regularly.

Lindsay wrote articles for the *Shaker* and contributed to the *Shaker Quarterly*. A paper she gave with Phelps in 1961, "Industries and Inventions of the Shakers: Shaker Music, a Brief History," was published in 1968. In 1987 she wrote a short piece, "The Shakers Face Their Last Amen," for *People Weekly* (2 Mar. 1987, p. 78). She recorded her memoirs and assisted in the preservation of the village. Her book, *Seasoned with Grace* (1987), edited by Mary Rose Boswell, combines recipes, photographs, and reminiscences that portray life as a Shaker in the twentieth century.

In 1967 Lindsay was appointed both as Canterbury eldress and as a member of the lead ministry. The conveyance of the deed of the site and properties to Shaker Village, Inc., a nonprofit educational institution, came about largely at her behest. She is remembered as a key force in the creation of the Canterbury Shaker Village Museum as it is today. In 1970 her vision failed entirely, but she continued her work for the village.

Lindsay loved cooking, music, and gardening. Even when she was in her late eighties and had lost her sight, it was not unusual to find her in the kitchen slicing apples for pie. Lindsay lived a life of prayer, love, and humility. She took seriously the Shaker tenet

"Hands to work and hearts to God" and so found herself in prayer throughout her day.

Lindsay was one of the most visible of the Canterbury Shakers, interpreting the Shaker experience for the general public, making it more accessible. She frequently said that she was "a witness for those who had gone before." Even in her last years she greeted as many of the hundreds of thousands of visitors to the Shaker Village Museum as she could, sitting daily for several hours in the entryway at the Trustees Building. She hoped that Shakerism would never die out but rather that it would take on new forms, touching the hearts of visitors who might then take Shaker ideas of union and community into the world. Lindsay died at Canterbury Shaker Village.

• Information on Lindsay is housed at the Canterbury Shaker Village Museum archives, Canterbury, N.H. Stephen J. Stein, *The Shaker Experience in America* (1992), is an excellent source of information. Cathy Newman, "The Shaker's Brief Eternity," *National Geographic*, Sept. 1989, pp. 302–25, and Ken Burns and Amy Stechler Burns, *Hands to Work and Hearts to God* (1985), a documentary film, both offer relevant visual images. An obituary is in the *Shaker Quarterly* 18 (Winter 1990): 117.

ERIKA M. BUTLER

LINDSAY, Howard (29 Mar. 1889–11 Feb. 1968), playwright, actor, and director, was born Herman Nelke in Waterford, New York, the son of Herman Siegmund Nelke, a salesman, natural healer, masseur, and newspaperman, and Susan Hall. When Herman Nelke's job hopping and stories of fantastic exploits exhausted the patience of his no-nonsense wife, she divorced him. Taking her four children and her mother, she moved to Atlantic City, New Jersey, where she worked as a typesetter on her brother's newspaper. Young Howard exhibited his father's dramatic flair and his mother's industry by selling newspapers and giving recitations on the boardwalk. His uncle passed on free tickets from theatrical advance men, and after seeing a melodrama when he was ten, Lindsay announced his ambition to be an actor.

His mother moved the family in 1902 to Boston, where Lindsay attended the Boston Latin School and developed an enthusiasm for writing. He received a scholarship to Harvard in 1907 but left after a year to study at the American Academy of Dramatic Arts in New York City.

When a stipend from his grandmother ran out after six months, he adopted her name for the stage and obtained his first professional engagement with a touring company of *Polly of the Circus*. In 1913 he won a place with Margaret Anglin's company and toured for five years as a minor actor and stage manager in a repertory of modern plays, Shakespeare, and Greek tragedy. This experience, Lindsay claimed, was his real schooling in the craft of acting.

When the United States entered World War I, Lindsay joined the army and spent thirteen months in Brest, France, where he organized entertainments for the troops. His success earned him an invitation to perform in Paris at the Théâtre des Champs-Elysées and a promotion from corporal to second lieutenant.

After the war Lindsay resumed his position with the Anglin company but left in 1919 when the management refused to recognize Actors' Equity, the newly formed actors' union. He went to New York and joined the staff of producer George C. Tyler as stage manager, head of casting, and occasional actor. His first directing assignment in 1921 was *Dulcy* by George S. Kaufman and Marc Connelly; it was his first Broadway success as a director, as well as the first for the playwrights and the leading actress, Lynn Fontanne.

In 1920 Lindsay married actress Virginia Frölich, whose mother had been wardrobe mistress for the Anglin company. The marriage ended in 1925. Two years later Lindsay began writing plays. In 1927 he married actress Dorothy Stickney. He had no children.

For his first writing partner Lindsay turned to Bertrand Robinson, a former actor who had written short plays and vaudeville sketches. Together they created three modest comedies: *Tommy* (1927), *Your Uncle Dudley* (1929), and *Oh Promise Me* (1930). Lindsay came into his own as a playwright in 1933 with *She Loves Me Not*, a successful farce that was dramatized from a novel by Edward Hope Coffey. "It compels you to laugh yourself blue in the face by the ceaseless invention of its writing," wrote John Mason Brown in the *New York Evening Post* (quoted in Skinner, p. 73).

In 1934 Lindsay began a collaboration with Russel Crouse that was to last twenty-eight years. Producer Vinton Freedly and composer Cole Porter had hired Lindsay to direct a musical for Ethel Merman about a ship that catches fire on its way to Europe. When the book by English authors Guy Bolton and P. G. Wodehouse arrived, Freedly was dismayed at its lack of stage-worthiness and appealed to Lindsay to rewrite it. He declined but reconsidered after a fire aboard a ship returning from Havana caused considerable loss of life, making the script's plot unsuitable for a comedy. Crouse, a former newspaperman working as a press agent for the Theatre Guild, was enlisted to assist. In two weeks the team had written a script titled *Anything Goes*. It ran for 420 performances.

After a play written with Damon Runyon in 1935 was unsuccessful, Lindsay returned to the partnership with Crouse. For length, productivity, and quality, their collaboration is unrivaled in American theater. From 1934 until 1962 they created fourteen scripts, including *Life with Father* (1939), which was based on Clarence Day's autobiographical *New Yorker* articles about his Victorian childhood. It ran for seven years, setting a record for the longest-running nonmusical on Broadway. They also won a Pulitzer Prize in 1946 for the political satire *State of the Union*. Other musicals included two for Ethel Merman, *Red, Hot, and Blue!* by Cole Porter (1936) and *Call Me Madam* by Irving Berlin (1950); and *The Sound of Music* for Mary Martin (1959), with lyrics by Richard Rodgers and music by Oscar Hammerstein.

According to Cornelia Otis Skinner's memoir *Life with Lindsay and Crouse* (1976) the two had solidified their method of working together by 1937. "Before putting a single word to paper . . . they'd meet for several hours a day and talk the project over—the plot, the situations, the characterizations, the opening and closing of each and every scene, just how the play must end. They'd talk for days, for weeks . . . for months. In the case of *Life with Father*, they talked for over two years—just about daily" (p. 167).

When they began writing, Crouse worked at the typewriter and Lindsay walked around the room acting out all the roles. Each suggested, rejected, and refined dialogue until, they claimed, neither could remember which lines were whose. In three or four months, after Lindsay had paced 5,000 miles according to Crouse's calculation, they had a new script.

After establishing his career as a playwright, Lindsay only occasionally acted, taking small roles in his own productions in the event of an emergency. However, when a suitable star could not be found to play Father in *Life with Father* opposite his wife as Mother, he consented to take the part. He played the role for five years. "To a generation of theater-goers," read the *New York Times* at his death, "he simply was Father Day and vice versa" (12 Feb. 1968).

Lindsay and Crouse also produced several plays, including *Arsenic and Old Lace*, which ran from 1941 to 1944, and *Detective Story* in 1949.

Lindsay's gentle wit, generosity, and modesty endeared him to colleagues and friends. In 1955 he was elected to a ten-year term as president of the Players, the club established by Edwin Booth. By tradition, the president was reelected for life, but illness forced Lindsay to retire in 1965. In his honor the dining room was named the Howard Lindsay Room. Expressing his thanks, Lindsay said, "I've had very little experience in being a room."

Lindsay was active in the Dramatists Guild and served as president of the Authors League. With Crouse, Rodgers, Hammerstein, and theatrical lawyer John Wharton, he also formed the New Dramatists Committee in 1940 to help young playwrights learn their craft. He frequently went to Washington, D.C., to testify in favor of legislation to establish the National Endowment for the Arts. A term on the grand jury aroused his interest in reform of the justice system, and he served as vice chair of the Committee for Modern Courts. He died in New York City.

• The Harvard Theatre Collection and the New York Public Library for the Performing Arts have clipping files on Lindsay. The Library of Congress has a sound recording of an interview. His recollections of his childhood are in Martin Levin, ed., *Five Boyhoods* (1962). An obituary is in the *New York Times*, 12 Feb. 1968.

ARNOLD WENGROW

LINDSAY, John (23 Aug. 1894–3 July 1950), jazz string bassist and trombonist, was born in New Orleans, Louisiana. Details of his parents are unknown. His nickname was Johnny, and his surname has often (and probably incorrectly) been spelled Lindsey. As a boy he played string bass with his family; his father played guitar, and his brother Herb, violin. In his teens the three men performed with cornetist Freddie Keppard at the Hanan Saloon in the Storyville district of New Orleans.

Lindsay was a member of songwriter and pianist Clarence William's group in 1916. From 1917 to 1918 he served in the army. On his return he took up trombone, working for a few months at the Lyric Theater with John Robichaux around 1920. In the fall of 1920 he joined violinist Armand J. Piron's orchestra, with which he toured to New York in 1923 and 1924 and recorded "West Indies Blues" (1923). In 1925 he was in trumpeter Dewey Jackson's band on the riverboat *Capitol*, touring between New Orleans and St. Paul, but that same year he settled in Chicago, Illinois, where he recorded "Black Bottom Stomp" and "Grandpa's Spells" as the bassist in Jelly Roll Morton's Red Hot Peppers (1926) and "Boar Hog Blues" as the trombonist in trumpeter Willie Hightower's band (1927).

By this time Lindsay was principally a string bassist. From March 1931 to March 1932 he toured nationally with Louis Armstrong's big band, with which he recorded "When It's Sleepy Time Down South" and "The Lonesome Road" (1931) and appeared in the film short *Rhapsody in Black and Blue* (1932). He later recorded with the Harlem Hamfats (1936–1937), singer Victoria Spivey (1936), reed player Sidney Bechet (1940), clarinetists Johnny Dodds and Jimmie Noone (both 1940), pianist Albert Ammons (1944), trumpeter Punch Miller (1944), and singer Chippie Hill (1946). Late in his career he led his own quartet at the Music Bar and also worked regularly with reed player Darnell Howard and guitarist Bob Tinsley. He died in Chicago.

Lindsay would be nothing more than yet another well-accomplished and little-known professional jazz accompanist were it not for the sessions with Morton. Here the tone of his instrument was tremendously well captured by Victor's studio engineers, in an era of low fidelity recording quality. On these few recordings, Lindsay summarizes the past and future of jazz bass, alternating a ragtime-based two-beat pattern (bass notes sounding on beats one and three of each measure) and an exaggeratedly percussive slapping attack with walking four-beat lines (sounding on each beat of the measure) and a smoothly plucked sound.

• Useful sources on Lindsay are Samuel B. Charters, *Jazz: New Orleans, 1885–1963: An Index to the Negro Musicians of New Orleans*, rev. ed. (1963; repr. 1983); Gunther Schuller, *Early Jazz: Its Roots and Musical Development* (1968); Albert McCarthy, *Big Band Jazz* (1974); and Humphrey Lyttelton, *The Best of Jazz*, vol. 1: *Basin Street to Harlem: Jazz Masters and Masterpieces, 1917–1930* (1978). See also John Chilton, *Who's Who of Jazz: Storyville to Swing Street*, 4th ed. (1985), and Barry Kernfeld, *What to Listen for in Jazz* (1995). Obituaries are in *Down Beat*, 11 Aug. 1950, and *Melody Maker*, 23 Sept. 1950.

BARRY KERNFELD

LINDSAY, Vachel (10 Nov. 1879–5 Dec. 1931), writer, was born Nicholas Vachel Lindsay in Springfield, Illinois, the son of Vachel Thomas Lindsay, a physician, and Esther Catherine Frazee. The Lindsays were devout Campbellites, a church founded in 1830 by the immigrant Scotch-Irish clergyman Alexander Campbell, whose emphasis on individual spiritual life, education, the missionary role of American democracy, and the hope for a nondenominational Christian church had a profound impact upon Lindsay, shaping his career as poet, pamphleteer, and performer.

From 1897 to 1899 Lindsay attended a Campbellite school, Hiram College in Ohio, but he never took a degree. There he kept notebooks and diaries, a practice he had begun when he was seven and continued throughout his life. He headed each diary with "This book belongs to Christ," consecrating himself to a lifelong project of spreading what he called "the gospel of beauty" devoted to the redemption of mankind through art.

In pursuit of this goal, Lindsay attended the Chicago Art Institute from 1901 to 1903. Although he was an undistinguished student, he held to his belief that art starts "with a *vision*, with a beautiful idealization of the thing you see." His drawings are fanciful illustrations of his poems and gospel and are imitative of William Blake and the pre-Raphaelites, but without the skill of either.

Lindsay next attended the New York School of Art (1903–1904). He spent a great deal of time at the Metropolitan Museum of Art, where he repeatedly visited the Egyptian sculptures, which began a lifelong interest in hieroglyphics, from which he drew inspiration for his symbols and theory of beauty. He also tried to publish his poems and illustrations but had little success.

In the summer of 1904 Lindsay experienced his first visions. At night, and again the next day, he saw Old Testament prophets. Afterward, he wrote his first mystical poem, "A Prayer in the Jungles of Heaven," and drew his "Map of the Universe," a source for symbols that appear in many of his poems and which he had reproduced in a slightly different version as the frontispiece to *Collected Poems* (1923). The map depicts Lindsay's moral "universe," with "The Throne of Mountains" standing atop "The Jungles of Heaven." At the bottom, lying by the "River Called Hate," is the tomb containing Lucifer; slightly above "The Gulfs of Silence" is his harp, from which issues "The Flame of Lucifer's Singing," which extends to heaven. Other symbols include "The Palace of Eve," "The Soul of a Butterfly" (Beauty), and a spider (Mammon). Lindsay also had a vision of his ideal bride, whom he called Psyche or Eve or Lady Romance. His tendency to idealize women, combined with his naïveté and his father's stern warnings against sex, may have contributed to his tendency to form one-sided romantic attachments that failed to develop into anything beyond infatuation.

On 23 and 24 March 1905 Lindsay had copies of two poems printed and tried to sell them on the streets of New York. These evenings spent peddling his poetry set the pattern for much of his career as a self-fashioned troubadour or wandering poet. His wandering began in earnest when he set sail for Florida on 3 March 1906 to begin the first of his tramps. Starting from Jacksonville, he walked through Georgia, the Carolinas, Kentucky, and home to Springfield. To pay his way, he gave recitals and lectures and sold copies of his poems. Shortly after his return home in June, he accompanied his family to Europe. On the night of 4 September, as the ship neared New York, he had a vision of Christ singing in Heaven. Between 10 November and Christmas he wrote "I Heard Immanuel Singing," expressing his millennerian vision.

On 21 April 1907 Lindsay left New York and set out on foot to Springfield. In August 1908 he lectured on race at the YMCA after witnessing race riots in Springfield, and in 1909 he lectured on behalf of the Anti-Saloon League. On 19 July 1909 he published at his own expense the first of five *War Bulletins*, which attacked greed, urbanization, and race prejudice. The third contained "The Creed of a Beggar," in which he declared himself a believer "in Christ the Socialist." The fourth, a collection of poems called *The Tramp's Excuses*, was published in September, and the fifth appeared in November.

From 1909 to 1912 Lindsay remained at home writing. In 1910 he published several hundred copies of *The Village Magazine*, consisting largely of editorials, with some poems and newspaper clippings, which brought him his first public notice when it was reviewed by *Current Literature*. Hamlin Garland, then a well-known novelist, ordered a copy and invited Lindsay to Chicago to address his club, the Cliff Dwellers, which he founded for regional writers, artists, and professional men.

On 29 May 1912 Lindsay set out on his most ambitious tramp, planning to walk to Los Angeles, then to Seattle, and back to Springfield, again carrying copies of his work to trade. He abandoned his plan in New Mexico and took a train to Los Angeles, where he spent a month writing "General William Booth Enters into Heaven," a tribute to the founder of the Salvation Army. The poem, which was set to music by Charles Ives in 1914, celebrates, with a vulgar pietism, Booth's militant Christianity in hectic rhythms derived from the hymn "The Blood of the Lamb." In the first part Booth leads a procession of outcasts into heaven where, in the second part, Christ heals them, followed by a chorus of celebration. This poem brought him instant fame when Harriet Monroe published it as the lead piece in the fourth issue of *Poetry* in January 1913. The *Review of Reviews* praised it as "perhaps the most remarkable poem of a decade." In his column for *Harper's*, William Dean Howells called it a "fine brave poem." Monroe was loyal in her devotion to Lindsay, and she was largely responsible for his association with Edgar Lee Masters, Carl Sandburg, and the Chicago renaissance. She saw to it that a $100 prize was given him for "General Booth" after Ezra Pound persuaded her that the first prize be given to William Butler Yeats for "The Grey Rock." Yeats himself praised "General Booth" as a poem "stripped bare of ornament." In the fall of 1913 Mitchell Kennerley published Lindsay's first book, *General William Booth Enters into Heaven and Other Poems.*

Lindsay's second most famous poem, "The Congo," was inspired by a sermon preached in October 1913 that detailed the drowning of a missionary in the Congo River. On 1 March 1914 he recited the poem at the *Poetry* banquet in Chicago, where Yeats and Sandburg were in attendance. Lindsay's recitations were the basis of his fame. He would rock on his feet and pump his arms as he shouted and sang his poems. Lindsay dubbed these compositions "the Higher Vaudeville," poems written in "a sort of ragtime manner that deceives them [his audience] into thinking they are at a vaudeville show." He wanted to bring poetry to the masses via his mix of song and oratory. Although the "Higher Vaudeville" makes up only a small portion of an oeuvre that includes nine books of poetry, five prose works, and numerous short stories and articles, Lindsay is remembered almost entirely for these two compositions and "The Chinese Nightingale," "The Santa Fé Trail" (which includes a blaring chorus of automobile horns), "Bryan, Bryan, Bryan, Bryan," and "The Kallyope Yell." Perhaps Lindsay summed up his career best when he wrote, "By that very act [the Higher Vaudeville] I persuaded the tired businessman to listen at last. But lo, my tiny reputation as a writer seemed wiped out by my new reputation as an entertainer." This remark reveals Lindsay's didactic aims as well as his appeal to middle-class men and women at a time when people in every American city formed business and women's clubs and arranged luncheons for the purpose of attaining culture. For the remainder of his life Lindsay struggled with the demand for his performances, his pleasure in giving them, and his knowledge that they took time away from his work. But the lure of the enthusiastic crowds and the never-ending need for money demanded that he maintain a life on the road.

In February 1914 Lindsay met Sara Teasdale in St. Louis following a period of correspondence. Together they traveled to New York, where he met William Rose Benét, Stephen Vincent Benét, Joyce Kilmer, Floyd Dell, Witter Bynner, Louis Untermeyer, Theodore Dreiser, and Upton Sinclair. In September Macmillan published Lindsay's second book, *The Congo and Other Poems.* The same month Kennerley published *Adventures While Preaching the Gospel of Beauty,* a prose account of Lindsay's tramps. In November 1914, while in Springfield, he read of Teasdale's engagement to a shoe manufacturer whom she married in December. He wrote to Harriet Moody that Teasdale was "the most intimate friend I had had for years and the best understander," and the news of her marriage left him feeling "baffled" and "rather empty and puzzled."

In February 1915 Lindsay recited before Woodrow Wilson's cabinet. He received the Levinson prize for "The Chinese Nightingale," published by *Poetry* in

November 1915. At this time also, upon the recommendation of Macmillan, he dropped "Nicholas" from his name. In the same year Lindsay received invitations to meet Jane Addams, Henry Ford, and D. W. Griffith. *The Art of the Moving Picture* (1915), Lindsay's classification and judgment of films, is notable for recognizing film's potential not only as an art, but as a medium for propaganda and cultural formation; the book closes with a prediction of an American millennium ushered in by movies.

Lindsay undertook extensive tours of the United States from 1916 through 1918, the year his father died. In January 1920 he published *The Golden Whales of California and Other Rhymes in the American Language,* which includes several poems inspired by Alexander Campbell. Now at the height of his fame, Lindsay undertook a tour of England, reading at Oxford, where he met Robert Bridges and Robert Graves, and at Cambridge and in London. He was well received and praised by *The Observer* (London) as "easily the most important living American poet." However, Lindsay's reputation began a precipitous decline with the publication of his utopian prose work, *The Golden Book of Springfield* (1920). The book opens in 1920 with a gathering of the "Prognosticators' Club," which consists, among others, of a Campbellite minister, a Jewish boy, a black woman, and a skeptic, who offer a vision of Springfield in 2018 in prose derived from such varied sources as the Bible, Swedenborg, and Marx. Although Lindsay continued to receive praise from English critics, American critics and readers dismissed him as tedious and incomprehensible. Opinion since has not changed.

Despite his desire to quit touring, Lindsay's financial difficulties required that he continue to earn money by giving recitals. His popularity with audiences did not abate despite the bad reviews. In 1921 he received an honorary degree from Mills College in Oakland, California, and delivered the Phi Beta Kappa poem at the Harvard commencement in 1922, the year of his mother's death. In January 1923, while in Mississippi for a recital at Gulf Park Junior College for Girls, he collapsed and was forced to cancel the remainder of his tour. He stayed in Gulf Park to teach contemporary poetry until July 1924. While there he began to suffer delusions of persecution that continued until his death.

In June 1924 Lindsay went to the Mayo Foundation in Rochester, Minnesota, where he was diagnosed as epileptic. In July 1924 he moved to Spokane, Washington, where he met Elizabeth Conner, a 23-year-old high school teacher. They married in 1925 and had two children. Suffering from paranoid delusions and spurred by resentment toward his audiences, Lindsay was given to sudden outbursts of rage at public functions, but his deteriorating financial situation forced him to go on tour in 1926.

A long tour, from October 1928 through March 1929, erased his debts but left him penniless. His financial burden was alleviated by a $500 prize awarded by *Poetry* in recognition of his life's work, but his reputation continued its decline. His family life also declined; he had delusions of persecution and unfounded suspicions of his wife's infidelity. Continuous money-raising tours were interrupted by brief visits at home. In 1930 he was made Doctor Honoris Causa by Hiram College, but his mental health continued to decline, and he threatened his wife and children with violence. On 5 December 1931 he committed suicide at home by drinking Lysol. His doctor decided that Lindsay's death should be reported as heart failure, and it was announced as such in the Springfield paper.

• Drafts and proofs of published and unpublished works, along with juvenilia, scrapbooks, letters, and personal possessions, are in the Vachel Lindsay Collection, Clifton Waller Barrett Library, University of Virginia. Major collections of his correspondence are in the Harriet Monroe Collection and the Harriet Moody Collection, University of Chicago; at Hiram College; and at the Vachel Lindsay Home in Springfield. The Teasdale-Lindsay correspondence is at the Beinecke Rare Book and Manuscript Library, Yale University. The best edition of his correspondence, which includes a useful chronology of his life, is *Letters of Vachel Lindsay*, ed. Marc Chénetier (1979). The *Collected Poems* (1923; rev. ed., 1925) has been superseded by *The Poetry of Vachel Lindsay*, ed. Dennis Camp (1984), a two-volume edition of his complete poetry and his accompanying drawings, along with a third volume of notes, Lindsay's prefaces, letters pertaining to his poetry, and a title index. Camp also edited the first of a two-volume edition of Lindsay's published prose along with drawings, *The Prose of Vachel Lindsay* (1988).

Important works by Lindsay not mentioned in the text are *The Chinese Nightingale and Other Poems* (1917); *The Daniel Jazz and Other Poems* (1920); *The Candle in the Cabin: A Weaving Together of Script and Singing* (1926); *Going-to-the-Stars* (1926); *Johnny Appleseed* (1928); *Every Soul Is a Circus* (1929); *Seleted Poems*, ed. Hazelton Spencer (1931), and ed. Mark Harris (1963); and *The Litany of Washington Street* (1929).

The first full-length biography, *Vachel Lindsay, a Poet in America* (1935), written by Edgar Lee Masters at the family's request, has been superseded by Mark Harris, *The City of Discontent: An Interpretative Biography of Vachel Lindsay* (1952), and Eleanor Ruggles, *The West-going Heart: A Life of Vachel Lindsay* (1959). Two more recent efforts to resuscitate Lindsay's literary reputation are Balz Engler, *Poetry and Community* (1990), and Ann Massa, *Vachel Lindsay: Fieldworker for the American Dream* (1970). Massa's is the best scholarly work on Lindsay, one that attempts to revise his reputation by presenting him as an eclectic but insightful writer on art and society. It also contains a useful bibliography of primary and secondary material.

JOSEPH G. KRONICK

LINDSEY, Ben B. (25 Nov. 1869–26 Mar. 1943), reformer and controversial Denver juvenile court founder, was born Benjamin Barr Lindsey in Jackson, Tennessee, the son of Landy Tunstall Lindsey, a former Confederate captain, and Letitia Barr, whose father owned a large plantation in Jackson. Lindsey's childhood on the Barr family plantation was carefree, marred only by his father's restlessness. A "rather moody and erratic character" (Larsen, p. 10), the elder Lindsey shocked the Barrs by converting his family from Episcopalianism to Catholicism when Ben was

five. Increased tension on the Barr plantation caused Ben's father to pursue a livelihood away from Jackson, as a telegrapher with the Denver and South Park Railroad. Ben was eleven when he and his brother joined his parents in Denver in 1880.

Religion influenced Lindsey's education and was a persistent element of his adult life. When he was twelve his parents sent him to board at a Catholic elementary school at Notre Dame University, where he excelled at debate. But after two years Lindsey's father lost his job, and the ensuing financial stress dictated that Lindsey leave the school and return to Tennessee to live again with his grandfather Barr, who assisted him through three years of college prep at Southwestern Baptist University. Ben eventually abandoned Catholicism, yet his later writings and public talks contained overt religious references.

In 1886 Lindsey went back to Denver and found that his family's financial difficulties had worsened. The next year, eighteen-year-old Lindsey was shattered by his father's suicide, which burdened him with the role of provider. He held numerous jobs simultaneously, one as a lawyer's aide. Lindsey's rising ambition to study law, even while trying to support his impoverished family, left him exhausted; one year later he also attempted suicide. The gun's failure to discharge, he subsequently remarked, prompted a vow "to crush the circumstances that had almost crushed me." Conquering his depression and profound self-doubt, Lindsey advanced in his legal studies and won admission to the Colorado bar in 1894. In 1896 he formed a partnership in Denver with F. W. Parks, who soon thereafter became a state legislator. Their brief partnership included a notable case in which Lindsey was the first to successfully argue for X-rays to be considered admissible court evidence.

Lindsey's legal career followed his passions for politics and social justice, which were also reflections of the rising social consciousness of the Progressive Era. He urged many reforms on turn-of-the-century Denver, a city whose political machinery and corruption "were among the worst in the nation" (DeLorme, p. 15). His energetic involvement in the Democratic party resulted in two appointments: one in 1899 as public guardian and administrator and another in 1901 to fill a vacated county judgeship in Arapahoe (now Denver) County. Lindsey was greatly disturbed by the troubled juveniles he encountered in court and believed that the legal system treated them unfairly.

Lindsey sought to establish a separate legal institution for juveniles, one he envisioned would protect, correct, and "save" young offenders, not punish them. This was the original premise behind the juvenile court. As county judge, asking the district attorney to refer all complaints involving children to his court, he organized a juvenile court on the basis of a school law that allowed the state to correct minors in its power as *parens patriae*. Lindsey's informal juvenile court predated that prescribed by the Illinois juvenile court act of 1899. And while other states had developed procedures such as probation and separate courtrooms for minors, Lindsey's dramatic flair, outspokenness, and obvious commitment to "saving" juvenile delinquents gave the Colorado court, officially established in 1907, worldwide recognition. He presided over the Denver juvenile court until 1927, when political controversies began to overshadow his work.

Lindsey's success in the juvenile court generated support for legislation known collectively as the Lindsey Bills, the most prominent being the Adult Delinquency Act of 1903, which introduced the idea that adults could be held legally accountable for contributing to the delinquency of a minor. His skillful use of the media energized the juvenile court movement; he tapped into radio and films and grandstanded in court, knowing that Denver's highly competitive newspapers would report it. His fame spread as accounts of his work appeared in national publications, including *McClure's*, *Redbook*, and *Charities*, and nearby states began to implement his ideas. He wrote many articles about his court, and in 1910 he published *The Beast*, which detailed his fight against corruption. Lindsey also spoke to admiring audiences nationwide, urging other states to adopt a juvenile court system.

Although his popularity did not carry a 1906 gubernatorial bid, Lindsey successfully ran for reelection to his judgeship as an independent in 1908. His growing public stature fueled larger political aspirations, though not without consequences. By 1912 he was a leading figure in the Progressive party and an active supporter and friend of Theodore Roosevelt. But Lindsey incurred criticism when he, accompanied by Henrietta Brevoort (whom he married in 1913 and with whom he later adopted a child), participated in Henry Ford's "Peace Party" mission to Europe in 1915. By the mid-1920s Lindsey's public career had included advocating controversial issues such as birth control, woman suffrage, and even "trial marriages," which he also wrote about in *The Revolt of Modern Youth* (1925) and *The Companionate Marriage* (1927). Lindsey clashed with the conservative Ku Klux Klan, a brief but significant political influence in Colorado, and was forced from his court in 1927. Having accepted payment for advice given in a New York case while still a judge, Lindsey gave his political foes superficial grounds for his disbarment in 1929.

Lindsey continued working for children after moving to Los Angeles in 1930, serving there as county judge, proposing children's laws, and founding the Children's Court of Conciliation in 1939. In 1935 Colorado's Supreme Court had acknowledged impropriety and reinstated Lindsey to the bar, but he remained in Los Angeles until his death there. Lindsey's effectiveness is apparent in the longevity of the institution he founded and the laws he wrote.

• Lindsey's voluminous papers and manuscripts are housed at the Library of Congress; some have been copied and stored at the University of California, Los Angeles. Period sources, such as Denver newspapers and some of the many articles he wrote, including "Some Experiences in the Juvenile Court of Denver," *Charities*, 7 Nov. 1903, pp. 403–13, reveal Lind-

sey's colorful character. Fundamental to understanding the early juvenile court is his *The Problem of the Children* (1904) and the autobiographic *The Dangerous Life* (1931). To date, Charles Larsen has written the only biography, *The Good Fight: The Life and Times of Ben B. Lindsey* (1972), but it does not capture the significance of Lindsey's contributions to law. Francis A. Huber, "The Progressive Career of Ben B. Lindsey, 1900–1920" (Ph.D. diss., Univ. of Michigan, 1963), provides more analysis of Lindsey's career. Lindsey should be depicted in the context of his time, and studies such as Lyle W. Dorsett's *The Queen City: A History of Denver* (1977), Roland DeLorme's "Turn-of-the-century Denver," *Colorado Magazine*, 45 (1968): pp. 1–15, and George Creel's autobiography, *Rebel At Large* (1947) are helpful though not always flattering. Sanford Withers's article "The Story of the First Roentgen Evidence," *Radiology*, July 1931, pp. 99–103, describes Lindsey's central role in the first use of the X-ray as evidence in court. The highlights of his life are described in his obituary in the *New York Times*, 27 Mar. 1943.

GINETTE T. ALEY

LINDSLEY, Philip (21 Dec. 1786–25 May 1855), university president, was born near Morristown, New Jersey, the son of Isaac Lindsley and Phebe Condict. He was educated in Presbyterian institutions, studying in Rev. Robert Finley's academy and the College of New Jersey (now Princeton University). After graduation in 1804 he taught school in the Morristown area for several years. In 1807 he returned to Princeton to work as a tutor while studying theology under the college's liberal Presbyterian president, Samuel Stanhope Smith. Licensed by the Presbytery of New Brunswick in 1810, he then preached for two years at several sites along the eastern seaboard.

In 1812 Lindsley returned permanently to higher education when he was appointed a senior tutor at Princeton. The next year he married Margaret Elizabeth Lawrence; they had five children. During his twelve years at Princeton, he quickly gained new responsibilities, serving as professor of languages, secretary of the board of trustees, librarian, vice president, and acting president. Despite this success, he had an ambivalent relationship with Princeton's trustees. Smith, Lindsley's mentor at Princeton, had followed the lead of his eminent predecessor, John Witherspoon, in broadening the curriculum and giving students more autonomy. Several student riots and resurgent piety in Presbyterianism brought Smith's downfall. Lindsley remained at Princeton after Smith's forced retirement but was discomforted by the change. Although Princeton Theological Seminary was separated from the college after one of the riots to protect the theologians' piety, the governing bodies of the two institutions cooperated to restore a more traditional curriculum and student piety. Uncomfortable with these changes, Lindsley alienated some of the trustees, and although the board elected him president, it did not offer him the enthusiastic support he wanted.

Declining the presidency of Princeton and of three other colleges, Lindsley agreed in 1824 to move to Nashville to lead the struggling Cumberland College, about to be renamed the University of Nashville. He spent the next quarter-century trying to turn it into an educational leader. At the time of his inaugural, the university was the only institution of higher education within two hundred miles of Nashville, yet support was difficult to find. Lindsley's commitment to creating a nondenominational institution precluded appeals for sectarian funds, and the Tennessee legislature was unenthusiastic. The founding of over twenty-five colleges in the Nashville region during Lindsley's presidency was testimony to his efforts to promote higher education, but the colleges quickly became rivals for funding and students. Most were denominational colleges that considered Nashville's nondenominationalism to be pernicious and worked to thwart Lindsley's hopes for state aid.

Lindsley had great ambitions for the University of Nashville, often citing Thomas Jefferson and his plans for the University of Virginia as a model. He wanted to create an institution where independent-minded students could study at an advanced level. His vision attracted some talented faculty but relatively few students. Although antebellum Nashville was a boom town, Lindsley could not garner sufficient civic support to implement his vision of a university. Despite the disappointment, he declined six other presidencies and the provostship of the University of Pennsylvania to remain at Nashville. During his tenure Nashville offered inspiration to a few, but Lindsley left behind a struggling institution, pieces of which were later absorbed by Vanderbilt University, the University of Tennessee, and George Peabody College for Teachers.

Although his institution building was relatively unsuccessful, Lindsley became a leading national spokesman for educational reform through his widely distributed baccalaureate and commencement addresses. Despite being an ordained minister who continued to be very involved in Presbyterian affairs, he vehemently criticized denominational colleges. In his 1829 baccalaureate he railed against the "barefaced impudence" of sectarian colleges that claimed to provide liberal education to the public when they included "partisans and bigots" who "are not fit to be the instructors of youth." He considered the quasi-public role of denominational colleges to be hypocritical. For him truly liberal institutions should be Christian only in the broadest sense; religion should be promoted by churches and theological seminaries, not by colleges.

Lindsley also rejected the assumption that colleges should act in loco parentis. He felt parents should "never look to a college for any miraculous moral regeneration or transformation of character." He wanted Nashville students to have the type of social and intellectual freedom offered by German universities, leaving students' moral development to other institutions. He also rejected the common Protestant prejudice that rural sites offered a morally superior atmosphere for colleges, charging that students in small town or rural colleges were "more boorish and savage in their manners, and more dissolute and licentious in their habits."

Lindsley promoted a meritocratic educational system as an antidote to Eastern elitism as well as to denominationalism. He declared in his 1825 inaugural that "the farmer, the mechanic, the manufacturer, the merchant, the sailor, the soldier . . . must be educated" and that anyone "who wishes to rise above the level of a mere labourer at task-work, ought to endeavour to obtain a liberal education." As his educational ideas failed to attract a large following, he became increasingly cynical, citing the biblical quotation, "Though the ass may make a pilgrimage to Mecca, yet an ass he will come back," in his 1848 commencement. In the same speech he also complained that "nearly all the preachers, teachers, editors, demagogues, and other friends of the people, are hostile to us and to Nashville."

Lindsley's first wife died in 1845, and in 1849 he married Mary Ann Silliman Ayers. The next year he resigned his position at Nashville to become a professor at New Albany (Indiana) Theological Seminary, retiring in 1853. He died in Nashville while attending the Presbyterian General Assembly.

A leading spokesman for reform in higher education in the 1820s and 1830s, Lindsley was a brilliant educator and intellect whose brand of educational reform did not find its audience. He upset traditionalists by rejecting denominationalism in collegiate life, and his high intellectual standards were alien in the heartland of Jacksonianism. The ideas of Lindsley and like-minded reformers of his generation, such as George Ticknor, James Marsh, and Jacob Abbott, became popular in the wave of university founding after the Civil War. However, in Lindsley's lifetime neither the intellectual nor economic conditions existed that could underwrite his vision.

• There is no full collection of Lindsley papers, but a small sampling is in the Princeton University Archives. Leroy J. Halsey published *A Memoir of Philip Lindsley* (1859) and edited *The Works of Philip Lindsley* (3 vols., 1866). Lindsley's writings are most easily sampled in Richard Hofstadter and Wilson Smith, eds., *American Higher Education: A Documentary History*, vol. 1 (1961), which includes four excerpts from his commencement and baccalaureate addresses. Frederick Rudolph, *The American College and University* (1962), locates Lindsley within the educational reform movement of the 1820s and 1830s. Thomas Wertenbaker, *Princeton 1746–1896* (1946), provides a laudatory view of his career at Princeton. Howard Miller, *The Revolutionary College: American Presbyterian Higher Education, 1707–1837* (1976), places his views of denominational colleges within the Presbyterian context. See also John E. Pomfret, "Philip Lindsley: Pioneer Educator in the Old Southwest," in *The Lives of Eighteen from Princeton*, ed. Willard Thorp (1946).

W. BRUCE LESLIE

LINDSTROM, Freddy (21 Nov. 1905–4 Oct. 1981), baseball player, manager, announcer, and coach, was born Frederick Anthony Lindstrom in Chicago, Illinois, the son of Frederick Lindstrom, a plumbing contractor, and Mary Sweeney. (His middle name was changed to Charles later on.) At Tilden High School and then at Loyola Academy, Lindstrom starred as an infielder and batter. In 1922 John McGraw, manager of the New York Giants, signed him to a professional contract and placed him with the Toledo club of the American Association.

Lindstrom spent the last part of 1922 and all of the 1923 season at Toledo. Although he batted creditably against strong minor-league pitching, he also led American Association third basemen in errors. McGraw nonetheless kept him on the Giants' roster for 1924. After getting into fifty-two games, mostly as a late-inning replacement, the eighteen year old started the opening game of the World Series because Henry "Heinie" Groh, the Giants' regular third baseman, was disabled. The youngest person ever to appear in the Series, Lindstrom played every game, made ten hits, and fielded errorlessly, yet he would always be remembered for what happened in the twelfth inning of game seven, at Washington, when a ground ball took a "bad hop" over his head and sent home the run that lost the Series for the Giants.

The tenth and last World Series for McGraw, the 1924 classic was really the beginning of a fine thirteen-year career for Lindstrom. Quick-witted and personable, the hustling youngster became a favorite of McGraw's and one of the few who got away with talking back to the "Little Napoleon." Besides making himself into one of the best major league infielders, Lindstrom was a consistently effective hitter during his Giants' career. On average, in five consecutive full seasons (1926–1930), he batted .334 and drove in close to 90 runs while scoring more than 104 runs per year. He enjoyed his best season in 1930, when he batted .379, made 231 hits (22 home runs), drove in 106 runs, and scored 127.

In June 1932, when McGraw resigned after thirty years as Giants' manager, he bitterly disappointed Lindstrom by naming first baseman Bill Terry to succeed him. When Lindstrom asked to be traded, Terry reluctantly obliged by arranging a three-way deal with the Pittsburgh Pirates and Philadelphia Phillies. Lindstrom ended up at Pittsburgh, where he played the outfield full time, putting in a solid 1933 season but missing much of 1934 because of injuries. Traded to the Chicago Cubs, Lindstrom appeared in ninety games in 1935; dividing his time between third and the outfield, he contributed key hits to the Cubs' late-season pennant drive and played in four of six World Series games (a Series the Cubs lost to the Detroit Tigers). That autumn, however, the Cubs unconditionally released him. Signed as a free agent by the Brooklyn Dodgers, Lindstrom played the outfield for twenty-six games and then retired at age thirty.

After two years of doing a radio sports program in Chicago (1937–1938), he managed in the minor leagues at Knoxville (Southern Association) in 1940–1941 and Fort Smith (Western Association) in 1942. He returned to the Chicago area for a four-year stint as baseball coach at Northwestern University, after which he served a total of seventeen years as postmas-

ter at Evanston, Illinois. After retiring from the U.S. Post Office in 1972, he resettled at New Port Richey, Florida, with his wife, the former Irene Kiedaisch, whom he had married in Chicago in 1928. They had three sons, of whom Charles, the youngest, reached the major leagues with the Chicago White Sox in 1958—for only one game and one at bat. (He got a hit—a triple.)

In the summer of 1976 Lindstrom made his last two public appearances—at an Oldtimers' Game at Shea Stadium in New York and at the induction ceremonies of the National Baseball Hall of Fame at Cooperstown. Lindstrom was chosen early in 1976 by the Hall of Fame Veterans Committee. He died in Chicago.

• For Lindstrom's full professional playing record, see Craig Carter, ed., *Daguerreotypes*, 8th ed. (1990), p. 164. For Lindstrom's time with the New York Giants, see Charles C. Alexander, *John McGraw* (1988), and Frank Graham, *McGraw of the Giants* (1944). Obituaries are in the *Sporting News*, 24 Oct. 1981, and the *New York Times*, 6 Oct. 1981.

CHARLES C. ALEXANDER

LINEN, James Alexander, III (20 June 1912–1 Feb. 1988), magazine publishing executive, was born in Waverly, Pennsylvania, the son of James Alexander Linen, Jr., and Genevieve Tuthill. He was educated at the Hotchkiss School (class of 1930). In 1934 he graduated from Williams College (A.B.) and married Sara Scranton; they had six children.

Linen's first job out of college came courtesy of family ties: his grandfather had helped to underwrite the fieldwork of Henry Robinson Luce's parents at Tengchow Missionary College in China. Luce gave Linen a job in New York City selling advertising for *Life* magazine. In 1937 he was transferred to Detroit, Michigan, where he outsold his predecessors and earned Luce's written applause. In 1938 he was promoted to advertising manager for *Life* and relocated to New York.

During World War II Linen served in the eastern Mediterranean as a specialist in psychological warfare at the Office of War Information. There he applied his keen knowledge of Byzantine culture and civilization, first acquired at Williams. Linen assumed he would return to *Life* after the war, but, instead, he was promoted in 1945 to publisher of *Time* magazine, a position he held for fifteen years. He immediately moved the publisher's desk away from the editorial floor.

Because of recent reorganization at the magazine, Linen assumed more responsibility than had his predecessors. Luce had convened the people in charge of the company's three publications—*Time*, *Life*, and *Fortune*—to entertain ideas to improve corporate structure. The veterans recommended centralizing the organization. Vertical management extended more authority to the publisher and clarified the relationship between publisher and managing editor.

Linen delegated responsibility well. He gathered a strong force of business managers from a roster of experienced comrades. He hired alumni of Williams College as general manager and circulation director

(Frederick S. Gilbert and Bernhard M. Auer, respectively). James A. Thomason, his business manager, had worked with Linen during the war. Linen chose John McLatchie as advertising director based on his sales experience.

Linen expanded *Time*, the flagship publication of Time Inc. The first color pages in an editorial section appeared the first year Linen was publisher, and by his last year an issue often included eight four-color editorial pages. He tripled the magazine's annual revenue from $4 million to $50 million. In 1960 marketers bought more than $50 million in advertising. In the early 1960s the Washington staff numbered seventeen with eleven bureaus; 113 "stringers" reported from across the nation. In the middle of Linen's run as publisher, the magazine employed seventeen people just to process letters to the editor.

In 1946 circulation rose above 1.5 million subscribers, and by 1950 *Time*'s circulation was twice that of *Newsweek*, its rival. In 1960, Linen's last year as publisher, the circulation of *Time*'s five international editions totaled 621,000. Despite the low number, Linen believed the international editions should continue; in his column for 27 May 1951, he wrote that readers of the Latin American edition proved they wanted news over propaganda.

Numbers were important to Linen because *Time* was important to Time Inc. Equally important, however, was maintaining a reputation for accuracy. Linen admitted in his weekly "Letter from the Publisher" that the magazine made errors, but he assured readers that corrections were recorded in a black book. With Linen as publisher and Andrew Heiskell as chair of Time Inc., the company moved into textbook publishing and film production.

Linen believed that his role as publisher necessitated that he visibly interact with the public. By being active in public service, Linen put a face on *Time*, especially in the business community. He worked with the United Community Funds and Councils of America (president, 1956–1958) and with the United States Council of the International Chamber of Commerce. He also volunteered with the American National Red Cross, worked with the Boys' Clubs of America, and served as president of the Urban League. He served on school boards, including the boards of Hotchkiss and Williams, Rockefeller University, and Athens College in Greece, and he chaired the board of trustees at Adelphi College.

Linen manifested his belief in worldwide communications by supporting international groups. He was vice chair of the Iran–United States Business Council, a member of the Emergency Committee for American Trade, and a trustee of the Asian Institute of Technology. He maintained his special interest in relations between the United States and Japan by serving as a member of the advisory councils for Japan–United States economic relations, the Japan Foundation, and the United States–Japan Conference on Cultural and Educational Exchange.

Redefining the role of publisher had begun to occur at *Time* when Linen became its publisher; the simultaneous redefining of the roles of senior executives eventually resulted in Linen's promotion to president of Time Inc. in 1960. Roy E. Larsen, who preceded Linen as president, was instrumental in encouraging Luce to promote Linen in order to exploit Linen's age and experience and, incidentally, to open the publisher's position to younger candidates. Larsen was also concerned that the company would lose Linen to politics: Sara Scranton Linen's family was energetic in Pennsylvania politics, and a cadre in Connecticut had talked to Linen about running for governor.

Linen became president of Time Inc. in the same year the parent company moved into the Time and Life Building at Rockefeller Center in New York City. Time Inc.'s net income was $9.3 million for 1960; by 1966 net income had grown to $37.2 million. Time Inc.'s total assets in 1960 were $230.6 million. In the first four years under Linen, net revenues rose from $287 million to $412.5 million, and net income increased from $9.3 million to $26.5 million. As president, Linen doubled the company's revenues to $600 million annually.

After suffering a stroke in 1969, Linen resigned as president but remained chair of Time Inc.'s executive committee. Mobilized by a wheelchair, he invested his considerable energy into being a consultant. He traveled all over the world, exploiting the contacts he had made with Time Inc. He concentrated on convening economic meetings among developers and heads of business and government with the goal of improving the finances of the nations he visited.

In semiretirement Linen continued to collect toy soldiers. Among the thousands he had acquired was reputedly the largest collection of toy soldiers from the era of Napoleon Bonaparte. Linen retired from Time Inc. in 1973. He died at the Greenwich (Conn.) Hospital, on whose board he had served, and is buried in Scranton, Pennsylvania.

• Biographical information about Linen can be found interwoven in histories of Time Inc., such as Robert T. Elson, *The World of Time Inc.: The Intimate History of a Publishing Enterprise, 1941–1960* (1973). Frank Luther Mott, *A History of American Magazines*, vol. 5 (1968), includes a chapter on *Time*. An obituary appears in the *New York Times*, 2 Feb. 1988, and in *Advertising Age*, 8 Feb. 1988.

MARTHA K. BAKER

LINFORTH, Ivan Mortimer (15 Sept. 1879–15 Dec. 1976), classical scholar, was born in San Francisco, California, the son of Edward William Linforth, a hardware dealer, and Emma Amanda French. His interest in antiquity appears to have been sparked by his maternal uncle, Heber Scollay Lyon, one of his teachers at Trinity School in San Francisco, which Linforth entered about 1890. There Lyon introduced him to the study of Latin. After graduating in 1894 from Trinity

School, he entered in 1895 the University of California at Berkeley, where he remained for all but a few years of his career.

While a Berkeley undergraduate, Linforth was influenced most profoundly by classics professor Isaac Flagg, with whom he first took a course in 1896 (in Homer), having already taught himself Greek. Flagg was presumably responsible for directing Linforth's later attention toward Greek rather than Latin. After 1905, when Linforth came to teach Greek himself, he adopted Flagg's characteristic insistence on the importance of correct phrasing and emphasis in reading. As a student, however, Linforth continued to focus on Latin. After receiving an A.B. in 1900, he went on to earn an M.A. in Latin in 1901. His thesis for this degree, "Adverb *iam* with Special Attention to the Usage of Lucretius," classified the various uses of this Latin word in the works of the Roman poet. After a somewhat unpleasant year at Harvard University (1902–1903), Linforth earned his Ph.D. at Berkeley in 1905. His Ph.D. thesis, "Semasiological Studies in Virgil," was similar to his M.A. thesis, devoted to the study of meanings of words in a Latin poet. Latin poetry also gave him his first publication ("Notes on the Pseudo-Virgilian *Ciris*," *American Philology Journal* 27 [1906]). After this, however, he ceased to work in the areas of Latin poetry or semantic studies.

In 1905 Linforth joined the faculty at Berkeley as an instructor in Greek. The next year he married Katherine Frances Storie; they had four children. In 1910 he became assistant professor of Greek and in 1916 was promoted to associate professor. In 1919, the same year that he published *Solon the Athenian*, he became full professor. Linforth's new work was favorably reviewed and established his reputation in his field. It opens with a study of the life of the sixth-century Greek statesman, which in its painstaking and judicious approach to the scant and problematic evidence for the subject's career, is typical of Linforth's scholarship. The second section is an edition of the surviving fragments of Solon's poetry, with translations and expert exegetical notes. Linforth's most important publications in the next decade were three papers on Herodotus.

In 1919–1920 Linforth was instrumental in instituting Berkeley's famous annual Sather Lectures in classics. He served as president of the Philological Association of the Pacific Coast for 1925–1926 and as president of the American Philological Association for 1932. In 1933 he was elected fellow of the American Academy of Arts and Letters. In 1934–1935 he was annual professor at the American School of Classical Studies at Athens.

Around 1930 Linforth began research on the topic of Orphism, which culminated in *The Arts of Orpheus* (1941), his most important work. The prevailing view at the time was that there had been among the ancient Greeks a religious movement associated with the mythical figure of Orpheus (hence "Orphism"). This religion was believed to have espoused coherent practices and doctrines and to have based these on particular religious texts, which, if true, would have made the movement highly unusual in the Greek world. Such an Orphic religion would have, according to Linforth's introduction, "set up a magnetic field which would profoundly affect the whole movement of thought" (p. ix). Lack of agreement as to the exact content or nature of Orphism led some scholars to doubt its existence as a distinct cult. *The Arts of Orpheus* was the most rigorous statement of this skeptical position. After thoroughly scrutinizing the surviving "Orphic" fragments and testimonies, Linforth concluded, first, that there had been no single Orphic entity in the ancient world, as had been supposed, but that, instead, Orpheus was the mythical founder of "teletai" (rites) in general and that religious practitioners known as "Orpheotelestai" had dispensed certain teletai to their customers. Finally, he deduced that there had been poems in circulation that were believed by the Greeks to have been composed by Orpheus. Although not everyone accepted Linforth's arguments, their effect on scholarly opinion can be gauged by classicist E. R. Dodds's statement that "the edifice reared by an ingenious scholarship" (i.e., the earlier view of Orphism) was "a house of dreams" (*The Greeks and the Irrational* [1951], p. 148).

In 1940 Linforth was chosen as annual faculty research lecturer at Berkeley. His most important works of that decade, "Soul and Sieve in Plato's Gorgias," "The Corybantic Rites in Plato," and "Telestic Madness in Plato," were all published in the *University of California Publications in Classical Philology* and were all particularly concerned with religious topics that related to Linforth's study of Orphism.

Linforth was an effective teacher—especially of Greek—whose students included the future Homerist Milman Parry. Linforth also took an active part in administration, chairing his department on three occasions (1924–1934, 1936–1939, 1948–1949). After retiring in 1949, he spent the following year as a member of the Institute for Advanced Study at Princeton. He continued to work during his retirement, publishing six papers on Sophocles in the *University of California Publications in Classical Philology* between 1951 and 1963. In 1968 he received Berkeley's University Citation. When the *Centennial Record* was published in 1967 to commemorate the hundredth anniversary (1968) of the founding of the University of California, Linforth was cited as one of the "distinguished faculty members." Although he lived for almost a century, he retained his mental vigor even in his later years. At Linforth's death in Berkeley, his record was one of the most distinguished possessed by any American Hellenist of the twentieth century, especially in the field of Greek religion. His publications in this area and in early Greek poetry and prose have permanently affected subsequent work in these fields.

• The fullest source for Linforth's life is Joseph Fontenrose's obituary in the *Classical Journal* 73 (1977–1978): 50–55, with a supplement in the *Classical Journal* 74 (1978–1979): 154. Together these give a full bibliography of Linforth's published works. A more up-to-date treatment is in the same author's *Classics at Berkeley: The First Century 1869–1970* (1982), which is also important for understanding Linforth's career in the context of Berkeley classics as a whole. Another obituary is in the *San Francisco Chronicle*, 17 Dec. 1976.

GAVIN WEAIRE

LINGELBACH, Anna Lane (10 Oct. 1873–14 July 1954), educator, historian, and civic leader, was born in Shelbyville, Illinois, the daughter of Oscar F. Lane, a farmer and minister of the Disciples of Christ, and Mary F. Wendling. Following her early education in private schools, she enrolled at Indiana University in Bloomington against strenuous objection from her father, who, like many of his era, felt higher education inappropriate for a woman. This early expression of Anna's force of character foreshadowed a life exhibiting similar determination and courage in a career of rich and diverse dimensions.

Lingelbach was graduated from Indiana University in 1895 and received an M.A. in history the following year. From 1896 to 1898 she studied history at the University of Chicago, where she met William Ezra Lingelbach. They married in Philadelphia in 1902, at which time her husband was professor of European history at the University of Pennsylvania. After giving birth to three children, Lingelbach resumed her studies at the Sorbonne in Paris during 1910–1911 and later at the University of Pennsylvania, where she received her Ph.D. in history in 1916. Her dissertation was entitled "Application of the British Navigation Acts to Intercourse with America, 1783–1815." In 1918–1919 Lingelbach accepted a one-year teaching appointment at Bryn Mawr College. In 1922 she was appointed professor of history at Temple University, where she remained until she retired in 1952.

Before obtaining her teaching position at Temple University, Lingelbach was appointed to the Philadelphia Board of Education in 1920, by which time she was becoming well known for her work in local civic affairs. She served as a member of the board until 1950 and as vice president from 1938 to 1948. As the first and only woman to serve in this capacity, she brought a strong and effective feminist consciousness to her responsibilities. Over the years she fought for, and eventually secured, equal pay for women teachers and for a single-salary schedule for the elementary and secondary levels. During the Great Depression she insisted that the salaries of school executives be cut before those of teachers. She also succeeded in changing the board's policies against hiring women who were married or who had children. As her own career testified, not only did she support the principle of women having careers outside the home, she argued effectively that "women lawyers and doctors are not restricted to celibacy, nor are men. Why should women teachers?" (*Philadelphia Evening Bulletin*, 19 July 1954). Politically savvy but always well mannered and professional, she thus succeeded in altering a number of policies and practices established by a board that had previously been dominated by older men with a patriarchal orientation. Her most important policy change stemmed from her deep conviction that there was an intrinsic linkage between good government and good schools, and she persuaded her male colleagues on the board to provide civic education to both girls and boys.

During World War I Lingelbach was an officer of the United Service Club for enlisted men, which provided social and recreational activities for military personnel. During the 1920s she served as the only female director of the Pennsylvania Crime Prevention Association. She also functioned for many years in an executive position on the Republican Women's Club of Pennsylvania and for six years as president of the New Century Club, a civic and cultural organization concerned with such causes as the continuing education of adult working women. From 1935 to 1945 she was chairperson of the West Philadelphia Women's Committee of the city's orchestra, and she served as president of the Philadelphia Federation of Women's Clubs from 1934 to 1938. As a result of her prominent civic activities, in 1934 she was appointed chairperson of a nationwide milk survey for the Philadelphia area, whose purpose was to study the relationship between illness and underconsumption of milk by children living in poverty. She also served as a member of the Presbyterian Board of Christian Education from 1923 to 1948 and as its vice president during her last five years. It is notable that her ongoing interest in religious education did not prevent her opposition to introducing religion into the Philadelphia public schools.

In her academic career as a professor of history at Temple University, Lingelbach served as a delegate to the international Anglo-American History Conference both in 1931 and 1936. The bulk of her publications—numbering more than forty—appeared in *Current History*, the *Dictionary of American Biography*, and the *American Historical Review*. Her historical contributions deal mainly with war-related issues involving Italy and Spain and were published in the period 1941–1945; her biographical entries focus on men and women of chiefly local significance in the Philadelphia area. Although her historical interests and expertise overlapped with those of her husband, they never jointly authored writings. Insofar as her husband was a prominent historian, they may have decided that to publish together might not have enhanced her reputation of scholarly independence as a woman. In reflecting on her career as a university professor and writer, she went on record with the view that "history is one field that men generally reserve for themselves" (*Philadelphia Sunday Bulletin*, 20 July 1947).

An austere matriarchal figure at home, Lingelbach provided her three children with high expectations concerning their own education. In recollecting Sunday dinners with the Lingelbachs, her granddaughter Anne Cook recalls: "More important than the meal was the intelligence and level of conversation expressed at the table." A frequent traveler to Europe and a devotee of classical music, fine art, and antiques, Lingelbach modeled at home her enthusiasm for and joy in learning even as she combined many public roles as an educator and champion of women's rights. On the campus of Indiana University a street—Lingelbach Lane—is named in her honor, and in Philadelphia a public school also carries her name. Lingelbach died in Philadelphia.

• The archives of the University of Pennsylvania, Temple University, Bryn Mawr College, Indiana University, and the Presbyterian Historical Society in Philadelphia all contain assorted materials about and by Lingelbach. The 1935 edition of the *Dictionary of American Biography* contains nineteen brief biographies authored by Lingelbach. She published twenty articles in *Current History* during World War II (1941–1945), all but one of which concern war issues in Italy and Spain. See also the *American Historical Review* 30, no. 4 (July 1925), and 43, no. 4 (July 1938), for articles by Lingelbach. Obituaries are in the *Philadelphia Evening Bulletin*, 15 July 1954, and the *New York Times* and the *Philadelphia Inquirer*, both 16 July 1954.

TIMOTHY H. SMITH
LAURIE S. MANDEL

LINING, John (Apr. 1708–21 Sept. 1760), physician and scientist, was born in Lanarkshire, Scotland, the son of Thomas Lining, a minister, and Anne Hamilton. Between 1697 and 1728 his native shire produced four of the leading figures of British medicine: William Smellie, William Cullen, William Hunter, and John Hunter. Given this fertile environment, it is not surprising that Lining turned to medicine as a career. In addition to studying medicine in Scotland, it is likely that he also studied at the University of Leyden but did not take a degree. He was a friend and most probably a student of Leyden resident D. Hermann Boerhaave, then the most influential medical educator and theorist in Europe (Waring, p. 255).

Around age twenty Lining emigrated to Charleston, South Carolina. There he became one of a small group of Scottish émigré physicians, scattered throughout the British mainland colonies during the first half of the eighteenth century, who played a major role in the early development of professional, scientific, and intellectual life in America.

While engaging in a large practice, which included serving as port physician and as physician to the poor of St. Philip's Parish, Lining also explored the fields of climatology, physiology, epidemiology, botany, and electricity. His most important work was in meteorology, metabolism, and yellow fever. At this time climatic factors were widely assumed to contribute greatly to the onset of poor health and disease. To test this assumption, Lining tried to establish a link between meteorological conditions in Charleston and the epidemic fevers which "as regularly return at their Stated Seasons as a good clock strikes 12 when the sun is in the Meridian" (Waring, p. 256). Beginning in April 1737, using a barometer, a Fahrenheit thermometer, and a hygroscope, Lining recorded each day's temperature, humidity, wind velocity, cloud cover, and rainfall. He continued to collect meteorological data for over fifteen years. Reports and tables of these studies were published in the *Philosophical Transactions of the Royal Society* in 1748 (vol. 45) and in 1753 (vol. 48, pt. 1). They were also reproduced in Governor James Glen's *A Description of South Carolina* (1761) and Lionel Chalmers's two-volume *Account of the Weather and Diseases of South Carolina* (1776).

In 1740–1741 Lining expanded his investigations on the relationship between weather and disease to include data on his own metabolism for a full year. He scrupulously kept an account of his daily weight, pulse rate, intake of food and liquids, and his bodily excretions. Earlier Sanctorious, a professor of medicine at the University of Padua, had conducted a similar study but, unlike Lining, published only aphorisms and not data. The results of Lining's investigations were published three times in the *Transactions*: volumes 42 (1743) and 43 (1744–1745), and an abridged volume of 1747. Despite his strenuous efforts, Lining was unable to establish any meaningful connection between the weather and the body's metabolism or disease.

In keeping with his interest in the epidemics that periodically descended upon Charleston, Lining wrote an important and pioneering study of yellow fever based on his experience with the epidemic that attacked Charleston in 1748. He described its symptoms and pathology, noting the distinctively low pulse that characterized the disease. He also correctly asserted that the disease was infectious, but he did not realize the intermediary role played by the *aëdes aegypti* mosquito. Other important observations were that people who were attacked once did not get the malady again, that blacks generally were immune, and that visitors from rural areas did not carry the disease home with them. Lining also recorded the weather conditions during the epidemic. He sent this account to Robert Whytt, a professor of medicine at the Edinburgh medical school, who had it published in the *Essays and Observations, Physical and Literary Read before a Society of Physicians in Edinburgh*, volume 2 (1756), and reproduced in the same work in 1770. In 1799 the study was reprinted in Philadelphia both as an independent pamphlet and as a supplement to Colin Chisholm's *An Essay on the Malignant Pestilential Fever*.

Lining's work in both botany and electricity was less significant, although botany was Lining's favorite branch of science. He wrote a paper on the Indian Pink that was published in the *Essays and Observations*, volume 1 (1754). The paper noted the plant's anthelminthic (worm-expelling) and poisonous properties but did not give a full botanical description of it. Lining also sent specimens of sugar cane, pineapple, and the rootbark of the magnolia, which he used as a substitute for cinchona bark (quinine) in treating "intermittent fever" (malaria), to Dr. Charles Alston of Edinburgh. Whytt also received plant specimens from Lining.

Lining and Benjamin Franklin corresponded regularly concerning various aspects of physics. They especially discussed the nature of electricity and lightning, and Lining early conducted a kite experiment similar to Franklin's. An account of his experiment appeared in the *Gentleman's Magazine* of London in 1753. An abstract of a letter of reply to Charles Pinckney, agent for South Carolina in London, relating to the dangers of the kite experiment and the necessity of proper grounding and insulation of the apparatus appeared in the *Transactions* (vol. 48, pt. 2) in 1754.

In addition to his large practice and scientific work, Lining, as was the case with many physicians of his era, was also active in civic affairs. He was a founder of the St. Andrew's Club, a senior warden of Solomon's Lodge of Masons, the president of the Charleston Library Society, and a justice of both the Court of Common Pleas and the Court of General Sessions.

Sometime after 1740 Lining entered into a partnership with Lionel Chalmers, a fellow Scottish émigré who shared many of Lining's scientific interests. In 1750 he married Sarah Hill, who had inherited several valuable pieces of property in South Carolina. They had no children. In 1754 the gout, as well as his aspirations to become a member of the planter elite, caused Lining to abandon his medical practice and turn to raising indigo and dabbling in science. He died in Charleston.

Versatile, industrious, astute, and painstaking, Lining well earned the prominent position he has held in the history of early American medicine and science.

• There is no known collection of Lining's papers. A complete list of his published writings is in Joseph I. Waring, *A History of Medicine in South Carolina, 1670–1825* (1964), which also contains the best brief account of his life and work. Early profiles of Lining are in David Ramsay, *The History of South Carolina from Its First Settlement in 1760 to the Year 1808*, vol. 2 (1809), pp. 111–12, 480–81; and James Thacher, *American Medical Biography*, vol. 1 (1828), pp. 357–58. See also Frederick P. Bowes, *The Culture of Early Charleston* (1942), pp. 75–84.

PHILIP CASH

LINK, Edwin Albert, Jr. (26 July 1904–7 Sept. 1981), inventor and businessman, was born in Huntington, Indiana, the youngest son of Edwin Albert Link, Sr., and Katherine Martin. In 1910 the family moved to Binghamton, New York, when Link's father purchased the bankrupt Binghamton Automatic Music Corporation. Renamed the Link Piano and Organ Company, the firm established a reputation for manufacturing theater organs, player pianos, and nickelodeons. Because he was less interested in academics than in tinkering with mechanical devices, Link's educational record was erratic. He spent a brief time at the Rockford Training High School (Ill.), Los Angeles Polytechnic High School, Bellefonte Academy (Pa.), and Lindsley Institute (W.Va.). In 1922 he returned to Binghamton and entered Central High School. He also worked for his father's company, where he rebuilt and repaired organs.

Like many in his generation, Link became interested in aviation because of World War I. He made his first flight in Los Angeles in 1920 with Sidney Chaplin, brother of the film comedian Charlie Chaplin. Although his father tried to discourage him from learning to fly, Link persisted, made his first solo flight in 1926, and earned his pilot's license the following year. In 1928 with the help of his mother he purchased his first airplane. While working for his father, Link got the idea for a rudimentary aircraft trainer that used parts of an organ and compressed air to mimic the motion of an airplane in flight. From 1927 to 1929, Link worked on his invention until it gave him the feel of the controls of a real aircraft. In April 1929 he filed for a patent and organized the Link Aeronautical Corporation to market the device. Early in its development the trainer was accepted only as a coin-operated amusement park ride, but convinced that it could be used in flight instruction, Link continued to refine the trainer's instrumentation. In 1930 he organized the Link Flying School, with the Link Trainer as the curriculum's central feature. As the depression deepened, however, the school attracted few students. Link was forced to augment his earnings from the flying school by managing small airports, flying, and servicing aircraft. In 1931 he married Marion Clayton, a reporter for the *Binghamton Press*, who helped him with his company's finances and wrote instructional material for the flight school. The couple had two children. During this time Link became acquainted with Charles S. "Casey" Jones, a former Curtiss test pilot. Jones's company, the J.V.W. Corporation, eventually became the sole sales representative for the Link Trainer.

Link received his first big break during the so-called Air Mail Crisis of 1934, when, after reports of corruption among private air-mail contractors, President Franklin D. Roosevelt canceled the existing airmail and ordered the Army Air Corps to deliver the mail. Link won a contract to develop a trainer for the Army Air Corps. In June 1934, Link sold his first six Model A trainers to the military. The Model A had a mock fuselage with wings and control surfaces that were installed on a turntable and mounted on a base. It also had a cockpit with a full instrument panel and set of controls. With the Army Air Corps order, Link's trainer had finally been taken seriously.

World War II brought more success for Link's company with the development of the ANT-18. Called "The Blue Box" because of the shape and color of its mocked-up fuselage, it became the standard military instrument trainer during the war. Link next produced a trainer that duplicated the flying characteristics of the North American AT-6/SNJ training aircraft. Another wartime development was the CNT (Celestial Navigation Trainer), which taught flight crews to navigate using the stars. Link also developed a Bubble Sextant that could be carried on aircraft for use in celestial navigation. By the war's end, instrument trainers were leaving the Binghamton assembly line at the rate of one every forty-five minutes.

After the war, the company's business dropped off, and Link needed something to take up the slack. The company worked to develop an all-electronic trainer and unsuccessfully sought to market a trainer that would teach high school students to fly. More successful were the C-11 in 1949, as well as the first device to simulate the handling of a jet-propelled aircraft and a simulator based on the Boeing B-47B bomber. Eventually, the company broke into the commercial aviation market and won the contract for a DC-8 simulator in the late 1950s. With the advent of computers and electronics-based simulators, however, Link became restless and in 1953, stepped down from the presidency. The company merged first with the General Precision Equipment Corporation (1954) and then with the Singer Company (1968).

After leaving the company, Link turned his attention to underwater exploration, which he believed offered the same kind of challenge that aviation had in its pioneering days. In 1955 he and his wife began a search for Columbus's *Santa Maria* off the Haitian coast and attempted to pinpoint where Columbus had first landed in the New World. In the early 1960s Link developed a submersible decompression chamber (SDC) that would allow divers to remain underwater longer and in deeper waters than had ever been attempted before. The SDC was part of Link's "Man-in-the-Sea," an idea to provide hospitable underwater habitats at unexplored depths of the ocean, and was later modified to include the submersible, portable, inflatable dwelling (SPID), another of Link's inventions.

In June 1964, using equipment designed by Link and others, divers Robert Stenuit and Jon Lindbergh (son of Charles A. Lindbergh) began the longest and deepest dive that had ever been attempted—432 feet. In the early 1970s Link and J. Seward Johnson developed the "Johnson-Sea-Link," a submersible that was capable of operating at a depth of three thousand feet. Link continued to work on underwater technology and in 1980 was honored by the Charles A. Lindbergh Fund for his work in science and technology in connection with preserving the environment. Other awards came from the Smithsonian Institution, Franklin Institute, and the Royal Aeronautical Society. Link died in Binghamton.

As the inventor of the first aircraft simulator, Link was a notable aviation pioneer. He devised a machine that made flight training safer and more efficient and enabled many pilots to be trained. He helped establish a multimillion dollar business enterprise that has become the core of modern aviation. During the last two decades of his life, he became a pioneer in developing underwater engineering and exploration systems, but he will most often be remembered as the father of modern aircraft simulation.

• Link's papers are in the Special Collections of the Glenn G. Bartle Library at Binghamton University, and in the Link Archival Collection of the Roberson Museum and Science Center in Binghamton. Although there is no standard biography of Link, Lloyd L. Kelly [as told to Robert B. Parke], *The Pilot Maker* (1970), chronicles Link's aviation career and the development of the trainer and devotes a small section to Link's interest in underwater exploration. Two books by Link's wife, Marion Clayton Link, *Sea Diver* (1959; repr. 1964) and *Windows in the Sea* (1973), record their mutual interest in oceanography. James I. Kilgore, "The Planes That Never Leave the Ground," *American Heritage of Invention and Technology* 4 (1989): 56–63, contains an excellent description of the development of Link trainers and simulators into recent times. An obituary is in the *New York Times*, 9 Sept. 1981.

DOMINICK A. PISANO

LINK, Henry Charles (27 Aug. 1889–9 Jan. 1952), psychologist, was born in Buffalo, New York, the son of George Link, a carpenter, and Martha Kraus. He enrolled at North Western (now North Central) College in Naperville, Illinois, in 1908. Finding its sectarian program "stifling," he transferred to Yale University. After graduating in 1913, Link remained at Yale to study philosophy. A progressivist history of philosophy course and William G. Sumner's relativist anthropology converted him to agnostic positivism, although Ernest Hocking's idealist ethics persuaded him to reserve some room for moral agency. Link's dissertation asserted that the active and causal quality of the "valuing process"—judgment—depended on and emerged from, but was not identical with, instincts. While concluding the Ph.D. in 1916, he married Carolyn Crosby Wilson; they had three children.

As employment psychologist at the Winchester Repeating Arms Company from 1916 to 1919 and at U.S. Rubber from 1919 to 1923, Link evaluated workers by analyzing the demands of the work environment before considering the adaptive qualities of the individual. Similar to Edward L. Thorndike's functionalist view of mental testing, Link did not promote "general intelligence," or IQ testing, as no single index of mentality corresponded to the skills needed for most jobs. He presented this position in *Employment Psychology* (1919), which promoted tests of "aptitudes" as combinations of inheritance and training. It also included some of the first systematic efforts to validate mental tests against external criteria, namely, abilities needed in the workplace.

Link believed that the mentally deficient could increasingly take over the unskilled jobs that were becoming more abundant under the division of labor. Winchester's management encouraged Link to develop ability tests to demonstrate that a group then considered to have lower intelligence, women—who were filling unskilled positions World War I had made available—could perform assembly tasks previously performed by men. Although Link accommodated the company's sexist view that higher-level assembly tasks required male "judgment," in one chapter he described a staff meeting of the future, in which two female psychological experts enlighten a pair of male executives by debunking "general intelligence."

Consistent with his testing of tests against real-world criteria, Link proposed in *Education and Industry* (1923) that public schools validate their curricula against the actual experiences of their graduates in industry. This was not to achieve John Dewey's integration of academic and vocational objectives but to promote the latter at the expense of the former. Less optimistic than in *Employment Psychology*, Link acknowledged that many normal workers might derive no more satisfaction from work than their wages.

The decline in Link's Progressive Era optimism occurred amid the highly publicized IQ debate of 1921–1923. Link found himself at a distance from the academic psychologists who drew invidious racial and social conclusions from World War I intelligence-test data. He attacked hereditarianism in an *Atlantic Monthly* article (1923) and recommended that general intelligence tests be redefined as "general attainment" tests, in part to preserve the ideal of equal educational opportunity.

Link's concerns shifted away from education when he became employed at Lord & Taylor and at Gimbel's between 1923 and 1930. While Link saw himself as a progressive mediator during the early 1920s, seeking common scientific grounds between workers and management and between education and business, now he sought a scientific ground for advertising, to improve communication between corporations and consumers. Link believed the integration of manufacturing and distribution in new chain stores required more standardized methods of breaking down consumer "resistance" to purchases.

After becoming secretary-treasurer of the Psychological Corporation in 1931, he invented one of the first market research surveys, the Psychological Barometer, as a basis for *The New Psychology of Selling and Advertising* (1932). Demonstrating how to measure the effect of particular appeals in the home environment of likely consumers, Link sent teams of interviewers to households in selected regions, classes, and other categories. By testing likely consumers for their association of a slogan with a brand name and applying statistical methods to minimize the error between a sample population and the entire nation, Link validated marketing appeals. Making advertising more effective was one way to combat a central cause of the Great Depression, the abundance of too many unpurchased products.

The solutions to the depression offered by Franklin D. Roosevelt's government, especially its commitments to labor unions and social welfare policies, disappointed Link greatly. With the exception of the Civilian Conservation Corps, he rejected the New Deal as a negative moral influence. Link adapted the Psychological Barometer to political issues in 1934 and exposed the bias of pro–New Deal opinion polls by demonstrating the effects of liberal question wording on liberals' poll results. Confident of his own objectivity, he believed the questions he asked were unbiased.

At the New Deal's high tide, Link published *The Return to Religion* (1936), which denounced modernist faith in rationality as a key to solving moral problems; it sold over a half-million copies. He asserted that higher education was producing self-centered individuals who were becoming obsessed with their own deficiencies—such as those diagnosed by psychoanalysts, among other determinists. Link advised that the ability to do things that were not immediately gratifying,

such as churchgoing, was the antidote to the modern poisons of introversion and narcissism. He also critiqued Progressive Era education, denouncing teachers who would abolish grades from the classroom. He believed the experience of being graded prepared students for the real world, not least because it taught them the real-world art of ingratiation!

While counseling young adults as director of the Psychological (Corporation's) Service Center, Link attempted to standardize the counseling process. In 1936 he developed an assessment device—to define normalcy—called the "PQ," or personality quotient, which he publicized in *The Rediscovery of Man* (1938). Essentially an interviewing survey, the PQ measured an individual's extroversion, based on amounts of social initiative, self-determination, economic independence, and "sex-adjustment . . . toward members of the opposite sex." Equating extroversion with selflessness, Link thus applied psychology to validate what was, for him, the most important principle of religious and commonsense values. Although extroversion itself could become a vice, he counseled vocation and marriage as safeguards against its disorderly expression.

Link resumed his jeremiad against modernism in the early Cold War. He believed the Nazi holocaust and nuclear weapons technology had provided ample evidence that science had betrayed human spirituality. He now denounced science and public education as "false gods" but saved his strongest reproach for a condition he had once anticipated optimistically, increased leisure. He blamed affluence for leading Americans to contemplate determinist theories similar to that which inspired the Soviet Union.

To combat socialist determinism, Link defined a consensus of American values. The same year Richard Hofstadter published *The American Political Tradition*, Link invoked Gunnar Myrdal's antiracist allusion to an "American creed" in *The Rediscovery of Morals* (1947). The core of American values, for Link, was the balance of equality and liberty. He attacked the materialist doctrine of absolute equality and the justification of envy under the rhetorical guise of "social justice." Foreshadowing late twentieth-century reactions to governmental affirmative action policies, Link opposed special treatment for any particular group and objected to, for example, the Supreme Court decisions in the 1940s favoring labor unions. To validate his consensus of American values empirically, he polled with questions such as "Is the closed union shop . . . good Americanism or bad Americanism?"

Opposition to special treatment led Link to attack the racism of Jim Crow laws, but he wondered whether the future might include "Jim Crowism in reverse" and "quotas" for hiring based on race. He linked racism and socialism as determinisms, which, in reducing behavior to group membership, destroyed individual responsibility. Link held that his social philosophy was thus not a "social" but a moral and family-based one. This was consistent with his early rejection of general intelligence and William McDougall's attempt to identify intelligence level with social class. Link believed that the IQ score difference between whites and blacks was mostly a result of unequal opportunities under Jim Crow and predicted the eventual disappearance of the difference.

Link blamed racial unrest on abundance, which allowed for an increasingly amoral public school system and welfare programs. In *The Way to Security* (1951), he cited research on the negative effect of state relief on families, fourteen years before Daniel P. Moynihan advocated "benign neglect." Middle-class families were also losing their traditional values, Link believed, as declining family size and the resulting increase in free time gave birth to insecurity and covetousness. Too much leisure was evident in a public school system that encouraged children to drift rather than to seek employment. Too much leisure was responsible for curricula given over to discussions of sex and race education. Worse yet, discussion, a means to an end, had become an end in itself. The resulting culture of "yakety-yak" offered words, not deeds, as solutions to social problems. This was nonetheless appropriate, Link felt, in a culture that valued verbal intelligence over morality and regularly discovered determinisms to excuse irresponsibility.

Consistent throughout Link's career was a concern for the valuing process, both in the method, as validation or verification, and in the content of his research, as judgment, desire, or active moral choice. What changed were his political and social opinions, whose development paralleled the trajectory of Republican party and business attitudes, from the scientific managerial visions of the Progressive Era to the neoconservatism of the Cold War period. Early in his career, he optimistically cast public education and science as emancipators not because they would liberate everyone but because they would inspire a few individuals to invent more labor-saving devices and so bring leisure to all. With the help of ostensibly objective aptitude tests, humankind, he believed, was initiating an era of merit-based justice, employment stability, and happiness for all. Later in his career, Link became pessimistic about the role of science in improving the human condition. This was due in some part to a need to ignore a cultural contradiction that his advertising career had encouraged: he developed an ethic of anti-intellectualism and idealized the selfless, outgoing personality just as he was deploying rational scientific methods to help mass producers appeal to nonrational desires and self-interest.

The extroverted, selfless type he promoted reflected his own professional experience. As one of the first research psychologists never to take a job in academia, he devoted his career to making science social, taking it into the workplace and homeplace and then into the more personal environs of politics and religion. The applied psychologist's concern to accommodate clients has an echo in Link's prescription to strengthen self-esteem by pleasing others first. His prescription to do the distasteful but necessary, written as he developed the science of advertising, signals the ascendancy of aesthetics over ethics—of the "well-liked" personality

over inner-directed character—in American culture. During the last ten years of his life, Link was a vice president and director of the Psychological Corporation. He died in Port Chester, New York.

• The annual reports of the Psychological Corporation disappeared during recent corporate moves. There are no other records of major manuscript collections relating to Link's life or career; scattered correspondence is in the archives of the History of American Psychology, University of Akron. Link published the abstract of his dissertation, "Instinct and Value," in the *American Journal of Psychology* 33 (1922): 1–18. He critiqued IQ testing in "What Is Intelligence?" *Atlantic Monthly*, Sept. 1923, pp. 374–85, and politicized his marketing survey in "A New Method for Testing Advertising and a Psychological Sales Barometer," *Journal of Applied Psychology* 18 (1934): 1–26. He unveiled the PQ in "A Test of Four Personality Traits of Adolescents," *Journal of Applied Psychology* 20 (1936): 527–34; see also *The Rediscovery of Man*, chap. 4. An obituary is in the *New York Times*, 10 Jan. 1952.

RICHARD T. VON MAYRHAUSER

LINK, Karl Paul Gerhardt (31 Jan. 1901–21 Nov. 1978), biochemist, was born in La Porte, Indiana, the son of George Link, a Lutheran minister, and Fredericka Mohr. His parents instilled in him the values of integrity, the work ethic, service to others, and love of nature, music, and literature. An aptitude for chemistry surfaced at La Porte High School. When the chemistry teacher was summoned for war duties in 1917, the school chose Link to teach his classes. In 1918 Link entered the University of Wisconsin, where he received a B.S. in 1922, an M.S. in 1923, and a Ph.D. in 1925, in agricultural chemistry. An International Education Board fellowship from 1925 to 1927 enabled him to study with the carbohydrate chemist, Sir James Irvine, at St. Andrews University, Scotland. A dispute with Irvine over the results of an experiment led to Link's expulsion when he suggested that Irvine change his interpretation of a phenomenon because of the experiment. Link then completed the fellowship with the Nobel laureates Paul Karrer at the University of Zurich and Fritz Pregl at the University of Graz. In 1927 he returned to Wisconsin as an assistant professor of agricultural chemistry, becoming full professor in 1931.

Link married Elizabeth Feldman in 1930; the couple had three children. He lived on a farm near Madison, sharing a kinship with farmers and dressing like one both on and off campus. Despite a robust appearance, his health was fragile, and in midlife he contracted tuberculosis, spending many months in sanatoria in 1945–1946 and 1958–1959. Faced with the ever-present prospect of relapse, his struggle against the disease made him a man of many moods and subject to periods of depression.

Link established a reputation as an outstanding carbohydrate chemist. His doctoral dissertation was on complex plant carbohydrates, and his research focused on the isolation and nature of plant polysaccharides. His reputation was, however, confined largely to the small group of experts in his field until the mid-

1930s, when that situation changed dramatically with his study of the sweet clover disease.

About 1923 a fatal bleeding of cattle appeared in North Dakota and Alberta. Veterinarians traced the malady to the spoiled sweet clover hay eaten by the cattle. In 1933 a Wisconsin farmer traveled to Madison in search of the state veterinarian. He came to the College of Agriculture and encountered Link instead. He brought with him a story of his cows dying after eating sweet clover hay as well as samples of the hay and milk cans full of blood that would not clot. Link immediately began a search for the substance responsible for sweet clover disease. He soon learned that it had no parallel in then known animal pathology, producing a progressive decrease over many days in the clotting power of blood.

Link first had to develop a bioassay to determine the anticoagulant activity of hay extracts. In 1934 he devised a quantitative method to determine the time needed for blood to clot. This served as a measure in the blood of the level of prothrombin, the protein necessary for coagulation. He then attempted to isolate the anticoagulant substance from hay extracts. In 1939 he obtained pure crystals of the substance. In 1940 he identified its nature and determined its structure, and in 1941 he synthesized it. The anticoagulant was a derivative of coumarin, the substance responsible for the fragrant odor of sweet clover. He established the biochemical reactions that took place during the spoilage of sweet clover, proving that the anticoagulant was an oxidized coumarin, two molecules of which had coupled, thus providing him with the generic name of "dicumarol" for the substance.

Animal feeding experiments proved that dicumarol destroyed prothrombin in the blood of susceptible animals. Would dicumarol also inhibit clotting in humans? Mayo Clinic scientists in Rochester, Minnesota, quickly picked up his findings and found dicumarol to be an excellent anticoagulant. Link assigned his 1941 patent and all subsequent ones to the Wisconsin Alumni Research Foundation (WARF), an agency founded in the 1920s to handle patents of Wisconsin University scientists. Dicumarol's major use was in the prevention of clot formation after surgery. It prevented coronary thrombosis and other deadly diseases associated with blood that was too thick.

Between 1941 and 1945 Link prepared more than 100 compounds related to dicumarol in search of new anticoagulants. He gave each compound a number based on structure. Struck with tuberculosis in 1945 in the midst of this research and confined for eight months to a sanitarium, he remembered during his convalescence that cattle with sweet clover disease died in a state of repose, seemingly unaware of their internal bleeding. He returned to research in 1946 with two goals. In addition to finding a superior anticoagulant for human therapy, he would search for a rat poison based on the physiological effects of dicumarol on cattle. He concentrated on compound 42, which exhibited high anticoagulant activity. In 1948 he found that it was not only an effective rat killer but had

the potential to revolutionize rodent control. Several patents ensued. He coined the name "Warfarin" for compound 42, a combination of WARF and the last four letters of coumarin. Warfarin became the most effective rat poison known following the more than 5,000 field tests by government and private agencies undertaken for its approval in 1950.

Link's quest for a superior anticoagulant also was successful. He prepared water-soluble warfarin sodium, and in 1953–1954 medical scientists found it to be five to ten times more potent than dicumarol. It was the only anticoagulant that could be administered orally, intravenously, and intramuscularly. Under the trade name "Coumadin" the anticoagulant became an important therapeutic drug and became well known in 1955 when, after a heart attack, President Dwight Eisenhower received Coumadin in order to prevent the formation of new blood clots and to control his prothrombin level. Coumadin combatted heart attack, strokes, and other afflictions that arose when blood vessels and organs became blocked by clots. New uses expanded its scope into the 1990s. In September 1995 came the announcement that Coumadin prevented strokes in persons with atrial fibrillation, an irregular heartbeat that makes sufferers susceptible to clot formation in the heart.

In 1953 Link discovered another valuable preventive medicine after losing laboratory rabbits to a diarrhea-like disease. He felt the disease was akin to calf scours, a malady that results in the death of about 15 percent of calves within a month of their birth. He learned that calves, being born with no protection through antibodies against disease organisms, were unable to cope with organisms that traveled through tiny hemorrhages in the stomach wall and entered the bloodstream. Since there were rich stocks of immunizing agents in cow's blood, he extracted the globulins from the blood, added vitamin K, a blood coagulant, to clot over the hemorrhages in the stomach wall, and fed milk containing globulin-vitamin K to calves. His formulation, which he named "plasmylac," received its first major field test in North Carolina. It proved to have no equal in preventing calf scours. Royalties from his patent and those for his anticoagulants generated many millions of dollars for the university.

Controversy marked Link's career. During his 1945–1946 stay in a sanitarium, he organized an insurrection among the patients and criticized the management for doing nothing to stimulate the patients. A state board of review dismissed his charges. When the relevant departments would not give him permission to use Wisconsin cows for his plasmylac tests, forcing him to go to North Carolina, he lambasted the university administration for failing to assist him. The university board of regents absolved the administration and censured Link. Among his many controversial actions, which ranged from a refusal to pose for a required university photoidentification card to suing the government to make it stop nuclear tests, the most disturbing for many was his serving as faculty advisor to leftist student groups. He was advisor to the Student

Youth League, a branch of the Young Communist League, during the anticommunist wave led by his own senator, Joseph McCarthy, and by the House Un-american Activities Committee. Link defended himself vigorously and claimed that he came from a staunch Republican background. No one really knew his political beliefs except that he revered the progressive Wisconsin senator Robert La Follette, Sr. Link retired in 1971, and he died in Madison.

Link was one of the most colorful and controversial figures at Wisconsin. He was also a creative and productive scientist of exceptionally high standards, who developed new anticoagulants that warded off heart attacks and strokes and promoted a new understanding of the diseases of the heart and blood vessels.

• The Link collection in the University of Wisconsin Archives includes correspondence, photographs, student and research records, speeches, patents, awards, a biographical file, and social and political material. Link provided two fascinating portrayals of his anticoagulant discoveries in "The Anticoagulant from Spoiled Sweet Clover Hay," *Harvey Lectures* 39 (1943–1944): 162–216 and "The Discovery of Dicumarol and Its Sequels," *Circulation* 19 (1959): 97–107. Robert H. Burris provides a comprehensive study of Link and a bibliography of his publications in "Karl Paul Link, January 31, 1901–November 21, 1978," National Academy of Sciences, *Biographical Memoirs* 65 (1994): 177–95. Clinton E. Ballou, a former Ph.D. student, wrote a detailed biographical and analytical study of Link, "Karl Paul Gerhardt Link 1901–1978," *Advances in Carbohydrate Chemistry* 39 (1981): 1–12. For popular accounts of dicumarol, see Marjorie Sacks, "Science Weaves Another Miracle," *Hygeia* 24 (May 1946): 356–57, and Lois Mattox Miller, "Dicumarol: The Miracle in the Haystack," *Reader's Digest*, Oct. 1948, pp. 22–24. On Warfarin, see Gardner Soule, "New Poison Fools Rats," *Popular Science Monthly* 159 (Nov. 1951): 201–4, and Paul de Kruif, "Sure Death to Rats," *Reader's Digest*, Mar. 1951, pp. 92–94. On Link's personality, see Donald G. Cooley, "Men Behind the Medical Miracles," *Today's Health* 37 (Jan. 1959): 21–22, 69.

ALBERT B. COSTA

LINN, John Blair (14 Mar. 1777–30 Aug. 1804), poet and clergyman, was born in Big Spring (now Newville), Pennsylvania, the eldest son among seven children of William Linn, pastor of the Presbyterian church there, and Rebecca Blair, the daughter of a theology professor at the College of New Jersey (later Princeton University). In the course of a distinguished career William Linn became president of Washington College in Maryland in 1784 and was appointed copastor of the Collegiate Dutch Reformed Church in New York in November 1786, moving there with his family.

Growing up in a home where learning and piety were valued and where prominent people were frequent visitors, John Blair Linn entered Columbia College at fourteen and at seventeen was contributing to the *New-York Magazine* pieces published in 1795 as *Miscellaneous Works, Prose and Poetical, by a Young Gentleman of New York*. Another anonymously issued subscription volume, *The Poetical Wanderer* (1796),

was conventional and imitative like the first. Upon graduation in 1795 Linn began to read law with his father's friend Alexander Hamilton (1755–1804), who had retired as secretary of the treasury earlier in the year; he found time to write a play, *Bourville Castle; or the Gallic Orphan*, which was performed three times in the John Street Theatre in January 1797 and received one notice, probably written by his friend Charles Brockden Brown, who had revised the manuscript.

Abandoning both the law and at least for the time being the literary life, Linn took up the study of theology at Union College in Schenectady, New York. With an M.A. from Union in 1797 and another granted *in absentia* by Columbia in 1798, he was elected copastor of Philadelphia's fashionable First Presbyterian Church in April 1799. In May he married Hester Bailey, daughter of Colonel John Bailey of Poughkeepsie, New York, and together they had three sons.

An outstanding preacher and the youngest man until that time to be awarded an honorary doctorate in divinity by the University of Pennsylvania, Linn was also active in the Tuesday Club, a literary group that included serious professional writers like Charles Brockden Brown and Joseph Dennie, editor of the *Port Folio*. Linn's first signed work, *The Death of Washington* (1800), a poem "in the manner of an imitation of Ossian," was criticized for being cast in a verse form ludicrously inappropriate for a panegyric on the revered late president. His next publication, *The Powers of Genius* (1801), an essay in heroic couplets filled with commonplaces of eighteenth-century criticism, was successful enough to appear in a second, revised edition that was also published in England. But in treating the familiar question of freedom and spontaneity versus judgment and taste, Linn hampered his argument with too many reservations and some outright contradictions, as when, after extravagantly praising Fielding's gift for creating characters in *Tom Jones*, Linn comments in a footnote that "his works contain many scenes of indecency! his works, therefore, I would by no means recommend." Later works were related to religious concerns: a eulogy (1802) on Linn's senior colleague John Ewing, two lengthy pamphlets (1803) in a controversial exchange with Joseph Priestley on the divinity of Jesus, and the posthumously published *Valerian, a Narrative Poem: Intended, in Part, to Describe the Early Persecutions of Christians, and Rapidly to Illustrate the Influence of Christianity on the Manners of Nations* (1805). Linn was still at work on this blank verse epic when he died of tuberculosis.

Charles Brockden Brown, who married Linn's sister Elizabeth three months later, remarked in his memoir of Linn prefixed to the unfinished poem that all of Linn's performances are best viewed as "preludes to future exertions, and indications of future excellence," thus tactfully recognizing that Linn's literary talent was not equal to his ambition. In nearly two centuries, this judgment has not been challenged. In their *Cyclopedia of American Literature* (1856), George Duyckinck and Evert Duyckinck remark that *The*

Powers of Genius "is smoothly written, but unfortunately exhibits slight indications of the 'powers' it celebrates"; a thirty-eight line extract allows the reader to consider the merit of such lines as

> What vast delights flow on that glowing breast,
> By virtue strengthen'd and by Genius blest!
> Whate'er in Nature beautiful or grand,
> In air, or ocean, or the teeming land,
> Meets its full view, excites a joy unknown,
> To those whom Genius dashes from her throne.

In *American Authors 1600–1900*, edited by Stanley J. Kunitz and Howard Haycraft (1938), Linn is pronounced "today . . . both unread and unreadable."

Never reprinted, Linn's poems are of interest chiefly to scholars looking for early intimations of a distinctly American literary consciousness. Linn can call on Genius to " . . . Sound [its] trump of fame, / And give to glory the Columbian name!" but in his own works he cannot respond. Lewis Leary, a historical critic fully aware of Linn's contradictory stance in celebrating spontaneity while at the same time calling for traditional correctness in form, concedes that "no line he wrote is significant today." Yet Leary believes that Linn is worthy of respect because "almost alone among his contemporaries, [he] applied himself seriously to the problem of determining what we in our day would call 'the function of the poet' as an artist and as a member of society" (*Soundings*, 1975). One of many places where Linn speaks about that function is in his explanation of "the Design" of *The Powers of Genius*; there he declares that "in union with religion, literature renders men more eminently useful, opens wider the gates of their intellect to the reception of divine light, banishes religious superstition, and bows the knee with purer adoration, before the throne of God." A clergyman's expression of hope rather than a writer's declaration of faith in his art, the passage may suggest why Linn was more successful in the pulpit than with the pen.

• Linn manuscripts, mostly letters, are at the Historical Society of Pennsylvania. There is no comprehensive biography, but substantial information can be found in Charles Brockden Brown's prefatory "A Sketch of the Life and Character of John Blair Linn" in Linn's *Valerian* (1805), reprinted without change in *Port Folio*, n.s., 1 (Jan. 1809): 21–29, 129–34, and 195–203. See also Lewis Leary, "John Blair Linn, 1777–1805," *William and Mary Quarterly*, n.s., 5 (Apr. 1947): 137–76, reprinted in Lewis Leary, *Soundings: Some Early American Writers* (1975). This article and Leary's earlier one, "The Writings of John Blair Linn," *Bulletin of Bibliography* 19 (1946): 18–19, name all of Linn's works, including contributions to the *New-York Mirror*, the *Literary Magazine and American Register*, and the *Port Folio*, the leading literary periodical of its day. For a convenient overview, see Alan Axelrod, "John Blair Linn," in Vol. 37 of the *Dictionary of Literary Biography*, ed. Emory Elliott (1985). In vol. 1 of *Annals of the New York Stage* (1927), George C. D. Odell documents the fact that *Bourville Castle* was performed three times in January 1797. No manuscript of Linn's play survives.

VINCENT FREIMARCK

LINN, Lewis Fields (5 Nov. 1795–3 Oct. 1843), U.S. senator, was born near Louisville, Kentucky, the son of Asahel Linn, who as a youth had escaped captivity by the Shawnee, and Nancy Ann Hunter. After both parents died, Linn was raised by his half-brother Henry Dodge, later a U.S. senator from Wisconsin. Early in his teens he began studying medicine with a Louisville physician, and during the War of 1812 he served as a surgeon with Dodge's mounted rifle volunteers. Linn finished his medical education in Philadelphia in 1816, thereafter establishing a practice near Dodge's home in Sainte Genevieve, Missouri Territory. In 1818 Linn married Elizabeth Relfe. He developed a reputation as a talented physician, particularly noted for his work in fighting the spread of cholera in southern Missouri early in the 1830s.

Linn, a Jacksonian Democrat, first entered political life in 1827, serving a term in the Missouri Senate. Named by President Andrew Jackson as a commissioner to arbitrate old French and Spanish land claims in Missouri, Linn moved to St. Louis in 1833. The same year the state's governor appointed him to the U.S. Senate to fill the vacancy created by the death of Alexander Buckner. Apparently less objectionable to Missouri Whigs than other prominent Democrats, Linn was thereafter twice returned to the Senate for full terms. He served there until his death.

Linn proved a devoted friend of Jackson and his administration, supporting the expunging of the Senate's censure of the president for his removal of federal funds from the Bank of the United States and later sponsoring a bill to aid the indebted Jackson. Early in his career the Missouri senator was noted by his colleagues for the assiduity with which he ushered through bills for the immediate advantage of his constituents and his home state. Many of these involved land claims—Linn chaired the Senate's Committee on Private Land Claims from 1835 to 1841—but the most significant was the Platte Purchase Bill, secured in partnership with Missouri's senior senator, Thomas Hart Benton. The purchase added nearly 2 million acres to the state's northwestern corner by pushing its boundaries to the Missouri River.

It was most likely Linn's constituents' interest in western trade and settlement that prodded the senator onto the national stage in the late 1830s. After 1837 he played a leading role in focusing the attention of Congress and the American public on U.S. claims in the Pacific Northwest. The Oregon country, sprawling from the northern border of Mexican California to the southeastern edge of Russian Alaska, had been under joint American-British occupation since 1818, but in 1838 Linn offered a bill establishing an American territory north of the Forty-second parallel and west of the Rockies, and providing for its occupation by U.S. forces, the maintenance of a port of entry, and the building of a fort on the Columbia River. The Senate declined to embrace Linn's bill but appointed him head of a special committee on Oregon. Later that year the committee produced a widely noted report (*Mr. Linn's Report, June 6, 1838*, 25th Cong., 2d sess.,

1838, S. Doc. 470) that affirmed the American claim at least as far north as the Forty-ninth parallel, while emphasizing the area's abundant resources and rich land and the potential for basing an Asian and Pacific trade there. The report helped to direct Americans' gaze to the Pacific Northwest, but Linn's subsequent efforts to provide for generous land grants to white settlers in Oregon probably did more than the document's exaggerated claims to turn citizens' thoughts toward the possibility of migrating there.

Through the later 1830s and the first years of the 1840s, a majority of Linn's colleagues in the Senate declined to press the Oregon claim as aggressively as he did. Many were unwilling to rile Great Britain, especially since the far less remote northeastern boundary with Canada had yet to be settled. But Linn kept a steady flow of bills and resolutions before the Senate, calling on the president to abrogate the joint occupation agreement with England and providing for the extension of U.S. laws over the territory, as well as the construction of a string of fortifications to protect settlers traveling from Missouri through the Rockies to Oregon. Linn became increasingly truculent in his attitude toward Britain and its agent in the Northwest, the Hudson's Bay Company; his demands with respect to Oregon began increasingly to be echoed in public meetings and petitions to Congress. Migration of Americans to Oregon's Willamette Valley was starting to grow, and the Webster-Ashburton Treaty of 1842 had settled the northeastern boundary but not the Oregon question; Linn's efforts began to fare better. In February 1843 Linn's comprehensive Oregon bill—promising expanded land grants, extending the jurisdiction of U.S. courts from the Rockies to the Pacific between the Forty-second and Fifty-fourth parallels, and providing for the fortifying of the route west—passed the Senate narrowly before running aground in the House of Representatives. In the fall of that year Linn died suddenly in Sainte Genevieve, Missouri, reportedly the victim of an aneurysm. He was survived by his wife and two children.

Barely a year after Linn's death, James Polk won the presidency on a platform that demanded—among other measures intended to help the nation realize its "manifest destiny"—the "reoccupation" of Oregon. After considerable diplomatic maneuvering, Polk secured the international boundary in the Pacific Northwest at the Forty-ninth parallel, confirming as American the territory of the present-day states of Oregon, Washington, and Idaho (as well as bits of Montana and Wyoming). Linn's role in agitating the question led some admirers to dub him the "father of Oregon."

• There is a collection of Lewis Linn material at the Missouri Historical Society in St. Louis. It has been some time since Linn's life received comprehensive treatment, but see Elizabeth Linn and N. Sargent, *The Life and Public Services of Dr. Lewis F. Linn* (1857); and James Robert Hartley, "The Political Career of Lewis Fields Linn" (M.A. thesis, Univ. of Missouri, 1951). A more recent and accessible discussion of the most significant aspect of Linn's career is Michael B. Husband, "Senator Lewis F. Linn and the Oregon Question," *Missouri Historical Review* 66 (1971–1972): 1–19.

PATRICK G. WILLIAMS

LINTON, Ralph (27 Feb. 1893–24 Dec. 1953), anthropologist, was born in Philadelphia, Pennsylvania, the son of Isaiah Waterman Linton, the proprietor of a chain of restaurants, and Mary Elizabeth Gillingham. He was christened Rolfe, named after John Rolfe, a distant ancestor who married Pocahontas, but to avoid confusion in school he changed his name to the more traditional spelling of Ralph. After completing his secondary education at Friends High School in Moorestown, New Jersey, Linton enrolled at Swarthmore College in 1911. He hoped to pursue biology, but his father, noting that not many job opportunities existed in that field, demanded that he study engineering. At the end of his freshmen year, Linton was failing half his subjects and was expelled. Although two professors recognized his abilities and persuaded school officials to let him reenter on probation, his father insisted that he quit school and go to work. Linton found work on a truck farm, saved his money, and returned for his sophomore year as a biology major.

Swarthmore did not offer courses on anthropology. However, Linton gained his first exposure to anthropology the following summer, when he accompanied an archaeological expedition to New Mexico and Colorado. During the winter of his junior year, he took some time off from school to join an expedition to Guatemala to make molds of the Mayan monuments. This was Linton's first contact with people of another culture.

In 1915 Linton graduated Phi Beta Kappa with a B.A. from Swarthmore. Shortly after graduation, he married his college sweetheart Josephine Foster; they had no children. Linton went to work excavating for the University Museum of the University of Pennsylvania and received his M.A. in anthropology from that university in 1916. That same year Linton enrolled in graduate studies at Columbia University to study under Professor Franz Boas. In April 1917, while Linton was studying at Columbia, the United States entered World War I. Linton enlisted in the U.S. Army and served two years with the Forty-second or Rainbow Division in France. He took part in the battles of Château-Thierry and St.-Mihiel and was gassed in November 1918. Despite the atrocities of war, he retained a romantic attitude toward the conflict, writing and publishing several war poems. The war did take its toll, however. His wife filed for divorce while he was fighting overseas. He ended the war as a liaison corporal.

After his return to the United States in 1919, Linton left Columbia for Harvard because of a conflict with Boaz. He earned his Ph.D. in 1925 despite the fact that he was only in residence for less than a year. In 1920 he had become associated with the Bernice P. Bishop Museum in Honolulu and for two years served as archaeologist and ethnologist on the museum's expedition to the Marquesas Islands in French Polynesia. While there Linton completed his Ph.D. dissertation, "The Material Culture of the Marquesas Islands," and began to cut back on his study of archaeology to concentrate more on cultural anthropology.

Upon arriving back in the United States in 1922, Linton joined the Field Museum of Natural History in Chicago, Illinois, as the assistant curator of North American ethnology. That year he married Margaret McIntosh; they had one child. In 1925 the Field Museum sent Linton to Madagascar, where he spent two and a half years studying native life. He resigned from the museum's staff in 1928 and took a position as an assistant professor of anthropology at the University of Wisconsin. He became a full professor in 1930 and remained on the faculty for the next eight years.

Linton's second marriage ended in divorce in 1934. In 1935 he married Adelin Sumner Briggs Hohlfield, a columnist and reviewer for the *Madison Capital Times*. They had no children. Adelin became an active partner in his projects. In 1936 he published *The Study of Man*, which proposed that a more functionalistic (the meaningful interrelation of sociocultural elements) approach to cultural studies. The book, although met with initial neglect, brought Linton the notice of his peers, leading to an invitation to join the teaching staff at Columbia.

While at Columbia, Linton continued his writings on the subject, focusing on psychological anthropology and personality. During World War II he served at Columbia's School of Military Government and Administration, a school started by the U.S. Navy to provide cultural training to potential military administrators. In 1945 Linton wrote *The Cultural Background of Personality* and edited *The Science of Man in the World Crisis*. The following year he left Columbia to become the Sterling Professor of Anthropology at Yale, a position he held until his death. He died in New Haven, Connecticut.

Even though Linton was one of the world's most distinguished anthropologists, he did not fit neatly into the role of academic scholar and researcher. One way in which he differed from the traditional anthropologist was his almost total disregard for the normal methods of scholarship. For example, *The Study of Man* had only one footnote and no references, a pattern followed in practically all of his books and articles. However, as John Gillen wrote in eulogizing Linton in *American Anthropologist* (Apr. 1954), "Despite his reluctance to put references down on paper, it was rare that Linton could be 'caught off base' with respect to his facts. There can be little doubt that much of his appeal, both to the academic world and to the general public, lay in his talent at one and the same time commanding the facts authoritatively and stating them, with a novel twist of his own, in terms that all could understand."

Tree of Culture, a book Linton had been working on at the time of his death, was published posthumously in 1955. In that monumental work he expressed his hope that the social sciences would use the existing time of unusual freedom to prepare some "solid platform from which the workers of the next civilization might go on." He was not, however, overly optimistic that this would happen. In the concluding paragraph of *The Study of Man* he wrote: "The signs are plain that this era of freedom is also drawing to a close, and there can be little doubt that the study of culture and society will be the first victim of the new order. . . . Unless all history is at fault, the social scientist will go the way of the Greek philosopher."

Despite this burst of pessimism, Linton had a genuine love for his profession and his relationship to his own society. In an account written for *Twentieth Century Authors* just three days before his death, he stated: "Fortunately, as an ethnologist I have always been able to combine business with pleasure and have found my greatest satisfaction in friendships with men of many different races and cultures. I consider as my greatest accomplishments that I am an adopted member of the Comanche tribe, was accepted as a master carver by the Marquesas natives . . . , am a member of the Native Church of North America . . . , became a properly accredited *ombiasy nkazo* (medicine man) in Madagascar, and was even invited to join the Rotary Club of a middle western city."

• No official Linton papers exist, but much of his work is in the archives and files of the various museums and schools at which he was employed. For a good biographical account of Linton's life, see Adelin Linton and Charles Wagely, *Ralph Linton* (1971), which also contains a complete list of his writings. See also the memoir by Charles Kluckhorn, in National Academy of Sciences, *Biographical Memoirs* 31 (1958): 236–53. Obituaries are in the *New York Times*, 25 Dec. 1953, and *American Anthropologist* 56 (Apr. 1954): 274–81.

FRANCESCO L. NEPA

LINTON, William James (7 Dec. 1812–29 Dec. 1897), wood engraver, printer, and poet, was born in London, England, the son of William Linton, an accountant and provision broker, and Mary Stephenson. In 1818 the Lintons moved to Stratford, where he attended Chigwell School, learning some Greek and Latin and reading illustrated miscellanies and novels, including those of Sir Walter Scott. He moved to London in 1828 in order to serve an apprenticeship with George Wilmot Bonner, a wood engraver. Subsequently he worked for two leading engravers, William Henry Powis and John Thompson, and then from 1840 to 1843 for John Orrin Smith. His work appeared in the *Illustrated London News*, the leading pictorial journal of the time.

In 1837 Linton married Laura Wade, the sister of the poet and dramatist Thomas Wade. She died of consumption the next year. He then lived with her sister Emily; they may never have married because of a law prohibiting marriage between in-laws, but they had seven children. Beginning in 1849 the family lived in the Lake District. Emily died in December 1856, and Linton subsequently married Eliza Lynn; they had no children.

Linton was active politically, espousing freedom of the press, free speech, universal suffrage, and women's rights. A member of the Chartist movement, he became interested in the activities of Mazzini and other Italian and Polish reformers. He was also involved in numerous publications, both as an editor and author. Among the works whose illustrations he engraved was an edition of Tennyson (1857) and Milton's *L'Allegro* (1859). He also illustrated his own poetry, published under the title *Claribel and Other Poems* (1865).

In 1866 he separated amicably from his wife. Heavily in debt because of his political activities and ill-fated investments in publications that failed to prosper, he moved to New York that same year.

Although Linton had not intended to remain long in the United States, he discovered that his skills as a wood engraver found a ready market there. He soon started working for Frank Leslie's *Illustrated News*. From 1868 to 1870 he also taught at the Ladies' School of Design at the Cooper Institute. Established in 1857, this institution trained about two hundred women as wood engravers by 1880. He also designed and engraved illustrations for American book publishers, including Ticknor and Fields of Boston, Massachusetts, and D. Appleton and Company, Charles Scribner & Co., and G. P. Putnam & Son of New York. D. Appleton and Company published William Cullen Bryant's *Picturesque America* in parts from 1872 to 1874. Linton was one of at least thirty-two wood engravers who transformed the artists' drawings and sketches into engravings that could be printed with the text.

During this period Linton also engraved literary illustrations for *Scribner's Monthly* and *Century Magazine*. For the *Aldine*, a fine art journal published in New York and edited by Richard H. Stoddard, he engraved reproductions of American landscape paintings. Linton considered these prints among his best.

In the 1870s the use of photographic technology transformed the work of wood engravers. No longer did the artist or engraver draw directly on the block; instead, designs were photographed onto treated blocks. Mechanical-looking lines and dots were used to create tonal qualities once provided by thinner or thicker lines. Engravers of what was called the New School were capable of producing greater realistic detail. The visual effect was very different, and Linton was foremost among the traditional engravers to critique the changes in technique and style. Participating in the debate between the practitioners of traditional techniques and those of the New School, Linton attacked the New School in the June 1879 issue of the *Atlantic Monthly*. The debate was subsequently taken up in the pages of *Scribner's Monthly*, which published many engravings by craftsmen skilled in the techniques of the New School. Linton responded in print with *Some Practical Hints on Wood-Engraving for the Instruction of Reviewers and the Public* (1879). The debate and his 1879 book led to the production of his *The History of Wood-Engraving in America*. First issued in the pages of Sylvester Koehler's *American Art Review*

in 1880, this book contains many valuable reminiscences and biographical sketches of engravers. Although contemporary commentary focused on Linton's criticism of the New School, the book was well received and remains a useful reference work.

During these first years in the United States, Linton continued his political activities, becoming involved in the Universal Republican Alliance, sympathetic to Mazzini and the Italian movement. He spoke before the Boston Radical Club in January 1869 on the topic of republican organization. The audience included John Greenleaf Whittier, Wendell Phillips, and Abby Kelly Foster. Linton also wrote pamphlets about the Irish Fenians and the uprising by revolutionaries in Cuba. He eventually became disillusioned by American politics and ceased any active engagement in reform activities after the mid-1870s.

In the spring of 1870 Linton moved to "Appledore Farm" in Hamden, Connecticut. Within a few years he had established his own printing press in his home and was able to continue supplying publishers with engraved blocks. Living near New Haven, he became a frequent reader in the Yale College libraries and eventually compiled several anthologies of British and American poetry. From 1878 he published a number of books and pamphlets at the Appledore Press, including collections of his own poems. An appreciation of Linton and a description of Appledore was published in the *New York Times* (29 Oct. 1893). The description includes information on the works of art hanging in Linton's drawing room, the books in his library, and the products of his printing press.

Linton found both wealth and an intellectual and artistic acceptance in his adopted land that had eluded him in his native England. Shortly after his arrival in New York, he was elected a member of the Century Club, and in 1870 he became a member of the National Academy of Design. He was also a founder of the American Society of Painters in Watercolors. He visited England several times in the 1870s and 1880s, including extended stays during 1872 and 1873 and from 1882 to 1884. During his final visit in 1889 he supervised the printing of his *Masters of Wood-Engraving* at the Chiswick Press. He worked at his printing press until a few months before his death at the home of his daughter in New Haven. He was undoubtedly the finest wood engraver of his generation, as well as an important figure in political and literary circles.

• The major collection of Linton's papers in the United States is at Yale University's Beinecke Library. The collection includes examples from the printing press that Linton established in his home, as well as manuscripts for his poetry, original sketches, correspondence, and diaries. The William James Linton Collection (about 100 items) at Brown University includes early poems and other literary works, sketches and photographs, letters from correspondents from his years in England and the United States, and five letters written by Linton.

Among the American works he illustrated are *The Boy's Picture Book of Boats* (c. 1866), Hans Christian Andersen's *Little Rudy and Other Stories* (1865), his own *The Flower and* the *Star* (1865), Dinah M. Craik's *Our Year: A Child's Book* (1866), Elizabeth Barrett Browning's *Lady Geraldine's Courtship* (1870), Julia Hatfield's *The Bryant Homestead Book* (1870), Charles Dickens's *A Child's Dream of a Star* (1871), *Songs of Nature* (1873), *The Bodley's Afoot* (1879), *Poetical Works of Henry Wadsworth Longfellow* (1879–1880), and *The Children's Book* (1881).

Francis Barrymore Smith, *Radical Artisan, William James Linton, 1812–97* (1973), is an excellent biography with an exhaustive bibliography; it focuses on Linton's political activities but also provides important insights into his career as a wood engraver, writer, and illustrator. Nancy Carlson Schrock's introduction to *American Wood Engraving: A Victorian History* (1976), which reprints Linton's *The History of Wood-Engraving in America*, provides an analysis of his wood engraving set in the context of his contemporaries. Schrock also lists fifteen essays and books by him on art, including his memoirs, *Threescore and Ten Years* (1894).

GEORGIA B. BARNHILL

LION, Jules (1809?–9 Jan. 1866), artist, was born in France, but the exact place of his birth is unknown. Nothing is known about his parents or his youth, but it seems likely that he received a traditional artistic education in Europe. Lion's lithographs were exhibited at the prestigious Paris Salons of 1831 (four prints, including *L'affût aux canards* [Duck blind], which won honorable mention), 1834 (four works, including a scene based on Victor Hugo's *Nôtre Dame de Paris*), and 1836 (lithographs after Van Dyck, Jacquand, Waltier, Boulanger, and others). In the mid-1830s Lion immigrated to New Orleans, where the 1837 city directory listed him as a free man of color and as a painter and lithographer; he worked in a lithography shop opened by the newspaper *L'Abeille* (The bee). Light-skinned, Lion often passed for white and appeared in other records as such. His studio was located at 56 Canal Street, a wide boulevard that divided Creole New Orleans from the flourishing American section of the city.

Lion returned to Paris during the summer of 1839, when Louis Jacques Daguerre distributed a pamphlet detailing his invention of early photographic methods. By 27 September Lion was back in New Orleans producing daguerrean views of the city. Newspapers praised the clear images he exhibited at the St. Charles Museum in March 1840; the *Bee* declared that "nothing can be more truly beautiful. . . . It is a wonderful discovery—one too, that will prove useful, as it is admirable" (14 Mar. 1840). Lion was celebrated for introducing the daguerreotype to New Orleans and for his charming personality: "Mr. Lion is a young French gentleman, after saying which we need not add that he is pleasing, courteous, and polite" (*Daily Picayune*, 20 Mar. 1840). Lion continued to take daguerreotypes of such landmarks as the Levee and the St. Louis Hotel, and in 1842 he advertised his services as a daguerreotypist of sick or deceased persons.

In 1843 Lion opened his own studio at 3, rue St. Charles, where he made lithographic portraits and miniatures and sold daguerreotypes from Paris. The *Bee* lauded his skill: "Mr. Lion is an artist of superior merit of which anyone can convince himself by an examination of the specimens before the office door" (25 Nov. 1843). Lion also made prints of local scenes, such as *The Cathedral, New Orleans* (1842) and *View of Canal Street* (1846). He exhibited and sold his works at book and frame shops.

Lion's best-known work is a series of more than 150 fine lithographs, executed between 1837 and 1847, of prominent Louisianians and other leaders. Among Lion's delicate and engaging portraits are those of the most popular Protestant minister in New Orleans, *Rev. Theodore Clapp* (1837); *Judge François Xavier Martin* (1837); the family of wealthy commission merchant Seaman Field, *Eliza Dubourg Field and Her Daughters Eliza and Odilie* (1838); *William Freret* (1839); *Andrew Jackson* (1840); and the legislator *James Dunwoody Bronson DeBow* (1847). Lion's sitters were Creoles and Americans and included physicians, historians, jurists, mayors, surveyors, and members of the Bringier and Villeré families. Other notable sitters were the artist John James Audubon, the lawyer Charles Conrad, the planter Victor Armand, the poet François Dominique Rouquette, and General Zachary Taylor. One newspaper called the last-named work "remarkable for its likeness and the beauty of the drawing" (*Gazette de Baton Rouge*, 12 Aug. 1837). Lion became the most prolific and admired artist of color in Louisiana in the nineteenth century. He tried to publish many of these portraits in one volume in the 1840s and again in 1860. Although he had numerous patrons, it would appear that he did not have sufficient funds, for the book was never produced. However, more than 150 of his portraits exist in a unique leather-bound volume in the Historic New Orleans Collection.

Lion's pastel work, *Asher Moses Nathan and Son* (1845, private collection), is a double portrait of a mulatto man and his white father. The youth may be Achille Lion, the illegitimate son of a woman of color (name unknown), who later became Jules Lion's wife, and Nathan, a Dutch Jewish immigrant and wealthy dry-goods merchant. Perhaps to spare his white wife embarrassment and to give his children a European education, Nathan sent Achille and his sister Anna to Paris. After Nathan's wife died, he legally adopted Achille Lion and left his fortune to him and Anna. Jules Lion portrayed his affluent stepson and natural father embracing; they seem to have had a cordial relationship. Thus, the composition may not only document the actual paternity of Lion's stepson but may also refer to the artist's own mixed heritage.

In the mid-1840s Lion was forced to sell property to pay debts. In 1848 he opened an art school with Dominique Canova, a noted muralist and ornamental painter. The *Louisiana Courier* (30 Nov. 1848) commended the undertaking by "two of our most talented artists," but the partnership dissolved after a year.

In 1850 Lion proposed a ceiling painting, altar picture, and pendentive decorations for the new St. Louis cathedral. He would have liked to paint them for the sake of his art but admitted he would need payment.

Lion assured the construction committee of his ardor: "For Gentlemen, after God, what I love the most is my art" (unpublished letter, trans. Samuel Wilson, Jr., Historic New Orleans Collection). It is not known whether Lion did the paintings.

Although Lion continued to work during the 1850s, the press published little about him. In 1852 he taught drawing at Louisiana Academy. The following year he moved from the French Quarter into the Third Municipality, perhaps to save money. It is not known when he married native New Orleanian Maria Ana Muñoz, but the two had a son in 1857.

During the Civil War Lion lithographed sheet music illustrations of Confederate subjects for several New Orleans music publishers. One work depicts the Free Market, which supplied Confederate New Orleans's indigents. Lion returned to portraiture when the city was occupied by Federal forces, then taught drawing at Louisiana Academy to local businessmen in the fall evenings of 1865. He died in New Orleans.

• Many of Lion's lithographic portraits of prominent Louisianians and some of his sheet music illustrations, as well as his letter to the St. Louis Cathedral committee, are in the Historic New Orleans Collection. His prints and pastels are also in the Louisiana State Museum collection. The most useful and thorough essays on Lion are Patricia Brady, "Black Artists in Antebellum New Orleans," *Louisiana History* (Winter 1991): 5–28, and Charles East, "Jules Lion's New Orleans," *Georgia Review* (Winter 1986): 914–16. Entries on Lion are also in the *Encyclopedia of New Orleans Artists, 1718–1918* (1987); Bertram Wallace Korn, *The Early Jews of New Orleans* (1969); and Robert R. Macdonald et al., eds., *Louisiana's Black Heritage* (1979). Speculations on *Asher Moses Nathan and Son* include Regenia A. Perry, *Selections of Nineteenth-Century Afro-American Art* (1976), and Judith Wilson, "Images of Miscegenation in Nineteenth- and Twentieth-Century Art," *American Art* (Summer 1991): 89–107. Lion's obituary is in *L'Abeille*, 10 Jan. 1866.

THERESA LEININGER-MILLER

LIPCHITZ, Jacques (22 Aug. 1891–26 May 1973), sculptor, was born Chaim Jacob Lipschitz in Druskieniki, Russia (now Poland), the son of Abraham Lipschitz, an engineer and building contractor, and Rachel Leah Krinsky. From 1906 to 1909 Lipchitz attended a state high school in Vilna, the capital of Lithuania, where he studied engineering. Against his father's wishes but with the support of his mother, he went to Paris in 1909 to pursue a career in art, studying at the École des Beaux-Arts under Jean-Antoine Ingalbert. He also attended drawing classes at the Académie Colarossi and the sculpture classes of Raoul Verlet at the Académie Julian. Originally unmoved by avant-garde art movements during his first years in Paris, Lipchitz's sculpture between 1909 and 1912 conformed to nineteenth-century Romantic-realist traditions.

In 1912 Lipchitz was called home for military service, but after receiving a medical discharge he returned to Paris in 1913 and established a studio in Montparnasse. Lipchitz's personal, mature style began to emerge in 1913–1914 under the influence of cubism. In fact, Lipchitz was among the earliest sculptors to extend into the third dimension the pictorial innovations first established in cubist paintings. *Sailor with Guitar* (1914; Philadelphia Museum of Art), for example, adopted in a predictable manner the rectilinear structure of the synthetic cubist paintings of Pablo Picasso and Georges Braque. More original were Lipchitz's *Bather* (1915), *Man with a Guitar* (1916; Museum of Modern Art, New York), and "detachable figures" of 1915–1916; these sculptures reflected the additional cubist influences of Juan Gris and Alexander Archipenko in the use of displaced planes and a reduced architectonic austerity, but they never lost touch with the human figure. This blending of abstract, geometric forms with the natural shapes and contours of the human body characterized Lipchitz's work until about 1925.

Lipchitz's growing reputation within the European art world led to his first large one-man show in 1920 at the Paris gallery of Léonce Rosenberg. In 1922 he attracted the patronage of the American collector Albert C. Barnes, who commissioned from the artist a series of bas-reliefs, a sculptural form with which Lipchitz had begun experimenting several years earlier. He became a French citizen in 1924 and soon after married Berthe Kitrosser, a Russian poet with whom he had been living since 1915.

Lipchitz continued his inventive approach to the application of cubist principles to sculpture into the mid-1920s, formulating an autonomous cubist sculpture through the discovery of formal and spatial solutions unique to three-dimensional art. In works such as *Pierrot with Clarinet* (1926), the sculptor rejected the solid geometric core that typified his earlier cubist figures for a constructivist approach in which space has been more successfully integrated as a major compositional element. About this time he also created his first "transparents," open, spatial structures originally modeled in wax, then cast in bronze. The transparents reflected not only Lipchitz's interest in exploring the inherent possibilities of casting in bronze but also his growing need to find new avenues of expression beyond the limitations of freestanding figural sculpture.

Lipchitz eventually abandoned the severe, blocklike style of his early phase of cubism for the freedom to experiment with movement and the expressionistic possibilities inherent in human form. One of the first sculptures to signal this shift was *Ploumanach* (1926). Seeking with this work an idiom that would allow a greater play of his emotions and imagination, Lipchitz adopted a more robust, fluid style. As such, *Ploumanach* anticipated the increasing subjectivity and sensitivity to feeling that characterized Lipchitz's work throughout the late 1920s and into the 1930s.

In contrast to the single-figure pieces typical of Lipchitz's cubist period, dual-figure sculptures such as *La Joie de vivre* (1927), *Mother and Child* (1929–1930; Cleveland Museum of Art), and *Return of the Prodigal Son* (1931) began to appear more regularly during these years. These works celebrated human fertility and continuity and asserted Lipchitz's belief in the triumph of the creative forces of life over death, themes that reflected the artist's emotional responses not only to personal events such as the death of his father and sister but also to the emergence of Hitler and Nazism and his own evolving self-awareness as a Jew.

Lipchitz's emotive style continued to evolve throughout the 1930s as he incorporated into his sculpture ever more aggressive elements, often resulting in expressionist abstract works of exceptional imagination and power. Reflecting his growing sense of anxiety regarding the current situation in Europe, he characteristically chose themes of conflict, resistance, and sexual violence derived from mythology and the Old Testament but bearing a metaphorical relationship to contemporary sociopolitical events. Typical examples include *Jacob and the Angel* (1932), *David and Goliath* (1933), and *Rape of Europa* (1938). Many of Lipchitz's statues from this period focused on the savage struggle between man and beast, metaphorical references to the growing brutality of the Nazi regime. *Prometheus Strangling the Vulture* (1936–1938), shown at the 1937 Paris World's Fair and later commissioned by the French government for the Grand Palais and the Brazilian government for the Ministry of Education and Health in Rio de Janeiro, perhaps captured best the artist's personal abhorrence of Fascism. Although in their modeling and construction sculptures such as *Prometheus* revealed Lipchitz's increasing debt to the powerful bronze aesthetics of Auguste Rodin and the fighting animal groups of Antoine-Louis Barye, they were imaginatively transformed by Lipchitz's unique expressionist vision and personal desire to comment on the world around him, often swelling to monumental scale and assuming the grotesque character of monsters.

Following Germany's invasion of France, Lipchitz and his wife fled Paris for Toulouse. They eventually immigrated to New York in 1941, leaving behind their art collection and most of the sculptor's work. Upon his arrival in America, Lipchitz, nearly broke, quickly set up a studio in Washington Square and began to re-create a body of work. Reacting positively to his new surroundings and feeling a sense of relief from the immediate threat of Nazism, he reduced his reliance on combat motifs, turning instead to more celebratory themes such as *Return of the Child* (1941; Solomon R. Guggenheim Museum, New York), *Blossoming* (1941–1942; Museum of Modern Art, New York), *Spring* (1942), and *Promise* (1942). The affirmative character of this kind of imagery dominated Lipchitz's work for the rest of his life.

Lipchitz's presence in the United States was felt immediately, especially in the wake of his first major exhibition after settling in New York, a one-man show held at Curt Valentin's Buchholz Gallery in 1942. Lipchitz also took part in a 1942 group show titled "Artists in Exile" held at the Pierre Matisse Gallery, where he shared space with notable European surrealists such as Yves Tanguy, Max Ernst, and André Masson. Not until after the war, however, did Lipchitz's work have a direct impact on the development of American art, influencing the more florid expressionism of leading American sculptors of the 1940s and 1950s such as Herbert Ferber, Theodore Roszak, and Seymour Lipton.

From the beginning, Lipchitz's work in America reflected a fuller play of his innate romantic sensibilities. *Mother and Child II* (1941–1945; Museum of Modern Art, New York), for example, revealed the sculptor's continuing reverence for Rodin in his use of the partial figure, a motif inherently expressionistic in its simplification and distortion of the human body. In 1943–1944 Lipchitz adopted the surrealist technique of automatism to create his "semiautomatics," works formed by modeling plasticine under water. Other key themes developed during these years include "Madonna" and "Hagar" motifs, the latter with probable autobiographical references to his forced expatriation, and a series of dancing figures.

Following the end of World War II, Lipchitz returned with his wife to France. But finding the atmosphere of postwar Paris too inhibiting, and after a split with Berthe, he returned to New York and established a new studio in Manhattan. Lipchitz's divorce from Berthe and marriage in 1948 to Yulla Halberstadt, also a sculptor, was quickly followed by the birth of a daughter. By 1950 Lipchitz had moved his new family to Hastings-on-Hudson. In January 1952 his New York studio was destroyed in a fire along with most of his American sculptures and models of works in progress. By the following year, however, Lipchitz was able, with the help of an aid committee sponsored by American museums, to set up a new studio at his home. In 1954 a major retrospective of Lipchitz's work was held at the Museum of Modern Art in New York.

Immediate postwar sculptures by Lipchitz included *Song of Songs* (1945–1948), the monumental *Sacrifice II* (1948–1952; Whitney Museum of American Art, New York), the *Variations on a Chisel* series, and *Birth of the Muses* (1950–1951), a bas-relief executed for Mrs. John D. Rockefeller III. Among Lipchitz's important public commissions of this period are a Madonna, *Notre Dame de Liesse* (1955), for the Church of Notre-Dame-de-Toute-Grâce in Assy, France (two additional versions of the figure were cast in 1958, one for Philip Johnson's Roofless Church in New Harmony, Indiana, and another for the Abbey of Saint Columba on the island of Iona, the Hebrides, Scotland), and *The Spirit of Enterprise*, completed in 1960 as part of the Samuel Memorial in Fairmount Park, Philadelphia. Amsterdam's Stedelijk Museum organized a major exhibition of Lipchitz's work in 1958. That same year Lipchitz became a U.S. citizen.

Following a trip to Italy in 1961, Lipchitz began spending his summers there, working at the Luigi Tommasi foundry in Pietrasanta. In 1963 he visited Israel for the first time. Important works by Lipchitz from the late 1960s and early 1970s included his *Images of Italy* series, posthumous busts of *John F. Kennedy* (1965), and *Bellerophon Taming Pegasus* (1970–1971), for Columbia University Law School. Ever more conscious in his later years of his Jewish heritage, Lipchitz designed a monument dedicated to the Jewish people, *Our Tree of Life* (1973), which was erected in Jerusalem on the grounds of the Hebrew University. A major retrospective of Lipchitz's art was held in 1972 at the Metropolitan Museum of Art in New York. Lipchitz died on the island of Capri.

• Important writings or statements by Lipchitz are *My Life in Sculpture* (1972); an interview published in Katherine Kuh, *The Artist's Voice: Talks with Seventeen Artists* (1962); and *Amedeo Modigliani* (1952). Monographs written on Lipchitz include A. M. Hammacher, *Jacques Lipchitz* (1975) and *Jacques Lipchitz: His Sculpture* (1960); Irene Patai, *Encounters: The Life of Jacques Lipchitz* (1961); and Henry R. Hope, *The Sculpture of Jacques Lipchitz* (1954). Other key works on Lipchitz are H. H. Arnason, *Jacques Lipchitz: Sketches in Bronze* (1969); Bert Van Bork, *Jacques Lipchitz: The Artist at Work* (1966); Pierre Schneider, "Lipchitz: Cubism, the School for Baroque," *ArtNews* 58 (Oct. 1959): 46; Albert Elsen, "The Humanism of Rodin and Lipchitz," *Art Journal* 17 (Spring 1958): 247–65; and Robert Goldwater, *Jacques Lipchitz* (1954; English trans., 1959). An obituary is in the *New York Times*, 28 May 1973.

THOMAS P. SOMMA

LIPMANN, Fritz Albert (12 June 1899–24 July 1986), biochemist, was born in Königsberg, Germany, the son of Leopold Lipmann, a lawyer, and Gertrud Lachmanski. After a year of army service during World War I in 1918–1919, Lipmann earned an M.D. from the University of Berlin in 1924. Having completed his exams, he questioned a career in medicine and decided to enroll in a three-month course in biochemistry given by Peter Rona. This, in turn, led to a fellowship spent in a pharmacology laboratory in Amsterdam. "This experience," he wrote in his autobiography, "was the turning point; it made me decide seriously to become a biochemist" (*Wanderings of a Biochemist*, p. 5). He went on to complete a Ph.D. in chemistry at the University of Berlin in 1927. From 1927 to 1931 he was a research assistant working with renowned chemists Albert Fischer and Otto Meyerhof in Berlin. Lipmann later noted that Meyerhof, a Nobel Prize winner, was one of "the influences of greatest consequence" (*Wanderings of a Biochemist*, p. 7). In 1931 Lipmann married Elfreda "Freda" M. Hall; they had one son.

Lipmann first came to the United States in 1932, as a researcher at the Rockefeller Institute for Medical Research in New York City, but he returned to Europe within a year to take up a position as an investigator at the Biological Institute of the Carlsbad Laboratories in Copenhagen, Denmark. His desire to return eventually to his native Germany was undermined by the political climate under the Hitler regime, which made it dangerous and unwise for Lipmann, a Jew, to go back. Instead, he returned in 1939 to the United States as a research associate at the Cornell Medical School and became a naturalized U.S. citizen in 1944.

In 1940 Lipmann's contribution to science was noted in the *New York Times*, which described him and a group of other scientists as having debunked a new discovery that heralded hope for understanding cancer. Lipmann was one of the researchers who "digested" healthy and abnormal cells by treating them with hydrochloric acid; after up to fifteen hours they tested the tissues with an enzyme that affected only unnatural amino acids and found "that the quality of so-called unnatural amino acids is about the same both in cancers and in good muscle. We have to write off another disappointment in cancer research," the newspaper reported (7 Jan. 1940).

After two years at Cornell, Lipmann moved in 1941 to Massachusetts General Hospital as head of the Biochemical Research Laboratory and research fellow at the Harvard Medical School. Although his affiliation at the hospital—with the Department of Surgery— seemed at the time "rather strange" for a biochemist, in retrospect Lipmann noted it was "one of the really lucky breaks in my life" (*Wanderings of a Biochemist*, p. 39).

Lipmann is best known for his work in the 1940s on carbohydrate metabolism and his discovery of a compound he named coenzyme A. In 1945 he isolated coenzyme A and explained its fundamental role in body chemistry when it combined with another two-carbon compound to form acetylcoenzyme A. He then went on to show how the compound contributes to the building of fatty acids and other components integral to growth and renewal in the body. In 1948 Lipmann received both the Carl Neuberg Medal and a Mead-Johnson & Co. award. The following year, he became professor of biological chemistry at the Harvard Medical School.

One of the highlights of Lipmann's scientific career was the 1953 Nobel Prize for medicine and physiology, which he shared with Hans Adolf Krebs, then professor of biochemistry at Sheffield, England. Lipmann was recognized for his work on the mechanism of biosynthesis and his discovery of coenzyme A. Commenting on the prize in the *New York Times* (23 Oct. 1953), Lipmann said, "If I made a contribution in the field, it was to open up an understanding of what metabolism is." He went on to say that his discovery of the mechanism of biosynthesis was made through some trial and error. "You have to follow your nose; you don't map it out," he said. "You try one experiment, then another, and bring some sense into it." In describing their postannouncement celebration, Lipmann's wife observed that "more than a hundred people roamed around in the little house—the police came three times for disturbing the peace" (*The Roots of Modern Biochemistry*, p. 7).

In addition to his scientific work, Lipmann was one of a number of scientists who were vocal about world political events. In 1955 he joined seventeen other Nobel Prize winners from around the world in cautioning against the use of nuclear weapons. A scientific meeting in Germany resulted in a declaration appealing to all nations to forsake nuclear force or risk destroying the world as a result of radioactive fallout.

In 1957 Lipmann became a member of the Rockefeller Institute and a faculty member of Rockefeller University. New laboratories were built for him in the New York City facility. An article in the *New York Times* (24 Jan. 1962) heralded "new gains" in understanding heredity. At a symposium at Indiana University Lipmann reported on his experiments on organisms as different as bacteria and rabbits. He found that although the experimental specimens and their cells were very different, they used the same coded information. Lipmann's contribution was reported as one of the first indicators that the genetic code was universal throughout nature.

Lipmann was elected to Britain's Royal Society in 1962 and was awarded the National Medal of Science by President Lyndon Johnson in 1966 for his "fundamental contributions to the conceptual structure of modern biochemistry" and for his discoveries of the molecular mechanisms that are part of the transformation and transfer of energy in living cells. He was a member of the National Academy of Sciences as well as a fellow of the New York Academy of Science and of the Danish Royal Academy of Sciences.

In his last twenty years, Lipmann continued to do research and take a stand for political causes. In 1982 he joined literary, cultural, and scientific leaders calling for an end to martial law in Poland. He died in Poughkeepsie, New York.

Lipmann was deemed by colleagues and observers of biochemistry to be a scientific genius, in part because of his ability to break complicated problems down into more understandable components. A postdoctoral associate who worked in Lipmann's lab at Rockefeller University, Robert Roskoski, Jr., observed of Lipmann in an obituary in *Trends in Biochemical Sciences*, "On the basis of his achievements, he was unquestionably, a biochemical genius. . . . I believe that this constant striving to simplify contributed to his success" (12 [1987]: 136).

• Lipmann's autobiography is *Wanderings of a Biochemist* (1971). Horst Kleinkauf et al., eds., *The Roots of Modern Biochemistry* (1988), features both biographical and autobiographical articles on Lipmann's life; a bibliography of Lipmann's work from 1924 to 1985, totaling 560 publications; and a series of recollections of the scientist at various points in his career in Europe and the United States written by colleagues; one, "Life with Fritz" was written by Freda Hall-Lipmann, his wife. This lengthy text also includes articles on the history and major developments in biochemistry and molecular biology and is reviewed in *Science* 242 (11 Nov. 1988). Dietmar Richter, ed., *Energy, Regulation and Biosynthesis in Molecular Biology*, was published in 1974 to celebrate the 12 June 1974 symposium held in Berlin-Dahlem in honor of Lipmann's seventy-fifth birthday. An obituary is in the *New York Times*, 25 July 1986.

MARIANNE FEDUNKIW STEVENS

LIPPARD, George (10 Apr. 1822–9 Feb. 1854), novelist and social reformer, was born on his father's farm in West Nantmeal Township in Chester County, Pennsylvania, the son of Daniel B. Lippard and Jemima Ford. His father, an erstwhile schoolteacher and local official, sold his farm in 1824 and moved the family to nearby Germantown, where George's German-speaking grandfather was living. Having become physically incapable of supporting a large family, the parents moved to Philadelphia, leaving George and his sisters in Germantown in the care of their grandfather and two maiden aunts. A sickly and intense youth, Lippard was considered a "queer" fellow "of no account" by some of his mates at the Concord School across from his home, which he attended from around 1829 to 1832.

Shortly after his mother's death in 1831, Lippard moved with his aunts and sisters to Philadelphia. In 1837 he was sent to a private school in Rhinebeck, New York, with the aim of studying for the Methodist ministry. Disgusted by the school's administrative hierarchy and the hypocrisy of its director, he returned to Philadelphia that October. He worked from 1838 to 1841 as a lawyers' assistant, an occupation that he said exposed him to "social life, hidden sins, and iniquities covered with the cloak of authority." Impoverished and shabby, he lived for a time like a bohemian in the studios of artist friends and in vacant buildings.

Soon disillusioned with the law, Lippard in 1842 gained visibility as a trenchant satirical columnist for a lively Philadelphia newspaper, the *Spirit of the Times*. He also wrote a Gothic novel, *The Ladye Annabel; or, The Doom of the Poisoner* (1844), a witches' brew of medieval torture, live burials, alchemy, and necrophilia. His close friend Edgar Allan Poe found the novel "richly inventive and imaginative—indicative of *genius* in its author."

The novel that made Lippard famous was *The Quaker City; or, The Monks of Monk-Hall* (1844–1845), which sensationally detailed secret sexual depravity and drunken excess among Philadelphia's ruling class. Nightmarish, erotic, and fiercely egalitarian, *The Quaker City* had instant appeal for the masses. It sold some 60,000 copies in its first year, passed through many American "editions" by 1849, and became, Lippard happily claimed, "more attacked, and more read, than any other work of American fiction ever published." Lippard went on to produce several more urban-exposé novels, including *The Empire City* (1850), *Memoirs of a Preacher* (1849), and *New York: Its Upper Ten and Lower Million* (1853), all of which luridly dramatized social injustice and upper-class corruption in America's rapidly expanding cities. He also wrote many semifanciful "legends" of American history, mythologizing the founding fathers and retelling key moments of the American Revolution so vividly that several of the legends (most famously the one describing the ringing of the Liberty Bell on 4 July 1776) became part of American folklore. In addition, he was a peripatetic lecturer, the editor of a short-lived reform newspaper, the *Quaker City* (1849), and the founder and "Supreme Washington" of the Brotherhood of the Union, a secret labor organization with 142 branches in nineteen states in 1850.

Though feverishly active, Lippard was rarely happy for long periods. He married Rose Newman in 1847; neither of their two children reached the age of two. After Rose died in 1851, Lippard devoted himself mainly to traveling and writing for his labor group. He died in Philadelphia of tuberculosis. For literary critics Lippard is chiefly studied as an important figure of popular culture, one whose novels represent the wildly subversive underside of the antebellum literary scene. Historians study him as a fiery social critic and working-class advocate.

• In addition to works mentioned in this article, Lippard was the author of *Blanche of Brandywine* (1846); *Legends of Mexico* (1847); *Washington and His Generals* (1847); *Paul Ardenheim, the Monk of Wissahikon* (1848); *The Killers* (1850); *Thomas Paine, Author-Soldier of the American Revolution* (1852); "The Heart-Broken" [tribute to Charles Brockden Brown] (1848); *The White Banner* (1851); and numerous pieces in the Philadelphia *Citizen Soldier*, the Philadelphia *Saturday Courier*, the Philadelphia *Nineteenth Century*, and other newspapers. A file of newspaper clippings, letters, and other assorted writings related to Lippard's career is held by the American Antiquarian Society in Worcester, Mass. The Joseph Jackson Collection at the Historical Society of Pennsylvania contains some sixteen letters in Lippard's hand; also at the Historical Society is a file of the *Spirit of the Times* and Lippard's newspaper the *Quaker City*. A representative selection of his works is David S. Reynolds, ed., *George Lippard, Prophet of Protest: Writings of an American Radical, 1822–1854* (1986). Brief obituaries appeared in the Philadelphia *Public Ledger*, 10 Feb. 1854, and the Philadelphia *Sunday Mercury*, 5 Mar. 1854. John Bell Bouton, *The Life and Choice Writings of George Lippard* (1855), is a flattering biography, authorized by Lippard. A chronology of his life, analyses of his fiction, and a set of annotated bibliographies may be found in David S. Reynolds, *George Lippard* (1982). See also Emilio DeGrazia, "The Life and Works of George Lippard" (Ph.D. diss., Ohio State Univ., 1969), and David S. Reynolds, *Beneath the American Renaissance: The Subversive Imagination in the Age of Emerson and Melville* (1988).

DAVID S. REYNOLDS

LIPPINCOTT, Joshua Ballinger (18 Mar. 1813–5 Jan. 1886), publisher, was born in Juliustown, Burlington County, New Jersey, the only child of Quakers Jacob Lippincott, who died when his son was very young, and Sarah Ballinger. After receiving a common school education, Lippincott moved in 1827 to Philadelphia to work as a clerk for "Clarke, the bookseller." He apparently did his job well, for when the business went bankrupt in 1831 Clarke's creditors asked the eighteen-year-old Lippincott to take charge of the business. In 1836 Lippincott bought the business and renamed it J. B. Lippincott & Company; he expanded into publishing and specialized in Bibles and prayer books. By 1849 he was successful enough to buy Grigg, Elliot & Company, the nation's (and probably the world's) largest book distributor and America's foremost medical publisher. John Grigg had started in the industry as a clerk for the Philadelphia publishers Benjamin Warner and Jacob Johnson, the latter of whom had begun business in 1792. By assuming Grigg, Elliot &

Company's "publishing tradition" with his purchase of the firm, Lippincott was able to date his company back to the eighteenth century.

Lippincott married Josephine Craige in 1845; they had four children, and all three sons went into their father's business. His second son, Craige, became president of the company after his father's death and was succeeded upon his death in 1911 by the youngest son, Joseph Bertram. Lippincott thus began a family publishing tradition that has continued to the present.

Lippincott was called the "Napoleon of the book trade" by his contemporaries, perhaps because he thought on a grand scale and took gambles in publishing. As he later said of his predecessor's business, "Mr. Grigg was considered a giant of a bookseller, yet his whole stock could be packed in one of the smallest of our rooms. We made more books in one month than he made in a year" (*Publishers Weekly*, 13 Dec. 1879, p. 834). By the time Lippincott died, his firm was publishing more than 2,500 volumes. The company became known for large projects that took years to complete and that were expensive to print; for example, Lippincott's most popular books included the 2,000-page *Lippincott's Pronouncing Gazetteer of the World* (1855) and the 2,300-page *Universal Pronouncing Dictionary of Biography and Mythology* (1870).

When the Civil War erupted in 1861, J. B. Lippincott & Company lost hundreds of thousands of dollars in unpaid debts owed by southern retailers. Many publishers went bankrupt during the war. Fortunately for Lippincott's firm, after the economic crisis of 1857 he had developed a policy of cash purchases, so the company had no outstanding debts, except to Lippincott himself, for money advanced to the firm. He also made up for his southern losses by developing new markets in the North and West and taking on government publications, including military and professional works. Indeed, he managed to expand during the war by erecting in 1861–1863 a new marble-fronted store on Market Street, a building that housed the entire operations of the firm and was so magnificent that it became a prominent Philadelphia tourist attraction. In 1862 Lippincott was one of the leading men of Philadelphia who formed the Union Club, a social organization of the city's elite intended to provide a "refuge for loyalty" in the midst of the border city's southern sympathies. He signed the articles of association from his sick bed, where he was recovering from typhoid fever.

Lippincott traveled a great deal, making five international trips during which he completed what he called "a survey, to a greater or less extent, of every country of Europe." During his trip in 1851 he vastly improved trade relations with English publishers, who had until then been fairly cold toward their American counterparts. As a result, J. B. Lippincott & Company began specializing in fine editions of British authors and became the American distributor for British publishers William and Robert Chambers, including their *Chambers Cyclopaedia of English Literature*. By 1875 the company had a large enough foreign distribution that Lippincott traveled to London to set up an import-export office. During that trip he also journeyed up the Nile and to Syria, where he contracted a fever that permanently weakened him and may have led to his death.

Lippincott believed that one could not succeed in both business and fashionable society, so he did not mingle in the Philadelphia social world. He was, however, friends with many of the leading authors of the day. Furthermore, as one contemporary noted, "He has ever manifested a deep interest in the welfare of his adopted city, and his business policy has always comprehended a strenuous endeavor to attract trade to Philadelphia, and to retain it. In the same spirit he has liberally invested his capital in whatever schemes promised to assist in the development of its resources and prosperity" (*Manufactories*, p. 259). In 1876 Lippincott was elected to the board of trustees of the University of Pennsylvania. He helped found, through his generous support, the University of Pennsylvania Department of Veterinary Medicine and was for a while the president of the Society for the Prevention of Cruelty to Animals. For the last twenty years of his life he sat on the board of managers of the Philadelphia and Reading Railroad Company. As his obituary in *Publishers Weekly* noted, "Mr. Lippincott was constantly beset with importunities to remove his [business] interests to New York. But he believed in Philadelphia and the possibility of a great publishing and booktrade there, and could not be persuaded to leave." After 1878 Lippincott took a much less active role in the day-to-day operations of the business, and in February 1885, perhaps anticipating his death, he reorganized the firm into a stock company, renamed it the J. B. Lippincott Company, and retained 9,970 of the 10,000 shares. His estate was worth more than $3 million when he died in Philadelphia.

Almost twenty years before his death Lippincott had told a friend, pointing to his private office, "Could I relate the scenes that have occurred in that room you would fully appreciate the annoyances and trials of a publisher's life. But its mysteries are sacred; and the blank, sad histories of would-be authors and the little foibles of the really great authors must all slumber there untold." In appreciation of Lippincott's "publisher's life," all of the bookstores in Philadelphia closed for the hour of his funeral.

• Information about Lippincott can be found in Joseph W. Lippincott, Jr.'s foreword to J. B. Lippincott Company, *The Author and His Audience* (1967); *The Manufactories and Manufacturers of Pennsylvania of the Nineteenth Century* (1875); W. S. W., *Joshua B. Lippincott: A Memorial Sketch* (1888); and "A Philadelphia Publisher," *Publishers Weekly*, 13 Dec. 1879, p. 834. Most histories of J. B. Lippincott Company include valuable information about the founder. See Margaret Becket, "J. B. Lippincott Company," in *American Literary Publishing Houses, 1638–1899*, vol. 1, ed. Peter Dzwonkoski (1986); J. Stuart Freeman, Jr., *Toward a Third Century of Excellence: An Informal History of the J. B. Lippincott Company on the Occasion of Its Two-Hundredth Anniversary* (1992); "J. B. Lippincott Company, 1792–1936," *Publishers Weekly*, 7 Nov. 1936, pp. 1840–43; George Thomas Kurian, *The Directory of American Book Publishing from Founding Fathers to Today's Conglomerates* (1975); "The Lippincotts of Philadelphia," *American Library Association Bulletin* 51, no. 6 (June 1957): 428–31; and Edith M. Stern, "J. B. Lippincott Co.," *Saturday Review of Literature* 24, no. 8 (14 June 1941): 11–12. An obituary is in *Publishers Weekly*, 9 Jan. 1886, pp. 49–50.

KAREN A. KEELY

LIPPINCOTT, Sara Jane Clarke (23 Sept. 1823–20 Apr. 1904), writer, was born in Pompey, New York, the daughter of Thaddeus Clarke, a physician, and Deborah Baker. Not long after her birth, the family moved to nearby Fabius and later to Rochester, where she was educated. While in her teens, she started contributing verse to the local papers. In 1842 the family moved to New Brighton, Pennsylvania, and she joined them there the following year.

In 1844 Lippincott began contributing letters to the New York Mirror and *Home Journal*, signing them "Grace Greenwood," a name she started using socially as well. These contributions secured her literary reputation, and she was soon writing for some of the most important periodicals of the day: *Godey's Lady's Book*, *Graham's American Monthly Magazine*, *Sartain's Union Magazine of Literature and Art*, and the *Saturday Evening Post*. Her contributions ranged from sentimental fiction and verse to comments on the current state of literature and politics. Perhaps most noteworthy are her remarks concerning the international copyright issue, written as burlesques of contemporary authors such as Edgar Allan Poe and Herman Melville. In 1849 she became an editorial assistant for *Godey's Lady's Book*, but Louis Godey dismissed her the following year for an antislavery essay she contributed to the abolitionist *National Era*. Gamaliel Bailey, the editor of the *National Era*, subsequently offered her a position and asked her to move to Washington, D.C. She accepted the offer and simultaneously became the Washington correspondent for the *Saturday Evening Post*. She continued her association with the *Post* until the late 1890s.

Starting in 1850, Lippincott began gathering and publishing her periodical contributions as separate works. *Greenwood Leaves*, a collection of sentimental sketches, literary burlesques, and journalistic letters, was the earliest of her many popular books. John Greenleaf Whittier found the letters the best part of the book. In them her "freedom, freshness, and strong individuality" were "fully developed" (*National Era* 3 [1849]: 197). She included proportionately more letters in *Greenwood Leaves: A Collection of Sketches and Letters: Second Series* (1852). *Poems*, a collection of periodical verse, and *History of My Pets*, her first work of juvenile literature, also appeared during the early 1850s. A European tour allowed her to contribute numerous travel reports to the *National Era* and the *Saturday Evening Post*. Her European sojourn also prompted a travel narrative, *Haps and Mishaps of a Tour in Europe* (1854), and another work for children,

Merrie England: Travels, Descriptions, Tales and Historical Sketches (1855).

In 1853 she married Leander K. Lippincott, with whom she had one daughter. That same year, she and her husband began the *Little Pilgrim*, one of America's first children's magazines, an effort that one reviewer called "the best work of the kind we have ever seen" (*Graham's* 44 [1854]: 234). Though their periodical venture was a success, their marriage proved unhappy. Lippincott's husband was often rumored to be unfaithful, and his association with the U.S. government was fraught with controversy. He acquired a government position and rose to the chief clerkship of the General Land Office only to be dismissed from the post and indicted on a charge concerning fraudulent Indian land claims in 1876. After the indictment, he fled prosecution and incidentally abandoned his wife and daughter.

Throughout the 1850s Lippincott continued to publish a steady stream of books, mostly collections gathered from the *Little Pilgrim* and from her numerous other periodical contributions. Late in the decade she joined the lecture circuit and spoke for various humanitarian reforms. Before the Civil War she argued vigorously for abolition. After the war she argued for prison reform and against capital punishment, among many other causes. She frequently vacationed overseas and out West from the 1870s. Her overseas journeys prompted *Stories and Sights of France and Italy* (1867), and another work for children, *Bonnie Scotland: Tales of Her History, Heroes, and Poets* (1861). Lippincott's excursions to Colorado inspired *New Life in New Lands: Notes of Travel* (1873), a collection of letters that originally appeared in the *New York Times* extolling the charm and beauty of the Rocky Mountains. The work provides memorably vivid descriptions of Chicago, Colorado, Utah, Nevada, and California. From 1870 she served as correspondent for the New York *Tribune* and the *New York Times* as well as for other newspapers in Philadelphia and Chicago. Before her death in New Rochelle, New York, she lived alternately in New York and Washington, continued to travel, and continued to write.

While Lippincott deserves credit as one of America's early female newspaper correspondents, she never really escaped the pervasive sentimentalism of her day. Reviewing one of her early works, a writer for *Graham's Magazine* (40 [1852]: 219) found that she had "not yet obtained the faculty of viewing things as they are in themselves, independent of the feelings they excite in her own soul." Though Lippincott's works remained popular throughout the nineteenth century, her sentimentality has doomed much of her work to obscurity. Her most lasting works are those that transcend the literary commonplaces of the day: her burlesque of contemporary literati, her tough-minded journalistic correspondence, and her appreciation of the landscape of the American West.

• Some of Lippincott's letters may be found at the Henry Huntington Library, San Marino, Calif., and at the Houghton Library, Harvard University. For additional information, see Maurine Beasley, "Pens and Petticoats: Early Women Washington Correspondents," *Journalism History* 1 (Winter 1974–1975): 112–15; A. Cheree Carlson, "Limitations on the Comic Frame: Some Witty American Women of the Nineteenth Century," *Quarterly Journal of Speech* 74 (1988): 310–22; Frank Luther Mott, *History of American Magazines* (5 vols., 1957–1968); Fred Lewis Pattee, *The Feminine Fifties* (1940), pp. 276–82; Margaret Farrand Thorp, *Female Persuasion: Six Strong-Minded Women* (1949), pp. 143–78; and Willard Thorp, "'Grace Greenwood' Parodies *Typee*," *American Literature* 9 (Jan. 1938): 455–57. An obituary is in the *New York Times*, 21 Apr. 1904.

KEVIN J. HAYES

LIPPMANN, Walter (23 Sept. 1889–14 Dec. 1974), journalist and author, was born in New York City, the son of Jacob Lippmann, an investor, and Daisy Baum. Born into a family of wealth and leisure, Lippmann traveled yearly to Europe with his art-loving parents, attended private schools in New York City, and entered Harvard in the illustrious class of 1910. Among his classmates were Heywood Broun, T. S. Eliot, and John Reed, who hailed him, to no one's surprise, as a future president of the United States. An idealistic young man, Lippmann worked with the poor of Boston, founded the student Socialist Club, and wrote for college journals pledged to social reform.

At Harvard the brilliant student made a strong impression on three men who influenced him greatly: the philosophers William James and George Santayana, and the British socialist Graham Wallas. From James, Lippmann learned to value experimentation, pluralism, and action; from Santayana, the opposite virtues of detachment, measure, and restraint; and from Wallas, a respect for an unpredictable human nature over the rigidities of political theories and institutions.

Chosen by Santayana as his assistant and expected one day to follow in his footsteps, Lippmann instead left Harvard in May 1910, just a few weeks before receiving his master's degree in philosophy, to be a reporter on the *Boston Common*, a socialist newspaper in Boston. At the time journalism was not considered to be a proper profession for gentlemen. But young Lippmann was fired by a need to be a part of the action. This tension between a life of contemplation and a yearning for involvement was a hallmark of his career.

Older men were attracted to Lippmann for his brilliance and he to them for what he could learn. After a few months with the reformist Boston editor Ralph Albertson (who in 1917 became his father-in-law when Lippmann married Albertson's daughter Faye), he won the coveted post of assistant to one of the great muckrakers and political debunkers of the age, Lincoln Steffens. From Steffens he learned irreverence and skepticism, qualities that he took with him in 1912 to Schenectady, New York, where he went to work for the newly elected socialist mayor. But what attracted Lippmann to socialism was less concern for the poor and downtrodden, as was the case with his friend John

Reed, than an impatience with how badly society was organized.

Lippmann's experience with socialists, along with his evenings in Greenwich Village among poets and pamphleteers intent on transforming the world, only intensified his skepticism about romantic reformers. In the summer of 1912 he retreated to the Maine woods and within a few months produced a short, opinionated book bristling with iconoclasm. *A Preface to Politics* was a young man's potpourri, combining James's hymn to experimentation with the Progressives' call to action, and spiced with Henri-Louis Bergson and a bit of Sigmund Freud, whose psychoanalytic theories had only begun to cross the Atlantic.

This cheeky tract caught the attention of Lippmann's political idol Theodore Roosevelt and also of Herbert Croly, who was launching a weekly magazine to promote Roosevelt's idea of a "New Nationalism." The 24-year-old Lippmann, talented and self-assured, struck Croly as perfect for an editorship at the *New Republic*. Even before the first issue appeared in November 1914, Lippmann brought out his second book—one sharply at odds with his first. In *Drift and Mastery* he cut his last ties to the socialists and extolled a scientifically managed society run by a public-minded elite. Roosevelt, who hoped to run for president again in 1916, saw this as a description of himself and pronounced Lippmann to be the "most brilliant young man of his age in all the United States."

Although the *New Republic* was meant to be a journal of Bull Moose domestic reform, its launching coincided with the outbreak of war in Europe, and the subject of foreign affairs became unavoidable. Lippmann, who was at the House of Commons when Britain declared war on Germany in 1914 and had cultivated such Fabian socialists as H. G. Wells, Bernard Shaw, Sidney Webb, and Beatrice Webb, began writing on the issues of the war, and more urgently on whether the United States should be drawn in.

In 1915 he published his first book on foreign policy, *The Stakes of Diplomacy*, and by the following year, convinced that the United States could not allow Britain to be defeated, began a series of editorials designed to bring the United States into the war. Developing close ties with Colonel Edward House, Woodrow Wilson's éminence grise, he gained privileged access to the White House. When the United States entered the war in 1917 Lippmann joined the government as part of a secret team known as the Inquiry. Its assignment was no less than to draw the geographic and political outlines of the postwar world. With Lippmann as coordinator, the group drafted the territorial provisions of Wilson's Fourteen Points.

In the spring of 1918 House sent Lippmann to London to conduct intelligence gathering and disseminate propaganda behind German lines. This experience proved to be critical in his intellectual development. Impressed by how easily public opinion could be molded and distorted, Lippmann returned from the war to examine, in a series of articles and then in the book *Liberty and the News* (1920), the role of the press.

This led him to write the far deeper and more sweeping study *Public Opinion* (1922). Behind its bland title lay disturbing conclusions.

If, he argued, the average person's perception of reality was governed by propaganda, prejudice, inattention, and even unconscious stereotypes ingrained by the culture, how could such a person make an informed political decision? Yet the very theory of democracy assumed that ordinary citizens could make intelligent decisions. If they could not, what was the virtue of democracy? Unwilling to give up on democratic government, Lippmann proposed to remedy the problem by training unbiased experts to filter the news and pass on the "truth."

But in *The Phantom Public* (1925), he abandoned even this device. Taking his analysis to its logical conclusion, he decided that the public should leave the experts alone to make decisions. When they made mistakes the public could kick them out and bring in new experts. The public could say "yes" or "no," but "with the substance of the problem it can do nothing but meddle ignorantly or tyrannically." A distressed John Dewey described Lippmann's thesis as "perhaps the most effective indictment of democracy ever penned."

The manipulations of the war and the compromises of the peace had disillusioned Lippmann in more ways than one. He had put his faith in Wilson's idealism and then felt betrayed by the vindictive peace imposed on Germany. The *New Republic*, having urged the United States into the war, now denounced the peace treaty and with it the proposed League of Nations. Lippmann did not join the "lost generation" of Paris, but he shared its disillusion, and for a time he retreated from the ardent internationalism that he had preached.

In 1922 Lippmann left the magazine to join the *World*, New York's leading liberal newspaper. As head of the editorial page he set the paper's position on the leading issues of the day, such as prohibition, disarmament, the financial crash, the Sacco-Vanzetti affair, and the Scopes trial. At the *World* his stinging editorials reached a far wider audience and established his reputation as a leading opinion maker.

Even while editing the paper and writing daily editorials Lippmann found time for another book. This one, however, concerned not politics, but ethics and values. *A Preface to Morals* (1929) was meant for those, like himself, who had lost their faith, but not their search for meaning in life. Lippmann was born into a Jewish family but rejected this religious and cultural identity. Although (or perhaps because) his analysis was gloomy—he praised the "disinterested" man who would find solace not in revelation but in stoicism—he captured the anxieties of the age, and with it a large new public.

When the *World* shut down in 1931, Lippmann joined its conservative rival, the *New York Herald-Tribune*, as a syndicated columnist. The switch distressed many readers but was not illogical. Lippmann had grown more conservative during the 1920s, and his new post offered not only full independence but a nationwide audience. At the time there were virtually no serious political columnists. Yet papers across the nation needed a knowledgeable authority to interpret the news. Writing simply and directly, but conveying great learning without ideological slant, he became America's guru. Within a short time his "Today and Tomorrow" column was syndicated to more than 200 papers with millions of readers. "To read, if not to comprehend, Lippmann was suddenly the thing to do," sourly commented an envious rival, Arthur Krock.

Through syndication Lippmann became an international figure. At least once a year he toured the capitals of Europe, meeting with heads of state as a matter of course, and pronouncing on the wisdom or follies of their policies. He scrupulously avoided scoops and instead concentrated on the meaning behind the news. As he had demonstrated in *Public Opinion*, facts were not the same as truth. By putting the facts into a coherent perspective—by telling his readers what to make of the cacaphonous onslaught of news—he made himself virtually indispensable. Even those who disagreed with him had to know what he had said.

Lippmann owed his success not only to the fact that he was the first serious political columnist and began in an era long before television, but also because he wrote with such grace, clarity, and authority. His audience was the kind of person who cared about public affairs but did not want to be bombarded with details. To read Lippmann was not only the thing to do, but marked one as a thoughtful person. Oliver Wendell Holmes captured part of his appeal by describing his prose as being like flypaper, "if I touch it, I am stuck till I finish it."

During his thirty-six years as a newspaper columnist, Lippmann was not always right nor universally popular. His rare gaffes—such as his early dismissal of Franklin D. Roosevelt as a well-meaning playboy—were memorable. His occasional enmities—such as his bitter feud with Lyndon Johnson over the Vietnam War—were monumental. Nor was he invariably consistent. His views changed with the times and with his own reading of events.

The young man who was a mild socialist in the early years of the century and an ardent interventionist in World War I became in the 1920s and 1930s a skeptic about the wisdom of the average man and an advocate of a hands-off policy toward Europe and Asia, even as the fragile peace began to crack. Although he supported the recovery programs of the early New Deal, once the worst of the economic crisis seemed over he turned against FDR's more ambitious reform programs.

Yet even though his views in the mid-1930s were often closer to Wall Street than to the White House, it would not be correct to label him simply a conservative. His 1934 book *The Method of Freedom* introduced his friend John Maynard Keynes's views on deficit spending to a wide American audience, while his learned study *The Good Society* (1937) was an earnest attempt to find a middle way between laissez-faire conservatism and conformist collectivism. Lippmann la-

bored to show that opposition to collectivism did not make him an enemy of social progress, and he drew up an "agenda of liberalism" that contained heavy components of the welfare state. But the times were not conducive to a nuanced approach, and the book was widely criticized by both the right and the left. Later generations, however, found much of merit in his effort to salvage liberalism without surrendering to a collectivist authoritarianism.

In 1938 Lippmann moved from New York to Washington, D.C., in part because government had become more centralized in the capital. But more importantly it stemmed from the uproar in his social world caused by his 1937 divorce from Faye Albertson and his marriage in 1938 to Helen Byrne, the wife of his close friend and colleague Hamilton Fish Armstrong. Although this double divorce provoked an emotional crisis in Lippmann's life, his second marriage brought him great happiness over the remaining years of his life. Lippmann had no children with either of his wives.

Lippmann's personal crisis coincided almost exactly with the European political crisis at the time of the Munich conference that led to the destruction of Czechoslovakia. All during the 1930s, in the face of the mounting belligerence of the fascist powers, Lippmann had urged a policy of armed neutrality for the United States. But after Munich he became alarmed that Britain and France could not keep Nazi Germany in check. In the fall of 1939, following the German invasion of Poland, he urged the lifting of the arms embargo to the democracies. With the fall of France in June 1940, he pleaded in his column and conspired behind the scenes to supply the British with surplus American destroyers and heavy military equipment under lend-lease. The German onslaught had destroyed his hope that the United States could stand apart. Never again would he put his faith in such Wilsonian notions as disarmament, neutrality, or international forums. Henceforth he would become a hardheaded "realist" concerned with power, alliances, and military balances.

Within a few years, as the German and Japanese armies were being turned back, this view brought Lippmann into conflict with those who believed that the defeat of the aggressors would bring about a peaceful "One World" under the benevolent guidance of the United Nations. To combat what he considered to be dangerous illusions, Lippmann in 1943 wrote a short, argumentative book titled *U.S. Foreign Policy: Shield of the Republic*. Coming at a time when Americans wanted to know what to think about the postwar world over the horizon, it was a bestseller. The core of his argument was that isolation was not possible for the United States, good intentions could not substitute for military force and alliances, and peace in the postwar world required a continuation of the wartime alliance of America and Britain with Russia. "The failure to form an alliance of the victors will mean the formation of alliances between the vanquished and some of the victors," he wrote presciently. A year later he followed this up with another short book, *U.S. War Aims* (1944).

But the wartime alliance did, of course, fall apart. For this Lippmann blamed London and Washington as well as Moscow. Although concerned by Soviet behavior in Eastern Europe, he urged that lines be kept open to Moscow. Lippmann always believed in negotiation, although from positions of strength. For that reason he wrote a series of columns in 1947, also published as a book, *The Cold War* (1947), denouncing the "containment doctrine" as enunciated by George Kennan and pursued by the Harry Truman administration. As the Cold War consensus hardened in Washington, Lippmann remained one of the few skeptics.

But the Moscow-engineered coup in February 1948 by Czech communists and the political disappearance of Czechoslovakia behind the Iron Curtain shattered his lingering hopes that somehow the wartime alliance could be maintained. As the Cold War hardened, Lippmann became an elucidator—always perceptive and authoritative, and often original—rather than a critic of the prevailing foreign policy consensus. Not until the mid-1960s, with the crisis over the Vietnam War, would he move again into the opposition.

In 1955 Lippmann published his last major book, *Essays in the Public Philosophy*. In it he attempted to distill his thinking about politics and come to terms with the weakness of democracies in confronting unpopular social and political problems. Consistent with the skepticism of mass democracy that he had first evidenced in *Public Opinion* more than thirty years earlier, but unwilling to seek refuge in undemocratic methods, he proposed that popular sovereignty be limited according to the tenets of "natural law." To Lippmann's great distress, the book on which he had worked for many years was tepidly received by critics.

For all his eminence and his reputation as the ultimate insider, Lippmann had a rocky relationship with most presidents. Even those he supported at the beginning, such as both Roosevelts, Wilson, Kennedy, and Johnson, ultimately disappointed him. This was in part because he tended to idealize strong leaders and thus was inevitably disillusioned when they failed to fulfill his exaggerated expectations. The only exceptions were De Gaulle and Churchill. But of course he never had to live under them. But beyond the waning of infatuations, he had a temperamental need to stand apart. All his life he wavered between the two poles of involvement and detachment, just as he was torn between the active life of writing for newspapers and the more contemplative life of writing books. "It is a fact," Lippmann once wrote of Santayana, "that a man can't see the play and be in it too." Yet Lippmann wanted both: to be spectator and actor, observer and insider. To a remarkable degree he succeeded.

Lippmann's last working years were spent alternately in embrace and opposition. After John F. Kennedy's assassination in 1963 he rallied immediately to Lyndon Johnson and for two years praised his leadership. He once again became the favored insider at the White House, courted by Johnson and awarded the

Presidential Medal of Freedom in September 1964. During this period he became a television celebrity, appearing on the CBS network in seven one-hour interviews over a five-year period (1960–1965). This brought him to an entirely new audience, and the programs drew very high ratings.

Had Lippmann retired in 1965 it would have been with every accolade that government could provide. But he kept writing his column for two more years, and they proved to be the most tempestuous of his entire career. In the end he was bitterly estranged from the White House and left Washington with sorrow in his heart.

The cause was that of so many sorrows: the Vietnam War. Lippmann, who had always tried to draw a distinction between areas of primary concern in foreign policy, like Europe and Japan, and those he considered to be marginal in the balance of power, like most of the small states of the Third World. For this reason he never was enthusiastic about U.S. aid to South Vietnam and in 1964 supported General de Gaulle's plan for neutralization of Indochina.

But the administration's scornful rejection of this exit plan and its intensification of the war against North Vietnam early in 1965 put Lippmann on a collision course with the White House. As he became convinced that Johnson was intent on a military victory rather than a negotiated peace, and as the casualties of the war mounted, Lippmann moved further into opposition. With mounting frustration over the steadily expanding war, he abandoned his carefully measured prose for the language of combat. The president he had earlier praised as "a man for this season" became a "primitive frontiersman" who had "betrayed and abandoned" the American promise.

Cut off from the administration and denounced as a "defeatist" by those who had so deferentially courted him earlier, Lippmann became an intellectual leader and elder statesman of the antiwar movement. Not since his youth had he thrown himself so passionately into a political struggle. But by the spring of 1967, distressed by the poisonous political climate in Washington and weary of battle after so many fights, he decided to draw an end to the newspaper column he had begun writing nearly thirty-six years earlier. He and his wife returned to New York, which was not the city they remembered from the 1930s, and where they found little peace in their retirement. There Lippmann died.

Although Lippmann is generally described as a journalist, the term does not encompass the full range of his talents and influence. In addition to writing a syndicated column, he was both a magazine and a newspaper editor, a promoter of causes and leaders, and the author of nearly two dozen books on politics, ethics, philosophy, perception, and governance. Considered to be the most influential political writer of his age, his authority rested on his personal relations with statesmen, an intellectual grounding in philosophy and history, an ability to synthesize and explain complex information, and a graceful literary style. Political figures sought him out for the privilege of being interviewed. As a colleague once said, his was "the name that opened every door." During his long career Lippmann had written about nearly every major event that touched Americans. Van Wyck Brooks expressed a widely held view of Lippmann when he wrote that his was the "most brilliant career ever devoted in America to political writing."

But Lippmann would have described his role differently. "Responsibility," he once wrote of a renowned editor, "consists in sharing the burden of men directing what is to be done, or the burden of offering some other course of action in the mood of one who has realized what it would mean to undertake it." This is the task that Lippmann set for himself, and it expresses much of what made him unique.

• Lippmann's papers, including private correspondence and many original manuscripts, are at Sterling Memorial Library, Yale University. A major portion of his published works is available from the library on microfilm. An important part of his correspondence can be found in *Public Philosopher: Selected Letters of Walter Lippmann*, ed. John Morton Blum (1985). Gilbert Harrison compiled both *Early Writings* (1970), a selection of Lippmann's articles for the *New Republic*, and *Public Persons* (1976), a collection of portraits by Lippmann of figures ranging from William James to John F. Kennedy. The transcripts of Lippmann's seven network television broadcasts from 1960 to 1965 are compiled under the title *Conversations with Walter Lippmann* (1965). The most complete biography, based on the private papers and conversations with Lippmann, is Ronald Steel, *Walter Lippmann and the American Century* (1980). A number of significant books have been written about different aspects of Lippmann's thought and career, including Stephen Blum, *Walter Lippmann: Cosmopolitanism in the Century of Total War* (1984); Barry Riccio, *Walter Lippmann: Odyssey of a Liberal* (1994); Anwar Seyd, *Walter Lippmann's Philosophy of International Politics* (1963); Hari Dam, *Intellectual Odyssey of Walter Lippmann* (1973); Charles Wellborn, *Twentieth Century Pilgrimage: Walter Lippmann and the Public Philosophy* (1969); Edward L. Schapsmeier and Frederick H. Schapsmeier, *Walter Lippmann: Philosopher-Journalist* (1969); Benjamin Wright, *Five Public Philosophies of Walter Lippmann* (1973); and Francine Curro Cary, *Influence of War on Walter Lippmann: 1914-1944* (1967). Clinton Rossiter and James Lare, *The Essential Lippmann* (1963), is a spotty collection of Lippmann's writings, focusing on the books and largely ignoring the articles and columns.

RONALD STEEL

LIPSCOMB, Big Daddy (9 Nov. 1931–10 May 1963), professional football player and wrestler, was born Eugene Alan Lipscomb in Detroit, Michigan. He never knew his father, who reportedly died in a Civilian Conservation Corps camp when Gene was very young; his mother was stabbed to death by a male acquaintance while she waited for a bus in Detroit in 1942. Gene was raised by his maternal grandfather, who, according to Lipscomb, "did the best he knew how. But for some reason it was always hard for us to talk together. Instead of telling me what I was doing wrong and how to correct it, my grandfather would holler and whip me." As a youth, Lipscomb held a variety of odd jobs to support himself, including a midnight-to-eight shift at a steel mill in Detroit, which he worked before attending classes at Miller High School. He quit school at age sixteen and joined the U.S. Marine Corps.

At Camp Pendleton, California, Lipscomb began to develop his football talents. Having played only one season at Miller High, Lipscomb learned the fundamentals of the game at a relatively high level of play while in the marines. With 280 pounds filling out his 6'6" frame and with unusual speed for a man his size, he soon made a reputation for himself in service football. He got his nickname, "Big Daddy," in the marines because he could not remember his teammates' names and called them all "little daddy." The Los Angeles Rams of the National Football League signed Lipscomb for $4,800 in 1953. He was one of the first extremely large interior linemen with exceptional mobility. But, as an unseasoned lineman engulfed with personal problems, including marital discord and alcohol abuse, his play was inconsistent, and Los Angeles put him on waivers in 1955.

Sought by several teams, Lipscomb signed with the Baltimore Colts in 1956 as a defensive tackle and came under the tutelage of head coach Weeb Ewbank, who described him as a "project." Under Ewbank's guidance, Lipscomb learned how to better utilize his size and mobility in interior line play and became one of the outstanding defensive linemen in the NFL. Lipscomb was one of the first black linemen to be widely recognized and acclaimed by fans around the league. While with Baltimore from 1955 to 1960, he was named to the all-NFL team twice and played in two Pro Bowl games. In 1958 and 1959, Lipscomb helped lead the Colts to consecutive NFL championships while anchoring an impressive defensive line that included Art Donovan, Gino Marchetti, and Don Joyce. Baltimore traded Lipscomb to the Pittsburgh Steelers in 1961. He continued to be one of the league's outstanding linemen and played one of his best games in the 1963 Pro Bowl, his third. At the height of his career, Lipscomb earned over $15,000 per season. During the off-season, he earned considerably more money as a professional wrestler, a sideline he had begun while in the marines in California.

Although unusually large and aggressive in line play, Lipscomb went out of his way to cultivate an image as a gentle giant. After a tackle, for example, he would help a ball carrier to his feet. "I don't want people or kids to think Big Daddy is a cruel man," he explained. Lipscomb also had the reputation of being something of a homespun philosopher both on and off the field. One of the few NFL players who did not attend college, Lipscomb liked to tell teammates he had played at "Miller Tech," and he once summarized his football technique by saying, "I just grab me an armful of men, pick them over until I find the one with the ball, then I throw them down." On another occasion he remarked, "New York, New York. So big they had to say it twice."

Despite his size, air of confidence, and genial manner, Lipscomb had a difficult personal life. "I've been scared most of my life," he once said. "You wouldn't think so to look at me." In the wake of his dismal childhood, Lipscomb was divorced three times and by the 1950s had a serious drinking problem. He died in Baltimore of an acute reaction to an overdose of heroin. An autopsy showed that a nonintoxicating amount of liquor in his body also contributed to his death. Despite the discovery of a number of recent needle marks on his arms, some of his friends, including Pittsburgh Steelers owner Dan Rooney, suspected foul play. They could not imagine Lipscomb being a drug abuser. Baltimore medical authorities ruled, however, that Lipscomb died of a self-administered overdose of heroin. Lipscomb was one of the first widely known defensive linemen in the NFL. He was also one of the first prominent professional athletes to be linked with drug addiction.

• There is no biography of Lipscomb, and there are few sources on his pre-NFL career. The best available sources are Weeb Ewbank, *Goal to Go: The Greatest Football Games I Have Coached* (1972); Dan Daily and Bob O'Donnell, *The Pro Football Chronicle* (1990); David L. Porter, ed., *Biographical Dictionary of American Sports: Football* (1987); Daniel Schwartz, "A Requiem for Big Daddy," *Esquire*, Sept. 1963, pp. 88–89; and Eugene Lipscomb file, Professional Football Hall of Fame, Canton, Ohio. Obituaries are in the *New York Times*, 11 May 1963, and *Time*, 17 May 1963, p. 101.

JOHN M. CARROLL

LIPSCOMB, Mance (9 Apr. 1895–30 Jan. 1976), songster and guitarist, was born on a farm near Navasota, Texas, the son of Charlie Lipscomb, a former slave who became a professional fiddler, and Janie Pratt. Mance learned to play fiddle and guitar at an early age, learning mainly by ear because his musician father was seldom home to teach him. While still a preteen, Mance supposedly traveled with his father for a time, accompanying him on guitar. However, when Mance was around eleven years old, his father stopped coming home altogether, and the youngster went to work on the farm to help his mother.

For the next half century Lipscomb worked full time as a farmer. He took jobs as a farm hand until he was sixteen, then began sharecropping on a twenty-acre tract, raising mainly corn and cotton. Two years later he married Elnora (maiden name unknown); they had one son but raised two sets of grandchildren and several great grandchildren as well. As a sharecropper and later as a rent farmer, Lipscomb worked from before dawn to well past dusk to eke out a slender living for his family. He lived this way until 1956, when he moved to Houston and went to work for a lumber company. Within a year, however, he was injured when a load of lumber fell on him, and he moved back to Navasota, using an insurance settlement to buy a parcel of land and build a small house where he planned to spend his retirement.

As a farmer, Lipscomb was never too far from music. In his early twenties he traveled to the northeastern part of the state to pick cotton, and on a Saturday night in Dallas he heard Texas blues virtuoso Blind Lemon Jefferson playing guitar on the street. He recalled hearing another Texas native, slide-guitar evangelist Blind Willie Johnson, when Johnson came through Navasota. He also heard obscure local musicians such as Robert Timm, said to be the first Navasota artist to play blues, and Hamp Walker, described by Lipscomb as "about the best guitar man and songster as I ever met," according to researcher Mack McCormick. At some point Lipscomb began playing guitar and singing at weekend country dances and picnics. Although he became an accomplished musician, his reputation was limited to the Brazos River farming community where he lived.

In the summer of 1960 two field researchers, Mack McCormick and Chris Strachwitz, heard about Lipscomb when they traveled out from Houston in search of folk musicians. They went to his house and were waiting for him when he got home after a full day in the fields. "So I came out on the porch with my guitar," Lipscomb later told author Bruce Cook, "and I played the worst one I could think of just to get rid of them." McCormick and Strachwitz requested more tunes, however, and that night recorded Lipscomb for almost five hours in his home—field recordings that formed the basis for Lipscomb's debut LP on Arhoolie Records.

A farmer all his life, Lipscomb became an overnight celebrity on the folk- and blues-revival circuits at age sixty-five. The year of his first field recordings, he played at the Texas Heritage Festival in Houston, initiating a steady schedule of festivals, campus and club bookings, recording sessions, film appearances, and oral-history interviews that continued into the early 1970s. His credits included all the major folk and blues festivals—Berkeley in 1961–1963, Monterey in 1963, Newport in 1965, the Festival of American Folklife in Washington, D.C., in 1968, Ann Arbor in 1970, Philadelphia in 1972—and a long list of lesser events. In addition to further recordings for Strachwitz's Arhoolie label, he was featured in the 1971 Les Blank film *A Well Spent Life*. His late-life success as a musician made it possible for Lipscomb to buy a bigger house, where he lived with his wife and one grandchild. As Lipscomb neared eighty, though, failing health curtailed his music career. He died at a hospital near his home and was buried at Rest Haven Cemetery in Navasota.

Discovered well past his prime as a musician, Mance Lipscomb nonetheless possessed both formidable skill as a guitarist and a repertoire of songs that was said to number in the hundreds. As a performer on the folk- and blues-revival circuits during the 1960s, Lipscomb was often regarded as a blues artist—a misnomer that, according to author Bruce Cook, caused some young audiences to react with impatience when Lipscomb trotted out such hoary standards as "You Are My Sunshine" and "Shine On, Harvest Moon." In fact, Lipscomb belonged to a Texas songster tradition that drew material from many sources, old and new. Lipscomb sang blues, to be sure; but as researcher Mack McCormack noted, he sang them as part of an unbroken musical stream that included ballads, work songs, breakdowns, and religious songs, in addition to the nineteenth-century standards and dance tunes he had learned in childhood. Lipscomb, who labeled himself a songster, adorned all of this material with a precise finger-picking style on guitar and delivered it with dignified yet intense vocals. He was among the most influential country performers of the revival era.

• For an oral autobiography (in printed dialect), see Mance Lipscomb, *I Say Me for a Parable*, comp. Glen Alyn (1993). For additional biographical information see Bruce Cook, *Listen to the Blues* (1973); Mack McCormack's extended liner notes accompanying Arhoolie album F1001, *Mance Lipscomb: Texas Sharecropper and Songster* (1960); and Sheldon Harris, *Blues Who's Who: A Biographical Dictionary of Blues Singers* (1989). For discographical information, see Paul Oliver, ed., *The Blackwell Guide to Blues Records* (1989), and Mike Leadbitter and Neil Slaven, *Blues Records, 1943–1970: A Selective Discography*, vol. 2 (1994). For a sample of his music, try his first Arhoolie album, referenced above.

BILL MCCULLOCH
BARRY LEE PEARSON

LISA, Manuel (8 Sept. 1772–12 Aug. 1820), fur trader, was born in New Orleans, Louisiana, the son of Christobal Lisa, a Spanish government employee, and Maria Ignacia Rodriguez. Lisa began trading along the Mississippi and Ohio rivers in the 1790s. In 1796 at Vincennes, on the Wabash River in the Northwest Territory, he opened a mercantile business. While at Vincennes, he married Polly Charles Chew, a widow and mother of an infant daughter. They had three children together, but none survived to adulthood. In 1798 Lisa moved his family to St. Louis where the energetic and wily newcomer engaged in the mercantile business, land speculation, and slave trading. Committed to the principle of free trade, Lisa joined other disgruntled traders in seeking an end to the Spanish government's monopolistic trade grants with the Indians.

Lisa was always willing to bend or ignore regulations and, when necessary, resort to devious methods to achieve his goals. In 1802 he convinced the Spanish governor general to prematurely revoke the lucrative Osage Indian trade monopoly that the Chouteaus, a prominent old-line St. Louis family, had enjoyed for eight years. Lisa's success in this instance angered the entrenched businessmen of St. Louis. Undaunted, he continued to trade along the lower Mississippi River, then turned to the upper Missouri Indian and fur trade after the purchase of Louisiana by the United States.

Lisa learned more about the Rocky Mountain fur trade's rich potential when the Lewis and Clark expedition returned to St. Louis in 1804. By then Lisa was enjoying success from his mercantile enterprises in Vincennes and St. Louis and his trading ventures along the Mississippi, Ohio, and Wabash rivers. Lisa

spent most of 1805–1806 trying to collect debts owed to him. In 1806 he also entered into a partnership that unsuccessfully tried to open trade with the Spanish Southwest. Abandoning that enterprise a year later, Lisa and two merchants from Kaskaskia (now in Ill.) financed the first commercial trading-trapping expedition up the Missouri to the Rocky Mountains. For Lisa, who led the expedition into the field, this would be the first of thirteen trips up or down the upper Missouri during his lifetime. The expedition returned a modest profit, and St. Louis businessmen, including rivals like the Chouteaus, decided to join Lisa rather than compete against him. This ten-man partnership formed the St. Louis Missouri Fur Company. Due to the indefatigable Lisa's expertise in Indian cultures, he led the company's traders and trappers into the field.

Lisa used gifts and, when necessary, a show of force to influence the Indians. He also understood the importance of constructing forts, such as Fort Mandan in the Gros Ventres–Mandan country, as bases of operations for the company's trappers. Utilizing the trappers rather than relying solely on the Indians for skins proved to be essential in his design for a profitable operation. The trappers also would provide valuable information about unexplored areas.

The venture proved profitable, and Lisa returned to St. Louis to raise more money and buy trade goods for another expedition up the Missouri to the Rocky Mountains. Problems occurred early on. A fire at the Cedar Island post caused some $12,000 in losses. Blackfeet killed eight company men. Equipment and furs were lost or stolen. In addition, the United States Embargo Act disrupted the delivery of supplies to company men in the field. Despite these problems, the 1809–1810 expedition returned a profit. The partners, however, had expected a better return on their investment.

For Lisa's next expedition the partners invested only $2,000 in supplies and equipment. To further complicate matters, John Jacob Astor sent his Pacific Fur Company, led by Wilson Price Hunt, from St. Louis up the Missouri three weeks before Lisa's party could leave. Worried that Hunt would turn the Sioux against him, Lisa and his men embarked on an exhausting two-month chase that became known as one of the great keelboat races in American history. On 2 June 1811 Lisa's men sighted the Astorians. An uneasy truce between the competitors ensued despite Lisa's underhanded attempt to hire away the Astorian interpreter.

The fur company's expedition once again netted only a small profit, and the partners reorganized. Unable to obtain company funds to purchase goods and equipment, Lisa signed personal notes for $13,000, and another $11,000 was raised so that an expedition for the reorganized Missouri Fur Company could start in the spring of 1812. Trade for the 1812–1813 season was poor. No profit was realized, and a majority of the partners voted on 17 January 1814 to disband the company.

Despite this setback Lisa did not abandon the fur trade. By the fall of 1814 he had found another partner, Theodore Hunt. William Clark, the Indian agent, provided Lisa with trade goods and appointed him subagent for the Indian tribes on the upper Missouri, above the Kansas River. During this tenure, Lisa married an Omaha Indian chief's daughter; they had two children. The marriage secured the tribe as allies for the United States. Clark also wanted Lisa to keep the Yankton and Teton Sioux as allies to neutralize the Santee Sioux, who were allied with the British. His success in this mission and his ability to get chiefs from various tribes to sign treaties with the United States made Lisa a man of importance during the War of 1812.

With Hunt as his partner, Lisa led an expedition to the Rocky Mountains in 1816. When he returned to St. Louis in 1817, the furs he brought earned $35,000. Despite this success, no investors would share the costs of a venture during the 1817–1818 season. In 1819 Jean Cabanne and Company became Lisa's partner, but a disagreement over Lisa's compensation caused Cabanne to dismiss him from the assignment in June 1819. Lisa quickly planned another fur trade expedition. Taking supplies upriver to his Omaha Indian post, Lisa spent part of the season in the company of the Yellowstone expedition at Council Bluffs. After the death of Polly Lisa in early 1818, Lisa had soon remarried. His second Anglo wife, Mary Hempstead Keeney, and another woman accompanied Lisa on this trip, becoming the first white women to travel the upper Missouri. Lisa became ill while on this expedition. Not long after his return to St. Louis in May 1820, Lisa died, almost penniless. Although Lisa had never been sufficiently capitalized to become a huge success in the fur trade, his methods would be copied more profitably after his death. As Chittenden wrote, Lisa had been "the ablest of traders" (p. 129).

• A small collection of Lisa's papers is housed at the Missouri Historical Society, St. Louis, where other important papers concerning early St. Louis business history, including the fur trade, exist. The most valuable work about Lisa is Richard Edward Oglesby, *Manuel Lisa and the Opening of the Missouri Fur Trade* (1963). In addition, students of Lisa should consult Walter B. Douglas, *Manuel Lisa* (1964). Oglesby also contributed a brief biography of Lisa to LeRoy R. Hafen, ed., *The Mountain Men and the Fur Trade of the Far West*, Vol. 5 (1968), pp. 180–201. Another valuable source on Lisa and the fur trade in general is Hiram Martin Chittenden, *The American Fur Trade of the Far West* (1935).

JAMES W. GOODRICH

LISAGOR, Peter Irvin (5 Aug. 1915–10 Dec. 1976), journalist, was born in Keystone, West Virginia, the son of Paris Lisagor, the manager of a general store, and Fanny Simpkins. He enrolled at Northwestern University in 1933, then transferred to the University of Michigan, where he received a bachelor's degree in political science in 1939. Along the way, he played baseball in the Midwest "for $65 a month and hamburgers." He worked for the campus newspaper at Michigan and was correspondent for three dailies.

Lisagor joined the *Chicago Daily News* as a sports reporter in 1939, switched to the United Press wire service as a general assignment reporter in 1941, then went back to the *Daily News*. He married Myra K. Murphy of Wabash, Indiana, in 1942; they had two children. Lisagor enlisted in the army in 1942 during World War II and was managing editor (1944–1945) of the London edition of the armed forces newspaper, *Stars and Stripes*, and Paris editor (1945) of *Stars and Stripes* magazine. After the army, he worked briefly in 1945 as news editor of the civilian *Paris Post*, before returning to the *Chicago Daily News* in 1945 as a reporter and feature writer. His February 1947 series of investigative articles on Illinois mental health hospitals brought reform for those institutions and a reputation for Lisagor. In 1948 he was awarded a Nieman Fellowship at Harvard, where he studied international affairs.

The *Daily News* named Lisagor its United Nations correspondent in 1949, then sent him to Washington in 1950 as diplomatic correspondent. He was promoted to chief of the newspaper's Washington bureau in 1959 and served in that capacity for the remainder of his career. Lisagor covered Presidents Dwight Eisenhower, John Kennedy, Lyndon Johnson, Richard Nixon, and Gerald Ford. He was only a few cars behind Kennedy when the president was assassinated in Dallas in 1963, and he accompanied Nixon to Russia and China in 1972.

Lisagor was often courted by the nation's chief executives, who couldn't understand why such a seemingly nice fellow was unpersuaded by their wooing. Johnson once bolted from a conversation with reporters, complaining that a Lisagor profile didn't show the "proper respect" for the president. But soon thereafter LBJ called in Lisagor to try to persuade him of the merits of yet another new policy. When Nixon was vice president, he repeatedly offered Lisagor private interviews during a Latin American trip. But Lisagor declined because he suspected Nixon was offering propaganda rather than legitimate news. Lisagor loved to razz his competitors when President Kennedy would call him aside for private conversations. "We talked in corridors, under wings of planes, any place away from the crowd," Lisagor recalled. "I always told the other reporters it was a privileged conversation about Berlin or Cuba or the Cold War and that I couldn't divulge any part of it" (*Chicago Daily News*, 31 Dec. 1966). In fact, Kennedy and Lisagor both suffered from back pain, and the president always wanted to know if Lisagor had found a cure.

Lisagor's syndicated column was published in ninety newspapers, but he seldom appeared in New York or Washington. Although he was the first to report during the Korean War that President Syngman Rhee had refused an offer of military help from India, he had to leak the story to the *New York Herald Tribune* before the rest of the press took note. He also scooped his colleagues with the first reliable account of Jacqueline Kennedy's demand that William Manchester remove several passages she considered private from the author's book on President Kennedy's assassination. The Kennedy-Manchester spat, however, was soon widely known because the *New York Times*, Associated Press, and United Press International picked up the story, attributing it to Lisagor. Although his principal occupation was always print journalism, Lisagor probably was best known to the public for his frequent television appearances on NBC's *Meet the Press* and Public Broadcasting System's *Washington Week in Review*, where he enhanced his reputation for incisive questions and a quick wit.

Secretary of State Henry Kissinger once remarked on what a "strange phenomenon" it was that Lisagor was so highly regarded: "You write for a newspaper that virtually no one in Washington reads. Yet you are one of the most influential newsmen in the nation's capital. You never makes heroes out of public officials—that is perhaps an understatement—yet they respect you, they seek your advice, and consider you their friend. You are the Renaissance man of the Washington press—equally adept at writing, reporting, television and commentary."

Lisagor also was popular and influential within the Washington press corps, serving as president of the Gridiron Club, the White House Correspondents Association, the State Department Correspondents Association, and the Overseas Writers Club and as a member of the board of governors of the National Press Club. He received numerous awards in journalism. Among them were the Page One Award of the American Newspaper Guild in 1948, 1949, and 1972; the National Headliners Club Award in 1974; the Peabody Broadcasting Award in 1974; the Harrid Foundation Award in 1974; the Marshall Field Award in 1974; the William Allen White Foundation Award for Journalistic Merit in 1976; and the Edward Weintal Prize for Diplomatic Reporting in 1976.

His reputation in the nation's capital was due largely to the perception that he was scrupulously fair in his reporting and commentary. "An old editor once told me to walk down the middle of the street and shoot windows out on both sides," he said. "I guess that's about what I try to do" ("Horizontal in Washington," p. 42). When he died in Arlington, Virginia, he was eulogized by many of his colleagues, including John Chancellor of NBC News, who described him as the "conscience" of the profession. Lisagor was buried in Arlington National Cemetery by order of President Ford.

• Lisagor was co-author, with Marguerite Higgins, of *Overtime in Heaven: Adventures in the Foreign Service*, a 1964 volume of nine stories about courage and bravery by State Department employees. For one of the best assessments of Lisagor's career as a journalist, see "Horizontal in Washington," *Time*, 17 Aug. 1970, p. 42. Notable obituaries are in the *New York Times*, the *Washington Post*, the *Chicago Tribune*, and the *Chicago Daily News*, all 11 Dec. 1976.

DANIEL J. FOLEY

LISTON, Emil Sycamore (21 Aug. 1890–26 Oct. 1949), coach and athletic administrator, was born in Stockton, Missouri, the son of George M. Liston, a physician. His mother's name is not known. He grew up in Baldwin City, Kansas. Liston graduated with a B.A. from Baker University in Baldwin in 1913. He starred on the basketball team and also won letters in football, baseball, and soccer. As a college student he volunteered to coach the Baldwin High School basketball team for three years, 1911–1913, and the football team in 1912. His 1912 basketball team won the state championship. After graduating, Liston moved to Fort Scott, Kansas, where from 1913 to 1915 he was director of physical education, coached that town's high school basketball team, and revived its football program. One of his basketball teams captured the district and Southeast Kansas tournament championships. In 1915–1916 Liston moved to Kemper Military School in Boonville, Missouri, where he coached several sports and led his basketball team to the championship of military schools. For the next two years, 1916–1918, Liston served as director of athletics for the Michigan College of Mines in Houghton. He reestablished the school's basketball program and founded a basketball tournament for upper peninsula high schools. From 1918 to 1920 Liston coached football and basketball and taught physical education at Wesleyan University in Middletown, Connecticut. In 1920 he returned to Baker University to direct athletics and coach football, basketball, and baseball.

Liston coached football from 1920 to 1937 and from 1940 to 1942. He compiled a win, loss, and tie record of 97–66 and 18, respectively. Between 1926 and 1928 Liston's teams played twenty-one games without a loss. In 1942, his last season in football, Baker had a perfect 7–0 record. Liston's football teams won conference titles in 1922, 1927, 1928, 1934, and 1942. Liston coached basketball at Baker from 1920 through 1945. His teams won championships in the old Kansas Conference in 1935 and 1937 and tied for the Heart of America Athletic Conference championships between 1941 and 1943. Liston's baseball teams won more than half their games.

As an administrator Liston established a major in physical education, developed an intramural athletic program, and raised money for a new athletic field and stadium. He founded the Baker University Relays and organized the Kansas Conference Coaches Association, serving as its president for three years. Liston was active in the Amateur Athletic Union (AAU) and served on the Missouri Valley AAU Records Committee (1935–1937) and National AAU Records Committee (1936–1937). He officiated at high school events as well. In the summer of 1928–1929 Liston taught football at Harvard University, where he earned a Master of Education degree in 1930.

In 1937 Liston joined with James Naismith, the retired inventor of basketball, and several Kansas City businessmen to organize an eight-team small college basketball tournament. The purpose of the tournament was, in part, to fill a gap in the Kansas City sports community caused by the Amateur Athletic Union's decision to move its national basketball tournament from Kansas City to Denver after the 1934 season. Liston and others also wanted to provide a format for small colleges and universities to determine a national champion, analogous to the National Collegiate Athletic Association (NCAA) tournament for universities that was initiated in 1939. In 1938 and 1939 the organizers of this small college tournament in Kansas City called it the National Intercollegiate Basketball Tournament and invited thirty-two teams to compete. In 1940 the founders of the event created the National Association of Intercollegiate Basketball (NAIB); Liston became its first executive secretary-treasurer. He worked diligently to recruit colleges to enlarge the organization, which three years after his death became the National Association of Intercollegiate Athletics. The organization gave small colleges an opportunity to design a structure of competition among schools without the resources of major universities.

Liston was married to Marie Thogmartin; they had no children. In 1944 he suffered a heart attack that forced him to retire from Baker University in 1945. In the last four years of his life, he devoted all of his energy to NAIB activities. He died in Baldwin City.

Liston was an outstanding representative of the coaching profession during the first half of the twentieth century. He was a model of those who worked tirelessly for their college and community. In 1974 he was named to the Naismith Basketball Hall of Fame.

• There is no single good source of information on Liston. See the Emil Liston Files at the Naismith Memorial Basketball Hall of Fame, Springfield, Mass., and in the Office of Alumni Relations at Baker University, Baldwin City, Kan. Obituaries are in the *Kansas City Times* and the *New York Times*, 27 Oct. 1949.

ADOLPH H. GRUNDMAN

LISTON, Sonny (8 May 1932–30 Dec. 1970), heavyweight boxer, was born Charles Liston in St. Francis County, Arkansas, the ninth of ten children of Tobe Liston, a sharecropper, and Helen Baskin. He received almost no formal education, working on his father's farm until he was thirteen years old. In later years, he claimed that his father worked him hard and whipped and verbally degraded him almost daily. His mother left the farm after a crop failure, going to St. Louis, Missouri, during the Second World War, and young Liston followed her there in 1945.

Liston grew up on the streets of St. Louis without supervision. Although he sometimes held legitimate jobs, mainly on construction gangs, he was frequently in trouble. At age sixteen he was arrested for breaking and entering but given probation. By 1950 he had been arrested six times for muggings, and he finally received a sentence of five years in the Missouri State Penitentiary after being convicted on two counts each of robbery and larceny.

Liston started boxing while in the penitentiary, through the encouragement of the prison chaplain, Father Alois Stevens. During this time he received the nickname "Sonny" from a fellow inmate. At 6'1" and 200 pounds, the broad-shouldered and powerful Liston improved rapidly. Before Liston was paroled on 30 October 1952, Father Stevens contacted Robert Burnes, sports editor of the *St. Louis Globe-Democrat*; Burnes found a trainer for Liston in Monroe Harrison, a former sparring partner to Joe Louis. Lacking money, Harrison secured a manager for Liston, Frank Mitchell, and together they launched him on a brief but highly successful amateur career. He won several amateur titles, including the 1953 Midwestern Golden Gloves heavyweight championship in Chicago, but lost for the first time in the National American Athletic Union tournament in Boston.

On 2 September 1953 Liston started his professional boxing career, winning his first five fights in St. Louis. In 1954 he went to Detroit for a series of fights and sustained his first loss to Marty Marshall, who broke Liston's jaw and outpointed him. Returning to action in March 1955, he won all six of his fights that year, including a knockout of Marshall, and in March 1956 he defeated Marshall again. During this period, Liston became involved with John Vitale, who had an extensive criminal record and connections to organized crime. Vitale used Liston as a labor "enforcer" and acquired a managerial interest in him.

On the night of 6 May 1956 Liston was involved in an incident that led to his being convicted of assaulting a police officer. In January 1957 he was sentenced to nine months in the city workhouse. Upon leaving prison, Liston was sent by Mitchell to Chicago to continue his career. There he won several fights, including two that were broadcast on national television. He also attracted the attention of Frank "Blinky" Palermo, a Mafia figure with a long police record and an interest in boxing. Palermo, who knew Vitale, selected a new manager for Liston, whose career then began to advance rapidly. Whereas previously he had difficulty in getting highly rated opponents, he became quickly matched with a succession of contenders. In 1959 he knocked out Mike DeJohn, Cleveland Williams, and Nino Valdes; and in 1960 he knocked out Williams again, Zora Folley, and Roy Harris, and he defeated Eddie Machen. By 1961 he was undisputably the leading contender for the heavyweight championship, held by Floyd Patterson.

In boxing style, Liston somewhat resembled Joe Louis, possessing an equally powerful left jab and left hook but a less forceful right hand. Powerfully built, he appeared to be a ponderous plodder, but in the ring he delivered blows with surprising quickness and was faster afoot than many other heavyweights. He attacked relentlessly and rarely seemed troubled by the hardest blows of his adversaries.

Patterson's manager, Cus D'Amato, was not eager to accept Liston as an opponent. He cited Liston's criminal record and his shady managerial connections as factors that should disqualify him from fighting for the championship. Indeed, Liston had been called to testify before the Kefauver Committee in the U.S.

Senate, which investigated the connections between organized crime and boxing. Moreover, the New York State Boxing Commission refused to give Liston a license to fight in that state. But Liston finally acquired respectable new managers and taunted Patterson into accepting him as an opponent.

Liston met Patterson twice for the heavyweight championship, on 25 September 1962 in Chicago and on 22 July 1963 in Las Vegas, Nevada; each time Liston scored a one-round knockout and looked almost unbeatable in doing so. Boxing authorities predicted that he would be the heavyweight champion for a long time, and he was heavily favored to retain the title when he defended it against Cassius Clay (Muhammad Ali) in Miami Beach, Florida, 25 February 1964. However, Clay proved much faster and cleverer and outboxed the champion. Liston refused to answer the bell for the seventh round, claiming he had an injured shoulder. On 25 May 1965 Liston fought Clay again before a small audience in Lewiston, Maine; the fight was televised nationally on a closed circuit to theaters. Liston went down for the count in the first round from a right hand that landed on his cheek. Few persons who saw the fight could believe that the blow was sufficient to knock out a man noted for his ability to take hard punches.

From 1966 to 1970 Liston won 14 consecutive fights, all but one of them by knockout. However, his reputation as a boxer was destroyed, and he could not regain the respect of boxing authorities. On 6 December 1969 he was knocked out by Leotis Martin in Las Vegas, but he returned to win one fight in 1970. In these years he lived comfortably in Las Vegas with his wife Geraldine Chambers, whom he probably married in 1954. However, rumors connected him with the selling of narcotics. On 5 January 1971 he was found dead by his wife upon her return from a Christmas trip to St. Louis. The condition of his body showed that he had been dead for about a week. Authorities found heroin in the house, needle marks on his arm, and narcotics in his body, although apparently insufficient to cause his death.

Liston was illiterate; he could count money and sign his name, but little more. Ordinarily he had little to say, although friends claimed that he was intelligent and sometimes witty. To many he seemed sullen and dangerous, to others merely shy. His arrival as heavyweight champion coincided with the civil rights revolution, and most African Americans deplored him as a setback to their cause. To Cassius Clay, he was "the ugly bear" and the perfect contrast to his own good looks, ebullient personality, and graceful ring style. Liston won 50 of his 54 fights, 39 by knockout, and lost only four times. He was inducted into the International Boxing Hall of Fame in 1991.

• The chief source of information on Liston's life until his winning of the heavyweight championship is A. S. Young, *Sonny Liston: The Champ Nobody Wanted* (1963). His boxing record is in Herbert G. Goldman, ed., *The Ring 1986–87 Record Book and Boxing Encyclopedia* (1986). Useful magazine articles include Robert L. Burnes, "Heavyweight with a Past," *Saturday Evening Post*, 13 Aug. 1960, pp. 28, 56–58; Joe Flaherty, "A Right to the Jaw—That's Black Power," *Esquire*, March 1969, pp. 112–14; and Bruce Jay Friedman, "Requiem for a Heavy," *Esquire*, Aug. 1971, pp. 55–57. Accounts of his major fights can be found in *The Ring* and *Sports Illustrated* magazines. An obituary is in the *New York Times*, 7 Jan. 1971.

LUCKETT V. DAVIS

LITCHFIELD, Electus Backus (15 Feb. 1813–12 May 1889), railroad pioneer, was born in Delphi Falls, New York, the son of Elisha Litchfield, a merchant, and Percy Tiffany. Litchfield married Hannah Maria Breed of Norwich, New York, in 1836; they had five children. Litchfield apprenticed in his father's store in Delphi and then partnered as a merchant with an older brother, Elisha Cleveland Litchfield, at Cazenovia. In 1844 Litchfield moved from the southern tier of New York State to New York City, already booming as the nation's commercial capital, where he operated a wholesale grocery enterprise until 1854.

The coming of the railroad attracted Litchfield, as it did so many other aspirants to fame and fortune. His firm of E. B. Litchfield & Co. acted as agent, banker, and broker for various railroads under construction. He and his brothers—Edwin C. Litchfield, a partner in the New York corporate law firm of Litchfield and Tracy and a railroad contractor; Elisha C. Litchfield, by then a Detroit attorney; and E. Darwin Litchfield, a London financier—started their enterprise by investing in the Michigan Southern.

By 1846 the state of Michigan had partially completed the railroad and looked for buyers to complete it, an example of state-in state-out public enterprise. In that year they sold it for less than half the state's investment to New York promoters and capitalists headed by George Bliss, a financier; John B. Jervis, a railroad engineer and executive; and the Litchfield family. Although Litchfield remained in the background in the Michigan Southern, his brothers had leading parts: Edwin served as treasurer from 1850 to 1855 and briefly as president in 1857, and Elisha was a director during the early 1850s. Fellow insiders alleged conflict of interest, and in 1862 Elisha unsuccessfully sued for commissions for financial services. The new board members, led by Henry Keep, a New York financier, were tough antagonists; in 1857 they ousted the Litchfield family from the management of the Michigan Southern, weakened by the 1857 panic.

The so-called developmental railroad was a midwestern phenomenon of the time. A developmental railroad was built in advance of sufficient traffic to be immediately profitable but was expected to stimulate economic growth and become profitable. The Litchfield brothers collaborated on several: the Northern Indiana, acquired by the Michigan Southern in 1850, and portions of the Terre Haute & Alton, the Lake Shore, and the Cleveland & Toledo. They cobbled together a through route from Chicago to Cleveland by 1852 and to Buffalo by 1857, which collapsed with the default of the Michigan Southern & Northern Indiana in the wake of the panic in that year. In 1869 this line became part of the New York Central system.

When the Civil War began, the railroad network in the old Northwest was largely in place, thanks to the efforts of the Litchfields and other railroad financiers who had mobilized both domestic and foreign capital. It is not surprising that Litchfield's eyes gazed further westward, since the railroad frontier had barely penetrated west of the Mississippi.

Litchfield owned the St. Paul & Pacific during 1862–1870 and 1873–1879. In 1862 he guaranteed the building and equipping of seventy miles of track for the railroad from near St. Paul, Minnesota, northwest to the Red River. In exchange, his payment was to consist of all stock on that construction in addition to cash. By 1864 the railroad no longer paid as stipulated, Litchfield balked, and he demanded and received additional stock. The First Division was organized in that year to further construction; eventually Litchfield owned all its common stock. Litchfield had already advanced much by 1866, declined to risk more, and consequently refused to pay interest due on the St. Paul & Pacific's bonds, his financial resources no doubt having been stretched to the limit.

In 1866 Litchfield convinced Lippmann, Rosenthal & Co., Amsterdam private bankers, to sell St. Paul & Pacific bonds in the Netherlands. The sale encouraged Litchfield to continue construction. Two years later, the First Division sold more stock, mostly to Litchfield and his family. The overcommitted Litchfield reduced his risk by selling the First Division to his brother, E. Darwin Litchfield, who had already invested in this financially shaky railroad and was willing to risk more to achieve control.

In 1870 the Litchfields conditionally sold control of the St. Paul & Pacific to the Northern Pacific. The default of the Northern Pacific in 1873 caused the St. Paul & Pacific to revert to the Litchfields.

Having exhausted their financial resources, the Litchfields then contended for control of the First Division with the Dutch bondholders represented by John Stewart Kennedy, a New York private banker. In 1875 the parties hammered out a compromise; however, the following year the Dutch bondholders failed to ratify the Litchfield agreement, but, nevertheless, the bondholders managed to assert effective control of the defaulted line.

In 1878 a group of investors bought the defaulted Dutch bonds and the following year purchased the essentially worthless stock and dubious claims of the Litchfields for $200,000 in cash and $300,000 in bonds. Reorganized as the St. Paul, Minneapolis & Manitoba, the line became the initial component of James J. Hill's Great Northern Railway, an unusually successful and well-constructed transcontinental system.

In addition to his western railroad ventures, Litchfield invested in real estate in largely rural Brooklyn, New York, where he had resided since 1846, and also constructed street railroads. He built the Atlantic Avenue and Fifth Avenue surface roads, purchased the Brooklyn, Bath & West End and became its president, and helped to develop Bay Ridge and to open the Thirty-ninth Street Ferry. Having lost one fortune in 1857, delay in building an elevated road on Fifth Avenue made him lose another in 1873.

Litchfield's family's estate comprised nearly all the region around Prospect Park, Brooklyn. With James Samuel T. Stranahan—president of the Brooklyn Park Board, merchant, investor, and one of Brooklyn's richest men—Litchfield laid out Prospect Park. The city purchased the land in piecemeal fashion between 1859 and 1869 from the Litchfield family, including Litchfield Villa, completed in 1856 and already contained within the precincts of the park.

Litchfield died in Brooklyn leaving an estate worth only about $100,000, despite the vast sums he had commanded during his life. An exemplar of the dictum that the reach should exceed the grasp, his penchant for speculative investments caused him to overreach and thereby dissipate his wealth. Enterprises he began became key components of important national rail systems, but only after he had lost control of them.

• The Litchfield family papers are deposited at the New-York Historical Society. Several books focus on Litchfield's railroad enterprises. Arthur M. Johnson and Barry Supple, *Boston Investors in Western Railroads* (1967), and Alvin F. Harlow, *The Road of the Century: The Story of the New York Central* (1947), examine the capital mobilization process and treat the Litchfields and the Michigan Southern in some detail. Ralph W. Hidy et al., *The Great Northern Railway: A History* (1988); Albro Martin, *James J. Hill and the Opening of the Northwest* (1976); and Saul Engelbourg and Leonard Bushkoff, *The Man Who Found the Money: John Stewart Kennedy and the Financing of the Western Railroads* (1996), explore the interaction between Litchfield and the St. Paul & Pacific. Obituaries in the *New York Times*, 14 May 1889, and the *Railroad Gazette*, 17 May 1889, shed light on other aspects of Litchfield's life.

SAUL ENGELBOURG

LITCHFIELD, Paul Weeks (26 July 1875–18 Mar. 1959), business executive, was born in Roxbury, a section of Boston, Massachusetts, the son of Charles Litchfield and Julia Weeks. His father was a salesman who later opened a photographic studio, and the family apparently had a comfortable middle-class life. Litchfield graduated with a degree in chemical engineering from the Massachusetts Institute of Technology in 1896. Over the next four years he moved through several short-term jobs, including spells in low-level managerial positions with three rubber manufacturing firms in Massachusetts and New Jersey. In this fashion he gained experience on the production side of an industry benefiting, in the form of tire sales, from the peak of the bicycle craze of the 1890s. In 1900 Litchfield moved to Akron, Ohio, to become factory superintendent with the recently formed Goodyear Tire & Rubber Company. He remained with the firm for the rest of his career.

After 1900 rubber manufacturing was transformed by the rapidly expanding demand for automobile tires. The tiny Goodyear business developed into the leading U.S. tire manufacturer during the first two decades of the twentieth century and has retained this position. Litchfield's initial responsibility was to design a reliable pneumatic tire for automobile use. However, he also exercised control over all aspects of manufacturing, including hiring and firing, purchasing, and the compounding of rubber and chemicals. Starting in 1908 Litchfield converted his personal control into a managerial hierarchy characterized by functional divisions and staffed by a cadre of middle managers operating under Litchfield's central direction. Final authority rested with Frank A. Seiberling, the founder, chairman, and chief stockholder of the firm, but Litchfield provided the basis of Goodyear's manufacturing strength. He joined the Goodyear board in 1908 and in 1915 was appointed a vice president in the burgeoning organization.

Litchfield promoted a variety of employee welfare schemes ranging from a factory magazine to pensions, paid vacations, and some plant medical care as well as some housing, educational, and recreational facilities. Litchfield's major innovation was to establish the Industrial Assembly, a forum for employee representation, which operated between 1919 and 1937. Litchfield's influence placed Goodyear among the leading practitioners of welfare capitalism in U.S. manufacturing between 1910 and 1930.

In 1904 Litchfield married Florence Brinton, an office worker from Ashland, Ohio. The couple had two daughters. The family's wealth, based on Goodyear stockholdings, expanded rapidly after 1910, and Litchfield purchased houses in Akron, New England, and Arizona. He spent part of his summer vacations on fishing trips in Canada and beginning in 1911 was a committed supporter of the Boy Scout movement. He was a mason and an Episcopalian.

The 1920–1921 recession had a severe impact on automobile-related industries and triggered a financial crisis at Goodyear. Although the threat of bankruptcy was averted, the eventual refinancing, organized by the Dillon, Read investment bank, was accompanied by the resignation of Frank Seiberling. Litchfield retained his position, however, and in 1926 was appointed company president.

In 1927 Litchfield resolved a dispute between the Dillon, Read investors and Goodyear's other major shareholders. This financial settlement ended the investment bank's effective control without reinstating the Seiberling family's earlier dominant position and, in effect, left Litchfield as the most experienced and powerful personality in the firm. As Goodyear president and as chairman, which he became in 1930, Litchfield also had a major role in rubber industry associations in the 1920s and 1930s and in local Akron society. In addition, he served on the Business Advisory Council in 1936.

Litchfield's business strategy was to make maximum use of Goodyear's manufacturing capacity. In 1926 he signed a contract to supply tires to Sears, Roebuck & Company, the mail-order firm, and this marked the beginning of a substantial expansion of tire retailing by mass distributors. The major tire producers (including Goodyear) also entered the tire retail business in the late 1920s. Both in this approach to marketing and in his response to the depression, Litchfield's emphasis on market share was an important influence in shaping the competitive character of the interwar tire business. Another aspect of Litchfield's leadership was an extension of Goodyear's multinational activities, particularly in manufacturing, in response to the spread of protective tariffs overseas. Between 1927 and 1938 the firm established six overseas factories (in Australia, England, Argentina, Java, Brazil, and Sweden) as well as several rubber plantations (in Sumatra, the Philippines, Panama, and Costa Rica). Throughout his career Litchfield traveled frequently both on company business to these sites and on vacations.

In the mid-1930s the emergence of labor unrest, sit-down strikes, and the United Rubber Workers union all fundamentally challenged Litchfield's approach to industrial relations. His earlier promotion of welfare capitalism fostered a bitter and emotional resistance to the notion of collective bargaining with independent unions. Only in 1941, a year after Litchfield had retired as Goodyear's president, did the firm reach an agreement with the United Rubber Workers.

The advent of World War II ensured Litchfield a continuation of a full-time business career in a war-related role. Litchfield, who had enthusiastically supported Goodyear's airship building, directed the formation of the Goodyear Aircraft Corporation to supply aircraft and components during the war. Litchfield remained chairman of Goodyear until 1958, when he was appointed honorary chairman, though effective control had passed to E. J. Thomas, his chosen successor, in the 1940s. He died in Phoenix, Arizona.

Photographs of Litchfield reveal a tall, thin, and rather diffident youth who in later life became a portly, patrician figure. His autobiography discloses that he was a teetotaler whose hair turned white abruptly during Goodyear's financial crisis of 1920–1921. His career suggests an astute, energetic, and hard-working man who had developed a rather autocratic streak by the 1930s, but who had thought earlier and more carefully than most other executives about the nature and implications of the new managerial capitalism that he embodied.

• The archives of the Goodyear Tire & Rubber Company include a printed collection of Litchfield's speeches. Litchfield's views on industrial relations and the role of professional managers are summarized in *The Industrial Republic* (1919; rev. ed. 1946). His autobiography is *Industrial Voyage: My Life as an Industrial Lieutenant* (1954). For a survey of the development of tire manufacturing and a further bibliography, see Michael J. French, *The US Tire Industry: A History* (1991). The various company histories of Goodyear contain further material on Litchfield's role and the firm's general fortunes; the best is Maurice O'Reilly, *The Goodyear Story*

(1983). See also Hugh Allen, *The House of Goodyear: A Story of Rubber and of Modern Business* (1937), from which O'Reilly's early chapters are derived; and the various "Histories of the Goodyear Tire and Rubber Company" in the W. D. Shilts Papers, University of Akron Archives, on which Allen's work is based. For the nature and impact of Litchfield's industrial relations policies, see Daniel Nelson, "The Company Union Movement, 1900–1937: A Re-examination," *Business History Review* 56 (Autumn 1982): 347–57, and *American Rubber Workers and Organized Labor, 1900–1941* (1988). An obituary is in the *Akron Beacon Journal*, 19 Mar. 1959.

MICHAEL J. FRENCH

LITCHMAN, Charles Henry (8 Apr. 1849–20 May 1902), labor reformer and editor, was born in Marblehead, Massachusetts, the son of William Litchman and Sarah Bartlett. He attended Marblehead public schools and made shoes in his father's factory, where he worked as a salesman from 1864 to 1870. He married Annie Shirley in February 1868; the couple had several children.

In 1870 he cofounded his own shoe factory and started studies in law. Both endeavors ended when the panic of 1873 bankrupted his firm. Litchman became a journeymen shoemaker and joined their national trade union, the Knights of St. Crispin. In 1876 he was elected Grand Scribe of the order, and the next year he became a salaried lecturer on its behalf.

Litchman's involvement with the Crispins coincided with a widespread decline in trade unionism in the wake of depression and capitalist repression following nationwide railroad strikes in 1877. As the Crispins declined, Litchman moved into the Knights of Labor (KOL). Insulated by the secrecy under which it operated and fortified by a complex ritual that demanded high commitment from members, only the KOL emerged from the 1870s as a stronger organization. Litchman, like the Knights' cofounder Uriah Stephens, shared a love of ritual fraternalism. He was an inveterate joiner who also held memberships in ritualistic fraternal associations such as the Freemasons, the Odd Fellows, the Order of Red Men, the Massachusetts Legion of Honor, and the Order of the Holy Cross.

In 1877 Litchman joined New York City Local Assembly 221, and he served as a delegate to the KOL's first grand assembly held in Reading, Pennsylvania, in 1878. That convention wrote the KOL's first platform and constitution; it also absorbed the Crispins into the KOL and chose Litchman as Grand Secretary. Appropriately, Litchman also oversaw the committee charged with revising the *Adelphon Kruptos*, the Knights' secret ritual book.

Litchman also took an active role in the political battles of the 1870s. He served on the Marblehead school committee from 1873 to 1878 and was outspoken in town meetings, where his defense of unions and cooperative production shocked the town's conservative business establishment. On the state level, Litchman joined the Greenback Labor party and, in 1877, lost a race for the Massachusetts Senate. In 1878 he won a seat on the Massachusetts General Court. His term was undistinguished, and the party did not renominate him. Litchman attended the party's convention in 1880, but he soon retreated to the Republican party politics of his youth. For much of the rest of his life, Litchman sought party patronage jobs.

With political ambitions on hold, Litchman turned his full attention to the Knights of Labor. In 1879 Uriah Stephens resigned as Grand Master Workman and was succeeded by Terence Powderly, a man troubled by the KOL's secrecy and determined to make the Knights a public, more bureaucratic organization. In 1880 Litchman became editor of the KOL's new national newspaper, the *Journal of United Labor*, which he published from his home in Marblehead. Membership increased by nearly 300 percent from 1879 to 1880, and Litchman credited the *JUL* for much of the growth. Controversy erupted when Litchman drained a KOL fund set aside for education and strike support by overestimating projected revenues for 1881, a year in which membership declined by nearly one-third. Critics charged Litchman with a deliberate strategy to justify the purchase of expensive printing equipment; others saw it as an attempt to discourage strikes. The 1881 grand assembly replaced him as Grand Secretary and *JUL* editor, and only Powderly's intervention saved Litchman from expulsion.

From 1881 through 1885 Litchman devoted his attentions to local and state KOL affairs. In 1881 he served as the chief administrative officer (Master Workman) for Massachusetts District Assembly 30. In 1882 the KOL became a public organization, and Litchman took an organizer's commission and established several new locals. He also controlled Marblehead Local Assembly 500 and published several short-lived labor papers, the best known of which was the *American Statesman*. Editorial content revealed Litchman to be a cautious man, though he embraced a wide spectrum of reform ranging from a call for cooperative production to support for racial equality and women's rights. Litchman's enemies charged nepotism and antiunion hiring practices in his ventures, but the papers failed largely because they were undercapitalized.

By 1886 the Knights of Labor had grown to over 729,000 members, and Litchman's District Assembly 30 was the largest single district. In 1886 he reassumed the post of General Secretary, but again he became the center of a controversy. By then a loose federation of radicals, ritualists, and anti–trade unionists controlled the Knights, and they moved to limit Litchman's power as they associated him with the bureaucratic policies of Powderly and thought both men to be middle-class poseurs seeking accommodation with capital. Litchman's District Assembly 30 background made him suspect as well; the bulk of the district's locals were trade assemblies. Litchman lost his editorship of the *Journal of United Labor* in early 1887. He also grew unpopular in District Assembly 30 where, ironically, he was unfairly accused of anti–trade unionism. This time Powderly did not save him; he allied himself with Litchman's enemies in order to save his own job. Devoid of supporters, Litchman resigned as General Secretary on 25 August 1887 and worked on Benjamin Harrison's (1833–1901) presidential campaign.

Litchman was rewarded when Harrison appointed him an immigration inspector for the Treasury Department in Boston, a post he held from 1888 to 1892. He continued to seek power within the Knights of Labor, but his self-aggrandizing behavior and tendency to write rash, angry letters led to a split with Powderly. He was equally frustrated on the district and local levels. Although he organized new assemblies and served as State Master Workman in 1890 and 1891, he was unceremoniously dropped from the Knights in 1892, when enemies discovered that his local did not have enough members to hold a charter.

Litchman also lost his government post when Harrison was not reelected. He retained ties with the KOL in the 1890s but never again held an important post. He eked out a modest living as a printer until William McKinley was elected president and appointed Litchman to the U.S. Industrial Commission, a position he held until early 1902 when the commission was disbanded. Shortly thereafter he visited Washington, D.C., where he contracted typhoid and died.

Litchman's career illustrates the inchoate structures of Gilded Age labor organizations, systems in which charisma and power politics could circumvent bureaucratic procedures. It also highlights internal debates within the Knights of Labor and the ideological tensions resulting from an incomplete move away from ritual fraternalism. As a ritualist Litchman had few peers, but as an administrator he was irascible and made more enemies than friends. Likewise, he was a decent writer but a poor businessman. His cautious approach to reform and conservative politics made him suspect among politicized Knights in the 1880s. Although Litchman held numerous positions of authority, his lack of personal charm, his penchant for bickering, and his inability to build coalitions often cost him those positions. In the end, Charles Litchman stands as an example of the failure of Gilded Age reform and of the way in which the Knights of Labor's structural flaws allowed members to battle each other with as much ferocity as they battled entrenched power elites.

• Litchman's official Knights of Labor correspondence is contained in the Terence V. Powderly Papers held by the Catholic University, Washington, D.C., and is available in microfilm editions. A short profile can also be found in the *Journal of United Labor*, June 1880. More details of Litchman's difficulties within the Knights of Labor can be found in Robert Weir, "When Friends Fall Out: Charles Litchman and the Role of Personality in the Knights of Labor," in *Labor in Massachusetts*, ed. Martin Kaufman and Kenneth Fones-Wolf (1990). That work includes detailed periodical references to Litchman. See also Norman Ware, *The Labor Movement in the United States, 1865–1900: A Study in Democracy* (1929). The June 1902 edition of the *Journal of the Knights of Labor* contains a short obituary.

ROBERT E. WEIR

LITTELL, William (1768–26 Sept. 1824), lawyer and author, was born in New Jersey, probably near Burlington, the son of parents whose names are unknown. Littell's life before he moved to Kentucky in 1801 is mostly a mystery; it is known only that he moved with his father to western Pennsylvania sometime before settling in Kentucky. After briefly practicing medicine in Mount Sterling, Kentucky, he studied and then practiced law. In 1816 Littell married Martha Irwin McCracken; they had one child, who died in 1824. After the death of his first wife, Littell married Eliza P. Hickman in 1823; that union produced one son.

Littell's legal expertise reportedly was confined to conflicts involving real property. Whatever the deficiencies of his skills as a lawyer, however, he excelled as a compiler and digester of statutes. Between 1809 and 1819 he published *The Statute Law of Kentucky*, a five-volume annotated collection of the state's legislation. Littell's compilation, the second and most successful early effort to codify Kentucky's statutes, proved to be an invaluable resource. The work demonstrated thorough knowledge of the relevant legislation and uncommon editorial skill. The digest's fourth volume, for example, provided useful guides for the practicing lawyer—among them, a review of legislation relative to conveyances, wills, promissory notes, and assignment of bonds, along with an outline of the duties of justices of the peace and sheriff and a short dissertation on proceedings in chancery against absentee defendants in land cases. The collection also included certain acts of Parliament and of Virginia's legislature that Littell deemed still to be in force as common law.

With a fellow lawyer, John Swigert, Littell published an improved *Digest of the Statute Law of Kentucky* in 1822. In this updated compilation, Littell and his coeditor supplemented the digest with relevant cases of the Kentucky Court of Appeals and the U.S. Supreme Court. In 1823 and 1824 Littell published six volumes of the decisions of the Kentucky Court of Appeals, one of which had not been published previously. So exhaustive were his searches for precedent and so extensive were his revisions of deficiently drawn legislation that Littell can be viewed as a law *maker*.

Littell's histories, *A Narrative of the Settlement of Kentucky* and *Political Transactions in and concerning Kentucky*, both published in 1806, elicited praise from contemporaries. His attempts at satire, however, were ridiculed; these included *Epistles of William, Surnamed Littell, to the People of the Realm of Kentucky* (1806) and *Festoons of Fancy, Consisting of Compositions Amatory, Sentimental and Humorous in Verse and Prose* (1814). Colleagues viewed these satires as proofs of his eccentricity, frivolousness, and immorality. Today they are acknowledged as important first examples of frontier humor. Littell died in Frankfort, Kentucky.

• There is no collection of Littell's papers, but valuable insights into his abilities and techniques as a legal digester and scholar can be obtained by examining his digests, especially the preface to *The Statute Law of Kentucky*. See also Littell's well-regarded legal treatise, *Principles of Law and Equity* (1808). In his introduction to a new edition of *Festoons of Fancy* (1940), Thomas D. Clark discusses Littell's place as a frontier humorist.

ROBERT M. IRELAND

LITTLE, Arthur (29 Nov. 1852–28 Mar. 1925), architect, was born in Boston, Massachusetts, the son of James Lovell Little, a wealthy financier, and Julia Augusta Cook. He received his architectural training at the Massachusetts Institute of Technology from 1871 to 1876 and as a draftsman in the Boston architectural firm of Peabody and Stearns from 1876 to 1878. In 1879 he opened his own architectural office in Boston.

Little played an important role in the promotion of the historic architecture of the United States, interest in which became popular with architects, artists, and the general public following the nation's centennial celebrations of 1876. His major contributions to the so-called colonial revival consisted of his book *Early New England Interiors* (1877) and his many architectural projects that incorporated motifs drawn from eighteenth- and nineteenth-century buildings.

Early New England Interiors was among the first published sketchbooks of American architecture. In it are images of historic buildings in Massachusetts, New Hampshire, and Maine that, he wrote, are "the relics of a style fast disappearing." The somewhat stiff execution of the drawings was criticized in an anonymous review in the *American Architect* (12 Jan. 1878), but the author nevertheless considered *Early New England Interiors* to be an indication of a sensitivity to colonial buildings that was just starting to emerge among American architects.

Little also expressed his admiration for colonial buildings in his first independent commission, a house for George Dudley Howe in Manchester, Massachusetts, in 1879. The house features doors, windows, and decorative details that recalled New England architecture of the Federal period. Known as "The Cliffs," the house established Little as a designer of residences for wealthy clients, especially those who were building summer homes in the new seaside resorts around Boston. In the early 1880s he began designing "cottages" for family members and others in Swampscott and Marblehead, Massachusetts, all of which included colonial-style elements as well as aspects of the equally popular "shingle style."

In 1889 he formed a partnership with Herbert Browne that continued until Little's death. The two designed numerous large houses in the Boston area, although their most extensive and elaborate commission was located in northwest Washington, D.C., a residence for Larz Anderson and his wife Isabel. The exterior treatment of their house (1902–1905) was based on eighteenth-century neoclassical British models, while the interior featured rooms in a number of historic styles with period-appropriate furnishings. (The house survives today as the headquaters of the Society of the Cincinnati.)

From the 1890s onward, Little spent much time in Europe, where he visited historic buildings and purchased antique furnishings for clients in the United States. He became especially fascinated with the Renaissance palaces of Rome. In 1894 he wrote to a friend of having had "a most enchanting dream of old furniture and marble mantles." He was also known for having incorporated paneling and other materials salvaged from early American buildings into the new houses he designed in the Boston area. Among these houses was the residence he designed for himself in 1890 at 2 Raleigh Street in Boston's fashionable Back Bay neighborhood. By 1892 he contemplated selling his house and building another in which he "should have no Colonial things and should have it Italian." His skill in the design and furnishing of interiors earned him the reputation among his family as "the best little fitter-upper in town."

In 1903 Little married Jessie Means Whitman, a widow and mother of five children; they had no children together. He endeared himself to the family, who remembered him as kind and affable. He designed the family home in Wenham, Massachusetts, which he christened "Spartivento." In keeping with its name, the house incorporated Italian motifs and materials, including an Italian stucco exterior that was considered a novelty on Boston's North Shore. Little died in Wenham.

Little's work demonstrated a broad interest in historic styles as the bases of architectural and interior design. This was a concern he shared with friends among Boston's elite. He knew Isabella Stewart Gardner, who established a museum of period rooms filled with medieval, Renaissance, and modern paintings in her Italian palazzo on Boston's Fenway. He was also closely associated with Ogden Codman, coauthor with novelist Edith Wharton of *The Decoration of Houses* (1897). Thus Little can be counted among the group of Boston aesthetes who at the end of the nineteenth century sought to "reform" interior design and formulate a post-Victorian aesthetic of the home by returning to the forms of early American and Italian Renaissance architecture and decoration.

• A collection of drawings, photographs, and firm records for Little and Browne are in the archives of the Society for the Preservation of New England Antiquities in Boston, which also has Little's correspondence with Ogden Codman in its Codman Family Collection. See also Vincent J. Scully, Jr., *The Shingle Style and the Stick Style* (1955); Walter Knight Sturges, "Arthur Little and the Colonial Revival," *Journal of the Society of Architectural Historians* 32, no. 2 (May 1973): 147–63; and Kevin D. Murphy, "A Stroll Thro' the Past: Three Architects of the Colonial Revival" (M.A. thesis, Boston Univ., 1985).

KEVIN D. MURPHY

LITTLE, Arthur Dehon (15 Dec. 1863–1 Aug. 1935), chemical engineer and industrial researcher, was born in Boston, Massachusetts, the son of Thomas Jones Little, a U.S. Army captain who was wounded during the Civil War, and Amelia Hixon. When the war ended, his father was granted a modest pension, and the family relocated to Portland, Maine. As a young boy Little demonstrated an unusual talent for both writing and chemistry; an essay he wrote about the marine life in Portland's Casco Bay won second prize in a contest sponsored by Harvard University, and at age thirteen he and a friend built a rudimentary chemical laboratory in the Littles' basement after nearly blowing up the house the year before. Recognizing their son's giftedness, in 1877 his parents sent him to New York City to obtain his high school education at the privately run Berkeley School. In 1881 he matriculated at the Massachusetts Institute of Technology (MIT), where he became cofounder and editor in chief of the student newspaper while majoring in chemistry. In 1884, when his family's deteriorating financial situation precluded his continuing his formal education, he went to work for the Richmond Paper Company's wood pulp mill in Rumford, Rhode Island.

Having studied papermaking during summer vacation in 1882, Little was able to obtain a position as an apprentice chemist at the mill, the first in the United States to use the sulfite process. This process involves softening the wood by "cooking" it in an acid bisulfite solution until the lignin, which cannot be made into paper, separates from the cellulose, the basic constituent of paper pulp. Six weeks later he was running the plant by himself after his immediate supervisors, the two plant superintendents, got into an argument and quit. He quickly realized that, while nothing was wrong with the sulfite process per se, the mill had been constructed in such a way that it took far longer than necessary to make a batch of paper pulp. He remedied this situation by rearranging the equipment, fine-tuning its operation, and inventing the "Little Digester," a steel pressure vessel with an acid-resistant lining wherein the wood could be cooked. For the "Little Digester" he received his first patent. Little's modifications worked so well that the company sent him to convert a mill it was building in New Bern, North Carolina, to the sulfite process.

In 1886 Little and Roger Burrill Griffin, his replacement at Rumford, returned to Boston to start the chemical analysis and consulting firm of Griffin & Little. One of their first steady clients was a Boston spice-milling company that hired them to test the purity of raw ingredients that the company purchased from merchants around the world. In time the firm began to specialize in papermill operations and became expert in matters of plant construction, product and process analysis, and general troubleshooting. Little was granted patents on both waxed and waterproofed paper and began to look for uses for lignin and other waste byproducts of the pulpmaking process. The two partners coauthored *The Chemistry of Paper Making* (1894), for many years the definitive text on the subject, and were named the official chemists of the American Pulp and Paper Association. They also began exploring opportunities in other industries. When artificial silk made from cellulose nitrate, a highly flammable substance, was displayed at the Paris Exposition in 1889, Little began looking for safer methods by which to convert cellulose into artificial silk; the result was the fabric known today as rayon. In 1892 his firm purchased from three British chemists the American patent rights to the viscose process, whereby cellulose is reduced to a nonflammable viscous solution by combining it with caustic soda and carbon bisulfide. In 1893 he began working with a new process for tanning leather whereby the hides are soaked in chromium sulfate solutions rather than tannin. Having also discovered the financial rewards available to expert witnesses in civil suits, the two partners seemed to be on the verge of achieving great success together when Griffin accidentally set himself on fire in the laboratory and died in 1893.

Stunned by his partner's sudden death, Little was further discouraged shortly thereafter when two pulp mills, the firm's most important clients, unexpectedly cancelled their contracts. Without a partner or a major account, he managed to eke out a living, mostly by performing routine chemical analyses. In 1894 he organized the American Viscose Company, consisting entirely of a small mill in Waltham, Massachusetts, that produced cellulose by the viscose process. The following year he was granted a patent for a process to make shades for incandescent lamps from cellulose acetate, a compound that was first produced in 1869 but was thought to have no commercial potential because it was both difficult and expensive to make. His plans to make cellulose acetate at his Waltham plant failed when the mill closed because of lack of capital. In 1899 he tried again, this time doing business as the Cellulose Products Company, but the result was the same as before. In 1900 he and William Hultz Walker, an instructor of analytical chemistry at MIT, reorganized the consulting firm to offer expertise in the areas of analytical chemistry, coal, lubrication, biology, textiles, engineering, and forest products. They also increased the staff of chemists and engineers to seven and named the new firm Little & Walker. In 1901 Little, plagued with debt, sold his rayon patent rights at auction; he also married Henriette Rogers Anthony, with whom he had no children. In 1903 the partners developed a safe and inexpensive way to produce from cellulose acetate the first commercial textile fiber, but the fiber never gained widespread industry acceptance.

In 1905 the partnership came to an end when Walker accepted an appointment as director of an applied chemistry research laboratory at MIT. Instead of taking on a new partner, Little decided to add to his growing staff of scientists and engineers and devote the efforts of the new firm, renamed the Arthur D. Little Company, to industrial research. He chose to do so at a time when chemists in general and industrial research in particular were held in low esteem by American manufacturers, who refused to believe that anything other than the old tried-and-true methods held any opportunity for increased profits. By contrast, it was Little's belief, which he expressed best in *The Handwriting on the Wall: A Chemist's Interpretation*

(1928), that "the price of progress is research, which alone assures the security of dividends." Henceforth, it would be his mission to preach the gospel of industrial research.

In 1906 Little's new company was retained by the U.S. Forestry Service to determine whether or not paper pulp could be made from pine trees. His conclusion that these species could indeed be converted into satisfactory paper pulp led to the creation in 1908 of the U.S. Forest Products Laboratory in Madison, Wisconsin, and the economic resuscitation of the pine-growing regions of the American South. In 1908 he became a founder of the American Institute of Chemical Engineers. In 1911 he designed and had built for the United Fruit Company a machine that could make paper out of bagasse, the waste fiber from sugarcane. That same year, Little negotiated a contract with General Motors to design and staff a research laboratory in Detroit, Michigan, where the automaker could test materials before incorporating them into their vehicles. In 1912 he was elected president of the American Chemical Society and for the next two years gave a number of speeches and wrote several articles regarding the many benefits that applied chemistry offered to American industry. In 1916 Little reached an agreement with the Canadian Pacific Railway to conduct a survey of Canada's natural resources. The survey resulted in 165 separate reports concerning everything from the production of paper from waste flax and cereal straw to the recovery of gasoline from natural gas. It also led to the creation by the Canadian government of an industrial research council, which was responsible for implementing the findings of the survey. During World War I his company contributed significantly to the American war effort by developing new chemicals for use in airplane dope, which was used to coat the wings of biplanes, and new sources of charcoal and fiber filters for gas masks. Perhaps his most impressive accomplishment, if not his most useless one, came in 1921 when he devised a method to make a silk purse out of a sow's ear. One hundred pounds of sow's ears were rendered into glue, combined with various chemicals, and then strained into gelatinous fibers from which two purses were sewn. The purses were made to demonstrate unequivocally to American businessmen the tremendous capabilities that industrial research in general and his research firm in particular offered American industry. Before long this development became the centerpiece of conversation at trade shows across the United States.

Little possessed a remarkably intriguing personality. A fastidious dresser and a chain smoker, he was quite actively involved in the Boston social scene and was described by many of his colleagues as the quintessential proper Bostonian. He was an excellent and prolific writer and public speaker, and he never missed an opportunity to proselytize in print or from the rostrum about the blessings of industrial research. Although he was an accomplished chemist and researcher, his business acumen was mediocre at best. As he preached tirelessly about the salutary effect of industrial research on a company's bottom line, his own firm often struggled from day to day to meet operating expenses and rarely paid a dividend to its stockholders. In fact, Little had a rather cavalier attitude toward money, particularly his own. He often refused to charge clients when his work on their behalf failed to yield the desired results, and he fervently believed that "a professional man starts to fail the moment he permits money to shape his career."

Although Little never graduated from MIT, he remained affiliated with the school until his death. He lectured there on the chemistry of papermaking from 1893 to 1916. In 1917 he moved his company from Boston to Cambridge, just to be closer to MIT, and he hired virtually every new member of his research staff from among its graduates. He served the school as a life member of the Corporation of the Massachusetts Institute of Technology and as president of the alumni association from 1921 to 1922. In addition, he made two major contributions to MIT's academic excellence. The first involved founding the School of Chemical Engineering Practices and developing its unique method of teaching chemical engineering as a discipline separate from either chemistry or mechanical engineering. He was also the first to conceptualize unit operations, a structure of logic that teaches process design by consolidating all the functions required to effect a particular physical or chemical change into a single step. Unit operations proved to be so powerful a teaching tool that by the mid-1920s it formed the basis of chemical engineering instruction and practice throughout the United States. The second involved saving the school from imminent death twice, once in 1905 by campaigning assiduously against a proposed merger between MIT and Harvard University and again in 1935 by bequesting to the school a majority interest in Arthur D. Little Inc. under terms that preserved the integrity and independence of both school and company.

Little received a number of honors and awards for his contributions to industrial research. He received honorary doctorates from five universities in the United States and England and was awarded the Society of the Chemical Industry's Perkin Medal in 1931. He was president of the American Chemical Society from 1912 to 1914, president of the American Institute of Chemical Engineers in 1919, and president of the Society of the Chemical Industry from 1928 to 1929. He died in Northeast Harbor, Maine.

Little was a pioneer in the fields of applied chemistry and industrial research. His research company, Arthur D. Little Inc., was the first independent industrial research laboratory in the United States to offer expertise to industry and government in the areas of marketing, energy, manufacturing, information, and environmental consulting; ninety years after its founding it employed more than 2,500 people in facilities around the world. His chemical know-how led to the discovery, invention, or improvement of many important chemical processes and the concept of unit operations. His ideas revolutionized chemical engineering instruction, particularly in the School of Chemical Engineering Practices, founded at MIT. His essays and speeches convinced many captains of American industry that the key to a profitable future could only be found through the research and development of innovative products and methods.

• Little's papers have not been located. Good biographies of Little can be found in E. J. Kahn, Jr., *The Problem Solvers: A History of Arthur D. Little Inc.* (1986), John F. Magee, *Arthur D. Little Inc.: At the Moving Frontier* (1985), and Williams Haynes, "Arthur Dehon Little," in *Great Chemists*, ed. Eduard Farber (1961). His obituary is in the *New York Times*, 3 August 1935.

CHARLES W. CAREY, JR.

LITTLE, Charles Joseph (21 Sept. 1840–11 Mar. 1911), Methodist minister and seminary president, was born in Philadelphia, Pennsylvania, the son of Thomas Rowell and Ann Zimmermann. Raised in a bilingual family (German and English), Little developed an excellent facility for languages and eventually became proficient in Greek, Latin, Italian, and French. Following his graduation with a B.A. from the University of Pennsylvania in 1861, he joined the Philadelphia Conference of the Methodist church the next year. Prevented from serving in the Union army during the Civil War because of poor health, he served as pastor of Methodist congregations in Newark, Delaware (1862–1863), and Philadelphia (1863–1865); he also visited thousands of wounded and dying soldiers on battlefields and comforted many who lost loved ones in the war. In 1864 he completed an M.A. at the University of Pennsylvania. After serving Methodist parishes in Springfield, Pennsylvania (1865–1866), and Chestnut Hill in Philadelphia (1866–1867), he accepted a position as a professor of mathematics at Dickinson Seminary (later Lycoming College) in Williamsport, Pennsylvania, a decision prompted in part by his fear that he did not have the physical stamina the ministry required. While doing graduate study in Europe from 1869 to 1872 he met Anna Marina Schultze, whom he married in Berlin, Germany, in 1872; they had four children.

Soon after his wedding, Little became the minister of Christ Methodist Church in Philadelphia. In 1874 he accepted a position as a professor of philosophy and history at Dickinson College. While teaching at Dickinson, he also served for three years as the librarian of the Pennsylvania State Library. In 1882 he received a Ph.D. from DePauw University in Indiana. In 1885 Syracuse University, a Methodist institution, appointed him professor of logic and history. After six years in this position, Little moved to Evanston, Illinois, in 1891 to become professor of church history at Garrett Biblical Institute, one of the three leading Methodist seminaries.

In 1895 Little was elected president of Garrett, a position he occupied until his death. As president, he continued to teach church history, increased the size and improved the quality of both the faculty and the student body, strengthened the facilities, especially the library, and developed a reputation as an able administrator and an excellent scholar. According to a historian of Methodism, Little "brought a spirit of intellectual discipline and scholarship, which extended in influence beyond the seminary into the whole church" (Norwood, p. 47).

In addition to helping shape the theology and ministry of the Methodist pastors who studied at Garrett, Little had a significant impact upon his denomination through his work at its quadrennial general conferences, his lectures, and his publications. Elected as a delegate to the conferences held from 1888 to 1908, he served on committees, dealing with education, the church's constitution, fraternal relations with other denominations, the eligibility of women as delegates to the conference, the admission of lay delegates, and the restatement of Methodist doctrine. An inspiring orator, he addressed the Methodist Centennial Conference in Baltimore, Maryland, in 1884 and gave the Fernley Lecture at the British Wesleyan Conference in 1900. He also spoke at the semicentennial celebration of Garrett in 1905.

Little was reluctant to put his lectures and thoughts into writing because he wanted to be able to reassess his conclusions in light of more thorough research and deeper reflection. He frequently responded to colleagues who urged him to publish more, remarking that "Jesus didn't write any books." Nevertheless, he contributed many review articles to theological journals. The stipulations of the Fernley Lecture required the publication of his *Christianity and the Nineteenth Century* (1900), a compelling defense of evangelical Christianity and the importance of personal spirituality against various forms of nationalism. The Methodist Book Concern persuaded him in 1904 to publish *The Angel in the Flame*, a series of sermons he had preached at the First Methodist Church of Evanston. A memorial volume prepared in his honor (1912) contains eight of his addresses and essays, including an analysis of work of pioneering Methodist pastors in America, an appreciative summary of John Wesley's life and expository preaching style, laudatory accounts of the contributions of John Milton and Abraham Lincoln, and an explanation of the breadth and quality of historic Christian thought. Five years after his death, his successor as Garrett's president, Charles Macaulay Stewart, published a collection of Little's essays on historical, religious, and literary topics as *Biographical and Literary Studies* (1916). These essays display the breadth of his intellectual interests as they analyze religious leaders (Paul, Savonarola, Luther), statesmen (Hildebrand), poets (Dante), scientists (Galileo), and dramatists (Shakespeare, Ibsen), as well as the place of Christ in modern thought.

Little was somewhat reserved and occasionally was so conscientious that he appeared aloof. Not a diplomat in either instinct or practice, he sometimes repelled people by freely speaking his mind. Although he was tenderhearted by nature, his criticism was at times caustic and severe. Nevertheless, he developed deep and enduring friendships and often delighted social gatherings with his wit and repartee. Contemporaries praised "comprehensive learning, exact scholarship, . . . peerless gifts of exposition," administrative talent, literary gifts, and religious enthusiasm (*In Memoriam*, pp. 72, 74). His colleague at Garrett, Milton Terry, labeled his sermons "eloquent, inspiring, instructive, and convincing." Herbert Welch, the president of Ohio Wesleyan University, lauded him as Methodism's best scholar.

One reason Little was so highly esteemed in his denomination was because his wide interests and broad understanding made him sympathetic with both its progressive and conservative wings. While strongly committed to Christian orthodoxy, he encouraged the use of critical methods to study the Bible. Although his life was spent primarily in theological reflection, Little constantly reminded Christians that "our theories, improve them how we may, have value only as they save souls, and homes and communities; only as we destroy saloons, and brothels, abolish wantonness, and greed, and graft; only as they make men love truth and hate lies, only as they make men do justice and love mercy and walk humbly with their God" (*Semi-Centennial Celebration*, p. 159). He died in Evanston.

• Little's papers are at Garrett Theological Seminary in Evanston, Ill. *Garrett Biblical Institute; Semi-Centennial Celebration* (1906) contains several of his addresses. The best source of information about Little's life and work is Charles M. Stuart, ed., *In Memoriam: Charles Joseph Little* (1912). This volume contains tributes and testimonies to Little by colleagues, friends, prominent Protestants from the Chicago area, and Methodist leaders from across the country. "President Charles J. Little," *Christian Advocate*, 16 Mar. 1911, pp. 3–4, is useful. Some biographical information is included in Charles J. Little, *Biographical and Literary Studies*, ed. Charles Macaulay Stewart (1916). See also "Charles Joseph Little," in *Minutes of the Rock River Annual Conference of the Methodist Episcopal Church* (1911), pp. 124–26, and *Journals of the General Conferences of the Methodist Episcopal Church,* (1888–1908). Frederick Norwood assesses Little's administration at the seminary in *From Dawn to Midday at Garrett* (1978). Obituaries are in the *New York Times* and the *Chicago Tribune*, both 12 Mar. 1911, and in *Northwestern Christian Advocate*, 15 Mar. 1911.

GARY SCOTT SMITH

LITTLE, Clarence Cook (6 Oct. 1888–22 Dec. 1971), scientist and educator, was born in Brookline, Massachusetts, the son of James Lovell Little, a Boston merchant, and Mary Robbins Revere. Little enrolled at Harvard University in 1906 to study zoology. He obtained a B.A. in 1910 with Phi Beta Kappa honors, and took a masters degree (M.S., 1912) and a doctorate (Sc.D., 1914) in the same subject under William Castle at Harvard's Bussey Institute of Applied Biology.

Throughout his life Little displayed extreme pride in his upper-class Boston heritage. His mother was a great-granddaughter of Paul Revere, and he held this bloodline in such esteem that in 1952 he contemplated writing a biography of his famous colonial relative.

Little was equally dedicated to Harvard, an institution with which he was academically and administratively involved for nearly twelve years. During his senior year at Harvard, "Pete" Little, as his friends nicknamed him, was captain of the track team and a popular student leader. His charismatic demeanor and his Cambridge connections combined to gain him a position as secretary to the Harvard Corporation during his first two years of graduate school (1910–1912). In 1911 Little married Katherine Day Andrews, the daughter of a Boston architect; they had three children before divorcing in 1929. From 1911 to 1913, Little was appointed research associate in genetics at Harvard's Bussey Institution. Despite the self-described embarrassment he experienced after initially failing his doctoral qualifying exams in 1913, Little stayed on at Harvard in both scientific and organizational capacities well after finishing his final degree; he held positions as research fellow in genetics from 1913 to 1917 and assistant dean of the college and acting university marshall from 1916 to 1917.

Little's first scientific research and writings focused on two main areas: mammalian genetics and the genetics of cancer. As Castle's graduate student, he had worked with one of the Mendelian theory of heredity's earliest and most influential American adherents. Castle's breeding experiments on small mammals were considered one of the greatest contributions to the developing science of genetics, and they provided important intellectual resources for Little. Little's own dissertation research explored the basic genetics of mouse coat color inheritance, with reference to the problems of dominance and epistasis.

From 1913 to 1916 Little performed pioneering work on the more complicated multifactorial inheritance of tumor susceptibility in mice, sometimes in collaboration with Ernest Everett Tyzzer of the Harvard Medical School. In 1914 Little published a theoretical paper ("A Possible Mendelian Explanation for a Type of Inheritance Apparently Non-Mendelian in Nature," *Science* 42: 904–6) suggesting that "certain characteristics of an organism depend for their visible manifestation . . . upon the simultaneous presence of more than one mendelizing factor" (p. 904). In such cases, Little asserted, a Mendelian statistical analysis demonstrated that as the number of factors involved in a trait's expression increased, the ratio of observed F2 (or second generation) animals that do *not* show the trait to those that do would also increase rapidly. Little concluded that this interpretation could explain data from his mouse-breeding experiments as well as data from previous cancer heredity studies, in which a tumor condition dominant in the F1 (or first) generation appeared to "almost completely disappear in the F2" (p. 906). His working hypothesis with regard to the genetics of tumor susceptibility, as he restated it in a 1931 paper ("The Role of Heredity in Determining the Incidence and Growth of Cancer," p. 2785), was

Since [genetic factors] segregate independently and recombine in the F2 according to the laws of chance, it would naturally follow that the more factors there were, the *fewer* of the gametes in F2 there would be which received the whole number necessary for susceptibility.

Little never completely abandoned mammalian genetics for cancer research. As a hobby, he began breeding dogs for show in the late 1910s. During the 1950s, he unsuccessfully attempted to establish four distinct pure dog breeds for behavioral genetic research, and in 1957, as the capstone to his research career, Little completed a canine coat color genetics textbook, which drew heavily on his years of practical experience with these pedigreed animals.

Little's primary scientific achievement was his development of the first healthy inbred mouse strain. Inbreeding was a method for producing genetically uniform (or highly homozygous) organisms that was practiced by plant and animal breeders in the early 1900s. In 1909, while he was an undergraduate, Little had begun the brother-sister inbreeding of a house mouse (*Mus musculus*) genetic type known as *dba*. He had noticed that mice descended from *dba* parents typically displayed a high frequency of tumor development, and by inbreeding them, he hoped to stabilize the genetic factors responsible for tumor incidence. Through persistence, careful selection of healthy organisms, and large-scale breeding, Little overcame the loss of vigor and fertility that usually plagued inbred animals. Because these organisms represented a predictable and replicable source of experimental material for biologists, Little believed that inbred mice from the *dba* and other strains would be invaluable for mammalian genetics research, and he strongly advocated their use throughout his subsequent career.

After graduate school, Little continued in scientific research while also developing his career as an administrator. Following two years of service (1917–1918) as a reserve officer in the U.S. Army's Aviation Section, he returned briefly to laboratory work as a research fellow in comparative pathology at the Harvard Medical School. Then in 1919 he became a research associate at the Carnegie Institution's Station for Experimental Evolution (SEE) at Cold Spring Harbor, New York. There Little supervised student research and published his own work on genetic topics, including mammalian coat color, transplantable tumors in mice, and human sex ratios. He also started another inbred mouse strain, *C57BL*, which displayed a low mammary cancer incidence. In 1922 he was appointed to the Eugenics Committee of the United States, the organizational forerunner to the American Eugenics Society, of which he was later elected president (1928). Little was promoted to assistant director of the SEE in 1921, but his brash personality led to administrative squabbling with director Charles B. Davenport. When Little was offered the presidency of the University of Maine in 1922—after giving a speech on education at the Orono campus—he quickly accepted.

Little soon developed a controversial reputation as the nation's then-youngest university president. At Maine, Little sought to transform the provincial campus by securing building improvements and implementing several innovative student programs, such as Freshman Week and women's athletics. But after encountering stiff opposition from Governor Percival Baxter and the state legislature, Little left Maine in 1925 and accepted the presidency of the University of Michigan. At Ann Arbor he was praised by faculty for his support of research, but he also drew criticism from students and alumni for his ban of automobiles on campus, his enforcement of alcohol prohibition at fraternity parties, and his insistence that any surplus revenues generated by Michigan's 1925–1926 Big Ten championship football team be used to build athletic fields for use by all men and women of the university.

An ardent eugenicist and birth control advocate, Little served as scientific director of the American Birth Control League from 1925 to 1945. In 1925 he gained national attention in a well-publicized debate on birth control with Michigan religious leaders. Soon thereafter, Little battled the Michigan regents over his plan to institute the University College, a basic core curriculum for all students, which would have effectively made degree requirements more stringent. In 1928, becoming frustrated and impatient with these highly politicized clashes, Little resigned his Michigan presidency. Years later many of Little's ideas would become widely accepted policies on American college campuses.

Little, who insisted on maintaining his inbred mice and his mouse cancer research while he was a university president, had established a small personal laboratory next door to his presidential offices at Maine. During summers he taught a field course in biology on Maine's Mount Desert Island. He also gave public lectures on cancer to wealthy Bar Harbor summer residents. Several of his listeners, including Detroit automobile industrialists Edsel Ford and Roscoe B. Jackson, later endorsed his Michigan presidency and contributed substantially to his cancer research there. When Little resigned from Michigan, his patrons agreed to continue supporting his scientific work. In 1929, shortly after Jackson's untimely death, Little founded the Roscoe B. Jackson Memorial Laboratory (the name of which was officially shortened to the Jackson Laboratory in 1963), and he relocated his mice and his entire Michigan lab staff to this new independent research institute in Bar Harbor.

As the Jackson Laboratory's director for the next twenty-seven years (1929–1956), Little achieved national prominence as a scientific administrator, and he oversaw the early development of the institution's research reputation. Officially dedicated to research on mammalian genetics and cancer, from 1933 to 1936 Little and his staff published a series of surprising mouse breeding results that indicated that "extra-chromosomal influences" were involved in the inheritance of mammary cancers. Despite the fact that Little himself held steadfastly to a genetic interpretation of these data, later researchers considered this work to be suggestive of a viral theory of cancer transmission. Shortly after its founding, the Jackson Laboratory also became an international center of large-scale inbred mouse production and distribution for all types of biological research. Little began selling so-called JAX mice (named for the institution's abbreviated cable address) in order to make financial ends meet during the depression. By the 1990s, worldwide circulation of JAX mice had exceeded two million organisms a year.

In 1930 Little married Beatrice Johnson, a former research student and ABCL secretary, with whom he had two children. From 1929 to 1945 he served as managing director of the American Society for the Control of Cancer, and he was twice president of the American Society for Cancer Research (1930–1931 and 1940–1941). In 1932 he acted as general secretary to the Sixth International Congress of Genetics. When the National Cancer Institute was initially created by Congress in 1937, Little addressed a joint committee on the importance of mouse material for cancer research, and he was appointed an original member of the National Advisory Cancer Council (1937–1939). In 1945 he was elected to the National Academy of Sciences.

Two years before retiring from the Jackson Laboratory in 1956, Little accepted a controversial position as chairman of the Tobacco Industry Research Committee's Scientific Advisory Board. Several Jackson Lab trustees worried that this association might seriously hamper their institution's ability to raise cancer research funds, and they immediately enacted measures to insure the Lab's fiscal and intellectual independence from its founder's latest patron. Little himself believed there was no contradiction; he consistently maintained that the cause and effect relationship between smoking and lung cancer needed further scientific investigation (as he put it in a March 1954 media statement) "on a basis that meets the requirements of definiteness, extent, and specificity of the data which the seriousness and implications of the problem deserve." A lifelong advocate of increased governmental funding for cancer research, Little testified before Congress again on this issue during the 1965 hearings on cigarette labeling and advertising. Ironically, Little died of a heart attack in Ellsworth, Maine, just one day before the 1971 U.S. National Cancer Institute Act was signed into law.

Little's commitment to the mouse as a valuable genetic research tool remains his most important legacy to experimental biology and medicine. But his forcefully worded ideals, his charismatic personality, and his administrative talents also combined to render him a uniquely effective early leader in the fields of American university education and cancer research.

• Most of Little's papers, including his presidential papers from the University of Maine, are housed at the Raymond Fogler Library, University of Maine, Orono. The C. C. Little University of Michigan Presidential Papers are at the Bentley Historical Library, University of Michigan, Ann Arbor. Harvard University's Pusey Library holds a significant collection of biographical material on Little. The Jackson Laboratory in Bar Harbor, Maine, also maintains its own historical archive

that dates back to 1929. Little's *The Awakening College* (1930) is an important source on his educational ideas, his *Civilization Against Cancer* (1939) details his scientific and political views on cancer research, and the series of articles he did for *The Birth Control Review* from 1926 to 1930 (especially "Unnatural Selection and its Resulting Obligations," 10 (Aug. 1926): 243–44) nicely summarizes his position on birth control. Little's important scientific publications include "The Role of Heredity in Determining the Incidence and Growth of Cancer," *American Journal of Cancer*, 15 (1931): 2780–89, and "The Existence of Non-Chromosomal Influence in the Incidence of Mammary Tumors in Mice," *Science*, 78 (1933): 465–66 (coauthored with the staff of the Jackson Memorial Laboratory). A virtually complete bibliography of Little's scientific work can be found in George D. Snell's memoir in National Academy of Sciences *Biographical Memoirs*, 46 (1975): 240–63. See also Jean Holstein, *The First Fifty Years at the Jackson Laboratory* (1979). On Little's college presidencies, see the relevant chapters in David C. Smith, *The First Century: A History of the University of Maine, 1865–1965* (1979), and Howard H. Peckham, *The Making of the University of Michigan, 1817–1967* (1967). Little's obituary is in the *New York Times*, 23 Dec. 1971.

KAREN RADER

LITTLE, George (10 or 15 Apr. 1754–22 July 1809), naval officer, was born in Marshfield, Massachusetts, the son of Lemuel Little and Penelope Eames (or Ames). Growing up near the Massachusetts seacoast, he was drawn to maritime life and became a merchant seaman. He also purchased a farm near his home town and in 1779 married a local woman, Rachel Rogers, with whom he had a son.

Shortly after the outbreak of the revolutionary war in 1775, Little was given command of the *Boston*, an armed vessel belonging to the Massachusetts state navy. Captured by the British, he was confined in the prison ship *Lord Sandwich*, anchored at Newport, Rhode Island, but he effected his escape on 7 March 1778. Later in the year he rejoined the Massachusetts navy as a second lieutenant on the brigantine *Active*, then was appointed master of the brigantine *Hazard*. On 3 May 1779 he was promoted to lieutenant and during the summer participated in the disastrous Penobscot expedition, in which Commodore Dudley Saltonstall almost managed to destroy the Massachusetts navy. He joined the crew of the Massachusetts ship *Protector* in 1780 and was with that vessel on 9 June when it captured the British privateer *Admiral Duff* after a hard-fought gunnery duel. The following year he was again taken prisoner by the British when the vastly outgunned *Protector* was captured by the warships *Roebuck* and *Medea*. Shut up in Mill Prison, Plymouth, England, he and some other American officers managed to bribe their way out and escape to France. In 1782 he returned to America, was promoted to captain in the Massachusetts navy, and was given command of the *Winthrop*. Ordered to raid enemy shipping in Penobscot Bay, he captured a number of British ships, thus partially avenging his state's earlier disgrace there. He cruised off the Massachusetts coast for the remainder of the war. On 23 June 1783 he resigned his commission and returned to his wife and farm at Marshfield.

Little's bucolic life was interrupted in the late 1790s when growing tensions between France and America on the high seas led to outright conflict. Although Congress never formally declared war with France, in 1798 it abrogated the Franco-American treaty of 1778, created a Navy Department, appropriated enough money to expand both the army and navy, and commenced undeclared naval war against France. On 4 March 1799 Little was commissioned a captain in the U.S. Navy by President John Adams and appointed commander of the newly built frigate *Boston*, which had twenty-eight guns. Benjamin Stoddert, secretary of the navy, approved of the president's choice, believing Little a man of "spirit & enterprize"; as for Adams, he said that Little was "one of the bravest men in one of the finest ships in the world." Little was delighted with his new command, declaring to the citizens of Boston, who had paid for the construction of the vessel, that his frigate outsailed every other ship on the ocean. Ordered to join an American squadron that was protecting American commerce off Cape François, on the northern coast of Santo Domingo, he sailed on 24 July for his new station. His next few months of service consisted of routine cruising, interrupted occasionally by the seizure of a few small French prizes.

On 1 December 1799 Little's military fortunes began to improve. While sailing in company with the cutter *General Greene*, Captain Christopher R. Perry commanding, he seized a Danish brig, the *Flying Fish*, laden with flour, beef, and dry goods, and also retook the schooner *Weymouth*, which had been captured earlier by a French privateer. A day or two later he and the *Norfolk*, Master Commandant William Bainbridge commanding, captured a French privateer and the cutter *Le Gourdie Le Pelican*. In early February 1800 he forced the surrender of the French privateer *Deux Anges*, which carried twenty guns. He stopped the French merchant sloop *La Fortune* on 4 March and relieved it of $3,382.20, although its captain had tried to secrete the money in "the well of the pump." Seven days later he was attacked by nine barge loads of enemy soldiers, about 300 in all, near the island of Gonave. After a fight of two hours, he destroyed three of the barges with their crews and forced the rest to flee "in a most shattered condition." He took the French sloop *Happy*, carrying a cargo of coffee, on 26 March and on 2 April the sloop *L'Heureux*. He seized a suspicious-looking schooner on 9 June, believing it to be a French ship even though it was flying the Danish flag. On 25 June he and his crew, tired after almost eleven months of unremitting sea duty, sailed for Boston, putting in at Havana, Cuba, where several British frigates gave the *Boston* "every mark of respect and esteem." He reached home in late July.

Little refitted the *Boston* during August, then on 7 September returned to sea, with orders to patrol off the American coast and protect merchant shipping. After a month of uneventful cruising, except for the capture of the brig *L'Espoir*, on 12 October he met and engaged the French corvette *Le Berceau*, which had twenty-four guns, Citizen Louis Andre Senes commanding. For two hours Captain Senes, although outgunned, valiantly defended his ship, killing four of Little's crew, wounding eight others, and inflicting considerable injury to the *Boston*'s, masts, rigging, and sails. Finally, Senes was compelled to surrender when his fore and main masts went over the side. Both warships limped into Boston harbor on 15 November.

Little's seafaring service was at an end, but he suffered much vexation in the next few months from court proceedings relating to his previous voyages. Earlier, on 4 February 1800, he had been sued by the owners of *Le Gourdie Le Pelican* for supposedly destroying ship's records but had been acquitted. After his return to Boston the owners of the *Flying Fish* sued him for damages, claiming he had acted beyond his orders in seizing a Danish ship, despite the fact that Edward Stevens, U.S. consul general at Santo Domingo, had approved the action at the time. When the case was appealed to the Supreme Court, the justices held that Little had to pay damages. Finally, on 7 September 1801 Little was court-martialed, supposedly for having allowed the crew of the *Boston* to pillage prisoners taken on *Le Berceau*, but he was honorably acquitted. He resigned his commission on 20 October 1801, retiring to Weymouth, Massachusetts, where he lived quietly with his wife until his death there.

• Primary sources on Little's part in the undeclared naval war with France are in Dudley Knox, ed., *Naval Documents Related to the Quasi-War between the United States and France, 1797–1801*, vols. 2–6 (1935–1938). Other sources on his life are in the Massachusetts Historical Society, *Collections* 20 (1884). For his role in the revolutionary war and for general background see Charles O. Paullin, *The Navy of the American Revolution* (1906); Gardner W. Allen, *The Naval History of the American Revolution* (2 vols., 1913); and William M. Fowler, Jr., *Rebels under Sail: The American Navy during the Revolution* (1976). His part in the undeclared war with France is surveyed in Gardner W. Allen, *Our Naval War with France* (1909); Howard P. Nash, *The Forgotten Wars: The Role of the U.S. Navy in the Quasi-War with France and the Barbary Wars, 1798–1805* (1968); and William M. Fowler, *Jack Tars and Commodores: The American Navy, 1783–1815* (1984). An obituary is in the *New-England Palladium*, 28 July 1809.

PAUL DAVID NELSON

LITTLE, Sophia Louisa Robbins (1799–1893), writer and reformer, was born in Newport, Rhode Island, the daughter of U.S. senator Asher Robbins, an attorney, and Mary Ellery. Educated locally, she married William Little, Jr., of Boston in 1824; they had three children. Her first publication was a poem, "Thanksgiving," included in a Boston gift book, *The Token* (1828).

By the mid-1830s Little was widowed, and her finances and sense of moral purpose were strained. Because most Newporters were proud of cordial relations with southerners who vacationed and sometimes resettled there, Little felt constrained from speaking openly about her antislavery convictions. Still she contrived to help slaves whom she saw as eager to leave their owners, and she contacted Dorothea Dix for help in freeing a mentally ill man chained in the Newport jail. Little began to write antislavery pieces as a form of religious expression and to promote reform and gain income.

The Robbins family was Episcopalian, but the pious Little had absorbed the Moravian emphasis on suffering and salvation through the atoning power of Christ's blood, which she cited as the basis of her work for the oppressed. African Americans, including a branch of the famous Remond family, allowed Little to speak at their local churches and in 1840 worked with Little to raise funds to send Charles Remond to the World Anti-Slavery Convention in London. Boston reformers also encouraged Little's inclinations, so much so that she, rather than confiding in her distinguished but disapproving father and brothers, sought legal and literary advice from Boston reformers. She contributed to gift books like the Pawtucket (R.I.) Juvenile Emancipation Society's *Envoy* and Maria Chapman's *Liberty Bell*, an annual sold at the Boston Anti-Slavery Fair. While not sharing Little's Moravian piety, local blacks and more distant white abolitionists were her readers and sponsors. Little disliked the militant, increasingly secular arguments of white abolitionists, but she remained loyal to these radicals, including William Lloyd Garrison, whom she had witnessed being attacked by a Boston mob in 1835.

Her Boston contacts led to Little's friendship with Ray Potter, an independent minister and printer who published many of her writings. She often visited Potter's home in Pawtucket, a town she found more tolerant of eccentric reformers than Newport, which Little described to Wendell Phillips in 1842 as "this frost bound moral Iceland."

Little experimented with poetry, short stories, dialogues, and the novel. Modern readers might enjoy the colorful characters and meandering plot of Little's temperance melodrama, *The Reveille* (1854), more than "Thanksgiving," which Rufus W. Griswold in *Female Poets of America* (1849) pronounced Little's best work. Her writings were often allegorical, including a prose piece, *Pilgrim's Progress in the Last Days* (1843), and several epic poems that focused on piety more than on reform; see, for example, *The Annunciation and Birth of Jesus* (1842), *The Resurrection* (1842), *The Betrothed* (1844), and *The Last Days of Jesus* (1893).

Little's letters to antislavery newspapers like the *Liberator* and *Herald of Freedom* show the forceful spirit of her piety, but her most powerful writing is her antislavery fiction. Contact with slaves visiting Newport with their masters, the Baltimore imprisonment of the Reverend Charles T. Torrey for aiding runaways, the Florida authorities' 1844 branding of Jonathan Walker "SS," meaning slave stealer, and the 1850 Fugitive Slave Act provided inspiration and often the plots for Little's writings. Her response to Walker's treatment, for example, was *The Branded Hand* (1845), a drama in verse that shows whites, North and South, as indifferent to the horrors of plantation life and its effects on slave families. When a slave mother begs her master to stop beating a daughter who has resisted his sexual advances, Little's fictional master is heartless:

> No! I'll not spare her! I will tear her flesh—
> I'll spoil her beauty—I will mar her pride—
> I'll make her but one hideous heap of scars!

One of Little's best works is her novel, *Thrice through the Furnace* (1852), which combines the lyricism of her poetry with her religious and political sensibilities. Like *Uncle Tom's Cabin*, Little's novel protested the Fugitive Slave Act by narrating the trials of several youths trying to escape from slavery. Even more than Harriet Beecher Stowe, Little saturates her plot with biblical language and characters, several of whom pray more than did Uncle Tom while suffering "through the furnace" of three failed escapes.

In her political comments *in Thrice through the Furnace*, Little was more forthright than Stowe, a quality that surely undermined her popularity. She showed whites on a southern plantation celebrating the Fugitive Slave Act by parading illuminated images of authors of the new, proslavery legislation, whom Little dubbed the "Gods of the new dispensation of death, Webster, Cass and Clay." Also displayed were images of slave catchers, cotton fields and factories, and approving clergymen. Those celebrating presented each image as an ingredient of national harmony, although Little's narrator comments that one banner, a motto adopted from the Bible, was an inversion of Christian teaching; "Righteousness and peace have met together—the North and South have kissed each other" (p. 129).

Little's speaking, writing, fundraising, and petitioning for antislavery, temperance, women's rights, and prison reform made her prominent among New England reformers. By 1865, however, she focused on temperance and prison reform, particularly when women were affected, and she even preached to inmates in the state prison. Her preaching and writing led to political organizing, and she used the skills she had honed in the antislavery crusade to found the state chapter of the Woman's Christian Temperance Union and to orchestrate the collection of 15,000 signatures on a petition presented to the state legislature. William Lloyd Garrison noted in 1870 that Little still displayed great energy and her "usual fervid and devotional frame of mind," qualities that made her among the most prominent and persistent of those leaders whose evangelical piety fueled reform movements both before and after the Civil War. Little died in Boston, Massachusetts.

• Letters from Little are in the antislavery collections of the Boston Public Library and the Wendell Phillips Papers at the Houghton Library, Harvard University. See also Deborah Van Broekhoven, "'A Determination to Labor . . . ': Female Antislavery Activity in Rhode Island," *Rhode Island History* 44 (May 1985): 35–45, and Van Broekhoven, "'Let Your Name Be Enrolled': Process and Ideology in Female Antislavery Petitioning," in *The Abolitionist Sisterhood: Women's Political Culture in Antebellum America*, ed. John Van Home and Jean Yellin (1994).

DEBORAH BINGHAM VAN BROEKHOVEN

LITTLE CROW (1812?–3 July 1863), Mdewakanton Dakota chief of the Kaposia band and principal leader of the Dakota (or Santee) in the War of 1862 in Minnesota, was the son of chief Big Thunder (Wakinyantanka) and a Mdewakanton woman believed to be Woman Planting in Water (Minio Kadawin). He was also known as His Scarlet People (Taoyateduta). Little Crow was descended from several generations of influential chieftains. His grandfather, Hawk that Hunts Walking (Chetanwakuamani), was considered the "first war chief" of the Dakotas by the British in the War of 1812; he died in 1833 or 1834 and was succeeded by his son Big Thunder, who died of accidental gunshot wounds in 1845. While his father was chief, Little Crow was exiled from his band—apparently for illicit affairs. During the 1830s he served the American cause in the Black Hawk War and married several daughters of a Wahpekute chief. About 1836 he left his Wahpekute wives and lived among the Wahpetons of Lac qui Parle; he eventually married four daughters of Chief Running Walker. Little Crow had twenty-two children. In a dispute with his half brothers in 1846 over who would become the next chief of the band, Little Crow was severely wounded in his forearm.

Already distinguished as a warrior and hunter, Little Crow soon became the leading orator of the eastern Dakota tribes. He was prominent in the negotiations of the Treaty of 1851 by which the Dakotas ceded all of their remaining land holdings in Minnesota, except for a reserve running on both sides of the Minnesota River. After removal to the reservation on the Minnesota River, he surpassed Wapahasha III, the principal chief, in influence. He went alone to Washington in 1854 to try to have the new reservation extended to the south and in 1857 commanded the Dakota expedition against the outlawed chief, Inkpaduta, who had committed atrocities against the whites. Agent Charles Flandrau called him "a man of greater parts than any Indian in the tribe." Minnesota legislator James Lynd wrote, "He possesses shrewd judgement, great foresight, and a comprehensive mind. . . . As an orator he has not an equal."

Little Crow was also the leading spokesman for his tribe in the Treaty of 1858 negotiations. By this treaty, the Dakotas ceded the northern half of their reserve, known as the "ten-mile strip." Coerced into signing the treaty, he said valiantly, "That is the way you all do. You use very good language, but we never receive half what is promised or which we ought to get." He refused to accept the government's acculturation policies and told President James Buchanan that he was born an Indian and would die one.

While still awaiting payment for the land cession of 1858, councils were held with Little Crow and other chiefs regarding debt payments to traders. Superintendent William Cullen submitted reports which stated that the Dakotas would pay whatever debts were deemed fair. As a result the government disbursed the entire amount of the treaty money to claimants. Little Crow afterward denied that he had given Cullen this authority, but his credibility in the tribe was severely damaged.

Resentment against the whites was increased when it was rumored in the spring of 1862 that the tribe's annuity money had been reduced by one-half as a result of claims mostly made by traders for money supposed due them from the Dakotas. To make matters worse, an annuity payment, planned for early July, was aborted when the Dakotas refused to consider taking greenbacks for their payment instead of gold. A warriors' soldiers' lodge was formed to take political and military control of the tribe effectively negating the authority of Little Crow and other civil chiefs. In early August, with no payment in sight, Little Crow asked agent Thomas Galbraith to issue annuity provisions to prevent his people from starving. He concluded with the apparent threat, "When men are hungry they help themselves." Galbraith promised to issue annuities but then left the reservation with a company of recruits for the Union army on 15 August. Two days later several Dakotas killed five white settlers, and the soldiers' lodge pressured Little Crow into broadening the war. Little Crow acquiesced, feeling that it was his patriotic duty to abide by the lodge's demands: "You will die like rabbits when the hungry wolves hunt them in the Hard Moon. [But] Taoyateduta is not a coward. He will die with you!"

On 18 August 1862 the Redwood Agency was destroyed, and in the following days Little Crow masterminded several attacks on Fort Ridgely and New Ulm. Failing in these attempts, he fought Colonel Henry H. Sibley's army at Wood Lake (23 Sept. 1862). Defeated again, he fled westward to Devil's Lake and actively sought allies who would join him in continuing the war. In May 1863 he asked for assistance from the English at Fort Garry (Winnipeg) but was refused help by Governor Alexander Dallas. All else failing, he resorted to a horse raid in Minnesota but was ambushed and killed by two farmers. His skull, armbones, and scalp ended up on display at the Minnesota state capitol but were finally buried at Flandreau, South Dakota, in 1971.

Little Crow was the most brilliant Dakota chief of his day and the tribe's most outstanding orator. However, his life has remained highly controversial on account of his participation in the Dakota War of 1862. Some of the bad publicity he received was a result of lies told by white officials who were covering up their own culpability in not averting the trouble. Little Crow ought to be viewed as a patriot, willing to submit to the authority of the soldiers' lodge and to fight and die for what he considered a just cause.

• Little Crow has received full-length biographical treatment in Gary C. Anderson, *Little Crow: Spokesman for the Sioux* (1986); see also Mark Diedrich, *Famous Chiefs of the Eastern Sioux* (1987). Many of Little Crow's speeches are available in

Mark Diedrich, comp., *Dakota Oratory* (1989). An early sympathetic view of Little Crow is Asa W. Daniels, "Reminiscences of Little Crow," *Minnesota Historical Collections* 12 (1908): 513–30. The quotation by James Lynd is in his "History . . . of the Dakota Nation," an unpublished manuscript, c. 1860, in Minnesota Historical Society, St. Paul. There is much literature on the Dakota War, but most accounts have vilified the chief. A good general account is in Roy W. Meyer, *History of the Santee Sioux* (1967).

MARK F. DIEDRICH

LITTLEDALE, Clara Savage (31 Jan. 1891–9 Jan. 1956), magazine editor, was born in Belfast, Maine, the daughter of John Arthur Savage, a Unitarian minister, and Emma Morrison. Her lifelong interest in journalism began as early as high school, where she worked on the school magazine, and by the time she received her B.A. from Smith College in 1913 she had already sold short feature articles to newspapers such as the *New York Times*. Shortly after graduating, she discarded the more usual "woman's occupation" of teaching and applied for a position at the *New York Evening Post*. She was one of the first two women reporters hired at the paper, and she shortly earned acceptance from her male colleagues.

In 1914, after extensive assignments to cover woman suffrage conventions and demonstrations, Savage became press chairperson of the National American Woman Suffrage Association, a position she held for a year, before leaving to become associate editor for *Good Housekeeping*. This post allowed her to seek assignments in Washington, D.C., reporting on national politics from a woman's perspective, with a focus on issues such as education and health and human services. Late in World War I (about June 1918) Savage went to Europe to cover the war, and she experienced the bombardment of Paris with its residents in addition to observing it as a journalist. Her stories—including observations on Chateau-Thierry—provided *Good Housekeeping*'s editor, William Bigelow, with "some of the best articles I have ever printed." In order to remain in Europe after the war ended, Savage resigned from *Good Housekeeping* and became a freelance writer, a career she continued to pursue after her return to the United States in 1920. Articles with her byline appeared during this period in the pages of many magazines, including the *New Republic* and *McCall's*. She often used her 1920 marriage to fellow journalist Harold Aylmer Littledale and the subsequent birth of their daughter, the first of two children, as source material for these articles.

Littledale's articles led publisher George Hecht in 1926 to seek her services as editor of his new magazine, *Children: The Magazine for Parents*. He had to convince her to accept a full-time job, because she insisted her duty was to home and family, but at last Hecht prevailed, and Littledale accepted the position she was to hold until her death. Her early dedication to the job was shown by the fact that she retained her position, with only a six months' leave of absence, through her 1927 pregnancy and the birth of her son.

The new magazine, retitled *Parents Magazine* in 1929, reached 400,000 subscribers by 1946 with spirited, informative articles addressing research in child development, which formerly was available only in technical language of little interest to lay readers. Littledale's editorial focus included varied aspects of child rearing, from prenatal care through the child's education and political rights. She wrote articles during much of her tenure and solicited material from authorities in the field. Her goals were, in her own words, "to give parents a realization of what underlies successful living—understanding between husbands and wives as well as between parents and children," and an awareness of "national problems and developments which affect the security of homes and the future of youth." The magazine tackled such issues as child labor laws, children's health, and federal aid to education.

Littledale's thinking on some issues was progressive for its time. She deemed punishment as necessary only if parents failed to teach and direct their children with caring and wisdom. She wanted the parenting role to stress education rather than chastisement or control, and much of her work on the magazine was aimed at showing parents the kind of resources available to them. She took her philosophy beyond the magazine, joining such organizations as the National Council on Parent Education, the Child Study Association of America, the National Commission for Mental Hygiene, and the American Association for Adult Education. She frequently attended conferences of these and other political and scholarly organizations, sometimes as a featured speaker. She also made numerous radio appearances and often met with parent-education trainers and representatives of child-welfare agencies in the magazine's offices in New York. Littledale also moved beyond the scope of the magazine, which became known as the "Family Bible" for the American home, by producing study outlines for Parent-Teacher Association meetings and women's clubs as well as advice books on child rearing.

In 1941 the plane in which Littledale and her husband were traveling crashed, and though she recovered from her injuries, he was paralyzed. Their marriage had for some time been unstable, and his disability seems to have damaged it irreparably, leading to their divorce in 1945. Both of her children were nearly grown, and from this point she concentrated on the magazine. With a circulation of more than a million by the end of World War II and with wider distribution of its study guides, *Parents Magazine* continued to have significant influence on the American family, and Littledale was firmly in charge of its direction. In 1951 she was diagnosed with cancer. She continued to work, often in pain, contributing not only to the magazine but also faithfully sending pieces to the class notes of her college alumnae journal, a relationship she had maintained for more than forty years. Littledale died in New York City.

• Autobiographical material on Littledale may be found in the Clara Savage Littledale Collection, Schlesinger Library,

Radcliffe College. For the best source of her writing and opinions, see *Parents Magazine* between its inception in 1926 and her death in January 1956. She also made continuing contributions to the *Smith Alumnae Quarterly* from 1913 to 1955; these can be found in the Alumnae Association Archives at Smith College. Obituaries are in the *New York Times* and the *New York Herald Tribune*, 10 Jan. 1956.

BARBARA STRAUS REED

LITTLEFIELD, Catherine (16 Sept. 1905–19 Nov. 1951), choreographer and artistic director, was born in Philadelphia, Pennsylvania, the daughter of James E. Littlefield, a newsreel pioneer, and Caroline Doebele. At the age of three she began study in her mother's newly opened ballet school. Despite limited formal training, Littlefield's mother was a prolific choreographer. In 1919 she was engaged to stage the production numbers for a musical called *Why Not?* sponsored by the Philadelphia Junior League. Impresario Florenz Ziegfeld, who had loaned the costumes for the production, attended the performance and saw Catherine dance. The confident youngster, with a strong mouth and glinting, deep-set eyes, vastly impressed Ziegfeld; her technique was noticeably secure.

Littlefield studied not only with her mother but also with several prominent teachers of the time, including Mikhail Mordkin, Luigi Albertieri, and Ivan Tarasov in New York City; and Leo Staats and Lubov Egorova in Paris, where James Littlefield took his family for summer vacations. In 1920 Littlefield was engaged for Ziegfeld's production of *Sally*, starring Marilyn Miller. Between 1922 and 1925 Littlefield appeared in five other Ziegfeld productions: *Follies* (1922, 1923), *Kid Boots* (1923), *Annie Dear* (1924), and *Louie the 14th* (1925).

In 1925 Littlefield's mother, who was called "Mommie" by her children and by all who studied and worked with her, became ballet director of the Philadelphia Civic Opera. She selected Littlefield as her principal dancer and assistant choreographer. By 1928 mother and daughter had also taken on the staging of movie prologues at Philadelphia's Fox, Earle, Mastbaum, and Stanley theaters.

In 1932 the Philadelphia Grand Opera gave Littlefield her first opportunity to work on her own as choreographer, of *H.P.* (horsepower), a lavish production with ninety-seven dancers. It was a major challenge for the young choreographer to work in collaboration with noted Mexican composer Carlos Chavez and painter Diego Rivera. The ballet, which had a propagandistic theme extolling Mexican-American trade relations, was overburdened with costumes and props. It did, however, earn Littlefield an invitation to work as a choreographer at New York's Roxy Theatre. Littlefield returned to Philadelphia in 1933 to marry Philip Ludwell Leidy, an attorney and the son of Helen C. Leidy, who had been a principal benefactor of the Philadelphia Grand Opera. Throughout their marriage, Leidy was extremely supportive of Littlefield's career and generously contributed funds to many of her projects. They had no children.

In 1934 Mommie and Littlefield began planning the establishment of a ballet company. Mommie was to be the director, Littlefield the choreographer and premiere danseuse, and her sister Dorothie Littlefield the first soloist. The Littlefield Ballet, the first American regional company to achieve both national and international status, was founded in 1935. Its initial performance took place on 25 October 1935 at Haverford High School, in the Philadelphia suburb where the Littlefields resided. By the following year Mommie had adopted the title of executive director, while Littlefield was listed as director, ballet mistress, and premiere danseuse. The only non-American in the company was Alexis Dolinoff, the premier danseur and ballet master. The repertoire was on the light side, including Littlefield's version of Michel Fokine's Chopin reverie *Les Sylphides* and a group of brief story ballets: *The Minstrels*, *The Snow Maiden*, and *Die Puppenfee* (*The Fairy Doll*). Three months after its opening the company was named the Philadelphia Ballet, a name it retained until 1940, when it reverted to its original name.

By the end of its first year, the company boasted a repertoire of eighteen complete ballets and twenty-two divertissements. Most had been choreographed by Littlefield and subsidized by Leidy. In 1937 the company performed the first American staging of *The Sleeping Beauty*, a nineteenth-century Russian classic. Most of the choreography was Littlefield's; she and Dolinoff danced the principal roles of Princess Aurora and Prince Désiré. Despite its magnitude, the ballet, which *New York Times* critic John Martin found "charming within its limitations," was meticulously rehearsed and reflected Littlefield's abiding respect for the niceties of *dance d'école*, or classical finish.

Littlefield's natural bent was for choreographing character works, genre ballets in which individuals were exuberantly conceived and portrayed. Concerning her style, Littlefield remarked in a 1937 interview, "I don't know what my style or school of dancing should be called. I feel our work is modern in the best sense of the word. I mean that it is free and fresh in approach and viewpoint. We use classical ballet technique, but only as a means to the end of unhampered expression." Her best-known works in the character genre, *Barn Dance* and *Terminal*, were both premiered in 1937. They were to form the kernel of the company's repertoire when it traveled to Europe during the late spring of that year, appearing in Paris, Brussels, The Hague, and London. The performances earned Littlefield the medal of the Archives Internationales de la Danse, and on the company's return to the United States she was similarly honored by the Philadelphia Academy of Arts and Sciences.

Littlefield enjoyed appearing in public. She dressed simply but so tastefully that she was named one of the country's ten best-dressed women. She was a persuasive speaker, with a low, vibrant voice and a ready wit. Both at work and at leisure Littlefield crackled with energy, while simultaneously exuding cool purposefulness; one of her contemporaries commented, "She was dry ice—fiery and cool."

While the company was touring in Europe in 1937, Littlefield encountered Paul Longone, the director of the Chicago City Opera; he engaged the Philadelphia Ballet for the 1938 season. Littlefield was in charge of her company's seven-week Chicago season and was responsible for the opera ballets. In 1939 the company performed a second Chicago season and then went on to appear at the Hollywood Bowl. Philip Leidy paid for the salaries and transportation of the fifty dancers.

In 1940 Littlefield was invited to set the dances for the Oscar Hammerstein II–Arthur Schwartz musical *American Jubilee*, to be performed at the New York World's Fair. The Littlefield Ballet was absorbed into the production; the most clever number was a turn-of-the-century bicycle romp for ninety dancers. Although the show opened in the pouring rain, the dancers were so securely rehearsed that they did not miss a beat on the waterlogged stage.

Between 1940 and 1950 Littlefield made significant contributions to musical theater. She was often assisted by her sister Dorothie and her brother Carl, who was also a member of the Littlefield Ballet. Olympic skater Sonja Henie produced a series of ice shows that involved Littlefield as choreographer, even though she had never learned to skate. The shows included *It Happens on Ice* (1940), *Stars on Ice* (1943), *Hats off to Ice* (1944), *Icetime* (1946), *Icetime '47*, and *Howdy, Mr. Ice* (1948).

Littlefield was unusually disciplined, and her ideas almost always proved theatrically viable. Consequently, Littlefield was able to devote time to other shows as well as to her company, although the latter did not receive much new choreography during the 1940s. In 1940 she staged the dances for *Hold onto Your Hats* and *Crazy with the Heat*, both of which were relative successes. Littlefield's choreography for *A Kiss for Cinderella* (1941) met with little critical acclaim, however. In 1941 the company traveled to Chicago, but without any new ballets in their repertoire and without Littlefield as premiere danseuse—she had retired from dancing. After the Pearl Harbor attack, most of the men in the company, including Carl Littlefield, were drafted. Littlefield decided to disband the company until after the war; it was never revived.

Always interested in promoting works by American choreographers, Ballet Theater (now American Ballet Theater) revived Littlefield's *Barn Dance* in 1944, with Dorothie Littlefield guesting in her original role as the country girl who returns home with her city-slicker lover. Littlefield continued her Broadway career by choreographing the dances for *Firebrand of Florence* in 1945 and *Sweethearts* in 1947. Also in 1947 she divorced Leidy; the following year she married Sterling Noel, the editor of the Sunday edition of the *New York Journal-American*.

Littlefield's health began to fail in the late 1940s; she was battling liver cancer. She died in Chicago while preparing the *Hollywood Ice Revue*. Work on the revue, which was performed in 1953–1954, was contin-ued by Dorothie Littlefield and completed by Carl Littlefield.

Though Catherine Littlefield's career was brief, she was responsible for the first American production of *The Sleeping Beauty*, and hers was the first American ballet company to travel to Europe and to perform on both coasts of the United States. In addition, Littlefield's *Barn Dance* popularized the use of American rural themes before Eugene Loring's *Billy the Kid* (1938) and Agnes de Mille's *Rodeo* (1942).

• The Dance Collection at the Lincoln Center Library of the Performing Arts contains Littlefield scrapbooks (1935–1941); souvenir programs of the Littlefield Ballet and Philadelphia Ballet (1935–1941) can be found in the Philadelphia Free Library. Biographical information about Littlefield is in Nancy Brooks Schmitz, "A Profile of Catherine Littlefield" (Ph.D. diss., Temple Univ., 1986). For an extensive article on the Littlefield family, see the following by Doris Hering: "An American Original, Part One: The Rise of Littlefield Ballet," *Dance Magazine*, Aug. 1993, pp. 42–46, and "An American Original, Part Two: The Littlefield Legacy," *Dance Magazine*, Sept. 1993, pp. 48–51. Other sources include Ann Barzel, "The Littlefields," *Dance Magazine*, May 1945, pp. 10–11, and June 1945, pp. 8–9; and George Amberg, *Ballet in America* (1949). An obituary by Barzel, "Valedictory to Catherine Littlefield," is in *Dance Magazine*, Jan. 1952, p. 11.

DORIS HERING

LITTLEFIELD, Dorothie (16 Sept. 1912–24 Aug. 1953), dancer, was born in Philadelphia, Pennsylvania, the daughter of James E. Littlefield, a businessman, and Caroline Doebele. Her parents' abiding interest in music and dance strongly influenced Dorothie and her three siblings. Caroline Littlefield opened the Littlefield School of Ballet in 1908 and began training her two daughters as soon as they were old enough. Dorothie demonstrated natural talent: her body was flexible and she moved easily, using her arms and head in a fluid, poetic fashion. One of her earliest stage appearances was as the principal female dancer in the ballet *H.P.* (horsepower), created by her sister Catherine in 1932 under the sponsorship of the Philadelphia Grand Opera.

In 1934 Lincoln Kirstein, George Balanchine, and Edward Warburg established the School of American Ballet in New York City. The school's two principal faculty members were Balanchine and the Russian premier danseur Pierre Vladimiroff. Littlefield was invited to be the third faculty member, in charge of the children's division. Balanchine and Vladimiroff received $100 and $150 per week, respectively, while Littlefield received only $25. Her meager salary reflected the low esteem in which American-trained dancers were held at that time. Nonetheless, Kirstein characterized the school as having "an atmosphere of Prussian grimness shot through with gaiety and affection (the latter provided by Dorothie)" (quoted in Jennifer Dunning, *But First a School* [1985]).

Littlefield's mother and sister decided in 1934 to establish a ballet company, with Catherine as prima ballerina and choreographer and her mother as director. After a brief stint in Balanchine's American Ballet, Littlefield returned to Philadelphia to become first soloist in her family's troupe. The company made its debut as the Littlefield Ballet in 1935 at Haverford High School, in the Philadelphia suburb where the Littlefields lived. By the end of that year they had also performed at the Academy of Music in Philadelphia.

The following year Catherine Littlefield became director of the company. She was also responsible for most of the repertoire, which in 1937 included an ambitious, full-length version of *The Sleeping Beauty*. Dorothie Littlefield danced as one of the fairies in the production. She also assisted Catherine with rehearsals, a task she often performed in the years ahead. Also in 1937, the company premiered Catherine's *Barn Dance*, a romping bit of Americana about a country girl who returns home from the big city with her city-slicker lover. Dorothie Littlefield earned immediate acclaim for her performance as the vivacious girl, and her success continued during the company's European tour later that year.

Between 1938 and 1941, when the Pearl Harbor attack and the American entrance into World War II forced the company to close, Littlefield continued to perform with the Littlefield Ballet in Chicago, Los Angeles, and eventually at the New York World's Fair, where the entire company was absorbed into a musical called *American Jubilee*. She also became director of the Littlefield Ballet's student company.

In 1940 Catherine Littlefield, whose career helped to shape not only Dorothie's but that of their younger brother Carl, staged *It Happens on Ice*, the first of a series of ice shows. Catherine never learned to skate, but Dorothie and Carl did, so they assisted her in rehearsals.

Dorothie Littlefield began to strike out on her own in 1943, and she danced in the Broadway revival of *The Vagabond King*. The following year, when Ballet Theatre staged a revival of Catherine's *Barn Dance*, Littlefield performed as guest artist in her original role. Because of her mother's training and summers spent in carefully selected Paris studios, Dorothie Littlefield had a far more secure technique than many of the dancers of her day and was extremely attractive, with luxuriant, dark hair, a small tilted nose, and a cleft chin. These attributes helped to make her an especially appealing soubrette.

In the meantime, Littlefield had also continued to assist Catherine with the staging of dances, including those for *Hold Onto Your Hats* and *Crazy With the Heat* in 1940, and *Hats Off to Ice* in 1944. During her relatively brief career Littlefield danced with the best-known companies of the day, including the American Ballet (1935), the Ballet Russe de Monte Carlo (1944), and Ballet Theatre (1944). But she always preferred to return to projects connected with her family.

In 1946 Littlefield married ice skater Harper Flaherty; they had one child. Littlefield died of a heart attack in Evanston, Illinois. She is best remembered as an endearing example of what is known today as the American classical style, dancing that combines the best in Russian, French, and Italian theory with an energy, vivacity, and freedom that are uniquely American.

• Information on Littlefield and her family is in the Littlefield scrapbooks (1935–1941) in the Dance Library at Lincoln Center, and in souvenir programs of the Littlefield Ballet and the Philadelphia Ballet (1935–1941) in the Philadelphia Free Library and at Lincoln Center. She is briefly discussed in Nancy Brooks Schmitz, "A Profile of Catherine Littlefield" (Ed.D. diss., Temple Univ., 1986). See also George Amberg, *Ballet in America* (1949); Ann Barzel, "The Littlefields," *Dance Magazine*, May/June 1945; and Doris Hering, "An American Original," *Dance Magazine*, Aug./Sept. 1993.

DORIS HERING

LITTLEFIELD, George Washington (21 June 1842–10 Nov. 1920), cattle dealer, banker, and philanthropist, was born in Panola County, Mississippi, the son of Fleming Littlefield and Mildred Terrell Satterwhite White, plantation owners. At the age of nine he moved with his family to a 1,500-acre plantation on the Guadalupe River, north of Gonzales, Texas. A year after his father's death in 1853, George's mother inventoried the family's holdings and divided them among her children. Consequently, George received five slaves, mules, horses, cattle, oxen, hogs, tools, and a carriage at the young age of twelve. After attending Baylor University in Independence, Texas, in 1857 and 1858, Littlefield returned to work on his mother's expanding plantation. He then joined the Eighth Texas Cavalry, also known as Terry's Texas Rangers, in August 1861. He fought as a lieutenant at Shiloh and as a captain in both Tennessee and Kentucky, most notably at the battle of Chickamauga. While returning to battle from a recruiting trip to Texas, Littlefield married Alice P. Tiller, whom he had known in Gonzales, in January 1863 in Houston. The couple had no children. He became major of his regiment, but while replacing a wounded lieutenant colonel at Mossy Creek, he sustained a life-threatening wound in December 1863. Acting on the advice of a surgeon, Littlefield resigned from service in late summer of the next year.

In October 1864 Littlefield and his wife moved to their own plantation near Gonzales and produced a profitable cotton crop the next year. Littlefield promptly began increasing his holdings by buying out various relatives, although floods, drought, and boll weevils eventually convinced him of the need to diversify. In addition to his struggles with the land, Littlefield occasionally struggled with his neighbors. In the spring of 1871, as he was preparing to drive 1,100 head of cattle to market in Abilene, Kansas, Littlefield shot and killed rancher John Watson in an argument over a former slave. The trial was held after his return from Abilene, and early in 1872 a Gonzales County jury acquitted him of murder.

Littlefield's financial success on his first attempt at cattle trading made it possible for him to hire men to conduct the drives, and he never went on another one. By buying low, fattening cattle over the winter, and selling high, he reaped profits even during the depression of 1873. Littlefield traded cattle with various partners and also owned a store with Doc Dilworth and Hugh Lewis in Gonzales, which slowly expanded its services to include a modest banking enterprise.

Seeking fresh grasslands, Littlefield established the open-range LIT ranch near the newly settled town of Tascosa in the Texas Panhandle, which he operated for five years before selling out for more than a quarter of a million dollars to a Scottish syndicate in 1881. The next year he established the LFD ranch on the Pecos River in New Mexico, and two years later he began shipping cattle to market by rail rather than trail.

Because his business dealings had resulted in both a surplus of cash and an awareness of the problems involved in carrying gold over long distances under risky conditions, Littlefield decided to go into banking in Austin, moving there in 1883 and establishing the American National Bank in 1890. Various friends and family members quickly took advantage of their acquaintance with Littlefield; his biographer J. Evetts Haley wrote, "He put them through school in youth, promoted them in business in maturity, backed them in adversity, wrote off their losses, plied them with patient advice, and backed them again" (pp. 205–6).

From his office in Austin, Littlefield continued to negotiate land and cattle deals, and in 1901 he purchased a quarter of a million acres in the Yellow Houses division of the Capitol Syndicate's holdings in Hockley, Lamb, Bailey, and Cochran counties in Texas, paying two dollars an acre. Eleven years later, with the new Santa Fe Railroad track running across his property, Littlefield purchased more land, established the town of Littlefield on the rail line, and created the Littlefield Lands Company to sell tracts to farmers at $15 to $35 an acre.

In 1911 Governor O. B. Colquitt appointed Littlefield to the board of regents of the University of Texas at Austin. Eugene C. Barker of the university's history department suggested to the Confederate veteran that he donate funds to establish a southern historical collection. The result was an endowment of $25,000, known as the Littlefield Fund for Southern History, the income of which was and has continued to be used to acquire library materials "for the full and impartial study of the South and its part in American History." Littlefield continued to supplement the gift, and his will added $100,000 to the original endowment. Littlefield's gifts to the university, ultimately totaling almost $2 million, included the purchase of the John Henry Wrenn Library of rare books, the creation of a monument commemorating southern heroes, and the erection of both a dormitory and a main building.

Littlefield died in Austin. He was a loyal southerner who attended reunions of Confederate veterans long after the Civil War had ended. Still, Littlefield looked to the West as the land of the future and of opportunity. His activities in Texas and New Mexico introduced ranching, farming, and Anglo settlement to the plains of the Southwest, and the profits he reaped furthered the fortunes of higher education in his adopted state.

• Littlefield's papers are in the Center for American History at the University of Texas at Austin. Some materials related to the Littlefield Lands Company are in the Southwest Collection at Texas Tech University. The dated but still essential biography is J. Evetts Haley, *George W. Littlefield, Texan* (1943). See also David B. Gracy II, *Littlefield Lands: Colonization on the Texas Plains, 1912–1920* (1968). An obituary is in the *Dallas Morning News*, 11 Nov. 1920.

CHERYL KNOTT MALONE

LITTLE TURTLE (1752–July 1812), military leader of the Miami Indians of the late eighteenth century, was born on the Eel River some twenty miles northeast of Fort Wayne, Indiana, the son of Aquenackque, war chief of the Miami, and (probably) an unnamed Mahican woman. A lover of good companionship, fine food, and good humor, Little Turtle was a powerful orator who counseled moderation at all times. Six feet in height, he was noteworthy for his subtlety and circumspectness. Little Turtle became one of the most successful woodland military commanders of his time, but after the treaty of Greenville (1795) he tried to keep his tribe at peace and at the same time protect its land from an imperialist United States. During his last two decades he worked closely with William Wells, a former captive from a prominent Kentucky family who became Little Turtle's son-in-law. In some aspects, both men had accepted each other's cultures. A few months after Little Turtle's death at Wells's house in Fort Wayne, Wells (dressed as an Indian) heroically died in defense of a Kentucky relative at Fort Dearborn (present-day Chicago). How one judges that unusual partnership determines whether one regards Little Turtle as a great American Indian or as a venal dupe of expansionist America.

Little Turtle's father was famous for organizing the Miami in a counterattack against Iroquois raiders from New York, and he signed a treaty with the English at Lancaster, Pennsylvania, three years before Little Turtle's birth. Although some authorities hold that his mother was partly French, she probably belonged to another anti-Iroquois group, the Mahicans of the Hudson River Valley. Little Turtle's sister married a French trader and was the mother of John B. Richardville, who became chief of the Miami after Little Turtle's death. It appears that Little Turtle married twice (names of wives and dates unknown) and had four children with his first wife and one child with his second.

Little Turtle was undoubtedly helped by the importance of his family but rose to prominence through his military abilities. During the American Revolution the Miami gave some assistance to the British, and Little Turtle may have participated in the defeat of a detachment led by Augustin de La Balme on its way to attack the British post of Detroit in 1780. After the Peace of Paris (1783) the Indians continued to resist American expansion north of the Ohio, and Little Turtle probably led small forays against the white settlements. By 1790 he had become the chief military leader of the Miami, serving under a civil chief, Le Gris.

Before 1790 the Miami villages at the head of the Maumee (near present-day Fort Wayne) had become the focus for many Indians displaced by fighting with the Kentuckians farther east, particularly Shawnees and Delawares. When Brigadier General Josiah Harmar led almost 1,500 troops to attack this concentration in October 1790, burning the Indian villages, Little Turtle was one of the chiefs orchestrating the defense. In the first Harmar defeat, a mostly Miami force ambushed Colonel John Hardin's force of militia and regulars. Along with Blue Jacket (Shawnee) and Buckongehelas (Delaware), Little Turtle was involved in the bitterly contested second battle where regulars under Major J. P. Wyllys were nearly annihilated and militia under Hardin barely saved themselves from disaster. The following year an American army general, Arthur St. Clair, advanced upon the Miami towns, but his troops were overwhelmingly defeated in November 1791 by a multitribal force. Miami accounts credit Little Turtle with being the overall Indian commander on this occasion, although a number of other sources name Blue Jacket.

While Little Turtle's influence was at its apogee, the triumph was overshadowed by General James Wilkinson's unexpected 1791 expedition, which not only destroyed Little Turtle's village on the Eel River but also captured his daughter. There followed an ill-conceived Indian assault on Fort Recovery (Ohio) in 1794, after which Little Turtle voiced the view that further resistance against the forces of General Anthony Wayne, the new American commander, would not be successful. His advice was overruled by other Indians, and Little Turtle dutifully helped defend the Indian position at Fallen Timbers, on the Maumee River, on 20 August 1794 and witnessed their defeat. When he signed the treaty of Greenville, ending the war, he reputedly said that he was one of the last to sign and that he would be the last to break the treaty.

Thereafter, Little Turtle held that the Miami would have to adapt to reality. He strongly urged abstinence from alcohol on his fellow Miami and made efforts to have them learn the principles of farming. On one of several trips to the East Coast, he visited Quakers in Pennsylvania in a successful attempt to get farming instructors. This accommodating attitude led him to sign three other major land-losing treaties with America. The resultant land cessions made many Miami suspect his integrity, and it is a fact that his nephew Richardville died a very rich man. Moreover, some of his critics were right in stating that the Americans wanted nearly all of the Native-American land. Little Turtle's tribal strategy was also doomed by the reluctance of the Miami to alter their older lifestyle. On the other hand, the marked displeasure of Little Turtle (and Wells) at American land hunger also caused American officials, such as William Henry Harrison, governor of Indian Territory, and the Indian agent John Jonston, to distrust him. Nevertheless, Little Turtle's counsels kept the majority of Miami from actively joining Tecumseh's anti-American confederation. In addition, Kentucky relatives of Wells fought prominently in the Battle of Tippecanoe (1811), which severely checked Tecumseh's progress. Little Turtle's reputation began to recover after this military defeat of the hostile confederation, and it was with good reason that the American government buried Little Turtle with full military honors.

The clash of personalities, tribal policies, and pantribal strategies that Little Turtle and the Shawnee leaders Blue Jacket and Tecumseh personified in their generation continued to be reflected in twentieth-century tribal discussions and in the general history of the Native American.

• Relatively little documentary evidence exists for Little Turtle. Most American newspapers published material on Harmar's expedition. See, for example, *The Providence Gazette and Country Journal*, 4 Dec. 1790 to 12 Mar. 1791. Hendrick Aupaumut's "Narrative," in *Pennsylvania Historical Society Memoirs* 2 (1827): 61–131, suggests the intertribal politics of Little Turtle's time, while an insight into the woodland Indians can be gained from James Smith's *Scoouwa* (1799; repr. 1978). C. F. Volney, *A View of the Soil and Climate of the United States of America* (1804; repr. 1968), contains details of an interview with Little Turtle and Wells. For military papers, see Gayle Thornbrough, ed., *Outpost on the Wabash, 1787–1791* (1957) and *The Military Journal of Major Ebenezer Denny* (1971). Harvey Lewis Carter, *The Life and Times of Little Turtle* (1987), contains a bibliography. B. B. Thatcher, *Indian Biography* (1832), presents a balanced chapter on Little Turtle. Later historians of Indiana also stress his career, including Wallace A. Brice, *History of Fort Wayne* (1868), and John B. Dillon, *History of Indiana* (1859). Twentieth-century local historians have discussed Little Turtle in Jacob Piatt Dunn, *True Indian Stories* (1909); Calvin Young, *Little Turtle* (1917); and Otho Winger, *The Last of the Miamis* (1935).

LEROY V. EID

LITTLE WOLF (1821?–1904), North Cheyenne chief, was born in Montana near the juncture of the Eel and Blue Rivers; his parents' names are not known. Called Two Tails as a child, Little Wolf (Oh-kom Kakit) gained a reputation for his prowess as a warrior and his skill as the fastest long-distance runner. After joining the society of Elk warriors known as Elkhorn Scrapers, he surpassed the other members in acts of bravery and quickly advanced to head chief. As a war leader who prepared in advance for battles, Little Wolf was reputed never to have sent anyone ahead of him in the fight.

In 1851 the Cheyenne signed the Big Treaty, also known as the Treaty of Horse Creek, which guaranteed wagon trains safe passage through Cheyenne territory. Relations remained relatively peaceful until 1856 when Major William Hoffman, commandant of Fort Laramie, learned that a group of Cheyennes were encamped nearby with four stray horses. Stating that the horses belonged to whites, Hoffman ordered the animals returned. An Indian delegation including Little Wolf arrived at the fort with three horses. Maintaining that the fourth horse had been found elsewhere, Little Wolf refused to surrender it. Angry at the rebuff, Hoffman ordered the Indians placed under arrest, but the Cheyennes bolted. One Indian was killed and another captured. Little Wolf made it to safety.

Over the next ten years other isolated incidents occurred between soldiers and Indians. Tensions further increased as whites began killing excessive numbers of buffalo, the Indians' prime food source, reducing many tribes to starvation. During these turbulent times the Northern Cheyenne looked to Chief Little Wolf for guidance and leadership. Named sweet medicine chief in 1864, he became the head chief of the Council of the Forty-four. The Forty-four were representatives from four warrior bands comprising four head chiefs and forty lesser chiefs. In addition to being named sweet medicine chief, Little Wolf became the first chief to also retain his position as head of the Elk warriors. By 1866 he was a prominent figure on the plains and was considered the most influential tribal chief.

On 10 May 1868 Little Wolf signed the Fort Laramie Treaty, which called for peace between all warring Indian and white factions and granted the Black Hills land and western half of South Dakota to the Cheyenne and the Ogallala Sioux. After rumors circulated that the Black Hills were rich with gold, fortune hunters flocked to the region. Attempting to block whites from entering the area, Little Wolf accompanied an Indian delegation to Washington, D.C., in 1873. He met with President Ulysses S. Grant, who told the Indians that when they signed the Treaty of 1868 they had given up all rights to the land north of the Platte River and had agreed to move south. Little Wolf's vehement protest delayed the Cheyenne removal. But by 1876 the government, determined to relocate all northern tribes, declared that any Indian found outside a reservation was considered hostile. Indians retaliated against the ruling with skirmishes and raids against the soldiers and settlers.

The deciding factor over land ownership came to a head in 1876 when Lieutenant Colonel George Armstrong Custer and the Seventh Calvary were defeated by the Sioux and Northern Cheyenne at Little Big Horn. Realizing that Indian survival meant peace, Little Wolf did not participate. Nevertheless, soldiers seeking reprisal attacked his village. Although wounded seven times, Little Wolf rescued the women and children and brought them to shelter in the bluffs. Unable to stop the soldiers, he watched his village burn before retreating into the mountains with his people. In an attempt at conciliation the Cheyenne made peace only to be once again ordered to move to the Oklahoma reservation land. Little Wolf and Chief Dull Knife refused to leave, but when soldiers withheld food rations from the starving Cheyenne, they relented. Guaranteed their move to the south would be on a trial basis, the Indians left, traveling south for seventy days to reach Darlington Agency in the Oklahoma region.

One thousand Indians arrived in August 1877; soon after, 600 of them took ill and 43 died. Rations and medicines had been delayed, and the land was insufficient for growing crops. Discouraged, the Cheyenne

requested to be returned to their homeland or to be sent to Washington to plead their case. When their pleas went unanswered, Little Wolf decided to take action. "Our hearts looked and longed for this country where we were born," Little Wolf said as he departed from the reservation with Dull Knife and over 350 people in September 1878.

Heading toward the Bighorn, Rosebud, Tongue, and Powder Rivers, the Cheyenne eluded the soldiers until the Platte River. On the other side of the river, Little Wolf and Dull Knife separated. For a time they succeeded in evading the soldiers, but eventually Little Wolf's band and the soldiers clashed. Although only a few whites and Indians lost their lives, Little Wolf surrendered when he saw that capture was inevitable. In March 1879 Little Wolf reported to Lieutenant William P. Clark (called White Hat by the Cheyenne), a man he trusted, and Little Wolf's Northern Cheyenne were sent to the Tongue River Indian Reservation in Montana. Dull Knife's group was also captured, but he escaped with his family to the Pine Ridge Agency, where he died in the early 1880s.

Little Wolf and his people were allowed to remain in Montana after signing on as army scouts. In 1880 Little Wolf killed Starving Elk, following a drunken encounter over the latter's mistreatment of Little Wolf's daughter. Having broken tribal rules, Little Wolf gave up his title as chief and voluntarily exiled himself. He lived the remainder of his life with his two wives along the Rosebud River until his death. One source places Little Wolf's age at the time of his death at eighty-four. Wooden Leg states that Little Wolf died at age eighty-three.

The Northern Cheyenne revered their tribal chief Little Wolf and had faith in what he said. His feats brought distinction and honor to his Elk warrior society. A compassionate man, he was also quick to defend himself and fought to control his explosive anger. After his exile Little Wolf gave away his horses and roamed the land. He was buried standing upright encased in stones on a hill. His body remained there for twenty-four years facing the Rosebud valley and the houses of the Cheyenne.

• Some details of Little Wolf can be found in reminiscences of Cheyennes as told to and interpreted by others. These accounts should be used with caution and include Thomas B. Marquis, *Wooden Leg: A Warrior Who Fought Custer* (1931); Mari Sandoz, *Cheyenne Autumn* (1953); and Father Peter John Powell, *People of the Sacred Mountain: A History of the Northern Cheyenne Chiefs and Warrior Societies, 1830–1879*, vol. 1 (1981). Portions of Little Wolf's life are recorded in *Report of the Commissioner of Indian Affairs* (1856); *Report of the Secretary of War* (1878); *Testimony Concerning the Removal of the Northern Cheyenne Indians*, Senate Report No. 78, 46th Cong., 2d sess. (1880); George Bird Grinnell, *The Cheyenne Indians: Their History and Ways of Life* (2 vols., 1923); *The Fighting Cheyennes* (1956); George E. Hyde, *Life of George Bent Written from His Letters* (1967); and Joe Starita, *The Dull Knifes of Pine Ridge: A Lakota Odyssey* (1995). An account of Little Wolf's and Dull Knife's journey to return north can be found in the *New York Times*, 5 Oct. 1878. Little Wolf's account is also retold in Dee Brown, *Bury My Heart at Wounded Knee* (1970), and Stan Hoig, *The Peace Chiefs of the Cheyennes* (1980).

MARILYN ELIZABETH PERRY

LIVERIGHT, Horace Brisbane (10 Dec. 1886–24 Sept. 1933), publisher, was born in Osceola Mills, Pennsylvania, the son of Henry Liveright, a merchant, and Henrietta Fleisher. The family moved to Philadelphia when Horace was thirteen. The next year, just short of completing his first year in high school, he dropped out to work with a local stockbroker. Shortly thereafter he left for New York, where he sold securities and bonds for Sutro Brothers and then managed the bond department at Day, Adams, and Company. His only foray into literature during this time was his book and lyrics for "John Smith," a comic opera written when he was seventeen, which he unsuccessfully attempted to see staged in New York. In 1911 Liveright married Lucile Elsas; they had two children. That same year he started a toilet paper company backed by Lucile's father, an executive with the International Paper Company. Although Liveright's product, "pick-quick paper," failed shortly after its inception, his father-in-law supplied him with capital for one more venture.

With this money on tap, Liveright in late 1916 fortuitously met Albert Boni. Boni and his brother Charles had recently sold the rights to their mass-marketing success, the Little Leather Library, and Albert had gone to work at Alfred Wallerstein's advertising agency, where Liveright had a temporary office. At their first encounter, Liveright bounced new product concepts off Boni, who responded with his vision of reprinting classic-yet-modern European writers in inexpensive formats. Taken with Boni's idea, Liveright decided to enter into an equal partnership with him, and in the spring of 1917 they began their Modern Library.

The new firm, Boni & Liveright (after 1928, Horace Liveright, Inc.), would become one of the most important American publishing houses to introduce and cultivate literary modernism. Although at first the house followed the original plan of reprinting European works, it soon expanded its scope to include original publications, American fiction, and books on psychology, economics, and sociology. Much of this direction can be attributed to Liveright: in July 1918, after several disputes among him, Boni, and a new partner (the firm's editor, Thomas Seltzer), a literal flip of the coin made Liveright the majority owner. Soon afterward, Boni retired from the firm, followed by Seltzer. Liveright subsequently published a range of genres and authors, utilizing his sharp instinct for marketable yet unconventional literature. For example, in 1917 Liveright established what would be a long, fruitful, but rocky relationship with Theodore Dreiser. He later published Sherwood Anderson, Gertrude Atherton, Hart Crane, E. E. Cummings, William Faulkner, Ernest Hemingway, Anita Loos, and Eugene O'Neill.

Liveright gained respect within the publishing world as a champion of free speech. Throughout his career he challenged and sometimes defeated attempts to censor his publications, including Petronius's *The Satyricon* (1922) and Maxwell Bodenheim's *Replenishing Jessica* (1925), both accused of being obscene by the New York Society for the Suppression of Vice.

Liveright's willingness to take a chance on new or unappreciated American talent largely explains the firm's success. But he also had a keen eye for recruiting gifted staff, among them several men who later distinguished themselves in the field of publishing: Julian Messner, Thomas R. Smith, Bennett Cerf, Louis Kronenberger, Dick Simon, Manuel Komroff, Arthur M. Pell, and Donald Friede. As chief editor, Liveright encouraged the creativity and contributions of employees at all levels; in many ways his office reflected his own colorful, flamboyant manner. Above all, publishers like Liveright (and his contemporary Alfred A. Knopf) injected much-needed energy into American publishing, which by the beginning of the twentieth century had become stale, ingrown, and overly genteel.

Liveright's downfall coincided with the close of the Jazz Age and came about through a variety of causes. He pointed to poor sales in a sluggish economy and price cutting by competitors, but others blamed his foolishly generous author advances and staff pay raises. He perennially had trouble translating his knack for literary gambling to his speculations in stocks and theater productions (an unusual hit came in 1927 with Bela Lugosi in *Dracula*). As these losses mounted during the late twenties, his father-in-law pressed him to pay back a longstanding series of personal loans. The combination led Liveright to sell the Modern Library in 1925 to Cerf, then a partner. Although Boni & Liveright, despite the sale, grossed the highest profits ever during 1927–1928, the loss damaged the firm's ability to weather future economic turbulence, and his authors began to desert him. Liveright went further into debt in 1928 to buy out the shares of his departing vice president, Donald Friede. In the same year, Liveright was sued for divorce by his then-estranged wife, adding further to his financial stress. His second marriage in December 1931, to Elise Bartlett Porter, an actress, ended in divorce less than a year later.

In July 1930 he announced that he was no longer president of Liveright, Inc. He then left for Hollywood in a futile attempt to sell movie rights to his properties. Until 1931 he advised the production department of Paramount Publix Corporation on novels and plays. Liveright then returned to New York and once more failed as a Broadway impresario.

He died of pneumonia in New York after months of hospitalization, still remembered by many writers and theater artists for his daring and outspoken loyalty to artistic freedom of expression. When asked in a 1923 interview with the *Literary Digest International Book Review* if he was a "radical publisher," Liveright replied, referring to his disregard for superficial and sanitized literature: "If you mean by 'radical,' getting at the roots of things, I cheerfully plead guilty."

• Liveright's papers are at the Univ. of Pennsylvania, although important letters of his can be found scattered in collections of his principal writers, especially those of Theodore Dreiser, also at the Univ. of Pennsylvania, and Sherwood Anderson, at the Newberry Library. Walker Gilmer *Horace Liveright: Publisher of the Twenties* (1970), gives an overview of his publishing activity and his censorship fights but skimps on details of his private life; see also Tom Dardis, *Firebrand: The Life of Horace Liveright* (1995). Personal accounts include Bennett Cerf, "Horace Liveright: An Obituary—Unedited," *Publishers Weekly* 124 (7 Oct. 1933): 1229–30; Edith Stern, "A Man Who Was Unafraid," *Saturday Review of Literature* 10 (28 June 1941): 10, 14; and Louis Kronenberger, "Gambler in Publishing: Horace Liveright," *Atlantic*, Jan. 1965, pp. 94–104. Liveright's obituary appears in the *New York Times*, 25 and 29 Sept. 1933, and in *Publishers Weekly*, 30 Sept. 1933.

RONALD J. ZBORAY

LIVERMORE, George (10 July 1809–30 Aug. 1865), merchant, book collector, and supporter of libraries, was born in Cambridge, Massachusetts, the son of Deacon Nathaniel Livermore and Elizabeth Gleason. He attended public and private schools at Cambridgeport until the age of fourteen. He abandoned the idea of college on health grounds, but he did attend Deerfield Academy in 1827–1828. After employment in the retail business of his older brothers, a stint as a salesman in a dry-goods store in Waltham from 1829 to 1831, and two subsequent years of running that business on his own account, he established a shoe and leather business in 1834. Then in 1838 he became a wool merchant, in partnership with his older brother Isaac. Livermore later wrote to Charles Eliot Norton that he was dependent on the annual earnings of that business and that it continued to require his "best efforts," but from the early 1840s he increasingly devoted himself to book collecting and service to cultural institutions in Boston and its environs. In October 1839 Livermore married Elizabeth Cunningham Odiorne; they had three sons.

From his youth he had purchased books with the scant funds available to him, but in 1842 and 1843 he systematically began to learn about books, especially Bibles and biblical works. In June 1842 he visited the Harvard College Library and was shown many old books by its assistant librarian, John Langdon Sibley. In July he visited the American Antiquarian Society, and in March 1843 he went to the Boston Athenaeum for the first time. Later that month he attended a meeting of the Massachusetts Historical Society. During this period he made several important acquaintances, including Henry Wadsworth Longfellow, George Hillard, and Harvard professor Charles Eliot Norton; he also became friendly with another book collector, Charles Sumner. In 1845 he visited Europe, where in the course of buying books, some from the Duke of Sussex, he met Alexander Everett. By 1846 Livermore had, according to Sibley's diary entry, an "exceedingly

choice library" of about 2,000 volumes, possibly containing "more gems than any one of the size in America."

In 1847 Alexander Everett, now Harvard's president, invited Livermore to become a member of the Overseers' Committee to Visit the Library. Livermore accepted and served until his death, during most of those years as the committee's secretary.

In October 1849 he was elected a member of the American Antiquarian Society and in November a member of the Massachusetts Historical Society. Its *Proceedings* were issued under his "superintending care," and he was a lifelong member of the committee of publication. Livermore was also a "most influential member" of the Society's standing committee. A neighbor and friend of Thomas Dowse, Livermore played a major role in obtaining material for the MHS Dowse's Library, which contemporaries highly valued.

Livermore became a proprietor of the Boston Athenaeum in 1843. As chairman of its library committee, he worked from 1848 to 1855 to acquire George Washington's library for the Athenaeum. He himself contributed significantly to its purchase, and subsequently, as a trustee of the Dowse estate, he made a contribution toward the cost of a catalog of Washington's library. From 1851 to 1859 he was a trustee of the Athenaeum, and from 1860 to 1865 he served as its vice president.

In 1850 Livermore became a trustee of the State Library. The same year he was awarded an honorary master of arts degree by Harvard, and he was also admitted to membership in Phi Beta Kappa. The American Academy of Arts and Sciences elected him a member in 1855, and he was treasurer of the Academy at the time of his death.

Livermore provided singular service to all libraries when in 1850 he published at the request of the editor of the *North American Review* a forty-page article titled "Remarks on Public Libraries," which is an early American statement of the importance of research libraries. Although Americans had been congratulating themselves on the number of books in their libraries, Livermore argued that the books were largely the same and that the country needed libraries in which research would not be "abandoned in despair on account of the meagreness of materials for pursuing the necessary investigations." Some copies of the article were separately issued, and it was twice reprinted.

Livermore's services to libraries were recognized outside Boston, for he was a member of the Smithsonian's committee to review Charles Coffin Jewett's plan for stereotyping book titles in order to create a catalog. The organizers of the librarians' conference of 1853, the first conference of its kind, invited Livermore to give a paper, though he did not accept.

Livermore gave a few books to Harvard and deposited others that were later partially or entirely removed. Instead of donating his library of about 6,000 volumes to any institution, he left it to his widow, perhaps to guarantee her financial well-being. Sold in

1891 by the auction house of Charles F. Libbie & Co., it was notable for its Bibles, New Testaments, Psalters, hymnals, and catechisms. It also contained a number of manuscripts, early printed books, and rarities, among them the *Souldiers Pocket Bible*, published in 1663 for Cromwell's soldiers, which Livermore had reprinted. It was then reprinted for sale by northern organizations seeking to raise funds. Livermore's *Historical Research respecting the Opinions of the Founders of the Republic on Negroes as Slaves, as Citizens, and as Soldiers* (1862) was also reprinted several times and is said to have been responsible for adding thousands of men to the Union forces.

Livermore took seriously his responsibilities to the numerous institutions with which he was connected, and he attended meetings, worked on committees, and wrote or edited a number of reports and other publications of these institutions. In a letter to Charles Deane on 2 February 1864, he stated that "a man is *rich*, not according to the amount of money he *keeps* but to the amount he has *used* for unselfish purposes." Livermore's acting out of that credo, combined with his book collecting and service to institutions, made him prominent among Boston's cultural elite.

• No Livermore papers have been located in a public institution, but there is extensive correspondence with Charles Deane, among others, in the Massachusetts Historical Society, and with Charles Eliot Norton in the Houghton Library, Harvard University. Correspondence with Hale is recorded as being in the New York State Library. After Livermore's death a funeral discourse by his minister, Henry C. Badger, and an address by Edward Everett Hale were delivered and printed. They show the respect and affection with which he was held by contemporaries, but the best biographical account is the *Memoir* by his friend Charles Deane (1869). An obituary is in the *Boston Daily Advertiser*, 2 Sept. 1865.

KENNETH E. CARPENTER

LIVERMORE, Harriet (14 Apr. 1788–30 Mar. 1868), evangelist and author, was born in Concord, New Hampshire, the daughter of Edward St. Loe Livermore, a judge and U.S. Congressman, and his first wife, Mehitable Harris. As an infant Harriet displayed a strong emotional temperament that became one of her hallmarks in later life. She was five when her mother died and at age eight young Harriet was sent to boarding schools, first at Haverhill, Massachusetts, and later to the Byfield Seminary in Newburyport, Massachusetts, and Atkinson Academy in New Hampshire.

In 1811, while still attending Atkinson, Livermore fell in love and became engaged to Moses Elliott of East Haverhill, Massachusetts. Elliott's parents found the strong-willed Livermore unacceptable and pressured their son into calling off the engagement. Livermore's response, at age twenty-three, was to turn to a solitary life of religious intensity, for which she became widely known both in the United States and abroad.

Beginning in 1812 Livermore spent several years studying the Bible in search of her faith. Although raised in an Episcopalian family, she was attracted to the quiet simplicity of the Quakers and the doctrinal orthodoxy of Congregationalism. She joined the Baptists in 1821, but after a nervous collapse a few years later, Livermore renounced organized denominations. She became a self-appointed missionary calling herself the "Pilgrim Stranger." Her first book, *Scriptural Evidence in favour of Female Testimony* (1824), justified the role of women in religious leadership. She gave her first public sermon the following year.

As her fame spread south from New England to New York and Philadelphia, she was invited to speak in Washington at a Sunday worship service held in the House chamber in January 1827. She wore plain Quaker dress, and her eloquence as well as her musical ability made a strong impression on those present, including President John Quincy Adams. She also spoke before Congress in 1832, 1838, and 1843, and at statehouses in Massachusetts and Pennsylvania.

Like many of her contemporaries, Livermore believed that Native Americans were descendants of the lost tribes of ancient Israel. Following her conviction that the second advent of Christ was also at hand, she journeyed west thousands of miles in 1832 with plans to evangelize the Indians. Federal agents at Fort Leavenworth, Kansas, however, forced her to turn back. Out of this experience came *The Harp of Israel* (1835), a collection of poems, hymns, and thoughts on the millennium, the second return of Christ and the restoration of Israel in Jerusalem prophesied in the New Testament.

Thus thwarted, Harriet resolved to go to Jerusalem to await Christ's second coming, arriving there in 1837. The need for income, however, forced her to continue to preach, lecture, write, and travel. In all she visited the Holy Land four times with millennialist expectations, and she made several trips to Europe as well. John Greenleaf Whittier describes how in Lebanon she befriended Lady Hester Stanhope, who then lived on Mt. Libanus. They fell out, however, following a disagreement over which of them was to ride alongside Christ to Jerusalem as the *bride* of the Bridegroom upon his return. Harriet as the "not unfeared, half-welcome guest" and Lady Stanhope, the "crazy Queen of Lebanon," both are immortalized in Whittier's poem "Snowbound" (1866).

Livermore lived off the sale of her tracts and books, none of which sold well. After the death of her father in 1832, a trust fund provided a meager annual income of $250. When she called on John Quincy Adams in 1842 in search of subscriptions for her latest book (*A Testimony for the Times* 1843), he found her aged and nearly impoverished. In vain she hoped that income from her last book, *Thoughts on Important Subjects* (1864), written when she was seventy-six, might allow her to return to Jerusalem to live out her final days. Her numerous books and pamphlets, like her preaching, were largely devotional and emphasized God's love for sinners. Yet her writings were also fervent in their expectation of the imminent return of Christ.

Earlier in her life Livermore had become acquainted with the Dunker fraternity (today Church of the Brethren) in Philadelphia. She preached in Brethren churches and in 1826 converted Sarah Righter Major, who later became their first woman preacher. When Livermore died destitute in a West Philadelphia poorhouse, another Brethren woman, Margaret Worrell, arranged to have the "Pilgrim Stranger" buried in her cemetery plot at the Dunker meetinghouse in Germantown. Although outspoken, sometimes controversial, and often eccentric, Harriet Livermore paved the way for other women to search out public leadership roles in the church.

• Major works by Livermore not cited above: *A Narration of Religious Experience* (1826); a novel, *A Wreath from Jessamine Lawn* (2 vols., 1831); *Millenial Tidings* (4 issues, 1831–1839); *The Counsel of God* (1844); *An Address to Judah* (1849); and *The Model Prayer* (1857). An important treatment is Samuel T. Livermore, *Harriet Livermore: the "Pilgrim Stranger"* (1884), which contains many letters to the author from prominent people who knew Livermore, as well as some autobiographical material. Walter E. Thwing, *The Livermore Family of America* (1902), contains a brief summary of her life. Two insightful scholarly studies are Elizabeth Hoxie, "Harriet Livermore: 'Vixen and Devotee,'" *New England Quarterly* (Mar. 1945): 39–50; and Catherine A. Brekus, "Harriet Livermore, the pilgrim stranger; Female Preaching and Biblical Feminism, *Church History*, Feb. 1996, pp. 388–404. See also Rebecca I. Davis, *Gleanings from Merrimac Valley* (1881); Roland L. Howe, *History of a Church (Dunker)* (1943), pp. 152, 457–58; and John Quincy Adams's *Memoirs*, ed. C. F. Adams, vol. 10 (1876), pp. 6–8; and vol. 12 (1877), pp. 9–10.

DAVID B. ELLER

LIVERMORE, Mary (19 Dec. 1820–23 May 1905), reformer, writer, and suffrage leader, was born Mary Ashton Rice in Boston, Massachusetts, the daughter of Timothy Rice, a laborer, and Zebiah Vose Glover Ashton. Mary's family had a strong sense of patriotism and adhered to the strict tenets of a Calvinist Baptist faith. Fear of eternal damnation caused Mary such great pain that she found passages in the Bible to disprove this doctrine. She often pretended to be a preacher by delivering sermons to playmates. At the age of fourteen she attended a Baptist female seminary in Charlestown, Massachusetts, where she studied French, Latin, and metaphysics. Following her graduation in 1836 she joined the teaching faculty of the school.

Although initially not a woman suffrage advocate, in 1838 Mary heard a speech by Angelina Grimké, an abolitionist and feminist, which convinced her that "women ought to be free" to live up to their capabilities. A year later she accepted a tutoring position on a Virginia plantation and witnessed the beating of slaves. When she returned to Massachusetts in 1842 to head a private school, she had become a radical abolitionist.

On 6 May 1845 Mary Rice married Daniel Parker Livermore, a Universalist minister. They had three daughters. Her husband's optimistic view of salvation helped her overcome the fears of her strict religious

upbringing. The Livermores served in several New England pastorates before moving to Chicago in 1857. Mary Livermore continued a writing career begun in 1844 when *The Children's Army*, a series of short stories dealing with the evils of drink, was published. In 1848 she published *A Mental Transformation*, a novel depicting a woman's religious rejection of Baptist beliefs. In Chicago she became the associate editor for her husband's Universalist newspaper *New Covenant*, often overseeing operations and staff in her husband's absence. In 1860 she attended the national Republican convention as the only female reporter.

In addition to church work and writing, Livermore immersed herself in charitable causes. In 1861 she helped found the Home for Aged Women and the Hospital for Women and Children, and she served on the board of directors at the Home for the Friendless, which aided impoverished women and children. When the Civil War began, she joined the Chicago branch of the Sanitary Commission, which coordinated volunteer workers, distributed medical and other supplies, and conducted fundraising. Livermore journeyed to army camps and attended women's councils in Washington to assess the needs of Union armies.

In conjunction with the Sanitary Commission, in 1862 Livermore was appointed as an agent of the Northwest Commission for six midwestern states. Organized and business-minded, sympathetic and zealous, she possessed remarkable physical strength and unwavering energy and provided strong leadership. She traveled throughout the Midwest bringing together women in more than 3,000 aid societies. The women learned how to collect money and supplies, how to assemble bandages, and where to send packages to soldiers.

In 1863 Livermore organized the Northwestern Sanitary Fair hoping to raise $25,000 to aid societies in procuring, coordinating, and shipping needed supplies. Visitors from six surrounding states attended the fair where livestock, sewing machines, and stoves were sold. Women served dinner, gave concerts, and held an art exhibition. The fair exceeded expectations and silenced critics who had ridiculed her idea. In addition to donations of food, between $86,000 and $100,000 was collected. Livermore was described as "fearful and wonderful" and a woman of "great and real power." The Sanitary Fair became the first of many held in northern cities, which collectively raised more than $1 million.

Following the Civil War Livermore decided that the vote would give women the power to fight poverty, drunkenness, and prostitution. In *The Story of My Life* (1897) she recalled that "a large portion of the nation's work was badly done . . . because woman was not recognized as a factor in the political world." Her articles supporting woman suffrage appeared in numerous papers. As the first president of the Illinois Woman Suffrage Association in 1868 she aided in passage of a bill in the Illinois legislature giving women rights to their own earnings. She founded a newspaper, the *Agitator*, a short-lived but nationally recognized voice for women's rights.

In 1869, through the encouragement of her husband, who gave up his newspaper and his position in Chicago and moved the family to Boston, Livermore became editor of the *Woman's Journal*, the weekly paper of the American Woman Suffrage Association (AWSA), merging it with the *Agitator*. In 1872 she resigned to join the lecture circuit as a speaker. Two of her most popular lectures, "What Shall We Do with Our Daughters?" and "Superfluous Women," stressed the importance of a young woman's education in becoming independent. American and European audiences alike enjoyed her lectures, which averaged 150 per year and covered a variety of topics. In 1873 she became president of the Association for the Advancement of Women, an organization of moderate feminists promoting "Women as thinkers." From 1875 to 1878 she served as president of the AWSA; in 1870 she founded the Massachusetts Woman Suffrage Association and in 1893 became its president, a position she held until 1903. Lecturing became a lucrative career for Livermore, and she remained on tour until 1895.

Livermore's writing also continued. *My Story of the War: A Woman's Narrative of Four Years of Personal Experience as Nurse in the Union Army* (1887) told of women and nursing during the Civil War. The publication of *The Story of My Life* produced a narrative of Livermore's life with a vivid depiction of her years on the Virginia plantation. Her articles appeared in the *North American Review*, the *Independent*, the *Chautauquan*, and other publications. Her interest in phrenology caused her to believe that a healthy regimen was related to the welfare of the mind and the soul. After her husband's death in 1899 she longed to reunite with him and embraced spiritualism as a means of contact. Within a year she confirmed that she had spoken to him through a medium. Livermore died in Melrose, Massachusetts.

Although remembered most for her volunteer work during the Civil War, Livermore was highly visible in women's rights, suffrage, temperance, abolitionism, and moral reforms. Although seeking to empower women with "new powers and aspirations," Livermore's attitude was generally conservative for she knew that women ultimately married and primarily functioned in the home. Still she did much to bring about change for women and created a powerful impression as she captivated her audiences with her logic and her forceful speaking.

• Mary Livermore's correspondence can be found in the antislavery Kate Field Collection, Boston Public Library, the Mary Livermore Collection at the Melrose Public Library, the Schlesinger Library, Radcliffe College; and the Sophia Smith Collection, Smith College. Additional writings by Livermore include *Thirty Years Too Late: A Temperance Story* (1845) and *Nineteen Pen Pictures* (1863). She also edited *A Woman of the Century* (1893). Details of her life and works are in L. P. Brockett, *Woman's Work in the Civil War* (1867); Elizabeth Cady Stanton et al., *History of Woman Suffrage*, vol. 4, *1883–1900* (1902); Eleanor Flexner, *Century of Strug-*gle: *The Woman's Rights Movement in the United States* (1975); Blanche Glassman Hersh, *The Slavery of Sex: Feminist-Abolitionists in America* (1978); Robert H. Bremner, *The Public Good: Philanthropy and Welfare in the Civil War Era* (1980); Ruth Bordin, *Woman and Temperance: The Quest for Power and Liberty, 1873–1900* (1981); Steven M. Buechler, *The Transformation of the Woman Suffrage Movement: The Case of Illinois, 1850–1920* (1986); and Carolyn DeSwarte Gifford, "Frances Willard and the Woman's Christian Temperance Union's Conversion to Woman Suffrage," in *One Woman, One Vote: Rediscovering the Woman Suffrage Movement*, ed. Marjorie Spruill Wheeler (1995). An obituary appears in the *New York Times*, 24 May 1905.

MARILYN ELIZABETH PERRY

LIVERMORE, Samuel (25 May 1732–18 May 1803), chief justice of New Hampshire and U.S. senator, was born in Waltham, Massachusetts, the son of Samuel Livermore, a farmer who held numerous town offices, and Hannah Brown. Refused admission to Harvard, Livermore taught school in Chelsea, Massachusetts, then in 1751 attended the College of New Jersey (later Princeton University), where after a year's attendance he received his degree. Livermore returned to Massachusetts, studied law under Edmund Trowbridge, and was admitted to the bar in 1756.

A year later Livermore moved north to Portsmouth, New Hampshire, and quickly cast his lot with the provincial elite dominated by the Wentworth family. In 1759 he married Jane Browne, daughter of the Reverend Arthur Browne, who served as rector of the Anglican church attended by most of the Wentworths; it is possible that Livermore had met Jane earlier and moved to Portsmouth because of her. They had five children. Meanwhile he developed an active legal practice and a reputation for both aggressiveness and competence in the courtroom. Among his friends were John Wentworth, nephew of Governor Benning Wentworth, and Wyseman Claggett, attorney general of the province. In 1767 John Wentworth succeeded his uncle as governor. Two years later he appointed Livermore judge-advocate in the admiralty court and soon thereafter attorney general to succeed Claggett, who had resigned. Livermore by then was also a member of the General Court representing Londonderry, a nearby community where he and his wife had moved temporarily. The two appointments necessitated their return to Portsmouth.

The American Revolution seriously disrupted Livermore's life. A cautious and pragmatic man, he recognized the dangers of being too closely identified with royal government and acted accordingly. He started accumulating property in the frontier town of Holderness. He moved his family back to Londonderry in 1774 and during the winter of 1775–1776 migrated out of harm's way to his undeveloped land in Holderness. When he arrived, only nine families resided in the town. For the next two years Livermore exerted most of his energies raising his children and developing a country estate.

Livermore reentered public life soon after the American victory at Saratoga in 1777. Before leaving for Holderness he had made clear to leaders of the independence movement in New Hampshire that his old Wentworth and Church of England ties did not make him a Loyalist. John Sullivan, who had read law under Livermore, respected him, as did Meshech Weare, the state's most prominent revolutionary leader. Livermore, in fact, received a justice of the peace commission from revolutionary authorities and may have been asked to continue as attorney general as early as the fall of 1776. In 1778 he was formally appointed to his old office. The next year, towns in the Holderness area elected him as representative to the General Court, and the court asked him to serve as a special agent at the Continental Congress to represent New Hampshire in its dispute with New York over what eventually became Vermont. He left immediately for Philadelphia.

For the next two decades Livermore continued his dual role as country squire and public servant. His dominance in Holderness was rarely questioned. He became owner of more than half the land in the town, ran the local mills, conducted Anglican church services at his home, mediated local disputes, and served off and on as legislative representative. Livermore's influence reached into neighboring towns as well, in part through the power he wielded in the Grafton County judicial system.

Livermore's political life outside Grafton County was both state and national in its scope. When the aging Meshech Weare retired as chief justice of New Hampshire, he arranged to have Livermore replace him. Livermore served six years, until 1789, and became well known for his willingness to exercise personal judgment and ignore legal precedent in deciding cases. The General Court appointed him five different times as a regular Continental Congress representative; he attended every session but one. Livermore sat in both the 1779 and 1791 state constitutional conventions, serving as president of the latter. He was a major organizer of the successful effort to have New Hampshire ratify the proposed federal Constitution. In 1787 he was among the leading vote-getters in the state presidential elections even though he never sought the office.

After adoption of the federal Constitution, Livermore spent more time on national than on state affairs. He was elected to Congress in 1789 and 1791, appointed U.S. senator by the General Court in 1793, and reappointed in 1799. Two principles guided his behavior at the federal level. Although an advocate of erecting a national government, he feared that it might end up dominating the individual states. When the Judiciary Act of 1789 was proposed, Livermore not only argued against adoption but said there was no need for any federal judiciary. He took an active role in the debate over proposed constitutional amendments, siding often with the few antifederalists in Congress. His second principle was to avoid close involvement with either of the emerging political parties. His fellow senators, in part out of respect for his evenhandedness, chose him president pro tempore in 1797 and again in

1799. Livermore's senatorial career ended in 1801 when rapidly deteriorating health forced him to retire. He returned to Holderness after resigning from the Senate and died at home. He was buried in the cemetery of the Episcopal church he had helped found a decade earlier.

• Unpublished Livermore papers are scattered throughout several collections in the New Hampshire Historical Society. Published primary material is concentrated in vols. 7, 8, 10, 21, and 22 of the *New Hampshire Provincial and State Papers* (1873–1893), and Edmund Burnett, ed., *Letters of the Members of the Continental Congress*, vols. 5–8 (1931–1936). The best biographical sketches are Charles R. Corning, *Address before the Grafton and Coos Bar Association* (1888), and Charles H. Bell, *Bench and Bar of New Hampshire* (1894), pp. 34–38. For Livermore's life in Holderness see Fred M. Colby, "Holderness and the Livermores," *Granite Monthly* 4 (1881): 175–81, and George Hodges, *Holderness: An Account of the Beginnings of a New Hampshire Town* (1907). Livermore's career in state government is traced in Jere R. Daniell, *Experiment in Republicanism: New Hampshire Politics and the American Revolution* (1970), and Lynn W. Turner, *The Ninth State: New Hampshire's Formative Years* (1983). See Daniell, "Frontier and Constitution: Why Grafton County Delegates Voted 10–1 for Ratification," *Historical New Hampshire* 45, no. 3 (Fall 1990): 207–29, for a close examination of Livermore's activities in the ratification process. No good literature on Livermore's role in national affairs exists, though for some guidance see Helen E. Veit et al., *Creating the Bill of Rights* (1991), and Roy Swanshaw, *The United States Senate, 1787–1801*, 99th Cong., 1st sess., 1985, S. Doc. 19.

JERE R. DANIELL

LIVERMORE, Samuel (26 Aug. 1786–11 July 1833), lawyer and legal scholar, was born in Concord, New Hampshire, the son of Edward St. Loe Livermore, a lawyer, and Mehitable Harris. His paternal grandfather, Samuel Livermore, was chief justice of New Hampshire and a congressman and senator from that state. His father moved to Massachusetts in 1802, represented Essex County in Congress for four years (1807–1811), and then took up residence in Boston, where he was a prominent critic of the War of 1812.

Livermore graduated from Harvard College in 1804, read law, and was admitted to the Essex County bar. Afterward he moved to Boston and practiced there, apparently specializing in maritime and commercial cases. In November 1811 he published at Boston the first American book on agency—the part of the law dealing with situations in which one person is authorized to act on behalf of another. It was titled *A Treatise on the Law Relative to Principals, Agents, Factors, Auctioneers, and Brokers*. While the work mainly relied on common law cases, occasional notes drew comparisons to European, especially French, law. Livermore wrote in the preface that he was also working on a book on the law of maritime insurance, but this work was never published.

During the War of 1812 Livermore volunteered for service on board the frigate *Chesapeake* just as it was leaving Boston on 1 June 1813 for its ill-fated encounter with the British ship the *Shannon*. He was designated acting chaplain by his friend Captain James Lawrence. Livermore was on deck when the British boarded the *Chesapeake*; he fired his pistol at the British captain, Sir Philip Broke, missed, and was severely wounded in the arm by an upward thrust from Broke's sabre. With the surviving crew of the *Chesapeake*, he was taken as a prisoner to Halifax and returned to Boston in late June 1813. In March 1814 he testified for the prosecution at the court-martial of Lieutenant William S. Cox, who was made the scapegoat for the loss of the *Chesapeake* (although ultimately rehabilitated by President Harry Truman in 1952).

After the war Livermore moved to Baltimore while his father and family temporarily moved west to Ohio. In Baltimore he is said to have assisted the ultra-Federalist Alexander Contee Hanson in publishing the *Federal Republican* at a time when Hanson was losing a bitter struggle with Roger Taney for control of the Maryland Federalist party.

In June 1818 Livermore published at Baltimore an expanded two-volume edition of his work on agency, now titled *A Treatise on the Law of Principal and Agent and of Sales by Auction*. This edition, even more so than the first, emphasized the importance of civilian authorities; Livermore said in the preface that he had "stated the rules of civil law to confirm and illustrate the principles of our own law," had tried to show how the two systems agreed and differed, and, in questions that appeared "to be doubtful or undecided at common law," had "had recourse to the opinions of the great *Roman* jurists, as the surest guide to a correct solution."

Shortly afterward he moved south again, to New Orleans, where civil law was in force and his recondite civilian learning actually seemed useful in law practice. From June 1819 he was regularly appearing before the Louisiana Supreme Court. Lawyers all over the country sought his opinions on matters of international jurisprudence.

Livermore's use of civilian authorities sometimes seemed precious even in Louisiana. In the landmark case of *Saul v. His Creditors* (1827), the Louisiana Supreme Court refused to adopt the methods of the continental "statutists," whose authority Livermore invoked in a printed brief running to some eighty pages. The court's opinion, by Judge Alexander Porter, not only decided against Livermore's position, which would have made the law of Virginia, a noncommunity property state where a couple resided when first married, continue to control their respective rights in property acquired after they moved to Louisiana; the opinion also dismissed the continental authorities on whom Livermore relied as practically worthless.

Livermore responded to this humiliation by writing a 170-page tract, *Dissertations on the Questions Which Arise from the Contrariety of the Positive Laws of Different States and Nations*, published in New Orleans in 1828. The first American book on the subject of conflict of laws, it was not a comprehensive treatise, and the text indicates that Livermore contemplated pub-

lishing further "dissertations." The two contained in his 1828 work constitute an introduction to the techniques and divergent views of the continental "statutists" who had spun out pedantic distinctions between "real statutes" (which apply only within the territory of the legislator) and "personal statutes" (which follow the person of subjects wherever they go abroad). The book provided an elaborate and profound discussion of an obscure and already obsolete body of learning; and, while it scored palpable hits against Judge Porter's insistence that mere "comity" (or courtesy) is the basis for giving effect to foreign law, it failed to provide the kind of easily applied rules that were needed to settle questions about which state's law governs transactions between citizens who are constantly moving from one state to another in a federal union.

Four years later Justice Joseph Story published the first edition of his enormously influential *Commentaries on the Conflict of Laws* (1834). Livermore's book went into complete eclipse, just as his treatise on agency was largely superseded when Story published his *Commentaries on the Law of Agency* in 1839. Story several times expressed appreciation for Livermore's learning but at bottom rejected Livermore's antiquated approach to the conflict of laws and also his attack on "comity"; indeed Story, like Porter, made "comity" the cornerstone of his theory of conflicts.

Livermore never married. He died at Florence, Alabama, while traveling back from New Orleans for a visit to New England. In his will he left Harvard his valuable library of some 300 titles (comprising more than 400 volumes) of the works of European jurists printed between 1500 and 1800. This bequest immediately put the Harvard law library in first place among American collections on Roman and civil law. It is often said to have provided the material for Story's researches, although the library only reached Harvard after the first edition of Story's commentaries on conflicts already had appeared early in 1834.

Livermore's books on agency and conflicts were the first of their kind published in the United States. They represented a deliberate effort to fuse common and civil law that was not uncommon among legal treatise writers during the first half of the nineteenth century but was then largely forgotten for more than a hundred years. More recently, with renewal of interest in evidence of interpenetration between civil and common law systems, Livermore appears as a notable figure in what is now seen as a perennial process of exchange between legal cultures.

• Livermore's cast of mind has to be reconstructed largely through his published writings and arguments summarized in the early *Louisiana Reports*. For basic biographical information, see Walter Eliot Thwing, *The Livermore Family of America* (1902). On the bequest of his library to Harvard, see Charles Warren, *History of the Harvard Law School and of Early Legal Conditions in America* (1908). For his service on the *Chesapeake*, see H. F. Pullen, *The* Shannon *and the* Chesapeake (1970), and Albert Gleaves, *James Lawrence* (1904). Further information about Livermore appears in the historical essays in the first part of Kurt H. Nadelmann, *Conflict of*

Laws: International and Interstate (1972). He is mentioned, usually in connection with Story, in most accounts of the history of conflict of laws doctrine; his 1828 book is briefly discussed in Alan Watson, *Joseph Story and the Comity of Errors* (1992), R. Kent Newmyer, *Supreme Court Justice Joseph Story* (1985), and William R. Leslie, "The Influence of Joseph Story's Theory of the Conflict of Laws on Constitutional Nationalism," *Mississippi Valley Historical Review* 35 (1948): 203–20. The only essay-length assessments devoted solely to Livermore are two articles by Italian scholars of conflicts and comparative law: Rodolfo de Nova, "The First American Book on Conflict of Laws," *American Journal of Legal History* 8 (1964): 136–56, and Gino Gorla, "Samuel Livermore (1786–1833): An American Forerunner to the Modern 'Civil Law—Common Law Dialogue,'" in *Comparative and Private International Law: Essays in Honor of John Henry Merryman*, ed. David S. Clark (1990).

EDWARD M. WISE

LIVINGSTON, Edward (28 May 1764–23 May 1836), lawyer and politician, was born at "Clermont," his family's estate in Columbia County, New York, the youngest son of Robert R. Livingston (1718–1775), a lawyer, judge, and wealthy landowner, and Margaret Beekman. Edward was educated at the College of New Jersey (now Princeton University), graduating in 1781. After spending a year learning French and German, he studied law in the office of John Lansing in Albany, New York. Livingston was admitted to the bar in 1785 and then practiced in New York City, where he quickly attained social prominence. In 1788 he married Mary McEvers, a merchant's daughter; they had three children.

Livingston entered politics as a Jeffersonian Republican, becoming a staunch party man in a district that just recently had converted to Republicanism. After unsuccessfully seeking several offices, he was elected to the U.S. House of Representatives in 1794 and reelected in 1796 and 1798. There he led the unsuccessful effort to kill Jay's Treaty by trying to withhold appropriations for it. He opposed the Quasi-War with France, voting against all war measures, and attacked the Alien and Sedition Acts. He became known as a temperamental radical who lived "like a nabob" and talked "like a Jacobin."

Early in 1801, when the task of choosing between Thomas Jefferson and Aaron Burr (1756–1836) for president passed to the House, Livingston supported Jefferson. In March, shortly after the death of Mary Livingston from scarlet fever, Jefferson rewarded him with the appointment as U.S. attorney for the District of New York, which then included the whole state. Several months later a council of state officials, as a second reward, appointed him mayor of New York City. He held the two offices concurrently.

In June 1803 a federal investigation revealed that a substantial sum of tax money the U.S. Treasury had placed in the keeping of Livingston's office was missing. Although careless in the management of finances, Livingston was innocent of wrongdoing. Unknown to him, a clerk had stolen the funds. Nonetheless, he was officially responsible for the loss; he accepted account-

ability but lacked the means for immediate payment. In August he resigned as U.S. attorney under pressure. Within a month he caught yellow fever, then raging in New York City. Two months later, when he had recovered his health, he resigned also as mayor and placed his property in the hands of a trustee to be sold to help satisfy his debt to the Treasury. In February 1804 he moved to New Orleans, hoping to reconstruct his ruined career in the Louisiana Territory that his brother, Chancellor Robert R. Livingston (1746–1813), had helped recently to acquire for the United States.

Livingston again built a successful law practice, again became active in politics, and in June 1805 married Louise Moreau de Lassy, the widowed daughter of a French planter from St. Domingue who had lost his fortune and fled the island after the French Revolution. This union produced one child. In the following year Livingston was wrongly accused of treason for allegedly conspiring with Burr in his schemes on the Mississippi. Soon after Livingston cleared himself of these charges he became locked in a bitter controversy with President Jefferson over the ownership of Batture St. Marie, land on the Mississippi shore adjacent to New Orleans that Livingston had acquired in payment for legal services. After losing title to most of this property, Livingston complained of his treatment to the courts and Congress; he also published pamphlets to explain his side of the dispute.

During the War of 1812 Livingston tried to recoup his fortunes by supplying timber from his land to the federal government for military use. When the British attempted to capture New Orleans in 1814, he chaired the city's committee of public defense, which organized the popular resistance. At the battle of New Orleans he served as General Andrew Jackson's aide-de-camp, interpreter, and adviser.

In 1820 Livingston was elected to the Louisiana state legislature, which in February of the following year commissioned him to prepare a code of criminal law for the state, a task he completed in 1824. Just after he had prepared the manuscript for the printer, a fire destroyed it. He spent about two years reconstructing it. Although the state did not adopt his code, which was designed to prevent rather than punish crime, it brought him widespread fame after it was published.

In 1822 Livingston had again been elected to the House of Representatives, where he remained until 1829. After being defeated in 1828, he was elected to the U.S. Senate by the Louisiana legislature. In 1826 the courts had awarded him a portion of the disputed Batture property, and from its proceeds he finally paid off his debt to the government in 1830.

When President Jackson broke up his first cabinet in April 1831, Livingston came under consideration for secretary of state. Although Jackson and Livingston had been friends since serving together in the Fourth Congress, when Martin Van Buren urged Livingston's candidacy the president at first resisted, asserting that "he knows nothing of mankind" and is "ill-qualified for the performance of executive duties." The president also valued Livingston's friendship, however, respected "his talents," regarded him as "a polished scholar, an able writer, and most excellent man," and in the end, on 24 May, he appointed him to the post.

Jackson made most foreign policy decisions on his own, and he relied more on the counsel of Van Buren than on that of the new secretary. Yet Livingston drafted the nationalistic Nullification Proclamation of 10 December 1832 as well as several other state papers. As secretary, Livingston strove to resolve the still-bothersome issue of impressment with Great Britain, negotiated with the British over the northeastern boundary between Maine and New Brunswick, and pressed claims with Britain for payment for American-owned slaves that authorities in the Caribbean had freed. Livingston also attempted to secure reparations from France for maritime spoliations suffered under Napoleon's Berlin and Milan decrees. In a treaty of 4 July 1831, the two nations had reached agreement, but still the French did not pay. Livingston pressed similar claims with the Kingdom of the Two Sicilies. Under threat of retaliation, the Two Sicilies agreed in a treaty of October 1832 to pay the American claimants, who thus received about 94 percent of what they had sought. He pushed the negotiation, completed in December 1832, of a commercial treaty with Russia that remained in force into the next century. The secretary took a hand in pressuring Mexico over American claims against Mexico and maneuvered for the possible purchase of Texas. These efforts accomplished little.

In a dispute with Argentina involving fishing and other rights in the waters of the Falkland (Malvinas) Islands, Livingston and the president took a notably bellicose stance. In 1831 Louis Vernet, an Argentine military officer who had taken possession of the islands, seized three American vessels. In retaliation Jackson ordered a naval frigate to the Falklands. Its crew invaded the islands, captured practically the whole population of forty people, and deported them. The Argentine government protested the intrusion, demanded reparation, and severed relations with Washington, but Livingston defended the action as a proper defense of the rights of American fishermen and traders. When the British occupied the islands in 1833, Argentina appealed to the United States for help against what Argentines termed a violation of the Monroe Doctrine. Jackson sided with the British.

On 29 May 1833, Livingston resigned as secretary to become minister to France, an office he had previously declined. "This is," he wrote, "the first time I have taken leave of my native land." Despite his reluctance to assume the post, he enjoyed France because intellectuals there honored him for his legal and literary accomplishments. For well over a year he strove to obtain payment of the spoliation claims as provided by treaty. He then urged the president to take a tough stance to bring the issue to a satisfactory conclusion. In December 1834 Jackson asked Congress for authority to proceed with reprisals if the French legislature did not appropriate funds for payment. The message produced a furor in France, created a diplomatic crisis, and stiffened French resistance on the matter of payment. The French offered Livingston his passports, which he at first refused, but in May 1835 he took them and returned to the United States. In June, after reaching Washington, he resigned his post. The following year he sought unsuccessfully to return to France. He then retired to "Montgomery Place," his estate on the Hudson River, in Dutchess County, New York, which he had inherited from his sister. He died there while still eager to return to public service.

Contemporaries regarded Livingston with fascination because he had a brilliant mind, an eloquent tongue, a fondness for female companionship, and a taste for high living. In his youth these qualities earned him the nickname "Beau Ned." His penal system and codification of criminal law, which was reprinted in London, Paris, and elsewhere, received the plaudits of men in civil and political life, gained him worldwide recognition, and even praise as a "legal genius." He worked zealously for the abolition of the death penalty, a pioneering effort in social reform. He is best remembered, however, for his political and diplomatic activities.

• The Edward Livingston Papers are in possession of the family at Montgomery Place in New York. His official papers as secretary of state are in the National Archives. The Livingston Family Papers are in the New York Public Library, and the Miscellaneous Livingston Manuscripts are in the New-York Historical Society. Livingston's legal writings are printed in *The Complete Works of Edward Livingston on Criminal Jurisprudence* (2 vols., 1873; repr. 1968). There are two biographies: Charles Havens Hunt, *Life of Edward Livingston* (1864), and William B. Hatcher, *Edward Livingston: Jeffersonian Republican and Jacksonian Democrat* (1940), which is fuller and more reliable. See also Louise Livingston Hunt, *Memoir of Mrs. Edward Livingston* (1886); Eugene Smith, "Edward Livingston and the Louisiana Codes," *Columbia Law Review* 2 (Jan. 1902): 25–36; Carleton Hunt, "The Life and Services of Edward Livingston," *Proceedings of the Louisiana Bar Association* (1903), pp. 7–50; Edwin Brockholst Livingston, *The Livingstons of Livingston Manor* (1910); and Francis Rawle, "Edward Livingston," in *The American Secretaries of State and Their Diplomacy*, ed. Samuel F. Bemis (1927–1929).

ALEXANDER DECONDE

LIVINGSTON, Henry Brockholst (25 Nov. 1757–18 Mar. 1823), U.S. Supreme Court justice, was born in New York City, the son of William Livingston, an attorney and later the first governor of the state of New Jersey, and Susanna French. The Livingstons were a large, politically and economically prominent New York family with several children named Henry, so Harry, as he was called as a child, later took his middle name to distinguish himself from his cousins. He grew up at "Liberty Hall" on his father's estate near Elizabethtown, New Jersey. He attended the College of New Jersey (subsequently Princeton) and was a classmate of James Madison. He actively supported the patriot cause and was commissioned a captain in the Continental army. Serving on the staffs of Generals Philip Schuyler, Arthur St. Clair, and Benedict Arnold, he rose to the rank of lieutenant colonel. In 1779 he accompanied John Jay, his brother-in-law, on a diplomatic mission to Spain. His sister warned him not to irritate the punctilious Spaniards, so instead the hot-tempered youth quarreled with Jay, beginning a lifelong antipathy. Captured by the British on his return voyage to the United States in 1782, Livingston managed to destroy the diplomatic papers in his possession. After accepting parole from Sir Guy Carleton, the commander of the British forces in North America, he began the study of law under Peter Yates in Albany.

Admitted to the bar in 1783, Livingston moved to New York at the war's end and began the practice of law. He served three terms in the state assembly, where he was known as a fierce partisan, moving from federalism to the Jeffersonian persuasion. Political tensions in New York ran high. In 1785 he survived an assassination attempt, and in 1798, after being assaulted by an obscure Federalist on the Battery, he killed the man in a duel fought in New Jersey. No indictment, however, resulted. In 1789, in the company of President George Washington, members of Congress, and the Order of the Cincinnati, Livingston gave a noted Independence Day address, the first after the adoption of the Constitution.

Livingston's activities included the publication, under the pseudonym of Aquiline Nimble-Chops, of *Democracy: An Epic Poem* (1794). Livingston was proud of his work and responded with a second canto, which, owing to the hostile reception accorded the first canto, could not be published. Another of his important works was *A Vindication of Mr. Randolph's Resignation* (1795), written with Edmund Randolph and explaining the attorney general's forced resignation. As a politician Livingston assumed leadership of the "Manor" branch of the Livingston family in their contentious lawsuits with the "Clermont" side. He remained especially hostile toward John Jay. One of his early partisan acts was in defense of the ambassador from the French Republic, Edmond "Citizen" Genet. John Jay was among those who claimed Genet had disparaged George Washington, a charge Genet denied. Livingston, as Genet's lawyer, began the prosecution of the then chief justice in his own court. The case collapsed when Genet was recalled and forced to seek asylum in the United States. Livingston's hostility to Jay continued in 1792 when Jay ran for governor of New York against George Clinton. Livingston played a central role in disposing of some inconvenient election returns and so defeating Jay. Later he orchestrated demonstrations against Jay for his work in obtaining the treaty with England that bears his name.

Livingston had a varied law practice. Early in his career he worked with Alexander Hamilton. In the noted Tory confiscation case of *Rutgers v. Waddington* (1784) they defended a Tory whose property had been taken under New York law but in violation of the peace treaty between the United States and Great Britain. Later he collaborated with Hamilton and Aaron Burr on the sensational "Manhattan Well Mystery" case, in which a man was acquitted of the murder of his fiancée.

After Livingston, Burr, and De Witt Clinton helped Thomas Jefferson carry New York in the election of 1800, Livingston was rewarded by an appointment as puisne judge on the New York Supreme Court in 1802. Notable among his 149 state opinions was a display of judicial humor in *Pierson v. Post* (1805), the famous fox hunting case in which, in dissent, Livingston argued that a hunter pursuing a fox on uninhabited ground and on the point of taking the creature had acquired a legal interest and therefore a right of action when another man killed the animal. Legally significant was *Palmer v. Mulligan* (1805), a water-rights case in which he favored industrial over agrarian usage. On the New York Council of Revision, a body charged with vetoing unconstitutional or defective legislative acts, Livingston agreed with the majority that a corporation could not be established without the consent of all the parties involved.

In 1806 Livingston was appointed to the U.S. Supreme Court. Given his strong personality and long record of Republican service, Jefferson hoped he would undermine the leadership of Chief Justice John Marshall. At first, Livingston rebelled against Marshall's practice of having the court issue per curiam decisions (i.e., decisions rendered in the name of the court, as opposed to opinions of individual judges), but Marshall's diplomatic courtship soon won Livingston over. Livingston's radicalism probably had more to do with New York's factionalism than with philosophical orientation. Freed from his New York environment, he grew increasingly conservative, a process assisted by his close friend, Chancellor James Kent. Producing only thirty-eight majority opinions and dissenting only eight times, Livingston reluctantly supported Marshall on most major issues. Joseph Story, after observing the Supreme Court in 1808, pronounced Livingston "a very able and independent judge. He is luminous, decisive, earnest and impressive on the bench."

New York had been in the vanguard of emerging American commercial law, and this became Livingston's area of expertise on the court. Although most of the issues were highly technical, the constitutionality of state bankruptcy legislation bedeviled the late years of the Marshall court. In the federal circuit court case of *Adams v. Storey* (1817), Livingston issued a sweeping opinion upholding a New York law that covered both retroactive contracts (those made before the law's passage) and extraterritorial application (to out-of-state parties). When these issues reached the Supreme Court later in *Sturges v. Crowninshield* (1819), Livingston in conference disagreed mightily with Marshall's voiding of the retroactive part of the New York statute, an opposition recorded not in public but only in Joseph Story's letters. Marshall's labored decision, which saved at least the theory of the principle of state bankruptcy, reflected concessions made to Livingston's position. Livingston, in turn, assented in the decision and published no dissent.

Perhaps the most widely cited in recent times of Livingston's cases, *United States v. Hoxie* (1808), was also given while on circuit. Here he held that a private person's violation of the Embargo Act for no further purpose than private gain did not constitute treason. The case has long remained an important precedent by virtue of its narrow definition of treason.

Livingston was charged with three ethical lapses while on the court. First, in 1813 a newspaper editorial claimed that a conspiracy existed to advance a case of Edward Livingston's, the family's black sheep in Louisiana. Actually Brockholst had taken no part in the decision. However, it was a breach of judicial ethics when he told John Quincy Adams of the Court's unannounced decision in *Fletcher v. Peck* (1810), the famous Yazoo land frauds case in which the court invalidated a Georgia state law as being in conflict with the Constitution's contract clause. In *Dartmouth College v. Woodward* (1819), which pitted the state legislature against the board of the college and tested whether such corporations were private or public, Livingston was apparently undecided even after Daniel Webster's great oration in defense of the college. Allegedly, a paper on the issues prepared by Chancellor James Kent reached him extrajudicially, while two other colleges likewise threatened, Princeton and Harvard, bestowed timely honorary degrees upon him. What might have loomed as a major question of conflict of interest was contained in the famous steamboat monopoly case of *Gibbons v. Ogden* (1824), for the Clermont branch of the Livingston family shared the monopoly with Robert Fulton. On circuit in 1811 in *Livingston v. Van Ingen* Livingston dismissed the initial proceedings, citing a lack of federal jurisdiction. He died, however, before the issue reached the Supreme Court. Livingston's death marked the end of an era on the Supreme Court. Chief Justice Marshall lost his control as divisions once hidden became open fissures.

Off the bench Livingston was a passionate advocate of public education and served as treasurer and trustee of Columbia University. He was a cofounder in 1804 and vice president of the New-York Historical Society. He fathered eleven children, five by his first wife, Catherine Keteltas, three by his second, Ann Ludlow, and three by his third, Catherine Kortright. Physically impressive on the bench, Livingston authored state and Supreme Court opinions marked by terse and pointed language and closely reasoned arguments. He was known as "a finished gentleman" in private life (*New York Evening Post*, 24 Mar. 1823). He died in Washington, D.C.

• The most complete account of Livingston's life is Gerald T. Dunne, "Brockholst Livingston," in *The Justices of the United States Supreme Court, 1789–1969*, ed. Leon Friedman and Fred L. Israel (1969). Livingston's Supreme Court days are covered in Charles Warren, *The Supreme Court in United States History* (1928). William W. Story, *Life and Letters of*

Joseph Story, vol. 1 (1851), offers an assessment of Livingston as a Supreme Court justice. Eight of Livingston's letters, along with two from Joseph Story, appear in Gerald T. Dunne, ed., "The Story-Livingston Correspondence," *American Journal of Legal History* 10 (July 1966): 224–36. No collection of his papers apparently exists, but some of his speeches and some decisions were bound under the title *Livingston's Speeches, Cases 1800* (Hamilton College Library, Clinton, N.Y.). Eulogies can be found in the *New York Evening Post*, 24 Mar. 1823, and the *Washington Daily National Intelligencer*, 19 Mar. 1823.

MICHAEL B. DOUGAN

LIVINGSTON, James (27 Mar. 1747–29 Nov. 1832), Continental army officer, was born to John Livingston and Catherine Ten Broeck. The location of his birth is unknown. A scion of a lesser line of the aristocratic Livingston family of New York, James Livingston entered King's College in 1763 but left without a degree. He became a lawyer by clerking for William Smith, Jr. (1728–1793). Livingston was among those colonials who settled in Canada after its absorption into the British empire. He resided near Chambly, learned French, and engaged in trade. During 1770, while living in Canada, he wed Elizabeth Simpson, like himself a New Yorker. They would have nine children.

Livingston kept in touch with his in-law, Philip Schuyler. After the American Revolution erupted, Livingston vigorously supported it. Assuming that there was much Canadian backing for the American cause, he informed Schuyler about the situation in Canada. On 5 September 1775 Schuyler sent him an address to the people of Canada, urging them to revolt against the British. Together with some followers, Livingston began to attack the British. When American general Richard Montgomery and his invading army entered Canada, Livingston joined them. He raised approximately 200 to 300 Canadian allies for the Americans.

During the siege of Fort St. Jean, Livingston commanded artillery pieces that had little effect on the outcome. However, Livingston's artillery was more effective in dealing with Fort Chambly. Barrages from the cannons brought the surrender of the post, with its substantial supply of gunpowder intact, on 18 October 1775. Chambly's surrender helped bring about the fall of St. Jean.

On 20 November 1775 Montgomery, obviously pleased by Livingston's activities, made him a colonel and authorized him to form a Continental force of Canadians. This unit became known as the First Canadian Regiment. Livingston's troops took part in the assault on Quebec (31 Dec. 1775). Ordered to attack St. John's Gate to divert attention from the main objective, the Canadians approached their target but ran away during the battle.

After the American retreat from Canada during 1776, Livingston continued with the patriot army. The Continental Congress gave him permission to recruit outside of Canada, and he raised many soldiers from New York. Livingston and his men fought in the Saratoga campaign, participating in the battles of

Freeman's Farm (19 Sept. 1777) and Bemis Heights (7 Oct. 1777), which is sometimes called Stillwater. A much more petty battle—an argument over military rank with another Canadian, Moses Hazen—was won by Livingston in 1780.

Because Livingston's soldiers were very poorly supplied, they could not serve in the field. Therefore, in August 1780 they were ordered into garrison duty along the Hudson River. Livingston commanded the post at King's Ferry, south of West Point. A French officer, the marquis de Chastellux, visited him there and praised Livingston as "a very amiable and well-informed young man" in his *Travels in North America* (1963 ed., vol. 1, pp. 97–98).

This posting involved Livingston, unwittingly, in Benedict Arnold's treason. The British ship, *Vulture*, which had brought John André to Arnold, had stayed near Livingston. The ship's officers planned to take André safely back to New York City, but Livingston, drawing on his artillery experience in Canada, thought he could easily drive the vessel away. He managed to obtain the necessary supplies from John Lamb, who commanded the artillery at West Point, despite Lamb's feeling that shelling the *Vulture* was a waste of scarce stores. On 22 September 1780 Livingston fired at the *Vulture* and forced it to leave. André, deprived of his transport, went by land, which resulted in his capture and Arnold's exposure. Although Livingston himself came under suspicion, he was quickly cleared.

Colonel Livingston's Continental army career ceased soon after. At the end of 1780 the Continental Congress reorganized the army, and Livingston's unit was slated for elimination. His men were distributed among the various state lines, and on 1 January 1781 he was retired.

Livingston settled in New York and became a state officeholder, serving as an assemblyman of Tryon (now Montgomery) County, 1784–1787 and 1789–1791. When the University of the State of New York was created in 1784, Livingston became a regent and was only replaced in 1797.

On 2 April 1787 Livingston was appointed to the congressional position of deputy superintendent of Indian affairs for the Northern District. His superior, General Richard Butler, was not resident in New York. The Iroquois had been accustomed to having a nearby Indian agent, and they had requested that the practice be continued. When the Iroquois' own preferred candidate, Schuyler, turned it down, Livingston received the office. He served as an intermediary between the Iroquois on one side and Butler and the Continental Congress on the other, thereby making communications easier for all concerned. When the new federal government was established in 1789, Livingston wanted to remain in this office and solicited the aid of Alexander Hamilton, who on 19 May 1790 wrote to Arthur St. Clair on Livingston's behalf. Despite Hamilton's intercession, Livingston was not reappointed.

In 1784, as compensation for his losses in Canada, New York State gave Livingston 1,000 acres. In 1798 the Congress awarded him another 1,000 acres in Ohio. By the end of Livingston's long life, he was the last surviving revolutionary colonel in New York. He died in Schuylerville, New York.

• Livingston's letters are in the Horatio Gates Papers and other collections at the New-York Historical Society and in the Emmet collection and the Philip Schuyler Papers at the New York Public Library. Miscellaneous items are at the New York State Library, Albany. Relevant material in the microfilmed Continental Congress Papers is listed in John P. Butler, ed., *Index: The Papers of the Continental Congress*, vol. 3 (1978). The published papers of revolutionary figures, such as George Washington and Alexander Hamilton, have letters or references to Livingston, as do the *American Archives* volumes. Worthington C. Ford, ed., *Journals of the Continental Congress* (34 vols., 1904–1937), is also useful. Genealogical information is in Florence Van Rensselaer, *The Livingston Family in America and Its Scottish Origins* (1949). Other sources for Livingston are Edgar A. Werner, *Civil List and Constitutional History of the Colony and State of New York* (1884); Allan S. Everest, *Moses Hazen and the Canadian Refugees in the American Revolution* (1976); Robert M. Hatch, *Thrust for Canada* (1979); Hal T. Shelton, *General Richard Montgomery and the American Revolution* (1994); and Richard J. Koke, *Accomplice in Treason* (1973). An obituary is in the *Daily Albany Argus*, 8 Dec. 1832.

PHILIP RANLET

LIVINGSTON, John Henry (30 May 1746–20 Jan. 1825), Dutch Reformed pastor and educator, was born in Poughkeepsie, New York, the son of Henry Livingston, a business assistant to his uncle Henry Beekman, a member of the provincial assembly, and the clerk of Dutchess County, and Susanna Conklin. He was the great-grandson of Robert Livingston, the original lord of the manor along the Hudson River, and a cousin both to Philip Livingston, a signer of the Declaration of Independence, and to William Livingston, governor of New Jersey. After private study in Dutchess County and schooling in New Milford, Connecticut, John entered Yale at age twelve and graduated with a B.A. in 1762. From 1762 to 1764 he studied law with Bartholomew Crannel, a Poughkeepsie lawyer, but after an illness precipitated his religious conversion, Livingston abandoned the study of law.

Seeking to improve his health, Livingston and a friend planned to visit the West Indies. At the last minute Livingston changed his mind and consequently was spared a certain death, for two crew members seized the ship and killed everyone on board except for a young boy who later told authorities of the tragedy.

This incident convinced Livingston that God had a plan for his life, so he made plans to continue his education and enter the ministry in the Dutch Reformed church. While he had some attraction to the Episcopal and Presbyterian churches, Livingston chose to serve the church of his upbringing. In the summer of 1765 he met the Reverend Archibald Laidlie, pastor of the Collegiate Church in New York City and the first English-speaking minister in the Dutch Reformed church in America. At Laidlie's urging and with his father's financing, Livingston pursued theological studies at the University of Utrecht in Holland. He studied under orthodox Reformed pastors such as Gijsbertus Bonnet, a defender of the Canons of Dort and "the last genuine Voetian."

In March 1769 the Collegiate Church in New York City issued a pastoral call to Livingston. In April 1770 Livingston finished his doctoral dissertation, a short work in Latin on the Sinaitic covenant, accepted the call from the Collegiate Church, and received ordination from the Classis of Amsterdam. After a successful defense of his dissertation in May, Livingston was awarded a doctorate and immediately set sail for America. Arriving in September 1770, Livingston commenced what became a forty-year ministry at the Collegiate Church.

Livingston's lineage, education, and irenicism equipped him to assume leadership in the struggling Dutch Reformed denomination. In 1772 he repaired the long-smoldering division between the church's Coetus and Conferentie parties—a mid-eighteenth-century schism rooted in the controversy over whether the American church should become self-sufficient or remain dependent on Holland. During his sojourn in Holland, Livingston had consulted with members of the Classis of Amsterdam and the Synod of North Holland on how to end the schism. Subsequently, soon after his arrival in New York, he persuaded his consistory to invite all Dutch Reformed churches to send delegates for the purpose of reuniting the church. At a meeting in October 1771, Livingston—a mere twenty-five years old—was chosen president and with a committee produced a Plan of Union (previously prepared and approved by ecclesiastical authorities in Holland) that gave virtual independence to the Dutch Reformed church in America. Ratified in 1772, the plan created an independent classis in America and permitted the training, examination, and ordination of ministers in America.

In 1775 Livingston married Sarah Livingston, his second cousin and the daughter of Philip Livingston. They had one child.

With the coming of the American Revolution and the British occupation of New York, the patriot Livingston fled the city to the upper Hudson Valley, where he served churches in Kingston, Albany, Livingston Manor, Poughkeepsie, and Red Hook. In 1783 he returned to his New York pastorate and decisively influenced the formation of an independent Dutch Reformed church in America. Livingston compiled its Constitution (1793)—an English translation of the Church Order of Dort, accompanied by a Livingston-authored set of "explanatory articles" that attempted to clarify the Reformed church's adaptation to American life. Drawing from the writings of Locke (whose influence can be seen in his doctoral dissertation), Livingston argued that conscience must not be coerced and rejected any references in the Church Order of Dort relating to direct involvement of the state in church matters. In addition, he translated and revised the liturgy of the Dutch church for American use, prepared the church's first hymnal, *Psalms and Hymns* (1793), and during 1812 and 1813 produced a considerably revised second edition of this work.

One of the most pressing denominational needs in which Livingston made a signal contribution was in the training of ministers. With his 1784 appointment as professor of theology by the Classis of Amsterdam, Livingston became the first theological educator in America under the direct aegis of a denomination. During the next forty years Livingston prepared nearly 150 men for the ministry—first as an independent professor in New York and Long Island (all the while continuing his pastoral labors), and then, following the merger of his theological school with Queen's College (now Rutgers University) in New Brunswick, New Jersey, as president and professor of theology from 1810 to 1825. Livingston referred to his move to New Brunswick as "a species of martyrdom," and yet he went, enduring inadequate financial support (undoubtedly, his financial independence enabled him to live on half his promised salary) and the separation from lifelong parishioners.

In addition to his direct involvement in denominational affairs, Livingston expressed an abiding interest in missions. He was instrumental in founding several missionary societies, served as vice president of the New York Missionary Society, and published a sermon, *The Triumph of the Gospel* (1804), that aroused missionary fervor and thus contributed to the launching of the Protestant foreign missionary movement in America. Livingston embraced a commonly held postmillennial eschatology, though unlike others such as Cotton Mather and Jonathan Edwards, he did not view America's place as unique in the divine scheme. He argued that the end of the world would come in the year 1999, which left Christians with less than 200 years to evangelize the world and help to fulfill this prophecy. Livingston's sermon not only influenced his own ministerial students but was widely circulated at Williams College, an institution often referred to as "the birthplace of modern missions." He died in New Brunswick, New Jersey.

In his own day, Livingston was aptly recognized as the "father of the Dutch Reformed church in America," for no other single individual of his time contributed to the development of the church in so many significant ways. During the colonial period he united a faction-riven church; following the revolution, he ensured the church's survival as an independent body by compiling or authoring its constitution and liturgy; finally, he bequeathed to future generations a trained ministry.

• Livingston's papers and manuscript sermons are in the New Brunswick Seminary library. His publications include *Oratio Inauguralis de Veritate Religionis Christianae* (1785); *The Glory of the Redeemer* (1789); *An Address Delivered at the Commencement Held in Queen's College in New-Jersey, Sept. 25, 1810* (1810); *A Funeral Service, or Meditations Adapted to Funeral Addresses* (1812); *A Dissertation on the Marriage of a Man with his Sister-in-law* (1816); and *An Address to Reformed German Churches in the United States* (1819).

Alexander Gunn, *Memoirs of the Rev. John Henry Livingston* (1856), remains an important biographical source, but see also Elton J. Bruins, "John Henry Livingston: His Life and Work, a Re-Interpretation" (master's thesis, Union Theological Seminary, 1957). See also John Coakley, "John Henry Livingston and the Liberty of Conscience," *Reformed Review* 46 (1992): 119–35, and Daniel J. Meeter, *Meeting Each Other* (1993), on his denominational contributions; John Beardslee, "John Henry Livingston and the Rise of the American Mission Movement," *Historical Highlights* 8 (1989): 1–21, and Earl William Kennedy, "From Providence to Civil Religion: Some 'Dutch' Reformed Interpretations of America in the Revolutionary Era," *Reformed Review* 29 (1976): 111–23, on his views of missions and civil religion; and Gerald De Jong, *The Dutch Reformed Church in the American Colonies* (1978), on the broader context of his life.

DAVID W. KLING

LIVINGSTON, Milton Stanley (25 May 1905–25 Aug. 1986), physicist, was born in Brodhead, Wisconsin, the son of Milton McWhorter Livingston, a minister, rancher, and teacher, and Sarah Jane Ten Eyck. He grew up in Pomona, California. In 1917 his mother died, and thereafter he was raised by a stepmother. Livingston attended high schools in Pomona and La Verne, California, graduating in 1921. He then entered Pomona College in Claremont, California, and supported himself by washing dishes and clerking in a store. In addition, he joined the gymnastics team and made the honor roll, receiving his bachelor's degree in 1926. He went on to Dartmouth College in Hanover, New Hampshire, receiving his master's degree in physics in 1928; he taught there until 1929. In August 1930 he married Lois Robinson; they had a son and a daughter.

In September 1930, after moving to the University of California at Berkeley, Livingston visited physics professor Ernest O. Lawrence. Livingston needed a subject for a doctoral thesis, while Lawrence needed someone to help him build a bigger version of his cyclotron, a device for accelerating subatomic particles to high velocities. "Lawrence was young, he was bursting with energy, his enthusiasm swept me off my feet," Livingston later recalled (Davis, p. 33). Thus began one of the century's crucial scientific collaborations, which was sometimes marked by what Livingston called "violent conflicts" between the two men (Davis, p. 352).

Lawrence had already built a small cyclotron that resembled a four-inch pillbox. He had gotten the idea for the cyclotron by reading a scheme (based on an older idea) proposed by a Norwegian engineer, Rolf Wideröe. Wideröe proposed building a linear (straight-line) accelerator that would accelerate ions by giving them small, repeated electric nudges to faster and faster speeds. Lawrence modified the idea by envisioning a device shaped like a manhole cover. Within it, a magnetic field would make particles spin around, while an oscillating electric field repeatedly pushed them to ever-higher speeds until they escaped in a beam.

Livingston examined the innards of Lawrence's primitive cyclotron and was distressed to conclude that it did not work as Lawrence assumed. The alleged increase in particle acceleration was an illusion caused by a mathematical error, Livingston believed. "Lawrence and [his student Niels E.] Edlefsen had made an error in their calibration of the magnetic field," he observed later (Davis, p. 33). Livingston modified the design until he had a device that worked. By March 1931 the cyclotron accelerated ions to energies of 80,000 electron volts.

During the next year Livingston managed to accelerate ions to an energy of one million volts within a nine-inch-wide cyclotron. He wrote the figure of one million volts "on the blackboard. Lawrence came in late one evening. He saw the board, looked at the microammeter to check the resonance current, and literally danced around the room. . . . We were busy all that [next] day demonstrating million-volt protons to eager viewers" (Davis, p. 42). Livingston's doctoral thesis was "The Production of High-Velocity Hydrogen Ions without the Use of High Voltage" (1931).

Their work attracted press attention. The Associated Press speculated about using the device to "break up" the atom. A *New York Times* headline suggested that cyclotrons might transmute atomic nuclei into gold. Others envisioned unleashing atomic energy.

Nevertheless, the Berkeley team missed the chance to be the first to disintegrate an atom. Two scientists in England, John Douglas Cockcroft and Ernest Walton, beat them to that feat by using a weaker, 710,000-volt device to fire protons at lithium (the third lightest element). Their beam disintegrated the lithium atoms into helium (the second lightest element). Eager to catch up, in September 1932 the Berkeley team used a cyclotron to trigger nuclear disintegration within a lithium crystal. The crystal glowed blue as the particles shattered its atomic lattices.

In 1934 Livingston moved to Cornell University in Ithaca, New York, where he worked with the physicist Hans Bethe and built the first cyclotron outside of Berkeley. At Cornell, far from the high-pressure Lawrence, Livingston found time to think. In 1936 and 1937 at Cornell, Livingston, Bethe, and Robert Bacher wrote the first complete review of nuclear physics. In 1938 Livingston moved to the Massachusetts Institute of Technology, where he built another cyclotron and served as associate professor of physics. He taught at MIT from 1938 to 1970.

Lawrence won the 1939 Nobel Prize in physics for inventing and developing the cyclotron. In his speech at the award ceremony, he did not mention Livingston. Livingston was hurt by such incidents, and later that hurt "turned into a lasting bitterness" (Davis, p. 44). However, in a letter, Livingston expressed a calm, balanced view of Lawrence, noting that while others had conceived of the cyclotron before Lawrence, "Lawrence was the first and only one to have enough confidence in it to try it out." He praised his colleague's "optimistic and inspirational attitude," his "ability as a director and organizer and his inspirational leadership," but added, "the bulk of the development was done by others" (quoted in Heilbron, p. 486).

From 1946 to 1948 Livingston chaired an accelerator project at Brookhaven National Laboratory on Long Island, New York. In 1952, working with Ernest D. Courant and Hartland Snyder, he developed the principle of alternating gradient focusing. This technique permitted the use of cheaper, smaller magnets and led to more powerful accelerators.

Livingston and his wife divorced in 1949. In 1952 he married Margaret Hughes.

In the 1950s, as chair of the Federation of American Scientists, Livingston publicly criticized excessive military secrecy. From 1967 until his retirement from MIT in 1970, he served as associate director of the Fermi National Accelerator Laboratory in Batavia, Illinois. He was a member of the National Academy of Sciences.

Livingston spent his last years in Santa Fe, New Mexico, where he died. In December 1986 the U.S. Department of Energy, which funded the nation's particle accelerator laboratories, awarded its top scientific prize, the Enrico Fermi Award, to Courant and, posthumously, to Livingston. Livingston was thus recognized for his key role in pioneering the modern age of particle accelerators that explore the underlying fabric of matter and energy.

• Extensive biographical details on Livingston appear in Nuel Pharr Davis, *Lawrence and Oppenheimer* (1968). See also J. L. Heilbron and Robert W. Seidel, *Lawrence and His Laboratory: A History of the Lawrence Berkeley Laboratory*, vol. 1 (1989). Livingston's personal account of cyclotron development is "History of the cyclotron," 12 (Oct. 1959): 18–23. He also wrote *High Energy Accelerators* (1954); *Particle Accelerators*, with J. P. Blewett (1962); and *Particle Accelerators: A Brief History* (1969). An obituary is in the *New York Times*, 20 Sept. 1986, and a brief item about his work with Courant is in the *Times*, 10 Dec. 1986.

KEAY DAVIDSON

LIVINGSTON, Peter Van Brugh (Oct. 1710–28 Dec. 1792), merchant and revolutionary leader, was born in Albany, New York, the son of Philip Livingston, a merchant and proprietor of Livingston Manor, and Catrina Van Brugh. The second of six brothers, Livingston spent his childhood in Albany among his predominantly Dutch relatives. He graduated from Yale College in 1731 and then embarked on a career in trade.

Family networks and connections shaped Livingston's early mercantile career. First, he traveled with his brother John to London, where the two served apprenticeships with merchant Samuel Storke, their father's longtime trading partner. By 1734 Peter Van Brugh Livingston returned to New York and formed a business partnership with his elder brother, Robert Livingston, Jr. Two years later Peter went to Jamaica to learn the sugar trade and to act as his father's commercial agent in the sugar islands.

By November 1739 Livingston was back in New York, where he married Mary Alexander, daughter of James Alexander, the province's leading lawyer, and of the merchant Mary Spratt Provoost. The couple had fifteen children, five of whom died young. After Mary's death in 1769, Livingston married Elizabeth Ricketts. They had no children.

During the French and Indian War (1754–1763), Livingston made a fortune in privateering and military contracts. With his brother-in-law William Alexander (1726–1783), he held contracts to provision the British expeditions to Niagara and Crown Point during the war's early years, though he and Alexander later engaged in a protracted lawsuit over the terms of their business partnership. Successful in trade, Livingston built a mansion in Manhattan, a country house at Dobbs Ferry in Westchester County, and one of eight sugar refineries in New York City during the colonial era. He owned land in the Hudson and Mohawk valleys and in 1773 purchased a township in Florida. When John Adams (1735–1826) visited New York in 1775, he reported to his diary that Livingston "is rich, and now lives upon his income."

Although Peter Van Brugh Livingston's brothers William Livingston and Philip Livingston exceeded him in civic activism, he was among a circle of public-spirited men who undertook many projects to improve their growing urban community. Like his brothers, Livingston was active in the effort to establish King's College (later Columbia) in New York, organizing lotteries to raise money for the proposed institution once it received its charter. Between 1748 and 1761 he also served as a trustee of the College of New Jersey. With his brothers and cousin Robert R. Livingston (1718–1775), he was a founding member of New York's Society for the Promotion of Useful Knowledge in 1748 and, in 1754, a charter member of the New York Society Library. In 1771 he became a member of the first board of governors of the Society of the New York Hospital.

Although Livingston did not hold public office until the 1770s, he was active behind the scenes of New York's factional politics, aligning himself with his brothers in a coalition of religious dissenters, landowners, and moderate Whigs that opposed a faction of merchants, Anglicans, and future Tories led by James De Lancey (1732–1800). In 1763 and 1764 Livingston signed the New York merchants' memorials protesting British plans to raise revenue in America and, unlike his more cautious brothers, he supported the radicals' strenuous resistance to British imperial policies.

The imperial crisis brought the aging Livingston to political prominence. He served on all three of New York's prerevolutionary committees. In May 1774 he was a member of the Committee of Fifty-one, which nominated candidates for the First Continental Congress; in July, however, Livingston and other radicals resigned from that committee when conservative merchants attempted to insulate its deliberations from the pressures of an increasingly radical populace. In November Livingston was elected to the new Committee of Sixty, formed to enforce the Continental Association. In May 1775 he served on the Committee of One Hundred, which effectively governed New York until July, when the first Provincial Congress convened in Manhattan.

One of few New Yorkers who commanded respect among both radicals and moderates, Livingston was elected president and later treasurer of New York's Provincial Congress. When the British bombarded New York City in November 1775, however, he fled upriver to Westchester County. Livingston retired from politics the following year, pleading ill health. He spent the war years and their aftermath quietly among kin in Basking Ridge and Elizabethtown, New Jersey, where he died.

Livingston's role in the revolutionary movement was short-lived but significant. His ability to appeal to both radicals and moderates helped solidify New York's Whig coalition at a critical juncture.

• Livingston's papers are in the New-York Historical Society and the Franklin D. Roosevelt Library, Hyde Park, N.Y. Cynthia A. Kierner, *Traders and Gentlefolk: The Livingstons of New York, 1675–1790* (1992), examines his early career and civic activities. Virginia D. Harrington, *The New York Merchant on the Eve of the Revolution* (1935), describes the mercantile community of which Livingston was a prominent member. Carl Lotus Becker, *The History of Political Parties in the Province of New York, 1760–1776* (1909), and Edward Countryman, *A People in Revolution: The American Revolution in New York, 1760–1790* (1981), discuss factional alignments in revolutionary New York, as well as the province's prerevolutionary committees.

CYNTHIA A. KIERNER

LIVINGSTON, Philip (15 Jan. 1716–12 June 1778), merchant and political leader, was born in Albany, New York, the son of Philip Livingston, a merchant and proprietor of "Livingston Manor," and Catrina Van Brugh. Livingston enjoyed the benefits of membership in one of New York's leading families. At a time when most Americans lacked formal education, four of six surviving Livingston brothers earned Yale degrees. Upon graduation in 1737, Philip Livingston returned to Albany to serve a mercantile apprenticeship with his father. Livingston learned the Albany trade and, through his father's efforts, obtained potentially valuable clerkships in Albany's local government. In 1740 he married Christina Ten Broeck, daughter of Colonel Dirck Ten Broeck, mayor of Albany. They had nine children, of whom eight survived infancy.

After several years in Albany, Livingston moved downriver to New York, where he established himself as a general merchant. He traded mainly with the British sugar islands although, like many New York merchants, he probably engaged in illicit trade with the French and Spanish island colonies. During King George's War (1744–1748), Livingston made his fortune provisioning and privateering. During the French and Indian War (1754–1763), he owned shares in six privateers, making him one of the colony's leading investors. Livingston also speculated heavily in real estate, accumulating more than 120,000 acres of unimproved land in New York and lesser holdings in New Jersey and Connecticut. He owned urban property in Albany and New York City, including his Manhattan home on Duke Street and a country estate in Brooklyn Heights.

The financially secure Livingston was a leader in the civic life of his community. In 1746 he endowed a professorship of divinity at Yale College. In 1754 he was one of six founders of the New York Society Library. Two years later he was president and founding member of the St. Andrew's Society, New York's first benevolent organization. Livingston also participated in efforts to establish a college in New York and, in 1766, was one of the original trustees of Queen's College in New Jersey. He helped organize the New York Chamber of Commerce in 1768 and, in 1771, was cofounder of the New York Hospital and a member of its first board of governors. An elder and a deacon of the Dutch Reformed church, Livingston was also a benefactor of New York's Anglican King's College and of the city's Presbyterian and Methodist congregations.

By the 1750s Livingston was also increasingly active in politics at both the local and provincial levels. Between 1754 and 1763 he served as alderman for New York's East Ward. In 1758 New Yorkers elected him to the provincial assembly, where in 1764 he helped pen a remonstrance against Parliament's unprecedented attempt to raise revenue in America. The following year he represented New York at the Stamp Act Congress.

Livingston's career in colonial politics culminated in 1768 with his election as the assembly's Speaker. By 1769 new factional alignments pitted an alliance of merchants, Anglicans, and radical Sons of Liberty against a coalition of landowners, religious dissenters, and more moderate opponents of British imperial policies. Livingston followed most of his relatives into the latter party and did not win reelection. His party remained in opposition for the rest of the colonial era.

Livingston and his allies were, however, prominent in the extralegal committees that orchestrated New York's firm but orderly resistance to British imperial policies. In May 1774 Livingston was one of the Committee of Fifty-One that nominated candidates—of which he was one—for the First Continental Congress. In November he was a member of the Committee of Sixty that enforced the Continental Association. In May 1775 he served on the Committee of One Hundred, which was New York's de facto government until the meeting of the first provincial Congress. That autumn, fearing naval bombardment of Manhattan, Livingston fled to Kingston in Ulster County. In 1776 he was mentioned as a possible candidate for governor. When New Yorkers enacted their state constitution in 1777, Livingston represented the British-occupied city of New York in the new state senate.

Between 1774 and 1778 Livingston was far more active in continental than provincial politics. He regularly attended the Continental Congress, where his business experience made him a valued member of several key committees. In September 1775 he was one of nine men appointed to the Secret Committee—later known as the Committee on Commerce—charged with arranging the importation of arms and gunpowder for the patriot forces. Livingston remained a member of this committee throughout his time in Congress, and, with other merchant congressmen, he advanced funds to the government in the course of filling its military contracts. Livingston also served on the Marine Committee and the Committee on Provisioning. In 1777 he was one of three members of Congress chosen to investigate complaints in the commissary's department.

In 1776 Livingston signed the Declaration of Independence, but he was absent when Congress debated the independence resolution. Like many conservative Whigs, Livingston accepted independence reluctantly, dreading the resulting social upheaval. In his 1774 pamphlet, *The Other Side of the Question*, Livingston had invoked both historical precedent and Lockean political theory to defend colonial opposition to parliamentary taxation, but he deemed American independence "the most vain, empty, shallow, and ridiculous project." In 1774 John Adams (1735–1826) confided to his *Diary* that Livingston was a "rough, rapid mortal," who "says if England should turn us adrift, we should go instantly to civil wars among ourselves." Livingston feared the "levelling spirit" of revolution. In 1777 he disparaged the abilities of New York's new leaders, regretting the state's lack of experienced governors.

Livingston was an exemplar of conservative patriotism in revolutionary America. A conscientious leader, possessed of an aristocrat's sense of social responsibility, he accepted republicanism without embracing its democratic implications. He died in York, Pennsylvania, while attending the Continental Congress.

• Many of Livingston's papers are in the New York Public Library. *Letters of Delegates to Congress, 1774–1789* (1976–), contains some of Livingston's wartime papers and is an important source for his career in Congress. Cynthia A. Kierner, *Traders and Gentlefolk: The Livingstons of New York, 1675–1790* (1992), examines the economic activities and political ideals of Livingston and his family. Patricia U. Bonomi, *A Factious People: Politics and Society in Colonial New York* (1971), and Carl Lotus Becker, *The History of Political Parties in the Province of New York, 1760–1776* (1909), are the standard political histories. William H. W. Sabine, ed., *Historical Memoirs . . . of William Smith . . .* (2 vols., 1956–1958), includes contemporary observations on Livingston's political attitudes and activities.

Cynthia A. Kierner

LIVINGSTON, Robert (13 Dec. 1654–1 Oct. 1728), colonial merchant, landowner, and politician, was born in Ancrum, Scotland, the son of the Reverend John Livingstone, a minister of the Church of Scotland, and Janet Fleeming. Livingston's father faced the threat of prosecution as a noted Presbyterian minister in a Scottish church that was moving strongly toward Episcopacy in the aftermath of the Restoration of Charles II,

and in 1663 the family fled Scotland for the Protestant haven at Rotterdam. The city of Rotterdam had a large community of Scottish merchants in the seventeenth century, and at a young age Livingston began to engage in commerce, possibly under the tutelage of two brothers-in-law who were active traders in that city.

On the death of Livingston's father in 1672, the family returned to Scotland. Livingston did not remain there long; the following year he departed for another haven for Reformed Protestants, the Puritan colony at Massachusetts Bay, where his father had considered moving the family some decades before. After forming an association with the Boston merchant John Hull, Livingston moved again in 1674, this time to the frontier city of Albany, in a New York colony that had recently been recaptured from the Dutch. Despite England's possession of the colony, the city of Albany and especially its flourishing fur trade remained firmly under the control of a Dutch commercial clique. It proved an ideal spot for one with Livingston's cosmopolitan background, as few outsiders had a sufficient mastery of either the Dutch language or their commercial ways to penetrate the city's cultural barriers.

Livingston quickly began to put his skills and connections to use. His first employment made use of his linguistic abilities, in the joint posts of secretary to Nicholas van Rensselaer of "Rensselaerswyck Manor" and clerk of the town of Albany and the board of Indian commissioners. None were especially important posts, but Livingston managed to parlay them into much more, making his way into the tight circle of Albany traders. In 1679, following the death of his employer, Livingston married his widow, Alida Schuyler van Rensselaer. The marriage gave him instant prominence and aligned him with several of the most important families in the province, including the Schuylers and van Cortlands.

Livingston's new connections provided the opportunity to expand his personal fortune. After his marriage he put in a dubious claim for the manor at Rensselaerswyck. Probably at the request of the governor, who wanted to keep the peace among powerful provincial families, Livingston eventually withdrew his suit. He was quickly rewarded with properties almost as vast, receiving patents from Governor Thomas Dongan for an indeterminate tract, eventually encompassing 2,000 acres, along the eastern shore of the Hudson River in 1684, another for up to 600 acres at Taconic in 1685, and, most spectacularly, a 1686 patent for what was to be the lordship and manor of "Livingston," which silently added all of the land in between, for a total of 160,000 acres. At the same time he was able to use both his distinct background and his family connections to establish a unique commercial position, incorporating both fur trading among the Dutch at Albany and overseas commerce through his mercantile connections, including a Scottish associate, James Graham, and his brother-in-law Stephan van Cortland.

Livingston also began to move into positions of power. In 1689 the Glorious Revolution that ousted James II from the English throne left a leadership vacuum in New York, which had belonged to James as proprietor since his days as duke of York. Into the vacuum stepped the New York merchant Jacob Leisler, affiliated with that city's Dutch Protestant community, who led a Protestant rebellion against the remnants of James's government in the colony. The Albany community was suspicious of Leisler's intentions and resisted his efforts to take control of the city, and Livingston assumed a leadership role in drafting their statement of resistance. This action necessitated his retreat to New England, from which he did not return until 1691, to wait out the Leislerian's seizure of power. In the following decade Livingston extended his influence to the provincial level and was appointed to the governor's council in 1698. He served in the New York Assembly from 1709 to 1711 and again after 1715, when a new patent for Livingston manor gave its freeholders the right to elect their own assemblyman. In 1718 he was chosen Speaker of the assembly, where he worked with Governors Robert Hunter and William Burnet in providing one of the more stable and effective periods of governmental administration in the colony's factious history.

Livingston's special province was Indian affairs; he had begun advising governors as early as 1678 in his role on the board of Indian affairs. In 1699 Livingston presented the governor, Lord Bellomont (Richard Coote), with an extensive report on Anglo-Iroquois relations. The document advocated using the Indian trade—in which Livingston himself had a considerable interest—to foster peace between the Five Nations and their western neighbors, who France was inciting to attack the frontiers of English America. The Iroquois alliance would become a cornerstone of English policy, and in 1700 Livingston undertook a 500-mile diplomatic expedition through Iroquois country. In 1720 he worked with Governor Burnet to suppress a Canadian fur trade that was helping support the French alliance with the western tribes. In 1722 he hosted a conference at Albany on Iroquois affairs involving three broadly imperial-minded governors: Burnet, William Keith of Pennsylvania, and Alexander Spotswood of Virginia. Like their host, all were of Scots ancestry, as the aftermath of the British Union of 1707 drew Scottish elites ever more deeply into imperial affairs.

A consistent factor in Livingston's rise to wealth was his ability to profit from serving the government at a time when governments relied quite regularly on the influence and resources of their well-to-do citizens. During the 1690s he aligned himself politically with Governors Henry Sloughter and Benjamin Fletcher, who were allies of influential imperial officials such as Sir William Blathwayt and Edward Randolph and who obtained for him the profitable office of commissary, with the responsibility of providing food and supplies for the military, a responsibility he would keep for most of his career. In 1695, while in London

attempting to collect money still owed him by the government, he broke with Fletcher and aligned himself with Fletcher's political opponents, who secured for him an appointment as secretary of Indian affairs, a post for which his bilingual skills made him particularly fit and that provided both a salary and commercial advantages. In 1710 he accepted a contract from Governor Hunter, a fellow Scots, to settle and provision several thousand Palatine refugees who had arrived in the colony with Hunter. Even when Livingston quarreled with governors, which the promotion of his own interests frequently caused, they still needed his ability to raise money and to secure supplies for troops at critical moments in strife-ridden times and his general knowledge of Indian affairs.

Livingston retired from the assembly in 1725 and spent his remaining years at Livingston manor, where he is presumed to have died. He was succeeded on the manor, in New York politics, and on the board of Indian affairs by his son Philip, the oldest surviving male among nine children. Their continuing possession of the manor would underwrite the continuing prominence of Livingstons in New York affairs for several generations.

In several respects, Livingston epitomized a particular type of immigrant who appeared in the seventeenth-century English colonial world, one who was well connected in the Protestant communities of Western Europe, experienced in foreign languages and commercial or military affairs, and having an ability to move freely among the different ethnic and commercial enclaves that developed along the increasingly diverse mid-Atlantic frontier. Within the Dutch settlement at Albany, New York, Livingston possessed an almost unique ability to maneuver between that colony's Dutch and English political and commercial circles, which he used to develop a vast landed estate, a substantial trading network, and an impressive personal fortune. Like a number of others from the British peripheries, he was also skillful at negotiating commercial and trade relations with the native peoples of the region. Together those skills made him an important and stabilizing political force in the emerging political order of provincial New York.

• The most significant collection of Livingston papers are in the Livingston-Redmond Manuscripts in the Gilder-Lehrman Collection in the Morgan Library, New York. The best biographical treatment is Lawrence H. Leder, *Robert Livingston, 1654–1728, and the Politics of Colonial New York* (1961). See also Edwin Brockholst Livingston, *The Livingstons of Livingston Manor* (1910), and Cynthia A. Kierner, *Traders and Gentlefolk: The Livingstons of New York, 1675–1790* (1992). His wife's business activities are discussed in Linda Biemer, ed., "Business Letters of Alida Schuyler Livingston, 1680–1726," *New York History* 63 (1982): 183–207. On his fellow Scotsman and New York political ally Robert Hunter, with much on Livingston, see Mary Lou Lustig, *Robert Hunter, 1666–1734: New York's Augustan Statesman* (1983). The best treatment of colonial New York is Michael Kammen, *Coloni-

al New York: A History (1975); on Albany, see Donna Merwick, *Possessing Albany, 1630–1710: The Dutch and English Experiences* (1990).

NED LANDSMAN

LIVINGSTON, Robert R. (27 Nov. 1746–26 Feb. 1813), statesman, and amateur scientist, was born Robert Robert Livingston, Jr., in New York City, the eldest son of ten surviving children of Robert Robert Livingston, a lawyer, merchant, and provincial supreme court judge, and Margaret Beekman. Raised mostly in New York City, where he kept a residence throughout his life, Livingston graduated from King's (Columbia) College in 1765. After studying law with his cousin William Livingston, and Judge William Smith, Jr., he joined the bar probably in 1768. In 1770 he married Mary, the daughter of John Stevens, a great New Jersey landowner for whom the Stevens Institute in Hoboken is named. The couple had two daughters, both of whom married cousins. In fact, the complex cousinage of New York's landed families, to the chief of which—Schuylers, Van Rensselaers, and Van Cortlandts—Livingston was related by blood, as well as the sometimes impenetrable factionalism, not unrelated to clan ties, of New York politics, were the principal settings of Livingston's personal and public life.

After practicing law from 1768 to 1770 with John Jay, a relative by marriage and a friend from King's College, Livingston entered colonial political office in 1773 when Governor William Tryon appointed him recorder of the city of New York. In that post, he served as secretary and member of the mayor's council when it sat as the mayor's court. Because of his sympathy for the developing revolution, signaled by his signing the Articles of Association drawn up by the First Continental Congress, he was removed from the recordership in 1775. Elected that same year to the New York Provincial Congress from Dutchess County, he also became one of twelve New York delegates to the Second Continental Congress, in which he served until 1776 and again from 1779 to 1781.

The year 1775–1776 gave mature and lasting form to Livingston's life. After the death in 1775 of his father, he inherited "Clermont," a vast, tenanted Hudson Valley estate, and the 500,000-acre Hardenburgh patent in the Catskills. He thus became de facto head of the "Lower Manor," or Clermont, branch of the Livingston family. That same year, the deaths of his grandfather and father-in-law brought him the extensive Beekman and Stevens landholdings (roughly 250,000 acres in Dutchess County).

His learning, intelligence, and oratorical skills also made him leader of the critical New York delegation in Congress. Looking on revolution as unfortunate yet necessary, Livingston urged postponement of the vote on Richard Henry Lee's resolutions for independence, whose passage on 2 July 1776 marked the colonies' formal break with Great Britain. His caution was no doubt due to the fact that, without instructions from the provincial Congress, New York's delegation could not vote. Nevertheless, to help cement New York to the cause, Congress named Livingston a member of the committee appointed to draft the Declaration of Independence. The surviving record, however, shows no evidence of his influence either on the committee or on Thomas Jefferson's celebrated text. Having left Philadelphia to participate in the New York Convention, he was not even present to sign the Declaration.

From this time on, Livingston combined service in both the state and national arenas. Even before the Declaration of Independence, he had been a member of a secret committee planning the defense of the Hudson, and of the New York Committee of Safety. He also served in the 1777 convention that wrote a constitution for the state. Largely the work of John Jay, whom he closely advised, the constitution, much to Livingston's liking, left intact much of the old system of elite government. Livingston is usually credited with proposing its most distinctive feature, the Council of Revision, a small group of officials collectively empowered to veto legislation. The same constitutional convention elected Livingston chancellor of the state and one of fifteen members of the Council of Safety that temporarily governed New York State. As chancellor, by which title Livingston has ever since been known, he not only sat on the Council of Revision but was chief judge of the state's court of equity. Because of the absence of any court records from his chancellorship, however, it is not possible to evaluate his jurisprudence.

During the American Revolution, Livingston suffered directly. The British, marching through the Hudson Valley in 1777, burned Clermont and his own family's residence, "Belvedere" (both of which he subsequently rebuilt); and Livingston's finances became seriously straitened despite his two official salaries. A prohibition against concurrent service in state and national offices not yet in force, the chancellor replaced Jay in the Continental Congress in 1779 while also serving in the New York legislature for the 1779–1780 term. Perhaps because he resented the taxes levied by Governor George Clinton's administration, he worked strenuously to increase congressional power, to enact duties on imports and exports, and to strengthen the revolutionary nation's military command and administrative structure. He was also instrumental in 1779 in settling disputes over New York's eastern and western boundaries.

After ratification in 1781 of the Articles of Confederation, Congress elected Livingston secretary of foreign affairs. A strong nationalist, he laid early claim to sole American control of the Mississippi, an issue that would vex the nation until the Louisiana Purchase of 1803, which he negotiated. Yet Livingston had little directly to do with the epochal 1783 Treaty of Peace, some of whose provisions violated his instructions to its American negotiators, resident in Paris, to negotiate only with the advice and consent of the French. In fact, his distress over their conduct widened a breach with Jay, one of the treaty's negotiators, which, begun in envy over Jay's election as president of Congress in

1778 and appointment as minister plenipotentiary to Spain in 1779, never healed. It no doubt contributed to Livingston's subsequent opposition to the Federalist party, of which Jay became a leading member.

After resigning as secretary in 1783, Livingston served briefly as a member of the Temporary Council that governed New York City after its evacuation by the British. He then returned in 1784 for another year in the New York legislature and in Congress, which appointed him a commissioner to settle the boundary dispute, finally resolved in 1786, between Massachusetts and New York. Elected to represent New York County in 1788 at the convention that met in Poughkeepsie to debate ratification of the new federal constitution, Livingston was among the leading figures who, arguing for government by the "disinterested" gentry, secured ratification, by a narrow vote of 30 to 27. By then one of the leading figures of state and nation, in 1789 as chancellor he administered the presidential oath of office to George Washington, on the steps of Federal Hall in New York, the nation's temporary capital.

A nationalist opposed to the antifederalism of Governor Clinton, Livingston had to seek appointive office, if it was to be his, at the national level. Yet he became quickly estranged from Washington, who named him neither chief justice nor treasury secretary, both of which positions he sought. Out of deep distrust of speculation, he also opposed Alexander Hamilton's plan to assume the state's revolutionary war debts, most of which seemed to have fallen into speculators' hands. Furthermore, believing that land, not commerce, was the source of wealth and credit, his views were consonant with those of Jefferson and the emerging Democratic-Republican opposition.

For these reasons then, soon after the new government began operations, Livingston was siding politically against Hamilton, Philip Schuyler, and most of his Livingston relatives, with some of whom he was then involved in a long dispute over the ownership of a gristmill on family lands. He sympathized early with the French Revolution, even to the point of supporting the outfitting of French privateers in American ports. He also publicly opposed the Jay Treaty with Great Britain, writing in 1795 as "Cato" in the New York *Argus* against it. When Washington offered him the ministry to France, he declined, privately citing differences with the administration. Apparently not done with Jay, Livingston accepted nomination to oppose him for governor in 1798. Yet, not making any effort to win, perhaps because those who nominated him were also backing his old political enemy (and kinsman) Stephen van Rensselaer for lieutenant governor, he lost resoundingly.

Following Jefferson's election to the presidency in 1801, Livingston refused the post of navy secretary but agreed to succeed Gouverneur Morris as minister to France, for which he resigned the chancellorship. The principal issue between the two nations concerned control of the Mississippi and by implication possession of Louisiana and the Floridas. Spain was known by then to have retroceded Louisiana secretly to France in 1801; the Floridas' status was unclear. Livingston was instructed to secure either permanent trading rights at New Orleans or possession of another port on the Mississippi. Imperturbable and artful, playing on French fears of British intentions in North America and of an American attack on New Orleans, and dealing firmly with Napoleon and Talleyrand, Livingston took the lead in suggesting the cession of all of Louisiana to the United States. Joined by James Monroe, Livingston won France's agreement to sell the young republic the entire Louisiana Territory for $15 million, which exceeded their instructions. The Purchase, which doubled the nation's territorial extent, was arguably the greatest real estate transaction in history. Livingston termed it "the noblest work of our lives" (Dangerfield, p. 376).

Unfortunately for his reputation, the Louisiana Purchase did not settle the Florida issue, which was not resolved until 1819; and the claims commission established by it caused severe difficulties. Moreover, Livingston's unsuccessful effort to conceal his backdating of the agreement to hide Monroe's contribution embarrassed him and contributed to his being passed over as Republican candidate for governor when he resigned his ministerial post in 1804.

Livingston maintained a lifelong involvement in agricultural experimentation and other amateur, though serious, "projecting," applying his innovations in farming and Merino sheep culture to his extensive acreage. Known throughout the Anglo-American world for his projects, in 1793 Livingston founded with others the New York Society for the Promotion of Agriculture, Manufactures, and the Useful Arts, of which he was elected first president and in whose *Transactions* he wrote of his many endeavors. In 1809 he published an *Essay on Sheep*. In 1801–1802, he was founding president of the American Academy of Fine Arts, which later became part of the National Academy of Design.

In 1797 Livingston joined Nicholas Roosevelt and his brother-in-law John Stevens in a partnership to develop steam navigation. Being prevented from obtaining a British steam engine but holding a legislative monopoly grant that enhanced their potential rewards, the partners built their own steam engine. They got a ship under power in 1798, although its defects were such as to make the continuance of this initial endeavor impracticable. By 1802, however, Livingston agreed to back Robert Fulton, whom he had met in Paris and supported in his experiments on the Seine, in building another Hudson steamship. This *North River Steamboat* (later known as the *Clermont*) made its maiden voyage north from New York to Albany in 1807, thus inaugurating regularly scheduled sailings and opening a new era in American transportation, commerce, and travel. Despite his monopoly of steamboating on the Mississippi as well as on the Hudson (a monopoly broken only by the Supreme Court's 1824 decision in *Gibbons v. Ogden*), Livingston gained little from his efforts, which troubled him financially until shortly before his death at Clermont.

A republican aristocrat, a revolutionary who improved his land with other's labor, and an ambitious leisure grandee, Livingston embodied the contradictions of the new nation. Neither a feudal baron exploiting his domains and tenants, nor a fully modern capitalist, he was something in between: an entrepreneurial agrarian projector who improved, rather than enlarged, his landholdings, who merchandised his products, and who seriously pursued and financed scientific and technological innovation. Through his association with the two great international triumphs of the young republic, Livingston deserves to be ranked among the nation's foremost diplomats, a nationalist whose endeavors helped create a new continental power among the nations of the world.

• The principal collection of Livingston papers is in the New-York Historical Society. The best biography of Livingston is George Dangerfield, *Chancellor Robert R. Livingston of New York, 1746–1813* (1960). A scholarly analysis of the history of the Livingston family in the eighteenth century is Cynthia A. Kierner, *Traders and Gentlefolk: The Livingstons of New York, 1675–1790* (1992). Two works that investigate the economic and social context of the Livingston landholdings are David Maldwyn Ellis, *Landlords and Farmers in the Hudson-Mohawk Region, 1790–1850* (1946), and, especially, Sung Bok Kim, *Landlord and Tenant in Colonial New York, 1664–1775* (1978). On Livingston's formative contributions to the New York ratifying convention, see Linda Grant DePauw, *The Eleventh Pillar: New York State and the Federal Constitution* (1966). The tangled politics of New York in the early nation, in which Livingston played such a major role, is fully explored in Alfred F. Young, *The Democratic Republicans of New York: The Origins, 1763–1797* (1967).

JAMES M. BANNER, JR.

LIVINGSTON, Robert Robert (Aug. 1718–9 Dec. 1775), landowner, attorney, and politician, was born in New York, the only son and heir of Robert Livingston and Margaret Howarden. His father, a younger son of manor lord Robert Livingston, was given a portion of land, called "Clermont," at the southern end of Livingston Manor. In 1742 Livingston married Margaret Beekman, the heir of Colonel Henry Beekman of Rhinebeck and Janet Livingston, a daughter of the first manor lord. The couple had nine children.

A dual inheritance of more than 100,000 acres made Livingston one of the most influential landowners in New York. Trained as an attorney, by 1742 he had established a practice in New York City and was active in city affairs. In 1754 Robert Livingston and other members of the Livingston family raised funds to establish the first circulating library in New York. In 1755 Livingston was named a commissioner to settle a boundary dispute with Massachusetts. Earlier that decade boundary uncertainty led to riots as New York tenant farmers sought to buy the land they farmed from Massachusetts. The New York landlords insisted the land was theirs, bought by direct purchase from the Indians. The tenants' refusal to accept that ownership led to extensive rioting on Livingston and other New York manors.

Like most members of his family, Livingston was also active in the province's politics. In 1756 he was named to the council by Governor Sir Thomas Hardy but was not confirmed by the royal government. Two years later the Livingstons tried to wrest control of the assembly from the influential DeLancey family by using the press as their principal tool to swing New York's voters to their candidates. Livingston was one of the family's most effective propagandists. Calling attention to Lieutenant Governor James DeLancey's lack of support for the ongoing French and Indian War, the Livingstons successfully weakened support for the DeLanceys. Livingston ran for and won an assembly seat from Dutchess County. Three other members of the Livingston family won elections that year, shifting the balance of power to their family for the next decade. In 1759 Livingston's prestige, and his income, increased when he was named a judge on the vice admiralty court.

In the assembly Livingston and other representatives continued their struggle to diminish the power of the royal prerogative as personified in the executive. These efforts accelerated following the 1760 death of Lieutenant Governor DeLancey when senior councillor Cadwallader Colden became acting governor. That same year George II died. As was customary, the province's judges resigned with the expectation that the governor would reappoint them with lifelong commissions, as was the practice in both England and New York. Colden reappointed them but, following the letter of his instructions, offered the judges commissions to serve at the king's pleasure, subject to dismissal. Irritated by this stipulation and by Colden's refusal to offer the chief justiceship of New York to Livingston ally William Smith, Sr., Livingston and other members of his family mobilized a massive propaganda campaign against Colden's attack on local privilege.

The campaign enjoyed temporary success; Colden found it impossible to get a New York attorney to serve on the supreme court. Few judges were willing to accept the diminished commissions, and the colony's courts remained closed. The situation changed with the 1761 arrival of Governor Robert Monckton, who allied with the Livingston family. Monckton, like Colden, appointed judges with untenured commissions, which were now accepted by the same men who had previously rejected them, as much a reflection of the scorn they held for Colden as it was their acceptance of the inevitable under Monckton. In 1763 Livingston was offered and accepted a post on the supreme court.

When Colden resumed the governorship following Monckton's recall in 1763, Livingston and other members of his family quickly found reason to differ with the governor over the *Forsey v. Cunningham* appeal. Cunningham, ordered to pay damages of £1,500 to Forsey, immediately asked his attorneys to appeal the verdict, contrary to English custom. The practice in both England and its colonies dictated that civil suits could be heard by the appeals court only in cases of error. Colden, the chief appellate judge, wanted to hear the appeal despite the advice of his council and the supreme court judges, including Livingston. At stake, the Livingstons pointed out, was the right of trial by jury. Colden's stance was later rejected by the attorney and solicitor generals in England.

Constitutional principles were again cited in 1765 by Livingston and other opponents of the Stamp Act, scheduled to go into effect on 1 November. Livingston was the chairman of New York's Committee of Correspondence, and as a member of the Stamp Act Congress he drafted petitions to the king and led debates protesting the act. Like most members of New York's elite, he was appalled by the riots that racked the colony for two days when the Stamp Act was to go into effect. With family member James Duane, Livingston walked New York's streets during the riots trying unsuccessfully to disband the lower-class mobs. In the spring of 1766, the riots spread to tenant farmers, still discontented at their inferior status. The uncertain border caused several tenants to buy from Massachusetts, land New York manor lords considered theirs. Tenants refused to pay rents or taxes to New York landlords who used British regular soldiers and the courts to pacify rebels. In 1767 and 1773 Livingston was again named to committees to settle the boundary dispute.

The increasing determination of the lower classes to think and act for themselves, as evidenced by the Stamp Act and tenant riots, along with rising alienation against the Livingstons, caused Robert Livingston and other members of his family to lose their assembly seats in 1768. Running for Dutchess County, he was soundly defeated because discontented tenants, brutally suppressed in the land riots of 1766, refused to vote for him.

Despite his ouster, Livingston remained active in the colony's affairs. In April 1768 he was named to the council by Governor Sir Henry Moore but was again rejected by the royal government. In 1769 Livingston, a member of the Church of England, defended his church against attacks by members of his own family. Most of the Livingston family, with the notable exception of Robert Livingston, were members of the Dutch Reformed or Presbyterian churches. Nonconformists feared that the intent of the British ministry was to deprive them of religious toleration, thereby excluding them from political office. The controversy erupted over a letter written by John Ewer, bishop of Landaff, who criticized Americans for opposing a resident bishop. Landaff was answered by Livingston's cousin, William Livingston, an ardent Presbyterian. In 1769 Robert R. Livingston wrote in defense of the Church of England.

Also in 1769 Livingston ran again for and won an assembly seat as a candidate for Livingston Manor. To prevent him from serving, the assembly, now under the control of the rival DeLancey family, quickly passed a bill excluding supreme court judges from that body. Livingston ran and was elected five more times,

but the assembly continued to refuse to let him serve. Livingston appealed the decision to authorities in England, who found no precedent for the actions of the New York assembly in English law. Their order to the assembly to permit Livingston to take his seat was ignored. Livingston died just months before independence from Great Britain was declared.

Robert R. Livingston made significant contributions to American colonial society. He embodied Whig principles of republican government. Even though he feared the rule of the masses, he recognized and encouraged rising republican tendencies. He took an active part in informing the lower classes of political events and in instructing them of their rights. In 1769, despite his election defeat the previous year at the hands of tenant farmers, Livingston supported the ballot bill, which would guarantee a secret vote rather than the customary oral ballot in the presence of the candidates. The bill was narrowly defeated by the DeLancey-controlled assembly. While determined to protect traditional and natural rights of New Yorkers, Livingston's primary concern was the economic well-being of the colony, and that concern underlay much of his opposition to British tax measures in the 1760s and 1770s.

• Correspondence and records for Robert R. Livingston and the Livingston family are included in the Schuyler papers and Yates papers, New York Public Library; Livingston papers, Museum of the City of New York; Livingston-Redmond papers, Franklin Delano Roosevelt Library, Hyde Park, N.Y.; Thomas Gage Papers, William L. Clements Library, University of Michigan; and the Livingston Account Book, Clermont, 1761–1781, 1772–1784, Robert R. Livingston Collection, Uncatalogued Livingston Manuscripts, James Duane Papers, 1752–1796, New-York Historical Society.

Information about Robert Livingston and the Livingston family can be found in various published sources, including E. B. O'Callaghan and B. Fernow, eds., *Documents Relative to the Colonial History of the State of New-York* (14 vols., 1853–1887); O'Callaghan, ed., *Documentary History of the State of New York* (4 vols., 1849–1851); *Journal of the Votes and Proceedings of the General Assembly of the Colony of New York, 1691–1765* (2 vols., 1764–1766); *Journal of the Votes and Proceedings of the General Assembly of the Colony of New York, from 1766 to 1776* (1820); *Journal of the Legislative Council of the Colony of New-York, 1691–1765* (2 vols., 1910); "The Letters and Papers of Cadwallader Colden," New-York Historical Society, *Collections* (1918–1937); and William Smith, Jr., *Historical Memoirs*, ed. William H. W. Sabine (1956).

For a contemporary history see Smith, *History of the Province of New York*, ed. Michael Kammen (2 vols., 1972). On Livingston's attempts to win an assembly seat, see Roger Champagne, "Family Politics versus Constitutional Principles: The New York Assembly Elections of 1768 and 1769," *William and Mary Quarterly* 20 (1963): 57–79.

For studies of New York and the Livingston family see Alice M. Keys, *Cadwallader Colden: A Representative Eighteenth Century Official* (1906); Sung Bok Kim, *Landlord and Tenant in Colonial New York: Manorial Society, 1664–1775* (1978); Lawrence H. Leder, *Robert Livingston (1654–1728) and the Politics of Colonial New York* (1961); Irving Mark, *Agrarian*

Conflicts in Colonial New York, 1711–1775 (1940); and Sean Wilentz, *Chants Democratic: New York City and the Rise of the American Working Class, 1788–1850* (1984).

MARY LOU LUSTIG

LIVINGSTON, William (Nov. 1723–25 July 1790), colonial politician, governor of New Jersey, and political satirist, was born in Albany, New York, the son of Philip Livingston, the second lord of Livingston Manor, and Catherine Van Brugh. As the scion of an elite New York clan, he headed the family faction that successfully challenged the rival DeLancey family for dominance in the colony. Rarely holding public office himself, Livingston nevertheless masterminded his faction's protracted battles with the DeLanceys. His success rested in part on his abilities with the pen. He wrote on the model provided by the English Whig pamphleteers, and his essays in the *Independent Reflector* in the 1750s and 1760s emulated, among others, those of Joseph Addison and Richard Steele. Livingston's penchant for political intrigue behind the legislative scenes was augmented immeasurably by his barbed assaults on the DeLanceys written under the pseudonyms of "American Whig," "Sentinel," and "Watch Tower." Livingston, who had graduated from Yale in 1741, also vociferously defended colonial American religious liberties, emerging as a major Presbyterian reformer advocating religious pluralism. This posture very early in his political career placed him at odds with the English Anglican establishment and helped him to move into the ranks of revolutionary Whigs.

Continuing involvement in the politics of prerevolutionary New York, however, was both distracting and unnerving to Livingston, who was by nature introverted. The emotional, highly charged personalized character of New York politics drained him, and in 1770 he prepared to leave both mainstream politics and his active law practice and retire to New Jersey. He made the move in 1772 and built "Liberty Hall," a magnificent estate in Elizabethtown that still stands.

A man of Livingston's prominence, elite status, and political stature could not long escape the blandishments of New Jersey's budding revolutionary leaders. Livingston brought with him a reputation as a persistent critic of the mother country's heavy economic and political hand. In the 1770s he came to reject British efforts to transform the American colonies into true economic and political subordinates within the empire.

Livingston was thus drawn into the web of revolutionary politics that spread across provincial New Jersey before 1776. One Whig leader put it succinctly, asking his compatriots to get "Mr. L" involved by informing him that "it is his duty." "If the trifling disputes of the Colony of New York were capable of Rousing him, then certainly the present times should." Livingston went to New Jersey with political pedigree in hand, and the familiar revolutionary issues proved irresistible to him.

Livingston was elected to the first and second Continental Congresses (1774–1776). He went on to command the East Jersey militia until elected governor of the new state, serving during its most turbulent years, 1776–1790. He was also a delegate to the federal Constitutional Convention in 1787. As governor of a state that from 1776 to 1781 was a major battleground of the war, he emerged as the executive on whom George Washington most relied. Livingston came to harbor a deep and visceral hatred of Loyalists, whose numbers and military operations posed a real civil threat in New Jersey. The governor's jaundiced reaction undermined his otherwise deep commitment to due process and his remarkable concern for the social and economic welfare of his constituents.

Livingston was by nature and education a man of conservative political leanings, forced into the personally distasteful role of flamboyant revolutionary. Indeed, throughout the war he was a rebel with a price on his head. Exiled New Jersey Loyalists several times tried to arrange his assassination by offering a reward for his murder. This threat caused the governor to stay continuously on the move for five years; he avoided spending more than a week in one place and rarely passed a night at Liberty Hall. Moving from town to town and tavern to tavern brought Livingston into close contact with his constituents: farmers, artisans, laborers, and even slaves. This continuous proximity resulted in a communion between Livingston and the populace that was as remarkable as it was improbable. It sensitized him to their needs and fears in ways that were rare to the eighteenth-century landed gentry. He became an early and vigorous opponent of slavery, a strong supporter of the yeoman tradition, and even slightly aware of the civil disabilities from which women suffered (evident more in the raising of his five daughters than in public policy). Governor Livingston made a real effort to redistribute Loyalist land by means of a strong pioneering confiscation act, a reform that did not work well in practice, but was intended by the governor to expand New Jersey's social revolution.

As a result of all these factors, Livingston's popularity was astounding. Adhering to the wishes of his personal constituency, the deeply divided New Jersey legislature reelected him annually for a decade and a half, usually with near unanimity. A part of that popularity was also rooted in the common knowledge that he was a forceful propagandist for the revolutionary, and later the Federalist, cause. Historians rank only Thomas Paine as a more influential American polemicist during the generation in which the country achieved independence. He early took on a variety of sacred cows, launching some of the most telling anonymous assaults on George III, his advisers, and his generals. In the growing American press, he also went on to disparage English military prowess generally, fiercely attack Loyalists, and condemn American wartime avarice.

In essays, written under his various pseudonyms, Livingston charted a visionary republican future for the new nation that rested on agrarian virtue combined with growing commerce and westward expansion. During the war the guises under which he wrote included that of a French count visiting America ("De-

Lisle"), a Pennsylvania Dutch farmer ("Adolphus"), a New Jersey gentryman ("Hortentius"), and New Jersey commoners (for example, "Cato" and "Camillus"). On occasion he would publish under the names of women, writing, for example, as "Belinda." After the Revolution he emerged as an important proponent of Federalist reform and an implacable enemy of antifederalism, particularly in multiple essays under the names "Primitive Whig" and "Scipio." In all, Livingston left behind at his death more than a hundred propaganda pieces written under at least twenty pseudonyms; they were published and republished for a generation in a score of American newspapers and periodicals. In about 1745 he had married M. Susannah French; they had thirteen children. Livingston died at his Liberty Hall estate.

Livingston's reputation among contemporaries at his death (during his fourteenth term as governor) was much higher than it would be two hundred years later, but he deserves to be remembered as one of the most accomplished among the second rank of founding fathers. No less importantly, he remains an articulate early interpreter of the new American republic he helped to found.

• The most comprehensive source for Livingston is *The Papers of William Livingston*, ed. Carl E. Prince et al. (5 vols., 1979–1988), also available on microfilm. The published volumes contain essays dealing with all the various phases of Livingston's long life and career, as well as a comprehensive collection of extant Livingston documents, exclusively limited to his New Jersey years. The best source for his life and career in New York is Milton M. Klein, ed., *The Independent Reflector* (1963). This publication has a fine introductory essay; Klein as well has published extensively on Livingston's New York years in a variety of essays. Also worthy of note for his New Jersey period is the extended interpretation of Livingston's role in the confederation era found in Richard P. McCormick, *Experiment in Independence: New Jersey in the Critical Period, 1781–1789* (1950).

CARL E. PRINCE

LIVINGSTONE, Belle (20 Jan. 1875?–7 Feb. 1957), showgirl, adventuress, and Prohibition Era saloonkeeper, was a foundling, purportedly discovered under a clump of sunflowers in Emporia, Kansas, in the summer of 1875 at approximately six months of age. She was adopted by newspaperman John Ramsey Graham and his wife, Anne M. Likly, and they named her Isabelle Graham.

Even Livingstone admitted that the sunflower story sounded a bit far-fetched. "Of course, I bedeviled my foster parents with questions," she wrote in her memoirs. "But they always clung to the sunflower story, and since it's a good story I may as well cling to it too." She had a conventional upbringing in Emporia. Her father was the editor and co-owner of the *Emporia News*, and he later founded the *Emporia Gazette*. When speculative business ventures caused him to lose the *Gazette*, he took a job with the *Chicago Dispatch*, and the family moved to Chicago. After her

family's move, Livingstone attended a convent school in Oldenburg, Indiana.

After she left school, Livingstone frequently attended theatrical productions with her father. She became stage-struck and began making audition rounds. She eventually landed a job in the chorus of the second road company of the comic opera *Wang* and left home on the sly, knowing that her parents would never give her permission.

Livingstone's father followed her to the company's first stop, Saginaw, Michigan, and told her that he and her mother would never allow their unmarried daughter to live away from home. She circumvented that edict by asking a newfound acquaintance, Chicago-based paint salesman Richard Wherry, to marry her. After a ceremony in Saginaw, Livingstone and Wherry went their separate ways. To avoid embarrassing her family, Livingstone adopted the stage name of Belle Livingstone, after missionary-explorer David Livingstone.

Livingstone appeared as a member of the chorus in several stage productions, settled in New York, and was dubbed "the girl with the poetic legs." She also showed a flair for making herself known. Among her acquaintances were Diamond Jim Brady and Theodore Roosevelt. Then, legend has it, her in-name-only husband died, and Livingstone unexpectedly inherited $150,000 from his estate. According to Livingstone's memoirs, Wherry had reluctantly divorced her a year earlier, which makes the unexpected inheritance seem even more unlikely. Whatever the true story, Livingstone did receive enough of a windfall to set sail for Europe in the summer of 1897. She settled in London, where she used her looks, her money, and the novelty of her forthright American ways to establish herself in London society. It was during her years in London that she coined the phrase "Spend it while you've got it," a dictum that she followed throughout her life.

In 1902, after being swindled with forged stock certificates and discovering that her investments in an Australian mine were worthless, Livingstone found herself broke. She bet friends £5,000 that she could make her way around the world on nothing more than a £5 note. Traveling east, she got as far as Japan. In March 1903, in Yokohama, she married Count Florentino Ghiberti Laltazzi, an Italian diplomat; they had one daughter. After their marriage, they headed in opposite directions, she to the United States to visit her family, he to Europe to resume his diplomatic duties. He died shortly thereafter in St. Petersburg, Russia. When Livingstone returned to Europe, she learned that his family had had their marriage declared invalid.

To support herself, Livingstone published her first volume of memoirs, *Letters of a Bohemian* (1906). In 1906 she married an American millionaire, Edward Mohler of Cleveland, Ohio. They lived in Paris and had a son. She divorced Mohler in 1911 and married Walter James Hutchins, a British engineer, in 1912. They lived in Paris, and Livingstone became a prominent hostess, noted for ignoring social barriers. It was during this period that a journalist dubbed her "the most dangerous woman in Europe."

In 1923 Livingstone learned that she had gone through virtually all of Hutchins's money. They separated with vague plans to resume their marriage once they had recovered financially. In 1925 Livingstone was paid well by *Cosmopolitan* magazine for a series of memoirs that were the basis of her second book, *Belle of Bohemia* (1927), and the marriage temporarily resumed, but they once again found themselves broke in 1927 and separated again. They were still separated when Hutchins died some five years later.

In 1927 Livingstone returned to the United States after thirty years abroad. She declared New York dull and announced an antidote: she would open a salon where luminaries could meet. Her salon proved to be a thinly disguised speakeasy. One Man House, membership for which cost $200, opened shortly after her return to New York and failed in 1928. A new "salon," the Silver Room, opened in the fall of 1929. By April 1930 Livingstone had been arrested three times in three months for violating the Volstead Act, which prohibited the sale, manufacture, and transportation of alcoholic beverages, and the colorful Livingstone's flip attitude and ability to turn a phrase had made her a newspaper favorite. Throughout 1930 and into 1931, federal agents would raid her saloons, rounds of court appearances would begin, and Livingstone would settle into another location. In 1931, however, she spent thirty days in prison.

After filing for bankruptcy, Livingstone left New York and moved to Reno, Nevada. Problems with liquor deliveries put an end to that venture, and she had subsequent short-lived clubs in Dallas, San Francisco, Phoenix, and East Hampton, New York. "Those who operate outside the law of the land find themselves perforce under the law of the jungle, where the strong prey on the weak and the fittest survive," she wrote in her final memoir, *Belle Out of Order* (1959). "The idea was finally being borne in upon me that perhaps I was not one of the fittest."

The repeal of Prohibition put an end to her career as saloon hostess and headline grabber. Her last nightclub, the Reno, opened in New York City in December 1934 and closed ten days later. After that, she lived modestly in a small New York City apartment and worked on her final memoirs, which were published posthumously. She suffered a heart attack in 1949, and after a second heart attack in 1955 she moved to a nursing home in the Bronx, where she died.

Belle Livingstone is one of those historical curiosities—a woman undeniably famous in her own era but for reasons subsequent generations cannot quite fathom. Throughout her life, Livingstone showed a knack for keeping her name in the limelight. Her ability to embellish, however, has made it difficult to ascertain what parts of the Livingstone legend are fact and what parts are fiction.

• Although they are to be approached with some skepticism, Livingstone's memoirs are the best sources on her life. Livingstone's Prohibition battles were covered thoroughly by all the New York City newspapers during 1930–1931. Useful obituaries appear in the *New York Times* and the *New York Herald Tribune*, both 8 Feb. 1957.

LYNN HOOGENBOOM

LIVINGSTONE, Mary (22 June 1908–30 June 1983), wife and longtime collaborator of radio and television comedian Jack Benny, was born Sadya Marks in Seattle, Washington, the daughter of David Marks, a prosperous scrap metal dealer, and Ester (maiden name unknown). Raised in Vancouver, British Columbia, Canada, she first met Jack Benny there in 1921 or 1922 when Benny, already an experienced vaudevillian, played at the Orpheum Theatre in Vancouver. Zeppo Marx took Benny to the home of David Marks, where they enjoyed a quiet and comfortable gathering. Marks's youngest daughter, Sadie (her name was anglicized), was very impressed by this comedian who played a violin as part of his act. By her own testimony she made up her mind that she would grow up and marry Jack Benny someday. Benny himself took no notice of the young teenager and was unreceptive when she wanted to perform on the violin—he did not like the idea of auditioning girl violinists.

The paths of Jack Benny and Sadie Marks did not cross again for a number of years, not until after she had graduated from King George High School in Vancouver. She encountered him once in San Francisco after her family moved there, but Benny did not recognize the young woman and brushed right by her. In 1926, however, the two met again in Los Angeles, where Marks was selling hosiery in the May Company Department Store. This time Benny was smitten (although he did not remember that he had met her some years before in Vancouver; she remembered very well). He made regular and preposterous excuses to buy silk stockings at Marks's counter; the two dated and were eventually married on 14 January 1927. By her own account, Sadie Marks had no desire to be anything other than the wife of Jack Benny, and although she filled in once or twice for some missing performer in his vaudeville act, she was paralyzed by stage fright and remained determined not to go into show business.

Nonetheless, she was eventually to play a major role in Benny's career. Like some other successful vaudevillians, Benny was reluctant to go into radio: he believed that this new form was a flash in the pan and that people would get tired of it when the novelty wore off. After several early stabs at the medium he got his own show in 1932. At first he experimented with several on-the-air personae (he tried for a time being a woman chaser and a drunk); it was only with the passage of time that he worked up the image of the vain 39-year-old skinflint, a routine that seemed to fit his talents to perfection.

Benny's wife had no role in the early shows and sought none. She got in by accident one day. In 1933 the writers of Benny's program developed a skit involving a seventeen-year-old girl from Plainfield, New Jersey, who was supposed to be president of the Jack Benny Fan Club there—a girl named Mary Livingstone. The skit involved having the girl on the program during a visit to California, so the NBC casting office sent over an actress good at doing the voices of teenage girls. But when the program went on the air the actress did not show up, so the part was read by Benny's wife. She did so well with this impersonation that the part was written into the following week's show, after which the character was dropped. The following year she and Benny adopted a two-week-old girl, their only child.

Following the disappearance of "Mary Livingstone," a multitude of letters were received at the studio asking, "What happened to that cute little Mary Livingstone from Plainfield, New Jersey? Couldn't you get her back?" To answer these demands, "Mary Livingstone" was restored with Mrs. Jack Benny playing the role. She turned out to be an ideal radio actress, with very distinctive voice qualities, and remained a regular on the "Jack Benny Show" as long as it was on the radio. With the passage of time she played Benny's secretary or girlfriend (the nature of their relationship was never made explicit), and in the show's credits both the actress and her character were known as Mary Livingstone. Indeed, so well identified were the two that Sadie Marks Benny eventually had her name changed legally to Mary Livingstone.

Livingstone turned out to be a very gifted comedian in her own right. She did not have to play the "dizzy dame" character that was typical of the wives of most radio comedians who had come over from vaudeville, especially the wives of George Burns (Gracie Allen) and Fred Allen (Portland Hoffa). Livingstone was a practical, no-nonsense woman with a delicious sense of humor, always able to puncture Benny's vanity and other peculiar character traits in a jeering but totally good-natured way. She had a wonderful sense of merriment in her voice and a laugh that Benny himself described as being "like the music of a rippling arpeggio of silvery notes." Hers was one of the great voices of radio and always immediately recognizable to listeners.

When Benny moved over into television, Livingstone only occasionally appeared on his show. She did not like the new medium and eventually retired. However, she remained a potent force in the Benny comic style. Livingstone was a much more important element in the success of the "Jack Benny Show" than might be assumed by those who remember the limited exposure given to her on-air character. She was a very good judge of material that fitted her husband, sat in on conferences with the writers, and, like Benny himself, was a superlative comedy "editor." Few shows in either radio or television were as well crafted and polished as the "Jack Benny Show," and much of this was due to the keen perception and eternal vigilance of Mary Livingstone. She died in Halmby Hills, California.

• Autobiographical details are in Mary Livingstone, *Jack Benny* (1978). There are no biographies of Livingstone herself, but several biographies of Jack Benny exist. Benny once attempted an autobiography that he intended to call "I Always Wore Shoes," but it was never published. (The significance of the title was the desire to point out that he did not grow up in poverty, as was rumored, but rather in middle-class comfort.) Joan Benny, the adopted daughter of Jack Benny and Mary Livingstone, unearthed this manuscript and published it along with extensive memories of her own in a book entitled *Sunday Nights at Seven* (1990). This book contains a great deal of information about the life and character of Mary Livingstone from both a husband's and a daughter's perspective. See also Mary Unterbrink, *Funny Women: American Comediennes* (1987). For a further idea of the contribution of Mary Livingstone to the "Jack Benny Show," see *The Jack Benny Show* (1977) by Milt Josefsberg, a longtime writer on the program. An obituary is in the *New York Times*, 1 July 1983.

GEORGE H. DOUGLAS

LLEWELLYN, Karl Nickerson (22 May 1893–13 Feb. 1962), legal theorist and law reformer, was born in Seattle, Washington, the son of William Henry Llewellyn, a businessman of Welsh ancestry, and Janet George, an ardent Congregationalist and late-Victorian reformer. His mother marched for woman suffrage and for Prohibition, and Llewellyn inherited her vigor and intelligence. Not long after Llewellyn's birth, his family moved to Brooklyn, where he attended Boys' High School. When Llewellyn was sixteen, his father decided his son would benefit from a period in Germany. He was enrolled in the Realgymnasium at Schwerin in Mecklenburg, where he became fully bilingual and was able later in life to publish in both English and German.

Llewellyn completed his secondary education in 1911, briefly attended the University of Lausanne, and in the fall of 1911 entered Yale College. He was an honors student and, despite his slight physical stature, avidly took up boxing. In 1914 he left Yale and studied for four months at the Sorbonne. When World War I began, the fondness Llewellyn had developed in Mecklenburg for German culture and discipline led him to join the German army. As a member of the Seventy-eighth Prussian Infantry, he was wounded near Ypres and spent three months in a military hospital. In February 1915 he was awarded the Iron Cross.

When Llewellyn returned to the United States in 1915, he completed his studies at Yale College and enrolled at the Yale Law School. He complained that the war had deprived the school of many superior students, and he was friendlier not with his classmates but with his instructors, in particular Arthur Corbin and Wesley Hohfeld. Earning an LL.B. in 1918 and a J.D. in 1920, he graduated near the top of his class and served as editor in chief of the *Yale Law Journal*. He was invited to join the faculty on a part-time basis to teach commercial law and jurisprudence, subjects that would dominate throughout his subsequent career. He also offered a course in the Department of Anthropology and Sociology named "Law in Society."

Llewellyn worked during the early 1920s in the legal department of the National City Bank in New York City and in the Wall Street law firm of Shearman and Sterling. In 1924 he married Elizabeth Sanford. For ten years the Yale Law School held open an offer for him to join its faculty on a full-time basis, but accommodating the preferences of his wife, Llewellyn in 1924 became a visiting lecturer at Columbia Law School and the following year became a full-time associate professor there.

At Columbia, Llewellyn was on the losing side in an internal power struggle concerning the designation of a new dean in 1928. He stayed on nevertheless, saying the school needed him now more than ever. Faculty colleagues and students apparently were of two minds about him. Some considered him brash, insensitive, and unpredictable; others found him spirited, brilliant, and creative. A later faculty colleague probably captured Llewellyn best when he described him as an "extraordinary piece of radioactive material."

In the years 1929–1930 Llewellyn rose dramatically from the ranks of American law professors to the very top of his profession. He was appointed the first Betts Professor of Jurisprudence at Columbia, and he published in rapid succession two much-discussed volumes, *Cases and Materials in the Law of Sales* (1930) and *The Bramble Bush* (1930).

Almost 1,100 pages in length, *Cases and Materials in the Law of Sales* was a groundbreaking text that eschewed the conceptualism and emphasis on general principles that had previously reigned in the subject area. Llewellyn proffered instead historical materials, detailed analysis, and the digests of literally hundreds of often contradictory cases. His goal was to explode the bogus unity of sales law.

The Bramble Bush grew out of a series of lectures Llewellyn gave to first-year students. His shortest but most-read work, the volume warned against teaching and studying law as if it were merely a matter of established rules. Rules, or formal prescriptions and proscriptions of the state, could be important in predicting what a judge would do, but he added, "That is all their importance, except as pretty playthings." To emphasize rules above all else ran the risk of "developing the technician at the cost of the whole man."

The two volumes and a dozen articles, including "A Realistic Jurisprudence: The Next Step" in the *Columbia Law Review* (1930), established Llewellyn as a leader of the "legal realist" movement. Although multifaceted and less coherent than a unified jurisprudential theory, legal realism in general called for the study of law not on the page but rather in action. What was important, the realists insisted, was the actual handling of disputes and negotiations by police, lawyers, judges, and citizens. In Llewellyn's opinion, the movement never meant to be a philosophy. Legal realism, he felt, was at its core "a methodology."

Despite a painful divorce from his first wife in 1930 and recurrent struggles with alcoholism, Llewellyn remained extremely productive during the pre–World War II years. In 1933 he married Emma Corstvet;

they adopted a son. His provocative *The Cheyenne Way* (1941), coauthored with anthropologist E. Adamson Hoebel, was a major contribution to the anthropological study of primitive law. Contemplating the Cheyenne approach to law, Llewellyn said later, enabled him to put aside the assumption that law and justice stood inherently in conflict.

During World War II and after, Llewellyn turned his attention increasingly to the drafting and promotion of the Uniform Commercial Code, an effort to standardize American commercial law sponsored jointly by the American Law Institute and the Conference of Commissioners on Uniform State Laws. He was chief reporter for this massive project, and although he worked with dozens of others, few doubted his influence. Scholar Grant Gilmore said, "Make no mistake: this Code was Llewellyn's Code; there is not a section, there is hardly a line, which does not bear his stamp and impress; from beginning to end he inspired, directed and controlled it." The first draft of the code was completed by 1949. Fifteen states formally adopted it before Llewellyn's death, and in subsequent years thirty-four more states adopted it. It was, stated simply, one of the most successful and pervasive law reforms in American legal history.

Consistent with Llewellyn's earlier disdain for conceptualism and rule-driven system building, the code used loose, open-ended language. Article Two concerned the law of sales and looked in particular to questions of fact, reasonableness, good faith, and usage of trade for answers to legal controversies. The commercial community was approached almost as modern-day Cheyenne and was trusted to derive legal fairness from its own norms.

Llewellyn divorced his second wife in 1946 and that same year married Soia Mentschikoff, who had been his student, research assistant, and associate chief reporter on the Uniform Commercial Code project. In 1951 he resigned from Columbia, where, because of his difficult and demanding personality, his relationship with faculty colleagues and the school administration had deteriorated badly. Llewellyn and Mentschikoff accepted a joint appointment at the University of Chicago Law School, the first time a major American law school had appointed spouses to its faculty.

A particular reason for Llewellyn's move to Chicago was his admiration for Dean Edward Levi, whose talents in Llewellyn's opinion would enable the University of Chicago Law School to compete with prestigious eastern schools. Levi thought just as highly of Llewellyn, authorized a salary even larger than his own, and was extremely pleased with the work of both Llewellyn and Mentschikoff. The two energized the school and raised its scholarly standards. They held weekly parties at their home, inviting all students to attend, and many later cited their contacts with Llewellyn and Mentschikoff as the high points of their legal educations.

In 1960 Llewellyn published his magnum opus, *The Common Law Tradition: Deciding Appeals*. Echoing the skepticism concerning rules in his earlier scholarship, he argued in this volume that rules alone do not decide cases. The law, he thought, was in perpetual motion, and in most appeals judges exercised judicial creativity. However, forces also channeled this creativity and prevented it from becoming mere arbitrariness.

Following the publication of *The Common Law Tradition*, Llewellyn planned to lecture in Germany and use his lecture series to synthesize his jurisprudential views. Unfortunately, poor health intervened, and he died in Chicago. One of the greatest figures of twentieth-century legal academics, Llewellyn uniquely combined originality and theoretical sophistication with a hands-on commitment to practical and enduring law reform.

• Llewellyn's papers are at the University of Chicago Law School Library. In addition to the works already mentioned, he also wrote *Jurisprudence: Realism in Theory and Practice*, which was published posthumously in 1962. The most extensive study of Llewellyn and his thought is William Twining, *Karl Llewellyn and the Realist Movement* (1973). Memorial tributes to Llewellyn by various authors are in the *University of Chicago Law Review* (Summer 1962) and the *Yale Law Journal* (Apr. 1962). An obituary is in the *New York Times*, 15 Feb. 1962.

DAVID RAY PAPKE

LLOYD, Alfred Henry (3 Jan. 1864–11 May 1927), philosopher and university administrator, was born in Montclair, New Jersey, the son of Henry Huggins Lloyd and Anna Mary Badger. After refusing an offer of financial support to prepare for the Congregationalist ministry, the religion in which he was born and reared, Lloyd chose Harvard and supported himself by fellowships and tutoring. He graduated in 1886. He taught for a year at Phillips Academy in Andover, Massachusetts, before returning to Harvard for graduate work in philosophy. He received his doctorate in 1893, writing a dissertation on freedom. Lloyd's main teachers at Harvard were William James, Josiah Royce, and George Herbert Palmer. In 1889–1891 he studied philosophy in Göttingen, Berlin, and Heidelberg.

In 1891 Lloyd became an instructor at the University of Michigan, where for three years he was a colleague of John Dewey and George Herbert Mead. When Dewey and Mead left for the University of Chicago in 1894, Lloyd became an assistant professor. He was promoted to associate professor in 1899 and to full professor in 1906. From 1915 to 1924 he was dean of the graduate school of the University of Michigan and in 1925 served as acting president of the university. Lloyd also was president of the Western Division of the American Philosophical Association in 1915–1916.

On the surface, Lloyd was an austere thinker, the author of short books on timeless metaphysical truths, seemingly divorced from the intellectual developments of his time. Posterity has tended to accept William James's verdict that Lloyd was "unassimilably obscure." Yet Lloyd was Dewey's intellectual companion during Dewey's years at Michigan and was included by James among the thinkers who, from differ-

ent starting points, were converging toward a common center and completely rearranging the philosophical landscape of the early twentieth century. For Lloyd, Darwin and evolutionary theory did not merely explain certain phenomenal facts but provided a "real insight into the character of the universe as a whole." This broader conception of evolution Lloyd shared with the American pragmatists, although he remained separated from most of them by his philosophical terminology, mostly derived from philosophical idealism.

For him, the task of philosophy was to generalize to the highest degree. In opposition to the dominant experimental psychology of his time, he argued that "real psychology" as the science of the soul was not only based on metaphysics but was metaphysics. Taking the relations between parts and wholes as his fundamental problem, Lloyd concluded that the category of relation was central and declared that reality is a system of relations. As such, the "world of things is an organism, a spontaneously changing, living, intelligent organism." The soul or self is the "world's *activity*," that which in its acts shows "the meaning of the world, the inner truth of the natural universe." This system, which he outlined in *Dynamic Idealism: An Elementary Course in the Metaphysics of Psychology* (1898), Lloyd called dynamic idealism. Because for this idealism ideas are "liberating plans," not static forms but forces, its natural allies are the pragmatists who argued that the meaning of ideas is to be found not in their origins but in experiences to which they lead.

Lloyd sought to overcome the separations and dualisms of traditional philosophy, the dualisms between body and soul, between the psychological and the physical sciences, between philosophy and the sciences. In many respects, he belongs with James and Dewey to the anticartesian strain of modern philosophy.

Lloyd early abandoned orthodox religious beliefs. He attacked religion with its creeds and liturgies as the source of bigotry, sectarianism, and authoritarianism. Organized religion, by isolating men from nature and other men, makes genuine religious life impossible. God, when properly understood, is that which is "inspiring or animating the natural with unlimited freedom and possibility." Lloyd shared with Dewey the desire to secularize religion and turn it into a reflective guide of social action. But unlike Dewey, Lloyd limited his own social action to lecturing and writing.

His emphasis on sociality and community led Lloyd to a critique of nationalism, to which he devoted a number of newspaper articles. He claimed that World War I should end in a negotiated truce rather than in the victory of one side. A supporter of the League of Nations, he criticized the choice of name, arguing that the word *league* is too suggestive of artificial separations. Lloyd preferred to speak of the united nations.

In 1892 Lloyd had married Margaret Elizabeth Crocker. They had four children. He collapsed while addressing the University of Michigan graduating class on "Some Factors of a Life Worth While" and died the next day in Detroit, Michigan.

• In addition to books already mentioned, Lloyd's publications include *Citizenship and Salvation; or, Greek and Jew: A Study in the Philosophy of History* (1897); *Philosophy of History: An Introduction to the Philosophical Study of Politics* (1899); *The Will to Doubt: An Essay in Philosophy for the General Thinker* (1907); and *Leadership and Progress and Other Essays of Progress* (1922). While recognized in his time as an important philosopher, Lloyd has received very little scholarly attention. A study of his life and thought is Evelyn Urban Shirk, *Adventurous Idealism: The Philosophy of Alfred Lloyd* (1952).

IGNAS K. SKRUPSKELIS

LLOYD, Alice Spencer Geddes (13 Nov. 1876–4 Sept. 1962), educator, was born in Athol, Massachusetts, the daughter of William Edwin Geddes, a merchant and ship owner, and Ella Mary Ainsworth. After graduating from the select Chauncey Hall School in 1894, she attended Radcliffe College, but her father's death in 1896 caused her to leave Radcliffe before earning her degree. Turning to newspaper work to support her mother and grandmother, Lloyd served as editor of the *Cambridge Press* in 1904 and the following year as managing editor of the *Wakefield Citizen and Banner* in Wakefield, Massachusetts. After her February 1914 marriage to Arthur Lloyd, she gave up newspaper work to concentrate on freelance writing. The couple moved to Gilmanton, New Hampshire, in 1915. Lloyd moved again the following year when her deteriorating health, which stemmed from a childhood case of meningitis, caused doctors to warn her that the harsh New England winters would hasten her death. Separating from her husband in 1916, Lloyd settled with her mother in an abandoned church mission in Ivis, a village located in Knott County, Kentucky.

Knott County claimed only two literate people out of every 100 and only one college graduate in its entire population. No high schools existed either in Knott or the surrounding counties, and the most men in the area could hope for was to spend their lives working in the local coal mines. County residents' incomes averaged about $25 a year. In 1917 Lloyd and her mother moved from Ivis to nearby Caney Creek at the request of local resident Abisha Johnson, who promised them fifty acres and a house if Lloyd would educate his children. This unexpected opportunity suited Lloyd's intention to use her life "to some good purpose," since her health problems led her to believe that she had only a few remaining years to live. Lloyd supervised the construction of a six-room schoolhouse and the Caney Creek Community Center, which became the site of educational activities. In 1919 Lloyd opened the area's first high school and in 1923 founded Caney Creek Junior College. As the community grew during the 1920s, Lloyd obtained mail delivery for Caney Creek and selected the name "Pippapass" (later altered to Pippa Passes in the 1950s) as its postal identity. Lloyd hoped that her students, like Pippa, the girl in Robert Browning's poem, "Pippa Passes," would do good as they traveled in the area.

Beginning in 1916 with letters to forty friends in Boston and elsewhere, Lloyd successfully raised over $2 million for her students and their schools during her tenure at Caney Creek. Her method of financing schools through public donations was necessary because the willingness to learn, not the ability to pay, was the criterion for admission. Although by the 1950s grade and high school teachers were paid with state and county money, Caney College still offered free housing to them and to some of the high school students. To offset expenses, college students worked part-time on the campus and promised to settle in the mountains after earning their degrees. Lloyd never drew a paycheck as president of the college, and she welcomed from those people who could not afford monetary donations contributions of time and skill. She encouraged not only her students, but also community members to work together to improve living conditions in the Kentucky hills. In daily discussions, teachers urged students to develop a purpose in their lives and to identify ways they could aid their own people. This philosophy, known as the "Purpose Road," was intertwined with most subjects taught at Caney. Lloyd also maintained a rigid behavior code that prohibited smoking, drinking, card playing, cursing, and dancing. She sought to keep girls and boys separated both socially and academically, teaching them in sex-segregated classrooms.

Caney College continued to grow despite constant financial shortages. By the 1960s the 175-acre campus included over forty-four buildings and an enrollment of approximately 250 students. The school earned accreditation from the Southern Association of Colleges and Secondary Schools in the mid-1950s, was renamed Alice Lloyd College in 1962, and was elevated to a four-year institution in 1980. Though many Caney graduates went on to earn bachelor's, law, and medical degrees at institutions outside Caney Creek, most students fulfilled their pledge to return to the mountains; an estimated 80 percent of Caney graduates taught in the hill country by the 1960s.

Although Lloyd had no formal training as a teacher, her work at Caney College contributed greatly to the expansion of educational and vocational opportunities for residents in the mountains of eastern Kentucky. At the core of her educational program was a belief that mountain people should help themselves to alleviate the harshness of their lives. Lloyd kept her word never to interfere in the politics, moonshining, or religion of the region. She focused instead on creating an institution that offered training to future community leaders while it preserved much of the mountain culture. She died in Pippa Passes.

• Information on Lloyd and on the origins and development of Alice Lloyd College may be found in the extensive clipping files of the Special Collections and Archives at the University of Kentucky, Lexington. The Alice Lloyd College Archives are housed in the Ethel Muller Barrett Memorial Library,

Pippa Passes, Ky. See also "School at Caney Valley," *Time*, 8 Apr. 1940, pp. 52–53; William S. Dutton, *Stay on Stranger* (1954); Laurel Anderson, "The School at Pippa Passes," *Appalachian Heritage* (Fall–Winter 1974–1975): 108–116; Jerry C. Davis, *Miracle at Caney Creek* (1982); and Robert W. Sloane, ed., *Alice Lloyd: Boston's Gift to Caney Creek* (1982).

JANICE M. LEONE

LLOYD, David (1656–6 Apr. 1731), leading Quaker legislator and jurist of early Pennsylvania, was born in Manafon, Montgomeryshire, Wales, the son of Thomas Lloyd. (His mother's name is unknown.) After grammar school, Lloyd studied law with George Jeffries, the Welshman who later became lord chief justice of the King's Bench and lord chancellor of England. On the basis of this legal training, William Penn engaged Lloyd in the early 1680s to assist land transactions among First Purchasers in London and to manage other legal affairs related to Pennsylvania.

Penn gained confidence in Lloyd and named him attorney general of Pennsylvania on 24 April 1686. With this commission, Lloyd and his wife, Sarah, sailed for Philadelphia aboard the *Amity*, arriving on 15 July of the same year. Soon after, he was named clerk of the Provincial Council, deputy master of the Rolls, and clerk of the Philadelphia County Court. These appointments placed him among the Quaker provincial elite. Lloyd was apparently a close relation to another Thomas Lloyd (not his father), who served as president of the Provincial Court and deputy governor of Pennsylvania, and to the wealthy and influential Lloyds of Dolobran Hall, Montgomeryshire. Led by Thomas Lloyd, many of the provincial elite had become disillusioned with the policies of Penn and his deputies in Pennsylvania. David Lloyd came to the assistance of Thomas Lloyd in his 1689 confrontation with Deputy Governor John Blackwell, by refusing Blackwell's request for Philadelphia County Court records in an appeals case, stating that powers of requisition were reserved for judges. This obstructionist tactic earned Lloyd expulsion from the clerk's office in February, but Thomas Lloyd, as keeper of the Great Seal, recommissioned him.

In 1693 Lloyd was elected to the Assembly from Chester County, where he established himself as a leading opponent of the royal governor, Benjamin Fletcher; in the next session, he was elected Speaker. With the restoration of Penn's charter in 1694, Lloyd was renamed attorney general, and in 1695 he was elected to the Provincial Council from Chester County for a three-year term. Lloyd resisted Markham's effort to secure legislation to aid the defense of New York, and he modeled a new Frame of Government that gave the Assembly exclusive control over the initiation of bills as well as the right to sit at its own adjournment, establish qualifications for assemblymen, and conduct business in closed session. Lloyd's early efforts in provincial government to limit metropolitan control—proprietary or imperial—brought him into conflict with Robert Quary, judge of vice admiralty, when in 1698, Attorney General Lloyd refused to prosecute

two bonds that apparently were forfeited to the crown. Before the Provincial Council, Lloyd argued in high-toned language against admiralty jurisdiction, claiming that Quary and others who would extend imperial authority over the colonial judiciary "ware greater Enemies to the rights and Liberties of the people" than ship money advocates during the reign of Charles I. Lloyd's efforts to weaken the Navigation Acts in Pennsylvania provoked the Board of Trade to recommend his removal from office, to which Penn acquiesced in 1700. Lloyd also was suspended from the Provincial Council and stripped of his Philadelphia County Court clerkship. From that point on he became an inexorable opponent of proprietary prerogative.

Lloyd's energies shifted to the Assembly, which he and scores of other residents petitioned in 1701 for changes to proprietary land policy and a new Frame of Government. This new frame, signed by Penn under the title charter of Privileges, confirmed many of the rights the Assembly had acquired during the preceding decade. Lloyd was elected to the Assembly in 1703 from Philadelphia County and chosen as its Speaker, a position he held in 1704, 1706 through 1709, 1714, 1723, and 1725 through 1728. He also held a number of offices in the Corporation of Philadelphia. Relations between Lloyd and Penn's allies, namely Governors John Evans and Charles Gookin and the proprietor's American secretary, James Logan, worsened through the years 1704 through 1710, owing largely to a Lloydian plan for judicial reorganization that substantially favored the Assembly. In 1704 Lloyd also authored a bitter remonstrance that historian Roy Lokken called "the boldest attack ever made on the Proprietor in the history of the Province" (p. 146). Heightening the tensions, the Assembly tried but ultimately failed to impeach Logan beginning in 1707. Tired of the rancor between Lloydian and proprietary factions and shocked at Lloyd's implication in a fraudulent scheme to buy 1,000 acres of Frankfurt Company land for £60 in 1708, the electorate voted Lloyd and his supporters out of the Assembly in 1710. Though he was reelected in 1711 and served during thirteen of the next twenty-one years, his spirited leadership of the antiproprietary faction had ended.

Poor economic conditions in 1722 and 1723 stimulated a demand for paper money, which Governor William Keith championed against the opposition of wealthy merchants. Roused by Keith's call for support, Lloyd returned to the Assembly in 1723 and became speaker, pushing through a bill for £30,000 in paper notes. This provoked an exchange on constitutional issues between Keith and Logan, which Lloyd joined with his *Vindication of the Legislative Power* (1725) and *A Further Vindication of the Rights and Privileges of the People of This Province of Pennsylvania* (1726). In the former he expressed confidence in popular government, stating that "a mean Man, of small Interest, devoted to the faithful discharge of his Trust and Duty to the Government, may do more good to the State, than a Richer or more Learned Man, who by his ill Temper and aspiring Mind becomes an opposer of the Constitution by which he should act" (p. 3). These pamphlets articulated a doctrine of legislative supremacy, defending the unicameral legislature he helped to fashion with the frame of 1701; they were written from the perspective of chief justice of the supreme court, a position Lloyd had held since 1717 and would hold until his death in Chester in 1731.

At various points in his life Lloyd was the richest resident of Chester County and one of the wealthiest landowners in the province. Having sold much of this property by the time of his death, he left his second wife, Grace Growdon, whom he had married in 1697, a large library, a spacious house in Chester, and ten slaves. Political opponents' portrayal of Lloyd as pugnacious and vengeful encouraged earlier historians of the period to view him as something of a rogue and a destabilizing element in government, though this view later gave way to a more generous depiction of him as architect of incipient democracy and self-government in the American colonies. More recent studies have stressed changes in social and economic configurations that strengthened his base of support, and the effects of his leadership, unintended perhaps, that politicized colonists from the middling and lower ranks. All agree, however, that Lloyd was one of the most influential lawmakers and jurists in the first half of colonial Pennsylvania's history.

• Manuscript materials relating to Lloyd's early career can be found in the Proud papers, James Logan Papers, and the papers of William Penn (microfilm), all at the Historical Society of Pennsylvania. His contribution to early Pennsylvania law and politics is evident in the public records of the colony, many of which are published, including *Votes and Proceedings of the House of Representatives of the Province of Pennsylvania* (1752) and *Minutes of the Provincial Council of Pennsylvania*, vols. 1–2 (1852). Other printed materials of interest include David Lloyd, "Correspondence with Thomas Lower," *The Friend* 39 (Nov. 1865); Edward Armstrong, ed., "Correspondence between William Penn and James Logan," *Memoirs of the Historical Society of Pennsylvania*, vols. 9–10 (1870–1872); and *The Papers of William Penn* (5 vols., 1981–1987), ed. Mary Maples Dunn and Richard S. Dunn. Lloyd received extensive biographical treatment in Roy Lokken, *David Lloyd: Colonial Lawmaker* (1959), and Craig W. Horle et al., *Lawmaking and Legislators in Pennsylvania: A Biographical Dictionary*, vol. 1 (1991). Earlier reviews of Lloyd's contribution to the movement for colonial self-government include William R. Shepherd, *History of Proprietary Government in Pennsylvania* (1896); H. Frank Eshleman, *The Constructive Genius of David Lloyd in Early Colonial Pennsylvania Legislation and Jurisprudence, 1686 to 1731* (1910); Isaac Sharpless, *Political Leaders of Provincial Pennsylvania* (1919); and Frank H. Eastman, *Courts and Lawyers of Pennsylvania*, vol. 1 (1922). More recent analyses of his legislative record and the nature of colonial Pennsylvania politics include Sister Joan de Lourdes Leonard, "The Organization and Procedure of the Pennsylvania Assembly, 1682–1776," *Pennsylvania Magazine of History and Biography* 72 (July and Oct. 1948); Gary B. Nash, *Quakers and Politics: Pennsylvania, 1681–1726* (1968); and Alan Tully, *Forming American Politics: Ideals, Interests, and Institutions in Colonial New York and Pennsylvania* (1994).

JEFFREY B. WEBB

LLOYD, Edward (22 July 1779–2 June 1834), politician and farmer, was born in Maryland, the son of Edward Lloyd, a Maryland official and planter, and Elizabeth Tayloe. Lloyd received his education primarily from private tutors but also from exposure to his father's political activities and plantation management. Upon his father's death in 1796, Lloyd, as the only son, inherited all of his father's land, principally over 11,000 acres in Talbot County, and more than two hundred slaves. In 1797 he married Sally Scott Murray; they had three sons and four daughters.

In 1800 Talbot voters elected Lloyd, barely of legal age, to the House of Delegates. A member of the Republican party despite his substantial wealth, Lloyd became a spokesman for the successful effort to eliminate property requirements for voting. He moved from the House of Delegates to the U.S. House of Representatives in 1806, when he was elected to fill the unexpired term of Joseph Nicholson, his brother-in-law, who had resigned to accept a judgeship. He served in Congress from December of that year until 1809. As a congressman, Lloyd expressed strong skepticism about conspiracy charges leveled against Aaron Burr, opposed 1807 legislation intended to outlaw the African slave trade, and supported federal efforts to resist British interference with American shipping and trade.

In 1809 the general assembly overwhelmingly elected Lloyd governor of Maryland to fill the unexpired term of Governor Robert Wright, who resigned in the expectation of a judicial appointment. He was reelected for two successive one-year terms, the maximum allowed. The most notable accomplishment of his tenure of office was passage of legislation that removed all property qualifications for officeholding. Even before he left his gubernatorial position, Lloyd was elected to the state senate. There he was an active supporter of the James Madison administration, favoring a military solution to the conflict with Britain and, in the War of 1812, assisting in the defense of Talbot County as a colonel in the militia. Lloyd left the senate in January 1815 but was elected to the House of Delegates the following October. Lloyd was defeated for reelection as a delegate in 1816, but after the Republican party regained control of the Maryland legislature in 1818, he was chosen as U.S. senator and took his seat on 21 December 1819.

While in the Senate, Lloyd abstained when the Missouri Compromise faced a vote. He also opposed Henry Clay's American System and efforts to bar slavery from territories north of 36 degrees 30 minutes, but he spoke in favor of simultaneous admission to the Union of Maine and Missouri. In addition he advocated granting public lands for educational purposes. Lloyd resigned from the Senate in January 1826 for health reasons. His political retirement was short-lived, however, as he was elected to the state senate in the same year and held that office until 1831, serving two terms as that body's president.

Despite the demands of his political career, Lloyd actively supervised the management of his vast agricultural interests. He continued to cultivate tobacco on his Wye farms, but like his father before him he was considered the largest grower of wheat in Maryland. He followed his father's example in specializing in agricultural production and livestock raising on his estates. With few exceptions, he hired free workers for the craft work needed to operate his farms, which numbered fifteen by 1834. He continued to consign his tobacco to merchants in England, who shipped cargoes of luxury goods back to Maryland in return, but he marketed his wheat and surplus corn in Baltimore. In 1818 Lloyd was a founding member of the Maryland Agricultural Society and its first vice president. He was an experimental breeder of imported merino sheep and horned cattle. A member of the Annapolis Jockey Club, he took pride in the quality of his racing stable, stud horses, and fighting gamecocks. In his youth he wagered with friends on both cockfights and billiards.

At the time of his death, Lloyd was the owner of 652 slaves. He is more noted, however, for being the employer of the master of Frederick Douglass. Douglass spent much of his youth at Lloyd's Wye House and vividly described the household and the estate in his autobiography. Lloyd died of gout in Annapolis. According to the *Baltimore American*:

In the various private and domestic relations of life Col. Lloyd so discharged the duties of his station as to gather around him and to bind in the bonds of social affection a large circle of friends and admirers, and in public, the estimation placed by the people upon his services is best evinced by the frequent calls made upon him to fill the most elevated dignities.

Lloyd began his political career at the earliest possible age and filled all major offices within the electoral control of Maryland voters as governor, U.S. senator, representative, state senator, and delegate. During his career, he favored the interests of the public over those of the political elite to which he belonged by supporting removal of property qualifications for voting and officeholding. He did not, however, exhibit the same independence with regard to his economic interests when he opposed federal legislation that would have limited the rights of slaveholders.

• The major primary documentation for Lloyd, as for other members of his family, is in the Lloyd papers, MS 2001, Maryland Historical Society. Gary Arnold, *A Guide to the Microfilm Edition of the Lloyd Papers* (1973), provides a concise summary of Lloyd's career, drawn from the fuller portrait available in Oswald Tilghman, *History of Talbot County, Maryland*, vol. 1 (1915), but without the romanticized view of the patriarch espoused by Tilghman. Frank F. White, Jr., *The Governors of Maryland, 1777–1970* (1970), contains a summary that relies on Tilghman but offers a more objective assessment. Tilghman provides the most complete account of Lloyd's career but embellishes it with assertions about Lloyd's beliefs and views that are unsupported by any evidence. For a very different view of Lloyd, see Frederick Douglass, *My Bondage and My Freedom*, chap. 8 (1855). Christopher Johnston, "Lloyd Family," *Maryland Historical Magazine*, Dec. 1912, pp. 420–30, supplies the basic genealogical information. Obituaries are in the *Baltimore Patriot and Mercantile Advertiser*, 3 June 1834; the *Baltimore Republican*, 4 June 1834; and the *Easton Gazette*, 7 June 1834.

JEAN B. RUSSO

LLOYD, Harold (20 Apr. 1893–8 Mar. 1971), film comedian, was born Harold Clayton Lloyd in Burchard, Nebraska, the son of James Darsie Lloyd, a shoe salesman, and Elizabeth Fraser. A chance meeting on a street in Omaha with theatrical producer John Lane Connor led the ten-year-old Lloyd to a lifelong concern with the theater. Connor taught the boy the art of makeup and began using him in minor roles. At eighteen, the now seasoned Lloyd became an instructor in the San Diego School of Expression, a later Connor enterprise, where he taught fencing, dancing, and elocution. In 1913 the Edison Film Company, based in Hollywood, arrived in San Diego to shoot some scenes for one of their westerns. Lloyd and a dozen or so students at the school were hired as extras. Using his makeup skills, he played a variety of roles for Edison.

Short of money during the summer break, Lloyd went to Los Angeles to find work as an extra at Universal Pictures, where he met Hal Roach, the man most directly responsible for his film career. With a small inheritance as capital, Roach began grinding out a series of one-reel comedies starring his new young friend. Most of the early Roach/Lloyd films no longer exist, but we know that they were slapstick comedies of the kind that Mack Sennett had introduced to American film audiences—films that starred Fatty Arbuckle, Mabel Normand, and, most importantly, Charlie Chaplin. Lloyd's first attempts at film comedy in 1915 featured a poor imitation of Chaplin who he called Willie Work. The films were successful only because of the public's insatiable desire for Chaplin. After a quarrel over money, Lloyd left Roach briefly in April 1915 to work for Sennett, where he picked up invaluable experience in creating slapstick. Upon rejoining Roach in June 1915 for considerably more money, Lloyd created his second character, Lonesome Luke, another tramp type whose attire was the exact opposite of Chaplin's. The costar of the Luke comedies was the teenage actress Bebe Daniels, who served an apprenticeship with Lloyd before beginning her own career as a comedienne. In later years Lloyd asserted that he had overheard two small boys dismiss his work in the Luke films as pure Chaplin imitation. Their contempt was so powerful that Lloyd told Roach that he would never make another Luke film. At this point he created the persona that made him world famous.

Lloyd stated that he conceived his "boy with horn-rimmed glasses and a straw hat" character (named Harold) in 1917 after seeing an early film about a quiet, shy churchman who, when provoked, suddenly asserts himself by becoming a savage fighter and destroying his enemies. Lloyd discovered that wearing the horn-rimmed glasses (always without lenses) gave him the chance to play an astonishingly wide range of characters and allowed him to sustain a love interest.

Audiences saw in Lloyd's Harold the living embodiment of hidden strength in a young man whose main attributes were ambition, perseverance, and eventual success. The character was the ultimate clean-cut "boy next door" who rose to all challenges.

Differing from Chaplin's pathos, Lloyd's plots involved comic suspense twists that always placed his character in physical danger. His best-known film, *Safety Last* (1923), made him the master of "daredevil" comedy. In it Lloyd found himself climbing the side of a tall building in downtown Los Angeles as part of his determination to gain success as a department store executive. Using a series of artful trick camera angles, Lloyd appeared to be in extreme peril as he climbed ever higher. At one moment he is forced to cling to the hands of a giant four-sided clock near the top of the building. The entire side of the clock face suddenly falls forward and Harold dangles helplessly on one of the hands. The image of Lloyd on the clock has become one of the most familiar in all film history. Lloyd actually performed all his own stunts, despite a major accident to his right hand during a promotional shoot that resulted in the loss of thumb and forefinger. A sports enthusiast, he had high standards in every area of his life. His passion for perfection had him spending far more on his production costs than other silent comedians to get things just right.

Lloyd's leading lady after 1920 was Mildred Davis, whom he married in 1923; they had three children, one of whom was adopted. Following the immense success of *Safety Last*, Lloyd left Roach to set up his own production firm and during the rest of the 1920s made the other films by which he is best remembered: *Girl Shy* (1924), *The Freshman* (1925), *For Heaven's Sake* (1926), *The Kid Brother* (1927), and *Speedy* (1928).

Lloyd, along with Chaplin and Buster Keaton, was one of the three great silent film comedians. And, like theirs, his career faltered with the coming of sound. With the possible exception of Chaplin's *Modern Times* (1936), Lloyd's *Movie Crazy* (1932), came closest to attaining in sound what the threesome had so brilliantly achieved in silent times. James Agee described Lloyd as a master film craftsman who had the extraordinary ability to create a gag, bring it to a successful conclusion, and then link it up with the next one. Agee asserted that few people in films came close to equaling Lloyd's art and that "nobody has ever beaten him" in creating laughter.

In his personal life, especially in terms of ambition and work ethic, Lloyd bore a resemblance to his glasses character. Like Chaplin, he started life poor, saved his money, invested wisely, and died a very wealthy man. Toward the end of his life he became active in the children's hospital charitable work of the Shriners, a branch of the Masons, and was on the cover of *Time* magazine when he was elected imperial potentate. He died in Los Angeles.

• Additional information on Lloyd's life and career can be found in Tom Dardis, *Harold Lloyd: The Man on the Clock* (1983), and Adam Reilly, *Harold Lloyd— "The King of Daredevil Comedy"* (1977). See also Kevin Brownlow, *The Parade's Gone By* (1969), Walter Kerr, *The Silent Clowns* (1975), and Richard Schickel, *The Shape of Laughter* (1974). An obituary is in the *New York Times*, 9 Mar. 1971.

THOMAS A. DARDIS

LLOYD, Henry Demarest (1 May 1847–28 Sept. 1903), journalist and social reformer, was born in New York City, the son of Aaron Lloyd, a pastor of the Dutch Reformed church, and Marie Christie Demarest. Lloyd grew up in impoverished rural parishes in New York, New Jersey, and Illinois. But in 1860 his father gave up the ministry and returned to New York City to move in with his father-in-law, a customs house official, and run a small book shop. A scholarship student at Columbia College, Lloyd graduated with a B.A. in 1867 and entered Columbia Law School. In 1869, after passing the New York bar exam, he became assistant secretary to the New York-based American Free-Trade League and for three years served as its public relations agent.

In 1872 he moved to Chicago to become literary editor of the *Chicago Tribune*. In December 1873 he married Jessie Louise Bross, daughter of William Bross, wealthy part-owner of that newspaper. They had four children. The next year Lloyd became financial editor and six years later chief editorial writer. Until he resigned in 1885, after political differences with Joseph Medill, the *Tribune*'s principal owner, Lloyd concentrated much of his editorial attention on the commercial, industrial, and financial ethics of the Gilded Age.

In March 1881 the *Atlantic Monthly* published as its lead article his "The Story of a Great Monopoly," an analysis of the widespread collusion of railroad financiers with officers of corporate combinations. Specifically, he traced the connections of the Pennsylvania Railroad with the Standard Oil Company in the ruinous rate wars of the 1870s and called for effective national regulation of the common carriers. That article caused the *Atlantic* to run an unprecedented seven printings and earned Lloyd, posthumously, the title "the first muckraker." It also inspired him to write, in addition to his newspaper contributions, a total of 105 subsequent magazine or journal articles, innumerable speeches and lectures, and five books. Five more book compilations of his works were published after his death.

After his resignation from the *Tribune* he traveled several months in Europe, where he suffered an emotional breakdown. During recuperation he followed an extensive program of reading and study, which eventually led him to an eclectic philosophy for social reform, both transcendental and pragmatic. In 1887 he was well enough to participate vigorously in the clemency movement for the Haymarket anarchists, accused in an 1886 Chicago bombing—so much so that he permanently alienated his multimillionaire father-in-law, who as a result left his estate to Lloyd's sons. But by this time Lloyd had invested shrewdly in Chicago real estate to be financially secure and was able to devote himself to social and political causes. Thus both his Winnetka, Illinois, home, "The Wayside," and his Sakonnet Point, Rhode Island, summer home, "The Watch House," served as rallying points for many in those causes.

In its September 1888 issue the *North American Review* published Lloyd's "The New Conscience; or, The Religion of Labor" in which he posited the moral imperative of a social brotherhood, much like the nascent Fabian socialism of his British friend William Clarke, as opposed to the doctrine of social Darwinism. In doing so, Lloyd became a "prophet-counselor" for social qua moral reform in America and one who during the 1890s sought unsuccessfully to fuse midwestern rural and urban populism into a viable political coalition. Thus he ran unsuccessfully for Congress in 1894 on a Chicago Labor–Populist ticket, in the aftermath excitement of the failed Pullman strike.

While speaking before Chicago labor groups in 1889, he became aware of the plight of coal miners locked out at Spring Valley, Illinois, by a company headed by William L. Scott, a lieutenant of the infamous financier Jay Gould. Lloyd publicized the exploited conditions of the miners in a series of newspaper stories and in 1890 published a book-length report of that lockout entitled *A Strike of Millionaires against Miners,* in which he defended staunchly the rights of laborers, faced by cynical combinations of capital, to unionize and bargain collectively. Then for several years Lloyd worked on a book about big-business ethics, using the Standard Oil Company as his touchstone, which he published in 1894 as *Wealth against Commonwealth.* The first thoroughly documented exposé of the socially destructive practices and effects of a representative trust, it was his most important contribution to the reform movement and the work for which most remember him.

Disheartened in 1896 by the fusion of the People's party with the Free Silver Democrats, Lloyd abandoned his attempt to bring about social reform via national political reform and turned instead to the cooperative movement as a vehicle for change. After personally studying American, British, and European cooperatives, he published his impressions in the book *Labour Copartnership* (1898). In 1899 he toured New Zealand and Australia to investigate their controversial experiments in social democracy. From his findings he published two books in 1900. One, *Country without Strikes,* is a brief but enthusiastic report about compulsory arbitration in New Zealand; the other, *Newest England,* is a more comprehensive study of socialist programs in both countries. At this time he began wintering in Cambridge, Massachusetts, where his sons attended Harvard, though he retained his Winnetka home. In both 1901 and 1902 he traveled several months in Europe to study the progress of socialism and cooperatives there. Afterward he wrote a book-length analysis of Switzerland's successful democratic control of the forces of industrialization, which was published posthumously in 1907 as *A Sovereign People.*

In May 1902 the United Mine Workers Union struck the Pennsylvania coal trust, which refused to negotiate. With the nation gripped by a severe fuel shortage that fall, President Theodore Roosevelt (1858–1919) convened a commission to resolve the dispute. Lloyd joined his friend Clarence Darrow, the famous Chicago lawyer, and John Mitchell (1870–1919), president of the union, to prepare and argue successfully labor's case. Heartened by that precedent for compulsory arbitration, Lloyd campaigned actively for municipal ownership of public transportation in Chicago late the following summer. While doing so he contracted a bronchial cold that turned into pneumonia, from which he died. Chicago labor and civic groups organized a memorial service at the auditorium, which was attended by 5,000 ticket holders, a testament to his popularity as a selfless social reformer.

Lloyd made a lasting impression on American social and intellectual history as a pioneering theorist and publicist of modern social science, for he was the first to explain to the general public the profound changes that were taking place in American business methods during the Gilded Age as well as the implications of those changes. He is remembered, therefore, as the first muckraker, the one who established for those who followed a mutual touchstone—a firm belief in democratic values—and several standard techniques—sincere outrage, dramatic exposé, substantial documentation, and critical inferences. He was also an effective apologist for the American labor movement and for nondoctrinaire Christian socialism. In brief, he helped provide late nineteenth-century American reform with both a theoretical and pragmatic intellectual base.

• The prolific Henry Demarest Lloyd Papers, indexed and available on microfilm, are held by the State Historical Society of Wisconsin. Caro Lloyd, Henry's sister, published a two-volume laudatory biography that contains an excellent primary bibliography: *Henry Demarest Lloyd, 1847–1903, a Biography* (1912). The definitive biography, extensively detailed and documented, is by Chester Destler, *Henry Demarest Lloyd and the Empire of Reform* (1963). A briefer assessment is by E. Jay Jernigan, *Henry Demarest Lloyd* (1976). See also Daniel Aaron, *Men of Good Hope* (1951), for a general review of Lloyd's role as a moral prophet of reform; Sidney Fine, *Laissez Faire and the General-Welfare State* (1956), for Lloyd's contributions to American socioeconomic theory; Joseph Furnas, *The Americans: A Social History of the United States, 1587–1914* (1969), for a comparison of Lloyd's reform theories to those of Henry George, Laurence Gronlund, and Edward Bellamy; Howard Quint, *The Forging of American Socialism* (1953), for Lloyd's contributions in the 1890s to that movement; and Peter Frederick, *Knights of the Golden Rule* (1976), for a comparison of the similar "Christian socialism" of William Dean Howells and Lloyd. An obituary is in the *New York Times,* 29 Sept. 1903.

E. JAY JERNIGAN

LLOYD, James, II (24 Mar. 1728–14 Mar. 1810), pioneer surgeon, was born at the Manor of Queens Village on Long Island, New York, the son of Henry Lloyd, a Boston merchant, and Rebecca Nelson.

Lloyd attended the New Haven Grammar school. His father, who had a fine collection of medical books, may have provided the stimulus for Lloyd's medical career. His great-great-great grandfather had been a doctor in physick in the court of Queen Elizabeth I. In 1745 Lloyd apprenticed with Sylvester Gardiner, a well-known Boston surgeon, and then studied with John Clark, in Boston, from 1746 until 1748. In 1749 Lloyd became a dresser (surgical resident) to Joseph Warner at Guy's Hospital in London. While there he attended lectures given by the famous obstetrician William Smellie, the renowned surgeon John Hunter, considered the founder of experimental and surgical pathology, and the well-known surgeon William Cheselden, originator of several new surgical procedures.

Lloyd returned to Boston in 1752, opening a practice in obstetrics and surgery. He delivered lectures in obstetrics from 1752 until 1755. Considered to be the first physician in America to specialize in obstetrics, Lloyd is also credited with being the first surgeon in America to use ligatures to control hemorrhage in place of searing vessels. He also introduced Cheselden's method of flap amputation.

In 1759 Lloyd married Sarah Comrin. They had six children (one, James Lloyd III, was elected a U.S. senator from Massachusetts, 1808–1813). Between 1760 and 1790 Lloyd apprenticed ten physicians, which represented more than a fifth of the Boston practitioners. Most prominent among his students were John Clark VI, Isaac Foster, Jr., John Jefferies, Andrew Oliver, Theodore Parsons, Isaac Rand, Jr., and Joseph Warren. He was also a strong advocate of Edward Jenner's smallpox vaccination and "inoculated as many as 500 in one day."

Lloyd, a Tory, served as the surgeon to the British Garrison on Castle William (an island in Boston harbor) from 1764 to 1777. After the British left Boston Lloyd was listed as a traitor and jailed. However, the need for his obstetrical skills, in particular, outweighed his political beliefs, and he was released to care for Americans in Boston.

In 1781 Lloyd, with thirty other physicians, was instrumental in founding the Massachusetts Medical Society. He presented the society's bill of incorporation to the legislature, helped draw up the bylaws, served on the original board of counselors, and was a censor as well. In April 1782 he was chosen as the first president of the society but declined, allowing his friend Edward Holyoke to assume the job.

During the war the Lloyds' Long Island estate was decimated. In 1789 the English offered Lloyd recompense for the property if he would become a British citizen. He refused, becoming a staunch Federalist.

His wife died in 1797 and he thirteen years later in Boston. He left no written materials behind but is immortalized in a "speaking likeness" pencil drawing by Gilbert Stuart (Frick Reference Library, Washington, D.C.).

• Two important sources on the life of James Lloyd are George Bowen, *James Lloyd II, M.D. (1728–1810) and His Family in Lloyd Neck* (1988), and Dorothy C. Barck, ed., *Papers of the Lloyd Family of the Manor of Queens Village, Lloyd's Neck, Long Island, New York* (2 vols., 1926–1927). There are general references to Lloyd in James Thacher's *American Medical Biography or Memoirs of Eminent Physicians* (1828), pp. 359–76; *Sibley's Harvard Graduates*, vol. 12, pp. 184–93; and H. R. Viets, "The Medical Education of James Lloyd in Colonial America," *Yale Journal of Biology and Medicine* 31 (1958–1959): 1–14.

PAUL BERMAN

LLOYD, John Henry (25 Apr. 1884–19 Mar. 1965), African-American baseball player and manager, known as Pop, was born in Palatka, Florida. His father died during Lloyd's infancy, and Lloyd was raised by his grandmother after his mother remarried. A grade school dropout, he began his career on the sandlots of Jacksonville, Florida, at age nineteen.

Mild-mannered, clean-living, and genial, Lloyd had high cheek bones, a lantern jaw, and piercing eyes. Similarities in physique, temperament, style, and talent led to comparisons with white baseball's preeminent shortstop, and Lloyd was often called the black Honus Wagner. Connie Mack felt the two were of equal caliber, and Wagner remarked: "After I saw him, I felt honored that they should name such a great ballplayer after me." Like Wagner, Lloyd was a big man for a shortstop (5'11", 180 pounds), with long arms and large, strong hands. Both had wide range in the field and scooped up unusual amounts of dirt while fielding groundballs, their strong throws to first base emerging from clouds of dust. Thus, in Cuba Lloyd earned the nickname "El Cuchara" ("The Scoop"). He was a devastating left-handed hitter. Setting himself at the plate with the bat in the crook of his left elbow, Lloyd unleashed a fluid, powerful swing, hitting line drives to all fields. On the bases his loping, awkward gait generated surprising speed.

Lloyd's hitting prowess gained him great fame among black fans, both in the United States and in Cuba, where he played many winters. In November 1910 he matched skills with Ty Cobb, whose Detroit Tigers played against two Cuban teams that included several African-American players. Not only was Cobb outhit by Lloyd, .500 to .369, but he was thrown out three times attempting to steal bases, prompting him to storm off the field, vowing never to compete against black players again. Lloyd twice hit above .400, and as late as 1928, at age forty-four, he led Negro League hitters with an astonishing .564 batting average, hitting 11 home runs and stealing 10 bases in only 37 games.

A list of cities in which Lloyd played illustrates the peripatetic nature of a black ballplayer's career: Macon, Georgia (Acmes); Philadelphia (Cuban X Giants, Philadelphia Giants, Hilldales); Chicago (Leland Giants, Chicago American Giants); New York (Lincoln Giants, Lincoln Stars, Black Yankees); Brooklyn (Royal Giants); Atlantic City, New Jersey (Bacharach Giants); and Columbus, Ohio (Buckeyes). He rarely stayed with a team as long as three seasons, and he often left after only one year. "Where the money was," Lloyd said, "that's where I was."

Lloyd was a key player on some of the greatest African-American teams. The 1910 Leland Giants compiled a record of 123–6, and the following year the Lincoln Giants were 105–7. Between 1914 and 1919 he played in three postseason series to determine the unofficial champion of black baseball.

During his early years Lloyd played shortstop, forming outstanding combinations with second basemen Grant Johnson and Bingo DeMoss. In 1924 he shifted to second base, teaming with shortstop Dick Lundy, and thereafter he played increasingly at first base. As his career progressed, the African-American baseball community affectionately bestowed on him the nickname "Pop." In 1918 he was named player-manager of the Brooklyn Royal Giants, his first of more than ten years as a manager. The best team he managed was the 1923 Hilldales of Philadelphia, champions of the Eastern Colored League's first season.

After retiring from organized Negro baseball in 1931, Lloyd worked as a janitor in the Atlantic City post office and public schools, although he continued as a semipro player-manager until 1942. He and his wife, Nan, had no children, but Lloyd became active in Little League baseball, even serving as commissioner in Atlantic City. A community ballpark built in Atlantic City in 1949 was named after him in recognition of his contributions to the city's youth. At the dedication ceremony Lloyd disclaimed any regrets for having played before Jackie Robinson broke organized baseball's color line. "I do not consider that I was born at the wrong time," he said. "I felt it was the right time, for I had a chance to prove the ability of our race in this sport, and because many of us did our very best to uphold the traditions of the game and of the world of sport, we have given the Negro a greater opportunity now to be accepted into the major leagues with other Americans."

Lloyd died in Atlantic City. In 1977 he was inducted into the National Baseball Hall of Fame by a committee created to examine the merits of Negro League veterans.

Playing at a time when unprecedented black migration to northern cities fostered a vibrant African-American baseball community, Lloyd became its first great star. Yet the racism that plagued baseball throughout his brilliant career deprived him of the recognition and acclaim his uncommon ability would have garnered among organized baseball's mainstream of white fans. Not only was one of the game's greatest players relegated to the underground of apartheid baseball, but the game itself was diminished.

• Accounts of Lloyd's career can be found in John Holway, *Voices from the Great Black Baseball Leagues* (1975); Robert W. Peterson, *Only the Ball Was White* (1970); and James A. Riley, *The All-Time Stars of Black Baseball* (1983). For statistical data, see Rick Wolff, ed., *The Baseball Encyclopedia*, 8th ed. (1990).

JERRY MALLOY

LLOYD, John Uri (19 Apr. 1849–9 Apr. 1936), pharmacist and author, was born in West Bloomfield, New York, the son of Nelson Marvin Lloyd, an engineer, and Sophia Webster, a schoolteacher. The eldest of three sons who would become leading manufacturers of botanical medicines, Lloyd left the Genesee Valley with his parents when he was only four to settle in northern Kentucky. In this rustic environment he evinced an early interest in the flora around him and developed the habit of surreptitiously borrowing his mother's kitchenware to fashion crude but instructive experiments with natural products.

From these rural roots Lloyd pursued a career in pharmacy. Cincinnati became his home for his adult life, as he established himself in the city as a pharmacy apprentice under W. J. M. Gordon and later under George Eger. His instruction included attendance at chemistry lectures by the famous Roberts Bartholow at the Ohio Medical College. While some biographers have made much of his "humble" and "self-taught" beginnings (Corinne Simons, *John Uri Lloyd, His Life and His Works* [1972], p. 331; Mayo, pp. 36–37), Lloyd's professional preparation equaled or exceeded that of many of his colleagues during the same period.

Lloyd's career took an extraordinary turn when he met John King and John Milton Scudder, leading figures in the American eclectic medical movement, a group opposed to the harsh heroics of the regular physicians in favor of botanical medications. King, noticing the keen intellect and promise of the young apprentice, offered Lloyd a position with the pharmaceutical house of H. M. Merrell, and with this Lloyd's professional career became permanently linked to these sectarian practitioners. When Merrell retired in 1881, Lloyd was able to bring his younger brother Nelson Ashley Lloyd into the firm as Thorp & Lloyd Brothers. Finally the two brothers obtained the financial assistance needed from Scudder and several others to buy out Thorp's interest, and in 1885 Lloyd Brothers was established (after 1924, Lloyd Brothers Pharmacists, Inc.). When the youngest of the Lloyd brothers, Curtis Gates, joined the business one year later, the stage was set for the firm to become the preeminent manufacturer of eclectic preparations until its sale to the S. B. Penick Co. in 1938.

Although Nelson Ashley demonstrated indispensable business acumen and Curtis rose to prominence in mycological studies, it was John Uri Lloyd who led the family. His insatiable curiosity and persistent laboratory work won him three Ebert Prizes from the American Pharmaceutical Association (1882, 1891, 1916) for original research in alkaloidal and colloidal chemistry. So impressed was Wolfgang Ostwald, the eminent authority on colloid chemistry, that he hailed Lloyd's work on "mass action" and reprinted the prize-winning essays on "Precipitates in Fluid Extracts" in his prestigious *Kolloidchemische Beihefte* (1916).

Whatever the theoretical implications of his work, Lloyd's prominence stems in no small part from the practical applications of his innovations to the pharmaceutical industry. This is evidenced in his technique for adsorption of alkaloids from solutions with hydrous aluminum silicate (Lloyd's reagent) and his method for soluble vegetable product extraction without the heat-altering characteristics of conventional processes. This latter invention (patented 1904) became known as Lloyd's "cold still" and was used in the industry for the next sixty years. In addition to these were numerous other successful products and processes developed by Lloyd, such as an atropine sulfate preparation for eye wounds used during World War I, an improved eye dropper, and an array of manufacturing apparatus for concentrating solutions, processing alkaloids, purifying volatile oils, and percolating and condensing fluids.

Lloyd was also a noted teacher and author. He taught at the Cincinnati College of Pharmacy from 1883 to 1887, but his lifelong connections remained with Cincinnati's Eclectic Medical Institute. He taught pharmacy and chemistry at that school from 1878 to 1895 and eventually rose to the presidency of its board of trustees. Perhaps Lloyd's most significant contribution to American pharmaceutical education rests in his *Chemistry of Medicines* (8 editions, 1881–1897), one of the first American textbooks on the subject. He also published hundreds of articles in the *Eclectic Medical Journal*, several important book-length pharmacognostic studies, and the eclectic *American Dispensatory*, coauthored first with John King (1886) and later with Harvey Wickes Felter (1898, 1909). He contributed regularly to the *Eclectic Medical Gleaner*, which he published from 1904 to 1912, and to the *Journal of the American Pharmaceutical Association*.

Lloyd's interest in research and scholarship helped found the Lloyd Library & Museum, which still stands in Cincinnati. Although Curtis Lloyd established the financial security of the library with his bequest and trust in 1917, there is no doubt that the core collection itself stems from John Uri Lloyd's research and development needs and his professional associations. Well before Lloyd's death, his library had gained fame for its rare botanical and pharmaceutical holdings.

Faithful to his eclectic connections, Lloyd wore the appellation "rebel" proudly. His extensive publications, his scholarship, and his notoriety as an innovative pharmaceutical manufacturer assured Lloyd's prominence in his profession. His fame launched him into the presidency of the American Pharmaceutical Association (1887–1888), and his many contributions to the field were acknowledged in 1920 with the American Pharmaceutical Association's highest honor, the Remington Medal.

Lloyd's life outside of pharmacy was equally remarkable. He wrote eight novels and numerous short stories, the six "Stringtown" novels about his northern Kentucky boyhood—*Stringtown on the Pike* (1900), *Warwick of the Knobs* (1901), *Red-Head* (1903), *Scroggins* (1904), *Felix Moses* (1930), and *Our Willie* (1934)—being the most popular in their day. This activity also put him into close contact with leading literary figures like James Lane Allen and James Whitcomb Riley.

Lloyd led a more tranquil personal life. He was married twice: briefly to Addie Meader who died of peritonitis on 7 January 1876, eleven days after their wedding; and in 1880 to Emma Rouse, with whom he had three children. Lloyd died while visiting his daughter's home in Van Nuys, California.

• Lloyd's papers are held primarily in the Lloyd Library & Museum, Cincinnati, Ohio, and the Kremers Reference Files at the University of Wisconsin School of Pharmacy, Madison. Lloyd's "Pharmacy Series" in the *Bulletin of the Lloyd Library* includes some of his most important work: *References to Capillarity* (1902), *The Eclectic Alkaloids* (1910), and the *History of the Vegetable Drugs of the Pharmacopeia of the United States*, with Curtis Gates Lloyd (1911; expanded ed., 1921). Also coauthored with Curtis is the two-volume *Drugs and Medicines of North America* (1884–1885). Lloyd's fiction includes *Etidorhpa* (1895), a hollow earth adventure of speculative philosophy, and the novelette *The Right Side of the Car* (1897), a sentimental tale written in part to defray the expense of erecting a monument to his departed friend and colleague John King.

A brief but authoritative source on Lloyd is *Kremers and Urdang's History of Pharmacy*, 4th ed., rev. by Glenn Sonnedecker (1976), and Caswell A. Mayo, *The Lloyd Library and Its Makers* (1928), is still useful. Michael A. Flannery, "John Uri Lloyd: The Life and Legacy of an Illustrious Heretic," *Queen City Heritage* 50 (1992): 2–14, provides a critical review of secondary sources. For an appraisal of Lloyd's Stringtown novels see Flannery's "The Local Color of John Uri Lloyd: A Critical Survey of the Stringtown Novels," *Register of the Kentucky Historical Society* 91 (1993): 24–50.

MICHAEL A. FLANNERY

LLOYD, Marshall Burns (10 Mar. 1858–10 Aug. 1927), inventor and manufacturer, was born in St. Paul, Minnesota, the son of John Lloyd and Margaret Commee. Lloyd's parents were English immigrants who initially had settled in Canada and moved back to a farm in Meaford, Ontario, shortly after their son's birth. As a youth, Lloyd had a limited formal education but exhibited an inventive bent and keen ambition. At age fourteen he worked in a country store. Then he invented a fish spear, caught fish, and sold them door-to-door, devised a clothes hamper and a spring bed, worked in a grocery store in Toronto, peddled soap, delivered mail by dogsled, and finally joined a land rush in Winnipeg. Speculating in land using his savings from waiting tables, he accumulated several thousand dollars. He was eighteen years old.

In 1880 Lloyd bought a farm for his family in Grafton, North Dakota, but within two years he left the farm and moved into town. While selling insurance he devised a combination grain-sack holder and scale in 1883 and manufactured it in a St. Thomas, North Dakota, blacksmith shop. After a fire destroyed the shop in 1886, he went to Minneapolis seeking capital to rebuild, but he was soon reduced to selling shoes. A wire doormat and a wire-weaving machine he invented in 1890, however, attracted the attention of the C. O. White Company. In exchange for his patents, Lloyd received an interest in the firm, and in 1894 he became president. Now a rising businessman, he was elected councillor in Minneapolis in 1896–1897. His next invention was a technique for weaving wire spring mattresses that proved enormously successful; the patent was licensed in Europe, Australia, New Zealand, and South Africa. With that money, Lloyd bought the firm in 1900 and renamed it the Lloyd Manufacturing Company.

Lloyd continued inventing. His next idea, in 1906, was a wire wheel for baby carriages and wagons, which he began to manufacture the following year in a new factory in Menominee, Michigan. In 1910 he devised and patented a system for making light-gauge seamless steel tubing. His machinery rolled, shaped, and then welded steel flats into tubing using oxyacetylene torches. By 1912 he was using this tubing to make steel beds; two years later he sold the patent rights for at least $800,000 to an automobile manufacturer.

Lloyd's next invention was his most famous—a mechanized process for producing wicker carriage bodies and later furniture. Until this time, wicker items were expensive because the cane had to be woven by hand around the frame of the object. Lloyd divided the labor and cut costs by separating frame production from the carriage body. At first, workers simply fabricated the wicker carriage bodies on removable frames; these wicker baskets were then joined to the carriage frame at final assembly. But in 1917, faced by demands for higher wages and a workers' strike, Lloyd took the crucial step toward the mechanization of wicker production, substituting twisted brown kraft paper for the difficult-to-handle cane and devising a series of machines to prepare and weave the paper fiber, thereby replacing skilled workers. In its final form, this process began by shearing large rolls of kraft paper into thin sections. Strips of paper were pulled off these rolls and twisted into fibers that could be mechanically woven. Lloyd's use of kraft paper as wicker fiber was not new; his contribution was to wrap the paper around metal wire, a material with which he was very familiar. The resulting wicker carriage bodies, after being dipped in a glue solution and painted, were very strong. By 1920 Lloyd, "the baby carriage king," was the largest maker of baby carriages in the world and had doubled the size of his factory.

Lloyd's process threatened traditional wicker furniture makers, and in 1921 a leading manufacturer, Washburn & Heywood Chair Company, bought Lloyd's patents for about $3 million. The resulting merger, the Heywood-Wakefield Company, retained Lloyd as "advisory engineer," and he began to devise mechanical means of producing wicker for furniture. The result was a machine that wove flat sheets of wicker that were cut to size and nailed to the bentwood furniture frames. A machine-woven braid covered the nails and edges of the wicker sheets. Like the carriages, this furniture was enormously durable. Additional improvements followed, including a loom in 1925 that wove decorative motifs, such as diamond shapes, into the wicker fabric.

Lloyd's inventions revolutionized wicker furniture production by removing it from the luxury category, and the Heywood-Wakefield Company introduced its successful Lloyd Loom line in 1922. The Menominee factory was expanded again in 1924, and the process was licensed in Australia, France, Germany, and, most successfully, to W. Lusty & Sons, in England. By 1940, 10 million pieces of Lloyd Loom wicker furniture had been sold in the United States and Great Britain.

Clearly, Lloyd's forte was invention, and the motto on his office wall read, "I never do what anyone else can do." Lloyd acquired 200 patents in his lifetime, aided by a team of six individuals who moved with him from Minneapolis to Menominee and built and operated the inventions that Lloyd envisioned. These men guided the company's furniture operations after Lloyd's death.

Lloyd's life sounds like a Horatio Alger story, but his path to success—combining invention and manufacturing into a business career—was far from unique. During this period, American business perfected manufacturing technologies and processes that permitted efficient production of consumer goods in quantity, perhaps the most important American contribution to technology. Lloyd's inventions and factories were part of this process. At the same time, they reflected, along with his activities outside of business, the powerful rhetoric of efficiency embraced by many turn-of-the-century Americans.

Twice elected mayor of Menominee, Lloyd served from 1913 to 1917 with the goal of cleaning up and beautifying the city. He earned the nickname "Efficiency Lloyd," although he seems to have encountered some resistance to his program. He also helped build—and pay for—a public water-supply system and in the 1920s a cooperative department store and the Lloyd Theater. After retiring from the factory in 1924, Lloyd and a dozen workers in his personal workshop devised prefabricated insulated housing for workers. A bequest from his $2 million estate later supported the Lloyd Memorial Hospital.

Lloyd was married three times: in 1894 (wife's name unknown), only to divorce two years later; in 1899 to Margaret Isadora (maiden name unknown); and a third time, in 1922, to Henriette Pollen. He and his first wife adopted his only child in 1894.

• Some information on Lloyd and his company can be found in the Menominee County (Mich.) Historical Society, including a scrapbook of newspaper clippings. (The author of this entry is indebted to librarian Elizabeth L. E. Brown.) The most comprehensive source of information on Lloyd is Lee J. Curtis, *Lloyd Loom Woven Fiber Furniture* (1991), a book that deals extensively with Lloyd Loom wicker furniture but also treats Lloyd's life and career. George W. Rowell, "Wicker Weaving by Machine," *Scientific American* 122 (6 Mar. 1920): 242, discusses the machinery developed by Lloyd. See also *A Completed Century, 1826–1926: The Story of Heywood-Wakefield Company* (1926), published by the company. A brief note that one of Lloyd's wives sued him for a share of his estate in 1928 appears in the *New York Times*, 6 May 1928. An obituary is in the *New York Times*, 11 Aug. 1927.

BRUCE E. SEELY

LLOYD, Pop. *See* Lloyd, John Henry.

LLOYD, Thomas (? Feb. 1640–10 Sept. 1694), lawyer and statesman, was born at Dolobran, Montgomeryshire, Wales, the son of Charles Lloyd, a land-rich gentleman, and Elizabeth Stanley. He was baptized on 17 February 1640. Like his older brother Charles, Lloyd had been attracted to the Society of Friends while at Jesus College, Oxford, where he studied law and medicine, probably between 1658 and 1663. An outspoken advocate of Quakerism, he suffered fines and imprisonment like so many Quakers of the Restoration era, including his brother. He married Mary Jones, a fellow Quaker, in 1665. They had ten children.

By the 1680s Lloyd intended to emigrate to Pennsylvania, probably convinced by William Penn, who had recruited many supporters in Wales. Lloyd stood out among middling farmers and artisans by dint of his knowledge of the law, his social prominence, and his sturdy efforts to defend Quakers, who rejected the worship and sacraments of the Church of England. Shortly after he arrived in Philadelphia in August 1683, Lloyd was selected as foreman of the provincial grand jury, and Penn appointed him master of the rolls in December 1683—a position that entrusted him with enrolling laws, commissions, deeds, and patents. Three months later he was elected a member of the council, where he played a central role in drafting laws for the legislative assembly.

Lloyd remained a firm member of Penn's inner circle during 1683 and 1684, and Penn relied on him to maintain proprietary policy and insulate proprietary privileges from jealous encroachers. When he left Philadelphia in August 1684, Penn included Lloyd among a coterie that he counted on to hold together a strong proprietary presence. Accepting Penn's appointments as keeper of the seal, commissioner of [proprietary] property, and president of the council, Lloyd became the most influential officeholder and politician in the infant colony. In Penn's absence, Lloyd acted as de facto governor until December 1688 except for his removal in December 1684 to New York. His first wife having died, he there married Patience Story and stayed for about two years. They had no children.

Lloyd's pivotal position after Penn's departure proved difficult. Many settlers resented proprietary quitrents, became annoyed at what seemed a distant and unresponsive proprietor, and harbored jealousy of the select proprietary circle. Lloyd found himself caught between the elected assembly and the council; between the Lower Counties (now Delaware) and Pennsylvania; and amid divisions among the inner group of councillors on whom Penn depended.

Penn hoped that men such as Lloyd could reconcile the various factions that embroiled politics in early Pennsylvania. Though Lloyd saw himself as a good faith conciliator, he disappointed the proprietor because Penn believed from afar the letters from his main confidants, Thomas Holme and William Markham, who argued that Lloyd was curbing Penn's power by enlarging the authority of the council and dismantling the machinery of proprietary quitrents. By about 1686, Penn was convinced that Lloyd was overbearing, hungry for power, and unfaithful to some of his instructions and policies. Deeply frustrated, Penn reorganized the executive arm of government in 1687, creating a commission of five deputies, which he hoped would end factional struggles and obtain strict conformity to proprietary policy.

Despite Penn's suspicions, he retained Lloyd in the colony's leadership. By charging Lloyd, James Claypoole, John Eckley, Robert Turner, and Nicholas More to act as his commissioners of state, Penn compounded rather than cured the province's ills. Deeply disappointed with the inability of the executive commissioners of state to achieve "a mutual simplicity, an entire confidence in one another," Penn abruptly invited Lloyd to serve as deputy governor. When Lloyd refused—apparently unwilling to accept responsibility for executing the proprietor's long-distasteful policies—Penn appointed John Blackwell, a Puritan and military officer, as deputy governor in 1688.

From the moment of Blackwell's arrival, Lloyd attempted to subvert the Puritan's governorship by blocking his power to resume judicial and sheriff appointments that earlier had been absorbed by the council. Blackwell responded by attempting to impeach Lloyd—in effect, an effort to neutralize the leader of the independent-minded Quaker merchants and landowners who had wrung autonomous power piecemeal from Penn. Amid tempestuous petitions, attempted boycotts of legislative assemblies, and angry threats, the Lloydians were able to bring about an impasse in government. Convinced that Lloyd had paralyzed his governorship, Blackwell resigned. By now under attack as a crypto-Catholic in England during the Glorious Revolution, Penn allowed the council to assume the authority of the executive branch, and the council promptly chose Lloyd as their president—tantamount to a deputy governorship. Lloyd quickly removed strong supporters of Penn's proprietary privileges from government positions. In a final attempt to win Lloyd over, Penn formally appointed him deputy governor in 1691.

Lloyd's leadership in the strained relations in early Pennsylvania became evident again in the Keithian controversy that spread civil strife to the religious sphere in 1691. Lloyd rallied many Quakers against George Keith's charges that Quakers needed greater definition of doctrine, a tightening of the structural relationships of the various monthly meetings, and a greater emphasis on Christian fundamentals. Moreover, Keith charged that the Quakers' profession of nonresistance rendered them incapable of performing the duties of civil government. To the already apprehensive Lloydian faction, Keith's incendiary behavior was the most dangerous threat to its position because Keith gathered many supporters from the Lower Counties, dissident Quakers, Anglicans, and many shopkeepers and master craftsmen who earlier had opposed an attempt by Lloyd to impose a tax to pay for his salary. Lloyd led the attempt to silence Keith by arresting William Bradford, Pennsylvania's only printer, who published Keith's fiery pamphlets against Lloyd. The Keithian controversy reached a climax in 1693, when the English government suspended Penn's right to govern and placed his colony under Benjamin Fletcher, the royal governor of New York. Lloyd died a year later in Philadelphia, his political power eclipsed.

Like many others who expected the western side of the Atlantic to promote their fortunes, Lloyd was disappointed by not prospering economically in early Pennsylvania. Wealthy enough to acquire five slaves and buy more than 7,000 acres of land in Pennsylvania, the Lower Counties of Delaware, and West New Jersey in the early years, Lloyd watched his position gradually slip. Practicing law and medicine and dabbling in trade proved unprofitable—so much so that the executors of his estate thought that his widow would be left with little money, if any, after Lloyd's creditors had been satisfied. Among Lloyd's ten children, three of his daughters married prominent merchants in Philadelphia.

Lloyd was one of a small number of first-generation immigrants who established and maintained the machinery of government in an era when the Quaker experiment had more than its share of divisiveness. While not always able to mediate among different factions in the context of an absentee leader and proprietor, Lloyd nonetheless exercised a moderating influence and a stabilizing effect as Quakers struggled to govern a colony of their own for the first and only time.

• The papers of Lloyd are not plentiful; most of those that exist are at the Historical Society of Pennsylvania, and many of these can be found in Mary Maples Dunn et al., eds., *The Papers of William Penn*, vols. 1–5 (1981–1987). The most recent and complete assessment is in Craig W. Horle et al., eds., *Lawmaking and Legislators in Pennsylvania: A Biographical Dictionary*, vol. 1: *1682–1709* (1991), pp. 505–17. Other assessments of Lloyd's role in early Pennsylvania are Gary B. Nash, *Quakers and Politics: Pennsylvania, 1681–1726* (1968), and Edwin B. Bronner, *William Penn's "Holy Experiment"* (1962).

GARY B. NASH

LLOYD-JONES, Eleanor (24 Dec. 1845–19 Nov. 1919), and **Jane Lloyd-Jones** (15 Apr. 1848–23 May 1917), educators, were both born near Ixonia, Wisconsin, the daughters of Richard Lloyd Jones and Mallie "Mary" Thomas James, farmers. Unlike most other members of the family, Eleanor, who was usually called Ellen (or Nell), and Jane (or Jennie) regularly wrote their surname as Lloyd-Jones. Ellen graduated from Platteville (Wisc.) State Normal School in 1870 and taught in various schools in Wisconsin. By the time she was in her early forties, she had left the classroom to be a teacher of teachers as head of the history department at River Falls (Wisc.) State Normal School. Jane graduated from Platteville in the same year as her sister. After some teaching in neighboring towns, she became interested in a new development, the kindergarten, and she went to St. Louis to study at the Kindergarten Training School. In her late thirties she went to St. Paul, Minnesota, as the director of Kindergarten Training Schools there. Neither sister ever married. Each woman had a significant career in education as an individual. Their major accomplishment, however, was the joint establishment of Hillside Home School, across the river from Spring Green, Wisconsin.

When their father died in 1885, he bequeathed the family farm to Ellen and Jane, his only unmarried children. In 1887 the two undertook to turn the farm into Hillside Home School, a boarding school for wealthy city children and a school for their many nieces and nephews as well as neighboring farm children. They were helped in getting established by the contacts and reputation of their brother Jenkin, a well-known Unitarian minister in Chicago. In their turn they assisted their young nephew Frank Lloyd Wright, who was just beginning his career. Wright designed and built the classrooms and the dormitory buildings. His famous windmill "Romeo and Juliet" was raised to supply the school with water.

The school, one of the first coeducational boarding schools, developed a regional reputation as a place of good teaching that promoted growth in children. It was never a secure financial enterprise, though, and faced money problems from the beginning. Besides a solid academic foundation the school stressed the whole development of the child. Outdoor activities were prominent: gardening, bird and flower identification, hikes, sleigh rides, and picnics. There was a dancing master and regular dances. Mary Ellen Chase, who taught at Hillside as a young woman, wrote that it was a "progressive" school before the term was coined or the idea articulated and that it was unself-consciously so because of the training and intuition of the two directors. Jane often attributed the school's approach to the nurturing and teaching given them by their mother.

The students were integrated into the life of nearby Valley, where five Jones family farms were located. All the students and staff addressed the Jones men as uncle and the women as aunts, especially Aunt Nell and Aunt Jane. On Sundays the school gathered in Unity Chapel, the little family church, for worship led by members of the family, Uncle Jenkin from Chicago, or some noted friend of Jenkin from farther away.

The Aunts intended that the school be continued by the next generation, and several nieces and nephews taught in the school. In 1903 Frank Lloyd Wright, now an established architect, designed and built a new stone classroom building with a gymnasium, a theater, and a memorial room dedicated to Richard and Mallie Jones. Ellen and Jane were not good businesswomen and let the money side of the school be managed by their brothers. The new building overextended the school's finances and caused a crippling debt. There was much acrimony within the family over responsibility for the situation and ways to deal with it. The next generation of Jones teachers did not come forward to replace Nell and Jane. In 1913 they had to give up the school. Frank Lloyd Wright took over the building, which became the architectural school still used by the Wright Foundation. Without personal resources and somewhat dependent on Wright, the sisters moved to California and then back to Chicago. Jane died in her old room at Hillside and Ellen in Chicago.

• The collected papers of the two women are in the State Historical Society of Wisconsin, Madison. There are brief, but good, biographical studies in Mary Ellen Chase, *A Goodly Fellowship* (1939), and Maginel Wright Barney, *The Valley of the God-Almighty Joneses* (1965). *Unity* (Chicago) printed a lengthy obituary and tribute to Jane on 31 May 1917. Ellen's death was barely noticed. Her obituary in the Madison (Wisc.) *Democrat* for 21 Nov. 1919 is a scant paragraph.

THOMAS E. GRAHAM

LOCKE, Alain Leroy (13 Sept. 1885–9 June 1954), philosopher and literary critic, was born in Philadelphia, Pennsylvania, the son of Pliny Ishmael Locke, a lawyer, and Mary Hawkins, a teacher and member of the Felix Adler Ethical Society. Locke graduated from Central High School and the Philadelphia School of Pedagogy in Philadelphia in 1904. That same year he published his first editorial, "Moral Training in Elementary Schools," in *The Teacher*, and entered undergraduate school at Harvard University. He studied at Harvard under such scholars as Josiah Royce, George H. Palmer, Ralph B. Perry, and Hugo Munsterberg before graduating in 1907 and becoming the first African-American Rhodes scholar, at Hertford College, Oxford. While in Europe, he also attended lectures at the University of Berlin (1910–1911) and studied the works of Franz Brentano, Alexius Meinong, and C. F. von Ehrenfels. Locke associated with other Rhodes scholars, including Horace M. Kallen, author of the concept of cultural pluralism; H. E. Alaily, president of the Egyptian Society of England; Pa Ka Isaka Seme, a black South African law student and eventual founder of the African National Congress of South Africa; and Har Dayal from India—each concerned with national liberation in their respective homelands. The formative years of Locke's education and early career were the years just proceeding and during World War I—years of nationalist uprising and wars between the world's major nation-states. Locke joined the Howard University faculty in 1912, to eventually form the most prestigious department of philosophy at a historically African-American university.

In the summer of 1915 Locke began a lecture series sponsored by the Social Science Club of the National Association for the Advancement of Colored People, titled "Race Contacts and Interracial Relations: A Study of the Theory and Practice of Race." Locke argued against social Darwinism, which held that distinct races exist and are biologically determined to express peculiar cultural traits. Locke believed that races were socially constructed and that cultures are the manifestation of stressed values, values always subject to transvaluation and revaluation. Locke introduced a new way of thinking about social entities by conceiving of race as a socially formed category, which, despite its foundation in social history, substantively affected material reality.

Locke received his doctorate in philosophy from Harvard in 1918 and shortly thereafter wrote "The Role of the Talented Tenth," which supported W. E. B. Du Bois's idea that the upward mobility of approximately one-tenth of a population is crucial for the improvement of the whole population. Locke also became interested in the Baha'i faith, finding particularly attractive its emphasis on racial harmony and the interrelatedness of all religious faiths. Locke attended the 1921 Inter-Racial Amity conference on 19–21 May in Washington, D.C., and as late as 1932 published short editorials in the *Baha'i World*. Although he did not formally join the Baha'i faith, he remained respectful of its practices.

Locke went on to help initiate the Harlem Renaissance, 1925–1939, a period of significant cultural contributions by African Americans. The years 1924–1925 were a major turning point in Locke's life. He edited a special edition of the magazine *Survey* titled the *Survey Graphic*, on the district of Harlem in Manhattan, New York. The editor of *Survey* was Paul U. Kellogg, and the associate editor was Jane Addams. That edition became the source for his seminal work reflecting the nature of valuation and the classicism of African-American culture, *The New Negro: An Interpretation of Negro Life*, published in 1925. *The New Negro* was a collage of art by Winold Reiss and Aaron Douglas and representations of African artifacts; articles by J. A. Rogers, E. Franklin Frazier, Charles S. Johnson, Melville J. Herskovits, and W. E. B. Du Bois; poetry by Countee Cullen, Langston Hughes, Arna Bontemps, and Angelina Grimke; spirituals; and bibliographies. *The New Negro* was intended as a work "by" rather than "about" African Americans, a text exuding pride, historical continuity, and a new spirit of self-respect not because a metamorphosis had occurred in the psychology of African Americans, "but because the Old Negro had long become more of a myth than a man." *The New Negro* embodied Locke's definition of essential features of African-American culture, themes such as the importance of self-respect in the face of social denigration, ethnic pride; overcoming racial stereotypes and idioms, such as call-and-response in the spirituals or discord and beats in jazz; and the importance that cultural hybridity, traditions, and revaluations play in shaping cross-cultural relationships. Locke promoted those features of African-American folk culture that he believed could be universalized and thus become classical idioms, functioning, for Locke, as cultural ambassadors encouraging cross-cultural and racial respect. As debates over how to characterize American and African-American cultural traits in literature became less a source of intellectual conflict, Locke's interests moved on to issues in education.

In 1936 Locke began work on a book series, the Bronze Booklets on the History, Problems, and Cultural Contributions of the Negro, under the auspices of the Associates in Negro Folk Education. Eight booklets were published in the series, which became a standard reference for the teaching of African-American history. In one of his frequent book reviews of African-American literature for *Opportunity: A Journal of Negro Life*, Locke supported the controversial novel by Richard Wright, *Native Son*, in 1941. The novel was controversial because Wright did not portray the lead character, Bigger Thomas, as a peace-loving, passive, and victimized African American, but as a critic of liberals and radicals. Locke's support for Wright's novel represented his belief that race divided America.

Locke published his first extensive article on his philosophy in 1935, "Values and Imperatives," in *American Philosophy: Today and Tomorrow*, edited by Horace M. Kallen and Sidney Hook. Locke argued that values are inherently unstable, always subject to transvaluation and transposition. Locke contended that "All philosophies, it seems to me, are in ultimate derivation philosophies of life and not of abstract, disembodied 'objective' reality; products of time, place, and situation, and thus systems of timed history rather than timeless eternity" (p. 313). Rather than believe that science is an adequate model for reasoning about social reality, Locke presented the view that knowledge is a function of experience and the categories of logic, science, math, and social science are heuristic value fields or distinctions.

Locke published his landmark work on education, "The Need for a New Organon in Education," in *Findings of the First Annual Conference on Adult Education and the Negro* (1938), based on a lecture before the American Association for Adult Education, the Extension Department of Hampton Institute, and the Associates in Negro Folk Education, in Hampton, Virginia, on 20–22 October 1938. Locke proposed the concept critical relativism (the view that there are no absolutely true propositions, but that we can have standards and criteria for critical evaluations). Locke warned against believing that all relevant knowledge can be acquired through application of formal logic and argued for the need to apply functional methods of reasoning and the importance of value judgments in considering defensible beliefs. Locke actively promoted adult education, working with the American Association of Adult Education in Washington, D.C., from 1948 to 1952.

In 1942 Locke edited, along with Bernard J. Stern, *When Peoples Meet: A Study of Race and Culture*. This anthology used a concept of ethnicity to account for both ethnic and racial contacts. Locke's approach continued his view that racial identities were socially created and were not based on substantive biological categories.

In 1944 Locke became a founding conference member of the Conference on Science, Philosophy and Religion, which published its annual proceedings of debates on the relationship of these areas of thought. He promoted the idea that cultural pluralism was an analog for why one knowledge field was an insufficient reasoning model for sure knowledge, i.e., different cultures and civilizations supported laudable values just as different disciplines could sustain different spheres of knowledge. For Locke, there was no reason to believe in a unified theory of knowledge, i.e., a theory that would tell us about the nature of all forms of knowledge. Rather, a plurality of fields of knowledge and cultural values was a preferable perspective on Locke's account.

Locke was a controversial figure. His aesthetic views contrasted with those of the Black Aesthetic Movement of the 1970s. He was satirized in novels, criticized by Zora Neale Hurston as an elitist interested in controlling the definition of African-American culture, reproached for failing to acknowledge the largest Pan-African movement of the 1920s, the Marcus Garvey–led United Negro Improvement Association, and denounced for placing too great a value on African-American literature as a text representing a unique cultural texture.

Locke died in New York City. He lived a controversial life because his ideas of values, race, and culture often went against popular ideas. His concept of pragmatism was critical of, and different from, the dominant forms represented by William James and John Dewey. Locke's effort to shape the Harlem Renaissance and define the "New Negro" went against those that believed folk culture should not be changed, and his advocacy of value-oriented education within the adult education movement was viewed as a new orientation. Locke's philosophy, promoted by the Alain L. Locke Society, remains a source of controversy and debate.

• Locke's personal correspondence and unfinished articles are in the Alain L. Locke Archives, Howard University, Washington, D.C. In addition to those works cited in the text, a number of Locke's most important writings are available in Jeffrey C. Stewart, ed., *The Critical Temper of Alain Locke: A Selection of His Essays on Art and Culture* (1983), and Leonard Harris, *The Philosophy of Alain Locke: Harlem Renaissance and Beyond* (1989). The largest anthology of articles about Locke's philosophy is Russell J. Linneman, *Alain Locke: Reflections on a Modern Renaissance Man* (1982). Excellent biographies of Locke include Eugene C. Holmes, "Alain L. Locke—Philosopher, Critic, Spokesman," *Journal of Philosophy* 54 (Feb. 1957): 113–18, and Douglas K. Stafford, "Alain Locke: The Child, the Man, and the People," *June* (Winter 1961): 25–34. Locke's method and ideas are compared to those of Jacques Derrida and Derrida's philosophy of deconstruction in Ernest D. Mason, "Deconstruction in the Philosophy of Alain Locke," *Transactions of the Charles S. Peirce Society* 24 (1988): 85–106, and Leonard Harris, "Identity: Alain Locke's Atavism," *Transactions of the Charles S. Peirce Society*, 26, no. 1 (Winter 1988): 65–84. An argument for interpreting Locke's role in American history as unique is presented by Houston A. Baker, Jr., *Modernism and the Harlem Renaissance* (1987), and Johnny Washington, *Alain Locke and His Philosophy: A Quest for Cultural Pluralism* (1986). An argument for interpreting Locke's role in American history as similar to other pragmatists such as William James and John Dewey is presented by George Hutchinson, *The Harlem Renaissance in Black and White* (1995). David L. Lewis, *When Harlem Was in Vogue* (1981), discusses Locke's personal influence on novelists and political activists. Locke's career is also assessed in Archie Epps et al., "The Alain L. Locke Symposium," *Harvard Advocate*, 1 Dec. 1973, pp. 9–29, and LaVerne Gyant, "Alain Leroy Locke: More than an Adult Educator," in *Freedom Road: Adult Education of African Americans* (1996), pp. 67–88.

LEONARD HARRIS

LOCKE, Bessie (7 Aug. 1865–9 Apr. 1952), educator and organizational director, was born in West Cambridge (now Arlington), Massachusetts, the daughter of William Henry Locke, a printer, and Jane MacFarland Schoulder. Locke's father lost his print works business in Passaic, New Jersey, as a result of the panic of 1869. He then opened a fabric-printing business in Brooklyn, New York, where Bessie Locke went to a private kindergarten that was one of the very few English-speaking kindergartens in the country at that time. She attended the Brooklyn public schools and worked as a bookkeeper while still a teenager. She took business courses at Columbia University but did not earn a degree. Locke assisted the pastor of All Souls Church in Brooklyn for two years before managing a millinery store owned by an uncle in North Carolina for two and a half years.

Like many others who became involved in the kindergarten movement, Locke was transformed by seeing a kindergarten in operation. Having read the works of Charles Dickens and others who described the miseries of poor children in heartrending detail, Locke was eager to engage in some form of social work to alleviate crime, delinquency, and poverty. When she visited, reportedly in 1892, a charity kindergarten in New York City run by a friend who had studied under Maria Kraus-Boelté, a follower of German kindergarten originator Friedrich Froebel, she was fascinated by what she saw but dubious that the program could have a permanent impact on the lives of impoverished and immigrant children. Locke returned six months later and was deeply moved by the positive changes she observed in the children. Converted to the kindergarten cause, Locke thought of the kindergarten as a religious mission and vocation. She began raising money to start more free kindergartens and founded the East End Kindergarten Union of Brooklyn.

Locke became an extremely effective kindergarten organizer and fundraiser. She was financial secretary of the Brooklyn Free Kindergarten Association from 1896 to 1923 and held the same position in the New York Kindergarten Society beginning in 1899. She raised some $700,000 for charity kindergartens in New York City and arranged for a donation of $250,000 from John D. Archbold, president of Standard Oil of New Jersey, to pay for housing the New York Kindergarten Society in a building that included a community center for mothers' meetings and other functions. In 1906 she began extending this organization's activities to promote the establishment of public kindergartens nationwide. With the support of prominent educators and kindergarten advocates such as John Dewey and Kate Douglas Wiggin, as well as wealthy patrons from business and society, the National Association for the Promotion of Kindergarten Education began in 1909; in 1911 it became the National Kindergarten Association, which Locke directed until nearly the end of her life. The National Kindergarten Association was a highly successful advocacy and lobbying group that developed extensive public relations materials, including press releases, surveys, articles, and films, one of which was produced in association with Thomas Edison's company and was titled "At the Threshold of Life." A clever marketing device, the film focused on an upper-class young businessman whose fiancée teaches in a charity kindergarten and refuses to marry him unless he contributes financially to the kindergarten cause. The National Kindergarten Association also authored model statutes that helped many states pass enabling legislation for kindergartens.

Locke and the National Kindergarten Association were also instrumental in the founding in 1912 of a Kindergarten Division of the U.S. Bureau of Education. Commissioner Philander P. Claxton asked Locke to help start the division, and she served as its director from 1913 to 1919, during which time the division published a series of influential circulars on topics such as kindergartens and Americanization, supervision, and standards for teacher training. The division reported on the efforts of manufacturers who sponsored industry-based kindergartens for the children of workers and began publishing home kindergarten articles for parents. In 1919 the National Kindergarten Association assumed responsibility for these articles, and in 1923 Locke's close colleague Florence Jane Ovens took on the editorship of these publications. By the time of Locke's death the home kindergarten articles had reached more than 38 million people through study groups in the United States and international distribution in forty-three countries.

Locke was also involved in the parent education movement and in other women's organizations that flourished in the early part of the twentieth century. She was chair of the kindergarten division of the National Congress of Parents and Teachers from 1913 to 1922 and director of the National Council of Women from 1921 to 1946. She was a member from 1920 of the governing board of the National College of Education, the kindergarten training college founded by Elizabeth Harrison in Evanston, Illinois, and a life member of the International Council of Women and of the Association for Childhood Education, one of the main professional organizations in early childhood education.

Aided by Locke and the National Kindergarten Association, the number of kindergartens in the United States grew steadily in the early twentieth century. In 1899–1900 public and private kindergarten enrollment totaled 93,737 students; by 1929–1930 it was 777,899, an increase of more than 700 percent. In 1899–1900, when Locke was beginning her work, 32 states had public kindergartens. By 1929–1930, toward the end of her career, 40 states had public kindergartens. Her organizational skills greatly enhanced the expansion of the American kindergarten movement from a private charity to a public institution and helped publicize the benefits of the kindergarten throughout the world. Locke's interests included anthropology and collecting paintings. She never married and died in New York City.

• Locke's papers are held in the records of the National Kindergarten Association in the archives of Teachers College, Columbia University. Her publications include "Kindergarten as an Agency for the Prevention of Crime," *American Federationist* (May 1934): 523–26; U.S. Bureau of Education, *Manufacturers Indorse* [sic] *Kindergartens* (July 1919); and Kindergarten Circular 4, *Bulletin of the Bureau of Education* (1920). An obituary is in the *New York Times*, 11 Apr. 1952.

BARBARA BEATTY

LOCKE, David Ross (20 Sept. 1833–15 Feb. 1888), literary comedian and newspaper editor, was born in Vestal, Broome County, New York, the son of Nathaniel Reed Locke, a laborer, tanner, and farmer, and Hester Ross. He was apprenticed as a printer to the *Cortland (N.Y.) Democrat*, in 1845, at the age of twelve, after five years of formal schooling in a one-room schoolhouse. The Locke family was never well-to-do, but the household was characterized by Locke's father's strong egalitarianism and deeply held moral convictions. Locke's mother was a strong moral influence on him, in conjunction with the opposition to alcohol of his father, a failed teetotaler who was never able to fully stop drinking.

In October 1853 Locke began his successful career as an editor with the *Plymouth (Ohio) Advertiser*. Sometime during this period, as his father had before him, the hard-drinking Locke declared himself a temperance man and courted Martha Hannah Bodine, to whom he was married in 1855 and with whom he had three sons. In September 1855 he entered into a partnership running the *Mansfield (Ohio) Republican*, moving four months later to the *Bucyrus (Ohio) Journal*, where he published the first of what became a series of letters written by Locke in the guise of an antiabolitionist postmaster, Petroleum Vesuvius Nasby.

The first Nasby letter actually appeared on 25 April 1862 in the *Findlay (Ohio) Hancock Jeffersonian*, which Locke owned and edited from the previous December. After a brief stint at the *Bellefontaine (Ohio) Republican* in 1865 Locke became editor of the *Toledo (Ohio) Blade* in October 1865, the newspaper with which he was closely identified for the rest of his career and from which he profited financially, becoming a partner in 1867.

Locke reorganized the Blade Co., a printing and paper company, in 1873, becoming its president in 1874 and sole owner in 1876. He also contributed to *The Index* and the *New York Evening Mail*, where he served as managing editor from 1871 through 1878. Throughout his career as a journalist Locke, or Nasby, as he was known to most readers, carried on an extensive public career as humorist-satirist writer and public lecturer. One of his proudest moments, however, was his election as an alderman for the Third Ward in Toledo in 1886. However, he became ill in November 1887, printed his last Nasby letter on 26 December 1887, and died, reportedly of tuberculosis, two months later in Toledo.

Locke's greatest impact was through his writings and lectures as Petroleum Vesuvius Nasby. The Nasby letters acridly satirized the plight of blacks in the South and the complicity of northern politicians in that plight. Both Abraham Lincoln and Ulysses S. Grant, admirers of Nasby themselves, identified Nasby as a major source of support for their presidencies. Lincoln and Grant offered Locke political patronage, possibly because of his writings or possibly because of his early and strong defense of Republican party principles. A copy of one of his books is supposed to have been the last thing Lincoln read before his assassination. Charles Sumner reported in his introduction to *The Struggles (Social, Financial and Political) of Petroleum V. Nasby* (1872) that Lincoln said to him in 1865, "For the genius to write these things I would gladly give up my office" (p. 15); in the same book, Nasby's "Prefis" proclaimed, "I woodn't give a ten-cent postal currency for wat the next generashen will do for me. It's this generashen I'm goin for" (p. 7). Thomas Nast became Nasby's illustrator, further increasing the power of his work. Mark Twain marveled at the graceless, forthright didactic power of Locke's lectures demanding equal rights for blacks.

The Nasby Papers: Letters and Sermons Containing the Views on the Topics of the Day of Petroleum V. Nasby, Pastor uv the Church uv the Noo Dispensashun appeared in book form in 1864, published in Indianapolis. Although the newspaper letters were widely circulated in the West and East, Locke was unsuccessful in selling rights to them to New York newspapers. The satires of southern bigotry, written in the guise of a redneck postmaster from Confederit X-Roads, Kentucky, attacked southern xenophobes and northern Copperheads embroiled in the Civil War and the complexities and ambiguities of the campaigns for the Fourteenth and Fifteenth amendments to the Constitution. Nasby gloated over the physical violence done to African Americans to reveal the horrible plight of blacks at the hands of their oppressors, a theme Locke developed in lectures as well, beginning with "Cussed Be Canaan" in 1867. Southerners and their northern sympathizers (his special target) were deeply antagonized by his writings. His lectures were extremely popular.

Various collections of letters followed. *Divers Views, Opinions, and Prophecies of Yoors Trooly Petroleum V.*

Nasby and *Swinging Round the Circle; or, Andy's Trip to the West* came in 1866. *Swingin' Round the Cirkle* (1867) holds some of Nasby's most profound moral statements. The letters composing the book were written in response to a phrase by Andrew Johnson on an uninspired tour of the country. In "A Vison of the Next World," Satan proclaims, "It takes a modritly smart man to be vishus enuff to come to me; he hez to have sense enuff to distinguish between good and evil, cussednis enuff to deliberately choose the latter, and brains enuff to do suthin startlin in that line" (p. 70). Nasby allowed that a number of major American politicians fell into those categories, although some southerners were more honest than their Copperhead counterparts in the North, and rank and file "ignorant wretches . . . ain't accountable, no how" (p. 70). The evils of failed Reconstruction are satirized in stark portraits. One southern deacon laments: "John Brown's karkis . . . took possession of seward, and thro his ugly mouth it spoke the words 'The nigger is free'" (p. 42). Selling off his own children he laments to one beautiful mulatto, "Farewell, Looizer, my daughter, farewell! I loved yoor mother ez never man loved nigger. . . . She I sold to pay orf a mortgage on the place. . . . Farewell! I hed hoped to hev sold yoo this winter (for yoo are still young), and bought out Jinkins. . . . Oh! it is hard for father to part with child, even when the market's high; but, Oh God! to part thus" (p. 44).

More devastating pictures identify the horrors of lynchings, schoolhouse burnings, and a wide array of brutality and violence clothed in sanctimonious false piety and garbled social doctrine. Dialect and cacophony, coupled with Locke's power with succinct description, give each letter its own power, frequently revealing both a political and an economic program: "Uv course the edecated and refined democrasy wood never consent to be carried up to the polls alongside uv a nigger—uv course no Democratic offis-seeker wood hoomiliate himself to treatin a nigger afore a election, it bein a article uv faith with us never to drink with a nigger, onless he pays for it" (p. 27). *Ekkoes from Kentucky* (1868) reprinted descriptions of the plight of African Americans as the North lost its grip on southern reform in 1866.

In 1872 *Struggles* appeared, including letters from the previous volumes and ending with Locke's lectures on "Canaan," the woman question (1868), and temperance (1870). *Nasby in Exile*, a book of travel critiques on Europe, followed in 1882. American backwoods stories and attitudes were mixed with European observations. Later works included *The Morals of Abou Ben Adhem* (1875), a collection of moral stories told by a Yankee swindler located in a small New Jersey town, setting up shop as a Persian mystic. Sarcastic about young men of "culcha," the stories featured characters such as old rats who survived drowning in water barrels to counsel their offspring to keep their eyes peeled, ears open, and claws sharp. But Locke's voice, speaking through his satiric spokesman, saw the Whipping Post in Delaware as an obvious obstacle to progress and wars as evidence that man was only partly along the progressive march to true civilization. His essay on progress, "Old Times and New," offered a characteristic position; Abou counsels his interviewer, "Instead of mourning for a miserable past, tackle the splendid present, and try to do something for a more splendid future."

Two of Locke's three later novels were published: *A Paper City* (1879) exposed small-town greed and speculation as sources of economic hardship; *The Demagogue* (1891), published three years after Locke's death, depicted a strong figure abusing political opportunity in a regionalist framework; and the third, *Strong Heart and Steady Hand* (1888), appeared only as a newspaper serial. A modest local color poem "Hannah Jane" (1882) was a popular presentation of the self-sacrificing virtues of Locke's wife as well as a statement on her narrowness, responding to Whittier's "Maud Muller." The importance of Locke's influence as Nasby during the Civil War is probably now underrated because of the topicality of his humor, but his comments and observations on the race question remain substantial and significant.

• Locke's extant papers are held in the Rutherford B. Hayes Library (Fremont, Ohio), with minor collections elsewhere, and the Ohio Historical Society holds related material and files of newspapers. John M. Harrison, *The Man Who Made Nasby, David Ross Locke* (1969), is the definitive analytic study, in company with James C. Austin, *Petroleum V. Nasby* (1965), a survey with a useful bibliography. Both replace Cyril Clemens's largely anecdotal *Petroleum Vesuvius Nasby* (1936). Brief and cogent is Dennis E. Minor, "David Ross Locke," in *American Humorists, 1800–1950*, ed. Stanley Trachtenberg, vol. 1 (1982), pp. 270–75. Obituaries and memorial articles are in the *Toledo Blade*, 15–20 Feb. 1888, and the *Toledo Weekly Blade*, 23 Feb. 1888.

DAVID E. E. SLOANE

LOCKE, John (19 Feb. 1792–10 July 1856), educator, scientist, and inventor, was born in Lempster, New Hampshire, the son of Samuel Barron Locke, a farmer and miller, and Hannah Russell. He was raised in Maine on his family's settlement, now known as Locke Mills. In 1815 Locke studied chemistry and natural philosophy with Benjamin Silliman at Yale. From 1816 to 1818 he studied botany and medicine with several doctors in New Hampshire, gave lectures on botany around New England, and served as curator of plants for the Botanical Garden of Cambridge. He joined the U.S. Navy in 1818 as an assistant surgeon. On his first voyage, his ship, the *Macedonian*, assigned to explore the Columbia River, was damaged by a storm in the West Indies. Locke withdrew from the navy, returned to Yale, and finished his M.D. in 1819. He also completed and published a popular textbook, *Outlines of Botany* (1819).

Locke taught in a female academy in Windsor, Vermont, and supervised a female academy for a year in Lexington, Kentucky. In 1822 he settled in Cincinnati, Ohio, and that year established the Cincinnati Female Academy, which he supervised until 1835. He also lectured at the Mechanics' Institute and was active in local scientific societies. In 1825 he married Mary Morris; they had ten children. In 1835 Locke was appointed professor of chemistry in the Medical College of Ohio, where he served for eighteen years. He was also employed in geological surveys by the state of Ohio and the federal government. His report on mineral resources in Iowa, Illinois, and Wisconsin was published as a congressional document. He also published pamphlets on local issues such as an analysis of water quality near Cincinnati.

Locke's interest in electricity and magnetism developed in early childhood and continued throughout his life. He invented a "thermoscopic galvanometer," which displayed electrical phenomena to a large audience. He also made some of the earliest observations of terrestrial magnetism west of the Allegheny Mountains. He published papers on the topic in several important journals, including the *American Journal of Science*, the American Philosophical Society's *Transactions*, and the Smithsonian *Contributions to Knowledge*. Locke held several patents, including those for a portable compass and a botanical press. His most significant invention was the "electro-chronograph," developed at the request of the U.S. Coast Survey in 1848. When attached to the second hand of a clock and connected to a telegraphic circuit, the electro-chronograph made clocks beat simultaneously all along the telegraph line and produced a paper strip chart that recorded events with an accuracy of one hundredth of a second. In an era before the development of time standards, this instrument was invaluable for determining longitudes and for precise observations in physics, geophysics, and astronomy. He received an award of $10,000 from Congress for his invention.

Medical education in Cincinnati was in a state of flux in the 1830s and 1840s. At least seven medical colleges in the city were founded, realigned, or closed their doors during Locke's tenure at the Medical College of Ohio. The Reformed Medical School closed in 1845, the Cincinnati Medical College merged with Locke's institution in 1846, and the Botanico-Medical College of Ohio failed in 1850. In the winter of 1849–1850, at the height of his success as a scientist and inventor, Locke was removed from his professorship, then quickly reinstated after his friends intervened. Nevertheless, the shock of losing his position, even temporarily, took a heavy toll. Locke resigned his professorship in 1853 and established a preparatory school in Lebanon, Ohio. His health failing, he returned in 1855 to Cincinnati, where he died.

• There is no central repository for Locke's personal papers. Some are located in the American Philosophical Society Library; others are scattered among the papers of scientists of his day. Copies of his lectures are located in the Erasmus Gest Papers of the Ohio Historical Society Library in Columbus. Locke's bibliography was published in *American Geologist* 14 (1894): 354–56. A list of his papers also appears in the Royal Society's *Catalogue of Scientific Papers*. His most important invention is described in "On the Electro-chronograph," *American Journal of Science*, 2d ser., 8 (1849): 231–52. Biographical sketches include M. B. Wright, *An Address on the Life and Character of the Late Professor John Locke* (1857), and Adolph E. Waller, "Dr. John Locke, Early Ohio Scientist," *Ohio Archaeological and Historical Quarterly* 55 (1946): 346–73.

JAMES RODGER FLEMING

LOCKHART, Charles (2 Aug. 1818–26 Jan. 1905), petroleum producer and refiner, was born in Cairn Heads, Wigtownshire, Scotland, the son of John Lockhart and Sarah Walker, prosperous farmers. At the age of seven he went to live with one of his mother's uncles, John Marshall, in Garliestown. There he attended local schools and at the age of twelve began to assist his relative in his importing-exporting business. After two years the firm was sold, and Lockhart returned home. He opened a grocery business in nearby Whithorn where, following four years of modest success, he learned of his father's plans to relocate to the United States. Accordingly, Lockhart sold out his interest in the grocery in May 1836 and emigrated with his family the following month.

Following their arrival in New York, the family proceeded to Pittsburgh, Pennsylvania, where his father sought a suitable farmstead in vain. Seeking better prospects, his family continued westward and settled in Trumbull County, Ohio. Lockhart remained in Pittsburgh after finding employment with the firm of James McCully, a wholesale and retail dealer in dry goods and produce. Initially working long hours for low wages as an errand boy, he rose to the position of clerk, and by the winter of 1844–1845 had earned sufficient respect from his employer to take charge of the entire operation while McCully took an extended business trip. In 1855 Lockhart earned a partnership, along with fellow clerk William Frew, in the renamed firm of James McCully & Company; the firm later profited immensely from the Civil War.

While still employed with McCully, Lockhart turned his attention in 1852 to a new opportunity—oil. In that year Isaac Huff, a salt producer, appeared at McCully's store with three barrels of crude petroleum (then known as "rock oil" or "Seneca oil") that he had previously attempted to sell to Samuel Kier, an early pioneer in oil refining. While oil had been used in a limited fashion as both a lubricant and a luminant, it was considered more of a nuisance than anything else; a byproduct of salt well operations, its most common consumer use was in the form of patent medicine. Recent advances in refining technology, however, had opened the door to a wide range of potential uses for oil, and entrepreneurs, including Lockhart, were determined to take advantage of the opportunity.

Through a set of shrewd negotiations, Lockhart agreed to purchase all the oil that Huff could produce for the next five years at 31¼ cents a gallon; he then arranged to sell the oil to Kier at 62½ cents a gallon. Sensing the potential profit, Lockhart bought a quarter interest in the salt works later that year and in the following year assumed full ownership. Still employed by McCully, he initially produced both salt and oil from the well, located near Tarentum, Pennsylvania. Lockhart's interest in oil was confirmed in 1859, when Colonel Edwin L. Drake struck oil at a well near Titusville, Pennsylvania. In that same year Lockhart, along with William Phillips, John Vanausdall, A. V. Kipp, and Frew, leased land in a desolate section of Pennsylvania along Oil Creek, organized the firm of Phillips, Frew & Company, and drilled their first well. Yielding forty-five barrels of oil a day, the partners soon sank additional wells nearby.

While most of their oil was shipped to Pittsburgh for refining, the partners sought additional markets. In May 1860 Lockhart traveled to Liverpool with two gallon cans, one filled with crude oil and the other with distilled oil, and stimulated trade with England by lighting the first petroleum lamp. A byproduct of the trip was his first meeting with Jane Walker of Scotland. The couple married during a return trip he made to Scotland in 1862; they had five children. Impressed with English oil refineries, Lockhart decided to enter refining himself. The partnership of Lockhart & Frew opened the Brilliant Refinery in Pittsburgh in the summer of 1861; it was the first major oil refinery in the United States. Lockhart & Frew bought out the interests of Phillips, Vanausdall, and Kipp in the summer of 1863 and later in 1865 expanded operations into Philadelphia. There they operated the Atlantic Refinery and a commission house with William G. Warden. Following the dissolution of his partnership with McCully in April 1865, Lockhart focused all his energies on the oil business.

By 1872 Lockhart owned seven refineries in the Pittsburgh area. The oil industry, after experiencing rapid growth in all facets of its operations, was troubled by excess refining capacity and fierce rivalry among the refining regions of Cleveland, Pittsburgh, and Oil Creek. Lockhart became a stockholder in the South Improvement Company in 1872. Formed in secrecy with the goal of dominating the refining industry, the company—backed by John D. Rockefeller—attempted to force out of business all refiners who refused to join it, using illegal railroad rate rebates as leverage. The resulting "oil war" (led by the oilmen of the Oil Creek region, who also coveted the potential profits of refining) led to the defeat of South Improvement. Lockhart and others then proposed another refiner alliance (the "Pittsburgh Plan") that also failed. Finally, at a meeting in 1874 with Rockefeller, Warden, and Henry M. Flagler, Lockhart agreed to accept stock in the Standard Oil Company in exchange for his refineries. Beginning in 1874 he served as president of Standard Oil Company of Pittsburgh and continued to buy and lease refineries in the surrounding area.

Resentment created by the South Improvement experience still lingered, however, and in 1879 Lockhart was indicted, along with several other Standard officials, for conspiracy. Instigated by the Petroleum Producers Union, a compromise settlement was reached in 1880, and the case never came to trial. Serving as a director of the Standard Oil Trust at its 1882 forma-

tion, Lockhart later became president of the Atlantic Refining Company when the trust dissolved in 1892.

Although respected by his peers at Standard—Rockefeller called him "one of the most experienced, self-contained, and self-controlled men in business" (Nevins, p. 508)—Lockhart was never a driving force in the trust, preferring to remain in Pittsburgh and diversify his interests. Prior to his retirement in 1900 he served as president of Lockhart Iron and Steel Company (1892–1900), helped to found the American and Red Star Steamship Lines, maintained gold-mining interests in Colorado and Idaho, and held lumbering interests in Alabama. Closer to home, he served as a director of the Pittsburgh Locomotive Works and the Pittsburgh National Bank of Commerce.

Following his death numerous local charities, including four hospitals, received the benefits of his largess. Although largely forgotten today, Charles Lockhart played a critical role in the early formation of the modern oil industry and the Standard Oil Company, now known as Exxon.

• While no collection of Lockhart's papers appears to have survived, some of the correspondence relating to the Standard Oil Company operations can be found in the Rockefeller Archive Center in North Tarrytown, N.Y. A "Short Autobiographical Sketch: Charles Lockhart, 1818–1905" (n.d.) is at the Historical Society of Western Pennsylvania, Pittsburgh. In addition to Ida M. Tarbell, *The History of the Standard Oil Company* (2 vols., 1904), other secondary sources containing information on Lockhart's life and career include Allan Nevins, *Study in Power: John D. Rockefeller, Industrialist and Philanthropist* (2 vols., 1953), and Ralph W. Hidy and Muriel E. Hidy, *Pioneering in Big Business* (1955). Obituaries are in the *Pittsburgh Post*, *Pittsburgh Dispatch*, and *Pittsburgh Press*, all 27 Jan. 1905.

EDWARD L. LACH, JR.

LOCKHEED, Allan Haines (20 Jan. 1889–26 May 1969), aeronautical engineer and airplane manufacturing executive, was born Allan Haines Loughead in Niles, California, the son of John Loughead, a truck gardener and fruit grower, and Flora Haines, a writer. Lockheed and his older brother Malcolm legally changed their name late in life to Lockheed to reflect pronunciation. Lockheed and his brothers grew up on a farm within ten miles of where he started his aircraft business at Sunnyvale, California. Lockheed received a common school education. His interest in aviation arose in 1909 when his older half-brother Victor returned from the East, where he had been working, with a new book he had written on aviation. Victor had been working for James E. Plew, the Chicago distributor of White automobiles, but he wanted to get into airplane manufacturing and sales. Victor thrilled Lockheed with his stories of flight, and the younger brother decided to enter the field. By 1910 Lockheed was also employed in the automotive business, learning quickly about the inner workings of complex engines and equipment.

Lockheed entered the aviation business in mid-1910 when Plew hired him as a mechanic for two aircraft, a

Montgomery glider and a Glenn Curtiss pusher biplane, he had purchased for study in Chicago. Lockheed sold his automobile for traveling expenses and traveled to Chicago, where he went to work for Plew. When chided by his friends for such a decision, Lockheed retorted, "I expect to see the time when aviation will be the safest means of transportation, at 40 to 50 mph, and the cheapest, and I'm not going to have long white whiskers when that happens." He predicted that the airplane would "take over land and water travel—flying has no barriers."

Once in Chicago, Lockheed taught himself to fly, soloing for the first time in December 1910. Not really a pilot at the time, on a frozen, wind-swept Hawthorne racetrack on the outskirts of Chicago, Lockheed bet two friends $20 that he could get the Curtiss pusher into the air. He later wrote, "I had to circle to stay inside the track area, and believe me, I made some very jerky turns. But I landed in the infield without cracking up. It was partly nerve, partly confidence, and partly damn foolishness." He added, however, that from that day "I was now an aviator."

For more than a year Lockheed was essentially a daredevil, giving airplane shows on any occasion and for almost no money. When Plew decided that the aviation business was not for him, mostly because it was so deadly, he sold his airplanes and went back to working exclusively for White Automobiles. Lockheed lost his job at that point, but he found another with the International Aviation Company of Chicago as a flight instructor. He also took the time to court and marry Dorothy Watts of Chicago in June 1911; they had two children. Dorothy Watts Lockheed died in 1922, and Lockheed married Evelyn Starr in 1924. After divorcing her in 1936, he married for a third time, to Helen Kundert, in 1938; they had one son.

While Lockheed flew as an instructor and barnstormer, he designed an aircraft of his own. By the time that Lockheed's work in Chicago ended and he had returned to the West Coast, he was ready to begin his own aircraft company. With his brother Malcolm, in early 1912 Lockheed completed the design of a seaplane, this type of craft having sales potential to boating enthusiasts in the San Francisco Bay area, called the Model G. They decided on that name to give the impression that they had completed several models preceding this one. For the next eighteen months they worked at wage jobs by day and aircraft construction in a rented garage on the San Francisco waterfront by night to complete the Model G. Early on 13 June 1913 the Lockheed brothers took the Model G out for their first flight. They spent the next two years demonstrating the plane at shows and giving rides to anyone with a few spare dollars.

In 1916 the Lockheed brothers established the Loughead Aircraft Manufacturing Company in a garage near the Santa Barbara waterfront. Berton R. Rodman, a Santa Barbara businessman interested in aviation, bankrolled the company and became its president. Lockheed served as vice president, Malcolm as secretary and treasurer, Norman S. Hall as sales manager, and Anthony Stadlman as factory superintendent. They hired as an engineer and draftsman John K. Northrop, who later founded his own aircraft firm. These men worked together to design a new flying boat as their first product. Since the Lockheed brothers were self-taught engineers, much of the early design work was Northrop's. The F-1 seaplane that emerged from this effort was a monstrous twin-engine, triple-fin tail aircraft that could carry ten passengers at a cruising speed of 70 mph.

Lockheed demonstrated the F-1 for the U.S. Navy on 28 March 1918, hoping to obtain sales during World War I, but the effort came to nothing. Thereafter, Lockheed reconfigured the F-1 as a land-based aircraft and attempted to sell it to commercial aviation firms. It proved too large and expensive in the nascent air transportation business, however, and the F-1 never found a market.

Lockheed's next venture was only a bit more successful; his firm built the S-1 single-engine monocoque biplane in 1919. This aircraft found a champion in Army Air Service lieutenant—later general—Henry H. Arnold, who endorsed its use in the army. Lockheed undertook an aggressive advertising campaign based on Arnold's enthusiasm, but in the post–World War I demobilization there was little opportunity for new aircraft sales either to the military or to commercial firms glutted with war-surplus equipment. The S-1 was a successful design but did not make enough sales to warrant an assembly line. Because of this lack of success, in 1919 Malcolm, who had never been as committed to aviation as Lockheed, left the firm to enter the automobile business.

Lockheed reentered the aviation business in late 1926 and soon made it into the black with its next design, the celebrated Vega airplane. Moving to Hollywood, California, after obtaining additional investment backing, Lockheed Aircraft Company was formally incorporated in Nevada in December 1926 and went to work manufacturing the Vega. A single-engine monocoque fuselage with an enclosed cabin, it was a version of this plane that Charles A. Lindbergh flew during his nonstop transatlantic flight in 1927. It suddenly became the plane of choice for a large number of high-profile fliers such as explorer Richard E. Byrd and dilettantes such as newspaper magnate George Hearst.

Beginning in 1927 a flood of orders for Lockheed Vegas came streaming into the corporate offices and the firm had to hire more workers to keep up with demand. For example, in 1928 Air Associates of New York placed an order for twenty Vegas, more than $250,000 worth, that forced a second shift in the Lockheed plant. The head of Western Air Express, predecessor of TWA, approached Lockheed in 1928 to purchase Vegas with upgraded engines, and the result was a new model of aircraft with a cruising speed of 150 mph. Using the marketing slogan of "It Takes a Lockheed to Beat a Lockheed," the aircraft firm worked hard to expand its markets during the rest of 1928 and 1929.

Because of this success, Lockheed Aircraft Company became a target for acquisition by the ambitious Detroit Aircraft Corporation, a holding company organized as a "General Motors of the Air." Although Lockheed was reluctant to sell out to the larger corporation, his stockholders had waited a long time to see returns on their investments and they ultimately forced him to merge. In July 1929 Detroit Aircraft purchased 87 percent interest in Lockheed by exchanging one and a half shares of its own stock for one Lockheed share. When this took place, Lockheed resigned as vice president and sold his holdings at $23 a share.

Lockheed was not a part of the company when it went into receivership later in the year after the stock market crash of 1929, and he remained outside aviation manufacturing until 1937, when he organized the Alcor Aircraft Corporation to build a twin-engine cabin monoplane. This effort went awry, however, when the plane was lost during a test flight over San Francisco Bay. His company quickly thereafter went out of business. He then tried to start the Loughead Brothers Aircraft Corporation, but it soon failed as well. Lockheed remained with aviation, however, working during World War II as a general manager of the aircraft division of a Grand Rapids, Michigan, company, making parts for navy fighters. After the war he moved to California's San Fernando Valley and entered the real-estate business. He died in Tucson, Arizona.

• There is no formal collection of Lockheed's papers. Material by and about him can be found at the Lockheed Aircraft Co., Burbank, Calif., but access is restricted. Some archival material is also available at the National Air and Space Museum, Smithsonian Institution, Washington, D.C. A short biography can be found in Spanish in *Enciclopedia de Aviación y Astronautica*, vol. 5 (1984). Additional information about Lockheed can be found in *Of Men and Stars: A History of Lockheed Aircraft Corporation, 1913–1957* (1957), and John B. Rae, *Climb to Greatness: The American Aircraft Industry, 1920–1960* (1968).

ROGER D. LAUNIUS

LOCKHEED, Malcolm (1887–13 Aug. 1958), aircraft engineer and inventor, was born Malcolm Loughead in Niles, California, the son of John Loughead, a hardware store owner, and Flora Haines, a fruit grower and writer. (He later started using a phonetic spelling of his Scottish name, which people had persisted in pronouncing "log-head" or "loaf-head.") His mother, long separated from her husband, was a college graduate and a former schoolteacher who supported her family by growing and marketing fruit and writing feature articles for the *San Francisco Chronicle*. Malcolm left school at the age of seventeen to take a job as a handyman at the White Steam Car Factory in San Francisco, where his mechanical aptitude earned him a promotion to foreman of the car-testing department within a year. Around 1904 he developed a four-wheel hydraulic brake system, which he worked on sporadically until he patented it in 1917.

In 1906 Lockheed was joined in San Francisco by his brother Allan, two years his junior, who took a job in a small car repair garage. Inspired by their older half-brother Victor, already an authority on the new science of aviation, the two became fascinated with the subject of flight. Allan found work as a mechanic with a builder of airplanes and went on to become a flying instructor with the International Aviation Company of Chicago. He returned to San Francisco in 1912, and Lockheed joined him in working on a new design for a seaplane. Supporting themselves with daytime jobs as automobile mechanics, they obtained financial assistance from the head of the Alco Cab Company and organized the Alco Hydroaeroplane Company. Together they produced a wood and fabric biplane, called the Model G in order to suggest they had built several planes previously. On 15 June 1913 they made their maiden flight, staying aloft for twenty minutes over San Francisco Bay. The Model G was one of the first aircraft capable of carrying more than one person. Its thirty-foot fuselage and 46-foot wingspan made it one of the largest planes of its time.

Finding no commercial opportunities for their work with aircraft, Lockheed and his brother tried their hand at prospecting in the California gold country, but they had little success and returned to their jobs as auto mechanics. In 1914 Lockheed briefly held the post of chief engineer of the Mexican air force (actually one battered biplane) for the government of President Venustiano Carranza in its battle with Pancho Villa. In August of that year he attempted to transport a Curtiss biplane to Hong Kong to establish a sales and service agency there, but the enterprise collapsed when a British warship confiscated the plane. He returned to San Francisco, where the brothers found a backer who enabled them to buy the Model G from Alco Hydroaeroplane Company and obtain the passenger-flying concession at the Panama-Pacific Exposition in 1915. Charging $10 for a ten-minute ride, they grossed $6,000 over fifty days.

Lockheed and his brother Allan moved to Santa Barbara the next year and established the Laughead Aircraft Manufacturing Company in the rear of a garage. Their backer, a local financier and machine-shop owner named Burton R. Rodman, served as president, Allan was first vice president, and Malcolm was secretary-treasurer. With the help of garage mechanic and architectural draftsman John K. Northrop, they designed a new airplane, called the F-1, in 1917. The world's largest seaplane at the time, it had a 74-foot upper wingspan and was built to hold ten people. It was rejected for use in World War I, but Lockheed and his brother were commissioned to build two seaplanes patterned on the Curtiss HS2L. Charging cost plus 12½ percent, the firm lost money on the contract. In 1918 the company rebuilt the F-1 as a land plane and renamed it the F-1A, but the plane went down on a transcontinental promotional flight. Rebuilt as the F-1, it was used successfully in a charter service in 1919. In October it carried the king and queen of Belgium on a sightseeing flight to an island in San Francisco Bay. The royal couple were so impressed by the experience that they awarded Lockheed and his brother the Belgian Order of the Golden Crown. The only plane on the West Coast large enough to carry a motion picture camera, the F-1 was chartered by several film studios at the unprecedented rate of $150 an hour.

In 1919 Lockheed and his brother Allan introduced a single-engine biplane called the S-1. The plane had several new features, including the first successful single-shell fuselage, moulded of plywood by a patented process, and folding wings that saved parking space on the ground. Compact and economical, it was advertised as "within the reach of every automobile owner," but a glut of war-surplus planes available for as little as $350 made it unmarketable, and in 1921 the Laughead Aircraft Manufacturing Company went out of business.

Lockheed withdrew from the business in 1919 and moved to Detroit in order to be close to the center of automobile manufacture. There he devoted himself to his automobile braking system and formed the Lockheed Hydraulic Brake Company. At first he had trouble selling his hydraulic brakes to the industry, but in 1923 Walter P. Chrysler bought them for the Maxwell and Chalmers cars he was then producing and included them in the first Chrysler the next year. Orders came quickly after that, and in 1929 the inventor sold the company for $1 million and retired. He changed his legal name to Lockheed in 1934.

Always a very private man, Lockheed withdrew from public life in the 1930s and moved to his remote mining property in Mokelumne Hill, California, where he died. A pioneer in the aviation and automotive industries, he made important contributions to the technology of both.

• Information about Lockheed is in Denholm S. Scott, "The Lockheed Story, 1911 to 1932," *Southern California Industrial News*, 24 Apr., 1 May, and 8 May 1967. These articles are reprinted in Ted Coleman, *Jack Northrop and the Flying Wing* (1988). His life and work are mentioned in *Of Men and Stars: A History of Lockheed Aircraft Corporation* (1957); René J. Francillon, *Lockheed Aircraft since 1913* (1985); and Richard Allen Sanders, *Revolution in the Sky: The Lockheeds of Aviation's Golden Age* (1988). An obituary is in the *New York Times*, 14 Aug. 1958.

DENNIS WEPMAN

LOCKRIDGE, Richard (26 Sept. 1898–19 June 1982), writer, was born Richard Orson Lockridge in St. Joseph, Missouri, the son of Ralph David L. Lockridge and Mary Olive Notson. After attending Kansas City Junior College (1916–1918), he served in the U.S. Navy in 1918. After the First World War he studied journalism at the University of Missouri (1920) before becoming a reporter for the *Kansas City Kansan* (1920–1921) and the *Kansas City Star* (1922).

Lockridge married Frances Davis in 1922; the couple had no children. They made one abortive attempt to relocate from Kansas City to New York before Lockridge found regular employment with the *New York Sun*, first (1922–1929) as a reporter whose assignments included the crime beat and later (1929–1943) as a drama critic. He also became a frequent contributor of "casuals" to the *New Yorker*.

In the early 1930s Lockridge wrote a series of light, nongenre domestic sketches, initially for the *Sun* and then for the *New Yorker*, which were subsequently collected and published under the title *Mr. and Mrs. North* (1936). These sketches were the beginning of a lifelong career for both Lockridges. The Norths, who are given no first names or occupations in these original sketches, are a vague, bumbling couple whose family name, as Lockridge later explained, came from the "amorphous and frequently inept" players assigned the "North" hand in newspaper bridge problems. In 1937, when Frances Lockridge conceived a plot for a detective novel, her husband offered his ready-made characters and mileu for its implementation. The result was *The Norths Meet Murder* (1940), the first in the highly successful series of mystery novels about the amateur detective couple that the Lockridges coauthored.

Between 1940 and Frances Lockridge's death in 1963 the couple published fifty-eight murder mysteries under their combined signature. Other works in the North series include *Death on the Aisle* (1942), *Murder Is Served* (1948), *The Long Skeleton* (1958), and *Murder Has its Points* (1961). Another series features Merton Heimrich, the police detective with whom the Norths worked, and includes such novels as *I Want to Go Home* (1948), *Foggy, Foggy Death* (1950), *Death by Association* (1952, also published as *Trial by Terror*), *Accent on Murder* (1958), and *The Distant One* (1963). During Frances Lockridge's lifetime the Heimrich novels were also joint efforts, as were the shorter series, such as the one featuring Nathan Shapiro and including such novels as *The Drill Is Death* (1961), the one featuring Paul Lane and including *Night of Shadows* (1962), or the one featuring Bernie Simmons and including *And Left for Dead* (1962). They were also coauthors of nonseries mysteries such as *Catch As Catch Can* (1958) and *The Ticking Clock* (1962).

Richard Lockridge frequently took pains to emphasize that, while he and his wife worked together plotting the overall structure of the books, all the actual writing was his own. The novels are generally considered weakest in the area of plot and strongest in characterization and evocation of atmosphere, particularly the moods of Greenwich Village in the years between the two world wars. The North series is noteworthy for the fact that it is the rather dizzy housewife, Pam North, who solves the crimes, although in the process she often needs to be rescued from the clutches of the villain. This convention became so familiar that critic Howard Haycraft remarked in 1946, "Someday, I'd like to read a North story in which Mrs. North does not wander alone and unprotected into the murderer's parlor in the last chapter."

In 1941, the year after the Norths' appearance in print as amateur detectives, they were introduced to a wider audience through a Broadway stage play and a movie, both mysteries entitled *Mr. and Mrs. North*. The film version starred Gracie Allen as Pam North. A short-lived nondetective situation comedy featuring the couple was also broadcast that year. The more famous radio detective series debuted in 1942 and ran for thirteen years, while a TV series ran concurrently between 1952 and 1954. In the 1940s and 1950s, therefore, the characters were present, often simultaneously, in a number of different sectors of the American cultural scene.

The Lockridges' fruitful collaboration was interrupted only briefly in those years, when Richard Lockridge, a member of the U.S. Naval Reserve, returned to active service (1942–1945) as a public relations officer for the navy. After Frances's death, Richard Lockridge did not continue the series about the famous detective couple, although he added new volumes to the other series he and Frances had inaugurated together and wrote several nonseries novels. Merton Heimrich novels from the later period include *Murder Roundabout* (1966), *With Option to Die* (1967), and *The Tenth Life* (1977). Solo Nathan Shapiro novels include *Murder Can't Wait* (1964), *Murder for Art's Sake* (1967), *Write Murder Down* (1972), and *The Old Die Young* (1980). Bernie Simmons is featured in such individually authored novels as *Squire of Death* (1965), *Twice Retired* (1970), and *Death on the Hour* (1974). Nonseries solo efforts include *The Empty Day* (1965) and *Encounter in Key West* (1966). Lockridge's only other collaborative work on a mystery, undertaken during Frances's lifetime, was with psychology professor G. H. Estabrooks, with whom he wrote the espionage thriller *Death in the Mind* (1945).

Lockridge married freelance writer Hildegarde Dolson in 1965. He apparently converted her to mystery writing, since she published four detective novels after their marriage. Their only collaboration, however, was *One Lady, Two Cats* (1967), an account of their courtship and marriage. Cats also figure prominently in the adventures of the Norths, and Lockridge collaborated with his first wife on *Cats and People*, published in 1950, as well as on such children's books as *The Proud Cat* (1951), *The Lucky Cat* (1954), and *The Cat Who Rode Cows* (1955).

Richard Lockridge wrote several biographies, the best known of which, *Darling of Misfortune: Edwin Booth, 1833–1893* (1932), predates his involvement with either the Norths or the mystery genre but draws on his knowledge of the theater and its denizens. By the time of his death in Tryon, North Carolina, he was primarily known, however, as a detective novelist, particularly as part of the writing couple that created the detective couple Pam and Jerry North.

• In addition to the books mentioned above, Lockridge's other noteworthy works include the North novels *A Pinch of Poison* (1941), *Death of a Tall Man* (1946), *Curtain for a Jester* (1953), and *The Judge Is Reversed* (1960), as well as *Think of Death* (1947), *A Client Is Cancelled* (1951), and *First Come, First Kill* (1962), all coauthored with Frances Lockridge, and written by himself, *A Risky Way to Kill* (1969), *Not I, Said the Sparrow* (1973), and *Death in a Sunny Place* (1972). Lock-

ridge's only autobiographical writing is included in the memoir of his relationship with his second wife and in the descriptions of his life and work collected in Otto Penzler, ed., *The Great Detectives* (1978). Intelligent plot summaries of several of the novels may be found in Bill Pronzini and Marcia Muller, eds., *1001 Midnights: The Aficionado's Guide to Mystery and Detective Fiction* (1986). An interview with Lockridge by Chris and Jane Filstrup was published in *Armchair Detective* 11 (Oct. 1978): 382–93. Useful discussions of Lockridge's life and works are contained in the entries on him and on the Norths in Chris Steinbrunner and Otto Penzler, eds., *Encyclopedia of Mystery and Detection* (1976), and, on Lockridge alone, in Fred N. Magill, ed., *Critical Survey of Mystery and Detective Fiction*, vol. 3 (1988). Important critical articles include R. Jeff Banks in *Armchair Detective* 9 (June 1976): 182–83, and Jane Filstrup in the *New Republic*, 22 July 1978, pp. 33–38. An obituary is in the *New York Times*, 21 June 1982.

LILLIAN S. ROBINSON

LOCKRIDGE, Ross Franklin, Jr. (25 Apr. 1914–6 Mar. 1948), author, was born in Bloomington, Indiana, the son of Ross Franklin Lockridge and Elsie Lillian Shockley. Variously employed as a country schoolteacher, a high school principal, a public defender, and a book salesman, his father also wrote a number of biographies of historical figures and lectured widely on Indiana history. He introduced Ross, Jr., at an early age to local myths as well as to family and national history. And young Lockridge's mother frequently entertained him with old family stories.

While a student at Bloomington High School, Lockridge wrote gothic and satiric stories and was president of his junior and senior classes, a thespian, and a member of the National Honor Society. After he graduated in 1931 he entered Indiana University, where he majored in English. His junior year, financed in part by a scholarship, was spent abroad. He studied at the Sorbonne in Paris, completing a thesis comparing modern French and British drama, and traveled in France, England, Italy, and Switzerland. In Paris Lockridge came to realize that the stories he had heard of rural Indiana and his mother's family were the materials from which he could create a great American novel.

Elected to Phi Beta Kappa and chosen first alternate for a Rhodes scholarship, Lockridge graduated from Indiana University in 1935, his grade average the highest of any student in the school's history. Determined to be the best at his chosen work, writing, he was confident of his own creative genius. Shortly before his graduation he fell ill with scarlet fever. Eight months of severe illness gave him time to reflect further on the novel that had first occurred to him in Paris. Choosing his mother and her two brothers as central characters, Lockridge planned to follow them from their childhood in rural Indiana during the 1890s through the great changes in American life at the turn of the century to the industrialized present of the 1930s.

Recovering his health, Lockridge became a popular instructor in English at Indiana University. In 1937 he wrote a pageant designed for performance to celebrate the history of Robert Owen's nineteenth-century utopian experiment at New Harmony, Indiana. On 11 July 1937 he married his high school sweetheart, Vernice Baker; they would have four children. Making no headway on the novel about his family, Lockridge abandoned the project in 1938 and began work on an epic poem entitled "The Dream of the Flesh of Iron." In its ultimate form, "The Dream" assumes cosmic scope as The Dreamer, the poem's central figure and narrator, pursues life's meaning across vast expanses of time.

Taking his master's degree from Indiana University in 1939, Lockridge accepted a graduate fellowship from Harvard University the following year. By the end of 1940 he had finished 400 typed pages of "The Dream of the Flesh of Iron." In February 1941 Lockridge submitted his epic poem to Houghton Mifflin, where it was quickly rejected. Still confident of his abilities, he put the poem aside and began work on the novel that six years later brought him wealth and fame.

As he took up the new project to which he had now committed himself, Lockridge was influenced by such writers as Thomas Wolfe and Thomas Mann and by such films as Orson Welles's *Citizen Kane* and D. W. Griffith's *Intolerance*. He was also attracted to the structure of James Joyce's *Ulysses*. Reading *Ulysses* and *Portrait of the Artist as a Young Man*, Lockridge found his literary home in Joyce's fresh poetic language and in his classical erudition and allusion. Already impressed by the new understanding of human behavior that he believed Freud had provided, he was especially taken with Joyce's exploration of the subconscious. Using the various insights gained from these sources, Lockridge was able to set his novel during a single day, 4 July 1892, and still bring together dream sequences and historical materials from nineteenth-century America, Indiana, and the Shockley family.

To support himself and his family while working on his novel, Lockridge taught at Simmons College in Boston from 1941 to 1945. During the late summer of 1943, he abandoned a 2,000-page draft of his novel and started over. He had come to realize that his best material was to be found in the Civil War days of his maternal grandfather, John Wesley Shockley: Shockley, in the fictional guise of John Wickliff Shawnessy, would be the main character; the novel would be dominated by his coming of age. Through a sequence of flashbacks from 4 July 1892—the holiday provided pageantry and patriotic fervor, the year a national election and the opportunity for political speculation— Lockridge would trace Shawnessy's efforts to understand his world and reveal the nature of the political and spiritual history of the American republic. Selecting events in the domestic and public life of twelve individuals from 1844 to 1892, he would show how people see themselves in relation to the region in which they live. Describing the democratic faith of nineteenth-century American life, he would examine its sexual characteristics and the dualism that existed between its political and religious rites and its idealism and realism.

With a working title of "The Riddle of Raintree County," Lockridge's final draft, weighing twenty pounds and containing more than 600,000 words (more than the published version of *Gone with the Wind*), was submitted to Houghton Mifflin on 24 April 1946. A year of revisions followed its acceptance for publication in June. Awaiting publication, Lockridge attempted to begin a new novel, but failed. The tension between his confidence that he had created a masterpiece and his fear of failure exacerbated his emotional problems, soon diagnosed as clinical depression, which led to a series of electric shock treatments. Winner of a much-publicized prize offered by Metro-Goldwyn-Mayer for new novels (a film version of *Raintree County* would be released by MGM in 1957) and chosen as the main selection of the Book-of-the-Month-Club, *Raintree County* appeared in January 1948.

Praise lavished on the novel by such critics as Howard Mumford Jones, John Marquand, James Hilton, and Charles Lee was tempered by harsh attacks by Hamilton Basso, M. P. Corcoran, and the Reverend Alfred J. Barrett of Fordham University, who saw the book falling within the general prohibition of the Roman Catholic Index. The negative reviews, some of which accused Lockridge of moral laxity and obscenity, appeared at a time when Lockridge was on the verge of mental collapse. Writing a great American novel had exhausted him. Though John Shawnessy's dreams continued to beckon to Lockridge, his own apparently did not. Two months after his novel's publication, Lockridge committed suicide by asphyxiating himself in the closed garage of his new Bloomington, Indiana, home, where he had left his car running.

• Biographical information and critical materials dealing with Lockridge's life and work can be found in Larry Lockridge, *Shade of the Raintree: The Life and Death of Ross Lockridge, Jr.* (1944); Joseph L. Blotner, "*Raintree County* Revisited," *Western Humanities Review* 10 (Winter 1956): 57–64; Leonard Lutwack, "*Raintree County* and the Epicising Poet in American Fiction," *Ball State University Forum* 13 (Winter 1972): 14–28; Lawrence J. Desner, "Value in Popular Fiction: The Case of *Raintree County*," *Junction* 1, no. 3 (1973): 147–52; John Leggett, *Ross and Tom: Two American Tragedies* (1974); Gerald C. Nemanic, "Ross Lockridge, *Raintree County*, and the Epic of Iron," *MidAmerica* 2 (1975): 35–46; Donald J. Greiner, "Ross Lockridge and the Tragedy of *Raintree County*," *Critique: Studies in Modern Fiction* 20 (Apr. 1979): 51–63; and Daniel Aaron, "On Ross Lockridge's *Raintree County*," in *Classics of Civil War Fiction*, ed. David Madden and Peggy Bach (1991), pp. 204–14. Obituaries are in *Time* and *Newsweek*, 15 Mar. 1948.

L. MOODY SIMMS, JR.

LOCKWOOD, Belva Ann Bennett McNall (24 Oct. 1830–19 May 1917), teacher, lawyer, and social activist, was born on a farm in Royalton, Niagara County, New York, the second child of Hannah Green and Lewis Johnson Bennett. Lockwood began teaching in the rural one-room schools of Niagara County at age fifteen.

She made her first public comments against gender discrimination after learning that male teachers were earning twice as much for similar work. In 1848 she married Uriah H. McNall, a local farmer and sawmill operator. McNall's death in 1853 left his 22-year-old widow with the responsibility of raising their young daughter. Lockwood enrolled at Genesee College (now Syracuse University), receiving a bachelor of science degree in 1857. In September of that year she accepted a position as principal of the Lockport Union School, again experiencing wage discrimination because she was a woman. After listening to woman's rights activist Susan B. Anthony, Lockwood introduced the then-radical subjects of public speaking, gymnastics, and botanical walks into the curriculum for women students. During these years she also attended a course in law given by a local attorney.

In 1866 Lockwood and her daughter moved to Washington, D.C. Combining her belief in independence and educational innovation, the young teacher opened one of the first private coeducational academies in the nation's capital. Curious about the nature of public power, she began observing congressional debates and local and federal court sessions.

In 1868 she married Dr. Ezekiel Lockwood, a 65-year-old Baptist minister and dentist. Their only child died at eighteen months. Shortly after their marriage, Dr. Lockwood assumed responsibility for the academy so that his wife could pursue a law degree, but Lockwood, now forty, found it impossible to gain admission to any of the law schools in the capital. In the words of one local law school administrator, Rev. G. W. Samson, "the attendance of ladies would be an injurious diversion of the attention of the students." In 1871, however, Lockwood and several other women were accepted into Washington's new National University Law School. In 1873 the school tried to deny Lockwood and another graduating woman student their diplomas because male students did not wish to graduate with women. Lockwood was also told that the Supreme Court of the District of Columbia would block her admission to its bar. After Lockwood wrote to President Ulysses S. Grant, ex officio president of the law school, he arranged for Lockwood to receive her diploma and be admitted to the District of Columbia bar.

For the next five years, Lockwood fought for the right of women lawyers to argue cases in state and national courts, lobbying until Congress passed a bill authorizing women to be admitted to the U.S. Supreme Court bar. On 3 March 1879 Lockwood became the first woman admitted to practice law before the Supreme Court of the United States. During these years in Washington Lockwood also joined other women in organizations designed to break down gender barriers. In 1867 she cofounded the capital's first suffrage organization, the Universal Franchise Association, and was later active in the National Woman Suffrage Association. She spoke regularly at political conventions and suffrage meetings and testified before congressional committees on such women's rights issues as an 1872 equal pay bill for government employees, legislation to liberalize the property rights of married women in the District of Columbia, and a bill to empower widows to claim full guardianship of their children in probate courts.

In 1884, Susan B. Anthony and Elizabeth Cady Stanton decided to continue to work for women's rights through an established national political party (Republican). Lockwood, then fifty-four, broke with them and accepted the nomination of the Equal Rights party as its presidential candidate. Her running mate was Marietta L. B. Stow. Their platform supported women's rights, including suffrage and reform of marriage and divorce laws; assimilation of Native Americans; veterans' benefits; civil service reform; prohibition of alcohol; greater action on behalf of universal peace; and a variety of economic measures to reduce public debt, improve trade, revive the expansion of industry in the East and the South, and limit monopolies. Victoria Woodhull had run for president in 1872 but had not reached the constitutionally mandated age of thirty-five, and she did not campaign formally because she was in jail. Lockwood thus was the first viable woman candidate for the U.S. presidency. Her ticket received 4,149 votes and the entire electoral vote of Indiana. She was renominated for president by the Equal Rights party in 1888.

Lockwood continued to lecture and also maintained her law practice, handling many pension claims and domestic law cases. She was one of the attorneys responsible for a $5-million United States land claim settlement in favor of the Eastern Cherokee. She was a member of the Universal Peace Union executive committee and represented it during the 1880s and 1890s at meetings on disarmament and arbitration in the United States and Europe.

Lockwood received numerous honors, including membership on the nominating committee for the Nobel Peace Prize, honorary academic degrees, and the presidency of the Woman's National Press Association. Ironically, however, twenty years after Lockwood's admission to the United States Supreme Court bar, that court, relying upon its decision in *Bradwell v. Illinois*, upheld the state of Virginia in denying her the right to practice law because she was a woman (*In re Lockwood*). Belva Lockwood died in Washington, D.C.

• Lockwood's papers are in the Peace Collection at Swarthmore College. The bibliographical citations in the chapter on Lockwood in Madeleine B. Stern, *We the Women: Career Firsts of Nineteenth-Century America* (1962; repr. 1974), are the most comprehensive available. See also Belva Lockwood, "My Efforts to Become a Lawyer," *Lippincott's Monthly Magazine*, Feb. 1888, pp. 215–29; Julia Davis, "Belva Ann Lockwood: Remover of Mountains," *American Bar Association Journal* 65 (1979): 924–28, and "Feisty Schoolmarm: May the Lawyers Sit Up and Take Notice," *Smithsonian*, Dec. 1981, pp. 133–50; Julia Hull Winner, "Belva A. Lockwood—That Extraordinary Woman," *New York History* 39, no. 1 (1958): 321–40; Karen B. Morello, *The Invisible Bar: The Woman Lawyer in America, 1638 to the Present* (1986); and Merle Eugene Curti, *Peace or War: The American Struggle, 1636–1936* (1936; repr. 1972). Cases cited: *Bradwell v. Illinois*, 83 U.S. (16 Wall.) 130 (1873); *In re Lockwood*, 154 U.S. 116 (1893).

JILL NORGREN

LOCKWOOD, Lorna Elizabeth (24 Mar. 1903–23 Sept. 1977), state supreme court justice, was born in Douglas, Arizona, the daughter of Alfred Collins Lockwood, an attorney and state supreme court justice, and Daisy Maude Lincoln. After completing high school in Tombstone, Arizona, she attended the University of Arizona, from which she received her bachelor's degree in 1923 and her law degree in 1925. She was only the second woman to attend the University of Arizona College of Law, and the dean was reluctant to admit her on account of her gender. Lockwood's decision to become an attorney at a time when very few women were admitted to the bar was originally inspired by her father and Sarah Soren, Arizona's first woman lawyer, who had practiced law with him in Globe, Arizona.

Although Lockwood was admitted to the Arizona bar shortly after graduating from law school, opportunities for women lawyers were so limited that she worked as a legal stenographer and secretary for fourteen years before entering the private practice of law in Phoenix in a partnership with Loretta Savage. Lockwood served in the Arizona House of Representatives from 1939 until 1942, when she resigned to go to Washington, D.C., to become an assistant to Arizona representative John R. Murdock. Lockwood returned to Arizona in 1943 to serve for two years as the district price attorney for the Office of Price Administration. In 1945 she returned to private practice with her father, who had retired from the state supreme court. From 1947 to 1949, she served another term in the state legislature, where she became chair of the House Judiciary Committee. Although a Democrat she was never elected on a partisan basis.

Lockwood began her judicial career in 1951, serving for ten years as a trial judge on the Maricopa County Superior Court in Phoenix. For three of those years, she served as a juvenile court judge and became known as a lifelong advocate of the rights of children. Active in many civic organizations, she helped form the Big Brothers and Big Sisters of Arizona.

In 1960 Lockwood was elected to the supreme court of Arizona. In 1965 she became chief justice when the court's process of rotating the chief justiceship gave her a turn to serve for one year as chief justice of the five-member court. She was the first woman to serve as chief justice of a state supreme court. Five years later, from 1970 to 1971, she served another one-year term as chief justice. Reelected to the court in 1966 and 1972, Lockwood resigned in September 1975 because of ill health.

Senator Carl Hayden of Arizona unsuccessfully urged President Lyndon B. Johnson to nominate Lockwood to the U.S. Supreme Court in 1965, after the resignation of Arthur J. Goldberg, and in 1967, after the resignation of Tom C. Clark. It was not until 1981 that another Phoenix judge, Sandra Day O'Connor, became the first woman justice of the Supreme Court. Lockwood's distinguished judicial career in Arizona may have facilitated the judicial success of O'Connor, who served as a judge on the Maricopa County Superior Court and the Arizona Court of Appeals before her appointment to the U.S. Supreme Court. O'Connor and many other women lawyers in Arizona paid tribute to Lockwood's efforts to nurture the careers of her fellow women at the bar. Lockwood organized a group of women attorneys in Phoenix that met regularly during the 1960s and early 1970s to discuss common problems that they encountered in a predominantly male profession. Upon becoming chief justice for the second time in 1970, Lockwood observed that "it is still more difficult for a woman to be accepted on the same basis as a man. She has to work a little harder at it."

Lockwood was well respected for her abilities as a jurist. As a member of the state supreme court, she authored a number of significant opinions. Although she was a firm advocate of stiff sentences for criminals, she also emphasized the importance of procedural fairness in numerous criminal law decisions. She wrote a number of opinions expanding the legal rights of women. In *City of Glendale v. Bradshaw* (1972), for example, she authored an opinion that changed the existing common law by granting women the right to claim the loss of consortium of their spouse in personal injury actions, a right that previously only men could claim. Lockwood observed sardonically in her opinion that until this alteration in the law, "upon marriage, the husband and wife became one, for many purposes, and the husband was that one."

Lockwood also was the author of significant opinions in which Arizona expanded the scope of consumer protection. In 1963 she authored a landmark opinion that rejected the state's immunity from tort liability, and in 1968 she wrote an opinion in which Arizona adopted strict liability in cases involving defective products. Lockwood also wrote a landmark decision on freedom of the press in 1974 in which the court invalidated the University of Arizona's regulations prohibiting the on-campus distribution of a controversial newspaper that was published off-campus.

Lockwood believed that her most significant opinion was *Shirley v. Superior Court* (1973), in which the court upheld the right of a Native American who was domiciled on a reservation to hold political office in the county in which he resided.

Lockwood, who never married, died in Phoenix two years after her resignation from the Arizona Supreme Court.

• Lockwood is the subject of two unpublished manuscripts that are located at the Arizona Historical Society in Tucson: David M. Quantz, "Lorna Lockwood: A Dynamic Woman in Changing Times" (1986), and Nancy L. Matte and Thomas A. Jacobs, "Justice Was a Lady: A Biography of the Public Life of Lorna E. Lockwood" (1985). Lockwood was also the subject of several tributes published in the *Arizona State Law Journal* (1975): iii–xii. An obituary is in the *New York Times*, 25 Sept. 1977.

WILLIAM G. ROSS

LODGE, George Cabot (10 Oct. 1873–21 Aug. 1909), poet, was born in Nahant, Massachusetts, the son of Henry Cabot Lodge, a Republican politician, and Anna Cabot Mills Davis. Called "*Ba*-by" by his older sister, Lodge was always known familiarly as "Bay." He attended private schools in Boston and then in Washington after his father was elected to Congress in 1886. Lodge frequently interacted with his parents' prominent friends, including Theodore Roosevelt, who took a strong mentorial interest in the young George. But Lodge was attracted less to Roosevelt's strenuous life of public service than to the private and contemplative life of another friend of his father's, William Sturgis Bigelow, who was a collector of oriental art and a proponent of Buddhism. On Tuckernuck Island near Nantucket, Bigelow owned a luxuriously idyllic estate, open exclusively to male guests, where Lodge and his father often retreated.

Lodge attended Harvard College (1891–1895) when the elective system was in its heyday and the humanities faculty was especially luminous. Never an outstanding student, he carried the burden of following in his distinguished father's footsteps, and he developed academic problems during his freshman year. Drawn initially to philosophy and literature, Lodge ultimately majored in French. Through the influence of his classmate Joseph Trumbull Stickney, equally gifted as a classicist and a poet, Lodge joined the Harvard literati and began to imagine a literary career for himself. During his senior year he wrote a good deal of verse; his first publication was a sonnet in the May 1895 issue of the *Harvard Monthly*, founded in 1885 by George Santayana, to which all the Harvard poets of this era contributed.

After graduation, Lodge enrolled at the Sorbonne in Paris to prepare for an academic post that might support his literary endeavors. He was appalled, however, by the philological scholarship required for a graduate degree in French literature, and he soon abandoned his plans and instead pursued reading and writing on his own. During his year abroad, Lodge suffered an emotional crisis that arose from his sense of failure and alienation. As he confided to his mother in a letter written in 1896,

I said to myself that I ought to go home in order to get into the tide of American life if for nothing else that I oughtn't to be dreaming & shrieking inside & poetizing & labouring on literature here in Paris supported by my father & that I ought to go home & live very hard making money. . . . But somehow all the while my soul refused to believe the plain facts & illogically clung to the belief that I might do some good & creative work in the world after all.

Lodge's letter captures the enduring tensions of his life: between deeds and words, business and litera-

ture, autonomy and dependence, immersion in the tide of American life and rejection of its prevailing values. Lodge bitterly came to accept that if he wished to be a poet, he had little choice but to be financially supported by his father. After a year of desultory study in Berlin, he came home in 1897 to a sinecure as secretary to his father, then in his first term as a U.S. senator from Massachusetts. After serving briefly as a gunnery officer in the Spanish-American War, Lodge settled in Washington and cultivated friendships with such older persons as Theodore Roosevelt, John Hay, Brooks Adams, Henry Adams, Charles Warren Stoddard, and Edith Wharton, all of whom delighted in what Wharton called Lodge's "abundance," his combination of "a joyous physical life" with "intellectual power": "I have seldom seen any one in whom the natural man was so wholesomely blent with the reflecting intelligence."

Lodge's first book, *The Song of the Wave and Other Poems* (1898), was issued, like all his later volumes, in a small, subsidized edition and was greeted by tepid reviews that noted the poetry's derivativeness and magniloquence. In 1900 Lodge married Matilda Elizabeth Frelinghuysen Davis; they had three children. At about this time Lodge tried his hand at other genres (drama, short stories, novels) in an attempt to earn something from his writing. Nothing came of these experiments, however, and he returned exclusively to poetry in a 1902 volume imitative of Walt Whitman, *Poems (1899–1902)*. The book contains the earliest expression of Lodge's philosophy of Conservative Christian Anarchism, an admixture of American Transcendentalism with the radicalism of Friedrich Nietzsche and the pessimism of Arthur Schopenhauer.

Like other Harvard poets (Santayana, Stickney, William Vaughn Moody), Lodge essayed blank verse drama on heroic subjects and on an equally heroic scale in *Cain: A Drama* (1904) and *Herakles* (1908). These poetic vehicles for Lodge's philosophizing, which did not elicit acclaim even from his friends, were less successful than *The Great Adventure* (1905), a book of sonnets inspired by his grief over the loss of Stickney, who had died at the age of thirty from a brain tumor. With his brother, John Ellerton Lodge, and William Vaughn Moody, Lodge also coedited *The Poems of Trumbull Stickney* (1905).

In 1907 Lodge discovered that a weakening heart placed his own life in jeopardy, and he husbanded his energy by working on shorter poems, such as "The Noctambulist" (1909), in which he effectively combined the elements of the sonnet and dramatic blank verse. Once more on Tuckernuck Island in the summer of 1909, Lodge contracted ptomaine poisoning and died suddenly of heart failure in his father's arms. Senator Lodge, who championed the cause of his son's literary reputation for the remainder of his own life, oversaw the posthumous publication of *The Soul's Inheritance and Other Poems* (1909) and *Poems and Dramas of George Cabot Lodge* (1911).

Dying as he did on the eve of a revolution in the arts, Lodge had no opportunity to develop beyond his formative literary influences. His poetry embraced the high culture of the European nineteenth century, but it lacked both originality and vitality. His importance is mainly historical, as one of the Harvard poets who came of age in the 1890s and then died young and whose work evinced the exhaustion of the literary traditions they had inherited as it foreshadowed the modernist innovations to come.

• Lodge's papers, including correspondence and manuscripts of published and unpublished work, are in the Massachusetts Historical Society, Boston. Henry Adams, *The Life of George Cabot Lodge* (1911), was written at the family's request. It is reprinted in Edmund Wilson, ed., *The Shock of Recognition* (1943), and was reissued in a 1978 facsimile edition, edited by John W. Crowley. Crowley has also written the only modern biography, *George Cabot Lodge* (1976), and he edited *George Cabot Lodge: Selected Fiction and Verse* (1976), in which *The Genius of the Commonplace* (1902), one of Lodge's novels, first appears. Lodge is warmly remembered and his career shrewdly assessed in Edith Wharton, "George Cabot Lodge," *Scribner's Magazine* 47 (Feb. 1910): 236–39, and in Wharton, *A Backward Glance* (1934). See also Frederick W. Conner, *Cosmic Optimism* (1949), on Lodge's philosophical heritage; Thomas Riggs, "Prometheus 1900," *American Literature* 22 (Jan. 1951): 399–423, on the Harvard poets' use of blank verse drama; and Howard Mumford Jones, *The Bright Medusa* (1952), Larzer Ziff, *The American 1890s* (1966), and T. J. Jackson Lears, *No Place of Grace* (1981), on Lodge's culturally symptomatic significance.

JOHN W. CROWLEY

LODGE, Henry Cabot (12 May 1850–9 Nov. 1924), senator and historian, was born in Boston, Massachusetts, the son of John Ellerton Lodge, a wealthy merchant and shipowner, and Anna Cabot. He graduated from Harvard College in 1871 and on that day married Anna "Nannie" Davis, daughter of a naval officer; they had three children.

After a year-long honeymoon in Europe, Lodge, at the suggestion of Henry Adams, whose history course was one of the few he had done well in at Harvard, undertook a "historico-literary" career. He enrolled at Harvard Law School and at the same time studied German and Anglo-Saxon in preparation for taking Adams's graduate seminar in medieval history, first offered in 1873. He received his law degree in 1874 and a Ph.D., one of the first granted in history in the United States, in 1876. His dissertation on Anglo-Saxon land law was published in the Adams-edited *Anglo-Saxon Law* (1876). At the same time he served without pay as assistant editor of the *North American Review*, of which Adams was editor. In 1877 he began teaching a course in American colonial history at Harvard, and the next year he published the *Life and Letters of George Cabot*, his great-grandfather. He was soon turning out books and articles at a rapid pace, among them biographies of Alexander Hamilton (1882), Daniel Webster (1883), and George Washington (2 vols., 1889).

Lodge also, again at the suggestion of Henry Adams, became involved in politics. Like many eastern intellectuals, Adams was appalled by the sordid state of national politics in the General Grant era. He hoped to create a "party of the centre" in order to compel either the Democrats or the Republicans to substitute competitive civil service examinations for the spoils system. Lodge, however, discovering that few practical politicians would consider joining the Independent movement, voted (reluctantly) for the 1876 Republican presidential candidate, Rutherford B. Hayes.

In 1878 Lodge was elected to the lower house of the Massachusetts General Court as a Republican. Two years later he was a delegate to the Republican presidential convention, and in 1883 he managed the successful campaign of George D. Robinson for governor of Massachusetts. In 1884 he was again a delegate to the Republican National Convention, where the leading candidates were President Chester A. Arthur and James G. Blaine, a former secretary of state. Lodge disapproved of Arthur because he was a machine politician and Blaine because he considered him corrupt. When Blaine won the nomination, Lodge "could only rage impotently." Yet in the end he supported Blaine, thereby cementing his own position with Republican politicians but losing the respect of Independents and most of his upper-class Boston friends.

Lodge was a combative person who made enemies easily. When people he respected turned against him, he hid his resentment, but his apparent aloofness only made their anger more intense. "I have grown callous to the abuse & slander which have poured out on me," he recorded in his journal in 1890. Actually he was both deeply hurt and reinforced in his decision to stand by the Republican party. After 1884, when partisan issues were involved, he had something close to a closed mind.

Party loyalty won Lodge nomination to a seat in the House of Representatives in 1884. He was defeated, but two years later he ran again and won. In Congress he was assiduous in attending to the needs of his constituents, in participating in House debates, in working on committees, and in conducting an extensive political correspondence. He followed the Republican line on the protective tariff and most other matters but adopted a middle-of-the-road position on the silver issue, favoring bimetallism rather than a single gold standard. He worked hard for the expansion of the civil service system and, being an author, for effective copyright legislation. In 1890 he took the lead in the fight for the Federal Elections (Force) Bill providing for federal supervision of elections in the South. The measure passed the House easily but was filibustered to death by southern senators. Lodge served in the House continuously until 1893, when he was elected to fill the seat of Senator Henry L. Dawes, who had retired.

In the Senate Lodge was basically conservative on domestic issues, but foreign affairs was his major interest. From early on his greatest ambition was to be chairman of the Senate Foreign Relations Committee. He favored building a modern steel navy and what became known as the "large" policy. "We are dominant in this hemisphere," he boasted in a Senate speech

(*Cong. Rec.* 53:3, pp. 3082–84). While not primarily interested in colonial expansion, he quickly adopted the ideas of Captain Alfred Thayer Mahan about the value of sea power in advancing the national interest.

During the 1895 boundary dispute between Venezuela and Great Britain, Lodge supported President Grover Cleveland's threat to intervene, arguing that the British position was "a direct violation of the Monroe Doctrine." He favored the annexation of Hawaii and was an all-out supporter of the Spanish-American War and the annexation of Puerto Rico and the Philippines. Indeed, he would have preferred taking Cuba as well.

During the Progressive Era Lodge went along with most of President Theodore Roosevelt's (1858–1919) domestic initiatives. He did so partly because Roosevelt and he were close friends. But he also believed that moderate changes in government economic policy were necessary to prevent more drastic ones, such as government ownership of public utilities. And although rich by any standard, he had an aristocratic disdain for what were called in that day "robber barons," men, he wrote, who "pay no regard to the laws of the land or the laws and customs of society if the laws are in their way" (*Early Memories*, p. 217). He opposed, however, the progressives' efforts to make government more responsive to public opinion, such as the direct election of senators and the initiative, referendum, and recall.

Lodge was an enthusiastic supporter of Roosevelt's foreign policy. The maintenance of an "Open Door" policy in China and the construction of a canal across Central America received his hearty approval. In 1903 Roosevelt appointed him to the joint commission that determined the disputed boundary between Canada and Alaska on terms favorable to the United States. But he was mildly alarmed by some of Roosevelt's more radical domestic policies in the last year of his second term and was relieved when Roosevelt decided against seeking a third term.

In the controversies that developed between progressive Republicans and the Old Guard during the administration of William Howard Taft, Lodge tried to steer a middle course. He objected to the progressives' refusal to go along with party decisions, and he considered Taft an inept chief executive. For a time he hoped that Roosevelt would seek the Republican nomination in 1912 in order to preserve party unity. But after Roosevelt, moving further to the left, came out for the recall of state judicial decisions and, having failed to win the Republican nomination, ran on a Progressive party ticket, Lodge voted for Taft.

Lodge had a low opinion of Woodrow Wilson, who won the presidential election, chiefly because he believed that the formerly conservative Wilson had adopted progressive policies to win political favor. But Lodge was away from the capital a good deal during 1913 and early 1914 because of illness and played little part in the debates on the president's New Freedom domestic program. He supported Wilson's request for the repeal of a law exempting American vessels from tolls on ships passing through the Panama Canal, arguing that it was the president's prerogative to determine American foreign policy, and during the early stages of the Mexican revolution he did not object to Wilson's refusal to recognize the government of the dictator Victoriano Huerta. But he soon decided that the Wilson administration's handling of Mexican relations was "incompetent," the president himself alarmingly timid.

When war broke out in Europe in 1914, Lodge (like Wilson and nearly everyone in the United States) believed that the United States should maintain its neutrality, but he also believed that Germany was the aggressor and that Great Britain and France were fighting for freedom and democracy. In the fall of 1914 Wilson proposed relieving the war-induced shortage of shipping by purchasing German merchant vessels pinned in American ports by fear of Allied warships. Lodge took the lead in opposing the administration's Ship Purchase Bill in the Senate. "I had to sit there like a terrier at the mouth of a trap waiting for . . . the rat to come out," he explained (Lodge to Sturgis Bigelow, 9 Mar. 1915, Lodge papers). He denounced Wilson as pro-German, his argument being that the ships were currently useless to the Germans and that since the Allies would not recognize the transfer of title, war might result if they seized or fired upon the vessels on the high seas. After months of debate, the bill was defeated.

The president's reluctance to strengthen the armed forces further angered Lodge, who by 1915 was convinced that a German victory would threaten American security. So did Wilson's failure to take strong action against Germany after a U-boat sank the British liner *Lusitania* without warning in May 1915. The president's insistence that both sides were violating America's rights as a neutral and his call for a "peace without victory" in early 1917 appalled Lodge.

When Wilson finally asked Congress to declare war in April 1917, as he put it, to make the world safe for democracy, Lodge praised his decision. He commented privately, however, that if that decision was correct, "everything [Wilson] has done for two years and a half is fundamentally wrong" (to Roosevelt, 23 Apr. 1917, Lodge papers). He also supported most of the administration's war policies. But he favored demanding the unconditional surrender of the Central Powers, and, like all Republican politicians, he resented deeply Wilson's 1918 "Appeal" unsuccessfully asking voters who "have approved of my leadership" to elect Democratic majorities to both houses of Congress.

Lodge approved of many of the terms negotiated by Wilson at the Paris Peace Conference, including the return of Alsace-Lorraine to France and the principle of self-determination in Central Europe. He also had no objection to the creation of some kind of international organization, but he thought the League of Nations as described in the peace treaty that Wilson negotiated "loose, involved, and full of dangers." By this time his dislike of Wilson had turned to hatred. This certainly influenced his attitude toward the league, as did his partisan wish to prevent the Democrats from converting the popular enthusiasm for peace into victory in the 1920 presidential election. But above all he believed that the league charter required sacrifices of national sovereignty that he (and in his opinion the Senate and most citizens) would not support. He insisted that Article X of the covenant, guaranteeing the territorial integrity of all members, usurped the constitutional power of Congress to declare war. "We are asked," Lodge told the Senate, "[to] subject our own will to the will of other nations. . . . That guarantee we must maintain at any cost when our word is once given" (*Cong. Rec.* 65:3, pp. 4520–28).

When the Versailles Treaty came before the Senate, Lodge, now chairman of the Foreign Relations Committee, drafted fourteen "reservations" to the league covenant. Some were designed for purely political purposes, and others were probably unnecessary. By far the most important stated that Article X should not apply "unless in any particular case the Congress . . . shall by act or joint resolution so provide."

A solid majority of the Senate, far more than the one-third needed to prevent ratification of the treaty, was committed to this position. Yet the president, who had suffered a severe stroke while the treaty was before the Senate, refused to accept the Lodge reservations or to make any compromise whatsoever. "Let Lodge compromise," he told Senate minority leader Gilbert Hitchcock. With Wilson adamant and Lodge and most of the Republican senators unwilling to accept the league as it was, the Versailles Treaty was rejected on 19 November 1919, thirty-five ayes to fifty-five nays. A second vote the following March produced a majority (but not the required two-thirds) for the league with Lodge's reservations.

The 1920 election was a sweeping Republican victory, but Lodge's role in the defeat of the League of Nations hurt him badly when he ran for a seventh term in the Senate two years later. He won reelection by a mere 7,000 votes in a total of nearly 900,000. Thereafter the Massachusetts Republican party was dominated by the supporters of Vice President (later President) Calvin Coolidge.

Lodge's last important public service was as a delegate to the Washington Disarmament Conference, the ratification of which he shepherded through the Senate successfully in March 1922. He died in Boston after a prostate operation.

Lodge was in many ways a model legislator. He was fiercely patriotic and devoted to public service. During his long career he spoke out clearly on public issues, worked hard at committee assignments, and attended assiduously to the legitimate requests of his constituents. He scrupulously avoided conflict-of-interest situations, always disposing in advance of stock and other assets that might be affected by legislation under discussion. Both his intelligence and his knowledge of politics were of a high order.

His weaknesses were primarily temperamental. The reaction of his set to his support of Blaine in 1884 seems at this distance to have been unjustified—Blaine for all his faults was a valuable public servant and far more creative than most of the leading men of the period. But the enduring bitterness, the cynicism, and the extreme partisanship that the episode inspired in Lodge are reflections of his haughty and combative nature. He lacked the warmheartedness of his even-more-combative friend Theodore Roosevelt, and this goes far toward explaining why he was so widely unloved.

• The Lodge papers are in the Massachusetts Historical Society. They contain masses of political and family letters and other material, including Lodge's journals and scrapbooks, and the manuscripts of many of his books and articles. The society also houses the papers of many of Lodge's contemporaries, as does the Library of Congress, where the most useful collection is the Theodore Roosevelt Papers. Lodge's autobiography, *Early Memories* (1913), is an essential source for his early life and shows Lodge's personality at its best. His *The Senate and the League of Nations* (1925) is useful but biased. (Lodge insists in it that he had no personal hostility toward Wilson.) Lodge edited *Selections from the Correspondence of Theodore Roosevelt and Henry Cabot Lodge* (2 vols., 1925), but this work must be used with caution because he altered many of the letters. The most complete biography is John A. Garraty, *Henry Cabot Lodge* (1953), but the fullest discussion of Lodge's ideas about foreign policy, and the most up-to-date listing of Lodge's published works, is in William C. Widenor, *Henry Cabot Lodge and the Search for an American Foreign Policy* (1980).

JOHN A. GARRATY

LODGE, Henry Cabot (5 July 1902–27 Feb. 1985), U.S. senator and diplomat, was born in Nahant, Massachusetts, the son of George Cabot Lodge, a poet, and Mathilda Frelinghuysen Davis. Named Henry Cabot Lodge, Junior, after his famous grandfather, the U.S. senator, he was educated in Paris and at Harvard, where he graduated cum laude in 1924. In 1926 he married Emily Sears; they had two children. From 1924 until 1933 Lodge worked as a journalist, spending three years with the Boston *Transcript* and six with the New York *Herald-Tribune*. During this period he also became an officer in the army reserve.

In 1933, he entered politics as a Republican state representative in Massachusetts. In 1936 he was elected to the U.S. Senate. Although he began his political career as a conservative Republican, perilous world conditions and the New Deal convinced him that if the Republican party wished to prevail, it must abandon isolationism in international affairs and embrace a more progressive domestic agenda. As a senator he occasionally supported limited prolabor and other "liberal" welfare measures, both to lure Democratic voters and to modify traditional Republican politics.

After the outbreak of World War II he took temporary leave from the Senate to serve with American tank units in Libya. Reelected in 1942, he resigned from the Senate in 1944 and served with the army in Europe, where he rose from captain to lieutenant colonel and earned a Bronze Star, six battle stars, and other citations.

In 1946 he won reelection to the Senate, where he continued to vote as a moderate Republican, particularly between 1949 and 1952, when he opposed the majority of his party in over 40 percent of his Senate votes. In the early 1950s Lodge was one of the moderate Republicans who engineered Dwight Eisenhower's successful bid for the presidency. He early saw General Eisenhower as a leader who could win the office for the Republicans. He worked assiduously, first to convince Eisenhower to run and then to win the Republican nomination for him over the opposition of Senator Robert Taft. Lodge was Eisenhower's manager at the 1952 Republican convention, served as his liaison with the outgoing Truman administration, and continued to advise him on political strategy throughout his presidency.

While guiding Eisenhower to victory in 1952, Senator Lodge, ironically, lost his own campaign for reelection by a narrow margin to young Massachusetts congressman John F. Kennedy. Lodge had spent too much time on presidential politics as the Kennedy family organized an innovative, expensive campaign that appealed to a broad spectrum of voters, including (fatally for Lodge) those conservative Republicans who had supported Taft over Eisenhower.

Eisenhower appointed Lodge as ambassador to the United Nations and elevated the position to cabinet rank. Lodge served as UN ambassador until 1960, during which time he met a succession of difficult crises that included the Guatemalan coup (1954), the Suez crisis and the Hungarian revolution (1956), the Castro revolution in Cuba (1957–1958), creation of the UN emergency force in Palestine (1956–1957), U.S. intervention in Lebanon (1958), and UN intervention in the Congo and the U-2 spy plane incident (1960). During these episodes Lodge, following the lead of President Eisenhower and his secretary of state, John Foster Dulles, hewed to an aggressive line against the Soviets, swiftly meeting their criticisms with counterarguments. He also dealt in these years with the politics of the newly independent states of Africa and Asia, in particular the neutralist bloc led by India. Within the Eisenhower administration, Lodge was the leading advocate of international development initiatives in Africa and Asia. While tough in his public opposition to the Soviet Union, Lodge could be more engaging in private. His fluency in French and his working knowledge of other languages, plus his imposing stature, humor, and patrician manners, helped him win allies in the United Nations.

In 1960 Lodge was Richard Nixon's vice presidential running mate. Because he had achieved high visibility and popularity as UN ambassador, he gave Nixon's campaign valuable support, though not enough to bring victory in the close contest won by John F. Kennedy and Lyndon B. Johnson.

In 1963 Kennedy appointed Lodge ambassador to Vietnam. He arrived in Saigon during a period of turmoil and rebellion within the South Vietnamese government and society. The decision by Lodge and the Kennedy administration to acquiesce in the South Vietnamese army's removal, if not murder, of President Ngo Dinh Diem did little to improve the nation's war effort, despite Lodge's strenuous efforts to bring order and direction to the struggle against Communist expansion. Lodge served until 1964 and returned as ambassador again in 1965 under President Johnson. He believed strongly that the United States should not permit a Communist victory in South Vietnam, and as ambassador until 1967 he helped plan and carry out Johnson's escalation of U.S. troop involvement and the air war against North Vietnam.

In 1967 Lodge was briefly an ambassador-at-large, working to prepare the ground for a negotiated settlement in Vietnam. In 1968–1969 he became U.S. ambassador to Germany. In 1969 he headed the U.S. delegation to the unsuccessful Paris peace talks with North Vietnam. From 1969 to 1977, Lodge served occasionally as envoy to the Vatican for Presidents Richard Nixon and Gerald Ford. In his last years he retired to Beverly, Massachusetts, where he lectured at local colleges and wrote his memoirs. He died in Beverly.

Lodge's two assignments in Vietnam proved more frustrating and less successful than his UN ambassadorship. His decision to continue in such controversial diplomatic service under successive Democratic administrations probably also prevented whatever chances he might have had to win the Republican presidential nomination, for which he had some support in 1964. Lodge's most productive and successful years as a politician and a diplomat began and ended with Eisenhower's presidency.

• Lodge's personal papers are at the Massachusetts Historical Society in Boston. He wrote *The Cult of Weakness* (1932) and two memoirs, *The Storm Has Many Eyes: A Personal Narrative* (1973) and *As It Was: An Inside View of Politics and Power in the '50s and '60s* (1976). The only biography is William J. Miller, *Henry Cabot Lodge: A Biography* (1967). Obituaries are in the Boston *Globe* and the *New York Times*, 28 Feb. 1985.

CAROL MORRIS PETILLO

LOEB, Jacques (7 Apr. 1859–11 Feb. 1924), biologist, was born Isaak Loeb in Mayen, a town in the Prussian Rhineland, the son of Benedict (Baruch) Loeb, a merchant, and Barbara Isay. Loeb's parents, observant Jews who were intellectually and politically liberal, both died when he was an adolescent, leaving him financially independent but not wealthy. In 1876 Loeb joined relatives of his mother in Berlin, where he completed secondary school, took the name Jacques, and began the study of medicine, first at the universities of Berlin and Munich, and from 1881 to 1885 at the University of Strassburg. His first scientific research, under the tutelage of the Strassburg physiologist Friedrich Goltz, concerned the psychological characteristics of brain-damaged dogs. He continued to explore problems of psychophysiology at the Berlin Agricultural College in 1885–1886 as an assistant to Nathan Zuntz and from 1886 to 1888 at the University of Wurzburg, where he worked under Adolf Fick.

Loeb was most important as an advocate and exemplar of the transformation of biology from the study of nature into an engineering science. In the late 1880s he was strongly influenced by the writings of the Austrian physicist-philosopher Ernst Mach, and by his contact at Wurzburg with the botanist Julius Sachs. Mach provided Loeb with a positivist philosophy of science that privileged the goals of prediction and control over a "metaphysical" concern for explanation. Sachs's studies of plant tropisms induced Loeb to investigate similar phenomena in animals and to search for ways to manipulate behavior. In 1889, after a year as a privatdocent at Strassburg, Loeb pursued research as an independent scientist at the Naples Zoological Station. When he succeeded the next year in experimentally producing two-headed hydroids (sessile marine animals related to jellyfish), he explained to Mach that his aim as a biologist was to develop "a technology of living substance"—to create new living forms.

Lack of professional opportunity, the repressive German political climate, and marriage in 1890 to Anne Louise Leonard, a graduate of Smith College who was studying in Zurich, induced Loeb to search for work in the United States. Hired as an instructor at Bryn Mawr College, he immigrated in 1891. The following year he joined the new University of Chicago as assistant professor of physiology. He became associate professor at Chicago in 1894, and professor in 1900. During summers he worked at the Marine Biological Laboratory in Woods Hole, Massachusetts, where he initiated an influential course in physiology. Loeb became a U.S. citizen in 1898 and did not revisit Europe until 1909, yet he maintained his visibility in European science by publishing much of his work in German journals until 1914. He and Anne Leonard had five children, three of whom survived infancy.

During the 1890s Loeb was a significant yet singular presence among such University of Chicago evolutionists as Charles O. Whitman, Thomas C. Chamberlin, John Dewey, and Albion Small. Loeb was a fervent and successful experimentalist, and his view, expressed in the preface to his *Studies in General Physiology* (1905), that "it is possible to get the life-phenomena under our control, and that such a control and nothing else is the aim of biology" seemed in accord with the pragmatism espoused, most notably, by Dewey. Yet as an immigrant Jew he remained on the margins of the American academic world, and he alienated colleagues with biting comments on the pretensions he perceived both in American society and in academic affairs. Moreover, he rejected as "metaphysical" the efforts of Chicago scientists and philosophers to construct a world view that was grounded in evolutionism. Claiming that "every philosopher is either a swindler or a fool," he focused instead on the power of the biologist to manipulate behavior and development and, ultimately, to transform species and create life.

Loeb's work on the factors influencing the behavior of invertebrates culminated in *Comparative Physiology of the Brain and Comparative Psychology* (1900), in which he sought to separate the concept of the reflex from the details of neuroanatomy and to define it as any regular relation between stimulus and response. The psychologist John B. Watson studied physiology under Loeb and was influenced by him in his development of behaviorism. In the early 1900s Loeb's views on behavior were critiqued by the evolutionary zoologist Herbert Spencer Jennings, who argued that Loeb paid insufficient attention to structure, diversity, and adaptation.

By the mid-1890s Loeb's research focus had shifted from invertebrate behavior to the ways that changes to the environments of cells could alter cellular functions. Recent advances in the understanding of the physical chemistry of aqueous solutions provided simple means for influencing processes within living cells. Loeb explored how changes in the osmotic pressure and chemical composition of solutions surrounding cells influenced membrane permeability, muscle contraction, and cell division.

Loeb's major scientific innovation, artificial parthenogenesis, was part of this research program. Between 1892 and 1899 he had investigated how changes in the concentration and composition of salts in seawater influenced the segmentation of sea urchin eggs and had been engaged in an ongoing dispute with T. H. Morgan, who also worked at Woods Hole, over the relative importance of environmental and structural factors in early development. This dispute led Loeb in 1899 to realize that by altering the composition of seawater he could initiate development in eggs that normally required activation by sperm.

The invention of artificial parthenogenesis brought Loeb scientific fame and public notoriety. In 1901 he was a finalist for the first Nobel Prize in physiology or medicine and became a head professor at Chicago. Newspapers and popular magazines such as *McClure's* compared him to Faust and Frankenstein. Discussions of possible parthenogenesis in humans, abetted by comments attributed to Loeb, ranged from vindications of the virgin birth of Jesus Christ to speculations about the future reproductive superfluousness of men. In 1902 Loeb accepted a physiology professorship at the University of California, Berkeley. Funded largely by the Hearst family, the post carried with it no teaching duties. Loeb was able to pursue experiments on marine organisms throughout the year at a small laboratory near Monterey.

At Berkeley, Loeb worked to improve artificial parthenogenesis, to hybridize distantly related species, and (unsuccessfully) to produce mutations by exposing organisms to radioactivity. He concentrated particularly on the ways ionic changes altered the properties of cell membranes, utilizing the Swedish chemist Svante Arrhenius's application of principles of chemical equilibrium and kinetics to immune responses. This work was summarized in *Artificial Parthenogenesis and Fertilization* (1913). Loeb worked to make Berkeley an international science center, bringing such eminent European scientists as Arrhenius, Wilhelm Ostwald, and Hugo De Vries to Berkeley for extended visits. He also attracted research students, mostly non-American. A number of biological scientists at the university, including W. J. V. Osterhout and A. E. Taylor, reoriented their work along lines Loeb pursued. He continued to publicize his vision of biology as an engineering science, in *The Dynamics of Living Matter* (1906), and at both the 1904 St. Louis World's Fair and the 1909 Cambridge University Darwin Centennial.

Loeb, however, never established deep roots at the University of California. Shuttling back and forth between Berkeley and Monterey, his was not a visible presence on campus, and he was too iconoclastic to be a successful institutional entrepreneur. Moreover, retrenchment following the 1906 San Francisco earthquake led to cancellation of plans to build a major marine laboratory in Monterey, the departure of junior colleagues, and friction between Loeb and his colleagues at the University of California medical school. In 1910 Loeb accepted medical research leader Simon Flexner's offer to become a member of the Rockefeller Institute for Medical Research in New York City. This appointment began the gradual broadening of the Rockefeller Institute's mission from medical research to biomedical science.

In New York, Loeb came into contact with progressive reformers, including Lilian Wald, William English Walling, and W. E. B. Du Bois, and became active in cultural affairs for the first time. In 1911 he addressed the International Monist Congress in Hamburg, Germany, and a year later published *The Mechanistic Conception of Life*, a volume of essays and lectures. He protested the arrest of the leaders of the Lawrence, Massachusetts, textile strike. His exclusion from the Century Association in 1913 symbolized the ethnic and political divisions within the New York cultural elite. With the beginning of World War I, he attacked biological racism, arguing in *The Crisis* (1914) that "there is absolutely no basis for saying that the color of the skin or the shape of the eyes, or any other bodily characteristic has anything to do with the intellectual or moral inferiority of an individual or a race."

At the same time, Loeb's scientific perspective was changing. He had encountered considerable difficulty in shifting from marine work to an urban laboratory; his research in the early 1910s involved a combination of the routine extension of earlier work (most notably the raising of parthenogenetic frogs to maturity) and bold failures (attempts to detect brain waves, to demonstrate the inheritance of acquired characters, and to induce sperm to develop into organisms). In 1915 Loeb rejected his earlier positivism and announced that the aim of science was to determine the "hidden processes" underlying visible phenomena. In *The Organism as a Whole* (1916), he argued that the basic determinants of harmonious development were located in the cytoplasm.

By combining this new commitment to reductionist analysis with his hatred of romanticism, Loeb in 1917 created a program to advance "physicochemical biology." He initiated a series of monographs on experimental biology that included *Forced Movements, Tropisms, and Animal Conduct* (1918), and in 1918 he established the *Journal of General Physiology*. His new research, on the chemistry of gelatin, was designed to demonstrate that the properties of biological materials could be understood in straightforward chemical terms, and that there was no basis for vague claims about the operation of unknown forces in biological materials. This work was summarized in *Proteins and the Theory of Colloidal Behavior* (1922).

Loeb suffered from coronary problems during the last two years of his life. He died in Hamilton, Bermuda, where he was attempting to recuperate from a heart attack. His intellectual legacy was divided. The novelist Sinclair Lewis, on the suggestion of the Rockefeller Institute bacteriologist Paul De Kruif, used Loeb as the basis for Max Gottlieb, the stereotyped German-Jewish, analytic, pure scientist in *Arrowsmith*. Loeb's program for an engineering biology, on the other hand, influenced psychologist John B. Watson, geneticist Hermann J. Muller, birth control pill inventor Gregory Pincus, and psychologist B. F. Skinner, and thus became part of the life sciences in twentieth-century America.

• Loeb's papers are at the Library of Congress. In addition to the books mentioned above, many of which appeared in different editions in German and French, he was the author of nearly 400 scientific papers, written in both German and English. Many early papers were compiled in English in the two-volume *Studies in General Physiology* (1905). A complete bibliography, along with much biographical information, can be found in his protégé W. J. V. Osterhout's "Jacques Loeb," National Academy of Sciences, *Biographical Memoirs* 13 (1930): 318–401. The fullest assessment of his life and work is Philip J. Pauly, *Controlling Life: Jacques Loeb and the Engineering Ideal in Biology* (1987). See also Donald Fleming's introduction to a 1964 reprint of *The Mechanistic Conception of Life*; Jerry Hirsch's introduction to a 1973 reprint of *Forced Movements, Tropisms, and Animal Conduct*; and Kenneth R. Manning, *Black Apollo of Science: The Life of Ernest Everett Just* (1983), chap. 3.

PHILIP J. PAULY

LOEB, James (6 Aug. 1867–27 May 1933), philanthropist and classicist, was born in New York City, the son of Solomon Loeb, a banker, and Betty Gallenberg. He was the brother-in-law of Jacob H. Schiff and Paul M. Warburg, whose brother was the art historian Aby Warburg. Loeb learned Greek and Latin at Julius Sach's Collegiate Institute in New York and earned his A.B. at Harvard in 1888, where his most influential teachers were the classical scholar John Williams White and the art historian Charles Eliot Norton. His courses in business and economics he later dismissed as wasted time; he was set on a career in classics. Norton candidly advised him that a university career in classics was not open to a Jew. In spite of this humiliating disappointment, Loeb became the greatest benefactor of classics in America and particularly at Harvard.

Upon graduation he joined his father's investment banking firm, Kuhn, Loeb & Co., becoming a partner, not unexpectedly, in 1894. The work was never congenial. He retired in 1901 to begin the career of a Maecenas. His practical business experience made his endowments secure. He instructed lawyers; he was not at their mercy. In 1902 he founded the Charles Eliot Norton Fellowship for a Harvard or Radcliffe student to attend the American School of Classical Studies in Athens. An accomplished cellist, Loeb founded and endowed in 1905 the Institute of Musical Art in New York, absorbed in 1926 by the Juilliard Musical Foundation.

For reasons that remain unclear, Loeb suffered a nervous breakdown in 1905 and (allegedly on the advice of Sigmund Freud) by 1906 was in Munich under the care of Emil Kraepelin. For the rest of his life Loeb was subject to recurrent depression. His gratitude to the psychiatric clinic at Munich was demonstrated by the considerable bequest he was to make to it. Also in 1906, the architect Carl Settler designed Loeb's estate "Hochried" at Murnau in Bavaria, where he would live as a recluse, devoting his remaining years to art, music, philanthropy, and scholarship, what he called "*res dulciores et humaniores.*" He passed World War I in Germany. Between 1906 and 1931 he published his translations into English of four French scholarly books on Greek literature. In 1921 Loeb married Marie Antonie (Schmidt) Hambuechen, his nurse and the widow of his parents' physician.

In 1912, alarmed by the rising neglect of the Greek and Latin authors, Loeb, at the suggestion of the wealthy French Jewish scholar Solomon Reinach, provided the considerable capital to establish the Loeb Classical Library, which in his words was "to include all that is of value and of interest in Greek and Latin literature from the time of Homer to the Fall of Constantinople." Each volume would contain an authoritative text and facing English translation with introduction and minimal notes. Numerous American and English scholars contributed. Often the Americans did better: one need only recall H. W. Smyth's *Aeschylus*, William Abbott Oldfather's *Epictetus*, and Paul Shorey's *Republic of Plato*. Surely his most enduring memorial, the library has been a commercial and cultural success. Profits pour into the Harvard Classics Department annually and finance the prestigious Loeb Lectures and Loeb Classical Monographs. By 1990 there were 473 volumes, including numerous revised reprints.

Loeb received honorary degrees from Cambridge (1925) and Munich (1923), never from his alma mater. He left generous bequests to the American School of Classical Studies in Athens (this eased purchase of the agora, the ancient marketplace of Athens, which became the most famous excavation in Europe), the Loeb Library, the Harvard Classics Department, and $1 million to the German Institute for Psychiatric Research. He endowed the Norton Lectureship for the Archaeological Institute of America (the organization of professional classical archaeologists). His magnificent collection of Greek vases, bronzes, jewelry and

terra-cottas went to Munich, where today it may be seen in the Glyptothek.

Loeb was a shy, enigmatic, sensitive, modest aristocrat. In 1927 the city of Munich presented him with a gold medal that bore his portrait and the inscription: "*vir hum. Iacobus Loeb artium et literarum cultor fautor conservator pauperum patronus dignatatis honestae probitat. modestae exemplar.*" ("James Loeb, a humane man, who cultivated, encouraged and preserved arts and letters, a patron of the poor, an exemplar of honest worth and modest probity.") There could not be a finer or a more sincere epitaph. Loeb died in Murnau.

• Loeb translated the following from French into English: Paul Decharme, *Euripides and the Spirit of His Dramas* (1906); Maurice Croiset, *Aristophanes and the Political Parties at Athens* (1909; repr. 1973); Philippe E. Legrand, *The New Greek Comedy* (1917); and Auguste Couat, *Alexandrian Poetry under the First Three Ptolemies 324–222 B.C.* (1931). The most revealing autobiographical document is a letter of Loeb published in F. W. Kelsey, ed., *Latin and Greek in American Education* (1911), pp. 211–17. Two letters of Charles Eliot Norton to Loeb are published in Sara Norton and M. A. De Wolfe Howe, *Letters of Charles Eliot Norton with Biographical Comment*, vol. 2 (1913), pp. 375–76, 389–90. Other published sources for Loeb's life include William M. Calder III, "Ulrich von Wilamowitz-Moellendorff to James Loeb: Two Unpublished Letters," *Illinois Classical Studies*, vol. 2 (1977), pp. 315–32; Friedrich Wilhelm Hamdorf, *James Loeb, Mäzen von Beruf* (1983); James Loeb, *Our Father: A Memorial* (1929); and "The Loeb Classical Library: A Word about Its Purpose and Its Scope," in *St. Augustine's Confessions with an English Translation by William Watts 1631*, vol. 1 (1912), pp. i–vii; Paul Shorey, "The Loeb Classics," *Harvard Graduates Magazine* 36, no. 143 (1928): 333–43; Frieda Schiff Warburg, *Reminiscences of a Long Life* (1956), pp. 19–20. Other valuable sources of information are Ron Chernow, *The Warbugs: A Family Saga* (1993), and Max Hall, *Harvard University Press: A History* (1986). Obituaries are in the *New York Times*, 29 May 1933, and the London *Times*, 2 June 1933.

WILLIAM M. CALDER III

LOEB, Morris (23 May 1863–8 Oct. 1912), chemist and philanthropist, was born in Cincinnati, Ohio, the son of Solomon Loeb, a financier, and Betty Gallenberg. As the son of one of the founders of Kuhn, Loeb & Company, Morris enjoyed access to the best general education available in New York, where the family had moved in his early years. In 1879 he enrolled at Harvard College, where, influenced by chemists Charles Loring Jackson, Henry Barker Hill, and Wolcott Gibbs, he decided to study chemistry. Jackson, who had studied with Robert Bunsen in Heidelberg and August von Hofmann in Berlin, imparted his enthusiasm for organic chemistry to Loeb, who soon after his graduation with magna cum laude distinction in both English and chemistry in 1883 went to Berlin and Hofmann's laboratory. For his dissertation on the use of phosgene and its derivatives in organic chemistry, Harvard awarded Loeb a Ph.D. in 1887. A further year of study spent in Germany at Heidelberg and Leipzig changed the direction of his career. At Leipzig, Loeb became the first American student of future

(1909) Nobel laureate Wilhelm Ostwald, one of the founders of the infant science of physical chemistry. Working directly with Ostwald's assistant Walther Nernst (Nobel Prize, 1920), who would become one of the foremost chemists of the twentieth century, Loeb undertook several research projects, which resulted in three papers that dealt with reactions of phosgene and were published in German journals.

Returning to the United States in the fall of 1888, Loeb spent a year as a volunteer assistant to Wolcott Gibbs, who had recently retired from Harvard and established a private laboratory near his home in Newport, Rhode Island. The American Chemical Society held its first national meeting in Newport in 1889, and Loeb had the distinction of presenting a paper at it. This gave him an opportunity to become familiar with the leaders in American chemistry and led to an appointment at Clark University in Worcester, Massachusetts, established in 1887 to emulate the German model of graduate education in the sciences. Loeb was invited in 1889 to become the docent in physical chemistry. His tenure at Clark, however, was very brief; in 1891 he was elected professor of chemistry and director of the chemical laboratory at New York University. He held this post until 1906, when he resigned to devote more time to his many scientific, civic, and philanthropic interests. He had married Eda Kuhn in 1895; they had no children.

One of the major activities that occupied Loeb in the last six years of his life was the Chemists Club of New York, of which he was twice president, in 1909 and 1912. The club offered chemists a congenial atmosphere in which to exchange ideas and socialize, as well as access to a first-class library. Loeb contributed large sums to the building fund for the club's permanent home in a ten-story building on East Forty-first Street. Opening on 17 March 1911, the club building, which contained laboratories as well as accommodations for visiting chemists, was a unique institution at this time.

Loeb was a founding member in 1891 of the New York Section (the second oldest) of the American Chemical Society and served as its first secretary and later as its chairman in 1909. His service to his alma mater included providing his expertise and financial assistance in building the Wolcott Gibbs Memorial Laboratory for physical and inorganic chemical research as well as a bequest of $500,000 to advance physics and chemistry.

Loeb, who never forgot his roots and the responsibility he bore as a result of his family's good fortune, was very active in Jewish organizations devoted to the poor in New York. He served on the boards of many Jewish institutions in New York, including the Hebrew Technical School, Jewish Agricultural and Industrial Aid Society, Jewish Theological Seminary, and the Education Alliance among others.

Loeb's active scientific career lasted principally from 1888 to 1906. During this time he was able to publish thirty papers and essays in the developing discipline of physical chemistry. In his 1889 inaugural lecture at Clark, Loeb stated that "too many chemists hurry in their studies toward the El Dorado of carbon synthesis; striving to obtain at the earliest moment tangible results in the shape of a new substance." To Loeb, physical chemistry was a way to understand the basic principles that guide the transformations of matter. Ostwald had earlier expressed a similar view, and he exerted considerable influence on Loeb and others who worked with him.

Early in the course of his career Loeb had studied molecular weights in solution. Starting with that of iodine and using various methods such as vapor-tension and freezing point depression, Loeb concluded that the molecular weight of iodine increased with increasing concentration. This varied from extreme dilution and saturation, where the molecular weight was constant and was correct. Another area of interest, begun in collaboration with Nernst, was an effort to prove the electrolytic theory of Friedrich Kohlrausch, who investigated the behavior of ions in solution and found that each type of ion behaved independently. Loeb became one of the major American proponents of the new ionist school of electrolytic dissociation as proposed by Svante Arrhenius. He believed that the mass of experimental evidence supporting ionization as a general phenomenon in solution could not be ignored. Loeb was able to improve the method of measuring electric currents by the technique of silver voltametry (by which the amount of current that passes through a solution is measured by the amount of silver deposited) by using a Gooch crucible that he modified with a glass mat that would prevent the solution from leaking and causing errors.

By all accounts Loeb's teaching was inspiring to his students because of his enthusiasm and love of chemistry. His sense of professional duty may have been responsible for his untimely death from typhoid fever and double pneumonia, contracted after his return from South America as a representative of the Eighth International Congress of Applied Chemistry, of which he had been an organizer in New York in 1912. He died at his estate in Sea Bright, New Jersey.

• Among Loeb's most significant papers are "Osmotic Pressure and the Determination of Molecular Weights," *American Chemical Journal* 12 (1890): 130–35; "Electrolytic Dissociation: A Review of the Hypothesis of Svante Arrhenius," *American Chemical Journal* 12 (1890): 506–16; "The Molecular Weight of Iodine in its Solutions," *Journal of the Chemical Society* 53 (1888): 805–12; "The Rates of Transference and the Conducting Power of Certain Silver Salts," *American Chemical Journal* 11 (1889): 106–21 (with Walther Nernst); and "The Use of the Gooch Crucible as a Silver Voltameter," *Journal of the American Chemical Society* 12 (1890): 300–301. An excellent biography is Theodore William Richards, ed., *The Scientific Work of Morris Loeb* (1913), which also reprints all of Loeb's scientific papers. An obituary is in the *New York Times*, 9 Oct. 1912.

MARTIN D. SALTZMAN

LOEB, Sophie Irene Simon (4 July 1876–18 Jan. 1929), author, journalist, and welfare worker, was born in Rovno, Russia, the daughter of Samuel Simon, a jeweler, and Mary Carey. Both of her parents were Jewish. Loeb emigrated to the United States with her family at the age of six; they settled in McKeesport, Pennsylvania, near Pittsburgh. Upon the death of her father ten years later, she began part-time work in a local store while finishing high school. Sophie was teaching grade school when in 1896, at the age of nineteen, she married Anselm Loeb, an older man who owned the store where she had worked. She stopped teaching and lived the life of a middle-class married woman, concentrating on entertaining, music, art, and poetry. She wrote epigrams, which she later published, and sympathetic essays about the poor. Unhappy with her married life, and seeking to serve society, Loeb obtained a divorce in 1910 and moved to New York City.

Loeb's essays, submitted earlier to the *New York Evening World* on the discontent in the society of McKeesport's industrial sector, secured her a position as a *World* reporter and feature writer. Her own experience as a fatherless child, coupled with her interviews with widowed mothers who had been forced to place their children in state-supported orphanages or to rely on private charity, inspired her to work for the allocation of public funds for "pensions," which would allow poor widows to maintain their families at home. Loeb publicized the movement for "widows' pensions," joining forces with such figures as Hannah Bachman Einstein.

In 1913 Loeb served with Einstein on the newly created State Commission on Relief for Widowed Mothers. Loeb visited England, Scotland, France, Switzerland, Germany, and Denmark for comparative studies of welfare policies. The commission report proposed a bill for state-funded relief for widows with children. Her work on this report, as well as her campaign in the pages of the *World*, contributed greatly to the New York legislature's passage in 1915 of a bill creating child welfare boards in every New York county. These boards were authorized to distribute public funds to widowed mothers.

Loeb was appointed to New York City's Child Welfare Board in 1915 and for eight years served as the board's president. She achieved stunning efficiency in the board's work, keeping administrative costs to a bare minimum while increasing New York City's appropriation to the board from $100,000 to $4,500,000 in seven years. Loeb employed trained social workers to conduct investigations in order to avoid political influence in the contest for funds. She lent her efforts to urban housing reform and opened public schools for civic centers and community forums. During these same years, she worked on a commission appointed by her friend, Governor Alfred E. Smith, to codify child welfare legislation in New York State.

Loeb extended her campaign for child welfare nationally and internationally. Her book *Everyman's Child* (1920) addressed the themes of her campaign, stating that if Everyman's child fails to receive proper food and clothing, "the Government must stand in place of his parents." Loeb included statistics, photo-

graphs, anecdotes, and an appendix to chart the progress of mothers' pension legislation in the United States and to demonstrate the government's responsibility to give every child "not charity, but a chance," "homes instead of institutions." She spoke before state legislatures throughout the country and in 1924 helped to found the Child Welfare Committee of America, which lobbied for state child welfare laws; she also served as its first president. Her resolution calling for family home life as opposed to the placement of children in institutions was endorsed by the First International Congress on Child Welfare at Geneva in 1925, and her report on blind children in the United States was accepted by the League of Nations in 1926. Loeb consistently spoke of mothers' aid as a right, not as charity, and she fought vigorously to remove the word illegitimate in references to children born out of wedlock. Her travels, speeches, and articles contributed to the passage of widows' aid legislation in forty-two states.

Loeb's observations of the problems of urban living motivated her to work for many other areas of reform. In 1917, as the first woman appointed as a New York City strike mediator, she settled a taxicab industry strike in seven hours. She lent her voice to crusades for penny lunches in the schools, sanitation and fire laws for motion picture establishments, maternity services for poor mothers, and public play areas for children living in congested areas. Her call for an investigation into corruption within the Public Service Commission resulted in the appointment of a new body. Loeb was a member of the National Institute of Social Sciences, the League of American Pen Women, the Women's City Club, the Civic Club, and the Twilight Club.

She had continued to write for the *Evening World*, and in 1925 the paper sent Loeb to Palestine to report on settlements there. She became a passionate Zionist, and her reports to the *World* were both investigative and romantic, full of arguments for welfare measures needed in the "pilgrimage center of all peoples." The next year she published *Palestine Awake: The Rebirth of a Nation*, a compilation of these articles, and she donated all royalties to the Palestine Fund. In addition to magazine and newspaper articles, Loeb published *Epigrams of Eve* (1913) and *Fables of Everyday Folks* (1919), collections of often biting stories and witticisms about city life, love, marriage, divorce, and money.

At the age of fifty-two, Loeb fell victim to cancer in New York City. Rabbi Stephen S. Wise, Lieutenant Governor Herbert H. Lehman, and Mayor James J. Walker paid tribute to her work at her funeral. The members of the Child Welfare Committee of America, including Governor Alfred E. Smith, presented a testimonial praising her as "one of America's most distinguished public servants, an indefatigable worker during more than two decades." Sophie Loeb's epitaph reads "Not charity, but a chance for every child." Her work for scores of reform causes, particularly for new public policies of relief, served as a foundation for more expansive policies of welfare in the United States.

• The B'nai Brith Committee on Jewish Americana has a collection of obituaries on Sophie Loeb, as well as medals and papers donated by a brother, A. M. Simon of McKeesport, Pa. Her articles can be found in the *New York Evening World* and in *Harper's Weekly*; a reprint of one *World* article was published as *The Basis of Marriage: An Interview* (1910). Accounts of her life include Eleanor M. Sickels, *Twelve Daughters of Democracy* (1941), and Blythe Sherwood, "She Mothers Many Millions," *National Magazine*, Dec. 1923. Indexed under her name and under "Child Welfare Board," the *New York Times* contains articles on her work from 1914 to 1923; see also the New York State Commission on Relief for Widowed Mothers Report (1914) and the *Annual Reports* of the Board of Child Welfare of the City of New York, 1915–1927. Obituaries are in the *New York Times*, 19, 21, and 26 Jan. 1929; the *New York World*, 19 and 22 Jan. 1929; and the *New York Evening World*, 19 Jan. 1929.

MARJORIE N. FELD

LOEB, William, III (26 Dec. 1905–13 Sept. 1981), conservative publisher, was born in Washington, D.C., the son of William Loeb, Jr., executive secretary to Theodore Roosevelt, and Katharine (born Catherine) Wilhelmina Dorr, a former stenographer. The elder Loeb, born in 1866, was stenographer to the New York State Assembly when he caught the eye of Governor Roosevelt in 1899. The two grew close when the governor's regular secretary fell ill and Loeb filled in for a summer at Roosevelt's Sagamore Hill home at Oyster Bay, New York. Loeb's career rose when Roosevelt was elected vice president in 1900 and became president after the assassination of William McKinley a year later. The elder Loeb eventually took on the duties of press relations for the Roosevelt White House.

Theodore and Edith Roosevelt acted as godparents at the 1906 baptism of the Loebs' only child by the Episcopal bishop of Washington, D.C. William Loeb III grew up playing at the White House and Sagamore Hill, and his life of ease continued after his father left Washington to become collector of customs for the Port of New York and a vice president of the American Smelting and Refining Co.

William Loeb III attended the exclusive Allen-Stevenson School in New York City and the Hotchkiss School in Lakeville, Connecticut. He graduated from Williams College with a bachelor of arts in 1927 and then attended Harvard Law School for two years. Loeb participated in debate and gun clubs at his schools but had few close friends. Classmates sometimes taunted him about his Jewish-sounding name. Biographer Kevin Cash suggests that Loeb's sensitivity about his name was the reason he occasionally printed copies of his baptism certificate after he became a newspaper publisher.

While at Williams, in 1926 Loeb married Elizabeth V. Nagy, a philosophy teacher eight years his senior. The match was contrary to his parents' wishes and ended in a 1932 divorce. Loeb wed Eleanore McAllister in 1942. That marriage produced one daughter and

ended in a 1952 divorce. That year Loeb married Mrs. Nackey Scripps Gallowhur, the granddaughter of newspaper magnate E. W. Scripps. They had one daughter.

While a student, Loeb had contributed articles to papers in Springfield, Massachusetts, and after his father died in 1937 he pursued his goal of becoming a publisher. His mother loaned him $40,000 to purchase the *St. Albans* (Vermont) *Daily Messenger* in 1941, and five years later he bought a share of the *Manchester Union Leader*, the only paper with statewide circulation in New Hampshire. Loeb took full control of it in 1948.

The papers quickly reflected the independent views of their owner. Three days after Loeb assumed control of the Vermont paper, it ran a page one story attacking the duchess of Windsor's visit to the White House as a "sad waste of ammunition money." And on 12 December 1946, a month after changing owners, the Manchester paper carried an editorial in which Loeb promised to be "independent and fearless." He also printed a quotation from Daniel Webster that subsequently appeared everyday atop the front page: "There is nothing so powerful as truth."

Truth was black-and-white to Loeb. "Things are either right or they are wrong," he once said in explaining a personal philosophy that his editors described as "radical conservative." Although he seldom interfered with the *Daily Messenger* and other small New England papers he came to own, Loeb used the *Manchester Union Leader* to crusade against official waste and corruption, to frame the issues of the day, and to build up or tear down state and national public figures—often in front-page editorials.

Loeb called Harry Truman "the little dictator" and "General Incompetence." Dwight Eisenhower, whom Loeb disliked for outmaneuvering Robert Taft for the 1952 Republican nomination, became "that stinking hypocrite" and "Dopey Dwight." He called John F. Kennedy "the No. 1 liar in the United States" and Nelson A. Rockefeller a "wife swapper." Loeb approved of Richard Nixon until the United States made diplomatic overtures to China, which Loeb said "devalued our chances of victory against the Communists by cuddling up to the Chinese Reds and the killers in the Kremlin."

Loeb's outspokenness would have had little impact outside New Hampshire if not for the state's leadoff position in the quadrennial presidential primaries. By owning the state's only major paper, Loeb shaped the way many New Hampshire voters perceived the candidates. Thus Republicans gave Loeb's choice, Henry Cabot Lodge, a write-in victory in 1964 even though he was not on the ballot. After Jimmy Carter won the 1976 presidential election, Loeb urged Ronald Reagan to bring together the conservatives of both major parties, and he devotedly backed Reagan in 1980.

Loeb's biggest impact on the presidential campaigns undoubtedly occurred in 1972. He published a letter—now believed to have been fabricated as a political dirty trick by the Nixon White House—that quoted

Democratic front-runner Edmund Muskie as making disparaging remarks about French Canadians in New England. A follow-up editorial, not written by Loeb, taunted Muskie's wife, Jane. Muskie cried while defending her, and news media coverage of his emotional response further damaged his presidential hopes.

Although Loeb angered some readers, others looked to him for guidance. Loeb's Manchester paper opposed state sales and income taxes and endorsed the nuclear power plant at Seabrook, New Hampshire. It probably printed more letters to the editor than any other American paper. It encouraged investigative reporting and published telephone records that raised questions about Senator Edward Kennedy's actions after a 1969 drowning at Chappaquiddick. Circulation of the Manchester Union Leader rose from 40,000 in the late 1940s to 65,000 at Loeb's death in Burlington, Massachusetts. Control of the paper passed to his widow.

Reporting on Loeb's funeral, at which a Baptist preacher officiated, the New York Times quoted a New Hampshire resident as saying, "I never met the man, but I considered him one of my best friends. I felt secure having him around. He was like a junkyard dog protecting me and my family from things that were evil." Three years later, the liberal New Republic said it would be a mistake to dismiss Loeb as an eccentric and called him a "vicious bigot."

For good or ill, Loeb helped set the political agenda for a state and, every four years, a nation. Few felt neutral about him; his Manchester editor in chief, Paul H. Tracy, undoubtedly was correct that Loeb was "loved, hated, respected, feared, never ignored." The presidential primaries are calmer in his absence.

• Loeb's personal papers are privately held. Loeb's correspondence with Charles W. Tobey, who served New Hampshire as governor, senator, and representative, is in the Tobey papers of the Baker Library at Dartmouth College. A former reporter for the Manchester Union Leader, Kevin Cash, produced an unauthorized 472-page biography, Who the Hell Is William Loeb? (1975). The book, unevenly written and highly critical, documents Loeb's influence in politics and includes an eye-opening glossary of the insulting names that Loeb called public figures in print. A profile appears in the New York Times, 12 Dec. 1971, which also carries Loeb's obituary and a memorial, 14 and 18 Sept. 1981.

MICHAEL S. SWEENEY

LOEFFLER, Charles Martin (30 Jan. 1861–19 May 1935), composer and violinist, was born near Berlin, Germany, the son of Dr. Karl Löffler, a writer and agricultural scientist, and Helena Schwerdtmann. His father's professional expertise was in demand in various sugar-producing regions of Europe. Thus, as he was growing up, Loeffler lived with his family in several towns in Germany and in France, Hungary, and Russia. As a child he was educated principally at home, although he recalled receiving his first violin lessons in Smela in Ukraine. Loeffler attended the Hochschule für Musik in Berlin from 1874 to 1877; there he studied violin with Joseph Joachim. In Paris

he studied violin with Lambert Joseph Massart and composition with Ernest Guiraud. Loeffler played for one year in the Pasdeloup Orchestra in Paris, after which he was a member of the private orchestra of Baron Paul von Derwies in France and Switzerland from 1879 to 1881.

In 1881 Loeffler emigrated to the United States. He played for one year in the New York Symphony Orchestra, after which he became assistant concertmaster of the Boston Symphony Orchestra (BSO). During the summer of 1884 he lived again in Paris while studying with Hubert Léonard, and he returned to Europe during a few additional summers. However, because his father had been subjected to political imprisonment during which he had suffered a fatal stroke, Loeffler disavowed his native country and allied his sentiments, tastes, and style with France and the United States. A self-professed "true and good republican," he adored the United States and became a citizen in 1887. "This country," he said, as reported in Hampton's Magazine (Jan. 1911), "is quick to reward genuine musical merit, and to reward it far more generously than Europe."

Loeffler often performed as a soloist with the BSO. He also appeared on Boston recital stages and achieved a reputation as a violinist of flawless and elegant technique and exquisite interpretation. He was a champion of modern French compositions and premiered several new French works in Boston.

In 1891 the BSO premiered Loeffler's first orchestral work, Les veillées de l'Ukraine. This tone poem and his first chamber works—a quartet, quintet, and sextet—met with critical and popular success. With his cello concerto, violin divertimento, and other works of the 1890s, however, he acquired a controversial reputation as an avant-garde composer. His eclectic style became increasingly allied with the French symbolist aesthetic; works such as his symphonic poem La mort de Tintagiles (1897), based on a play by Maeterlinck; his Rapsodies for viola, oboe, and piano (1901), based on poems by Maurice Rollinat; his choral work L'archet (c. 1899), based on a medieval legend; and his songs to verses by Verlaine, Baudelaire, and Gustave Kahn, were judged to be "decadent." Though Loeffler's tone poetry was considered to be refreshing and beautiful by those who admired his ability to evoke mood through color and effect, it was vague and difficult to others.

Despite mixed critical response to his music, Loeffler became something of a cult figure in Boston, and his compositions formed part of the city's culture for a half century. His works were performed repeatedly by the BSO and leading choral and chamber ensembles, such as the Cecilia Society and the Kneisel Quartette. He frequently appeared in the salons of such patrons as Isabella Stewart Gardner, where he was highly regarded for his keen intellect and sharp wit along with his musical talent.

Loeffler retired from the BSO in 1903, the same year that G. Schirmer began publishing his music. His national and international reputation steadily grew.

He spent a year in Paris, where he strengthened his ties to French musicians and culture. Loeffler returned to the United States in 1905 and settled on a farm in Medfield, Massachusetts, where he continued to teach violin and to compose. In 1908 he formed the American String Quartette, which he coached. He married Elise Burnett Fay in 1910. The couple did not have children.

Loeffler served on a number of juries and committees, including the Board of Directors of the Boston Opera Company. He acted as an adviser to the BSO, recommending players and conductors, until the Koussevitzky era. During World War I he organized several benefit concerts. Although he continued occasionally to perform his own works in concert through the war years, he left the public concert stage after the war.

Loeffler's most famous orchestral work, *A Pagan Poem*, was premiered by the BSO in 1907. Characterized by the inventiveness and sensuousness common to his compositions, the emotional passion of the piece signaled a departure from his early predilection for somber and macabre subjects, which had alienated conservative critics. No longer a "decadent," Loeffler became known as a mystic who evoked moving and beautiful musical visions. He then composed his only completed, but never staged, opera, *The Passion of Hilarion* (1913); his second string quartet, *Music for Four Stringed Instruments* (1917–1919); *Five Irish Fantasies* for tenor and orchestra (1920); and Partita for violin and piano (1930), among other works. His tone poem *Memories of My Childhood* won the Chicago North Shore Festival Association prize in 1924. His *Canticum fratris solis* was commissioned for the opening of the new music hall at the Library of Congress in 1925, and *Evocation* was commissioned for the opening of Severance Hall in Cleveland in 1930.

During his lifetime Loeffler was the most important liaison between the musical cultures of France and the United States. He received several honors from France. He was named an *officier* (1906) and a correspondent (1920) of the Académie des Beaux-Arts, received the palms of Officer of Public Instruction (1917), and was elected a chevalier of the Légion d'honneur (1919). Loeffler received several American honors as well, including a gold medal from the National Institute of Arts and Letters (1920), an honorary doctor of music from Yale (1926), and election to the American Academy of Arts and Letters (1931).

During the last years of his life, Loeffler became increasingly reclusive as a victim of angina pectoris. He died in Medfield. Through the terms of his will, a Charles Martin Loeffler composition prize was established at the Conservatoire de Musique in Paris.

After an early reputation as a modernist and a "decadent" composer, Loeffler became established as a leading composer of his time. His style was acknowledged to be individual and distinctive. At a time when adherents to French impressionism or symbolism were rare in American musical culture, Loeffler was the leading proponent of the symbolist aesthetic in music in the United States.

• The principal collection of Loeffler manuscripts, including musical manuscripts and correspondence, is located at the Library of Congress. Other manuscripts are at the Isabella Stewart Gardner Museum in Boston, Boston Public Library, New England Conservatory, and Yale University. The first comprehensive biography, with a complete, annotated catalog of works is Ellen Knight, *Charles Martin Loeffler: A Life Apart in American Music* (1993). Interviews with Loeffler include Olin Downes, "Originality in Composer's Art Means Sophistication, Says Loeffler," *Musical America*, 16 Apr. 1910, p. 3, and "The Music of Charles Martin Loeffler," *Christian Science Monitor*, 29 Jan. 1910. Valuable articles by Loeffler's contemporaries include Carl Engel, "Charles Martin Loeffler," *Musical Quarterly* 11 (1925): 311–30, which was revised for Oscar Thompson, ed., *Great Modern Composers* (1940); Walter Damrosch, "Charles Martin Loeffler," *American Academy of Arts and Letters Publication* no. 88 (1936); Lawrence Gilman, "The Music of Loeffler," *North American Review* 193 (1911): 47–59; and Edward Burlingame Hill, "Charles Martin Loeffler," *Modern Music* 13 (1935): 26–31.

ELLEN KNIGHT

LOENING, Grover Cleveland (12 Sept. 1888–29 Feb. 1976), aeronautical engineer and author, was born in Bremen, Germany, the son of Albert Loening and Hermine R. Rubino. After spending his first year in Bremen, where his father was U.S. consul, Loening returned to the family home in New York. Educated in private schools in New York and New Jersey, he received a B.S. degree from Columbia University in 1908. In his senior year, Loening went to Morris Park, New York, to see the flight of an airplane. Although the machine never made it off the ground, Loening came away with an enthusiasm for aviation that would last a lifetime. He helped to organize the Columbia University Aero Club and designed a flying boat glider (which never became airborne). He remained at Columbia to take a M.A. in aeronautics, studying fluid dynamics under visiting professor Karl Runge of the University of Göttingen. In 1910 he was awarded the first degree in aeronautical engineering ever conferred by a university in the United States. His thesis—a study of the aerodynamic basis of contemporary airplanes—was published under the title *Monoplanes and Biplanes* (1911). Loening continued his graduate education for an additional year, earning a degree in civil engineering in 1911.

In 1912 Loening became chief engineer for the Queen Aeroplane Company of New York, where he worked on a flying boat that used a French Blériot fuselage. The following year, Orville Wright hired Loening as assistant engineer—later, plant manager—for the Wright Company factory at Dayton, Ohio. Loening went on to serve in 1914–1915 as the first chief aeronautical engineer of the U.S. Army Signal Corps. His lectures on airplane design and construction were published in 1915 as *Military Aeroplanes*, a textbook that was adopted by the military services in the United States and Great Britain and sold 43,000 copies. In 1916 he became vice president and general manager of the Sturtevant Aeroplane Company in Hyde Park, Mass., where he introduced a new method of steel frame construction and spot welding in the manufacture of biplane fuselages.

In 1917 Loening organized and became president of the Loening Aeronautical Engineering Corporation at Long Island City, New York. The next year he received a development contract from the army that led to the M-8 pursuit plane. A two-seat monoplane featuring a rigid-strut bracing system that Loening had invented, the M-8 was hailed as the fastest pursuit ship in the world, with an operational top speed of 145 miles per hour. For his achievement, Loening received a distinguished service award from the secretary of war. The war ended, however, before a production contract could be drawn. He sold only a handful of the speedy airplanes to the financially strapped military services in the postwar years.

Hoping to tap the civilian market, in 1921 Loening designed and built the five-seat Loening Flying Yacht. The monoplane flying boat, powered by a single 400-horsepower Liberty pusher engine, won the prestigious Collier Trophy for the year's "greatest achievement in aviation." Although a few Flying Yachts were sold to rich sportsmen, the lack of demand for civil aircraft in early postwar years forced Loening to discontinue production.

Loening believed that at least part of the problem in marketing his aircraft lay in a widespread prejudice against strut-braced monoplanes. As a result, Loening later recalled, he "lost his nerve and succumbed to popular pressure" by adopting a biplane design for his next flying boat. The six-passenger Loening amphibian made its first flight in 1924 and featured the first practical retractable landing gear for such airplanes. The versatile amphibian proved a great success and sold well to the military services and to a variety of civilian aviation enterprises. In 1928, at a time of consolidation in the aircraft industry, Loening sold his firm for a handsome profit to the giant Curtiss-Wright Company, where it was merged into the Keystone Aircraft Corporation.

In 1930 Loening married Marka Truesdale. The marriage produced three children before ending in divorce in 1940.

Loening developed a thriving consulting practice during the 1930s that provided engineering advice to the Grumman Aircraft Corporation and other aircraft manufacturers. He also served on the board of directors of Pan American Airways. Between 1937 and 1938 he acted as an aeronautical adviser to the U.S. Maritime Commission, surveying the projected role of aircraft in transoceanic travel and arguing against monopolistic practices.

During the war years, Loening was adviser on aircraft to the chairman of the War Production Board. He reported on the problems in developing adequate cargo airplanes and suggested ways in which the situation could be improved. "I think the one job you did in connection with cargo aircraft," Chairman Donald M.

Nelson informed Loening in 1945, "contributed tremendously to the rapid winning of the war."

Developing an interest in rotary-wing and short-takeoff-and-landing (STOL) aircraft after the war, Loening served as chairman of the helicopter committee of the National Advisory Committee for Aeronautics from 1945 to 1949. Later he was a consulting engineer and board chairman of New York Airways, a pioneering helicopter airline. He also devoted a good deal of time to aviation safety as a director of the Flight Safety Foundation.

In his eighties, Loening turned once again to writing and produced three works: *Takeoff Into Greatness* (1968), a history of the aviation industry; *Conquering Wing* (1970), a novel set in aviation's pre–World War I era; and *Amphibian: The Story of the Loening Biplane* (1973), an account of his most famous airplane. He retired to Key Biscayne, Florida, but died in Miami.

• The Loening papers are in the Manuscript Division of the Library of Congress, Washington, D.C. In addition to the informative *Amphibian*, Loening wrote an episodic autobiography, *Our Wings Grow Faster* (1935). An obituary is in the *New York Times*, 1 Mar. 1976.

WILLIAM M. LEARY

LOESSER, Frank (29 June 1910–28 July 1969), composer and lyricist, was born Francis Henry Loesser in New York City, the son of Henry Loesser, a piano teacher, and Julia Ehrlich, a professional accompanist. His parents were natives of Prussia and Austria, respectively, and the household was culturally and musically sophisticated in the European fashion. Young Frank, however, aggressively resisted his father's highbrow tastes, dabbling in songwriting and playing the harmonica. He attended a New York City school for gifted children through his high school years, then at age fifteen demonstrated his rebelliousness by getting himself expelled from the City College of New York for failing every subject except gym and English. He entered the workforce, trying various jobs with indifferent success. Among other things, he labored as a city editor for a short-lived New Rochelle, New York, newspaper, as a sketch writer for the Keith vaudeville circuit, as a knit-goods editor for *Women's Wear Daily*, and as a press representative for a small movie company.

Loesser's first published song—and first published failure—was the 1931 "In Love with a Memory of You," with a melody composed by William Schuman (later president of the Juilliard School of Music and of Lincoln Center for the Performing Arts). By the mid-1930s Loesser and a composer-collaborator, Irving Actman, were singing for their suppers at the Back Drop, an East Fifty-second Street night spot. During the day, he continued working at various jobs, including a staff position with the firm of Leo Feist, writing lyrics to Joseph Brandfon's melodies for forty dollars a week. These songs failed to attract the attention of either publishers or performers, and after a year Loesser was fired.

The Back Drop connection led to a first attempt at a Broadway musical, *The Illustrator's Show*, in 1936. It ran only four nights. But Loesser, through a music publishing house, had come to the attention of Hollywood and was contracted by Universal Studios in 1936. He moved to California, bringing along radio vocalist Lynn Garland (born Mary Alice Blankenbaker), whom he had met at the Back Drop. They married in 1936 and had two children. Although Universal used several of Loesser's lyrics, the studio allowed his contract to run out.

After some time spent freelancing, Loesser signed a contract with Paramount Studios and there—beginning with "Moon of Manakoora" written for Dorothy Lamour in *The Hurricane* (1937)—began the climb from obscurity to become one of Hollywood's most productive and successful lyricists. Working with major composers such as Alfred Newman, Hoagy Carmichael, Frederick Hollander, and Joseph Lilley, Loesser wrote more than seventy lyrics (and in many instances also composed the music) for more than thirty motion pictures. These include "Small Fry" and "Two Sleepy People," written with Carmichael; "Jingle, Jangle, Jingle," with Lilley; "See What the Boys in the Back Room Will Have," with Hollander, which was made famous by Marlene Dietrich; and "I Don't Want to Walk without You, Baby," written with Jule Styne. His efforts yielded him a five-figure income. He hired a chauffeur, which allowed the songwriter to concentrate on his lyrics as he was hurried through Los Angeles traffic.

Loesser responded to the Japanese attack on Pearl Harbor with a lyric inspired by the words of a navy chaplain, William Maguire: "Praise the Lord and Pass the Ammunition." In common with most lyricists, Loesser customarily wrote to a "dummy" tune intended to fill in until suitable music could be composed. When he tried out the new song, friends were impressed by the lyrics but even more enthusiastic about the melody and urged Loesser to publish both. He thereafter worked as both lyricist and composer.

During the Second World War Loesser served in the army air force and supplied lyrics and tunes at the request of the armed forces. He wrote "They're Either Too Young or Too Old" for the film *Stage Door Canteen*. When the war ended he returned to Hollywood to complete his contract, now working alone. "Baby, It's Cold Outside," written for the film *Neptune's Daughter*, won him the 1949 Academy Award for Best Song. However, Loesser increasingly wished to express himself in an entire score, rather than with a single song. He managed this with the film *Hans Christian Andersen* (1952), which contained at least a half dozen notable compositions, including "Wonderful Copenhagen," "Inch Worm," "Anywhere I Wander," and "Thumbelina."

After the war Loesser also made a triumphant return to Broadway. He formed an association with Cy Feuer and Ernest Martin to produce a musical for Ray Bolger based on Brandon Thomas's nineteenth-century farce *Charley's Aunt*. Retitled *Where's Charley?* and

directed for the stage by George Abbott, the show opened on Broadway on 11 October 1948. It received mixed notices but succeeded with audiences, running 729 performances. A film version was released in 1952. Loesser's songs were praised for their direct emotional appeal and "intricate, clever lyrics sung to complex music" (*New York Times*, 29 July 1969). *Where's Charley?* was the first of five musicals in a row for Feuer and Martin.

The next was *Guys and Dolls*, based on a Damon Runyon short story and adapted for the stage by Abe Burrows, with stage direction by George S. Kaufman, choreography by Michael Todd, and musical direction by Loesser. The show opened in 1950, ran for 1,200 performances, and was revived on Broadway in 1976 and again in 1992 to great acclaim. A movie version was made in 1955. Not only did the lyrics, perfectly tailored to suit each character, attest to Loesser's versatility, but so did the music. The show included a Bach-like fugue, college-style anthems, religious music, and vaudeville songs. Particularly outstanding compositions include "Sit Down, You're Rocking the Boat," "Adelaide's Lament," "A Bushel and a Peck," "I've Never Been in Love Before," "If I Were a Bell," "Fugue for Tin Horns," and "Take Back Your Mink." Bob Fosse termed *Guys and Dolls* "the greatest American musical of all time."

In 1952, at the suggestion of Samuel Taylor, Loesser began the process of converting Sidney Howard's 1924 Pulitzer Prize–winning play *They Knew What They Wanted* into the "extended musical comedy" *The Most Happy Fella*. Excising from the play what he referred to as "all this political talk, the labor talk, the religious talk," Loesser crafted a tender tale of an elderly Italian winemaker in California who falls in love with a waitress. It ranked with George Gershwin's *Porgy and Bess* as one of Broadway musical theater's most musically serious works, virtually operatic in scope. The score includes recitatives, arias, duets, trios, choral passages, canons, folk hymns, and excellent show tunes. Lyrics, melodies, and libretto were the result of more than four years' work on Loesser's part. Running for 676 performances, *The Most Happy Fella* won the Drama Critics Circle Award as the Best Musical of the 1956–1957 season.

In 1957 Loesser and Lynn Garland divorced. Two years later he married Jo Sullivan, who had created the role of Rosabella, one of the leads in *The Most Happy Fella*. The marriage produced two children.

The delicate B. J. Chute story of Greenwillow, "somewhere along the banks of the Meander River," moved Loesser to create a pastoral world through his music and lyrics. He based his score on a variety of folk themes, demonstrating his ability to re-create familiar musical styles while endowing his songs with his own individual touch. Opening on 8 March 1960, *Greenwillow* ran a disappointing ninety-five performances. Walter Kerr wrote in the *New York Times*, "Folklore may be just one dish that can't be cooked over." It nevertheless became something of a cult musical, probably due to the richness of the score.

Loesser's longest-running Broadway hit (excluding revivals of *Guys and Dolls*), *How to Succeed in Business without Really Trying*, opened in 1961 and ran for 1,417 performances. This satire on corporate ladder–climbing was a return for Loesser to the more colloquial musical but not a relaxation of his high standards. The show benefited greatly from the collaboration of Abe Burrows as stage director and Bob Fosse as choreographer. *New York Times* critic Howard Taubman wrote, "Frank Loesser has written lyrics with an edge and tunes with a grin." Robert Morse performed the show's most remarkable song, "I Believe in You." Although described by some as musically sparse, the show won the Drama Critics Circle Award, the Tony, and was only the fourth musical to be awarded a Pulitzer Prize for Drama. Like *Guys and Dolls*, it was successfully revived on Broadway in subsequent decades.

How to Succeed was Loesser's last Broadway show. *Pleasures and Palaces* (1965) closed before reaching New York. The work of his final years, *Señor Indiscretion*, was not produced before his death.

"I don't write slowly," Loesser had said in explaining why he turned out only a relative handful of shows. "It's just that I throw out fast." Observers confirmed his hard-driving work habits. According to the *New York Times*, "He was consumed by nervous energy and as a result slept only four hours a night, spending the rest of the time working." In addition to his musicals, he developed his own publishing company and spent considerable time introducing new talent to Broadway. His hard work was attended by heavy smoking. Loesser died of cancer in New York City.

• A clipping file, along with manuscripts, can be found in the Billy Rose Theatre Collection at the New York Public Library for the Performing Arts, Lincoln Center. See also Jack Burton, *Tin Pan Alley Blue Book* (1965); David Ewen, *Great Men of American Popular Song* (1972) and *New Complete Book of the American Musical Theatre* (1970); Martin Gottfried, *Broadway Musicals* (1979); Goddard Lieberson, "Guys and Dolls and Frank Loesser," *Saturday Review*, 30 Dec. 1950, pp. 38; and Ewen, "He Passes the Ammunition for Hits," *Theatre Arts*, May 1956, pp. 73–75. The *New York Times* printed an obituary on 29 July 1969.

JOHN L. COGDILL

LOEW, Marcus (7 May 1870–5 Sept. 1927), motion picture pioneer, was born in New York City, the son of Herman Loew, a waiter, and Ida Lewinstein. The son of immigrants from Vienna, Loew dropped out of school before his tenth birthday and took odd jobs to help support his family. In 1894 he married Caroline Rosenheim; their twin sons, Arthur M. Loew and David L. Loew, both of whom would become movie producers, were born in 1897. Marcus Loew worked in various occupations—including newspapers, furs, and real estate—until he was thirty-five and entered the entertainment business in his native Manhattan.

Loew began his formal career as a show business entrepreneur with the 1905 opening of a nickelodeon. A couple of years earlier Adolph Zukor had persuaded Loew (and others) to invest in a New York City penny arcade, but liking the quick profits of the nickelodeon, Loew abandoned his alliance with Zukor and started his own operation. He made his move into small-time vaudeville when he bought a deserted burlesque theater in Brooklyn and reopened it as the Royal in January 1908. Two years later Loew had a circuit covering the New York boroughs. By 1911 the now incorporated Loew's business included forty theaters throughout New York City and ranked as one of the largest theater chains in the nation.

During the 1910s movie exhibition replaced vaudeville as the dominant mass entertainment form preferred by Americans. Skillfully Loew used his position in small-time vaudeville to fashion the dominant chain for motion pictures in the nation's largest city. From 1912 to 1924 Loew's, Inc. moved from managing cut-rate vaudeville theaters to being the owner and operator of a string of movie palaces. By 1919 Loew's, Inc., ranked as a $25 million corporation traded on the New York Stock Exchange.

Loew's most important innovation was bridging the gap between the nickelodeon and the movie palace by offering customers a nearly equal mix of vaudeville and film entertainment. In his chain of thousand-seat theaters, Loew sought to provide something better than the purely movie nickel show, but something not as expensive as the top talent mix of big-time vaudeville offered by the Keith's and Orpheum chains.

Loew ran his ever growing entertainment empire with a conservative hand. He saw Loew's, Inc., as simply a combination of two proven forms: vaudeville and movies. He ran the whole operation as a real estate business in which the show could fail but the land would still be his. He stuck to what he knew had worked—opening well-sited theaters. George M. Cohan properly called Loew the "Henry Ford of show business." Loew's plan was always to tender popular entertainment at low prices.

In the years immediately after World War I, Loew began to move his successful formula into other markets. Soon his empire stretched from Montreal, Canada, to New Orleans, Louisiana. Loew skillfully took advantage of changing cityscapes. For example, trapped within the long, narrow island of Manhattan, Loew recognized that it was important to build outside Times Square. Second- and third-generation Americans, educated far in excess of the norm and holding well-paying jobs, had moved away from the central city and wanted to spend their time and money on entertainment near their new homes. They lived in Queens, Brooklyn, the Bronx, and Staten Island, so Loew built three-thousand-seat movie palaces in these boroughs, close to the customers.

But the expansion of his theater chain presented Loew with a problem. The stronger he grew in exhibition, the more he needed a guaranteed supply of quality films, especially those featuring top Hollywood stars. Toward that end Loew first fashioned a deal with the Metro Film Corporation, owned by producer Louis B. Mayer. Then, in 1924, he acquired Goldwyn Pictures and all the remaining assets of Louis B.

Mayer and merged his movie-making operations into Metro-Goldwyn-Mayer. One of the most renowned movie-making companies of the Hollywood studio era, MGM would never have come into being if Loew had not needed films to supply his chain of theaters.

Loew created carefully crafted packages of pleasure designed to generate consistently high profits. Hollywood's top movies were only part of what he offered his customers. His strategy was multilayered. First it depended on finding a location at a mass transit crossroads: no complaints about getting to a Loew house. Then the movie building was made so spectacular that it served as an attraction on its own; there just was nothing like the lobby and auditorium of one of his baroque theaters. Finally, once inside you were waited on, led to your seat, and made to feel comfortable—cozy in the winter, cool in the summer.

Loew did not live to enjoy the fruits of his labors. Before the Golden Age of Hollywood commenced, while talkies were still being perfected, he died at his home in Glen Cove, Long Island, New York, leaving an estate of over $10 million. Others, principally Nicholas M. Schenck, would operate the Loew's, Inc., empire through Hollywood's Golden Age of the 1930s and 1940s.

• Marcus Loew left no private papers and very few writings. For a rare example see Loew's essay, "The Motion Picture and Vaudeville," in *The Story of Films*, ed. Joseph P. Kennedy (1927). The best survey of Loew's career can be found in Robert Sobel, *The Entrepreneurs* (1974). See also Bosley Crowther, *The Lion's Share* (1957); Benjamin B. Hampton, *A History of the Movies* (1931); Robert C. Allen, *Vaudeville and Film* (1980); and "Loew's, Inc.," originally published in *Fortune*, Aug. 1939, and found in Tino Balio, ed., *The American Film Industry*, rev. ed. (1985).

DOUGLAS GOMERY

LOEWE, Frederick (10 June 1901–14 Feb. 1988), theatrical composer, was born in Berlin, Germany, the son of Edmund Loewe, an actor, and Rosa Baumeister, an actress who claimed to have been a mistress to the Austrian archduke Ferdinand. Although many details of Loewe's early life are obscure, before World War I he apparently studied music at the (Berlin) Stern Academy. Loewe's father starred in such tuneful operettas as *The Merry Widow* and *The Chocolate Soldier*, and Loewe later claimed to have written at age nine a song his father sang onstage. He also claimed that when he was fifteen years old, his saucy "Katrina" sold more than 2 million copies of sheet music in Germany and Austria.

Although Loewe may have previously visited the United States, he arrived in 1923 with his mother and his father, who was booked to appear in a Broadway play. His father died before the show opened, but his family decided to stay. Their whereabouts between 1924 and 1931 are undocumented. Loewe claimed to have boxed in New York, instructed in horseback riding in New Hampshire, and prospected for gold and punched cattle in Montana. By 1931 he was playing piano in New York theater-district nightclubs. That

year he married Ernestine Zwerleine; they had no children and were divorced in 1957. By 1934 Loewe was playing in theater orchestras and writing songs for the annual gambols at the theatrical club, The Lambs.

From the beginning, Loewe's compositions reflected his Viennese background, but the 1930s Broadway stage was still dominated by jazz-influenced composers such as George Gershwin and Cole Porter, while fluent melody remained the province of Jerome Kern and Richard Rodgers. In 1935 Loewe sold "Love Tiptoed through My Heart" (lyrics by Irene Alexander) to singing actor Dennis King for the drama *Petticoat Fever* (1936). In 1936 Loewe teamed with lyricist Earle Crooker on "A Waltz Was Born in Vienna" for *The Illustrators' Show*, a revue that lasted five performances.

With Crooker, Loewe wrote the full score of *Salute to Spring* (1937), a successful revue at the St. Louis Municipal Opera. Loewe's operetta with Crooker, *Great Lady* (1938), closed on Broadway after twenty performances. The partners' version of the English *Patricia*, called *The Life of the Party*, toured in 1941–1942. Loewe's Carnegie Hall recital in 1942 was uneventful. But when an opportunity came to use the songs from *Salute to Spring* in another show as well as providing new ones, Crooker was in the navy. Loewe met Alan Jay Lerner at The Lambs and invited him to collaborate. This production, *The Patsy*, only toured, but Lerner and Loewe arrived on Broadway in 1943 (the year of Rodgers and Oscar Hammerstein II's *Oklahoma!*) with *What's Up?*, a flippant musical comedy directed by George Balanchine. It ran for sixty-three performances, and Loewe's score was called "bright . . . not overwhelming."

Lerner and Loewe brought out the best in each other and became the most successful musical theater team of their era. Loewe's estimation of himself ("I was never a songwriter; I was a dramatic composer, one who could illustrate any emotion") accurately foretold his contributions to the character-based musicals that followed *Oklahoma!* Further, Lerner's intellect and cosmopolitan wit counterbalanced Loewe's schmaltz, rather as the astringency of Lerner's idol, Lorenz Hart, cut Rodgers's sweetness.

The partners were both great raconteurs, and their collaborations were hectic. Lerner called Loewe a "finger composer," meaning that he could not or would not think out an idea before sitting down at the keyboard. For his part, the neurotic perfectionist Lerner could sometimes take months to write a single line. Loewe eventually broke up the partnership, claiming that the passion of composing was hard on his heart.

The Day before Spring (1945), a somewhat experimental work giving each principal a ballet, ran 165 performances, and Loewe's score, called evocative of Rodgers, was acclaimed. Lerner sold the rights to *The Day before Spring* to MGM for $250,000; Loewe, by heritage and inclination a sensualist who had spent a "very hungry" World War I, said the sale enabled him to eat properly for the first time.

Brigadoon (1947) established Lerner and Loewe as natural inheritors and rivals of Rodgers and Hammerstein. A fey fantasy of love conquering time, *Brigadoon* ran 581 New York performances, continuing its success in London and on film (1954). In *Brigadoon* Loewe, lauded by Lerner for "wistful tenderness . . . plus a soaring quality," extended his talent for pastiche, mimicking Scottish rhythms. After *Brigadoon*, Lerner wrote for films, but Loewe, commenting that his ambition was life on a tropical island, lost heavily on gambling.

Lerner and Loewe reunited for *Paint Your Wagon* (1951), a tale of the California gold rush and their only musical set in the United States. Loewe's "They Call the Wind Maria" successfully evoked a lush Western openness. *Paint Your Wagon* achieved 289 performances; much altered, it became a film in 1969, but Loewe declined writing its new songs. When the partners separated again, Loewe and Harold Rome attempted unsuccessfully to create a new show.

Having boasted in 1934 that he intended to write "the best musical on Broadway," Loewe surely achieved his ambition in 1956 with Lerner in *My Fair Lady*, whose 2,717 performances set a long-run record. *My Fair Lady* continued its success around the world and on film (1965). Loewe's score was somehow English yet redolent of czardas and serenades and Weimar cabaret. Its "Embassy Waltz" was pure Vienna. Lerner's acerbic lyrics remarkably evoked George Bernard Shaw, the author of its source, *Pygmalion*. *My Fair Lady* has been called the greatest of musicals.

The string of Lerner-Loewe successes continued with *Gigi* (1958), a film based upon the stories of Collette filled with waltzes, tetchy monologues, and lush melody. Having suffered his first heart attack, Loewe accepted the Academy Award for best song ("Gigi") in 1959 "from the bottom of my somewhat damaged heart." Another semiretirement ended in near-traumatic collaboration with Lerner on *Camelot* (1960), the unsettling comic-tragic tale of King Arthur, Guinevere, and Lancelot. Loewe's most varied score helped the show achieve 873 performances. Shortly thereafter, Loewe was handed the keys to West Berlin by its mayor Willy Brandt. With that honor, Loewe truly retired.

Although Lerner and Loewe's music did not become "standard" like the detachable songs from earlier musical comedies, it was widely recorded and contributed to their huge royalties. In his Sybaritic retirement, Loewe eventually built a remarkable home in Palm Springs, California, and became a part of the desert's celebrity community, donating large amounts of money to its hospitals.

When *Gigi* became a stage musical in 1973, Lerner coaxed Loewe into collaborating on four new songs. Despite a pre-Broadway cross-country run, *Gigi* closed in three months. The old partners wrote once more, for the film *The Little Prince* (1975), whose failure Lerner blamed on director Stanley Donen's tampering with Loewe's rhythms. In 1978 rumors arose of a concerto by Loewe, but it never materialized. In 1979 he told an interviewer that contemporary music

was so loud because contemporary life had become so loud. Loewe died in Palm Springs.

• Gene Lees, *Inventing Champagne: The Musical Worlds of Lerner and Loewe* (1990), is based on excellent detective work. Stephen Citron, *The Wordsmiths: Oscar Hammerstein 2nd and Alan Jay Lerner* (1995), touches lightly upon Loewe. Lerner's partial autobiography, *The Street Where I Live* (1978), is wonderfully anecdotal. Benny Green, *Let's Face the Music* (1989), contains a perceptive chapter on Lerner and Loewe. An obituary is in *Variety*, 17 Feb. 1988.

JAMES ROSS MOORE

LOEWI, Otto (3 June 1873–25 Dec. 1961), pharmacologist, was born in Frankfurt am Main, Germany, the son of Jacob Loewi, a wine merchant, and Anna Willstädter. After spending his early years at a family home in the Hardt Mountains, Loewi entered the Frankfurt gymnasium at age nine. He found mathematics and physics difficult but excelled in the humanities and initially desired to be an art historian. At the urging of his parents, however, he decided to study medicine and in 1891 entered the University of Strasbourg. There Loewi was influenced by such greats as Gustave Schwalbe in anatomy, Bernhard Naunyn in medicine and experimental pathology, and Oswald Schmiedeberg in pharmacology. Loewi's research for his dissertation was directed by Schmiedeberg and was concerned with the effects of hydrocyanic acid, arsenic, and phosphorus on the isolated heart of the frog.

Loewi's interest in biology and physiology was also stimulated by Oscar Minkowski, who was investigating the role of insulin in diabetes, and by Friedrich Miescher, the Swiss biologist who had described nucleic acids. After graduating with an M.D. in 1896 and a brief visit to Italy, Loewi received a short period of training in Franz Hofmeister's clinic, where he increased his knowledge of experimental biochemistry. He worked in the medical department of the city hospital of Frankfurt with pneumonia and tuberculosis patients. However, the high incidence of fatal pneumonia and tuberculosis among his young and vigorous colleagues discouraged him from further pursuit of clinical medicine. He then obtained an assistantship at the University of Marburg in pharmacologist Hans Meyer's department. Meyer soon became Loewi's friend and patron, and they collaborated in the years between 1898 and 1905. Loewi made his first step up the academic ladder at Marburg to privatdocent in 1900, and two years later he published his first important research—a number of papers on the action of diuretics on kidney function. In 1903 Loewi spent several months at University College, London, in physiologist Ernst Starling's laboratory. Here he met Sir Henry H. Dale, with whom he would later receive a Nobel Prize. Also while in England he met J. W. Langley and H. K. Anderson, who had worked out the anatomy, function, and interrelationship of the two parts of the autonomic nervous system—the sympathetic and the parasympathetic divisions. Around 1901, a number of scientists were investigating the possibility that nerve impulses were transmitted by chemicals. In 1904 Meyer moved to the University of Vienna, and Loewi became acting chairman at Marburg. A year later Loewi joined Meyer, serving as the latter's assistant until 1907, when Loewi became assistant professor of pharmacology.

In 1907, while vacationing in Switzerland, Loewi met Guida Goldschmidt, daughter of the professor of chemistry at the University of Prague. The couple married in 1908 and had four children. Loewi published papers in this period on a number of subjects in collaboration with various colleagues. Among the topics he studied were the effect of adrenaline and noradrenaline on the action of insulin and the effect of stimulating the vagus on the heart. Loewi was appointed professor of pharmacology at the University of Graz in 1908 and remained in this position until 1938, when the Nazis occupied Austria.

Although T. R. Elliot had suggested that nerve impulses were carried by chemical transmitters, no decisive evidence proving this speculation had been obtained. During the night of Easter Sunday in 1921, Loewi "awoke from a dream and jotted down a few notes on a tiny slip of (toilet) paper. In the morning," he writes (quoted in Wasson), "I was unable to decipher the scrawl. The next night, at three o'clock, the idea returned. It was of the design of an experiment to determine whether or not the hypothesis of chemical transmission, that I had uttered seventeen years ago, was correct. I got up immediately and went to the laboratory and performed a simple experiment on a frog heart according to nocturnal design."

Isolating two frog hearts, one with its nervous innervation intact and the other denervated, Loewi attached both hearts to cannulas in a manner that allowed them to be perfused with Ringer's solution (an artificial physiological salt solution). He then stimulated the vagus nerve of the undenervated heart and took the perfusion fluid that flowed from this heart and injected it into the fluid perfusing the denervated heart. When the perfusion fluid containing fluid from the stimulated heart passed into the denervated heart, the latter heart acted as if the vagus nerve had been stimulated. Loewi next stimulated a nerve known to increase heart rate, transferred the perfusion fluid to the denervated heart, and it also increased the heart rate. With this experiment Loewi demonstrated that it was not the nerve but the chemicals released on stimulation that affected the heart.

Loewi named the material that slowed the heart Vagusstoff and the substance that accelerated the heart Acceleransstoff. By 1928 he and Ernst Navratil had identified the Vagusstoff as acetylcholine. Shortly thereafter they found that the action of chemical transmission was terminated by an enzyme, choline esterase, which split acetylcholine into the inactive substances, acetate and choline. Other investigators had difficulty, at first, reproducing Loewi's experiments. To settle this doubt, Loewi was asked to perform the experiment at the International Congress of Physiology in Stockholm. In this demonstration Loewi successfully reproduced the vagus effect eighteen times

before a critical audience. Loewi gave the 1933 Harvey Lecture in New York and at that time expressed his doubts that a chemical transmitter existed in the voluntary nervous system. Henry H. Dale, however, subsequently demonstrated chemical transmission in the voluntary nervous system. Loewi also published a paper identifying adrenaline as the sympathetic chemical transmitter; however, it was later shown that norepinephrine was the main sympathetic transmitter. Their research laid the groundwork for a better understanding of how the sympathetic and parasympathetic divisions of the nervous system function. In 1936 Loewi and Dale were awarded the Nobel Prize in medicine or physiology for their discoveries related to nervous transmission.

In 1938, when the Nazis occupied Austria, Loewi and his two sons were imprisoned. He and his sons were released after the Nobel Prize money was transferred to Nazi-controlled banks. Loewi was allowed to go to Brussels, where he served as visiting professor at the Free University. World War II broke out in 1939, while Loewi was visiting England, and after spending several months at Oxford University, he was appointed research professor at the New York University School of Medicine. Loewi arrived in New York in 1940, his wife and children joined him a year later, and in 1946 he became a U.S. citizen. Loewi continued working in the laboratory until 1958, the year his wife suddenly died. The last years of his life were spent writing articles, compiling his memoirs, and giving lectures. He died in New York City.

• Loewi's "An Autobiographical Sketch" is in *Perspectives in Biology and Medicine* 4 (Autumn 1960): 3–25. For biographical accounts see H. H. Dale, *Biographical Memoirs of the Royal Society* 8 (1962): 67–90; Webb Haymaker and Francis Schiller, *The Founders of Neurology* (1970); G. H. Bishop et al., *The Excitement and Fascination of Science* (1965); D. W. Ingle, ed., *A Dozen Doctors* (1963), pp. 109–31; Tyler Wasson, ed., *Nobel Prize Winners: An H. W. Wilson Biographical Dictionary* (1987), pp. 640–42; and Victor W. Chen, "Otto Loewi," in *The Nobel Prize Winners: Physiology or Medicine*, vol. 1, ed. Frank N. Magill (1991), pp. 425–31. An obituary is in the *New York Times*, 27 Dec. 1961.

DAVID Y. COOPER

LOEWY, Raymond Fernand (5 Nov. 1893–14 July 1986), industrial designer, was born in Paris, France, the son of Maximilian Loewy, the managing editor of a financial journal, and Marie Labalme. Loewy grew up in Paris, where he saw the introduction of the automobile, airplane, telephone, and phonograph and became an enthusiastic apologist for the machine age, no matter its ills. After studying at the Université de Paris from 1910, serving in the French Corps of Engineers from 1914 until 1918 as a liaison officer with the American Expeditionary Force in World War I, and being awarded the croix de guerre four times, he received an engineering degree from the École de Laneau in 1918.

In September of the next year Loewy sailed on the S.S. *France* for New York City, where he began working as a freelance window decorator for Bonwit Teller,

Saks Fifth Avenue, and Macy's stores. Having drawn locomotives and automobiles at an early age may have helped him become a success in selling his fashion illustrations to *Vogue*, *Vanity Fair*, and *Harper's Bazaar* magazines. In 1929 he opened his own design office with the advent of his first industrial-design commission, the housing for the Gestetner duplicating machine.

For this project, assigned to him by British industrialist Sigmund Gestetner himself, Loewy heaped $100 worth of Plasticine clay onto the mechanical workings of the machine to form a new housing shape, in much the same way automobile-body designers create housing today. The mechanics of the duplicator were concealed within a smooth, flowing unit, unlike the previous version, which featured exposed mechanics mounted on an awkward base with twisted legs. In 1931 the machine-style predominated at the Brooklyn Museum exhibition of the first designer consortium in the United States, the American Union of Decorative Artists and Craftsmen. That same year Loewy married Jean Thomson.

Having achieved some success, Loewy spent his money lavishly, buying a villa in St. Tropez in 1930 and the chateau "La Cense" near Paris in 1933. Loewy received his first commissions in 1933 from the Sears, Roebuck & Co.; the Pennsylvania Railroad Company; and the Greyhound Corporation. His "Coldspot" refrigerator (1934) for Sears, with its innovative "feather touch" door latch, was a resounding commercial success; 275,000 units were sold annually compared to the previous model's 65,000. The same year, receiving favorable publicity for the "Designer's Office and Studio" model room (1934, with Lee Simonson) installed at one of the seminal industrial design venues at New York's Metropolitan Museum of Art, Loewy opened an office in London at about the time his Hupmobile (1932) for the Hupp Motor Company went into serial production. By 1939, in addition to London and New York, he had offices in Chicago and South Bend in North America and São Paulo in South America.

Loewy also set up an architecture and interior design department within his New York firm in 1937, and important commissions followed in rapid succession, including the redesign of the Lord & Taylor fashion store in New York (1937) and the bullet-shaped "S1" locomotive (1938) for Pennsylvania Railroad. From 1938, when he became a naturalized citizen of the United States, his roster of clients for ongoing assignments included the Studebaker Company and Coca-Cola. For the latter Loewy designed ice-box coolers, dispensing machines, and graphics. It is untrue that he designed a version of the Coke bottle, but an article in *Life* (May 1949) was a major contributor to the fallacy.

Loewy's "GG1" locomotive shown at the Paris Exposition Internationale des Arts et Techniques Dans la Vie Moderne (1937) won a gold medal. At another seminal fair, the New York World of Tomorrow (1939), where Loewy and James Gamble Rogers's Chrysler Motors building was a main feature, Lowey's "S1" locomotive and Rocketport attracted attention. Having become the most prominent industrial designer in the world through his own self promotion, Loewy was recognized by *Architectural Forum* (Oct. 1940) as "the only designer in the United States who can cross the country in cars, buses, trains, and aircraft he has designed himself."

With the United States' involvement in World War II beginning and metal (like that used in green ink) becoming scarce, Loewy redesigned a red-and-white pack (1942) for Lucky Strike cigarettes. In 1944, two years after he was made an officer of the Legion d'honneur in Paris, he and five partners reorganized his firm as Raymond Loewy Associated in New York, and his corporate-identity program for the International Harvester Company began. Loewy became a skilled designer of corporate emblems, which in addition to Lucky Strike embraced image programs for Pepsodent, Coca-Cola, and the National Biscuit Company. Jean Thomson, who remained a partner in the firm until 1950, divorced Loewy in 1945. The American Society of Industrial Designers (founded in 1943) elected Loewy president in 1946.

Following the war Loewy's designs became simpler, incorporating long, flowing arcs. These streamlined features were exemplified by Loewy's Studebaker "Champion" car (1947), the first postwar automobile produced in the United States and one that incorporated fenders that receded into the body and featured a long, low trunk. Due to the back and front ends' duplicating projected forms, the joke of the time was that you could not tell if the automobile was coming or going. Concurrent with the introduction of the "Champion," in 1947 Loewy reopened his London office, which been closed earlier because of the war. Loewy married Viola Erickson in 1948. They had one child. He established the Raymond Loewy corporation as a separate entity for mainly architectural commissions in 1950, shortly after *Time* magazine (Oct. 1949) had published a cover story to recognize the stature he had achieved.

As a result of constraining governmental economic regulations in Britain, the London office was closed again in 1951, the year Loewy's autobiography, *Never Leave Well Enough Alone*, was published. A collection of insights and reminiscences, the book did not pretend to be a systematic study. Some critics have accused Loewy of attempting to rid everyday objects of their familiarity, not just their lack of aesthetic appeal, while others credit him with having simplified shapes. About his quest for simplicity, Loewy claimed that "as a child he had experienced pure aesthetic pleasure on seeing the streamlined locomotives of the Paris-Lyon-Mediterranée run and he assumes that his readers will also have [had] such a primary experience of beauty; it is the secondary element that is the principal subject-matter of the book [*Never Leave Well Enough Alone*]—how to communicate beauty to the public and the manufacturers and condition them to appreciate it" (Lichtenstein, p. 144). At the time of its publication, the functionalists of the formidable Hochschule für

Gestaltung (College of Design) in Ulm, Germany, denounced the tenets of the book, which had been given the misleadingly and absurdly translated title *HäBlichkeit verkauft sich schlecht* ("Ugliness Sells Poorly") and accused Loewy of lacking moral integrity. Other detractors have suggested that his streamlining was superficial, altering only the skin of a product with no regard to its relationship to function. But a 31 October 1949 *Time* cover offered an insight into Loewy's successful relationship with industry: "He streamlines the sales curve." Nevertheless, the book's tremendous success in Germany (including worldwide with its publication in numerous other languages such as French, Dutch, Arabic, and Japanese) encouraged a laudatory cover story in the magazine *Der Spiegel* (9 Dec. 1953).

In 1952 Loewy, who spoke with a French accent in the United States and an American one in France, founded the CEI (Compagnie de l'Esthetique Industrielle) in Paris, which went on to produce corporate identity programs for BP (British Petroleum) (1957) and Shell (1967). Continuing his three-decade relationship with Studebaker, the "Starliner" automobile (1953) was thought by the public (encouraged by its immodest designer) to be a "dream" car, and many critics considered its proportions perfect and its form noble. Unfortunately, Loewy's efforts did not save Studebaker from bankruptcy in 1962, the year of his last body design, the "Avanti" sports car, for the ill-fated manufacturer.

Loewy's high-profile work continued with the "Scenicruiser" bus (1954) for Greyhound. His list of commissiones grew to include those from clients in Europe, such as the "2000" tableware produced by Rosenthal Porzellan in Germany. The New York firm was reorganized as Raymond Loewy/William Snaith, Inc., in 1961, when Loewy traveled to Moscow on the invitation of the Soviet Committee for Science and Technology. The trip proved fruitful; his CEI office in Paris was commissioned to design the Moskvich car, the first Soviet design to be commissioned from a westerner.

Loewy's proudest moment came in 1967, when he was hired as a consultant to the National Aeronautics and Space Administration (NASA), an association that lasted until 1974. In the Skylab space station, astronauts were being required to stay up in space longer than in the Gemini and Apollo flights. Because NASA's own staff design for the station was far too stark and inhospitable, George Mueller, head of the Office of Manned Spaceflight, suggested that an industrial designer be appointed to solve the problem. The builder of the station, the Martin Marietta Corporation, recommended the Loewy/Snaith firm. Having ceased some of his activities at the firm by this time, the 75-year-old Loewy leaped at the opportunity and garnered "Skylab" as his own personal project. He bragged, "My first opportunity to express a deep interest in the future of spatial exploration occurred thirty-seven years ago, at a time when such matters were generally ignored. It happened at the New York World's

Fair . . . ; [my] huge rocket intended for 'international transportation of passengers and mail' . . . left the spectators deeply impressed; it was dramatic and a hit of the World's Fair" (Schonberger, p. 188). This and other flights of braggadocio frequently peppered his speeches and interviews subsequent to his receiving the NASA assignment. Even when the self-appointed visionary was nearing age eighty, further NASA commissions included the design of the interior of the "Space Shuttle" (from 1970). Prior to the NASA work, his most prestigious design, at least to him, was the interior of Air Force One, John F. Kennedy's presidential jet airliner.

In 1975 the Loewy/Snaith partnership was transformed into Raymond Loewy International, Inc., with offices in London and Paris only, and both offices closed finally in 1984, two years before the designer's death in Monte Carlo, Monaco. With a career spanning sixty years, outspoken Raymond Loewy became the highly visible spokesperson of the prominent group of four (who included Henry Dreyfuss, Walter Dorwin Teague, and Norman Bel Geddes) for the new profession of industrial design.

Loewy's flamboyance should not overshadow his important contributions, both tangible and theoretical, which shaped material culture of the twentieth century—from the amazingly popular Sears "Coldspot" refrigerator of the early 1930s to the interior of the elitist "Concorde" jet airplane of the early 1970s. His name is virtually synonymous with twentieth-century American business and its products, and his influence on international consumer culture continues to be appreciable.

• Loewy's other publications include *Industrial Design* (1979; repr. 1988), *The Locomotive: Its Esthetics* (1937, repr. 1987), and *Looking Back to the Future: Raymond Loewy* [video recording], PBS Video (1985). Annie E. S. Beard, *Our Foreign-Born Citizens*, 6th ed. (1968), and Joseph Lee Cook and Earleen H. Cook, *Raymond Fernand Loewy, Industrial Designer* (1984), are good sources. *The Designs of Raymond Loewy* is an exhibition catalog for the Renwick Gallery, the National Collection of Fine Arts (1975). Paul Jodard, *Raymond Loewy* (1992), is a biography. Karl Lagerfeld, *Karl Lagerfeld: Off the Record*, ed. Gerhard Steidl and Walter Keller (1994), and *Raymond Loewy Foundation for the Promotion of Industrial Design* (1995), are also valuable. See Angela Schonberger, ed., *Raymond Loewy: Pioneer of American Industrial Design* (1990), and Jerry Streichler, *The Consultant Industrial Design in American Industry 1927–1960* (1962) for more information. An obituary is Jeffrey L. Meikle, "Raymond Loewy 1893–1986," *Industrial Design* (Nov.–Dec. 1986), pp. 25ff.

MEL BYARS

LOFTUS, Cissie (22 Oct. 1876–12 July 1943), actress and mimic, was born Marie Cecilia Loftus Brown in Glasgow, Scotland, the daughter of Ben Brown, a music hall comedian, and Marie Loftus, a music hall singer. Her childhood was spent at boarding schools and backstage at the theaters where her mother played. She left the Convent of the Holy Child, Blackpool, England, in 1892 to become her mother's dressing room maid.

Her own career began later in 1892 at a music hall in Belfast, Ireland. Taking the stage name of Cissie Loftus, she performed songs and gave impersonations of other entertainers with uncanny accuracy. An immediate success, she was booked into a London music hall in July 1893, where she was an even greater sensation. An obituary says her salary at the music hall jumped from five pounds the first week to £500 for the third week (*New York Herald Tribune*, 13 July 1943). Her gift of mimicry was aided by a singing voice of unusual range, encompassing both female and male registers. In London she was advised that her voice was suitable for opera, but Loftus chose to remain a music hall performer. She did, however, venture into acting during the 1893–1894 season, playing in light entertainments at the Gaiety Theatre, London.

In 1894, at age seventeen, Loftus eloped with Justin Huntly McCarthy, dramatic critic and playwright; they had no children, and the marriage would end in divorce in 1899. She brought her music hall act to American vaudeville in 1895, repeating her English success. Thereafter, for many years, she regularly toured both England and the United States. To an interviewer she defined her technique as not "imitation, it is *absorption* . . . " (*Broadway Magazine*, May 1899). She would observe another performer closely, soaking in every intonation, every movement of the body, every indication of temperament, even the breathing pattern—then "when my work is complete . . . all that is left for me is to present the mental photograph as I have received it." She claimed she temporarily became that person.

By the end of the century, Loftus yearned to be a dramatic star herself, not merely an impersonator of such stars. In New York she had an acting role in *The Highwayman* (1895) and in London played in *The Children of the King* (1897). In 1900 she became a member of Mme. Modjeska's company in New York and played the Shakespearean roles of Viola and Hero. At this time she began to be billed as Cecilia Loftus, though remaining Cissie in vaudeville. After playing some modern parts for Daniel Frohman's stock company (1900–1901), she became leading lady to E. H. Sothern in two successful historical romances, *Richard Lovelace* (1901) and *If I Were King* (1901). In 1902 she played in *Faust* and *The Merchant of Venice* with Sir Henry Irving in London. Then she returned for another New York season (1903–1904) with Sothern, playing Ophelia to his Hamlet as well as the earlier roles, until illness forced her to withdraw.

At no time was she hailed as a great dramatic actress, though well liked by the public. The *New York Times* praised her demeanor as "charming and womanly and gracious" (15 Oct. 1901), but gave her performances the faint praise of "sometimes effective but . . . uneven" (27 Apr. 1902) and "never in any respect inadequate" (31 Dec. 1902). She starred in *The Serio-Comic Governess* (1904) in New York, but the height of her acting career came in London in 1905, when she played the title role in *Peter Pan* to great acclaim.

After that, Loftus's career as an actress began to decline. There were physical problems: an accident during rehearsals in 1908 resulted in a major operation; her voice failed in 1911. A problem for both her health and her stage work was her increasing addiction to alcohol. Though many theater people loved her personally, she became known as unreliable professionally. A second marriage to physician Alonzo Higbee Waterman came in 1909 and produced a son before ending in divorce. Loftus never remarried, but formed romantic attachments that were sometimes reported as engagements. She was still in demand for road companies and toured with William Faversham in a Shakespearean repertory in 1913–1914, playing Juliet and Desdemona. She made a motion picture, *A Lady of Quality* (1914), but the silent screen was unsuited to her talents. When she needed money, she resorted to short vaudeville tours, where she remained as highly paid a headliner as ever.

In 1915 Loftus returned to London, but poor health made it difficult for her to maintain a rigorous performing schedule. Her finances became precarious: she made a few stage and music hall appearances but for the most part lapsed into obscurity. In 1922 she was indicted on narcotics charges. Her attorneys admitted her addiction to drugs but argued that it was due to inept nursing after she had suffered a late miscarriage (no date was given). She was placed on probation for a year and after a bout of illness returned to work and live in New York.

There in 1923 her career began an upswing when she headlined the bill at the Palace, America's premier vaudeville house. Loftus received an ovation and was declared as astonishing in her mimicry as when she first appeared in the United States almost thirty years before. Still unstable, she had to withdraw after two weeks but went into the current Ziegfeld *Follies* as a specialty act and continued to give one-night "concert" appearances. She was being applauded as a gallant trouper and survivor, as well as a performer: the review of one concert notes that she was "uproariously greeted" by her celebrity-filled audience, and there were "frequent interruptions of cheers and frenzied applause" during her performance (*New York Times*, 9 Dec. 1923).

In 1928 and the following decade, Loftus found her second wind in the theater as a character actress, beginning with her role as a noble lady of Spain who could not pay her hotel bill in a revival of *Diplomacy* (1928). The *New York Times* reviewer, while he applauded her "lively and engaging comic quality" in the role, also hailed her as part of theater history: she was still "the Cecilia Loftus—otherwise Cissy [*sic*]—who was Francois Villon's romantic lady in 'If I Were King' . . . and the same Cissy also who did imitations and Ophelia" (29 Mar. 1928).

Loftus could be comic, as in *Diplomacy*, or grim, when playing one of the more unpleasant Crawleys in a revival of *Becky Sharpe* (1929). In 1930 she went into talking pictures successfully, appearing in various character roles, sometimes mean, sometimes grandmotherly: her films include *East Lynne* (1930), *The Old Maid* (1939), *The Blue Bird* (1940), and *Lucky Partners* (1940). She made a hit on Broadway in *Three-Cornered Moon* (1933) and on tour in *Reunion in Vienna* (1934) and *Tonight at 8:30* (1938). When she opened in *There's Always a Breeze* (1938), the *New York Times* reviewer praised her, ambiguously, as "the best scattered, grandmotherly alcoholic in the business" (3 Mar. 1938). She had a final triumph as an impersonator in a solo show, *An Evening with Cecilia Loftus*, in 1938. Her last stage appearance was with a touring company of *Arsenic and Old Lace* (1942). She died in a New York City hotel.

Loftus is described by theater historian Daniel C. Blum as "a frail little woman with blue eyes, who never lost her trusting quality of a child." She figures in theatrical history as a performer of astounding versatility, who maintained her appeal over a fifty-year career. She also came to embody the "grand old trouper" who can struggle out of personal depths to make comeback after comeback, until she ends as a living legend.

• Materials on Loftus are in the Billy Rose Theatre Collection at the New York Public Library for the Performing Arts, Lincoln Center. A substantial biographical article is John Anderson, "Miss Cecilia Loftus," *Harper's Bazaar*, June 1938. Her career in vaudeville is sketched in Anthony Slide, *The Encyclopedia of Vaudeville* (1994). Daniel C. Blum, *Great Stars of the American Stage* (1952), contains portraits together with a biographical paragraph. Obituaries are in the *New York Times* and the *New York Herald Tribune*, both 13 July 1943.

WILLIAM STEPHENSON

LOGAN, Benjamin (c. 1742–11 Dec. 1802), military and civil officer, was born in Augusta County in the Shenandoah Valley of Virginia, the son of David Logan and Jane McKinley, farmers. His parents, Anglo-Irish immigrants to Pennsylvania, moved to Virginia in the late 1730s, where David Logan purchased an 860-acre tract. Benjamin Logan apparently received little formal schooling, but a commanding physical presence together with an aptitude for hunting and wrestling earned the young man the respect of his backcountry peers. Following the death of his father in 1757, Benjamin, the oldest living son, inherited the family's Shenandoah Valley lands. Seeking more and better land, Logan relocated to the Holston River Valley in southwestern Virginia in the fall of 1771. There he married twenty-year-old Ann Montgomery in 1772. They had nine children.

Logan soon realized that his future lay farther west. In 1764 Logan had gained his first military seasoning and his first appreciation of trans-Appalachian lands as a sergeant in Colonel Henry Bouquet's campaign against the Shawnee Indians. A decade later, in the 1774 war between Virginia and the Shawnees called Lord Dunmore's War after the governor of Virginia, Logan served as a lieutenant in the Fincastle County militia, an experience that added to his knowledge of Indian fighting and western lands. By the spring of 1775, he was ready to move his family across the mountains into the still-unsettled Kentucky country.

According to one tradition, Logan set out for Kentucky in the company of the North Carolina speculator Richard Henderson. Supposedly a disagreement with Henderson led Logan to separate and start his own settlement, called St. Asaph's. Other evidence suggests, however, that Logan came to Kentucky a few weeks after Henderson. While Logan was not likely the founder, he quickly assumed a prominent role at St. Asaph's.

During the years when Kentucky was part of Virginia, Logan's civil and military authority expanded. In 1776 he was appointed a sheriff and justice of the peace. Five years later, Logan was elected, as representative of Lincoln County, to the Virginia General Assembly, a position he occupied for two more terms, from 1785 to 1787. Logan was also a member of most of the official conclaves concerning Kentucky's separation from Virginia, as well as a participant at Kentucky's first constitutional convention in 1792. But it was military rather than civil service that gained Logan fame. Appointed in 1776 a captain in the militia of Kentucky County, Logan became the second ranking officer in the Kentucky militia after he was promoted to colonel in 1779. Logan commanded a number of retaliatory expeditions across the Ohio River that destroyed Ohio Indian villages and cornfields to punish Ohio Indians for their raids into Kentucky. He frequently clashed with George Rogers Clark, his superior during 1782, about the best strategy for winning the war in the West and defending Kentucky settlements. Clark considered the defense of Falls of Ohio (now Louisville) absolutely crucial, whereas Logan was committed to defending more densely settled districts of Central Kentucky, including St. Asaph's. Logan, too, came in for severe criticism for failing to get his troops to the battle of Blue Licks in time to avert a disastrous defeat. Following the Revolution, Logan emerged as the foremost military figure in Kentucky. In command of a 1786 raid against Ohio Indians, Logan directed the devastation of seven villages. Unfortunately, these "retaliations" did not distinguish between friendly and hostile Indians. Instead of quieting the Kentucky frontier, the murder of the Shawnee chief Moluntha, an advocate of peaceful relations, stirred up more enmity, further eroding the positions of Ohio Indian "accommodationists" and leading to new rounds of retaliatory violence.

After Kentucky achieved statehood in 1792, Logan increasingly turned his attention to political affairs. He served in the Kentucky lower house from 1793 to 1795 and ran for governor in 1796. Although he received a plurality of the electoral vote on the first ballot, he was denied election in a disputed second ballot. His supporters flung charges of a corrupt bargain on the part of the rich and powerful, and historians often interpreted Logan's defeat as a victory of wealthy Bluegrass planters over poorer farmers. But Logan, a moderate Republican of substantial means, was no radical egalitarian. In the mid-1790s he owned nearly 6,000 acres of land, fourteen slaves, and numerous livestock. Against the calls of radicals, he remained dedicated to the preservation of slavery in Kentucky. In his second attempt to secure the governorship in 1800, Logan finished third in a four-man field, ending his political career. He died shortly after in Shelbyville, Kentucky.

No longer as well known as some pioneers, Logan's contributions to the settling and securing of Kentucky were certainly equal to those of the better remembered. Unlike so many of his fellow pioneers, Logan died a wealthy man, still in control of the lands that had lured him to Kentucky.

• Manuscript sources on Logan's life are widely scattered. The most valuable documentary evidence is in the Draper manuscripts at the State Historical Society of Wisconsin. Letters from Logan to Va.'s governors regarding military and civil matters in frontier Ky. are in the Executive Papers Collection at the Virginia State Library. A book-length biography is Charles Gano Talbert, *Benjamin Logan: Kentucky Frontiersman* (1962).

STEPHEN ARON

LOGAN, C. A. (4 May 1806–22 Feb. 1853), actor and playwright, was born Cornelius Ambrosius Logan on a farm near Baltimore, Maryland. He was descended on his father's side from a line of upper-class Irish families who held large estates and figured prominently as officials both in the church and in government; but when his parents (whose names are unknown) immigrated to America, they took up farming. In 1814 his father was killed by British troops moving through Maryland, and Cornelius, one of eight children, was brought up by his mother. He prepared for the priesthood in the Roman Catholic faith at St. Mary's College, where he learned some Latin and some principles of writing. When he was severely reproved by an older priest, he left the college and worked in a shipping house. From there he went to sea, a venture that took him to China. Returning to New York, Logan worked as a reporter and critic for a newspaper. With this experience—later he was characterized as a "man of letters"—Logan turned to the theater for a career.

Philadelphians first saw him at the Tivoli Garden in July 1825 and then at the Walnut Street Theatre. New Yorkers saw him the following year at the Bowery Theatre as a member of the stock company. There he played roles in *The Road to Ruin* and *School for Scandal* and appeared as Claudio in Shakespeare's *Much Ado about Nothing*. With his theater career underway, he married Eliza Akeley and, with his family (which eventually included ten children) in tow, took up the life of an itinerant actor in search of what he could do best. This took him west to Pittsburgh and from there to the river towns along the Ohio and Mississippi, where he found success as a comedian, a line of acting he continued throughout his life.

Logan never achieved stardom as an actor. His short stature and round, fleshy face fully declared him a comedian in looks, and he was warmly received wherever he played. As reported in the *New Orleans Delta*, "[H]is dry, quaint manner would almost elicit laughter from a dead elephant." "He stands at the head of his profession," said the *Nashville American*, "the most original genius on the American stage." To some, this seemed like an overblown puff, but there was no question that while he did not have the drawing power of a star, his acting was much admired. When he played stock for two seasons with his daughter in St. Louis in 1848–1849, he met only moderate success, though in 1850 they were announced there as stars. Noah Ludlow, comanager with Sol Smith of the St. Louis, New Orleans, and Mobile theaters, described Logan as possessing the kind of face "on whose features Momus had placed such an indelible stamp that he could not on the stage express the most serious sentiments without creating a laugh."

Logan's playwriting, however, gave him another stance in the theater of his day. Arthur Hobson Quinn, in his *A History of the American Drama*, considered Logan's plays as constituting "a school of American playwriting, which would probably have had little notice given to it, had it not been caricature." Quinn's view certainly eliminated Logan's plays as drama, but they still qualified as acting pieces with merit in the realm of low comedy. A few plays had been written in this genre before Logan tried his hand at it, but his contribution was that of helping other comedians with dramatic structures and credible plots that they could flesh out with their unique talents, thus giving them in performance a vibrant stage life. In 1834 he wrote *The Wag of Maine* for James Hackett. When that comedian neglected the piece, Logan rewrote it for Dan Marble under the title *Yankee Land; or, The Foundling of the Apple Orchard*. With this play a success, he wrote *The Vermont Wool Dealer; or, The Yankee Traveler* (1840), again for Marble. If his daughter Olive Logan is to be believed, he wrote the first version of *The People's Lawyer* (1842), which J. S. Jones then rewrote for George Hill, who made it a major part of his career repertoire. These plays are still available in print and are still playable, a testimonial to Logan's talents, for they held the stage in one version or another for many years, and taken together, they set the style for the much more highly developed Yankee plays of the 1870s and 1880s.

The plots of Logan's plays—all that we have—make us wonder how the actors who played them could turn them into substantial, even hilarious, entertainments. In *Yankee Land*, for example, the plot is certainly conventional for its day: an orphan boy, Lot Sap Sago, brought up by a wicked Mr. Malson, is involved in a string of incidents, from the threat of a mortgage foreclosure, a forced marriage, and a thwarted attempt to murder Malson to a discovery that wealthy Englishman Lord Oglesby, in search of his long-lost son, is really the orphan's father. The role of Lot required the unique talents of an actor-comedian, and this Marble was. It is just possible, in view of its wide performance and warm reception wherever Marble played it, that *Yankee Land*, in showing a native American in a situation in which his astuteness, slickness, and country charm could hoodwink others, and then having him turn out to be the long-lost son of an English nobleman, was a symbolic recapitulation of the reunion of

England and America two decades after the War of 1812. Making an audience laugh was easy, Logan had found out as an actor, but making it aware that one was laughing at not only his neighbor but also at himself was a singular achievement.

Three of Logan's daughters also took up acting. One of them, Olive, also became a writer, publishing three books on the theater.

When Logan died of apoplexy on an Ohio River steamboat in February 1853, he was on his way to Louisville to perform in the theater there. He was buried in Spring Grove Cemetery in Cincinnati. At forty-six he ended a busy career of entertaining Americans, both as an actor and a playwright, with a view of themselves. Though his name has long been forgotten, any recounting of Logan's life recaptures in depth the very spirit, variety, and energy of nineteenth-century comedy in the United States.

• No extended treatment of C. A. Logan's life and work is available, nor are any papers extant. Consequently, his story must be pieced together from fragments, such as Olive Logan's brief treatment in *The Mimic World and Public Exhibitions* (1871), the record of performances, a vignette in Noah Ludlow's *Dramatic Life as I Found It* (repr. with index, 1966), and mentions in Sol Smith's *Theatrical Management in the West and South for Thirty Years* (1868). Montrose Moses includes him in *The American Dramatist* (1925), H. P. Phelps in *Players of a Century* (1880), and Joseph Ireland in *Records of the New York Stage* (1866–1867). *The Vermont Wool Dealer* and *Yankee Land* were both published by Samuel French (n.d.) and are available in print. For specifics on Logan's work for actors of the New England folk character see Francis Hodge, *Yankee Theatre* (1964).

FRANCIS HODGE

LOGAN, George (9 Sept. 1753–9 Apr. 1821), innovative gentleman farmer and politician, was born at the family estate of "Stenton" near Philadelphia, Pennsylvania, the son of William Logan, gentleman farmer, and Hannah Emlen. He attended the Friends Public School from age eight to fourteen and continued his education in England from 1768 to 1771. After an apprenticeship to a Philadelphia Quaker merchant, Logan was allowed to pursue medicine and obtained the M.D. from Edinburgh in 1779. Having already become master of Stenton due to the recent demise of his parents, he returned to Philadelphia in 1780. He married Deborah Norris in 1781; they had three sons. Logan actively practiced medicine only briefly. By the mid-1780s he was devoting himself to making Stenton a model, scientific farm. Over time, for example, he conducted and reported on fourteen experiments to determine the best way to rotate crops. In 1793 Thomas Jefferson proclaimed Logan "the best farmer in Pensylv*ᵃ* both in theory & practice." He helped form agricultural societies, produced numerous tracts on scientific farming, and was an advocate of raising Merino sheep.

Although disowned by the Society of Friends in 1791 for serving in the militia, Logan hated war. Indeed, he is best remembered for undertaking a private

diplomatic mission to France in 1798 to try to resolve disputes between that country and the United States. His actions led to the passage of the still extant 1799 law, commonly called the Logan Act, that made such unauthorized private diplomacy a crime. Logan had an extensive political career. He served in the Pennsylvania Assembly (1785–1789) and in the 1790s authored numerous political tracts espousing physiocratic ideas that marked him as a spokesman for the emerging Jeffersonian Republicans. He again served in the state assembly (1796–1801) and was appointed to the U.S. Senate in 1801 where he served until 1807 as a Jeffersonian Republican who nevertheless increasingly questioned many of Jefferson's policies. Logan detested indirect taxes and most commercial regulations but did come to advocate internal improvements and the creation of a national university. He supported the elimination of the slave trade and the effort to keep slavery out of the territories. Disregarding the possibility that the Logan Act might be invoked against him, Logan undertook private citizen diplomacy a second time in 1810, when he journeyed to England in an unsuccessful effort to derail the movement toward war between Great Britain and the United States.

Five feet eight inches tall, Logan was small of frame and, according to his historian wife Deborah, handsome. For most of his adult life he dressed in plain homespun. A shy person who nevertheless had a sharp temper, he so disliked public speaking that he rarely spoke as a legislator. Although praised as a good and kind person, Logan was chastised by many as a shallow, doctrinaire thinker who acted inconsistently. He was, for example, charged with being a Tory during the Revolution who in the 1790s embraced radical ideas about the rights of men. Moreover, as noted, he was a Quaker pacifist who, nevertheless, joined the militia. Logan's willingness to admit past errors of analysis and his penchant for attempting to act as a mediator do not explain away his inconsistencies. Still, Logan consistently advocated the rule of law, and he steadfastly believed that the United States should remain a nation of farmers. Indeed, to the day he died at Stenton, he never wavered in his efforts to champion agrarianism.

• The bulk of Logan's papers are housed at the Historical Society of Pennsylvania (HSP) in two collections: the Logan Family Papers (1664–1871) and the Logan Family Business Papers (1808–1836). The HSP also has Logan's diaries. The records of the many societies to which Logan belonged contain important material, and numerous Logan letters exist in the papers of major American figures of the period. The one scholarly biography is Frederick B. Tolles, *George Logan of Philadelphia* (1953). Deborah Norris Logan, *Memoir of Dr. George Logan of Stenton . . . with Selections from his Correspondence*, ed. Frances A. Logan (1899), is essential but slights his extensive political career. For information on the Logan Act, see Charles Warren, *History of Laws Prohibiting Correspondence with a Foreign Government and Acceptance of a Commission* (1917).

JOHN K. ALEXANDER

LOGAN, James (20 Oct. 1674–31 Oct. 1751), provincial councilor, scholar, and William Penn's secretary in America, was born in Lurgan, County Armagh, Ireland, the son of Scottish Quakers Patrick Logan, a minister and teacher, and Isabel Hume. His father, who earned an A.M. from Edinburgh University, taught him Latin, Greek, and Hebrew, and at age thirteen he was apprenticed to Edward Webb, a Quaker linen draper in Dublin. Logan returned to Lurgan six months later, then moved with his family to Bristol when his father was appointed master of the Friar Meetinghouse School. He replaced his father in this position in 1693 and later earned the respect of William Penn when the colonial proprietor served on the school's supervisory board. Penn invited Logan to be his secretary in Pennsylvania, and he was with the Penn family aboard the *Canterbury* when they arrived in Philadelphia on 3 December 1699.

In America, Logan served as Penn's chief steward in land transactions and the collection of proprietary revenues. To execute these tasks, he was named commissioner of property in 1701 and receiver general in 1703. He also served as clerk of the Provincial Council beginning in 1701 and became a full voting member in 1703, sitting until his retirement in 1747. In 1701 Logan represented Penn in negotiations with David Lloyd to revise the 1696 Frame of Government. Those meetings produced the Charter of Privileges, an instrument of government Logan criticized for divesting the council of legislative power. In a letter to Penn in 1705, he commented, "Most are of opinion it is not worth so many pence, and if mine were asked, I should still rate it much lower" (Armstrong, vol. 2, p. 10). In 1706 Logan resisted the assembly's effort, led by Speaker Lloyd, to control fines and forfeitures and to invest local courts with ultimate jurisdiction over land titles—traditionally considered the right of the proprietor and his deputy. Lloyd initiated impeachment proceedings against Logan in early 1707. Although all charges were dropped in March 1712 following Logan's return from a two-year trip to England, his identification as leader of the Proprietary party was thereafter unquestioned.

As a proprietary placeman, Logan prospered, acquiring a great deal of wealth and social privilege. As Penn's land agent and ambassador to local American Indians, Logan gained knowledge of the interior and established himself in the "skin trade." By 1715 he built a large trading station on the Susquehanna River and began to send £1,000 in furs per year to England. He engaged in other ventures as well, shipping provisions to the Carolinas, rum to Newfoundland, and lumber to the Mediterranean and investing heavily in real estate. In 1714 he married Sarah Read; they had four children.

Logan became the object of popular resentment, however, during the recession of 1722, when he objected to Governor William Keith's plan to issue paper money, which had broad support among the middling and lower ranks. He then callously suggested that the paper money advocate determine "whether he has

been as industrious and frugal in the management of his affairs as their circumstances required" (Tolles, p. 127). The paper money exchange occasioned Logan's most extensive public reflection on the nature of government. He wrote in *Charge Delivered from the Bench to the Grand-Jury* (1723):

RELIGION and JUSTICE will necessarily induce a *Regular Administration in the Government*: when the Magistrate of every Rank, having a sense of GOD's Omnipresence, and Omniscience before him, considers that his Power is from GOD: That he Acts for HIM on Earth, and is to be Judged as he Judges: And the Private Man, from a sense of the Obedience to higher Powers, enjoyned on him by GOD, will not fail of paying that Submission to the Magistrate, and the Laws, that both *Religion* and *Reason* indispensibly require him. (p. 5)

His ideas of balanced government and the reciprocal duties of rulers and subjects were cemented by his appointment to the Philadelphia County bench in 1726 and his tenure as chief justice of the Pennsylvania Supreme Court in 1731–1739.

If Logan gained little but frustration in his struggles with the assembly and the governor, he achieved many of his objectives in the sphere of Indian affairs, especially territorial expansion in the Delaware, Schuylkill, and Susquehanna watersheds. In several of his dealings, including dispossessing the Tulpehocken Lenapes of their lands in the Schuylkill basin in 1732 and the infamous "Walking Purchase" of 1737, Logan employed questionable tactics that several historians have condemned as motivated by pecuniary interest. As an imperialist, though, Logan believed that Pennsylvania's frontier was vulnerable to French encroachment, leading him to appreciate the strategic importance of the Iroquois Confederacy. To strengthen the colony's diplomatic ties to the Six Nations, Logan favored Iroquois assertions of suzerainty over the region, which also provided Logan with leverage against the local tribes' territorial claims in treaty negotiations. As a result, he ended whatever autonomy the Shawnees and Lenapes enjoyed in negotiations with Penn, hastening their political subordination to the Six Nations and improving the Iroquois Confederacy's situation on the eve of the French and Indian War.

In 1726 Logan moved from Philadelphia to "Stenton," his large plantation near Germantown, to advance his scholarly pursuits. In a series of experiments in 1727, he proved definitively that maize reproduced sexually. Peter Collinson of London's Royal Society was impressed with his findings, and in 1736 Logan's research was published in the society's *Philosophical Transactions*. With the cooperation of Dutch botanist John F. Gronovius, his studies of plant reproduction were published in Leiden in 1739. Swedish naturalist Carl Linnaeus was sufficiently indebted to Logan's work that he named the order Loganiaceae in his honor, the genera of which numbers thirty, in species over three hundred. Logan's other pieces in *Philosophical Transactions* defended Thomas Godfrey's priority over

John Hadley in improvements on the standard mariner's quadrant and attempted to explain why the Sun and Moon appear larger to the human eye at the horizons than at their zeniths. He also published comments on Pythagoras in Hamburg in 1737 and on Euclid in Amsterdam in 1740. Logan encouraged the research of John Bartram, Benjamin Franklin, and others and thus helped to give shape to the developing scientific community in Philadelphia. Animated by Lockean epistemology, Newtonian physics, and other intellectual currents of the Enlightenment, Logan believed, like other gentlemen scholars of the age, that the cosmos is "governed by laws steady and unalterable," which he attributed to the "supreme and divine Author of all things."

After Logan's death at Stenton, his library of more than 3,000 books was bequeathed to the public and later merged into the holdings of the Library Company of Philadelphia. A wealthy country gentleman, influential officeholder, and internationally known scholar, he was principal among the "Quaker grandees" or the aristocratic Quaker gentry who dominated colonial Pennsylvania politics and culture. He thus was one of the leading statesmen and intellectuals in America in the prerevolutionary period.

• Logan's papers at the Historical Society of Pennsylvania include his letterbooks and several manuscript treatises. Some of his letters are printed in Edward Armstrong, ed., *Correspondence between William Penn and James Logan, Secretary of the Province of Pennsylvania, and Others, 1700–1750* (2 vols., 1870–1872); Wilson Armistead, ed., *Memoirs of James Logan* (1851); and Norman Penney, ed., *The Correspondence of James Logan and Thomas Story, 1724–1741* (1927). Logan's political ideas are summarized in his *The Antidote* (1725) and *Charge Delivered from the Bench to the Grand Inquest* (1736). Logan assessed the Anglo-French imperial rivalry and remarked on frontier defense and Indian affairs in "A Memorial" (1732), which is printed with an introduction in Joseph E. Johnson, "A Quaker Imperialist's View of the British Colonies in America: 1732," *Pennsylvania Magazine of History and Biography* 60 (1936): 97–130. Logan's scholarly writings on mathematics, astronomy, optics, and botany along with commentary are in Roy N. Lokken, ed., "The Scientific Papers of James Logan," *Transactions of the American Philosophical Society* 62 (1972): 5–94. Logan also translated two works of Marcus Tullius Cicero from Latin, *Cato's Moral Distiches, Englished in Couplets* (1735) and *M. T. Cicero's Cato Major; or, His Discourse of Old Age* (1744). Frederick B. Tolles, *James Logan and the Culture of Provincial America* (1957), is a standard biography. The nature of Logan's scientific and philosophical inquiry is appraised in Edwin Wolf II, *The Library of James Logan of Philadelphia, 1674–1751* (1974); Lokken, "The Social Thought of James Logan," *William and Mary Quarterly*, 3d ser., 27 (1970): 68–89; and Dennis Barone, "James Logan and Gilbert Tennent: Enlightenment Classicist versus Awakened Evangelist," *Early American Literature* 21 (1986): 103–117.

JEFFREY B. WEBB

LOGAN, James (c. 1725–1780), Mingo Indian, famous in his own time as an ally of English colonials; succeeding generations remember the tragedy that befell him and the lament he made in response. He was probably born at the village of Shamokin (Sunbury, Pa.), the son of the Oneida chief Shikellamy and a Cayuga woman. Known as Soyechtowa, Tocaniadorogon, or Logan the Mingo, historians have incorrectly called him Tàh-gah-jute.

He is worth notice for his role in processes and relationships peculiar to the frontier region where colonials and tribesmen mingled. Firmly loyal to Pennsylvania and its Iroquois allies, Logan's father served as intermediary between the colony and its tribes. Soyechtowa admired his father's Pennsylvania friend, Secretary James Logan (1674–1751), so much that he followed a widely practiced Indian custom and took James Logan as his own name.

Almost nothing is known about him until the climactic tragedy of his life. The botanist John Bartram described "Shikellamy's son" as tall and commanding, but in context Bartram seems to have referred to the older brother Tachnechdorus, who had inherited Shikellamy's mantle as Iroquois head man in the province. Nonspecific sources hint that Logan the Mingo was lame. He was certainly not Shikellamy's political successor.

Brother Tachnechdorus told the Pennsylvania Council in 1756 that Logan and his family were living near Shamokin and were in jeopardy from hostile Delawares. The brothers tried to persuade the Delawares to resume friendship with Pennsylvania but were rebuffed angrily. Logan was "led astray" by those Delawares, according to his brother, but repented and desired to rejoin the Pennsylvanians. In August 1762, he attended the important treaty at Lancaster, but he did not speak.

He became known as Logan the Mingo when he moved his family to the "Ohio Country," where he settled in a community of emigrants from the Iroquois Six Nations called "Mingoes." These emigrants acted independently of the Iroquois Grand Council, which accepted no responsibility for them.

At the climactic moment of his life, Logan was living at the mouth of Yellow Creek on the right bank of the Ohio River about thirty miles north of modern Wheeling, West Virginia. He became involved unwittingly in a dispute between Virginia and Pennsylvania concerning overlapping jurisdictions when British troops evacuated Fort Pitt in 1774. Virginia's governor, Lord John Dunmore, immediately seized the fort to establish Virginia's jurisdiction and appointed Dr. John Connolly (1743–1813) as commandant. Their behavior indicates that Connolly and Dunmore hoped to make personal fortunes by snapping up Shawnee Indian lands. When the Shawnees failed to cooperate, Connolly whipped up propaganda for war against them.

Numerous homesteaders swarmed into the region, also intending to take over Shawnee lands. A large company of seventy to ninety men congregated at Wheeling and hired veteran frontiersman Michael Cresap as their leader.

Logan the Mingo and his family had the misfortune to be the Indians nearest to these bellicose "settlers," living so close because they were formally allies. Hot-heads among the expansionists wanted to attack immediately, but Cresap momentarily dissuaded them by insisting that the Mingoes were "friendlies." Nevertheless, he organized the party for war.

After Connolly wrote him, arguing that war with the Shawnees was inevitable, Cresap took it as "the signal for open hostilities against the Indians" (Mayer, p. 93). Cresap's men, who made no distinction between one Indian and another, declared war on all of them. On 26 April, they took two scalps despite Cresap's opposition.

Accounts of what followed are confused by obvious efforts to shift blame, especially to blame the Indians for their own victimization; Brantz Mayer's shiftily tendentious book, which remained standard much too long, denigrated Indians in order to exculpate Cresap. One must go back to the documents assembled by Thomas Jefferson in the appendix to *Notes on the State of Virginia*.

It appears that the countryside had been alarmed by Connolly's letter predicting war. A party of armed men assembled across the Ohio from Logan's camp at the house of a liquor dealer named Baker. One of the party, called Daniel Greathouse, invited the Indians for a drinking party at Baker's. Four men, three women, and an infant girl canoed to Baker's without weapons, and the men became staggeringly drunk. When they turned to go, John Sappington shot Logan's brother in the back. (Sappington testified later that Cresap did not rebuke him.) All the others except the infant girl were killed. Indians on the opposite shore heard the gunfire and tried to escape, but they were pursued and shot to death. Logan was away, but his sister as well as his brother were among the thirteen dead.

These Indians were not the Shawnees against whom Virginia declared war. They were Mingo friends of the English. Later, James Chalmers testified that he had been solicited but had refused to participate in the massacre, and that it was premeditated to "get a great deal of plunder" (1825 ed., p. 320). The Iroquois Grand Council shrugged off the incident and the subsequent war. Pennsylvania was in the throes of a domestic revolution. Virginia was the enemy. No recourse for justice was open to Logan except reprisal. This was easier because the massacre had aroused the Indians so that the predicted war broke out. Logan avenged himself with scalps numbering between thirteen and seventy depending on the source.

But the incident demoralized Logan; he became a violent sot and was killed, perhaps by his nephew in self-defense.

Logan is famous now because Thomas Jefferson described his tragedy in *Notes on the State of Virginia* and printed Logan's eloquent lament, which became a favorite of elocutionists in the nineteenth century:

I appeal to any white man to say, if ever he entered Logan's cabin hungry, and he gave him not meat; if ever he came cold and naked, and he clothed him not. During the course of the last long and bloody war [the Seven Years' War] Logan remained idle in his cabin, an advocate for peace. Such was my love for the whites, that my countrymen pointed as they passed, and said, "Logan is the friend of white men." I had even thought to have lived with you, but for the injuries of one man. Colonel Cresap, the last spring, in cold blood, and unprovoked, murdered all the relations of Logan, not even sparing my women and children. There runs not a drop of my blood in the veins of any living creature. This called on me for revenge. I have sought it: I have killed many: I have fully glutted my vengeance: for my country I rejoice at the beams of peace. But do not harbour a thought that mine is the joy of fear. Logan never felt fear. He will not turn on his heel to save his life. Who is there to mourn for Logan?—Not one. (1788 ed., pp. 67–68)

• Logan's "lament" was treated variously by successive editors of Thomas Jefferson's *Notes on the State of Virginia*. Jefferson picked it up from Dixon and Hunter's *Virginia Gazette* of 4 Apr. 1775. He put the Logan story in the *Notes* text of the first American edition in 1788. (The book had been published in Paris in 1784 and 1786, and again in London, 1787.) Responding to hostile critics, Jefferson added an appendix of documents about the Logan episode but kept the lament in the main text in the 1801 edition. By 1825, an editor had moved the lament back with the documents in the appendix. Logan's family is the subject of Rev. W. M. Beauchamp, "Shikellamy and His Son Logan," verifiably based on a search of Pennsylvania's colonial records, in *Twenty-first Annual Report of the American Scenic and Historic Preservation Society* (1916), pp. 599–611. Probably the most cited, and certainly the least reliable, study is Brantz Mayer, *Tah-gah-jute: or Logan and Cresap* (1851). It is erroneous from the first word of the title and crafted as anti-Indian propaganda. For the political background and land speculations, see Thomas Perkins Abernethy, *Western Lands and the American Revolution* (1937).

FRANCIS JENNINGS

LOGAN, James (1776?–23 Nov. 1812), Shawnee warrior whose Indian name was Spemica Lawba, the High Horn, and who became an American hero in the War of 1812, was born in Ohio. His parentage is unknown. According to a friend, John Allen, he was a mixed-blood whose Indian mother was related to Tecumseh. Logan's mother may have been an aunt or cousin to Tecumseh, but she assuredly was not his sister, as is sometimes reported. John Johnston, an Indian agent who knew Logan, denied that there was any blood relationship between the latter and Tecumseh. In the 1840s several veteran pioneers, including members of the Renick family, maintained that Logan was one of two sons of Joshua Renick, a white man captured about 1761 and raised by Indians, and that Logan was named James. Since he spent much of his life about U.S. settlements, however, it is surprising that the connection with Renick, if true, did not surface earlier. It is even possible that the view that Logan was a mixed-blood was nothing more than a fallacious inference based on Logan's rudimentary command of English and his imbibing of American customs and attitudes.

As a boy Logan was captured when Kentuckians under Benjamin Logan attacked the Shawnee town of Mackachack, situated on a tributary of the Mad River (Logan County, Ohio) in October 1786. Among the thirty or so other prisoners was Logan's mother, who enjoyed a reputation as an Indian doctor. The Indians were held at Danville and Lexington in Kentucky and North Bend in Ohio, but all were released in exchanges of prisoners held at Maysville in August 1787 and the mouth of the Miami in September 1789. From his captivity Logan acquired the name by which he was thereafter known by whites (apparently taken from Benjamin Logan, who befriended the boy) and some facility in the English tongue.

Between 1789 and 1795 Logan fought with his fellow Shawnees against the United States in the war that closed with the treaty of Greenville. Afterward he remained friendly to Americans and was one of those Shawnees who believed that their remaining lands in Ohio could be best protected by a policy of peace and the development of the Indian economy on lines recommended by the U.S. and Quaker missionaries, namely, dispensing with hunting and intensifying agriculture. He married a Shawnee named Rebecca, who herself had been captured by Kentuckians as a child—apparently in John Hardin's expedition against the Wabash Indians in August 1789—and raised by Hardin before her release, probably in 1795. Logan fathered four children and latterly lived just outside the Shawnee town of Wapakoneta on the upper Auglaize. He was a skilled hunter but also became a trader, purchasing goods at Cincinnati for resale to other Indians.

In maturity Logan was impressive, handsome, muscular, and tall, excelling in Indian wrestling. Although noisy when drunk, he was good-natured and had a powerful reputation for honesty. John Johnston remembered that he "never knew a more sincere friend or a truer-hearted man" than Logan. The trust in which he was held is evident in 1809 when the Quaker missionary at Wapakoneta, William Kirk, having been compelled to abandon his mission, left the considerable equipment in Logan's care. Logan had influential relations, including the war chief Black Snake, who was a first cousin, but Logan never became a village chief of his people, possibly because he apparently belonged to the Mekoche division of the tribe, in which such positions were generally hereditary. He was popular with the young warriors, however, and by 1812 was sitting in the Wapakoneta councils as a top war chief.

Logan's reliability and his grasp of English made him useful during difficulties between the Shawnees and U.S. settlements. In August 1806 he accompanied Blue Jacket and Tecumseh to Chillicothe to reassure the citizens of Shawnee goodwill. The following year he was carrying messages between Wapakoneta and local settlers. He interpreted Shawnee protests at the closure of Kirk's mission in 1809, and in September 1810 he attended an intertribal conference at Brownstown, on the Detroit River.

The War of 1812 divided the Shawnees. The Wabash band under Tecumseh joined the British, while those in Ohio nominally remained neutral, although they gave occasional support to the United States. Logan was the most important Shawnee to serve with American forces. He carried Brigadier general William Hull's proclamation, which advised the Indian tribes to stay out of the war, from Urbana (Ohio) to the Wabash, and then helped guide Hull's army in its march through Ohio to Detroit. In July he visited Tecumseh at Fort Malden (Amherstburg, Ontario) in an unsuccessful attempt to persuade the chief to abandon his British alliance. After Hull's surrender in August, Logan was recruited by John Johnston to withdraw twenty-five women and children from the endangered outpost of Fort Wayne, Indiana Territory, and to bring them to Piqua, Ohio.

Johnston also recruited Logan to serve under the new American commander in chief, William Henry Harrison, for $45 a month, the use of a horse, and the provision of rations and forage. Early in September Logan had again reached Fort Wayne, this time passing through the lines of British Indian forces that were moving up the Maumee River to attack the garrison. He successfully made the return trip to verify reports that Fort Wayne was under siege, and he helped guide the army under Harrison that relieved the post on 12 September. From Fort Wayne Harrison launched forays against neighboring Indian villages, but unconvinced that these were hostile to the United States, Logan refused to participate. Nevertheless, with a few followers he continued to scout for the American army and in one reconnaissance in November was surprised by a superior force near the Maumee rapids. Logan's party was dispersed, but Logan reached a camp of James Winchester's wing of the U.S. Army, situated on the Maumee, six miles below Defiance.

At Winchester's camp some reservations were expressed about the reliability of the Shawnee "spies," in view of Tecumseh's alliance with the British, Logan's disapproval of Harrison's attacks on Indian communities, and the quitting of the camp by two of Logan's Shawnee associates. Partly to quench such suspicions, Logan and two of his three remaining followers (the younger Captain Johnny and Bright Horn) left the camp on the morning of 22 November to reconnoiter downstream toward British-Indian positions at the rapids. The trio were on foot but had proceeded some ten miles when they were intercepted by an enemy party consisting of the British agent Alexander Elliott, the Potawatomi chief Winamec, and four other Indians, all armed and on horseback. Outnumbered, Logan bluffed that he was on his way to join the British forces and allowed his party to be escorted downstream while awaiting an opportunity to make a surprise attack.

After several miles Logan judged that he could delay his attack no longer. In a fierce exchange of fire three or four of his opponents were killed or fatally wounded, including Elliott and Winamec, the latter shot and then tomahawked by Logan himself. The other British allied Indians were driven to a thicket, but then Bright Horn and Logan were both hit, Logan shot through the upper abdomen. Catching two enemy horses, the wounded men returned to Winchester's camp about ten o'clock at night, while Captain Johnny came in on foot the following morning.

Logan's wounds were dressed, and he was kept in comfortable tents. He asked his friend Major Martin D. Hardin to see that his children were educated and raised as whites. Although in pain, he fell asleep close to midnight and died shortly thereafter. The body was taken to Fort Winchester (Defiance) and buried with the military honors of a captain.

Logan's death caused genuine grief among his Shawnee and American associates. Hardin remarked, "Logan, by all who knew him well, was considered a man of the first probity. His death is very much regretted in the army. His last act has wiped off all suspicion from his tribe." His exploits at Fort Wayne and his final engagement gave him a place in histories of the War of 1812 as the foremost Indian hero on the American side of that conflict.

• Robert B. McAfee, *History of the Late War in the Western Country* (1816), pp. 122–23, 125, 149, 172–76, and Benjamin Drake, *Life of Tecumseh* (1841), pp. 49–60, are the most reliable accounts. The sources on which they were based have been preserved in the Draper manuscripts, State Historical Society of Wisconsin, Madison, U (Frontier Wars) ser., vol. 7. The letters of John Bickley (23 Nov. 1812), John Allen (1 Dec. 1812), and Martin D. Hardin (2 Dec. 1812) are particularly valuable. Leslie Combs, "The Last Battle and Death of Logan," *Southern and Western Literary Messenger and Review* 13 (1847): 119–25, is written by someone who knew Logan. Examples of the scattered additional references to Logan are *Virginia Argus*, 6 Sept. 1806; Logan Esarey, ed., *Messages and Letters of William Henry Harrison*, vol. 2 (1922), pp. 246–48; Gayle Thornbrough, ed., *Letter Book of the Indian Agency at Fort Wayne, 1809–1815* (1961), pp. 61, 63; and papers in the Draper manuscripts, including Black Hoof to Benjamin Whiteman, 15 June 1807, U ser., vol. 5, p. 182; James Galloway to Benjamin Drake, 12–23 Jan. 1839, J ser., vol. 8, pp. 245–59; John Johnston to people of Cincinnati, 18 Dec. 1838, YY ser., vol. 11, p. 20; and Benjamin Logan interviewed by Lyman C. Draper (1863), S ser., vol. 18, pp. 168–77. The Letters Received by the Secretary of War (Record Group 107) in the National Archives, Washington, D.C., contain such pertinent documents as Shawnees to John Johnston, 30 Apr. 1812 and the agreement between Shawnees and William Hull, 8 June 1812.

JOHN SUGDEN

LOGAN, John Alexander (9 Feb. 1826–26 Dec. 1886), Union general and U.S. senator, was born in Jackson County, Illinois, the son of John Logan, a physician and politician, and Elizabeth Jenkins. He was educated in local schools and at an academy in adjoining Randolph County before serving as second lieutenant in an Illinois regiment during the Mexican War, service that took him as far as Santa Fe but involved no combat. Afterward he studied law at the University of Louisville (1850–1851), won election as prosecuting attorney for Jackson and Franklin counties, Illinois,

moved to Benton, Illinois, and then successfully campaigned for the Illinois legislature. At the age of twenty-six, the fiery Jacksonian Democrat won popularity as the chief proponent of legislation effectively banning blacks from Illinois. In 1855 he married Mary Simmerson Cunningham, who, well educated and vivacious, furthered his career with her charm and writing ability. The couple had three children. Prominence in the law, both in private practice and as prosecutor, and another term in the legislature (1857) prepared the way for his election to Congress in 1858.

Congressman Logan was a staunch ally of Stephen A. Douglas, whom he exceeded in deference to the South. Logan responded to charges that returning fugitive slaves was "dirty work" by asserting that his constituents welcomed such work and won himself the enduring nickname of "Dirty Work" Logan. During the presidential campaign of 1860, the owners of a Democratic newspaper in Benton considered defecting to the Republicans. Backed by a menacing crowd of political supporters, Logan forced the owners to sell, an act reinforcing the dirty work image. During the secession crisis following the election, Logan turned compromiser because his district in southernmost Illinois (called Egypt) divided its support between North and South. "The election of Mr. Lincoln, deplorable as it may be," he wrote, "affords no justification or excuse for overthrowing the republic."

Even after the war began, Logan remained silent, declining to echo Douglas's support of the North. When Logan's young brother-in-law joined a company from southern Illinois that was recruited for Confederate service, Logan's silence was interpreted as approval. Two months into the war Logan finally spoke out for the Union, denounced secessionists and abolitionists equally, and decided to recruit a regiment. Logan's tardy announcement had considerable effect on public sentiment in Egypt, thereafter more closely tied to the North, and gave Logan national recognition as a patriotic convert.

As colonel of the Thirty-first Illinois, Logan fought in the early battles of Brigadier General Ulysses S. Grant: at Belmont, Missouri (7 Nov. 1861) and Fort Donelson (15 Feb. 1862), where Logan received severe wounds and won promotion to brigadier general. He resigned from Congress, committed himself to military service, and avoided politics even when his former law partner, William Joshua Allen, a Peace Democrat and strong opponent of the war, replaced him in Congress. During the Vicksburg campaign Logan, now a major general, enhanced his reputation for fierce fighting and dramatic leadership. His swarthy complexion and walrus mustache gave him the new nickname "Black Jack." During the summer of 1863 he made patriotic speeches in Egypt as a War Democrat and Unionist. He appeared to edge toward the Republicans by accepting the desirability of emancipation.

Campaigning in Georgia in 1864, Logan led the Fifteenth Corps of the Army of the Tennessee, commanded by Major General James B. McPherson.

When McPherson fell before Atlanta in July, Logan succeeded to command by seniority. William T. Sherman quickly replaced Logan with a professional soldier, Oliver O. Howard, who had been educated at West Point. Logan never forgave the slight and for the rest of his life sang the praises of volunteers and denigrated professionals. Sherman thought Logan more politician than soldier, an opinion that was vindicated when Logan returned to southern Illinois in the fall of 1864 to campaign for Abraham Lincoln's reelection and Congressman Allen's Unionist opponent. Friends ascribed Republican victories in the district and state to Logan's oratory. He returned to the army, where he might have replaced George H. Thomas at Nashville had not the dilatory Thomas won a smashing victory. Logan accompanied Sherman's campaign through the Carolinas and ended the war a military hero with bright political prospects.

Wavering between parties after the war, Logan played a major role in organizing the Grand Army of the Republic (GAR), a politically potent veterans' group. Nominated by Republicans for a statewide congressional seat in 1866, Logan broke all former political ties, denied reports of his disloyalty in 1861, and swept to victory. During four years in the House, Logan affiliated with the radical Republicans and displayed the fervor of a convert. He achieved a reputation for ruthless denunciation of former Confederates and merciless attacks on President Andrew Johnson, culminating in service as a manager during the impeachment trial. Reelected twice, he finally won a long-coveted Senate seat in 1871. He broadened his political base that year by moving from sparsely populated Egypt to flourishing Chicago. A stalwart supporter of the Grant presidency (1869–1877), Logan reaped rewards of patronage and power. Buoyed by support from officeholders and veterans, Logan began to play a role in national politics until his career received a setback through defeat for reelection in 1877. He returned to the Senate in 1879, more powerful than before among Republican chieftains, and tried strenuously but fruitlessly to secure Grant a third-term nomination in 1880.

Logan had some support for the Republican nomination for president in 1884, but James G. Blaine won the prize, and Logan took second place. The vice presidential nominee campaigned energetically and stridently in a close election won by Grover Cleveland. In 1885 Logan nearly lost his Senate seat again, when the Illinois legislature deadlocked for weeks, mired in corruption. When a Democratic legislator died, Republicans nominated no candidate in that district and lulled Democrats into failing to vote; carefully organized Republicans rushed to the polls late in the day. This disreputable trick brought a new Republican legislator to Springfield to reelect Logan.

In his last years Logan compiled a massive manuscript, *The Great Conspiracy*, published in 1886. Criticized as "a narrative stump speech," the book blamed the Civil War on sinister southern plotting to strengthen slaveholders' power and to defeat beneficent tariffs.

In his final year Logan wrote *The Volunteer Soldier of America* (1887), a lengthy argument extolling citizen soldiers and exaggerating the follies of the professional military. Both books illustrate the depths of Logan's passion and the shallowness of his thought.

When Logan died in Washington, D.C., veterans mourned. He had always protected their interests and promoted their pensions. As commander of the GAR, he had proclaimed the first formal Memorial Day in 1868, a day originally consecrated to perpetuating wartime emotions and Republican voting. Many considered him a political opportunist and spoilsman, but none could deny that in wartime he had been an inspiring commander, a ferocious fighter, and among Grant's ablest subordinates.

• A massive collection of Logan family manuscripts, possibly weeded by his widow to enhance his reputation, is in the Library of Congress. Another large collection in the Illinois State Historical Library consists largely of congratulatory letters, but the library also has papers of his father, Dr. John Logan. *The Volunteer Soldier* (1887), published posthumously, includes biographical material and selections from Logan's wartime journals. A spate of contemporary campaign biographies culminated with George Francis Dawson, *Life and Services of Gen. John A. Logan as Soldier and Statesman* (1887), a book read and vetted by both Logan and his wife. Mary S. C. Logan, *Reminiscences of a Soldier's Wife* (1913), is readable, adulatory, and unreliable. James P. Jones has written the only modern published biographies, *"Black Jack": John A. Logan and Southern Illinois in the Civil War Era* (1967) and *John A. Logan: Stalwart Republican from Illinois* (1982). Lengthy obituaries filled with adulation and reminiscence appear in the Springfield *Illinois State Journal* and the *Chicago Tribune*, both 27 Dec. 1886.

JOHN Y. SIMON

LOGAN, Joshua (5 Oct. 1908–12 July 1988), director, producer, playwright, lyricist, and actor, was born Joshua Lockwood Logan in Texarkana, Texas. His lumberman father, Joshua Lockwood Logan, Sr., died when Logan was only three years old. He was raised in Louisiana by his mother, Susan Nabors, and stepfather, Howard F. Noble, an officer on the staff of the Culver Military Academy, where Logan attended school. Logan began his theatrical career in 1928 as a student at Princeton University, where he was a founder of the University Players, a summer stock group that performed on Cape Cod and that also included Henry Fonda, Margaret Sullavan, Myron McCormick, and James Stewart. Another member of the troupe, actress Barbara O'Neil, and Logan were married in 1939; they had one child and divorced in 1945. In 1931 Logan received a grant to travel to Moscow to study with the great Russian actor-director Constantin Stanislavsky. On his return to the United States he spent some time in Hollywood as dialogue director for the films *The Garden of Allah* (1936) and *History Is Made at Night* (1937) and as the codirector of *I Met My Love Again* (1938).

It was to be in the theater, however, that Logan would make his name. He made his New York City directing debut with E. M. Delafield's *To See Our-*

selves (1935) but truly arrived with his highly praised direction of Paul Osborn's *On Borrowed Time* (1938) and the popular Rodgers and Hart musical *I Married an Angel* (1938). From the late 1930s to the mid-1960s, Logan was perhaps the most admired theatrical director of the American theater. His love of the theater and the process of getting a play on stage was obvious. In his first memoir, *Josh, My Up and Down, In and Out Life*, he wrote that "the theater is a kaleidoscope, a hall of mirrors, a kangaroo, a Roman candle. A director must change hats and even costumes constantly: a preacher's collar, a trainer's turtleneck, a doctor's stethoscope, a cheerleader's megaphone. He must encourage, persuade, bully gently, argue, convince, inspire, flatter, fight, and above all he must win." Logan was particularly noted for his extraordinary ability to unify all aspects of production, even in the most extravagant circumstances, and to bring out the best in his collaborators, both onstage and off.

Among the most significant directorial achievements of his career were some of the outstanding musicals and dramas of the era: *Knickerbocker Holiday* (1938), starring Walter Huston; *Stars in Your Eyes* (1939), his first musical with Ethel Merman; *Morning's at Seven* (1939) by Paul Osborn, a failure despite critical approval; a revival of the 1890s British farce *Charley's Aunt* (1940) that first brought Jose Ferrer to prominence; Rodgers and Hart's *By Jupiter* (1942); Irving Berlin's all-soldier show *This Is the Army* (1942); Berlin's classic musical comedy *Annie Get Your Gun* (1946), with Ethel Merman; John Van Druten's popular wartime comedy *John Loves Mary* (1947); Harold Rome's popular musical *Wish You Were Here* (1952); Mary Martin's nonmusical performance in *Kind Sir* (1953); William Inge's Pulitzer Prize–winning *Picnic* (1953); Harold Rome and S. N. Behrman's musical *Fanny* (1954), starring opera great Ezio Pinza; Paddy Chayefsky's *Middle of the Night* (1956), with a memorable performance by Edward G. Robinson; Irving Berlin's last original musical *Mr. President* (1962); and the failed musical adaptation of *Lilies of the Field* called *Look to the Lilies* (1970), starring Shirley Booth. Remembered for strongly defined characterizations and lusty mixtures of comedy and drama, Logan's stage work provided the Broadway stage with expert productions of enduring classics.

Logan's military service during World War II was a significant factor in the great success of two productions he directed. With *Mister Roberts* (1948), adapted from Thomas Heggen's novel by Logan and Heggen, Logan was able to strengthen the novel's characters and sharpen the dramatic conflict with an effective mixture of comedy and tragedy. The highly successful Broadway production starred Logan's friend Henry Fonda in a role that would become permanently associated with the actor. As colibrettist of *South Pacific* (1949), Logan collaborated with Richard Rodgers and Oscar Hammerstein in adapting James A. Michener's *Tales of the South Pacific* stories to the musical stage. Logan successfully heightened all of the values of this dramatic musical in a colorful and sensual production

featuring Ezio Pinza, Mary Martin, Juanita Hall, and Myron McCormick. Logan also directed the successful English production of *South Pacific*. For his work in the theater, Logan won four Tony Awards, two for *Mister Roberts*, one each for *South Pacific* and *Picnic*.

In films Logan directed *Picnic* (1956); *Bus Stop* (1956), featuring a well-regarded performance by Marilyn Monroe; a touching wartime drama *Sayonara* (1957), starring Marlon Brando and Red Buttons in a supporting actor Academy Award performance; *South Pacific* (1958); and two of the last large-scale musical films made by Hollywood, *Camelot* (1967) and *Paint Your Wagon* (1969). Neither of the last two succeeded critically or commercially. He won a Golden Globe as best director for *Picnic* and was nominated for Academy Awards for *Picnic* and *Sayonara*. Logan's films were usually popular successes, but he was often criticized for a lack of subtlety in his screen directing. He also appeared as himself in the movie *Main Street to Broadway* (1953).

In the early 1940s, Logan suffered from exhaustion and spent more than a year in a psychiatric hospital, a situation that repeated itself in the 1950s. He was diagnosed a manic depressive, and counter to the practices of his time, Logan spoke openly about his battle with the illness in hopes of raising public consciousness. In the 1960s Logan learned to control his condition with lithium carbonate, but his peak years as a director were over. He had little theatrical luck in the last twenty years of his life. One major return to directing in 1974 with *Miss Moffat*, a musical version of Emlyn Williams's play *The Corn Is Green*, starred Bette Davis but closed before opening on Broadway when Davis withdrew from the production. However, Logan's two volumes of memoirs written in the mid-1970s, *Josh, My Up and Down, In and Out Life* (1976) and *Movie Stars, Real People, and Me* (1978), were critically acclaimed bestsellers. Logan also produced, directed, and performed in his first nightclub show at New York City's Rainbow Grill in 1977.

In 1945 Logan married Nedda Harrigan, daughter of turn-of-the-century actor and producer Edward "Ned" Harrigan. They had a son and a daughter. He died in New York City. Reflecting on his life, and his struggles with mental and physical ills, Logan wrote in his memoir, *Josh*: "Choose another life? Never. I believe that high, wild side, that manic side, has given me a daring I could never have learned, and that daring has made for me a life I could never have dreamed of living otherwise."

• In addition to his memoirs, Logan wrote "Co-Author of New Drama Tells How Bestselling Novel 'Mr. Roberts' Was Made into Broadway Hit," *Cue*, 6 Mar. 1948. For additional information on Logan, see John Mason Brown, "Louisiana Chekhov," *Saturday Review*, 15 Apr. 1950, p. 36; "Golddiggers of 1969: Joshua Logan Talks to Gordon Gow," *Films and Filming*, Dec. 1969, p. 12; Norris Houghton, "Bretaigne Windust and Joshua L. Logan," *Theatre Arts* 31 (Apr. 1947): 31; A. B. Lochheim, "Director Having Wonderful Time," *New York Times Magazine*, 15 June 1952; M. MacKaye, "Broadway Says He's a Genius," *Saturday Evening Post*, 20

Oct. 1951, p. 44; B. Miller, "Josh Logan, Watermelons and Sex," *Vision* (Spring 1962): 11; "Personality of the Month," *Films and Filming*, Oct. 1961, p. 5; Andrew Sarris, "Minor Disappointments," *Film Culture* (Spring 1963): 41; Gay Talese, "Soft Psyche of Joshua Logan," *Esquire*, Apr. 1963, p. 82; William A. Wellman, Jr., "Runnin' into Marlon," *Film Comment* 27 (July–Aug. 1991): 34–36; and Maurice Zolotow, "Josh-of-All-Theatre-Trades," *Theatre Arts*, Oct. 1954, p. 18.

JAMES FISHER

LOGAN, Martha Daniell (29 Dec. 1704–28 June 1779), horticulturist, was born in Charleston, South Carolina, the daughter of Robert Daniell and Martha Wainwright. Her father had traveled from Barbados to Charleston in 1679 and had quickly become involved in the commerce of the region. He held the title of "Landgrave," bestowed upon him by the Lords Proprietors, which permitted him to acquire 48,000 acres. In addition, he served two terms as lieutenant governor of South Carolina, having been appointed to the position by the Lords Proprietors. He died in 1718.

In July 1719, Martha married George Logan, Jr., and, about the same time, her mother married George Logan, Sr. During the next sixteen years, Logan and her husband had eight children. It is not known what George did for a living, but apparently he and Martha suffered financially, judging from the fact that Martha began her various enterprises more than twenty years before her husband's death in 1764. In 1742 she advertised in the local paper that she would board students and teach them to read and write. By the early 1750s the Logans had moved from their home on the Wando River about ten miles from Charleston to a place "on the green at Trotts point" in town. It was from this address that she began advertising her horticultural activities.

Soon she was publishing a "Gardeners Kalender," and she reported for sale "very good seed, flower roots, and fruit stones." During the spring of 1760, Logan met John Bartram of Philadelphia and gave him a tour of her garden in Charleston. Shortly thereafter she began exchanging both letters and plants with Bartram. In her first letter Logan presented a list of plants that she could send to Philadelphia, mostly woody shrubs grown in midcentury Charleston, a mixture of native and cultivated species. By 1761 Logan and Bartram were passing back and forth a small silk bag containing seeds.

Impressed with her garden and plants, Bartram, in 1761, mentioned her in a letter to a London merchant interested in botany. In this letter Bartram reported that he had the favor of an "elderly widow lady" who was remarkable in her correspondence though he visited with her for only about "4 minutes." During this visit to Charleston in 1760, Bartram also met Alexander Garden (1730–1791), the famous gardener and physician. In addition to Dr. Garden, several prominent Charlestonians of the time were known to both Bartram and Logan, including Dr. Lionel Chalmers, Logan's son-in-law. Although some of them had given

Logan seeds and roots from their gardens or assisted her in other ways, apparently Dr. Garden was not very friendly or helpful; Logan indicates in her letters to Bartram that "Dr. Garden has so much business he has not time to think of me." In another letter to Bartram she mentions her desire for specific plants not available to her but adds that Dr. Garden has these and they are doing well for him. She also requested that Bartram not bother Dr. Garden but rather send materials directly to her in care of her son. Previous letters sent by way of Dr. Garden appear to have been delivered belatedly or not at all.

In 1763 King George appointed Bartram the king's botanist for the purpose of visiting the newly acquired territory of Florida and writing a journal of his observations. Therefore, Bartram returned to Charleston in 1765 to begin his journey and may have visited Logan again; however, his later correspondence with her, if any, has been lost.

Several questions remain concerning the life and times of this extraordinary woman. Did she manage the Logan plantation before the death of her husband? Did she begin her boarding school because she needed the money, although her husband's father and her own had held positions of trust in the province and were considered financially secure? Did she sell the family home and other properties as advertised in 1749? And why did Bartram refer to her as an "elderly widow lady" in 1761 when her husband did not die until 1764? These questions suggest a fascinating life for this industrious pioneer female horticulturist and correspondent whose "garden was her delight." She died in Charleston, a year before the British retook the city during the American Revolution, and is buried in St. Philip's churchyard.

• Letters from Martha Logan to John Bartram are in the Bartram papers, Historical Society of Pennsylvania, Philadelphia. These letters are reprinted in "Letters of Martha Logan to John Bartram, 1760–1763," *South Carolina Historical Magazine*, Jan. 1958. She is also mentioned in David Duncan Wallace, *History of South Carolina* (4 vols., 1934); David Ramsay, *History of South Carolina* (2 vols., 1809); George W. Logan, *A Record of the Logan Family of Charleston* (1923); B. Hollingsworth, *Her Garden Was Her Delight* (1962); Idella Bodie, *South Carolina Women* (1991); and Edmund and Dorothy Smith Berkeley, *The Life and Travels of John Bartram* (1982).

DAVID H. REMBERT, JR.

LOGAN, Olive (22 Apr. 1839–27 Apr. 1909), actress and writer, was born in Elmira, New York, the daughter of Cornelius Ambrosius Logan, an actor, and Eliza Akeley, an actress. Logan's show business career began when, as a child, she appeared on stage with her parents. For most of her professional life in the theater she played leading and character roles on the New York stage and toured throughout the country, primarily in the company of John Augustin Daly. When Logan first began in his company, she was considered by him to be one of the most professional and solid, if not imaginative, character actors in the company. She never lost her respect for and appreciation of Daly, but her distaste for theatrical life and her unstable mental state seemed to take a toll on their relationship. She left the company as soon as she was financially able to. She received much of her formal education in France as a young adult and lived there for many years.

Logan left the stage for eight years after she married Henry A. DeLille in 1857; the couple had no children. She returned to the stage only once in that period, to star in her own play *Eveleen* in 1864. Her reasons for leaving the stage, rather than being prompted by the usual need to keep house and rear children, arose instead from her personal distaste for acting. After her divorce from DeLille in 1865, she reluctantly resumed acting and eagerly continued writing. Despite an upbringing in a theatrical family and success as an actress, especially in roles such as Laura Roslyn in *Sam* and the title role in *Eveleen*, Logan never had an abiding love for the stage.

Logan abandoned her acting career permanently in 1868, continuing her connection with the stage only as a playwright and a historian. Yet while criticizing what she saw as the sham and immorality of the theater, Logan acknowledged the rare benefits of money and independence provided by a theatrical career. She also drew heavily upon the theater as a source for her writing.

By the time she retired from the stage, Logan had launched two other careers. She wrote novels, plays, and lengthy feature articles in *Galaxy*, *Harper's*, and *Player's* magazines, chiefly on art, politics, and fashion in the Paris of 1862. She also became known as a speaker on the touring lecture circuit. Three of her plays met with success on stage, but, as was frequently the case in the nineteenth century, they were never published. Those that were performed in New York included *Armadale* (1866); *Surf*, a dramatization of a Wilkie Collins novel (1870); and *Newport* (1879).

Logan's nonfiction works include *Photographs of Paris Life* (1862), published under the pseudonym Chroniqueuse. She is also one of the unrecognized social historians of the American stage, with two books on theatrical life. The first, *Apropos of Women and the Theatres* (1869), expounds upon a theme that became one of Logan's preoccupations: the immorality of Lydia Thompson and her "British Blondes," a forerunner of the twentieth-century burlesque, and of the lavish 1866 burlesque extravaganza entitled *The Black Crook*. Logan believed that such performances, which featured seminudity and dancers in flesh-colored tights, served only to give respectable actresses like herself a bad name. Her second and most substantial work on the theater appeared first in 1870 under the title *Before the Footlights and Behind the Scenes* and then the next year as *The Mimic World*. This lengthy, often biased, but valuable study provides pictures of backstage life and of forms of entertainment other than the legitimate stage, as, for example, the circus. The work contains biographical sketches and anecdotes, arguments encouraging the respectful treatment of actors, and Logan's favorite briefs advocating the elimi-

nation of the theater's third tier of balconies, often reserved for prostitutes, as well as the elimination of stage "nudity."

Logan, always ready to express her strong opinions, published two other works of nonfiction, *Get Thee Behind Me, Satan: A Home-born Book of Home-Truths* (1872) and *The American Abroad* (1882). The first is a defense of the home as opposed to free love and love-less "mercantile" marriages. She warns women against accepting marriage as their only option in life and against allowing oneself to be treated as a commodity. Portraits of several types of unhappy women illustrate her feminist thesis. In *The American Abroad* (1883), Logan again mounts her soapbox, to decry the shameful way in which the British treat Americans.

Logan's first novel, *Chateau Frissac: Home Scenes in France* (1865), was also an attack on the Victorian marriage of convenience. It is a melodramatic treatment of love thwarted by inadequate dowries, family disapproval, and arranged alliances. Her second novel, *John Morris' Money* (1867), tells of a family that takes in and entertains an old aunt, who eventually rewards the family with an inheritance.

Two pieces of Logan's shorter fiction are worth noting for their use of her theatrical experiences. "The Good Mr. Bagglethorpe" (1870) is a Cinderella story of a poor, orphaned young actress appearing in "moral dramas" who is seen and loved by the wealthy Willie Gentry. To make the union between the two possible, the actress must be taken from the stage and educated for two years. Another story, "Carrie Lee, an American Debutante," illustrates the love-hate relationship that Logan had with the theater: for even though there were pitfalls to be encountered there, the stage offered young women one of the few chances to work with dignity. Her final novel, *They Met by Chance: A Society Novel* (1873), is about death and intrigue in high society.

Although Logan's writing never met with the acclaim or garnered her the living wage that any writer yearns for, it is valuable as a reflection of life and attitudes in nineteenth-century America, especially of that which she knew best, the theater. In 1871 she married William Wirt Sikes, who died in 1883. In 1892 she married James O'Neill; no children resulted from either marriage. Logan battled poverty and mental disorder all her life. In her fifties she began to succumb to both, dying at age seventy in a home for the insane in Banstead, England, where she had lived for most of her life.

• Information about Logan's life and career can be found in Thomas A. Brown, *History of the American Stage* (1903); Joseph N. Ireland, *Records of the New York Stage* (1866–1867); Noah Ludlow, *Dramatic Life as I Found It* (1913); and William Winter, *The Wallet of Time* (1913). An obituary is in the *New York Times*, 29 Apr. 1909.

CLAUDIA DURST JOHNSON

LOGAN, Rayford Whittingham (7 Jan. 1897–4 Nov. 1981), historian of the African diaspora, university professor, and civil rights and Pan-Africanist activist, was born in Washington, D.C., the son of Arthur Logan and Martha Whittingham, domestic workers. Two circumstances of Logan's parents are germane to his later life and work. Although he grew up in modest circumstances, his parents enjoyed a measure of status in the Washington black community owing to his father's employment as a butler in the household of Frederic Walcott, Republican senator from Connecticut. And the Walcotts took an interest in the Logan family, providing them with occasional gifts, including money to purchase a house. The Walcotts also took an interest in Rayford Logan's education, presenting him with books and later, in the 1920s and 1930s, introducing him to influential whites in government. Logan grew up on family lore about the antebellum free Negro heritage of the Whittinghams. It is open to question how much of what he heard was factual; nevertheless, he learned early to make class distinctions among African Americans and to believe that his elite heritage also imposed on him an obligation to help lead his people to freedom and equality.

Both lessons were reinforced by his secondary education at the prestigious M Street (later Dunbar) High School, a public but segregated institution in the District of Columbia. Jim Crow had narrowed the professional options of African-American educators, and the faculty included such first-rate intellectuals as Carter Woodson, Jessie Fauset, and Anna Julia Cooper; its goal was education for leadership, and among its distinguished alumni were Charles Houston, William Hastie, Charles Drew, and Benjamin O. Davis. Logan was the valedictorian of the class of 1913. He continued his academic career at Williams College, from which he was graduated Phi Beta Kappa in 1917. After he delivered one of three commencement speeches, he returned to Washington, where he enlisted in the military to fight in World War I.

The First World War was a turning point in Logan's life. Like most African Americans, he followed the lead of W. E. B. Du Bois and the National Association for the Advancement of Colored People in supporting the war effort with the expectation that blacks' discharging a patriotic duty would bring them full citizenship rights. Logan rose from private to the rank of lieutenant in the segregated 372d Infantry Regiment, one of only four combat units open to black American soldiers; most blacks were restricted to militarized labor units.

Logan saw combat in the Argonne campaign of June 1918 and was wounded; the "war neurosis" that accompanied the injury triggered a series of outbursts by Logan directed at white American officers in retaliation for the accumulated racial humiliation and harassment they visited on him and all black military personnel. He spent the next year fighting the racism of the U.S. military. There were two wars going on—Mr. Wilson's and Mr. Logan's—he asserted in his unpublished autobiography. When he was demobilized in August 1919, Logan chose to remain in France. "My experiences in the army left me so bitter . . . that I re-

mained an expatriate in Europe," he later wrote. "I *hated* white Americans."

Between 1919 and 1924 Logan lived in Paris and became a leading member of the Pan-African Congress movement based there. Logan worked closely with W. E. B. Du Bois, the movement's principal architect (it was the beginning of a collaboration that would last into the 1950s), as well as a number of prominent francophone blacks also resident in Paris. The Pan-African Congress, which met four times between 1919 and 1927, espoused the equality of the black race, an end to colonial abuses in Africa, eventual self-government for Europe's African possessions, and full civil rights for African Americans.

In many respects Pan-Africanism between the two world wars was a precursor to America's civil rights movement, as it was supported by the leading black Americans of the day. His five-year European expatriation introduced Logan to the international dimensions of the "race problem," and his interactions with Haitian diplomat Dantes Bellegarde laid the basis for a lifelong scholarly and political interest in the first independent black republic in the Western Hemisphere.

Having exorcised white Americans from his spirit—largely by avoiding them in Paris—Logan returned to the United States in 1924 determined to pursue the fight for civil rights as both a scholar and an activist. Between 1925 and 1938 he taught at two elite, historically black colleges: Virginia Union University in Richmond (1925–1931) and Atlanta University (1933–1938). In the interim he served for two years as Carter Woodson's assistant at the Association for the Study of Negro Life and History. At Virginia Union, Logan taught French and history, and introduced the college's first courses on black history and on imperialism; he earned a reputation as a serious scholar and an engaging teacher.

While on the Union faculty, Logan married Ruth Robinson in 1927; they had no children. He pursued advanced degrees in history, earning his A.M. from Williams College in 1929, and beginning in 1930 the residency and course requirements for his Ph.D. from Harvard University. (He completed them in 1932.) While at Atlanta he researched and wrote his doctoral dissertation, completed in 1936, on the diplomatic relations between the United States and Haiti, a groundbreaking work on race and diplomacy that was published in 1941 as *The Diplomatic Relations of the United States with Haiti, 1776–1891*. He visited Haiti twice, and was a firsthand witness to the 1934 end of the American occupation. In the 1920s and 1930s his scholarship on Haiti and colonial Africa earned him national recognition not only in the black diaspora—he was awarded Haiti's Order of Honor and Merit in 1941 for his scholarship and advocacy—but also from influential, predominantly white organizations such as the Foreign Policy Association.

In Richmond and Atlanta—and in Washington, where between 1938 and 1968 he taught at Howard University—Logan engaged in innovative civil rights activity. In the 1920s and 1930s in the first two cities he organized, in conjunction with other outspoken African Americans like Lugenia Hope, voter registration drives; the citizenship schools, which taught African Americans how to register to vote and anchored the campaigns, became models for similar activities in the 1960s. On the eve of World War II, he spearheaded a drive of mass rallies and organizing local African-American coalitions against the exclusion of African Americans from the U.S. military; the force of the campaign was such that in 1940 he was invited to meet with President Franklin D. Roosevelt on the matter and drafted for the president an order prohibiting the exclusion of blacks from the service.

In 1941 Logan was a leader of A. Philip Randolph's March on Washington Movement, which pressured Roosevelt issuing Executive Order 8802 banning racial discrimination in defense industries; Logan participated in the final negotiations over the order. The March on Washington Movement declared victory, and the march was canceled. Logan edited *What the Negro Wants* (1944), a collection of essays by fourteen prominent African Americans that helped to bring before the entire American public the demand for a total elimination of segregation. Turning his attention once again to international affairs in the postwar era, Logan, in close alliance with Du Bois, fought to orient the United Nations, the United States, and the European powers toward justice and decolonization in Africa. He spent the last decade of his life organizing and editing with Michael R. Winston the *Dictionary of American Negro Biography* (1982).

The central point of Logan's scholarship and activism was the promotion of the dignity and equality of black people throughout the world and the critical examination of American racial hypocrisy. But in an era dominated by the incipient Cold War, his scholarship and activism were too strident for the U.S. political establishment, and he often found it difficult to attain a hearing in the white mainstream. *What the Negro Wants* saw life only after he threatened to sue the publisher for breach of contract; two of his other important works, *The Negro and the Post–War World* (1945) and *The African Mandates and World Politics* (1948), were issued privately by Logan because no publisher would bring them out. His best-known work, *The Negro in American Life and Thought: The Nadir, 1877–1901* (1954; revised and republished as *The Betrayal of the Negro* [1965]), which established a useful framework for historians to analyze that period of African-American history, was turned down by one publisher, and Macmillan agreed to publish it only after Logan posted a $5,000 subvention.

Rayford Logan was a distinguished and talented intellectual. While he insisted on strict adherence to the historical record and was perhaps conservative in what he considered historical evidence, he knitted his scholarship together with a lifetime of activism. Just as he had hoped that his scholarship would reach a wide audience, he also wanted to be a major civil rights figure. He never reached this position, partly because he was often more strident than the mainstream race advancement organizations of the 1930s, 1940s, and 1950s. He was overlooked by the activists of the 1960s and 1970s in part, he believed, because that generation's impetuousness prevented it from learning from and about the sacrifices and efforts of earlier activists. (In fact, such staples of the 1960s as voter registration drives had been pioneered by Logan three decades earlier.) But there were other reasons, notably his abrasive personality and his chafing at organizational discipline. As a result, he often was on the sidelines, an incisive but little-recognized critic. He perhaps was comfortable in this marginal role because he did not have to implement his visionary, but neglected, plans, but marginality also prevented him from achieving the stature he believed he deserved in both white and black America. He died in Washington, D.C.

• The major part of Logan's papers, including a two-volume autobiographical manuscript, a comprehensive run of speeches, articles, and correspondence on civil rights and historical issues from the 1930s to the 1970s, are deposited at the Moorland-Spingarn Research Center at Howard University in Washington, D.C. His diaries, which he kept on a frequent basis between 1940 and 1982, are deposited in the Manuscript Division of the Library of Congress. Researchers should also consult the papers of W. E. B. Du Bois at the University of Massachusetts at Amherst; these are also on microfilm. Kenneth Robert Janken, *Rayford W. Logan and the Dilemma of the African-American Intellectual* (1993), is a complete assessment of Logan.

KENNETH ROBERT JANKEN

LOGAN, Stephen Trigg (24 Feb. 1800–17 July 1880), lawyer and jurist, was born in Franklin County, Kentucky, the son of David Logan and Mary Trigg. Logan received his early education in Frankfort, Kentucky, and at age thirteen served as clerk in the office of the secretary of state. In 1817 he went to Glasgow, the seat of Barren County, Kentucky, to study law under his uncle Judge Christopher Tompkins; he was admitted to the bar before age twenty-one. Logan also taught school and worked as a deputy in the office of the circuit clerk of the county. His work in the clerk's office gave him experience with various forms of legal procedure and the drafting of legal documents, skills for which he became noted in his professional life.

Soon after Logan began his law practice, he was appointed the commonwealth's attorney for the Glasgow circuit; he held this office from 1823 to 1832. He built up a clientele and earned a reputation for analytical power in dealing with evidence and for having an amazing command of complicated facts. On 25 June 1823 Logan married America T. Bush of Glasgow; they had eight children.

While establishing his professional reputation, Logan became financially impoverished by lending money to friends who failed in business. In the spring of 1832, seeking better means to provide for his family in the newer state of Illinois, he moved to Springfield. The family settled on a farm outside of town, and Logan considered agriculture as his life's work, but his inclination to the law was too strong. Within a year, he resettled in Springfield and began acquiring prominence in the growing legal circles and the rough-and-tumble politics of Illinois. The Illinois legislature elected Logan judge of the First Judicial Circuit in 1835; he presided at the court from January 1835 until March 1837, when he resigned because the salary was too low and returned to law practice.

In 1841 Logan formed a partnership with Abraham Lincoln, whom he had met when Lincoln ran for the state legislature in 1832. "He made a very considerable impression on me," Logan later recalled; nevertheless, he continued, "Lincoln's knowledge of the law was very small when I took him in" (Logan, p. 3). In his reminiscences, Logan claimed a substantial role in Lincoln's legal education. The two became partners not only in law but also in Whig politics. As members of the "Springfield junto" (so named by opposition Democrats), who met informally to influence Whig nominations and policies. Logan and Lincoln dissolved their partnership by mutual agreement in 1844, and Logan brought his son David into his firm.

Logan was elected in 1842 to represent Sangamon County in the Illinois legislature and was reelected in 1844 and 1846. In 1847 he was chosen a delegate to the state constitutional convention. In both bodies, Logan was influential in debates, promoting strict economy in public expenditures and opposing debt repudiation.

In 1848 Logan was the Whig candidate to succeed Lincoln as congressman from the capital district of Illinois. Logan had the opportunity to run in 1848 because Lincoln decided not to seek reelection. Although Congressman Lincoln's opposition to the war with Mexico had cost him support among some Illinois Whigs, historian Mark E. Neely, Jr., wrote that Lincoln's decision "had nothing to do with his record on the war," but was meant to keep good feeling among his political friends, including Logan, and share the opportunity to represent the only Whig district in Illinois (Neely, p. 194).

During the campaign Logan could not avoid addressing the Mexican War, as the issue that agitated many in Illinois. Logan pointed out that the war was unconstitutionally begun by the president when he ordered General Zachary Taylor to advance to the banks of the Rio Grande; the president did not consult Congress, even though it was in session. In spite of the clarity of his argument, Judge Logan was not an appealing candidate; he was a careless dresser, an ineffective public speaker, and a "poor man for the stump" (Boritt, p. 93). He lost the election to Democrat war hero Major Thomas Harris. His defeat was called by some a "repudiation of Lincoln as well as a defeat of the Whigs" (*Memorials*, p. 10). Many historians have accepted this interpretation, but recent analyses note other issues in the campaign and attribute greater weight to Logan's own weaknesses.

Logan was returned to the state legislature for one more term (1854–1856) and was chairman of the Judiciary Committee. In 1855 he lost an election for judge of the Supreme Court. By the time of the Republican National Convention of 1860, he had joined that new party. As a member of the Illinois delegation, he went to Chicago to help secure the presidential nomination for his former law partner.

Before Lincoln's inauguration, and with civil war threatening, Logan was chosen by the governor of Illinois as one of the state's five commissioners to the National Peace Conference, which convened in Washington on 4 February 1861. Called by Virginia, the conference worked out amendments to the Constitution which, if adopted by the Congress and the necessary number of states, might preserve the Union. A delegate from Ohio wrote of Logan's diligent efforts to prevent war: "While he was true to his convictions, he was conspicuous as a patriot and a peace-maker." Regretting that remarks made in the conference were not recorded, W. S. Groesbeck of Ohio recalled, "When we were feeling very much discouraged" near the end of the conference, Logan made a speech urging compromise between the North and the South that "touched every heart" (quoted in *Memorials*, p. 12).

President Lincoln appointed Logan in 1862 to a commission in Cairo, Illinois, charged with investigating claims against the government; this was Logan's last public service. He began gradually to discontinue his law practice. Logan had acquired sufficient means to enjoy retirement in a fine home near a park, but he lived unpretentiously as he always had, enjoying friends and family. He remained a close observer of public events. In 1872 Logan was chosen unanimously to preside over the Republican state convention, probably his last public appearance as a speaker. He died at his home in Springfield after a brief illness.

A small and unpretentious young man, unconcerned about his appearance, Logan had a thin voice and a nervous temperament, and he was reserved to the point of seeming cold; all these factors may have contributed to his failure to win high political office. Yet he achieved wealth and wide respect as a jurist and lawyer. Logan's thinking on political matters during his later years is not clear. Some contemporaries felt that he was not an enthusiastic supporter of the Civil War, or that he was troubled about Reconstruction; he is thought to have sympathized with the Democrats for a time, then returned to his Republicanism. There is more agreement on his excellent professional qualities. Lincoln regarded him as a thorough and accomplished lawyer. John T. Stuart spoke of Logan being "grounded in the law as a science" and presenting arguments with logic to enlighten both bench and jury (quoted in *Memorials*, p. 16–17). David Davis admired Logan as a great trial lawyer and a judge who spoke clearly and reasoned powerfully.

• A collection of Logan's papers is at the Illinois State Historical Library. *Memorials of the Life and Character of Stephen T. Logan* (1882) contains a lengthy biographical sketch as well as eulogies and resolutions by members of the Illinois legal profession, commemorative proceedings of courts and the City Council, and extracts from obituaries in Illinois newspapers. Joseph Wallace, *Past and Present of the City of Springfield and Sangamon County, Illinois* (1904), gives the historical setting and biographical sketches of Logan and his contemporaries.

Logan's "Stephen T. Logan Talks about Lincoln," *Bulletin of the Lincoln Centennial Association* 12 (1 Sept. 1928): 1–3, 5, is one of his few commentaries on Lincoln. Logan destroyed his correspondence with Lincoln. On his relationship with Lincoln, see Roy P. Basler, ed., *The Collected Works of Abraham Lincoln* (9 vols., 1955). Albert J. Beveridge, *Abraham Lincoln 1809–1858* (1928), is useful for contemporary newspaper opinions on Logan. For the Illinois political scene and the problems of the Whig party, see Willard L. King, *Lincoln's Manager: David Davis* (1960); Donald W. Riddle, *Lincoln Runs for Congress* (1948) and *Congressman Abraham Lincoln* (1957); Gabor S. Boritt, "Lincoln's Opposition to the Mexican War," *Journal of the Illinois State Historical Society* 67 (Feb. 1974): 79–100; and Mark E. Neely, Jr., "Lincoln and the Mexican War: An Argument by Analogy," *Civil War History* 24 (Mar. 1978): 5–24. Neely, *The Abraham Lincoln Encyclopedia* (1982), examines Logan's 1848 congressional campaign. An obituary is in the *New York Times*, 18 July 1880.

SYLVIA B. LARSON

LOGAN, Thomas Muldrup (3 Nov. 1840–11 Aug. 1914), Confederate general and railroad developer, was born in Charleston, South Carolina, the son of Judge George William Logan and Anna D'Oyley. Raised in a family that had a rich tradition of service in law and the military, Logan graduated at the head of his class from South Carolina College in 1860. When the Civil War began one year later there was no doubt as to where his loyalty lay; he served as a volunteer at the bombardment of Fort Sumter and soon afterward was elected first lieutenant of Company A of the Hampton Legion of the Confederate army.

Logan fought at the first battle of Manassas and was promoted to captain. He was wounded by a shell fragment at Gaines' Mill during the Seven Days' Battle in 1862. Still recovering from his wound, he was brought by military ambulance to the second battle of Manassas, where he commanded his company despite his injury. He was commended for bravery in the battle of Antietam and soon was promoted to major. Transferred to Micah Jenkins's South Carolina brigade, Logan served in the Suffolk and Knoxville campaigns and fought at the battle of Chickamauga. Promoted to colonel in the summer of 1864, he was shot from his horse near Riddles' Shop in Virginia. After an absence from the line for three months, he accompanied General Wade Hampton to South Carolina, where on 15 February 1865 he was made a Confederate brigadier general. During the last desperate actions that the Confederates fought against Union general William T. Sherman, Logan commanded M. C. Butler's cavalry brigade. During the battle of Bentonville, North Carolina, Logan led the last Confederate cavalry charge of the war. Logan and his men were cut off from the main body of Confederate troops for a time; only his quick thinking and skillful maneuvering saved the brigade from capture. All of the efforts of Logan, Hampton, General Joseph Johnston, and others came to naught however in the face of the size of the Union armies. On 26 April 1865 Logan surrendered with General Johnston to General Sherman at Durham Station, North Carolina.

Paroled soon after the surrender, Logan borrowed five dollars from a friend and married Kate Virginia Cox, the daughter of a Virginia judge, in May 1865. The couple had nine children, of whom five lived to maturity. Making his home in Virginia, Logan studied and practiced law for a few years. In 1881 he purchased an estate on the James River. At "Algoma" he lived the life of a southern gentleman, while he also maintained a business residence in New York City. According to one of his daughters, "Many have said that our home, Algoma, in its life resembled more nearly than any other of its time, the old 'befo de war,' country homes" (Logan and Morrill, p. 48).

In the mid-1870s Logan came upon the great passion of his business career: railroad development. He began to purchase stock in the Richmond and Danville Railroad, and in 1878 he was one of the organizers of a syndicate that obtained a charter for a new corporation and holding company, the Richmond and West Point Terminal Railway and Warehouse Company (incorporated 8 Mar. 1880). Logan was the second largest shareholder in the company, and he figured prominently in the leadership of the organization for a number of years.

The 1880s were a period of considerable economic expansion in the South. Logan directed the building of the Georgia Pacific Railroad, and the holding company acquired control of two more: the East Tennessee and Virginia and Georgia railroads. By 1890 his company held control of more than 8,000 miles of track and water lines and appeared to be destined to run the transportation affairs of the South. The company, however, was not prepared for the panic of 1893 and went into receivership soon after that event; it was sold and became the basis for J. P. Morgan's southern railroad empire. Logan appears not to have suffered much from this reverse. He had also purchased control of the Seattle, Lake Shore & Eastern Railroad in 1890 and sold it soon afterward, for a large profit, to the Northern Pacific.

Logan turned his hand for a time to inventions. He tried without success to have the new telautograph, which used electric signals to transmit and receive handwritten messages by wire, adapted to the American market and lost a large amount of money in his efforts. He also dabbled in politics, serving as chair of the Virginia Executive Democratic Committee in 1879 and of the Gold Democratic party in Virginia in 1896. He died in New York City and was buried in Richmond.

Logan's life and career stand as a testament to the strengths of the southern aristocratic class, that of the Tidewater section in particular. After serving with distinction in the Civil War, he turned his attention to railroad development and prospered to the extent that on his family estate he was able to reconstitute some measure of antebellum southern life. At the same time, his entry into the areas of capital, railroads, and the stock market indicated a clearly modern approach to life in the late nineteenth century. It is unclear whether Logan actually longed for a revival of the pre–

Civil War South; what seems certain is that he employed methods in business that brought areas of the South served by the Richmond Terminal Company more into line with the hard-driving capitalism of the North, a capitalism that was exemplified by men such as Jay Gould, John D. Rockefeller, and to a certain extent by Logan himself.

• Logan's military career is covered in some detail in Ellison Capers, *South Carolina*, vol. 5 of *Confederate Military History*, ed. Clement A. Evans (1889); Ezra J. Warner, *Generals in Gray: Lives of the Confederate Commanders* (1959); and Jay Luvaas, *The Battle of Bentonville: March 19–20–21, 1865* (1965). Logan's business career is given attention in Maury Klein, *The Great Richmond Terminal: A Study in Businessmen and Business Strategy* (1970), and is touched on in C. Vann Woodward, *Origins of the New South, 1877–1913* (1951), and Davis Burke, *The Southern Railway* (1985). His family background is described in G. W. Logan and Lily Logan Morrill, *A Record of the Logan Family of Charleston, South Carolina*, rev. ed. (1923). An obituary is in the *New York Times*, 12 Aug. 1914.

SAMUEL WILLARD CROMPTON

LOGAN THE MINGO. *See* Logan, James (c. 1725–1780).

LOGUEN, Jermain Wesley (c. 1813–30 Sept. 1872), bishop of the African Methodist Episcopal Zion church and abolitionist, was born Jarm Logue in Davidson County, Tennessee, the son of a slave mother, Cherry, and white slaveholder, David Logue. After David Logue sold his sister and mother to a brutal master, Jarm escaped through Kentucky and southern Indiana, aided by Quakers, and reached Hamilton, Upper Canada, about 1835. He tried his hand at farming, learned to read at the age of twenty-three, and worked as a hotel porter and lumberjack. It was in Canada that he added an *n* to the spelling of his name to distinguish it from that of his slave master. When creditors seized his farm in 1837, Loguen moved to Rochester, New York, and found employment as a hotel porter.

The black clergyman Elymus P. Rogers urged him to attend Beriah Green's abolitionist school, Oneida Institute, at Whitesboro, New York. Loguen enrolled there in 1839, despite his lack of formal education. He started a school in nearby Utica for African-American children and made a public profession of faith. He settled in Syracuse in 1841, opened another school, and married Caroline Storum of Busti, New York. They would have five children. One daughter, Amelia, married Lewis E. Douglass, the son of Frederick Douglass; Gerrit Smith Loguen became an accomplished artist; and Sarah Marinda Loguen graduated from the medical school of Syracuse University in 1876.

After being ordained by the AMEZ Church in 1842, Loguen served congregations in Syracuse, Bath, Ithaca, and Troy. He gave his first speech against slavery at Prattsburgh, Steuben County, in 1844 and was enlisted as an itinerant lecturer promoting the Liberty party. Loguen's sacred vocation now focused on aboli-

tionism, and he devoted less and less time to the local ministry. Working in cooperation with Frederick Douglass of Rochester, Unitarian minister Samuel May of Syracuse, and abolitionist and reformer Gerrit Smith of Peterboro in Madison County, Loguen actively aided fugitive slaves passing through upstate New York on their way to Canada. His home became the center of Underground Railroad activity in Syracuse, and in his autobiography (1859) he claimed to have assisted more than 1,500 runaway slaves.

Loguen was presiding elder of the AMEZ's Troy district when the Fugitive Slave Law of 1850 was passed. Loguen returned to Syracuse, where he publicly defied the law and vowed resistance. "I don't respect this law," he said, "I don't fear it, I won't obey it! It outlaws me, and I outlaw it, and the men who attempt to enforce it on me. I place the governmental officials on the ground that they place me. I will not live a slave, and if force is employed to re-enslave me, I shall make preparations to meet the crisis as becomes a man." With other members of the Fugitive Aid Society, Loguen participated in the famous rescue of William "Jerry" McHenry at Syracuse in October 1851; fearing arrest for his actions, he fled to St. Catharines, Canada West, where he conducted missionary work and spoke on behalf of the temperance cause among other fugitives. Despite the failure of his appeal of 2 December 1851 for safe passage to Governor Washington Hunt of New York, Loguen returned to Syracuse in late 1852 and renewed his labors on behalf of the Underground Railroad and the local Fugitive Aid Society. Loguen was indicted by a grand jury at Buffalo, New York, but was never tried.

By the 1840s Loguen had moved away from the moral suasion philosophy of William Lloyd Garrison and into the circle of central New York abolitionists who endorsed political means. After the demise of the Liberty party, Loguen supported a remnant known as the Liberty League. By 1854 Loguen had abandoned the nonviolent philosophy of many of his abolitionist colleagues and joined the Radical Abolition Society. After 1857 he devoted all of his time to the Fugitive Aid Society. He returned to Canada West to attend a convention led by John Brown (1800–1859) prior to the 1859 raid at Harpers Ferry but apparently did not know the details of Brown's plan.

In the early 1860s Loguen served as pastor of Zion Church in Binghamton, New York. He also recruited black troops for the Union army. After the Civil War, Loguen was active in establishing AMEZ congregations among the southern freedmen. He had a special interest in Tennessee, where he believed his mother and sister lived. (Earlier he had refused to purchase the freedom of his mother because her master, Manasseth Logue, his father's brother, demanded that Loguen also purchase his own freedom.) Loguen became bishop of the Fifth District of the AMEZ Church in 1868, with responsibilities for the Allegheny and Kentucky conferences. He supported the work of the Freedmen's Bureau and the American Missionary Association in the South. On the eve of leaving for a new post as organizer of AMEZ missions on the Pacific coast, he died in Saratoga Springs, New York.

• Loguen's letters are on microfilm in the *Black Abolitionist Papers*, ed. George E. Carter and C. Peter Ripley. Originals are in the Gerrit Smith Papers, George Arents Research Library, Syracuse University. Jermain W. Loguen, *The Rev. J. W. Loguen, as a Slave and as a Freeman* (1859), contains biographical information but was compiled by someone other than Loguen, most likely the Syracuse abolitionist John Thomas. The best recent account of Loguen's antislavery career is Carol M. Hunter, "To Set the Captives Free: Reverend Jermain Wesley Loguen and the Struggle for Freedom in Central New York, 1835–1872" (Ph.D. diss., SUNY, Binghamton, 1989). See also Milton C. Sernett, "A Citizen of 'No Mean City': Jermain W. Loguen and the Antislavery Reputation of Syracuse," *Syracuse University Library Associates Courier* 22 (Fall 1987): 33–55. An obituary is in the *Syracuse Journal*, 1 Oct. 1872.

MILTON C. SERNETT

LOHMAN, Ann Trow (6 May 1811–1 Apr. 1878), abortionist, also known as Madame Restell, was born in Painswick, Gloucestershire, England, the daughter of John Trow, a laborer; her mother's name is unknown. Lohman received very little formal education, and at age fifteen she took a job as a maid and at sixteen married Henry Summers of Wittshire, a 23-year-old tailor. In 1830 her only child, a daughter, was born. In 1831 the family immigrated to New York City in search of wealth and opportunity. In August of that year, however, Henry Summers died of "bilious fever" and left her alone with a young daughter to support, which she did by becoming a seamstress.

In 1836 Ann Trow met Charles Lohman, a printer. The couple were soon married, and both considered themselves freethinkers and atheists, bound by no particular religious admonitions. Eager to become rich, they began selling patent medicines for birth control and pregnancy termination, though it is a mystery how Ann Lohman learned to perform surgical abortions, a procedure she began offering soon thereafter. Charles Lohman, clever and well read, wrote the advertisements that began appearing about 1839 in the *New York Sun*, which instructed women to visit "Madame Restell" at 160 Greenwich Street. (Lohman tried, usually in vain, to disassociate herself from the persona of Restell, never admitting that she was the notorious abortionist, just her spokesperson.) These commercial notices asked prospective patients if it was "moral for parents to increase their families, regardless of consequences to themselves, or the well being of their offspring, when a simple, easy, healthy, and certain remedy is within our control" (quoted in Browder, p. 9).

It was a precarious time to begin a practice marketing abortion and birth control, as great debates were brewing over the topics throughout the United States. On one side were the moralists, who believed that preventing pregnancy amounted to tampering with God and Nature. They worried that women's easy access to contraception and abortion would make them less virtuous, for there would be no preventing them from being unchaste. On the other side was Ann Trow Lohman. She and her husband began mailing circulars that promoted Preventive Powders and Female Monthly Pills, which Charles Lohman maintained could cure anything from "derangement of the stomach" to "deathly, sallow, and inanimate complexion" but which probably were composed of substances either ineffective (oil of tansy) or dangerous (turpentine). When the pills did not work (and they often did not), Lohman's patients were told to return for a "simple and painless" operation, which usually involved using a wire to pierce the amniotic sac and which would cost them from $20 to $100, depending on their financial situation.

Publicity paid off for Lohman, and she soon became quite well known throughout the city. Her fame made her rich, but it also made her a target of attack by conservatives and moralists. Samuel Jenks Smith, the editor of the *New York Sunday Morning News*, proclaimed that her practice made the "institution of marriage a mere farce." The Lohmans responded to their critics with literate and sometimes eloquent defenses, declaring that birth control allowed men to marry earlier, perhaps before they were financially able to support a family, and that many women's lives were saved by abortions. Her first arrest in 1839 did not lead to a trial; the case against her, like many cases against abortionists and birth control advocates, relied on witnesses who were either dead or too ashamed to come forward.

In 1840 Ann Lohman expanded her business by opening a hospital in which single pregnant women could give birth. In 1846 a young woman alleged that Lohman had stolen her newborn baby from her after delivery. Cleared of the charges in court, on her return home Lohman faced an irate mob that dispersed only after New York City mayor William Havemeyer promised to have her imprisoned. Rumors of Lohman's stealing and selling infants persisted, as did gossip that she occasionally murdered babies and/or their mothers. Some stories even claimed the existence of a special sewer running directly from the abortionist's office to the Hudson River, which would enable her to dispose of the evidence.

The 1845 Abortion Law made abortion of a quickened fetus manslaughter, and little more than two years passed before Lohman was charged under the new legislation. In 1847 her sensational trial for performing an abortion on Maria Bodine, an impoverished young woman six months pregnant who was sent to Lohman by her lover, a widower who was also arrested, made numerous headlines and drew even more curiosity seekers. Though Lohman escaped the more serious manslaughter charge, she was sentenced to one year at Blackwell's Island, New York City's penitentiary, for the misdemeanor of performing an abortion on a fetus that had not quickened. During her stay at Blackwell's Island (1848–1849), Lohman, evidently buying her way out of incarceration's unpleasantries, slept on a feather bed, ate fine food, and managed to sew herself a few silk dresses. On her release in mid-

1849, she returned to a more expensive house on what is now West Broadway. After vowing never to return to prison, she resumed her practice.

The 1850s were relatively quiet for Lohman, as authorities, probably paid off handsomely, toned down their surveillance of her property and scrutiny of her business. In 1857 the Lohmans bought property farther north and soon constructed a grand house on the corner of Fifth Avenue and Fifty-second Street, in which they took up residence in 1864. Lohman never hid her wealth, and her mansion in this fashionable neighborhood appalled the neighbors (the houses on each side of her remained unoccupied). She entertained lavishly, and in 1867 she moved her office to her residence. Her clientele, always predominantly affluent, now became almost exclusively rich women (many married) who wanted to avoid the shame or inconvenience of an unwanted pregnancy; some reportedly paid up to $2,000 per case at a time when the cheapest abortionists were charging the paltry sum of $10.

In 1871 the *New York Times*, flush from the recent success of its injurious stories on William "Boss" Tweed, printed an electrifying exposé of abortionists after a reporter visited several, Lohman included. Then, to add to her problems, Charles Lohman, her husband, publicist, and business manager, died in early 1877. In late January 1878 Lohman crossed paths with Anthony Comstock, who had spent the preceding few years crusading against and seizing medicines used by abortionists, "obscene" books and pictures, and "articles made of rubber for immoral purposes," among other items. Serving as an agent to the post office and the New York Society for the Suppression of Vice and working under the authority of the Comstock Law of 1873, which made it a crime to sell or advertise obscene material or anything that could prevent or terminate a pregnancy, Comstock visited Lohman, and she sold him contraceptives. Armed with a search warrant, he returned on 11 February and, after a search of her house, arrested her for possessing medicines used for "immoral" aims. Lohman spent the next few weeks in and out of jail, becoming increasingly fearful and paranoid; she believed that the relatively minor charge against her would lead to more serious convictions and that she would die in jail. At home on 31 March, Lohman received word that her case had been transferred to the Court of Oyer and Terminer, a higher tribunal. Sure that her worst fears were coming true, in the early morning of 1 April Lohman lay down in her bathtub and sliced her throat from ear to ear with an ebony-handled kitchen knife. When word of her suicide reached the courthouse that morning, Comstock (and many others) at first believed it was all an April Fools' joke, but he later took credit for driving the abortionist to suicide, calling her death a "bloody ending to a bloody life." She left her family an estate valued between $600,000 and $1 million.

Ann Trow Lohman's fate made the perfect nineteenth-century morality lesson: apparent evil was punished by a horrific end. But what the reformers failed to foresee, as evidenced by the weekly *Puck*'s cartoon showing Fifth Avenue four years after Lohman's death as teeming with infants and toddlers, was that the death of Madame Restell did not end the demand for safe contraception and abortion. Labeled the "wickedest woman in New York," Lohman was greedy, vain, flamboyant, and, most importantly, a quack. Perhaps if she had been less ostentatious, with her mansion, diamonds, and team of horses, she might have escaped the wrath of the moralists. But, for the most part, New York society was willing to tolerate her, probably because she performed a service that middle- and upper-class women either used or at least felt more comfortable knowing was there if they needed it. The problem with understanding Lohman is that she left no record of her motives or convictions. All we know of her is what her adversaries thought of her, enemies sometimes more concerned with the "purity" of the woman than the life of the unborn child. An early voice in an ongoing debate, Lohman played an important role in legitimizing the discussion of birth control and abortion.

• Ann Lohman left no papers. For biographical details, see Clifford Browder, *The Wickedest Woman in New York: Madame Restell, the Abortionist* (1988). Most histories of New York City refer to her; for example, see Eric Homberger, *Corruption and Conscience in Old New York* (1995). Lohman is discussed briefly in Amy Gilman Srebnick, *The Mysterious Death of Mary Rogers* (1995); Rogers was a young New York City woman who died in the early 1840s, probably as a result of an abortion (not performed by Lohman). Information on Lohman and her practice can be found in New York newspapers around the times of her trials. Obituaries are in the major New York newspapers, including the *Tribune* and the *Times*, 2 Apr. 1878.

STACEY HAMILTON

LOMASNEY, Martin Michael (3 Dec. 1859–12 Aug. 1933), politician, was born in Boston, Massachusetts, the son of Maurice Lomasney, a tailor, and Mary Murray. His parents were refugees from the great Irish potato famine. His formal education was limited to elementary school; he attended the Mayhew School but stopped before eighth grade. After the premature deaths of both of his parents and two siblings, Martin and his brother Joseph lived with an aunt and struggled for survival at odd jobs. The leader of a street gang of tough, young Irishmen, Lomasney became a protégé of the local Democratic ward boss, who provided him with municipal employment as a lamplighter and an inspector for the Boston Board of Health.

Lomasney gradually ascended the partisan ladder, moving from precinct worker to captain to boss of the west side Eighth Ward by the mid-1880s. By 1888 he was powerful enough to secure the election of his brother to the common council; the following year he engineered Joseph's elevation to the lower house of the Massachusetts General Court. Ostensibly a real estate broker, Lomasney attained a national reputation as the "czar" or "mahatma" of Ward Eight because of his legendary ability to deliver a solid vote for candidates, regardless of party. In 1885 Lomasney organized the Hendricks Club, a social and political establishment named for Vice President Thomas A. Hendricks. Every day for nearly half a century Lomasney sat in his office, dispensing benefits, solving problems, adjudicating disputes, and performing services for his cohorts and constituents, including help with rent, food, and fuel; aid in dealing with law enforcement and other governmental agencies; and, above all, jobs in both the public and private sectors. "I think that there's got to be in every ward," he explained to muckraking journalist Lincoln Steffens, "somebody any bloke can come to—no matter what he's done—and get help. Help, you understand; none of your law and your justice, but help." Every Sunday before an election Tuesday, Lomasney gathered his followers and announced the endorsements that his constituents converted into overwhelming majorities. The keys to his success and longevity were accessibility and service. "The politician who thinks he can get away from the people who made him," Lomasney insisted, "usually gets what is coming to him—a swift kick in his political pants." Directed by good government reformers to Lomasney as "the worst, the most impossible man in Boston," Steffens ended by concluding that the mahatma was a man of integrity and vision. Lomasney was frequently accused of corruption or vote fraud, mostly by his political opponents, but neither Steffens nor anyone else ever found any incriminating evidence. Political scientist Harold Zink observed that "when he stands before the Hebrews, Irish, and Italians who throng Donovan Hall on Sunday afternoons, he talks to them not as a mere politician but rather as a father."

Because Boston Democratic politics was essentially internecine warfare among several ward bosses, Lomasney periodically endorsed Independents and Republicans against the candidates of his current antagonists. In 1917 he even supported Good Government Association candidate Andrew J. Peters for mayor. During the first three decades of the twentieth century, Lomasney, John F. Fitzgerald, and James Michael Curley interacted in the formation of a bewildering series of electoral coalitions. On the state level, such prominent Democratic governors as Eugene Foss, David I. Walsh, and Joseph B. Ely acknowledged Lomasney's significant role in their electoral victories. On the national scene, he controlled one of Boston's congressional seats for decades, served as a delegate to several Democratic National Conventions, and delivered impressive majorities for Alfred E. Smith, Franklin D. Roosevelt, and other Democratic presidential candidates. In both 1916 and 1920 he aroused great consternation at the Democratic National Conventions by introducing resolutions on behalf of Irish independence.

Lomasney's lengthy, intermittent, and generally distinguished legislative career began with his service on the Boston Board of Aldermen from 1893 to 1895. After serving a single term in the Massachusetts Senate in 1897–1898, Lomasney spent the next three decades alternately in and out of the General Court, as his political strategy dictated, filling terms in 1899, 1905–1909, 1911–1915, 1917, 1921–1922, and 1927–1928. In that capacity he compiled a record reflective of his status as a Democratic legislator representing an ethnic, working-class constituency, particularly in his support of labor and welfare measures, including strengthening organized labor; wages and hours legislation for women, children, and public employees; workmen's compensation; pensions for public employees; and state aid for public education. He was also an advocate of initiative and referendum, the direct election of U.S. senators, annual elections, the election of judges, and legislative reappointment. A fierce opponent of prohibition, he drank nothing stronger than tea; a confirmed bachelor, he opposed woman suffrage on the grounds that "you can't trust these women, they are apt to blab everything they know." Even some Republican legislators hailed him as "the most influential man in the legislature," and a Boston newspaper called him "the best informed man in the legislature on general and Boston legislation" and acknowledged that "no abler man ever served in the Massachusetts legislature." The official historian of the 1917 state constitutional convention, in which Lomasney served as a delegate, judged him to be fair, generous, sympathetic, respected, and "the most intense personal force in the convention." Republican governor Samuel McCall reportedly regarded him as one of the two convention delegates who stood out above all the rest in constructive work. He died in Boston.

• Frequently credited with coining the political maxim "Never write anything down when you can say it; never say anything when you can nod your head," Lomasney left no appreciable collection of personal papers. The cryptic notes that he kept in a file cabinet in his office, along with the public record and newspapers, provided much of the basis for his biography, *Boston Mahatma*, written by Leslie G. Ainley (1949). Lincoln Steffens's mutually enlightening encounter with Lomasney appears in *The Autobiography of Lincoln Steffens* (1931), pp. 604–27. An insightful portrait of the "czar" of Boston ward politics can be found in Harold Zink, *City Bosses in the United States: A Study of Twenty Municipal Bosses* (1930), pp. 69–84. John D. Buenker, "The Mahatma and Progressive Reform: Martin Lomasney as Lawmaker, 1911–1917," *New England Quarterly* 44 (Sept. 1971): 397–419, focuses on Lomasney's record as a state legislator and as a member of the Massachusetts Constitutional Convention of 1917. A useful contemporary account is "Martin Lomasney, the Story of His Life as Related by Him to Thomas Carens," *Boston Herald*, 5 Dec. 1928. An obituary is in the *New York Times*, 13 Aug. 1933.

JOHN D. BUENKER

LOMAX, John Avery (23 Sept. 1867–26 Jan. 1948), collector and publisher of folksongs, was born in Goodman, Mississippi, the son of James Avery Lomax and Susan Frances Cooper, farmers. The family moved to Bosque County, Texas, in 1869 and settled near Meridian, on land located next to a branch of the Chisholm Trail. There Lomax learned ballads from passing cowboys and spirituals from Nat Blythe, a local African American whom he taught to read and write. By his twentieth year Lomax had written down the lyrics of numerous songs on scraps of cardboard and paper.

Lomax attended Granbury College in Hood County, in 1887. He then taught for a year at Clifton Academy in Bosque County and for six years thereafter at Weatherford College. During that time he continued his education in summer sessions at Eastman Business College and at Chautauqua in New York state. Lomax completed his B.A. in 1897, after only two years at the University of Texas, and he acted as registrar there from 1897 through 1903. He also briefly attended the University of Chicago in 1895 and 1903.

Lomax taught English at the Agricultural and Mechanical College of Texas (now Texas A&M University) from 1903 through 1910. In 1904 he married Bess Baumann Brown; the couple had four children. He earned his M.A. at the University of Texas in 1906 and won a scholarship to Harvard University, where he received a second M.A. in 1907 after studying American literature under Barrett Wendell. Lomax also had contact at Harvard with George Lyman Kittredge, who, along with Wendell, encouraged Lomax to continue collecting cowboy songs. His efforts were funded by three Sheldon Fellowships from Harvard, and his first major publication, *Cowboy Songs and Other Frontier Ballads*, was released in 1910. Songs that were made popular by that publication include "Get Along, Little Dogies," "The Old Chisholm Trail," and "Home on the Range."

Lomax returned to the University of Texas as secretary of the Ex-Students' Association in 1910. In that year he also began lecturing on folksong—an activity that would continue, with some interruptions, for the rest of his life. In 1917 Lomax and several other persons lost their jobs at the University of Texas through the machinations of Governor James Ferguson. Following Ferguson's impeachment for improper conduct in office, Lomax and the others were offered their jobs back. He worked as a bond salesman in Chicago until he returned to the university in 1919. Lomax remained at the university until 1925, when he became manager of the bond department of Republic Savings and Trust in Dallas. In 1928, when Republic Savings and Trust was absorbed by Republic National Bank, Lomax became third vice president of the bank.

In 1931 the death of his wife and the Great Depression caused serious emotional difficulties that forced Lomax to resign his vice presidency. He then became a full-time folksong collector and undertook the work that ensured his fame. For the remainder of his life, he traveled to forty-seven states, often with his son Alan. Much of his work involved the collection of prison songs, mostly from African-American inmates in the South. Lomax even championed the early release of several of his informants, the most famous of whom was Huddie Ledbetter, or "Lead Belly," with whom he and Alan toured following Ledbetter's release from the Louisiana State Penitentiary.

After 1931 Lomax produced numerous publications, both large and small, working with the Archive of American Folksong at the Library of Congress. He also founded and served as president of the Texas Folklore Society and was a member of the Texas Academy of Arts and Letters and the Texas Philosophical Society. Lomax collaborated with folksong scholars George Herzog and Phillips Barry on projects involving song recording and transcription as well. Lomax married Ruby R. Terrill, dean of women at the University of Texas, in 1934. He died while on a song-collecting expedition in Greenville, Mississippi.

Lomax's principal importance lies in his vast compilation of folksongs spanning a wide idiomatic range. Many of his academic labors left much to be desired. He seems to have had a special fondness for romanticizing some purportedly factual accounts, and his acknowledgment of informants and sources was often either spotty or absent. Furthermore, it seems that many of the single tunes and texts that he reported were really composites of various renditions by diverse informants. All of these practices would now be considered by historians blatantly improper.

In Lomax's defense, however, it should be noted that in his time neither folklore study in general, nor ethnomusicology in particular, were marked by today's exceedingly strict guidelines, and some of his methods are less disturbing if they are evaluated within the appropriate context. In addition, Lomax's failings are partly offset by his important contributions to folksong scholarship. Perhaps the most important of which was his functional approach that included the consideration of extramusical events in the lives of the singers, an approach that involved his practice of seeking out and recording singers in their native habitats. Another contribution was Lomax's use of mechanical recording devices in fieldwork. All of those have become standard ethnomusicological procedures, and Lomax's recordings continue to be used by research scholars. Finally, it should be remembered that Lomax was aware of the looseness of some of his methods. His central objective was neither to leave a comprehensive, precise written record nor to analyze exhaustively what he had amassed. Instead, he sought to publicize and make widely popular an important aspect of American culture. Lomax, in using a broad-brush approach, both greatly and permanently facilitated Americans' heightened awareness and appreciation of their richly multifaceted musical heritage.

• The John Avery Lomax Family Papers are located in the Barker Manuscript Collection at the University of Texas at Austin's Center for American History. The collection is described in Chester V. Keilman, *University of Texas Archives* (1967). Lomax's principal publications include *The Book of Texas*, with H. W. Benedict (1916); *Songs of the Cattle Trail and Cow Camp* (1919); *American Ballads and Folk Songs*, with Alan Lomax (1934); *Our Singing Country*, with Alan Lomax and Ruth Crawford Seeger (1941); *The Adventures of a Ballad Hunter* (1947; repr. 1971); and *Folksong, U.S.A.* (1947). Lomax also contributed articles to *Musical Quarterly*, the *Jour-*

nal of American Folklore, and other periodicals. See also his "Governor Ferguson and the University of Texas," *Southwestern Review* 28 (1942): 11–29. The principal assessments of Lomax's work are Nolan Porterfield, *Last Cavalier: The Life and Times of John A. Lomax, 1867–1948* (1996); Kate Prude, "The Contribution of John Avery Lomax to American Folklore" (M.A. thesis, Hardin-Simmons Univ., 1950); Wade Gard, "Lomax, John Avery," in *The Handbook of Texas*, ed. Walter Prescott Webb, vol. 2 (3 vols., 1952); and D. K. Wilgus, *Anglo-American Folksong Scholarship since 1898* (1959). Obituaries are in the *Delta Democrat-Times*, 27 Jan. 1948; the Dallas *White Rocker*, 29 Jan. 1948; and the *Journal of American Folklore* 61 (July–Sept. 1948): 305–6.

J. MARSHALL BEVIL

LOMBARD, Carole (6 Oct. 1908–16 Jan. 1942), movie actress, was born Jane Alice Peters in Fort Wayne, Indiana, the daughter of Frederick C. Peters and Elizabeth "Bessie" Knight, members of socially prominent families in the city. Her parents separated in 1914, her mother moving to California with Jane and her two older brothers and eventually settling in Los Angeles.

Jane led a tomboy life with her brothers to such an extent that movie director Allan Dwan, who spotted her playing in the street, cast her as a tomboyish daughter in *A Perfect Crime* (1921). Although no further film assignments were forthcoming, after she graduated from junior high school, Jane decided, with her mother's approval, to attempt a career in the booming movie industry in nearby Hollywood. Always a pretty girl and rapidly maturing as a beauty, Jane was noticed by a Hollywood producer while she was dancing at the Cocoanut Grove nightclub. After a screen test she was signed to a contract by Fox, at which time she changed her name to Carol Lombard. Lombard was the name of a good friend of her mother. The "e" was added by a printing error to the advertisements for *Fast and Loose* (1930), and she decided to retain it.

In 1925–1926 Lombard made four films of routine interest. Then her career was almost ended when, as a result of an automobile accident, a sliver of glass lodged in her cheek. Fortunately, stitches made immediately and subsequent plastic surgery assured that her face was only slightly marred. Later, she learned how to eliminate the small scar by skillful lighting.

In 1927 Lombard signed with Mack Sennett for a series of two-reel comedies. Though her roles were mostly as one of his "bathing beauties," she nonetheless learned a great deal about comic playing and comic timing. In these years of apprenticeship (1926–1928), working with directors like Howard Hawks and Gregory La Cava with whom she would be associated later in her best work, she appeared in nine forgettable films, mostly for Pathé, but they were enough to establish her as a film actress and led to her being signed to a seven-year contract by Paramount in 1930. She was kept busy by the new studio, making seventeen films of no permanent interest between 1930 and 1933, although she starred in two with William Powell, *Man of the World* and *Ladies Man* (both 1931). She married Powell in 1931.

Showcasing her in white evening gowns, her blonde hair beautifully coiffed, the studio presented Lombard more or less as an image of 1930s glamour, not quite of the first rank. But her career took an upturn with a box-office hit, *Bolero* (1934), in which she danced sensually with George Raft to Ravel's music, and with *We're Not Dressing* (1934), a loosely adapted musical version of James M. Barrie's *The Admirable Crichton*, in which she shared billing with Bing Crosby, George Burns, Gracie Allen, and Ethel Merman.

Lombard's "breakthrough" film, *Twentieth Century*, was made while she was on loan to Columbia Pictures in 1934. Ben Hecht's and Charles MacArthur's stage farce, directed at a zippy pace by Howard Hawks, starred John Barrymore as Oscar Jaffe, a megalomaniac stage producer, and Lombard as Lily Garland, an actress born Mildred Plotka, whose flamboyant personality he himself had created. Lombard's Lily revealed her unsuspected comic gifts and caused Barrymore to call her "the finest actress I have worked with, bar none."

Lombard returned to Paramount to star opposite Gary Cooper in *Now and Forever* (1934), essentially a vehicle for the reigning box-office champion Shirley Temple, but the studio loaned her once again to Columbia for *Lady by Choice* (1934) and then to Metro-Goldwyn-Mayer for *The Gay Bride* (1934). Back at Paramount, she and George Raft were in *Rumba* (1935), a blatant rehash of *Bolero*, but then Ernst Lubitsch, the master director of comedy who had become head of production, designed Lombard's first star vehicle for Paramount, *Hands across the Table* (1935), "a film of divine facetiousness" in David Shipman's opinion, in which she played a gold-digging manicurist who mistakenly falls in love with an impoverished playboy, portrayed by Fred MacMurray in his first important role. So successful was this team that Lombard and MacMurray appeared together in three more films: *The Princess Comes Across* (1936) and *Swing High, Swing Low* and *True Confession* (both 1937).

Lombard divorced William Powell in 1933, citing incompatibility, but the divorce, in which she demanded no alimony, was amicable. They remained friends and costarred in what is a high point in both their careers, *My Man Godfrey* (1936), directed by Gregory La Cava. Powell asked specifically for her to play Irene Bullock, the daffy society girl who wins a prize in a charity scavenger hunt for finding Godfrey, a "forgotten man" living in a garbage dump on New York's East Side. She hires him to be the family butler. A supreme example of the incomparable 1930s genre labeled "screwball comedy"—stylized comedies of manners mixed with farce detailing the zany actions of the rich during the Great Depression—this film is the kind at which Carole Lombard excelled, and it is the only one for which she was nominated for an Academy Award. As the film reveals, Lombard's combination of beauty, eccentricity, and comic timing was unsurpassed; she was glamorous and funny, and although of her contemporaries two or three others also possessed these qualities (Jean Harlow, Claudette Colbert, Jean Arthur), Lombard had no peers. The other classic of this genre associated with Lombard is *Nothing Sacred* (1937), writer Ben Hecht's attack on American sentimentality and media exploitation in which Lombard as Hazel Flagg, a small-town girl supposedly dying of radium poisoning, is brought to New York for a final fling in a bogus publicity campaign conceived by a newspaper reporter (Fredric March). William Wellman, who directed the film, asserted, "She could do anything."

In the decade during which Lombard rose to stardom, she became a popular, even beloved, figure in Hollywood. Colleagues, particularly the working crews, admired her for her lack of pretension, her professionalism, and her decency. Stories abound (which she frequently tried to conceal) detailing her kindness, particularly to the temporarily downtrodden. She was also a popular hostess, giving unusual parties, such as one for which she rented an amusement pier and invited movie people—actors, cameramen, carpenters, electricians—to enjoy the rides and entertainment booths. She was noted for cursing immoderately, but her profanity was often witty and somehow seldom offensive. All in all, she was a regular sort of person, even when she looked like a glamorous star. She had brief affairs with several men, including screenwriter Robert Riskin and actors George Raft and Cesar Romero, and she was expected to marry the popular singer Russ Columbo when he died suddenly in 1934. In 1937 Lombard became the highest paid actress in Hollywood, earning $465,000, even though her listing on the box-office popularity polls had never been higher than twelfth.

The Lombard legend was heightened when she married Clark Gable, nicknamed "The King," in 1939. They had made *No Man of Her Own* in 1932 without being attracted to each other, but in 1936 they met again and began a love affair that led to marriage three years later when Gable's estranged wife finally consented to a divorce. For the Hollywood community and for movie fans, it was the romance of the decade. Despite some stress, Gable knew domestic happiness for the first time with a wife who was both lover and companion. Lombard adapted herself to his favorite activities, hunting and fishing, looking like a star even when roughing it beside a campfire or sitting in a duck blind. They bought a ranch in Encino and became serious movie-star farmers, calling each other "Ma" and "Pa." Although they made efforts to conceive, they remained childless.

To an extent Lombard curtailed her career after her marriage in order to make a comfortable life for her husband, but she also turned her abilities toward drama, appearing with James Stewart in a tear-jerker, *Made for Each Other*, and with Cary Grant in another, *In Name Only* (both 1939). She was very good in a grim hospital story, *Vigil in the Night*, and as Charles Laughton's mail-order bride in *They Knew What They Wanted* (both 1940). She returned to comedy in *Mr. and Mrs. Smith* (1941), directed by Alfred Hitchcock, and ended her career superbly in Ernst Lubitsch's black comedy *To Be or Not to Be* (1942), outwitting Nazis after Adolf Hitler's invasion of Poland. Its gallows humor mingled with farce was not immediately understood, but today's audiences are attuned to it.

The outbreak of war in 1941 stirred the patriotism of both Gables, but Lombard was among the first to devote time to selling war bonds. After a trip to her home state of Indiana where she sold $2 million worth of bonds in one day, Lombard died when her plane struck a mountain near Las Vegas, killing all the passengers instantly. Gable was inconsolable and, stirred by his wife's sacrifice in the fight for freedom, almost immediately enlisted. Lombard was truly Hollywood's first war hero, and President Franklin D. Roosevelt publicly recognized her contribution to the war effort. Jack Benny, her costar in *To Be or Not to Be* (which was released posthumously), canceled his weekly radio program, grief-stricken, as was the Hollywood community.

Lombard is remembered for the half-dozen superlative comedies in which she starred, and whenever a beautiful actress with comic skills emerges, Lombard's name is invoked as the standard to which the newcomer is compared.

• Book-length biographies of Carole Lombard include Frederick W. Ott, *The Films of Carole Lombard* (1972); Warren G. Harris, *Gable and Lombard* (1974); Larry Swindell, *Screwball: The Life of Carole Lombard* (1975); Leonard Maltin, *Carole Lombard* (1976); Joe Morella and Edward Z. Epstein, *Gable and Lombard and Powell and Harlow* (1976); and Robert D. Matzen, *Carole Lombard: A Bio-bibliography* (1988). James Robert Parish's discussion of Lombard in *The Paramount Pretties* (1972) is sometimes factually inaccurate. In *The Film Encyclopedia* (1994), Ephraim Katz cites President Roosevelt's tribute to Lombard in full. David Shipman's assessment of her career in *The Great Movie Stars: The Golden Years* (1979) is full of admiration. An obituary is in the *New York Times*, 17 Jan. 1942.

JAMES VAN DYCK CARD

LOMBARDI, Ernesto Natali (6 Apr. 1908–26 Sept. 1977), baseball player, was born in Oakland, California, the son of Italian immigrants. His father, Dominic Lombardi, operated a grocery store. (His mother's name is unknown.) In 1927, several years after graduating from Cole grade school, Lombardi, whom his teammates called "Ernie," "Schnozz," and "Bocci," began his professional baseball career with a tryout as a catcher for the Oakland Oaks of the Pacific Coast League (PCL). He did not make the Oakland team but was signed that season with Ogden of the Utah-Idaho League, for whom he batted .398 in 50 games. Lombardi then played for Oakland where, over the next three seasons, he punished the PCL pitchers with respective batting averages of .377, .366, and .370. In 1931 he joined the Brooklyn Dodgers and hit .297 before the Dodgers traded him after one season to the Cincinnati Reds. During his ten seasons with Cincinnati Lombardi reached his career high, hitting .343 in 1935. The following two seasons he hit .333 and .334, respectively, and his .342 led the league in 1938, when he became the second catcher to win a batting title and was named as the National League's Most Valuable Player. Despite a drop to .287 in 1939, Lombardi hit 20 home runs and batted in 85 runs to help the Reds win the National League pennant. He then batted .319 in 1940, when Cincinnati again won the pennant as well as its first World Series title since its tainted victory in 1919.

Cincinnati sold Lombardi to the Boston Braves in 1942, and in his one season with Boston Lombardi hit .330, which earned him another batting crown and made him the first catcher to win two or more batting titles. In 1943 Lombardi was traded to the New York Giants for whom, over three seasons, he caught in more than 100 games and twice batted over .300. The Giants released Lombardi, and in 1948, following a single season with Sacramento of the PCL, he retired from baseball.

Lombardi used an interlocking grip on the bat, much like that of a golfer, to lessen the pressure on his little finger where a blister had developed. Although he was a power hitter, he struck out relatively few times. In 1938, for example, he struck out only 14 times in 489 times at bat, and he never fanned more than 25 times in any one season during his career. On the down side, Lombardi grounded into the most double plays in four different seasons, including a National League record of 30 in 1938. His batting ability, however, more than made up for the 6′3″ 230-pound catcher's lack of running speed. Ten times over the course of his career he batted over .300, and he compiled a lifetime average of .306. In 1,853 major league games he scored 601 runs and knocked in 990 runs. His 1,792 hits included 277 doubles, 27 triples, and 190 home runs; eleven times he compiled more than 100 hits in a season. On 8 May 1935 Lombardi hit four doubles in one game, tying the major league record, and in 1937 he tied the National League record of six hits in six consecutive times at bat. Almost as impressive, he made five hits in one game on five separate occasions. His World Series record was another story, however. Lombardi managed only a .235 batting average in six games, totaling only four hits and one run batted in seventeen times at bat. Lombardi attacked a baseball with extraordinary strength. Carl Hubbell, Hall of Fame pitcher for the New York Giants, later admitted that he feared Lombardi. "I thought he might hurt me, even kill me, with one of those liners. They were screamers."

An excellent defensive player, Lombardi caught more than 100 games in each of 14 seasons, for a total of 1,542, and appeared in five All-Star contests. He was behind the plate for Johnny Vander Meer's record of two consecutive no-hitters in 1938 and twice led the National League in fielding.

Money and salary negotiations, especially with Reds general manager Warren Giles, often interfered with his playing career. At a banquet in Cincinnati in 1938, a slightly inebriated Lombardi told a radio announcer, "As soon as I had a bad year, I was gone!" Lombardi earned his highest salary, $17,000, in 1939. In 1938,

his MVP award year, he was paid a mere $13,000. What embittered him more, though, was his failure to be inducted into the National Baseball Hall of Fame during his lifetime, as his accomplishments overshadowed those of other catchers who already had been so enshrined. A few months before his death Lombardi remarked, "If they elect me now, I wouldn't even show up. That sounds terrible but I'm bitter. All anybody wants to remember about me is that I couldn't run."

Lack of foot speed was in fact the single flaw in an otherwise perfect ball player. A dead-pull hitter, Lombardi caused infielders to favor the left side of the diamond, and generally they played him 10 to 15 feet deeper than the average runner. Sometimes he fooled them by bunting for base hits. Trying to put his lack of speed in perspective, Lombardi once quipped to Hall of Fame Brooklyn Dodger shortstop Pee Wee Reese, "It was five years before I learned you weren't an outfielder." Harry Craft, Lombardi's teammate with the Reds for five seasons, would have nodded in agreement. "Ernie was the best right-handed hitter I ever saw," Craft once said. "He was an exceptional player in every department except running. If he hadn't been so slow, he would have had an even better batting average."

Good natured but taciturn, Lombardi had an awkward-looking body and a big nose, both of which made him the foil of many bench jockeys. Perhaps the most unfair legend about Lombardi is that he allowed the New York Yankees to win the 1939 World Series because of a missed play at home plate that his critics called "Ernie's Swoon" (or "Snooze"). In the tenth inning of the fourth series game, with the Yankees enjoying a commanding three-game lead, Joe DiMaggio hit a single to right field, scoring Frank Crosetti from third and breaking the four-all deadlock. Ival Goodman's misplay of the hit in the outfield prompted "King Kong" Charlie Keller to attempt to score from first base. On the play, Keller violently crashed into Lombardi at home plate. Dazed by the collision, Lombardi had trouble finding the loose ball, allowing DiMaggio to score also for the 7 to 4 final tally. Lombardi was made to be the "goat," even though the additional two runs had little bearing on the outcome of the game. Bucky Walters, the Reds pitcher in the tenth inning, admitted, "I was to blame for not backing up the play."

Lombardi, married to Bernice Marie Ayers since 1944, experienced emotional difficulties after retiring from the game. Five years later, in 1953, in the midst of severe depression, he attempted suicide by slashing his throat. Later he worked as a press box custodian for the San Francisco Giants but quit after a young sportswriter insulted him. Lombardi then worked menial jobs and as a gas station attendant until his death in Santa Cruz, California. In 1986 the Veterans Committee elected him to the National Baseball Hall of Fame. His wife was his sole survivor.

• Information on Lombardi's career in baseball is housed at the National Baseball Hall of Fame in Cooperstown, N.Y., and the *Sporting News* archives in St. Louis, Mo. A nostalgic interview with Lombardi is Stan Hochman, "The Schnozz Remembers," *Philadelphia Daily News*, 15 Sept. 1961. His career is featured in Gene Karst and Martin Jones, Jr., *Who's Who In Professional Baseball* (1973); Paul McFarlane, ed., *TSN Daguerreotypes of Great Stars of Baseball* (1971); Lowell Reidenbaugh, *Cooperstown: When Baseball Legends Live Forever* (1983); Mike Shatzkin, ed., *The Ballplayers* (1990); and Frank Stevens, *Baseball's Forgotten Heroes* (1984). Obituaries are in the *New York Times*, 28 Sept. 1977, and the *Sporting News*, 15 Oct. 1977.

WILLIAM A. BORST

LOMBARDI, Vince (11 June 1913–3 Sept. 1970), professional football coach, was born Vincent Thomas Lombardi in Brooklyn, New York, the son of Italian immigrants Harry Lombardi, a butcher, Matilda Izzo. Originally hoping to become a Catholic priest, Lombardi studied at the Cathedral College of the Immaculate Conception, Preparatory Seminary, from 1929 to 1932. Abandoning that goal, he set his sights on winning a college scholarship by playing football. To this end, in 1932 Lombardi attended Brooklyn's St. Francis Academy, where he played both guard and fullback on the football team and played basketball and baseball. Named to the 1932 All-City football team, Lombardi was recruited by several colleges. He won a scholarship from Fordham University to play football under new coach Jim Crowley, a former member of Notre Dame's legendary "Four Horsemen" backfield of the 1920s.

Lombardi entered Fordham in 1933, majoring in business administration. After three years of limited action on the football team, he started in 1936 as a guard on the noted "Seven Blocks of Granite" line with two future College Football Hall of Famers, center Alex Wojciechowicz and tackle Ed Franco. A football power, Fordham lost only one game that year. Lombardi was a small lineman, standing at 5'10" and weighing only 180 pounds, but his toughness was a great asset that allowed him to excel.

After graduating in 1937 with a B.S. degree, Lombardi played some semiprofessional football for several eastern teams. Simultaneously, he spent one year working for a New York finance company before enrolling at Fordham Law School in 1938 for an academically unsuccessful semester. In 1939 he accepted a position as a teacher at St. Cecilia High School in Englewood, New Jersey. Besides teaching Latin, physics, chemistry, and physical education, Lombardi served as head basketball coach and as an assistant football coach. In 1942 Lombardi became the head football coach, and from 1942 to 1945 St. Cecilia's was unbeaten for 32 consecutive games. In 1940 Lombardi had married his college classmate Marie Planitz, with whom he had two children.

As he triumphed at the high school level, Lombardi dreamed of becoming a head football coach at a major university. His goal, however, proved to be elusive. In January 1947 Fordham made him its assistant director of physical education and assistant to head football coach Ed Danowski. In this capacity Lombardi coached both the freshman squad and the varsity backfield. The next year, Lombardi installed a T-formation offense, but the varsity team still struggled. After efforts by his supporters at the university failed to have him replace Danowski as head coach, Lombardi sought employment elsewhere. In 1949 Lombardi landed a job at the U.S. Military Academy at West Point, New York, as an assistant coach under Earl "Red" Blaik. He soon became coach of Army's offensive unit. Afterward Lombardi always believed that Blaik was a great teacher and motivator and considered him a tremendous personal influence. During Lombardi's five-year tenure as assistant coach, Army won 30 games while losing only 12 and tying two.

With Army's success Lombardi began to attract the attention of professional football teams. In 1954 former Fordham classmate Wellington Mara, an executive with the New York Giants, hired Lombardi as an offensive coach. Lombardi worked in this capacity for five years, during which the Giants won two Eastern Conference titles and one National Football League (NFL) championship. Although possessing a reputation as a top offensive coach, Lombardi was nonetheless passed over for several head coaching jobs, including the one at West Point.

In 1959 the Green Bay Packers, then a struggling NFL franchise, took a chance on Lombardi, making him head coach and general manager. Lombardi quickly introduced a harsh discipline in training camp, telling his players, "I've never been connected with a loser, and I don't intend to be." Lombardi also stressed to his team the fundamentals of the sport: blocking and tackling. Never a great innovator, he placed great emphasis on a rugged running game renowned for its end sweeps. He soon became famous for proclaiming, "Winning isn't everything, it's the only thing." Valuing hard work and discipline, the deeply religious Lombardi believed that one's faith in God and loyalty to family and team were imperative. In later years this philosophy would make Lombardi an icon of traditional values amidst the cultural unrest of the 1960s. In addition, Lombardi maintained that coaches played a vital role in a team's success. Acknowledging that every squad's coaches had approximately equal football knowledge, Lombardi claimed that organization, communication, and character made the difference. "Every coach's team is an extension of himself," he said, "and so the personality of the coach becomes the personality of his team."

Lombardi inherited a team that had won only a single game the previous year, but his hard-driving personal style demanded obedience and helped develop a winning attitude. He quickly inserted new faces into the Packer lineup: Bart Starr at quarterback, Paul Hornung at halfback, and Jim Taylor at fullback. The results were impressive: the Packers won seven of 12 contests in 1959, resulting in Lombardi's recognition as the NFL's Coach of the Year.

Green Bay began its domination of the NFL in 1960 as the Packers captured their first Western Conference title in 16 years. Only a loss to the Philadelphia Eagles in the championship game that season kept Lombardi from his ultimate goal. The following year, however, the Packers easily won the conference title and demolished the New York Giants in the NFL title game, 37–0. The 1962 Packers were perhaps Lombardi's strongest team. Losing only one regular season game, Green Bay defeated the Giants again in the championship game, giving Lombardi back-to-back titles. Hampered by the loss of Hornung through suspension, the Packers finished in second place in 1963, despite suffering only two regular season losses. Within two years, however, Lombardi had his team back on top. In 1965 he guided the Packers to their first of an unprecedented three consecutive NFL championships. Following the 1966 and 1967 seasons, Lombardi's Packers defeated the rival American Football League champions in the first two Super Bowl contests.

By the end of the 1967 season Lombardi had grown tired of the demands made upon him. He thus resigned as head coach but still kept his duties as general manager. Lombardi enjoyed his first off-season away from football. He found, however, that once training camp began in July 1968 he had made a mistake, for he missed the "closeness" of his football team.

In early 1969 Lombardi agreed to become the new head coach and general manager of the Washington Redskins. As part of his contract with the Redskins, he received 5 percent ownership of the team. Like the Packers of 1959, Washington was a team with losing tendencies. Lombardi immediately turned things around, bringing the Redskins their first winning season since 1955. Before he could make them dominant, however, Lombardi became ill during the 1970 training camp. He died in Washington, D.C., of intestinal cancer.

In Lombardi's professional coaching career his teams won 96 regular season games, while losing only 34 and tying six. In postseason play, his teams won nine of 10 games, including five NFL championships. Lombardi was inducted into the Pro Football Hall of Fame in 1971.

Despite his blustery personality and temper, Lombardi won the respect of his players. All-pro guard Jerry Kramer characterized him as a "cruel, kind, tough, gentle, miserable, wonderful man." Bart Starr believed that those who played on Lombardi's teams "are better people for it." Lombardi, after whom the NFL's Super Bowl Trophy was named, has become one of professional football's legendary figures and a symbol of excellence.

• Lombardi wrote one book, *Run to Daylight!*, with W. C. Heinz (1963), describing in detail his team's preparation for a particular game. He also is credited with co-writing several articles, including three for *Look* magazine, "Why the Pros Play Better Football," 24 Oct. 1961; "A Game for Madmen," 5 Sept. 1967; and "Green Bay's Coach Reveals His Secrets of Winning Football," 19 Sept. 1967. Lombardi is the subject of a number of books, notably Michael O'Brien, *Vince: A Per-*

sonal Biography of Vince Lombardi (1987); Robert Wells, *Lombardi: His Life and Times* (1971); and Tom Dowling, *Coach: A Season with Lombardi* (1970). Lombardi is profiled in Tim Cohane, *Bypaths of Glory* (1963); Denis J. Harrington, *The Pro Football Hall of Fame: Players, Coaches, Team Owners and League Officials, 1963–1991* (1991); Jerry Kramer, *Instant Replay: The Green Bay Diary of Jerry Kramer* (1968); and Leonard Shecter, "The Toughest Man in Pro Football," *Esquire*, Jan. 1968, pp. 68–71ff. Obituaries are in the *New York Times*, 4 Sept. 1970; *Newsweek*, 14 Sept. 1970, p. 123; *Time*, 14 Sept. 1970, p. 61; and *Sports Illustrated*, 14 Sept. 1970, p. 14.

MARC S. MALTBY

LOMBARDO, Guy (19 June 1902–5 Nov. 1977), dance-band leader and producer of musical extravaganzas, was born Gaetano Alberto Lombardo in London, Ontario, Canada, the son of Gaetano Lombardo, a tailor, and Angelina Paladino, a secretary. All of the Lombardo children were required to study a musical instrument and singing. At the age of nine Guy, the eldest, began violin lessons. Around 1915 the musical family appeared as the Lombardo Brothers Concert Company with Guy as the violinist; Carmen as the flutist, saxophonist, and singer; Lebert as the trumpeter and drummer; and Freddie Kreitzer as the pianist. This group played for church socials and other occasions in London, Ontario, and surrounding areas. Because the local communities had many Scottish descendents their repertoire included, among other songs, *Auld Lang Syne*. By 1919 the enlarged band with guitar and trombone played a summer engagement at Grand Bend, Ontario. During 1922 Carmen played in Detroit, Michigan, with the Pasternak-Rubinstein band, which used slower tempos for the dancers rather than the standard, fast, snappy "businessman's bounce."

The Guy Lombardo band began to make new arrangements based on ideas gathered from Carmen and the bands of Paul Whiteman and Isham Jones, with Lebert's idol Louis Panico on trumpet. Engagements at London's Springbank Park, six nights a week, and at the Winter Garden (1922–1923) were followed by a summer season in Port Stanley, Ontario, in 1923.

In 1924 the nine original members from London, including the three Lombardos, Freddie Kreitzer on piano, George Gowans on drums, Francis Henry on guitar, Eddie Mashurette on tuba, Jeff Dillon on trombone, and Archie Cunningham on saxophone, traveled to the United States to play a few engagements in Ohio. On 18 February 1924 they opened under their new name, Guy Lombardo and the Royal Canadians, at the Claremont in Cleveland. Its owner, Louis Bleet, advised them to play more softly (to allow talking and listening) and to play soft chords under the solos rather than clapping an accompaniment. To deal with all the requests, Bleet suggested that the choruses of several songs be strung together. Accordingly the medley with Guy calling out the next chorus as one was being played was formed with a bridge passage using a modulation on the piano and often a schottische rhythm, another identifying feature of the "Lombardo sound." The famous sax section was based on the flutelike vibrato used by Carmen. Lebert's trumpet sound had a vocal quality, while Gowans's drum gave a beat within the band but never dominated. The band also began to give daily hour-long concerts on radio station WTAM in Cleveland.

In 1927 Guy married Lilliebell Glenn Caldwell, who was supportive throughout their life together. The couple had no children. That same year Guy decided with his brothers Carmen and Lebert, the coowners of the band, to accept Al Quodbach's offer to play at the Granada Cafe in Chicago. On 16 November 1927 the new Chicago radio station WBBM first broadcast the band. The enthusiastic response resulted in two sponsors and the initiation of the first radio network, with St. Paul's KSTP broadcasting remotely from the Granada. Many bandleaders, including Louis Armstrong, who was smuggled in by Lebert one night to play with them, made a point of listening to these broadcasts in order to copy elements of the effective Lombardo formula. In *Variety* (28 Sept. 1949) Armstrong later wrote, "Guy Lombardo and his band has always been my favorite band." After hearing the band at the Palace Theatre in Chicago in 1928, Ashton Stevens, the critic of the *Chicago Herald and Examiner*, described Lombardo and company as "the softest and sweetest jazzmen on any stage this side of heaven." This was modified to be used as the band's identifying moniker: "the sweetest music this side of heaven."

On 3 October 1929 the band opened at the Roosevelt Grill in the Roosevelt Hotel in New York. Except for two winters at the Cocoanut Grove in Los Angeles in 1933 and 1934, the band played at the Roosevelt for over thirty years in its classic format. Varying in size from nine to sixteen members, its standard instrumentation was two trumpets and one trombone, three saxophones (no baritone), doubling clarinets, the twin pianos to provide a rippling background, guitar, tuba (no string bass), and drums. The core personnel remained members of the Lombardo family—Victor played as a clarinetist and saxophonist for over thirty years, and sister Rose Marie was a vocalist during the 1940s—plus associates from London.

In 1930 the "Robert Burns Panatella Cigar Show" of NBC broadcast across the continent a half-hour of Lombardo's performance every Monday night from the Roosevelt, including the Hit of the Week. Carmen and Guy became noted for picking successful songs, and the band introduced over 400 hit songs. Carmen himself wrote over 200 songs, including *Boo-Hoo* (1937) and *Seems Like Old Times* (1945)—the theme song for Arthur Godfrey's show—while Guy wrote some eight songs in the years 1928–1930. In 1933 Lombardo introduced a comedy team on the "Robert Burns Show" with a live audience and accordingly opened the world of radio to performers such as Jack Benny, George Burns, and Gracie Allen. From 1933 to 1977, the band also played at every presidential inauguration, except for John Kennedy's.

By sticking with his "Lombardo sound" in carefully crafted arrangements, usually by Dewey Bergman, and by focusing on the melody with the simplest of embellishment, Guy and his band made over a hundred albums, selling more than 450 million records for Columbia, Decca, and MCA. Their famed New Year's Eve broadcast, which was used by CBS before midnight and NBC after midnight, with the signature tune *Auld Lang Syne* played at midnight, began to be telecast from the Roosevelt to over 55 million viewers in 1954. This tradition continued from the Waldorf-Astoria in New York in 1964. In the mid-1950s the Royal Canadians also had a regular live telecast from the Roosevelt.

The band traveled up to 80,000 miles a year throughout North America and, from 1953 to 1977, played for three months at the Jones Beach Theatre in Wantagh, Long Island. The Lombardos produced sixteen different musical extravaganzas for the 8,200-seat amphitheatre. These were *Arabian Nights* (1954–1955), *Show Boat* (1956–1957), *Song of Norway* (1958–1959), *Hit the Deck* (1960), *Paradise Island* (1961–1962), *Around the World in 80 Days* (1963–1964), *Mardi Gras* (1965–1966), *Arabian Nights* (1967), *South Pacific* (1968–1969), *The Sound of Music* (1970–1971), *The King and I* (1972), *Carousel* (1973), *Fiddler on the Roof* (1974), *Oklahoma* (1975), *Show Boat* (1976), and *Finian's Rainbow* (1977).

From 1940 to 1963 as a sportsman in various boats usually named *Tempo*, Guy Lombardo broke several speedboat records and won the Gold Cup in 1946. He was awarded an honorary doctorate of music from the University of Western Ontario in 1971. After his death in Houston, Texas, the Royal Canadians, the longest surviving American dance orchestra, continued under the leadership of his nephew, Bill Lombardo.

• Memorabilia can be found in the Guy Lombardo Music Centre in London, Ontario, Canada. Lombardo wrote an autobiography with Jack Altshul titled *Auld Acquaintance: An Autobiography* (1975). For other biographical information, see Beverly Fink Cline, *The Lombardo Story* (1979); Gene Lees, "Guy Lombardo—The Melody Lingers On," *High Fidelity (Musical America)* 24, no. 4 (1974): 24, 29–32; and "Guy Lombardo's 25th Anniversary," *Variety*, 28 Sept. 1949, pp. 1, 37–51, 54, 71–72. Also useful is the entry "Guy Lombardo and His Royal Canadians" in *Encyclopedia of Music in Canada*, ed. Helmut Kallmann and Gilles Potvin (1992), pp. 768–69. See also John S. Wilson, "Guy Lombardo," *International Musician* 70 (1971): 5; Saul Richman, *Guy* (1978); and B. Herndon, *The Sweetest Music This Side of Heaven* (1964). An obituary is in the *New York Times*, 7 Nov. 1977.

ELAINE KEILLOR

LONDON, George (30 May 1920–24 Mar. 1985), operatic bass-baritone, was born George Burnstein in Montreal, Canada, the son of Louis Samuel Burnstein, the owner of a hat manufacturing and distributing firm, and Bertha Broad. In 1935 London's family moved to Los Angeles, where he sang in his high school glee club. Two years later he enrolled in the opera department at Los Angeles City College, which led to a position in 1938 in the chorus of a Los Angeles opera company that was sponsored by the Works Progress Administration.

London made his debut in 1941 in a concert performance of Albert Coates's *Gainsborough's Duchess* in Los Angeles. He made his professional debut later that same year as Dr. Grenvil in Verdi's *La traviata* at the Hollywood Bowl. Two years later he appeared with the San Francisco Opera as Monterone in Verdi's *Rigoletto*. In 1946 London went to New York, where he studied with Enrico Rosati and Paola Novikova and appeared in Romberg's *The Desert Song* at the City Center. That same year he sang as a soloist in the world premiere of the Hindemith *Requiem*, using the name George London. In 1947 London joined the Bel Canto Trio with soprano Frances Yeend and tenor Mario Lanza; they toured the United States for two seasons. During the second season London sang his first solo recital in Estherville, Iowa.

London signed a four-month contract with the Vienna State Opera Company in 1949. He later claimed that the Vienna engagement proved the turning point in his career. London's roles included Amonasro in Verdi's *Aida*, Escamillo in Bizet's *Carmen*, Mephistopheles in Gounod's *Faust*, all four villains in Offenbach's *The Tales of Hoffmann*, and the title role in Mussorgsky's *Boris Godunov*. In portraying Boris, he became the first American to sing the role in Russian. His performances in Vienna led to roles in the early 1950s at Glyndebourne, Bayreuth, the Metropolitan Opera, and La Scala. In 1954 London received the title of "Kammersänger" from Austrian President Theodor Koerner, becoming one of the youngest ever to be named a court singer.

London sang many times at the Metropolitan Opera, making his first and last appearances as Amonasro in *Aida* (13 Nov. 1951 and 10 Mar. 1966). He made a particularly fine impression there in 1953 as Boris Godunov, becoming the first American to sing the role at the Metropolitan. Other notable appearances included Mandryka in the 1956 Metropolitan premiere of Richard Strauss's *Arabella* and the title role in Menotti's *The Last Savage* in 1964.

London participated in an exchange program in 1960 that sent him to the Soviet Union for four weeks. While in Moscow, he became the first non-Russian to sing Boris Godunov at the Bolshoi Theater. After London received a standing ovation from the Moscow audience, news of his stunning performance made the front page of the *New York Times*. Two years later he recorded the role in Moscow with the Bolshoi, the first American to do so.

London achieved one of his greatest triumphs as Wotan in a celebrated complete Wagner *Ring* cycle staged by Wieland Wagner in Cologne between 1962 and 1964. Throughout this period he also made guest appearances at the important opera houses in Europe and in North and South America. Some of London's other notable roles included Amfortas in Wagner's *Parsifal*, the title role in Mozart's *Don Giovanni*, the title role in Wagner's *The Flying Dutchman*, and Scarpia in Puccini's *Tosca*. His performances were notable for a "rare dramatic individuality and vocal power," and his acting ability had considerable influence

on younger artists. Musical theater director Harold Prince was particularly impressed by London's keen sense of drama.

London's recorded legacy includes a widely admired *Flying Dutchman*, and he sang Wotan in the first complete *Ring* recording conducted by Sir Georg Solti in 1958. He also recorded selections from Broadway shows and considered such music the equal of contemporary American music for the opera.

At the height of his career London was forced to abandon singing in 1967 because of a paralyzed vocal cord that had atrophied. For the remainder of his career he devoted himself to arts administration and to producing and directing opera. In 1955 London had married Nora Shapiro. They had two children, and she had two children from a previous marriage.

In July 1968 London was appointed music administrator of the Kennedy Center for the Performing Arts in Washington, D.C., to develop programs for the center's opera house and concert hall. He resigned in 1971 to become general director of the Los Angeles Music Center Opera Association and executive director of the National Opera Institute, but he remained a consultant to the Kennedy Center. The Los Angeles project failed because of insufficient financial backing, but London remained with the National Opera Institute from 1971 to 1977 and was concurrently the executive and finally general director of the Opera Society of Washington from 1975 to 1977.

As a director London staged the first complete English-language production of Wagner's *Ring* in the United States with the Seattle Opera in 1975. The company was the first in the country to present the entire *Ring* cycle in less than one week (over six days) and became the first company in the world to offer complete German and English versions in tandem. The productions, part of the company's new Pacific Northwest Festival, constituted an effort by London to gain an international reputation for the company.

London wrote prolifically on a number of musically related subjects, including government-subsidized arts programs (for which he once spoke in 1961 at a congressional hearing), music education for children, and the role of opera in contemporary American life. London also became an articulate spokesman and advocate for artistic issues concerning musicians and artists connected with opera.

In August 1977 London suffered a heart attack that permanently ended his career in the arts. Numerous awards were bestowed on him in the late 1970s and 1980s, including a special citation from the National Opera Institute in 1978 for contributions as an artist, administrator, and teacher. Furthermore, a series of grants in his name was established for young singers. London died in Armonk, New York.

One critic asserted that London's enduring importance rests on his "preoccupation with accuracy of detail in the playing of an operatic role" and in his "almost obsessive corollary concern about linguistics." Both as a performer and an administrator, London will be remembered as one who believed that his mission was to maintain—or, if at all possible, to raise—the highest standards of his art.

• For a discussion by London of the current state of opera, see "Whither Opera in America," *Opera News* 36 (1972): 6–7. For examples of London's concern with operatic interpretation, see his "Current Techniques at Bayreuth," *Opera News* 18 (1954): 7–9; and "The World of Wieland Wagner," *Saturday Review* 50 (1967): 59–60+. See Nora London, *Aria for George* (1987), for his wife's remembrance of his career and life. For profiles, see Joseph Wechsberg, "The Vocal Mission," *New Yorker*, 26 Oct. 1957, pp. 49–50+, and 2 Nov. 1957, pp. 47–48+; and Thomas Stewart, "George London," *Opera News* 50 (1985): 32–33. A discography appears in Leo Riemens and Rodolfo Celletti, "London, George," *Le grand voci* (1964). An obituary is in the *New York Times*, 26 Mar. 1985.

WILLIAM THORNHILL

LONDON, Jack (12 Jan. 1876–22 Nov. 1916), writer, war correspondent, and agronomist, was born in San Francisco, California, the son of Flora Wellman and, allegedly, William Henry Chaney, a reformer and professor of astrology. Chaney separated from his common-law wife when he learned of her pregnancy, angrily denying his paternity and later insisting (in two 1897 letters written in response to London's inquiries) that he had been impotent at the time of the child's conception. Wellman nevertheless named her son "John Griffith Chaney" on his birth certificate.

Wellman was a headstrong social maverick whose emotional growth had been warped by the death of her mother during early childhood and whose physical growth had been stunted by typhoid fever during early adolescence. At age sixteen she ran away from her home in Massillon, Ohio, where her father had been the town's leading citizen. After several years of cross-country wandering, she eventually found a spiritual home with Chaney and other free-thinking reformers in San Francisco. Equipped neither physically nor emotionally to care for her unwanted child, she entrusted him for the first eight months of his life to Virginia Prentiss, an African-American woman who had recently lost her own baby in childbirth. "Mammy Jennie," as he fondly called her for the rest of his life, provided the maternal affection London never received from his biological mother. Wellman, a devoted spiritualist, seemed interested more in holding seances than in holding her infant son. On 7 September 1876 she married Civil War veteran and widower John London, whom she had met through the Prentisses, and changed her baby's surname from "Chaney" to "London."

Although a loving father and conscientious provider, John London was harried into several unsuccessful business and agricultural enterprises by the socially ambitious Flora. The family (including Eliza and Ida, daughters of London's first marriage) therefore moved often, from city to several farms and back, steadily declining in economic status, so that Jack was forced to work at an early age. In a 1900 letter to his first publisher, Houghton, Mifflin, he attested that "from my

ninth year, with the exception of the hours spent at school (and I earned them by hard labor), my life has been one of toil. It is worthless to give the long sordid list of occupations, none of them trades, all heavy manual labor."

What London neglected to mention were the adventurous interludes in his "sordid list of occupations." In fact, his entire life might be accurately described in terms of an alternating pattern of work and escape. Perhaps the supreme irony was that while he chose the career of writing as a means to escape the toilsome underworld of the "workbeast," he was ultimately driven to work himself to death. His spectacular success story—as fantastic as Jay Gatsby's rise from rags to riches—was an epitome of the American Dream. Notably, a decade and a half before F. Scott Fitzgerald created his famous character, London had written a mordant critique of the myth of success in his autobiographical bildungsroman, *Martin Eden* (1909).

There is little gainsaying Alfred Kazin's remark that the "greatest story Jack London ever wrote was the story he lived." Kazin's observation may be readily substantiated with a brief recounting of biographical highlights: As soon as he had graduated from grammar school at age fourteen, London was compelled to take a job in a factory, an ordeal on which he based his indictment of child labor in "The Apostate" (1906). He escaped at fifteen, with $300 borrowed from Jennie Prentiss, by buying French Frank's sloop the *Razzle Dazzle* and joining a gang of hard-drinking hoodlums known as "the Oyster Pirates" on San Francisco Bay; these escapades were fictionalized in *The Cruise of the Dazzler* (1902). Years afterward, London remarked that the miracle of his life was that he lived to be twenty-one, since most of his friends had by then wound up dead or in prison. At sixteen he switched sides to the law by joining the California Fish Patrol at Benecia—compare his *Tales of the Fish Patrol* (1905). Eight days after his seventeenth birthday he signed aboard the *Sophia Sutherland* as an able-bodied seaman and headed to the Northwest Pacific on a seal-hunting expedition, gathering the materials for his first publication, "Story of a Typhoon off the Coast of Japan" (which won first prize of $25 in a contest for young writers sponsored by the *San Francisco Morning Call* in Nov. 1893), and, later, for his popular classic *The Sea-Wolf* (1904).

These escapades were punctuated with periods of strenuous labor. After returning from his sea voyage, London worked during the fall and winter—sometimes for sixteen hours a day at ten cents an hour—in a jute mill, then quit and took a job at a local power plant with the idea of learning a respectable trade. "I still believed in the old myths which were the heritage of the American boy," he recollected in *John Barleycorn* (1913). "Any boy, who took employment with any firm, could, by thrift, energy, and sobriety, learn the business and rise from position to position until he was taken in as a junior partner. After that the senior partnership was only a matter of time. Very often—so ran the myth—the boy, by reason of his steadiness and application, married his employer's daughter." The superintendent of the power plant promised to make an electrician of Jack if he were willing to start at the bottom by shoveling coal for $30 a month. His boss's real aim, however—as Jack discovered after several days of back-breaking labor—was to make $50 a month out of him by firing two coal-passers who had been making $40 each. "Learning a trade could go hang," he decided after a fellow worker confided the ruse. "It was a whole lot better to royster and frolic over the world in the way I had previously done."

His roystering led him cross-country as a hobo in the spring of 1894 and then, fatefully that summer, into the Erie County Penitentiary, where he served thirty days for vagrancy. Sickened by what he saw in prison, London determined to raise himself out of society's "submerged tenth" by returning to school. He would later recount his hoboing and prison experiences in *The Road* (1907); meanwhile he returned to Oakland High School, where he published ten sketches and essays in *The Aegis*, the student literary magazine. In the spring of 1896 he joined the Socialist Labor party. That fall, after intensive cramming to pass the entrance examinations, he spent a semester at the University of California. Forced to withdraw in January because of inadequate finances, he decided to make his career in writing and plunged into this new work. "Heavens, how I wrote!" he reminisced in *John Barleycorn*. "I wrote everything—ponderous essays, scientific and sociological, short stories, humorous verse, verse of all sorts from triolets and sonnets to blank verse tragedy and elephantine epics in Spenserian stanzas. On occasion I composed steadily, day after day, for fifteen hours a day." His creative orgy earned him nothing but dozens of rejection slips, and he again resorted to manual labor, this time in the laundry at Belmont Academy (London dramatized both these episodes in *Martin Eden*).

He found a way to escape again in late July 1897 when he left for the Klondike Gold Rush with his stepsister Eliza's husband, J. H. Shepard, who mortgaged their Oakland home to finance the expedition. Although he spent less than a year in the Klondike, forced out by a severe case of scurvy the next spring, this was the most crucial experience in London's career: "It was in the Klondike that I found myself," he said. "There you get your true perspective. I got mine." Although he brought home less than five dollars in gold dust, the wealth of experience he had gained in the Northland, not only firsthand but also from listening to the argonauts and sourdoughs with whom he had spent the long winter, proved to be the richest investment of his life.

Starting in the early fall of 1898, confronted by mounting economic pressures (his stepfather had died while he was in the Klondike, leaving Jack with the burden of family support) and seemingly endless rejections, London worked with desperate energy to break into the literary marketplace. "I don't care if the whole present, all I possess, were swept away from me," he wrote on the last day of November to his sweetheart Mabel Applegarth (the model for Ruth

Morse in *Martin Eden*), "I will build a new present; if I am left naked and hungry to-morrow—before I give in I will go on naked and hungry; if I were a woman I would prostitute myself to all men but that I would succeed—in short, I will."

And, in short, he did. By January 1899 he had published his story "To the Man on Trail" in the *Overland Monthly*; by January 1900 more than a score of his works were in print. The following spring his first book, *The Son of the Wolf*, received unqualified praise from the reviewers. "Critics have complained about the swift education one of my characters, Martin Eden, achieved," London commented in *John Barleycorn*.

In three years, from a sailor with a common school education, I made a successful writer of him. The critics say this is impossible. Yet I was Martin Eden. At the end of three working years, two of which were spent in high school and the university and one spent at writing, and all three in studying immensely and intensely, I was publishing stories in magazines such as the *Atlantic Monthly*, was correcting proofs of my first book (issued by Houghton, Mifflin Co.), was selling sociological articles to *Cosmopolitan* and *McClure's*, had declined an associate editorship proffered me by telegraph from New York City, and was getting ready to marry.

London married Bessie Mae Maddern on 7 April 1900, the same day that *The Son of the Wolf* was released. They had two children. Because of the couple's incompatible personalities, however, the marriage was doomed from the outset. Their daughter Becky recollected, "Daddy wanted company and liked to do things on impulse; Mother didn't like company—liked guests maybe once a year—liked to plan out everything. They were as different as chalk and cheese." London found a more suitable companion in Anna Strunsky, a brilliant Stanford student and fellow socialist with whom he collaborated in writing a dialogue on love, *The Kempton-Wace Letters* (1902). While theirs was a brief romantic involvement and a lifelong friendship, the affair was never consummated.

During the summer of 1902, London spent six weeks in the slums of London's notorious East End, living with "the homeless ones," whose miseries he depicted in *The People of the Abyss* (1903). The following winter he wrote the novel that would bring him international fame, *The Call of the Wild* (1903). In the summer of 1903 he answered his own romantic call by falling in love with Charmian Kittredge, the niece of Ninetta Eames, whose husband, Roscoe, was business manager for the *Overland Monthly*. Kittredge—intelligent, vivacious, comely, and daringly independent—was the prototypal New Woman; she became London's ideal "Mate Woman" and served as the model for Maud Brewster in his popular classic *The Sea-Wolf* (1904) and also for the heroines in his agrarian trilogy: *Burning Daylight* (1910), *The Valley of the Moon* (1913), and *The Little Lady of the Big House* (1916).

In 1904, leaving his manuscript of *The Sea-Wolf* for Kittredge to edit, London sailed for Japan, Korea, and

Manchuria to report the Russo-Japanese War for the Hearst Syndicate. The next spring, after running unsuccessfully for mayor of Oakland on the Socialist ticket, he purchased a 130-acre ranch near Glen Ellen, California, and took up permanent residence in the Sonoma Valley. In June, following the publication of his boxing novel *The Game* (1905), he began writing his other classic dog story—"the Call of the Tame," he called it—*White Fang* (1906). That fall and winter, as president of the Intercollegiate Socialist Society, he delivered a series of cross-country lectures subsequently published in *Revolution and Other Essays* (1910). On 19 November 1905, two days after the final decree of Bessie's divorce, he married Charmian Kittredge in Chicago. His lecture tour climaxed that winter with addresses to students at Yale and Harvard. "I went to the University," he told them, "but I did not find the University alive. . . . Fight for us or fight against us! Raise your voices one way or the other; be alive!"

London's socialist fervor reached its highest creative peak in 1906 with the composition of his apocalyptic novel *The Iron Heel* (1908). The scenes of urban catastrophe at the end of this work were inspired by his reporting of the great San Francisco earthquake and fire in April. This controversial novel has been praised not only by such noteworthy historical figures as Leon Trotsky and Anatole France, but also by such respected literary scholars as Robert E. Spiller and Maxwell Geismar, who call it "a terrifying forecast of Fascism and its evils" and "a key work—perhaps a classic work—of American radicalism."

Along with the decline of his active involvement in the Socialist cause, the last decade of London's life and career was distinguished by four major factors: (1) his (and Charmian's) two-year Pacific voyage, dramatically recorded in *The Cruise of the Snark* (1911) and fictionally reflected in *Adventure* (1911), *South Sea Tales* (1911), *A Son of the Sun* (1912), *Jerry of the Islands* (1917), *Michael Brother of Jerry* (1917), and *The Red One (and Other Stories)* (1918); (2) his vigorous efforts "to make the land better for my having been" in building the 1,500-acre "Beauty Ranch," which inspired *The Acorn-Planter: A California Forest Play* (1916) as well as his three agrarian novels; (3) his deteriorating health, resulting from several tropical ailments contracted during the *Snark* voyage and from kidney disease and rheumatoid arthritis, exacerbated by financial stress, improper diet, excessive smoking, and lack of regular exercise and sleep (a recent medical theory maintains that he also suffered from lupus)—all of which is reflected indirectly and perhaps unconsciously in such fantasy writings as *The Scarlet Plague* (1915), *The Star Rover* (1915), and his haunting Melanesian version of Joseph Conrad's *Heart of Darkness*, "The Red One" (1918); and (4) his attempts during the last two years of his life to revitalize himself, spiritually as well as physically, through direct contact with Hawaii and its myths and, near the end, through the therapeutic psychology of C. G. Jung.

Charmian London reports in her biography that when her husband discovered Jung's recently translated *Psychology of the Unconscious* in the early summer of 1916, he excitedly confessed, "I tell you I am standing on the edge of a world so new, so terrible, so wonderful, that I am almost afraid to look over into it." But he dared to look, and the literary results of his discovery were a series of extraordinary stories published posthumously in *On the Makaloa Mat* (1919). These signified not only a remarkable advance in his own work but also a pioneering achievement in modern literature: London became the first American author to incorporate Jungian theory into his fiction. As Kohokumu, the wise old fisherman in "The Water Baby," tells his skeptical companion John Lakana (the Hawaiian name for Jack London), "This I know: as I grow old I seek less for the truth from without me, and find more of the truth from within me. Why have I thought this thought of my return to my mother [the Sea] and of my rebirth from my mother into the sun? . . . I do not know, save that without whisper of man's voice or printed word, without prompting from otherwhere, this thought has arisen from within me, from the deeps of me that are as deep as the sea." Completed just six weeks before London's death, "The Water Baby" indicates a radical transformation for a writer who had systematically disavowed all metaphysical pretensions—notwithstanding the fact that much of his best work was informed by what Jung called the "primordial [or archetypal] vision."

London died on his ranch in Glen Ellen: the cause of death, according to his four attendant physicians, was "uraemia following renal colic." However, careful medical scrutiny of his symptoms indicates stroke and heart failure as the more probable cause. There is no substantial evidence to support the suicide canard popularized by Irving Stone and some other biographers.

Jack London's historical significance is major. A legendary figure and front-page celebrity during his own lifetime, London was a personal epitome of America's Strenuous Age. His generation was the last fully possessed of that "coarseness and strength combined with acuteness and inquisitiveness, [that] restless nervous energy, [that] dominant individualism [and] buoyancy and exuberance" which Frederick Jackson Turner cited in defining the American character as shaped by the frontier experience. "He was a quick study and leapt on the history of his times like a man to the back of a horse," asserts E. L. Doctorow: "It was Jack London's capacity for really living in the world, for taking it on in self-conscious and often reckless acts of courage, that made him our first writer-hero."

London's literary achievement is manifold. During a career that lasted less than twenty years, he produced some four hundred nonfiction pieces, two hundred stories, twenty novels, and three full-length plays on an astonishing variety of topics (some of which had never before been considered proper belletristic subjects): agronomy, alcoholism, animal training, architecture, assassination, astral projection, big business, ecology, economics, folklore, gold hunting, greed, hoboing, mental retardation, penal reform, political corruption, prizefighting, psychology (animal as well as human), racial exploitation, revolution, science, seafaring, socialism, stockbreeding, war, wildlife, and the writing game.

Under the influence of Herbert Spencer's "Philosophy of Style" and Rudyard Kipling's "plain style," London predicated his techniques on sincerity, functionalism, and what he termed "impassioned realism." He ushered into American literature a new prose for the modern fictionist—clear, straightforward, unpretentious, imagistic—thereby exerting through his literary as well as his lifestyle a seminal influence on such later figures as Ernest Hemingway, James Jones, Jack Kerouac, and Norman Mailer. In *The Road* and in his stories, he made the tramp an authentic literary subject. In *The People of the Abyss*, he created the kind of New Journalism attributed to Tom Wolfe in the 1960s. He pioneered the modern agrarian novel as well as the fields of sports writing and social-science fiction. In his Northland saga and in his sea stories, he popularized the coarse, action-filled stuff of the new naturalism, bridging the wide cultural gap between saloon and salon. "Except for the similar sensation caused by the appearance of Mark Twain's mining-camp humor in the midst of Victorian America, nothing more disturbing to the forces of gentility had ever happened in our literature," says Kenneth Lynn, "and it decisively changed the course of American fiction." London's works have been translated into more than eighty languages, and foreign critics rank him among the nation's foremost literary figures.

• The largest collections of London's papers are housed at the Huntington Library, San Marino, Calif., and at Utah State University, with smaller but significant holdings at the University of Virginia, UCLA, University of Southern California, University of California at Berkeley, Stanford, Yale, Centenary College of Louisiana, the New York Public Library, and the Jack London State Historical Park and Jack London Research Center, both in Glen Ellen, Calif. The most useful bibliographical guides are Hensley C. Woodbridge's monumental *Jack London: A Bibliography* (1966, 1973); Dale Walker and James Sisson's *The Fiction of Jack London: A Chronological Bibliography* (1972); Joan Sherman's *Jack London: A Reference Guide* (1977); and Jacqueline Tavernier-Courbin's *Critical Essays on Jack London* (1983), which updates Sherman's *Guide* in addition to providing a score of important essays. David Mike Hamilton's *"The Tools of My Trade": Annotated Books in Jack London's Library* (1986) and Tony Williams's *Jack London, the Movies: An Historical Survey* (1992) are also excellent reference works. While no comprehensive collection of London's writings has been published, the Stanford editions of *The Letters of Jack London* (1988) and *The Complete Short Stories of Jack London* (1993), ed. Earle Labor et al. are basic. Additional important collections are *Jack London Reports: War Correspondence, Sports Articles, and Miscellaneous Writings*, ed. King Hendricks and Irving Shepard (1970); *Jack London on the Road: The Tramp Diary and Other Hobo Writings*, ed. Richard W. Etulain (1979); *No Mentor but Myself: A Collection of Articles, Essays, Reviews, and Letters, by Jack London, on Writing and Writers*,

ed. Dale L. Walker (1979); and the two Library of America volumes of *Novels & Stories* and *Novels & Social Writings*, ed. Donald Pizer (1982). In the absence of a definitive biography, the most reliable studies are Russ Kingman, *A Pictorial Life of Jack London* (1979) and *Jack London: A Definitive Chronology* (1992). Other helpful sources are Charmian K. London, *The Log of the Snark* (1915), *Our Hawaii* (1917), and *The Book of Jack London* (1921); Joan London, *Jack London and His Times: An Unconventional Biography* (1939); Clarice Stasz, *American Dreamers: Charmian and Jack London* (1988); and Mark E. Zamen, *Standing Room Only: Jack London's Controversial Career as a Public Speaker* (1990). Noteworthy critical studies are Franklin Walker, *Jack London and the Klondike: The Genesis of an American Writer* (1966); Earle Labor, *Jack London* (1974); James I. McClintock, *White Logic: Jack London's Short Stories* (1975); and Charles N. Watson, *The Novels of Jack London: A Reappraisal* (1983). An obituary is in the *San Francisco Chronicle*, 24 Nov. 1916.

EARLE LABOR

LONDON, Meyer (29 Dec. 1871–6 June 1926), socialist leader and labor lawyer, was born in Kalvarie, province of Suvalki, Poland, the son of Ephraim London, a printer, and Rebecca Berson. His father received a traditional Orthodox Jewish education but turned to radicalism under the influence of the enlightenment movement. His mother was born into a rabbinical family and retained her Orthodox views. London's father arrived in the United States in 1888 and set up a printing shop on the Lower East Side of New York City that published a Yiddish anarchist journal. In 1891 he sent for the rest of his family. Meyer entered New York University's law school in 1896 and was admitted to the bar two years later. In 1899 he married Anna Rosenson, a dentist; they had one child.

As a socialist leader, London belonged to the centrist faction of the party. Breaking away from the Daniel De Leon–dominated Socialist Labor party in 1897, he followed Eugene V. Debs into the new Social Democracy, which in 1901 became the Socialist Party of America. A perennial candidate for state office, London by 1910 had developed a reputation as a union lawyer and negotiator for a number of garment industry unions, and his immersion in the cultural and social life of the Lower East Side made him an ideal candidate for the district's congressional seat. After running strong races in 1910 and 1912, London was elected in 1914, the second member of the Socialist party to sit in Congress. He won reelection in 1916, was defeated in 1918, and was elected for his third and last term in 1920. London supported an array of progressive legislation, including national social insurance, prohibition of labor injunctions and child labor, and an antilynching law, and he opposed immigration restriction. True to the Socialist party's position, he opposed Woodrow Wilson's preparedness program, and he voted against the declaration of war, conscription, and the espionage laws. However, with the United States at war, he believed opposition to war measures was "impracticable, unrealizable . . . and essentially wrong and immoral in a democracy like the

United States," arousing the wrath of the radical wing of the Socialist party.

His undogmatic approach held him in good stead as legal counselor and negotiator for the garment unions. He was instrumental in formulating the "protocol of peace," which ended the 1910 general strike of the International Ladies Garment Workers Union, and he represented the union in the mediation machinery created by the agreement. In 1912 he represented the Furriers Union in reaching a similar agreement following a bitter strike. In both cases he was accused by radical trade unionists of giving into the manufacturers and compromising socialist principles. From 1905 to his death he served as legal adviser to the Workmen's Circle, a socialist fraternal order of Jewish workers. In the final years of his life London fought a losing battle against the left-wing takeover of the cloakmakers' and furriers' unions. He succeeded in thwarting a similar attempt to gain control of the Workmen's Circle.

Although as a socialist politician and labor leader London had a constituency composed of Jewish immigrants, he remained, for the most part, aloof from Jewish communal life. He opposed Zionism as chauvinistic and utopian and unrelated to the needs of the Jewish working class. However, when the outbreak of war placed millions of Jews in Eastern Europe in jeopardy, London accepted the leadership of the Jewish Relief Committee, which joined the relief organizations sponsored by German-Jewish philanthropists and Orthodox Jews to form the American Jewish Joint Distribution Committee, the major Jewish agency coordinating overseas relief. London also participated in the formation of the American Jewish Congress, whose purpose was to represent American Jewry in lobbying for Jewish group rights in Europe and Palestine at the Paris Peace Conference.

London died from injuries sustained when he was struck by a car in New York City. The public funeral following his death was one of the largest New York City witnessed and reflected the enormous affection felt for him. Half a million people lined the streets of the Lower East Side, and 50,000 marched behind the hearse. He was interred in the section of the Workmen's Circle in Mount Carmel Cemetery that is reserved for luminaries of the Jewish labor movement.

London's home and locus of activity throughout his life remained the Lower East Side. Unlike his fellow socialist and lawyer, Morris Hillquit, he had no desire to assume a national role in the party. The modesty of his lifestyle and his altruistic bent—refusing fees and making contributions beyond his means—were public knowledge. His moral stature and realistic nature combined to make him one of the most effective and influential figures of his generation in the Jewish labor movement, and he was highly respected in American radical circles. He used his public career as political campaigner and congressman to focus the attention of the large mass of immigrant Jews on the social issues facing American society and on the potential power they possessed as citizens to effect change.

• Additional information on London is in Harry Rogoff, *An East Side Epic: The Life and Work of Meyer London* (1930); Melech Epstein, *Profiles of Eleven* (1965); and Arthur Gorenstein (Goren), "A Portrait of Ethnic Politics: The Socialists and the 1908 and 1910 Congressional Elections on the East Side," *Publications of the American Jewish Historical Society* 50 (Mar. 1961): 202–38. Also see Gordon J. Goldberg, "Meyer London and the National Social Insurance Movement, 1914–1922," *American Jewish Historical Quarterly* 65 (Sept. 1975): 57–73, and Melvyn Dubofsky, *When Workers Organize: New York City in the Progressive Era* (1968).

ARTHUR A. GOREN

LONG, Breckinridge (16 May 1881–26 Sept. 1958), lawyer and diplomat, was born in St. Louis, Missouri, the son of William Strudwick Long, a lawyer and politician, and Margaret Miller Breckinridge. The son of two prominent families, the Longs of Virginia and North Carolina and the Breckinridges from Kentucky, Breckinridge Long graduated from Princeton University in 1904. He studied law at St. Louis Law School (now Washington University) from 1905 to 1906 and gained admission to the Missouri bar in 1906. He began his law career the following year, struggling with a small practice in civil and criminal law. Early on he demonstrated a strong interest in politics and international relations. Following a failed 1907 campaign for Democratic state assemblyman in a local primary, he wrote a master's thesis, "The Impossibility of India's Revolt from England," which was accepted by Princeton University in 1909. He resumed his modest law practice, and on 1 June 1912 he married the wealthy Christine Graham, granddaughter of Francis Preston Blair, Democratic nominee for vice president in 1868. The couple had one daughter. Having achieved some degree of financial independence, Long became increasingly involved in politics. He ardently worked for Woodrow Wilson's reelection in 1916 and made substantial financial contributions to the Democratic National Committee. Wilson rewarded Long on 29 January 1917 with an appointment as third assistant secretary of state.

Following America's entry into World War I, Long supervised the Bureau of Accounts for Far Eastern Affairs, but he never lost his desire for elected office. He continued to support the Democratic National Committee and resigned from the State Department in June 1920 to devote his full energies to politics. Long strongly supported the internationalist policies of Woodrow Wilson, under whom he had studied constitutional law at Princeton University. As the Democratic nominee for the Missouri Senate seat in 1920, Long endorsed approval of the Treaty of Versailles and the League of Nations. His campaign was doomed by isolationist sentiment and by intraparty squabbles, and Long lost the race to Republican incumbent Selden P. Spencer. Two years later he challenged James Reed for the Senate; again, Long was defeated.

"Breck" Long moved to Laurel, Maryland, and resumed his career in international law, but he also remained active in Democratic politics throughout the 1920s, contributing heavily to the Democratic National Committee and supporting Democratic candidates on the national level. During the decade he made important political contacts with Franklin D. Roosevelt and Cordell Hull. Long served as Roosevelt's floor manager in the 1932 presidential campaign and, immediately following Roosevelt's victory, was appointed Ambassador to Italy.

At first Long admired Benito Mussolini's fascist regime for its efficiency and compared some of its success to the achievements of the New Deal. His enthusiasm dampened just prior to Italy's invasion of Ethiopia in 1935, when Long characterized the fascisti as "obdurate, ruthless, and vicious" (*The War Diary of Breckinridge Long*, p. xix). During his tenure in Italy, Long warned of the likelihood of general European war and urged a policy of American neutrality. He was instrumental in persuading Roosevelt from imposing an oil embargo against Italy following that nation's invasion of Ethiopia. He resigned his post early in 1936, citing health reasons, although the decision may have been influenced by a reprimand accusing Long of bypassing the State Department when he attempted to mediate the Ethiopian dispute.

His semi-retirement ended in January 1940, when Roosevelt appointed Long assistant secretary of state for special problems, a position he held until January 1944. As assistant secretary, Long was in charge of twenty-three State Department divisions including the Visa Section, which was instrumental in determining American policy toward refugees. In such matters, Long wrote, "I have had the major part and have been the policy making officer and the executive agent of the Government" (*The War Diary of Breckinridge Long*, p. 166). His jurisdiction extended to the issuance of visas for entry into the United States, the dispatch of relief funds for immigrants, and policy concerning the rescue of refugees. A 1924 law restricted immigration to an annual entry of 150,000 aliens, but even the meager quota was not met during World War II when hundreds of thousands sought to flee from Nazi persecution. This would become the most controversial issue in Long's public life. In 1970 Henry Feingold charged that Long was an anti-Semite who deliberately impeded the influx of Jewish refugees into the United States. In 1984 David Wyman regarded Long not as an anti-Semite but rather a nativist indifferent to the tragedy of the European Jews. Long's defenders contended that he was interpreting the administration's policy toward Jewish refugees and that he believed he was serving the national interest by obstructing invasion by radicals and foreign agents. Long himself, in his writings, equated communism with Jewish internationalism and regarded Hitler's *Mein Kampf* "eloquent in opposition to Jewry and to Jews as exponents of Communism and chaos" (Long Diary, 6 Feb. 1938).

Long was a delegate to the Dumbarton Oaks conference and retired from the State Department on 28 November 1944. He devoted his remaining years to breeding race horses and serving as a trustee of Princeton University (1937–1941) and as director of the Jefferson Memorial Foundation. He died at his country home, Montpelier Manor, near Laurel, Maryland. As a confirmed internationalist, he was gratified by the U.S. participation in the United Nations. At the time of his death he was praised for his work as liaison between Congress and the State Department. He is also credited for persuading Japanese ambassador Admiral Kichisaburo Normura not to commit suicide during his wartime internment in Washington. More recent studies identify Long as a representative of a conservative elite whose nativist attitudes dominated the State Department before and during World War II. According to this view, Long defined Americans as those with lineage in the United States and was deeply suspicious of foreigners as enemy agents and carriers of alien idealogies. Holocaust scholars, in particular, hold Long and his associates responsible for preventing European Jews from finding safe haven in the United States during their time of gravest peril.

• Long's personal papers and diaries are located in the Library of Congress. See also *The War Diary of Breckinridge Long*, ed. Fred L. Israel (1966); James F. Watts, Jr., "The Public Life of Breckinridge Long, 1916–1944" (Ph.D. diss., Univ. of Missouri, 1964); Dale F. Smith, "Breckinridge Long: The State Department Years" (M.A. thesis, Western Connecticut State Univ., 1993); and Lee Patterson, "Breckinridge Long, the State Department, and the Refugee Problem" (M.A. thesis, Georgia Southern Univ., 1994). Studies critical of Long include Henry Feingold, *The Politics of Rescue: The Roosevelt Administration and the Holocaust, 1938–1945* (1970); Arthur Morse, *While Six Million Died* (1967); David Wyman, *The Abandonment of the Jews: America and the Holocaust, 1941–1945* (1984); and Wyman, *Paper Walls: America and the Refugee Crisis, 1938–1941* (1968).

DONALD SCHWARTZ

LONG, Crawford Williamson (1 Nov. 1815–16 June 1878), physician, surgeon, and pioneer anesthesiologist, was born in Danielsville, Georgia, the son of James Long and Elizabeth Ware. Long's father, a prosperous and public-spirited planter and merchant who was clerk of the local court and a member of the Georgia Senate, named his son in honor of his friend William H. Crawford, then secretary of war and a former minister to France.

After graduating with honors from the University of Georgia in 1835, Long taught for a year at the Danielsville Academy. Well educated and widely read, he was a man of refinement and catholic tastes. Beginning the study of medicine in 1836 under George Grant of Jefferson, Georgia, Long continued his medical studies, first at Transylvania University in Lexington, Kentucky, and then at the University of Pennsylvania, from which he received an M.D. in 1839. Following graduation, Long worked for more than a year in New York hospitals, where he was recognized for his proficiency in surgery. Returning to Georgia in 1841, Long succeeded Grant, his preceptor, as a general practitioner at Jefferson. In 1842 he married Caroline Swain, the niece of a former governor of North Carolina and president of the University of North Carolina;

the Longs had six children. Long removed to Atlanta in 1850, but the next year he settled in Athens, seat of the University of Georgia, where he maintained a large and lucrative practice until his death.

During the first winter of his practice in Jefferson, several of Long's friends asked him to prepare for use in their "frolics" the gas nitrous oxide, then commonly known as "laughing gas," because of its exhilarating effects. Long suggested that instead of nitrous oxide they use sulphuric ether, which was already available. When participants in these frolics inhaled ether, Long observed that they suffered no pain, even when severely bruised. In light of this observation, he resolved to use ether as an anesthetic in a surgical operation. On 30 March 1842 he removed a tumor from the neck of James M. Venable, who felt no pain during the operation. By September 1846 Long had administered ether in eight operations, six of which can be documented. Moreover, Long administered ether to his wife at the birth of their second child in December 1845.

Although Long was the first physician to use ether in surgical anesthesia, he did not report his experiences until 1849. The heavy demands of a rural practice far from a metropolitan center and natural diffidence largely accounted for his delay. His inaction probably also reflected the teaching of his revered preceptor at the University of Pennsylvania, George B. Wood, who condemned the premature reporting of medical discoveries. Long also deferred to Paul F. Eve and Louis A. Dugas, two older surgeons at the Medical College of Georgia, who advocated mesmerism as an anesthetic. Eve, nevertheless, invited Long in 1848 to lecture at the medical college on his use of ether anesthesia and, in December 1849, published Long's account of his work in the *Southern Medical and Surgical Journal*, which Eve edited. In April 1852 Long read a paper before the Medical Society of Georgia on his experiences with ether anesthesia, which was later published in the society's *Transactions* (June 1853).

In November 1846, three years before the appearance of Long's account, Boston surgeon Henry Jacob Bigelow had reported in the *Boston Medical and Surgical Journal* the use of ether anesthesia in an operation performed on 16 October 1846 by John C. Warren at the Massachusetts General Hospital. William T. G. Morton, a Boston dentist who had administered the ether used in that operation, later claimed that he had been the first to use ether in surgical anesthesia. Morton and his former dental partner Horace Wells had previously used nitrous oxide and ether anesthesia in their dental practice on the suggestion of Charles T. Jackson, an analytical chemist and geologist of Boston. Apparently Jackson, Morton, and Wells were unaware of Long's prior use of ether anesthesia in remote Georgia. The claim by Frank Kells Boland and others that Jackson's travels as a geologist had taken him in 1842 to Georgia, where he had become acquainted with Long's use of ether has not been substantiated.

When Morton petitioned Congress in 1849 for compensation as the discoverer of ether anesthesia, Jackson and the heirs of Wells advanced their claims.

Long's friends then persuaded him to come forward with his claim. To ascertain the validity of Long's challenge, Jackson visited him in 1854 and became convinced that in 1842 the Georgian had indeed been the first to use ether anesthesia in surgery. But while acknowledging Long's prior use, Jackson pointed out that he and others had published accounts of their independent work first. Amidst the confusion of these conflicting claims and growing sectional conflict in the nation, Congress did not act. Long's legitimate claim to have been the first to use ether in surgical anesthesia remained largely unrecognized until 1877, when the distinguished gynecologist James Marion Sims asserted the priority of Long's use of ether anesthesia in the *Virginia Medical Monthly*. Although Long's primacy has become generally acknowledged, his failure to report his experiences before other surgeons has diminished the significance of his contribution to the development of surgical anesthesia.

Long is remembered mainly for his pioneer use of ether in surgical anesthesia, but his contemporaries honored and cherished him as a dedicated and skillful physician and surgeon. Because of his skill in surgery and obstetrics, his fellow physicians frequently consulted him in difficult cases. He was especially noted for his success in operating for cancer of the breast. From his extensive medical practice, partnership in a large retail and wholesale drugstore, and holdings in lands and slaves, Long enjoyed considerable prosperity, though he suffered heavy pecuniary losses following the Civil War. Opposed to secession, he served nevertheless as surgeon to the Confederate hospital on the campus of the University of Georgia and in the Home Guard of the Georgia State Infantry. After the war, he was appointed surgeon to the Federal troops occupying Athens, Georgia. Active to the end, Long died of apoplexy in Athens, while delivering the child of a colleague.

Throughout his professional career, Long was strongly convinced of his calling to serve humanity. He said that his profession was a "ministry from God" and that "his highest ambition was to do good and leave the world better by his labors." His achievement is commemorated by statues to his memory in Statuary Hall in Washington, D.C., and at Danielsville, his birthplace, and by a monument at Jefferson, the site of his first use of ether as an anesthetic in surgery. There are also memorials at the Universities of Georgia and Pennsylvania, and his portrait hangs in the Georgia capitol. Long County, Georgia, and the Crawford W. Long Hospital in Atlanta are named in his honor.

• Long's professional papers and other material concerning his career are in the Division of Manuscripts of the Library of Congress, and a collection of Long family papers is in the University of Georgia Library in Athens. Other Long memorabilia are in the Crawford W. Long Medical Museum, Jefferson, Ga., and the Medical Museum at Crawford Long Hospital of Emory University. Publications by Long include "An Account of the First Use of Sulphuric Ether by Inhalation as an Anesthetic," *Southern Medical and Surgical Journal*, n.s., 5 (1849): 705–13, with further elaborations in 6 (1850):

63–64; 9 (1853): 254–55, 384; and 10 (1854): 257–58. A full-length biography of Long is by his daughter Frances Long Taylor, *Crawford Williamson Long and the Discovery of Ether Anesthesia* (1928). Authoritative accounts of Long's role in the discovery of ether anesthesia are Frank Kells Boland, *The First Anesthetic: The Story of Crawford Long* (1950); Joseph Krafka, Jr., "Long, Eve and Dugas," *Journal of the Medical Association of Georgia* 33 (1944): 330–34; and Hugh H. Young, "Crawford W. Long: The Pioneer in Anesthesia," *Bulletin of the History of Medicine* 12 (1942): 191–225. For the historical development of anesthesia, see Nicholas M. Greene, "A Consideration of Factors in the Discovery of Anesthesia and Their Effects on Its Development," *Anesthesiology* 35 (1971): 515–22.

MALCOLM LESTER

LONG, Cyril Norman Hugh (19 June 1901–6 July 1970), endocrinologist, was born in Wiltshire, England, the son of John Long, a civil servant, and Rose Fanny Langdill. Long spent many of his early years in the town of Wigan, near Manchester, and received his early education at the Wigan Grammar School. A voracious reader with an interest in history and literature, Long was a fan of Jules Verne and later shared a friendship with Joseph Conrad. Having varied interests, Long played soccer and cricket, built model buildings, and was a skilled amateur photographer. After completing grammar school, Long entered the Honors School of Chemistry at Manchester University, receiving a thorough education in inorganic and organic chemistry. He graduated with a B.S. in 1921, preparing his first two publications on the Friedel-Crafts reaction. While at the university, Long was recruited to work on a chemistry experiment in physiology professor A. V. Hill's laboratory, where he discovered his life's work.

Receiving a scholarship in 1921, Long immediately began to study for his M.S. in science, but with Hill's encouragement he also studied for his medical examinations. He and Hill collaborated on the publication of eight papers on their work describing the correlation between physiology and chemistry of isolated muscles. They later studied the clinical aspects of the same correlation. This experience convinced Long that "the greatest discoveries are made from astute observation as a matter of chance" and that the purpose of a scientific mind is to "accept conclusions in the light of newly discovered facts."

Long's conversion to physiologist was swift, and after receiving his M.S. in 1923 he went on to join the department at University College, London. There Long became interested in the role of the endocrine glands in diabetes and applied his chemical knowledge to physiology. This resulted in the publication of a paper with K. S. Hetzel from the Department of Medicine at the University of London titled "The Metabolism of the Diabetic Individual, during and after Muscular Exercise." Soon after, he read Graham Lusk's *The Science of Nutrition*, which influenced his work for the remainder of his life. Also during that period, collaboration with his friend Alan Parkes pro-

duced a clinical paper on fetal reabsorption, a study of Parkes's at the time.

In 1925 Hill arranged for Long to go to Canada and join Jonathon Meakins, a professor of experimental medicine at McGill University. For the next two years, Long lectured in the Department of Biochemistry in medical research. In 1928 he received his M.D.C.M. degree and assumed control of the medical laboratory at the Royal Victoria Hospital for the Department of Medicine, later becoming assistant professor of medical research. Also in 1928 he met and married Hilda Jarman; they had two daughters.

Long left McGill in 1932 and joined the George S. Cox Research Institute at the University of Pennsylvania as director. His goal was finding a cure for diabetes, and, with his assistant F. D. W. Lukens, he investigated the amelioration of diabetes by the Houssay procedure. The Houssay procedure involved the removal of the pituitary gland, "demonstrating the participation of at least one extrapancreatic factor in the diabetic syndrome." Realizing that adrenal atrophy occurred after hypophysectomy, Long and Lukens began an investigation of the role of the adrenal in the Houssay preparation. By 1934 Lukens had devised a method to prepare cats with no pancreas and no adrenal glands. These cats lived about twice as long as the usual diabetic cats, with blood sugars lower than normal, while receiving no insulin.

Further work revealed that the amelioration of diabetes was due to the removal of the adrenal cortex, not the medulla, and the lower sugar resulted from a decreased production of sugar from body proteins. Although this discovery resulted in no cure for diabetes, it demonstrated that the pituitary and other endocrine glands were involved in diabetes and that the balance of endocrine function was an important factor in body metabolism.

In 1936 Long moved to Yale as a professor of physiological chemistry. Neurophysiologist John Fulton, who was instrumental in Long's appointment, evaluated his work, saying that Long "perhaps more than any other contributed to the disentanglement of the confusion that reigned between the functions of the various endocrine glands and . . . metabolism and had put this on a sound scientific basis." Long stayed at Yale for thirty-three years, serving as professor and chairman of the Department of Physiological Chemistry and becoming Sterling Professor in 1938.

During World War II, with Frank Engel, Long investigated the role of adrenal cortex in hemorrhagic shock. Granted U.S. citizenship in 1942, Long spent many years advising the government on medical affairs. In 1952 his biochemistry department was the first of its kind in the United States. Long also served as chair of the Department of Pharmacology and the Division of Biological Sciences. He served briefly as dean of the School of Medicine (1947–1952) and was actively involved in the Yale community. During 1937 and 1938 his department published over fifty papers, including "Effect of Adrenal Cortical Hormone on Carbohydrate Stores of Fasted Hypophysectomized

Rats," "The Effect of the Adrenal Cortical Hormone on the Liver and Muscle Glycogen of Normal Fasting Mice and Rats," "Diabetes Mellitus in the Light of Our Present Knowledge of Metabolism," and many others.

During Long's tenure as dean of the medical school, he halved the school's deficit, broadened its responsibility in the community, and improved personal relations among the staff. When his term expired Long moved to the Department of Physiology. He chaired this department until 1964, then served as Sterling Professor, becoming emeritus in 1969. Long continued his research in the hypophyseal function in the diabetic syndrome. These studies led to the isolation of prolactin (in collaboration with A. White), of adrenocorticotrophic hormone (with George E. Sayers), and of growth hormone (with Alfred Wilhelmi and Jane Russell Wilhelmi). Later studies involving the development of adrenal ascorbic acid bioassay for pituitary adrenocortical hormones were significant contributions to this field of study. Appointed a fellow at the John B. Pierce Foundation at Yale in 1969, Long continued to work until his death at Pemaquid Beach, Maine.

Long enjoyed a close relationship with his family and was a known as a warm, compassionate man. His medical accomplishments, particularly in the study of diabetes, have led to many other studies and discoveries in the latter half of the twentieth century. The author or coauthor of more than two hundred papers, Long dedicated his life to medical research and advanced the study of diabetes considerably.

• A collection of Long's papers is at the American Philosophical Society, Philadelphia. A detailed memoir is O. L. Smith and J. D. Hardy, National Academy of Sciences, *Biographical Memoirs* 46 (1975): 265–309. Other important sources are A. V. Hill, *Trials and Trails in Physiology* (1965), and J. B. Priestley, *The Edwardians* (1970). A brief obituary is in the *New York Times*, 8 July 1970.

DAVID Y. COOPER
MICHELLE E. OSBORN

LONG, Earl Kemp (26 Aug. 1895–5 Sept. 1960), governor of Louisiana, was born in Winnfield, Louisiana, the son of Huey Pierce Long, Sr., and Caledonia Tison, farmers. His older brother, Huey P. Long, Jr., nicknamed "the Kingfish," became nationally prominent as Louisiana governor (1928–1932) and U.S. senator (1932–1935). Unlike his seven siblings (there were actually eight, but one died in infancy), Earl Long was a mediocre student and much preferred farming to school. Following Huey's example, he dropped out after finishing the eleventh grade and began a successful career as a traveling salesman. From 1912 to 1927 he sold kerosene cans, home remedies, baking powder, and boot polish in the rural areas of Louisiana, Texas, Arkansas, and Mississippi, earning lucrative commissions of over $10,000 a year by 1921. With his charming personality and gift of gab, Long could sell people on himself as well as on his wares,

with great success; when Huey's political fortunes began to rise, Earl felt the urge to embark on a political career of his own.

Earl Long's baptism in state politics was assisting Huey in winning the election to the Louisiana Railroad Commission in 1918 (in 1921, the state constitution changed the name to the Louisiana Public Service Commission). Earl gave Huey money, drove all over the district hustling votes, and rounded up local politicos to join the Long bandwagon. When Huey ran for governor, unsuccessfully in 1923 and successfully in 1927, Earl again gave him considerable help, especially by bringing into the Long camp such future stalwarts of the Kingfish's machine as Robert Maestri, Seymour Weiss, Allen Ellender, and Leander Perez. As a reward, Huey appointed his brother attorney for the inheritance tax collector, a choice patronage plum. Earl's main political task was to serve as Huey's chief legislative liaison in pushing his progressive program. In 1929 Earl performed yeoman work in helping Huey avert a senate trial on the impeachment charges brought against him by the lower house of the state legislature. But in the statewide elections of 1931, Earl ran for lieutenant governor on an independent ticket because Huey would not let him run on his own ticket. In his first try for elective office, Earl ran a poor third. The split between Earl and Huey persisted for three years, while Earl publicly campaigned for Huey's opponents. During this time Earl met Blanche Revere, whom he married on 7 February 1932. Finally, in 1934 the brothers reconciled. When Huey was assassinated in September 1935, Earl again found himself in the Long inner circle.

In 1936 Earl ran for lieutenant governor on the Long machine's ticket headed by Richard W. Leche, and because of popular sympathy for the fallen Kingfish, the ticket swept the elections. In his first position as an elected official, Earl played a key role in getting the Leche administration's political program through the legislature: state-funded old age pensions, a teachers' tenure law, a new state charity hospital, and increased funding for health, education, and welfare. Earl also helped reconcile the Louisiana state government with the administration of President Franklin D. Roosevelt, which had had a serious rift as a result of Huey's demagogic rhetorical assaults on establishment politics and his ambitions for national office. Thus federal jobs and money returned to the state. Although Earl engaged in bribery and graft, he distanced himself from the wholesale corruption of the Leche administration. After press revelations in June 1939 led to Leche's resignation, Earl Long served the remaining eleven months of the governor's term. But the scandals led to his defeat in 1940, as anti-Long reformer Sam H. Jones won the governorship. In 1944 Earl lost when he ran for lieutenant governor, prompting most experts to predict his demise as a state politician.

In 1948 Long surprised the experts, however, by successfully challenging Sam Jones. As governor from 1948 to 1952, Long raised state taxes to pay for large increases in state spending for old age pensions, schools, hospitals, roads and bridges, welfare, mental asylums, and a host of other social benefits. He also equalized pay scales for black and white teachers, and he dramatically increased black voter registration by more than 90,000, giving Louisiana the largest number and highest percentage of registered blacks in the South. The threat of lawsuits by NAACP attorney A. P. Tureaud strongly motivated Long to make the right to vote available to all citizens. To accomplish this, Long persuaded local registrars to abandon "literacy tests" and other obstacles typically used to bar blacks from the polls. Popular as these programs were, with particular constituencies, for the most part the poor, the governor lost general public support through his blatant attempts to revert to the dictatorial politics of the Huey Long era. Earl abolished the state civil service and fired hundreds of state employees for such reasons as "political halitosis." He attempted to wrest control over state universities from their governing boards, and he tried to destroy the municipal independence of the city of New Orleans, which was controlled by Mayor DeLesseps S. Morrison, his political enemy. Long also allowed organized crime figures like Frank Costello and Carlos Marcello to expand their illegal gambling and vice empire in Louisiana by opening up casinos and slot machines throughout the southern half of the state. This return to the politics of the past led to the election of anti-Long reformer Robert F. Kennon as governor in 1952. But in 1956 Earl Long triumphed again by winning the governor's race in the first primary.

During his 1956–1960 term Long made international headlines by being committed to mental institutions in Texas and Louisiana in the spring and summer of 1959. After having been married for twenty-six years, Earl and his wife, Blanche, separated in late 1958. During the first five months of 1959, Long went on wild sprees, drinking and carousing in New Orleans's French Quarter and conducting several highly publicized flings with Blaze Starr and other strippers. When the state legislature convened in May 1959, segregationist politicians led by state senator William Rainach attempted to disfranchise black voters. Enraged, the governor tried to stop that effort, but in a televised address to a joint legislative session he lost control of himself and began to curse and shout.

Confined to the John Sealy Clinic in Galveston, Texas, and then Southeast Louisiana Hospital in Mandeville, Long received psychiatric care for a mental problem that in all probability was manic depression. After securing his release from the Mandeville hospital through typically high-handed political maneuvers, he embarked on a whirlwind, eighteen-day vacation swing through several western states and Mexico. Disgraced by these episodes, Long lost another try for the lieutenant governorship in 1959. In the summer of 1960 he managed to upset incumbent congressman Harold McSween in a primary, but on the day of his victory Long suffered a massive heart attack and died several days later in an Alexandria, Louisiana, hospital.

The brother of Huey Long is remembered more for his personal eccentricities and his no-holds-barred political methods than for his actual achievements as the governor of a state in the Deep South of the mid-twentieth century. A classic populist, Earl Long championed the poor, and for providing them with relatively generous social welfare programs the disadvantaged gave him their votes. If he used government to curry favor with the masses, he nevertheless acted on a premise that in later decades was deemed discredited by most politicians in the South: that government can genuinely improve people's lives. Unlike other politicians of his region and era, Long also chose not to drive a wedge between the races, to pit poor whites against even more disadvantaged blacks. His successful bid to register tens of thousands of African Americans as voters helped him to consolidate a large constituency, but a tactic of that kind made Earl Long more than just another populist demagogue. And he went further in facilitating a modicum of racial justice: in 1958 he opened the first fully integrated public university in the South, Louisiana State University at New Orleans; he helped to enforce the peaceful desegregation of New Orleans's public transportation system; he publicly denounced segregationist politicians. His brother Huey—the grittier, more ruthless populist—never did anything so constructive. Earl Long, however, will always remain in the Kingfish's shadow.

• No collection of Earl Long manuscripts is known to exist. For a comprehensive bibliography on Long and the most reliable biography, see Michael L. Kurtz and Morgan D. Peoples, *Earl K. Long: The Saga of Uncle Earl and Louisiana Politics* (1990). For amusing and entertaining accounts of Long, see A. J. Liebling, *The Earl of Louisiana* (1961), and William J. Dodd, *Peapatch Politics: The Earl Long Era in Louisiana* (1991). See also T. Harry Williams, *Huey Long* (1969), and Allan J. Sindler, *Huey Long's Louisiana: State Politics, 1920–1952* (1956). An obituary is in the *Baton Rouge Morning Advocate*, 6 Sept. 1960.

MICHAEL L. KURTZ

LONG, Esmond (16 June 1890–11 Nov. 1979), physician and medical historian, was born in Chicago, Illinois, the son of John Harper Long, a professor of physiological chemistry, and Catherine Stoneman. On graduating from the University of Chicago with an A.B. in 1911, Long found a post there as a chemical assistant under the noted chemical pathologist H. Gideon Wells. Wells, a generous mentor, was probably the chief early influence on the development of Long's interests in characterizing the environmental conditions under which bacterial organisms, such as the causative organism of tuberculosis, might develop. Two years later, after a series of episodes of illness during which he had begun to cough up blood, Long stained his own sputum and found it teeming with tuberculosis organisms. What followed was a youthful period of several years of part-time medical education at the University of Chicago's Rush Medical School, interspersed with long stretches of convalescence between roughly 1914 and 1919 spent in "desert" and "rest" cures in Arizona and the famous sanatorium at Saranac Lake, New York. He ultimately earned an M.D. in 1926, eight years after receiving his Ph.D. from the University of Chicago in 1918.

While his lengthy bout of severe pulmonary tuberculosis was formative in shaping Long's career as well as his personal life and world view, other well-defined influences preceded his contraction of the disease. The young Long was particularly interested in humanities subjects and possessed a scholarly turn of mind. His early interest in languages, particularly Latin, led him in later life to turn to the study of historical medical subjects, notably the background of his chosen medical field, pathology. His father's example, too, may have influenced his decision to pursue research in medical science.

In his autobiographical writings and in personal accounts to colleagues Long always emphasized the extent to which his lengthy illness bred in him a sense of the contemplative and the inquiring, traits he later brought to the study of both pathology and medical history. Still at Chicago, he spent the early years of his career engaged in scholarly research in bacterial metabolism and, in his personal sphere, a complementary pursuit of the outdoor life, which he had come to value during his illness. On his return east from a mountaineering trip in 1921 Long renewed his friendship with a distant cousin, Marian Bock Adams. The relationship flowered into romance, and the two married in mid-1922; they had three children.

Following a long-standing nineteenth-century tradition of American medical scientists traveling abroad to work in the great laboratories of Central Europe, the Longs journeyed to Prague, Czechoslovakia, where Long learned the skills of pathological anatomy under the tutelage of the renowned pathologist Anton Ghon. The obligatory *Wanderjahr*, in which the traveler moved from capital to capital, followed Prague. When he returned with the newly acquired European credentials, Long took up a salaried post as an assistant professor in pathology at the University of Chicago, where he resumed a large range of studies of the experimental pathology of tuberculosis, investigating such problems as the protein chemistry of the disease's causative organism.

In 1932 Long accepted the invitation of the Phipps Institute in Philadelphia, associated with the University of Pennsylvania, to join its staff as director of laboratories, succeeding Eugene Opie. While the dean, William Pepper, announced to the local medical and scientific community that Long's chief preoccupation would be research, the latter now began in fact to move Long away from basic bench science and into epidemiological research. This research involved all aspects of TB treatment and control, including, prominently, clinical field trials of the substance known as PPD (purified protein derivative). In the 1930s and 1940s PPD, originally posited (under the name tuberculin) as a TB therapy by Robert Koch, was further refined and developed. It ultimately became, by 1952, the international standard, through the World Health Organization, for tuberculosis detection and monitoring.

Long became actively involved in a myriad of national organizations during and after the Second World War and, throughout the 1930s and 1940s, wrote scores of articles and books. Of these, his works in the history of pathological science, *History of Pathology* (1928) and *Selected Readings in Pathology* (1929), perhaps produced his most lasting legacy. Long's historical and scientific publications were coextensive and commingled over a striking sixty-year period. As late as the early 1970s, while in his eighties, Long continued to publish vital works, including such monograph-length historical studies as *History of the American Society for Experimental Pathology* (1972) and the *History of the American Association of Pathologists and Bacteriologists* (1974).

Long died in Devon, Pennsylvania. He was a member of what was probably the most remarkable generation of American medical scientists of the twentieth century, those who came of age between two world wars. They began their careers at a time when American medicine was just emerging from the Flexner reform era and when many aspiring young medical scientists were starting out with obligatory overseas study. By the end of their careers, medicine in the United States had gained pride of place in the world arena, and the flow of talent and resources had reversed. Long participated in all of this. A professor of pathology and an opinion leader at some of the nation's leading and most elite medical centers and universities, he was elected to the National Academy of Sciences and received virtually every other major honor in the pantheon of science and medicine. Yet he also stood outside this dramatic sweep of historical science, chronicling it while living it, as few others did, with both incision and concision.

• Long's papers are held primarily at the University of Pennsylvania Archives, while similar files can be found at the College of Physicians of Philadelphia (including a reasonably complete run of his published reprints) and the American Philosophical Society, Philadelphia, Pa. This last file includes correspondence between Long and several important figures, including Simon Flexner, Thomas Rivers, Richard Shryock, Eugene Opie, Florence Sabin, and others. While Long never wrote a book-length autobiography, he produced "A Pathologist's Recollections of the Control of Tuberculosis," in *A Dozen Doctors: Autobiographical Sketches*, ed. Dwight J. Ingle (1963). Peter Nowell and Louis B. Delpino provide a memoir of Long in the National Academy of Sciences, *Biographical Memoirs* 56 (1987): 258–310. Obituaries are in the *American Philosophical Society Yearbook* (1980), pp. 613–17; the *American Journal of Pathology* 100 (Aug. 1980): 323–25; the *Philadelphia Bulletin*, 13 Nov. 1979; and the *Philadelphia Inquirer*, 17 Nov. 1979.

RUSSELL C. MAULITZ

LONG, George S. (3 Dec. 1853–2 Aug. 1930), lumberman and business executive, was born in Claremont (near Indianapolis), Indiana, the son of Isaac Long, a merchant, and Sarah V. Smith. He attended local public schools before his father purchased a small lumbermill and relocated the family to Tipton County in northern Indiana about 1863. After gaining experience at the mill for about a year and a half, George Long and his family were sent back to Indianapolis by his father on account of an outbreak of malaria. There Long completed two years of high school and also continued to work for his father, who had remained in northern Indiana, as a local sales agent. His father, after working in the northern part of the state for an additional three years or so, relocated his mill to Indianapolis. Around 1872 his father's business collapsed, and Long was forced to leave high school. He then worked at a local real estate firm and enjoyed the fruits of a wartime boom period until the market collapsed in 1876. With the resulting real estate bust, Long lost both his job and his desire to remain in that line of work.

Returning to a field he knew well, Long went to work for the wholesale lumber firm of Holt and Buggee in Indianapolis. Although that firm landed in receivership as well after only three months, Long had found his true calling and subsequently went to work for the firm of H. C. Long (no relation). Under the tutelage of H. C. Long, whom he later credited for his business success, Long served as a field representative in Iowa, Missouri, and the Indian Territory (modern-day Okla.) with responsibilities that included locating, buying, logging, manufacturing, and shipping timber products. While in the field Long contracted malaria and swore never to venture south of the Mason-Dixon line again in pursuit of business.

In 1884 Long relocated to Eau Claire, Wisconsin, and served as a shipping clerk at the Northwestern Lumber Company. Within three months' time he became yard foreman and a year later rose to the position of sales manager. His responsibilities increased as the firm expanded, and he soon found himself in charge of five separate mills. Long made a major contribution to the industry as a whole during this period by virtue of his work with the Northwestern Lumber Manufacturers' Association. The newly founded (1881) association was struggling mightily to attain credibility among producers in the upper Midwest. Long served the organization, which sought voluntary controls on pricing and production, as secretary-treasurer, and in 1890 he also chaired a committee that sought to establish uniform standards for grading pine lumber. Although the resulting report was not fully accepted within the industry for nearly ten years, it did finally influence other producer groups and helped to create the long-sought industrywide standard.

The death of Northwestern's president, combined with a perception (on his part) that the firm's resources were becoming depleted, convinced Long to change jobs again. He became a manager with the firm of Brittingham and Hixon of Madison, Wisconsin, only to leave, three weeks later when he received an offer that would change his life, and the industry, forever—general manager of Weyerhaeuser Timber Company.

Upon relocating to Tacoma, Washington, Long was confronted with a task that might have floored another man. Weyerhaeuser had recently purchased 1 million acres of timberland in the Pacific Northwest from James J. Hill's Northern Pacific Railroad, and Long found himself responsible for managing the vast tract. He also saw the need to assuage fears on the part of small lumbermill operators, farmers, and settlers regarding the intentions of his huge and powerful employer. Blessed with a salesman's instincts, Long quickly bought additional lands (while at the same time yielding tracts to small operators where it would bring the firm goodwill) in order to increase the practical layout of the company's holdings. For similar reasons, he held back for many years in developing the company's own milling operations, preferring instead to sell timber to independent operators.

As general manager and director (and vice president after 1918) of Weyerhaeuser, Long faced many challenges. Confronted with the need to expand markets, he led the way in expanding the firm's fleet of ocean freighters, thereby decreasing Weyerhaeuser's dependence on railroad common carriers. He successfully avoided major labor disputes with the Industrial Workers of the World with the help of an industry-sponsored union, the Loyal Legion of Loggers and Lumbermen. Long brought the firm additional goodwill with the creation of the Logged Off Land Department, which helped farmers settle on otherwise useless former timberland. His greatest contribution, however, came in the areas of reforestation and fire control. His tireless lobbying of Congress led directly to the Clark-McNary Act of 1924, which provided tax incentives for private firms to replant cut-over land and also contributed to the creation of cooperative fire prevention efforts. Long had previously, in 1909, been instrumental in creating the Western Forestry and Conservation Association, which pioneered in combining public and private resources in the prevention of devastating forest fires.

During World War I Long served on the lumber committee of the Council of National Defense. He married Carrie B. Robinson of Bedford, Indiana, and their union produced three children before his wife's death in 1925. Long himself remained active with Weyerhaeuser until his death in Klamath Falls, Oregon.

George S. Long was a leader of the timber industry. While he helped make Weyerhaeuser the largest private lumbering firm in the United States, his greatest legacy may come from his efforts on behalf of forest fire control and reforestation; his accomplishments played a key part in the long-term development of the modern timber industry.

• The papers of George S. Long are held at the Weyerhaeuser Company archives in Tacoma, Wash. The best secondary source of information on his life and career is Ralph Willard Hidy et al., *Timber and Men: The Weyerhaeuser Story* (1963). He also receives mention in William B. Greeley, *Forests and Men* (1972).

EDWARD L. LACH, JR.

LONG, Huey Pierce (30 Aug. 1893–10 Sept. 1935), governor of Louisiana and U.S. senator, was born in the hill country of Winn Parish, Louisiana, the son of Huey Pierce Long and Caledonia Tison, modestly prosperous farmers who lived comfortably by the standards of their community and sent six of their ten children to college. Huey, however, was not one of them. Even while attending high school, he worked for several years as a traveling salesman. Later, he briefly studied law at the University of Oklahoma and Tulane University. He received no degree, but he equipped himself to pass the Louisiana bar exam. By the summer of 1915, he was practicing law in his home town of Winnfield and starting a family with his wife of two years, Rose McConnell. They would eventually have three children.

Long's first love, however, was always politics, and he quickly carved out a place for himself in the fractious political life of Louisiana. He was driven in part by the populist and agrarian-socialist traditions of Winn Parish, which led him to identify with the "common people" and to present himself as a scourge of privileged elites. But he was driven above all by extraordinary, even obsessive, ambition, honed at an early age, which led him to subordinate all other concerns—personal, financial, and when necessary ideological—to the demands of his public career.

In 1918 Long conducted a successful and well-publicized defense of a socialist state senator, S. J. Harper, against charges that Harper had violated the Espionage Act by opposing American intervention in World War I. His victory helped him win election in that year to the Louisiana Railroad Commission (soon renamed the Public Service Commission). Over the next eight years, during five of which he chaired the commission, Long established himself as a champion of popular interests against the powerful oil companies, the utilities, and the conservative political elite that had governed the state for decades. He ran unsuccessfully for governor in 1924 and spent the next four years preparing to run again. After a campaign of exceptional intensity, he won a decisive victory in 1928 by compiling enormous pluralities in the rural parishes to overcome a weak showing in New Orleans.

As governor from 1928 to 1932, Long channeled public money into roads, bridges, hospitals, schools, and the state university at Baton Rouge. He made modest reforms in the state tax codes, shifting some of the burden to corporations and wealthy individuals. He placed a few limits on the power of the large oil companies. In contrast to his staunchly conservative predecessors, Long was a remarkably progressive leader. By almost any other standard, however, his record was one of modest, conventional reform.

Long's methods, however, were anything but conventional. He created a statewide political organization without precedent in American history; within a few years he wielded so much power that his enemies exaggerated only slightly in calling him a "dictator." Even his supporters referred to him as the "Kingfish" (a nickname drawn from the popular radio show "Amos 'n' Andy"). He accumulated power brilliantly and ruthlessly by campaigning effectively to have his supporters elected to the legislature, by systematically filling state offices with loyal allies, by ramming through the compliant legislature laws concentrating more power in his own hands, and perhaps above all by retaining the loyalty—indeed the intense devotion—of the poor, rural voters who formed a majority of the Louisiana electorate.

In 1930 Long won election to the U.S. Senate, but he refused to resign the governorship and assume his Senate seat until after the 1932 gubernatorial election, in which he ensured that a docile ally, Oscar K. Allen, would replace him. As a senator, he dominated Louisiana politics almost as completely as he had when serving as governor. Long's enemies had demonstrated no capacity to challenge him after an unsuccessful impeachment attempt in 1929. They could do little more than watch, with growing fury and contempt, as he began to move beyond Louisiana and into national politics.

In Washington Long quickly established himself as a critic of Herbert Hoover's administration and a vocal advocate of redistributing the nation's wealth to end the Great Depression. In the 1932 presidential election he worked energetically on behalf of Franklin Roosevelt, both at the Democratic National Convention and in the fall campaign, and by the time Roosevelt took office, he had emerged as a significant force within the Democratic party. But Long quickly became disillusioned with the New Deal. Roosevelt, he believed, showed insufficient enthusiasm for redistribution of wealth and displayed a troubling inclination to create powerful national bureaucracies, such as the National Recovery Administration, which Long attacked as potentially tyrannical. The president also failed to allow Long to exercise as much influence in the administration as he thought he should have. In any event, Long's own thinly concealed presidential ambitions probably made a break with Roosevelt inevitable, and such a break was all but complete by the end of 1933.

For the next two years Long took little interest in the work of the Senate (except for occasionally launching filibusters against New Deal legislation he opposed). He concentrated instead on building a national political following of his own and laying the groundwork for an independent presidential bid in 1936 or 1940. He announced his own economic program, the Share Our Wealth Plan, and then he created his own political organization, the Share Our Wealth Society, to promote the plan. He published a national newspaper, the *American Progress*, and a brief autobiography, *Every Man a King* (1935). He spoke regularly to network radio audiences and traveled widely to address sympathetic audiences. He won publicity, too, through his blunt public statements, his ostentatious wardrobe, and his occasionally scandalous social escapades—some of them a result of political calculation, others, such as a celebrated episode in which he urinated on the trouser leg of another guest at a Long Island club, apparently of drunkenness. Long had become so fully a creature of politics that he had virtually no private life and no important personal relationships. He seldom saw his family. He lived almost entirely in hotels, even when he was in Louisiana a few blocks from his own home.

Opponents dismissed him as a demagogue, and indeed there was much in Long's message that was demagogic. His Share Our Wealth Plan, for example, was unworkable. Long called for steep income and inheritance taxes to scale down large fortunes and for redistributing the surplus wealth such taxes would bring into the treasury to the rest of the citizenry. Every family would be guaranteed a "homestead" of $5,000 and an annual income of $2,500. But confiscating great fortunes would not have been nearly enough to finance the plan.

Unworkable as Long's plan might be, the message behind it had some substance. The maldistribution of wealth he decried was real, and it was not unreasonable to argue that it had contributed to the nation's economic problems. The power of established financial and corporate interests was considerable, and Long's attacks on them had echoes in the rhetoric of many more conventional political figures of his time, including Franklin Roosevelt. Long's warnings of the tyrannical possibilities of great national bureaucracies (public or private), his call for the return of authority to individuals, and his evocation of the value of community in the face of concentrated power all resonated with a populist sensibility that survived with considerable strength among much of the American public.

By early 1935 Long was attracting substantial popular support. Polls commissioned by the Democratic National Committee suggested he might draw as much as 10 percent of the national vote in 1936, enough to throw a close election to the Republicans. Long himself seems never to have decided to be a candidate for president that year, but he clearly intended to support a third-party challenge to Roosevelt whether or not he ran himself. To that end, he began a modest public flirtation with other national dissident leaders such as Father Charles Coughlin and Dr. Francis Townsend, perhaps as a prelude to an election-year alliance.

The president took the threat seriously. He once called Long one of the "two most dangerous men in America" (the other was Douglas MacArthur), and he began trying to undermine Long by withholding patronage from his Louisiana organization and ordering IRS investigations of his associates. In the spring of 1935, when Roosevelt submitted a series of new legislative proposals to Congress, he included a revenue bill, denounced by critics as a "soak-the-rich tax," which many believed was designed to challenge Long's hold on the issue of the redistribution of wealth. Long simultaneously took credit for it and rejected it as an inadequate gesture.

In the meantime, Long was continuing to shore up his power within Louisiana. In a series of special legislative sessions in 1934 and 1935, he forced passage of laws that effectively eliminated local government and vitiated the courts. Every public employee in the state—from schoolteachers and police officers to members of the cabinet—needed the approval of the Long machine. All were required, moreover, to contribute a portion of their salaries to the organization's campaign fund, creating an enormous pool of cash for which there was almost no public accounting. Exactly how much financial corruption there was in the Long organization is difficult to determine, but it was substantial. Long himself seemed to have relatively little interest in accumulating personal wealth, however; IRS and FBI investigations into his own finances failed to produce a convincing case against him.

In September 1935, with his national political prospects apparently at their peak, Long returned to Louisiana to supervise another special session of the legislature. On the afternoon of 10 September, as he rushed down one of the marble corridors of the state capitol he had built for himself, he was fatally shot by a young New Orleans physician, Carl Austin Weiss, the son-in-law of one of Long's political opponents. Weiss apparently shared the almost obsessive hatred of the senator that had become common among the New Orleans elite, but his precise motives for shooting Long remain unknown, since he was gunned down on the spot by the senator's bodyguards. Indeed, speculation persists that Weiss was not the killer at all, although no credible alternative theory has emerged to explain the assassination. After Long's death, his frail national movement quickly evaporated, and his Louisiana organization soon made its peace with the Roosevelt administration.

Long's legacy in Louisiana was substantial. He compiled a considerable record of important public works, and he defined political divisions in the state for a generation to come. His brother, Earl Long, served several terms as governor; his son, Russell Long, served in the U.S. Senate for four decades; other relatives and allies played prominent roles in state politics for years. As late as the 1960s, political campaigns continued to reflect the rivalry between Long and anti-Long factions.

Beyond Louisiana he left no concrete legacy. He did, however, help reveal the survival of strong populist sentiments among much of the electorate. He may also have played a role in helping to sustain and strengthen those sentiments. And his effective attacks, not just on the wealthy, but also on the New Deal, suggested some of the ways in which many Americans attracted to populist ideas were beginning to fear the power of government as much as they had traditionally feared the power of private corporations.

• There is no significant body of Long's papers, but the Huey Long Collection at Louisiana State University contains some valuable material. In addition to the autobiography mentioned above, Long was the author of a fanciful account of his imagined presidency, *My First Days in the White House* (1935). T. Harry Williams, *Huey Long* (1969), and William Ivy Hair, *The Kingfish and His Realm* (1991), are the two most important biographies; the former is sympathetic, the latter hostile. Alan Brinkley, *Voices of Protest: Huey Long,*

Father Coughlin, and the Great Depression (1982), examines Long's national career. Robert Penn Warren's novel *All the King's Men* (1946) features a character, Willie Stark, modeled on Long.

ALAN BRINKLEY

LONG, James (10 Oct. 1792 or 1793–8 Apr. 1822), leader of two filibustering expeditions from the United States into Spanish Texas, was born probably in North Carolina or perhaps Culpeper County, Virginia. His parents' names and occupations are unknown. He moved at an early age to Rutherford and Maury counties, Tennessee, with his father. Nothing is known about his education, but he was reputedly a surgeon with William Carroll's Tennessee volunteers in 1814 and served at the battle of New Orleans on 8 January 1815.

In 1815 Long married the orphaned niece of General James Wilkinson, Jane Herbert Wilkinson. They had three children, one of whom died soon after birth. The pair lived at Port Gibson, Mississippi, where Long practiced medicine briefly before acquiring a plantation near Vicksburg late that same year. He was an unsuccessful planter for two years, and in 1817 the couple moved to Natchez, where Long opened a store.

In June 1819 Long was chosen to lead a filibustering expedition to Nacogdoches in Spanish Texas by a group of Mississippi merchants disgruntled by the Adams-Oñís Transcontinental Treaty of that year, which set the Sabine River as the western boundary of the Louisiana Purchase. Incensed that Secretary of State John Quincy Adams had relinquished U.S. claims to eastern Texas as part of the purchase in order to secure Florida from Spain, volunteers marched west from Natchitoches, Louisiana, and captured the Spanish outpost of Nacogdoches. A council of eleven investors chose Long president of the newly created Republic of Texas on 22 June 1819. Long sent agents to Galveston Island to enlist the aid of privateer Jean Laffite, not knowing that the corsair was a paid informant of the Spanish authorities at San Antonio.

In September the Spanish governor ordered an expedition against the Anglo-American invaders, and by 28 October 1819 all of Long's volunteers had been either captured, killed, or had fled east of the Sabine River. Long and his wife barely escaped capture but returned to her relatives at Alexandria. Thus ended the first Long expedition.

A small core of filibusterers, however, relocated at the end of 1819 on Bolivar Peninsula on the southeast corner of Galveston Bay. They erected a fort of flotsam overlooking the entrance to the bay opposite Galveston Island, where Laffite's men remained. Long and his wife and daughter, Ann, arrived in early 1820. But the character of this second expedition changed when New Orleans merchants and a band of republican Mexican refugees joined the effort to force the Spanish to give up Mexico. The struggle for Mexican independence had begun in 1810 but soon withered to spasmodic guerrilla warfare until 1820, when the movement was revitalized, leading to victory in 1821.

Long's role on Bolivar Peninsula was twofold: to command the Anglo-Americans and to seek financial support in New Orleans. Cultural misunderstandings with the Mexican republicans, rivalries between all factions, and a lack of financial support prevented launching an attack against Spanish forces to the south. Word reached the isolated peninsula in September 1821 that the Mexican republicans had been successful and controlled Mexico City. While the Mexican leaders sailed for Veracruz, Long and some fifty volunteers sailed to Copano Bay to ascertain if the Spanish troops at La Bahia (now Goliad) had taken the oath to the new republic. The garrison had acknowledged the new government, and the commandant arrested Long and his men in October as possible filibusterers. They were sent to Mexico City, where they remained on parole. Long was killed—probably intentionally—by a sentry in Mexico City.

Long had left perhaps sixty people on Bolivar Peninsula, including his pregnant wife, his daughter, and several married couples. When he failed to return in a few weeks as promised, many left the barren sandbar as winter approached. By December Jane and Ann Long and their servant girl were alone waiting for James to return. Jane gave birth to a daughter at the end of the month and by March 1822 was rescued by Anglo-American immigrants entering Galveston Bay to join Stephen F. Austin's new colony. She remained in the area until summer, when she learned of the death of her husband. In the fall of 1822 Jane journeyed to San Antonio, where she unsuccessfully petitioned the Texas governor for a pension, based on James's support for the revolutionary cause. She returned to relatives in Louisiana but moved to Austin's colony in 1824. Jane received the standard 4,428-acre headright from Austin, which she located in Fort Bend County. She never married again and was admired as a pioneer Texan until her death in 1880.

• No Long papers have survived, but in the late 1830s Jane Long told aspiring historian and politician Mirabeau Buonaparte Lamar her version of events in her and her husband's lives. Lamar also collected some documents pertaining to Long; thus Charles Adams Gulick, Jr., et al., eds., *The Papers of Mirabeau Buonaparte Lamar* (6 vols., 1921–1927), is the best source if used with caution. The originals are at the Texas State Library and Archives. Likewise the published papers associated with Austin's colony offer some differing information: Eugene C. Barker, ed., "The Austin Papers," *American Historical Association Annual Report 1919* (1924). The Lamar material was used verbatim by Henry Stuart Foote, *Texas and the Texans* (2 vols., 1841), with some romantic embellishment in interpretation. Other nineteenth-century Texas historians only added more myth to the Long story. Anne A. Brindley, "Jane Long," *Southwestern Historical Quarterly* 56 (Oct. 1952): 211–38, adds some details from genealogical researchers, but James Long's personal history remains obscure. Harris Gaylord Warren, *The Sword Was Their Passport* (1943), is still the standard work on filibustering in Texas.

MARGARET SWETT HENSON

LONG, Jefferson Franklin (3 Mar. 1836–4 Feb. 1901), Reconstruction era politician, was born a slave of mixed African and Caucasian ancestry in Knoxville, Crawford County, Georgia. The names of his parents and of his owners are unknown. Sometime before the beginning of the Civil War, Long was taken from rural Crawford County to nearby Macon, where he evidently taught himself to read and write and learned a trade. Freed at the end of the war, he opened a tailor shop in Macon, which he and his son operated for a number of years and which provided him a steady income and a position of some eminence in the black community there. He married Lucinda Carhart (marriage date unknown) and had seven children.

Like many who became involved in Republican party politics in the early years of Reconstruction, Long attended sessions of the Georgia Equal Rights Association and by the summer of 1867 was making speeches for that group's successor, the Georgia Equal Rights and Educational Association, urging blacks to register to vote under the terms of the congressional program launched in the spring. In 1868, while not a candidate for any office, Long campaigned diligently for the Grant ticket; although it failed to carry Georgia, he was rewarded for his efforts with a seat on the Republican state central committee. In 1869 Long and Henry McNeal Turner, a black minister-politician from Macon, summoned a convention of more than two hundred delegates who urged the creation of a public school system and called for higher wages for farm day laborers and for substantially more favorable terms for tenants in the emerging system of sharecropping.

Before 1870 Long appeared to have only limited roles—organizer, speaker, agitator—in the Reconstruction politics of Georgia. However, just as Republican power was ebbing in the state and at the same time as the Democrats regained control of the legislature, party leaders chose Long as a candidate for Congress from the Fourth District (located in the "black belt") in the elections of December 1870. But because Georgia had been denied representation in Congress before 15 July 1870, Long was elected only to the third session of the Forty-first Congress, which would meet early in 1871; a white Republican was chosen to represent the district for a full term in the Forty-second. It was the Republicans' rather manipulative strategy that year to attract black voters to their ticket by nominating black candidates for the short term and whites for the full one. Sworn in on 16 January 1871 and serving until the end of the session on 3 March, Long nevertheless was the only black congressman elected from Georgia in the nineteenth century. In his brief tenure, Long also was the first black member to address the House. His short but impassioned speech, widely commented on in the national press, was in opposition to a measure that would relax slightly the restrictions imposed on former Confederates who sought public office. He spoke not to the details of the measure but to the larger question of ongoing racial violence and resistance to Radical Reconstruction in the South. "Do we, then," he said, "really propose here to-day, when

the country is not ready for it, where those disloyal people still hate this Government, when loyal men dare not carry the 'stars and stripes' through our streets, for if they do they will be turned out of employment, to relieve from political disability the very men who have committed these Kuklux outrages?" Long evidently failed to persuade many congressmen, for the bill passed by a vote of 118 to 90.

Long returned to Macon when Congress adjourned and, while never again seeking or holding a public office, remained active in politics until 1884. He appeared regularly at Republican state and district gatherings and was a delegate to the national convention in 1872, 1876, and 1880. The remainder of his public career signified his rising dissatisfaction with the white leadership of his party (although he did not advocate black solidarity against all whites in it) and his repeated efforts to transform black voters into a more independent political force. He was particularly critical of the ring control of the state Republican party and its descent into patronage-brokering. At the same time Long realized that black voters would have to reach an accommodation with at least some of the white conservatives who had taken control of Georgia in December 1871.

Soon after Redemption, when the Democratic party showed signs of splitting between the Regulars and the Independents, who resisted the machine-like control of the party apparatus by powerful bosses, Long supported the Independents and campaigned for William H. Felton, an Independent congressman from a north Georgia district. In 1880, however, when the state Republican party did not put forth a candidate for governor, Long joined other prominent black Republicans in working vigorously for the incumbent, Alfred Holt Colquitt, a Bourbon Democrat and former Confederate general, instead of Thomas M. Norwood, an Independent Democrat supported by most white Republicans. Many blacks endorsed Colquitt, who was also a licensed Methodist preacher, partly because of his well-received sermons in black churches and his efforts as governor to protect blacks against white violence and partly because of their deep hostility to white manipulation of the Republican party apparatus. After Colquitt's victory, Long won enthusiastic commendations from the Democratic power brokers.

Within the Republican party, which was weakened by persisting divisions between white officeholders and federal appointees, on the one hand, and the black rank and file, on the other, Long was a steady opponent of what he believed was unprincipled white control. Black dissatisfaction with the party culminated at the state convention in 1880, when the black majority among the delegates, angry because choice nominations and federal appointments usually went to whites and hostile toward the party leaders' intentions to expand the Republican base by wooing white conservatives, seized control of the central committee, made William A. Pledger, a young black newspaperman from Athens, the committee chairman, and sent a majority black delegation to the national convention.

Two years later Pledger stepped down as chairman in favor of Alfred E. Buck, a white politician popular with blacks, who held the position until 1898 and adeptly fought off efforts to make the party lily-white. These convolutions in Republican affairs in Georgia left Long frustrated in his attempts to win meaningful influence for black voters and disillusioned with politics itself. In an open letter that he wrote as a parting shot in 1884, he spoke about schoolhouses and churches and about "Christianity, morality, education, and industry" in addressing the unresolved problem of racial advancement in the post–Reconstruction South.

Long lived in Macon the rest of his life, with his son running his tailor's shop and adding a drycleaning establishment. Long helped organize the Union Brotherhood Lodge, a black mutual aid society with headquarters in Macon and branches in other towns nearby. His daughter Annie Eunice was the wife of Henry Allan Rucker, collector of internal revenue for Georgia from 1897 to 1909. Far more than Long's brief tenure in Congress, his public career in the state illuminates the difficulties that confronted black politicians, the weaknesses of Republicanism, and the limitations of the political process in the protection and advancement of black people's interests in the Reconstruction period. Long died in Macon.

• No collection of Long's papers exists; the details of his life and career are pieced together mainly from newspaper articles of the period. For a published discussion of his career, see John M. Matthews, "Jefferson Franklin Long: The Public Career of Georgia's First Black Congressman," *Phylon* 42 (June 1981): pp. 145–56. Olive Hall Shadgett, *The Republican Party in Georgia from Reconstruction through 1900* (1964), is useful for the political context it provides. See also Edmund L. Drago, *Black Politicians and Reconstruction in Georgia* (1982), and the sketch on Long in Eric Foner, *Freedom's Lawmakers* (1993). Obituaries are in the Atlanta *Constitution* and the Atlanta *Journal*, 5 Feb. 1901.

JOHN M. MATTHEWS

LONG, John Davis (27 Oct. 1838–28 Aug. 1915), governor of Massachusetts, congressman, and secretary of the navy, was born in Buckfield, Maine, the son of Zadoc Long, a retired storekeeper, and Julia Temple Davis. After his initial education in the Buckfield public schools and at neighboring Hebron Academy, Long, not yet fifteen, enrolled at Harvard University in 1853. After graduating second in his class in 1857, he became headmaster of an academy in Westford, Massachusetts. While he enjoyed the rural setting and the congenial small-town life, he resisted the temptation to settle down. After two years at Westford, he read law in the office of Boston attorney Sidney Bartlett and continued his studies at Harvard Law School. He was admitted to the Massachusetts bar in January 1861.

Long "hung out his shingle" in Buckfield. When this produced but scant remuneration, he returned to Boston in October 1862. After brief stints with two law firms, he joined the office of Stillman B. Allen in May 1863. By the late 1860s Long, now an equal partner, was spending his summers in Hingham, a quiet town southeast of Boston on the South Shore. In 1870 he married Mary Woodward Glover; they had two children. Although busy with a successful law practice and a growing family, Long was drawn into local politics. By 1871 he was living in Hingham, where the local Democrats and the Independent Republicans nominated him as their candidate for the Massachusetts General Court that year. He did not campaign for office and was defeated. Losing again the following year under similar circumstances, he was elected as a Republican to the General Court in 1874. Soon thereafter he established a winter residence in Boston, where, James W. Hess has argued, Long's "social consciousness and ambition" seemingly intensified (Hess, p. 61).

During the 1875 session, Long presided over the house during the Speaker's absence. Proving an effective campaign orator for the Republican party, he was elected Speaker in 1876. He was unanimously reelected Speaker in 1877 and, with only a half-dozen in opposition, was given a third term in 1878. Later that year Long's supporters put forward his name for Republican candidate for governor. When that honor went to Thomas Talbot, Long was nominated by acclamation for lieutenant governor. After helping the ticket win election, he represented the executive at various official functions, and when Talbot declined a second term, Long became his party's gubernatorial nominee. He won the election against Democrat Benjamin F. Butler and was reelected with increased majorities in 1881 and 1882.

Long kept a journal throughout his life, but his record of these years is fragmentary. Only after the death of his ailing wife in February 1882 did he resume his journal. Looking back over his political career, he wrote in December 1882 that he had "tried to do my duty" and had "served no other than the public interest" (Margaret Long, p. 162). Long was respected by many of his contemporaries. George Frisbie Hoar, in his autobiography, described him as "a great public favorite, who had just ended a brilliant and most acceptable term of service as Governor" (vol. 2, p. 117). Long was not an aggressive reform governor. He recommended legislation exempting wages from attachment, and the Massachusetts legislature enacted laws providing for weekly payment of wages. In 1881 he proposed a constitutional amendment providing for woman suffrage, and he also advocated electoral reforms and restrictions on corporations. These were mild recommendations in response to the discontent of the period.

Long was elected to the U.S. House of Representatives in 1882 and was easily reelected in 1884 and 1886. In 1882–1883 his name was put forward as a strong candidate for the U.S. Senate against incumbent Republican senator Hoar. Long probably could have secured Hoar's seat had he been willing to accept an offer of support from Butler and the Democrats. Unfortunately, Long's strong appetite for fame and political advancement was offset by his inhibitions as a genteel reformer to promote his own candidacy. Hoar retained his seat. Long fared little better in 1886–1887, when his friends and supporters urged him to campaign for the seat of incumbent Senator Henry Laurens Dawes. This was a crucial juncture in his career. Although he was considered as a possible successor to Dawes, he refused to be a candidate. Henry Cabot Lodge, Long's former campaign manager, having no such inhibitions, secured the prize in early 1893. Subsequently Long's relationship with Lodge cooled considerably.

Long retired from Congress in 1889 and devoted himself to his law practice and his family. In 1886 he had married Agnes Peirce; they had one child. In early 1897 President-elect William McKinley offered Long a position in his cabinet. Possessing similar kindly dispositions, they had become close friends while serving in Congress together in the 1880s. Long selected the position of secretary of the navy. He had been retired from active politics for several years and this offer caught the senators from Massachusetts, Lodge and Hoar, by surprise. While Lodge acquiesced in the ex-governor's appointment after meeting with McKinley, he accomplished what Wendell D. Garrett has described as "a masterpiece of political management" by securing the appointment of Theodore Roosevelt, his close friend, as assistant secretary of the navy. This appointment "treated the country to a strange spectacle of the young, big-navy interventionist aligned with the elderly, small-navy pacifist—both attempting to steer the Navy in the troubled Spanish waters" (Garrett, p. 295).

Initially Long accepted Roosevelt as the best man for the job. A year later Long, who genuinely liked Roosevelt, reached a different conclusion. After the destruction of the *Maine* in Havana Harbor in mid-February, Long, who was hoping for a peaceful solution to the crisis and was exhausted by the pressure of events, went home on the afternoon of the 25th to rest. Roosevelt, in charge as acting secretary, sent off various instructions, including one to Commodore George Dewey to coal up and be ready for offensive actions in the Philippines. Returning to his office the next day, Long wrote in his journal that "Roosevelt, in his precipitate way, has come very near causing more of an explosion than happened to the *Maine*" and had "gone at things like a bull in a china shop." While Long felt Roosevelt "means to be thoroughly loyal," his actions had been "most discourteous to me, because it suggests that there had been a lack of attention, which he was supplying" (Margaret Long, pp. 216–17).

Although Roosevelt resigned his position a few months later and found military glory in Cuba, his shadow and the events of 25 February have loomed large over Long's reputation. By the 1930s some scholars concluded that the McKinley administration had been the victim of a "large policy," engineered by Lodge and Roosevelt, to bring the Philippines and other possessions within the American orbit. More recent scholarship, however, has deemphasized the role of Roosevelt and noted that the orders of 25 February reflected a war plan developed earlier envisioning only the temporary retention of Manila. What began as a military operation against the Spanish squadron in the Philippines, however, soon became a responsibility that the administration was unable or unwilling to relinquish. Long became a reluctant expansionist. He saw no feasible alternative to keeping the islands, a decision he sincerely hoped would benefit their inhabitants. "If in so doing, he erred, as many believe today," David F. Trask wrote in 1981, "it was not because he was a fool, coward, criminal, or dupe. Many others travelled a similar road, including the President of the United States" (Trask, p. 456).

Indeed, Long compiled a credible record as secretary of the navy. To be sure, he had not come to his office as qualified as his predecessor, Hilary A. Herbert, and as he noted in his journal, Long made it "a point not to trouble myself overmuch to acquire a thorough knowledge of the details," leaving such "matters to the bureau chiefs" and "limiting myself to the general direction of affairs." Yet his journals for 1898 reflect almost incessant activity and frequent counsel with the president. By the time the war concluded in August 1898, Long had purchased over one hundred vessels, chartered others, and saw Congress authorize a doubling of enlisted strength. "Whatever the situation elsewhere in the government, the Navy Department responded efficiently to the challenge of 1898" (Trask, pp. 88–89).

The historian Paolo E. Coletta wrote in 1980, "For one who knew nothing about the Navy and did not bother to learn about its details, Long proved to be a fairly competent secretary." In 1897 the U.S. Navy ranked sixth, but by the time Long left office, the United States was the fourth rated naval power in the world. During his tenure, massive dry docks had been constructed capable of handling the navy's largest ships, and there was significant new construction at the Naval Academy. Long settled a controversy with domestic manufacturers over the price of armored plate. The navy made significant technological advances: an expanded use of electricity both on ship and on shore, the utilization of wireless telegraphy, and the adoption of submarines. While he had rejected Roosevelt's pleas to prepare for war in 1897, Long generally accepted the advice of the Naval Board on matters of strategy and tactics. His administration of the navy had "well passed the supreme test, that of war" (Coletta, p. 454).

Long's final years in office were not particularly happy, as he was drawn into the controversy between supporters of Commodore Winfield Scott Schley and Rear Admiral William T. Sampson. In 1899 McKinley advanced both men to the permanent rank of rear admiral but made Sampson senior by one number. Long came under increasingly bitter attack by friends of the popular Schley. A month after McKinley's assassination in September 1901, Long's daughter Helen Long died of tuberculosis. In addition to grieving for his beloved daughter, Long missed the companionship of his old friend President McKinley. He grew restless under McKinley's successor Roosevelt, whose impulsiveness and interference with the Navy Department annoyed Long. In April 1902 he resigned as secretary and returned to his law practice in Boston.

Long remained active after leaving Washington. In 1903 he published a two-volume work, *The New American Navy*. Although he was careful to praise the accomplishments of his predecessor and his own bureau chiefs, he took credit for the appointment of Dewey as commander of the Asiatic Squadron, noted his own role in sending instructions to Dewey in April 1898, and defended his position in the Schley-Sampson controversy. He was elected president of the Harvard Chapter of Phi Beta Kappa, the Harvard College Board of Overseers, and the Harvard Alumni Association. Long spent much of his time in Hingham or puttering around in Buckfield, where he had purchased his grandfather's farm as a summer residence. In 1912 he made a brief return to politics when he campaigned for William Howard Taft. Long died in Hingham.

• Long's papers and those of his family are in the Massachusetts Historical Society in Boston; Gardner Weld Allen published on behalf of the society the *Papers of John Davis Long, 1897–1904* (1939). Long's journals have been an important resource for scholars of the McKinley administration and the Spanish-American War; extracts are in Lawrence Shaw Mayo, *America of Yesterday: As Reflected in the Journal of John Davis Long* (1923). See also *The Journal of John D. Long*, ed. Margaret Long (1956), which includes many of the same entries published by Mayo but provides more detail on Long's personal life. Long's own publications include a translation of Virgil's *Aeneid* into blank verse (1879); an edited volume, *The Republican Party: Its History, Principles, and Policies* (1888); *After-dinner and Other Speeches* (1895); and a collection of poems, *At the Fireside* (1892). Long's recollection of the deficiences of his education is in "Reminiscences of My Seventy Years' Education," *Proceedings of the Massachusetts Historical Society* 42 (1909): 348–58. James W. Hess has evaluated Long as a reformer in "John D. Long and Reform Issues in Massachusetts Politics, 1870–1889," *New England Quarterly* 33 (1960): 57–73. Somewhat more favorable assessments of Long's career in Mass. are in Samuel Leland Powers, *Portraits of a Half Century* (1925); Solomon Bulkley Griffin, *People and Politics: Observed by a Massachusetts Editor* (1923); and George F. Hoar, *Autobiography of Seventy Years* (2 vols., 1903). Philip Putnam Chase, "A Crucial Juncture in the Political Careers of Lodge and Long," *Proceedings of the Massachusetts Historical Society* 70 (1950): 102–27, emphasizes the importance of the 1886 senatorial contest on both men's careers. Wendell D. Garrett, "John Davis Long, Secretary of the Navy, 1897–1902: A Study in Changing Political Alignments," *New England Quarterly* 31 (1958): 291–311, focuses on the slowly deteriorating relationship between Long and Roosevelt. John A. S. Grenville and George Berkeley Young, *Politics, Strategy, and American Diplomacy: Studies in Foreign Policy, 1873–1917* (1966), notes that offensive operations in the Philippines were undertaken in accordance with existing war plans. Paolo E. Coletta ably analyzed Long's role as secretary of the navy, "John Davis Long," in *American Secretaries of the Navy*, vol. 1 (1980). David F. Trask, in his definitive study *The War with Spain in 1898* (1981), details the preparations for war, the military campaigns, and the decision to retain all of the Philippines.

Ephraim K. Smith summarizes scholarship on the latter question, "William McKinley's Enduring Legacy: The Historiographical Debate on the Taking of the Philippine Islands," in *Crucible of Empire: The Spanish American War & Its Aftermath*, ed. James C. Bradford (1993). Bradford's volume also includes perspectives on the Schley-Sampson dispute by Joseph G. Dawson III, "William T. Sampson and Santiago: Blockade, Victory, and Controversy," and Harold D. Langley, "Winfield S. Schley and Santiago: A New Look at an Old Controversy."

EPHRAIM K. SMITH

LONG, John Luther (1 Jan. 1855–31 Oct. 1927), author and playwright, was born in Hanover, Pennsylvania, the son of Henry Long, a silversmith and merchant, and Sarah Dickinson Mitchell. After teaching school in local townships, he studied law in Hanover and was admitted to the bar in York County on 7 March 1881 and in Philadelphia on 29 October 1881. Long married Mary Jane Sprenkle in Hanover in 1882; they had one child, a son. For many years, Long practiced law in association with a real estate office in Philadelphia while he pursued a second career as a writer. Since he published in magazines under a variety of pseudonyms, the nature and scope of his early writings remain unclear. A first novel, *Miss Cherry-Blossom of Tôkyô* (1895), enjoyed a modest success in the United States and England as a charming variation on the theme of East-West romances made popular by Pierre Loti's *Madame Chrysanthème*.

Long achieved lasting success with his next major work, "Madame Butterfly," which appeared in the *Century Magazine* in January 1898. In the wake of the Spanish-American War and an increased American presence in Asia, the pathetic story of Cho-Cho-San, the overtrusting Japanese "girl-woman" betrayed by Lieutenant Pinkerton, generated interest and controversy. It gave the title to a collection of stories published in October ("Madame Butterfly," "Purple Eyes," "A Gentleman of Japan and a Lady," "Kito," and "Glory"), which went through several editions in the next two decades. Initial responses to the story were mixed. While some reviewers were charmed by its pathos, others remained unconvinced, particularly by the pidgin English of the heroine ("I'm mos' bes' happy female woman in Japan—mebby in that whole worl'"). Long never visited Japan. The story was based on an incident witnessed by his sister, Sara Jane Correll, wife of a Methodist Episcopal missionary stationed in Nagasaki. While visiting Philadelphia in 1897, she related the event to her brother, then provided information and corrected drafts to keep the story true to life. This attention to detail as well as the factual basis of the story give "Madame Butterfly" a focus often lacking in Long's writings. His stance against the exploitation of women in treaty-port marriages, and especially Pinkerton's actions, emerges in the final chapter, on the heroine's attempted suicide: "She now first knew that it was sad to die. He had come, and substituted himself for everything; he had gone, and left her nothing—nothing but this."

The success of the story prompted David Belasco to undertake a one-act stage adaptation. *Madame Butterfly* opened to enthusiastic reviews at New York's Herald Square Theater on 5 March 1900; it received its British premiere on 28 April at the Duke of York's Theatre, London. Puccini, who was in London to assist with rehearsals for the Covent Garden premiere of *Tosca*, saw the play on 21 June and was entranced by the subject. As Belasco's demands for royalties at first stalled negotiations for an operatic treatment, Puccini's librettists began with a scenario based on Long's story, which became act 1, then used the Belasco-Long play for acts 2 and 3. Puccini attended the Metropolitan Opera premiere on 11 February 1907, making a special trip to Philadelphia to discuss another project with Long, from which nothing materialized. Long did collaborate with other composers, providing the text for Horatio Parker's *A Song of Times*, op. 73 (1911), and orientalizing libretti for Wassili Leps, such as *Hoshi-san*.

After the success of *Madame Butterfly*, Long's career as a novelist and writer of short stories burgeoned for a decade. His publications include tales and novels, such as *The Fox-Woman* (1900), *Naughty Nan* and *Little Miss Joy-Sing* (1902), *Billy-Boy* and *The Way of the Gods* (1906), *Felice* (1908), and *Baby Grand* (1912), and several collections of stories: *The Prince of Illusion* (1901), *Sixty Jane* (1903), and *Heimweh* (1905). Two main types of subject predominate in Long's writings: orientalized—usually Japanese—stories and tales with Pennsylvania local color, the former facilitated by his sister's acquaintance with Japan, the latter often with a German or Pennsylvania Dutch tenor ("Ein Nixnutz," "Heimweh," "The Strike on the Schlafeplatz Railroad").

Long also wrote for the stage, achieving early successes with two extravagant melodramas written in collaboration with Belasco, the orientalist *The Darling of the Gods* (1902) and *Adrea* (1904), set in the last days of the Roman empire. His later plays, often written for particular leading ladies, were not successful: *The Dragon Fly* (with E. C. Carpenter, 1905), *Dolce* (for Minnie Maddern Fiske, 1906), *Remembrance* (with Carpenter, 1909), *Kassa* (for Leslie Carter, 1909), *Baby Grand* (1912), *War—or What Happens When One Loves One's Enemy* (1913), *Lady Betty Martingale* (for Fiske, 1914), *Billy Boy* (1915), and *Crowns* (1922).

Long characterized himself as "a sentimentalist and a feminist, and proud of it," a description supported by the large number of plays and stories written around a central female character. The sentimentality of his plays did not survive changing tastes after World War I, and attempts to mine the orientalizing vein that had proved so successful in "Madame Butterfly" never matched the success of that work. In an interview published in the *New York Tribune* after the failure of his last play, Long lamented that theater audiences had been jaded by "too much bedroom drama and too much farce" and that his reading public resisted Japanese experiments too dissimilar from "Madame Butterfly": "They want you to do the same thing all along.

They don't want you to branch out into something different" (19 Dec. 1922). Long died in Clifton Springs, New York.

• The Harry Ransom Humanities Research Center at the University of Texas at Austin has the largest collection of Long papers, including general and literary correspondence, literary works (mostly unpublished versions of short stories, plays, poetry, and librettos), and a collection of reviews and photographs. The Theatre Collection at the Free Library of Philadelphia has a smaller collection of typescripts, outlines and fragments, and some correspondence.

Background on the Long family can be obtained from William Gabriel Long's *History of the Long Family of Pennsylvania* (1930), while the birthdate given in earlier studies has been corrected by Arnold T. Schwab, "John Luther Long's Birthdate: A Correction," *American Literature* 50 (1978): 119. Biographical information on Long is scarce, owing to his reticence; the best source is a typescript copy of newspaper articles—from the *Hanover* (Pa.) *Evening Sun* as well as national newspapers—compiled by relatives and now at the public library in Hanover. William Winter's *Life of David Belasco* (1918) contains a partisan account of the collaboration with Long, while the background and genesis of *Madame Butterfly* has been traced by Arthur Groos, "Madame Butterfly: The Story," *Cambridge Opera Journal* 3 (1991): 125–58.

ARTHUR GROOS

LONG, Lois (15 Dec. 1901–29 July 1974), fashion critic and columnist, was born in Stamford, Connecticut, the daughter of William J. Long, a Congregationalist minister and lexicographer, and Frances Marsh Bancroft. She earned an A.B. in English from Vassar College in 1922 and immediately moved to New York City to begin a job as a copywriter for *Vogue*. The following year, while still writing for *Vogue*, she toured as a bit player in the play *The Dancers*. She returned to *Vogue* for part of 1924, but she later moved on to *Vanity Fair*, where she remained until 1925. During this period, while trying unsuccessfully to launch a Broadway acting career, she was primarily known as a "girl about town," a fixture at nightclubs, tea dances, and parties.

In 1925 Harold Ross founded the *New Yorker* and hired Long that same year as the anonymous "Lipstick," the writer for the important "Tables for Two" column reporting on cafe society. Here, according to a memorial in the *New Yorker*, Long's "embodiment of the glamorous insider" gave the column its "in-the-know" tone and provided Long with a method of combining her party girl persona and writing talent into a steady income, something her acting and copy writing could not provide.

Long embodied the atmosphere of the "Roaring Twenties Jazz Age," and her stories of those days are similar to a Fitzgerald novel. Remembering the heady days of parties and drinking, she would tell the exemplary tale of heading home in the early hours of the morning and realizing that her copy was due at noon. She went straight to the office, still in her backless to the waist evening gown, and "threw up a few times," but she met her deadline. Her tone was dry, witty, and often tongue-in-cheek. Reviewing a new singer, she wrote, "In an attempt to throw personality around the room, he has a tendency to grimace constantly in a nerve-wracking way, but otherwise he seems like a nice enough lad. And I like his voice" (*New Yorker*, 12 Feb. 1927).

Even at the height of the depression, she continued her upbeat tone, albeit with an eye to finances. She was not above tweaking dinner clubs for getting every penny from their customers or complaining about what she saw as exorbitant prices.

She married *New Yorker* cartoonist Peter Arno in 1927. They had one daughter before their divorce in 1932. She later married businessman Harold A. "Huck" Fox in 1953.

In 1927 Ross named her fashion editor of the magazine, and she began writing the column "On and Off the Avenue." It was here that Long proved herself to be an innovator. Wallace Shawn, a later editor of the *New Yorker*, claims that she "invented fashion criticism." Until Long, fashion criticism tended to be puff pieces aimed at stirring up reader interest in advertisers' goods. But Ross's determination to avoid advertising "blackmail" and Long's innate honesty combined to make her column one that set the standard for fashion criticism.

In his memoirs Shawn notes that Long was "the first American fashion critic to approach fashion as an art and to criticize women's clothes with independence, intelligence, humor, and literary style." She wrote for women like herself, educated, practical, and independent: the "New Woman" who did not want to be treated as a second-class person or a brainless fashion plate. Her tastes were informed by a desire to look attractive and feminine, yet she always kept an eye on the wearability and practicality of clothes. She would often resort to scornful mocking of clothes that she felt were too trendy, blasting the "dictators" of high fashion as being too arbitrary in their "proclamations" on fashion.

Because the *New Yorker* did not use photographs to illustrate its stories, Long literally had to paint pictures with her words. Her descriptions would often be as detailed as they were chatty. She would not only list colors available, but offer commentary, for instance, on the "yellowish peach color known as Rose of the Jungle (marvelous with sunburned skins)." And she would give her opinions freely: "The lingerie is more elaborate than the severe fashion dictators tell us it should be, but we must be frivolous somewhere!" (29 Jan. 1927).

The column covered more than clothing, for Long would discuss accessories and even makeup trends. In these areas too her fashion sense was informed by good taste, not trendiness. She was vocal in her opposition to what she felt was vulgar. In the 1960s when bright and heavy eye makeup was in vogue, she wrote, "I am troubled by the much too theatrical makeup that I see on midday streets, even if it is not as prevalent as the high-fashion people would have us believe" (25 Sept. 1965).

Brendon Gill, her colleague at the *New Yorker*, recalls in his memoirs that Long's combination of taking fashion seriously and her honesty soon gained her column a huge following with the magazine's female readers—upper-middle-class women with the money to spend on clothes. She went on telling the truth about fashion until her retirement in 1970 "with a wit and a lack of rancor that made her career an enviable one" (Gill, p. 206).

A champion of American design, Long also set a precedent in her coverage of American designers and proved a boon to the American fashion industry by being the only fashion columnist to actually visit and report on ready-to-wear wholesalers.

Long retired to her Pennsylvania home in 1970 and died there. Her contributions to the development of the American fashion industry is currently being studied by scholars, but her high-quality writing for the *New Yorker* stands alongside that of her colleagues as among the wittiest of the early half of the century.

• Long's columns in the *New Yorker's* "Tables for Two" are signed "Lipstick," and her "On and Off the Avenue" column, usually signed "L.L." but occasionally signed with her full name, appears regularly between 1927 and 1970. She is found in the memoirs of her colleagues, most notably in Brendon Gill's *Here at the New Yorker* (1975) and Jane Grant's *Ross, the New Yorker, and Me* (1968). Thomas Kunkel discusses her briefly in *Genius in Disguise: Harold Ross of the New Yorker* (1995). Her contribution to American fashion is briefly discussed in Caroline Rennolds Milbank's *New York Fashion: The Evaluation of American Style* (1989). Obituaries are in the *New York Times*, 31 July 1974, and the *New Yorker*, 12 Sept. 1974.

MARGARETTE R. CONNOR

LONG, Perrin Hamilton (7 Apr. 1899–17 Dec. 1965), physician, was born in Bryan, Ohio, the son of James Wilkerson Long, a physician, and Wilhelmina Lillian Kautsky. Long received his early education in Bryan and, after graduating from high school, entered the University of Michigan in 1916. In 1917 he left Michigan to join the American Field Service and served in France as an ambulance driver during World War I. When the United States entered the war, Long joined the armed forces and began an association with the military that continued with occasional interruptions throughout his career. For bravery in action he was awarded the croix de guerre in 1918. In 1919 he returned to the University of Michigan, and in 1924 he received a B.S. and an M.D. He married fellow undergraduate Elizabeth D. Griswold in September 1922; they had two children.

Long spent the next three years in Boston, Massachusetts, first at the Thorndyke Memorial Laboratory and then as an intern and resident at the Boston City Hospital. He continued his training by spending the year 1927 as a voluntary assistant at the Hygiene Institute in Freiburg, Germany. The following year he began work under Simon Flexner and Peter Olitski at the Rockefeller Institute in New York City, where he began his study of infectious diseases. In 1929 he joined the faculty of the Johns Hopkins Medical School, where he began his pioneering studies in infectious diseases and bacteriology as an assistant to Dr. Eleanor Bliss. Later Long learned of Gerhard Domag's discovery that sulfa drugs were effective against streptococcal infection and brought back a supply of prontosil from Europe in 1936. Long and Bliss tried the experimental drugs first on mice and then on humans and reported their preliminary findings in the autumn of 1936. Their demonstration of the effectiveness and safety of the sulfa drugs effected a revolution in the management of bacterial infections in the United States. These positive results brought recognition to Long, and in 1940 he was made professor and chairman of the Department of Preventive Medicine at Johns Hopkins.

During World War II Long was chosen, for his knowledge of the use of chemotherapy in infectious diseases, as one of a few consultants who were flown to Hawaii to advise treatment of the casualties of the Japanese attack on Pearl Harbor of 7 December 1941. In 1942 Long returned to active duty in the army and served in the African and Mediterranean theaters of military operations. On Long's retirement from the service following the war, he was awarded the Legion of Merit. Later, in recognition for his service to the Allies, he was awarded the Order of the British Empire (1945) and elected to the Royal College of Physicians in 1946. In 1951 he was made a Chevalier of the Legion of Honor.

Long returned to Johns Hopkins after his discharge from the service. In 1951 he became chairman of the Department of Medicine of the newly organized State University of New York Downstate Medical Center in Brooklyn, New York. Here he devoted his time to running the department and teaching, an activity in which he excelled. He also served in many advisory capacities for the National Research Council, the Veterans Administration, the Public Health Service, the Food and Drug Administration, and the U.S. Army. For his military service he was promoted to brigadier general. He was editor of *Medical Times* and *Resident Physician*.

In 1958 Long had a laryngectomy, which curtailed his activities for a short time. He returned to his usual busy routine after the operation, having learned to speak ably with an artificial larynx. By 1961, however, he felt that he had become less effective as a physician as well as a teacher and retired from academic life. He continued his two editorships and wrote widely on both social and scientific aspects of medicine. He died in Chapaquiddick Island, Massachusetts.

Long was one of the first of a new generation of medical clinicians and investigators who spent his entire career in academic medicine. He is remembered for introducing the use of chemotherapy into the United States.

• A collection of biographies and newspaper clippings about Long are at the Johns Hopkins Archives. Numerous letters of Long's are in various collections at the American Philosophical Society. Articles by Long include "Sulfapyridine," *Journal of the American Medical Association* 112, no. 6 (11 Feb. 1939): 538–39; and "A Varray Parfit Praktisour," *Medical Times* 94, no. 6 (June 1966): 687–702. His collaborations with Eleaner Bliss include "Para-Amino-Benzene-Sulfonamide and Its Derivatives," *Journal of the American Medical Association* 108 (2 Jan. 1937): 32–37; "Observations of the Mode of Action of Sulfanitamide," *Journal of the American Medical Association* 109, no. 19 (6 Nov. 1937): 1524–28; and, with W. Harry Feinstein, "Mode of Action, Chemical Use, and Toxic Manifestations of Sulfanitamide," *Journal of the American Medical Association* 112, no. 2 (14 Jan. 1939): 115–21. An obituary is in the *New York Times*, 18 Dec. 1965.

DAVID Y. COOPER

LONG, Robert Cary (c. 1770–21 Feb. 1833), builder and architect, was perhaps born in Maryland. Little is known of his childhood, but the clarity of thought and expression in his few surviving writings testify to a good education. By 1791 he was enrolled in the Carpenters' Society in Baltimore, serving as temporary secretary in 1797. In 1796 Long was operating a carpentry shop, and a few years later he opened a lumberyard. He was the contractor for the Assembly Rooms (1797–1798) and the jail (1800–1802), both in Baltimore and both designed by Nicholas Rogers, a wealthy amateur; successful completion of these large masonry structures demonstrated Long's organizational ability. In 1797 Long married Sarah Carnaghan; two children reached adulthood. From 1804 to 1813 he served on the committee to erect a state penitentiary. Long was a founding board member of the Mechanics Bank in 1804 and of the Baltimore Fire Insurance Company in 1808. Although few of his domestic works can be identified, Long's first important commission was for the Robert Oliver House in Baltimore (1805–1807; burned 1904). His first wife having died in 1807, Long married Anna Hamilton in 1809; they had six children.

Long was best known for his public buildings, many of which became landmarks in the developing city of Baltimore. Reflecting eighteenth-century English architectural trends, they included the Union Bank (1806–1809; demolished 1859), which was influenced by Sir John Soane, and the Palladian Holliday Street Theatre (1811–1813; burned 1873). Still standing are the Medical College on Lombard and Greene streets (1812–1813), inspired by the Roman Pantheon and eighteenth-century neoclassical variations on it; and the Baltimore Museum (1813–1814), now the Peale Museum on Holliday Street. This building is a three-story, five-bay Federal structure of brick, individualized by the conversion of the central bay into a tripartite pavilion of masonry, with Doric and Ionic columns on the first two levels and a large panel on the third.

Long's most notable achievement, St. Paul's P. E. Church (1814–1817; burned 1854), was the first seat of a bishopric built in the United States after the Revolution. In this church Long introduced two rows of tall columns into an auditorium, the type of which was developed in the late seventeenth century by Sir Christopher Wren and was systematized in the early eighteenth century by James Gibbs; thus Long created a longitudinal axis that focused on high-church ritual. A monumental entrance and great tower carried pairs of columns in the traditional vertical sequence from Doric to Composite, but the ancient Greek proportions and form used in the Doric order foreshadowed the Greek revival style that became popular in the 1820s.

In 1814, during the War of 1812, Long constructed military barracks and improved Baltimore's defenses. His last known architectural work was a row of seven houses (c. 1817–1822; four remain) on Hamilton Street, one of which was his home. These were simple, small, inexpensive houses of brick, without stoops or backbuildings, the fronts marked only by a string course separating the three-bay ground floor from the upper two stories, each of which contained one large window.

Although Long was called "architect" as early as 1814, and despite the fact that he adopted that title in 1824, other interests superseded his architectural practice. In 1816 he was a founding director of the Gas Light Company of Baltimore, and in 1818 he became the operating officer of the company; in 1817 he became a director of the Peale Museum. Long owned a third of the Lanvale Woolen Factory, and by 1831 he was an official of the Canton Company, participating in the development of an industrial park in eastern Baltimore.

Always active in carpenters' affairs, Long aided young carpenters and served occasionally as a trustee for the property of deceased or bankrupt colleagues. He laid out streets and evaluated the performance of contractors of public works for both the city of Baltimore and the state of Maryland. In 1832 he was honored with an appointment as a city commissioner and port warden.

Long's career typified the rise of a craftsman to higher social and economic levels, a route taken by many during this period. His architectural designs began in a conservative vein, but he introduced modern elements, such as a proper Greek order or a compositional device derived from Soane. At a time when no trained architect resided in Baltimore, Long designed several major buildings of different types, all of them contributions toward the urbanization of the new city. Although his later years were devoted to business interests, following his death in Baltimore, Long was remembered in a *Baltimore American* obituary as "much esteemed . . . a most valuable architect."

• Manuscript materials by Long are in the Maryland Historical Society, the Baltimore City Archives, and the Maryland State Archives. Family information and legend appear in a letter by Long's grandson T. Buckler Ghequiere, "The Messrs. Long, Architects," *American Architect and Building News* 1 (1876): 207. The fullest account of Long is given in Claire Wittler Eckels, "Baltimore's Earliest Architects, 1785–1820" (Ph.D. diss., Johns Hopkins Univ., 1950). Eckels's work is the source for Richard Hubbard Howland and Eleanor Patterson Spencer, *The Architecture of Baltimore* (1953). For more specific studies of Long and his works see Robert L. Alexander, "The Union Bank, by Long after Soane," *Journal of the Society of Architectural Historians* 22 (1963): 135–38; Alexander, "Nicholas Rogers, Gentleman-Architect of Baltimore," *Maryland Historical Magazine* 78 (1983): 85–105; and Alexander, "'Wealth Well Bestowed in Worship': St. Paul's in Baltimore from Robert Cary Long, Sr., to Richard Upjohn," *Maryland Historical Magazine* 86 (1991): 122–49. For discussion of a work built, but not designed, by Long, see Paul F. Norton, "The Architect of Calverton," *Maryland Historical Magazine* 76 (1981): 113–23. An obituary is in the *Baltimore American*, 23 Feb. 1833.

ROBERT L. ALEXANDER

LONG, Stephen Harriman (30 Dec. 1784–4 Sept. 1864), army explorer and engineer, was born in Hopkinton, New Hampshire, the son of Moses Long, a farmer, tradesman, and local politician, and Lucy Harriman. In 1809 he graduated from Dartmouth College, and he spent the next five years teaching at Salisbury, New Hampshire, and Germantown, Pennsylvania. In those positions he demonstrated a high level of mathematical skill while becoming a surveyor and an inventor. Soon he came to the attention of U.S. army chief of engineers General Joseph Swift. Swift encouraged Long to join the Corps of Engineers, and on 12 December 1814 he accepted a commission as a second lieutenant. Shortly after that he became an assistant professor of mathematics at West Point, a position he held for the next year. In 1816 he received a promotion to the rank of brevet major and was assigned to the topographical engineers. He would remain in that organization for most of the next four decades.

A man of immense energy, Long wanted to explore the West and envisioned himself as the logical successor to Lewis and Clark. During 1816 and 1817 he crisscrossed Illinois, Iowa, Indiana, and Missouri, examining army garrisons and gathering general scientific data about the region. In 1817 he led a small party up the Mississippi River to the site of Minneapolis, where he dealt with the Indians and sought future sites for military posts. During the winter of 1817–1818 he traveled up the Arkansas River, choosing the site for what became Fort Smith, Arkansas. Later in 1818 Secretary of War John C. Calhoun decided to have Long organize and lead a scientific expedition up the Missouri River to the Rocky Mountains. He ordered the major to Pittsburgh, where Long designed and supervised the construction of a steamboat, the *Western Engineer*, that was to carry the scientists west.

While waiting for the final tests on the steamer, Long slipped away to Philadelphia, where on 3 March 1819 he married Martha Hodgkins. The couple had five children during their marriage. On 5 May 1819 the *Western Engineer* began its journey down the Ohio River to St. Louis. Long had assembled an impressive group of scientists for the expedition, including William Baldwin, Titian R. Peale, Thomas Say, and Samuel Seymour. Despite their long-awaited start, trouble with the steamboat design and machinery, a lack of efficient fuel, and the muddy Missouri River water all combined to slow the boat. Frequent breakdowns hindered upriver progress so that when the scientists halted near present Omaha, Nebraska, in September

1819, they had fallen far short of earlier expectations. As a result, the War Department ended its effort to explore the western rivers by steamboat.

The following summer Long and a much-reduced party of soldiers and scientists set out to explore the central plains. Drought, lack of horses, an inadequate supply of food, and faulty maps caused the explorers much difficulty. They traveled west to the Rocky Mountains and then south to the Arkansas River. There half of the party turned east while Long led the rest south in search of the headwaters of the Red River. They hunted in vain, and having depleted their food and water, they headed east along one of the branches of the Canadian River, having failed to locate the Red. The scientists dispersed at Fort Smith as they returned east. Long's negative description of the central plains as the Great American Desert appeared on maps for the next generation. The explorers published their findings in the three-volume *Account of an Expedition from Pittsburgh to the Rocky Mountains . . .* (1823), compiled by Edwin James.

In 1823 the War Department dispatched Long to explore the headwaters of the Mississippi River and the border between the United States and Canada. He led a small group of soldiers and scientists up the Mississippi and then up the Red River of the north to Lake of the Woods. From there they turned east along the north shore of Lake Superior. This trek produced fewer scientific results than had the plains expedition and essentially ended Long's career as an explorer. His companion William H. Keating published their findings as a *Narrative of an Expedition to the Source of St. Peter's River, Lake Winnepeek, Lake of the Woods . . .* (2 vols., 1824).

For the next four decades Long turned his efforts to transportation developments. In 1827 he went on detached duty to become a consulting engineer for the new Baltimore and Ohio Railroad. He helped select its route, served on its board of engineers, and wrote his *Rail Road Manual* (1829), which included many of the principles used in building the road through the mountains. For the next several years he remained on detached duty while serving as a consulting engineer for other eastern railroads. During these years he also published two treatises on bridge building. Back on active duty, he supervised efforts to dredge the navigation channels in the Ohio, Arkansas, Red, and Mississippi rivers. He also supervised the construction and operation of maritime hospitals for riverboatmen. When the Civil War broke out, he was called east to Washington, D.C., and on 9 September 1861 he was promoted to the rank of colonel. In 1863 he retired, and the next year he died at Alton, Illinois.

Stephen Long's career illustrates the basic contributions that the army engineers made to U.S. science and technology during the first half of the nineteenth century. Long's efforts to bring leading scientists into federal exploration laid the basis for much of later exploration in the West. He helped the young nation through his engineering work on early railroads and with his efforts to keep the rivers open for travel and economic development.

• There is no extensive collection of Long papers, but his official correspondence may be found in various record groups at the National Archives. The most thorough study of his life is Richard G. Wood, *Stephen Harriman Long, 1784–1864* (1966). For an examination of his contributions as an explorer, see Roger L. Nichols and Patrick L. Halley, *Stephen Long and American Frontier Exploration* (1980). An account written during Long's lifetime is John Livingston, "Colonel Stephen H. Long of the United States Army," in his *Portraits of Eminent Americans Now Living* (4 vols., 1853–1854). Harry B. Weiss and Grace M. Ziegler, *Thomas Say: Early American Naturalist* (1931), and Jessie Poesch, ed., *Titian Ramsay Peale, 1799–1885* (1961), focus on several of Long's scientific companions. Joseph A. Ewan, *Rocky Mountain Naturalists* (1950); Susan D. McKelvey, *Botanical Exploration of the Trans-Mississippi West, 1790–1850* (1955); and Carl I. Wheat, *Mapping the Trans-Mississippi West, 1540–1861* (5 vols., 1957–1963), all place Long's explorations in the context of broad scientific development during the middle of the nineteenth century.

ROGER L. NICHOLS

LONG, Sylvester Clark (1 Dec. 1890–20 Mar. 1932), writer and actor, was born in Winston (now Winston-Salem), North Carolina, the son of Joseph Long, a school janitor, and Sallie Carson. His family had a mixed-race background. His mother was part white, part Indian; his father, a former slave, was part Indian and probably part white and black. On reaching school age in 1897, Long learned the full meaning of his family's classification as "colored." Although the six-year-old lived just three blocks away from an elementary school, it was for whites, and he was forced to attend the school for blacks, which was two miles away. From an early age he longed to escape the segregationist system, and his appearance—he looked Indian rather than black or white—allowed him to do so. At age thirteen he left home to join a Wild West show, where he was accepted by the performers as an Indian. He returned home briefly in 1909, just long enough to apply to the Carlisle Indian School in Pennsylvania as part Cherokee and part Croatan (a Cherokee with the Wild West show had taught him some words in Cherokee). Carlisle accepted him.

Long entered grade six, but his teachers quickly accelerated him when they saw evidence of his abilities. At school his teachers helped him develop an appreciation for literature, and they encouraged him to write. He also excelled at sports. At age twenty-one Sylvester Long Lance, as he now called himself, graduated at the head of Carlisle's senior class. Carlisle immediately enrolled him at Conway Hall, the preparatory school for neighboring Dickinson College. The following year he won a scholarship to St. John's Military Academy, near Syracuse, New York, which he attended from 1913 to 1915.

In 1916 the United States had not yet entered the First World War. Anxious to fight, Long went north to Montreal and enlisted in the Canadian Expeditionary Force. He served overseas in the trenches and was twice seriously wounded. When asked after the war where he preferred his discharge, he selected Calgary, a city in Alberta, the last Canadian province to be settled.

Proudly identifying himself as an Oklahoma Cherokee, Long (going by the name Long Lance) worked as a reporter for the Calgary *Herald* from 1919 to 1922, writing a series in 1921 on the Indians of southern Alberta. Also during this period, while on a visit to the Blood Indians, members of the Blackfoot Confederacy, he made a special friend of the Reverend S. H. Middleton, the reservation's Anglican missionary. The following year, Middleton arranged for his guest to be adopted as a Blood Indian by the graduates and friends of St. Paul's, the Anglican residential school on the reservation. The old warrior Mountain Horse named the Cherokee journalist Buffalo Child.

Upon leaving Calgary in 1922, Long took his new Indian name and tribal identity as a Blood or Blackfoot Indian with him. He worked first on a series on the Indians of British Columbia for the Vancouver *Sun* and then wrote a series on the Indians of Saskatchewan for the Regina *Leader* and another series on the Indians of Manitoba for the Winnipeg *Tribune*. Now calling himself Chief Buffalo Child Long Lance, he wrote newspaper and magazine articles out of Winnipeg from 1923 to 1925. Major North American publications bought his stories on the North American Indians. Finally, in 1926, he decided to try and make it as a writer in New York City.

Throughout 1927 Long worked on what he claimed was his autobiography, which was published in 1928. Entitled *Long Lance*, the book began: "The first thing in my life that I can remember is the exciting aftermath of an Indian fight in northern Montana." Tales followed of his Blackfoot boyhood on the plains in the days of the last buffalo hunts and of his band's adventures on hunting expeditions in the Rocky Mountains. The critics loved it. Paul Radin, a well-known American anthropologist, praised the book in the New York *Herald-Tribune* (14 Oct. 1928) as an "unusually faithful account of his childhood and early manhood." A British edition of *Long Lance* followed, as did full translations into German and Dutch in 1929.

After Douglas Burden, a young naturalist and film producer, saw the striking portrait of Buffalo Child presented in the book, he approached Long and asked him to take the leading role in his new film, "The Silent Enemy," about the life of the Indians of northern Canada before the arrival of the Europeans. Long accepted. When the film was released in 1930, *Variety* praised his performance: "Chief Long Lance is an ideal picture Indian, because he is a full-blooded one . . . an author of Indian lore, and now an actor in fact."

Only one year later, however, Long's past caught up with him. In early 1931 his brother Walter contacted him in New York City. Their father was desperately sick in Winston-Salem, and the family needed money to pay his doctor and hospital bills. The two brothers had not met for twenty-two years. Long agreed to send money home, but he would not return himself and risk

the disclosure that his family was classified as "colored." He had spent over half his life lying about his background, and then lying again to cover up his lies.

Sylvester Long's love of his new identity as Chief Buffalo Child Long Lance won out over his love for his family. But the pain of his decision eventually killed him. In the year that followed he became more and more unstable. In the late spring of 1931 he took the job of secretary and bodyguard to Anita Baldwin, a wealthy philanthropist in California. In the library of her mansion in Arcadia, near Los Angeles, he shot himself fatally through the head.

• A substantial collection of materials written by and about Long is housed in the archives of the Glenbow Museum in Calgary, Alberta, Canada. For a fuller discussion, see Donald B. Smith, *Long Lance: The True Story of an Imposter* (1982).

DONALD B. SMITH

LONGACRE, James Barton (11 Aug. 1794–1 Jan. 1869), artist and engraver, was born in Delaware County, Pennsylvania, the son of Peter Longacre. He began drawing while still a boy, and his talent was noticed by the Philadelphia bookseller and antiquarian John Fanning Watson, whom he served as an apprentice. Watson subsequently apprenticed him to the Philadelphia engraver George Murray. Longacre established his own engraving business in 1819. His first important commission came the following year when he engraved the portraits of George Washington, Thomas Jefferson, and John Hancock that appeared on John Binns's facsimile of the Declaration of Independence. His next major project was to engrave the portraits for John Sanderson's *Biographies of the Signers to the Declaration of Independence*, published in nine volumes between 1820 and 1827 in Philadelphia. For this publication he engraved twenty-three plates by himself and two in conjunction with another engraver. He also supervised the other engravers and the printing of the plates. By the time the last volume was published, his skills both as an artist and an engraver had grown impressively, and he ranked among the leading engravers in the United States.

The success of Sanderson's publication gave Longacre the idea for another book of illustrated biographies, one that would consist of living Americans only. By his own account he had been planning this since 1824. A lack of financing prevented him from undertaking it immediately upon completion of the last of Sanderson's volumes, but by 1831 he had earned enough from his engraving business to begin work. Longacre was deeply interested in portraiture, and the primary purpose of his book was to disseminate first-rate engravings of the best portraits available of America's leading citizens. There would be brief biographies of these individuals, but they would be secondary to the portrait engravings. The United States at that time was caught up in sectional rivalries, and Longacre hoped his publication would "produce a community of feeling. . . . It introduces the Arts, as a peace offering to the angry and jealous passions, that are striking at our Nation's heart" (quoted in Marshall, p. 59). By early 1831 he had signed a contract to supply 1,500 copies of his book, which he entitled *American Portrait Gallery*, and he invested $1,000 of his own money in the project.

Longacre was brought up short, however, in October 1831 when he saw a prospectus for a similar undertaking by New York artist James Herring. Herring's proposed book, modeled on an English publication titled *National Portrait Gallery* then enjoying good sales in the United States, was called *The National Portrait Gallery of Distinguished Americans*. It differed from Longacre's in that it would include historical as well as living Americans and would have longer biographical sketches. As the market was not large enough for two similar works, the men joined forces, and Longacre easily adapted his ideas to Herring's. Herring oversaw the editorial side of the enterprise, commissioning—and sometimes writing—the biographical sketches, securing subscribers, and occasionally painting portraits to serve as models for the engravings. Longacre served as the art editor. He drew many of the portraits from life, copied historical portraits, and engraved both his own and others' work. He also had the daunting responsibility of locating original portraits to copy (which often involved travel to distant places), coordinating 144 plates by twenty-six different engravers, and supervising the printing of those plates. Despite the size and complexity of the task, Longacre achieved a high standard of quality, and the engravings were among the best produced in America up to that time. It is Longacre's great achievement that he both demanded such high quality and got it. Much of his own best work appeared in the book. He did a sepia drawing from life of William Wirt, U.S. attorney general, which he then engraved; critics then and art historians now consider both the drawing and the engraving to be his finest work in each medium. Other notables who sat for Longacre included John C. Calhoun, Andrew Jackson, James Madison, and Daniel Webster. His engravings, after other artists, of John Adams, Nicholas Biddle, Daniel Boone, Samuel Chase, Francis Hopkinson, John Paul Jones, Alexander Macomb, and David Rittenhouse also received favorable contemporary comment. One reviewer noted that they were "engraved on a style that would do credit to any work of art."

Longacre and Herring issued *The National Portrait Gallery of Distinguished Americans* in four volumes. The first was published in 1834, the second the next year. Until then there had been no major problems. But flagging subscriptions and difficulties in collecting money owed, coupled with a fire at the bindery in New York, delayed the publication of volume three; and the panic of 1837 and ensuing depression postponed publication of volume four until 1839. Longacre had gone deeply into debt in order to produce as high quality a publication as possible, and he voluntarily declared bankruptcy. By 1842, however, he had paid off all his creditors.

Longacre returned to engraving and executed a series of engraved likenesses (after originals by other artists) of prominent religious figures. These appeared in publications issued by the American Sunday School Union. In 1844 he was appointed chief engraver of the U.S. Mint, a post he held for the rest of his life. As chief engraver, he was responsible for the designs of coinage and currency, including the gold dollar and the first $3 gold piece, both produced in 1854. He continued to draw an occasional portrait, mainly of members of his family. Although he no longer controlled the rights to *The National Portrait Gallery of Distinguished Americans*, he continued to take an interest in its subsequent reissues and offered advice to the new publishers both on how to extend the life of the engraving plates and on additional persons to be included in the later editions.

Longacre married Eliza Stiles; they had at least two children. Longacre died in Philadelphia.

The National Portrait Gallery of Distinguished Americans was a milestone in American publishing. It remained in print for many years (the last edition was in 1868) and served as the model for other publications. (One of these, the *National Portrait Gallery of Eminent Americans*, not only had a similar title, but its illustrations were based on those in the Longacre and Herring work.) Longacre's own contribution was of immense importance. In striving for the highest quality, he reached a standard not seen before in American book illustration and seldom equaled afterward. Many of his own life portraits of prominent Americans became the best-known likenesses of those individuals and were still being reproduced late in the twentieth century.

• Longacre's papers are in the National Portrait Gallery, Smithsonian Institution, Washington, D.C., and the Library Company of Philadelphia. Most of his original drawings for *The National Portrait Gallery of Distinguished Americans* are now owned by the National Portrait Gallery. Others belong to the Library Company of Philadelphia. The National Portrait Gallery also owns three self-portrait drawings and an ambrotype portrait by Isaac Rehn. George C. Groce and David H. Wallace, *The New-York Historical Society's Dictionary of Artists in America, 1564–1860* (1957), and Robert G. Stewart, *A Nineteenth-century Gallery of Distinguished Americans* (1969), give accounts of Longacre's life and career. The best account of *The National Portrait Gallery of Distinguished Americans* project is Gordon M. Marshall, "The Golden Age of Illustrated Biographies: Three Case Studies," in *American Portrait Prints*, ed. Wendy Wick Reaves (1984).

DAVID MESCHUTT

LONGCOPE, Warfield Theobald (29 Mar. 1877–25 Apr. 1953), pathologist and educator, was born in Baltimore, Maryland, the son of George von S. Longcope and Ruth Theobald, whose occupations are unknown. After receiving his A.B. from Johns Hopkins University in 1897, he enrolled in the university's medical school, at the time the only one in the United States that required its students to ground themselves in laboratory work as well as the bedside examination of patients. He received his M.D. in 1901 and immediately accepted a position as resident pathologist at Philadelphia's Pennsylvania Hospital.

In 1904 Longcope became director of the hospital's Ayer Clinical Laboratory, a state-of-the-art facility that under his supervision developed considerable expertise in the study of bacteriology, biochemistry, and serology. His own laboratory investigations covered a number of topics including pneumococcal and streptococcal bacteria (thus earning for him the epithet "Bugs"), aortic insufficiency, and Hodgkin's disease, a form of cancer that attacks the lymphatic system. He took it upon himself to educate the hospital's medical staff, most of whom had no training in laboratory work and therefore did not appreciate its value as a diagnostic tool, to the importance of combining laboratory findings with clinical observations in order to arrive at a better understanding of a particular patient's condition. In 1909 he assumed the additional duties of assistant professor of applied medicine at the University of Pennsylvania, where he introduced the Hopkins method of imparting laboratory competence and a well-planned bedside manner to medical students.

In 1911 Longcope became an associate professor of the practice of medicine at Columbia University's College of Physicians and Surgeons, where he continued to develop in his students an appreciation for both laboratory and clinical skills. In 1914, the year before he married Janet Percy Dana with whom he had four children, he was appointed Bard Professor of the Practice of Medicine. He also assisted at New York City's Presbyterian Hospital as an associate physician between 1911 and 1914, and in the latter year he was made director of its medical service. While at Columbia he became interested in the susceptibility of humans to foreign proteins as a cause of many so-called natural diseases and in the process helped to initiate the study of allergies. To this end he examined several aspects of hypersensitivity including the effect of repeated injections of foreign protein on the heart muscle, the potential for chronic protein intoxication in animals to result in severe system shock, and the potential for urticaria, a vascular reaction of the skin caused by external irritants, to inhibit the functioning of the kidneys.

When the United States entered World War I in 1917 Longcope was commissioned a major in the Medical Officers Reserve Corps and assigned to the army's Office of the Surgeon General in Washington, D.C. In 1918 he was promoted to lieutenant colonel and went to France as part of the American Expeditionary Force's Medical Corps. The bulk of his wartime duties involved investigating the epidemics of influenza and pneumonia that broke out in the American trenches.

In 1919 Longcope returned to his duties at Columbia and Presbyterian. In 1922 he taught for a semester at Cornell University's Medical College and served as visiting physician at the second division of New York's Bellevue Hospital before returning that same year to Hopkins as chairman of the department of medicine

and chief physician of its hospital. Although he continued to investigate the causes of a number of diseases, he remained highly interested in hypersensitivity as a cause of disease, particularly nephritis. In 1929 he advanced the theory that this condition, a severe inflammation of the kidney that is often fatal, results from an allergic reaction by the kidney's tissue to streptococcal infection, a theory that enjoyed a great deal of currency for a number of years thereafter, but has since been discredited. During World War II he discovered that British Anti-Lewisite, an antidote for several forms of chemical warfare agents, was also useful for treating civilian patients who suffered from mercury or arsenic poisoning.

In 1946 Longcope retired from Hopkins and moved to the Berkshire Mountains in western Massachusetts. He spent the remaining years of his life consulting for several hospitals in the neighboring counties, conducting clinics for undergraduate students at Albany (N.Y.) Medical School, and serving as a research adviser for that school and the New York State Department of Health Laboratories.

Longcope was a founder of the American Academy for the Study of Allergy, served as president of the Society for Clinical Investigation in 1919, the American Association of Immunologists in 1935, and the Association of American Physicians (AAP) from 1945 to 1946; and was a member of the Board of Scientific Directors of the Rockefeller Institute for Medical Research. He received the AAP's George M. Kober Medal in 1948 and was elected to membership in the National Academy of Sciences, the American Association for the Advancement of Science, and the American Academy of Arts and Sciences. He died in Lee, Massachusetts.

Longcope made two important contributions to the development of American medicine. His role in "spreading the gospel" to physicians and medical students concerning the importance of laboratory work helped to elevate the general quality of medical diagnosis in the United States. His research shed much light on the role played by allergic reactions as a cause of disease.

• Longcope's papers are in the Alan Mason Chesney Medical Archives at Johns Hopkins University. A biography, including a bibliography, is William S. Tillett, "Warfield Theobald Longcope," in National Academy of Sciences, *Biographical Memoirs* 33 (1959): 205–25. Obituaries are in the *New York Times*, 26 Apr. 1953; *American Medical Association Journal* 13 (June 1953); and *School and Society*, 2 May 1953.

CHARLES W. CAREY, JR.

LONGFELLOW, Henry Wadsworth (27 Feb. 1807–24 Mar. 1882), poet and professor of modern languages, was born in Portland, Maine, then a part of the Commonwealth of Massachusetts, the son of Stephen Longfellow, a lawyer and legislator, and Zilpah Wadsworth. In 1825 he was graduated from Bowdoin College, in the same class with Nathaniel Hawthorne. Though primarily interested in writing, Longfellow was preparing for a legal career when Bowdoin offered him a professorship of modern languages, one of the first to be established in America. The position required that he first go to Europe to qualify himself further for his duties. The originally contemplated year's absence stretched out to three, involving visits to France, Spain, Italy, and Germany.

Longfellow taught at Bowdoin from 1829 to 1835, during which period he published several textbooks and contributed linguistic and literary articles to the *North American Review*. In 1833 he translated the *Coplas de Jorge Manrique*, but his independent career in belles lettres began with a prose work, *Outre-Mer: A Pilgrimage beyond the Sea*, published in parts in 1833 and 1834 and as a book in 1835. In 1831 he married Mary Storer Potter, the daughter of a Portland jurist.

In 1834 Longfellow accepted the Smith professorship of French and Spanish at Harvard College, succeeding George Ticknor, who had advised him about his earlier European sojourn. Before assuming his teaching duties, Longfellow was again required to go to Europe for further study. He and his wife sailed in April 1835. In Holland, in October, Mary had a miscarriage, and the next month she died at Rotterdam. She was, Longfellow later wrote in "Footsteps of Angels," "the Being Beauteous, / Who unto my youth was given." In December 1836 Longfellow returned to Cambridge and the next summer took lodging in the historic Craigie House, which once served as George Washington's headquarters.

Longfellow's career as a writer moved forward with the publication in 1839 of *Hyperion*, a prose romance that enjoyed a success not wholly comprehensible today; European travelers long used it as a kind of guidebook. More permanently significant was his first collection of lyrics, *Voices of the Night* (1839). Two years later *Ballads and Other Poems* brought the first revelation of his gifts as a storyteller. In 1842, on his way home from a water cure in Germany, he wrote *Poems on Slavery*, his most important contribution to the abolitionist movement.

While traveling in Switzerland during the summer of 1836, Longfellow had met Fanny Appleton, daughter of the wealthy Boston merchant Nathan Appleton. From their first meeting, Longfellow had been strongly attracted to her, but his courtship did not run smoothly. Among other things, he had offended her by making a veiled presentation of his passion in *Hyperion*, and he practically gave up hope of winning her. "The Bridge" preserves a record of his sufferings during this period. She had a change of heart, however, and the two were married in the summer of 1843. After their marriage they lived together in Craigie House, which Nathan Appleton had purchased for them as a wedding gift. It remained Longfellow's home for the rest of his life. Later designated the Longfellow National Historic Site, it has been kept as a shrine to his memory.

His second marriage, which produced six children, seems to have been as nearly ideal as any union can be. But it ended tragically in 1861: Fanny Longfellow was burned to death when hot sealing wax, with which she was doing up locks of her children's hair in packets, ignited her light summer dress.

In 1843 Longfellow published a closet drama, *The Spanish Student*, and in 1845 he published another collection of lyrics, *The Belfry of Bruges and Other Poems*, containing "The Arsenal at Springfield," "The Arrow and the Song," "The Old Clock on the Stairs," and his first important Indian poem, "To the Driving Cloud." In 1847 he further established his reputation with *Evangeline: A Tale of Acadie*. This story of the expulsion of the Acadians from their homeland by the British during the French and Indian War had been told to him by Hawthorne. Written in dactylic hexameter, it was not only Longfellow's first long poem, but the first long poem in American letters to live beyond its own time.

In 1845 Longfellow edited and translated material for a huge anthology, *The Poets and Poetry of Europe*, which fit his academic interests and performed an immensely important service in introducing many European writers to American readers. He had already edited and published a small anthology of verse, *The Waif* (1845), which was followed by another, *The Estray*, in 1846. After that he edited no more anthologies until 1876–1879, when he brought out *Poems of Places*, a kind of immense poetic gazeteer, in thirty-one volumes. In 1849 he produced his last piece of prose fiction, *Kavanagh*, a story of New England village life that presaged, if dimly, the coming local color movement.

The Seaside and the Fireside (1850), which included "The Building of the Ship," was Longfellow's most significant book reflecting public affairs. The long poem *The Golden Legend* (1851), set in the Middle Ages, failed to please Longfellow's usual admirers, but it was shortly followed by two resounding triumphs, *The Song of Hiawatha* (1855) and *The Courtship of Miles Standish* (1858).

Hiawatha was described by the poet as an "Indian Edda." Though it has some epic characteristics, it is essentially a collection of traditional tales derived mainly from the writings of the ethnologist and explorer Henry Rowe Schoolcraft, who hailed it as the first literary work in which the American Indian was treated seriously and respectfully, and the Moravian missionary John G. E. Heckewelder. The much ridiculed and easily imitated trochaic tetrameter of the poem came from the Finnish epic *Kalevala*; this meter made *Hiawatha* the most parodied poem in the English language. *Miles Standish*, also written in hexameter, is shorter, simpler, and much more unified, and the material of which it is composed was more familiar to Longfellow.

Tales of a Wayside Inn (1863), probably the most famous American poetic storybook and certainly Longfellow's largest collection of narrative poems, appeared serially. The *Tales* vary in type, derivation, quality, and popularity; some have achieved an independent life apart from the framework in which the poet placed them. The longest and most ambitious,

"The Saga of King Olaf," is Longfellow's boldest essay in the epic mood; "The Ballad of Carmilhan" is a successful venture into the supernatural; and "Emma and Eginhard" achieves a somewhat astonishing sexual frankness for Longfellow. Most famous is the opening tale, "Paul Revere's Ride," which was off to a running start from its initial appearance in the *Atlantic Monthly* just as the Civil War was beginning.

Much of Longfellow's energy following his wife's death went into his translation of Dante's *Divine Comedy*, published in three volumes in 1865–1867. Liberally annotated, it combined the interests of the poet and the scholar and long remained a standard work. In 1866 Longfellow published another miscellaneous collection, *Flower-de-Luce*, which included the grim Civil War poem "Killed at the Ford," a poetic tribute to Hawthorne, and a series of sonnets about *The Divine Comedy*. Other sonnets appeared in later volumes. Longfellow was by far the finest metrist among the poets of what Van Wyck Brooks would call "the flowering of New England." Even those who do not care much for some of his more ambitious works can generally be counted on to award his sonnets high praise. In 1867–1870 the Household Edition of Longfellow's collected poems was published.

Though he was only fifty-four when his second wife died, Longfellow never remarried. However, he did have many friendships with women, most of whom were much younger than he was. Among these were the Mississippi local color writer Sherwood Bonner and the singers Blanche Roosevelt and Frances Rowena Miller. How much interest he had in Cornelia Fitch, whom he met while summering at Nahant, Massachusetts, is not clear, but her family seems to have been sufficiently alarmed by the attentions she received both from him and from his son Charles to snatch her hurriedly away. Rather more is known about Alice Frere, to whom he may indeed have proposed marriage when she was in Boston in 1867.

During the later years of his life, Longfellow turned increasingly toward the dramatic or semidramatic form, for which he had no special gift. In 1868 *The New England Tragedies* appeared, comprising *John Endicott* and *Giles Corey of the Salem Farm*, followed in 1871 by his long-pondered but on the whole undistinguished treatment of scenes from the life of Christ, *The Divine Tragedy*. In 1872 *Judas Maccabeus*, based on the Old Testament Apocrypha, appeared in *Three Books of Song*. That same year, apparently undeterred by the comparatively cold reception *The Golden Legend* had already received, he gathered it, along with *The Divine Tragedy* and *The New England Tragedies*, into an immense trilogy called *Christus: A Mystery*. His announced purpose in producing the trilogy was to illustrate Christian faith and practice in ancient, medieval, and modern times, but few, if any, people have ever understood how Longfellow could have thought Salem witchcraft representative of modern Christianity. The rather Faustian medievalism of *The Golden Legend* is the best part of the trilogy. Longfellow was a Unitarian, but he was not doctrinaire about it, and his

Dante studies and other scholarly interests had given him an appreciation of Catholicism uncommon in the New England of his time.

The title piece in *The Masque of Pandora and Other Poems* (1875) is an opera, which was performed in Boston with Blanche Roosevelt, but the most distinguished piece in the volume is the "Morituri Salutamus," a fiftieth-anniversary poem for a Bowdoin College reunion. In comparison, "The Hanging of the Crane," Longfellow's most elaborate performance in his familiar role as the poet of the domestic affections, seems commonplace.

Like "The Hanging of the Crane," which had first been published separately in 1874, "Kéramos," a long poem about potters and pottery, first appeared alone in 1877. The next year it was published in *Kéramos and Other Poems*. *Ultima Thule*, published in 1880, was the last collection to appear during the poet's lifetime. His final collection, *In the Harbor* (1882), was published after his death, along with *Michael Angelo* (1882–1883), a dramatic poem into which he poured many of his most mature musings about art, life, and destiny.

Longfellow was enormously popular, especially during his later years; at the end of his life, his birthday was even being celebrated in schools. He was as beloved in England as in America; people from everywhere came to see him, and his last trip to Europe in 1868–1869 was virtually a triumphant processional. Queen Victoria received him in a private audience, and both Oxford and Cambridge gave him honorary degrees. He was the first front-ranking New England poet of his time to die, and his death in Cambridge, closely followed by that of Ralph Waldo Emerson, for many marked the end of an era.

Emerson, his mind almost gone, attended Longfellow's funeral. He could not remember the name of "the sleeper," but he was sure he had had "a beautiful soul," and to this judgment there have been virtually no dissenters. William Dean Howells's words, "all other men I have known had some foible, or pettiness, or bitterness, but Longfellow had none, nor the suggestion of any," may seem adulatory, but his claim has not been refuted.

Longfellow's literary reputation, like Tennyson's, has suffered from the inevitable changes in poetic style and taste. He has been called too didactic, but when he began writing he was widely blamed for sacrificing uplift to purely aesthetic considerations. "A Psalm of Life" (1839) seems one of his poorest poems, but his contemporaries, including the French poet Charles Baudelaire, found it deeply moving. An impatient reader and writer, Longfellow wanted everything stated as quickly and as plainly as possible, not left to implication and inference. Yet he was a scholar and far less simple than his work suggests. He admired the primitive, and in his Indian poems and elsewhere he introduced important native materials into American literature. Yet he also played an important part in establishing modern languages in the American educational curriculum, and he labored valiantly to introduce American readers to large aspects of the literature and art of Europe, encouraging them to enter into the common cultural inheritance of Western culture.

• The important depositories of Longfellow manuscripts and papers are the Houghton Library at Harvard University and the Longfellow National Historic Site in Cambridge. The authorized biography is by the poet's brother, Samuel Longfellow, *Life of Henry Wadsworth Longfellow, with Extracts from His Journals and Correspondence* (2 vols., 1886). *Final Memorials of Henry Wadsworth Longfellow* (1887), edited by Samuel Longfellow, was republished as *Life of Henry Wadsworth Longfellow* (3 vols., 1891). The only other early works still of interest are Thomas Wentworth Higginson, *Henry Wadsworth Longfellow* (1902), and George Rice Carpenter, *Henry Wadsworth Longfellow* (1901).

Andrew Hilen edited *The Letters of Henry Wadsworth Longfellow* (6 vols., 1966–1982), a storehouse of biographical information. At this writing, Longfellow's journals, long promised, still await publication. Lawrance Thompson, *Young Longfellow (1807–1843)* (1938), though unsympathetic, is fully researched and authoritative for the period covered. The only modern biographical work, based on original sources and covering the entire life, is Edward Wagenknecht, *Longfellow: A Full-Length Portrait* (1955), and its condensation, *Henry Wadsworth Longfellow: Portrait of an American Humanist* (1966); both contain extensive bibliographies. See also Wagenknecht, *Mrs. Longfellow: Selected Letters and Journals of Fanny Appleton Longfellow (1817–1861)* (1956). For modern critical reviews of Longfellow's writings, see Newton Arvin, *Longfellow: His Life and Work* (1963); Cecil B. Williams, *Henry Wadsworth Longfellow* (1964); and Wagenknecht, *Henry Wadsworth Longfellow: His Poetry and Prose* (1986).

EDWARD WAGENKNECHT

LONGFELLOW, Samuel (18 June 1819–3 Oct. 1892), Unitarian minister and author of belles lettres, was born in Portland, Maine, the son of Stephen Longfellow, an attorney and Federalist member of the House of Representatives, and Zilpah Wadsworth. Samuel was a younger brother of Henry Wadsworth Longfellow. He was raised in the First Parish of Portland, a church moving theologically from orthodox Congregationalism to Unitarianism. He attended Portland Academy and entered Harvard College in 1835. After graduating in 1839, he worked as a tutor until he began study at Harvard Divinity School in 1842.

Longfellow belonged to a cohort of students at the divinity school who would question the special authority of Christianity in the 1860s and 1870s, among them Octavius Brooks Frothingham, Thomas Wentworth Higginson, and Longfellow's lifelong friend, Samuel Johnson (1822–1882). Despite the eventual intellectual boldness that Longfellow shared with these contemporaries, he was too conservative in the 1840s to embrace uncritically the radical Transcendentalist theology of Ralph Waldo Emerson and Theodore Parker. Longfellow was probably influenced at least as much by the moderate Transcendentalism of his divinity school professor, Convers Francis. Some twentieth-century biographies, such as the sketch by J. W. Chadwick in *Heralds of a Liberal Faith* (1910), have emphasized Longfellow's affinity with Parker's theism. In contrast, Joseph May, Longfellow's first bi-

ographer in 1894, stressed Longfellow's loyalty as a divinity student to the Unitarianism of his youth, quoted reservations about Parker that Longfellow expressed in a letter to Johnson in 1846, and recorded the participation of Francis (and not Parker) at his ordination in 1848. The truth probably lies between these varying interpretations. Although Longfellow was attracted to Parker's theological defense of religious freedom and change, his cast of mind was less rationalistic and polemical than Parker's. Interested in awakening religious sensibility, Longfellow focused during his early career on liturgical reform. His attachment to Jesus as a figure capable of stirring piety and his concern with church ritual were positions that tied him to moderate Transcendentalists.

After Longfellow graduated from Harvard Divinity School in 1846, he served successively as minister to three Unitarian congregations in Fall River, Massachusetts (1848–1851), Brooklyn, New York (1853–1860), and Germantown, Pennsylvania (1878–1882). Unlike many contemporary Unitarian ministers, Longfellow was only marginally involved in social reform. He preached occasionally on political topics, such as John Brown's (1800–1859) raid on Harpers Ferry in 1859. But, according to May, Longfellow felt more comfortable with "simple themes" such as inner life, domestic relations, and mutual service (p. 187). In that spirit, Longfellow concentrated on pastoral work. He believed that a church must honor the intellectual freedom of its members without doctrinal restrictions, an idea best expressed in a sermon preached in Brooklyn, "A Spiritual and Working Church." Without theological consensus, congregations had an unprecedented need for new sources of community. Longfellow's most important contribution to religious liberalism was through liturgical revisions intended to unite people by means of aesthetic and affective experience. He and Johnson collaborated on two collections of hymns, *A Book of Hymns for Public and Private Devotion* (1846) and *Hymns of the Spirit* (1864). Both books contained original hymns by the editors as well as lyrics borrowed from many Protestant denominations and from contemporary poets. Longfellow's attention to religious feelings also led to his composition of the first Unitarian vespers service, a liturgical format that replaced the Sunday afternoon sermon with an evening meeting that included hymns, Bible readings, and an informal meditation by the preacher. The service was published as *Vespers* in 1859.

In the course of his career, Longfellow moved intellectually from liberal Christianity, a version of the Christian tradition that emphasized reason and toleration, to liberal religion, an affirmation of the universal presence of religious impulses in human nature. His mature position de-emphasized the importance of Jesus, even as a human moral exemplar, and cast Christianity as one of many historical expressions of humankind's religious ideas. Longfellow's essays on "Theism" (1872) and "The Unity and Universality of Religious Ideas" (1875) developed these themes.

After the Civil War, Longfellow joined the Radical Club and had some association with the Free Religious Association. Longfellow's religious rebellion, however, contained elements of persistent moderation. Philosophically, he retained the Unitarians' common sense realism and eschewed the intuitive epistemology and monism of romantic Transcendentalists such as Emerson. He demonstrated only a mild interest in the implications of science for religion in essays such as "Some Radical Doctrines" (1867). He was more comfortable with theism based on simple observation of the idea of God in human nature than on scientific evidence.

Like many Unitarians who accepted sources of revelation in human culture besides the Bible, Longfellow showed an interest in secular as well as theological writing. In 1853 he published a book of poems in collaboration with Higginson, *Thalatta: A Book for the Seaside.* Since Longfellow never married, he lived frequently near or with the family of his brother, Henry, in Cambridge, Massachusetts. After Henry's death, Samuel published a *Life of Henry Wadsworth Longfellow* (1886). He died in Portland, Maine.

Samuel Longfellow's life and thought highlight the ways in which the unprecedented intellectual freedom, cosmopolitanism, and secularism of mid-nineteenth-century American culture spurred revisions in traditional Christian ideas and institutions. Although Longfellow allied himself with the most radical Protestant thinkers among his contemporaries, both the underlying strain of moderation in his views and his continuing concern with the quality of church fellowship reveal the power of traditional Christianity to act as a brake on philosophical speculation.

• The principal manuscript collection of Samuel Longfellow's papers is located in Houghton Library, Harvard University, and consists primarily of letters to his brother, Henry. Longfellow's short works are collected in *Samuel Longfellow: Essays and Sermons,* ed. Joseph May (1894). The only full-length biography of Longfellow is Joseph May, *Samuel Longfellow: Memoir and Letters* (1894). See also J. W. Chadwick, "Samuel Longfellow," in *Heralds of a Liberal Faith,* ed. Samuel A. Eliot, vol. 3 (1910). The intellectual movements in which Longfellow was involved are discussed in Stow Persons, *Free Religion: An American Faith* (1947), and William R. Hutchison, *The Modernist Impulse in American Protestantism* (1976).

ANNE C. ROSE

LONGFELLOW, William Pitt Preble (25 Oct. 1836–3 Aug. 1913), architect and author, was born in Portland, Maine, the son of Stephen Longfellow V, a lawyer, and Marianne Preble. His parents' marriage was not a happy one, and at the age of three William went to live with his maternal grandmother Nancy Gale Tucker Preble. The Longfellows divorced in 1850, and William's mother eventually remarried. Graduating from Harvard College with a B.A. in 1855 and from Harvard's Lawrence Scientific School, where he was also an instructor in engineering, with an S.B. in 1859, Longfellow received his architectural training through

study abroad and while employed in the offices of Edward Clarke Cabot. Both Cabot and Longfellow were among the founders of the Boston Society of Architects, of which Cabot served as president and Longfellow as secretary in 1868–1869. From 1870 to 1872 he worked in Washington, D.C., at the Office of the Supervising Architect of the Treasury Department under Alfred B. Mullett, collaborating with him on the design and construction of the Boston Post Office and Sub-Treasury Building, completed in 1872 (demolished 1929). Returning to Boston, he was director of the newly established school of drawing and painting at the Boston Museum of Fine Arts, an institution for which he served as a trustee after 1882. He also designed a special commemorative chair, presented by the schoolchildren of Cambridge to his uncle Henry Wadsworth Longfellow, carved from the wood of the poet's "spreading chestnut tree."

Returning to Boston in 1875 from further European study, Longfellow was appointed the first editor of the *American Architect & Building News,* the first professional architectural journal in the United States to achieve a national audience and influence. Issued weekly and modeled after successful British counterparts, the *American Architect* sought to avoid critical judgment of individual buildings or designers through editorial concentration on educational matters and questions of professional interest to the trade. However, the four to eight full-page illustrations in each issue, which were the publication's most notable feature, and Longfellow's undeniable predilection for displaying the works of Ware & Van Brunt, H. H. Richardson, Peabody & Stearns, Richard Morris Hunt, Bruce Price, and, later, McKim, Mead & White and Carrère & Hastings, evinced a clear bias toward Boston and New York designers who embraced academic eclecticism. Indeed, Longfellow's weekly editorial comments continually stressed the need for the development of an American architecture based on classic precedent and American colonial models. As a result, the *American Architect* became a major influence in establishing H. H. Richardson as the acknowledged master of the profession, as well as in promoting the Romanesque and other revival styles of the 1880s and 1890s. Often bitterly criticized by architects from Chicago and the West for its eastern parochialism, the *American Architect* under Longfellow and his chosen successor, William Rotch Ware, was an increasingly powerful voice in defining the direction of American architectural theory and practice.

Subsequent to his departure from the *American Architect* in 1881, Longfellow became an adjunct professor of architecture at the Massachusetts Institute of Technology and devoted himself with heightened fervor to the writing of articles and books on architectural matters. Among these were *Abstract of Lectures on Perspective* (1889); the three-volume standard text *A Cyclopedia of Works in Architecture in Italy, Greece, and the Levant* (1895–1905), written in collaboration with the architect C. K. Cummings; *The Column and the Arch* (1899), a collection of essays on architectural history; and *Applied Perspective* (1901). He was also a frequent contributor of pieces on classic design to professional journals such as the *Architectural Record*, the *Architectural Review*, and the *Brickbuilder*, and to general periodicals such as *Scribner's Magazine*, which published his essay "The Architect's Point of View" (Jan. 1891). In 1893 he was a juror for the architectural awards at the World's Columbian Exposition in Chicago.

Married in 1870 to Susan Emily Daniell in Boston, Longfellow and his wife were longtime residents of Cambridge, Massachusetts, in a home adjacent to that of his famous uncle. Summers were spent in his native Maine with his bachelor cousin, architect Alexander W. Longfellow. An amateur composer, William Longfellow fashioned several competent, if uninspired, musical settings of the poems of Lord Tennyson. He died at East Gloucester, Massachusetts, during a visit to the summer art colony located there. The Longfellows had no children.

Although as an architect Longfellow's achievements were unremarkable, his influence as an educator and author played a significant role in late nineteenth-century architectural thought. A serious student of art, music, and literature, as well as architecture, he played a central role in the reaction against Victorian artisan design and in the advancement of professional academic training for the architect and of the beaux-arts eclecticism that dominated American architecture from the 1880s to the First World War.

• A manuscript biography of Longfellow can be found in the archives of the School of the Boston Museum of Fine Arts. For more information on Longfellow see Bainbridge Bunting, *Houses of Boston's Back Bay* (1967); Margaret H. Floyd, *Architecture after Richardson* (1994); Moses King, ed., *King's Handbook of Boston* (1889); Henry F. Withey and Elsie Rathburn Withey, *Biographical Dictionary of American Architects (Deceased)* (1970); Mary Woods, "The First American Architectural Journals: The Profession's Voice," *Journal of the Society of Architectural Historians* 48, no. 2 (June 1989): 117–38; and William David Barry, "William Pitt Preble Longfellow" in *A Biographical Dictionary of Architects in Maine* 4, no. 10 (1987): unpaginated. Obituaries are in the *New York Times*, 4 Aug. 1913, and *American Architect*, 13 Aug. 1913.

WILLIAM ALAN MORRISON

LONGHAIR, Professor. *See* Professor Longhair.

LONG LANCE. *See* Long, Sylvester Clark.

LONGSTREET, Augustus Baldwin (27 Sept. 1790–9 July 1870), author and educator, was born in Augusta, Georgia, the son of William Longstreet, an inventor and land speculator, and Hannah Randolph. In 1808 he began attending Dr. Moses Waddell's celebrated school in Willington, South Carolina, where he boarded with the family of John C. Calhoun, who had preceded him at the school by several years. In 1811 Longstreet entered Yale University as a junior. After graduating in 1813, he attended a law school in Litchfield, Connecticut, that was conducted by Judges Tapping Reeve and James Gould. In 1815 he returned to Georgia, was admitted to the bar, and began work as a circuit lawyer.

In 1817 Longstreet married Frances Eliza Parke; although the couple had eight children, only two survived childhood. In 1821 he was elected to the State Assembly, and the following year he was appointed Superior Court judge of Omalgee District, one of only five districts in the state. During a promising campaign for Congress in 1824, he withdrew shortly before the election due to the death of his oldest son. Distraught, Longstreet took solace in religion, eventually joining the Methodist Church in 1827. That year he also began a law partnership in Augusta and bought a plantation outside of town. The plantation was unsuccessful, and Longstreet sold his slaves shortly thereafter, a sale that he later wrote, "relieved me of the eternal torment of negroes, overseers, and creditors" (Wade, p. 118).

In 1830 Longstreet began to write the sketches of Georgia life that would make his name. Three years later he began publishing them in the Milledgeville *Southern Recorder*, and shortly thereafter he continued the series in the *State Rights' Sentinel*, an Augusta newspaper that he purchased in 1834 and used as a platform for commenting on state and national politics. The next year the *Sentinel's* press published *Georgia Scenes: Characters, Incidents, &c., in the First Half Century of the Republic* by "a Native Georgian." Generally regarded as the first major work of Southwest or backwoods humor, *Georgia Scenes* is a collection of nineteen sketches that combine literary realism with tall-tale exaggeration in a complex portrayal of a culture only recently evolved from the frontier. Longstreet later wrote that "the aim of the author was to supply a chasm in history which has always been overlooked—the manners, customs, amusements, wit, dialect, as they appear in all grades of society to an ear and eye witness of them" (Fitzgerald, p. 164). Despite his emphasis on the archival nature of the work, Longstreet's nuanced representation of a wide range of social groups and his sophisticated handling of his two narrative personae, Hall and Baldwin, show that he was a talented artist as well. Longstreet's colorful descriptions of horse swaps, dances, fights, gander pullings, horse races, and shooting matches made the work a popular success. Harper's brought out an edition of it in 1840, and it was regularly reprinted for the rest of the century. Discriminating critics recognized its literary value; in an appreciative review, Edgar Allan Poe called it "a sure omen of better days of the literature of the South" (p. 93). Although he later downplayed his literary efforts as the frivolous "amusement of my idle hours," his work was respected and sought after by readers and editors; the several sketches that he published during this period were later collected by his nephew, Fitz R. Longstreet, in *Stories with a Moral* (1912).

In 1838 Longstreet left the law and politics to enter the ministry. Although remembered as a mediocre preacher, he was active and influential in church politics. In 1839 the Methodist Church appointed him president of Emory College in Oxford, Georgia. Following the 1844 Methodist convention, Longstreet played a major role in the geographical division of the church over the question of slavery. In 1847 he published *A Voice from the South*, a vitriolic series of letters addressed to "Massachussetts," expressing proslavery, antiabolitionist arguments.

In 1848 Longstreet resigned as president of Emory College to accept what he thought was a forthcoming offer to serve as president of the University of Mississippi. When that position failed to materialize, he accepted a position as president of Centenary College in Jackson, Louisiana. Discouraged by his perceived lack of authority there, Longstreet accepted the presidency of the University of Mississippi in 1847. In 1856, following a bitter public dispute with the anti-Catholic Know-Nothing party, Longstreet resigned and shortly thereafter assumed the presidency of South Carolina College in Columbia. In his baccalaureate address of 1857, he heatedly called for secession and, if necessary, war. With war looming on the horizon in 1861, however, the erstwhile firebreather reversed his position in *Shall South Carolina Begin the War?* an antiwar pamphlet counselling prudence.

With the outbreak of the Civil War, Longstreet moved his family to Oxford, Mississippi, where, in 1862, his house was burned by General Grant's soldiers. After his return to Georgia, a Macon publisher brought out *Master William Mitten* (1864), a moralistic *bildungsroman* that Longstreet had begun at Centenary and published serially in 1859 in the *Southern Field and Fireside*. After the war ended Longstreet moved his family back to Oxford, where he died.

Although Longstreet wanted to be remembered as a lawyer, a minister, and an educator, his fame rests upon *Georgia Scenes*. While it has long been recognized that *Georgia Scenes* pointed the way for contemporary humorists such as Johnson Jones Hooper, Joseph Glover Baldwin, and Longstreet's friend and protégé William Tappan Thompson, the importance of the work to the broader tradition of Southern literature has been underestimated. Calling attention to Longstreet's precise observation of character, the poet and critic Allen Tate numbered *Georgia Scenes* with Mark Twain's *Adventures of Huckleberry Finn* as the two works that "are the beginning of modern Southern literature." "They are also," Tate continues, "important for American literature as a whole" (p. 147).

• For biographical material, see John Donald Wade's *Augustus Baldwin Longstreet: A Study in the Development of Culture in the South* (1924) and O. P. Fitzgerald's hagiographical *Judge Longstreet: A Life Sketch* (1891). Kimball King's *Augustus Baldwin Longstreet* (1984) contains a biographical overview and sound critical commentary on Longstreet's major works. For Poe's review of *Georgia Scenes*, see M. Thomas Inge, *The Frontier Humorists: Critical Views* (1975). Tate's interesting essay can be found in Allen Tate, *Memoirs and Opinions: 1926–1974* (1975). For information about Longstreet's relationship to literary realism and his handling of narrative personae, see James B. Meriwether, "Augustus Baldwin Longstreet: Realist and Artist," *Mississippi Quarterly* 35 (1982): 351–64; and James E. Kibler, Jr., "Introduction," *Georgia Scenes* (1992). See also Keith Newlin, "Georgia Scenes: The Satiric Artistry of Augustus Baldwin Longstreet," *Mississippi Quarterly* 41 (1987–1988): 21–37, for an examination of Longstreet's satire, and Scott Romine, "Negotiating Community in Augustus Baldwin Longstreet's *Georgia Scenes*," *Style* 29 (1996): 1–27, for a discussion of the role of community in Longstreet's work.

SCOTT ROMINE

LONGSTREET, James (8 Jan. 1821–2 Jan. 1904), Confederate general, was born in the Edgefield District of South Carolina, the son of James Longstreet and Mary Anne Dent, planters. He grew up in Gainesville, Georgia, and was educated at the Richmond Academy in Augusta, Georgia, where he lived with his uncle, Augustus Baldwin Longstreet, a well-known jurist, educator, and clergyman. Following the death of Longstreet's father in 1833, his mother moved to Somerville, Alabama, and Longstreet was appointed to the U.S. Military Academy at West Point from that state. Nicknamed "Old Pete" by his classmates, he graduated in 1842, fifty-fourth out of a class of fifty-six.

Longstreet served as a subaltern in Missouri, Louisiana, and Florida until 1845, when his unit, the Eighth Infantry, joined General Zachary Taylor's army at Corpus Christi, Texas. During the war with Mexico (1846–1848), Longstreet fought in almost every major battle, earning promotion to the ranks of first lieutenant and brevet major. A company officer and, later, regimental adjutant, he often displayed reckless bravery. At Chapultepec he was grievously wounded while carrying the regimental colors.

Invalided to the United States just as the war ended, Longstreet married Maria Louisa Garland, the daughter of Brevet Brigadier General John Garland of Virginia, in March 1848. The Longstreets had ten children, only five of whom lived to maturity.

Longstreet rejoined his regiment at San Antonio, Texas, in May 1849. During the twelve years of frontier service that followed, he usually served with or near his father-in-law, who commanded the Eighth Infantry and a military department embracing parts of Arizona, New Mexico, and Texas. He was chief of commissary for the Department of Texas in 1850 and 1851 and commander of Fort Bliss, Texas, for much of the period from 1855 to 1858. He made full captain in 1852 and became a full major in 1858 by transferring to the Paymaster Department. Longstreet was stationed in Albuquerque, New Mexico, when the shots fired on Fort Sumter in April 1861 prompted him to resign from the U.S. Army and offer his services to the Confederacy.

Appointed a brigadier general in June 1861, Longstreet served under P. G. T. Beauregard in Virginia. Promoted to major general in October, he led a division under Joseph E. Johnston during the Peninsula campaign. When Robert E. Lee replaced Johnston in June 1862, he selected Longstreet as his second-in-command. Longstreet led the First Corps, rising to the rank of lieutenant general in October 1862. He fought at Fredericksburg in December of that year and the next spring was detached to conduct semi-independent operations in southeastern Virginia. Following the Gettysburg campaign of July 1863, he went west with reinforcements, joining Braxton Bragg's Army of Tennessee for the battle of Chickamauga in September. He spent the winter of 1863–1864 attempting unsuccessfully to capture Knoxville, Tennessee. Returning to Lee's army in the spring of 1864, he was severely wounded by friendly fire in May at the Wilderness. By the time he returned to duty in October, Lee's forces were besieged at Petersburg. Longstreet headed the surrender commission at Appomattox in April 1865, and his corps was the last portion of the Army of Northern Virginia to lay down its arms.

Longstreet's soldiers held him in respect and great affection, nicknaming him "the Old Bulldog" for his tenacity in battle. As a combat commander, he had few peers. Prior to being wounded, he was physically indefatigable, requiring almost no sleep. He used his enormous energy to keep tight control over his troops, which he maneuvered with skill and speed. At Second Manassas and Chickamauga his troops fought aggressively, but he generally favored the tactical defensive as the best means of compensating for the Confederacy's manpower shortages. He argued that defensive tactics should, however, be tied to a strategic offensive whenever practicable.

Longstreet was a leading advocate of allocating greater resources to the western theater of the war. Realizing that the South could not achieve a purely military solution in its quarrel with the Union, he proposed strategic operations targeted against civilian morale in the North and Abraham Lincoln's reelection prospects rather than against northern soldiers. President Jefferson Davis, however, preferred the more sanguinary strategies of Robert E. Lee and John Bell Hood.

Longstreet's estrangement from Davis, which began late in 1861 for reasons that have never been clear, prevented him from attaining command of an army, a position to which he aspired with neither more nor less ambition than his peers. Not one to suffer fools gladly, Longstreet intrigued shamelessly for Bragg's removal after he went west. The mutual animosity between Bragg and Longstreet led to the decision to send Longstreet to attack Knoxville. During this, Longstreet's only completely independent period of command, competition between his subordinates hampered operations, and Davis's failure to support his disciplinary actions made matters much worse. Even so, Longstreet's difficulties in East Tennessee rightly call into question his potential as an army commander.

Longstreet made his greatest contributions serving under Lee, who called him "my Old War Horse" and "the Staff of my right hand." Contrary to myth, Longstreet, not Stonewall Jackson, was Lee's intimate confidant, close friend, and principal military adviser. Contemporaries described their relationship as one of brotherly affection. Their disagreement over military affairs—with Lee stressing the Virginia theater and the tactical offensive—caused friction, but it did not lessen their mutual regard. While Longstreet was dismayed by Lee's costly attacks at Gettysburg, preferring a tactical defensive, he was neither stubborn nor disobedient during the campaign. On the second day of the battle, Longstreet's poor reconnaissance delayed his attack, but by no more than an hour, and his overall movements were not slow. On the final day of the battle, Longstreet did take longer than necessary to implement Lee's orders for an assault on the Federal center, but this was not the reason "Pickett's Charge" failed. As the attack was both flawed in concept and doomed from the start, Longstreet's reluctance was both understandable and sensible.

At war's end, Longstreet settled in New Orleans, where he became a cotton broker and where he was acknowledged and honored as a hero. His status as a hero was effectively erased, however, when in 1867 he became a "scalawag," a native white southerner who supported the Republican party. Although he was a conservative and a white supremacist, Longstreet believed that cooperation with the Republican party would reduce the Reconstruction period to a minimum. Whether despite or because of the extreme wrath that descended upon him for this political heresy, Longstreet devoted much of the remainder of his life to the Republican party, enjoying its patronage at the federal and state level.

In Louisiana, Longstreet was surveyor of the port of New Orleans (1869–1872), adjutant general of Louisiana (1870–1872), major general commanding the Louisiana state militia (1872–1876), and president of the Levee Commission of Engineers (1873–1877). Returning to his hometown, Longstreet was deputy collector of internal revenue and postmaster of Gainesville, Georgia from 1878 to 1880. Named U.S. ambassador to Turkey in 1880, he served only a year in that assignment, returning in 1881 to become federal marshal of Georgia, a post he held until 1884. In old age, he received the sinecure position of U.S. commissioner of railroads (1898–1904), as a reward for his support of William McKinley.

Maria Louisa Longstreet died in 1889, and in 1897 Longstreet married Helen Dortch, who was more than forty years his junior.

In addition to politics, Longstreet's time was occupied by the farm and hotel he owned in Gainesville and, increasingly, by the need to defend his military record. Following Lee's death in 1870, a group of his former subordinates and staff officers—led by Jubal A. Early, William N. Pendleton, and Fitzhugh Lee—launched a campaign to enshrine him as the South's primary Confederate hero. One of the primary forces in creating the intense, nostalgic self-worship behind the myth of the Lost Cause, their deification of Lee rested in part upon the castigation of Longstreet for his alleged errors at Gettysburg.

In speeches delivered in 1872 and 1873, Early and Pendleton accused Longstreet of failing to attack on the second day of Gettysburg as early as Lee had desired. Longstreet's rebuttal of this and similar accusations leveled at him repeatedly for the next quarter-century failed for three reasons. The foremost of these was the fallout from his actions in September 1874, when, as commander of Louisiana's all-black state militia, he led former slaves into battle against the Crescent City White League's attempt to overthrow the state's carpetbagger government. As an apparent traitor to the white race, Longstreet was vulnerable to even the most farfetched accusations in regard to his military record leading some to believe, as Early and others contended, that Longstreet had willfully betrayed Lee at Gettysburg and that his betrayal cost the South its independence.

Secondly, Longstreet was overcome by the sophistication and sheer weight of the attack against him. Detesting Longstreet because of his political affiliation, and anxious to cover mistakes of his own at Gettysburg, Early forged a coherent anti-Longstreet faction whose members coordinated the production of books and articles with the avowed goal of writing Longstreet out of Confederate history.

Finally, Longstreet besmirched his own reputation. Frozen out of the circle of Confederate heroes, he wrote articles for the *Philadelphia Times* (1877–1878) and *Century* magazine (1885–1887) and an autobiography, *From Manassas to Appomattox* (1896), that shamelessly exaggerated his own accomplishments and displayed extreme jealously of Lee and Jackson. Historians have wrongly taken this bitter, self-promoting postwar prose as representative of Longstreet's wartime character and attitudes.

Longstreet died in Gainesville in 1904, having outlived almost every other high-ranking Confederate. A negative view of him has persisted, partly because almost all of Lee's biographers have accepted uncritically the historically inaccurate version of events at Gettysburg popularized by Jubal Early. Longstreet's Judas image contrasts strongly with the Christ imagery of Lee and continues to provide a temptingly simplistic explanation for the South's defeat. Significantly, there are no monuments to Longstreet's memory on any battlefield.

• Longstreet's most important military correspondence is preserved in *War of the Rebellion: A Compilation of the Official Records of the Union and Confederate Armies* (128 vols., 1880–1901). Almost all of his personal papers, however, perished when his home burned in 1899. Most extant material is from the post–Civil War period, providing information on his writings and political activities but almost nothing about his private life. Longstreet letters are located at the Chicago Historical Society; Duke University; Emory University; the Georgia Historical Society (which also has the extensive papers of his second wife, Helen); the Georgia State Department of Archives and History; Harvard University; the Historical Society of Pennsylvania; the Museum of the Confederacy, Richmond; the Rutherford B. Hayes Memorial Library, Fremont, Ohio; and the University of North Carolina. Longstreet's postwar activities, particularly his writings in defense of his reputation, are the subject of extensive comment in the John W. Daniel Papers, Jubal A. Early Papers, and Fitzhugh Lee Papers at Duke University; the Jubal A. Early Papers at the Library of Congress; and the A. L. Long Papers, Lafayette McLaws Papers, and William N. Pendleton Papers at the University of North Carolina.

Longstreet is the subject of four biographies. H. J. Eckenrode and Bryan Conrad, *James Longstreet: Lee's War Horse* (1936), reflects the extreme bias against him current in the early twentieth century. Donald Bridgman Sanger and Thomas Robson Hay, *James Longstreet: Soldier, Politician, Officeholder, and Writer* (1952), exonerates him with regard to his military career but is highly critical of his postwar politics. Wilbur Thomas, *General James "Pete" Longstreet: Lee's "Old War Horse," Scapegoat for Gettysburg* (1979), is an amateurish defense of his military record. William Garrett Piston, *Lee's Tarnished Lieutenant: James Longstreet and His Place in Southern History* (1987), analyzes Longstreet's wartime performance and his relations with Lee and chronicles his role and place in the evolution of the Lost Cause mythology. Jeffrey D. Wert, *General James Longstreet: The Confederacy's Most Controversial Soldier* (1993), focuses almost exclusively on Longstreet's military career, arguing that Longstreet was the greatest corps-level commander of the Civil War, North or South.

The best works on Longstreet at Gettysburg are Glenn Tucker, *Lee and Longstreet at Gettysburg* (1968), Edwin B. Coddington, *The Gettysburg Campaign: A Study in Command* (1968), and Harry W. Pfanz, *Gettysburg—The Second Day* (1987).

An obituary is in the *New York Times*, 7 Jan. 1904.

WILLIAM GARRETT PISTON

LONGSTREET, William (6 Oct. 1759–1 Sept. 1814), inventor, was born near Allentown, Monmouth County, New Jersey, the son of Stoffel Longstreet and Abigail Wooley. Longstreet received some local schooling and at an early age showed mechanical skill and an interest in the increasing talk of steam engines and steamboats. In 1783 he married Hannah Randolph of Allentown, with whom he had six children. She had inherited a sizable sum of money from her father, and sometime before the fall of 1786 the family had settled in Augusta, Georgia, where Longstreet made his living as an inventor of steam engines and steamboats.

Longstreet's sources of knowledge remain obscure, but he seems to have been influenced by the steamboat experiments of John Fitch and Oliver Evans. In February 1788 the General Assembly at Augusta passed an act that conferred on Longstreet and fellow inventor Isaac Briggs exclusive patent rights to their steam engine for fourteen years. The brief entry by Georgia's secretary of state described a globular boiler, double-acting horizontal piston, and a condenser. The condenser may have been an original attempt to avoid the inefficient cooling of the entire cylinder, one of the drawbacks of the heavy and fuel-hungry Newcomen engine, or an attempt by Longstreet to reproduce Scottish inventor James Watt's 1769 condenser. Though South Carolina had issued Longstreet and Briggs a similar patent in 1786, the two men apparently had not tried to build a boat at that time.

Briggs dropped out of the endeavor sometime between 1788 and 1790, and Longstreet continued fundraising efforts alone. In a 26 September 1790 letter to

Georgia governor Edward Telfair, Longstreet wrote that difficulties in obtaining proper materials and workmen had prevented him from actually building a steamboat but that he planned to move ahead "almost entirely with wooden materials, and by such workmen as may be gotten here." No doubt the difficulty of building a complicated mechanical device from wood continued to hamper him, though his engine was eventually constructed primarily of iron.

Longstreet's bid for financial assistance apparently went unheeded. In addition to these problems, Longstreet shared the common bane of most inventors by enduring public criticism of his awkward attempts at invention. The 22 September 1792 *Augusta Chronicle* contained an article advertising his newly invented steam engine, noting its usefulness for both grist and saw milling. Hinting at what was probably his ultimate goal, as well as the widespread public skepticism, Longstreet wrote, "I would add, if it was not *for fear* of being accused with a *baloon* or *steamboat project*, how easily could I apply it to *boating*!" Though concentrating on other endeavors for a time, Longstreet eventually amassed sufficient funds, materials, and workers so that sometime during 1806–1808 he propelled a small steamboat against the current of the Savannah River. What little is known about the boat indicates that it was propelled by long poles pushing against the bottom of the river; this was one popular experimental method before the paddle wheel became standard.

Long before his eventual steamboating success, Longstreet sought to apply the power of steam to other uses; he had been working on a cotton gin of his own invention since at least 1790. Many southern tinkerers, mechanics, and entrepreneurs sought to capitalize on the developing cotton economy by mechanizing the frustratingly time-consuming process of separating the seeds from the fibers, and their efforts resulted in a bewildering variety of inventions, patents, claims, and counterclaims. In 1793 Eli Whitney invented a gin that used teeth to separate the seeds from the cotton fibers. These saw gins revolutionized cotton agriculture by allowing the rapid expansion of the relatively easily cultivated but difficult to separate short-staple upland cotton. Earlier inventors had succeeded in ginning the less abundant but easier to separate long-staple, or Sea Island, cotton with gins utilizing rollers. Longstreet patented a variation on the roller gin and increased its efficiency by applying his steam engine as a power source. He appears to have profited from his marriage of an improved roller gin with an original steam engine, which became a valuable asset to Sea Island cotton growers. The 24 December 1796 *Augusta Chronicle* contained an ad for his soon-to-be-completed gin, and in the same issue eight prominent local men endorsed the device. Issues of the *Augusta Chronicle* in 1797 carried information about the gin as well as disputes over the origin of the improvements, which plagued nearly all early cotton gin manufacturers.

In around 1801, two of Longstreet's steam-powered gins were put into operation in Augusta, but both were destroyed by fire within a week. By at least 1802 Longstreet had also pioneered a portable steam sawmill, a few of which were used in Georgia. But fire, this time set by the British, destroyed a Longstreet steam mill (either grist or saw) near St. Mary's in 1812. A combination of the cumulative fatigue of fundraising, difficulties with workmen and materials, as well as the destruction of many of his inventions all helped lead to his death in Augusta two years later.

Longstreet's varied career reveals a multifaceted figure with many interests and a reasonably prestigious social standing. His penchant for entrepreneurial endeavors may have been one of the factors that led him to promote the controversial sale of land to private interests by the state of Georgia, known as the Yazoo Land Act, but this association did not prevent him from becoming president of the Augusta Association of Mechanics in 1794, justice of the peace in 1797, one of the commissioners during Augusta's incorporation in 1798, and town council member twice during the 1790s.

Later commentators made much out of the early date of Longstreet's steam engine experiments, several noting that his ideas preceded Robert Fulton's by many years. Fulton, one of the leading steamboat inventors, piloted his steamboat up the Hudson River in 1807. While it was true that up to a dozen different men—including Longstreet—had built experimental steamboats before that date, Fulton generally retains credit as the one to carry the idea through to practical application. Longstreet's success with his steamboat came late in his life and did not provide the income or notoriety he desired. Both time and geography hampered his achievements. Eighteenth-century Georgia was a difficult place to obtain the necessary materials and metal-working skills needed for steamboat production, and many of his mechanical ideas were ahead of the available technology. Historians of technology have given little space to Longstreet because his steamboat experiments were only one of several in the field. But the general perception of the antebellum South as bereft of technological innovation has obscured Longstreet's considerable achievements in applying his steam engine to ginning and milling. All of these factors have contributed to the relative historical anonymity of a man who foresaw the coming century as a true age of steam.

• No major collection of Longstreet's papers is known to exist, but the Georgia Department of Archives and History in Atlanta has Longstreet's letter to Governor Telfair and may possess some other scattered manuscript material. The Georgia Historical Society in Savannah has an extensive collection of Longstreet family papers. The Augusta-Richmond County Public Library in Augusta has a personal name index for the *Augusta Chronicle*, which will guide the researcher to the many places Longstreet appeared in that paper. Information about Longstreet is not extensive. Charles C. Jones and Salem Dutcher, *Memorial History of Augusta, Georgia* (1911); John Donald Wade, *Augustus Baldwin Longstreet: A Study of the Development of Culture in the South* (1924); and Edward J. Cashin, *The Story of Augusta* (1980), contain the lengthiest discussions of William Longstreet's life and work. In the context of Georgia history, W. H. Spark, *The Memories of Fifty Years* (1882), makes brief mention of Longstreet, while Lucian Lamar Knight, *Georgia's Landmarks, Memorials, and Legends*, vols. 1 and 2 (1913, 1914), contains more lengthy material about his inventions, including a transcript of his Georgia patent and his tombstone inscription. Thompson Westcott, *Life of John Fitch* (1857); George Henry Preble, *A Chronological History of the Origin and Development of Steam Navigation* (1883); and Victor S. Clark, *History of Manufactures in the United States*, vol. 1 (1929), each contain brief accounts of his efforts and steamboat inventions, but the best and most reliable source on Longstreet's steamboat is Carroll W. Pursell, Jr., *Early Stationary Steam Engines in America: A Study in the Migration of a Technology* (1969).

THOMAS A. KINNEY

LONGSWORTH, Lewis Gibson (16 Nov. 1904–9 Aug. 1981), physical and biological chemist, was born in Somerset, Kentucky, the son of Lawrence Roscoe and Sarah Elizabeth Nichols. He was educated at Southwestern College, from which he obtained a B.A. in 1925, and at the University of Kansas, which awarded him an M.A. in 1927 and a Ph.D. in 1928. Longsworth's graduate research, done under the direction of H. P. Cady, was a study of the motion of ions in an electric field. His first publication on that subject, "A Modification of the Moving-boundary Method for the Determination of Transference Numbers," which appeared in 1929 (*Journal of the American Chemical Society* 51: 1656–64), was followed by a series of papers on the mobility and the diffusion of ions. In 1929 he married Helen Frances Cady; they had three children.

Immediately after graduation, Longsworth obtained a National Research Council Fellowship and opted to go to the Rockefeller Institute for Medical Research, in New York City, to work in collaboration with D. A. MacInnes. Thus began a lifelong association with that institution: in 1930 he was appointed assistant; in 1945, was promoted to associate; and in 1949, was named a member of the institute. When the institute became a graduate university in 1954, he assumed the rank of professor. He became professor emeritus in 1970.

Longsworth's first paper on a biological subject, which was coauthored by MacInnes and appeared in 1935, dealt with the growth of *Lactobacillus acidophilus*. He is best known for his contributions to the analysis and the characterization of proteins in solution by electrochemical means. This approach to the study of proteins was introduced by Arne Tiselius, winner of the Nobel Prize in chemistry for 1948. In 1939 Longsworth perfected a method of visualizing the movement of proteins (schlieren photography), which made it possible to analyze blood plasma and other liquid samples of biological and clinical interest. This method was widely used for about a decade; since then, it has been almost completely displaced by analyses done in gels. Albeit more practical, the measurements done in solid media are not so easily amenable to physicochemical interpretation, and that was Longsworth's primary interest.

In recognition of his achievements, Longsworth was elected to membership in the National Academy of Sciences in 1947 and was the recipient of the 1968 American Chemical Society Award in Chromatography and Electrophoresis.

Although when queried about his hobbies, Longsworth stated that he had not pursued any one of them for long, he was a bicycle rider, hiker, and mountain climber, who ascended Long's Peak thirteen times, often in the company of his wife. He died in Estes Park, Colorado, the Longsworths' favorite vacation spot.

• A limited amount of information is held in the archives of Rockefeller University, North Terrytown, N.Y. An obituary is in the *New York Times*, 12 Aug. 1981.

GEORGE GORIN

LONGWORTH, Alice Lee Roosevelt (12 Feb. 1884– 21 Feb. 1980), socialite and celebrity, was born in New York City, the daughter of Theodore Roosevelt (1858–1919), the twenty-sixth president of the United States, and Alice Hathaway Lee, a Boston socialite. An only child, Alice was two days old when her mother and her paternal grandmother died. Her father left her with his sister, Anna Roosevelt (Cowles), and went west to assuage his double loss. For the next two years, Alice saw her father only occasionally. In 1887 Theodore returned with his new wife, Edith Kermit Carow, to take Alice to their new home, "Sagamore Hill," on Long Island. Theodore never spoke to her of her mother.

Alice felt like an orphan in the Roosevelt clan. She briefly had a governess and occasionally shared her brothers' tutors but was largely an autodidact. From a shy girl in leg braces (to offset childhood polio), she matured into an intelligent, spunky, and attractive young woman. Her youth was colored by an unmet desire: the assurance of her father's love. His burgeoning career precluded any closeness. Frequent pregnancies and illnesses prevented Edith Roosevelt from filling the void. Consequently, Alice rebelled. She demanded attention, refused to attend school, and joined an all-boys' club. She taught herself to bet and play poker, and she resisted religious confirmation.

Neither life in Albany as the governor's daughter (1899–1900) nor in Washington, D.C., as the vice president's daughter (1901) could prepare Alice for her new celebrity status as first daughter in September 1901. Her 1902 White House debut was the social event of the year. Before international cameras she embarked on public trips and performances, earning universal respect and the affectionate nickname "Princess Alice." She christened Kaiser Wilhelm's American-made yacht, stood in receiving lines with her parents, and was the guest of honor at balls and charity events. Crowds of thousands gathered to see her. The president sent her on goodwill tours of Cuba, Puerto Rico, Korea, Japan, China, and the Philippines. Foreign sovereigns treated her as royalty. She understood politics and protocol and dispensed American beneficence at orphanages, women's clubs, factories, and schools.

As a result, Alice widened the sphere of action for young women. She drove her own car, bet on horses, and smoked in public. President Roosevelt himself conceded that he could govern the country or govern his daughter, but he could not possibly do both. Yet fond Americans wrote songs for her and named their babies after her. "Alice blue," a color created for her by dressmakers, became a fashion rage. The *Washington Post* called her "the most widely discussed woman in America." Her diaries, however, testify to her lonesomeness and her fear that people befriended her to benefit from her position. In 1904 she fell in love with Ohio representative Nicholas Longworth (1869–1931), a man fourteen years her senior. Their 17 February 1906 White House wedding received international press coverage. Foreign governments sent gifts. After a celebrated European honeymoon, the Longworths returned to Washington, where Alice's wit and political sagacity cemented their position at the acme of society. Her famous dinner parties brought political foes together for intimate and amicable debate.

Politics became the focus of Alice Longworth's life. She helped her husband wage a successful campaign for his third term in the House of Representatives, but the 1912 election was difficult for her. She had finally become her father's confidante, but her loyalties were split between his new Progressive party and her husband's Republican party. They forbade her to choose sides or use her fame to campaign. Her dilemma was resolved when Roosevelt lost the presidency and Longworth suffered his only congressional defeat. The Longworths withdrew to their Cincinnati mansion, and their marriage suffered from his extramarital affairs.

Longworth reentered Congress in 1914 without his wife's help. She instead goaded the anti-Wilson forces, urging immediate American entry into World War I. She used her celebrity status to sell Liberty Bonds, but her real concern was to prevent American entry into the League of Nations. She won the title "Colonel" of the Irreconcilables' Battalion of Death for her successful efforts. In 1920 she campaigned for Warren G. Harding, whom she privately called "not a bad man, just a slob." In 1925 Nick Longworth was elected Speaker of the House, and Alice gave birth to her only child, fathered by Senator William E. Borah.

When Congressman Longworth died in 1931, Alice Longworth declined offers to run for his vacant seat. Financially strapped, she published her autobiography, *Crowded Hours*, in 1933. She campaigned for Herbert Hoover in 1932 and criticized her cousin President Franklin D. Roosevelt's New Deal, both privately and through her syndicated newspaper column. She served as delegate to the 1936 Republican National Convention and for sixty years attended both parties' conventions.

Still strongly isolationist, Longworth supported Republican candidate Robert Taft in 1940 and 1944 and served as an officer of America First's national committee and a director of its Washington chapter in the 1940s. Twelve years later, she raised money for Dwight D. Eisenhower's presidential campaign. She monitored the House Committee on Un-American Activities, taking no sides but delighting in seating adversaries beside each other at her parties. She enjoyed the comradeship of people as diverse as John L. Lewis, the Richard Nixons, the Lyndon Johnsons, and the Kennedys. As "Washington's other monument," "Mrs. L." maintained her celebrity status. Reporters sought her opinions on the political landscape throughout her life. Through the 1970s, her cachet was necessary for social success in Washington. She died in Washington, D.C.

Longworth's celebrity status rested on her father's legacy, her social status as first daughter, her political intelligence, and her biting wit. She liked Calvin Coolidge, who, she said, looked "as though he had been weaned on a pickle." Cousin Franklin was "one-third sap and two-thirds Eleanor"; the activist first lady was "a Trojan mare." She accused columnist Dorothy Thompson of being "the only woman who had her menopause in public and got paid for it." She cautioned about Douglas MacArthur, "Never trust a man who parts his hair straight from his left armpit." Of President Lyndon B. Johnson's televised display of his gall-bladder operation scars, she ventured, "We should be grateful it wasn't a prostate operation." Her pillow read, "If you haven't got anything nice to say, come and sit by me." "My speciality," she confessed, "is detached malevolence." Her words might disoblige, but her lifelong financial assistance to family members and her unpublicized donations to environmental and medical charities belied true bitterness.

Longworth ruled Washington society and decoded politics for nearly seventy years. Attendance at her Massachusetts Avenue salon conferred upon the powerful and influential an intangible but real legitimacy. At the turn of the century, as one of America's first female celebrities, she broadened women's options. Throughout her life she used her fame, contacts, acumen, and family name to sway politics and politicians.

• Longworth's correspondence, diaries, scrapbooks, clipping and photograph files, as well as Nicholas Longworth's papers, can be found at the Library of Congress. The Longworth family papers are located in the Cincinnati Historical Society, which also contains the courtship letters of Nicholas Longworth to Alice Roosevelt. The Theodore Roosevelt Collection, Harvard University, houses the majority of the Roosevelt family papers, while the rest are located at the Library of Congress. The Columbia University Oral History Collection contains transcripts of an interview with Longworth. In addition to her autobiography, Longworth coedited with her brother Theodore Roosevelt, Jr., *The Desk Drawer Anthology: Poems for the American People* (1937). Michael Teague, *Mrs. L: Conversations with Alice Roosevelt Longworth* (1981), is a biography based on oral interviews. See also Carol Felsenthal, *Alice Roosevelt Longworth* (1988); Howard Teichmann, *Alice: The Life and Times of Alice Roosevelt Longworth* (1979); and James Brough, *Princess Alice* (1975). Two articles by Stacy A. Rozek provide information about Longworth's life while her father was president: "'The First Daughter of the Land:' Alice Roosevelt as Presidential Celebrity, 1902–1906," *Presidential Studies Quarterly* 19 (Winter 1989): 51–

70, and "Theodore Roosevelt's Private Diplomat: Alice Roosevelt and the 1905 Far Eastern Junket," in *Theodore Roosevelt: Many-Sided American*, ed. Natalie A. Naylor et al. (1992), pp. 353–67. See also Sylvia Jukes Morris, *Edith Kermit Roosevelt: Portrait of a First Lady* (1980). The most important of the many obituaries published throughout the country are in the *New York Times* and the *Washington Post*, 21 Feb. 1980.

STACY A. CORDERY

LONGWORTH, Nicholas (16 Jan. 1782–10 Feb. 1863), horticulturist and philanthropist, was born in Newark, New Jersey, the son of Thomas Longworth and Apphia Vanderpoel. His grandfather, also named Thomas, was a Loyalist at the time of the Revolution, an allegiance that caused the considerable Longworth property to be confiscated. With nothing but an impressive wardrobe that included six coats with four pairs of silk and eight pairs of woolen breeches, Nicholas Longworth turned west to make his fortune, arriving in Cincinnati in May 1804, when it was little more than a village. After a short period of reading law in the office of Judge Jacob Burnet, he was admitted to the bar and practiced law until 1819. According to his own account, the foundation for his fortune was laid when he successfully defended an accused horse thief. After acquittal, the client was unable to pay his lawyer's fee, so Longworth accepted two copper whiskey stills, which in turn he bargained for thirty-three acres of what became prime urban real estate during Cincinnati's rapid growth. By 1850 the worth of this land was estimated at $2 million. Buying, selling, and renting Cincinnati town lots was thereafter Longworth's chief activity. By midcentury he was paying more real estate tax than any other American except William B. Astor.

Longworth's wealth exemplified Henry George's concept of the "unearned increment" that comes from the rise of land values, so it is no wonder the Marxist Gustavus Myers characterized him as one who "foreclosed with pitiless promptitude" and whose "adroit knowledge of the law, approaching if not reaching, that of an unscrupulous pettifogger, enabled him to get the upper hand in every transaction" (p. 185). However, Longworth contributed much to charity, though always on his own terms. Every Monday he distributed gifts to the poor, and anybody who applied at his house might receive the choice of a loaf of bread, a peck of corn, or ten cents in cash. But when a newspaper editor approached him to assist a poor "deserving" widow, Longworth flatly refused, saying that plenty of others were willing to help such persons: "I shall assist none but the idle, drunken, worthless vagabonds that nobody else will help" (quoted in Cist, p. 338).

He took pride in his eccentricities and slovenly dress. He would set out about town with several slips of paper pinned to his sleeve, each representing a piece of business he had to transact that day, tearing off each as the business was completed. According to a story often repeated, when Abraham Lincoln visited Cincinnati in connection with a law case, he went to see the Longworth estate, where he mistook its owner for a gardener. Longworth often pocketed the coins visitors offered him for a tour of his garden, but it is said that he remarked to Lincoln that his customary charge of ten cents was "the only really honest money I ever made, having been, by profession, a lawyer."

Three years after his arrival in Cincinnati, Longworth married the widow Susan Howell Conner, whom he met while visiting an artist's studio. They had three daughters and a son, and together they continued to enjoy the arts. Nicholas Longworth became the patron of several artists, the most notable being the sculptor Hiram Powers, who remained a lifelong friend and who named his son after his benefactor. Not all were as grateful. The painter Thomas Buchanan Read, who was given his own studio by Longworth, never forgave "Old Nick" for telling him, with some justice, that he was too impatient for fame to learn the rudiments of his art. And John Frankenstein, who fancied himself a poet, condemned "Nick Littleworth" in his *American Art: Its Awful Altitude* (1864) as a connoisseur who bought pictures at auction because he admired the smoothness of their canvas.

A better poet took a more favorable view—at least of Longworth's vintage. Longfellow's "Catawba Wine" praises the results of Longworth's lengthy experimentation with more than forty grape varieties; wine produced from the native Catawba proved good enough to export to Britain and Italy. From 1828 until about 1850, when the vines were killed by blight, Longworth produced as many as 150,000 bottles of sparkling Catawba a year from his 200 acres of terraced vines on the slopes of Mount Adams, where he had donated four acres as the site for an observatory. On this estate, which later became Cincinnati's Eden Park, he also experimented with strawberries by planting alternate rows of staminate and pistillate plants. This practice enabled Cincinnati market growers to take a leading role in the production of strawberries in the 1840s, and even after Longworth himself had introduced a hermaphrodite plant he continued to defend his original practice in the periodical press. One mark of the size and success of his horticultural work was his catalog, issued in 1825, of fruit trees for sale. It listed more than eighty varieties of apples, fifty varieties of peaches, seventy varieties of pears, twenty varieties of cherries, and numerous forms of quinces, apricots, grapes, currants, and gooseberries—all under cultivation in the twenty acres he had set aside as a nursery on his estate. He was author of numerous articles on practical horticulture, but his only publication still remembered is a nineteen-page pamphlet, *A Letter from N. Longworth to the Members of the Cincinnati Horticultural Society, on the Cultivation of the Grape . . . Also on the Character and Habits of the Strawberry Plant . . .* (1846).

Toward the end of his life in Cincinnati, where he died, Longworth was surrounded by grandchildren. It was his practice to fill a drawer in his desk with cash each day, so that his dependents could take what they needed without bothering to ask. It became a family tradition that the flight of their black butler, Harvey Young, rescued by Longworth from slave catchers before they could take him back across the river to servitude, was the inspiration for the character Eliza in *Uncle Tom's Cabin*. Harriet Beecher Stowe had heard the story when she lived in Cincinnati.

• The Cincinnati Historical Society has Longworth's will and five boxes of leases, deeds, and other documents pertaining to the Longworth estate that were copied from originals at the Hamilton County Courthouse before they were destroyed during a riot in 1884, as well as copies of a few letters addressed to him. Because there were three men named Nicholas Longworth (also his grandson the judge and his great-grandson the congressman) much confusion exists in the catalogs of their papers. The largest single collection of letters pertaining to the first of this name is one of about 200 items at the New Jersey Historical Society addressed to him by Catherine Longworth and to Marcus Ward, governor of New Jersey. Of interest are his letters to the painter Lily Martin Spencer, whose scattered papers have been gathered and filmed by the Archives of American Art; letters to him by the artist Hiram Powers remain in private hands, but copies are at the Cincinnati Historical Society. Clara Longworth de Chambrun, *The Making of Nicholas Longworth* (1933), is about the great-grandson, but one chapter, "Great-Grandfather Longworth," records some family traditions. Charles Cist, a newspaper editor who knew Longworth personally, left his reminiscences in *Sketches and Statistics of Cincinnati in 1851*, which gave an erroneous birth date often repeated in sketches based on it. Some of the "Letters of Hiram Powers" to Longworth were published in the *Quarterly Publication of the Historical and Philosophical Society of Ohio* 1 (1906): 33–59. His relationship with his most important protégé—whose marble bust of Longworth is at the Cincinnati Art Museum—is fully covered in Richard P. Wunder, *Hiram Powers, Vermont Sculptor* (1991). Gustavus Myers, *History of the Great American Fortunes*, rev. ed. (1936), gives a biased, but not uncommon, view of Longworth's financial success.

CHARLES BOEWE

LONGWORTH, Nicholas (5 Nov. 1869–9 Apr. 1931), Speaker of the House of Representatives, was born in Cincinnati, Ohio, the son of Nicholas Longworth, a lawyer, and Susan Walker. He was a fourth-generation member of one of Cincinnati's oldest and wealthiest families. His great grandfather, the first Nicholas Longworth, settled in Cincinnati in 1804 and established the family fortune by speculating in land. His grandfather and his father, the latter a judge of the Ohio Supreme Court for one year, were prominent in local civic and cultural affairs. After receiving his B.A. from Harvard University in 1891 and attending Harvard Law School for a year, he enrolled in Cincinnati Law School, earning his LL.B. in 1894. Supported by local Republican boss George B. Cox, he was elected to the Cincinnati Board of Education in 1898 and to the Ohio House of Representatives a year later. In 1901 he was elected to the Ohio Senate. The Longworth Act (1902), regulating the issuance of municipal bonds, was later acclaimed as one of the most successful laws in Ohio's history. In 1902 Cox offered Longworth the party's nomination for the U.S. House of Representatives. Longworth was easily elected, and he

served in the House from 1903 to 1913 and from 1915 until his death. He was among the many Republican incumbents defeated for reelection in 1912 as a result of a split between the party's mainstream members and its progressive wing, which deserted President William Howard Taft to support Theodore Roosevelt.

Initially assigned to the Committee on Foreign Affairs, Longworth became an advocate for better housing for U.S. ambassadors abroad. His bill to authorize the purchase of overseas residences for U.S. diplomats eventually became law. In 1907 he joined the Committee on Ways and Means, which provided him a platform for his views favoring limited government, moderately high import tariffs, and low domestic taxes. His work on the Payne-Aldrich Tariff Act of 1909 revealed an affinity for the political horse-trading that such legislation requires. Thereafter, he specialized in tariff law and was regarded by many as an expert in that area. A proponent of party government, he initially was a loyal follower of Speaker Joseph G. Cannon, whose autocratic style and vindictiveness rankled many Republicans as well as Democrats. However, in 1910, with Cannon's unpopularity threatening his party's prospects at the polls, Longworth broke ranks and became the first mainstream Republican to call for the election of a new Speaker. His action prompted some seventy Republicans to join him, ensuring that Cannon would not return as Speaker in the next Congress, but it failed to save the party from losing its House majority in the November elections.

Although usually labeled a conservative, Longworth often sided with his party's moderates on key issues, such as tariff policy. He had a streak of independence, which led him occasionally to take positions not shared by most of his House colleagues, such as when he denounced the seniority system for choosing committee chairmen. When the House Republicans returned to power in 1919, he emerged as one of his party's key leaders. In 1923 his fellow party members chose him to succeed Frank Mondell as the majority floor leader. His talent as a conciliator soon became evident in his negotiation of a delicate truce that kept disgruntled progressives from bolting the House Republican party and thereby reducing it to minority status. As majority leader, he worked harmoniously with the Calvin Coolidge administration to enact a tax reduction, a veterans' bonus, and an agreement to settle the European war debt. Under his leadership, the House in 1923–1925 passed 594 bills, double the number of the preceding two years. In April 1926 *Trend* magazine, praising the majority leader for a successful first term, said he had transformed a disorganized House into "one of the most efficient legislative machines in contemporary American history."

After serving for two years as majority leader, Longworth replaced Frederick Gillett as Speaker of the House when Gillett moved to the Senate on 7 December 1925. Longworth assumed an office that had been stripped of much of its defined authority. Under rules adopted following the House's 1910–1911 revolt against Speaker Cannon, the Speaker's role was reduced to that of a ceremonial officer, while the majority leader dominated the key party committees that set policy and managed the legislative agenda. Unwilling to give up his power as majority leader for the Speakership's prestige, Longworth maneuvered with his followers to accept the new office on his own terms, which included retaining his control over the party's governing committees. He thus managed, as he later explained, "to take the majority leadership from the floor to the chair, which most Speakers in recent years, except for [Thomas B.] Reed and Cannon, were not able to do." His achievement was extraordinary. Without changing the House rules, he took a weak and ineffectual office and overnight, by the force of his character and personality, restored it to dominance in the House. In demanding punishment for thirteen progressives who had refused to support the 1924 Republican candidate for president, he established his intent to command with a firm hand.

Throughout his three terms as Speaker (1925–1931), Longworth ruled as a benevolent czar. His influence over House affairs rivaled Cannon's at his peak. Unlike Cannon, however, he practiced the art of conciliation and accommodation so astutely that he got his way without sacrificing his popularity or his reputation for fairness. He gave much attention to the internal affairs of the House, introducing various reforms. He posted in advance the coming week's legislative calendar, information previously withheld from the minority; he made the *Congressional Record* more reliable by barring members from self-serving editing of their transcribed debates; and he ended House practices that discriminated against the women then beginning to enter Congress. Longworth was a top contender for the 1928 Republican presidential nomination until his anti-Prohibition record became an issue in the campaign.

Perpetually cheerful and outgoing, Longworth was an accomplished musician and comic performer and a highly popular figure on Capitol Hill and in Washington society. His marriage in 1906 to Alice Lee Roosevelt, daughter of then president Theodore Roosevelt, attracted worldwide attention and brought him instant fame. The Longworths had one daughter. Although he was a serious and talented lawmaker, Longworth's marriage caused many to dismiss him as a wealthy dilettante who owed his success more to a politically powerful father-in-law than to his own ability and hard work. Moreover, his joyous attitude toward life led some to doubt his seriousness as a leader. One of his House colleagues noted after Longworth's death, "His reputation as a good fellow and a charming companion rather obscured his real ability, which was very great." Consequently, he has never gained the recognition due him as one of the outstanding Speakers of the House. He died while visiting friends in Aiken, South Carolina.

• The bulk of Longworth's papers were lost or destroyed following his death. Most of his extant correspondence, speeches, articles, and scrapbooks are archived at the Cincinnati [Ohio] Historical Society. Additional papers are in the Nicholas Longworth and Alice Longworth collections of the Manuscript Division, Library of Congress, Washington, D.C. Clara Longworth De Chambrun, *The Making of Nicholas Longworth: Annals of an American Family* (1933), is a full-length biography of him, affectionately written by his sister, and is primarily an account of his early years in Cincinnati. Articles and other biographical sources are listed in Donald R. Kennon, ed., *The Speakers of the U.S. House of Representatives: A Bibliography, 1789–1984* (1986). Obituaries are in the *New York Times*, *New York Herald Tribune*, and *Washington Post*, all 10 Apr. 1931.

DONALD C. BACON

LOOKING GLASS (c. 1823–1877), Nez Percé war chief and buffalo hunter, known as Allalimya Tàkanin, or Looking Glass the Younger, was born in the Wallowa country in the Northwest Territory, the son of Apash Wyakaikt, chief of the Nez Percé. His mother's name is unknown. When his father, also known as Looking Glass the Elder, died, Allalimya Tàkanin removed the small, round trade mirror that his father had worn, placed it around his own neck, and thereafter called himself Looking Glass. As was the tradition, at about age ten the younger Looking Glass probably went on a solitary search to find his *Wyakin*, or guardian spirit, who, it was believed, gave protection and skills. As a young man he became a proficient hunter and horseman, spending much time away from his home in pursuit of buffalo, deer, and elk.

As a young warrior Looking Glass became caught in the struggle of landownership between the Nez Percé and the white settlers. He was part of a band of Indians who were referred to as "nontreaty" because they had refused to sign an 1863 treaty. He emerged as a leader and war chief because of his diplomacy, his eloquent speaking, and his decisive and persuasive manner in battles with the Sioux and Blackfeet. Although at times aggressive, and reputed to be antiwhite and anti-Christian, Looking Glass desired peace and did not want to begin an armed conflict with the settlers. He warned the Nez Percé that they could not succeed against the whites.

Following a lengthy history of treaties, the Indians were confined to a small reservation in the Wallowa Valley. In 1870 and 1871 settlers began straying onto their reservation lands. Looking Glass and the other chiefs protested but were informed that the U.S. government had purchased the land in the 1863 treaty. Conflicts heightened between Indians and whites and escalated when in 1877 a new commander, General Oliver Otis Howard, arrived at Fort Vancouver. Although sympathetic to the Indians, he nevertheless demanded they surrender a million acres of land and withdraw to a new reservation in Idaho. Looking Glass met with Howard to speak about the injustices done to them and to persuade him to change his mind. But Howard delivered an ultimatum that the Indians leave within thirty days.

Two days before the scheduled departure, three young Nez Percé avenged the death of one of the youth's fathers by killing four white settlers. Looking

Glass attempted to keep out of the conflict to no avail. Terrified settlers shrieked for justice. Chief Joseph, a respected Nez Percé, called for a truce and sent a delegation to the fort under a white flag. An anxious civilian opened fire, resulting in the wounding of three Indians. Howard sent 400 men to enclose the Nez Percé in White Bird Canyon. Rumors reached Howard that Looking Glass had decided to send reinforcements and then join "his people . . . on the first favorable opportunity." Howard sent two cavalry contingents to stop Looking Glass. The chief had no intention of entering the hostilities, but when a soldier fired his rifle, chaos ensued. Several tipis were burned, the village was looted, and soldiers rode off on Indian horses. Provoked, Looking Glass and his villagers escaped to join the more militant faction of the Nez Percé.

After ten days of pursuit, Howard discovered Looking Glass and the other Nez Percé, and fighting broke out. Called the battle of Clearwater, the skirmish lasted two days, after which the Indians scattered. Looking Glass and his band fled to Big Hole River in Montana, where he hoped to find a safe haven with the Plains Indians, the Crows. When they reached Montana, Looking Glass stopped, thinking they were out of danger. Several weeks later the Indians were attacked. They retaliated, resulting in large losses of life for both sides. Once again Looking Glass and his followers escaped. After another skirmish Looking Glass rested before taking flight to Canada, where he hoped to find refuge with Sitting Bull.

Blame for the Big Hole disaster and the deaths of many Indian women and children was placed on Looking Glass because of his overconfidence and failure at adequately protecting the encampment. The chief lost his authority to another in the band, and Looking Glass was designated as second in command. He later regained his position when he effectively spoke before the Indian council. Knowing that his people were tired and heartsick at their loss of relatives, he decided to slow the traveling pace.

Only forty miles short of the Canadian border, troops attacked the Indians again at the edge of the Bear Paw Mountains. Some Indians managed to escape and to reach Sitting Bull, who, it was reported, had gathered his Sioux warriors to aid the Nez Percé. In the meantime Looking Glass met in council with Chief Joseph. Joseph argued that they should surrender, and although Looking Glass desired to continue the fight, the chiefs agreed to at least talk to the whites.

Before any truce occurred, however, Looking Glass, who posted guard anticipating the arrival of Sitting Bull, saw an Indian on horseback and stood up from his hidden position on a bluff. Instantly Looking Glass was struck in the forehead by an army sharpshooter's bullet and died. Eyewitness accounts vary as to the exact date of the death of Looking Glass. Some set the date at 30 September 1877 and others contend it was 5 October 1877. Afterward, Chief Joseph surrendered, and the flight that had taken the Nez Percé 1,700 miles ended.

Other chiefs lost their lives in that final battle, but the loss of Looking Glass, a proud, eloquent, and forceful leader, was seen as the end of the traditions of the Nez Percé chiefs. In their flight to safety Looking Glass had been responsible for decisions that proved unwise, but his people continued to believe in his abilities to lead them to safety. Their confidence stemmed from the chief's knowledge of trails and Indians in the region gained from his extensive travels during hunts. Looking Glass never understood why the whites wanted "to separate my children and scatter them all over the country," for he wished only to have peace and a homeland for his people.

• No account exists of Looking Glass's origins, and few details can be found on his youth. The Nez Percé flight is included in military accounts and oral histories of the period. Information on the flight appears in O. O. Howard, *Nez Perce Joseph: An Account of His Ancestors, His Lands, His Confederates, His Enemies, His Murderers, His War, His Pursuit and Capture* (1881); Lucullus Virgil McWhorter, *Yellow Wolf: His Own Story* (1948) and *Hear Me My Chiefs!* (1952); Merrill D. Beal, *"I Will Fight No More Forever": Chief Joseph and the Nez Perce War* (1963); Alvin M. Josephy, Jr., *The Nez Perce Indians and the Opening of the Northwest* (1965); M. Gidley, *Kopet: A Documentary Narrative of Chief Joseph's Last Years* (1981); David Lavender, *Let Me Be Free: The Nez Perce Tragedy* (1992); Bruce Hampton, *Children of Grace: The Nez Perce War of 1877* (1994); and Lee Miller, ed., *From the Heart: Voices of the American Indian* (1995), p. 335.

MARILYN ELIZABETH PERRY

LOOKOUT, Fred (Nov. 1865–28 Aug. 1949), Native-American leader, was born near present Independence, Kansas, on the Osage reservation, the son of an Osage woman who died within weeks of his birth and Eagle-That-Dreams, warrior and hunter. Little is known of his childhood. He recalled accompanying his father on buffalo hunts when quite young and receiving the name Wy-hah-shah-shin-kah, Little-Eagle-That-Gets-What-He-Wants. The name "Lookout" came from a careless interpretation of the Osage terminology describing a perched eagle gazing into the distance and dreaming.

The Osages were removed from Kansas to a final reservation in Indian Territory (northern Oklahoma) in 1871. In 1881 Laban J. Miles, Quaker agent of the Bureau of Indian Affairs, chose Lookout and a few other tribal children to attend the Indian boarding school at Carlisle, Pennsylvania. In 1884 Lookout returned to be with his father, who was dying. Relatives advised him not to go back to school, and he stayed on the reservation to escape forced acculturation. In 1887 he married Julia Pryor (Mo-se-che-he), and the two worked a small farm near Pawhuska, the Osage national capital. When they lost the oldest of their four children, they grieved in the old way, giving away all their possessions and roaming the reservation, to be fed and sheltered by others.

In the 1890s many Osages followed the peyote religion, and Lookout became a Road Man, a principal figure in the ceremonies. He gave up his roached hair and plucked eyebrows, allowing his hair to grow long and wearing it in two braids. At the same time the tribe came under enormous pressure to allot their communal holdings to individual Osages, which they did in 1906, and in 1907, when Oklahoma became a state, the former reservation was incorporated as a county. The allotment act provided for an eight-man tribal council headed by a principal chief and an assistant chief. Lookout was elected assistant chief in 1908 for a two-year term and was appointed principal chief in 1914; he won election in 1916, again in 1924, and consecutively through 1946.

The Osages were wealthy due to oil and natural gas royalties earned from leasing their tribally owned mineral rights, which had been retained despite allotment of the surface area of their land. The council's business in the 1920s was primarily ratifying leases, but in the 1930s economic hardship hit the tribe as fuel prices fell. Lookout's leadership style was shrewdly effective. He relied heavily on younger, educated tribal members of mixed blood on the council to deal with the federal bureaucracy and the surrounding white majority. At the same time he urged moderation and restraint on the part of the older full-blood members in confronting modern realities. Tribal politics are complex and often tied to blood relationships. That Lookout could continue to be reelected is a tribute to his sagacity in remaining as a visible full-blood chief while allowing others of mixed blood to serve as cultural middlemen in protecting tribal rights. He died in Pawhuska, Osage County, Oklahoma.

• There is no collection of Lookout papers; however, the Osage Agency Collection housed at the Federal Records Center in Fort Worth, Tex., contains much about his political career. What little is known of his early life can be found in a newspaper article by Osage writer John Joseph Mathews in the *Sunday Oklahoman* (Oklahoma City), 23 Apr. 1939. Information on his beginnings as a tribal political power is in Orpha B. Russell, "Chief James Bigheart of the Osages," *Chronicles of Oklahoma* 32 (Winter 1954–1955): 384–94. A biographical sketch of his life and career is provided in Terry P. Wilson, "Chief Fred Lookout and the Politics of Osage Oil, 1906–1949," *Journal of the West* 23 (July 1984): 46–53.

TERRY P. WILSON

LOOMIS, Charles Battell (16 Sept. 1861–23 Sept. 1911), humorist, was born in Brooklyn, New York, the son of Charles Battell Loomis and Mary Worthington and the brother of composer Harvey Worthington Loomis. Orphaned in his teens, Loomis was educated at the Brooklyn Polytechnical Institute, though he left without receiving a degree. Between 1879 and 1891 he worked as an office clerk. In 1888 Loomis married Mary Charlotte Fullerton of New York; they had three children. For several years in the early 1890s he farmed the family estate in Torringford, Connecticut.

Loomis began to publish jokes and anecdotes in the humor magazine *Puck* in 1887, and he eventually became a regular contributor to such periodicals as *Harper's*, *Century*, *St. Nicholas*, *Criterion*, *Life*, *Bookman*, and the *Saturday Evening Post*. Among his humor

writings are "An Attempt to Translate Henry James," a gently mocking parody of James's late prolix style, published in the *Bookman* in July 1905, and "Earth Letter of a Martian," a fantastic send-up of early science fiction, which appeared in the same magazine in August 1907. In the latter article, for example, Loomis defined "artists" as "the people who interrupt conversation at receptions" and a professional as "one who does things for money that he couldn't be hired to do for love."

Over the years Loomis published *Just Rhymes* (1899), an edition of his occasional verse, and no less than thirteen other books, mostly collections of reprinted sketches, including *The Four-masted Cat-boat* (1899), *Yankee Enchantments* (1900), *A Partnership in Magic* (1903), *Cheerful Americans* (1903), *I've Been Thinking* (1905), *Cheer Up* (1906), the novel *Minerva's Manoeuvres* (1906), *A Bath in an English Tub* (1907), *Poe's "Raven" in an Elevator* (1907), *The Knack of It* (1908), *A Holiday Touch* (1908), *Just Irish* (1909), and *Little Maude and Her Mama* (1909). His brand of humor was ironical and whimsical domestic burlesque, not social or political satire. Of *Cheerful Americans*, Loomis's first major literary success, for example, the *Nation* (8 Oct. 1903) remarked that he "touches on a variety of life's little pleasantries, ranging from adventures of travel to ways and means of making presents to poor clergymen, and from fantastic incident to monologue portraits" (p. 287).

Loomis bolstered his reputation for humor as a popular platform speaker. As his friend and editor Jerome K. Jerome remembered, "His writings, as scattered through the magazines, were mildly amusing, but that was all. Until he stood up before an audience and read them: when at once they became the most humorous stories in American literature. He made no gestures; his face, but for the eyes, might have been carved out of wood; his genius was in his marvellous voice." In company with Jerome, in 1905 Loomis lectured across the United States and Canada and in England. His deadpan performances before the Salmagundi and Authors clubs of New York were the stuff of local legend. His friend the writer Stuart Henry remarked that "his lectures and readings, scintillating with amiable fun, never failed of their response of congenial laughter."

Preferring the suburbs to New York City, Loomis resided in New Jersey, living in Englewood and Fanwood and, after he earned his literary reputation, summering in Leonia. According to Henry, "His was the instinct of the people, for the mass." Through Loomis, Jerome "came to know the other America" outside the city—"the America of the dreamers, the thinkers, the idealists. He took me to see them in their shabby clubs; to dine with them in their fifty-cent restaurants; to spend fine Sundays with them in their wooden shanties, far away where the tram-lines end." Loomis died in Hartford, Connecticut, after a nine-month bout with stomach cancer.

• Few of Loomis's letters survive, though there are several small collections, the most significant of them at the Library of Congress, the University of Illinois, the University of Iowa, and the University of Virginia. Stuart Henry's memoir appears in the *Bookman* 35 (May 1912): 327–28; Jerome K. Jerome's reminiscence is in his autobiography, *My Life and Times* (1926). Obituaries are in the *New York Times*, 24 Sept. 1911, and the *Hartford Courant*, 25 Sept. 1911.

GARY SCHARNHORST

LOOMIS, Elias (7 Aug. 1811–15 Aug. 1889), educator, astronomer, and meteorologist, was born in Willington, Connecticut, the son of Hubbel Loomis, a Baptist minister, and Jerusha Burt. Loomis's father had studied at Union College and had received an honorary degree from Yale. As a child Loomis attended public school, studied Greek and mathematics with his father, and spent one winter at the academy at Monson, Massachusetts. He was admitted to Yale College at age fourteen, but he delayed his matriculation one year because of poor health. In addition to the classical curriculum at Yale, he took courses in natural philosophy and astronomy with Denison Olmsted. He graduated in 1830.

Loomis taught mathematics for one year at the Mount Hope Institute near Baltimore and attended Andover Theological Seminary for two years. From 1833 to 1836 he served as a tutor at Yale, first in Latin and subsequently in mathematics and natural philosophy. There, under Olmsted's mentorship, Loomis began to build his reputation as a scientist, primarily as a dedicated observer. According to his handwritten autobiographical sketch, for two weeks in November and December 1834, from 4:00 to 6:00 A.M., he joined Professor A. C. Twining at West Point in making observations for determining the altitude of shooting stars. "These are believed to have been the first concerted observations of the kind made in America." For fourteen months in 1834 and 1835 Loomis made hourly observations of the declination of the magnetic needle. Loomis and Olmsted were the first persons in America to identify Halley's comet on its return to perihelion in 1835, and Loomis computed the elements of its orbit from his own observations. During this period Loomis published his first scientific papers and became a member of the Connecticut Academy of Arts and Sciences.

In 1836 Loomis was appointed professor of mathematics and natural philosophy in Western Reserve College in Hudson, Ohio. He spent the first year of his appointment traveling in Great Britain and France, buying books and instruments, visiting scientists, and attending meetings and lectures. An account of his travels appeared as thirty-six "Letters from Europe" in the *Ohio* (later *Cleveland*) *Observer* between October 1836 and November 1837.

Loomis taught at Western Reserve from 1837 to 1844. There he built a small astronomical observatory and pursued his investigations in astronomy, meteorology, and terrestrial magnetism. In 1840 he married Julia Elmore Upson; the couple had two children. Loomis felt isolated in Hudson. The college was poor, its library was small, and he was its only professor of natural philosophy. Western Reserve had financial problems and often paid professors in part with merchandise or food. In 1844, when the college could not pay him at all, Loomis resigned and returned east. (When Loomis left, the college offered him the deed to unimproved lands as payment for his services.)

Loomis served as professor of mathematics and natural philosophy for fifteen years at New York University. He taught at Princeton for one year (1848) but then decided to return to New York. After the death of his wife in 1854, he lived a secluded life dedicated to teaching and research. Loomis was called to Yale in 1860 to replace Olmsted as professor of natural philosophy and astronomy and remained there for the rest of his life.

Between 1847 and 1869 Loomis published a series of standard textbooks on mathematics, natural philosophy, astronomy, and meteorology. Sales totaled over 600,000 copies, and the texts were reprinted many times. His well-known survey of astronomical observatories, *The Recent Progress of Astronomy, Especially in the United States*, was published in 1850. He was an authority in meteorology and a pioneer in the depiction of weather phenomena on maps. In 1869 one of his former students at Western Reserve, Wisconsin congressman Halbert E. Paine, sponsored legislation that inaugurated a national weather service. Between 1874 and 1889 Loomis, working with maps produced by the national weather service, published a series of twenty-three papers, "Contributions to Meteorology," in the *American Journal of Science*.

Loomis was interested in genealogy and traced his ancestors to Joseph Loomis of Braintree, England, who settled in Windsor, Connecticut, in 1639. He published a volume on the male branch in 1870 and a second edition in 1875. He also published a two-volume edition of the female descendents of Joseph Loomis in 1880.

He was a member of the U.S. National Academy of Sciences, American Philosophical Society, and American Academy of Arts and Sciences; a corresponding member of the British Association for the Advancement of Science; and an honorary member of the Philosophical Society of Glasglow, Royal Irish Academy, Royal Meteorological Society, and Societa Meteorologica Italiana. His textbooks were translated into French, Italian, Arabic, and Chinese.

Loomis was well respected by his students, who referred to him as "mathematics personified." According to an obituary notice from a Buffalo, New York, paper dated 17 August 1889, "Every word he uttered, every motion of his body, and even the arrangement of furniture in his room was as precise as if governed by the laws of geometry. . . . Prof. Loomis always appeared to wear the same clothes [a top hat and threadbare black frock coat] and it was the easiest thing in the world to imitate his angular manner." Loomis died of "Bright's disease" in New Haven, Connecticut. He bequeathed the bulk of his estate, valued at approximately $300,000, to Yale University.

• Yale University has two major collections of Loomis's papers, the Elias Loomis Papers in the Beinecke Rare Book and Manuscript Library and the Loomis Family Papers in Manuscripts and Archives. Correspondence from Loomis is found in the collections of most of the prominent scientists of his era, notably in the Edward Claudius Herrick Papers at Yale and in the Joseph Henry Collection at the Smithsonian Institution.

The standard biographies are by H. A. Newton, *Elias Loomis, LL.D., 1811–1889, Memorial Address Delivered in Osborn Hall, April 11, 1890* (1890) and "Memoir of Elias Loomis, 1811–1889," National Academy of Sciences, *Biographical Memoirs* 3 (1895): 213–52. A brief autobiographical sketch, written after 1883, is in the Marcus Benjamin Papers, Smithsonian Institution Archives.

On Loomis's work at Western Reserve see Bonnie S. Stadelman, "Elias Loomis and the Loomis Observatory," *Ohio Historical Quarterly* 69 (1960): 157–70, and E. R. Miller, "The Pioneer Meteorological Work of Elias Loomis at Western Reserve College, 1837–1844," *Monthly Weather Review* 59 (1931): 194–95. On Loomis as a professor at Yale see "An Old School Professor: Memoirs of Elias Loomis as a Man, Teacher, and Yale Benefactor," *Yale Alumni Weekly* 21 (1911–1912): 656–57, and Anson Phelps Stokes, *Memorials of Eminent Yale Men* (1914). James Rodger Fleming, *Meteorology in America, 1800–1870* (1990), contains an extended discussion of Loomis's role in meteorology and a comprehensive bibliography.

JAMES RODGER FLEMING

LOOMIS, Francis Butler (27 July 1861–4 Aug. 1948), journalist, diplomat, and foreign trade adviser, was born in Marietta, Ohio, the son of William Butler Loomis, an Ohio state judge, and Harriet Frances Wheeler. Francis Loomis graduated from Marietta College in 1883. After graduation Loomis worked with the *Marietta Leader* in 1883 and 1884 before moving to the *New York Tribune* in 1884 and 1885. He returned to serve as Ohio state librarian from 1885 to 1887 before reentering the world of journalism as Washington correspondent for the *Philadelphia Press* from 1887 to 1890.

Loomis frequently undertook political work for the Republican party, serving as press agent to Republican presidential candidate James G. Blaine in 1884 and to Benjamin Harrison (1833–1901) in 1888. President Harrison rewarded Loomis with an appointment as U.S. consul at St.-Étienne and Grenoble in France from 1890 to 1893. When Loomis returned to the United States, he assumed the post of editor in chief of the *Cincinnati Daily Tribune*. In 1896 he worked for William McKinley's successful presidential campaign. He married Elizabeth M. Mast in 1897; they had two children.

For this additional service to the Republican party and McKinley, the president named Loomis envoy extraordinary and minister plenipotentiary (EEMP) to Venezuela on 8 July 1897. He was recalled at the request of the Venezuelan government on 25 March 1901. He moved to Portugal as EEMP on 17 June 1901 and left that post on 16 September 1902. He returned to the United States to serve as first assistant secretary of state from 7 January 1903 until 10 October 1905.

When Secretary of State John Hay died, Loomis served briefly as acting secretary of state from 1 to 18 July 1905.

Loomis supported the objectives of the Open Door policy and the Roosevelt Corollary to the Monroe Doctrine. His most significant services were linked to U.S. commercial expansion, including efforts to secure the order and stability needed to promote investment and commerce. During his service in Venezuela, he worked on parcel post, extradition, and reciprocity trade treaties to facilitate trade, and in 1898 he traveled up the Orinoco River in Venezuela in search of opportunities for U.S. investors to participate in development projects.

Loomis played an instrumental role in generating U.S. support for Panama's separation from Colombia, the U.S. acquisition of French interoceanic canal company rights, and the signing of a treaty with the new Panamanian state. Although President Theodore Roosevelt (1858–1919) had encouraged the U.S. Senate to reject the first Hay-Pauncefote Treaty in 1900, he refused to concede Colombia's sovereign right to reject the Hay-Herrán convention in 1902. Philippe Bunau-Varilla, a French engineer and an official of the Universal Interoceanic Canal Company, was reportedly allied with Gustave Eiffel, Gerson Bleichröder, and other powerful French and German financial figures to extract gain from the collapse of the original canal company with the creation of the New Panama Canal Company. Bunau-Varilla used his friendship with Loomis to gain access to the U.S. government. In August 1903 Loomis asked John Bassett Moore, renowned international legal expert and frequent State Department legal counsel, whether the Bidlack-Mallarino Treaty of 1846 (which established U.S. and Colombian relations with regard to interoceanic transit) applied to the U.S.–Colombian canal negotiations. Moore's memorandum on this issue supplied the basis for aggressive U.S. policy and conduct in late 1903. Part of Loomis's value was his ability to organize ideas or rationalizations to pursue desired objectives.

Loomis became the intermediary between Bunau-Varilla (for the French interests) and the revolutionaries on the isthmus on one hand and Roosevelt's administration in 1903 on the other hand. He arranged several meetings for Bunau-Varilla with Secretary of State Hay and President Roosevelt. Apparently Loomis also advised Bunau-Varilla of U.S. policy and plans so that he could use Bunau-Varilla's connections with the disgruntled isthmian factions to coordinate the conduct of the revolutionary forces with U.S. military action and policy. Loomis arranged a meeting with Roosevelt on 29 October 1903, several days before Panama successfully revolted, to allow Bunau-Varilla to inform the isthmian revolutionaries about U.S. attitudes and activity. U.S. support was as circumspect as possible but direct when it had to be; U.S. naval vessels were sent to be present during the revolt, and when Colombian soldiers arrived to quell the uprising, the U.S. naval commander, under orders, denied them the right to land. The U.S.-Panamanian Treaty of 1903, negotiated and signed by Bunau-Varilla, not a Panamanian, conceded the U.S. government very favorable terms to build a canal and made Bunau-Varilla and his colleagues a large fortune. In 1904 the French government acknowledged Loomis's service to French interests by naming him a grand officer of the Legion of Honor.

Loomis was also an early supporter of establishing U.S. customs receiverships in Latin America as a means to prevent debt default problems from inducing foreign intervention into the Caribbean. In 1898 he made the unusual proposal of a U.S. customs receivership for Venezuela to resolve that country's debt default problems. Loomis also favored similar U.S. intervention into Santo Domingo in 1904 to avoid another crisis like the one that had followed the British-French-German-Italian intervention in Venezuela in 1902. He wanted to allow the Dominican government only 40 percent of its customs revenue to cover its budget, with the rest of the revenue diverted to debt payments and other essential foreign obligations. He drafted the final agreement formalizing U.S. intervention in Santo Domingo. He insisted that the pact should placate the U.S. Senate, which was uneasy about its prerogatives to approve such an agreement, rather than the Dominicans' concerns over having sufficient money to run their government. In the end, Loomis did accept a revision that allowed the Dominican government 45 percent of the customs revenue. His ideas and activity in the Santo Domingo negotiations were consistent with the Roosevelt Corollary to the Monroe Doctrine.

Loomis took an active role in U.S. policy toward Russia and the Far East. In mid-1903, when Secretary of State Hay was out of Washington, Roosevelt used Loomis to issue a statement condemning Russian pogroms against the Jews and protesting Russian conduct in Manchuria and China, which the president alleged undermined the Open Door. Loomis argued forcefully against conceding Japanese and Russian penetration in Manchuria. In 1905 he, Far Eastern expert William W. Rockhill, and U.S. minister to China Edwin Conger persuaded Roosevelt to resist a negotiated cancellation of the China Development Company contract (which was a J. P. Morgan [1837–1913] project), alleging that a cancellation would hamper future U.S. investment interests in China.

Loomis considered Japan a major player in the future of Asia. In 1905 he railed against the U.S. Pacific slope "idiots" (Californians) for their insensitivity in handling the matter of Japanese migration to California. In 1908 Roosevelt sent him as U.S. high commissioner to a proposed Japanese World Exposition. While in Japan, Loomis discussed with Japanese officials matters regarding the forthcoming visit of the U.S. fleet. During this mission, he expressed his personal conviction that Japan was not seeking world domination and that the country's leaders were level-headed and thoughtful men. In 1909 Japan granted him the Order of Sacred Treasure.

Loomis was named U.S. special ambassador to France in June 1905 to receive the remains of John Paul Jones (1747–1792) for reinterment in the United States. In 1912 he was named U.S. commissioner to the Turin (Italy) Exposition and the Berlin International Exposition Congress. In 1912 Italy awarded him the Grand Cordon, Crown of Italy, and he also received the Order of Bolívar from Venezuela.

Loomis was one of the original "incorporators" of the American Red Cross in 1905 and served on the Red Cross Board of Incorporators. About 1913 he made an unsuccessful attempt to purchase the *Oakland Tribune*. In 1914 he moved to Burlingame, California, and began a career as foreign trade adviser to Standard Oil of California. He became president of the Japanese Society of America in an effort to improve relations with Japan and to temper California attitudes toward Asians. Later he was president of the San Francisco chapter of the Italy America Society. In 1941 he retired from Standard Oil. He died in Burlingame.

Loomis succeeded as a newspaperman, as a public relations agent for the Republican party, and as a consultant in the oil industry. His most lasting impact upon U.S. history was his diplomatic labor in favor of U.S. expansion from the 1890s until World War I.

• The Francis Butler Loomis Papers, located in the Special Collections at Stanford University, are available on microfilm. Stanford University Libraries published a pamphlet, *Francis Butler Loomis and the Panama Crisis* (1965), which sketches his life and his role in the acquisition of the Panama Canal Treaty and briefly describes the material in the collection. There are hints of Loomis's role in Far Eastern affairs and in European diplomacy in Howard K. Beale, *Theodore Roosevelt and the Rise of America to World Power* (1956). Loomis's role in Latin America, the Panamanian Revolution, and the acquisition of canal rights on the isthmus is touched on in Richard H. Collin, *Theodore Roosevelt's Caribbean* (1990), David McCullough, *The Path between the Seas: The Creation of the Panama Canal, 1870–1914* (1977), and Thomas Schoonover, *The United States in Central America, 1860–1911: Episodes of Social Imperialism and Imperial Rivalry in the World System* (1991). Bunau-Varilla's relationship with Loomis is described in Gustavo Anguizola, *Philippe Bunau-Varilla* (1980). There are biographical sketches of Loomis in John E. Findling, ed., *Dictionary of American Diplomatic History* (1989), and the *Marietta Alumnus* 7 (June 1928): 177–78. Obituaries are in the *Marietta Alumnus* 28 (Oct.–Nov. 1948): 7–8, 14; the *New York Times*, 7 Aug. 1948; and the *Marietta Daily Times*, 10 Aug. 1948.

THOMAS SCHOONOVER

LOOMIS, Francis Wheeler (4 Aug. 1889–9 Feb. 1976), physicist, was born in Parkersburg, West Virginia, the son of Charles Wheeler Loomis and Miriam Linnell Nye. His father died when he was three years of age, and his mother held various jobs in Wisconsin and Massachusetts, being the sole provider for Loomis and his brother. Loomis attended Newton High School in Newton, Massachusetts, where one of his teachers excited his interest in physics and urged him to go to Harvard. In 1906 Loomis entered Harvard, from which he received his A.B. in 1910 and his A.M. in physics in 1913. From 1913 to 1915 he was an instructor in mathematics at Harvard, and in 1917 he was awarded his doctorate in physics. His dissertation, "The Heat of Vaporization in Mercury," was on experimental thermodynamics and was directed by Harvey N. Davis.

Loomis then worked as a research physicist at the lamp division of Westinghouse Electric Company in 1917 and in 1919–1920, with a two-year break for wartime service as a captain in the U.S. Army Ordnance Department. In 1920 he joined the faculty of New York University as an assistant professor. In July 1922 he married Edith Livingston Smith; they had three daughters. Later that year he went to the University of Illinois as an associate professor, and in 1929 he became professor and head of the physics department, serving in this capacity until two years before his retirement in 1959.

Upon returning to the university community in 1920, Loomis had switched his field of interest from thermodynamics to molecular spectroscopy, particularly the band spectra of diatomic molecules. In this field he rapidly gained an international reputation for his discovery of the influence of the isotopic composition of the constituent atoms upon the resulting band spectra. The initial work, done in 1920, was carried out with hydrogen chloride, allowing for the identification of several molecular species that in turn facilitated the discovery of important new isotopes of carbon and oxygen. In 1922 he refined the oil-drop technique for what was then a new precise measurement of the ratio of the charge on the electron and proton. He coauthored the National Research Council Report "Molecular Spectra in Gases," led by Edwin C. Kemble (1926). Finally, with Robert C. Wood, he discovered the nuclear spin of potassium (1931). A careful and ingenious experimenter, Loomis instilled these virtues in his students; one of them, Polykarp Kusch, won the 1955 Nobel Prize in physics.

Loomis's tenure at Illinois was interrupted by his study during 1928–1929 in Europe as a Guggenheim fellow in Göttingen and Zürich; at the latter, he attended the lectures of Wolfgang Pauli and found them to be very stimulating. Beginning with World War II Loomis became increasingly involved in the administration and direction of governmental research and development. This included his service as associate director of the Radiation Laboratory at the Massachusetts Institute of Technology (1941–1946), as well as organizer and first director of the Lincoln Laboratory at the same institution (1951–1952). He also founded (1952) and directed (1952–1959) the Control Systems Laboratory (later the Coordinated Science Laboratory) at the University of Illinois. His postwar activities included membership on numerous advisory boards and committees for the Atomic Energy Commission, the U.S. Air Force, the Ballistic Research Laboratories, the National Academy of Sciences, and the Na-

tional Science Foundation. Loomis conducted much of his advisory work on highly classified projects during the Cold War period, and his actual contributions and roles in them are not known to the general public. Loomis was elected a member of the National Academy of Sciences in 1949; that same year he was president of the American Physical Society. The Loomis Laboratory at the University of Illinois was named in his honor.

Throughout his career Loomis focused his attention on two objectives: the pursuit of research of the highest quality by himself and his staff; and the building of academic and research programs on firm foundations of excellence. His personal research was distinguished, and his government service was outstanding. The latter was no doubt due to the soundness of his scientific advice, to his excellent contacts, and to his unfailing ability to recruit top quality people to serve under him. Under Loomis's tutelage, the physics department at the University of Illinois flourished and developed into one of the most distinguished departments in the United States. Taking great pride in the accomplishments of his staff and students, Loomis was delighted when one of his colleagues, John Bardeen, shared the Nobel Prize in physics (1956), the first Nobel Prize to be awarded to a University of Illinois physicist. Bardeen was to share a second Nobel Prize in 1972. Loomis died in Urbana, Illinois.

• The University Archives at the University of Illinois at Urbana-Champaign holds a collection of Loomis's papers, including a transcript of an interview with him conducted in Nov. 1964. The major biographical reference on Loomis is in National Academy of Sciences, *Biographical Memoirs* 60 (1991): 116–26, which contains a portrait and a list of publications. Loomis apparently had little taste for reminiscing and preferred to speak of the present and his hopes for the future; consequently, little is known about his family life or personal life. In his final address as outgoing president of the American Physical Society in 1950, however, he indulged in a rare moment of introspection. This address, "Can Physics Serve Two Masters?" appeared in *Bulletin of the Atomic Scientists*, Apr. 1950, pp. 115–20 and 127. An obituary notice is in *Physics Today*, May 1977, pp. 83–85.

JOSEPH D. ZUND

LOOS, Anita (26 Apr. 1893–18 Aug. 1981), author and child actress, was born Corinne Anita Loos in Sissons (now called Mount Shasta), California, the daughter of Richard Beers Loos, a newspaper owner and editor, and Minnie Ellen Smith. "In my youth I never kept a diary, feeling that a girl who could sell her words for money had other fish to fry," Loos (pronounced Lohse) wrote in her 1974 autobiography, *Kiss Hollywood Good-by*. These words typify the writer who, from a very early age, kept herself busy making money. Her handsome, roving father moved the family to San Diego, California, as he pursued an erratic career in journalism. By the time Anita graduated from San Diego High School, she had already worked as a child actress in a number of productions, including *Quo Vadis? A Doll's House*, and *Little Lord Fauntleroy* (in which she played Fauntleroy). She began writing screen scenarios while still a teenager; her first sale was "The New York Hat," which was produced in 1912. Her first screenplay, *The Road to Plaindale*, appeared in the same year. She was paid $25 for each.

When, after a brief, unhappy marriage to Frank Pallma in 1915, Loos went to Hollywood with her mother to apply for a regular job, D. W. Griffith mistook the ninety-pound Loos for a child and assumed her mother to be the author. Properly informed, Griffith hired the young woman to write plots and subtitles for his silent films. During the years she worked in Hollywood, she created more than 200 film scripts, including more than 100 half-hour slapstick comedies, such as *The Deadly Glass of Beer* (1914), for which she wrote a one-page synopsis and earned $25. Pretty, sociable, talented, and amusing, Loos soon became an active part of the Hollywood scene. Her friends included Lillian and Dorothy Gish, Norma and Constance Talmadge, Douglas Fairbanks, and Mary Pickford. Loos traveled to New York, Palm Beach, and Europe. She married writer-director John Emerson in 1919 and collaborated with him on numerous films and plays. Neither of her marriages produced children. Although Emerson was nineteen years her senior and more experienced in the business, friends believed that Loos's wit was responsible for much of their continued success.

The publication of *Gentlemen Prefer Blondes* as a serial in *Harper's Bazaar* in 1925 elevated Loos to international fame. Protagonist Lorelei Lee (supposedly based on a companion of the author's friend H. L. Mencken) has often been viewed as the prototypical dumb blonde, but her insights are sharp enough to serve as criticism of American and European society. Lorelei is not what she would call "authrodox"; she says of herself, "I seem to be thinking practically all of the time. I mean it is my favorite recreation and sometimes I sit for hours and do not seem to do anything else but think." She explains that this is the reason she came to be writing a book instead of reading one. Lorelei's (and Loos's) combination of wit and wisdom made *Gentlemen* so popular that it had eighty-three American printings and was translated into thirteen languages. At least one source reports that Winston Churchill kept a copy of the book on his bedside table, and James Joyce is said to have read it when he was losing his eyesight. Aldous Huxley said he would like to keep Loos "as a pet," and Mencken claimed she was "the first American writer ever to poke fun at sex." Loos rewrote the book as a play that had tremendous popularity on stage with Carol Channing as Lorelei. It was later made into a movie starring Marilyn Monroe. Loos's sequel to the book, *But Gentlemen Marry Brunettes*, came out in 1928 and was widely read but did not achieve the fame of its predecessor.

In 1931, after the death of Griffith, Loos went to work at MGM for Irving Thalberg, continuing her screenwriting career. In 1931–1932 she wrote the screenplay for *Red-Headed Woman*, based on a bestselling novel by Katharine Brush. This was Loos's introduction to the "talkies," and it was so successful that it "instantly catapulted Jean Harlow into stardom." It also won *Vanity Fair*'s award as best film of the year but was considered rather scandalous because the heroine was a bad girl who gained success rather than recrimination for her sins. In 1932 Loos supplied dialogue for *Blondie of the Follies*. Her 1936 screenplay *San Francisco* was a showcase for Clark Gable. Other films included *Hold Your Man* (1933), *Social Register* (1934), and *Riffraff* (1935). Loos's last film credit was for *Gentlemen Prefer Blondes* in 1953. She acted as a troubleshooter on other scripts and also wrote a number of popular plays, including *The Whole Town's Talking* (1923), in collaboration with John Emerson; *Happy Birthday* (1947); and *Gigi* (1951), based on the novel by Collette.

In her two-volume autobiography, *A Girl Like I* (1966) and *Kiss Hollywood Good-by* (1974), Loos presents an irreverent, gossip-filled, readable picture of her life among the stars. Concurrently she coauthored *Twice Over Lightly* with Helen Hayes. This nonfiction work appeared in 1972 and recorded their 1970–1971 exploration of New York City, which lasted eighteen months and included such disparate adventures as a trip to the Staten Island zoo and a local bartenders' school. Hayes, noting Loos's preference for Balenciaga and high society, claimed that her friend's chief standard of judgment was chic and once said to her, "If you get to heaven and find St. Peter short on chic, you'll back away and head in the other direction." Another acquaintance remarked that "Anita's allegiance to high fashion has always been shared by a love for piquant company. Her idea of a pleasant evening is to trail a Halston ball gown across the sawdust floor of a saloon."

In spite of her taste for fun and her ability to make friends, life was not always smooth for Loos. She and Emerson spent years living separately while she supported both of them. Ignoring his reported infidelities, she maintained the marriage and took care of him when he became ill. She had a long-term (but apparently chaste) relationship with Wilson Mizner, whom she described as "slim, beautiful, and his voice was sexy to the ear," until his death. She spent the last years of her life alone except for the companionship of her housekeeper and the continued appreciation of friends and her many fans. She died in New York City.

• A list of screenplays by Anita Loos appears in *Kiss Hollywood Good-by*. In addition to the novels already named, Loos wrote *A Mouse Is Born* (1951) and *No Mother to Guide Her* (1961). Nonfiction works include *A Cast of Thousands* (1977), a large volume consisting mainly of photographs, and *The Talmadge Girls* (1979). Some additional plays are *The Fall of Eve*, *Cheri*, *All About Anne*, and *Lorelei* (based on *Gentlemen Prefer Blondes*). Also useful is the biography of Gary Carey, *Anita Loos* (1988), and Nancy Walker and Zita Dresner, eds., *Redressing the Balance* (1988), an anthology of American women's literary humor. An obituary is in the *New York Times*, 19 Aug. 1981.

ELAINE FREDERICKSEN

LOPEZ, Aaron (1731–28 May 1782), merchant, was born Duarte Lopez in Lisbon, Portugal, the son of Diego Lopez (mother's name unknown). Nothing is known of his childhood or education. He abandoned his Christian name Duarte, his parents, and his native land of Portugal when he left Lisbon in 1752 with his wife, Anna, setting sail for the British colony of Rhode Island. He followed in the footsteps of his older brother, Moses (born José), who had fled religious persecution in the 1730s, going first to New York, and then by 1749 to the seaport town of Newport, Rhode Island, a city known for its religious tolerance. By the time Aaron (as he now called himself) arrived in America, Moses had already established himself as a merchant in the thriving commercial entrepôt. When Aaron Lopez arrived in Newport, he was welcomed by the small Jewish community there, gained easy access to credit, and quickly began to develop a business that would make him Newport's "merchant prince" by 1770.

In 1761, having resided in Newport for over seven years, Lopez tried to gain status as a naturalized inhabitant of Rhode Island. His application was denied by the Rhode Island legislature and by the superior court. While his credentials were impeccable, his timing was not. He was a pawn in the rivalry between Newport and Providence, Rhode Island's two major cities. Stephen Hopkins (1707–1785), a leader of the Providence faction, was chief justice at the time of Lopez's application, and because he wanted to do nothing that would enhance the power of Newport, he used his influence to deny Lopez's application. Using connections he had developed in Boston, Lopez moved to Swansea, Massachusetts, established residence there, and received his naturalization papers in October 1762. While naturalization did not afford him political rights, it did guarantee him all commercial privileges accruing to any British colonist.

Lopez's fortunes rose and fell with the fortunes of his adopted home. He had arrived at a propitious time, at the beginning of the Seven Years' War (1755–1763), when commercial opportunities abounded. While the war disrupted trade, it also created work for ship builders, resulted in government contracts for well-connected artisans and victuallers, and stimulated the economy as English and American soldiers both became avid consumers of domestic and imported goods. Investments in privateers and flags of truce were risky, but they often proved extremely lucrative. Like all New England merchants, Lopez hedged his bets, diversifying his cargoes and sending his ships to a variety of destinations. He specialized in the sale of spermaceti, material from the head matter of sperm whales that was used to make candles. In 1761, he joined the United Company of Spermaceti Candlers, a consortium of nine firms—six of which were Jewish owned—designed to regulate the spermaceti trade, reduce competition, and lower the price of the precious head matter. By at least 1767, he was engaged in the manufacture as well as the sale of spermaceti candles.

By the end of the war, Lopez's personal and professional fortunes had taken a turn for the worse. His wife Anna (now the Jewish "Abigail") died in 1762 leaving him to care for their seven children; the following year he married Sarah Rodrieguez Rivera, daughter of commercial magnate Jacob Rodrieguez Rivera. But even this advantageous union did not help Lopez to prosper throughout the postwar depression that devastated Newport's merchant community. The contraction of trade, coupled with new, more strictly enforced shipping regulations emanating from London, made postwar Newport, in one merchant's words, "a world uncertain and strongly chequer'd."

Ironically, as his business prospects were at their gloomiest, Lopez decided to expand his operations. He availed himself of the seemingly limitless credit offered by Bristol merchant Henry Cruger to try to establish commercial connections in England. He was unsuccessful, and so turned his attentions to the West Indies, especially Jamaica, where, after a few false starts, he was more successful. By 1770, he had not only recouped his losses, but was one of Newport's leading merchants. No one profited more from the city's "golden age" than Aaron Lopez. He owned twenty vessels and traded throughout Europe, the West Indies, and Africa. He also moved into manufacturing, employing workers to make cloth, shoes, barrels, and ships. He was involved as well in the slave trade, rum distilling and chocolate grinding. In 1775 he was Newport's largest taxpayer and served on various committees created by Rhode Island's legislature.

Lopez's success was due in part to luck and in part to his conservative approach to business. He took no undue risks; he was a businessman, not a speculator. His techniques were those employed by all Newport merchants in the eighteenth century: he established sound personal connections with his trading partners, diversified his trading operations, and became involved in manufacturing and real estate ventures, never limiting himself to merchant affairs alone.

With the coming of the Revolution, Lopez's commercial empire collapsed. He was at best a lukewarm patriot, and he strove mightily to keep his merchant business afloat when war broke out. But with the British occupation of Newport from 1776 to 1779, Lopez fled the city with his family, first to Portsmouth, and ultimately to Leicester, Massachusetts, to await the end of the war. There he dabbled in real estate, built an "elegant mansion," and tried to continue his merchant activities in the face of a British blockade and the threat posed by American privateers, whose captains did not always take the trouble to distinguish between loyal and disloyal ships.

Lopez returned with his family to Newport in 1782. He was still young and had some reason to hope that he might duplicate his prewar successes. To be sure, Newport merchants had to contend with the increasingly sharp competition from merchants based in Providence, whose control of the colony's political machinery and greater access to Rhode Island's hinterland made them formidable rivals. Moreover, another postwar depression threatened everyone's immediate prospects. Still, Lopez's ability and connections made him optimistic.

He failed, however, to rebuild his commercial empire. On a family excursion to Providence, Lopez stopped at Smithfield to water his horses. As he drove his carriage into a pond, the carriage tipped over, and Lopez—who had never learned to swim—drowned in front of his horrified family. He was buried in Newport's Jewish cemetery.

• Most of Aaron Lopez's papers are located in the Newport Historical Society in Newport, Rhode Island. Some letters can also be found in *Commerce of Rhode Island* (2 vols., 1914–1915). The most recent biography is Stanley F. Chyet, *Lopez of Newport: Colonial American Merchant Prince* (1970). See also Morris A. Gutstein, *Aaron Lopez and Judah Touro: A Refugee and a Son of a Refugee* (1939), and David S. Lovejoy, *Rhode Island Politics and the American Revolution: 1760–1776* (1958).

SHEILA L. SKEMP

LÓPEZ, José Dolores (1 Apr. 1868–17 May 1937), farmer, carpenter, and woodcarver, was born in Córdova, Rio Arriba County, New Mexico, the son of Nasario Guadalupe López and María Teresa Bustos. Nasario López was a carpenter, and his son learned that trade as a child. As a young man he worked as a shepherd, but in 1893 he married Candelaria Trujillo and moved to a farm in Llano de Quemadeños, east of Córdova. They had seven children. Candelaria died in 1912, and in 1913 López moved back to Córdova and married Demetra Romero. That marriage was childless.

López began to carve and work in wood in 1917 to relieve his anxiety over his eldest son, who had been drafted into the army and sent to Europe. He made carved and painted picture frames, clock shelves, and stands, which he presented to his neighbors as gifts. He also made carved woodwork and religious images for the chapel of San Antonio, of which he was sacristan, and for the *morada* (meeting place) of the confraternity of the Brothers of Our Father Jesus the Nazarene, of which he was *hermano mayor* (spiritual leader). Most of this work was of highly original design, carved with floral, animal, and geometric patterns in shallow incised lines and brightly painted with commercial oil-based house paint.

In the early 1920s López's work came to the attention of Anglo-American art patrons in Santa Fe, including two of the founders of the Spanish Colonial Art Society, Frank Applegate and Mary Austin. Applegate invited López to show his woodcarving at the society's annual exhibit during the Santa Fe Fiesta, and in 1927 López won first prize in the furniture category for a carved shelf. His Anglo-American patrons soon influenced López to abandon his brightly painted furniture for an unpainted and richly carved style that conformed to their conception of Hispanic folk art. He made utilitarian objects such as record racks, lazy Susans, and screen doorframes in this style, as well as imaginative animals and religious figures, whose surfaces were ornamented with elaborate incised patterns. Many of his religious figures were carved in groups representing narrative themes such as Adam and Eve in the Garden of Eden, the Expulsion from the Garden, the Flight into Egypt, and the Nativity, and these groups are regarded by art historians as his most important works.

After 1927 all of López's carvings were made for the tourist trade, and many were sold at the annual Santa Fe Fiesta and through the Spanish Arts Shop and the Native Market, which were outlets for Hispanic crafts. López's lively wit and outgoing personality made his work extremely popular with Anglo-American patrons. While there are no records of his rate of production or income, family members have recalled that he worked all year long to fill orders, and he earned enough to live in his native village without doing other kinds of work. His small animal carvings sold for twenty-five to fifty cents each; chairs, from five to seven dollars; and tables, ten dollars. Applegate and Austin, in their unpublished manuscript on New Mexican folk art, said that López's work combined "the austere lines and expressiveness of the best modern sculpture" with the "authentic folk touch." Because of injuries received in an accident, López stopped carving in 1933. He died in Córdova.

López established woodcarving as an important cottage industry in the town of Córdova. His sons Nicudemas, Raphael, Ricardo, and George became well-known carvers, as did two grandchildren. Following the López family's example, several other Córdova families opened shops and began to sell carvings, which became a major source of income to the community and made Córdova famous for its woodcarving.

By the early 1930s López had become recognized as an important American folk artist. His work was included in an exhibition of southwestern arts and crafts at the Arden Gallery in New York in 1931, in the National Exhibition of Art by the Public Works of Art Project at the Corcoran Gallery of Art in Washington, D.C., in 1934, and in the National Rural Arts Exhibition organized by Allen Eaton in Washington in 1937. His work is in the collections of the Museum of International Folk Art in Santa Fe, the Denver Art Museum, the Taylor Museum of the Colorado Springs Fine Arts Center in Colorado Springs, and the Smithsonian Institution's National Museum of American Art.

• The most complete treatment of López's life and work is in Charles L. Briggs, *The Wood Carvers of Córdova, New Mexico* (1980). See also Sarah Nester, *The Native Market of the Spanish New Mexican Craftsmen, 1933–1940* (1978), and Lonn Taylor and Dessa Bokides, *New Mexican Furniture* (1987).

LONN TAYLOR

LOPEZ, Vincent (30 Dec. 1895–20 Sept. 1975), bandleader and jazz pianist, was born in Brooklyn, New York, the son of Antonio Lopez, a music teacher, and Virginia Gonsalves. Lopez's father, a former naval bandmaster who was a strict disciplinarian, made young Lopez practice the piano for three hours each day during the school year and for six hours per day during vacations. In spite of this attention to music, Lopez's father planned for his son to enter the Roman Catholic priesthood, and so the youngster was enrolled at age twelve in St. Mary's Passionist Monastery in Dunkirk, New York. After three years, Lopez left St. Mary's against his father's wishes and returned to Brooklyn, where he completed a nine-month course of study at Kissick's Business College. Lopez then accepted a clerical job for a local milk company, and he also began to play piano in the evenings at Clayton's, a Brooklyn saloon. By 1916 Lopez had left the milk company and was working full time as a professional pianist in various beer halls and restaurants in New York City.

In 1916 Lopez assumed the duties of bandleader at the famous Pekin Restaurant in Times Square, replacing Ed Fischelli. Lopez, exempt from service in the armed forces because of gout, remained at the Pekin throughout World War I. After employment at Ross Fenton's Farms in Asbury Park, in 1921 Lopez was hired as bandleader at the Grill of the Hotel Pennsylvania in Manhattan.

On 27 November 1921 Lopez and his band performed a live radio broadcast from the WJZ studios in Newark, New Jersey, and within several weeks were broadcasting regularly from the Hotel Pennsylvania. These performances are possibly the earliest remote (originating from a location other than the studio) broadcasts on commercial radio. During the WJZ broadcasts Lopez first introduced himself with "Hello everybody—Lopez speaking." He also began to use as his theme "Nola," a piano solo composed by Felix Arndt. He continued his distinctive introduction and the use of "Nola" as a theme for the remainder of his career.

The remote radio broadcasts earned Lopez so much fame that the band began to perform in concerts and appeared in two Broadway musicals, Sigmund Romberg's *Love Birds* (1921) and *Greenwich Village Follies* (1924). Performances during the next several years included an extended engagement at the Palace (Aug.–Oct. 1922), a concert at the Metropolitan Opera House (23 Nov. 1924), President Calvin Coolidge's inaugural ball (Jan. 1925), and a tour of England (summer 1925).

On 15 October 1925 Lopez opened his own nightclub, named Casa Lopez. After it was destroyed by fire in early 1927, he opened a second Casa Lopez, but it failed financially after only a few months of operation. Lopez appeared in another Broadway musical, *Earl Carroll's Vanities of 1928*. In June 1928 he was hired by the St. Regis Roof Garden. The St. Regis management was so delighted with his services that in 1930 they signed him to a ten-year, $10 million contract, but the Great Depression forced the St. Regis to cancel the contract in 1934.

During the next seven years, Lopez traveled frequently outside New York City to find work and performed everywhere "from Florida dog tracks to Buffalo gambling dens." He appeared on various radio shows, including Plough's "Musical Courier" (1934),

the "Speed Show" with Floyd Gibbons (1936), the "Nash Show" starring Grace Moore (1937), and the "Show of the Week" with Buddy Clark (1940); also in 1940 he appeared at Billy Rose's Aquacade at the New York World's Fair. In 1941 he was hired by the Grill Room of the Hotel Taft for what was originally intended to be a three-month engagement; Lopez remained at the Grill Room until the mid-1960s.

After the success of an appearance on the "Ed Sullivan Show" in 1949, Lopez hosted his own fifteen-minute daily television program that ran for more than two years on the Dumont network. In 1950 his "Dinner Date with Lopez" broadcast from the Grill Room became the first regularly scheduled television program to be broadcast remotely.

In 1921 Lopez married May Kenny, with whom he had one child. His first wife died in 1938, and Lopez married Bettye Long in 1951. The couple had no children. Lopez died in a nursing home in North Miami Beach.

Lopez developed an active interest in numerology. He published a book of predictions, *What's Ahead?* (1944), authored a column on numerology for the *San Francisco Chronicle*, wrote brief numerology articles for several magazines, including *American Astrology*, and presented lectures on the subject. His autobiography, *Lopez Speaking: My Life and How I Changed It* (1960), details his belief in numerology and the vicissitudes of his career. Lopez also wrote the four-volume *Modern Piano Method* (1931).

Songs for which Lopez is credited as composer or lyricist include "Knock Knock," "Rockin' Chair Swing," "Silver Head," "Piano Echoes," "Three Sisters," "Since Nellie Came Back from the City," "Sky Ride," "Capricorn," "What's Your Business," "Does a Duck Like Water?," "Clarabel," "The World Stands Still," "Bell Bottom Trousers," "Charlie Was a Sailor," and "Charlie Was a Boxer."

Lopez's significance lies foremost in his enormous popularity as a leader of sweet-styled dance bands. He is also remembered for scouting talent; notable musicians who worked with Lopez early in their careers include Glenn Miller, Artie Shaw, Charlie Spivak, Xavier Cugat, Abbe Lane, and Betty Hutton. Using numerology, he renamed Hutton from Betty Darling and recast Edna Mae Burbin as Deanna Durbin.

• Lopez's autobiography, *Lopez Speaking*, remains the most significant source of information on his career; a number of journal articles and reference works, including the detailed but somewhat hagiographic profile of Lopez in *Current Biography 1960*, pp. 242–44, merely recycle information from it. Obituaries are in *Newsweek* and *Time*, both 6 Oct. 1975.

MICHAEL COGSWELL

LORAS, John Mathias Peter (30 Aug. 1792–19 Feb. 1858), first Roman Catholic bishop of Dubuque, Iowa, was born in Lyons, France, the son of Jean Mathias Loras and Étiennete Michalet. His father, a prosperous merchant and councillor of the city of Lyons, was sent to the guillotine on 9 November 1793 for his part in that city's revolt against the Jacobin government in Paris. His mother continued to harbor priests, one of whom later founded a presbyteral school that Mathias attended. A classmate was Jean-Baptiste Vianney, the future curé d'Ars and saint. Mathias entered first the minor seminary at L'Argentière in 1807 and then the grand seminary of St. Irenaeus in Lyons, where he studied under Ambroise Maréchal and was a classmate of James Whitefield, two future archbishops of Baltimore. Ordained a priest on 12 November 1815, he was rector of the minor seminaries of Meximieux (1817–1824) and L'Argentière (1824–1827), at both of which he put up substantial buildings. When Bishop Michael Portier of Mobile, Alabama, invited him in 1829 to join his new and underdeveloped diocese, Loras was engaged in pastoral work in the archdiocese of Lyons.

On his arrival in Mobile, Loras was appointed vicar general and sent on a seven-month tour of Alabama to search out Catholics and devise plans for churches. His principal task, however, was the founding in 1830 of an academy and seminary, Spring Hill College, of which he was president until 1832. He served as head of the board of the college from 1833 to 1837. In 1833 he began, as rector, the construction of a cathedral. At the Third Provincial Council of Baltimore the American bishops proposed Loras as first bishop of the projected diocese of Dubuque, compromising that part of the Wisconsin Territory above the state of Missouri between the Mississippi and Missouri rivers. The choice was confirmed by Rome on 28 July 1837, and Loras was raised to the episcopacy on 10 December by Bishop Portier in Mobile. Loras immediately left for France to seek recruits. Two priests, including a friend and former pupil at Meximieux, Joseph Cretin, and four subdeacons responded.

In his extensive diocese he found only the Dominican missionary Samuel Charles Mazzuchelli, a newly built church, and a few hundred Catholics, mostly French-Canadian fur trappers near Fort Snelling and some Irish in his see city. The Black Hawk Purchase had, however, opened large parts of his diocese to settlement, and Irish and German Catholics were beginning to enter in great numbers. Loras placed advertisements in eastern newspapers and sent agents to promote immigration to Iowa. This placed him in contention with a number of eastern prelates, most notably Archbishop John Hughes of New York, who feared a loss of faith on the understaffed frontier. Loras's confidence, however, was justified; Iowa filled rapidly. Though the bishop purchased land and built churches in farming villages to attract Catholics, the Irish particularly preferred growing cities such as Dubuque, Davenport, Burlington, and Des Moines. A large rural Catholic population, however, pushed westward, reaching Council Bluffs on the western edge of the state in the 1850s. Loras also devoted a large part of the diocesan resources to the Indian missions in the north. A significant portion of the generous allocations of mission-aid societies in Lyons, Munich, and Vienna was devoted to this work. He was relieved of his Indian ministry in 1850 when the diocese of St. Paul was carved out of the northern portion of the diocese of Dubuque with Joseph Cretin, Loras's former vicar general, its first bishop. Until 1843, when the dioceses of Chicago and Milwaukee were created, Loras also had charge of Wisconsin east of the Mississippi and parts of northwest Illinois.

Loras was always in need of Irish and German priests, despite his many begging tours in Europe. In 1839 he opened a combination academy and seminary that today is Loras College. In 1851 he began a separate and larger seminary. Catholic education, a major concern of Loras, received a great boost in 1843 when the Sisters of Charity of the Blessed Virgin Mary of Philadelphia agreed to move their entire establishment to Dubuque. In 1850 a body of Trappist monks from Ireland established the Abbey of New Melleray near the see city and opened a free school for boys. Visitation sisters entered the diocese in 1852 to open an academy for girls. Communities of teaching brothers came twice to Dubuque but neither remained long.

Loras was a tireless worker but not the best of administrators. In 1850 and 1853 he conducted diocesan synods that brought sufficient order to his episcopal domain and a measure of harmony that compensated for earlier difficulties. An estrangement that had developed with Father Mazzuchelli and contention with the Irish of his see city, whom he finally put under interdict in 1853 for refusing to support the new cathedral he was raising, caused him to establish residence elsewhere for a few years. Loras became one of the foremost Catholic promoters of the temperance movement, refusing to touch even a glass of wine during visits to his native France. He lived simply. Though he never lost his French airs and accent, he was thoroughly American in his outlook, spurning the offer of a French see. In 1857, for reasons of health, he chose as his coadjutor with right of succession the Irish abbot of New Melleray. By the time of his death a year later in Dubuque, Loras had created one of the most flourishing dioceses west of the Mississippi River, counting sixty churches, forty-eight priests, an impressive number of schools, and a Catholic population of 54,000.

• The Loras papers are located in the archives of the archdiocese of Dubuque. Somewhat inadequate biographies are Louis de Cailly, *Memoirs of Bishop Loras, First Bishop of Dubuque, Iowa, and of Members of His Family from 1792 to 1858* (1897), and Sister Stanislaus Fleming, *Life of the Right Reverend Mathias Loras, D.D., First Bishop of Dubuque, Iowa, 1792–1858* (1933), but important material can be found in M. M. Hoffmann, *Church Founders of the Northwest: Loras and Cretin and Other Captains of Christ* (1937), and "Iowa's Early Catholic History," *Palimpsest* 34 (1953): 337–400.

THOMAS W. SPALDING

LORD, Asa Dearborn (17 June 1816–7 Mar. 1875), teacher, education reformer, and editor, was born in Madrid, New York, the son of Asa Lord, occupation unknown, and Lucretia Dearborn, a teacher. Unlike many men of his era, Lord received formal education in several areas. His early education was provided by his mother. He then attended the local district school and an academy, probably the St. Lawrence Academy in Potsdam, New York. In 1837, while teaching in Willoughby, Ohio, Lord returned to his studies at Western Reserve College in Hudson, Ohio. In 1838 he entered Oberlin as a sophomore and stayed for one year. Lord resumed his teaching duties at Willoughby, remaining in that position until 1839. He later studied medicine there, receiving a medical diploma in 1846. He also studied theology privately and was licensed to preach by the Presbytery of Franklin, Ohio. He married Elizabeth W. Russell in 1842; they had no children. She served as an assistant dean at Oberlin and worked with her husband in his many positions.

Interested in the profession of education, Lord served as the principal of the newly formed Western Reserve Teachers' Seminary in Kirtland, Ohio, from 1839 to 1847. He established a training program for 40 to 100 teachers who taught at common and other schools. While specific subjects are not known, the school provided instruction in pedagogy through lectures.

Along with his efforts at the seminary, Lord was the chief speaker at the Teachers' Institutes. These in-service courses, begun with Lord's help in Sandusky, Ohio, in 1845, were offered throughout the state. The institutes comprised a series of lectures, much like lyceum lectures, held throughout the area. They provided additional training for teachers by exposure to new ideas in education. One hundred students attended the first series.

Lord was a major organizer and promoter of the State Teachers' Association founded in 1847. The group held two meetings a year for the next ten years and supported improvement and professionalization of teaching. He left his position in the Columbus, Ohio, schools in 1854 to spend a year as an agent for the organization. In an early account of education in Ohio, Lord described the work of the association as being too extensive to mention. A partial list included the appointment of the first city and county superintendents of schools, the granting of aid to ten county teacher institutes, and the passage of a law requiring the testing of common school teachers in English grammar and geography. Through a committee of the State Teachers' Association, with Lord as chair, the organization published a report that assisted in the reorganization of and provision for free graded schools in about seventy towns and cities.

In another professional capacity, Lord acted as editor and publisher of the *Ohio School Journal* from 1846 to 1849. He also published the *Public School Advocate* during the same period, and from 1852 to 1855 he served as founder and editor of the *Ohio Journal of Education*. These publications were used as platforms to promote public education. Lord continued to work in the Columbus schools while serving as editor and publisher of the various journals.

Lord learned about education from men such as Calvin Stowe, who had visited the Prussian schools and worked to organize the Ohio schools by combining political and educational leadership. Henry Barnard, a former Connecticut school superintendent, visited Ohio in 1843, while on a fifteen-month U.S. tour, and again in 1846. Barnard helped to create in Columbus, Ohio, the first superintendency in the Midwest, lending the insight he had gleaned from his position as state superintendent of Connecticut and the material he had gathered for his history of American education. Lord filled the newly established position and, again influenced by Barnard, founded the first public high school in Columbus and the first graded school system in the state.

In 1856 Lord began his work in a different area in education, when he became the head of the Ohio Institution for the Education of the Blind; subsequently, in 1868 he became the head of the new State School for the Blind in Batavia, New York. With his background in education and his medical training, he was especially suited to the job. It was to the practical and vocational education of the blind that Lord devoted the remainder of his life, as did his wife, who replaced him as superintendent in Batavia after his death in that town.

Lord's career in education contributed to the professionalization of teaching through the Western Reserve Teacher's Seminary, which provided extensive and practical training for teachers, the Teachers' Institutes, and the numerous journals that he edited. His activities in the Ohio State Teachers' Association and his collaboration with men such as Barnard, Samuel Lewis, and Stowe helped to promote his ideas on the graded school and teacher preparation.

• The richest source of information is Lord's address "Twenty-five Years in the Schools of Ohio," delivered at the Ohio State Teachers' Association meeting in Cleveland, Ohio, on 1 July 1863. See also J. J. Burns, *Education History of Ohio* (1905), and William T. Goggeshall, "System of Common Schools in Ohio," *American Journal of Education* 6 (Mar. 1859): 81–168.

RITA S. SASLAW

LORD, Eleazar (9 Sept. 1788–3 June 1871), financier, railway president, and theologian, was born in Franklin, Connecticut, the son of Nathan Lord and Mary Nevins. After a local education, Lord began clerking in nearby Norwich. Four years later, in 1808, he prepared for college with the pastor of a nearby Congregational church. Lord entered Andover Theological Seminary in 1810. The Haverhill Association licensed him to preach in 1812, and he served a year as an itinerant. Lord later entered Princeton to complete his ordination studies. Failing eyesight thwarted his plans but did not keep him from enjoying a life of money-making, political lobbying, economic theorizing, and theological ruminating.

Lord returned to the United States after a European trip (1817–1818) to lobby in Washington, D.C. (1819, 1820, 1823–1824), for protective tariffs. He served as secretary of the National Institution for the Promotion of Industry and helped its organ, the New York–based

Patron of Industry. Lord was also a zealous advocate of internal improvements, backing the Grand Canal and investing heavily in canal bonds. As his interest in transportation and protection grew, Lord established the Manhattan Fire Insurance Company (1821). During his tenure as president (1821–1834), he initiated or extended important insurance practices, like reinsurance, which helped his firm pay 9 percent dividends. Lord married Elizabeth Pierson of Ramapo, New York, in 1824. The couple had seven children before her death in 1833.

Lord had good reason to champion the cause of transportation for New York's Southern Tier. His merchant brothers wanted to divert the region's trade, which floated downriver to Pennsylvania, to burgeoning New York City. His father-in-law, Jeremiah Pierson, sought a cheap way to connect his isolated Ramapo Iron Works to wider markets. Lord himself owned a substantial amount of land in Rockland County, near the Hudson River, and an inviting gap in the mountains. It was there that Lord imagined the terminus of an "Appian Way" to Lake Erie. Lord's first effort toward this goal was a conference at Newburgh in October 1826, aimed at the construction of a turnpike. He later looked into the feasibility of a canal. Technological advances and initial successes in the new railroad industry caught Lord's attention, however, and a railway was soon his main object. Lord was finally able to overcome political opposition to secure a rather unfavorable charter in 1833. Lord became the New York and Erie Railroad Company's first president (1833–1835; 1839–1841; 1844–1845). Rival groups of stockholders who disliked his business decisions ousted Lord from the presidency several times. Indeed, Lord made crucial errors. By one estimate his insistence on a six-foot gauge and a wooden pile roadbed eventually cost the railroad $70 million. Lord's financial innovations, on the other hand, saved the company from disaster. Lord proposed New York State match every dollar the company raised from local communities along the road route. Other railroads soon followed this successful example. Though long since retired from active management, Lord published *A Historical Review of the New York and Erie Railroad* (1855), which urged investors to buy the railroad's stock.

Lord's business ventures did not keep him from writing and scholarship. In 1825 he edited *Lemprière's Universal Biography*, contributing hundreds of short sketches of American notables. He was also a founder and a member of the council of the University of the City of New York (1831–1834).

Lord's most significant writings were his economic treatises. His first work in this field, *The Principles of Currency and Banking*, was published too late in 1829 to effect the adoption of New York's famous Safety Fund. The book was successful, however, and Lord published a revamped second edition, *On Credit, Currency, and Banking*, in 1834. Many of the ideas Lord put forth in these works were soon adopted in the "free banking" laws of more than a dozen states. Lord argued banks should store money for safekeeping and discount only self-liquidating commercial paper, not mere promissory notes. To achieve this ideal, Lord believed banks should be required to invest in permanent government bonds. Soon after the Civil War began, Lord published *A Letter on National Currency* (1861). He argued in favor of unredeemable fiat currency, noting that its "intrinsic value" lay in the faith of the nonexportable national securities backing it. In *Six Letters on the Necessity and Practicability of a National Currency* (1862), Lord more fully laid the foundations for the National Banking Act of 1863. Though the bill he advanced was modified before being passed, Lord deserves much credit for creating the basis of our banking system from the Civil War until the establishment of the Federal Reserve.

Lord never relinquished his religious and philanthropic activities. Although his *Compendious History of the Principal Protestant Missions to the Heathen* (2 vols., 1813) was largely a compilation of quotations, the book showed Lord's zeal for scholarship and evangelicalism. Lord was a founder (1815), secretary (1818–1826), and president (1826–1836) of the New York Sunday School Union Society. In his *Thoughts on the Practical Advantages of Those Who Hold the Doctrines of Peace over Those Who Vindicate War* (1816), Lord argued that the Bible frowned upon "retaliation and revenge." No one "but madmen" would defend property or honor with their lives. He concluded by arguing a "conquest of love" was necessary because "the Millennium is about to take place." Also in 1816 Lord played a role in the organization of the American Bible Society. In 1820 he helped found the Auburn Theological Seminary. The following year he helped write the fifth annual report of the Society for the Prevention of Pauperism. In 1826 his interest returned to missionary work, helping to form the American Home Mission Society, of which he was the first corresponding secretary. He helped to write a report for the New York City Temperance Society in 1829. Lord published the *Memoir of the Rev. Joseph Stibbs Christmas* (1831) to prove "the destruction of those who do not obey the Gospel, is to be attributed wholly to themselves." After retiring from business pursuits, Lord devoted much of his time to religious studies. The implications of the uniformitarian theories of English geologists James Hutton and Charles Lyell clearly troubled Lord. *Geological Cosmogony* (1843) and *The Epoch of Creation* (1851) were his attempts to reconcile Scripture with geological observations. They are extremely interesting because Lord unleashed a blistering, almost Feyerabendian attack on the "miracles" or assumptions of science. "The theory [of an ancient earth] is merely an inference, a supposition, a conjecture, derived from the construction which the geologist puts upon the facts of the science, the phenomena which he observes," Lord argued, pointing out that "such an assumption is not science. It is mere conjecture." Lord wrote several other book-length religious treatises.

In 1835 he married Ruth Thompson. Lord wrote a short account of the life of one of his children from this second marriage, Mary Thompson Lord Swift (1840–1866), after her early death. Lord, usually a stern disciplinarian, was deeply moved by her death. "Till Mary's last illness," an anonymous relative wrote, "her father had scarcely been known for many years to pay any attention to flowers. Within a few weeks he has several times walked tremblingly to a little border . . . and bending with caution over his staff, picked a white lily and carried it to the bedside" (*Memorial of Swift*, pp. 72–73, 113). Lord died at his home, "Lord Castle," in Piermont, New York, a potent economic and religious theorist rarely given enough credit for the profoundness of his thought.

• The Eleazar Lord Papers (1831–1860) at Rockland Community College Library in Suffern, N.Y., contain materials concerning the railroad business. The Pierson Family Papers at the Rockland County Historical Society in New City, N.Y., also contain some information on Lord. An unpublished "Autobiography of Eleazar Lord, LL.D." (1870), at the Connecticut Historical Society, is a major source. *Our Sister, Mrs. Ruth Thompson Lord* (1874) includes family information and a list of his published writings. Lord's writings not mentioned above include *Fifth Report of the Society for the Prevention of Pauperism in the City of New York* (1821), *An Address to Physicians, by the Executive Committee of the Board of Managers of the New-York City Temperance Society* (1829), *Second Report of the Directors of the New York and Erie Railroad Company, to the Stockholders* (1841), *The Messiah: In Moses and the Prophets* (1853), *Symbolic Prophecy* (1854), *Plenary Inspiration of the Holy Scriptures* (1857), *The Prophetic Office of Christ* (1859), *Analysis of the Book of Isaiah* (1861), and *Theories of Currency* (1864). Lord also contributed frequently to the *Theological and Literary Journal*, which was edited by his brother David, and wrote numerous reviews and essays for sundry publications. Primary sources relating to Lord include Lewis Tappan, *Letter to Eleazar Lord, Esq., in Defense of Measures for Promoting the Observance of the Christian Sabbath* (1831), which is an attack of Lord's "Recommendatory letter" of a British theological work. *Memorial of Mary T. L. Swift, Daughter of Eleazar and Ruth T. Lord* (1867), by an unnamed relative, gives glimpses into Lord's family life and personality. The two most comprehensive railroad histories include Edward Mott, *Between the Ocean and the Lakes: The Story of Erie* (1901), and Edward Hungerford, *Men of Erie: A Story of Human Effort* (1946). They contain biographical sketches and detailed treatments of Lord's railroad decisions. For the Manhattan Insurance Company, see the *New York Spectator*, 13 Apr. 1821, 4 Feb. 1823, 25 Nov. 1823. For Lord's tariff activities, see *New York Patron of Industry*, 28 June 1820, 12 July 1820, 31 Jan. 1824, 25 Apr. 1821. An obituary is in the *New York Tribune*, 6 June 1871.

ROBERT E. WRIGHT

LORD, Henry Curwen (17 Apr. 1866–15 Sept. 1925), astronomer, was born in Cincinnati, Ohio, the son of Henry Clark Lord and Elizabeth Burnet Wright. After attending public schools in Cincinnati, Lord entered Ohio State University in 1884. At the end of his third year he transferred to the University of Wisconsin, where he was an assistant at the college's Washburn Observatory of astronomy and received a B.S. in 1889.

For about two years Lord was employed by the Thompson-Huston Electric Company (city unknown). In 1891 he became assistant in mathematics and astronomy at Ohio State University, where he advanced to associate professor of astronomy in 1894 and to professor in 1900.

On a leave of absence in 1893 Lord served as astronomer on the United States and Great Britain Boundary Line Survey Commission to determine the boundary between Alaska and Canada. He did this at the request of Thomas Corwin Mendenhall, superintendent of the U.S. Coast and Geodetic Survey, who had been a professor at Ohio State when Lord was a student. In 1898 Lord married Edith Lelia Hudson; they had one child.

As soon as he had joined the faculty at Ohio State, Lord began urging that an astronomical observatory be built there. Through the generosity of philanthropist Emerson McMillin, this goal was achieved in 1895. During the planning stage, Lord visited observatories and instrument makers in the eastern United States to determine what kind of building and equipment was best suited to his new facility. He was "the happiest man on campus June 16, 1896, the opening day of the Observatory with himself its director," according to his biographer and colleague Joseph N. Bradford (p. 6). The Emerson McMillin Observatory was especially intended for student instruction and had considerable equipment for that purpose. It contained a telescope on a twelve and one-half-inch equatorial mount, in which the two axes of motion are at right angles with one parallel to the earth's axis. This feature allows for convenient tracking of specific stellar objects. Lord designed a spectroscope, based on what he considered the best features of instruments of the time. He noted that the carpentry work of the observatory was done by the university carpenter and the patterns for the dome mechanism were made by the students.

In 1897 Lord published papers on focusing a telescope on the slit of a spectroscope ("Notes on the Determination of the Focus of an Objective," *Astrophysical Journal* 5 [May 1897]: 305–9) and a mathematical treatise on "Curvature of the Spectral Lines" (*Astrophysical Journal* 5 [May 1897]: 348–50). Later that year he described a compound correcting lens for flattening the color curve ("The New Photographic Correcting Lens of the Emerson McMillin Observatory," *Astrophysical Journal* 6 [Aug. 1897]: 87–90), based on a suggestion by James Edward Keeler of Lick Observatory. His papers were well received by other astronomers. With his own spectroscope Lord began studies of the radial velocities of stars, in which their motion is determined by the shift in the wavelength of the star's light emission. This field of astronomy was advancing rapidly in the latter half of the nineteenth century after the introduction by Hermann Karl Vogel of Germany of a photographic method in spectroscopy. Limited by a small telescope and a location within a large city with industrial smoke, Lord could study only the brightest stars, but he was able to present the results of successful observations in various papers from 1898 to 1905. At that time he chose to abandon his efforts on velocities, because observatories with larger telescopes were better able to study them and because the night visibility in his location was steadily deteriorating.

A skilled mechanic, Lord built most of his own equipment in a workshop in the observatory. He designed and built a photographic lens. According to Bradford, "Some prominent optical designers said that a lens of his design would not be very successful," but it proved to be entirely so. At a solar eclipse that Lord observed at Barnesville, Georgia, in October 1900, with the U.S. Naval Observatory expedition, he used his lens to obtain excellent photographs of the flash spectrum at complete sun cover that had first been described by astronomer Charles Augustus Young in 1870, the existence of which had been doubted by other astronomers for some years. Lord's presentation helped to resolve the question, and in it he identified spectral lines and the elevations of various gases in the sun's atmosphere ("Observations of the Solar Eclipse of May 28, 1900," *Astrophysical Journal*, 13 [Mar. 1901]: 149–66). He also published on techniques of photographic astronomical observations and on double stars. In 1904 he published *The Elements of Geodetic Astronomy for Civil Engineers*, which he set in print himself on a manual printing press.

In 1910 Lord led an expedition to Hawaii to study the transit of Halley's comet, but clouds prevented the making of any observations.

Considered an excellent teacher, Lord was "painstaking and thorough himself and expected no less from his students," notes Bradford, who described him as "a genius of high order" and "a delightful companion" (p. 6).

Lord was an instructor in the School of Military Aeronautics at Ohio State during World War I. He was a member of the American Astronomical Society and a fellow of the Royal Astronomical Society. He died in Columbus, Ohio.

• Lord described the equipment of the McMillin Observatory in "The Spectroscope of the Emerson McMillin Observatory," *Astrophysical Journal* 4 (June 1896): 50–53. A description of the eclipse of October 1900 by S. J. Brown in *Astrophysical Journal* 12 (July 1900): 58–67, includes a section by Lord that describes his technique. A biography of Lord is Joseph N. Bradford, "Professor Lord Is Gone," *Ohio State University Monthly* 17 (Oct. 1925): 6–7, 26.

ELIZABETH NOBLE SHOR

LORD, Pauline (8 Aug. 1890–11 Oct. 1950), actress, was born in Hanford, California, the daughter of Edward Lord, a tinsmith, and Sarah Foster. The family had come from Delaware to live on a fruit farm in the San Joaquin valley but moved to San Francisco when she was a child. She attended Holy Rosary Academy in Woodland. Participation in a school play awakened her interest in theater, and she regularly spent her allowance on admission to Saturday matinees in San Francisco as well as taking acting lessons at the Alcazar Theatre. At thirteen she made her professional debut, playing the maid in *Are You a Mason?* with the Belasco Stock Company at the Alcazar Theatre in San Francisco. Noticed by comedian Nat Goodwin, she followed up his invitation to contact him in New York. She was sixteen when she traveled to the East Coast and joined his touring company.

After some difficult years of apprenticeship, including stints with stock companies in Springfield, Massachusetts, and Milwaukee, Wisconsin, Lord made her New York debut on 8 January 1912 in the supporting role of the seduced innocent in Marion Fairfax's hit play *The Talker*. Then followed several years of performing in vaudeville and acting in a string of unremarkable plays (she later admitted to poor judgment in the choice of scripts). A turning point came with her appearance as the streetwalker Sadie in *The Deluge* at New York's Hudson Theatre in August 1917, under the direction of Arthur Hopkins. It was Hopkins who rescued her from another series of mediocre works and cast her opposite Ben-Ami in *Samson and Delilah* in November 1920, and most importantly, as Anna Christopherson in Eugene O'Neill's *Anna Christie*. Alexander Woollcott's review of the latter (*New York Times*, 3 Nov. 1921) referred to Hopkins's "continuing direction of the career of that most gifted and interesting actress Pauline Lord. She gives a telling performance in a rich and salty play that grips the attention with the rise of the first curtain and holds it fiercely to the end. . . . The choice of the difficult Pauline Lord for the central role was an inspiration and those genuine and multitudinous cheers which followed the third act last night were for her." Woollcott did not say why he called her "difficult," but Elizabeth Shepley Sergeant wrote that "you cannot ignore her temperament." In their 1926 interview, Lord admitted to Sergeant that after struggling with a role and getting to the point at which "every word, every action, every intonation, every movement is clear to me," the normally soft-spoken actress would involuntarily take on an imperious attitude toward her fellow actors in rehearsal. Wistful-looking, with brown eyes and "a fascinating little face, mobile and sensitive," Lord was an intuitive actress who shaped her characters through a succession of mood changes. In the role of Anna, Lord toured successfully in the United States and won resounding success in London. The Strand Theatre opening on 10 April 1923 culminated in a half-hour ovation.

Lord's second great role was Amy, the waitress who becomes a "mail order" bride in *They Knew What They Wanted* by Sidney Howard, produced by the Theatre Guild. Stark Young's review (*New York Times*, 25 Nov. 1924) observed: "Her playing last night had that shy pathos and intensity that we saw in her *Launzi* last year. She is an actress that, when she finds a part within her range, has in that part a range and perfection at the top of all the realism in our theatre. Last night she never missed a shading or a point; she had always a wonderful, frail power in the scene, and throughout her performance a kind of beautiful, poignant accuracy." In 1928 she was cast as Nina Leeds in the Theatre Guild's road company of Eugene O'Neill's *Strange Interlude*. Comparing her performance with that of Lynn Fontanne, who had created the role, critics were "almost unanimous in preferring the more emotional, subjective, intuitive approach of Lord to the intelligent, technically polished performance of Fontanne" (Ranald, p. 390). The last important role she created, on 21 February 1936, was Zenobia Frome in a dramatization of Edith Wharton's *Ethan Frome*, opposite Raymond Massey and Ruth Gordon; Lord was able to find and project the humanity in the unsympathetic character of the wife.

Noteworthy among the other productions in which Lord appeared were *Out There* (1917), *Night Lodging* (1919), *Launzi* (1923), *Trelawney of the Wells* (1925), *Sandalwood* (1926), *Spellbound* (1927), *Salvation* (1928), *The Late Christopher Bean* (1932), and *The Glass Menagerie* (1946). In 1939 she performed in two productions in Australia. She also starred in two films, *Mrs. Wiggs of the Cabbage Patch* (1934) and *A Feather in Her Hat* (1935). She married once, on 27 April 1929 in Elkton, Maryland, to Owen B. Winters, an advertising executive. The marriage was kept secret until 17 May, after they had sailed for a European honeymoon. Winters divorced her on 26 October 1931, charging incompatibility; they had no children. Lord died at a hospital in Alamogordo, New Mexico, where she contracted bronchopneumonia during treatment for injuries received in an automobile accident.

Lord's acting was a special brand of realism. Offstage, the woman known to her friends as Polly was self-effacing and lacking in confidence, but on stage she seemed to absorb her character into herself with—as Arthur Hopkins told Elizabeth Sergeant—"the absolute sureness of a hypnotized person." Her gestures and movements were sparing, as if she were restraining some deeply felt emotion. According to Sergeant, "Pauline Lord is one who shows authentically that inferior frisson that lies at the heart of drama." She excelled in roles of women who had been battered by life, and she often transcended her material. Sometimes compared to Eleonora Duse, she came to represent an American ideal of art seemingly beyond technique.

• The Billy Rose Theatre Collection at the Lincoln Center Theatre Library branch of the New York Public Library has clippings files on Lord. Evocations of Lord's stage persona are included in many works on the theater of the period. See, for example, Brooks Atkinson, *Broadway* (1970); Joseph Wood Krutch, "Pauline Lord," *The Nation*, 30 Nov. 1927; Elizabeth Shepley Sargeant, "Pauline Lord: One Stung by the Gadfly," *New Republic*, 22 Sept. 1926; Ashton Stevens, *Actorviews* (1923); and Stark Young, *Immortal Shadows* (1948). Lord's two roles in Eugene O'Neill plays earned her an entry in *The Eugene O'Neill Companion* (1984) by Margaret Loftus Ranald, who calls her "the quintessential O'Neill heroine." An obituary is in the *New York Times*, 12 Oct. 1950.

FELICIA HARDISON LONDRÉ

LOREE, Leonor Fresnel (23 Apr. 1858–6 Sept. 1940), railroad executive, was born in Fulton City, Illinois, the son of William Mulford Loree, a shipbuilder and millwright, and Sarah Elizabeth Marsh. He attended Rutgers College, majored in mathematics and engineering, and graduated in 1877. Loree's characteristic ambition, direction, and determination to succeed were already evident when he finished college. Attracted to the expanding railroad industry, he sought employment with one of the major companies in the field, the Pennsylvania Railroad (PRR), where he began as an assistant in the engineering department. Two years later, in 1879, he broadened his expertise by working for the Army Corps of Engineers as a transitman. In 1881 he became an instrument man and topographer with the Mexican National Railway.

Loree returned to the PRR in 1883 as assistant engineer and began a rapid climb up the managerial ladder. His innovative approach to railroad engineering problems won him a promotion in 1884 to maintenance-of-way engineer on various divisions. In 1885 he married Jessie Tabor of Logansport, Indiana, and they raised two sons and a daughter. Loree distinguished himself by his efforts in dealing with the aftereffects of devastating floods along the Miami River in Ohio and in Johnstown, Pennsylvania. In 1901 he was elected fourth vice president of Lines West.

The Pennsylvania, which had been expanding its influence over northeastern railroads, arranged for Loree to be elected president of the Baltimore & Ohio (B&O) in June 1901. He remained at the B&O for only two and a half years before federal pressure forced the PRR to relinquish its interest, but while there Loree made notable physical improvements in the carrier. In January 1904 Loree became president of the Chicago, Rock Island & Pacific Railroad, also assuming the position of chairman of the executive committee of its affiliate, the St. Louis–San Francisco Railway (Frisco). Dissatisfied, he soon resigned.

One of the B&O's directors, financier Edward H. Harriman, who controlled the Union Pacific and the Southern Pacific, had been greatly impressed by Loree's energy and brilliance, and they became good friends. With Harriman's aid, Loree was elected chairman of the executive committee of the Kansas City Southern Railroad (KCS) in 1906, a position he maintained for the rest of his active life, until 1936. Harriman's influence helped Loree win the presidency, the chairmanship of the executive committee, and a membership on the board of managers of the Delaware & Hudson Company (D&H) in April 1907.

Chartered in 1823 as an anthracite-carrying canal company, the D&H by 1907 had evolved into a 900-mile system, with lines extending from Pennsylvania to Montreal, and with investments in steamboats, hotels, trolley lines, and coal mines. Loree improved operating efficiencies by extending double track, constructing new yards, centralizing the shops, and purchasing improved locomotives. Later, he was among the early users of centralized traffic control devices and continuous welded rail.

A firm believer in management control and in "a day's work for a day's pay," Loree scorned government interference. In 1922, when shop workers went on strike to prevent management from lowering wages that had been increased during the period of federal control, Loree led the railroads' resistance. He hired new workers, fired the strikers, and rejected President Warren Harding's peace proposals. The strike was broken, but business and efficiency suffered and bitterness lingered for years.

On the other hand, Loree felt employees should have "protection against the major hazards of life; these being unemployment, sickness, accident, superannuation and death." By the early 1920s he had established group insurance, accident insurance, and co-pension plans that were partly paid for by the company. In 1931 he temporarily replaced the industry's traditional mileage and hourly pay system with a monthly salary plan, but hard times and the threat of a strike forced the restoration of the old arrangement.

Loree's ambitions were too extensive to be contained by a regional carrier such as the D&H; he aspired to be a giant in the railway world. While he fell short in a positive sense, he did succeed in thwarting mergers that would have absorbed the D&H. He also earned substantial profits for the D&H through his investments in other roads. These were not enough to offset the effects of the depression. The D&H suspended dividends in 1934, bringing criticism from a minority of stockholders. Loree responded by denouncing New Deal legislation and the Interstate Commerce Commission, and he called for wage cuts, tax reductions, the closing of stations, and the abandonment of lines, although he underestimated the effects of highway competition.

Loree was active in other ways. In 1922 he published *Railroad Freight Transportation*, considered to be a thorough analysis of rail operations. Ten years later he wrote *The Story of Anthracite*. He served in various trade associations in several capacities, and in 1923 he founded The Newcomen Society in North America to promote "material history" rather than political history.

By the mid-1930s Loree, his health failing, began to curtail his activities. He presided over his last stockholders' meeting in 1935 and appeared less frequently in his office. The board became concerned over the D&H's continuing losses, and Loree resigned in March 1938. He retired to "Bowood," his estate in West Orange, New Jersey, where he died.

Loree was in some ways an anachronism and in others a prophet. He never abandoned his view that managers should run their enterprises and that government should not interfere in the economic processes. He accepted certain technological innovations readily, and he wrote off money-losing local trains long before his contemporaries or regulatory agencies would permit. He never lost interest in the mechanics of railroading. His labor policies seemed harsh at times; he urged reforms in work rules and procedures, but no man was laid off despite the depression. Only grudgingly would he admit labor's claim that it should share in a higher standard of living. He put a high price on his talents; for many years, his combined salaries from the D&H and KCS made him the nation's highest-paid rail executive. Nonetheless, his dream to be a top railroad magnate eluded him.

• Loree contributed significantly, if anonymously, to the Delaware & Hudson's centennial history, *A Century of Progress* (1925). His impact on the Baltimore & Ohio is ably described in Herbert Harwood, *Impossible Challenge* (1979) and "Nothing at the End of the Rainbow: The B&O in Western Pennsylvania," *Railroad History*, no. 129 (Autumn 1973): 56–70. Also treating his short but productive tenure with the B&O are Edward Hungerford, *The Story of the Baltimore & Ohio Railroad*, vol. 1 (1928), and John F. Stover, *History of the Baltimore and Ohio Railroad* (1987). Loree's later career is covered peripherally in Robert Archer, *History of the Lehigh Valley Railroad* (1972), and George Burgess and Miles Kennedy, *Centennial History of the Pennsylvania Railroad Company* (1949). Jim Shaughnessy, *Delaware and Hudson* (1967), describes his impact on the D&H. Details of his interest in motive power can be found in various articles in *Railway Age* and in *Trains* magazine, especially David P. Morgan, "Loree's Locomotives," *Trains* 12, no. 9 (July 1952): 20–25, and W. T. Coniff, "The Delaware & Hudson," *Trains* 5, no. 3 (Jan. 1945): 24–35. Charles Penrose paid tribute in a speech, published in pamphlet form by The American Newcomen Society, *L. F. Loree: Patriarch of the Rails!* (1955). Numerous articles on Loree can be found in the *New York Times*, including an obituary, 7 Sept. 1940.

JAMES N. J. HENWOOD

LORENTZ, Pare (11 Dec. 1905–4 Mar. 1992), documentary filmmaker, was born Leonard MacTaggart Lorentz in Clarksburg, West Virginia, the son of Alma MacTaggart Ruttencutter and Pare Hanson Lorentz, a printer. After studying at West Virginia Wesleyan College and the University of West Virginia, Lorentz moved to New York City in 1924, where he found employment as editor for the *Edison Mazda Lamp Sales Builder*, General Electric's house publication. In 1925 he adopted his father's given name, Pare, and in 1926 he became a film reviewer for the humor magazine *Judge*. Though his film reviews castigated Hollywood for its aesthetic superficiality and lack of moral courage, he praised certain directors including F. W. Murnau and King Vidor. Vidor later helped Lorentz procure studio stock footage for Lorentz's first directing effort. Lorentz continued to write for *Judge* until 1934.

In 1930 Lorentz co-authored, with civil-liberties attorney Morris L. Ernst, the book *Censored: A Private Life of the Movies* in 1930. The following year he married actress Sarah Richardson (Sally) Bates, with whom he later had a son, Pare, Jr., and a daughter, Matilda Grey. For the next several years Lorentz wrote film criticism for such publications as publisher William Randolph Hearst's *New York Evening Journal* (1931–1932), *Vanity Fair* (1932–1933), *Town and Country* (1933–1936), and *McCall's* (1935–1941). His film reviews were eventually published in a collection titled *Lorentz on Film* (1975).

An enthusiastic supporter of the New Deal, Lorentz wrote an account of Franklin D. Roosevelt's first year in the White House titled *The Roosevelt Year: 1933*, which was published in 1934. The following year he was hired by Roosevelt's U.S. Resettlement Administration to publicize the plight of American farmers during the depression. His first project was *The Plow That Broke the Plains* (1936), a stirring documentary about Oklahoma Dust Bowl farmers upon whom the country's economic policies and ecological irresponsibility weighed heavily. Made on a paltry budget with the help of photographers Paul Strand and Leo Hurwitz, among others, the film's artful orchestration of stunning landscape cinematography, symbolic montage, Virgil Thompson's lush score, and a poetic, sonorous voice-over commentary written by Lorentz and narrated by Thomas Chalmers drew critical acclaim and international recognition. Hollywood studios perceived the government-sponsored film as a threat to the market domination of their own commercial products; having denied assistance during its production, the major studios refused to screen the finished film in their national theaters. Despite this fact, the film was widely exhibited by independent theaters, schools, and private organizations.

His next film, *The River* (1938), was made for the Farm Security Administration and documented the effects of flooding on the Mississippi River; it was both a celebration of the river and a critique of ecological practices. Lorentz, who had once studied music, considered this film to be his "opera." In it he combined local folk music and another original Virgil Thompson score with his own lyrical commentary, which the novelist James Joyce proclaimed "the most beautiful prose I have heard in 10 years." The film took first prize for best documentary feature at the 1938 Venice International Film Festival.

In 1938 Roosevelt appointed Lorentz director of the U.S. Film Service, established that year to record the poverty and natural disasters of the 1930s. In addition to overseeing director Joris Ivens's *Power and the Land* (1940) and director Robert Flaherty's *The Land* (1941), Lorentz made *The Fight for Life* (1940), a searing account of the circumstances surrounding childbirth and malnutrition among Chicago's poverty-stricken underclass. The film earned the National Board of Review's best documentary film award. However, its critical tone and controversial subject angered many lawmakers, and that year the U.S. Film Service dissolved after Congress refused to grant it further funding. The withdrawal of financial support prevented the completion of *Ecce Homo!*, a planned film version of Lorentz's 1938 CBS radio production of the same name. Lorentz had begun work on the film, which was to examine American unemployment, in 1938 but never finished the project.

Following the collapse of the film unit, Lorentz ventured to Hollywood for a brief stint as producer and director for RKO, which ultimately reneged on Lorentz's contract to make two films. Lorentz successfully sued the studio for more than $1 million in damages as well as the rights to the completed footage for a film called *Name, Age, Occupation*.

Shortly thereafter he became a major in the army air corps, where he made over 200 briefing films for American pilots. In 1944 he earned the rank of lieutenant colonel and received the Legion of Merit. In 1946 he became chief of the film section of the War Department's Civil Affairs Division, where he oversaw film, theater, and music productions designed for exhibition in U.S.-occupied areas of Germany, Japan, Austria, and Korea. Following the release of his last feature-length documentary, *The Nuremberg Trials* (1946), he resigned from the War Department in 1947.

In 1948 Lorentz formed his own production company, whose first effort, a documentary about atomic bomb testing on Bikini Atoll to be called *Your Brother's Keeper*, was abandoned owing to lack of funds. In June 1949 he married his second wife, Elizabeth Meyer, daughter of *Washington Post* editor and publisher Eugene Meyer. Though Lorentz virtually disappeared from the public arena of film production, he remained politically active for many years. In 1955 he acted as special correspondent to the *Washington Post* and attended the First United Nations Conference on the Peaceful Uses of the Atom. In 1960 he served as a member of the Democratic Advisory Council on Natural Resources and co-authored, with environmentalist Rachel Carson, the Pollution Platform for the Democratic National Committee.

For the last three decades of his life, he worked as a freelance consultant to film production companies and lectured on documentary filmmaking at various universities. In 1981 he received a Special Salute from the Academy of Motion Picture Arts and Sciences for *The Plow That Broke the Plains* and *The River*, and in 1985 the International Documentary Association awarded him a career achievement award. The following year, the Washington Film Council gave him its First Annual Award of Honor, and the West Virginia Division of Culture and History presented him with a Lifetime Achievement Award in 1990. His memoirs and shooting scripts were published as *F. D. R.'s Moviemaker: Memoirs and Scripts* shortly after his death in Armonk, New York.

• Lorentz's film scripts and books are held at the Pare Lorentz Collection room at the University of Wisconsin–Oshkosh. For further information, see Robert L. Snyder, *Pare Lorentz and the Documentary Film* (1968). An obituary is in the *New York Times*, 5 Mar. 1992.

JENNIFER M. BARKER

LORIMER, George Horace (6 Oct. 1867–22 Oct. 1937), editor, was born in Louisville, Kentucky, the son of George Claude Lorimer, a minister, and Arabella Burford. He entered Yale in 1888, but in the summer of 1889, Chicago meatpacker Philip D. Armour persuaded Lorimer to come into his business. In 1892 Lorimer married Alma V. Ennis; they had four children, one of whom died almost immediately after birth. In 1896, although he had risen to department head at Armour, Lorimer decided to go into the wholesale grocery business for himself. That venture failed within the year, and he moved East to try journalism.

During 1897 and 1898, Lorimer held reporting jobs in Boston on the *Post* and the *Herald* and also enrolled briefly at Colby College to develop his writing skills. In 1898, learning that Cyrus Curtis, publisher of the *Ladies' Home Journal*, had purchased the old *Saturday Evening Post*, he wired asking for a position. Following a brief interview in Boston, Curtis hired Lorimer as the *Post*'s literary editor.

In March 1899, Curtis went abroad to offer the *Post* editorship to Arthur Sherburne Hardy, leaving Lorimer as acting editor. Seizing this opportunity, Lorimer set to work to put his stamp on the magazine. When copies reached Curtis overseas, he was sufficiently impressed to drop his pursuit of Hardy, return to Philadelphia, and appoint Lorimer editor. Lorimer's name first appeared on the masthead on 10 June 1899.

Lorimer chose to focus the *Post* on American business and businessmen, a term broad enough to encompass wealthy industrialists, ambitious young salesmen, small-scale farmers, and even ministers. Features provided model life stories of self-made men, instructed readers on how to succeed, explained the ins and outs of salesmanship, and offered information on how to invest.

Lorimer revolutionized the magazine market for freelance writing by offering a decision on all manuscripts within seventy-two hours of receipt and promising payment on acceptance rather than on publication. The results were particularly dramatic with fiction, which quickly became one of the *Post*'s strongest departments. The editor sought business fiction, but the most successful work in this line was his own *Letters from a Self-Made Merchant to His Son*, serialized anonymously in 1901–1902. The series was published as a book in 1902.

Post weekly circulation, less than two thousand at the time of Curtis's purchase of the magazine, reached one million in 1908, and in the years before the First World War, Lorimer's magazine, dedicated to progressive Republicanism and the support of Theodore Roosevelt (1858–1919), became the most popular and influential weekly in the country. The war in Europe found Lorimer committed to non-intervention; however, when the United States entered the war in 1917, the *Post* vigorously supported the country's war aims.

The principal effect of the war on Lorimer, and thus on the *Post*, was an infusion of nativist and isolationist beliefs that drastically altered the magazine. From 1919 on the *Post* argued for curbs on immigration, urged deportation of aliens considered undesirable, attacked the efforts of labor to achieve collective bargaining, contributed to red-baiting, and denigrated those ideas and art forms that Lorimer considered corrupted by European notions and aesthetics.

The *Post* reached its zenith in the 1920s. Issues were filled with pieces by celebrities, popular fiction writers, and well-known professional staffers. Circulation approached three million in the later years of the decade, and advertising typically filled 60 percent of issues that often exceeded two hundred pages. But despite its success, the magazine had lost the zest and quality of its earlier years and seemed mired in its own conservatism and complacency. Then, with the stock market crash, the depression, and the election of Franklin Delano Roosevelt, Lorimer was reinvigorated. In nearly every aspect of the New Deal he saw initiatives that ran counter to the old American values he held dear, especially self-reliance founded on hard work and thrift. The slimmed-down *Post* of these years was again vigorous and feisty, but now Lorimer was no longer in harmony with the country he believed his magazine had helped to create. Shortly after Roosevelt's 1936 landslide victory, Lorimer announced his retirement in the final issue for 1936.

During his years at the *Post*, Lorimer also assumed major responsibilities within the Curtis Corporation, the parent company for the *Post*, the *Ladies' Home Journal*, and *Country Gentleman*. He was elected to the positions of director in 1903, vice president and chairman of the executive committee in 1927, president in 1932, and chairman of the board in 1934. Lorimer died in Wyncote, Pennsylvania, only ten months after his retirement from the *Post*.

• Letters from Lorimer are scattered among several archives: the Lorimer papers and those of Adelaide Neall in the Historical Society of Pennsylvania, the Wesley Stout and the Albert Beveridge Archives at the Library of Congress, the Mary Roberts Rinehart Collection at the University of Pittsburgh Library, the archives of Julian Street and Booth Tarkington at the Princeton Library, the Kenneth Roberts Papers at the Dartmouth College Library, the Robert Herrick Papers at the University of Chicago Library, and the Hal G. Evarts Archive at the University of Oregon. Additional works by Lorimer include *Old Gorgon Graham: More Letters from a Self-Made Merchant to his Son* (1904), *The False Gods* (1906), and *Jack Spurlock, Prodigal* (1908).

The two biographies of Lorimer are John Tebbel, *George Horace Lorimer and the "Saturday Evening Post"* (1948), and Jan Cohn, *Creating America: George Horace Lorimer and the "Saturday Evening Post"* (1989). There are numerous references to Lorimer in Frank L. Mott, *A History of American Magazines*, vol. 4 (1968), and James Playsted Wood, *The Curtis Magazines* (1971), and in in-house histories published by the Curtis Corporation in 1923 and 1936. More recently, Lorimer's work is discussed in C. P. Wilson, "The Rhetoric of Consumption," in *The Culture of Consumption: Critical Essays in American History, 1880–1980*, ed. Richard Wightman Fox and T. J. Jackson Lears (1983). An obituary is in the *New York Times*, 23 Oct. 1937.

JAN COHN

LORIMER, William (27 Apr. 1861–13 Sept. 1934), Illinois Republican party boss, was born in Manchester, England, the son of William Lorimer, Sr., a Scotch Presbyterian minister, and Sarah Harley. He immigrated with his family to the United States in 1865, moving to the West Side of Chicago in 1870. Lorimer's father died soon after their arrival in Chicago, and from the ages of ten to twenty-one, Lorimer held a variety of jobs, including paperboy, stockyards laborer, and streetcar conductor. In 1884 he married Susan

K. Mooney, an Irish Catholic, and he converted to Roman Catholicism in 1914. They had eight children. He was a devoted family man and did not drink, smoke, or attend the theater.

Lorimer's career as a professional politician began in the presidential election of 1884, when he was unable to find a Republican ballot at his polling place in order to cast a vote for James G. Blaine. Perceiving the need for a Republican organization on Chicago's West Side, he began organizing the traditionally Democratic Irish, Bohemian, and Russian Jewish immigrants in the district. He won their support through the usual tools of the machine politician, using a network of friendships, patronage, and favors to develop a strong personal following. Holding membership in a Republican faction that had little sympathy with reform issues, he often formed alliances with Democratic machine politicians to do battle with Republican reformers over political as well as cultural issues such as prohibition.

The political machine that Lorimer organized brought together several factions within the Republican party that represented largely working-class and immigrant voters. He acquired great power in the Cook County Republican organization and gained considerable influence in Illinois State Republican politics. He frequently allied with downstate Republican politicians against Chicago reformers and was often the determining influence in nominations for state, federal, and city offices. From 1894 to 1905 he helped nominate and elect two governors, two U.S. senators, and numerous city, county, and state officials.

Lorimer was a "political entrepreneur" who regarded politics as a business and who used his power for personal as well as party gain. His organization had strong ties with such leading Chicago businessmen as traction magnate Charles Tyson Yerkes, electrical utility builder Samuel Insull, and banker John R. Walsh; and Lorimer played an important role in protecting and advancing their corporate interests in the Chicago City Council and in the Illinois General Assembly. Lorimer himself owned or was a partner in several construction companies that held city and county contracts on major projects, such as the Chicago Drainage Canal; a brick company; a coal company; and a bank, the La Salle Street Trust and Savings Company, which received large public deposits.

From 1895 to 1901, and again from 1903 to 1909, Lorimer represented the Illinois Second District in the Illinois House of Representatives. In the Illinois House, he worked for the interests of his Chicago constituents and of such Chicago industries as meat packing, steel, and lumber. Although he usually voted the party line, on two occasions—the war with Spain in 1898 and the Meat Inspection Bill of 1906—he broke with Republican presidents because he believed the positions they were taking were at odds with those of substantial Chicago interests.

In 1909 Lorimer masterminded a deadlock in the Illinois General Assembly to block the reelection of his former ally but now political foe, Republican senator Albert J. Hopkins. After a deadlock lasting for almost five months and involving ninety-four ballots, a coalition of 55 Republicans and 53 Democrats elected Lorimer to the Senate seat. A year later, however, a Democratic state legislator, Charles A. White, confessed to being paid for his vote, and the Chicago *Tribune* began a campaign to oust Lorimer from the Senate.

In 1910 the Burrows committee, a subcommittee of the Senate Committee on Privileges and Elections, investigated the bribery charge and concluded that Lorimer's election was not corrupt; the full committee concurred. Over the opposition of President William Howard Taft, former president Theodore Roosevelt (1858–1919), as well as all the "insurgent" senators, the Senate voted 46 to 40 to retain Lorimer in his seat, with 10 Democrats and 36 Republicans voting for Lorimer and 18 Democrats and 22 Republicans voting against him.

Lorimer's enemies, however, continued their attack, and in 1911 an Illinois state senate committee, the Helm committee, unanimously concluded that Lorimer had been elected because of "bribery and corruption." Later in the year, newly elected Republican and Democratic progressives in Congress reopened the investigation into the case. After extensive hearings by a committee chaired by Republican senator William P. Dillingham of Vermont, a majority held that the doctrine of res judicata applied and that the case should be dismissed because of the lack of new evidence. Lorimer, said the committee majority, was entitled to his seat. The full Senate, however, disagreed and voted 55 to 28 to oust him from the chamber. In this vote, only 8 Democrats and 20 Republicans voted for him, while 29 Democrats and 26 Republicans voted against him. Most significantly, 21 of the 23 freshman senators who cast a ballot voted to expel, including 6 Republicans and 15 Democrats. The Lorimer case undoubtedly played a role in the ratification in 1913 of the Seventeenth Amendment to the Constitution providing for the direct election of U.S. senators.

After his expulsion, Lorimer spent the rest of his life in politics and in business, but he never regained his former power. In 1914 Lorimer's bank and three affiliated banks failed. In 1916 Lorimer and his partner Charles B. Munday were indicted by the Chicago grand jury on charges of misappropriation of funds and conspiracy to defraud. At the trial, however, the jury found Munday guilty of the charges while Lorimer was acquitted. In the following years, Lorimer made several attempts at electoral office, but to no avail. More significant was his relationship to William Hale "Big Bill" Thompson, mayor of Chicago from 1915 to 1923 and from 1927 to 31, whose base of power was in the old Lorimer territory on Chicago's West Side. Lorimer had significant influence in the various Thompson administrations, helping Big Bill in the Chicago ethnic and African-American working-class wards. Lorimer's political career came to an end in 1931, when Democrat Anton J. Cermak defeated Thompson. Lorimer died in Chicago.

Lorimer's career is significant for two reasons: his organization and control of a major Republican faction that reflected the changing ethnic and cultural composition of Chicago at the turn of the century and his expulsion from the U.S. Senate. Lorimer stimulated within the Chicago GOP a conflict that outwardly appeared to pit "corrupt" professional politicians against "honest" reformers but in reality reflected deep-seated cultural and ethnic divisions. Lorimer's followers often came from ethnic and class groups skeptical of "reform" efforts who viewed politics from a practical and materialistic perspective. His critics, on the other hand, resented the power he wielded, questioned his followers' devotion to American ideals, opposed his use of government for patronage purposes, and distrusted his allies in the business community. Many of the reformers belonged to a cosmopolitan, professionally trained upper class that valued efficient and expert municipal government and advocated urban centralization. In his Senate expulsion, Lorimer fell victim to the antiboss feeling of the Progressive Era and to an ethos that emphasized reforms such as the direct primary and the popular election of U.S. senators. Whether he was truly corrupt, however, remains an open question.

• The most valuable source for understanding Lorimer's career is his testimony in the Dillingham Committee Hearings of the U.S. Senate in 1911. There is no collection of Lorimer papers, although many letters concerning his political career can be found in archival collections. Most useful are the Charles G. Dawes Papers at Northwestern University; the Frank O. Lowden Papers at the University of Chicago; the Shelby M. Cullom and Lawrence Y. Sherman papers at the Illinois State Historical Library; and the Theodore Roosevelt, William Howard Taft, and Albert J. Beveridge papers at the Library of Congress. For a full bibliography plus a detailed study of his life, see Joel A. Tarr, *A Study in Boss Politics: William Lorimer of Chicago* (1971). In addition, William T. Hutchinson, *Lowden of Illinois* (2 vols., 1957), is a valuable biography for understanding Illinois politics during this period. Obituaries and related articles are in the *Chicago Tribune*, 14 and 18 Sept. 1934, and the *New York Times*, 14, 16, and 18 Sept. 1934.

JOEL A. TARR

LORIMIER, Louis (Mar. 1748–26 June 1812), trader, Indian agent, and founder of Cape Girardeau, Missouri, was born probably in Lachine, Canada, the son of Claude-Nicolas de la Rivière de Lorimier, a French colonial officer and commander of La Présentation (Ogdensburg, N.Y.), and Marie-Louise Lepailleur de Laferté. Louis came west with his father in 1769 and at the outbreak of the American Revolution was trading with the Miami Indians on the Wabash. Because of his influence with and knowledge of the Indians, he was employed by the British to rally the tribes to the king's cause and to direct them against American settlements in Kentucky and elsewhere. At Christmas 1776 he moved to the Shawnee country in present-day Ohio and soon established a trading post on Lorimier's Creek at the headwaters of the Great Miami River. He acquired a facility with the Shawnee language and es-

tablished an unusual rapport with the tribesmen. In February 1778 Lorimier was one of two Frenchmen who accompanied Blackfish and eighty Shawnees on a raid against Boonesborough, Kentucky, but they got no further than the Licking River, where they captured Boone and twenty-seven men collecting salt. Lorimier also joined ten other whites and some three hundred Indians for Blackfish's unsuccessful siege of Boonesborough in September 1778. He continued to work among the Indians on behalf of the British, aiding Captain Henry Bird's invasion of Kentucky in 1780, but in November 1782 his store, along with three Shawnee villages on the Great Miami, was destroyed in a retaliatory campaign led by George Rogers Clark.

After the war Lorimier remained in the Indian country, rebuilding his business. About 1783 he strengthened his position among the Shawnees by marrying Pemanpich, also known as Charlotte Bougainville, a woman of mixed French and Shawnee parentage whose relations included an influential Shawnee chief named Blackbeard. With Pemanpich, Lorimier had six surviving children. Pemanpich died at Cape Girardeau in 1808, aged fifty years.

In 1785 Lorimier was trading with the Delaware Indians on the White River in what is now Indiana, and among these communities, too, he gained great influence. But in April 1787 he left for Illinois to escape creditors, apparently because of the sequestration of the goods of one of his suppliers, Antoine Lasselle. Subsequently he moved across the Mississippi onto Spanish territory, where he opened an Indian trade as a partner of the commandant at Ste. Genevieve (Mo.).

At that time the Spaniards wanted to strengthen their possessions on the Mississippi against threats from both the warlike Osages in the west and the ambitions of the United States to the east. Lorimier proved to be useful in establishing communities in Missouri. As early as the summer of 1787 Shawnees and Delawares were quitting Ohio and Indiana to settle in Missouri at Lorimier's invitation, hoping to free themselves from the interference of the United States. These Indians formed settlements, the Shawnees on Apple Creek (Perry County, Mo.) and later on the Meramec, and the Delawares on the St. Francis. Their land grants were confirmed by the Spanish government in 1793. The Delawares occupied the area until 1815, while the Shawnees did not exchange their territory for lands in Kansas until 1825.

Lorimier also encouraged industrious white settlers to join him, settling them about Cape Girardeau, where he lived and obtained grants of land from Spain. He received 6,000 arpens of land and in 1799 successfully petitioned for a further 30,000 arpens. By 1804 the district of Cape Girardeau contained 1,470 white settlers, nearly all of them Anglo-Americans. Although the United States secured this territory in 1804, Lorimier laid out the town of Cape Girardeau in 1808. In addition to building colonies, Lorimier traded with the Indians and served the Spaniards as an interpreter in many Indian councils at St. Louis and elsewhere, and he undertook difficult journeys on their behalf. He was entrusted with the command of the district of Cape Girardeau and made captain of militia.

After the Louisiana Purchase sovereignty of this area passed to the United States, and American troops took possession of St. Louis in 1804. The Territory of Louisiana was created in 1805. Lorimier viewed these proceedings with dismay and contemplated persuading the Shawnees and Delawares to accompany him to the Mexican frontier, where they could remain within Spanish jurisdiction. However, Lorimier's importance was immediately recognized by his new masters, and steps were taken to secure his loyalty. Although he was not successful during his lifetime in obtaining confirmation of his Spanish land grants, Lorimier was appointed a judge of the court of common pleas, and his son Louis, Jr., was awarded a cadetship at West Point despite his Indian blood.

After the death of Pemanpich, Lorimier married another mixed-blood Shawnee, Marie Berthiaume, with whom he had a child who died in infancy. Louis also had a son, Guillaume, born in 1791; the child's mother's name is unknown. Some of Lorimier's descendants followed him into Indian trade, and Louis, Jr., was employed by a St. Louis fur company to visit the Crows in 1812.

Lorimier cut a strange figure, eccentric and flamboyant. Sometimes he wore his hair in a long, ribboned queue that he used as a riding whip. In 1810 John James Audubon said that he looked "as if he had just been shot out of a popgun" and found him "the most ludicrous caricature that can be imagined." Courteous and well spoken in English, French, and a number of Indian languages, he combined Indian and European styles of dress. To an old-fashioned European coat, waistcoat, and shirt he added Indian leggings and moccasins. He was well formed and slim but was said to have been under five feet in height and with a large, aquiline nose was less than handsome. Few Europeans won greater confidence from Indian peoples, and throughout his life he enjoyed a reputation for honesty, efficiency, courage, and enterprise. He must be regarded as one of the builders of modern Missouri. Louis Lorimier died at Cape Girardeau.

• Lorimier's "Memoire de Service que Louis Lorimier," dated 28 Dec. 1782, can be found in the Frederick Haldimand Papers (British Library, London, Add. Ms. 21,831, ff. 57–60). Other references to Lorimier are in the Haldimand papers, the Lasselle papers (Indiana State Library, Indianapolis), and in various collections of the Missouri Historical Society, St. Louis. These last include Lorimier's wills of 1788 and 1808, filed in the Wills Collection and Rodney Family Papers, respectively. Reference to Lorimier is also made by the report of Joseph Jackson, 1 May 1799, in the Claus papers, Public Archives of Canada, Ottawa, MG19/fl, vol. 8, ff. 89–91. Published references include Louis Houck, *A History of Missouri* (1908); Houck, *The Spanish Regime in Missouri* (including a Lorimier journal) (1909); Houck, *Memorial Sketches of Pioneers* (1915); Edouard Zotique Massicotte, "La Famille de Lorimier," *Le Bulletin des Recherches Historiques* 21 (1915): 10–16, 33–45; John Francis McDermott, ed., "Audubon's Journey up the Mississippi," *Journal of the Illinois State Historical Society* 35 (1942): 148–73; and Abraham P. Nasatir, *Spanish War Vessels on the Mississippi, 1792–1796* (1968). Stella M. Drumm's designation of him as Pierre Louis Lorimier in the *Dictionary of American Biography*, vol. 6, appears to be erroneous.

JOHN SUGDEN

LORING, Charles Harding (26 Dec. 1828–5 Feb. 1907), naval officer and engineer, was born in Boston, Massachusetts, the son of William Price Loring and Elizabeth Harding. Charles had an elementary public school education and began working as a machine shop apprentice. However, he finished first among fourteen on competitive examinations and joined the navy on 26 February 1851. As the U.S. Navy became increasingly dependent on steam-propelled warships and with the American Civil War on the horizon, his engineering experience was a valuable asset. In 1852 he married Ruth Malbon; the couple had one daughter.

In the decade preceding the Civil War, Loring became familiar with the growing mechanization of naval propulsion systems and rose rapidly in rank and technical expertise. Involved in testing and developing experimental steam power plants, he was on the cutting edge of mechanical propulsion. By the time he was promoted to the position of chief engineer on 25 March 1861, he had mastered a number of steam power systems.

Loring was ideally situated when the Civil War broke out in the spring of 1861. The sudden need for large numbers of naval craft to blockade the southern coasts of the eastern United States spurred both a frantic naval building program and efforts to convert civilian shipping to combatants. Although the vast majority of available shipping in the United States was sail, steam-powered naval craft offered a considerable advantage. Without the need for labor intensive sail raising, lowering, and adjustment, the steamships promised Federal planners vast savings in manpower. Loring, of course, had just the expertise to manage, supervise, and direct this rapid naval conversion. At the war's outset, he was made the North Atlantic fleet engineer.

Loring was soon called on to oversee another aspect of rapid technological change in the U.S. Navy. By the 1860s armament had so advanced that wooden-hulled ships were increasingly vulnerable. Rifled cannon, rapid-firing breechloaders, and metallurgical techniques that permitted lighter but more powerful and longer range armament made armored hulls logical to some. The era of the ironclad had arrived, and Loring was appointed the U.S. Navy's general inspector of all ironclad, steam-propelled craft constructed west of the Alleghenies. He became the chief technician for the many monitors employed in the strategically vital campaign to secure the Mississippi River for the Union.

After the Civil War, Loring returned to his original area of expertise, steam propulsion, but as his reputation grew, his role in U.S. Navy technology became more all-encompassing. In 1872 he was a member of a board considering choices within a simmering dispute: whether or not the navy should accept compound steam engines or retain their simple power plants. Since compound steam engines involved higher pressures, the safety risks were greater. In 1873 Loring came down on the side of the compound designs, mainly because of their increased efficiency and higher levels of power. The navy accepted his recommendations and appointed him to a panel to consider an even more controversial question.

In 1881 Loring was a member of the First Naval Advisory Board, a high-ranking group of officers that debated the notion of abandoning wooden-hulled naval combatants altogether in favor of ships constructed of metal. With his mechanical engineering and metal working background, he argued for steel naval craft. The board agreed with his view, and a virtual firestorm of debate erupted among traditionalists and those who saw steel ships as the wave of the future.

Loring was promoted to rear admiral in 1884 and became the navy's engineer in chief, but he left that assignment the next year. A combination of unexpectedly increased federal revenues, the beginning of an intense international naval rivalry in Latin American and Pacific waters, and the desire of both major American political parties to commence a major naval building program had made naval construction and technology a much-debated issue in the early 1880s. Loring fell out of favor in some quarters, but his recommendations were followed as the United States began building a fleet of modern battleships and battle cruisers. He served on a number of important boards up until his retirement on 26 December 1890. During the Spanish-American War, he returned to active duty as the inspector of naval construction in New York. Well known in civilian engineering circles, he held offices in New York and national engineering societies. His central contribution was the long and faithful service he rendered in the cause of U.S. Navy technological modernization. He died in Hackettstown, New Jersey.

• The Lorings are traced in C. H. Pope and K. P. Loring, *Loring Genealogy* (1917). Loring's career is highlighted in L. R. Hamersly, *The Records of Living Officers of the U.S. Navy and Marine Corps*, 5th ed. (1894), and *Register of the Commissioned and Warrant Officers of the Navy of the United States and of the Marine Corps* (1907). The record of his Civil War service is in *The Official Records of the Union and Confederate Navies in the War of the Rebellion* (30 vols., 1894–1922). Obituaries are in the *Army and Navy Journal*, 9 Feb. 1907, the *Journal of the American Society of Naval Engineers*, Feb. 1907, the *Journal of the American Society of Mechanical Engineers* 29 (1907), and the *Army and Navy Register*, 9 Feb. 1907.

ROD PASCHALL

LORING, Eugene (2 Aug. 1911–30 Aug. 1982), choreographer, dancer, and teacher, was born Leroy Kerpestein in Milwaukee, Wisconsin, the son of Gilbert Kerpestein, a boxing trainer, and Anna Raddatz. Loring's early ambitions were focused upon becoming an actor. After graduating from high school in 1929, he joined an amateur theater group known as the Wisconsin Players. Here he met Boris S. Glagolin, a Russian theater director who followed Stanislavsky's principles. Because Loring's shortness in height restricted the roles in which he was cast, Glagolin encouraged the aspiring performer to turn instead to dance, and in 1934 he choreographed *The Gardener's Dog* followed by *Credentials* for the newly organized Civic Players. Members of the *Credentials* audience spoke with Loring afterward, advising him to go to New York where Lincoln Kirstein and Edward M. M. Warburg had founded the School of American Ballet.

Loring was awarded a scholarship and entered a circle of eminent dancers, teachers, and choreographers, including Pierre Vladimiroff, George Balanchine, and Michel Fokine. The young performer appeared in the school's student performance in June 1934, participating in the Procession section of Balanchine's *Dreams* at Felix Warburg's estate in White Plains, New York. Loring subsequently auditioned for Michel Fokine, dancing the role of a slave in *Schéhérazade* and Pantalon in *Carnaval* that summer at Lewisohn Stadium at the College of the City of New York. The following year he performed as the Photographer in Balanchine's *Alma Mater* with the American Ballet, at the time the resident company of the Metropolitan Opera House. Loring then joined Ballet Caravan, a small group formed by Lincoln Kirstein to present American works on summer tours, providing a springboard for young dancers.

The involvement with this venture afforded Loring his first major choreographic opportunities. *Harlequin for President*, a political satire in the manner of commedia dell'arte, premiered at Bennington College in July 1936. A year later *Yankee Clipper* christened Loring as one of America's most up-and-coming choreographers. Inspired by his visit to the Whaling Museums in Salem and New Bedford, Massachusetts, it told the story of a farmer boy who went to sea and visited many countries. The return home to his Quaker girl was marked by difficulties in reconciling his everyday life with his previous exotic travels. The ballet highlighted important features of Loring's work: his use of American-based themes and his interest in the psychological state of the characters. It was in the creation of *Billy the Kid* (1938) that both these strands were blended into a landmark work.

Kirstein had given Loring a book to read, *The Saga of Billy the Kid*, by Walter Noble Burns, suggesting its potential as the basis for a dance work. Loring's imagination was fired, and as additional preparation he read other books about the frontier, including Theodore Roosevelt's, from which he took inspiration. The first performance of *Billy the Kid* occurred at the Chicago Opera House in October 1938, with Loring dancing the title role. It was unlike any ballet previously witnessed by dance audiences. There were juxtaposed scenes from the life of the outlaw with panoramic depictions of the settling of the West, all set to Aaron Copland's first major commissioned ballet score. The Chicago critic Anne Barzel commented in *Dance* (Dec. 1938) that "Billy the Kid . . . marks a milestone in American Ballet . . . Loring's choreography is marked by inventiveness and imagination . . . yet his work is never obscure. Loring's inventiveness is shown in movements devised, whether it be to illustrate riding a horse or pushing West. His details are excellent" (Chujoy, p. 115). Loring had used balletic vocabulary for the purposes of creating a very modern dance drama. It set a precedent for works tackling American-based subject matter, freeing American ballet from the traditions of the Franco-Russian schools.

After leaving Ballet Caravan, Loring worked as a soloist and choreographer with Ballet Theatre from 1940 to 1941, producing *The Great American Goof*, which premiered at Center Theater in New York in January 1940. He also danced Peter in *Peter and the Wolf* there (1940) and the Devil in *Three Virgins and a Devil* at the Majestic Theater in February 1941. Loring then made his Broadway debut as Owen Webster in *The Beautiful People* at the Lyceum in April 1941.

In 1941 Loring established his own company, The Dance Players, whose members included Lew Christensen, Michael Kidd, Joan McCracken, and Janet Reed. The repertory consisted of new works—*City Portrait*, *The Duke of Sacramento*, *The Man from Midian* and *Prairie*—as well as some of his earlier works. The group remained in existence until 1942. Although full of undoubted talent, inexperience led to its disbandment.

Loring returned to the Broadway stage, choreographing *Carmen Jones* at the Broadway Theater in December 1943. His other shows included *Park Avenue* (1946), *Three Wishes for Jaimie* (1952), *Butrio Square* (1952), and *Silk Stockings* (1957).

As well as commercial theater, Loring's career ventured into films. He appeared in *National Velvet* (1944) and subsequently choreographed *Yolanda and the Thief* (1945). Here Loring worked with Fred Astaire and Vincente Minelli. The dream sequence titled "Will You Marry Me?"—in which Astaire's character is torn between his increasing love for Lucille Bremer's character and his desire to remain single—is a key example of Loring's film choreography. The sequence is comprised of several parts, each depicting aspects of Astaire's character's past, present, and potential future. It demonstrates Loring's interest in composing movement to further the plot, the dance being not merely to decorate but integral to the drama.

The most distinctive element of Loring's style was juxtaposing unusual rhythms and movement among a variety of dance forms within the same number. The "Coffee Time" sequence in *Yolanda and the Thief* has townspeople moving in a social dance style, with Astaire and Bremer also participating. The townsfolk step aside to marvel at the couple's dancing, clapping to the beat of the music. At one point only the clapping continues, yet Astaire and Bremer carry on dancing as if to castanets. The crowd rejoins the couple as the mu-

sic takes on a 1940s big band sound. There are further examples of combining unusual rhythms with distinctive choreographic segments, such as "The Flaming Flamenco" in *Fiesta* (1947), "One Alone" in *Deep in My Heart* (1954), "Let's Kiss and Make up" in *Funny Face* (1957), and "The Red Blues" in *Silk Stockings* (1957).

Loring also choreographed for television, working on a specially commissioned ballet for NBC's "Capital of the World" (1953), based on a short story by Ernest Hemingway. Loring also made television specials for Shirley Temple and Cyd Charisse. He was the subject of another TV program in 1961, *The Story of Eugene Loring—an American Dancer*. In 1976 he also produced a version of *Billy the Kid* for the Dance in America series.

Throughout Loring's career he continued to create a rich repertory of stage ballets including *The Sisters* (1966), *Prisms, Pinions, Paradox* (1968), *Polyphonica* (1970), *Who Am I? Where Do I Come from? What Am I Doing Here?* (1973), *The Tender Land* (1978), and *Time unto Time* (1980).

As well as choreographing, Loring's input into dance education was a significant part of his career. His American School of Dance in Hollywood, established in 1948, quickly became a prestigious training ground for performers on the West Coast. Among its graduates were George Chakiris, Mary Tyler Moore, and Max Mattox. Loring's eclecticism led to a unique "freestyle" form that blended various dance techniques—ballet, modern, and jazz—and he devised his own notation system, kineseography.

In 1965 Loring became chairman of dance and senior lecturer at the University of California at Irvine. The department sought to offer a comprehensive dance education, and Loring was rewarded with a Dance Magazine Award in 1967 in recognition of his work in the field. Having sold his American School of Dance in 1974, Loring was able to devote more time to university education, becoming a professor emeritus in 1979. Retiring in 1981, he died in Kingston, New York. His pioneering work, spanning over five decades, pushed forward the boundaries of choreography, dance performance and dance education in America.

• Recordings of Loring's work and other resources are available at the Dance Collection at the New York Public Library for the Performing Arts, Lincoln Center. Loring's reflections on his own career are featured in Jerome Delamater, *Dance in Hollywood Musical* (1981), and Olga Maynard, "Eugene Loring Talks to Olga Maynard," *Dance Magazine*, July 1966, pp. 35–39, and Aug. 1966, pp. 52, 72–74. Secondary sources include George Amberg, *Ballet: The Emergence of an American Art* (1949); Anatole Chujoy, *The New York City Ballet* (1977); and Charles Payne, *American Ballet Theatre* (1977). Analysis of Loring's *Billy the Kid* appears in a broad range of dance history texts, including Richard Philp, "Billy the Kid Turns Fifty: An American Dance Document," *Dance Magazine*, Nov. 1988, pp. 36–51; Grace Robert, *The Borzoi Book of Ballets* (1946); and Marcia Siegal, *The Shapes of Change: Images of American Dance* (1981). Loring's approach to dance education is featured in Margaret Lloyd and Selma Jeanne Cohen, "Eugene Loring's Very American School of Dance," *Dance Magazine*, Aug. 1956, pp. 30–33; Marian Horosko, "Loring the Teacher," *Dance Magazine*, Nov. 1988, p. 46; and Olga Maynard, "College Controversy: The University of California at Irvine Causes a Stir by Its Totally Professional Approach to Dance," *Dance Magazine*, Sept. 1966, pp. 62–65. An analysis of Loring's notation system is given in Ann Hutchinson Guest, "Selma Jeanne Cohen and Eugene Loring's Kinesiography," *Dance Chronicle* 18 (1995): 195–206. An obituary is in the *New York Times*, 1 Sept. 1982.

MELANIE TRIFONA CHRISTOUDIA

LORING, Joshua (3 Aug. 1716–5 Oct. 1781), British naval officer and Loyalist, was born in Boston, Massachusetts, the son of Joshua Loring, a tanner, and Hannah Jackson. Fatherless by the age of five, Joshua moved to Roxbury, where he was apprenticed to a tanner named James Mears. However, the continuing warfare between England and France attracted him, and when of age he went to sea and served on a privateer. In 1740 he married Mary Curtis; they had seven children. During the War of Austrian Succession (1740–1748), he became captain of his own privateer with 120 seamen under his command. In 1744, near Louisburg, Cape Breton Island, Nova Scotia, his ship was captured by two French men-of-war after a four-hour chase. He spent several months in a prison in Louisburg, then was released. When the French and Indian War began, Loring was commissioned a lieutenant in the British navy and by December 1757 was commissioned a captain in command of a twenty-gun vessel named the *Squirrel*. In 1759–1760 he was commanding officer during operations on Lake George, Champlain, and Ontario. It was during this time that he held the honorary title of "commodore." In 1760, during a naval campaign led by General Jeffrey Amherst to capture Montreal, Loring, in command of the *Onondaga* (twenty-two guns), went aground in the St. Lawrence River. There his military career ended when a cannonball tore the calf of his right leg.

At the end of the war, in the decade before the American Revolution, Loring retired to Massachusetts on a British pension of half pay for life and became a prosperous farmer and businessman. Earlier, in 1752, he had purchased sixty-acre Roxbury farm for £693, most likely using prize money from the war. In 1760 he built a two-story, eleven-room wood mansion at a cost of £2,000 currency. It was known to later generations as the Loring-Greenough House of Jamaica Plain. The house was filled with exquisite mahogany furniture and was staffed by three servants and a black slave named London. Loring also had a number of sleighs and coaches to take him into Boston. His neighbors were other wealthy men who also desired country estates, neighbors such as Sir Francis Bernard and Sir William Pepperell. He expanded his real estate holdings by buying a nearby 18-acre Roxbury farm, a 23-acre wood lot in Roxbury, 5 acres of salt meadows near Boston, and a house and garden on the South End of Boston near the Boston Common.

Loring was a man not only of wealth but also of status. He hired a private tutor for his children, and when his son Benjamin Loring attended Harvard in 1772, he was listed second in his class because of the Loring family status. As a member of the First Parish of Jamaica Plain, Commodore Loring was moderator and on the committee that arranged for Roxbury's first minister, William Gordon. Loring served as secretary and founding member of the local Masonic Lodge, St. Andrews Royal Arch Chapter of Masons, and was a member of the Boston Marine Society. In 1769 his friend, Governor Francis Bernard, appointed him justice of the peace for Suffolk County and later appointed him one of the five commissioners of revenue. In recognition of his past loyalty and prominence, General Thomas Gage appointed him a member of the council by writ of mandamus. Loring's appointment angered the populace, since all previous council members had been elected by the lower houses. After a town meeting, a prominent committeeman urged Loring to resign his seat on the council. Following a nightlong consultation with a neighbor, Deacon Joseph Brewer, on 31 August 1774 Loring and his family fled into British-occupied Boston. As he left he told a neighbor, "I have always eaten the king's bread, and always intend to." Loring displayed courage as one of the ten mandamus counsellors, out of thirty-six appointed, who did not yield to patriot pressure and resign his commission.

Like their father, the Loring sons became active Loyalists. Joshua Loring, Jr., was an addresser of Governor Thomas Hutchinson and General Gage. He became so greedy for lucrative offices that he purchased the title of high sheriff in Boston. He became infamous when he allowed the British general, Sir William Howe, to keep his wife, Elizabeth Lloyd Loring, as his mistress. In reward for services rendered, Howe appointed Joshua Loring, Jr., commissary of prisoners. The other sons of Commodore Loring served in either the British army or navy during the American Revolution.

For eighteen months the Loring family lived in Boston, surrounded by the hostile patriot army and unable to return home. When Howe evacuated Boston in March 1776, the Loring family sailed to London, where they lived on an allowance of £200 per year, the sum given to each of the mandamus counsellors. Since the family property was abandoned, Loring's fine stock of animals was soon running loose in the streets of Roxbury. The selectmen of the town took charge, allowing a company of patriot soldiers to barrack in the mansion. The troops plundered the furniture and animals, although they failed to find a stock of fine liquors that was discovered more than fifty years later hidden in the cellar behind a false wall. In June 1775 the Massachusetts Provincial Congress ordered that the mansion be made a hospital for the American army at Cambridge. A few American soldiers who died under the surgeon's scalpel or from disease were buried in the backyard. Properties abandoned by Loyalists were available for rental at an auction, and wealthy and prominent patriots benefited from the opportunity. Thus the Committee of Correspondence of Roxbury first rented Loring's Roxbury mansion to William Phillips, a representative from Boston, for £75 currency for the year. The next year Isaac Sears, the famous leader of the New York Sons of Liberty who had business dealings in Boston, leased the Loring mansion.

In 1778 the Massachusetts legislature named Commodore Loring in the Banishment Act, and in 1779 the legislature singled out twenty-nine Loyalists, including Loring, as "notorious conspirators," who immediately forfeited all property without a hearing or trial. The Massachusetts legislature wasted no time in ordering the immediate sale of the Suffolk estates of the "conspirators." Loring's property was quickly auctioned off, second only to former governor Hutchinson's mansion in Milton. In 1779 Sears bought the Roxbury mansion at public auction for £26,486 currency. At the auction, which took place at the mansion on 1 June 1779, the members of the Committee to Sell Conspirator Estates awarded themselves some questionable expenses. For example, one of the committee members deducted £1.13.0 for repair of the auctioneer's carriage, and the members spent £40.10.0 on liquor. The plunder of Loring's assets continued. By 1774 Commodore Loring had extended credit in the amount of £2,487 at 6 percent interest to many of his neighbors. Now these same debtors filed claims against Loring in the amount of £1,384. At first these claims were approved by a committee of ten "yeomanry farmers and mechanicks of the neighborhood," but this group allowed so many unjust claims that a special Massachusetts commission investigated and corrected some of the fraud.

When Commodore Loring died in exile, in Highgate (London), England, his widow filed a claim for £4,815 sterling with the Commission on American Loyalists, a board appointed by Parliament to recompense American Loyalists. The commission allowed her £3,356 sterling and an annual pension of £100.

• Loring's wife's claim for losses suffered is in American Loyalists Claims, Public Record Office, Kew, Greater London, England, Audit Office 12/105/107; AO 12/109/192. For short biographies of Loring see James H. Stark, *The Loyalists of Massachusetts and the Other Side of the American Revolution* (1910), and E. Alfred Jones, *The Loyalists of Massachusetts: Their Memorials, Petitions and Claims* (1930). For information on the house and property see Eva Boyd, "Jamaica Plain by Way of London," *Old-Time New England* 49 (1959): 85–103.

DAVID E. MAAS

LORING, Joshua (1 Nov. 1744–18 Sept. 1789), Loyalist, was born in Roxbury, Massachusetts, the son of Joshua Loring, a British naval officer, and Mary Curtis. He was commissioned as an ensign in the British army, 11 July 1761, and as a lieutenant in the 15th Regiment of Foot in America, 21 August 1765. He sold off his commission in June 1768 and returned to live in Boston. Meanwhile, in March 1767 he had been

appointed by Governor John Wentworth of New Hampshire as deputy surveyor of the King's Woods in North America, a sinecure worth £100 a year.

On 19 October 1769 he married a young heiress, Elizabeth Lloyd, daughter of the late Nathaniel Lloyd, a wealthy Boston merchant, by his wife Elizabeth Davenport and stepdaughter of Judge Nathaniel Hatch of Dorchester, Massachusetts. They attended Boston's Anglican Trinity Church, where Elizabeth's grandfather had been rector. Eventually the couple had six children; the eldest son became a rear admiral in the Royal Navy, while a younger son became archdeacon of Calcutta.

Loring supported the cause of the Crown by signing the memorial addressed to Governor Thomas Hutchinson, upon his departure from the province in May 1774. The family's links to the British administration were strengthened in August when both his own father and his wife's stepfather were named as mandamus councillors by the new governor, General Thomas Gage. Under the aegis of General Gage, Loring purchased the office of sheriff of Suffolk County for 500 guineas in 1775.

On 19 April 1775, the day of the battles at Lexington and Concord, Loring and his family fled from their 13-acre estate in Dorchester to nearby Boston and the protection of the king's troops. Loring signed the loyal address to General Gage upon his departure from Boston on 6 October 1775, and one of Gage's last acts as governor was to appoint Loring as "sole vendue master and auctioneer" for the town of Boston in charge of final execution of judgments, awards, and decrees awarded by the courts (*Massachusetts Gazette*, 26 Oct. 1775).

Upon the evacuation of Boston in March 1776, Loring and his family went with the British troops to Halifax, Nova Scotia, and then in June on to New York, where he was appointed commissary of prisoners by Sir William Howe. Elizabeth Loring also caught the eye of the womanizing commander-in-chief Howe, and their relationship became notorious during the New York winter of 1777.

Loring's historical reputation as commissary of prisoners has been largely constructed on the negative testimony of two men. Ethan Allen, whose primary complaint while in British custody was that he had not been treated as a gentleman, had no trouble in decrying Loring as a "monster" who collaborated with Howe in "murdering premeditately (in cold blood) near or quite 2000 helpless prisoners, and that in the most clandestine, mean and shameful manner (at N. York.)" (*The Narrative of Colonel Ethan Allen* [1961], 106–7). Likewise, the Whig *New York Journal* printed a second-hand report in which the British general James Robertson alleged that Loring profited from charging for rations issued to dead prisoners; or, as it was more poetically phrased, "feeding the dead and starving the living" (quoted in Frank Moore, *Diary of the American Revolution* [1865], 2: 110). However, Loring's American counterpart, Elias Boudinot, was reported to be "perfectly satisfied in the Treatment they meet with" following a visit to the hospitals, sugar house, and provost in New York (Loring to Gen. Sir William Howe, 7 Feb. 1778, *Royal Institution*). The correspondence of both Boudinot and General George Washington reflect a positive professional relationship with Loring despite insurmountable problems of supply. General Gold Selleck Silliman's letters to his wife commented on Loring's "complaisance, kindness, and friendship" in his own treatment. Loring continued as commissary of prisoners and arranged for prisoner exchanges throughout the balance of the war in America, including the exchanges that took place following the battle of Yorktown.

Elizabeth Loring and the children had gone to England in 1778, and Loring followed in November 1782. He petitioned the Loyalist Commissioners for a pension, which was denied, although he was awarded £830 against a loss of property valued at £1,050, in addition to a share in his father's estate. Shortly before his death, Loring unsuccessfully attempted to exchange 20,000 acres of land in New Hampshire, which he had received for "Services in America in the late French War" for land in either Nova Scotia or New Brunswick. Loring lived in exile at Englefield, near Reading, Berkshire, where he died.

Loring's career mirrored many others which aligned themselves with the British military establishment during the Revolution. Aside from his controversial role as commissary of prisoners, there is little to distinguish his life of disappointment.

• Loring's memorials to the American Loyalist Commissioners are at the Public Record Office, Kew, England, in the Audit Office series 12 and 13. Extracts of his official correspondence appear in *Report on American Manuscripts in the Royal Institution of Great Britain* (Historical Manuscript Commission), 4 vols. (1904–1909). A sympathetic view of Loring's activities as commissary of prisoners is given in Thomas Jones, *History of New York During the Revolutionary War*, 2 vols. (1879), pp. 423–26. The story of the family's Massachusetts home and English exile is told in Eva Phillips Boyd, "Jamaica Plain by Way of London," *Old-Time New England* 49 (1959): 85–103.

EDWARD W. HANSON

LORING, William Wing (7 Dec. 1818–30 Dec. 1886), soldier, was born in Wilmington, North Carolina, the son of Reuben Loring, a planter and native of Hingham, Massachusetts, and Hannah Kenan of North Carolina. The family moved to Florida when Loring was a child. The Second Seminole War erupted in December 1835, and William, age seventeen, enlisted in the Florida Volunteers and participated in the battles of Black Point (18 Dec. 1835) and Wahoo Swamp (21 Nov. 1836). By age nineteen he was a second lieutenant in the Second Florida Volunteers. Returning to civil life, Loring attended Episcopal Academy in Alexandria, Virginia, and Georgetown College. He graduated from Georgetown in 1842 with a law degree, was admitted to the Florida bar, and was elected to the territorial legislature, where he served three years.

"Educated in the true school of the soldier—active campaign life," Loring received a direct commission on 27 May 1846 into the U.S. Army as captain in the newly constituted Mounted Rifles. He was promoted to major on 16 February 1847 and participated in Major General Winfield Scott's famed campaign from Veracruz to Mexico City. He led a battalion at Contreras, and at the storming of Chapultepec (13 Sept.) he was badly wounded, losing his left arm. In recognition of his gallantry, Loring was breveted a lieutenant colonel on 20 August 1847 and a colonel on 13 September.

In 1849, in advance of hordes of gold seekers, Loring crossed the continent over the Oregon Trail with his regiment from Fort Leavenworth to the Pacific Coast—2,500 miles—taking with him a train of 600 wagons. After arriving in the Willamette Valley he assumed command of the newly constituted Department of Oregon, a position he held until 1851. The next five years found Loring and his regiment posted in Texas and New Mexico, where on several occasions he saw combat against Comanches and Kiowas on patrols into the Llano Estacado.

Transferred to the Department of New Mexico, Loring assumed command at Fort Union in September 1856, and on 30 December 1856 he was promoted, becoming the youngest colonel of the line in the "old army." In April 1858 he took his regiment into Utah Territory and participated in the Mormon War. Securing a year's leave of absence in April 1859, he traveled in Europe, Egypt, and the Ottoman Empire, studying the militaries of the region.

Loring returned to the United States in the winter of 1860–1861, and on 22 March 1861 he was named to command the Department of New Mexico. He did not sympathize with the secession, but, believing in states' rights, he resigned his commission on 13 May 1861, and traveled east to offer his service to the Confederacy. President Jefferson Davis, familiar with Loring's distinguished record, had him named brigadier general to rank from 20 May 1861.

After the death of Brigadier General Robert B. Garnett in the engagement at Corrick's Ford, Loring was named on 20 July to command the northwestern army and charged with the defense of the western approaches to the Shenandoah Valley. Within a week of Loring's arrival on site, he was joined at Huntersville by General Robert E. Lee. Loring had higher rank than Lee in the "old army" and had led troops into battle in Mexico when Lee was a staffer. The two officers did not work well together, and the Confederates, plagued by heavy rains and rugged terrain, botched Lee's ambitious plans to rout the enemy from Cheat Mountain and recover the Tygart Valley (10–17 Sept.).

Snow came to the mountains in November, and Loring, with most of his army, was redeployed, reporting to Major General Thomas J. "Stonewall" Jackson at Winchester on 26 December. Loring and his division—in frightful weather—participated in the Romney Expedition (31 Dec. 1861–21 Jan. 1862). When Jackson and the Stonewall brigade returned to Winchester, leaving Loring's division isolated at Romney,

Loring bypassed the chain of command and secured authority from the War Department to evacuate Romney and return to the Shenandoah Valley. The resulting brouhaha led Jackson to request relief of command, and Loring was reassigned to the Department of Norfolk. To salve Loring's bruised ego, President Jefferson Davis promoted him a major general to rank from 15 February 1862. Two days before Confederate forces evacuated Norfolk, on 8 May Loring was ordered to the western part of the state and designated commander of the newly constituted Department of Southwestern Virginia, with his headquarters at Dublin.

September 1862 found Confederate armies on the offensive from Tidewater to the Indian Territory. Loring, boldly seizing the initiative, struck northward on 6 September, beat the Federals at Fayetteville and Cotton Hill, and on 13 September occupied Charleston and hounded the retreating Union forces down the Kanawha Valley to Point Pleasant on the Ohio. Following up their Antietam victory, the Federals heavily reinforced their Point Pleasant forces, and Loring pulled back to the falls of the Kanawha, where, on 15 October he was relieved and ordered to Richmond.

In December Loring reported for duty in the Department of Mississippi and East Louisiana. Lieutenant General John C. Pemberton, his commanding officer, had been a captain of artillery in the prewar army. In February 1863 Loring rushed to Greenwood, Mississippi, where, with 2,000 men and eight guns emplaced behind the cotton-bale parapets of Fort Pemberton, he turned back a formidable amphibious force. On 11 March and again on 13 March he stood atop the parapet shouting: "Give them blizzards, boy!" From then on his nom de guerre was "Old Blizzards." While at Greenwood, Loring became disenchanted with Pemberton's leadership. This rift was a factor in the Confederates' defeat in the battle at Champion Hill on 16 May and the next day in the rout at Big Black Bridge, although Loring was not present at the bridge. Believing that it would be inviting disaster to rejoin Pemberton's army on its retreat into the Vicksburg defenses, Loring was en route to Jackson to join General Joseph E. Johnston. Loring and his division campaigned in Mississippi and western Alabama from June 1863 to May 1864.

Loring accompanied Lieutenant General Leonidas Polk and the Army of the Mississippi to northwestern Georgia, where at Resaca on 11 May 1864 he confronted Major General William T. Sherman's "army group." During the next four weeks Loring and his division marched, skirmished, and entrenched as Sherman inched his way forward. The death of General Polk at Pine Mountain on 14 June elevated Loring to command of the Army of the Mississippi, one of the three corps constituting Johnston's army. Loring and his troops easily repulsed Union forces sent against Little Kennesaw and Pigeon Hill on 27 June.

The Confederate War Department again demonstrated lack of confidence in Loring on 8 July when A. P. Stewart, having been promoted lieutenant general, replaced Loring as corps commander. Loring, a good soldier, returned to his division and fought at Peachtree Creek (20 July) and Ezra Church (28 July). Wounded at Ezra Church, Loring did not return to duty until early September, after the evacuation of Atlanta. On the campaign that took the Army of Tennessee, led since 18 July by John Bell Hood, from Palmetto, Georgia, to Florence, Alabama, Loring captured Big Shanty and Acworth on 3–4 October, taking 425 prisoners and tearing up the railroad. Loring was with the army on the advance to Nashville and the retreat to Tupelo. At Franklin, on 30 November, his division on the corps' right and pushed against the Big Harpeth River, suffered many casualties. At Nashville Loring and his people held their ground, but the retreat of units to their left compelled them to regroup on the night of 15 December and retreat late on the afternoon of 16 December. Loring's conduct and "skillful management" of his division during this disastrous campaign earned commendation from General Stewart.

Loring and his division, a shadow of itself, departed Mississippi for the Carolinas in late January 1865. At Bentonville (19–21 Mar.), for the last time he battled Sherman's troops. Writing of the Confederate attack, General Johnston noted that Loring "gallantly seconded" General Hardee's charge. Loring's service in behalf of the South ended at Greensboro on 2 May, when he was paroled.

After the war, Loring became a New York City banker and in 1869, along with other former Confederate officers, traveled to Egypt and entered the service of the Khedive as a Lewan Pasha (brigadier general). In 1870 he became commandant of Alexandria and was given charge of defending all Egyptian coasts. In 1875–1876 he commanded Egyptian forces engaged in the Sudan, and led them in the battle of Kaya-Khor. Loring earned promotion to the dignity of pasha and was awarded the orders of Osmanli and Grand Officer of the Medjidieh.

After ten years in Egypt, in 1879 Loring was mustered out of the Khedive's service. He returned to the United States and settled in Florida for a while before relocating to New York City, where during the next several years he wrote a number of articles and in 1884 wrote *A Confederate Soldier in Egypt*, the story of his ten year's service under the Khedive. A bachelor, he died in New York City and was buried in St. Augustine, Florida. At the time of his death, he had in preparation an autobiography, "Fifty Years a Soldier," which was not published. The location of the manuscript is unknown.

• For additional information on Loring, see John J. Dickison, *Confederate Military History*, Florida Extended Edition 16 (1989), pp. 203–06; Ezra J. Warner, *Generals in Gray: Lives of the Confederate Commanders* (1959), pp. 193–94; William L. Wessels, *Born to Be a Soldier: The Military Career of William Wing Loring* (1972); *The War of the Rebellion: A Compilation of the Official Records of the Union and Confederate Armies* (128 vols., 1880–1901); *Compiled Service Records of Confederate General and Staff Officers and Nonregimental Enlisted Men*, National Archives, M-331; and Leo E. Oliva, *Fort Un-*

ion and the Frontier Army in the Southwest (1993). See also C. H. Pope and R. P. Loring, *Loring Genealogy* (1912). An obituary is in the *New York Herald*, 31 Dec. 1886.

E. C. BEARSS

LORRE, Peter (26 June 1904–23 Mar. 1964), stage and film actor, was born Ladislav (or Laszlo) Loewenstein in Rózsahegy (or Rosenberg), Hungary, the son of Alois Loewenstein, a commercial manager, and Elvira (maiden name unknown). When Lorre was four, his mother died of blood poisoning, and shortly thereafter his father married her best friend, Melanie Klein, whom Lorre never accepted. In 1913 the family moved to the outskirts of Vienna. In school, Lorre was a disinterested student, rarely applying himself to his studies. Instead, he was drawn to the theater and acting. His family (his stepmother in particular) did not share his enthusiasm and imposed strict punishments for his nights at the theater, including locking him out of the house.

Lorre made his stage debut in Zurich, and in the early 1920s he became involved with avant-garde theater groups and performed in stock theater. From 1925 through 1928 Lorre completely immersed himself in the Viennese theater scene, playing a wide variety of roles. Leaving Vienna, he moved to Berlin where he made a name for himself overnight in Bertolt Brecht's *Die Pioniere von Ingolstadt* (1928). During this successful period in Berlin Lorre met and married Cecilia Lvovsky, an actress. They divorced in 1945, and Lorre married two more times: to Kaaren Verne in 1945 (divorced in 1953) and to Annemarie Stoldt, his press agent, in 1953. He had one daughter with Stoldt.

Lorre's stage presence caught the eye of Fritz Lang, who persuaded the young actor to play the lead role in his first sound film, *M* (1931). Lorre's portrayal of a child-murderer was a striking debut, giving him immediate international recognition. His performance was so believable that when he appeared in public, people would cross the street to avoid him. Lorre's physical stature made him immediately noticeable. He was short, described at one point as a pint-sized Boris Karloff, and his memorable eyes, described by one interviewer as "hard-boiled," protruded from his round face. He received critical acclaim for *M* and found himself typecast in similar villainous and psychotic roles for the rest of his film career.

With the rise of the Nazis, Lorre and other artists fled Germany in 1933. Traveling across Europe, he made a film in France in 1933 and eventually arrived in England. Despite the fact that Lorre spoke no English, Alfred Hitchcock cast him in *The Man Who Knew Too Much* (1934). On the strength of *M*, Lorre was then recruited by several Hollywood studios. In an effort to escape his sinister screen image, Lorre signed in 1934 with Columbia Pictures, since the studio indicated that they would not cast him in any horror films. Unfortunately, Lorre only made one film for Columbia during this time. In 1936 he worked again with Hitchcock in England in *Secret Agent*.

That same year, unhappy with Columbia, Lorre signed with 20th Century–Fox. Although the roles he received were unchallenging, he did appear in more films. In an effort to build on the popularity of the Charlie Chan pictures, Fox cast this Hungarian actor as the Japanese detective Mr. Moto in eight films. While Lorre enjoyed the unique character of the role at first, he later came to dread it. In fact, Lorre considered few of his roles in Hollywood worthwhile. He was cynical about the entire system and the limited importance of the actor. In a 1944 interview he remarked, "Dogs have been box-office bonanzas." Feeling that his career was stalling, Lorre left Fox and freelanced, but he could only find work as a villain in movies such as *Island of the Doomed Men* (1940) and *The Face behind the Mask* (1941).

In 1941 he made *The Maltese Falcon* for director John Huston. In the film he played thief Joel Cairo, a rather effeminate con who continually mothers his young cohort Wilmer and introduces himself with gardenia-scented calling cards. The next year he made *Casablanca*, in which he played a small but unforgettable role as Ugarte, again a thief but also a murderer—he kills two Germans for special letters of transit—who pleads for Rick Blaine (Humphrey Bogart) to save him just before being shot dead in Rick's Cafe. These two films stand as the work for which he is best known in American film lore. Not only did he work with Humphrey Bogart in both films, but he also worked with Sydney Greenstreet, who became Lorre's costar in seven other movies in the 1940s. On the strength of these two pictures, Warner Bros. hired Lorre as a character actor, providing him with steady employment, even though he continued to be typecast.

After the war, Lorre was slowly pushed out of the studio, since spy thrillers and mysteries, Lorre's perceived specialty, were no longer necessary. When it was acknowledged that the war was won, Hollywood turned to more escapist material for their films, such as musicals, melodramas, and film noir. However, Warner Bros., like other studios before them, found it extremely difficult to cast Lorre because of his typecasting and looks. Lorre also did not get along with Jack Warner, so there were financial as well as personal reasons for his dismissal. The last film he made for Warner Bros. during this period was *The Beast with Five Fingers* (1946), which, ironically, was the only true horror picture he made. He again crossed paths with Brecht in Hollywood in the 1940s, and the two tried unsuccessfully to sell joint film projects to the studios. In response to his lack of film work, Lorre created a vaudeville-like traveling show that included recitations and dramatizations of Edgar Allan Poe's works. He also hosted "Mystery in the Air" on the radio in 1947. The money he earned, though, was not enough to pay his bills, and he declared bankruptcy in May 1949.

In June 1949 Lorre returned to Europe where he toured the camps and devastated countryside. In Germany he decided to direct, produce, write, and act in his own film, *Der Verlorene* (1951). With this film,

Lorre finally acquired complete control over a project, which Hollywood studios had denied him. It was unsuccessful, even though a few critics hailed it as the film that could reawaken German cinema. Deflated and broke, Lorre returned to the United States.

He worked sporadically, appearing in John Huston's *Beat the Devil* and Walt Disney's *20,000 Leagues Under the Sea* (both 1954). He continued to play minor supporting roles in films of questionable quality, including Irwin Allen's *Voyage to the Bottom of the Sea* (1961). To supplement the money from his occasional film appearances, Lorre reluctantly turned to television, performing a number of sketches parodying his menacing screen persona. The comical depiction of his sinister image would continue long after his death. Lorre died of a stroke in Hollywood a few days before his scheduled divorce hearing from his third wife.

Even though Lorre is best known for his Hollywood films, he considered his work in the early 1930s with Bertolt Brecht and Fritz Lang in Berlin to be the pinnacle of his acting career. While he "acted" in Germany, in Hollywood he only "made faces." Lorre went to California with dreams of having complete artistic control over the films he made. This notion was quickly dispelled. Instead, he found himself typecast repeatedly as a villain, and with each role the deeper ingrained he became in the Hollywood system. Despite Lorre's disdain he was trapped because the financial rewards of the movies were incredibly attractive, and he embraced the glittering life of the Hollywood star. In essence, Lorre sacrificed his aesthetic dream for financial gain, and it was not until later in life that he truly came to realize what he lost in the exchange.

• Stephen D. Youngkin et al., *The Films of Peter Lorre* (1982), has in-depth bibliographic information, photos, and reviews of Lorre's movies. Another full-length study of Lorre is Ted Sennett, *Masters of Menace: Greenstreet and Lorre* (1979), which discusses not only the nine films the twosome made together but also the films they made separately. There are also numerous articles on Lorre, ranging from Paul Benedict's "Mild Mannered Maniac" in the fan magazine *Silver Screen*, Oct. 1944, pp. 26–27, 64–65, to Herbert Luft's biographical article, "Peter Lorre: Began His Film Career as a Psychopath and May End It as a Clown," in *Films in Review*, May 1960, pp. 278–84. An obituary is in the *New York Times*, 24 Mar. 1964.

WILLIAM C. BOLES

LOSEY, Joseph (14 Jan. 1909–22 June 1984), stage and film director, was born Joseph Walton Losey III in La Crosse, Wisconsin, the son of Joseph Walton Losey, Jr., a minor railway executive, and Ina Higbee. Losey attended Dartmouth College from 1925 to 1929 and was active with the Dartmouth Players; he graduated with a bachelor's degree. He then attended Harvard University, where he earned a master's degree in English literature in 1930. After his Harvard graduation, he tried a number of jobs, among them reviewing plays for *Theater Arts Monthly*, the *Saturday Review of Literature*, and the *New York Times*, and he became a roving reporter for *Variety*. He was stage manager for

the first live shows at Radio City Music Hall in 1932 and later served as stage manager for several Broadway plays.

He went on to direct several Broadway productions, beginning with the social problem play *Little Ol' Boy* in 1933. In 1935 Losey went to Moscow, where he attended film classes conducted by the eminent Russian director Sergei Eisenstein and directed an English-language stage production of Clifford Odets's *Waiting for Lefty*. In 1936 he helped found the Living Newspaper, a project of the Federal Theater. Foster Hirsch has written that each Living Newspaper play "was addressed to a particular social problem, usually a grievance of the working class. The politics of the plays were at least incipiently, if not actually and fully, Marxist; and the productions were designed to instruct Depression audiences and to encourage them to take action. The Living Newspaper dramas were . . . explicitly polemical—newspaper editorials brought vividly to life. . . . " Losey's artistic interests gradually changed from stage to screen in the late 1930s. In 1939 he was directing educational shorts in New York, beginning with *Pete Roleum and His Cousins*, a marionette play about the oil industry, which he made for the New York World's Fair. During the early 1940s he directed radio dramas for the National Broadcasting Company, then directed war relief shows before joining the U.S. Army Signal Corps in 1943. He went to Hollywood after the war; there he made another short, *A Gun in His Hand* (1945), which was part of the Metro-Goldwyn-Mayer "Crime Does Not Pay" series.

When MGM gave no indication that it intended to elevate Losey to feature production anytime soon, Losey accepted an offer from Dore Schary, the production chief at RKO, who encouraged independent filmmakers to direct with a degree of artistic freedom uncommon under the studio system of the time. Losey's first picture for RKO was *The Boy with Green Hair* (1948), but before it was finished, Howard Hughes had taken over the studio. Schary and his policies were out, and Losey's long struggle for creative control of his films was under way. Every day he received memos from Hughes about how he should shoot the movie, and Losey carried out Hughes's instructions as best he could.

The Boy with Green Hair is an allegory that uses the lad's green hair as a symbol of the need for international peace and understanding. The film is not akin to Losey's subsequent work, which is rooted in realism and which seeks to explore problems rather than to solve them. Losey preferred to make films that "disturb and stay with the viewer after he has seen them," not pictures that offer easy answers (author's interview). The film sounded a thematic chord that would reverberate in all of his work: "if I have one theme," he said, "it is the question of hypocrisy; people who condemn others without looking at themselves" (Milne, *Losey on Losey*, p. 128).

After his first feature, Losey was more determined than ever to find the creative freedom that had been promised to him at RKO but that had disappeared after Hughes's takeover. Hence, he turned to independent producers for work.

In the late 1940s suspicion surfaced that he might be a member of the Communist party. These were the Cold War years when the House Un-American Activities Committee (HUAC) held its hearings into purported leftist influences on Hollywood films and labor activities. The fears, suspicion, and cowardice of the time caused Losey to be blacklisted in the U.S. film industry, and in 1952, after avoiding a HUAC subpoena, he was forced into exile in England.

When Losey tracked down the reasons for his blacklisting, he found that he was suspect because he had openly supported the blacklisted Adrian Scott, producer of *The Boy with Green Hair* and a convicted member of the Hollywood Ten who had defied HUAC. Other reasons were Losey's involvement with the Living Newspaper project; his association with the blacklisted German writer Bertolt Brecht, whose play *Galileo* Losey had directed on Broadway in 1947; and a direct accusation by a former friend and colleague that he was a former Communist party member.

"Because his acclaimed work for the Living Newspaper had stamped him as a political activist," Foster Hirsch has noted, "Losey was chosen by Brecht to direct the American premiere of *Galileo*." HUAC considered the production politically suspect, "not only because of Brecht's Communist sympathies, but also because Losey was known to have left-wing associations." As Losey explained: "They were concerned about my association with people like Hanns Eisler, who wrote the music for Brecht's plays and for my films. He happened to be the brother of Gerhardt Eisler, the head of the German Communist party at the time, which made them suspect anyone associated with him. I had helped to bring Hanns Eisler into this country, and my sponsorship of him was one of the things mentioned in my dossier" (author's interview). (Interestingly enough, in *Guilty by Suspicion*, a 1991 film about the Hollywood blacklist, Losey himself was portrayed as "Joseph Lesser" by film director Martin Scorsese.)

In England Losey took whatever work he could find. He was initially hired to direct low-budget features, beginning with *The Sleeping Tiger* (1954), which he directed under the name Victor Hanbury to avoid risking loss of U.S. distribution. Of his early British films, Losey said: "I was still a foreigner in England—I'm a foreigner wherever I am and always will be—and my eye was foreign, seeing strange things which now would be quite ordinary to me" (Milne, *Losey on Losey*, p. 44). As a leftist outsider, Losey was fascinated by the class system in England, and the films he made there often explore how chaos and tragedy can result from the rigid maintenance of class barriers. For example, *The Sleeping Tiger* deals with an upper-class wife's love affair with a lower-class rogue. Losey's interest in British class consciousness also is closely related to his theme of hypocrisy. In discussing his film *Accident* (1967), Losey formulated this concept fully. The film focuses on marital infidelity among the faculty at Oxford University. Losey pointed out that it "is about a kind of moral bankruptcy, which is almost amoral, in contemporary society, among people who have every resource of our so-called civilization, and who are worse off than their grandfathers were in terms of coping with life. It is about conspiracy and betrayal between human beings, despite their declared loyalties. It is about people's failure to recognize themselves, what they are really like" (author's interview). Although Losey was thinking specifically of *Accident* when he articulated this triple theme—moral bankruptcy, human betrayal, and failure in self-knowledge—it underlies in varying degrees most of the films he made.

Losey's determination to make his films in his own way was illustrated during the shooting of *The Concrete Jungle* (1960). He refused to film a race track robbery in detail, as the film's distributors wanted. "It seemed to me the important thing was to see the exterior aspect," Losey explained, "to see how they got in, and then see them come out and escape. The fact that inside somebody points a gun at somebody else and someone puts lots of money into satchels is not to me interesting." Losey added that his attitude had sometimes caused distributors to complain, "He made his film; he didn't make ours." To this criticism, Losey responded, characteristically, "Well, I make my film; and I don't know what their film is" (Milne, *Losey on Losey*, p. 158).

Losey filmed *The Servant* in 1963, the first of three pictures he made in collaboration with playwright-screenwriter Harold Pinter, the others being *Accident* and *The Go-Between* (1971). All three films explore the moral bankruptcy of society, particularly among the upper class. *The Servant* reflects the class struggle in terms of a weak-willed young aristocrat, named Tony (played by James Fox), who allows himself to be dominated by his resentful manservant Barrett (Dirk Bogarde). Lacking moral convictions and realistic personal goals, Tony is methodically reduced by Barrett, through drugs and alcohol, to a total wreck. At film's end, when Barrett's triumph over Tony is complete, he locks the front door, sliding the bolts like a jailer. As the nominal servant ascends the stairs on his way to sleep in the master bedroom, he passes his degraded master, groveling on the stairs in a drunken stupor. Losey photographs Tony, imprisoned by his addictions to intoxicants as well as by his emotional dependence on Barrett, through the bars of the bannister railing. In essence, *The Servant* is a chilling parable, a film that ranks among Losey's finest achievements.

To those who felt that *The Servant* exemplified the pessimistic tone of many of Losey's films, he replied: "I don't regard my work as being pessimistic, because I think pessimism is an attitude that sees no hope in human beings or life in general, that has no compassion, therefore; and to have compassion, I strongly believe you have to examine the worst, the most tragic, the most crucifying aspects of life as well as the beautiful ones, and also the things that corrupt life, distort it, destroy it" (Leahy, p. 11).

Losey and Pinter's *The Go-Between*, which won the grand prize at the Cannes Film Festival, examines the love affair of an upper-class young woman with a working-class farmer. The production's opulent look belies the movie's stringent budget. "I think the degree of freedom in film making is in inverse proportion to the amount of money expended," Losey observed. "That's why I stay with a relatively low budget" (author's interview).

Losey had worked within an even tighter budget when he made *King and Country* (1964). More than an antiwar movie, it is a study of how the class divisions of the European social system have operated during wartime between officers and enlisted men. The film centers on Hamp (Tom Courtenay), a young soldier who is court-martialed and executed during World War I for desertion. The tribunal senses that the lad was driven to desertion, not by disloyalty, but by emotional fatigue and horror at the carnage of war. "I just started walking away from the guns," he explains at his trial. "I thought I was walking home." But the youth is sacrificed to an impersonal military code that recognizes no exceptions.

In *King and Country* Losey indicts the injustices of war by using imagery as potent as the spoken dialogue; thus he avoids the explicitly polemical approach to which this type of story lends itself. For example, a mock trial of a rat by a group of tired and tense soldiers is intercut with Hamp's trial. The false sense of values on which the tribunal bases its decision is made clear by the prosecuting attorney, who snaps at the well-meaning but ineffectual defense lawyer (Dirk Bogarde), "A proper court is concerned with law; it's a bit amateur to plead for justice." Yet how different the tribunal's action seems to the filmgoer when recorded by Losey's critical camera.

Losey fulfilled a long-cherished wish by bringing Brecht's *Galileo* to the screen in 1975. Central to the drama is the question of whether the seventeenth-century Italian astronomer Galileo (Topol) can retain his intellectual integrity in the face of the Vatican's condemnation of his scientific theories and findings. Like Brecht, Losey wanted to portray "individual responsibility" challenged by dogmatic authority. According to the director, the film implies that "the human race isn't going to survive if people consistently . . . allow themselves to be intimidated. That's the magnificence of that play" (Ciment, p. 339).

Losey took sick while making what would be his last film, *Steaming* (1985), which depicts a group of women who derive mutual support from sharing their common concerns. Shortly after completing the film, he died in London.

In interviews Losey was virtually silent about his domestic life. He mentioned to Michel Ciment that he was married three times, but neither the names of his wives nor the dates of the marriages are known. He had two children, one of whom was by his first marriage.

Like many film directors, Losey had to face great obstacles in achieving artistic control of his films. Yet he went on working until he won it, for he firmly believed that to be taken seriously, a director's films should be distinguished by a strong personal style. Throughout his career, first in Hollywood and later in England, he fought for the right to make films that would bear his stamp. "Working over the years," Losey reflected, "sacrificing the big, juicy jobs for the things I believe in, and doing it with no money and little encouragement, it's been exhausting" (author's interview). Yet with all of the obstacles in his path, he created a canon of intriguing films that bear the imprint of his thematic vision—films that should guarantee him a place in film history.

• Michel Ciment, *Conversations with Losey* (1985), is a book-length interview with the director. It updates an earlier interview book, Tom Milne, *Losey on Losey* (1968). James Leahy, *The Cinema of Joseph Losey* (1967), is an early critical study of the director's career, while Foster Hirsch, *Joseph Losey* (1980), surveys Losey's films almost to the end of his career. James Palmer and Michael Riley, *The Films of Joseph Losey* (1993), is an in-depth treatment of five of his major films. See Bernard Dick, *Radical Innocence* (1989), pp. 1–11, on the blacklisting era in Hollywood. Among critical essays available on Losey's major films, the following are noteworthy: Tom Milne, *"Accident," Sight and Sound* 36, no. 2 (1967): 56–59, and Richard Roud, "Going Between," *Sight and Sound* 40, no. 3 (1971): 158–59.

GENE D. PHILLIPS

LOSSING, Benson John (12 Feb. 1813–3 June 1891), author of illustrated books, was born in Beekman, New York, the son of John Lossing and Miriam Dorland, farmers. His father died before Lossing was one year old, and his mother died when he was eleven. At that time, with less than three years of schooling, he started his working career, on a farm. When he was fourteen he was apprenticed to Adam Henderson, a watchmaker and silversmith, in Poughkeepsie and in 1833, on completing his apprenticeship, became a partner in the firm and married Henderson's niece, Alice Barritt, who died in 1855. There were no children. The following year he married Helen Sweet, with whom he had four children.

Lossing left the partnership in 1835 to become editor and joint publisher of the *Poughkeepsie Telegraph*, a weekly newspaper with a circulation of 2,500, and a year later he founded the *Poughkeepsie Casket*, a semi-monthly journal "devoted exclusively to the different branches of polite literature and the arts." He then extended his training and experience as a watchmaker and silversmith into the study of wood engraving under J. A. Adams of New York City and in 1838 became editor and illustrator of *Family Magazine*, which several decades later was described by Nelson Rockefeller as "one of the first fully illustrated periodicals published in North America." At the same time, he and his brother-in-law, William Barritt, had gone into the business of wood engraving and soon became the foremost practitioners of that art in the state, providing engravings for the leading book and periodical publications of the time.

Lossing's first book, *An Outline History of the Fine Arts*, was published in 1840 as No. 105 of the Harper's Family Library. That would be followed by more than forty other books on American history and biography, all copiously illustrated and filled with anecdotes and even eyewitness accounts. In 1846 and 1847 he produced the two volumes of *Seventeen Hundred and Seventy-six; or, The War of Independence*, which he followed in 1852 with the massive two-volume *Pictorial Field-Book of the American Revolution*, the compilation of thirty pamphlets published the year before by Harper & Bros. With its 1,350 illustrations and roughly fifteen hundred pages of text, this work established the base from which Lossing launched himself as the leading author of illustrated histories and biographies on American subjects in the last half of the nineteenth century. *The Hudson: From the Wilderness to the Sea*, first published in the London *Art Journal* in 1860 and 1861 and, later, in 1866, by H. B. Nims & Co. of Troy, New York, is an excellent example of Lossing's method. He works his way from what was then thought to be the source of the Hudson River in the Adirondacks, downstream 300 miles to Sandy Hook, by canoe and rowboat, horse, and shank's mare, recording in words and 463 prints the most important features of the stream and its settlements in the late 1850s.

Lossing wrote and illustrated books covering almost every possible topic in American history: an edition of George Washington's diary, a history of New York State, a grammar school history of the United States, a book on the lives of the presidents, another on the life and times of revolutionary war officer Philip Schuyler. Lossing observed the one hundredth anniversary of the Declaration of Independence with a book entitled *The American Centenary: A History of the Progress of the Republic of the United States during the First One Hundred Years of Its Existence*. In 1890, the year before his death, he was the leading contributor to *The Achievements of Four Centuries; or The Wonderful Story of Our Great Continent within and beyond the States*. It was fitting, therefore, that in 1905, well over a decade after Lossing's death, Harper & Bros. published the *Harper's Encyclopaedia of United States History: Based upon the Plan of Benson John Lossing* and featured his name in large type, leading all other contributors, on the title pages of all ten volumes. He died at his home in Dover Plains, New York.

• Collections of Lossing papers and correspondence are in the Special Collections at Syracuse University and in the Rutherford B. Hayes Library, Fremont, Ohio. The Adriance Memorial Library in Poughkeepsie, N.Y., has a small file on Lossing, mostly genealogical, as well as a complete file of the *Year Book of the Dutchess County Historical Society*, which has several articles on him. The Apr. 1968 issue of *Antiques* magazine includes the article "Benson J. Lossing, Nineteenth-century Historian and Wood Engraver." The foreword written by John T. Cunningham to the 1976 edition of Lossing's *The Pictorial Fieldbook of the War of 1812* is an excellent critical discussion that can be applied to many of Lossing's other books. The 1972 edition of *The Hudson: From the Wilderness to the Sea* includes a foreword by Nelson Rockefeller.

ALFRED H. MARKS

LOTHROP, Alice Higgins (28 Mar. 1870–2 Sept. 1920), social worker, was born Alice Louise Higgins in Boston, Massachusetts, the daughter of Albert H. Higgins, a merchant, and Adelaide A. Everson. Alice attended private schools in Boston. As a young woman she volunteered as supervisor of Sunday school activities in the Unitarian church and as an aide with the local Children's Aid Society. In 1898 she joined the Associated Charities of Boston as a worker in training. Superiors, impressed with her "quiet efficiency" and comprehension of "facts," appointed her district secretary in 1900. Two years later she took a summer course at the New York School of Philanthropy, and in 1903 she was promoted to general secretary of the Associated Charities.

A leader who inspired and challenged social workers to put forth their best efforts, Alice Higgins set the example. She evaluated each individual case, looking closely at family and community relationships. She examined new data on each client to determine the best course of action for every individual. For Higgins, caseworkers were "of primary importance," and she never undermined their position but sought their information and advice on cases. She considered volunteers to be "sacred," but she also stressed the need for training and education in social work. When a formal training program was proposed, Higgins wholeheartedly promoted a campaign to fund the Boston School for Social Workers. She served as special assistant and lectured on a variety of subjects at the school from its inception in 1904 until 1920. The school provided expert training and gave social work greater respectability.

Higgins was skeptical initially of physicians' efforts to combine medical and social work, but her pessimism disappeared when she gained a deeper knowledge of the medical field. She then realized that correlating medical and social services would not only benefit the individual but also strengthen social services. When a medical-social work department was established at Massachusetts General Hospital in 1905 Higgins was on hand to guide caseworkers and medical experts in their evaluations of the best treatments.

Seeking "protection and rehabilitation of the family," Higgins broadened her roles within the community. She actively campaigned to pass mothers' aid laws to help widows and their children, supported alcohol prevention programs, and set up shelters for the homeless. She also sat on the boards of many committees, including the Massachusetts Child Labor Committee, the Massachusetts Association for Relief and Control of Tuberculosis, and the Massachusetts Civic League. In 1910 she was appointed to the Massachusetts Commission to Investigate Employment Agencies. In each organization she worked to keep communication open among numerous agencies and Associated Charities.

To form a network of cooperation among local social agencies, Higgins advocated the methods of field work used in other cities. To promote this effort she helped to found the National Association of Societies for Organizing Charity in 1910–1911. She chaired the association—which later changed its name to the American Association for Organizing Family Social Work—from 1914 to 1920. The association established social service agencies in cities with populations of 10,000 or more and set up guidelines and training programs for a nationwide system of social workers and relief work.

Higgins's organizational skills proved very helpful in responding to numerous disasters across the country. In 1906 she spent nine weeks aiding in the formation of a relief program following the San Francisco earthquake. This program laid the foundation for later relief programs such as those responding to fires in Chelsea, Massachusetts, in 1908 and in Salem, Massachusetts, in 1914. Following a 1917 explosion at Halifax, her intervention saved the eyesight of many victims cut by flying glass when she immediately brought eye specialists onto the scene to provide emergency measures.

After her marriage in 1913 to William Howard Lothrop, a Boston businessman, Alice Higgins resigned from her position as general secretary of Associated Charities, but she continued in the capacity of director. She also remained active in the Red Cross as secretary of the Plan and Scope Committee of the Boston Metropolitan Chapter, and she became director of the Civilian Relief Department in the New England Division of the Red Cross in 1917.

During her two years as director, Lothrop was responsible for developing home services to assist families in wartime. The Home Service Institute trained emergency workers to aid families of soldiers in hospitals and army camps. Lothrop extended home services into all division chapters of the Red Cross, and the service was employed both during and after World War I.

Only a few weeks after she was struck with a rare disease, Lothrop died in her home in Newtonville, Massachusetts. Having had no children of her own, she dedicated her life to the welfare of other children and their families. A woman who spent her few leisure hours gardening, she worked tirelessly to cultivate the best in social workers. Alice Higgins Lothrop foresaw that united efforts between agency, caseworker, and client brought the best results in forming an integrated and productive family unit.

• Material regarding Lothrop's work can be found in the archives of the Family Service Association of Greater Boston. See also her three articles in the *Proceedings of the National Conference of Charities and Correction*: "Comparative Advantages of Municipal and C.O.S. Lodging Houses," 31 (1904): 148–55; "Helping Widows to Bring Up Citizens" (with Florence Windom), 38 (1910): 138–44; and "The Responsibility of Medical Social Workers," 43 (1916): 502–7. Brief excerpts from her reports on cases are in Mary E. Richmond, *Social Diagnosis* (1917). The best information on her work with the Associated Charities of Boston is in its annual *Reports* (1904–1913). For other details of her work and activities, see the memorial issue of the *Family*, Dec. 1920. Additional information is in Elisabeth M. Herlihy, ed., *Fifty Years of Boston* (1932), Roy Lubove, *The Professional Altruist* (1965), and Frank Dekker Watson, *The Charity Organization Movement in the United States* (1922; repr. 1971). Obituaries appear in the *Boston Transcript*, 3 Sept. 1920, and *Survey*, 15 Sept. 1920.

MARILYN ELIZABETH PERRY

LOTHROP, Daniel (11 Aug. 1831–18 Mar. 1892), publisher, was born in Rochester, New Hampshire, the son of Daniel Lothrop and Sophia Horne. Lothrop abandoned formal schooling in 1845, when one of his older brothers, who wanted to leave New Hampshire to study medicine in Pennsylvania, asked him to "take charge" of his drugstore. A family acquaintance remembered in an article for the *Bay State Monthly* (Dec. 1884) that Lothrop's brother offered him "an equal division as to profits, and [said] that the firm should read 'D. Lothrop & Co.'" (p. 123). The "ambitious lad" accepted the proposal, thus forming a family partnership that eventually included his other brother and lasted for many years.

Perhaps inspired by regional drugstores, which tended to offer a wide variety of goods in addition to medicines, Lothrop decided to sell books in his shop. He was one of the first to implement this practice, now common in American drugstores and supermarkets. While it proved fairly successful for Lothrop, this tactic did not become widespread for many years. In the 1930s, when publishing houses tried to place their books in drugstores to boost sales, an observer called Lothrop's technique "the newest novelty in the . . . trade." However, writer Ellis Parker Butler decried the growing trend, loathe to see even cheap novels as "the chum of the hair-remover and cough-cure, and the pal of the ice-cream soda and the lettuce sandwich." The practice garnered little criticism at the time, however, and Lothrop soon opened other drugstores with book lines in eastern New Hampshire.

Lothrop expanded his commitment to the book trade in 1850, when he bought a popular bookstore in Dover, New Hampshire. He encouraged area residents to use the shop as an intellectual and social meeting place, displaying an interest in community development that would shape his later publishing house. Lothrop began to experiment with publishing, releasing a few titles while running the bookstore.

Encouraged by his success in New Hampshire, Lothrop went to Minnesota Territory in 1856 and opened a bank and a drugstore in St. Peter, then the capital. He offered an assortment of books in his western drugstore, as he did in his eastern shops. Both the bank and the drugstore quickly failed, however, victims of the 1857 financial panic and the decision to move the capital to St. Paul. Lothrop refused to let any of his ensuing debts go unpaid. Though he eventually settled all his accounts, the *Bay State Monthly* reported that he "broke in health" from the experience.

After leaving Minnesota Territory, Lothrop spent time in Florida, where he made a full recovery from his illness. He then returned to New Hampshire and concentrated on his Dover bookstore. He married Ellen Morrill in 1860; they had no children.

Lothrop closed his businesses after the Civil War ended, and he made plans to start a publishing house. Guided by an ideal one of his later authors described to *Lend a Hand* (Oct. 1892) as "the thought that literature must be of some use, and especially of use to the American community" (p. 263), he decided to target the Sunday school market. Lothrop consulted three men who had firsthand knowledge of American religious affairs. All agreed that he had little chance of success but conceded to work as reviewers, charmed by his enthusiasm for the project.

Ignoring their predictions, Lothrop opened D. Lothrop and Co. in Boston, Massachusetts, during 1867. He applied two rules to his work: "1. Never to publish a book purely sensational, no matter what the chances of money it has in it, [and] 2. To publish books which will make for a true, steadfast growth in right living" (McClintock, p. 126). Whether knowingly or not, these principles and Lothrop's other practices followed guidelines issued by the American Sunday School Union in the 1830s for its publication of children's literature—that material be moral, of accomplished style and interesting content, age appropriate, and American in character. Hoping to surpass competitors' material, Lothrop sponsored contests and offered prizes of up to $1,000 for good manuscripts.

Lothrop's approach succeeded. Mary Andrews Denison's *Andy Luttrell*, published in 1869, was one of the firm's first novels to become a bestseller. As his books enjoyed widespread popularity, Lothrop started to pursue a two-track publishing strategy, releasing general literature for children and families in addition to his Sunday school products. He became one of the most successful publishers of children's literature to that point. He also issued children's magazines. *Wide Awake*, started in 1874, featured authors such as Edward Everett Hale, Sarah Orne Jewett, Margaret Sidney, and Mary Mapes Dodge. The magazine sought to both educate and entertain, offering poems, short stories, serialized novels, and puzzles. Virtually all of the pieces taught some kind of moral lesson. Lothrop added to his stable of juvenile magazines with *Babyland*, *Our Little Men and Women*, and *Pansy*. He also published *The Chatauqua Young Folk's Journal*, which strengthened his ties to the growing New York–based movement. His publishing house expanded continuously, surviving economic depressions and a fire.

Lothrop's success in the Sunday school market inspired others to join the field, starting an eventual tidal wave of religious-moral literature for children. Some observers scorned the trend's products. In an 1873 speech Henry Ward Beecher told the audience "that the Sunday-school library has opened upon [children] as a flood, or rather a swarm, that can be compared to

little else than the locusts, the lice, and the frogs, often, of Egypt." He regarded the material as "an immense amount of wishy-washy stuff" (quoted in Tebbel, vol. 2, p. 596). The phrase "savored of the Sunday school" eventually became verbal shorthand for anything boring or overtly pedantic. Many supported Lothrop's contributions, however; *Publishers Weekly* (26 Mar. 1892) called them "the better class of this literature," and the *Boston Herald* labeled one of his magazines a "marvel of excellence."

In 1880 Lothrop furthered his desire to serve the community by creating the American Institute of Civics. Concentrating on the public realm of government rather than the private arena of moral development, the organization sought to teach people about the workings of the government. Lothrop's wife died the same year, and he married Harriett Mulford Stone in 1881; they had one child. An author who used the pseudonym Margaret Sidney, Stone gained enormous success after her *Five Little Peppers and How They Grew* appeared on the pages of *Wide Awake* in serialized form. Two years later the Lothrops bought "The Wayside," Nathaniel Hawthorne's former home in Concord, Massachusetts. The couple painstakingly preserved the house, and it became the site of many social and literary events. Lothrop died in Boston.

Even before the glow of eulogies and peer assessments deified Lothrop's contributions to children's publishing, the *Bay State Monthly* judged that he "interpenetrates the life of our whole people" and was "known by his name and his work to the entire English speaking world" (McClintock, p. 121). While undoubtedly containing elements of journalistic overstatement, the article's tone conveyed Lothrop's influence. He affected the public not with individual books but rather a body of work. Lothrop's efforts helped solidify a genre and set a standard for the field.

• John Tebbel, *A History of Book Publishing in the United States*, vol. 2 (1975), presents a thorough examination of Lothrop's publishing company and children's literature in general, and vol. 1 (1972), contains an evaluation of the field before 1865. For period reportage on Lothrop, see John McClintock, "Daniel Lothrop," *Bay State Monthly*, Dec. 1884, pp. 121–31. Edward Everett Hale assesses Lothrop's contributions in "An American Publisher," *Lend a Hand*, Oct. 1892, pp. 253–63. Lothrop's daughter, Margaret M. Lothrop, discusses her parents' life and work in *The Wayside: Home of Authors* (1940). A complete obituary appears in *Publishers Weekly*, Mar. 1892, pp. 494–95. Other obituaries are in the *Boston Daily Globe*, 20 Mar. 1892, and the *Boston Herald*, 19 Mar. 1892.

MARGARET THOMPSON

LOTHROPP, John (1584–8 Nov. 1653), Independent clergyman and colonizer in New Plymouth, was born in Yorkshire, England, and baptized in Etton, Yorkshire, the son of Thomas Lothropp or Lowthroppe, a landed gentleman, and Mary (maiden name unknown). His name is sometimes spelled Lathrop. His father had twenty-two children, and John was one of two sons who were sent to college. Nothing is known of John's youth, but in 1601 he matriculated at Queen's College, Cambridge, graduating in 1605 and receiving an M.A. in 1609. In 1610 he married Hannah House; they had six children. Ordained in the Anglican church by 1611, he was curate of a parish in Egerton, Kent, during the 1610s.

By 1623 Lothropp had renounced his orders. In 1624 he succeeded the well-known Henry Jacob as pastor of the first Independent or Congregational church in England, which Jacob had founded in Southwark (London) in 1616. Jacob immigrated to Virginia, where he soon died. Lothropp became prominent enough to attract the attention of John Cotton and the bishop of London. Cotton, before he left England for Massachusetts Bay, complained in a letter to Samuel Skelton of Salem on 2 October 1630 that the Salem leaders had been too strict when taking the position that "none of the congregations in England are particular Reformed Churches but Mr. Lathrop's and such as his" (Edmund Morgan, *Visible Saints* [1963], p. 86). Cotton was probably upset that the Salem church had admitted one of Lothropp's congregation into communion while refusing it to members of English parish churches, including Governor John Winthrop.

That Lothropp's congregation should have been deemed a true reformed church by the separatist-leaning authorities in Salem was shortly authenticated by the harassment experienced by Lothropp and his congregation. After meeting in secret for a number of years, Lothropp and forty-two of his congregation were jailed at the Clink and Newgate after being seized by the bishop's pursuivant on 29 April 1632. Two years later the followers were freed, but Lothropp was judged by the Star Chamber as too dangerous to be released. His wife died at this time. The authorities, apparently moved by her death and the poverty of Lothropp's petitioning children, released Lothropp on bail on 24 April 1634 with the admonition that he not frequent any conventicles. By 18 September he was in Boston, having arrived on the ship *Griffin* along with some thirty of his congregation.

Lothropp and his group quickly moved to Scituate, about twenty-five miles south of Boston in Plymouth Colony, probably upon previous invitation from the handful of settlers there. According to his records, the church was formed by covenant on 8 January 1635, and on 19 January he was chosen pastor by the congregation. It was appropriate that he and his group locate in Plymouth Colony, which was founded by separatists. This did not, however, preclude divisions within the new settlement. Lothropp's records indicate that over fifty new members were admitted to the church between January 1635 and February 1638, but the congregation ceased to grow after that. Scituate was the Plymouth town closest to the Massachusetts Bay Colony, which was then agitated by the expulsion of Roger Williams and the antinomian Ann Hutchinson. Lothropp's records refer to 22 February 1638, when new admissions abruptly declined, as a day of humiliation "for the remoueall of these Spreading opinions in

the churches att ye Bey, and alsoe for the preventing of any intended evill against the churches here" (*New England Historical and Genealogical Register* 10, p. 37). In 1637 he married Ann, whose last name was probably Hammond. They had four children.

Just what evil could have menaced the churches of Plymouth is highly conjectural, for Lothropp's records are cryptic, to say the least. As regards Scituate, Lothropp may have been criticized for liberalism in church polity. As early as 1637 he allowed children of parishioners not in full communion to be baptized, a point remarked upon by Ezra Stiles in a postscript to his transcription of Lothropp's church records. Not until 1662 did Massachusetts Bay uncomfortably resolve this knotty problem in the Half-Way Covenant. Further, the mode of baptism would shortly split the congregation during the ministry of Charles Chauncy, Lothropp's replacement and a total immersionist, unlike Lothropp. Quite possibly the division was not simply theological. Removal petitions to the Plymouth Court mentioned a scarcity of good land, although this quarrel did not prevent Scituate from growing into the second largest town in Plymouth Colony by 1643.

Soon after arriving in Scituate, Lothropp and his supporters began petitioning Governor Thomas Prence for removal to another location in the colony. The Plymouth Court granted permission for the Scituate settlers to move to a location on Cape Cod over fifty miles farther removed from Massachusetts Bay, Mattakeese, which became known as Barnstable. Lothropp recorded arriving there on 11 October 1639 along with a sizable segment of his congregation. Some early settlers led by Rev. Joseph Hull moved to Yarmouth, then Barnstable apparently grew peacefully during the remainder of Lothropp's ministry. Two of his sons became prominent in New England. Thomas Lothropp was a captain in the Connecticut militia and led an expedition against Deerfield. Barnabas Lothropp was appointed a representative of Plymouth in the short-lived Council for New England under Edmund Andros but did not serve.

Lothropp's career was anomalous in some respects. A significant figure in English Puritanism, he might have been expected to enter the theological controversies of New England. But although in 1641 he published a brief pamphlet on baptism that has not survived, he was active mostly as a leader of settlement in Plymouth Colony. Nathaniel Morton's description of him as "a man of a humble and broken heart and spirit" and "studious of peace" (p. 168) suggests that he was not inclined toward disputation so much as establishing the "peaceable kingdom" that was the elusive ideal of early New England towns. When that ideal proved unattainable in Scituate, Lothropp and his followers removed to Barnstable, where it seems to have been realized. He remained an active minister until he died in Barnstable.

• No Lothropp sermons, published or manuscript, survive. Two petitions to Thomas Prence are in the Edward Winslow manuscripts. The records of both of his churches survive only in notes of admissions, baptisms, and days of thanksgiving and humiliation as transcribed by Ezra Stiles, Beinecke Rare Book and Manuscript Library, Yale University. They were published as "Scituate and Barnstable Church Records" in the *New England Historical and Genealogical Register* 9 (July 1855): 279–87, and 10 (Jan. 1856): 37–43. For his English ministry see Daniel Neal, *History of the Puritans*, vol. 3 (1769), and John Waddington, "The Church in Southwark," in *The Works of John Robinson*, vol. 3, ed. Robert Ashton (1851). His years in New England are touched in Nathaniel Morton, *New England's Memorial* (1669). For more extended discussions see Samuel Deane, *History of Scituate* (1831), and Eugene Aubrey Stratton, *Plymouth Colony* (1986). Lothrop was the progenitor of a remarkable number of notable Americans, and the most useful genealogical notes and essays are E. B. Huntington, *A Genealogical Memoir of the Lo-Lathrop Family* (1884), and Amos Otis, *Genealogical Notes of Barnstable Families, Being a Reprint of the Amos Otis Papers*, revised by C. F. Swift, vol. 2 (1890).

H. JAMES HENDERSON

LOTKA, Alfred James (2 Mar. 1880–5 Dec. 1949), statistician and demographer, was born in Lemberg, Austria-Hungary (now Lwiw, Ukraine), the son of Jacques Lotka and Marie Doebely, religious missionaries who, although American citizens, lived most of their lives in Europe. Lotka's boyhood was spent in France and Germany. He attended the University of Birmingham (England), receiving his B.Sc. in 1901. He was broadly interested in physics, chemistry, and biology, and even at this period saw mathematical links between phenomena conventionally studied in independent disciplines.

Lotka spent the 1901–1902 academic year at the University of Leipzig, taking graduate courses in physics and developing his mathematical theory of evolution. In 1902 he came to the United States and worked as a chemist for General Chemical Co. In addition to papers of engineering interest on gas mixtures (1907, 1909), he published articles on human birth and death rates in *Science* (1907) and on the growth of material aggregates in the *American Journal of Science* (1907). In these early papers he noted the formal similarity between mathematical functions describing population dynamics and those describing purely physical processes.

Lotka left General Chemical Co. in 1908 to do further graduate work in physics, this time at Cornell University, obtaining his M.A. in 1909. From 1909 through 1911 he worked concurrently as an examiner in the U.S. Patent Office and as an assistant in physics at the National Bureau of Standards.

Lotka continued to publish papers on age distribution in populations as functions of birth and death rates, expanding his researches to include problems of evolutionary change. In an important paper written with Francis R. Sharpe, he showed that a closed population with fixed sex ratio at birth and fixed mortality and fertility rates acquires a stable age distribution and a characteristic rate of increase. The paper appeared in *Philosophical Magazine* in 1911. He received a D.Sc. from the University of Birmingham in 1912.

Lotka became editor of *Scientific American Supplement* in 1911, and in 1913 he published in its pages an English translation of his paper on evolution, which had appeared in German two years earlier. In 1914 he returned to General Chemical Co. as a chemist, remaining there until 1919. His numerous journal articles during this period, however, continued to reflect his interest in demography, including epidemiology and population fluctuations and their mathematical analogs in the fields of chemical reactions and natural selection.

Lotka was well-read and fluent in French, German, and English and wrote for both scholarly and popular publications. The depth of his understanding is evident in his article on Albert Einstein's theory of relativity (*Harper's Monthly*, Apr. 1920), a lucid exposition for the educated nontechnical reader. He noted, well in advance of the development of nuclear weapons, the extraordinary amount of energy that, according to Einstein's equation, a small amount of matter could release.

However, Lotka focused his main efforts on bringing his own mathematical conceptions of biological phenomena into a coherent, readable form. He spent two years (1922–1924) at Johns Hopkins University, where he completed his major work, *Elements of Physical Biology* (later retitled *Elements of Mathematical Biology*), published in 1925. Some of the subjects he investigated in it were growth and reproduction of organisms, equilibrium between organisms and their environment, evolutionary change, energy balance, the operations of the senses, and the problem of consciousness. For many biological phenomena, he offered mathematical analogies from chemistry and physics. Of the topics treated, only his discussions of population dynamics and evolution had significant influence on later investigators.

In 1924 Lotka joined Metropolitan Life Insurance Company as a supervisor of its statistical bureau. He was promoted to assistant statistician in 1934 and remained with Metropolitan until his retirement in 1948. In 1935 he married Romola Beattie; they had no children.

In the period between his leaving General Chemical Co. and joining Metropolitan Life, Lotka published about twenty technical papers. But his first paper associated with his new employer had repercussions on the American political scene. The United States had only recently adopted restrictive immigration policies, rationalized by census data on the nation's "natural increase" in population. Lotka and coauthor Louis I. Dublin showed the reported figure of 10.7 per 1,000 per annum to be misleading because of the unusually large portion of the population in the fertile 20–45-year age range. In the absence of immigration, the "intrinsic" rate of increase, useful in predicting population trends, was only 5.2. This finding had the effect, Dublin noted twenty-five years later, of converting Malthusian fears of overpopulation into fears of decline of Western populations.

Lotka's three books, published jointly with Dublin, are mainly of actuarial and insurance interest: *The Money Value of a Man* (1930), *Length of Life* (1936), and *Twenty-five Years of Health Progress* (1937).

Lotka's last book on population was *Analyse Démographique avec Application Particulière à L'Espèce Humaine*, published in France in 1939. In it he attempted to relate demographic phenomena to the physical structure of the organism.

Recognition of Lotka's stature as a statistician and demographer led to his election as president of the Population Association of America (1938–1939), president of the American Statistical Association (1942), and vice president of the International Union for the Study of Population (1948–1949).

Lotka wrote prolifically until the year of his death, often elaborating earlier views or defending them against criticism. In his "Evolution and Thermodynamics" in *Science and Society* 8 (1944), responding to Joseph Needham's criticism, he points out that evolutionary "progress" is not inconsistent with the second law of thermodynamics, since the evolution of higher orders of complexity (i.e., reduction in entropy) can be accomplished by the use of energy from the organism's environment. Lotka also noted that the evolution of photosynthetic plants, which are predominantly anabolic, differs from that of animals, which are primarily catabolic. Lotka died in Red Bank, New Jersey.

• A complete collection of Lotka's writings is in the Princeton University Library. The Dover edition (1956) of *Elements of Mathematical Biology* contains a list of Lotka's technical papers. Sewall Wright, *Evolution and the Genetics of Populations*, vol. 2: *The Theory of Gene Frequencies* (1969), pp. 30–31, cites Lotka's work on the evolutionary genetics of populations. Ludwig von Bertalanffy, *The Problems of Life* (1952), p. 52, acknowledges Lotka's contributions to systems theory.

CHARLES H. FUCHSMAN

LOUCKS, Henry Langford (24 May 1846–29 Dec. 1928), politician and economist, was born in Hull, Quebec, Canada, the son of William J. Loucks, a merchant, and Anna York. Henry received his education in the Canadian common schools. For a number of years after graduating he became involved, for varying lengths of time, in merchandizing and the lumber business. In 1878 Loucks married Florence Isabel McCraney, and they produced seven children, three of whom died before reaching adulthood.

In 1884, with money he had saved, Loucks bought a two-section farm in Dakota Territory's Deuel County. A seven-year period of economic expansion was about to end. Crop prices were falling; bank loans were scarce and interest rates high; and the railroad charges were exorbitant and service poor. Wishing to improve the situation, Loucks formed a farmers' club in 1884. The following year, it joined with other such clubs to create the Northern [National] Farmers' Alliance. In 1886 Loucks became president of the Dakota Farmers' Alliance and editor of its main organ, the *Dakota Ruralist*. Largely because of his drive and skill, by 1890

the organization had some 500 chapters and 40,000 members. To provide farmers with economic assistance, the Dakota Alliance, under Loucks's direction, established warehouses, elevators, cooperatives, and a joint-stock company, which provided members with coal, household goods, twine, and machinery at substantial savings. "Our remedy," he said, "lies not in abusing the railroad elevator, manufacturing or coal monopolies, trusts or combinations. That might relieve our feelings, but not our finances. So long as they gather the plums, they can laugh at the abuse." The Dakota Alliance also offered members several different types of insurance at low premiums and loans at reasonable interest rates and even sponsored railroad-building projects. When the economy collapsed in the early 1890s, however, all of these endeavors failed.

Under Loucks's leadership the Dakota Alliance also used political methods during the 1880s to gain broader reforms. The alliance worked as a pressure group in both parties and placed a farm bloc in every territorial legislature from 1885 to 1889. The alliance wanted laws to regulate railroads and elevators, control monopolies, create fairer taxation, and put into effect Prohibition and woman suffrage. Some reform legislation passed, but it was diluted because of the influence of a railroad lobby and Republican conservatives, who feared that the alliance would take over their party.

In June 1889 Loucks helped move the Dakota Alliance out of the Northern Farmers' Alliance and linked it, instead, with the more successful and radical Southern Farmers' Alliance. At the same time, Loucks expanded the Dakota Alliance's goals to include government ownership and operation of public utilities, popular election of senators, adoption of the Australian ballot, and the elimination of child labor.

Early in 1889, Congress passed an enabling act allowing South Dakota to join the Union. Loucks believed that the Republicans, who dominated Dakota politics, planned to exclude all alliance members from state offices. At the July 1889 Constitutional Convention in Sioux Falls, Loucks's alliance delegates joined the Democrats and Prohibitionists, and they almost passed their version of the new constitution. However, the conservative Republicans, by skillful use of persuasion and cajolery, ultimately defeated them. About a month later the South Dakota Republicans held their first state convention. The conservatives were able to nominate their candidate for governor, but the alliance's choice for lieutenant governor won nomination, and the party adopted a vaguely stated profarmer platform. Loucks asked alliance members to accept the outcome. In the September 1889 elections Republican candidates won handily. However, when the South Dakota legislature met in Pierre a month later to elect U.S. senators, the conservatives ignored the alliance and sent their own choices to Washington; nor did the Republicans fulfill their campaign promises to help the farmers.

In June 1890 a joint meeting of the Dakota Alliance and Knights of Labor, at Loucks's urging, agreed to create the Independent party. In July the new party's convention selected Loucks as its candidate for governor. Among other things, the party's platform called for national income and real estate taxes and the free and unlimited coinage of silver.

South Dakota's Republicans, fearing that the Independents and Democrats might fuse and oust them from power, adopted the Independent party's main planks and campaigned hard. The Republicans took the governorship, but Loucks's party garnered one-third of the total votes cast and elected many of its members to the state legislature. In early 1891, Independent and Democratic legislators temporarily combined to elect their candidate, James H. Kyle, to the U.S. Senate.

The next year proved to be equally eventful for Loucks. In the spring of 1892 the Southern Alliance's president, Leonidas L. Polk, died suddenly, and Loucks, as vice president, automatically succeeded him. At the same time, the National Farmers' Alliance was laying the foundation for the People's or Populist party. Loucks became chairman of the new party's convention, which met in Omaha in the summer of 1892. The convention selected James B. Weaver of Iowa as its presidential nominee and adopted a comprehensive reform platform that included a demand for inflation through the free and unlimited coinage of silver at a ratio of sixteen to one. As president of the Southern Alliance, Loucks was anxious for the Populist party to succeed. He was able to bring into the party about half of the southern Democrats, mostly poor farmers. However, when southern Republicans began joining the Populists, many of the Democratic Populists left. In the South, most of the Populist candidates were beaten in the 1892 election.

In June 1892 over 500 Populist delegates met in Redfield, South Dakota. Although Populists and Democrats fused to some degree in about thirty South Dakota counties, Loucks convinced the convention not to endorse the policy on the state level. Populists, Democrats, and Republicans in South Dakota all offered separate slates of candidates in 1892. The Republicans created a reform platform, passed a few reforms into law, and won overwhelmingly in November.

After the 1892 election, thousands of members quit both the Northern and Southern Alliances, and the Populists all but absorbed the Southern Alliance. Loucks encouraged this process because he now believed that the Populist party was the best instrument to promote the farmers' welfare. Despite this attitude, he was elected president of the Southern Alliance in a spirited contest at a meeting in Memphis and, in November, also became president of the newly formed National Farmers' Alliance and Industrial Union.

The collapse in farm prices during the depression of 1893 through 1895 hit South Dakota farmers hard. In South Dakota and in the nation, the Democrats, Populists, and free-silver Republicans joined to support William Jennings Bryan for president and a wide-ranging reform platform. Loucks, who had earlier opposed fusion, joined forces with U.S. Senator Richard Pettigrew, a powerful Republican, who had become increasingly interested in free silver and railroad regulation. In July, when the South Dakota Republican Convention rejected free silver, the senator and his followers bolted and joined the Populists at their convention in Huron, with Loucks in full control. Subsequently, Loucks also convinced the Democrats to fuse with his clearly dominant Populist party and to back a broad-based reform package. By very narrow margins the Populists elected railroad commissioners, the attorney general, both congressmen, and Andrew Lee as governor and took control of the state legislature.

Lee had severe difficulties holding his diverse coalition together. Loucks himself left the Populists in 1898. He simply could not tolerate long-term fusion with the Democrats; he was convinced that they were not genuinely devoted to Populist tenets. In March 1898, at a meeting of the South Dakota Populist party's Central Committee in Huron, members adopted a resolution to continue fusion, over his impassioned protests. Dismayed by the decision, that summer Loucks decided to address the state Republican convention in Mitchell. He offered to return to the Republican ranks and to deliver the Populist vote if the delegates adopted a plank favoring an initiative and referendum amendment. The Republicans cheered his speech and accepted his terms.

Loucks was the first South Dakota leader to advocate the initiative and referendum energetically and consistently. As early as 1888 he began using his newspaper to publicize the issue and, in 1892, helped to persuade the South Dakota Populists to list it second in their platform. The legislature failed to adopt the amendment in 1893 and again in 1895. However, by 1898 the measure passed, for by then all major parties had come to recognize both its virtues and popularity. The South Dakota voters approved it overwhelmingly in November 1898, and in March 1899 the state became the first to adopt these processes.

After 1900, Loucks remained active as an erstwhile office seeker and a prolific writer. In 1914 he ran unsuccessfully, as an independent, for the U.S. Senate and again in 1924, garnering only 1,378 votes and placing last in a field of eight candidates. His books continued to promote and extend the reform themes he began in the early 1890s with the publication of *The New Monetary System as Advocated by the National Farmers' Alliance and Industrial Union* (1893). Between 1916 and 1922 Loucks published several works, including *The Great Conspiracy of the House of Morgan Exposed and How to Defeat It* (1916). Loucks died in Clear Lake, South Dakota.

Loucks was an unfailingly affable man, incapable of hating his opponents or of advocating violence. He had a gift for analyzing complex subjects and presenting their essence cleverly and clearly to readers and listeners alike. Loucks was an important, greatly respected leader, who relied upon logic and humor to persuade the public and who used the existing governmental structure to implement his ideas and principles. His actions consistently showed that his devotion to ideas and principles far outweighed any desire for personal power or wealth.

• Loucks's family correspondence and copies of the *Dakota Ruralist* (1888–1900) can be found in the South Dakota Historical Archives in Pierre. Loucks wrote many works, including *Government Ownership of Railroads and Telegraph, as Advocated by the National Farmers' Alliance and Industrial Union* (1894), *Farm Problems and State Development* (1914), *Common Sense Rural Credits* (1915), *Our Daily Bread* (1919), *How to Restore and Maintain Our Government Bonds at Par* (1921), *The Mythical Gold Base, or Standard of the Federal Reserve System Compared with Our Farmers' Land Loan and Sub-Treasury Plan* (1922), and *The Soldier Bonus* (1922). No biography or scholarly article devoted exclusively to Loucks and his career, exists. Beyond Loucks's own writings, information must be gleaned from portions of a variety of books, articles, and theses. Among the most useful of these are Nelson A. Dunning, *The Farmers' Alliance and Agricultural Digest* (1891), which is an excellent contemporary account; Lawrence K. Fox, ed., *Foxes's Who's Who among South Dakotans* vol. 1 (1924–1925); Herbert S. Schell, *History of South Dakota*, (1975); Edwin C. Torrey, *Early Days in Dakota* (1925); Warren S. Tryon, "Agriculture and Politics in South Dakota, 1889 to 1900," in *South Dakota Historical Collections*, comp. State Department of History, vol. 13 (1926); H. Roger Grant, "Origins of a Progressive Reform: The Initiative and Referendum Movement in South Dakota," *South Dakota History* 3 (Fall 1973): 390–407; Burton E. Tiffany, "History of the Initiative and Referendum in South Dakota," in *South Dakota Historical Collections*, comp. State Department of History, vol. 12 (1924); and three works by Kenneth Elton Hendrickson, Jr.: "The Populist Movement in South Dakota, 1890–1900" (M.A. thesis, Univ. of S. Dak., 1958); "The Public Career of Richard F. Pettigrew of South Dakota, 1848–1926," in *South Dakota Report and Historical Collections*, comp. South Dakota State Historical Society, vol. 34 (1968); and "The Populist-Progressive Era: Richard Franklin Pettigrew, Andrew E. Lee, and Coe I. Crawford," in *South Dakota Leaders*, ed. Herbert T. Hoover and Larry J. Zimmerman (1989). Obituaries are in the *New York Times* and the Sioux Falls, S. Dak. *Argus Leader*, 30 Dec. 1928.

GERALD W. WOLFF

LOUDON, Samuel (1727?–24 Feb. 1813), printer and entrepreneur, was born probably in Scotland. He emigrated to New York in or before 1753, when he established a general store opposite the Old Slip Market. During the next decade and a half, he expanded his business and personal interests. On 24 January 1756 he married Sarah Oakes. By 1757 he had enlarged his trade to sell nautical goods. By 1768 Sarah had died, and Loudon had married his second wife, Lydia Griswold. He had a total of eight children. In the late 1760s and early 1770s he speculated in upper New York land with Philip Schuyler, selling properties to recent Scottish immigrants. Loudon's various business ventures show his versatility. He was a shrewd opportunist who could sense profit, and he had the easy assurance to switch from one venture to the next. In late 1771 he began selling books along with nautical goods and soon undertook publishing. In 1773 he published a work reflecting his business sensibilities, *The Religious Trader; or, Advice for the Trader's Prudent and Pious Conduct*, and an ambitious three-volume edition of Josephus's *Works*, which was probably printed in Glasgow, Scotland.

Bookselling proved financially hopeful, and Loudon, a shareholder in the New York Society Library, recognized other ways to make money from books. On 1 January 1774 he opened New York's second known circulating library. Loudon identified women as an important force in the literary marketplace, and he shaped his inventory to suit his growing clientele, actively purchasing old libraries and "well chosen novels." Advertising the circulating library's success ten months after it opened, Loudon wrote that the "ladies are his best customers, and shew a becoming delicacy of taste in their choice of books." By early 1776 the circulating library had grown to over two thousand volumes, making it the largest in America.

The book business thriving, Loudon next purchased some printing equipment from Frederick Shober, and the two men went into partnership. Before the end of 1775 Shober backed out of the partnership and sold his interest to Loudon, who then began printing on his own. Though his printing outfit, as Loudon himself admitted, was "by far the smallest" in New York City, he quickly became an active printer and publisher. On 4 January 1776 he established the *New-York Packet*. In his prospectus for the paper in the *New-York Journal* (14 Dec. 1775), Loudon explained that he had been persuaded to establish a newspaper by "a numerous circle of warm friends to our (at present much distressed) country." His printing activities were successful enough to make him remain in New York and risk the burgeoning hostilities. In March 1776 Loudon printed about fifteen hundred copies of Charles Inglis's answer to Thomas Paine, *Deceiver Unmasked; or, Loyalty and Interest United*, a somewhat unusual publication for a printer with Whiggish sympathies. A mob of angry New Yorkers stormed Loudon's house and took away nearly the whole impression (two copies survive) and burnt them. Loudon's printing of the tract was construed by the mob as a Loyalist action, but his devotion to the colonial cause never wavered. Rather, his entrepreneurial enthusiasm simply outpaced his discretion. Loudon recognized that the pamphlet would be profitable and attempted to capitalize on it. (James Humphreys's edition of Inglis's work, *True Interest of America Impartially Stated, in Certain Strictures on . . . Common Sense*, sold several thousand copies.) Other tracts on the revolutionary cause that Loudon printed in New York City are Richard Price's *Observations on the Nature of Civil Liberty* (1776) and Samuel Sherwood's *The Church's Flight into the Wilderness* (1776).

With British forces poised to enter the city, Loudon suspended the *New-York Packet* on 29 August 1776. He moved his press to Fishkill, New York, where the provincial congress was located. On 16 January 1777 Loudon, with an annual stipend from the New York Committee of Safety, commenced publishing the *New-York Packet* at Fishkill. He did much work for provincial New York, but his inadequate printing equipment made it difficult for him to keep up with business, and John Holt replaced him as New York printer during the summer of 1777. Nevertheless, Loudon continued to do some state printing. His most notable Fishkill imprints are four numbers of Thomas Paine's *American Crisis* (1777) and over two thousand copies of the first Constitution of New York State (1777). Loudon diversified his business activities by speculating in wartime supplies and captured British equipment. Despite chronic paper shortages, he continued to publish the *New-York Packet* at Fishkill until 28 August 1783. He then brought the newspaper back to New York City and, on 13 November 1783, published the first semiweekly issue after his return. Loudon also reestablished his New York circulating library.

After the revolutionary war, Loudon undertook a wide variety of printing jobs. His eye for profit, however, sometimes led to indiscretions. When the Continental treasurer asked for bids to print currency in 1786, both Loudon and fellow New York printer Shepard Kollock submitted bids. In confidence, Kollock told Loudon his bid, and Loudon subsequently underbid him and got the contract. Kollock lambasted him in the *New York Gazette*: "To good and evil equal bent, / He's both a Devil and a Saint" (quoted in Wall, p. 88). From December 1787 through November 1788, Loudon published Noah Webster's *American Magazine*, but he devoted his greatest efforts to his own newspaper. The *New-York Packet* became a triweekly on 5 May 1789, was reduced to a weekly on 3 February 1791, and ceased publication on 26 January 1792. Within three weeks (15 Feb. 1792) Loudon established the daily New-York *Diary; or, Loudon's Register*. He took his son, Samuel, into partnership at the beginning of 1793, and the *Diary* was published under Samuel Loudon & Son. One year later Abraham Brower was admitted to the partnership, and the paper's title was changed to the *Diary; or Evening Register*. The partnership with Brower lasted less than ten months, and in October 1794 the firm reverted to Loudon & Son. In February 1795 Loudon let his son take over the paper. After young Loudon's death in September of that year, his father no longer took an interest in the paper. After 1800 Loudon retired to Middletown Point, New Jersey, where he died.

Loudon's keen entrepreneurial ability allowed him to excel with each commercial venture he attempted. He deserves to be remembered for his circulating library, his wartime publications, and his newspaper activities.

• Some of Loudon's letters survive at the New-York Historical Society; the Peck Library, Norwich, Conn.; and the Hartford Seminary Foundation Library. For Loudon's imprints, see Charles Evans, *American Bibliography* (1903–1934). Information concerning Loudon within Evans is easily accessible using Roger Pattrell Bristol, *Index of Printers, Publishers, and Booksellers Indicated by Charles Evans in His American Bibliography* (1961). See also Bristol's *Supplement to Charles Evans' American Bibliography* (1970) and R. W. G. Vail, "A Patriotic Pair of Peripatetic Printers: The Up-State Imprints of John Holt and Samuel Loudon 1776–1783," in *Essays Honoring Lawrence C. Wroth* (1951). Loudon's newspapers are discussed in Clarence S. Brigham, *History and Bibliography of American Newspapers 1690–1820* (1947). Other sources include Isaiah Thomas, *The History of Printing in America*, ed. Marcus A. McCorison (1970); William McCulloch, "Additions to Thomas's History of Printing," *Proceedings of the American Antiquarian Society* 31 (1921); A. J. Wall, "Samuel Loudon (1727–1813): (Merchant, Printer and Patriot) With Some of His Letters," *New-York Historical Society Quarterly Bulletin* 6 (1922): 75–92; and David Kaser, *A Book for a Sixpence: The Circulating Library in America* (1980).

KEVIN J. HAYES

LOUDOUN, Earl of (5 May 1705–27 Apr. 1782), commander in chief of British forces in North America, was born John Campbell at Loudoun Castle in Ayrshire, Scotland, the son of Hugh Campbell, third earl of Loudoun and statesman, and Lady Margaret Dalrymple. Details of his early life and education are unavailable. Although Loudoun did not enter the British army until he was twenty-two, he had the talent, wealth, and political standing to advance steadily to high command. He began his military service in 1727 as a cornet in the prestigious Scots Greys. After succeeding his father as fourth earl of Loudoun in 1731 and being chosen a representative peer for Scotland three years later, he rose from captain in the Seventh Dragoons (1734) to captain and lieutenant colonel in the elite Third Foot Guards (1739) to governor of Stirling Castle (1741). His service in the ensuing War of the Austrian Succession and in the Scottish Rebellion of 1745–1746 against the Jacobites ensured the favor of King George II. He became colonel of the Fifty-fourth Regiment of Foot in 1745, colonel of the Thirtieth Regiment of Foot in 1749, and a major general in 1755.

In 1756, at the beginning of the Seven Years' War, Loudoun was appointed commander in chief in North America and given the daunting task of persuading British colonists to work together under his direction to defeat the French and American Indians. The colonists outnumbered the French 1,042,000 to 55,000 and had the support of small regular forces. Yet they had such trouble cooperating with each other and accepting military discipline that they were losing the war. The British government, wishing to secure the colonies without burdening England itself, directed Loudoun to ask the colonial assemblies to cooperate not just in raising, paying, and supporting provincial forces but also in providing recruits for his regular units and in placing all forces under his command. The assemblies, fearing a standing army and knowing that provincials expected to serve under their own officers, were reluctant to yield command of their troops to Loudoun and refused to recruit men for service in regular regiments.

With little real authority over the colonists, Loudoun soon decided he could not rely on them to win the war. Provincial troops were dirty, undisciplined, and ignorant of basic military duties. Because they refused to be integrated into regular units or obey British officers and because they usually served for only one campaign, Loudoun despaired of shaping them into an effective army. He also found individual colonists unwilling to enlist in regular units. Colonists who were interested in becoming soldiers clearly preferred to serve in provincial forces, where the pay was higher, the period of enlistment shorter, and the discipline less strict. By the winter of 1756, Loudoun had decided to reduce the size of provincial forces for the ensuing campaign and to recommend that the British government depend mainly on regulars to defeat the French.

While he awaited reinforcements from Britain, Loudoun did succeed by concessions, threats, and persuasion in getting some control over provincial forces and in creating the logistical system that would be needed for an Anglo-American victory. By agreeing to let provincial officers rank after British majors and keep their men separate from regulars, he was able to take loose command of provincials. By seizing and threatening to seize quarters for his troops, he was able to persuade the colonial assemblies either to build barracks or to quarter troops in public or private houses, and by buying horses and wagons and employing drivers and carpenters on a regular basis, he was able to develop transportation independent of the colonists. His provisions, bought and paid for mainly in Britain and assembled by contractors in America, were usually ample and of reasonable quality.

Nevertheless, Loudoun was not successful campaigning against the French. During the autumn of 1756 he developed a plan for winning the war in 1757. While provincials and a detachment of regulars defended the upper Hudson River, he would sail from New York early in the spring with some 5,000 regulars to join with a fleet and another 6,000 regulars from Britain in attacking Quebec via the St. Lawrence River, destroying the main French army. His plan soon began to unravel. Provincials were more than a month late in assembling at Albany, thereby delaying the release and embarkation of his regulars from New York. By the time he was ready to sail, he had to wait another two weeks while cruisers made sure that there were not, as he had heard, French warships awaiting him off the coast of New England. When at last he reached Halifax on 30 June, he found that the fleet and army he was expecting from Britain had not yet arrived and that a powerful French fleet had already reached Louisbourg, the fortified harbor on Cape Breton that guarded the approaches to the St. Lawrence. Loudoun now knew that he would have to take Louisbourg by siege before going on to Quebec and that a siege would probably consume the remainder of the campaign. So late were his reinforcements in arriving and so unfavorable were the winds through the remainder of July that on 4 August he decided to abandon the campaign against Louisbourg and return to Albany for a thrust toward Montreal. Again, he was too late. On 9 August the French captured Fort William Henry on Lake George and preempted any British offensive from Albany in 1757. The ministry, exasperated with the results of the campaign, recalled Loudoun in March

1758. Loudoun had not been a bold or aggressive commander, yet during his service in America, he had created the kind of army and logistical system that would be needed to conquer Canada.

After returning from America, Loudoun commanded British troops in Portugal, 1762–1763, and received regular promotions: to lieutenant general (1758), governor of Edinburgh Castle (1763), colonel of the Third Foot Guards (1770), and general (1770). After 1763 he was occupied increasingly with improving the trees, shrubs, and crops of his Scottish estates. He died, unmarried, at Loudoun Castle.

• Because Loudoun was meticulous in keeping records and sustaining his correspondence, the manuscript sources for his military career are unusually rich. The best collections for his service in North America are the Loudoun papers in the Huntington Library, San Marino, Calif.; the Colonial Office and War Office Papers in the Public Record Office; the Newcastle papers in the British Library; and the Cumberland papers at Windsor Castle. Manuscripts for the remainder of his military career are in the Loudoun papers in the British Library. Some of his American correspondence has been published among the colonial records of Conn., Md., N.C., N.J., N.H., N.Y., Pa., and R.I. and in Stanley Pargellis, ed., *Military Affairs in North America 1748–1765* (1936). The best study of Loudoun is Pargellis, *Lord Loudoun in North America* (1933). Other works of quality dealing with his command in America are Guy Frégault, *Canada: The War of the Conquest* (1969), John A. Schutz, *William Shirley King's Governor of Massachusetts* (1961), and Fred Anderson, *A People's Army: Massachusetts Soldiers and Society in the Seven Years' War* (1984).

IRA D. GRUBER

LOUIS, Joe (13 May 1914–12 Apr. 1981), boxer, was born Joseph Louis Barrow near Lafayette, in Chambers County, Alabama, the son of Munroe Barrow, a farmer, and Lillie Reese. His father was committed to a mental institution in 1916, and his mother later married again to Pat Brooks. The family, which included eight children, moved to Detroit, Michigan, when Louis was ten years old, and he attended school there until dropping out at age seventeen. As a boy he worked in a food market and delivered ice and coal. A friend, Thurston McKinney, introduced him to boxing, and he had his first amateur fight in 1932. Discouraged after a bad beating, he worked briefly at the Ford Motor Company but soon returned to boxing and became a highly successful amateur. He won fifty of fifty-four amateur fights and, in April 1934, became the American Athletic Union national light heavyweight champion. He dropped the name "Barrow" by accident, by incorrectly filling out an amateur application card, and was always known thereafter in boxing as simply "Joe Louis."

Under the management of John Roxborough and Julian Black, and trained by a former great lightweight boxer, Jack Blackburn, Louis moved to Chicago and turned professional there in July 1934. He was fighting ten-round main events by September and won all of his twelve fights that year. After winning six more fights in 1935, four of them by knockout, Louis and his managers signed a contract to fight for a rising New York promoter, Mike Jacobs. Jacobs, who would promote almost all of Louis's fights thereafter, quickly brought him to New York City for the first time. On 25 June 1935, at Yankee Stadium, Louis scored an impressive six-round knockout over the former heavyweight champion, Primo Carnera. Before the end of the year he knocked out three contenders, King Levinsky, Paulino Uzcudun, and former heavyweight champion Max Baer. His hard hitting and rapid progress made Louis the sensation of the boxing world, the idol of the African-American community, and the foremost contender for the heavyweight championship.

On 18 June 1936 in New York City, Louis fought another former heavyweight champion, Max Schmeling of Germany, and suffered his first professional defeat. Unable to avoid Schmeling's right-hand punches, he received a bad beating and was knocked out in twelve rounds. But he returned to action just two months later and scored a quick knockout over another former heavyweight champion, Jack Sharkey, in New York City. He knocked out three more opponents in 1936, and in 1937 he outpointed Bob Pastor and knocked out Natie Brown. Finally, on 22 June 1937, Louis fought Jim Braddock for the world heavyweight championship in Chicago, survived a first-round knockdown, and then won the title by knocking out the champion in the eighth round. Louis's victory prompted parades and other demonstrations of pride in black communities throughout the United States.

Louis stood nearly 6′2″ and weighed a little more than two hundred pounds in his prime. His light brown skin color came from his mixed racial background, mainly white and Native American from his father and African American from his mother. His skin color and terrific punching power earned him the nickname "Brown Bomber" early in his career. Nat Fleischer described his style thus:

Joe Louis, as he starts into action, moves slowly, almost mechanically . . . as he shuffles along . . . but once he gets his bearings, all that is gone. The legs become springy and the arms . . . suddenly dart out. . . . The secret of Louis' punching power is rhythm. All of his muscles and his faculties are perfectly adjusted. He has an amazing sense of timing and that is what makes his punches so tremendously effective.

His face was expressionless as he unrelentingly stalked an opponent. His left jab was one of the best in the history of boxing and produced the openings for his powerful straight right and left hook.

Louis's first title defense proved to be one of his most difficult, against Welshman Tommy Farr in New York City on 30 August 1937. Farr proved to be rugged and resourceful, and he made Louis fight hard for a fifteen-round win by decision. In early 1938 Louis won his next two defenses with quick knockouts of Nathan Mann and Harry Thomas.

Louis said that he did not really feel himself to be heavyweight champion until his rematch with Schmel-

ing, which occurred on 22 June 1938 in New York. As important as the fight was to Louis personally, it was also given racial and national overtones by the prefight publicity of Mike Jacobs and the writings of many others, with both Louis and Schmeling being made symbols of their respective peoples and homelands. It was over in less than a round after Louis launched a devastating attack; his bewildered opponent scarcely landed a punch before suffering a knockout defeat. Louis's victory was interpreted by some as a blow against the Nazi doctrine of European racial superiority.

In 1939 Louis made four successful defenses of his title, winning all by knockout. John Henry Lewis, Jack Roper, and Bob Pastor were easy victims for the Brown Bomber, but the short, fat Tony Galento provided surprising opposition by staggering Louis in the first round and knocking him down in the second, before Louis administered a bad beating and knocked out Galento in round four.

Louis made four more successful defenses in 1940. The first of these proved to be the most difficult, as Arturo Godoy of Chile lasted the full fifteen rounds by using an exaggerated crouching style. Later in the year Louis knocked out Godoy in eight rounds in a rematch, Johnny Paycheck in two rounds, and Al McCoy in six rounds. In 1941 Louis defended his title monthly from January to May; he knocked out Red Burman, Gus Dorazio, Abe Simon, and Tony Musto and then defeated Buddy Baer by disqualification in seven rounds after being knocked down in the first round.

In June 1941 Louis met Billy Conn, the most difficult opponent he had faced since becoming champion. Smaller than Louis, but a much faster and a more clever boxer, Conn dominated the fight for twelve rounds and appeared to be well on his way to victory. However, in the thirteenth round he made the mistake of swapping punches with Louis, who knocked him out. Later in the year Louis defended his title again, knocking out Lou Nova in six rounds.

In January 1942, just before receiving his notice of induction into the U.S. Army, Louis knocked out Buddy Baer in one round and donated most of his earnings to the Navy Relief Society. After his induction he was allowed to make one more title defense, a rematch with Abe Simon, with proceeds going to the Army Emergency Relief Fund. Simon, who had lasted thirteen rounds with Louis in their first fight, was knocked out in six. Louis's army career consisted mostly of boxing exhibitions and morale-boosting visits to military bases and hospitals around the world. Despite his fame he experienced racial discrimination while in the service, but he was too unassuming to make a serious protest.

Throughout the war there was great anticipation of a return fight between Louis and Billy Conn. After both were discharged from military service, they fought again in New York City on 19 June 1946, before an audience of about 45,000 who paid gate proceeds of nearly $2 million. The fight was a disappointment because Conn had lost his speed and confidence, and he failed to make it a serious contest before Louis knocked him out in the eighth round. Louis made another defense in 1946 against Tami Mauriello, scoring a one-round knockout after almost being knocked down himself.

Louis's personal affairs now began to direct the course of his boxing career. In 1935 he had married Marva Trotter, a part-time student at the University of Chicago. Later, he became involved in numerous extramarital affairs, most notably with singer Lena Horne, that finally led to divorce in 1945. He remarried Marva in 1946 but divorced her again in 1949, with a large financial settlement. Throughout his career he spent money and gave it away freely to his many friends and acquaintances. He became an avid golfer and lost large bets to other players. He started several business ventures but lost interest each time, and the resulting failures cost him severely. Extremely careless in his income tax payments, he owed $150,000 in back taxes upon his discharge from the service, a debt that increased greatly during the next several years. He was also heavily in debt to Jacobs and Roxborough. Though seeming to have lost some of his enthusiasm in the sport, he had to continue boxing because he had no other income and no other way to pay his debts.

On 5 December 1947 in New York City, Louis risked his title against Jersey Joe Walcott, a man even older than himself but a clever, quick boxer. Walcott scored knockdowns in the first and fourth rounds, but Louis won a highly disputed split decision. A rematch took place in New York City, and Louis scored an eleven-round knockout. On 1 March 1949 Louis announced his retirement, but his debts soon forced him to return to the ring. While he was retired, Ezzard Charles had become heavyweight champion, and the two were matched to fight for the title. On 27 September 1950, again in New York City, Charles gave Louis a severe beating over fifteen rounds to retain the heavyweight championship. Nevertheless, Louis decided to continue his comeback. In 1950 and 1951 he won eight consecutive victories against good opponents, but his reactions had slowed and he hit less powerfully. On 26 October 1951 Louis was knocked out by Rocky Marciano in eight rounds at Madison Square Garden in New York City and retired immediately afterward.

Still heavily in debt to the Internal Revenue Service (IRS), Louis began working in public relations for the Louis-Rowe Publicity Agency, run by his friend Billy Rowe. Paid by the job, his duties mainly involved dining with clients and mixing with them at social functions. In 1955 he married Rose Morgan, owner of a New York beauty salon. Their marriage ended in 1958, and the next year he married Martha Malone Jefferson, a Los Angeles lawyer, who convinced the IRS to cease trying to collect his back taxes because he had no more earning power.

In 1966 Louis and his wife moved to Las Vegas, Nevada, where he spent most of his remaining years as a greeter and debt collector for gambling casinos. He became addicted to cocaine and also turned to smoking and drinking. By 1977 he had developed a heart condition. As his physical health declined, so did his mental processes; as a result, he spent a short time in a mental hospital. Wheelchair bound in his last years, he died in Las Vegas. Few others have had more good times, seen more of the world, enjoyed so much adulation, and known so many other famous persons. Not long before his death he wrote, "Well, like the man said, 'If you dance you got to pay the piper.' Believe me, I danced, I paid the piper, and left him a big fat tip."

Perhaps because of a slight speech impediment, the quiet Louis seldom initiated a conversation. He hardly ever made any emotional display, either in the ring or out. He had two children from his marriages to Marva Trotter, but he was not involved in the raising of either of them. Although capable of wit, as when he remarked of Billy Conn that "He can run, but he can't hide" in the ring, he never derided an opponent, and his behavior was dignified and friendly at all times. He thereby avoided antagonizing white people, as the earlier heavyweight champion Jack Johnson had, but was nevertheless embraced by African Americans as their champion. His popularity with all races undoubtedly was a major factor in opening the door to African-American participation in professional and amateur sports from which they had previously been excluded.

Louis won sixty-three of his sixty-six professional fights, forty-nine by knockout. His twelve-year reign as heavyweight champion set a record as the longest in the history of that division. He was an inaugural inductee into the International Boxing Hall of Fame in 1990.

• Louis's complete record is available in Herbert G. Goldman, ed., *The 1986–87 Ring Record Book and Boxing Encyclopedia* (1986). The most useful sources of information on his life and career are his autobiography, *Joe Louis: My Life*, with Edna and Art Rust, Jr. (1978), and a biography by his son, Joe Louis Barrow, Jr., with Barbara Munder, *Joe Louis: 50 Years an American Hero* (1988). "Jolting Joe: the Amazing Story of Joe Louis and His Rise to World Heavyweight Title," in Nat Fleischer, *Black Dynamite*, vol. 2 (1938), has remained a useful account of his early career. Other autobiographies are *Born to Fight: Joe Louis' Own Story* (1935), *My Life Story* (1947), and a second book entitled *My Life Story*, written with the editorial aid of Chester L. Washington and Haskell Cohen (1953). He also authored *How to Box* (1948). He was the subject of numerous magazine articles, including Richard Wright, "High Tide in Harlem: Joe Louis as a Symbol of Freedom," *New Masses*, 5 July 1938, pp. 18–20. An obituary is in the *New York Times*, 13 Apr. 1981.

LUCKETT V. DAVIS

LOUIS, Morris (28 Nov. 1912–7 Sept. 1962), painter, was born Morris Louis Bernstein in Baltimore, Maryland, the son of Louis Bernstein, a Russian-born factory worker who later owned a small grocery store, and Cecelia Luckman. Pressured by his family to follow his brothers into college, Louis briefly attended Baltimore City College, leaving in 1929 to attend the Maryland Institute of Fine and Applied Arts, which he left without a degree in 1932. Louis held various odd jobs and became active in local art affairs. In 1935 he was elected president of the Baltimore Artists' Union.

In 1936 Louis moved to the Chelsea district of New York City. It was at this time that he legally changed his name. He met and worked with a number of artists, including David Alfaro Siqueiros, Jack Tworkov, and Arshile Gorky. Louis was a worker for the Works Progress Administration's Federal Art Project in the easel painting division. One of his works, *Broken Bridge*, was included in the 1939 New York World's Fair exhibition of WPA paintings. His painting from this time is a figurative nature, influenced by the work of Max Beckmann, whose work Louis saw at the Museum of Modern Art. He also assisted other artists on mural projects. Louis was an intensely private individual, and, except for a fellow female WPA artist with whom he lived for a time, he formed no close relationships in New York.

In 1943 Louis returned to Baltimore to live with his parents. He continued to paint and gave private art lessons to support himself. In 1947 he married Marcella Siegel, a writer and editor for the U.S. Public Health Service, and the couple moved into her Silver Spring, Maryland, apartment near Washington, D.C. The couple had no children.

Working as an instructor at the Washington Workshop Center of the Arts, Louis showed his paintings at local exhibitions and served on the Artists' Committee of the Baltimore Museum of Art. Isolated from the New York art world, he was a successful but provincial artist. This situation changed in 1952 when he met Kenneth Noland, who had joined the staff of the Washington Workshop. Louis and the younger, more cosmopolitan Noland quickly became friends; Louis would later say, "Suddenly I wasn't alone."

In April 1953 Louis and Noland traveled to New York to visit Noland's friend, the influential critic Clement Greenberg. In a few short days, Louis saw firsthand the works of Jackson Pollock and Franz Kline. Visiting the studio of Helen Frankenthaler, Louis enthusiastically reacted to her *Mountains and Sea*, created with a poured-paint, stained method. Returning to Washington, he had his first solo exhibition at the Washington Workshop Art Center Gallery on 12 April 1953 but was dissatisfied with his work after being exposed to that done by the New York artists.

Early in 1954 Greenberg came to Washington to select works by Louis and Noland for a show at Samuel M. Kootz Gallery in New York City. Greenberg encouraged the dealer Pierre Matisse to look at more of Louis's work. Louis sent Matisse nine paintings, most of which were in a dramatically different style from those shown at the Kootz Gallery. The items sent to New York included some of the earliest works in what would be termed Louis's "Veil" series, large canvases with large swatches of acrylic paint "staining" the surface. Though Matisse was not impressed with the work, Greenberg was. Louis and Greenberg continued to meet both in Washington and in New York on

an occasional basis throughout the rest of 1955 and 1956, with Greenberg encouraging Louis to avoid the style of second-generation abstract expressionism.

In November 1957 Louis had his first major one-man show at the Martha Jackson Gallery in New York City. Dissatisfied with much of his work, with Greenberg's concurrence Louis destroyed most of the 300 paintings he had completed between 1954 and 1957, excluding those in his signature style of the "Veil" series. Over the next two years, in 1957 and 1958, Louis completed his second "Veil" series, which was exhibited at French & Company in New York in 1959.

Reviews of Louis's work were positive, and he began receiving widespread coverage in the art press as well as exhibitions in New York and Europe. In 1960 Louis had solo exhibitions at French & Co., the Institute of Contemporary Art in London, Galleria dell'Ariete in Milan, and Bennington College in Vermont, as well as group shows at Galerie Neufville in Paris and the New York Art Foundation in Rome. The next year he had solo shows at Galerie Neufville and André Emmerich Gallery in New York and group shows at Marlborough Fine Art Ltd. in London, the Solomon R. Guggenheim Museum in New York, and the Art Institute of Chicago.

At age forty-nine, in July 1962, just as he was achieving prominence in the art world, Louis was diagnosed with lung cancer. A few days after the diagnosis, his left lung was removed. Louis was able to oversee the initial planning for his 1962 exhibition at the André Emmerich Gallery, but he never regained the strength to paint. He died in Washington.

Louis showed little interest in titling his works, particularly from 1954 onwards. After his death, the "Veil" series were given names from letters of the Hebrew alphabet, the "Unfurleds" (a series begun in 1960) letters from the Greek alphabet, and paintings from the "Stripe" series (begun in 1961) the names of stars. The series names themselves were not given by Louis.

Emmerich Gallery continued to exhibit Louis's work, and memorial exhibitions were held at the Guggenheim Museum (1963) and at the Stedelijk Museum in Amsterdam (1965). The 1967 exhibition "Morris Louis 1912–62" traveled across the United States, and a major retrospective was organized by the Museum of Modern Art, New York, in 1986.

Though associated with Greenberg and fellow "color school" painters Noland and Gene Davis, Louis was very private about his work. He preferred not to look at the work of other painters, reputedly saying, "They get in my eyes." His own work was not hung in his house but kept rolled and stored so as not to influence his current work.

• Louis's works are in the collections of the National Gallery of Art, Washington, D.C.; the Solomon R. Guggenheim Museum, New York; the Hirshhorn Museum and Sculpture Garden, Smithsonian Institution; the Museum of Modern Art, New York; the Nationalgalerie, Berlin; and the Whitney Museum of American Art, New York. Microfilm copies of

Louis's papers are held by the Archives of American Art, Smithsonian Institution. Biographical information is included in John Elderfield, *Morris Louis* (1987). Diane Upright, *Morris Louis: The Complete Paintings: A Catalogue Raisonné* (1985), is a complete listing of his paintings. See also William Rubin, "Younger American Artists," in *Art International* 4, no. 1 (Jan. 1960): 25–30. An obituary is in the *Washington Post*, 8 Sept. 1962.

MARTIN R. KALFATOVIC

LOUNSBURY, Thomas Raynesford (1 Jan. 1838–9 Apr. 1915), literary historian and linguist, was born in Ovid, New York, the son of Thomas Lounsbury, a Presbyterian minister, and Mary Janette Woodward. Admitted to Yale in 1855, he excelled in his studies, earned Phi Beta Kappa honors, and received a B.A. in 1859. He won prizes in English composition, debate, and oratory and served on the editorial staff of the *Yale Literary Magazine*. After graduation Lounsbury worked for three years in New York City as an editor of Appleton's *New American Cyclopaedia*. Since his father was a fervent abolitionist who had written *Pro-Slavery Overthrown* (1847), it is hardly surprising that in 1862 Lounsbury volunteered for service in the Union army. Appointed a first lieutenant, he was on active duty throughout the Civil War despite his capture at Harpers Ferry. Following an exchange of prisoners, he fought at Gettysburg, where he was one of the few officers in his regiment to survive the battle unscathed. Discharged from military service in June 1865, Lounsbury became a teacher of Greek and Latin in New York City at Lespinasse's French Institute; and then turned to private tutoring in New Jersey. During these four years of teaching classical languages, he taught himself to read Old and Middle English and mastered the rudiments of English philology. This program of self-education proved timely, for Yale needed an instructor of English on the modern languages faculty of its innovative Sheffield Scientific School and appointed Lounsbury to the position in January 1870. Promoted the next year from instructor to professor of English, he married Jane D. Folwell in 1871. He taught for thirty-six years at "Sheff," where he was a pioneer in the burgeoning new discipline of English.

In 1870 the classical liberal arts curriculum was still largely intact in American colleges. Bliss Perry recalled in *And Gladly Teach* (1935) that when he began his freshman Latin lessons at Williams in 1877, "We were doing, literally, what our fathers had done before us." But in Yale's Scientific School the forward-looking Lounsbury found striking departures from the traditional course of study in which he had been educated. There he contributed importantly to the expansion of a curriculum that was an early model of the modern liberal arts college. In the Scientific School, which had developed at Yale out of efforts during the 1850s to assimilate chemistry and engineering into a college until then fully committed to the classical curriculum, modern languages were substituted for Greek and Latin. Accordingly, the Yale Sanskrit scholar and pioneer linguistic scientist William Dwight Whitney had moved from the College to the Scientific School where he taught French and German during the decade preceding Lounsbury's appointment. The enactment of the elective system in the 1870s assured the eventual triumph of modern over classical languages in American colleges; and, by the same process, the growth of English as a formal discipline soon outstripped that of the other modern languages.

The position offered Lounsbury had been defined initially as an instructorship in English composition, but Lounsbury made his acceptance contingent on the Scientific School's allowing him to devise and offer an extensive course in English literature from Chaucer to Pope. Within several months of his appointment, Lounsbury had written for the *New Englander* (predecessor of the *Yale Review*) his influential article on "The Study of English Literature," a foundational document for the new departments of English that had begun to appear in the nation's colleges. The article made a case for the intrinsic value of great literature as the justification for its proposed movement to the center of English studies in place of the preponderant attention then given to an elaborate formal rhetoric and an arbitrarily rules-oriented grammar, neither of which Lounsbury judged pedagogically useful. Confronting this division, he proposed that both writing instruction and the study of the English language become more productively allied to a close, genuinely responsive reading of the best authors. Although Francis Andrew March of Lafayette College was given the title professor of the English language in 1857 and Francis James Child at Harvard was made a professor of English literature in 1876, Lounsbury was arguably the first to preside over an English curriculum that undertook to integrate the teaching of literature, language, and composition into a single discipline. As such, he is clearly a founder of the modern English department.

Lounsbury possessed the personal strength and forcefulness essential to a reformer acting within a community of scholars largely inimical to change. Moreover, the expertness and comprehensiveness of Lounsbury's English scholarship gave the new subject much of its early distinction, and thereby narrowed the difference in status at Yale and elsewhere between the Scientific School and the College. Classically educated like most of his contemporaries, he was never a captive of the classical tradition. In his approach to literary history, linguistics, and composition he was consistently skeptical of arbitrary beliefs, however long established, and sensibly utilitarian in his devotion to rational inquiry and the disinterested search for truth. His classroom methods were studied across the nation by those of his colleagues interested in developing modern forms of instruction for the increasingly diverse schools of late nineteenth-century America. His numerous writings, often based upon exhaustive research, remained useful and reliable a half-century or more after they were published.

Having noted in his 1870 article that English was a neglected subject and that even the little instruction given was of unsatisfactory quality, only rarely "carried on in a scientific spirit," Lounsbury vigorously criticized the grammarians of his time for positing rules of correctness without any factual basis in historical English usage. His *History of the English Language* (1879), revised in 1894 and often reissued, became the standard introduction in colleges throughout the nation for more than thirty years. It provided a solid foundation for questioning the judgments of grammarians who equated linguistic change with the violation of good manners. Like his Scientific School colleague Whitney, Lounsbury turned away from the moralistic prescriptivism deriving from metaphysical and religious conceptions of language toward the scientific view of languages as organic, naturally evolving systems to be studied descriptively. Whitney's *Language and the Study of Language* (1867) and *The Life and Growth of Language* (1875) represent the beginnings of linguistic science in America. By building his *History* upon the most advanced general linguistics available during the 1870s, Lounsbury endowed students of English with a then invaluable resource. In the swelling post–Civil War debate over the effort of scholars to legitimate common usage against the "authoritative" corrections of popular language in books like Richard Grant White's *Words and Their Uses* (1870), Lounsbury's democratic, empirical perspective led him to defend "unrefined" speech and to anticipate the view of more recent linguistic scientists that in speech and writing the usage of the many is rightly dominant. With Brander Matthews, he asserted the progressive view that the American language has been enriched by the speech of immigrants. Lounsbury seconded Fitzedward Hall's erudite attacks on White's dogmatic prescriptions of the "best" English, but he gained a wider audience by writing in a more easily understood scholarly style than Hall had managed. Published in various journals throughout his career, Lounsbury's articles on American English usage were collected in *The Standard of Pronunciation in English* (1904), *The Standard of Usage in English* (1908), and *English Spelling and Spelling Reform* (1909).

Lounsbury's commitment to scientific inquiry and his readiness to challenge conventional beliefs also informed his studies of English and American literature. Contemptuous of the manuals of literary history still commonly substituted in the classrooms of the 1870s for the reading of literature itself, he promptly extended his survey of English literature to a two-year course in which close reading of complete works by great writers replaced the superficial and frequently inaccurate plot summaries and catalogues of authors and titles that had before constituted literary study. Meaningful literary study, according to Lounsbury, brought students into a "close and constant intimacy with the words and ideas of a great writer." It probed the relationship, if any, between the author's life and work in place of merely requiring memorization of a manual. He maintained that useful literary study involved examination of an author's language for the literary meaning it might reveal, not for the philological interest it might possess. Like his *History of the English*

Language, Lounsbury's scholarship in the fields of English and American literary history broke new ground. His research typically exposed old errors and pseudo-scholarship by painstaking investigations from which more credible explanations might be inferred and disputed points settled.

Published in 1882 and within three years already in its fifth edition, Lounsbury's *James Fenimore Cooper* was the first full-length biography of the first American author to gain fame in Europe and Great Britain. More than seventy years later, Robert Spiller referred to this "classic" biography as the one to which we owe, "and still owe, most of our fundamental concepts" of Cooper and his art. Despite the fierce disputes that marked Cooper's life and the difficulty of ascertaining the facts of that life owing to the inaccessibility of Cooper's personal records, Lounsbury's thorough research and independent judgment produced a balanced, reliable portrait that separates fact from distortion, distinguishes both the novelist's virtues and deficiencies, and accurately characterizes the public reception of the author and his works. At a time when the emergent literary scholarship in America was almost entirely preoccupied with British authors, Lounsbury's biography of Cooper contributed importantly to the growth of a scholarly tradition in the field of American literary history.

Of even greater significance to the advance of literary scholarship was Lounsbury's three-volume *Studies in Chaucer: His Life and Writings* (1892), a magisterial work described by Brander Matthews as "the most important contribution yet made by an American scholar to the great unwritten history of English literature." As in his biography of Cooper and his later volumes on Shakespeare's critics, Lounsbury's study of Chaucer focused upon the reception of the author and his works in order to separate facts from familiar legends. Ever the scientific historian, he filtered Chaucer's biographical records, literary sources, and textual history through his extensive knowledge and skeptical intelligence to reveal an intensely human, irreverent Chaucer who spoke "the language of common life."

In *Shakespeare as a Dramatic Artist* (1901) and *Shakespeare and Voltaire* (1902), Lounsbury recognized that the critical debates over the nature of Shakespeare's genius and those over the establishment of the best texts of his plays and poems were "inextricably bound together" in that the critics' conceptions of Shakespeare's art had often influenced the emendations introduced into his texts. These two volumes moved beyond previous biographies of Shakespeare by tracing both the powerful renewal of classical poetics and the efforts of writers to moderate or escape such regulation and by demonstrating the uses to which Shakespeare was put in the progress of that conflict. In portraying the savagery with which neoclassical critics like Thomas Rymer and Voltaire responded to Shakespeare's violations of the unities and mixing of comic with tragic scenes, Lounsbury exhibited the same disapproval of arbitrary rules and appeals to authority that is evident in his linguistic scholarship. *The*

Text of Shakespeare (1906), Lounsbury's third volume in a series he called the "Shakespearean Wars," is a microscopic examination of the controversy generated by the editions of Alexander Pope and Lewis Theobald. By his close and objective scrutiny of all the literature associated with the controversy, Lounsbury became the first scholar to understand fully the meaning of the 1729 *Dunciad* as part of the debate between Pope and Theobald; and his corrected account of Theobald's position was an important revision of eighteenth-century literary history. W. S. Lewis noted in 1949 that the celebrated Yale school of eighteenth-century scholars, commonly thought to have begun with Cross, Nettleton, and Tinker, actually began with Lounsbury, and his contributions to Chaucerian and Shakespearean studies are insufficiently remembered landmarks of nineteenth-century literary scholarship. Citing the names of those responsible for Yale's growing literary distinction, Van Wyck Brooks in *New England: Indian Summer* rightly placed Lounsbury's name first.

By 1906, the year of his retirement from teaching, Lounsbury's poor health and failing vision had seriously reduced his remarkable capacity for research and prevented him from writing a projected fourth volume of the "Shakespearean Wars" dealing with the controversies of the later eighteenth century. However, research conducted during the previous decade provided the groundwork for both *The Early Literary Career of Robert Browning* (1911) and his unfinished *The Life and Times of Tennyson*, an edited version of which was published posthumously in 1915.

At Yale and elsewhere by the 1920s, English faculties had evolved into large, increasingly specialized departments; whereas Lounsbury, during most of his long career, had been by himself a veritable English department. In addition to his teaching and research in the history of the English language and the full sweep of English and American literature, a "distinctly recognizable share" of his time "was spent in reading and correcting college themes." Lounsbury's own scholarly writing was conspicuous for its wit and Johnsonian resonance. His gift for the well-formed sentence, expressive diction, and vivid images produced a style that combined eloquence, precision, and force. Lounsbury was a founding member of the American Academy of Arts and Letters and a fellow of the American Academy of Arts and Sciences. He died in New Haven.

• Lounsbury's papers are located in Manuscripts and Archives in the Sterling Memorial Library at Yale. His innovative conception of English as a discipline is memorably stated in "The Study of English Literature," *New Englander* 29 (1870): 572–601; and in "Compulsory Composition in Colleges," *Harper's Monthly* 123 (1911): 866–80. His academic setting has been definitively portrayed in Russell H. Chittenden, *History of the Sheffield Scientific School of Yale University, 1846–1922*, vol. 1 (1928). Lounsbury's personal qualities are well described in Brander Matthews, "An American Scholar," *Century* 55 (1898): 561–65; and in Wilbur L. Cross, *Connecticut Yankee* (1943). Discussions of his scholarship may be found in Edward Finegan, *Attitudes toward English Usage* (1980); Kenneth Cmiel, *Democratic Eloquence* (1990); and Linda Georgianna, "The Protestant Chaucer," in *Chaucer's Religious Tales*, ed. C. David Benson and Elizabeth Robertson (1990). An obituary is in the *New York Times*, 10 Apr. 1915.

MYRON SIMON

LOUVIN, Ira (21 Apr. 1924–20 June 1965), country music singer and composer, was born Ira Lonnie Loudermilk in Section, on Sand Mountain in northeast Alabama, the son of Colonel Monero Allen Loudermilk and Georgianne Elizabeth Wootten, farmers. The Woottens were heavily involved in the shape note Sacred Harp religious singing on the mountain, while Colonel Loudermilk won regional fame as an old-time clawhammer style banjo player. Ira and his younger brother Charlie were steeped in both types of music while they were growing up; in 1929 the family relocated to Henagar, Alabama, where the brothers actually came to age. The Loudermilk farm yielded products such as cotton and sorghum, and the brothers' early days were spent in harvesting and taking these products to markets.

Sand Mountain was also a center for the newer type of southern gospel singing, one based on a seven-shape note system (i.e., where the shape of the note, not especially the position on the staff, determines its pitch). Dozens of quartets and composers came from the region, and "singing schools" were often held in rural communities during the summer. The 1930s, when the Loudermilk brothers were growing up, was also an age of country styled duet singing on the radio, and the boys listened intently to the music of stars such as the Blue Sky Boys (the Bolick Brothers), the Monroe Brothers, Mac and Bob, and the Delmore Brothers. The last named were especially appealing, since they also came from the Sand Mountain gospel tradition and had even written the hit song "Sand Mountain Blues."

The Loudermilks began to experiment with their own harmony singing, and Ira soon acquired a mandolin from a pawn shop in nearby Chattanooga, Tennessee. Fascinated with the way Bill Monroe played the instrument, he soon became more than adept at playing it. On 4 July 1940 the boys made their first money entertaining, playing at a county fair at Flat Rock, Alabama. By 1942 the pair had relocated to Chattanooga, where Ira held down a day job at a woolen mill and the brothers were on local station WDEF as the Radio Twins. A few months later Ira was drafted—in spite of the fact that he had married Annie Lou Roberts and had a new baby—but a back injury soon led to his dismissal, and the brothers joined Chattanooga's most popular radio band, Bob Douglas and his Foggy Mountain Boys. Performing over the more powerful station WDOD, the Loudermilks soon won a regional reputation as singers of sentimental and gospel songs. Before they could capitalize on it, though, Charlie was drafted; in his absence, Ira took a job as a mandolin player and singer with radio and record star Charlie

Monroe. It was with Monroe that he made his first records, for RCA Victor, in 1947; included was a blistering mandolin feature called "Bringing in the Georgia Mail."

In the fall of 1946 Charlie returned from the army, and the brothers decided to try to make it in the music business. They began by changing their name to Louvin, a name created by taking the first three letters of "Loudermilk" and adding a simple suffix. They began working over Knoxville radio stations but soon met a genial promoter and singer, Eddie Hill. With him, they moved to WMPS in Memphis, where they spent the next four years on the air as the Lonesome Valley Trio. These years solidified their reputation as gospel singers, and they were amazed at the amount of money and fame they could win by singing at area churches and revivals. Also by this time, Ira had found that he had a talent for writing songs and was producing pieces like "Robe of White," "Seven Year Blues," "Are You Afraid to Die," and "Alabama." The last-named became their first recording as members of Eddie Hill's band on the independent Apollo label in 1947. It also helped win them a contract with the Acuff-Rose company, Nashville's premier country-music publishing house. With the music industry contacts of Fred Rose, the Louvins soon found their songs being widely recorded by artists like Roy Acuff and Red Sovine. Though the songs usually bore composer credits to both Charlie and Ira, Charlie confirmed that most were in fact the work of Ira.

It was through Rose that the Louvins got their own recording contract, first with Decca, then with MGM, and finally, in 1952, with Capitol, where they began a relationship that would last for the rest of Ira's life and win them nationwide fame. At first producer Ken Nelson saw them as strictly gospel singers and was reluctant to let them try their hand at secular material. The brothers persisted, however, and he finally let them cut a song of Ira's called "When I Stop Dreaming" in 1955. The result was a national hit and a piece that would become the brothers' signature song. A series of chart-topping singles quickly followed, including "I Don't Believe You've Met My Baby," "Hoping That You're Hoping," "You're Running Wild," and "Cash on the Barrelhead" (all 1956).

In the meantime, the brothers had been unable to capitalize on their record and songwriting success. They bounced around from Memphis to Greensboro, North Carolina, to Danville Virginia, to Fort Payne, Alabama, and to Birmingham; finally their Capitol producer got them signed on the Grand Ole Opry. They held forth there throughout the late 1950s (with a year's detour to Wheeling, West Va.) and continued to produce memorable singles and albums such as *Tragic Songs of Life* (1956) and the Pentecostal-flavored *Satan Is Real* (1960). They toured widely with most of the stars of the day, including a young Elvis Presley, who expressed open admiration for their gospel harmonies. By this time Ira had divorced his first wife and had gone through a second marriage, with Bobbie Lowery; by the late 1950s he had married Faye

Cunningham, a union that turned turbulent, partly because of Ira's volatile temper and drinking problems. In 1961 things reached a crisis stage when Faye shot Ira five times with a pistol. He survived, but the story reached the national news media. In later years Ira was married a fourth time, to western singer Anne Young. He had three children overall.

In August 1963 the brothers decided to split up and start separate solo careers. Both began work on albums for their old label, Capitol, and Charlie retained his post on the Opry. Ira built a home on Sand Mountain and planned to do instrument repair work on the side (he had invented a number of instruments, including a "high G" guitar and an electric Spanish guitar). But all of those plans ended on 20 June 1965, when Ira and his wife were killed in a grinding automobile crash near Williamsburg, Missouri.

Charlie went on to have a successful solo career after Ira's death but never really found anyone who could sing the kind of piercing tenor harmony that had so characterized the Louvin sound. Through the 1970s and 1980s, the Louvin brothers' songs continued to remain in the repertoires of country and bluegrass singers from Bill Monroe to Emmylou Harris.

• For a biographical and musical analysis, see Charles K. Wolfe, *In Close Harmony: The Story of the Louvin Brothers* (1996). A complete discography of Louvin Brothers recordings can be found in the booklet notes to the Bear Family CD boxed set of the Louvins' complete works, BCS 15561.

CHARLES K. WOLFE

LOVE, Alfred Henry (7 Sept. 1830–29 June 1913), peace activist, was born in Philadelphia, Pennsylvania, the son of William Henry Love, a merchant, and Rachel Evans. After graduation from Philadelphia Central High School, Love began work as a woolen commission merchant, a profession he followed until his death. In 1853 he married Susan Henry Brown, with whom he had three children.

Although raised in the Society of Friends by his parents, Love himself never officially joined the denomination. The society splintered in the antebellum period into two major factions and several smaller bodies, one of which, the Progressive Friends, initially attracted Love. Love's liberal religious views later led the Hicksites, one of the two major bodies of Friends, to reject his request for membership, though he continued to attend their meetings throughout his life. Regardless of doctrinal disputes, his Quaker faith inspired his broad social activism and his specific commitment to peace.

Love rose to a position of national leadership in the peace movement as a result of the Civil War. Both wings of the prewar peace movement supported the Union cause. The more moderate American Peace Society (APS) characterized the conflict as a battle within a nation and, since it opposed only offensive wars between nations, openly endorsed the North. The New England Non-Resistance Society, led by William Lloyd Garrison, had broken from the APS in the

1830s over that group's failure to condemn defensive wars. Yet Garrison and most nonresisters rejected their earlier absolute prohibition against violence and supported the Union. The Civil War had become, for them, a divinely ordained retribution against the evils of slavery.

Love, who had been a follower of Garrison, parted from his mentor and most of his fellow peace activists by asserting that no matter how noble the aims of a war, religious doctrine prohibited his support. In his 1862 *An Appeal in Vindication of Peace Principles and against Resistance by Force*, Love argues that though "a pure non-resistance by carnel weapons politically considered, may seem at this time impracticable, yet as Christians we must know nothing of expediency." Love believed that southerners could be convinced of slavery's immorality and that northerners should accept a temporary disunion until such a moral transformation occurred. Love himself refused to cooperate with the draft; he did not serve, hire a substitute, or pay a commutation fee, even though Garrison counseled him that the latter would not compromise Love's principles. During the war Love also refused to accept any military contracts, a decision that cost him considerable business opportunities. Though Love's God was the forgiving deity shared by all liberal Protestants, his God also ordained absolute laws, one of which forbade killing under any circumstance.

In 1865 and 1866 Love helped organize a series of conferences of his fellow absolute nonresisters. Following an 1866 conference in Providence, the participants formed the Universal Peace Union (UPU) (at first named the Universal Peace Society), of which Love served as the first and only president. The group's initial declaration asserted, "War is a sin against God and opposed to the best interests of mankind, and its immediate abandonment is alike a religious duty, the wisest expediency and an imperative necessity."

The UPU's budget never exceeded $1,500 a year, and its journal—variously titled *Bond of Peace* (1868–1874), *Voice of Peace* (1874–1882), and *Peacemaker and Court of Arbitration* (1883–1913), which was edited by Love—averaged only a few hundred subscribers. The UPU, which never had more than 4,000 supporters, comprised representatives of such small sects as the Shakers and the Bible Christians as well as such liberal Protestants as the Society of Friends. The UPU convened periodic public meetings and lectures and urged its members to write letters to politicians and the press. The UPU's views after the Civil War paralleled the APS on such matters as arbitration and international law, yet the UPU also advocated domestic reform, including opposition to capital punishment, corporal punishment, war toys, and the violence of American football. The group also supported women's rights, and women constituted one-third of its supporters, including such prominent women's rights advocates as Susan B. Anthony, Lucretia Mott, and Belva Lockwood.

The slight interest in international affairs by government and populace alike after the Civil War provided the UPU with little impetus for growth. In the 1890s the UPU enjoyed a brief revival, and as many as 5,000 people attended its annual four-day conventions in Mystic, Connecticut. Yet compared to the new organizations of the 1890s peace movement, the UPU's eclectic combination of social reform and international concern gained few new followers. The peace movement was becoming more practical as various political and economic elites entered the movement in hope of directing the United States' increasingly global power toward free trade, international engagement, and an end to war. Love responded to the peace movement's growing popularity by adding as UPU vice presidents such public figures as William Taft, Elihu Root, and President Porfirio Díaz of Mexico, men who embraced little of Love's international or domestic agenda.

The U.S. war with Spain in 1898 allowed Love a brief twilight renown, while he suffered public vilification for opposing the conflict. Urging peaceful alternatives, Love wrote letters in vain to diplomats worldwide, including President William McKinley, the American ambassador to Spain, the Spanish premier, and even the queen regent of Spain. With war declared, Love continued his dissent, even as most of the practical peace activists urged quietude and some even supported U.S. military intervention. Having long ago made his stand, Love remained resolute. He died in Philadelphia in 1913, and the UPU died with him, too early to oppose yet another war that would rend the increasingly conservative prewar peace movement and destroy the old nonresister ideology as a political force.

Although some scholars label Love and the UPU with the twentieth-century word pacifist, other scholars apply the term "nonresister," which the participants themselves universally used. Based on the biblical injunction "resist not evil," nonresisters were divided between religious sects whose pessimism about worldly change prompted a withdrawal from the world and their more optimistic counterparts, like those in the UPU, who believed that setting a moral example could inspire other individuals to change. This approach differed from modern American pacifism, which often stressed how tactical disobedience to laws could force changes in institutions and public policy, a difference Love highlighted in his 1862 address, "Let us seek to convert rather than coerce."

Also unlike their pacifist progeny, Love and the UPU considered the United States a potential model for proper international conduct, in part because the Civil War had narrowed their differences with the government but primarily because nonresisters universally believed that free trade—a canon of late nineteenth-century American foreign policy—would prevent war and preserve world order. Love's isolated and limited dissent from free-trade orthodoxy rested on his personal experience with the effects of international competition on the woolen industry, not from any awareness that great power market competition might itself lead to war or from a recognition of the consequences of capitalist commerce on the nonindustrial world. In this, Love and his supporters focused perhaps too narrowly on European matters to fully deserve the name "internationalists."

The same classical liberal distrust of government's economic action also helped support a belief among pacifists in the necessity of individual moral action to reform the country, although Love's economic views and class experiences left him far too little to say about the central issue of his time, the conflict between labor and capital. As the late nineteenth- and early twentieth-century peace movements became increasingly conservative, Love kept alive a belief that peace meant domestic social reform and international cooperation, a connection that appeared to die with him even though others would soon forge the alliance anew.

• The papers of Alfred Love and the Universal Peace Union are part of the Swarthmore College Peace Collection. David Patterson edited a microfiche reproduction of the UPU journal from 1883 to 1913, *Peacemaker and Court of Arbitration*, (1982). Love's other published works include *Address Before the Peace Convention, Held in Boston, March 14 & 15, 1866* (1866) and *A Brief Synopsis of Work Proposed, Aided, and Accomplished by the Universal Peace Union* (1897). The most authoritative account of Love's life is Robert Wesley Doherty, "Alfred H. Love and the Universal Peace Union" (Ph.D. diss., Univ. of Pennsylvania, 1962), while Peter Brock's many works attempt to place Love's efforts in relation to other pacifist groups. See especially Brock's encyclopedic *Pacifism in the United States from the Colonial Era to the First World War* (1968). For Love's place within the larger and more practical peace movement, see David S. Patterson, *Toward a Warless World: The Travail of the American Peace Movement, 1887–1914* (1976). For essential background material on the pre–Civil War peace movement in a work sensitive to the nuances of nonresister ideology, see Valarie H. Ziegler, *The Advocates of Peace in Antebellum America* (1992). The entry on Love in the 1927 edition of the *DAB* by renowned historian Merle E. Curti as well as the 1929 publication of his dissertation, *The American Peace Crusade, 1815–1860*, created the field of peace history. An obituary is in the *New York Times*, 30 June 1913.

R. ALLEN SMITH

LOVE, James Spencer (6 July 1896–20 Jan. 1962), founder of Burlington Mills (renamed Burlington Industries in 1955), was born in Cambridge, Massachusetts, the son of James Lee Love, a college professor, and Julia James Spencer, called "June" from an early age. His maternal grandmother was Cornelia Phillips Spencer, a North Carolina journalist known for her support of the state university, public schools, and education for women. Educated at Harvard, Love attended its business school before receiving a commission in 1917 as a lieutenant in the U.S. Army. In France he first served as a division adjutant during the battle for St. Mihiel and then transferred to the general staff for the Argonne offensive. His work earned him promotions to captain and then to major.

Discharged in 1919, he settled in his father's hometown, Gastonia, North Carolina, to work in a textile mill started by his grandfather, Grier Love, and still owned by the family. Within a year, using the credit of a New York commission house, he bought the mill for himself only to discover that its small size and aging equipment gave him little flexibility. Realizing that his factory sat on valuable real estate, Love sold it in order to raise capital and moved his operations to Burlington, North Carolina, where local investors offered him assistance.

Love's new company, Burlington Mills, chartered in 1923, also proved to be too small and too old-fashioned to compete with other larger, more modernized cotton mills. Looking for an alternative, Love experimented with the first man-made fiber, rayon, starting with bedspreads, then turning to dress goods. By 1937 Love had built his company into the nation's largest rayon weaver; 80 percent of its output was unfinished rayon cloth sold to the women's apparel industry, and 20 percent was bedspreads and draperies distributed to retail and catalog outlets. Its success was due to the popularity of rayon as a substitute for silk during the depression, assistance from rayon yarn and loom manufacturers, and the rural South's cheap labor force. Unlike the North's smaller and older silk mills, Burlington used the latest and fastest looms to produce a higher quality rayon cloth in larger volume. By 1937 it had expanded to nineteen mills employing 6,750 workers with sales of over $27 million.

In 1937 Love transformed Burlington Mills into a public company with shares sold on the New York Stock Exchange. Gaining access to more capital, he diversified into hosiery, carpets, cotton, wool, and, after 1950, a new generation of synthetics, particularly blends of Dacron polyester and Orlon acrylic with natural fibers. Hosiery proved profitable because of the growing popularity of seamless nylon stockings for women. Burlington Mills also led in the vertical integration of the textile industry, controlling more of its own yarn processing, dyeing and finishing, and marketing. Love pursued an aggressive policy of acquisitions that by 1954 made his firm the largest textile company in the world with sixty-six factories and 44,000 employees and with sales of over $347 million. Just after his death in 1962, the company grew to 122 factories and 62,000 workers and passed the $1-billion mark in sales, twice those of its nearest competitor, J. P. Stevens.

In labor relations Love always expressed intense hostility toward unions, characterizing them as "a large scale racket" that "outside of the Russian threat . . . [was] by far the most insidious menace facing our country and our civilization." Immediately after the general strike of 1934 Love employed labor spies to report to him on union activity and saw to it that workers accused of attempting to dynamite mills in Burlington were vigorously prosecuted. This opposition to unions did not abate after the Second World War, but Love took care to create a reputation for himself as a "forward-looking" business leader. He endorsed increases in the minimum wage in 1947 and 1953 and supported a pardon in 1961 for a labor official, Boyd Paxton, who had been imprisoned for conspiracy after leading a textile strike in Henderson, North Carolina. While adopting a more conciliatory public position after the war, Love continued to select labor managers who were adept at suppressing union activity through the creation of a highly centralized personnel department that could closely monitor workers. Love's company was also among the first southern textile firms to sell its mill village housing because its cost became unnecessary when paved roads and cheaper automobiles made commuting easier for workers. Because Burlington had become the nation's largest textile firm, its success at defeating unions proved to be a significant roadblock to organized labor in the industry.

Love moved to Washington, D.C., in 1943 to serve as head of the textile bureau of the War Production Board, and after World War II he took a more active role in public affairs and became more involved in Democratic party politics. He served on the boards of trustees of the University of North Carolina, Davidson College, and Harvard's business school. Politically more moderate than many other textile manufacturers, he worked for the election of Frank Porter Graham to the Senate in 1950, publicly criticized Senator Joseph McCarthy, and in 1960 endorsed John Kennedy for president and the liberal candidate for governor of North Carolina, Terry Sanford.

Wiry, intense, and tireless, Love commuted almost weekly among New York's textile markets, company headquarters in North Carolina, and his winter home in Florida, using his personal airplane as an office. Devoted to the company he created, he married three times before he found personal stability. His first wife (and first cousin) Elizabeth Love was eighteen when they married in 1922; they had four children. After their divorce in 1940, he married Dorothy Beattie in 1941. They soon found themselves incompatible and divorced in 1943. In 1944 he married Martha Eskridge; they also had four children. Love died of a heart attack while playing tennis in Palm Beach, Florida.

Love belongs to that part of North Carolina's elite that V. O. Key described as the "progressive plutocracy." Although relentless in his opposition to unions and meaningful social reform, he devoted his time and energy to fostering "progress" for North Carolina and envisioned his company as a force for building a better South.

• The major collection of Love's papers is in the Southern Historical Collection, University of North Carolina at Chapel Hill, which also holds the papers of his father, sister, and grandmother. Substantial treatments of Love's life appear in Jacquelyn Dowd Hall et al., *Like a Family: The Making of a Southern Cotton Mill World* (1987), and Allen Tullos, *Habits of Industry: White Culture and the Transformation of the Carolina Piedmont* (1989). The best early account of his company is "Who Will Weave It?," *Fortune*, July, 1937, pp. 44–48, 114–18. Obituaries are in the *New York Times* and *Durham Morning Herald*, both 21 Jan. 1962, and in *Time*, 26 Jan. 1962.

ANNETTE C. WRIGHT

LOVE, Nat (June 1854–1921), cowboy and author, was born in Davidson County, Tennessee, the son of Sampson Love and a mother whose name is unknown. Both were slaves owned by Robert Love, whom Nat described as a "kind and indulgent Master." Nat

Love's father was a foreman over other slaves; his mother, a cook. The family remained with Robert Love after the end of the Civil War.

In February 1869 Nat struck out on his own. He left because Robert Love's plantation was in desperate economic straits after the war, and he sensed that there were few opportunities other than agricultural work for young former slaves in the defeated South. Although his father had died the year before, leaving him the head of the family, Nat nevertheless left because, as he admitted, "I wanted to see more of the world."

After a short stay in Kansas, Love worked for three years on the ranch of Sam Duval in the Texas panhandle. For the next eighteen years (1872–1890) Love was a cowboy on the giant Gallinger Ranch in southern Arizona. He traveled all the western trails herding cattle to market and, as his autobiography reveals, engaged in the drinking, gambling, and violence typical of western cow towns. He became an expert in identifying cattle brands and learned to speak fluent Spanish on trips to Mexico. In 1889 he married a woman named Alice (maiden name unknown), with whom he had one child.

The cowboy business was doomed by the westward movement of the railroads. Love recognized this situation and in 1890 secured employment with the Denver and Rio Grande Railroad as a Pullman car porter, one of the few occupations open to black men in the West. For fifteen years Love held this position on various western railroads. His last job, beginning in 1907, was as a bank guard with the General Securities Company in Los Angeles, where he died.

Most of what is known of Love's life is from his 1907 autobiography, *The Life and Adventures of Nat Love, Better Known in the Cattle Country as "Deadwood Dick," by Himself*. The 100-page work seems to have been inspired by the popular and melodramatic dime novels of the day and likely contains more than a bit of fiction itself. Love certainly portrayed himself as a larger-than-life figure. He claimed he could outdrink any man in the West without it affecting him in any way. He depicted himself as one of the most expert cowboys, who could outrope, outshoot, and outride the best of them. He reported that he single-handedly broke up a robbery at an isolated Union Pacific railroad station. "I carry the marks of fourteen bullet wounds on different part [sic] of my body, most any one of which would be sufficient to kill an ordinary man," he boasted," "but I am not even crippled. . . . I have had five horses shot from under me. . . . Yet I have always managed to escape with only the mark of a bullet or knife as a reminder." Shot and captured by Indians in 1876, he said he was nursed back to health by them and adopted into the tribe; he was offered the chief's daughter in marriage. But Love had other plans and made his escape one night. He claimed as close acquaintances many western notables such as William F. "Buffalo Bill" Cody, Frank and Jesse James, Kit Carson, and "Billy the Kid" (William H. Bonney). Even as a railroad porter Love made himself out to be one of the best.

The legendary "Deadwood Dick" was created by the western dime novelist Edward L. Wheeler in the 1870s. Several men claimed to be the prototype for the character, including Love, whose autobiography places him in Deadwood in the Dakota Territory on the Fourth of July 1876. In a roping contest, he "roped, threw, tied, bridled, saddled and mounted my mustang in exactly nine minutes," a championship record he said he held until his retirement as a cowboy fourteen years later and a feat, so he claimed, that instantly won him the title of "Deadwood Dick."

The autobiography is consistently upbeat, with the author invariably winning out over those skeptical of his abilities. He mentions no incidents of racial discrimination, although they are known to have occurred in the West. While his accounts of heroic achievements and derring-do are certainly possible, he seems to have stretched the truth, not unlike other western reminiscences. And some of his claims are not verified in other sources. As one student of the West, William Loren Katz, commented, Love's autobiography is "easy to read but hard to believe" (p. 323). Yet his life and work do illustrate how a black man of the late nineteenth century could rise from slavery to a satisfying life in the cowboy world, where ability and fortitude did serve to mitigate race prejudice.

• The fullest account of Love's life is his autobiography, *The Life and Adventures of Nat Love, Better Known in the Cattle Country as "Deadwood Dick," by Himself* (1907; repr. 1968), though it must be used with caution, given his penchant for glorifying his achievements. Philip Durham and Everett L. Jones, *The Negro Cowboys* (1965), summarizes the autobiography and critically analyzes it within the dime novel tradition. William Loren Katz, *The Black West* (1971), also is skeptical of Love's hyperbole. Harold W. Felton, *Nat Love: Negro Cowboy* (1969), is a children's book drawn largely from the autobiography.

WILLIAM F. MUGLESTON

LOVECRAFT, H. P. (20 Aug. 1890–15 Mar. 1937), author, was born Howard Phillips Lovecraft in Providence, Rhode Island, the son of Winfield Scott Lovecraft, a traveling salesman, and Sarah Susan Phillips. Lovecraft's father died in 1898 of tertiary syphilis, and the boy's upbringing fell to his overprotective mother, his two aunts, and his grandfather Whipple Van Buren Phillips, a wealthy industrialist.

Lovecraft was a precocious youth: he was reading by age two, writing poems and tales at seven, and learning Latin and Greek at eight. Early readings in the brothers Grimm, the *Arabian Nights*, and Edgar Allan Poe gave him a lifelong interest in the weird and the supernatural; he also read avidly in classical literature, eighteenth-century poetry and belles lettres, and the sciences. His first appearance in print was a letter to the *Providence Journal* for 3 June 1906, on a point of astronomy, and shortly thereafter he began contributing astronomy columns to several local papers. The death of Lovecraft's grandfather in 1904, and the subsequent mismanagement of his estate by relatives, spelled financial disaster for the family, and Lovecraft and his mother were forced to move from

their spacious family home to a smaller one in Providence.

Lovecraft's formal schooling was sporadic because of ill health: he later claimed to have suffered mysterious nervous breakdowns at various points in his youth, and one of these, in 1908, forced him to leave high school just before receiving his diploma. At this time he destroyed nearly all of his early writing. For five years he was essentially a hermit, doing little save reading, studying astronomy, and sporadically taking correspondence courses in chemistry.

In 1914 Lovecraft discovered the amateur journalism movement. He was initially recruited into the United Amateur Press Association; later he joined the National Amateur Press Association. He held several offices in both associations and edited his own amateur journal, the *Conservative*, between 1915 and 1923. He contributed poetry, essays, and reviews voluminously to many amateur papers and is regarded as a leading figure in the field. In 1917 he resumed the writing of fiction. "The Outsider" (1921) and "The Rats in the Walls" (1923) are regarded as among his best early tales.

The death of Lovecraft's mother on 24 May 1921 caused him great trauma. Gradually, however, he recovered and began to emerge from his hermitry. At an amateur convention in Boston on 4 July 1921, he met Sonia Haft Greene, a Russian Jew. They married on 3 March 1924. The couple moved to Sonia's apartment in Brooklyn, but Lovecraft's inability to find work in New York, along with the bankruptcy of the Manhattan hat shop in which she worked and her subsequent ill health, put great strain on the relationship. Lovecraft yearned to return to Providence and finally did so on 17 April 1926. When Sonia wished to set up a business there, however, Lovecraft's aunts refused to allow a tradeswoman wife for their nephew, and Lovecraft meekly acquiesced in their decision. A divorce was inevitable, and papers were filed in 1929, although Lovecraft never signed the final decree.

Living first with his elder aunt, Lillian Clark, then with his younger aunt, Annie E. P. Gamwell, Lovecraft matured into a recognized figure in weird fiction. His return from New York impelled an enormous outburst of fiction, including "The Call of Cthulhu" (1926), "The Colour out of Space" (1927), and two short novels, *The Dream-Quest of Unknown Kadath* (1926–1927) and *The Case of Charles Dexter Ward* (1927); he also completed his important critical essay, "Supernatural Horror in Literature" (1927), a historical survey of horror fiction from antiquity to the 1920s and a defense of the "weird tale" as an aesthetically significant literary form. He became a tireless traveler, seeking antiquarian locales along the eastern seaboard, from Quebec to Key West. The establishment in 1923 of the pulp magazine *Weird Tales* provided a regular market for his work, although some of his later tales were rejected because of their length or their nonconformity to pulp standards. Never a prolific writer of fiction, Lovecraft made the bulk of his income, from as early as 1916, by literary revision and ghostwriting, which ran the gamut from poetry to textbooks to novels. He had difficulty marketing his tales to standard book publishers, and, aside from several amateur press pamphlets, he saw only one volume of his work—the crudely produced *The Shadow over Innsmouth* (1936)—before his death in Providence of intestinal cancer and kidney failure.

Upon his death, Lovecraft's many friends set about rescuing his work from the oblivion of the pulps. August Derleth and Donald Wandrei founded their own company, Arkham House, for the expressed purpose of publishing Lovecraft's tales in hardcover; their first volume, *The Outsider and Others* (1939), is a landmark in weird fiction. Many other volumes from Arkham House followed, and Lovecraft's work has been widely disseminated in paperback and translated into more than a dozen languages. Many of his tales have been adapted for radio, film, and television. Although still largely unknown to academics, he has a wide popular following and is regarded by many European critics as a significant American writer.

Lovecraft's place in literary history currently resides in his pivotal role in the development of modern weird fiction. His tales are an outgrowth of his philosophical thought. An atheistic materialist, Lovecraft came to feel that human beings occupied an insignificant place in the boundless realms of space and time; in his fiction this conception was expressed by his frequently used term *cosmicism*. He wrote in a letter of 1927: "Now all my tales are based on the fundamental premise that common human laws and interests and emotions have no validity or significance in the vast cosmos-at-large. . . . To achieve the essence of real externality, whether of time or space or dimension, one must forget that such things as organic life, good and evil, love and hate, and all such local attributes of a negligible and temporary race called mankind, have any existence at all." This philosophical perspective led him to effect a union between conventional supernaturalism and the then-nascent field of science fiction (*At the Mountains of Madness* [1931] and "The Shadow out of Time" [1934–1935] appeared in *Astounding Stories*), transferring the locus of horror from the human realm to the vast and unknowable cosmos. Some of his most powerful tales employ a pseudomythology (labeled the Cthulhu Mythos by Derleth) to convey his cosmicism.

Lovecraft can also be regarded as a New England local colorist: such tales as "The Colour out of Space," "The Whisperer in Darkness" (1930), and "The Shadow over Innsmouth" (1931) capture with great richness and subtlety the sinister atmosphere of the untamed woods of Massachusetts and Vermont and of the decaying backwaters along the North Shore. He created an imaginary geography of New England, similar to that of William Faulkner's Yoknapatawpha County.

In addition to fiction, essays, and poetry, Lovecraft was one of the most prolific letter writers in literary history. He wrote tens of thousands of letters to amateur colleagues and fellow writers (Derleth, Frank Belknap Long, Clark Ashton Smith, Robert E. Howard, Robert Bloch, Fritz Leiber). These letters may be seen as Lovecraft's greatest literary accomplishment, for they reveal him to be a prodigious autodidact, a keen commentator on the political and cultural scene, a provocative theorist on the nature and purpose of weird fiction, and a tirelessly patient tutor and mentor to his friends and colleagues.

As a person, Lovecraft had both great virtues and some significant failings. On the negative side, the intolerance and dogmatism of his early opinions, his shabby treatment of his wife, and, most seriously, a lifelong racism, expressed extensively in his letters but only indirectly in his stories, that led him to believe in the biological inferiority of blacks and to be hostile to all "unassimilated" aliens and culture streams. On the positive side, however, are the testimonials of many of his friends who saw in him a prodigally generous and humane person whose devotion to the aesthetic integrity of his writing was matched by the natural dignity of his personal comportment. As Ernest A. Edkins wrote in 1940, "I think that the most lasting impression Lovecraft left me was one of essential nobility, of dauntless integrity. . . . He remains enshrined in my memory as a great gentleman, in the truest sense of that much abused term."

• Lovecraft's papers (including manuscripts, letters, memorabilia, and an extensive collection of published work) are in the John Hay Library of Brown University. His *Selected Letters*, ed. August Derleth et al., have been published in five volumes (1965–1976); several smaller editions of letters to individual correspondents also have appeared. The standard bibliography is S. T. Joshi, *H. P. Lovecraft and Lovecraft Criticism: An Annotated Bibliography* (1981). The only full-length biography—replacing Derleth's inadequate *H. P. L.: A Memoir* (1945)—is L. Sprague de Camp, *Lovecraft: A Biography* (1975), which embodies a great deal of research but has been criticized for its failure to sympathize with Lovecraft's beliefs and motivations. Many colleagues have written memoirs, the most notable of them being W. Paul Cook, *In Memoriam: Howard Phillips Lovecraft* (1941), and Frank Belknap Long, *Howard Phillips Lovecraft: Dreamer on the Nightside* (1975). Also valuable is Sonia (Greene) Davis, *The Private Life of H. P. Lovecraft* (1985). Kenneth W. Faig, Jr., *The Parents of Howard Phillips Lovecraft* (1990), is a brilliant monograph.

A useful overview of criticism from 1944 to 1978 can be found in Joshi, *H. P. Lovecraft: Four Decades of Criticism* (1980). There are three competent critical introductions: Joshi, *H. P. Lovecraft* (1982); Donald R. Burleson, *H. P. Lovecraft: A Critical Study* (1983); and Peter Cannon, *H. P. Lovecraft* (1989). Maurice Lévy, *Lovecraft ou du fantastique* (1972; trans. in 1988 as *Lovecraft: A Study in the Fantastic*), is a masterful thematic interpretation. Burleson has written a challenging deconstructionist study, *Lovecraft: Disturbing the Universe* (1990), and Joshi has written a philosophical analysis, *H. P. Lovecraft: The Decline of the West* (1990). A valuable collection of original essays by leading scholars can be found in David E. Schultz and Joshi, *An Epicure in the Terrible: A Centennial Anthology of Essays in Honor of H. P. Lovecraft* (1991). Obituaries are in the *Providence Journal* and the *New York Times*, 16 Mar. 1937.

S. T. JOSHI